BUTTERWORTHS
COMPETITION LAW
HANDBOOK

Eighth edition

Edited by

GARTH LINDRUP, BA, LLM, *Solicitor*
Partner, Addleshaw Booth & Co, Manchester

Butterworths
A Member of the LexisNexis Group

Members of the LexisNexis Group worldwide

United Kingdom	LexisNexis Butterworths Tolley, a Division of Reed Elsevier (UK) Ltd, Halsbury House, 35 Chancery Lane, LONDON, WC2A 1EL, and 4 Hill Street, EDINBURGH EH2 3JZ
Argentina	LexisNexis Argentina, BUENOS AIRES
Australia	LexisNexis Butterworths, CHATSWOOD, New South Wales
Austria	LexisNexis Verlag ARD Orac GmbH & Co KG, VIENNA
Canada	LexisNexis Butterworths, MARKHAM, Ontario
Chile	LexisNexis Chile Ltda, SANTIAGO DE CHILE
Czech Republic	Nakladatelství Orac sro, PRAGUE
France	Éditions du Juris-Classeur SA, PARIS
Hong Kong	LexisNexis Butterworths, HONG KONG
Hungary	HVG-Orac, BUDAPEST
India	LexisNexis Butterworths, NEW DELHI
Ireland	Butterworths (Ireland) Ltd, DUBLIN
Italy	Giuffré Editore, MILAN
Malaysia	Malayan Law Journal Sdn Bhd, KUALA LUMPUR
New Zealand	LexisNexis Butterworths, WELLINGTON
Poland	Wydawnictwo Prawnicze LexisNexis, WARSAW
Singapore	LexisNexis Butterworths, SINGAPORE
South Africa	LexisNexis Butterworths, DURBAN
Switzerland	Stämpfli Verlag AG, BERNE
USA	LexisNexis, DAYTON, Ohio

© Reed Elsevier (UK) Ltd 2002

A CIP Catalogue record for this book is available from the British Library.

ISBN 0 406 95762 2

Printed and bound in Great Britain by Clays Ltd, St Ives Plc

Visit Butterworths LexisNexis *direct* at www.butterworths.com

PREFACE

To many competition law practitioners it came as a surprise to discover that the Competition Act 1998 did not satisfy, at least for the time being, all the Government's aspirations for competition law reform outside the field of merger control. UK regulators may have been stung by the 'so what ?' reaction to the 1998 Act in certain quarters (notably the USA), coupled with comment to the effect that no antitrust system will earn respect until it has the capacity to send people to jail. In any event, barely 16 months after the commencement of the Competition Act, the DTI published its proposals for a "world class" competition regime, the *sine qua non* of any such being (apparently) the criminalisation of participation in cartels. The final destination of those proposals was the Enterprise Act 2002, which received Royal Assent on 7 November 2002, and the competition provisions of which are reproduced in this edition.

In addition to the criminalisation of certain conduct, by the creation of the cartel offence, and the disqualification of directors, the Act also makes substantial changes in relation to the structure and functions of the OFT and in relation to the areas of merger control, market investigations, super-complaints, appeals and Competition Commission procedures. In relation to merger control, the Act changes not only the jurisdictional thresholds but also the substantive test, which is now to be whether or not the merger has caused or may be expected to cause a substantial lessening of competition (SLC), a test applied in US merger control. The European Commission has also been considering the SLC test in its review of the EC Merger Regulation. However, the latest indication is that the ECMR will retain the dominance test, possibly coupled with new guidelines on how that will be applied going forward. As with criminalisation, the SLC test will therefore set the UK apart from the rest of the EU/EEA—harmonisation among member states was plainly not uppermost in the Government's mind here.

The competition and consumer provisions of the Enterprise Act are all expected to come into force by the summer of 2003, and different provisions may well come into force on different dates by virtue of separate Commencement Orders. This edition incorporates the prospective amendments made by the Act to prior legislation.

The lists of statutory instruments and of OFT Guidelines have been updated, although it was not possible to include in this edition the OFT's overview of the Enterprise Act. The revocation of the Beer Orders has been anticipated by a month or two.

The EC material includes the new de minimis notice, the new leniency notice and the new Block Exemption Regulation in relation to motor vehicles. This Block Exemption entered into force on 1 October 2002, but there is transitional relief up to 30 September 2003 in respect of agreements already in force which satisfied the conditions for exemption under Regulation (EC) 1475/95. For the "old" Block Exemption, readers will have to refer to the seventh edition.

The EC section has also been improved by the introduction of a new section on Rights of the Defence. The State Aids material has also been expanded by the inclusion of the Notice on state guarantees and the two sets of guidelines on rescuing/restructuring aid and regional aid.

The published proposal for the Modernisation Regulation to replace Regulation 17/62 remains as an Appendix to this edition. However, the final form of that Regulation is expected to be adopted before the end of November 2002, to come into effect on 1 May 2004. The next edition will deal with that and with other changes on the horizon such as the revision of the EC Merger Regulation and the replacement Block Exemption for the insurance sector.

Garth Lindrup
November 2002

CONTENTS

D. Exclusions and Exemptions

E. Merger Control

PART III OFT GUIDELINES (COMPETITION ACT 1998)

PART IV EC MATERIALS

A. General

B. Transport

F. Mergers and Joint Ventures

G. Enforcement

PART I
STATUTES

FAIR TRADING ACT 1973

(1973 c 41)

ARRANGEMENT OF SECTIONS

PART I
INTRODUCTORY

PART IV
FUNCTIONS OF DIRECTOR AND COMMISSION IN RELATION TO MONOPOLY SITUATIONS AND UNCOMPETITIVE PRACTICES

Powers for Director to require information

Monopoly references

Undertakings as alternative to monopoly reference by Director

PART V
MERGERS

Newspaper merger references

PART VI
REFERENCES TO COMMISSION OTHER THAN MONOPOLY AND MERGER REFERENCES

PART VII
PROVISIONS RELATING TO REFERENCES TO ADVISORY COMMITTEE OR TO COMMISSION

PART VIII
ADDITIONAL PROVISIONS RELATING TO REFERENCES TO COMMISSION

PART IX
AMENDMENTS OF RESTRICTIVE TRADE PRACTICES ACTS

PART XII
MISCELLANEOUS AND SUPPLEMENTARY PROVISIONS

An Act to provide for the appointment of a Director General of Fair Trading and of a Consumer Protection Advisory Committee, and to confer on the Director General and the Committee so appointed, on the Secretary of State, on the Restrictive Practices Court and on certain other courts new functions for the protection of consumers; to make provisions, in substitution for the Monopolies and Restrictive Practices (Inquiry and Control) Act 1948 and the Monopolies and Mergers Act 1965, for the matters dealt with in those Acts and related matters, including restrictive labour practices; to amend the Restrictive Trade Practices Act 1956 and the Restrictive Trade Practices Act 1968, to make provision for extending the said Act of 1956 to agreements relating to services, and to transfer to the Director

General of Fair Trading the functions of the Registrar of Restrictive Trading Agreements; to make provision with respect to pyramid selling and similar trading schemes; to make new provision in place of section 30(2) to (4) of the Trade Descriptions Act 1968; and for purposes connected with those matters

[25 July 1973]

NOTES

The subject-matter of Pts I–III, XI of this Act is a "reserved matter" for the purposes of the Scotland Act 1998, which by virtue of s 29(2)(b) of that Act, is outside the legislative competence of the Scottish Parliament; see s 30 of and Sch 5, Pt II, Head C, para C7, Pt III, para 5 to that Act. For restrictions upon the ability of the Scottish Parliament to modify the law on reserved matters, see s 29 of and Sch 4, Pt I, paras 2, 3 to that Act.

PART I
INTRODUCTORY

1 Director General of Fair Trading

(1)   The Secretary of State shall appoint an officer to be known as the Director General of Fair Trading (in this Act referred to as "the Director") for the purpose of performing the functions assigned or transferred to the Director by or under this Act.

(2)   An appointment of a person to hold office as the Director shall not be for a term exceeding five years; but previous appointment to that office shall not affect eligibility for re-appointment.

(3)   The Director may at any time resign his office as the Director by notice in writing addressed to the Secretary of State; and the Secretary of State may remove any person from that office on the ground of incapacity or misbehaviour.

(4)   Subject to subsections (2) and (3) of this section, the Director shall hold and vacate office as such in accordance with the terms of his appointment.

(5)   The Director may appoint such staff as he may think fit, subject to the approval of the Minister for the Civil Service as to numbers and as to terms and conditions of service.

(6)   The provisions of Schedule 1 to this Act shall have effect with respect to the Director.

[1]

NOTES

Repealed by the Enterprise Act 2002, s 278(2), Sch 26, as from a day to be appointed.

Director General of Fair Trading: the Enterprise Act 2002, s 2(1), at **[255]**, provides that, as from the coming into force of that section in accordance with s 279 at **[463]**, the functions of the Director General of Fair Trading, his property, rights and liabilities are transferred to the Office of Fair Trading. Accordingly, (by virtue of s 2(2), (3) of the 2002 Act) the office of the Director is abolished, and any reference to the Director in any enactment, instrument or other document passed or made before the commencement of s 2(1) shall have effect as if it were a reference to the Office of Fair Trading. For transitional provisions in connection with the transfer, see s 276(1) of, and Sch 24, para 6 to, the 2002 Act at **[477]**.

Minister of Civil Service: functions transferred to the Treasury by the Transfer of Functions (Minister for the Civil Service and Treasury) Order 1981, SI 1981/1670.

2 General functions of Director

(1)   Without prejudice to any other functions assigned or transferred to him by or under this Act, it shall be the duty of the Director, so far as appears to him to be practicable from time to time,—

(a) to keep under review the carrying on of commercial activities in the United Kingdom which relate to goods supplied to consumers in the United

Kingdom or produced with a view to their being so supplied, or which relate to services supplied for consumers in the United Kingdom, and to collect information with respect to such activities, and the persons by whom they are carried on, with a view to his becoming aware of, and ascertaining the circumstances relating to, practices which may adversely affect the economic interests of consumers in the United Kingdom, and

(b) to receive and collate evidence becoming available to him with respect to such activities as are mentioned in the preceding paragraph and which appears to him to be evidence of practices which may adversely affect the interests (whether they are economic interests or interests with respect to health, safety or other matters) of consumers in the United Kingdom.

(2)   It shall also be the duty of the Director, so far as appears to him to be practicable from time to time, to keep under review the carrying on of commercial activities in the United Kingdom, and to collect information with respect to those activities, and the persons by whom they are carried on, with a view to his becoming aware of, and ascertaining the circumstances relating to, monopoly situations or uncompetitive practices.

(3)   It shall be the duty of the Director, where either he considers it expedient or he is requested by the Secretary of State to do so,—

(a) to give information and assistance to the Secretary of State with respect to any of the matters in respect of which the Director has any duties under subsections (1) and (2) of this section, or

(b) subject to the provisions of Part II of this Act in relation to recommendations under that Part of this Act, to make recommendations to the Secretary of State as to any action which in the opinion of the Director it would be expedient for the Secretary of State or any other Minister to take in relation to any of the matters in respect of which the Director has any such duties.

(4)   It shall also be the duty of the Director to have regard to evidence becoming available to him with respect to any course of conduct on the part of a person carrying on a business which appears to be conduct detrimental to the interests of consumers in the United Kingdom and (in accordance with the provisions of Part III of this Act) to be regarded as unfair to them, with a view to considering what action (if any) he should take under Part III of this Act.

(5)   It shall be the duty of the Director to have regard to the needs of regional development and to the desirability of dispersing administrative offices from London in making decisions on the location of offices for his staff.

[2]

NOTES

Repealed by the Enterprise Act 2002, s 278(2), Sch 26, as from a day to be appointed.

The Director: see the note "Director General of Fair Trading" to s 1 at **[1]**.

3, 4   *(S 3 outside the scope of this work; s 4 repealed by the Competition Act 1998, s 74(1), (3), Sch 12, para 1(1), (2), Sch 14, Pt I.)*

5   Principal functions of Commission

(1)   Without prejudice to any other functions assigned to the Commission by or under this Act, it shall be the duty of the Commission, subject to and in accordance with the following provisions of this Act, to investigate and report on any question which may be referred to the Commission under this Act—

(a) with respect to the existence, or possible existence, of a monopoly situation, or

(b) with respect to a transfer of a newspaper or of newspaper assets (within the meaning of Part V of this Act), *or*

(c) *with respect to the creation, or possible creation, of a merger situation qualifying for investigation (within the meaning of Part V of this Act).*

(2) It shall be the duty of *the Director*, for the purpose of assisting the Commission in carrying out an investigation on a reference made to them under this Act, to give to the Commission—

(a) any information which is in *his* possession and which relates to matters falling within the scope of the investigation, and which is either requested by the Commission for that purpose or is information which in *his* opinion it would be appropriate for that purpose to give to the Commission without any such request, and

(b) any other assistance which the Commission may require, and which it is within *his* power to give, in relation to any such matters,

and the Commission, for the purpose of carrying out any such investigation, shall take account of any information given to them for that purpose under this subsection.

(3)   In this Act "monopoly reference" means any reference to the Commission under this Act which falls within paragraph (a) of subsection (1) of this section; "merger reference" (subject to section 63 of this Act) means any reference to the Commission under this Act which falls within paragraph (b) or paragraph (c) of that subsection; and "monopoly situation" (except in sections 6 to 8 of this Act) means circumstances in which, in accordance with the following provisions of this Part of this Act, a monopoly situation is for the purposes of this Act to be taken to exist in relation to any matters specified in section 6(1), section 7(1) or section 8 of this Act.

[3]

NOTES

Sub-s (1): paras (a), (c) and the word preceding para (c), repealed by the Enterprise Act 2002, s 278(2), Sch 26, as from a day to be appointed.

Sub-s (2): for the first words in italics there are substituted the words "the Office of Fair Trading", and for the second, third and fourth words in italics there are substituted the word "its" by the Enterprise Act 2002, s 278(1), Sch 25, para 5(1), (2), as from a day to be appointed.

Sub-s (3): repealed by the Enterprise Act 2002, s 278(2), Sch 26, as from a day to be appointed.

The Director: see the note "Director General of Fair Trading" to s 1 at **[1]**.

6   Monopoly situation in relation to supply of goods

(1)   For the purposes of this Act a monopoly situation shall be taken to exist in relation to the supply of goods of any description in the following cases, that is to say, if—

(a) *at least one-quarter of all the goods of that description which are supplied in the United Kingdom are supplied by one and the same person, or are supplied to one and the same person, or*

(b) *at least one-quarter of all the goods of that description which are supplied in the United Kingdom are supplied by members of one and the same group of interconnected bodies corporate, or are supplied to members of one and the same group of interconnected bodies corporate, or*

(c) *at least one-quarter of all the goods of that description which are supplied in the United Kingdom are supplied by members of one and the same group consisting of two or more such persons as are mentioned in subsection (2) of this section, or are supplied to members of one and the same group consisting of two or more such persons, or*

(d) *one or more agreements are in operation, the result or collective result of which is that goods of that description are not supplied in the United Kingdom at all.*

(2)   The two or more persons referred to in subsection (1)(c) of this section, in relation to goods of any description, are any two or more persons (not being a group of interconnected bodies corporate) who whether voluntarily or not, and whether by agreement or not, so conduct their respective affairs as in any way to prevent, restrict or distort competition in connection with the production or supply of goods of that description, whether or not they themselves are affected by the competition and whether the competition is between persons interested as producers or suppliers or between persons interested as customers of producers or suppliers.

[4]

NOTES
Repealed by the Enterprise Act 2002, s 278(2), Sch 26, as from a day to be appointed.

7   Monopoly situation in relation to supply of services

(1)   For the purposes of this Act a monopoly situation shall be taken to exist in relation to the supply of services of any description in the following cases, that is to say, if—

(a) the supply of services of that description in the United Kingdom is, to the extent of at least one-quarter, supply by one and the same person, or supply for one and the same person, or

(b) the supply of services of that description in the United Kingdom is, to the extent of at least one-quarter, supply by members of one and the same group of interconnected bodies corporate, or supply for members of one and the same group of interconnected bodies corporate, or

(c) the supply of services of that description in the United Kingdom is, to the extent of at least one-quarter, supply by members of one and the same group consisting of two or more such persons as are mentioned in subsection (2) of this section, or supply for members of one and the same group consisting of two or more such persons, or

(d) one or more agreements are in operation, the result or collective result of which is that services of that description are not supplied in the United Kingdom at all.

(2)   The two or more persons referred to in subsection (1)(c) of this section, in relation to services of any description, are any two or more persons (not being a group of interconnected bodies corporate) who whether voluntarily or not, and whether by agreement or not, so conduct their respective affairs as in any way to prevent, restrict or distort competition in connection with the supply of services of that description, whether or not they themselves are affected by the competition, and whether the competition is between persons interested as persons by whom, or as persons for whom, services are supplied.

(3)   In the application of this section for the purposes of a monopoly reference, the Commission, or the person or persons making the reference, may, to such extent as the Commission, or that person or those persons, think appropriate in the circumstances, treat services as supplied in the United Kingdom if the person supplying the services—

(a) has a place of business in the United Kingdom, or

(b) controls the relevant activities from the United Kingdom, or

(c) being a body corporate, is incorporated under the law of Great Britain or of Northern Ireland,

and may do so whether or not those services would otherwise be regarded as supplied in the United Kingdom.

[5]

8   Monopoly situation in relation to exports

   (1)   For the purposes of this Act a monopoly situation shall be taken to exist in relation to exports of goods of any description from the United Kingdom in the following cases, that is to say, if—
>   *(a)   at least one-quarter of all the goods of that description which are produced in the United Kingdom are produced by one and the same person, or*
>   *(b)   at least one-quarter of all the goods of that description which are produced in the United Kingdom are produced by members of one and the same group of interconnected bodies corporate;*

and in those cases a monopoly situation shall for the purposes of this Act be taken to exist both in relation to exports of goods of that description from the United Kingdom generally and in relation to exports of goods of that description from the United Kingdom to each market taken separately.

   (2)   In relation to exports of goods of any description from the United Kingdom generally, a monopoly situation shall for the purposes of this Act be taken to exist if—
>   *(a)   one or more agreements are in operation which in any way prevent or restrict, or prevent, restrict or distort competition in relation to, the export of goods of that description from the United Kingdom, and*
>   *(b)   that agreement is or (as the case may be) those agreements collectively are operative with respect to at least one-quarter of all the goods of that description which are produced in the United Kingdom.*

   (3)   In relation to exports of goods of any description from the United Kingdom to any particular market, a monopoly situation shall for the purposes of this Act be taken to exist if—
>   *(a)   one or more agreements are in operation which in any way prevent or restrict, or prevent, restrict or distort competition in relation to, the supply of goods of that description (whether from the United Kingdom or not) to that market, and*
>   *(b)   that agreement is or (as the case may be) those agreements collectively are operative with respect to at least one-quarter of all the goods of that description which are produced in the United Kingdom.*

                                                                              [6]

9   Monopoly situation limited to part of United Kingdom

   (1)   For the purposes of a monopoly reference, other than a reference relating to exports of goods from the United Kingdom, the person or persons making the reference may, if it appears to him or them to be appropriate in the circumstances to do so, determine that consideration shall be limited to a part of the United Kingdom.

   (2)   Where such a determination is made, then for the purposes of that monopoly reference the provisions of sections 6 and 7 of this Act, or such of those provisions as are applicable for those purposes, shall have effect as if, wherever those provisions refer to the United Kingdom, they referred to that part of the United Kingdom to which, in accordance with that determination, consideration is to be limited.

(3) The preceding provisions of this section shall have effect subject to subsection (4) of section 50 of this Act in cases to which that subsection applies.

[7]

NOTES

Repealed by the Enterprise Act 2002, s 278(2), Sch 26, as from a day to be appointed.

10 Supplementary provisions relating to ss 6 to 9

(1) In the application of any of the provisions of sections 6 to 9 of this Act for the purposes of a monopoly reference, those provisions shall have effect subject to the following provisions of this section.

(2) ...

(3) In relation to goods or services of any description which are the subject of different forms of supply—
   (a) references in paragraphs (a) to (d) of subsection (1), and in subsection (2), of section 6 or in section 8(3) of this Act to the supply of goods, or
   (b) references in paragraphs (a) to (d) of subsection (1), and in subsection (2), of section 7 of this Act to the supply of services,

shall for those purposes be construed in whichever of the following ways the Commission, or the person or persons making the monopoly reference, think appropriate in all the circumstances, that is to say, as references to any of those forms of supply taken separately, to all those forms of supply taken together, or to any of those forms of supply taken in groups.

(4) For the purposes of subsection (3) of this section the Commission, or the person or persons making the monopoly reference in question, may treat goods or services as being the subject of different forms of supply whenever the transactions in question differ as to their nature, their parties, their terms or their surrounding circumstances, and the difference is one which, in the opinion of the Commission, or the person or persons making the reference, ought for the purposes of that subsection to be treated as a material difference.

(5) For the purposes of a monopoly reference made by the Director, subsections (3) and (4) of this section shall have effect subject to section 50(3) and (4) of this Act.

(6) In determining, for the purposes of a monopoly reference, whether the proportion of one-quarter mentioned in any provision of section 6, section 7 or section 8 of this Act is fulfilled with respect to goods or services of any description, the Commission, or the person or persons making the reference, shall apply such criterion (whether it be value or cost or price or quantity or capacity or number of workers employed or some other criterion, of whatever nature) or such combination of criteria as may appear to them or him to be most suitable in all the circumstances.

(7) The criteria for determining when goods or services can be treated, for the purposes of a monopoly reference, as goods or services of a separate description shall be such as the person or persons making the reference may think most suitable in the circumstances.

(8) In construing the provisions of section 7(3) and section 9 of this Act and the provisions of subsections (1) [and (3) to (7)] of this section, the purposes of a monopoly reference shall be taken to include the purpose of enabling the Director, or the Secretary of State or any other Minister, to determine in any particular circumstances—
   (a) whether a monopoly reference could be made under Part IV of this Act, and

(b) *if so, whether in those circumstances such a reference could be made by the Director,*

and references in those provisions to the person or persons making a monopoly reference shall be construed accordingly.

[8]

NOTES

Repealed by the Enterprise Act 2002, s 278(2), Sch 26, as from a day to be appointed.

Sub-s (2): repealed by the Competition Act 1998, s 74(1), (3), Sch 12, para 1(1), (3)(a), Sch 14, Pt I, subject to savings in Sch 13, Pt V, para 40 of the 1998 Act at **[246]**. Original text, as amended by the Restrictive Trade Practices Act 1976, s 44, Sch 5, read as follows—

"(2) No account shall for those purposes be taken of any provisions of an agreement in so far as they are provisions by virtue of which it is an agreement to which [the Act of 1976] applies."

Sub-s (8): words in square brackets substituted by the Competition Act 1998, s 74(1), Sch 12, para 1(1), (4).

The Director: see the note "Director General of Fair Trading" to s 1 at **[1]**.

11   Meaning of "complex monopoly situation"

(1)   In this Act "complex monopoly situation" means circumstances in which, in accordance with the preceding provisions of this Act, a monopoly situation is for the purposes of this Act to be taken to exist in relation to the supply of goods or services of any description, or in relation to exports of goods of any description from the United Kingdom, by reason that the condition specified in paragraph (c) or in paragraph (d) of section 6(1) or of section 7(1) of this Act is fulfilled, or that the conditions specified in subsection (2) or in subsection (3) of section 8 of this Act are fulfilled.

(2)   Any reference in the preceding subsection to paragraph (c) or paragraph (d) of section 6(1) or of section 7(1) of this Act shall be construed as including a reference to that paragraph as modified by section 9(2) of this Act.

[9]

NOTES

Repealed by the Enterprise Act 2002, s 278(2), Sch 26, as from a day to be appointed.

12   Powers of Secretary of State in relation to functions of Director

(1)   The Secretary of State may give general directions indicating considerations to which the Director should have particular regard in determining the order of priority in which—

(a) *matters are to be brought under review in the performance of his duty under section 2(1) of this Act, or*

(b) *classes of goods or services are to be brought under review by him for the purpose of considering whether a monopoly situation exists or may exist in relation to them.*

(2)   The Secretary of State may also give general directions indicating—

(a) *considerations to which in cases where it appears to the Director that a practice may adversely affect the interests of consumers in the United Kingdom, he should have particular regard in determining whether to make a recommendation to the Secretary of State under section 2(3)(b) of this Act, or*

(b) *considerations to which, in cases where it appears to the Director that a consumer trade practice may adversely affect the economic interests of consumers in the United Kingdom, he should have particular regard in determining whether to make a reference to the Advisory Committee under Part II of this Act, or*

   (c) *considerations to which, in cases where it appears to the Director that a monopoly situation exists or may exist, he should have particular regard in determining whether to make a monopoly reference to the Commission under Part IV of this Act.*

  (3)   *The Secretary of State, on giving any directions under this section, shall arrange for those directions to be published in such manner as the Secretary of State thinks most suitable in the circumstances.*

[10]

NOTES

Repealed by the Enterprise Act 2002, ss 9, 278(2), Sch 26, as from a day to be appointed.
The Director: see the note "Director General of Fair Trading" to s 1 at **[1]**.

13–43   (*(Pts II, III) outside the scope of this work.*)

PART IV
FUNCTIONS OF DIRECTOR AND COMMISSION IN RELATION TO MONOPOLY SITUATIONS AND UNCOMPETITIVE PRACTICES

Powers for Director to require information

44   General power for Director to require information

  (1)   Where it appears to the Director that there are grounds for believing—
    (a)   that a monopoly situation may exist in relation to the supply of goods or services of any description, or in relation to exports of goods of any description from the United Kingdom, and
    (b)   that in accordance with the following provisions of this Part of this Act he would not be precluded from making a monopoly reference to the Commission with respect to the existence or possible existence of that situation,

[the Director may exercise the powers conferred by subsection (2) below for the purpose of assisting him in determining whether to take either of the following decisions with regard to that situation.]

  [(1A) Those decisions are—
    (a)   whether to make a monopoly reference with respect to the existence or possible existence of the situation;
    (b)   whether, instead, to make a proposal under section 56A below for the Secretary of State to accept undertakings.]

  [(2)   In the circumstances and for the purpose mentioned in subsection (1) above, the Director may—
    (a)   require any person within subsection (3) below to produce to the Director, at a specified time and place—
      (i)   any specified documents, or
      (ii)   any document which falls within a specified category,
    which are in his custody or under his control and which are relevant;
    (b)   require any person within subsection (3) below who is carrying on a business to give the Director specified estimates, forecasts, returns, or other information, and specify the time at which and the form and manner in which the estimates, forecasts, returns or information are to be given;
    (c)   enter any premises used by a person within subsection (3) below for business purposes, and—
      (i)   require any person on the premises to produce any documents on the premises which are in his custody or under his control and which are relevant;

    (ii) *require any person on the premises to give the Director such explanation of the documents as he may require.*

   (3)   *A person is within this subsection if—*
    (a) *he produces goods of the description in question in the United Kingdom;*
    (b) *he supplies goods or (as the case may be) services of the description in question in the United Kingdom; or*
    (c) *such goods (or services) are supplied to him in the United Kingdom.*

   (4)   *The power to impose a requirement under subsection (2)(a) or (b) above is to be exercised by notice in writing served on the person on whom the requirement is imposed; and "specified" in those provisions means specified or otherwise described in the notice, and "specify" is to be read accordingly.*

   (5)   *The power under subsection (2)(a) above to require a person ("the person notified") to produce a document includes power—*
    (a) *if the document is produced—*
      (i) *to take copies of it or extracts from it;*
      (ii) *to require the person notified, or any person who is a present or past officer of his, or is or was at any time employed by him, to provide an explanation of the document;*
    (b) *if the document is not produced, to require the person notified to state, to the best of his knowledge and belief, where it is.*

   (6)   *Nothing in this section confers power to compel any person—*
    (a) *to produce any document which he could not be compelled to produce in civil proceedings before the High Court or, in Scotland, the Court of Session; or*
    (b) *in complying with any requirement for the giving of information, to give any information which he could not be compelled to give in evidence in such proceedings.*

   (7)   *No person has to comply with a requirement imposed under subsection (2) above by a person acting under an authorisation under paragraph 7 of Schedule 1 to this Act unless evidence of the authorisation has, if required, been produced.*

   (8)   *For the purposes of subsection (2) above—*
    (a) *a document is relevant if—*
      (i) *it is relevant to a decision mentioned in subsection (1A) above; and*
      (ii) *the powers conferred by this section are exercised in relation to the document for the purpose of assisting the Director in determining whether to take that decision;*
    (b) *"document" includes information recorded in any form; and*
    (c) *in relation to information recorded otherwise than in legible form, the power to require its production includes power to require production of it in legible form, so far as the means to do so are within the custody or under the control of the person on whom the requirement is imposed.]*

[11]

NOTES

    Repealed by the Enterprise Act 2002, s 278(2), Sch 26, as from a day to be appointed; for a saving in relation to any monopoly reference made under s 50 or s 51 of this Act before such day or days as the Secretary of State may appoint, see s 276(1) of, and Sch 24, para 14 to, the 2002 Act at **[477]**.

    Sub-s (1): words in square brackets substituted by the Competition Act 1998, s 66(1), (2).

    Sub-s (1A): inserted by the Competition Act 1998, s 66(1), (3).

    Sub-ss (2)–(8): substituted for original sub-s (2) by the Competition Act 1998, s 66(1), (4).

    Functions of the Director General of Fair Trading: the functions under this section and ss 50, 52, 53, 86 and 88 of this Act, were partly transferred to the following industry regulators (so as to be exercisable concurrently with the Director General of Fair Trading), and the references in Pt IV (ss 44–56G, Schs 7, 8) and ss 86, 88 and 133 of this Act to the Director are to be construed accordingly: (i) the Director General of Telecommunications, so far as relating to monopoly situations which exist or may exist in relation to commercial activities connected with telecommunications (see the Telecommunications Act 1984, s 50(2, (4), (7)); (ii) the Director General of Water Services, so far as relating to monopoly situations which exist in relation to commercial activities connected with the supply of water or the provision of sewerage services (see the Water Industry Act 1991, s 31(2), (4), (5)–(9)); (iii) the Gas and Electricity Markets Authority, so far as relating to monopoly situations which exist or may exist in relation to commercial activities connected with the generation, transmission or supply of electricity (see the Electricity Act 1989, s 43(2), (4)–(7)) and so far as relating to monopoly situations which exist or may exist in relation to commercial activities connected with the carrying on of activities to which the Gas Act 1986, s 36A(2) applies (see the Gas Act 1986, s 36A(2), (4)–(7), (10)); (iv) the Rail Regulator, so far as relating to monopoly situations which exist or may exist in relation to the supply of railway services (see the Railways Act 1993, s 67(2), (4)–(8)); and (v) the Civil Aviation Authority, so far as relating to monopoly situations which exist or may exist in relation to the supply of air traffic services (see the Transport Act 2000, s 86(1), (2), (4), (5), (7)).

The amendments made to this section and to s 46 by the Competition Act 1998, ss 66, 67 are to have effect not only in relation to the jurisdiction of the Director under this section and s 46, but also in relation to sectoral regulators in accordance with s 66(5), Sch 10, para 1 of the 1998 Act at **[223]**.

As to the furnishing of false or misleading information, generally, to the Director under this Part, see s 93B of this Act at **[79]** (as inserted by the Companies Act 1989, s 151).

As to the Director, see also the note "Director General of Fair Trading" to s 1 at **[1]**.

45　(*Repealed by the Competition Act 1998, s 74(1), (3), Sch 12, para 1(1), (8), Sch 14, Pt I.*)

46　Supplementary provisions as to requirements to furnish information

(1)–(3) . . .

[(4)　Any person who refuses or wilfully neglects to comply with a requirement imposed under section 44(2) above is guilty of an offence and liable—
　　(a)　on summary conviction, to a fine not exceeding the prescribed sum, or
　　(b)　on conviction on indictment, to imprisonment for a term not exceeding two years or to a fine or to both.

(5)　If a person is charged with an offence under subsection (4) in respect of a requirement to produce a document, it is a defence for him to prove—
　　(a)　that the document was not in his possession or under his control; and
　　(b)　that it was not reasonably practicable for him to comply with the requirement.

(6)　If a person is charged with an offence under subsection (4) in respect of a requirement—
　　(a)　to provide an explanation of a document, or
　　(b)　to state where a document is to be found,

it is a defence for him to prove that he had a reasonable excuse for failing to comply with the requirement.

(7)　A person who intentionally obstructs the Director in the exercise of his powers under section 44 is guilty of an offence and liable—
　　(a)　on summary conviction, to a fine not exceeding the prescribed sum;
　　(b)　on conviction on indictment, to a fine.

(8)　A person who wilfully alters, suppresses or destroys any document which he has been required to produce under section 44(2) is guilty of an offence and liable—
　　(a)　on summary conviction, to a fine not exceeding the prescribed sum;
　　(b)　on conviction on indictment, to imprisonment for a term not exceeding two years or to a fine or to both.]

[12]

NOTES
　Repealed by the Enterprise Act 2002, s 278(2), Sch 26, as from a day to be appointed; for a saving in relation to any monopoly reference made under s 50 or s 51 of this Act before such day or days as the Secretary of State may appoint, see s 276(1) of, and Sch 24, para 14 to, the 2002 Act at **[477]**.

Sub-ss (1), (2): repealed by the Competition Act 1998, s 67(1), (2).
Sub-s (3): repealed by the Companies Act 1989, ss 153, 212, Sch 20, para 1, Sch 24.
Sub-ss (4)–(8): inserted by the Competition Act 1998, s 67(1), (3).
The Director: see the note "Director General of Fair Trading" to s 1 at **[1]**.
See also the notes to s 44 at **[11]**.

Monopoly references

47   General provisions as to monopoly references

(1)   A monopoly reference—
  (a) shall specify the description of goods or services to which it relates;
  (b) in the case of a reference relating to goods, shall state whether it relates to the supply of goods or to exports of goods from the United Kingdom or to both; and
  (c) if, for the purposes of the reference, consideration is to be limited to a part of the United Kingdom, shall specify the part of the United Kingdom to which consideration is to be limited,

and (subject to the next following subsection) shall be framed in one or other of the ways specified in section 48 or section 49 of this Act.

(2)   A monopoly reference (whether it falls within section 48 or within section 49 of this Act) may be so framed as to require the Commission to exclude from consideration, or to limit consideration to,—
  (a) such agreements as are mentioned in paragraph (d) of section 6(1) or paragraph (d) of section 7(1) of this Act (or in either of those paragraphs as modified by section 9(2) of this Act) or as are mentioned in subsection (2) or subsection (3) of section 8 of this Act, or
  (b) agreements or practices whereby persons conduct their affairs as mentioned in section 6(2) or section 7(2) of this Act,

or to exclude from consideration, or to limit consideration to, such one or more agreements or practices falling within paragraph (a) or paragraph (b) of this subsection as are specified in the reference.

[13]

NOTES
    Repealed by the Enterprise Act 2002, s 278(2), Sch 26, as from a day to be appointed; for a saving in relation to any monopoly reference made under s 50 or s 51 of this Act before such day or days as the Secretary of State may appoint, see s 276(1) of, and Sch 24, para 14 to, the 2002 Act at **[477]**.

48   Monopoly reference limited to the facts

A monopoly reference may be so framed as to require the Commission only to investigate and report on the questions whether a monopoly situation exists in relation to the matters set out in the reference in accordance with section 47 of this Act and, if so—
  (a) by virtue of which provisions of sections 6 to 8 of this Act that monopoly situation is to be taken to exist;
  (b) in favour of what person or persons that monopoly situation exists;
  (c) whether any steps (by way of uncompetitive practices or otherwise) are being taken by that person or those persons for the purpose of exploiting or maintaining the monopoly situation and, if so, by what uncompetitive practices or in what other way; and
  (d) whether any action or omission on the part of that person or those persons is attributable to the existence of the monopoly situation and, if so, what action or omission and in what way it is so attributable;

and a monopoly reference so framed is in this Act referred to as a "monopoly reference limited to the facts".

[14]

NOTES
    Repealed by the Enterprise Act 2002, s 278(2), Sch 26, as from a day to be appointed; for a saving in relation to any monopoly reference made under s 50 or s 51 of this Act before such day or days as the Secretary of State may appoint, see s 276(1) of, and Sch 24, para 14 to, the 2002 Act at **[477]**.

49 Monopoly reference not limited to the facts

(1)   A monopoly reference may be so framed as to require the Commission to investigate and report on the question whether a monopoly situation exists in relation to the matters set out in the reference in accordance with section 47 of this Act and, if so, to investigate and report—

(a) on the questions mentioned in paragraphs (a) to (d) of section 48 of this Act, and

(b) on the question whether any facts found by the Commission in pursuance of their investigations under the preceding provisions of this subsection operate, or may be expected to operate, against the public interest.

(2)   A monopoly reference may be so framed as to require the Commission to investigate and report on the questions whether a monopoly situation exists in relation to the matters set out in the reference in accordance with section 47 of this Act and, if so,—

(a) by virtue of which provisions of sections 6 to 8 of this Act that monopoly situation is to be taken to exist;

(b) in favour of what person or persons that monopoly situation exists; and

(c) whether any action or omission on the part of that person or those persons in respect of matters specified in the reference for the purposes of this paragraph operates, or may be expected to operate, against the public interest.

(3)   For the purposes of subsection (2)(c) of this section any matter may be specified in a monopoly reference if it relates to any of the following, that is to say—

(a) prices charged, or proposed to be charged, for goods or services of the description specified in the reference;

(b) any recommendation or suggestion made as to such prices;

(c) any refusal to supply goods or services of the description specified in the reference;

(d) any preference given to any person (whether by way of discrimination in respect of prices or in respect of priority of supply or otherwise) in relation to the supply of goods or services of that description;

and any matter not falling within any of the preceding paragraphs may be specified for those purposes in a monopoly reference if, in the opinion of the person or persons making the reference, it is of a kind such that (if a monopoly situation is found to exist) that matter might reasonably be regarded as a step taken for the purpose of exploiting or maintaining that situation or as being attributable to the existence of that situation.

(4)   A monopoly reference framed in either of the ways mentioned in subsections (1) and (2) of this section is in this Act referred to as a "monopoly reference not limited to the facts".

[15]

NOTES
    Repealed by the Enterprise Act 2002, s 278(2), Sch 26, as from a day to be appointed; for a saving in relation to any monopoly reference made under s 50 or s 51 of this Act before such day or days as the Secretary of State may appoint, see s 276(1) of, and Sch 24, para 14 to, the 2002 Act at **[477]**.

50 Monopoly references by Director

(1)   Where it appears to the Director that a monopoly situation exists or may exist in relation to—

(a) the supply of goods of any description, or

(b) the supply of services of any description, or16

(c) exports of goods of any description from the United Kingdom, either generally or to any particular market,

the Director, subject to section 12 of this Act and to the following provisions of this section, may if he thinks fit make a monopoly reference to the Commission with respect to the existence or possible existence of such a monopoly situation.

(2)   [Subject to subsection (2A) of this section] no monopoly reference shall be made by the Director with respect to the existence or possible existence of a monopoly situation in relation to the supply of goods or services of any description specified in Part I of Schedule 5 or in Part I of Schedule 7 to this Act.

[(2A) Subsection (2) of this section shall not preclude the making of a monopoly reference by the Director with respect to the existence or possible existence of a monopoly situation in relation to the supply of such services as are specified in paragraph 5 of Schedule 5 to this Act in Great Britain, except in relation to the supply of any such services by—

(a) a body corporate to which section 16 of this Act applies;

(b) a subsidiary, within the meaning of section 736 of the Companies Act 1985, of any such body corporate; or

(c) a publicly owned railway company, within the meaning of the Railways Act 1993.]

(3)   Notwithstanding anything in subsections (3) and (4) of section 10 of this Act—

(a) for the purposes of any monopoly reference made by the Director the supply of goods or services of any description specified in the first column . . . of Part II of Schedule 7 to this Act in any manner specified in relation to that description of goods or services in the second column of Part II of the relevant Schedule shall be taken to be a separate form of supply, and

(b) any monopoly reference made by the Director in relation to the supply of goods or services of any such description shall be limited so as to exclude that form of supply.

(4)   For the purposes of any monopoly reference made by the Director in relation to goods of any description specified in the first column of Part III of Schedule 7 to this Act—

(a) the supply of goods of that description in Northern Ireland in any manner specified in relation to that description of goods in the second column of that Part of that Schedule shall be taken to be a separate form of supply, and, notwithstanding anything in section 10(3) and (4) of this Act, any monopoly reference so made in relation to the supply of goods of any such description in Northern Ireland shall be limited so as to exclude that form of supply, and

(b) for the purposes of any such monopoly reference the Director shall so exercise his powers under section 9 of this Act as to comply with the requirements of the preceding paragraph.

(5)   The Secretary of State may by order made by statutory instrument vary any of the provisions of Schedule 7 to this Act, either by adding one or more further entries or by altering or deleting any entry for the time being contained in it; and any reference in this Act to that Schedule shall be construed as a reference to that Schedule as for the time being in force.

(6)   *On making a monopoly reference to the Commission, the Director shall send a copy of it to the Secretary of State; and if, before the end of the period of fourteen days from the day on which the reference is first published in the Gazette in accordance with section 53 of this Act, the Secretary of State directs the Commission not to proceed with the reference,—*

(a)   *the Commission shall not proceed with that reference, but*

(b)   *nothing in the preceding paragraph shall prevent the Commission from proceeding with any subsequent monopoly reference, notwithstanding that it relates wholly or partly to the same matters.*

[16]

NOTES

Repealed by the Enterprise Act 2002, s 278(2), Sch 26, as from a day to be appointed; for a saving in relation to any monopoly reference made under this section or s 51 of this Act before such day or days as the Secretary of State may appoint, see s 276(1) of, and Sch 24, para 14 to, the 2002 Act at **[477]**.

Sub-s (2): words in square brackets inserted by the Railways Act 1993, s 66(1).

Sub-s (2A): inserted by the Railways Act 1993, s 66(1).

Sub-s (3): words omitted from para (a) repealed by the Telecommunications Act 1984, s 109(6), Sch 7, Pt I.

Functions of the Director General of Fair Trading: see the note to s 44 at **[11]**. See also the note "Director General of Fair Trading" to s 1 at **[1]**.

See further, as to the powers exercisable in consequence of a report of the Competition Commission which concludes that a monopoly situation operating against the public interest exists in relation to patented products, the Patents Act 1977, s 51.

Orders: the Monopoly References (Alteration of Exclusions) Order 1984, SI 1984/1887; the Monopoly References (Deletion of Exclusions) Order 1998, SI 1998/2253.

51   Monopoly references by Ministers

(1)   *Subject to the following provisions of this section, the Secretary of State, or the Secretary of State and any other Minister acting jointly, where it appears to him or them that a monopoly situation exists or may exist in relation to—*

(a)   *the supply of goods of any description, or*

(b)   *the supply of services of any description, or*

(c)   *export of goods of any description from the United Kingdom, either generally or to any particular market,*

may, if the Secretary of State (or, in the case of joint action by the Secretary of State and another Minister, each of them) thinks fit, make a monopoly reference to the Commission with respect to the existence or possible existence of such a monopoly situation.

(2)   *Where it appears to the Secretary of State that a monopoly situation exists or may exist as mentioned in the preceding subsection, and that the goods or services in question are of a description specified in Part I of, . . . , Schedule 5 or Schedule 7 to this Act, the Secretary of State shall not make a monopoly reference with respect to the existence or possible existence of that situation except jointly with such one or more of the Ministers mentioned in the next following subsection as appear to him to have functions directly relating—*

(a)   *to the supply of goods or services of that description in the area (whether consisting of the whole or part of the United Kingdom) in relation to which the question arises, or*

(b)   *to exports of goods of that description from the United Kingdom, as the case may be.*

(3)   *The Ministers referred to in subsection (2) of this section are the Secretary of State for Scotland, the Secretary of State for Wales, the Secretary of State for Northern Ireland, [the Secretary of State for Transport, Local Government and the Regions] the Minister of Agriculture, Fisheries and Food, the Minister of Agriculture for Northern Ireland, the Minister of Commerce for Northern Ireland . . .*

(4)   Where it appears to the Secretary of State that a monopoly situation exists or may exist as mentioned in subsection (1) of this section in relation to the supply in Northern Ireland of goods of a description specified in the first column of Part III of Schedule 7 to this Act, the Secretary of State shall not make a monopoly reference with respect to the existence or possible existence of that situation except jointly with the Minister of Agriculture for Northern Ireland.

[17]

NOTES

Repealed by the Enterprise Act 2002, s 278(2), Sch 26, as from a day to be appointed; for a saving in relation to any monopoly reference made under this section or s 50 of this Act before such day or days as the Secretary of State may appoint, see s 276(1) of, and Sch 24, para 14 to, the 2002 Act at **[477]**.

Sub-s (2): words omitted repealed by the Telecommunications Act 1984, s 109(6), Sch 7, Pt I.

Sub-s (3): words in square brackets substituted by the Secretaries of State for Transport, Local Government and the Regions and for Environment, Food and Rural Affairs Order 2001, SI 2001/2568, art 16, Schedule, para 5; words omitted repealed by the Ministry of Posts and Telecommunications (Dissolution) Order 1974, SI 1974/691, art 4(1), Schedule.

Minister of Agriculture, Fisheries and Food: now the Secretary of State for Environment, Food and Rural Affairs: see the Secretaries of State for Transport, Local Government and the Regions and for Environment, Food and Rural Affairs Order 2001, SI 2001/2568.

See the Competition Act 1980, s 21 at **[118]**, as to the power of the Secretary of State to make a monopoly reference acting alone.

See, also, the note to s 50 at **[16]** as to the powers exercisable under the Patents Act 1977, s 51.

---

52   Variation of monopoly reference

(1)   Subject to the following provisions of this section, the Director may at any time vary a monopoly reference made by him, and the Secretary of State (or, in the case of a monopoly reference made by the Secretary of State jointly with one or more other Ministers, the Secretary of State and that Minister or those Ministers acting jointly) may vary a monopoly reference made by him or them.

(2)   A monopoly reference not limited to the facts shall not be varied so as to become a monopoly reference limited to the facts; but (subject to the following provisions of this section) a monopoly reference limited to the facts may be varied so as to become a monopoly reference not limited to the facts, whether the Commission have already reported on the reference as originally made or not.

(3)   A monopoly reference made by the Director shall not be varied so as to become a reference which he is precluded from making by any provisions of section 50 of this Act.

(4)   On varying a monopoly reference made by him, the Director shall send a copy of the variation to the Secretary of State; and if, before the end of the period of fourteen days from the day on which the variation is first published in the Gazette in accordance with the next following section, the Secretary of State directs the Commission not to give effect to the variation,—

   (a)   the Commission shall proceed with the reference as if that variation had not been made, but

   (b)   nothing in the preceding paragraph shall prevent the Commission from proceeding with any subsequent monopoly reference, or from giving effect to any subsequent variation, notwithstanding that it relates wholly or partly to the matters to which that variation related.

(5)   In this section and in sections 53 to 55 of this Act "Ministers" includes the Minister of Agriculture for Northern Ireland and the Minister of Commerce for Northern Ireland.

[18]

PART I
STATUTES

NOTES

Repealed by the Enterprise Act 2002, s 278(2), Sch 26, as from a day to be appointed; for a saving in relation to any monopoly reference made under s 50 or s 51 of this Act before such day or days as the Secretary of State may appoint, see s 276(1) of, and Sch 24, para 14 to, the 2002 Act at **[477]**.

Functions of the Director General of Fair Trading: see the note to s 44 at **[11]**. See also the note "Director General of Fair Trading" to s 1 at **[1]**.

53 Publication of monopoly references and variations, and of directions relating to them

(1) On making a monopoly reference, or a variation of a monopoly reference, the Director or, as the case may be, the Secretary of State (or, in the case of a monopoly reference or variation made by the Secretary of State acting jointly with one or more other Ministers, the Secretary of State and that Minister or those Ministers acting jointly) shall arrange for the reference or variation to be published in full in the Gazette, and shall arrange for the reference or variation to be published in such other manner as he or they may think most suitable for bringing it to the attention of persons who, in his or their opinion, would be affected by it.

(2) Where the Secretary of State gives a direction under section 50(6) of this Act with respect to a monopoly reference, or gives a direction under section 52(4) of this Act with respect to a variation of a monopoly reference, the Secretary of State shall arrange for the direction to be published in the Gazette and otherwise in the same manner as the monopoly reference or variation was published in accordance with the preceding subsection.

(3) In this section "the Gazette" means the London, Edinburgh and Belfast Gazettes, except that, in relation to a monopoly reference under which consideration is limited to a particular part of the United Kingdom in accordance with section 9 of this Act (including a reference under which consideration is required to be so limited by section 50(4)(b) of this Act), it means such one or more of those Gazettes as are appropriate to that part of the United Kingdom.

(4) In sections 50 and 52 of this Act any reference to publication in the Gazette is a reference to publication in the London Gazette, the Edinburgh Gazette or the Belfast Gazette, whichever first occurs.

[19]

NOTES

Repealed by the Enterprise Act 2002, s 278(2), Sch 26, as from a day to be appointed; for a saving in relation to any monopoly reference made under s 50 or s 51 of this Act before such day or days as the Secretary of State may appoint, see s 276(1) of, and Sch 24, para 14 to, the 2002 Act at **[477]**.

Functions of the Director General of Fair Trading: see the note to s 44 at **[11]**. See also the note "Director General of Fair Trading" to s 1 at **[1]**.

54 Report of Commission on monopoly reference

(1) A report of the Commission on a monopoly reference—
  (a) if the reference was made by the Director, shall be made to the Secretary of State, and
  (b) in any other case, shall be made to the Minister or Ministers by whom the reference was made.

(2) In making their report on a monopoly reference, the Commission shall include in it definite conclusions on the questions comprised in the reference, together with—
  (a) such an account of their reasons for those conclusions, and
  (b) such a survey of the general position with respect to the subject-matter of the reference, and of the developments which have led to that position,

as in their opinion are expedient for facilitating a proper understanding of those questions and of their conclusions.

(3)   Where, on a monopoly reference not limited to the facts, the Commission find that a monopoly situation exists and that facts found by the Commission in pursuance of their investigations under subsection (1) or subsection (2) of section 49 of this Act operate, or may be expected to operate, against the public interest, the report shall specify those facts, and the conclusions to be included in the report, in so far as they relate to the operation of those facts, shall specify the particular effects, adverse to the public interest, which in their opinion those facts have or may be expected to have; and the Commission—

(a)   shall, as part of their investigations, consider what action (if any) should be taken for the purpose of remedying or preventing those adverse effects, and

(b)   may, if they think fit, include in their report recommendations as to such action.

(4)   In paragraph (a) of subsection (3) of this section the reference to action to be taken for the purpose mentioned in that paragraph is a reference to action to be taken for that purpose either—

(a)   by one or more Ministers (including Ministers or departments of the Government of Northern Ireland) or other public authorities, or

(b)   by the person or (as the case may be) one or more of the persons in whose favour, in accordance with the findings of the Commission, the monopoly situation in question exists.

(5)   . . .

[20]

NOTES

Repealed by the Enterprise Act 2002, s 278(2), Sch 26, as from a day to be appointed; for a saving in relation to any monopoly reference made under s 50 or s 51 of this Act before such day or days as the Secretary of State may appoint, see s 276(1) of, and Sch 24, para 14 to, the 2002 Act at **[477]**.

Sub-s (5): repealed by the Competition Act 1998, s 74(1), (3), Sch 12, para 1(1), (3)(b), Sch 14, Pt I, subject to savings in Sch 13, Pt V, para 40 of the 1998 Act at **[231]**. Original text, as amended by the Restrictive Trade Practices Act 1976, s 44, Schs 5, 6, read as follows—

"(5)   Where, on a monopoly reference not limited to the facts, the Commission find—

(a)   that a monopoly situation exists, and

(b)   that the person (or, if more than one, any of the persons) in whose favour it exists is a party to an agreement to which [the Act of 1976] applies,

the Commission, in making their report on that reference, shall exclude from their consideration the question whether the provisions of that agreement, in so far as they are provisions by virtue of which it is an agreement to which . . . that Act applies, operate, or may be expected to operate, against the public interest; and subsection (3) of this section, in so far as it refers to facts found by the Commission in pursuance of their investigations, shall have effect subject to the provisions of this subsection."

Director: see the note "Functions of the Director General of Fair Trading" to s 44 at **[11]**. See also the note "Director General of Fair Trading" to s 1 at **[1]**.

---

55   Time-limit for report on monopoly reference

(1)   A monopoly reference shall specify a period within which the Commission are to report on the reference; and, if a report of the Commission on the reference—

(a)   is not made before the end of the period so specified, or

(b)   if one or more extended periods are allowed under the next following subsection, is not made before the end of that extended period or of the last of those extended periods, as the case may be,

the reference shall cease to have effect and no action, or (if action has already been taken) no further action, shall be taken in relation to that reference under this Act.

(2) *Directions may be given—*

   (a) *in the case of a monopoly reference made by the Director or by the Secretary of State otherwise than jointly with one or more Ministers, by the Secretary of State, or*

   (b) *in the case of a monopoly reference made by the Secretary of State jointly with one or more other Ministers, by the Secretary of State and that Minister or those Ministers acting jointly,*

allowing to the Commission such extended period for the purpose of reporting on the reference as may be specified in the directions, or, if the period has already been extended once or more than once by directions under this subsection, allowing to the Commission such further extended period for that purpose as may be so specified.

[21]

NOTES

Repealed by the Enterprise Act 2002, s 278(2), Sch 26, as from a day to be appointed; for a saving in relation to any monopoly reference made under s 50 or s 51 of this Act before such day or days as the Secretary of State may appoint, see s 276(1) of, and Sch 24, para 14 to, the 2002 Act at **[477]**.

Director: see the note "Functions of the Director General of Fair Trading" to s 44 at **[11]**. See also the note "Director General of Fair Trading" to s 1 at **[1]**.

56 Order of appropriate Minister on report on monopoly reference

(1) The provisions of this section shall have effect where a report of the Commission on a monopoly reference not limited to the facts has been laid before Parliament in accordance with the provisions of Part VII of this Act, and the conclusions of the Commission set out in the report, as so laid,—

   (a) *include conclusions to the effect that a monopoly situation exists and that facts found by the Commission in pursuance of their investigations under section 49 of this Act operate, or may be expected to operate, against the public interest, and*

   (b) *specify particular effects, adverse to the public interest, which in their opinion those facts have or may be expected to have.*

(2) In the circumstances mentioned in the preceding subsection the appropriate Minister may (subject to subsection (6) of this section) by order made by statutory instrument exercise such one or more of the powers specified in Parts I and II of Schedule 8 to this Act as he considers it requisite to exercise for the purpose of remedying or preventing the adverse effects specified in the report as mentioned in the preceding subsection; and those powers may be so exercised to such extent and in such manner as the appropriate Minister considers requisite for that purpose.

(3) In determining whether, or to what extent or in what manner, to exercise any of those powers, the appropriate Minister shall take into account any recommendations included in the report of the Commission in pursuance of section 54(3)(b) of this Act and any advice given by the Director under section 88 of this Act.

(4) Subject to the next following subsection, in this section "the appropriate Minister" means the Secretary of State.

(5) Where, in any such report as is mentioned in subsection (1) of this s22ection, the person or one of the persons specified as being the person or persons in whose favour the monopoly situation in question exists is a body corporate fulfilling the following conditions, that is to say—

   (a) *that the affairs of the body corporate are managed by its members, and*

   (b) *that by virtue of an enactment those members are appointed by a Minister,*

then for the purpose of making any order under this section in relation to that body corporate (but not for the purpose of making any such order in relation to any other person) "the appropriate Minister" in this section means the Minister by whom members of that body corporate are appointed.

(6)   In relation to any such body corporate as is mentioned in subsection (5) of this section, the powers exercisable by virtue of subsection (2) of this section shall not include the powers specified in Part II of Schedule 8 to this Act.

[22]

NOTES

Repealed by the Enterprise Act 2002, s 278(2), Sch 26, as from a day to be appointed; for a saving in relation to any monopoly reference made under s 50 or s 51 of this Act before such day or days as the Secretary of State may appoint, see s 276(1) of, and Sch 24, para 14 to, the 2002 Act at **[477]**.

Director: see the note "Functions of the Director General of Fair Trading" to s 44 at **[11]**. See also the note "Director General of Fair Trading" to s 1 at **[1]**.

Transitional provisions: for transitional provisions in relation to any order made (whether before, on or after the appointed day) by a Minister of the Crown under this section, see s 276(1) of, and Sch 24, paras 15(2)–(5), 17(1), (3)–(5) to, the Enterprise Act 2002 at **[477]**.

Orders: the Restriction on Agreements (Manufacturers and Importers of Motor Cars) Order 1982, SI 1982/1146; the Restriction on Agreement and Conduct (Tour Operators) Order 1987, SI 1987/1131, as amended by SI 2000/2031; the Restriction on Conduct (Specialist Advertising Services) Order 1988, SI 1988/1017; the Films (Exclusivity Agreements) Order 1989, SI 1989/271, as amended by SI 2000/2031; the Supply of Beer (Loan Ties, Licensed Premises and Wholesale Prices) Order 1989, SI 1989/2258, as amended by SI 2000/2031; the Supply of Beer (Tied Estate) Order 1989, SI 1989/2390, as amended by SI 1997/1740, SI 2000/2031; the Credit Cards (Merchant Acquisition) Order 1990, SI 1990/2158, as amended by SI 2000/2031; the Credit Cards (Price Discrimination) Order 1990, SI 1990/2159, as amended by SI 2000/2031; the Electrical Contracting (London Exhibition Halls) Order 1995, SI 1995/3299, as amended by SI 2000/2031; the Films (Exhibition Periods) Order 1996, SI 1996/3140; the Restriction on Agreements and Conduct (Specified Domestic Electrical Goods) Order 1998, SI 1998/1271, as amended by SI 2000/2031; the Supply of New Cars Order 2000, SI 2000/2088; the Foreign Package Holidays (Tour Operators and Travel Agents) Order 2000, SI 2000/2110; and the Foreign Package Holidays (Tour Operators and Travel Agents) Order 2001, SI 2001/2581. In addition, the following orders also have effect, by virtue of s 139(2), Sch 11, para 1 at **[92]**, **[103]**, as if made under this section: the Monopolies and Restrictive Practices (Dental Goods) Order 1951, SI 1951/1200; the Monopolies and Restrictive Practices (Imported Hardwood and Softwood Timber) Order 1960, SI 1960/1211; the Restriction on Agreements (Estate Agents) Order 1970, SI 1970/1696.

[Undertakings as alternative to monopoly reference by Director

56A   Proposals by Director

(1)   The Director may propose that the Secretary of State accept undertakings in lieu of the Director making a monopoly reference if—

> *(a) he considers that a monopoly situation exists and that there are facts relating to the monopoly situation which may now or in future operate against the public interest,*
> *(b) he intends, apart from the question of undertakings being accepted in lieu, to make a monopoly reference with respect to the existence of the monopoly situation and that the reference should be a monopoly reference not limited to the facts, and*
> *(c) he considers that undertakings offered to be given by particular persons would be sufficient to deal with such of the relevant adverse effects of the monopoly situation as he thinks need to be dealt with.*

(2)   A proposal under this section shall include—

> *(a) a statement of the terms of the proposed undertakings and the persons by whom they are proposed to be given,*
> *(b) a statement of the facts relating to the monopoly situation which the Director considers may now or in future operate against the public interest, and*

   (c) *a statement of the effects identified by the Director as the relevant adverse effects of the monopoly situation.*

   (3) For the purposes of the law relating to defamation, absolute privilege shall attach to anything included in a proposal under this section pursuant to subsection (2)(b) or (c) of this section.

   (4) In this section, references to the relevant adverse effects of a monopoly situation are to the particular effects, adverse to the public interest, which the facts relating to the monopoly situation may now or in future have.]

[23]

NOTES

   Inserted, together with preceding cross-heading, and ss 56B–56G, by the Deregulation and Contracting Out Act 1994, s 7(1).

   Repealed by the Enterprise Act 2002, s 278(2), Sch 26, as from a day to be appointed; for a saving in relation to any monopoly reference made under s 50 or s 51 of this Act before such day or days as the Secretary of State may appoint, see s 276(1) of, and Sch 24, para 14 to, the 2002 Act at **[477]**.

   Functions of the Director General of Fair Trading: references to the Director General of Fair Trading in this section and ss 56B–56G of this Act, so far as relating to certain activities are to be construed as including: (i) the Director General of Telecommunications (see the Deregulation and Contracting Out Act 1994, Sch 2, para 1(1)); (ii) the Gas and Electricity Markets Authority (see Sch 2, para 4(1) to that Act); (iii) the Director General of Electricity Supply for Northern Ireland (see Sch 2, para 5(1) to that Act); (iv) the Director General of Water Services (see Sch 2, para 8(1), 9, to that Act), and (v) the Rail Regulator (see Sch 2, para 11(1) to that Act). See also the note "Director General of Fair Trading" to s 1 at **[1]**.

   Transitional provisions: for transitional provisions in relation to undertakings accepted (whether before, on or after the appointed day) by a Minister of the Crown in pursuance of a proposal under this section, see s 276(1) of, and Sch 24, paras 15(1), (4), (5), 16 to, the Enterprise Act 2002 at **[477]**.

[56B   Proposals under section 56A: preparatory steps

   (1) The Director may only make a proposal under section 56A of this Act if—
   (a) *the first or second condition is met, and*
   (b) *the third condition is met.*

   (2) The first condition is that the Director has published in an appropriate manner a notice containing—
   (a) *each of the matters mentioned in subsection (5) of this section, and*
   (b) *the invitation mentioned in subsection (6) of this section.*

   (3) The second condition is that the Director has published in an appropriate manner—
   (a) *a notice containing the matters mentioned in paragraphs (a) and (b) of subsection (5) of this section, and*
   (b) *a notice containing—*
      (i) *the matters mentioned in paragraphs (c), (d), (e) and (f) of that subsection, and*
      (ii) *the invitation mentioned in subsection (6) of this section.*

   (4) The third condition is that the Director has considered any representations made to him in accordance with the notice under this section which contains the invitation mentioned in subsection (6) of this section.

   (5) The matters referred to above are—
   (a) *the identity of the person or persons in whose favour the Director considers the monopoly situation exists,*
   (b) *the terms of the proposed monopoly reference,*
   (c) *the facts relating to the monopoly situation which the Director considers may now or in future operate against the public interest,*

  (d) the effects identified by the Director as the particular effects, adverse to the public interest, which the facts relating to the monopoly situation may now or in future have,

  (e) the terms of the undertakings which the Director is, at the time of the notice, considering proposing the Secretary of State accept in lieu of the Director making the proposed monopoly reference ("the potential undertakings"), and

  (f) the identity of the persons by whom the potential undertakings would be given.

(6) The invitation referred to above is an invitation to make representations to the Director, within such time as he may specify, about the potential undertakings being the subject of a proposal under section 56A of this Act.

(7) For the purposes of the law relating to defamation, absolute privilege shall attach to anything contained in a notice published under this section.

(8) In this section, references to an appropriate manner, in relation to the publication of a notice by the Director, are to such manner as he considers most suitable for the purpose of bringing the notice to the attention of persons who, in his opinion, are likely to be interested in it.]

                      [24]

NOTES

 Inserted as noted to s 56A at **[23]**.

 Repealed by the Enterprise Act 2002, s 278(2), Sch 26, as from a day to be appointed; for a saving in relation to any monopoly reference made under s 50 or s 51 of this Act before such day or days as the Secretary of State may appoint, see s 276(1) of, and Sch 24, para 14 to, the 2002 Act at **[477]**.

 Functions of the Director General of Fair Trading: see the note to s 56A at **[23]**. See also the note "Director General of Fair Trading" to s 1 at **[1]**.

[56C Proposals under section 56A: exclusion of sensitive information

(1) The Director shall—

  (a) in formulating the statement required by section 56A(2)(b) or (c) of this Act, and

  (b) in publishing a notice under section 56B of this Act containing the matters mentioned in subsection (5)(c) and (d) of that section,

have regard to the need for excluding, so far as practicable, any matter to which subsection (2) or (3) of this section applies.

(2) This subsection applies to any matter which relates to the private affairs of an individual, where publication of that matter would or might, in the opinion of the Director, seriously and prejudicially affect the interests of that individual.

(3) This subsection applies to any matter which relates specifically to the affairs of a particular body of persons, whether corporate or unincorporate, where publication of that matter would or might, in the opinion of the Director, seriously and prejudicially affect the interests of that body, unless in his opinion the inclusion of that matter relating specifically to that body is necessary for the purposes of the statement or notice, as the case may be.]

                     [25]

NOTES

 Inserted as noted to s 56A at **[23]**.

 Repealed by the Enterprise Act 2002, s 278(2), Sch 26, as from a day to be appointed; for a saving in relation to any monopoly reference made under s 50 or s 51 of this Act before such day or days as the Secretary of State may appoint, see s 276(1) of, and Sch 24, para 14 to, the 2002 Act at **[477]**.

 Functions of the Director General of Fair Trading: see the note to s 56A at **[23]**. See also the note "Director General of Fair Trading" to s 1 at **[1]**.

[56D Acceptance by Secretary of State of proposals under section 56A

(1) Where the Secretary of State accepts a proposal under section 56A of this Act, then, within the period of twelve months from the date of acceptance of the undertakings to which the proposal relates, no monopoly reference may be made in the same, or substantially the same, terms as those published by the Director under section 56B of this Act preparatory to making the proposal.

(2) Subsection (1) of this section shall not prevent a reference being made if the Director—

 (a) considers that any of the undertakings has been breached, or needs to be varied or superseded, and

 (b) has given notice of that fact to the person responsible for giving the undertaking.

(3) The Secretary of State shall send to the Director a copy of every undertaking accepted pursuant to a proposal under section 56A of this Act.

(4) For the purposes of subsection (1) of this section, the Secretary of State shall be treated as accepting a proposal under section 56A of this Act if he accepts the undertakings to which the proposal relates, either in the form in which they were proposed or with such modifications as he thinks fit; and references in this Act to an undertaking accepted pursuant to a proposal under that section shall be construed accordingly.]

[26]

NOTES

Inserted as noted to s 56A at **[23]**.

Repealed by the Enterprise Act 2002, s 278(2), Sch 26, as from a day to be appointed; for a saving in relation to any monopoly reference made under s 50 or s 51 of this Act before such day or days as the Secretary of State may appoint, see s 276(1) of, and Sch 24, para 14 to, the 2002 Act at **[477]**.

Functions of the Director General of Fair Trading: see the note to s 56A at **[23]**. See also the note "Director General of Fair Trading" to s 1 at **[1]**.

[56E Review of undertakings

(1) The Director shall keep the carrying out of an undertaking to which this section applies under review, and from time to time consider whether, by reason of any change of circumstances, the undertaking is no longer appropriate and either—

 (a) one or more of the parties to it can be released from it, or

 (b) it needs to be varied or to be superseded by a new undertaking.

(2) If it appears to the Director—

 (a) that any one or more of the parties to an undertaking to which this section applies can be released from it,

 (b) that such an undertaking needs to be varied or to be superseded by a new undertaking, or

 (c) that there has been any failure to carry out such an undertaking,

he shall give to the Secretary of State such advice as he may think proper in the circumstances.

(3) Where the Director advises the Secretary of State under subsection (2) of this section that an undertaking needs to be varied or to be superseded by a new undertaking, he shall propose the terms of variation or, as the case may be, the new undertaking.

(4) The Director shall, if the Secretary of State so requests, give him advice with respect to the release, variation or superseding of an undertaking to which this section applies.

(5)   In this section, references to an undertaking to which this section applies are to an undertaking accepted—
    (a)   pursuant to a proposal under section 56A of this Act, or
    (b)   under section 56F of this Act.]

[27]

NOTES

Inserted as noted to s 56A at **[23]**.

Repealed by the Enterprise Act 2002, s 278(2), Sch 26, as from a day to be appointed; for a saving in relation to any monopoly reference made under s 50 or s 51 of this Act before such day or days as the Secretary of State may appoint, see s 276(1) of, and Sch 24, para 14 to, the 2002 Act at **[477]**.

Functions of the Director General of Fair Trading: see the note to s 56A at **[23]**. See also the note "Director General of Fair Trading" to s 1 at **[1]**.

[56F   Release, variation and replacement of undertakings

(1)   The Secretary of State may only—
    (a)   accept a new undertaking in place of an undertaking to which this section applies,
    (b)   release a person from such an undertaking, or
    (c)   agree to the variation of such an undertaking,
after considering the advice of the Director on the subject.

(2)   The Secretary of State shall send to the Director—
    (a)   a copy of every undertaking accepted under this section,
    (b)   particulars of every variation of an undertaking agreed under this section, and
    (c)   particulars of every release of a person from an undertaking under this section.

(3)   In this section, references to an undertaking to which this section applies are to an undertaking accepted—
    (a)   pursuant to a proposal under section 56A of this Act, or
    (b)   under this section.]

[28]

NOTES

Inserted as noted to s 56A at **[23]**.

Repealed by the Enterprise Act 2002, s 278(2), Sch 26, as from a day to be appointed; for a saving in relation to any monopoly reference made under s 50 or s 51 of this Act before such day or days as the Secretary of State may appoint, see s 276(1) of, and Sch 24, para 14 to, the 2002 Act at **[477]**.

Functions of the Director General of Fair Trading: see the note to s 56A at **[23]**. See also the note "Director General of Fair Trading" to s 1 at **[1]**.

Transitional provisions: for transitional provisions in relation to undertakings accepted (whether before, on or after the appointed day) by a Minister of the Crown under this section, see s 276(1) of, and Sch 24, paras 15(1), (4), (5), 16 to, the Enterprise Act 2002 at **[477]**.

[56G   Publication of undertakings etc

(1)   The Secretary of State shall arrange for the publication in such manner as he considers appropriate of—
    (a)   every undertaking accepted—
        (i)   pursuant to a proposal under section 56A of this Act, or
        (ii)   under section 56F of this Act, and
    (b)   every variation or release under that section.

(2)   Where the Secretary of State accepts undertakings pursuant to a proposal under section 56A of this Act, he shall arrange for the statements included in the

proposal under subsection (2)(b) and (c) of that section to be published in such manner as he considers appropriate.

(3) If it appears to the Secretary of State that the publication of any matter contained in a statement which falls to be published under subsection (2) of this section would be against the public interest, he shall exclude that matter from the statement as published under that subsection.

(4) Without prejudice to subsection (3) of this section, if the Secretary of State considers that it would not be in the public interest to disclose—

> *(a) any matter contained in a statement which falls to be published under subsection (2) of this section relating to the private affairs of an individual whose interests would, in the opinion of the Secretary of State, be seriously and prejudicially affected by the publication of that matter, or*
>
> *(b) any matter contained in such a statement relating specifically to the affairs of a particular person whose interests would, in the opinion of the Secretary of State, be seriously and prejudicially affected by the publication of that matter,*

the Secretary of State shall exclude that matter from the statement as published under subsection (2) of this section.]

[29]

NOTES

Inserted as noted to s 56A at **[23]**.

Repealed by the Enterprise Act 2002, s 278(2), Sch 26, as from a day to be appointed; for a saving in relation to any monopoly reference made under s 50 or s 51 of this Act before such day or days as the Secretary of State may appoint, see s 276(1) of, and Sch 24, para 14 to, the 2002 Act at **[477]**.

Functions of the Director General of Fair Trading: see the note to s 56A at **[23]**. See also the note "Director General of Fair Trading" to s 1 at **[1]**.

PART V
MERGERS

NOTES

Fees: The Secretary of State may by order require the payment to him or the OFT of such fees as may be prescribed in connection with the exercise by the Secretary of State, the OFT and the Competition Commission of their functions under, or by virtue of, Part V of this Act: see the Enterprise Act 2002, s 121 at **[367]**.

Newspaper merger references

57 Meaning of "newspaper", "transfer of newspaper or of newspaper assets" and related expressions

(1) In this Part of this Act—

> (a) "newspaper" means a daily, Sunday or local (other than daily or Sunday) newspaper circulating wholly or mainly in the United Kingdom or in a part of the United Kingdom;
>
> [(b) "newspaper proprietor" includes (in addition to an actual proprietor of a newspaper) any member of a group of persons of which another member is an actual proprietor of a newspaper.

(1A) In this Part of this Act, any reference to the newspapers of a newspaper proprietor ("NP") is to—

> (a) all newspapers of which NP is an actual proprietor, and
>
> (b) all newspapers of which a member of a group of persons of which NP is a member is an actual proprietor.]

(2) In this Part of this Act "transfer of a newspaper or of newspaper assets" means any of the following transactions, that is to say—

(a) any transaction (whether involving a transfer or not) by virtue of which a person would become, or would acquire the right to become[—

(i) an actual proprietor of a newspaper, or

(ii) a person with a primary or secondary controlling interest in an actual proprietor of a newspaper;]

(b) any transfer of assets necessary to the continuation of a newspaper as a separate newspaper (including goodwill or the right to use the name of the newspaper);

(c) any transfer of plant or premises used in the publication of a newspaper, other than a transfer made without a view to a change in the ownership or control of the newspaper or to its ceasing publication;

and "the newspaper concerned in the transfer", in relation to any transaction falling within paragraph (a), paragraph (b) or paragraph (c) of this subsection, means the newspaper in relation to which (as mentioned in that paragraph) the transaction is or is to be effected.

(3) In this Part of this Act "average circulation per day of publication" in relation to a newspaper, means its average circulation for the appropriate period, ascertained by dividing the number of copies to which its circulation amounts for that period by the number of days on which the newspaper was published during that period (circulation being calculated on the basis of actual sales in the United Kingdom of the newspaper as published on those days); and for the purposes of this subsection "the appropriate period"—

(a) in a case in which an application is made for consent under the next following section, means the period of six months ending six weeks before the date of the application, or

(b) in a case in which a transfer or purported transfer is made without any such application for consent, means the period of six months ending six weeks before the date of the transfer or purported transfer.

(4) For the purposes of this section a person has a [primary] controlling interest in a body corporate if (but only if) he can, directly or indirectly, determine the manner in which one-quarter of the votes which could be cast at a general meeting of the body corporate are to be cast on matters, and in circumstances, not of such a description as to bring into play any special voting rights or restrictions on voting rights.

(5) For the purposes of this section a person ("A") has a secondary controlling interest in a body corporate ("B") if, without having a primary controlling interest in B—

(a) A has a primary controlling interest in a body corporate which has a primary controlling interest in B, or

(b) A is connected to B by a chain of any number of other bodies corporate, in the first of which A has a primary controlling interest, in the second of which the first has a primary controlling interest, and so on, the last such body corporate having a primary controlling interest in B.

(6) For the purposes of this section a group of persons consists of any number of persons of whom the first is—

(a) a person other than a body corporate, or

(b) a body corporate in which no other person has a primary controlling interest,

and the others are the bodies corporate in which the first has a primary or secondary controlling interest.

(7) In determining for the purposes of subsection (6)(b) of this section whether a body corporate ("X") is one in which another person has a primary controlling

interest, there shall be disregarded any body corporate in which X has a primary or secondary controlling interest.]

NOTES

Sub-s (1): para (b) substituted, together with sub-s (1A), for original para (b) by the Deregulation and Contracting Out Act 1994, s 8(1), (2), (6), and is deemed always to have had effect.

Sub-s (1A): substituted as noted above.

Sub-s (2): words in square brackets substituted by the Deregulation and Contracting Out Act 1994, s 8(1), (3), (6), and are deemed always to have had effect.

Sub-s (4): words in square brackets inserted by the Deregulation and Contracting Out Act 1994, s 8(1), (4), (6), and are deemed always to have had effect.

Sub-ss (5)–(7): inserted by the Deregulation and Contracting Out Act 1994, s 8(1), (5), (6), and deemed always to have had effect.

Application: the Monopolies and Mergers Act 1965, s 8 (repealed by this Act) is deemed never to have applied to transactions to which it would not have applied had there been in force at the time of the transaction amendments of that Act corresponding to the amendments made to this Act by the Deregulation and Contracting Out Act 1994, s 8; see s 8(7) of the 1994 Act.

Transfer of a newspaper or of newspaper assets: the prohibition imposed by the Competition Act 1998, s 2(1) at **[134]**, does not apply to an agreement to the extent to which it constitutes, or would if carried out constitute, a transfer of a newspaper or of newspaper assets for the purposes of this section (see s 3(1)(a) of, Sch 1, para 3(1) to, that Act at **[135]**, **[207]**); and the prohibition imposed by s 18(1) of the 1998 Act at **[149]**, does not apply to conduct to the extent to which it constitutes such a transfer, or it is directly related and necessary to the implementation of the transfer (see s 19(1)(a) of, and Sch 1, para 3(2) to, the 1998 Act, at **[150]**, **[207]**).

58   Prohibition of certain newspaper mergers

(1)   Subject to the following provisions of this section, a transfer of a newspaper or of newspaper assets to a newspaper proprietor whose newspapers have an average circulation per day of publication amounting, together with that of the newspaper concerned in the transfer, to 500,000 or more copies shall be unlawful and void, unless the transfer is made with written consent given (conditionally or unconditionally) by the Secretary of State.

(2)   Except as provided by subsections (3) and (4) of this section and by section 60(3) of this Act, the consent of the Secretary of State under the preceding subsection shall not be given in respect of a transfer until after the Secretary of State has received a report on the matter from the Commission.

(3)   Where the Secretary of State is satisfied that the newspaper concerned in the transfer is not economic as a going concern and as a separate newspaper, then—

    (a)   if he is also satisfied that, if the newspaper is to continue as a separate newspaper, the case is one of urgency, he may give his consent to the transfer without requiring a report from the Commission under this section;

    (b)   if he is satisfied that the newspaper is not intended to continue as a separate newspaper, he shall give his consent to the transfer, and shall give it unconditionally, without requiring such a report.

(4)   If the Secretary of State is satisfied that the newspaper concerned in the transfer has an average circulation per day of publication of not more than [50,000] copies, he may give his consent to the transfer without requiring a report from the Commission under this section.

(5)   The Secretary of State may by order made by statutory instrument provide, subject to any transitional provisions contained in the order, that for any number specified in subsection (1) or subsection (4) of this section (whether as originally enacted or as previously varied by an order under this subsection) there shall be substituted such other number as is specified in the order.

(6)   In this section "satisfied" means satisfied by such evidence as the Secretary of State may require.

[31]

NOTES

Sub-s (4): figure in square brackets substituted by the Fair Trading Act (Amendment) (Newspaper Mergers) Order 1995, SI 1995/1351, art 2.

Orders: the Fair Trading Act (Amendment) (Newspaper Mergers) Order 1995, SI 1995/1351.

59 Newspaper merger reference

(1)   Where an application is made to the Secretary of State for his consent to a transfer of a newspaper or of newspaper assets, the Secretary of State, subject to the next following subsection, shall, within one month after receiving the application, refer the matter to the Commission for investigation and report.

(2)   The Secretary of State shall not make a reference to the Commission under the preceding subsection in a case where—
  (a) by virtue of subsection (3) of section 58 of this Act he is required to give his consent unconditionally without requiring a report from the Commission under this section, or
  (b) by virtue of subsection (3) or subsection (4) of that section he has power to give his consent without requiring such a report from the Commission, and determines to exercise that power,

or where the application is expressed to depend on the operation of subsection (3) or subsection (4) of that section.

(3)   On a reference made to them under this section (in this Act referred to as a "newspaper merger reference") the Commission shall report to the Secretary of State whether the transfer in question may be expected to operate against the public interest, taking into account all matters which appear in the circumstances to be relevant and, in particular, the need for accurate presentation of news and free expression of opinion.

[32]

60 Time-limit for report on newspaper merger reference

(1)   A report of the Commission on a newspaper merger reference shall be made before the end of [such period (not being longer than three months beginning with the date of the reference) as may be specified in the] reference or of such further period (if any) as the Secretary of State may allow for the purpose in accordance with the next following subsection.

(2)   The Secretary of State shall not allow any further period for a report on such a reference except on representations made by the Commission and on being satisfied that there are special reasons why the report cannot be made within the [period specified in the newspaper merger reference]; and the Secretary of State shall allow only one such further period on any one reference, and no such further period shall be longer than three months.

(3)   If on such a reference the Commission have not made their report before the end of the period specified in [the newspaper merger reference] or of any further period allowed under subsection (2) of this section, the Secretary of State may, without waiting for the report, give his consent to the transfer to which the reference relates.

[33]

NOTES

Sub-ss (1)–(3): words in square brackets substituted by the Companies Act 1989, s 133, Sch 20, para 2, in relation to newspaper merger references made on or after 16 November 1989.

61   Report on newspaper merger reference

(1)   In making their report on a newspaper merger reference, the Commission shall include in it definite conclusions on the questions comprised in the reference, together with—

(a) such an account of their reasons for those conclusions, and

(b) such a survey of the general position with respect to the transfer of a newspaper or of newspaper assets to which the reference relates, and of the developments which have led to that position,

as in their opinion are expedient for facilitating a proper understanding of those questions and of their conclusions.

(2)   Where on such a reference the Commission find that the transfer of a newspaper or of newspaper assets in question might operate against the public interest, the Commission shall consider whether any (and, if so, what) conditions might be attached to any consent to the transfer in order to prevent the transfer from so operating, and may, if they think fit, include in their report recommendations as to such conditions.

[34]

62   Enforcement provisions relating to newspaper mergers

(1)   Any person who is knowingly concerned in, or privy to, a purported transfer of a newspaper or of newspaper assets which is unlawful by virtue of section 58 of this Act shall be guilty of an offence.

(2)   Where under that section the consent of the Secretary of State is given to a transfer of a newspaper or of newspaper assets, but is given subject to one or more conditions, any person who is knowingly concerned in, or privy to, a breach of that condition, or of any of those conditions, as the case may be, shall be guilty of an offence.

(3)   A person guilty of an offence under this section shall be liable, on conviction on indictment, to imprisonment for a term not exceeding two years or to a fine or to both.

(4)   No proceedings for an offence under this section shall be instituted—

(a) in England or Wales, except by, or with the consent of, the Director of Public Prosecutions, or

(b) in Northern Ireland, except by, or with the consent of, the Director of Public Prosecutions for Northern Ireland.

[35]

Other merger references

63   Merger references to which ss 64 to 75 apply

(1)   Sections 64 [to 75K of this Act shall not have effect in relation to] newspaper merger references; and accordingly in those sections "merger reference" shall be construed—

(a) as not including a reference made under section 59 of this Act, but

(b) as including any merger reference relating to a transfer of a newspaper or of newspaper assets, if the reference is made under section 64 or section 75 of this Act in a case falling within section 59(2) of this Act.

(2)   In the following provisions of this Part of this Act "enterprise" means the activities, or part of the activities, of a business.

[36]

NOTES

Repealed by the Enterprise Act 2002, s 278(2), Sch 26, as from a day to be appointed; for savings in relation to cases where two or more enterprises ceased to be distinct enterprises (within the meaning of Part V of this Act) before such day or days as the Secretary of State may appoint, see s 276(1) of, and Sch 24, para 13 to, the 2002 Act at **[477]**.

Sub-s (1): words in square brackets substituted by the Companies Act 1989, s 153, Sch 20, para 3.

64 Merger situation qualifying for investigation

(1)   A merger reference may be made to the Commission by the Secretary of State where it appears to him that it is or may be the fact that two or more enterprises (in this section referred to as "the relevant enterprises"), of which one at least was carried on in the United Kingdom or by or under the control of a body corporate incorporated in the United Kingdom, have, at a time or in circumstances falling within subsection (4) of this section, ceased to be distinct enterprises, and that either—

(a) as a result, the condition specified in subsection (2) or in subsection (3) of this section prevails, or does so to a greater extent, with respect to the supply of goods or services of any description, or

(b) the value of the assets taken over exceeds [£70 million].

(2)   The condition referred to in subsection (1)(a) of this section, in relation to the supply of goods of any description, is that at least one-quarter of all the goods of that description which are supplied in the United Kingdom, or in a substantial part of the United Kingdom, either—

(a) are supplied by one and the same person or are supplied to one and the same person, or

(b) are supplied by the persons by whom the relevant enterprises (so far as they continue to be carried on) are carried on, or are supplied to those persons.

(3)   The condition referred to in subsection (1)(a) of this section, in relation to the supply of services of any description, is that the supply of services of that description in the United Kingdom, or in a substantial part of the United Kingdom, is, to the extent of at least one-quarter, either—

(a) supply by one and the same person, or supply for one and the same person, or

(b) supply by the persons by whom the relevant enterprises (so far as they continue to be carried on) are carried on, or supply for those persons.

(4)   For the purposes of subsection (1) of this section enterprises shall be taken to have ceased to be distinct enterprises at a time or in circumstances falling within this subsection if either—

(a) they did so not earlier than [four months] before the date on which the merger reference relating to them is to be made, or

(b) they did so under or in consequence of arrangements or transactions which were entered into without prior notice being given to the Secretary of State or to the Director of material facts about the proposed arrangements or transactions and in circumstances in which those facts had not been made public, and notice of those facts was not given to the Secretary of State or to the Director or made public more than [four months] before the date mentioned in the preceding paragraph.

(5)   In determining whether to make a merger reference to the Commission the Secretary of State shall have regard, with a view to the prevention or removal of uncertainty, to the need for making a determination as soon as is reasonably practicable.

(6)   On making a merger reference, the Secretary of State shall arrange for it to be published in such manner as he thinks most suitable for bringing it to the attention of persons who in his opinion would be affected by it.

(7)   The Secretary of State may by order made by statutory instrument provide, subject to any transitional provisions contained in the order, that for the sum specified in subsection (1)(b) of this section (whether as originally enacted or as previously varied by an order under this subsection) there shall be substituted such other sum (not being less than £5 million) as is specified in the order.

(8)   The fact that two or more enterprises have ceased to be distinct enterprises in the circumstances described in subsection (1) of this section (including in those circumstances the result specified in paragraph (a), or fulfilment of the condition specified in paragraph (b), of that subsection) shall, for the purposes of this Act, be regarded as creating a merger situation qualifying for investigation; and in this Act "merger situation qualifying for investigation" and any reference to the creation of such a situation shall be construed accordingly.

(9)   In this section "made public" means so publicised as to be generally known or readily ascertainable.

[37]

NOTES

Repealed by the Enterprise Act 2002, s 278(2), Sch 26, as from a day to be appointed; for savings in relation to cases where two or more enterprises ceased to be distinct enterprises (within the meaning of Part V of this Act) before such day or days as the Secretary of State may appoint, see s 276(1) of, and Sch 24, para 13 to, the 2002 Act at **[477]**.

Sub-s (1): words in square brackets in para (b) substituted by the Merger References (Increase in Value of Assets) Order 1994, SI 1994/72, art 2.

Sub-s (4): words in square brackets in paras (a), (b) substituted by the Deregulation (Fair Trading Act 1973) (Amendment) (Merger Reference Time Limits) Order 1996, SI 1996/345, art 2.

A merger reference may be made under this section in a case in which the relevant enterprises ceased to be distinct enterprises at a time and in circumstances not falling within sub-s (4) if by reason of Council Regulation 4064/89/EEC of 21 December 1989 on the Control of Concentrations between Undertakings or anything done under or in accordance with that Regulation the reference could not have been made earlier than six months before the date on which it is to be made: see the EEC Merger Control (Consequential Provisions) Regulations 1990, SI 1990/1563 at **[2175]**.

The Director: see the note "Director General of Fair Trading" to s 1 at **[1]**.

Orders: the Merger References (Increase in Value of Assets) Order 1994, SI 1994/72 (increased the sum specified in sub-s (1)(b) from £30 million to £70 million, with effect from 9 February 1994, but not so as to have effect in relation to any merger reference made to the Monopolies and Mergers Commission before that date).

65   Enterprises ceasing to be distinct enterprises

(1)   For the purposes of this Part of this Act any two enterprises shall be regarded as ceasing to be distinct enterprises if either—

(a)   they are brought under common ownership or common control (whether or not the business to which either of them formerly belonged continues to be carried on under the same or different ownership or control), or

(b)   either of the enterprises ceases to be carried on at all and does so in consequence of any arrangements or transaction entered into to prevent competition between the enterprises.

(2)   For the purposes of the preceding subsection enterprises shall (without prejudice to the generality of the words "common control" in that subsection) be regarded as being under common control if they are—

(a)   enterprises of interconnected bodies corporate, or

(b)   enterprises carried on by two or more bodies corporate of which one and the same person or group of persons has control, or

(c) an enterprise carried on by a body corporate and an enterprise carried on by a person or group of persons having control of that body corporate.

(3)   A person or group of persons able, directly or indirectly, to control or materially to influence the policy of a body corporate, or the policy of any person in carrying on an enterprise, but without having a controlling interest in that body corporate or in that enterprise, may for the purposes of subsections (1) and (2) of this section be treated as having control of it.

(4)   For the purposes of subsection (1)(a) of this section, in so far as it relates to bringing two or more enterprises under common control, a person or group of persons may be treated as bringing an enterprise under his or their control if—

(a) being already able to control or materially to influence the policy of the person carrying on the enterprise, that person or group of persons acquires a controlling interest in the enterprise or, in the case of an enterprise carried on by a body corporate, acquires a controlling interest in that body corporate, or

(b) being already able materially to influence the policy of the person carrying on the enterprise, that person or group of persons becomes able to control that policy.

[38]

NOTES

Repealed by the Enterprise Act 2002, s 278(2), Sch 26, as from a day to be appointed; for savings in relation to cases where two or more enterprises ceased to be distinct enterprises (within the meaning of Part V of this Act) before such day as the Secretary of State may appoint, see s 276(1) of, and Sch 24, para 13 to, the 2002 Act at **[477]**.

Shall be regarded as ceasing to be distinct enterprises: the prohibition imposed by the Competition Act 1998, s 2(1) at **[134]**, does not apply to the extent to which an agreement results, or if carried out would result, in any two enterprises ceasing to be distinct enterprises for the purposes of Pt V of this Act (see s 3(1)(a) of, and Sch 1, para 1(1) to, the 1998 Act, at **[135]**, **[207]**, and see further Sch 1, paras 1(2)–(4), 4, 5 thereto at **[207]**); and the prohibition imposed by s 18(1) of the 1998 Act, does not apply to the extent to which conduct results in any two enterprises ceasing to be distinct enterprises for the purposes of Pt V of this Act, or is directly related and necessary to the attainment of that result (see s 19(1)(a) of, and Sch 1, para 2(1) to, the 1998 Act, at **[150]**, **[207]**, and see further Sch 1, para 2(2) thereto at **[207]**).

66   Time when enterprises cease to be distinct

(1)   Where under or in consequence of the same arrangements or transaction, or under or in consequence of successive arrangements or transactions between the same parties or interests, successive events to which this subsection applies occur within a period of two years, then for the purposes of a merger reference those events may, if the Secretary of State [or the Commission] thinks fit, be treated as having occurred simultaneously on the date on which the latest of them occurred.

(2)   The preceding subsection applies to any event whereby, under or in consequence of the arrangements or the transaction or transactions in question, any enterprises cease as between themselves to be distinct enterprises.

(3)   For the purposes of subsection (1) of this section any arrangements or transactions may be treated by the Secretary of State [or the Commission] as arrangements or transactions between the same interests if it appears to him to be appropriate that they should be so treated, having regard to the persons who are substantially concerned in them.

(4)   Subject to the preceding provisions of this section [and to section 66A of this Act], the time at which any two enterprises cease to be distinct enterprises, where they do so under or in consequence of any arrangements or transaction not having immediate effect, or having immediate effect in part only, shall be taken to be the

time when the parties to the arrangements or transaction become bound to such extent as will result, on effect being given to their obligations, in the enterprises ceasing to be distinct enterprises.

(5)　In accordance with subsection (4) of this section (but without prejudice to the generality of that subsection) for the purpose of determining the time at which any two enterprises cease to be distinct enterprises no account shall be taken of any option or other conditional right until the option is exercised or the condition is satisfied.

[39]

NOTES

Repealed by the Enterprise Act 2002, s 278(2), Sch 26, as from a day to be appointed; for savings in relation to cases where two or more enterprises ceased to be distinct enterprises (within the meaning of Part V of this Act) before such day as the Secretary of State may appoint, see s 276(1) of, and Sch 24, para 13 to, the 2002 Act at **[477]**.

Sub-ss (1), (3), (4): words in square brackets inserted by the Companies Act 1989, s 153, Sch 20, paras 4, 10, except in relation to any merger reference made before 16 November 1989.

[66A　Obtaining control by stages

(1)　Where an enterprise is brought under the control of a person or group of persons in the course of two or more transactions (referred to in this section as a "series of transactions") falling within subsection (2) of this section, those transactions may, if the Secretary of State or, as the case may be, the Commission thinks fit, be treated for the purposes of a merger reference as having occurred simultaneously on the date on which the latest of them occurred.

(2)　The transactions falling within this subsection are—
(a)　any transaction which—
　　(i)　enables that person or group of persons directly or indirectly to control or materially to influence the policy of any person carrying on the enterprise,
　　(ii)　enables that person or group of persons to do so to a greater degree, or
　　(iii)　is a step (whether direct or indirect) towards enabling that person or group of persons to do so, and
(b)　any transaction whereby that person or group of persons acquires a controlling interest in the enterprise or, where the enterprise is carried on by a body corporate, in that body corporate.

(3)　Where a series of transactions includes a transaction falling within subsection (2)(b) of this section, any transaction occurring after the occurrence of that transaction is to be disregarded for the purposes of subsection (1) of this section.

(4)　Where the period within which a series of transactions occurs exceeds two years, the transactions that may be treated as mentioned in subsection (1) of this section are any of those transactions that occur within a period of two years.

(5)　Sections 65(2) to (4) and 77(1) and (4) to (6) of this Act apply for the purposes of this section to determine whether an enterprise is brought under the control of a person or group of persons and whether a transaction falls within subsection (2) of this section as they apply for the purposes of section 65 of this Act to determine whether enterprises are brought under common control.

(6)　In determining for the purposes of this section the time at which any transaction occurs, no account shall be taken of any option or other conditional right until the option is exercised or the condition is satisfied.]

[40]

67 Valuation of assets taken over

(1)   The provisions of this section shall have effect for the purposes of section 64(1)(b) of this Act.

(2)   Subject to subsection (4) of this section, the value of the assets taken over—
(a) shall be determined by taking the total value of the assets employed in, or appropriated to, the enterprises which cease to be distinct enterprises, except
[(i) any enterprise which remains under the same ownership and control, or
(ii) if none of the enterprises remains under the same ownership and control, the enterprise having the assets with the highest value, and]
(b) shall be so determined by reference to the values at which, on the enterprises ceasing to be distinct enterprises or (if they have not then done so) on the making of the merger reference to the Commission, the assets stand in the books of the relevant business, less any relevant provisions for depreciation, renewals or diminution in value.

(3)   For the purposes of subsection (2) of this section any assets of a body corporate which, on a change in the control of the body corporate or of any enterprise of it, are dealt with in the same way as assets appropriated to any such enterprise shall be treated as appropriated to that enterprise.

(4)   Where in accordance with subsection (1) of section 66 [or subsection (1) of section 66A] of this Act events to which [either of those subsections] applies are treated as having occurred simultaneously, subsection (2) of this section shall apply with such adjustments as appear to the Secretary of State or to the Commission to be appropriate.

[41]

68 Supplementary provisions as to merger situations qualifying for investigation

(1)   In relation to goods or services of any description which are the subject of different forms of supply—
(a) references in subsection (2) of section 64 of this Act to the supply of goods, or
(b) references in subsection (3) of that section to the supply of services,

shall be construed in whichever of the following ways appears to the Secretary of State or the Commission, as the case may be, to be appropriate in all the

PART I
STATUTES

circumstances, that is to say, as references to any of those forms of supply taken separately, to all those forms of supply taken together, or to any of those forms of supply taken in groups.

(2) For the purposes of the preceding subsection the Secretary of State or the Commission may treat goods or services as being the subject of different forms of supply whenever the transactions in question differ as to their nature, their parties, their terms or their surrounding circumstances, and the difference is one which, in the opinion of the Secretary of State or of the Commission, as the case may be, ought for the purposes of that subsection to be treated as a material difference.

(3) For the purpose of determining whether the proportion of one-quarter mentioned in subsection (2) or subsection (3) of section 64 of this Act is fulfilled with respect to goods or services of any description, the Secretary of State or the Commission, as the case may be, shall apply such criterion (whether it be value or cost or price or quantity or capacity or number of workers employed or some other criterion, of whatever nature) or such combination of criteria as may appear to the Secretary of State or the Commission to be most suitable in all the circumstances.

(4) The criteria for determining when goods or services can be treated, for the purposes of section 64 of this Act, as goods or services of a separate description shall be such as in any particular case the Secretary of State [or, as the case may be, the Commission] thinks most suitable in the circumstances of that case.

[42]

NOTES

Repealed by the Enterprise Act 2002, s 278(2), Sch 26, as from a day to be appointed; for savings in relation to cases where two or more enterprises ceased to be distinct enterprises (within the meaning of Part V of this Act) before such day as the Secretary of State may appoint, see s 276(1) of, and Sch 24, para 13 to, the 2002 Act at **[477]**.

Sub-s (4): words in square brackets inserted by the Companies Act 1989, s 153, Sch 20, paras 6, 10, except in relation to any merger reference made before 16 November 1989.

---

69   Different kinds of merger references

(1) Subject to the following provisions of this Part of this Act, on a merger reference the Commission shall investigate and report on the questions—

    (a) whether a merger situation qualifying for investigation has been created, and

    (b) if so, whether the creation of that situation operates, or may be expected to operate, against the public interest.

(2) A merger reference may be so framed as to require the Commission, in relation to the question whether a merger situation qualifying for investigation has been created, to exclude from consideration paragraph (a) of subsection (1) of section 64 of this Act, or to exclude from consideration paragraph (b) of that subsection, or to exclude one of those paragraphs if the Commission find the other satisfied.

(3) In relation to the question whether any such result as is mentioned in section 64(1)(a) of this Act has arisen, a merger reference may be so framed as to require the Commission to confine their investigation to the supply of goods or services in a specified part of the United Kingdom.

(4) A merger reference may require the Commission, if they find that a merger situation qualifying for investigation has been created, to limit their consideration thereafter to such elements in, or possible consequences of, the creation of that

situation as may be specified in the reference, and to consider whether, in respect only of those elements or possible consequences, the situation operates, or may be expected to operate, against the public interest.

[43]

NOTES

Repealed by the Enterprise Act 2002, s 278(2), Sch 26, as from a day to be appointed; for savings in relation to cases where two or more enterprises ceased to be distinct enterprises (within the meaning of Part V of this Act) before such day as the Secretary of State may appoint, see s 276(1) of, and Sch 24, para 13 to, the 2002 Act at **[477]**.

70   Time-limit for report on merger reference

(1)   Every merger reference shall specify a period (not being longer than six months beginning with the date of the reference) within which a report on the reference is to be made; and a report of the Commission on a merger reference shall not have effect, and no action shall be taken in relation to it under this Act, unless the report is made before the end of that period or of such further period (if any) as may be allowed by the Secretary of State in accordance with the next following subsection.

(2)   The Secretary of State shall not allow any further period for a report on a merger reference except on representations made by the Commission and on being satisfied that there are special reasons why the report cannot be made within the period specified in the reference; and the Secretary of State shall allow only one such further period on any one reference, and no such further period shall be longer than three months.

[44]

NOTES

Repealed by the Enterprise Act 2002, s 278(2), Sch 26, as from a day to be appointed; for savings in relation to cases where two or more enterprises ceased to be distinct enterprises (within the meaning of Part V of this Act) before such day as the Secretary of State may appoint, see s 276(1) of, and Sch 24, para 13 to, the 2002 Act at **[477]**.

71   Variation of certain merger references

(1)   Subject to the following provisions of this section, the Secretary of State may at any time vary a merger reference . . .

(2)   . . .

(3)   Without prejudice to the powers of the Secretary of State under section 70 of this Act, a merger reference shall not be varied so as to specify a period within which a report on the reference is to be made which is different from the period specified in the reference in accordance with that section.

[45]

NOTES

Repealed by the Enterprise Act 2002, s 278(2), Sch 26, as from a day to be appointed; for savings in relation to cases where two or more enterprises ceased to be distinct enterprises (within the meaning of Part V of this Act) before such day as the Secretary of State may appoint, see s 276(1) of, and Sch 24, para 13 to, the 2002 Act at **[477]**.

Sub-s (1): words omitted repealed by the Companies Act 1989, ss 153, 212, Sch 20, paras 7(a), 10, Sch 24, except in relation to any merger reference made before 16 November 1989.

Sub-s (2): repealed by the Companies Act 1989, ss 153, 212, Sch 20, paras 7(b), 10, Sch 24, except in relation to any merger reference made before 16 November 1989.

72   Report of Commission on merger reference

(1)   In making their report on a merger reference, the Commission shall include in it definite conclusions on the questions comprised in the reference, together with—

   (a)   such an account of their reasons for those conclusions, and

   (b)   such a survey of the general position with respect to the subject-matter of the reference, and of the developments which have led to that position,

as in their opinion are expedient for facilitating a proper understanding of those questions and of their conclusions.

(2)   Where on a merger reference the Commission find that a merger situation qualifying for investigation has been created and that the creation of that situation operates or may be expected to operate against the public interest (or, in a case falling within subsection (4) of section 69 of this Act, find that one or more elements in or consequences of that situation which were specified in the reference in accordance with that subsection so operate or may be expected so to operate) the Commission shall specify in their report the particular effects, adverse to the public interest, which in their opinion the creation of that situation (or, as the case may be, those elements in or consequences of it) have or may be expected to have; and the Commission—

   (a)   shall, as part of their investigations, consider what action (if any) should be taken for the purpose of remedying or preventing those adverse effects, and

   (b)   may, if they think fit, include in their report recommendations as to such action.

(3)   In paragraph (a) of subsection (2) of this section the reference to action to be taken for the purpose mentioned in that paragraph is a reference to action to be taken for that purpose either—

   (a)   by one or more Ministers (including Ministers or departments of the Government of Northern Ireland) or other public authorities, or

   (b)   by one or more persons specified in the report as being persons carrying on, owning or controlling any of the enterprises which, in accordance with the conclusions of the Commission, have ceased to be distinct enterprises.

[46]

NOTES

Repealed by the Enterprise Act 2002, s 278(2), Sch 26, as from a day to be appointed; for savings in relation to cases where two or more enterprises ceased to be distinct enterprises (within the meaning of Part V of this Act) before such day as the Secretary of State may appoint, see s 276(1) of, and Sch 24, para 13 to, the 2002 Act at **[477]**.

73   Order of Secretary of State on report on merger reference

(1)   The provisions of this section shall have effect where a report of the Commission on a merger reference has been laid before Parliament in accordance with the provisions of Part VII of this Act, and the conclusions of the Commission set out in the report, as so laid,—

   (a)   include conclusions to the effect that a merger situation qualifying for investigation has been created and that its creation, or particular elements in or consequences of it specified in the report, operate or may be expected to operate against the public interest, and

   (b)   specify particular effects, adverse to the public interest, which in the opinion of the Commission the creation of that situation, or (as the case may be) those elements in or consequences of it, have or may be expected to have.

(2)   In the circumstances mentioned in the preceding subsection the Secretary of State may by order made by statutory instrument exercise such one or more of the powers specified in Parts I and II of Schedule 8 to this Act as he may consider it requisite to exercise for the purpose of remedying or preventing the adverse effects specified in the report as mentioned in the preceding subsection; and those powers may be so exercised to such extent and in such manner as the Secretary of State considers requisite for that purpose.

(3)   In determining whether, or to what extent or in what manner, to exercise any of those powers, the Secretary of State shall take into account any recommendations included in the report of the Commission in pursuance of section 72(2)(b) of this Act and any advice given by the Director under section 88 of this Act.

[47]

NOTES

Repealed by the Enterprise Act 2002, s 278(2), Sch 26, as from a day to be appointed; for savings in relation to cases where two or more enterprises ceased to be distinct enterprises (within the meaning of Part V of this Act) before such day as the Secretary of State may appoint, see s 276(1) of, and Sch 24, para 13 to, the 2002 Act at **[477]**.

The Director: see the note "Director General of Fair Trading" to s 1 at **[1]**.

Transitional provisions: for transitional provisions in relation to any order made (whether before, on or after the appointed day) by a Minister of the Crown under this section, see s 276(1) of, and Sch 24, paras 15(2)–(5), 17(1), (3)–(5) to, the Enterprise Act 2002 at **[477]**.

74   Interim order in respect of merger reference

(1)   Where a merger reference has been made to the Commission, . . . , then, with a view to preventing action to which this subsection applies, the Secretary of State, subject to subsection (3) of this section, may by order made by statutory instrument—

(a)   prohibit or restrict the doing of things which in his opinion would constitute action to which this subsection applies, or

(b)   impose on any person concerned obligations as to the carrying on of any activities or the safeguarding of any assets, or

(c)   provide for the carrying on of any activities or the safeguarding of any assets either by the appointment of a person to conduct or supervise the conduct of any activities (on such terms and with such powers as may be specified or described in the order) or in any other manner, or

(d)   exercise any of the powers which, by virtue of [paragraphs 12 and 12A] of Schedule 8 to this Act, are exercisable by an order under section 73 of this Act.

(2)   In relation to a merger reference the preceding subsection applies to any action which might prejudice the reference or impede the taking of any action under this Act which may be warranted by the Commission's report on the reference.

(3)   No order shall be made under this section in respect of a merger reference after whichever of the following events first occurs, that is to say—

(a)   the time (including any further period) allowed to the Commission for making a report on the reference expires without their having made such a report;

(b)   the period of forty days beginning with the day on which a report of the Commission on the reference is laid before Parliament expires.

(4)   An order under this section made in respect of a merger reference (if it has not previously ceased to have effect) shall cease to have effect on the occurrence of whichever of those events first occurs, but without prejudice to anything previously done under the order.

(5) Subsection (4) of this section shall have effect without prejudice—

(a) to the operation, in relation to any such order, of section 134(1) of this Act, or

(b) to the operation of any order made under section 73 of this Act which exercises the same or similar powers to those exercised by the order under this section.

[48]

NOTES

Repealed by the Enterprise Act 2002, s 278(2), Sch 26, as from a day to be appointed; for savings in relation to cases where two or more enterprises ceased to be distinct enterprises (within the meaning of Part V of this Act) before such day as the Secretary of State may appoint, see s 276(1) of, and Sch 24, para 13 to, the 2002 Act at **[477]**.

Sub-s (1): words omitted repealed and words in square brackets substituted by the Companies Act 1989, ss 153, 212, Sch 20, paras 8, 10, Sch 24, except in relation to any merger reference made before 16 November 1989.

Transitional provisions: for transitional provisions in relation to any order made (whether before, on or after the appointed day) by a Minister of the Crown under this section, see s 276(1) of, and Sch 24, paras 15(2)–(5), 17(1), (3)–(5) to, the Enterprise Act 2002 at **[477]**.

Orders: the Merger Reference (Interbrew SA and Bass PLC) (Interim Provisions) Order 2000, SI 2000/2566 (which purported to be made under s 64 of this Act at **[37]**, but this is thought to be an error and it was intended to be made under this section).

75   Reference in anticipation of merger

(1)   A merger reference may be made to the Commission by the Secretary of State where it appears to him that it is or may be the fact that arrangements are in progress or in contemplation which, if carried into effect, will result in the creation of a merger situation qualifying for investigation.

(2)   Subject to the following provisions of this section, on a merger reference under this section the Commission shall proceed in relation to the prospective and (if events so require) the actual results of the arrangements proposed or made as, in accordance with the preceding provisions of this Part of this Act, they could proceed if the arrangements in question had actually been made, and the results in question had followed immediately before the date of the reference under this section.

(3)   A merger reference under this section may require the Commission, if they find that a merger situation qualifying for investigation has been created, or will be created if the arrangements in question are carried into effect, to limit their consideration thereafter to such elements in, or possible consequences of, the creation of that situation as may be specified in the reference, and to consider whether, in respect only of those elements or possible consequences, the situation might be expected to operate against the public interest.

(4)   In relation to a merger reference under this section, sections 66, [66A,] 67, 69, 71, 72, 73 and 74 of this Act shall apply subject to the following modifications, that is to say—

[(a) section 66 shall apply, where an event by which any enterprises cease as between themselves to be distinct enterprises will occur if the arrangements are carried into effect, as if the event had occurred immediately before the date of the reference;

(aa) section 66A shall apply, where a transaction falling within subsection (2) of that section will occur if the arrangements are carried into effect, as if the transaction had occurred immediately before the date of the reference;

(b) in section 67(4) the references to subsection (1) of section 66 and subsection (1) of section 66A shall be construed as references to those subsections as modified in accordance with paragraph (a) or (aa) of this subsection;]

(c) in section 69, subsection (1) shall be construed as modified by subsection (2) of this section; in subsections (2) and (3) any reference to the question whether a merger situation qualifying for investigation has been created, or whether a result mentioned in section 64(1)(a) of this Act has arisen, shall be construed as including a reference to the question whether such a situation will be created or such a result will arise if the arrangements in question are carried into effect; and subsection (4) of that section shall not apply;

(d) in section 71, in section 72(2) and in section 74(1), the references to section 69(4) of this Act shall be construed as references to subsection (3) of this section; and

(e) in section 73(1), the reference to conclusions to the effect that a merger situation qualifying for investigation has been created shall be construed as including a reference to conclusions to the effect that such a situation will be created if the arrangements in question are carried into effect.

[(4A) Where a merger reference is made under this section, it shall be unlawful, except with the consent of the Secretary of State under subsection (4C) of this section—

(a) for any person carrying on any enterprise to which the reference relates or having control of any such enterprise or for any subsidiary of his, or

(b) for any person associated with him or for any subsidiary of such a person,

directly or indirectly to acquire, at any time during the period mentioned in subsection (4B) of this section, an interest in shares in a company if any enterprise to which the reference relates is carried on by or under the control of that company.

(4B) The period referred to in subsection (4A) of this section is the period beginning with the announcement by the Secretary of State of the making of the merger reference concerned and ending—

(a) where the reference is laid aside at any time, at that time,

(b) where the time (including any further period) allowed to the Commission for making a report on the reference expires without their having made such a report, on the expiration of that time,

(c) where a report of the Commission on the reference not including such conclusions as are referred to in section 73(1)(b) of this Act is laid before Parliament, at the end of the day on which the report is so laid,

(d) where a report of the Commission on the reference including such conclusions is laid before Parliament, at the end of the period of forty days beginning with the day on which the report is so laid,

and where such a report is laid before each House on different days, it is to be treated for the purposes of this subsection as laid on the earlier day.

(4C) The consent of the Secretary of State—

(a) may be either general or special,

(b) may be revoked by the Secretary of State, and

(c) shall be published in such way as, in the opinion of the Secretary of State, to give any person entitled to the benefit of it an adequate opportunity of getting to know of it, unless in the Secretary of State's opinion publication is not necessary for that purpose.

(4D) Section 93 of this Act applies to any contravention or apprehended contravention of subsection (4A) of this section as it applies to a contravention or apprehended contravention of an order to which section 90 of this Act applies.

(4E) Subsections (4F) to (4K) of this section apply for the interpretation of subsection (4A).

(4F) The circumstances in which a person acquires an interest in shares include those where—

(a) he enters into a contract to acquire the shares (whether or not for cash),

(b) not being the registered holder, he acquires a right to exercise, or to control the exercise of, any right conferred by the holding of the shares, or

(c) he acquires a right to call for delivery of the shares to himself or to his order or to acquire an interest in the shares or assumes an obligation to acquire such an interest,

but does not include those where he acquires an interest in pursuance of an obligation assumed before the announcement by the Secretary of State of the making of the merger reference concerned.

(4G) The circumstances in which a person acquires a right mentioned in subsection (4F) of this section—

(a) include those where he acquires a right or assumes an obligation the exercise or fulfilment of which would give him that right, but

(b) does not include those where he is appointed as proxy to vote at a specified meeting of a company or of any class of its members or at any adjournment of the meeting or he is appointed by a corporation to act as its representative at any meeting of the company or of any class of its members,

and references to rights and obligations in this subsection and subsection (4F) of this section include conditional rights and conditional obligations.

(4H) Any reference to a person carrying on or having control of any enterprise includes a group of persons carrying on or having control of an enterprise and any member of such a group.

(4J) Sections 65(2) to (4) and 77(1) and (4) to (6) of this Act apply to determine whether any person or group of persons has control of any enterprise and whether persons are associated as they apply for the purposes of section 65 of this Act to determine whether enterprises are brought under common control.

(4K) "Subsidiary" has the meaning given by section 736 of the Companies Act 1985, but that section and section 736A of that Act also apply to determine whether a company is a subsidiary of an individual or of a group of persons as they apply to determine whether it is a subsidiary of a company and references to a subsidiary in subsections (8) and (9) of section 736A as so applied are to be read accordingly.

(4L) In this section—
"company" includes any body corporate, and
"share" means share in the capital of a company, and includes stock.

(4M) Nothing in subsection (4A) of this section makes anything done by a person outside the United Kingdom unlawful unless he is—

(a) a British citizen, a British Dependent Territories citizen, a British Overseas citizen or a British National (Overseas),

(b) a body corporate incorporated under the law of the United Kingdom or of a part of the United Kingdom, or

(c) a person carrying on business in the United Kingdom, either alone or in partnership with one or more other persons.]

(5)   If, in the course of their investigations on a merger reference under this section, it appears to the Commission that the proposal to make arrangements such as are mentioned in the reference has been abandoned, the Commission—

(a) shall, if the Secretary of State consents, lay the reference aside, but

(b) shall in that case furnish to the Secretary of State such information as he may require as to the results until then of the investigations.

NOTES

Repealed by the Enterprise Act 2002, s 278(2), Sch 26, as from a day to be appointed; for savings in relation to cases where two or more enterprises ceased to be distinct enterprises (within the meaning of Part V of this Act) before such day as the Secretary of State may appoint, see s 276(1) of, and Sch 24, para 13 to, the 2002 Act at **[477]**.

Sub-s (4): figure in square brackets inserted and paras (a), (aa), (b) substituted for original paras (a), (b) by the Companies Act 1989, s 153, Sch 20, paras 9, 10, except in relation to any merger reference made before 16 November 1989.

Sub-ss (4A)–(4M): inserted by the Companies Act 1989, s 149, except in relation to any merger reference made before 16 November 1989.

British Dependent Territories citizen: to be read as a reference to "British overseas territories citizen" by virtue of the British Overseas Territories Act 2002, s 2(3).

[Restriction on power to make merger reference where prior notice has been given

75A   General rule where notice given by acquirer and no reference made within period for considering notice

(1)   Notice may be given to the Director by a person authorised by regulations to do so of proposed arrangements which might result in the creation of a merger situation qualifying for investigation.

(2)   The notice must be in the prescribed form and state that the existence of the proposal has been made public.

(3)   If the period for considering the notice expires without any reference being made to the Commission with respect to the notified arrangements, no reference may be made under this Part of this Act to the Commission with respect to those arrangements or to the creation or possible creation of any merger situation qualifying for investigation which is created in consequence of carrying those arrangements into effect.

(4)   Subsection (3) of this section is subject to sections 75B(5) and 75C of this Act.

(5)   A notice under subsection (1) of this section is referred to in sections 75B to 75F of this Act as a "merger notice".]

[50]

NOTES

Inserted, together with preceding cross-heading, and ss 75B–75F, by the Companies Act 1989, s 146.

Repealed by the Enterprise Act 2002, s 278(2), Sch 26, as from a day to be appointed; for savings in relation to cases where two or more enterprises ceased to be distinct enterprises (within the meaning of Part V of this Act) before such day as the Secretary of State may appoint, see s 276(1) of, and Sch 24, para 13 to, the 2002 Act at **[477]**.

The Director: see the note "Director General of Fair Trading" to s 1 at **[1]**.

Regulations: the Merger (Prenotification) Regulations 1990, SI 1990/501, as amended by SI 1994/1934 at **[2162]**.

[75B   The role of the Director

(1)   The Director shall, when the period for considering any merger notice begins, take such action as he considers appropriate to bring the existence of the proposal, the fact that the merger notice has been given and the date on which the period for considering the notice may expire to the attention of those who in his opinion would be affected if the arrangements were carried into effect.

(2)   The period for considering a merger notice is the period of twenty days, determined in accordance with subsection (9) of this section, beginning with the first day after—

(a) the notice has been received by the Director, and

(b) any fee payable to the Director in respect of the notice has been paid.

(3) The Director may, and shall if required to do so by the Secretary of State, by notice to the person who gave the merger notice [extend the period mentioned in subsection (2) of this section by a further fifteen days].

(4) The Director may by notice to the person who gave the merger notice request him to provide the Director within such period as may be specified in the notice with such information as may be so specified.

(5) If the Director gives to the person who gave the merger notice (in this subsection referred to as "the relevant person") a notice stating that the Secretary of State is seeking undertakings under section 75G of this Act, section 75A(3) of this Act does not prevent a reference being made to the Commission unless—

(a) after the Director has given that notice, the relevant person has given a notice to the Director stating that he does not intend to give such undertakings, and

(b) the period of ten days beginning with the first day after the notice under paragraph (a) of this subsection was received by the Director has expired.

(6) A notice by the Director under subsection (3), (4) or (5) of this section must either be given to the person who gave the merger notice before the period for considering the merger notice expires or be sent in a properly addressed and pre-paid letter posted to him at such time that, in the ordinary course of post, it would be delivered to him before that period expires.

(7) The Director may, at any time before the period for considering any merger notice expires, reject the notice if—

(a) he suspects that any information given in respect of the notified arrangements, whether in the merger notice or otherwise, by the person who gave the notice or any connected person is in any material respect false or misleading,

(b) he suspects that it is not proposed to carry the notified arrangements into effect, . . .

(c) any prescribed information is not given in the merger notice or any information requested by notice under subsection (4) of this section is not provided within the period specified in the notice [or,

(d) it appears to him that the notified arrangements are, or if carried into effect would result in, a concentration with a Community dimension within the meaning of Council Regulation (EEC) No 4064/89 of 21st December 1989 on the control of concentrations between undertakings.]

(8) If—

(a) under subsection [(3)] of this section the period for considering a merger notice has been extended by a further fifteen days, but

(b) the Director has not made any recommendation to the Secretary of State under section 76(b) of this Act as to whether or not it would in the Director's opinion be expedient for the Secretary of State to make a reference to the Commission with respect to the notified arrangements,

then, during the last five of those fifteen days, the power of the Secretary of State to make a reference to the Commission with respect to the notified arrangements is not affected by the absence of any such recommendation.

(9) In determining any period for the purposes of subsections (2), (3) and (5) of this section no account shall be taken of—

(a) Saturday, Sunday, Good Friday and Christmas Day, and

(b) any day which is a bank holiday in England and Wales.]

PART I
STATUTES

NOTES

Inserted as noted to s 75A at **[50]**.

Repealed by the Enterprise Act 2002, s 278(2), Sch 26, as from a day to be appointed; for savings in relation to cases where two or more enterprises ceased to be distinct enterprises (within the meaning of Part V of this Act) before such day as the Secretary of State may appoint, see s 276(1) of, and Sch 24, para 13 to, the 2002 Act at **[477]**.

The Director: see the note "Director General of Fair Trading" to s 1 at **[1]**.

Sub-s (3): words in square brackets substituted by the Fair Trading Act (Amendment) (Merger Prenotification) Regulations 1994, SI 1994/1934, regs 1(3), 2.

Sub-s (7): word omitted from para (b) repealed and para (d) and word immediately preceding it added by the EEC Merger Control (Consequential Provisions) Regulations 1990, SI 1990/1563, reg 2.

Sub-s (8): figure in square brackets substituted, in relation to notices under s 75A(1) of this Act given on or after 1 August 1994, by SI 1994/1934, reg 3.

[75C   Cases where power to refer unaffected

(1)   Section 75A(3) of this Act does not prevent any reference being made to the Commission if—

   (a)   before the end of the period for considering the merger notice, it is rejected by the Director under section 75B(7) of this Act,

   (b)   before the end of that period, any of the enterprises to which the notified arrangements relate cease to be distinct from each other,

   (c)   any information (whether prescribed information or not) that—

      (i)   is, or ought to be, known to the person who gave the merger notice or any connected person, and

      (ii)   is material to the notified arrangements;

   is not disclosed to the Secretary of State or the Director by such time before the end of that period as may be specified in regulations,

   (d)   at any time after the merger notice is given but before the enterprises to which the notified arrangements relate cease to be distinct from each other, any of those enterprises ceases to be distinct from any enterprise other than an enterprise to which those arrangements relate,

   (e)   the six months beginning with the end of the period for considering the merger notice expires without the enterprises to which the notified arrangements relate ceasing to be distinct from each other,

   (f)   the merger notice is withdrawn, or

   (g)   any information given in respect of the notified arrangements, whether in the merger notice or otherwise, by the person who gave the notice or any connected person is in any material respect false or misleading.

(2)   Where—

   (a)   two or more transactions which have occurred or, if any arrangements are carried into effect, will occur may be treated for the purposes of a merger reference as having occurred simultaneously on a particular date, and

   (b)   subsection (3) of section 75A of this Act does not prevent such a reference with respect to the last of those transactions,

that subsection does not prevent such a reference with respect to any of those transactions which actually occurred less than six months before—

   (i)   that date, or

   (ii)   the actual occurrence of another of those transactions with respect to which such a reference may be made (whether or not by virtue of this subsection).

(3)   In determining for the purposes of subsection (2) of this section the time at which any transaction actually occurred, no account shall be taken of any option or other conditional right until the option is exercised or the condition is satisfied.]

NOTES

Repealed by the Enterprise Act 2002, s 278(2), Sch 26, as from a day to be appointed; for savings in relation to cases where two or more enterprises ceased to be distinct enterprises (within the meaning of Part V of this Act) before such day as the Secretary of State may appoint, see s 276(1) of, and Sch 24, para 13 to, the 2002 Act at **[477]**.

The Director: see the note "Director General of Fair Trading" to s 1 at **[1]**.

Regulations: the Merger (Prenotification) Regulations 1990, SI 1990/501, as amended by SI 1994/1934 at **[2162]**.

[75D Regulations

(1) The Secretary of State may make regulations for the purposes of sections 75A to 75C of this Act.

(2) The regulations may, in particular—
  (a) *provide for section 75B(2) or (3) or section 75C(1)(e) of this Act to apply as if any reference to a period of days or months were a reference to a period specified in the regulations for the purposes of the provision in question,*
  (b) *provide for the manner in which any merger notice is authorised or required to be given, rejected or withdrawn, and the time at which any merger notice is to be treated as received or rejected,*
  (c) *provide for the manner in which any information requested by the Director or any other material information is authorised or required to be provided or disclosed, and the time at which such information is to be treated as provided or disclosed,*
  (d) *provide for the manner in which any notice under section 75B of this Act is authorised or required to be given,*
  (e) *provide for the time at which any notice under section 75B(5)(a) of this Act is to be treated as received,*
  (f) *provide for the address which is to be treated for the purposes of section 75B(6) of this Act and of the regulations as a person's proper address,*
  (g) *provide for the time at which any fee is to be treated as paid, and*
  (h) *provide that a person is, or is not, to be treated, in such circumstances as may be specified in the regulations, as acting on behalf of a person authorised by regulations to give a merger notice or a person who has given such a notice.*

(3) The regulations may make different provision for different cases.

(4) Regulations under this section shall be made by statutory instrument.]

[53]

NOTES

Inserted as noted to s 75A at **[50]**.

Repealed by the Enterprise Act 2002, s 278(2), Sch 26, as from a day to be appointed; for savings in relation to cases where two or more enterprises ceased to be distinct enterprises (within the meaning of Part V of this Act) before such day as the Secretary of State may appoint, see s 276(1) of, and Sch 24, para 13 to, the 2002 Act at **[477]**.

The Director: see the note "Director General of Fair Trading" to s 1 at **[1]**.

Regulations: the Merger (Prenotification) Regulations 1990, SI 1990/501, as amended by SI 1994/1934 at **[2162]**.

[75E Interpretation of sections 75A to 75D

In this section and sections 75A to 75D of this Act—
  "connected person", in relation to the person who gave a merger notice, means—
    (a) *any person who, for the purposes of section 77 of this Act, is associated with him, or*

    (b) any subsidiary of the person who gave the merger notice or of any person so associated with him,

"merger notice" is to be interpreted in accordance with section 75A(5) of this Act,

"notified arrangements" means the arrangements mentioned in the merger notice or arrangements not differing from them in any material respect,

"prescribed" means prescribed by the Director by notice having effect for the time being and published in the London, Edinburgh and Belfast Gazettes,

"regulations" means regulations under section 75D of this Act, and

"subsidiary" has the meaning given by section 75(4K) of this Act,

and references to the enterprises to which the notified arrangements relate are references to those enterprises that would have ceased to be distinct from one another if the arrangements mentioned in the merger notice in question had been carried into effect at the time when the notice was given.]

                                                    [54]

NOTES

Inserted as noted to s 75A at **[50]**.

Repealed by the Enterprise Act 2002, s 278(2), Sch 26, as from a day to be appointed; for savings in relation to cases where two or more enterprises ceased to be distinct enterprises (within the meaning of Part V of this Act) before such day as the Secretary of State may appoint, see s 276(1) of, and Sch 24, para 13 to, the 2002 Act at **[477]**.

The Director: see the note "Director General of Fair Trading" to s 1 at **[1]**.

Regulations: the Merger (Prenotification) Regulations 1990, SI 1990/501, as amended by SI 1994/1934 at **[2162]**.

[75F   Power to amend sections 75B to 75D

(1)   The Secretary of State may, for the purpose of determining the effect of giving a merger notice and the steps which may be or are to be taken by any person in connection with such a notice, by regulations made by statutory instrument amend sections 75B to 75D of this Act.

(2)   The regulations may make different provision for different cases and may contain such incidental and supplementary provisions as the Secretary of State thinks fit.

(3)   No regulations shall be made under this section unless a draft of the regulations has been laid before and approved by resolution of each House of Parliament.]

                                                    [55]

NOTES

Inserted as noted to s 75A at **[50]**.

Repealed by the Enterprise Act 2002, s 278(2), Sch 26, as from a day to be appointed; for savings in relation to cases where two or more enterprises ceased to be distinct enterprises (within the meaning of Part V of this Act) before such day as the Secretary of State may appoint, see s 276(1) of, and Sch 24, para 13 to, the 2002 Act at **[477]**.

Regulations: the Fair Trading Act (Amendment) (Merger Prenotification) Regulations 1994, SI 1994/1934.

[Undertakings as alternative to merger reference

75G   Acceptance of undertakings

(1)   Where—

    (a) the Secretary of State has power to make a merger reference to the Commission under section 64 or 75 of this Act,

   (b) the Director has made a recommendation to the Secretary of State under section 76 of this Act that such a reference should be made, and

   (c) the Director has (in making that recommendation or subsequently) given advice to the Secretary of State specifying particular effects adverse to the public interest which in his opinion the creation of the merger situation qualifying for investigation may have or might be expected to have,

the Secretary of State may, instead of making a merger reference to the Commission, accept from such of the parties concerned as he considers appropriate undertakings . . . to take specified action which the Secretary of State considers appropriate to remedy or prevent the effects adverse to the public interest specified in the advice.

   (2), (3). . .

   (4) If the Secretary of State has accepted one or more undertakings under this section, no reference may be made to the Commission with respect to the creation or possible creation of the merger situation qualifying for investigation by reference to which the undertakings were accepted, except in a case falling within subsection (5) of this section.

   (5) Subsection (4) of this section does not prevent a reference being made to the Commission if material facts about the arrangements or transactions, or proposed arrangements or transactions, in consequence of which the enterprises concerned ceased or may cease to be distinct enterprises were not—

   (a) notified to the Secretary of State or the Director, or

   (b) made public,

before the undertakings were accepted.

   (6) In subsection (5) of this section "made public" has the same meaning as in section 64 of this Act.]

[56]

NOTES

   Inserted, together with preceding cross-heading, and ss 75H–75K, by the Companies Act 1989, s 147.

   Repealed by the Enterprise Act 2002, s 278(2), Sch 26, as from a day to be appointed; for savings in relation to cases where two or more enterprises ceased to be distinct enterprises (within the meaning of Part V of this Act) before such day as the Secretary of State may appoint, see s 276(1) of, and Sch 24, para 13 to, the 2002 Act at **[477]**.

   Sub-s (1): words omitted repealed by the Deregulation and Contracting Out Act 1994, s 81(1), Sch 17.

   Sub-ss (2), (3): repealed by the Deregulation and Contracting Out Act 1994, ss 9(1), 81(1), Sch 17.

   See further, the Competition Act 1980, s 29(1) at **[122]**.

   The Director: see the note "Director General of Fair Trading" to s 1 at **[1]**.

   Transitional provisions: for transitional provisions in relation to undertakings accepted (whether before, on or after the appointed day) by a Minister of the Crown under this section, see s 276(1) of, and Sch 24, paras 15(1), (4), (5), 16 to, the Enterprise Act 2002 at **[477]**.

[75H   Publication of undertakings

   (1) The Secretary of State shall arrange for—

   (a) any undertaking accepted by him under section 75G of this Act,

   (b) the advice given by the Director for the purposes of subsection (1)(c) of that section in any case where such an undertaking has been accepted, and

   (c) any variation or release of such an undertaking,

to be published in such manner as he may consider appropriate.

   (2) In giving advice for the purposes of section 75G(1)(c) of this Act the Director shall have regard to the need for excluding, so far as practicable, any matter to which subsection (4) of this section applies.

(3)   The Secretary of State shall exclude from any such advice as published under this section—

(a)   any matter to which subsection (4) of this section applies and in relation to which he is satisfied that its publication in the advice would not be in the public interest, and

(b)   any other matter in relation to which he is satisfied that its publication in the advice would be against the public interest.

(4)   This subsection applies to—

(a)   any matter which relates to the private affairs of an individual, where publication of that matter would or might, in the opinion of the Director or the Secretary of State, as the case may be, seriously and prejudicially affect the interests of that individual, and

(b)   any matter which relates specifically to the affairs of a particular body of persons, whether corporate or unincorporate, where publication of that matter would or might, in the opinion of the Director or the Secretary of State, as the case may be, seriously and prejudicially affect the interests of that body, unless in his opinion the inclusion of that matter relating specifically to that body is necessary for the purposes of the advice.

(5)   For the purposes of the law relating to defamation, absolute privilege shall attach to any advice given by the Director for the purposes of section 75G(1)(c) of this Act.]

[57]

NOTES

Inserted as noted to s 75G at **[56]**.

Repealed by the Enterprise Act 2002, s 278(2), Sch 26, as from a day to be appointed; for savings in relation to cases where two or more enterprises ceased to be distinct enterprises (within the meaning of Part V of this Act) before such day as the Secretary of State may appoint, see s 276(1) of, and Sch 24, para 13 to, the 2002 Act at **[477]**.

The Director: see the note "Director General of Fair Trading" to s 1 at **[1]**.

[75J   Review of undertakings

Where an undertaking has been accepted by the Secretary of State under section 75G of this Act, it shall be the duty of the Director—

(a)   to keep under review the carrying out of that undertaking, and from time to time consider whether, by reason of any change of circumstances, the undertaking is no longer appropriate and either—

(i)   one or more of the parties to it can be released from it, or

(ii)   it needs to be varied or to be superseded by a new undertaking, and

(b)   if it appears to him that the undertaking has not been or is not being fulfilled, that any person can be so released or that the undertaking needs to be varied or superseded, to give such advice to the Secretary of State as he may think proper in the circumstances.]

[58]

NOTES

Inserted as noted to s 75G at **[56]**.

Repealed by the Enterprise Act 2002, s 278(2), Sch 26, as from a day to be appointed; for savings in relation to cases where two or more enterprises ceased to be distinct enterprises (within the meaning of Part V of this Act) before such day as the Secretary of State may appoint, see s 276(1) of, and Sch 24, para 13 to, the 2002 Act at **[477]**.

The Director: see the note "Director General of Fair Trading" to s 1 at **[1]**.

[75K   Order of Secretary of State where undertaking not fulfilled

(1)   The provisions of this section shall have effect where it appears to the Secretary of State that an undertaking accepted by him under section 75G of this Act has not been, is not being or will not be fulfilled.

(2)   The Secretary of State may by order made by statutory instrument exercise such one or more of the [relevant powers] as he may consider it requisite to exercise for the purpose of remedying or preventing the adverse effects specified in the advice given by the Director for the purposes of section 75G(1)(c) of this Act; and those powers may be so exercised to such extent and in such manner as the Secretary of State considers requisite for that purpose.

(3)   In determining whether, or to what extent or in what manner, to exercise any of those powers, the Secretary of State shall take into account any advice given by the Director under section 75J(b) of this Act.

(4)   The provision contained in an order under this section may be different from that contained in the undertaking.

(5)   On the making of an order under this section, the undertaking and any other undertaking accepted under section 75G of this Act by reference to the same merger situation qualifying for investigation are released by virtue of this section.

[(6)   In subsection (2) of this section, "the relevant powers" means—
(a)   in relation to an undertaking to which subsection (7) of this section applies ("a divestment undertaking"), the powers specified in paragraphs 9A and 12 to 12C and Part II of Schedule 8 to this Act, and
(b)   in relation to an undertaking which is not a divestment undertaking, the powers specified in that Schedule.

(7)   This subsection applies to an undertaking which provides for—
(a)   the division of a business by the sale of any part of the undertaking or assets or otherwise (for which purpose all the activities carried on by way of business by any one person or by any two or more interconnected bodies corporate may be treated as a single business),
(b)   the division of a group of interconnected bodies corporate, or
(c)   the separation, by the sale of any part of the undertaking or assets concerned or other means, of enterprises which are under common control otherwise than by reason of their being enterprises of interconnected bodies corporate.

(8)   Schedule 8 to this Act shall, to such extent as is necessary for the purpose of giving effect to subsection (2) of this section, have effect as if, in paragraph 1 of that Schedule, after "section 73" there were inserted "or section 75K".]]

[59]

NOTES

Inserted as noted to s 75G at **[56]**.

Repealed by the Enterprise Act 2002, s 278(2), Sch 26, as from a day to be appointed; for savings in relation to cases where two or more enterprises ceased to be distinct enterprises (within the meaning of Part V of this Act) before such day as the Secretary of State may appoint, see s 276(1) of, and Sch 24, para 13 to, the 2002 Act at **[477]**.

Sub-s (2): words in square brackets substituted by the Deregulation and Contracting Out Act 1994, s 9(2).

Sub-ss (6)–(8): inserted by the Deregulation and Contracting Out Act 1994, s 9(3).

The Director: see the note "Director General of Fair Trading" to s 1 at **[1]**.

Transitional provisions: for transitional provisions in relation to any order made (whether before, on or after the appointed day) by a Minister of the Crown under this section, see s 276(1) of, and Sch 24, paras 15(2), 17(2)–(5) to, the Enterprise Act 2002 at **[477]**.

Supplementary

76 Functions of Director in relation to merger situations

[(1)] It shall be the duty of the Director—

(a) *to take all such steps as are reasonably practicable for keeping himself informed about actual or prospective arrangements or transactions which may constitute or result in the creation of merger situations qualifying for investigation, and*

(b) *to make recommendations to the Secretary of State as to any action under this Part of this Act which in the opinion of the Director it would be expedient for the Secretary of State to take in relation to any such arrangements or transactions.*

[(2) In exercising his duty under this section the Director shall take into consideration any representations made to him by persons appearing to him to have a substantial interest in any such arrangements or transactions or by bodies appearing to him to represent substantial numbers of persons who have such an interest.]

[60]

NOTES

Repealed by the Enterprise Act 2002, s 278(2), Sch 26, as from a day to be appointed; for savings in relation to cases where two or more enterprises ceased to be distinct enterprises (within the meaning of Part V of this Act) before such day as the Secretary of State may appoint, see s 276(1) of, and Sch 24, para 13 to, the 2002 Act at **[477]**.

Sub-s (2): added by the Companies Act 1989, s 153, Sch 20, para 11. In the interest of consistency the original section has been numbered as sub-s (1).

The Director: see the note "Director General of Fair Trading" to s 1 at **[1]**.

As to the furnishing of false or misleading information, generally, to the Director under this Part, see s 93B of this Act at **[79]**.

77 Associated persons

(1) For the following purposes, that is to say—

(a) for the purpose of determining under section 57(1) [or (1A)] of this Act whether a person is a newspaper proprietor and, if so, which newspapers are his newspapers;

(b) *for the purpose of determining under section 65 of this Act whether any two enterprises have been brought under common ownership or common control; and*

(c) *for the purpose of determining what activities are carried on by way of business by any one person, in so far as that question arises in the application, by virtue of an order under section 73 of this Act, of paragraph 14 of Schedule 8 to this Act,*

associated persons, and any bodies corporate which they or any of them control, shall (subject to the next following subsection) be treated as one person.

(2) The preceding subsection shall not have effect—

(a) for the purpose mentioned in paragraph (a) of that subsection so as to exclude from section 58 of this Act any case which would otherwise fall within that section, *or*

(b) *for the purpose mentioned in paragraph (b) of the preceding subsection so as to exclude from section 65 of this Act any case which would otherwise fall within that section.*

(3) A merger reference other than a newspaper merger reference (whether apart from this section the reference could be made or not) may be so framed as to exclude from consideration, either altogether or for any specified purpose or to any specified extent, any matter which, apart from this section, would not have been taken into account on that reference.

(4)   For the purposes of this section the following persons shall be regarded as associated with one another, that is to say—

(a) any individual and that individual's husband or wife and any relative, or husband or wife of a relative, of that individual or of that individual's husband or wife;

(b) any person in his capacity as trustee of a settlement and the settlor or grantor and any person associated with the settlor or grantor;

(c) persons carrying on business in partnership and the husband or wife and relatives of any of them;

(d) any two or more persons acting together to secure or exercise control of a body corporate or other association or to secure control of any enterprise or assets.

(5)   The reference in subsection (1) of this section to bodies corporate which associated persons control shall be construed as follows, that is to say—

(a) in its application for the purpose mentioned in paragraph (a) of that subsection, "control" in that reference means having a [primary] controlling interest within the meaning of section 57(4) of this Act, *and*

(b) *in its application for any other purpose mentioned in subsection (1) of this section, "control" in that reference shall be construed in accordance with section 65(3) and (4) of this Act.*

(6)   In this section "relative" means a brother, sister, uncle, aunt, nephew, niece, lineal ancestor or descendant (the stepchild or illegitimate child of any person, or anyone adopted by a person, whether legally or otherwise, as his child, being taken into account as a relative or to trace a relationship in the same way as that person's child); and references to a wife or husband shall include a former wife or husband and a reputed wife or husband.

[61]

NOTES

Sub-s (1): words in square brackets inserted by the Deregulation and Contracting Out Act 1994, s 39, Sch 11, para 2(1), (2); paras (b), (c) repealed by the Enterprise Act 2002, s 278(2), Sch 26, as from a day to be appointed, for savings in relation to cases where two or more enterprises ceased to be distinct enterprises (within the meaning of Part V of this Act) before such day as the Secretary of State may appoint, see s 276(1) of, and Sch 24, para 13 to, the 2002 Act at **[477]**.

Sub-s (2): para (b) and the word preceding it repealed by the Enterprise Act 2002, s 278(2), Sch 26, as from a day to be appointed; for savings in relation to cases where two or more enterprises ceased to be distinct enterprises (within the meaning of Part V of this Act) before such day as the Secretary of State may appoint, see s 276(1) of, and Sch 24, para 13 to, the 2002 Act at **[477]**.

Sub-s (3): repealed by the Enterprise Act 2002, s 278(2), Sch 26, as from a day to be appointed; for savings in relation to cases where two or more enterprises ceased to be distinct enterprises (within the meaning of Part V of this Act) before such day as the Secretary of State may appoint, see s 276(1) of, and Sch 24, para 13 to, the 2002 Act at **[477]**.

Sub-s (5): word in square brackets inserted by the Deregulation and Contracting Out Act 1994, s 39, Sch 11, para 2(1), (2); para (b) and word preceding it repealed by the Enterprise Act 2002, s 278(2), Sch 26, as from a day to be appointed, for savings in relation to cases where two or more enterprises ceased to be distinct enterprises (within the meaning of Part V of this Act) before such day as the Secretary of State may appoint, see s 276(1) of, and Sch 24, para 13 to, the 2002 Act at **[477]**.

PART VI
REFERENCES TO COMMISSION OTHER THAN MONOPOLY AND MERGER REFERENCES

78   General references

(1)   The Secretary of State, or the Secretary of State and any other Minister acting jointly, may at any time require the Commission to submit to him or them a report on the general effect on the public interest—

    (a) of practices of a specified class which, in his or their opinion, are commonly adopted as a result of, or for the purpose of preserving, monopoly situations, or

    (b) of any specified practices which appear to him or them to be uncompetitive practices.

(2) The Secretary of State, or the Secretary of State and any other Minister acting jointly, may also at any time require the Commission to submit to him or them a report on the desirability of action of any specified description for the purpose of remedying or preventing effects, adverse to the public interest, which result or might result from monopoly situations or from any such practices as are mentioned in the preceding subsection.

(3) ...

[62]

NOTES

    Repealed by the Enterprise Act 2002, ss 208, 278(2), Sch 26, as from a day to be appointed.

    Sub-s (3): repealed by the Competition Act 1998, s 74(1), (3), Sch 12, para 1(1), (3)(c), Sch 14, Pt I, subject to savings in Sch 13, Pt V, para 40 of the 1998 Act at **[231]**. Original sub-s (3), as amended by the Restrictive Trade Practices Act 1976, s 44, Sch 5, read as follows—

    "(3) The matters to be taken into consideration by the Commission on any reference under this section shall not include any provisions of any agreement in so far as they are provisions by virtue of which it is an agreement to which [the Act of 1976] applies.".

79 References as to restrictive labour practices

(1) The Secretary of State, or the Secretary of State and any other Minister acting jointly, may at any time refer to the Commission the questions—

    (a) whether a practice of a description specified in the reference exists and, if so, whether it is a restrictive labour practice, and

    (b) if it exists and is a restrictive labour practice, whether it operates or may be expected to operate against the public interest and, if so, what particular effects, adverse to the public interest, it has or may be expected to have.

(2) A reference under this section may refer those questions to the Commission either—

    (a) in relation to commercial activities in the United Kingdom generally, or

    (b) in relation to such commercial activities in the United Kingdom as consist of the supply of goods of a description specified in the reference, or of the supply of services of a description so specified, or of the export from the United Kingdom of goods of a description so specified.

(3) The Commission shall examine any questions referred to them under this section and shall report to the Minister or Ministers who referred them to the Commission.

(4) For the purposes of their functions under subsection (3) of this section the Commission shall disregard anything which appears to them to have been done, or omitted to be done, in contemplation or furtherance of an industrial dispute within the meaning of the Industrial Relations Act 1971.

(5) In this section "restrictive labour practice" means any practice whereby restrictions or other requirements, not being restrictions or requirements relating exclusively to rates of remuneration, operate in relation to the employment of workers in any commercial activities in the United Kingdom or in relation to work done by any such workers, and are restrictions or requirements which—

    (a) could be discontinued without thereby contravening the provisions of an enactment or of any instrument having effect by virtue of an enactment, and

PART I
STATUTES

(b) are not necessary for, or are more stringent than is necessary for, the efficient conduct of those activities.

[63]

NOTES

Repealed by the Enterprise Act 2002, ss 208, 278(2), Sch 26, as from a day to be appointed.

Industrial Relations Act 1971: repealed by the Trade Union and Labour Relations Act 1974, ss 1(1), 25(3), Sch 5, itself repealed and replaced by the Trade Union and Labour Relations (Consolidation) Act 1992.

80   Variation of reference under Part VI

A reference made under this Part of this Act may at any time be varied by the Minister or Ministers by whom the reference was made.

[64]

NOTES

Repealed by the Enterprise Act 2002, ss 208, 278(2), Sch 26, as from a day to be appointed.

PART VII
PROVISIONS RELATING TO REFERENCES TO ADVISORY COMMITTEE OR TO COMMISSION

81   Procedure in carrying out investigations

(1)   The Advisory Committee, in carrying out an investigation on a reference to which section 17 of this Act applies, . . . —
  (a) shall take into consideration any representations made to them by persons appearing to them to have a substantial interest in the subject-matter of the reference, or by bodies appearing to them to represent substantial numbers of persons who have such an interest, and
  (b) unless in all the circumstances they consider it not reasonably necessary or not reasonably practicable to do so, shall permit any such person or body to be heard orally by the Advisory Committee . . . , or by a member of the Committee . . . nominated by them for that purpose.

(2)   Subject to subsection (1) of this section, the Advisory Committee . . . may determine their own procedure for carrying out any investigation on a reference under this Act, and in particular may determine—
  (a) the extent, if any, to which persons interested or claiming to be interested in the subject-matter of the reference are allowed to be present or to be heard, either by themselves or by their representatives, or to cross-examine witnesses or otherwise take part in the investigation, and
  (b) the extent, if any, to which the sittings of the Advisory Committee . . . are to be held in public.

(3)   In determining their procedure under subsection (2) of this section, . . . , the Advisory Committee . . . , shall act in accordance with any general directions which may from time to time be given to them by the Secretary of State.

(4)   The Secretary of State shall lay before each House of Parliament a copy of any directions given by him under subsection (3) of this section.

[65]

NOTES

Repealed by the Enterprise Act 2002, s 278(2), Sch 26, as from a day to be appointed.

Sub-ss (1)–(3): words omitted repealed by the Competition Act 1998, s 74(1), (3), Sch 12, para 1(1), (9), Sch 14, Pt I.

82 General provisions as to reports

(1) In making any report under this Act *the Advisory Committee or* the Commission shall have regard to the need for excluding, so far as that is practicable,—

    (a) any matter which relates to the private affairs of an individual, where the publication of that matter would or might, in their opinion, seriously and prejudicially affect the interests of that individual, and

    (b) any matter which relates specifically to the affairs of a particular body of persons, whether corporate or uncorporate, where publication of that matter would or might, in the opinion of *the Advisory Committee or of* the Commission, *as the case may be,* seriously and prejudicially affect the interests of that body, unless in their opinion the inclusion of that matter relating specifically to that body is necessary for the purposes of the report.

(2) For the purposes of the law relating to defamation, absolute privilege shall attach to any report of *the Advisory Committee or of* the Commission under this Act.

(3) [If]—

    (a) on a reference to the Advisory Committee under this Act, . . .

    (b) . . .

a member of the Advisory Committee . . . , dissents from any conclusions contained in the report on the reference as being conclusions of the Committee . . . , the report shall, if that member so desires, include a statement of his dissent and of his reasons for dissenting.

[(4) If, on a reference to the Commission, *other than a monopoly reference limited to the facts,* a member of the group selected for the purpose pursuant to paragraph 15 of Schedule 7 to the Competition Act 1998 dissents from any conclusions contained in the report as being conclusions of the Commission, the report shall, if that member so desires, include a statement of his dissent and of his reasons for dissenting.]

[66]

NOTES

    Sub-ss (1), (2): words in italics repealed by the Enterprise Act 2002, s 278(2), Sch 26, as from a day to be appointed.

    Sub-s (3): repealed by the Enterprise Act 2002, s 278(2), Sch 26, as from a day to be appointed; word in square brackets substituted and words omitted repealed by the Competition Act 1998 (Transitional, Consequential and Supplemental Provisions) Order 2000, SI 2000/311, art 9(1), (2)(a), (b).

    Sub-s (4): substituted by SI 2000/311, art 9(1), (2)(c); words in italics repealed by the Enterprise Act 2002, s 278(2), Sch 26, as from a day to be appointed.

---

83 Laying before Parliament and publication of reports

(1) . . . the Minister or Ministers to whom *any report of the Advisory Committee on a reference to which section 17 of this Act applies, or* any report of the Commission under this Act, is made shall lay a copy of the report before each House of Parliament, and shall arrange for the report to be published in such manner as appears to the Minister or Ministers to be appropriate.

[(1A) . . .]

(2) If such a report is presented by command of Her Majesty to either House of Parliament otherwise than at or during the time of a sitting of that House, the presentation of the report shall for the purposes of this section be treated as the laying of a copy of it before that House by the Minister or Ministers to whom the report was made.

(3)   If it appears to the Minister or Ministers to whom any report *of the Advisory Committee or* of the Commission under this Act is made that the publication of any matter in the report would be against the public interest, the Minister or Ministers shall exclude that matter from the copies of the report as laid before Parliament and from the report as published under this section.

[(3A)   Without prejudice to subsection (3) above, if the Minister or Ministers to whom any such report is made consider that it would not be in the public interest to disclose—

(a) any matter contained in the report relating to the private affairs of an individual whose interests would, in the opinion of the Minister or Ministers, be seriously and prejudicially affected by the publication of that matter, or

(b) any matter contained in the report relating specifically to the affairs of a particular person whose interests would, in the opinion of the Minister or Ministers, be seriously and prejudicially affected by the publication of that matter,

the Minister or Ministers shall exclude that matter from the copies of the report as laid before Parliament and from the report as published under this section.]

(4)   Any reference in this Act to a report *of the Advisory Committee or* of the Commission as laid before Parliament shall be construed as a reference to the report in the form in which copies of it are laid (or by virtue of subsection (2) of this section are treated as having been laid) before each House of Parliament under this section.

[67]

NOTES

Sub-s (1): words omitted repealed by the Competition Act 1998, ss 69(a), 74(3), Sch 14, Pt I; words in italics repealed by the Enterprise Act 2002, s 278(2), Sch 26, as from a day to be appointed.

Sub-s (1A): inserted by the Competition Act 1980, s 22(b); repealed by the Competition Act 1998, ss 69(b), 74(3), Sch 14, Pt I.

Sub-ss (3), (4): words in italics repealed by the Enterprise Act 2002, s 278(2), Sch 26, as from a day to be appointed.

Sub-s (3A): inserted by the Companies Act 1989, s 153, Sch 20, para 12, except in relation to any report made before 16 November 1989.

PART VIII
ADDITIONAL PROVISIONS RELATING TO REFERENCES TO COMMISSION

84   Public interest

(1)   In determining for any purposes to which this section applies whether any particular matter operates, or may be expected to operate, against the public interest, the Commission shall take into account all matters which appear to them in the particular circumstances to be relevant and, among other things, shall have regard to the desirability—

(a) *of maintaining and promoting effective competition between persons supplying goods and services in the United Kingdom;*

(b) *of promoting the interests of consumers, purchasers and other users of goods and services in the United Kingdom in respect of the prices charged for them and in respect of their quality and the variety of goods and services supplied;*

(c) *of promoting, through competition, the reduction of costs and the development and use of new techniques and new products, and of facilitating the entry of new competitors into existing markets;*

(d) *of maintaining and promoting the balanced distribution of industry and employment in the United Kingdom; and*

(e) *of maintaining and promoting competitive activity in markets outside the United Kingdom on the part of producers of goods, and of suppliers of goods and services, in the United Kingdom.*

(2) *This section applies to the purposes of any functions of the Commission under this Act other than functions to which section 59(3) of this Act applies.*

[68]

NOTES

Repealed by the Enterprise Act 2002, s 278(2), Sch 26, as from a day to be appointed.

85   Attendance of witnesses and production of documents

(1)   For the purposes of any investigation on a reference made to them under this Act the Commission may, by notice in writing signed on their behalf by any of their members or by their secretary,—

(a) require any person to attend at a time and place specified in the notice, and to give evidence to the Commission or a member of the Commission nominated by them for the purpose, or

(b) require any person to produce, at a time and place specified in the notice, to the Commission or to any person nominated by the Commission for the purpose,

[(i)] any documents which are specified or described in the notice, [or

(ii) any document which falls within a category of document which is specified, or described, in the notice,]

and which are documents in his custody or under his control and relating to any matter relevant to the investigation, or

(c) require any person carrying on any business to furnish to the Commission such estimates [forecasts], returns or other information as may be specified or described in the notice, and specify the time, the manner and the form in which any such estimates [forecasts], returns or information are to be furnished.

[(1A) For the purposes of subsection (1) above—

(a) "document" includes information recorded in any form;

(b) the power to require the production of documents includes power to take copies of, or extracts from, any document produced; and

(c) in relation to information recorded otherwise than in legible form, the power to require it to be produced includes power to require it to be produced in legible form, so far as the means to do so are within the custody or under the control of the person on whom the requirement is imposed.]

(2)   For the purposes of [an investigation of the kind mentioned in subsection (1)] the Commission, or a member of the Commission nominated by them for that purpose, may take evidence on oath, and for that purpose may administer oaths.

(3)   No person shall be compelled for the purpose of any such investigation to give any evidence or produce any document which he could not be compelled to give or produce in civil proceedings before the court or, in complying with any requirement for the furnishing of information, to give any information which he could not be compelled to give in evidence in such proceedings.

(4)   No person shall be required, in obedience to a notice under subsection (1) of this section, to go more than ten miles from his place of residence unless the necessary expenses of his attendance are paid or tendered to him.

(5)   . . .

(6)   Any person who—
    (a)   wilfully alters, suppresses or destroys any document which he has been required by any such notice to produce, . . .
    (b)   . . .

shall be guilty of an offence and liable on summary conviction to a fine not exceeding [the prescribed sum] or, on conviction on indictment, to imprisonment for a term not exceeding two years or to a fine or to both.

[(7)   If any person (referred to in subsection (7A) of this section as "the defaulter") refuses or otherwise fails to comply with any notice under subsection (1) of this section, any one of those who, in relation to the investigation in question, are performing the functions of the Commission may certify that fact in writing to the court and the court may enquire into the case.

(7A)   If, after hearing any witness who may be produced against or on behalf of the defaulter and any statement which may be offered in defence, the court is satisfied that the defaulter did without reasonable excuse refuse or otherwise fail to comply with the notice, the court may punish the defaulter (and, in the case of a body corporate, any director or officer) in like manner as if the defaulter had been guilty of contempt of court.]

(8)   In this section "the court"—
    (a)   in relation to England and Wales, means the High Court;
    (b)   in relation to Scotland, means the Court of Session; and
    (c)   in relation to Northern Ireland, means the High Court or a judge of the High Court.

[69]

NOTES

Sub-s (1): para (b)(i) numbered as such, and words in square brackets inserted, by the Competition Act 1998, s 74(1), Sch 12, para 1(1), (10), (11).

Sub-s (1A): inserted by the Competition Act 1998, s 74(1), Sch 12, para 1(1), (12).

Sub-s (2): words in square brackets substituted by the Competition Act 1998, s 74(1), Sch 12, para 1(1), (13).

Sub-s (5): repealed by the Companies Act 1989, ss 153, 212, Sch 20, para 13(2), Sch 24.

Sub-s (6): para (b) and word immediately preceding it repealed by the Companies Act 1989, ss 153, 212, Sch 20, para 13(2), Sch 24; words in square brackets substituted by virtue of the Magistrates' Courts Act 1980, s 32(2).

Sub-ss (7), (7A): substituted for original sub-s (7) by the Companies Act 1989, s 153, Sch 20, para 13(1).

86   Director to receive copies of reports

(1)   Subject to the next following subsection, a copy of every report of the Commission on a monopoly reference, or on a merger reference other than a newspaper merger reference, shall be transmitted by the Commission to the Director; and the Minister or Ministers to whom any such report is made shall take account of any advice given to him or them by the Director with respect to a report of which a copy is transmitted to the Director under this section.

(2)   The preceding subsection shall not apply to a report made on a monopoly reference, where the reference was made by a Minister or Ministers and (by virtue of any of the provisions of section 50 of this Act) could not have been made by the Director.

(3)   In this section "Minister" includes the Minister of Agriculture for Northern Ireland and the Minister of Commerce for Northern Ireland.

[70]

NOTES

Repealed by the Enterprise Act 2002, s 278(2), Sch 26, as from a day to be appointed.

The Director: see the note "Functions of the Director General of Fair Trading" to s 44 at **[11]**. See also the note "Director General of Fair Trading" to s 1 at **[1]**.

87   Supplementary provisions as to laying reports before Parliament

(1)   Where under section 83 of this Act the Secretary of State lays before Parliament a copy of a report of the Commission on a newspaper merger reference, then—

   (a) if before laying it the Secretary of State has consented to the transfer of a newspaper or of newspaper assets to which the report relates, he shall annex a copy of that consent to the copy of the report laid before Parliament, or

   (b) if he subsequently consents to that transfer, he shall thereupon lay before Parliament a copy of that consent.

(2)   Where the persons to whom a report of the Commission is made under this Act include the Minister of Agriculture for Northern Ireland, that Minister shall lay a copy of the report before the Senate and House of Commons of Northern Ireland, and shall arrange for it to be published in Northern Ireland in such manner as appears to him to be appropriate.

(3)   If a report to which subsection (2) of this section applies is presented by command of the Governor of Northern Ireland to the Senate or House of Commons of Northern Ireland otherwise than at or during the time of a sitting of the Senate or of that House, as the case may be, the presentation of the report shall for the purposes of that subsection be treated as the laying of a copy of it before the Senate or that House as required by that subsection.

[71]

88   Action by Director in consequence of report of Commission on monopoly or merger reference

(1)   Where a report of the Commission on a monopoly reference, or on a merger reference other than a newspaper merger reference, as laid before Parliament,—

   (a) in the case of a monopoly reference, sets out such conclusions as are mentioned in section 56(1) of this Act, or

   (b) in the case of a merger reference, sets out such conclusions as are mentioned in section 73(1) or in section 75(4)(e) of this Act,

and a copy of the report is transmitted to the Director under section 86 of this Act, it shall be the duty of the Director, [to comply with any request of the appropriate Minister or Ministers to consult with any persons mentioned in the request (referred to below in this section as "the relevant parties")] with a view to obtaining from them undertakings to take action indicated in the request made to the Director as being action requisite, in the opinion of the appropriate Minister or Ministers, for the purpose of remedying or preventing the adverse effects specified in the report.

(2)   The Director shall report to the appropriate Minister or Ministers the outcome of his consultations under the preceding subsection; and if any undertaking is given by any of the relevant parties to take action indicated in the request made to the Director as mentioned in that subsection (in this section referred to as an "appropriate undertaking") the Minister to whom the undertaking is given shall furnish particulars of it to the Director.

[(2A)   Where—

   (a) an undertaking is given under this section after the commencement of this subsection, or

(b) an undertaking given under this section is varied or released after that time,

the Minister to whom the undertaking is or was given shall cause the undertaking or, as the case may be, the variation or release to be published in such manner as the Minister may consider appropriate.]

(3) Where in his consultations under subsection (1) of this section the Director seeks to obtain an appropriate undertaking from any of the relevant parties, and either—

(a) he is satisfied that no such undertaking is likely to be given by that party within a reasonable time, or

(b) having allowed such time as in his opinion is reasonable for the purpose, he is satisfied that no such undertaking has been given by that party,

the Director shall give such advice to the appropriate Minister or Ministers as he may think proper in the circumstances (including, if the Director thinks fit, advice with respect to the exercise by the appropriate Minister or Ministers of his or their powers under section 56 or section 73 of this Act, as the case may be).

(4) Where the Director has made a report under subsection (2) of this section, and particulars of an undertaking given by any of the relevant parties have been furnished to the Director in accordance with that subsection, it shall be the duty of the Director—

(a) to keep under review the carrying out of that undertaking, and from time to time to consider whether, by reason of any change of circumstances, [the undertaking is no longer appropriate and either the relevant parties (or any of them) can be released from the undertaking or the undertaking] needs to be varied or to be superseded by a new undertaking, and

(b) if it appears to him [that any person can be so released or that an undertaking] has not been or is not being fulfilled, or needs to be varied or superseded, to give such advice to the appropriate Minister or Ministers as he may think proper in the circumstances.

(5) Where, in consequence of a report of which a copy is transmitted to the Director under section 86 of this Act, an order is made under section 56 or section 73 of this Act in relation to any of the matters to which the report relates it shall be the duty of the Director to keep under review the action (if any) taken in compliance with that order, and from time to time to consider whether, by reason of any change of circumstances, the order should be varied [or revoked] or should be superseded by a new order, and—

(a) if it appears to him that the order has in any respect not been complied with, to consider whether any action (by way of proceedings in accordance with section 93 of this Act or otherwise) should be taken for the purpose of securing compliance with the order, and (where in his opinion it is appropriate to do so) to take such action himself or give advice to any Minister or other person by whom such action might be taken, or

(b) if it appears to him that the order needs to be varied [or revoked], or to be superseded by a new order, to give such advice to the appropriate Minister or Ministers as he may think proper in the circumstances.

(6) In this section . . . , in relation to a report of the Commission, "the appropriate Minister or Ministers" means the Minister or Ministers to whom the report is made, "undertaking" means an undertaking given to that Minister or to one of those Ministers, as the case may be, and, in subsections (3) and (5) of this section, the references to section 73 of this Act shall be construed as including references to that section as applied by section 75(4) of this Act.

NOTES

Repealed by the Enterprise Act 2002, s 278(2), Sch 26, as from a day to be appointed.

Sub-s (1): words in square brackets substituted by the Companies Act 1989, s 153, Sch 20, para 14(1), (5), except in relation to any report made before 16 November 1989.

Sub-s (2A): inserted by the Companies Act 1989, s 153, Sch 20, para 14(2), except in relation to any report made before 16 November 1989.

Sub-s (4): words in square brackets substituted by the Companies Act 1989, s 153, Sch 20, para 14(1), (3), except in relation to any report made before 16 November 1989.

Sub-s (5): words in square brackets inserted by the Companies Act 1989, s 153, Sch 20, para 14(3), except in relation to any report made before 16 November 1989.

Sub-s (6): words omitted repealed by the Companies Act 1989, ss 153, 212, Sch 20, para 14(4), (5), Sch 24, except in relation to any report made before 16 November 1989.

The Director: see the note "Functions of the Director General of Fair Trading" to s 44 at **[11]**. See also the note "Director General of Fair Trading" to s 1 at **[1]**.

See further the Competition Act 1980, s 29(1) at **[122]**.

Transitional provisions: for transitional provisions in relation to undertakings accepted (whether before, on or after the appointed day) by a Minister of the Crown under this section, see s 276(1) of, and Sch 24, paras 15, 16 to, the Enterprise Act 2002 at **[477]**.

89   Interim order after report of Commission under s 54 or s 72

(1)   The provisions of this section shall have effect where—

[(a)   in the circumstances specified in subsection (1) of any of the following sections—

  (i)   sections 56, 73 and 75K of this Act, ...

  (ii) . . .

  the Secretary of State makes, has made, or has under consideration the making of, an order under the section in question exercising any of the powers specified in Schedule 8 to this Act, or

(b)   in the circumstances specified in subsection (1) of section 12 of the Competition Act 1980 the Secretary of State makes, has made, or has under consideration the making of, an order under subsection (5) of that section exercising any of those powers and in those provisions "the principal order" means the order which the Secretary of State makes, or has it under consideration to make, as mentioned in paragraph (a) or paragraph (b) of this subsection.]

(2)   With a view to achieving the purpose for which any of the powers specified in . . . that Schedule are, or are proposed to be, exercised by the principal order, the Secretary of State may by order made by statutory instrument exercise any of the powers mentioned in the next following subsection.

(3)   An order under this section may—

(a)   prohibit or restrict the doing of things which, in the opinion of the Secretary of State, might impede the operation of the principal order or, where it has not yet been made, might be an impediment to making it;

(b)   impose on any person concerned obligations as to the carrying on of any activities or the safeguarding of any assets;

[(bb) require any person to furnish any such information to the Director as may be specified or described in the order;]

(c)   provide for the carrying on of any activities or the safeguarding of any assets either by the appointment of a person to conduct or supervise the conduct of any activities (on such terms and with such powers as may be specified or described in the order under this section) or in any other manner.

NOTES

Repealed by the Enterprise Act 2002, s 278(2), Sch 26, as from a day to be appointed.

Sub-s (1): words in square brackets substituted by the Companies Act 1989, s 153, Sch 20, para 15(1), (4), in relation to the making of any order under this section after 16 November 1989, whether the principal order was made before or after that date, words omitted therefrom repealed by the Competition Act 1998 (Transitional, Consequential and Supplemental Provisions) Order 2000, SI 2000/311, art 9(1), (3).

Sub-s (2): words omitted repealed by the Companies Act 1989, ss 153, 212, Sch 20, para 15(2), (4), Sch 24, in relation to the making of any order under this section after 16 November 1989, whether the principal order was made before or after that date.

Sub-s (3): para (bb) inserted by the Companies Act 1989, s 153, Sch 20, para 15(3), (4), in relation to the making of any order under this section after 16 November 1989, whether the principal order was made before or after that date.

The Director: see the note "Director General of Fair Trading" to s 1 at **[1]**.

Transitional provisions: for transitional provisions in relation to any order made (whether before, on or after the appointed day) by a Minister of the Crown under this section, see s 276(1) of, and Sch 24, paras 15(2)–(5), 17(1), (3)–(5) to, the Enterprise Act 2002 at **[477]**.

90 General provisions as to orders under ss 56, 73, 74 and 89

(1) This section applies to any order under section 56, section 73, section 74[, section 75K] or section 89 of this Act.

(2) Any such order declaring anything to be unlawful may declare it to be unlawful either for all persons or for such persons as may be specified or described in the order.

(3) Nothing in any such order shall have effect so as to apply to any person in relation to his conduct outside the United Kingdom unless that person is—

    (a) a citizen of the United Kingdom and Colonies, or

    (b) a body corporate incorporated under the law of the United Kingdom or of a part of the United Kingdom, or

    (c) a person carrying on business in the United Kingdom, either alone or in partnership with one or more other persons,

but, in the case of a person falling within paragraph (a), paragraph (b) or paragraph (c) of this subsection, any such order may extend to acts or omissions outside the United Kingdom.

(4) An order to which this section applies may extend so as to prohibit the carrying out of agreements already in existence on the date on which the order is made.

[(5) Nothing in any order to which this section applies shall have effect so as to—

    (a) cancel or modify conditions in licences granted—

        (i) under a patent granted under the Patents Act 1949 or the Patents Act 1977 or a European patent (UK) (within the meaning of the Patents Act 1977), or

        (ii) in respect of a design registered under the Registered Designs Act 1949,

    by the proprietor of the patent or design, or

    (b) require an entry to be made in the register of patents or the register of designs to the effect that licences under such a patent or such a design are to be available as of right.]

(6) Nothing in any such order shall affect the conduct of a board established under a scheme made under the Agricultural Marketing Act 1958 . . . [or the Agricultural Marketing (Northern Ireland) Order 1982].

(7)   An order to which this section applies may authorise the Minister making the order to give directions to a person specified in the directions, or to the holder for the time being of an office so specified in any company or association,—

> *(a) to take such steps within his competence as may be specified or described in the directions for the purpose of carrying out, or securing compliance with, the order, or*
>
> *(b) to do or refrain from doing anything so specified or described which he might be required by the order to do or refrain from doing,*

and may authorise that Minister to vary or revoke any directions so given.

[74]

NOTES

   Repealed by the Enterprise Act 2002, s 278(2), Sch 26, as from a day to be appointed.
   Sub-s (1): words in square brackets inserted by the Companies Act 1989, s 153, Sch 20, para 16(1), (2).
   Sub-s (5): substituted by the Companies Act 1989, s 153, Sch 20, para 16(1), (3).
   Sub-s (6): words omitted repealed and words in square brackets added by the Agricultural Marketing (Northern Ireland) Order 1982, SI 1982/1080, art 46(1), (2), Sch 8, Sch 9.
   This section is extended (subject to specified exceptions) to orders made under the Competition Act 1980, ss 10, 12: see s 12(6)(a) of that Act at **[110]**.

91   Procedure relating to orders to which s 90 applies

(1)   No order to which section 90 of this Act applies and which exercises any of the powers specified in Part II of Schedule 8 to this Act, and no order varying or revoking any such order, shall be made unless a draft of the order has been laid before Parliament and approved by a resolution of each House of Parliament; and the provisions of Schedule 9 to this Act shall have effect with respect to the procedure to be followed before laying before Parliament a draft of any such order.

(2)   Before making any order under section 56 or section 73 of this Act other than any such order as is mentioned in the preceding subsection, the Minister proposing to make the order shall publish, in such manner as appears to him to be appropriate, a notice—

> *(a) stating his intention to make the order;*
>
> *(b) indicating the nature of the provisions to be embodied in the order; and*
>
> *(c) stating that any person whose interests are likely to be affected by the order, and who is desirous of making representations in respect of it, should do so in writing (stating his interest and the grounds on which he wishes to make the representations) before a date specified in the notice (that date being not earlier than the end of the period of thirty days beginning with the day on which publication of the notice is completed);*

and the Minister shall not make the order before the date specified in the notice in accordance with paragraph (c) of this subsection and shall consider any representations duly made to him in accordance with the notice before that date.

[75]

NOTES

   Repealed by the Enterprise Act 2002, s 278(2), Sch 26, as from a day to be appointed.
   Sub-s (2) is extended to orders made under the Competition Act 1980, ss 10, 12: see s 12(6)(b) of that Act at **[110]**.

92   Investigation of company or association with reference to order to which s 90 applies

(1)   For the purpose of determining whether to make an order to which section 90 of this Act applies whereby any powers are to be exercised in relation to a

company or association, or for the purpose of obtaining information on which to exercise by or under any such order any powers in relation to a company or association, the Secretary of State may appoint an inspector to investigate and report to him on any such matters falling within the next following subsection as are specified or described in the appointment.

[(2) The matters which may be so specified or described are any matters which in the case of a company registered under the Companies Act 1985 (or the previous corresponding legislation)—

  (a) could in accordance with sections 432 and 433 of that Act be investigated by an inspector appointed under section 432, or

  (b) could in accordance with section 442 of that Act, or in accordance with any provisions as applied by section 443(1), be investigated by an inspector appointed under section 442.

(3) For purposes connected with any investigation made by an inspector appointed under this section—

  (a) sections 434 to 436 of the Companies Act 1985 (or those sections as applied by section 443(1)) shall have effect as they do for the purposes of any investigation under section 432 or 442 of that Act, and

  (b) the provisions of that Act referred to in this and the last preceding subsection shall be taken to extend throughout the United Kingdom.]

[76]

NOTES

Repealed by the Enterprise Act 2002, s 278(2), Sch 26, as from a day to be appointed.

Sub-ss (2), (3): substituted by the Companies Consolidation (Consequential Provisions) Act 1985, s 30, Sch 2.

93 Enforcement of orders to which s 90 applies

(1) No criminal proceedings shall, by virtue of the making of an order to which section 90 of this Act applies, lie against any person on the grounds that he has committed, or aided, abetted, counselled or procured the commission of, or conspired or attempted to commit, or incited others to commit, any contravention of the order.

(2) Nothing in the preceding subsection shall limit any right of any person to bring civil proceedings in respect of any contravention or apprehended contravention of any such order, and (without prejudice to the generality of the preceding words) compliance with any such order shall be enforceable by civil proceedings by the Crown for an injunction or interdict or for any other appropriate relief.

(3) If any person makes default in complying with any directions given under section 90(7) of this Act, the court may, on the application of the Secretary of State, make an order requiring him to make good the default within a time specified in the order, or, if the directions related to anything to be done in the management or administration of a company or association, requiring the company or association or any officer of it to do so.

(4) Any order of the court under subsection (3) of this section may provide that all the costs or expenses of or incidental to the application for the order shall be borne by any person in default or by any officers of a company or association who are responsible for its default.

(5) In this section "the court"—

  (a) in relation to England and Wales, means the High Court;

  (b) in relation to Scotland, means the Court of Session; and

(c) in relation to Northern Ireland, means the High Court or a judge of the High Court.

[77]

NOTES

Repealed by the Enterprise Act 2002, s 278(2), Sch 26, as from a day to be appointed.

This section is extended to orders made under the Competition Act 1980, ss 10, 12: see s 12(6)(c) of that Act at [110].

[93A Enforcement of undertakings

(1) This section applies where a person (in this section referred to as "the responsible person") has given an undertaking which—
  (a) has been accepted by the Secretary of State [pursuant to a proposal under section 56A of this Act or under section 56F or] 75G of this Act,
  (b) has been accepted by the appropriate Minister or Ministers under section 88 of this Act after the commencement of this section, . . .
  (c) . . .

(2) Any person may bring civil proceedings in respect of any failure, or apprehended failure, of the responsible person to fulfil the undertaking, as if the obligations imposed by the undertaking on the responsible person had been imposed by an order to which section 90 of this Act applies.]

[78]

NOTES

Inserted by the Companies Act 1989, s 148.

Repealed by the Enterprise Act 2002, s 278(2), Sch 26, as from a day to be appointed.

Sub-s (1): words in square brackets substituted by the Deregulation and Contracting Out Act 1994, s 39, Sch 11, para 2(1), (3); para (c) and word immediately preceding it repealed by the Competition Act 1998 (Transitional, Consequential and Supplemental Provisions) Order 2000, SI 2000/311, art 9(1), (4).

[93B False or misleading information

(1) If a person furnishes any information—
  (a) to the Secretary of State, *the Director* or the Commission in connection with any of their functions under *Parts IV, V, VI* or this Part of this Act *or under the Competition Act 1980*, or
  (b) to the Commission in connection with the functions of the Commission under the Telecommunications Act 1984 or the Airports Act 1986,

and either he knows the information to be false or misleading in a material particular, or he furnishes the information recklessly and it is false or misleading in a material particular, he is guilty of an offence.

(2) A person who—
  (a) furnishes any information to another which he knows to be false or misleading in a material particular, or
  (b) recklessly furnishes any information to another which is false or misleading in a material particular,

knowing that the information is to be used for the purpose of furnishing information as mentioned in subsection (1)(a) or (b) of this section, is guilty of an offence.

(3) A person guilty of an offence under subsection (1) or (2) of this section is liable—
  (a) on summary conviction, to a fine not exceeding the statutory maximum, and
  (b) on conviction on indictment, to imprisonment for a term not exceeding two years or to a fine or to both.

(4)   Section 129(1) of this Act does not apply to an offence under this section.]

[(5) This section shall not have effect in relation to the furnishing of information to the Commission in connection with its functions under any provision of the Enterprise Act 2002 as applied by virtue of section 13B of the Telecommunications Act 1984 or section 44B of the Airports Act 1986.]

[79]

NOTES

Inserted by the Companies Act 1989, s 151.

Sub-s (1): for the first words in italics there are substituted the words "the Office of Fair Trading", for the second words in italics there are substituted the words "Part 5", and the third words in italics are repealed, by the Enterprise Act 2002, s 278, Sch 25, para 5(4)(a), Sch 26, as from a day to be appointed.

Sub-s (5): added by the Enterprise Act 2002, s 278(1), Sch 25, para 5(4)(b), as from a day to be appointed.

Functions of the Director General of Fair Trading: in the case of functions which, under ss 44, 45, 50, 52, 53, 86, 88 of this Act, are jointly exercisable by the Director General of Fair Trading and the Rail Regulator by virtue of the Railways Act 1993, s 67(2), and the Competition Act 1998, Sch 10, Pt I, para 1, this section has effect as if the reference in sub-s (1)(a) to the Director included a reference to the Rail Regulator; see s 67(9) of the 1993 Act.

This section has effect: (i) so far as it relates to functions exercisable by the Rail Regulator by virtue of the Deregulation and Contracting Out Act 1994, Sch 2, para 11, as if the reference in sub-s (1)(a) to the Director included a reference to the Rail Regulator (see s 7(2) of, and Sch 2, para 14 to, the 1994 Act); (ii) so far as it relates to functions exercisable by the Director General of Telecommunications by virtue of the Telecommunications Act 1984, s 50(2), and the Competition Act 1998, Sch 10, Pt I, para 1, or the Deregulation and Contracting Out Act 1994, Sch 2, para 1, as if the reference in sub-s (1)(a) to the Director included a reference to the Director General of Telecommunications (see s 50(6A) of the 1984 Act); (iii) so far as it relates to functions exercisable by the Gas and Electricity Markets Authority by virtue of the Gas Act 1986, s 36A(2), and the Competition Act 1998, Sch 10, Pt I, para 1, as if the reference in sub-s (1)(a) to the Director included a reference to the Authority (see s 36A(8) of the 1986 Act); (iv) so far as it relates to functions exercisable by the Gas and Electricity Markets Authority by virtue of the Electricity Act 1989, s 43(2), and the Competition Act 1998, Sch 10, Pt I, para 1, or the Deregulation and Contracting Out Act 1994, Sch 2, para 4, as if the reference in sub-s (1)(a) to the Director General of Fair Trading included a reference to the Authority (see s 43(6A) of the 1989 Act); and (v) so far as it relates to functions exercisable by the Director General of Water Services by virtue of the Water Industry Act 1991, s 31(2), and the Competition Act 1998, Sch 10, Pt I, para 1, or the Deregulation and Contracting Out Act 1994, Sch 2, para 8, as if the reference in sub-s (1)(a) to the Director included a reference to the Director General of Water Services (see s 31(8A) of the 1991 Act). As to the Director, see also the note "Director General of Fair Trading" to s 1 at **[1]**.

PART IX
AMENDMENTS OF RESTRICTIVE TRADE PRACTICES ACTS

94   Transfer of functions of Registrar to Director

(1)   Subject to the transitional provisions having effect by virtue of section 139 of this Act, the functions of the Registrar of Restrictive Trading Agreements are hereby transferred to the Director, and the office of Registrar of Restrictive Trading Agreements is hereby abolished.

(2)   . . .

[80]

NOTES

Sub-s (2): repealed by the Resale Prices Act 1976, s 29, Sch 3, Pt I.

The Director: see the note "Director General of Fair Trading" to s 1 at **[1]**.

95–123   (*Ss 95–106, ss 107–117 (Pt X) repealed and consolidated by the Restrictive Trade Practices Act 1976; ss 118–123 (Pt XI) outside the scope of this work.*)

PART XII
MISCELLANEOUS AND SUPPLEMENTARY PROVISIONS

124   Publication of information and advice

(1)   With respect to any matter in respect of which the Director has any duties under section 2(1) of this Act, he may arrange for the publication, in such form and in such manner as he may consider appropriate, of such information and advice as it may appear to him to be expedient to give to consumers in the United Kingdom.

(2)   In arranging for the publication of any such information or advice, the Director shall have regard to the need for excluding, so far as that is practicable,—

(a)   any matter which relates to the private affairs of an individual, where the publication of that matter would or might, in the opinion of the Director, seriously and prejudicially affect the interests of that individual, and

(b)   any matter which relates specifically to the affairs of a particular body of persons, whether corporate or unincorporate, where publication of that matter would or might, in the opinion of the Director, seriously and prejudicially affect the interests of that body.

(3)   Without prejudice to the exercise of his powers under subsection (1) of this section, it shall be the duty of the Director to encourage relevant associations to prepare, and to disseminate to their members, codes of practice for guidance in safeguarding and promoting the interests of consumers in the United Kingdom.

(4)   In this section "relevant association" means any association (whether incorporated or not) whose membership consists wholly or mainly of persons engaged in the production or supply of goods or in the supply of services or of persons employed by or representing persons so engaged and whose objects or activities include the promotion of the interests of persons so engaged.

[81]

NOTES

Repealed by the Enterprise Act 2002, s 278(2), Sch 26, as from a day to be appointed.

By virtue of the Telecommunications Act 1984, s 109(1), Sch 4, para 57(1), the Gas Act 1986, s 67(1), Sch 7, para 15(1), the Electricity Act 1989, s 48(3), the Water Consolidation (Consequential Provisions) Act 1991, s 2(1), Sch 1, para 24(1), the Railways Act 1993, s 71(3) and the Transport Act 2000, s 90(6), the Director General of Fair Trading is to consult with the Director General of Telecommunications, the Gas and Electricity Markets Authority, the Director General of Water Services, the Rail Regulator or the Civil Aviation Authority, as appropriate, before publishing under this section any information or advice which they have power to publish under s 48(1) of the 1984 Act, s 35(1) of the 1986 Act, s 48 of the 1989 Act, s 201(2) of the 1991 Act, s 71 of the 1993 Act and s 90 of the 2000 Act.

The Director: see the note "Director General of Fair Trading" to s 1 at **[1]**.

---

125   Annual and other reports of Director

(1)   The Director shall, as soon as practicable after the end of the year 1974 and of each subsequent calendar year, make to the Secretary of State a report on his activities, and the activities of the Advisory Committee and of the Commission, during that year.

(2)   Every such report shall include a general survey of developments, during the year to which it relates, in respect of matters falling within the scope of the Director's duties under any enactment (including any enactment contained in this Act, other than this section) [and shall set out any directions given to the Director under section 2(2) of the Consumer Credit Act 1974 during that year].

(3)　The Secretary of State shall lay a copy of every report made by the Director under subsection (1) of this section before each House of Parliament, and shall arrange for every such report to be published in such manner as he may consider appropriate.

(4)　The Director may also prepare such other reports as appear to him to be expedient with respect to such matters as are mentioned in subsection (2) of this section, and may arrange for any such report to be published in such manner as he may consider appropriate.

(5)　In making any report under this Act the Director shall have regard to the need for excluding, so far as that is practicable, any such matter as is specified in paragraph (a) or paragraph (b) of section 124(2) of this Act.

(6)　For the purposes of this section any period between the commencement of this Act and the end of the year 1973 shall be treated as included in the year 1974.

[82]

NOTES

Repealed by the Enterprise Act 2002, s 278(2), Sch 26, as from a day to be appointed.

Sub-s (2): words in square brackets added by the Consumer Credit Act 1974, s 5.

By virtue of the Telecommunications Act 1984, s 109(1), Sch 4, para 57(2), the Water Industry Act 1991, s (2)(1), Sch 1, para 24(2), the Railways Act 1993, s 74, and the Utilities Act 2000, s 5(9), sub-s (1) above does not apply to activities of the Competition Commission on which the Director General of Telecommunications, the Director General of Water Services, the Rail Regulator or the Gas and Electricity Markets Authority are required to report by s 55(1) of the 1984 Act, s 193(1) of the 1991 Act, s 74(7) of the 1993 Act, or s 5 of the 2000 Act.

The Director: see the note "Director General of Fair Trading" to s 1 at **[1]**.

See further, as to the last annual report of the Director, the Enterprise Act 2002, s 276(1), Sch 24, para 5 at **[477]**.

126–128　*(S 126 repealed by the Patents Act 1977, s 132(7), Sch 6; s 127 inserts the Agricultural Marketing Act 1958, s 19A; s 128 repealed and consolidated by the Restrictive Trade Practices Act 1976.)*

129　Time-limit for prosecutions

(1)　No prosecution for an offence under this Act shall be commenced after the expiration of three years from the commission of the offence or one year from its discovery by the prosecutor, whichever is the earlier.

(2)　Notwithstanding anything in [section 127(1) of the Magistrates' Courts Act 1980], a magistrates' court may try an information for an offence under this Act if the information was laid within twelve months from the commission of the offence.

(3)　Notwithstanding anything in [section 136 of the Criminal Procedure (Scotland) Act 1995], summary proceedings in Scotland for an offence under this Act may be commenced within twelve months from the commission of the offence, and [subsection (3) of the said section 136] shall apply for the purposes of this subsection as it applies for the purposes of that section.

(4)　In the application of this section to Northern Ireland, for the references in subsection (2) to [section 127(1) of the Magistrates' Courts Act 1980], and to the trial and laying of an information there shall be substituted respectively references to [Article 19(1) of the Magistrates' Courts (Northern Ireland) Order 1981] and to the hearing and determination and making of a complaint [and as if in that subsection for the words "an offence under this Act" there were substituted the words "an offence under section 30(1) *or 46(2)* of this Act"].

[83]

NOTES

Sub-s (2): words in square brackets substituted by the Magistrates' Courts Act 1980, s 154, Sch 7, para 118.

Sub-s (3): words in square brackets substituted by the Criminal Procedure (Consequential Provisions) (Scotland) Act 1995, s 5, Sch 4, para 9.

Sub-s (4): words in first pair of square brackets substituted by the Magistrates' Courts Act 1980, s 154, Sch 7, para 118; words in second pair of square brackets substituted by the Magistrates' Courts (Northern Ireland) Order 1981, SI 1981/1675, art 170(2), Sch 6, Pt I; words in final pair of square brackets added by the Criminal Justice (Northern Ireland) Order 1980, SI 1980/704, art 12, Sch 1, Pt II and words in italics therein repealed by the Enterprise Act 2002, s 278(2), Sch 26, as from a day to be appointed.

130 Notice to Director of intended prosecution

(1) Where a local weights and measures authority in England or Wales proposes to institute proceedings for an offence under section 23 of this Act, or for an offence under the Trade Descriptions Act 1968, other than an offence under section 28(5) or section 29 of that Act, [or for an offence under any provision made by or under Part III of the Consumer Protection Act 1987,] [or for an offence under section 1 of, or paragraph 6 of the Schedule to, the Property Misdescriptions Act 1991,] [or for an offence under [any of sections 1A to 2 or 5B of the Timeshare Act 1992]] it shall, as between the authority and the Director, be the duty of the authority to give to the Director notice of the intended proceedings, together with a summary of the facts on which the charges are to be founded, and to postpone institution of the proceedings until either—

(a) twenty-eight days have elapsed since the giving of that notice, or

(b) the Director has notified the authority that he has received the notice and the summary of the facts.

(2) In relation to offences under the Trade Descriptions Act 1968, the preceding subsection shall have effect subject to the transitional provisions having effect by virtue of section 139 of this Act.

[84]

NOTES

Repealed by the Enterprise Act 2002, s 278(2), Sch 26, as from a day to be appointed.

Sub-s (1): words in first pair of square brackets inserted by the Consumer Protection Act 1987, s 48, Sch 4, para 3; words in second pair of square brackets inserted by the Property Misdescriptions Act 1991, s 3, Schedule, para 2(1); words in third (outer) pair of square brackets inserted by the Timeshare Act 1992, s 10, Schedule, para 2(1); words in final (inner) pair of square brackets substituted by the Timeshare Regulations 1997, SI 1997/1081, reg 13(5).

The Director: see the note "Director General of Fair Trading" to s 1 at **[1]**.

131 Notification of convictions and judgments to Director

(1) Where in any criminal proceedings a person is convicted of an offence by or before a court in the United Kingdom, or a judgment is given against a person in civil proceedings in any such court, and it appears to the court—

(a) having regard to the functions of the Director under Part III of this Act [or under the Estate Agents Act 1979], that it would be expedient for the conviction or judgment to be brought to his attention, and

(b) that it may not be brought to his attention unless arrangements for the purpose are made by the court,

the court may make arrangements for that purpose notwithstanding that the proceedings have been finally disposed of by the court.

(2) In this section "judgment" includes any order or decree, and any reference to the giving of a judgment shall be construed accordingly.

[85]

NOTES

Repealed by the Enterprise Act 2002, s 278(2), Sch 26, as from a day to be appointed.

Sub-s (1): words in square brackets in para (a) inserted by the Estate Agents Act 1979, s 9(5).

The Director: see the note "Director General of Fair Trading" to s 1 at **[1]**.

132   Offences by bodies corporate

(1) Where an offence under section 23, *section 46,* section 85(6) [section 93B] or Part XI of this Act, which has been committed by a body corporate, is proved to have been committed with the consent or connivance of, or to be attributable to any neglect on the part of, any director, manager, secretary or other similar officer of the body corporate, or any person who was purporting to act in any such capacity, he as well as the body corporate shall be guilty of that offence and be liable to be proceeded against and punished accordingly.

(2) Where the affairs of a body corporate are managed by its members, subsection (1) of this section shall apply in relation to the acts and defaults of a member in connection with his functions of management as if he were a director of the body corporate.

[86]

NOTES

Sub-s (1): words in italics repealed by the Enterprise Act 2002, s 278(2), Sch 26, as from a day to be appointed; words in square brackets inserted by the Companies Act 1989, s 153, Sch 20, para 17.

133   General restrictions on disclosure of information

(1)   Subject to subsections (2) to (4) of this section, no information with respect to any particular business which has been obtained under or by virtue of the provisions (other than Part II) of this Act . . . shall, so long as that business continues to be carried on, be disclosed without the consent of the person for the time being carrying on that business.

(2)   The preceding subsection does not apply to any disclosure of information which is made—

    (a) for the purpose of facilitating the performance of any functions of the Director, [the Director General of Telecommunications,] [the Gas and Electricity Markets Authority] [the Civil Aviation Authority,] [the Director General of Water Services,] [. . .] [the Director General of Electricity Supply for Northern Ireland] [or the Director General of Gas for Northern Ireland] [the Rail Regulator] [the Authorised Conveyancing Practitioners Board, the Coal Authority] the Commission, the Secretary of State or any other Minister under this Act, . . . [the Estate Agents Act 1979, or] [the Competition Act 1980,] [or the Telecommunications Act 1984,] [. . .] [or the Gas Act 1986,] [or the Airports Act 1986,] [or the Water Act 1989,] [or the Water Industry Act 1991 or any of the other consolidation Acts (within the meaning of section 206 of that Act of 1991)] [or the Electricity Act 1989,] [or the Electricity (Northern Ireland) Order 1992] [or the Gas (Northern Ireland) Order 1996] [or Part IV of the Airports (Northern Ireland) Order 1994] [or the Broadcasting Act 1990,] or [the Control of Misleading Advertisements Regulations 1988] [or the Courts and Legal Services Act 1990] [or the Railways Act 1993] [or the Coal Industry Act 1994] [or the Competition Act 1998] [or the EC Competition Law (Articles 84 and 85) Enforcement Regulations 2001] or] [Part I of the Transport Act 2000 or] [or Chapter 2 of Part 18 of the Financial Services and Markets Act 2000]

  *(b) in pursuance of a Community obligation within the meaning of the
       European Communities Act 1972.*

  *(3)   Subsection (1) of this section does not apply to any disclosure of information
which is made for the purposes of any proceedings before the Restrictive Practices
Court or of any other legal proceedings, whether civil or criminal, under this Act,
the [. . .] [or the Control of Misleading Advertisements Regulations 1988].*

  (4)   Nothing in subsection (1) of this section shall be construed—

  *(a) as limiting the matters which may be included in, or made public as part
       of, a report of the Advisory Committee or of the Commission [or a notice
       published by the Director under section 56B of this Act];*
  (b) . . .
  *(c) as applying to any information which has been made public as part of such
       a report or as part of that register.*

  *(5)   Any person who discloses any information in contravention of this section
shall be guilty of an offence and shall be liable—*

  (a) on summary conviction, to a fine not exceeding [the prescribed sum],
  *(b) on conviction on indictment, to imprisonment for a term not exceeding two
       years or to a fine or to both.*

  *(6)   In this section references to this Act shall be construed as including
references to any enactment repealed by this Act.*

                                                                              [87]

NOTES

    Repealed by the Enterprise Act 2002, ss 247(b), 278(2), Sch 26, as from a day to be appointed; the
repeal of sub-s (3) does not affect any right to disclose information for the purposes of proceedings before
the Restrictive Practices Court to which the Competition Act 1998, Sch 13, para 42 applies (see s 276(1)
of, and Sch 24, para 21 to, the 2002 Act at **[477]**).

    Sub-ss (1), (4): words omitted repealed by the Restrictive Trade Practices Act 1976, s 44, Sch 6.

    Sub-s (2): words in square brackets in para (a) added or substituted by the Estate Agents Act 1979,
s 10(4)(a), the Competition Act 1980, s 19(4)(c), the Telecommunications Act 1984, s 109(1), Sch 4,
para 57(3), the Financial Services Act 1986, s 182, Sch 13, para 1, the Gas Act 1986, s 67(1), Sch 7,
para 15(3), the Airports Act 1986, s 83(1), Sch 4, para 3, the Control of Misleading Advertisements
Regulations 1988, SI 1988/915, reg 7(6)(a), the Water Act 1989, s 190(1), Sch 25, para 45(3), the
Electricity Act 1989, s 112(1), Sch 16, para 16(1), (4), the Broadcasting Act 1990, s 203(1), Sch 20,
para 20, the Courts and Legal Services Act 1990, s 125(3), Sch 18, para 4, as from a day to be appointed,
the Water Consolidation (Consequential Provisions) Act 1991, s 2(1), Sch 1, para 24(3), the Electricity
(Northern Ireland) Order 1992, SI 1992/231 (NI 1), art 95(1), Sch 12, para 10, the Railways Act 1993,
s 152, Sch 12, para 7, the Coal Industry Act 1994, s 67(1), Sch 9, para 14, the Airports (Northern Ireland)
Order 1994, SI 1994/426, art 71(2), Sch 9, para 2, the Gas (Northern Ireland) Order 1996, SI 1996/275,
art 71(1), Sch 6, the Competition Law (Articles 88 and 89) Enforcement Regulations 1996, SI 1996/2199,
reg 29(1), the Competition Act 1998, s 74(1), Sch 12, para 1(1), (14), the Transport Act 2000, s 97, Sch 8,
Pt IV, para 11, the Utilities Act 2000, s 3(2), the EC Competition Law (Articles 84 and 85) Enforcement
Regulations 2001, SI 2001/2916, reg 35(1), the Financial Services and Markets Act 2000 (Consequential
Amendments and Repeals) Order 2001, SI 2001/3649, art 285(1), (3); words omitted in the first place
repealed by virtue of the Utilities Act 2000, s 3(2); words omitted in the second place originally inserted
by the Restrictive Trade Practices Act 1976, s 44, Sch 5, repealed by the Competition Act 1998
(Transitional, Consequential and Supplemental Provisions) Order 2000, SI 2000/311, art 9(1), (5); words
omitted in the second place repealed by the Financial Services and Markets Act 2000 (Consequential
Amendments and Repeals) Order 2001, SI 2001/3649, art 285(1), (2).

    Sub-s (3): words omitted in first pair of square brackets substituted by the Restrictive Trade Practices
Act 1976, s 44, Sch 5, repealed by SI 2000/311, art 9(1), (5); words in second pair of square brackets added
by SI 1988/915, reg 7(6)(a)(ii).

    Sub-s (4): words in square brackets in para (a) inserted by the Deregulation and Contracting Out
Act 1994, s 39, Sch 11, para 2(1), (4).

    Sub-s (5): words in square brackets substituted by virtue of the Magistrates' Courts Act 1980, s 32(2).

Disclosure of information: sub-s (3), so far as it relates to information obtained under or by virtue of any provision of Part III of this Act, has effect in relation to the disclosure of information by or on behalf of a public authority, as if the purposes for which the disclosure of information is authorised included the purposes mentioned in the Anti-terrorism, Crime and Security Act 2001, s 17; see Sch 4, Pt 1 of the 2001 Act.

The Director: see the note "Functions of the Director General of Fair Trading" to s 44 at **[11]**. See also the note "Director General of Fair Trading" to s 1 at **[1]**.

134　　Provisions as to orders

(1)　Any statutory instrument whereby any order is made under any of the preceding provisions of this Act, other than a provision which requires a draft of the order to be laid before Parliament before making the order, or whereby any regulations are made under this Act, shall be subject to annulment in pursuance of a resolution of either House of Parliament.

(2)　Any power conferred by any provision of this Act to make an order by statutory instrument shall include power to revoke or vary the order by a subsequent order made under that provision.

[88]

135　　Financial provisions

(1)　The Secretary of State shall pay all remuneration, allowances or other sums payable under this Act to or in respect of persons who are or have been members of the Advisory Committee *or the Commission*, and shall defray—
　(a)　. . .
　(b)　to such amount as the Secretary of State with the approval of the Minister for the Civil Service may determine, all other expenses duly incurred by the Advisory Committee . . . .

(2)　There shall be defrayed out of moneys provided by Parliament—
　(a)　all expenses incurred by the Secretary of State in consequence of the provisions of this Act;
　(b)　any expenses incurred in consequence of those provisions by any other Minister of the Crown or government department, not being a Minister or department of the Government of Northern Ireland;
　(c)　the remuneration of, and any travelling or other allowances payable under this Act to, the Director and any staff of the Director, any other sums payable under this Act to or in respect of the Director, and any expenses duly incurred by the Director or by any of his staff in consequence of the provisions [of this or any other Act];
　(d)　any increase attributable to this Act in the sums payable out of moneys so provided under the Superannuation Act 1972.

(3)　. . .

[89]

NOTES

Sub-s (1): words omitted repealed by the Competition Act 1998, s 74(1), (3), Sch 12, para 1(1), (15), Sch 14, Pt I, with continuing effect in respect of any pension, allowance, gratuity or sum by way of compensation in respect of which a determination has been made prior to 1 April 1999.

Sub-s (2): words in square brackets in para (c) inserted by the Competition Act 1980, s 32(2).

Sub-s (3): repealed by the Northern Ireland (Modification of Enactments—No 1) Order 1973, SI 1973/2163, art 14(2), Sch 6.

Minister for the Civil Service: now the Treasury, by virtue of the Transfer of Functions (Civil Service and Treasury) Order 1981, SI 1981/1670.

The Director: see the note "Director General of Fair Trading" to s 1 at **[1]**.

136　*(Repealed by the Statute Law (Repeals) Act 1977.)*

137   General interpretation provisions

(1)   In this Act—
"the Act of 1948" means the Monopolies and Restrictive Practices (Inquiry and
     Control) Act 1948;

                              . . . . .

"the Act of 1965" means the Monopolies and Mergers Act 1965;

                              . . . . .

"contract of employment" means a contract of service or of apprenticeship,
     whether it is express or implied, and (if it is express) whether it is oral or in
     writing;
"scale" (where the reference is to the scale on which any services are, or are to
     be, made available, supplied or obtained) means scale measured in terms of
     money or money's worth or in any other manner.

(2)   Except in so far as the context otherwise requires, in this Act, ... , the
following expressions have the meanings hereby assigned to them respectively, that
is to say—
"the Advisory Committee" means the Consumer Protection Advisory Committee;
"agreement" means any agreement or arrangement, in whatever way and in
     whatever form it is made, and whether it is, or is intended to be, legally
     enforceable or not;
"business" includes a professional practice and includes any other undertaking
     which is carried on for gain or reward or which is an undertaking in the
     course of which goods or services are supplied otherwise than free
     of charge;
"commercial activities in the United Kingdom" means any of the following,
     that is to say, the production and supply of goods in the United Kingdom,
     the supply of services in the United Kingdom and the export of goods from
     the United Kingdom;
"the Commission" means the [Competition Commission];
"complex monopoly situation" has the meaning assigned to it by section 11 of
     this Act;
"consumer" (subject to subsection (6) of this section) means any person who is
     either—
     (a) a person to whom goods are or are sought to be supplied (whether by
          way of sale or otherwise) in the course of a business carried on by the
          person supplying or seeking to supply them, or
     (b) a person for whom services are or are sought to be supplied in the
          course of a business carried on by the person supplying or seeking to
          supply them,
     and who does not receive or seek to receive the goods or services in the
     course of a business carried on by him;
"the Director" means the Director General of Fair Trading;
"enactment" includes an enactment of the Parliament of Northern Ireland;
"goods" includes buildings and other structures, and also includes ships,
     aircraft and hovercraft, . . . ;
"group" (where the reference is to a group of persons fulfilling specified
     conditions, other than the condition of being interconnected bodies
     corporate) means any two or more persons fulfilling those conditions,
     whether apart from fulfilling them they would be regarded as constituting a
     group or not;
"merger reference" has the meaning assigned to it by section 5(3) of this Act;
"merger situation qualifying for investigation" has the meaning assigned to it
     by section 64(8) of this Act;

"Minister" includes a government department but shall not by virtue of this provision be taken to include the establishment consisting of the Director and his staff, and, except where the contrary is expressly provided, does not include any Minister or department of the Government of Northern Ireland;

"monopoly reference" and "monopoly situation" have the meanings assigned to them by section 5(3) of this Act;

"newspaper merger reference" has the meaning assigned to it by section 59(3) of this Act;

"practice" means any practice, whether adopted in pursuance of an agreement or otherwise;

"price" includes any charge or fee, by whatever name called;

"produce", in relation to the production of minerals or other substances, includes getting them, and, in relation to the production of animals or fish, includes taking them;

"supply", in relation to the supply of goods, includes supply by way of sale, lease, hire or hire-purchase, and, in relation to buildings or other structures, includes the construction of them by a person for another person;

"uncompetitive practices" means practices having the effect of preventing, restricting or distorting competition in connection with any commercial activities in the United Kingdom;

"worker" (subject to subsection (7) of this section) has the meaning assigned to it by section 167 of the Industrial Relations Act 1971.

(3)   In the provisions of this Act . . . "the supply of services" does not include the rendering of any services under a contract of employment but, . . .

(a) includes the undertaking and performance for gain or reward of engagements (whether professional or other) for any matter other than the supply of goods, and

(b) includes both the rendering of services to order and the provision of services by making them available to potential users; [and

(c) includes the making of arrangements for a person to put or keep on land a caravan (within the meaning of Part I of the Caravan Sites and Control of Development Act 1960) other than arrangements by virtue of which the person may occupy the caravan as his only or main residence] [and

(d) includes the making of arrangements for the use by public service vehicles (within the meaning of the Public Passenger Vehicles Act 1981) of a parking place which is used as a point at which passengers on services provided by means of such vehicles may be taken up or set down] [and

(e) includes the making of arrangements permitting use of the tunnel system (within the meaning of the Channel Tunnel Act 1987) by a person operating services for the carriage of passengers or goods by rail] [and

(f) includes the making of arrangements, by means of such an agreement as is mentioned in section 189(2) of the Broadcasting Act 1990, for the sharing of the use of any telecommunication apparatus (within the meaning of Schedule 2 to the Telecommunications Act 1984)] [and

(g) includes the supply of network services and station services, within the meaning of Part I of the Railways Act 1993;]

and any reference in those provisions to services supplied or to be supplied, or to services provided or to be provided, shall be construed accordingly.

[(3A) The Secretary of State may by order made by statutory instrument—

(a) provide that "the supply of services" in the provisions of this Act is to include, or to cease to include, any activity specified in the order which consists in, or in making arrangements in connection with, permitting the use of land; and

(b) for that purpose, amend or repeal any of paragraphs (c), (d), (e) or (g) of subsection (3) above.

(3B) No order under subsection (3A) above is to be made unless a draft of the order has been laid before Parliament and approved by a resolution of each House of Parliament.

(3C) The provisions of Schedule 9 to this Act apply in the case of a draft of any such order as they apply in the case of a draft of an order to which section 91(1) above applies.]

(4)   . . .

(5)   For the purposes of the provisions of this Act . . . , any two bodies corporate are to be treated as interconnected if one of them is a body corporate of which the other is a subsidiary (within the meaning of [section 736 of the Companies Act 1985]) or if both of them are subsidiaries (within the meaning of that section) of one and the same body corporate; and in those provisions "interconnected bodies corporate" shall be construed accordingly, and "group of interconnected bodies corporate" means a group consisting of two or more bodies corporate all of whom are interconnected with each other.

(6)   For the purposes of the application of any provision of this Act in relation to goods or services of a particular description or to which a particular practice applies, "consumers" means persons who are consumers (as defined by subsection (2) of this section) in relation to goods or services of that description or in relation to goods or services to which that practice applies.

(7)   For the purposes of the application of this Act to Northern Ireland, the definition of "worker" in subsection (2) of this section shall apply as if the Industrial Relations Act 1971 extended to Northern Ireland but, in section 167(2)(a) of that Act, references to general medical services, pharmaceutical services, general dental services or general ophthalmic services provided under the enactments mentioned in that subsection were references to the corresponding services provided in Northern Ireland under the corresponding enactments there in force.

(8)   Except in so far as the context otherwise requires, any reference in this Act to an enactment shall be construed as a reference to that enactment as amended or extended by or under any other enactment, including this Act.

[90]

NOTES

Sub-s (1): words omitted in the first place repealed by the Resale Prices Act 1976, s 29, Sch 3, Pt I and by the Competition Act 1998 (Transitional, Consequential and Supplemental Provisions) Order 2000, SI 2000/311, art 9(1), (6); words omitted in the second place repealed by the Restrictive Trade Practices Act 1976, s 44, Sch 6.

Sub-s (2): words omitted in the first place repealed by the Restrictive Trade Practices Act 1976, s 44, Sch 6; definitions "the Advisory Committee" and "the Director" repealed by the Enterprise Act 2002, s 278(2), Sch 26, as from a day to be appointed; words in square brackets in definition "the Commission" substituted by the Competition Act 1998 (Competition Commission) Transitional, Consequential and Supplemental Provisions Order 1999, SI 1999/506, art 14; words omitted in the second place repealed by the Electricity Act 1989, s 112(4), Sch 18.

Sub-s (3): words omitted repealed by the Restrictive Trade Practices Act 1976, s 44, Sch 6; para (c) and word immediately preceding it inserted by the Competition Act 1980, s 23; para (d) and word immediately preceding it inserted by the Transport Act 1985, s 116(1); para (e) and word immediately preceding it inserted by the Channel Tunnel Act 1987, s 33(10); para (f) and word immediately preceding it inserted by the Broadcasting Act 1990, s 192(1); para (g) and word immediately preceding it inserted by the Railways Act 1993, s 66(4).

Sub-ss (3A)–(3C): inserted by the Competition Act 1998, s 68.

Sub-s (4): repealed by the Electricity Act 1989, s 112(4), Sch 18.

Sub-s (5): words omitted repealed by the Restrictive Trade Practices Act 1976, s 44, Sch 6; words in square brackets substituted by the Companies Consolidation (Consequential Provisions) Act 1985, s 30, Sch 2.

The Director: see the note "Director General of Fair Trading" to s 1 at **[1]**.

Industrial Relations Act 1971, s 167: whole Act repealed by the Trade Union and Labour Relations Act 1974, ss 1(1), 25(3), Sch 5 (repealed); see now the Trade Union and Labour Relations (Consolidation) Act 1992, s 296(1).

Monopolies and Mergers Act 1965; Monopolies and Restrictive Practices (Inquiry and Control) Act 1948: repealed by s 139(1) of, and Sch 13 to, this Act.

138   Supplementary interpretation provisions

(1)   This section applies to the following provisions of this Act, that is to say, section 2(4), *Parts II and III,* section 137(6), and the definition of "consumer" contained in section 137(2).

(2)   For the purposes of any provisions to which this section applies it is immaterial whether any person supplying goods or services has a place of business in the United Kingdom or not.

(3)   For the purposes of any provisions to which this section applies any goods or services supplied wholly or partly outside the United Kingdom, if they are supplied in accordance with arrangements made in the United Kingdom, whether made orally or by one or more documents delivered in the United Kingdom or by correspondence posted from and to addresses in the United Kingdom, shall be treated as goods supplied to, or services supplied for, persons in the United Kingdom.

(4)   In relation to the supply of goods under a hire-purchase agreement, a credit-sale agreement or a conditional sale agreement, the person conducting any antecedent negotiations, as well as the owner or seller, shall for the purposes of any provisions to which this section applies be treated as a person supplying or seeking to supply the goods.

[(5)   In subsection (4) of this section, the following expressions have the meanings given by, or referred to in, section 189 of the Consumer Credit Act 1974—
   "antecedent negotiations",
   "conditional sale agreement",
   "credit-sale agreement",
   "hire-purchase agreement".]

(6)   In any provisions to which this section applies—
   (a) any reference to a person to or for whom goods or services are supplied shall be construed as including a reference to any guarantor of such a person, and
   (b) any reference to the terms or conditions on or subject to which goods or services are supplied shall be construed as including a reference to the terms or conditions on or subject to which any person undertakes to act as such a guarantor;

and in this subsection "guarantor", in relation to a person to or for whom goods or services are supplied, includes a person who undertakes to indemnify the supplier of the goods or services against any loss which he may incur in respect of the supply of the goods or services to or for that person.

(7)   For the purposes of any provisions to which this section applies goods or services supplied by a person carrying on a business shall be taken to be supplied in the course of that business if payment for the supply of the goods or services is made or (whether under a contract or by virtue of an enactment or otherwise) is required to be made.

[91]

NOTES
Sub-s (1): words in italics repealed by the Enterprise Act 2002, s 278(2), Sch 26, as from a day to be appointed.

Sub-s (5): substituted by the Consumer Credit Act 1974, s 192(3)(a), Sch 4, Pt I, para 37.

139   Amendments, repeals and transitional provisions

(1)   Subject to the transitional provisions and savings contained in Schedule 11 to this Act—

   (a) the enactments specified in Schedule 12 to this Act shall have effect subject to the amendments specified in that Schedule (being minor amendments or amendments consequential upon the preceding provisions of this Act), and

   (b) the enactments specified in Schedule 13 to this Act are hereby repealed to the extent specified in the third column of that Schedule.

(2)   The provisions of Schedule 11 to this Act shall have effect for the purposes of this Act.

[92]

140   Short title, citation, commencement and extent

(1)   This Act may be cited as the Fair Trading Act 1973.

(2)   . . .

(3)   This Act shall come into operation on such day as the Secretary of State may by order made by statutory instrument appoint: and different dates may be so appointed for, or for different purposes of, any one or more of the provisions of this Act (including, in the case of section 139 of this Act, the amendment or repeal of different enactments specified in Schedule 12 or Schedule 13 to this Act or of different provisions of any enactment so specified).

(4)   Where any provision of this Act, other than a provision contained in Schedule 11, refers to the commencement of this Act, it shall be construed as referring to the day appointed under this section for the coming into operation of that provision.

(5)   This Act extends to Northern Ireland.

[93]

_____

NOTES

   Sub-s (2): repealed by the Restrictive Trade Practices Act 1976, s 44, Sch 6.
   Orders: the Fair Trading Act 1973 (Commencement No 1) Order 1973, SI 1973/1545; the Fair Trading Act 1973 (Commencement No 2) Order 1973, SI 1973/1652.

_____

SCHEDULES

SCHEDULE 1

Section 1

DIRECTOR GENERAL OF FAIR TRADING

1.   There shall be paid to the Director such remuneration, and such travelling and other allowances, as the Secretary of State with the approval of the Minister for the Civil Service may determine.

2.   In the case of any such holder of the office of the Director as may be determined by the Secretary of State with the approval of the Minister for the Civil Service, there shall be paid such pension, allowance or gratuity to or in respect of him on his retirement or death, or such contributions or payments towards provision for such a pension, allowance or gratuity, as may be so determined.

3.   If, when any person ceases to hold office as the Director, it appears to the Secretary of State with the approval of the Minister for the Civil Service that there are special circumstances which make it right that he should receive compensation, there may be paid to him a sum by way of compensation of such amount as may be so determined.

4.   . . .

5.   The Director shall have an official seal for the authentication of documents required for the purposes of his functions.

6.   The Documentary Evidence Act 1868 shall have effect as if the Director were included in the first column of the Schedule to that Act, as if the Director and any person authorised to act on behalf of the Director were mentioned in the second column of that Schedule, and as if the regulations referred to in that Act included any document issued by the Director or by any such person.

7.   Anything authorised or required by or under this Act or any other enactment to be done by the Director, other than the making of a statutory instrument, may be done by any member of the staff of the Director who is authorised generally or specially in that behalf in writing by the Director.

[94]

NOTES

Repealed by the Enterprise Act 2002, s 278(2), Sch 26, as from a day to be appointed.

Para 4: repealed by the House of Commons Disqualification Act 1975, s 10(2), Sch 3 and the Northern Ireland Assembly Disqualification Act 1975, s 5(2), Sch 3, Pt I.

Transfer of functions: by the Transfer of Functions (Treasury and Minister for the Civil Service) Order 1995, SI 1995/269, art 3, Schedule, para 9, the Minister for the Civil Service's functions under paras 1–3 of this Schedule (which were transferred to the Treasury by the Transfer of Functions (Minister for the Civil Service and Treasury) Order 1981, SI 1981/1670), became functions of the Minister with effect from 1 April 1995.

The Director: see the note "Director General of Fair Trading" to s 1 at [1].

(Sch 2 outside the scope of this work; Sch 3 repealed by the Competition Act 1998, s 74(1), (3), Sch 12, para 1(1), (2), Sch 14, Pt I (paras 6, 8, 9 have continuing effect in respect of any pension, allowance, gratuity or sum by way of compensation in respect of which a determination has been made prior to 1 April 1999).)

SCHEDULE 4

Sections 14 and 109

SERVICES EXCLUDED FROM SECTIONS 14 AND 109

1.   Legal services (that is to say, the services of barristers, advocates or solicitors in their capacity as such).

2.   Medical services (that is to say, the provision of medical or surgical advice or attendance and the performance of surgical operations).

3.   Dental services (that is to say, any services falling within the practice of dentistry within the meaning of the Dentists Act [1984]).

4.   Ophthalmic services (that is to say, the testing of sight).

5.   Veterinary services (that is to say, any services which constitute veterinary surgery within the meaning of the Veterinary Surgeons Act 1966).

[6.   The services of registered nurses or midwives in their capacity as such.]

7.   The services of . . . physiotherapists or chiropodists in their capacity as such.

8.   The services of architects in their capacity as such.

9.   *Accounting and auditing services (that is to say, the making or preparation of accounts or accounting records and the examination, verification and auditing of financial statements).*

[10.   The services of registered patent agents (within the meaning of Part V of the Copyright, Designs and Patents Act 1988) in their capacity as such.]

[10A.   The services of persons carrying on for gain in the United Kingdom the business of acting as agents or other representatives of other persons for the purpose of applying for or obtaining European patents or for the purpose of conducting proceedings [in relation to applications for or otherwise] in connection with such patents before the European Patent Office or the comptroller and whose names appear on the European list (within the meaning of [Part V of the Copyright, Designs and Patents Act 1988]) in their capacity as such persons.]

11.   *The services of parliamentary agents entered in the register in either House of Parliament as agents entitled to practise both in promoting and in opposing Bills, in their capacity as such parliamentary agents.*

12.   *The services of surveyors (that is to say, of surveyors of land, of quantity surveyors, of surveyors of buildings or other structures and of surveyors of ships) in their capacity as such surveyors.*

13.   *The services of professional engineers or technologists (that is to say, of persons practising or employed as consultants in the field of—*
   (a) civil engineering;
   (b) mechanical, aeronautical, marine, electrical or electronic engineering;
   (c) mining, quarrying, soil analysis or other forms of minerology or geology;
   (d) agronomy, forestry, livestock rearing or ecology;
   (e) metallurgy, chemistry, biochemistry or physics; or
   (f) any other form of engineering or technology analogous to those mentioned in the preceding sub-paragraphs),
in their capacity as such engineers or technologists.

14.   *Services consisting of the provision—*
   (a) of primary, secondary or further education within the meaning of [the Education Act 1996,] the Education (Scotland) Acts 1939 to 1971 or the Education and Libraries (Northern Ireland) Order 1972, or
   (b) of university or other higher education not falling within the preceding sub-paragraph.

15.   *The services of ministers of religion in their capacity as such ministers.*

NOTES

Repealed by the Enterprise Act 2002, s 278(2), Sch 26, as from a day to be appointed.

Para 3: date in square brackets substituted by the Dentists Act 1984, s 54(1), Sch 5, para 6.

Para 6: substituted by the Nursing and Midwifery Order 2001, SI 2002/253, art 54(3), Sch 5, para 3(a).

Para 7: word omitted repealed by SI 2002/253, art 54(3), Sch 5, para 3(b).

Para 10: substituted by the Copyright, Designs and Patents Act 1988, s 303(1), Sch 7, para 15.

Para 10A: inserted by the Patents Act 1977, s 132(6), Sch 5, para 7; words in first pair of square brackets inserted by the Administration of Justice Act 1985, s 60(2)(a), (6); words in second pair of square brackets substituted by the Copyright, Designs and Patents Act 1988, s 303(1), Sch 7, para 15.

Para 14: words in square brackets substituted by the Education Act 1996, s 582(1), Sch 37, Pt I, para 26.

Nurses Act 1957: repealed by the Nurses, Midwives and Health Visitors Act 1979, s 23(5), Sch 8.

Modification: the reference to solicitors in para 1 includes a reference to bodies recognised under the Administration of Justice Act 1985, s 9, by virtue of the Solicitors' Incorporated Practices Order 1991, SI 1991/2684, arts 2–5, Sch 1.

SCHEDULE 5
Sections 16, 50, 51

GOODS AND SERVICES REFERRED TO IN SECTION 16

PART I
GENERAL RESTRICTION

[1.], 3.   ...

[4.   The carriage of passengers by road in Northern Ireland.]

[5.   Services for the carriage of passengers, or of goods, by railway, network services and station services, within the meaning of Part I of the Railways Act 1993, but excluding the carriage of passengers or goods on shuttle services (within the meaning of the Channel Tunnel Act 1987).]

6.   The services of conveying, receiving, collecting, despatching and delivering letters.

7.   The running of any system for the conveyance, through the agency of electric, magnetic, electro-magnetic, electro-chemical or electro-mechanical energy, of any of the matters specified *[in paragraphs (a) to (d) of section 4(1) of the Telecommunications Act 1984].*

[96]

NOTES
Repealed by the Enterprise Act 2002, s 278(2), Sch 26, as from a day to be appointed.
Para 1: (as substituted for original paras 1, 2 by the Gas Act 1986, s 67(1), Sch 7, para 15(4)) repealed by the Gas Act 1995, s 17(5), Sch 6.
Para 3: repealed by the Electricity Act 1989, s 112(1), (4), Sch 16, para 16(5), Sch 18 and the Electricity (Northern Ireland) Order 1992, SI 1992/231, art 95(1), (4), Sch 12, para 11, Sch 14.
Para 4: substituted by the Transport Act 1985, s 114(2)(a).
Para 5: substituted by the Railways Act 1993, s 66(5).
Para 7: words in square brackets substituted by the Telecommunications Act 1984, s 109, Sch 4, para 57(4).

(*Sch 5, Pt II repealed by the Telecommunications Act 1984, s 109(6), Sch 7, Pt I; Sch 6 outside the scope of this work.*)

SCHEDULE 7
Sections 50 and 51

GOODS AND SERVICES (IN ADDITION TO THOSE IN SCHEDULE 5) WHOLLY OR PARTLY EXCLUDED FROM SECTION 50

PART I
GOODS AND SERVICES WHOLLY EXCLUDED

1.   Raw cane or beet sugar.

2.   Sugar beet.

3.   Hops.

4.   Water.

5.   Port facilities (as defined by section 92(1) of the Transport Act 1962).

6.   Air navigation services (as defined by section 64(1) of the Civil Aviation Act 1971).

[7.   International carriage by air, otherwise than on a charter flight (that is to say, a flight on which the whole capacity of the aircraft is available for purchase by one or more charterers for his or their own use or for resale).]

8.   ...

[9.   ...]

[97]

NOTES
Repealed by the Enterprise Act 2002, s 278(2), Sch 26, as from a day to be appointed.
Para 4: repealed in relation to England and Wales by the Water Act 1989, s 190(1), (3), Sch 25, para 45(4), Sch 27, Pt I.
Para 7: substituted by the Monopoly References (Alteration of Exclusion) Order 1984, SI 1984/1887, art 2.
Para 8: repealed by the Broadcasting Act 1990, ss 192(4), 203(3), Sch 21.
Para 9: added by the Cable and Broadcasting Act 1984, s 57(1), Sch 5, para 29; repealed by the Broadcasting Act 1990, ss 192(4), 203(3), Sch 21.
Civil Aviation Act 1971, s 92(1): repealed by the Civil Aviation Act 1982, s 109, Sch 16; replaced by s 105(1) of that Act.

PART II
GOODS AND SERVICES PARTLY EXCLUDED

Description of goods or services	*Form of supply excluded*
9. ...	...
10. Refined sugar.	Supply otherwise than by way of retail sale.
11. Fleece wool.	Supply under a scheme for the time being in force under the Agricultural Marketing Act 1958.
12., 13 ...	...

[98]

NOTES
Repealed by the Enterprise Act 2002, s 278(2), Sch 26, as from a day to be appointed.
Paras 9, 12: repealed by the Monopoly References (Deletion of Exclusions) Order 1998, SI 1998/2253, art 2.
Para 13: repealed by the Airports Act 1986, s 83(5), Sch 6, Pt II.

PART III
GOODS PARTLY EXCLUDED IN RELATION TO NORTHERN IRELAND ONLY

Description of goods	*Form of supply excluded*
14. Live pigs.	Supply for slaughter.
15. Fresh uncured carcases or parts of carcases of pigs.	Supply otherwise than by way of retail sale.

[99]

NOTES
Repealed by the Enterprise Act 2002, s 278(2), Sch 26, as from a day to be appointed.

SCHEDULE 8
Sections 56, 73, 74, 77, 89 and 91
POWERS EXERCISABLE BY ORDERS UNDER SECTIONS 56 AND 73

PART I
POWERS EXERCISABLE IN ALL CASES

1.   Subject to paragraph 3 of this Schedule, an order under section 56 or section 73 of this Act (in this Schedule referred to as an "order") may declare it to be unlawful, except to such extent and in such circumstances as may be provided by or under the order, to make or to carry out any such agreement as may be specified or described in the order.

2.   Subject to the next following paragraph, an order may require any party to any such agreement as may be specified or described in the order to terminate the agreement within such time as may be so specified, either wholly or to such extent as may be so specified.

3.—(1), (2)   . . .

(3)   An order shall not by virtue of either of those paragraphs declare it to be unlawful to make or to carry out, or require any person to terminate, an agreement in so far as, if made, it would relate, (or as the case may be) in so far as it relates, to the terms and conditions of employment of any workers, or to the physical conditions in which any workers are required to work.

(4)   In this paragraph "terms and conditions of employment" has the meaning assigned to it by section 167(1) of the Industrial Relations Act 1971.

4.   An order may declare it to be unlawful, except to such extent and in such circumstances as may be provided by or under the order, to withhold or to agree to withhold or to threaten to withhold, or to procure others to withhold or to agree to withhold or threaten to withhold, from any such persons as may be specified or described in the order, any supplies or services so specified or described or any orders for such supplies or services (whether the withholding is absolute or is to be effectual only in particular circumstances).

5.   An order may declare it to be unlawful, except to such extent and in such circumstances as may be provided by or under the order, to require, as a condition of the supplying of goods or services to any person,—

   (a)   the buying of any goods, or

   (b)   the making of any payment in respect of services other than the goods or services supplied, or

   (c)   the doing of any other such matter as may be specified or described in the order.

6.   An order may declare it to be unlawful, except to such extent and in such circumstances as may be provided by or under the order,—

   (a)   to discriminate in any manner specified or described in the order between any persons in the prices charged for goods or services so specified or described, or

   (b)   to do anything so specified or described which appears to the appropriate Minister to amount to such discrimination,

or to procure others to do any of the things mentioned in sub-paragraph (a) or sub-paragraph (b) of this paragraph.

7.   An order may declare it to be unlawful, except to such extent and in such circumstances as may be provided by or under the order,—

   (a)   to give or agree to give in other ways any such preference in respect of the supply of goods or services, or the giving of orders for goods or services, as may be specified or described in the order, or

   (b)   to do anything so specified or described which appears to the appropriate Minister to amount to giving such preference,

or to procure others to do any of the things mentioned in sub-paragraph (a) or sub-paragraph (b) of this paragraph.

8.   An order may declare it to be unlawful, except to such extent and in such circumstances as may be provided by or under the order, to charge for goods or services supplied prices differing from those in any published list or notification, or to do anything specified or described in the order which appears to the appropriate Minister to amount to charging such prices.

9.   An order may require a person supplying goods or services to publish a list of or otherwise notify prices, with or without such further information as may be specified or described in the order.

[9A.—(1)   An order may require a person supplying goods or services to publish—

   (a)   any such accounting information in relation to the supply of the goods or services, and

   (b)   any such information in relation to—

      (i)   the quantities of goods or services supplied, or

      (ii)   the geographical areas in which they are supplied,

as may be specified or described in the order.

PART I
STATUTES

(2)   In this paragraph "accounting information", in relation to a supply of goods or services, means information as to—
    (a)   the costs of the supply, including fixed costs and overheads,
    (b)   the manner in which fixed costs and overheads are calculated and apportioned for accounting purposes of the supplier, and
    (c)   the income attributable to the supply.]

10.—(1)   Subject to the following provisions of this paragraph, an order may, to such extent and in such circumstances as may be provided by or under the order, regulate the prices to be charged for any goods or services specified or described in the order.

(2)   An order shall not exercise the power conferred by the preceding sub-paragraph in respect of goods or services of any description unless the matters specified in the relevant report as being those which in the opinion of the Commission operate, or may be expected to operate, against the public interest relate, or include matters relating, to the prices charged for goods or services of that description.

(3)   In this paragraph "the relevant report", in relation to an order, means the report of the Commission in consequence of which the order is made, in the form in which that report is laid before Parliament.

11.   An order may declare it to be unlawful, except to such extent and in such circumstances as may be provided by or under the order, for any person, by publication or otherwise, to notify, to persons supplying goods or services, prices recommended or suggested as appropriate to be charged by those persons for those goods or services.

12.—(1)   An order may prohibit or restrict the acquisition by any person of the whole or part of the undertaking or assets of another person's business, or the doing of anything which will or may have a result to which this paragraph applies, or may require that, if such an acquisition is made or anything is done which has such a result, the persons concerned or any of them shall thereafter observe any prohibitions or restrictions imposed by or under the order.

(2)   This paragraph applies to any result which consists in two or more bodies corporate becoming interconnected bodies corporate.

(3)   Where an order is made in consequence of a report of the Commission under section 72 of this Act, or is made under section 74 of this Act, this paragraph also applies to any result (other than that specified in sub-paragraph (2) of this paragraph) which, in accordance with section 65 of this Act, consists in two or more enterprises ceasing to be distinct enterprises.

[12A.   An order may require any person to furnish any such information to the Director as may be specified or described in the order.

12B.   An order may require any activities to be carried on separately from any other activities.

12C.   An order may prohibit or restrict the exercise of any right to vote exercisable by virtue of the holding of any shares, stock or securities.]

13.   In this Part of this Schedule "the appropriate Minister", in relation to an order, means the Minister by whom the order is made.

                                                               [100]

NOTES
    Repealed by the Enterprise Act 2002, s 278(2), Sch 26, as from a day to be appointed; for a saving in relation to any monopoly reference made under s 50 or s 51 of this Act before such day or days as the Secretary of State may appoint, see s 276(1) of, and Sch 24, para 14 to, the 2002 Act at **[477]**.
    Para 3: sub-paras (1), (2) repealed by the Competition Act 1998, s 74(1), (3), Sch 12, para 1(1), (3)(d), Sch 14, Pt I, subject to savings and transitional provisions in Sch 13, Pt V, paras 40, 41 of the 1998 Act at **[246]**. Original text of sub-paras (1), (2), as amended by the Restrictive Trade Practices Act 1976, s 44, Sch 5, read as follows—
    "(1)   An order shall not by virtue of paragraph 1 of this Schedule declare it to be unlawful to make any agreement in so far as, if made, it would be an agreement to which [the Act of 1976] would apply.

(2)   An order shall not by virtue of paragraph 1 or paragraph 2 of this Schedule declare it to be unlawful to carry out, or require any person to terminate, an agreement in so far as it is an agreement to which [the Act of 1976] applies."

Paras 9A, 12A–12C: inserted by the Companies Act 1989, s 153, Sch 20, para 19.

This Part is extended (subject to a limited exception) to orders made under the Competition Act 1980, ss 10, 12: see s 12(6)(d) thereof at **[110]**.

The powers conferred by this Part are: (a) further exercisable by orders under the Competition Act 1980, ss 10(2)(b), 12(5); and (b) extended, in relation to copyright and design right, by the Copyright Designs and Patents Act 1988, ss 144, 238.

Modification: para 1 has effect, to such extent as is necessary for the purpose of giving effect to s 75K(2) of this Act, as if after the words "section 73" there were inserted the words "or section 75K"; see s 75K(8) of this Act at **[59]**.

The Director: see the note "Director General of Fair Trading" to s 1 at **[1]**.

Industrial Relations Act 1971, s 167(1). The whole Act was repealed by the Trade Union and Labour Relations Act 1974, s 1(1), 25(3), Sch 5, itself repealed and replaced by the Trade Union and Labour Relations (Consolidation) Act 1992.

PART II
POWERS EXERCISABLE EXCEPT IN CASES FALLING WITHIN SECTION 56(6)

14. *An order may provide for the division of any business by the sale of any part of the undertaking or assets or otherwise (for which purpose all the activities carried on by way of business by any one person or by any two or more interconnected bodies corporate may be treated as a single business), or for the division of any group of interconnected bodies corporate, and for all such matters as may be necessary to effect or take account of the division, including—*

    (a) the transfer or vesting of property, rights, liabilities or obligations;

    (b) the adjustment of contracts, whether by discharge or reduction of any liability or obligation or otherwise;

    (c) the creation, allotment, surrender or cancellation of any shares, stock or securities;

    (d) the formation or winding up of a company or other association, corporate or unincorporate, or the amendment of the memorandum and articles or other instruments regulating any company or association;

    (e) the extent to which, and the circumstances in which, provisions of the order affecting a company or association in its share capital, constitution or other matters may be altered by the company or association, and the registration under any enactment of the order by companies or associations so affected;

    (f) the continuation, with any necessary change of parties, of any legal proceedings.

15. *In relation to an order under section 73 of this Act, the reference in paragraph 14 of this Schedule to the division of a business as mentioned in that paragraph shall be construed as including a reference to the separation, by the sale of any part of any undertaking or assets concerned or other means, of enterprises which are under common control otherwise than by reason of their being enterprises of interconnected bodies corporate.*

[101]

NOTES

Repealed by the Enterprise Act 2002, s 278(2), Sch 26, as from a day to be appointed; for a saving in relation to any monopoly reference made under s 50 or s 51 of this Act before such day or days as the Secretary of State may appoint, see s 276(1) of, and Sch 24, para 14 to, the 2002 Act at **[477]**.

SCHEDULE 9
Section 91

PROCEDURE PRELIMINARY TO LAYING DRAFT OF ORDER TO WHICH
SECTION 91(1) APPLIES

1. *The provisions of this Schedule shall have effect where the Secretary of State proposes to lay before Parliament a draft of any such order as is mentioned in section 91(1) of this Act.*

2.   The Secretary of State shall cause notice of his intention to lay a draft of the order before Parliament to be published in the London Gazette, the Edinburgh Gazette and the Belfast Gazette and in two or more daily newspapers (other than local newspapers), and shall not lay a draft of the order until the end of the period of forty-two days beginning with the day on which the publication of the notice in accordance with this paragraph is completed.

3.   A notice under this Schedule shall—
  (a)   state that it is proposed to lay a draft of the order before Parliament;
  (b)   indicate the nature of the provisions to be embodied in the order;
  (c)   name a place where a copy of the draft will be available to be seen at all reasonable times; and
  (d)   state that any person whose interests are likely to be affected by the order, and who is desirous of making representations in respect of it, should do so in writing (stating his interest and the grounds on which he wishes to make the representations) before the date on which the period mentioned in paragraph 2 of this Schedule is due to expire (specifying that date).

4.   The Secretary of State shall consider any representation that is duly made with respect to the draft order and is not withdrawn, and, at any time after the date specified in the notice in accordance with sub-paragraph (d) of paragraph 3 of this Schedule, may lay the draft order . . .

[102]

NOTES
   Repealed by the Enterprise Act 2002, s 278(2), Sch 26, as from a day to be appointed.
   Para 4: words omitted repealed by the Companies Act 1989, ss 153, 212, Sch 20, para 20, Sch 24, in relation to the laying of any draft order under that paragraph after 16 November 1989, whether the notice was published before or after that date.

(Sch 10 repealed by the Restrictive Trade Practices Act 1976, s 44, Sch 6.)

SCHEDULE 11

Sections 139, 140

TRANSITIONAL PROVISIONS AND SAVINGS

General provisions

1.—(1)   Subject to the following provisions of this Schedule, in so far as anything done under an enactment repealed by this Act could have been done under a corresponding provision of this Act, it shall not be invalidated by the repeal but shall have effect as if done under that provision.

   (2)   In relation to the Commission (by whichever of the names mentioned in section 4(1) of this Act it was for the time being called) sub-paragraph (1) of this paragraph applies, in particular, to any appointment of a member of the Commission (including any appointment, or extension of the term of service, of a chairman or deputy chairman of the Commission) or of any of the staff of the Commission, any reference made to the Commission, any proceedings or report of the Commission on such a reference, and any order made in consequence of any such report.

   (3)   A provision of this Act shall, for the purposes of this Schedule, be regarded as corresponding to an enactment repealed by this Act if (notwithstanding that it differs, whether to a small extent or substantially, from that enactment) it fulfils in this Act a purpose similar to that which that enactment fulfilled in the repealed enactments; and any reference in this Schedule to provisions of the repealed enactments corresponding to any provisions of this Act shall be construed accordingly.

   (4)   In this Schedule "the repealed enactments" means the enactments repealed by this Act, and "the commencement of this Act", where that expression occurs in any provision of this Schedule,—
  (a)   if the same day is appointed under section 140 of this Act for the repeal of all those enactments, means the day so appointed, or

(b) if different days are appointed under that section for the repeal of different enactments, means such day as may be specified for the purposes of this sub-paragraph in an order made by the Secretary of State by statutory instrument;

and different days may be so specified in relation to different provisions of this Schedule.

2. For the purposes of the operation of paragraph 1 of this Schedule, anything done by or in relation to the Board of Trade shall be treated as having been done by or in relation to the Secretary of State, whether apart from this paragraph it would fall to be so treated or not.

3. Without prejudice to any express amendment made by this Act, where an Act (whether passed before, or in the same Session as, this Act) or any document refers, either expressly or by implication, to an enactment repealed by this Act, the reference shall, except where the context otherwise requires, be construed as, or as including, a reference to any corresponding provision of this Act.

4. Where any period of time specified in an enactment repealed by this Act is current at the commencement of this Act, and there is a corresponding provision in this Act, this Act shall have effect as if that corresponding provision had been in force when that period began to run.

5. Without prejudice to paragraph 1 of this Schedule, any reference in this Act (whether express or implied) to a thing done or required or authorised to be done, or omitted to be done, or to an event which has occurred, under or for the purposes of or by reference to or in contravention of any provisions of this Act shall, except where the context otherwise requires, be construed as including a reference to the corresponding thing done or required or authorised to be done, or omitted, or to the corresponding event which occurred, as the case may be, under or for the purposes of or by reference to or in contravention of any corresponding provisions of the repealed enactments.

6. Nothing in this Act shall affect the repealed enactments in their operation in relation to offences committed before the commencement of this Act.

Reference made to Commission before commencement of Act

7.—(1) Any reference made to the Commission under the repealed enactments, and any report of the Commission made before the commencement of this Act on any such reference, shall have effect in accordance with paragraph 1 of this Schedule if made in accordance with such of the repealed enactments as were applicable to it, and shall so have effect notwithstanding that the reference or report was not made in accordance with the corresponding provisions of this Act.

(2) In the case of any such reference on which the Commission have not made their report before the commencement of this Act—

(a) any proceedings of the Commission on that reference after the commencement of this Act shall be conducted in accordance with the repealed enactments as if they had not been repealed, and

(b) any report of the Commission on that reference shall be made in accordance with those enactments and not in accordance with any corresponding provisions of this Act;

but nothing in this sub-paragraph shall be construed as excluding the operation of any provisions of this Act relating to any functions of the Director in relation to the Commission, to the transmission to the Director of copies of reports of the Commission, or to any other action authorised or required to be taken in relation to or in consequence of a report made by the Commission.

(3) In particular, but without prejudice to the generality of the preceding sub-paragraphs, any reference, proceedings or report to which either of those sub-paragraphs applies shall have effect, or shall be conducted or made, as mentioned in that sub-paragraph notwithstanding that the reference or report related or relates to the question whether conditions to which the Act of 1948 applied prevailed or prevail, and not to the existence or possible existence of a monopoly situation within the meaning of this Act.

(4)   For the purposes of the operation of sub-paragraph (2) of this paragraph in relation to a report made by the Commission after the commencement of this Act, section 29(1) of the Act of 1956 (whereby conditions to which the Act of 1948 applied were not to be considered to prevail by reason of any agreement to which Part I of the Act of 1956 applied) shall be construed as if section 6(1) of the Act of 1956 had been originally enacted as amended by section 95 of this Act.

Report of Commission made before 5th August 1965

8.   An order made under section 56 of this Act in consequence of a report made by the Commission before the commencement of the Act of 1965 shall not exercise any of the powers specified in Part II of Schedule 8 to this Act; and accordingly the powers conferred by section 89 of this Act shall not be exercisable in consequence of any such report.

Undertaking given in consequence of report on reference made under repealed enactments

9.—(1)   This paragraph applies to any undertaking given to a Minister which is certified by the Secretary of State to have been given in relation to matters dealt with in a report made by the Commission on a reference under section 2 of the Act of 1948 or on a reference under section 6 of the Act of 1965 and which either—
 (a) was given before the commencement of this Act, or
 (b) is given after the commencement of this Act in a case where no request under subsection (1) of section 88 of this Act has been made to the Director to carry out consultations in accordance with that subsection.

    (2)   A copy of any certificate given by the Secretary of State under the preceding sub-paragraph shall be furnished to the Director and the Minister to whom any such undertaking was or is given shall furnish particulars of it to the Director.

    (3)   Subsection (4) of section 88 of this Act shall have effect in relation to any undertaking to which this paragraph applies as if—
 (a) it were an undertaking of which particulars have been furnished to the Director under subsection (2) of that section, and
 (b) any reference in subsection (4) of that section to the report of the Director were a reference to a report made by the Commission as mentioned in sub-paragraph (1) of this paragraph.

    (4)   The preceding provisions of this paragraph shall have effect without prejudice—
 (a) to the duty of the Commission under section 86 of this Act to transmit to the Director copies of reports which were made by the Commission before the commencement of this Act and which, by virtue of paragraphs 1 and 7 of this Schedule, have effect as if made under this Act, or
 (b) to any duty of the Director, where requested by the appropriate Minister or Ministers to do so with respect to any such report, to carry out such consultations as are mentioned in section 88(1) of this Act.

Functions of Director in relation to orders made under Acts of 1948 and 1965

10.   Subsection (5) of section 88 of this Act shall have effect in relation to any order which was made under section 10 of the Act of 1948 or under section 3 or section 6 of the Act of 1965 and which, by virtue of paragraph 1 of this Schedule, has effect as if made under this Act, as that subsection has effect in relation to orders made under this Act in the circumstances specified in that subsection.

Provisions consequential upon transfer of functions from Registrar to Director

11.—(1) Except as provided by paragraph 15 of this Schedule, in relation to any time after the commencement of this Act, anything which has before the commencement of this Act been done by or in relation to the Registrar shall have effect as if it had been done by or in relation to the Director.

    (2)   Sub-paragraph (1) of this paragraph applies, in particular, to any regulations made by the Registrar, any register kept or document issued by the Registrar, any particulars furnished to the Registrar, and any application to or proceedings before the Restrictive Practices Court,

PART I
STATUTES

or any other court, tribunal or authority, made or instituted by or against the Registrar or to which the Registrar was otherwise a party; and any such proceedings, if pending at the commencement of this Act, may accordingly be continued by or against the Director, or with the Director being otherwise treated as a party to them, as the circumstances may require, and for the purpose of so continuing them anything done by or in relation to the Registrar in connection with any such proceedings shall be treated as having been done by or in relation to the Director.

(3) In this Schedule "the Registrar" means the Registrar of Restrictive Trading Agreements.

12., 13. ...

Pension benefits

14. The repeal by this Act of the following enactments, that is to say, Part II of Schedule 1 to the Act of 1965 and section 3(4)(d) of the Superannuation (Miscellaneous Provisions) Act 1967, shall not affect the operation of those enactments in relation to any person who was appointed to be chairman or deputy chairman of the Commission before the commencement of this Act; and, in relation to any such person, a recommendation made under paragraph 5 of that Schedule shall have effect whether made before or after the commencement of this Act.

15.—(1) The repeal by this Act of subsections (7) and (8) of section 1 of the Act of 1956 shall not affect the operation of those subsections in relation to any person who was appointed to be the Registrar before the commencement of this Act; and, in relation to any such person, a determination made under subsection (7) of that section shall have effect whether made before or after the commencement of this Act.

(2) Paragraph 11 of this Schedule shall not have effect for the purposes of the operation of subsection (7) or subsection (8) of section 1 of the Act of 1956 in accordance with the preceding sub-paragraph.

Trade Descriptions Act 1968, s 30

16. The repeal by this Act of subsections (2) to (4) of section 30 of the Trade Descriptions Act 1968 shall not affect the operation of those subsections in their application to any case where a notice under subsection (2) of that section, or a certificate under subsection (4) of that section or a document purporting to be such a certificate, has been given or issued before the commencement of this Act; and the duty imposed by section 130(1) of this Act shall not apply where such a notice has been so given.

[103]

NOTES

Paras 12, 13: repealed and consolidated by the Restrictive Trade Practices Act 1976, s 44, Sch 6.

See further, in relation to para 9, the Competition Act 1980, s 29(1) at **[121]**.

The Director: see the note "Director General of Fair Trading" to s 1 at **[1]**.

Act of 1948: the Monopolies and Restrictive Practices (Inquiry and Control) Act 1948: repealed by this Act, s 139(1), Sch 13.

Act of 1956: the Restrictive Trade Practices Act 1956: repealed by the Restrictive Practices Court Act 1976, s 11, Schedule, the Restrictive Trade Practices Act 1976, s 44, Sch 6, and the Resale Prices Act 1976, s 29, Sch 3.

Act of 1965: the Monopolies and Mergers Act 1965: repealed by this Act, s 139(1), Sch 13.

Superannuation (Miscellaneous Provisions) Act 1967, s 3(4)(d); Trade Descriptions Act 1968, s 30(2)–(4): repealed by s 139(1) of, and Sch 13 to, this Act.

(Sch 12, in so far as unrepealed, contains miscellaneous amendments; Sch 13 contains repeals.)

COMPETITION ACT 1980

(1980 c 21)

ARRANGEMENT OF SECTIONS

An Act to abolish the Price Commission; to make provision for the control of anti-competitive practices in the supply and acquisition of goods and the supply and securing of services; to provide for references of certain public bodies and other persons to the Monopolies and Mergers Commission; to provide for the investigation of prices and charges by the Director General of Fair Trading; to provide for the making of grants to certain bodies; to amend and provide for the amendment of the Fair Trading Act 1973; to make amendments with respect to the Restrictive Trade Practices Act 1976; to repeal the remaining provisions of the Counter-Inflation Act 1973; and for purposes connected therewith

[3 April 1980]

NOTES

Monopolies and Mergers Commission: the Monopolies and Mergers Commission was dissolved by the Competition Act 1998, s 45(3) at **[177]**, which also transferred the functions of the Monopolies and Mergers Commission to the Competition Commission.

Director General of Fair Trading: the Enterprise Act 2002, s 2(1), at **[255]**, provides that, as from the coming into force of that section in accordance with s 279 at **[463]**, the functions of the Director General of Fair Trading, his property, rights and liabilities are transferred to the Office of Fair Trading. Accordingly, (by virtue of s 2(2), (3) of the 2002 Act) the office of the Director is abolished, and any reference to the Director in any enactment, instrument or other document passed or made before the commencement of s 2(1) shall have effect as if it were a reference to the Office of Fair Trading. For transitional provisions in connection with this transfer, see s 276(1) of, and Sch 24, para 6 to, the 2002 Act at **[477]**.

1   *(Repealed by the Statute Law (Repeals) Act 1989.)*

Control of anti-competitive practices

2–10   *(Repealed by the Competition Act 1998, ss 17, 74(3), Sch 14, Pt I.)*

Further references and investigations

11   References of public bodies and certain other persons to the Commission

(1)   The Secretary of State may at any time refer to the Commission any question relating to—
  (a) the efficiency and costs of, [or]
  (b) the service provided by, *or*
  (c) *possible abuse of a monopoly situation by,*
a person falling within subsection (3) below and specified in the reference, including any question whether, in relation to a matter falling within *paragraph (a), (b) or (c)* above, the person is pursuing a course of conduct which operates against the public interest.

(2)   *For the purposes of subsection (1)(c) above "monopoly situation" includes a monopoly situation which is limited to a part of the United Kingdom and, accordingly, for those purposes references to the United Kingdom in sections 6 and 7 of the Fair Trading Act 1973 shall be taken to include references to a part of the United Kingdom.*

(3)   The persons referred to in subsection (1) above are—
  (a) any body corporate—
      (i) which supplies goods or services by way of business,
      (ii) the affairs of which are managed by its members, and
      (iii) the members of which hold office as such by virtue of their appointment to that or another office by a Minister under any enactment; or
  [(aa) any publicly owned railway company, within the meaning of the Railways Act 1993, which supplies network services or station services, within the meaning of Part I of that Act; or]
  [(b) any person (not falling within paragraph (a) above) who provides in Northern Ireland a bus service within the meaning of section 14 of the Finance Act (Northern Ireland) 1966; or]
  [(bb) any person who provides a railway passenger service in pursuance of an agreement entered into by London Regional Transport by virtue of [section 3(2) or (2A)(a)] of the [London Regional Transport Act 1984]; or]
  [(c) the [Environment Agency];] or
  [(cc) . . .]

    (d) any board administering a scheme under the Agricultural Marketing Act 1958 [or the Agricultural Marketing (Northern Ireland) Order 1982]; or

    (e) any body corporate with a statutory duty to promote and assist the maintenance and development of the efficient supply of any goods or services by a body falling within paragraphs (a) to (d) above; or

    (f) any subsidiary, within the meaning of [section 736 of] the [Companies Act 1985], of a body falling within paragraphs (a) to (e) above.

(4) The Secretary of State may by order exclude from subsection (3)(b) [or (bb)] above persons of such descriptions as may be specified in the order.

(5) No question concerning a person falling within subsection (3)(b) [or (bb)] above or a subsidiary of a body falling within [either of those paragraphs] may be referred to the Commission under this section unless it relates to the carriage of passengers by the person or, as the case may be, the subsidiary.

(6) The Secretary of State may at any time by notice given to the Commission vary a reference under this section.

(7) On making a reference under this section or on varying such a reference under subsection (6) above the Secretary of State shall arrange for the reference or, as the case may be, the variation to be published in such manner as he considers most suitable for bringing it to the attention of persons who in his opinion would be affected by it or be likely to have an interest in it.

(8) On a reference under this section the Commission shall investigate and report on any question referred to them but shall exclude from their investigation and report consideration of—

    (a) any question relating to the appropriateness of any financial obligations or guidance as to financial objectives (however expressed) imposed on or given to the person in question by or under any enactment, or otherwise by a Minister; . . .

    (b) . . .

[(9) The provisions mentioned in subsection (9A) are to apply in relation to a reference under this section as if—

    (a) the functions of the Competition Commission under this section were functions under the Fair Trading Act 1973;

    (b) the expression "merger reference" included a reference to the Commission under this section; and

    (c) in paragraph 20(2)(a) of Schedule 7 to the Competition Act 1998, the reference to section 56 of the Fair Trading Act 1973 were a reference to section 12 below.

(9A) The provisions are—

    (a) sections 70 (time limit for report on merger), 84 (public interest) and 85 (attendance of witnesses and production of documents) of the Fair Trading Act 1973; and

    (b) Part II of Schedule 7 to the Competition Act 1998 (performance of the Competition Commission's general functions).]

(10) A report of the Commission on a reference under this section shall be made to the Secretary of State and shall state, with reasons, the conclusions of the Commission with respect to any question referred to them and, where the Commission conclude that the person specified in the reference is pursuing a course of conduct which operates against the public interest, the report may include recommendations as to what action (if any) should be taken by the person for the purpose of remedying or preventing what the Commission consider are the adverse effects of that course of conduct.

(11) In this section "Minister" includes a Northern Ireland department and the head of such a department.

[104]

NOTES

Sub-s (1): word in square brackets in para (a) inserted, para (c) and word immediately preceding it repealed, and for the final words in italics there are substituted the words "paragraph (a) or (b)", by the Enterprise Act 2002, s 278, Sch 25, para 10(1), (2)(a), Sch 26, as from a day to be appointed.

Sub-s (2): repealed by the Enterprise Act 2002, s 278, Sch 25, para 10(1), (2)(b), Sch 26, as from a day to be appointed.

Sub-s (3): para (aa) inserted by the Railways Act 1993, s 152(1), Sch 12, para 12(1); para (b) substituted by the Transport Act 1985, s 114(1); para (bb) inserted by the London Regional Transport Act 1984, s 71(3)(a), Sch 6, para 15, words in first pair of square brackets substituted by the London Regional Transport Act 1996, s 4(2)(a), words in second pair of square brackets substituted by the Transport Act 1985, s 114(1); para (c) substituted by the Water Act 1989, s 190(1), Sch 25, para 59(1), words in square brackets substituted by the Environment Act 1995 (Consequential Amendments) Regulations 1996, SI 1996/593, reg 2, Sch 1; para (cc) inserted, in relation to Scotland only, by the Local Government etc (Scotland) Act 1994, s 72, repealed by the Water Industry (Scotland) Act 2002, s 71, Sch 7, para 10; words in square brackets in para (d) substituted by the Agricultural Marketing (Northern Ireland) Order 1982, SI 1982/1080, art 46, Schs 8, 9; words in first pair of square brackets in para (f) inserted by the Companies Act 1989, s 144(4), Sch 18, para 22, words in second pair of square brackets substituted by the Companies Consolidation (Consequential Provisions) Act 1985, s 30, Sch 2.

Sub-s (4): words in square brackets inserted by the London Regional Transport Act 1984, s 71(3)(a), Sch 6, para 15.

Sub-s (5): words in first pair of square brackets inserted and words in second pair of square brackets substituted by the London Regional Transport Act 1984, s 71(3)(a), Sch 6, para 15.

Sub-s (8): words omitted repealed by the Competition Act 1998, s 74(1), (3), Sch 12, para 4(1), (2), Sch 14, Pt I, subject to savings in Sch 13, Pt V, para 40 of the 1998 Act at **[246]**. The original text read as follows—

"and

    (b)   the question whether any course of conduct required or envisaged as mentioned in section 2(2) above operates against the public interest."

Sub-ss (9), (9A): substituted, for original sub-s (9), by the Competition Act 1998, s 74(1), Sch 12, para 4(1), (3); repealed by the Enterprise Act 2002, s 278, Sch 25, para 10(1), (2)(b), Sch 26, as from a day to be appointed.

Monopoly reference: see further, as to the duty of the Rail Regulator to disclose information and provide assistance to the Competition Commission in carrying out an investigation on certain references under this section, the Railways Act 1993, s 67.

London Regional Transport Act 1984: repealed by the Greater London Authority Act 1999, s 423, Sch 24, Pt II, as from a day to be appointed; as to the abolition of London Regional Transport and the transition to Transport for London, see ss 297–303 of the 1999 Act.

Orders: the Competition (Exclusion of Bus Operators) Order 1980, SI 1980/981 (now spent, following the substitution of sub-s (3)(b), as noted above).

[11A   References under section 11: time-limits

(1)   Every reference under section 11 above shall specify a period (not longer than six months beginning with the date of the reference) within which a report on the reference is to be made.

(2)   A report of the Commission on a reference under section 11 above shall not have effect (and no action shall be taken in relation to it under section 12 below) unless the report is made before the end of the period specified in the reference or such further period (if any) as may be allowed by the Secretary of State under subsection (3) below.

(3)   The Secretary of State may, if he has received representations on the subject from the Commission and is satisfied that there are special reasons why the report cannot be made within the period specified in the reference, extend that period by no more than three months.

(4)   No more than one extension is possible under subsection (3) above in relation to the same reference.

(5)   The Secretary of State shall publish any extension made by him under subsection (3) above in such manner as he considers most suitable for bringing it to the attention of persons who in his opinion would be affected by it or be likely to have an interest in it.]

[105]

NOTES
Commencement: to be appointed.
Inserted by the Enterprise Act 2002, s 278(1), Sch 25, para 10(3), as from a day to be appointed.
Ministers of the Crown: the Enterprise Act 2002, Sch 25, para 10(10) provides that for the purposes of the Scotland Act 1998, the amendments made by Sch 25, para 10(1)–(9) shall be taken to be pre-commencement enactments within the meaning of the 1998 Act; references to a Minister of the Crown in this section should be construed accordingly.

[11B References under section 11: powers of investigation and penalties

(1)   The following sections of Part 3 of the Enterprise Act 2002 shall apply, with the modifications mentioned in subsections (2) and (3) below, for the purposes of references under section 11 above as they apply for the purposes of references under that Part—
   (a) section 109 (attendance of witnesses and production of documents etc);
   (b) section 110 (enforcement of powers under section 109: general);
   (c) section 111 (penalties);
   (d) section 112 (penalties: main procedural requirements);
   (e) section 113 (payments and interest by instalments);
   (f) section 114 (appeals in relation to penalties);
   (g) section 115 (recovery of penalties); and
   (h) section 116 (statement of policy).

(2)   Section 110 shall, in its application by virtue of subsection (1) above, have effect as if—
   (a) subsection (2) were omitted;
   (b) in subsection (4), for the word "publication" there were substituted "laying before both Houses of Parliament"; and
   (c) in subsection (9) the words from "or section" to "section 65(3))" were omitted.

(3)   Section 111(5)(b)(ii) shall, in its application by virtue of subsection (1) above, have effect as if—
   (a) for the words "published (or, in the case of a report under section 50 or 65, given)" there were substituted "made";
   (b) for the words "published (or given)", in both places where they appear, there were substituted "made"; and
   (c) the words "by this Part" were omitted.]

[106]

NOTES
Commencement: to be appointed.
Inserted as noted to s 11A at [105].

[11C References under section 11: further supplementary provisions

(1)   Section 117 of the Enterprise Act 2002 (false or misleading information) shall apply in relation to functions under this Act as it applies in relation to functions under Part 3 of that Act but as if, in subsections (1)(a) and (2), the words "the OFT," were omitted.

(2)   Section 125 of the Enterprise Act 2002 (offences by bodies corporate) shall apply for the purposes of this Act as it applies for the purposes of Part 3 of that Act.

(3)   For the purposes of section 12 below, a conclusion contained in a report of the Commission is to be disregarded if the conclusion is not that of at least two-thirds of the members of the group constituted in connection with the reference concerned in pursuance of paragraph 15 of Schedule 7 to the Competition Act 1998.]

[107]

NOTES

Commencement: to be appointed.

Inserted as noted to s 11A at **[105]**.

[11D   Interim orders

(1)   Subsection (2) below applies where, in the circumstances specified in subsection (1) of section 12 below, the Secretary of State has under consideration the making of an order under subsection (5) of that section.

(2)   The Secretary of State may by order, for the purpose of preventing pre-emptive action—

  (a)   prohibit or restrict the doing of things which the Secretary of State considers would constitute pre-emptive action;

  (b)   impose on any person concerned obligations as to the carrying on of any activities or the safeguarding of any assets;

  (c)   provide for the carrying on of any activities or the safeguarding of any assets either by the appointment of a person to conduct or supervise the conduct of any activities (on such terms and with such powers as may be specified or described in the order) or in any other manner;

  (d)   do anything which may be done by virtue of paragraph 19 of Schedule 8 to the Enterprise Act 2002 (information powers).

(3)   An order under this section shall come into force at such time as is determined by or under the order.

(4)   An order under this section shall, if it has not previously ceased to be in force, cease to be in force on the making of the order under section 12(5) below or (as the case may be) on the making of the decision not to make such an order.

(5)   The Secretary of State shall publish any decision made by him not to make an order under section 12(5) below in such manner as he considers most suitable for bringing it to the attention of persons who in his opinion would be affected by it or would be likely to have an interest in it.

(6)   The Secretary of State shall, as soon as reasonably practicable, consider any representations received by him in relation to varying or revoking an order under this section.

(7)   The following provisions of Part 3 of the Enterprise Act 2002 shall apply in relation to orders under this section as they apply in relation to orders under paragraph 2 of Schedule 7 to that Act—

  (a)   section 86(2) and (3) (enforcement orders: general provisions);

  (b)   section 87 (delegated power of directions); and

  (c)   section 94(1) to (5), (8) and (9) (rights to enforce orders).

(8)   In this section "pre-emptive action" means action which might impede the making of an order under section 12(5) below.]

12   Orders following report under section 11

(1)   This section applies where a report of the Commission on a reference under
section 11 above concludes that the person specified in the reference is pursuing a
course of conduct which operates against the public interest.

(2)   If it appears to the Secretary of State that any other Minister has functions
directly relating to the person specified in the reference or, in the case of a reference
only concerning the activities of the person in a part of the United Kingdom,
functions directly relating to the person in respect of his activities in that part, he
shall send a copy of the report of the Commission on the reference to that Minister;
and in subsection (3) below "the relevant Minister" means—

    (a)   in a case where it appears to the Secretary of State that any Minister
(including himself) has such functions, that Minister, and

    (b)   in a case where it appears to the Secretary of State that no Minister has
such functions, the Secretary of State.

(3)   If—

    (a)   the relevant Minister considers it appropriate for the purpose of remedying
or preventing what he considers are the adverse effects of the course of
conduct specified in the report of the Commission as operating against the
public interest, and

    (b)   the person specified in the reference does not fall within paragraph (d) of
section 11(3) above and is not a subsidiary of a body falling within that
paragraph,

he may by order direct the person to prepare within such time, if any, as may be
specified in the order a plan for remedying or preventing such of those effects as are
so specified; but where there is more than one relevant Minister no such order shall
be made except by all the relevant Ministers acting jointly and where none of the
relevant Ministers is the Secretary of State no such order shall be made except after
consultation with him.

(4)   It shall be the duty of a person to whom a direction is given under
subsection (3) above to prepare such a plan as is mentioned in that subsection and to
send a copy of that plan to the Minister or Ministers by whom the order containing
the direction was made who shall lay it before Parliament; and, in a case where the
plan involves the use by a body of its powers in relation to any subsidiary within the
meaning of [section 736 of] the [Companies Act 1985], the plan shall specify the
manner in which the body proposes using those powers.

(5)   Whether or not an order has been or may be made under subsection (3)
above, the Secretary of State may, if he considers it appropriate for the purpose of
remedying or preventing what he considers are the adverse effects of the course of
conduct specified in the report of the Commission as operating against the public
interest, *by order exercise one or more of the powers specified in Part I, excluding
paragraph 10, of Schedule 8 to the Fair Trading Act 1973, to such extent and in such
manner as he considers appropriate.*

[(5A) An order under subsection (5) above may contain anything permitted by Schedule 8 to the Enterprise Act 2002, except paragraphs 8, 13 and 14 of that Schedule.

(5B) An order under subsection (5) above shall come into force at such time as is determined by or under the order.]

(6) *In the Fair Trading Act 1973—*

    (a) *section 90 (general provisions as to orders under section 56 etc) except subsections (2) and (3),*

    (b) *section 91(2) (publication of proposals to make an order),*

    (c) *section 93 (enforcement of certain orders), and*

    (d) *Part I (except paragraph 10) of Schedule 8 (powers exercisable by orders under section 56 etc),*

shall have effect as if any reference in those provisions to an order under section 56 of that Act included a reference to an order under subsection (5) above.

[109]

NOTES

Sub-s (4): words in first pair of square brackets inserted by the Companies Act 1989, s 144(4), Sch 18, para 22; words in second pair of square brackets substituted by the Companies Consolidation (Consequential Provisions) Act 1985, s 30, Sch 2.

Sub-s (5): for the words in italics there are substituted the words "make an order under this subsection", by the Enterprise Act 2002, s 278(1), Sch 25, para 10(4)(a), as from a day to be appointed.

Sub-ss (5A), (5B) inserted by the Enterprise Act 2002, s 278(1), Sch 25, para 10(4)(b), as from a day to be appointed.

Sub-s (6): substituted by the Enterprise Act 2002, s 278(1), Sch 25, para 10(4)(c), as from a day to be appointed as follows—

"(6) The following provisions of Part 3 of the Enterprise Act 2002 shall apply in relation to orders under subsection (5) above as they apply in relation to orders under paragraph 11 of Schedule 7 to that Act—

    (a) section 86(2) and (3) (enforcement orders: general provisions);

    (b) section 87 (delegated power of directions);

    (c) section 88 (contents of certain enforcement orders);

    (d) section 94(1) to (5), (8) and (9) (rights to enforce orders); and

    (e) Schedule 10 (procedural requirements for orders).

(7) The Secretary of State shall publish any decision made by him to dispense with the requirements of Schedule 10 to the Enterprise Act 2002 as applied by subsection (6) above; and shall do so in such manner as he considers most suitable for bringing the decision to the attention of persons who in his opinion would be affected by it or be likely to have an interest in it.".

Ministers of the Crown: the Enterprise Act 2002, Sch 25, para 10(10) provides that for the purposes of the Scotland Act 1998, the amendments made by Sch 25, para 10(1)–(9) shall be taken to be pre-commencement enactments within the meaning of the 1998 Act; references to a Minister of the Crown should be construed accordingly.

Secretary of State may . . . by order exercise: see further, the Copyright, Designs and Patents Act 1988, ss 144, 238 (powers in relation to licences granted or refused by copyright owner or design right owner).

13   Investigations of prices directed by Secretary of State

(1) *If so directed by the Secretary of State, the Director shall carry out an investigation into any price specified in the direction with a view to providing the Secretary of State with information of a description so specified relating to that price: . . .*

(2) *The Secretary of State shall not give a direction under this section unless he is satisfied that the price in question is one of major public concern and, in this connection, he shall have regard to whether—*

    (a) *the provision or acquisition of the goods or services in question is of general economic importance; or*

    (b) *consumers are significantly affected, whether directly or indirectly, by the price.*

(3)   The Secretary of State may at any time vary or revoke a direction given under this section, but he shall not exercise his power to vary such a direction unless he is satisfied that the direction as proposed to be varied would be such as he could have given, having regard to subsection (2) above.

(4)   On giving a direction under this section or on varying or revoking such a direction, the Secretary of State shall arrange for the direction, variation or revocation to be published in such manner as he considers most suitable for bringing it to the attention of persons who, in his opinion, would be affected by, or be likely to have an interest in, the investigation to which the direction, variation or revocation relates.

(5)   A direction under this section shall specify a period within which the Director is to report on his investigation to the Secretary of State, and, before the expiry of the period specified in the direction (whether as originally given or as varied under subsection (3) above), the Director shall make a report on the investigation to the Secretary of State—

  (a)   stating his findings of fact which are material to the information which he is required to provide in accordance with the direction; and

  (b)   containing such additional observations (if any) as the Director considers should be brought to the attention of the Secretary of State as a result of the investigation.

[(6)   For the purposes of an investigation under this section the Director may, by notice in writing signed by him—

  (a)   require any person to produce—

    (i)   at a time and a place specified in the notice,

    (ii)   to the Director or to any person appointed by him for the purpose,

    any documents which are specified or described in the notice and which are documents in his custody or under his control and relating to any matter relevant to the investigation; or

  (b)   require any person carrying on any business to—

    (i)   furnish to the Director such estimates, forecasts, returns or other information as may be specified or described in the notice; and

    (ii)   specify the time, manner and form in which any such estimates, forecasts, returns or information are to be furnished.

(7)   No person shall be compelled, for the purpose of any investigation under this section—

  (a)   to produce any document which he could not be compelled to produce in civil proceedings before the High Court or, in Scotland, the Court of Session; or

  (b)   in complying with any requirement for the furnishing of information, to give any information which he could not be compelled to give in evidence in such proceedings.

(8)   Subsections (6) to (8) of section 85 of the Fair Trading Act 1973 (enforcement provisions relating to notices requiring production of documents etc) shall apply in relation to a notice under subsection (6) above as they apply in relation to a notice under section 85(1) but as if, in section 85(7), for the words from "any one" to "the Commission" there were substituted "the Director."]

[110]

NOTES

Repealed by the Enterprise Act 2002, ss 9, 278(2), Sch 26, as from a day to be appointed.

Sub-s (1): words omitted repealed by the Competition Act 1998, s 74(1), (3), Sch 12, para 4(1), (4)(a), Sch 14, Pt I.

Sub-ss (6)–(8): substituted for original sub-s (6) by the Competition Act 1998, s 74(1), Sch 12, para 4(1), (4)(b).

The Director: see the note "Director General of Fair Trading" at the beginning of this Act.

Patents and agricultural schemes

14 *(Repealed by the Copyright, Designs and Patents Act 1988, s 303(2), Sch 8.)*

15 Agricultural schemes: special provisions

(1) ...

(2) The Secretary of State shall not—
(a), (b) ...
(c) make or vary a reference under section 11 above,

in a case where the person to whom or to whose conduct or activities the investigation or reference relates falls within section 11(3)(d) above unless he has first consulted the relevant Minister.

(3), (4) ...

(5) In this section "the relevant Minister" means—
(a) in the case of a board administering a scheme under the said Act of 1958, the Minister who would have power to make an order under section 19 of that Act in relation to that board or the board administering that scheme, and
(b) in the case of a board administering a scheme under [the said Order of 1982], the Department of Agriculture for Northern Ireland.

[111]

NOTES

Sub-s (1): amends the Agricultural Marketing Act 1958, s 19A(1).

Sub-s (2): para (a) and word immediately following it repealed by the Deregulation and Contracting Out Act 1994, s 81(1), Sch 17; para (b) repealed by the Competition Act 1998, s 74(1), (3), Sch 12, para 4(1), (5), Sch 14, Pt I.

Sub-ss (3), (4): repealed by the Competition Act 1998, s 74(1), (3), Sch 12, para 4(1), (5), Sch 14, Pt I.

Sub-s (5): words in square brackets substituted by the Agricultural Marketing (Northern Ireland) Order 1982, SI 1982/1080, art 46(1), Schs 8, 9.

General provisions about references and investigations

16 General provisions as to reports

(1) In making any report under this Act the Commission or the Director shall have regard to the need for excluding, so far as that is practicable—
(a) any matter which relates to the private affairs of an individual, where the publication of that matter would or might, in the opinion of the Commission or the Director, as the case may be, seriously and prejudicially affect the interests of that individual, and
(b) any matter which relates specifically to the affairs of a body of persons, whether corporate or unincorporate, where publication of that matter would or might, in the opinion of the Commission or the Director, as the case may be, seriously and prejudicially affect the interests of that body, unless in the opinion of the Commission or the Director, as the case may be, the inclusion of that matter relating specifically to that body is necessary for the purposes of the report.

(2) For the purposes of the law relating to defamation, absolute privilege shall attach to any report of the Commission *or of the Director* under this Act.

[(3) ....]

NOTES

Sub-s (1): repealed by the Enterprise Act 2002, s 278, Sch 25, para 10(5)(a), Sch 26, as from a day to be appointed.

Sub-s (2): words in italics repealed by the Enterprise Act 2002, s 278, Sch 25, para 10(5)(b), Sch 26, as from a day to be appointed.

Sub-s (3): added by the Deregulation and Contracting Out Act 1994, s 39, Sch 11, para 4(1), (5); repealed by the Competition Act 1998, s 74(1), (3), Sch 12, para 4(1), (6), Sch 14, Pt I.

The Director: see the note "Director General of Fair Trading" at the beginning of this Act.

17   Laying before Parliament and publication of reports

(1)   Subject to subsection (2) below, the Secretary of State shall lay a copy of any report made to him under section . . . , 11(10) *or 13(5)* above before each House of Parliament and shall arrange for the report to be published in such manner as appears to him appropriate.

(2)   The Secretary of State shall not lay a copy of a report made to him under section . . . 11(10) above before either House of Parliament unless at least twenty-four hours before doing so he has transmitted to every person specified in the reference a copy of the report in the form in which it is laid (or by virtue of subsection (3) below is treated as being laid) before each House of Parliament.

(3)   If a report made to him under section . . . , 11(10) *or 13(5)* above is presented by command of Her Majesty to either House of Parliament otherwise than at or during the time of a sitting of that House, the presentation of the report shall for the purposes of this section be treated as the laying of a copy of it before that House by the Secretary of State.

(4)   If it appears to the Secretary of State that the publication of any matter in a report made to him under section . . . , 11(10) *or 13(5)* above would be *against the public interest*, he shall exclude that matter from the copies of the report as laid before Parliament and from the report as published under this section.

(5)   Without prejudice to subsection (4) above, if the Secretary of State considers that it would not be in the public interest to disclose—

   (a)   any matter contained in a report made to him under section . . . , 11(10) or 13(5) above relating to the private affairs of an individual whose interests would, in the opinion of the Secretary of State, be seriously and prejudicially affected by the publication of that matter, or

   (b)   any matter contained in such a report relating specifically to the affairs of a particular person whose interests would, in the opinion of the Secretary of State, be seriously and prejudicially affected by the publication of that matter,

the Secretary of State shall exclude that matter from the copies of the report as laid before Parliament and from the report as published by virtue of subsection (1) above.

(6)   Any reference in [section] 12 above to a report of the Commission shall be construed as a reference to the report in the form in which copies of it are laid (or by virtue of subsection (3) of this section are treated as having been laid) before each House of Parliament under this section.

NOTES

Sub-ss (1), (3): words omitted repealed by the Competition Act 1998, s 74(1), (3), Sch 12, para 4(1), (7)(a), (b), Sch 14, Pt I; words in italics repealed by the Enterprise Act 2002, s 278, Sch 25, para 10(6)(a), Sch 26, as from a day to be appointed.

Sub-s (2): word omitted repealed by the Competition Act 1998, s 74(1), (3), Sch 12, para 4(1), (7)(b), Sch 14, Pt I.

Sub-s (4): word omitted repealed by the Competition Act 1998, s 74(1), (3), Sch 12, para 4(1), (7)(a), (b), Sch 14, Pt I; first words in italics repealed, and for the second words in italics there is substituted the word "inappropriate", by the Enterprise Act 2002, s 278, Sch 25, para 10(6)(a), (b), Sch 26, as from a day to be appointed.

Sub-s (5): substituted by the Enterprise Act 2002, s 278(1), Sch 25, para 10(6)(c), as from a day to be appointed as follows—

"(5) In deciding what is inappropriate for the purposes of subsection (4) the Secretary of State shall have regard to the considerations mentioned in section 244 of the Enterprise Act 2002.".

Word omitted repealed by the Competition Act 1998, s 74(1), (3), Sch 12, para 4(1), (7)(a), Sch 14, Pt I.

Ministers of the Crown: the Enterprise Act 2002, Sch 25, para 10(10) provides that for the purposes of the Scotland Act 1998, the amendments made by Sch 25, para 10(1)–(9) shall be taken to be pre-commencement enactments within the meaning of the 1998 Act; references to a Minister of the Crown should be construed accordingly.

Sub-s (6): word in square brackets substituted by the Competition Act 1998, s 74(1), Sch 12, para 4(1), (7)(c).

18 Information and advice about operation of Act

The Director shall arrange for the dissemination in such form and manner as he considers appropriate of such information and advice as it may appear to him expedient to give the public in the United Kingdom about the operation of this Act.

[114]

NOTES

Repealed by the Enterprise Act 2002, s 278, Sch 25, para 10(7), Sch 26, as from a day to be appointed.
The Director: see the note "Director General of Fair Trading" at the beginning of this Act.

19 Restriction on disclosure of information

(1) Subject to subsection (2) below, no information obtained under or by virtue of the preceding provisions of this Act about any business shall, so long as the business continues to be carried on, be disclosed without the consent of the person for the time being carrying it on.

(2) Subsection (1) above does not apply to any disclosure of information made—
(a) for the purpose of facilitating the performance of any functions under this Act or any of the enactments [or subordinate legislation] specified in subsection (3) below of any Minister, any Northern Ireland department, the head of any such department, the Director, [the Director General of Telecommunications,] [the Gas and Electricity Markets Authority,] [the Civil Aviation Authority,] [the Director General of Water Services,] [. . .] [the Director General of Electricity Supply for Northern Ireland] [or the Director General for Gas for Northern Ireland] [the Rail Regulator,] [the Authorised Conveyancing Practitioners Board] [the Coal Authority] the Commission or a local weights and measures authority in Great Britain; or
(b) in connection with the investigation of any criminal offence or for the purposes of any criminal proceedings; or
(c) for the purposes of any civil proceedings brought under or by virtue of this Act or any of the enactments [or subordinate legislation] specified in subsection (3) below; or
(d) in pursuance of a Community obligation.

(3) The enactments [and subordinate legislation] referred to in subsection (2) above are—
(a) the Trade Descriptions Act 1968;
(b) the Fair Trading Act 1973;
(c) the Consumer Credit Act 1974;
(d), (e) . . .
(f) the Estate Agents Act 1979

[(g)   the Telecommunications Act 1984]
[(h)   the Gas Act 1986]
[(hh) Chapter III of Part X (competition scrutiny of regulating provisions and practices of the Authority), and Chapter II of Part XVII (competition scrutiny of regulatory provisions and practices of recognised clearing houses and recognised investment exchanges), of the Financial Services and Markets Act 2000;]
[(i)   the Airports Act 1986]
[(j)   the Consumer Protection Act 1987]
[(k)   the Control of Misleading Advertisements Regulations 1988]
[(l)   the Water Act 1989 [the Water Industry Act 1991 or any of the other consolidation Acts (within the meaning of section 206 of that Act of 1991)]]
[(m) the Electricity Act 1989]
[(m) the Courts and Legal Services Act 1990]
[(n)   the Broadcasting Act 1990]
[(n)   the Electricity (Northern Ireland) Order 1992]
[(nn) Part IV of the Airports (Northern Ireland) Order 1994]
[(nn) the Gas (Northern Ireland) Order 1996]
[(o)   the Railways Act 1993]
[(p)   the Coal Industry Act 1994]
[(q)   [the EC Competition Law (Articles 84 and 85) Enforcement Regulations 2001]]
[(r)   the Competition Act 1998]
[(s)   Part I of the Transport Act 2000].

(4)   . . .

(5)   *Nothing in subsection (1) above shall be construed—*
   (a)   as limiting the matters which may be included in any report of the Director or of the Commission made under this Act [. . .]; or
   (b)   as applying to any information which has been made public as part of such a report or as part of the register kept for the purposes of the Act of 1976.

(6)   *Any person who discloses information in contravention of this section shall be liable on summary conviction to a fine not exceeding the statutory maximum and, on conviction on indictment, to imprisonment for a term not exceeding two years or to a fine or both.*

(7)   . . .

                                                                        [115]

NOTES

Sub-s (1): repealed by the Enterprise Act 2002, ss 247(f), 278(2), Sch 26, as from a day to be appointed.

Sub-s (2): repealed by the Enterprise Act 2002, ss 247(f), 278(2), Sch 26, as from a day to be appointed; words in first pair of square brackets in para (a), and words in square brackets in para (c), inserted by the Control of Misleading Advertisements Regulations 1988, SI 1988/915, reg 7(6)(e)(i); entry "the Director General of Telecommunications" inserted by the Telecommunications Act 1984, s 109, Sch 4, para 73; entry "the Gas and Electricity Markets Authority" substituted by virtue of the Utilities Act 2000, s 3(2); entry "the Civil Aviation Authority" inserted by the Airports Act 1986, s 83(1), Sch 4, para 7; entry "the Director General of Water Services" inserted by the Water Act 1989, s 190, Sch 25, para 59(2); entry omitted originally inserted by the Electricity Act 1989, s 112(1), Sch 16, para 25, repealed by virtue of the Utilities Act 2000, s 3(2); entry "the Director General of Electricity Supply for Northern Ireland" inserted by the Electricity (Northern Ireland) Order 1992, SI 1992/231, art 95(1), Sch 12, para 21(a); entry "or the Director General of Gas for Northern Ireland" inserted by the Gas (Northern Ireland) Order 1996, SI 1996/275, art 71(1), Sch 6; entry "the Rail Regulator" inserted by the Railways Act 1993, s 152, Sch 12, para 12(2); entry "the Authorised Conveyancing Practitioners Board" inserted by the Courts and Legal Services Act 1990, s 125(3), Sch 18, para 23, as from a day to be appointed; entry "the Coal Authority" inserted by the Coal Industry Act 1994, s 67, Sch 9, para 23(1).

Sub-s (3): repealed by the Enterprise Act 2002, ss 247(f), 278(2), Sch 26, as from a day to be appointed; words in first pair of square brackets, and para (k), added by SI 1988/915, reg 7(6)(e); paras (d), (e) repealed, and para (r) added, by the Competition Act 1998, s 74(1), (3), Sch 12, para 4(1), (8), (9), Sch 14, Pt I; para (g) added by the Telecommunications Act 1984, s 109, Sch 4, para 73; para (h) added by the Gas Act 1986, s 67(1), Sch 7, para 28; para (hh) substituted for a second para (h) (as originally added by the Financial Services Act 1986, s 182, Sch 13, para 5) by the Financial Services and Markets Act 2000 (Consequential Amendments) Order 2002, SI 2002/1555, art 8; para (i) added by the Airports Act 1986, s 83(1), Sch 4, para 7; para (j) added by the Consumer Protection Act 1987, s 48, Sch 4; para (l) added by the Water Act 1989, s 190, Sch 25, para 59(2), words in square brackets therein inserted by the Water Consolidation (Consequential Provisions) Act 1991, s 2(1), Sch 1, para 34; first para (m) added by the Electricity Act 1989, s 112(1), Sch 16, para 25; second para (m) added by the Courts and Legal Services Act 1990, s 125(3), Sch 18, para 23, as from a day to be appointed; first para (n) added by the Broadcasting Act 1990, s 203(1), Sch 20, para 28; second para (n) added by SI 1992/231, art 95(1), Sch 12, para 21(b); first para (nn) added by the Airports (Northern Ireland) Order 1994, SI 1994/426, art 71(2), Sch 9, para 8; second para (nn) added by SI 1996/275, art 71(1), Sch 6; para (o) added by the Railways Act 1993, s 152, Sch 12, para 12(3); para (p) added by the Coal Industry Act 1994, s 67, Sch 9, para 23(2); para (q) added by the EC Competition Law (Articles 88 and 89) Enforcement Regulations 1996, SI 1996/2199, reg 29(3), words in square brackets therein substituted by EC Competition Law (Articles 84 and 85) Enforcement Regulations 2001, SI 2001/2916, reg 35(2); para (s) added by the Transport Act 2000, s 97, Sch 8, Pt IV, para 12.

Sub-s (4): paras (a), (e) amend the Agricultural Marketing Act 1958, s 47(2) and the Restrictive Trade Practices Act 1976, s 41(1)(a); para (b) repealed by the Agricultural Marketing (Northern Ireland) Order 1982, SI 1982/1080, art 46(2), Sch 9; paras (c), (d), (f) amend the Fair Trading Act 1973, s 133(2)(a), at **[88]**, the Consumer Credit Act 1974, s 174(3)(a), the Estate Agents Act 1979, s 10(3)(a), and are repealed by the Enterprise Act 2002, ss 247(f), 278(2), Sch 26, as from a day to be appointed.

Sub-s (5): repealed by the Enterprise Act 2002, ss 247(f), 278(2), Sch 26, as from a day to be appointed; words omitted originally inserted by the Deregulation and Contracting Out Act 1994, s 39, Sch 11, para 4(1), (6), repealed by the Competition Act 1998, s 74(1), (3), Sch 12, para 4(1), (10), Sch 14, Pt I.

Sub-s (6): repealed by the Enterprise Act 2002, ss 247(f), 278(2), Sch 26, as from a day to be appointed

Sub-s (7): repealed by the Statute Law (Repeals) Act 1993.

General restrictions on disclosure of information: see the Water Industry Act 1991, s 206, Sch 15, the Water Resources Act 1991, s 204, Sch 24, the Railways Act 1993, s 145, and the Coal Industry Act 1994, s 59.

The Director: see the note "Director General of Fair Trading" at the beginning of this Act.

Act of 1976: ie the Restrictive Trade Practices Act 1976; repealed by the Competition Act 1998, ss 1, 74(3), Sch 14, Pt I, subject to savings in Sch 13 of the 1998 Act at **[247]**.

Grants

20   Power to make grants to certain bodies

If the Secretary of State is satisfied that—

(a) the general advice of any body on matters of interest to users of goods and services would be useful to him in the formulation of policy concerning those matters and

(b) the body disseminates information of such interest,

he may make a grant to the body on such terms as he thinks fit.

                                                            [116]

NOTES

Repealed by the Enterprise Act 2002, s 278(2), Sch 26, as from a day to be appointed.

Amendments of Fair Trading Act 1973

21   Monopoly references by Secretary of State alone

It is hereby declared that where it appears to the Secretary of State that—

(a) a monopoly situation exists or may exist as mentioned in subsection (1) of section 51 of the Fair Trading Act 1973 (monopoly references by Ministers), and

   (b) *the goods or services in question are of a description mentioned in subsection (2) of that section, and*

   (c) *none of the Ministers mentioned in subsection (3) of that section has such functions as are mentioned in subsection (2) of that section in relation to goods or services of that description,*

the Secretary of State may make a monopoly reference with respect to the existence or possible existence of that situation acting alone; and accordingly any reference which has been made in such circumstances by the Secretary of State acting alone has been made in compliance with that section.

[117]

NOTES

    Repealed by the Enterprise Act 2002, s 278, Sch 25, para 10(7), Sch 26, as from a day to be appointed.

22, 23 *(S 22 repealed by the Competition Act 1998, s 74(1), (3), Sch 12, para 4(1), (11), Sch 14, Pt I; s 23 amends the Fair Trading Act 1973, s 137(3) at* **[90]**.*)*

24 Modification of provisions about performance of Commission's functions

(1) The Secretary of State may by order make such modifications in [Part II of Schedule 7 to the Competition Act 1998 (performance of the Competition Commission's general functions)] as appear to him to be appropriate for improving the performance by the Commission of their functions.

(2) An order under this section may contain such transitional, incidental or supplementary provisions as the Secretary of State thinks fit.

[118]

NOTES

    Repealed by the Enterprise Act 2002, s 278, Sch 25, para 10(7), Sch 26, as from a day to be appointed.

    Sub-s (1): words in square brackets substituted by the Competition Act 1998, s 74(1), Sch 12, para 4(1), (12).

Amendments of Restrictive Trade Practices Act 1976

25 Suspension of declarations under section 1(3) of Restrictive Trade Practices Act 1976 pending appeals

Where on an application under section 1(3) of the Restrictive Trade Practices Act 1976 the Court declares at any time after the coming into force of this section that any restrictions or information provisions are contrary to the public interest, that declaration shall not have effect—

   (a) *until the expiration of the period of 21 days beginning with the expiration of the period within which any party to that application may appeal against the declaration, and*

   (b) *in a case where such an appeal is brought, until the expiration of the period of 21 days after the date on which the appeal has been finally determined or withdrawn.*

[119]

NOTES

    Repealed by the Competition Act 1998, s 74(1), (3), Sch 12, para 4(1), (13), Sch 14, Pt I, subject to savings in Sch 13, Pt VI, para 44(a) of the 1998 Act at **[247]**.

    Restrictive Trade Practices Act 1976: repealed by the Competition Act 1998, ss 1, 74(3), Sch 14, Pt I, subject to savings in Sch 13 of the 1998 Act at **[247]**.

26   Suspension of declarations under section 1(3) of Restrictive Trade Practices Act 1976 pending revision of agreements

(1)   Where the Court has declared under section 1(3) of the Restrictive Trade Practices Act 1976 that any restrictions or information provisions in an agreement are contrary to the public interest, any party to the agreement or to the proceedings in which the declaration was made may, at any time before the declaration comes into effect, submit a revised agreement or a draft of a revised agreement to the Court and the Court may declare that any restrictions or information provisions contained in the revised agreement by virtue of which the said Act of 1976 applies or would apply to that agreement are not contrary to the public interest.

(2)   Variations of the agreement in relation to which the declaration under section 1(3) of the said Act of 1976 was made may not be submitted to the Court under subsection (1) above unless particulars of them have been furnished to the Director under section 24(2) of that Act and a new agreement may not be so submitted unless it has been registered under that Act and particulars of any variation of it have been so furnished.

(3)   The duty of taking proceedings before the Court imposed on the Director by section 1(2)(c) of the said Act of 1976 shall not apply in respect of an agreement if the Court has declared under subsection (1) above that all the restrictions or information provisions by virtue of which that Act applies to the agreement are not contrary to the public interest.

(4)   Where any person who may make an application under subsection (1) above in relation to a declaration applies to the Court at any time before the declaration comes into effect for an extension of the period after which it will come into effect to enable an application to be made to the Court under subsection (1) above and it appears to the Court reasonable to do so, it may extend that period by such period (not exceeding six months on a first application under this subsection or three months on a second such application) as it thinks fit, but no more than two extensions may be made in respect of any declaration.

(5)   Where, following a declaration under section 1(3) of the said Act of 1976, an application is made under subsection (1) or (4) above, the declaration shall not come into effect until the application has been determined.

(6)   The Court may, if it thinks fit, grant an extension under subsection (4) above in relation to some but not all of the restrictions and information provisions in question and in that event—

(a)   the period within which an application under subsection (1) above or a second application under subsection (4) above may be made shall not expire until the declaration has come into effect in relation to all the restrictions or information provisions, and

(b)   subsection (5) above shall not prevent a declaration coming into effect in relation to any restriction or information provision in relation to which no extension was granted.

(7)   Notice of an application made under subsection (1) or (4) above shall be served on the Director in accordance with rules of court and the Director shall be entitled in accordance with such rules to appear and to be heard on the application.

(8)   Where a declaration is made under subsection (1) above the Director shall cause notice of it to be entered in the register kept by him under section 23 of the said Act of 1976—

(a)   in the case of a declaration in relation to restrictions or information provisions contained in an agreement registered under the Act, on the making of the declaration, and

(b) in the case of a declaration in relation to restrictions or information
     provisions contained in a draft agreement, on the registration of an
     agreement in the form of the draft.

(9)   Sections 10 and 19 of the said Act of 1976 (public interest) shall apply to
proceedings under this section as they apply to proceedings under Part I of that Act.

[120]

NOTES

Repealed by the Competition Act 1998, s 74(1), (3), Sch 12, para 4(1), (13), Sch 14, Pt I, subject to savings in Sch 13, Pt VI, para 44(b) of the 1998 Act at **[247]**.

Rules of court: see the Restrictive Practices Court Rules 1976, SI 1976/1897, rr 57A–57F, laying down the procedures to be followed when applications are made under sub-ss (1), (4), above.

The Director: see the note "Director General of Fair Trading" at the beginning of this Act.

Restrictive Trade Practices Act 1976: repealed by the Competition Act 1998, ss 1, 74(3), Sch 14, Pt I, subject to savings in Sch 13 of the 1998 Act at **[247]**.

27, 28   *(Repealed by the Competition Act 1998, s 74(1), (3), Sch 12, para 4(1), (13), Sch 14, Pt I.)*

29   Exemption of certain undertakings from Restrictive Trade Practices Acts

(1)   The Restrictive Trade Practices Act 1976 shall not apply in relation to any
agreement by virtue only of restrictions being accepted or information provisions
being made under it which are comprised in undertakings which have been—
   [(za) accepted pursuant to a proposal under section 56A of the Fair Trading
          Act 1973 (within the meaning of that Act) or under section 56F of that
          Act, or]
   (a)   given pursuant to section [75G or] 88 of [the said Act of 1973], or
   (b)   certified by the Secretary of State under paragraph 9 of Schedule 11 to the
         said Act of 1973, or
   (c)   accepted under section 4 or 9 above.

(2)   The said Act of 1976 and Part I of the Restrictive Trade Practices Act 1956
shall be deemed never to have applied in relation to any agreement by virtue only of
restrictions being accepted or information provisions being made under it which are
comprised in undertakings falling within paragraph (a) or (b) of subsection (1) above.

[121]

NOTES

Repealed by the Competition Act 1998, s 74(1), (3), Sch 12, para 4(1), (13), Sch 14, Pt I, subject to savings in Sch 13, Pt VI, para 43 of the 1998 Act at **[247]**.

Sub-s (1): para (za) inserted, and words in second pair of square brackets in para (a) substituted, by the Deregulation and Contracting Out Act 1994, s 39, Sch 11, para 4(1), (7); words in first pair of square brackets in para (a) inserted by the Companies Act 1989, s 153, Sch 20, para 24.

Restrictive Trade Practices Act 1976: repealed by the Competition Act 1998, ss 1, 74(3), Sch 14, Pt I, subject to savings in Sch 13 of the 1998 Act at **[247]**.

Restrictive Trade Practices Act 1956, Pt I: largely repealed by the Restrictive Trade Practices Act 1976, s 44, Sch 6 (the 1976 Act is repealed as noted above).

30   *(Repealed by the Competition Act 1998, s 74(1), (3), Sch 12, para 4(1), (13), Sch 14, Pt I.)*

Supplementary

31   Orders and regulations

(1)   Any power of the Secretary of State to make orders *or regulations* under this
Act shall be exercisable by statutory instrument.

(2)   . . .

(3)   Any statutory instrument containing *regulations under this Act or* an order under section . . . , 11(4)[, 11D] or 12(3) or (5) above[, or section 111(4) or (6) or 114(3)(b) or (4)(b) of the Enterprise Act 2002 as applied by section 11B(1)(c) or (f) above,] shall be subject to annulment in pursuance of a resolution of either House of Parliament.

(4)   No order shall be made under section 24(1) above unless a draft of the order has been laid before, and approved by a resolution of, each House of Parliament.

[(5)   Any power of the Secretary of State to make an order under this Act—
  (a)   may be exercised so as to make different provision for different cases or different purposes; and
  (b)   includes power to make such incidental, supplementary, consequential, transitory, transitional or saving provision as the Secretary of State considers appropriate.]

[122]

NOTES

Sub-s (1): words in italics repealed by the Enterprise Act 2002, s 278, Sch 25, para 10(8)(a), Sch 26, as from a day to be appointed.

Sub-s (2): repealed by the Competition Act 1998, s 74(1), (3), Sch 12, para 4(1), (14)(a), Sch 14, Pt I.

Sub-s (3): words in italics repealed, and words in square brackets inserted, by the Enterprise Act 2002, s 278, Sch 25, para 10(8)(b), Sch 26, as from a day to be appointed; number omitted repealed by the Competition Act 1998, s 74(1), (3), Sch 12, para 4(1), (14)(b), Sch 14, Pt I.

Sub-s (4): repealed by the Enterprise Act 2002, s 278, Sch 25, para 10(8)(c), Sch 26, as from a day to be appointed.

Sub-s (5): added by the Enterprise Act 2002, s 278(1), Sch 25, para 10(8)(d), as from a day to be appointed.

Ministers of the Crown: the Enterprise Act 2002, Sch 25, para 10(10) provides that for the purposes of the Scotland Act 1998, the amendments made by Sch 25, para 10(1)–(9) shall be taken to be pre-commencement enactments within the meaning of the 1998 Act; references to a Minister of the Crown should be construed accordingly.

32   Financial provisions

(1)   There shall be defrayed out of moneys provided by Parliament—
  (a)   any expenses incurred by the Secretary of State in consequence of the provisions of this Act; and
  (b)   any increase attributable to this Act in the sums payable out of moneys so provided under any other Act.

(2)   . . .

[123]

NOTES

Sub-s (2): amends the Fair Trading Act 1973, s 135(2)(c) at **[89]**.

33   Short title, interpretation, repeals, commencement and extent

(1)   This Act may be cited as the Competition Act 1980.

(2)   Except in so far as any provision of this Act otherwise provides, section 137 of the Fair Trading Act 1973 (general interpretation provisions) shall have effect in relation to [sections 1 to 13 and sections 15 to 24] above as if those sections were contained in that Act; and for ease of reference the expressions which are used in those sections and have meanings assigned to them by the said section 137 are—

. . .

> *"agreement"*
> *"business"*
> *"the Commission"*
> *"consumer"*
> *"the Director"*
> *"enactment"*
> *"goods"*
> *"group"*
> *"group of inter-connected bodies corporate"*
> *"inter-connected bodies corporate"*
> *"Minister"*
> *"monopoly situation"*
> *"practice"*
> *"price"*
> *"services"*
> *"supply"*
> *"the supply of services".*

(3), (4) ...

(5)   This Act shall come into operation on such day as the Secretary of State may by order appoint, and different days may be so appointed for different provisions and for different purposes.

(6)   An order under this section appointing a day for the coming into operation of any provision of Schedule 2 to this Act may contain such savings with respect to the operation of that provision and such incidental and transitional provisions as appear to the Secretary of State to be appropriate.

(7)   Any reference in any provision of this Act to the appointed day shall be construed as a reference to the day appointed or, as the case may require, first appointed under this section for the coming into operation of that provision.

(8)   This Act extends to Northern Ireland.

[124]

NOTES

Sub-s (2): substituted by the Enterprise Act 2002, s 278(1), Sch 25, para 10(9), as from a day to be appointed as follows—

"(2) Unless the context otherwise requires, in this Act "Minister" includes a government department and the following expressions shall have the same meanings as they have in Part 3 of the Enterprise Act 2002—
   "business"
   "the Commission"
   "enactment"
   "goods"
   "services"
   "supply (in relation to the supply of goods)"
   "the supply of services".".

Words in square brackets substituted by the Competition Act 1998, s 74(1), Sch 12, para 4(1), (15)(a); words omitted repealed by the Competition Act 1998 (Transitional, Consequential and Supplemental Provisions) Order 2000, SI 2000/311, art 11.

Sub-ss (3), (4): repealed by the Competition Act 1998, s 74(1), (3), Sch 12, para 4(1), (15)(b), Sch 14, Pt I.

The Director: see the note "Director General of Fair Trading" at the beginning of this Act.

Orders: the Competition Act 1980 (Commencement No 1) Order 1980, SI 1980/497; the Competition Act 1980 (Commencement No 2) Order 1980, SI 1980/978.

(Sch 1 repealed by the Statute Law (Repeals) Act 1989; Sch 2 contains repeals.)

COMPANIES ACT 1989

(1989 c 40)

ARRANGEMENT OF SECTIONS

PART II
ELIGIBILITY FOR APPOINTMENT AS COMPANY AUDITOR

Supplementary provisions

PART VI
MERGERS AND RELATED MATTERS

PART X
MISCELLANEOUS AND GENERAL PROVISIONS

General

1–23   ((*Pt I*) *outside the scope of this work.*)

PART II
ELIGIBILITY FOR APPOINTMENT AS COMPANY AUDITOR

24–44   (*Outside the scope of this work.*)

Supplementary provisions

45   (*Outside the scope of this work.*)

46   Delegation of functions of Secretary of State

(1)   The Secretary of State may by order (a "delegation order") establish a body corporate to exercise his functions under this Part.

(2)   A delegation order has the effect of transferring to the body established by it, subject to such exceptions and reservations as may be specified in the order, all the functions of the Secretary of State under this Part except—

(a) such functions under Part I of Schedule 14 (prevention of restrictive practices) as are excepted by regulations under section 47, and

(b) his functions in relation to the body itself;

and the order may also confer on the body such other functions supplementary or incidental to those transferred as appear to the Secretary of State to be appropriate.

(3)   Any transfer of the functions under the following provisions shall be subject to the reservation that they remain exercisable concurrently by the Secretary of State—

(a) section 38 (power to call for information), and

(b) section 40 (directions to comply with international obligations);

and any transfer of the function of refusing to approve an overseas qualification, or withdrawing such approval, on the grounds referred to in section 33(3) (lack of reciprocity) shall be subject to the reservation that the function is exercisable only with the consent of the Secretary of State.

(4)   A delegation order may be amended or, if it appears to the Secretary of State that it is no longer in the public interest that the order should remain in force, revoked by a further order under this section.

(5)   Where functions are transferred or resumed, the Secretary of State may by order confer or, as the case may be, take away such other functions supplementary or incidental to those transferred or resumed as appear to him to be appropriate.

(6)   The provisions of Schedule 13 have effect with respect to the status, constitution and proceedings of a body established by a delegation order, the exercise by it of certain functions transferred to it and other supplementary matters.

(7)   An order under this section shall be made by statutory instrument.

(8)   An order which has the effect of transferring or resuming any functions shall not be made unless a draft of it has been laid before and approved by resolution of each House of Parliament; and any other description of order shall be subject to annulment in pursuance of a resolution of either House of Parliament.

[125]

NOTES

Commencement: to be appointed.

47 Restrictive practices

(1)   The provisions of Schedule 14 have effect with respect to certain matters relating to restrictive practices and competition law.

(2)   The Secretary of State may make provision by regulations as to the discharge of the functions under paragraphs 1 to 7 of that Schedule when a delegation order is in force.

(3)   The regulations may—

(a) except any function from the effect of the delegation order,

(b) modify any of the provisions mentioned in subsection (2), and

(c) impose such duties on the body established by the delegation order, the Secretary of State and *Director General of Fair Trading* as appear to the Secretary of State to be appropriate.

(4)   The regulations shall contain such provision as appears to the Secretary of State to be necessary or expedient for reserving to him the decision—

(a) to refuse recognition on the ground mentioned in paragraph 1(3) of that Schedule, or

(b) to exercise the powers conferred by paragraph 6 of that Schedule.

(5)   For that purpose the regulations may—

(a) prohibit the body from granting a recognition order without the leave of the Secretary of State, and

(b) empower the Secretary of State to direct the body to exercise its powers in such manner as may be specified in the direction.

(6)   Regulations under this section shall be made by statutory instrument which shall be subject to annulment in pursuance of a resolution of either House of Parliament.

[126]

NOTES

Commencement: 1 March 1990 (sub-s (1)); to be appointed (sub-ss (2)–(6)).

Sub-s (3): for the words in italics there are substituted the words "the Office of Fair Trading" by the Enterprise Act 2002, s 278(1), Sch 25, para 21(1), (2), as from a day to be appointed.

Director General of Fair Trading: the Enterprise Act 2002, s 2(1), at **[255]**, provides that, as from the coming into force of that section in accordance with s 279 at **[463]**, the functions of the Director General of Fair Trading, his property, rights and liabilities are transferred to the Office of Fair Trading. Accordingly, (by virtue of s 2(2), (3) of the 2002 Act) the office of the Director is abolished, and any reference to the Director in any enactment, instrument or other document passed or made before the commencement of s 2(1) shall have effect as if it were a reference to the Office of Fair Trading. For transitional provisions in connection with this transfer, see s 276(1) of, and Sch 24, para 6 to, the 2002 Act.

48   Exemption from liability for damages

(1)   Neither a recognised supervisory body, nor any of its officers or employees or members of its governing body, shall be liable in damages for anything done or omitted in the discharge or purported discharge of functions to which this subsection applies, unless the act or omission is shown to have been in bad faith.

(2)   Subsection (1) applies to the functions of the body so far as relating to, or to matters arising out of—

     (a)   such rules, practices, powers and arrangements of the body to which the requirements of Part II of Schedule 11 apply, or

     (b)   the obligations with which paragraph 16 of that Schedule requires the body to comply,

     (c)   any guidance issued by the body, or

     (d)   the obligations to which the body is subject by virtue of this Part.

(3)   Neither a body established by a delegation order, nor any of its members, officers or employees, shall be liable in damages for anything done or omitted in the discharge or purported discharge of the functions exercisable by virtue of an order under section 46, unless the act or omission is shown to have been in bad faith.

[127]

NOTES

Commencement: 1 March 1990 (sub-ss (1), (2)); to be appointed (sub-s (3)).

49   Service of notices

(1)   This section has effect in relation to any notice, direction or other document required or authorised by or under this Part to be given to or served on any person other than the Secretary of State.

(2)   Any such document may be given to or served on the person in question—

     (a)   by delivering it to him,

     (b)   by leaving it at his proper address, or

     (c)   by sending it by post to him at that address.

(3)   Any such document may—

     (a)   in the case of a body corporate, be given to or served on the secretary or clerk of that body;

     (b)   in the case of a partnership, be given to or served on any partner;

     (c)   in the case of an unincorporated association other than a partnership, be given to or served on any member of the governing body of the association.

(4)   For the purposes of this section and section 7 of the Interpretation Act 1978 (service of documents by post) in its application to this section, the proper address of any person is his last known address (whether of his residence or of a place where he carries on business or is employed) and also—

    (a) in the case of a person who is eligible under the rules of a recognised supervisory body for appointment as company auditor and who does not have a place of business in the United Kingdom, the address of that body;

    (b) in the case of a body corporate, its secretary or its clerk, the address of its registered or principal office in the United Kingdom;

    (c) in the case of an unincorporated association (other than a partnership) or a member of its governing body, its principal office in the United Kingdom.

[128]

50–145   *(Ss 50–54, ss 55–145 (Pts III–V) outside the scope of this work.)*

PART VI
MERGERS AND RELATED MATTERS

146–151   *(Ss 146, 147, 148 insert the Fair Trading Act 1973, ss 75A–75H, 75J, 75K, 93A at* **[50]**–**[59]**, **[78]**, *and are repealed by the Enterprise Act 2002, s 278(2), Sch 26, as from a day to be appointed; s 149 inserts s 75(4A)–(4M) of the 1973 Act at* **[49]**, *except in relation to any merger reference made before 16 November 1989, and is repealed by the Enterprise Act 2002, s 278(2), Sch 26 as from a day to be appointed; s 150 inserts s 66A of the 1973 Act at* **[40]**, *except in relation to any merger reference made before 16 November 1989, and is repealed by the Enterprise Act 2002, s 278(2), Sch 26 as from a day to be appointed; s 151 inserts s 93B of the 1973 Act at* **[79]**.*)*

152 Fees

(1)   The Secretary of State may by regulations made by statutory instrument require the payment to him or to the Director of such fees as may be prescribed by the regulations in connection with the exercise by the Secretary of State, the Director and the Commission of their functions under Part V of the Fair Trading Act 1973.

(2)   The regulations may provide for fees to be payable—
    (a) in respect of—
        (i) an application for the consent of the Secretary of State under section 58(1) of the Fair Trading Act 1973 to the transfer of a newspaper or of newspaper assets, and
        (ii) a notice under section 75A(1) of that Act, and
    (b) on the occurrence of any event specified in the regulations.

(3)   The events that may be specified in the regulations by virtue of subsection (2)(b) above include—
    (a) the making by the Secretary of State of a merger reference to the Commission under section 64 or 75 of the Fair Trading Act 1973,
    (b) the announcement by the Secretary of State of his decision not to make a merger reference in any case where, at the time the announcement is made, he would under one of those sections have power to make such a reference.

(4)   The regulations may also contain provision—
    (a) for ascertaining the persons by whom fees are payable,
    (b) specifying whether any fee is payable to the Secretary of State or to the Director,

(c) for the amount of any fee to be calculated by reference to matters which may include—

   (i) in a case involving functions of the Secretary of State under sections 57 to 61 of the Fair Trading Act 1973, the number of newspapers concerned, the number of separate editions (determined in accordance with the regulations) of each newspaper and the average circulation per day of publication (within the meaning of Part V of that Act) of each newspaper, and

   (ii) in any other case, the value (determined in accordance with the regulations) of any assets concerned,

(d) as to the time when any fee is to be paid, and

(e) for the repayment by the Secretary of State or the Director of the whole or part of any fee in specified circumstances.

(5)   The regulations may make different provision for different cases.

(6)   Subsections (2) to (5) above do not prejudice the generality of subsection (1) above.

(7)   In determining the amount of any fees to be prescribed by the regulations, the Secretary of State may take into account all costs incurred by him and by the Director in respect of the exercise by him, by the Commission and by the Director of their respective functions—

(a) under Part V of the Fair Trading Act 1973, and

(b) under Parts I, VII and VIII of that Act in relation to merger references or other matters arising under Part V.

(8)   A statutory instrument containing regulations under this section shall be subject to annulment in pursuance of a resolution of either House of Parliament.

(9)   Fees paid to the Secretary of State or the Director under this section shall be paid into the Consolidated Fund.

(10)   In this section—
   "the Commission",
   "the Director", and
   "merger reference",

have the same meaning as in the Fair Trading Act 1973, and "newspaper" has the same meaning as in Part V of that Act.

(11)   References in this section to Part V of the Fair Trading Act 1973 and to merger references under section 64 or 75 of that Act or under that Part [include sections 32 and 34 of the Water Industry Act 1991 and any reference under section 32 of that Act.]

                                                                              [129]

NOTES

   Repealed by the Enterprise Act 2002, s 278(2), Sch 26, as from a day to be appointed.

   Sub-s (11): words in square brackets substituted by the Water Consolidation (Consequential Provisions) Act 1991, s 2(1), Sch 1, para 52.

   The Director: see the note "Director General of Fair Trading" to s 47 at **[126]**.

   Regulations: the Merger (Fees) Regulations 1990, SI 1990/1660 at **[2178]**, as amended by SI 2001/1199.

153–207   (S 153, ss 154–207 (Pts VII–IX) outside the scope of this work.)

PART X
MISCELLANEOUS AND GENERAL PROVISIONS

208–211   (Outside the scope of this work.)

General

212–215   (*Outside the scope of this work.*)

216 Short title

This Act may be cited as the Companies Act 1989.

SCHEDULES

(*Schs 1–13 outside the scope of this work.*)

SCHEDULE 14

Section 47(1)

SUPERVISORY AND QUALIFYING BODIES: RESTRICTIVE PRACTICES

PART I
PREVENTION OF RESTRICTIVE PRACTICES

Refusal of recognition on grounds related to competition

1.—(1)   The Secretary of State shall before deciding whether to make a recognition order in respect of a supervisory body or professional qualification send to *the Director General of Fair Trading (in this Schedule referred to as "the Director")* a copy of the rules and of any guidance which the Secretary of State is required to consider in making that decision together with such other information as the Secretary of State considers will assist the *Director*.

(2)   The *Director* shall consider whether the rules or guidance have, or are intended or likely to have, to any significant extent the effect of restricting, distorting or preventing competition, and shall report to the Secretary of State; and the Secretary of State shall have regard to *his* report in deciding whether to make a recognition order.

(3)   The Secretary of State shall not make a recognition order if it appears to him that the rules and any guidance of which copies are furnished with the application have, or are intended or likely to have, to any significant extent the effect of restricting, distorting or preventing competition, unless it appears to him that the effect is reasonably justifiable having regard to the purposes of this Part of this Act.

Notification of changes to rules or guidance

2.—(1)   Where a recognised supervisory or qualifying body amends, revokes or adds to its rules or guidance in a manner which may reasonably be regarded as likely—
>   (a) to restrict, distort or prevent competition to any significant extent, or
>   (b) otherwise to affect the question whether the recognition order granted to the body
>   should continue in force,
it shall within seven days give the Secretary of State written notice of the amendment, revocation or addition.

(2)   Notice need not be given under sub-paragraph (1) of the revocation of guidance not intended to have continuing effect or issued otherwise than in writing or other legible form, or of any amendment or addition to guidance which does not result in or consist of guidance which is intended to have continuing effect and is issued in writing or other legible form.

Continuing scrutiny by the Director General of Fair Trading

3.—(1)   The *Director* shall keep under review the rules made or guidance issued by a recognised supervisory or qualifying body, and if *he* is of the opinion that any rules or guidance of such a body have, or are intended or likely to have, to any significant extent the effect of restricting, distorting or preventing competition, *he* shall report *his* opinion to the Secretary of State, stating what in *his* opinion the effect is or is likely to be.

(2)   The Secretary of State shall send to the *Director* copies of any notice received by him under paragraph 2, together with such other information as he considers will assist the *Director*.

(3)   The *Director* may report to the Secretary of State *his* opinion that any matter mentioned in such a notice does not have, and is not intended or likely to have, to any significant extent the effect of restricting, distorting or preventing competition.

(4)   The *Director* may from time to time consider whether—

    (a) any practices of a recognised supervisory or qualifying body in its capacity as such, or

    (b) any relevant practices required or contemplated by the rules or guidance of such a body or otherwise attributable to its conduct in its capacity as such,

have, or are intended or likely to have, to any significant extent the effect of restricting, distorting or preventing competition and, if so, what that effect is or is likely to be; and if *he* is of that opinion *he* shall make a report to the Secretary of State stating *his* opinion and what the effect is or is likely to be.

(5)   The practices relevant for the purposes of sub-paragraph (4)(b) in the case of a recognised supervisory body are practices engaged in for the purposes of, or in connection with, appointment as a company auditor or the conduct of company audit work by persons who—

    (a) are eligible under its rules for appointment as a company auditor, or

    (b) hold an appropriate qualification and are directors or other officers of bodies corporate which are so eligible or partners in, or employees of, partnerships which are so eligible.

(6)   The practices relevant for the purposes of sub-paragraph (4)(b) in the case of a recognised qualifying body are—

    (a) practices engaged in by persons in the course of seeking to obtain a recognised professional qualification from that body, and

    (b) practices engaged in by persons approved by the body for the purposes of giving practical training to persons seeking such a qualification and which relate to such training.

Investigatory powers of the Director

4.—(1) The following powers are exercisable by the *Director* for the purpose of investigating any matter in connection with *his* functions under paragraph 1 or 3.

(2)   The *Director* may by a notice in writing require any person to produce, at a time and place specified in the notice, to the *Director* or to any person appointed by *him* for the purpose, any documents which are specified or described in the notice and which are documents in his custody or under his control and relating to any matter relevant to the investigation.

(3)   The *Director* may by a notice in writing require any person to furnish to the *Director* such information as may be specified or described in the notice, and specify the time within which and the manner and form in which any such information is to be furnished.

(4)   A person shall not under this paragraph be required to produce any document or disclose any information which he would be entitled to refuse to produce or disclose on grounds of legal professional privilege in proceedings in the High Court or on the grounds of confidentiality as between client and professional legal adviser in proceedings in the Court of Session.

(5)   Subsections (6) to (8) of section 85 of the Fair Trading Act 1973 (enforcement provisions) apply in relation to a notice under this paragraph as they apply in relation to a notice under subsection (1) of that section but as if, in subsection (7) of that section, for the words from "any one" to "the Commission" there were substituted "the Director".

[Enforcement

4A.—(1) The court may, on an application by the OFT, enquire into whether any person ("the defaulter") has refused or otherwise failed, without reasonable excuse, to comply with a notice under paragraph 4.

(2)   An application under sub-paragraph (1) shall include details of the possible failure which the OFT considers has occurred.

(3)   In enquiring into a case under sub-paragraph (1), the court shall hear any witness who may be produced against or on behalf of the defaulter and any statement which may be offered in defence.

(4)   Sub-paragraphs (5) and (6) apply where the court is satisfied, after hearing any witnesses and statements as mentioned in sub-paragraph (3), that the defaulter has refused or otherwise failed, without reasonable excuse, to comply with the notice under paragraph 4.

(5)   The court may punish the defaulter as it would have been able to punish him had he been guilty of contempt of court.

(6)   Where the defaulter is a body corporate, the court may punish any director or officer of the defaulter as it would have been able to punish that director or officer had the director or officer been guilty of contempt of court.

(7)   In this section "the court"—
    (a)   in relation to England and Wales, means the High Court, and
    (b)   in relation to Scotland, means the Court of Session.

4B.—(1)   A person commits an offence if he intentionally alters, suppresses or destroys a document which he has been required to produce by a notice under paragraph 4.

(2)   A person who commits an offence under sub-paragraph (1) shall be liable—
    (a)   on summary conviction, to a fine not exceeding the statutory maximum;
    (b)   on conviction on indictment, to imprisonment for a term not exceeding two years or to a fine or to both.]

Publication of Director's reports

5.—(1)   The *Director* may, if *he* thinks fit, publish any report made by *him* under paragraph 1 or 3.

(2)   *He* shall exclude from a published report, so far as practicable, any matter which relates to the affairs of a particular person (other than the supervisory or qualifying body concerned) the publication of which would or might in *his* opinion seriously and prejudicially affect the interests of that person.

Powers exercisable by the Secretary of State in consequence of report

6.—(1)   The powers conferred by this section are exercisable by the Secretary of State if, having received and considered a report from the *Director* under paragraph 3(1) or (4), it appears to him that—
    (a)   any rules made or guidance issued by a recognised supervisory or qualifying body, or
    (b)   any such practices as are mentioned in paragraph 3(4),
have, or are intended or likely to have, to any significant extent the effect of restricting, distorting or preventing competition and that that effect is greater than is reasonably justifiable having regard to the purposes of this Part of this Act.

(2)   The powers are—
    (a)   to revoke the recognition order granted to the body concerned;
    (b)   to direct it to take specified steps for the purpose of securing that the rules, guidance or practices in question do not have the effect mentioned in sub-paragraph (1), and
    (c)   to make alterations in the rules of the body for that purpose.

(3)   The provisions of paragraph 3(2) to (5), (7) and (9) of Schedule 11 or, as the case may be, Schedule 12 have effect in relation to the revocation of a recognition order under sub-paragraph (2)(a) above as they have effect in relation to the revocation of such an order under that Schedule.

(4)   Before the Secretary of State exercises the power conferred by sub-paragraph (2)(b) or (c) above he shall—
    (a)   give written notice of his intention to do so to the body concerned and take such steps (whether by publication or otherwise) as he thinks appropriate for bringing the notice to the attention of any other person who in his opinion is likely to be affected by the exercise of the power, and

(b)　have regard to any representation made within such time as he considers reasonable by the body or any such other person.

(5)　A notice under sub-paragraph (4) shall give particulars of the manner in which the Secretary of State proposes to exercise the power in question and state the reasons for which he proposes to act; and the statement of reasons may include matters contained in any report received by him under paragraph 4.

Supplementary provisions

7.—(1)　A direction under paragraph 6 is, on the application of the Secretary of State, enforceable by injunction or, in Scotland, by an order under section 45 of the Court of Session Act 1988.

(2)　The fact that any rules made by a recognised supervisory or qualifying body have been altered by the Secretary of State, or pursuant to a direction of the Secretary of State, under paragraph 6 does not preclude their subsequent alteration or revocation by that body.

(3)　In determining for the purposes of this Part of this Schedule whether any guidance has, or is likely to have, any particular effect the Secretary of State and the *Director* may assume that the persons to whom it is addressed will act in conformity with it.

[131]

NOTES

Para 1: for the first words in italics there are substituted the words "the Office of Fair Trading (in this Schedule referred to as "the OFT")", for the second and third words in italics there is substituted the word "OFT", and for the fourth word in italics there is substituted the word "its", by the Enterprise Act 2002, s 278(1), Sch 25, para 21(1), (4)(a), as from a day to be appointed.

Para 3: for the words "Director", "he" and "his" in italics, there are substituted the words "OFT", "it" and "its" respectively, and in the cross-heading preceding para 3, for the words "Director General of Fair Trading", there are substituted the words "Office of Fair Trading", by the Enterprise Act 2002, s 278(1), Sch 25, para 21(1), (4)(b), as from a day to be appointed.

Para 4: for the words "Director" (including where it appears in the cross-heading preceding para 4), "his" and "him" in italics, there are substituted the words "OFT", "its" and "it" respectively, and sub-para (5) is repealed, by the Enterprise Act 2002, s 278, Sch 25, para 21(1), (4)(c), Sch 26, as from a day to be appointed.

Paras 4A, 4B: inserted by the Enterprise Act 2002, s 278(1), Sch 25, para 21(1), (4)(d), as from a day to be appointed.

Para 5: for the words "Director", "he", "him" and "his" in italics, there are substituted the words "OFT", "it", "it" and "its" respectively, and in the cross-heading preceding para 5, for the word "Director's", there is substituted the word "OFT's" by the Enterprise Act 2002, s 278(1), Sch 25, para 21(1), (4)(e), as from a day to be appointed.

Paras 6, 7: for the word "Director" in italics, there is substituted the word "OFT" by the Enterprise Act 2002, s 278(1), Sch 25, para 21(1), (4)(f), as from a day to be appointed.

The Director: see the note "Director General of Fair Trading" to s 47 at **[126]**.

PART II
CONSEQUENTIAL EXEMPTIONS FROM COMPETITION LAW

Fair Trading Act 1973 (c 41)

8.—(1)　*For the purpose of determining whether a monopoly situation within the meaning of the Fair Trading Act 1973 exists by reason of the circumstances mentioned in section 7(1)(c) of that Act (supply of services by or for group of two or more persons), no account shall be taken of—*

(a)　*the rules of or guidance issued by a recognised supervisory or qualifying body, or*

(b)　*conduct constituting such a practice as is mentioned in paragraph 3(4) above.*

(2)　*Where a recognition order is revoked there shall be disregarded for the purpose mentioned in sub-paragraph (1) any such conduct as is mentioned in that sub-paragraph which occurred while the order was in force.*

(3)   Where on a monopoly reference under section 50 or 51 of the Fair Trading Act 1973 falling within section 49 of that Act (monopoly reference not limited to the facts) the [Competition Commission] find that a monopoly situation within the meaning of that Act exists and—

  (a)   that the person (or, if more than one, any of the persons) in whose favour it exists is—

   (i)   a recognised supervisory or qualifying body, or

   (ii) a person of a description mentioned in paragraph 3(5) or (6) above, or

  (b)   that any such person's conduct in doing anything to which the rules of such a body relate is subject to guidance issued by the body,

the Commission in making their report on that reference shall exclude from their consideration the question whether the rules or guidance of the body concerned, or the acts or omissions of that body in its capacity as such, operate or may be expected to operate against the public interest.

[The Competition Act 1998

9.—(1)   The Chapter I prohibition does not apply to an agreement for the constitution of a recognised supervisory or qualifying body to the extent to which it relates to—

  (a)   rules of, or guidance issued by, the body; and

  (b)   incidental matters connected with the rules or guidance.

(2)   The Chapter I prohibition does not apply to an agreement the parties to which consist of or include—

  (a)   a recognised supervisory or qualifying body, or

  (b)   any person mentioned in paragraph 3(5) or (6) above,

to the extent to which the agreement consists of provisions the inclusion of which in the agreement is required or contemplated by the rules or guidance of that body.

(3)   The Chapter I prohibition does not apply to the practices mentioned in paragraph 3(4)(a) and (b) above.

(4)   Where a recognition order is revoked, sub-paragraphs (1) to (3) above are to continue to apply for a period of six months beginning with the day on which the revocation takes effect, as if the order were still in force.

(5)   In this paragraph—

  (a)   "the Chapter I prohibition" means the prohibition imposed by section 2(1) of the Competition Act 1998,

  (b)   references to an agreement are to be read as applying equally to, or in relation to, a decision or concerted practice,

and expressions used in this paragraph which are also used in Part I of the Competition Act 1998 are to be interpreted in the same way as for the purposes of that Part of that Act.

(6)   In the application of this paragraph to decisions and concerted practices, references to provisions of an agreement are to be read as references to elements of a decision or concerted practice.]

10.   . . .

[132]

NOTES

   Para 8: repealed by the Enterprise Act 2002, s 278, Sch 25, para 21(1), (4)(g), Sch 26, as from a day to be appointed; words in square brackets in sub-para (3) substituted by the Competition Act 1998 (Competition Commission) Transitional, Consequential and Supplemental Provisions Order 1999, SI 1999/506, art 26.
   Para 9: substituted by the Competition Act 1998, s 3(1)(b), Sch 2, Pt II, para 2(1), (2).
   Para 10: repealed by the Competition Act 1998 (Transitional, Consequential and Supplemental Provisions) Order 2000, SI 2000/311, art 24(a).
   The Director: see the note "Director General of Fair Trading" to s 47 at **[126]**.

(Schs 15–24 outside the scope of this work.)

COMPETITION ACT 1998

(1998 c 41)

ARRANGEMENT OF SECTIONS

PART I
COMPETITION

CHAPTER I
AGREEMENTS

Introduction

CHAPTER II
ABUSE OF DOMINANT POSITION

The prohibition

CHAPTER III
INVESTIGATION AND ENFORCEMENT

Investigations

Enforcement

Offences

CHAPTER IV
THE COMPETITION COMMISSION AND APPEALS

The Commission

Appeals

CHAPTER V
MISCELLANEOUS

Vertical agreements and land agreements

Director's rules, guidance and fees

Regulators

An Act to make provision about competition and the abuse of a dominant position in the market; to confer powers in relation to investigations conducted in connection with Article 85 or 86 of the treaty establishing the European Community; to amend the Fair Trading Act 1973 in relation to information which may be required in connection with investigations under that Act; to make provision with respect to the meaning of "supply of services" in the Fair Trading Act 1973; and for connected purposes

[9 November 1998]

NOTES

Substitution of references to the Director General of Fair Trading: the Enterprise Act 2002, s 2(1), at **[255]**, provides that, as from the coming into force of that section in accordance with s 279 at **[463]**, the functions of the Director General of Fair Trading, his property, rights and liabilities are transferred to the Office of Fair Trading. Accordingly, (by virtue of s 2(2), (3) of the 2002 Act) the office of the Director is abolished, and amendments are made to this Act by the 2002 Act to take account of this (see Sch 25, para 38). Consequently, throughout this Act, unless noted otherwise, for the words "Director", "Director's", "he", "him" and "his" in italics, there are substituted the words "OFT", "OFT's", "it", "it" and "its" respectively.

PART I
COMPETITION

CHAPTER I
AGREEMENTS

Introduction

1 Enactments replaced

The following shall cease to have effect—
   (a) the Restrictive Practices Court Act 1976 (c 33),
   (b) the Restrictive Trade Practices Act 1976 (c 34),
   (c) the Resale Prices Act 1976 (c 53), and
   (d) the Restrictive Trade Practices Act 1977 (c 19).

[133]

NOTES

Commencement: 1 March 2000 (paras (b)–(d)); to be appointed (remainder).

The prohibition

2 Agreements etc preventing, restricting or distorting competition

(1) Subject to section 3, agreements between undertakings, decisions by associations of undertakings or concerted practices which—
   (a) may affect trade within the United Kingdom, and
   (b) have as their object or effect the prevention, restriction or distortion of competition within the United Kingdom,
are prohibited unless they are exempt in accordance with the provisions of this Part.

(2)   Subsection (1) applies, in particular, to agreements, decisions or practices which—

(a) directly or indirectly fix purchase or selling prices or any other trading conditions;

(b) limit or control production, markets, technical development or investment;

(c) share markets or sources of supply;

(d) apply dissimilar conditions to equivalent transactions with other trading parties, thereby placing them at a competitive disadvantage;

(e) make the conclusion of contracts subject to acceptance by the other parties of supplementary obligations which, by their nature or according to commercial usage, have no connection with the subject of such contracts.

(3)   Subsection (1) applies only if the agreement, decision or practice is, or is intended to be, implemented in the United Kingdom.

(4)   Any agreement or decision which is prohibited by subsection (1) is void.

(5)   A provision of this Part which is expressed to apply to, or in relation to, an agreement is to be read as applying equally to, or in relation to, a decision by an association of undertakings or a concerted practice (but with any necessary modifications).

(6)   Subsection (5) does not apply where the context otherwise requires.

(7)   In this section "the United Kingdom" means, in relation to an agreement which operates or is intended to operate only in a part of the United Kingdom, that part.

(8)   The prohibition imposed by subsection (1) is referred to in this Act as "the Chapter I prohibition".

[134]

NOTES

Commencement: 1 March 2000.

Excluded agreements

3   Excluded agreements

(1)   The Chapter I prohibition does not apply in any of the cases in which it is excluded by or as a result of—

(a) Schedule 1 (mergers and concentrations);

(b) Schedule 2 (competition scrutiny under other enactments);

(c) Schedule 3 (planning obligations and other general exclusions); *or*

(d) *Schedule 4 (professional rules).*

(2)   The Secretary of State may at any time by order amend Schedule 1, with respect to the Chapter I prohibition, by—

(a) providing for one or more additional exclusions; or

(b) amending or removing any provision (whether or not it has been added by an order under this subsection).

(3)   The Secretary of State may at any time by order amend Schedule 3, with respect to the Chapter I prohibition, by—

(a) providing for one or more additional exclusions; or

(b) amending or removing any provision—

(i) added by an order under this subsection; or

(ii) included in paragraph 1, 2, 8 or 9 of Schedule 3.

(4)   The power under subsection (3) to provide for an additional exclusion may be exercised only if it appears to the Secretary of State that agreements which fall within the additional exclusion—

(a) do not in general have an adverse effect on competition, or

(b) are, in general, best considered under Chapter II or *the Fair Trading Act 1973.*

(5)   An order under subsection (2)(a) or (3)(a) may include provision (similar to that made with respect to any other exclusion provided by the relevant Schedule) for the exclusion concerned to cease to apply to a particular agreement.

(6)   Schedule 3 also gives the Secretary of State power to exclude agreements from the Chapter I prohibition in certain circumstances.

[135]

NOTES

Commencement: 11 January 1999 (sub-s (1), certain purposes, sub-ss (2)–(6)); 1 March 2000 (sub-s (1), remaining purposes).

Sub-s (1): para (d) and the word immediately preceding it repealed by the Enterprise Act 2002, ss 207, 278(2), Sch 26, as from a day to be appointed, subject to savings in s 276(1) of, and Sch 24, para 20 to, that Act at **[477]**.

Sub-s (4): for the words in italics in para (b) there are substituted the words "the Enterprise Act 2002" by the Enterprise Act 2002, s 278(1), Sch 25, para 38(1), (2), as from a day to be appointed.

Exemptions

4   Individual exemptions

(1)   The *Director* may grant an exemption from the Chapter I prohibition with respect to a particular agreement if—

(a) a request for an exemption has been made to *him* under section 14 by a party to the agreement; and

(b) the agreement is one to which section 9 applies.

(2)   An exemption granted under this section is referred to in this Part as an individual exemption.

(3)   The exemption—

(a) may be granted subject to such conditions or obligations as the *Director* considers it appropriate to impose; and

(b) has effect for such period as the *Director* considers appropriate.

(4)   That period must be specified in the grant of the exemption.

(5)   An individual exemption may be granted so as to have effect from a date earlier than that on which it is granted.

(6)   On an application made in such way as may be specified by rules under section 51, the *Director* may extend the period for which an exemption has effect; but, if the rules so provide, *he* may do so only in specified circumstances.

[136]

NOTES

Commencement: 1 March 2000.

Director: as to the abolition of the office of the Director General of Fair Trading and the substitution of references to the Director and related expressions, see the note preceding s 1 at **[133]**.

PART I
STATUTES

5 Cancellation etc of individual exemptions

(1) If the *Director* has reasonable grounds for believing that there has been a material change of circumstance since *he* granted an individual exemption, *he* may by notice in writing—

 (a) cancel the exemption;

 (b) vary or remove any condition or obligation; or

 (c) impose one or more additional conditions or obligations.

(2) If the *Director* has a reasonable suspicion that the information on which *he* based *his* decision to grant an individual exemption was incomplete, false or misleading in a material particular, *he* may by notice in writing take any of the steps mentioned in subsection (1).

(3) Breach of a condition has the effect of cancelling the exemption.

(4) Failure to comply with an obligation allows the *Director*, by notice in writing, to take any of the steps mentioned in subsection (1).

(5) Any step taken by the *Director* under subsection (1), (2) or (4) has effect from such time as may be specified in the notice.

(6) If an exemption is cancelled under subsection (2) or (4), the date specified in the notice cancelling it may be earlier than the date on which the notice is given.

(7) The *Director* may act under subsection (1), (2) or (4) on *his* own initiative or on a complaint made by any person.

[137]

NOTES

Commencement: 1 March 2000.

Director: as to the abolition of the office of the Director General of Fair Trading and the substitution of references to the Director and related expressions, see the note preceding s 1 at **[133]**.

6 Block exemptions

(1) If agreements which fall within a particular category of agreement are, in the opinion of the *Director*, likely to be agreements to which section 9 applies, the *Director* may recommend that the Secretary of State make an order specifying that category for the purposes of this section.

(2) The Secretary of State may make an order ("a block exemption order") giving effect to such a recommendation—

 (a) in the form in which the recommendation is made; or

 (b) subject to such modifications as he considers appropriate.

(3) An agreement which falls within a category specified in a block exemption order is exempt from the Chapter I prohibition.

(4) An exemption under this section is referred to in this Part as a block exemption.

(5) A block exemption order may impose conditions or obligations subject to which a block exemption is to have effect.

(6) A block exemption order may provide—

 (a) that breach of a condition imposed by the order has the effect of cancelling the block exemption in respect of an agreement;

 (b) that if there is a failure to comply with an obligation imposed by the order, the *Director* may, by notice in writing, cancel the block exemption in respect of the agreement;

 (c) that if the *Director* considers that a particular agreement is not one to which section 9 applies, *he* may cancel the block exemption in respect of that agreement.

(7)   A block exemption order may provide that the order is to cease to have effect at the end of a specified period.

(8)   In this section and section 7 "specified" means specified in a block exemption order.

NOTES
   Commencement: 1 March 2000.
   Director: as to the abolition of the office of the Director General of Fair Trading and the substitution of references to the Director and related expressions, see the note preceding s 1 at **[133]**.
   Orders: the Competition Act 1998 (Public Transport Ticketing Schemes Block Exemption) Order 2001, SI 2001/319 at **[2138]**.

7   Block exemptions: opposition

(1)   A block exemption order may provide that a party to an agreement which—
   (a) does not qualify for the block exemption created by the order, but
   (b) satisfies specified criteria,
may notify the *Director* of the agreement for the purposes of subsection (2).

(2)   An agreement which is notified under any provision included in a block exemption order by virtue of subsection (1) is to be treated, as from the end of the notice period, as falling within a category specified in a block exemption order unless the *Director*—
   (a) is opposed to its being so treated; and
   (b) gives notice in writing to the party concerned of *his* opposition before the end of that period.

(3)   If the *Director* gives notice of *his* opposition under subsection (2), the notification under subsection (1) is to be treated as both notification under section 14 and as a request for an individual exemption made under subsection (3) of that section.

(4)   In this section "notice period" means such period as may be specified with a view to giving the *Director* sufficient time to consider whether to oppose under subsection (2).

NOTES
   Commencement: 1 March 2000.
   Director: as to the abolition of the office of the Director General of Fair Trading and the substitution of references to the Director and related expressions, see the note preceding s 1 at **[133]**.

8   Block exemptions: procedure

(1)   Before making a recommendation under section 6(1), the *Director* must—
   (a) publish details of *his* proposed recommendation in such a way as *he* thinks most suitable for bringing it to the attention of those likely to be affected; and
   (b) consider any representations about it which are made to *him*.

(2)   If the Secretary of State proposes to give effect to such a recommendation subject to modifications, he must inform the *Director* of the proposed modifications and take into account any comments made by the *Director*.

(3)   If, in the opinion of the *Director*, it is appropriate to vary or revoke a block exemption order *he* may make a recommendation to that effect to the Secretary of State.

(4)   Subsection (1) also applies to any proposed recommendation under subsection (3).

(5)   Before exercising his power to vary or revoke a block exemption order (in a case where there has been no recommendation under subsection (3)), the Secretary of State must—

(a) inform the *Director* of the proposed variation or revocation; and

(b) take into account any comments made by the *Director*.

(6)   A block exemption order may provide for a block exemption to have effect from a date earlier than that on which the order is made.

[140]

NOTES

Commencement: 1 March 2000.

Director: as to the abolition of the office of the Director General of Fair Trading and the substitution of references to the Director and related expressions, see the note preceding s 1 at **[133]**.

Orders: the Competition Act 1998 (Public Transport Ticketing Schemes Block Exemption) Order 2001, SI 2001/319 at **[2138]**.

9   The criteria for individual and block exemptions

This section applies to any agreement which—

(a) contributes to—

(i) improving production or distribution, or

(ii) promoting technical or economic progress,

while allowing consumers a fair share of the resulting benefit; but

(b) does not—

(i) impose on the undertakings concerned restrictions which are not indispensable to the attainment of those objectives; or

(ii) afford the undertakings concerned the possibility of eliminating competition in respect of a substantial part of the products in question.

[141]

NOTES

Commencement: 1 March 2000.

10   Parallel exemptions

(1)   An agreement is exempt from the Chapter I prohibition if it is exempt from the Community prohibition—

(a) by virtue of a Regulation,

(b) because it has been given exemption by the Commission, or

(c) because it has been notified to the Commission under the appropriate opposition or objection procedure and—

(i) the time for opposing, or objecting to, the agreement has expired and the Commission has not opposed it; or

(ii) the Commission has opposed, or objected to, the agreement but has withdrawn its opposition or objection.

(2)   An agreement is exempt from the Chapter I prohibition if it does not affect trade between Member States but otherwise falls within a category of agreement which is exempt from the Community prohibition by virtue of a Regulation.

(3)   An exemption from the Chapter I prohibition under this section is referred to in this Part as a parallel exemption.

(4)   A parallel exemption—

(a) takes effect on the date on which the relevant exemption from the Community prohibition takes effect or, in the case of a parallel exemption under subsection (2), would take effect if the agreement in question affected trade between Member States; and

(b) ceases to have effect—
    (i) if the relevant exemption from the Community prohibition ceases to have effect; or
    (ii) on being cancelled by virtue of subsection (5) or (7).

(5)   In such circumstances and manner as may be specified in rules made under section 51, the *Director* may—
    (a) impose conditions or obligations subject to which a parallel exemption is to have effect;
    (b) vary or remove any such condition or obligation;
    (c) impose one or more additional conditions or obligations;
    (d) cancel the exemption.

(6)   In such circumstances as may be specified in rules made under section 51, the date from which cancellation of an exemption is to take effect may be earlier than the date on which notice of cancellation is given.

(7)   Breach of a condition imposed by the *Director* has the effect of cancelling the exemption.

(8)   In exercising *his* powers under this section, the *Director* may require any person who is a party to the agreement in question to give *him* such information as *he* may require.

(9)   For the purpose of this section references to an agreement being exempt from the Community prohibition are to be read as including references to the prohibition being inapplicable to the agreement by virtue of a Regulation or a decision by the Commission.

(10) In this section—
"the Community prohibition" means the prohibition contained in—
    (a) paragraph 1 of Article 85;
    (b) any corresponding provision replacing, or otherwise derived from, that provision;
    (c) such other Regulation as the Secretary of State may by order specify; and
"Regulation" means a Regulation adopted by the Commission or by the Council.

(11) This section has effect in relation to the prohibition contained in paragraph 1 of Article 53 of the EEA Agreement (and the EFTA Surveillance Authority) as it has effect in relation to the Community prohibition (and the Commission) subject to any modifications which the Secretary of State may by order prescribe.

[142]

NOTES
    Commencement: 1 March 2000.
    Director: as to the abolition of the office of the Director General of Fair Trading and the substitution of references to the Director and related expressions, see the note preceding s 1 at **[133]**.

---

11 Exemption for certain other agreements

(1)   The fact that a ruling may be given by virtue of Article 88 of the Treaty on the question whether or not agreements of a particular kind are prohibited by Article 85 does not prevent such agreements from being subject to the Chapter I prohibition.

(2)   But the Secretary of State may by regulations make such provision as he considers appropriate for the purpose of granting an exemption from the Chapter I prohibition, in prescribed circumstances, in respect of such agreements.

(3)   An exemption from the Chapter I prohibition by virtue of regulations under this section is referred to in this Part as a section 11 exemption.

[143]

NOTES

Commencement: 1 March 2000.

Regulations: the Competition Act 1998 (Section 11 Exemption) Regulations 2001, SI 2001/2993 at **[2159]**.

Notification

12   Requests for *Director* to examine agreements

(1)   Sections 13 and 14 provide for an agreement to be examined by the *Director* on the application of a party to the agreement who thinks that it may infringe the Chapter I prohibition.

(2)   Schedule 5 provides for the procedure to be followed—
   (a) by any person making such an application; and
   (b) by the *Director*, in considering such an application.

(3)   The Secretary of State may by regulations make provision as to the application of sections 13 to 16 and Schedule 5, with such modifications (if any) as may be prescribed, in cases where the *Director*—
   (a) has given a direction withdrawing an exclusion; or
   (b) is considering whether to give such a direction.

[144]

NOTES

Commencement: 11 January 1999 (sub-s (3)); 1 March 2000 (remainder).

Director: as to the abolition of the office of the Director General of Fair Trading and the substitution of references to the Director and related expressions, see the note preceding s 1 at **[133]**.

Regulations: the Competition Act 1998 (Notification of Excluded Agreements and Appealable Decisions) Regulations 2000, SI 2000/263 at **[2015]**.

13   Notification for guidance

(1)   A party to an agreement who applies for the agreement to be examined under this section must—
   (a) notify the *Director* of the agreement; and
   (b) apply to *him* for guidance.

(2)   On an application under this section, the *Director* may give the applicant guidance as to whether or not, in *his* view, the agreement is likely to infringe the Chapter I prohibition.

(3)   If the *Director* considers that the agreement is likely to infringe the prohibition if it is not exempt, *his* guidance may indicate—
   (a) whether the agreement is likely to be exempt from the prohibition under—
      (i) a block exemption;
      (ii) a parallel exemption; or
      (iii) a section 11 exemption; or
   (b) whether *he* would be likely to grant the agreement an individual exemption if asked to do so.

(4)   If an agreement to which the prohibition applies has been notified to the *Director* under this section, no penalty is to be imposed under this Part in respect of any infringement of the prohibition by the agreement which occurs during the period—
   (a) beginning with the date on which notification was given; and

(b) ending with such date as may be specified in a notice in writing given to the applicant by the *Director* when the application has been determined.

(5)   The date specified in a notice under subsection (4)(b) may not be earlier than the date on which the notice is given.

[145]

NOTES

Commencement: 1 March 2000.

Sub-s (1): for the word in italics in para (b) there is substituted the words "the OFT" by the Enterprise Act 2002, s 278(1), Sch 25, para 38(1), (10), as from a day to be appointed.

Director: as to the abolition of the office of the Director General of Fair Trading and the substitution of references to the Director and related expressions, see the note preceding s 1 at [133].

14   Notification for a decision

(1)   A party to an agreement who applies for the agreement to be examined under this section must—
  (a) notify the *Director* of the agreement; and
  (b) apply to *him* for a decision.

(2)   On an application under this section, the *Director* may make a decision as to—
  (a) whether the Chapter I prohibition has been infringed; and
  (b) if it has not been infringed, whether that is because of the effect of an exclusion or because the agreement is exempt from the prohibition.

(3)   If an agreement is notified to the *Director* under this section, the application may include a request for the agreement to which it relates to be granted an individual exemption.

(4)   If an agreement to which the prohibition applies has been notified to the *Director* under this section, no penalty is to be imposed under this Part in respect of any infringement of the prohibition by the agreement which occurs during the period—
  (a) beginning with the date on which notification was given; and
  (b) ending with such date as may be specified in a notice in writing given to the applicant by the *Director* when the application has been determined.

(5)   The date specified in a notice under subsection (4)(b) may not be earlier than the date on which the notice is given.

[146]

NOTES

Commencement: 1 March 2000.

Sub-s (1): for the word in italics in para (b) there is substituted the words "the OFT" by the Enterprise Act 2002, s 278(1), Sch 25, para 38(1), (11), as from a day to be appointed.

Director: as to the abolition of the office of the Director General of Fair Trading and the substitution of references to the Director and related expressions, see the note preceding s 1 at [133].

15   Effect of guidance

(1)   This section applies to an agreement if the *Director* has determined an application under section 13 by giving guidance that—
  (a) the agreement is unlikely to infringe the Chapter I prohibition, regardless of whether or not it is exempt;
  (b) the agreement is likely to be exempt under—
    (i) a block exemption;
    (ii) a parallel exemption; or
    (iii) a section 11 exemption; or

(c) *he* would be likely to grant the agreement an individual exemption if asked to do so.

(2)   The *Director* is to take no further action under this Part with respect to an agreement to which this section applies, unless—

    (a) *he* has reasonable grounds for believing that there has been a material change of circumstance since *he* gave *his* guidance;

    (b) *he* has a reasonable suspicion that the information on which *he* based *his* guidance was incomplete, false or misleading in a material particular;

    (c) one of the parties to the agreement applies to *him* for a decision under section 14 with respect to the agreement; or

    (d) a complaint about the agreement has been made to *him* by a person who is not a party to the agreement.

(3)   No penalty may be imposed under this Part in respect of any infringement of the Chapter I prohibition by an agreement to which this section applies.

(4)   But the *Director* may remove the immunity given by subsection (3) if—

    (a) *he* takes action under this Part with respect to the agreement in one of the circumstances mentioned in subsection (2);

    (b) *he* considers it likely that the agreement will infringe the prohibition; and

    (c) *he* gives notice in writing to the party on whose application the guidance was given that *he* is removing the immunity as from the date specified in *his* notice.

(5)   If the *Director* has a reasonable suspicion that information—

    (a) on which *he* based *his* guidance, and

    (b) which was provided to *him* by a party to the agreement,

was incomplete, false or misleading in a material particular, the date specified in a notice under subsection (4)(c) may be earlier than the date on which the notice is given.

[147]

NOTES

    Commencement: 1 March 2000.

    Director: as to the abolition of the office of the Director General of Fair Trading and the substitution of references to the Director and related expressions, see the note preceding s 1 at **[133]**.

16   Effect of a decision that the Chapter I prohibition has not been infringed

(1)   This section applies to an agreement if the *Director* has determined an application under section 14 by making a decision that the agreement has not infringed the Chapter I prohibition.

(2)   The *Director* is to take no further action under this Part with respect to the agreement unless—

    (a) *he* has reasonable grounds for believing that there has been a material change of circumstance since *he* gave *his* decision; or

    (b) *he* has a reasonable suspicion that the information on which *he* based *his* decision was incomplete, false or misleading in a material particular.

(3)   No penalty may be imposed under this Part in respect of any infringement of the Chapter I prohibition by an agreement to which this section applies.

(4)   But the *Director* may remove the immunity given by subsection (3) if—

    (a) *he* takes action under this Part with respect to the agreement in one of the circumstances mentioned in subsection (2);

    (b) *he* considers that it is likely that the agreement will infringe the prohibition; and

(c) gives notice in writing to the party on whose application the decision was made that *he* is removing the immunity as from the date specified in *his* notice.

(5) If the *Director* has a reasonable suspicion that information—
  (a) on which *he* based *his* decision, and
  (b) which was provided to *him* by a party to the agreement,

was incomplete, false or misleading in a material particular, the date specified in a notice under subsection (4)(c) may be earlier than the date on which the notice is given.

[148]

NOTES

Commencement: 1 March 2000.

Director: as to the abolition of the office of the Director General of Fair Trading and the substitution of references to the Director and related expressions, see the note preceding s 1 at **[133]**.

CHAPTER II
ABUSE OF DOMINANT POSITION

17 (*Repeals the Competition Act 1980, ss 2–10.*)

The prohibition

18   Abuse of dominant position

(1)   Subject to section 19, any conduct on the part of one or more undertakings which amounts to the abuse of a dominant position in a market is prohibited if it may affect trade within the United Kingdom.

(2)   Conduct may, in particular, constitute such an abuse if it consists in—
  (a) directly or indirectly imposing unfair purchase or selling prices or other unfair trading conditions;
  (b) limiting production, markets or technical development to the prejudice of consumers;
  (c) applying dissimilar conditions to equivalent transactions with other trading parties, thereby placing them at a competitive disadvantage;
  (d) making the conclusion of contracts subject to acceptance by the other parties of supplementary obligations which, by their nature or according to commercial usage, have no connection with the subject of the contracts.

(3)   In this section—
  "dominant position" means a dominant position within the United Kingdom; and "the United Kingdom" means the United Kingdom or any part of it.

(4)   The prohibition imposed by subsection (1) is referred to in this Act as "the Chapter II prohibition".

[149]

NOTES

Commencement: 1 March 2000.

Excluded cases

19   Excluded cases

(1)   The Chapter II prohibition does not apply in any of the cases in which it is excluded by or as a result of—
  (a) Schedule 1 (mergers and concentrations); or
  (b) Schedule 3 (general exclusions).

(2)   The Secretary of State may at any time by order amend Schedule 1, with respect to the Chapter II prohibition, by—

    (a) providing for one or more additional exclusions; or

    (b) amending or removing any provision (whether or not it has been added by an order under this subsection).

(3)   The Secretary of State may at any time by order amend paragraph 8 of Schedule 3 with respect to the Chapter II prohibition.

(4)   Schedule 3 also gives the Secretary of State power to provide that the Chapter II prohibition is not to apply in certain circumstances.

[150]

NOTES

Commencement: 11 January 1999.

Notification

20   Requests for *Director* to consider conduct

(1)   Sections 21 and 22 provide for conduct of a person which that person thinks may infringe the Chapter II prohibition to be considered by the *Director* on the application of that person.

(2)   Schedule 6 provides for the procedure to be followed—

    (a) by any person making an application, and

    (b) by the *Director*, in considering an application.

[151]

NOTES

Commencement: 1 March 2000.

Director: as to the abolition of the office of the Director General of Fair Trading and the substitution of references to the Director and related expressions, see the note preceding s 1 at **[133]**.

21   Notification for guidance

(1)   A person who applies for conduct to be considered under this section must—

    (a) notify the *Director* of it; and

    (b) apply to *him* for guidance.

(2)   On an application under this section, the *Director* may give the applicant guidance as to whether or not, in *his* view, the conduct is likely to infringe the Chapter II prohibition.

[152]

NOTES

Commencement: 1 March 2000.

Sub-s (1): for the word in italics in para (b) there is substituted the words "the OFT" by the Enterprise Act 2002, s 278(1), Sch 25, para 38(1), (15), as from a day to be appointed.

Director: as to the abolition of the office of the Director General of Fair Trading and the substitution of references to the Director and related expressions, see the note preceding s 1 at **[133]**.

22   Notification for a decision

(1)   A person who applies for conduct to be considered under this section must—

    (a) notify the *Director* of it; and

    (b) apply to *him* for a decision.

(2)   On an application under this section, the *Director* may make a decision as to—

    (a) whether the Chapter II prohibition has been infringed; and

(b) if it has not been infringed, whether that is because of the effect of an exclusion.

NOTES

Commencement: 1 March 2000.

Sub-s (1): for the word in italics in para (b) there is substituted the words "the OFT" by the Enterprise Act 2002, s 278(1), Sch 25, para 38(1), (16), as from a day to be appointed.

Director: as to the abolition of the office of the Director General of Fair Trading and the substitution of references to the Director and related expressions, see the note preceding s 1 at **[133]**.

23   Effect of guidance

(1)   This section applies to conduct if the *Director* has determined an application under section 21 by giving guidance that the conduct is unlikely to infringe the Chapter II prohibition.

(2)   The *Director* is to take no further action under this Part with respect to the conduct to which this section applies, unless—
  (a) *he* has reasonable grounds for believing that there has been a material change of circumstance since *he* gave *his* guidance;
  (b) *he* has a reasonable suspicion that the information on which *he* based *his* guidance was incomplete, false or misleading in a material particular; or
  (c) a complaint about the conduct has been made to *him*.

(3)   No penalty may be imposed under this Part in respect of any infringement of the Chapter II prohibition by conduct to which this section applies.

(4)   But the *Director* may remove the immunity given by subsection (3) if—
  (a) *he* takes action under this Part with respect to the conduct in one of the circumstances mentioned in subsection (2);
  (b) *he* considers that it is likely that the conduct will infringe the prohibition; and
  (c) *he* gives notice in writing to the undertaking on whose application the guidance was given that *he* is removing the immunity as from the date specified in *his* notice.

(5)   If the *Director* has a reasonable suspicion that information—
  (a) on which *he* based *his* guidance, and
  (b) which was provided to *him* by an undertaking engaging in the conduct,

was incomplete, false or misleading in a material particular, the date specified in a notice under subsection (4)(c) may be earlier than the date on which the notice is given.

NOTES

Commencement: 1 March 2000.

Director: as to the abolition of the office of the Director General of Fair Trading and the substitution of references to the Director and related expressions, see the note preceding s 1 at **[133]**.

24   Effect of a decision that the Chapter II prohibition has not been infringed

(1)   This section applies to conduct if the *Director* has determined an application under section 22 by making a decision that the conduct has not infringed the Chapter II prohibition.

(2)   The *Director* is to take no further action under this Part with respect to the conduct unless—
  (a) *he* has reasonable grounds for believing that there has been a material change of circumstance since *he* gave *his* decision; or

(b) *he* has a reasonable suspicion that the information on which *he* based *his* decision was incomplete, false or misleading in a material particular.

(3) No penalty may be imposed under this Part in respect of any infringement of the Chapter II prohibition by conduct to which this section applies.

(4) But the *Director* may remove the immunity given by subsection (3) if—
    (a) *he* takes action under this Part with respect to the conduct in one of the circumstances mentioned in subsection (2);
    (b) *he* considers that it is likely that the conduct will infringe the prohibition; and
    (c) *he* gives notice in writing to the undertaking on whose application the decision was made that *he* is removing the immunity as from the date specified in *his* notice.

(5) If the *Director* has a reasonable suspicion that information—
    (a) on which *he* based *his* decision, and
    (b) which was provided to *him* by an undertaking engaging in the conduct,

was incomplete, false or misleading in a material particular, the date specified in a notice under subsection (4)(c) may be earlier than the date on which the notice is given.

[155]

NOTES
Commencement: 1 March 2000.
Director: as to the abolition of the office of the Director General of Fair Trading and the substitution of references to the Director and related expressions, see the note preceding s 1 at **[133]**.

CHAPTER III
INVESTIGATION AND ENFORCEMENT

Investigations

25 *Director's* power to investigate

The *Director* may conduct an investigation if there are reasonable grounds for suspecting—
    (a) that the Chapter I prohibition has been infringed; or
    (b) that the Chapter II prohibition has been infringed.

[156]

NOTES
Commencement: 1 March 2000.
Director: as to the abolition of the office of the Director General of Fair Trading and the substitution of references to the Director and related expressions, see the note preceding s 1 at **[133]**.

26 Powers when conducting investigations

(1) For the purposes of an investigation under section 25, the *Director* may require any person to produce to *him* a specified document, or to provide *him* with specified information, which *he* considers relates to any matter relevant to the investigation.

(2) The power conferred by subsection (1) is to be exercised by a notice in writing.

(3) A notice under subsection (2) must indicate—
    (a) the subject matter and purpose of the investigation; and
    (b) the nature of the offences created by sections 42 to 44.

(4) In subsection (1) "specified" means—
(a) specified, or described, in the notice; or
(b) falling within a category which is specified, or described, in the notice.

(5) The *Director* may also specify in the notice—
(a) the time and place at which any document is to be produced or any information is to be provided;
(b) the manner and form in which it is to be produced or provided.

(6) The power under this section to require a person to produce a document includes power—
(a) if the document is produced—
(i) to take copies of it or extracts from it;
(ii) to require him, or any person who is a present or past officer of his, or is or was at any time employed by him, to provide an explanation of the document;
(b) if the document is not produced, to require him to state, to the best of his knowledge and belief, where it is.

[157]

NOTES

Commencement: 1 March 2000.

Director: as to the abolition of the office of the Director General of Fair Trading and the substitution of references to the Director and related expressions, see the note preceding s 1 at **[133]**.

27 Power to enter premises without a warrant

(1) Any officer of the *Director* who is authorised in writing by the *Director* to do so ("an investigating officer") may enter any premises in connection with an investigation under section 25.

(2) No investigating officer is to enter any premises in the exercise of his powers under this section unless he has given to the occupier of the premises a written notice which—
(a) gives at least two working days' notice of the intended entry;
(b) indicates the subject matter and purpose of the investigation; and
(c) indicates the nature of the offences created by sections 42 to 44.

(3) Subsection (2) does not apply—
(a) if the *Director* has a reasonable suspicion that the premises are, or have been, occupied by—
(i) a party to an agreement which *he* is investigating under section 25(a); or
(ii) an undertaking the conduct of which *he* is investigating under section 25(b); or
(b) if the investigating officer has taken all such steps as are reasonably practicable to give notice but has not been able to do so.

(4) In a case falling within subsection (3), the power of entry conferred by subsection (1) is to be exercised by the investigating officer on production of—
(a) evidence of his authorisation; and
(b) a document containing the information referred to in subsection (2)(b) and (c).

(5) An investigating officer entering any premises under this section may—
(a) take with him such equipment as appears to him to be necessary;
(b) require any person on the premises—
(i) to produce any document which he considers relates to any matter relevant to the investigation; and
(ii) if the document is produced, to provide an explanation of it;

(c) require any person to state, to the best of his knowledge and belief, where any such document is to be found;

(d) take copies of, or extracts from, any document which is produced;

(e) require any information which is *held in a computer* and is accessible from the premises and which the investigating officer considers relates to any matter relevant to the investigation, to be produced in a form—

　(i) in which it can be taken away, and

　(ii) in which it is visible and legible [or from which it can readily be produced in a visible and legible form].

[158]

NOTES

Commencement: 1 March 2000.

Sub-s (5): in para (e), for the words in italics there are substituted the words "stored in any electronic form", and the words in square brackets are added, by the Criminal Justice and Police Act 2001, s 70, Sch 2, Pt 2, para 21, as from a day to be appointed.

Director: as to the abolition of the office of the Director General of Fair Trading and the substitution of references to the Director and related expressions, see the note preceding s 1 at **[133]**.

28　Power to enter premises under a warrant

(1) On an application made by the *Director* to the court in accordance with rules of court, a judge may issue a warrant if he is satisfied that—

(a) there are reasonable grounds for suspecting that there are on any premises documents—

　(i) the production of which has been required under section 26 or 27; and

　(ii) which have not been produced as required;

(b) there are reasonable grounds for suspecting that—

　(i) there are on any premises documents which the *Director* has power under section 26 to require to be produced; and

　(ii) if the documents were required to be produced, they would not be produced but would be concealed, removed, tampered with or destroyed; or

(c) an investigating officer has attempted to enter premises in the exercise of his powers under section 27 but has been unable to do so and that there are reasonable grounds for suspecting that there are on the premises documents the production of which could have been required under that section.

(2) A warrant under this section shall authorise a named officer of the *Director*, and any other of *his officers whom he* has authorised in writing to accompany the named officer—

(a) to enter the premises specified in the warrant, using such force as is reasonably necessary for the purpose;

(b) to search the premises and take copies of, or extracts from, any document appearing to be of a kind in respect of which the application under subsection (1) was granted ("the relevant kind");

(c) to take possession of any documents appearing to be of the relevant kind if—

　(i) such action appears to be necessary for preserving the documents or preventing interference with them; or

　(ii) it is not reasonably practicable to take copies of the documents on the premises;

(d) to take any other steps which appear to be necessary for the purpose mentioned in paragraph (c)(i);

(e) to require any person to provide an explanation of any document appearing to be of the relevant kind or to state, to the best of his knowledge and belief, where it may be found;

(f) to require any information which is *held in a computer* and is accessible from the premises and which the named officer considers relates to any matter relevant to the investigation, to be produced in a form—
    (i) in which it can be taken away, and
    (ii) in which it is visible and legible [or from which it can readily be produced in a visible and legible form].

(3) If, in the case of a warrant under subsection (1)(b), the judge is satisfied that it is reasonable to suspect that there are also on the premises other documents relating to the investigation concerned, the warrant shall also authorise action mentioned in subsection (2) to be taken in relation to any such document.

[(3A) A warrant under this section may authorise persons specified in the warrant to accompany the named officer who is executing it.]

(4) Any person entering premises by virtue of a warrant under this section may take with him such equipment as appears to him to be necessary.

(5) On leaving any premises which he has entered by virtue of a warrant under this section, the named officer must, if the premises are unoccupied or the occupier is temporarily absent, leave them as effectively secured as he found them.

(6) A warrant under this section continues in force until the end of the period of one month beginning with the day on which it is issued.

(7) Any document of which possession is taken under subsection (2)(c) may be retained for a period of three months.

[159]

NOTES
Commencement: 1 March 2000.
Sub-s (2): for the second words in italics there are substituted the words "the OFT's officers whom the OFT", by the Enterprise Act 2002, s 278(1), Sch 25, para 38(1), (22)(b)(ii), as from a day to be appointed; in para (f), for the words in italics there are substituted the words "stored in any electronic form", and the words in square brackets are added, by the Criminal Justice and Police Act 2001, s 70, Sch 2, Pt 2, para 21, as from a day to be appointed.
Sub-s (3A): inserted by the Enterprise Act 2002, s 203(1), (2), as from a day to be appointed.
Director: as to the abolition of the office of the Director General of Fair Trading and the substitution of references to the Director and related expressions, see the note preceding s 1 at **[133]**.

29 Entry of premises under warrant: supplementary

(1) A warrant issued under section 28 must indicate—
    (a) the subject matter and purpose of the investigation;
    (b) the nature of the offences created by sections 42 to 44.

(2) The powers conferred by section 28 are to be exercised on production of a warrant issued under that section.

(3) If there is no one at the premises when the named officer proposes to execute such a warrant he must, before executing it—
    (a) take such steps as are reasonable in all the circumstances to inform the occupier of the intended entry; and
    (b) if the occupier is informed, afford him or his legal or other representative a reasonable opportunity to be present when the warrant is executed.

(4) If the named officer is unable to inform the occupier of the intended entry he must, when executing the warrant, leave a copy of it in a prominent place on the premises.

(5) In this section—
"named officer" means the officer named in the warrant; and

"occupier", in relation to any premises, means a person whom the named officer reasonably believes is the occupier of those premises.

[160]

NOTES
Commencement: 1 March 2000.

30 Privileged communications

(1)   A person shall not be required, under any provision of this Part, to produce or disclose a privileged communication.

(2)   "Privileged communication" means a communication—
  (a) between a professional legal adviser and his client, or
  (b) made in connection with, or in contemplation of, legal proceedings and for the purposes of those proceedings,

which in proceedings in the High Court would be protected from disclosure on grounds of legal professional privilege.

(3)   In the application of this section to Scotland—
  (a) references to the High Court are to be read as references to the Court of Session; and
  (b) the reference to legal professional privilege is to be read as a reference to confidentiality of communications.

[161]

NOTES
Commencement: 1 March 2000.

[30A Use of statements in prosecution

A statement made by a person in response to a requirement imposed by virtue of any of sections 26 to 28 may not be used in evidence against him on a prosecution for an offence under section 188 of the Enterprise Act 2002 unless, in the proceedings—
  (a) in giving evidence, he makes a statement inconsistent with it, and
  (b) evidence relating to it is adduced, or a question relating to it is asked, by him or on his behalf.]

[162]

NOTES
Commencement: to be appointed.
Inserted by the Enterprise Act 2002, s 198, as from a day to be appointed.

31 Decisions following an investigation

(1)   Subsection (2) applies if, as the result of an investigation conducted under section 25, the *Director* proposes to make—
  (a) a decision that the Chapter I prohibition has been infringed, or
  (b) a decision that the Chapter II prohibition has been infringed.

(2)   Before making the decision, the *Director* must—
  (a) give written notice to the person (or persons) likely to be affected by the proposed decision; and
  (b) give that person (or those persons) an opportunity to make representations.

[163]

NOTES
Commencement: 1 March 2000.
Director: as to the abolition of the office of the Director General of Fair Trading and the substitution
of references to the Director and related expressions, see the note preceding s 1 at **[133]**.

Enforcement

32 Directions in relation to agreements

(1)   If the *Director* has made a decision that an agreement infringes the Chapter I prohibition, *he* may give to such person or persons as *he* considers appropriate such directions as *he* considers appropriate to bring the infringement to an end.

(2)   Subsection (1) applies whether the *Director's* decision is made on *his* own initiative or on an application made to *him* under this Part.

(3)   A direction under this section may, in particular, include provision—
   (a) requiring the parties to the agreement to modify the agreement; or
   (b) requiring them to terminate the agreement.

(4)   A direction under this section must be given in writing.

[164]

NOTES
Commencement: 1 March 2000.
Director: as to the abolition of the office of the Director General of Fair Trading and the substitution
of references to the Director and related expressions, see the note preceding s 1 at **[133]**.

33 Directions in relation to conduct

(1)   If the *Director* has made a decision that conduct infringes the Chapter II prohibition, *he* may give to such person or persons as *he* considers appropriate such directions as *he* considers appropriate to bring the infringement to an end.

(2)   Subsection (1) applies whether the *Director's* decision is made on *his* own initiative or on an application made to *him* under this Part.

(3)   A direction under this section may, in particular, include provision—
   (a) requiring the person concerned to modify the conduct in question; or
   (b) requiring him to cease that conduct.

(4)   A direction under this section must be given in writing.

[165]

NOTES
Commencement: 1 March 2000.
Director: as to the abolition of the office of the Director General of Fair Trading and the substitution
of references to the Director and related expressions, see the note preceding s 1 at **[133]**.

34 Enforcement of directions

(1)   If a person fails, without reasonable excuse, to comply with a direction under section 32 or 33, the *Director* may apply to the court for an order—
   (a) requiring the defaulter to make good his default within a time specified in the order; or
   (b) if the direction related to anything to be done in the management or administration of an undertaking, requiring the undertaking or any of its officers to do it.

(2)   An order of the court under subsection (1) may provide for all of the costs of, or incidental to, the application for the order to be borne by—
  (a) the person in default; or
  (b) any officer of an undertaking who is responsible for the default.

(3)   In the application of subsection (2) to Scotland, the reference to "costs" is to be read as a reference to "expenses".

[166]

NOTES

Commencement: 1 March 2000.

Director: as to the abolition of the office of the Director General of Fair Trading and the substitution of references to the Director and related expressions, see the note preceding s 1 at **[133]**.

35   Interim measures

(1)   This section applies if the *Director*—
  (a) has a reasonable suspicion that the Chapter I prohibition has been infringed, or
  (b) has a reasonable suspicion that the Chapter II prohibition has been infringed,
but has not completed *his* investigation into the matter.

(2)   If the *Director* considers that it is necessary for *him* to act under this section as a matter of urgency for the purpose—
  (a) of preventing serious, irreparable damage to a particular person or category of person, or
  (b) of protecting the public interest,
he may give such directions as *he* considers appropriate for that purpose.

(3)   Before giving a direction under this section, the *Director* must—
  (a) give written notice to the person (or persons) to whom *he* proposes to give the direction; and
  (b) give that person (or each of them) an opportunity to make representations.

(4)   A notice under subsection (3) must indicate the nature of the direction which the *Director* is proposing to give and *his* reasons for wishing to give it.

(5)   A direction given under this section has effect while subsection (1) applies, but may be replaced if the circumstances permit by a direction under section 32 or (as appropriate) section 33.

(6)   In the case of a suspected infringement of the Chapter I prohibition, sections 32(3) and 34 also apply to directions given under this section.

(7)   In the case of a suspected infringement of the Chapter II prohibition, sections 33(3) and 34 also apply to directions given under this section.

[167]

NOTES

Commencement: 1 March 2000.

Director: as to the abolition of the office of the Director General of Fair Trading and the substitution of references to the Director and related expressions, see the note preceding s 1 at **[133]**.

36   Penalty for infringing Chapter I or Chapter II prohibition

(1)   On making a decision that an agreement has infringed the Chapter I prohibition, the *Director* may require an undertaking which is a party to the agreement to pay *him* a penalty in respect of the infringement.

(2) On making a decision that conduct has infringed the Chapter II prohibition, the *Director* may require the undertaking concerned to pay *him* a penalty in respect of the infringement.

(3) The *Director* may impose a penalty on an undertaking under subsection (1) or (2) only if *he* is satisfied that the infringement has been committed intentionally or negligently by the undertaking.

(4) Subsection (1) is subject to section 39 and does not apply if the *Director* is satisfied that the undertaking acted on the reasonable assumption that that section gave it immunity in respect of the agreement.

(5) Subsection (2) is subject to section 40 and does not apply if the *Director* is satisfied that the undertaking acted on the reasonable assumption that that section gave it immunity in respect of the conduct.

(6) Notice of a penalty under this section must—
    (a) be in writing; and
    (b) specify the date before which the penalty is required to be paid.

(7) The date specified must not be earlier than the end of the period within which an appeal against the notice may be brought under section 46.

(8) No penalty fixed by the *Director* under this section may exceed 10% of the turnover of the undertaking (determined in accordance with such provisions as may be specified in an order made by the Secretary of State).

(9) Any sums received by the *Director* under this section are to be paid into the Consolidated Fund.

[168]

NOTES
    Commencement: 1 March 2000.
    Sub-ss (1)–(3): for the second word in italics there is substituted the words "the OFT" by the Enterprise Act 2002, s 278(1), Sch 25, para 38(1), (28)(b), (c), as from a day to be appointed.
    Director: as to the abolition of the office of the Director General of Fair Trading and the substitution of references to the Director and related expressions, see the note preceding s 1 at **[133]**.
    Orders: the Competition Act 1998 (Determination of Turnover for Penalties) Order 2000, SI 2000/309, as amended by SI 2000/2952, SI 2002/765 at **[2085]**.

37 Recovery of penalties

(1) If the specified date in a penalty notice has passed and—
    (a) the period during which an appeal against the imposition, or amount, of the penalty may be made has expired without an appeal having been made, or
    (b) such an appeal has been made and determined,

the *Director* may recover from the undertaking, as a civil debt due to *him*, any amount payable under the penalty notice which remains outstanding.

(2) In this section—
    "penalty notice" means a notice given under section 36; and
    "specified date" means the date specified in the penalty notice.

[169]

NOTES
    Commencement: 1 March 2000.
    Sub-s (1): for the second word in italics there is substituted the words "the OFT" by the Enterprise Act 2002, s 278(1), Sch 25, para 38(1), (29), as from a day to be appointed.
    Director: as to the abolition of the office of the Director General of Fair Trading and the substitution of references to the Director and related expressions, see the note preceding s 1 at **[133]**.

38   The appropriate level of a penalty

(1)   The *Director* must prepare and publish guidance as to the appropriate amount of any penalty under this Part.

(2)   The *Director* may at any time alter the guidance.

(3)   If the guidance is altered, the *Director* must publish it as altered.

(4)   No guidance is to be published under this section without the approval of the Secretary of State.

(5)   The *Director* may, after consulting the Secretary of State, choose how *he* publishes *his* guidance.

(6)   If the *Director* is preparing or altering guidance under this section *he* must consult such persons as *he* considers appropriate.

(7)   If the proposed guidance or alteration relates to a matter in respect of which a regulator exercises concurrent jurisdiction, those consulted must include that regulator.

(8)   When setting the amount of a penalty under this Part, the *Director* must have regard to the guidance for the time being in force under this section.

(9)   If a penalty or a fine has been imposed by the Commission, or by a court or other body in another Member State, in respect of an agreement or conduct, the *Director*, an appeal tribunal or the appropriate court must take that penalty or fine into account when setting the amount of a penalty under this Part in relation to that agreement or conduct.

(10) In subsection (9) "the appropriate court" means—
    (a) in relation to England and Wales, the Court of Appeal;
    (b) in relation to Scotland, the Court of Session;
    (c) in relation to Northern Ireland, the Court of Appeal in Northern Ireland;
    (d) the House of Lords.

[170]

NOTES
    Commencement: 1 March 2000 (sub-ss (8)–(10)); 11 January 1999 (remainder).
    Director: as to the abolition of the office of the Director General of Fair Trading and the substitution of references to the Director and related expressions, see the note preceding s 1 at **[133]**.

39   Limited immunity for small agreements

(1)   In this section "small agreement" means an agreement—
    (a) which falls within a category prescribed for the purposes of this section; but
    (b) is not a price fixing agreement.

(2)   The criteria by reference to which a category of agreement is prescribed may, in particular, include—
    (a) the combined turnover of the parties to the agreement (determined in accordance with prescribed provisions);
    (b) the share of the market affected by the agreement (determined in that way).

(3)   A party to a small agreement is immune from the effect of section 36(1); but the *Director* may withdraw that immunity under subsection (4).

(4)   If the *Director* has investigated a small agreement, *he* may make a decision withdrawing the immunity given by subsection (3) if, as a result of *his* investigation, *he* considers that the agreement is likely to infringe the Chapter I prohibition.

(5)   The *Director* must give each of the parties in respect of which immunity is withdrawn written notice of *his* decision to withdraw the immunity.

(6)   A decision under subsection (4) takes effect on such date ("the withdrawal date") as may be specified in the decision.

(7)   The withdrawal date must be a date after the date on which the decision is made.

(8)   In determining the withdrawal date, the *Director* must have regard to the amount of time which the parties are likely to require in order to secure that there is no further infringement of the Chapter I prohibition with respect to the agreement.

(9)   In subsection (1) "price fixing agreement" means an agreement which has as its object or effect, or one of its objects or effects, restricting the freedom of a party to the agreement to determine the price to be charged (otherwise than as between that party and another party to the agreement) for the product, service or other matter to which the agreement relates.

[171]

NOTES

Commencement: 1 March 2000.

Director: as to the abolition of the office of the Director General of Fair Trading and the substitution of references to the Director and related expressions, see the note preceding s 1 at **[133]**.

Regulations: the Competition Act 1998 (Small Agreements and Conduct of Minor Significance) Regulations 2000, SI 2000/262, as amended by SI 2000/2952, SI 2002/765 at **[2079]**.

40   Limited immunity in relation to the Chapter II prohibition

(1)   In this section "conduct of minor significance" means conduct which falls within a category prescribed for the purposes of this section.

(2)   The criteria by reference to which a category is prescribed may, in particular, include—
   (a) the turnover of the person whose conduct it is (determined in accordance with prescribed provisions);
   (b) the share of the market affected by the conduct (determined in that way).

(3)   A person is immune from the effect of section 36(2) if his conduct is conduct of minor significance; but the *Director* may withdraw that immunity under subsection (4).

(4)   If the *Director* has investigated conduct of minor significance, *he* may make a decision withdrawing the immunity given by subsection (3) if, as a result of *his* investigation, *he* considers that the conduct is likely to infringe the Chapter II prohibition.

(5)   The *Director* must give the person, or persons, whose immunity has been withdrawn written notice of *his* decision to withdraw the immunity.

(6)   A decision under subsection (4) takes effect on such date ("the withdrawal date") as may be specified in the decision.

(7)   The withdrawal date must be a date after the date on which the decision is made.

(8)   In determining the withdrawal date, the *Director* must have regard to the amount of time which the person or persons affected are likely to require in order to secure that there is no further infringement of the Chapter II prohibition.

[172]

NOTES

Commencement: 1 March 2000.

Director: as to the abolition of the office of the Director General of Fair Trading and the substitution of references to the Director and related expressions, see the note preceding s 1 at **[133]**.

Regulations: the Competition Act 1998 (Small Agreements and Conduct of Minor Significance) Regulations 2000, SI 2000/262, as amended by SI 2000/2952, SI 2002/765 at **[2079]**.

41 Agreements notified to the Commission

(1)   This section applies if a party to an agreement which may infringe the Chapter I prohibition has notified the agreement to the Commission for a decision as to whether an exemption will be granted under Article 85 with respect to the agreement.

(2)   A penalty may not be required to be paid under this Part in respect of any infringement of the Chapter I prohibition after notification but before the Commission determines the matter.

(3)   If the Commission withdraws the benefit of provisional immunity from penalties with respect to the agreement, subsection (2) ceases to apply as from the date on which that benefit is withdrawn.

(4)   The fact that an agreement has been notified to the Commission does not prevent the *Director* from investigating it under this Part.

(5)   In this section "provisional immunity from penalties" has such meaning as may be prescribed.

[173]

NOTES

Commencement: 1 March 2000.

Director: as to the abolition of the office of the Director General of Fair Trading and the substitution of references to the Director and related expressions, see the note preceding s 1 at **[133]**.

Regulations: the Competition Act 1998 (Provisional Immunity from Penalties) Regulations 1999, SI 1999/2281 at **[2072]**.

Offences

42 Offences

(1)   A person is guilty of an offence if he fails to comply with a requirement imposed on him under section 26, 27 or 28.

(2)   If a person is charged with an offence under subsection (1) in respect of a requirement to produce a document, it is a defence for him to prove—
   (a) that the document was not in his possession or under his control; and
   (b) that it was not reasonably practicable for him to comply with the requirement.

(3)   If a person is charged with an offence under subsection (1) in respect of a requirement—
   (a) to provide information,
   (b) to provide an explanation of a document, or
   (c) to state where a document is to be found,

it is a defence for him to prove that he had a reasonable excuse for failing to comply with the requirement.

(4)   Failure to comply with a requirement imposed under section 26 or 27 is not an offence if the person imposing the requirement has failed to act in accordance with that section.

(5)   A person is guilty of an offence if he intentionally obstructs an officer acting in the exercise of his powers under section 27.

(6)   A person guilty of an offence under subsection (1) or (5) is liable—
   (a) on summary conviction, to a fine not exceeding the statutory maximum;
   (b) on conviction on indictment, to a fine.

(7)   A person who intentionally obstructs an officer in the exercise of his powers under a warrant issued under section 28 is guilty of an offence and liable—

    (a) on summary conviction, to a fine not exceeding the statutory maximum;

    (b) on conviction on indictment, to imprisonment for a term not exceeding two years or to a fine or to both.

[174]

NOTES

    Commencement: 1 March 2000.

43 Destroying or falsifying documents

(1)   A person is guilty of an offence if, having been required to produce a document under section 26, 27 or 28—

    (a) he intentionally or recklessly destroys or otherwise disposes of it, falsifies it or conceals it, or

    (b) he causes or permits its destruction, disposal, falsification or concealment.

(2)   A person guilty of an offence under subsection (1) is liable—

    (a) on summary conviction, to a fine not exceeding the statutory maximum;

    (b) on conviction on indictment, to imprisonment for a term not exceeding two years or to a fine or to both.

[175]

NOTES

    Commencement: 1 March 2000.

44 False or misleading information

(1)   If information is provided by a person to the *Director* in connection with any function of the *Director* under this Part, that person is guilty of an offence if—

    (a) the information is false or misleading in a material particular, and

    (b) he knows that it is or is reckless as to whether it is.

(2)   A person who—

    (a) provides any information to another person, knowing the information to be false or misleading in a material particular, or

    (b) recklessly provides any information to another person which is false or misleading in a material particular,

knowing that the information is to be used for the purpose of providing information to the *Director* in connection with any of *his* functions under this Part, is guilty of an offence.

(3)   A person guilty of an offence under this section is liable—

    (a) on summary conviction, to a fine not exceeding the statutory maximum;

    (b) on conviction on indictment, to imprisonment for a term not exceeding two years or to a fine or to both.

[176]

NOTES

    Commencement: 1 March 2000.

    Director: as to the abolition of the office of the Director General of Fair Trading and the substitution of references to the Director and related expressions, see the note preceding s 1 at **[133]**.

CHAPTER IV
THE COMPETITION COMMISSION AND APPEALS

The Commission

45   The Competition Commission

(1)   There is to be a body corporate known as the Competition Commission.

(2)   The Commission is to have such functions as are conferred on it by or as a result of this Act.

(3)   The Monopolies and Mergers Commission is dissolved and its functions are transferred to the Competition Commission.

(4)   In any enactment, instrument or other document, any reference to the Monopolies and Mergers Commission which has continuing effect is to be read as a reference to the Competition Commission.

(5)   The Secretary of State may by order make such consequential, supplemental and incidental provision as he considers appropriate in connection with—
    (a)   the dissolution of the Monopolies and Mergers Commission; and
    (b)   the transfer of functions effected by subsection (3).

(6)   An order made under subsection (5) may, in particular, include provision—
    (a)   for the transfer of property, rights, obligations and liabilities and the continuation of proceedings, investigations and other matters; or
    (b)   amending any enactment which makes provision with respect to the Monopolies and Mergers Commission or any of its functions.

(7)   *Schedule 7 makes* further provision about the Competition Commission.

[(8)   The Secretary of State may by order make such modifications in Part 2 of Schedule 7 and in Schedule 7A (performance of the Competition Commission's general functions) as he considers appropriate for improving the performance by the Competition Commission of its functions.]

[177]

NOTES

Commencement: 1 April 1999.

Sub-s (7): for the words in italics there are substituted the words "Schedules 7 and 7A make" by the Enterprise Act 2002, s 187(1), as from a day to be appointed.

Sub-s (8): added by the Enterprise Act 2002, s 278(1), Sch 25, para 38(1), (35), as from a day to be appointed.

Orders: the Competition Act 1998 (Competition Commission) Transitional, Consequential and Supplemental Provisions Order 1999, SI 1999/506 at **[2028]**; the Competition Act 1998 (Transitional, Consequential and Supplemental Provisions) Order 2000, SI 2000/311, as amended by SI 2000/2031; the Competition Act 1998 (Consequential and Supplemental Provisions) Order 2000, SI 2000/2031.

Appeals

46   Appealable decisions

(1)   Any party to an agreement in respect of which the *Director* has made a decision may appeal to *the Competition Commission* against, or with respect to, the decision.

(2)   Any person in respect of whose conduct the *Director* has made a decision may appeal to *the Competition Commission* against, or with respect to, the decision.

(3)   In this section "decision" means a decision of the *Director*—
    (a)   as to whether the Chapter I prohibition has been infringed,
    (b)   as to whether the Chapter II prohibition has been infringed,

(c) as to whether to grant an individual exemption,
(d) in respect of an individual exemption—
  (i) as to whether to impose any condition or obligation under section 4(3)(a) or 5(1)(c),
  (ii) where such a condition or obligation has been imposed, as to the condition or obligation,
  (iii) as to the period fixed under section 4(3)(b), or
  (iv) as to the date fixed under section 4(5),
(e) as to—
  (i) whether to extend the period for which an individual exemption has effect, or
  (ii) the period of any such extension,
(f) cancelling an exemption,
(g) as to the imposition of any penalty under section 36 or as to the amount of any such penalty,
(h) *withdrawing or varying any of the decisions in paragraphs (a) to (f) following an application under section 47(1),*

and includes a direction given under section 32, 33 or 35 and such other decision [under this Part] as may be prescribed.

(4) Except in the case of an appeal against the imposition, or the amount, of a penalty, the making of an appeal under this section does not suspend the effect of the decision to which the appeal relates.

(5) Part I of Schedule 8 makes further provision about appeals.

[178]

NOTES
Commencement: 1 March 2000.
Sub-ss (1), (2): for the second words in italics there are substituted the words "the Tribunal" by the Enterprise Act 2002, s 21, Sch 5, paras 1, 2(a), as from a day to be appointed.
Sub-s (3): para (h) repealed, and words in square brackets inserted, by the Enterprise Act 2002, ss 21, 278(2), Sch 5, paras 1, 2(b), (c), Sch 26, as from a day to be appointed.
Director: as to the abolition of the office of the Director General of Fair Trading and the substitution of references to the Director and related expressions, see the note preceding s 1 at **[133]**.
Regulations: the Competition Act 1998 (Notification of Excluded Agreements and Appealable Decisions) Regulations 2000, SI 2000/263 at **[2015]**.

47 Third party appeals

(1) A person who does not fall within section 46(1) or (2) may apply to the Director asking him to withdraw or vary a decision ("the relevant decision") falling within paragraphs (a) to (f) of section 46(3) or such other decision as may be prescribed.

(2) The application must—
  (a) be made in writing, within such period as the Director may specify in rules under section 51; and
  (b) give the applicant's reasons for considering that the relevant decision should be withdrawn or (as the case may be) varied.

(3) If the Director decides—
  (a) that the applicant does not have a sufficient interest in the relevant decision,
  (b) that, in the case of an applicant claiming to represent persons who have such an interest, the applicant does not represent such persons, or
  (c) that the persons represented by the applicant do not have such an interest,
he must notify the applicant of his decision.

(4) If the Director, having considered the application, decides that it does not show sufficient reason why he should withdraw or vary the relevant decision, he must notify the applicant of his decision.

(5) Otherwise, the Director must deal with the application in accordance with such procedure as may be specified in rules under section 51.

(6) The applicant may appeal to the Competition Commission against a decision of the Director notified under subsection (3) or (4).

(7) The making of an application does not suspend the effect of the relevant decision.

[179]

NOTES

Commencement: 1 March 2000.

Substituted by the Enterprise Act 2002, s 17, as from a day to be appointed, as follows—

"47 Third party appeals

(1) A person who does not fall within section 46(1) or (2) may appeal to the Tribunal with respect to a decision falling within paragraphs (a) to (f) of section 46(3) or such other decision of the OFT under this Part as may be prescribed.

(2) A person may make an appeal under subsection (1) only if the Tribunal considers that he has a sufficient interest in the decision with respect to which the appeal is made, or that he represents persons who have such an interest.

(3) The making of an appeal under this section does not suspend the effect of the decision to which the appeal relates.".

The Director: the Enterprise Act 2002, s 2(1), at **[255]**, provides that, as from the coming into force of that section in accordance with s 279 at **[463]**, the functions of the Director General of Fair Trading, his property, rights and liabilities are transferred to the Office of Fair Trading. Accordingly, (by virtue of s 2(2), (3) of the 2002 Act) the office of the Director is abolished, and any reference to the Director in any enactment, instrument or other document passed or made before the commencement of s 2(1) shall have effect as if it were a reference to the Office of Fair Trading. For transitional provisions in connection with this transfer, see s 276(1) of, and Sch 24, para 6 to, the 2002 Act.

Regulations: the Competition Act 1998 (Notification of Excluded Agreements and Appealable Decisions) Regulations 2000, SI 2000/263 at **[2015]**.

[47A Monetary claims before Tribunal

(1) This section applies to—
    (a) any claim for damages, or
    (b) any other claim for a sum of money,

which a person who has suffered loss or damage as a result of the infringement of a relevant prohibition may make in civil proceedings brought in any part of the United Kingdom.

(2) In this section "relevant prohibition" means any of the following—
    (a) the Chapter I prohibition;
    (b) the Chapter II prohibition;
    (c) the prohibition in Article 81(1) of the Treaty;
    (d) the prohibition in Article 82 of the Treaty;
    (e) the prohibition in Article 65(1) of the Treaty establishing the European Coal and Steel Community;
    (f) the prohibition in Article 66(7) of that Treaty.

(3) For the purpose of identifying claims which may be made in civil proceedings, any limitation rules that would apply in such proceedings are to be disregarded.

(4) A claim to which this section applies may (subject to the provisions of this Act and Tribunal rules) be made in proceedings brought before the Tribunal.

(5)   But no claim may be made in such proceedings—

    (a) until a decision mentioned in subsection (6) has established that the relevant prohibition in question has been infringed; and

    (b) otherwise than with the permission of the Tribunal, during any period specified in subsection (7) or (8) which relates to that decision.

(6)   The decisions which may be relied on for the purposes of proceedings under this section are—

    (a) a decision of the OFT that the Chapter I prohibition or the Chapter II prohibition has been infringed;

    (b) a decision of the OFT that the prohibition in Article 81(1) or Article 82 of the Treaty has been infringed;

    (c) a decision of the Tribunal (on an appeal from a decision of the OFT) that the Chapter I prohibition, the Chapter II prohibition or the prohibition in Article 81(1) or Article 82 of the Treaty has been infringed;

    (d) a decision of the European Commission that the prohibition in Article 81(1) or Article 82 of the Treaty has been infringed; or

    (e) a decision of the European Commission that the prohibition in Article 65(1) of the Treaty establishing the European Coal and Steel Community has been infringed, or a finding made by the European Commission under Article 66(7) of that Treaty.

(7)   The periods during which proceedings in respect of a claim made in reliance on a decision mentioned in subsection (6)(a), (b) or (c) may not be brought without permission are—

    (a) in the case of a decision of the OFT, the period during which an appeal may be made to the Tribunal under section 46, section 47 or the EC Competition Law (Articles 84 and 85) Enforcement Regulations 2001 (SI 2001/2916);

    (b) in the case of a decision of the OFT which is the subject of an appeal mentioned in paragraph (a), the period following the decision of the Tribunal on the appeal during which a further appeal may be made under section 49 or under those Regulations;

    (c) in the case of a decision of the Tribunal mentioned in subsection (6)(c), the period during which a further appeal may be made under section 49 or under those Regulations;

    (d) in the case of any decision which is the subject of a further appeal, the period during which an appeal may be made to the House of Lords from a decision on the further appeal;

and, where any appeal mentioned in paragraph (a), (b), (c) or (d) is made, the period specified in that paragraph includes the period before the appeal is determined.

(8)   The periods during which proceedings in respect of a claim made in reliance on a decision or finding of the European Commission may not be brought without permission are—

    (a) the period during which proceedings against the decision or finding may be instituted in the European Court; and

    (b) if any such proceedings are instituted, the period before those proceedings are determined.

(9)   In determining a claim to which this section applies the Tribunal is bound by any decision mentioned in subsection (6) which establishes that the prohibition in question has been infringed.

(10) The right to make a claim to which this section applies in proceedings before the Tribunal does not affect the right to bring any other proceedings in respect of the claim.]

NOTES

Commencement: to be appointed.

Inserted by the Enterprise Act 2002, s 18(1), as from a day to be appointed; by virtue of s 18(2) of the 2002 Act, this section applies to claims arising before the commencement of s 18 of the 2002 Act as it applies to claims arising after that time.

[47B Claims brought on behalf of consumers

(1) A specified body may (subject to the provisions of this Act and Tribunal rules) bring proceedings before the Tribunal which comprise consumer claims made or continued on behalf of at least two individuals.

(2) In this section "consumer claim" means a claim to which section 47A applies which an individual has in respect of an infringement affecting (directly or indirectly) goods or services to which subsection (7) applies.

(3) A consumer claim may be included in proceedings under this section if it is—

    (a) a claim made in the proceedings on behalf of the individual concerned by the specified body; or

    (b) a claim made by the individual concerned under section 47A which is continued in the proceedings on his behalf by the specified body;

and such a claim may only be made or continued in the proceedings with the consent of the individual concerned.

(4) The consumer claims included in proceedings under this section must all relate to the same infringement.

(5) The provisions of section 47A(5) to (10) apply to a consumer claim included in proceedings under this section as they apply to a claim made in proceedings under that section.

(6) Any damages or other sum (not being costs or expenses) awarded in respect of a consumer claim included in proceedings under this section must be awarded to the individual concerned; but the Tribunal may, with the consent of the specified body and the individual, order that the sum awarded must be paid to the specified body (acting on behalf of the individual).

(7) This subsection applies to goods or services which—

    (a) the individual received, or sought to receive, otherwise than in the course of a business carried on by him (notwithstanding that he received or sought to receive them with a view to carrying on a business); and

    (b) were, or would have been, supplied to the individual (in the case of goods whether by way of sale or otherwise) in the course of a business carried on by the person who supplied or would have supplied them.

(8) A business includes—

    (a) a professional practice;

    (b) any other undertaking carried on for gain or reward;

    (c) any undertaking in the course of which goods or services are supplied otherwise than free of charge.

(9) "Specified" means specified in an order made by the Secretary of State, in accordance with criteria to be published by the Secretary of State for the purposes of this section.

(10) An application by a body to be specified in an order under this section is to be made in a form approved by the Secretary of State for the purpose.]

PART I
STATUTES

NOTES

Commencement: to be appointed.

Inserted by the Enterprise Act 2002, s 19, as from a day to be appointed.

48 Appeal tribunals

(1) Any appeal made to the Competition Commission under section 46 or 47 is to be determined by an appeal tribunal.

(2) The Secretary of State may, after consulting the President of the Competition Commission Appeal Tribunals and such other persons as he considers appropriate, make rules with respect to appeals and appeal tribunals.

(3) The rules may confer functions on the President.

(4) Part II of Schedule 8 makes further provision about rules made under this section but is not to be taken as restricting the Secretary of State's powers under this section.

[182]

NOTES

Commencement: 1 April 1999.

Repealed by the Enterprise Act 2002, ss 21, 278(2), Sch 5, paras 1, 3, Sch 26, as from a day to be appointed; for a saving in relation to rules made under this section, see s 276(1) of, and Sch 24, para 12 to, the 2002 Act at **[477]**.

Rules: the Competition Commission Appeal Tribunal Rules 2000, SI 2000/261 at **[2035]**.

49 Appeals on point of law etc

(1) An appeal lies—
    (a) on a point of law arising from a decision of an appeal tribunal, or
    (b) from any decision of an appeal tribunal as to the amount of a penalty.

(2) An appeal under this section may be made only—
    (a) to the appropriate court;
    (b) with leave; and
    (c) at the instance of a party or at the instance of a person who has a sufficient interest in the matter.

(3) Rules under section 48 may make provision for regulating or prescribing any matters incidental to or consequential upon an appeal under this section.

(4) In subsection (2)—
    "the appropriate court" means—
        (a) in relation to proceedings before a tribunal in England and Wales, the Court of Appeal;
        (b) in relation to proceedings before a tribunal in Scotland, the Court of Session;
        (c) in relation to proceedings before a tribunal in Northern Ireland, the Court of Appeal in Northern Ireland;
    "leave" means leave of the tribunal in question or of the appropriate court; and
    "party", in relation to a decision, means a person who was a party to the proceedings in which the decision was made.

[183]

NOTES

Commencement: 1 March 2000 (sub-ss (1), (2), (4)); 1 April 1999 (remainder).

Substituted by the Enterprise Act 2002, s 21, Sch 5, paras 1, 4, as from a day to be appointed, as follows—

"49 Further appeals

(1) An appeal lies to the appropriate court—

(a) from a decision of the Tribunal as to the amount of a penalty under section 36;

(b) from a decision of the Tribunal as to the award of damages or other sum in respect of a claim made in proceedings under section 47A or included in proceedings under section 47B (other than a decision on costs or expenses) or as to the amount of any such damages or other sum; and

(c) on a point of law arising from any other decision of the Tribunal on an appeal under section 46 or 47.

(2) An appeal under this section—

(a) may be brought by a party to the proceedings before the Tribunal or by a person who has a sufficient interest in the matter; and

(b) requires the permission of the Tribunal or the appropriate court.

(3) In this section "the appropriate court" means the Court of Appeal or, in the case of an appeal from Tribunal proceedings in Scotland, the Court of Session.".

Rules: the Competition Commission Appeal Tribunal Rules 2000, SI 2000/261 at **[2035]**.

CHAPTER V
MISCELLANEOUS

Vertical agreements and land agreements

50 Vertical agreements and land agreements

(1) The Secretary of State may by order provide for any provision of this Part to apply in relation to—

(a) vertical agreements, or

(b) land agreements,

with such modifications as may be prescribed.

(2) An order may, in particular, provide for exclusions or exemptions, or otherwise provide for prescribed provisions not to apply, in relation to—

(a) vertical agreements, or land agreements, in general; or

(b) vertical agreements, or land agreements, of any prescribed description.

(3) An order may empower the *Director* to give directions to the effect that in prescribed circumstances an exclusion, exemption or modification is not to apply (or is to apply in a particular way) in relation to an individual agreement.

(4) Subsections (2) and (3) are not to be read as limiting the powers conferred by section 71.

(5) In this section—

"land agreement" and "vertical agreement" have such meaning as may be prescribed; and

"prescribed" means prescribed by an order.

[184]

NOTES

Commencement: 11 January 1999.

Director: as to the abolition of the office of the Director General of Fair Trading and the substitution of references to the Director and related expressions, see the note preceding s 1 at **[133]**.

Orders: the Competition Act 1998 (Land and Vertical Agreements Exclusion) Order 2000, SI 2000/310 at **[2130]**.

Director's rules, guidance and fees

51 Rules

(1) The *Director* may make such rules about procedural and other matters in connection with the carrying into effect of the provisions of this Part as *he* considers appropriate.

(2) Schedule 9 makes further provision about rules made under this section but is not to be taken as restricting the *Director's* powers under this section.

(3) If the *Director* is preparing rules under this section *he* must consult such persons as *he* considers appropriate.

(4) If the proposed rules relate to a matter in respect of which a regulator exercises concurrent jurisdiction, those consulted must include that regulator.

(5) No rule made by the *Director* is to come into operation until it has been approved by an order made by the Secretary of State.

(6) The Secretary of State may approve any rule made by the *Director*—
    (a) in the form in which it is submitted; or
    (b) subject to such modifications as he considers appropriate.

(7) If the Secretary of State proposes to approve a rule subject to modifications he must inform the *Director* of the proposed modifications and take into account any comments made by the *Director*.

(8) Subsections (5) to (7) apply also to any alteration of the rules made by the *Director*.

(9) The Secretary of State may, after consulting the *Director*, by order vary or revoke any rules made under this section.

(10) If the Secretary of State considers that rules should be made under this section with respect to a particular matter he may direct the *Director* to exercise *his* powers under this section and make rules about that matter.

[185]

NOTES
  Commencement: 26 November 1998.
  Director: as to the abolition of the office of the Director General of Fair Trading and the substitution of references to the Director and related expressions, see the note preceding s 1 at **[133]**.
  Orders: the Competition Act 1998 (Director's rules) Order 2000, SI 2000/293 at **[2025]**.

---

52 Advice and information

(1) As soon as is reasonably practicable after the passing of this Act, the Director must prepare and publish general advice and information about—
    (a) the application of the Chapter I prohibition and the Chapter II prohibition, and
    (b) the enforcement of those prohibitions.

(2) The *Director* may at any time publish revised, or new, advice or information.

(3) Advice and information published under this section must be prepared with a view to—
    (a) explaining provisions of this Part to persons who are likely to be affected by them; and
    (b) indicating how the *Director* expects such provisions to operate.

(4)   Advice (or information) published by virtue of subsection (3)(b) may include advice (or information) about the factors which the *Director* may take into account in considering whether, and if so how, to exercise a power conferred on *him* by Chapter I, II or III.

(5)   Any advice or information published by the *Director* under this section is to be published in such form and in such manner as *he* considers appropriate.

(6)   If the *Director* is preparing any advice or information under this section *he* must consult such persons as *he* considers appropriate.

(7)   If the proposed advice or information relates to a matter in respect of which a regulator exercises concurrent jurisdiction, those consulted must include that regulator.

(8)   In preparing any advice or information under this section about a matter in respect of which he may exercise functions under this Part, a regulator must consult—

   (a) the *Director*;

   (b) the other regulators; and

   (c) such other persons as he considers appropriate.

[186]

NOTES

Commencement: 26 November 1998.

Director: as to the abolition of the office of the Director General of Fair Trading and the substitution of references to the Director and related expressions, see the note preceding s 1 at **[133]**.

53   Fees

(1)   The *Director* may charge fees, of specified amounts, in connection with the exercise by *him* of specified functions under this Part.

(2)   Rules may, in particular, provide—

   (a) for the amount of any fee to be calculated by reference to matters which may include—

      (i)   the turnover of any party to an agreement (determined in such manner as may be specified);

      (ii) the turnover of a person whose conduct the *Director* is to consider (determined in that way);

   (b) for different amounts to be specified in connection with different functions;

   (c) for the repayment by the *Director* of the whole or part of a fee in specified circumstances;

   (d) that an application or notice is not to be regarded as duly made or given unless the appropriate fee is paid.

(3)   In this section—

   (a) "rules" means rules made by the *Director* under section 51; and

   (b) "specified" means specified in rules.

[187]

NOTES

Commencement: 11 January 1999.

Director: as to the abolition of the office of the Director General of Fair Trading and the substitution of references to the Director and related expressions, see the note preceding s 1 at **[133]**.

Regulators

54   Regulators

(1)   In this Part "regulator" means *any person mentioned in paragraphs (a) to (g) of paragraph 1 of Schedule 10 [and the Civil Aviation Authority]*.

(2)   Parts II and III of Schedule 10 provide for functions of the *Director* under this Part to be exercisable concurrently by regulators.

(3)   Parts IV and V of Schedule 10 make minor and consequential amendments in connection with the regulators' competition functions.

(4)   The Secretary of State may make regulations for the purpose of co-ordinating the performance of functions under this Part ("Part I functions") which are exercisable concurrently by two or more competent persons as a result of any provision made by Part II or III of Schedule 10 [or by Chapter V of Part I of the Transport Act 2000].

(5)   The regulations may, in particular, make provision—

    (a) as to the procedure to be followed by competent persons when determining who is to exercise Part I functions in a particular case;

    (b) as to the steps which must be taken before a competent person exercises, in a particular case, such Part I functions as may be prescribed;

    (c) as to the procedure for determining, in a particular case, questions arising as to which competent person is to exercise Part I functions in respect of the case;

    (d) for Part I functions in a particular case to be exercised jointly—

        (i) by the *Director* and one or more regulators, or

        (ii) by two or more regulators,

    and as to the procedure to be followed in such cases;

    (e) as to the circumstances in which the exercise by a competent person of such Part I functions as may be prescribed is to preclude the exercise of such functions by another such person;

    (f) for cases in respect of which Part I functions are being, or have been, exercised by a competent person to be transferred to another such person;

    (g) for the person ("A") exercising Part I functions in a particular case—

        (i) to appoint another competent person ("B") to exercise Part I functions on A's behalf in relation to the case; or

        (ii) to appoint officers of B (with B's consent) to act as officers of A in relation to the case;

    (h) for notification as to who is exercising Part I functions in respect of a particular case.

(6)   Provision made by virtue of subsection (5)(c) may provide for questions to be referred to and determined by the Secretary of State or by such other person as may be prescribed.

(7)   "Competent person" means the *Director* or any of the regulators.

[188]

NOTES

    Commencement: 1 March 2000 (sub-s (1), sub-ss (2), (3), certain purposes); 1 April 1999 (sub-s (3), certain purposes); 11 January 1999 (sub-s (3), remaining purposes, sub-ss (4)–(7)); 26 November 1998 (sub-s (2), remaining purposes).

    Sub-s (1): words in square brackets added by the Transport Act 2000, s 97, Sch 8, Pt IV, para 14; for the words in italics there are substituted the following words, by the Enterprise Act 2002, s 278(1), Sch 25, para 38(41)(a), as from a day to be appointed—

    "—

        (a) the Director General of Telecommunications;

        (b) the Gas and Electricity Markets Authority;

        (c) the Director General of Electricity Supply for Northern Ireland;

        (d) the Director General of Water Services;

        (e) the Rail Regulator;

        (f) the Director General of Gas for Northern Ireland;

        (g) the Civil Aviation Authority.".

Sub-s (4): words in square brackets added by the Transport Act 2000, s 97, Sch 8, Pt IV, para 14.
Director: as to the abolition of the office of the Director General of Fair Trading and the substitution of references to the Director and related expressions, see the note preceding s 1 at **[133]**.
Regulations: the Competition Act 1998 (Concurrency) Regulations 2000, SI 2000/260 at **[2005]**.

Confidentiality and immunity from defamation

55 General restrictions on disclosure of information

(1) No information which—
  (a) has been obtained under or as a result of any provision of this Part, and
  (b) relates to the affairs of any individual or to any particular business of an undertaking,
is to be disclosed during the lifetime of that individual or while that business continues to be carried on, unless the condition mentioned in subsection (2) is satisfied.

(2) The condition is that consent to the disclosure has been obtained from—
  (a) the person from whom the information was initially obtained under or as a result of any provision of this Part (if the identity of that person is known); and
  (b) if different—
    (i) the individual to whose affairs the information relates, or
    (ii) the person for the time being carrying on the business to which the information relates.

(3) Subsection (1) does not apply to a disclosure of information—
  (a) made for the purpose of—
    (i) facilitating the performance of any relevant functions of a designated person;
    (ii) facilitating the performance of any functions of the Commission in respect of Community law about competition;
    (iii) facilitating the performance by the Comptroller and Auditor General of any of his functions;
    (iv) criminal proceedings in any part of the United Kingdom;
  (b) made with a view to the institution of, or otherwise for the purposes of, civil proceedings brought under or in connection with this Part;
  (c) made in connection with the investigation of any criminal offence triable in the United Kingdom or in any part of the United Kingdom; or
  (d) which is required to meet a Community obligation.

(4) In subsection (3) "relevant functions" and "designated person" have the meaning given in Schedule 11.

(5) Subsection (1) also does not apply to a disclosure of information made for the purpose of facilitating the performance of specified functions of any specified person.

(6) In subsection (5) "specified" means specified in an order made by the Secretary of State.

(7) If information is disclosed to the public in circumstances in which the disclosure does not contravene subsection (1), that subsection does not prevent its further disclosure by any person.

(8) A person who contravenes this section is guilty of an offence and liable—
  (a) on summary conviction, to a fine not exceeding the statutory maximum; or
  (b) on conviction on indictment, to imprisonment for a term not exceeding two years or to a fine or to both.

NOTES
Commencement: 1 March 2000 (sub-ss (1)–(5), (7), (8)); 11 January 1999 (remainder).
Repealed by the Enterprise Act 2002, ss 247(j), 278(2), Sch 26, as from a day to be appointed.

56 Director and Secretary of State to have regard to certain matters in relation to the disclosure of information

(1) This section applies if the Secretary of State or the Director is considering whether to disclose any information acquired by him under, or as a result of, any provision of this Part.

(2) He must have regard to the need for excluding, so far as is practicable, information the disclosure of which would in his opinion be contrary to the public interest.

(3) He must also have regard to—
   (a) the need for excluding, so far as is practicable—
      (i) commercial information the disclosure of which would, or might, in his opinion, significantly harm the legitimate business interests of the undertaking to which it relates, or
      (ii) information relating to the private affairs of an individual the disclosure of which would, or might, in his opinion, significantly harm his interests; and
   (b) the extent to which the disclosure is necessary for the purposes for which the Secretary of State or the Director is proposing to make the disclosure.

[190]

NOTES
Commencement: 1 March 2000.
Repealed by the Enterprise Act 2002, ss 247(j), 278(2), Sch 26, as from a day to be appointed.
The Director: see the note to s 47 at **[179]**.

57 Defamation

For the purposes of the law relating to defamation, absolute privilege attaches to any advice, guidance, notice or direction given, or decision made, by the *Director* in the exercise of any of *his* functions under this Part.

[191]

NOTES
Commencement: 11 January 1999.
Director: as to the abolition of the office of the Director General of Fair Trading and the substitution of references to the Director and related expressions, see the note preceding s 1 at **[133]**.

Findings of fact by Director

58 Findings of fact by Director

(1) Unless the court directs otherwise or the *Director* has decided to take further action in accordance with section 16(2) or 24(2), *a Director's* finding which is relevant to an issue arising in Part I proceedings is binding on the parties if—
   (a) the time for bringing an appeal [under section 46 or 47] in respect of the finding has expired and the relevant party has not brought such an appeal; or
   (b) the decision of *an appeal tribunal* on such an appeal has confirmed the finding.

(2)   In this section—

"*a Director's* finding" means a finding of fact made by the *Director* in the course of—

    (a) determining an application for a decision under section 14 or 22, or

    (b) conducting an investigation under section 25;

"Part I proceedings" means proceedings—

    (a) in respect of an alleged infringement of the Chapter I prohibition or of the Chapter II prohibition; but

    (b) which are brought otherwise than by the *Director*;

"relevant party" means—

    (a) in relation to the Chapter I prohibition, a party to the agreement which is alleged to have infringed the prohibition; and

    (b) in relation to the Chapter II prohibition, the undertaking whose conduct is alleged to have infringed the prohibition.

(3)   Rules of court may make provision in respect of assistance to be given by the *Director* to the court in Part I proceedings.

[192]

NOTES

Commencement: 1 March 2000.

Sub-s (1): for the second words in italics there are substituted the words "an OFT's", the words in square brackets in para (a) are inserted, and for the words in italics in para (b) there are substituted the words "the Tribunal", by the Enterprise Act 2002, ss 21, 2783(1), Sch 5, paras 1, 5, Sch 25, para 38(1), (43)(b), as from a day to be appointed.

Sub-s (2): for the first words in italics there are substituted the words "an OFT's" by the Enterprise Act 2002, s 278(1), Sch 25, para 38(1), (43)(b), as from a day to be appointed.

Director: as to the abolition of the office of the Director General of Fair Trading and the substitution of references to the Director and related expressions, see the note preceding s 1 at **[133]**.

[Findings of infringements

58A Findings of infringements

(1)   This section applies to proceedings before the court in which damages or any other sum of money is claimed in respect of an infringement of—

    (a) the Chapter I prohibition;

    (b) the Chapter II prohibition;

    (c) the prohibition in Article 81(1) of the Treaty;

    (d) the prohibition in Article 82 of the Treaty.

(2)   In such proceedings, the court is bound by a decision mentioned in subsection (3) once any period specified in subsection (4) which relates to the decision has elapsed.

(3)   The decisions are—

    (a) a decision of the OFT that the Chapter I prohibition or the Chapter II prohibition has been infringed;

    (b) a decision of the OFT that the prohibition in Article 81(1) or Article 82 of the Treaty has been infringed;

    (c) a decision of the Tribunal (on an appeal from a decision of the OFT) that the Chapter I prohibition or the Chapter II prohibition has been infringed, or that the prohibition in Article 81(1) or Article 82 of the Treaty has been infringed.

(4)   The periods mentioned in subsection (2) are—

    (a) in the case of a decision of the OFT, the period during which an appeal may be made to the Tribunal under section 46 or 47 or the EC Competition Law (Articles 84 and 85) Enforcement Regulations 2001 (SI 2001/2916);

(b) in the case of a decision of the Tribunal mentioned in subsection (3)(c), the period during which a further appeal may be made under section 49 or under those Regulations;

(c) in the case of any decision which is the subject of a further appeal, the period during which an appeal may be made to the House of Lords from a decision on the further appeal;

and, where any appeal mentioned in paragraph (a), (b) or (c) is made, the period specified in that paragraph includes the period before the appeal is determined.]

[193]

NOTES

Commencement: to be appointed.

Inserted, together with the preceding cross-heading, by the Enterprise Act 2002, s 20(1), as from a day to be appointed; by s 20(2) of the 2002 Act, this section does not apply in relation to decisions made before the commencement of the said s 20.

Interpretation and governing principles

59 Interpretation

(1) In this Part—

"appeal tribunal" means an appeal tribunal established in accordance with the provisions of Part III of Schedule 7 for the purpose of hearing an appeal under section 46 or 47;

"Article 85" means Article 85 of the Treaty;

"Article 86" means Article 86 of the Treaty;

"block exemption" has the meaning given in section 6(4);

"block exemption order" has the meaning given in section 6(2);

"the Chapter I prohibition" has the meaning given in section 2(8);

"the Chapter II prohibition" has the meaning given in section 18(4);

"the Commission" (except in relation to the Competition Commission) means the European Commission;

"the Council" means the Council of the European Union;

"the court", except in sections 58[, 58A] and 60 and the expression "European Court", means—

(a) in England and Wales, the High Court;

(b) in Scotland, the Court of Session; and

(c) in Northern Ireland, the High Court;

"the Director" means the Director General of Fair Trading;

"document" includes information recorded in any form;

"the EEA Agreement" means the Agreement on the European Economic Area signed at Oporto on 2nd May 1992 as it has effect for the time being;

"the European Court" means the Court of Justice of the European Communities and includes the Court of First Instance;

"individual exemption" has the meaning given in section 4(2);

"information" includes estimates and forecasts;

"investigating officer" has the meaning given in section 27(1);

"Minister of the Crown" has the same meaning as in the Ministers of the Crown Act 1975;

"officer", in relation to a body corporate, includes a director, manager or secretary and, in relation to a partnership in Scotland, includes a partner;

["the OFT" means the Office of Fair Trading;]

"parallel exemption" has the meaning given in section 10(3);

"person", in addition to the meaning given by the Interpretation Act 1978, includes any undertaking;

"premises" does not include domestic premises unless—

(a) they are also used in connection with the affairs of an undertaking, or

(b) documents relating to the affairs of an undertaking are kept there,
but does include any vehicle;
"prescribed" means prescribed by regulations made by the Secretary of State;
"regulator" has the meaning given by section 54;
"section 11 exemption" has the meaning given in section 11(3); and
"the Treaty" means the treaty establishing the European Community.
["the Tribunal" means the Competition Appeal Tribunal;
"Tribunal rules" means rules under section 15 of the Enterprise Act 2002.]

(2)   The fact that to a limited extent the Chapter I prohibition does not apply to
an agreement, because of an exclusion provided by or under this Part or any other
enactment, does not require those provisions of the agreement to which the
exclusion relates to be disregarded when considering whether the agreement
infringes the prohibition for other reasons.

(3)   For the purposes of this Part, the power to require information, in relation to
information recorded otherwise than in a legible form, includes power to require a
copy of it in a legible form.

(4)   Any power conferred on the *Director* by this Part to require information
includes power to require any document which *he* believes may contain that
information.

[194]

NOTES

Commencement: 26 November 1998 (certain purposes); 11 January 1999 (remaining purposes).

Sub-s (1): definitions "appeal tribunal" and "the Director" repealed, figure in square brackets in
definition "the court" and definitions "the OFT", "the Tribunal" and "Tribunal rules" inserted, by the
Enterprise Act 2002, ss 20(3), 21, 278, Sch 5, paras 1, 6, Sch 25, para 38(1), (44)(a), Sch 26, as from a day
to be appointed.

Director: as to the abolition of the office of the Director General of Fair Trading and the substitution
of references to the Director and related expressions, see the note preceding s 1 at **[133]**.

60   Principles to be applied in determining questions

(1)   The purpose of this section is to ensure that so far as is possible (having
regard to any relevant differences between the provisions concerned), questions
arising under this Part in relation to competition within the United Kingdom are dealt
with in a manner which is consistent with the treatment of corresponding questions
arising in Community law in relation to competition within the Community.

(2)   At any time when the court determines a question arising under this Part, it
must act (so far as is compatible with the provisions of this Part and whether or not it
would otherwise be required to do so) with a view to securing that there is no
inconsistency between—

(a) the principles applied, and decision reached, by the court in determining
    that question; and
(b) the principles laid down by the Treaty and the European Court, and any
    relevant decision of that Court, as applicable at that time in determining
    any corresponding question arising in Community law.

(3)   The court must, in addition, have regard to any relevant decision or
statement of the Commission.

(4)   Subsections (2) and (3) also apply to—

(a) the *Director*; and
(b) any person acting on behalf of the *Director*, in connection with any matter
    arising under this Part.

(5)   In subsections (2) and (3), "court" means any court or tribunal.

(6)   In subsections (2)(b) and (3), "decision" includes a decision as to—
  (a) the interpretation of any provision of Community law;
  (b) the civil liability of an undertaking for harm caused by its infringement of
       Community law.

[195]

NOTES
Commencement: 11 January 1999.
Director: as to the abolition of the office of the Director General of Fair Trading and the substitution
of references to the Director and related expressions, see the note preceding s 1 at **[133]**.

PART II
INVESTIGATIONS IN RELATION TO ARTICLES 85 AND 86

61 Introduction

(1)   In this Part—
  "Article 85" and "Article 86" have the same meaning as in Part I;
  "authorised officer", in relation to the *Director*, means an officer to whom an
       authorisation has been given under subsection (2);
  "the Commission" means the European Commission;
  "the Director" means the Director General of Fair Trading;
  "Commission investigation" means an investigation ordered by a decision of
       the Commission under a prescribed provision of Community law relating
       to Article 85 or 86;
  ["the OFT" means the Office of Fair Trading;]
  "Director's investigation" means an investigation conducted by the Director at
       the request of the Commission under a prescribed provision of Community
       law relating to Article 85 or 86;
  "Director's special investigation" means a Director's investigation conducted
       at the request of the Commission in connection with a Commission
       investigation;
  "prescribed" means prescribed by order made by the Secretary of State;
  "premises" means—
       (a) in relation to a Commission investigation, any premises, land or
            means of transport which an official of the Commission has power to
            enter in the course of the investigation; and
       (b) in relation to *a Director's* investigation, any premises, land or means
            of transport which an official of the Commission would have power to
            enter if the investigation were being conducted by the Commission.

(2)   For the purposes of *a Director's* investigation, an officer of the *Director* to
whom an authorisation has been given has the powers of an official authorised by the
Commission in connection with a Commission investigation under the relevant
provision.

(3)   "Authorisation" means an authorisation given in writing by the *Director*
which—
  (a) identifies the officer;
  (b) specifies the subject matter and purpose of the investigation; and
  (c) draws attention to any penalties which a person may incur in connection
       with the investigation under the relevant provision of Community law.

[196]

NOTES
Commencement: 1 March 2000.
Sub-s (1): definition "the Director" repealed, definition "the OFT" inserted, for the third words in
italics there are substituted the words ""OFT's investigation" means an investigation conducted by the
OFT", for the fourth words in italics there are substituted the words ""OFT's special investigation" means

an OFT's", and for the fifth words in italics (in definition "premises") there are substituted the words "an OFT's", by the Enterprise Act 2002, s 278, Sch 25, para 38(1), (46)(a), Sch 26, as from a day to be appointed.

Sub-s (2): for the first words in italics there are substituted the words "an OFT's", by the Enterprise Act 2002, s 278(1), Sch 25, para 38(1), (46)(b)(i), as from a day to be appointed.

Director: as to the abolition of the office of the Director General of Fair Trading and the substitution of references to the Director and related expressions, see the note preceding s 1 at **[133]**.

Orders: the Competition Act 1998 (Commission Investigation and Director's Investigation) Order 1999, SI 1999/3027 at **[2076]**.

62   Power to enter premises: Commission investigations

(1)   A judge of the High Court may issue a warrant if satisfied, on an application made to the High Court in accordance with rules of court by the *Director*, that a Commission investigation is being, or is likely to be, obstructed.

(2)   A Commission investigation is being obstructed if—
- (a)   an official of the Commission ("the Commission official"), exercising his power in accordance with the provision under which the investigation is being conducted, has attempted to enter premises but has been unable to do so; and
- (b)   there are reasonable grounds for suspecting that there are books or records on the premises which the Commission official has power to examine.

(3)   A Commission investigation is also being obstructed if there are reasonable grounds for suspecting that there are books or records on the premises—
- (a)   the production of which has been required by an official of the Commission exercising his power in accordance with the provision under which the investigation is being conducted; and
- (b)   which have not been produced as required.

(4)   A Commission investigation is likely to be obstructed if—
- (a)   an official of the Commission ("the Commission official") is authorised for the purpose of the investigation;
- (b)   there are reasonable grounds for suspecting that there are books or records on the premises which the Commission official has power to examine; and
- (c)   there are also reasonable grounds for suspecting that, if the Commission official attempted to exercise his power to examine any of the books or records, they would not be produced but would be concealed, removed, tampered with or destroyed.

(5)   A warrant under this section shall authorise—
- (a)   a named officer of the *Director*,
- (b)   any other of *his officers whom he* has authorised in writing to accompany the named officer, and
- (c)   any official of the Commission authorised for the purpose of the Commission investigation,

to enter the premises specified in the warrant, and search for books and records which the official has power to examine, using such force as is reasonably necessary for the purpose.

[(5A)   A warrant under this section may authorise persons specified in the warrant to accompany the named officer who is executing it.]

(6)   Any person entering any premises by virtue of a warrant under this section may take with him such equipment as appears to him to be necessary.

(7)   On leaving any premises entered by virtue of the warrant the named officer must, if the premises are unoccupied or the occupier is temporarily absent, leave them as effectively secured as he found them.

(8)   A warrant under this section continues in force until the end of the period of one month beginning with the day on which it is issued.

(9)   In the application of this section to Scotland, references to the High Court are to be read as references to the Court of Session.

NOTES

Commencement: 1 March 2000.

Sub-s (5): for the words in italics in para (b) there are substituted the words "the OFT's officers whom the OFT" by the Enterprise Act 2002, s 278(1), Sch 25, para 38(1), (47)(b)(ii), as from a day to be appointed.

Sub-s (5A): inserted by the Enterprise Act 2002, s 203(1), (3), as from a day to be appointed.

Director: as to the abolition of the office of the Director General of Fair Trading and the substitution of references to the Director and related expressions, see the note preceding s 1 at [133].

---

63   Power to enter premises: *Director's* special investigations

(1)   A judge of the High Court may issue a warrant if satisfied, on an application made to the High Court in accordance with rules of court by the *Director, that a Director's* special investigation is being, or is likely to be, obstructed.

(2)   *A Director's* special investigation is being obstructed if—
   (a) an authorised officer of the *Director* has attempted to enter premises but has been unable to do so;
   (b) the officer has produced his authorisation to the undertaking, or association of undertakings, concerned; and
   (c) there are reasonable grounds for suspecting that there are books or records on the premises which the officer has power to examine.

(3)   *A Director's* special investigation is also being obstructed if—
   (a) there are reasonable grounds for suspecting that there are books or records on the premises which an authorised officer of the *Director* has power to examine;
   (b) the officer has produced his authorisation to the undertaking, or association of undertakings, and has required production of the books or records; and
   (c) the books and records have not been produced as required.

(4)   *A Director's* special investigation is likely to be obstructed if—
   (a) there are reasonable grounds for suspecting that there are books or records on the premises which an authorised officer of the *Director* has power to examine; and
   (b) there are also reasonable grounds for suspecting that, if the officer attempted to exercise his power to examine any of the books or records, they would not be produced but would be concealed, removed, tampered with or destroyed.

(5)   A warrant under this section shall authorise—
   (a) a named authorised officer of the *Director*,
   (b) any other authorised officer accompanying the named officer, and
   (c) any named official of the Commission,
to enter the premises specified in the warrant, and search for books and records which the authorised officer has power to examine, using such force as is reasonably necessary for the purpose.

[(5A) A warrant under this section may authorise persons specified in the warrant to accompany the named authorised officer who is executing it.]

(6)   Any person entering any premises by virtue of a warrant under this section may take with him such equipment as appears to him to be necessary.

(7)   On leaving any premises which he has entered by virtue of the warrant the named officer must, if the premises are unoccupied or the occupier is temporarily absent, leave them as effectively secured as he found them.

(8)   A warrant under this section continues in force until the end of the period of one month beginning with the day on which it is issued.

(9)   In the application of this section to Scotland, references to the High Court are to be read as references to the Court of Session.

[198]

NOTES

Commencement: 1 March 2000.

Sub-s (1): for the words in italics there are substituted the words "OFT, that an OFT's" by the Enterprise Act 2002, s 278(1), Sch 25, para 38(1), (48)(a), as from a day to be appointed.

Sub-ss (2)–(4): for the first words in italics there are substituted the words "An OFT's" by the Enterprise Act 2002, s 278(1), Sch 25, para 38(1), (48)(b), as from a day to be appointed.

Sub-s (5A): inserted by the Enterprise Act 2002, s 203(1), (4), as from a day to be appointed.

Director: as to the abolition of the office of the Director General of Fair Trading and the substitution of references to the Director and related expressions, see the note preceding s 1 at **[133]**.

64   Entry of premises under sections 62 and 63: supplementary

(1)   A warrant issued under section 62 or 63 must indicate—
  (a)   the subject matter and purpose of the investigation;
  (b)   the nature of the offence created by section 65.

(2)   The powers conferred by section 62 or 63 are to be exercised on production of a warrant issued under that section.

(3)   If there is no one at the premises when the named officer proposes to execute such a warrant he must, before executing it—
  (a)   take such steps as are reasonable in all the circumstances to inform the occupier of the intended entry; and
  (b)   if the occupier is informed, afford him or his legal or other representative a reasonable opportunity to be present when the warrant is executed.

(4)   If the named officer is unable to inform the occupier of the intended entry he must, when executing the warrant, leave a copy of it in a prominent place on the premises.

(5)   In this section—
  "named officer" means the officer named in the warrant; and
  "occupier", in relation to any premises, means a person whom the named officer reasonably believes is the occupier of those premises.

[199]

NOTES

Commencement: 1 March 2000.

65   Offences

(1)   A person is guilty of an offence if he intentionally obstructs any person in the exercise of his powers under a warrant issued under section 62 or 63.

(2)   A person guilty of an offence under subsection (1) is liable—
  (a)   on summary conviction, to a fine not exceeding the statutory maximum;
  (b)   on conviction on indictment, to imprisonment for a term not exceeding two years or to a fine or to both.

[200]

NOTES
Commencement: 1 March 2000.

PART III
MONOPOLIES

66–69 (*Ss 66, 67 amend the Fair Trading Act 1973, ss 44, 46 at* **[11]**, **[12]**, *and are repealed by the Enterprise Act 2002, s 278(2), Sch 26, as from a day to be appointed; s 68 inserts s 137(3A)–(3C) of the 1973 Act at* **[91]**; *s 69 amends s 83 of the 1973 Act at* **[67]**.)

PART IV
SUPPLEMENTAL AND TRANSITIONAL

70 (*Repeals the Patents Act 1977, ss 44, 45.*)

71 Regulations, orders and rules

(1) Any power to make regulations or orders which is conferred by this Act is exercisable by statutory instrument.

(2) The power to make rules which is conferred by section 48 is exercisable by statutory instrument.

(3) Any statutory instrument made under this Act may—
  (a) contain such incidental, supplemental, consequential and transitional provision as the Secretary of State considers appropriate; and
  (b) make different provision for different cases.

(4) No order is to be made under—
  (a) section 3,
  (b) section 19,
  (c) section 36(8),
  [(ca) section 45(8),]
  (d) section 50, or
  (e) paragraph 6(3) of Schedule 4,

unless a draft of the order has been laid before Parliament and approved by a resolution of each House.

(5) Any statutory instrument made under this Act, apart from one made—
  (a) under any of the provisions mentioned in subsection (4), or
  (b) under section 76(3),

shall be subject to annulment by a resolution of either House of Parliament.

[201]

NOTES
Commencement: 9 November 1998.
Sub-s (4): para (ca) inserted by the Enterprise Act 2002, s 278(1), Sch 25, para 38(1), (49), as from a day to be appointed.

72 Offences by bodies corporate etc

(1) This section applies to an offence under any of sections 42 to 44, 55(8) or 65.

(2) If an offence committed by a body corporate is proved—
  (a) to have been committed with the consent or connivance of an officer, or
  (b) to be attributable to any neglect on his part,

the officer as well as the body corporate is guilty of the offence and liable to be proceeded against and punished accordingly.

(3)   In subsection (2) "officer", in relation to a body corporate, means a director, manager, secretary or other similar officer of the body, or a person purporting to act in any such capacity.

(4)   If the affairs of a body corporate are managed by its members, subsection (2) applies in relation to the acts and defaults of a member in connection with his functions of management as if he were a director of the body corporate.

(5)   If an offence committed by a partnership in Scotland is proved—
    (a)   to have been committed with the consent or connivance of a partner, or
    (b)   to be attributable to any neglect on his part,
the partner as well as the partnership is guilty of the offence and liable to be proceeded against and punished accordingly.

(6)   In subsection (5) "partner" includes a person purporting to act as a partner.

                                                                 [202]

NOTES

Commencement: 1 March 2000.

73   Crown application

(1)   Any provision made by or under this Act binds the Crown except that—
    (a)   the Crown is not criminally liable as a result of any such provision;
    (b)   the Crown is not liable for any penalty under any such provision; and
    (c)   nothing in this Act affects Her Majesty in her private capacity.

(2)   Subsection (1)(a) does not affect the application of any provision of this Act in relation to persons in the public service of the Crown.

(3)   Subsection (1)(c) is to be interpreted as if section 38(3) of the Crown Proceedings Act 1947 (interpretation of references in that Act to Her Majesty in her private capacity) were contained in this Act.

(4)   If, in respect of a suspected infringement of the Chapter I prohibition or of the Chapter II prohibition otherwise than by the Crown or a person in the public service of the Crown, an investigation is conducted under section 25—
    (a)   the power conferred by section 27 may not be exercised in relation to land which is occupied by a government department, or otherwise for purposes of the Crown, without the written consent of the appropriate person; and
    (b)   section 28 does not apply in relation to land so occupied.

(5)   In any case in which consent is required under subsection (4), the person who is the appropriate person in relation to that case is to be determined in accordance with regulations made by the Secretary of State.

(6)   Sections 62 and 63 do not apply in relation to land which is occupied by a government department, or otherwise for purposes of the Crown, unless the matter being investigated is a suspected infringement by the Crown or by a person in the public service of the Crown.

(7)   In subsection (6) "infringement" means an infringement of Community law relating to Article 85 or 86 of the Treaty establishing the European Community.

(8)   If the Secretary of State certifies that it appears to him to be in the interests of national security that the powers of entry—
    (a)   conferred by section 27, or
    (b)   that may be conferred by a warrant under section 28, 62 or 63,

should not be exercisable in relation to premises held or used by or on behalf of the Crown and which are specified in the certificate, those powers are not exercisable in relation to those premises.

(9)   Any amendment, repeal or revocation made by this Act binds the Crown to the extent that the enactment amended, repealed or revoked binds the Crown.

[203]

NOTES
Commencement: 1 March 2000.
Regulations: the Competition Act 1998 (Definition of Appropriate Person) Regulations 1999, SI 1999/2282 at **[2074]**.

74   Amendments, transitional provisions, savings and repeals

(1)   The minor and consequential amendments set out in Schedule 12 are to have effect.

(2)   The transitional provisions and savings set out in Schedule 13 are to have effect.

(3)   The enactments set out in Schedule 14 are repealed.

[204]

NOTES
Commencement: 1 March 2000 (certain purposes); 10 November 1999 (certain purposes); 1 April 1999 (certain purposes); 11 January 1999 (certain purposes); 9 November 1998 (certain purposes): to be appointed (remainder).

75   Consequential and supplementary provision

(1)   The Secretary of State may by order make such incidental, consequential, transitional or supplemental provision as he thinks necessary or expedient for the general purposes, or any particular purpose, of this Act or in consequence of any of its provisions or for giving full effect to it.

(2)   An order under subsection (1) may, in particular, make provision—
    (a)   for enabling any person by whom any powers will become exercisable, on a date specified by or under this Act, by virtue of any provision made by or under this Act to take before that date any steps which are necessary as a preliminary to the exercise of those powers;
    (b)   for making savings, or additional savings, from the effect of any repeal made by or under this Act.

(3)   Amendments made under this section shall be in addition, and without prejudice, to those made by or under any other provision of this Act.

(4)   No other provision of this Act restricts the powers conferred by this section.

[205]

NOTES
Commencement: 9 November 1998.
Orders: the Competition Act 1998 (Competition Commission) Transitional, Consequential and Supplemental Provisions Order 1999, SI 1999/506 at **[2028]**; the Judicial Pensions (Qualifying Judicial Offices) (President of the Competition Commission Appeal Tribunals) Order 1999, SI 1999/2283; the Competition Act 1998 (Transitional, Consequential and Supplemental Provisions) Order 2000, SI 2000/311, as amended by SI 2000/2031; the Competition Act 1998 (Consequential and Supplemental Provisions) Order 2000, SI 2000/2031; the Competition Act 1998 (Public Transport Ticketing Schemes Block Exemption) Order 2001, SI 2001/319 at **[2138]**.

76   Short title, commencement and extent

(1)   This Act may be cited as the Competition Act 1998.

(2)   Sections 71 and 75 and this section and paragraphs 1 to 7 and 35 of Schedule 13 come into force on the passing of this Act.

(3)   The other provisions of this Act come into force on such day as the Secretary of State may by order appoint; and different days may be appointed for different purposes.

(4)   This Act extends to Northern Ireland.

[206]

NOTES

Commencement: 9 November 1998.

Orders: the Competition Act 1998 (Commencement No 1) Order 1998, SI 1998/2750; the Competition Act 1998 (Commencement No 2) Order 1998, SI 1998/3166; the Competition Act 1998 (Commencement No 3) Order 1999, SI 1999/505; the Competition Act 1998 (Commencement No 4) Order 1999, SI 1999/2859; the Competition Act 1998 (Commencement No 5) Order 2000, SI 2000/344.

SCHEDULES

SCHEDULE 1

Sections 3(1)(a) and 19(1)(a)

EXCLUSIONS: MERGERS AND CONCENTRATIONS

PART I
MERGERS

Enterprises ceasing to be distinct: the Chapter I prohibition

1.—(1)   To the extent to which an agreement (either on its own or when taken together with another agreement) results, or if carried out would result, in any two enterprises ceasing to be distinct enterprises for the purposes of *Part V of the Fair Trading Act 1973 ("the 1973 Act")*, the Chapter I prohibition does not apply to the agreement.

(2)   The exclusion provided by sub-paragraph (1) extends to any provision directly related and necessary to the implementation of the merger provisions.

(3)   In sub-paragraph (2) "merger provisions" means the provisions of the agreement which cause, or if carried out would cause, the agreement to have the result mentioned in sub-paragraph (1).

(4)   *Section 65 of the 1973 Act* applies for the purposes of this paragraph as if—
   (a) in subsection (3) (circumstances in which a person or group of persons may be treated as having control of an enterprise), and
   (b) in subsection (4) (circumstances in which a person or group of persons may be treated as bringing an enterprise under their control),

for "may" there were substituted "must".

Enterprises ceasing to be distinct: the Chapter II prohibition

2.—(1)   To the extent to which conduct (either on its own or when taken together with other conduct)—
   (a) results in any two enterprises ceasing to be distinct enterprises for the purposes of *Part V of the 1973 Act)*, or
   (b) is directly related and necessary to the attainment of the result mentioned in paragraph (a),

the Chapter II prohibition does not apply to that conduct.

(2)   *Section 65 of the 1973 Act* applies for the purposes of this paragraph as it applies for the purposes of paragraph 1.

Transfer of a newspaper or of newspaper assets

3.—(1)   The Chapter I prohibition does not apply to an agreement to the extent to which it constitutes, or would if carried out constitute, a transfer of a newspaper or of newspaper assets for the purposes of section 57 of the 1973 Act.

(2)   The Chapter II prohibition does not apply to conduct (either on its own or when taken together with other conduct) to the extent to which—

(a) it constitutes such a transfer, or

(b) it is directly related and necessary to the implementation of the transfer.

(3)   The exclusion provided by sub-paragraph (1) extends to any provision directly related and necessary to the implementation of the transfer.

Withdrawal of the paragraph 1 exclusion

4.—(1)   The exclusion provided by paragraph 1 does not apply to a particular agreement if the *Director* gives a direction under this paragraph to that effect.

(2)   If the *Director* is considering whether to give a direction under this paragraph, *he* may by notice in writing require any party to the agreement in question to give *him* such information in connection with the agreement as *he* may require.

(3)   The *Director* may give a direction under this paragraph only as provided in sub-paragraph (4) or (5).

(4)   If at the end of such period as may be specified in rules under section 51 a person has failed, without reasonable excuse, to comply with a requirement imposed under sub-paragraph (2), the *Director* may give a direction under this paragraph.

(5)   The *Director* may also give a direction under this paragraph if—

(a) *he* considers—

(i) that the agreement will, if not excluded, infringe the Chapter I prohibition; and

(ii) that *he* is not likely to grant it an unconditional individual exemption; and

(b) the agreement is not a protected agreement.

(6)   For the purposes of sub-paragraph (5), an individual exemption is unconditional if no conditions or obligations are imposed in respect of it under section 4(3)(a).

(7)   A direction under this paragraph—

(a) must be in writing;

(b) may be made so as to have effect from a date specified in the direction (which may not be earlier than the date on which it is given).

Protected agreements

5.   An agreement is a protected agreement for the purposes of paragraph 4 if—

(a) *the Secretary of State has announced his decision not to make a merger reference to the Competition Commission under section 64 of the 1973 Act in connection with the agreement;*

(b) *the Secretary of State has made a merger reference to the Competition Commission under section 64 of the 1973 Act in connection with the agreement and the Commission has found that the agreement has given rise to, or would if carried out give rise to, a merger situation qualifying for investigation;*

(c) *the agreement does not fall within sub-paragraph (a) or (b) but has given rise to, or would if carried out give rise to, enterprises to which it relates being regarded under section 65 of the 1973 Act as ceasing to be distinct enterprises (otherwise than as the result of subsection (3) or (4)(b) of that section); or*

(d) *the Secretary of State has made a merger reference to the Competition Commission under section 32 of the Water Industry Act 1991 in connection with the agreement and the Commission has found that the agreement has given rise to, or would if carried out give rise to, a merger of the kind to which that section applies.*

NOTES

Commencement: 11 January 1999.

Para 1: for the words in italics in sub-para (1) there are substituted the words "Part 3 of the Enterprise Act 2002 ("the 2002 Act")", and for the words in italics in sub-para (4) there are substituted the words "Section 26 of the 2002 Act", by the Enterprise Act 2002, s 278(1), Sch 25, para 38(1), (50)(a), as from a day to be appointed.

Para 2: for the words in italics in sub-para (1)(a) there are substituted the words "Part 3 of the 2002 Act", and for the words in italics in sub-para (2) there are substituted the words "Section 26 of the 2002 Act", by the Enterprise Act 2002, s 278(1), Sch 25, para 38(1), (50)(b), as from a day to be appointed.

Para 4: for the third word in italics in sub-para (2) there is substituted the words "the OFT" by the Enterprise Act 2002, s 278(1), Sch 25, para 38(1), (50)(c)(ii), as from a day to be appointed.

Para 5: sub-paras (a)–(d) substituted by the Enterprise Act 2002, s 278(1), Sch 25, para 38(1), (50)(d), as from a day to be appointed, as follows—

"(a) the OFT or (as the case may be) the Secretary of State has published its or his decision not to make a reference to the Competition Commission under section 22, 33, 45 or 62 of the 2002 Act in connection with the agreement;

(b) the OFT or (as the case may be) the Secretary of State has made a reference to the Competition Commission under section 22, 33, 45 or 62 of the 2002 Act in connection with the agreement and the Commission has found that the agreement has given rise to, or would if carried out give rise to, a relevant merger situation or (as the case may be) a special merger situation;

(c) the agreement does not fall within paragraph (a) or (b) but has given rise to, or would if carried out give rise to, enterprises to which it relates being regarded under section 26 of the 2002 Act as ceasing to be distinct enterprises (otherwise than as the result of subsection (3) or (4)(b) of that section); or

(d) the OFT has made a reference to the Competition Commission under section 32 of the Water Industry Act 1991 in connection with the agreement and the Commission has found that the agreement has given rise to, or would if carried out give rise to, a merger of any two or more water enterprises of the kind to which that section applies.".

Director: as to the abolition of the office of the Director General of Fair Trading and the substitution of references to the Director and related expressions, see the note preceding s 1 at **[133]**.

PART II
CONCENTRATIONS SUBJECT TO EC CONTROLS

6.—(1) To the extent to which an agreement (either on its own or when taken together with another agreement) gives rise to, or would if carried out give rise to, a concentration, the Chapter I prohibition does not apply to the agreement if the Merger Regulation gives the Commission exclusive jurisdiction in the matter.

(2) To the extent to which conduct (either on its own or when taken together with other conduct) gives rise to, or would if pursued give rise to, a concentration, the Chapter II prohibition does not apply to the conduct if the Merger Regulation gives the Commission exclusive jurisdiction in the matter.

(3) In this paragraph—

"concentration" means a concentration with a Community dimension within the meaning of Articles 1 and 3 of the Merger Regulation; and

"Merger Regulation" means Council Regulation (EEC) No 4064/89 of 21st December 1989 on the control of concentrations between undertakings as amended by Council Regulation (EC) No 1310/97 of 30th June 1997.

[208]

NOTES

Commencement: 11 January 1999.

(Sch 2: Pt I substitutes the Financial Services Act 1986, ss 125, 127 (repealed), and repeals s 126 of that Act; Pt II amends the Companies Act 1989, Sch 14 at **[131]** *and the Companies (Northern Ireland) Order 1990, SI 1990/593; Pts III, IV outside the scope of this work.)*

SCHEDULE 3

GENERAL EXCLUSIONS

Planning obligations

1.—(1)   The Chapter I prohibition does not apply to an agreement—
   (a)   to the extent to which it is a planning obligation;
   (b)   which is made under section 75 (agreements regulating development or use of land) or 246 (agreements relating to Crown land) of the Town and Country Planning (Scotland) Act 1997; or
   (c)   which is made under Article 40 of the Planning (Northern Ireland) Order 1991.

   (2)   In sub-paragraph (1)(a), "planning obligation" means—
   (a)   a planning obligation for the purposes of section 106 of the Town and Country Planning Act 1990; or
   (b)   a planning obligation for the purposes of section 299A of that Act.

Section 21(2) agreements

2.—(1)   The Chapter I prohibition does not apply to an agreement in respect of which a direction under section 21(2) of the Restrictive Trade Practices Act 1976 is in force immediately before the coming into force of section 2 ("a section 21(2) agreement").

   (2)   If a material variation is made to a section 21(2) agreement, sub-paragraph (1) ceases to apply to the agreement on the coming into force of the variation.

   (3)   Sub-paragraph (1) does not apply to a particular section 21(2) agreement if the *Director* gives a direction under this paragraph to that effect.

   (4)   If the *Director* is considering whether to give a direction under this paragraph, *he* may by notice in writing require any party to the agreement in question to give *him* such information in connection with the agreement as *he* may require.

   (5)   The *Director* may give a direction under this paragraph only as provided in sub-paragraph (6) or (7).

   (6)   If at the end of such period as may be specified in rules under section 51 a person has failed, without reasonable excuse, to comply with a requirement imposed under sub-paragraph (4), the *Director* may give a direction under this paragraph.

   (7)   The *Director* may also give a direction under this paragraph *if he* considers—
   (a)   that the agreement will, if not excluded, infringe the Chapter I prohibition; and
   (b)   that *he is* not likely to grant it an unconditional individual exemption.

   (8)   For the purposes of sub-paragraph (7) an individual exemption is unconditional if no conditions or obligations are imposed in respect of it under section 4(3)(a).

   (9)   A direction under this paragraph—
   (a)   must be in writing;
   (b)   may be made so as to have effect from a date specified in the direction (which may not be earlier than the date on which it is given).

EEA Regulated Markets

3.—(1)   The Chapter I prohibition does not apply to an agreement for the constitution of an EEA regulated market to the extent to which the agreement relates to any of the rules made, or guidance issued, by that market.

   (2)   The Chapter I prohibition does not apply to a decision made by an EEA regulated market, to the extent to which the decision relates to any of the market's regulating provisions.

   (3)   The Chapter I prohibition does not apply to—
   (a)   any practices of an EEA regulated market; or
   (b)   any practices which are trading practices in relation to an EEA regulated market.

   (4)   The Chapter I prohibition does not apply to an agreement the parties to which are or include—

   (a) an EEA regulated market, or

   (b) a person who is subject to the rules of that market,

to the extent to which the agreement consists of provisions the inclusion of which is required or contemplated by the regulating provisions of that market.

   (5)   In this paragraph—

"EEA regulated market" is a market which—

   (a) is listed by an EEA State other than the United Kingdom pursuant to article 16 of Council Directive No 93/22/EEC of 10th May 1993 on investment services in the securities field; and

   (b) operates without any requirement that a person dealing on the market should have a physical presence in the EEA State from which any trading facilities are provided or on any trading floor that the market may have;

"EEA State" means a State which is a contracting party to the EEA Agreement;

"regulating provisions", in relation to an EEA regulated market, means—

   (a) rules made, or guidance issued, by that market,

   (b) practices of that market, or

   (c) practices which, in relation to that market, are trading practices;

"trading practices", in relation to an EEA regulated market, means practices of persons who are subject to the rules made by that market, and—

   (a) which relate to business in respect of which those persons are subject to the rules of that market, and which are required or contemplated by those rules or by guidance issued by that market; or

   (b) which are otherwise attributable to the conduct of that market as such.

Services of general economic interest etc

4.   Neither the Chapter I prohibition nor the Chapter II prohibition applies to an undertaking entrusted with the operation of services of general economic interest or having the character of a revenue-producing monopoly in so far as the prohibition would obstruct the performance, in law or in fact, of the particular tasks assigned to that undertaking.

Compliance with legal requirements

5.—(1)   The Chapter I prohibition does not apply to an agreement to the extent to which it is made in order to comply with a legal requirement.

   (2)   The Chapter II prohibition does not apply to conduct to the extent to which it is engaged in an order to comply with a legal requirement.

   (3)   In this paragraph "legal requirement" means a requirement—

   (a) imposed by or under any enactment in force in the United Kingdom;

   (b) imposed by or under the Treaty or the EEA Agreement and having legal effect in the United Kingdom without further enactment; or

   (c) imposed by or under the law in force in another Member State and having legal effect in the United Kingdom.

Avoidance of conflict with international obligations

6.—(1)   If the Secretary of State is satisfied that, in order to avoid a conflict between provisions of this Part and an international obligation of the United Kingdom, it would be appropriate for the Chapter I prohibition not to apply to—

   (a) a particular agreement, or

   (b) any agreement of a particular description,

he may by order exclude the agreement, or agreements of that description, from the Chapter I prohibition.

   (2)   An order under sub-paragraph (1) may make provision for the exclusion of the agreement or agreements to which the order applies, or of such of them as may be specified, only in specified circumstances.

   (3)   An order under sub-paragraph (1) may also provide that the Chapter I prohibition is to be deemed never to have applied in relation to the agreement or agreements, or in relation to such of them as may be specified.

   (4)   If the Secretary of State is satisfied that, in order to avoid a conflict between provisions of this Part and an international obligation of the United Kingdom, it would be

appropriate for the Chapter II prohibition not to apply in particular circumstances, he may by order provide for it not to apply in such circumstances as may be specified.

(5)   An order under sub-paragraph (4) may provide that the Chapter II prohibition is to be deemed never to have applied in relation to specified conduct.

(6)   An international arrangement relating to civil aviation and designated by an order made by the Secretary of State is to be treated as an international obligation for the purposes of this paragraph.

(7)   In this paragraph and paragraph 7 "specified" means specified in the order.

Public policy

7.—(1)   If the Secretary of State is satisfied that there are exceptional and compelling reasons of public policy why the Chapter I prohibition ought not to apply to—
    (a) a particular agreement, or
    (b) any agreement of a particular description,
he may by order exclude the agreement, or agreements of that description, from the Chapter I prohibition.

(2)   An order under sub-paragraph (1) may make provision for the exclusion of the agreement or agreements to which the order applies, or of such of them as may be specified, only in specified circumstances.

(3)   An order under sub-paragraph (1) may also provide that the Chapter I prohibition is to be deemed never to have applied in relation to the agreement or agreements, or in relation to such of them as may be specified.

(4)   If the Secretary of State is satisfied that there are exceptional and compelling reasons of public policy why the Chapter II prohibition ought not to apply in particular circumstances, he may by order provide for it not to apply in such circumstances as may be specified.

(5)   An order under sub-paragraph (4) may provide that the Chapter II prohibition is to be deemed never to have applied in relation to specified conduct.

Coal and steel

8.—(1)   The Chapter I prohibition does not apply to an agreement which relates to a coal or steel product to the extent to which the ECSC Treaty gives the Commission exclusive jurisdiction in the matter.

(2)   Sub-paragraph (1) ceases to have effect on the date on which the ECSC Treaty expires ("the expiry date").

(3)   The Chapter II prohibition does not apply to conduct which relates to a coal or steel product to the extent to which the ECSC Treaty gives the Commission exclusive jurisdiction in the matter.

(4)   Sub-paragraph (3) ceases to have effect on the expiry date.

(5)   In this paragraph—
    "coal or steel product" means any product of a kind listed in Annex I to the ECSC
        Treaty; and
    "ECSC Treaty" means the Treaty establishing the European Coal and Steel Community.

Agricultural products

9.—(1)   The Chapter I prohibition does not apply to an agreement to the extent to which it relates to production of or trade in an agricultural product and—
    (a) forms an integral part of a national market organisation;
    (b) is necessary for the attainment of the objectives set out in Article 39 of the
        Treaty; or
    (c) is an agreement of farmers or farmers' associations (or associations of such
        associations) belonging to a single member State which concerns—
            (i) the production or sale of agricultural products, or
            (ii) the use of joint facilities for the storage, treatment or processing of
                agricultural products,
    and under which there is no obligation to charge identical prices.

(2)   If the Commission determines that an agreement does not fulfil the conditions specified by the provision for agricultural products for exclusion from Article 85(1), the exclusion provided by this paragraph ("the agriculture exclusion") is to be treated as ceasing to apply to the agreement on the date of the decision.

(3)   The agriculture exclusion does not apply to a particular agreement if the *Director* gives a direction under this paragraph to that effect.

(4)   If the *Director* is considering whether to give a direction under this paragraph, *he* may by notice in writing require any party to the agreement in question to give *him* such information in connection with the agreement as *he* may require.

(5)   The *Director* may give a direction under this paragraph only as provided in sub-paragraph (6) or (7).

(6)   If at the end of such period as may be specified in rules under section 51 a person has failed, without reasonable excuse, to comply with a requirement imposed under sub-paragraph (4), the *Director* may give a direction under this paragraph.

(7)   The *Director* may also give a direction under this paragraph if *he* considers that an agreement (whether or not *he* considers that it infringes the Chapter I prohibition) is likely, or is intended, substantially and unjustifiably to prevent, restrict or distort competition in relation to an agricultural product.

(8)   A direction under this paragraph—
    (a) must be in writing;
    (b) may be made so as to have effect from a date specified in the direction (which may not be earlier than the date on which it is given).

(9)   In this paragraph—
    "agricultural product" means any product of a kind listed in Annex II to the Treaty; and
    "provision for agricultural products" means Council Regulation (EEC) No 26/62 of 4th April 1962 applying certain rules of competition to production of and trade in agricultural products.

[209]

NOTES

Commencement: 11 January 1999.

Para 2: for the third word in italics in sub-para (4) there is substituted the words "the OFT", for the second words in italics in sub-para (7) there are substituted the words "if it", and for the third words in italics there are substituted the words "the OFT is", by the Enterprise Act 2002, s 278(1), Sch 25, para 38(1), (51)(a)(ii), (iii), as from a day to be appointed.

Para 9: for the third word in italics in sub-para (4) there is substituted the words "the OFT" by the Enterprise Act 2002, s 278(1), Sch 25, para 38(1), (51)(b)(ii), as from a day to be appointed.

Director: as to the abolition of the office of the Director General of Fair Trading and the substitution of references to the Director and related expressions, see the note preceding s 1 at **[133]**.

Restrictive Trade Practices Act 1976: repealed.

SCHEDULE 4

Section 3(1)(d)

PROFESSIONAL RULES

PART I
EXCLUSION

General

1.—(1)   *To the extent to which an agreement (either on its own or when taken together with another agreement)—*
    (a) constitutes a designated professional rule,
    (b) imposes obligations arising from designated professional rules, or
    (c) constitutes an agreement to act in accordance with such rules,
the Chapter I prohibition does not apply to the agreement.

(2)   In this Schedule—
"*designated*" means designated by the Secretary of State under paragraph 2;
"*professional rules*" means rules regulating a professional service or the persons providing, or wishing to provide, that service;
"*professional service*" means any of the services described in Part II of this Schedule; and
"*rules*" includes regulations, codes of practice and statements of principle.

Designated rules

2.—(1)   The Secretary of State must establish and maintain a list designating, for the purposes of this Schedule, rules—
(a)   which are notified to him under paragraph 3; and
(b)   which, in his opinion, are professional rules.

(2)   The list is to be established, and any alteration in the list is to be effected, by an order made by the Secretary of State.

(3)   The designation of any rule is to have effect from such date (which may be earlier than the date on which the order listing it is made) as may be specified in that order.

Application for designation

3.—(1)   Any body regulating a professional service or the persons who provide, or wish to provide, that service may apply to the Secretary of State for rules of that body to be designated.

(2)   An application under this paragraph must—
(a)   be accompanied by a copy of the rules to which it relates; and
(b)   be made in the prescribed manner.

Alterations

4.—(1)   A rule does not cease to be a designated professional rule merely because it is altered.

(2)   If such a rule is altered (whether by being modified, revoked or replaced), the body concerned must notify the Secretary of State and the Director of the alteration as soon as is reasonably practicable.

Reviewing the list

5.—(1)   The Secretary of State must send to the Director—
(a)   a copy of any order made under paragraph 2; and
(b)   a copy of the professional rules to which the order relates.

(2)   The Director must—
(a)   retain any copy of a professional rule which is sent to him under sub-paragraph (1)(b) so long as the rule remains in force;
(b)   maintain a copy of the list, as altered from time to time; and
(c)   keep the list under review.

(3)   If the Director considers—
(a)   that, with a view to restricting the exclusion provided by this Schedule, some or all of the rules of a particular body should no longer be designated, or
(b)   that rules which are not designated should be designated,
he must advise the Secretary of State accordingly.

Removal from the list

6.—(1)   This paragraph applies if the Secretary of State receives advice under paragraph 5(3)(a).

(2)   If it appears to the Secretary of State that another Minister of the Crown has functions in relation to the professional service concerned, he must consult that Minister.

(3)   If it appears to the Secretary of State, having considered the Director's advice and the advice of any other Minister resulting from consultation under sub-paragraph (2), that the rules in question should no longer be designated, he may by order revoke their designation.

(4)   Revocation of a designation is to have effect from such date as the order revoking it may specify.

Inspection

7.—*(1)   Any person may inspect, and take a copy of—*
  (a) any entry in the list of designated professional rules as kept by the Director under paragraph 5(2); or
  (b) any copy of professional rules retained by him under paragraph 5(1).

  (2)   The right conferred by sub-paragraph (1) is to be exercised only—
  (a) at a time which is reasonable;
  (b) on payment of such fee as the Director may determine; and
  (c) at such offices of his as the Director may direct.

[210]

NOTES
Commencement: 11 January 1999.

Repealed by the Enterprise Act 2002, ss 207, 278(2), Sch 26, as from a day to be appointed, subject to savings in relation to designation orders in s 276(1) of, and Sch 24, para 20 to, that Act at **[477]**.

The Director: see the note to s 47 at **[179]**.

Regulations: the Competition Act 1998 (Application for Designation of Professional Rules) Regulations 1999, SI 1999/2546 at **[2001]**.

PART II
PROFESSIONAL SERVICES

Legal

8.   *The services of barristers, advocates or solicitors.*

Medical

9.   *The provision of medical or surgical advice or attendance and the performance of surgical operations.*

Dental

10. *Any services falling within the practice of dentistry within the meaning of the Dentists Act 1984.*

Ophthalmic

11. *The testing of sight.*

Veterinary

12. *Any services which constitute veterinary surgery within the meaning of the Veterinary Surgeons Act 1966.*

Nursing

13. *The services of nurses.*

Midwifery

14. *The services of midwives.*

Physiotherapy

15. *The services of physiotherapists.*

Chiropody

16. The services of chiropodists.

Architectural

17. The services of architects.

Accounting and auditing

18. The making or preparation of accounts or accounting records and the examination, verification and auditing of financial statements.

Insolvency

19. Insolvency services within the meaning of section 428 of the Insolvency Act 1986.

Patent agency

20. The services of registered patent agents (within the meaning of Part V of the Copyright, Designs and Patents Act 1988).

21. The services of persons carrying on for gain in the United Kingdom the business of acting as agents or other representatives for or obtaining European patents or for the purpose of conducting proceedings in relation to applications for or otherwise in connection with such patents before the European Patent Office or the comptroller and whose names appear on the European list (within the meaning of Part V of the Copyright, Designs and Patents Act 1988).

Parliamentary agency

22. The services of parliamentary agents entered in the register in either House of Parliament as agents entitled to practise both in promoting and in opposing Bills.

Surveying

23. The services of surveyors of land, of quantity surveyors, of surveyors of buildings or other structures and of surveyors of ships.

Engineering and technology etc

24. The services of persons practising or employed as consultants in the field of—
   (a) civil engineering;
   (b) mechanical, aeronautical, marine, electrical or electronic engineering;
   (c) mining, quarrying, soil analysis or other forms of mineralogy or geology;
   (d) agronomy, forestry, livestock rearing or ecology;
   (e) metallurgy, chemistry, biochemistry or physics; or
   (f) any other form of engineering or technology analogous to those mentioned in sub-paragraphs (a) to (e).

Educational

25. The provision of education or training.

Religious

26. The services of ministers of religion.

NOTES
   Commencement: 11 January 1999.
   Repealed by the Enterprise Act 2002, ss 207, 278(2), Sch 26, as from a day to be appointed, subject to savings (in relation to designation orders under para 2 of this Schedule at **[210]**) in s 276(1) of, and Sch 24, para 20 to, that Act at **[477]**.

SCHEDULE 5

NOTIFICATION UNDER CHAPTER I: PROCEDURE

Terms used

1. In this Schedule—
"applicant" means the person making an application to which this Schedule applies;
"application" means an application under section 13 or an application under section 14;
"application for guidance" means an application under section 13;
"application for a decision" means an application under section 14;
"rules" means rules made by the *Director* under section 51; and
"specified" means specified in the rules.

General rules about applications

2.—(1) An application must be made in accordance with rules.

(2) A party to an agreement who makes an application must take all reasonable steps to notify all other parties to the agreement of whom he is aware—
(a) that the application has been made; and
(b) as to whether it is for guidance or a decision.

(3) Notification under sub-paragraph (2) must be in the specified manner.

Preliminary investigation

3.—(1) If, after a preliminary investigation of an application, the *Director* considers that it is likely—
(a) that the agreement concerned will infringe the Chapter I prohibition, and
(b) that it would not be appropriate to grant the agreement an individual exemption,
he may make a decision ("a provisional decision") under this paragraph.

(2) If the *Director* makes a provisional decision—
(a) the *Director* must notify the applicant in writing of *his* provisional decision; and
(b) section 13(4) or (as the case may be) section 14(4) is to be taken as never having applied.

(3) When making a provisional decision, the *Director* must follow such procedures as may be specified.

(4) A provisional decision does not affect the final determination of an application.

(5) If the *Director* has given notice to the applicant under sub-paragraph (2) in respect of an application for a decision, he may continue with the application under section 14.

Procedure on application for guidance

4. When determining an application for guidance, the *Director* must follow such procedure as may be specified.

Procedure on application for a decision

5.—(1) When determining an application for a decision, the *Director* must follow such procedure as may be specified.

(2) The *Director* must arrange for the application to be published in such a way as *he thinks* most suitable for *bringing it* to the attention of those likely to be affected by it, unless *he is* satisfied that it will be sufficient *for him* to seek information from one or more particular persons other than the applicant.

(3) In determining the application, the *Director* must take into account any representations made to *him* by persons other than the applicant.

Publication of decisions

6.   If the *Director* determines an application for a decision *he* must publish *his* decision, together with *his* reasons for making it, in such manner as may be specified.

Delay by the Director

7.—(1)   This paragraph applies if the court is satisfied, on the application of a person aggrieved by the failure of the *Director* to determine an application for a decision in accordance with the specified procedure, that there has been undue delay on the part of the *Director* in determining the application.

(2)   The court may give such directions to the *Director* as it considers appropriate for securing that the application is determined without unnecessary further delay.

[212]

NOTES

Commencement: 1 March 2000 (paras 1–6); to be appointed (remainder).

Para 5: for the second words in italics in sub-para (2) there are substituted the words "it thinks", for the third words in italics there are substituted the words "bringing the application", for the fourth words in italics there are substituted the words "the OFT is", and the fifth words in italics are repealed, by the Enterprise Act 2002, s 278, Sch 25, para 38(1), (52)(c), Sch 26, as from a day to be appointed.

Director: as to the abolition of the office of the Director General of Fair Trading and the substitution of references to the Director and related expressions, see the note preceding s 1 at **[133]**.

SCHEDULE 6

Section 20(2)

NOTIFICATION UNDER CHAPTER II: PROCEDURE

Terms used

1.   In this Schedule—

"applicant" means the person making an application to which this Schedule applies;

"application" means an application under section 21 or an application under section 22;

"application for guidance" means an application under section 21;

"application for a decision" means an application under section 22;

"other party", in relation to conduct of two or more persons, means one of those persons other than the applicant;

"rules" means rules made by the *Director* under section 51; and

"specified" means specified in the rules.

General rules about applications

2.—(1)   An application must be made in accordance with rules.

(2)   If the conduct to which an application relates is conduct of two or more persons, the applicant must take all reasonable steps to notify all of the other parties of whom he is aware—

(a)   that the application has been made; and

(b)   as to whether it is for guidance or a decision.

(3)   Notification under sub-paragraph (2) must be in the specified manner.

Preliminary investigation

3.—(1)   If, after a preliminary investigation of an application, the *Director* considers that it is likely that the conduct concerned will infringe the Chapter II prohibition, *he* may make a decision ("a provisional decision") under this paragraph.

(2)   If the *Director* makes a provisional decision, *he* must notify the applicant in writing of that decision.

(3)   When making a provisional decision, the *Director* must follow such procedure as may be specified.

(4)   A provisional decision does not affect the final determination of an application.

(5)   If the *Director* has given notice to the applicant under sub-paragraph (2) in respect of an application for a decision, he may continue with the application under section 22.

Procedure on application for guidance

4.   When determining an application for guidance, the *Director* must follow such procedure as may be specified.

Procedure on application for a decision

5.—(1)   When determining an application for a decision, the *Director* must follow such procedure as may be specified.

(2)   The *Director* must arrange for the application to be published in such a way as *he thinks* most suitable for *bringing it* to the attention of those likely to be affected by it, unless *he is* satisfied that it will be sufficient *for him* to seek information from one or more particular persons other than the applicant.

(3)   In determining the application, the *Director* must take into account any representations made to *him* by persons other than the applicant.

Publication of decisions

6.   If the *Director* determines an application for a decision *he* must publish *his* decision, together with his reasons for making it, in such manner as may be specified.

Delay by the Director

7.—(1)   This paragraph applies if the court is satisfied, on the application of a person aggrieved by the failure of the *Director* to determine an application for a decision in accordance with the specified procedure, that there has been undue delay on the part of the *Director* in determining the application.

(2)   The court may give such directions to the *Director* as it considers appropriate for securing that the application is determined without unnecessary further delay.

[213]

NOTES

Commencement: 1 March 2000 (paras 1–6); to be appointed (remainder).

Para 5: for the second words in italics in sub-para (2) there are substituted the words "it thinks", for the third words in italics there are substituted the words "bringing the application", for the fourth words in italics there are substituted the words "the OFT is", and the fifth words in italics are repealed, by the Enterprise Act 2002, s 278, Sch 25, para 38(1), (53)(c), Sch 26, as from a day to be appointed.

Director: as to the abolition of the office of the Director General of Fair Trading and the substitution of references to the Director and related expressions, see the note preceding s 1 at **[133]**.

SCHEDULE 7

Section 45(7)

THE COMPETITION COMMISSION

PART I
GENERAL

Interpretation

1.   In this Schedule—
  "the 1973 Act" means the Fair Trading Act 1973;
  "appeal panel member" means a member appointed under paragraph 2(1)(a);
  "Chairman" means the chairman of the Commission;
  "the Commission" means the Competition Commission;

"Council" has the meaning given in paragraph 5;

"general functions" means any functions of the Commission other than functions—

    (a) *in connection with appeals under this Act; or*

    (b) which are to be discharged by the Council;

"member" means a member of the Commission;

"newspaper merger reference" means a newspaper merger reference under section 59 of the 1973 Act;

["newspaper panel member" means a member of the panel maintained under paragraph 22;]

"President" has the meaning given by paragraph 4(2);

"reporting panel member" means a member appointed under paragraph 2(1)(b);

"secretary" means the secretary of the Commission appointed under paragraph 9; and

"specialist panel member" means a member appointed under any of the provisions mentioned in paragraph 2(1)(d).

Membership of the Commission

2.—(1) The Commission is to consist of—

    (a) *members appointed by the Secretary of State to form a panel for the purposes of the Commission's functions in relation to appeals;*

    (b) members appointed by the Secretary of State to form a panel for the purposes of the Commission's general functions;

    (c) members appointed (in accordance with paragraph 15(5)) from the panel maintained under paragraph 22;

    (d) members appointed by the Secretary of State under or by virtue of—

        (i) section 12(4) or 14(8) of the Water Industry Act 1991;

        [(ii) section 104 of the Utilities Act 2000;]

        (iii) section 13(10) of the Telecommunications Act 1984;

        (iv) Article 15(9) of the Electricity (Northern Ireland) Order 1992;

    [(e) one or members appointed by the Secretary of State to serve on the Council].

[(1A) A person may not be, at the same time, a member of the Commission and a member of the Tribunal.]

(2) A person who is appointed as a member of a kind mentioned in one of paragraphs *(a)* to (c) of sub-paragraph (3) may also be appointed as a member of either or both of the other kinds mentioned in those paragraphs.

(3) The kinds of member are—

    (a) *an appeal panel member;*

    [(aa) a newspaper panel member;]

    (b) a reporting panel member;

    (c) a specialist panel member.

(4) Before appointing a person who is qualified for appointment to the panel of chairmen (see paragraph 26(2)), the Secretary of State must consult the Lord Chancellor or [Secretary of State], as he considers appropriate.

(5) The validity of the Commission's proceedings is not affected by a defect in the appointment of a member.

Chairman and deputy chairmen

3.—(1) The Commission is to have a chairman appointed by the Secretary of State from among the reporting panel members.

(2) The Secretary of State may appoint one or more of the reporting panel members to act as deputy chairman.

(3) The Chairman, and any deputy chairman, may resign that office at any time by notice in writing addressed to the Secretary of State.

(4) If the Chairman (or a deputy chairman) ceases to be a member he also ceases to be Chairman (or a deputy chairman).

(5) If the Chairman is absent or otherwise unable to act, or there is no chairman, any of his functions may be performed—

    (a) if there is one deputy chairman, by him;

    (b) if there is more than one—
         (i) by the deputy chairman designated by the Secretary of State; or
        (ii) if no such designation has been made, by the deputy chairman designated by the deputy chairmen;
    (c) if there is no deputy chairman able to act—
         (i) by the member designated by the Secretary of State; or
        (ii) if no such designation has been made, by the member designated by the Commission.

President

4.—*(1)* *The Secretary of State must appoint one of the appeal panel members to preside over the discharge of the Commission's functions in relation to appeals.*

(2) *The member so appointed is to be known as the President of the Competition Commission Appeal Tribunals (but is referred to in this Schedule as "the President").*

(3) *The Secretary of State may not appoint a person to be the President unless that person—*
    (a) *has a ten year general qualification within the meaning of section 71 of the Courts and Legal Services Act 1990,*
    (b) *is an advocate or solicitor in Scotland of at least ten years' standing, or*
    (c) *is—*
         (i) *a member of the Bar of Northern Ireland of at least ten years' standing, or*
        (ii) *a solicitor of the Supreme Court of Northern Ireland of at least ten years' standing,*

and appears to the Secretary of State to have appropriate experience and knowledge of competition law and practice.

(4) *Before appointing the President, the Secretary of State must consult the Lord Chancellor or [Secretary of State], as he considers appropriate.*

(5) *If the President ceases to be a member he also ceases to be President.*

The Council

5.—(1) The Commission is to have a *management* board to be known as the Competition Commission Council (but referred to in this Schedule as "the Council").

    (2) The Council is to consist of—
    (a) the Chairman [and any deputy chairmen of the Commission];
    (b) *the President;*
  [(bb) the member or members appointed under paragraph 2(1)(e);]
    (c) such other members as the Secretary of State may appoint; and
    (d) the secretary.

    (3) In exercising its functions under paragraphs 3 and 7 to 12 *and paragraph 5 of Schedule 8*, the Commission is to act through the Council.

[(3A) Without prejudice to the question whether any other functions of the Commission are to be so discharged, the functions of the Commission under sections 106, 116, and 171 of the Enterprise Act 2002 (and under section 116 as applied for the purposes of references under Part 4 of that Act by section 176 of that Act) are to be discharged by the Council.]

    (4) The Council may determine its own procedure including, in particular, its quorum.

    (5) The Chairman (and any person acting as Chairman) is to have a casting vote on any question being decided by the Council.

Term of office

6.—(1) Subject to the provisions of this Schedule, each member is to hold and vacate office in accordance with the terms of his appointment.

    (2) A person is not to be appointed as a member for more than *five years at a time*.

    (3) Any member may at any time resign by notice in writing addressed to the Secretary of State.

(4)   The Secretary of State may remove a member on the ground of incapacity or misbehaviour.

(5)   No person is to be prevented from being appointed as a member merely because he has previously been a member.

Expenses, remuneration and pensions

7.—(1)   The Secretary of State shall pay to the Commission such sums as he considers appropriate to enable it to perform its functions.

(2)   The Commission may pay, or make provision for paying, to or in respect of each member such salaries or other remuneration and such pensions, allowances, fees, expenses or gratuities as the Secretary of State may determine.

(3)   If a person ceases to be a member otherwise than on the expiry of his term of office and it appears to the Secretary of State that there are special circumstances which make it right for him to receive compensation, the Commission may make a payment to him of such amount as the Secretary of State may determine.

(4)   The approval of the Treasury is required for—
   (a) any payment under sub-paragraph (1);
   (b) any determination of the Secretary of State under sub-paragraph (2) or (3).

[7A. The Commission may publish advice and information in relation to any matter connected with the exercise of its functions.]

The Commission's powers

8.   Subject to the provisions of this Schedule, the Commission has power to do anything (except borrow money)—
   (a) calculated to facilitate the discharge of its functions; or
   (b) incidental or conducive to the discharge of its functions.

Staff

9.—(1)   The Commission is to have a secretary, appointed by the Secretary of State on such terms and conditions of service as he considers appropriate.

(2)   The approval of the Treasury is required as to those terms and conditions.

(3)   Before appointing a person to be secretary, the Secretary of State must consult the Chairman *and the President.*

(4)   Subject to obtaining the approval of—
   (a) the Secretary of State, as to numbers, and
   (b) the Secretary of State and Treasury, as to terms and conditions of service,
the Commission may appoint such staff as it thinks appropriate.

Procedure

10.   Subject to any provision made by or under this Act, the Commission may regulate its own procedure.

Application of seal and proof of instruments

11.—(1)   The application of the seal of the Commission must be authenticated by the signature of the secretary or of some other person authorised for the purpose.

(2)   Sub-paragraph (1) does not apply in relation to any document which is or is to be signed in accordance with the law of Scotland.

(3)   A document purporting to be duly executed under the seal of the Commission—
   (a) is to be received in evidence; and
   (b) is to be taken to have been so executed unless the contrary is proved.

Accounts

12.—(1) The Commission must—
   (a) keep proper accounts and proper records in relation to its accounts;
   (b) prepare a statement of accounts in respect of each of its financial years; and
   (c) send copies of the statement to the Secretary of State and to the Comptroller and Auditor General before the end of the month of August next following the financial year to which the statement relates.

   (2)   The statement of accounts must comply with any directions given by the Secretary of State with the approval of the Treasury as to—
   (a) the information to be contained in it,
   (b) the manner in which the information contained in it is to be presented, or
   (c) the methods and principles according to which the statement is to be prepared,

and must contain such additional information as the Secretary of State may with the approval of the Treasury require to be provided for informing Parliament.

   (3)   The Comptroller and Auditor General must—
   (a) examine, certify and report on each statement received by him as a result of this paragraph; and
   (b) lay copies of each statement and of his report before each House of Parliament.

   (4)   In this paragraph "financial year" means the period beginning with the date on which the Commission is established and ending with March 31st next, and each successive period of twelve months.

[Annual reports

12A.—(1) The Commission shall make to the Secretary of State a report for each financial year on its activities during the year.

   (2)   The annual report must be made before the end of August next following the financial year to which it relates.

   (3)   The Secretary of State shall lay a copy of the annual report before Parliament and arrange for the report to be published.]

Status

13.—(1) The Commission is not to be regarded as the servant or agent of the Crown or as enjoying any status, privilege or immunity of the Crown.

   (2)   The Commission's property is not to be regarded as property of, or held on behalf of, the Crown.

[214]

NOTES
   Commencement: 1 April 1999.
   Para 1: definitions "appeal panel member" and "President", and words in italics in definition "general functions" repealed, and definition "newspaper panel member" inserted, by the Enterprise Act 2002, ss 21, 185, 278(2), Sch 5, paras 1, 7(1), (2), Sch 11, paras 1, 2, Sch 26, as from a day to be appointed.
   Para 2: sub-paras (1)(a), (3)(a), (4) repealed, for words in italics in sub-para (1)(c) there are substituted the words "the members of", sub-paras (1)(e), (1A), (3)(aa) inserted, and for letter in italics in sub-para (2) there is substituted "(aa)", by the Enterprise Act 2002, ss 21, 185, 278(2), Sch 5, paras 1, 7(1), (3), Sch 11, paras 1, 3, Sch 26, as from a day to be appointed; sub-para (1)(d)(ii) substituted by the Utilities Act 2000, s 104(3); words in square brackets in sub-para (4) substituted by virtue of the Transfer of Functions (Lord Advocate and Secretary of State) Order 1999, SI 1999/678, art 2(1), Schedule.
   Para 4: repealed by the Enterprise Act 2002, ss 21, 278(2), Sch 5, paras 1, 7(1), (4), Sch 26, as from a day to be appointed; words in square brackets in sub-para (4) substituted by virtue of SI 1999/678, art 2(1), Schedule.
   Para 5: words in italics in sub-paras (1), (3), and sub-para (2)(b), repealed, and words in square brackets in sub-para (2)(a) and sub-paras (2)(bb), (3A) inserted, by the Enterprise Act 2002, ss 21, 185, 278(2), Sch 5, paras 1, 7(1), (5), Sch 11, paras 1, 4, Sch 26, as from a day to be appointed.
   Para 6: for words in italics in sub-para (2) there are substituted the words "eight years (but this does not prevent a re-appointment for the purpose only of continuing to act as a member of a group selected under paragraph 15 before the end of his term of office)", and sub-para (5) repealed, by the Enterprise Act 2002, ss 185, 278(2), Sch 11, paras 1, 5, Sch 26, as from a day to be appointed.

Para 7: sub-para (4) repealed by the Enterprise Act 2002, ss 185, 278(2), Sch 11, paras 1, 6, Sch 26, as from a day to be appointed.

Para 7A: inserted by the Enterprise Act 2002, s 185, Sch 11, paras 1, 7, as from a day to be appointed.

Para 9: sub-para (2), and words in italics in sub-para (3) repealed, and for sub-paras (4)(a), (b) there are substituted the words "the Secretary of State as to numbers and terms and conditions of service", by the Enterprise Act 2002, ss 185, 278(2), Sch 11, paras 1, 8, Sch 26, as from a day to be appointed.

Para 10: repealed by the Enterprise Act 2002, ss 185, 278(2), Sch 11, paras 1, 9, Sch 26, as from a day to be appointed.

Para 12A: inserted by the Enterprise Act 2002, s 186, as from a day to be appointed.

President of the Competition Commission Appeal Tribunals: the person who is President of the Competition Commission Appeal Tribunals under para 4 immediately before the commencement of the Enterprise Act 2002, s 12 at **[264]**, is on that date to become the President of the Competition Appeal Tribunal; see s 276(1), Sch 24, para 7 of the 2002 Act at **[477]**.

Competition Commission appeal panel: any person who is a member of the Competition Commission appeal panel (but not a member of the panel of chairmen) immediately before the commencement of the Enterprise Act 2002, s 12 at **[264]**, is on that date to become a member of the Competition Appeal Tribunal; see s 276(1), Sch 24, para 9 of the 2002 Act at **[477]**.

PART II
PERFORMANCE OF THE COMMISSION'S GENERAL FUNCTIONS

Interpretation

14. In this Part of this Schedule "group" means a group selected under paragraph 15.

Discharge of certain functions by groups

15.—(1) Except where sub-paragraph (7) [or (8)] gives the Chairman power to act on his own, any general function of the Commission must be performed through a group selected for the purpose by the Chairman.

(2)   The group must consist of at least three persons one of whom may be the Chairman.

(3)   In selecting the members of the group, the Chairman must comply with any requirement as to its constitution imposed by any enactment applying to specialist panel members.

(4)   If the functions to be performed through the group relate to a newspaper merger reference, the group must, subject to sub-paragraph (5), consist of such reporting panel members as the Chairman may select.

(5)   *The Secretary of State may appoint one, two or three persons from the panel maintained under paragraph 22 to be members and, if he does so, the group—*
  (a) must include that member or those members; and
  (b) if there are three such members, may (if the Chairman so decides) consist entirely of those members.

(6)   Subject to sub-paragraphs (2) to (5), a group must consist of reporting panel members or specialist panel members selected by the Chairman.

(7)   While a group is being constituted to perform a particular general function of the Commission, the Chairman may—
  (a) take such steps (falling within that general function) as he considers appropriate to facilitate the work of the group when it has been constituted; *or*
  (b) *exercise the power conferred by section 75(5) of the 1973 Act (setting aside references).*

[(8)   The Chairman may exercise the power conferred by section 37(1), 48(1) or 64(1) of the Enterprise Act 2002 while a group is being constituted to perform a relevant general function of the Commission or, when it has been so constituted, before it has held its first meeting.]

Chairmen of groups

16. The Chairman must appoint one of the members of a group to act as the chairman of the group.

Replacement of member of group

17.—(1) If, during the proceedings of a group—

    (a) a member of the group ceases to be a member of the Commission,

    (b) the Chairman is satisfied that a member of the group will be unable for a substantial period to perform his duties as a member of the group, or

    (c) it appears to the Chairman that because of a particular interest of a member of the group it is inappropriate for him to remain in the group,

the Chairman may appoint a replacement.

    (2)   The Chairman may also at any time appoint any reporting panel member to be an additional member of a group.

Attendance of other members

18.—(1) At the invitation of the chairman of a group, any reporting panel member who is not a member of the group may attend meetings or otherwise take part in the proceedings of the group.

    (2)   But any person attending in response to such an invitation may not—

    (a) vote in any proceedings of the group; or

    (b) have a statement of his dissent from a conclusion of the group included in a report made by them.

    (3)   Nothing in sub-paragraph (1) is to be taken to prevent a group, or a member of a group, from consulting any member of the Commission with respect to any matter or question with which the group is concerned.

Procedure

19.—(1) Subject to any special or general directions given by the Secretary of State, each group may determine its own procedure.

    (2)   Each group may, in particular, determine its quorum and determine—

    (a) the extent, if any, to which persons interested or claiming to be interested in the subject-matter of the reference are allowed—

        (i) to be present or to be heard, either by themselves or by their representatives;

        (ii) to cross-examine witnesses; or

        (iii) otherwise to take part; and

    (b) the extent, if any, to which sittings of the group are to be held in public.

    (3)   In determining its procedure a group must have regard to any guidance issued by the Chairman.

    (4)   Before issuing any guidance for the purposes of this paragraph the Chairman must consult the members of the Commission.

    [(5)   This paragraph does not apply to groups for which rules must be made under paragraph 19A.]

[19A.—(1) The Chairman must make rules of procedure in relation to merger reference groups, market reference groups and special reference groups.

    (2)   Schedule 7A makes further provision about rules made under this paragraph but is not to be taken as restricting the Chairman's powers under this paragraph.

    (3)   The Chairman must publish rules made under this paragraph in such manner as he considers appropriate for the purpose of bringing them to the attention of those likely to be affected by them.

    (4)   The Chairman must consult the members of the Commission and such other persons as he considers appropriate before making rules under this paragraph.

    (5)   Rules under this paragraph may—

    (a) make different provision for different cases or different purposes;

    (b) be varied or revoked by subsequent rules made under this paragraph.

    (6)   Subject to rules made under this paragraph, each merger reference group, market reference group and special reference group may determine its own procedure.

(7)   In determining how to proceed in accordance with rules made under this paragraph and in determining its procedure under sub-paragraph (6), a group must have regard to any guidance issued by the Chairman.

(8)   Before issuing any guidance for the purposes of this paragraph the Chairman shall consult the members of the Commission and such other persons as he considers appropriate.

(9)   In this paragraph and in Schedule 7A—
"market reference group" means any group constituted in connection with a reference under section 131 or 132 of the Enterprise Act 2002 (including that section as it has effect by virtue of another enactment);
"merger reference group" means any group constituted in connection with a reference under section 59 of the Fair Trading Act 1973 (c 41), section 32 of the Water Industry Act 1991 (c 56) or section 22, 33, 45 or 62 of the Enterprise Act 2002; and
"special reference group" means any group constituted in connection with a reference or (in the case of the Financial Services and Markets Act 2000 (c 8)) an investigation under—
  (a)   section 11 of the Competition Act 1980 (c 21);
  (b)   section 13 of the Telecommunications Act 1984 (c 12);
  (c)   section 43 of the Airports Act 1986 (c 31);
  (d)   section 24 or 41E of the Gas Act 1986 (c 44);
  (e)   section 12 or 56C of the Electricity Act 1989 (c 29);
  (f)   Schedule 4 to the Broadcasting Act 1990 (c 42);
  (g)   section 12 or 14 of the Water Industry Act 1991 (c 56);
  (h)   article 15 of the Electricity (Northern Ireland) Order 1992 (SI 1992/231 (NI 1));
  (i)   section 13 of, or Schedule 4A to, the Railways Act 1993 (c 43);
  (j)   article 34 of the Airports (Northern Ireland) Order 1994 (SI 1994/426 (NI 1));
  (k)   article 15 of the Gas (Northern Ireland) Order 1996 (SI 1996/275 (NI 2));
  (l)   section 15 of the Postal Services Act 2000 (c 26);
  (m)   section 162 or 306 of the Financial Services and Markets Act 2000 (c 8); or
  (n)   section 12 of the Transport Act 2000 (c 38).]

Effect of exercise of functions by group

20.—(1) Subject to *sub-paragraph (2)*, anything done by or in relation to a group in, or in connection with, the performance of functions to be performed by the group is to have the same effect as if done by or in relation to the Commission.

(2)   For the purposes of—
  (a)   *sections 56 and 73 of the 1973 Act,*
  (b)   *section 19A of the Agricultural Marketing Act 1958,*
  (c)   *Articles 23 and 42 of the Agricultural Marketing (Northern Ireland) Order 1982,*
a conclusion contained in a report of a group is to be disregarded if the conclusion is not that of at least two-thirds of the members of the group.

Casting votes

21.   The chairman of a group is to have a casting vote on any question to be decided by the group.

Newspaper merger references

22.   *The Secretary of State must maintain a panel of persons whom he regards as suitable* for selection as members of a group constituted in connection with a newspaper merger reference.
[215]

NOTES
Commencement: 1 April 1999.
Para 15: words in square brackets in sub-para (1), and sub-para (8) inserted, sub-para (7)(b) and the word preceding it repealed, and for sub-para (5) there is substituted the following paragraph, by the Enterprise Act 2002, ss 185, 278(2), Sch 11, paras 1, 10, Sch 26, as from a day to be appointed—

"(5) The Chairman must select one or more newspaper panel members to be members of the group dealing with functions relating to a newspaper merger reference and, if he selects at least three such members, the group may consist entirely of those members.".

Para 19: sub-para (5) inserted by the Enterprise Act 2002, s 187(2), as from a day to be appointed.

Para 19A: inserted by the Enterprise Act 2002, s 187(3), as from a day to be appointed.

Para 20: for words in italics in sub-para (1) there are substituted the words "sub-paragraphs (2) to (9)" and sub-para (2) is substituted, by the Enterprise Act 2002, ss 185, Sch 11, paras 1, 11, as from a day to be appointed, as follows—

"(2) For the purposes of Part 3 of the Enterprise Act 2002 (mergers) any decision of a group under section 35(1) or 36(1) of that Act (questions to be decided on non-public interest merger references) that there is an anti-competitive outcome is to be treated as a decision under that section that there is not an anti-competitive outcome if the decision is not that of at least two-thirds of the members of the group.

(3) For the purposes of Part 3 of the Act of 2002, if the decision is not that of at least two-thirds of the members of the group—

    (a)   any decision of a group under section 47 of that Act (questions to be decided on public interest merger references) that a relevant merger situation has been created is to be treated as a decision under that section that no such situation has been created;

    (b)   any decision of a group under section 47 of that Act that the creation of a relevant merger situation has resulted, or may be expected to result, in a substantial lessening of competition within any market or markets in the United Kingdom for goods or services is to be treated as a decision under that section that the creation of that situation has not resulted, or may be expected not to result, in such a substantial lessening of competition;

    (c)   any decision of a group under section 47 of that Act that arrangements are in progress or in contemplation which, if carried into effect, will result in the creation of a relevant merger situation is to be treated as a decision under that section that no such arrangements are in progress or in contemplation; and

    (d)   any decision of a group under section 47 of that Act that the creation of such a situation as is mentioned in paragraph (c) may be expected to result in a substantial lessening of competition within any market or markets in the United Kingdom for goods or services is to be treated as a decision under that section that the creation of that situation may be expected not to result in such a substantial lessening of competition.

(4) For the purposes of Part 3 of the Act of 2002, if the decision is not that of at least two-thirds of the members of the group—

    (a)   any decision of a group under section 63 of that Act (questions to be decided on special public interest merger references) that a special merger situation has been created is to be treated as a decision under that section that no such situation has been created; and

    (b)   any decision of a group under section 63 of that Act that arrangements are in progress or in contemplation which, if carried into effect, will result in the creation of a special merger situation is to be treated as a decision under that section that no such arrangements are in progress or in contemplation.

(5) For the purposes of Part 4 of the Act of 2002 (market investigations), if the decision is not that of at least two-thirds of the members of the group, any decision of a group under section 134 or 141 (questions to be decided on market investigation references) that a feature, or combination of features, of a relevant market prevents, restricts or distorts competition in connection with the supply or acquisition of any goods or services in the United Kingdom or a part of the United Kingdom is to be treated as a decision that the feature or (as the case may be) combination of features does not prevent, restrict or distort such competition.

(6) Accordingly, for the purposes of Part 4 of the Act of 2002, a group is to be treated as having decided under section 134 or 141 that there is no adverse effect on competition if—

    (a)   one or more than one decision of the group is to be treated as mentioned in sub-paragraph (5); and

    (b)   there is no other relevant decision of the group.

(7) In sub-paragraph (6) "relevant decision" means a decision which is not to be treated as mentioned in sub-paragraph (5) and which is that a feature, or combination of features, of a relevant market prevents, restricts or distorts competition in connection with the supply or acquisition of any goods or services in the United Kingdom or a part of the United Kingdom.

(8) Expressions used in sub-paragraphs (2) to (7) shall be construed in accordance with Part 3 or (as the case may be) 4 of the Act of 2002.

(9) Sub-paragraph (1) is also subject to specific provision made by or under other enactments about decisions which are not decisions of at least two-thirds of the members of a group.".

Para 22: for words in italics there are substituted the words "There are to be members of the Commission appointed by the Secretary of State to form a panel of persons available" by the Enterprise Act 2002, ss 185, Sch 11, paras 1, 12, as from a day to be appointed.

PART III
APPEALS

Interpretation

23. In this Part of this Schedule—
  "panel of chairmen" means the panel appointed under paragraph 26; and
  "tribunal" means an appeal tribunal constituted in accordance with paragraph 27.

Training of appeal panel members

24. The President must arrange such training for appeal panel members as he considers appropriate.

Acting President

25. If the President is absent or otherwise unable to act, the Secretary of State may appoint as acting president an appeal panel member who is qualified to act as chairman of a tribunal.

Panel of tribunal chairmen

26.—(1) There is to be a panel of appeal panel members appointed by the Secretary of State for the purposes of providing chairmen of appeal tribunals established under this Part of this Schedule.

  (2)   A person is qualified for appointment to the panel of chairmen only if—
    (a) he has a seven year general qualification within the meaning of section 71 of the Courts and Legal Services Act 1990,
    (b) he is an advocate or solicitor in Scotland of at least seven years' standing, or
    (c) he is—
        (i) a member of the Bar of Northern Ireland of at least seven years' standing, or
        (ii) a solicitor of the Supreme Court of Northern Ireland of at least seven years' standing,
and appears to the Secretary of State to have appropriate experience and knowledge of competition law and practice.

Constitution of tribunals

27.—(1) On receipt of a notice of appeal, the President must constitute an appeal tribunal to deal with the appeal.

  (2)   An appeal tribunal is to consist of—
    (a) a chairman, who must be either the President or a person appointed by him to be chairman from the panel of chairmen; and
    (b) two other appeal panel members appointed by the President.

[216]

NOTES
Commencement: 1 April 1999.
Repealed by the Enterprise Act 2002, ss 21, 278(2), Sch 5, paras 1, 7(6), Sch 26, as from a day to be appointed.
Competition Commission appeal panel: any member of the Competition Commission appeal panel who is, immediately before the commencement of the Enterprise Act 2002, s 12 at **[264]**, a member of the panel of chairmen under para 26 is on that date to become a chairman of the Competition Appeal Tribunal; see s 276(1), Sch 24, para 10 of the 2002 Act at **[477]**.

PART IV
MISCELLANEOUS

Disqualification of members for House of Commons

28. In Part II of Schedule 1 to the House of Commons Disqualification Act 1975 (bodies of which all members are disqualified) insert at the appropriate place—

  "The Competition Commission".

Disqualification of members for Northern Ireland Assembly

29. In Part II of Schedule 1 to the Northern Ireland Assembly Disqualification Act 1975 (bodies of which all members are disqualified) insert at the appropriate place—

"The Competition Commission".

[217]

NOTES

Commencement: 1 April 1999.

PART V
TRANSITIONAL PROVISIONS

Interpretation

30. In this Part of this Schedule—
    "commencement date" means the date on which section 45 comes into force; and
    "MMC" means the Monopolies and Mergers Commission.

Chairman

31.—(1) The person who is Chairman of the MMC immediately before the commencement date is on that date to become both a member of the Commission and its chairman as if he had been duly appointed under paragraphs 2(1)(b) and 3.

(2)   He is to hold office as Chairman of the Commission for the remainder of the period for which he was appointed as Chairman of the MMC and on the terms on which he was so appointed.

Deputy chairmen

32. The persons who are deputy chairmen of the MMC immediately before the commencement date are on that date to become deputy chairmen of the Commission as if they had been duly appointed under paragraph 3(2).

Reporting panel members

33.—(1) The persons who are members of the MMC immediately before the commencement date are on that date to become members of the Commission as if they had been duly appointed under paragraph 2(1)(b).

(2)   Each of them is to hold office as a member for the remainder of the period for which he was appointed as a member of the MMC and on the terms on which he was so appointed.

Specialist panel members

34.—(1) The persons who are members of the MMC immediately before the commencement date by virtue of appointments made under any of the enactments mentioned in paragraph 2(1)(d) are on that date to become members of the Commission as if they had been duly appointed to the Commission under the enactment in question.

(2)   Each of them is to hold office as a member for such period and on such terms as the Secretary of State may determine.

Secretary

35. The person who is the secretary of the MMC immediately before the commencement date is on that date to become the secretary of the Commission as if duly appointed under paragraph 9, on the same terms and conditions.

Council

36.—(1) The members who become deputy chairmen of the Commission under paragraph 32 are also to become members of the Council as if they had been duly appointed under paragraph 5(2)(c).

(2)   Each of them is to hold office as a member of the Council for such period as the Secretary of State determines.

───────────────

NOTES
    Commencement: 1 April 1999.

───────────────

[SCHEDULE 7A

THE COMPETITION COMMISSION: PROCEDURAL RULES FOR MERGERS AND MARKET REFERENCES ETC

1.   In this Schedule—
    "market investigation" means an investigation carried out by a market reference group in connection with a reference under section 131 or 132 of the Enterprise Act 2002 (including that section as it has effect by virtue of another enactment);
    "market reference group" has the meaning given by paragraph 19A(9) of Schedule 7 to this Act;
    "merger investigation" means an investigation carried out by a merger reference group in connection with a reference under section 59 of the Fair Trading Act 1973 (c 41), section 32 of the Water Industry Act 1991 (c 56) or section 22, 33, 45 or 62 of the Act of 2002;
    "merger reference group" has the meaning given by paragraph 19A(9) of Schedule 7 to this Act;
    "relevant group" means a market reference group, merger reference group or special reference group;
    "special investigation" means an investigation carried out by a special reference group—
        (a)   in connection with a reference under a provision mentioned in any of paragraphs (a) to (l) and (n) of the definition of "special reference group" in paragraph 19A(9) of Schedule 7 to this Act; or
        (b)   under a provision mentioned in paragraph (m) of that definition; and
    "special reference group" has the meaning given by paragraph 19A(9) of Schedule 7 to this Act.

2.   Rules may make provision—
    (a)   for particular stages of a merger investigation, a market investigation or a special investigation to be dealt with in accordance with a timetable and for the revision of that timetable;
    (b)   as to the documents and information which must be given to a relevant group in connection with a merger investigation, a market investigation or a special investigation;
    (c)   as to the documents or information which a relevant group must give to other persons in connection with such an investigation.

3.   Rules made by virtue of paragraph 2(a) and (b) may, in particular, enable or require a relevant group to disregard documents or information given after a particular date.

4.   Rules made by virtue of paragraph 2(c) may, in particular, make provision for the notification or publication of, and for consultation about, provisional findings of a relevant group.

5.   Rules may make provision as to the quorum of relevant groups.

6.   Rules may make provision—
    (a)   as to the extent (if any) to which persons interested or claiming to be interested in a matter under consideration which is specified or described in the rules are allowed—
        (i)   to be (either by themselves or by their representatives) present before a relevant group or heard by that group;
        (ii)   to cross-examine witnesses; or
        (iii)   otherwise to take part;
    (b)   as to the extent (if any) to which sittings of a relevant group are to be held in public; and

(c) generally in connection with any matters permitted by rules made under paragraph (a) or (b) (including, in particular, provision for a record of any hearings).

7. Rules may make provision for—
    (a) the notification or publication of information in relation to merger investigations, market investigations or special investigations;
    (b) consultation about such investigations.]

[219]

NOTES

    Commencement: to be appointed.
    Inserted by the Enterprise Act 2002, s 187(4), Sch 12, as from a day to be appointed.

SCHEDULE 8

Sections 46(5) and 48(4)

APPEALS

PART I
GENERAL

Interpretation

1. In this Schedule—
    "the chairman" means a person appointed as chairman of a tribunal in accordance with paragraph 27(2)(a) of Schedule 7;
    "the President" means the President of the Competition Commission Appeal Tribunals appointed under paragraph 4 of Schedule 7;
    "rules" means rules made by the Secretary of State under section 48;
    "specified" means specified in rules;
    "tribunal" means an appeal tribunal constituted in accordance with paragraph 27 of Schedule 7.

General procedure

2.—(1) An appeal to the *Competition Commission must be made by sending a notice of appeal to the Commission* within the specified period.

    (2) The notice of appeal must set out the grounds of appeal in sufficient detail to indicate—
        (a) under which provision of this Act the appeal is brought;
        (b) to what extent (if any) the appellant contends that the decision against, or with respect to which, the appeal is brought was based on an error of fact or was wrong in law; and
        (c) to what extent (if any) the appellant is appealing against the *Director's exercise of his* discretion in making the disputed decision.

    (3) The *tribunal* may give an appellant leave to amend the grounds of appeal identified in the notice of appeal.

    [(4) In this paragraph references to the Tribunal are to the Tribunal as constituted (in accordance with section 14 of the Enterprise Act 2002) for the purposes of the proceedings in question.

    (5) Nothing in this paragraph restricts the power under section 15 of the Enterprise Act 2002 (Tribunal rules) to make provision as to the manner of instituting proceedings before the Tribunal.]

Decisions of the tribunal

3.—(1) The *tribunal* must determine the appeal on the merits by reference to the grounds of appeal set out in the notice of appeal.

    (2) The *tribunal* may confirm or set aside the decision which is the subject of the appeal, or any part of it, and may—
        (a) remit the matter to the *Director*,

    (b) impose or revoke, or vary the amount of, a penalty,

    (c) grant or cancel an individual exemption or vary any conditions or obligations imposed in relation to the exemption by the *Director*,

    (d) give such directions, or take such other steps, as the *Director* could *himself* have given or taken, or

    (e) make any other decision which the *Director* could *himself* have made.

(3)   Any decision of the *tribunal* on an appeal has the same effect, and may be enforced in the same manner, as a decision of the *Director*.

(4)   If the *tribunal* confirms the decision which is the subject of the appeal it may nevertheless set aside any finding of fact on which the decision was based.

4.—*(1)* *A decision of the tribunal may be taken by a majority.*

  (2) *The decision must—*
    (a) *state whether it was unanimous or taken by a majority; and*
    (b) *be recorded in a document which—*
        (i) *contains a statement of the reasons for the decision; and*
       (ii) *is signed and dated by the chairman of the tribunal.*

(3) *When the tribunal is preparing the document mentioned in sub-paragraph (2)(b), section 56 is to apply to the tribunal as it applies to the Director.*

(4) *The President must make such arrangements for the publication of the tribunal's decision as he considers appropriate.*

[220]

NOTES

Commencement: 1 March 2000 (para 2–4); 1 April 1999 (remainder).

Paras 1, 4: repealed by the Enterprise Act 2002, ss 21, 278(2), Sch 5, paras 1, 8(1), (2), (5), Sch 26, as from a day to be appointed.

Para 2: for the words in italics in sub-para (1) there are substituted the words "Tribunal under section 46 or 47 must be made by sending a notice of appeal to it", for the words in italics in sub-para (2)(c) there are substituted the words "OFT's exercise of its", for the word in italics in sub-para (3) there is substituted the word "Tribunal", and sub-paras (4), (5) are inserted, by the Enterprise Act 2002, ss 21, 278(1), Sch 5, paras 1, 8(1), (3), Sch 25, para 38(1), (54)(b), as from a day to be appointed.

Para 3: for the first word in italics in sub-paras (1)–(4) there is substituted the word "Tribunal" and for the second word in italics in sub-paras (2)(d), (e) there is substituted the word "itself", by the Enterprise Act 2002, ss 21, 278(1), Sch 5, paras 1, 8(1), (4), Sch 25, para 38(1), (54)(c), as from a day to be appointed.

Director: as to the abolition of the office of the Director General of Fair Trading and the substitution of references to the Director and related expressions, see the note preceding s 1 at **[133]**.

PART II
RULES

Registrar of Appeal Tribunals

5.—*(1)* *Rules may provide for the appointment by the Competition Commission, with the approval of the Secretary of State, of a Registrar of Appeal Tribunals.*

  (2) *The rules may, in particular—*
    (a) *specify the qualifications for appointment as Registrar; and*
    (b) *provide for specified functions relating to appeals to be exercised by the Registrar in specified circumstances.*

Notice of appeal

6. *Rules may make provision—*
    (a) *as to the period within which appeals must be brought;*
    (b) *as to the form of the notice of appeal and as to the information which must be given in the notice;*
    (c) *with respect to amendment of a notice of appeal;*
    (d) *with respect to acknowledgement of a notice of appeal.*

Response to the appeal

7.   *Rules may provide for the tribunal to reject an appeal if—*
  (a) *it considers that the notice of appeal reveals no valid ground of appeal; or*
  (b) *it is satisfied that the appellant has habitually and persistently and without any reasonable ground—*
    (i)   *instituted vexatious proceedings, whether against the same person or against different persons; or*
    (ii) *made vexatious applications in any proceedings.*

Pre-hearing reviews and preliminary matters

8.—*(1) Rules may make provision—*
  (a) *for the carrying-out by the tribunal of a preliminary consideration of proceedings (a "pre-hearing review"); and*
  (b) *for enabling such powers to be exercised in connection with a pre-hearing review as may be specified.*

  (2)   If rules make provision of the kind mentioned in sub-paragraph (1), they may also include—
  (a) *provision for security; and*
  (b) *supplemental provision.*

  (3)   In sub-paragraph (2) "provision for security" means provision authorising a tribunal carrying out a pre-hearing review under the rules, in specified circumstances, to make an order requiring a party to the proceedings, if he wishes to continue to participate in them, to pay a deposit of an amount not exceeding such sum—
  (a) *as may be specified; or*
  (b) *as may be calculated in accordance with specified provisions.*

  (4)   In sub-paragraph (2) "supplemental provision" means any provision as to—
  (a) *the manner in which the amount of such a deposit is to be determined;*
  (b) *the consequences of non-payment of such a deposit; and*
  (c) *the circumstances in which any such deposit, or any part of it, may be—*
    (i)   *refunded to the person who paid it; or*
    (ii) *paid to another party to the proceedings.*

Conduct of the hearing

9.—*(1) Rules may make provision—*
  (a) *as to the manner in which appeals are to be conducted, including provision for any hearing to be held in private if the tribunal considers it appropriate because it may be considering information of a kind to which section 56 applies;*
  (b) *as to the persons entitled to appear on behalf of the parties;*
  (c) *for requiring persons to attend to give evidence and produce documents and for authorising the administration of oaths to witnesses;*
  (d) *as to the evidence which may be required or admitted in proceedings before the tribunal and the extent to which it should be oral or written;*
  (e) *allowing the tribunal to fix time limits with respect to any aspect of the proceedings before it and to extend any time limit (whether or not it has expired);*
  (f) *for enabling the tribunal to refer a matter back to the Director if it appears to the tribunal that the matter has not been adequately investigated;*
  (g) *for enabling the tribunal, on the application of any party to the proceedings before it or on its own initiative—*
    (i)   *in England and Wales or Northern Ireland, to order the disclosure between, or the production by, the parties of documents or classes of documents;*
    (ii) *in Scotland, to order such recovery or inspection of documents as might be ordered by a sheriff;*
  (h) *for the appointment of experts for the purposes of any proceedings before the tribunal;*
  (i) *for the award of costs or expenses, including any allowances payable to persons in connection with their attendance before the tribunal;*
  (j) *for taxing or otherwise settling any costs or expenses directed to be paid by the tribunal and for the enforcement of any such direction.*

(2)   A person who without reasonable excuse fails to comply with—
  (a) any requirement imposed by virtue of sub-paragraph (1)(c), or
  (b) any requirement with respect to the disclosure, production, recovery or inspection of documents which is imposed by virtue of sub-paragraph (1)(g),

is guilty of an offence and liable on summary conviction to a fine not exceeding level 3 on the standard scale.

Interest

10.—(1) Rules may make provision—
  (a) as to the circumstances in which the tribunal may order that interest is payable;
  (b) for the manner in which and the periods by reference to which interest is to be calculated and paid.

(2)   The rules may, in particular, provide that compound interest is to be payable if the tribunal—
  (a) upholds a decision of the Director to impose a penalty, or
  (b) does not reduce a penalty so imposed by more than a specified percentage,

but in such a case the rules may not provide that interest is to be payable in respect of any period before the date on which the appeal was brought.

Fees

11.—(1) Rules may provide—
  (a) for fees to be chargeable in respect of specified costs of proceedings before the tribunal;
  (b) for the amount of such costs to be determined by the tribunal.

(2)   Any sums received in consequence of rules under this paragraph are to be paid into the Consolidated Fund.

Withdrawing an appeal

12. Rules may make provision—
  (a) that a party who has brought an appeal may not withdraw it without the leave of—
    (i) the tribunal, or
    (ii) in specified circumstances, the President or the Registrar;
  (b) for the tribunal to grant leave to withdraw the appeal on such conditions as it considers appropriate;
  (c) enabling the tribunal to publish any decision which it could have made had the appeal not been withdrawn;
  (d) as to the effect of withdrawal of an appeal;
  (e) as to any procedure to be followed if parties to proceedings on an appeal agree to settle.

Interim orders

13.—(1) Rules may provide for the tribunal to make an order ("an interim order") granting, on an interim basis, any remedy which the tribunal would have power to grant in its final decision.

(2)   An interim order may, in particular, suspend the effect of a decision made by the Director or vary the conditions or obligations attached to an exemption.

(3)   Rules may also make provision giving the tribunal powers similar to those given to the Director by section 35.

Miscellaneous

14. Rules may make provision—
  (a) for a person who is not a party to proceedings on an appeal to be joined in those proceedings;
  (b) for appeals to be consolidated on such terms as the tribunal thinks appropriate in such circumstances as may be specified.

NOTES

Commencement: 1 April 1999.

Repealed by the Enterprise Act 2002, ss 21, 278(2), Sch 5, paras 1, 8(1), (5), Sch 26, as from a day to be appointed.

Registrar of Appeal Tribunals: the person who is Registrar of Appeal Tribunals under para 5 immediately before the commencement of the Enterprise Act 2002, s 12 at **[264]**, is on that date to become the Registrar of the Competition Appeal Tribunal; see s 276(1), Sch 24, para 8 of the 2002 Act at **[477]**.

The Director: see the note to s 47 at **[179]**.

SCHEDULE 9

Section 51(2)

DIRECTOR'S RULES

General

1. In this Schedule—

    "application for guidance" means an application for guidance under section 13 or 21;

    "application for a decision" means an application for a decision under section 14 or 22;

    "guidance" means guidance given under section 13 or 21;

    "rules" means rules made by the *Director* under section 51; and

    "specified" means specified in rules.

Applications

2. Rules may make provision—

    (a) as to the form and manner in which an application for guidance or an application for a decision must be made;

    (b) for the procedure to be followed in dealing with the application;

    (c) for the application to be dealt with in accordance with a timetable;

    (d) as to the documents and information which must be given to the *Director* in connection with the application;

    (e) requiring the applicant to give such notice of the application, to such other persons, as may be specified;

    (f) as to the consequences of a failure to comply with any rule made by virtue of sub-paragraph (e);

    (g) as to the procedure to be followed when the application is subject to the concurrent jurisdiction of the *Director* and a regulator.

Provisional decisions

3. Rules may make provision as to the procedure to be followed by the *Director* when making a provisional decision under paragraph 3 of Schedule 5 or paragraph 3 of Schedule 6.

Guidance

4. Rules may make provision as to—

    (a) the form and manner in which guidance is to be given;

    (b) the procedure to be followed if—

        (i) the *Director* takes further action with respect to an agreement after giving guidance that it is not likely to infringe the Chapter I prohibition; or

        (ii) the *Director* takes further action with respect to conduct after giving guidance that it is not likely to infringe the Chapter II prohibition.

Decisions

5.—(1) Rules may make provision as to—

    (a) the form and manner in which notice of any decision is to be given;

    (b) the person or persons to whom the notice is to be given;

    (c) the manner in which the *Director* is to publish a decision;

(d) the procedure to be followed if—
  (i) the *Director* takes further action with respect to an agreement after having decided that it does not infringe the Chapter I prohibition; or
  (ii) the *Director* takes further action with respect to conduct after having decided that it does not infringe the Chapter II prohibition.

(2) In this paragraph "decision" means a decision of the *Director* (whether or not made on an application)—
  (a) as to whether or not an agreement has infringed the Chapter I prohibition, or
  (b) as to whether or not conduct has infringed the Chapter II prohibition,

and, in the case of an application for a decision under section 14 which includes a request for an individual exemption, includes a decision as to whether or not to grant the exemption.

Individual exemptions

6. Rules may make provision as to—
  (a) the procedure to be followed by the *Director* when deciding whether, in accordance with section 5—
    (i) to cancel an individual exemption that *he* has granted,
    (ii) to vary or remove any of its conditions or obligations, or
    (iii) to impose additional conditions or obligations;
  (b) the form and manner in which notice of such a decision is to be given.

7. Rules may make provision as to—
  (a) the form and manner in which an application under section 4(6) for the extension of an individual exemption is to be made;
  (b) the circumstances in which the *Director* will consider such an application;
  (c) the procedure to be followed by the *Director* when deciding whether to grant such an application;
  (d) the form and manner in which notice of such a decision is to be given.

Block exemptions

8. Rules may make provision as to—
  (a) the form and manner in which notice of an agreement is to be given to the *Director* under subsection (1) of section 7;
  (b) the procedure to be followed by the *Director* if *he* is acting under subsection (2) of that section;
  (c) as to the procedure to be followed by the *Director* if *he* cancels a block exemption.

Parallel exemptions

9. Rules may make provision as to—
  (a) the circumstances in which the *Director* may—
    (i) impose conditions or obligations in relation to a parallel exemption,
    (ii) vary or remove any such conditions or obligations,
    (iii) impose additional conditions or obligations, or
    (iv) cancel the exemption;
  (b) as to the procedure to be followed by the *Director* if *he* is acting under section 10(5);
  (c) the form and manner in which notice of a decision to take any of the steps in sub-paragraph (a) is to be given;
  (d) the circumstances in which an exemption may be cancelled with retrospective effect.

Section 11 exemptions

10. Rules may, with respect to any exemption provided by regulations made under section 11, make provision similar to that made with respect to parallel exemptions by section 10 or by rules under paragraph 9.

Directions withdrawing exclusions

11. Rules may make provision as to the factors which the *Director* may take into account when *he* is determining the date on which a direction given under paragraph 4(1) of Schedule 1 or paragraph 2(3) or 9(3) of Schedule 3 is to have effect.

Disclosure of information

12.—(1) Rules may make provision as to the circumstances in which the *Director* is to be required, before disclosing information given to *him* by a third party in connection with the exercise of any of the *Director's* functions under Part I, to give notice, and an opportunity to make representations, to the third party.

(2) In relation to the agreement (or conduct) concerned, "third party" means a person who is not a party to the agreement (or who has not engaged in the conduct).

Applications under section 47

13. Rules may make provision as to—
    (a) the period within which an application under section 47(1) must be made;
    (b) the procedure to be followed by the *Director* in dealing with the application;
    (c) the person or persons to whom notice of the *Director's* response to the application is to be given.

Enforcement

14. Rules may make provision as to the procedure to be followed when the *Director* takes action under any of sections 32 to 41 with respect to the enforcement of the provisions of this Part.

[222]

NOTES
    Commencement: 26 November 1998.
    Director: as to the abolition of the office of the Director General of Fair Trading and the substitution of references to the Director and related expressions, see the note preceding s 1 at **[133]**.

SCHEDULE 10

Sections 54 and 66(5)

REGULATORS

PART I
MONOPOLIES

1. The amendments of the Fair Trading Act 1973 made by sections 66 and 67 of this Act are to have effect, not only in relation to the jurisdiction of the Director under the provisions amended, but also in relation to the jurisdiction under those provisions of each of the following—
    (a) the Director General of Telecommunications;
    [(b) the Gas and Electricity Markets Authority;]
    (c) the Director General of Electricity Supply for Northern Ireland;
    (d) the Director General of Water Services;
    (e) the Rail Regulator;
    (f) . . . ; and
    (g) the Director General of Gas for Northern Ireland.

[223]

NOTES
    Commencement: 1 April 1999.
    Repealed by the Enterprise Act 2002, s 278(2), Sch 26, as from a day to be appointed; para (b) substituted and words omitted from para (f) repealed, by virtue of the Utilities Act 2000, s 3(2).
    The Director: see the note to s 47 at **[179]**.

PART II
THE PROHIBITIONS

Telecommunications

2.—(1) In consequence of the repeal by this Act of provisions of the Competition Act 1980, the functions transferred by subsection (3) of section 50 of the Telecommunications Act 1984 (functions under 1973 and 1980 Acts) are no longer exercisable by the Director General of Telecommunications.

(2)–(10) ...

Gas

3.—(1) In consequence of the repeal by this Act of provisions of the Competition Act 1980, the functions transferred by subsection (3) of section 36A of the Gas Act 1986 (functions with respect to competition) are no longer exercisable by the Director General of Gas Supply.

(2)–(11) ...

Electricity

4.—(1) In consequence of the repeal by this Act of provisions of the Competition Act 1980, the functions transferred by subsection (3) of section 43 of the Electricity Act 1989 (functions with respect to competition) are no longer exercisable by the Director General of Electricity Supply.

(2)–(9) ...

Water

5.—(1) In consequence of the repeal by this Act of provisions of the Competition Act 1980, the functions exercisable by virtue of subsection (3) of section 31 of the Water Industry Act 1991 (functions of Director with respect to competition) are no longer exercisable by the Director General of Water Services.

(2)–(13) ...

Railways

6.—(1) In consequence of the repeal by this Act of provisions of the Competition Act 1980, the functions transferred by subsection (3) of section 67 of the Railways Act 1993 (respective functions of the Regulator and the Director etc) are no longer exercisable by the Rail Regulator.

(2)–(9) ...

[224]

NOTES

Commencement: 1 March 2000 (certain purposes); 26 November 1998 (otherwise).

Para 2: sub-paras (2)–(10) amend the Telecommunications Act 1984, ss 3, 50; repealed in part by the Enterprise Act 2002, s 278(2), Sch 26, as from a day to be appointed.

Para 3: sub-paras (2)–(11) amend the Gas Act 1986, ss 4, 36A; repealed in part by the Utilities Act 2000, s 108, Sch 8, and the Enterprise Act 2002, s 278(2), Sch 26, as from a day to be appointed.

Para 4: sub-paras (2)–(9) amend the Electricity Act 1989, ss 3, 43; repealed in part by the Utilities Act 2000, s 108, Sch 8, and the Enterprise Act 2002, s 278(2), Sch 26, as from a day to be appointed.

Para 5: sub-paras (2)–(13) amend the Water Industry Act 1991, ss 2, 31; repealed in part by the Enterprise Act 2002, s 278(2), Sch 26, as from a day to be appointed.

Para 6: sub-paras (2)–(9) amend the Railways Act 1993, ss 4, 67; repealed in part by the Enterprise Act 2002, s 278(2), Sch 26, as from a day to be appointed.

Director General of Gas Supply and the Director General of Electricity Supply: the functions of the Director General of Gas Supply and the Director General of Electricity Supply are transferred to the Gas and Electricity Markets Authority by virtue of the Utilities Act 2000, s 3(2). References in paras 3 and 4 above to either of those Directors should be construed accordingly.

PART III
THE PROHIBITIONS: NORTHERN IRELAND

Electricity

7.—(1)   In consequence of the repeal by this Act of provisions of the Competition Act 1980, the functions transferred by paragraph (3) of Article 46 of the Electricity (Northern Ireland) Order 1992 (functions with respect to competition) are no longer exercisable by the Director General of Electricity Supply for Northern Ireland.

(2)–(9)   . . .

Gas

8.—(1)   In consequence of the repeal by this Act of provisions of the Competition Act 1980, the functions transferred by paragraph (3) of Article 23 of the Gas (Northern Ireland) Order 1996 (functions with respect to competition) are no longer exercisable by the Director General of Gas for Northern Ireland.

(2)–(11)   . . .

[225]

NOTES
Commencement: 1 March 2000 (certain purposes); 26 November 1998 (otherwise).
Para 7: sub-paras (2)–(9) amend the Electricity (Northern Ireland) Order 1992, SI 1992/231 (NI 1), arts 6, 46; repealed in part by the Enterprise Act 2002, s 278(2), Sch 26, as from a day to be appointed.
Para 8: sub-paras (2)–(11) amend the Gas (Northern Ireland) Order 1996, SI 1996/275 (NI 2), arts 5, 23; repealed in part by the Enterprise Act 2002, s 278(2), Sch 26, as from a day to be appointed.

(Pt IV (minor and consequential amendments), Pt V (minor and consequential amendments in relation to Northern Ireland) outside the scope of this work.)

SCHEDULE 11
Section 55(4)

INTERPRETATION OF SECTION 55

Relevant functions

1.   *In section 55(3) "relevant functions" means any function under—*
   (a)   Part I or any enactment repealed in consequence of Part I;
   (b)   the Fair Trading Act 1973 (c 41) or the Competition Act 1980 (c 21);
   (c)   the Estate Agents Act 1979 (c 38);
   (d)   the Telecommunications Act 1984 (c 12);
   (e)   the Gas Act 1986 (c 44) or the Gas Act 1995 (c 45);
   (f)   the Gas (Northern Ireland) Order 1996;
   (g)   the Airports Act 1986 (c 31) or Part IV of the Airports (Northern Ireland) Order 1994;
   [(h)   the Financial Services and Markets Act 2000 (c 11);]
   (i)   the Electricity Act 1989 (c 29) or the Electricity (Northern Ireland) Order 1992;
   (j)   the Broadcasting Act 1990 (c 42) or the Broadcasting Act 1996 (c 55);
   (k)   the Courts and Legal Services Act 1990 (c 41);
   (l)   the Water Industry Act 1991 (c 56), the Water Resources Act 1991 (c 57), the Statutory Water Companies Act 1991 (c 58), the Land Drainage Act 1991 (c 59) and the Water Consolidation (Consequential Provisions) Act 1991 (c 60);
   (m)   the Railways Act 1993 (c 43);
   (n)   the Coal Industry Act 1994 (c 21);
   (o)   [the EC Competition Law (Articles 84 and 85) Enforcement Regulations 2001];
   (p)   any subordinate legislation made (whether before or after the passing of this Act) for the purpose of implementing Council Directive No 91/440/EEC of 29th July 1991 on the development of the Community's railways, Council Directive No 95/18/EC of 19th June 1995 on the licensing of railway undertakings or Council

Directive No 95/19/EC of 19th June 1995 on the allocation of railway infrastructure capacity and the charging of infrastructure fees
[(q) Part I of the Transport Act 2000].

Designated persons

2. In section 55(3) "designated person" means any of the following—
    (a) the Director;
    (b) the Director General of Telecommunications;
    (c) the Independent Television Commission;
    [(d) the Gas and Electricity Markets Authority;]
    (e) the Director General of Gas for Northern Ireland;
    (f) the Civil Aviation Authority;
    (g) the Director General of Water Services;
    (h) ...
    (i) the Director General of Electricity Supply for Northern Ireland;
    (j) the Rail Regulator;
    [(k) the Strategic Rail Authority;]
    (l) the International Rail Regulator;
    (m) the Authorised Conveyancing Practitioners Board;
    (n) the Scottish Conveyancing and Executry Services Board;
    (o) the Coal Authority;
    (p) the Monopolies and Mergers Commission;
    (q) the Competition Commission;
    [(r) the Financial Services Authority;]
    (s) any Minister of the Crown or any Northern Ireland department.

[226]

NOTES
Commencement: 1 March 2000.

Repealed by the Enterprise Act 2002, ss 247(j), 278(2), Sch 26, as from a day to be appointed.

Para 1: sub-para (h) substituted by the Financial Services and Markets Act 2000 (Consequential Amendments) Order 2002, SI 2002/1555, art 24(1), (2); words in square brackets in sub-para (o) substituted by EC Competition Law (Articles 84 and 85) Enforcement Regulations 2001, SI 2001/2916, reg 35(5); sub-para (q) added by the Transport Act 2000, s 97, Sch 8, Pt IV, para 15.

Para 2: sub-para (d) substituted, sub-para (h) repealed, by virtue of the Utilities Act 2000, s 3(2); sub-para (k) substituted by the Transport Act 2000, s 215, Sch 16, para 57; sub-para (r) substituted by SI 2002/1555, art 24(1), (3).

The Director: see the note to s 47 at **[179]**.

(*Sch 12 (minor and consequential amendments) outside the scope of this work.*)

SCHEDULE 13
Section 74(2)

TRANSITIONAL PROVISIONS AND SAVINGS

PART I
GENERAL

Interpretation

1.—(1) In this Schedule—
    "RPA" means the Resale Prices Act 1976;
    "RTPA" means the Restrictive Trade Practices Act 1976;
    "continuing proceedings" has the meaning given by paragraph 15;
    "the Court" means the Restrictive Practices Court;
    "Director" means the Director General of Fair Trading;
    "document" includes information recorded in any form;
    "enactment date" means the date on which this Act is passed;
    "information" includes estimates and forecasts;

"interim period" means the period beginning on the enactment date and ending immediately before the starting date;

"prescribed" means prescribed by an order made by the Secretary of State;

"regulator" means any person mentioned in paragraphs (a) to (g) of paragraph 1 of Schedule 10 [and the Civil Aviation Authority];

"starting date" means the date on which section 2 comes into force;

"transitional period" means the transitional period provided for in Chapters III and IV of Part IV of this Schedule.

(2)   Sections 30, 44, 51, 53, 55, 56, 57 and 59(3) and (4) and paragraph 12 of Schedule 9 ("the applied provisions") apply for the purposes of this Schedule as they apply for the purposes of Part I of this Act.

(3)   Section 2(5) applies for the purposes of any provisions of this Schedule which are concerned with the operation of the Chapter I prohibition as it applies for the purposes of Part I of this Act.

(4)   In relation to any of the matters in respect of which a regulator may exercise powers as a result of paragraph 35(1), the applied provisions are to have effect as if references to the Director included references to the regulator.

(5)   The fact that to a limited extent the Chapter I prohibition does not apply to an agreement, because a transitional period is provided by virtue of this Schedule, does not require those provisions of the agreement in respect of which there is a transitional period to be disregarded when considering whether the agreement infringes the prohibition for other reasons.

General power to make transitional provision and savings

2.—(1)   Nothing in this Schedule affects the power of the Secretary of State under section 75 to make transitional provisions or savings.

(2)   An order under that section may modify any provision made by this Schedule.

Advice and information

3.—(1)   The Director may publish advice and information explaining provisions of this Schedule to persons who are likely to be affected by them.

(2)   Any advice or information published by the Director under this paragraph is to be published in such form and manner as he considers appropriate.

[227]

NOTES

Commencement: 9 November 1998.

Para 1: in sub-para (1) words in square brackets in definition "regulator" inserted by the Transport Act 2000, s 97, Sch 8, Pt IV, para 16(1), (2).

The Director: see the note to s 47 at **[179]**.

PART II
DURING THE INTERIM PERIOD

Block exemptions

4.—(1)   The Secretary of State may, at any time during the interim period, make one or more orders for the purpose of providing block exemptions which are effective on the starting date.

(2)   An order under this paragraph has effect as if properly made under section 6.

Certain agreements to be non-notifiable agreements

5.   An agreement which—

(a)   is made during the interim period, and

(b)   satisfies the conditions set out in paragraphs (a), (c) and (d) of section 27A(1) of the RTPA,

is to be treated as a non-notifiable agreement for the purposes of RTPA.

6.   In relation to agreements made during the interim period—

    (a)   the Director is no longer under the duty to take proceedings imposed by section 1(2)(c) of the RTPA but may continue to do so;

    (b)   section 21 of that Act has effect as if subsections (1) and (2) were omitted; and

    (c)   section 35(1) of that Act has effect as if the words "or within such further time as the Director may, upon application made within that time, allow" were omitted.

Guidance

7.—(1)   Sub-paragraphs (2) to (4) apply in relation to agreements made during the interim period.

    (2)   An application may be made to the Director in anticipation of the coming into force of section 13 in accordance with directions given by the Director and such an application is to have effect on and after the starting date as if properly made under section 13.

    (3)   The Director may, in response to such an application—

    (a)   give guidance in anticipation of the coming into force of section 2; or

    (b)   on and after the starting date, give guidance under section 15 as if the application had been properly made under section 13.

    (4)   Any guidance so given is to have effect on and after the starting date as if properly given under section 15.

[228]

NOTES

Commencement: 9 November 1998.

The Director: see the note to s 47 at **[179]**.

Orders: the Competition Act 1998 (Director's rules) Order 2000, SI 2000/293 at **[2025]**.

PART III
ON THE STARTING DATE

Applications which fall

8.—(1)   Proceedings in respect of an application which is made to the Court under any of the provisions mentioned in sub-paragraph (2), but which is not determined before the starting date, cease on that date.

    (2)   The provisions are—

    (a)   sections 2(2), 35(3), 37(1) and 40(1) of the RTPA and paragraph 5 of Schedule 4 to that Act;

    (b)   section 4(1) of the RTPA so far as the application relates to an order under section 2(2) of that Act; and

    (c)   section 25(2) of the RPA.

    (3)   The power of the Court to make an order for costs in relation to any proceedings is not affected by anything in this paragraph or by the repeals made by section 1.

Orders and approvals which fall

9.—(1)   An order in force immediately before the starting date under—

    (a)   section 2(2), 29(1), 30(1), 33(4), 35(3) or 37(1) of the RTPA; or

    (b)   section 25(2) of the RPA,

ceases to have effect on that date.

    (2)   An approval in force immediately before the starting date under section 32 of the RTPA ceases to have effect on that date.

[229]

NOTES

Commencement: 1 March 2000.

PART IV
ON AND AFTER THE STARTING DATE

CHAPTER I
GENERAL

Duty of Director to maintain register etc

10.—(1) This paragraph applies even though the relevant provisions of the RTPA are repealed by this Act.

(2)   The Director is to continue on and after the starting date to be under the duty imposed by section 1(2)(a) of the RTPA to maintain a register in respect of agreements—
  (a) particulars of which are, on the starting date, entered or filed on the register;
  (b) which fall within sub-paragraph (4);
  (c) which immediately before the starting date are the subject of proceedings under the RTPA which do not cease on that date by virtue of this Schedule; or
  (d) in relation to which a court gives directions to the Director after the starting date in the course of proceedings in which a question arises as to whether an agreement was, before that date—
      (i) one to which the RTPA applied;
      (ii) subject to registration under that Act;
      (iii) a non-notifiable agreement for the purposes of that Act.

(3)   The Director is to continue on and after the starting date to be under the duties imposed by section 1(2)(a) and (b) of the RTPA of compiling a register of agreements and entering or filing certain particulars in the register, but only in respect of agreements of a kind referred to in paragraph (b), (c) or (d) of sub-paragraph (2).

(4)   An agreement falls within this sub-paragraph if—
  (a) it is subject to registration under the RTPA but—
      (i) is not a non-notifiable agreement within the meaning of section 27A of the RTPA, or
      (ii) is not one to which paragraph 5 applies;
  (b) particulars of the agreement have been provided to the Director before the starting date; and
  (c) as at the starting date no entry or filing has been made in the register in respect of the agreement.

(5)   Sections 23 and 27 of the RTPA are to apply after the starting date in respect of the register subject to such modifications, if any, as may be prescribed.

(6)   In sub-paragraph (2)(d) "court" means—
  (a) the High Court;
  (b) the Court of Appeal;
  (c) the Court of Session;
  (d) the High Court or Court of Appeal in Northern Ireland; or
  (e) the House of Lords.

RTPA section 3 applications

11.—(1) Even though section 3 of the RTPA is repealed by this Act, its provisions (and so far as necessary that Act) are to continue to apply, with such modifications (if any) as may be prescribed—
  (a) in relation to a continuing application under that section; or
  (b) so as to allow an application to be made under that section on or after the starting date in respect of a continuing application under section 1(3) of the RTPA.

(2)   "Continuing application" means an application made, but not determined, before the starting date.

RTPA section 26 applications

12.—(1) Even though section 26 of the RTPA is repealed by this Act, its provisions (and so far as necessary that Act) are to continue to apply, with such modifications (if any) as may be prescribed, in relation to an application which is made under that section, but not determined, before the starting date.

(2)   If an application under section 26 is determined on or after the starting date, this Schedule has effect in relation to the agreement concerned as if the application had been determined immediately before that date.

Right to bring civil proceedings

13.—(1) Even though section 35 of the RTPA is repealed by this Act, its provisions (and so far as necessary that Act) are to continue to apply in respect of a person who, immediately before the starting date, has a right by virtue of section 27ZA or 35(2) of that Act to bring civil proceedings in respect of an agreement (but only so far as that right relates to any period before the starting date or, where there are continuing proceedings, the determination of the proceedings).

(2)   Even though section 25 of the RPA is repealed by this Act, the provisions of that section (and so far as necessary that Act) are to continue to apply in respect of a person who, immediately before the starting date, has a right by virtue of subsection (3) of that section to bring civil proceedings (but only so far as that right relates to any period before the starting date or, where there are continuing proceedings, the determination of the proceedings).

CHAPTER II
CONTINUING PROCEEDINGS

The general rule

14.—(1) The Chapter I prohibition does not apply to an agreement at any time when the agreement is the subject of continuing proceedings under the RTPA.

(2)   The Chapter I prohibition does not apply to an agreement relating to goods which are the subject of continuing proceedings under section 16 or 17 of the RPA to the extent to which the agreement consists of exempt provisions.

(3)   In sub-paragraph (2) "exempt provisions" means those provisions of the agreement which would, disregarding section 14 of the RPA, be—
  (a) void as a result of section 9(1) of the RPA; or
  (b) unlawful as a result of section 9(2) or II of the RPA.

(4)   If the Chapter I prohibition does not apply to an agreement because of this paragraph, the provisions of, or made under, the RTPA or the RPA are to continue to have effect in relation to the agreement.

(5)   The repeals made by section 1 do not affect—
  (a) continuing proceedings; or
  (b) proceedings of the kind referred to in paragraph 11 or 12 of this Schedule which are continuing after the starting date.

Meaning of "continuing proceedings"

15.—(1) For the purposes of this Schedule "continuing proceedings" means proceedings in respect of an application made to the Court under the RTPA or the RPA, but not determined, before the starting date.

(2)   But proceedings under section 3 or 26 of the RTPA to which paragraph 11 or 12 applies are not continuing proceedings.

(3)   The question whether (for the purposes of Part III, or this Part, of this Schedule) an application has been determined is to be decided in accordance with sub-paragraphs (4) and (5).

(4)   If an appeal against the decision on the application is brought, the application is not determined until—
  (a) the appeal is disposed of or withdrawn; or
  (b) if as a result of the appeal the case is referred back to the Court—
      (i) the expiry of the period within which an appeal ("the further appeal") in respect of the Court's decision on that reference could have been brought had this Act not been passed; or
      (ii) if later, the date on which the further appeal is disposed of or withdrawn.

(5)   Otherwise, the application is not determined until the expiry of the period within which any party to the application would have been able to bring an appeal against the decision on the application had this Act not been passed.

RTPA section 4 proceedings

16.   Proceedings on an application for an order under section 4 of the RTPA are also continuing proceedings if—
  (a) leave to make the application is applied for before the starting date but the proceedings in respect of that application for leave are not determined before that date; or
  (b) leave to make an application for an order under that section is granted before the starting date but the application itself is not made before that date.

RPA section 16 or 17 proceedings

17.   Proceedings on an application for an order under section 16 or 17 of the RPA are also continuing proceedings if—
  (a) leave to make the application is applied for before the starting date but the proceedings in respect of that application for leave are not determined before that date; or
  (b) leave to make an application for an order under section 16 or 17 of the RPA is granted before the starting date, but the application itself is not made before that date.

Continuing proceedings which are discontinued

18.—(1) On an application made jointly to the Court by all the parties to any continuing proceedings, the Court must, if it is satisfied that the parties wish it to do so, discontinue the proceedings.

(2)   If, on an application under sub-paragraph (1) or for any other reason, the Court orders the proceedings to be discontinued, this Schedule has effect (subject to paragraphs 21 and 22) from the date on which the proceedings are discontinued as if they had never been instituted.

CHAPTER III
THE TRANSITIONAL PERIOD

The general rule

19.—(1) Except where this Chapter or Chapter IV provides otherwise, there is a transitional period, beginning on the starting date and lasting for one year, for any agreement made before the starting date.

(2)   The Chapter I prohibition does not apply to an agreement to the extent to which there is a transitional period for the agreement.

(3)   The Secretary of State may by regulations provide for sections 13 to 16 and Schedule 5 to apply with such modifications (if any) as may be specified in the regulations, in respect of applications to the Director about agreements for which there is a transitional period.

Cases for which there is no transitional period

20.—(1) There is no transitional period for an agreement to the extent to which, immediately before the starting date, it is—
  (a) void under section 2(1) or 35(1)(a) of the RTPA;
  (b) the subject of an order under section 2(2) or 35(3) of the RTPA; or
  (c) unlawful under section 1, 2 or 11 of the RPA or void under section 9 of that Act.

(2)   There is no transitional period for an agreement to the extent to which, before the starting date, a person has acted unlawfully for the purposes of section 27ZA(2) or (3) of the RTPA in respect of the agreement.

(3)   There is no transitional period for an agreement to which paragraph 25(4) applies.

(4)   There is no transitional period for—
  (a) an agreement in respect of which there are continuing proceedings, or
  (b) an agreement relating to goods in respect of which there are continuing proceedings,

to the extent to which the agreement is, when the proceedings are determined, void or unlawful.

Continuing proceedings under the RTPA

21. In the case of an agreement which is the subject of continuing proceedings under the RTPA, the transitional period begins—
  (a) if the proceedings are discontinued, on the date of discontinuance;
  (b) otherwise, when the proceedings are determined.

Continuing proceedings under the RPA

22.—(1) In the case of an agreement relating to goods which are the subject of continuing proceedings under the RPA, the transitional period for the exempt provisions of the agreement begins—
  (a) if the proceedings are discontinued, on the date of discontinuance;
  (b) otherwise, when the proceedings are determined.

  (2)   In sub-paragraph (1) "exempt provisions" has the meaning given by paragraph 14(3).

Provisions not contrary to public interest

23.—(1) To the extent to which an agreement contains provisions which, immediately before the starting date, are provisions which the Court has found not to be contrary to the public interest, the transitional period lasts for five years.

  (2)   Sub-paragraph (1) is subject to paragraph 20(4).

  (3)   To the extent to which an agreement which on the starting date is the subject of continuing proceedings is, when the proceedings are determined, found by the Court not to be contrary to the public interest, the transitional period lasts for five years.

Goods

24.—(1) In the case of an agreement relating to goods which, immediately before the starting date, are exempt under section 14 of the RPA, there is a transitional period for the agreement to the extent to which it consists of exempt provisions.

  (2)   Sub-paragraph (1) is subject to paragraph 20(4).

  (3)   In the case of an agreement relating to goods—
  (a) which on the starting date are the subject of continuing proceedings, and
  (b) which, when the proceedings are determined, are found to be exempt under section 14 of the RPA,

there is a transitional period for the agreement, to the extent to which it consists of exempt provisions.

  (4)   In each case, the transitional period lasts for five years.

  (5)   In sub-paragraphs (1) and (3) "exempt provisions" means those provisions of the agreement which would, disregarding section 14 of the RPA, be—
  (a) void as a result of section 9(1) of the RPA; or
  (b) unlawful as a result of section 9(2) or 11 of the RPA.

Transitional period for certain agreements

25.—(1) This paragraph applies to agreements—
  (a) which are subject to registration under the RTPA but which—
    (i) are not non-notifiable agreements within the meaning of section 27A of the RTPA, or
    (ii) are not agreements to which paragraph 5 applies; and
  (b) in respect of which the time for furnishing relevant particulars as required by or under the RTPA expires on or after the starting date.

(2)   "Relevant particulars" means—
  (a) particulars which are required to be furnished by virtue of section 24 of the RTPA; or
  (b) particulars of any variation of an agreement which are required to be furnished by virtue of sections 24 and 27 of the RTPA.

(3)   There is a transitional period of one year for an agreement to which this paragraph applies if—
  (a) relevant particulars are furnished before the starting date; and
  (b) no person has acted unlawfully (for the purposes of section 27ZA(2) or (3) of the RTPA) in respect of the agreement.

(4)   If relevant particulars are not furnished by the starting date, section 35(1)(a) of the RTPA does not apply in relation to the agreement (unless sub-paragraph (5) applies).

(5)   This sub-paragraph applies if a person falling within section 27ZA(2) or (3) of the RTPA has acted unlawfully for the purposes of those subsections in respect of the agreement.

Special cases

26.—(1) In the case of an agreement in respect of which—
  (a) a direction under section 127(2) of the Financial Services Act 1986 ("the 1986 Act") is in force immediately before the starting date, or
  (b) a direction under section 194A(3) of the Broadcasting Act 1990 ("the 1990 Act") is in force immediately before the starting date,
the transitional period lasts for five years.

(2)   To the extent to which an agreement is the subject of a declaration—
  (a) made by the Treasury under section 127(3) of the 1986 Act, and
  (b) in force immediately before the starting date,
the transitional period lasts for five years.

(3)   Sub-paragraphs (1) and (2) do not affect the power of—
  (a) the Treasury to make a declaration under section 127(2) of the 1986 Act (as amended by Schedule 2 to this Act),
  (b) the Secretary of State to make a declaration under section 194A of the 1990 Act (as amended by Schedule 2 to this Act),
in respect of an agreement for which there is a transitional period.

CHAPTER IV
THE UTILITIES

General

27. In this Chapter "the relevant period" means the period beginning with the starting date and ending immediately before the fifth anniversary of that date.

Electricity

28.—(1) For an agreement to which, immediately before the starting date, the RTPA does not apply by virtue of a section 100 order, there is a transitional period—
  (a) beginning on the starting date; and
  (b) ending at the end of the relevant period.

(2)   For an agreement which is made at any time after the starting date and to which, had the RTPA not been repealed, that Act would not at the time at which the agreement is made have applied by virtue of a section 100 order, there is a transitional period—
  (a) beginning on the date on which the agreement is made; and
  (b) ending at the end of the relevant period.

(3)   For an agreement (whether made before or after the starting date) which, during the relevant period, is varied at any time in such a way that it becomes an agreement which, had the RTPA not been repealed, would at that time have been one to which that Act did not apply by virtue of a section 100 order, there is a transitional period—
  (a) beginning on the date on which the variation is made; and
  (b) ending at the end of the relevant period.

(4)   If an agreement for which there is a transitional period as a result of sub-paragraph (1), (2) or (3) is varied during the relevant period, the transitional period for the agreement continues if, had the RTPA not been repealed, the agreement would have continued to be one to which that Act did not apply by virtue of a section 100 order.

(5)   But if an agreement for which there is a transitional period as a result of sub-paragraph (1), (2) or (3) ceases to be one to which, had it not been repealed, the RTPA would not have applied by virtue of a section 100 order, the transitional period ends on the date on which the agreement so ceases.

(6)   Sub-paragraph (3) is subject to paragraph 20.

(7)   In this paragraph and paragraph 29—
   "section 100 order" means an order made under section 100 of the Electricity Act 1989; and
   expressions which are also used in Part I of the Electricity Act 1989 have the same meaning as in that Part.

Electricity: power to make transitional orders

29.—(1) There is a transitional period for an agreement (whether made before or after the starting date) relating to the generation, transmission or supply of electricity which—
   (a)   is specified, or is of a description specified, in an order ("a transitional order") made by the Secretary of State (whether before or after the making of the agreement but before the end of the relevant period); and
   (b)   satisfies such conditions as may be specified in the order.

(2)   A transitional order may make provision as to when the transitional period in respect of such an agreement is to start or to be deemed to have started.

(3)   The transitional period for such an agreement ends at the end of the relevant period.

(4)   But if the agreement—
   (a)   ceases to be one to which a transitional order applies, or
   (b)   ceases to satisfy one or more of the conditions specified in the transitional order,
the transitional period ends on the date on which the agreement so ceases.

(5)   Before making a transitional order, the Secretary of State must consult [the Gas and Electricity Markets Authority].

(6)   The conditions specified in a transitional order may include conditions which refer any matter to the Secretary of State for determination after such consultation as may be so specified.

(7)   In the application of this paragraph to Northern Ireland, the reference in sub-paragraph (5) to [the Gas and Electricity Markets Authority] is to be read as a reference to the Director General of Electricity Supply for Northern Ireland.

Gas

30.—(1) For an agreement to which, immediately before the starting date, the RTPA does not apply by virtue of section 62 or a section 62 order, there is a transitional period—
   (a)   beginning on the starting date; and
   (b)   ending at the end of the relevant period.

(2)   For an agreement which is made at any time after the starting date and to which, had the RTPA not been repealed, that Act would not at the time at which the agreement is made have applied by virtue of section 62 or a section 62 order, there is a transitional period—
   (a)   beginning on the date on which the agreement is made; and
   (b)   ending at the end of the relevant period.

(3)   For an agreement (whether made before or after the starting date) which, during the relevant period, is varied at any time in such a way that it becomes an agreement which, had the RTPA not been repealed, would at that time have been one to which that Act did not apply by virtue of section 62 or a section 62 order, there is a transitional period—
   (a)   beginning on the date on which the variation is made; and
   (b)   ending at the end of the relevant period.

(4)   If an agreement for which there is a transitional period as a result of sub-paragraph (1), (2) or (3) is varied during the relevant period, the transitional period for the agreement continues if, had the RTPA not been repealed, the agreement would have continued to be one to which that Act did not apply by virtue of section 62 or a section 62 order.

(5)   But if an agreement for which there is a transitional period as a result of sub-paragraph (1), (2) or (3) ceases to be one to which, had it not been repealed, the RTPA would not have applied by virtue of section 62 or a section 62 order, the transitional period ends on the date on which the agreement so ceases.

(6)   Sub-paragraph (3) also applies in relation to a modification which is treated as an agreement made on or after 28th November 1985 by virtue of section 62(4).

(7)   Sub-paragraph (3) is subject to paragraph 20.

(8)   In this paragraph and paragraph 31—
"section 62" means section 62 of the Gas Act 1986;
"section 62 order" means an order made under section 62.

Gas: power to make transitional orders

31.—(1) There is a transitional period for an agreement of a description falling within section 62(2)(a) and (b) or section 62(2A)(a) and (b) which—
  (a) is specified, or is of a description specified, in an order ("a transitional order") made by the Secretary of State (whether before or after the making of the agreement but before the end of the relevant period); and
  (b) satisfies such conditions as may be specified in the order.

(2)   A transitional order may make provision as to when the transitional period in respect of such an agreement is to start or to be deemed to have started.

(3)   The transitional period for such an agreement ends at the end of the relevant period.

(4)   But if the agreement—
  (a) ceases to be one to which a transitional order applies, or
  (b) ceases to satisfy one or more of the conditions specified in the transitional order,
the transitional period ends on the date when the agreement so ceases.

(5)   Before making a transitional order, the Secretary of State must consult [the Gas and Electricity Markets Authority] and the Director.

(6)   The conditions specified in a transitional order may include—
  (a) conditions which are to be satisfied in relation to a time before the coming into force of this paragraph;
  (b) conditions which refer any matter (which may be the general question whether the Chapter I prohibition should apply to a particular agreement) to the Secretary of State, the Director or [the Gas and Electricity Markets Authority] for determination after such consultation as may be so specified.

Gas: Northern Ireland

32.—(1) For an agreement to which, immediately before the starting date, the RTPA does not apply by virtue of an Article 41 order, there is a transitional period—
  (a) beginning on the starting date; and
  (b) ending at the end of the relevant period.

(2)   For an agreement which is made at any time after the starting date and to which, had the RTPA not been repealed, that Act would not at the time at which the agreement is made have applied by virtue of an Article 41 order, there is a transitional period—
  (a) beginning on the date on which the agreement is made; and
  (b) ending at the end of the relevant period.

(3)   For an agreement (whether made before or after the starting date) which, during the relevant period, is varied at any time in such a way that it becomes an agreement which, had the RTPA not been repealed, would at that time have been one to which that Act did not apply by virtue of an Article 41 order, there is a transitional period—
  (a) beginning on the date on which the variation is made; and
  (b) ending at the end of the relevant period.

(4)   If an agreement for which there is a transitional period as a result of sub-paragraph (1), (2) or (3) is varied during the relevant period, the transitional period for the agreement continues if, had the RTPA not been repealed, the agreement would have continued to be one to which that Act did not apply by virtue of an Article 41 order.

(5)   But if an agreement for which there is a transitional period as a result of sub-paragraph (1), (2) or (3) ceases to be one to which, had it not been repealed, the RTPA would not have applied by virtue of an Article 41 order, the transitional period ends on the date on which the agreement so ceases.

(6)   Sub-paragraph (3) is subject to paragraph 20.

(7)   In this paragraph and paragraph 33—
    "Article 41 order" means an order under Article 41 of the Gas (Northern Ireland) Order 1996;
    "Department" means the Department of Economic Development.

Gas: Northern Ireland—power to make transitional orders

33.—(1) There is a transitional period for an agreement of a description falling within Article 41(1) which—
    (a) is specified, or is of a description specified, in an order ("a transitional order") made by the Department (whether before or after the making of the agreement but before the end of the relevant period); and
    (b) satisfies such conditions as may be specified in the order.

(2)   A transitional order may make provision as to when the transitional period in respect of such an agreement is to start or to be deemed to have started.

(3)   The transitional period for such an agreement ends at the end of the relevant period.

(4)   But if the agreement—
    (a) ceases to be one to which a transitional order applies, or
    (b) ceases to satisfy one or more of the conditions specified in the transitional order,
the transitional period ends on the date when the agreement so ceases.

(5)   Before making a transitional order, the Department must consult the Director General of Gas for Northern Ireland and the Director.

(6)   The conditions specified in a transitional order may include conditions which refer any matter (which may be the general question whether the Chapter I prohibition should apply to a particular agreement) to the Department for determination after such consultation as may be so specified.

Railways

34.—(1) In this paragraph—
    "section 131" means section 131 of the Railways Act 1993 ("the 1993 Act");
    "section 131 agreement" means an agreement—
        (a) to which the RTPA does not apply immediately before the starting date by virtue of section 131(1); or
        (b) in respect of which a direction under section 131(3) is in force immediately before that date;
    "non-exempt agreement" means an agreement relating to the provision of railway services (whether made before or after the starting date) which is not a section 131 agreement; and
    "railway services" has the meaning given by section 82 of the 1993 Act.

(2)   For a section 131 agreement there is a transitional period of five years.

(3)   There is a transitional period for a non-exempt agreement to the extent to which the agreement is at any time before the end of the relevant period required or approved—
    (a) by the Secretary of State or the Rail Regulator in pursuance of any function assigned or transferred to him under or by virtue of any provision of the 1993 Act;
    (b) by or under any agreement the making of which is required or approved by the Secretary of State or the Rail Regulator in the exercise of any such function; or
    (c) by or under a licence granted under Part I of the 1993 Act.

(4)   The transitional period conferred by sub-paragraph (3)—
    (a) is to be taken to have begun on the starting date; and
    (b) ends at the end of the relevant period.

(5)   Sub-paragraph (3) is subject to paragraph 20.

(6)   Any variation of a section 131 agreement on or after the starting date is to be treated, for the purposes of this paragraph, as a separate non-exempt agreement.

The regulators

35.—(1) Subject to sub-paragraph (3), each of the regulators may exercise, in respect of sectoral matters and concurrently with the Director, the functions of the Director under paragraph 3, 7, 19(3), 36, 37, 38 or 39.

(2)   In sub-paragraph (1) "sectoral matters" means—
     (a) in the case of the Director General of Telecommunications, the matters referred to in section 50(3) of the Telecommunications Act 1984;
     (b) in the case of [the Gas and Electricity Markets Authority], the matters referred to in section 36A(3) and (4) of the Gas Act 1986;
     (c) in the case of [the Gas and Electricity Markets Authority], the matters referred to in section 43(3) of the Electricity Act 1989;
     (d) in the case of the Director General of Electricity Supply for Northern Ireland, the matters referred to in Article 46(3) of the Electricity (Northern Ireland) Order 1992;
     (e) in the case of the Director General of Water Services, the matters referred to in section 31(3) of the Water Industry Act 1991;
     (f) in the case of the Rail Regulator, the matters referred to in section 67(3) of the Railways Act 1993;
     (g) in the case of the Director General of Gas for Northern Ireland, the matters referred to in Article 23(3) of the Gas (Northern Ireland) Order 1996.
     [(h) in the case of the Civil Aviation Authority, the supply of air traffic services within the meaning given by section 98 of the Transport Act 2000.]

(3)   The power to give directions in paragraph 7(2) is exercisable by the Director only but if the Director is preparing directions which relate to a matter in respect of which a regulator exercises concurrent jurisdiction, he must consult that regulator.

(4)   Consultations conducted by the Director before the enactment date, with a view to preparing directions which have effect on or after that date, are to be taken to satisfy sub-paragraph (3).

(5)   References to enactments in sub-paragraph (2) are to the enactments as amended by or under this Act.

CHAPTER V
EXTENDING THE TRANSITIONAL PERIOD

36.—(1) A party to an agreement for which there is a transitional period may apply to the Director, not less than three months before the end of the period, for the period to be extended.

(2)   The Director may (on his own initiative or on an application under sub-paragraph (1))—
     (a) extend a one-year transitional period by not more than twelve months;
     (b) extend a transitional period of any period other than one year by not more than six months.

(3)   An application under sub-paragraph (1) must—
     (a) be in such form as may be specified; and
     (b) include such documents and information as may be specified.

(4)   If the Director extends the transitional period under this paragraph, he must give notice in such form, and to such persons, as may be specified.

(5)   The Director may not extend a transitional period more than once.

(6)   In this paragraph—
    "person" has the same meaning as in Part I; and
    "specified" means specified in rules made by the Director under section 51.

CHAPTER VI
TERMINATING THE TRANSITIONAL PERIOD

General

37.—(1) Subject to sub-paragraph (2), the Director may by a direction in writing terminate the transitional period for an agreement, but only in accordance with paragraph 38.

(2)   The Director may not terminate the transitional period, nor exercise any of the powers in paragraph 38, in respect of an agreement which is excluded from the Chapter I prohibition by virtue of any of the provisions of Part I of this Act other than paragraph 1 of Schedule 1 or paragraph 2 or 9 of Schedule 3 [or the Competition Act 1998 (Land and Vertical Agreements Exclusion) Order 2000].

Circumstances in which the Director may terminate the transitional period

38.—(1) If the Director is considering whether to give a direction under paragraph 37 ("a direction"), he may in writing require any party to the agreement concerned to give him such information in connection with that agreement as he may require.

(2)   If at the end of such period as may be specified in rules made under section 51, a person has failed, without reasonable excuse, to comply with a requirement imposed under sub-paragraph (1), the Director may give a direction.

(3)   The Director may also give a direction if he considers—
    (a) that the agreement would, but for the transitional period or a relevant exclusion, infringe the Chapter I prohibition; and
    (b) that he would not be likely to grant the agreement an unconditional individual exemption.

(4)   For the purposes of sub-paragraph (3) an individual exemption is unconditional if no conditions or obligations are imposed in respect of it under section 4(3)(a).

(5)   In this paragraph—
    "person" has the same meaning as in Part I;
    "relevant exclusion" means an exclusion under paragraph 1 of Schedule 1 or paragraph 2 or 9 of Schedule 3 [or the Competition Act 1998 (Land and Vertical Agreements Exclusion) Order 2000].

Procedural requirements on giving a paragraph 37 direction

39.—(1) The Director must specify in a direction under paragraph 37 ("a direction") the date on which it is to have effect (which must not be less than 28 days after the direction is given).

(2)   Copies of the direction must be given to—
    (a) each of the parties concerned, and
    (b) the Secretary of State,
not less than 28 days before the date on which the direction is to have effect.

(3)   In relation to an agreement to which a direction applies, the transitional period (if it has not already ended) ends on the date specified in the direction unless, before that date, the direction is revoked by the Director or the Secretary of State.

(4)   If a direction is revoked, the Director may give a further direction in respect of the same agreement only if he is satisfied that there has been a material change of circumstance since the revocation.

(5)   If, as a result of paragraph 24(1) or (3), there is a transitional period in respect of provisions of an agreement relating to goods—
    (a) which immediately before the starting date are exempt under section 14 of the RPA, or
    (b) which, when continuing proceedings are determined, are found to be exempt under section 14 of the RPA,
the period is not affected by paragraph 37 or 38.

[230]

NOTES

Commencement: 9 November 1998 (para 35); 11 January 1999 (paras 10(5), 19(3), paras 11, 12(1), certain purposes); 1 March 2000 (paras 10(1)–(4), (6), 12(2), 13–18, 19(1), (2), 20–34, 36–39, para 12(1) remaining purposes); to be appointed (remainder).

Para 29: words in square brackets in sub-paras (5), (7) substituted by virtue of the Utilities Act 2000, s 3(2).

Para 31: words in square brackets in sub-paras (5), (6)(b) substituted by virtue of the Utilities Act 2000, s 3(2).

Para 35: words in square brackets in sub-para (2)(b), (c) substituted by virtue of the Utilities Act 2000, s 3(2)(2); sub-para (2)(h) added by the Transport Act 2000, s 97, Sch 8, Pt IV, para 16(1), (3).

Para 37: words in square brackets in sub-para (2) added by the Competition Act 1998 (Transitional, Consequential and Supplemental Provisions) Order 2000, SI 2000/311, art 2.

Para 38: words in square brackets in sub-para (5) inserted by the Competition Act 1998 (Consequential and Supplemental Provisions) Order 2000, SI 2000/2031, art 2.

The Director: see the note to s 47 at **[179]**.

Financial Services Act 1986, s 127: repealed.

Orders: the Competition Act 1998 (Director's rules) Order 2000, SI 2000/293 at **[2025]**.

Regulations: the Competition Act 1998 (Notification of Excluded Agreements and Appealable Decisions) Regulations 2000, SI 2000/263 at **[2015]**.

PART V
THE FAIR TRADING ACT 1973

References to the Monopolies and Mergers Commission

40.—(1) If, on the date on which the repeal by this Act of a provision mentioned in sub-paragraph (2) comes into force, the Monopolies and Mergers Commission has not completed a reference which was made to it before that date, continued consideration of the reference may include consideration of a question which could not have been considered if the provision had not been repealed.

(2) The provisions are—
  (a) sections 10(2), 54(5) and 78(3) and paragraph 3(1) and (2) of Schedule 8 to the Fair Trading Act 1973 (c 41);
  (b) section 11(8)(b) of the Competition Act 1980 (c 21);
  (c) section 14(2) of the Telecommunications Act 1984 (c 12);
  (d) section 45(3) of the Airports Act 1986 (c 31);
  (e) section 25(2) of the Gas Act 1986 (c 44);
  (f) section 13(2) of the Electricity Act 1989 (c 29);
  (g) section 15(2) of the Water Industry Act 1991 (c 56);
  (h) article 16(2) of the Electricity (Northern Ireland) Order 1992;
  (i) section 14(2) of the Railways Act 1993 (c 43);
  (j) article 36(3) of the Airports (Northern Ireland) Order 1994;
  (k) article 16(2) of the Gas (Northern Ireland) Order 1996.

Orders under Schedule 8

41.—(1) In this paragraph—
  "the 1973 Act" means the Fair Trading Act 1973;
  "agreement" means an agreement entered into before the date on which the repeal of the limiting provisions comes into force;
  "the order" means an order under section 56 or 73 of the 1973 Act;
  "the limiting provisions" means sub-paragraph (1) or (2) of paragraph 3 of Schedule 8 to the 1973 Act (limit on power to make orders under paragraph 1 or 2 of that Schedule) and includes any provision of the order included because of either of those sub-paragraphs; and
  "transitional period" means the period which—
    (a) begins on the day on which the repeal of the limiting provisions comes into force; and
    (b) ends on the first anniversary of the starting date.

(2) Sub-paragraph (3) applies to any agreement to the extent to which it would have been unlawful (in accordance with the provisions of the order) but for the limiting provisions.

(3) As from the end of the transitional period, the order is to have effect in relation to the agreement as if the limiting provisions had never had effect.

Part III of the Act

42.—(1) The repeals made by section 1 do not affect any proceedings in respect of an application which is made to the Court under Part III of the Fair Trading Act 1973, but is not determined, before the starting date.

(2) The question whether (for the purposes of sub-paragraph (1)) an application has been determined is to be decided in accordance with sub-paragraphs (3) and (4).

(3)   If an appeal against the decision on the application is brought, the application is not determined until—

(a) the appeal is disposed of or withdrawn; or

(b) if as a result of the appeal the case is referred back to the Court—

(i) the expiry of the period within which an appeal ("the further appeal") in respect of the Court's decision on that reference could have been brought had this Act not been passed; or

(ii) if later, the date on which the further appeal is disposed of or withdrawn.

(4)   Otherwise, the application is not determined until the expiry of the period within which any party to the application would have been able to bring an appeal against the decision on the application had this Act not been passed.

(5)   Any amendment made by Schedule 12 to this Act which substitutes references to a relevant Court for references to the Court is not to affect proceedings of the kind referred to in sub-paragraph (1).

[231]

NOTES

Commencement: 10 November 1999 (paras 40, 41); 1 March 2000 (para 42).

Monopolies and Mergers Commission: the Monopolies and Mergers Commission was dissolved by s 45(3) of this Act at **[184]**, which also transferred the functions of the Monopolies and Mergers Commission to the Competition Commission.

PART VI
THE COMPETITION ACT 1980

Undertakings

43.—(1) Subject to sub-paragraph (2), an undertaking accepted by the Director under section 4 or 9 of the Competition Act 1980 ceases to have effect on the coming into force of the repeal by this Act of that section.

(2)   If the undertaking relates to an agreement which on the starting date is the subject of continuing proceedings, the undertaking continues to have effect for the purposes of section 29 of the Competition Act 1980 until the proceedings are determined.

Application of sections 25 and 26

44. The repeals made by section 1 do not affect—

(a) the operation of section 25 of the Competition Act 1980 in relation to an application under section 1(3) of the RTPA which is made before the starting date;

(b) an application under section 26 of the Competition Act 1980 which is made before the starting date.

[232]

NOTES

Commencement: 1 March 2000.

The Director: see the note to s 47 at **[179]**.

PART VII
MISCELLANEOUS

Disclosure of information

45.—(1) Section 55 of this Act applies in relation to information which, immediately before the starting date, is subject to section 41 of the RTPA as it applies in relation to information obtained under or as a result of Part I.

(2)   But section 55 does not apply to any disclosure of information of the kind referred to in sub-paragraph (1) if the disclosure is made—

(a) for the purpose of facilitating the performance of functions of a designated person under the Control of Misleading Advertisements Regulations 1988; or

(b) for the purposes of any proceedings before the Court or of any other legal proceedings under the RTPA or the Fair Trading Act 1973 or the Control of Misleading Advertisements Regulations 1988.

(3)   Section 56 applies in relation to information of the kind referred to in sub-paragraph (1) if particulars containing the information have been entered or filed on the special section of the register maintained by the Director under, or as a result of, section 27 of the RTPA or paragraph 10 of this Schedule.

(4)   Section 55 has effect, in relation to the matters as to which section 41(2) of the RTPA had effect, as if it contained a provision similar to section 41(2).

The Court

46.   If it appears to the Lord Chancellor that a person who ceases to be a non-judicial member of the Court as a result of this Act should receive compensation for loss of office, he may pay to him out of moneys provided by Parliament such sum as he may with the approval of the Treasury determine.

[233]

NOTES

Commencement: 1 March 2000.
The Director: see the note to s 47 at **[179]**.

(Sch 14 contains repeals and revocations.)

FINANCIAL SERVICES AND MARKETS ACT 2000

(2000 c 8)

ARRANGEMENT OF SECTIONS

An Act to make provision about the regulation of financial services and markets; to provide for the transfer of certain statutory functions relating to building societies, friendly societies, industrial and provident societies and certain other mutual societies; and for connected purposes

[14 June 2000]

NOTES

Only the provisions of this Act relevant to Competition law are reproduced here.

Substitution of references to the Director General of Fair Trading: the Enterprise Act 2002, s 2(1), at **[255]**, provides that, as from the coming into force of that section in accordance with s 279 at **[463]**, the functions of the Director General of Fair Trading, his property, rights and liabilities are transferred to the Office of Fair Trading. Accordingly, (by virtue of s 2(2), (3) of the 2002 Act) the office of the Director is abolished, and amendments are made to this Act by the 2002 Act to take account of this (see Sch 25, para 40). Consequently, throughout the provisions of this Act reproduced here, unless noted otherwise, for the words "Director", "Director's", "he", "him" and "his" in italics, there are substituted the words "OFT", "OFT's", "the OFT", "it" and "its" respectively.

PART VI
OFFICIAL LISTING

Competition

95 Competition scrutiny

(1) The Treasury may by order provide for—
    (a) regulating provisions, and
    (b) the practices of the competent authority in exercising its functions under this Part ("practices"),
to be kept under review.

(2) Provision made as a result of subsection (1) must require the person responsible for keeping regulating provisions and practices under review to consider—
    (a) whether any regulating provision or practice has a significantly adverse effect on competition; or
    (b) whether two or more regulating provisions or practices taken together have, or a particular combination of regulating provisions and practices has, such an effect.

(3)   An order under this section may include provision corresponding to that made by any provision of Chapter III of Part X.

(4)   Subsection (3) is not to be read as in any way restricting the power conferred by subsection (1).

(5)   Subsections (6) to (8) apply for the purposes of provision made by or under this section.

(6)   Regulating provisions or practices have a significantly adverse effect on competition if—
   (a) they have, or are intended or likely to have, that effect; or
   (b) the effect that they have, or are intended or likely to have, is to require or encourage behaviour which has, or is intended or likely to have, a significantly adverse effect on competition.

(7)   If regulating provisions or practices have, or are intended or likely to have, the effect of requiring or encouraging exploitation of the strength of a market position they are to be taken to have, or be intended or be likely to have, an adverse effect on competition.

(8)   In determining whether any of the regulating provisions or practices have, or are intended or likely to have, a particular effect, it may be assumed that the persons to whom the provisions concerned are addressed will act in accordance with them.

(9)   "Regulating provisions" means—
   (a) listing rules,
   (b) general guidance given by the competent authority in connection with its functions under this Part.

                                                                      [233A]

NOTES
   Commencement: 1 December 2001.

PART X
RULES AND GUIDANCE

CHAPTER III
COMPETITION SCRUTINY

159 Interpretation

(1) In this Chapter—
   "Director" means the Director General of Fair Trading;
   "practices", in relation to the Authority, means practices adopted by the Authority in the exercise of functions under this Act;
   "regulating provisions" means any—
      (a) rules;
      (b) general guidance (as defined by section 158(5));
      (c) statement issued by the Authority under section 64;
      (d) code issued by the Authority under section 64 or 119.

(2) For the purposes of this Chapter, regulating provisions or practices have a significantly adverse effect on competition if—
   (a) they have, or are intended or likely to have, that effect; or
   (b) the effect that they have, or are intended or likely to have, is to require or encourage behaviour which has, or is intended or likely to have, a significantly adverse effect on competition.

(3) If regulating provisions or practices have, or are intended or likely to have, the effect of requiring or encouraging exploitation of the strength of a market position they are to be taken, for the purposes of this Chapter, to have an adverse effect on competition.

(4) In determining under this Chapter whether any of the regulating provisions have, or are likely to have, a particular effect, it may be assumed that the persons to whom the provisions concerned are addressed will act in accordance with them.

[234]

NOTES

Commencement: 18 June 2001.

Sub-s (1): for the definition in italics there is substituted the definition ""OFT" means the Office of Fair Trading" by the Enterprise Act 2002, s 278(1), Sch 25, para 40(1), (2), as from a day to be appointed.

160 Reports by *Director General of Fair Trading*

(1) The *Director* must keep the regulating provisions and the Authority's practices under review.

(2) If at any time the *Director* considers that—
  (a) a regulating provision or practice has a significantly adverse effect on competition, or
  (b) two or more regulating provisions or practices taken together, or a particular combination of regulating provisions and practices, have such an effect,

he must make a report to that effect.

(3) If at any time the *Director* considers that—
  (a) a regulating provision or practice does not have a significantly adverse effect on competition, or
  (b) two or more regulating provisions or practices taken together, or a particular combination of regulating provisions and practices, do not have any such effect,

he may make a report to that effect.

(4) A report under subsection (2) must include details of the adverse effect on competition.

(5) If the *Director* makes a report under subsection (2) *he* must—
  (a) send a copy of it to the Treasury, the Competition Commission and the Authority; and
  (b) publish it in the way appearing to *him* to be best calculated to bring it to the attention of the public.

(6) If the *Director* makes a report under subsection (3)—
  (a) *he* must send a copy of it to the Treasury, the Competition Commission and the Authority; and
  (b) *he* may publish it.

(7) Before publishing a report under this section the *Director* must, so far as practicable, exclude any matter which relates to the private affairs of a particular individual the publication of which, in the opinion of the *Director*, would or might seriously and prejudicially affect his interests.

(8) Before publishing such a report the *Director* must, so far as practicable, exclude any matter which relates to the affairs of a particular body the publication of which, in the opinion of the *Director*, would or might seriously and prejudicially affect its interests.

(9) Subsections (7) and (8) do not apply in relation to copies of a report which the *Director* is required to send under subsection (5)(a) or (6)(a).

(10) For the purposes of the law of defamation, absolute privilege attaches to any report of the *Director* under this section.

[235]

NOTES

Commencement: 18 June 2001.

Section heading: for the words in italics there are substituted the word "OFT" by the Enterprise Act 2002, s 278(1), Sch 25, para 40(1), (3)(b), as from a day to be appointed.

Director: as to the abolition of the office of the Director General of Fair Trading and the substitution of references to the Director and related expressions, see the note preceding s 95 at [233A].

161 Power of *Director* to request information

(1) For the purpose of investigating any matter with a view to its consideration under section 160, the *Director* may exercise the powers conferred on *him* by this section.

(2) The *Director* may by notice in writing require any person to produce to *him* or to a person appointed by *him* for the purpose, at a time and place specified in the notice, any document which—
(a) is specified or described in the notice; and
(b) is a document in that person's custody or under his control.

(3) The *Director* may by notice in writing—
(a) require any person carrying on any business to provide *him* with such information as may be specified or described in the notice; and
(b) specify the time within which, and the manner and form in which, any such information is to be provided.

(4) A requirement may be imposed under subsection (2) or (3)(a) only in respect of documents or information which relate to any matter relevant to the investigation.

(5) If a person ("the defaulter") refuses, or otherwise fails, to comply with a notice under this section, the *Director* may certify that fact in writing to the court and the court may enquire into the case.

(6) If, after hearing any witness who may be produced against or on behalf of the defaulter and any statement which may be offered in defence, the court is satisfied that the defaulter did not have a reasonable excuse for refusing or otherwise failing to comply with the notice, the court may deal with the defaulter as if he were in contempt.

(7) "Court" means—
(a) the High Court; or
(b) in relation to Scotland, the Court of Session.

[236]

NOTES

Commencement: 18 June 2001.

Director: as to the abolition of the office of the Director General of Fair Trading and the substitution of references to the Director and related expressions, see the note preceding s 95 at [233A].

162 Consideration by Competition Commission

(1) If the *Director*—
(a) makes a report under section 160(2), or
(b) asks the Commission to consider a report that *he* has made under section 160(3),
the Commission must investigate the matter.

(2) The Commission must then make its own report on the matter unless it considers that, as a result of a change of circumstances, no useful purpose would be served by a report.

(3) If the Commission decides in accordance with subsection (2) not to make a report, it must make a statement setting out the change of circumstances which resulted in that decision.

(4) A report made under this section must state the Commission's conclusion as to whether—

    (a) the regulating provision or practice which is the subject of the report has a significantly adverse effect on competition; or

    (b) the regulating provisions or practices, or combination of regulating provisions and practices, which are the subject of the report have such an effect.

(5) A report under this section stating the Commission's conclusion that there is a significantly adverse effect on competition must also—

    (a) state whether the Commission considers that that effect is justified; and

    (b) if it states that the Commission considers that it is not justified, state its conclusion as to what action, if any, ought to be taken by the Authority.

(6) Subsection (7) applies whenever the Commission is considering, for the purposes of this section, whether a particular adverse effect on competition is justified.

(7) The Commission must ensure, so far as that is reasonably possible, that the conclusion it reaches is compatible with the functions conferred, and obligations imposed, on the Authority by or under this Act.

(8) A report under this section must contain such an account of the Commission's reasons for its conclusions as is expedient, in the opinion of the Commission, for facilitating proper understanding of them.

(9) Schedule 14 supplements this section.

(10) If the Commission makes a report under this section it must send a copy to the Treasury, the Authority and the *Director*.

[237]

NOTES

Commencement: 18 June 2001.

Director: as to the abolition of the office of the Director General of Fair Trading and the substitution of references to the Director and related expressions, see the note preceding s 95 at **[233A]**.

163 Role of the Treasury

(1) This section applies if the Competition Commission makes a report under section 162(2) which states its conclusion that there is a significantly adverse effect on competition.

(2) If the Commission's conclusion, as stated in the report, is that the adverse effect on competition is not justified, the Treasury must give a direction to the Authority requiring it to take such action as may be specified in the direction.

(3) But subsection (2) does not apply if the Treasury consider—

    (a) that, as a result of action taken by the Authority in response to the Commission's report, it is unnecessary for them to give a direction; or

    (b) that the exceptional circumstances of the case make it inappropriate or unnecessary for them to do so.

(4) In considering the action to be specified in a direction under subsection (2), the Treasury must have regard to any conclusion of the Commission included in the report because of section 162(5)(b).

(5) Subsection (6) applies if—
  (a) the Commission's conclusion, as stated in its report, is that the adverse effect on competition is justified; but
  (b) the Treasury consider that the exceptional circumstances of the case require them to act.

(6) The Treasury may give a direction to the Authority requiring it to take such action—
  (a) as they consider to be necessary in the light of the exceptional circumstances of the case; and
  (b) as may be specified in the direction.

(7) The Authority may not be required as a result of this section to take any action—
  (a) that it would not have power to take in the absence of a direction under this section; or
  (b) that would otherwise be incompatible with any of the functions conferred, or obligations imposed, on it by or under this Act.

(8) Subsection (9) applies if the Treasury are considering—
  (a) whether subsection (2) applies and, if so, what action is to be specified in a direction under that subsection; or
  (b) whether to give a direction under subsection (6).

(9) The Treasury must—
  (a) do what they consider appropriate to allow the Authority, and any other person appearing to the Treasury to be affected, an opportunity to make representations; and
  (b) have regard to any such representations.

(10) If, in reliance on subsection (3)(a) or (b), the Treasury decline to act under subsection (2), they must make a statement to that effect, giving their reasons.

(11) If the Treasury give a direction under this section they must make a statement giving—
  (a) details of the direction; and
  (b) if the direction is given under subsection (6), their reasons for giving it.

(12) The Treasury must—
  (a) publish any statement made under this section in the way appearing to them best calculated to bring it to the attention of the public; and
  (b) lay a copy of it before Parliament.

[238]

NOTES

Commencement: 18 June 2001.

164 The Competition Act 1998

(1) The Chapter I prohibition does not apply to an agreement the parties to which consist of or include—
  (a) an authorised person, or
  (b) a person who is otherwise subject to the Authority's regulating provisions,

to the extent to which the agreement consists of provisions the inclusion of which in the agreement is encouraged by any of the Authority's regulating provisions.

(2) The Chapter I prohibition does not apply to the practices of an authorised person or a person who is otherwise subject to the regulating provisions to the extent to which the practices are encouraged by any of the Authority's regulating provisions.

(3) The Chapter II prohibition does not apply to conduct of—
    (a) an authorised person, or
    (b) a person who is otherwise subject to the Authority's regulating provisions,
to the extent to which the conduct is encouraged by any of the Authority's regulating provisions.

(4) "The Chapter I prohibition" means the prohibition imposed by section 2(1) of the Competition Act 1998.

(5) "The Chapter II prohibition" means the prohibition imposed by section 18(1) of that Act.

[239]

NOTES

Commencement: 18 June 2001.

PART XVIII
RECOGNISED INVESTMENT EXCHANGES AND CLEARING HOUSES

CHAPTER II
COMPETITION SCRUTINY

302 Interpretation

(1) In this Chapter and Chapter III—
    "practices" means—
        (a) in relation to a recognised investment exchange, the practices of the exchange in its capacity as such; and
        (b) in relation to a recognised clearing house, the practices of the clearing house in respect of its clearing arrangements;
    "regulatory provisions" means—
        (a) the rules of an investment exchange or a clearing house;
        (b) any guidance issued by an investment exchange or clearing house;
        (c) in the case of an investment exchange, the arrangements and criteria mentioned in section 287(3);
        (d) in the case of a clearing house, the arrangements and criteria mentioned in section 288(3).

(2) For the purposes of this Chapter, regulatory provisions or practices have a significantly adverse effect on competition if—
    (a) they have, or are intended or likely to have, that effect; or
    (b) the effect that they have, or are intended or likely to have, is to require or encourage behaviour which has, or is intended or likely to have, a significantly adverse effect on competition.

(3) If regulatory provisions or practices have, or are intended or likely to have, the effect of requiring or encouraging exploitation of the strength of a market position they are to be taken, for the purposes of this Chapter, to have an adverse effect on competition.

(4) In determining under this Chapter whether any regulatory provisions have, or are intended or likely to have, a particular effect, it may be assumed that persons to whom the provisions concerned are addressed will act in accordance with them.

[240]

NOTES

Commencement: 3 September 2001.

Role of Director General of Fair Trading

303 Initial report by *Director*

(1) The Authority must send to the Treasury and to the *Director* a copy of any regulatory provisions with which it is provided on an application for recognition under section 287 or 288.

(2) The Authority must send to the *Director* such information in its possession as a result of the application for recognition as it considers will assist *him* in discharging *his* functions in connection with the application.

(3) The *Director* must issue a report as to whether—

(a) a regulatory provision of which a copy has been sent to *him* under subsection (1) has a significantly adverse effect on competition; or

(b) a combination of regulatory provisions so copied to *him* have such an effect.

(4) If the *Director's* conclusion is that one or more provisions have a significantly adverse effect on competition, *he* must state *his* reasons for that conclusion.

(5) When the *Director* issues a report under subsection (3), *he* must send a copy of it to the Authority, the Competition Commission and the Treasury.

[241]

NOTES

Commencement: 3 September 2001.

In the cross-heading preceding this section, for the words "Director General of Fair Trading" there are substituted the words "Office of Fair Trading" by the Enterprise Act 2002, s 278(1), Sch 25, para 40(1), (10), as from a day to be appointed.

Sub-s (2): for the second word in italics there is substituted the words "the OFT" by the Enterprise Act 2002, s 278(1), Sch 25, para 40(1), (10)(b), as from a day to be appointed.

Sub-s (4): for the second word in italics there is substituted the word "it" by the Enterprise Act 2002, s 278(1), Sch 25, para 40(1), (10)(d), as from a day to be appointed.

Director: as to the abolition of the office of the Director General of Fair Trading and the substitution of references to the Director and related expressions, see the note preceding s 95 at **[233A]**.

304 Further reports by *Director*

(1) The *Director* must keep under review the regulatory provisions and practices of recognised bodies.

(2) If at any time the *Director* considers that—

(a) a regulatory provision or practice has a significantly adverse effect on competition, or

(b) regulatory provisions or practices, or a combination of regulating provisions and practices have such an effect,

he must make a report.

(3) If at any time the *Director* considers that—

    (a) a regulatory provision or practice does not have a significantly adverse effect on competition, or

    (b) regulatory provisions or practices, or a combination of regulatory provisions and practices do not have any such effect,

he may make a report to that effect.

(4) A report under subsection (2) must contain details of the adverse effect on competition.

(5) If the *Director* makes a report under subsection (2), *he* must—

    (a) send a copy of it to the Treasury, to the Competition Commission and to the Authority; and

    (b) publish it in the way appearing to *him* to be best calculated to bring it to the attention of the public.

(6) If the *Director* makes a report under subsection (3)—

    (a) *he* must send a copy of it to the Treasury, to the Competition Commission and to the Authority; and

    (b) *he* may publish it.

(7) Before publishing a report under this section, the *Director* must, so far as practicable, exclude any matter which relates to the private affairs of a particular individual the publication of which, in the opinion of the *Director*, would or might seriously and prejudicially affect his interests.

(8) Before publishing such a report, the *Director* must exclude any matter which relates to the affairs of a particular body the publication of which, in the opinion of the *Director*, would or might seriously and prejudicially affect its interests.

(9) Subsections (7) and (8) do not apply to the copy of a report which the *Director* is required to send to the Treasury, the Competition Commission and the Authority under subsection (5)(a) or (6)(a).

(10) For the purposes of the law of defamation, absolute privilege attaches to any report of the *Director* under this section.

                                                       [242]

NOTES

    Commencement: 1 December 2001.

    Sub-s (5): for the word in italics in para (b) there is substituted the words "the OFT" by the Enterprise Act 2002, s 278(1), Sch 25, para 40(1), (11)(b), as from a day to be appointed.

    Director: as to the abolition of the office of the Director General of Fair Trading and the substitution of references to the Director and related expressions, see the note preceding s 95 at **[233A]**.

305 Investigations by *Director*

(1) For the purpose of investigating any matter with a view to its consideration under section 303 or 304, the *Director* may exercise the powers conferred on *him* by this section.

(2) The *Director* may by notice in writing require any person to produce to *him* or to a person appointed by *him* for the purpose, at a time and place specified in the notice, any document which—

    (a) is specified or described in the notice; and

    (b) is a document in that person's custody or under his control.

(3) The *Director* may by notice in writing—

    (a) require any person carrying on any business to provide *him* with such information as may be specified or described in the notice; and

(b) specify the time within which, and the manner and form in which, any such information is to be provided.

(4) A requirement may be imposed under subsection (2) or (3)(a) only in respect of documents or information which relate to any matter relevant to the investigation.

(5) If a person ("the defaulter") refuses, or otherwise fails, to comply with a notice under this section, the *Director* may certify that fact in writing to the court and the court may enquire into the case.

(6) If, after hearing any witness who may be produced against or on behalf of the defaulter and any statement which may be offered in defence, the court is satisfied that the defaulter did not have a reasonable excuse for refusing or otherwise failing to comply with the notice, the court may deal with the defaulter as if he were in contempt.

(7) In this section, "the court" means—
(a) the High Court; or
(b) in Scotland, the Court of Session.

[243]

NOTES
Commencement: 3 September 2001 (for the purposes of s 303); 1 December 2001 (remaining purposes).
Director: as to the abolition of the office of the Director General of Fair Trading and the substitution of references to the Director and related expressions, see the note preceding s 95 at **[233A]**.

Role of Competition Commission

306 Consideration by Competition Commission

(1) If subsection (2) or (3) applies, the Commission must investigate the matter which is the subject of the *Director's* report.

(2) This subsection applies if the *Director* sends to the Competition Commission a report—
(a) issued by *him* under section 303(3) which concludes that one or more regulatory provisions have a significantly adverse effect on competition, or
(b) made by *him* under section 304(2).

(3) This subsection applies if the *Director* asks the Commission to consider a report—
(a) issued by *him* under section 303(3) which concludes that one or more regulatory provisions do not have a significantly adverse effect on competition, or
(b) made by *him* under section 304(3).

(4) The Commission must then make its own report on the matter unless it considers that, as a result of a change of circumstances, no useful purpose would be served by a report.

(5) If the Commission decides in accordance with subsection (4) not to make a report, it must make a statement setting out the change of circumstances which resulted in that decision.

(6) A report made under this section must state the Commission's conclusion as to whether—
(a) the regulatory provision or practice which is the subject of the report has a significantly adverse effect on competition, or
(b) the regulatory provisions or practices or combination of regulatory provisions and practices which are the subject of the report have such an effect.

(7) A report under this section stating the Commission's conclusion that there is a significantly adverse effect on competition must also—

(a) state whether the Commission considers that that effect is justified; and

(b) if it states that the Commission considers that it is not justified, state its conclusion as to what action, if any, the Treasury ought to direct the Authority to take.

(8) Subsection (9) applies whenever the Commission is considering, for the purposes of this section, whether a particular adverse effect on competition is justified.

(9) The Commission must ensure, so far as that is reasonably possible, that the conclusion it reaches is compatible with the obligations imposed on the recognised body concerned by or under this Act.

(10) A report under this section must contain such an account of the Commission's reasons for its conclusions as is expedient, in the opinion of the Commission, for facilitating proper understanding of them.

(11) The provisions of Schedule 14 (except paragraph 2(b)) apply for the purposes of this section as they apply for the purposes of section 162.

(12) If the Commission makes a report under this section it must send a copy to the Treasury, the Authority and the *Director*.

[244]

NOTES

Commencement: 3 September 2001 (for the purposes of reports issued by the Director under s 303); 1 December 2001 (remaining purposes).

Sub-ss (2), (3): for the words in italics in paras (a), (b) there are substituted the words "the OFT" by the Enterprise Act 2002, s 278(1), Sch 25, para 40(1), (13), as from a day to be appointed.

Director: as to the abolition of the office of the Director General of Fair Trading and the substitution of references to the Director and related expressions, see the note preceding s 95 at **[233A]**.

Role of the Treasury

307 Recognition orders: role of the Treasury

(1) Subsection (2) applies if, on an application for a recognition order—

(a) the *Director* makes a report under section 303 but does not ask the Competition Commission to consider it under section 306;

(b) the Competition Commission concludes—

(i) that the applicant's regulatory provisions do not have a significantly adverse effect on competition; or

(ii) that if those provisions do have that effect, the effect is justified.

(2) The Treasury may refuse to approve the making of the recognition order only if they consider that the exceptional circumstances of the case make it inappropriate for them to give their approval.

(3) Subsection (4) applies if, on an application for a recognition order, the Competition Commission concludes—

(a) that the applicant's regulatory provisions have a significantly adverse effect on competition; and

(b) that that effect is not justified.

(4) The Treasury must refuse to approve the making of the recognition order unless they consider that the exceptional circumstances of the case make it inappropriate for them to refuse their approval.

[245]

PART I
STATUTES

NOTES

Commencement: 3 September 2001.

   Director: as to the abolition of the office of the Director General of Fair Trading and the substitution of references to the Director and related expressions, see the note preceding s 95 at **[233A]**.

308 Directions by the Treasury

(1) This section applies if the Competition Commission makes a report under section 306(4) (other than a report on an application for a recognition order) which states the Commission's conclusion that there is a significantly adverse effect on competition.

(2) If the Commission's conclusion, as stated in the report, is that the adverse effect on competition is not justified, the Treasury must give a remedial direction to the Authority.

(3) But subsection (2) does not apply if the Treasury consider—
   (a) that, as a result of action taken by the Authority or the recognised body concerned in response to the Commission's report, it is unnecessary for them to give a direction; or
   (b) that the exceptional circumstances of the case make it inappropriate or unnecessary for them to do so.

(4) In considering the action to be specified in a remedial direction, the Treasury must have regard to any conclusion of the Commission included in the report because of section 306(7)(b).

(5) Subsection (6) applies if—
   (a) the Commission's conclusion, as stated in its report, is that the adverse effect on competition is justified; but
   (b) the Treasury consider that the exceptional circumstances of the case require them to act.

(6) The Treasury may give a direction to the Authority requiring it to take such action—
   (a) as they consider to be necessary in the light of the exceptional circumstances of the case; and
   (b) as may be specified in the direction.

(7) If the action specified in a remedial direction is the giving by the Authority of a direction—
   (a) the direction to be given must be compatible with the recognition requirements applicable to the recognised body in relation to which it is given; and
   (b) subsections (3) and (4) of section 296 apply to it as if it were a direction given under that section.

(8) "Remedial direction" means a direction requiring the Authority—
   (a) to revoke the recognition order for the body concerned; or
   (b) to give such directions to the body concerned as may be specified in it.

[246]

NOTES

Commencement: 1 December 2001.

309 Statements by the Treasury

(1) If, in reliance on subsection (3)(a) or (b) of section 308, the Treasury decline to act under subsection (2) of that section, they must make a statement to that effect, giving their reasons.

(2) If the Treasury give a direction under section 308 they must make a statement giving—
    (a) details of the direction; and
    (b) if the direction is given under subsection (6) of that section, their reasons for giving it.

(3) The Treasury must—
    (a) publish any statement made under this section in the way appearing to them best calculated to bring it to the attention of the public; and
    (b) lay a copy of it before Parliament.

[247]

NOTES
    Commencement: 1 December 2001.

310 Procedure on exercise of certain powers by the Treasury

(1) Subsection (2) applies if the Treasury are considering—
    (a) whether to refuse their approval under section 307;
    (b) whether section 308(2) applies; or
    (c) whether to give a direction under section 308(6).

(2) The Treasury must—
    (a) take such steps as they consider appropriate to allow the exchange or clearing house concerned, and any other person appearing to the Treasury to be affected, an opportunity to make representations—
      (i) about any report made by the *Director* under section 303 or 304 or by the Competition Commission under section 306;
      (ii) as to whether, and if so how, the Treasury should exercise their powers under section 307 or 308; and
    (b) have regard to any such representations.

[248]

NOTES
    Commencement: 3 September 2001 (for the purposes of s 307); 1 December 2001 (remaining purposes).
    Director: as to the abolition of the office of the Director General of Fair Trading and the substitution of references to the Director and related expressions, see the note preceding s 95 at [233A].

CHAPTER III
EXCLUSION FROM THE COMPETITION ACT 1998

311 The Chapter I prohibition

(1) The Chapter I prohibition does not apply to an agreement for the constitution of a recognised body to the extent to which the agreement relates to the regulatory provisions of that body.

(2) If the conditions set out in subsection (3) are satisfied, the Chapter I prohibition does not apply to an agreement for the constitution of—
    (a) an investment exchange which is not a recognised investment exchange, or
    (b) a clearing house which is not a recognised clearing house,
to the extent to which the agreement relates to the regulatory provisions of that body.

(3) The conditions are that—

    (a) the body has applied for a recognition order in accordance with the provisions of this Act; and

    (b) the application has not been determined.

(4) The Chapter I prohibition does not apply to a recognised body's regulatory provisions.

(5) The Chapter I prohibition does not apply to a decision made by a recognised body to the extent to which the decision relates to any of that body's regulatory provisions or practices.

(6) The Chapter I prohibition does not apply to practices of a recognised body.

(7) The Chapter I prohibition does not apply to an agreement the parties to which consist of or include—

    (a) a recognised body, or

    (b) a person who is subject to the rules of a recognised body,

to the extent to which the agreement consists of provisions the inclusion of which is required or encouraged by any of the body's regulatory provisions or practices.

(8) If a recognised body's recognition order is revoked, this section is to have effect as if that body had continued to be recognised until the end of the period of six months beginning with the day on which the revocation took effect.

(9) "The Chapter I prohibition" means the prohibition imposed by section 2(1) of the Competition Act 1998.

(10) Expressions used in this section which are also used in Part I of the Competition Act 1998 are to be interpreted in the same way as for the purposes of that Part of that Act.

[249]

NOTES

Commencement: 3 September 2001.

312 The Chapter II prohibition

(1) The Chapter II prohibition does not apply to—

    (a) practices of a recognised body;

    (b) the adoption or enforcement of such a body's regulatory provisions;

    (c) any conduct which is engaged in by such a body or by a person who is subject to the rules of such a body to the extent to which it is encouraged or required by the regulatory provisions of the body.

(2) The Chapter II prohibition means the prohibition imposed by section 18(1) of the Competition Act 1998.

[250]

NOTES

Commencement: 3 September 2001.

PART XXX
SUPPLEMENTAL

431 Commencement

(1) The following provisions come into force on the passing of this Act—

    (a) this section;

    (b), (c) . . .

(2)　The other provisions of this Act come into force on such day as the Treasury may by order appoint; and different days may be appointed for different purposes.

[251]

NOTES
Commencement: 14 June 2000.
Sub-s (1): paras (b), (c) outside the scope of this work.
Orders: the Financial Services and Markets Act 2000 (Commencement No 1) Order 2001, SI 2001/516; the Financial Services and Markets Act 2000 (Commencement No 2) Order 2001, SI 2001/1282; the Financial Services and Markets Act 2000 (Commencement No 3) Order 2001, SI 2001/1820; the Financial Services and Markets Act 2000 (Commencement No 4 and Transitional Provision) Order 2001, SI 2001/2364; the Financial Services and Markets Act 2000 (Commencement No 5) Order 2001, SI 2001/2632; the Financial Services and Markets Act 2000 (Commencement No 6) Order 2001, SI 2001/3436; the Financial Services and Markets Act 2000 (Commencement No 7) Order 2001, SI 2001/3538.

433 Short title

This Act may be cited as the Financial Services and Markets Act 2000.

[252]

NOTES
Commencement: 14 June 2000.

SCHEDULE 14

Section 162

ROLE OF THE COMPETITION COMMISSION

Provision of information by Treasury

1.—(1)　The Treasury's powers under this paragraph are to be exercised only for the purpose of assisting the Commission in carrying out an investigation under section 162.

(2)　The Treasury may give to the Commission—
    (a)　any information in their possession which relates to matters falling within the scope of the investigation; and
    (b)　other assistance in relation to any such matters.

(3)　In carrying out an investigation under section 162, the Commission must have regard to any information given to it under this paragraph.

Consideration of matters arising on a report

2.　In considering any matter arising from a report made by the *Director* under section 160, the Commission must have regard to—
    (a)　any representations made to *it* in connection with the matter by any person appearing to the Commission to have a substantial interest in the matter; and
    (b)　any cost benefit analysis prepared by the Authority (at any time) in connection with the regulatory provision or practice, or any of the regulatory provisions or practices, which are the subject of the report.

[Investigations under section 162: application of Enterprise Act 2002

2A.—(1)　The following sections of Part 3 of the Enterprise Act 2002 shall apply, with the modifications mentioned in sub-paragraphs (2) and (3), for the purposes of any investigation by the Commission under section 162 of this Act as they apply for the purposes of references under that Part—
    (a)　section 109 (attendance of witnesses and production of documents etc);
    (b)　section 110 (enforcement of powers under section 109: general);
    (c)　section 111 (penalties);
    (d)　section 112 (penalties: main procedural requirements);
    (e)　section 113 (payments and interest by instalments);
    (f)　section 114 (appeals in relation to penalties);
    (g)　section 115 (recovery of penalties); and
    (h)　section 116 (statement of policy).

(2)   Section 110 shall, in its application by virtue of sub-paragraph (1), have effect as if—
    (a) subsection (2) were omitted; and
    (b) in subsection (9) the words from "or section" to "section 65(3))" were omitted.

(3)   Section 111(5)(b) shall, in its application by virtue of sub-paragraph (1), have effect as if for sub-paragraph (ii) there were substituted—

> "(ii) if earlier, the day on which the report of the Commission on the investigation concerned is made or, if the Commission decides not to make a report, the day on which the Commission makes the statement required by section 162(3) of the Financial Services and Markets Act 2000."

(4)   Section 117 of the Enterprise Act 2002 (false or misleading information) shall apply in relation to functions of the Commission in connection with an investigation under section 162 of this Act as it applies in relation to its functions under Part 3 of that Act but as if, in subsections (1)(a) and (2), the words "the OFT," and "or the Secretary of State" were omitted.

(5)   Provisions of Part 3 of the Enterprise Act 2002 which have effect for the purposes of sections 109 to 117 of that Act (including, in particular, provisions relating to offences and the making of orders) shall, for the purposes of the application of those sections by virtue of sub-paragraph (1) or (4) above, have effect in relation to those sections as applied by virtue of those sub-paragraphs.

(6)   Accordingly, corresponding provisions of this Act shall not have effect in relation to those sections as applied by virtue of those sub-paragraphs.

Section 162: modification of Schedule 7 to the Competition Act 1998

2B. For the purposes of its application in relation to the function of the Commission of deciding in accordance with section 162(2) of this Act not to make a report, paragraph 15(7) of Schedule 7 to the Competition Act 1998 (power of the Chairman to act on his own while a group is being constituted) has effect as if, after paragraph (a), there were inserted

"; or
  (aa) in the case of an investigation under section 162 of the Financial Services and Markets Act 2000, decide not to make a report in accordance with subsection (2) of that section (decision not to make a report where no useful purpose would be served).

Reports under section 162: further provision

2C.—(1) For the purposes of section 163 of this Act, a conclusion contained in a report of the Commission is to be disregarded if the conclusion is not that of at least two-thirds of the members of the group constituted in connection with the investigation concerned in pursuance of paragraph 15 of Schedule 7 to the Competition Act 1998.

(2)   If a member of a group so constituted disagrees with any conclusions contained in a report made under section 162 of this Act as the conclusions of the Commission, the report shall, if the member so wishes, include a statement of his disagreement and of his reasons for disagreeing.

(3)   For the purposes of the law relating to defamation, absolute privilege attaches to any report made by the Commission under section 162.]

Applied provisions

3.—*(1) The provisions mentioned in sub-paragraph (2) are to apply in relation to the functions of the Commission under section 162 as they apply in relation to the functions of the Commission in relation to a reference to the Commission under the Fair Trading Act 1973.*

  (2) The provisions are—
    (a) section 82(2), (3) and (4) of the Fair Trading Act 1973 (general provisions about reports);
    (b) section 85 of that Act (attendance of witnesses and production of documents);
    (c) section 93B of that Act (false or misleading information);
    (d) section 24 of the Competition Act 1980 (modifications of provisions about the performance of the Commission's functions);
    (e) Part II of Schedule 7 to the Competition Act 1998 (performance by the Commission of its general functions).

PART I
STATUTES

(3) But the reference in paragraph 15(7)(b) in Schedule 7 to the 1998 Act to section 75(5) of that Act is to be read as a reference to the power of the Commission to decide not to make a report in accordance with section 162(2).

Publication of reports

4.—(1) If the Commission makes a report under section 162, it must publish it in such a way as appears to it to be best calculated to bring it to the attention of the public.

(2) Before publishing the report the Commission must, so far as practicable, exclude any matter which relates to the private affairs of a particular individual the publication of which, in the opinion of the Commission, would or might seriously and prejudicially affect his interests.

(3) Before publishing the report the Commission must, so far as practicable, also exclude any matter which relates to the affairs of a particular body the publication of which, in the opinion of the Commission, would or might seriously and prejudicially affect its interests.

(4) Sub-paragraphs (2) and (3) do not apply in relation to copies of a report which the Commission is required to send under section 162(10).

[253]

NOTES

Commencement: 18 June 2001.

Para 2: for the word in italics in para (a) there is substituted the words "the Commission" by the Enterprise Act 2002, s 278(1), Sch 25, para 40(1), (20)(a), as from a day to be appointed.

Paras 2A–2C: inserted by the Enterprise Act 2002, s 278(1), Sch 25, para 40(1), (20)(b), as from a day to be appointed.

Para 3: repealed by the Enterprise Act 2002, s 278, Sch 25, para 40(1), (20)(c), Sch 26, as from a day to be appointed.

Director: as to the abolition of the office of the Director General of Fair Trading and the substitution of references to the Director and related expressions, see the note preceding s 95 at **[233A]**.

ENTERPRISE ACT 2002

(2002 c 40)

ARRANGEMENT OF SECTIONS

PART 1
THE OFFICE OF FAIR TRADING

Establishment of OFT

PART 2
THE COMPETITION APPEAL TRIBUNAL

The Competition Appeal Tribunal

PART 3
MERGERS

CHAPTER 1
DUTY TO MAKE REFERENCES

Duty to make references: completed mergers

Duty to make references: anticipated mergers

Determination of references

CHAPTER 2
PUBLIC INTEREST CASES

Power to make references

Reports on references

CHAPTER 3
OTHER SPECIAL CASES

Special public interest cases

CHAPTER 4
ENFORCEMENT

Powers exercisable before references under section 22 or 33

CHAPTER 5
SUPPLEMENTARY

PART 4
MARKET INVESTIGATIONS

CHAPTER 1
MARKET INVESTIGATION REFERENCES

Making of references

Determination of references

CHAPTER 2
PUBLIC INTEREST CASES

Intervention notices

Intervention notices under section 139(1)

Intervention notices under section 139(2)

Other

CHAPTER 3
ENFORCEMENT

Undertakings and orders

Enforcement functions of OFT

Supplementary

CHAPTER 4
SUPPLEMENTARY

Regulated markets

Consultation, information and publicity

Investigation powers

Reports

Other

PART 6
CARTEL OFFENCE

Cartel offence

Establish and provide for the functions of the Office of Fair Trading, the Competition Appeal Tribunal and the Competition Service; to make provision about mergers and market structures and conduct; to amend the constitution and functions of the Competition Commission; to create an offence for those entering into certain anti-competitive agreements; to provide for the disqualification of directors of companies engaging in certain anti-competitive practices; to make other provision about competition law; to amend the law relating to the protection of the collective interests of consumers; to make further provision about the disclosure of information obtained under competition and consumer legislation; to amend the Insolvency Act 1986 and make other provision about insolvency; and for connected purposes

[7 November 2002]

PART 1
THE OFFICE OF FAIR TRADING

Establishment of OFT

1 The Office of Fair Trading

(1)   There shall be a body corporate to be known as the Office of Fair Trading (in this Act referred to as "the OFT").

(2)   The functions of the OFT are carried out on behalf of the Crown.

(3)   Schedule 1 (which makes further provision about the OFT) has effect.

(4)   In managing its affairs the OFT shall have regard, in addition to any relevant general guidance as to the governance of public bodies, to such generally accepted principles of good corporate governance as it is reasonable to regard as applicable to the OFT.

[254]

NOTES

Commencement: to be appointed.

2 The Director General of Fair Trading

(1)   The functions of the Director General of Fair Trading (in this Act referred to as "the Director"), and his property, rights and liabilities, are transferred to the OFT.

(2)   The office of the Director is abolished.

(3)   Any enactment, instrument or other document passed or made before the commencement of subsection (1) which refers to the Director shall have effect, so far as necessary for the purposes of or in consequence of anything being transferred, as if any reference to the Director were a reference to the OFT.

[255]

NOTES

Commencement: to be appointed.

3 Annual plan

(1)   The OFT shall, before each financial year, publish a document (the "annual plan") containing a statement of its main objectives and priorities for the year.

(2)   The OFT shall for the purposes of public consultation publish a document containing proposals for its annual plan at least two months before publishing the annual plan for any year.

(3)   The OFT shall lay before Parliament a copy of each document published under subsection (2) and each annual plan.

[256]

NOTES

Commencement: to be appointed.

4 Annual and other reports

(1)   The OFT shall, as soon as practicable after the end of each financial year, make to the Secretary of State a report (the "annual report") on its activities and performance during that year.

(2)   The annual report for each year shall include—
  (a) a general survey of developments in respect of matters relating to the OFT's functions;
  (b) an assessment of the extent to which the OFT's main objectives and priorities for the year (as set out in the annual plan) have been met;
  (c) a summary of the significant decisions, investigations or other activities made or carried out by the OFT during the year;
  (d) a summary of the allocation of the OFT's financial resources to its various activities during the year; and
  (e) an assessment of the OFT's performance and practices in relation to its enforcement functions.

(3)   The OFT shall lay a copy of each annual report before Parliament and arrange for the report to be published.

(4)   The OFT may—
  (a) prepare other reports in respect of matters relating to any of its functions; and
  (b) arrange for any such report to be published.

[257]

NOTES

Commencement: to be appointed.

General functions of OFT

5 Acquisition of information etc

(1)   The OFT has the function of obtaining, compiling and keeping under review information about matters relating to the carrying out of its functions.

(2)   That function is to be carried out with a view to (among other things) ensuring that the OFT has sufficient information to take informed decisions and to carry out its other functions effectively.

(3)   In carrying out that function the OFT may carry out, commission or support (financially or otherwise) research.

[258]

NOTES
Commencement: to be appointed.

6 Provision of information etc to the public

(1)   The OFT has the function of—
  (a)   making the public aware of the ways in which competition may benefit consumers in, and the economy of, the United Kingdom; and
  (b)   giving information or advice in respect of matters relating to any of its functions to the public.

(2)   In carrying out those functions the OFT may—
  (a)   publish educational materials or carry out other educational activities; or
  (b)   support (financially or otherwise) the carrying out by others of such activities or the provision by others of information or advice.

[259]

NOTES
Commencement: to be appointed.

7 Provision of information and advice to Ministers etc

(1)   The OFT has the function of—
  (a)   making proposals, or
  (b)   giving other information or advice,

on matters relating to any of its functions to any Minister of the Crown or other public authority (including proposals, information or advice as to any aspect of the law or a proposed change in the law).

(2)   A Minister of the Crown may request the OFT to make proposals or give other information or advice on any matter relating to any of its functions; and the OFT shall, so far as is reasonably practicable and consistent with its other functions, comply with the request.

[260]

NOTES
Commencement: to be appointed.

8 Promoting good consumer practice

(1)   The OFT has the function of promoting good practice in the carrying out of activities which may affect the economic interests of consumers in the United Kingdom.

(2)   In carrying out that function the OFT may (without prejudice to the generality of subsection (1)) make arrangements for approving consumer codes and may, in accordance with the arrangements, give its approval to or withdraw its approval from any consumer code.

(3)   Any such arrangements must specify the criteria to be applied by the OFT in determining whether to give approval to or withdraw approval from a consumer code.

(4)   Any such arrangements may in particular—
  (a) specify descriptions of consumer code which may be the subject of an application to the OFT for approval (and any such description may be framed by reference to any feature of a consumer code, including the persons who are, or are to be, subject to the code, the manner in which it is, or is to be, operated and the persons responsible for its operation); and
  (b) provide for the use in accordance with the arrangements of an official symbol intended to signify that a consumer code is approved by the OFT.

(5)   The OFT shall publish any arrangements under subsection (2) in such manner it considers appropriate.

(6)   In this section "consumer code" means a code of practice or other document (however described) intended, with a view to safeguarding or promoting the interests of consumers, to regulate by any means the conduct of persons engaged in the supply of goods or services to consumers (or the conduct of their employees or representatives).

[261]

NOTES

Commencement: to be appointed.

Miscellaneous

9 (*Repeals the Fair Trading Act 1973, s 12, at* **[10]**, *and the Competition Act 1980, s 13, at* **[110]**.)

10 Part 2 of the 1973 Act

(1)   The following provisions of the 1973 Act shall cease to have effect—
  (a) section 3 and Schedule 2 (which establish, and make provision with respect to, the Consumer Protection Advisory Committee);
  (b) sections 13 to 21 (which relate to references made to, and reports of, that Committee); and
  (c) section 22 (power of Secretary of State to make orders in pursuance of a report of that Committee).

(2)   But subsection (1)(c) does not affect—
  (a) any order under section 22 of the 1973 Act which is in force immediately before the commencement of this section;
  (b) the continued operation of that section so far as applying to the revocation of any such order.

(3)   If the orders saved by subsection (2)(a) have been revoked, the Secretary of State may by order—
  (a) repeal any unrepealed provision of Part 2 of the 1973 Act and subsection (2) above; and
  (b) make such other consequential modifications of any Act or subordinate legislation (whenever passed or made) as he thinks fit.

(4)   An order under subsection (3)—

(a)   may make transitional or saving provision in connection with any modification made by the order; and

(b)   shall be made by statutory instrument subject to annulment in pursuance of a resolution of either House of Parliament.

[262]

NOTES

Commencement: to be appointed.

11 Super-complaints to OFT

(1)   This section applies where a designated consumer body makes a complaint to the OFT that any feature, or combination of features, of a market in the United Kingdom for goods or services is or appears to be significantly harming the interests of consumers.

(2)   The OFT must, within 90 days after the day on which it receives the complaint, publish a response stating how it proposes to deal with the complaint, and in particular—

(a)   whether it has decided to take any action, or to take no action, in response to the complaint, and

(b)   if it has decided to take action, what action it proposes to take.

(3)   The response must state the OFT's reasons for its proposals.

(4)   The Secretary of State may by order amend subsection (2) by substituting any period for the period for the time being specified there.

(5)   "Designated consumer body" means a body designated by the Secretary of State by order.

(6)   The Secretary of State—

(a)   may designate a body only if it appears to him to represent the interests of consumers of any description, and

(b)   must publish (and may from time to time vary) other criteria to be applied by him in determining whether to make or revoke a designation.

(7)   The OFT—

(a)   must issue guidance as to the presentation by the complainant of a reasoned case for the complaint, and

(b)   may issue such other guidance as appears to it to be appropriate for the purposes of this section.

(8)   An order under this section—

(a)   shall be made by statutory instrument, and

(b)   shall be subject to annulment in pursuance of a resolution of either House of Parliament.

(9)   In this section—

(a)   references to a feature of a market in the United Kingdom for goods or services have the same meaning as if contained in Part 4, and

(b)   "consumer" means an individual who is a consumer within the meaning of that Part.

[263]

NOTES

Commencement: to be appointed.

PART 2
THE COMPETITION APPEAL TRIBUNAL

The Competition Appeal Tribunal

12 The Competition Appeal Tribunal

(1)   There shall be a tribunal, to be called the Competition Appeal Tribunal (in this Part referred to as "the Tribunal").

(2)   The Tribunal shall consist of—
    (a)   a person appointed by the Lord Chancellor to preside over the Tribunal (in this Part referred to as "the President");
    (b)   members appointed by the Lord Chancellor to form a panel of chairmen; and
    (c)   members appointed by the Secretary of State to form a panel of ordinary members.

(3)   The Tribunal shall have a Registrar appointed by the Secretary of State.

(4)   The expenses of the Tribunal shall be paid by the Competition Service.

(5)   Schedule 2 (which makes further provision about the Tribunal) has effect.
[264]

NOTES
    Commencement: to be appointed.

13 The Competition Service

(1)   There shall be a body corporate called the Competition Service (in this Part referred to as "the Service").

(2)   The purpose of the Service is to fund, and provide support services to, the Competition Appeal Tribunal.

(3)   In subsection (2) "support services" includes the provision of staff, accommodation and equipment and any other services which facilitate the carrying out by the Tribunal of its functions.

(4)   The activities of the Service are not carried out on behalf of the Crown (and its property is not to be regarded as held on behalf of the Crown).

(5)   The Secretary of State shall pay to the Service such sums as he considers appropriate to enable it to fund the activities of the Tribunal and to carry out its other activities.

(6)   Schedule 3 (which makes further provision about the Service) has effect.
[265]

NOTES
    Commencement: to be appointed.

14 Constitution of Tribunal for particular proceedings and its decisions

(1)   For the purposes of any proceedings before it the Tribunal shall consist of a chairman and two other members.

(2)   The chairman must be the President or a member of the panel of chairmen.

(3)   The other members may be chosen from either the panel of chairmen or the panel of ordinary members.

(4)   If the members of the Tribunal as constituted in accordance with this section are unable to agree on any decision, the decision is to be taken by majority vote.

(5)   This section has effect subject to paragraph 18 of Schedule 4 (consequences of a member of the Tribunal being unable to continue after the proceedings have begun to be heard).

(6)   Part 1 of Schedule 4 (which makes further provision about the decisions of the Tribunal and their enforcement) has effect.

[266]

PART I
STATUTES

NOTES
Commencement: to be appointed.

15 Tribunal rules

(1)   The Secretary of State may, after consulting the President and such other persons as he considers appropriate, make rules (in this Part referred to as "Tribunal rules") with respect to proceedings before the Tribunal.

(2)   Tribunal rules may make provision with respect to matters incidental to or consequential upon appeals provided for by or under any Act to the Court of Appeal or the Court of Session in relation to a decision of the Tribunal.

(3)   Tribunal rules may—
   (a) specify qualifications for appointment as Registrar;
   (b) confer functions on the President or the Registrar in relation to proceedings before the Tribunal; and
   (c) contain incidental, supplemental, consequential or transitional provision.

(4)   The power to make Tribunal rules is exercisable by statutory instrument subject to annulment in pursuance of a resolution of either House of Parliament.

(5)   Part 2 of Schedule 4 (which makes further provision about the rules) has effect, but without prejudice to the generality of subsection (1).

[267]

NOTES
Commencement: to be appointed.

16 Transfers of certain proceedings to and from Tribunal

(1)   The Lord Chancellor may by regulations—
   (a) make provision enabling the court—
       (i) to transfer to the Tribunal for its determination so much of any proceedings before the court as relates to an infringement issue; and
       (ii) to give effect to the determination of that issue by the Tribunal; and
   (b) make such incidental, supplementary, consequential, transitional or saving provision as the Lord Chancellor may consider appropriate.

(2)   The power to make regulations under subsection (1) is exercisable by statutory instrument subject to annulment in pursuance of a resolution of either House of Parliament.

(3)   Rules of court may prescribe the procedure to be followed in connection with a transfer mentioned in subsection (1).

(4)   The court may transfer to the Tribunal, in accordance with rules of court, so much of any proceedings before it as relates to a claim to which section 47A of the 1998 Act applies.

(5) Rules of court may make provision in connection with the transfer from the Tribunal to the High Court or the Court of Session of a claim made in proceedings under section 47A of the 1998 Act.

(6) In this section—

"the court" means—

(a) the High Court or a county court; or

(b) the Court of Session or a sheriff court; and

"infringement issue" means any question relating to whether or not an infringement of—

(a) the Chapter I prohibition or the Chapter II prohibition; or

(b) Article 81 or 82 of the Treaty,

has been or is being committed;

but otherwise any terms used in this section and Part 1 of the 1998 Act have the same meaning as they have in that Part.

[268]

NOTES

Commencement: to be appointed.

17–21 (*S 17 substitutes the Competition Act 1998, s 47, at* **[179]**; *s 18 inserts s 47A of the 1998 Act, at* **[180]**, *in relation to claims arising both before and after the commencement of s 18; s 19 inserts s 47B of the 1998 Act, at* **[181]**; *s 20 inserts s 58A of the 1998 Act, at* **[193]**, *except in relation to decisions made before the commencement of s 20, and amends 59(1) of that Act, at* **[194]**; *s 21 introduces Sch 5 to this Act (further amendments of the 1998 Act).*)

PART 3
MERGERS

CHAPTER 1
DUTY TO MAKE REFERENCES

Duty to make references: completed mergers

22 Duty to make references in relation to completed mergers

(1) The OFT shall, subject to subsections (2) and (3), make a reference to the Commission if the OFT believes that it is or may be the case that—

(a) a relevant merger situation has been created; and

(b) the creation of that situation has resulted, or may be expected to result, in a substantial lessening of competition within any market or markets in the United Kingdom for goods or services.

(2) The OFT may decide not to make a reference under this section if it believes that—

(a) the market concerned is not, or the markets concerned are not, of sufficient importance to justify the making of a reference to the Commission; or

(b) any relevant customer benefits in relation to the creation of the relevant merger situation concerned outweigh the substantial lessening of competition concerned and any adverse effects of the substantial lessening of competition concerned.

(3) No reference shall be made under this section if—

(a) the making of the reference is prevented by section 69(1), 74(1) or 96(3) or paragraph 4 of Schedule 7;

(b) the OFT is considering whether to accept undertakings under section 73 instead of making such a reference;

(c) the relevant merger situation concerned is being, or has been, dealt with in connection with a reference made under section 33;

(d) a notice under section 42(2) is in force in relation to the matter or the matter to which such a notice relates has been finally determined under Chapter 2 otherwise than in circumstances in which a notice is then given to the OFT under section 56(1); or

(e) the European Commission is considering a request made, in relation to the matter concerned, by the United Kingdom (whether alone or with others) under article 22(3) of the European Merger Regulations, is proceeding with the matter in pursuance of such a request or has dealt with the matter in pursuance of such a request.

(4) A reference under this section shall, in particular, specify—

(a) the enactment under which it is made; and

(b) the date on which it is made.

(5) The references in this section to the creation of a relevant merger situation shall be construed in accordance with section 23, the reference in subsection (2) of this section to relevant customer benefits shall be construed in accordance with section 30 and the reference in subsection (3) of this section to a matter to which a notice under section 42(2) relates being finally determined under Chapter 2 shall be construed in accordance with section 43(4) and (5).

(6) In this Part "market in the United Kingdom" includes—

(a) so far as it operates in the United Kingdom or a part of the United Kingdom, any market which operates there and in another country or territory or in a part of another country or territory; and

(b) any market which operates only in a part of the United Kingdom;

and references to a market for goods or services include references to a market for goods and services.

(7) In this Part "the decision-making authority" means—

(a) in the case of a reference or possible reference under this section or section 33, the OFT or (as the case may be) the Commission; and

(b) in the case of a notice or possible notice under section 42(2) or 59(2) or a reference or possible reference under section 45 or 62, the OFT, the Commission or (as the case may be) the Secretary of State.

[269]

NOTES

Commencement: to be appointed.

23 Relevant merger situations

(1) For the purposes of this Part, a relevant merger situation has been created if—

(a) two or more enterprises have ceased to be distinct enterprises at a time or in circumstances falling within section 24; and

(b) the value of the turnover in the United Kingdom of the enterprise being taken over exceeds £70 million.

(2) For the purposes of this Part, a relevant merger situation has also been created if—

(a) two or more enterprises have ceased to be distinct enterprises at a time or in circumstances falling within section 24; and

(b) as a result, one or both of the conditions mentioned in subsections (3) and (4) below prevails or prevails to a greater extent.

(3) The condition mentioned in this subsection is that, in relation to the supply of goods of any description, at least one-quarter of all the goods of that description which are supplied in the United Kingdom, or in a substantial part of the United Kingdom—

(a) are supplied by one and the same person or are supplied to one and the same person; or

(b) are supplied by the persons by whom the enterprises concerned are carried on, or are supplied to those persons.

(4) The condition mentioned in this subsection is that, in relation to the supply of services of any description, the supply of services of that description in the United Kingdom, or in a substantial part of the United Kingdom, is to the extent of at least one-quarter—

(a) supply by one and the same person, or supply for one and the same person; or

(b) supply by the persons by whom the enterprises concerned are carried on, or supply for those persons.

(5) For the purpose of deciding whether the proportion of one-quarter mentioned in subsection (3) or (4) is fulfilled with respect to goods or (as the case may be) services of any description, the decision-making authority shall apply such criterion (whether value, cost, price, quantity, capacity, number of workers employed or some other criterion, of whatever nature), or such combination of criteria, as the decision-making authority considers appropriate.

(6) References in subsections (3) and (4) to the supply of goods or (as the case may be) services shall, in relation to goods or services of any description which are the subject of different forms of supply, be construed in whichever of the following ways the decision-making authority considers appropriate—

(a) as references to any of those forms of supply taken separately;

(b) as references to all those forms of supply taken together; or

(c) as references to any of those forms of supply taken in groups.

(7) For the purposes of subsection (6) the decision-making authority may treat goods or services as being the subject of different forms of supply whenever—

(a) the transactions concerned differ as to their nature, their parties, their terms or their surrounding circumstances; and

(b) the difference is one which, in the opinion of the decision-making authority, ought for the purposes of that subsection to be treated as a material difference.

(8) The criteria for deciding when goods or services can be treated, for the purposes of this section, as goods or services of a separate description shall be such as in any particular case the decision-making authority considers appropriate in the circumstances of that case.

(9) For the purposes of this Chapter, the question whether a relevant merger situation has been created shall be determined as at—

(a) in the case of a reference which is treated as having been made under section 22 by virtue of section 37(2), such time as the Commission may determine; and

(b) in any other case, immediately before the time when the reference has been, or is to be, made.

NOTES

Commencement: to be appointed.

24 Time-limits and prior notice

(1)   For the purposes of section 23 two or more enterprises have ceased to be distinct enterprises at a time or in circumstances falling within this section if—
- (a) the two or more enterprises ceased to be distinct enterprises before the day on which the reference relating to them is to be made and did so not more than four months before that day; or
- (b) notice of material facts about the arrangements or transactions under or in consequence of which the enterprises have ceased to be distinct enterprises has not been given in accordance with subsection (2).

(2)   Notice of material facts is given in accordance with this subsection if—
- (a) it is given to the OFT prior to the entering into of the arrangements or transactions concerned or the facts are made public prior to the entering into of those arrangements or transactions; or
- (b) it is given to the OFT, or the facts are made public, more than four months before the day on which the reference is to be made.

(3)   In this section—
  "made public" means so publicised as to be generally known or readily ascertainable; and
  "notice" includes notice which is not in writing.

[271]

NOTES
Commencement: to be appointed.

25 Extension of time-limits

(1)   The OFT and the persons carrying on the enterprises which have or may have ceased to be distinct enterprises may agree to extend by no more than 20 days the four month period mentioned in section 24(1)(a) or (2)(b).

(2)   The OFT may by notice to the persons carrying on the enterprises which have or may have ceased to be distinct enterprises extend the four month period mentioned in section 24(1)(a) or (2)(b) if it considers that any of those persons has failed to provide, within the period stated in a notice under section 31 and in the manner authorised or required, information requested of him in that notice.

(3)   An extension under subsection (2) shall be for the period beginning with the end of the period within which the information is to be provided and which is stated in the notice under section 31 and ending with—
- (a) the provision of the information to the satisfaction of the OFT; or
- (b) if earlier, the cancellation by the OFT of the extension.

(4)   The OFT may by notice to the persons carrying on the enterprises which have or may have ceased to be distinct enterprises extend the four month period mentioned in section 24(1)(a) or (2)(b) if it is seeking undertakings from any of those persons under section 73.

(5)   An extension under subsection (4) shall be for the period beginning with the receipt of the notice under that subsection and ending with the earliest of the following events—
- (a) the giving of the undertakings concerned;
- (b) the expiry of the period of 10 days beginning with the first day after the receipt by the OFT of a notice from the person who has been given a notice under subsection (4) and from whom the undertakings are being sought stating that he does not intend to give the undertakings; or
- (c) the cancellation by the OFT of the extension.

(6)   The OFT may by notice to the persons carrying on the enterprises which have or may have ceased to be distinct enterprises extend the four month period mentioned in section 24(1)(a) or (2)(b) if the European Commission is considering a request made, in relation to the matter concerned, by the United Kingdom (whether alone or with others) under article 22(3) of the European Merger Regulations (but is not yet proceeding with the matter in pursuance of such a request).

(7)   An extension under subsection (6) shall be for the period beginning with the receipt of the notice under that subsection and ending with the receipt of a notice under subsection (8).

(8)   The OFT shall, in connection with any notice given by it under subsection (6), by notice inform the persons carrying on the enterprises which have or may have ceased to be distinct enterprises of the completion by the European Commission of its consideration of the request of the United Kingdom.

(9)   Subject to subsections (10) and (11), where the four month period mentioned in section 24(1)(a) or (2)(b) is extended or further extended by virtue of this section in relation to a particular case, any reference to that period in section 24 or the preceding provisions of this section shall have effect in relation to that case as if it were a reference to a period equivalent to the aggregate of the period being extended and the period of the extension (whether or not those periods overlap in time).

(10)   Subsection (11) applies where—
   (a)   the four month period mentioned in section 24(1)(a) or (2)(b) is further extended;
   (b)   the further extension and at least one previous extension is made under one or more of subsections (2), (4) and (6); and
   (c)   the same days or fractions of days are included in or comprise the further extension and are included in or comprise at least one such previous extension.

(11)   In calculating the period of the further extension, any days or fractions of days of the kind mentioned in subsection (10)(c) shall be disregarded.

(12)   No more than one extension is possible under subsection (1).

[272]

NOTES
Commencement: to be appointed.

26 Enterprises ceasing to be distinct enterprises

(1)   For the purposes of this Part any two enterprises cease to be distinct enterprises if they are brought under common ownership or common control (whether or not the business to which either of them formerly belonged continues to be carried on under the same or different ownership or control).

(2)   Enterprises shall, in particular, be treated as being under common control if they are—
   (a)   enterprises of interconnected bodies corporate;
   (b)   enterprises carried on by two or more bodies corporate of which one and the same person or group of persons has control; or
   (c)   an enterprise carried on by a body corporate and an enterprise carried on by a person or group of persons having control of that body corporate.

(3)   A person or group of persons able, directly or indirectly, to control or materially to influence the policy of a body corporate, or the policy of any person in carrying on an enterprise but without having a controlling interest in that body

corporate or in that enterprise, may, for the purposes of subsections (1) and (2), be treated as having control of it.

(4) For the purposes of subsection (1), in so far as it relates to bringing two or more enterprises under common control, a person or group of persons may be treated as bringing an enterprise under his or their control if—

(a) being already able to control or materially to influence the policy of the person carrying on the enterprise, that person or group of persons acquires a controlling interest in the enterprise or, in the case of an enterprise carried on by a body corporate, acquires a controlling interest in that body corporate; or

(b) being already able materially to influence the policy of the person carrying on the enterprise, that person or group of persons becomes able to control that policy.

[273]

NOTES

Commencement: to be appointed.

27 Time when enterprises cease to be distinct

(1) Subsection (2) applies in relation to any arrangements or transaction—

(a) not having immediate effect or having immediate effect only in part; but

(b) under or in consequence of which any two enterprises cease to be distinct enterprises.

(2) The time when the parties to any such arrangements or transaction become bound to such extent as will result, on effect being given to their obligations, in the enterprises ceasing to be distinct enterprises shall be taken to be the time at which the two enterprises cease to be distinct enterprises.

(3) In accordance with subsections (1) and (2) (but without prejudice to the generality of those subsections) for the purpose of determining the time at which any two enterprises cease to be distinct enterprises no account shall be taken of any option or other conditional right until the option is exercised or the condition is satisfied.

(4) Subsections (1) to (3) are subject to subsections (5) to (8) and section 29.

(5) The decision-making authority may, for the purposes of a reference, treat successive events to which this subsection applies as having occurred simultaneously on the date on which the latest of them occurred.

(6) Subsection (5) applies to successive events—

(a) which occur within a period of two years under or in consequence of the same arrangements or transaction, or successive arrangements or transactions between the same parties or interests; and

(b) by virtue of each of which, under or in consequence of the arrangements or the transaction or transactions concerned, any enterprises cease as between themselves to be distinct enterprises.

(7) The decision-making authority may, for the purposes of subsections (5) and (6), treat such arrangements or transactions as the decision-making authority considers appropriate as arrangements or transactions between the same interests.

(8) In deciding whether it is appropriate to treat arrangements or transactions as arrangements or transactions between the same interests the decision-making authority shall, in particular, have regard to the persons substantially concerned in the arrangements or transactions concerned.

[274]

PART I
STATUTES

NOTES
Commencement: to be appointed.

28 Turnover test

(1)   For the purposes of section 23 the value of the turnover in the United Kingdom of the enterprise being taken over shall be determined by taking the total value of the turnover in the United Kingdom of the enterprises which cease to be distinct enterprises and deducting—

    (a)   the turnover in the United Kingdom of any enterprise which continues to be carried on under the same ownership and control; or

    (b)   if no enterprise continues to be carried on under the same ownership and control, the turnover in the United Kingdom which, of all the turnovers concerned, is the turnover of the highest value.

(2)   For the purposes of this Part (other than section 121(4)(c)(ii)) the turnover in the United Kingdom of an enterprise shall be determined in accordance with such provisions as may be specified in an order made by the Secretary of State.

(3)   An order under subsection (2) may, in particular, make provision as to—

    (a)   the amounts which are, or which are not, to be treated as comprising an enterprise's turnover;

    (b)   the date or dates by reference to which an enterprise's turnover is to be determined;

    (c)   the connection with the United Kingdom by virtue of which an enterprise's turnover is turnover in the United Kingdom.

(4)   An order under subsection (2) may, in particular, make provision enabling the decision-making authority to determine matters of a description specified in the order (including any of the matters mentioned in paragraphs (a) to (c) of subsection (3)).

(5)   The OFT shall—

    (a)   keep under review the sum for the time being mentioned in section 23(1)(b); and

    (b)   from time to time advise the Secretary of State as to whether the sum is still appropriate.

(6)   The Secretary of State may by order amend section 23(1)(b) so as to alter the sum for the time being mentioned there.

[275]

NOTES
Commencement: to be appointed.

29 Obtaining control by stages

(1)   Where an enterprise is brought under the control of a person or group of persons in the course of two or more transactions (in this section a "series of transactions") to which subsection (2) applies, those transactions may, if the decision-making authority considers it appropriate, be treated for the purposes of a reference as having occurred simultaneously on the date on which the latest of them occurred.

(2)   This subsection applies to—

    (a)   any transaction which—

        (i)   enables that person or group of persons directly or indirectly to control or materially to influence the policy of any person carrying on the enterprise;

        (ii)   enables that person or group of persons to do so to a greater degree; or

PART I
STATUTES

    (iii) is a step (whether direct or indirect) towards enabling that person or group of persons to do so; and

  (b) any transaction by virtue of which that person or group of persons acquires a controlling interest in the enterprise or, where the enterprise is carried on by a body corporate, in that body corporate.

(3) Where a series of transactions includes a transaction falling within subsection (2)(b), any transaction occurring after the occurrence of that transaction is to be disregarded for the purposes of subsection (1).

(4) Where the period within which a series of transactions occurs exceeds two years, the transactions that may be treated as mentioned in subsection (1) are any of those transactions that occur within a period of two years.

(5) Sections 26(2) to (4) and 127(1), (2) and (4) to (6) shall apply for the purposes of this section to determine—

  (a) whether an enterprise is brought under the control of a person or group of persons; and

  (b) whether a transaction is one to which subsection (2) applies;

as they apply for the purposes of section 26 to determine whether enterprises are brought under common control.

(6) In determining for the purposes of this section the time at which any transaction occurs, no account shall be taken of any option or other conditional right until the option is exercised or the condition is satisfied.

[276]

___

NOTES

Commencement: to be appointed.

___

30 Relevant customer benefits

(1) For the purposes of this Part a benefit is a relevant customer benefit if—

  (a) it is a benefit to relevant customers in the form of—

    (i) lower prices, higher quality or greater choice of goods or services in any market in the United Kingdom (whether or not the market or markets in which the substantial lessening of competition concerned has, or may have, occurred or (as the case may be) may occur); or

    (ii) greater innovation in relation to such goods or services; and

  (b) the decision-making authority believes—

    (i) in the case of a reference or possible reference under section 22 or 45(2), as mentioned in subsection (2); and

    (ii) in the case of a reference or possible reference under section 33 or 45(4), as mentioned in subsection (3).

(2) The belief, in the case of a reference or possible reference under section 22 or section 45(2), is that—

  (a) the benefit has accrued as a result of the creation of the relevant merger situation concerned or may be expected to accrue within a reasonable period as a result of the creation of that situation; and

  (b) the benefit was, or is, unlikely to accrue without the creation of that situation or a similar lessening of competition.

(3) The belief, in the case of a reference or possible reference under section 33 or 45(4), is that—

  (a) the benefit may be expected to accrue within a reasonable period as a result of the creation of the relevant merger situation concerned; and

  (b) the benefit is unlikely to accrue without the creation of that situation or a similar lessening of competition.

(4)   In subsection (1) "relevant customers" means—
   (a) customers of any person carrying on an enterprise which, in the creation of the relevant merger situation concerned, has ceased to be, or (as the case may be) will cease to be, a distinct enterprise;
   (b) customers of such customers; and
   (c) any other customers in a chain of customers beginning with the customers mentioned in paragraph (a);

and in this subsection "customers" includes future customers.

[277]

NOTES
Commencement: to be appointed.

31 Information powers in relation to completed mergers

(1)   The OFT may by notice to any of the persons carrying on the enterprises which have or may have ceased to be distinct enterprises request him to provide the OFT with such information as the OFT may require for the purpose of deciding whether to make a reference under section 22.

(2)   The notice shall state—
   (a) the information required;
   (b) the period within which the information is to be provided; and
   (c) the possible consequences of not providing the information within the stated period and in the authorised or required manner.

[278]

NOTES
Commencement: to be appointed.

32 Supplementary provision for purposes of sections 25 and 31

(1)   The Secretary of State may make regulations for the purposes of sections 25 and 31.

(2)   The regulations may, in particular—
   (a) provide for the manner in which any information requested by the OFT under section 31 is authorised or required to be provided, and the time at which such information is to be treated as provided (including the time at which it is to be treated as provided to the satisfaction of the OFT for the purposes of section 25(3));
   (b) provide for the persons carrying on the enterprises which have or may have ceased to be distinct enterprises to be informed, in circumstances in which section 25(3) applies—
      (i)   of the fact that the OFT is satisfied as to the provision of the information requested by it or (as the case may be) of the OFT's decision to cancel the extension; and
      (ii) of the time at which the OFT is to be treated as so satisfied or (as the case may be) of the time at which the cancellation is to be treated as having effect;
   (c) provide for the persons carrying on the enterprises which have or may have ceased to be distinct enterprises to be informed, in circumstances in which section 25(5) applies—
      (i)   of the OFT's decision to cancel the extension; and
      (ii) of the time at which the cancellation is to be treated as having effect;
   (d) provide for the time at which any notice under section 25(4), (5)(b), (6) or (8) is to be treated as received;

(e) provide that a person is, or is not, to be treated, in such circumstances as may be specified in the regulations, as acting on behalf of a person carrying on an enterprise which has or may have ceased to be a distinct enterprise.

(3)   A notice under section 25(2)—
 (a) shall be given within 5 days of the end of the period within which the information is to be provided and which is stated in the notice under section 31; and
 (b) shall inform the person to whom it is addressed of—
  (i) the OFT's opinion as mentioned in section 25(2); and
  (ii) the OFT's intention to extend the period for considering whether to make a reference.

(4)   In determining for the purposes of section 25(1) or (5)(b) or subsection (3)(a) above any period which is expressed in the enactment concerned as a period of days or number of days no account shall be taken of—
 (a) Saturday, Sunday, Good Friday and Christmas Day; and
 (b) any day which is a bank holiday in England and Wales.

[279]

NOTES

Commencement: to be appointed.

Duty to make references: anticipated mergers

33 Duty to make references in relation to anticipated mergers

(1)   The OFT shall, subject to subsections (2) and (3), make a reference to the Commission if the OFT believes that it is or may be the case that—
 (a) arrangements are in progress or in contemplation which, if carried into effect, will result in the creation of a relevant merger situation; and
 (b) the creation of that situation may be expected to result in a substantial lessening of competition within any market or markets in the United Kingdom for goods or services.

(2)   The OFT may decide not to make a reference under this section if it believes that—
 (a) the market concerned is not, or the markets concerned are not, of sufficient importance to justify the making of a reference to the Commission;
 (b) the arrangements concerned are not sufficiently far advanced, or are not sufficiently likely to proceed, to justify the making of a reference to the Commission; or
 (c) any relevant customer benefits in relation to the creation of the relevant merger situation concerned outweigh the substantial lessening of competition concerned and any adverse effects of the substantial lessening of competition concerned.

(3)   No reference shall be made under this section if—
 (a) the making of the reference is prevented by section 69(1), 74(1) or 96(3) or paragraph 4 of Schedule 7;
 (b) the OFT is considering whether to accept undertakings under section 73 instead of making such a reference;
 (c) the arrangements concerned are being, or have been, dealt with in connection with a reference made under section 22;
 (d) a notice under section 42(2) is in force in relation to the matter or the matter to which such a notice relates has been finally determined under Chapter 2 otherwise than in circumstances in which a notice is then given to the OFT under section 56(1); or

(e) the European Commission is considering a request made, in relation to the matter concerned, by the United Kingdom (whether alone or with others) under article 22(3) of the European Merger Regulations, is proceeding with the matter in pursuance of such a request or has dealt with the matter in pursuance of such a request.

(4) A reference under this section shall, in particular, specify—
   (a) the enactment under which it is made; and
   (b) the date on which it is made.

[280]

NOTES
   Commencement: to be appointed.

34 Supplementary provision in relation to anticipated mergers

(1) The Secretary of State may by order make such provision as he considers appropriate about the operation of sections 27 and 29 in relation to—
   (a) references under this Part which relate to arrangements which are in progress or in contemplation; or
   (b) notices under section 42(2), 59(2) or 67(2) which relate to such arrangements.

(2) An order under subsection (1) may, in particular—
   (a) provide for sections 27(5) to (8) and 29 to apply with modifications in relation to such references or notices or in relation to particular descriptions of such references or notices;
   (b) enable particular descriptions of events, arrangements or transactions which have already occurred—
      (i) to be taken into account for the purposes of deciding whether to make such references or such references of a particular description or whether to give such notices or such notices of a particular description;
      (ii) to be dealt with under such references or such references of a particular description or under such notices or such notices of a particular description.

[281]

NOTES
   Commencement: to be appointed.

Determination of references

35 Questions to be decided in relation to completed mergers

(1) Subject to subsections (6) and (7) and section 127(3), the Commission shall, on a reference under section 22, decide the following questions—
   (a) whether a relevant merger situation has been created; and
   (b) if so, whether the creation of that situation has resulted, or may be expected to result, in a substantial lessening of competition within any market or markets in the United Kingdom for goods or services.

(2) For the purposes of this Part there is an anti-competitive outcome if—
   (a) a relevant merger situation has been created and the creation of that situation has resulted, or may be expected to result, in a substantial lessening of competition within any market or markets in the United Kingdom for goods or services; or

(b) arrangements are in progress or in contemplation which, if carried into effect, will result in the creation of a relevant merger situation and the creation of that situation may be expected to result in a substantial lessening of competition within any market or markets in the United Kingdom for goods or services.

(3) The Commission shall, if it has decided on a reference under section 22 that there is an anti-competitive outcome (within the meaning given by subsection (2)(a)), decide the following additional questions—

(a) whether action should be taken by it under section 41(2) for the purpose of remedying, mitigating or preventing the substantial lessening of competition concerned or any adverse effect which has resulted from, or may be expected to result from, the substantial lessening of competition;

(b) whether it should recommend the taking of action by others for the purpose of remedying, mitigating or preventing the substantial lessening of competition concerned or any adverse effect which has resulted from, or may be expected to result from, the substantial lessening of competition; and

(c) in either case, if action should be taken, what action should be taken and what is to be remedied, mitigated or prevented.

(4) In deciding the questions mentioned in subsection (3) the Commission shall, in particular, have regard to the need to achieve as comprehensive a solution as is reasonable and practicable to the substantial lessening of competition and any adverse effects resulting from it.

(5) In deciding the questions mentioned in subsection (3) the Commission may, in particular, have regard to the effect of any action on any relevant customer benefits in relation to the creation of the relevant merger situation concerned.

(6) In relation to the question whether a relevant merger situation has been created, a reference under section 22 may be framed so as to require the Commission to exclude from consideration—

(a) subsection (1) of section 23;

(b) subsection (2) of that section; or

(c) one of those subsections if the Commission finds that the other is satisfied.

(7) In relation to the question whether any such result as is mentioned in section 23(2)(b) has arisen, a reference under section 22 may be framed so as to require the Commission to confine its investigation to the supply of goods or services in a part of the United Kingdom specified in the reference.

[282]

NOTES
Commencement: to be appointed.

36 Questions to be decided in relation to anticipated mergers

(1) Subject to subsections (5) and (6) and section 127(3), the Commission shall, on a reference under section 33, decide the following questions—

(a) whether arrangements are in progress or in contemplation which, if carried into effect, will result in the creation of a relevant merger situation; and

(b) if so, whether the creation of that situation may be expected to result in a substantial lessening of competition within any market or markets in the United Kingdom for goods or services.

(2) The Commission shall, if it has decided on a reference under section 33 that there is an anti-competitive outcome (within the meaning given by section 35(2)(b)), decide the following additional questions—

    (a) whether action should be taken by it under section 41(2) for the purpose of remedying, mitigating or preventing the substantial lessening of competition concerned or any adverse effect which may be expected to result from the substantial lessening of competition;

    (b) whether it should recommend the taking of action by others for the purpose of remedying, mitigating or preventing the substantial lessening of competition concerned or any adverse effect which may be expected to result from the substantial lessening of competition; and

    (c) in either case, if action should be taken, what action should be taken and what is to be remedied, mitigated or prevented.

(3)   In deciding the questions mentioned in subsection (2) the Commission shall, in particular, have regard to the need to achieve as comprehensive a solution as is reasonable and practicable to the substantial lessening of competition and any adverse effects resulting from it.

(4)   In deciding the questions mentioned in subsection (2) the Commission may, in particular, have regard to the effect of any action on any relevant customer benefits in relation to the creation of the relevant merger situation concerned.

(5)   In relation to the question whether a relevant merger situation will be created, a reference under section 33 may be framed so as to require the Commission to exclude from consideration—

    (a) subsection (1) of section 23;

    (b) subsection (2) of that section; or

    (c) one of those subsections if the Commission finds that the other is satisfied.

(6)   In relation to the question whether any such result as is mentioned in section 23(2)(b) will arise, a reference under section 33 may be framed so as to require the Commission to confine its investigation to the supply of goods or services in a part of the United Kingdom specified in the reference.

[283]

NOTES

Commencement: to be appointed.

37 Cancellation and variation of references under section 22 or 33

(1)   The Commission shall cancel a reference under section 33 if it considers that the proposal to make arrangements of the kind mentioned in the reference has been abandoned.

(2)   The Commission may, if it considers that doing so is justified by the facts (including events occurring on or after the making of the reference concerned), treat a reference made under section 22 or 33 as if it had been made under section 33 or (as the case may be) 22; and, in such cases, references in this Part to references under those sections shall, so far as may be necessary, be construed accordingly.

(3)   Where, by virtue of subsection (2), the Commission treats a reference made under section 22 or 33 as if it had been made under section 33 or (as the case may be) 22, sections 77 to 81 shall, in particular, apply as if the reference had been made under section 33 or (as the case may be) 22 instead of under section 22 or 33.

(4)   Subsection (5) applies in relation to any undertaking accepted under section 80, or any order made under section 81, which is in force immediately before the Commission, by virtue of subsection (2), treats a reference made under section 22 or 33 as if it had been made under section 33 or (as the case may be) 22.

(5)   The undertaking or order shall, so far as applicable, continue in force as if—

   (a) in the case of an undertaking or order which relates to a reference made under section 22, accepted or made in relation to a reference made under section 33; and

   (b) in the case of an undertaking or order which relates to a reference made under section 33, accepted or made in relation to a reference made under section 22;

and the undertaking or order concerned may be varied, superseded, released or revoked accordingly.

(6)   The OFT may at any time vary a reference under section 22 or 33.

(7)   The OFT shall consult the Commission before varying any such reference.

(8)   Subsection (7) shall not apply if the Commission has requested the variation concerned.

(9)   No variation by the OFT under this section shall be capable of altering the period permitted by section 39 within which the report of the Commission under section 38 is to be prepared and published.

[284]

NOTES

Commencement: to be appointed.

38 Investigations and reports on references under section 22 or 33

(1)   The Commission shall prepare and publish a report on a reference under section 22 or 33 within the period permitted by section 39.

(2)   The report shall, in particular, contain—

   (a) the decisions of the Commission on the questions which it is required to answer by virtue of section 35 or (as the case may be) 36;

   (b) its reasons for its decisions; and

   (c) such information as the Commission considers appropriate for facilitating a proper understanding of those questions and of its reasons for its decisions.

(3)   The Commission shall carry out such investigations as it considers appropriate for the purposes of preparing a report under this section.

(4)   The Commission shall, at the same time as a report prepared under this section is published, give it to the OFT.

[285]

NOTES

Commencement: to be appointed.

39 Time-limits for investigations and reports

(1)   The Commission shall prepare and publish its report under section 38 within the period of 24 weeks beginning with the date of the reference concerned.

(2)   Where article 9(6) of the European Merger Regulations applies in relation to the reference under section 22 or 33, the Commission shall prepare and publish its report under section 38—

   (a) within the period of 24 weeks beginning with the date of the reference; or

   (b) if it is a shorter period, within such period as is necessary to ensure compliance with that article.

(3)   The Commission may extend, by no more than 8 weeks, the period within which a report under section 38 is to be prepared and published if it considers that there are special reasons why the report cannot be prepared and published within that period.

(4)   The Commission may extend the period within which a report under section 38 is to be prepared and published if it considers that a relevant person has failed (whether with or without a reasonable excuse) to comply with any requirement of a notice under section 109.

(5)   In subsection (4) "relevant person" means—
    (a) any person carrying on any of the enterprises concerned;
    (b) any person who (whether alone or as a member of a group) owns or has control of any such person; or
    (c) any officer, employee or agent of any person mentioned in paragraph (a) or (b).

(6)   For the purposes of subsection (5) a person or group of persons able, directly or indirectly, to control or materially to influence the policy of a body of persons corporate or unincorporate, but without having a controlling interest in that body of persons, may be treated as having control of it.

(7)   An extension under subsection (3) or (4) shall come into force when published under section 107.

(8)   An extension under subsection (4) shall continue in force until—
    (a) the person concerned provides the information or documents to the satisfaction of the Commission or (as the case may be) appears as a witness in accordance with the requirements of the Commission; or
    (b) the Commission publishes its decision to cancel the extension.

(9)   References in this Part to the date of a reference shall be construed as references to the date specified in the reference as the date on which it is made.

(10) This section is subject to section 40.

                                                            [286]

NOTES
    Commencement: to be appointed.

40 Section 39: supplementary

(1)   No extension is possible under subsection (3) or (4) of section 39 where the period within which the report is to be prepared and published is determined by virtue of subsection (2)(b) of that section.

(2)   Where the period within which the report is to be prepared and published is determined by virtue of subsection (2)(a) of section 39, no extension is possible under subsection (3) or (4) of that section which extends that period beyond such period as is necessary to ensure compliance with article 9(6) of the European Merger Regulations.

(3)   A period extended under subsection (3) of section 39 may also be extended under subsection (4) of that section and a period extended under subsection (4) of that section may also be extended under subsection (3) of that section.

(4)   No more than one extension is possible under section 39(3).

(5)   Where a period within which a report under section 38 is to be prepared and published is extended or further extended under section 39(3) or (4), the period as extended or (as the case may be) further extended shall, subject to subsections (6) and (7), be calculated by taking the period being extended and adding to it the period of the extension (whether or not those periods overlap in time).

(6)   Subsection (7) applies where—

    (a) the period within which the report under section 38 is to be prepared and published is further extended;

    (b) the further extension and at least one previous extension is made under section 39(4); and

    (c) the same days or fractions of days are included in or comprise the further extension and are included in or comprise at least one such previous extension.

(7)   In calculating the period of the further extension, any days or fractions of days of the kind mentioned in subsection (6)(c) shall be disregarded.

(8)   The Secretary of State may by order amend section 39 so as to alter any one or more of the following periods—

    (a) the period of 24 weeks mentioned in subsection (1) of that section or any period for the time being mentioned in that subsection in substitution for that period;

    (b) the period of 24 weeks mentioned in subsection (2)(a) of that section or any period for the time being mentioned in that subsection in substitution for that period;

    (c) the period of 8 weeks mentioned in subsection (3) of that section or any period for the time being mentioned in that subsection in substitution for that period.

(9)   No alteration shall be made by virtue of subsection (8) which results in the period for the time being mentioned in subsection (1) or (2)(a) of section 39 exceeding 24 weeks or the period for the time being mentioned in subsection (3) of that section exceeding 8 weeks.

(10) An order under subsection (8) shall not affect any period of time within which the Commission is under a duty to prepare and publish its report under section 38 in relation to a reference under section 22 or 33 if the Commission is already under that duty in relation to that reference when the order is made.

(11) Before making an order under subsection (8) the Secretary of State shall consult the Commission and such other persons as he considers appropriate.

(12) The Secretary of State may make regulations for the purposes of section 39(8).

(13) The regulations may, in particular—

    (a) provide for the time at which information or documents are to be treated as provided (including the time at which they are to be treated as provided to the satisfaction of the Commission for the purposes of section 39(8));

    (b) provide for the time at which a person is to be treated as appearing as a witness (including the time at which he is to be treated as appearing as a witness in accordance with the requirements of the Commission for the purposes of section 39(8));

    (c) provide for the persons carrying on the enterprises which have or may have ceased to be, or may cease to be, distinct enterprises to be informed, in circumstances in which section 39(8) applies, of the fact that—

       (i) the Commission is satisfied as to the provision of the information or documents required by it; or

       (ii) the person concerned has appeared as a witness in accordance with the requirements of the Commission;

    (d) provide for the persons carrying on the enterprises which have or may have ceased to be, or may cease to be, distinct enterprises to be informed, in circumstances in which section 39(8) applies, of the time at which the

Commission is to be treated as satisfied as mentioned in paragraph (c)(i) above or the person concerned is to be treated as having appeared as mentioned in paragraph (c)(ii) above.

[287]

NOTES

Commencement: to be appointed.

41 Duty to remedy effects of completed or anticipated mergers

(1)   Subsection (2) applies where a report of the Commission has been prepared and published under section 38 within the period permitted by section 39 and contains the decision that there is an anti-competitive outcome.

(2)   The Commission shall take such action under section 82 or 84 as it considers to be reasonable and practicable—

  (a) to remedy, mitigate or prevent the substantial lessening of competition concerned; and

  (b) to remedy, mitigate or prevent any adverse effects which have resulted from, or may be expected to result from, the substantial lessening of competition.

(3)   The decision of the Commission under subsection (2) shall be consistent with its decisions as included in its report by virtue of section 35(3) or (as the case may be) 36(2) unless there has been a material change of circumstances since the preparation of the report or the Commission otherwise has a special reason for deciding differently.

(4)   In making a decision under subsection (2), the Commission shall, in particular, have regard to the need to achieve as comprehensive a solution as is reasonable and practicable to the substantial lessening of competition and any adverse effects resulting from it.

(5)   In making a decision under subsection (2), the Commission may, in particular, have regard to the effect of any action on any relevant customer benefits in relation to the creation of the relevant merger situation concerned.

[288]

NOTES

Commencement: to be appointed.

CHAPTER 2
PUBLIC INTEREST CASES

Power to make references

42 Intervention by Secretary of State in certain public interest cases

(1)   Subsection (2) applies where—

  (a) the Secretary of State has reasonable grounds for suspecting that it is or may be the case that a relevant merger situation has been created or that arrangements are in progress or in contemplation which, if carried into effect, will result in the creation of a relevant merger situation;

  (b) no reference under section 22 or 33 has been made in relation to the relevant merger situation concerned;

  (c) no decision has been made not to make such a reference (other than a decision made by virtue of subsection (2)(b) of section 33 or a decision to accept undertakings under section 73 instead of making such a reference); and

(d) no reference is prevented from being made under section 22 or 33 by virtue
of—
  (i) section 22(3)(a) or (e) or (as the case may be) 33(3)(a) or (e); or
  (ii) Community law or anything done under or in accordance with it.

(2) The Secretary of State may give a notice to the OFT (in this Part "an
intervention notice") if he believes that it is or may be the case that one or more than
one public interest consideration is relevant to a consideration of the relevant merger
situation concerned.

(3) For the purposes of this Part a public interest consideration is a
consideration which, at the time of the giving of the intervention notice concerned,
is specified in section 58 or is not so specified but, in the opinion of the Secretary of
State, ought to be so specified.

(4) No more than one intervention notice shall be given under subsection (2) in
relation to the same relevant merger situation.

(5) For the purposes of deciding whether a relevant merger situation has been
created or whether arrangements are in progress or in contemplation which, if
carried into effect, will result in the creation of a relevant merger situation,
sections 23 to 32 (read together with section 34) shall apply for the purposes of this
Chapter as they do for the purposes of Chapter 1 but subject to subsection (6).

(6) In their application by virtue of subsection (5) sections 23 to 32 shall have
effect as if—
  (a) for paragraph (a) of section 23(9) there were substituted—
    "(a) in relation to the giving of an intervention notice, the time when
        the notice is given;
    (aa) in relation to the making of a report by the OFT under section 44,
        the time of the making of the report;
    (ab) in the case of a reference which is treated as having been made
        under section 45(2) or (3) by virtue of section 49(1), such time as
        the Commission may determine; and";
  (b) the references to the OFT in sections 25(1) to (3), (6) and (8) and 31
      included references to the Secretary of State;
  (c) the references to the OFT in section 25(4) and (5) were references to the
      Secretary of State;
  (d) the reference in section 25(4) to section 73 were a reference to paragraph 3
      of Schedule 7;
  (e) after section 25(5) there were inserted—

    "(5A) The Secretary of State may by notice to the persons carrying on the
    enterprises which have or may have ceased to be distinct enterprises extend
    the four month period mentioned in section 24(1)(a) or (2)(b) if, by virtue of
    section 46(5) or paragraph 3(6) of Schedule 7, he decides to delay a decision
    as to whether to make a reference under section 45.

    (5B) An extension under subsection (5A) shall be for the period of the
    delay.";
  (f) in section 25(10)(b) after the word "(4)" there were inserted ", (5A)";
  (g) the reference in section 25(12) to one extension were a reference to one
      extension by the OFT and one extension by the Secretary of State;
  (h) the powers to extend time-limits under section 25 as applied by subsection
      (5) above, and the power to request information under section 31(1) as so
      applied, were not exercisable by the OFT or the Secretary of State before
      the giving of an intervention notice but the existing time-limits in relation
      to possible references under section 22 or 33 were applicable for the
      purposes of the giving of that notice;

    (i) the existing time-limits in relation to possible references under section 22 or 33 (except for extensions under section 25(4)) remained applicable on and after the giving of an intervention notice as if any extensions were made under section 25 as applied by subsection (5) above but subject to further alteration by the OFT or the Secretary of State under section 25 as so applied;

    (j) in subsection (1) of section 31 for the words "section 22" there were substituted "section 45(2) or (3)" and, in the application of that subsection to the OFT, for the word "deciding" there were substituted "enabling the Secretary of State to decide";

    (k) in the case of the giving of intervention notices, the references in sections 23 to 32 to the making of a reference or a reference were, so far as necessary, references to the giving of an intervention notice or an intervention notice; and

    (l) the references to the OFT in section 32(2)(a) to (c) and (3) were construed in accordance with the above modifications.

(7)   Where the Secretary of State has given an intervention notice mentioning a public interest consideration which, at that time, is not finalised, he shall, as soon as practicable, take such action as is within his power to ensure that it is finalised.

(8)   For the purposes of this Part a public interest consideration is finalised if—

    (a) it is specified in section 58 otherwise than by virtue of an order under subsection (3) of that section; or

    (b) it is specified in that section by virtue of an order under subsection (3) of that section and the order providing for it to be so specified has been laid before, and approved by, Parliament in accordance with subsection (7) of section 124 and within the period mentioned in that subsection.

        [289]

NOTES

Commencement: to be appointed.

43 Intervention notices under section 42

(1)   An intervention notice shall state—

    (a) the relevant merger situation concerned;

    (b) the public interest consideration or considerations which are, or may be, relevant to a consideration of the relevant merger situation concerned; and

    (c) where any public interest consideration concerned is not finalised, the proposed timetable for finalising it.

(2)   Where the Secretary of State believes that it is or may be the case that two or more public interest considerations are relevant to a consideration of the relevant merger situation concerned, he may decide not to mention in the intervention notice such of those considerations as he considers appropriate.

(3)   An intervention notice shall come into force when it is given and shall cease to be in force when the matter to which it relates is finally determined under this Chapter.

(4)   For the purposes of this Part, a matter to which an intervention notice relates is finally determined under this Chapter if—

    (a) the time within which the OFT is to report to the Secretary of State under section 44 has expired and no such report has been made;

    (b) the Secretary of State decides to accept an undertaking or group of undertakings under paragraph 3 of Schedule 7 instead of making a reference under section 45;

(c) the Secretary of State otherwise decides not to make a reference under that section;

(d) the Commission cancels such a reference under section 48(1) or 53(1);

(e) the time within which the Commission is to prepare a report under section 50 and give it to the Secretary of State has expired and no such report has been prepared and given to the Secretary of State;

(f) the time within which the Secretary of State is to make and publish a decision under section 54(2) has expired and no such decision has been made and published;

(g) the Secretary of State decides under section 54(2) to make no finding at all in the matter;

(h) the Secretary of State otherwise decides under section 54(2) not to make an adverse public interest finding;

(i) the Secretary of State decides under section 54(2) to make an adverse public interest finding but decides neither to accept an undertaking under paragraph 9 of Schedule 7 nor to make an order under paragraph 11 of that Schedule; or

(j) the Secretary of State decides under section 54(2) to make an adverse public interest finding and accepts an undertaking under paragraph 9 of Schedule 7 or makes an order under paragraph 11 of that Schedule.

(5)   For the purposes of this Part the time when a matter to which an intervention notice relates is finally determined under this Chapter is—

(a) in a case falling within subsection (4)(a), (e) or (f), the expiry of the time concerned;

(b) in a case falling within subsection (4)(b), the acceptance of the undertaking or group of undertakings concerned;

(c) in a case falling within subsection (4)(c), (d), (g) or (h), the making of the decision concerned;

(d) in a case falling within subsection (4)(i), the making of the decision neither to accept an undertaking under paragraph 9 of Schedule 7 nor to make an order under paragraph 11 of that Schedule; and

(e) in a case falling within subsection (4)(j), the acceptance of the undertaking concerned or (as the case may be) the making of the order concerned.

[290]

NOTES

Commencement: to be appointed.

44 Investigation and report by OFT

(1)   Subsection (2) applies where the Secretary of State has given an intervention notice in relation to a relevant merger situation.

(2)   The OFT shall, within such period as the Secretary of State may require, give a report to the Secretary of State in relation to the case.

(3)   The report shall contain—

(a) advice from the OFT on the considerations relevant to the making of a reference under section 22 or 33 which are also relevant to the Secretary of State's decision as to whether to make a reference under section 45; and

(b) a summary of any representations about the case which have been received by the OFT and which relate to any public interest consideration mentioned in the intervention notice concerned and which is or may be relevant to the Secretary of State's decision as to whether to make a reference under section 45.

(4)   The report shall, in particular, include decisions as to whether the OFT believes that it is, or may be, the case that—

(a) a relevant merger situation has been created or arrangements are in progress or in contemplation which, if carried into effect, will result in the creation of a relevant merger situation;

(b) the creation of that situation has resulted, or may be expected to result, in a substantial lessening of competition within any market or markets in the United Kingdom for goods or services;

(c) the market or markets concerned would not be of sufficient importance to justify the making of a reference to the Commission under section 22 or 33;

(d) in the case of arrangements which are in progress or in contemplation, the arrangements are not sufficiently far advanced, or not sufficiently likely to proceed, to justify the making of such a reference;

(e) any relevant customer benefits in relation to the creation of the relevant merger situation concerned outweigh the substantial lessening of competition and any adverse effects of the substantial lessening of competition; or

(f) it would be appropriate to deal with the matter (disregarding any public interest considerations mentioned in the intervention notice concerned) by way of undertakings under paragraph 3 of Schedule 7.

(5) If the OFT believes that it is or may be the case that it would be appropriate to deal with the matter (disregarding any public interest considerations mentioned in the intervention notice concerned) by way of undertakings under paragraph 3 of Schedule 7, the report shall contain descriptions of the undertakings which the OFT believes are, or may be, appropriate.

(6) The report may, in particular, include advice and recommendations on any public interest consideration mentioned in the intervention notice concerned and which is or may be relevant to the Secretary of State's decision as to whether to make a reference under section 45.

(7) The OFT shall carry out such investigations as it considers appropriate for the purposes of producing a report under this section.

[291]

NOTES

Commencement: to be appointed.

45 Power of Secretary of State to refer matter to Commission

(1) Subsections (2) to (5) apply where the Secretary of State—

(a) has given an intervention notice in relation to a relevant merger situation; and

(b) has received a report of the OFT under section 44 in relation to the matter.

(2) The Secretary of State may make a reference to the Commission if he believes that it is or may be the case that—

(a) a relevant merger situation has been created;

(b) the creation of that situation has resulted, or may be expected to result, in a substantial lessening of competition within any market or markets in the United Kingdom for goods or services;

(c) one or more than one public interest consideration mentioned in the intervention notice is relevant to a consideration of the relevant merger situation concerned; and

(d) taking account only of the substantial lessening of competition and the relevant public interest consideration or considerations concerned, the creation of that situation operates or may be expected to operate against the public interest.

(3) The Secretary of State may make a reference to the Commission if he believes that it is or may be the case that—

    (a) a relevant merger situation has been created;

    (b) the creation of that situation has not resulted, and may be expected not to result, in a substantial lessening of competition within any market or markets in the United Kingdom for goods or services;

    (c) one or more than one public interest consideration mentioned in the intervention notice is relevant to a consideration of the relevant merger situation concerned; and

    (d) taking account only of the relevant public interest consideration or considerations concerned, the creation of that situation operates or may be expected to operate against the public interest.

(4) The Secretary of State may make a reference to the Commission if he believes that it is or may be the case that—

    (a) arrangements are in progress or in contemplation which, if carried into effect, will result in the creation of a relevant merger situation;

    (b) the creation of that situation may be expected to result in a substantial lessening of competition within any market or markets in the United Kingdom for goods or services;

    (c) one or more than one public interest consideration mentioned in the intervention notice is relevant to a consideration of the relevant merger situation concerned; and

    (d) taking account only of the substantial lessening of competition and the relevant public interest consideration or considerations concerned, the creation of the relevant merger situation may be expected to operate against the public interest.

(5) The Secretary of State may make a reference to the Commission if he believes that it is or may be the case that—

    (a) arrangements are in progress or in contemplation which, if carried into effect, will result in the creation of a relevant merger situation;

    (b) the creation of that situation may be expected not to result in a substantial lessening of competition within any market or markets in the United Kingdom for goods or services;

    (c) one or more than one public interest consideration mentioned in the intervention notice is relevant to a consideration of the relevant merger situation concerned; and

    (d) taking account only of the relevant public interest consideration or considerations concerned, the creation of the relevant merger situation may be expected to operate against the public interest.

(6) For the purposes of this Chapter any anti-competitive outcome shall be treated as being adverse to the public interest unless it is justified by one or more than one public interest consideration which is relevant.

(7) This section is subject to section 46.

NOTES

Commencement: to be appointed.

46 References under section 45: supplementary

(1) No reference shall be made under section 45 if—

    (a) the making of the reference is prevented by section 69(1), 74(1) or 96(3) or paragraph 4 of Schedule 7; or

    (b) the European Commission is considering a request made, in relation to the matter concerned, by the United Kingdom (whether alone or with others) under article 22(3) of the European Merger Regulations, is proceeding with the matter in pursuance of such a request or has dealt with the matter in pursuance of such a request.

(2)   The Secretary of State, in deciding whether to make a reference under section 45, shall accept the decisions of the OFT included in its report by virtue of subsection (4) of section 44 and any descriptions of undertakings as mentioned in subsection (5) of that section.

(3)   Where the decision to make a reference under section 45 is made at any time on or after the end of the period of 24 weeks beginning with the giving of the intervention notice concerned, the Secretary of State shall, in deciding whether to make such a reference, disregard any public interest consideration which is mentioned in the intervention notice but which has not been finalised before the end of that period.

(4)   Subject to subsection (5), where the decision to make a reference under section 45(2) or (4) is made at any time before the end of the period of 24 weeks beginning with the giving of the intervention notice concerned, the Secretary of State shall, in deciding whether to make such a reference, disregard any public interest consideration which is mentioned in the intervention notice but which has not been finalised if its effect would be to prevent, or to help to prevent, an anti-competitive outcome from being adverse to the public interest.

(5)   The Secretary of State may, if he believes that there is a realistic prospect of the public interest consideration mentioned in subsection (4) being finalised within the period of 24 weeks beginning with the giving of the intervention notice concerned, delay deciding whether to make the reference concerned until the public interest consideration is finalised or, if earlier, the period expires.

(6)   A reference under section 45 shall, in particular, specify—
   (a) the subsection of that section under which it is made;
   (b) the date on which it is made; and
   (c) the public interest consideration or considerations mentioned in the intervention notice concerned which the Secretary of State is not under a duty to disregard by virtue of subsection (3) above and which he believes are or may be relevant to a consideration of the relevant merger situation concerned.

[293]

NOTES

Commencement: to be appointed.

Reports on references

47 Questions to be decided on references under section 45

(1)   The Commission shall, on a reference under section 45(2) or (3), decide whether a relevant merger situation has been created.

(2)   If the Commission decides that such a situation has been created, it shall, on a reference under section 45(2), decide the following additional questions—
   (a) whether the creation of that situation has resulted, or may be expected to result, in a substantial lessening of competition within any market or markets in the United Kingdom for goods or services; and
   (b) whether, taking account only of any substantial lessening of competition and the admissible public interest consideration or considerations concerned, the creation of that situation operates or may be expected to operate against the public interest.

(3)   If the Commission decides that a relevant merger situation has been created, it shall, on a reference under section 45(3), decide whether, taking account only of the admissible public interest consideration or considerations concerned, the creation of that situation operates or may be expected to operate against the public interest.

(4)   The Commission shall, on a reference under section 45(4) or (5), decide whether arrangements are in progress or in contemplation which, if carried into effect, will result in the creation of a relevant merger situation.

(5)   If the Commission decides that such arrangements are in progress or in contemplation, it shall, on a reference under section 45(4), decide the following additional questions—
  (a) whether the creation of that situation may be expected to result in a substantial lessening of competition within any market or markets in the United Kingdom for goods or services; and
  (b) whether, taking account only of any substantial lessening of competition and the admissible public interest consideration or considerations concerned, the creation of that situation may be expected to operate against the public interest.

(6)   If the Commission decides that arrangements are in progress or in contemplation which, if carried into effect, will result in the creation of a relevant merger situation, it shall, on a reference under section 45(5), decide whether, taking account only of the admissible public interest consideration or considerations concerned, the creation of that situation may be expected to operate against the public interest.

(7)   The Commission shall, if it has decided on a reference under section 45 that the creation of a relevant merger situation operates or may be expected to operate against the public interest, decide the following additional questions—
  (a) whether action should be taken by the Secretary of State under section 55 for the purpose of remedying, mitigating or preventing any of the effects adverse to the public interest which have resulted from, or may be expected to result from, the creation of the relevant merger situation;
  (b) whether the Commission should recommend the taking of other action by the Secretary of State or action by persons other than itself and the Secretary of State for the purpose of remedying, mitigating or preventing any of the effects adverse to the public interest which have resulted from, or may be expected to result from, the creation of the relevant merger situation; and
  (c) in either case, if action should be taken, what action should be taken and what is to be remedied, mitigated or prevented.

(8)   Where the Commission has decided by virtue of subsection (2)(a) or (5)(a) that there is or will be a substantial lessening of competition within any market or markets in the United Kingdom for goods or services, it shall also decide separately the following questions (on the assumption that it is proceeding as mentioned in section 56(6))—
  (a) whether action should be taken by it under section 41 for the purpose of remedying, mitigating or preventing the substantial lessening of competition concerned or any adverse effect which has resulted from, or may be expected to result from, the substantial lessening of competition;
  (b) whether the Commission should recommend the taking of action by other persons for the purpose of remedying, mitigating or preventing the substantial lessening of competition concerned or any adverse effect which has resulted from, or may be expected to result from, the substantial lessening of competition; and

(c) in either case, if action should be taken, what action should be taken and what is to be remedied, mitigated or prevented.

(9) In deciding the questions mentioned in subsections (7) and (8) the Commission shall, in particular, have regard to the need to achieve as comprehensive a solution as is reasonable and practicable to—
  (a) the adverse effects to the public interest; or
  (b) (as the case may be) the substantial lessening of competition and any adverse effects resulting from it.

(10) In deciding the questions mentioned in subsections (7) and (8) in a case where it has decided by virtue of subsection (2)(a) or (5)(a) that there is or will be a substantial lessening of competition, the Commission may, in particular, have regard to the effect of any action on any relevant customer benefits in relation to the creation of the relevant merger situation concerned.

(11) In this section "admissible public interest consideration" means any public interest consideration which is specified in the reference under section 45 and which the Commission is not under a duty to disregard.

[294]

NOTES
  Commencement: to be appointed.

48 Cases where references or certain questions need not be decided

(1) The Commission shall cancel a reference under section 45(4) or (5) if it considers that the proposal to make arrangements of the kind mentioned in that reference has been abandoned.

(2) In relation to the question whether a relevant merger situation has been created or the question whether a relevant merger situation will be created, a reference under section 45 may be framed so as to require the Commission to exclude from consideration—
  (a) subsection (1) of section 23;
  (b) subsection (2) of that section; or
  (c) one of those subsections if the Commission finds that the other is satisfied.

(3) In relation to the question whether any such result as is mentioned in section 23(2)(b) has arisen or the question whether any such result will arise, a reference under section 45 may be framed so as to require the Commission to confine its investigation to the supply of goods or services in a part of the United Kingdom specified in the reference.

[295]

NOTES
  Commencement: to be appointed.

49 Variation of references under section 45

(1) The Commission may, if it considers that doing so is justified by the facts (including events occurring on or after the making of the reference concerned), treat—
  (a) a reference made under subsection (2) or (3) of section 45 as if it had been made under subsection (4) or (as the case may be) (5) of that section; or
  (b) a reference made under subsection (4) or (5) of section 45 as if it had been made under subsection (2) or (as the case may be) (3) of that section;

and, in such cases, references in this Part to references under those enactments shall, so far as may be necessary, be construed accordingly.

(2)   Where, by virtue of subsection (1), the Commission treats a reference made under subsection (2) or (3) of section 45 as if it had been made under subsection (4) or (as the case may be) (5) of that section, paragraphs 1, 2, 7 and 8 of Schedule 7 shall, in particular, apply as if the reference had been made under subsection (4) or (as the case may be) (5) of that section instead of under subsection (2) or (3) of that section.

(3)   Where, by virtue of subsection (1), the Commission treats a reference made under subsection (4) or (5) of section 45 as if it had been made under subsection (2) or (as the case may be) (3) of that section, paragraphs 1, 2, 7 and 8 of Schedule 7 shall, in particular, apply as if the reference had been made under subsection (2) or (as the case may be) (3) of that section instead of under subsection (4) or (5) of that section.

(4)   Subsection (5) applies in relation to any undertaking accepted under paragraph 1 of Schedule 7, or any order made under paragraph 2 of that Schedule, which is in force immediately before the Commission, by virtue of subsection (1), treats a reference as mentioned in subsection (1).

(5)   The undertaking or order shall, so far as applicable, continue in force as if—
  (a) in the case of an undertaking or order which relates to a reference under subsection (2) or (3) of section 45, accepted or made in relation to a reference made under subsection (4) or (as the case may be) (5) of that section; and
  (b) in the case of an undertaking or order which relates to a reference made under subsection (4) or (5) of that section, accepted or made in relation to a reference made under subsection (2) or (as the case may be) (3) of that section;

and the undertaking or order concerned may be varied, superseded, released or revoked accordingly.

(6)   The Secretary of State may at any time vary a reference under section 45.

(7)   The Secretary of State shall consult the Commission before varying any such reference.

(8)   Subsection (7) shall not apply if the Commission has requested the variation concerned.

(9)   No variation by the Secretary of State under this section shall be capable of altering the public interest consideration or considerations specified in the reference or the period permitted by section 51 within which the report of the Commission under section 50 is to be prepared and given to the Secretary of State.

[296]

NOTES

Commencement: to be appointed.

50 Investigations and reports on references under section 45

(1)   The Commission shall prepare a report on a reference under section 45 and give it to the Secretary of State within the period permitted by section 51.

(2)   The report shall, in particular, contain—
  (a) the decisions of the Commission on the questions which it is required to answer by virtue of section 47;
  (b) its reasons for its decisions; and
  (c) such information as the Commission considers appropriate for facilitating a proper understanding of those questions and of its reasons for its decisions.

(3)   The Commission shall carry out such investigations as it considers appropriate for the purpose of producing a report under this section.

[297]

NOTES
    Commencement: to be appointed.

51 Time-limits for investigations and reports by Commission

(1)   The Commission shall prepare its report under section 50 and give it to the Secretary of State under that section within the period of 24 weeks beginning with the date of the reference concerned.

(2)   Where article 9(6) of the European Merger Regulations applies in relation to the reference under section 45, the Commission shall prepare its report under section 50 and give it to the Secretary of State—
   (a) within the period of 24 weeks beginning with the date of the reference; or
   (b) if it is a shorter period, within such period as is necessary to ensure compliance with that article.

(3)   The Commission may extend, by no more than 8 weeks, the period within which a report under section 50 is to be prepared and given to the Secretary of State if it considers that there are special reasons why the report cannot be prepared and given to the Secretary of State within that period.

(4)   The Commission may extend the period within which a report under section 50 is to be prepared and given to the Secretary of State if it considers that a relevant person has failed (whether with or without a reasonable excuse) to comply with any requirement of a notice under section 109.

(5)   In subsection (4) "relevant person" means—
   (a) any person carrying on any of the enterprises concerned;
   (b) any person who (whether alone or as a member of a group) owns or has control of any such person; or
   (c) any officer, employee or agent of any person mentioned in paragraph (a) or (b).

(6)   For the purposes of subsection (5) a person or group of persons able, directly or indirectly, to control or materially to influence the policy of a body of persons corporate or unincorporate, but without having a controlling interest in that body of persons, may be treated as having control of it.

(7)   An extension under subsection (3) or (4) shall come into force when published under section 107.

(8)   An extension under subsection (4) shall continue in force until—
   (a) the person concerned provides the information or documents to the satisfaction of the Commission or (as the case may be) appears as a witness in accordance with the requirements of the Commission; or
   (b) the Commission publishes its decision to cancel the extension.

(9)   This section is subject to sections 52 and 53.

[298]

NOTES
    Commencement: to be appointed.

52 Section 51: supplementary

(1)   No extension is possible under subsection (3) or (4) of section 51 where the period within which the report is to be prepared and given to the Secretary of State is determined by virtue of subsection (2)(b) of that section.

(2)   Where the period within which the report is to be prepared and given to the Secretary of State is determined by virtue of subsection (2)(a) of section 51, no extension is possible under subsection (3) or (4) of that section which extends that period beyond such period as is necessary to ensure compliance with article 9(6) of the European Merger Regulations.

(3)   A period extended under subsection (3) of section 51 may also be extended under subsection (4) of that section and a period extended under subsection (4) of that section may also be extended under subsection (3) of that section.

(4)   No more than one extension is possible under section 51(3).

(5)   Where a period within which a report under section 50 is to be prepared and given to the Secretary of State is extended or further extended under section 51(3) or (4), the period as extended or (as the case may be) further extended shall, subject to subsections (6) and (7), be calculated by taking the period being extended and adding to it the period of the extension (whether or not those periods overlap in time).

(6)   Subsection (7) applies where—
  (a) the period within which the report under section 50 is to be prepared and given to the Secretary of State is further extended;
  (b) the further extension and at least one previous extension is made under section 51(4); and
  (c) the same days or fractions of days are included in or comprise the further extension and are included in or comprise at least one such previous extension.

(7)   In calculating the period of the further extension, any days or fractions of days of the kind mentioned in subsection (6)(c) shall be disregarded.

(8)   The Secretary of State may by order amend section 51 so as to alter any one or more of the following periods—
  (a) the period of 24 weeks mentioned in subsection (1) of that section or any period for the time being mentioned in that subsection in substitution for that period;
  (b) the period of 24 weeks mentioned in subsection (2)(a) of that section or any period for the time being mentioned in that subsection in substitution for that period;
  (c) the period of 8 weeks mentioned in subsection (3) of that section or any period for the time being mentioned in that subsection in substitution for that period.

(9)   No alteration shall be made by virtue of subsection (8) which results in the period for the time being mentioned in subsection (1) or (2)(a) of section 51 exceeding 24 weeks or the period for the time being mentioned in subsection (3) of that section exceeding 8 weeks.

(10)   An order under subsection (8) shall not affect any period of time within which the Commission is under a duty to prepare and give to the Secretary of State its report under section 50 in relation to a reference under section 45 if the Commission is already under that duty in relation to that reference when the order is made.

(11)   Before making an order under subsection (8) the Secretary of State shall consult the Commission and such other persons as he considers appropriate.

(12)   The Secretary of State may make regulations for the purposes of section 51(8).

(13)   The regulations may, in particular—
  (a) provide for the time at which information or documents are to be treated as provided (including the time at which they are to be treated as provided to the satisfaction of the Commission for the purposes of section 51(8));

(b) provide for the time at which a person is to be treated as appearing as a witness (including the time at which he is to be treated as appearing as a witness in accordance with the requirements of the Commission for the purposes of section 51(8));

(c) provide for the persons carrying on the enterprises which have or may have ceased to be, or may cease to be, distinct enterprises to be informed, in circumstances in which section 51(8) applies, of the fact that—

 (i) the Commission is satisfied as to the provision of the information or documents required by it; or

 (ii) the person concerned has appeared as a witness in accordance with the requirements of the Commission;

(d) provide for the persons carrying on the enterprises which have or may have ceased to be, or may cease to be, distinct enterprises to be informed, in circumstances in which section 51(8) applies, of the time at which the Commission is to be treated as satisfied as mentioned in paragraph (c)(i) above or the person concerned is to be treated as having appeared as mentioned in paragraph (c)(ii) above.

[299]

NOTES

Commencement: to be appointed.

53 Restrictions on action where public interest considerations not finalised

(1) The Commission shall cancel a reference under section 45 if—

(a) the intervention notice concerned mentions a public interest consideration which was not finalised on the giving of that notice or public interest considerations which, at that time, were not finalised;

(b) no other public interest consideration is mentioned in the notice;

(c) at least 24 weeks has elapsed since the giving of the notice; and

(d) the public interest consideration mentioned in the notice has not been finalised within that period of 24 weeks or (as the case may be) none of the public interest considerations mentioned in the notice has been finalised within that period of 24 weeks.

(2) Where a reference to the Commission under section 45 specifies a public interest consideration which has not been finalised before the making of the reference, the Commission shall not give its report to the Secretary of State under section 50 in relation to that reference unless—

(a) the period of 24 weeks beginning with the giving of the intervention notice concerned has expired;

(b) the public interest consideration concerned has been finalised; or

(c) the report must be given to the Secretary of State to ensure compliance with article 9(6) of the European Merger Regulations.

(3) The Commission shall, in reporting on any of the questions mentioned in section 47(2)(b), (3), (5)(b), (6) and (7), disregard any public interest consideration which has not been finalised before the giving of the report.

(4) The Commission shall, in reporting on any of the questions mentioned in section 47(2)(b), (3), (5)(b), (6) and (7), disregard any public interest consideration which was not finalised on the giving of the intervention notice concerned and has not been finalised within the period of 24 weeks beginning with the giving of the notice concerned.

(5) Subsections (1) to (4) are without prejudice to the power of the Commission to carry out investigations in relation to any public interest consideration to which it might be able to have regard in its report.

[300]

NOTES

Commencement: to be appointed.

Decisions of the Secretary of State

54 Decision of Secretary of State in public interest cases

(1)   Subsection (2) applies where the Secretary of State has received a report of the Commission under section 50 in relation to a relevant merger situation.

(2)   The Secretary of State shall decide whether to make an adverse public interest finding in relation to the relevant merger situation and whether to make no finding at all in the matter.

(3)   For the purposes of this Part the Secretary of State makes an adverse public interest finding in relation to a relevant merger situation if, in relation to that situation, he decides—

(a) in connection with a reference to the Commission under subsection (2) of section 45, that it is the case as mentioned in paragraphs (a) to (d) of that subsection or subsection (3) of that section;

(b) in connection with a reference to the Commission under subsection (3) of that section, that it is the case as mentioned in paragraphs (a) to (d) of that subsection;

(c) in connection with a reference to the Commission under subsection (4) of that section, that it is the case as mentioned in paragraphs (a) to (d) of that subsection or subsection (5) of that section; and

(d) in connection with a reference to the Commission under subsection (5) of that section, that it is the case as mentioned in paragraphs (a) to (d) of that subsection.

(4)   The Secretary of State may make no finding at all in the matter only if he decides that there is no public interest consideration which is relevant to a consideration of the relevant merger situation concerned.

(5)   The Secretary of State shall make and publish his decision under subsection (2) within the period of 30 days beginning with the receipt of the report of the Commission under section 50.

(6)   In making a decision under subsections (2) to (4), the Secretary of State shall disregard any public interest consideration not specified in the reference under section 45 and any public interest consideration disregarded by the Commission for the purposes of its report.

(7)   In deciding whether to make an adverse public interest finding under subsection (2), the Secretary of State shall accept—

(a) in connection with a reference to the Commission under section 45(2) or (4), the decision of the report of the Commission under section 50 as to whether there is an anti-competitive outcome; and

(b) in connection with a reference to the Commission under section 45(3) or (5)—

(i) the decision of the report of the Commission under section 50 as to whether a relevant merger situation has been created or (as the case may be) arrangements are in progress or in contemplation which, if carried into effect, will result in the creation of a relevant merger situation; and

(ii) the decision of the report of the OFT under section 44 as to the absence of a substantial lessening of competition.

(8)   In determining for the purposes of subsection (5) the period of 30 days no account shall be taken of—
  (a) Saturday, Sunday, Good Friday and Christmas Day; and
  (b) any day which is a bank holiday in England and Wales.

[301]

NOTES
  Commencement: to be appointed.

55 Enforcement action by Secretary of State

(1)   Subsection (2) applies where the Secretary of State has decided under subsection (2) of section 54 within the period required by subsection (5) of that section to make an adverse public interest finding in relation to a relevant merger situation and has published his decision within the period so required.

(2)   The Secretary of State may take such action under paragraph 9 or 11 of Schedule 7 as he considers to be reasonable and practicable to remedy, mitigate or prevent any of the effects adverse to the public interest which have resulted from, or may be expected to result from, the creation of the relevant merger situation concerned.

(3)   In making a decision under subsection (2) the Secretary of State shall, in particular, have regard to the report of the Commission under section 50.

(4)   In making a decision under subsection (2) in any case of a substantial lessening of competition, the Secretary of State may, in particular, have regard to the effect of any action on any relevant customer benefits in relation to the creation of the relevant merger situation concerned.

[302]

NOTES
  Commencement: to be appointed.

Other

56 Competition cases where intervention on public interest grounds ceases

(1)   Where the Secretary of State decides not to make a reference under section 45 on the ground that no public interest consideration to which he is able to have regard is relevant to a consideration of the relevant merger situation concerned, he shall by notice require the OFT to deal with the matter otherwise than under this Chapter.

(2)   Where a notice is given to the OFT in the circumstances mentioned in subsection (1), the OFT shall decide whether to make a reference under section 22 or 33; and any time-limits in relation to the Secretary of State's decision whether to make a reference under section 45 (including any remaining powers of extension) shall apply in relation to the decision of the OFT whether to make a reference under section 22 or 33.

(3)   Where the Commission cancels under section 53(1) a reference under section 45 and the report of the OFT under section 44 contains the decision that it is or may be the case that there is an anti-competitive outcome in relation to the relevant merger situation concerned, the Commission shall proceed under this Part as if a reference under section 22 or (as the case may be) 33 had been made to it by the OFT.

(4)   In proceeding by virtue of subsection (3) to prepare and publish a report under section 38, the Commission shall proceed as if—

(a) the reference under section 22 or 33 had been made at the same time as the reference under section 45;

(b) the timetable for preparing and giving its report under section 50 (including any remaining powers of extension and as extended by an additional period of 20 days) were the timetable for preparing and publishing its report under section 38; and

(c) in relation to the question whether a relevant merger situation has been created or the question whether arrangements are in progress or in contemplation which, if carried into effect, will result in the creation of a relevant merger situation, the Commission were confined to the questions on the subject to be investigated by it under section 47.

(5) In determining the period of 20 days mentioned in subsection (4) no account shall be taken of—

(a) Saturday, Sunday, Good Friday and Christmas Day; and

(b) any day which is a bank holiday in England and Wales.

(6) Where the Secretary of State decides under section 54(2) to make no finding at all in the matter in connection with a reference under section 45(2) or (4), the Commission shall proceed under this Part as if a reference under section 22 or (as the case may be) 33 had been made to it instead of a reference under section 45 and as if its report to the Secretary of State under section 50 had been prepared and published by it under section 38 within the period permitted by section 39.

(7) In relation to proceedings by virtue of subsection (6), the reference in section 41(3) to decisions of the Commission as included in its report by virtue of section 35(3) or 36(2) shall be construed as a reference to decisions which were included in the report of the Commission by virtue of section 47(8).

(8) Where the Commission becomes under a duty to proceed as mentioned in subsection (3) or (6), references in this Part to references under sections 22 and 33 shall, so far as may be necessary, be construed accordingly; and, in particular, sections 77 to 81 shall apply as if a reference has been made to the Commission by the OFT under section 22 or (as the case may be) 33.

[303]

NOTES

Commencement: to be appointed.

57 Duties of OFT and Commission to inform Secretary of State

(1) The OFT shall, in considering whether to make a reference under section 22 or 33, bring to the attention of the Secretary of State any case which it believes raises any consideration specified in section 58 unless it believes that the Secretary of State would consider any such consideration immaterial in the context of the particular case.

(2) The OFT and the Commission shall bring to the attention of the Secretary of State any representations about exercising his powers under section 58(3) which have been made to the OFT or (as the case may be) the Commission.

[304]

NOTES

Commencement: to be appointed.

58 Specified considerations

(1) The interests of national security are specified in this section.

(2)   In subsection (1) "national security" includes public security; and in this subsection "public security" has the same meaning as in article 21(3) of the European Merger Regulations.

(3)   The Secretary of State may by order modify this section for the purpose of specifying in this section a new consideration or removing or amending any consideration which is for the time being specified in this section.

(4)   An order under this section may, in particular—

(a)   provide for a consideration to be specified in this section for a particular purpose or purposes or for all purposes;

(b)   apply in relation to cases under consideration by the OFT, the Commission or the Secretary of State before the making of the order as well as cases under consideration on or after the making of the order.

[305]

NOTES
Commencement: to be appointed.

CHAPTER 3
OTHER SPECIAL CASES

Special public interest cases

59 Intervention by Secretary of State in special public interest cases

(1)   Subsection (2) applies where the Secretary of State has reasonable grounds for suspecting that it is or may be the case that a special merger situation has been created or arrangements are in progress or in contemplation which, if carried into effect, will result in the creation of a special merger situation.

(2)   The Secretary of State may give a notice to the OFT (in this Part "a special intervention notice") if he believes that it is or may be the case that one or more than one consideration specified in section 58 is relevant to a consideration of the special merger situation concerned.

(3)   For the purposes of this Part a special merger situation has been created if—

(a)   no relevant merger situation has been created because of section 23(1)(b) and (2)(b); but

(b)   a relevant merger situation would have been created if those enactments were disregarded;

and the conditions mentioned in subsection (4) are satisfied.

(4)   The conditions mentioned in this subsection are that, immediately before the enterprises concerned ceased to be distinct—

(a)   at least one of the enterprises concerned was carried on in the United Kingdom or by or under the control of a body corporate incorporated in the United Kingdom; and

(b)   a person carrying on one or more of the enterprises concerned was a relevant government contractor.

(5)   For the purposes of deciding whether a relevant merger situation has been created or whether arrangements are in progress or in contemplation which, if carried into effect, will result in the creation of a relevant merger situation, sections 23 to 32 (read together with section 34) shall apply for the purposes of this Chapter as they do for the purposes of Chapter 1 but subject to subsection (6).

(6)   In their application by virtue of subsection (5) sections 23 to 32 shall have effect as if—

(a)   for paragraph (a) of section 23(9) there were substituted—

"(a)   in relation to the giving of a special intervention notice, the time when the notice is given;

(aa)   in relation to the making of a report by the OFT under section 61, the time of the making of the report;

(ab)   in the case of a reference which is treated as having been made under section 62(2) by virtue of section 64(2), such time as the Commission may determine; and";

(b)   the references to the OFT in section 24(2)(a) and (b) included references to the Secretary of State;

(c)   the references to the OFT in sections 25(1) to (3), (6) and (8) and 31 included references to the Secretary of State;

(d)   the references to the OFT in section 25(4) and (5) were references to the Secretary of State;

(e)   the reference in section 25(4) to section 73 were a reference to paragraph 3 of Schedule 7;

(f)   the reference in section 25(12) to one extension were a reference to one extension by the OFT and one extension by the Secretary of State;

(g)   the powers to extend time-limits under section 25 as applied by subsection (5) above, and the power to request information under section 31(1) as so applied, were not exercisable by the OFT or the Secretary of State before the giving of a special intervention notice;

(h)   in subsection (1) of section 31 for the words "section 22" there were substituted "section 62(2)" and, in the application of that subsection to the OFT, for the word "deciding" there were substituted "enabling the Secretary of State to decide";

(i)   in the case of the giving of special intervention notices, the references in sections 23 to 32 to the making of a reference or a reference were, so far as necessary, references to the giving of a special intervention notice or a special intervention notice; and

(j)   the references to the OFT in section 32(2)(a) to (c) and (3) were construed in accordance with the above modifications.

(7)   No more than one special intervention notice shall be given under subsection (2) in relation to the same special merger situation.

(8)   In this section "relevant government contractor" means—

(a)   a government contractor—

(i)   who has been notified by or on behalf of the Secretary of State of information, documents or other articles relating to defence and of a confidential nature which the government contractor or an employee of his may hold or receive in connection with being such a contractor; and

(ii)   whose notification has not been revoked by or on behalf of the Secretary of State; or

(b)   a former government contractor who was so notified when he was a government contractor and whose notification has not been revoked by or on behalf of the Secretary of State.

(9)   In this section—

"defence" has the same meaning as in section 2 of the Official Secrets Act 1989 (c 6); and

"government contractor" has the same meaning as in the Act of 1989 and includes any sub-contractor of a government contractor, any sub-contractor of that sub-contractor and any other sub-contractor in a chain of sub-contractors which begins with the sub-contractor of the government contractor.

[306]

NOTES

Commencement: to be appointed.

60 Special intervention notices under section 59

(1)   A special intervention notice shall state—

    (a) the special merger situation concerned; and

    (b) the consideration specified in section 58 or considerations so specified which are, or may be, relevant to the special merger situation concerned.

(2)   Where the Secretary of State believes that it is or may be the case that two or more considerations specified in section 58 are relevant to a consideration of the special merger situation concerned, he may decide not to mention in the special intervention notice such of those considerations as he considers appropriate.

(3)   A special intervention notice shall come into force when it is given and shall cease to be in force when the matter to which it relates is finally determined under this Chapter.

(4)   For the purposes of this Part, a matter to which a special intervention notice relates is finally determined under this Chapter if—

    (a) the time within which the OFT is to report to the Secretary of State under section 61 has expired and no such report has been made;

    (b) the Secretary of State decides to accept an undertaking or group of undertakings under paragraph 3 of Schedule 7 instead of making a reference under section 62;

    (c) the Secretary of State otherwise decides not to make a reference under that section;

    (d) the Commission cancels such a reference under section 64(1);

    (e) the time within which the Commission is to prepare a report under section 65 and give it to the Secretary of State has expired and no such report has been prepared and given to the Secretary of State;

    (f) the time within which the Secretary of State is to make and publish a decision under section 66(2) has expired and no such decision has been made and published;

    (g) the Secretary of State decides under subsection (2) of section 66 otherwise than as mentioned in subsection (5) of that section;

    (h) the Secretary of State decides under subsection (2) of section 66 as mentioned in subsection (5) of that section but decides neither to accept an undertaking under paragraph 9 of Schedule 7 nor to make an order under paragraph 11 of that Schedule; or

    (i) the Secretary of State decides under subsection (2) of section 66 as mentioned in subsection (5) of that section and accepts an undertaking under paragraph 9 of Schedule 7 or makes an order under paragraph 11 of that Schedule.

(5)   For the purposes of this Part the time when a matter to which a special intervention notice relates is finally determined under this Chapter is—

    (a) in a case falling within subsection (4)(a), (e) or (f), the expiry of the time concerned;

    (b) in a case falling within subsection (4)(b), the acceptance of the undertaking or group of undertakings concerned;

    (c) in a case falling within subsection (4)(c), (d) or (g), the making of the decision concerned;

    (d) in a case falling within subsection (4)(h), the making of the decision neither to accept an undertaking under paragraph 9 of Schedule 7 nor to make an order under paragraph 11 of that Schedule; and

(e) in a case falling within subsection (4)(i), the acceptance of the undertaking concerned or (as the case may be) the making of the order concerned.

    [307]

NOTES
    Commencement: to be appointed.

61 Initial investigation and report by OFT

(1) Subsection (2) applies where the Secretary of State has given a special intervention notice in relation to a special merger situation.

(2) The OFT shall, within such period as the Secretary of State may require, give a report to the Secretary of State in relation to the case.

(3) The report shall contain—
  (a) advice from the OFT on the considerations relevant to the making of a reference under section 22 or 33 which are also relevant to the Secretary of State's decision as to whether to make a reference under section 62; and
  (b) a summary of any representations about the case which have been received by the OFT and which relate to any consideration mentioned in the special intervention notice concerned and which is or may be relevant to the Secretary of State's decision as to whether to make a reference under section 62.

(4) The report shall include a decision as to whether the OFT believes (disregarding section 59(4)(b)) that it is, or may be, the case that a special merger situation has been created or (as the case may be) arrangements are in progress or in contemplation which, if carried into effect, will result in the creation of a special merger situation.

(5) The report may, in particular, include advice and recommendations on any consideration mentioned in the special intervention notice concerned and which is or may be relevant to the Secretary of State's decision as to whether to make a reference under section 62.

(6) The OFT shall carry out such investigations as it considers appropriate for the purposes of producing a report under this section.

    [308]

NOTES
    Commencement: to be appointed.

62 Power of Secretary of State to refer the matter

(1) Subsection (2) applies where the Secretary of State—
  (a) has given a special intervention notice in relation to a special merger situation; and
  (b) has received a report of the OFT under section 61 in relation to the matter.

(2) The Secretary of State may make a reference to the Commission if he believes that it is or may be the case that—
  (a) a special merger situation has been created;
  (b) one or more than one consideration mentioned in the special intervention notice is relevant to a consideration of the special merger situation concerned; and
  (c) taking account only of the relevant consideration or considerations concerned, the creation of that situation operates or may be expected to operate against the public interest.

(3)   The Secretary of State may make a reference to the Commission if he believes that it is or may be the case that—

   (a) arrangements are in progress or in contemplation which, if carried into effect, will result in the creation of a special merger situation;

   (b) one or more than one consideration mentioned in the special intervention notice is relevant to a consideration of the special merger situation concerned; and

   (c) taking account only of the relevant consideration or considerations concerned, the creation of that situation may be expected to operate against the public interest.

(4)   No reference shall be made under this section if the making of the reference is prevented by section 69(1) or paragraph 4 of Schedule 7.

(5)   The Secretary of State, in deciding whether to make a reference under this section, shall accept the decision of the OFT included in its report under section 61 by virtue of subsection (4) of that section.

(6)   A reference under this section shall, in particular, specify—

   (a) the subsection of this section under which it is made;

   (b) the date on which it is made; and

   (c) the consideration or considerations mentioned in the special intervention notice which the Secretary of State believes are, or may be, relevant to a consideration of the special merger situation concerned.

[309]

NOTES

Commencement: to be appointed.

63 Questions to be decided on references under section 62

(1)   The Commission shall, on a reference under section 62(2), decide whether a special merger situation has been created.

(2)   The Commission shall, on a reference under section 62(3), decide whether arrangements are in progress or in contemplation which, if carried into effect, will result in the creation of a special merger situation.

(3)   If the Commission decides that a special merger situation has been created or that arrangements are in progress or in contemplation which, if carried into effect, will result in the creation of a special merger situation, it shall, on a reference under section 62, decide whether, taking account only of the consideration or considerations mentioned in the reference, the creation of that situation operates or may be expected to operate against the public interest.

(4)   The Commission shall, if it has decided on a reference under section 62 that the creation of a special merger situation operates or may be expected to operate against the public interest, decide the following additional questions—

   (a) whether action should be taken by the Secretary of State under section 66 for the purpose of remedying, mitigating or preventing any of the effects adverse to the public interest which have resulted from, or may be expected to result from, the creation of the special merger situation concerned;

   (b) whether the Commission should recommend the taking of other action by the Secretary of State or action by persons other than itself and the Secretary of State for the purpose of remedying, mitigating or preventing any of the effects adverse to the public interest which have resulted from, or may be expected to result from, the creation of the special merger situation concerned; and

(c) in either case, if action should be taken, what action should be taken and what is to be remedied, mitigated or prevented.

NOTES

Commencement: to be appointed.

64 Cancellation and variation of references under section 62

(1)   The Commission shall cancel a reference under section 62(3) if it considers that the proposal to make arrangements of the kind mentioned in that reference has been abandoned.

(2)   The Commission may, if it considers that doing so is justified by the facts (including events occurring on or after the making of the reference concerned), treat a reference made under subsection (2) or (3) of section 62 as if it had been made under subsection (3) or (as the case may be) (2) of that section; and, in such cases, references in this Part to references under those enactments shall, so far as may be necessary, be construed accordingly.

(3)   Where, by virtue of subsection (2), the Commission treats a reference made under subsection (2) or (3) of section 62 as if it had been made under subsection (3) or (as the case may be) (2) of that section, paragraphs 1, 2, 7 and 8 of Schedule 7 shall, in particular, apply as if the reference had been made under subsection (3) or (as the case may be) (2) of that section instead of under subsection (2) or (3) of that section.

(4)   Subsection (5) applies in relation to any undertaking accepted under paragraph 1 of Schedule 7, or any order made under paragraph 2 of that Schedule, which is in force immediately before the Commission, by virtue of subsection (2), treats a reference made under subsection (2) or (3) of section 62 as if it had been made under subsection (3) or (as the case may be) (2) of that section.

(5)   The undertaking or order shall, so far as applicable, continue in force as if—

(a) in the case of an undertaking or order which relates to a reference under subsection (2) of section 62, accepted or made in relation to a reference made under subsection (3) of that section; and

(b) in the case of an undertaking or order which relates to a reference made under subsection (3) of that section, accepted or made in relation to a reference made under subsection (2) of that section;

and the undertaking or order concerned may be varied, superseded, released or revoked accordingly.

(6)   The Secretary of State may at any time vary a reference under section 62.

(7)   The Secretary of State shall consult the Commission before varying any such reference.

(8)   Subsection (7) shall not apply if the Commission has requested the variation concerned.

(9)   No variation by the Secretary of State under this section shall be capable of altering the consideration or considerations specified in the reference or the period permitted by virtue of section 65 within which the report of the Commission under that section is to be prepared and given to the Secretary of State.

NOTES

Commencement: to be appointed.

65 Investigations and reports on references under section 62

(1)   The Commission shall prepare a report on a reference under section 62 and give it to the Secretary of State within the period permitted by virtue of this section.

(2)   The report shall, in particular, contain—
  (a) the decisions of the Commission on the questions which it is required to answer by virtue of section 63;
  (b) its reasons for its decisions; and
  (c) such information as the Commission considers appropriate for facilitating a proper understanding of those questions and of its reasons for its decisions.

(3)   Sections 51 and 52 (but not section 53) shall apply for the purposes of a report under this section as they apply for the purposes of a report under section 50.

(4)   The Commission shall carry out such investigations as it considers appropriate for the purpose of producing a report under this section.

[312]

NOTES

Commencement: to be appointed.

---

66 Decision and enforcement action by Secretary of State

(1)   Subsection (2) applies where the Secretary of State has received a report of the Commission under section 65 in relation to a special merger situation.

(2)   The Secretary of State shall, in connection with a reference under section 62(2) or (3), decide the questions which the Commission is required to decide by virtue of section 63(1) to (3).

(3)   The Secretary of State shall make and publish his decision under subsection (2) within the period of 30 days beginning with the receipt of the report of the Commission under section 65; and subsection (8) of section 54 shall apply for the purposes of this subsection as it applies for the purposes of subsection (5) of that section.

(4)   In making his decisions under subsection (2), the Secretary of State shall accept the decisions of the report of the Commission under section 65 as to whether a special merger situation has been created or whether arrangements are in progress or in contemplation which, if carried into effect, will result in the creation of a special merger situation.

(5)   Subsection (6) applies where the Secretary of State has decided under subsection (2) that—
  (a) a special merger situation has been created or arrangements are in progress or in contemplation which, if carried into effect, will result in the creation of a special merger situation;
  (b) at least one consideration which is mentioned in the special intervention notice concerned is relevant to a consideration of the special merger situation concerned; and
  (c) taking account only of the relevant consideration or considerations concerned, the creation of that situation operates or may be expected to operate against the public interest;

and has so decided, and published his decision, within the period required by subsection (3).

(6) The Secretary of State may take such action under paragraph 9 or 11 of Schedule 7 as he considers to be reasonable and practicable to remedy, mitigate or prevent any of the effects adverse to the public interest which have resulted from, or may be expected to result from, the creation of the special merger situation concerned.

(7) In making a decision under subsection (6), the Secretary of State shall, in particular, have regard to the report of the Commission under section 65.

[313]

NOTES

Commencement: to be appointed.

European mergers

67 Intervention to protect legitimate interests

(1) Subsection (2) applies where—

  (a) the Secretary of State has reasonable grounds for suspecting that it is or may be the case that—

     (i) a relevant merger situation has been created or that arrangements are in progress or in contemplation which, if carried into effect, will result in the creation of a relevant merger situation; and

     (ii) a concentration with a Community dimension (within the meaning of the European Merger Regulations), or a part of such a concentration, has thereby arisen or will thereby arise;

  (b) a reference which would otherwise be possible under section 22 or 33 is prevented from being made under that section in relation to the relevant merger situation concerned by virtue of Community law or anything done under or in accordance with it; and

  (c) the Secretary of State is considering whether to take appropriate measures to protect legitimate interests as permitted by article 21(3) of the European Merger Regulations.

(2) The Secretary of State may give a notice to the OFT (in this section "a European intervention notice") if he believes that it is or may be the case that one or more than one public interest consideration is relevant to a consideration of the relevant merger situation concerned.

(3) A European intervention notice shall state—

  (a) the relevant merger situation concerned;

  (b) the public interest consideration or considerations which are, or may be, relevant to a consideration of the relevant merger situation concerned; and

  (c) where any public interest consideration concerned is not finalised, the proposed timetable for finalising it.

(4) Where the Secretary of State believes that it is or may be the case that two or more public interest considerations are relevant to a consideration of the relevant merger situation concerned, he may decide not to mention in the intervention notice such of those considerations as he considers appropriate.

(5) No more than one European intervention notice shall be given under subsection (2) in relation to the same relevant merger situation.

(6) Where the Secretary of State has given a European intervention notice mentioning a public interest consideration which, at that time, is not finalised, he shall, as soon as practicable, take such action as is within his power to ensure that it is finalised.

(7) For the purposes of deciding whether a relevant merger situation has been created or whether arrangements are in progress or in contemplation which, if

carried into effect, will result in the creation of a relevant merger situation, sections 23 to 32 (read together with section 34) shall apply for the purposes of this section as they do for the purposes of Chapter 1 but subject to subsection (8).

(8)   In their application by virtue of subsection (7) sections 23 to 32 shall have effect as if—

    (a) references in those sections to the decision-making authority were references to the Secretary of State;

    (b) for paragraphs (a) and (b) of section 23(9) there were substituted ", in relation to the giving of a European intervention notice, the time when the notice is given";

    (c) the references to the OFT in section 24(2)(a) and (b) included references to the Secretary of State;

    (d) sections 25, 31 and 32 were omitted; and

    (e) the references in sections 23 to 29 to the making of a reference or a reference were, so far as necessary, references to the giving of a European intervention notice or a European intervention notice.

(9)   Section 42(3) shall, in its application to this section and section 68, have effect as if for the words "intervention notice" there were substituted "European intervention notice".

[314]

NOTES

Commencement: to be appointed.

---

68 Scheme for protecting legitimate interests

(1)   The Secretary of State may by order provide for the taking of action, where a European intervention notice has been given, to remedy, mitigate or prevent effects adverse to the public interest which have resulted from, or may be expected to result from, the creation of a European relevant merger situation.

(2)   In subsection (1) "European relevant merger situation" means a relevant merger situation—

    (a) which has been created or will be created if arrangements which are in progress or in contemplation are carried into effect;

    (b) by virtue of which a concentration with a Community dimension (within the meaning of the European Merger Regulations), or a part of such a concentration, has arisen or will arise; and

    (c) in relation to which a reference which would otherwise have been possible under section 22 or 33 was prevented from being made under that section by virtue of Community law or anything done under or in accordance with it.

(3)   Provision made under subsection (1) shall include provision ensuring that considerations which are not public interest considerations mentioned in the European intervention notice concerned may not be taken into account in determining whether anything operates, or may be expected to operate, against the public interest.

(4)   Provision made under subsection (1) shall include provision—

    (a) applying with modifications sections 23 to 32 for the purposes of deciding for the purposes of this section whether a relevant merger situation has been created or whether arrangements are in progress or in contemplation which, if carried into effect, will result in the creation of a relevant merger situation;

    (b) requiring the OFT to make a report to the Secretary of State before a reference is made;

    (c) enabling the Secretary of State to make a reference to the Commission;

    (d) requiring the Commission to investigate and report to the Secretary of State on such a reference;

    (e) enabling the taking of interim and final enforcement action.

    (5) An order under this section may include provision (including provision for the creation of offences and penalties, the payment of fees and the delegation of functions) corresponding to any provision made in, or in connection with, this Part in relation to intervention notices or special intervention notices and the cases to which they relate.

    (6) In this section "European intervention notice" has the same meaning as in section 67.

[315]

NOTES

    Commencement: to be appointed.

Other

69 Newspaper mergers

    (1) No reference shall, subject to subsection (2), be made under section 22, 33, 45 or 62 in relation to a transfer of a newspaper or of newspaper assets to which section 58(1) of the Fair Trading Act 1973 (c 41) applies.

    (2) Subsection (1) does not apply in a case falling within section 59(2) of the Act of 1973.

    (3) In this section "transfer of a newspaper or of newspaper assets" has the meaning given by section 57(2) of the Act of 1973.

[316]

NOTES

    Commencement: to be appointed.

70 *(Outside the scope of this work.)*

CHAPTER 4
ENFORCEMENT

Powers exercisable before references under section 22 or 33

71 Initial undertakings: completed mergers

    (1) Subsection (2) applies where the OFT is considering whether to make a reference under section 22.

    (2) The OFT may, for the purpose of preventing pre-emptive action, accept from such of the parties concerned as it considers appropriate undertakings to take such action as it considers appropriate.

    (3) No undertaking shall be accepted under subsection (2) unless the OFT has reasonable grounds for suspecting that it is or may be the case that a relevant merger situation has been created.

    (4) An undertaking under this section—

      (a) shall come into force when accepted;

      (b) may be varied or superseded by another undertaking; and

      (c) may be released by the OFT.

(5)   An undertaking which—

    (a)   is in force under this section in relation to a possible reference or reference under section 22; and

    (b)   has not been adopted under section 80 or paragraph 1 of Schedule 7;

shall cease to be in force if an order under section 72 or 81 comes into force in relation to that reference or an order under paragraph 2 of that Schedule comes into force in relation to the matter.

(6)   An undertaking under this section shall, if it has not previously ceased to be in force and if it has not been adopted under section 80 or paragraph 1 of Schedule 7, cease to be in force—

    (a)   where the OFT has decided to make the reference concerned under section 22, at the end of the period of 7 days beginning with the making of the reference;

    (b)   where the OFT has decided to accept an undertaking under section 73 instead of making that reference, on the acceptance of that undertaking;

    (c)   where an intervention notice is in force, at the end of the period of 7 days beginning with the giving of that notice; and

    (d)   where the OFT has otherwise decided not to make the reference concerned under section 22, on the making of that decision.

(7)   The OFT shall, as soon as reasonably practicable, consider any representations received by it in relation to varying or releasing an undertaking under this section.

(8)   In this section and section 72 "pre-emptive action" means action which might prejudice the reference concerned or impede the taking of any action under this Part which may be justified by the Commission's decisions on the reference.

[317]

NOTES

    Commencement: to be appointed.

72   Initial enforcement orders: completed mergers

(1)   Subsection (2) applies where the OFT is considering whether to make a reference under section 22.

(2)   The OFT may by order, for the purpose of preventing pre-emptive action—

    (a)   prohibit or restrict the doing of things which the OFT considers would constitute pre-emptive action;

    (b)   impose on any person concerned obligations as to the carrying on of any activities or the safeguarding of any assets;

    (c)   provide for the carrying on of any activities or the safeguarding of any assets either by the appointment of a person to conduct or supervise the conduct of any activities (on such terms and with such powers as may be specified or described in the order) or in any other manner;

    (d)   do anything which may be done by virtue of paragraph 19 of Schedule 8.

(3)   No order shall be made under subsection (2) unless the OFT has reasonable grounds for suspecting that it is or may be the case that—

    (a)   a relevant merger situation has been created; and

    (b)   pre-emptive action is in progress or in contemplation.

(4)   An order under this section—

    (a)   shall come into force at such time as is determined by or under the order; and

    (b)   may be varied or revoked by another order.

(5) An order which—

    (a) is in force under this section in relation to a possible reference or a reference under section 22; and

    (b) has not been adopted under section 81 or paragraph 2 of Schedule 7;

shall cease to be in force if an undertaking under section 71 or 80 comes into force in relation to that reference or an undertaking under paragraph 1 of that Schedule comes into force in relation to the matter.

(6) An order under this section shall, if it has not previously ceased to be in force and if it is not adopted under section 81 or paragraph 2 of Schedule 7, cease to be in force—

    (a) where the OFT has decided to make the reference concerned under section 22, at the end of the period of 7 days beginning with the making of the reference;

    (b) where the OFT has decided to accept an undertaking under section 73 instead of making that reference, on the acceptance of that undertaking;

    (c) where an intervention notice is in force, at the end of the period of 7 days beginning with the giving of that notice; and

    (d) where the OFT has otherwise decided not to make the reference concerned under section 22, on the making of that decision.

(7) The OFT shall, as soon as reasonably practicable, consider any representations received by it in relation to varying or revoking an order under this section.

[318]

NOTES

Commencement: to be appointed.

73 Undertakings in lieu of references under section 22 or 33

(1) Subsection (2) applies if the OFT considers that it is under a duty to make a reference under section 22 or 33 (disregarding the operation of section 22(3)(b) or (as the case may be) 33(3)(b) but taking account of the power of the OFT under section 22(2) or (as the case may be) 33(2) to decide not to make such a reference).

(2) The OFT may, instead of making such a reference and for the purpose of remedying, mitigating or preventing the substantial lessening of competition concerned or any adverse effect which has or may have resulted from it or may be expected to result from it, accept from such of the parties concerned as it considers appropriate undertakings to take such action as it considers appropriate.

(3) In proceeding under subsection (2), the OFT shall, in particular, have regard to the need to achieve as comprehensive a solution as is reasonable and practicable to the substantial lessening of competition and any adverse effects resulting from it.

(4) In proceeding under subsection (2), the OFT may, in particular, have regard to the effect of any action on any relevant customer benefits in relation to the creation of the relevant merger situation concerned.

(5) An undertaking under this section—

    (a) shall come into force when accepted;

    (b) may be varied or superseded by another undertaking; and

    (c) may be released by the OFT.

(6) An undertaking under this section which is in force in relation to a relevant merger situation shall cease to be in force if an order comes into force under section 75 or 76 in relation to that undertaking.

PART I
STATUTES

(7)   The OFT shall, as soon as reasonably practicable, consider any representations received by it in relation to varying or releasing an undertaking under this section.

NOTES
   Commencement: to be appointed.

74 Effect of undertakings under section 73

(1)   The relevant authority shall not make a reference under section 22, 33 or 45 in relation to the creation of a relevant merger situation if—
   (a)   the OFT has accepted an undertaking or group of undertakings under section 73; and
   (b)   the relevant merger situation is the situation by reference to which the undertaking or group of undertakings was accepted.

(2)   Subsection (1) does not prevent the making of a reference if material facts about relevant arrangements or transactions, or relevant proposed arrangements or transactions, were not notified (whether in writing or otherwise) to the OFT or made public before any undertaking concerned was accepted.

(3)   For the purposes of subsection (2) arrangements or transactions, or proposed arrangements or transactions, are relevant if they are the ones in consequence of which the enterprises concerned ceased or may have ceased, or may cease, to be distinct enterprises.

(4)   In subsection (2) "made public" means so publicised as to be generally known or readily ascertainable.

(5)   In this section "relevant authority" means—
   (a)   in relation to a possible reference under section 22 or 33, the OFT; and
   (b)   in relation to a possible reference under section 45, the Secretary of State.

NOTES
   Commencement: to be appointed.

75 Order-making power where undertakings under section 73 not fulfilled etc

(1)   Subsection (2) applies where the OFT considers that—
   (a)   an undertaking accepted by it under section 73 has not been, is not being or will not be fulfilled; or
   (b)   in relation to an undertaking accepted by it under that section, information which was false or misleading in a material respect was given to the OFT by the person giving the undertaking before the OFT decided to accept the undertaking.

(2)   The OFT may, for any of the purposes mentioned in section 73(2), make an order under this section.

(3)   Subsections (3) and (4) of section 73 shall apply for the purposes of subsection (2) above as they apply for the purposes of subsection (2) of that section.

(4)   An order under this section may contain—
   (a)   anything permitted by Schedule 8; and
   (b)   such supplementary, consequential or incidental provision as the OFT considers appropriate.

(5)   An order under this section—
   (a)   shall come into force at such time as is determined by or under the order;

(b) may contain provision which is different from the provision contained in the undertaking concerned; and

(c) may be varied or revoked by another order.

(6) The OFT shall, as soon as reasonably practicable, consider any representations received by it in relation to varying or revoking an order under this section.

[321]

NOTES

Commencement: to be appointed.

76 Supplementary interim order-making power

(1) Subsection (2) applies where—

(a) the OFT has the power to make an order under section 75 in relation to a particular undertaking and intends to make such an order; or

(b) the Commission has the power to make an order under section 83 in relation to a particular undertaking and intends to make such an order.

(2) The OFT or (as the case may be) the Commission may, for the purpose of preventing any action which might prejudice the making of that order, make an order under this section.

(3) No order shall be made under subsection (2) unless the OFT or (as the case may be) the Commission has reasonable grounds for suspecting that it is or may be the case that action which might prejudice the making of the order under section 75 or (as the case may be) 83 is in progress or in contemplation.

(4) An order under subsection (2) may—

(a) prohibit or restrict the doing of things which the OFT or (as the case may be) the Commission considers would prejudice the making of the order under section 75 or (as the case may be) 83;

(b) impose on any person concerned obligations as to the carrying on of any activities or the safeguarding of any assets;

(c) provide for the carrying on of any activities or the safeguarding of any assets either by the appointment of a person to conduct or supervise the conduct of any activities (on such terms and with such powers as may be specified or described in the order) or in any other manner;

(d) do anything which may be done by virtue of paragraph 19 of Schedule 8.

(5) An order under this section—

(a) shall come into force at such time as is determined by or under the order; and

(b) may be varied or revoked by another order.

(6) An order under this section shall, if it has not previously ceased to be in force, cease to be in force on—

(a) the coming into force of an order under section 75 or (as the case may be) 83 in relation to the undertaking concerned; or

(b) the making of the decision not to proceed with such an order.

(7) The OFT or (as the case may be) the Commission shall, as soon as reasonably practicable, consider any representations received by it in relation to varying or revoking an order under this section.

[322]

NOTES

Commencement: to be appointed.

Interim restrictions and powers

77 Restrictions on certain dealings: completed mergers

(1)   Subsections (2) and (3) apply where—
  (a) a reference has been made under section 22 but not finally determined; and
  (b) no undertakings under section 71 or 80 are in force in relation to the relevant merger situation concerned and no orders under section 72 or 81 are in force in relation to that situation.

(2)   No relevant person shall, without the consent of the Commission—
  (a) complete any outstanding matters in connection with any arrangements which have resulted in the enterprises concerned ceasing to be distinct enterprises;
  (b) make any further arrangements in consequence of that result (other than arrangements which reverse that result); or
  (c) transfer the ownership or control of any enterprises to which the reference relates.

(3)   No relevant person shall, without the consent of the Commission, assist in any of the activities mentioned in paragraphs (a) to (c) of subsection (2).

(4)   The prohibitions in subsections (2) and (3) do not apply in relation to anything which the person concerned is required to do by virtue of any enactment.

(5)   The consent of the Commission under subsection (2) or (3)—
  (a) may be general or special;
  (b) may be revoked by the Commission; and
  (c) shall be published in such manner as the Commission considers appropriate for the purpose of bringing it to the attention of any person entitled to the benefit of it.

(6)   Paragraph (c) of subsection (5) shall not apply if the Commission considers that publication is not necessary for the purpose mentioned in that paragraph.

(7)   Subsections (2) and (3) shall apply to a person's conduct outside the United Kingdom if (and only if) he is—
  (a) a United Kingdom national;
  (b) a body incorporated under the law of the United Kingdom or of any part of the United Kingdom; or
  (c) a person carrying on business in the United Kingdom.

(8)   In this section "relevant person" means—
  (a) any person who carries on any enterprise to which the reference relates or who has control of any such enterprise;
  (b) any subsidiary of any person falling within paragraph (a); or
  (c) any person associated with any person falling within paragraph (a) or any subsidiary of any person so associated.

NOTES

Commencement: to be appointed.

78 Restrictions on certain share dealings: anticipated mergers

(1)   Subsection (2) applies where—
  (a) a reference has been made under section 33; and
  (b) no undertakings under section 80 are in force in relation to the relevant merger situation concerned and no orders under section 81 are in force in relation to that situation.

(2)   No relevant person shall, without the consent of the Commission, directly or indirectly acquire during the relevant period an interest in shares in a company if any enterprise to which the reference relates is carried on by or under the control of that company.

(3)   The consent of the Commission under subsection (2)—
  (a) may be general or special;
  (b) may be revoked by the Commission; and
  (c) shall be published in such manner as the Commission considers appropriate for bringing it to the attention of any person entitled to the benefit of it.

(4)   Paragraph (c) of subsection (3) shall not apply if the Commission considers that publication is not necessary for the purpose mentioned in that paragraph.

(5)   Subsection (2) shall apply to a person's conduct outside the United Kingdom if (and only if) he is—
  (a) a United Kingdom national;
  (b) a body incorporated under the law of the United Kingdom or of any part of the United Kingdom; or
  (c) a person carrying on business in the United Kingdom.

(6)   In this section and section 79—
"company" includes any body corporate;
"relevant period" means the period beginning with the making of the reference concerned and ending when the reference is finally determined;
"relevant person" means—
  (a) any person who carries on any enterprise to which the reference relates or who has control of any such enterprise;
  (b) any subsidiary of any person falling within paragraph (a); or
  (c) any person associated with any person falling within paragraph (a) or any subsidiary of any person so associated; and
"share" means share in the capital of a company, and includes stock.

[324]

NOTES
Commencement: to be appointed.

79 Sections 77 and 78: further interpretation provisions

(1)   For the purposes of this Part a reference under section 22 or 33 is finally determined if—
  (a) the reference is cancelled under section 37(1);
  (b) the time within which the Commission is to prepare and publish a report under section 38 in relation to the reference has expired and no such report has been prepared and published;
  (c) the report of the Commission under section 38 contains the decision that there is not an anti-competitive outcome;
  (d) the report of the Commission under section 38 contains the decision that there is an anti-competitive outcome and the Commission has decided under section 41(2) neither to accept an undertaking under section 82 nor to make an order under section 84; or
  (e) the report of the Commission under section 38 contains the decision that there is an anti-competitive outcome and the Commission has decided under section 41(2) to accept an undertaking under section 82 or to make an order under section 84.

(2)   For the purposes of this Part the time when a reference under section 22 or 33 is finally determined is—

(a) in a case falling within subsection (1)(a), the making of the decision concerned;

(b) in a case falling within subsection (1)(b), the expiry of the time concerned;

(c) in a case falling within subsection (1)(c), the publication of the report;

(d) in a case falling within subsection (1)(d), the making of the decision under section 41(2); and

(e) in a case falling within subsection (1)(e), the acceptance of the undertaking concerned or (as the case may be) the making of the order concerned.

(3)   For the purposes of section 78 and subject to subsection (4) below, the circumstances in which a person acquires an interest in shares include those where—

(a) he enters into a contract to acquire the shares (whether or not for cash);

(b) he is not the registered holder but acquires the right to exercise, or to control the exercise of, any right conferred by the holding of the shares; or

(c) he—

(i) acquires a right to call for delivery of the shares to himself or to his order or to acquire an interest in the shares; or

(ii) assumes an obligation to acquire such an interest.

(4)   The circumstances in which a person acquires an interest in shares for the purposes of section 78 do not include those where he acquires an interest in pursuance of an obligation assumed before the publication by the OFT of the reference concerned.

(5)   The circumstances in which a person acquires a right mentioned in subsection (3)—

(a) include those where he acquires a right, or assumes an obligation, whose exercise or fulfilment would give him that right; but

(b) do not include those where he is appointed as proxy to vote at a specified meeting of a company or of any class of its members or at any adjournment of the meeting or he is appointed by a corporation to act as its representative at any meeting of the company or of any class of its members.

(6)   References to rights and obligations in subsections (3) to (5) include conditional rights and conditional obligations.

(7)   References in sections 77 and 78 to a person carrying on or having control of any enterprise includes a group of persons carrying on or having control of an enterprise and any member of such a group.

(8)   Sections 26(2) to (4) and 127(1), (2) and (4) to (6) shall apply for the purposes of sections 77 and 78 to determine whether any person or group of persons has control of any enterprise and whether persons are associated as they apply for the purposes of section 26 to determine whether enterprises are brought under common control.

(9)   Sections 736 and 736A of the Companies Act 1985 (c 6) shall apply for the purposes of sections 77 and 78 to determine whether a company is a subsidiary of an individual or of a group of persons as they apply to determine whether it is a subsidiary of a company; and references to a subsidiary in subsections (8) and (9) of section 736A as so applied shall be construed accordingly.

[325]

NOTES

Commencement: to be appointed.

80 Interim undertakings

(1) Subsections (2) and (3) apply where a reference under section 22 or 33 has been made but is not finally determined.

(2) The Commission may, for the purpose of preventing pre-emptive action, accept from such of the parties concerned as it considers appropriate undertakings to take such action as it considers appropriate.

(3) The Commission may, for the purpose of preventing pre-emptive action, adopt an undertaking accepted by the OFT under section 71 if the undertaking is still in force when the Commission adopts it.

(4) An undertaking adopted under subsection (3)—
    (a) shall continue in force, in accordance with its terms, when adopted;
    (b) may be varied or superseded by an undertaking under this section; and
    (c) may be released by the Commission.

(5) Any other undertaking under this section—
    (a) shall come into force when accepted;
    (b) may be varied or superseded by another undertaking; and
    (c) may be released by the Commission.

(6) References in this Part to undertakings under this section shall, unless the context otherwise requires, include references to undertakings adopted under this section; and references to the acceptance or giving of undertakings under this section shall be construed accordingly.

(7) An undertaking which is in force under this section in relation to a reference under section 22 or 33 shall cease to be in force if an order under section 81 comes into force in relation to that reference.

(8) An undertaking under this section shall, if it has not previously ceased to be in force, cease to be in force when the reference under section 22 or 33 is finally determined.

(9) The Commission shall, as soon as reasonably practicable, consider any representations received by it in relation to varying or releasing an undertaking under this section.

(10) In this section and section 81 "pre-emptive action" means action which might prejudice the reference concerned or impede the taking of any action under this Part which may be justified by the Commission's decisions on the reference.

[326]

NOTES

Commencement: to be appointed.

81 Interim orders

(1) Subsections (2) and (3) apply where a reference has been made under section 22 or 33 but is not finally determined.

(2) The Commission may by order, for the purpose of preventing pre-emptive action—
    (a) prohibit or restrict the doing of things which the Commission considers would constitute pre-emptive action;
    (b) impose on any person concerned obligations as to the carrying on of any activities or the safeguarding of any assets;

(c) provide for the carrying on of any activities or the safeguarding of any assets either by the appointment of a person to conduct or supervise the conduct of any activities (on such terms and with such powers as may be specified or described in the order) or in any other manner;

(d) do anything which may be done by virtue of paragraph 19 of Schedule 8.

(3) The Commission may, for the purpose of preventing pre-emptive action, adopt an order made by the OFT under section 72 if the order is still in force when the Commission adopts it.

(4) An order adopted under subsection (3)—

(a) shall continue in force, in accordance with its terms, when adopted; and

(b) may be varied or revoked by an order under this section.

(5) Any other order under this section—

(a) shall come into force at such time as is determined by or under the order; and

(b) may be varied or revoked by another order.

(6) References in this Part to orders under this section shall, unless the context otherwise requires, include references to orders adopted under this section; and references to the making of orders under this section shall be construed accordingly.

(7) An order which is in force under this section in relation to a reference under section 22 or 33 shall cease to be in force if an undertaking under section 80 comes into force in relation to that reference.

(8) An order under this section shall, if it has not previously ceased to be in force, cease to be in force when the reference under section 22 or 33 is finally determined.

(9) The Commission shall, as soon as reasonably practicable, consider any representations received by it in relation to varying or revoking an order under this section.

[327]

NOTES

Commencement: to be appointed.

Final powers

82 Final undertakings

(1) The Commission may, in accordance with section 41, accept, from such persons as it considers appropriate, undertakings to take action specified or described in the undertakings.

(2) An undertaking under this section—

(a) shall come into force when accepted;

(b) may be varied or superseded by another undertaking; and

(c) may be released by the Commission.

(3) An undertaking which is in force under this section in relation to a reference under section 22 or 33 shall cease to be in force if an order under section 76(1)(b) or 83 comes into force in relation to the subject-matter of the undertaking.

(4) No undertaking shall be accepted under this section in relation to a reference under section 22 or 33 if an order has been made under—

(a) section 76(1)(b) or 83 in relation to the subject-matter of the undertaking; or

(b) section 84 in relation to that reference.

(5)   The Commission shall, as soon as reasonably practicable, consider any representations received by it in relation to varying or releasing an undertaking under this section.

[328]

NOTES
Commencement: to be appointed.

83 Order-making power where final undertakings not fulfilled

(1)   Subsection (2) applies where the Commission considers that—
  (a) an undertaking accepted by it under section 82 has not been, is not being or will not be fulfilled; or
  (b) in relation to an undertaking accepted by it under that section, information which was false or misleading in a material respect was given to the Commission or the OFT by the person giving the undertaking before the Commission decided to accept the undertaking.

(2)   The Commission may, for any of the purposes mentioned in section 41(2), make an order under this section.

(3)   Subsections (3) to (5) of section 41 shall apply for the purposes of subsection (2) above as they apply for the purposes of subsection (2) of that section.

(4)   An order under this section may contain—
  (a) anything permitted by Schedule 8; and
  (b) such supplementary, consequential or incidental provision as the Commission considers appropriate.

(5)   An order under this section—
  (a) shall come into force at such time as is determined by or under the order;
  (b) may contain provision which is different from the provision contained in the undertaking concerned; and
  (c) may be varied or revoked by another order.

(6)   No order shall be varied or revoked under this section unless the OFT advises that such a variation or revocation is appropriate by reason of a change of circumstances.

[329]

NOTES
Commencement: to be appointed.

84 Final orders

(1)   The Commission may, in accordance with section 41, make an order under this section.

(2)   An order under this section may contain—
  (a) anything permitted by Schedule 8; and
  (b) such supplementary, consequential or incidental provision as the Commission considers appropriate.

(3)   An order under this section—
  (a) shall come into force at such time as is determined by or under the order; and
  (b) may be varied or revoked by another order.

(4)   No order shall be varied or revoked under this section unless the OFT advises that such a variation or revocation is appropriate by reason of a change of circumstances.

(5)   No order shall be made under this section in relation to a reference under section 22 or 33 if an undertaking has been accepted under section 82 in relation to that reference.

[330]

NOTES

Commencement: to be appointed.

Public interest and special public interest cases

85 Enforcement regime for public interest and special public interest cases

(1)   Schedule 7 (which provides for the enforcement regime in public interest and special public interest cases) shall have effect.

(2)   The OFT may advise the Secretary of State in relation to the taking by him of enforcement action under Schedule 7.

[331]

NOTES

Commencement: to be appointed.

Undertakings and orders: general provisions

86 Enforcement orders: general provisions

(1)   An enforcement order may extend to a person's conduct outside the United Kingdom if (and only if) he is—
  (a) a United Kingdom national;
  (b) a body incorporated under the law of the United Kingdom or of any part of the United Kingdom; or
  (c) a person carrying on business in the United Kingdom.

(2)   Nothing in an enforcement order shall have effect so as to—
  (a) cancel or modify conditions in licences granted—
    (i) under a patent granted under the Patents Act 1977 (c 37) or a European patent (UK) (within the meaning of the Act of 1977); or
    (ii) in respect of a design registered under the Registered Designs Act 1949 (c 88);
  by the proprietor of the patent or design; or
  (b) require an entry to be made in the register of patents or the register of designs to the effect that licences under such a patent or such a design are to be available as of right.

(3)   An enforcement order may prohibit the performance of an agreement already in existence when the order is made.

(4)   Schedule 8 (which provides for the contents of certain enforcement orders) shall have effect.

(5)   Part 1 of Schedule 9 (which enables certain enforcement orders to modify licence conditions etc in regulated markets) shall have effect.

(6)   In this Part "enforcement order" means an order made under section 72, 75, 76, 81, 83 or 84 or under paragraph 2, 5, 6, 10 or 11 of Schedule 7.

[332]

NOTES

Commencement: to be appointed.

87 Delegated power of directions

(1)   An enforcement order may authorise the person making the order to give directions falling within subsection (2) to—

    (a) a person specified in the directions; or

    (b) the holder for the time being of an office so specified in any body of persons corporate or unincorporate.

(2)   Directions fall within this subsection if they are directions—

    (a) to take such action as may be specified or described in the directions for the purpose of carrying out, or ensuring compliance with, the enforcement order concerned; or

    (b) to do, or refrain from doing, anything so specified or described which the person might be required by that order to do or refrain from doing.

(3)   An enforcement order may authorise the person making the order to vary or revoke any directions so given.

(4)   The court may by order require any person who has failed to comply with directions given by virtue of this section to comply with them, or otherwise remedy his failure, within such time as may be specified in the order.

(5)   Where the directions related to anything done in the management or administration of a body of persons corporate or unincorporate, the court may by order require the body of persons concerned or any officer of it to comply with the directions, or otherwise remedy the failure to comply with them, within such time as may be specified in the order.

(6)   An order under subsection (4) or (5) shall be made on the application of the person authorised by virtue of this section to give the directions concerned.

(7)   An order under subsection (4) or (5) may provide for all the costs or expenses of, or incidental to, the application for the order to be met by any person in default or by any officers of a body of persons corporate or unincorporate who are responsible for its default.

(8)   In this section "the court" means—

    (a) in relation to England and Wales or Northern Ireland, the High Court; and

    (b) in relation to Scotland, the Court of Session.

[333]

NOTES

Commencement: to be appointed.

88 Contents of certain enforcement orders

(1)   This section applies in relation to any order under section 75, 83 or 84 or under paragraph 5, 10 or 11 of Schedule 7.

(2)   The order or any explanatory material accompanying the order shall state—

    (a) the actions that the persons or description of persons to whom the order is addressed must do or (as the case may be) refrain from doing;

    (b) the date on which the order comes into force;

    (c) the possible consequences of not complying with the order; and

    (d) the section of this Part under which a review can be sought in relation to the order.

[334]

NOTES

Commencement: to be appointed.

89 Subject-matter of undertakings

(1)   The provision which may be contained in an enforcement undertaking is not limited to the provision which is permitted by Schedule 8.

(2)   In this Part "enforcement undertaking" means an undertaking under section 71, 73, 80 or 82 or under paragraph 1, 3 or 9 of Schedule 7.

[335]

NOTES

Commencement: to be appointed.

90 Procedural requirements for certain undertakings and orders

Schedule 10 (which provides for the procedure for accepting certain enforcement undertakings and making certain enforcement orders and for their termination) shall have effect.

[336]

NOTES

Commencement: to be appointed.

91 Register of undertakings and orders

(1)   The OFT shall compile and maintain a register for the purposes of this Part.

(2)   The register shall be kept in such form as the OFT considers appropriate.

(3)   The OFT shall ensure that the following matters are entered in the register—
  (a) the provisions of any enforcement undertaking accepted under this Part;
  (b) the provisions of any enforcement order made under this Part;
  (c) the details of any variation, release or revocation of such an undertaking or order; and
  (d) the details of any consent given by the Commission under section 77(2) or (3) or 78(2) or by the Secretary of State under paragraph 7(2) or (3) or 8(2) of Schedule 7.

(4)   The duty in subsection (3) does not extend to anything of which the OFT is unaware.

(5)   The Commission and the Secretary of State shall inform the OFT of any matters which are to be included in the register by virtue of subsection (3) and which relate to enforcement undertakings accepted by them, enforcement orders made by them or consents given by them.

(6)   The OFT shall ensure that the contents of the register are available to the public—
  (a) during (as a minimum) such hours as may be specified in an order made by the Secretary of State; and
  (b) subject to such reasonable fees (if any) as the OFT may determine.

(7)   If requested by any person to do so and subject to such reasonable fees (if any) as the OFT may determine, the OFT shall supply the person concerned with a copy (certified to be true) of the register or of an extract from it.

[337]

NOTES

Commencement: to be appointed.

Enforcement functions of OFT

92 Duty of OFT to monitor undertakings and orders

(1)   The OFT shall keep under review—
  (a) the carrying out of any enforcement undertaking or any enforcement order; and
  (b) compliance with the prohibitions in sections 77(2) and (3) and 78(2) and in paragraphs 7(2) and (3) and 8(2) of Schedule 7.

(2)   The OFT shall, in particular, from time to time consider—
  (a) whether an enforcement undertaking or enforcement order has been or is being complied with;
  (b) whether, by reason of any change of circumstances, an enforcement undertaking is no longer appropriate and—
    (i)   one or more of the parties to it can be released from it; or
    (ii) it needs to be varied or to be superseded by a new enforcement undertaking; and
  (c) whether, by reason of any change of circumstances, an enforcement order is no longer appropriate and needs to be varied or revoked.

(3)   The OFT shall give the Commission or (as the case may be) the Secretary of State such advice as it considers appropriate in relation to—
  (a) any possible variation or release by the Commission or (as the case may be) the Secretary of State of an enforcement undertaking accepted by it or (as the case may be) him;
  (b) any possible new enforcement undertaking to be accepted by the Commission or (as the case may be) the Secretary of State so as to supersede another enforcement undertaking given to the Commission or (as the case may be) the Secretary of State;
  (c) any possible variation or revocation by the Commission or (as the case may be) the Secretary of State of an enforcement order made by the Commission or (as the case may be) the Secretary of State;
  (d) any possible enforcement undertaking to be accepted by the Commission or (as the case may be) the Secretary of State instead of an enforcement order or any possible enforcement order to be made by the Commission or (as the case may be) the Secretary of State instead of an enforcement undertaking;
  (e) the enforcement by virtue of section 94(6) to (8) of any enforcement undertaking or enforcement order; or
  (f) the enforcement by virtue of section 95(4) and (5) of the prohibitions in sections 77(2) and (3) and 78(2) and in paragraphs 7(2) and (3) and 8(2) of Schedule 7.

(4)   The OFT shall take such action as it considers appropriate in relation to—
  (a) any possible variation or release by it of an enforcement undertaking accepted by it;
  (b) any possible new enforcement undertaking to be accepted by it so as to supersede another enforcement undertaking given to it;
  (c) any possible variation or revocation by it of an enforcement order made by it;
  (d) any possible enforcement undertaking to be accepted by it instead of an enforcement order or any possible enforcement order to be made by it instead of an enforcement undertaking;
  (e) the enforcement by it by virtue of section 94(6) of any enforcement undertaking or enforcement order; or
  (f) the enforcement by it by virtue of section 95(4) and (5) of the prohibitions in sections 77(2) and (3) and 78(2) and in paragraphs 7(2) and (3) and 8(2) of Schedule 7.

(5)   The OFT shall keep under review the effectiveness of enforcement undertakings accepted under this Part and enforcement orders made under this Part.

(6)   The OFT shall, whenever requested to do so by the Secretary of State and otherwise from time to time, prepare a report of its findings under subsection (5).

(7)   The OFT shall—
    (a) give any report prepared by it under subsection (6) to the Commission;
    (b) give a copy of the report to the Secretary of State; and
    (c) publish the report.

[338]

NOTES
Commencement: to be appointed.

93 Further role of OFT in relation to undertakings and orders

(1)   Subsections (2) and (3) apply where—
    (a) the Commission is considering whether to accept undertakings under section 80 or 82; or
    (b) the Secretary of State is considering whether to accept undertakings under paragraph 1, 3 or 9 of Schedule 7.

(2)   The Commission or (as the case may be) the Secretary of State (in this section "the relevant authority") may require the OFT to consult with such persons as the relevant authority considers appropriate with a view to discovering whether they will offer undertakings which the relevant authority would be prepared to accept under section 80 or 82 or (as the case may be) paragraph 1, 3 or 9 of Schedule 7.

(3)   The relevant authority may require the OFT to report to the relevant authority on the outcome of the OFT's consultations within such period as the relevant authority may require.

(4)   A report under subsection (3) shall, in particular, contain advice from the OFT as to whether any undertakings offered should be accepted by the relevant authority under section 80 or 82 or (as the case may be) paragraph 1, 3 or 9 of Schedule 7.

(5)   The powers conferred on the relevant authority by subsections (1) to (4) are without prejudice to the power of the relevant authority to consult the persons concerned itself.

(6)   If asked by the relevant authority for advice in relation to the taking of enforcement action (whether or not by way of undertaking) in a particular case, the OFT shall give such advice as it considers appropriate.

[339]

NOTES
Commencement: to be appointed.

Other

94 Rights to enforce undertakings and orders

(1)   This section applies to any enforcement undertaking or enforcement order.

(2)   Any person to whom such an undertaking or order relates shall have a duty to comply with it.

(3)   The duty shall be owed to any person who may be affected by a contravention of the undertaking or (as the case may be) order.

(4)   Any breach of the duty which causes such a person to sustain loss or damage shall be actionable by him.

(5)   In any proceedings brought under subsection (4) against a person to whom an enforcement undertaking or an enforcement order relates it shall be a defence for that person to show that he took all reasonable steps and exercised all due diligence to avoid contravening the undertaking or (as the case may be) order.

(6)   Compliance with an enforcement undertaking or an enforcement order shall also be enforceable by civil proceedings brought by the OFT for an injunction or for interdict or for any other appropriate relief or remedy.

(7)   Compliance with an undertaking under section 80 or 82, an order made by the Commission under section 76 or an order under section 81, 83 or 84, shall also be enforceable by civil proceedings brought by the Commission for an injunction or for interdict or for any other appropriate relief or remedy.

(8)   Compliance with an undertaking under paragraph 1, 3 or 9 of Schedule 7, an order made by the Secretary of State under paragraph 2 of that Schedule or an order under paragraph 5, 6, 10 or 11 of that Schedule, shall also be enforceable by civil proceedings brought by the Secretary of State for an injunction or for interdict or for any other appropriate relief or remedy.

(9)   Subsections (6) to (8) shall not prejudice any right that a person may have by virtue of subsection (4) to bring civil proceedings for contravention or apprehended contravention of an enforcement undertaking or an enforcement order.

[340]

NOTES
Commencement: to be appointed.

95 Rights to enforce statutory restrictions

(1)   The obligation to comply with section 77(2) or (3) or 78(2) or paragraph 7(2) or (3) or 8(2) of Schedule 7 shall be a duty owed to any person who may be affected by a contravention of the enactment concerned.

(2)   Any breach of the duty which causes such a person to sustain loss or damage shall be actionable by him.

(3)   In any proceedings brought under subsection (2) against a person who has an obligation to comply with section 77(2) or (3) or 78(2) or paragraph 7(2) or (3) or 8(2) of Schedule 7 it shall be a defence for that person to show that he took all reasonable steps and exercised all due diligence to avoid contravening the enactment concerned.

(4)   Compliance with section 77(2) or (3) or 78(2) shall also be enforceable by civil proceedings brought by the OFT or the Commission for an injunction or for interdict or for any other appropriate relief or remedy.

(5)   Compliance with paragraph 7(2) or (3) or 8(2) of Schedule 7 shall also be enforceable by civil proceedings brought by the OFT or the Secretary of State for an injunction or for interdict or for any other appropriate relief or remedy.

(6)   Subsections (4) and (5) shall not prejudice any right that a person may have by virtue of subsection (2) to bring civil proceedings for contravention or apprehended contravention of section 77(2) or (3) or 78(2) or paragraph 7(2) or (3) or 8(2) of Schedule 7.

[341]

NOTES
Commencement: to be appointed.

CHAPTER 5
SUPPLEMENTARY

Merger notices

96 Merger notices

(1) A person authorised to do so by regulations under section 101 may give notice to the OFT of proposed arrangements which might result in the creation of a relevant merger situation.

(2) Any such notice (in this Part a "merger notice")—

    (a) shall be in the prescribed form; and

    (b) shall state that the existence of the proposal has been made public.

(3) No reference shall be made under section 22, 33 or 45 in relation to—

    (a) arrangements of which notice is given under subsection (1) above or arrangements which do not differ from them in any material respect; or

    (b) the creation of any relevant merger situation which is, or may be, created in consequence of carrying such arrangements into effect;

if the period for considering the merger notice has expired without a reference being made under that section in relation to those arrangements.

(4) Subsection (3) is subject to section 100.

(5) In this section and sections 99(5)(c) and 100(1)(c) "prescribed" means prescribed by the OFT by notice having effect for the time being and published in the London, Edinburgh and Belfast Gazettes.

(6) In this Part "notified arrangements" means arrangements of which notice is given under subsection (1) above or arrangements not differing from them in any material respect.

[342]

NOTES

    Commencement: to be appointed.

97 Period for considering merger notices

(1) The period for considering a merger notice is, subject as follows, the period of 20 days beginning with the first day after—

    (a) the notice has been received by the OFT; and

    (b) any fee payable by virtue of section 121 to the OFT in respect of the notice has been paid.

(2) Where no intervention notice is in force in relation to the matter concerned, the OFT may by notice to the person who gave the merger notice extend by a further 10 days the period for considering the merger notice.

(3) Where an intervention notice is in force in relation to the matter concerned and there has been no extension under subsection (2), the OFT may by notice to the person who gave the merger notice extend by a further 20 days the period for considering the merger notice.

(4) Where an intervention notice is in force in relation to the matter concerned and there has been an extension under subsection (2), the OFT may by notice to the person who gave the merger notice extend the period for considering the merger notice by a further number of days which, including any extension already made under subsection (2), does not exceed 20 days.

(5) The OFT may by notice to the person who gave the merger notice extend the period for considering a merger notice if the OFT considers that the person has failed to provide, within the period stated in a notice under section 99(2) and in the authorised or required manner, information requested of him in that notice.

(6) An extension under subsection (5) shall be for the period until the person concerned provides the information to the satisfaction of the OFT or, if earlier, the cancellation by the OFT of the extension.

(7) The OFT may by notice to the person who gave the merger notice extend the period for considering a merger notice if the OFT is seeking undertakings under section 73 or (as the case may be) the Secretary of State is seeking undertakings under paragraph 3 of Schedule 7.

(8) An extension under subsection (7) shall be for the period beginning with the receipt of the notice under that subsection and ending with the earliest of the following events—

(a) the giving of the undertakings concerned;
(b) the expiry of the period of 10 days beginning with the first day after the receipt by the OFT of a notice from the person from whom the undertakings are being sought stating that he does not intend to give the undertakings; or
(c) the cancellation by the OFT of the extension.

(9) The Secretary of State may by notice to the person who gave the merger notice extend the period for considering a merger notice if, by virtue of paragraph 3(6) of Schedule 7, he decides to delay a decision as to whether to make a reference under section 45.

(10) An extension under subsection (9) shall be for the period of the delay.

(11) The OFT may by notice to the person who gave the merger notice extend the period for considering a merger notice if the European Commission is considering a request made, in relation to the matter concerned, by the United Kingdom (whether alone or with others) under article 22(3) of the European Merger Regulations (but is not yet proceeding with the matter in pursuance of such a request).

(12) An extension under subsection (11) shall be for the period beginning with the receipt of the notice under that subsection and ending with the receipt of a notice under subsection (13).

(13) The OFT shall, in connection with any notice given by it under subsection (11), by notice inform the person who gave the merger notice of the completion by the European Commission of its consideration of the request of the United Kingdom.

[343]

NOTES

Commencement: to be appointed.

98 Section 97: supplementary

(1) A notice under section 97(2), (3), (4), (5), (7), (9) or (11) shall be given, before the end of the period for considering the merger notice, to the person who gave the merger notice.

(2) A notice under section 97(5)—

(a) shall also be given within 5 days of the end of the period within which the information is to be provided and which is stated in the notice under section 99(2); and

(b) shall also inform the person who gave the merger notice of—
　　　(i) the OFT's opinion as mentioned in section 97(5); and
　　　(ii) the OFT's intention to extend the period for considering a merger notice.

(3) In determining for the purposes of section 97(1), (2), (3), (4) or (8)(b) or subsection (2)(a) above any period which is expressed in the enactment concerned as a period of days or number of days no account shall be taken of—
　(a) Saturday, Sunday, Good Friday and Christmas Day; and
　(b) any day which is a bank holiday in England and Wales.

(4) Any reference in this Part (apart from in section 97(1) and section 99(1)) to the period for considering a merger notice shall, if that period is extended by virtue of any one or more of subsections (2), (3), (4), (5), (7), (9) and (11) of section 97 in relation to a particular case, be construed in relation to that case as a reference to that period as so extended; but only one extension is possible under section 97(2), (3) or (4).

(5) Where the period for considering a merger notice is extended or further extended by virtue of section 97, the period as extended or (as the case may be) further extended shall, subject to subsections (6) and (7), be calculated by taking the period being extended and adding to it the period of the extension (whether or not those periods overlap in time).

(6) Subsection (7) applies where—
　(a) the period for considering a merger notice is further extended;
　(b) the further extension and at least one previous extension is made under one or more of subsections (5), (7), (9) and (11) of section 97; and
　(c) the same days or fractions of days are included in or comprise the further extension and are included in or comprise at least one such previous extension.

(7) In calculating the period of the further extension, any days or fractions of days of the kind mentioned in subsection (6)(c) shall be disregarded.

[344]

NOTES

Commencement: to be appointed.

99 Certain functions of OFT and Secretary of State in relation to merger notices

(1) The OFT shall, so far as practicable and when the period for considering any merger notice begins, take such action as the OFT considers appropriate to bring—
　(a) the existence of the proposal;
　(b) the fact that the merger notice has been given; and
　(c) the date on which the period for considering the notice may expire;

to the attention of those whom the OFT considers would be affected if the arrangements were carried into effect.

(2) The OFT may by notice to the person who gave the merger notice request him to provide the OFT with such information as the OFT or (as the case may be) the Secretary of State may require for the purpose of carrying out its or (as the case may be) his functions in relation to the merger notice.

(3) A notice under subsection (2) shall state—
　(a) the information required;
　(b) the period within which the information is to be provided; and
　(c) the possible consequences of not providing the information within the stated period and in the authorised or required manner.

(4) A notice by the OFT under subsection (2) shall be given, before the end of the period for considering the merger notice, to the person who gave the merger notice.

(5) The OFT may, at any time before the end of the period for considering any merger notice, reject the notice if—

(a) the OFT suspects that any information given in respect of the notified arrangements (whether in the merger notice or otherwise) by the person who gave the notice or any connected person is in any material respect false or misleading;

(b) the OFT suspects that it is not proposed to carry the notified arrangements into effect;

(c) any prescribed information is not given in the merger notice or any information requested by notice under subsection (2) is not provided as required; or

(d) the OFT considers that the notified arrangements are, or if carried into effect would result in, a concentration with a Community dimension within the meaning of the European Merger Regulations.

(6) In this section and section 100 "connected person", in relation to the person who gave a merger notice, means—

(a) any person who, for the purposes of section 127, is associated with him; or

(b) any subsidiary of the person who gave the merger notice or of any person so associated with him.

[345]

NOTES

Commencement: to be appointed.

100 Exceptions to protection given by merger notices

(1) Section 96(3) does not prevent any reference being made to the Commission if—

(a) before the end of the period for considering the merger notice, the OFT rejects the notice under section 99(5);

(b) before the end of that period, any of the enterprises to which the notified arrangements relate cease to be distinct from each other;

(c) any information (whether prescribed information or not) that—

(i) is, or ought to be, known to the person who gave the merger notice or any connected person; and

(ii) is material to the notified arrangements;

is not disclosed to the OFT by such time before the end of that period as may be specified in regulations under section 101;

(d) at any time after the merger notice is given but before the enterprises to which the notified arrangements relate cease to be distinct from each other, any of those enterprises ceases to be distinct from any enterprise other than an enterprise to which those arrangements relate;

(e) the six months beginning with the end of the period for considering the merger notice expires without the enterprises to which the notified arrangements relate ceasing to be distinct from each other;

(f) the merger notice is withdrawn; or

(g) any information given in respect of the notified arrangements (whether in the merger notice or otherwise) by the person who gave the notice or any connected person is in any material respect false or misleading.

(2) Subsection (3) applies where—

(a) two or more transactions which have occurred, or, if any arrangements are carried into effect, will occur, may be treated for the purposes of a reference under section 22, 33 or 45 as having occurred simultaneously on a particular date; and

(b) section 96(3) does not prevent such a reference in relation to the last of those transactions.

(3) Section 96(3) does not prevent such a reference in relation to any of those transactions which actually occurred less than six months before—

(a) that date; or

(b) the actual occurrence of another of those transactions in relation to which such a reference may be made (whether or not by virtue of this subsection).

(4) In determining for the purposes of subsections (2) and (3) the time at which any transaction actually occurred, no account shall be taken of any option or other conditional right until the option is exercised or the condition is satisfied.

(5) In this section references to the enterprises to which the notified arrangements relate are references to those enterprises that would have ceased to be distinct from one another if the arrangements mentioned in the merger notice concerned had been carried into effect at the time when the notice was given.

[346]

NOTES

Commencement: to be appointed.

101 Merger notices: regulations

(1) The Secretary of State may make regulations for the purposes of sections 96 to 100.

(2) The regulations may, in particular—

(a) provide for section 97(1), (2), (3) or (4) or section 100(1)(e) to apply as if any reference to a period of days or months were a reference to a period specified in the regulations for the purposes of the enactment concerned;

(b) provide for the manner in which any merger notice is authorised or required to be rejected or withdrawn, and the time at which any merger notice is to be treated as received or rejected;

(c) provide for the time at which any notice under section 97(7), (8)(b), (11) or (13) is to be treated as received;

(d) provide for the manner in which any information requested by the OFT or any other material information is authorised or required to be provided or disclosed, and the time at which such information is to be treated as provided or disclosed (including the time at which it is to be treated as provided to the satisfaction of the OFT for the purposes of section 97(6));

(e) provide for the person who gave the merger notice to be informed, in circumstances in which section 97(6) applies—

 (i) of the fact that the OFT is satisfied as to the provision of the information requested by the OFT or (as the case may be) of the OFT's decision to cancel the extension; and

 (ii) of the time at which the OFT is to be treated as so satisfied or (as the case may be) of the time at which the cancellation is to be treated as having effect;

(f) provide for the person who gave the merger notice to be informed, in circumstances in which section 97(8) applies—

 (i) of any decision by the OFT to cancel the extension; and

 (ii) of the time at which such a cancellation is to be treated as having effect;

(g) provide for the time at which any fee is to be treated as paid;

(h) provide that a person is, or is not, to be treated, in such circumstances as may be specified in the regulations, as acting on behalf of a person authorised by regulations under this section to give a merger notice or a person who has given such a notice.

[347]

NOTES

Commencement: to be appointed.

102   Power to modify sections 97 to 101

The Secretary of State may, for the purposes of determining the effect of giving a merger notice and the action which may be or is to be taken by any person in connection with such a notice, by order modify sections 97 to 101.

[348]

NOTES

Commencement: to be appointed.

General duties in relation to references

103   Duty of expedition in relation to references

(1) In deciding whether to make a reference under section 22 or 33 the OFT shall have regard, with a view to the prevention or removal of uncertainty, to the need for making a decision as soon as reasonably practicable.

(2) In deciding whether to make a reference under section 45 or 62 the Secretary of State shall have regard, with a view to the prevention or removal of uncertainty, to the need for making a decision as soon as reasonably practicable.

[349]

NOTES

Commencement: to be appointed.

104   Certain duties of relevant authorities to consult

(1) Subsection (2) applies where the relevant authority is proposing to make a relevant decision in a way which the relevant authority considers is likely to be adverse to the interests of a relevant party.

(2) The relevant authority shall, so far as practicable, consult that party about what is proposed before making that decision.

(3) In consulting the party concerned, the relevant authority shall, so far as practicable, give the reasons of the relevant authority for the proposed decision.

(4) In considering what is practicable for the purposes of this section the relevant authority shall, in particular, have regard to—

(a) any restrictions imposed by any timetable for making the decision; and

(b) any need to keep what is proposed, or the reasons for it, confidential.

(5) The duty under this section shall not apply in relation to the making of any decision so far as particular provision is made elsewhere by virtue of this Part for consultation before the making of that decision.

(6) In this section—

"the relevant authority" means the OFT, the Commission or the Secretary of State;

PART I
STATUTES

"relevant decision" means—

(a) in the case of the OFT, any decision by the OFT—

    (i) as to whether to make a reference under section 22 or 33 or accept undertakings under section 73 instead of making such a reference; or

    (ii) to vary under section 37 such a reference;

(b) in the case of the Commission, any decision on the questions mentioned in section 35(1) or (3), 36(1) or (2), 47 or 63; and

(c) in the case of the Secretary of State, any decision by the Secretary of State—

    (i) as to whether to make a reference under section 45 or 62; or

    (ii) to vary under section 49 or (as the case may be) 64 such a reference; and

"relevant party" means any person who appears to the relevant authority to control enterprises which are the subject of the reference or possible reference concerned.

[350]

NOTES

Commencement: to be appointed.

Information and publicity requirements

105 General information duties of OFT and Commission

(1) Where the OFT decides to investigate a matter so as to enable it to decide whether to make a reference under section 22 or 33, or so as to make a report under section 44 or 61, it shall, so far as practicable, take such action as it considers appropriate to bring information about the investigation to the attention of those whom it considers might be affected by the creation of the relevant merger situation concerned or (as the case may be) the special merger situation concerned.

(2) Subsection (1) does not apply in relation to arrangements which might result in the creation of a relevant merger situation if a merger notice has been given in relation to those arrangements under section 96.

(3) The OFT shall give the Commission—

(a) such information in its possession as the Commission may reasonably require to enable the Commission to carry out its functions under this Part; and

(b) any other assistance which the Commission may reasonably require for the purpose of assisting it in carrying out its functions under this Part and which it is within the power of the OFT to give.

(4) The OFT shall give the Commission any information in its possession which has not been requested by the Commission but which, in the opinion of the OFT, would be appropriate to give to the Commission for the purpose of assisting it in carrying out its functions under this Part.

(5) The OFT and the Commission shall give the Secretary of State—

(a) such information in their possession as the Secretary of State may by direction reasonably require to enable him to carry out his functions under this Part; and

(b) any other assistance which the Secretary of State may by direction reasonably require for the purpose of assisting him in carrying out his functions under this Part and which it is within the power of the OFT or (as the case may be) the Commission to give.

(6) The OFT shall give the Secretary of State any information in its possession which has not been requested by the Secretary of State but which, in the opinion of the OFT, would be appropriate to give to the Secretary of State for the purpose of assisting him in carrying out his functions under this Part.

(7) The Commission shall have regard to any information given to it under subsection (3) or (4); and the Secretary of State shall have regard to any information given to him under subsection (5) or (6).

(8) Any direction given under subsection (5)—
   (a) shall be in writing; and
   (b) may be varied or revoked by a subsequent direction.

[351]

NOTES

Commencement: to be appointed.

106 Advice and information about references under sections 22 and 33

(1) As soon as reasonably practicable after the passing of this Act, the OFT shall prepare and publish general advice and information about the making of references by it under section 22 or 33.

(2) The OFT may at any time publish revised, or new, advice or information.

(3) As soon as reasonably practicable after the passing of this Act, the Commission shall prepare and publish general advice and information about the consideration by it of references under section 22 or 33 and the way in which relevant customer benefits may affect the taking of enforcement action in relation to such references.

(4) The Commission may at any time publish revised, or new, advice or information.

(5) Advice and information published under this section shall be prepared with a view to—
   (a) explaining relevant provisions of this Part to persons who are likely to be affected by them; and
   (b) indicating how the OFT or (as the case may be) the Commission expects such provisions to operate.

(6) Advice (or information) published by virtue of subsection (1) or (3) may include advice (or information) about the factors which the OFT or (as the case may be) the Commission may take into account in considering whether, and if so how, to exercise a function conferred by this Part.

(7) Any advice or information published by the OFT or the Commission under this section shall be published in such manner as the OFT or (as the case may be) the Commission considers appropriate.

(8) In preparing any advice or information under this section, the OFT shall consult the Commission and such other persons as it considers appropriate.

(9) In preparing any advice or information under this section, the Commission shall consult the OFT and such other persons as it considers appropriate.

[352]

NOTES

Commencement: to be appointed.

PART I STATUTES

107 Further publicity requirements

(1)   The OFT shall publish—

(a)   any reference made by it under section 22 or 33 or any decision made by it not to make such a reference (other than a decision made by virtue of subsection (2)(b) of section 33);

(b)   any variation made by it under section 37 of a reference under section 22 or 33;

(c)   such information as it considers appropriate about any decision made by it under section 57(1) to bring a case to the attention of the Secretary of State;

(d)   any enforcement undertaking accepted by it under section 71;

(e)   any enforcement order made by it under section 72 or 76 or paragraph 2 of Schedule 7;

(f)   any variation, release or revocation of such an undertaking or order;

(g)   any decision made by it as mentioned in section 76(6)(b); and

(h)   any decision made by it to dispense with the requirements of Schedule 10.

(2)   The Commission shall publish—

(a)   any cancellation by it under section 37(1) of a reference under section 33;

(b)   any decision made by it under section 37(2) to treat a reference made under section 22 or 33 as if it had been made under section 32 or (as the case may be) 22;

(c)   any extension by it under section 39 of the period within which a report under section 38 is to be prepared and published;

(d)   any decision made by it to cancel an extension as mentioned in section 39(8)(b);

(e)   any decision made by it under section 41(2) neither to accept an undertaking under section 82 nor to make an order under section 84;

(f)   any decision made by it that there has been a material change of circumstances as mentioned in subsection (3) of section 41 or there is another special reason as mentioned in that subsection of that section;

(g)   any cancellation by it under section 48(1) or 53(1) of a reference under section 45 or any cancellation by it under section 64(1) of a reference under section 62;

(h)   any decision made by it under section 49(1) to treat—

(i)   a reference made under subsection (2) or (3) of section 45 as if it had been made under subsection (4) or (as the case may be) (5) of that section; or

(ii)   a reference made under subsection (4) or (5) of section 45 as if it had been made under subsection (2) or (as the case may be) (3) of that section;

(i)   any extension by it under section 51 of the period within which a report under section 50 is to be prepared and published;

(j)   any decision made by it under section 51(8)(b) to cancel such an extension;

(k)   any extension by it under section 51 as applied by section 65(3) of the period within which a report under section 65 is to be prepared and published;

(l)   any decision made by it under section 51(8)(b) as applied by section 65(3) to cancel such an extension;

(m)   any decision made by it under section 64(2) to treat a reference made under subsection (2) or (3) of section 62 as if it had been made under subsection (3) or (as the case may be) (2) of that section;

(n)   any decision made by it as mentioned in section 76(6)(b);

(o)   any enforcement order made by it under section 76 or 81;

(p)   any enforcement undertaking accepted by it under section 80;

(q)   any variation, release or revocation of such an order or undertaking; and

(r)   any decision made by it to dispense with the requirements of Schedule 10.

(3)   The Secretary of State shall publish—
- (a) any intervention notice or special intervention notice given by him;
- (b) any report of the OFT under section 44 or 61 which has been received by him;
- (c) any reference made by him under section 45 or 62 or any decision made by him not to make such a reference;
- (d) any variation made by him under section 49 of a reference under section 45 or under section 64 of a reference under section 62;
- (e) any report of the Commission under section 50 or 65 which has been received by him;
- (f) any decision made by him neither to accept an undertaking under paragraph 9 of Schedule 7 nor to make an order under paragraph 11 of that Schedule;
- (g) any notice given by him under section 56(1);
- (h) any enforcement undertaking accepted by him under paragraph 1 of Schedule 7;
- (i) any variation or release of such an undertaking;
- (j) any decision made by him as mentioned in paragraph 6(6)(b) of Schedule 7; and
- (k) any decision made by him to dispense with the requirements of Schedule 10.

(4)   Where any person is under a duty by virtue of subsection (1), (2) or (3) to publish the result of any action taken by that person or any decision made by that person, the person concerned shall, subject to subsections (5) and (6), also publish that person's reasons for the action concerned or (as the case may be) the decision concerned.

(5)   Such reasons need not, if it is not reasonably practicable to do so, be published at the same time as the result of the action concerned or (as the case may be) as the decision concerned.

(6)   Subsections (4) and (5) shall not apply in relation to any information published under subsection (1)(c).

(7)   The Secretary of State shall publish his reasons for—
- (a) any decision made by him under section 54(2) or 66(2); or
- (b) any decision to make an order under section 58(3) or vary or revoke such an order.

(8)   Such reasons may be published after—
- (a) in the case of subsection (7)(a), the publication of the decision concerned; and
- (b) in the case of subsection (7)(b), the making of the order or of the variation or revocation;

if it is not reasonably practicable to publish them at the same time as the publication of the decision or (as the case may be) the making of the order or variation or revocation.

(9)   The Secretary of State shall publish—
- (a) the report of the OFT under section 44 in relation to a matter no later than publication of his decision as to whether to make a reference under section 45 in relation to that matter; and
- (b) the report of the Commission under section 50 in relation to a matter no later than publication of his decision under section 54(2) in relation to that matter.

(10) The Secretary of State shall publish—
- (a) the report of the OFT under section 61 in relation to a matter no later than publication of his decision as to whether to make a reference under section 62 in relation to that matter; and

(b) the report of the Commission under section 65 in relation to a matter no later than publication of his decision under section 66(2) in relation to that matter.

(11) Where the Secretary of State has decided under section 55(2) or 66(6) to accept an undertaking under paragraph 9 of Schedule 7 or to make an order under paragraph 11 of that Schedule, he shall (after the acceptance of the undertaking or (as the case may be) the making of the order) lay details of his decision and his reasons for it, and the Commission's report under section 50 or (as the case may be) 65, before each House of Parliament.

[353]

NOTES

Commencement: to be appointed.

108 Defamation

For the purposes of the law relating to defamation, absolute privilege attaches to any advice, guidance, notice or direction given, or decision or report made, by the OFT, the Commission or the Secretary of State in the exercise of any of their functions under this Part.

[354]

NOTES

Commencement: to be appointed.

Investigation powers

109 Attendance of witnesses and production of documents etc

(1) The Commission may, for the purpose of any investigation on a reference made to it under this Part, give notice to any person requiring him—
    (a) to attend at a time and place specified in the notice; and
    (b) to give evidence to the Commission or a person nominated by the Commission for the purpose.

(2) The Commission may, for the purpose of any investigation on a reference made to it under this Part, give notice to any person requiring him—
    (a) to produce any documents which—
        (i) are specified or described in the notice, or fall within a category of document which is specified or described in the notice; and
        (ii) are in that person's custody or under his control; and
    (b) to produce them at a time and place so specified and to a person so specified.

(3) The Commission may, for the purpose of any investigation on a reference made to it under this Part, give notice to any person who carries on any business requiring him—
    (a) to supply to the Commission such estimates, forecasts, returns or other information as may be specified or described in the notice; and
    (b) to supply it at a time and place, and in a form and manner, so specified and to a person so specified.

(4) A notice under this section shall include information about the possible consequences of not complying with the notice.

(5) The Commission or any person nominated by it for the purpose may, for the purpose of any investigation on a reference made to it under this Part, take evidence on oath, and for that purpose may administer oaths.

(6)   The person to whom any document is produced in accordance with a notice under this section may, for the purpose of any investigation on a reference made to the Commission under this Part, copy the document so produced.

(7)   No person shall be required under this section—
     (a)   to give any evidence or produce any documents which he could not be compelled to give or produce in civil proceedings before the court; or
     (b)   to supply any information which he could not be compelled to supply in evidence in such proceedings.

(8)   No person shall be required, in compliance with a notice under this section, to go more than 10 miles from his place of residence unless his necessary travelling expenses are paid or offered to him.

(9)   Any reference in this section to the production of a document includes a reference to the production of a legible and intelligible copy of information recorded otherwise than in legible form.

(10)   In this section "the court" means—
     (a)   in relation to England and Wales or Northern Ireland, the High Court; and
     (b)   in relation to Scotland, the Court of Session.

[355]

NOTES
Commencement: to be appointed.

110 Enforcement of powers under section 109: general

(1)   Where the Commission considers that a person has, without reasonable excuse, failed to comply with any requirement of a notice under section 109, it may impose a penalty in accordance with section 111.

(2)   The Commission may proceed (whether at the same time or at different times) under subsection (1) and section 39(4) or (as the case may be) 51(4) (including that enactment as applied by section 65(3)) in relation to the same failure.

(3)   Where the Commission considers that a person has intentionally obstructed or delayed another person in the exercise of his powers under section 109(6), it may impose a penalty in accordance with section 111.

(4)   No penalty shall be imposed by virtue of subsection (1) or (3) if more than 4 weeks have passed since the publication of the report of the Commission on the reference concerned; but this subsection shall not apply in relation to any variation or substitution of the penalty which is permitted by virtue of this Part.

(5)   A person, subject to subsection (6), commits an offence if he intentionally alters, suppresses or destroys any document which he has been required to produce by a notice under section 109.

(6)   A person does not commit an offence under subsection (5) in relation to any act which constitutes a failure to comply with a notice under section 109 if the Commission has proceeded against that person under subsection (1) above in relation to that failure.

(7)   A person who commits an offence under subsection (5) shall be liable—
     (a)   on summary conviction, to a fine not exceeding the statutory maximum;
     (b)   on conviction on indictment, to imprisonment for a term not exceeding two years or to a fine or to both.

(8)   The Commission shall not proceed against a person under subsection (1) in relation to an act which constitutes an offence under subsection (5) if that person has been found guilty of that offence.

(9)   In deciding whether and, if so, how to proceed under subsection (1) or (3) or section 39(4) or 51(4) (including that enactment as applied by section 65(3)), the Commission shall have regard to the statement of policy which was most recently published under section 116 at the time when the failure concerned or (as the case may be) the obstruction or delay concerned occurred.

(10) The reference in this section to the production of a document includes a reference to the production of a legible and intelligible copy of information recorded otherwise than in legible form; and the reference to suppressing a document includes a reference to destroying the means of reproducing information recorded otherwise than in legible form.

[356]

NOTES
Commencement: to be appointed.

111 Penalties

(1)   A penalty imposed under section 110(1) or (3) shall be of such amount as the Commission considers appropriate.

(2)   The amount may, in the case of a penalty imposed under section 110(1), be a fixed amount, an amount calculated by reference to a daily rate or a combination of a fixed amount and an amount calculated by reference to a daily rate.

(3)   The amount shall, in the case of a penalty imposed under section 110(3), be a fixed amount.

(4)   No penalty imposed under section 110(1) shall—
   (a) in the case of a fixed amount, exceed such amount as the Secretary of State may by order specify;
   (b) in the case of an amount calculated by reference to a daily rate, exceed such amount per day as the Secretary of State may so specify; and
   (c) in the case of a fixed amount and an amount calculated by reference to a daily rate, exceed such fixed amount and such amount per day as the Secretary of State may so specify.

(5)   In imposing a penalty by reference to a daily rate—
   (a) no account shall be taken of any days before the service of the notice under section 112 on the person concerned; and
   (b) unless the Commission determines an earlier date (whether before or after the penalty is imposed), the amount payable shall cease to accumulate at the beginning of—
      (i) the day on which the requirement of the notice concerned under section 109 is satisfied or (as the case may be) the obstruction or delay is removed; or
      (ii) if earlier, the day on which the report of the Commission on the reference concerned is published (or, in the case of a report under section 50 or 65, given) or, if no such report is published (or given) within the period permitted for that purpose by this Part, the latest day on which the report may be published (or given) within the permitted period.

(6)   No penalty imposed under section 110(3) shall exceed such amount as the Secretary of State may by order specify.

(7)   An order under subsection (4) or (6) shall not specify—
   (a) in the case of a fixed amount, an amount exceeding £30,000;
   (b) in the case of an amount calculated by reference to a daily rate, an amount per day exceeding £15,000; and

(c) in the case of a fixed amount and an amount calculated by reference to a daily rate, a fixed amount exceeding £30,000 and an amount per day exceeding £15,000.

(8) Before making an order under subsection (4) or (6) the Secretary of State shall consult the Commission and such other persons as he considers appropriate.

[357]

NOTES

Commencement: to be appointed.

112 Penalties: main procedural requirements

(1) As soon as practicable after imposing a penalty under section 110(1) or (3), the Commission shall give notice of the penalty.

(2) The notice shall state—
  (a) that the Commission has imposed a penalty on the person concerned;
  (b) whether the penalty is of a fixed amount, of an amount calculated by reference to a daily rate or of both a fixed amount and an amount calculated by reference to a daily rate;
  (c) the amount or amounts concerned and, in the case of an amount calculated by reference to a daily rate, the day on which the amount first starts to accumulate and the day or days on which it might cease to accumulate;
  (d) the failure or (as the case may be) the obstruction or delay which the Commission considers gave it the power to impose the penalty;
  (e) any other facts which the Commission considers justify the imposition of a penalty and the amount or amounts of the penalty;
  (f) the manner in which, and place at which, the penalty is required to be paid to the Commission;
  (g) the date or dates, no earlier than the end of the relevant period beginning with the date of service of the notice on the person concerned, by which the penalty or (as the case may be) different portions of it are required to be paid;
  (h) that the penalty or (as the case may be) different portions of it may be paid earlier than the date or dates by which it or they are required to be paid; and
  (i) that the person concerned has the right to apply under subsection (3) below or to appeal under section 114 and the main details of those rights.

(3) The person against whom the penalty was imposed may, within 14 days of the date of service on him of a notice under subsection (1), apply to the Commission for it to specify a different date or (as the case may be) different dates by which the penalty or (as the case may be) different portions of it are to be paid.

(4) A notice under this section shall be given by—
  (a) serving a copy of the notice on the person on whom the penalty was imposed; and
  (b) publishing the notice.

(5) In this section "relevant period" means the period of 28 days mentioned in subsection (3) of section 114 or, if another period is specified by the Secretary of State under that subsection, that period.

[358]

NOTES

Commencement: to be appointed.

113 Payments and interest by instalments

(1) If the whole or any portion of a penalty is not paid by the date by which it is required to be paid, the unpaid balance from time to time shall carry interest at the rate for the time being specified in section 17 of the Judgments Act 1838 (c 110).

(2) Where an application has been made under section 112(3), the penalty shall not be required to be paid until the application has been determined, withdrawn or otherwise dealt with.

(3) If a portion of a penalty has not been paid by the date required for it, the Commission may, where it considers it appropriate to do so, require so much of the penalty as has not already been paid (and is capable of being paid immediately) to be paid immediately.

(4) Any sums received by the Commission in or towards the payment of a penalty, or interest on a penalty, shall be paid into the Consolidated Fund.

[359]

NOTES
Commencement: to be appointed.

114 Appeals in relation to penalties

(1) This section applies if a person on whom a penalty is imposed under section 110(1) or (3) is aggrieved by—
    (a) the imposition or nature of the penalty;
    (b) the amount or amounts of the penalty; or
    (c) the date by which the penalty is required to be paid or (as the case may be) the different dates by which portions of the penalty are required to be paid.

(2) The person aggrieved may apply to the Competition Appeal Tribunal.

(3) If a copy of the notice under section 112(1) was served on the person on whom the penalty was imposed, the application to the Competition Appeal Tribunal shall, subject to subsection (4), be made within—
    (a) the period of 28 days starting with the day on which the copy was served on the person concerned; or
    (b) such other period as the Secretary of State may by order specify.

(4) If the application relates to a decision of the Commission on an application by the person on whom the penalty was imposed under section 112(3), the application to the Competition Appeal Tribunal shall be made within—
    (a) the period of 28 days starting with the day on which the person concerned is notified of the decision; or
    (b) such other period as the Secretary of State may by order specify.

(5) On an application under this section, the Competition Appeal Tribunal may—
    (a) quash the penalty;
    (b) substitute a penalty of a different nature or of such lesser amount or amounts as the Competition Appeal Tribunal considers appropriate; or
    (c) in a case falling within subsection (1)(c), substitute for the date or dates imposed by the Commission an alternative date or dates;
if it considers it appropriate to do so.

(6) The Competition Appeal Tribunal shall not substitute a penalty of a different nature under subsection (5)(b) unless it considers that the person on whom the penalty is imposed will, or is likely to, pay less under the substituted penalty than he would have paid under the original penalty.

(7) Where an application has been made under this section—
  (a) the penalty shall not be required to be paid until the application has been determined, withdrawn or otherwise dealt with; and
  (b) the Commission may agree to reduce the amount or amounts of the penalty in settlement of the application.

(8) Where the Competition Appeal Tribunal substitutes a penalty of a different nature or of a lesser amount or amounts it may require the payment of interest on the substituted penalty at such rate or rates, and from such date or dates, as it considers appropriate.

(9) Where the Competition Appeal Tribunal specifies as a date by which the penalty, or a portion of the penalty, is to be paid a date before the determination of the application under this section it may require the payment of interest on the penalty, or portion, from that date at such rate as it considers appropriate.

(10) An appeal lies to the appropriate court—
  (a) on a point of law arising from a decision of the Tribunal in proceedings under this section; or
  (b) from a decision of the Tribunal in such proceedings as to the amount or amounts of a penalty.

(11) An appeal under subsection (10)—
  (a) may be brought by a party to the proceedings before the Tribunal; and
  (b) requires the permission of the Tribunal or the appropriate court.

(12) In this section "the appropriate court" means the Court of Appeal or, in the case of Tribunal proceedings in Scotland, the Court of Session.

[360]

NOTES

Commencement: to be appointed.

115 Recovery of penalties

Where a penalty imposed under section 110(1) or (3), or any portion of such a penalty, has not been paid by the date on which it is required to be paid and—
  (a) no application relating to the penalty has been made under section 114 during the period within which such an application may be made, or
  (b) any such application which has been made has been determined, withdrawn or otherwise dealt with,

the Commission may recover from the person on whom the penalty was imposed any of the penalty and any interest which has not been paid; and in England and Wales and Northern Ireland such penalty and interest may be recovered as a civil debt due to the Commission.

[361]

NOTES

Commencement: to be appointed.

116 Statement of policy

(1) The Commission shall prepare and publish a statement of policy in relation to the enforcement of notices under section 109.

(2) The statement shall, in particular, include a statement about the considerations relevant to the determination of the nature and amount of any penalty imposed under section 110(1) or (3).

(3)   The Commission may revise its statement of policy and, where it does so, it shall publish the revised statement.

(4)   The Commission shall consult such persons as it considers appropriate when preparing or revising its statement of policy.

[362]

NOTES

Commencement: to be appointed.

117 False or misleading information

(1)   A person commits an offence if—
  (a) he supplies any information to the OFT, the Commission or the Secretary of State in connection with any of their functions under this Part;
  (b) the information is false or misleading in a material respect; and
  (c) he knows that it is false or misleading in a material respect or is reckless as to whether it is false or misleading in a material respect.

(2)   A person commits an offence if he—
  (a) supplies any information to another person which he knows to be false or misleading in a material respect; or
  (b) recklessly supplies any information to another person which is false or misleading in a material respect;

knowing that the information is to be used for the purpose of supplying information to the OFT, the Commission or the Secretary of State in connection with any of their functions under this Part.

(3)   A person who commits an offence under subsection (1) or (2) shall be liable—
  (a) on summary conviction, to a fine not exceeding the statutory maximum;
  (b) on conviction on indictment, to imprisonment for a term not exceeding two years or to a fine or to both.

[363]

NOTES

Commencement: to be appointed.

Reports

118 Excisions from reports

(1)   Subsection (2) applies where the Secretary of State is under a duty to publish—
  (a) a report of the OFT under section 44 or 61; or
  (b) a report of the Commission under section 50 or 65.

(2)   The Secretary of State may exclude a matter from the report concerned if he considers that publication of the matter would be inappropriate.

(3)   In deciding what is inappropriate for the purposes of subsection (2) the Secretary of State shall have regard to the considerations mentioned in section 244.

(4)   The body which has prepared the report shall advise the Secretary of State as to the matters (if any) which it considers should be excluded by him under subsection (2).

(5)   References in sections 38(4) and 107(11) to the giving or laying of a report of the Commission shall be construed as references to the giving or laying of the report as published.

[364]

NOTES

Commencement: to be appointed.

119 Minority reports of Commission

(1)   Subsection (2) applies where, on a reference to the Commission under this Part, a member of a group constituted in connection with the reference in pursuance of paragraph 15 of Schedule 7 to the Competition Act 1998 (c 41), disagrees with any decisions contained in the report of the Commission under this Part as the decisions of the Commission.

(2)   The report shall, if the member so wishes, include a statement of his disagreement and of his reasons for disagreeing.

[365]

NOTES

Commencement: to be appointed.

Miscellaneous

120 Review of decisions under Part 3

(1)   Any person aggrieved by a decision of the OFT, the Secretary of State or the Commission under this Part in connection with a reference or possible reference in relation to a relevant merger situation or a special merger situation may apply to the Competition Appeal Tribunal for a review of that decision.

(2)   For this purpose "decision"—
- (a) does not include a decision to impose a penalty under section 110(1) or (3); but
- (b) includes a failure to take a decision permitted or required by this Part in connection with a reference or possible reference.

(3)   Except in so far as a direction to the contrary is given by the Competition Appeal Tribunal, the effect of the decision is not suspended by reason of the making of the application.

(4)   In determining such an application the Competition Appeal Tribunal shall apply the same principles as would be applied by a court on an application for judicial review.

(5)   The Competition Appeal Tribunal may—
- (a) dismiss the application or quash the whole or part of the decision to which it relates; and
- (b) where it quashes the whole or part of that decision, refer the matter back to the original decision maker with a direction to reconsider and make a new decision in accordance with the ruling of the Competition Appeal Tribunal.

(6)   An appeal lies on any point of law arising from a decision of the Competition Appeal Tribunal under this section to the appropriate court.

(7)   An appeal under subsection (6) requires the permission of the Tribunal or the appropriate court.

(8)   In this section—

"the appropriate court" means the Court of Appeal or, in the case of Tribunal proceedings in Scotland, the Court of Session; and

"Tribunal rules" has the meaning given by section 15(1).

[366]

NOTES

Commencement: to be appointed.

121 Fees

(1)   The Secretary of State may by order require the payment to him or the OFT of such fees as may be prescribed by the order in connection with the exercise by the Secretary of State, the OFT and the Commission of their functions under or by virtue of this Part, Part V of the Fair Trading Act 1973 (c 41) and sections 32 to 34 of, and Schedule 4ZA to, the Water Industry Act 1991 (c 56).

(2)   An order under this section may, in particular, provide for fees to be payable—

(a) in respect of a merger notice;

(b) in respect of an application for the consent of the Secretary of State under section 58(1) of the Act of 1973 to the transfer of a newspaper or of newspaper assets; or

(c) on the occurrence of any event specified in the order.

(3)   The events that may be specified in an order under this section by virtue of subsection (2)(c) include, in particular—

(a) the decision by the OFT in relation to a possible reference under section 22 or 33 that it is or may be the case that a relevant merger situation has been created or (as the case may be) that arrangements are in progress or in contemplation which, if carried into effect, will result in the creation of a relevant merger situation;

(b) the decision by the Secretary of State in relation to a possible reference under section 45 that it is or may be the case that a relevant merger situation has been created or (as the case may be) that arrangements are in progress or in contemplation which, if carried into effect, will result in the creation of a relevant merger situation;

(c) the decision by the Secretary of State in relation to a possible reference under section 62 that—

(i) it is or may be the case that a special merger situation has been created or (as the case may be) that arrangements are in progress or in contemplation which, if carried into effect, will result in the creation of a special merger situation; and

(ii) one or more than one consideration mentioned in the special intervention notice is relevant to a consideration of the special merger situation concerned; and

(d) the decision by the OFT in relation to a possible reference under section 32 of the Act of 1991 that it is or may be the case that arrangements are in progress which, if carried into effect, will result in a merger of any two or more water enterprises or that such a merger has taken place otherwise than as a result of the carrying into effect of arrangements that have been the subject of a reference by virtue of paragraph (a) of that section.

(4)   An order under this section may, in particular, contain provision—

(a) for ascertaining the persons by whom fees are payable;

(b) specifying whether any fee is payable to the Secretary of State or the OFT;

PART I
STATUTES

(c) for the amount of any fee to be calculated by reference to matters which may include—

    (i) in a case involving functions of the Secretary of State under sections 57 to 61 of the Act of 1973, the number of newspapers concerned, the number of separate editions (determined in accordance with the order) of each newspaper and the average circulation per day of publication (within the meaning of Part V of that Act) of each newspaper; and

    (ii) in any other case, the value of the turnover of the enterprises concerned;

(d) as to the time when any fee is to be paid; and

(e) for the repayment by the Secretary of State or the OFT of the whole or part of any fee in specified circumstances.

(5) For the purposes of subsection (4)(c)(ii) the turnover of an enterprise shall be determined in accordance with such provisions as may be specified in an order under this section.

(6) Provision made by virtue of subsection (5) may, in particular, include provision—

(a) as to the amounts which are, or which are not, to be treated as comprising an enterprise's turnover;

(b) as to the date or dates by reference to which an enterprise's turnover is to be determined;

(c) restricting the turnover to be taken into consideration to turnover which has a connection of a particular description with the United Kingdom.

(7) An order under this section may, in particular, in connection with provisions of the kind mentioned in subsection (5) make provision enabling the Secretary of State or the OFT to determine matters of a description specified in the order (including any of the matters mentioned in paragraphs (a) to (c) of subsection (6)).

(8) In determining the amount of any fees to be prescribed by an order under this section, the Secretary of State may take into account all costs incurred by him and by the OFT in respect of the exercise by him, the OFT and the Commission of their respective functions under or by virtue of this Part, Part V of the Act of 1973 and sections 32 to 34 of, and Schedule 4ZA to, the Act of 1991.

(9) Fees paid to the Secretary of State or the OFT under this section shall be paid into the Consolidated Fund.

(10) In this section "newspaper" has the same meaning as in Part V of the Act of 1973.

[367]

NOTES

Commencement: to be appointed.

122 Primacy of Community law

(1) Advice and information published by virtue of section 106(1) or (3) shall include such advice and information about the effect of Community law, and anything done under or in accordance with it, on the provisions of this Part as the OFT or (as the case may be) the Commission considers appropriate.

(2) Advice and information published by the OFT by virtue of section 106(1) shall, in particular, include advice and information about the circumstances in which the duties of the OFT under sections 22 and 33 do not apply as a result of the European Merger Regulations or anything done under or in accordance with them.

(3)   The duty or power to make a reference under section 22 or 45(2) or (3), and the power to give an intervention notice under section 42, shall apply in a case in which the relevant enterprises ceased to be distinct enterprises at a time or in circumstances not falling within section 24 if the condition mentioned in subsection (4) is satisfied.

(4)   The condition mentioned in this subsection is that, because of the European Merger Regulations or anything done under or in accordance with them, the reference, or (as the case may be) the reference under section 22 to which the intervention notice relates, could not have been made earlier than 4 months before the date on which it is to be made.

(5)   Where the duty or power to make a reference under section 22 or 45(2) or (3), or the power to give an intervention notice under section 42, applies as mentioned in subsection (3), references in this Part to the creation of a relevant merger situation shall be construed accordingly.

[368]

NOTES
Commencement: to be appointed.

123 Power to alter share of supply test

(1)   The Secretary of State may by order amend or replace the conditions which determine for the purposes of this Part whether a relevant merger situation has been created.

(2)   The Secretary of State shall not exercise his power under subsection (1)—
  (a) to amend or replace the conditions mentioned in paragraphs (a) and (b) of subsection (1) of section 23;
  (b) to amend or replace the condition mentioned in paragraph (a) of subsection (2) of that section.

(3)   In exercising his power under subsection (1) to amend or replace the condition mentioned in paragraph (b) of subsection (2) of section 23 or any condition which for the time being applies instead of it, the Secretary of State shall, in particular, have regard to the desirability of ensuring that any amended or new condition continues to operate by reference to the degree of commercial strength which results from the enterprises concerned having ceased to be distinct.

(4)   Before making an order under this section the Secretary of State shall consult the OFT and the Commission.

(5)   An order under this section may provide for the delegation of functions to the decision-making authority.

[369]

NOTES
Commencement: to be appointed.

Other

124 Orders and regulations under Part 3

(1)   Any power of the Secretary of State to make an order or regulations under this Part shall be exercisable by statutory instrument.

(2) Any power of the Secretary of State to make an order or regulations under this Part—

(a) may be exercised so as to make different provision for different cases or different purposes; and

(b) includes power to make such incidental, supplementary, consequential, transitory, transitional or saving provision as the Secretary of State considers appropriate.

(3) The power of the Secretary of State under section 34 or 123 (including that power as extended by subsection (2) above) may be exercised by modifying any enactment comprised in or made under this Act, or any other enactment.

(4) The power of the Secretary of State under section 40(8), 52(8) (including that enactment as applied by section 65(3)), 58(3), 68 or 102 as extended by subsection (2) above may be exercised by modifying any enactment comprised in or made under this Act, or any other enactment.

(5) An order made by the Secretary of State under section 28 (including that enactment as applied by section 42(5), 59(5) and 67(7)), 40(8), 52(8) (including that enactment as applied by section 65(3)), 111(4) or (6), 114(3)(b) or (4)(b) or 121 or Schedule 7 shall be subject to annulment in pursuance of a resolution of either House of Parliament.

(6) No order shall be made by the Secretary of State under section 34, 68, 102, 123 or 128(6) unless a draft of it has been laid before, and approved by a resolution of, each House of Parliament.

(7) An order made by the Secretary of State under section 58(3) shall be laid before Parliament after being made and shall cease to have effect unless approved, within the period of 28 days beginning with the day on which it is made, by a resolution of each House of Parliament.

(8) In calculating the period of 28 days mentioned in subsection (7), no account shall be taken of any time during which Parliament is dissolved or prorogued or during which both Houses are adjourned for more than four days.

(9) If an order made by the Secretary of State ceases to have effect by virtue of subsection (7), any modification made by it of an enactment is repealed (and the previous enactment revived) but without prejudice to the validity of anything done in connection with that modification before the order ceased to have effect and without prejudice to the making of a new order.

(10) If, apart from this subsection, an order made by the Secretary of State under section 58(3) would be treated for the purposes of the standing orders of either House of Parliament as a hybrid instrument, it shall proceed in that House as if it were not such an instrument.

[370]

NOTES

Commencement: to be appointed.

---

125 Offences by bodies corporate

(1) Where an offence under this Part committed by a body corporate is proved to have been committed with the consent or connivance of, or to be attributable to any neglect on the part of—

(a) a director, manager, secretary or other similar officer of the body corporate, or

(b) a person purporting to act in such a capacity,

he as well as the body corporate commits the offence and shall be liable to be proceeded against and punished accordingly.

(2)   Where the affairs of a body corporate are managed by its members, subsection (1) applies in relation to the acts and defaults of a member in connection with his functions of management as if he were a director of the body corporate.

(3)   Where an offence under this Part is committed by a Scottish partnership and is proved to have been committed with the consent or connivance of a partner, or to be attributable to any neglect on the part of a partner, he as well as the partnership commits the offence and shall be liable to be proceeded against and punished accordingly.

(4)   In subsection (3) "partner" includes a person purporting to act as a partner.

[371]

NOTES

Commencement: to be appointed.

126 Service of documents

(1)   Any document required or authorised by virtue of this Part to be served on any person may be served—
- (a) by delivering it to him or by leaving it at his proper address or by sending it by post to him at that address;
- (b) if the person is a body corporate other than a limited liability partnership, by serving it in accordance with paragraph (a) on the secretary of the body;
- (c) if the person is a limited liability partnership, by serving it in accordance with paragraph (a) on a member of the partnership; or
- (d) if the person is a partnership, by serving it in accordance with paragraph (a) on a partner or a person having the control or management of the partnership business.

(2)   For the purposes of this section and section 7 of the Interpretation Act 1978 (c 30) (service of documents by post) in its application to this section, the proper address of any person on whom a document is to be served shall be his last known address, except that—
- (a) in the case of service on a body corporate (other than a limited liability partnership) or its secretary, it shall be the address of the registered or principal office of the body;
- (b) in the case of service on a limited liability partnership or a member of the partnership, it shall be the address of the registered or principal office of the partnership;
- (c) in the case of service on a partnership or a partner or a person having the control or management of a partnership business, it shall be the address of the principal office of the partnership.

(3)   For the purposes of subsection (2) the principal office of a company constituted under the law of a country or territory outside the United Kingdom or of a partnership carrying on business outside the United Kingdom is its principal office within the United Kingdom.

(4)   Subsection (5) applies if a person to be served under this Part with any document by another has specified to that other an address within the United Kingdom other than his proper address (as determined under subsection (2)) as the one at which he or someone on his behalf will accept documents of the same description as that document.

(5) In relation to that document, that address shall be treated as his proper address for the purposes of this section and section 7 of the Interpretation Act 1978 in its application to this section, instead of that determined under subsection (2).

(6) Any notice in writing or other document required or authorised by virtue of this Part to be served on any person may be served on that person by transmitting the text of the notice or other document to him by means of a telecommunication system (within the meaning of the Telecommunications Act 1984 (c 12)) or by other means but while in electronic form provided the text is received by that person in legible form and is capable of being used for subsequent reference.

(7) This section does not apply to any document if rules of court make provision about its service.

(8) In this section references to serving include references to similar expressions (such as giving or sending).

[372]

NOTES

Commencement: to be appointed.

127 Associated persons

(1) Associated persons, and any bodies corporate which they or any of them control, shall be treated as one person—
  (a) for the purpose of deciding under section 26 whether any two enterprises have been brought under common ownership or common control; and
  (b) for the purpose of determining what activities are carried on by way of business by any one person so far as that question arises in connection with paragraph 13(2) of Schedule 8.

(2) Subsection (1) shall not exclude from section 26 any case which would otherwise fall within that section.

(3) A reference under section 22, 33, 45 or 62 (whether or not made by virtue of this section) may be framed so as to exclude from consideration, either altogether or for a specified purpose or to a specified extent, any matter which, apart from this section, would not have been taken into account on that reference.

(4) For the purposes of this section—
  (a) any individual and that individual's spouse or partner and any relative, or spouse or partner of a relative, of that individual or of that individual's spouse or partner;
  (b) any person in his capacity as trustee of a settlement and the settlor or grantor and any person associated with the settlor or grantor;
  (c) persons carrying on business in partnership and the spouse or partner and relatives of any of them; or
  (d) two or more persons acting together to secure or exercise control of a body of persons corporate or unincorporate or to secure control of any enterprise or assets,

shall be regarded as associated with one another.

(5) The reference in subsection (1) to bodies corporate which associated persons control shall be construed in accordance with section 26(3) and (4).

(6) In this section "relative" means a brother, sister, uncle, aunt, nephew, niece, lineal ancestor or descendant (the stepchild of any person, or anyone adopted by a person, whether legally or otherwise, as his child being regarded as a relative or

PART I
STATUTES

taken into account to trace a relationship in the same way as that person's child); and references to a spouse or partner shall include a former spouse or partner.

[373]

NOTES

Commencement: to be appointed.

128 Supply of services and market for services etc

(1)   References in this Part to the supply of services shall be construed in accordance with this section; and references in this Part to a market for services and other related expressions shall be construed accordingly.

(2)   The supply of services does not include the provision of services under a contract of service or of apprenticeship whether it is express or implied and (if it is express) whether it is oral or in writing.

(3)   The supply of services includes—
    (a) performing for gain or reward any activity other than the supply of goods;
    (b) rendering services to order;
    (c) the provision of services by making them available to potential users.

(4)   The supply of services includes making arrangements for the use of computer software or for granting access to data stored in any form which is not readily accessible.

(5)   The supply of services includes making arrangements by means of a relevant agreement (within the meaning of section 189(2) of the Broadcasting Act 1990 (c 42)) for sharing the use of telecommunications apparatus.

(6)   The supply of services includes permitting or making arrangements to permit the use of land in such circumstances as the Secretary of State may by order specify.

[374]

NOTES

Commencement: to be appointed.

129 Other interpretation provisions

(1)   In this Part, unless the context otherwise requires—
    "action" includes omission; and references to the taking of action include references to refraining from action;
    "agreement" means any agreement or arrangement, in whatever way and whatever form it is made, and whether it is, or is intended to be, legally enforceable or not;
    "business" includes a professional practice and includes any other undertaking which is carried on for gain or reward or which is an undertaking in the course of which goods or services are supplied otherwise than free of charge;
    "change of circumstances" includes any discovery that information has been supplied which is false or misleading in a material respect;
    "Community law" means—
        (a) all the rights, powers, liabilities, obligations and restrictions from time to time created or arising by or under the Community Treaties; and
        (b) all the remedies and procedures from time to time provided for by or under the Community Treaties;

"consumer" means any person who is—
    (a) a person to whom goods are or are sought to be supplied (whether by way of sale or otherwise) in the course of a business carried on by the person supplying or seeking to supply them; or
    (b) a person for whom services are or are sought to be supplied in the course of a business carried on by the person supplying or seeking to supply them;

and who does not receive or seek to receive the goods or services in the course of a business carried on by him;

"customer" includes a customer who is not a consumer;

"enactment" includes an Act of the Scottish Parliament, Northern Ireland legislation and an enactment comprised in subordinate legislation, and includes an enactment whenever passed or made;

"enterprise" means the activities, or part of the activities, of a business;

"the European Merger Regulations" means Council Regulation (EEC) No 4064/89 of 21st December 1989 on the control of concentrations between undertakings as amended by Council Regulation (EC) No 1310/97 of 30th June 1997;

"goods" includes buildings and other structures, and also includes ships, aircraft and hovercraft;

"modify" includes amend or repeal;

"notice" means notice in writing;

"price" includes any charge or fee (however described);

"subordinate legislation" has the same meaning as in the Interpretation Act 1978 (c 30) and also includes an instrument made under an Act of the Scottish Parliament and an instrument made under Northern Ireland legislation;

"subsidiary" has the meaning given by section 736 of the Companies Act 1985 (c 6);

"supply", in relation to the supply of goods, includes supply by way of sale, lease, hire or hire-purchase, and, in relation to buildings or other structures, includes the construction of them by a person for another person; and

"United Kingdom national" means an individual who is—
    (a) a British citizen, a British overseas territories citizen, a British National (Overseas) or a British Overseas citizen;
    (b) a person who under the British Nationality Act 1981 (c 61) is a British subject; or
    (c) a British protected person within the meaning of that Act.

(2)   For the purposes of this Part any two bodies corporate are interconnected if—
    (a) one of them is a body corporate of which the other is a subsidiary; or
    (b) both of them are subsidiaries of one and the same body corporate;

and in this Part "interconnected bodies corporate" shall be construed accordingly and "group of interconnected bodies corporate" means a group consisting of two or more bodies corporate all of whom are interconnected with each other.

(3)   References in this Part to a person carrying on business include references to a person carrying on business in partnership with one or more other persons.

(4)   Any duty to publish which is imposed on a person by this Part shall, unless the context otherwise requires, be construed as a duty on that person to publish in such manner as he considers appropriate for the purpose of bringing the matter concerned to the attention of those likely to be affected by it.

[375]

NOTES

Commencement: to be appointed.

130 Index of defined expressions

In this Part, the expressions listed in the left-hand column have the meaning given by, or are to be interpreted in accordance with, the provisions listed in the right-hand column.

Expression	Provision of this Act
Action (and the taking of action)	Section 129(1)
Adverse public interest finding	Section 54(3)
Agreement	Section 129(1)
Anti-competitive outcome	Section 35(2)
Business (and carrying on business)	Section 129(1) and (3)
Change of circumstances	Section 129(1)
The Commission	Section 273
Community law	Section 129(1)
Consumer	Section 129(1)
Customer	Section 129(1)
Date of reference	Section 39(9)
The decision-making authority	Section 22(7)
Enactment	Section 129(1)
Enforcement order	Section 86(6)
Enforcement undertaking	Section 89(2)
Enterprise	Section 129(1)
Enterprises ceasing to be distinct	Section 26(1)
European Merger Regulations	Section 129(1)
Final determination of matter to which intervention notice relates	Section 43(4) and (5)
Final determination of matter to which special intervention notice relates	Section 60(4) and (5)
Final determination of reference under section 22 or 33	Section 79(1) and (2)
Goods	Section 129(1)

Expression	*Provision of this Act*
Interconnected bodies corporate (and a group of interconnected bodies corporate)	Section 129(2)
Intervention notice	Section 42(2)
Market for goods or services	Section 22(6)
Market in the United Kingdom	Section 22(6)
Merger notice	Section 96(2)
Modify	Section 129(1)
Notice	Section 129(1)
Notified arrangements	Section 96(6)
The OFT	Section 273
Orders under section 81	Section 81(6)
Orders under paragraph 2 of Schedule 7	Paragraph 2(7) of Schedule 7
The period for considering a merger notice	Sections 97 and 98
Price	Section 129(1)
Public interest consideration	Sections 42(3) and 67(9)
Public interest consideration being finalised	Section 42(8)
Publish	Section 129(4)
References under section 22, 33, 45 or 62	Sections 37(2), 49(1), 56(8) and 64(2)
Relevant customer benefit	Section 30
Relevant merger situation	Section 23 (as read with other enactments)
Reports of the Commission	Section 118(5)
Special intervention notice	Section 59(2)
Special merger situation	Section 59(3)
Subordinate legislation	Section 129(1)
Subsidiary	Section 129(1)

Expression	Provision of this Act
Supply (in relation to the supply of goods)	Section 129(1)
The supply of services (and a market for services etc)	Section 128
The turnover in the United Kingdom of an enterprise	Section 28(2)
Undertakings under section 80	Section 80(6)
Undertakings under paragraph 1 of Schedule 7	Paragraph 1(7) of Schedule 7
United Kingdom national	Section 129(1)

[376]

NOTES

Commencement: to be appointed.

PART 4
MARKET INVESTIGATIONS

CHAPTER 1
MARKET INVESTIGATION REFERENCES

Making of references

131 Power of OFT to make references

(1)   The OFT may, subject to subsection (4), make a reference to the Commission if the OFT has reasonable grounds for suspecting that any feature, or combination of features, of a market in the United Kingdom for goods or services prevents, restricts or distorts competition in connection with the supply or acquisition of any goods or services in the United Kingdom or a part of the United Kingdom.

(2)   For the purposes of this Part any reference to a feature of a market in the United Kingdom for goods or services shall be construed as a reference to—
   (a) the structure of the market concerned or any aspect of that structure;
   (b) any conduct (whether or not in the market concerned) of one or more than one person who supplies or acquires goods or services in the market concerned; or
   (c) any conduct relating to the market concerned of customers of any person who supplies or acquires goods or services.

(3)   In subsection (2) "conduct" includes any failure to act (whether or not intentional) and any other unintentional conduct.

(4)   No reference shall be made under this section if—
   (a) the making of the reference is prevented by section 156(1); or
   (b) a reference has been made under section 132 in relation to the same matter but has not been finally determined.

(5)   References in this Part to a market investigation reference being finally determined shall be construed in accordance with section 183(3) to (6).

(6)   In this Part—
   "market in the United Kingdom" includes—
> (a) so far as it operates in the United Kingdom or a part of the United Kingdom, any market which operates there and in another country or territory or in a part of another country or territory; and
> (b) any market which operates only in a part of the United Kingdom;
   "market investigation reference" means a reference under this section or section 132;

and references to a market for goods or services include references to a market for goods and services.

[377]

NOTES

Commencement: to be appointed.

132 Ministerial power to make references

(1)   Subsection (3) applies where, in relation to any goods or services, the appropriate Minister is not satisfied with a decision of the OFT not to make a reference under section 131.

(2)   Subsection (3) also applies where, in relation to any goods or services, the appropriate Minister—
> (a) has brought to the attention of the OFT information which the appropriate Minister considers to be relevant to the question of whether the OFT should make a reference under section 131; but
> (b) is not satisfied that the OFT will decide, within such period as the appropriate Minister considers to be reasonable, whether to make such a reference.

(3)   The appropriate Minister may, subject to subsection (4), make a reference to the Commission if he has reasonable grounds for suspecting that any feature, or combination of features, of a market in the United Kingdom for goods or services prevents, restricts or distorts competition in connection with the supply or acquisition of any goods or services in the United Kingdom or a part of the United Kingdom.

(4)   No reference shall be made under this section if the making of the reference is prevented by section 156(1).

(5)   In this Part "the appropriate Minister" means—
> (a) the Secretary of State; or
> (b) the Secretary of State and one or more than one other Minister of the Crown acting jointly.

[378]

NOTES

Commencement: to be appointed.

133 Contents of references

(1)   A market investigation reference shall, in particular, specify—
> (a) the enactment under which it is made;
> (b) the date on which it is made; and
> (c) the description of goods or services to which the feature or combination of features concerned relates.

(2)   A market investigation reference may be framed so as to require the Commission to confine its investigation into the effects of features of markets in the United Kingdom for goods or services of a description specified in the reference to the effects of features of such of those markets as exist in connection with—

(a) a supply, of a description specified in the reference, of the goods or services concerned; or

(b) an acquisition, of a description specified in the reference, of the goods or services concerned.

(3)   A description of the kind mentioned in subsection (2)(a) or (b) may, in particular, be by reference to—

(a) the place where the goods or services are supplied or acquired; or

(b) the persons by or to whom they are supplied or by or from whom they are acquired.

[379]

NOTES

Commencement: to be appointed.

Determination of references

134 Questions to be decided on market investigation references

(1)   The Commission shall, on a market investigation reference, decide whether any feature, or combination of features, of each relevant market prevents, restricts or distorts competition in connection with the supply or acquisition of any goods or services in the United Kingdom or a part of the United Kingdom.

(2)   For the purposes of this Part, in relation to a market investigation reference, there is an adverse effect on competition if any feature, or combination of features, of a relevant market prevents, restricts or distorts competition in connection with the supply or acquisition of any goods or services in the United Kingdom or a part of the United Kingdom.

(3)   In subsections (1) and (2) "relevant market" means—

(a) in the case of subsection (2) so far as it applies in connection with a possible reference, a market in the United Kingdom—

(i) for goods or services of a description to be specified in the reference; and

(ii) which would not be excluded from investigation by virtue of section 133(2); and

(b) in any other case, a market in the United Kingdom—

(i) for goods or services of a description specified in the reference concerned; and

(ii) which is not excluded from investigation by virtue of section 133(2).

(4)   The Commission shall, if it has decided on a market investigation reference that there is an adverse effect on competition, decide the following additional questions—

(a) whether action should be taken by it under section 138 for the purpose of remedying, mitigating or preventing the adverse effect on competition concerned or any detrimental effect on customers so far as it has resulted from, or may be expected to result from, the adverse effect on competition;

(b) whether it should recommend the taking of action by others for the purpose of remedying, mitigating or preventing the adverse effect on competition concerned or any detrimental effect on customers so far as it has resulted from, or may be expected to result from, the adverse effect on competition; and

(c) in either case, if action should be taken, what action should be taken and what is to be remedied, mitigated or prevented.

(5) For the purposes of this Part, in relation to a market investigation reference, there is a detrimental effect on customers if there is a detrimental effect on customers or future customers in the form of—

    (a) higher prices, lower quality or less choice of goods or services in any market in the United Kingdom (whether or not the market to which the feature or features concerned relate); or

    (b) less innovation in relation to such goods or services.

(6) In deciding the questions mentioned in subsection (4), the Commission shall, in particular, have regard to the need to achieve as comprehensive a solution as is reasonable and practicable to the adverse effect on competition and any detrimental effects on customers so far as resulting from the adverse effect on competition.

(7) In deciding the questions mentioned in subsection (4), the Commission may, in particular, have regard to the effect of any action on any relevant customer benefits of the feature or features of the market concerned.

(8) For the purposes of this Part a benefit is a relevant customer benefit of a feature or features of a market if—

    (a) it is a benefit to customers or future customers in the form of—

        (i) lower prices, higher quality or greater choice of goods or services in any market in the United Kingdom (whether or not the market to which the feature or features concerned relate); or

        (ii) greater innovation in relation to such goods or services; and

    (b) the Commission, the Secretary of State or (as the case may be) the OFT believes that—

        (i) the benefit has accrued as a result (whether wholly or partly) of the feature or features concerned or may be expected to accrue within a reasonable period as a result (whether wholly or partly) of that feature or those features; and

        (ii) the benefit was, or is, unlikely to accrue without the feature or features concerned.

[380]

NOTES

Commencement: to be appointed.

135 Variation of market investigation references

(1) The OFT or (as the case may be) the appropriate Minister may at any time vary a market investigation reference made by it or (as the case may be) him.

(2) The OFT or (as the case may be) the appropriate Minister shall consult the Commission before varying any such reference.

(3) Subsection (2) shall not apply if the Commission has requested the variation concerned.

(4) No variation under this section shall be capable of altering the period permitted by section 137 within which the report of the Commission under section 136 is to be prepared and published or (as the case may be) the period permitted by section 144 within which the report of the Commission under section 142 is to be prepared and published or given.

[381]

NOTES

Commencement: to be appointed.

136 Investigations and reports on market investigation references

(1)   The Commission shall prepare and publish a report on a market investigation reference within the period permitted by section 137.

(2)   The report shall, in particular, contain—
    (a) the decisions of the Commission on the questions which it is required to answer by virtue of section 134;
    (b) its reasons for its decisions; and
    (c) such information as the Commission considers appropriate for facilitating a proper understanding of those questions and of its reasons for its decisions.

(3)   The Commission shall carry out such investigations as it considers appropriate for the purposes of preparing a report under this section.

(4)   The Commission shall, at the same time as a report under this section is published—
    (a) in the case of a reference under section 131, give it to the OFT; and
    (b) in the case of a reference under section 132, give it to the appropriate Minister and give a copy of it to the OFT.

(5)   Where a reference has been made by the OFT under section 131 or by the appropriate Minister under section 132 in circumstances in which a reference could have been made by a relevant sectoral regulator under section 131 as it has effect by virtue of a relevant sectoral enactment, the Commission shall, at the same time as the report under this section is published, give a copy of it to the relevant sectoral regulator concerned.

(6)   Where a reference has been made by a relevant sectoral regulator under section 131 as it has effect by virtue of a relevant sectoral enactment, the Commission shall, at the same time as the report under this section is published, give a copy of it to the OFT.

(7)   In this Part "relevant sectoral enactment" means—
    (a) in relation to the Director General of Telecommunications, section 50 of the Telecommunications Act 1984 (c 12);
    (b) in relation to the Gas and Electricity Markets Authority, section 36A of the Gas Act 1986 (c 44) or (as the case may be) section 43 of the Electricity Act 1989 (c 29);
    (c) in relation to the Director General of Water Services, section 31 of the Water Industry Act 1991 (c 56);
    (d) in relation to the Director General of Electricity Supply for Northern Ireland, article 46 of the Electricity (Northern Ireland) Order 1992 (SI 1992/231 (NI 1));
    (e) in relation to the Rail Regulator, section 67 of the Railways Act 1993 (c 43);
    (f) in relation to the Director General of Gas for Northern Ireland, article 23 of the Gas (Northern Ireland) Order 1996 (SI 1996/275 (NI 2)); and
    (g) in relation to the Civil Aviation Authority, section 86 of the Transport Act 2000 (c 38).

(8)   In this Part "relevant sectoral regulator" means the Director General of Telecommunications, the Gas and Electricity Markets Authority, the Director General of Water Services, the Director General of Electricity Supply for Northern Ireland, the Rail Regulator, the Director General of Gas for Northern Ireland or the Civil Aviation Authority.

(9)   The Secretary of State may by order modify subsection (7) or (8).

[382]

NOTES
Commencement: to be appointed.

137 Time-limits for market investigations and reports

(1)   The Commission shall prepare and publish its report under section 136 within the period of two years beginning with the date of the market investigation reference concerned.

(2)   Subsection (1) is subject to section 151(3) and (5).

(3)   The Secretary of State may by order amend subsection (1) so as to alter the period of two years mentioned in that subsection or any period for the time being mentioned in that subsection in substitution for that period.

(4)   No alteration shall be made by virtue of subsection (3) which results in the period for the time being mentioned in subsection (1) exceeding two years.

(5)   An order under subsection (3) shall not affect any period of time within which the Commission is under a duty to prepare and publish its report under section 136 in relation to a market investigation reference if the Commission is already under that duty in relation to that reference when the order is made.

(6)   Before making an order under subsection (3) the Secretary of State shall consult the Commission and such other persons as he considers appropriate.

(7)   References in this Part to the date of a market investigation reference shall be construed as references to the date specified in the reference as the date on which it is made.

[383]

NOTES
Commencement: to be appointed.

138 Duty to remedy adverse effects

(1)   Subsection (2) applies where a report of the Commission has been prepared and published under section 136 within the period permitted by section 137 and contains the decision that there is one or more than one adverse effect on competition.

(2)   The Commission shall, in relation to each adverse effect on competition, take such action under section 159 or 161 as it considers to be reasonable and practicable—

(a)   to remedy, mitigate or prevent the adverse effect on competition concerned; and

(b)   to remedy, mitigate or prevent any detrimental effects on customers so far as they have resulted from, or may be expected to result from, the adverse effect on competition.

(3)   The decisions of the Commission under subsection (2) shall be consistent with its decisions as included in its report by virtue of section 134(4) unless there has been a material change of circumstances since the preparation of the report or the Commission otherwise has a special reason for deciding differently.

(4)   In making a decision under subsection (2), the Commission shall, in particular, have regard to the need to achieve as comprehensive a solution as is reasonable and practicable to the adverse effect on competition concerned and any

detrimental effects on customers so far as resulting from the adverse effect on competition.

(5)   In making a decision under subsection (2), the Commission may, in particular, have regard to the effect of any action on any relevant customer benefits of the feature or features of the market concerned.

(6)   The Commission shall take no action under subsection (2) to remedy, mitigate or prevent any detrimental effect on customers so far as it may be expected to result from the adverse effect on competition concerned if—

    (a) no detrimental effect on customers has resulted from the adverse effect on competition; and

    (b) the adverse effect on competition is not being remedied, mitigated or prevented.

[384]

NOTES

Commencement: to be appointed.

CHAPTER 2
PUBLIC INTEREST CASES

Intervention notices

139 Public interest intervention by Secretary of State

(1)   The Secretary of State may give a notice to the Commission if—
    (a) a market investigation reference has been made to the Commission;
    (b) no more than four months has passed since the date of the reference;
    (c) the reference is not finally determined; and
    (d) the Secretary of State believes that it is or may be the case that one or more than one public interest consideration is relevant to the case.

(2)   The Secretary of State may give a notice to the OFT if—
    (a) the OFT is considering whether to accept—
       (i) an undertaking under section 154 instead of making a reference under section 131; or
      (ii) an undertaking varying or superseding any such undertaking;
    (b) the OFT has published a notice under section 155(1) or (4); and
    (c) the Secretary of State believes that it is or may be the case that one or more than one public interest consideration is relevant to the case.

(3)   In this Part "intervention notice" means a notice under subsection (1) or (2).

(4)   No more than one intervention notice shall be given under subsection (1) in relation to the same market investigation reference and no more than one intervention notice shall be given under subsection (2) in relation to the same proposed undertaking or in relation to proposed undertakings which do not differ from each other in any material respect.

(5)   For the purposes of this Part a public interest consideration is a consideration which, at the time of the giving of the intervention notice concerned, is specified in section 153 or is not so specified but, in the opinion of the Secretary of State, ought to be so specified.

(6)   Where the Secretary of State has given an intervention notice mentioning a public interest consideration which, at that time, is not finalised, he shall, as soon as practicable, take such action as is within his power to ensure that it is finalised.

(7)   For the purposes of this Part a public interest consideration is finalised if—

     (a)   it is specified in section 153 otherwise than by virtue of an order under subsection (3) of that section; or

     (b)   it is specified in that section by virtue of an order under subsection (3) of that section and the order providing for it to be so specified has been laid before, and approved by, Parliament in accordance with subsection (6) of section 181 and within the period mentioned in that subsection.

[385]

NOTES

Commencement: to be appointed.

Intervention notices under section 139(1)

140   Intervention notices under section 139(1)

(1)   An intervention notice under section 139(1) shall state—

     (a)   the market investigation reference concerned;

     (b)   the date of the market investigation reference concerned;

     (c)   the public interest consideration or considerations which are, or may be, relevant to the case; and

     (d)   where any public interest consideration concerned is not finalised, the proposed timetable for finalising it.

(2)   Where the Secretary of State believes that it is or may be the case that two or more public interest considerations are relevant to the case, he may decide not to mention in the intervention notice such of those considerations as he considers appropriate.

(3)   The Secretary of State may at any time revoke an intervention notice which has been given under section 139(1) and which is in force.

(4)   An intervention notice under section 139(1) shall come into force when it is given and shall cease to be in force when the matter to which it relates is finally determined under this Chapter.

(5)   For the purposes of subsection (4) a matter to which an intervention notice under section 139(1) relates is finally determined under this Chapter if—

     (a)   the period permitted by section 144 for the preparation of the report of the Commission under section 142 and for action to be taken in relation to it under section 143(1) or (3) has expired and no such report has been so prepared or no such action has been taken;

     (b)   the Commission decides under section 145(1) to terminate its investigation;

     (c)   the report of the Commission has been prepared under section 142 and published under section 143(1) within the period permitted by section 144;

     (d)   the Secretary of State fails to make and publish a decision under subsection (2) of section 146 within the period required by subsection (3) of that section;

     (e)   the Secretary of State decides under section 146(2) that no eligible public interest consideration is relevant;

     (f)   the Secretary of State decides under section 147(2) neither to accept an undertaking under section 159 nor to make an order under section 161;

     (g)   the Secretary of State accepts an undertaking under section 159 or makes an order under section 161; or

     (h)   the Secretary of State decides to revoke the intervention notice concerned.

PART I
STATUTES

(6)   For the purposes of subsections (4) and (5) the time when a matter to which an intervention notice under section 139(1) relates is finally determined under this Chapter is—

(a) in a case falling within subsection (5)(a) or (d), the expiry of the period concerned;

(b) in a case falling within subsection (5)(b), (e), (f) or (h), the making of the decision concerned;

(c) in a case falling within subsection (5)(c), the publication of the report concerned; and

(d) in a case falling within subsection (5)(g), the acceptance of the undertaking concerned or (as the case may be) the making of the order concerned.

(7)   In subsection (6)(d) the reference to the acceptance of the undertaking concerned or the making of the order concerned shall, in a case where the enforcement action under section 147(2) involves the acceptance of a group of undertakings, the making of a group of orders or the acceptance and making of a group of undertakings and orders, be treated as a reference to the acceptance or making of the last undertaking or order in the group; but undertakings or orders which vary, supersede or revoke earlier undertakings or orders shall be disregarded for the purposes of subsections (5)(g) and (6)(d).

[386]

NOTES

Commencement: to be appointed.

141 Questions to be decided by Commission

(1)   This section applies where an intervention notice under section 139(1) is in force in relation to a market investigation reference.

(2)   The Commission shall decide whether any feature, or combination of features, of each relevant market (within the meaning given by section 134(3)) prevents, restricts or distorts competition in connection with the supply or acquisition of any goods or services in the United Kingdom or a part of the United Kingdom.

(3)   The Commission shall, if it has decided that there is an adverse effect on competition, decide the following additional questions—

(a) whether action should be taken by the Secretary of State under section 147 for the purpose of remedying, mitigating or preventing the adverse effect on competition concerned or any detrimental effect on customers so far as it has resulted from, or may be expected to result from, the adverse effect on competition;

(b) whether the Commission should recommend the taking of other action by the Secretary of State or action by persons other than itself and the Secretary of State for the purpose of remedying, mitigating or preventing the adverse effect on competition concerned or any detrimental effect on customers so far as it has resulted from, or may be expected to result from, the adverse effect on competition; and

(c) in either case, if action should be taken, what action should be taken and what is to be remedied, mitigated or prevented.

(4)   The Commission shall, if it has decided that there is an adverse effect on competition, also decide separately the following questions (on the assumption that it is proceeding as mentioned in section 148(1))—

(a) whether action should be taken by it under section 138 for the purpose of remedying, mitigating or preventing the adverse effect on competition concerned or any detrimental effect on customers so far as it has resulted from, or may be expected to result from, the adverse effect on competition;

(b) whether the Commission should recommend the taking of action by other persons for the purpose of remedying, mitigating or preventing the adverse effect on competition concerned or any detrimental effect on customers so far as it has resulted from, or may be expected to result from, the adverse effect on competition; and

(c) in either case, if action should be taken, what action should be taken and what is to be remedied, mitigated or prevented.

(5) In deciding the questions mentioned in subsections (3) and (4), the Commission shall, in particular, have regard to the need to achieve as comprehensive a solution as is reasonable and practicable to the adverse effect on competition concerned and any detrimental effects on customers so far as resulting from the adverse effect on competition.

(6) In deciding the questions mentioned in subsections (3) and (4), the Commission may, in particular, have regard to the effect of any action on any relevant customer benefits of the feature or features of the market concerned.

[387]

NOTES

Commencement: to be appointed.

142 Investigations and reports by Commission

(1) Where an intervention notice under section 139(1) is in force in relation to a market investigation reference, the Commission shall prepare a report on the reference and take action in relation to it under section 143(1) or (3) within the period permitted by section 144.

(2) The report shall, in particular, contain—

(a) the decisions of the Commission on the questions which it is required to answer by virtue of section 141;

(b) its reasons for its decisions; and

(c) such information as the Commission considers appropriate for facilitating a proper understanding of those questions and of its reasons for its decisions.

(3) The Commission shall carry out such investigations as it considers appropriate for the purposes of preparing a report under this section.

[388]

NOTES

Commencement: to be appointed.

143 Publication etc of reports of Commission

(1) The Commission shall publish a report under section 142 if it contains—

(a) the decision of the Commission that there is no adverse effect on competition; or

(b) the decisions of the Commission that there is one or more than one adverse effect on competition but, on the question mentioned in section 141(4)(a) and in relation to each adverse effect on competition, that no action should be taken by it.

(2) The Commission shall, at the same time as the report is published under subsection (1)—

(a) in the case of a reference under section 131, give it to the OFT; and

(b) in the case of a reference under section 132, give it to the appropriate Minister and give a copy of it to the OFT.

(3)   Where a report under section 142 contains the decisions of the Commission that there is one or more than one adverse effect on competition and, on the question mentioned in section 141(4)(a) and in relation to at least one such adverse effect, that action should be taken by it, the Commission shall give the report to the Secretary of State.

(4)   The Secretary of State shall publish, no later than publication of his decision under section 146(2) in relation to the case, a report of the Commission given to him under subsection (3) and not required to be published by virtue of section 148(2).

(5)   The Secretary of State shall, at the same time as a report of the Commission given to him under subsection (3) is published under subsection (4), give a copy of it—
  (a) in the case of a reference under section 131, to the OFT; and
  (b) in the case of a reference under section 132, to any other Minister of the Crown who made the reference and to the OFT.

(6)   Where a reference has been made by the OFT under section 131 or by the appropriate Minister under section 132 in circumstances in which a reference could have been made by a relevant sectoral regulator under section 131 as it has effect by virtue of a relevant sectoral enactment, the relevant authority shall, at the same time as the report under section 142 is published under subsection (1) or (4), give a copy of it to the relevant sectoral regulator concerned.

(7)   Where a reference has been made by a relevant sectoral regulator under section 131 as it has effect by virtue of a relevant sectoral enactment, the relevant authority shall, at the same time as the report under section 142 is published under subsection (1) or (4), give a copy of it to the OFT.

(8)   In subsections (6) and (7) "the relevant authority" means—
  (a) in the case of a report published under subsection (1), the Commission; and
  (b) in the case of a report published under subsection (4), the Secretary of State.

[389]

NOTES

Commencement: to be appointed.

144 Time-limits for investigations and reports: Part 4

(1)   The Commission shall, within the period of two years beginning with the date of the reference, prepare its report under section 142 and publish it under subsection (1) of section 143 or (as the case may be) give it to the Secretary of State under subsection (3) of that section.

(2)   The Secretary of State may by order amend subsection (1) so as to alter the period of two years mentioned in that subsection or any period for the time being mentioned in that subsection in substitution for that period.

(3)   No alteration shall be made by virtue of subsection (2) which results in the period for the time being mentioned in subsection (1) exceeding two years.

(4)   An order under subsection (2) shall not affect any period of time within which, in relation to a market investigation reference, the Commission is under a duty to prepare its report under section 142 and take action in relation to it under section 143(1) or (3) if the Commission is already under that duty in relation to that reference when the order is made.

(5)   Before making an order under subsection (2) the Secretary of State shall consult the Commission and such other persons as he considers appropriate.

[390]

PART I
STATUTES

NOTES
Commencement: to be appointed.

145 Restrictions where public interest considerations not finalised: Part 4

(1) The Commission shall terminate its investigation under section 142 if—

    (a) the intervention notice concerned mentions a public interest consideration which was not finalised on the giving of that notice or public interest considerations which, at that time, were not finalised;

    (b) no other public interest consideration is mentioned in the notice;

    (c) at least 24 weeks has elapsed since the giving of the notice; and

    (d) the public interest consideration mentioned in the notice has not been finalised within that period of 24 weeks or (as the case may be) none of the public interest considerations mentioned in the notice has been finalised within that period of 24 weeks.

(2) Where the intervention notice concerned mentions a public interest consideration which is not finalised on the giving of the notice, the Commission shall not give its report under section 142 to the Secretary of State in accordance with section 143(3) unless the period of 24 weeks beginning with the giving of the intervention notice concerned has expired or the public interest consideration concerned has been finalised.

(3) The Commission shall, in reporting on any of the questions mentioned in section 141(3), disregard any public interest consideration which has not been finalised before the giving of the report.

(4) The Commission shall, in reporting on any of the questions mentioned in section 141(3), disregard any public interest consideration which was not finalised on the giving of the intervention notice concerned and has not been finalised within the period of 24 weeks beginning with the giving of the notice concerned.

(5) Subsections (1) to (4) are without prejudice to the power of the Commission to carry out investigations in relation to any public interest consideration to which it might be able to have regard in its report.

[391]

NOTES
Commencement: to be appointed.

146 Decision of Secretary of State

(1) Subsection (2) applies where the Secretary of State has received a report of the Commission which—

    (a) has been prepared under section 142;

    (b) contains the decisions that there is one or more than one adverse effect on competition and, on the question mentioned in section 141(4)(a) and in relation to at least one such adverse effect, that action should be taken by it; and

    (c) has been given to the Secretary of State as required by section 143(3).

(2) The Secretary of State shall decide whether—

    (a) any eligible public interest consideration is relevant; or

    (b) any eligible public interest considerations are relevant;

to any action which is mentioned in the report by virtue of section 141(4)(a) and (c) and which the Commission should take for the purpose of remedying, mitigating or preventing any adverse effect on competition concerned or any detrimental effect on customers so far as it has resulted or may be expected to result from any adverse effect on competition.

(3)   The Secretary of State shall make and publish his decision under subsection (2) within the period of 90 days beginning with the receipt of the report of the Commission under section 142.

(4)   In this section "eligible public interest consideration" means a public interest consideration which—

    (a) was mentioned in the intervention notice concerned; and

    (b) was not disregarded by the Commission for the purposes of its report under section 142.

[392]

NOTES

    Commencement: to be appointed.

147 Remedial action by Secretary of State

(1)   Subsection (2) applies where the Secretary of State—

    (a) has decided under subsection (2) of section 146 within the period required by subsection (3) of that section that an eligible public interest consideration is relevant as mentioned in subsection (2) of that section or eligible public interest considerations are so relevant; and

    (b) has published his decision within the period required by subsection (3) of that section.

(2)   The Secretary of State may, in relation to any adverse effect on competition identified in the report concerned, take such action under section 159 or 161 as he considers to be—

    (a) reasonable and practicable—

        (i) to remedy, mitigate or prevent the adverse effect on competition concerned; or

        (ii) to remedy, mitigate or prevent any detrimental effect on customers so far as it has resulted from, or may be expected to result from, the adverse effect on competition; and

    (b) appropriate in the light of the eligible public interest consideration concerned or (as the case may be) the eligible public interest considerations concerned.

(3)   In making a decision under subsection (2), the Secretary of State shall, in particular, have regard to—

    (a) the need to achieve as comprehensive a solution as is reasonable and practicable to the adverse effect on competition concerned and any detrimental effects on customers so far as resulting from the adverse effect on competition; and

    (b) the report of the Commission under section 142.

(4)   In having regard by virtue of subsection (3) to the report of the Commission under section 142, the Secretary of State shall not challenge the decision of the Commission contained in the report that there is one or more than one adverse effect on competition.

(5)   In making a decision under subsection (2), the Secretary of State may, in particular, have regard to the effect of any action on any relevant customer benefits of the feature or features of the market concerned.

(6)   The Secretary of State shall take no action under subsection (2) to remedy, mitigate or prevent any detrimental effect on customers so far as it may be expected to result from the adverse effect on competition concerned if—

    (a) no detrimental effect on customers has resulted from the adverse effect on competition; and

    (b) the adverse effect on competition is not being remedied, mitigated or prevented.

(7)   In this section "eligible public interest consideration" has the same meaning as in section 146.

[393]

NOTES

    Commencement: to be appointed.

148　Reversion of the matter to the Commission

(1)   If—

    (a) the Secretary of State fails to make and publish his decision under subsection (2) of section 146 within the period required by subsection (3) of that section; or

    (b) the Secretary of State decides that no eligible public interest consideration is relevant as mentioned in subsection (2) of that section;

the Commission shall proceed under section 138 as if the report had been prepared and published under section 136 within the period permitted by section 137.

(2)   The Commission shall publish the report which has been prepared by it under section 142 (if still unpublished) as soon as it becomes able to proceed by virtue of subsection (1).

(3)   The Commission shall, at the same time as its report is published under subsection (2), give a copy of it—

    (a) in the case of a reference under section 131, to the OFT; and

    (b) in the case of a reference under section 132, to any Minister of the Crown who made the reference (other than the Secretary of State) and to the OFT.

(4)   Where a reference has been made by the OFT under section 131 or by the appropriate Minister under section 132 in circumstances in which a reference could have been made by a relevant sectoral regulator under section 131 as it has effect by virtue of a relevant sectoral enactment, the Commission shall, at the same time as its report is published under subsection (2), give a copy of it to the relevant sectoral regulator concerned.

(5)   Where a reference has been made by a relevant sectoral regulator under section 131 as it has effect by virtue of a relevant sectoral enactment, the Commission shall, at the same time as its report is published under subsection (2), give a copy of it to the OFT.

(6)   In relation to proceedings by virtue of subsection (1), the reference in section 138(3) to decisions of the Commission included in its report by virtue of section 134(4) shall be construed as a reference to decisions which were included in the report of the Commission by virtue of section 141(4).

(7)   Where the Commission, in proceeding by virtue of subsection (1), intends to proceed in a way which is not consistent with its decisions as included in its report by virtue of section 141(4), it shall not so proceed without the consent of the Secretary of State.

(8)   The Secretary of State shall not withhold his consent under subsection (7) unless he believes that the proposed alternative way of proceeding will operate against the public interest.

(9)   For the purposes of subsection (8) a proposed alternative way of proceeding will operate against the public interest only if any eligible public interest consideration or considerations outweigh the considerations which have led the Commission to propose proceeding in that way.

(10) In deciding whether to withhold his consent under subsection (7), the Secretary of State shall accept the Commission's view of what, if the only relevant consideration were how to remedy, mitigate or prevent the adverse effect on competition concerned or any detrimental effect on customers so far as resulting from the adverse effect on competition, would be the most appropriate way to proceed.

(11) In this section "eligible public interest consideration" has the same meaning as in section 146.

[394]

NOTES
Commencement: to be appointed.

Intervention notices under section 139(2)

149 Intervention notices under section 139(2)

(1)   An intervention notice under section 139(2) shall state—
   (a) the proposed undertaking which may be accepted by the OFT;
   (b) the notice under section 155(1) or (4);
   (c) the public interest consideration or considerations which are, or may be, relevant to the case; and
   (d) where any public interest consideration concerned is not finalised, the proposed timetable for finalising it.

(2)   Where the Secretary of State believes that it is or may be the case that two or more public interest considerations are relevant to the case, he may decide not to mention in the intervention notice such of those considerations as he considers appropriate.

(3)   The Secretary of State may at any time revoke an intervention notice which has been given under section 139(2) and which is in force.

(4)   An intervention notice under section 139(2) shall come into force when it is given and shall cease to be in force on the occurrence of any of the events mentioned in subsection (5).

(5)   The events are—
   (a) the acceptance by the OFT with the consent of the Secretary of State of an undertaking which is the same as the proposed undertaking mentioned in the intervention notice by virtue of subsection (1)(a) or which does not differ from it in any material respect;
   (b) the decision of the OFT to proceed neither with the proposed undertaking mentioned in the intervention notice by virtue of subsection (1)(a) nor a proposed undertaking which does not differ from it in any material respect; or
   (c) the decision of the Secretary of State to revoke the intervention notice concerned.

[395]

NOTES
Commencement: to be appointed.

150 Power of veto of Secretary of State

(1)   Where an intervention notice under section 139(2) is in force, the OFT shall not, without the consent of the Secretary of State, accept the proposed undertaking concerned or a proposed undertaking which does not differ from it in any material respect.

(2)   The Secretary of State shall withhold his consent if he believes that it is or may be the case that the proposed undertaking will, if accepted, operate against the public interest.

(3)   For the purposes of subsection (2) a proposed undertaking will, if accepted, operate against the public interest only if any public interest consideration which is mentioned in the intervention notice concerned and has been finalised, or any public interest considerations which are so mentioned and have been finalised, outweigh the considerations which have led the OFT to propose accepting the undertaking.

(4)   In making his decision under subsection (2) the Secretary of State shall accept the OFT's view of what undertakings, if the only relevant consideration were how to remedy, mitigate or prevent the adverse effect on competition concerned or any detrimental effect on customers so far as resulting from the adverse effect on competition, would be most appropriate.

(5)   Where a public interest consideration which is mentioned in the intervention notice concerned is not finalised on the giving of the notice, the Secretary of State shall not make his decision as to whether to give his consent under this section before—

(a) the end of the period of 24 weeks beginning with the giving of the intervention notice; or

(b) if earlier, the date on which the public interest consideration concerned has been finalised.

(6)   Subject to subsections (2) to (5), the Secretary of State shall not withhold his consent under this section.

[396]

NOTES

Commencement: to be appointed.

Other

151 Further interaction of intervention notices with general procedure

(1)   Where an intervention notice under section 139(1) comes into force in relation to a market investigation reference, sections 134(1), (4), (6) and (7), 136(1) to (6), 137(1) to (6) and 138 shall cease to apply in relation to that reference.

(2)   Where the Secretary of State revokes an intervention notice which has been given under section 139(1), the Commission shall instead proceed under sections 134 and 136 to 138.

(3)   Where the Commission is proceeding by virtue of subsection (2), the period within which the Commission shall prepare and publish its report under section 136 shall be extended by an additional period of 20 days.

(4)   Where the Commission terminates its investigation under section 145(1), the Commission shall proceed under sections 134 and 136 to 138.

(5)   Where the Commission is proceeding by virtue of subsection (4), the period within which the Commission shall prepare and publish its report under section 136 shall be extended by an additional period of 20 days.

(6)   In determining the period of 20 days mentioned in subsection (3) or (5) no account shall be taken of—

    (a) Saturday, Sunday, Good Friday and Christmas Day; and

    (b) any day which is a bank holiday in England and Wales.

[397]

NOTES

    Commencement: to be appointed.

152 Certain duties of OFT and Commission

(1)   The OFT shall, in considering whether to make a reference under section 131, bring to the attention of the Secretary of State any case which it believes raises any consideration specified in section 153 unless it believes that the Secretary of State would consider any such consideration immaterial in the context of the particular case.

(2)   The Commission shall, in investigating any reference made to it under section 131 or 132 within the previous four months, bring to the attention of the Secretary of State any case which it believes raises any consideration specified in section 153 unless it believes that the Secretary of State would consider any such consideration immaterial in the context of the particular case.

(3)   The OFT and the Commission shall bring to the attention of the Secretary of State any representations about exercising his power under section 153(3) which have been made to the OFT or (as the case may be) the Commission.

[398]

NOTES

    Commencement: to be appointed.

153 Specified considerations: Part 4

(1)   The interests of national security are specified in this section.

(2)   In subsection (1) "national security" includes public security; and in this subsection "public security" has the same meaning as in article 21(3) of Council Regulation (EEC) No 4064/89 of 21st December 1989 on the control of concentrations between undertakings as amended by Council Regulation (EC) No 1310/97 of 30th June 1997.

(3)   The Secretary of State may by order modify this section for the purpose of specifying in this section a new consideration or removing or amending any consideration which is for the time being specified in this section.

(4)   An order under this section may apply in relation to cases under consideration by the OFT, by the Secretary of State, by the appropriate Minister (other than the Secretary of State acting alone) or by the Commission before the making of the order as well as cases under consideration on or after the making of the order.

[399]

NOTES

    Commencement: to be appointed.

CHAPTER 3
ENFORCEMENT

Undertakings and orders

154 Undertakings in lieu of market investigation references

(1)   Subsection (2) applies if the OFT considers that it has the power to make a reference under section 131 and otherwise intends to make such a reference.

(2)   The OFT may, instead of making such a reference and for the purpose of remedying, mitigating or preventing—

(a)   any adverse effect on competition concerned; or

(b)   any detrimental effect on customers so far as it has resulted from, or may be expected to result from, the adverse effect on competition;

accept, from such persons as it considers appropriate, undertakings to take such action as it considers appropriate.

(3)   In proceeding under subsection (2), the OFT shall, in particular, have regard to the need to achieve as comprehensive a solution as is reasonable and practicable to the adverse effect on competition concerned and any detrimental effects on customers so far as resulting from the adverse effect on competition.

(4)   In proceeding under subsection (2), the OFT may, in particular, have regard to the effect of any action on any relevant customer benefits of the feature or features of the market concerned.

(5)   The OFT shall take no action under subsection (2) to remedy, mitigate or prevent any detrimental effect on customers so far as it may be expected to result from the adverse effect on competition concerned if—

(a)   no detrimental effect on customers has resulted from the adverse effect on competition; and

(b)   the adverse effect on competition is not being remedied, mitigated or prevented.

(6)   An undertaking under this section—

(a)   shall come into force when accepted;

(b)   may be varied or superseded by another undertaking; and

(c)   may be released by the OFT.

(7)   The OFT shall, as soon as reasonably practicable, consider any representations received by it in relation to varying or releasing an undertaking under this section.

(8)   This section is subject to sections 150 and 155.

[400]

NOTES

Commencement: to be appointed.

155 Undertakings in lieu: procedural requirements

(1)   Before accepting an undertaking under section 154 (other than an undertaking under that section which varies an undertaking under that section but not in any material respect), the OFT shall—

(a)   publish notice of the proposed undertaking; and

(b)   consider any representations made in accordance with the notice and not withdrawn.

(2)   A notice under subsection (1) shall state—
   (a) that the OFT proposes to accept the undertaking;
   (b) the purpose and effect of the undertaking;
   (c) the situation that the undertaking is seeking to deal with;
   (d) any other facts which the OFT considers justify the acceptance of the undertaking;
   (e) a means of gaining access to an accurate version of the proposed undertaking at all reasonable times; and
   (f) the period (not less than 15 days starting with the date of publication of the notice) within which representations may be made in relation to the proposed undertaking.

(3)   The matters to be included in a notice under subsection (1) by virtue of subsection (2) shall, in particular, include—
   (a) the terms of the reference under section 131 which the OFT considers that it has power to make and which it otherwise intends to make; and
   (b) the adverse effect on competition, and any detrimental effect on customers so far as resulting from the adverse effect on competition, which the OFT has identified.

(4)   The OFT shall not accept the undertaking with modifications unless it—
   (a) publishes notice of the proposed modifications; and
   (b) considers any representations made in accordance with the notice and not withdrawn.

(5)   A notice under subsection (4) shall state—
   (a) the proposed modifications;
   (b) the reasons for them; and
   (c) the period (not less than 7 days starting with the date of the publication of the notice under subsection (4)) within which representations may be made in relation to the proposed modifications.

(6)   If, after publishing notice under subsection (1) or (4), the OFT decides—
   (a) not to accept the undertaking concerned; and
   (b) not to proceed by virtue of subsection (8) or (9);
it shall publish notice of that decision.

(7)   As soon as practicable after accepting an undertaking to which this section applies, the OFT shall—
   (a) serve a copy of the undertaking on any person by whom it is given; and
   (b) publish the undertaking.

(8)   The requirements of subsection (4) (and those of subsection (1)) shall not apply if the OFT—
   (a) has already published notice under subsection (1) but not subsection (4) in relation to the proposed undertaking; and
   (b) considers that the modifications which are now being proposed are not material in any respect.

(9)   The requirements of subsection (4) (and those of subsection (1)) shall not apply if the OFT—
   (a) has already published notice under subsections (1) and (4) in relation to the matter concerned; and
   (b) considers that the further modifications which are now being proposed do not differ in any material respect from the modifications in relation to which notice was last given under subsection (4).

(10) Paragraphs 6 to 8 (but not paragraph 9) of Schedule 10 (procedural requirements before terminating undertakings) shall apply in relation to the proposed release of undertakings under section 154 (other than in connection with

accepting an undertaking under that section which varies or supersedes an undertaking under that section) as they apply in relation to the proposed release of undertakings under section 73.

[401]

NOTES
  Commencement: to be appointed.

156 Effect of undertakings under section 154

(1) No market investigation reference shall be made by the OFT or the appropriate Minister in relation to any feature, or combination of features, of a market in the United Kingdom for goods or services if—

  (a) the OFT has accepted an undertaking or group of undertakings under section 154 within the previous 12 months; and
  (b) the goods or services to which the undertaking or group of undertakings relates are of the same description as the goods or services to which the feature, or combination of features, relates.

(2) Subsection (1) does not prevent the making of a market investigation reference if—

  (a) the OFT considers that any undertaking concerned has been breached and has given notice of that fact to the person responsible for giving the undertaking; or
  (b) the person responsible for giving any undertaking concerned supplied, in connection with the matter, information to the OFT which was false or misleading in a material respect.

[402]

NOTES
  Commencement: to be appointed.

157 Interim undertakings: Part 4

(1) Subsection (2) applies where—

  (a) a market investigation reference has been made;
  (b) a report has been published under section 136 within the period permitted by section 137 or (as the case may be) a report prepared under section 142 and given to the Secretary of State under section 143(3) within the period permitted by section 144 has been published; and
  (c) the market investigation reference concerned is not finally determined.

(2) The relevant authority may, for the purpose of preventing pre-emptive action, accept, from such persons as the relevant authority considers appropriate, undertakings to take such action as the relevant authority considers appropriate.

(3) An undertaking under this section—

  (a) shall come into force when accepted;
  (b) may be varied or superseded by another undertaking; and
  (c) may be released by the relevant authority.

(4) An undertaking under this section shall, if it has not previously ceased to be in force, cease to be in force when the market investigation reference is finally determined.

(5) The relevant authority shall, as soon as reasonably practicable, consider any representations received by the relevant authority in relation to varying or releasing an undertaking under this section.

(6)   In this section and section 158—

"pre-emptive action" means action which might impede the taking of any action under section 138(2) or (as the case may be) 147(2) in relation to the market investigation reference concerned; and

"the relevant authority" means—

(a) where an intervention notice is in force in relation to the market investigation reference, the Secretary of State;

(b) in any other case, the Commission.

[403]

NOTES

Commencement: to be appointed.

158 Interim orders: Part 4

(1)   Subsection (2) applies where—

(a) a market investigation reference has been made;

(b) a report has been published under section 136 within the period permitted by section 137 or (as the case may be) a report prepared under section 142 and given to the Secretary of State under section 143(3) within the period permitted by section 144 has been published; and

(c) the market investigation reference concerned is not finally determined.

(2)   The relevant authority may by order, for the purpose of preventing pre-emptive action—

(a) prohibit or restrict the doing of things which the relevant authority considers would constitute pre-emptive action;

(b) impose on any person concerned obligations as to the carrying on of any activities or the safeguarding of any assets;

(c) provide for the carrying on of any activities or the safeguarding of any assets either by the appointment of a person to conduct or supervise the conduct of any activities (on such terms and with such powers as may be specified or described in the order) or in any other manner;

(d) do anything which may be done by virtue of paragraph 19 of Schedule 8.

(3)   An order under this section—

(a) shall come into force at such time as is determined by or under the order; and

(b) may be varied or revoked by another order.

(4)   An order under this section shall, if it has not previously ceased to be in force, cease to be in force when the market investigation reference is finally determined.

(5)   The relevant authority shall, as soon as reasonably practicable, consider any representations received by the relevant authority in relation to varying or revoking an order under this section.

[404]

NOTES

Commencement: to be appointed.

159 Final undertakings: Part 4

(1)   The Commission may, in accordance with section 138, accept, from such persons as it considers appropriate, undertakings to take action specified or described in the undertakings.

(2)   The Secretary of State may, in accordance with section 147, accept, from such persons as he considers appropriate, undertakings to take action specified or described in the undertakings.

(3)   An undertaking under this section shall come into force when accepted.

(4)   An undertaking under subsection (1) or (2) may be varied or superseded by another undertaking under that subsection.

(5)   An undertaking under subsection (1) may be released by the Commission and an undertaking under subsection (2) may be released by the Secretary of State.

(6)   The Commission or (as the case may be) the Secretary of State shall, as soon as reasonably practicable, consider any representations received by it or (as the case may be) him in relation to varying or releasing an undertaking under this section.

[405]

NOTES

Commencement: to be appointed.

160   Order-making power where final undertakings not fulfilled: Part 4

(1)   Subsection (2) applies where the relevant authority considers that—
- (a) an undertaking accepted by the relevant authority under section 159 has not been, is not being or will not be fulfilled; or
- (b) in relation to an undertaking accepted by the relevant authority under that section, information which was false or misleading in a material respect was given to the relevant authority or the OFT by the person giving the undertaking before the relevant authority decided to accept the undertaking.

(2)   The relevant authority may, for any of the purposes mentioned in section 138(2) or (as the case may be) 147(2), make an order under this section.

(3)   Subsections (3) to (6) of section 138 or (as the case may be) 147 shall apply for the purposes of subsection (2) above as they apply for the purposes of that section.

(4)   An order under this section may contain—
- (a) anything permitted by Schedule 8; and
- (b) such supplementary, consequential or incidental provision as the relevant authority considers appropriate.

(5)   An order under this section—
- (a) shall come into force at such time as is determined by or under the order;
- (b) may contain provision which is different from the provision contained in the undertaking concerned; and
- (c) may be varied or revoked by another order.

(6)   No order shall be varied or revoked under this section unless the OFT advises that such a variation or revocation is appropriate by reason of a change of circumstances.

(7)   In this section "the relevant authority" means—
- (a) in the case of an undertaking accepted under section 159 by the Commission, the Commission; and
- (b) in the case of an undertaking accepted under that section by the Secretary of State, the Secretary of State.

[406]

NOTES

Commencement: to be appointed.

161 Final orders: Part 4

(1)   The Commission may, in accordance with section 138, make an order under this section.

(2)   The Secretary of State may, in accordance with section 147, make an order under this section.

(3)   An order under this section may contain—
  (a) anything permitted by Schedule 8; and
  (b) such supplementary, consequential or incidental provision as the person making it considers appropriate.

(4)   An order under this section—
  (a) shall come into force at such time as is determined by or under the order; and
  (b) may be varied or revoked by another order.

(5)   No order shall be varied or revoked under this section unless the OFT advises that such a variation or revocation is appropriate by reason of a change of circumstances.

[407]

NOTES

Commencement: to be appointed.

Enforcement functions of OFT

162 Duty of OFT to monitor undertakings and orders: Part 4

(1)   The OFT shall keep under review the carrying out of any enforcement undertaking or any enforcement order.

(2)   The OFT shall, in particular, from time to time consider—
  (a) whether an enforcement undertaking or enforcement order has been or is being complied with;
  (b) whether, by reason of any change of circumstances, an enforcement undertaking is no longer appropriate and—
    (i) one or more of the parties to it can be released from it; or
    (ii) it needs to be varied or to be superseded by a new enforcement undertaking; and
  (c) whether, by reason of any change of circumstances, an enforcement order is no longer appropriate and needs to be varied or revoked.

(3)   The OFT shall give the Commission or (as the case may be) the Secretary of State such advice as it considers appropriate in relation to—
  (a) any possible variation or release by the Commission or (as the case may be) the Secretary of State of an enforcement undertaking accepted by it or (as the case may be) him;
  (b) any possible new enforcement undertaking to be accepted by the Commission or (as the case may be) the Secretary of State so as to supersede another enforcement undertaking given to the Commission or (as the case may be) the Secretary of State;
  (c) any possible variation or revocation by the Commission or (as the case may be) the Secretary of State of an enforcement order made by the Commission or (as the case may be) the Secretary of State;

(d) any possible enforcement undertaking to be accepted by the Commission or (as the case may be) the Secretary of State instead of an enforcement order or any possible enforcement order to be made by the Commission or (as the case may be) the Secretary of State instead of an enforcement undertaking; or

(e) the enforcement by virtue of section 167(6) to (8) of any enforcement undertaking or enforcement order.

(4) The OFT shall take such action as it considers appropriate in relation to—

(a) any possible variation or release by it of an undertaking accepted by it under section 154;

(b) any possible new undertaking to be accepted by it under section 154 so as to supersede another undertaking given to it under that section; or

(c) the enforcement by it by virtue of section 167(6) of any enforcement undertaking or enforcement order.

(5) The OFT shall keep under review the effectiveness of enforcement undertakings accepted under this Part and enforcement orders made under this Part.

(6) The OFT shall, whenever requested to do so by the Secretary of State and otherwise from time to time, prepare a report of its findings under subsection (5).

(7) The OFT shall—

(a) give any report prepared by it under subsection (6) to the Commission;

(b) give a copy of the report to the Secretary of State; and

(c) publish the report.

(8) In this Part—

"enforcement order" means an order made under section 158, 160 or 161; and
"enforcement undertaking" means an undertaking accepted under section 154, 157 or 159.

[408]

NOTES

Commencement: to be appointed.

---

163 Further role of OFT in relation to undertakings and orders: Part 4

(1) Subsections (2) and (3) apply where the Commission or the Secretary of State (in this section "the relevant authority") is considering whether to accept undertakings under section 157 or 159.

(2) The relevant authority may require the OFT to consult with such persons as the relevant authority considers appropriate with a view to discovering whether they will offer undertakings which the relevant authority would be prepared to accept under section 157 or (as the case may be) 159.

(3) The relevant authority may require the OFT to report to the relevant authority on the outcome of the OFT's consultations within such period as the relevant authority may require.

(4) A report under subsection (3) shall, in particular, contain advice from the OFT as to whether any undertakings offered should be accepted by the relevant authority under section 157 or (as the case may be) 159.

(5) The powers conferred on the relevant authority by subsections (1) to (4) are without prejudice to the power of the relevant authority to consult the persons concerned itself.

(6)   If asked by the relevant authority for advice in relation to the taking of enforcement action (whether or not by way of undertakings) in a particular case, the OFT shall give such advice as it considers appropriate.

[409]

NOTES

Commencement: to be appointed.

Supplementary

164 Enforcement undertakings and orders under this Part: general provisions

(1)   The provision which may be contained in an enforcement undertaking is not limited to the provision which is permitted by Schedule 8.

(2)   The following enactments in Part 3 shall apply in relation to enforcement orders under this Part as they apply in relation to enforcement orders under that Part—

    (a)   section 86(1) to (5) (enforcement orders: general provisions); and

    (b)   section 87 (power of directions conferred by enforcement order).

(3)   An enforcement order under section 160 or 161 or any explanatory material accompanying the order shall state—

    (a)   the actions that the persons or description of persons to whom the order is addressed must do or (as the case may be) refrain from doing;

    (b)   the date on which the order comes into force;

    (c)   the possible consequences of not complying with the order; and

    (d)   the section of this Part under which a review can be sought in relation to the order.

[410]

NOTES

Commencement: to be appointed.

165 Procedural requirements for certain undertakings and orders: Part 4

Schedule 10 (procedural requirements for certain undertakings and orders), other than paragraph 9 of that Schedule, shall apply in relation to undertakings under section 159 and orders under section 160 or 161 as it applies in relation to undertakings under section 82 and orders under section 83 or 84.

[411]

NOTES

Commencement: to be appointed.

166 Register of undertakings and orders: Part 4

(1)   The OFT shall compile and maintain a register for the purposes of this Part.

(2)   The register shall be kept in such form as the OFT considers appropriate.

(3)   The OFT shall ensure that the following matters are entered in the register—

    (a)   the provisions of any enforcement undertaking accepted by virtue of this Part (whether by the OFT, the Commission, the Secretary of State or a relevant sectoral regulator);

    (b)   the provisions of any enforcement order made by virtue of this Part (whether by the Commission, the Secretary of State or a relevant sectoral regulator); and

(c) the details of any variation, release or revocation of such an undertaking or order.

(4) The duty in subsection (3) does not extend to anything of which the OFT is unaware.

(5) The Commission, the Secretary of State and any relevant sectoral regulator shall inform the OFT of any matters which are to be included in the register by virtue of subsection (3) and which relate to enforcement undertakings accepted by them or enforcement orders made by them.

(6) The OFT shall ensure that the contents of the register are available to the public—

(a) during (as a minimum) such hours as may be specified in an order made by the Secretary of State; and

(b) subject to such reasonable fees (if any) as the OFT may determine.

(7) If requested by any person to do so and subject to such reasonable fees (if any) as the OFT may determine, the OFT shall supply the person concerned with a copy (certified to be true) of the register or of an extract from it.

[412]

_____

NOTES
Commencement: to be appointed.
_____

167 Rights to enforce undertakings and orders under this Part

(1) This section applies to any enforcement undertaking or enforcement order.

(2) Any person to whom such an undertaking or order relates shall have a duty to comply with it.

(3) The duty shall be owed to any person who may be affected by a contravention of the undertaking or (as the case may be) order.

(4) Any breach of the duty which causes such a person to sustain loss or damage shall be actionable by him.

(5) In any proceedings brought under subsection (4) against a person to whom an enforcement undertaking or enforcement order relates it shall be a defence for that person to show that he took all reasonable steps and exercised all due diligence to avoid contravening the undertaking or (as the case may be) order.

(6) Compliance with an enforcement undertaking or an enforcement order shall also be enforceable by civil proceedings brought by the OFT for an injunction or for interdict or for any other appropriate relief or remedy.

(7) Compliance with an undertaking accepted under section 157 or 159, or an order under section 158, 160 or 161, shall also be enforceable by civil proceedings brought by the relevant authority for an injunction or for interdict or for any other appropriate relief or remedy.

(8) In subsection (7) "the relevant authority" means—

(a) in the case of an undertaking accepted by the Commission or an order made by the Commission, the Commission; and

(b) in the case of an undertaking accepted by the Secretary of State or an order made by the Secretary of State, the Secretary of State.

(9) Subsections (6) to (8) shall not prejudice any right that a person may have by virtue of subsection (4) to bring civil proceedings for contravention or apprehended contravention of an enforcement undertaking or an enforcement order.

[413]

NOTES
Commencement: to be appointed.

CHAPTER 4
SUPPLEMENTARY

Regulated markets

168 Regulated markets

(1)   Subsection (2) applies where the Commission or the Secretary of State is considering for the purposes of this Part whether relevant action would be reasonable and practicable for the purpose of remedying, mitigating or preventing an adverse effect on competition or any detrimental effect on customers so far as resulting from such an effect.

(2)   The Commission or (as the case may be) the Secretary of State shall, in deciding whether such action would be reasonable and practicable, have regard to the relevant statutory functions of the sectoral regulator concerned.

(3)   In this section "relevant action" means—
  (a) modifying the conditions of a licence granted under section 7 of the Telecommunications Act 1984 (c 12);
  (b) modifying conditions in force under Part 4 of the Airports Act 1986 (c 31) other than any conditions imposed or modified in pursuance of section 40(3) or (4) of that Act;
  (c) modifying the conditions of a licence granted under section 7 or 7A of the Gas Act 1986 (c 44);
  (d) modifying the conditions of a licence granted under section 6 of the Electricity Act 1989 (c 29);
  (e) modifying networking arrangements (within the meaning given by section 39(1) of the Broadcasting Act 1990 (c 42));
  (f) modifying the conditions of a company's appointment under Chapter 1 of Part 2 of the Water Industry Act 1991 (c 56);
  (g) modifying the conditions of a licence granted under article 10 of the Electricity (Northern Ireland) Order 1992 (SI 1992/231 (NI 1));
  (h) modifying the conditions of a licence granted under section 8 of the Railways Act 1993 (c 43);
  (i) modifying an access agreement (within the meaning given by section 83(1) of the Act of 1993) or a franchise agreement (within the meaning given by section 23(3) of that Act);
  (j) modifying conditions in force under Part 4 of the Airports (Northern Ireland) Order 1994 (SI 1994/426 (NI 1)) other than any conditions imposed or modified in pursuance of article 40(3) or (4) of that Order;
  (k) modifying the conditions of a licence granted under article 8 of the Gas (Northern Ireland) Order 1996 (SI 1996/275 (NI 2));
  (l) modifying the conditions of a licence granted under section 11 of the Postal Services Act 2000 (c 26); or
  (m) modifying the conditions of a licence granted under section 5 of the Transport Act 2000 (c 38).

(4)   In this section "relevant statutory functions" means—
  (a) in relation to any licence granted under section 7 of the Telecommunications Act 1984, the duties and obligations of the Director General of Telecommunications imposed on him by or in pursuance of any enactment or other provision mentioned in section 7(5)(a) of that Act;

(b) in relation to conditions in force under Part 4 of the Airports Act 1986 (c 31) other than any conditions imposed or modified in pursuance of section 40(3) or (4) of that Act, the duties of the Civil Aviation Authority under section 39(2) and (3) of that Act;

(c) in relation to any licence granted under section 7 or 7A of the Gas Act 1986 (c 44), the objectives and duties of the Gas and Electricity Markets Authority under section 4AA and 4AB(2) of that Act;

(d) in relation to any licence granted under section 6 of the Electricity Act 1989 (c 29), the objectives and duties of the Gas and Electricity Markets Authority under section 3A and 3B(2) of that Act;

(e) in relation to any networking arrangements (within the meaning given by section 39(1) of the Broadcasting Act 1990 (c 42)), the duties of the Independent Television Commission under section 2(2) of that Act;

(f) in relation to a company's appointment under Chapter 1 of Part 2 of the Water Industry Act 1991 (c 56), the duties of the Director General of Water Services under section 2 of that Act;

(g) in relation to any licence granted under article 10 of the Electricity (Northern Ireland) Order 1992 (SI 1992/231 (NI 1)), the duty of the Director General of Electricity Supply for Northern Ireland under article 6 of that Order;

(h) in relation to any licence granted under section 8 of the Railways Act 1993 (c 43) where none of the conditions of the licence relate to consumer protection, the duties of the Rail Regulator under section 4 of that Act;

(i) in relation to any licence granted under section 8 of the Act of 1993 where one or more than one condition of the licence relates to consumer protection, the duties of the Rail Regulator under section 4 of that Act and the duties of the Strategic Rail Authority under section 207 of the Transport Act 2000 (c 38);

(j) in relation to any access agreement (within the meaning given by section 83(1) of the Act of 1993), the duties of the Rail Regulator under section 4 of the Act of 1993;

(k) in relation to any franchise agreement (within the meaning given by section 23(3) of the Act of 1993), the duties of the Strategic Rail Authority under section 207 of the Act of 2000;

(l) in relation to conditions in force under Part 4 of the Airports (Northern Ireland) Order 1994 (SI 1994/426 (NI 1)) other than any conditions imposed or modified in pursuance of article 40(3) or (4) of that Order, the duties of the Civil Aviation Authority under article 30(2) and (3) of that Order;

(m) in relation to any licence granted under article 8 of the Gas (Northern Ireland) Order 1996 (SI 1996/275 (NI 2)), the duties of the Director General of Gas for Northern Ireland under article 5 of that Order;

(n) in relation to any licence granted under section 11 of the Postal Services Act 2000 (c 26), the duties of the Postal Services Commission under sections 3 and 5 of that Act; and

(o) in relation to any licence granted under section 5 of the Transport Act 2000, the duties of the Civil Aviation Authority under section 87 of that Act.

(5) In this section "sectoral regulator" means—

(a) the Civil Aviation Authority;

(b) the Director General of Electricity Supply for Northern Ireland;

(c) the Director General of Gas for Northern Ireland;

(d) the Director General of Telecommunications;

(e) the Director General of Water Services;

(f) the Gas and Electricity Markets Authority;

(g) the Independent Television Commission;

(h) the Postal Services Commission;

(i) the Rail Regulator; or

(j) the Strategic Rail Authority.

(6)   Subsection (7) applies where the Commission or the Secretary of State is considering for the purposes of this Part whether modifying the conditions of a licence granted under section 7 or 7A of the Gas Act 1986 (c 44) or section 6 of the Electricity Act 1989 (c 29) would be reasonable and practicable for the purpose of remedying, mitigating or preventing an adverse effect on competition or any detrimental effect on customers so far as resulting from such an effect.

(7)   The Commission or (as the case may be) the Secretary of State may, in deciding whether modifying the conditions of such a licence would be reasonable and practicable, have regard to those matters to which the Gas and Electricity Markets Authority may have regard by virtue of section 4AA(4) of the Act of 1986 or (as the case may be) section 3A(4) of the Act of 1989.

(8)   The Secretary of State may by order modify subsection (3), (4), (5), (6) or (7).

(9)   Part 2 of Schedule 9 (which makes provision for functions under this Part to be exercisable by various sectoral regulators) shall have effect.

[414]

NOTES

Commencement: to be appointed.

Consultation, information and publicity

169 Certain duties of relevant authorities to consult: Part 4

(1)   Subsection (2) applies where the relevant authority is proposing to make a relevant decision in a way which the relevant authority considers is likely to have a substantial impact on the interests of any person.

(2)   The relevant authority shall, so far as practicable, consult that person about what is proposed before making that decision.

(3)   In consulting the person concerned, the relevant authority shall, so far as practicable, give the reasons of the relevant authority for the proposed decision.

(4)   In considering what is practicable for the purposes of this section the relevant authority shall, in particular, have regard to—

(a) any restrictions imposed by any timetable for making the decision; and

(b) any need to keep what is proposed, or the reasons for it, confidential.

(5)   The duty under this section shall not apply in relation to the making of any decision so far as particular provision is made elsewhere by virtue of this Part for consultation before the making of that decision.

(6)   In this section—

"the relevant authority" means the OFT, the appropriate Minister or the Commission; and

"relevant decision" means—

(a) in the case of the OFT, any decision by the OFT—

(i) as to whether to make a reference under section 131 or accept undertakings under section 154 instead of making such a reference; or

(ii) to vary under section 135 such a reference;

(b) in the case of the appropriate Minister, any decision by the appropriate Minister—

(i) as to whether to make a reference under section 132; or

(ii) to vary under section 135 such a reference; and

(c) in the case of the Commission, any decision on the questions mentioned in section 134 or 141.

[415]

NOTES

Commencement: to be appointed.

170 General information duties

(1) The OFT shall give the Commission—

    (a) such information in its possession as the Commission may reasonably require to enable the Commission to carry out its functions under this Part; and

    (b) any other assistance which the Commission may reasonably require for the purpose of assisting it in carrying out its functions under this Part and which it is within the power of the OFT to give.

(2) The OFT shall give the Commission any information in its possession which has not been requested by the Commission but which, in the opinion of the OFT, would be appropriate to give to the Commission for the purpose of assisting it in carrying out its functions under this Part.

(3) The OFT and the Commission shall give the Secretary of State or the appropriate Minister so far as he is not the Secretary of State acting alone—

    (a) such information in their possession as the Secretary of State or (as the case may be) the appropriate Minister concerned may by direction reasonably require to enable him to carry out his functions under this Part; and

    (b) any other assistance which the Secretary of State or (as the case may be) the appropriate Minister concerned may by direction reasonably require for the purpose of assisting him in carrying out his functions under this Part and which it is within the power of the OFT or (as the case may be) the Commission to give.

(4) The OFT shall give the Secretary of State or the appropriate Minister so far as he is not the Secretary of State acting alone any information in its possession which has not been requested by the Secretary of State or (as the case may be) the appropriate Minister concerned but which, in the opinion of the OFT, would be appropriate to give to the Secretary of State or (as the case may be) the appropriate Minister concerned for the purpose of assisting him in carrying out his functions under this Part.

(5) The Commission shall have regard to any information given to it under subsection (1) or (2); and the Secretary of State or (as the case may be) the appropriate Minister concerned shall have regard to any information given to him under subsection (3) or (4).

(6) Any direction given under subsection (3)—

    (a) shall be in writing; and

    (b) may be varied or revoked by a subsequent direction.

[416]

NOTES

Commencement: to be appointed.

171 Advice and information: Part 4

(1) As soon as reasonably practicable after the passing of this Act, the OFT shall prepare and publish general advice and information about the making of references by it under section 131.

(2) The OFT may at any time publish revised, or new, advice or information.

(3)   As soon as reasonably practicable after the passing of this Act, the Commission shall prepare and publish general advice and information about the consideration by it of market investigation references and the way in which relevant customer benefits may affect the taking of enforcement action in relation to such references.

(4)   The Commission may at any time publish revised, or new, advice or information.

(5)   Advice and information published under this section shall be prepared with a view to—
    (a)   explaining relevant provisions of this Part to persons who are likely to be affected by them; and
    (b)   indicating how the OFT or (as the case may be) the Commission expects such provisions to operate.

(6)   Advice and information published by virtue of subsection (1) or (3) shall include such advice and information about the effect of Community law, and anything done under or in accordance with it, on the provisions of this Part as the OFT or (as the case may be) the Commission considers appropriate.

(7)   Advice (or information) published by virtue of subsection (1) or (3) may include advice (or information) about the factors which the OFT or (as the case may be) the Commission may take into account in considering whether, and if so how, to exercise a function conferred by this Part.

(8)   Any advice or information published by the OFT or the Commission under this section shall be published in such manner as the OFT or (as the case may be) the Commission considers appropriate.

(9)   In preparing any advice or information under this section, the OFT shall consult the Commission and such other persons as it considers appropriate.

(10)   In preparing any advice or information under this section, the Commission shall consult the OFT and such other persons as it considers appropriate.

(11)   In this section "Community law" means—
    (a)   all the rights, powers, liabilities, obligations and restrictions from time to time created or arising by or under the Community Treaties; and
    (b)   all the remedies and procedures from time to time provided for by or under the Community Treaties.

[417]

NOTES
    Commencement: to be appointed.

172   Further publicity requirements: Part 4

(1)   The OFT shall publish—
    (a)   any reference made by it under section 131;
    (b)   any variation made by it under section 135 of a reference under section 131;
    (c)   any decision of a kind mentioned in section 149(5)(b); and
    (d)   such information as it considers appropriate about any decision made by it under section 152(1) to bring a case to the attention of the Secretary of State.

(2)   The Commission shall publish—
    (a)   any decision made by it under section 138(2) neither to accept an undertaking under section 159 nor to make an order under section 161;
    (b)   any decision made by it that there has been a material change of circumstances as mentioned in section 138(3) or there is another special reason as mentioned in that section;

    (c) any termination under section 145(1) of an investigation by it;

    (d) such information as it considers appropriate about any decision made by it under section 152(2) to bring a case to the attention of the Secretary of State;

    (e) any enforcement undertaking accepted by it under section 157;

    (f) any enforcement order made by it under section 158; and

    (g) any variation, release or revocation of such an undertaking or order.

(3)   The Secretary of State shall publish—

    (a) any reference made by him under section 132;

    (b) any variation made by him under section 135 of a reference under section 132;

    (c) any intervention notice given by him;

    (d) any decision made by him to revoke such a notice;

    (e) any decision made by him under section 147(2) neither to accept an undertaking under section 159 nor to make an order under section 161;

    (f) any enforcement undertaking accepted by him under section 157;

    (g) any variation or release of such an undertaking; and

    (h) any direction given by him under section 170(3) in connection with the exercise by him of his functions under section 132(3).

(4)   The appropriate Minister (other than the Secretary of State acting alone) shall publish—

    (a) any reference made by him under section 132;

    (b) any variation made by him under section 135 of a reference under section 132; and

    (c) any direction given by him under section 170(3) in connection with the exercise by him of his functions under section 132(3).

(5)   Where any person is under an obligation by virtue of subsection (1), (2), (3) or (4) to publish the result of any action taken by that person or any decision made by that person, the person concerned shall, subject to subsections (6) and (7), also publish that person's reasons for the action concerned or (as the case may be) the decision concerned.

(6)   Such reasons need not, if it is not reasonably practicable to do so, be published at the same time as the result of the action concerned or (as the case may be) as the decision concerned.

(7)   Subsections (5) and (6) shall not apply in relation to any case falling within subsection (1)(d) or (2)(d).

(8)   The Secretary of State shall publish his reasons for—

    (a) any decision made by him under section 146(2); or

    (b) any decision to make an order under section 153(3) or vary or revoke such an order.

(9)   Such reasons may be published after—

    (a) in the case of subsection (8)(a), the publication of the decision concerned; and

    (b) in the case of subsection (8)(b), the making of the order or of the variation or revocation;

if it is not reasonably practicable to publish them at the same time as the publication of the decision or (as the case may be) the making of the order or variation or revocation.

(10) Where the Secretary of State has decided under section 147(2) to accept an undertaking under section 159 or to make an order under section 161, he shall (after the acceptance of the undertaking or (as the case may be) the making of the order) lay details of his decision and his reasons for it, and the Commission's report under section 142, before each House of Parliament.

[418]

NOTES

Commencement: to be appointed.

173 Defamation: Part 4

For the purposes of the law relating to defamation, absolute privilege attaches to any advice, guidance, notice or direction given, or decision or report made, by the OFT, by the Secretary of State, by the appropriate Minister (other than the Secretary of State acting alone) or by the Commission in the exercise of any of their functions under this Part.

[419]

NOTES

Commencement: to be appointed.

Investigation powers

174 Investigation powers of OFT

(1)   The OFT may exercise any of the powers in subsections (3) to (5) for the purpose of assisting it in deciding whether to make a reference under section 131 or to accept undertakings under section 154 instead of making such a reference.

(2)   The OFT shall not exercise any of the powers in subsections (3) to (5) for the purpose of assisting it as mentioned in subsection (1) unless it already believes that it has power to make such a reference.

(3)   The OFT may give notice to any person requiring him—
    (a) to attend at a time and place specified in the notice; and
    (b) to give evidence to the OFT or a person nominated by the OFT for the purpose.

(4)   The OFT may give notice to any person requiring him—
    (a) to produce any documents which—
        (i) are specified or described in the notice, or fall within a category of document which is specified or described in the notice; and
        (ii) are in that person's custody or under his control; and
    (b) to produce them at a time and place so specified and to a person so specified.

(5)   The OFT may give notice to any person who carries on any business requiring him—
    (a) to supply to the OFT such estimates, forecasts, returns or other information as may be specified or described in the notice; and
    (b) to supply it at a time and place, and in a form and manner, so specified and to a person so specified.

(6)   A notice under this section shall include information about the possible consequences of not complying with the notice.

(7)   The person to whom any document is produced in accordance with a notice under this section may, for the purpose mentioned in subsection (1), copy the document so produced.

(8)   No person shall be required under this section—
    (a) to give any evidence or produce any documents which he could not be compelled to give or produce in civil proceedings before the court; or
    (b) to supply any information which he could not be compelled to supply in evidence in such proceedings.

(9)   No person shall be required, in compliance with a notice under this section, to go more than 10 miles from his place of residence unless his necessary travelling expenses are paid or offered to him.

(10)   Any reference in this section to the production of a document includes a reference to the production of a legible and intelligible copy of information recorded otherwise than in legible form.

(11)   In this section "the court" means—

    (a)   in relation to England and Wales or Northern Ireland, the High Court; and

    (b)   in relation to Scotland, the Court of Session.

[420]

NOTES

Commencement: to be appointed.

175   Enforcement of powers under section 174: offences

(1)   A person commits an offence if he, intentionally and without reasonable excuse, fails to comply with any requirement of a notice under section 174.

(2)   A person commits an offence if he intentionally and without reasonable excuse alters, suppresses or destroys any document which he has been required to produce by a notice under section 174.

(3)   A person who commits an offence under subsection (1) or (2) shall be liable—

    (a)   on summary conviction, to a fine not exceeding the statutory maximum;

    (b)   on conviction on indictment, to imprisonment for a term not exceeding two years or to a fine or to both.

(4)   A person commits an offence if he intentionally obstructs or delays—

    (a)   the OFT in the exercise of its powers under section 174; or

    (b)   any person in the exercise of his powers under subsection (7) of that section.

(5)   A person who commits an offence under subsection (4) shall be liable—

    (a)   on summary conviction, to a fine not exceeding the statutory maximum;

    (b)   on conviction on indictment, to a fine.

[421]

NOTES

Commencement: to be appointed.

176   Investigation powers of the Commission

(1)   The following sections in Part 3 shall apply, with the modifications mentioned in subsections (2) and (3) below, for the purposes of references under this Part as they apply for the purposes of references under that Part—

    (a)   section 109 (attendance of witnesses and production of documents etc);

    (b)   section 110 (enforcement of powers under section 109: general);

    (c)   section 111 (penalties);

    (d)   section 112 (penalties: main procedural requirements);

    (e)   section 113 (payments and interest by instalments);

    (f)   section 114 (appeals in relation to penalties);

    (g)   section 115 (recovery of penalties); and

    (h)   section 116 (statement of policy).

(2) Section 110 shall, in its application by virtue of subsection (1) above, have effect as if—

(a) subsection (2) were omitted; and

(b) in subsection (9) the words from "or section" to "section 65(3))" were omitted.

(3) Section 111(5)(b)(ii) shall, in its application by virtue of subsection (1) above, have effect as if—

(a) for the words "section 50 or 65, given" there were substituted "section 142, published or given under section 143(1) or (3)"; and

(b) for the words "(or given)", in both places where they appear, there were substituted "(or published or given)".

[422]

NOTES

Commencement: to be appointed.

Reports

177 Excisions from reports: Part 4

(1) Subsection (2) applies where the Secretary of State is under a duty to publish a report of the Commission under section 142.

(2) The Secretary of State may exclude a matter from the report if he considers that publication of the matter would be inappropriate.

(3) In deciding what is inappropriate for the purposes of subsection (2) the Secretary of State shall have regard to the considerations mentioned in section 244.

(4) The Commission shall advise the Secretary of State as to the matters (if any) which it considers should be excluded by him under subsection (2).

(5) References in sections 136(4) to (6), 143(2) and (5) to (7), 148(3) to (5) and 172(10) to the giving or laying of a report of the Commission shall be construed as references to the giving or laying of the report as published.

[423]

NOTES

Commencement: to be appointed.

178 Minority reports of Commission: Part 4

(1) Subsection (2) applies where, on a market investigation reference, a member of a group constituted in connection with the reference in pursuance of paragraph 15 of Schedule 7 to the Competition Act 1998 (c 41), disagrees with any decisions contained in the report of the Commission under this Part as the decisions of the Commission.

(2) The report shall, if the member so wishes, include a statement of his disagreement and of his reasons for disagreeing.

[424]

NOTES

Commencement: to be appointed.

Other

179 Review of decisions under Part 4

(1)   Any person aggrieved by a decision of the OFT, the appropriate Minister, the Secretary of State or the Commission in connection with a reference or possible reference under this Part may apply to the Competition Appeal Tribunal for a review of that decision.

(2)   For this purpose "decision"—
  (a) does not include a decision to impose a penalty under section 110(1) or (3) as applied by section 176; but
  (b) includes a failure to take a decision permitted or required by this Part in connection with a reference or possible reference.

(3)   Except in so far as a direction to the contrary is given by the Competition Appeal Tribunal, the effect of the decision is not suspended by reason of the making of the application.

(4)   In determining such an application the Competition Appeal Tribunal shall apply the same principles as would be applied by a court on an application for judicial review.

(5)   The Competition Appeal Tribunal may—
  (a) dismiss the application or quash the whole or part of the decision to which it relates; and
  (b) where it quashes the whole or part of that decision, refer the matter back to the original decision maker with a direction to reconsider and make a new decision in accordance with the ruling of the Competition Appeal Tribunal.

(6)   An appeal lies on any point of law arising from a decision of the Competition Appeal Tribunal under this section to the appropriate court.

(7)   An appeal under subsection (6) requires the permission of the Tribunal or the appropriate court.

(8)   In this section—
    "the appropriate court" means the Court of Appeal or, in the case of Tribunal proceedings in Scotland, the Court of Session; and
    "Tribunal rules" has the meaning given by section 15(1).

[425]

NOTES
Commencement: to be appointed.

180 Offences

(1)   Sections 117 (false or misleading information) and 125 (offences by bodies corporate) shall apply, with the modifications mentioned in subsection (2) below, for the purposes of this Part as they apply for the purposes of Part 3.

(2)   Section 117 shall, in its application by virtue of subsection (1) above, have effect as if references to the Secretary of State included references to the appropriate Minister so far as he is not the Secretary of State acting alone.

[426]

NOTES
Commencement: to be appointed.

181 Orders under Part 4

(1)   Any power of the Secretary of State to make an order under this Part shall be exercisable by statutory instrument.

(2)   Any power of the Secretary of State to make an order under this Part—
  (a) may be exercised so as to make different provision for different cases or different purposes;
  (b) includes power to make such incidental, supplementary, consequential, transitory, transitional or saving provision as the Secretary of State considers appropriate.

(3)   The power of the Secretary of State under section 136(9), 137(3), 144(2), 153(3) or 168(8) as extended by subsection (2) above may be exercised by modifying any enactment comprised in or made under this Act, or any other enactment.

(4)   An order made by the Secretary of State under section 137(3), 144(2), 158, 160 or 161, or under section 111(4) or (6) or 114(3)(b) or (4)(b) as applied by section 176, shall be subject to annulment in pursuance of a resolution of either House of Parliament.

(5)   No order shall be made by the Secretary of State under section 136(9) or 168(8), or section 128(6) as applied by section 183(2), unless a draft of it has been laid before, and approved by a resolution of, each House of Parliament.

(6)   An order made by the Secretary of State under section 153(3) shall be laid before Parliament after being made and shall cease to have effect unless approved, within the period of 28 days beginning with the day on which it is made, by a resolution of each House of Parliament.

(7)   In calculating the period of 28 days mentioned in subsection (6), no account shall be taken of any time during which Parliament is dissolved or prorogued or during which both Houses are adjourned for more than four days.

(8)   If an order made by the Secretary of State ceases to have effect by virtue of subsection (6), any modification made by it of an enactment is repealed (and the previous enactment revived) but without prejudice to the validity of anything done in connection with that modification before the order ceased to have effect and without prejudice to the making of a new order.

(9)   If, apart from this subsection, an order made by the Secretary of State under section 153(3) would be treated for the purposes of the standing orders of either House of Parliament as a hybrid instrument, it shall proceed in that House as if it were not such an instrument.

(10) References in this section to an order made under this Part include references to an order made under section 111(4) or (6) or 114(3)(b) or (4)(b) as applied by section 176 and an order made under section 128(6) as applied by section 183(2).

[427]

NOTES

Commencement: to be appointed.

182 Service of documents: Part 4

Section 126 shall apply for the purposes of this Part as it applies for the purposes of Part 3.

[428]

NOTES

Commencement: to be appointed.

183 Interpretation: Part 4

(1)   In this Part, unless the context otherwise requires—

"action" includes omission; and references to the taking of action include references to refraining from action;

"business" includes a professional practice and includes any other undertaking which is carried on for gain or reward or which is an undertaking in the course of which goods or services are supplied otherwise than free of charge;

"change of circumstances" includes any discovery that information has been supplied which is false or misleading in a material respect;

"consumer" means any person who is—

(a) a person to whom goods are or are sought to be supplied (whether by way of sale or otherwise) in the course of a business carried on by the person supplying or seeking to supply them; or

(b) a person for whom services are or are sought to be supplied in the course of a business carried on by the person supplying or seeking to supply them;

and who does not receive or seek to receive the goods or services in the course of a business carried on by him;

"customer" includes a customer who is not a consumer;

"enactment" includes an Act of the Scottish Parliament, Northern Ireland legislation and an enactment comprised in subordinate legislation, and includes an enactment whenever passed or made;

"goods" includes buildings and other structures, and also includes ships, aircraft and hovercraft;

"Minister of the Crown" means the holder of an office in Her Majesty's Government in the United Kingdom and includes the Treasury;

"modify" includes amend or repeal;

"notice" means notice in writing;

"subordinate legislation" has the same meaning as in the Interpretation Act 1978 (c 30) and also includes an instrument made under an Act of the Scottish Parliament and an instrument made under Northern Ireland legislation; and

"supply", in relation to the supply of goods, includes supply by way of sale, lease, hire or hire-purchase, and, in relation to buildings or other structures, includes the construction of them by a person for another person.

(2)   Sections 127(1)(b) and (4) to (6) and 128 shall apply for the purposes of this Part as they apply for the purposes of Part 3.

(3)   For the purposes of this Part a market investigation reference is finally determined if—

(a) where no intervention notice under section 139(1) has been given in relation to it—

(i) the period permitted by section 137 for preparing and publishing a report under section 136 has expired and no such report has been prepared and published;

(ii) such a report has been prepared and published within the period permitted by section 137 and contains the decision that there is no adverse effect on competition;

(iii) the Commission has decided under section 138(2) neither to accept undertakings under section 159 nor to make an order under section 161; or

     (iv) the Commission has accepted an undertaking under section 159 or made an order under section 161;

  (b) where an intervention notice under section 139(1) has been given in relation to it—

     (i) the period permitted by section 144 for the preparation of the report of the Commission under section 142 and for action to be taken in relation to it under section 143(1) or (3) has expired while the intervention notice is still in force and no such report has been so prepared or no such action has been taken;

     (ii) the Commission has terminated under section 145(1) its investigation and the reference is finally determined under paragraph (a) above (disregarding the fact that the notice was given);

    (iii) the report of the Commission has been prepared under section 142 and published under section 143(1) within the period permitted by section 144;

     (iv) the intervention notice was revoked and the reference is finally determined under paragraph (a) above (disregarding the fact that the notice was given);

     (v) the Secretary of State has failed to make and publish a decision under subsection (2) of section 146 within the period permitted by subsection (3) of that section and the reference is finally determined under paragraph (a) above (disregarding the fact that the notice was given);

     (vi) the Secretary of State has decided under section 146(2) that no eligible public interest consideration is relevant and the reference is finally determined under paragraph (a) above (disregarding the fact that the notice was given);

    (vii) the Secretary of State has decided under 146(2) that a public interest consideration is relevant but has decided under section 147(2) neither to accept an undertaking under section 159 nor to make an order under section 161; or

    (viii) the Secretary of State has decided under section 146(2) that a public interest consideration is relevant and has accepted an undertaking under section 159 or made an order under section 161.

(4)   For the purposes of this Part the time when a market investigation reference is finally determined is—

  (a) in a case falling within subsection (3)(a)(i) or (b)(i), the expiry of the time concerned;

  (b) in a case falling within subsection (3)(a)(ii) or (b)(iii), the publication of the report;

  (c) in a case falling within subsection (3)(a)(iv) or (b)(viii), the acceptance of the undertaking concerned or (as the case may be) the making of the order concerned; and

  (d) in any other case, the making of the decision or last decision concerned or the taking of the action concerned.

(5)   The references in subsection (4) to subsections (3)(a)(i), (ii) and (iv) include those enactments as applied by subsection (3)(b)(ii), (iv), (v) or (vi).

(6)   In subsection (4)(c) the reference to the acceptance of the undertaking concerned or the making of the order concerned shall, in a case where the enforcement action concerned involves the acceptance of a group of undertakings, the making of a group of orders or the acceptance and making of a group of undertakings and orders, be treated as a reference to the acceptance or making of the last undertaking or order in the group; but undertakings or orders which vary, supersede or revoke earlier undertakings or orders shall be disregarded for the purposes of subsections (3)(a)(iv) and (b)(viii) and (4)(c).

(7)   Any duty to publish which is imposed on a person by this Part shall, unless the context otherwise requires, be construed as a duty on that person to publish in such manner as that person considers appropriate for the purpose of bringing the matter concerned to the attention of those likely to be affected by it.

[429]

NOTES

Commencement: to be appointed.

184 Index of defined expressions: Part 4

In this Part, the expressions listed in the left-hand column have the meaning given by, or are to be interpreted in accordance with, the provisions listed in the right-hand column.

Expression	Provision of this Act
Action (and the taking of action)	Section 183(1)
Adverse effect on competition	Section 134(2)
Appropriate Minister	Section 132(5)
Business	Section 183(1)
Change of circumstances	Section 183(1)
The Commission	Section 273
Consumer	Section 183(1)
Customer	Section 183(1)
Date of market investigation reference	Section 137(7)
Detrimental effect on customers	Section 134(5)
Enactment	Section 183(1)
Enforcement order	Section 162(8)
Enforcement undertaking	Section 162(8)
Feature of a market	Section 131(2)
Final determination of market investigation reference	Section 183(3) to (6)
Goods	Section 183(1)
Intervention notice	Section 139(3)
Market for goods or services	Section 131(6)
Market in the United Kingdom	Section 131(6)

PART I STATUTES

Expression	Provision of this Act
Market investigation reference	Section 131(6)
Minister of the Crown	Section 183(1)
Modify	Section 183(1)
Notice	Section 183(1)
The OFT	Section 273
Public interest consideration	Section 139(5)
Public interest consideration being finalised	Section 139(7)
Publish	Section 183(7)
Relevant customer benefit	Section 134(8)
Relevant sectoral enactment	Section 136(7)
Relevant sectoral regulator	Section 136(8)
Reports of the Commission	Section 177(5)
Subordinate legislation	Section 183(1)
Supply (in relation to the supply of goods)	Section 183(1)
The supply of services (and a market for services etc)	Section 183(2)

[430]

NOTES

   Commencement: to be appointed.

PART 5
THE COMPETITION COMMISSION

185–187 *((Pt 5) s 185 introduces Sch 11 to this Act (amendments to the Competition Act 1998 relating to the constitution and powers of the Competition Commission); s 186 inserts the Competition Act 1998, Sch 7, para 12A, at* **[214]***; s 187 amends s 46 of the 1998 Act, at* **[178]***, inserts Sch 7, paras 19(5), 19A, to that Act, at* **[215]***, and introduces Sch 12 to this Act (insertion of the Competition Act 1998, Sch 7A, at* **[219]***).)*

PART 6
CARTEL OFFENCE

Cartel offence

188 Cartel offence

(1)   An individual is guilty of an offence if he dishonestly agrees with one or more other persons to make or implement, or to cause to be made or implemented, arrangements of the following kind relating to at least two undertakings (A and B).

(2)   The arrangements must be ones which, if operating as the parties to the agreement intend, would—

    (a) directly or indirectly fix a price for the supply by A in the United Kingdom (otherwise than to B) of a product or service,

    (b) limit or prevent supply by A in the United Kingdom of a product or service,

    (c) limit or prevent production by A in the United Kingdom of a product,

    (d) divide between A and B the supply in the United Kingdom of a product or service to a customer or customers,

    (e) divide between A and B customers for the supply in the United Kingdom of a product or service, or

    (f) be bid-rigging arrangements.

(3)   Unless subsection (2)(d), (e) or (f) applies, the arrangements must also be ones which, if operating as the parties to the agreement intend, would—

    (a) directly or indirectly fix a price for the supply by B in the United Kingdom (otherwise than to A) of a product or service,

    (b) limit or prevent supply by B in the United Kingdom of a product or service, or

    (c) limit or prevent production by B in the United Kingdom of a product.

(4)   In subsections (2)(a) to (d) and (3), references to supply or production are to supply or production in the appropriate circumstances (for which see section 189).

(5)   "Bid-rigging arrangements" are arrangements under which, in response to a request for bids for the supply of a product or service in the United Kingdom, or for the production of a product in the United Kingdom—

    (a) A but not B may make a bid, or

    (b) A and B may each make a bid but, in one case or both, only a bid arrived at in accordance with the arrangements.

(6)   But arrangements are not bid-rigging arrangements if, under them, the person requesting bids would be informed of them at or before the time when a bid is made.

(7)   "Undertaking" has the same meaning as in Part 1 of the 1998 Act.

[431]

NOTES

   Commencement: to be appointed.

189 Cartel offence: supplementary

(1)   For section 188(2)(a), the appropriate circumstances are that A's supply of the product or service would be at a level in the supply chain at which the product or service would at the same time be supplied by B in the United Kingdom.

(2)   For section 188(2)(b), the appropriate circumstances are that A's supply of the product or service would be at a level in the supply chain—

    (a) at which the product or service would at the same time be supplied by B in the United Kingdom, or

    (b) at which supply by B in the United Kingdom of the product or service would be limited or prevented by the arrangements.

(3) For section 188(2)(c), the appropriate circumstances are that A's production of the product would be at a level in the production chain—

    (a) at which the product would at the same time be produced by B in the United Kingdom, or

    (b) at which production by B in the United Kingdom of the product would be limited or prevented by the arrangements.

(4) For section 188(2)(d), the appropriate circumstances are that A's supply of the product or service would be at the same level in the supply chain as B's.

(5) For section 188(3)(a), the appropriate circumstances are that B's supply of the product or service would be at a level in the supply chain at which the product or service would at the same time be supplied by A in the United Kingdom.

(6) For section 188(3)(b), the appropriate circumstances are that B's supply of the product or service would be at a level in the supply chain—

    (a) at which the product or service would at the same time be supplied by A in the United Kingdom, or

    (b) at which supply by A in the United Kingdom of the product or service would be limited or prevented by the arrangements.

(7) For section 188(3)(c), the appropriate circumstances are that B's production of the product would be at a level in the production chain—

    (a) at which the product would at the same time be produced by A in the United Kingdom, or

    (b) at which production by A in the United Kingdom of the product would be limited or prevented by the arrangements.

                                                         [432]

NOTES

Commencement: to be appointed.

190 Cartel offence: penalty and prosecution

(1) A person guilty of an offence under section 188 is liable—

    (a) on conviction on indictment, to imprisonment for a term not exceeding five years or to a fine, or to both;

    (b) on summary conviction, to imprisonment for a term not exceeding six months or to a fine not exceeding the statutory maximum, or to both.

(2) In England and Wales and Northern Ireland, proceedings for an offence under section 188 may be instituted only—

    (a) by the Director of the Serious Fraud Office, or

    (b) by or with the consent of the OFT.

(3) No proceedings may be brought for an offence under section 188 in respect of an agreement outside the United Kingdom, unless it has been implemented in whole or in part in the United Kingdom.

(4) Where, for the purpose of the investigation or prosecution of offences under section 188, the OFT gives a person written notice under this subsection, no proceedings for an offence under section 188 that falls within a description specified in the notice may be brought against that person in England and Wales or Northern Ireland except in circumstances specified in the notice.

                                                           [433]

NOTES
Commencement: to be appointed.

191 Extradition

The offences to which an Order in Council under section 2 of the Extradition Act 1870 (c 52) (arrangements with foreign states) can apply include—

    (a) an offence under section 188,

    (b) conspiracy to commit such an offence, and

    (c) attempt to commit such an offence.

[434]

NOTES
Commencement: to be appointed.

Criminal investigations by OFT

192 Investigation of offences under section 188

(1) The OFT may conduct an investigation if there are reasonable grounds for suspecting that an offence under section 188 has been committed.

(2) The powers of the OFT under sections 193 and 194 are exercisable, but only for the purposes of an investigation under subsection (1), in any case where it appears to the OFT that there is good reason to exercise them for the purpose of investigating the affairs, or any aspect of the affairs, of any person ("the person under investigation").

[435]

NOTES
Commencement: to be appointed.

193 Powers when conducting an investigation

(1) The OFT may by notice in writing require the person under investigation, or any other person who it has reason to believe has relevant information, to answer questions, or otherwise provide information, with respect to any matter relevant to the investigation at a specified place and either at a specified time or forthwith.

(2) The OFT may by notice in writing require the person under investigation, or any other person, to produce, at a specified place and either at a specified time or forthwith, specified documents, or documents of a specified description, which appear to the OFT to relate to any matter relevant to the investigation.

(3) If any such documents are produced, the OFT may—

    (a) take copies or extracts from them;

    (b) require the person producing them to provide an explanation of any of them.

(4) If any such documents are not produced, the OFT may require the person who was required to produce them to state, to the best of his knowledge and belief, where they are.

(5) A notice under subsection (1) or (2) must indicate—

    (a) the subject matter and purpose of the investigation; and

    (b) the nature of the offences created by section 201.

[436]

NOTES
Commencement: to be appointed.

194 Power to enter premises under a warrant

(1)   On an application made by the OFT to the High Court, or, in Scotland, by the procurator fiscal to the sheriff, in accordance with rules of court, a judge or the sheriff may issue a warrant if he is satisfied that there are reasonable grounds for believing—

(a) that there are on any premises documents which the OFT has power under section 193 to require to be produced for the purposes of an investigation; and

(b) that—

(i) a person has failed to comply with a requirement under that section to produce the documents;

(ii) it is not practicable to serve a notice under that section in relation to them; or

(iii) the service of such a notice in relation to them might seriously prejudice the investigation.

(2)   A warrant under this section shall authorise a named officer of the OFT, and any other officers of the OFT whom the OFT has authorised in writing to accompany the named officer—

(a) to enter the premises, using such force as is reasonably necessary for the purpose;

(b) to search the premises and—

(i) take possession of any documents appearing to be of the relevant kind, or

(ii) take, in relation to any documents appearing to be of the relevant kind, any other steps which may appear to be necessary for preserving them or preventing interference with them;

(c) to require any person to provide an explanation of any document appearing to be of the relevant kind or to state, to the best of his knowledge and belief, where it may be found;

(d) to require any information which is stored in any electronic form and is accessible from the premises and which the named officer considers relates to any matter relevant to the investigation, to be produced in a form—

(i) in which it can be taken away, and

(ii) in which it is visible and legible or from which it can readily be produced in a visible and legible form.

(3)   Documents are of the relevant kind if they are of a kind in respect of which the application under subsection (1) was granted.

(4)   A warrant under this section may authorise persons specified in the warrant to accompany the named officer who is executing it.

(5)   . . .

NOTES
Commencement: to be appointed.
Sub-s (5): inserts the Criminal Justice and Police Act 2001, Sch 1, Pt 1, para 73A.

195 Exercise of powers by authorised person

(1)   The OFT may authorise any competent person who is not an officer of the OFT to exercise on its behalf all or any of the powers conferred by section 193 or 194.

(2)   No such authority may be granted except for the purpose of investigating the affairs, or any aspect of the affairs, of a person specified in the authority.

(3)   No person is bound to comply with any requirement imposed by a person exercising powers by virtue of any authority granted under this section unless he has, if required to do so, produced evidence of his authority.

[438]

NOTES

Commencement: to be appointed.

196   Privileged information etc

(1)   A person may not under section 193 or 194 be required to disclose any information or produce any document which he would be entitled to refuse to disclose or produce on grounds of legal professional privilege in proceedings in the High Court, except that a lawyer may be required to provide the name and address of his client.

(2)   A person may not under section 193 or 194 be required to disclose any information or produce any document in respect of which he owes an obligation of confidence by virtue of carrying on any banking business unless—

  (a)   the person to whom the obligation of confidence is owed consents to the disclosure or production; or

  (b)   the OFT has authorised the making of the requirement.

(3)   In the application of this section to Scotland, the reference in subsection (1)—

  (a)   to proceedings in the High Court is to be read as a reference to legal proceedings generally; and

  (b)   to an entitlement on grounds of legal professional privilege is to be read as a reference to an entitlement by virtue of any rule of law whereby—

    (i)   communications between a professional legal adviser and his client, or

    (ii)   communications made in connection with or in contemplation of legal proceedings and for the purposes of those proceedings,

  are in such proceedings protected from disclosure on the ground of confidentiality.

[439]

NOTES

Commencement: to be appointed.

197   Restriction on use of statements in court

(1)   A statement by a person in response to a requirement imposed by virtue of section 193 or 194 may only be used in evidence against him—

  (a)   on a prosecution for an offence under section 201(2); or

  (b)   on a prosecution for some other offence where in giving evidence he makes a statement inconsistent with it.

(2)   However, the statement may not be used against that person by virtue of paragraph (b) of subsection (1) unless evidence relating to it is adduced, or a question relating to it is asked, by or on behalf of that person in the proceedings arising out of the prosecution.

[440]

NOTES

Commencement: to be appointed.

198–200 (*S 198 inserts the Competition Act 1998, s 30A, at* **[162]**; *s 199 amends the Regulation of Investigatory Powers Act 2000, ss 32–37, 40, 46, 48; s 200 amends the Police Act 1997, ss 93, 94.*)

201 Offences

(1)   Any person who without reasonable excuse fails to comply with a requirement imposed on him under section 193 or 194 is guilty of an offence and liable on summary conviction to imprisonment for a term not exceeding six months or to a fine not exceeding level 5 on the standard scale or to both.

(2)   A person who, in purported compliance with a requirement under section 193 or 194—

   (a) makes a statement which he knows to be false or misleading in a material particular; or

   (b) recklessly makes a statement which is false or misleading in a material particular,

is guilty of an offence.

(3)   A person guilty of an offence under subsection (2) is liable—

   (a) on conviction on indictment, to imprisonment for a term not exceeding two years or to a fine or to both; and

   (b) on summary conviction, to imprisonment for a term not exceeding six months or to a fine not exceeding the statutory maximum, or to both.

(4)   Where any person—

   (a) knows or suspects that an investigation by the Serious Fraud Office or the OFT into an offence under section 188 is being or is likely to be carried out; and

   (b) falsifies, conceals, destroys or otherwise disposes of, or causes or permits the falsification, concealment, destruction or disposal of documents which he knows or suspects are or would be relevant to such an investigation,

he is guilty of an offence unless he proves that he had no intention of concealing the facts disclosed by the documents from the persons carrying out such an investigation.

(5)   A person guilty of an offence under subsection (4) is liable—

   (a) on conviction on indictment, to imprisonment for a term not exceeding 5 years or to a fine or to both; and

   (b) on summary conviction, to imprisonment for a term not exceeding six months or to a fine not exceeding the statutory maximum, or to both.

(6)   A person who intentionally obstructs a person in the exercise of his powers under a warrant issued under section 194 is guilty of an offence and liable—

   (a) on conviction on indictment, to imprisonment for a term not exceeding 2 years or to a fine or to both; and

   (b) on summary conviction, to a fine not exceeding the statutory maximum.

                                              [441]

NOTES

Commencement: to be appointed.

202 Interpretation of sections 192 to 201

In sections 192 to 201—

     "documents" includes information recorded in any form and, in relation to information recorded otherwise than in a form in which it is visible and legible, references to its production include references to producing it in a form in which it is visible and legible or from which it can readily be produced in a visible and legible form;

"person under investigation" has the meaning given in section 192(2).

[442]

NOTES

Commencement: to be appointed.

PART 7
MISCELLANEOUS COMPETITION PROVISIONS

203 (*Inserts the Competition Act 1998, ss 28(3A), 62(5A), 63(5A), at* **[159]**, **[197]**, **[198]**.)

Directors disqualification

204 Disqualification

(1)   The Company Directors Disqualification Act 1986 (c 46) is amended as follows.

(2)   The following sections are inserted after section 9 (matters for determining unfitness in certain cases)—

"Disqualification for competition infringements

9A Competition disqualification order

(1)   The court must make a disqualification order against a person if the following two conditions are satisfied in relation to him.

(2)   The first condition is that an undertaking which is a company of which he is a director commits a breach of competition law.

(3)   The second condition is that the court considers that his conduct as a director makes him unfit to be concerned in the management of a company.

(4)   An undertaking commits a breach of competition law if it engages in conduct which infringes any of the following—

    (a)   the Chapter 1 prohibition (within the meaning of the Competition Act 1998) (prohibition on agreements, etc preventing, restricting or distorting competition);

    (b)   the Chapter 2 prohibition (within the meaning of that Act) (prohibition on abuse of a dominant position);

    (c)   Article 81 of the Treaty establishing the European Community (prohibition on agreements, etc preventing, restricting or distorting competition);

    (d)   Article 82 of that Treaty (prohibition on abuse of a dominant position).

(5)   For the purpose of deciding under subsection (3) whether a person is unfit to be concerned in the management of a company the court—

    (a)   must have regard to whether subsection (6) applies to him;

    (b)   may have regard to his conduct as a director of a company in connection with any other breach of competition law;

    (c)   must not have regard to the matters mentioned in Schedule 1.

(6)   This subsection applies to a person if as a director of the company—

    (a)   his conduct contributed to the breach of competition law mentioned in subsection (2);

(b)   his conduct did not contribute to the breach but he had reasonable grounds to suspect that the conduct of the undertaking constituted the breach and he took no steps to prevent it;

(c)   he did not know but ought to have known that the conduct of the undertaking constituted the breach.

(7)   For the purposes of subsection (6)(a) it is immaterial whether the person knew that the conduct of the undertaking constituted the breach.

(8)   For the purposes of subsection (4)(a) or (c) references to the conduct of an undertaking are references to its conduct taken with the conduct of one or more other undertakings.

(9)   The maximum period of disqualification under this section is 15 years.

(10) An application under this section for a disqualification order may be made by the OFT or by a specified regulator.

(11) Section 60 of the Competition Act 1998 (c 41) (consistent treatment of questions arising under United Kingdom and Community law) applies in relation to any question arising by virtue of subsection (4)(a) or (b) above as it applies in relation to any question arising under Part 1 of that Act.

9B   Competition undertakings

(1)   This section applies if—

(a)   the OFT or a specified regulator thinks that in relation to any person an undertaking which is a company of which he is a director has committed or is committing a breach of competition law,

(b)   the OFT or the specified regulator thinks that the conduct of the person as a director makes him unfit to be concerned in the management of a company, and

(c)   the person offers to give the OFT or the specified regulator (as the case may be) a disqualification undertaking.

(2)   The OFT or the specified regulator (as the case may be) may accept a disqualification undertaking from the person instead of applying for or proceeding with an application for a disqualification order.

(3)   A disqualification undertaking is an undertaking by a person that for the period specified in the undertaking he will not—

(a)   be a director of a company;

(b)   act as receiver of a company's property;

(c)   in any way, whether directly or indirectly, be concerned or take part in the promotion, formation or management of a company;

(d)   act as an insolvency practitioner.

(4)   But a disqualification undertaking may provide that a prohibition falling within subsection (3)(a) to (c) does not apply if the person obtains the leave of the court.

(5)   The maximum period which may be specified in a disqualification undertaking is 15 years.

(6)   If a disqualification undertaking is accepted from a person who is already subject to a disqualification undertaking under this Act or to a disqualification order the periods specified in those undertakings or the undertaking and the order (as the case may be) run concurrently.

(7)   Subsections (4) to (8) of section 9A apply for the purposes of this section as they apply for the purposes of that section but in the application of subsection (5) of that section the reference to the court must be construed as a reference to the OFT or a specified regulator (as the case may be).

9C Competition investigations

(1)   If the OFT or a specified regulator has reasonable grounds for suspecting that a breach of competition law has occurred it or he (as the case may be) may carry out an investigation for the purpose of deciding whether to make an application under section 9A for a disqualification order.

(2)   For the purposes of such an investigation sections 26 to 30 of the Competition Act 1998 (c 41) apply to the OFT and the specified regulators as they apply to the OFT for the purposes of an investigation under section 25 of that Act.

(3)   Subsection (4) applies if as a result of an investigation under this section the OFT or a specified regulator proposes to apply under section 9A for a disqualification order.

(4)   Before making the application the OFT or regulator (as the case may be) must—
  (a)   give notice to the person likely to be affected by the application, and
  (b)   give that person an opportunity to make representations.

9D Co-ordination

(1)   The Secretary of State may make regulations for the purpose of co-ordinating the performance of functions under sections 9A to 9C (relevant functions) which are exercisable concurrently by two or more persons.

(2)   Section 54(5) to (7) of the Competition Act 1998 (c 41) applies to regulations made under this section as it applies to regulations made under that section and for that purpose in that section—
  (a)   references to Part 1 functions must be read as references to relevant functions;
  (b)   references to a regulator must be read as references to a specified regulator;
  (c)   a competent person also includes any of the specified regulators.

(3)   The power to make regulations under this section must be exercised by statutory instrument subject to annulment in pursuance of a resolution of either House of Parliament.

(4)   Such a statutory instrument may—
  (a)   contain such incidental, supplemental, consequential and transitional provision as the Secretary of State thinks appropriate;
  (b)   make different provision for different cases.

9E Interpretation

(1)   This section applies for the purposes of sections 9A to 9D.

(2)   Each of the following is a specified regulator for the purposes of a breach of competition law in relation to a matter in respect of which he or it has a function—
  (a)   the Director General of Telecommunications;
  (b)   the Gas and Electricity Markets Authority;
  (c)   the Director General of Water Services;
  (d)   the Rail Regulator;
  (e)   the Civil Aviation Authority.

(3)   The court is the High Court or (in Scotland) the Court of Session.

(4)   Conduct includes omission.

(5)   Director includes shadow director."

(3)   In section 1(1) (general provision about disqualification orders) for "section 6" substitute "sections 6 and 9A".

(4)   In section 8A (variation etc of disqualification undertaking) after subsection (2) there is inserted the following subsection—

"(2A) Subsection (2) does not apply to an application in the case of an undertaking given under section 9B, and in such a case on the hearing of the application whichever of the OFT or a specified regulator (within the meaning of section 9E) accepted the undertaking—

    (a)   must appear and call the attention of the court to any matters which appear to it or him (as the case may be) to be relevant;

    (b)   may give evidence or call witnesses."

(5)   In section 8A for subsection (3) there is substituted—

"(3) In this section "the court"—

    (a)   in the case of an undertaking given under section 9B means the High Court or (in Scotland) the Court of Session;

    (b)   in any other case has the same meaning as in section 7(2) or 8 (as the case may be)."

(6)   In section 16(3) for "the Secretary of State or the official receiver or the liquidator" substitute "a person falling within subsection (4)".

(7)   In section 16 after subsection (3) there is inserted the following subsection—

"(4) The following fall within this subsection—

    (a)   the Secretary of State;

    (b)   the official receiver;

    (c)   the OFT;

    (d)   the liquidator;

    (e)   a specified regulator (within the meaning of section 9E)."

(8)   In section 17 (applications for leave under an order or undertaking) after subsection (3) there is inserted the following subsection—

"(3A) Where a person is subject to a disqualification undertaking accepted at any time under section 9B any application for leave for the purposes of section 9B(4) must be made to the High Court or (in Scotland) the Court of Session."

(9)   In section 17(4) for "or 1A(1)(a)" substitute "1A(1)(a) or 9B(4)".

(10) In section 17 after subsection (5) there are inserted the following subsections—

"(6) Subsection (5) does not apply to an application for leave for the purposes of section 1(1)(a) if the application for the disqualification order was made under section 9A.

(7)   In such a case and in the case of an application for leave for the purposes of section 9B(4) on the hearing of the application whichever of the OFT or a specified regulator (within the meaning of section 9E) applied for the order or accepted the undertaking (as the case may be)—

    (a)   must appear and draw the attention of the court to any matters which appear to it or him (as the case may be) to be relevant;

    (b)   may give evidence or call witnesses."

(11) In section 18 (register of disqualification orders and undertakings) for subsection (2A) substitute—

"(2A) The Secretary of State must include in the register such particulars as he considers appropriate of—

(a) disqualification undertakings accepted by him under section 7 or 8;

(b) disqualification undertakings accepted by the OFT or a specified regulator under section 9B;

(c) cases in which leave has been granted as mentioned in subsection (1)(d)."

[443]

Miscellaneous

205 Super-complaints to regulators other than OFT

(1) The Secretary of State may by order provide that section 11 is to apply to complaints made to a specified regulator in relation to a market of a specified description as it applies to complaints made to the OFT, with such modifications as may be specified.

(2) An order under this section—

(a) shall be made by statutory instrument, and

(b) shall be subject to annulment in pursuance of a resolution of either House of Parliament.

(3) In this section—

"regulator" has the meaning given in section 54(1) of the 1998 Act; and

"specified" means specified in the order.

[444]

NOTES
Commencement: to be appointed.

206 Power to modify Schedule 8

(1) The Secretary of State may by order made by statutory instrument modify Schedule 8.

(2) An order under this section may make—

(a) different provision for different cases or different purposes;

(b) such incidental, supplementary, consequential, transitory, transitional or saving provision as the Secretary of State considers appropriate.

(3) An order under this section may, in particular, modify that Schedule in its application by virtue of Part 3 of this Act, in its application by virtue of Part 4 of this Act, in its application by virtue of any other enactment (whether by virtue of Part 4 of this Act as applied by that enactment or otherwise) or in its application by virtue of every enactment that applies it.

(4) An order under this section as extended by subsection (2) may modify any enactment comprised in or made under this Act, or any other enactment.

(5) No order shall be made under this section unless a draft of it has been laid before, and approved by a resolution of, each House of Parliament.

(6) No modification of Schedule 8 in its application by virtue of Part 3 of this Act shall be made by an order under this section if the modification relates to a relevant merger situation or (as the case may be) a special merger situation which has been created before the coming into force of the order.

(7) No modification shall be made by an order under this section of Schedule 8 in its application in relation to references made under section 22, 33, 45 or 62 before the coming into force of the order.

(8) No modification shall be made by an order under this section of Schedule 8 in its application in relation to references made under section 131 or 132 before the coming into force of the order (including references made under section 131 as applied by another enactment).

(9) Before making an order under this section, the Secretary of State shall consult the OFT and the Commission.

(10) Expressions used in this section which are also used in Part 3 of this Act have the same meaning in this section as in that Part.

[445]

NOTES

Commencement: to be appointed.

207, 208 (*S 207 repeals the Competition Act 1998, s 3(1)(d), Sch 4, at* **[135]**, **[210]**; *s 208 repeals the Fair Trading Act 1973, ss 78–80, at* **[62]–[64]**.)

209 Reform of Community competition law

(1) The Secretary of State may by regulations make such modifications of the 1998 Act as he considers appropriate for the purpose of eliminating or reducing any differences between—
   (a) the domestic provisions of the 1998 Act, and
   (b) European Community competition law,
which result (or would otherwise result) from a relevant Community instrument made after the passing of this Act.

(2) In subsection (1)—
   "the domestic provisions of the 1998 Act" means the provisions of the 1998 Act so far as they do not implement or give effect to a relevant Community instrument;
   "European Community competition law" includes any Act or subordinate legislation so far as it implements or gives effect to a relevant Community instrument;
   "relevant Community instrument" means a regulation or directive under Article 83 of the Treaty establishing the European Community.

(3) The Secretary of State may by regulations repeal or otherwise modify any provision of an Act (other than the 1998 Act) which excludes any matter from the Chapter I prohibition or the Chapter II prohibition (within the meaning of Part 1 of the 1998 Act).

(4) The power under subsection (3) may not be exercised—
   (a) before the power under subsection (1) has been exercised; or
   (b) so as to extend the scope of any exclusion that is not being removed by the regulations.

(5) Regulations under this section may—
   (a) confer power to make subordinate legislation;
   (b) make such consequential, supplementary, incidental, transitory, transitional or saving provision as the Secretary of State considers appropriate (including provision modifying any Act or subordinate legislation); and
   (c) make different provision for different cases or circumstances.

(6)   The power to make regulations under this section is exercisable by statutory instrument.

(7)   No regulations may be made under this section unless a draft of them has been laid before and approved by a resolution of each House of Parliament.

(8)   Paragraph 1(1)(c) of Schedule 2 to the European Communities Act 1972 (c 68) (restriction on powers to legislate) shall not apply to regulations which implement or give effect to a relevant Community instrument made after the passing of this Act.

[446]

NOTES

Commencement: to be appointed.

210–236 ((*Pt 8: Enforcement of certain consumer legislation) outside the scope of this work.*)

PART 9
INFORMATION

Restrictions on disclosure

237 General restriction

(1)   This section applies to specified information which relates to—
  (a) the affairs of an individual;
  (b) any business of an undertaking.

(2)   Such information must not be disclosed—
  (a) during the lifetime of the individual, or
  (b) while the undertaking continues in existence,
unless the disclosure is permitted under this Part.

(3)   But subsection (2) does not prevent the disclosure of any information if the information has on an earlier occasion been disclosed to the public in circumstances which do not contravene—
  (a) that subsection;
  (b) any other enactment or rule of law prohibiting or restricting the disclosure of the information.

(4)   Nothing in this Part authorises a disclosure of information which contravenes the Data Protection Act 1998 (c 29).

(5)   Nothing in this Part affects the Competition Appeal Tribunal.

(6)   This Part (except section 244) does not affect any power or duty to disclose information which exists apart from this Part.

[447]

NOTES

Commencement: to be appointed.

238 Information

(1)   Information is specified information if it comes to a public authority in connection with the exercise of any function it has under or by virtue of—
  (a) Part 1, 3, 4, 6, 7 or 8;
  (b) an enactment specified in Schedule 14;

(c) such subordinate legislation as the Secretary of State may by order specify for the purposes of this subsection.

(2)   It is immaterial whether information comes to a public authority before or after the passing of this Act.

(3)   Public authority (except in the expression "overseas public authority") must be construed in accordance with section 6 of the Human Rights Act 1998 (c 42).

(4)   In subsection (1) the reference to an enactment includes a reference to an enactment contained in—
    (a) an Act of the Scottish Parliament;
    (b) Northern Ireland legislation;
    (c) subordinate legislation.

(5)   The Secretary of State may by order amend Schedule 14.

(6)   The power to make an order under subsection (5) includes power to add, vary or remove a reference to any provision of—
    (a) an Act of the Scottish Parliament;
    (b) Northern Ireland legislation.

(7)   An order under this section must be made by statutory instrument subject to annulment in pursuance of a resolution of either House of Parliament.

(8)   This section applies for the purposes of this Part.

[448]

NOTES
Commencement: to be appointed.

Permitted disclosure

239 Consent

(1)   This Part does not prohibit the disclosure by a public authority of information held by it to any other person if it obtains each required consent.

(2)   If the information was obtained by the authority from a person who had the information lawfully and the authority knows the identity of that person the consent of that person is required.

(3)   If the information relates to the affairs of an individual the consent of the individual is required.

(4)   If the information relates to the business of an undertaking the consent of the person for the time being carrying on the business is required.

(5)   For the purposes of subsection (4) consent may be given—
    (a) in the case of a company by a director, secretary or other officer of the company;
    (b) in the case of a partnership by a partner;
    (c) in the case of an unincorporated body or association by a person concerned in the management or control of the body or association.

[449]

NOTES
Commencement: to be appointed.

240 Community obligations

This Part does not prohibit the disclosure of information held by a public authority to another person if the disclosure is required for the purpose of a Community obligation.

[450]

PART I
STATUTES

NOTES

Commencement: to be appointed.

241 Statutory functions

(1) A public authority which holds information to which section 237 applies may disclose that information for the purpose of facilitating the exercise by the authority of any function it has under or by virtue of this Act or any other enactment.

(2) If information is disclosed under subsection (1) so that it is not made available to the public it must not be further disclosed by a person to whom it is so disclosed other than with the agreement of the public authority for the purpose mentioned in that subsection.

(3) A public authority which holds information to which section 237 applies may disclose that information to any other person for the purpose of facilitating the exercise by that person of any function he has under or by virtue of—
  (a) this Act;
  (b) an enactment specified in Schedule 15;
  (c) such subordinate legislation as the Secretary of State may by order specify for the purposes of this subsection.

(4) Information disclosed under subsection (3) must not be used by the person to whom it is disclosed for any purpose other than a purpose relating to a function mentioned in that subsection.

(5) In subsection (1) the reference to an enactment includes a reference to an enactment contained in—
  (a) an Act of the Scottish Parliament;
  (b) Northern Ireland legislation;
  (c) subordinate legislation.

(6) The Secretary of State may by order amend Schedule 15.

(7) The power to make an order under subsection (6) includes power to add, vary or remove a reference to any provision of—
  (a) an Act of the Scottish Parliament;
  (b) Northern Ireland legislation.

(8) An order under this section must be made by statutory instrument subject to annulment in pursuance of a resolution of either House of Parliament.

[451]

NOTES

Commencement: to be appointed.

242 Criminal proceedings

(1) A public authority which holds information to which section 237 applies may disclose that information to any person—
  (a) in connection with the investigation of any criminal offence in any part of the United Kingdom;
  (b) for the purposes of any criminal proceedings there;
  (c) for the purpose of any decision whether to start or bring to an end such an investigation or proceedings.

(2) Information disclosed under this section must not be used by the person to whom it is disclosed for any purpose other than that for which it is disclosed.

(3)   A public authority must not make a disclosure under this section unless it is satisfied that the making of the disclosure is proportionate to what is sought to be achieved by it.

[452]

NOTES
Commencement: to be appointed.

243 Overseas disclosures

(1)   A public authority which holds information to which section 237 applies (the discloser) may disclose that information to an overseas public authority for the purpose mentioned in subsection (2).

(2)   The purpose is facilitating the exercise by the overseas public authority of any function which it has relating to—

    (a) carrying out investigations in connection with the enforcement of any relevant legislation by means of civil proceedings;

    (b) bringing civil proceedings for the enforcement of such legislation or the conduct of such proceedings;

    (c) the investigation of crime;

    (d) bringing criminal proceedings or the conduct of such proceedings;

    (e) deciding whether to start or bring to an end such investigations or proceedings.

(3)   But subsection (1) does not apply to any of the following—

    (a) information which is held by a person who is designated by virtue of section 213(4) as a designated enforcer for the purposes of Part 8;

    (b) information which comes to a public authority in connection with an investigation under Part 4, 5 or 6 of the 1973 Act or under section 11 of the Competition Act 1980 (c 21);

    (c) competition information within the meaning of section 351 of the Financial Services and Markets Act 2000 (c 8);

    (d) information which comes to a public authority in connection with an investigation under Part 3 or 4 or section 174 of this Act.

(4)   The Secretary of State may direct that a disclosure permitted by this section must not be made if he thinks that in connection with any matter in respect of which the disclosure could be made it is more appropriate—

    (a) if any investigation is to be carried out, that it is carried out by an authority in the United Kingdom or in another specified country or territory;

    (b) if any proceedings are to be brought, that they are brought in a court in the United Kingdom or in another specified country or territory.

(5)   The Secretary of State must take such steps as he thinks are appropriate to bring a direction under subsection (4) to the attention of persons likely to be affected by it.

(6)   In deciding whether to disclose information under this section a public authority must have regard in particular to the following considerations—

    (a) whether the matter in respect of which the disclosure is sought is sufficiently serious to justify making the disclosure;

    (b) whether the law of the country or territory to whose authority the disclosure would be made provides appropriate protection against self-incrimination in criminal proceedings;

    (c) whether the law of that country or territory provides appropriate protection in relation to the storage and disclosure of personal data;

(d) whether there are arrangements in place for the provision of mutual assistance as between the United Kingdom and that country or territory in relation to the disclosure of information of the kind to which section 237 applies.

(7) Protection is appropriate if it provides protection in relation to the matter in question which corresponds to that so provided in any part of the United Kingdom.

(8) The Secretary of State may by order—
  (a) modify the list of considerations in subsection (6);
  (b) add to those considerations;
  (c) remove any of those considerations.

(9) An order under subsection (8) must be made by statutory instrument subject to annulment in pursuance of a resolution of either House of Parliament.

(10) Information disclosed under this section—
  (a) may be disclosed subject to the condition that it must not be further disclosed without the agreement of the discloser, and
  (b) must not otherwise be used by the overseas public authority to which it is disclosed for any purpose other than that for which it is first disclosed.

(11) An overseas public authority is a person or body in any country or territory outside the United Kingdom which appears to the discloser to exercise functions of a public nature in relation to any of the matters mentioned in paragraphs (a) to (e) of subsection (2).

(12) Relevant legislation is—
  (a) this Act, any enactment specified in Schedule 14 and such subordinate legislation as is specified by order for the purposes of section 238(1);
  (b) any enactment or subordinate legislation specified in an order under section 211(2);
  (c) any enactment or subordinate legislation specified in an order under section 212(3);
  (d) legislation in any country or territory outside the United Kingdom which appears to the discloser to make provision corresponding to this Act or to any such enactment or subordinate legislation.

[453]

NOTES

Commencement: to be appointed.

244 Specified information: considerations relevant to disclosure

(1) A public authority must have regard to the following considerations before disclosing any specified information (within the meaning of section 238(1)).

(2) The first consideration is the need to exclude from disclosure (so far as practicable) any information whose disclosure the authority thinks is contrary to the public interest.

(3) The second consideration is the need to exclude from disclosure (so far as practicable)—
  (a) commercial information whose disclosure the authority thinks might significantly harm the legitimate business interests of the undertaking to which it relates, or
  (b) information relating to the private affairs of an individual whose disclosure the authority thinks might significantly harm the individual's interests.

(4)   The third consideration is the extent to which the disclosure of the information mentioned in subsection (3)(a) or (b) is necessary for the purpose for which the authority is permitted to make the disclosure.

[454]

NOTES
Commencement: to be appointed.

Offences

245 Offences

(1)   A person commits an offence if he discloses information to which section 237 applies in contravention of section 237(2).

(2)   A person commits an offence if he discloses information in contravention of a direction given under section 243(4).

(3)   A person commits an offence if he uses information disclosed to him under this Part for a purpose which is not permitted under this Part.

(4)   A person who commits an offence under this section is liable—
   (a) on summary conviction to imprisonment for a term not exceeding three months or to a fine not exceeding the statutory maximum or to both;
   (b) on conviction on indictment to imprisonment for a term not exceeding two years or to a fine or to both.

[455]

NOTES
Commencement: to be appointed.

General

246 Subordinate legislation

In this Part "subordinate legislation" has the same meaning as in section 21(1) of the Interpretation Act 1978 (c 30) and includes an instrument made under—
   (a) an Act of the Scottish Parliament;
   (b) Northern Ireland legislation.

[456]

NOTES
Commencement: to be appointed.

247–272 (*S 247 repeals the Trade Descriptions Act 1968, s 28(5), (5A), the Fair Trading Act 1973, s 30(3), 133, at* **[87]**, *the Prices Act 1974, Schedule, para 12, the Consumer Credit Act 1974, s 174, the Estate Agents Act 1979, s 10, the Competition Act 1980, s 19(1)–(3), (4)(c), (d), (f), (5), (6), at* **[115]**, *the Consumer Protection Act 1987, s 38, the Property Misdescriptions Act 1991, Schedule, para 7, the Timeshare Act 1992, Sch 2, para 5, the Competition Act 1998, ss 55, 56, Sch 11, at* **[189]**, **[190]**, **[226]**, *and the Financial Services and Markets Act 2000, s 351(1)–(3), (7), Sch 19; ss 248–272 (Pt 10: Insolvency) outside the scope of this work.*)

PART 11
SUPPLEMENTARY

273 Interpretation

In this Act—
    "the 1973 Act" means the Fair Trading Act 1973 (c 41);
    "the 1998 Act" means the Competition Act 1998 (c 41);
    "the Commission" means the Competition Commission;
    "the Director" means the Director General of Fair Trading; and
    "the OFT" means the Office of Fair Trading.

[457]

NOTES
Commencement: to be appointed.

274 Provision of financial assistance for consumer purposes

The Secretary of State may give financial assistance to any person for the purpose of assisting—
    (a) activities which the Secretary of State considers are of benefit to consumers; or
    (b) the provision of—
        (i) advice or information about consumer matters;
        (ii) educational materials relating to consumer matters; or
        (iii) advice or information to the Secretary of State in connection with the formulation of policy in respect of consumer matters.

[458]

NOTES
Commencement: to be appointed.

275 Financial provision

There shall be paid out of money provided by Parliament—
    (a) any expenditure incurred by the OFT, the Secretary of State, any other Minister of the Crown or a government department by virtue of this Act; and
    (b) any increase attributable to this Act in the sums payable out of money so provided by virtue of any other Act.

[459]

NOTES
Commencement: to be appointed.

276 Transitional or transitory provision and savings

    (1) Schedule 24 (which makes transitional and transitory provisions and savings) has effect.

    (2) The Secretary of State may by order made by statutory instrument make such transitional or transitory provisions and savings as he considers appropriate in connection with the coming into force of any provision of this Act.

    (3) An order under subsection (2) may modify any Act or subordinate legislation.

(4)   Schedule 24 does not restrict the power under subsection (2) to make other transitional or transitory provisions and savings.

[460]

NOTES

Commencement: to be appointed.

277 Power to make consequential amendments etc

(1)   The Secretary of State may by order make such supplementary, incidental or consequential provision as he thinks appropriate—

    (a) for the general purposes, or any particular purpose, of this Act; or

    (b) in consequence of any provision made by or under this Act or for giving full effect to it.

(2)   An order under this section may—

    (a) modify any Act or subordinate legislation (including this Act);

    (b) make incidental, supplementary, consequential, transitional, transitory or saving provision.

(3)   The power to make an order under this section is exercisable by statutory instrument subject to annulment in pursuance of a resolution of either House of Parliament.

(4)   The power conferred by this section is not restricted by any other provision of this Act.

[461]

NOTES

Commencement: to be appointed.

278 Minor and consequential amendments and repeals

(1)   Schedule 25 (which contains minor and consequential amendments) has effect.

(2)   Schedule 26 (which contains repeals and revocations) has effect.

[462]

NOTES

Commencement: to be appointed.

279 Commencement

The preceding provisions of this Act shall come into force on such day as the Secretary of State may by order made by statutory instrument appoint; and different days may be appointed for different purposes.

[463]

NOTES

Commencement: 7 November 2002.

280 Extent

(1)   Sections 256 to 265, 267, 269 and 272 extend only to England and Wales.

(2)   Sections 204, 248 to 255 and 270 extend only to England and Wales and Scotland (but subsection (3) of section 415A as inserted by section 270 extends only to England and Wales).

(3)   Any other modifications by this Act of an enactment have the same extent as the enactment being modified.

(4)   Otherwise, this Act extends to England and Wales, Scotland and Northern Ireland.

[464]

NOTES

    Commencement: 7 November 2002.

281   Short title

This Act may be cited as the Enterprise Act 2002.

[465]

NOTES

    Commencement: 7 November 2002.

SCHEDULES

SCHEDULE 1

Section 1

THE OFFICE OF FAIR TRADING

Membership

1.—(1)   The OFT shall consist of a chairman and no fewer than four other members, appointed by the Secretary of State.

(2)   The Secretary of State shall consult the chairman before appointing any other member.

Terms of appointment, remuneration, pensions etc

2.—(1)   Subject to this Schedule, the chairman and other members shall hold and vacate office in accordance with the terms of their respective appointments.

(2)   The terms of appointment of the chairman and other members shall be determined by the Secretary of State.

3.—(1)   An appointment of a person to hold office as chairman or other member shall be for a term not exceeding five years.

(2)   A person holding office as chairman or other member—

    (a)   may resign that office by giving notice in writing to the Secretary of State; and

    (b)   may be removed from office by the Secretary of State on the ground of incapacity or misbehaviour.

(3)   A previous appointment as chairman or other member does not affect a person's eligibility for appointment to either office.

4.—(1)   The OFT shall pay to the chairman and other members such remuneration, and such travelling and other allowances, as may be determined by the Secretary of State.

(2)   The OFT shall, if required to do so by the Secretary of State—

    (a)   pay such pension, allowances or gratuities as may be determined by the Secretary of State to or in respect of a person who holds or has held office as chairman or other member; or

    (b)   make such payments as may be so determined towards provision for the payment of a pension, allowances or gratuities to or in respect of such a person.

(3)   If, where any person ceases to hold office as chairman or other member, the Secretary of State determines that there are special circumstances which make it right that he should receive compensation, the OFT shall pay to him such amount by way of compensation as the Secretary of State may determine.

Staff

5.—(1) The Secretary of State shall, after consulting the chairman, appoint a person (who may, subject to sub-paragraph (2), also be a member of the OFT) to act as chief executive of the OFT on such terms and conditions as the Secretary of State may think appropriate.

(2)   A person appointed as chief executive after the end of the transitional period may not at the same time be chairman.

(3)   In sub-paragraph (2) "the transitional period" means the period of two years beginning with the day on which this paragraph comes into force.

6.   The OFT may, with the approval of the Minister for the Civil Service as to numbers and terms and conditions of service, appoint such other staff as it may determine.

Membership of committees or sub-committees of OFT

7.   The members of a committee or sub-committee of the OFT may include persons who are not members of the OFT (and a sub-committee may include persons who are not members of the committee which established it).

Proceedings etc

8.—(1) The OFT may regulate its own procedure (including quorum).

(2)   The OFT shall consult the Secretary of State before making or revising its rules and procedures for dealing with conflicts of interest.

(3)   The OFT shall from time to time publish a summary of its rules and procedures for dealing with conflicts of interest.

9.   The validity of anything done by the OFT is not affected by a vacancy among its members or by a defect in the appointment of a member.

10.—(1) The application of the seal of the OFT shall be authenticated by the signature of—
  (a) any member; or
  (b) some other person who has been authorised for that purpose by the OFT, whether generally or specially.

(2)   Sub-paragraph (1) does not apply in relation to any document which is, or is to be, signed in accordance with the law of Scotland.

11. A document purporting to be duly executed under the seal of the OFT, or signed on its behalf, shall be received in evidence and, unless the contrary is proved, be taken to be so executed or signed.

Performance of functions

12.—(1) Anything authorised or required to be done by the OFT (including exercising the power under this paragraph) may be done by—
  (a) any member or employee of the OFT who is authorised for that purpose by the OFT, whether generally or specially;
  (b) any committee of the OFT which has been so authorised.

(2)   Sub-paragraph (1)(b) does not apply to a committee whose members include any person who is not a member or employee of the OFT.

Supplementary powers

13. The OFT has power to do anything which is calculated to facilitate, or is conducive or incidental to, the performance of its functions.

14–16 ...

NOTES
  Commencement: to be appointed.
  Paras 14–16: amend the Parliamentary Commissioner Act 1967, Sch 2, the House of Commons Disqualification Act 1975, Sch 1, and the Northern Ireland Assembly Disqualification Act 1975, Sch 1.

SCHEDULE 2

Section 12

THE COMPETITION APPEAL TRIBUNAL

Appointment, etc of President and chairmen

1.—(1) A person is not eligible for appointment as President unless—

    (a) he has a 10 year general qualification;

    (b) he is an advocate or solicitor in Scotland of at least 10 years' standing; or

    (c) he is a member of the Bar of Northern Ireland or solicitor of the Supreme Court of Northern Ireland of at least 10 years' standing;

and he appears to the Lord Chancellor to have appropriate experience and knowledge of competition law and practice.

(2) A person is not eligible for appointment as a chairman unless—

    (a) he has a 7 year general qualification;

    (b) he is an advocate or solicitor in Scotland of at least 7 years' standing; or

    (c) he is a member of the Bar of Northern Ireland or solicitor of the Supreme Court of Northern Ireland of at least 7 years' standing;

and he appears to the Lord Chancellor to have appropriate experience and knowledge (either of competition law and practice or any other relevant law and practice).

(3) Before appointing an advocate or solicitor in Scotland under this paragraph, the Lord Chancellor must consult the Lord President of the Court of Session.

(4) In this paragraph "general qualification" has the same meaning as in section 71 of the Courts and Legal Services Act 1990 (c 41).

2.—(1) The members appointed as President or as chairmen shall hold and vacate office in accordance with their terms of appointment, subject to the following provisions.

(2) A person may not be a chairman for more than 8 years (but this does not prevent a temporary re-appointment for the purpose of continuing to act as a member of the Tribunal as constituted for the purposes of any proceedings instituted before the end of his term of office).

(3) The President and the chairmen may resign their offices by notice in writing to the Lord Chancellor.

(4) The Lord Chancellor may remove a person from office as President or chairman on the ground of incapacity or misbehaviour.

3. If the President is absent or otherwise unable to act the Lord Chancellor may appoint as acting President any person qualified for appointment as a chairman.

Appointment, etc of ordinary members

4.—(1) Ordinary members shall hold and vacate office in accordance with their terms of appointment, subject to the following provisions.

(2) A person may not be an ordinary member for more than 8 years (but this does not prevent a temporary re-appointment for the purpose of continuing to act as a member of the Tribunal as constituted for the purposes of any proceedings instituted before the end of his term of office).

(3) An ordinary member may resign his office by notice in writing to the Secretary of State.

(4) The Secretary of State may remove a person from office as an ordinary member on the ground of incapacity or misbehaviour.

Remuneration etc for members

5.—(1) The Competition Service shall pay to the President, the chairmen and the ordinary members such remuneration (whether by way of salaries or fees), and such allowances, as the Secretary of State may determine.

(2) The Competition Service shall, if required to do so by the Secretary of State—

    (a) pay such pension, allowances or gratuities as may be determined by the Secretary of State to or in respect of a person who holds or has held office as President, a chairman or an ordinary member; or

(b)   make such payments as may be so determined towards provision for the payment of a pension, allowance or gratuities to or in respect of such a person.

Compensation for loss of office

6.   If, where any person ceases to hold office as President, a chairman or ordinary member, the Secretary of State determines that there are special circumstances which make it right that he should receive compensation, the Competition Service shall pay to him such amount by way of compensation as the Secretary of State may determine.

Staff, accommodation and property

7.   Any staff, office accommodation or equipment required for the Tribunal shall be provided by the Competition Service.

Miscellaneous

8.   The President must arrange such training for members of the Tribunal as he considers appropriate.

9.   In this Schedule "chairman" and "ordinary member" mean respectively a member of the panel of chairmen, or a member of the panel of ordinary members, appointed under section 12.

10., 11.   ....

[467]

NOTES

Commencement: to be appointed.

Paras 10, 11: amend the House of Commons Disqualification Act 1975, Sch 1, and the Northern Ireland Assembly Disqualification Act 1975, Sch 1.

SCHEDULE 3

Section 13

THE COMPETITION SERVICE

PART 1
CONSTITUTION ETC

Membership of the Service

1.—(1)   The Service shall consist of—
    (a)   the President of the Competition Appeal Tribunal;
    (b)   the Registrar of the Competition Appeal Tribunal; and
    (c)   one or more appointed members.

    (2)   An appointed member shall be appointed by the Secretary of State after consulting the President.

Chairman of Service

2.—(1)   Subject to sub-paragraph (2), the members shall choose one of their number to be chairman of the Service.

    (2)   The Secretary of State shall designate one of the members to be the first chairman of the Service for such period as the Secretary of State may determine.

Appointed members

3.   An appointed member shall hold and vacate office in accordance with the terms of his appointment (and is eligible for re-appointment).

Allowances, etc for members

4.—(1)   The Service shall pay—
    (a)   such travelling and other allowances to its members, and
    (b)   such remuneration to any appointed member,

as may be determined by the Secretary of State.

  (2)   The Service shall, if required to do so by the Secretary of State—
    (a) pay such pension, allowances or gratuities as may be determined by the Secretary of State to or in respect of a person who holds or has held office as an appointed member; or
    (b) make such payments as may be so determined towards provision for the payment of a pension, allowances or gratuities to or in respect of such a person.

5.   If, where any person ceases to hold office as an appointed member, the Secretary of State determines that there are special circumstances which make it right that he should receive compensation, the Service shall pay to him such amount by way of compensation as the Secretary of State may determine.

Staff

6.—(1) The Service may, with the approval of the Secretary of State as to numbers and terms and conditions of service, appoint such staff as it may determine.

  (2)   The persons to whom section 1 of the Superannuation Act 1972 (c 11) (persons to or in respect of whom benefits may be provided by schemes under that section) applies shall include the staff of the Service.

  (3)   The Service shall pay to the Minister for the Civil Service, at such times as he may direct, such sums as he may determine in respect of any increase attributable to sub-paragraph (2) in the sums payable out of money provided by Parliament under the Superannuation Act 1972.

Procedure

7.—(1) The Service may regulate its own procedure (including quorum).

  (2)   The validity of anything done by the Service is not affected by a vacancy among its members or by a defect in the appointment of a member.

8.—(1) The application of the seal of the Service shall be authenticated by the signature of—
    (a) any member; or
    (b) some other person who has been authorised for that purpose by the Service, whether generally or specially.

  (2)   Sub-paragraph (1) does not apply in relation to any document which is, or is to be, signed in accordance with the law of Scotland.

9.   A document purporting to be duly executed under the seal of the Service, or signed on its behalf, shall be received in evidence and, unless the contrary is proved, be taken to be so executed or signed.

The Service's powers

10. The Service has power to do anything which is calculated to facilitate, or is conducive or incidental to, the performance of its functions.

Accounts

11.—(1) The Service shall keep proper accounts and proper records in relation to its accounts.

  (2)   In performing that duty the Service shall, in addition to accounts and records relating to its own activities (including the services provided to the Tribunal), keep separate accounts and separate records in relation to the activities of the Tribunal.

12.—(1) The Service shall—
    (a) prepare a statement of accounts in respect of each of its financial years; and
    (b) prepare a statement of accounts for the Tribunal for each of its financial years.

  (2)   The Service must send copies of the accounts required by sub-paragraph (1) to the Secretary of State and to the Comptroller and Auditor General before the end of August following the financial year to which they relate.

  (3)   Those accounts must comply with any directions given by the Secretary of State with the approval of the Treasury as to—
    (a) the information to be contained in them;

(b) the manner in which that information is to be presented; and

(c) the methods and principles according to which they are to be prepared.

(4) The Comptroller and Auditor General shall—

(a) examine, certify and report on each statement of accounts received by him; and

(b) lay copies of each statement before Parliament.

(5) In this paragraph "financial year" means the period of 12 months ending with 31st March.

[468]

NOTES

Commencement: to be appointed.

PART 2
TRANSFERS OF PROPERTY ETC BETWEEN THE COMMISSION AND THE SERVICE

13.—(1) The Secretary of State may make one or more schemes for the transfer to the Service of defined property, rights and liabilities of the Commission (including rights and liabilities relating to contracts of employment).

(2) A scheme may define the property, rights and liabilities to be transferred by specifying or describing them or by referring to all (or all except anything specified or described) of the property, rights and liabilities comprised in a specified part of the undertaking of the transferor.

(3) The property, rights and liabilities which may be transferred include any that would otherwise be incapable of being transferred or assigned.

(4) A scheme may include supplementary, incidental, transitional and consequential provision.

14.—(1) On the day appointed by a scheme under paragraph 13, the property, rights and liabilities which are the subject of the scheme shall, by virtue of this sub-paragraph, be transferred in accordance with the provisions of the scheme.

(2) If, after that day, the Commission and the Service so agree in writing, the scheme shall for all purposes be deemed to have come into force on that day with such modification as may be agreed.

(3) An agreement under sub-paragraph (2) may, in connection with giving effect to modifications to the scheme, include supplemental, incidental, transitional and consequential provision.

15. The transfer by paragraph 14(1) of the rights and liabilities relating to an individual's contract of employment does not break the continuity of his employment and, accordingly—

(a) he is not to be regarded for the purposes of Part 11 of the Employment Rights Act 1996 as having been dismissed by virtue of the transfer; and

(b) his period of employment with the transferor counts as a period of employment with the transferee for the purposes of that Act.

16.—(1) Anything done by or in relation to the transferor for the purposes of or in connection with anything transferred by paragraph 14(1) which is in effect immediately before it is transferred shall be treated as if done by or in relation to the transferee.

(2) There may be continued by or in relation to the transferee anything (including legal proceedings) relating to anything so transferred which is in the process of being done by or in relation to the transferor immediately before it is transferred.

(3) A reference to the transferor in any document relating to anything so transferred shall be taken (so far as necessary for the purposes of or in consequence of the transfer) as a reference to the transferee.

(4) A transfer under paragraph 14(1) does not affect the validity of anything done by or in relation to the transferor before the transfer takes effect.

[469]

NOTES

Commencement: to be appointed.

(Pt 3 amends the House of Commons Disqualification Act 1975, Sch 1, and the Northern Ireland Assembly Disqualification Act 1975, Sch 1.)

SCHEDULE 4

Sections 14 and 15

TRIBUNAL: PROCEDURE

PART 1
GENERAL

Decisions of the Tribunal

1.—(1) A decision of the Tribunal in any proceedings before it must—
- (a) state the reasons for the decision and whether it was unanimous or taken by a majority;
- (b) be recorded in a document signed and dated by the chairman of the Tribunal dealing with the proceedings.

(2)   In preparing that document the Tribunal shall have regard to the need for excluding, so far as practicable—
- (a) information the disclosure of which would in its opinion be contrary to the public interest;
- (b) commercial information the disclosure of which would or might, in its opinion, significantly harm the legitimate business interests of the undertaking to which it relates;
- (c) information relating to the private affairs of an individual the disclosure of which would, or might, in its opinion, significantly harm his interests.

(3)   But the Tribunal shall also have regard to the extent to which any disclosure mentioned in sub-paragraph (2) is necessary for the purpose of explaining the reasons for the decision.

(4)   The President shall make such arrangements for the publication of the decisions of the Tribunal as he considers appropriate.

Enforcement of decisions in Great Britain

2.   If a decision of the Tribunal is registered in England and Wales in accordance with rules of court or any practice direction—
- (a) payment of damages which are awarded by the decision;
- (b) costs or expenses awarded by the decision; and
- (c) any direction given as a result of the decision,

may be enforced by the High Court as if the damages, costs or expenses were an amount due in pursuance of a judgment or order of the High Court, or as if the direction were an order of the High Court.

3.   If a decision of the Tribunal awards damages, costs or expenses, or results in any direction being given, the decision may be recorded for execution in the Books of Council and Session and shall be enforceable accordingly.

4.   Subject to rules of court or any practice direction, a decision of the Tribunal may be registered or recorded for execution—
- (a) for the purpose of enforcing a direction given as a result of the decision, by the Registrar of the Tribunal or a person who was a party to the proceedings;
- (b) for the purpose of enforcing a decision to award damages, costs or expenses (other than a decision to which paragraph (c) applies), by the person to whom the sum concerned was awarded; and
- (c) for the purpose of enforcing a decision to award damages which is the subject of an order under section 47B(6) of the 1998 Act, by the specified body concerned.

Enforcement of decisions in Northern Ireland

5.—(1) A decision of the Tribunal may be enforced in Northern Ireland with the leave of the High Court in Northern Ireland—
- (a) in the case of a direction given as a result of the decision, by the Registrar of the Tribunal or a person who was a party to the proceedings;

(b) for the purpose of enforcing a decision to award damages, costs or expenses (other than a decision to which paragraph (c) applies), by the person to whom the sum concerned was awarded; and

(c) for the purpose of enforcing a decision to award damages which is the subject of an order under section 47B(6) of the 1998 Act, by the specified body concerned.

(2) For the purpose of enforcing in Northern Ireland a decision to award damages, costs or expenses—

(a) payment may be enforced as if the damages, costs or expenses were an amount due in pursuance of a judgment or order of the High Court in Northern Ireland; and

(b) a sum equal to the amount of damages, costs or expenses shall be deemed to be payable under a money judgment within the meaning of Article 2(2) of the Judgments Enforcement (Northern Ireland) Order 1981 (SI 1981/226 (NI 6)) (and the provisions of that Order apply accordingly).

(3) For the purpose of enforcing in Northern Ireland a direction given as a result of a decision of the Tribunal, the direction may be enforced as if it were an order of the High Court in Northern Ireland.

Miscellaneous

6. A decision of the Tribunal in proceedings under section 47B of the 1998 Act which—

(a) awards damages to an individual in respect of a claim made or continued on his behalf (but is not the subject of an order under section 47B(6)); or

(b) awards costs or expenses to an individual in respect of proceedings in respect of a claim made under section 47A of that Act prior to its being continued on his behalf in the proceedings under section 47B,

may only be enforced by the individual concerned with the permission of the High Court or Court of Session.

7. An award of costs or expenses against a specified body in proceedings under section 47B of the 1998 Act may not be enforced against any individual on whose behalf a claim was made or continued in those proceedings.

8. In this Part of this Schedule any reference to damages includes a reference to any sum of money (other than costs or expenses) which may be awarded in respect of a claim made under section 47A of the 1998 Act or included in proceedings under section 47B of that Act.

[470]

NOTES

Commencement: to be appointed.

PART 2
TRIBUNAL RULES

General

9. In this Schedule "the Tribunal", in relation to any proceedings before it, means the Tribunal as constituted (in accordance with section 14) for the purposes of those proceedings.

10. Tribunal rules may make different provision for different kinds of proceedings.

Institution of proceedings

11.—(1) Tribunal rules may make provision as to the period within which and the manner in which proceedings are to be brought.

(2) That provision may, in particular—

(a) provide for time limits for making claims to which section 47A of the 1998 Act applies in proceedings under section 47A or 47B;

(b) provide for the Tribunal to extend the period in which any particular proceedings may be brought; and

(c) provide for the form, contents, amendment and acknowledgement of the documents by which proceedings are to be instituted.

12. Tribunal rules may provide for the Tribunal to reject any proceedings (other than proceedings under section 47A or 47B of the 1998 Act) if it considers that—

    (a) the person instituting them does not have a sufficient interest in the decision with respect to which the proceedings are brought; or

    (b) the document by which he institutes them discloses no valid grounds for bringing them.

13. Tribunal rules may provide for the Tribunal—

    (a) to reject the whole of any proceedings under section 47B of the 1998 Act if it considers that the person bringing the proceedings is not entitled to do so or that the proceedings do not satisfy the requirements of section 47B(1);

    (b) to reject any claim which is included in proceedings under section 47B if it considers that—

        (i) the claim is not a consumer claim (within the meaning of section 47B(2)) which may be included in such proceedings; or

        (ii) the individual concerned has not consented to its being made or continued on his behalf in such proceedings; or

    (c) to reject any claim made under section 47A of the 1998 Act or included in proceedings under section 47B of that Act if it considers that there are no reasonable grounds for making it.

14. Tribunal rules may provide for the Tribunal to reject any proceedings if it is satisfied that the person instituting the proceedings has habitually and persistently and without any reasonable ground—

    (a) instituted vexatious proceedings (whether against the same person or against different persons); or

    (b) made vexatious applications in any proceedings.

15. Tribunal rules must ensure that no proceedings are rejected without giving the parties the opportunity to be heard.

Pre-hearing reviews and preliminary matters

16.—(1) Tribunal rules may make provision for the carrying out by the Tribunal of a preliminary consideration of proceedings (a "pre-hearing review").

  (2)   That provision may include—

    (a) provision enabling such powers to be exercised on a pre-hearing review as may be specified in the rules;

    (b) provision for security and supplemental provision relating to security.

  (3)   For the purposes of sub-paragraph (2)(b)—

    (a) "provision for security" means provision authorising the Tribunal, in specified circumstances, to order a party to the proceedings, if he wishes to continue to participate in them, to pay a deposit not exceeding such sum as may be specified or calculated in a specified manner; and

    (b) "supplemental provision", in relation to security, means provision as to—

        (i) the manner in which the amount of a deposit is to be determined;

        (ii) the consequences of non-payment of a deposit;

        (iii) the circumstances in which the deposit, or any part of it, may be refunded to the person who paid it or paid to another party to the proceedings.

Conduct of the hearing

17.—(1) Tribunal rules may make provision—

    (a) as to the manner in which proceedings are to be conducted, including provision for any hearing to be held in private if the Tribunal considers it appropriate because it is considering information of a kind mentioned in paragraph 1(2);

    (b) as to the persons entitled to appear on behalf of the parties;

    (c) for requiring persons to attend to give evidence and produce documents, and for authorising the administration of oaths to witnesses;

    (d) as to the evidence which may be required or admitted and the extent to which it should be oral or written;

    (e) allowing the Tribunal to fix time limits with respect to any aspect of proceedings and to extend any time limit (before or after its expiry);

    (f) enabling the Tribunal, on the application of any party or on its own initiative, to order—

        (i) the disclosure between, or the production by, the parties of documents or classes of documents; or

        (ii) such recovery or inspection of documents as might be ordered by a sheriff;

    (g) for the appointment of experts for the purposes of proceedings;

    (h) for the award of costs or expenses, including allowances payable to persons in connection with attendance before the Tribunal;

    (i) for taxing or otherwise settling any costs or expenses awarded by the Tribunal or for the enforcement of any order awarding costs or expenses.

(2)   Rules under sub-paragraph (1)(h) may provide, in relation to a claim made under section 47A of the 1998 Act which is continued on behalf of an individual in proceedings under section 47B of that Act, for costs or expenses to be awarded to or against that individual in respect of proceedings on that claim which took place before it was included in the proceedings under section 47B of that Act.

(3)   Otherwise Tribunal rules may not provide for costs or expenses to be awarded to or against an individual on whose behalf a claim is made or continued in proceedings under section 47B of the 1998 Act.

(4)   Tribunal rules may make provision enabling the Tribunal to refer any matter arising in any proceedings (other than proceedings under section 47A or 47B of the 1998 Act) back to the authority that made the decision to which the proceedings relate, if it appears that the matter has not been adequately investigated.

(5)   A person who without reasonable excuse fails to comply with—

    (a) any requirement imposed by virtue of sub-paragraph (1)(c); or

    (b) any requirement with respect to the disclosure, production, recovery or inspection of documents which is imposed by virtue of sub-paragraph (1)(f),

is guilty of an offence and liable on summary conviction to a fine not exceeding level 3 on the standard scale.

Quorum

18.—(1) Tribunal rules may make provision as to the consequences of a member of the Tribunal being unable to continue after part of any proceedings have been heard.

(2)   The rules may allow the Tribunal to consist of the remaining members for the rest of the proceedings.

(3)   The rules may enable the President, if it is the chairman of the Tribunal who is unable to continue—

    (a) to appoint either of the remaining members to chair the Tribunal; and

    (b) if that person is not a member of the panel of chairmen, to appoint himself or some other suitably qualified person to attend the proceedings and advise the remaining members on any questions of law arising.

(4)   For the purpose of sub-paragraph (3) a person is "suitably qualified" if he is, or is qualified for appointment as, a member of the panel of chairmen.

Interest

19.—(1) Tribunal rules may make provision allowing the Tribunal to order that interest is payable on any sum awarded by the Tribunal or on any fees ordered to be paid under paragraph 20.

(2)   That provision may include provision—

    (a) as to the circumstances in which such an order may be made;

    (b) as to the manner in which, and the periods in respect of which, interest is to be calculated and paid.

Fees

20.—(1) Tribunal rules may provide—

    (a) for fees to be chargeable in respect of specified costs of proceedings; and

    (b) for the amount of such costs to be determined by the Tribunal.

(2)   Any sums received in respect of such fees shall be paid into the Consolidated Fund.

Withdrawal of proceedings

21.—(1) Tribunal rules may make provision—

  (a) preventing a party who has instituted proceedings from withdrawing them without the permission of the Tribunal or, in specified circumstances, the President or the Registrar;

  (b) for the Tribunal to grant permission to withdraw proceedings on such conditions as it considers appropriate;

  (c) enabling the Tribunal to publish any decision which it would have made in any proceedings, had the proceedings not been withdrawn;

  (d) as to the effect of withdrawal of proceedings; and

  (e) as to the procedure to be followed if parties to proceedings agree to settle.

  (2) Tribunal rules may make, in relation to a claim included in proceedings under section 47B of the 1998 Act, any provision which may be made under sub-paragraph (1) in relation to the whole proceedings.

Interim orders

22.—(1) Tribunal rules may provide for the Tribunal to make an order, on an interim basis—

  (a) suspending the effect of any decision which is the subject matter of proceedings before it;

  (b) in the case of an appeal under section 46 or 47 of the 1998 Act, varying the conditions or obligations attached to an exemption;

  (c) granting any remedy which the Tribunal would have had power to grant in its final decision.

  (2) Tribunal rules may also make provision giving the Tribunal powers similar to those given to the OFT by section 35 of the 1998 Act.

Miscellaneous

23.—(1) Tribunal rules may make provision enabling the Tribunal to decide where to sit for the purposes of, or of any part of, any proceedings before it.

  (2) Tribunal rules may make provision enabling the Tribunal to decide that any proceedings before it are to be treated, for purposes connected with—

  (a) any appeal from a decision of the Tribunal made in those proceedings; and

  (b) any other matter connected with those proceedings,

as proceedings in England and Wales, Scotland or Northern Ireland (regardless of the decision made for the purposes of sub-paragraph (1)).

  (3) For the purposes of sub-paragraph (2), Tribunal rules may provide for each claim made or continued on behalf of an individual in proceedings under section 47B of the 1998 Act to be treated as separate proceedings.

24. Tribunal rules may make provision—

  (a) for a person who is not a party to be joined in any proceedings;

  (b) for hearing a person who is not a party where, in any proceedings, it is proposed to make an order or give a direction in relation to that person;

  (c) for proceedings to be consolidated on such terms as the Tribunal thinks appropriate in such circumstances as may be specified.

25. Tribunal rules may make provision for the Tribunal to transfer a claim made in proceedings under section 47A of the 1998 Act to—

  (a) the High Court or a county court in England and Wales or Northern Ireland; or

  (b) the Court of Session or a sheriff court in Scotland.

26. Tribunal rules may make provision in connection with the transfer of any proceedings from a court mentioned in paragraph 25 to the Tribunal under section 16.

[471]

NOTES

Commencement: to be appointed.

(*Sch 5 amends the Competition Act 1998, Pt I, at* **[133]**, *et seq; Sch 6 outside the scope of this work.*)

SCHEDULE 7

Section 85

ENFORCEMENT REGIME FOR PUBLIC INTEREST AND SPECIAL PUBLIC INTEREST CASES

Pre-emptive undertakings and orders

1.—(1) Sub-paragraph (2) applies where an intervention notice or special intervention notice is in force.

(2)   The Secretary of State may, for the purpose of preventing pre-emptive action, accept from such of the parties concerned as he considers appropriate undertakings to take such action as he considers appropriate.

(3)   Sub-paragraph (4) applies where an intervention notice is in force.

(4)   The Secretary of State may, for the purpose of preventing pre-emptive action, adopt an undertaking accepted by the OFT under section 71 if the undertaking is still in force when the Secretary of State adopts it.

(5)   An undertaking adopted under sub-paragraph (4)—
   (a) shall continue in force, in accordance with its terms, when adopted;
   (b) may be varied or superseded by an undertaking under this paragraph; and
   (c) may be released by the Secretary of State.

(6)   Any other undertaking under this paragraph—
   (a) shall come into force when accepted;
   (b) may be varied or superseded by another undertaking; and
   (c) may be released by the Secretary of State.

(7)   References in this Part to undertakings under this paragraph shall, unless the context otherwise requires, include references to undertakings adopted under this paragraph; and references to the acceptance or giving of undertakings under this paragraph shall be construed accordingly.

(8)   An undertaking which is in force under this paragraph in relation to a reference or possible reference under section 45 or (as the case may be) 62 shall cease to be in force if an order under paragraph 2 or an undertaking under paragraph 3 comes into force in relation to that reference.

(9)   An undertaking under this paragraph shall, if it has not previously ceased to be in force, cease to be in force when the intervention notice concerned or (as the case may be) special intervention notice concerned ceases to be in force.

(10) No undertaking shall be accepted by the Secretary of State under this paragraph before the making of a reference under section 45 or (as the case may be) 62 unless the undertaking relates to a relevant merger situation which has been, or may have been, created or (as the case may be) a special merger situation which has been, or may have been, created.

(11) The Secretary of State shall, as soon as reasonably practicable, consider any representations received by him in relation to varying or releasing an undertaking under this paragraph.

(12) In this paragraph and paragraph 2 "pre-emptive action" means action which might prejudice the reference or possible reference concerned under section 45 or (as the case may be) 62 or impede the taking of any action under this Part which may be justified by the Secretary of State's decisions on the reference.

2.—(1) Sub-paragraph (2) applies where an intervention notice or special intervention notice is in force.

(2)   The Secretary of State or the OFT may by order, for the purpose of preventing pre-emptive action—
   (a) prohibit or restrict the doing of things which the Secretary of State or (as the case may be) the OFT considers would constitute pre-emptive action;
   (b) impose on any person concerned obligations as to the carrying on of any activities or the safeguarding of any assets;
   (c) provide for the carrying on of any activities or the safeguarding of any assets either by the appointment of a person to conduct or supervise the conduct of any activities (on such terms and with such powers as may be specified or described in the order) or in any other manner;

(d) do anything which may be done by virtue of paragraph 19 of Schedule 8.

(3) Sub-paragraph (4) applies where an intervention notice is in force.

(4) The Secretary of State or the OFT may, for the purpose of preventing pre-emptive action, adopt an order made by the OFT under section 72 if the order is still in force when the Secretary of State or (as the case may be) the OFT adopts it.

(5) An order adopted under sub-paragraph (4)—
   (a) shall continue in force, in accordance with its terms, when adopted; and
   (b) may be varied or revoked by an order under this paragraph.

(6) Any other order under this paragraph—
   (a) shall come into force at such time as is determined by or under the order; and
   (b) may be varied or revoked by another order.

(7) References in this Part to orders under this paragraph shall, unless the context otherwise requires, include references to orders adopted under this paragraph; and references to the making of orders under this paragraph shall be construed accordingly.

(8) An order which is in force under this paragraph in relation to a reference or possible reference under section 45 or (as the case may be) 62 shall cease to be in force if an undertaking under paragraph 1 or 3 comes into force in relation to that reference.

(9) An order under this paragraph shall, if it has not previously ceased to be in force, cease to be in force when the intervention notice concerned or (as the case may be) special intervention notice concerned ceases to be in force.

(10) No order shall be made by the Secretary of State or the OFT under this paragraph before the making of a reference under section 45 or (as the case may be) 62 unless the order relates to a relevant merger situation which has been, or may have been, created or (as the case may be) a special merger situation which has been, or may have been, created.

(11) The Secretary of State or (as the case may be) the OFT shall, as soon as reasonably practicable, consider any representations received by that person in relation to varying or revoking an order under this paragraph.

Undertakings in lieu of reference under section 45 or 62

3.—(1) Sub-paragraph (2) applies if the Secretary of State has power to make a reference to the Commission under section 45 or 62 and otherwise intends to make such a reference.

(2) The Secretary of State may, instead of making such a reference and for the purpose of remedying, mitigating or preventing any of the effects adverse to the public interest which have or may have resulted, or which may be expected to result, from the creation of the relevant merger situation concerned or (as the case may be) the special merger situation concerned, accept from such of the parties concerned as he considers appropriate undertakings to take such action as he considers appropriate.

(3) In proceeding under sub-paragraph (2), the Secretary of State shall, in particular—
   (a) accept the decisions of the OFT included in its report under section 44 so far as they relate to the matters mentioned in subsections (4) and (5) of that section; or
   (b) (as the case may be) accept the decisions of the OFT included in its report under section 61 so far as they relate to the matters mentioned in subsections (3)(a) and (4) of that section.

(4) In proceeding under sub-paragraph (2) in relation to an anti-competitive outcome, the Secretary of State may, in particular, have regard to the effect of any action on any relevant customer benefits in relation to the creation of the relevant merger situation concerned.

(5) No undertaking shall be accepted by the Secretary of State under this paragraph in connection with a possible reference under section 45 if a public interest consideration mentioned in the intervention notice concerned has not been finalised and the period of 24 weeks beginning with the giving of that notice has not expired.

(6) The Secretary of State may delay making a decision as to whether to accept any such undertaking (and any related decision as to whether to make a reference under section 45) if he considers that there is a realistic prospect of the public interest consideration being finalised within the period of 24 weeks beginning with the giving of the intervention notice concerned.

(7)   A delay under sub-paragraph (6) shall not extend beyond—
(a) the time when the public interest consideration is finalised; or
(b) if earlier, the expiry of the period of 24 weeks mentioned in that sub-paragraph.

(8)   An undertaking under this paragraph—
(a) shall come into force when accepted;
(b) may be varied or superseded by another undertaking; or
(c) may be released by the Secretary of State.

(9)   An undertaking under this paragraph which is in force in relation to a relevant merger situation or (as the case may be) a special merger situation shall cease to be in force if an order comes into force under paragraph 5 or 6 in relation to that undertaking.

(10)   The Secretary of State shall, as soon as reasonably practicable, consider any representations received by him in relation to varying or releasing an undertaking under this section.

4.—(1) The relevant authority shall not make a reference under section 22, 33 or 45 in relation to the creation of a relevant merger situation or (as the case may be) a reference under section 62 in relation to the creation of a special merger situation if—
(a) the Secretary of State has accepted an undertaking or group of undertakings under paragraph 3; and
(b) the relevant merger situation or (as the case may be) the special merger situation is the situation by reference to which the undertaking or group of undertakings was accepted.

(2)   In sub-paragraph (1) "the relevant authority" means—
(a) in relation to a possible reference under section 22 or 33, the OFT; and
(b) in relation to a possible reference under section 45 or 62, the Secretary of State.

(3)   Sub-paragraph (1) does not prevent the making of a reference if material facts about relevant arrangements or transactions, or relevant proposed arrangements or transactions, were not notified (whether in writing or otherwise) to the Secretary of State or the OFT or made public before any undertaking concerned was accepted.

(4)   For the purposes of sub-paragraph (3) arrangements or transactions, or proposed arrangements or transactions, are relevant if they are the ones in consequence of which the enterprises concerned ceased or may have ceased, or may cease, to be distinct enterprises.

(5)   In sub-paragraph (3) "made public" means so publicised as to be generally known or readily ascertainable.

5.—(1) Sub-paragraph (2) applies where the Secretary of State considers that—
(a) an undertaking accepted by him under paragraph 3 has not been, is not being or will not be fulfilled; or
(b) in relation to an undertaking accepted by him under that paragraph, information which was false or misleading in a material respect was given to him or the OFT by the person giving the undertaking before he decided to accept the undertaking.

(2)   The Secretary of State may, for any of the purposes mentioned in paragraph 3(2), make an order under this paragraph.

(3)   Sub-paragraphs (3) and (4) of paragraph 3 shall apply for the purposes of sub-paragraph (2) above as they apply for the purposes of sub-paragraph (2) of that paragraph.

(4)   An order under this paragraph may contain—
(a) anything permitted by Schedule 8; and
(b) such supplementary, consequential or incidental provision as the Secretary of State considers appropriate.

(5)   An order under this paragraph
(a) shall come into force at such time as is determined by or under the order; and
(b) may contain provision which is different from the provision contained in the undertaking concerned.

(6)   No order shall be varied or revoked under this paragraph unless the OFT advises that such a variation or revocation is appropriate by reason of a change of circumstances.

6.—(1) Sub-paragraph (2) applies where—
(a) the Secretary of State has the power to make an order under paragraph 5 in relation to a particular undertaking and intends to make such an order; or

(b) the Secretary of State has the power to make an order under paragraph 10 in relation to a particular undertaking and intends to make such an order.

(2) The Secretary of State may, for the purpose of preventing any action which might prejudice the making of that order, make an order under this paragraph.

(3) No order shall be made under sub-paragraph (2) unless the Secretary of State has reasonable grounds for suspecting that it is or may be the case that action which might prejudice the making of the order under paragraph 5 or (as the case may be) 10 is in progress or in contemplation.

(4) An order under sub-paragraph (2) may—
  (a) prohibit or restrict the doing of things which the Secretary of State considers would prejudice the making of the order under paragraph 5 or 10;
  (b) impose on any person concerned obligations as to the carrying on of any activities or the safeguarding of any assets;
  (c) provide for the carrying on of any activities or the safeguarding of any assets either by the appointment of a person to conduct or supervise the conduct of any activities (on such terms and with such powers as may be specified or described in the order) or in any other manner;
  (d) do anything which may be done by virtue of paragraph 19 of Schedule 8.

(5) An order under this paragraph shall come into force at such time as is determined by or under the order.

(6) An order under this paragraph shall, if it has not previously ceased to be in force, cease to be in force on—
  (a) the coming into force of an order under paragraph 5 or (as the case may be) 10 in relation to the undertaking concerned; or
  (b) the making of the decision not to proceed with such an order.

(7) The Secretary of State shall, as soon as reasonably practicable, consider any representations received by him in relation to varying or revoking an order under this paragraph.

Statutory restrictions following reference under section 45 or 62

7.—(1) Sub-paragraphs (2) and (3) apply where—
  (a) a reference has been made under section 45(2) or (3) or 62(2) but not finally determined; and
  (b) no undertakings under paragraph 1 are in force in relation to the relevant merger situation concerned or (as the case may be) the special merger situation concerned and no orders under paragraph 2 are in force in relation to that situation.

(2) No relevant person shall, without the consent of the Secretary of State—
  (a) complete any outstanding matters in connection with any arrangements which have resulted in the enterprises concerned ceasing to be distinct enterprises;
  (b) make any further arrangements in consequence of that result (other than arrangements which reverse that result); or
  (c) transfer the ownership or control of any enterprises to which the reference relates.

(3) No relevant person shall, without the consent of the Secretary of State, assist in any of the activities mentioned in paragraphs (a) to (c) of sub-paragraph (2).

(4) The prohibitions in sub-paragraphs (2) and (3) do not apply in relation to anything which the person concerned is required to do by virtue of any enactment.

(5) The consent of the Secretary of State under sub-paragraph (2) or (3)—
  (a) may be general or specific;
  (b) may be revoked by the Secretary of State; and
  (c) shall be published in such manner as the Secretary of State considers appropriate for bringing it to the attention of any person entitled to the benefit of it.

(6) Paragraph (c) of sub-paragraph (5) shall not apply if the Secretary of State considers that publication is not necessary for the purpose mentioned in that paragraph.

(7) Sub-paragraphs (2) and (3) shall apply to a person's conduct outside the United Kingdom if (and only if) he is—
  (a) a United Kingdom national;

(b) a body incorporated under the law of the United Kingdom or of any part of the United Kingdom; or

(c) a person carrying on business in the United Kingdom.

(8) For the purpose of this paragraph a reference under section 45(2) or (3) is finally determined if—

(a) the time within which the Commission is to prepare a report under section 50 in relation to the reference and give it to the Secretary of State has expired and no such report has been so prepared and given;

(b) the Commission decides to cancel the reference under section 53(1);

(c) the time within which the Secretary of State is to make and publish a decision under section 54(2) has expired and no such decision has been made and published;

(d) the Secretary of State decides under section 54(2) to make no finding at all in the matter;

(e) the Secretary of State otherwise decides under section 54(2) not to make an adverse public interest finding;

(f) the Secretary of State decides under section 54(2) to make an adverse public interest finding but decides neither to accept an undertaking under paragraph 9 of this Schedule nor to make an order under paragraph 11 of this Schedule; or

(g) the Secretary of State decides under section 54(2) to make an adverse public interest finding and accepts an undertaking under paragraph 9 of this Schedule or makes an order under paragraph 11 of this Schedule.

(9) For the purpose of this paragraph a reference under section 62(2) is finally determined if—

(a) the time within which the Commission is to prepare a report under section 65 in relation to the reference and give it to the Secretary of State has expired and no such report has been so prepared and given;

(b) the time within which the Secretary of State is to make and publish a decision under section 66(2) has expired and no such decision has been made and published;

(c) the Secretary of State decides under subsection (2) of section 66 otherwise than as mentioned in subsection (5) of that section;

(d) the Secretary of State decides under subsection (2) of section 66 as mentioned in subsection (5) of that section but decides neither to accept an undertaking under paragraph 9 of this Schedule nor to make an order under paragraph 11 of this Schedule; or

(e) the Secretary of State decides under subsection (2) of section 66 as mentioned in subsection (5) of that section and accepts an undertaking under paragraph 9 of this Schedule or makes an order under paragraph 11 of this Schedule.

(10) For the purposes of this paragraph the time when a reference under section 45(2) or (3) or (as the case may be) 62(2) is finally determined is—

(a) in a case falling within sub-paragraph (8)(a) or (c) or (as the case may be) (9)(a) or (b), the expiry of the time concerned;

(b) in a case falling within sub-paragraph (8)(b), (d) or (e) or (as the case may be) (9)(c), the making of the decision concerned;

(c) in a case falling within sub-paragraph (8)(f) or (as the case may be) (9)(d), the making of the decision neither to accept an undertaking under paragraph 9 of this Schedule nor to make an order under paragraph 11 of this Schedule; and

(d) in a case falling within sub-paragraph (8)(g) or (as the case may be) (9)(e), the acceptance of the undertaking concerned or (as the case may be) the making of the order concerned.

(11) In this paragraph "relevant person" means—

(a) any person who carries on any enterprise to which the reference relates or who has control of any such enterprise;

(b) any subsidiary of any person falling within paragraph (a); or

(c) any person associated with any person falling within paragraph (a) or any subsidiary of any person so associated.

8.—(1) Sub-paragraph (2) applies where—

(a) a reference has been made under section 45(4) or (5) or 62(3); and

(b) no undertakings under paragraph 1 are in force in relation to the relevant merger situation concerned or (as the case may be) special merger situation concerned and no orders under paragraph 2 are in force in relation to that situation.

(2) No relevant person shall, without the consent of the Secretary of State, directly or indirectly acquire during the relevant period an interest in shares in a company if any enterprise to which the reference relates is carried on by or under the control of that company.

(3) The consent of the Secretary of State under sub-paragraph (2)—
  (a) may be general or specific;
  (b) may be revoked by the Secretary of State; and
  (c) shall be published in such manner as the Secretary of State considers appropriate for bringing it to the attention of any person entitled to the benefit of it.

(4) Paragraph (c) of sub-paragraph (3) shall not apply if the Secretary of State considers that publication is not necessary for the purpose mentioned in that paragraph.

(5) Sub-paragraph (2) shall apply to a person's conduct outside the United Kingdom if (and only if) he is—
  (a) a United Kingdom national;
  (b) a body incorporated under the law of the United Kingdom or of any part of the United Kingdom; or
  (c) a person carrying on business in the United Kingdom.

(6) In this paragraph—
  "company" includes any body corporate;
  "relevant period" means the period beginning with the publication of the decision of the Secretary of State to make the reference concerned and ending when the reference is finally determined;
  "relevant person" means—
    (a) any person who carries on any enterprise to which the reference relates or who has control of any such enterprise;
    (b) any subsidiary of any person falling within paragraph (a); or
    (c) any person associated with any person falling within paragraph (a) or any subsidiary of any person so associated; and
  "share" means share in the capital of a company, and includes stock.

(7) For the purposes of the definition of "relevant period" in sub-paragraph (6), a reference under section 45(4) or (5) is finally determined if—
  (a) the Commission cancels the reference under section 48(1) or 53(1);
  (b) the time within which the Commission is to prepare a report under section 50 in relation to the reference and give it to the Secretary of State has expired and no such report has been so prepared and given;
  (c) the time within which the Secretary of State is to make and publish a decision under section 54(2) has expired and no such decision has been made and published;
  (d) the Secretary of State decides under section 54(2) to make no finding at all in the matter;
  (e) the Secretary of State otherwise decides under section 54(2) not to make an adverse public interest finding;
  (f) the Secretary of State decides under section 54(2) to make an adverse public interest finding but decides neither to accept an undertaking under paragraph 9 of this Schedule nor to make an order under paragraph 11 of this Schedule; or
  (g) the Secretary of State decides under section 54(2) to make an adverse public interest finding and accepts an undertaking under paragraph 9 of this Schedule or makes an order under paragraph 11 of this Schedule.

(8) For the purposes of the definition of "relevant period" in sub-paragraph (6), a reference under section 62(3) is finally determined if—
  (a) the Commission cancels the reference under section 64(1);
  (b) the time within which the Commission is to prepare a report under section 65 in relation to the reference and give it to the Secretary of State has expired and no such report has been so prepared and given;
  (c) the time within which the Secretary of State is to make and publish a decision under section 66(2) has expired and no such decision has been made and published;
  (d) the Secretary of State decides under subsection (2) of section 66 otherwise than as mentioned in subsection (5) of that section;
  (e) the Secretary of State decides under subsection (2) of section 66 as mentioned in subsection (5) of that section but decides neither to accept an undertaking under paragraph 9 of this Schedule nor to make an order under paragraph 11 of this Schedule; or

(f) the Secretary of State decides under subsection (2) of section 66 as mentioned in subsection (5) of that section and accepts an undertaking under paragraph 9 of this Schedule or makes an order under paragraph 11 of this Schedule.

(9)   For the purposes of the definition of "relevant period" in sub-paragraph (6) above, the time when a reference under section 45(4) or (5) or (as the case may be) 62(3) is finally determined is—

    (a) in a case falling within sub-paragraph (7)(a), (d) or (e) or (as the case may be) (8)(a) or (d), the making of the decision concerned;

    (b) in a case falling within sub-paragraph (7)(b) or (c) or (as the case may be) (8)(b) or (c), the expiry of the time concerned;

    (c) in a case falling within sub-paragraph (7)(f) or (as the case may be) (8)(e), the making of the decision neither to accept an undertaking under paragraph 9 of this Schedule nor to make an order under paragraph 11 of this Schedule; and

    (d) in a case falling within sub-paragraph (7)(g) or (as the case may be) (8)(f), the acceptance of the undertaking concerned or (as the case may be) the making of the order concerned.

(10)   Section 79 shall apply for the purposes of paragraph 7 and this paragraph in relation to a reference under section 45 or 62 as it applies for the purposes of sections 77 and 78 in relation to a reference under section 22 or 33.

(11)   In its application by virtue of sub-paragraph (10) section 79 shall have effect as if—

    (a) subsections (1) and (2) were omitted; and

    (b) for the reference in subsection (4) to the OFT there were substituted a reference to the Secretary of State.

Final undertakings and orders

9.—(1) The Secretary of State may, in accordance with section 55 or (as the case may be) 66(5) to (7), accept, from such persons as he considers appropriate, undertakings to take action specified or described in the undertakings.

(2)   An undertaking under this paragraph—

    (a) shall come into force when accepted;

    (b) may be varied or superseded by another undertaking; and

    (c) may be released by the Secretary of State.

(3)   An undertaking which is in force under this paragraph in relation to a reference under section 45 or 62 shall cease to be in force if an order under paragraph 6(1)(b) or 10 comes into force in relation to the subject-matter of the undertaking.

(4)   No undertaking shall be accepted under this paragraph in relation to a reference under section 45 or 62 if an order has been made under—

    (a) paragraph 6(1)(b) or 10 in relation to the subject-matter of the undertaking; or

    (b) paragraph 11 in relation to that reference.

(5)   The Secretary of State shall, as soon as reasonably practicable, consider any representations received by him in relation to varying or releasing an undertaking under this section.

10.—(1) Sub-paragraph (2) applies where the Secretary of State considers that—

    (a) an undertaking accepted by him under paragraph 9 has not been, is not being or will not be fulfilled; or

    (b) in relation to an undertaking accepted by him under that paragraph, information which was false or misleading in a material respect was given to him or the OFT by the person giving the undertaking before he decided to accept the undertaking.

(2)   The Secretary of State may, for any purpose mentioned in section 55(2) or (as the case may be) 66(6), make an order under this paragraph.

(3)   Subsections (3) and (4) of section 55 or (as the case may be) subsection (7) of section 66 shall apply for the purposes of sub-paragraph (2) above as they or it applies for the purposes of section 55(2) or (as the case may be) 66(6).

(4)   An order under this paragraph may contain—

    (a) anything permitted by Schedule 8; and

    (b) such supplementary, consequential or incidental provision as the Secretary of State considers appropriate.

(5)   An order under this paragraph—
     (a)   shall come into force at such time as is determined by or under the order; and
     (b)   may contain provision which is different from the provision contained in the undertaking concerned.

(6)   No order shall be varied or revoked under this paragraph unless the OFT advises that such a variation or revocation is appropriate by reason of a change of circumstances.

11.—(1) The Secretary of State may, in accordance with section 55 or (as the case may be) 66(5) to (7), make an order under this paragraph.

(2)   An order under this paragraph may contain—
     (a)   anything permitted by Schedule 8; and
     (b)   such supplementary, consequential or incidental provision as the Secretary of State considers appropriate.

(3)   An order under this paragraph shall come into force at such time as is determined by or under the order.

(4)   No order shall be made under this paragraph in relation to a reference under section 45 or (as the case may be) 62 if an undertaking has been accepted under paragraph 9 in relation to that reference.

(5)   No order shall be varied or revoked under this paragraph unless the OFT advises that such a variation or revocation is appropriate by reason of a change of circumstances.

[472]

NOTES

Commencement: to be appointed.

SCHEDULE 8

Section 86(4)

PROVISION THAT MAY BE CONTAINED IN CERTAIN ENFORCEMENT ORDERS

Introductory

1.   This Schedule applies in relation to such orders, and to such extent, as is provided by this Part and Part 4 and any other enactment; and references in this Schedule to an order shall be construed accordingly.

General restrictions on conduct

2.—(1)   An order may—
     (a)   prohibit the making or performance of an agreement;
     (b)   require any party to an agreement to terminate the agreement.

(2)   An order made by virtue of sub-paragraph (1) shall not—
     (a)   prohibit the making or performance of; or
     (b)   require any person to terminate,

an agreement so far as, if made, the agreement would relate, or (as the case may be) so far as the agreement relates, to the terms and conditions of employment of any workers or to the physical conditions in which any workers are required to work.

3.—(1) An order may prohibit the withholding from any person of—
     (a)   any goods or services;
     (b)   any orders for any such goods or services.

(2)   References in sub-paragraph (1) to withholding include references to—
     (a)   agreeing or threatening to withhold; and
     (b)   procuring others to withhold or to agree or threaten to withhold.

4.   An order may prohibit requiring as a condition of the supply of goods or services to any person—
     (a)   the buying of any goods;
     (b)   the making of any payment in respect of services other than the goods or services supplied;
     (c)   the doing of any other such matter or the refraining from doing anything mentioned in paragraph (a) or (b) or any other such matter.

5.   An order may prohibit—
   (a) discrimination between persons in the prices charged for goods or services;
   (b) anything which the relevant authority considers to be such discrimination;
   (c) procuring others to do anything which is such discrimination or which the relevant authority considers to be such discrimination.

6.   An order may prohibit—
   (a) giving, or agreeing to give in other ways, any preference in respect of the supply of goods or services or in respect of the giving of orders for goods or services;
   (b) giving, or agreeing to give in other ways, anything which the relevant authority considers to be a preference in respect of the supply of goods or services or in respect of the giving of orders for goods or services;
   (c) procuring others to do anything mentioned in paragraph (a) or (b).

7.   An order may prohibit—
   (a) charging, for goods or services supplied, prices differing from those in any published list or notification;
   (b) doing anything which the relevant authority considers to be charging such prices.

8.—(1) An order may regulate the prices to be charged for any goods or services.

   (2)   No order shall be made by virtue of sub-paragraph (1) unless the relevant report in relation to the matter concerned identifies the prices charged for the goods or services as requiring remedial action.

   (3)   In this paragraph "the relevant report" means the report of the Commission which is required by the enactment concerned before an order can be made under this Schedule.

9.   An order may prohibit the exercise of any right to vote exercisable by virtue of the holding of any shares, stock or securities.

General obligations to be performed

10.—(1) An order may require a person to supply goods or services or to do anything which the relevant authority considers appropriate to facilitate the provision of goods or services.

   (2)   An order may require a person who is supplying, or is to supply, goods or services to supply such goods or services to a particular standard or in a particular manner or to do anything which the relevant authority considers appropriate to facilitate the provision of such goods or services to that standard or in that manner.

11.   An order may require any activities to be carried on separately from any other activities.

Acquisitions and divisions

12.—(1) An order may prohibit or restrict—
   (a) the acquisition by any person of the whole or part of the undertaking or assets of another person's business;
   (b) the doing of anything which will or may result in two or more bodies corporate becoming interconnected bodies corporate.

   (2)   An order may require that if—
   (a) an acquisition of the kind mentioned in sub-paragraph (1)(a) is made; or
   (b) anything is done which results in two or more bodies corporate becoming interconnected bodies corporate;
the persons concerned or any of them shall observe any prohibitions or restrictions imposed by or under the order.

   (3)   This paragraph shall also apply to any result consisting in two or more enterprises ceasing to be distinct enterprises (other than any result consisting in two or more bodies corporate becoming interconnected bodies corporate).

13.—(1) An order may provide for—
   (a) the division of any business (whether by the sale of any part of the undertaking or assets or otherwise);
   (b) the division of any group of interconnected bodies corporate.

   (2)   For the purposes of sub-paragraph (1)(a) all the activities carried on by way of business by any one person or by any two or more interconnected bodies corporate may be treated as a single business.

(3)   An order made by virtue of this paragraph may contain such provision as the relevant authority considers appropriate to effect or take account of the division, including, in particular, provision as to—

(a)   the transfer or creation of property, rights, liabilities or obligations;

(b)   the number of persons to whom the property, rights, liabilities or obligations are to be transferred or in whom they are to be vested;

(c)   the time within which the property, rights, liabilities or obligations are to be transferred or vested;

(d)   the adjustment of contracts (whether by discharge or reduction of any liability or obligation or otherwise);

(e)   the creation, allotment, surrender or cancellation of any shares, stock or securities;

(f)   the formation or winding up of any company or other body of persons corporate or unincorporate;

(g)   the amendment of the memorandum and articles or other instruments regulating any such company or other body of persons;

(h)   the extent to which, and the circumstances in which, provisions of the order affecting a company or other body of persons corporate or unincorporate in its share capital, constitution or other matters may be altered by the company or other body of persons concerned;

(i)   the registration of the order under any enactment by a company or other body of persons corporate or unincorporate which is affected by it as mentioned in paragraph (h);

(j)   the continuation, with any necessary change of parties, of any legal proceedings;

(k)   the approval by the relevant authority or another person of anything required by virtue of the order to be done or of any person to whom anything is to be transferred, or in whom anything is to be vested, by virtue of the order; or

(l)   the appointment of trustees or other persons to do anything on behalf of another person which is required of that person by virtue of the order or to monitor the doing by that person of any such thing.

14. The references in paragraph 13 to the division of a business as mentioned in sub-paragraph (1)(a) of that paragraph shall, in the case of an order under section 75, 83, 84, 160 or 161, or an order under paragraph 5, 10 or 11 of Schedule 7, be construed as including references to the separation, by the sale of any part of any undertaking or assets concerned or other means, of enterprises which are under common control (within the meaning of section 26) otherwise than by reason of their being enterprises of interconnected bodies corporate.

Supply and publication of information

15.—(1) An order may require a person supplying goods or services to publish a list of prices or otherwise notify prices.

(2)   An order made by virtue of this paragraph may also require or prohibit the publication or other notification of further information.

16. An order may prohibit any person from notifying (whether by publication or otherwise) to persons supplying goods or services prices recommended or suggested as appropriate to be charged by those persons for those goods or services.

17.—(1) An order may require a person supplying goods or services to publish—

(a)   accounting information in relation to the supply of the goods or services;

(b)   information in relation to the quantities of goods or services supplied;

(c)   information in relation to the geographical areas in which they are supplied.

(2)   In sub-paragraph (1) "accounting information", in relation to a supply of goods or services, means information as to—

(a)   the costs of the supply, including fixed costs and overheads;

(b)   the manner in which fixed costs and overheads are calculated and apportioned for accounting purposes of the supplier; and

(c)   the income attributable to the supply.

18. An order made by virtue of paragraph 15 or 17 may provide for the manner in which information is to be published or otherwise notified.

19. An order may—

(a)   require any person to supply information to the relevant authority;

(b)   where the OFT is not the relevant authority, require any person to supply information to the OFT;

(c) provide for the publication, by the person who has received information by virtue of paragraph (a) or (b), of that information.

National security

20.—(1) An order may make such provision as the person making the order considers to be appropriate in the interests of national security (within the meaning of section 58(1)).

(2)   Such provision may, in particular, include provision requiring a person to do, or not to do, particular things.

Supplementary

21.—(1) An order, as well as making provision in relation to all cases to which it may extend, may make provision in relation to—
    (a) those cases subject to specified exceptions; or
    (b) any particular case or class of case.

(2)   An order may, in relation to the cases in relation to which it applies, make the full provision which may be made by it or any less provision (whether by way of exception or otherwise).

(3)   An order may make provision for matters to be determined under the order.

(4)   An order may—
    (a) make different provision for different cases or classes of case or different purposes;
    (b) make such transitional, transitory or saving provision as the person making it considers appropriate.

22.—(1) An order which may prohibit the doing of anything (or the refraining from doing anything) may in particular by virtue of paragraph 21(2) prohibit the doing of that thing (or the refraining from doing of it) except to such extent and in such circumstances as may be provided by or under the order.

(2)   Any such order may, in particular, prohibit the doing of that thing (or the refraining from doing of it)—
    (a) without the agreement of the relevant authority or another person; or
    (b) by or in relation to a person who has not been approved by the relevant authority or another person.

Interpretation

23. References in this Schedule to the notification of prices or other information are not limited to the notification in writing of prices or other information.

24. In this Schedule "the relevant authority" means—
    (a) in the case of an order to be made by the OFT, the OFT;
    (b) in the case of an order to be made by the Commission, the Commission; and
    (c) in the case of an order to be made by the Secretary of State, the Secretary of State.

[473]

NOTES

Commencement: to be appointed.

(Sch 9 (amendments of sectoral enactments) outside the scope of this work.)

SCHEDULE 10

Section 90

PROCEDURAL REQUIREMENTS FOR CERTAIN ENFORCEMENT UNDERTAKINGS
AND ORDERS

Requirements for accepting undertakings and making orders

1.   Paragraph 2 applies in relation to—
    (a) any undertaking under section 73 or 82 or paragraph 3 or 9 of Schedule 7 (other than an undertaking under the enactment concerned which varies an undertaking under that enactment but not in any material respect); and

(b) any order under section 75, 83 or 84 or paragraph 5, 10 or 11 of Schedule 7 (other than an order under the enactment concerned which is a revoking order of the kind dealt with by paragraphs 6 to 8 below).

2.—(1) Before accepting an undertaking to which this paragraph applies or making an order to which this paragraph applies, the OFT, the Commission or (as the case may be) the Secretary of State (in this Schedule "the relevant authority") shall—

    (a) give notice of the proposed undertaking or (as the case may be) order; and

    (b) consider any representations made in accordance with the notice and not withdrawn.

(2) A notice under sub-paragraph (1) shall state—

    (a) that the relevant authority proposes to accept the undertaking or (as the case may be) make the order;

    (b) the purpose and effect of the undertaking or (as the case may be) order;

    (c) the situation that the undertaking or (as the case may be) order is seeking to deal with;

    (d) any other facts which the relevant authority considers justify the acceptance of the undertaking or (as the case may be) the making of the order;

    (e) a means of gaining access to an accurate version of the proposed undertaking or (as the case may be) order at all reasonable times; and

    (f) the period (not less than 15 days starting with the date of publication of the notice in the case of an undertaking and not less than 30 days starting with that date in the case of an order) within which representations may be made in relation to the proposed undertaking or (as the case may be) order.

(3) A notice under sub-paragraph (1) shall be given by—

    (a) in the case of a proposed order, serving on any person identified in the order as a person on whom a copy of the order should be served a copy of the notice and a copy of the proposed order; and

    (b) in every case, publishing the notice.

(4) The relevant authority shall not accept the undertaking with modifications or (as the case may be) make the order with modifications unless the relevant authority—

    (a) gives notice of the proposed modifications; and

    (b) considers any representations made in accordance with the notice and not withdrawn.

(5) A notice under sub-paragraph (4) shall state—

    (a) the proposed modifications;

    (b) the reasons for them; and

    (c) the period (not less than 7 days starting with the date of the publication of the notice under sub-paragraph (4)) within which representations may be made in relation to the proposed modifications.

(6) A notice under sub-paragraph (4) shall be given by—

    (a) in the case of a proposed order, serving a copy of the notice on any person identified in the order as a person on whom a copy of the order should be served; and

    (b) in every case, publishing the notice.

3.—(1) If, after giving notice under paragraph 2(1) or (4), the relevant authority decides—

    (a) not to accept the undertaking concerned or (as the case may be) make the order concerned; and

    (b) not to proceed by virtue of paragraph 5;

the relevant authority shall give notice of that decision.

(2) A notice under sub-paragraph (1) shall be given by—

    (a) in the case of a proposed order, serving a copy of the notice on any person identified in the order as a person on whom a copy of the order should be served; and

    (b) in every case, publishing the notice.

4. As soon as practicable after accepting an undertaking to which paragraph 2 applies or (as the case may be) making an order to which that paragraph applies, the relevant authority shall (except in the case of an order which is a statutory instrument)—

    (a) serve a copy of the undertaking on any person by whom it is given or (as the case may be) serve a copy of the order on any person identified in the order as a person on whom a copy of the order should be served; and

    (b) publish the undertaking or (as the case may be) the order.

5.—(1) The requirements of paragraph 2(4) (and those of paragraph 2(1)) shall not apply if the relevant authority—

(a) has already given notice under paragraph 2(1) but not paragraph 2(4) in relation to the proposed undertaking or order; and

(b) considers that the modifications which are now being proposed are not material in any respect.

(2) The requirements of paragraph 2(4) (and those of paragraph 2(1)) shall not apply if the relevant authority—

(a) has already given notice under paragraphs 2(1) and (4) in relation to the matter concerned; and

(b) considers that the further modifications which are now being proposed do not differ in any material respect from the modifications in relation to which notice was last given under paragraph 2(4).

Termination of undertakings and orders

6. Paragraph 7 applies where the relevant authority is proposing to—

(a) release any undertaking under section 73 or 82 or paragraph 3 or 9 of Schedule 7 (other than in connection with accepting an undertaking under the enactment concerned which varies or supersedes an undertaking under that enactment); or

(b) revoke any order under section 75, 83 or 84 or paragraph 5, 10 or 11 of Schedule 7 (other than in connection with making an order under the enactment concerned which varies or supersedes an order under that enactment).

7.—(1) Before releasing an undertaking to which this paragraph applies or (as the case may be) revoking an order to which this paragraph applies, the relevant authority shall—

(a) give notice of the proposed release or (as the case may be) revocation; and

(b) consider any representations made in accordance with the notice and not withdrawn.

(2) A notice under sub-paragraph (1) shall state—

(a) the fact that a release or (as the case may be) revocation is proposed;

(b) the reasons for it; and

(c) the period (not less than 15 days starting with the date of publication of the notice in the case of an undertaking and not less than 30 days starting with that date in the case of an order) within which representations may be made in relation to the proposed release or (as the case may be) revocation.

(3) If after giving notice under sub-paragraph (1) the relevant authority decides not to proceed with the release or (as the case may be) the revocation, the relevant authority shall give notice of that decision.

(4) A notice under sub-paragraph (1) or (3) shall be given by—

(a) serving a copy of the notice on the person who gave the undertaking which is being released or (as the case may be) on any person identified in the order being revoked as a person on whom a copy of the order should be served; and

(b) publishing the notice.

8. As soon as practicable after releasing the undertaking or making the revoking order, the relevant authority shall (except in the case of an order which is a statutory instrument)—

(a) serve a copy of the release of the undertaking on the person who gave the undertaking or (as the case may be) serve a copy of the revoking order on any person identified in the order being revoked as a person on whom a copy of that order should be served; and

(b) publish the release or (as the case may be) the revoking order.

Power to dispense with the requirements of the Schedule

9. The relevant authority may dispense with any or all of the requirements of this Schedule if the relevant authority considers that the relevant authority has special reasons for doing so.

[474]

NOTES

Commencement: to be appointed.

(Sch 11 amends the Competition Act 1998 Sch 7, at **[214]***; Sch 12 inserts Sch 7A to the 1998 Act, at* **[219]***; Sch 13 outside the scope of this work.)*

SCHEDULE 14

Sections 238 and 243

SPECIFIED FUNCTIONS

Parts 2, 3, 4, 5, 6, 7, 8 and 11 of the Fair Trading Act 1973 (c 41).

Trade Descriptions Act 1968 (c 29).

Prices Act 1974 (c 24).

Consumer Credit Act 1974 (c 39).

Estate Agents Act 1979 (c 38).

Competition Act 1980 (c 21).

Consumer Protection Act 1987 (c 43).

Property Misdescriptions Act 1991 (c 29).

Timeshare Act 1992 (c 35).

Competition Act 1998 (c 41).

Chapter 3 of Part 10 and Chapter 2 of Part 18 of the Financial Services and Markets Act 2000 (c 8).

An order made under section 95 of that Act.

[475]

NOTES

Commencement: to be appointed.

SCHEDULE 15

Section 241

ENACTMENTS CONFERRING FUNCTIONS

Gun Barrel Proof Act 1868 (cap 113).

Gun Barrel Proof Act 1950 (cap 3).

Trade Descriptions Act 1968.

Unsolicited Goods and Services Act 1971 (c 30).

Fair Trading Act 1973.

Hallmarking Act 1973 (c 43).

Prices Act 1974.

Consumer Credit Act 1974.

Gun Barrel Proof Act 1978 (c 9).

Estate Agents Act 1979.

Competition Act 1980.

National Audit Act 1983 (c 44).

Telecommunications Act 1984 (c 12).

Companies Act 1985 (c 6).

Weights and Measures Act 1985 (c 72).

Airports Act 1986 (c 31).

Gas Act 1986 (c 44).

Financial Services Act 1986 (c 60).

Consumer Protection Act 1987 (c 43).

Copyright, Designs and Patents Act 1988 (c 48).

Water Act 1989 (c 15).

Electricity Act 1989 (c 29).

Courts and Legal Services Act 1990 (c 41).

Broadcasting Act 1990 (c 42).

Property Misdescriptions Act 1991 (c 29).

Water Industry Act 1991 (c 56).

Water Resources Act 1991 (c 57).

Statutory Water Companies Act 1991 (c 58).

Land Drainage Act 1991 (c 59).

Timeshare Act 1992 (c 35).

Railways Act 1993 (c 43).

Coal Industry Act 1994 (c 21).

Trade Marks Act 1994 (c 26).

Gas Act 1995 (c 45).

Broadcasting Act 1996 (c 55).

Competition Act 1998 (c 41).

Financial Services and Markets Act 2000 (c 8).

Government Resources and Accounts Act 2000 (c 20).

Postal Services Act 2000 (c 26).

Utilities Act 2000 (c 27).

Part 1 of the Transport Act 2000 (c 38).

NOTES

Commencement: to be appointed.

(Schs 16–23 (insolvency provisions) outside the scope of this work.)

SCHEDULE 24

Section 276

TRANSITIONAL AND TRANSITORY PROVISIONS AND SAVINGS

Operation of references to OFT before commencement of section 2(3)

1.—(1) This paragraph applies to any provision contained in this Act, or made by virtue of this Act, which contains a reference to the OFT but comes into force before the time at which section 2(3) comes into force.

(2)   Until that time any reference to the OFT is to be taken as a reference to the Director.

Pensions etc of former Directors

2.   In the case of any such person who has held the office of the Director as may be determined by the Secretary of State with the approval of the Minister for the Civil Service—
   (a)   such pension, allowance or gratuity shall be paid to or in respect of him on his retirement or death, or
   (b)   such contributions or payments shall be paid towards provision for such a pension, allowance or gratuity,
as may be so determined.

First financial year of the OFT

3.—(1) If the period beginning with the day on which the OFT is established and ending with the next 31st March is six months or more, the first financial year of the OFT is that period.

(2)   Otherwise the first financial year of the OFT is the period beginning with the day on which it is established and ending with 31st March in the following year.

First annual plan of the OFT

4.—(1) The OFT's first annual plan (as required by section 3(1)) shall be published within the period of three months beginning with the day on which it is established.

(2)   Subject to sub-paragraph (3), that annual plan shall relate to the period beginning with the date of publication and ending with the next 31st March.

(3)   If the period mentioned in sub-paragraph (2) is three months or less, that annual plan shall relate to the period beginning with the date of publication and ending with the 31st March in the following year.

Last annual report of the Director General of Fair Trading

5.—(1) After the abolition of the office of the Director, any duty of his to make an annual report, in relation to any calendar year for which such a report has not been made, shall be performed by the OFT.

(2)   The period between the abolition of that office and the end of the preceding calendar year (if less than 12 months) shall be treated as the calendar year for which the last annual report is required.

(3)   If that period is nine months or more, the OFT shall make the last annual report as soon as practicable after the end of that period.

(4)   Otherwise the OFT shall make the last annual report no later than the making of its first report under section 4(1).

(5)   In this paragraph "annual report" means a report required by section 125(1) of the 1973 Act.

Effect of transfers under section 2

6.—(1) In this paragraph—
   "commencement" means the commencement of section 2(1);
   "transferred" means transferred by section 2(1).

(2)   Anything which—
   (a) has been done by or in relation to the Director for the purposes of or in connection with anything transferred; and
   (b) is in effect immediately before commencement,
shall be treated as if done by or in relation to the OFT.

(3)   Anything (including legal proceedings) which—
   (a) relates to anything transferred; and
   (b) is in the process of being done by or in relation to the Director immediately before it is transferred,
may be continued by or in relation to the OFT.

(4)   Nothing in section 2 or this paragraph affects the validity of anything done by or in relation to the Director before commencement.

First President and Registrar of the Competition Appeal Tribunal

7.   The person who is President of the Competition Commission Appeal Tribunals (under paragraph 4 of Schedule 7 to the 1998 Act) immediately before the commencement of section 12 is on that date to become the President of the Competition Appeal Tribunal as if duly appointed under that section, on the same terms.

8.   The person who is Registrar of Appeal Tribunals (under paragraph 5 of Schedule 8 to the 1998 Act) immediately before the commencement of section 12 is on that date to become the Registrar of the Competition Appeal Tribunal as if duly appointed under that section, on the same terms.

9.   Any person who is a member of the Competition Commission appeal panel (but not a member of the panel of chairmen) immediately before the commencement of section 12 is on that date to become a member of the Competition Appeal Tribunal, on such terms and for such a period as the Secretary of State may determine.

10. Any member of the Competition Commission appeal panel who is, immediately before the commencement of section 12, a member of the panel of chairmen under paragraph 26 of

Schedule 7 to the 1998 Act is on that date to become a chairman of the Competition Appeal Tribunal, on such terms and for such a period as the Lord Chancellor may determine.

11. Nothing in paragraph 7, 8, 9 or 10 applies to any person who, before the commencement of section 12, gives notice to the Secretary of State stating that he does not wish that paragraph to apply to him.

Tribunal rules

12.—(1) Any rules made under section 48 of the 1998 Act which are in force immediately before the commencement of section 15 above shall be treated after that commencement as having been made under section 15.

(2)   The Secretary of State may treat any consultation carried out with the President of the Competition Commission Appeal Tribunals (before the appointment of the President of the Competition Appeal Tribunal) as being as effective for the purposes of section 15(1) as if it had been carried out with the President of the Competition Appeal Tribunal.

Merger references

13.—(1) Subject to paragraphs 15 to 18, the old law shall continue to apply where—
    (a) two or more enterprises have ceased to be distinct enterprises (within the meaning of Part 5 of the 1973 Act); and
    (b) the cessation has occurred before the appointed day.

(2)   Subject to sub-paragraphs (3), (4) and (5) and paragraphs 15 to 18, the old law shall continue to apply in relation to any relevant arrangements which were in progress or in contemplation before the appointed day and are in progress or in contemplation on that day and (if events so require) the actual results of those arrangements where, before the appointed day—
    (a) a merger notice was given, and not rejected under section 75B(7) of the 1973 Act or withdrawn, in relation to the arrangements;
    (b) no merger notice was so given but, in relation to the arrangements—
        (i) a reference was made under section 75 of the 1973 Act;
        (ii) undertakings were accepted under section 75G of that Act; or
        (iii) a decision was made by the Secretary of State neither to make a reference under section 75 of that Act nor to accept undertakings under section 75G of that Act; or
    (c) a merger notice was so given, was rejected under section 75B(7) of the 1973 Act or withdrawn, paragraph (a) does not apply in relation to a different merger notice given in relation to the arrangements and, in relation to the arrangements, paragraph (b)(i), (ii) or (iii) applies.

(3)   Subject to sub-paragraph (8), the new law shall, in a case of the kind mentioned in sub-paragraph (2)(a), apply in relation to any relevant arrangements and (if events so require) the actual results of those arrangements if, on or after the appointed day, a merger notice is rejected under section 75B(7) of the 1973 Act or withdrawn in relation to the arrangements.

(4)   Subject to sub-paragraph (8), the new law shall, in a case of the kind mentioned in sub-paragraph (2)(a), apply in relation to any relevant arrangements and (if events so require) the actual results of those arrangements if—
    (a) the making of a reference under section 64 or 75 of the 1973 Act in relation to those arrangements and (if events so require) the actual results of those arrangements was, immediately before the appointed day and by virtue of section 75C(1)(c), (e) or (g) of that Act, not prevented;
    (b) the period for considering the merger notice has expired (whether before, on or after the appointed day); and
    (c) no reference has been made under section 64 or 75 of the 1973 Act and no undertakings have been accepted under section 75G of that Act.

(5)   Subject to sub-paragraph (8), the new law shall, in a case of the kind mentioned in sub-paragraph (2)(a), apply in relation to any relevant arrangements and (if events so require) the actual results of those arrangements if—
    (a) the making of a reference under section 64 or 75 of the 1973 Act in relation to those arrangements and (if events so require) the actual results of those arrangements becomes, on or after the appointed day and by virtue of section 75C(1)(b), (c), (d), (e) or (g) of that Act, not prevented;

    (b) the period for considering the merger notice has expired (whether before, on or after the appointed day); and

    (c) no reference has been made under section 64 or 75 of the 1973 Act and no undertakings have been accepted under section 75G of that Act.

  (6)   Subject to sub-paragraph (8), the new law shall apply in relation to relevant arrangements and (if events so require) the actual results of those arrangements if—

    (a) the arrangements were in progress or in contemplation before the appointed day and are in progress or in contemplation on that day;

    (b) before the appointed day and in relation to the arrangements—

       (i) no reference was made under section 75 of the 1973 Act;

     (ii) no undertakings were accepted under section 75G of that Act; and

    (iii) a decision neither to make a reference under section 75 of that Act nor to accept undertakings under section 75G of that Act was not made by the Secretary of State; and

    (c) no merger notice was given to the Director or the OFT before that day in relation to the arrangements.

  (7)   Subject to sub-paragraph (8), the new law shall, in a case of the kind mentioned in sub-paragraph (2)(c) (excluding the words from "and" to the end), apply in relation to any relevant arrangements and (if events so require) the actual results of those arrangements if, in relation to the arrangements, sub-paragraph (2)(b)(i), (ii) and (iii) do not apply.

  (8)   Subject to paragraphs 15 to 18, the old law shall continue to apply in relation to concentrations with a Community dimension (within the meaning of the European Merger Regulations) notified before the appointed day to the European Commission under article 4 of those Regulations.

  (9)   In this paragraph references to relevant arrangements which are in progress or in contemplation on the appointed day include references to the actual results of those arrangements if the arrangements were in progress or in contemplation immediately before the appointed day and have, at the beginning of the appointed day, resulted in two or more enterprises ceasing to be distinct enterprises (within the meaning of Part 5 of the 1973 Act).

  (10) In this paragraph—

    "the European Merger Regulations" has the meaning given by section 129(1);

    "merger notice" means a notice under section 75A(1) of the 1973 Act;

    "the new law" means Part 3 of this Act and any related provision of law (including, in particular, any modification made under section 276(2) to that Part or any such provision);

    "the old law" means sections 64 to 75K of the 1973 Act and any related provision of law (including, in particular, any modification made under section 276(2) to those sections or any such provision); and

    "relevant arrangements" means arrangements which might result in two or more enterprises ceasing to be distinct enterprises (within the meaning of Part 5 of the 1973 Act).

Monopoly references

14.—(1) Subject to paragraphs 15 to 18, the old law shall continue to apply in relation to any monopoly reference made before the appointed day under section 50 or 51 of the 1973 Act.

  (2)   No person has to comply on or after the appointed day with a requirement imposed before that day under section 44 of the 1973 Act.

  (3)   In this paragraph—

    "monopoly reference" has the meaning given by section 5(3) of the 1973 Act; and

    "the old law" means Part 4 of the 1973 Act and any related provision of law (including, in particular, any modification made under section 276(2) to that Part or any such provision).

Enforcement undertakings and orders

15.—(1) Section 94(1) to (6) shall apply in relation to any undertaking—

    (a) accepted (whether before, on or after the appointed day) by a Minister of the Crown—

       (i) in pursuance of a proposal under section 56A of the 1973 Act; or

     (ii) under section 56F, 75G or 88 of that Act; and

(b) of a description specified in an order made by the Secretary of State under this paragraph;

as it applies in relation to enforcement undertakings under Part 3.

(2)   Section 94(1) to (6) shall apply in relation to any order made by a Minister of the Crown under section 56, 73, 74, 75K or 89 of the 1973 Act (whether before, on or after the appointed day) and of a description specified in an order made by the Secretary of State under this paragraph as it applies in relation to enforcement orders under Part 3.

(3)   Compliance with—
  (a) an undertaking accepted by a Minister of the Crown under section 88 of the 1973 Act (whether before, on or after the appointed day) and of a description specified in an order made by the Secretary of State under this paragraph; or
  (b) an order made by a Minister of the Crown under section 56, 73, 74 or 89 of the 1973 Act (whether before, on or after the appointed day) and of a description specified in an order made by the Secretary of State under this paragraph;

shall also be enforceable by civil proceedings brought by the Commission for an injunction or for interdict or for any other appropriate relief or remedy.

(4)   Sub-paragraph (3) and section 94(6) as applied by virtue of sub-paragraph (1) or (2) shall not prejudice any right that a person may have by virtue of section 94(4) as so applied to bring civil proceedings for contravention or apprehended contravention of an undertaking or order.

(5)   Sections 93 and 93A of the 1973 Act shall accordingly cease to apply in relation to undertakings and orders to which sub-paragraphs (1) to (3) above apply.

16.—(1) Sub-paragraph (2) applies to any undertaking—
  (a) accepted (whether before, on or after the appointed day) by a Minister of the Crown—
    (i) in pursuance of a proposal under section 56A of the 1973 Act; or
    (ii) under section 56F, 75G or 88 of that Act; and
  (b) of a description specified in an order made by the Secretary of State under this paragraph.

(2)   An undertaking to which this sub-paragraph applies may be—
  (a) superseded by a new undertaking accepted by the relevant authority under this paragraph;
  (b) varied by an undertaking accepted by the relevant authority under this paragraph; or
  (c) released by the relevant authority.

(3)   Subject to sub-paragraph (4) and any provision made under section 276(2), the power of the relevant authority under this paragraph to supersede, vary or release an undertaking is exercisable in the same circumstances, and on the same terms and conditions, as the power of the Minister concerned to supersede, vary or release the undertaking would be exercisable under the 1973 Act.

(4)   The duty under section 75J(b) of the 1973 Act to give advice shall be a duty of the OFT to consider what action (if any) it should take.

(5)   Where the relevant authority has the power by virtue of this paragraph to supersede, vary or release an undertaking accepted by a Minister of the Crown—
  (a) in pursuance of a proposal under section 56A of the 1973 Act; or
  (b) under section 56F, 75G or 88 of that Act;

the Minister concerned shall accordingly cease to have the power under that Act to supersede, vary or release the undertaking.

(6)   In this paragraph "the relevant authority" means—
  (a) in the case of an undertaking accepted in pursuance of a proposal under section 56A of the 1973 Act or an undertaking under section 56F or 75G of that Act, the OFT; and
  (b) in the case of an undertaking accepted under section 88 of that Act, the Commission.

17.—(1) Any order made by a Minister of the Crown under section 56, 73, 74 or 89 of the 1973 Act (whether before, on or after the appointed day) and of a description specified in an order made by the Secretary of State under this paragraph may be varied or revoked by an order made by the Commission under this paragraph.

(2)   Any order made by a Minister of the Crown under section 75K of the 1973 Act (whether before, on or after the appointed day) and of a description specified in an order made by the Secretary of State under this paragraph may be varied or revoked by an order made by the OFT under this paragraph.

(3)   Subject to sub-paragraph (4) and any provision made under section 276(2), the power of the Commission to make an order under sub-paragraph (1), and the power of the OFT to make an order under sub-paragraph (2), is exercisable in the same circumstances, and on the same terms and conditions, as the power of the Minister concerned to make a corresponding varying or revoking order under the 1973 Act would be exercisable.

(4)   The power of the Commission to make an order under sub-paragraph (1), and the power of the OFT to make an order under sub-paragraph (2), shall not be exercisable by statutory instrument and shall not be subject to the requirements of section 134(1) of the 1973 Act.

(5)   Where the Commission or the OFT has the power by virtue of this paragraph to vary or revoke an order made by a Minister of the Crown under section 56, 73, 74, 75K or 89 of the 1973 Act, the Minister concerned shall accordingly cease to have the power to do so under that Act.

18.—(1) Section 94(1) to (6) shall apply in relation to undertakings accepted under paragraph 16 and orders made under paragraph 17 as it applies in relation to enforcement undertakings and enforcement orders under Part 3.

(2)   Compliance with an undertaking accepted by the Commission under paragraph 16 or an order made by it under paragraph 17 shall also be enforceable by civil proceedings brought by the Commission for an injunction or for interdict or for any other appropriate relief or remedy.

(3)   Sub-paragraph (2) and section 94(6) as applied by virtue of sub-paragraph (1) shall not prejudice any right that a person may have by virtue of section 94(4) as so applied to bring civil proceedings for contravention or apprehended contravention of an undertaking or order.

Paragraphs 13 to 18: supplementary provision

19.—(1) In paragraphs 13 to 18 "the appointed day" means such day as the Secretary of State may by order made by statutory instrument appoint; and different days may be appointed for different purposes.

(2)   An order made by the Secretary of State under paragraph 15, 16 or 17—
    (a) may make different provision for different purposes; and
    (b) shall be made by statutory instrument which shall be subject to annulment in pursuance of a resolution of either House of Parliament.

Designation orders under Schedule 4 to the 1998 Act

20.—(1) Subject to sub-paragraph (2), the repeals made by section 207 do not affect—
    (a) the operation of Schedule 4 to the 1998 Act in relation to any application for designation of a professional rule which is made before the commencement date;
    (b) the operation of section 3(1)(d) of and Schedule 4 to the 1998 Act in relation to any designation effected by an order made before the commencement date or on an application mentioned in paragraph (a).

(2)   No designation order (whenever made) shall have any effect in relation to any period of time after the end of the transitional period.

(3)   Subject to sub-paragraph (2) a designation order may be made after the end of the transitional period on an application mentioned in sub-paragraph (1)(a).

(4)   For the purposes of this paragraph—
    "commencement date" means the day on which section 207 comes into force;
    "designation" means designation under paragraph 2 of Schedule 4 to the 1998 Act; and
    "the transitional period" means the period of three months beginning with the commencement date.

Proceedings under Part 3 of the 1973 Act

21. The repeal of section 133(3) of the 1973 Act does not affect any right to disclose information for the purposes of any proceedings before the Restrictive Practices Court to which paragraph 42 of Schedule 13 to the 1998 Act applies.

PART I
STATUTES

Supplementary

22.—Any provision made by any of paragraphs 1 to 21 shall not apply if, and to the extent that, an order under section 276(2) makes alternative provision or provides for it not to apply.

[477]

NOTES

Commencement: to be appointed.

(Sch 25 contains minor and consequential amendments; in so far as these are relevant to this work, they have been incorporated at the appropriate place.)

SCHEDULE 26

Section 278

REPEALS AND REVOCATIONS

Reference	Extent of repeal or revocation
Registered Designs Act 1949 (c 88)	In section 11A(1), paragraphs (a) and (b)
Agricultural Marketing Act 1958 (c 47)	In section 19A(2), the words from the beginning of the subsection to "this section"
Public Records Act 1958 (c 51)	In Schedule 1, in Part 2, the entry relating to the Office of the Director General of Fair Trading
Parliamentary Commissioner Act 1967 (c 13)	In Schedule 2, the entry relating to the Office of the Director General of Fair Trading
Trade Descriptions Act 1968 (c 29)	Section 28(5) and (5A)
Local Government Act 1972 (c 70)	Section 81(1) and (2)
Fair Trading Act 1973 (c 41)	Sections 1 to 3 In section 5— in subsection (1), paragraph (a) and the word "or" at the end of it, and paragraph (c) and the word "or" before it; subsection (3) Sections 6 to 22 In section 30, subsection (3) and, in subsection (5), the words ", subsection (3)" Sections 34 to 42 Sections 44 to 56G Sections 63 to 76 In section 77— subsection (1)(b) and (c); in subsection (2), paragraph (b) and the word "or" before it; subsection (3) in subsection (5), paragraph (b) and the word "and" before it Sections 78 to 81 In section 82— in subsection (1), the words "the Advisory Committee or", and, in paragraph (b), the words "the Advisory Committee or of" and the words ", as the case may be,"; in subsection (2), the words "the Advisory Committee or of"; subsection (3);

Reference	Extent of repeal or revocation
Fair Trading Act 1973 (c 41)—*contd*	in subsection (4), the words "other than a monopoly reference limited to the facts" In section 83— in subsection (1), the words from "any report of the Advisory Committee" to "applies, or"; in subsections (3) and (4), the words "of the Advisory Committee or" Section 84 Section 86 Sections 88 to 93A In section 93B(1), the words "or under the Competition Act 1980" Sections 124 and 125 In section 129(4), the words "or 46(2)" Sections 130 and 131 In section 132(1), the words "section 46," Section 133 In section 137(2), the definitions of "the Advisory Committee" and "the Director" In section 138, the words "Parts II and III," Schedules 1, 2 and 4 to 9 In Schedule 12, the entry relating to the Public Records Act 1958
Prices Act 1974 (c 24)	In the Schedule, paragraph 12
Consumer Credit Act 1974 (c 39)	Section 5 Section 161(2) Section 174 In section 189(1), the definition of "Director" In Schedule 4, paragraph 28
House of Commons Disqualification Act 1975 (c 24)	In Schedule 1, in Part 3, the entry relating to the Director General of Fair Trading
Northern Ireland Assembly Disqualification Act 1975 (c 25)	In section 51(1), paragraphs (a) and (b)
Patents Act 1977 (c 37)	In Schedule 5, paragraph 7
Estate Agents Act 1979 (c 38)	Section 9(5) Section 10 Section 26(2) In section 33(1), the definition of "Director"
Competition Act 1980 (c 21)	In section 11, in subsection (1), paragraph (c) and the word "or" before it, and subsections (2), (9) and (9A) Section 13 In section 16, subsection (1) and, in subsection (2), the words "or of the Director" In section 17, in subsections (1), (3) and (4), the words "or 13(5)" Section 18 In section 19, subsections (1) to (3), (4)(c), (d) and (f) and (5) and (6) Sections 20, 21 and 24 In section 31, in subsection (1), the words "or regulations", in subsection (3), the words "regulations under this Act or", and subsection (4)

PART I
STATUTES

Reference	Extent of repeal or revocation
Telecommunications Act 1984 (c 12)	In section 13, subsections (9) and (9A) In section 50— subsection (1); in subsection (6), the words from "or paragraph" to "Act 1994"; subsection (7) In Schedule 4, paragraphs 57, 60(2), 72 and 73
Dentists Act 1984 (c 24)	In Schedule 5, paragraph 6
Companies Consolidation (Consequential Provisions) Act 1985 (c 9)	In Schedule 2, the entry relating to section 92 of the Fair Trading Act 1973
Administration of Justice Act 1985 (c 61)	In section 60(6), the words "in paragraph 10A of Schedule 4 to the Fair Trading Act 1973 and"
Insolvency Act 1985 (c 65)	In Schedule 8, paragraph 22
Bankruptcy (Scotland) Act 1985 (c 66)	In Schedule 3, paragraphs 1 to 3 and 8 to 8C
Weights and Measures Act 1985 (c 72)	In Schedule 12, paragraph 6
Airports Act 1986 (c 31)	In section 44, subsections (3) and (3A) In section 54, subsection (3) In Schedule 4, paragraphs 3, 4, 6 and 7
Gas Act 1986 (c 44)	In section 24, subsections (7) and (7A) In section 26A, subsections (12) and (13) Section 27(3) and (4) In section 36A, subsections (1) and (9) In section 41E, subsections (7) and (8) In Schedule 7, paragraphs 15, 19, 27 and 28
Insolvency Act 1986 (c 45)	In section 212— in subsection (1)(b), the word ", administrator"; in subsection (2), in each place, the words "or administrator"; in subsection (4), the words "or administrator" Section 230(1) In section 231, in each place, the word "administrator," In section 232, the word "administrator," In section 240(1), the word "and" before paragraph (c) In section 245(3), the word "or" before paragraph (c) Section 275 Section 282(5) In section 292(1)(a), the words "except at a time when a certificate for the summary administration of the bankrupt's estate is in force," In section 293(1), the words "and no certificate for the summary administration of the bankrupt's estate has been issued," In section 294(1), paragraph (b) and the word "and" before it

Reference	Extent of repeal or revocation
Insolvency Act 1986 (c 45)—*contd*	In section 297— subsections (2) and (3); in subsection (4), the words "but no certificate for the summary administration of the estate is issued" Section 298(3) In section 300— subsection (5); in subsections (6) and (7), the words "or (5)" In section 310(1), the words ", on the application of the trustee," Sections 361 and 362 Section 405 In section 427— in subsection (1), the words "England and Wales or"; subsection (7) In Schedule 6, paragraphs 1 to 7 In Schedule 10— the entry for section 12(2); the entry for section 15(8); the entry for section 18(5); the entry for section 21(3); the entry for section 22(6); the entry for section 23(3); the entry for section 24(7); the entry for section 27(6); in the entry for section 31, the word "Undischarged"; the entries for sections 361 and 362
Consumer Protection Act 1987 (c 43)	Section 38 In Schedule 4, paragraphs 2(2), 3, 4 and 7
Consumer Protection (Northern Ireland) Order 1987 (SI 1987/2049 (NI 20))	In Schedule 3, paragraphs 2 and 4
Income and Corporation Taxes Act 1988 (c 1)	In Schedule 29, in paragraph 32, in the Table, the references relating to the Insolvency Act 1986
Criminal Justice Act 1988 (c 33)	Section 62(2)(a)
Copyright, Designs and Patents Act 1988 (c 48)	In Schedule 7, paragraph 15
Control of Misleading Advertisements Regulations 1988 (SI 1988/915)	Regulation 7(6)(a), (b), (d) and (e)
Water Act 1989 (c 15)	In Schedule 25, paragraphs 45(3), 47, 57 and 59(2)
Electricity Act 1989 (c 29)	In section 12, subsections (8) and (8A) In section 14A, subsections (12) and (13) In section 43— subsection (1); in subsection (6), the words from "or paragraph" to "Act 1994"; subsection (7) In section 56C, subsections (7) and (8) In Schedule 16, paragraphs 16, 17(2), 24, 25 and 36
Companies Act 1989 (c 40)	Sections 146 to 150 Section 152

Reference	Extent of repeal or revocation
Companies Act 1989 (c 40)—*contd*	In Schedule 14, paragraphs 4(5) and 8 In Schedule 20, paragraphs 3 to 11, 14 to 16 and 19
Courts and Legal Services Act 1990 (c 41)	Section 46(3) In section 119(1), the definition of "the Director" In Schedule 18, paragraphs 4, 6, 22 and 23
Broadcasting Act 1990 (c 42)	Section 187(3) Section 192 In section 194A(9), the definition of "Director" In Schedule 4, in paragraph 4, sub-paragraphs (7) and (7A), in paragraph 5, sub-paragraph (5), in paragraph 8, sub-paragraphs (3) and (4) and, in paragraph 10, the definition of "the Director" In Schedule 20, paragraphs 20 and 28
EEC Merger Control (Consequential Provisions) Regulations 1990 (SI 1990/ 1563)	Regulation 2
Property Misdescriptions Act 1991 (c 29)	In the Schedule, paragraphs 2 and 7
Finance Act 1991 (c 31)	In Schedule 2, paragraphs 21A and 22
Water Industry Act 1991 (c 56)	In section 14, subsections (7) and (7A) In section 31— subsection (1); in subsection (8), the words from "or paragraph" to "Act 1994"; subsection (9) In section 36(1), the definition of "the 1973 Act" and the word "and" at the end of it
Water Consolidation (Consequential Provisions) Act 1991 (c 60)	In Schedule 1, paragraphs 24, 26, 33, 34 and 52
Social Security (Consequential Provisions) Act 1992 (c 6)	In Schedule 2, paragraph 73
Timeshare Act 1992 (c 35)	In Schedule 2, paragraphs 2(1) and 5
Electricity (Northern Ireland) Order 1992 (SI 1992/ 231 (NI 1))	Article 15(8) and (8A) In Article 46, paragraph (1), in paragraph (6), the words from "or paragraph" to "Act 1994", and paragraph (7) In Schedule 12, paragraphs 9, 10, 14, 20, 21 and 31
Finance Act 1993 (c 34)	Section 36(1) to (3)
Railways Act 1993 (c 43)	In section 4, in subsection (2)(a), the words from "in cases where" to "market", and subsection (8) Section 13(8) and (8A) Section 66(1) and (2) In section 67— subsection (1); in subsection (7), the words from "was made" to "that it"; in subsection (8), the words from "or paragraph" to "Act 1994"; subsection (10)

Reference	Extent of repeal or revocation
Railways Act 1993 (c 43)—*contd*	In section 83(1), the definition of "the Director" In Schedule 12, paragraphs 7, 8, 11, 12(2) and (3) and 26
Finance Act 1994 (c 9)	In Schedule 6, paragraph 13(1) and (2) In Schedule 7, paragraph 7(2)
Coal Industry Act 1994 (c 21)	In Schedule 9, paragraphs 14, 15, 21 and 23
Value Added Tax Act 1994 (c 23)	In Schedule 14, paragraph 8
Deregulation and Contracting Out Act 1994 (c 40)	Section 7(1) Section 9 Schedule 2 In Schedule 4, paragraph 2 In Schedule 11, paragraphs 2(3) and (4) and 4(6)
Airports (Northern Ireland) Order 1994 (SI 1994/426)	Article 35(3) and (3A) In Article 45, paragraph (3) In Schedule 9, paragraphs 2, 4, 7 and 8
Finance Act 1995 (c 4)	In section 17, the words "section 386(1) of the Insolvency Act 1986) (categories of preferential debts) and"
Finance Act 1996 (c 8)	In Schedule 5, paragraph 12(1) and (2)
Employment Rights Act 1996 (c 18)	In sections 166(7)(a) and 183(3)(a), the words "or an administration order." Section 189(4)
Channel Tunnel Rail Link Act 1996 (c 61)	Section 22(1)
Gas (Northern Ireland) Order 1996 (SI 1996/ 275 (NI 2))	Article 15(9) and (9A) Article 18(3) Article 23(1) and (8) In Schedule 6, the entries relating to sections 16 and 133 of the Fair Trading Act 1973, the entry relating to the Estate Agents Act 1979, the entry relating to the Competition Act 1980 and the entries relating to section 38 of the Consumer Protection Act 1987
Deregulation (Fair Trading Act 1973) (Amendment) (Merger Reference Time Limits) Order 1996 (SI 1996/345)	The whole Order
Finance Act 1997 (c 16)	In Schedule 2, paragraph 6
Justices of the Peace Act 1997 (c 25)	Section 65
Competition Act 1998 (c 41)	In section 3(1), paragraph (d) and the word "or" before it Section 46(3)(h) Section 48 Sections 55 and 56 In section 59(1), the definitions of "appeal tribunal" and "the Director" In section 61(1), the definition of "the Director" Sections 66 and 67 Schedule 4 In Schedule 5, in paragraph 5(2), the words "for him"

Reference	Extent of repeal or revocation
Competition Act 1998 (c 41)—*contd*	In Schedule 6, in paragraph 5(2), the words "for him"
	In Schedule 7—
	in paragraph 1, the definitions of "appeal panel member" and "President" and, in the definition of "general functions", paragraph (a) and the word "or" at the end of it;
	paragraph 2(1)(a), (3)(a) and (4);
	paragraph 4;
	in paragraph 5, in sub-paragraph (1), the word "management", sub-paragraph (2)(b) and, in sub-paragraph (3), the words "and paragraph 5 of Schedule 8";
	paragraph 6(5);
	paragraph 7(4);
	in paragraph 9, sub-paragraph (2) and in sub-paragraph (3), the words "and the President"
	paragraph 10;
	in paragraph 15(7), paragraph (b) and the word "or" before it;
	paragraphs 23 to 27
	In Schedule 8, paragraphs 1 and 4 to 14
	In Schedule 10—
	paragraph 1;
	paragraph 2(7) and (10);
	paragraph 3(6) and (9) to (11);
	paragraph 4(6) and (9);
	paragraph 5(7), (9), (10) and (13);
	paragraph 6(6) and (9);
	paragraph 7(6) and (9);
	paragraph 8(6) and (9) to (11);
	paragraph 9(5);
	paragraph 10(4);
	paragraph 12(4) and (6);
	paragraph 13(8);
	paragraph 15(4);
	paragraph 17(6)
	Schedule 11
	In Schedule 12—
	paragraph 1(4) to (7) and (14);
	paragraph 3;
	paragraph 4(3), (4), (9), (10), (12) and (15)(a);
	paragraph 10
Competition Act 1998 (Competition Commission) Transitional, Consequential and Supplemental Provisions Order 1999 (SI 1999/ 506)	Article 22
Financial Services and Markets Act 2000 (c 8)	Section 351(1) to (3) and (7)
	In Schedule 14, paragraph 3
	Schedule 19
Finance Act 2000 (c 17)	In Schedule 7, paragraphs 2 and 3
Regulation of Investigatory Powers Act 2000 (c 23)	In section 32(6), the word "and" at the end of paragraph (l)
	In section 35(10), the word "or" at the end of paragraph (b)

Reference	Extent of repeal or revocation
Regulation of Investigatory Powers Act 2000 (c 23)—*contd*	In section 36— in subsection (1), the word "or" at the end of paragraph (c); in subsection (6), the word "and" at the end of paragraph (f) In section 37(1), the word "or" at the end of paragraph (c)
Postal Services Act 2000 (c 26)	Section 20
Utilities Act 2000 (c 27)	Section 40(2), (4) and (5) In Schedule 6, paragraph 9
Transport Act 2000 (c 38)	Section 12(9), (10) and (11) In section 85(3), the words "the 1973 Act or" Section 90(8) Section 91(5) In Schedule 8, paragraphs 11 and 12 In Schedule 10, in paragraph 4(3), the words "for him"
Insolvency Act 2000 (c 39)	Section 9 In Schedule 4, paragraph 13(3)
Competition Act 1998 (Transitional, Consequential and Supplemental Provisions) Order 2000 (SI 2000/311)	Article 9(5)
Finance Act 2001 (c 9)	In Schedule 5, paragraphs 17(1) and (2) and 18
Anti-terrorism, Crime and Security Act 2001 (c 24)	In Schedule 4, paragraphs 5, 9, 10, 11, 17, 27, 30 and 33
Stop Now Orders (EC Directive) Regulations 2001 (SI 2001/1422)	The whole Regulations
EC Competition Law (Articles 84 and 85) Enforcement Regulations 2001 (SI 2001/2916)	Regulation 35(1) and (2)

[478]

NOTES

Commencement: to be appointed.

PART II
STATUTORY INSTRUMENTS

PART II
STATUTORY INSTRUMENTS

A. PROCEDURAL MATTERS

COMPETITION ACT 1998 (APPLICATION FOR DESIGNATION OF PROFESSIONAL RULES) REGULATIONS 1999

(SI 1999/2546)

NOTES

Made: 9 September 1999.
Authority: Competition Act 1998, ss 59(1), 71, Sch 4, para 3(2)(b).
Commencement: 1 October 1999.

1 Citation and commencement

These Regulations may be cited as the Competition Act 1998 (Application for Designation of Professional Rules) Regulations 1999 and shall come into force on 1st October 1999.

[2001]

NOTES

Commencement: 1 October 1999.

2 Applications for designation

An application for designation of the rules of a body regulating a professional service or the persons who provide or wish to provide that service shall be made in writing to the Secretary of State for Trade and Industry, 1 Victoria Street, London SW1H 0ET accompanied by a copy of the rules to which the application relates.

[2002]

NOTES

Commencement: 1 October 1999.

3   The application shall state—
  (a) the name of the applicant body;
  (b) to which type of professional service listed in Part II of Schedule 4 of the Act the rules relate;
  (c) the date on which the rules and any amendments which they include were adopted; and
  (d) an address and telephone number for correspondence.

[2003]

NOTES

Commencement: 1 October 1999.

4   The application shall be signed by an officer of the body who shall certify that he is authorised by the body to make the application on its behalf.

[2004]

NOTES

Commencement: 1 October 1999.

COMPETITION ACT 1998 (CONCURRENCY) REGULATIONS 2000

(SI 2000/260)

NOTES
Made: 7 February 2000.
Authority: Competition Act 1998, ss 54(4), (5), (6), 71.
Commencement: 1 March 2000.

ARRANGEMENT OF REGULATIONS

1 Citation

These Regulations may be cited as the Competition Act 1998 (Concurrency) Regulations 2000 and shall come into force on 1st March 2000.

[2005]

NOTES
Commencement: 1 March 2000.

2 Interpretation

In these Regulations—
  (a) "the Act" means the Competition Act 1998;
  (b) "applicant" means a person who has submitted an application;
  (c) "application" means an application made under section 4(6), 13, 14, 21 or 22 of the Act or made under sections 13 or 14 of the Act, as extended by Regulations made pursuant to section 12(3) of the Act;
  (d) "Director's rules" means rules made by the Director and approved by an order made by the Secretary of State in accordance with section 51 of the Act;
  (e) "prescribed functions" means—
      (i) the exercise by any competent person of any of the functions of the Director under the provisions of sections 25, 26, 27, 28 and 29 of the Act;
      (ii) making a decision, as defined in section 46(3) of the Act;
      (iii) giving written notification in accordance with the Director's rules that a competent person proposes to make a decision that either the Chapter I prohibition or the Chapter II prohibition has been infringed and considering any representations made pursuant to that notification;
      (iv) giving written notification in accordance with the Director's rules that a competent person proposes to grant an individual exemption subject to condition or obligations in accordance with section 4(3) of the Act and considering any representations made pursuant to that notification;
      (v) issuing guidance in accordance with either section 13 or section 21 of the Act;
      (vi) making a provisional decision in accordance with the Director's rules;

(vii)   exercising functions under paragraph 4 of Schedule 1 or paragraph 2 of Schedule 3 or in accordance with an order made pursuant to section 50 of the Act;

(f)   "Part I functions" means any functions of the Director under the provisions of Part I of the Act which can be exercised by a regulator;

(g)   "working day" means a day which is not a Saturday, Sunday or an official holiday on which the Office of Fair Trading is closed.

[2006]

NOTES

Commencement: 1 March 2000.

Director: the Enterprise Act 2002, s 2(1), at **[255]**, provides that, as from the coming into force of that section in accordance with s 279 at **[463]**, the functions of the Director General of Fair Trading, his property, rights and liabilities are transferred to the Office of Fair Trading. Accordingly, (by virtue of s 2(2), (3) of the 2002 Act) the office of the Director is abolished, and any reference to the Director in any enactment, instrument or other document passed or made before the commencement of s 2(1) shall have effect as if it were a reference to the Office of Fair Trading. For transitional provisions in connection with the transfer, see s 276(1) of, and Sch 24, para 6 to, the 2002 Act at **[477]**.

3 Information

For the purposes of determining which competent persons have jurisdiction to exercise Part I functions in relation to a case—

(a)   the Director General of Fair Trading may send to any other competent person details of information submitted as an application;

(b)   a competent person may send to any other competent person details of information he receives in relation to a proposed application; and

(c)   a competent person may send to any other competent person details of any information he receives that an infringement of the Chapter I or the Chapter II prohibition may have taken place.

[2007]

NOTES

Commencement: 1 March 2000.

Director General of Fair Trading: see the note "Director" to reg 2 at **[2006]**.

4 Applications

All applications shall be submitted to the Director General of Fair Trading in accordance with the Director's rules.

[2008]

NOTES

Commencement: 1 March 2000.

Director General of Fair Trading: see the note "Director" to reg 2 at **[2006]**.

5 Determination of the exercise of prescribing functions

(1)   If the Director General of Fair Trading considers that a regulator has or may have concurrent jurisdiction to exercise Part I functions in relation to an agreement or conduct in respect of which an application has been submitted, he shall—

(a)   send one copy of the information submitted as that application to that regulator; and

(b)   inform the applicant in writing that he has done so.

(2)   If a competent person proposes to exercise any of the prescribed functions in relation to a case which is not the subject of an application and he considers that another competent person has or may have concurrent jurisdiction to exercise Part I

functions in relation to that case, he shall inform that other competent person of his intention to exercise prescribed functions in relation to that case.

(3) Where either—
- (a) the Director General of Fair Trading has sent information submitted as an application to another competent person in accordance with paragraph (1) above; or
- (b) a competent person has informed another competent person of his intention to exercise prescribed functions in accordance with paragraph (2) above in relation to a case

all such competent persons (together "the relevant competent persons") shall agree who shall exercise prescribed functions in relation to that case.

(4) When agreement has been reached in accordance with paragraph (3) above, the case shall be transferred to the competent person who is to exercise prescribed functions in relation to that case and the Director General of Fair Trading shall as soon as practicable inform in writing—
- (a) the relevant competent persons; and
- (b) in cases where an application has been submitted, the applicant,

which competent person is to exercise prescribed functions in relation to the case.

[2009]

NOTES

Commencement: 1 March 2000.

Director General of Fair Trading: see the note "Director" to reg 2 at **[2006]**.

6 Dispute

(1) If the relevant competent persons are not able to reach agreement in accordance with regulation 5(3) above within a reasonable time, the Director General of Fair Trading shall inform the Secretary of State in writing.

(2) Any relevant competent person may make representations in writing to the Secretary of State no later than the date upon which the Director General of Fair Trading informs the Secretary of State in accordance with paragraph (1) above of the failure to reach agreement.

(3) The Secretary of State shall within 8 working days of receipt of a communication made in accordance with paragraph (1) above—
- (a) determine which competent person shall exercise prescribed functions in relation to the case and direct that the case shall be transferred to that competent person; and
- (b) inform in writing—
  - (i) all relevant competent persons; and
  - (ii) in cases where an application has been made, the applicant which competent person is to exercise jurisdiction in relation to the case and the date of transfer of the case.

(4) In making a determination in accordance with paragraph (3)(a) above the Secretary of State shall take into consideration any representations made in accordance with paragraph (2) above.

[2010]

NOTES

Commencement: 1 March 2000.

Director General of Fair Trading: see the note "Director" to reg 2 at **[2006]**.

7 Avoidance of double jeopardy

(1) Where two or more competent persons may have concurrent jurisdiction in relation to a case, no competent person shall exercise any prescribed functions in relation to that case before agreement has been reached in accordance with regulation 5(3) or a determination has been made in accordance with regulation 6(3)(a) above as to which competent person is to exercise prescribed functions in relation to a case.

(2) Subject to regulation 8 below, once agreement has been reached in accordance with regulation 5(3) or a determination has been made in accordance with regulation 6(3)(a) above as to which competent person is to exercise prescribed functions in relation to a case, no other competent person shall exercise any of the prescribed functions in relation to that case.

[2011]

NOTES

Commencement: 1 March 2000.

8 Transfer

(1) Subject to paragraphs (2), (5) and (6) below, a competent person who has exercised any Part I functions in relation to a case ("the transferor") may agree with another competent person who has concurrent jurisdiction to exercise Part I functions in relation to that case ("the transferee") to transfer the case to the transferee.

(2) If the transferor and the transferee propose to agree a transfer in accordance with paragraph (1) above, the transferor shall notify in writing either—
  (a) in the case of an application, the applicant, or
  (b) in other cases, subject to paragraph (5) below, the undertaking which is the subject of the exercise of Part I functions in that case,

of the proposed transfer and shall invite the recipient of the notice to make written representations upon the proposal within seven working days of the date of that notice.

(3) If, after taking into consideration any representations made in accordance with paragraph (2) above, a transfer is agreed in accordance with paragraph (1) in respect of a case which is the subject of an application the transferor shall—
  (a) send the original application, together with all supporting documents which have been supplied to the transferor to support that application, to the transferee, and
  (b) inform the applicant in writing—
    (i) that the transferee is to exercise jurisdiction in relation to the case and of the reasons for the transfer; and
    (ii) of the date of the transfer.

(4) Subject to paragraph (5) below, if a transfer is agreed in accordance with paragraph (1) for a case which is not the subject of an application, the transferor shall inform the undertaking which is the subject of the exercise of Part I functions in that case in writing that the transferee is to exercise jurisdiction in relation to the case from the date of the transfer and of the reasons for this transfer.

(5) The transferor shall not be under any obligation to notify an undertaking in accordance with paragraph (2)(b) above or to inform an undertaking in accordance with paragraph (4) above if—
  (a) the transfer takes place before agreement has been reached in accordance with regulation 5(3) or a determination has been made in accordance with regulation 6(3)(a) above as to which competent person is to exercise prescribed functions in relation to a case; or
  (b) the transferor has not informed that undertaking that he has exercised Part I functions in relation to the case; or

(c) that undertaking is not an applicant but is a party to an agreement or conduct which is the subject of an application.

(6) Where a transfer of an application takes place in accordance with regulation 5(4) or 6(3)(a) above—

(a) paragraphs (1), (2) and (3) above shall have no application;

(b) the Director General of Fair Trading shall as soon as reasonably practicable send the original application, together with all supporting documents which have been supplied to him to support that application to the competent person who is to exercise prescribed functions in relation to the case.

[2012]

NOTES

Commencement: 1 March 2000.
Director General of Fair Trading: see the note "Director" to reg 2 at **[2006]**.

9 Use of staff

(1) A competent person who wishes to exercise Part I functions in relation to a case ("the appointor") may appoint an officer of another competent person ("the appointee") to act as his officer in relation to that case provided that the competent person of which the appointee is an officer gives his written consent to the appointment on or prior to the date upon which the appointment commences.

(2) An appointee shall be an officer of the appointor for the purposes of sections 27 to 29 inclusive of the Act.

(3) Any act or omission of the appointee within the terms of the appointment shall be deemed to be an act or omission of the appointor.

[2013]

NOTES

Commencement: 1 March 2000.

10 Service of notices

Any notice to be served on any person under these Regulations may be served by post, and a letter containing that notice shall be deemed to be properly addressed if it is addressed to that person at its registered office or last known residence or last known place of business in the United Kingdom.

[2014]

NOTES

Commencement: 1 March 2000.

COMPETITION ACT 1998 (NOTIFICATION OF EXCLUDED AGREEMENTS AND APPEALABLE DECISIONS) REGULATIONS 2000

(SI 2000/263)

NOTES

Made: 7 February 2000.
Authority: Competition Act 1998, ss 12(3), 46(3), 47(1), 59(1), 71, Sch 13, para 19(3).
Commencement: 1 March 2000.

ARRANGEMENT OF REGULATIONS

1 Citation and commencement

These Regulations may be cited as the Competition Act 1998 (Notification of Excluded Agreements and Appealable Decisions) Regulations 2000 and shall come into force on 1st March 2000.

[2015]

NOTES

Commencement: 1 March 2000.

2 Interpretation

In these Regulations "the Act" means the Competition Act 1998 and references to sections and Schedules are references to sections of and Schedules to the Act.

[2016]

NOTES

Commencement: 1 March 2000.

3 General

Sections 13 (notification for guidance), 14 (notification for a decision), 15 (effect of guidance) and 16 (effect of a decision) and Schedule 5 (notification under Chapter I: procedure) shall apply, with the modifications set out below, to an application for guidance or a decision in respect of an agreement to which the Chapter I prohibition does not apply by reason of—

(a) an exclusion in respect of which the Director has given a direction withdrawing the exclusion or is considering whether to give such a direction, or

(b) a transitional period under Schedule 13.

[2017]

NOTES

Commencement: 1 March 2000.

Director: the Enterprise Act 2002, s 2(1), at **[255]**, provides that, as from the coming into force of that section in accordance with s 279 at **[463]**, the functions of the Director General of Fair Trading, his property, rights and liabilities are transferred to the Office of Fair Trading. Accordingly, (by virtue of s 2(2), (3) of the 2002 Act) the office of the Director is abolished, and any reference to the Director in any enactment, instrument or other document passed or made before the commencement of s 2(1) shall have effect as if it were a reference to the Office of Fair Trading. For transitional provisions in connection with the transfer, see s 276(1) of, and Sch 24, para 6 to, the 2002 Act at **[477]**.

4 Notification for guidance

Section 13 shall apply with the addition at the end of subsection (2) of the words "or would be likely to if the prohibition applied.".

[2018]

NOTES
   Commencement: 1 March 2000.

5 Notification for a decision

Section 14 shall apply with the insertion in subsection (2) after paragraph (b) of—

   "; or
   (c)   if it has not been infringed, whether the Chapter I prohibition
         would be infringed if it applied to the agreement."

                                                                      [2019]

NOTES
   Commencement: 1 March 2000.

6 Effect of guidance

Section 15 shall apply with the insertion in subsection (1) at the end of paragraph (a) of—

   "(aa)   the agreement would be unlikely to infringe the Chapter I prohibition
           if it applied;".

                                                                      [2020]

NOTES
   Commencement: 1 March 2000.

7 Effect of a decision that the Chapter I prohibition has not been infringed

Section 16 shall apply with the insertion at the end of subsection (1) of the words "or would not do so if the prohibition applied to the agreement."

                                                                      [2021]

NOTES
   Commencement: 1 March 2000.

8 Schedule 5

Schedule 5 shall apply to notifications of agreements under sections 13 and 14 as applied by these Regulations, subject to the modifications set out in regulation 9, save that an applicant shall not be required under Schedule 5 to do any act or supply any information to the Director in respect of an application for guidance or a decision that he has already done or supplied to the Director in respect of a direction withdrawing an exclusion or terminating the transitional period in respect of an agreement or of the Director's consideration of whether to give such a direction.

                                                                      [2022]

NOTES
   Commencement: 1 March 2000.
   Director: see the note to reg 3 at **[2017]**.

9   Paragraph 3 shall apply with the insertion in subparagraph (1)(a) after "prohibition," of—

   "(aa)   or that the agreement concerned would infringe the Chapter I
           prohibition if it applied.".

                                                                      [2023]

10 Appealable decisions

The following are prescribed as decisions for the purpose of sections 46 and 47—

(a) a decision of the Director imposing conditions or obligations subject to which a parallel exemption is to have effect, or varying or removing any such conditions or obligations; and

(b) a decision of the Director under section 14, as applied by Regulation 5 of these Regulations, that the Chapter I prohibition would be infringed if it applied to the agreement.

[2024]

COMPETITION ACT 1998 (DIRECTOR'S RULES) ORDER 2000

(SI 2000/293)

1 Citation and Commencement

This Order may be cited as the Competition Act 1998 (Director's rules) Order 2000 and shall come into force on 1st March 2000.

[2025]

2 Approval of the Director's Rules

The Secretary of State hereby approves without modification the rules made by the Director which are set out in the Schedule hereto.

[2026]

PART II
STATUTORY INSTRUMENTS

SCHEDULE
DIRECTOR'S RULES

1. Form of application

(1)   An application under section 13 or 14 for an agreement to be examined, or under section 21 or 22 for conduct to be considered, shall consist of—

(a) Form N;

(b) the copies of Form N required by rule 3 below; and

(c) the fee payable under rule 6 below.

(2)   The documents referred to in sub-paragraphs (1)(a) and (b) above shall be submitted to the Director General of Fair Trading, and the fee referred to in sub-paragraph (1)(c) above shall be paid in accordance with rule 6 below.

2. Joint applications

Where a joint application is submitted, Form N shall be submitted to the Director General of Fair Trading by or on behalf of all the applicants, and a joint representative may be appointed as authorised to act on behalf of some or all of the applicants for the purposes of these rules.

3. Copies

(1)   Subject to paragraph (2) below, two copies of Form N, in addition to the original, shall be submitted to the Director General of Fair Trading.

(2)   If, in the applicant's opinion, a regulator, or more than one regulator, has or may have concurrent jurisdiction with the Director General of Fair Trading under Part I, one extra copy of Form N shall be submitted to the Director General of Fair Trading for each such regulator.

(3)   Supporting documents submitted as part of Form N shall be either originals or true copies, and the applicant shall certify that each copy is a true copy of the original.

4. Content of application

(1)   The information submitted as Form N shall, subject to paragraph (3) below, be correct and complete.

(2)   If the applicant considers that the Director would find any part of the information contained in the application to be confidential, in the sense given to that word by sub-paragraph (1)(c) of rule 30 below, he shall set out that part of the information in a separate annex to the application marked "confidential information" and provide a written explanation as to why he considers that the Director should treat it as such.

(3)   The Director General of Fair Trading may, by giving notice in writing to the applicant, dispense with the obligation to submit any particular information, including any supporting document, forming part of Form N, if he considers that such information or document is unnecessary for the examination of the agreement, or the consideration of the conduct, which is the subject of the application.

(4)   Where the applicant knows of material changes in the information contained in the application he shall without delay communicate those changes to—

    (a)   the Director General of Fair Trading; or

    (b)   if the Director General of Fair Trading has informed the applicant, in accordance with regulations made under section 54 (concurrency), that a regulator will be exercising prescribed functions (as defined in such regulations) in relation to the agreement or conduct which is the subject of the application, that regulator.

5. Date of application

(1)   Except where paragraph (3) below applies, an application is made (and notification for the purposes of sections 13, 14, 21 or 22, whichever is applicable, is given) on the date on which—

    (a)   Form N is received by the Director General of Fair Trading; and

    (b)   any fee payable in respect of the application has been paid in accordance with rule 6 below.

(2)   The Director General of Fair Trading shall acknowledge receipt of an application by giving notice in writing to the applicant without delay.

(3)   Where—

    (a)   the Director General of Fair Trading; or

    (b)   if the Director General of Fair Trading has informed the applicant, in accordance with regulations made under section 54 (concurrency), that a regulator will be exercising prescribed functions (as defined in such regulations) in relation to the agreement or conduct which is the subject of the application, that regulator,

finds that the information submitted as Form N is incomplete he shall, without delay and in any event within one month from the date on which that information was received by the Director General of Fair Trading and any fee payable in respect of the application has been paid in accordance with rule 6 below, give notice in writing to the applicant of which information, by reference to Annex 1 hereto, is outstanding.

(4)   Where the Director has invoked paragraph (3) above he shall give notice in writing to the applicant of such time limit as that Director considers is appropriate for the outstanding information to be received by him.

(5)   Where the Director has invoked paragraph (3) above the application shall be made (and notification for the purposes of sections 13, 14, 21 or 22, whichever is applicable, shall be given) on the date on which he receives the outstanding information and any fee payable in respect of the application has been paid in accordance with rule 6 below.

(6)   If the Director who has invoked paragraph (3) above has not received the outstanding information by the date of expiry of the time limit notified to the applicant under paragraph (4) above, or of such further period, if any, as he considers appropriate, he shall return the information submitted as Form N to the applicant and shall inform him in writing that his application has not been made in accordance with this rule.

6. Fees for applications

(1)   A fee of the amount referred to in paragraph (2) below shall be payable by the applicant in connection with the exercise by the Director of any of the following functions—

    (a) examining an agreement in respect of which an application under section 13 has been made;

    (b) examining an agreement in respect of which an application under section 14 has been made;

    (c) considering conduct in respect of which an application under section 21 has been made; and

    (d) considering conduct in respect of which an application under section 22 has been made.

(2)   The amount of the fee payable under paragraph (1) above shall be—

    (a) in a case falling within sub-paragraph (a) or (c) of that paragraph, the amount specified in Part 1 of Annex 2 hereto; and

    (b) in a case falling within sub-paragraph (b) or (d) of that paragraph, the amount specified in Part 2 of Annex 2 hereto.

(3)   Where a joint application is submitted the applicants shall be jointly and severally liable for any fee payable in respect of the application.

(4)   The fee shall be paid to the Director General of Fair Trading.

(5)   The fee shall be payable when Form N is submitted to the Director General of Fair Trading.

(6)   The Director General of Fair Trading shall repay the whole of the fee to the applicant if—

    (a) the Director returns the information submitted as Form N to the applicant under rule 5(6) above; or

    (b) the Director determines the application by exercising his discretion not to give guidance or make a decision.

(7)   A fee payable under this rule shall be treated as having been paid to the Director General of Fair Trading on the day on which the correct amount of the fee has been transferred to the bank account of the Office of Fair Trading.

7. Notification of application to other parties

Notification by an applicant under paragraph 2(2) of Schedule 5 or 6 shall be written and shall be given within seven working days from the date on which the applicant receives acknowledgement of receipt of his application by the Director General of Fair Trading; the applicant shall provide a copy of the notification to the Director General of Fair Trading without delay.

8. Public register

(1)   The Director General of Fair Trading shall maintain a register in which there shall be entered, in respect of every application made under section 14 or 22, a summary of the nature and objectives of the agreement or conduct which is the subject of the application (as referred to in Part 4 of Annex 1 hereto) and an indication of the final outcome of the application.

(2)   The register shall be open to public inspection—

    (a) at the Office of Fair Trading, between 10.00 am and 4.30 pm on every working day; and

    (b) on the Office of Fair Trading's website on the Internet.

9. Provisional decision

(1)   If the Director proposes to make a provisional decision he shall consult the applicant and those persons whom the applicant has identified in the application as being the other parties to the agreement, or the other persons, if any, who are engaged in the conduct, as the case may be.

(2)   If the Director makes a provisional decision he shall state, in the written notification of the decision to the applicant, the facts on which he bases the decision and his reasons for it.

(3)   Subject to rule 25 below, if the Director makes a provisional decision he shall give written notice of it to those persons whom the applicant has identified in the application as

being the other parties to the agreement, or the other persons, if any, who are engaged in the conduct, as the case may be, stating the facts on which he bases the decision and his reasons for it.

10. Giving guidance

(1)   Where the Director gives guidance, he shall do so in writing to the applicant, stating the facts on which he bases the guidance and his reasons for it.

(2)   Where the Director determines an application for guidance by exercising his discretion not to give guidance, he shall give written notice to the applicant of that fact and shall repay the whole of the fee in accordance with rule 6(6)(b) above.

11. Further action after guidance

If, having given guidance of the kind referred to in section 15(1) or 23(1), the Director proposes to take further action under Part I, he shall consult the person to whom he gave the guidance.

12. Consultation of public following certain applications

(1)   On an application under section 14 for an agreement to be examined—
    (a) if the Director proposes to grant an individual exemption, whether or not subject to conditions or obligations, he shall consult the public; and
    (b) if the Director proposes to make a decision that the Chapter I prohibition has not been infringed, he may consult the public.

(2)   If, on an application under section 22 for conduct to be considered, the Director proposes to make a decision that the Chapter II prohibition has not been infringed, he may consult the public.

13. Investigations

(1)   An officer shall grant a request of the occupier of premises entered by the officer ("the occupier") to allow a reasonable time for the occupier's legal adviser to arrive at the premises before the investigation continues, if the officer considers it reasonable in the circumstances to do so and if he is satisfied that such conditions as he considers it appropriate to impose in granting the occupier's request are, or will be, complied with.

(2)   For the purposes of paragraph (1) above, "a reasonable time" means such period of time as the officer considers is reasonable in the circumstances.

(3)   A person required by the Director under section 26(6)(a)(ii) to provide an explanation of a document may be accompanied by a legal adviser.

14. Proposed infringement and conditional exemption decisions

(1)   If the Director proposes to make a decision that the Chapter I prohibition or the Chapter II prohibition has been infringed he shall give written notice—
    (a) where an application has been made, to the applicant and, subject to rules 25 and 26 below, to those persons whom the applicant has identified in the application as being the other parties to the agreement, or the other persons, if any, who are engaged in the conduct, as the case may be, which that Director considers has led to the infringement; and
    (b) where no application has been made, subject to rules 25 and 26 below, to each person who that Director considers is a party to the agreement, or is engaged in the conduct, as the case may be, which that Director considers has led to the infringement.

(2)   If the Director proposes to grant an individual exemption subject to conditions or obligations, he shall give written notice to the applicant and, subject to rules 25 and 26 below, to those persons whom the applicant has identified in the application as being the other parties to the agreement to which the application relates.

(3)   A written notice given under paragraph (1) or (2) above shall state the facts on which the Director relies, the matters to which he has taken objection, the action he proposes and his reasons for it.

(4)   A written notice given under paragraph (1) or (2) above shall specify a period within which each person referred to in sub-paragraph (1)(a) or (b) or paragraph (2) above,

whichever is applicable, may indicate to the Director any part of the information contained in the notice which he considers the Director would find to be confidential, in the sense given to that word by sub-paragraph (1)(c) of rule 30 below.

(5)   Subject to paragraph (6) below, the Director shall give each person referred to in sub-paragraph (1)(a) or (b) or paragraph (2) above, whichever is applicable, a reasonable opportunity to inspect the documents in that Director's file relating to the proposed decision.

(6)   The Director may withhold any document—
- (a) to the extent that it contains information which a person has stated to that Director to be, and which that Director has found to be, confidential, in the sense given to that word by sub-paragraph (1)(c) of rule 30 below;
- (b) which is, in the opinion of that Director, otherwise confidential; or
- (c) which is internal, in the sense given to that word by sub-paragraph (1)(f) of rule 30 below.

(7)   Subject to rules 25 and 26 below, the Director shall give each person referred to in sub-paragraph (1)(a) or (b) or paragraph (2) above, whichever is applicable, written notice of the period within which that person may make written representations to him on the information referred to in paragraph (3) above.

(8)   The Director shall give each person referred to in sub-paragraph (1)(a) or (b) or paragraph (2) above, whichever is applicable, a reasonable opportunity to make oral representations to him on the information referred to in paragraph (3) above.

15. Notice of decision

(1)   If the Director has made a decision as to whether or not an agreement has infringed the Chapter I prohibition, or as to whether or not conduct has infringed the Chapter II prohibition, he shall, without delay—
- (a) give written notice of the decision—
  - (i)   where the decision was made following an application, to the applicant and, subject to rules 25 and 26(2) below, to those persons whom the applicant has identified in the application as being the other parties to the agreement, or the other persons, if any, who are engaged in the conduct, as the case may be; and
  - (ii) where no application has been made, subject to rules 25 and 26(2) below, to each person who that Director considers is a party to the agreement, or is engaged in the conduct, as the case may be,

  stating in the decision the facts on which he bases it and his reasons for making it; and
- (b) publish the decision.

(2)   Where the Director determines an application for a decision by exercising his discretion not to give a decision, he shall—
- (a) give written notice of that fact to—
  - (i)   the applicant; and
  - (ii) subject to rules 25 and 26 below, those persons whom the applicant has identified in the application as being the other parties to the agreement, or the other persons, if any, who are engaged in the conduct, as the case may be; and
- (b) repay the whole of the fee in accordance with rule 6(6)(b) above.

16. Further action after a decision

If, having made a decision that an agreement has not infringed the Chapter I prohibition, or that conduct has not infringed the Chapter II prohibition, the Director proposes to take further action under Part I, he shall—
- (a) where the decision was made following an application, consult the applicant and, subject to rules 25 and 26 below, those persons whom the applicant has identified in the application as being the other parties to the agreement, or the other persons, if any, who are engaged in the conduct, as the case may be, which is the subject of the decision; and
- (b) where no application has been made, subject to rules 25 and 26 below, consult each person who that Director considers is a party to the agreement, or is engaged in the conduct, as the case may be, which is the subject of the decision.

17. Directions and penalties

(1)   Where the Director gives a direction to a person under section 32 or 33, he shall at the same time inform that person in writing of the facts on which he bases the direction and his reasons for giving it.

(2)   Where the Director requires an undertaking to pay a penalty under section 36, he shall at the same time inform that undertaking in writing of the facts on which he bases the penalty and his reasons for requiring that undertaking to pay it.

(3)   The Director shall publish directions given under section 32, 33 or 35.

18. Interim measures

(1)   Subject to paragraph (2) below, if the Director proposes to give a direction under section 35, he shall give each person to whom he proposes to give the direction a reasonable opportunity to inspect the documents in that Director's file relating to the proposed direction.

(2)   The Director may withhold any document—
  (a) to the extent that it contains information which a person has stated to that Director to be, and which that Director has found to be, confidential, in the sense given to that word by sub-paragraph (1)(c) of rule 30 below;
  (b) which is, in the opinion of that Director, otherwise confidential; or
  (c) which is internal, in the sense given to that word by sub-paragraph (1)(f) of rule 30 below.

(3)   Where the Director gives a direction to a person under section 35, he shall at the same time inform that person in writing of the facts on which he bases the direction and his reasons for giving it.

19. Application for extension of individual exemption

(1)   An application under section 4(6) for an extension of the period for which an individual exemption has effect shall consist of Form N, and the copies of Form N required under paragraph (4) below, and shall be submitted to the Director General of Fair Trading.

(2)   If the Director proposes to grant the application, he shall consult the public.

(3)   If the Director has made a decision as to whether or not to grant the application, he shall—
  (a) give written notice of the decision to—
      (i)   the applicant; and
      (ii) subject to rules 25 and 26(2) below, those persons whom the applicant has identified in the application as being the other parties to the agreement; and
  (b) publish the decision,
stating in the decision the facts on which he bases it, his reasons for it and, if appropriate, the period of extension granted.

(4)   Rules 2 (joint applications), 3 (copies), 4 (content of application), 5 (date of application) and 8 (public register) above shall apply to an application submitted under this rule as they apply, to the extent that they apply, to an application submitted under rule 1 above; rule 5(1) and (5) above shall also apply as if the parts in brackets were omitted from them.

20. Cancellation etc of individual exemption

(1)   If the Director proposes to take any of the steps mentioned in section 5(1), he shall consult the public, the person who applied for the exemption and, subject to rules 25 and 26 below, those persons whom that person identified in his application as being the other parties to the agreement to which the exemption relates.

(2)   If the Director issues a notice in writing under section 5(1), he shall—
  (a) give notice in writing of his decision to do so to—
      (i)   the person who applied for the exemption; and
      (ii) subject to rules 25 and 26(2) below, those persons whom the person who applied for the exemption identified in his application as being the other parties to the agreement; and
  (b) publish the decision,
stating in the decision the facts on which he bases it and his reasons for it.

21. Cancellation etc of parallel exemption

(1)   The circumstances in which the Director may exercise the powers in section 10(5) are where he finds that an agreement which benefits from a parallel exemption nevertheless has effects in the United Kingdom, or a part of it, which are incompatible with the conditions laid down in section 9.

(2)   If the Director proposes to exercise any of the powers in section 10(5) he shall, subject to rules 25 and 26 below, consult each person who he considers is a party to the agreement, and he may consult the public.

(3)   Subject to rules 25 and 26(2) below, if the Director has decided to exercise any of the powers in section 10(5), he shall give notice in writing of his decision to each person who he considers is a party to the agreement, stating in the decision the facts on which he bases it and his reasons for it, and he shall publish the decision.

(4)   Subject to rules 25 and 26 below the Director shall exercise the powers in section 10(5) by giving notice in writing to each person who he considers is a party to the agreement.

22. Withdrawal of exclusions

(1)   Subject to rules 25 and 26 below, if the Director proposes to give a direction under paragraph 4 of Schedule 1 or paragraph 2 or 9 of Schedule 3, or in accordance with an order made under section 50, to the effect that an exclusion made by a provision specified in paragraph (2) below does not apply to an agreement, he shall consult each person who he considers is a party to the agreement.

(2)   The provisions specified for the purposes of paragraph (1) above are—
   (a) paragraph 1 of Schedule 1 (mergers);
   (b) paragraph 2(1) of Schedule 3 (section 21(2) agreements);
   (c) paragraph 9(1) of Schedule 3 (agricultural products); and
   (d) an order made under section 50 (vertical agreements and land agreements).

(3)   The period specified for the purposes of paragraph 4(4) of Schedule 1 and paragraphs 2(6) and 9(6) of Schedule 3 is ten working days from the date on which the person in question receives notice in writing requiring him to give information to the Director.

(4)   If the Director has given a direction referred to in paragraph (1) above, he shall publish it.

23. Termination of transitional period

(1)   Subject to rules 25 and 26 below, if the Director proposes to give a direction under paragraph 37 of Schedule 13, he shall consult each person who he considers is a party to the agreement.

(2)   The period specified for the purposes of paragraph 38(2) of Schedule 13 is ten working days from the date on which the person in question receives the requirement in writing to give information to the Director.

(3)   The Director shall publish a direction given under paragraph 37 of Schedule 13 after the date on which the direction takes effect; if the direction is revoked, he shall publish a notice of that fact.

24. Application for extension of transitional period

(1)   An application under paragraph 36 of Schedule 13 for the extension of transitional period shall—
   (a) be submitted in writing either to the Director General of Fair Trading or to a regulator who, in the applicant's opinion, has concurrent jurisdiction with the Director General of Fair Trading under paragraph 36 of Schedule 13 ("the appropriate Director");
   (b) comply with paragraph (2) below; and
   (c) include the documents specified in paragraph (3) below.

(2)   An application submitted under paragraph (1) above shall—
   (a) be signed by the applicant or by a duly authorised representative of the applicant;
   (b) contain an explanation of—
       (i) the purpose of the agreement;

     (ii) the basis for the applicant's belief that there is a transitional period;

    (iii) the need for an extension of the transitional period; and

    (iv) the likely application of the Chapter I prohibition to the agreement at the end of the transitional period, including any grounds for believing that an exemption from that prohibition is likely; and

  (c) specify the length of the transitional period, the date of its expiry and the period of extension applied for.

(3)   The documents specified for the purposes of paragraph (1) above are the following—

  (a) two copies of the application;

  (b) three copies of the agreement, each copy certified by the applicant to be a true copy of the original; and

  (c) where the application is signed by a solicitor or other representative of an applicant, written proof of that representative's authority to act on that applicant's behalf.

(4)   If either the Director General of Fair Trading or a regulator—

  (a) refuses an application submitted to him under paragraph (1) above; or

  (b) grants the application, or grants an extension which is of shorter duration than that applied for,

he shall give written notice of his decision to the applicant not less than one month before the date of expiry of the transitional period, specifying, if appropriate, the period of extension granted.

(5)   Where the appropriate Director finds that he does not have jurisdiction to determine an application submitted to him under paragraph (1) above, he shall without delay return it to the applicant.

(6)   Subject to rules 25 and 26(2) below, if the Director General of Fair Trading or a regulator extends a transitional period on his own initiative, he shall give written notice of his decision to each person who he considers is a party to the agreement, specifying the period of extension granted.

(7)   Rules 2 (joint applications), 4 (content of application) and 5(1) and (2) (date of application) above shall apply to an application under this rule with the following modifications—

  (a) Rule 2 shall apply as if the reference to "Form N" were a reference to "the application", and as if the reference to "Director General of Fair Trading" were a reference to "appropriate Director";

  (b) Rule 4 shall apply as if—

    (i) the reference in paragraph (1) to "information submitted as Form N" were a reference to "application";

    (ii) the references in paragraph (2) to "Director" were references to "appropriate Director";

    (iii) in paragraph (3) the reference to "Director General of Fair Trading" were a reference to "appropriate Director", the words "forming part of Form N" were replaced with the words "required by these rules for an application under paragraph 36 of Schedule 13", and "the agreement, or the consideration of the conduct, which is the subject of" were omitted; and

    (iv) sub-paragraphs (4)(a) and (b) were replaced with the words "the appropriate Director"; and

  (c) Rule 5(1) shall apply as if the words "Except where paragraph (3) below applies, an" were replaced with the word "The", and the part in brackets were omitted, and as if in sub-paragraph (1)(a) the reference to "Form N" were a reference to "the application" and the reference to "Director General of Fair Trading" were a reference to "appropriate Director"; rule 5(2) shall apply as if the reference to "Director General of Fair Trading" were a reference to "appropriate Director".

(8)   If the Director General of Fair Trading or a regulator extends a transitional period, he shall publish a notice of that fact, specifying the period of extension granted.

25. Associations of undertakings

(1)   Where a rule requires the Director to give written notice, or notice in writing, of any matter to an association of undertakings and the notice does not relate to an agreement or to conduct which is the subject of an application to that Director by that association, he shall give such notice to the director, secretary, manager or other similar officer of the association on its behalf.

(2)   Where a rule requires the Director to give written notice, or notice in writing, of any matter to each of more than fifty members of an association of undertakings, he may, instead of giving such notice to any such member, give such notice to the director, secretary, manager or other similar officer of the association on that member's behalf, provided that individual notice shall be given to any member who has made an application to that Director in respect of the agreement or the conduct to which the notice relates.

26. Time limits and giving notices

(1)   Where it is not reasonably practicable for the Director to give—
-   (a)   written notice to a person—
    -   (i)   other than the applicant, under rule 14(1), (2) or (7) or rule 15(2)(a) above;
    -   (ii)   other than the applicant, in order to consult that person under rule 16 above;
    -   (iii)   other than the person who applied for the exemption and the public, in order to consult that person under rule 20(1) above; or
    -   (iv)   in order to consult that person under rule 21(2) (in the case of this rule, other than the public), 22(1) or 23(1) above, or rule 28(6) below; or
-   (b)   notice in writing to a person under rule 21(4) above,

in particular having regard to the number of persons to whom such notice is required to be given, he may, instead of so doing, take all the steps mentioned in paragraph (3) below.

(2)   Where it is not reasonably practicable for the Director to give—
-   (a)   written notice of the decision to a person, other than the applicant, under rule 15(1)(a) or 19(3)(a) above;
-   (b)   written notice of his decision under rule 24(6) above;
-   (c)   written notice of his decision to a person, other than the applicant, under rule 28(7) below;
-   (d)   notice in writing of his decision to a person under rule 20(2)(a), in the case of this rule, other than the person who applied for the exemption, or 21(3) above; or
-   (e)   written notice in order to consult a third party under rule 30(3) below,

in particular having regard to the number of persons to whom such notice is required to be given, he may, instead of so doing, take all the steps mentioned in sub-paragraph (3)(b) below.

(3)   The steps mentioned for the purposes of paragraphs (1) and (2) above are the following—
-   (a)   publish the notice by means of entry in the register maintained by the Director General of Fair Trading under rule 8 above; and
-   (b)   cause the notice to be published in—
    -   (i)   the London, Edinburgh and Belfast Gazettes;
    -   (ii)   at least one national daily newspaper; and
    -   (iii)   if there is in circulation an appropriate trade journal which is published at intervals not exceeding one month, in such trade journal.

(4)   Except where paragraph (1) or (2) above is invoked, where these rules allow or require written notice, or notice in writing, to be given to a person, such notice shall be treated as having been given on the date on which that person receives it.

(5)   Where paragraph (1) or (2) above is invoked, the notice shall be treated as having been given on the date of its publication in accordance with the paragraph invoked.

(6)   Where the time prescribed by these rules for doing any act expires on a day which is not a working day, the act is in time if done before 6 pm on the next following working day.

(7)   Where an act done in accordance with these rules is done on a day which is not a working day, or after 6 pm on a working day, the act shall be treated as done on the next following working day.

27. Confidential third party information

(1)   If a person gives information to the Director in connection with the exercise of any of the Director's functions under Part I, or under paragraphs 36 or 37 of Schedule 13, in relation to an agreement to which that person is not a party, or in relation to conduct in which that person has not engaged, and that person considers that the Director would find any part of the information to be confidential, in the sense given to that word by sub-paragraph (1)(c) of rule

30 below, he shall set out that part of the information in a separate annex marked "confidential information" and provide a written explanation as to why he considers that the Director should treat it as such.

(2)   The Director shall, if he proposes to disclose, in connection with the exercise of any of his functions under Part I, or under paragraph 36 or 37 of Schedule 13, any of the information contained in an annex provided in accordance with paragraph (1) above, give the person who provided the information—

(a) written notice of his proposed action; and

(b) a reasonable opportunity to make representations to him,

if it is reasonably practicable for him to do so.

28. Third party appeals

(1)   An application under section 47(1) asking the Director to withdraw or vary a decision shall—

(a) be submitted in writing to that Director within one month from the date of publication of that decision by means of entry in the register maintained by the Director General of Fair Trading under rule 8 above;

(b) comply with paragraph (2) below; and

(c) include the documents specified in paragraph (3) below.

(2)   An application submitted under paragraph (1) above shall be signed by the applicant, or by a duly authorised representative of the applicant, and shall state the applicant's reasons—

(a) for considering that he has a sufficient interest in the decision referred to in paragraph (1) above; or

(b) where he claims to represent persons who have a sufficient interest in that decision—

(i) for claiming that he represents those persons; and

(ii) for claiming that those persons have a sufficient interest in that decision.

(3)   The documents specified for the purposes of paragraph (1) above are the following—

(a) three copies of the application; and

(b) where the application is signed by a solicitor or other representative of an applicant, written proof of that representative's authority to act on that applicant's behalf.

(4)   The application is made on the date on which it is received by the Director to whom the appeal is made; that Director shall acknowledge receipt of the application by giving notice in writing to the applicant without delay.

(5)   Where the applicant knows of material changes in the information contained in the application he shall without delay communicate those changes to the Director to whom the application is made.

(6)   If the Director proposes to grant the application, he shall, subject to rules 25 and 26 above, consult all persons whom he was required by these rules to notify of the decision referred to in paragraph (1) above.

(7)   If the Director grants the application, he shall give written notice of his decision to the applicant, and, subject to rules 25 and 26(2) above, to all persons whom he was required by these rules to notify of the decision referred to in paragraph (1) above, stating in his decision the facts on which he bases it and his reasons for it, and he shall publish his decision.

29. Modification of rules for notification of excluded agreements

These rules shall apply, with the following modifications, to an application made under section 13 or 14 as modified by regulations made under section 12(3) and paragraph 19(3) of Schedule 13 (notification of excluded agreements)—

(a) rule 14 shall apply with the insertion in paragraph (1) after the word "infringed" of: ", or that the Chapter I prohibition would be infringed if it applied to the agreement," and with the insertion in sub-paragraph (1)(a) after the words "has led" of: "or, in the case of an agreement which would infringe the Chapter I prohibition if it applied to the agreement, would lead,";

(b) rule 15 shall apply with the insertion in paragraph (1) after the words "Chapter I prohibition" of: ", or as to whether or not the Chapter I prohibition would be infringed if it applied to the agreement"; and

(c) rule 16 shall apply with the insertion after the words "Chapter I prohibition" of: ", or would not do so if the Chapter I prohibition applied to the agreement".

30. Interpretation and supplemental

(1)   In these rules—

(a) "agreement" shall be construed by reference to section 2(5);

(b) "applicant" means—

(i) in rules 2, 3(2) and (3), 4(2) and (3), 5(2), (3), (4) and (6), 6(1), (3) and (6), 7, 24(1) to (3), and 28(2) and (3)(b) above, person who is making the application; and

(ii) in rules 4(4), 9, 10, 14, 15, 16, 19(3)(a), 24(4) and (5), and 28(4), (5) and (7) above, person who has made the application;

(c) information is confidential if it is—

(i) commercial information the disclosure of which would, or might, significantly harm the legitimate business interests of the undertaking to which it relates; or

(ii) information relating to the private affairs of an individual the disclosure of which would, or might, significantly harm his interests;

(d) "the Director" means the Director General of Fair Trading or a regulator who has concurrent jurisdiction to exercise the functions of the Director General of Fair Trading under Part I;

(e) "Form N" means, subject to rule 4(3) above—

(i) the information, including any supporting document, required by Annex 1 hereto; and

(ii) the declaration made in the form set out in Part 2A of Annex 1 hereto;

(f) "internal" document includes the following—

(i) a document produced within the office of either the Director General of Fair Trading or a regulator concerning a case;

(ii) correspondence between the Director General of Fair Trading and a regulator, or between regulators, concerning a case; and

(iii) correspondence between the Director General of Fair Trading, or a regulator, and a government department or another competition authority, concerning a case;

(g) "an officer" means an investigating officer within the meaning of section 27(1) or a named officer of the Director authorised by a warrant issued under section 28;

(h) "regulator" has the meaning given to it by section 54; and

(i) "working day" means day which is not Saturday, Sunday or any other day on which the Office of Fair Trading is closed for business.

(2)   Where the Director, if he proposes to take action, is required to consult a person, he shall—

(a) except where otherwise indicated, give written notice to that person; and

(b) state in that notice the action he proposes, his reasons for it and the period within which that person may make written representations to him on these matters.

(3)   Where the Director, if he proposes to take action—

(a) is required to consult the public; or

(b) proposes to consult the public in exercise of his discretion to do so,

he shall publish a notice stating the action he proposes, his reasons for it and the period within which written representations may be made to him on these matters, and shall, subject to rules 25 and 26(2) above, consult any third party, within the meaning of paragraph 12(2) of Schedule 9, who appears to him likely to be affected by the action he proposes.

(4)   Where the Director is required to publish a decision, a proposal or any other information, he shall do so by means of entry in the register maintained by the Director General of Fair Trading under rule 8 above.

(5)   References in these rules to numbered Parts, sections, Schedules or paragraphs are, unless the contrary intention appears, to the Parts, sections, Schedules or paragraphs so numbered in the Competition Act 1998.

ANNEX 1

FORM N
**INFORMATION REQUIRED FOR APPLICATIONS FOR GUIDANCE OR A
DECISION UNDER CHAPTERS I AND II OF THE COMPETITION ACT 1998**

PART 1: INTRODUCTION

This document lists the information and supporting documents which must be provided when making an application for guidance under section 13 or 21 or an application for a decision under section 14 or 22.

If the Applicant(s) considers that the Director would find any part of the information contained in the application to be confidential, in the sense given to that word by rule 30(1), he must set out that part of the information in a separate annex to the application marked "confidential information" and provide a written explanation as to why he considers that the Director should treat it as such.

This document must also be used when making an application under section 4(6) (see rule 19).

PART 2: INFORMATION TO BE PROVIDED BY THE UNDERTAKING(S) MAKING THE APPLICATION

1   *INFORMATION ABOUT THE UNDERTAKING(S) SUBMITTING THE APPLICATION (THE "APPLICANT(S)") AND THE OTHER PARTIES TO THE AGREEMENT*

    1.1   Please give the full name, address (by registered office, where appropriate, and principal place of business, if different), telephone and fax numbers and e-mail address (where available) of the Applicant(s) and a brief description of the nature of its business. If the Applicant(s) is a partnership, sole trader or other unincorporated body trading under a business name, give the name(s) and address(es) of the partners or proprietor(s). Please quote any reference which should be used.

    1.2   Please give the full name, address, telephone and fax numbers and e-mail address (where available) of any representative(s) who has been authorised to act for the Applicant(s), indicating whom they represent and in what capacity (eg a solicitor).

    1.3   Where the declaration to be made in the form set out in Part 2A is signed by a solicitor or other representative of the Applicant(s), please provide written proof of that representative's authority to act on the Applicant(s)'s behalf.

    1.4   If a joint application is being submitted, indicate whether or not a joint representative has been appointed. If a joint representative has been appointed, give his full name, address (by registered office, where appropriate, and principal place of business, if different), telephone and fax numbers and e-mail address (where available), and indicate whom he represents.

    1.5   Please provide the Standard Industrial Classification code (as listed in the United Kingdom Standard Industrial Classification of Economic Activities 1992, produced by the Office for National Statistics and published by The Stationery Office in 1997 with ISBN code 011620923–2 (to supersede the 1992 edition)) for the goods or services to which the agreement or conduct that is the subject of the application relates, if the code is known. If the code is not known, describe the goods or services involved as fully and accurately as possible.

    1.6   Please give the full names, addresses (by registered office, where appropriate, and principal place of business, if different), telephone and fax numbers, nature of business, and brief description of the other parties to the agreement and any other persons engaging in the conduct which is the subject of the application, together with the name of a contact at each undertaking concerned, their address, telephone and fax numbers and details of their position in the undertaking.

    1.7   Please provide details of the steps taken or to be taken to notify all the other parties to the agreement or conduct which is the subject of the application of whom the Applicant(s) is aware that the application is being submitted. Indicate whether those parties have received a copy of the application and if so, whether confidential information (as defined in rule 30(1)) was included in the copy of the application. If the Applicant(s) considers that it is not practicable to notify the other parties of the application, please give the reasons why it is not practicable.

1.8 Please identify the groups to which each party to the agreement or conduct which is the subject of the application belongs. For the purposes of the information required by this form, a group relationship exists where one undertaking—
— owns more than half the capital or business assets of another undertaking; or
— has the power to exercise more than half the voting rights in another undertaking; or
— has the power to appoint more than half the members of the supervisory board, board of directors or bodies legally representing the undertaking; or
— has the right to manage the affairs of another undertaking.

An undertaking which is jointly controlled by several other undertakings (eg a joint venture) forms part of the group of each of these undertakings.

2   PURPOSE OF THE APPLICATION

2.1 Specify whether the application is being made in relation to the Chapter I prohibition, the Chapter II prohibition or both.

2.2 Specify whether the application is for guidance or a decision.

2.3 If the application is for a decision in relation to the Chapter I prohibition and an individual exemption is sought (see further 9 below), specify the date from which the exemption is required to have effect, giving reasons.

2.4 State which provisions or effects of the agreement or conduct which is the subject of the application might in the Applicant's view raise questions of compatibility with the Chapter I prohibition and/or the Chapter II prohibition, and give reasons for that view.

2.5 If the application is for an extension of an individual exemption, state the date of expiry of the existing exemption and the reasons why an extension is sought. Please also give details of any changes that have occurred in the relevant market(s) (see 6.2 and 6.3 below) and in the agreement itself since the grant of the exemption. Specify how any such changes impact on the fulfilment by the agreement of the conditions set out in section 9 of the Act. Please also enclose a copy of the decision letter granting the exemption.

2.6 If the agreement which is the subject of the application is considered to qualify for an exemption (other than an individual exemption), specify the exemption and give reasons why the Applicant(s) is unsure whether the agreement is covered by the exemption and why the application is considered appropriate.

2.7 If the agreement or conduct which is the subject of the application is considered to benefit from any exclusion from the Chapter I prohibition and/or Chapter II prohibition, specify the exclusion and give reasons why the Applicant(s) is unsure whether the agreement or conduct is covered by the exclusion and why the application is considered appropriate.

3   JURISDICTION

3.1 Please state whether the Applicant(s) considers that the agreement or conduct which is the subject of the application may affect trade between Member States of the European Community.

3.2 Please state whether the agreement or conduct which is the subject of the application has been notified to the European Commission under Regulation 17. If so, it would assist consideration of the application if a copy of the completed Form A/B (including supporting documents) and, if appropriate, of any decision or comfort letter received from the European Commission were provided to the DGFT.

3.3 Please state whether the agreement relates to transport by rail, road, inland waterway or to services ancillary to transport and is the subject of a notification to the European Commission under Regulation 1017/68. If so, it would assist consideration of the application if a copy of the completed Form II (including supporting documents) and, if appropriate, of any decision or comfort letter received from the European Commission, were provided to the DGFT.

3.4 Please state whether the agreement or conduct which is the subject of the application is also the subject of an application to any national competition authority outside the United Kingdom. If so, please provide brief details (where applicable) of the outcome of such application, if known.

3.5 Please provide details of any previous contacts of which the Applicant(s) is aware with the Office of Fair Trading or a regulator relating to the agreement or conduct which is the subject of the application.

3.6 Please state whether, in the Applicant(s) opinion, a regulator, or more than one regulator, has or may have concurrent jurisdiction with the DGFT to deal with the application. If so, please identify the relevant regulator(s).

4   DETAILS OF THE AGREEMENT OR CONDUCT

4.1 Please provide a brief description of the agreement or conduct which is the subject of the application (including the nature, content, purpose, date(s) and duration).

4.2 If the application is made in relation to a written agreement, attach either an original of the most recent text of that agreement, or a copy certified by the applicant to be a true copy of the original. If the application is made in relation to an agreement which is not written, provide a full description of the agreement. If the application is made in relation to conduct, provide a full description of that conduct.

4.3 Identify any provisions in the agreement or aspects of the conduct which may restrict the parties in their freedom to take independent commercial decisions or to act on those decisions.

4.4 If the application relates to standard form terms and conditions, indicate the number of agreements expected to be entered into on those terms and conditions.

5   INFORMATION ON THE PARTIES TO THE AGREEMENT OR CONDUCT AND THE GROUPS TO WHICH THEY BELONG

5.1 Please give the applicable turnover in the last business year of each party to the agreement or conduct which is the subject of the application and the consolidated applicable turnover for the group (within the meaning of 1.8 above) to which each party belongs. For the purposes of this form, "applicable turnover" and "business year" shall have the meaning given to them in an Order made pursuant to section 36(8). Please attach one copy of the most recent annual report and accounts (or equivalent for unincorporated bodies) for each party to the agreement or conduct and of the most recent annual report and accounts for the ultimate parent company of these undertakings.

5.2 Please list the product and/or services market(s) in which each party to the agreement or conduct and each member of the groups (within the meaning of 1.8 above) to which they belong are active.

6   THE RELEVANT PRODUCT AND GEOGRAPHIC MARKET(S)

6.1 A "*relevant product market*" comprises all those products and/or services regarded by the consumer of the products or acquirer of the services as interchangeable or substitutable by reason of the products' characteristics, price and intended use. The "*relevant geographic market*" comprises the area in which the undertakings concerned are involved in the supply of products or services, in which the conditions of competition are sufficiently homogeneous and which can be distinguished from neighbouring areas because, in particular, conditions of competition are appreciably different in those areas.

6.2 Please supply and explain the definition of the relevant product market(s) which in the Applicant(s)'s opinion should form the basis of the analysis of the application. State the specific products or services directly or indirectly affected by the agreement or conduct which is the subject of the application and other goods or services that may be viewed as substitutable. Give reasons for all assumptions or findings.

6.3 Please supply and explain the definition of the relevant geographic market(s) which in the Applicant(s)'s opinion should form the basis of the analysis of the application. Please identify the geographic scope of the relevant market(s), with reasons. Give reasons for all assumptions or findings.

6.4 For each of the relevant product and geographic market(s) identified in 6.2 and 6.3 above, give details of—

a the level of concentration in the markets;

b the nature and extent of vertical integration;

c the direction and extent of trade within the UK and/or between the UK and abroad;

d the prevailing methods of distributing goods and services, including the extent of the involvement of undertakings which are not party to the agreement or conduct which is the subject of the application (ie third parties), and their significance;

e the prevailing service networks (for example for repair and maintenance), including the extent to which these services are provided by third parties;

f the significance of customer preferences, in terms of brand loyalty, product differentiation and the provision of a full range of products;

g the categories and relative strengths of different types of customer, including private and public sector purchasers; and

h the extent to which customers have long-term relationships with suppliers.

Where available, please provide a copy of the most recent long-term market studies (produced by the Applicant(s) in-house or commissioned by the Applicant(s) from outside consultants) which assess and/or analyse the relevant product market(s) and/or the relevant geographic market(s). Please supply references to any external published studies of the relevant product market(s) and/or the relevant geographic market(s) or, where available, please supply a copy of each such study with the application.

6.5 For each of the parties to the agreement or conduct which is the subject of the application, provide a list of all undertakings belonging to the same group (within the meaning of 1.8 above) which are active in the relevant product market(s) identified in 6.2 above, and those active in markets neighbouring the relevant product market(s)—that is, active in products and/or services which are regarded by the consumer as imperfect and partial substitutes for those products and/or included in the relevant product market(s) as defined in 6.2 above. Such undertakings must be identified even if they sell the product or service in question in geographic areas other than those in which the parties to the agreement or conduct which is the subject of the application operate. Please list the name, place of incorporation, exact product manufactured and the geographic scope of operation of each member of the group.

7 THE POSITION OF THE UNDERTAKINGS IN THE RELEVANT PRODUCT MARKET(S)

7.1 Please provide the following information in respect of each of the previous three calendar or financial years, as available—

a the Applicant(s)'s best estimates of the market shares of each party to the agreement or conduct which is the subject of the application, in the goods or services in the relevant product market(s) on the relevant geographic market(s), as identified in 6.2 and 6.3 above, and, if different, in the UK, and in the European Community;

b identify the five main competitors of each party to the agreement or conduct which is the subject of the application in the relevant product and geographic market(s), and give the Applicant(s)'s best estimates of their market shares in the goods or services in the relevant product and geographic market(s); provided each competitor's name, address, telephone and fax numbers, and, where possible, a contact name;

c identify the five main customers of each party to the agreement or conduct which is the subject of the application, in the relevant product and geographic market(s), giving the customer's name, address, telephone and fax numbers, and, where possible, a contact name; and

d details of each party to the agreement or conduct's interests in, and agreements with, any other undertakings competing in the relevant product and geographic market(s), together with the Applicant(s)'s best estimates of those other undertakings' market shares in the goods or services in the relevant product and geographic market(s), if known.

Information requested in this section must be provided for the group to which each party to the agreement or conduct which is the subject of the application belongs (within the meaning of 1.8 above) and not in relation to the individual undertakings which are party to the agreement or conduct which is the subject of the application.

Justification for the figures provided in response to the above must be given. Thus, for each answer to (a), (b) and (d), total market value or volume must be stated, together with the sales or turnover of each of the undertakings in question. The source or sources of the information should also be given and one copy should be provided of any document, where available, from which information has been taken.

8   MARKET ENTRY AND POTENTIAL COMPETITION IN THE RELEVANT PRODUCT AND GEOGRAPHIC MARKET(S)

8.1   For each of the relevant product and geographic market(s) identified in 6.2 and 6.3 above, describe—

a   the factors influencing entry in product terms into the relevant product market(s); that is, the barriers which exist to prevent undertakings not presently manufacturing goods or providing services within the relevant product market(s) from entering the market(s), taking account of, in particular but not exclusively, the extent to which—

— entry is influenced by the requirements of government authorisation or standard-setting, in any form, and any legal or regulatory controls on entry to the market(s);

— entry is influenced by the availability of raw materials;

— entry is influenced by the length of contracts between an undertaking and its suppliers and customers; and

— research and development and licensing patents, know-how and other intellectual property rights are important; and

b   the factors influencing entry in geographic terms into the relevant geographic market(s); that is, the barriers which exist to prevent undertakings already manufacturing and/or marketing goods or providing services within the relevant product market(s) outside the relevant geographic market(s) from extending sales into the relevant geographic market(s), taking account of, in particular but not exclusively, the importance of—

— trade barriers imposed by law, such as tariffs, quotas etc;

— local specifications or technical requirements;

— procurement policies;

— the existence of adequate and available local distribution and retailing facilities;

— transport costs; and

— strong consumer preference for local brands or products.

8.2   Estimate the amount of time required for entry into the relevant product and geographic market(s), taking account of the individual barriers to entry referred to in the answer to 8.1 above.

8.3   State whether any new undertakings have entered the relevant product market(s) in geographic areas where the parties to the agreement or conduct which is the subject of the application sell, during the last three years. Identify these undertakings by full name, address (by registered office, where appropriate, and principal place of business, if different), telephone and fax numbers and, where possible, a contact name. Please give the Applicant(s)'s best estimates of the market shares of each such undertaking in the goods or services in the relevant product and geographic market(s).

9   EXEMPTION

If exemption from the Chapter I prohibition is sought, or guidance on the likelihood of exemption from the Chapter I prohibition is sought, explain how the agreement contributes to improving production or distribution and/or promoting technical or economic progress, and how consumers will be allowed a fair share of the resulting benefit. Explain how each restriction imposed by the agreement is indispensable to the attainment of those objectives, and how the agreement does not afford the undertakings concerned the possibility of eliminating competition in respect of a substantial part of the products in question (as identified in 6.2 and 6.3 above).

PART II
STATUTORY INSTRUMENTS

10 TRANSITIONAL PERIODS

If the Applicant(s) considers that the agreement benefits from any transitional periods (during which the Chapter I prohibition does not apply), indicate the duration of the relevant transitional periods by reference to Schedule 13.

11 OTHER INFORMATION:

11.1 Where the application is for a decision under section 14 or 22, please provide details of trade publications in which advertisements seeking the views of third parties might be placed.

11.2 Please give any other information which the Applicant(s) considers may be helpful.

11.3 Please specify how the fee payable under rule 6 has been paid and complete the details on the relevant payment slip at Part 5 of this form.

12 SUPPORTING DOCUMENTS

Please ensure that the Applicant(s) has attached the following documents (where relevant) to the application—

(a) if 1.3 above applies, written proof of the representative's authority to act on the Applicant(s) behalf;

(b) if 2.5 above applies, a copy of the decision letter granting the exemption;

(c) if 3.2 above applies, a copy of Form A/B (including supporting documents) and, if appropriate, of any decision or comfort letter;

(d) if 3.3 above applies, a copy of Form II (including supporting documents) and, if appropriate, of any decision or comfort letter;

(e) if 4.2 above applies with regard to a written agreement, either an original or certified copy, of the most recent version of the text of the agreement which is the subject of the application;

(f) one copy of the most recent annual report and accounts (or equivalent for unincorporated bodies) for each party to the agreement or conduct and of the most recent annual report and accounts for the ultimate parent company of these undertakings (see 5.1 above);

(g) where available, one copy of the most recent long-term market studies which assess and/or analyse the relevant market(s) (in-house studies produced by the Application(s) or commissioned by the Applicant(s) from outside consultants) (see 6.4 above);

(h) where available, one copy of any external studies of the relevant product and/or the relevant geographic market(s) (see 6.4 above); and

(i) where available, one copy of any document from which information has been taken and provided in answer to 7.1 above.

Part 2A:

> Under section 44 of the Act, it is an offence, punishable by a fine or imprisonment or both, to provide information which is false or misleading in a material particular if the undertaking or person providing it knows that it is false or misleading, or is reckless as to whether it is. If the undertaking or person is a body corporate, under section 72 of the Act its officers may be guilty of an offence

DECLARATION

The undersigned declare that all the information given above and in the . . . . pages annexed hereto is correct to the best of their knowledge and belief, and that all estimates are identified as such and are their best estimates of the underlying facts.

Place and date . . . .

Signatures . . . .

. . . .

Status. . . . .

. . . . name(s) in block capitals

PART 3: ACKNOWLEDGEMENT OF RECEIPT

This acknowledgement of receipt will be returned to the address inserted below if the Applicant(s) provides the information requested below.

To be completed by the Applicant(s)

To: . . . . (name and address of Applicant(s))

. . . .

. . . .

. . . .

The application dated. . . . .

concerning. . . . .

involving the following undertakings:

1. . . . .

2. . . . .[and others]

To be completed by the Office of Fair Trading

was received on . . . .

and registered under reference number

. . . .**Please quote this number in all correspondence with the Office of Fair Trading or the office of a regulator.**

PART 4—TO BE COMPLETED BY THE APPLICANT(S)

Information for the OFT public register

1. Please give the full names of the parties to the agreement(s) or conduct which is the subject of the application, as in the response to 1.1 and 1.6 above.

2. Please provide a short summary which does not contain any confidential information (no more than 250 words) of the nature and objectives of the agreement(s) or conduct which is the subject of the application.

3. Please identify the Standard Industrial Classification code (as referred to in 1.5 above) for the relevant good(s) or service(s), if known. If the code is not known, describe the goods or services involved as fully and accurately as possible.

PART 5: PAYMENT DETAILS FOR FEES PAYABLE UNDER RULE 6

For payment by cheque

Co-ordination Unit
Office of Fair Trading
Fleetbank House
2–6 Salisbury Square
London EC4Y 8JX

I enclose cheque no .... for the amount of .... made payable to "The Office of Fair Trading".

Name (Block Letters)—

. . . .

Address (Block Letters)—

. . . .
. . . .
. . . .
. . . .

Signature. . . . .

Date. . . . .

For payment by BACS

Co-ordination Unit
Office of Fair Trading
Fleetbank House
2–6 Salisbury Square
London EC4Y 8JX

I confirm that payment by BACS for the amount of .... has been processed on .... to be paid into the following account—

Account Name: The Office of Fair Trading

Account Number: 11673000

Sort Code: 10—14—99

Reference Number: [..................]-**CP/CA1998**

ANNEX 2

PART 1

The amount specified for the purposes of rule 6(2)(a) above is £5,000.

PART 2

The amount specified for the purposes of rule 6(2)(b) above is £13,000.

[2027]

NOTES

Commencement: 1 March 2000.
Director General of Fair Trading: see the note "Director" to art 2 at **[2026]**.

B. COMPETITION COMMISSION

COMPETITION ACT 1998 (COMPETITION COMMISSION) TRANSITIONAL, CONSEQUENTIAL AND SUPPLEMENTAL PROVISIONS ORDER 1999

(SI 1999/506)

NOTES
Made: 25 February 1999.
Authority: Competition Act 1998, ss 45, 71, 75.
Commencement: 1 April 1999.

1 Citation and commencement

This Order may be cited as the Competition Act 1998 (Competition Commission) Transitional, Consequential and Supplemental Provisions Order 1999 and shall come into force on 1st April 1999.

[2028]

NOTES
Commencement: 1 April 1999.

PART I

2 Interpretation

In Part I of this Order—

(a) the "MMC" means the Monopolies and Mergers Commission;

(b) the "Commission" means the Competition Commission; and

(c) the "commencement date" means the date on which the MMC is dissolved and its functions are transferred to the Competition Commission by virtue of section 45(3) of the Competition Act 1998 coming into force.

[2029]

NOTES
Commencement: 1 April 1999.

3 General

(1) Anything having any continuing effect done by or in relation to the MMC before the commencement date, including (without prejudice to the generality of the foregoing) anything done by or in relation to the MMC in respect of a reference made to the MMC, is deemed from the commencement date to have been done by or in relation to the Commission and is not to be invalidated by the repeal of the provision under which or by relation to which it was done.

(2) Any proceedings by, against or in respect of the MMC which are in existence immediately prior to the commencement date are from that date to continue as proceedings by, against or in respect of the Commission.

[2030]

NOTES
Commencement: 1 April 1999.

4 Transfer of assets, rights, obligations and liabilities

(1) All property, rights, obligations and liabilities of the MMC immediately prior to the commencement date are on that date transferred to the Commission.

(2) The liability of the Secretary of State for the payment of pensions of former Chairmen and deputy chairmen of the MMC is transferred to the Commission on the commencement date.

(3) On the commencement date the liability of the Secretary of State for the payment of the following are transferred to the Commission—

   (a) remuneration, allowances, or gratuities to persons who immediately before the commencement date were members of the MMC and who from that date become members of the Commission; and

   (b) pensions of the persons who immediately before the commencement date were Chairman and deputy chairmen of the MMC and who from that date become Chairman and deputy chairmen of the Commission.

[2031]

NOTES

Commencement: 1 April 1999.

5 Members of the MMC and the Commission

Subject to article 4(2) and (3), the repeal by the Competition Act 1998 of section 135(1) of, and paragraphs 6, 8 and 9 of Schedule 3 to, the Fair Trading Act 1973 is not to affect the continuing application of those provisions in respect of any pension, allowance, gratuity or sum by way of compensation in respect of which a determination has been made prior to the commencement date.

[2032]

NOTES

Commencement: 1 April 1999.

6 Deputy chairmen

Subject to article 4(3) each person who immediately prior to the commencement date is a deputy chairman of the MMC is to hold office as a deputy chairman of the Commission for the remainder of the term for which he was appointed as a deputy chairman of the MMC and on the terms on which he was so appointed.

[2033]

NOTES

Commencement: 1 April 1999.

7 Transfer of employees

(1) A contract of employment between the MMC and a person who is employed by the MMC immediately before the commencement date is to have effect from the commencement date as if originally made between him and the Commission.

(2) All rights, powers, duties and liabilities of the MMC under or in connection with a contract to which paragraph (1) applies are transferred to the Commission on the commencement date.

(3) Anything done before the commencement date by or in relation to the MMC in respect of such a contract, or in respect of a person employed under such a contract, is to be deemed from that date to have been done by or in relation to the Commission.

(4)   Paragraphs (1) to (3) are without prejudice to the right of an employee to terminate his contract of employment if his working conditions are changed substantially to his detriment; but such a change is not to be taken to have occurred by reason only of the application of this article.

(5)   Articles 3(1) and 4(1) do not apply where the preceding provisions of this article apply.

[2034]

NOTES
Commencement: 1 April 1999.

8–45   (*Art 8 modifies the Competition Act 1980, ss 5, 7, which are now repealed; arts 9–45 contain consequential amendments, repealed in part by the Enterprise Act 2002, s 278(2), Sch 26, as from a day to be appointed.*)

COMPETITION COMMISSION APPEAL TRIBUNAL RULES 2000

(SI 2000/261)

NOTES
Made: 7 February 2000.
Authority: Competition Act 1998, ss 48(2)–(4), 49(3), 71, Sch 8, Pt II.
Commencement: 1 March 2000.

ARRANGEMENT OF RULES

PART I
INTRODUCTION

PART II
COMMENCING PROCEEDINGS

PART III
RESPONSE TO THE APPLICATION

PART IV
INTERVENTION, CONSOLIDATION AND LOCATION OF PROCEEDINGS

PART I
INTRODUCTION

1   Citation and commencement

These rules may be cited as the Competition Commission Appeal Tribunal Rules 2000 and shall come into force on 1st March 2000.

[2035]

NOTES

Commencement: 1 March 2000.

2   The Registrar of Appeal Tribunals

(1)   A Registrar of Appeal Tribunals shall be appointed by the Competition Commission with the approval of the Secretary of State.

(2)   Any person appointed to be the Registrar shall—

(a) have a seven year general qualification within the meaning of section 71 of the Courts and Legal Services Act 1990;

(b) be an advocate or solicitor in Scotland of at least seven years standing; or

(c) be—

(i) a member of the Bar of Northern Ireland; or

(ii) a solicitor of the Supreme Court of Northern Ireland

of at least seven years standing.

(3)   The Registrar shall act in accordance with the instructions of the President and shall, in particular, be responsible for—

(a) the establishment and maintenance of a register in which all pleadings and supporting documents and all orders and decisions of the tribunal shall be registered; and

(b) the acceptance, transmission, service and custody of documents in accordance with these rules.

(4)   The President may delegate to the Registrar the power to abridge or extend the time prescribed by these rules for the doing of any act.

(5)   Any function of the Registrar may be performed on his behalf by any other member of his staff whom the President may authorise for the purpose.

[2036]

NOTES

Commencement: 1 March 2000.

3   Tribunal address for service

For the purposes of proceedings under sections 46 and 47 of the Competition Act 1998 ("the Act") the address for service of documents on the Competition Commission (referred to in these rules as "the Tribunal address for service") is: The Registrar, The Competition Commission Appeal Tribunals, New Court, 48 Carey Street, London WC2A 2JT or such other address as may be notified in the London, Edinburgh and Belfast Gazettes.

[2037]

NOTES

Commencement: 1 March 2000.

4   Constitution of Tribunals

(1)   The President shall publish the arrangements for constituting tribunals to determine appeals.

(2)   If a member of a tribunal constituted by the President in accordance with paragraph 27 of Schedule 7 to the Act ceases to be an appeal panel member or is otherwise unable to act before that tribunal has commenced hearing the appeal in

accordance with rules 23 and 24 below, the President may attribute the hearing of that appeal to a differently constituted tribunal.

[2038]

NOTES
Commencement: 1 March 2000.

5   Representation

In proceedings before the tribunal, a party may be represented by—
  (a) a qualified lawyer having rights of audience before a court in the United Kingdom; or
  (b) any other person allowed by the tribunal to appear on his behalf.

[2039]

NOTES
Commencement: 1 March 2000.

PART II
COMMENCING PROCEEDINGS

6 Time and manner of commencing proceedings

(1)   In these rules the notice of appeal referred to in Schedule 8 to the Act is referred to as "the application" and "the applicant" means the person making the appeal.

(2)   An appeal to the Competition Commission under sections 46 and 47 of the Act must be made by sending an application to the Registrar so that it is received not later than two months after the date upon which the applicant was notified of the disputed decision.

(3)   The tribunal may not extend the time limit provided under paragraph (2) unless satisfied that the circumstances are exceptional.

(4)   The application shall state—
  (a) the name and address of the applicant;
  (b) the name and address of the applicant's legal representative, if appropriate;
  (c) an address for service in the United Kingdom;
  (d) in which part of the United Kingdom the applicant requests that the proceedings take place; and
  (e) the name and address of the respondent to the proceedings
and shall be signed and dated by the applicant or his legal representative.

(5)   The application shall contain—
  (a) a brief statement of the facts;
  (b) a summary of the principal grounds for contesting the decision, which shall include the information required by paragraph 2(2) of Schedule 8 to the Act;
  (c) a succinct presentation of the arguments supporting each of those grounds;
  (d) the relief sought by the applicant, and any directions sought pursuant to rule 17 below; and
  (e) a schedule listing all the documents annexed to the application.

(6)   There shall be annexed to the application—
  (a) a copy of the disputed decision; and
  (b) as far as practicable, a copy of every document on which the applicant relies including the written statements of all witnesses of fact, or expert witnesses, if any.

(7) The signed original of the application (and its annexes) must be accompanied by seven copies certified by the applicant or his legal representative as conforming to the original.

(8) If the applicant wishes to request confidential treatment for any part of his application, or the annexes, he must indicate in the application, or within 14 days after sending it to the Registrar, the relevant passages or documents, together with the reasons, and, if so directly the Registrar, supply a non-confidential version of the application.

[2040]

NOTES
Commencement: 1 March 2000.

7 Defective applications

(1) If the tribunal considers that the application does not comply with rule 6 above, or is materially incomplete, or is unduly prolix or lacking in clarity, the tribunal may give such directions as may be necessary to ensure that the application is put in order and dealt with justly.

(2) The tribunal may, if satisfied that the efficient conduct of the proceedings so require, instruct the Registrar to defer service of the application on the respondent until after the directions referred to in paragraph (1) above have been complied with.

[2041]

NOTES
Commencement: 1 March 2000.

8 Power to strike out applications

(1) The tribunal may, after hearing the parties, strike out an application at any stage in the proceedings if—

  (a) it considers that the application discloses no valid ground of appeal;

  (b) it is satisfied that the applicant has habitually and persistently and without any reasonable ground—

    (i) instituted vexatious proceedings, whether against the same person or different persons; or

    (ii) made vexatious applications in any proceedings; or

  (c) the application does not comply with rule 6 in a substantial respect, and the applicant has not remedied the defect pursuant to a direction under rule 7(1); or

  (d) the applicant fails to comply with a direction of the tribunal.

(2) When the tribunal strikes out an application it may make any consequential order it considers appropriate.

[2042]

NOTES
Commencement: 1 March 2000.

9 Amendment of application

(1) The applicant may amend the application only with the permission of the tribunal.

(2) Where the tribunal grants permission under paragraph (1) it may do so on such terms as it thinks fit, and shall give such further or consequential directions as may be necessary.

(3)   The tribunal shall not grant permission to amend in order to add a new ground for contesting the decision unless—
  (a) such ground is based on matters of law or fact which have come to light since the application was made; or
  (b) it was not practicable to include that ground in the application; or
  (c) the circumstances are exceptional.

[2043]

NOTES
Commencement: 1 March 2000.

10 Withdrawal of application

(1)   The applicant may withdraw his application only with the permission of the tribunal, or if the application has not yet proceeded to a hearing, the President.

(2)   Where the tribunal gives permission under paragraph (1) it may—
  (a) do so on such terms as it thinks fit; and
  (b) instruct the Registrar to publish notice of the withdrawal in one issue of the London, Edinburgh and Belfast Gazettes and in such other manner as the tribunal may direct.

(3)   Where an application is withdrawn—
  (a) any interim order made under rule 32, other than an order made in respect of costs, shall immediately cease to have effect; and
  (b) a fresh application may not be brought by the applicant in relation to the decision which was the subject of the application withdrawn.

[2044]

NOTES
Commencement: 1 March 2000.

PART III
RESPONSE TO THE APPLICATION

11 Acknowledgement and notification

On receiving an application the Registrar shall—
  (a) send an acknowledgement of its receipt to the applicant; and
  (b) subject to rules 7(2) and 8 above, send a copy of the application to the respondent who made the disputed decision.

[2045]

NOTES
Commencement: 1 March 2000.

12 Defence

(1)   The respondent shall send to the Registrar a defence in the form required by this rule so that the defence is received within six weeks, (or such further time as the tribunal may allow), of the date on which the respondent received a copy of the application sent in accordance with rule 11(b) above.

(2)   The defence shall state—
  (a) the name and address of the respondent;
  (b) the name and address of the respondent's legal representative, if appropriate;
  (c) an address for service in the United Kingdom;

(d) in which part of the United Kingdom the respondent requests that the proceedings take place

and shall be signed and dated by the respondent, or on his behalf by his duly authorised officer or his legal representative.

(3) The defence shall contain—

   (a) a succinct presentation of the arguments of fact and law upon which the respondent will rely in opposing the application;

   (b) the relief sought by the respondent and any directions sought pursuant to rule 17 below; and

   (c) a schedule listing all the documents annexed to the defence.

(4) There shall be annexed to the defence a copy of every document upon which the respondent relies including the written statements of all witnesses of fact, and where practicable expert witnesses, if any.

(5) The signed original of the defence (and its annexes) must be accompanied by seven copies certified by the respondent or on his behalf by his duly authorised officer or his legal representative as conforming to the original.

(6) Rules 6(8), 7, 8 (except rule 8(1)(b)) and 9 shall apply to the defence as if references to "rule 6" were references to "rule 12", references to "the applicant" were references to "the respondent", references to "the application" were references to "the defence", the reference in rule 8(1)(a) above to "ground of appeal" were a reference to "ground for opposing the application" and the reference in rule 9(3) above to "the decision" were a reference to "the application".

(7) On receiving the defence, the Registrar shall send a copy to the applicant.

[2046]

NOTES

Commencement: 1 March 2000.

PART IV
INTERVENTION, CONSOLIDATION AND LOCATION OF PROCEEDINGS

13 Publication of notice of application

(1) Upon receipt of an application the Registrar shall, subject to any directions or order of the tribunal pursuant to rule 7 or 8, as soon as practicable publish a notice in the London, Edinburgh and Belfast Gazettes and in any other manner as the President may think fit.

(2) The notice referred to in paragraph (1) above shall state—

   (a) that an application has been received;

   (b) the name of the applicant;

   (c) the disputed decision to which the application relates and the person by whom it was made;

   (d) the particulars of the relief sought by the applicant;

   (e) a summary of the principal grounds relied on; and

   (f) that any person who considers that he has sufficient interest may apply to intervene in the proceedings, in accordance with rule 14 below, within one month of publication of the notice.

[2047]

NOTES

Commencement: 1 March 2000.

14 Addition of parties to the proceedings

(1)   Any person who considers he has sufficient interest in the outcome of any proceedings may make a request to the tribunal, in the form required by this rule, for permission to intervene.

(2)   The request must be sent to the Registrar within one month of the date upon which the notice in respect of the relevant proceedings is published in accordance with rule 13(1).

(3)   The Registrar shall give notice of the request for permission to intervene to all the other parties to the proceedings and invite their observations on that request within a time limit specified in the notice.

(4)   A request for permission to intervene shall state—
  (a) the title of the proceedings to which that request relates;
  (b) the name and address of the person wishing to intervene;
  (c) the name and address of his legal representative, if appropriate;
  (d) an address for service in the United Kingdom.

(5)   The request shall contain—
  (a) a concise statement of the matters in issue in the proceedings which affect the person making the request;
  (b) the name of any party whose position the person making the request intends to support; and
  (c) a succinct presentation of the reasons for making the request.

(6)   If the tribunal is satisfied, having taken into account the observations of the parties, that the person wishing to intervene has a sufficient interest, it may permit the intervention on such terms and conditions as it thinks fit.

(7)   On granting permission in accordance with paragraph (6) of this rule, the tribunal shall give all such consequential directions as it considers necessary with regard, in particular, to the service on the intervener of documents lodged with the Registrar, the submission by the intervener of a statement of intervention and, if appropriate, the submission by the principal parties of a response to the statement of intervention.

(8)   In making any order under this rule, section 56 of the Act shall apply to the tribunal as it applies to the Director.

(9)   The statement of intervention shall contain—
  (a) a succinct presentation of the facts and arguments supporting the intervention;
  (b) the relief sought by the intervener; and
  (c) a schedule listing all documents annexed to the intervention and, as far as possible shall have annexed, a copy of every document on which the intervener relies including the written statement of witnesses of fact or expert witnesses, if any.

(10) Rules 6(8), 7, 8 (except 8(1)(b)) and 9 shall apply to the statement of intervention as if references to "rule 6" were references to "rule 14(9)", references to "the applicant" were references to "the intervener", references to "the application" were references to "the statement of intervention", the reference in rule 8(1)(a) above to "ground of appeal" were a reference to "ground for intervention" and the reference in rule 9(3) above to "contesting the decision" were a reference to "supporting the intervention".

NOTES
  Commencement: 1 March 2000.
  Director: the Enterprise Act 2002, s 2(1), at **[255]**, provides that, as from the coming into force of that section in accordance with s 279 at **[463]**, the functions of the Director General of Fair Trading, his property, rights and liabilities are transferred to the Office of Fair Trading. Accordingly, (by virtue of s 2(2), (3) of the 2002 Act) the office of the Director is abolished, and any reference to the Director in any enactment, instrument or other document passed or made before the commencement of s 2(1) shall have effect as if it were a reference to the Office of Fair Trading. For transitional provisions in connection with the transfer, see s 276(1) of, and Sch 24, para 6 to, the 2002 Act at **[477]**.

15 Consolidation of applications

(1)   Where two or more applications have been made in respect of the same decision or which involve the same or similar issues, the tribunal may, on the request of a party or of its own motion, order that the applications or any particular issue or matter raised in the applications be consolidated or heard together.

(2)   Before making an order under this rule, the tribunal shall invite the parties to the relevant proceedings to submit their observations on the consolidation of the proceedings.

[2049]

NOTES
  Commencement: 1 March 2000.

16 Location of the proceedings

(1)   The tribunal shall, as soon as practicable, taking account of the observations of the parties in the application and defence, determine whether the proceedings are proceedings before a tribunal in England and Wales, in Scotland or in Northern Ireland and shall instruct the Registrar to notify the parties of its determination.

(2)   In making this determination, the tribunal shall have regard to all matters which appear to it to be relevant and in particular, the part of the United Kingdom where—

  (a) the applicant is habitually resident or has his principal place of business;
  (b) the majority of the parties are habitually resident or have their principal places of business;
  (c) any agreement, decision or concerted practice to which the disputed decision relates was made or implemented or intended to be implemented;
  (d) any conduct to which the disputed decision relates took place.

(3)   The tribunal may hold any meeting, case conference, pre-hearing review or hearing or give any directions in such place as it thinks fit having regard to the just, expeditious and economical conduct of the proceedings.

[2050]

NOTES
  Commencement: 1 March 2000.

PART V
PREPARATION FOR DECIDING THE APPLICATION

17 Directions

(1)   The tribunal may at any time, on the request of a party or of its own motion, at the pre-hearing review or otherwise, give such directions as are provided for in paragraph (2) below or such other directions as it thinks fit to secure the just, expeditious and economical conduct of the proceedings.

(2)   The tribunal may give directions—

  (a) as to the manner in which the proceedings are to be conducted, including any time limits to be observed in the conduct of the oral hearing;

  (b) that the parties file a reply to the defence or other additional pleadings;

  (c) for holding a pre-hearing review;

  (d) requiring persons to attend and give evidence or to produce documents;

  (e) as to the evidence which may be required or admitted in proceedings before the tribunal and the extent to which it shall be oral or written, including, where a witness statement has been submitted, whether the witness is to be called to give oral evidence;

  (f) as to the submission in advance of a hearing of any witness statements or expert reports;

  (g) as to the examination or cross-examination of witnesses;

  (h) as to the fixing of time limits with respect to any aspect of the proceedings;

  (i) as to the abridgement or extension of any time limits, whether or not expired;

  (j) to enable a disputed decision to be referred back (or in Scotland, remitted) to the person by whom it was taken;

  (k) for the disclosure between, or the production by, the parties of documents or classes of documents; or in the case of proceedings taking place in Scotland, for such recovery or inspection of documents as might be ordered by a sheriff;

  (l) for the appointment and instruction of experts, whether by the tribunal or by the parties and the manner in which expert evidence is to be given; and

  (m) for the award of costs or expenses, including any allowances payable to persons in connection with their attendance before the tribunal.

(3)   The tribunal may, in particular, of its own motion—

  (a) put questions to the parties;

  (b) invite the parties to make written or oral submissions on certain aspects of the proceedings;

  (c) ask the parties or third parties for information or particulars;

  (d) ask for documents or any papers relating to the case to be produced;

  (e) summon the parties' representatives or the parties in person to meetings or case conferences.

(4)   A request by a party for directions shall be made, as far as practicable, in the application or defence, or on notice at the pre-hearing review. A request made at any other time shall be made in writing and shall be served by the Registrar on any other party who might be affected by such directions and determined by the tribunal taking into account the observations of the parties.

[2051]

NOTES

Commencement: 1 March 2000.

18 Pre-hearing review

(1)   Where it appears to the tribunal that any proceedings would be facilitated by holding a pre-hearing review, taking into account the criteria set out in paragraph (3) below, the tribunal may on the request of a party or of its own motion, give directions for such a review to be held. The Registrar shall give the parties not less than fourteen days notice, or such shorter notice as the parties agree, of the time and place of the pre-hearing review.

(2)   The pre-hearing review shall be in private unless the tribunal otherwise directs.

(3)   The purpose of the pre-hearing review shall be—

  (a) to ensure the efficient conduct of the proceedings;

  (b) to determine the points on which the parties must present further argument or which call for further evidence to be produced;

(c) to clarify the forms of order sought by the parties, their arguments on fact and law and the points at issue between them;

(d) to ensure that all agreements that can be reached between the parties about the matters in issue and the conduct of the proceedings are made and recorded;

(e) to facilitate the settlement of the proceedings.

(4) The tribunal may authorise a person qualified for appointment to the panel of chairmen to carry out on its behalf the pre-hearing review or any other preparatory measure relating to the organisation or disposal of the proceedings.

[2052]

NOTES

Commencement: 1 March 2000.

19 Timetable for the oral hearing

As soon as practicable, the tribunal shall—

(a) set a timetable outlining the steps to be taken by the parties pursuant to the directions of the tribunal in preparation for the oral hearing;

(b) fix the date for the oral hearing;

(c) notify the parties in writing of the date and place for the oral hearing and send them a copy of the timetable for that hearing; and

(d) if it considers it necessary for the expeditious disposal of the proceedings, send the parties a report for the hearing summarising the factual context of the case and the parties' principal submissions.

[2053]

NOTES

Commencement: 1 March 2000.

20 Evidence

(1) The tribunal may control the evidence by giving directions as to—

(a) the issues on which it requires evidence;

(b) the nature of the evidence which it requires to decide those issues; and

(c) the way in which the evidence is to be placed before the tribunal.

(2) The tribunal may admit or exclude evidence, whether or not the evidence was available to the respondent when the disputed decision was taken and notwithstanding any enactment or rule of law relating to the admissibility of evidence in proceedings before a court.

(3) The tribunal may require any witness to give evidence on oath or affirmation or if in writing by way of affidavit.

(4) The tribunal may allow a witness to give evidence through a video link or by other means.

[2054]

NOTES

Commencement: 1 March 2000.

21 Summoning or citing of witnesses

(1) Subject to paragraphs (2) and (3) below, the tribunal may at any time, either of its own motion or on the request of any party, issue a summons, (or in relation to proceedings taking place in Scotland, a citation), requiring any person wherever he may be in the United Kingdom to do one or both of the following—

(a) to attend as a witness before the tribunal at the time and place set out in the summons or citation; and

   (b) to answer any questions or produce any documents or other material in his possession or under his control which relate to any matter in question in the proceedings.

(2)   A request by a party for the issue of a summons or citation or for directions under this rule shall state with reasons—

   (a) upon which facts the witness is to be questioned and the reasons for the examination;

   (b) the documents required to be produced.

(3)   No person may be required to attend in compliance with a summons or citation under this rule unless—

   (a) he has been given at least 7 days notice of the hearing; and

   (b) he is paid—

      (i) if the proceedings are taking place before a tribunal in England and Wales, such sum as would be recoverable by that witness in respect of his attendance in proceedings before the Supreme Court of England and Wales;

      (ii) if the proceedings are taking place before a tribunal in Scotland, such sum as would be recoverable by that witness in respect of his attendance in proceedings before the Court of Session; and

      (iii) if the proceedings are taking place before a tribunal in Northern Ireland, such sum as would be recoverable by that witness in respect of his attendance in proceedings before the Supreme Court of Northern Ireland.

(4)   The tribunal may make the summoning or citation of a witness in accordance with paragraph (1) above conditional upon the deposit with the Registrar of a sum determined by the tribunal as sufficient to cover—

   (a) the costs of the summons or citation;

   (b) the sum referred to in sub-paragraph (3)(b) of this rule.

(5)   The Registrar shall advance the funds necessary in connection with the examination of any witnesses summoned by the tribunal on its own motion.

[2055]

NOTES
   Commencement: 1 March 2000.

22 Failure to comply with directions

If any party fails to comply with any direction given in accordance with these rules, the tribunal may if it considers that the justice of the case so requires, order that such party be debarred from taking any further part in the proceedings without the permission of the tribunal.

[2056]

NOTES
   Commencement: 1 March 2000.

PART VI
THE HEARING

23 Hearing to be in public

The hearing shall be in public except as to any part where the tribunal is satisfied that it will be considering information which is, in its opinion, confidential information.

[2057]

24 Procedure at the hearing

(1)   The proceedings shall be opened and directed by the President or Chairman who shall be responsible for the proper conduct of the hearing.

(2)   The tribunal shall, so far as it appears to it appropriate, seek to avoid formality in its proceedings and shall conduct the hearing in such manner as it considers most appropriate for the clarification of the issues before it and generally to the just handling of the proceedings.

(3)   If, after the commencement of any hearing, a member other than the President or Chairman, is absent, the application may, with the consent of the parties, be heard by the other two members and, in that event, the tribunal shall be deemed to be properly constituted. A decision of a tribunal so constituted must be unanimous.

(4)   Unless the tribunal otherwise directs, no witness of fact or expert shall be heard unless the relevant witness statement or expert report has been submitted in advance of the hearing and in accordance with any directions of the tribunal.

(5)   The tribunal may limit cross-examination of witnesses to any extent or in any manner it deems appropriate, having regard to the just, expeditious and economical conduct of the proceedings.

[2058]

PART VII
DECISION OF THE TRIBUNAL

25 Delivery of the decision

(1)   The decision of the tribunal shall be delivered in public on the date fixed for that purpose.

(2)   The Registrar shall send a copy of the document recording the decision to each party and shall enter it on the register.

(3)   The decision of the tribunal shall be treated as having been notified on the date on which a copy of the document recording it is sent to the parties under paragraph (2) of this rule.

[2059]

26 Costs

(1)   For the purposes of these rules "costs" means—
   (a) if the proceedings are taking place before a tribunal in England and Wales, costs and expenses recoverable in proceedings before the Supreme Court of England and Wales;
   (b) if the proceedings are taking place before a tribunal in Scotland, costs and expenses recoverable in proceedings before the Court of Session; and

(c) if the proceedings are taking place before a tribunal in Northern Ireland, costs and expenses recoverable in proceedings before the Supreme Court of Northern Ireland.

(2) The tribunal may at its discretion, at any stage of the proceedings, make any order it thinks fit in relation to the payment of costs by one party to another in respect of the whole or part of the proceedings and, in determining how much the party is required to pay, the tribunal may take account of the conduct of all parties in relation to the proceedings.

(3) Any party against whom an order for costs is made shall, if the tribunal so directs, pay to any other party a lump sum by way of costs, or such proportion of the costs as may be just. The tribunal may assess the sum to be paid pursuant to any order made under paragraph (2) above or may direct that it be assessed by the President or Chairman or dealt with by the detailed assessment of the costs by a costs officer of the Supreme Court or a taxing officer of the Supreme Court of Northern Ireland or by the Auditor of the Court of Session.

(4) Unless the tribunal otherwise directs, any order or direction made pursuant to paragraphs (2) and (3) above may be made in the decision, if the parties so consent, or immediately following delivery of the decision.

(5) The power to award costs pursuant to this rule includes the power to direct any party to pay to the tribunal such sum as may be appropriate in reimbursement of any costs incurred by the tribunal in connection with the summoning or citation of witnesses or the instruction of experts on the tribunal's behalf.

(6) If a party against whom an order for costs has been made fails to pay those costs within 28 days of the later of—
(a) the date of that order, or,
(b) where costs are assessed in accordance with paragraph (3) above, the date of that assessment

the person to whom the outstanding amount is due may recover that amount from the debtor as a civil debt due to him.

[2060]

NOTES
Commencement: 1 March 2000.

27 Interest on penalties

If it imposes confirms or varies any penalty, the tribunal may, in addition, order that interest is to be payable on the amount of any such penalty from such date, not being a date earlier than the date upon which the application was made in accordance with rule 6 above, and at such rate, as the tribunal considers appropriate. Unless the tribunal otherwise directs, the rate of interest shall not exceed the rate specified in any Order made pursuant to section 44 of the Administration of Justice Act 1970. Such interest is to form part of the penalty and be recoverable as a civil debt in addition to the amount payable on any outstanding penalty notice issued in accordance with section 36 of the Act.

[2061]

NOTES
Commencement: 1 March 2000.

28 Consent orders

(1) If all the parties agree the terms on which to settle all or any part of the proceedings, they may request the tribunal to make a consent order.

(2)   A request for a consent order shall be made by sending to the Registrar—
  (a) a draft consent order;
  (b) a consent order impact statement; and
  (c) a statement signed by all the parties to the proceedings or their legal representatives requesting that an order be made in the form of the draft.

(3)   A consent order impact statement shall provide an explanation of the draft consent order, including an explanation of the circumstances giving rise to the draft order, the relief to be obtained if the order is made and the anticipated effects on competition of that relief.

(4)   If the tribunal considers that a proposed consent order may have a significant effect on competition, it shall direct the Registrar as soon as practicable following receipt of the request to publish a notice in one issue of the London, Edinburgh and Belfast Gazettes and in such other manner as the tribunal may direct.

(5)   The notice referred to in paragraph (4) above shall state—
  (a) that a request for a consent order has been received;
  (b) the name of each of the parties to the proceedings;
  (c) the particulars of the relief sought by those parties; and
  (d) that the draft consent order and consent order impact statement may be inspected at the Tribunal address for service or such other place as may be mentioned in the notice

and shall exclude any information of a confidential nature.

(6)   Any person may send his comments upon a request for a consent order to the Registrar within one month of the date upon which the notice was published in accordance with paragraph (4) above.

(7)   Comments supplied in accordance with paragraph (6) above shall be in writing, signed by the commentator and shall state the title of the proceedings to which the comments relate and the name and address of the commentator.

(8)   The Registrar shall send all comments received in accordance with paragraph (6) above to all parties to the proceedings. Any party to the proceedings may within 14 days of receipt of the comments send a response to the comments to the Registrar.

(9)   In respect of any request for a consent order the tribunal may, as it thinks fit, after hearing the parties and considering the comments of third parties—
  (a) make the order in the terms requested;
  (b) invite the parties to vary the terms; or
  (c) refuse to make any order.

[2062]

NOTES

Commencement: 1 March 2000.

PART VIII
APPEALS

29 Request for permission to appeal

(1)   A request to the tribunal for permission to appeal from a decision of the tribunal may be made—
  (a) orally at any hearing at which the decision is delivered by the tribunal; or
  (b) in writing to the Registrar within one month of the notification of that decision.

(2)   Where a request for permission to appeal is made in writing, it shall be signed and dated by the party or his representative and shall—

(a) state the name and address of the party and of any representative of the party;

(b) identify the tribunal decision to which the request relates;

(c) state the grounds on which the party intends to rely in his appeal; and

(d) state whether the party seeks a hearing of his request and any special circumstances relied on.

[2063]

NOTES

Commencement: 1 March 2000.

30 Decision of the tribunal on request for permission to appeal

(1)   Where a request for permission to appeal is made orally the tribunal shall give its decision either orally or in writing, stating its reasons.

(2)   Where a request for permission to appeal is made in writing, the tribunal shall decide whether to grant such permission on consideration of the party's request and, unless it considers that special circumstances render a hearing desirable, in the absence of the parties.

(3)   The decision of the tribunal on a written request for permission to appeal together with the reasons for that decision shall be recorded in writing and the Registrar shall notify the parties of such decision.

[2064]

NOTES

Commencement: 1 March 2000.

PART IX
REFERENCES TO THE EUROPEAN COURT

31 Reference to the European Court

(1)   An order may be made by the tribunal of its own motion at any stage in the proceedings or on application by a party before or at the oral hearing.

(2)   An order shall set out in a schedule the request for the preliminary ruling of the European Court and the tribunal may give directions as to the manner and form in which the schedule is to be prepared.

(3)   The proceedings in which an order is made shall, unless the tribunal otherwise orders, be stayed (or in Scotland, sisted) until the European Court has given a preliminary ruling on the question referred to it.

(4)   When an order has been made, the Registrar shall send a copy thereof to the Registrar of the European Court.

(5)   In this rule—

"European Court" means the Court of Justice of the European Communities;

"order" means an order referring a question to the European Court for a preliminary ruling under Article 234 of the Treaty establishing the European Community, Article 150 of the Treaty establishing the European Atomic Energy Community or Article 41 of the Treaty establishing the European Coal and Steel Community.

[2065]

NOTES
Commencement: 1 March 2000.

PART X
INTERIM ORDERS AND MEASURES

32 Power to make interim orders and to take interim measures

(1) The tribunal may make an order granting on an interim basis any remedy which the tribunal would have the power to grant in its final decision.

(2) Without prejudice to the generality of the foregoing, if the tribunal considers that it is necessary as a matter of urgency for the purpose of—

    (a) preventing serious, irreparable damage to a particular person or category of person, or

    (b) protecting the public interest

the tribunal may make an order giving such directions as it considers appropriate for that purpose.

(3) The tribunal may make an order—

    (a) suspending the effect of the disputed decision in whole or part; or

    (b) varying any or all of the conditions or obligations attached to an exemption.

(4) The tribunal shall exercise its power under this rule taking into account all the relevant circumstances, including—

    (a) the urgency of the matter;

    (b) the effect on the party making the request if the interim order is not made; and

    (c) the effect on competition if the interim order is made.

(5) Any order or direction under this rule is subject to the tribunal's further order or final decision.

(6) A person shall apply for an order under this rule by sending a request for interim relief in the form required by paragraph (7) below to the Registrar.

(7) The request for interim relief shall state—

    (a) the subject matter of the proceedings;

    (b) in the case of a request for an order pursuant to paragraph (2) of this rule, the circumstances giving rise to the urgency;

    (c) the factual and legal grounds establishing a prima facie case for the interim order being made by the tribunal;

    (d) the relief sought;

    (e) if no application has been made in accordance with rule 6, in respect of the decision which is the subject of the request for interim relief, the information required by rule 6(4) above.

(8) On receiving a request for interim relief the Registrar shall send a copy to all the other parties to the proceedings (and where no application has been made in accordance with rule 6, to the competent person who made the decision to which the request for interim relief relates) and shall inform them of the date by which they may submit written or oral observations to the tribunal.

(9) The tribunal shall fix a date for the hearing of the request for interim relief and give the parties any directions as may be necessary for disposing of that request.

(10) If the urgency of the case so requires, the tribunal may dispense with a written request for interim relief or grant the request for interim relief before the observations of the other parties have been submitted.

(11) Unless the context otherwise requires, these rules apply to requests for interim relief.

[2066]

NOTES
Commencement: 1 March 2000.

PART XI
SUPPLEMENTARY

33 Power of President and Chairman to exercise powers of tribunal

(1)   Any act required or authorised by these rules, not being one required or authorised by the following rules—

(a) rule 8	*(power to strike out applications);*
(b) rule 9	*(amendment of application);*
(c) rule 10	*(as regards withdrawal of an application during or after the hearing);*
(d) rule 17 (except sub-paragraphs (2)(h) and (2)(i))	*(directions);*
(e) rule 18	*(pre hearing review);*
(f) rule 24	*(procedure at the hearing);*
(g) rule 25	*(delivery of the decision);*
(h) rule 26	*(costs);*
(i) rule 28	*(consent orders);*
(j) rules 29 and 30	*(appeals);*
(k) rule 31	*(references to the European Court);*

may be done by the President acting alone.

(2)   In relation to particular proceedings, the powers of the President may be exercised by a Chairman of the tribunal constituted to deal with those proceedings except the powers conferred by rule 32 *(interim orders and measures).*

[2067]

NOTES
Commencement: 1 March 2000.

34 Documents etc

(1)   Any document required to be sent to or served on any person in accordance with these rules may be—
  (a) delivered personally at his appropriate address;
  (b) sent to him at his appropriate address by first class post;
  (c) served through a document exchange;
  (d) where authorised by the tribunal, sent to him by facsimile or electronic mail or other similar means.

(2)   A document which is sent to or served in accordance with these rules shall be treated as if it had been received by or served on that person—
  (a) in the case of personal delivery, on the day of delivery;

(b) when sent by first class post or through a document exchange, on the second day after it was posted or left at the document exchange;

(c) in the case of a facsimile transmitted before 4 pm on a business day, on that day and in any other case on the business day after it is transmitted;

(d) in the case of electronic mail or similar means, on the second day after the day on which it is transmitted.

(3)   Subject to paragraph (2)(c) above, if a document is served after 5 pm on any day, the document shall be treated as having been served on the next business day.

(4)   For the purposes of these rules "business day" means any day except Saturday, Sunday or a Bank Holiday, and Bank Holiday includes Christmas Day and Good Friday.

(5)   A person's appropriate address for the purposes of paragraph (1) is—

(a) in the case of a document directed to the tribunal or to the Registrar, the Tribunal address for service;

(b) in the case of a document directed to the applicant or to his representative, the address stated in the application in accordance with rule 6(4)(c) or such other address as may be subsequently notified to the tribunal;

(c) in the case of a document addressed to the respondent, the address stated in the defence in accordance with rule 12(2)(c) or such other address as may be subsequently notified to the tribunal;

(d) in the case of an intervener, the address stated in the request to intervene in accordance with rule 14(4)(d) or such other address as may be subsequently notified to the tribunal.

(6)   Anything required to be sent to or served on a company is duly sent or served if it is sent to or served on the secretary of the company at its principal place of business or registered address on the date of service.

(7)   Anything required to be sent or delivered to or served on a partnership is duly sent or served if it is sent to or served on any one of the partners for the time being.

[2068]

NOTES

Commencement: 1 March 2000.

---

35 Time

(1)   Where a period expressed in days, weeks or months is to be calculated from the moment at which an event occurs or an action takes place, the day during which that event occurs or that action takes place shall not be counted as falling within the period in question.

(2)   A period expressed in weeks or months shall end with the expiry of whichever day in the last week or month is that same day of the week or falls on the same date in the month, as the day during which the event or action from which the period is to be calculated occurred or took place. If, in a period expressed in months, the day on which it should expire does not occur in the last month, the period shall end with the last day of that month.

(3)   Where the time prescribed by the President, a Chairman, the Registrar or the tribunal or by these rules for doing any act expires on a day which is not a business day, the act is in time if done on the next following business day.

[2069]

PART II
STATUTORY INSTRUMENTS

NOTES
Commencement: 1 March 2000.

36 Irregularities

(1) Any irregularity resulting from failure to comply with any provision of these rules before the tribunal has reached its decision shall not of itself render the proceedings void.

(2) Where any such irregularity comes to the attention of the tribunal, the tribunal may, and must if it considers any person may have been prejudiced by the irregularity, give such directions as it thinks just to cure or waive the irregularity before reaching its decision.

(3) Clerical mistakes in any document recording a direction, order or decision of the President, Registrar, a Chairman or tribunal, or errors arising in such a document from an accidental slip or omission, may be corrected by the President, Registrar or Chairman by certificate under his hand.

[2070]

NOTES
Commencement: 1 March 2000.

37 General power of the tribunal

(1) Subject to the provisions of these rules, the tribunal may regulate its own procedure.

(2) The President may issue practice directions in relation to the procedures provided for by these rules.

[2071]

NOTES
Commencement: 1 March 2000.

C. INVESTIGATIONS AND PENALTIES

COMPETITION ACT 1998 (PROVISIONAL IMMUNITY FROM PENALTIES) REGULATIONS 1999

(SI 1999/2281)

NOTES
Made: 10 August 1999.
Authority: Competition Act 1998, ss 41(5), 59(1), 71.
Commencement: 1 March 2000.

1 Citation

These Regulations may be cited as the Competition Act 1998 (Provisional Immunity from Penalties) Regulations 1999 and shall come into force on 1st March 2000.

[2072]

NOTES
Commencement: 1 March 2000.

2 Provisional immunity from penalties

For the purposes of section 41 of the Competition Act 1998 the expression "provisional immunity from penalties" means immunity from fines for breach of the prohibition contained in Article 81(1) of the Treaty by reason of—

  (i) Article 15(5)(a) of Council Regulation (EEC) No 17/62 the First Regulation implementing Articles 85 and 86 of the Treaty;
 (ii) Article 19(4) of Council Regulation (EEC) No 4056/86 laying down detailed rules for the application of Articles 85 and 86 of the Treaty to maritime transport; and
(iii) Article 12(5) of Council Regulation (EEC) No 3975/87 laying down the procedure for the application of the rules on competition to undertakings in the air transport sector.

[2073]

NOTES
Commencement: 1 March 2000.

COMPETITION ACT 1998 (DEFINITION OF APPROPRIATE PERSON) REGULATIONS 1999

(SI 1999/2282)

NOTES
Made: 10 August 1999.
Authority: Competition Act 1998, ss 71, 73(5).
Commencement: 1 March 2000.

1 Citation and commencement

These Regulations may be cited as the Competition Act 1998 (Definition of Appropriate Person) Regulations 1999 and shall come into force on 1st March 2000.

[2074]

2 Definition of appropriate person

For the purposes of section 73(4)(a) of the Competition Act 1998 "appropriate person" means—
  (a) in relation to any land which is occupied by a government department that department; and
  (b) in relation to any other land which is otherwise occupied for purposes of the Crown the person occupying the land for such purposes.

[2075]

COMPETITION ACT 1998 (COMMISSION INVESTIGATION AND DIRECTOR'S INVESTIGATION) ORDER 1999

(SI 1999/3027)

1 Citation and commencement

This Order may be cited as the Competition Act 1998 (Commission Investigation and Director's Investigation) Order 1999 and shall come into force on 1st March 2000.

[2076]

2 Prescribed provisions of Community law

For the purposes of the meaning of "Commission investigation" given in section 61(1) of the Competition Act 1998 each of the following is a prescribed provision of Community law relating to Article 85 or 86—
  (i) Article 14 of Council Regulation (EEC) No 17/62 the First Regulation implementing Articles 85 and 86 of the Treaty;
  (ii) Article 21 of Council Regulation (EEC) No 1017/68 applying rules of competition to transport by rail, road and inland waterway;
  (iii) Article 18 of Council Regulation (EEC) No 4056/86 laying down detailed rules for the application of Articles 85 and 86 of the Treaty to maritime transport; and
  (iv) Article 11 of Council Regulation (EEC) No 3975/87 laying down the procedure for the application of the rules on competition to undertakings in the air transport sector.

[2077]

3 For the purposes of the meaning of "Director's investigation" given in section 61(1) of the Competition Act 1998 each of the following is a prescribed provision of Community law relating to Article 85 or 86—

  (i) Article 13 of Council Regulation (EEC) No 17/62 the First Regulation implementing Articles 85 and 86 of the Treaty;

  (ii) Article 20 of Council Regulation (EEC) No 1017/68 applying rules of competition to transport by rail, road and inland waterway;

  (iii) Article 17 of Council Regulation (EEC) No 4056/86 laying down detailed rules for the application of Articles 85 and 86 of the Treaty to maritime transport; and

  (iv) Article 10 of Council Regulation (EEC) No 3975/87 laying down the procedure for the application of the rules on competition to undertakings in the air transport sector.

[2078]

NOTES
Commencement: 1 March 2000.

Director: the Enterprise Act 2002, s 2(1), at **[255]**, provides that, as from the coming into force of that section in accordance with s 279 at **[463]**, the functions of the Director General of Fair Trading, his property, rights and liabilities are transferred to the Office of Fair Trading. Accordingly, (by virtue of s 2(2), (3) of the 2002 Act) the office of the Director is abolished, and any reference to the Director in any enactment, instrument or other document passed or made before the commencement of s 2(1) shall have effect as if it were a reference to the Office of Fair Trading. For transitional provisions in connection with the transfer, see s 276(1) of, and Sch 24, para 6 to, the 2002 Act at **[477]**.

COMPETITION ACT 1998 (SMALL AGREEMENTS AND CONDUCT OF MINOR SIGNIFICANCE) REGULATIONS 2000

(SI 2000/262)

NOTES
Made: 7 February 2000.
Authority: Competition Act 1998, ss 39, 40, 59(1), 71.
Commencement: 1 March 2000.

1 Citation and commencement

These Regulations may be cited as the Competition Act 1998 (Small Agreements and Conduct of Minor Significance) Regulations 2000 and shall come into force on 1st March 2000.

[2079]

NOTES
Commencement: 1 March 2000.

2 Interpretation

In these Regulations—

  "the Act" means the Competition Act 1998;

  "applicable turnover" means the turnover of an undertaking for a business year determined in accordance with the Schedule to this Order; and where a business year does not equal twelve months the applicable turnover shall be the amount which bears the same proportion to the applicable turnover during that business year as twelve months does to that period;

  "business year" means a period of more than six months in respect of which an undertaking publishes accounts or, if no such accounts have been published for the period, prepares accounts.

[2080]

NOTES
Commencement: 1 March 2000.

3 Small agreements

The category of agreements prescribed for the purposes of section 39(1) of the Act is all agreements between undertakings the combined applicable turnover of which for the business year ending in the calendar year preceding one during which the infringement occurred does not exceed £20 million.

[2081]

NOTES
Commencement: 1 March 2000.

4 Conduct of minor significance

The category of conduct prescribed for the purposes of section 40(1) of the Act is conduct by an undertaking the applicable turnover of which for the business year ending in the calendar year preceding one during which the infringement occurred does not exceed £50 million.

[2082]

NOTES
Commencement: 1 March 2000.

5 Where in the application of regulation 3 or 4 there is a calendar year in respect of which an undertaking has no business year ending in the preceding calendar year then the applicable turnover shall be the turnover for the preceding calendar year.

[2083]

NOTES
Commencement: 1 March 2000.

SCHEDULE

Article 2

APPLICABLE TURNOVER

1. Interpretation

In this Schedule:
- ["credit institution" means a credit institution for the purposes of [Article 1(1)(a)] of Directive 2000/12/EC of the European Parliament and of the Council of 20 March 2000 relating to the taking up and pursuit of the business of credit institutions;
- "financial institution" means a financial institution for the purposes of Article 1 of Directive 2000/12/EC of the European Parliament and of the Council of 20 March 2000 relating to the taking up and pursuit of the business of credit institutions;]
- "insurance undertaking" means an insurance undertaking carrying on the business of direct insurance of a class set out in the Annex to Council Directive (EEC) 73/239 the First Council Directive on the coordination of laws, regulations and administrative provisions relating to the taking up and pursuit of the business of direct insurance other than life assurance or in Article 1 of Council Directive (EEC) 79/267 the First Council Directive on the coordination of laws, regulations and administrative provisions relating to the taking up and pursuit of the business of direct life assurance; and

terms used in this Schedule in respect of the determination of the applicable turnover of credit institutions, financial institutions and insurance undertakings shall (except where the contrary intention appears) have the same meaning as in the relevant Directive.

2. The provisions of this Schedule shall be interpreted in accordance with generally accepted accounting principles and practices.

3. General

The applicable turnover of an undertaking, other than a credit institution, financial institution, insurance undertaking, or an association of undertakings, shall be limited to the amounts derived by the undertaking from the sale of products and the provision of services falling within the undertaking's ordinary activities after deduction of sales rebates, value added tax and other taxes directly related to turnover.

4. Where an undertaking consists of two or more undertakings that each prepare accounts then the applicable turnover shall be calculated by adding together the respective applicable turnover of each, save that no account shall be taken of any turnover resulting from the sale of products or the provision of services between them.

5. Credit institutions and financial institutions

The applicable turnover of a credit institution or financial institution shall be limited to the sum of the following income items listed in Council Directive (EEC) 86/635 received by that institution after deductions of value added tax and other taxes directly related to those items:

   (i)   interest income and similar income;
   (ii) income from securities:
     — income from shares and other variable yield securities,
     — income from participating interests,
     — income from shares in affiliated undertakings,
  (iii) commissions receivable;
  (iv) net profit on financial operations; and
   (v) other operating income.

6. Insurance undertakings

The applicable turnover of an insurance undertaking shall be limited to the value of gross premiums received which shall comprise all amounts received and receivable in respect of insurance contracts issued by or on behalf of the undertaking, including outgoing reinsurance premiums, and after deduction of taxes and parafiscal contributions or levies charged by reference to the amounts of individual premiums or the total volume of premiums.

7. Turnover of associations of undertakings

The turnover of an association of undertakings shall be the aggregate applicable turnover of the undertakings that are members of the association.

8. Aid granted to undertakings

Any aid granted by a public body to an undertaking which relates to one of the undertaking ordinary activities shall be included in the calculation of turnover if the undertaking is itself the recipient of the aid and if the aid is directly linked to the sale of products or the provision of services by the undertaking and is therefore reflected in the price.

[2084]

NOTES

  Commencement: 1 March 2000.

  Para 1: definitions "credit institution" and "financial institution" substituted by the Banking Consolidation Directive (Consequential Amendments) Regulations 2000, SI 2000/2952, reg 15; words in square brackets in definition "credit institution" substituted by the Electronic Money (Miscellaneous Amendments) Regulations 2002, SI 2002/765, reg 8.

PART II
STATUTORY INSTRUMENTS

COMPETITION ACT 1998 (DETERMINATION OF TURNOVER FOR PENALTIES) ORDER 2000

(SI 2000/309)

NOTES

Made: 10 February 2000.
Authority: Competition Act 1998, ss 36(8), 71.
Commencement: 1 March 2000.

1 Citation and commencement

(1)   This Order may be cited as the Competition Act 1998 (Determination of Turnover for Penalties) Order 2000 and shall come into force on 1st March 2000.

[2085]

NOTES

Commencement: 1 March 2000.

2 Interpretation

(1)   In this Order—

"the Act" means the Competition Act 1998;

"applicable turnover" means the turnover of an undertaking for a business year determined in accordance with the Schedule to this Order; and where a business year does not equal 12 months the applicable turnover shall be the amount which bears the same proportion to the applicable turnover during that business year as 12 months does to that period;

"business year" means a period of more than six months in respect of which an undertaking publishes accounts or, if no such accounts have been published for the period, prepares accounts;

"length of the infringement" means the period in a decision made under section 36 of the Act during which an undertaking is determined to have infringed the Chapter I or the Chapter II prohibition, and the "date when the infringement ended" means the end of that period.

[2086]

NOTES

Commencement: 1 March 2000.

3 Determination of turnover for the purposes of section 36(8)

The turnover of an undertaking for the purposes of section 36(8) is—

(1)   the applicable turnover for the business year preceding the date when the infringement ended;

(2)   where the length of the infringement is more than 12 months, in addition the amount of the applicable turnover for the business year preceding that identified under paragraph (1) which bears the same proportion to the applicable turnover for that business year as the period by which the length of infringement exceeds 12 months bears to 12 months; and

(3)   where the length of the infringement is more than 24 months, in addition the amount of the applicable turnover for the business year preceding that identified under paragraph (2) which bears the same proportion to the applicable turnover for that business year as the period by which the length of infringement exceeds 24 months bears to 12 months;

save that the amount added under paragraph (2) or (3) shall not exceed the amount of the applicable turnover for the preceding business year in question.

[2087]

NOTES

Commencement: 1 March 2000.

---

4   Where in the application of article 3 there is any period in respect of which there is no preceding business year then the applicable turnover shall be the turnover for that period.

[2088]

NOTES

Commencement: 1 March 2000.

SCHEDULE

Article 2

APPLICABLE TURNOVER

1. Interpretation

(1)   In this Schedule—

"branch" means a place of business in the United Kingdom which forms a legally dependent part of a credit institution or financial institution and which conducts directly all or some of the operations inherent in the business of the undertaking and any number of branches set up in the United Kingdom shall for the purposes of this Order be regarded as a single branch;

["credit institution" means a credit institution for the purposes of [Article 1(1)(a)] of Directive 2000/12/EC of the European Parliament and of the Council of 20 March 2000 relating to the taking up and pursuit of the business of credit institutions;

"financial institution" means a financial institution for the purposes of Article 1 of Directive 2000/12/EC of the European Parliament and of the Council of 20 March 2000 relating to the taking up and pursuit of the business of credit institutions;]

"insurance undertaking" means an insurance undertaking carrying on the business of direct insurance of a class set out in the Annex to Council Directive (EEC) 73/239 the First Council Directive on the co-ordination of laws, regulations and administrative provisions relating to the taking-up and pursuit of the business of direct insurance other than life assurance or in Article 1 of Council Directive (EEC) 79/267 the First Council Directive on the co-ordination of laws, regulations and administrative provisions relating to the taking up and pursuit of the business of direct life assurance; and

terms used in this Schedule in respect of the determination of the applicable turnover of credit institutions, financial institutions and insurance undertakings shall (except where the contrary intention appears) have the same meaning as in the relevant Directive.

2.   The provisions of this Schedule shall be interpreted in accordance with generally accepted accounting principles and practices.

3. General

The applicable turnover of an undertaking, other than a credit institution, financial institution, insurance undertaking, or an association of undertakings, shall be limited to the amounts derived by the undertaking from the sale of products and the provision of services falling within the undertaking's ordinary activities to undertakings or consumers in the United Kingdom after deduction of sales rebates, value added tax and other taxes directly related to turnover.

4.   Where an undertaking consists of two or more undertakings that each prepare accounts then the applicable turnover shall be calculated by adding together the respective applicable turnover of each, save that no account shall be taken of any turnover resulting from the sale of products or the provision of services between them.

5. Credit institutions and financial institutions

The applicable turnover of a credit institution or financial institution shall be limited to the sum of the following income as defined in Council Directive (EEC) 86/635 received by the branch or division of that institution established in the United Kingdom after deduction of value added tax and other taxes directly related to those items—

   (i) interest income and similar income;
   (ii) income from securities—
      — income from shares and other variable yield securities;
      — income from participating interests;
      — income from shares in affiliated undertakings;
   (iii) commissions receivable;
   (iv) net profit on financial operations;
   (v) other operating income.

6. Insurance undertakings

The applicable turnover of an insurance undertaking shall be limited to the value of gross premiums received from residents of the United Kingdom which shall comprise all amounts received and receivable in respect of insurance contracts issued by or on behalf of the undertaking, including outgoing reinsurance premiums, and after deduction of taxes and parafiscal contributions or levies charged by reference to the amounts of individual premiums or the total volume of premiums.

7. Turnover of associations of undertakings

The turnover of an association of undertakings shall be the aggregate applicable turnover of the undertakings that are members of the association.

8. Aid granted to undertakings

Any aid granted by a public body to an undertaking which relates to one of the undertaking's ordinary activities shall be included in the calculation of turnover if the undertaking is itself the recipient of the aid and if the aid is directly linked to the sale of products or the provision of services by the undertaking and is therefore reflected in the price.

[2089]

NOTES
Commencement: 1 March 2000.
Para 1: definitions "credit institution" and "financial institution" substituted by the Banking Consolidation Directive (Consequential Amendments) Regulations 2000, SI 2000/2952, reg 16; words in square brackets in definition "credit institution" substituted by the Electronic Money (Miscellaneous Amendments) Regulations 2002, SI 2002/765, reg 9.

EC COMPETITION LAW (ARTICLES 84 AND 85) ENFORCEMENT REGULATIONS 2001

(SI 2001/2916)

NOTES
Made: 15 August 2001.
Authority: European Communities Act 1972, s 2(2).
Commencement: 17 August 2001.

ARRANGEMENT OF REGULATIONS

1 Citation, commencement and extent

(1)   These Regulations may be cited as the EC Competition Law (Articles 84 and 85) Enforcement Regulations 2001 and shall come into force on the day after the day on which they are laid before Parliament.

(2)   These Regulations shall extend to Northern Ireland.

[2090]

NOTES

Commencement: 17 August 2001.

2 Interpretation

(1)   In these Regulations—
    "the Act" means the Competition Act 1998;
    "the court" means—
        (a) in England and Wales, the High Court;
        (b) in Scotland, the Court of Session; and
        (c) in Northern Ireland, the High Court;
    "the Director" means the Director General of Fair Trading;

"document" includes information recorded in any form;

"information" includes estimates and forecasts;

"investigating officer" has the meaning given in regulation 13(1);

"officer", in relation to a body corporate, includes a director, manager or secretary and, in relation to a partnership in Scotland, includes a partner;

"person", in addition to the meaning given by the Interpretation Act 1978, includes any undertaking;

"premises" does not include domestic premises unless—

    (a) they are also used in connection with the affairs of an undertaking, or

    (b) documents relating to the affairs of an undertaking are kept there,

but does include any vehicle;

"President" means the person appointed under paragraph 4 of Schedule 7 to the Act;

"the 1996 Regulations" means the EC Competition Law (Articles 88 and 89) Enforcement Regulations 1996;

"tribunal" means an appeal tribunal established in accordance with the provisions of Part III of Schedule 7 to the Act; and

"tribunal rules" means the rules made in accordance with section 48(2) of the Act.

(2)   References in these Regulations to Articles are references to Articles of the treaty establishing the European Community.

(3)   Any provision of these Regulations which is expressed to apply to, or in relation to, an agreement is to be read as applying equally to, or in relation to, a decision by an association of undertakings or a concerted practice (but with any necessary modifications).

(4)   Paragraph (3) above does not apply where the context otherwise requires.

(5)   For the purposes of these Regulations, the power to require information, in relation to information recorded otherwise than in a legible form, includes power to require a copy of it in a legible form.

(6)   Any power conferred on the Director by these Regulations to require information includes the power to require any document which he believes may contain that information.

[2091]

NOTES

Commencement: 17 August 2001.

Director General of Fair Trading: the Enterprise Act 2002, s 2(1), at **[255]**, provides that, as from the coming into force of that section in accordance with s 279 at **[463]**, the functions of the Director General of Fair Trading, his property, rights and liabilities are transferred to the Office of Fair Trading. Accordingly, (by virtue of s 2(2), (3) of the 2002 Act) the office of the Director is abolished, and any reference to the Director in any enactment, instrument or other document passed or made before the commencement of s 2(1) shall have effect as if it were a reference to the Office of Fair Trading. For transitional provisions in connection with the transfer, see s 276(1) of, and Sch 24, para 6 to, the 2002 Act at **[477]**.

---

3 Commencement of investigations by the Director

(1)   If it appears to the Director that the United Kingdom might have a duty under Article 84 to rule on the question—

    (a) whether or not there is or has been in existence an agreement which infringes or has infringed the prohibition in Article 81(1), or

    (b) whether or not conduct constitutes an infringement of the prohibition in Article 82,

he may commence an investigation under these Regulations.

(2)   The Director may conclude that the United Kingdom might have such a duty if—

(a) there are reasonable grounds for suspecting that there is or has been in existence an agreement which may infringe the prohibition in Article 81(1),

(b) there are reasonable grounds for suspecting that the prohibition in Article 82 has been infringed,

(c) a party to an agreement applies for an agreement to be considered under regulation 7, or

(d) a person applies for conduct to be considered under regulation 10.

[2092]

NOTES

Commencement: 17 August 2001.

Director: see the note "Director General of Fair Trading" to reg 2 at **[2091]**.

4 Exemptions

(1)   The Director may grant an exemption from the prohibition in Article 81(1) with respect to a particular agreement if—

(a) a request for an exemption has been made to him under regulation 7 by a party to the agreement; and

(b) the conditions for application of Article 81(3) are met.

(2)   The exemption—

(a) may be granted subject to such conditions or obligations as the Director considers it appropriate to impose; and

(b) has effect for such period as the Director considers appropriate.

(3)   That period must be specified in the grant of the exemption.

(4)   On an application in accordance with the rules set out in Schedule 1, the Director may, in accordance with those rules, extend the period for which an exemption has effect.

[(5) If an exemption granted under this regulation is subject to conditions or obligations concerning slots, the Director may (for the purpose of that exemption) give to such person or persons as he considers appropriate such directions as he considers appropriate in relation to the allocation or use of those slots.

(6)   A direction under paragraph (5) must be given in writing.

(7)   In this regulation, "slot" means the scheduled time of arrival or departure available or allocated to an aircraft movement on a specific date at an airport co-ordinated under the terms of Council Regulation (EEC) No 95/93 on common rules for the allocation of slots at Community airports.]

[2093]

NOTES

Commencement: 17 August 2001.

Paras (5)–(7): inserted by the EC Competition Law (Articles 84 and 85) Enforcement (Amendment) Regulations 2002, SI 2002/42, regs 2, 3.

Director: see the note "Director General of Fair Trading" to reg 2 at **[2091]**.

5 Cancellation etc of exemptions

(1)   If the Director has reasonable grounds for believing that there has been a material change of circumstance since he granted an exemption, he may by notice in writing—

(a) cancel the exemption;

(b) vary or remove any condition or obligation; or

(c) impose one or more additional conditions or obligations.

(2)   If the Director has a reasonable suspicion that the information on which he based his decision to grant an exemption was incomplete, false or misleading in a material particular, he may by notice in writing take any of the steps mentioned in paragraph (1).

(3)   Breach of a condition has the effect of cancelling the exemption.

(4)   Failure to comply with an obligation allows the Director, by notice in writing, to take any of the steps mentioned in paragraph (1).

(5)   Any step taken by the Director under paragraph (1), (2) or (4) has effect from such time as may be specified in the notice.

(6)   If an exemption is cancelled under paragraph (2) or (4), the date specified in the notice cancelling it may be earlier than the date on which the notice is given.

(7)   The Director may act under paragraph (1), (2) or (4) on his own initiative or on a complaint made by any person.

[2094]

NOTES

Commencement: 17 August 2001.

Director: see the note "Director General of Fair Trading" to reg 2 at **[2091]**.

6 Notification in relation to agreements

(1)   Regulation 7 provides for an agreement to be examined by the Director on the application of a party to the agreement who thinks that it may infringe the prohibition in Article 81(1).

(2)   Schedule 1 provides for the procedure to be followed—
    (a) by any person making such an application; and
    (b) by the Director, in considering such an application.

[2095]

NOTES

Commencement: 17 August 2001.

Director: see the note "Director General of Fair Trading" to reg 2 at **[2091]**.

7 Notification for a decision in relation to agreements

(1)   A party to an agreement who applies for the agreement to be examined under this regulation must—
    (a) notify the Director of the agreement; and
    (b) apply to him for a decision.

(2)   On an application under this regulation, the Director may make a decision as to whether the prohibition in Article 81(1) has been infringed.

(3)   If an agreement is notified to the Director under this regulation, the application may include a request for the agreement to which it relates to be granted an exemption.

[2096]

NOTES

Commencement: 17 August 2001.

Director: see the note "Director General of Fair Trading" to reg 2 at **[2091]**.

8 Effect of a decision that the prohibition in Article 81(1) has not been infringed

(1)   This regulation applies to an agreement if the Director has determined an application under regulation 7 by making a decision that the agreement has not infringed the prohibition in Article 81(1).

(2)   The Director is to take no further action under these Regulations with respect to the agreement unless—

(a) he has reasonable grounds for believing that there has been a material change of circumstance since he gave his decision; or

(b) he has a reasonable suspicion that the information on which he based his decision was incomplete, false or misleading in a material particular; or

(c) pursuant to Article 85(2), the European Commission has taken a reasoned decision recording an infringement of Article 81(1) and has authorised the United Kingdom to take measures needed to remedy the situation.

[2097]

NOTES

Commencement: 17 August 2001.

Director: see the note "Director General of Fair Trading" to reg 2 at **[2091]**.

9 Notification in relation to conduct

(1)   Regulation 10 provides for conduct of a person which that person thinks may infringe the prohibition in Article 82 to be considered by the Director on the application of that person.

(2)   Schedule 1 provides for the procedure to be followed—

(a) by any person making an application, and

(b) by the Director, in considering an application.

[2098]

NOTES

Commencement: 17 August 2001.

Director: see the note "Director General of Fair Trading" to reg 2 at **[2091]**.

10 Notification for a decision in relation to conduct

(1)   A person who applies for conduct to be considered under this regulation must—

(a) notify the Director of it; and

(b) apply to him for a decision.

(2)   On an application under this regulation the Director may make a decision as to whether the prohibition in Article 82 has been infringed.

[2099]

NOTES

Commencement: 17 August 2001.

Director: see the note "Director General of Fair Trading" to reg 2 at **[2091]**.

11 Effect of a decision that the prohibition in Article 82 has not been infringed

(1)   This regulation applies to conduct if the Director has determined an application under regulation 10 by making a decision that the conduct has not infringed the prohibition in Article 82.

(2)   The Director is to take no further action under these Regulations with respect to the conduct unless—

(a) he has reasonable grounds for believing that there has been a material change of circumstance since he gave his decision; or

(b) he has a reasonable suspicion that the information on which he based his decision was incomplete, false or misleading in a material particular; or

(c) pursuant to Article 85(2), the European Commission has taken a reasoned decision recording an infringement of Article 82 and has authorised the United Kingdom to take measures needed to remedy the situation.

[2100]

NOTES

Commencement: 17 August 2001.

Director: see the note "Director General of Fair Trading" to reg 2 at **[2091]**.

12 Powers when conducting investigations

(1) For the purposes of an investigation under regulation 3, the Director may require any person to produce to him a specified document, or to provide him with specified information, which he considers relates to any matter relevant to the investigation.

(2) The power conferred by paragraph (1) is to be exercised by a notice in writing.

(3) A notice under paragraph (2) must indicate—
(a) the subject matter and purpose of the investigation; and
(b) the nature of the offences created by regulations 22 to 24.

(4) In paragraph (1) "specified" means—
(a) specified, or described, in the notice; or
(b) falling within a category which is specified, or described, in the notice.

(5) The Director may also specify in the notice—
(a) the time and place at which any document is to be produced or any information is to be provided;
(b) the manner and form in which it is to be produced or provided.

(6) The power under this paragraph to require a person to produce a document includes power—
(a) if the document is produced—
    (i) to take copies of it or extracts from it;
    (ii) to require him, or any person who is a present or past officer of his, or is or was at any time employed by him, to provide an explanation of the document;
(b) if the document is not produced, to require him to state, to the best of his knowledge and belief, where it is.

[2101]

NOTES

Commencement: 17 August 2001.

Director: see the note "Director General of Fair Trading" to reg 2 at **[2091]**.

13 Power to enter premises without a warrant

(1) Any officer of the Director who is authorised in writing by the Director to do so ("an investigating officer") may enter any premises in connection with an investigation under regulation 3.

(2) No investigating officer is to enter any premises in the exercise of his powers under this regulation unless he has given to the occupier of the premises a written notice which—
(a) gives at least two working days' notice of the intended entry;
(b) indicates the subject matter and purpose of the investigation; and
(c) indicates the nature of the offences created by regulations 22 to 24.

(3)   Paragraph (2) does not apply—

   (a)   if the Director has a reasonable suspicion that the premises are, or have been, occupied by—

     (i)   a party to an agreement which he is investigating under regulation 3; or

     (ii)   an undertaking the conduct of which he is investigating under regulation 3; or

   (b)   if the investigating officer has taken all such steps as are reasonably practicable to give notice but has not been able to do so.

(4)   In a case falling within paragraph (3), the power of entry conferred by paragraph (1) is to be exercised by the investigating officer on production of—

   (a)   evidence of his authorisation; and

   (b)   a document containing the information referred to in paragraph (2)(b) and (c).

(5)   An investigating officer entering any premises under this regulation may—

   (a)   take with him such equipment as appears to him to be necessary;

   (b)   require any person on the premises—

     (i)   to produce any document which he considers relates to any matter relevant to the investigation; and

     (ii)   if the document is produced, to provide an explanation of it;

   (c)   require any person to state, to the best of his knowledge and belief, where any such document is to be found;

   (d)   take copies of, or extracts from, any document which is produced;

   (e)   require any information which is held in a computer and is accessible from the premises and which the investigating officer considers relates to any matter relevant to the investigation, to be produced in a form—

     (i)   in which it can be taken away, and

     (ii)   in which it is visible and legible.

[2102]

NOTES

Commencement: 17 August 2001.

Director: see the note "Director General of Fair Trading" to reg 2 at **[2091]**.

14   Powers to enter premises under a warrant

(1)   On an application made by the Director to the court in accordance with rules of court, a judge may issue a warrant if he is satisfied that—

   (a)   there are reasonable grounds for suspecting that there are on any premises documents—

     (i)   the production of which has been required under regulation 12 or 13; and

     (ii)   which have not been produced as required;

   (b)   there are reasonable grounds for suspecting that—

     (i)   there are on any premises documents which the Director has power under regulation 12 to require to be produced; and

     (ii)   if the documents were required to be produced, they would not be produced but would be concealed, removed, tampered with or destroyed; or

   (c)   an investigating officer has attempted to enter premises in the exercise of his powers under regulation 13 but has been unable to do so and that there are reasonable grounds for suspecting that there are on the premises documents the production of which could have been required under that regulation.

(2)   A warrant under this regulation shall authorise a named officer of the Director, and any other of his officers whom he has authorised in writing to accompany the named officer—

    (a) to enter the premises specified in the warrant, using such force as is reasonably necessary for the purpose;

    (b) to search the premises and take copies of, or extracts from, any document appearing to be of a kind in respect of which the application under paragraph (1) was granted ("the relevant kind");

    (c) to take possession of any documents appearing to be of the relevant kind if—

        (i) such action appears to be necessary for preserving the documents or preventing interference with them; or

        (ii) it is not reasonably practicable to take copies of the documents on the premises;

    (d) to take any other steps which appear to be necessary for the purpose mentioned in sub-paragraph (c)(i);

    (e) to require any person to provide an explanation of any document appearing to be of the relevant kind or to state, to the best of his knowledge and belief, where it may be found;

    (f) to require any information which is held in a computer and is accessible from the premises and which the named officer considers relates to any matter relevant to the investigation, to be produced in a form—

        (i) in which it can be taken away, and

        (ii) in which it is visible and legible.

(3)   If, in the case of a warrant under paragraph (1)(b), the judge is satisfied that it is reasonable to suspect that there are also on the premises other documents relating to the investigation concerned, the warrant shall also authorise action mentioned in paragraph (2) to be taken in relation to any such document.

(4)   Any person entering premises by virtue of a warrant under this regulation may take with him such equipment as appears to him to be necessary.

(5)   On leaving any premises which he has entered by virtue of a warrant under this regulation, the named officer must, if the premises are unoccupied or the occupier is temporarily absent, leave them as effectively secured as he found them.

(6)   A warrant under this regulation continues in force until the end of the period of one month beginning with the day on which it is issued.

(7)   Any document of which possession is taken under paragraph (2)(c) may be retained for a period of three months.

                                                      [2103]

NOTES

Commencement: 17 August 2001.

Director: see the note "Director General of Fair Trading" to reg 2 at **[2091]**.

---

15 Entry of premises under warrant—supplementary

(1)   A warrant issued under regulation 14 must indicate—

    (a) the subject matter and purpose of the investigation;

    (b) the nature of the offences created by regulations 22 to 24.

(2)   The powers conferred by regulation 14 are to be exercised on production of a warrant issued under that regulation.

(3)   If there is no one at the premises when the named officer proposes to execute such a warrant he must, before executing it—

(a) take such steps as are reasonable in all the circumstances to inform the occupier of the intended entry; and

(b) if the occupier is informed, afford him or his legal or other representative a reasonable opportunity to be present when the warrant is executed.

(4)   If the named officer is unable to inform the occupier of the intended entry he must, when executing the warrant, leave a copy of it in a prominent place on the premises.

(5)   In this regulation—

"named officer" means the officer named in the warrant; and

"occupier", in relation to any premises, means a person whom the named officer reasonably believes is the occupier of those premises.

[2104]

NOTES

Commencement: 17 August 2001.

16 Privileged communications

(1)   A person shall not be required, under any provision of these Regulations, to produce or disclose a privileged communication.

(2)   "Privileged communication" means a communication—

(a) between a professional legal adviser and his client, or

(b) made in connection with, or in contemplation of, legal proceedings and for the purposes of those proceedings,

which in proceedings in the High Court would be protected from disclosure on grounds of legal professional privilege.

(3)   In the application of this regulation to Scotland—

(a) references to the High Court are to be read as references to the Court of Session; and

(b) the reference to legal professional privilege is to be read as a reference to confidentiality of communications.

[2105]

NOTES

Commencement: 17 August 2001.

17 Decisions following an investigation

(1)   Paragraph (2) applies if, as the result of an investigation conducted under regulation 3, the Director proposes to make—

(a) a decision that the prohibition in Article 81(1) has been infringed, or

(b) a decision that the prohibition in Article 82 has been infringed.

(2)   Before making the decision, the Director must—

(a) give written notice to the person (or persons) likely to be affected by the proposed decision; and

(b) give that person (or those persons) an opportunity to make representations.

[2106]

NOTES

Commencement: 17 August 2001.

Director: see the note "Director General of Fair Trading" to reg 2 at **[2091]**.

18 Directions in relation to agreements

(1) If—
   (a) the Director has made a decision that an agreement infringes the prohibition in Article 81(1), or
   (b) pursuant to Article 85(2) the European Commission has taken a reasoned decision recording an infringement of Article 81(1) and has authorised the United Kingdom to take measures needed to remedy the situation,

the Director may give to such person or persons as he considers appropriate such directions as he considers appropriate to bring the infringement to an end.

(2) Paragraph (1)(a) applies whether the Director's decision is made on his own initiative or on an application made to him under these Regulations.

(3) A direction under this regulation may, in particular, include provision—
   (a) requiring the parties to the agreement to modify the agreement; or
   (b) requiring them to terminate the agreement.

(4) A direction under this regulation must be given in writing.

[2107]

NOTES
Commencement: 17 August 2001.
Director: see the note "Director General of Fair Trading" to reg 2 at **[2091]**.

19 Directions in relation to conduct

(1) If—
   (a) the Director has made a decision that conduct infringes the prohibition in Article 82, or
   (b) pursuant to Article 85(2) the European Commission has taken a reasoned decision recording an infringement of Article 82 and has authorised the United Kingdom to take measures needed to remedy the situation,

the Director may give to such person or persons as he considers appropriate such directions as he considers appropriate to bring the infringement to an end.

(2) Paragraph (1)(a) applies whether the Director's decision is made on his own initiative or on an application made to him under these regulations.

(3) A direction under this regulation may, in particular, include provision—
   (a) requiring the person concerned to modify the conduct in question; or
   (b) requiring him to cease that conduct.

(4) A direction under this regulation must be given in writing.

[2108]

NOTES
Commencement: 17 August 2001.
Director: see the note "Director General of Fair Trading" to reg 2 at **[2091]**.

20 Enforcement of Directions

(1) If a person fails, without reasonable excuse, to comply with a direction under regulation [4, 18 or 19], the Director may apply to the court for an order—
   (a) requiring the defaulter to make good his default within a time specified in the order; or
   (b) if the direction related to anything to be done in the management or administration of an undertaking, requiring the undertaking or any of its officers to do it.

(2)   An order of the court under paragraph (1) may provide for all of the costs of, or incidental to, the application for the order to be borne by—

(a) the person in default; or

(b) any officer of an undertaking who is responsible for the default.

(3)   In the application of paragraph (2) to Scotland, the reference to "costs" is to be read as a reference to "expenses".

[2109]

NOTES

Commencement: 17 August 2001.

Para (1): words in square brackets substituted by the EC Competition Law (Articles 84 and 85) Enforcement (Amendment) Regulations 2002, SI 2002/42, regs 2, 4.

Director: see the note "Director General of Fair Trading" to reg 2 at **[2091]**.

21 Interim measures

(1)   This regulation applies if the Director—

(a) has a reasonable suspicion that an agreement is or has been in existence which may infringe the prohibition in Article 81(1), or

(b) has a reasonable suspicion that the prohibition in Article 82 has been infringed,

but has not completed his investigation into the matter.

(2)   If the Director considers that it is necessary for him to act under this regulation as a matter of urgency for the purpose—

(a) of preventing serious, irreparable damage to a particular person or category of person, or

(b) of protecting the public interest,

he may give such directions as he considers appropriate for that purpose.

(3)   Before giving a direction under this regulation, the Director must—

(a) give written notice to the person (or persons) to whom he proposes to give the direction; and

(b) give that person (or each of them) an opportunity to make representations.

(4)   A notice under paragraph (3) must indicate the nature of the direction which the Director is proposing to give and his reasons for wishing to give it.

(5)   A direction given under this regulation has effect while paragraph (1) applies, but may be replaced if the circumstances permit by a direction under regulation 18 or, as appropriate, regulation 19.

(6)   In a case where it is suspected that there may be an infringement of the prohibition in Article 81(1), regulations 18(3) and 20 also apply to directions given under this regulation.

(7)   In the case of a suspected infringement of the prohibition in Article 82, regulations 19(3) and 20 also apply to directions given under this regulation.

[2110]

NOTES

Commencement: 17 August 2001.

Director: see the note "Director General of Fair Trading" to reg 2 at **[2091]**.

22 Offences

(1)   A person is guilty of an offence if he fails to comply with a requirement imposed on him under regulations 12, 13 or 14.

(2)   If a person is charged with an offence under paragraph (1) in respect of a requirement to produce a document, it is a defence for him to prove—

(a) that the document was not in his possession or under his control; and

(b) that it was not reasonably practicable for him to comply with the requirement.

(3)   If a person is charged with an offence under paragraph (1) in respect of a requirement—

(a) to provide information,

(b) to provide an explanation of a document, or

(c) to state where a document is to be found,

it is a defence for him to prove that he had a reasonable excuse for failing to comply with the requirement.

(4)   Failure to comply with a requirement imposed under regulation 12 or 13 is not an offence if the person imposing the requirement has failed to act in accordance with that regulation.

(5)   A person is guilty of an offence if he intentionally obstructs an officer acting in the exercise of his powers under regulation 13.

(6)   A person guilty of an offence under paragraph (1) or (5) is liable—

(a) on summary conviction, to a fine not exceeding the statutory maximum;

(b) on conviction on indictment, to a fine.

(7)   A person who intentionally obstructs an officer in the exercise of his powers under a warrant issued under regulation 14 is guilty of an offence and liable—

(a) on summary conviction, to a fine not exceeding the statutory maximum;

(b) on conviction on indictment, to imprisonment for a term not exceeding two years or to a fine or to both.

[2111]

NOTES

Commencement: 17 August 2001.

23 Destroying or falsifying documents

(1)   A person is guilty of an offence if, having been required to produce a document under regulation 12, 13 or 14—

(a) he intentionally or recklessly destroys or otherwise disposes of it, falsifies it or conceals it, or

(b) he causes or permits its destruction, disposal, falsification or concealment.

(2)   A person guilty of an offence under paragraph (1) is liable—

(a) on summary conviction, to a fine not exceeding the statutory maximum;

(b) on conviction on indictment, to imprisonment for a term not exceeding two years or to a fine or to both.

[2112]

NOTES

Commencement: 17 August 2001.

24 False or misleading information

(1)   If information is provided by a person to the Director in connection with any function of the Director under these Regulations, that person is guilty of an offence if—

(a) the information is false or misleading in a material particular, and

(b) he knows that it is or is reckless as to whether it is.

(2)   A person who—

(a) provides any information to another person, knowing the information to be false or misleading in a material particular, or

    (b) recklessly provides any information to another person which is false or misleading in a material particular,

knowing that the information is to be used for the purpose of providing information to the Director in connection with any of his functions under these Regulations, is guilty of an offence.

    (3) A person guilty of an offence under this regulation is liable—
      (a) on summary conviction, to a fine not exceeding the statutory maximum;
      (b) on conviction on indictment, to imprisonment for a term not exceeding two years or to a fine or to both.

[2113]

NOTES

Commencement: 17 August 2001.

Director: see the note "Director General of Fair Trading" to reg 2 at **[2091]**.

25 Appeals

    (1) Any party to an agreement in respect of which the Director has made a decision may appeal to the tribunal against, or with respect to, the decision.

    (2) Any person in respect of whose conduct the Director has made a decision may appeal to the tribunal against, or with respect to, the decision.

    (3) In this regulation "decision" means a decision of the Director—
      (a) as to whether the prohibition in Article 81(1) has been infringed,
      (b) as to whether the prohibition in Article 82 has been infringed,
      (c) as to whether to grant an exemption,
      (d) in respect of an exemption—
        (i) as to whether to impose any condition or obligation under regulation 4(2)(a) or 5(1)(c),
        (ii) where such a condition or obligation has been imposed, as to the condition or obligation,
        (iii) as to the period fixed under regulation 4(2)(b),
        [(iv) as to whether to give a direction under regulation 4, or as to the terms of any such direction,]
      (e) as to—
        (i) whether to extend the period for which an exemption has effect, or
        (ii) the period of any such extension,
      (f) cancelling an exemption,
      (g) withdrawing or varying a decision in paragraph (a) to (f) following an application under regulation 26,

and includes a direction given under regulation 18, 19 or 21.

    [(3A)Any person to whom a direction has been given under regulation 4 may appeal to the tribunal against, or with respect to, the direction.]

    (4) The making of an appeal under this regulation does not suspend the effect of the decision to which the appeal relates.

    (5) Schedule 2 makes further provision about appeals.

[2114]

NOTES

Commencement: 17 August 2001.

Para (3): sub-para (d)(iv) inserted by the EC Competition Law (Articles 84 and 85) Enforcement (Amendment) Regulations 2002, SI 2002/42, regs 2, 5(1).

Para (3A): inserted by SI 2002/42, regs 2, 5(2).

Director: see the note "Director General of Fair Trading" to reg 2 at **[2091]**.

26 Third party appeals

(1)   A person who does not fall within regulation 25(1) or (2) may apply to the Director asking him to withdraw or vary a decision ("the relevant decision") falling within paragraphs (a) to (f) of regulation 25.

(2)   The application must—
  (a) be made in writing, within such period as is specified in the rules in Schedule 1; and
  (b) give the applicant's reasons for considering that the relevant decision should be withdrawn or (as the case may be) varied.

(3)   If the Director decides—
  (a) that the applicant does not have a sufficient interest in the relevant decision,
  (b) that, in the case of an applicant claiming to represent persons who have such an interest, the applicant does not represent such persons, or
  (c) that the persons represented by the applicant do not have such an interest,

he must notify the applicant of his decision.

(4)   If the Director, having considered the application, decides that it does not show sufficient reason why he should withdraw or vary the relevant decision, he must notify the applicant of his decision.

(5)   Otherwise, the Director must deal with the application in accordance with the rules in Schedule 1.

(6)   The applicant may appeal to the tribunal against a decision of the Director notified under paragraph (3) or (4).

(7)   The making of an application does not suspend the effect of the relevant decision.

[2115]

NOTES
  Commencement: 17 August 2001.
  Director: see the note "Director General of Fair Trading" to reg 2 at **[2091]**.

27 Appeal tribunals

(1)   Any appeal made to the tribunal under regulation 25 or 26 is to be determined by a tribunal constituted by the President in accordance with paragraph 27 of Schedule 7 to the Act.

(2)   The tribunal rules shall apply to an appeal under regulation 25 or 26 save that any reference in the tribunal rules to the provisions of the Act shall be deemed to be to the equivalent provisions in these Regulations.

[2116]

NOTES
  Commencement: 17 August 2001.

28 Appeals on point of law etc

(1)   An appeal lies on a point of law arising from a decision of the tribunal.

(2)   An appeal under this regulation may be made only—
  (a) to the appropriate court;
  (b) with permission and in accordance with the requirements of the tribunal rules; and

(c) at the instance of a party or at the instance of a person who has a sufficient interest in the matter.

(3)   In paragraph (2)—
"the appropriate court" means—
  (a) in relation to proceedings before a tribunal in England and Wales, the Court of Appeal;
  (b) in relation to proceedings before a tribunal in Scotland, the Court of Session;
  (c) in relation to proceedings before a tribunal in Northern Ireland, the Court of Appeal in Northern Ireland;
"party", in relation to a decision, means a person who was a party to the proceedings in which the decision was made; and
"permission" means permission of the tribunal in question or of the appropriate court.

[2117]

NOTES
Commencement: 17 August 2001.

29 General restrictions on disclosure of information

(1)   No information which—
  (a) has been obtained under or as a result of any provision of these Regulations, and
  (b) relates to the affairs of any individual or to any particular business of an undertaking, is to be disclosed during the lifetime of that individual or while that business continues to be carried on, unless the condition mentioned in paragraph (2) is satisfied.

(2)   The condition is that consent to the disclosure has been obtained from—
  (a) the person from whom the information was initially obtained under or as a result of any provision of these Regulations (if the identity of that person is known); and
  (b) if different—
    (i) the individual to whose affairs the information relates, or
    (ii) the person for the time being carrying on the business to which the information relates.

(3)   Paragraph (1) does not apply to a disclosure of information—
  (a) made for the purpose of—
    (i) facilitating the performance of any functions of the Director, the Civil Aviation Authority, the Competition Commission, or the Secretary of State under these Regulations, or the Fair Trading Act 1973, or the Competition Act 1980, or the Civil Aviation Act 1982, or the Airports Act 1986; or the Licensing of Air Carriers Regulations 1992, or Part IV of the Airports (Northern Ireland) Order 1994, or Part I of the Transport Act 2000 or the Act;
    (ii) facilitating the performance of any functions of the European Commission in respect of Community law about competition;
    (iii) facilitating the performance by the Comptroller and Auditor General of any of his functions;
    (iv) criminal proceedings in any part of the United Kingdom;
  (b) made with a view to the institution of, or otherwise for the purposes of, civil proceedings brought under or in connection with these Regulations;
  (c) made in connection with the investigation of any criminal offence triable in the United Kingdom or in any part of the United Kingdom; or
  (d) which is required to meet a Community obligation.

(4)   If information is disclosed to the public in circumstances in which the disclosure does not contravene paragraph (1), that paragraph does not prevent its further disclosure by any person.

(5)   A person who contravenes this regulation is guilty of an offence and liable—
   (a) on summary conviction, to a fine not exceeding the statutory maximum; or
   (b) on conviction on indictment, to imprisonment for a term not exceeding two years or to a fine or to both.

[2118]

NOTES
   Commencement: 17 August 2001.
   Director: see the note "Director General of Fair Trading" to reg 2 at **[2091]**.

30 Director to have regard to certain matters in relation to the disclosure of information

(1)   This regulation applies if the Director is considering whether to disclose any information acquired by him under, or as a result of, any provision of these Regulations.

(2)   He must have regard to the need for excluding, so far as is practicable, information the disclosure of which would in his opinion be contrary to the public interest.

(3)   He must also have regard to—
   (a) the need for excluding, so far as is practicable—
      (i) commercial information the disclosure of which would, or might, in his opinion, significantly harm the legitimate business interests of the undertaking to which it relates, or
      (ii) information relating to the private affairs of an individual the disclosure of which would, or might, in his opinion, significantly harm his interests; and
   (b) the extent to which the disclosure is necessary for the purposes for which the Director is proposing to make the disclosure.

[2119]

NOTES
   Commencement: 17 August 2001.
   Director: see the note "Director General of Fair Trading" to reg 2 at **[2091]**.

31 Defamation

For the purposes of the law relating to defamation, absolute privilege attaches to any advice, notice or direction given, or decision made, by the Director in the exercise of any of his functions under these Regulations.

[2120]

NOTES
   Commencement: 17 August 2001.
   Director: see the note "Director General of Fair Trading" to reg 2 at **[2091]**.

32 Findings of fact by the Director

(1)   Unless the court directs otherwise or the Director has decided to take further action in accordance with regulation 8(2) or 11(2), a Director's finding which is relevant to an issue arising in proceedings which are brought otherwise than by the Director in respect of an alleged infringement under these Regulations of the prohibition in Article 81(1) or of the prohibition in Article 82 is binding on the parties if—

(a) the time for bringing an appeal in respect of the finding has expired and the relevant party has not brought such an appeal; or

(b) the decision of a tribunal on such an appeal has confirmed the finding.

(2) In this regulation—

"a Director's finding" means a finding of fact made by the Director in the course of—

(a) determining an application for a decision under regulation 7 or 10, or

(b) conducting an investigation under regulation 3;

"relevant party" means—

(a) in relation to the prohibition in Article 81(1), a party to the agreement which is alleged to have infringed the prohibition; and

(b) in relation to the prohibition in Article 82, the undertaking whose conduct is alleged to have infringed the prohibition.

(3) Rules of court may make provision in respect of assistance to be given by the Director to the court in the proceedings referred to in paragraph (1).

[2121]

NOTES

Commencement: 17 August 2001.

Director: see the note "Director General of Fair Trading" to reg 2 at **[2091]**.

33 Offences by bodies corporate etc

(1) This regulation applies to an offence under any of regulations 22 to 24 or 29(5).

(2) If an offence committed by a body corporate is proved—

(a) to have been committed with the consent or connivance of an officer, or

(b) to be attributable to any neglect on his part,

the officer as well as the body corporate is guilty of the offence and liable to be proceeded against and punished accordingly.

(3) In paragraph (2) "officer", in relation to a body corporate, means a director, manager, secretary or other similar officer of the body, or a person purporting to act in any such capacity.

(4) If the affairs of a body corporate are managed by its members, paragraph (2) applies in relation to the acts and defaults of a member in connection with his functions of management as if he were a director of the body corporate.

(5) If an offence committed by a partnership in Scotland is proved—

(a) to have been committed with the consent or connivance of a partner, or

(b) to be attributable to any neglect on his part,

the partner as well as the partnership is guilty of the offence and liable to be proceeded against and punished accordingly.

(6) In paragraph (5) "partner" includes a person purporting to act as a partner.

[2122]

NOTES

Commencement: 17 August 2001.

34 Crown application

(1) Any provision made by or under these Regulations binds the Crown except that—

(a) the Crown is not criminally liable as a result of any such provisions; and

(b) nothing in these Regulations affects Her Majesty in her private capacity.

(2)   Paragraph (1)(a) does not affect the application of any provision of these Regulations in relation to persons in the public service of the Crown.

(3)   Paragraph (1)(b) is to be interpreted as if section 38(3) of the Crown Proceedings Act 1947 (interpretation of references in that Act to Her Majesty in her private capacity) were contained in these Regulations.

(4)   If, in a case where it is suspected that there may be an infringement of the prohibition in Article 81(1) or in respect of a suspected infringement of the prohibition in Article 82 otherwise than by the Crown or a person in the public service of the Crown, an investigation is conducted under regulation 3—

(a)   the power conferred by regulation 13 may not be exercised in relation to land which is occupied by a government department, or otherwise for purposes of the Crown, without the written consent of the appropriate person; and

(b)   regulation 14 does not apply in relation to land so occupied.

(5)   In any case in which consent is required under paragraph (4), the person who is the appropriate person in relation to that case is—

(a)   in relation to any land which is occupied by a government department that department; and

(b)   in relation to any other land which is otherwise occupied for purposes of the Crown the person occupying the land for such purposes.

(6)   If the Secretary of State certifies that it appears to him to be in the interests of national security that the powers of entry—

(a)   conferred by regulation 13, or

(b)   that may be conferred by a warrant under regulation 14,

should not be exercisable in relation to premises held or used by or on behalf of the Crown and which are specified in the certificate, those powers are not exercisable in relation to those premises.

(7)   Any amendment of an enactment made by these Regulations binds the Crown to the extent that the enactment amended binds the Crown.

[2123]

NOTES

Commencement: 17 August 2001.

35 Amendments to other enactments

(1)   In section 133(2)(a) of the Fair Trading Act 1973 for the words "EC Competition Law (Articles 88 and 89) Enforcement Regulations 1996" there shall be substituted the words "EC Competition Law (Articles 84 and 85) Enforcement Regulations 2001".

(2)   In section 19(3)(q) of the Competition Act 1980 for the words "the EC Competition Law (Articles 88 and 89) Enforcement Regulations 1996" there shall be substituted the words "the EC Competition Law (Articles 84 and 85) Enforcement Regulations 2001".

(3)   In section 74(3)(o) of the Airports Act 1986 for the words "the EC Competition Law Enforcement Regulations 1996" there shall be substituted the words "the EC Competition Law (Articles 84 and 85) Enforcement Regulations 2001".

(4)   In article 49(3)(r) of the Airports (Northern Ireland) Order 1994 for the words "the EC Competition Law (Articles 88 and 89) Enforcement Regulations 1996" there shall be substituted the words "the EC Competition Law (Articles 84 and 85) Enforcement Regulations 2001".

(5)   In paragraph 1(o) of Schedule 11 to the Act for the words "the EC Competition Law (Articles 88 and 89) Enforcement Regulations 1996" there shall be substituted the words "the EC Competition Law (Articles 84 and 85) Enforcement Regulations 2001".

[2124]

NOTES

Commencement: 17 August 2001.

Paras (1), (2): repealed by the Enterprise Act 2002, s 278(2), Sch 26, as from a day to be appointed.

36 Past agreements and infringements

Nothing in these Regulations shall enable or require the Director to investigate or make a decision in relation to an agreement which was determined, or on conduct which has ceased, before 28th August 1996 being the date on which the 1996 Regulations came into force.

[2125]

NOTES

Commencement: 17 August 2001.

Director: see the note "Director General of Fair Trading" to reg 2 at **[2091]**.

37 Revocation and transitional provision

(1)   Subject to paragraph (2), the 1996 Regulations are hereby revoked.

(2)   Any information which was obtained under or by virtue of the provisions of the 1996 Regulations and which was subject to the restrictions on disclosure of information in regulation 28 of the 1996 Regulations shall be treated as if it was information obtained under or as a result of a provision of these Regulations.

[2126]

NOTES

Commencement: 17 August 2001.

SCHEDULE 1

Regulations 4, 6, 9 and 26

RULES

1   Form of application
2   Joint applications
3   Copies
4   Content of application
5   Date of application
6   Notification of application to other parties
7   Public register
8   Consultation of public following applications
9   Investigations
10   Proposed infringement and conditional exemption decisions
11   Notice of decision
12   Further action after a decision
13   Directions
14   Interim measures
15   Application for extension of exemption
16   Cancellation etc of exemption
17   Associations of undertakings
18   Time limits and giving notices

PART II
STATUTORY INSTRUMENTS

1. Form of application

(1)   An application under regulation 7 for an agreement to be examined, or under regulation 10 for conduct to be considered, shall consist of—

(a)   Form ERN; and

(b)   the copies of Form ERN required by rule 3 below.

(2)   The documents referred to in sub-paragraphs (1)(a) and (b) above shall be submitted to the Director.

2. Joint applications

Where a joint application is submitted, Form ERN shall be submitted to the Director by or on behalf of all the applicants, and a joint representative may be appointed as authorised to act on behalf of some or all of the applicants for the purposes of these rules.

3. Copies

(1)   Two copies of Form ERN, in addition to the original, shall be submitted to the Director.

(2)   Supporting documents submitted as part of Form ERN shall be either originals or true copies, and the applicant shall certify that each copy is a true copy of the original.

4. Content of application

(1)   The information submitted as Form ERN shall, subject to paragraph (3) below, be correct and complete.

(2)   If the applicant considers that the Director would find any part of the information contained in the application to be confidential, in the sense given to that word by sub-paragraph (1)(c) of rule 21 below, he shall set out that part of the information in a separate annex to the application marked "confidential information" and provide a written explanation as to why he considers that the Director should treat it as such.

(3)   The Director may, by giving notice in writing to the applicant, dispense with the obligation to submit any particular information, including any supporting document, forming part of Form ERN, if he considers that such information or document is unnecessary for the examination of the agreement, or the consideration of the conduct, which is the subject of the application.

(4)   Where the applicant knows of material changes in the information contained in the application he shall without delay communicate those changes to the Director.

5. Date of application

(1)   Except where paragraph (3) below applies, an application is made (and notification for the purposes of regulations 7 or 10, whichever is applicable, is given) on the date on which Form ERN is received by the Director.

(2)   The Director shall acknowledge receipt of an application by giving notice in writing to the applicant without delay.

(3)   Where the Director finds that the information submitted as Form ERN is incomplete he shall, without delay and in any event within one month from the date on which that information was received by the Director, give notice in writing to the applicant of which information, by reference to the Annex hereto, is outstanding.

(4)   Where the Director has invoked paragraph (3) above he shall give notice in writing to the applicant of such time limit as the Director considers is appropriate for the outstanding information to be received by him.

(5)   Where the Director has invoked paragraph (3) above the application shall be made (and notification for the purposes of regulations 7 or 10, whichever is applicable, shall be given) on the date on which he receives the outstanding information.

(6)   If the Director has invoked paragraph (3) above and has not received the outstanding information by the date of expiry of the time limit notified to the applicant under paragraph (4) above, or of such further period, if any, as he considers appropriate, he shall return the information submitted as Form ERN to the applicant and shall inform him in writing that his application has not been made in accordance with this rule.

6. Notification of application to other parties

(1)   An applicant who is a party to an agreement must take all reasonable steps to notify all other parties to the agreement of whom he is aware that an application has been made for a decision.

(2)   If the conduct to which an application relates is conduct of two or more persons, the applicant must take all reasonable steps to notify all of the other parties of whom he is aware that an application has been made for a decision.

(3)   Notification by an applicant under paragraphs (1) or (2) above shall be written and shall be given within seven working days from the date on which the applicant receives acknowledgement of receipt of his application by the Director; the applicant shall provide a copy of the notification to the Director without delay.

7. Public register

(1)   The Director shall maintain a register in which there shall be entered, in respect of every application made under regulation 7 or 10, a summary of the nature and objectives of the agreement or conduct which is the subject of the application (as referred to in Part 4 of the Annex hereto) and an indication of the final outcome of the application.

(2)   The register shall be open to public inspection—
    (a) at the Office of Fair Trading, between 10.00 am and 4.30 pm on every working day; and
    (b) on the Office of Fair Trading's website on the Internet.

(3)   In determining an application under regulation 7 or 10, the Director must take into account any representations made to him by persons other than the applicant.

8. Consultation of public following applications

(1)   On an application under regulation 7 for an agreement to be examined—
    (a) if the Director proposes to grant an exemption, whether or not subject to conditions or obligations, he shall consult the public; and
    (b) if the Director proposes to make a decision that the prohibition in Article 81(1) has not been infringed, he may consult the public.

(2)   If, on an application under regulation 10 for conduct to be considered, the Director proposes to make a decision that the prohibition in Article 82 has not been infringed, he may consult the public.

9. Investigations

(1)   An officer shall grant a request of the occupier of premises entered by the officer ("the occupier") to allow a reasonable time for the occupier's legal adviser to arrive at the premises before the investigation continues, if the officer considers it reasonable in the circumstances to do so and if he is satisfied that such conditions as he considers it appropriate to impose in granting the occupier's request are, or will be, complied with.

(2)   For the purposes of paragraph (1) above, "a reasonable time" means such period of time as the officer considers is reasonable in the circumstances.

(3)   A person required by the Director under regulation 12(6)(a)(ii) to provide an explanation of a document may be accompanied by a legal adviser.

10. Proposed infringement and conditional exemption decisions

(1)   If the Director proposes to make a decision that the prohibition in Article 81(1) or the prohibition in Article 82 has been infringed he shall give written notice—
    (a) where an application has been made, to the applicant and, subject to rules 17 and 18 below, to those persons whom the applicant has identified in the application as

being the other parties to the agreement, or the other persons, if any, who are engaged in the conduct, as the case may be, which the Director considers has led to the infringement; and

(b) where no application has been made, subject to rules 17 and 18 below, to each person who the Director considers is a party to the agreement, or is engaged in the conduct, as the case may be, which the Director considers has led to the infringement.

(2)   If the Director proposes to grant an exemption subject to conditions or obligations, he shall give written notice to the applicant and, subject to rules 17 and 18 below, to those persons whom the applicant has identified in the application as being the other parties to the agreement to which the application relates.

(3)   A written notice given under paragraph (1) or (2) above shall state the facts on which the Director relies, the matters to which he has taken objection, the action he proposes and his reasons for it.

(4)   A written notice given under paragraph (1) or (2) above shall specify a period within which each person referred to in sub-paragraph (1)(a) or (b) or paragraph (2) above, whichever is applicable, may indicate to the Director any part of the information contained in the notice which he considers the Director would find to be confidential, in the sense given to that word by sub-paragraph (1)(c) of rule 21 below.

(5)   Subject to paragraph (6) below, the Director shall give each person referred to in sub-paragraph (1)(a) or (b) or paragraph (2) above, whichever is applicable, a reasonable opportunity to inspect the documents in the Director's file relating to the proposed decision.

(6)   The Director may withhold any document—

(a) to the extent that it contains information which a person has stated to the Director to be, and which the Director has found to be, confidential, in the sense given to that word by sub-paragraph (1)(c) of rule 21 below;

(b) which is, in the opinion of the Director, otherwise confidential; or

(c) which is internal, in the sense given to that word by sub-paragraph (1)(e) of rule 21 below.

(7)   Subject to rules 17 and 18 below, the Director shall give each person referred to in sub-paragraph (1)(a) or (b) or paragraph (2) above, whichever is applicable, written notice of the period within which that person may make written representations to him on the information referred to in paragraph (3) above.

(8)   The Director shall give each person referred to in sub-paragraph (1)(a) or (b) or paragraph (2) above, whichever is applicable, a reasonable opportunity to make oral representations to him on the information referred to in paragraph (3) above.

11. Notice of decision

(1)   If the Director has made a decision as to whether or not an agreement has infringed the prohibition in Article 81(1), or as to whether or not conduct has infringed the prohibition in Article 82, he shall, without delay—

(a) give written notice of the decision—

(i) where the decision was made following an application, to the applicant and, subject to rules 17 and 18(2) below, to those persons whom the applicant has identified in the application as being the other parties to the agreement, or the other persons, if any, who are engaged in the conduct, as the case may be; and

(ii) where no application has been made, subject to rules 17 and 18(2) below, to each person who the Director considers is a party to the agreement, or is engaged in the conduct, as the case may be,

stating in the decision the facts on which he bases it and his reasons for making it; and

(b) publish the decision.

(2)   Where the Director determines an application for a decision by exercising his discretion not to give a decision, he shall give written notice of that fact to—

(a) the applicant; and

(b) subject to rules 17 and 18 below, those persons whom the applicant has identified in the application as being the other parties to the agreement, or the other persons, if any, who are engaged in the conduct, as the case may be.

12. Further action after a decision

If, having made a decision that an agreement has not infringed the prohibition in Article 81(1), or that conduct has not infringed the prohibition in Article 82, the Director proposes to take further action under the Regulations, he shall—

   (a) where the decision was made following an application, consult the applicant and, subject to rules 17 and 18 below, those persons whom the applicant has identified in the application as being the other parties to the agreement, or the other persons, if any, who are engaged in the conduct, as the case may be, which is the subject of the decision; and

   (b) where no application has been made, subject to rules 17 and 18 below, consult each person who the Director considers is a party to the agreement, or is engaged in the conduct, as the case may be, which is the subject of the decision.

13. Directions

   (1)   Where the Director gives a direction to a person under regulation 18 or 19, he shall at the same time inform that person in writing of the facts on which he bases the direction and his reasons for giving it.

   (2)   The Director shall publish directions given under regulation [4, 18, 19 or 21].

14. Interim measures

   (1)   Subject to paragraph (2) below, if the Director proposes to give a direction under regulation 21, he shall give each person to whom he proposes to give the direction a reasonable opportunity to inspect the documents in the Director's file relating to the proposed direction.

   (2)   The Director may withhold any document—

   (a) to the extent that it contains information which a person has stated to the Director to be, and which the Director has found to be, confidential, in the sense given to that word by sub-paragraph (1)(c) of rule 21 below;

   (b) which is, in the opinion of the Director, otherwise confidential; or

   (c) which is internal, in the sense given to that word by sub-paragraph (1)(e) of rule 21 below.

   (3)   Where the Director gives a direction to a person under regulation 21, he shall at the same time inform that person in writing of the facts on which he bases the direction and his reasons for giving it.

15. Application for extension of exemption

   (1)   An application under regulation 4(4) for an extension of the period for which an exemption has effect shall consist of Form ERN, and the copies of Form ERN required under paragraph (4) below, and shall be submitted to the Director.

   (2)   If the Director proposes to grant the application, he shall consult the public.

   (3)   If the Director has made a decision as to whether or not to grant the application, he shall—

   (a) give written notice of the decision to—
        (i) the applicant; and
        (ii) subject to rules 17 and 18(2) below, those persons whom the applicant has identified in the application as being the other parties to the agreement; and
   (b) publish the decision,

stating in the decision the facts on which he bases it, his reasons for it and, if appropriate, the period of extension granted.

   (4)   Rules 2 (joint applications), 3 (copies), 4 (content of application), 5 (date of application) and 7 (public register) above shall apply to an application submitted under this rule as they apply, to the extent that they apply, to an application submitted under rule 1 above; rule 5(1) and (5) above shall also apply as if the parts in brackets were omitted from them.

16. Cancellation etc of exemption

   (1)   If the Director proposes to take any of the steps mentioned in regulation 5(1), he shall consult the public, the person who applied for the exemption and, subject to rules 17

and 18 below, those persons whom that person identified in his application as being the other parties to the agreement to which the exemption relates.

(2) If the Director issues a notice in writing under regulation 5(1), he shall—
    (a) give notice in writing of his decision to do so to—
        (i) the person who applied for the exemption; and
        (ii) subject to rules 17 and 18(2) below, those persons whom the person who applied for the exemption identified in his application as being the other parties to the agreement; and
    (b) publish the decision,

stating in the decision the facts on which he bases it and his reasons for it.

17. Associations of undertakings

(1) Where a rule requires the Director to give written notice, or notice in writing, of any matter to an association of undertakings and the notice does not relate to an agreement or to conduct which is the subject of an application to the Director by that association, he shall give such notice to the director, secretary, manager or other similar officer of the association on its behalf.

(2) Where a rule requires the Director to give written notice, or notice in writing, of any matter to each of more than fifty members of an association of undertakings, he may, instead of giving such notice to any such member, give such notice to the director, secretary, manager or other similar officer of the association on that member's behalf, provided that individual notice shall be given to any member who has made an application to the Director in respect of the agreement or the conduct to which the notice relates.

18. Time limits and giving notices

(1) Where it is not reasonably practicable for the Director to give written notice to a person—
    (a) other than the applicant, under rule 10(1), (2) or (7) or rule 11(2) above;
    (b) other than the applicant, in order to consult that person under rule 12 above;
    (c) other than the person who applied for the exemption and the public, in order to consult that person under rule 16(1) above; or
    (d) in order to consult that person under rule 20(6) below,

in particular having regard to the number of persons to whom such notice is required to be given, he may, instead of so doing, take all the steps mentioned in paragraph (3) below.

(2) Where it is not reasonably practicable for the Director to give—
    (a) written notice of the decision to a person, other than the applicant, under rule 11(1)(a) or 15(3)(a) above;
    (b) written notice of his decision to a person, other than the applicant, under rule 20(7) below;
    (c) notice in writing of his decision to a person under rule 16(2)(a), other than the person who applied for the exemption; or
    (d) written notice in order to consult a third party under rule 21(3) below,

in particular having regard to the number of persons to whom such notice is required to be given, he may, instead of so doing, take all the steps mentioned in sub-paragraph (3)(b) below.

(3) The steps mentioned for the purposes of paragraphs (1) and (2) above are the following—
    (a) publish the notice by means of entry in the register maintained by the Director under rule 7 above; and
    (b) cause the notice to be published in—
        (i) the London, Edinburgh and Belfast Gazettes;
        (ii) at least one national daily newspaper; and
        (iii) if there is in circulation an appropriate trade journal which is published at intervals not exceeding one month, in such trade journal.

(4) Except where paragraph (1) or (2) above is invoked, where these rules allow or require written notice, or notice in writing, to be given to a person, such notice shall be treated as having been given on the date on which that person receives it.

(5) Where paragraph (1) or (2) above is invoked, the notice shall be treated as having been given on the date of its publication in accordance with the paragraph invoked.

(6)   Where the time prescribed by these rules for doing any act expires on a day which is not a working day, the act is in time if done before 6 pm on the next following working day.

(7)   Where an act done in accordance with these rules is done on a day which is not a working day, or after 6 pm on a working day, the act shall be treated as done on the next following working day.

19. Confidential third party information

(1)   If a person gives information to the Director in connection with the exercise of any of the Director's functions under the Regulations, in relation to an agreement to which that person is not a party, or in relation to conduct in which that person has not engaged, and that person considers that the Director would find any part of the information to be confidential, in the sense given to that word by sub-paragraph (1)(c) of rule 21 below, he shall set out that part of the information in a separate annex marked "confidential information" and provide a written explanation as to why he considers that the Director should treat it as such.

(2)   The Director shall, if he proposes to disclose, in connection with the exercise of any of his functions under the Regulations, any of the information contained in an annex provided in accordance with paragraph (1) above, give the person who provided the information—
(a)   written notice of his proposed action; and
(b)   a reasonable opportunity to make representations to him,
if it is reasonably practicable for him to do so.

20. Third party appeals

(1)   An application under regulation 26(1) asking the Director to withdraw or vary a decision shall—
(a)   be submitted in writing to the Director within one month from the date of publication of that decision by means of entry in the register maintained by the Director under rule 7 above;
(b)   comply with paragraph (2) below; and
(c)   include the documents specified in paragraph (3) below.

(2)   An application submitted under paragraph (1) above shall be signed by the applicant or by a duly authorised representative of the applicant, and shall state the applicant's reasons—
(a)   for considering that he has a sufficient interest in the decision referred to in paragraph (1) above; or
(b)   where he claims to represent persons who have a sufficient interest in that decision—
(i)   for claiming that he represents those persons; and
(ii)   for claiming that those persons have a sufficient interest in that decision.

(3)   The documents specified for the purposes of paragraph (1) above are the following—
(a)   three copies of the application; and
(b)   where the application is signed by a solicitor or other representative of an applicant, written proof of that representative's authority to act on that applicant's behalf.

(4)   The application is made on the date on which it is received by the Director; the Director shall acknowledge receipt of the application by giving notice in writing to the applicant without delay.

(5)   Where the applicant knows of material changes in the information contained in the application he shall without delay communicate those changes to the Director.

(6)   If the Director proposes to grant the application, he shall, subject to rules 17 and 18 above, consult all persons whom he was required by these rules to notify of the decision referred to in paragraph (1) above.

(7)   If the Director grants the application, he shall give written notice of his decision to the applicant, and, subject to rules 17 and 18(2) above, to all persons whom he was required by these rules to notify of the decision referred to in paragraph (1) above, stating in his decision the facts on which he bases it and his reasons for it, and he shall publish his decision.

21. Interpretation and supplemental

(1) In these rules—

    (a) "agreement" shall be construed by reference to regulation 2(3);

    (b) "applicant" means—

        (i) in rules 2, 3(2), 4(2) and (3), 5(2), (3), (4) and (6), 6, 7(3) and 20(2) and (3)(b) above and paragraph (1)(i) below, person who is making the application; and

        (ii) in rules 4(4), 10, 11, 12, 15(3)(a) and 20(4), (5) and (7) above, person who has made the application;

    (c) information is confidential if it is—

        (i) commercial information the disclosure of which would, or might, significantly harm the legitimate business interests of the undertaking to which it relates; or

        (ii) information relating to the private affairs of an individual the disclosure of which would, or might, significantly harm his interests;

    (d) "Form ERN" means, subject to rule 4(3) above—

        (i) the information, including any supporting document, required by the Annex hereto; and

        (ii) the declaration made in the form set out in Part 2A of the Annex hereto;

    (e) "internal" document includes the following—

        (i) a document produced within the office of either the Director or a regulator concerning a case; and

        (ii) correspondence between the Director and a regulator, or between regulators, concerning a case; and

        (iii) correspondence between the Director, or a regulator, and a government department or another competition authority, concerning a case;

    (f) "an officer" means an investigating officer within the meaning of regulation 13(1) or a named officer of the Director authorised by a warrant issued under regulation 14;

    (g) "regulator" has the meaning given to it by section 54 of the Act;

    (h) "working day" means day which is not Saturday, Sunday or any other day on which the Office of Fair Trading is closed for business; and

    (i) "other party" in relation to conduct of two or more persons, means one of those persons other than the applicant.

(2) Where the Director, if he proposes to take action, is required to consult a person, he shall—

    (a) except where otherwise indicated, give written notice to that person; and

    (b) state in that notice the action he proposes, his reasons for it and the period within which that person may make written representations to him on these matters.

(3) Where the Director, if he proposes to take action—

    (a) is required to consult the public; or

    (b) proposes to consult the public in exercise of his discretion to do so,

he shall publish a notice stating the action he proposes, his reasons for it and the period within which written representations may be made to him on these matters, and shall, subject to rules 17 and 18(2) above, consult any third party (being in relation to the agreement or conduct concerned, a person who is not a party to the agreement or who has not engaged in the conduct) who appears to him likely to be affected by the action he proposes.

(4) Where the Director is required to publish a decision, a proposal or any other information, he shall do so by means of entry in the register maintained by him under rule 7 above.

NOTES

    Commencement: 17 August 2001.

    Rule 13: words in square brackets in para (2) substituted by the EC Competition Law (Articles 84 and 85) Enforcement (Amendment) Regulations 2002, SI 2002/42, regs 2, 6.

    Director: see the note "Director General of Fair Trading" to reg 2 at **[2091]**.

ANNEX

FORM ERN
INFORMATION REQUIRED FOR APPLICATIONS FOR A DECISION UNDER THE EC COMPETITION LAW (ARTICLES 84 AND 85) ENFORCEMENT REGULATIONS 2001

PART 1—INTRODUCTION

This document lists the information and supporting documents which must be provided when making an application for a decision under regulation 7 or 10.

If the Applicant(s) considers that the Director would find any part of the information contained in the application to be confidential, in the sense given to that word by rule 21(1), he must set out that part of the information in a separate annex to the application marked "confidential information" and provide a written explanation as to why he considers that the Director should treat it as such.

This document must also be used when making an application under regulation 4(4) (see rule 15).

PART 2—INFORMATION TO BE PROVIDED BY THE UNDERTAKING(S) MAKING THE APPLICATION

1 *INFORMATION ABOUT THE UNDERTAKING(S) SUBMITTING THE APPLICATION (THE "APPLICANT(S)") AND THE OTHER PARTIES TO THE AGREEMENT*

1.1   Please give the full name, address (by registered office, where appropriate, and principal place of business, if different), telephone and fax numbers and e-mail address (where available) of the Applicant(s) and a brief description of the nature of its business. If the Applicant(s) is a partnership, sole trader or other unincorporated body trading under a business name, give the name(s) and address(es) of the partners or proprietor(s). Please quote any reference which should be used.

1.2   Please give the full name, address, telephone and fax numbers and e-mail address (where available) of any representative(s) who has been authorised to act for the Applicant(s), indicating whom they represent and in what capacity (e.g. a solicitor).

1.3   Where the declaration to be made in the form set out in Part 2A is signed by a solicitor or other representative of the Applicant(s), please provide written proof of that representative's authority to act on behalf of the Applicant(s).

1.4   If a joint application is being submitted, indicate whether or not a joint representative has been appointed. If a joint representative has been appointed, give his full name, address (by registered office, where appropriate, and principal place of business, if different), telephone and fax numbers and e-mail address (where available), and indicate whom he represents.

1.5   Please give full names, addresses (by registered office, where appropriate, and principal place of business, if different), telephone and fax numbers, nature of business, and brief description of the other parties to the agreement and any other persons engaging in the conduct which is the subject of the application, together with the name of a contact at each undertaking concerned, their address, telephone and fax numbers and details of their position in the undertaking.

1.6   Please provide details of the steps taken or to be taken to notify all the other parties to the agreement or conduct which is the subject of the application of whom the Applicant(s) is aware that the application is being submitted. Indicate whether those parties have received a copy of the application and if so, whether confidential information (as defined in rule 21(1)) was included in the copy of the application. If the Applicant(s) considers that it is not practicable to notify the other parties of the application, please give the reasons why it is not practicable.

1.7   Please identify the groups to which each party to the agreement or conduct which is the subject of the application belongs. For the purposes of the information required by this form, a group relationship exists where one undertaking—

— owns more than half the capital or business assets of another undertaking; or
— has the power to exercise more than half the voting rights in another undertaking; or

— has the power to appoint more than half the members of the supervisory board, board of directors or bodies legally representing the undertaking; or
— has the right to manage the affairs of another undertaking.
— An undertaking which is jointly controlled by several other undertakings (eg a joint venture) forms part of the group of each of these undertakings.

2   PURPOSE OF THE APPLICATION

2.1   Specify whether the application is being made in relation to the prohibition in Article 81(1), the prohibition in Article 82 or both.

2.2   State which provisions or effects of the agreement or conduct which is the subject of the application might in the Applicant's view raise questions of compatibility with the prohibition in Article 81(1) and/or the prohibition in Article 82, and give reasons for that view.

2.3   If the application is for an extension of an exemption, state the date of expiry of the existing exemption and the reasons why an extension is sought. Please also give details of any changes that have occurred in the relevant market(s) (see 6.2 and 6.3 below) and in the agreement itself since the grant of the exemption. Specify how any changes impact on the fulfilment by the agreement of the conditions set out in Article 81(3). Please also enclose a copy of the decision granting the exemption.

3   JURISDICTION

3.1   Please state whether the agreement or conduct which is the subject of the application is also the subject of an application to any competition authority outside the United Kingdom. If so, please provide brief details (where applicable) of the outcome of such application, if known.

3.2   Please provide details of any previous contacts of which the Applicant(s) is aware with the Office of Fair Trading or the European Commission relating to the agreement or conduct which is the subject of the application.

4   DETAILS OF THE AGREEMENT OR CONDUCT

4.1   Please provide a brief description of the agreement or conduct which is the subject of the application (including the nature, content, purpose, date(s) and duration).

4.2   If the application is made in relation to a written agreement, attach either an original of the most recent text of that agreement, or a copy certified by the applicant to be a true copy of the original. If the application is made in relation to an agreement which is not written, provide a full description of the agreement. If the application is made in relation to conduct, provide a full description of that conduct.

4.3   Identify any provisions in the agreement or aspects of the conduct which may restrict the parties in their freedom to take independent commercial decisions or to act on those decisions.

4.4   If the application relates to standard form terms and conditions, indicate the number of agreements expected to be entered into on those terms and conditions.

4.5   Please identify those Member States of the European Community trade between which may be affected by the arrangements. Please give reasons for your reply to this question, giving data on trade flows where relevant. Furthermore please state whether trade between the Community and any third countries is affected, again giving reasons for your reply.

5   INFORMATION ON THE PARTIES TO THE AGREEMENT OR CONDUCT AND THE GROUPS TO WHICH THEY BELONG

5.1   Please attach one copy of the most recent annual report and accounts (or equivalent for unincorporated bodies) for each party to the agreement or conduct and of the most recent annual report and accounts for the ultimate parent company of these undertakings.

5.2   Please list the product and/or services market(s) in which each party to the agreement or conduct and each member of the groups (within the meaning of 1.7 above) to which they belong are active.

6   THE RELEVANT PRODUCT AND GEOGRAPHIC MARKET(S)

6.1   A *"relevant product market"* comprises all those products and/or services regarded by the consumer of the products or acquirer of the services as interchangeable or substitutable by reason of the products' characteristics, price and intended use. The *"relevant geographic market"* comprises the area in which the undertakings concerned are involved in the supply of products or services, in which the conditions of competition are sufficiently homogeneous and which can be distinguished from neighbouring areas because, in particular, conditions of competition are appreciably different in those areas.

6.2   Please supply and explain the definition of the relevant product market(s) which in the opinion of the Applicant(s) should form the basis of the analysis of the application. State the specific products or services directly or indirectly affected by the agreement or conduct which is the subject of the application and other products or services that may be viewed as substitutable. Give reasons for all assumptions or findings.

6.3   Please supply and explain the definition of the relevant geographic market(s) which in the opinion of the Applicant(s) should form the basis of the analysis of the application. Please identify the geographic scope of the relevant market(s), with reasons. Give reasons for all assumptions or findings.

6.4   For each of the relevant product and geographic market(s) identified in 6.2 and 6.3 above, give details of—

   (a)   the level of concentration in the markets;
   (b)   the nature and extent of vertical integration;
   (c)   the direction and extent of trade within the European Community and/or between the Community and third countries;
   (d)   the prevailing methods of distributing products and services, including the extent of the involvement of undertakings which are not party to the agreement or conduct which is the subject of the application (i.e. third parties), and their significance;
   (e)   the significance of customer preferences, in terms of brand loyalty, product differentiation and the provision of a full range of products;
   (f)   the categories and relative strengths of different types of customer, including private and public sector purchasers; and
   (g)   the extent to which customers have long-term relationships with suppliers.

Where available, please provide a copy of the most recent long-term market studies (produced by the Applicant(s) in-house or commissioned by the Applicant(s) from outside consultants) which assess and/or analyse the relevant product market(s) and/or the relevant geographic market(s). Please supply references to any external published studies of the relevant product market(s) and/or the relevant geographic market(s) or, where available, please supply a copy of each such study with the application.

6.5   For each of the parties to the agreement or conduct which is the subject of the application, provide a list of all undertakings belonging to the same group (within the meaning of 1.7 above) which are active in the relevant product market(s) identified in 6.2 above, and those active in markets neighbouring the relevant product market(s)—that is, active in products and/or services which are regarded by the consumer as imperfect and partial substitutes for those products and/or services included in the relevant product market(s) as defined in 6.2 above. Such undertakings must be identified even if they sell the product or service in question in geographic areas other than those in which the parties to the agreement or conduct which is the subject of the application operate. Please list the name, place of incorporation, exact product and/or service provided and the geographic scope of operation of each member of the group.

7   THE POSITION OF THE UNDERTAKINGS IN THE RELEVANT PRODUCT MARKET(S)

7.1   Please provide the following information in respect of each of the previous three calendar or financial years, as available—

   (a)   the best estimates of the Applicant(s) of the market shares of each party to the agreement or conduct which is the subject of the application, in the products or services in the relevant product market(s) on the relevant geographic market(s), as identified in 6.2 and 6.3 above, and, if different, in the European Community, and in each Member State of the Community (for this section, where market shares are less than 20%, please simply state which of the following bands are relevant—less than 5%, less than 10%, less than 15%, less than 20%);

   (b) identify the five main competitors of each party to the agreement or conduct which is the subject of the application in the relevant product and geographic market(s), and give the best estimates of the Applicant(s) of their market shares in the products or services in the relevant product and geographic market(s); provide each competitor's name, address, telephone and fax numbers, and, where possible, a contact name—

   (c) identify the five customers of each party to the agreement or conduct which is the subject of the application, in the relevant product and geographic market(s), giving the customer's name, address, telephone and fax numbers, and, where possible, a contact name; and

   (d) details of each party to the agreement or conduct's interests in, and agreements with, any other undertakings competing in the relevant product and geographic market(s), together with the best estimates of the Applicant(s) of those other undertakings' market shares in the products or services in the relevant product and geographic market(s), if known.

Information requested in this section must be provided for the group to which each party to the agreement or conduct which is the subject of the application belongs (within the meaning of 1.7 above) and not in relation to the individual undertakings which are party to the agreement or conduct which is the subject of the application.

Justification for the figures provided in response to the above must be given. Thus, for each answer to (a), (b) and (d), total market value or volume must be stated, together with the sales or turnover of each of the undertakings in question. The source or sources of the information should also be given and one copy should be provided of any document, where available, from which information has been taken.

8 MARKET ENTRY AND POTENTIAL COMPETITION IN THE RELEVANT PRODUCT AND GEOGRAPHIC MARKET(S)

   8.1   For each of the relevant product and geographic market(s) identified in 6.2 and 6.3 above, describe—

   (a) the factors influencing entry in product terms into the relevant product market(s); that is, the barriers which exist to prevent undertakings not presently manufacturing products or providing services within the relevant product market(s) from entering the market(s), taking account of, in particular but not exclusively, the extent to which—

      — entry is influenced by the requirements of government authorisation or standard-setting, in any form, and any legal or regulatory controls on entry to the market(s);

      — entry is influenced by the need to have access to transport infrastructure;

      — entry is influenced by the availability of aircraft, vessels or other vehicles required for providing services;

      — entry is influenced by the length of contracts between an undertaking and its suppliers and customers; and

      — research and development and licensing patents, know-how and other intellectual property rights are important; and

   (b) the factors influencing entry in geographic terms into the relevant geographic market(s); that is, the barriers which exist to prevent undertakings already marketing or providing products or services within the relevant product market(s) outside the relevant geographic market(s) from extending sales into the relevant geographic market(s), taking account of, in particular but not exclusively, the importance of—

      — trade barriers imposed by law;

      — local specifications or technical requirements;

      — procurement policies;

      — the existence of adequate and available local distribution and retailing facilities;

      — the need to have access to transport infrastructure; and

      — strong consumer preference for local brands or products.

   8.2   Estimate the amount of time required for entry into the relevant product and geographic market(s), taking account of the individual barriers to entry referred to in the answer to 8.1 above.

   8.3   State whether any new undertakings have entered the relevant product market(s) in geographic areas where the parties to the agreement or conduct which is the subject of the application sell, during the last three years. Identify these undertakings by full name, address (by registered office, where appropriate, and principal place of business, if different), telephone and fax numbers and, where possible, a contact name. Please give the best estimates of the Applicant(s) of the market shares of each such undertaking in the products or services in the relevant product and geographic market(s).

9 *EXEMPTION*

If exemption from the prohibition in Article 81(1) is sought, explain how the agreement contributes to improving production or distribution and/or promoting technical or economic progress, and how consumers will be allowed a fair share of the resulting benefit. Explain how each restriction imposed by the agreement is indispensable to the attainment of those objectives, and how the agreement does not afford the undertakings concerned the possibility of eliminating competition in respect of a substantial part of the products in question (as identified in 6.2 and 6.3 above).

10 *OTHER INFORMATION*

10.1 Please provide details of trade publications in which advertisements seeking the views of third parties might be placed.

10.2 Please give any other information which the Applicant(s) considers may be helpful.

11 *SUPPORTING DOCUMENTS*

Please ensure that the Applicant(s) has attached the following documents (where relevant) to the application—

(a) if 1.3 above applies, written proof of the representative's authority to act on the Applicant(s) behalf;

(b) if 2.3 above applies, a copy of the decision granting the exemption;

(c) if 4.2 above applies with regard to a written agreement, either an original or certified copy, of the most recent version of the text of the agreement which is the subject of the application;

(d) one copy of the most recent annual report and accounts (or equivalent for unincorporated bodies) for each party to the agreement or conduct and of the most recent annual report and accounts for the ultimate parent company of these undertakings (see 5.1 above);

(e) where available, one copy of the most recent long-term market studies which assess and/or analyse the relevant market(s) (in-house studies produced by the Application(s) or commissioned by the Applicant(s) from outside consultants) (see 6.4 above);

(f) where available, one copy of any external studies of the relevant product and/or the relevant geographic market(s) (see 6.4 above); and

(g) where available, one copy of any document from which information has been taken and provided in answer to 7.1 above.

PART 2A

Under regulation 24, it is an offence, punishable by a fine or imprisonment or both, to provide information which is false or misleading in a material particular if the undertaking or person providing it knows that it is false or misleading, or is reckless as to whether it is. If the undertaking or person is a body corporate, under regulation 33 its officers may be guilty of an offence.

Declaration

The undersigned declare that all the information given above and in the .. .. pages annexed hereto is correct to the best of their knowledge and belief, and that all estimates are identified as such and are their best estimates of the underlying facts.

Place and date .. ..

Signatures .. ..

Status .. ..

Name(s) in block capitals .. ..

PART 3—ACKNOWLEDGEMENT OF RECEIPT

This acknowledgement of receipt will be returned to the address inserted below if the Applicant(s) provides the information requested below.

To be completed by the Applicant(s)

To: ....

(name and address of Applicant(s))

....

....

....

The application dated ....

concerning ....

involving the following undertakings:

1. ....

2. ....

[and others]

To be completed by the Office of Fair Trading

was received on ....

and registered under reference number ....

Please quote this number in all correspondence with the Office of Fair Trading

PART 4—TO BE COMPLETED BY THE APPLICANT(S)

Information for the OFT public register

1.   Please give the full names of the parties to the agreement(s) or conduct which is the subject of the application, as in the response to 1.1 and 1.5 above.

2.   Please provide a short summary which does not contain any confidential information (no more than 250 words) of the nature and objectives of the agreement(s) or conduct which is the subject of the application.

3.   Please describe the relevant product(s) or services(s) involved.

[2128]

NOTES

Commencement: 17 August 2001.
Director: see the note "Director General of Fair Trading" to reg 2 at **[2091]**.

SCHEDULE 2

Regulation 25

APPEALS

1. Interpretation

In this Schedule—
> "the chairman" means a person appointed as chairman of a tribunal in accordance with
> paragraph 27(2)(a) of Schedule 7 to the Act;
> "specified" means specified in rules.

2. General procedure

(1)   An appeal to the tribunal must be made by sending a notice of appeal to the tribunal within the specified period.

(2)   The notice of appeal must set out the grounds of appeal in sufficient detail to indicate—
    (a) under which provision of these regulations the appeal is brought;

(b) to what extent (if any) the appellant contends that the decision against, or with respect to which, the appeal is brought was based on an error of fact or was wrong in law; and

(c) to what extent (if any) the appellant is appealing against the Director's exercise of his discretion in making the disputed decision.

(3)   The tribunal may give an appellant permission to amend the grounds of appeal identified in the notice of appeal.

3. Decisions of the tribunal

(1)   The tribunal must determine the appeal on the merits by reference to the grounds of appeal set out in the notice of appeal.

(2)   The tribunal may confirm or set aside the decision which is the subject of the appeal, or any part of it, and may—

    (a) remit the matter to the Director,

    (b) give such directions, or take such other steps, as the Director could himself have given or taken,

    (c) grant or cancel an exemption or vary any conditions or obligations imposed in relation to the exemption by the Director, or

    (d) make any other decision which the Director could himself have made.

(3)   Any decision of the tribunal on an appeal has the same effect, and may be enforced in the same manner, as a decision of the Director.

(4)   If the tribunal confirms the decision which is the subject of the appeal it may nevertheless set aside any finding of fact on which the decision was based.

4.—(1)   A decision of the tribunal may be taken by a majority.

(2)   The decision must—

    (a) state whether it was unanimous or taken by a majority; and

    (b) be recorded in a document which—

        (i) contains a statement of the reasons for the decision; and

        (ii) is signed and dated by the chairman of the tribunal.

(3)   When the tribunal is preparing the document mentioned in sub-paragraph (2)(b), regulation 30 is to apply to the tribunal as it applies to the Director.

(4)   The President must make such arrangements for the publication of the tribunal's decision as he considers appropriate.

5. A person who without reasonable excuse fails to comply with any requirement imposed pursuant to tribunal rules which make provision for the matters referred to in—

    (a) paragraph 9(1)(c) of Schedule 8 to the Act; or

    (b) paragraph 9(1)(g) of Schedule 8 to the Act

is guilty of an offence and liable on summary conviction to a fine not exceeding level 3 on the standard scale.

[2129]

NOTES

Commencement: 17 August 2001.

Director: see the note "Director General of Fair Trading" to reg 2 at **[2091]**.

D. EXCLUSIONS AND EXEMPTIONS

COMPETITION ACT 1998 (LAND AND VERTICAL AGREEMENTS EXCLUSION) ORDER 2000

(SI 2000/310)

NOTES
Made: 10 February 2000.
Authority: Competition Act 1998, ss 50, 71.
Commencement: 1 March 2000.

ARRANGEMENT OF ARTICLES

1 Citation and commencement

This Order may be cited as the Competition Act 1998 (Land and Vertical Agreements Exclusion) Order 2000 and shall come into force on 1st March 2000.

[2130]

NOTES
Commencement: 1 March 2000.

2 Definitions

In this Order—

"the Act" means the Competition Act 1998;

"interest in land" includes any estate, interest, easement, servitude or right in or over land (including any interest or right created by a licence), and in Scotland also includes any interest under a lease and other heritable right in or over land including a heritable security;

"land" includes buildings and other structures and land covered with water;

"land agreement" means an agreement between undertakings which creates, alters, transfers or terminates an interest in land, or an agreement to enter into such an agreement, together with any obligation and restriction to which Article 6 applies; and to the extent that an agreement is a vertical agreement it is not a land agreement;

"party to an agreement" in respect of a land agreement includes a successor in title to a party to the agreement;

"relevant land" means the land in respect of which a land agreement creates, alters, transfers or terminates an interest, or in respect of which it constitutes an agreement to do so; and "other relevant land" means other land in which a party to a land agreement has an interest; and

"vertical agreement" means an agreement between undertakings, each of which operates, for the purposes of the agreement, at a different level of the production or distribution chain, and relating to the conditions under which the parties may purchase, sell or resell certain goods or services and includes provisions contained in such agreements which relate to the assignment to the buyer or use by the buyer of intellectual property rights, provided that those provisions do not constitute the primary object of the agreement and are directly related to the use, sale or resale of goods or services by the buyer or its customers.

[2131]

3 Exclusion of vertical agreements from the Chapter I prohibition

The Chapter I prohibition shall not apply to an agreement to the extent that it is a vertical agreement.

[2132]

4   Article 3 shall not apply where the vertical agreement, directly or indirectly, in isolation or in combination with other factors under the control of the parties has the object or effect of restricting the buyer's ability to determine its sale price, without prejudice to the possibility of the supplier imposing a maximum sale price or recommending a sale price, provided that these do not amount to a fixed or minimum sale price as a result of pressure from, or incentives offered by, any of the parties.

[2133]

5 Exclusion of land agreements from the Chapter I prohibition

The Chapter I prohibition shall not apply to an agreement to the extent that it is a land agreement.

[2134]

6 Obligations and restrictions

(1)   This article applies to an obligation which is accepted by a party to a land agreement in his capacity as holder of an interest—
  (a) in the relevant land or other relevant land and is for the benefit of another party to the agreement in his capacity as holder of an interest in the relevant land; or
  (b) in other relevant land and relates to the imposition in respect of that land of—
    (i) restrictions of a kind described in paragraph (2)(a) which correspond to those accepted by a party to the agreement in his capacity as holder of an interest in the relevant land; or
    (ii) obligations which correspond to those accepted by a party to the agreement in his capacity as holder of an interest in the relevant land.

(2)   This article applies to a restriction which—
  (a) restricts the activity that may be carried out on, from, or in connection with the relevant land or other relevant land and is accepted by a party to the agreement in his capacity as holder of an interest in the relevant land or other relevant land and is for the benefit of another party to the agreement in his capacity as holder of an interest in the relevant land;

(b) is accepted by a party to the agreement in his capacity as holder of an interest in other relevant land and relates to the imposition of restrictions on the activity that may be carried out on, from, or in connection with the other relevant land which correspond to those accepted by a party to the agreement in his capacity as holder of an interest in the relevant land; or

(c) restricts the freedom of a party to the agreement to create or transfer an interest in the relevant land to another person.

[2135]

NOTES
Commencement: 1 March 2000.

7 Withdrawal of exclusion etc

The power in paragraph 4 of Schedule 1 to the Act to withdraw the benefit of the exclusion from the Chapter I prohibition applies (with the exception of sub-paragraph (5)(b)) to the exclusion provided by Articles 3 and 5 as it applies to the exclusion provided by paragraph 1 of Schedule 1.

[2136]

NOTES
Commencement: 1 March 2000.

8   Articles 3 and 5 do not apply to an agreement to the extent that it takes effect between the same parties and is to the like object or effect as an agreement which has been the subject of a direction under Article 7.

[2137]

NOTES
Commencement: 1 March 2000.

COMPETITION ACT 1998 (PUBLIC TRANSPORT TICKETING SCHEMES BLOCK EXEMPTION) ORDER 2001

(SI 2001/319)

NOTES
Made: 8 February 2001.
Authority: Competition Act 1998, ss 6(2), (5)–(7), 8(6), 71(3), 75.
Commencement: 1 March 2001.

ARRANGEMENT OF ARTICLES

Citation, Commencement, Duration and Interpretation

1   This Order may be cited as the Competition Act 1998 (Public Transport Ticketing Schemes Block Exemption) Order 2001 and shall come into force on 1st March 2001.

[2138]

NOTES
Commencement: 1 March 2001.

2 This Order shall have effect from the beginning of 1st March 2000 and shall cease to have effect at the end of the period of five years commencing on 1st March 2001.

[2139]

NOTES

Commencement: 1 March 2001.

3 In this Order—
  "the Act" means the Competition Act 1998;
  "block exemption" means the exemption from the Chapter I prohibition arising by virtue of this Order for the category of agreements specified in this Order;
  "bus service" has the meaning given in section 159(1) of the Transport Act 1968 but excludes a bus service which is a tourist service;
  "chartered service" means a public transport service:
  (a) for which the whole capacity of the vehicle, vessel or craft supplying that service has been purchased by one or more charterers for his or their own use or for resale;
  (b) which is a journey or trip organised privately by any person acting independently of the person operating the vehicle, vessel or craft supplying that service; or
  (c) on which the passengers travel together on a journey, with or without breaks, from one or more places to one or more places and back;
  "complementary services" means local public transport services which are not in competition with each other over a substantial part of the route covered by the ticket in question;
  "connecting service" means a service (other than a bus service, a chartered service or a tourist service) for the carriage of passengers by road, tramway, railway, inland waterway or air which is a long distance service and which runs between—
  (a) a station or stopping place at or in the vicinity of which the relevant local public transport service stops; and
  (b) any other place;
  "inland waterway" includes both natural and artificial waterways, and waterways within parts of the sea that are in the United Kingdom;
  "journey" means any journey made by an individual passenger and includes a return journey;
  "local public transport service" means:
  (a) a bus service; or
  (b) a scheduled public transport service (other than a bus service) using one or more vehicles or vessels for the carriage of passengers by road, railway, tramway or inland waterway at separate fares other than a long distance service, a chartered service or a tourist service;
  "long distance add-on" means:
  (a) a ticket (or tickets) entitling the holder to make a journey solely on the local public transport services of any one operator;
  (b) a multi-operator travelcard; or
  (c) a through ticket,
  each being purchased as an add-on to a ticket (or tickets) entitling the holder to make a particular journey on one or more connecting services;
  "long distance operator" means an undertaking (other than an operator) supplying a scheduled long distance service using one or more vehicles, vessels or craft for the carriage of passengers by road, railway, tramway, inland waterway or air at separate fares other than a chartered service or a tourist service;

"long distance service" means a public transport service in relation to which (except in an emergency) one or both of the following conditions are met with respect to every passenger using the service:

(a) the place where he is set down is fifteen miles or more, measured in a straight line, from the place where he was taken up;

(b) some point on the route between those places is fifteen miles or more, measured in a straight line, from either of those places,

and where a public transport service consists of one or more parts with respect to which one or both of these conditions are met, and one or more parts with respect to which neither of them is met, each of those parts shall be treated as a separate public transport service;

"members of the public" means any person other than an operator, potential operator, long distance operator or potential long distance operator;

"multi-operator individual ticket" means a ticket (or tickets) entitling the holder, where a particular journey could be made on local public transport services provided by any of two or more operators, to make that journey or any part of it on whichever service the holder chooses;

"multi-operator travel card" means a ticket (or tickets) entitling the holder to make three or more journeys on three or more specified local public transport services operating on three or more routes provided that:

(a) these routes are not substantially the same;

(b) these local public transport services are not substantially the same; and

(c) for each of these routes and local public transport services, the passenger usage and revenue received from the ticket and other such tickets purchased as a result of the relevant agreement, demonstrate that the ticket is not, in practice, a multi-operator individual ticket or a through ticket;

"operator" means an undertaking supplying local public transport services;

"posted price" means, where a ticket is purchased from one undertaking (the seller), a wholesale price set independently by another undertaking ("the creditor") for the carriage of passengers bearing that ticket on the public transport services of the creditor;

"public transport ticketing scheme" has the meaning given in Article 4(2);

"the register" means the register maintained by the Director under rule 8 of the Director's rules set out in the Schedule to the Competition Act 1998 (Director's rules) Order 2000;

"short distance add-on" means a multi-operator travelcard purchased as an add-on to a ticket (or tickets) entitling the holder to make a particular journey on a local public transport service pursuant to an agreement which provides for onward travel connections for passengers on complementary services;

"stopping place" means a point at which passengers are taken up or set down in the course of a public transport service;

"through ticket" means a ticket (or tickets) entitling the holder to make a particular journey on two or more local public transport services provided that such a journey is made on complementary services;

"ticket" means evidence of a contractual right to travel;

"tourist service" means a public transport service where the price charged for that service includes payment for a live or recorded commentary about the locality being a service primarily for the benefit of tourists;

"vehicle" includes vehicles constructed or adapted to run on flanged wheels but excludes hackney carriages, taxis, cabs, hire cars and any vehicle propelled by an animal; and

"working day" means a day which is not a Saturday, Sunday or any other day on which the Office of Fair Trading is closed for business.

NOTES

Commencement: 1 March 2001.

Director: the Enterprise Act 2002, s 2(1), at **[255]**, provides that, as from the coming into force of that section in accordance with s 279 at **[463]**, the functions of the Director General of Fair Trading, his property, rights and liabilities are transferred to the Office of Fair Trading. Accordingly, (by virtue of s 2(2), (3) of the 2002 Act) the office of the Director is abolished, and any reference to the Director in any enactment, instrument or other document passed or made before the commencement of s 2(1) shall have effect as if it were a reference to the Office of Fair Trading. For transitional provisions in connection with the transfer, see s 276(1) of, and Sch 24, para 6 to, the 2002 Act at **[477]**.

Block Exemption

4.—(1) The category of agreements identified in paragraph (2) as public transport ticketing schemes is hereby specified for the purposes of section 6 of the Act.

(2)   For the purpose of this Order a public transport ticketing scheme is one or more of the following:

(a)   a written agreement between operators to the extent that it provides for members of the public to purchase, in a single transaction, a multi-operator travelcard;

(b)   a written agreement between operators to the extent that it provides for members of the public to purchase, in a single transaction, a through ticket;

(c)   a written agreement between operators to the extent that it provides for members of the public to purchase, in a single transaction, a multi-operator individual ticket;

(d)   a written agreement between operators to the extent that it provides for members of the public to purchase, in a single transaction, a short distance add-on;

(e)   a written agreement between one or more operators and one or more long distance operators to the extent that it provides for members of the public to purchase, in a single transaction, a long distance add-on.

[2141]

NOTES

Commencement: 1 March 2001.

5   This block exemption has effect subject to the conditions and the obligation specified in Articles 6 to 17.

[2142]

NOTES

Commencement: 1 March 2001.

Conditions and consequences of breach of conditions

6   Unless there is an objective, transparent and non-discriminatory reason, a public transport ticketing scheme shall not, directly or indirectly, in isolation or in combination with other factors under the control of the parties:

(a)   have the object or effect of preventing any operator or potential operator from participating in that public transport ticketing scheme; or

(b)   to the extent that the scheme provides for members of the public to purchase a long distance add-on, have the object or effect of preventing any operator, potential operator, long distance operator or potential long distance operator from participating in that public transport ticketing scheme.

[2143]

NOTES
Commencement: 1 March 2001.

7 A public transport ticketing scheme shall not, directly or indirectly, in isolation or in combination with other factors under the control of the parties, have the object or effect of limiting:

    (a) the variety or number of routes on which any operator or long distance operator provides or may provide public transport services; or

    (b) the freedom of operators or long distance operators to set the price or availability of, the fare structure relating to, or the zones or geographical validity applicable for, any ticket entitling the holder to make a journey solely on the public transport services of any one operator or any one long distance operator.

    [2144]

NOTES
Commencement: 1 March 2001.

8 A public transport ticketing scheme shall not, directly or indirectly, in isolation or in combination with other factors under the control of the parties, have the object or effect or limiting the frequency or timing of any public transport services operated by any operator or long distance operator, unless such restriction is indispensable to the effective operation of that scheme, pursuant to an agreement which provides for onward travel connections for passengers.

    [2145]

NOTES
Commencement: 1 March 2001.

9.—(1) Subject to paragraph (2), a public transport ticketing scheme shall not, directly or indirectly, in isolation or in combination with other factors under the control of the parties, have the object or effect of facilitating an exchange of information between the parties to that public transport ticketing scheme.

    (2) Paragraph (1) shall not prevent an exchange of information between the parties to a public transport ticketing scheme which is directly related and indispensable to the effective operation of that scheme, provided that the relevant provision under which the information is exchanged is objective, transparent and non-discriminatory and that it does not breach any of the other conditions imposed by this Order.

    [2146]

NOTES
Commencement: 1 March 2001.

10 Breach of any of the conditions imposed by any of Articles 6, 7, 8 or 9 shall have the effect of cancelling the block exemption in respect of that public transport ticketing scheme.

    [2147]

NOTES
Commencement: 1 March 2001.

11 The parties to a public transport ticketing scheme which provides for members of the public to purchase a multi-operator travelcard shall not distribute between themselves the revenue received by virtue of the operation of that scheme other than pursuant to terms contained in that scheme which reflect, as far as is reasonably practicable, the actual passenger miles travelled on the vehicles or vessels of each party by passengers using tickets issued under that scheme during the accounting period in which such revenue was received.

[2148]

NOTES
Commencement: 1 March 2001.

12 Breach of the condition imposed by Article 11 shall have the effect of cancelling the block exemption in respect of the relevant public transport ticketing scheme to the extent that such scheme provides for members of the public to purchase a multi-operator travelcard.

[2149]

NOTES
Commencement: 1 March 2001.

13.—(1) Subject to paragraph (2), a public transport ticketing scheme which provides for members of the public to purchase a through ticket, multi-operator individual ticket, short distance add-on or long distance add-on, shall not directly or indirectly, in isolation or in combination with other factors under the control of the parties have the object or effect of fixing a price at which the respective through ticket, multi-operator individual ticket, short distance add-on or long distance add-on is offered for sale.

(2)   Paragraph (1) shall not prevent—
  (a) the parties to a public transport ticketing scheme from agreeing to charge each other non-discriminatory posted prices for sales of the respective through ticket, short distance add-on or long distance add-on; or
  (b) operators from fixing the price of a multi-operator travelcard which may be purchased as a short distance add-on or long distance add-on

provided that such action does not breach any of the other conditions imposed by this Order.

[2150]

NOTES
Commencement: 1 March 2001.

14 Breach of the condition imposed by Article 13 shall have the effect of cancelling the block exemption in respect of the relevant public transport ticketing scheme to the extent that such scheme provides for members of the public to purchase the relevant through ticket, multi-operator individual ticket, short distance add-on or long distance add-on.

[2151]

NOTES
Commencement: 1 March 2001.

15 The parties to a public transport ticketing scheme which provides for members of the public to purchase a multi-operator individual ticket, shall not:
  (a) include an operator as a party to that scheme unless that operator also makes available, concurrently with making available that multi-operator individual ticket, single and return tickets entitling the holder to make the particular journey covered by that multi-operator individual ticket solely on the local public transport services of that operator; or

(b) distribute between themselves the revenue received by virtue of the operation of that scheme other than pursuant to terms contained in that scheme whereby the operator which sells any particular multi-operator individual ticket retains exclusively all the revenue received from that sale.

[2152]

NOTES
Commencement: 1 March 2001.

16 Breach of the condition imposed by Article 15 shall have the effect of cancelling the block exemption in respect of the relevant public transport ticketing scheme to the extent that such scheme provides for members of the public to purchase a multi-operator individual ticket.

[2153]

NOTES
Commencement: 1 March 2001.

Obligation

17 A person shall, within ten working days from the date on which it receives notice in writing under this Article, supply to the Director such information in connection with those public transport ticketing schemes to which it is a party as the Director may require.

[2154]

NOTES
Commencement: 1 March 2001.
Director: see the note to art 3 at **[2140]**.

Cancellation by notice

18 If there is a failure to comply with the obligation imposed by Article 17 without reasonable excuse, the Director may, subject to Article 20, by notice in writing cancel this block exemption in respect of any public transport ticketing scheme to which the relevant request for information under Article 17 relates.

[2155]

NOTES
Commencement: 1 March 2001.
Director: see the note to art 3 at **[2140]**.

19 If the Director considers that a particular public transport ticketing scheme is not one to which section 9 of the Act applies, he may, subject to Article 20, by notice in writing cancel this block exemption in respect of that scheme.

[2156]

NOTES
Commencement: 1 March 2001.
Director: see the note to art 3 at **[2140]**.

20 If the Director proposes to cancel the block exemption in accordance with Article 18 or Article 19, he shall first give notice in writing of his proposal and shall consider any representations made to him.

[2157]

NOTES
Commencement: 1 March 2001.
Director: see the note to art 3 at **[2140]**.

21 For the purpose of Articles 18, 19 and 20, notice in writing is given by—

    (a) the Director giving notice in writing of his decision or proposal to those persons whom he can reasonably identify as being parties to the relevant public transport ticketing scheme; or

    (b) where it is not reasonably practicable for the Director to comply with paragraph (a), the Director publishing his decision or proposal in the register and—

        (i) the London, Edinburgh and Belfast Gazettes;

        (ii) at least one national daily newspaper; and

        (iii) if there is in circulation an appropriate trade journal which is published at intervals not exceeding one month, in such trade journal,

stating the facts on which he bases it and his reasons for making it.

[2158]

NOTES
Commencement: 1 March 2001.
Director: see the note to art 3 at **[2140]**.

COMPETITION ACT 1998 (SECTION 11 EXEMPTION) REGULATIONS 2001

(SI 2001/2993)

NOTES
Made: 28 August 2001.
Authority: Competition Act 1998, ss 11(2), 71.
Commencement: 30 September 2001.

1 Citation

These Regulations may be cited as the Competition Act 1998 (Section 11 Exemption) Regulations 2001 and shall come into force on 30th September 2001.

[2159]

NOTES
Commencement: 30 September 2001.

2 Interpretation

In these Regulations—

    "the Act" means the Competition Act 1998;

    "the Community prohibition" means the prohibition contained in—

        (a) paragraph 1 of Article 81 of the Treaty;

        (b) any corresponding provision replacing, or otherwise derived from, that provision;

    "the Director's rules" means the Director's rules set out in the Schedule to the Competition Act 1998 (Director's rules) Order 2000;

    "the enforcement regulations" means the EC Competition Law (Articles 84 and 85) Enforcement Regulations 2001.

[2160]

PART II
STATUTORY INSTRUMENTS

NOTES

Commencement: 30 September 2001.

Director: the Enterprise Act 2002, s 2(1), at **[255]**, provides that, as from the coming into force of that section in accordance with s 279 at **[463]**, the functions of the Director General of Fair Trading, his property, rights and liabilities are transferred to the Office of Fair Trading. Accordingly, (by virtue of s 2(2), (3) of the 2002 Act) the office of the Director is abolished, and any reference to the Director in any enactment, instrument or other document passed or made before the commencement of s 2(1) shall have effect as if it were a reference to the Office of Fair Trading. For transitional provisions in connection with the transfer, see s 276(1) of, and Sch 24, para 6 to, the 2002 Act at **[477]**.

3 Exemption

(1) The prescribed circumstances in which agreements in relation to which a ruling may be given by virtue of Article 84 of the Treaty are exempt from the Chapter I prohibition are—

(a) that an agreement is exempt from the Community prohibition by virtue of a decision by the Director under the enforcement regulations; and

(b) that the Director has not found that an agreement which would otherwise benefit from a section 11 exemption has effects in the United Kingdom, or a part of it, which are incompatible with the conditions laid down in section 9 of the Act.

(2) A section 11 exemption—

(a) subject to paragraph (3), takes effect on the date on which the relevant exemption from the Community prohibition takes effect, and

(b) ceases to have effect on the date on which—

(i) a cancellation of the relevant exemption from the Community prohibition pursuant to the enforcement regulations takes effect;

(ii) the relevant exemption from the Community prohibition otherwise ceases to have effect; or

(iii) a finding is made by the Director that the agreement to which the relevant exemption relates has effects in the United Kingdom, or a part of it, which are incompatible with the conditions laid down in section 9 of the Act.

(3) A section 11 exemption may, if the Director considers it appropriate and so determines, take effect from a date specified by the Director which is earlier than the date on which the exemption from the Community prohibition takes effect.

(4) The Director shall not make a finding that the agreement to which the relevant exemption relates has effects in the United Kingdom, or a part of it, which are incompatible with the conditions laid down in section 9 of the Act unless he does so in the manner specified in rule 21 of the Director's rules.

[2161]

NOTES

Commencement: 30 September 2001.

Director: see the note to reg 2 at **[2160]**.

E. MERGER CONTROL

MERGER (PRENOTIFICATION) REGULATIONS 1990

(SI 1990/501)

NOTES

Made: 7 March 1990.
Authority: Fair Trading Act 1973, ss 75A(1), 75C(1)(c), 75D(1), (2)(b)–(h), (3), (4), 75E.
Commencement: 1 April 1990.

ARRANGEMENT OF REGULATIONS

1   Citation, commencement and interpretation

(1)   These Regulations may be cited as the Merger (Prenotification) Regulations 1990 and shall come into force on 1st April 1990.

(2)   In these Regulations—
"the Act" means the Fair Trading Act 1973;
"the Director" means the Director General of Fair Trading;
"working day" means any day which is not—
     (a)   Saturday, Sunday, Good Friday or Christmas Day, or
     (b)   a bank holiday in England and Wales.

(3)   A reference in these Regulations to a person who does anything on behalf of a person who is authorised to give a merger notice or who has given such notice shall be construed as limited to a reference to a person who does so having been authorised so to act in accordance with regulation 13 of these Regulations.

[2162]

NOTES

Director General of Fair Trading: the Enterprise Act 2002, s 2(1), at **[255]**, provides that, as from the coming into force of that section in accordance with s 279 at **[463]**, the functions of the Director General of Fair Trading, his property, rights and liabilities are transferred to the Office of Fair Trading. Accordingly, (by virtue of s 2(2), (3) of the 2002 Act) the office of the Director is abolished, and any reference to the Director in any enactment, instrument or other document passed or made before the commencement of s 2(1) shall have effect as if it were a reference to the Office of Fair Trading. For transitional provisions in connection with the transfer, see s 276(1) of, and Sch 24, para 6 to, the 2002 Act at **[477]**.

2   Person authorised to give merger notice

A merger notice may be given under section 75A(1) of the Act by any person carrying on an enterprise to which the notified arrangements relate.

[2163]

3   Time limit for disclosure of material information

The time specified for the purpose of section 75C(1)(c) of the Act (the time before the end of the period for considering a merger notice within which material information must be disclosed) is [five working days].

[2164]

NOTES
   Words in square brackets substituted by the Fair Trading Act (Amendment) (Merger Prenotification) Regulations 1994, SI 1994/1934, reg 4.

4   Time and manner of the giving of a merger notice

(1)   A merger notice shall be given by being delivered in writing to the office of the Director by hand or by post.

(2)   Subject to paragraph (3) below, a merger notice shall be treated as having been received at the office of the Director on the day on which it is in fact delivered to that office.

(3)   Where a merger notice is delivered to the office of the Director on any day which is not a working day or after 5.00 pm on any working day, it shall be treated as having been received on the next working day.

(4)   Section 7 of the Interpretation Act 1978 shall not apply to the giving of a merger notice in accordance with this regulation.

[2165]

NOTES
   Director: see the note "Director General of Fair Trading" to reg 1 at **[2162]**.

5   Rejection of a merger notice

A rejection of a merger notice under section 75B(7) of the Act shall be given in writing (including by facsimile or other form of electronic transmission) and such a notice shall be treated as having been rejected at the time when the rejection is sent to the person who gave the merger notice or a person acting on his behalf.

[2166]

6   Withdrawal of a merger notice

A merger notice may be withdrawn by or on behalf of the person who gave the notice by a notice in writing delivered to the office of the Director (including a notice delivered by facsimile or other form of electronic transmission).

[2167]

NOTES
   Director: see the note "Director General of Fair Trading" to reg 1 at **[2162]**.

7   Provision of information to the Director

(1)   Any information which—
   (a)   is, or ought to be, known to the person who gave the merger notice or any connected person, and
   (b)   is material to the notified arrangements,

or any information requested by the Director under section 75B(4) of the Act shall be provided or disclosed in writing (including by facsimile or other form of electronic transmission).

(2)   Subject to paragraph (3) below, any information provided or disclosed to the Director under this regulation shall be treated as having been so provided or disclosed on the day on which it is in fact delivered to the office of the Director.

(3)   Where information is delivered to the office of the Director on any day, which is not a working day or after 5.00 pm on any working day, it shall be treated as having been provided or disclosed to the Director on the next working day.

(4)   Section 7 of the Interpretation Act 1978 shall not apply to the provision or disclosure of any information under this regulation.

[2168]

NOTES

Director: see the note "Director General of Fair Trading" to reg 1 at **[2162]**.

8   Notice to extend period for consideration of merger notice

A notice to extend the period mentioned in section 75B(2) of the Act (period for consideration of merger notice) may be given orally or in writing (including by facsimile or other form of electronic transmission).

[2169]

9   Notice requesting further information

Any notice under section 75B(4) of the Act requesting information from the person who gave a merger notice may be given in writing (including by facsimile or other form of electronic transmission).

[2170]

10   Time at which notices relating to undertakings are to be treated as received

A notice given to the Director under section 75B(5)(a) of the Act shall be treated as having been received by him—
- (a)   subject to paragraph (b) below, on the day on which it is in fact delivered to his office (including by facsimile or other form of electronic transmission);
- (b)   where it is delivered to his office on any day which is not a working day or after 5.00 pm on any working day, on the next working day,

and section 7 of the Interpretation Act 1978 shall not apply.

[2171]

NOTES

Director: see the note "Director General of Fair Trading" to reg 1 at **[2162]**.

11   Address to be treated as a person's proper address

(1)   For the purposes of section 75B(6) and of these Regulations, the address provided or disclosed in writing to the Director as a person's proper address by or on behalf of the person giving a merger notice shall, subject to paragraph (2) below, be treated as that person's proper address.

(2)   Where an address is provided or disclosed in writing to the Director as a person's proper address by or on behalf of a person in respect of whom a different address has previously been provided or disclosed in accordance with paragraph (1)

above, the new address shall be treated as that person's proper address with effect from 9.00 am on the working day following the day on which it is delivered to the office of the Director.

[2172]

NOTES
 Director: see the note "Director General of Fair Trading" to reg 1 at **[2162]**.

12 Time at which fees are to be treated as paid

(1)   Subject to paragraphs (2) and (3) below, any fee payable in accordance with a merger notice shall be treated as having been paid on the day on which a valid cheque or other instrument for the correct amount is received at the office of the Director.

(2)   Where a cheque or other instrument received as payment for a fee referred to in paragraph (1) above is dishonoured on presentation, the fee shall, subject to paragraph (3) below, nevertheless be treated as having been paid on the day on which that cheque or other instrument is received if the condition specified in paragraph (4) below is subsequently satisfied.

(3)   Where a cheque or other instrument in respect of a fee referred to in paragraph (1) above is delivered to the office of the Director on any day which is not a working day or after 5.00 pm on any working day, it shall be treated as having been received on the next working day.

(4)   The condition referred to in paragraph (2) above is that, within the period of 20 days determined in accordance with section 75B(9) of the Act and beginning with the first day after the merger notice is, in accordance with regulation 4 of these Regulations, treated as having been received at the office of the Director, the correct amount of the fee has been properly paid by a valid cheque or other instrument.

(5)   Section 7 of the Interpretation Act 1978 shall not apply to the giving or sending of a cheque or other instrument in respect of a fee referred to in paragraph (1) above.

[2173]

NOTES
 Director: see the note "Director General of Fair Trading" to reg 1 at **[2162]**.

13 Circumstances in which a person is or is not to be treated as acting on behalf of the giver of a merger notice

(1)   A person shall be treated as acting on behalf of a person who is authorised to give a merger notice or who has given such a notice only if the person on whose behalf he is to be treated as acting has authorised him so to act in accordance with paragraph (2) below.

(2)   An authorisation to act on behalf of another person for the purposes of paragraph (1) above shall be given to the Director in writing and an authorisation to act on behalf of a company shall be signed by a director or other officer of that company.

(3)   A person who has given an authorisation in accordance with paragraph (1) above may revoke it by a notice in writing given to the Director and, where that person is a company, the notice shall be signed by a director or other officer of that company.

[2174]

NOTES
 Director: see the note "Director General of Fair Trading" to reg 1 at **[2162]**.

EEC MERGER CONTROL (CONSEQUENTIAL PROVISIONS) REGULATIONS 1990

(SI 1990/1563)

NOTES
Made: 27 July 1990.
Authority: European Communities Act 1972, s 2(2), and the Fair Trading Act 1973, s 75F(1), (2).
Commencement: 21 September 1990.

1.—(1) These Regulations may be cited as the EEC Merger Control (Consequential Provisions) Regulations 1990 and shall come into force on 21st September 1990.

(2) In these Regulations, "the Merger Control Regulation" means Council Regulation (EEC) No 4064/89 on the control of concentrations between undertakings, and expressions used in that Regulation shall bear the same meaning in these Regulations.

[2175]

2 For the purpose of determining the effect of giving a merger notice and the steps which may be or are to be taken by any person in connection with such a notice in a case in which the arrangements in question are or would result in a concentration with a Community dimension, . . .

[2176]

NOTES
Repealed by the Enterprise Act 2002, s 278(2), Sch 26, as from a day to be appointed; words omitted amend the Fair Trading Act 1973, s 75B.

3 A merger reference may be made under section 64 of the Fair Trading Act 1973 in a case in which the relevant enterprises ceased to be distinct enterprises at a time and in circumstances not falling within subsection (4) of that section if by reason of the Merger Control Regulation or anything done under or in accordance with it the reference could not have been made earlier than six months before the date on which it is to be made.

[2177]

MERGER (FEES) REGULATIONS 1990

(SI 1990/1660)

NOTES
Made: 9 August 1990.
Authority: Companies Act 1989, s 152.
Commencement: 1 October 1990.

ARRANGEMENT OF REGULATIONS

PART II
DATA PROTECTION; HUMAN RIGHTS

1   Citation, commencement and interpretation

(1)   These Regulations may be cited as the Merger (Fees) Regulations 1990 and shall come into force on 1st October 1990.

(2)   In these Regulations—
  (a) "the Act" means the Fair Trading Act 1973;
  (b) a reference to a numbered Regulation shall be construed as a reference to the Regulation bearing that number in these Regulations.

(3)   These Regulations shall be construed as one with Part V of the Act and as if sections 67 and 77 of the Act applied for the purpose of construing these Regulations.

[2178]

2   Matters in respect of which fees are payable

A fee of the amount specified in Regulation 4 shall be payable in respect of—
  (a) subject to Regulation 3(1), an application for the consent of the Secretary of State under section 58(1) of the Act to the transfer of a newspaper or of newspaper assets;
  (b) the giving of a merger notice under section 75A(1) of the Act;
  (c) the making by the Secretary of State of a merger reference to the Commission under [section 32(1) of the Water Industries Act 1991];
  (d) subject to Regulation 3(2), the making by the Secretary of State of a merger reference to the Commission under section 64 or 75 of the Act;
  (e) subject to Regulation 3(2), the announcement by the Secretary of State of his decision not to make a merger reference in any case where, at the time the announcement is made, he would, under section 64 or 75 of the Act, have the power to make such a reference.

[2179]

NOTES

   Para (c): words in square brackets substituted by the Merger (Fees) (Amendment) Regulations 2001, SI 2001/1199, reg 2(1), (4). It is thought that the reference to the Water Industries Act 1991 is intended to be a reference to the Water Industry Act 1991.

3   Circumstances in which certain fees are not payable

(1)   A fee shall not be payable under Regulation 2(a) in respect of an application for the consent of the Secretary of State under section 58(1) of the Act to the transfer of a newspaper or of newspaper assets—
  (a) where an application has been made by the same person within the previous six months in relation to the transfer to the same person of the same newspaper or the same newspaper assets and that application was expressed to depend on the operation of section 58(3) or (4) of the Act; or
  (b) the value of the newspaper or newspaper assets transferred is less than £100,000.

(2)   A fee shall not be payable under Regulation 2(d) in respect of a merger reference or under Regulation 2(e) in respect of the announcement by the Secretary of State of his decision not to make a merger reference—
  (a) where a fee has been paid under Regulation 2(b) in respect of a merger notice given in relation to proposed arrangements and either—
    (i) the merger reference or, as the case may be, the Secretary of State's decision not to make a merger reference is made in relation to those arrangements, or
    (ii) if the fee under Regulation 2(b) became due within the previous six months, the result of carrying those arrangements into effect is the

creation or possible creation of the merger situation qualifying for investigation which is the subject of the merger reference or, as the case may be, the Secretary of State's decision not to make a merger reference;

(b) where the creation or possible creation of the merger situation depends or would depend on the operation of section 65(3) or (4)(b) of the Act.

[2180]

4 Amount of fees

The amount of the fee payable under Regulation 2 shall be—

(a) in a case falling within paragraph (a) of that Regulation—

    (i) where the average circulation per day of publication of any of the newspapers concerned in the transfer is more than 25,000, £10,000, and

    (ii) where sub-paragraph (i) above does not apply, £5,000;

(b) in a case falling within paragraph (b), (c), (d) or (e) of that Regulation—

    (i) where the value of the assets which have been taken over, or, as the case may be, which it is proposed or contemplated should be taken over, does not exceed £30 million, £5,000,

    (ii) where the value of such assets exceeds £30 million but does not exceed £100 million, £10,000,

    (iii) where the value of such assets exceeds £100 million, £15,000.

[2181]

5 Person by whom fees are payable

(1) In a case falling within Regulation 2(a), the fee shall be payable by the person who makes the application for the consent of the Secretary of State under section 58(1) of the Act.

(2) In a case falling within Regulation 2(b), the fee shall be payable by the person who gives the merger notice.

(3) Subject to paragraph (5) [or (6)] below, in a case falling within Regulation 2(c), (d) or (e), the fee shall be payable—

(a) where it appears to the Secretary of State that it is or may be the fact that—

    (i) there is a merger situation to which section 65(1)(a) of the Act applies, or

    (ii) arrangements are in progress or in contemplation which if carried into effect would result in the creation of a merger situation to which that provision of the Act would apply, or

    (iii) there is a situation to which either paragraph (a) or (b) of subsection (1) of [section 32 of the Water Industries Act 1991] applies,

by the person, or group of persons, who has or have acquired or will, if those arrangements are carried into effect, acquire either—

    (iv) a controlling interest in one of the enterprises which was or is involved in the merger or prospective merger and in which he or they did not previously have such an interest, or

    (v) in the case of such an enterprise carried on by a body corporate in which he or they did not previously have a controlling interest, a controlling interest in that body corporate; or

(b) where it appears to the Secretary of State that it is or may be the fact that—

    (i) there is a merger situation to which section 65(1)(b) of the Act applies, or

    (ii) arrangements are in progress or in contemplation which if carried into effect would result in the creation of a merger situation to which that provision of the Act would apply,

by the person or group of persons who—

    (iii) carried on or are carrying on the enterprise involved in the merger or prospective merger which did not cease or will not, if those arrangements are carried into effect, cease to be carried on at all, or

    (iv) had or have a controlling interest in that enterprise, or

    (v) in the case where that enterprise was or is carried on by a body corporate, had or have a controlling interest in that body corporate.

(4)   In a case where paragraph (3) above applies to more than one person, whether by virtue of them being treated as one by the operation of section 77 of the Act or otherwise, the persons to whom it applies shall be jointly and severally liable for the fee in that case.

(5)   Where a fee is payable under Regulation 2(c) in respect of a merger reference under [section 32(1) of the Water Industries Act 1991], under Regulation 2(d) in respect of a merger reference under section 64 or 75 of the Act or under Regulation 2(e) in respect of the announcement by the Secretary of State of his decision not to make such a merger reference but the person specified in subparagraph (3) above is not—

    (a) a British citizen, a [British overseas territories citizen], a British Overseas citizen or a British National (Overseas); or

    (b) a body corporate incorporated under the law of the United Kingdom or of a part of the United Kingdom; or

    (c) a person carrying on business in the United Kingdom, either alone or in partnership with one or more persons;

he shall not be liable to pay the fee unless the merger situation or, as the case may be, the arrangements in progress or in contemplation result, wholly or partially, from anything done by him within the United Kingdom.

[(6) In a case falling within regulation 2(b) to (e), the person or group of persons specified in paragraph (2) or (3) above shall not be liable to pay the fee if:

    (a) being a person of the kind described in paragraph (2) above, the enterprise carried on by him or under his control is one to which the notified arrangements relate and he will, if the notified arrangements are carried into effect, be in the position of a person or group of persons described in subparagraphs (b) or (c) below; or

    (b) being a person or group of persons of the kind described in paragraph (3)(a) above, the relevant enterprise carried on by him or them or under his or their control will if the arrangements are carried into effect, or did if the arrangements have been carried into effect, cease to be distinct from the enterprises described in paragraph 3(a)(iv) or (v) above; or

    (c) in the circumstances described in paragraph (3)(b)(i) or (ii) above he is a person or group of persons to whom paragraph (3)(b)(iii), (iv) or (v) above applies;

and the relevant enterprise carried on by that person or group of persons or under his or their control qualifies as small or medium sized.

(7)   For the purposes of paragraph (6):—

    (a) an enterprise qualifies as small or medium sized if, immediately before the time at which the fee would otherwise become payable—

        (i) it satisfies the requirements to be small or medium sized set out in subsections (3) to (6) of section 247 of the Companies Act 1985 ("the Act of 1985") in its most recent financial year, whether or not the enterprise is a company; and

        (ii) where it is a member of a group as defined in section 262 of the Act of 1985 (whether or not the enterprise is a company), that group qualifies as small or medium sized within the meaning of subsections (3) to (5) of section 249 of the Act of 1985 in its most recent financial year;

    (b) a "relevant enterprise" is, in a case falling within paragraph (3)(a) above one to which the circumstances described in paragraph (3)(a)(i), (ii) or (iii) relate, or, in a case falling within paragraph (3)(b) above one to which the circumstances described in paragraph (3)(b)(i) or (ii) relate.

(8) Paragraph (6) shall not apply to fees becoming payable before 1st June 2001.]

[2182]

NOTES

Para (3): words in square brackets substituted by the Merger (Fees) (Amendment) Regulations 2001, SI 2001/1199, reg 2(1), (2), (4).

Para (5): first words in square brackets substituted by SI 2001/1199, reg 2(1), (4); words in square brackets in sub-para (a) substituted by virtue of the British Overseas Territories Act 2002, s 2(3).

Paras (6)–(8): added by SI 2001/1199, reg 2(1), (3).

It is thought that the references in paras (3), (5) to the Water Industries Act 1991 are intended to be references to the Water Industry Act 1991.

6 Person to whom fees are payable

(1) In a case falling within Regulation 2(a), the fee shall be payable to the Secretary of State.

(2) In a case falling within Regulation 2(b), (c), (d) or (e), the fee shall be payable to the Director.

[2183]

NOTES

Director: the Enterprise Act 2002, s 2(1), at **[255]**, provides that, as from the coming into force of that section in accordance with s 279 at **[463]**, the functions of the Director General of Fair Trading, his property, rights and liabilities are transferred to the Office of Fair Trading. Accordingly, (by virtue of s 2(2), (3) of the 2002 Act) the office of the Director is abolished, and any reference to the Director in any enactment, instrument or other document passed or made before the commencement of s 2(1) shall have effect as if it were a reference to the Office of Fair Trading. For transitional provisions in connection with the transfer, see s 276(1) of, and Sch 24, para 6 to, the 2002 Act at **[477]**.

7 Time when fees are payable

(1) In a case falling within Regulation 2(b), the fee shall be payable at the time when the application for the consent of the Secretary of State under section 58(1) of the Act is made.

(2) In a case falling within Regulation 2(b), the fee shall be payable at the time when the merger notice is given.

(3) In a case falling within Regulation 2(c), (d) or (e), the fee shall be payable when the Secretary of State publishes the merger reference or, as the case may be, announces his decision not to make a merger reference.

[2184]

8 Repayment of fees

In a case falling within Regulation 2(b)—

(a) the Director may repay the whole of the fee where the notified arrangements would not, if they were carried into effect, result in the creation of a merger situation qualifying for investigation; and

(b) the Director shall repay the whole of the fee where he rejects the merger notice under section 75B(7)(d) of the Act (rejection of merger notice where the notified arrangements are or would result in a concentration with a Community dimension).

[2185]

NOTES

Director: see the note to reg 6 at **[2183]**.

EEC MERGER CONTROL (DISTINCT MARKET INVESTIGATIONS) REGULATIONS 1990

(SI 1990/1715)

NOTES
Made: 20 August 1990.
Authority: European Communities Act 1972, s 2(2).
Commencement: 21 September 1990.

1.—(1) These Regulations may be cited as the EEC Merger Control (Distinct Market Investigations) Regulations 1990 and shall come into force on 21 September 1990.

(2) In these Regulations, "the Merger Control Regulation" means Council Regulation (EEC) No 4064/89 on the control of concentrations between undertakings, and expressions used in that Regulation shall bear the same meaning in these Regulations.

[2186]

2 At any time after the Commission has transmitted to the competent authorities of the United Kingdom a copy of the notification to the Commission of a concentration with a Community dimension, the Director General of Fair Trading ("the Director") may, for the purpose of furnishing information to the Commission under the second sentence of Article 19(2) of the Merger Control Regulation, and by notice in writing signed by him—

(a) require any person to produce, at a time and place specified in the notice, to the Director or to any person appointed by him for the purpose, any documents which are specified or described in the notice and which are documents in his custody or under his control and relating to any matter relevant to the furnishing of information as aforesaid, or

(b) require any person carrying on any business to furnish to the Director such estimates, returns or other information as may be specified or described in the notice, and specify the time, the manner and the form in which such estimates, returns or information are to be furnished;

but no person shall be compelled by virtue of this regulation to produce any documents which he could not be compelled to produce in civil proceedings before the High Court or, in Scotland, the Court of Session or, in complying with any requirement for the furnishing of information, to give any information which he could not be compelled to give in evidence in such proceedings.

[2187]

NOTES
Director General of Fair Trading: the Enterprise Act 2002, s 2(1), at **[255]**, provides that, as from the coming into force of that section in accordance with s 279 at **[463]**, the functions of the Director General of Fair Trading, his property, rights and liabilities are transferred to the Office of Fair Trading. Accordingly, (by virtue of s 2(2), (3) of the 2002 Act) the office of the Director is abolished, and any reference to the Director in any enactment, instrument or other document passed or made before the commencement of s 2(1) shall have effect as if it were a reference to the Office of Fair Trading. For transitional provisions in connection with the transfer, see s 276(1) of, and Sch 24, para 6 to, the 2002 Act at **[477]**.

3.—(1) Subsections (6) to (8) of section 85 of the Fair Trading Act 1973 (enforcement provisions relating to notices under subsection (1) of that section requiring production of documents etc) shall, subject to paragraph (2) below, apply in relation to a notice under regulation 2 above as they apply in relation to a notice under subsection (1) of that section, but as if—

(a) the reference in subsection (6) of that section to a fine not exceeding the prescribed sum were a reference to a fine not exceeding an amount equal to level 5 on the standard scale, and

(b) in subsection (7) of that section, for the words from "any one" to "the Commission" there were substituted "the Director".

(2)   In punishing a defaulter under subsection (7A) of the said section 85, the court shall not impose any penalty which could not be imposed on summary conviction for an offence created in exercise of the powers conferred by section 2(2) of the European Communities Act 1972.

[2188]

NOTES

Director: see the note to reg 2 at **[2187]**.

4   Sections 93B (furnishing false or misleading information to the Director) and 133 (restrictions on disclosure of information) of the Fair Trading Act 1973 shall apply as if these Regulations were contained in Part V of that Act and the references in—

(a) subsection (3)(a) of the said section 93B to a fine not exceeding the statutory maximum, and

(b) subsection (5)(a) of the said section 133 to a fine not exceeding the prescribed sum

were references to a fine not exceeding an amount equal to level 5 on the standard scale.

[2189]

NOTES

Director: see the note to reg 2 at **[2187]**.

PART III
OFT GUIDELINES
(COMPETITION ACT 1998)

CURRENT LIST OF GUIDELINES

THE MAJOR PROVISIONS

(OFT 400, March 1999)

1 What this guideline is about

1.1 Competition lies at the heart of any successful market economy and is crucial to the protection of consumers' interests and the efficient allocation of resources. It is a process whereby undertakings constantly try to gain an advantage over their rivals and win more business by offering more attractive terms to customers or by developing better products or more effective ways of meeting their requirements. Competition has several dimensions of which price is only one, albeit in many markets the most important. It encourages the development of new or improved products or processes and enhances economic growth and living standards. The Director General will apply and enforce the provisions of the Competition Act 1998 (**'the Act'**) in order to ensure that the competition process is unhindered by anti-competitive activity.

1.2 The Act replaces or amends legislation including the Restrictive Trade Practices Act 1976, the Resale Prices Act 1976 and the majority of the Competition Act 1980. The old legislation was unduly technical, and did not contain sufficient sanctions against genuinely harmful anti-competitive conduct, while unnecessarily catching many innocuous agreements. It did not prohibit any particular kinds of conduct and had become a burden for businesses and cumbersome for the authorities to operate.

1.3 The new legislation introduces two prohibitions: one of agreements (whether written or not) which prevent, restrict or distort competition and which may affect trade within the United Kingdom (**'the Chapter I prohibition'**); the other of conduct by undertakings which amounts to an abuse of a dominant position in a market and which may affect trade within the United Kingdom (**'the Chapter II prohibition'**).

1.4 This guideline gives an overall summary of the Act's provisions. Parts 2, 3 and 4 explain the basic elements of the Chapter I and Chapter II prohibitions which are based on Articles 85 and 86 of the EC Treaty[1] (Articles 85 and 86, respectively). Part 5 of this guideline describes the exclusions provided for in the Act.

1.5 Section 60 of the Act sets out principles which provide for the United Kingdom authorities to handle cases in such a way as to ensure consistency with Community law. This is considered in more detail in part 6 of this guideline.

1.6 Explanations of the procedure for notifications and for complaints can be found in parts 7 and 8 and a description of the provisions relating to confidentiality and disclosure of information appears in part 9. The Act provides for certain fees to be charged by the Director General, as explained in part 10. The powers under the Act of investigation of undertakings believed to be involved in anti-competitive activities, and of enforcement, are described in part 11 of this guideline. The consequences of breach and the power to impose financial penalties on undertakings is discussed in part 12. Part 13 explains the continuing relevance of the Fair Trading Act 1973 and the new Competition Commission established by the Act and the appeal system is discussed in part 14.

1.7 Other guidelines provide more details on specific areas. The guidelines will be revised and reissued from time to time and new ones may be published.

1.8 The two prohibitions come into force on 1 March 2000. Until then, the legislation which the Act replaces continues to operate in a modified form. In particular, under the Restrictive Trade Practices Act 1976 all new agreements except those involving price-fixing are non-notifiable. After 1 March 2000, many existing agreements which complied with previous competition legislation will benefit from further transitional periods (in most cases one year, but five years for some) during which the prohibition on anti-competitive agreements will not apply. Agreements which are the subject of a direction under section 21(2) of the Restrictive Trade Practices Act benefit from an exclusion from the prohibition on anti-competitive agreements (see part 5 below). Further details of the transitional provisions are given in the Competition Act guideline *Transitional Arrangements*.

Terms used in this guideline

1.9   **Agreement** covers agreements between undertakings, decisions by associations of undertakings and concerted practices. These may be spoken, as well as written, and need not necessarily be legally binding (for example unwritten 'gentlemen's agreements'). It may cover co-operation without any agreement or decision.

Undertaking includes any natural or legal person capable of carrying on commercial or economic activities relating to goods or services, irrespective of its legal status. It includes companies, firms, businesses, partnerships, individuals operating as sole traders, agricultural cooperatives, trade associations and non-profit making organisations. A parent company and its subsidiaries will usually be treated as a single undertaking if they operate as a single economic unit, depending on the facts of each case.

These concepts are discussed further in the Competition Act guideline *The Chapter I Prohibition*.

[3001]

NOTES

   [1]   [Now] renumbered Articles 81 and 82 following ratification of the Treaty of Amsterdam.

---

2   The prohibitions

2.1   The Chapter I and Chapter II prohibitions in the Act are based on Articles 85 and 86. Articles 85 and 86 continue to apply to agreements or conduct which may affect trade between EC Member States. The Act applies to agreements or conduct that affect trade within the United Kingdom. Issues arising in relation to the overlap between the United Kingdom and Community prohibitions are dealt with in the Competition Act guidelines *The Chapter I Prohibition* and *The Chapter II Prohibition*.

2.2   The prohibitions in the Act apply to business in the same way as the Community models in Articles 85 and 86. As far as possible, agreements and practices which are prohibited under one regime are therefore prohibited under the other, and those that are permitted are permitted under both. The Act therefore provides for the United Kingdom authorities to handle cases in such a way as to ensure consistency with Community law (see part 6 below).

2.3   The Act has two main features—

    —   **a prohibition of agreements between undertakings, decisions by associations of undertakings or concerted practices which have the object or effect of preventing, restricting or distorting competition in the United Kingdom (or a part thereof) and which may affect trade within the United Kingdom (the Chapter I prohibition).**

The Chapter I prohibition is subject to certain exclusions and exemptions. Anti-competitive effects may occur without any clearly expressed or overt agreement and the prohibition therefore covers decisions by associations of undertakings, and concerted practices, whether written or not. The anti-competitive nature of the agreement is judged according to its effects on competition, or its objective, rather than its wording or form; and

— **a prohibition of conduct by one or more undertakings which amounts to the abuse of a dominant position, in a market in the United Kingdom (or a part thereof), which may affect trade within the United Kingdom (the Chapter II prohibition).**

The Chapter II prohibition is subject to certain limited exclusions. There is no possibility of an exemption. The prohibition is on the *abuse* of the dominant position: there is no prohibition on the holding or acquisition of a dominant position.

[3002]

3   The Chapter I prohibition—anti-competitive agreements

The Prohibition

3.1   The Chapter I prohibition covers agreements between undertakings that have the object or effect of preventing, restricting or distorting competition in the United Kingdom and which may affect trade within the United Kingdom, or a part thereof.

3.2   The Act gives examples of the sorts of agreements that will be caught by the Chapter I prohibition—those which—

'(a) *directly or indirectly fix purchase or selling prices or any other trading conditions;*

(b) *limit or control production, markets, technical development or investment;*

(c) *share markets or sources of supply;*

(d) *apply dissimilar conditions to equivalent transactions with other trading parties, thereby placing them at a competitive disadvantage;*

(e) *make the conclusion of contracts subject to acceptance by the other parties of supplementary obligations which, by their nature or according to commercial usage, have no connection with the subject of such contracts.'*

3.3   **This list is not exhaustive and is for illustration only.** More detailed examples of agreements which may be considered to be prohibited by the Act are given in the Competition Act guideline *The Chapter I Prohibition.*

Appreciable effect

3.4   An agreement will infringe the Chapter I prohibition only if it has as its object or effect an appreciable prevention, restriction or distortion of competition in the United Kingdom. This follows from established case law of the European Court which the Director General and the United Kingdom courts will be bound to follow under section 60 of the Act. Any agreement which does not have an appreciable effect on competition in the United Kingdom should not be notified to the Director General.

3.5   The Director General takes the view that an agreement will generally have no appreciable effect on competition if the parties' combined share of the relevant market does not exceed 25 per cent, although there will be circumstances in which this is not the case.

3.6 The Director General will, in addition, generally regard any agreement between undertakings which—

— directly or indirectly fixes prices or shares markets; or

— imposes minimum resale prices; or

— is one of a network of similar agreements which have a cumulative effect on the market in question

as being capable of having appreciable effect even where the combined market share falls below the 25 per cent threshold. Further details on networks of agreements are given in the Competition Act guideline *Vertical Agreements and Restraints*.

3.7 Even where the parties' combined market share is higher than 25 per cent, the Director General may find that the effect on competition is not appreciable. This will depend on other factors such as the content of the agreement and the structure of the market affected.

3.8 Further details on defining the relevant market are given in the Competition Act guideline *Market Definition* and further guidance on appreciability is given in the Competition Act guideline *The Chapter I Prohibition*.

Exemptions

3.9 The Act provides for exemption from the prohibition of agreements which satisfy certain exemption criteria. There are three kinds of exemption—

— an **individual exemption** may be granted in respect of an individual agreement where it can be shown to contribute to improving production or distribution, or to promoting technical or economic progress, and which allows consumers a fair share of the resulting benefit. Any restrictions contained in the agreement must be indispensable to the attainment of those objectives, and the overall agreement must not afford the possibility of eliminating competition in a substantial part of the products concerned. An agreement must be notified to the Director General in order to receive an individual exemption;

— a **block exemption** covers particular categories of agreements which meet the same exemption criteria as for an individual exemption. An agreement which falls within a block exemption will be exempt automatically and does not need to be notified in order to benefit from the exemption;

— a **parallel exemption** applies to agreements that benefit from individual or block exemption under Article 85(3).[1] This exemption also covers agreements which fall within the terms of a European Commission block exemption but which are not subject to Article 85 because they do not affect inter-state trade. These are automatically exempted under the Act without the need for individual notification. In certain circumstances the Director General may impose conditions on a parallel exemption, or vary or cancel the parallel exemption, following procedures specified in the *Director General of Fair Trading's Procedural Rules*.

3.10 Exemptions are time limited and may be granted subject to certain specified conditions or obligations. The exemption can have effect from a date which is earlier than that on which it is granted.

[3003]

NOTES

[1] Agreements covering exclusive distribution, exclusive purchasing, motor vehicle distribution and servicing, specialisation, research and development cooperation, franchises, technology transfer, and certain types of agreement in the insurance sector are currently the subject of European Commission block exemptions.

4 The Chapter II prohibition—abuse of a dominant position

The prohibition

4.1 The Chapter II prohibition covers conduct by one or more undertakings which amounts to the abuse of a dominant position in a market in the United Kingdom (or a part thereof) which may affect trade within the United Kingdom.

4.2 The Act gives examples of conduct which may amount to abuse of a dominant position—

'(a) *directly or indirectly imposing unfair purchase or selling prices or other unfair trading conditions;*

(b) *limiting production, markets or technical development to the prejudice of consumers;*

(c) *applying dissimilar conditions to equivalent transactions with other trading parties, thereby placing them at a competitive disadvantage;*

(d) *making the conclusion of contracts subject to acceptance by the other parties of supplementary obligations which, by their nature or according to commercial usage, have no connection with the subject of the contracts.'*

4.3 **This list is not exhaustive and is for illustration only.** More detailed examples of conduct which may be considered to be an abuse of a dominant position are given in the Competition Act guideline *The Chapter II Prohibition.*

Dominance and market definition

4.4 An undertaking will be dominant if it can behave *'to an appreciable extent independently of its competitors and customers and ultimately of consumers'* when making commercial decisions.[1] This must be judged against the background of a properly defined relevant market through assessment of—

— the goods or services which form part of the market (the product market); and

— the geographic extent of the market.

4.5 Further details are available in the Competition Act guidelines *The Chapter II Prohibition* and *Market Definition.*

Exemption

4.6 There is no possibility of exemption from the prohibition of abuse of a dominant position.

[3004]

NOTES

[1] Case 27/76 *United Brands v Commission* [1978] ECR 207, [1978] 1 CMLR 429.

5 Exclusions

5.1 The Act provides for certain exclusions from the Chapter I and Chapter II prohibitions in Schedules 1 to 4. Broadly, these are as follows—

Agreements excluded from the Chapter I prohibition—

— an agreement which is subject to competition scrutiny under the Financial Services Act 1986, the Companies Act 1989, the Broadcasting Act 1990, or the Environment Act 1995;

— an agreement which is required in order to comply with, and to the extent that it is, a planning obligation;

— an agreement which is the subject of a direction under section 21(2) of the Restrictive Trade Practices Act 1976;

— an agreement for the constitution of a European Economic Area regulated market, to the extent that it relates to the rules made or guidance issued by that market;

— an agreement where it relates to production of or trade in **'agricultural products'** as defined in the EC Treaty and in Council Regulation (EEC) No 26/62, or to farmers' co-operatives;

— an agreement which constitutes a designated professional rule, imposes obligations arising from such a rule, or constitutes an agreement to act in accordance with such rules.

Agreements and/or conduct excluded from the Chapter I and/or Chapter II prohibition—

— to the extent to which an agreement/conduct would result in a merger or joint venture within the merger provisions of the Fair Trading Act 1973 (see the Competition Act guideline *Mergers and Ancillary Restrictions* for further detail);

— an agreement/conduct which would result in a concentration with a Community dimension and thereby be subject to the EC Merger Regulation;

— an agreement/conduct to the extent to which it is made/engaged in to comply with a specified legal requirement;

— an agreement/conduct which is necessary to avoid conflict with international obligations and which is also the subject of an order by the Secretary of State;

— an agreement/conduct which is necessary for compelling reasons of public policy and which is also the subject of an order by the Secretary of State;

— an agreement/conduct which relates to a coal or steel product within the ECSC Treaty;

— an agreement made or conduct engaged in by an undertaking entrusted with the operation of services of general economic interest or of a revenue producing monopoly, insofar as the prohibition would obstruct the performance of those tasks (see the Competition Act guideline *General Economic Interest*).

5.2   The Secretary of State has the power to add, amend or remove exclusions in certain circumstances.

5.3   Section 50 provides for special treatment under the Chapter I prohibition for certain types of vertical agreements and agreements relating to land. It is intended that orders will be introduced whereby the Chapter I prohibition will not apply to agreements falling into either of these categories, although subject to a **clawback** provision (see the Competition Act guidelines *Vertical Agreements and Restraints* and *Land Agreements*).

[3005]

6   Community law

Section 60

6.1   Section 60 of the Act sets out certain principles with a view to ensuring that the United Kingdom authorities handle cases in such a way as to ensure consistency with Community law.

6.2   The Act therefore places a dual obligation on the United Kingdom authorities in considering and dealing with the application of the Chapter I and Chapter II prohibitions. First they must ensure that there is no inconsistency with either the principles laid down by the EC Treaty and the European Court or any relevant decision of the European Court. Secondly, the United Kingdom authorities must have regard to any relevant decision or statement of the European Commission. In the Director General's view this is limited to decisions or statements which have the authority of the European Commission as a whole, such as, for example, decisions on individual cases under Articles 85 and 86. It would also include clear statements about its policy approach which the European Commission has published in the Annual Report on Competition Policy.

6.3   The obligation to ensure consistency applies only to the extent that this is possible, having regard to any relevant differences between the provisions concerned. This means that there will be certain areas where the Community principles will not be relevant. For example, the Community single market objectives designed to establish a European common market would not be relevant to the domestic prohibition system.

6.4   The provisions of section 60 apply to all United Kingdom authorities which are involved with the administration and enforcement of the Act: the Director General, the Competition Commission and the domestic courts.

Direct application of Community law

6.5   Community law applies to anti-competitive agreements and abuses of a dominant position where they may affect trade between EC Member States. United Kingdom undertakings may, therefore, be subject to Community law as well as the prohibitions in the Act.

6.6   **There is a considerable volume of Community law, and, while the relevant principles and provisions are reflected in this and other guidelines, the guidelines should not be regarded as a substitute for, or as an authoritative interpretation of, Community law.**

Interrelationship between Community law and the Act

6.7   There are provisions in the Act designed to reduce the possibility of investigation of the same issue by both the European Commission and by the Director General—

— agreements which are exempt from the Article 85 prohibition (whether under an individual exemption or by virtue of a European Commission block exemption Regulation) benefit from an automatic **parallel exemption** under the Act (see paragraph 3.9 above);

— an agreement which has been notified to the European Commission is provisionally immune from penalties under the Act, in the same way as it is provisionally immune from European Commission fines, until the European Commission formally determines the matter or withdraws the immunity. This will be the case whether or not it has also been notified to the Director General under the Act. The Director General can, however, still investigate the agreement, notwithstanding that it has been notified to the European Commission.

6.8   The relevance of Community law to the operation of the Act is also discussed in the Competition Act guideline *The Chapter I Prohibition*.

                                                  [3006]

7   Procedures

Notification

7.1   There is no statutory requirement to notify agreements or conduct to the Director General of Fair Trading. It is for the parties to an agreement or conduct themselves to take on the responsibility of ensuring that their agreements and conduct are lawful and to decide whether notification is appropriate in any particular case.

7.2   Notification may be made for guidance or for a decision, but cannot be made in respect of prospective agreements (that is, those into which the parties have not yet entered) or prospective conduct. Notification to the Director General of Fair Trading is necessary if a decision is sought granting an individual exemption. Notification provides the parties with provisional immunity from financial penalties in respect of an agreement from the time a valid notification is received by the Director General of Fair Trading. Provisional immunity from financial penalties does **not** apply to conduct notified under the Chapter II prohibition.

7.3   **Guidance** may indicate whether or not the agreement or conduct would be likely to infringe the relevant prohibition and, in the case of agreements only, whether or not it would be likely to be granted an exemption if application were made for a decision. Favourable guidance provides immunity from financial penalties. The Director General is not able to reopen a case once guidance has been given unless he has reasonable grounds for believing that there has been a material change of circumstance since the guidance was given; or he has a reasonable suspicion that materially incomplete, misleading or false information had been given; or a complaint is received from a third party, or, in respect of the Chapter I prohibition only, where one of the parties to the agreement applies for a decision with respect to the agreement.

7.4   A **decision** may be that the agreement or conduct is (i) outside the relevant prohibition (including those covered by an exclusion), or (ii) that it is prohibited, or (iii) in the case of agreements only, that it is exempt. The decision entails an assessment of the relevant market and of the individual circumstances of the case, including the economic effects, and any views received from third parties. The Director General is not able to reopen a case once a decision has been given that the prohibition has not been infringed unless he has reasonable grounds for believing that there has been a material change in circumstances or he has a reasonable suspicion that materially incomplete, misleading or false information had been given. Unlike guidance, a decision cannot be reopened simply because a complaint is made by a third party.

7.5   In all decision cases a notice is published containing details of the notification (the parties involved, a brief summary of the provisions of the agreement and the goods or services) on the register at the Office of Fair Trading and on the Office of Fair Trading's website on the Internet. This notice corresponds to the 250 word summary required in Part 4 of Form N. The Director General of Fair Trading will also publish a weekly gazette containing summaries of notifications for decisions as well as the results of notifications for decisions.

7.6   In the case of exemption decisions, the Director General will invite further comments by third parties before reaching a final decision. Such an invitation will be published on the register kept at the Office of Fair Trading and its website on the Internet, and will usually be published in the weekly gazette and in the relevant trade press or national press.

7.7   If, after a preliminary investigation, the Director General considers that it is likely that an agreement will infringe the Chapter I prohibition, and that it would not be appropriate to grant an individual exemption, he may make a provisional decision notifying the parties of his preliminary conclusion. The decision means that the provisional immunity from financial penalties which arose as a consequence of notification will be treated as never having applied in respect of that agreement. A similar procedure will be followed where the Director General considers that conduct will infringe the Chapter II prohibition (although in such cases there is no immunity from financial penalties to be removed).

7.8   If the Director General proposes to make an infringement decision, he will send the party or parties a written statement setting out the matters to which he has taken objection, the action he proposes to take and the reasons for it. The Director General must allow the person receiving the notice an opportunity to make representations to him. The person receiving the notice may request a meeting with officials of the office of the Director General to make oral representations to elaborate on his written representations already made in this regard. If requested, the Director General must give the party or parties or an authorised representative an opportunity to inspect the Director General's file relating to the proposed decision. The Director General's file will not include documents to the extent that they contain confidential information or the Director General's internal documents.

Notification forms

7.9   All notifications must be made to the Director General of Fair Trading, even if the notification relates to a market which is subject to sectoral regulation. The original Form N plus two copies should be sent to the Office of Fair Trading. An original or certified copy of any relevant agreement and annexes plus two further copies should also be sent. Where the market is subject to the concurrent jurisdiction of another regulator or regulators, one further copy of the Form N (together with its annexes and copies of agreements) for each of those regulators must be sent to the Office of Fair Trading. A copy of the Form N (together with its annexes and copies of agreements) should also be sent direct to the relevant regulator(s). A notification will not be deemed incomplete simply because the notifier fails to send an additional copy of the form to or for a relevant regulator.

7.10   Form N contains the checklist of information which must be supplied to the Director General to enable him to determine a notification. It is available from the Director General of Fair Trading and from the regulators.

7.11   Form N is similar to Form A/B used for notifications to the European Commission. If a simultaneous notification is being made to the Director General of Fair Trading and to the European Commission, parties may choose to send three copies of the completed Form A/B and supporting documents (and a further copy, if information has been given in response to question 3.5 of Part 2 of Form N relating to concurrent jurisdiction, both to the Director General of Fair Trading and direct to the relevant regulator) as well as the Form N. In this way it will be unnecessary for the parties to repeat information given on Form A/B in the Form N, although cross-references to the relevant information on Form A/B should be given. Further, information specific to the United Kingdom market will still be necessary (following the format in question 7.1 of Part 2 of Form N) to the extent that it has not been given on Form A/B, and should be provided separately. Simultaneous notifications to both the European Commission and to the Director General are, however, undesirable in terms of the compliance costs for undertakings and the duplication of effort by the competition authorities. Dual notifications are also dealt with in Part 7 of the Competition Act guideline *The Chapter I Prohibition*.

7.12   In some limited circumstances, it may be possible to dispense with some of the information requirements on Form N. This should be discussed, in advance, with the Office of Fair Trading or the relevant regulator where appropriate.

7.13   The party notifying an agreement must take all reasonable steps to notify the other party or parties to the agreement that it is doing so. If a party is notifying conduct and the conduct in question is being carried on by more than one party, the party notifying should inform the other(s).

7.14 Notifications must be sent to—
The Office of Fair Trading
Competition Act Notifications
Field House
Bream's Buildings
London
EC4A 1PR

The addresses of the regulators are set out [at **[3130]**.]

Public register

7.15 The Director General of Fair Trading will maintain a public register containing details of each notification for a decision and an indication of the outcome of the notification. The register will contain a summary of the nature and objectives of the agreement or conduct. Parties are asked at Part 4 of Form N to provide the details which will appear on the public register. The register will be accessible via the Internet and may be inspected at the Office of Fair Trading during office hours. Applications for guidance will not appear on the register.

Confidentiality

7.16 Parties are asked in completing Form N to set out any information that they consider to be confidential in a separate annex and explain why it is to be so regarded. Confidentiality and disclosure of information are discussed further in part 9 below.

Procedural rules

7.17 Fuller details relating to procedural matters are contained in, and reference should be made to, the ***Director General of Fair Trading's Procedural Rules*** which are available from the Office of Fair Trading.

[3007]

8 Complaints

Procedure

8.1 Complaints alleging breach of either prohibition may be made to the Director General of Fair Trading or, if appropriate, to a regulator. Where the complaint relates to issues falling within the concurrent jurisdiction of a regulator, the complaint will usually be dealt with by that regulator rather than by the Office of Fair Trading.

8.2 There is no form to complete to make a complaint. Guidance about the information likely to be required is available from the Office of Fair Trading and each of the regulators. While the Office of Fair Trading or regulator will do its best to pursue even anonymous complaints, there may be practical difficulties in doing so where full information is not available and clarification cannot be sought from the complainant. Information should be given as to whether, for example, the complainant is a competitor or customer of the undertaking complained about or a final consumer, together with an explanation of the reasons for and details of the complaint (including, if appropriate, copies of relevant correspondence or notes of telephone conversations). If possible and appropriate, information should also be provided about the market concerned (its annual value, the undertakings involved in it, together with information about their market shares, and details of any recent independent studies of the market). Officials of the Office of Fair Trading or of one of the regulators will always be willing to discuss the situation before a complaint is made.

8.3   The Director General may pursue the complaint or he may consider that the complaint does not reveal a possible breach of either of the prohibitions. If he intends to take no further action he will inform the complainant as soon as possible and the matter will be closed or redirected to another body if appropriate. If the complaint does provide grounds for further investigation of a possible breach of the prohibitions, he may need to seek further information from the complainant before he can pursue the matter. If the Director General concludes that either of the prohibitions has been infringed, appropriate enforcement action will be taken.

Confidentiality of complaints

8.4   If the Director General decides to pursue a complaint, he will seek further information from the undertaking which has been complained about. At that stage it may be necessary to divulge the source of the complaint in order to provide the undertaking with full details of the agreement or conduct about which the complaint has been made and in order to verify details. In some cases, a complainant may not want to be identified to the undertaking which has been complained about and, in such cases, this should be made clear at the earliest opportunity. In addition, to facilitate the speedy handling of complaints, it is sometimes necessary for letters from complainants to be shown or copied to the target of the complaint. Complainants should therefore put any confidential material into an annex clearly marked as containing such material and explain why it should be treated as confidential. The amount of such material should be kept to a minimum to enable the complaint to be pursued effectively.

8.5   The Director General recognises the importance of complainants voluntarily supplying information and also recognises their interest in confidentiality. If he proposes to disclose any of the information in the annex he will, if it is practicable to do so, consult the person who provided the information. Confidentiality and disclosure of information is also discussed in part 9 below.

[3008]

9   Confidentiality and disclosure of information

9.1   The Act imposes limits on the disclosure of information obtained under or as a result of Part I of the Act that relates to the affairs of any individual or to any particular business of an undertaking. This will not be limited to information supplied in the context of a notification for guidance or a decision, but will include information obtained during the course of an investigation by the Director General. The Act requires that such information is not to be disclosed during the lifetime of that individual or while the business is carried on unless consent has been obtained from the person who originally provided the information and, if different, the individual to whose affairs the information relates or the person carrying on the business to which the information relates.

9.2   There are several exceptions to this requirement. These include, but are not limited to, where the disclosure is—

— made for the purpose of facilitating the performance by the Director General of Fair Trading or by the regulators of any of their functions under Part I of the Act;

— made for the purpose of facilitating the performance by the regulators of their functions under the sector-specific legislation;

— made with a view to the institution of civil proceedings under Part I of the Act or otherwise in connection with such proceedings;

— made for the purpose of criminal proceedings or the investigation of any criminal offence in any part of the United Kingdom;

— made for the purpose of facilitating the performance of any of the European Commission's functions in respect of Community competition law; and

— required to meet a Community obligation.

9.3 In addition, when the Secretary of State or the Director General is considering whether to disclose any information acquired under or as a result of Part I, he must have regard to the need for excluding, so far as is practicable, information the disclosure of which would in his opinion be contrary to the public interest.

9.4 The Director General and Secretary of State must also consider the need to exclude, so far as is practicable—

— commercial information which, if disclosed, would, or might, significantly harm the legitimate business interests of the undertaking to which it relates; or

— information relating to the private affairs of an individual which, if disclosed would, or might, significantly harm his interests.

9.5 When considering whether information should be excluded, the Director General must also consider the extent to which the disclosure of such information is necessary for the purposes for which it is to be disclosed.

[3009]

10 Fees

10.1 The Act provides for the Director General to charge fees for notifications and for other designated functions of the Director General. These will be explained further in a separate booklet.

[3010]

11 Investigation and enforcement

Powers of investigation

11.1 The Act gives the Director General powers to investigate suspected infringements of the prohibitions. This part sets out the powers that can be exercised by authorised officials if the Director General has reasonable grounds for suspecting that an undertaking is infringing either of the prohibitions. Details of related offences are also provided below. Further details are given in the Competition Act guideline *Powers of Investigation*.

Production of documents and information

11.2 The Director General or authorised officials can—

— require the production of any document or information that is specified or that falls within a specified category, which he considers relates to any matter relevant to the investigation, at a time and place, and in the manner or form, specified;

— take copies of, or extracts from, any document produced;

— require an explanation of any such document; and

— if a document is not produced, require a statement as to where it can be found.

Entry without a warrant

11.3 The Director General or authorised officials can enter premises without a warrant and—

— require the production of any document that he considers relates to any matter relevant to the investigation;

— take copies of, or extracts from, documents produced;
— require any person to provide an explanation of any document produced or to state where it may be found; and
— require any relevant information held in a computer to be produced in a form in which it can be read and can be taken away.

11.4 At least two working days' written notice must be given to the occupier, unless the Director General has a reasonable suspicion that premises are, or have been, occupied by a party to the agreement or conduct under investigation, or if the investigating officer has been unable to give notice to the occupier, despite taking all reasonably practicable steps to do so. The notice must state the subject matter and purpose of the investigation and the nature of the offences committed if a person fails to comply when the powers of investigation are exercised (see paragraph 11.8 below).

Entry with a warrant

11.5 On the authority of a High Court or Court of Session warrant, the Director General or authorised officials can enter premises without notice, subject to taking certain steps if the premises are unoccupied, using such force as is reasonably necessary, and search the premises, if there are reasonable grounds for suspecting that there are on the premises documents which—

— have previously been required to be produced by written notice or during an investigation without a warrant and which have not been produced;
— could be required to be produced, but if they were so required, would be concealed, removed, tampered with or destroyed; or
— could have been required to be produced during an investigation without a warrant but the investigating officer has been unable to enter the premises.

11.6 The warrant must specify the subject matter and purpose of the investigation and the nature of the offences committed if a person fails to comply when the powers of investigation are exercised (see paragraph 11.8 below).

11.7 Having obtained the warrant, the Director General or an authorised official can—

— search the premises and take copies of, or extracts from, any documents appearing to be of the kind in respect of which the warrant was granted;
— take possession of any documents appearing to be of the kind in respect of which the warrant was granted if such action appears to be necessary for preserving the documents or preventing interference with them, or if it is not reasonably practicable to take copies of the documents on the premises. They can also take any other steps which appear necessary in order to preserve the documents or prevent interference with them;
— require any person to provide an explanation of any such document or to state where it may be found; and
— require any relevant information held on computer to be produced in a form in which it can be read and can be taken away.

Offences

11.8 Any person who—
— fails to comply with a requirement imposed under the investigation powers (subject to certain defences);
— intentionally obstructs an investigator carrying out an investigation;
— intentionally or recklessly destroys, disposes of, falsifies or conceals documents; or

PART III
OFT GUIDELINES

— knowingly or recklessly supplies materially false or misleading information either to the Director General, or to another person, knowing that the information is to be used for the purpose of providing information to the Director General;

commits an offence.

11.9 No person can be required to produce a privileged communication, that is a communication—

— between a professional legal adviser (including an in-house legal adviser) and a client; or

— made in connection with or in contemplation of legal proceedings;

which would be protected from disclosure on grounds of legal professional privilege in the High Court or the Court of Session.

Enforcement powers

Provisional decisions

11.10 Where the Director General has conducted a preliminary investigation of an application and considers that it is likely that an agreement will infringe the Chapter I prohibition, and that it would not be appropriate to grant an individual exemption, he may make a provisional decision notifying the parties of his preliminary conclusion (see paragraph 7.7 above).

Infringement decision and directions

11.11 Where the Director General proposes to make a decision that a breach of either prohibition has occurred (an infringement decision), he will send the party or parties a written statement setting out the matters to which he has taken objection, the action he proposes to take and the reasons for it. The Director General must allow the person receiving the notice an opportunity to make representations to him. The person receiving the notice may request a meeting with officials of the office of the Director General to make oral representations to elaborate on his written representations already made in this regard and, if he requests it, will be given an opportunity to inspect the Director General's file on the case.

11.12 Where the Director General has made an infringement decision, he may give a direction to the parties concerned, or to such persons as he considers appropriate, to bring the infringement to an end. This may include a direction to modify or terminate the agreement, or to modify or cease the conduct in question. Any directions given by the Director General will set out the facts on which the direction is based and the reasons for it. The directions will be published on the register that will be kept at the Office of Fair Trading and on a website on the Internet. The Director General may seek a court order to enforce the direction if a person fails to comply. Breach of such an order would be punishable as a contempt of court.

Interim measures directions

11.13 The Director General has the power to impose interim measures directions during an investigation. Interim measures directions may be imposed when the Director General has a reasonable suspicion that one of the prohibitions has been infringed and he considers that it is necessary for him to act as a matter of urgency to prevent serious, irreparable damage to a person or category of persons or to protect the public interest. He may give such directions as he considers appropriate, which may include modification or termination of the agreement or conduct.

11.14 Before he gives an interim measures direction, the Director General must give written notice to the person(s) to whom he proposes to give the direction, indicating the nature of the proposed direction and stating the reasons for wishing to give it. The Director General must allow such person(s) the opportunity to make representations to him. They may request a meeting with the Director General to make oral representations to elaborate on their written representations already made in this regard. If requested, they will be given an opportunity to inspect the Director General's file on the case.

11.15 An interim measures direction may last for as long as the Director General continues to have a reasonable suspicion that there has been an infringement and until the investigation is completed. It can be replaced by final directions when the investigation is completed.

11.16 Powers of enforcement are addressed in more detail in the Competition Act guideline *Enforcement*.

[3011]

12 Consequences of breach

Penalties

12.1 Financial penalties of up to a maximum of 10 per cent of the turnover of an undertaking in the United Kingdom may be imposed for an infringement of either of the prohibitions. Further guidance on penalties (and other consequences of breach of the prohibitions) is available in the Competition Act guideline *Enforcement*.

Immunity from penalties for small businesses

12.2 In order to avoid the prohibition regime being unduly burdensome on small businesses, the Act provides limited immunity from financial penalties for **'small agreements'** in relation to infringements of the Chapter I prohibition and for **'conduct of minor significance'** in relation to infringements of the Chapter II prohibition. The immunity does not apply to price-fixing agreements.

12.3 Small agreements and conduct of minor significance can be defined (among other ways) by the turnover or the market share of the undertaking(s). The criteria to be used will be defined by the Secretary of State by order and are expected to be based on the turnover of the undertaking(s) in the United Kingdom. Undertakings which are immune from financial penalties are not exempt either from other enforcement action by the Director General or from third party actions for damages in the courts.

12.4 The Director General may still investigate small agreements or conduct of minor significance and can decide to withdraw the immunity from financial penalties if, having investigated the agreement or conduct, he considers that it is likely to infringe the relevant prohibition. Withdrawal of the immunity in this way cannot precede the date of this decision.

Other consequences of breach

12.5 Any agreement which infringes the Chapter I prohibition is void and cannot be enforced.

12.6 Third parties who consider that they have suffered loss as a result of any unlawful agreement or conduct have a claim for damages in the courts.

[3012]

13 The Fair Trading Act 1973

13.1 The United Kingdom competition law framework which deals with monopolies in the Fair Trading Act 1973 is retained in addition to the Competition Act.

13.2 The Fair Trading Act allows scale or complex monopolies to be examined by the Director General (which includes the regulators, who have concurrent jurisdiction to exercise such powers under the Fair Trading Act). He may make a reference to the Competition Commission (which is established by the Act and assumes this role of the Monopolies and Mergers Commission—see part 14 of this guideline) in order to establish whether a monopoly situation operates, or may be expected to operate, against the public interest. A scale monopoly situation exists where a single company (or a group of interconnected companies) supplies or acquires at least one quarter of the goods or services of a particular type in all or part of the United Kingdom. A complex monopoly situation exists where a group of companies which are not connected and which together account for at least one quarter of the supply or acquisition of any particular description of goods or services in all or part of the United Kingdom engage in conduct which has or is likely to have the effect of restricting, distorting or preventing competition.

13.3 It is not intended that the prohibitions in the Competition Act and the retained complex monopoly and scale monopoly provisions in the Fair Trading Act should be used in parallel to investigate the same matters. A suspected infringement of one of the Competition Act prohibitions will normally be investigated under the Competition Act rather than under the monopoly provisions of the Fair Trading Act.

13.4 The complex monopoly provisions are retained for activities which are not caught by the Competition Act prohibitions: where, for example, a group of companies all adopt similar practices or engage in parallel behaviour which appears to be anti-competitive, but there is no evidence of collusion or agreement. The scale monopoly provisions are intended for dealing with the situation where a prior infringement of the prohibitions in the Competition Act has already been proven but where the Director General believes that there is a real prospect of further abuse by the same company. The structural remedies available under the scale monopoly powers may be the only effective means of preventing those further abuses.

13.5 Because of the special circumstances of the utility sectors, and the difficulty of establishing competition, the full use of the scale monopoly provisions is retained for the regulated utility sectors. This means that the scale monopoly provisions may be used in respect of those sectors whether or not there has been a prior infringement of the prohibitions in the Competition Act.

13.6 The provisions in the Fair Trading Act which deal with mergers remain unchanged. Further details are found in the Competition Act guideline *Mergers and Ancillary Restraints*.

[3013]

14 The Competition Commission and appeals

14.1 Appeals against decisions of the Director General are heard by the Competition Commission which is established by the Act. In addition to acting as an appeals tribunal, the Competition Commission has also assumed the previous reporting role of the Monopolies and Mergers Commission under the monopoly and mergers provisions in the Fair Trading Act 1973.

Appealable decisions

14.2 Any party to an agreement in respect of which the Director General has made a decision, and any person in respect of whose conduct the Director General has made a decision, may appeal to the Competition Commission against, or with respect to, the decision. Appeals against decisions made under the Act are possible on both the substance of the decision and on any penalties imposed. The making of an appeal against a decision does not suspend the effect of that decision, unless the appeal is against the imposition or level of a penalty, in which case the penalty only is suspended.

Appeals

14.3 Any appeal made to the Competition Commission against a decision of the Director General will be determined by an appeal tribunal. The Secretary of State may make rules with respect to appeals and appeal tribunals.

14.4 The appeal tribunal can—
— confirm the decision;
— remit the matter to the Director General;
— impose or revoke, or vary (either higher or lower) the amount of a penalty;
— grant or cancel an individual exemption or vary any conditions or obligations;
— give such directions or take other steps as the Director General himself could have taken;
— make any other decision which the Director General himself could have made.

14.5 The appeal tribunal will not carry out investigation work: if substantial new evidence comes to light at the appeal stage, the case will be referred back to the Director General.

14.6 Any decision of the appeal tribunal of the Competition Commission has the same effect and is enforced in the same way as a decision of the Director General. Decisions of the appeal tribunal are subject to appeal to the Court of Appeal (or the Court of Appeal in Northern Ireland or Court of Session in Scotland) on points of law and levels of penalty only.

Third party appeals

14.7 A person who is not the subject of a decision may apply to the Director General asking him to withdraw or vary any decisions made by him, except those concerning the imposition of any penalty or the withdrawing or varying of a decision following an appeal by a third party. Such third party appeals may be made either by individuals or by a representative organisation. These appeals may be made only by third parties that either have **'sufficient interest'** in the decision themselves, or represent those with 'sufficient interest' in the decision, as judged by the Director General. Parties should explain in their application why they consider that they (or their representatives) have sufficient interest. The application must be made within one month of publication of the relevant decision.

14.8 If the Director General rejects a third party application for an appeal, the third party may appeal to the Competition Commission against that decision. The original decision will remain in force during the appeal process.

[3014]

THE CHAPTER I PROHIBITION

(OFT 401, March 1999)

1 Introduction

1.1 The Competition Act 1998 (**'the Act'**) prohibits agreements[1] which prevent, restrict or distort competition and may affect trade within the United Kingdom (**'The Chapter I prohibition'**).[2]

1.2 The terms used in the Chapter I prohibition and the concepts relevant to its application are considered in part 2 of this guideline. Section 60 of the Act sets out principles which provide for the United Kingdom authorities to handle cases in such as way as to ensure consistency with Community law. This provision is also considered in part 2.

1.3   Types of anti-competitive agreements to which the Chapter I prohibition may apply are considered in part 3. Certain types of agreements caught by the Chapter I prohibition may be exempted where they satisfy certain statutory criteria. The types of exemption available and the criteria which need to be satisfied are dealt with in part 4. Certain categories of agreement are excluded from the scope of the Chapter I prohibition. These are set out in part 5.

1.4   Breach of the Chapter I prohibition means that the agreement is void and that the offending parties may be liable to financial penalties of up to 10 per cent of their turnover in the United Kingdom. In addition, third parties who consider that they have been harmed may have a claim for damages in the courts. These consequences of infringement are considered in part 6.

1.5   Some agreements can be caught by both Article 85 of the EC Treaty (**'Article 85'**)[3] and the Chapter I prohibition. Part 7 of this guideline deals with the relationship between Article 85 and the Chapter I prohibition.

[3015]

NOTES

[1]   References in this guideline to 'agreement' should, unless otherwise stated or the context demands it, be taken to include decisions by associations of undertakings and concerted practices.

[2]   Section 2.

[3]   [Now] renumbered Article 81 following ratification of the Treaty of Amsterdam.

2   Relevant terms

2.1   The Chapter I prohibition is modelled on Article 85. Section 60 of the Act sets out certain principles with a view to ensuring that the United Kingdom authorities handle cases in such a way as to ensure consistency with Community law. The Act therefore places a dual obligation on the United Kingdom authorities in considering and dealing with the application of the Chapter I prohibition. First, they must ensure that there is no inconsistency with either the principles laid down by the EC Treaty and the European Court or any relevant decision of the European Court. Secondly, the United Kingdom authorities must have regard to any relevant decision or statement of the European Commission. In the Director General's view this is limited to decisions or statements which have the authority of the European Commission as a whole, such as for example, decisions on individual cases under Article 85 and Article 86 of the EC Treaty (**'Article 86'**).[1] It would also include any clear statements which the European Commission has published about its policy approach in the Annual Report on Competition Policy.

2.2   The obligation to ensure consistency applies only to the extent that this is possible, having regard to any relevant differences between the provisions concerned. This means that there will be certain areas where the Community principles will not be relevant. For example the community single market objectives designed to establish a European common market would not be relevant to the domestic prohibition system.

2.3   The provisions of section 60 apply to all United Kingdom authorities which are involved with the administration and enforcement of the Act: the Director General, the Competition Commission and the domestic Courts.

2.4   The terms used in the Act in section 2 and the concepts relevant to the application of the Chapter I prohibition are dealt with below. These terms and concepts are used consistently throughout the guideline.

Terms used in the Chapter I prohibition

Undertakings

2.5   Undertaking includes any natural or legal person capable of carrying on commercial or economic activities relating to goods or services, whatever its legal status. It includes companies, firms, businesses, partnerships, individuals operating as sole traders, agricultural co-operatives, trade associations and non profit-making organisations.

2.6   The Chapter I prohibition does not apply to agreements where there is only one undertaking: that is, between undertakings which form a single economic unit. In particular, an agreement between a parent and its subsidiary company or between two companies which are under the control of a third will not be agreements between undertakings if the subsidiary has no real freedom to determine its course of action on the market and, although having a separate legal personality, enjoys no economic independence.[2] Whether or not the undertakings form a single economic unit will depend on the facts of each case.

Agreement

2.7   Agreement has a wide meaning and covers agreements whether legally enforceable or not, written or oral; it includes so-called **gentlemen's agreements**. There does not have to be a physical meeting of the parties for an agreement to be reached: an exchange of letters or telephone calls may suffice if a consensus is arrived at as to the action each party will, or will not, take.

2.8   The fact that a party may have played only a limited part in the setting up of the agreement, or may not be fully committed to its implementation, or participated only under pressure from other parties does not mean that it is not party to the agreement (although the fact may be taken into account in deciding the level of any financial penalty).

Decisions by associations of undertakings

2.9   The Chapter I prohibition also covers decisions by associations of undertakings. Trade associations are the most common form of associations of undertakings but the provisions are not limited to any particular type of association. A decision may cover the constitution or rules of an association, decisions which are binding on its members and recommendations. A decision may be a resolution of the management committee of an association or of the full membership in general meeting, the effect of which is to limit the commercial freedom of action of the members in some respect. It will also cover any coordination of the members' conduct in accordance with its constitution even if that recommendation is not binding on the members, and may not have been fully complied with. It will be a question of fact in each case whether an association of undertakings is itself a party to an agreement.

2.10 The Competition Act guideline *Trade Associations, Professions and Self-Regulating Bodies* elaborates on the application and enforcement of the Act in respect of both trade associations and the rules of self-regulating bodies. Agreements constituting the rules regulating certain specified professional services are excluded from the prohibition; details are included in the same guideline.

Concerted practices

2.11 The Chapter I prohibition applies to concerted practices as well as to agreements. The boundary between the two concepts is imprecise. The key difference is that a concerted practice may exist where there is informal co-operation without any formal agreement or decision.

2.12 In considering if a concerted practice exists, the Director General will follow relevant Community precedents established under Article 85. An economic assessment of the relevant market will need to be made in each case and two main elements will need to be established—

— the existence of positive contacts between the parties; and
— the contact has the object or effect of changing the market behaviour of the undertakings in a way which may not be dictated by market forces.

2.13 The following are examples of factors which the Director General may consider in establishing if a concerted practice exists—

— whether the parties knowingly enter into practical co-operation;
— whether behaviour in the market is influenced as a result of direct or indirect contact between undertakings;
— whether parallel behaviour is a result of contact between undertakings which leads to conditions of competition which do not correspond to normal conditions of the market;
— the structure of the relevant market and the nature of the product involved;
— the number of undertakings in the market, and where there are only a few undertakings whether they have similar cost structures and outputs.

The United Kingdom

2.14 The Chapter I prohibition applies only if the agreement is, or is intended to be, implemented in the United Kingdom.

2.15 The United Kingdom means Great Britain (England, Wales and Scotland and the subsidiary islands, excluding the Isle of Man and the Channel Islands) and Northern Ireland. For the purposes of the Chapter I prohibition, the United Kingdom includes any part of the United Kingdom where an agreement operates or is intended to operate.

2.16 Although the prohibition refers to a dual test, **'affect trade'** and **'restrict competition'**, in practice it is very unlikely that an agreement which restricts competition in the United Kingdom does not also affect trade in the United Kingdom. In applying the Chapter I prohibition the focus will be on the effect on competition.

The prevention, restriction or distortion of competition

2.17 The Chapter I prohibition applies where the object or effect of the agreement is to prevent, restrict or distort competition within the United Kingdom. Any agreement between undertakings might be said to restrict competition to some degree, in that it restricts the freedom of action of the parties. That does not necessarily mean that the agreement has or will have an appreciable effect on competition, however, and the Director General does not adopt such a narrow approach. He will assess the effect of an agreement on competition in the United Kingdom or a part of it, by examining it in its market and economic context.

The appreciable effect test

2.18 An agreement will infringe the Chapter I prohibition only if it has as its object or effect an appreciable prevention, restriction or distortion of competition in the United Kingdom. This follows from established case law of the European Court which the Director General and the United Kingdom courts will be bound to follow under Section 60 of the Act. **Any agreement which does not have an appreciable effect on competition in the United Kingdom should not be notified to the Director General.**

2.19 The Director General takes the view that an agreement will generally have no appreciable effect on competition if the parties' combined share of the relevant market does not exceed 25 per cent, although there will be circumstances in which this is not the case.

2.20 The Director General will, in addition, generally regard any agreement between undertakings which—

— directly or indirectly fixes prices or shares markets (referred to further in paragraphs 3.5–3.8 and 3.10–3.11 below); or

— imposes minimum resale prices; or

— is one of a network of similar agreements which have a cumulative effect on the market in question

as being capable of having an appreciable effect even where the combined market share falls below the 25 per cent threshold. Further details on networks of agreements are given in the Competition Act guideline *Vertical Agreements and Restraints*.

Other factors

2.21 Even where the parties' combined market share is higher than 25 per cent, the Director General may find that the effect on competition is not appreciable. Other factors, for example, the content of the agreement and the structure of the market or markets affected by the agreement, such as entry conditions or the characteristics of buyers and the structure of the buyers' side of the market, will be considered in determining whether the agreement has an appreciable effect (see the Competition Act guideline *Assessment of Market Power*).

Calculating market share

2.22 When applying the market share thresholds discussed in paragraphs 2.19–2.21 above, the relevant market share will be the combined market share not only of the parties to the agreement but also of other undertakings belonging to the same group of undertakings as the parties to the agreement. These will include, in the case of each party to the agreement, (i) undertakings over which it exercises control, and (ii) both undertakings which exercise control over it and any other undertakings which are controlled by those undertakings. Further details on defining the relevant market are given in the Competition Act guideline *Market Definition*.

[3016]

NOTES

1   [Now] renumbered Article 82 following ratification of the Treaty of Amsterdam.

2   Case 22/71 *Beguelin Import v GL Import Export* [1972] CMLR 81, [1971] ECR 949.

3   Examples of anti-competitive agreements

3.1   The Chapter I prohibition applies to—

'*agreements between undertakings, decisions by associations of undertakings or concerted practices which—*

(a) *may affect trade within the United Kingdom, and*

(b) *have as their object or effect the prevention, restriction or distortion of competition within the United Kingdom*'

PART III
OFT GUIDELINES

3.2   Section 2(2) provides a list of agreements to which, in particular, the prohibition is to apply, namely those which—

'(a) *directly or indirectly fix purchase or selling prices or any other trading conditions;*

(b) *limit or control production, markets, technical development or investment;*

(c) *share markets or sources of supply;*

(d) *apply dissimilar conditions to equivalent transactions with other trading parties, thereby placing them at a competitive disadvantage;*

(e) *make the conclusion of contracts subject to acceptance by the other parties of supplementary obligations which, by their nature or according to commercial usage, have no connection with the subject of such contracts.'*

3.3   The list is identical to that in Article 85. It is a non-exhaustive, illustrative, list and does not set a limit on the investigation and enforcement activities of the Director General. Some guidance on the Director General's attitude towards these types of agreement, and other potentially anti-competitive agreements, follows. It should be noted, however, that any agreement that has an appreciable effect on competition is likely to fall within the Chapter I prohibition irrespective of whether or not it is of a type described in the illustrative list in the statute or in this guideline, although it may be subject to exemption. The possibility of exemption is considered in part 4.

3.4   **The examples that follow are not exhaustive: they include** *types* **of agreements which would generally fall within the prohibition, but the particular circumstances of a given agreement may mean that it does not do so. Equally, there will clearly be instances of agreements not listed in the types shown below which are prohibited because of their particular conditions or restrictions.**

Directly or indirectly fixing purchasing or selling prices

3.5   Agreements which explicitly and directly fix prices, or the resale prices of any product or service are likely to infringe the prohibition. The Director General believes that such price-fixing agreements have appreciable effects on competition.

3.6   There are many ways in which prices can be fixed. It may involve fixing the components of a price, setting a minimum price below which prices are not to be reduced, establishing the amount or percentage by which prices are to be increased, or establishing a range outside which prices are not to move. There are other types of agreements which may have an effect on the prices charged; these are considered separately below.

3.7   An agreement may affect the price to be charged only indirectly. It may cover the discounts or allowances to be granted, transport charges, payments for additional services, credit terms or the terms of guarantees, for example. The agreement may relate to the charges or allowances quoted themselves or to the ranges within which they fall or to the formulae by which ancillary terms are to be calculated. Such an agreement may have an appreciable effect on competition. This is, in particular, likely to be the case in concentrated markets with standardised products, where direct price competition may be inhibited.

3.8   Any agreement which seeks to restrict, or has the effect of restricting, price competition will also infringe the prohibition. This will include not only a price-fixing agreement between undertakings but also an agreement to adhere to published price lists, for example, or not to quote a price without consulting potential competitors, or not to charge less than any other price in the market. This is likely to be so even if price competition is not entirely eliminated by the agreement. Competition may, for example, remain in the ability to grant discounts or special deals on a published list price or ruling price. Recommendations of a trade association in relation to price are dealt with in the Competition Act guideline *Trade Associations, Professions and Self-Regulating Bodies*.

Agreements to fix trading conditions

3.9 Undertakings may agree to regulate the terms and conditions on which goods or services are to be supplied, in addition to prices. Use of standard terms and conditions are dealt with in the Competition Act guideline *Trade Associations, Professions and Self-Regulating Bodies*.

Agreements to share markets

3.10 Undertakings may agree to share markets, whether by territory, type or size of customer, or in some other way. This may be as well as or instead of the price to be charged, especially where the product is reasonably standardised. Such an agreement is likely to have an appreciable effect on competition.

3.11 There can be agreements, however, which have the effect of sharing the market to some degree but where that effect is no more than a consequence of the main object of the agreement. Parties may agree, for example, each to specialise in the manufacture of certain products in a range, or of certain components of a product, in order to be able to produce in longer runs and therefore more efficiently. Such an agreement is caught by the prohibition where there is, or is likely to be, an appreciable effect on competition.

Agreements to limit or control production or investment

3.12 An agreement to limit or control production may appreciably affect competition. Such an agreement may be the way in which prices are fixed, or it may relate to production levels or quotas or it may be intended to deal with structural overcapacity. In some cases, it will be linked to other agreements which may affect competition.

3.13 Competitive pressures may be reduced if undertakings in an industry agree to limit or at least to coordinate future investment plans. It is likely that any agreement to limit or control investment will restrict competition to an appreciable extent.

Collusive tendering ('bid-rigging')

3.14 Tendering procedures are designed to provide competition in areas where it might otherwise be absent. An essential feature of the system is that prospective suppliers prepare and submit tenders or bids independently. Any tenders submitted as a result of joint activities are likely to have an appreciable effect on competition.

Joint buying/selling

3.15 An agreement between buyers to fix (directly or indirectly) the price that they are prepared to pay, or to purchase only through agreed arrangements, limits competition between them. An example of the type of agreement which might be made between purchasers is an agreement as to those with whom they will deal. Such an arrangement may be caught by the Chapter I prohibition if it has an appreciable effect on competition.

3.16 The same issues potentially arise in agreements between sellers, in particular, where sellers agree to boycott certain customers. This type of agreement may have an appreciable effect on competition.

Information-sharing agreements

3.17 As a general principle, the more information made publicly available to market participants, the more effective competition is likely to be. In the normal course of business, undertakings exchange information on a variety of matters legitimately and with no risk to the competitive process. Indeed, competition may be enhanced by the sharing of information, for example, on new technologies or market opportunities.

3.18 There are circumstances where there can be no objection to the exchange of information, whoever the exchange is made by, even between competitors and whether or not under the aegis of a trade association (see the Competition Act guideline *Trade Associations, Professions and Self-Regulating Bodies*).

3.19 The exchange of information may however have an effect on competition where it serves to remove any uncertainties in the market and therefore eliminate any competition between undertakings. This will be the case even though the exchange of information might appear to be innocuous. It does not matter that the information could have been obtained from other sources. Whether or not the information exchange has an appreciable effect on competition will depend on the circumstances of each individual case: the market characteristics, the type of information and the way in which it is exchanged. As a general principle, the Director General will consider that there is more likely to be an appreciable effect on competition the smaller the number of undertakings operating in the market, the more frequent the exchange and the more sensitive and confidential the nature of the information which is exchanged.

3.20 The Director General's general approach to information exchange, based on the relevant Community precedents[1] as appropriate, is set out below.

Exchange of price information

3.21 The exchange of information on prices may lead to price co-ordination and therefore eliminate any competition which would otherwise be present between the undertakings. This will be the case whether the information exchanged relates directly to the prices charged or to the elements of a pricing policy, for example including discounts, costs, terms of trade and rates and dates of change.

3.22 The circulation of historical information or the collation of price trends may be less likely to have an appreciable effect on competition. An example may be where it forms part of a structured scheme of inter-business comparison which is intended to spread best industrial practice, in particular if the information is collected, aggregated and disseminated by an independent body, for example a bench-marking exercise.

Exchange of non-price information

3.23 The exchange of information on matters other than price may have an appreciable effect on competition depending on the type of information exchanged and the market to which it relates. The exchange of statistical data, market research, and general industry studies for example are unlikely to have an appreciable effect on competition provided that the information exchanged relates to what the European Commission has called **'opinion and experience'**[2] and does not enable confidential or sensitive business information to be shared.

3.24 In general, the exchange of information on output and sales should not affect competition provided that it is sufficiently historic and cannot influence future competitive market behaviour. There may however be an appreciable effect on competition if it is possible to disaggregate the information and identify the participants. This may also be the case if the exchange relates to recent, current or future information.

Advertising

3.25 Restrictions on advertising, whether relating to the amount, nature or form of advertising, restrict competition to some degree. Whether the effect is appreciable depends on the purpose and nature of the restriction, and on the market in which it is to apply. Decisions aimed at curbing misleading advertising, or at ensuring that advertising is legal, truthful and decent are unlikely to have an appreciable effect on competition (see the Competition Act guideline *Trade Associations, Professions and Self-Regulating Bodies*).

Standardisation agreements

3.26 An agreement on technical or design standards may lead to an improvement in production by reducing costs or raising quality, or it may promote technical or economic progress by reducing waste and consumers' search costs. The agreement may, however, have an appreciable effect on competition if it includes restrictions on what the parties may produce or is, in effect, a means of limiting competition from other sources, for example by raising entry barriers.

Other anti-competitive agreements

3.27 Competition in a market can be restricted in less direct ways than by the fixing of prices or the sharing of markets or the other examples set out above—for example, an **'aggregated rebate'** scheme under which a customer obtains better terms the more business he places with all the parties to the scheme. Each case will need to be considered in its own circumstances.

3.28 Other agreements where the parties agree to cooperate may fall within the Chapter I prohibition if they have an appreciable effect on competition. These include, for example, agreements for specialisation where each party agrees to produce particular products and supply them to the other, or to co-operate in research and development, and many joint venture agreements in particular for the development of new products or markets.

[3017]

NOTES

[1] For example, *United Kingdom Agricultural Tractor Registration Exchange* OJ [1992] L 68/19, [1993] 4 CMLR 358, upheld by the Court of First Instance, case T34/92; Case C–8/95 *New Holland Ford Limited v Commission* [1998] 5 CMLR 311, Case T–35/92 *John Deere v Commission* [1994] II ECR 957.

[2] Notice on Co-operation Agreements OJ 1968 C 75/3.

4 Exemptions

4.1 **An agreement which falls within the scope of the Chapter I prohibition may be exempted if it satisfies the criteria in section 9 of the Act. There are three types of exemption.**

Types of exemption

Individual exemption

4.2 An individual exemption must be applied for by way of a notification on Form N and may be granted for individual agreements which satisfy the statutory exemption criteria. An individual exemption may be granted subject to conditions or obligations and/or for a specified period. The exemption can have effect from a date which is earlier than that on which it is granted.

Block exemption

4.3 Under the Act the Director General may, by order, make domestic block exemptions which exempt particular categories of agreement which he considers are likely to satisfy the statutory exemption criteria. An agreement which falls within a category specified in the block exemption will be automatically exempt from the Chapter I prohibition, and there is no need to notify such an agreement to the Director General. Any such block exemption may impose conditions or obligations subject to which the block exemption will have effect.

4.4 The breach of a *condition* imposed by the block exemption cancels the block exemption in respect of an agreement. The failure to comply with an *obligation* imposed by the block exemption enables the Director General to cancel the block exemption in respect of an agreement. Furthermore if the Director General thinks that an agreement does not satisfy the statutory exemption criteria he may cancel the block exemption in respect of an agreement.

4.5 The Act provides that a block exemption order may include an opposition procedure. This will enable an agreement which falls outside the scope of the block exemption to be treated as falling within it where—
— the agreement satisfies the specified criteria;
— the agreement has been notified to the Director General; and
— the Director General does not oppose it being so treated before the end of a specified period by giving notice in writing to the parties. If he does exercise that right, the notification made is automatically treated as a notification for decision in the normal way, and as a request for individual exemption (see paragraph 4.2 above).

Parallel exemption

4.6 A parallel exemption applies to an agreement which is covered by a European Commission individual or block exemption under Article 85(3), or would be covered by a European Commission block exemption if the agreement had an effect on trade between EC Member States.[1] These types of agreement are automatically exempted under the Act without the need for individual exemption.

4.7 Where an agreement which benefits from a parallel exemption has produced, or may produce, significantly adverse effects on a market in the United Kingdom or part of it, the Director General may impose conditions on a parallel exemption or vary or cancel the exemption following procedures specified in rule 21 of the *Director General of Fair Trading's Procedural Rules*.

Exemption criteria

4.8 Section 9 of the Act sets out the criteria which must be met if an exemption is to be granted. That is any agreement which—
'(a) contributes to
   (i) improving production or distribution, or
   (ii) promoting technical or economic progress, while allowing consumers a fair share of the resulting benefit; but
(b) does not
   (i) impose on the undertakings concerned restrictions which are not indispensable to the attainment of those objectives; or
   (ii) afford the undertakings concerned the possibility of eliminating competition in respect of a substantial part of the products in question.'

4.9 The wording of the section is identical to that of Article 85(3) except that the latter refers to **'improving production or distribution of goods'**. The intention of the section is to make clear that (consistently with European Commission practice in relation to Article 85(3)) the domestic exemption provisions apply also to agreements which contribute to improvements in the provision of services.

4.10 The exemption criteria require that four conditions, two positive, two negative, are satisfied (see paragraphs 4.11–4.16 below). All of the conditions must be met. The objective and appreciable advantages must be sufficient to outweigh any disadvantages to competition. This must be judged objectively. The onus of demonstrating that the conditions are met falls upon the parties to an agreement.

The agreement contributes to improving production or distribution or promoting technical or economic progress . . .

4.11 Examples of improvements in production or distribution include lower costs from longer production or delivery runs, or from changes in the methods of production or distribution; improvements in product quality; increases in the range of products produced or services provided. In each case the nature of the improvement claimed must be clearly identified and justified.

4.12 Examples of the promotion of technical or economic progress include efficiency gains from economies of scale and specialisation in research and development with the prospect of an enhanced flow or speed of innovation, and technical progress.

. . . while allowing consumers a fair share of the resulting benefits

4.13 The second positive condition is not limited to final consumers. It can include the customers of the parties to the agreement. If an improvement, for example, a cost reduction, is seen as benefiting only the shareholders of the parties to the agreement, the condition would not be satisfied. The views of customers and consumers are likely to be important in the consideration of the case for exemption, and, in appropriate cases, they will be sought.

4.14 The resulting benefits are likely to be those which flow from improvements in production or distribution. An agreement may lead, for example, to the faster development of new products or of new markets or better distribution systems, so that the benefits to consumers also lie in the future. The Director General takes account of the dynamics of market conduct and competition in assessing whether or not this condition for exemption is satisfied.

Restrictions which are not indispensable to the attainment of the objectives set out in the two positive criteria

4.15 To qualify for exemption, agreements may not include restrictions beyond those necessary for the attainment of the benefits which the parties demonstrate are likely to flow from the agreement. The agreement should contain the least restrictive means of achieving its aims. The Director General will look carefully for any restrictions beyond those necessary to securing those benefits.

The possibility of eliminating competition in respect of a substantial part of the products in question

4.16 The Director General's assessment will consider this second negative condition in the overall context of the effect of the agreement on competition. If, after an appropriate market analysis, he concludes that it is not satisfied, there can be no possibility of an exemption. An application for an individual exemption is unlikely to succeed if the parties are unable to show that there will continue to be effective competition in the market(s) for the goods or services with which the agreement is concerned.

[3018]

NOTES

   1 The most relevant European Commission block exemptions are: Commission Regulation (EEC) No 417/85 on the application of Article 85(3) to categories of specialisation agreements; Commission Regulation (EEC) No 418/85 on the application of Article 85(3) to categories of research and development agreements as amended and extended by Regulation No 151/93; Commission Regulation (EEC) No 1983/83 on the application of Article 85(3) to categories of agreements concerning exclusive distribution agreements; Commission Regulation (EEC) No 1984/83 on the application of Article 85(3) to categories of exclusive purchasing agreements; Commission Regulation (EEC) No 4087/88 on the application of Article 85(3) to categories of franchise agreements; Commission Regulation (EEC) No 1475/95 on the application of Article 85(3) to certain categories of motor vehicle distribution and servicing agreements; and Commission Regulation (EEC) No 240/96 on the application of Article 85(3) to certain categories of technology transfer agreements.

5 Exclusions

   5.1 Schedules 1–4 of the Act specifically exclude from the Chapter I prohibition certain categories of agreement—

   — to the extent to which an agreement would result in a merger or joint venture within the merger provisions of the Fair Trading Act 1973 (see the Competition Act guideline *Mergers and Ancillary Restrictions* for further detail);

   — an agreement which would result in a concentration with a Community dimension and thereby be subject to the EC Merger Regulation;

   — an agreement which is subject to competition scrutiny under the Financial Services Act 1986, the Companies Act 1989, the Broadcasting Act 1990, or the Environment Act 1995;

   — an agreement which is required in order to comply with, and to the extent that it is, a planning obligation;

   — an agreement which is the subject of a direction under section 21(2) of the Restrictive Trade Practices Act 1976;

   — an agreement for the constitution of a European Economic Area regulated market, to the extent that it relates to the rules made or guidance issued by that market;

   — an agreement made by an undertaking entrusted with the operation of services of general economic interest or of a revenue producing monopoly, insofar as the prohibition would obstruct the performance of those tasks (see the Competition Act guideline *General Economic Interest*);

   — an agreement to the extent to which it is made to comply with a specified legal requirement;

   — an agreement which is necessary to avoid conflict with international obligations and which is also the subject of an order by the Secretary of State;

   — an agreement which is necessary for compelling reasons of public policy and which is also the subject of an order by the Secretary of State;

   — an agreement which relates to a coal or steel product within the ECSC Treaty;

   — an agreement where it relates to production of or trade in '**agricultural products**' as defined in the EC Treaty and in Council Regulation (EEC) No 26/62, or to farmers' co-operatives;

   — an agreement which constitutes a designated professional rule, imposes obligations arising from such a rule or constitutes an agreement to act in accordance with such rules.

   5.2 The Secretary of State has the power to add, amend or remove exclusions in certain circumstances.

   5.3 Section 50 provides for special treatment under the Chapter I prohibition for certain types of vertical agreements or to agreements relating to land. It is intended that Orders will be introduced whereby the Chapter I prohibition will not apply to agreements falling into either of these categories, although subject to a **clawback** provision (see the Competition Act guidelines *Vertical Agreements and Restraints* and *Land Agreements*).

[3019]

6 Consequences of infringement

Voidness

6.1   Any agreement which infringes the Chapter I prohibition is void and cannot be enforced.

Financial penalties

6.2   Financial penalties of up to a maximum of 10 per cent of turnover in the United Kingdom of an undertaking may be imposed for an infringement of the Chapter I prohibition (see the Competition Act guideline *Enforcement*).

6.3   The Act provides limited immunity from financial penalties for 'small agreements' in relation to infringements of the Chapter I prohibition. This immunity does not apply to price-fixing agreements. Section 39 of the Act provides that 'small agreements' can be defined (among other things) by the turnover or the market share of the undertaking(s). The criteria to be used will be defined by the Secretary of State in an order and are expected to be based on the turnover of the undertaking(s) in the United Kingdom.

6.4   The Director General retains the right to investigate such small agreements and can withdraw the immunity if, as a result of his investigation, he considers the agreement is likely to infringe the Chapter I prohibition.

Third party claims

6.5   Third parties who consider that they have suffered loss as a result of an unlawful agreement have a claim for damages in the courts.

[3020]

7 The relationship between the Chapter I prohibition and Article 85

Introduction

7.1   If an agreement has an effect on trade and an appreciable effect on competition in the United Kingdom, it may be caught both by Article 85 and by the Chapter I prohibition. In such cases the parties to an agreement could notify the agreement to both the European Commission and the Director General. Notifications to both the European Commission and the Director General are, however, undesirable in terms of the compliance costs for undertakings and the duplication of effort by competition authorities. The Director General considers that the European Commission is the more appropriate authority to whom notification should be made if the agreement is caught by Article 85.

Overlap of Article 85 and the Chapter I prohibition

7.2   Article 85 applies to agreements which **'may affect trade between Member States'**. The case law of the European Court has interpreted this phrase broadly: 'the agreement in question may have an influence, direct or indirect, actual or potential, on the pattern of trade between Member States',[1] and has found that even where the parties to an agreement are confined to the same country, inter-state trade may still be affected.[2] The term **'trade'** has itself been interpreted broadly and covers the right of establishment and free movement of suppliers as well as the movement of goods and services.[3] Given the breadth of this interpretation, many agreements will be caught both by Article 85 and the Chapter I prohibition where trade within the United Kingdom may be affected.

7.3   Because of the overlap, parties to such agreements will need to consider which authority to notify. The starting point in determining which is the more appropriate authority for notifications is to assess whether or not the agreement may affect trade between Member States. In practice, parties would be advised to consider fully the application of Article 85 before notifying agreements to the Director General under Chapter I. This part considers the issues in deciding which is the appropriate authority to notify.

The appropriate authority to notify

7.4   In considering the appropriate authority to notify, there are several advantages in notifying agreements to the European Commission under Article 85 rather than to the Director General under the Chapter I prohibition—

— only the European Commission can give an exemption from Article 85(1). This exemption automatically exempts the agreement from the Chapter I prohibition (a **'parallel exemption,'** referred to in paragraphs 4.6 and 4.7 above).[4] By contrast, however, exemption from the Chapter I prohibition does not preclude the application of Article 85(1);

— European Commission Article 85(3) exemption has effect in all the EC Member States, but exemption by the Director General has effect only in the United Kingdom;

— provisional immunity from financial penalties under the Chapter I prohibition is available without notification to the Director General; he may not impose a penalty under the Chapter I prohibition if an agreement has been notified to the European Commission and the European Commission has not yet determined the matter. It should be noted, however, that if the European Commission withdraws the benefit of provisional immunity from penalties with respect to the agreement before determining the matter, the immunity from penalty under the Chapter I prohibition will automatically cease on the same date.

7.5   The European Commission does not have the power to grant retroactive exemptions in all cases. The parties to an agreement may, therefore, consider it commercially beneficial to notify the European Commission at the earliest possible date. The Director General, however, does have the power to grant retroactive exemptions in all cases.

7.6   If the inter-state trade criterion is not met but the agreement does have an appreciable effect on competition in the United Kingdom, the Director General is the appropriate authority for notification. Where it is unclear whether the inter-state trade criterion is satisfied, the parties to an agreement may wish to consult with the Director General's officials as to the more appropriate authority to notify.

7.7   Where the parties to an agreement notify the European Commission and the European Commission takes the view that the agreement does not affect trade between Member States, the parties may choose to notify the Director General if the agreement has an appreciable effect on competition. The Director General will endeavour to give priority to such cases, and may grant individual exemptions where the agreements satisfy the section 9 exemption criteria.

Treatment of dual notifications

7.8   There are clear advantages in notifying to only one competition authority. However in the event of dual notifications the following points should be noted.

7.9   The Director General's officials will liaise closely with those of the European Commission in determining the more appropriate authority to assess the agreement. Where it is clear that the European Commission will deal with the agreement either by formal decision or by informal means, the Director General will generally take no action until the European Commission has completed its assessment and informed the parties. Where the European Commission formally exempts the agreement from Article 85 by a decision under Article 85(3), the agreement is automatically exempt from the Chapter I prohibition. If the case is closed by informal means, as a general policy the Director General will follow the European Commission's assessment of the agreement (see paragraphs 7.11 and 7.12 below). If the Director General does intend to depart from the European Commission's assessment of an agreement he will consult the European Commission before doing so.

7.10   The Director General may, however, proceed to consider a notification that has been made to both authorities and is already being considered by the European Commission, in particular where—
- the agreement raises particular concerns in relation to competition in the United Kingdom;
- he considers the agreement involves important legal, economic or policy developments.

EC comfort letters

7.11   Many agreements notified to the European Commission receive an informal indication of the European Commission's likely assessment by means of a **comfort letter** rather than a formal decision. EC comfort letters are not legally binding but it is clear that the European Commission will re-open the file only in certain limited circumstances. The Act does not make provision for the informal procedures of the European Commission.

7.12   As a general policy, the Director General will not depart from the European Commission's assessment of an agreement as set out in an EC comfort letter, but the following exceptions to this policy should be noted—
- an agreement may raise particular concerns in relation to competition in the United Kingdom;
- the European Commission may indicate that there is an infringement of Article 85 which would not qualify for exemption, but that as a matter of its internal priorities it will not consider the matter further (a **discomfort letter**);
- the European Commission may indicate that the agreement does not have an **appreciable effect** on inter-state trade for the purposes of the application of Article 85(1).

In these circumstances, the parties will need to consider the application of the Chapter I prohibition and, if the agreement is subject to the prohibition, whether notification to the Director General is appropriate.

Proceedings in the United Kingdom courts

7.13   In the cases where an undertaking that has already received a European Commission comfort letter in respect of an agreement faces a challenge to that agreement in the United Kingdom courts on the basis that it infringes the Chapter I prohibition, it may notify the agreement to the Director General at the time when the agreement is challenged in court proceedings. The Director General will endeavour to give priority to such cases and considers that an agreement in this situation, if capable of exemption, would be likely to receive exemption with retroactive effect.

[3021]

NOTES
¹   Case 56/65 *Société Technique Minière v Maschinenbau Ulm GmbH* [1966] ECR 235.
²   Case 8/72 *Vereeniging van Cementhandelaren v Commission* [1972] ECR 977, [1973] CMLR 7.
³   Case 161/84 *Pronuptia de Paris GmbH v Pronuptia de Paris Irmgard Schillgalis* [1986] ECR 353, [1986] 1 CMLR 414.
⁴   A parallel exemption may be revoked by the Director General in certain specified circumstance.

THE CHAPTER II PROHIBITION

(OFT 402, March 1999)

1   What this guideline is about

1.1   The Competition Act 1998 prohibits conduct which amounts to abusive behaviour by a dominant **undertaking**.¹ This guideline sets out some of the circumstances in which behaviour will or may be regarded as **abusive**. It is intended that it should be of assistance not only to those undertakings which are dominant in their market or markets, but also to their customers and other businesses.

1.2   Some of the situations explained in this guideline may also be covered by the monopoly provisions of the Fair Trading Act. The potential overlap between the two regimes is explained in the Competition Act guideline *The Major Provisions*.

1.3   The Director General of Fair Trading has a duty under section 60 to handle cases in such a way as to ensure consistency with Community law. This is described further in the Competition Act guideline *The Major Provisions*.

[3022]

NOTES
¹   The term **undertaking** includes not only companies but the full range of business entities including sole traders, partnerships, trade associations, and non-profit making organisations. See the Competition Act guideline *The Major Provisions*.

2   Abuse of a dominant position: the prohibition

Scope of the prohibition

2.1   Any conduct in a market by one or more undertakings which amounts to the abuse of a dominant position, and which may affect trade in the United Kingdom, is prohibited by section 18(1) of the Act (**the Chapter II prohibition**) and may be subject to financial penalties. This is a two stage test: whether an undertaking is dominant in a relevant market; and, if so, whether it is abusing that dominant position. The prohibition is of the abuse of the dominant position, not the *holding* of the position. The Director General would find an undertaking's behaviour an abuse only after a detailed examination of the market concerned and the effects of the undertaking's conduct. Third parties adversely affected by the conduct of a dominant company may, in addition to making a complaint to the Director General, take action in the courts to stop the behaviour, and to seek damages.

2.2   The prohibition is based on Article 86 of the EC Treaty (Article 86).¹ Like Article 86, section 18(2) of the Act states that conduct may constitute an abuse if it consists in—

'*(a) directly or indirectly imposing unfair purchase or selling prices or other unfair trading conditions;*

(b) limiting production, markets or technical development to the prejudice of consumers;

(c) applying dissimilar conditions to equivalent transactions with other trading parties, thereby placing them at a competitive disadvantage;

(d) making the conclusion of contracts subject to acceptance by the other parties of supplementary obligations which, by their nature or according to commercial usage, have no connection with the subject of the contracts.'

2.3   These are no more than examples, and are not exhaustive. The important issue is whether the dominant undertaking is using its dominant position in an abusive way. This may occur if it uses practices different from those normally adopted in the course of competition in the market, with the effect of restricting the degree of competition which it faces, or of exploiting its market position unjustifiably.

Exclusions

2.4   There are specific exclusions for conduct—

— to the extent to which it would result in a merger or joint venture within the merger provisions of the Fair Trading Act 1973 (see the Competition Act guideline *Mergers and Ancillary Restrictions* for further detail);

— which would result in a concentration with a Community dimension and thereby be subject to the EC Merger Regulation;

— which is carried out by an undertaking entrusted with the operation of services of general economic interest or of a revenue producing monopoly, insofar as the prohibition would obstruct the performance of those tasks (see the Competition Act guideline *General Economic Interest*);

— to the extent to which it is engaged in order to comply with a specified legal requirement;

— which is necessary to avoid conflict with international obligations and which is also the subject of an order by the Secretary of State;

— which relates to a coal or steel product within the ECSC Treaty;

— where there are compelling reasons of public policy and it is also the subject of an order by the Secretary of State.

2.5   The Secretary of State has the power to add, amend or remove exclusions in certain circumstances.

Exemptions

2.6   There is no power to grant exemptions from the Chapter II prohibition.

2.7   If an undertaking's behaviour involves an agreement which is exempt from the Chapter I prohibition, the position under Chapter II will depend on the type of exemption—

— if the agreement has an **individual exemption** granted by the Director General it cannot be looked at again under the Chapter II prohibition in the absence of any change in circumstances. The same position applies if the agreement benefits from a parallel exemption because it has an individual exemption under Article 85(3) of the EC Treaty;[2] but

— the benefit of a **block exemption** does not prevent the undertaking's behaviour from being an abuse under the Chapter II prohibition. This position also applies when the agreement benefits from a parallel exemption because the agreement falls within a category of agreements which is covered by a European Commission block exemption.

Conduct of minor significance

2.8 The Act provides that financial penalties cannot be imposed in respect of **conduct of minor significance**. Conduct of minor significance can be defined (among other ways) by the turnover or market share of the undertaking. The criteria to be used will be defined by the Secretary of State in an order, and are expected to be based on the turnover of the undertaking. The immunity applies only to penalties: abusive conduct by such undertakings is still an infringement of the Act, and it does not prevent third parties from claiming damages for such conduct.

2.9 The Director General still has the right to investigate such conduct and can withdraw the immunity if, as a result of his investigation, he considers the conduct is likely to infringe the Chapter II prohibition.

[3023]

NOTES
1 [Now] re-numbered Article 82 following ratification of the Treaty of Amsterdam.
2 [Now] re-numbered Article 81(3) following ratification of the Treaty of Amsterdam.

3 Dominance

3.1 There are two tests in assessing whether the Chapter II prohibition applies—
— whether an undertaking is dominant;
— and, if it is, whether it is abusing that dominant position.

3.2 The first test raises two questions which are considered below: the definition of the market in which the undertaking is alleged to be dominant, and whether it is dominant within that market.

Market definition

3.3 Before assessing whether an undertaking is dominant, the relevant market must be determined. This relevant market will have two dimensions—
— the relevant goods or services (**the product market**); and
— the geographic extent of the market (**the geographic market**).

3.4 Further details on the Director General's approach to market definition are available in the Competition Act guideline *Market Definition*, but the following is a brief summary.

The product market

3.5 The boundaries of the market are determined by taking the products or services relevant to the investigation and looking at the closest substitute products, those products which consumers would switch to if prices of the relevant products or services rose. These substitute products are included in the market if substitution by consumers would prevent prices of the products relevant to the investigation from rising above competitive levels. The alternative products do not need to be perfect substitutes, but alternatives which would fill a similar role to the goods or services in question, and to which consumers would be prepared to switch in the event of a price increase. If such similar goods or services would prevent price-setting above competitive levels, they should be included in the definition of the relevant product market.

3.6 In addition to this substitution by customers (**demand-side substitution**), prices can also be constrained by the potential behaviour of suppliers producing other products (**supply-side substitution**). Businesses which are not currently supplying a particular product might switch some of their existing facilities to supplying that product (or close substitutes) if prices rose significantly.

The geographic market

3.7   Similar methods are used to define the geographic boundaries of a market. The geographic market will sometimes be the area supplied by the complainant, or the party or parties to the conduct concerned, but the Director General also considers whether customers could easily obtain similar products from suppliers in other areas on reasonable terms. If so, those other areas may form part of the geographic market. The geographic market may be a part of the United Kingdom, the whole of it, or it may extend beyond the United Kingdom. Under the Chapter II prohibition, a dominant position can occur in any part of the United Kingdom.

3.8   In some cases a market may previously have been investigated and defined by the Director General or by another competition authority. While such precedents can provide useful insights, the market definition used in a previous case may not always be the correct one to use in subsequent cases.

Assessing dominance

3.9   An undertaking may be dominant if it possesses a substantial level of market power. The essence of dominance is the power to behave independently of competitive pressures. This can allow a dominant undertaking to charge higher prices profitably (or, if it is a dominant buyer, extract lower prices) than if it faced effective competition. It can also use its market power to engage in anti-competitive conduct and exclude or deter competitors from the market.

3.10   The European Court has defined a dominant market position as—

'... *a position of economic strength enjoyed by an undertaking which enables it to prevent effective competition being maintained on the relevant market by affording it the power to behave to an appreciable extent independently of its competitors, customers and ultimately of consumers.*' [1]

3.11   In assessing whether there is dominance the Director General considers whether and to what extent an undertaking will face constraints on its ability to behave independently. Those constraints might be—

— existing competitors, according to their strength in the market: this may be shown by market shares;

— potential competitors: this may be shown by a lack of significant entry barriers and the existence of other undertakings which might easily enter the market; and

— other constraints such as strong buyer-power from the undertaking's customers (which may include distributors, processors and commercial users).

3.12   These issues are explained in more detail in the Competition Act guideline *Assessment of Market Power*. The following is a summary explaining the assessment of market power in the context of the Chapter II prohibition.

Market shares

3.13   The Act does not set any market share thresholds for defining dominance. Market share is an important factor but does not, on its own, determine whether an undertaking is dominant. For example, it is also necessary to consider the position of other undertakings operating in the same market and how market shares have changed over time. An undertaking is more likely to be dominant if its competitors enjoy relatively weak positions or if it has enjoyed both a high, and relatively stable, market share. The European Court has stated that dominance can be presumed in the absence of evidence to the contrary if an undertaking has a market share persistently above 50 per cent.[2] The Director General considers it unlikely that an undertaking will be individually dominant if its market share is below 40 per cent, although dominance could be established below that figure if other relevant factors (such as the weak position of competitors in that market) provided strong evidence of dominance.

Entry barriers

3.14 The other main factor in establishing dominance is whether the undertaking faces, or is likely to face, competition from new entrants. An attempt to raise prices may prompt entry to the market and force prices down to their original level. The Director General will look carefully to see whether there are any barriers which will prevent entry into the market. These barriers exist when incumbent undertakings would have a significant advantage over new entrants, although an advantage created by superior efficiency is not treated as an entry barrier.

3.15 There are many ways in which different types of entry barrier can be classified, but it is useful to distinguish between three sources—

— **absolute advantages**—undertakings may not have equal access to important assets or rights. For example there may be regulations which restrict new entry, such as requirements to possess licences or permits. Copyright, patents and other intellectual property rights can be examples of these regulatory barriers, although such rights do not automatically imply that an undertaking is dominant: it may be possible to innovate around these rights or there may be competition between holders of rival rights within the same market. Alternatively, undertakings may have preferential access to important inputs, such as raw materials. For example denial of access to a port might be an absolute barrier to entry if other ports could not serve the same market;

— **strategic advantages**—advantages which an undertaking enjoys from being already active in a market (**first-mover advantages**). They can arise when new entrants would face **sunk costs**, those which must be incurred when entering a market but which cannot be recovered on exit. The importance of sunk costs in deterring new entry depends on whether new entrants expect to recover them from the revenues that they will earn operating in the market. If new entrants expect to face vigorous competition from existing undertakings in the market, sunk costs are more likely to deter new entry. The importance of sunk costs will therefore depend at least to some extent on the conduct (or expected conduct) of the allegedly dominant undertaking. (If the incumbent itself has incurred sunk costs that may make it more likely to respond vigorously to new entry.) A strategic advantage might also arise if new entrants find it more difficult to fund the necessary investments than incumbents;

— **exclusionary behaviour**—for example an undertaking may build up a reputation for predatory behaviour, which will deter new entrants. Undertakings can also conclude contracts which tie up distribution: a manufacturer might tie up all the retailers within a market exclusively to its products, for example. Such behaviour can increase the impact of an absolute or strategic advantage.

3.16 It is also important to take account of the rate of innovation within the market. In markets where high rates of innovation occur, or are expected, barriers to entry may quickly be eroded. It is important that competition policy does not undermine the incentives for such innovation.

Other constraints

3.17 Lastly, consideration is given to whether there are other factors, apart from existing or potential competition, which will constrain the undertaking's behaviour. The principal example is strong buyer power which might arise if customers were large relative to the undertaking—a large retail chain may be able to resist any attempts by a supplier with a high market share to abuse its position on the market, for example. The key issue is whether the buyer will have a stronger bargaining position than the seller. (On the other hand an undertaking with strong buyer-power may itself be dominant. If it exploits its sellers this could itself be an abuse, particularly if the undertaking also enjoys market power in downstream markets.)

3.18 Undertakings may also be constrained by government regulations. In this situation the undertaking may still be considered to be dominant although regulation may prevent it abusing that dominant position.

Joint dominance

3.19 The Chapter II prohibition prohibits conduct on the part of *one or more* undertakings which amounts to the abuse of a dominant position (a collective dominant position). This means that the behaviour of undertakings within the same corporate group may be dealt with together even if they are not considered to operate as a single economic unit.

3.20 In addition, a dominant position may be collective when two or more legally independent undertakings are linked in such a way that they adopt the same conduct in the market. The Court of First Instance confirmed the principle of joint dominance in the *Italian Flat Glass* case—

'There is nothing, in principle, to prevent two or more independent economic entities from being, on a specific market, united by such economic links that, by virtue of that fact, together they hold a dominant position vis à vis the other operators on the same market.'[3]

3.21 The links may be structural or they may be such that the undertakings adopt the same conduct on the market.

————————————   **[3024]**

NOTES
[1]   Case 27/76 *United Brands v EC Commission* [1978] ECR 207, [1978] 1 CMLR 429; it has been used in other cases.
[2]   Case C62/86, *AKZO Chemie BV v Commission* [1993] 5 CMLR 215.
[3]   Cases T-68/69 etc *Società Italiano Vetro SpA v Commission*, [1992] II ECR 1403, [1992] 5 CMLR 302.
————————————

4 Abuse

4.1   The following paragraphs give some guidance on the second part of the test: when an undertaking's behaviour might be regarded as crossing the line into **abuse of a dominant position**.

4.2   The Act lists broad categories of business behaviour within which particular examples of abusive conduct are most likely to be found rather than specifically prohibited business practices. Conduct may be abusive when, through the effects of conduct on the competitive process, it adversely affects consumers directly (through the prices charged, for example) or indirectly (for example, conduct which raises or enhances entry barriers or increases competitors' costs).

4.3   As with Article 86, there is no provision in the Act under which an abuse can be exempted because it produces benefits, but conduct for which there is an objective justification is not regarded as an abuse even if it does restrict competition. For example a refusal to supply might be justified by the poor creditworthiness of the customer. It will still be necessary for a dominant undertaking to show that the behaviour is proportionate to the justification. Conduct which stems from the superior efficiency of an undertaking is not an abuse—the purpose of competition policy is to encourage, not to penalise, efficiency.

4.4 As referred to at paragraph 3.15 above, the exclusive rights provided by an intellectual property right (IPR) do not necessarily give rise to a dominant position (depending on the nature of the protected right and the extent of the relevant product market). In addition, even where an undertaking is dominant, the legitimate exercise of an IPR is not an abuse. The Director General recognises the role of IPRs in encouraging creative and innovative activity. It is, however, possible that the way in which an IPR is exercised may give rise to concern if it goes beyond the legitimate exploitation of the IPR—if it is used to leverage market power from one market to another, for example (see the Competition Act guideline *Intellectual Property Rights* and paragraph 4.5 opposite).

4.5 Abusive conduct generally falls into one of the following categories—

conduct which *exploits* customers or suppliers through, for example—
— excessively high prices; or
— discriminatory prices, or other terms or conditions; or

conduct which is *anti-competitive* (sometimes called **'exclusionary behaviour'**), because it removes or limits competition from existing competitors, or because it excludes new undertakings from entering the market by, for example—
— **predatory** behaviour;
— vertical restraints; or
— refusing to supply existing or potential competitors.

4.6 The following explanations do not constitute an exhaustive list of behaviour which the Director General might regard as an abuse. They are likely to cover many potential cases, but each case will be considered on its own merits.

Excessively high prices

4.7 Perhaps the most obvious form of abuse is where a dominant undertaking charges prices higher than it would do if it faced effective competition.[1] The European Court has held that—

'charging a price which is excessive because it has no reasonable relation to the economic value of the product supplied is ... an abuse.'[2]

4.8 The essential issue is when a price becomes **excessively high**: in general to be excessively high the price must be higher than it would normally be in a competitive market. Clearly all companies must earn some level of profits in order to finance investments. The profits of a dominant undertaking in the relevant market consistently exceeding its relevant cost of capital (the return which could be earned from investing elsewhere having regard to the risks incurred by investing in the particular company) might, however, indicate that its prices were excessive.

4.9 There may, however, be many objective justifications for prices which are apparently 'excessively high'. First, in competitive markets, prices and costs vary over time and there are likely to be periods when high profits can be earned. This is an important part of the competitive process since it can encourage increased output or entry to a market. Secondly, undertakings in competitive markets may be able to sustain high profits for a period of time if they are more efficient than their competitors. This might occur if an undertaking has developed lower-cost techniques of production, supplies higher quality products or is more effective at identifying market opportunities. (Exclusive access to low-cost inputs, such as exclusive rights to certain raw materials, is not, however, the same thing as superior efficiency.) To be an abuse, prices would have to be *persistently* excessive without stimulating new entry or innovation.

4.10 Given the uncertainties in estimating what an undertaking's cost of capital should be, prices would have to allow profits which *significantly* and persistently exceeded its cost of capital before an abuse could be established. The assessment of this question is explained in more detail in the Competition Act guideline *Assessment of Individual Agreements and Conduct*.

Individual agreements and conduct

4.11 In markets where there is a high rate of innovation it may be natural to see high prices for a period of time. Persistently high profits which result from successive innovations will provide both a return on previous innovations and incentives for further innovation. In these circumstances high profits will not indicate an abuse.

4.12 In applying the Chapter II prohibition the Director General will therefore be mindful of the need not to interfere in natural market mechanisms where high prices will encourage new entry or innovation and thereby serve to increase competition. Excessive prices are likely to be regarded as an abuse only in markets where an undertaking is so dominant, and new entry so unlikely, that it is clear that high profits will not stimulate successful new entry or innovation within a reasonable period.

4.13 Where joint dominance exists, undertakings might engage in some form of **tacit collusion**—failing to compete on price even though there is no agreement between them. In some cases this type of behaviour may be prohibited under Chapter I as a concerted practice, but if the level of collusion falls short of a concerted practice, it might in principle be considered under the Chapter II prohibition if the undertakings were jointly dominant. The fact that different undertakings charge the same price is not, of itself, however, an abuse: in competitive markets, undertakings which sell similar products and incur similar costs will tend to charge the same price. To show that tacit collusion was an abuse of joint dominance would usually require other evidence—that opportunities to cut prices following a significant fall in input costs were deliberately ignored, or that prices were excessive (as defined above), for example.

Price discrimination

4.14 Price discrimination involves applying different conditions (normally different prices) to equivalent transactions. It can take two basic forms—

— the charging of different prices to different customers, or categories of customers, for the same product—where the differences in prices do not reflect the quantity, quality or any other characteristics of the items supplied. The pricing structure would not be considered discriminatory, however, where there were objective and proportionate reasons for an undertaking charging different prices to different customers—for instance, where there were different transport costs; or

— the charging of the same price to different customers, or categories of customers, even though the costs of supplying the product were very different. A policy of uniform delivered prices throughout the country could be discriminatory if differences in transport costs were significant, for example.

4.15 Price discrimination raises complex economic issues and is not automatically an abuse. There are many areas of business where it is a usual and legitimate commercial practice. For example it might be objectively justified in industries where there are large fixed costs and low marginal costs (the cost of supplying each additional unit of output is very small compared to the initial investment to set up the business). In most markets undertakings are normally expected to set prices equal to their marginal cost, but in industries with high fixed costs an undertaking which did so might never be able to recover its fixed costs. It may therefore be more efficient to set higher prices to customers with a higher willingness to pay. In general, price discrimination will not be an abuse in such industries if it leads to higher levels of output than an undertaking could achieve by charging every customer the same price.

4.16 The Director General anticipates that he would consider price discrimination to be an abuse only if there were evidence that prices were excessive (as discussed above) or that it was used to exclude competitors (for example, because it was predatory or because it involved discounts designed to foreclose markets—these issues are explained in the sections on predation and vertical restraints below). It would clearly not be an abuse if it resulted from a pricing obligation imposed by a regulator. More details on the assessment of price discrimination are given in the Competition Act guideline *Assessment of Individual Agreements and Conduct*.

Discounts

4.17 The offering of discounts to certain customers is a form of price competition and is generally to be encouraged. As with price discrimination, discounts will infringe the Chapter II prohibition only if they are anti-competitive: if prices are set at predatory levels, or if they are used to foreclose a market, for example. Foreclosure can occur when discounts are conditional on customers buying all or a large proportion of their purchases from the dominant undertaking (**fidelity discounts**), or where they are conditional on the purchase of tied products.

Predation

4.18 Predatory behaviour constitutes a class of anti-competitive behaviour where prices are set so low as to eliminate some undertakings and threaten the competitive process itself. In these circumstances consumers may benefit in the short run from lower prices, but, in the longer term, weakened competition will lead to higher prices, reduced quality and less choice. Distinguishing predatory behaviour from legitimate competition is difficult. Since the main objective of competition policy is to create conditions where consumers benefit from effective competition, the distinction must be drawn between low prices which result from predatory behaviour, and low prices which result from legitimate competitive behaviour.

4.19 This is not an easy distinction to make and there have been relatively few European cases where predation has been proved. The European Court has stated that where prices are below the average variable cost of production (**variable costs** are costs which vary with the amount of output produced), predation should be presumed.[3] The Court held also that if prices are above average variable costs but below average total costs, conduct is to be regarded as predatory where it can be established that the purpose of the conduct was to eliminate a competitor.[4] In these cases a key issue was whether the dominant undertakings were covering their costs, but evidence on the undertakings' intentions was also relevant. Both issues are considered below.

Costs

4.20 The following broad guidelines can be drawn from the judgments of the European Court cited above:

Price below average variable costs	Predation can be assumed
Price above average variable costs, but below average total costs	Evidence on costs may indicate predation, but the Director General would need to establish evidence that the dominant undertaking intended to eliminate a competitor before predation could be found
Price above average total cost	Evidence does not indicate predation

4.21 In the normal course of business, selling at below average variable costs is unlikely to be rational and could be taken as conclusive proof of predation. An undertaking failing to cover its variable costs (or pricing below its *average* variable costs) is, on average, making losses on each unit of output it supplies. The undertaking could increase its profitability by reducing its output, increasing its price, or ceasing supply altogether.

4.22 The Director General would of course consider any evidence that the undertaking's behaviour was objectively justified. For example, a policy of loss leading might be objectively justified and would not therefore normally be predatory.

4.23 Where prices are above average variable costs but below average total costs the Director General may consider other evidence on costs. For example he might consider whether the undertaking is covering its **long-run avoidable costs**, which are costs which could be avoided if the undertaking were to cease the activity in question (the **activity** being the part of the business accused of predating). They include both fixed costs and variable costs, but they do not include—

— **common costs** (costs which can be attributed to a number of different activities)—the Director General may, however, expect the undertaking to cover common costs through the activities to which these costs contribute; or

— **sunk costs**—although sunk costs may be included in avoidable costs if they are incurred as part of the alleged predatory strategy, since the undertaking could then have avoided them by not incurring them.

4.24 Prices below average avoidable costs might be evidence of predation (although not as strong as where price is below average variable costs).

4.25 In its *Notice on the Application of Agreements in the Telecommunications Sector* (March 1998), the European Commission indicated that it would often need to examine long-run incremental costs (the cost of increasing output by one unit) as the appropriate cost floor in the telecommunications sector (see the Competition Act guideline **Application in the Telecommunications Sector**).

Intentions

4.26 Evidence on the intentions of the undertaking may be relevant. In the *AKZO* and *Tetra Pak II* judgments the fact that undertakings set prices below average variable costs was, in the circumstances of each case, evidence of an intent to remove competitors.

4.27 In contrast, where prices fall between average variable and average total costs the Director General would need to consider other evidence on the intentions of the dominant undertaking before establishing whether its behaviour would be predatory. Pricing in this range for short-run periods will often be a rational strategy for an undertaking and represent legitimate competition. In that case, it would not be an abuse. If, however, prices were set at this level as part of a strategy to eliminate a competitor this conduct would be an abuse.

4.28 In addition to the evidence on costs explained above, the following areas of evidence on the undertakings' intentions may be relevant—

— **whether there is evidence of incremental losses**—predation is *strategic* behaviour where an undertaking accepts short run losses in order to eliminate a competitor so as to charge higher prices in the future. The alleged predatory strategy should therefore lead to *incremental* losses for the undertaking in the short run. If the alleged behaviour results in the undertaking making higher profits (or lower losses) than it otherwise would, then that behaviour would be legitimate competition and would not be an abuse. Thus where an undertaking could demonstrate that its behaviour was increasing its profits (or reducing its losses) that particular behaviour would not be predatory. In *Compagnie Maritime Belge* the Court of First Instance cited the fact that the parties 'admit having reduced their earnings' as evidence of an abuse;[5]

— the assessment of whether an action has resulted in higher or lower profits can be very complicated. Difficulties can arise in determining the appropriate comparison. Where the action is a straightforward price cut the best comparison is between the undertaking's profits before and after the price cut. Where the price cut occurs at the same time as a new entrant enters the market, however, the incumbent undertaking's profitability prior to the price cut is less useful, as its profitability would have been reduced by the new entrant in any case;

— **other evidence on the behaviour of the undertaking**—in some cases the behaviour of the undertaking will indicate whether there is intent to predate against a rival. The actions of an undertaking which targeted its price cuts against a new entrant, while maintaining its prices elsewhere, would be consistent with predation. Conversely, price-cutting across the board, not just in the areas where it competes with the new entrant, is not evidence of intent. Other evidence might include the timing of the action, whether the action follows a pattern of aggressive pricing or is a one-off, whether the undertaking engages in **dirty tricks**, or any other relevant evidence;

— **documentary evidence**—in some instances documentary evidence may determine whether an undertaking intended to predate.

Feasibility of recouping losses

4.29 Predation involves undertakings incurring short run losses so that they can increase profits in the long run. In the short run, the undertaking incurs losses in order to eliminate competitors. In the long run, it will expect to recoup the losses by charging higher prices (or offering less favourable terms). Predation works only if the undertaking will be able to recoup its short run losses by charging higher prices in the future—which will be possible only if the undertaking will not face significant competition in the future, from new entrants, for example. This raises the question of whether the Director General needs to establish that an undertaking will be able to recoup its losses before concluding that predation is occurring.

4.30 Predation is an abuse only if it is practised by a dominant undertaking, possessing a substantial level of market power which allows it to act independently of competitors and customers. This is normally shown by high market shares and significant barriers to entry, as explained above. A dominant undertaking can therefore be expected to be able to recoup losses in a market where it is already dominant. Consequently, the question of feasibility is likely to arise only where a dominant undertaking is alleged to be engaging in predation in a related market where it is not currently dominant. In *AKZO* and *Tetra-Pak II* the European Court found the undertakings' conduct to be an abuse without explicitly considering whether recouping losses would be feasible. The Director General therefore does not consider that he would necessarily be required to establish that predation was feasible.

Vertical restraints

4.31 Vertical restraints are arrangements between suppliers and purchasers which restrict the commercial freedom of one or more party. They differ from horizontal agreements because they are agreements between undertakings at different stages in the economic process. This guideline refers to agreements between a manufacturer and a retailer, but the same principles apply to agreements between any two parties operating at different stages in the supply chain. The same principles apply in the supply of services or property rights.

4.32 Vertical restraints can produce anti-competitive effects but they may also produce benefits which can outweigh any anti-competitive effects they produce. Any assessment of the effects of a vertical restraint needs to take account of both its potential anti-competitive effects and of any countervailing benefits. More details of the potential positive and negative effects of vertical restraints are contained in the Competition Act guideline *Assessment of Individual Agreements and Conduct.*

4.33 Vertical restraints are often part of an agreement and would therefore fall within the scope of the Chapter I prohibition in the United Kingdom. The majority of vertical agreements do not raise competition concerns, however, and provisions for **special treatment** for most vertical agreements will therefore be introduced to take them out of the scope of the Chapter I prohibition, although subject to a **clawback** provision. This special treatment will not apply to the Chapter II prohibition so vertical restraints involving dominant undertakings may still be prohibited. (They may also be examined by the Competition Commission following a reference made under the monopoly provisions of the Fair Trading Act 1973: see the Competition Act guideline *Vertical Agreements and Restraints*.) The following paragraphs explain the circumstances in which a vertical restraint imposed by a dominant undertaking might infringe the Chapter II prohibition.

4.34 There is a wide range of restrictions that may constitute vertical restraints and which potentially reduce competition; the following non-exhaustive list covers the main types—

— **resale price maintenance (RPM)**—where the manufacturer specifies the resale price of the product. Commonly the manufacturer will specify only a minimum or a maximum price;

— **selective distribution**—where a manufacturer supplies only a limited number of retailers who are restricted in their ability to re-sell products. They may, for example, have to meet certain standards of service;

— **exclusive distribution**—a particular form of selective distribution where the manufacturer supplies only one retailer in a particular territory. Alternatively, the manufacturer might allow only one retailer to supply a particular class of customer, such as wholesale or retail customers;

— **exclusive purchasing or dealing**—where the retailer agrees to purchase, or 'deal' in, goods from only one manufacturer;

— **tie-in sales and bundling**—where the manufacturer makes the purchase of one product (the **tying** product) conditional on the purchase of a second (**tied**) product. A set of tied products is sometimes called a **bundle**;

— **full-line forcing**—an extreme form of tie-in sale where the retailer must stock the full range of the manufacturer's product range. This may be an absolute requirement, or the manufacturer may charge higher prices if only part of the range is stocked;

— **quantity forcing**—where the retailer is required to purchase a minimum quantity of a certain product;

— **'fidelity' discounts**—where the retailer receives discounts based on the proportion of its sales which come from the manufacturer; and

— **non-linear pricing:**—where, for example, the retailer must pay a franchise fee in addition to the price of each unit sold, or the manufacturer may be required to pay the retailer a **'slotting'** fee in order to get its products stocked.

4.35 These arrangements are common business practices and will be an abuse only if they lead to a reduction in competition.

Competition effects

4.36 RPM can have direct effects on competition. Where prices are fixed absolutely, or minimum prices are specified, there will be no price competition between the retailers affected. Maximum RPM is less likely to be a problem since it allows retailers to compete by charging lower prices, providing it is not used to facilitate collusion between retailers. RPM is more likely to be investigated under the Chapter I prohibition than the Chapter II prohibition.

4.37 The main competition effects of other vertical restraints are market foreclosure, raising rivals' costs, and competition dampening. Foreclosure effects occur when undertakings are completely or partially prevented from entering a market. For example a market will be partially foreclosed if competing undertakings end up with a much lower market share than they would have in the absence of the vertical restraint, or if smaller undertakings are prevented from entering the market. Partial foreclosure often results when the vertical restraint raises rivals' costs, thereby raising entry barriers or forcing existing competitors out of the market.

4.38 Vertical restraints can foreclose markets at either the manufacturer or retailer level. The following restraints might foreclose the market to manufacturers—

— **exclusive purchasing or dealing** may foreclose the market if a significant proportion of potential retail outlets are tied to existing manufacturers. A particular form of this restriction was found to be an abuse in *Hoffman-La Roche*;[6]

— **tie-in sales, full-line forcing, quantity forcing and fidelity discounts** can have similar effects. The Court of First Instance found tying restrictions to be an abuse under Article 86 in *Hilti*.[7] Fidelity rebates were found to be an abuse in *Hoffman-La Roche* (even though the rebates were demanded by large customers), the European Court affirming the European Commission's decision. In *Michelin*[8] the European Court stated that a similar abuse may occur where non-transparent discounts were dependent on dealers meeting sales targets and were based on their previous year's sales;

— **'slotting' fees** can also foreclose markets since they may represent a sunk cost; franchise fees can produce the same effects as exclusive dealing by making small purchases of products from other manufacturers relatively expensive.

4.39 The following restraints might foreclose markets to retailers—

— **exclusive distribution** can foreclose the market if practised by a sufficient proportion of manufacturers. **Selective distribution** can also foreclose markets to retailers, depending on the conditions which retailers have to meet;

— **tie-in sales** and **full-line forcing** can restrict entry by smaller retailers or undertakings that wish to specialise in more limited product ranges. **Quantity forcing** can also prevent entry by small-scale retailers;

— **non-linear pricing** can be used to raise the costs of new entry—by providing noncost-related discounts to existing retailers, for example; and

— **franchise fees** can have similar effects on retailers as slotting fees have on manufacturers, since they may raise the sunk costs of entry.

4.40 These effects involve establishing whether the restraints create an absolute bar to new entry, or force existing competitors out of the market. Vertical restraints can also affect competition by reducing its intensity, or **dampening** competition. The effects described at paragraph 4.38 above can reduce competition between manufacturers (*inter*-brand competition) while those at paragraph 4.39 can similarly reduce competition between retailers of the same product (*intra*-brand competition).

4.41 This list is not exhaustive and vertical restraints can have other anti-competitive effects, particularly when they reinforce other competition problems. For example, tie-in sales can be used to extend the scope of excessive prices, perhaps in a way designed to evade price regulation. The key issues in establishing whether such practices infringe the prohibition will be the extent to which the restraint forecloses a market, raises rivals' costs or dampens competition between existing competitors.

Benefits of vertical restraints

4.42 While vertical restraints imposed by dominant undertakings can lead to anti-competitive effects, the same vertical restraints can also produce economic benefits which outweigh the anti-competitive effects. Such benefits may provide an objective justification which would prevent the imposition of the restraint being an abuse of dominance under Chapter II.

4.43 Vertical restraints are often used to overcome failures in the operation of the market. The most frequently cited benefits of vertical restraints are overcoming **free-rider** problems which arise in the distribution of certain products: there is a clear benefit to consumers if retailers provide services such as demonstrating products, and providing advice to potential purchasers. These services help to increase sales of the product but their benefits can spill over to other retailers: **discount** retailers can **free-ride** on the demonstration services of the high-cost retailers who then lose sales and cut back on their demonstration services. The supply of demonstration services then falls below the manufacturer's preferred level. Manufacturers can use vertical restraints to overcome this problem, by, for example, imposing selective distribution conditions requiring retailers to provide the necessary demonstration services. Similar issues can arise when retailers invest in advertising or promotion which will generate sales for rival retailers.

4.44 A similar problem may arise when a manufacturer provides support to a retailer. This might include providing information on potential customers, financing investment in equipment, providing technical support or providing staff training. Other manufacturers may be able to free-ride on this investment and support.

4.45 In addition to these free-riding effects, manufacturers may also wish to limit the numbers of retailers to ensure that economies of scale in distribution are achieved. This may lead them to impose selective distribution. They may wish to ensure that retailers stock a full range of products in order to achieve certain economies of scope between these products in production or distribution, perhaps by imposing tie-ins or full-line forcing. They may also wish to control retail margins to prevent retailers exploiting any downstream market power, which can be achieved by imposing maximum RPM. Lastly, a manufacturer may wish to reduce the risks retailers incur from distributing its products, for example by setting non-linear prices (which might involve paying a slotting fee and charging a higher unit price).

4.46 If a vertical restraint were considered to be having anti-competitive effects the Director General would expect the dominant undertaking to establish that its behaviour could be objectively justified, and that the benefits could not be achieved without producing such anti-competitive effects. Any restriction of competition would need to be proportionate to the benefits produced.

Refusal to supply

4.47 The European Court established in *Commercial Solvents*[9] that refusal to supply an existing customer by a dominant undertaking can be an abuse if no objective justification for the behaviour can be provided. Obvious justifications for a refusal to supply might be that the customer had poor creditworthiness, or that supplies were cut for a temporary period due to capacity constraints. Refusal to supply might also be used to impose a vertical restraint: a manufacturer imposing a selective distribution system is, by definition, refusing to supply outlets outside the system, in which case the principles explained above would apply. In other cases, refusal to supply may be used to exclude certain competitors, particularly in upstream or down-stream markets.

4.48 In some limited circumstances the refusal to supply a new customer might be an abuse. This was the case in *Magill*[10] which involved the refusal to license copyright. In general, refusal to license an intellectual property right is not an abuse. The limited circumstances where it would be are explained in the Competition Act guideline *Intellectual Property Rights*.

4.49 More recent cases of this type have raised the question of whether the dominant undertaking is abusing ownership of an **essential facility**. A facility can be viewed as essential if access to it is indispensable in order to compete in the market and duplication is impossible or extremely difficult owing to physical, geographic or legal constraints (or is highly undesirable for reasons of public policy).[11] Potential examples include ports, bus stations, utility distribution networks and some telecommunications networks. In general, ownership of an essential facility confers a dominant position. The refusal of access may then constitute an abuse. More details on the assessment of such cases is given in the Competition Act guideline *Assessment of Individual Agreements and Conduct*.

Abuse in related markets

4.50 As explained at paragraph 3.1 above, the Chapter II prohibition implies two tests: whether an undertaking is dominant, and whether it is abusing that dominant position. It is not necessary to show that the abuse was committed in the market which the undertaking dominates. In certain circumstances, the Chapter II prohibition may apply where an undertaking that is dominant in one market commits an abuse in a different but closely associated market. This principle was set out by the European Court in the case of *Tetra Pak II*. In this case the Court found that Tetra Pak's activities in relation to the markets in non-aseptic machines and cartons constituted an abuse of its dominant position in the distinct, but closely associated, markets for aseptic machines and cartons intended for the packaging of liquid foods.

Other abuses

4.51 The examples described above illustrate areas where abuses might occur, but they do not constitute an exhaustive list. When other forms of behaviour by dominant undertakings are considered, the main question, as with all forms of behaviour, will be whether the conduct either exploits the undertaking's customers or reduces existing or potential competition (or whether, on the other hand, there is an objective justification).

[3025]

NOTES

1   Authority for the principle that charging unfairly high prices is an abuse is found in the *General Motors* case (Case 26/75, *General Motors Continental NV v Commission*, [1975] ECR 1367; [1976] 1 CMLR 95), in which the European Commission found the pricing strategy of the dominant undertaking to be excessive and imposed a fine. The Commission's decision was annulled by the European Court on the basis of the facts, but the principle was upheld.

2   Case 27/76 *United Brands v Commission* [1978] ECR 207, [1978] 1 CMLR 429.

3   Case C62/86 AKZO *Chemie BV v Commission* [1993] 5 CMLR 215, and Tetra Pak II [1997] 4 CMLR 662.

4   A further case involving the use of 'fighting ships' (*Compagnie Maritime Belge Transports SA and Others v EC Commission*, [1997] 4 CMLR 273) is currently on appeal to the ECJ.

5   *Compagnie Maritime Belge Transports SA and Others v EC Commission*, [1997] 4 CMLR 273, at point 141. This case is currently on appeal to the ECJ.

6   Case 85/76 *Hoffman-La Roche & Co AG v EC Commission* [1979] ECR 461, [1979] 3 CMLR 211.

7   Case T-30/89 *Hilti AG v Commission* [1991] II ECR 1439, [1992] 4 CMLR 16.

8   Case 322/81 *Michelin NV v Commission* [1983] ECR 3461, [1985] 1 CMLR 282.

9   Cases 6 and 7/73 *Commercial Solvents v Commission* [1974] ECR 223, [1974] 1 CMLR 309.

10   Cases C-241 and 242/91 *RTE and ITP v Commission ('Magill')*, [1995] 1 ECR 743, [1995] 4 CMLR 718.

11   See, for example, the judgment of the ECJ in Case C-7/79 *Oscar Bronner v Mediaprint and Others*, [1998] and in particular the opinion of AG Jacobs, paras 47 & 65.

MARKET DEFINITION

(OFT 403, March 1999)

1 Introduction

1.1 This guideline provides advice and information on how the Director General of Fair Trading defines markets when investigating cases under the Competition Act 1998. The techniques described in this guideline are not new. They reflect current practice by the Director General of Fair Trading, and by competition authorities throughout Europe, North America and elsewhere.

1.2 The Director General has a duty under section 60 to handle cases in such a way as to ensure consistency with Community law. This is described further in the Competition Act guideline *The Major Provisions*.

1.3 In general, this guideline follows the same approach as the European Commission's Notice on market definition.[1]

1.4 Market definition and the measurement of market shares form only one part of an investigation. An investigation will normally look at the potential for new entry, other evidence on market power, and the individual behaviour of undertakings. Assessment of these issues are discussed in other Competition Act guidelines *Assessment of Market Power* and *Assessment of Individual Agreements and Conduct*.

1.5 The approach described in this guideline is not mechanical, it is a conceptual framework within which evidence can be organised. The Director General will not follow every step described below in every case. Instead, he will look at the areas of evidence which are relevant to the case in question—and will often be constrained by the extent to which evidence is available. Market definition is not an end in itself, but rather a step which helps in the process of determining whether undertakings possess, or will possess, market power.

1.6 In particular, in some cases it may be clear that on any sensible market definition the undertakings under investigation will not possess any market power. In that case it will not normally be necessary to establish which of the potential market definitions is correct.

[3026]

NOTES

[1] European Commission, *Commission Notice on the definition of the relevant market for the purposes of Community competition law*, 1997. The same approach is also used in the US Department of Justice and Federal Trade Commission, *Horizontal Merger Guidelines*, revised 1992 and in OFT Research Paper 1 (OFT049): National Economic Research Associates, *Market Definition in UK Competition Policy*, 1992.

2 Market definition

The purpose of market definition

2.1 The prohibitions in the Act are designed primarily to prevent undertakings from exploiting **market power**. Market power exists where undertakings can consistently charge higher prices, or supply goods and services of a lower quality, than they would if they faced effective competition.[1] Market power can exist when an undertaking has a high market share or when undertakings which together have high market shares do not actively compete with each other.

2.2 Some agreements between undertakings, such as price-fixing agreements, might be prohibited even if the undertakings involved did not possess market power (see the Competition Act guideline *The Chapter I prohibition*). Apart from those cases, an investigation under the Act normally begins by considering whether particular undertakings possess market power. High market shares, combined with other evidence, may indicate that undertakings possess market power. Where an undertaking has a high market share there may be a lack of strong competitors, in which case it may be able to raise prices above competitive levels without fear of losing sales. It may also be easier for undertakings to collude. High market shares do not always convey market power—for example, there may be a strong threat of competition from new entrants. If, however, the relevant market has been defined appropriately, undertakings with very low market shares will almost certainly not possess market power, and an investigation can normally be dropped at an early stage.

2.3   Market definition is important because, first, market shares can be calculated only after the boundaries of a market have been defined. Secondly, it is important in the rest of the Director General's analysis under the Competition Act, because it sets the stage on which competition takes place. For example, when considering the potential for new entry it is necessary to identify the market being entered.

2.4   Thirdly, market definition is important for establishing whether or not particular undertakings fall within the scope of the prohibitions—

— the Chapter I prohibition applies only to agreements which have an **'appreciable'** effect on competition. The appreciability test requires definition of a relevant market and demonstration that the agreement would have an appreciable effect on competition within that market (see the Competition Act guideline *The Chapter I prohibition*);

— under Chapter II, undertakings with very low market shares are unlikely to be dominant so their behaviour will not be caught by the prohibition (see the Competition Act guideline *The Chapter II prohibition*).

2.5   High market shares are not themselves prohibited, and do not necessarily indicate a competition problem. The main purpose in measuring market shares is to establish at an early stage those cases where it is clear that no market power is present and that no further action by the Director General is necessary.

The main concept

2.6   The idea of a **market** is familiar. Annual reports, business plans and other documents often refer to the market in which the undertaking operates. This will normally include other undertakings which the undertaking views as its competitors. The Director General starts from the same position, trying to identify products which are substitutes for each other, so that competing undertakings can be identified.

2.7   The boundaries of a market are not always obvious, however. Does a manufacturer of colas compete in the market for cola-flavoured drinks, the market for carbonated or 'fizzy' drinks, the market for soft drinks, the market for non-alcoholic beverages, or some other collection of products? Clearly its market share could vary significantly depending on which definition was used. Market shares cannot be measured until that question has been resolved: that involves identifying the products which are the closest substitutes for the products at the centre of the investigation. If an undertaking supplying the products set prices above competitive levels would its consumers still buy its products, or would they switch to substitutes? In particular, would so many switch to substitutes that it would be unprofitable to raise prices above competitive levels?

2.8   One way to look at this problem is to consider an undertaking that was the only supplier of the products (or group of products) at the centre of the investigation and use the conceptual framework of whether a **hypothetical monopolist** of these products would maximise its profits by consistently charging higher prices than it would if it faced competition.[2] The assumption is that this hypothetical undertaking would not be constrained by the threat of new entry, which would be considered in any overall assessment of an undertaking's market power—see the Competition Act guideline ***Assessment of Market Power.*** (Defining the market therefore cannot demonstrate on its own that an undertaking possesses market power.)[3]

2.9   If the undertaking would be prevented from setting prices above competitive levels by substitution to certain products, those substitutes can then be added to the potential market and the test applied again. This involves asking whether an undertaking which was the only supplier of this larger group of products would maximise profits by charging prices above competitive levels. By repeating the process a definition can eventually be reached where, under the assumptions above, a 'hypothetical monopolist' *could* maintain prices above competitive levels. This will usually be the market definition used. If the market were to be expanded further, the same condition should be met: a 'hypothetical monopolist' could set higher prices than an undertaking facing competition. The Director General would usually use the narrowest potential market definition.[4] This will not always be the case, however; the relevant market may be wider in the case of a horizontal agreement, for example.

2.10   A market definition should normally contain two dimensions: a **product** and a **geographic area**.[5] Taking a recent example, when looking at a complaint regarding ice cream cabinets in Ireland the European Commission defined the relevant market as *impulse ice cream in Ireland.* The product market was *impulse ice cream* (ice creams bought from convenience outlets on the spur of the moment rather than from a supermarket) and the geographic market was *Ireland* (rather than, say, Western Europe). The market definition analysis has to be applied separately to determine both the product and the geographic area. In the case of the geographic market the question is whether an increase in price would cause customers to switch to suppliers in neighbouring areas. The geographic market could be wider than the United Kingdom or it could be any part of the United Kingdom.

2.11   The issue in market definition is usually to determine products to which *consumers* might switch. However, substitution can also take place by suppliers. If prices rise, undertakings which do not currently supply the product might be able to start supplying it at short notice. This will prevent undertakings charging monopoly prices, so any supply-side substitutes should also be included in the market.

[3027]

NOTES

[1]   Competition problems often involve other forms of conduct, such as vertical restraints or predation, rather than high profits, but it is the ability to raise prices above competitive levels which demonstrates that undertakings possess market power.

[2]   The term **monopolist** here merely means that the undertaking is the only supplier of these products or services, not that it necessarily possesses any market power.

[3]   It is also assumed that the Government does not regulate the undertaking's prices, and that the undertaking does not reduce prices to avoid future regulation. This does not mean that the test cannot be applied to products supplied by regulated undertakings. The test poses a hypothetical question and is not meant to represent reality. However, the existence of Government regulations, or a statutory monopoly, may affect the scope for supply-side substitution (see paras 3.13 to 3.22). Any assessment of a regulated undertaking's conduct will take account of the fact that its behaviour is regulated.

[4]   The test can be thought of as looking at a group of hypothetical oligopolists rather than a single monopolist. According to the 'hypothetical monopolist' test, if the narrowest possible market is identified and the undertakings do not collude, then, by definition, only an undertaking with 100 per cent of that market would possess market power. A group of undertakings acting together could, however, behave as if they were a hypothetical monopolist, and thus one of the undertakings would hold market power without having 100 per cent of the narrowest conceivable market. In practice, the narrowest theoretical market might be one for which no disaggregated data existed, so that the market may be defined to be larger than the narrowest theoretically possible market. Part 5 of this guideline describes how the relevant market may sometimes be wider than the narrowest conceivable market.

[5]   Throughout these guidelines, the term **product** includes services and property rights.

3 The product market

The demand-side

3.1   The process starts by looking at a relatively narrow potential definition. This would normally be the products which two parties to an agreement both produce or the products which are the subject of a complaint. Common sense will normally indicate the narrowest potential market definition. The Director General then considers how customers would react if prices were raised a small but significant amount above competitive levels.

3.2   Common practice in both Europe and the US is to consider a price 5–10 per cent above competitive levels. This will normally be the Director General's approach, although, in practice, it is often difficult to quantify a potential price rise. The 5–10 per cent test is a rough guide rather than a rule.[1]

3.3   If significant numbers of customers would switch to substitutes (known as **demand-side substitution**), the market definition should be widened to include the substitutes. It is not necessary for all customers, or even the majority, to switch. The important factor is whether the number of customers likely to switch is large enough to prevent a 'hypothetical monopolist' exercising market power.

3.4   Substitutes do not have to be identical products to be included in the same market. For example, in its report on *Matches and Disposable Lighters*,[2] the Monopolies and Mergers Commission included matches and disposable lighters in the same market because consumers viewed them as close substitutes. The products' prices do not have to be identical. For example, if two products perform the same purpose, but one is of a higher quality, they might be included in the same market. This depends on whether the price of one constrains the price of the other. Although one is of a lower quality, customers might still switch to this product if the price of the more expensive product rose and if they no longer felt that the higher quality justified the price differential.

3.5   The important issue is whether the undertaking could *maintain* prices above competitive levels. The products will still be included in the same market if the delay before substitution takes place is so short it would never be worthwhile to raise prices in the first place. As a rough rule of thumb, if substitution took longer than one year the products would not be included in the same market. However, the answer will vary from case to case. Substitution that was possible within one year might not be included if customers would have to incur significant switching costs, for example.

3.6   The Director General considers evidence on substitution from a number of different sources. The information used will vary from case to case, but the following areas are likely to be important—

— customers and competitors will often be interviewed. In particular, customers can be asked directly how they would react to a hypothetical price rise, but because of the hypothetical nature of the question, answers may need to be treated with a degree of caution;

— a significant factor determining whether substitution takes place is whether customers would incur costs in substituting products. High switching costs relative to the value of the product will make substitution less likely;

— patterns in price changes can provide strong evidence, when combined with other evidence. For example, two products showing the same pattern of price changes, for reasons not connected to costs, could be strong evidence that they were close substitutes. The Director General may also look at the effects of any past price changes to see how customers reacted. Price divergence over time, without significant levels of substitution, provides evidence that the two products may be in separate markets.

However, if the absence of substitution could be explained by a divergence in both price and quality, the products could still be in the same market (see paragraph 3.4 above);

— evidence on price elasticities may also be examined. These measure the rate at which demand for a product changes when its price (or the price of substitutes) goes up or down. OFT Research Paper 1[3] provides information on how price elasticities can be used to define markets.

Captive customers and price discrimination

3.7   In many cases some customers will be able to switch between product A and product B while others cannot, and are therefore **captive**. As noted at paragraph 3.3, the market might still be wider than product A if there are a significant number of customers who could substitute to product B. The important question is whether substitution by the non-captive customers will prevent a monopolist charging prices above competitive levels.

3.8   Even if the proportion of captive customers is small, the monopolist may be able to set monopolistic prices if it can discriminate between different customers, charging high prices to those who are captive, and lower (competitive) prices to those who are not. For example, on a particular hypothetical route, commuters travelling by train might be keen to minimise the time they spend travelling, in which case they might not view coaches as close substitutes. They might also need to travel before 9.00am. Leisure travellers might be willing to travel later in the day and may view coaches as a close substitute. If this were the case, commuters might be captive while leisure travellers were not, and a train operating company could price discriminate against the (captive) commuters by charging higher fares before 9.00am. After 9.00am fares might be constrained by competition from coaches while before 9.00am they could be set at a monopoly level.

Chains of substitution

3.9   Two products do not have to be direct substitutes to be included in the same market. There may be a **chain of substitution** between them. A large luxury car is unlikely to be a *direct* substitute for a small hatchback, for example. If the price of one manufacturer's small hatchback rose, customers would be more likely to switch to a different small hatchback rather than to a large luxury model. The hatchback and the luxury car are not likely to be direct substitutes for most customers.

3.10   If the price of all small hatchbacks rose, however, customers might hypothetically switch to slightly larger cars (a medium-sized hatchback, for example), since the price differential would narrow. These cars might then be included in the same market. Similarly, if the price of medium-sized hatchbacks rose customers might either switch to small hatchbacks or to slightly larger cars. If this were the case, there might then be a chain of substitution linking together cars of different sizes.

3.11   The Director General will sometimes look at chains of substitution when defining markets. However, he will look carefully to ensure that there are no breaks in the chain which would suggest that separate markets exist. In the hypothetical example above, the Director General might find that a monopolist in large luxury cars would not be constrained by substitution to smaller models, because there is a gap in the chain of substitution. It might then hypothetically decide that a chain of substitution existed between small and medium-sized cars, but that large cars formed a separate market.

3.12   A chain of substitution is a useful concept, but it does not necessarily define the boundaries of a market. The Director General often needs to identify the narrowest potential market, so part of the chain might still be treated as a separate market. For example, if there was a chain linking products A to Z, and the issue was in which market a supplier of product F operated, it might be found that F alone would not be a relevant market due to substitution to E and G. If, however, there was a sole supplier of E, F and G, customers buying F would only substitute to products E or G, where the same undertaking would be the only supplier. So it might be worthwhile for the undertaking to raise the prices of E, F and G above competitive levels together. In that case the group of products E to G might be defined as a separate market from others in the chain. The main issue then is whether substitution to D and H would prevent the undertaking from raising the prices of the intervening products.

The supply-side

3.13 Substitution can also take place by suppliers (known as **supply-side substitution**). If prices rise, undertakings which do not currently supply a product might be able to supply it at short notice. This will prevent undertakings charging monopoly prices, so any supply-side substitutes should also be included in the market.

3.14 An example is the supply of paper for use in publishing.[4] Paper is produced in various different grades dependent on the coating used. From a customer's point of view, the different types of paper are not viewed as substitutes, but because they are produced using the same plant and raw materials, it is relatively easy for manufacturers to switch production between different grades. If a 'hypothetical monopolist' in one grade of paper tried to set prices above competitive levels, manufacturers currently producing other grades could easily start supplying that grade—the ability to exploit market power is thus constrained by substitution by suppliers.

3.15 Analysing supply-side substitution raises similar issues to the analysis of barriers to entry (discussed further in the Competition Act guideline *Assessment of Market Power*). In both cases the question is whether undertakings would start supplying a particular product if prices rose. The distinction is timing: supply-side substitution occurs when undertakings start supplying the market in the short run (for example, within one year), whereas new entry into the market occurs over a longer time scale.

3.16 As with the demand-side, substitution should be relatively quick. If substitution took longer than one year these undertakings would not normally be included in the market. Since the issue is identifying opportunities for short-run substitution, undertakings would not normally be included if they had to make a significant investment in new production capacity or other fixed assets.

3.17 Even if substitution were technically possible, there may be other barriers. It may be necessary to advertise products or incur other marketing costs. For example, if two consumer products are produced using similar technology, and substitution is technically feasible, an undertaking switching between them might still need to spend time establishing a brand in a new product area, in which case substitution could not occur in the short run. There might also be other barriers to distribution, for example if supply chains were foreclosed to new suppliers.

3.18 Some competition authorities prefer to define markets solely on the demand-side, leaving supply-side issues to the analysis of new entry. In practice both approaches should produce the same conclusions on the question of market power, provided that supply-side issues are examined at some point. However, the Director General will define markets on the supply-side in some circumstances. In the paper example above there would be little value in analysing competition in each grade of paper if it was clear that supply-side substitution would undermine any potential market power in a particular grade. Defining markets on the supply-side can allow early determination that an undertaking has no market power, thus avoiding the need for further analysis.

3.19 Supply-side substitutes will therefore be included within the market definition when it is clear that substitution would take place quickly and easily. If there is any serious doubt on this point, they will not be included but will be considered when analysing potential entry.

3.20 The Director General might look at evidence from some or all of the following sources—

— potential suppliers might be asked whether substitution was technically possible, and about the costs of switching production between products, and the time it would take to switch production. The key question is whether it would be economic to switch production given a small (ie 5–10 per cent) price increase;

— undertakings might be asked whether they had spare capacity or were free to switch production. Undertakings may be prevented from switching production because all their existing capacity was tied up—they may be committed to long-term contracts. There might also be difficulties obtaining necessary inputs or finding distribution outlets;

— although new undertakings may be able to supply the market, there may be reasons why customers would not use their products, so the views of customers might be sought.

3.21 Supply-side substitutes are included in market shares by identifying a set of products whose suppliers would switch to selling the relevant product if prices rose. It is the products rather than the undertakings which are added to the market definition. Market shares should then be calculated by adding up supplies of all the products which are included within the market, although this can prove difficult. Part 4 of the Competition Act guideline *Assessment of Market Power* explains more fully how market shares are calculated. If there are practical difficulties in estimating market shares when supply-side substitutes are included, the suppliers of the substitutes may be treated as potential entrants that will constrain market power, rather than as existing competitors.

3.22 Where supply-side substitutes are included there may still be constraints on the capacity that an undertaking might switch into supplying the relevant product. In that case the market shares might be adjusted to reflect this, or substitutable capacity could be used as a measure of market shares.

　　　　　　　　　　　　　　　　　　　　　　　　　　　　　　　[3028]

NOTES

1　　Arguably, the test should be applied to the value added by the undertaking, not its selling price. In practice, selling prices are more easily seen and are usually the price which will be considered. This is one reason why some flexibility in the size of price differential considered must be retained.

2　　Cm 1854, 1992.

3　　See footnote [to para 1.3].

4　　Where the Commission defined the market based on supply-side substitution in *Torras/Sarrio*, Case IV/M166 OJ (1992) C58/20, [1992] 4 CMLR 341.

4　The geographic market

4.1 The geographic market is the area over which substitution takes place. Geographic markets are defined using the same process as that used to define the product market. This part outlines some issues which are particularly relevant to geographic market definition—

— demand-side issues;

— supply-side issues; and

— imports.

4.2 The approach often depends on whether the product is retailing, wholesaling or manufacturing. Retailing markets are more likely to be defined on the demand-side, while wholesaling and manufacturing markets are more likely to be defined on the supply-side.

The demand-side

4.3　As with the product market, the objective is to identify substitutes which are so close that they would prevent a 'hypothetical monopolist' in one area from charging monopolistic prices. The process starts by looking at a relatively narrow area, which would normally be the area supplied by the parties to an agreement or the subject of a complaint. Examination is then broadened to consider whether consumers would switch to suppliers in neighbouring areas in response to a small increase in price. If substitution is potentially so significant that it would prevent an undertaking from raising prices, the area is added to the market definition.

4.4　Chains of substitution can be an important factor in geographic markets, particularly retail markets. Consumers in any one location might not be willing to travel more than, say, two or three miles to purchase a particular product, but there may be a chain of substitution creating a much larger geographic market. In principle, this could create a market covering the whole of the United Kingdom but it would depend on whether there were areas where the chain broke. Chains of substitution often break down in rural areas—that between Northern England and Central Scotland, for example—or in the peripheries of the British Isles. Even if most of the United Kingdom formed a single market, areas such as the Highlands of Scotland might form separate markets; the answer will vary from case to case.

4.5　If an undertaking with a monopoly in several neighbouring areas could raise prices across those areas, the total area might form a separate market (see paragraph 3.12 above on chains of substitution in product markets).

4.6　The evidence used to define geographic markets on the demand-side will usually be similar to the information used to define the product market (see paragraph 3.6), but the value of a product is often an important factor in defining geographic markets. The higher the value, the more likely customers are to travel further in search of cheaper supplies. The mobility of customers may be a relevant factor: whether most customers have access to cars, for example.

The supply-side

4.7　This entails looking at the potential for undertakings to supply customers in neighbouring territories. As with product-market definition, substitution should be possible in the short run (for example, within one year). Supply-side substitution may not be possible within one year if undertakings need to spend significant sums on advertising or marketing, or if distribution channels are foreclosed.

4.8　Again the main evidence will usually mirror the information gathered on product market definition, but the level of transport costs relative to the price of a product is also an important issue. Higher relative transport costs normally mean a narrower geographic market. This has often led to regional market definitions for building products, for example, although the regions may be linked together by a chain of substitution (which led the European Commission to widen the geographic market in *Pilkington Techint/SIV*).[1]

Imports

4.9　Significant imports of a particular product may indicate that the market is international, although it is not always the case. Imports may come only from subsidiaries of domestic suppliers, for example, or there may be quotas which limit the volume of imports.

4.10　Conversely a lack of imports does not necessarily mean that the market cannot be international. The potential for imports may still be an important source of substitution should prices rise: when the European Commission looked at a merger between bus manufacturers in Germany it found that although imports were low at the time, there were no significant barriers to imports from the rest of the Community should prices in Germany rise.[2]

[3029]

NOTES
[1]   Case IV/M358, 1993, CMLR 4 [1994] 405, CCH 2 [1994] 2 031.
[2]   *Mercedes-Benz/Kassbohrer*, Case IV/M477, 1995, OJ [1995] L211/1, CMLR 4 [1995] 573.

5   Other issues

Temporal markets

5.1   A third dimension to market definition is time. Examples of temporal markets include—

— peak and off-peak services. This can be a factor in transport services or utilities such as electricity supply;

— seasonal variations, such as summer *versus* winter months; and

— inter-generational products. Customers may defer expenditure on present products because they believe innovation will soon produce better substitutes.

5.2   Markets can be defined by time when—

— It is not possible for customers to substitute between time periods. Customers might not view peak and off-peak train tickets as substitutes, for example, or they might not be able to store fruit from one season to another; and

— suppliers' capacity varies between time periods. Fresh fruit supplies may vary depending on the season of the year.

5.3   To some extent, temporal markets are simply an extension of the product dimension: the product can be defined as the supply of train services at a certain time of day.

Complements and secondary products

5.4   Market definition normally involves identifying groups of substitutes, but markets can be defined to include groups of **complements**. Complements are products which are consumed together (coffee and milk) or produced together (petrol and diesel oil). Complements are included in the same market when competition to supply one product constrains the prices charged for the other. The most common area when they arise is for secondary markets—sometimes called **after markets**.

5.5   Secondary products are those purchased only if the customer has already purchased a primary product. The main examples are spare parts and servicing: car tyres (a secondary product) are not bought unless the buyer already owns a car (the primary product). Manufacturers of primary products sometimes have a monopoly or high market share in the supply of secondary products or services. They might be accused of exploiting this dominant position. However, the secondary product is not always a relevant market, because any exploitation of a manufacturer's monopoly in the secondary product can affect its position in the market for the primary product. An aircraft engine manufacturer, for example, might have a monopoly supplying spare parts for its engines, but an increase in the price of the spare parts might be taken into account by airlines when purchasing engines in the future.

5.6   Where secondary products exist there are three possible market definitions—

— **a single market**—including both the primary and secondary products (cars plus their spare parts);

— **multiple markets**—where there is one market for the primary product but separate markets for secondary products for each brand of primary product (Ford spare parts, Fiat spare parts, Volkswagen spare parts etc); or

— **dual markets**—one for the primary product and one for all brands of secondary product (a market for new cars and a separate market for spare parts for all types of car).

5.7 The main issue is whether customers take account of the whole-life cost of a product before purchasing. This occurs if customers look at both the cost of the primary product and the costs of expected secondary product purchases when deciding which product to buy. A significant number of car buyers looking at spare part costs when choosing which car to buy might prevent a manufacturer from exploiting any monopoly in spare parts. Not all consumers need to do so, however, as long as the manufacturer cannot discriminate between those who do and those who do not.

5.8 The following factors may indicate whether customers will whole-life cost—

— customers are more likely to whole-life cost if the secondary product is a higher proportion of the primary product's price;

— large companies may be better able to whole-life cost than smaller companies or final consumers;

— if customers lack information on the costs of spare parts and servicing, and the reliability of products, whole-life costing will be more difficult. The availability of specialist publications may be a factor here; and

— if there is uncertainty about how often spare parts or servicing will be required it will be difficult to whole-life cost.

5.9 In 1995, the European Commission rejected a complaint that Kyocera, a manufacturer of computer printers, was abusing its dominant position in the supply of secondary products for its printers. One reason for rejection was that Kyocera was not dominant. The Commission concluded that Kyocera was constrained by competition in the primary market for computer printers, because customers were well informed about the costs of secondary products which were significant relative to the printer's price.[1]

5.10 A further factor is how often the primary product is replaced, and whether there are switching costs from changing suppliers. If replacement is very infrequent or switching costs are high there may be a significant number of secondary product customers who are captive. Depending on the relative size of the primary market, even if new customers whole-life cost, the supplier may find it profitable to exploit these captive customers, implying that the secondary products will be a separate market.

5.11 Suppliers of the primary product may reduce prices below cost in order to increase profits from future sales of secondary products. It has been argued that in this situation the market should be defined to include both products. However, this behaviour might itself be considered undesirable (for example, it may lead to *over-supply* of the primary product, and *under-supply* of the secondary product). In this situation it may be more appropriate to treat the primary and secondary products as separate markets and consider separately whether or not the undertaking's behaviour in either market might be an abuse under the Chapter II prohibition.

Identifying the competitive price

5.12 A remaining difficulty is how to identify the competitive price. When assessing a new agreement the Director General might assume that the current price was competitive: even if it was not at the competitive level in practice, it might be appropriate to use it as the benchmark price. The agreement could have an appreciable effect on competition if it would allow the undertakings to raise prices further above competitive levels than they could at present.

5.13 When assessing an undertaking's position under the Chapter II prohibition, consideration has to be given to whether the current price was above competitive levels—a dominant undertaking could already have raised prices above competitive levels to its profit-maximising level. In that situation, it will be constrained from raising prices further by substitution from its closest substitutes—even a monopolist would find it unprofitable to raise prices further at some level. If the question was whether or not the undertaking could raise prices above *current* levels, the answer would be that it could not due to substitution from other products. If prices already exceeded the competitive level, however, it would clearly be wrong to include those products in the relevant market and argue that they prevented the undertaking from exercising market power. This problem is sometimes known as the **cellophane fallacy** after a US case involving cellophane products.[2] The Director General must make some judgement on whether or not the current price is likely to be significantly above competitive levels already.

5.14 This is a difficult question to answer. Evidence that prices are above competitive levels might include excess profits or past price movements (see part 2 of the Competition Act guideline *Assessment of Individual Agreements or Conduct*). In these cases, the process of defining the market will not be carried out in isolation but would be considered alongside other evidence on market power and the undertaking's conduct, reflecting the fact that market definition is a tool for assessing whether undertakings possess market power, not an end in itself.

Previous cases

5.15 In many cases a market may have already been investigated and defined by the Director General or by another competition authority. Sometimes, earlier definitions can provide a useful short cut. Although previous cases can provide useful information, the market definition used may not always be the correct one to use in future cases. Most obviously, competitive conditions may change over time. In particular, innovation may make substitution between products easier, or more difficult, and therefore change the market definition. Secondly, a previous product market definition may relate to a particular area, such as another part of the European Union, where substitution is more, or less, likely. A product market definition may therefore be different in different locations. In assessing cases in markets which have already been considered by the European Commission and the European Court, the Director General will ensure that the question of market definition is dealt with in a manner which is consistent with its treatment in Community law.

Market definitions are not unique

5.16 A third reason why precedents may be of limited value is that many markets contain differentiated products where there is no clear cut-off point delineating the boundary of the market. This means that, in practice, even within the same area at the same time, the market definition is not unique and can vary depending on the competition problem under investigation. The two following hypothetical examples illustrate how market definition can be affected by the nature of the competition issue.

Definition varies depending on the parties

5.17 If, hypothetically, there were three versions of the same product, A, B and C, and each was produced using different technology and were therefore not supply-side substitutes, and each version varied slightly in performance so that A was the best, B the second best and C the worst, some consumers would view A and B as substitutes, some would view B and C as substitutes, but A and C would not be *direct* substitutes. It might be concluded that a monopolist that supplied only one version would not be able to set prices above competitive levels because of substitution by consumers. None of A, B or C forms a separate market, because to some extent they are linked by a chain of substitution. However, a monopolist that supplied both A and B could set prices above competitive levels, as could a monopolist which supplied both B and C. The market definition is not unique: it could be A plus B or B plus C. The definition used in any particular case will depend on the parties being investigated. If an agreement existed between undertakings which manufactured products A and B, the relevant market would be A plus B. If the agreement was between manufacturers of B and C, the relevant market would be B plus C. If the market had been defined as A plus B in one case, undertakings should not assume that B and C could never be included in the same market in future cases. This example shows that the market definition can vary depending on where the test starts (with product A or product C).

Definition varies depending on the type of alleged infringement

5.18 Again hypothetically, if Airways operated an air service between two cities and Trainco operated a train service between the same two cities, an allegation might be received that Airways had used predatory pricing tactics or some other form of anti-competitive conduct to remove a rival airline. Airways' conduct would be found to contravene the Chapter II prohibition only if a number of tests were met. One aspect would be whether it possessed a dominant position, depending in part on whether air services were a separate market from train services. The Director General might conclude that air services were a separate market—perhaps because train services were slower and did not constrain Airway's prices. The relevant market might change, however, if Airways and Trainco entered into an agreement to coordinate timetables so that their services did not directly compete.[3]

5.19 Looking at a hypothetical monopoly supplier of air and train services, a supplier might be able to set prices of both services above existing levels because trains and aeroplanes are substitutes at the margin. Although air fares might already be above competitive levels, they might still be constrained to some extent by competition from trains. In the future, if that competition were to be removed, fares could increase. So because the competition problem is different the relevant market definition would then be different.

5.20 This hypothetical example also shows that the relevant market will not necessarily be the narrowest economic market. This is particularly so in cases involving horizontal agreements where there might be a perceived loss of competition between two undertakings where their products were the closest substitutes at the margin; this would apply even if they could be defined as separate markets using the narrowest potential market definition.

The role of market definition

5.21 This guideline explains how the Director General delineates the boundaries of a market by identifying existing competitors and thus the calculation of market shares. However, the question is only part of a full competition analysis. In particular, an undertaking with a high share within a properly defined market might still face other constraints which will prevent it from exercising market power. This is explained further in the Competition Act guideline *Assessment of Market Power*.

5.22 Market definition is most useful as a way of identifying relatively quickly those cases where undertakings clearly will not possess market power because they face significant competition from existing competitors. This is likely to be the case where undertakings possess low market shares within a properly defined market. The Competition Act guidelines **The Chapter I prohibition** and **The Chapter II prohibition** indicate market shares where, depending on the issue involved, the Director General does not generally expect undertakings to be affected by the prohibitions in the Act.

[3030]

NOTES

1   *Pelikan/Kyocera* European Commission, *XXVth Report on Competition Policy*: 1995 p140.
2   *US v El Du Pont de Nemours & Co*, [1956] 351 US 377.
3   The agreement might qualify for an individual exemption, but the Director General would still have to define the relevant market to assess whether there was an appreciable effect on competition and the agreement was caught by the Chapter I prohibition in the first place.

POWERS OF INVESTIGATION

(OFT 404, March 1999)

1 Introduction

1.1   The Competition Act 1998 (**'the Act'**) gives the Director General powers of investigation to determine whether there has been an infringement of the Chapter I or Chapter II prohibition in the Act. Effective powers of investigation are a key element of deterring anti-competitive behaviour. The purpose of these powers is to enable the Director General to obtain the information which he needs to apply and enforce the prohibitions in the Act.

1.2   The powers of investigation set out in the Act[1] to investigate suspected infringements of the Chapter I and Chapter II prohibitions are described in this guideline. The Act gives the Director General the power—
   — to require the production of specified documents or specified information;[2]
   — to enter premises without a warrant;[3] and
   — to enter and search premises with a warrant.[4]

1.3   Parts 3 to 5 of this guideline describe when each of these powers can be used, the extent of each power and the procedures that must be followed. The limitations on the use of these powers are described in part 6 and the offences committed by a person who fails to comply when these powers are exercised are described in part 7. The power to require information when determining whether to withdraw the benefit of a transitional period or an exclusion is described in part 8.

1.4   The Act also amends the existing powers of investigation in the Fair Trading Act 1973 in relation to the investigation of monopolies. These amended powers are described in part 9. The powers of investigation available to the Director General of Fair Trading when assisting the European Commission in investigations carried out in relation to Article 85 or Article 86 of the EC Treaty (Article 85 and Article 86)[5] are described in part 10.

1.5   The powers of investigation can be delegated to an officer authorised to act on the Director General's behalf.

[3031]

NOTES

1   Sections 25–29.
2   Section 26.
3   Section 27.
4   Section 28.
5   [Now] renumbered Articles 81 and 82 respectively following ratification of the Treaty of Amsterdam.

2 Trigger for the use of the powers of investigation

2.1 The Director General can carry out an investigation if there are **reasonable grounds for suspecting** that either the Chapter I prohibition or the Chapter II prohibition has been infringed. The formal powers of investigation cannot be used unless this requirement is met. Whether there are reasonable grounds for suspicion will depend upon the information available and the judgment of the Director General. Examples of information that may be sources of reasonable grounds for suspicion include copies of secret agreements provided by disaffected members of a cartel, statements from employees or ex-employees, or a complaint.

2.2 The Director General expects that the power to require the production of specified documents or information or to carry out an on-site investigation will be used most frequently to obtain further information following the receipt of a complaint or where a suspected infringement has otherwise come to his attention, rather than following a notification.

2.3 The Director General may obtain information about undertakings, agreements, practices and markets at any time through informal enquiries. Such enquiries, which may be made at a meeting, in written correspondence or in a telephone conversation, may be made in addition to, or instead of, using the formal investigation powers set out in the Act. The Director General cannot compel an undertaking to respond to an informal enquiry which is not backed by statutory powers. Undertakings are encouraged to cooperate.

[3032]

3 Production of specified documents and information

When the power can be used

3.1 If the Director General has reasonable grounds for suspecting that either the Chapter I or the Chapter II prohibition has been infringed he can, for the purposes of an investigation, require a person to produce specified documents or to provide specified information at any stage of an investigation. This is the investigation power that the Director General will tend to rely on most frequently. The power is exercised by written notice the contents of which are set out in paragraph 3.8 below.

3.2 It is not necessary for the power to be used before carrying out an on-site investigation (described in parts 4 and 5 below). For example, it may be used for the first time following an on-site investigation to clarify facts that have emerged. There may be cases where the Director General uses the power if further information is needed to assess an application for guidance or a decision.

3.3 A person may receive a notice requiring the production of documents or information on more than one occasion during the course of an investigation. For example, the Director General may require a person to produce further information after considering the material produced in response to an earlier notice.

The scope of the power

3.4 The Director General can require any person to produce documents or information that he considers relates to any matter relevant to the investigation. The Director General is not limited to approaching the undertakings alleged to have infringed one of the prohibitions. For example, the notice may be addressed to third parties such as complainants, suppliers, customers and competitors.

3.5 The Director General can also—
— take copies or extracts from any document produced;
— require the person required to produce the document or any past or present officer or employee of that person to provide an explanation of the document if it is produced;

— require the person required to produce the document to state, to the best of his knowledge or belief, where the document can be found, if the document is not produced.

3.6   The term **'document'** includes **'information recorded in any form'**.[1] This definition includes records, such as invoices or sales figures, held on computer. **'Specified'** means documents or information that are specified or described in a written notice or that fall within a category which is so specified or described. A category of documents may include, for example, invoices, agreements and minutes of meetings.

3.7   The Director General can use the power to require the production of specified information to require the compilation and production of information that is not already in recorded form. For example, a person may be asked to provide market share information or to provide a description of a particular market using the knowledge or experience of the sales manager.

The procedure

3.8   The power to require the production of documents or information using section 26 is exercised by serving a written notice. The written notice will usually be sent by post or by fax. The written notice must—

— state the subject matter and the purpose of the investigation;

— specify or describe the documents or information, or categories of documents or information, required; and

— set out the nature of the offences created by the Act, including the offences that may be committed when the addressee of the notice: fails to comply with the requirement; destroys, disposes of, falsifies or conceals a document; or provides false or misleading information.

The Director General can also require the production of documents when carrying out an on-site investigation with or without a warrant (described in parts 4 and 5 of this guideline).

3.9   The notice may also state the time and place at which a document or information must be produced and the manner and form in which it is to be produced. For example, a person may be required to produce the documents or information at a specified address on a designated date at a particular time. If a document is produced the Director General may require that an explanation of the document is provided. A person required by the Director General to provide an explanation of a document may be accompanied by a legal adviser (rule 13 of the *Director General of Fair Trading's Procedural Rules*).

3.10   When setting the appropriate time limit for the production of documents or information the Director General will consider the amount and the complexity of the information required and the urgency of the case.

3.11   The notice may be addressed to individuals, undertakings or associations of undertakings. Where a notice is addressed to an undertaking or association of undertakings, the appropriate person to respond is the person who is authorised by the undertaking or association of undertakings to respond on behalf of the undertaking or association of undertakings.

[3033]

_____

NOTES

   [1]   Section 59.

_____

4 Power to enter premises without a warrant

4.1 If the Director General has reasonable grounds for suspecting that either the Chapter I prohibition or the Chapter II prohibition has been infringed he may conduct an investigation and has the power to enter premises to carry out on-site investigations, either with or without a warrant. This power enables the Director General to enter premises and require the production of documents relevant to an investigation. The power to carry out on-site investigations without a warrant is described in this part. The power to carry out on-site investigations when a warrant has been obtained is described in part 5.

When the power can be used

4.2 Any officer of the Director General who is authorised in writing by the Director General to enter premises (**'an investigating officer'**) may enter premises in connection with an investigation if he has given the occupier of the premises at least two working days' written notice of the intended entry. The occupier of the premises need not be suspected of an infringement. For example, the premises of a supplier or customer may be entered using this power.

4.3 An investigating officer may enter premises in connection with an investigation without a warrant and without notice if—

— the Director General has a reasonable suspicion that the premises are, or have been, occupied by a party to an agreement which he is investigating or an undertaking whose conduct he is investigating; or

— the investigating officer has been unable to give notice to the occupier, despite taking all reasonably practicable steps to give notice.

The scope of the power

4.4 An investigating officer entering premises without a warrant may require—

— any person on the premises to produce any document that he considers relates to any matter relevant to the investigation. For example, an employee may be asked to produce minutes of any meetings with competitors, the diaries of specified directors, sales data or invoices. The investigating officer can take copies of, or extracts from, any document produced;

— any person on the premises to provide an explanation of any document produced. For example, an employee may be requested to provide an explanation of the entries or codes on an invoice or spreadsheet;

— any person to state, to the best of his knowledge and belief, where any document that the investigating officer considers relates to any matter relevant to the investigation can be found; and

— any information held on computer that the investigating officer considers relates to any matter relevant to the investigation, and which is accessible from the premises, to be produced in a form in which it can be read and can be taken away.

4.5 The investigating officer may take with him any equipment that he deems necessary when entering any premises. For example, the investigating officer may take portable computer equipment and tape recording equipment.

4.6 **'Premises'** generally refers to business premises, but includes domestic premises only if the home is used in connection with the business or if business documents are kept there. 'Premises' also includes any vehicle.

The procedure

4.7   If the investigating officer is carrying out an on-site investigation without a warrant after giving at least two working days' written notice, the written notice must state—

— the subject matter and purpose of the investigation. The notice will identify the type of infringement that is suspected and will set out in general terms the matters which the investigation is intended to investigate; and

— the nature of the offences that may be committed if a person fails to comply when the powers of investigation are exercised (described in part 7 below).

4.8   If the investigating officer is entering the premises without a warrant and without written notice, he may enter only on production of evidence of his authorisation by the Director General and a document indicating—

— the subject matter and purpose of the investigation; and

— the nature of the offences that may be committed if a person fails to comply when the powers of investigation are exercised (described in part 7 below).

4.9   The investigating officer will normally arrive at the premises during office hours. On entering the premises, the investigating officer will produce evidence of his identity. He will also hand over a separate document which sets out the powers of the investigating officer and states that the occupier may request that his legal adviser is present. Where possible, the person in charge at the premises should designate an appropriate person to be a point of contact for the investigating officer during his investigation.

Access to legal advice

4.10   An undertaking being investigated will be able to contact its legal advisers during the course of an on-site investigation. The investigating officer will grant a request to wait a short time for legal advisers to arrive at the premises before the investigation continues if he considers that it is reasonable to do so in the circumstances.[1] It is intended that the practice of the Director General will go no further than the practice of the European Commission when determining how long to wait for the legal advisers to arrive.

4.11   The exercise of the right to consult a legal adviser must not unduly delay or impede the investigation. Any delay must be kept to a strict minimum. The main concern is that any delay might provide an opportunity for evidence to be tampered with or for other parties to a suspected infringement to be warned about the investigation, for example, by telephone or e-mail. To reduce this concern, when agreeing a reasonable time to wait, the investigating officer may attach such conditions as he considers appropriate in the circumstances. The conditions could include, for example, the sealing of cabinets, keeping business records in the same state and place as when the investigating officer arrived, suspending external e-mail and allowing the investigating officer to enter and remain in occupation of offices of his choice. If an undertaking has an in-house legal adviser on the premises, or if the undertaking has been given notice of the investigation, the investigating officer will not wait for an external legal adviser to arrive.

                                                                     [3034]

NOTES

[1]   Rule 13 of the *Director General of Fair Trading's Procedural Rules.*

PART III
OFT GUIDELINES

5 Power to enter and search premises with a warrant

5.1 An application can be made to a judge of the High Court or Court of Session for a warrant for a named officer of the Director General and other officers authorised in writing by the Director General to enter and search premises.

When the power can be used

5.2 The Act identifies three circumstances in which a judge of the High Court or Court of Session may issue a warrant to authorise a named officer of the Director General to enter and search premises specified in the warrant. The judge must be satisfied that there are reasonable grounds for suspecting that there are on the premises documents—

— which the Director General has required to be produced, either by written notice (section 26) or in the course of an on-site investigation without a warrant (section 27), and which have not been produced;

— which the Director General has the power to require to be produced by written notice (section 26), but that if they were required to be produced they would be concealed, removed, tampered with or destroyed; or

— which the investigating officer could have required to be produced in an on-site investigation without a warrant (section 27); the judge must also be satisfied that the investigating officer has attempted but has been unable to enter the premises without a warrant.

5.3 The second ground for obtaining a warrant identified above (that documents are likely to be destroyed or tampered with etc if required to be produced) is the only ground that will enable the Director General to carry out an on-site investigation with a warrant without using one of the other investigatory powers first.

The scope of the power

5.4 The warrant will authorise a named officer of the Director General, and any other of his officers whom he has authorised in writing, to—

— enter the premises specified in the warrant using such force as reasonably necessary. The officer entering the premises will be entitled to use force only if he is prevented from entering the premises. The officer may use only such force as is reasonably necessary for the purpose of gaining entry. The officer cannot use force against any person;

— search the premises and take copies of, or extracts from, any documents appearing to be of the kind in respect of which the warrant was granted (identified in paragraph 5.6 below). The officer can search offices, desks and filing cabinets etc. to find such documents;

— take possession of any documents appearing to be of the kind in respect of which the warrant was granted (identified in paragraph 5.6 below) if such action appears to be necessary for preserving the documents or preventing interference with them, or if it is not reasonably practicable to take copies of the documents on the premises. The officer can also take any other steps which appear necessary in order to preserve the documents or prevent interference with them. In most cases the officer will take copies of documents. Original documents that are taken will be returned within three months;

— require any person to provide an explanation of any document appearing to be of the kind in respect of which the warrant was granted or to state to the best of his knowledge and belief where it may be found;

— require any information held on computer that the named officer considers relates to any matter relevant to the investigation, and which is accessible from the premises, to be produced in a form in which it can be read and can be taken away.

5.5   Any person entering premises under a warrant may take with him such equipment as he deems necessary. This will include equipment that can be used to enter the premises using reasonable force (for example, equipment that can be used to break locks) as well as equipment that can be used to facilitate the search (for example, computer equipment).

5.6   The category of documents that the named officer can take copies of etc depends on the ground under which the warrant was obtained—

— where the warrant was granted because a person failed to produce documents, the named officer can take copies etc of any documents which were required to be produced and were not produced under section 26 or 27;

— where the warrant was granted because there were reasonable grounds for suspecting that the documents would have been tampered with etc, the named officer can take copies etc of any documents which he had power to require to be produced under section 26. In addition, if the judge is satisfied that it is reasonable to suspect that there are also other documents relating to the investigation on the premises the warrant will also authorise the named officer to take copies etc of any such document;

— where the warrant was granted because the investigating officer was unable to enter premises, the named officer can take copies etc of any document which could have been required to be produced under section 27 had he been able to enter the premises.

5.7   The premises that can be entered using these powers are described in paragraph 4.6 above.

The procedure

5.8   The officer named in the warrant may exercise the powers set out in paragraphs 5.4–5.7 only on producing the warrant.

5.9   The warrant must indicate—

— the subject matter and purpose of the investigation; and

— the nature of the offences committed if a person fails to comply when the powers of investigation are exercised.

The warrant continues in force for one month from the date of issue.

5.10   The Director General's officer or officers will normally arrive at the premises during office hours. On entering the premises, the officer will produce evidence of his identity. He will also hand over a document which sets out the powers of the officer and states that the occupier may request that his legal adviser is present. Where possible, the person in charge at the premises should designate an appropriate person to be a point of contact for the officer during his investigation.

5.11   If there is no one at the premises, the officer named in the warrant must take reasonable steps to inform the occupier of the premises of the intended entry. If the occupier is informed, the occupier, his legal advisers or other representatives must be given a reasonable opportunity to be present when the warrant is executed. If the officer has been unable to inform the occupier of the intended entry, he is under a duty to leave a copy of the warrant in a prominent place on the premises. On leaving premises that are unoccupied the officer must leave them secured as effectively as he found them.

Access to legal advice

5.12   See paragraphs 4.10–4.11 above.

6 Limitations on the use of the powers of investigation

Privileged communications

6.1 The power to require the production of documents, either on written notice or during an on-site investigation, does not extend to privileged communications.[1] A person can refuse to produce or disclose a document that is a privileged communication. A privileged communication is defined by the Act to mean a communication—

— between a professional legal adviser and his client; or
— made in connection with, or in contemplation of, legal proceedings and for the purposes of those proceedings

which would be protected from disclosure in proceedings in the High Court on grounds of legal professional privilege or in the Court of Session on grounds of confidentiality of communications.

6.2 The categories of communication which attract privilege under the Act are wider than the categories of communication that the European Court[2] has recognised as being privileged. The definition in the Act refers to a **'professional legal adviser'**, which has been interpreted by the United Kingdom courts as including in-house lawyers as well as lawyers in private practice. When the powers of investigation set out in the Act are used to investigate suspected infringements of the Chapter I and Chapter II prohibitions the interpretation of privileged information under Community law will not apply (see paragraph 10.7 below).

Self-incrimination

6.3 The defence against self-incrimination which has been recognised under EC jurisprudence will apply. Section 60 of the Act sets out principles which provide for the United Kingdom authorities to handle cases in such a way as to ensure consistency with Community law.

6.4 Applying EC jurisprudence,[3] the Director General may compel an undertaking to provide specified documents or specified information but cannot compel the provision of answers which might involve an admission on its part of the existence of an infringement, which it is incumbent upon the Director General to prove. The Director General will, however, request documents or information relating to facts, for example, whether a particular employee attended a particular meeting.

Disclosure of confidential information

6.5 The Act imposes limits on the disclosure of information obtained under or as a result of Part I of the Act (which includes information obtained during the course of an investigation) that relates to the affairs of any individual or to any particular business of an undertaking. The Act requires that such information is not to be disclosed during the lifetime of that individual or while the business is carried on unless consent has been obtained from the person who originally provided the information and, if different, the individual to whose affairs the information relates or the person carrying on the business to which the information relates. There are several exceptions to this requirement, including where disclosure is made for the purpose of facilitating any function of the Director General under Part I of the Act.

6.6 If the person supplying a document or information in response to a written notice to produce a specified document or specified information considers that any part of the document or information supplied is confidential, that part should be clearly marked as confidential and should be put in a separate confidential annex. It is suggested that where possible the occupier of premises entered by an officer of the Director General during an investigation should, after the site visit, identify any information in the documents produced or copied that he considers is confidential. It is for the Director General to determine whether or not the information is to be disclosed.

6.7   When the Director General is considering whether to disclose any information acquired by him under or as a result of Part I (for example, where such information is included in material to be published or otherwise made available to third parties), he must have regard to the need for excluding, so far as is practicable, information the disclosure of which would in his opinion be contrary to the public interest.[4]

6.8   The Director General must also consider the need to exclude, so far as is practicable—

— commercial information which, if disclosed, would, or might, significantly harm the legitimate business interests of the undertaking to which it relates; or

— information relating to the private affairs of an individual which, if disclosed would, or might, significantly harm his interests.

6.9   When considering whether information should be excluded, the Director General must also consider the extent to which the disclosure of such information is necessary for the purposes for which it is to be disclosed. The Director General may have to edit documents he proposes to disclose to remove such information, for example, by blanking out parts of documents or by aggregating sales figures.

6.10   A person who is not a party to the agreement or has not engaged in the conduct that is being investigated and who supplies information to the Director General in connection with the exercise of any of the Director General's functions under Part I of the Act is required to identify any information that he considers is confidential and to set it out in a separate annex marked **'confidential information'**.[5] The Director General will consult the third party before disclosing the information where it is practicable to do so.

[3036]

NOTES

[1]   Section 30.

[2]   Case 155/79 *AM&S v Commission* [1982] ECR 1575 and see paragraph 10.7 below.

[3]   Case 374/87 *Orkem v Commission* [1989] ECR 3283.

[4]   Section 56.

[5]   Rule 25 of the *Director General of Fair Trading's Rules*.

7   Offences created by the Act relating to the powers of investigation

7.1   The Act sets out a number of criminal offences which may be committed where a person fails to cooperate when the investigation powers set out in the Act are exercised. It is an offence for a person—

— to fail to comply with a requirement imposed under the investigation powers in the Act (subject to certain defences, see below);

— intentionally to obstruct an officer carrying out an on-site investigation either with or without a warrant;

— intentionally or recklessly to destroy or otherwise dispose of or falsify or conceal a document that he has been required to produce or cause or permit its destruction, disposal, falsification or concealment; or

— to provide information that is false or misleading in a material particular if he knows, or is reckless as to whether, it is false or misleading, either to the Director General or to another person, for example, an employee or legal adviser, knowing that it will be used for the purpose of providing information to the Director General.

7.2   A person who fails to comply with a requirement to produce a document has a defence if he can prove that the document was not in his possession or control and that it was not reasonably practicable for him to comply with this requirement. It is a defence for a person who fails to comply with a requirement to provide information or an explanation of a document or to state where a document is to be found if he can prove that he had a reasonable excuse for failing to comply with the requirement.

7.3   Failing to comply with a requirement imposed under section 26 or 27 is not an offence if the person imposing the requirement fails to act in accordance with the provision in question.

7.4   The officer as well as the body corporate is guilty of any of the offences described above if the offence that is committed by a body corporate is proved to have been committed with the consent or connivance of an officer or to be attributable to his neglect. An **'officer'** is defined to mean a director, manager, secretary or other similar officer of the company or a person purporting to act in any such capacity. Where the affairs of the body corporate are managed by its members, a member is also guilty of an offence if the offence of the body corporate is proved to have been committed with the consent or connivance of the member or to be attributable to his neglect as if he were a director. In Scotland a partner or person purporting to be a partner, as well as the partnership, may be guilty of the offence.

7.5   Offences will be tried either summarily in the Magistrates' Court or Sheriff Court or, in the case of more serious offences, on indictment in the Crown Court or the High Court of the Justiciary. Factors that will be taken into account when determining where to commence proceedings include the gravity of the alleged offence and the complexity of the matter.

7.6   A person convicted of intentionally obstructing an officer carrying out an on-site investigation without a warrant will be liable to a fine. The consequences for intentionally obstructing an officer exercising his powers under a warrant are more serious. Conviction on indictment may lead to a fine, to imprisonment for up to two years, or both.

7.7   The sanctions that may be imposed by the courts on a person found guilty of each offence described in paragraph 7.1 are set out in the table below. The sanctions that are available for each offence differ according to whether the person is found guilty on summary conviction or on indictment.

Offence	Sanction on summary conviction	Sanction on conviction on indictment
Fail to comply with a requirement imposed under the investigation powers	Fine of up to the statutory maximum (currently £5000)	Unlimited fine
Intentionally obstruct an officer carrying out an on-site investigation *without* a warrant	Fine of up to the statutory maximum	Unlimited fine
Intentionally obstruct an officer carrying out an on-site investigation *with* a warrant	Fine of up to the statutory maximum	Unlimited fine and/or up to two years' imprisonment

Offence	Sanction on summary conviction	Sanction on conviction on indictment
Intentionally or recklessly destroy, dispose of, falsify or conceal document the production of which has been required or cause or permit its destruction etc.	Fine of up to the statutory maximum	Unlimited fine and/or up to two years' imprisonment
Knowingly or recklessly provide information that is false or misleading in a material particular	Fine of up to the statutory maximum	Unlimited fine and/or up to two years' imprisonment

[3037]

8   Transitional arrangements and exclusions

Transitional arrangements

8.1   The transitional periods that apply in respect of the Chapter I prohibition are described in the Competition Act guideline *Transitional Arrangements*. The Director General has the power to terminate transitional periods early if he considers that the agreement would infringe the Chapter I prohibition and that he would be unlikely to grant it an unconditional individual exemption.[1]

8.2   If the Director General is considering whether to give a direction to terminate the transitional period he may in writing require any party to the agreement to provide such information in connection with that agreement as he may require.[2] The Director General may terminate the transitional period if the party fails to provide the information within the time period specified in the *Director General of Fair Trading's Procedural Rules* without reasonable excuse.[3] The Director General may terminate the transitional period of an agreement excluded from the Chapter I prohibition only where the agreement falls within one of the categories of excluded agreements that are identified in paragraph 8.3.[4]

Exclusions

8.3   The Act specifically excludes certain categories of agreements and/or conduct from the prohibitions (see the Competition Act guideline *The Major Provisions*).[5] The Director General may issue a direction to withdraw the application of an exclusion from a particular agreement falling within one of the following categories if he considers that the agreement would infringe the Chapter I prohibition and that he would be unlikely to grant it an unconditional individual exemption—

— certain agreements falling within the mergers exclusion;[6]
— agreements which are the subject of a direction under section 21(2) of the Restrictive Trade Practices Act 1976;[7]
— agreements which relate to production of or trade in **'agricultural products'** as defined in the EC Treaty and in Council Regulation (EEC) No 26/62, or to certain farmers' cooperatives;[8] and
— certain vertical agreements and land agreements which fall within the relevant orders made pursuant to section 50.

8.4   If the Director General is considering withdrawing an exclusion he may require any party to the agreement in question to give him such information in connection with the agreement as he may require. This must be done by sending a written notice. If the party fails to provide the information required within the time period specified in the *Director General of Fair Trading's Procedural Rules* without reasonable excuse, the Director General may give a direction withdrawing the exclusion.[9]

8.5   The Director General must follow a special procedure before exercising the powers of investigation in the Act in relation to an agreement that falls within the following categories of excluded agreement—

— agreements in relation to recognised professional bodies subject to competition scrutiny under section 127 of the Financial Services Act 1986;[10] and

— agreements subject to competition scrutiny under section 194A of the Broadcasting Act 1990.[11]

8.6   Before exercising the investigatory powers in relation to agreements for the constitution of recognised professional bodies or agreements relating to investment business falling within section 127 of the Financial Services Act 1986 (as amended by the Competition Act), the Director General must notify the Treasury of his intention to use the powers and provide the Treasury with information about the agreement in question. The Director General may not use the powers of investigation unless the Treasury confirms that: (i) it has not made, and does not intend to make, a declaration the effect of which is that the Chapter I prohibition does not apply; or (ii) that it revoked such a declaration at least six months earlier. The Director General must notify the Secretary of State, rather than the Treasury, and follow the same procedure if he wishes to exercise the powers of investigation in relation to agreements subject to competition scrutiny under the Broadcasting Act 1990.

[3038]

NOTES
  [1]   A direction may be revoked prior to it taking effect, either by the Director General or by the Secretary of State.
  [2]   Schedule 13, paragraph 38.
  [3]   Rule 23.
  [4]   Schedule 13, paragraph 37(2).
  [5]   Schedules 1–4.
  [6]   Schedule 1.
  [7]   Schedule 3.
  [8]   Schedule 3.
  [9]   Rule 22(3).
  [10]   Schedule 2.
  [11]   Schedule 2.

9   Investigation powers in the Fair Trading Act 1973

9.1   The Act repeals most of the existing competition law regime in the United Kingdom although some has been retained. The complex monopoly and scale monopoly provisions of the Fair Trading Act 1973 have been retained (see the Competition Act guideline *The Major Provisions*).

9.2   The Act amends the Fair Trading Act[1] to strengthen the Director General's investigation powers in relation to complex and scale monopolies to bring them broadly into line with the powers of investigation available to enforce the Chapter I and Chapter II prohibitions in the Act, with the exception that a power to enter and search premises with a warrant has not been added.

9.3   The Act strengthens the Director General's power to seek information in connection with a monopoly reference under the Fair Trading Act or when seeking undertakings as an alternative to a monopoly reference. The amendments under the Act give the Director General the power—

— to require the production of specified documents, estimates, forecasts,

returns and other information from certain producers, suppliers and customers;[2] and
— to enter business premises without notice and to require the production of relevant documents and to provide an explanation of the documents produced.

9.4   The occupier of premises being entered using this power will be given the same opportunity set out in paragraphs 4.10 to 4.11 to request that a legal adviser be present as he would if his premises were being entered under the investigation powers used to enforce the prohibitions in the Act.

9.5   The amendments under the Act create the offences that can be committed and the sanctions that apply for failing to comply with the amended investigation powers in the Fair Trading Act. The Act creates the following offences: refusing or wilfully neglecting to comply with a requirement to produce documents or other information; wilfully interfering with documents; and intentionally obstructing the Director General in the exercise of his powers. On conviction on indictment the sanction for obstruction is an unlimited fine. The sanction on conviction on indictment for not complying with a requirement to produce documents or information or interfering with documents is an unlimited fine, a maximum imprisonment of two years, or both.

[3039]

NOTES
1   Sections 44, 46 and 137 of the Fair Trading Act.
2   Amended section 44(3) of the Fair Trading Act.

10   Power to assist the European Commission in its investigations

10.1   Each Member State is required to assist the European Commission when European Commission officials are carrying out on-site investigations in its territory and encounter opposition from the undertakings in question, and may be required to carry out an on-site investigation on behalf of the European Commission. The Act sets out the new powers of the Director General of Fair Trading to discharge this obligation.

10.2   In relation to investigations carried out in the United Kingdom in connection with Article 85 or 86 the Act confers powers of investigation on the Director General of Fair Trading that are similar to the power to enter and search premises with a warrant described in part 5.

10.3   The Director General of Fair Trading may be given powers of entry and search when assisting the European Commission in an investigation relating to Article 85 or 86 ordered by a European Commission decision or carrying out an investigation at the request of the European Commission in connection with an investigation relating to Article 85 or 86 ordered by a European Commission decision.

10.4   When assisting the European Commission in an investigation, the Director General of Fair Trading may obtain a warrant where a European Commission investigation is being obstructed or is likely to be obstructed. The warrant will authorise a named authorised officer of the Director General of Fair Trading, other authorised officers of the Director General of Fair Trading and the relevant European Commission officials to enter the premises in question and to search for books and records that the officials have the power to examine, using such force as is reasonably necessary for the purpose.

10.5   When the Director General of Fair Trading is carrying out an investigation at the request of the European Commission, he may obtain a warrant where his investigation is being, or is likely to be, obstructed. The warrant will authorise a named officer of the Director General of Fair Trading, other officers of the Director General of Fair Trading and any relevant European Commission officials to enter the premises in question and to search for books and records that the officer of the Director General of Fair Trading has the power to examine, using such force as is reasonably necessary for the purpose. The officer will have the powers of an official authorised by the European Commission. The authorisation will identify the officer, the subject matter and purpose of the investigation and draw attention to the penalties which a person may incur in connection with the investigation under the relevant provision of Community law.[1]

10.6 The warrant that may be obtained by the Director General of Fair Trading when assisting or carrying out an investigation at the request of the European Commission must indicate the subject matter and purpose of the investigation and the nature of the offence described in paragraph 10.9.

10.7 As described in paragraph 6.2, the categories of documents that the European Court has recognised as being privileged is narrower than the definition of privileged communications in the Act. The European Court has recognised that correspondence between a client and an external legal adviser, entitled to practice in one of the Member States, is privileged where: (i) the correspondence follows the initiation of proceedings by the European Commission and concerns the defence of the client; or (ii) the correspondence existed before the initiation of proceedings but is closely linked with the subject-matter of the proceedings. Correspondence between a client and an external legal adviser who is not entitled to practice in one of the Member States[2] or between a client and an in-house legal adviser (unless the in-house legal adviser is simply reporting the statement of an external legal adviser) is not recognised by the European Court as being protected by legal privilege.

10.8 Where the Director General of Fair Trading assists in an investigation carried out by the European Commission or carries out an investigation at the request of the European Commission, privilege can be claimed only for documents that fall within the category of correspondence that the European Court has recognised as being privileged. In order to claim legal privilege for certain documents during an on-site investigation the occupier must make a case to the European Commission demonstrating why the documents are covered by legal privilege. If the European Commission rejects the occupier's arguments, the European Commission may adopt a decision requiring the documents to be handed over. The occupier can challenge this decision in the Court of First Instance.

10.9 A person will be guilty of an offence if he intentionally obstructs any person in the exercise of his powers under a warrant issued in relation to an investigation relating to Article 85 or 86. The sanction is a fine of up to the statutory maximum on summary conviction or an unlimited fine and/or a maximum of two years' imprisonment on conviction on indictment.

[3040]

NOTES
  1   Regulation 17/62 Article 15(1)(c) (fines) and Article 16(1)(d) (periodic penalty payments).
  2   The Commission has indicated that such correspondence may be protected if suitable reciprocity agreements are negotiated.

CONCURRENT APPLICATION TO REGULATED INDUSTRIES

(OFT 405, January 2001)

1 Introduction

1.1   For a number of industries the enforcement of the Competition Act 1998 ('the Act') is carried out by the sector regulator concurrently with the Director General of Fair Trading.

1.2   This guideline provides information about which industry sectors are affected by the concurrency provisions and the scope of the concurrent powers. Part 3 describes the procedures for making notifications and complaints, the way in which notifications and complaints are dealt with under concurrent powers and how the regulators work with the Director General of Fair Trading and with each other, using the powers in the Act, including under the Competition Act 1998 (Concurrency) Regulations SI 2000/260) ('the Regulations').[1] Part 4 explains how the use of these powers interacts with the regulators' sectoral powers and duties and the powers under the Fair Trading Act 1973. Finally, Part 5 describes the restrictions on the disclosure of information contained within the Act. This guideline does not set out the detailed procedure for the operation of concurrent jurisdiction or the procedure to be adopted by the Concurrency Working Party.

1.3   Sector-specific guidelines have been produced and reference should be made to those guidelines, where appropriate.

[3041]

NOTES
  [1]   SI 2000/260 is reproduced at **[2005]**.

2 The concurrent powers

2.1   The industry sectors where a regulator has concurrent powers with the Director General of Fair Trading are:

Agreements or conduct relating to:	Statute	Regulatory body
commercial activities connected with telecommunications	The Telecommunications Act 1984	OFTEL
the shipping, conveyance or supply of gas and activities ancillary thereto	The Gas Act 1986	OFGEM
commercial activities connected with the generation, transmission or supply of electricity	The Electricity Act 1989	OFGEM
commercial activities in England and Wales connected with the supply of water or securing a supply of water or with the provision or securing of sewerage services	The Water Industry Act 1991	OFWAT
the supply of railway services	The Railways Act 1993	ORR

Agreements or conduct relating to:	Statute	Regulatory body
commercial activities connected with the generation, transmission or supply of electricity in Northern Ireland	The Electricity (Northern Ireland) Order 1992	OFREG
the conveyance, storage or supply of gas in Northern Ireland	The Gas (Northern Ireland) Order 1996	OFREG

The addresses of the regulators are given [at **[3130]**.]

2.2   With the exceptions noted in paragraph 2.4 below, the regulators have all the powers of the Director General of Fair Trading to apply and enforce the Act to deal with anti-competitive agreements or abuses of a dominant position which, in each case, relate to their designated sectors. In many cases, the undertakings whose agreement or conduct is relevant will be licencees, franchisees or similar right holders under one of the statutes listed above, although it is the subject matter to which the agreement or conduct relates rather than the identity of the undertakings involved which will determine whether there is concurrent jurisdiction.

2.3   A regulator may—
— give guidance on the application of the Act;
— consider complaints about breach of the prohibitions;
— impose interim measures to prevent serious and irreparable damage;
— consider notifications for a decision and give decisions on the application of the Act;
— grant exemptions to the Chapter I prohibition (subject, where appropriate, to conditions);
— carry out investigations both on the regulator's own initiative and in response to complaints. Regulators have the same powers to require the production of documents and information and to search premises as the Director General of Fair Trading. Further details about these powers are given in the Competition Act guideline *Powers of Investigation;*
— impose financial penalties, taking account of the statutory guidance on penalties issued by the Director General of Fair Trading;[1]
— give and enforce directions to bring an infringement to an end; and
— issue general advice and information on how the Act applies to his sector.

2.4   The Director General of Fair Trading alone, however, has powers to issue guidance on penalties and to make and amend the Director's rules (now in the form of a statutory instrument, SI 2000/293), which set out the procedures to be followed by the Director General of Fair Trading, the sector regulators and third parties carrying into effect the provisions of Part I of the Act. In each case, the Director General of Fair Trading is required to consult with the regulators.

2.5   Once it has been decided which authority will exercise certain prescribed functions in relation to a case, the Regulations prevent another authority from doing so unless the case is formally transferred under the Regulations to that authority (Regulation 7). "Prescribed functions" are defined in Regulation 2 of the Regulations. They include—
— the exercise of the formal powers of investigation in sections 25 to 29 of the Act;
— the withdrawal of an exclusion from the Chapter I prohibition;
— the making of certain formal decisions, including as to whether there has been an infringement;

— the giving of written notice prior to the making of an infringement decision or the grant of an exemption subject to conditions; and
— the giving of formal guidance.

NOTES

1   See Director General's guidance as to the appropriate amount of a penalty (OFT 423) [at **[3113]**].

3   Concurrency in practice

3.1   The Regulations contain provisions for the co-ordination of the performance by the Director General of Fair Trading and the regulators of their concurrent functions under the Act.

These provisions include—

— allowing for the exchange of information between the Director General of Fair Trading and the regulators for the purposes of determining who has jurisdiction to exercise concurrent functions in relation to a case (Regulation 3);
— provisions for determining who should exercise prescribed functions in relation to a case (Regulation 5);
— provisions for resolving disputes as to who should exercise prescribed functions in relation to a case (Regulation 6);
— provisions to prevent the simultaneous exercise by more than one authority of prescribed functions in relation to a case (Regulation 7);
— provision for the transfer of cases from one authority to another (Regulation 8); and
— provision for the Director General of Fair Trading or a regulator for the use of the staff of another regulator or of the Director General of Fair Trading (Regulation 9).

3.2   The Regulations are not intended to deal comprehensively with all aspects of the relationship between the Director General of Fair Trading and the regulators. Matters which are not addressed specifically in the Regulations are dealt with by means of informal arrangements between the Director General of Fair Trading and the regulators.

Ensuring consistency of decision-making

3.3   The Director General of Fair Trading and each regulator are represented on the Concurrency Working Party, chaired by a representative of the Office of Fair Trading. The Working Party was formed in 1997 to ensure full co-ordination between regulators and the Director General of Fair Trading, to consider the practical working arrangements between them, including ensuring that a single case would not be investigated by more than one authority, to ensure consistency of approach in casework, to co-ordinate the use of the concurrent powers, and to prepare the guidelines issued under section 52 of the Act. The Concurrency Working Party's Terms of Reference are at Annexe 2.

3.4   The Working Party has continued in operation following implementation of the Act and the making of the Regulations. It deals with, among other things, the issues set out below.

These are—

— **general principles and information sharing**—where necessary, information about complaints received and investigations in progress or contemplated will be shared to ascertain whether there is concurrent jurisdiction. This will include any matters that are also capable of being investigated under sector-specific legislation. Information about cases in progress, including matters of general policy and the way in which the Act is interpreted and applied, will also be shared, in each case with a view to ensuring consistency in decision-making;

— **guidelines**—the Working Party will keep under review the existing guidelines, both general and sector-specific, and will consider the necessity for revision or replacement in the light of developments in the application of the Act (or other relevant legislation);

— **disagreement over who should exercise jurisdiction**—members of the Working Party may be called upon to advise if the Director General of Fair Trading and a regulator or two or more regulators are unable in the first instance to reach agreement under Regulation 5 as to who should exercise prescribed functions in relation to a case (for the procedure in cases where agreement can still not be reached, see 3.9 below).

The Working Party will not, however, discuss any matter which would constitute a breach of the confidentiality provisions in sections 55 and 56 of the Act (see paragraph 5.2 below).

3.5   The Director General of Fair Trading and the regulators have a duty under section 60 to handle cases in such a way as to ensure consistency with Community law. This is described further in the Competition Act guideline *The Major Provisions.*

3.6   All decisions, whether of the Director General of Fair Trading or of a regulator, are subject to appeal to the appeals tribunal of the Competition Commission on both the substance of the decision and on any penalties imposed, with a further appeal to the Court of Appeal, or (in the case of Scotland) to the Court of Session or (in the case of Northern Ireland) to the Court of Appeal in Northern Ireland on points of law or on the level of financial penalties imposed. Further details are given in the Competition Act guideline *The Major Provisions.*

Case-handling

3.7   Regulators and the Director General of Fair Trading will always consult with each other before acting on a case where it appears that they may have concurrent jurisdiction. They must consult under the Regulations on receipt of an application[1] or, in the absence of such an application, before exercising prescribed functions. Such consultation will include the circulation of details submitted in actual or proposed applications or complaints.

3.8   In general, an agreement or conduct which relates to the industry sector of a regulator (listed above) will be dealt with by that regulator, although in some cases the Director General of Fair Trading will deal with such a case. The general principle will be that a case will be dealt with by whichever of the Director General of Fair Trading or the relevant regulator is better, or best, placed to do so. The factors considered in determining which of the Director General or regulators deals with the matter include the sectoral knowledge of a regulator; any previous contacts between the parties or complainants and a regulator, or with the Director General of Fair Trading, and any recent experience in dealing with any of the undertakings or similar issues which may be involved in the proceedings. In the case of an application, applicants must be informed which authority is handling the application (Regulations 5 and 6). In the case of a complaint, the complainant will, as a matter of policy, be informed which authority is handling the complaint.

3.9   It is expected that an agreement will generally be reached as to which authority is better or best placed to deal with a particular notification or complaint within one month of receipt. In circumstances where Regulation 5 of the Regulations applies and agreement cannot be reached between the relevant authorities within a reasonable time the matter will be referred to the Secretary of State for him to decide which authority should deal with a case (Regulation 6).

3.10 Neither the Director General of Fair Trading nor the regulators may exercise prescribed functions in relation to a case until the matter has been determined under Regulations 5 or 6 of the Regulations (Regulation 7). Once the matter has been determined under Regulations 5 or 6, Regulation 7 also prohibits any other authority from exercising prescribed functions in relation to that case unless it is formally transferred to that authority under the procedures laid down in Regulation 8.

3.11 Even where Regulation 7 does not apply (because a determination has not been made under Regulations 5 or 6 and it is not yet proposed to exercise prescribed functions), it is the policy of the Director General of Fair Trading and the regulators that, once it has been decided which authority should deal with a case, only that authority will, unless the case is subsequently transferred from that authority to another, handle the investigation, decision-making and enforcement for that case. The Director General of Fair Trading and other relevant regulators will be consulted, as appropriate, however.

3.12 The Regulations set out the procedure which must be followed in the cases of transfers under Regulation 8. In the case of an application, the applicant will be given the opportunity to make representations, and notified of the outcome (Regulation 8). There is no right to make representations in relation to the initial decision under Regulation 5 or 6 as to which authority will exercise prescribed functions in relation to the application. In the case of complaints, the undertaking which is the subject of the investigation will in certain circumstances be given an opportunity to make representations on the proposed transfer, and notified of the outcome. This will not be the case where the undertaking has not yet been informed that it is the subject of the investigation (Regulation 8). Those making such representations should assume that such representations will be seen by both or all of the competent persons concerned. The complainant will also be notified of any transfer.

Notifications[2] and complaints

3.13 **Notifications for guidance** under the Act must, in all cases, be sent to the Director General of Fair Trading (Regulation 4) together with the relevant fee. If the matter falls within one of the industry sectors listed in the table on page 2, an additional copy of the notification form (Form N, the same as that used for notifications for decisions, for which see below) should be provided to the Director General of Fair Trading for each relevant regulator. The applicant should also send a further copy of the form direct to each relevant regulator, but failure to send an additional copy of the form to or for the relevant regulator will not render the notification incomplete. Applicants will be told as soon as practicable who is dealing with the case, and will also be informed if the case is subsequently transferred to another regulator or to the Director General of Fair Trading. Where it is subsequently proposed that a case should be transferred, the applicant will be notified in writing of the proposal and invited to make written representations within seven working days of the date of the notice. Following such a transfer the applicant will be notified of the transfer and given reasons for it.

3.14 **Notifications for decisions** (including applications for an individual exemption from the Chapter I prohibition) must also, in all cases, be sent to the Director General of Fair Trading (Regulation 4) together with the relevant fee. As with notifications for guidance, if the matter falls within one of the industry sectors listed in the table on page 2, an additional copy of the Form N should be provided to the Director General of Fair Trading for each relevant regulator. The applicant should also send a further copy of the form direct to each relevant regulator, but failure to send an additional copy of the form to or for the relevant regulator will not render the notification incomplete. Applicants will be told as soon as practicable who is dealing with the case, and if the case is subsequently transferred to another regulator or the Director General of Fair Trading. Where a case is subsequently transferred, the applicant will, as in the case of notifications for guidance, be given an opportunity to make written representations before the transfer takes place and will be notified of the transfer and given reasons for it.

3.15 **Complaints** may be made either to the Director General of Fair Trading or direct to the relevant regulator. The principles relating to case-handling will apply as outlined above. Further, complaints alleging breach both of the prohibitions in the Act and of licence conditions (or equivalent) in sector-specific legislation in relation to the same subject matter would normally be considered by the regulator. Complainants should, however, make one complaint only, sent either to the Director General of Fair Trading or to a regulator, but not to both (but complaints about licence conditions only should continue to be sent direct to the regulator). Complainants will be told as soon as is practicable which authority is dealing with the case. They will also be notified of any subsequent changes. Submitting substantially the same complaint to a different authority will not lead to a re-examination of the complaint under the Act. Substantial new factual evidence (not known at the time of the original complaint) which subsequently comes to light should be submitted to the authority which dealt with the initial complaint. Further guidance on making a complaint and on confidentiality of information is available in the Competition Act guideline *The Major Provisions*.

3.16 Submissions that urgent **interim measures** are needed to prevent 'serious, irreparable damage' as a result of a breach of the prohibitions of the Act will be treated in the same way as complaints and the same comments apply. Further guidance on interim measures is given in the Competition Act guideline *Enforcement*.

[3043]

NOTES

1   The term "application" in the Regulations includes notifications for guidance or a decision under sections 13, 14, 21 or 22 of the Act and applications for an extension of the period for which an individual exemption has effect.

2   See: The Competition Act 1998 (Director's rules) Order 2000, Form N (OFT 409) and Guidance Notes on completing Form N (OFT 431) [at **[2025]**, **[3123]** respectively].

---

4   Regulators' other powers and duties

Statutory sectoral duties

4.1   The general duties of regulators are set out in the individual statutes listed in the table on page 2. In general, regulators must ensure that there is sufficient provision of the regulated service throughout the United Kingdom, must promote or facilitate competition, and must protect the interests of customers and consumers. The Act amends the statutes shown in the table so that, while regulators should continue to have regard to their sectoral duties when carrying out utility functions, they should not do so when exercising concurrent functions under the Act. Regulators may, however, have regard to matters covered by their sectoral duties provided they are matters to which the Director General of Fair Trading could have regard in exercising his powers under the Act.

Relationship with sector-specific legislation

4.2   In some circumstances, a particular agreement or practice may fall within the scope of a regulator's sector-specific legislation as well as within the prohibitions contained in the Act. Regulated companies may, for example, have licences which prevent them from showing undue preference to, or undue discrimination against, any class of persons: some types of price discrimination, for example, may also infringe the prohibition in Chapter II of the Act. Further details are given in the Competition Act guideline *The Chapter II Prohibition*.

4.3   In some circumstances, sector-specific legislation requires a regulator to enforce a licence condition; sometimes, however, it may be more effective or more efficient to use the powers available under the Act. The Act therefore amends the sector-specific legislation to provide that a regulator's duty to take licence enforcement action does not apply where he is satisfied that, in a particular case, it is more appropriate to proceed under the Act. If it appears during an investigation by a regulator using his sector-specific powers that action under the Act is more appropriate (or, as the case may be, under his sector-specific powers), the parties will be informed. Information gathered using sector-specific powers can be used for the purposes of an investigation under the Act or vice versa.

Exceptions for services of 'general economic interest'

4.4   In line with Article 86(2) (ex Article 90(2)) of the EC Treaty, the Act provides, in Schedule 3, an exclusion from the Chapter I and Chapter II prohibitions, whether applied by the Director General of Fair Trading or by a regulator—

— where an undertaking has either been entrusted with a service of 'general economic interest', or is a 'revenue-producing monopoly' (that is, an undertaking that has been granted monopoly powers by the state to raise money for the state); and

— insofar as the application of the prohibition in the Act would obstruct the performance of the particular task assigned to the undertaking.

4.5   The Director General of Fair Trading and the regulators will be required to apply these principles when applying the exclusion in Schedule 3.

4.6   The fact that the Act may not apply to certain activities of a regulated business in these circumstances does not, however, mean that regulators cannot apply their sectoral powers to those activities. Indeed it is precisely in these situations that the regulators' ability to ensure that services are available to consumers throughout the United Kingdom on reasonable terms by using their sector powers is particularly relevant.

The Fair Trading Act 1973

4.7   The competition law framework which deals with monopolies in the Fair Trading Act 1973 has been retained in addition to the Competition Act. This allows scale or complex monopolies to be examined by the Director General (which includes the regulators who have concurrent jurisdiction to exercise such powers under the Fair Trading Act) who may then make a reference to the Competition Commission for it to investigate whether a monopoly situation operates, or may be expected to operate, against the public interest. In general, a suspected infringement of one of the Competition Act prohibitions will normally be investigated under the Competition Act rather than the monopoly provisions of the Fair Trading Act.

4.8   The retained scale monopoly provisions in the Fair Trading Act are generally intended for dealing with a situation where a prior infringement of the prohibitions in the Competition Act has already been proven, but where the Director General believes that there is a real prospect of further abuse by the same company. However, because of the special circumstances of the utility sectors, and the difficulty of establishing competition, the full use of the scale monopoly provisions is retained for the regulated utility sectors. This means that the scale monopoly provisions may be used in respect of those sectors whether or not there has been a prior infringement of the prohibitions in the Competition Act.

4.9 Further details concerning these powers under the Fair Trading Act can be found in the Competition Act guideline *The Major Provisions*.

5 Confidentiality and disclosure of information

5.1 In the course of any investigation, the Director General of Fair Trading or the regulator will indicate the purposes for which any requested documents or information are required, and under which powers they are sought. Further information on the information-seeking powers is given in the Competition Act guideline *Powers of Investigation*.

5.2 The Act imposes limits on the disclosure of information obtained by the Director General of Fair Trading or a regulator under, or as a result of, Part I of the Act (see Competition Act guideline *The Major Provisions*). The Act does, however, allow for the disclosure of information in certain circumstances. These include, but are not limited to, where the disclosure is—

— made for the purpose of facilitating the performance by the Director General of Fair Trading or by the regulators of any of their functions under Part I of the Act;

— made for the purpose of facilitating the performance by the regulators (and certain other designated persons) of their functions under Part I of the Act, or sector-specific legislation (or certain other legislation listed in Schedule 11 of the Act);

— made with a view to the institution of civil proceedings under Part I of the Act or otherwise in connection with such proceedings;

— made for the purpose of facilitating the performance of any of the European Commission's functions in respect of Community competition law.

5.3 The Director General of Fair Trading or regulator must also have regard to the need for excluding (so far as is practicable) commercial information whose disclosure might significantly harm the legitimate business interests of the undertaking to which it relates and the extent to which disclosure is necessary for the purpose for which it is made. A similar obligation arises in relation to information relating to the private affairs of an individual whose disclosure might significantly harm his or her interests.

5.4 Where information obtained under the Act is used for sector-specific regulatory purposes, subsequent disclosure of the information is subject to the restrictions in the Act rather than the provisions of the sector-specific legislation: any such information passed to any other regulator will be subject to the same restrictions on disclosure as those applying to the Director General of Fair Trading or the regulator to whom the information was first given.

(Annexe 1 contains the Competition Act 1998 (Concurrency) Regulations 2000, SI 2000/260, which are reproduced at **[2005]**.*)*

ANNEXE 2

Terms of Reference for the Concurrency Working Party

A. Introduction

1 The Competition Act 1998 (the Act) is applied and enforced by the Director General of Fair Trading (DGFT) and, in relation to the regulated utility sectors, concurrently with the Director General of Telecommunications, the Directors General of Gas and Electricity Supply, the Directors General of Gas and Electricity Supply for Northern Ireland, the Director General of Water Services and the Rail Regulator (the Regulators).

2   The Concurrency Working Party (CWP) was formed in 1997. Membership consists of the DGFT and the Regulators named in paragraph 1 above, and includes the Independent Television Commission (ITC) and the Civil Aviation Authority (CAA) who sit as observers but do not have concurrent powers. The CWP is chaired by a representative of the Office of Fair Trading (OFT).

3   The aims of the CWP are—
   — To facilitate, to the greatest extent possible, a consistent approach by the Regulators and the DGFT to the exercise of their functions under the Act,
   — To consider the practical working arrangements between them,
   — To provide a vehicle for the discussion of matters of common interest, and the sharing of information where appropriate and where legally permitted, and
   — To co-ordinate the provision of advice and information on the Act to the public.

4   This document represents a commitment by the members of the CWP to work together to achieve the aims outlined. **It does not in any way fetter the discretion of the DGFT or the Regulators in the exercise of their functions under the Act.**

B. Legal requirements

5   It is desirable that powers under the Act should be exercised so as to ensure consistency of approach in casework. The Act itself imposes the following legal requirements.

Section 60: Consistency with EC law

6   So far as is possible, the DGFT and the Regulators are required by section 60 to deal with questions arising under Part I of the Act in relation to competition in a manner which is consistent with the treatment of corresponding questions under EC competition law.

Section 52: Provision of advice and information

7   The DGFT is required by section 52 of the Act to prepare and publish general advice and information about the application of the Chapter I and Chapter II prohibitions and their enforcement. In preparing such advice or information the DGFT is required to consult the Regulators. The Regulators can also provide advice or information under section 52 and must consult the DGFT and other Regulators when doing so.

Sections 55 and 56: Confidentiality requirements

8   The Act imposes certain restrictions on the disclosure of information obtained under or as a result of its provisions. The DGFT and the Regulators need to comply with these restrictions, as well as any common law duty of confidentiality to which they may be subject, and to take care in deciding the level of information which is disclosed between them, both when discussing policy issues and, in particular, individual cases.

9   Members of the CWP will need to be satisfied when disclosing information which was obtained under or as a result of any provision of Part I of the Act and which relates to the affairs of any living individual or to any particular business of an undertaking which is still being carried on, either that the requisite consents have been obtained under section 55(2) of the Act or that one of the gateways in section 55(3) applies.

10   Members of the CWP will also need to ensure that they have regard to the matters in section 56 of the Act, in particular, the extent to which disclosure of the information is necessary for the purpose for which it is proposed to make the disclosure.

The Competition Act 1998 (Concurrency) Regulations 2000 (the Regulations)

11   The Regulations contain provisions for the co-ordination of the performance of concurrent functions under the Act by the DGFT and the Regulators. In particular, the Regulations require the DGFT and the Regulators—
   — to agree who shall exercise prescribed functions in relation to a case,
   — to refer the case to the Secretary of State, where agreement cannot be reached, in order that he may determine the matter,
   — to agree when they wish to transfer a case between each other.

C. Areas of co-operation

12   The DGFT and the Regulators believe that the CWP is a means of facilitating compliance with the requirements of the Act and to meet the common objective of achieving, as far as

possible, a consistent approach to casework. The DGFT and the Regulators recognise that there are benefits to be derived from co-operation and consistency of approach, where possible, in administering a new legal framework.

Determining who shall exercise jurisdiction on a case

13 The Regulations anticipate co-operation between the DGFT and the Regulators in determining who should exercise jurisdiction. It is not practical for the CWP to deal with day to day administrative matters. Appropriate procedures will be agreed to ensure compliance with the Regulations and facilitate efficient case handling, eg by identifying relevant contacts to ensure there will be no undue delays in processing cases, agreeing timetables for action where appropriate, and providing for written confirmation where a case is transferred under the Regulations.

14 Notifications for guidance or a decision are received by OFT who will identify issues of concurrent jurisdiction. Any Regulator receiving a complaint or initiating an investigation will have responsibility for identifying such issues and contacting OFT and any other Regulator who may have concurrent jurisdiction.

15 A case will be dealt with by whichever of the DGFT or the relevant Regulator(s) is better, or best, placed to do so. In general, an agreement or conduct which falls within the industry sector of a Regulator will be dealt with by that Regulator, although in some cases DGFT will deal with such a case. The factors to be taken into account in reaching that decision include—

— the sectoral knowledge of a Regulator,
— whether the case affects more than one regulatory sector (for these purposes gas and electricity are considered to be one regulatory sector),
— any previous contacts between the parties or complainants and a Regulator, or with OFT,
— any recent experience in dealing with any of the undertakings or similar issues which may be involved in the proceedings.

16 Discussions will take place initially between OFT and the relevant Regulator(s) with a view to determining who has jurisdiction on a case and who shall exercise it. Such agreements will be confirmed in writing between OFT and the relevant Regulator(s). Where agreement cannot be reached between OFT and the relevant Regulator(s) the CWP will have an advisory role in assisting them to agree the matter amongst themselves.

Information sharing

17 The CWP will share information with regard to general policy and precedent relating to the application and interpretation of the Act in order to facilitate a consistency of approach and compliance with section 60. At the monthly CWP meeting OFT and each Regulator will provide wherever possible and in an appropriate form, having regard to any legal restrictions on disclosure, a brief summary of policy issues arising from current cases. Where a case raises new issues of general policy or of precedent in respect of the application or interpretation of the Act, the CWP member who is dealing with the case will endeavour to bring these issues to the attention of the CWP for discussion before they are decided. Where a case has been decided the CWP may wish to discuss any issues of common interest arising from the case.

18 OFT will produce an internal monthly bulletin which includes decisions on relevant UK cases, European Commission and Court cases, references to articles and publications of note, knowledge of which will assist consistency and compliance with section 60 of the Act. Members of the CWP may contribute to the bulletin and issues arising may be discussed at CWP meetings.

19 Internal case-handling procedures of OFT and the Regulators will be influenced by caseloads and the resources available. However, information relating to procedures will be shared and common procedures may be used where that is considered appropriate.

20 OFT and the Regulators have between them considerable knowledge, experience, and expertise across a wide range of sectors and this should be shared where appropriate and possible. The particular sectoral knowledge of the ITC and the CAA is noted in this respect.

21 Members of the CWP may at their discretion identify relevant cases that raise issues which could be usefully shared with the CWP, eg the reasons why a Regulator has dealt with a case under licensing provisions rather than under the CA98.

General advice and information

22   A consistent approach is desirable in respect of general advice or information which is published by the DGFT or a Regulator.

23   In the case of general advice or information which falls under section 52, consultation amongst the DGFT and the Regulators will take place through the CWP. The text will be circulated for discussion at a CWP meeting and comments invited. The DGFT and the Regulators will aim to reach agreement on the text of such advice or information prior to publication.

24   What constitutes advice or information falling under section 52 will need to be determined on a case by case basis but will normally include—

— The series of guidelines which have been produced by the DGFT and the Regulators. The form and content of these were agreed by the CWP prior to publication. It will be necessary to revise the existing guidelines in due course and to devise new ones. These will also fall under section 52,

— Additional advice produced by the DGFT or the Regulators in the form of guidance booklets or leaflets which deal generally with the application or enforcement of the Act,

— Publications which make a new statement about the application or enforcement of the Act, eg about a development in EC case law, or which deviate from advice or information which has already been published.

25   Where the DGFT or a Regulator is preparing a new publication which includes general advice or information which has previously been published (eg as part of one of the guidelines) this will not fall under section 52. However, the CWP should, so far as is practicable, be invited to comment on the draft. It would be helpful in such cases if the CWP could be made aware in advance of the thinking behind the publication, its target audience, and the likely messages in any documentation. In the case of general advice and information which falls outside section 52, consideration should be given as to whether it would be appropriate to refer the matter to a CWP meeting for discussion.

26   The time agreed for comment needs to allow for the complexity of the matter, the length of the document, and the timescales for publication. Before the document is circulated it should be checked for consistency with the guidelines and specific areas highlighted where comments might be appropriate with reasons given as to why this is the case. In the case of general advice or information which falls outside section 52, consideration should be given as to whether it would be appropriate to refer the matter to a CWP meeting for discussion.

Working arrangements

27   The CWP will normally meet every month and, to aid efficient handling of business, attendance will generally be limited to one or two persons from each authority. There will be flexibility to ensure that additional meetings to deal with specific issues can be called at short notice where necessary. Ad hoc groups can be formed where appropriate.

28   Co-operation on training programmes is desirable to aid liaison and to make effective use of resources. Common training needs may be identified and proposals made to address them, where appropriate. In principle members will aim to make any relevant in-house training they develop available to each other's staff.

29   The use by the DGFT or a Regulator of the staff of another Regulator or the DGFT is provided for in the Regulations and is supported as an aid to effective case-handling through shared knowledge and expertise, eg to assist the carrying out of on-site investigations.

30   Common performance targets for handling notifications, complaints, and enquiries will be agreed in the light of experience where possible. Any proposed changes will be discussed by the CWP. Publication of targets is at the discretion of the individual members of the CWP.

PART III
OFT GUIDELINES

TRANSITIONAL ARRANGEMENTS

(OFT 406, March 1999)

1 Introduction

1.1 Provisions for the transition from existing competition legislation to the Competition Act 1998 (**'the Act'**) are set out in Schedule 13 to the Act. The purpose of this guideline is to explain the effect that the transitional arrangements now in place will have on agreements prior to the introduction of the Chapter I prohibition.

1.2 There are no transitional periods available in respect of the Chapter II prohibition. It will apply to the behaviour of dominant undertakings immediately from the starting date.

1.3 The transitional arrangements in Schedule 13 are intended to allow businesses a reasonable time to modify their agreements and practices in order to comply with the new regime under the Act. Consequently, following enactment of the Act on 9 November 1998 (**'the enactment date'**), there is a period of approximately sixteen months (**'the interim period'**) before the Chapter I and Chapter II prohibitions come into force on 1 March 2000 (**'the starting date'**).

1.4 In addition, most agreements made prior to the starting date which comply with existing laws will benefit from certain further concessionary periods of transition during which the Chapter I prohibition will not apply (**'transitional periods'**). In most cases, these transitional periods will run from the starting date and last one or five years (they should not be confused with the interim period, which ends immediately before the starting date). For agreements made in the interim period, it is possible to obtain guidance prior to the starting date on the forthcoming application of the Chapter I prohibition (**'early guidance'**).

1.5 The Restrictive Trade Practices Act 1976 and the Resale Prices Act 1976 will be repealed as from the starting date. For agreements in existence prior to that, those Acts continue to apply until their repeal at that time. However, in order to allow undertakings to concentrate on preparing themselves for the new regime, the Restrictive Trade Practices Act now operates in modified form as regards agreements made in the interim period. In particular, all agreements that are subject to registration under the Restrictive Trade Practices Act, except those that involve price-fixing, are non-notifiable, and there will be no need to furnish particulars of them to the Director General of Fair Trading.

1.6 There are two key points to be taken into account when considering the application of the transitional arrangements to potentially anti-competitive agreements—

— the first is to keep in mind the date on which the agreement is made—prior to the enactment date (on or before 8 November 1998), during the interim period (9 November 1998 to 29 February 2000, both dates inclusive), or on or after the starting date (from 1 March 2000);

— the second is to distinguish between the continuing application of existing legislation on one hand, and the application of the new legislation on the other.

1.7 The table on page 4 of this guideline summarises the transitional provisions on the basis of these two key considerations—it shows, by reference to the time when agreements are made, both the continuing application of the Restrictive Trade Practices Act in the interim period and the introduction of the Chapter I prohibition. It should be noted that the table does not purport to be a comprehensive illustration of all of the transitional provisions, but rather is intended to set out the main elements relevant in the case of most agreements. It should be used in conjunction with the rest of this guideline and Schedule 13 itself.

1.8   The application of existing competition legislation to agreements made prior to the starting date is explained in part 2 of this guideline, and the procedure for early guidance on the application of the new legislation is dealt with in part 3. The operation of the transitional periods and related procedures are explained in parts 4 and 5.

1.9   Schedule 13 makes further provision for Restrictive Practices Court proceedings undetermined at the starting date, Restrictive Practices Court orders and the public register of restrictive trading agreements. This is dealt with in parts 6 and 7. It also provides for the treatment after the starting date of various matters under the Fair Trading Act 1973 and the Competition Act 1980, including continuing investigations, orders and undertakings, as explained in part 8. Part 9 deals with the introduction of the Chapter II prohibition.

1.10 The Director General of Fair Trading exercises his powers under Schedule 13 relating to the Chapter I prohibition concurrently with the regulators in respect of sectoral matters, as explained in part 10. References to the Director General in this guideline and to the Director in the relevant provisions of the Schedule are to be taken to include references to the regulators for those purposes.

1.11 Much of Schedule 13 is concerned with agreements. In the case of provisions of the Schedule relating to the operation of the Chapter I prohibition, the term **'agreement'** includes decisions of associations of undertakings and concerted practices.[1] Where provisions are concerned with the operation of the Restrictive Trade Practices Act or the Resale Prices Act, the meaning of the term under that legislation applies.

1.12 Finally, it should be noted that a number of provisions in Part I of the Act are applied to Schedule 13, including those relating to legal professional privilege, provision of false or misleading information, and disclosure of information.[2]

Application of the Restrictive Practices Act (RTPA)

Agreements		◄— **Interim period** —►	**Starting date**
		┌─ **Enactment date**	┌─ **Starting date**
Made prior to the enactment date	RTPA continues to operate as before, until its repeal (variations remain notifiable)		RTPA repealed on the starting date, but continuation of— ■ Pre-repeal voidness ■ Pre-repeal rights for breach of statutory duty
Made in the interim period		RTPA applies but— ■ All agreements except price-fixing non-notifiable ■ The Director General of Fair Trading's duty to refer to RPC replaced by discretion ■ S 21(2) directions not possible	■ Certain undetermined RPC applications ■ RTPA register (but only added to or varied in limited circumstances)
Made after the starting date			No RTPA

Application of Chapter I

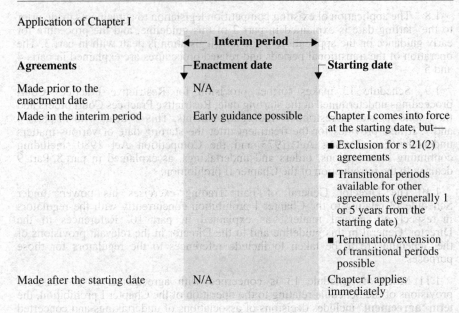

Agreements	Interim period	
	Enactment date	**Starting date**
Made prior to the enactment date	N/A	
Made in the interim period	Early guidance possible	Chapter I comes into force at the starting date, but—
		■ Exclusion for s 21(2) agreements
		■ Transitional periods available for other agreements (generally 1 or 5 years from the starting date)
		■ Termination/extension of transitional periods possible
Made after the starting date	N/A	Chapter I applies immediately

[3047]

NOTES
¹ Schedule 13, paragraph 1(3).
² Schedule 13, paragraph 1(2).

2 Transition from the Restrictive Trade Practices Act 1976 and the Resale Prices Act 1976

2.1 The application of existing competition legislation under the Restrictive Trade Practices Act and the Resale Prices Act is determined by whether the agreement in question was made prior to the enactment date, or is made in the interim period. At the starting date the Restrictive Trade Practices Act and the Resale Prices Act will be repealed by order of the Secretary of State bringing into force the relevant parts of section 1 of the Competition Act. They will not apply at all to agreements made on or after the starting date. Instead, the prohibition in Chapter I will apply immediately to such agreements.

Agreements made prior to the enactment date

2.2 For agreements made prior to the enactment date (that is on or before 8 November 1998), the Restrictive Trade Practices Act continues to operate as it did prior to the enactment date up until its repeal at the starting date. Particulars of pre-enactment date agreements which are registrable and which do not benefit from the non-notifiable derogation under the Restrictive Trade Practices Act should be duly furnished to the Director General of Fair Trading as required by that Act. The normal time limits for notification set out in Schedule 2 to the Restrictive Trade Practices Act (in most cases three months from the date of the making of the agreement) continue to apply. This still applies to agreements made in the last three months before the enactment date. That the deadline for furnishing falls after the enactment date does not mean that such agreements benefit from the non-notifiability rules outlined in paragraph 2.5 below. It is the date on which the agreement is made that determines whether the new rules on non-notifiability apply.

2.3   Likewise, variations to pre-enactment date agreements which are registrable and not non-notifiable should continue to be furnished as normal in accordance with sections 24 and 27 of the Restrictive Trade Practices Act, and regulation 5 of the Registration of Restrictive Trading Agreements Regulations 1984. This includes variations to these agreements which are made in the interim period, as well as variations made prior to the enactment date.

2.4   Parties to agreements made before the enactment date where the deadline for furnishing particulars falls after that date (that is agreements made less than three months before the enactment date, and any variations to pre-enactment date agreements) should be aware that the Director General of Fair Trading will not extend the time limits for furnishing other than in the most exceptional circumstances.

Agreements made in the Interim Period

Non-notifiable agreements

2.5   In respect of agreements made in the interim period (9 November 1998 to 29 February 2000, both dates inclusive), the Restrictive Trade Practices Act continues to apply. The only agreements which remain notifiable, however, are registrable agreements in which one of the relevant restrictions or information provisions relates to price—that is price-fixing agreements within the meaning of section 27A(3) of the Restrictive Trade Practices Act (which definition encompasses an agreement only one party to which accepts a price restriction).[1] All other agreements will be non-notifiable under the Restrictive Trade Practices Act. This concession is intended to assist undertakings in readying themselves for compliance with the new regime. It is not a moratorium on the pursuit of anti-competitive agreements. The Director General of Fair Trading intends to keep an active watch for anti-competitive agreements during the interim period and will not hesitate to call in agreements for competition scrutiny under his powers in section 36 of the Restrictive Trade Practices Act if necessary. The Director General of Fair Trading also has discretion to institute Restrictive Practices Court proceedings up to the starting date[2] and in urgent cases interim orders to restrain parties from giving effect to anti-competitive agreements may be obtained from the Court (see paragraph 6.2 below).

Notifiable agreements

2.6   For any agreements made in the interim period that remain notifiable under the Restrictive Trade Practices Act, the rules laid down in that Act on the time limits for notification and related conditions continue to apply (in particular, section 27ZA on the non-operation of restrictions prior to furnishing). The Director General of Fair Trading no longer has the power to extend the time limits for furnishing particulars of such agreements, however,[3] and there is therefore no possibility of the parties obtaining an extension. As with non-notifiable agreements, the Director General of Fair Trading still has discretion to institute proceedings in the Restrictive Practices Court.

2.7   Variations made in the interim period to pre-enactment date agreements continue to be notifiable as they were prior to the enactment date—see paragraph 2.3 above.

2.8   It is possible to apply for early guidance on the compatibility of agreements made in the interim period with the Chapter I prohibition, as explained in part 3 below.

Particulars with a deadline for furnishing which would fall after the starting date

2.9 Finally, special rules apply where the deadline for furnishing particulars of agreements or variations would fall on or after the starting date.[4] These rules will apply to the small category of interim period agreements that are still notifiable (because they are price-fixing agreements) and which are made in the final three months before the starting date. They will also apply to any variations made in those three months which are still notifiable—both variations to the small category of interim period price-fixing agreements themselves, and interim period variations to pre-enactment date agreements (which continue to require furnishing as they did before—see paragraph 2.3 above). The rules are as follows—

— parties will not have to furnish particulars of these types of agreement or variations; neither voidness of the relevant restrictions nor third party liability will arise if the particulars are not furnished, provided that the parties do not give effect to the restrictions (that is they do not breach section 27ZA of the Restrictive Trade Practices Act) prior to the starting date. However, the agreement concerned will not receive the benefit of a transitional period if particulars are not furnished[5] (see paragraph 4.1 below);

— parties who do choose to furnish particulars should do so before the starting date. This will make the agreement concerned eligible for a one year transitional period (see paragraph 4.1 below). Again, the parties must not give effect to the restrictions prior to furnishing.

2.10 The day before the starting date will therefore be the last possible day on which particulars can be furnished under the Restrictive Trade Practices Act.

[3048]

NOTES
1   Schedule 13, paragraph 5.
2   Schedule 13, paragraph 6(a).
3   Schedule 13, paragraph 6(c).
4   Schedule 13, paragraph 25.
5   Schedule 13, paragraph 20(2).

3 Early guidance on the Chapter I Prohibition

3.1 When entering into agreements in the interim period, undertakings should consider carefully whether they are likely to comply with the Chapter I prohibition. Parties to agreements made in the interim period also have the option of applying to the Director General of Fair Trading (in the first instance) for early guidance as to whether the agreement is likely to infringe the Chapter I prohibition when it comes into force and, if so, whether exemption is likely.[1]

3.2 As with the notification of agreements for guidance or a decision under the full procedures which will apply after the starting date, applications for early guidance are optional. The Government intends that the Chapter I prohibition will not apply to most types of vertical and land agreements (by virtue of orders made under section 50 of the Act), so in most cases there will be no need to notify such agreements. It is also unnecessary to notify an agreement unless there are grounds for believing that it has as its object or effect an appreciable restriction on competition caught by the prohibition (further detail is given in the Competition Act guideline *The Chapter I Prohibition*). There may, nevertheless, be cases where parties wish to obtain advance comfort that an existing agreement is unlikely to infringe the Chapter I prohibition or would be likely to qualify for exemption, in which case the early guidance procedure is available.

3.3 Early guidance is possible only for agreements made in the interim period (9 November 1998 to 29 February 2000, both dates inclusive); agreements made before the enactment date may not be notified until after the starting date, when the full procedures for notification come into force.

3.4 The *Director General of Fair Trading's Procedural Rules*, setting out the procedure for notifications, will apply only after the starting date to notifications under sections 13 and 14 of the Act (under section 51 of the Act a period of consultation is required after the enactment date before the Rules can come into force). In order to provide the necessary procedure for early guidance applications, the Director General of Fair Trading has therefore given early guidance directions (for further information see *Early Guidance Directions*).

3.5 Applications for early guidance must be made on Form EG, in accordance with the notes attached to that form and with the procedures laid down in the *Early Guidance Directions*. Form EG should be used for all applications made before the starting date. The only applications that it will be possible to make before the starting date are those for early guidance. Applications for a decision cannot be made until after the starting date. No early guidance is available on the Chapter II prohibition.

3.6 Any early guidance given is to have the same effect on and after the starting date as guidance given under section 15 of the Act. After the starting date, favourable early guidance will be binding on the Director General and will provide immunity from financial penalties to the same extent as guidance given under section 15. Applications for early guidance still being considered by the Director General at the starting date will then be treated by him as if they had properly been made under section 13, so applicants in such cases will have the benefit of provisional immunity from penalties until the application is determined by the Director General.

[3049]

NOTES
¹ Schedule 13, paragraph 7.

4   Introduction of the Chapter I Prohibition (the transitional periods)

The time from which Chapter I will apply

4.1 For agreements made before the starting date, there will be a number of transitional periods provided during which the Chapter I prohibition will not apply. The following transitional periods will be available—

(a) the general rule is that all agreements not falling within (**b**) to (**f**) below will receive a one year transitional period.[1] In practice, the two main examples of agreement benefiting from this one year transitional period will be non-notifiable agreements made during the interim period, and agreements made prior to the enactment date to which the Restrictive Trade Practices Act did not apply;

(b) agreements will receive no transitional period to the extent to which, immediately before the starting date, under the Restrictive Trade Practices Act they are void or subject to a restraining order, or a person has unlawfully given effect to restrictions prior to furnishing particulars of an agreement or variations. Similarly, agreements receive no transitional period to the extent to which, immediately before the starting date, they are unlawful or void under the Resale Prices Act;[2]

(c) agreements and variations in the small category where the deadline for furnishing particulars under the Restrictive Trade Practices Act falls after the starting date, but particulars are not furnished by that date, will receive no transitional period[3] (see paragraph 2.9 above);

(d) agreements will receive a five year transitional period to the extent to which, immediately before the starting date, they have been found not to be contrary to the public interest by the Restrictive Practices Court[4] or relate to goods which fall within the scope of an exemption order under section 14 of the Resale Prices Act;[5]

(e) in the special case of certain agreements which have been subject to scrutiny under the Financial Services Act 1986 or the Broadcasting Act 1990, there will be a five year transitional period;[6]

(f) certain agreements in the electricity, gas and railway industries will receive transitional periods of up to five years, as explained in paragraph 4.8 below.

4.2   In addition, agreements which, immediately before the starting date, benefit from a section 21(2) Restrictive Trade Practices Act direction will be excluded from the Chapter I prohibition for their duration.[7] This exclusion will be available for many agreements made prior to the enactment date. The exclusion and the circumstances where its benefit will be lost are explained further in paragraphs 4.13 to 4.16 and 5.6 to 5.12 below.

4.3   Except in the limited case of certain utilities agreements explained in paragraph 4.8 below, there will be no transitional period available for agreements made after the starting date: the Chapter I prohibition has immediate effect.

The operation of the transitional periods

4.4   Generally, transitional periods will begin on the starting date.[8] There are two exceptions to this rule: first, for certain agreements relating to the utilities (see paragraphs 4.8 to 4.12 below) and, secondly, for agreements subject to certain Restrictive Practices Court proceedings continuing after the starting date (see paragraphs 6.3 to 6.8 below). In the case of these latter agreements, any transitional period available will begin when the proceedings end.[9] This is important, as the outcome of continuing proceedings may affect the transitional period applicable to the agreement. For example, to the extent to which an agreement as found by the Restrictive Practices Court in continuing proceedings not to be contrary to the public interest, it would receive a five year transitional period,[10] starting from the end of those proceedings. Conversely, to the extent to which an agreement was found to be contrary to the public interest, it would receive no transitional period,[11] and would instead be immediately subject to the Chapter I prohibition at the conclusion of the proceedings.

4.5   The Chapter I prohibition will not apply **'to the extent to which'** a transitional period is available.[12] Similarly, a number of the transitional periods set out in paragraph 4.1 above will apply 'to the extent to which' an agreement meets the relevant criteria. Therefore a particular transitional period may apply only to certain provisions of an agreement rather than its entirety. Consequently, it will be possible for some provisions in an agreement to benefit from transitional periods of different lengths from others. For example, those provisions of an agreement made before the enactment date and duly notified within the time limits under the Restrictive Trade Practices Act which were found by the Restrictive Practices Court not to be contrary to the public interest would receive a five year transitional period, whereas the rest of the agreement would receive a one year transitional period.

4.6   Where an agreement is only partly covered by a transitional period and the Director General has competition concerns about the provisions not covered, he will still be able to have regard to the whole agreement in order to assess whether the Chapter I prohibition has been breached[13] (rather than assess only the provisions not covered by a transitional period in an artificial vacuum which does not take account of the surrounding circumstances). However, in the event of an infringement finding, those provisions benefiting from a transitional period will not be prohibited or subject to the consequences of infringement for the duration of that period.

4.7   Further procedures for agreements benefiting from a transitional period are explained in part 5 below.

Utilities agreements

4.8   Schedule 13 provides further transitional periods for particular agreements in the electricity, gas and railway industries.[14] In summary, the existing arrangements under the Restrictive Trade Practices Act will be retained for a further five years from the starting date, in that agreements currently exempt from the application of the Restrictive Trade Practices Act and similar future agreements will benefit from transitional periods excluding them from the Chapter I prohibition during that period. The operation of the transitional provisions relating to utilities agreements is explained below. The relevant regulators will issue further, sector-specific advice in due course if the need arises.[15]

4.9   There are three categories of agreement that will benefit from sector-specific transitional periods in the electricity and gas sectors—

— agreements to which, immediately before the starting date, the Restrictive Trade Practices Act does not apply by virtue of the section 100 of the Electricity Act 1989 or section 62 of the Gas Act 1986 respectively or orders made thereunder. These will receive a five year transitional period running from the starting date;

— agreements made during the five year period beginning at the starting date which are of a type such that, even if the Restrictive Trade Practices Act had not been repealed, it would not have applied to them (because they would have been like those agreements in the category above), and agreements, whether made before or after the starting date, that are varied to become of that type in the five year period. These will receive a transitional period applying from the date that the agreement or variation is made and for the remaining part of the five year period;

— agreements of a description specified in a transitional order by the Secretary of State. These will receive a transitional period beginning at such time as is specified in the order and, again, applying for the remaining part of the five year period beginning at the starting date.

4.10   The benefit of these transitional periods will be lost if the agreement is varied in such a way that it ceases to be one to which the Restrictive Trade Practices Act would not have applied or one to which a transitional order applies.

4.11   There are two categories of agreement which will benefit from sector-specific transitional periods in the railway sector—

— as with the gas and electricity sectors, there will be a five year transitional period beginning at the starting date for agreements to which, immediately before the starting date, the Restrictive Trade Practices Act does not apply by virtue of section 131 of the Railways Act 1993 and directions made thereunder;

— other rail sector agreements (whether made before or after the starting date) will receive a five year transitional period taken to have begun at the starting date, to the extent to which they are required or approved under the Railways Act 1993 in that period.

4.12 Any variation of an agreement falling within the first category in paragraph 4.9 above during the five year period is to be treated as falling within the second category. It should be noted as regards railway agreements that, whereas disapplication of the Restrictive Trade Practices Act to an agreement under section 131(1) of the Railways Act (which would put the agreement in the first category) is available only if all of the provisions in the agreement are required or approved, under the second category, transitional periods will be available for individual provisions of agreements. This will include provisions in agreements made prior to the starting date even though those agreements did not previously benefit from disapplication of the Restrictive Trade Practices Act because not all of their provisions met the criteria in section 131(1) of the Railways Act (this is the effect of the wording 'to the extent to which'—see paragraph 4.5).

Section 21(2) of the Restrictive Trade Practices Act

4.13 Section 3 of the Competition Act provides for a number of exclusions from the Chapter I prohibition, one of which is of particular relevance in the context of the transitional arrangements: the exclusion for agreements benefiting from directions by the Secretary of State under section 21(2) of the Restrictive Trade Practices Act that the restrictions or information provisions they contain are not of such significance as to call for investigation by the Restrictive Practices Court. This is an important category of agreements; the majority of agreements made prior to the enactment date which have been furnished to the Director General under the Restrictive Trade Practices Act have the benefit of section 21(2) directions and will generally not be of concern under the new regime.

4.14 Consequently, all agreements which, immediately before the starting date, benefit from a direction under section 21(2) will be excluded from the Chapter I prohibition for their duration.[16] It should, however, be noted that it will not be possible to obtain section 21(2) directions for any agreement made on or after the enactment date, so the exclusion is available only for agreements made prior to 9 November 1998.[17]

4.15 Where particulars of subsequent variations to an agreement which has the benefit of section 21(2) directions have been duly furnished and the Secretary of State has not withdrawn the section 21(2) directions, the exclusion will cover the agreement as varied. This is the case for variations made in the interim period to pre-enactment date agreements (which remain notifiable as before) as well as variations furnished prior to the enactment date.

4.16 The Director General will have the power to clawback the exclusion, as explained in paragraphs 5.6 to 5.12 below. In addition, the benefit of this exclusion from the Chapter I prohibition is lost if, after the starting date, there is a **'material variation'** to such an agreement.[18] The criterion of whether or not an agreement is varied in a 'material' manner is intended to allow parties flexibility to alter their day-to-day arrangements but without permitting the addition or extension of provisions that might be appreciably restrictive of competition. The Director General will consider variations to be material for the purposes of this provision only if the agreement then has an appreciable effect on competition within the meaning of the Chapter I prohibition. In the case of a typical commercial agreement, therefore, minor adjustments to the parties' trading relationship—such as a change in delivery dates, mode of transportation, credit terms or manner of payment—would not be caught by the test. On the other hand, variations to such an agreement involving the conversion of a joint marketing area into partitioned markets, or the addition of a significant competitor as a party to the agreement, are likely to be considered material.

NOTES

1   Schedule 13, paragraph 19.
2   Schedule 13, paragraph 20(1) to 20(2).
3   Schedule 13, paragraph 20(3).
4   Schedule 13, paragraph 23(1).
5   Schedule 13, paragraph 24(1).
6   Schedule 13, paragraph 26.
7   Schedule 3, paragraph 2.
8   Schedule 13, paragraph 19(1).
9   Schedule 13, paragraphs 21–22.
10 Schedule 13, paragraph 23(3).
11 Schedule 13, paragraph 20(3).
12 Schedule 13, paragraph 19(2).
13 Schedule 13, paragraph 1(5).
14 Schedule 13, paragraph 27–34.
15 Schedule 13, paragraph 3 and 35.
16 Schedule 3, paragraph 2(1).
17 Schedule 13, paragraph 6(b).
18 Schedule 3, paragraph 2(2).

5   Transitional procedures

5.1   This part deals with procedures applicable to agreements benefiting from a transitional period.

Extension of transitional periods

5.2   The Director General will be able to extend transitional periods either on application by one of the parties to the agreement or on his own initiative.[1] In respect of one year transitional periods, the Director General of Fair Trading may grant a single extension of up to one year. In respect of transitional periods of other lengths (usually five years), the Director General may grant a single extension of up to six months.

5.3   Applicants for an extension should apply to the Director General of Fair Trading (in the first instance) in writing not less than three months before the end of the transitional period, enclosing the agreement and other relevant information, as required by the *Director General of Fair Trading's Procedural Rules*. As set out in the Rules, the Director General must give written notice to the applicant of his decision on the application within two months of the effective date of the application. If he refuses the application there should therefore be at least one month before the transitional period expires for the parties to apply for guidance or a decision under Chapter I if that is necessary. If, however, the Director General has not informed the applicant to the contrary within two months following the effective date of the application, then the transitional period will be extended by the maximum permitted period or, if shorter, the period of extension applied for.

5.4   The Director General will not grant extensions as a matter of course. He is likely to grant them only where—

— it appears from the information provided that the agreement may infringe the Chapter I prohibition if it were not for the transitional period, but not seriously infringe it; and

— there are good reasons why an extension is required—for example, the agreement is being re-negotiated, the agreement is due to expire shortly after the end of the unextended transitional period, or the parties have a legitimate need for more time to prepare a notification.

5.5   Agreements involving what would be serious infringements of the Chapter I prohibition (for example, price-fixing or market-sharing) which would be unlikely to be granted an exemption, or which would only be exemptible with conditions, will not be granted an extension.

Termination of transitional periods

5.6   The transitional periods are intended to assist business in adjusting to the new regime, not as a means for seriously anti-competitive behaviour to escape competition scrutiny. The Director General of Fair Trading therefore plans to keep under review the operation of agreements benefiting from transitional periods and has clawback powers in relation to such agreements. As explained below, he will be able to require parties to provide information about an agreement subject to a transitional period and to terminate transitional periods early.[2] The *Director General of Fair Trading's Procedural Rules* set out the procedural requirements for the termination of transitional periods in addition to those in Schedule 13.

5.7   In order to reach a view about the possible exercise of his power to withdraw the benefit of a transitional period, the Director General has power to require information from parties in connection with an agreement the subject of a transitional period. Failure to provide the information required within the time limit specified in the *Director General of Fair Trading's Procedural Rules* without reasonable excuse may in itself result in the Director General giving a direction to terminate the transitional period.

5.8   The Director General will also be able to give a direction terminating the transitional period if he considers the agreement would infringe the Chapter I prohibition and that he would be unlikely to grant it an unconditional exemption. A direction must be given by notice in writing to the parties not less than 28 days before it is to have effect. The Director General will consider any representations made by the parties during the notice period. A direction may be revoked prior to it taking effect, either by the Director General or by the Secretary of State.

5.9   Where parties to an agreement have received notice from the Director General of a direction to terminate the transitional period, it will still be possible for them to make an application for an exemption (see paragraphs 5.13–5.15 below).

5.10   The Director General is likely to exercise his power of clawback where he is concerned that an agreement may be having an appreciable effect on competition, such that it is appropriate for him to review it under the Chapter I prohibition immediately rather than wait for the transitional period to run its course. He will consider carefully complaints from third parties in respect of agreements subject to transitional periods.

5.11   The above powers do not apply in relation to transitional periods for provisions in agreements relating to goods which immediately before the starting date fall within the scope of an exemption order under section 14 of the Resale Prices Act.[3]

5.12   The Director General has equivalent information-gathering and clawback powers in respect of agreements benefiting from a direction under section 21(2) of the Restrictive Trade Practices Act and consequently excluded from the Chapter I prohibition.[4] The *Director General of Fair Trading's Procedural Rules* set out the procedural requirements for the exercise of his powers to withdraw the section 21(2) and other exclusions.

Applications for guidance or a decision

5.13   On the starting date, the full notification procedures under the Act will come into force, replacing the early guidance procedure which applies in the interim period. Parties to agreements benefiting from a transitional period will be able to notify the agreement under section 13 of the Act during the currency of the transitional period for guidance as to whether the agreement is likely to infringe the Chapter I prohibition when the transitional period ends, and, if so, whether exemption is likely.[5] Notification for a decision, including a request for an individual exemption, where the transitional period in respect of the agreement in question has been terminated, may be made under section 14. Notification must be made in accordance with the ***Director General of Fair Trading's Procedural Rules***, but should not be made if the agreement does not have an appreciable effect on competition.

5.14 Parties should also bear in mind that where an agreement is also subject to Article 85 of the EC Treaty,[6] there will be many cases where notification under Article 85 is more advantageous to them than notification under Chapter I. For advice on the effect of parallel exemptions under section 10 of the Act, EC notifications, EC comfort letters and the treatment of dual notifications, see the Competition Act guideline ***The Chapter I Prohibition***. The Director General considers that the European Commission is the more appropriate authority to whom notification should be made if the agreement is caught by Article 85.

5.15 Parties who do decide to notify should indicate in paragraph 11 in part 2 of Form N the duration of any transitional period they consider relevant by reference to schedule 13.

[3051]

NOTES

1   Schedule 13, paragraph 36.
2   Schedule 13, paragraphs 37–39.
3   Schedule 13, paragraph 39(5).
4   Schedule 3, paragraph 2(3)–(9).
5   Subject to any modifications made by Regulations made by the Secretary of State under paragraph 19 of Schedule 13 to the Act.
6   [Now] renumbered Article 81 following ratification of the Treaty of Amsterdam.

---

6   Restrictive Practices Court orders and proceedings

Court orders of the Restrictive Practices Court

6.1   During the interim period orders of the Restrictive Practices Court under the Restrictive Trade Practices Act and the Resale Prices Act will remain in force and parties should continue to comply with them. From the starting date, however, most orders of the Court will cease to have effect.[1] This includes in particular restraining orders under sections 2(2) and 35(3) of the Restrictive Trade Practices Act (and undertakings *in lieu* of those orders). Nevertheless, orders in existence before the starting date will remain important because—

— breach of orders committed before the starting date will still constitute contempt of court and the Director General of Fair Trading may take action accordingly. The possibility of taking action for contempt will not lapse at the starting date;

— parties to private actions for breach of statutory duty brought after the starting date will be able to rely, under section 35(7) of the Restrictive Trade Practices Act, on issues of fact and law determined in proceedings brought by the Director General of Fair Trading for a section 35(3) order.[2]

6.2   A significant exception to the general rule that Court orders cease to have effect on the starting date relates to interim orders under section 3 of the Restrictive Trade Practices Act, which remain relevant in the context of agreements subject to continuing proceedings. As explained in paragraph 6.6 below, such agreements are not subject to the Chapter I prohibition while the proceedings continue; instead, the Restrictive Trade Practices Act is deemed to continue to apply. The continuing application of interim orders is therefore necessary to prevent the operation of seriously anti-competitive agreements which are the subject of continuing proceedings. With this aim, interim orders do not cease to have effect on the starting date. In addition, applications for interim orders made but not determined at the starting date will remain effective after that date. It will also be possible to make applications for interim orders on or after the starting date in relation to continuing proceedings under section 1(3) of the Restrictive Trade Practices Act.[3]

Proceedings before the Restrictive Practices Court

6.3 Proceedings before the Restrictive Practices Court may be instituted at any time before the starting date. Schedule 13 makes detailed provision in respect of proceedings under the Restrictive Trade Practices Act and the Resale Prices Act which are not determined by the starting date, the main features of which are as follows.

Proceedings which cease

6.4 As with orders which will fall at the starting date, proceedings under a number of provisions of the Restrictive Trade Practices Act and Resale Prices Act will cease at the starting date,[4] in particular those for restraining orders under sections 2(2) and 35(3) of the Restrictive Trade Practices Act.

Proceedings which remain ongoing

6.5 Certain Restrictive Practices Court applications made but not yet determined by the starting date may, however, remain ongoing past the starting date to their conclusion.[5] Appeals form part of those applications—the application is not determined until the expiry of the period in which the relevant party is able to appeal or until any appeal brought has been disposed of or withdrawn.[6]

6.6 Certain of these undetermined applications are to be treated as **'continuing proceedings'**.[7] These include proceedings instituted by the Director General of Fair Trading under section 1(3) of the Restrictive Trade Practices Act for a declaration as to whether or not restrictions or information provisions in an agreement are contrary to the public interest. Under the Resale Prices Act, applications under section 16 for a class of goods to be exempted by an order under section 14, and applications under section 17 for the Restrictive Practices Court to review its previous exemption decisions, are also 'continuing proceedings'.

6.7 Continuing proceedings may continue to their conclusion, during which time the application of the Chapter I prohibition and the start of any relevant transitional period will be affected. The Chapter I prohibition does not apply to an agreement subject to continuing proceedings[8] and any transitional period available for the agreement will run from the end of the continuing proceedings (see paragraph 4.4 above).

6.8 Other proceedings which are undetermined at the starting date will be allowed to continue to their conclusion but will not be 'continuing proceedings',[9] and so the application of the Chapter I prohibition is not suspended: subject to any transitional period or other exclusion, the Chapter I prohibition will apply to the agreement from the starting date. Proceedings of this type are applications under section 3 of the Restrictive Trade Practices Act for interim orders (see paragraph 6.2 above) and applications under section 26 of the Restrictive Trade Practices Act for a declaration of the Court as to whether or not an agreement is registrable or non-notifiable and for rectification of the register.[10]

Private actions/void agreements

6.9 The repeal of the Restrictive Trade Practices Act and Resale Prices Act at the starting date will not prevent third parties seeking damages for breach of statutory duty in respect of the period before that date where a right to do so by virtue of those Acts has arisen before repeal,[11] nor will it validate provisions in agreements made void by those Acts prior to repeal.

6.10 **The transition from the Restrictive Trade Practices Act and Resale Prices Act to the Chapter I prohibition will not be a moratorium on the pursuit of anti-competitive agreements.** The discovery of anti-competitive activity by the Director General of Fair Trading, even though shortly before the starting date, may, therefore, still lead to full Restrictive Practices Court proceedings.

[3052]

NOTES
  1   Schedule 13, paragraph 9.
  2   Schedule 13, paragraph 13(1).
  3   Schedule 13, paragraph 11.
  4   Schedule 13, paragraph 8.
  5   Schedule 13, paragraphs 11–12 and 14–17.
  6   Schedule 13, paragraph 15(3)–(5).
  7   Schedule 13, paragraph 15(1)–(2).
  8   Schedule 13, paragraph 14(1)–(2).
  9   Schedule 13, paragraph 15(2).
  10 Schedule 13, paragraph 12.
  11 Schedule 13, paragraph 13.

7   The Restrictive Trade Practices Act Public Register

7.1   The public register of restrictive trading agreements is to continue in existence after the starting date, although the Director General of Fair Trading will from then add further particulars of agreements to it in only a limited number of cases—

— particulars of notifiable agreements which have been furnished but not entered on the register before the starting date;

— particulars of agreements subject to continuing proceedings determined after the starting date; and

— particulars of agreements in relation to which a court gives directions to the Director General of Fair Trading after the starting date as to the application of the Restrictive Trade Practices Act prior to its repeal.[1]

7.2   It is intended that parties seeking to discover the effect of the Restrictive Trade Practices Act on an agreement (for example, whether that agreement benefits from a direction under section 21(2) of the Restrictive Trade Practices Act) should have access to the register. For an initial period after the starting date the register will remain accessible to the general public on the same basis as at present. Following that, and when the level of requests for access to the register no longer justifies the costs involved, it is likely that regulations reducing access will be made.[2]

[3053]

NOTES
  1   Schedule 13, paragraph 10(2)–(4).
  2   Schedule 13, paragraph 10(5).

8   Transition from the Fair Trading Act 1973 and the Competition Act 1980

The Fair Trading Act 1973

8.1   Investigations by the Monopolies and Mergers Commission (MMC) under the Fair Trading Act 1973 continuing at the starting date will, as of that date, be allowed to take into account agreements which could not previously have been considered by the MMC because they fell instead to be dealt with under the Restrictive Trade Practices Act.[1] Similarly, remedial orders of the Secretary of State following monopoly or merger references under the Fair Trading Act which, by virtue of paragraphs 3(1) and (2) of Schedule 8 to that Act, are restricted from applying to agreements covered by the Restrictive Trade Practices Act, will have that restriction lifted one year after the starting date, from which time they will have effect as if they had never been limited.[2] Applications to the Restrictive Practices Court under Part III of the Fair Trading Act which are made but not determined before the starting date will continue in the Restrictive Practices Court unaffected,[3] and new applications under Part III will be assigned to the High Court (in Scotland, the Court of Session).[4]

The Competition Act 1980

8.2   At the starting date the provisions of the Competition Act 1980 dealing with the control of anti-competitive practices will be repealed by order of the Secretary of State bringing into force section 17 of the Competition Act 1998. Any ongoing investigations by the Director General or the MMC under those provisions of the 1980 Act will cease at that time. Undertakings accepted by the Director General under sections 4 or 9 of the 1980 Act will also cease to have effect on its repeal, except where the undertaking relates to an agreement subject to 'continuing proceedings' under the Restrictive Trade Practices Act 1976 or the Resale Prices Act 1976, in which case it continues to have effect until the end of the proceedings (so that the disapplication of the Restrictive Trade Practices Act from agreements comprised in undertakings given under the 1980 Act is retained).[5]

[3054]

NOTES
[1]   Schedule 13, paragraph 40.
[2]   Schedule 13, paragraph 41.
[3]   Schedule 13, paragraph 42.
[4]   Schedule 12, paragraph 1(5)–(7).
[5]   Schedule 13, paragraph 43.

9   Introduction of the Chapter II prohibition

9.1   The Chapter II prohibition will come into force on the starting date. It will apply to abuses of a dominant position immediately. There are no transitional periods available in respect of the Chapter II prohibition. Where an agreement entered into by a dominant undertaking is operated in such a way as to constitute an abuse, the undertaking cannot claim the benefit of any Chapter I transitional period the agreement may have to exclude it from the Chapter II prohibition. There will be no early guidance possible in respect of the Chapter II prohibition either.

9.2   For further advice on the introduction of the Chapter II prohibition, see the Competition Act guideline *The Chapter II Prohibition*.

[3055]

10 Concurrency

10.1 As explained in paragraph 4.8 to 4.12 above, the transitional arrangements make specific provision for certain agreements relating to electricity, gas and railways. The powers of the Director General of Fair Trading under Schedule 13 relating to the Chapter I prohibition are, in respect of sectoral matters, functions exercised concurrently with the other regulators.[1] For those purposes, references to the Director General of Fair Trading in this guideline and to the Director in the relevant provisions of the Schedule are to be taken to include references to the other regulators.[2] Powers exercised concurrently include those for—
    — the provision of advice and information about the transitional provisions, such as this guideline, which the other regulators will do in due course if the need arises (see paragraph 4.8 to 4.12 above);

— the giving of early guidance in relation to agreements made during the interim period (see part 3 above). Directions on the procedure for early guidance have been issued by the Director General of Fair Trading alone, but following consultation with the regulators in respect of matters where they exercise concurrent jurisdiction;[3]

— the extension and termination of transitional periods (see paragraphs 5.2 to 5.12 above).

[3056]

NOTES
1   Schedule 13, paragraph 35.
2   Schedule 13, paragraph 1(4).
3   Schedule 13, paragraph 35(3).

ENFORCEMENT

(OFT 407, March 1999)

1 Introduction

1.1   The Competition Act 1998 (**'the Act'**) gives the Director General powers to enforce the Chapter I and Chapter II prohibitions. The enforcement of the Act to ensure competitive markets that will benefit both consumers and business will be one of the main functions of the Director General.

1.2   The Chapter I and Chapter II prohibitions will be enforced by the Director General using the powers set out in Chapter III of the Act. This guideline describes the power of the Director General—

— to give directions to bring an infringement to an end (part 2);

— to give interim measures directions during an investigation (part 3); and

— to impose penalties on undertakings for infringing the Chapter I or the Chapter II prohibition (part 4).

1.3   Private remedies arising from breach of the prohibitions are described in part 5 of this guideline. The new powers of investigation of the Director General are described in the Competition Act guideline *Powers of Investigation*.

[3057]

2 Directions

2.1   The Act gives the Director General the power to give such directions as he considers appropriate to bring an infringement to an end where he has made a decision that the Chapter I prohibition or the Chapter II prohibition has been infringed.

2.2   The directions may be given to such person or persons as he considers appropriate, which includes individuals and undertakings. The Director General is not limited to giving directions to the infringing parties. For example, directions may be addressed to the parent company which, though not the actual instigator of the infringement, has a subsidiary which is the immediate party to the infringement.

2.3   Directions may in particular require the person concerned to modify the agreement or conduct, or to terminate the agreement or cease the conduct in question. Directions may require positive action, such as informing third parties that an infringement has been brought to an end and reporting back periodically to the Director General on certain matters such as prices charged.

Procedure

2.4 The directions must be in writing and may be given to such person or persons as the Director General considers appropriate. They are likely to form part of the infringement decision in cases where the decision and the directions are addressed to the same person. If the Director General proposes to make an infringement decision, he will send the party or parties a written statement setting out the matters to which he has taken objection, the action he proposes to take and the reasons for it. The Director General must allow the person receiving the notice an opportunity to make representations to him. The person receiving the notice may request a meeting with officials of the office of the Director General to make oral representations to elaborate on his written representations already made in this regard.

2.5 The *Director General of Fair Trading's Procedural Rules* provide that if requested, the Director General must give the party or parties or an authorised representative an opportunity to inspect the Director General's file relating to the proposed decision. The Director General's file will not include documents to the extent to which they contain confidential information or the Director General's internal documents.

2.6 Any directions given by the Director General will set out the facts on which the direction is based and the reasons for it. The directions will be published on the register that will be kept at the Office of Fair Trading and on a website on the Internet.

2.7 Directions can be appealed to an appeal tribunal of the Competition Commission. The making of an appeal will not suspend the effect of the direction. The rules of the appeal tribunal may provide that the tribunal can make an interim order to suspend the effect of a direction.

Enforcement of directions

2.8 In most cases directions will have immediate effect. In some cases the Director General may allow the undertakings a period of time within which to comply with a direction.

2.9 The Director General may apply to the court for an order requiring compliance with a direction within a specified time limit if a person fails to comply with it without reasonable excuse. The Director General will actively seek to enforce directions in the courts. The court can require the person in default, or any officer of an undertaking who is responsible for the default, to pay the costs of obtaining the order. If a direction relates to something to be done in the management or administration of the undertaking the order can compel the undertaking or its officers to take action to comply with it. Any person who fails to comply with an order enforcing a direction will be in contempt of court. The sanction for contempt of court is a fine or imprisonment.

[3058]

3 Interim measures directions

3.1 One of the weaknesses of the previous competition regime was that serious damage could be inflicted on a company before the competition authorities could intervene. The Act gives the Director General the power to give interim measures directions pending his final decision as to whether or not there has been an infringement of the Chapter I or Chapter II prohibition. Interim measures directions will not affect the final decision.

3.2 The Act gives the Director General the power to give interim measures directions before he has completed his investigation of the suspected infringement if (i) he has a reasonable suspicion that the Chapter I or the Chapter II prohibition has been infringed and (ii) he considers that it is necessary for him to act urgently either to prevent serious, irreparable damage to a particular person or category of persons, or to protect the public interest. The opportunity to give interim measures directions if these tests are satisfied enables the Director General to take action to tackle anti-competitive behaviour quickly before serious damage has been inflicted.

3.3   The European Court has held that the European Commission has the power to impose interim measures.[1] The European Commission has not used this power very often. This may be because the first part of the test that the European Commission must satisfy before imposing interim measures is that it has established a prima facie case of an infringement of Articles 85 or 86 of the EC Treaty (Article 85 and Article 86).[2]

3.4   Whether the Director General has a reasonable suspicion that the Chapter I or the Chapter II prohibition has been infringed will depend upon the information available and the judgment of the Director General. Examples of information that may give rise to a reasonable suspicion include copies of secret agreements provided by disaffected members of a cartel; statements from employees or ex-employees and a complaint.

3.5   The Director General may consider that it is necessary to act urgently to prevent serious, irreparable damage to a particular person or category of persons where, for example, as a result of what appears to be abusive conduct on the part of another, dominant, undertaking, a smaller competitor is being put out of business or is suffering a considerable competitive disadvantage.

3.6   The Director General may also impose interim measures directions where he has a reasonable suspicion that the Chapter I or Chapter II prohibition has been infringed and he considers that it is necessary to act urgently to protect the public interest, for example, to prevent damage being caused to an industry.

3.7   Interim measures directions may be given by the Director General on his own initiative or after receiving a request from a complainant provided that the tests in paragraph 3.2 above are satisfied. Any complainant requesting an interim measures direction should provide as much evidence as possible, demonstrating that the alleged infringement is causing serious, irreparable damage. The complainant should also indicate as precisely as possible the nature of the interim measure that he is seeking.

3.8   The Director General may give such interim measures directions as he considers appropriate. He may in particular require the person concerned to terminate the agreement or cease the conduct in question, or to modify the agreement or conduct.

3.9   Once an interim measures direction has been made it has effect for as long as the Director General continues to have a reasonable suspicion that there has been an infringement of the Chapter I or Chapter II prohibition and until the investigation is complete. When the investigation is complete and the Director General has decided that an infringement has taken place, he may replace the interim measures direction with a direction described in part 2 above.

Procedure

3.10   Before giving an interim measures direction the Director General must give written notice to the person to whom he proposes to give the direction, indicating the nature of the direction he proposes to give and his reasons for deciding to give it. The Director General must allow the person receiving the notice an opportunity to make representations to him. The person receiving the notice may request a meeting with officials of the office of the Director General to make oral representations to elaborate on his written representations already made in this regard.

3.11 The person who receives written notice from the Director General about the proposed interim measures direction may ask to inspect the Director General's file on the case. The *Director General of Fair Trading's Procedural Rules* provide that, if requested, the Director General must give such a person or his authorised representative an opportunity to inspect all the documents in the Director General's file relating to the proposed direction. The Director General's file will not include documents to the extent to which they contain confidential information or the Director General's internal documents.

3.12 The interim measures direction will be published on the register maintained by the Director General at the Office of Fair Trading and on a website on the Internet. The Director General may also consider publishing the interim measures direction in an appropriate trade journal.

3.13 An interim measures direction can be appealed to an appeal tribunal of the Competition Commission. The making of an appeal will not suspend the effect of the interim measures direction.

Enforcement of interim measures directions

3.14 Interim measures directions can be enforced following the procedure set out in paragraph 2.9.

[3059]

NOTES
1 Case 792/79R *Camera Care v Commission* [1980] ECR 119.
2 [Now] renumbered Articles 81 and 82 following ratification of the Treaty of Amsterdam.

4 Penalties

General powers

4.1 The Act gives the Director General the power to impose financial penalties of up to 10 per cent of turnover in the United Kingdom on an undertaking which has infringed the Chapter I prohibition or the Chapter II prohibition. The Director General can impose penalties for infringements that have already stopped as well as for ongoing infringements.

4.2 The Director General intends to use this power to ensure that penalties have the necessary deterrent effect to prevent the occurrence and repetition of infringements. Subject to the maximum penalty of 10 per cent of an undertaking's turnover, where appropriate, the Director General may increase levels of penalties to ensure that deterrence is achieved.[1] The deterrent is not aimed solely at the undertakings which are subject to the decision, but also to other undertakings which might be considering similar activities that are contrary to the Chapter I and Chapter II prohibitions.

Intentionally or negligently

4.3 Before exercising the power to impose a penalty, the Director General must be satisfied that the infringement has been committed intentionally or negligently.[2] For intention or negligence to be found it is not necessary for there to have been action by, or even knowledge on the part of, the partners or principal managers of the undertaking concerned; action by a person who is authorised to act on behalf of the undertaking suffices.[3]

4.4 The Director General may consider the existence of past Restrictive Practice Court orders made against and undertakings *in lieu* given by an undertaking when considering whether or not an infringement of the Chapter I prohibition by similar anti-competitive activities of that undertaking was committed intentionally or negligently.

4.5   Parties will not be able to rely on the newness of the regime as a reason against a finding of intention or negligence.

Intention

4.6   The circumstances in which the Director General might find that an infringement has been committed intentionally include the following—
— the agreement or conduct has as its object the restriction of competition;
— the undertaking in question is aware that its actions will be, or are reasonably likely to be, restrictive of competition but still wants, or is prepared, to carry them out; or
— the undertaking could not have been unaware that its agreement or conduct had as its object the restriction of competition, even if it did not know that it would infringe either prohibition in the Act.

4.7   Ignorance or a mistake of law is no bar to a finding of intentional infringement.

4.8   In establishing whether or not there is intention, the Director General may consider internal documents generated by the undertakings in question. The Director General may regard deliberate concealment of an agreement or practice by the parties as strong evidence of an intentional infringement.

Negligence

4.9   The Director General is likely to find that an infringement of the Chapter I or Chapter II prohibition has been committed negligently where an undertaking knew or ought to have known that its actions would result in infringement of the prohibition.[4]

4.10   The fact that a particular type of agreement or conduct has not previously been found to be in breach of the Chapter I or Chapter II prohibitions does not mean that the infringement cannot be committed negligently.

Involuntary infringement

4.11   Where an undertaking participates in an infringement under pressure, it may still be held to have acted intentionally or negligently, although, depending on the circumstances, the penalty may be reduced.[5]

Turnover

4.12   The definition of turnover in respect of the maximum penalty of 10 per cent that can be imposed will be set out in an order made by the Secretary of State pursuant to section 36(8) of the Act. This order will establish, among other things, that turnover for the purposes of penalties means turnover in the United Kingdom. Factors that will be considered by the Director General in setting the level of a penalty are set out in the *Guidance on Penalties*, details of which are given in paragraphs 4.32–4.34 below.

Tax deductibility of penalties

4.13   It is the view of the Inland Revenue that penalties imposed under the Act will not be deductible in computing trading profits for tax purposes.[6] This is because civil or criminal penalties imposed by or under the authority of an Act of Parliament are not deductible: they are **'losses not connected with or arising out of the trade'** and so not deductible by virtue of section 74(1)(e) of the Income and Corporation Taxes Act 1988.

PART III
OFT GUIDELINES

Limited immunity for 'small agreements' and 'conduct of minor significance'

4.14 To ensure that smaller enterprises are not unduly burdened with the operation of the prohibitions the Act provides limited immunity from financial penalties for **'small agreements'** in relation to infringements of the Chapter I prohibition and **'conduct of minor significance'** in relation to infringements of the Chapter II prohibition. This immunity does not apply to price fixing agreements. 'Small agreements' and 'conduct of minor significance' can be defined (among other ways) by the turnover and/or the market share of the undertaking(s). The criteria to be used will be defined by the Secretary of State by order, and are expected to be based on the turnover of the undertaking(s) in the United Kingdom.

4.15 Undertakings will benefit from immunity if the Director General is satisfied that they acted on the reasonable assumption that they qualified for the limited immunity for 'small agreements' or 'conduct of minor significance'.

4.16 This concession confers provisional immunity from penalties only. The other possible sanctions (voidness of agreements or third party actions for breach of statutory duty) are still applicable.

Withdrawal notice

4.17 The Director General still has the right to investigate such agreements and conduct and can withdraw the immunity if, as a result of his investigation, he considers the agreement or conduct is likely to infringe the Chapter I or Chapter II prohibition.

4.18 Where the Director General has withdrawn the immunity from penalties for infringement of the Chapter I or Chapter II prohibition, he must give written notice of his decision to the person or persons from whom the immunity has been withdrawn. The notice will specify the date on which the withdrawal of immunity is to take effect. When determining that date, the Director General must have regard to the amount of time which the person or persons affected are likely to need in order to secure that there is no further infringement of the Chapter I or Chapter II prohibition, as the case may be. That date must follow the date of the Director General's decision.

Provisional immunity from penalties arising from notification to the European Commission

4.19 If a party to an agreement which may infringe the Chapter I prohibition has notified the agreement to the European Commission for an individual exemption under Article 85(3), the Director General may not require the payment of a penalty for any infringement of the Chapter I prohibition which occurs after the date of notification but before the date on which the European Commission determines the matter either formally or informally through a **comfort** letter. The Director General can still investigate an agreement, notwithstanding that it has been notified to the European Commission. No such immunity exists under the Chapter II prohibition.

4.20 If the European Commission grants an individual exemption for an agreement, the agreement will be automatically exempt from the Chapter I prohibition by virtue of a parallel exemption under section 10 of the Act. However, while the Director General has no power to withdraw an exemption from Article 85, where he finds that an agreement which benefits from a parallel exemption has produced, or may produce, significantly adverse effects on a market in the United Kingdom he may impose conditions or obligations subject to which the parallel exemption is to have effect, vary or remove any such condition or obligation, impose one or more additional conditions or obligations or cancel the parallel exemption (rule 21 of the *Director General of Fair Trading's Procedural Rules*).

4.21 If the European Commission withdraws the benefit of provisional immunity from fines for breach of Article 85 with respect to the agreement, provisional immunity from penalties for breach of the Chapter I prohibition will automatically cease to apply as from the date on which the immunity is withdrawn by the European Commission.

Provisional immunity from penalties under the Chapter I prohibition from the date of notification to the Director General

4.22 The Act provides for parties to notify their agreements to the Director General for guidance or a decision; these aspects are dealt with in the Competition Act guideline *The Major Provisions*. Where an agreement to which the Chapter I prohibition applies has been notified, the Director General cannot impose a penalty in respect of any infringement of the Chapter I prohibition by the agreement which occurs in the period beginning with the date of notification and ending on such date as may be specified in a notice given in writing to the applicant by the Director General on determination of the application. The date specified in the notice may not precede the date on which the notice is given. No such immunity exists for notifications under the Chapter II prohibition.

4.23 An application for early guidance will, on and after the starting date (1 March 2000), have the same effect as an application for full guidance. Consequently, the application will confer the same immunity from penalties as an application for guidance made after the starting date.

4.24 Provisional immunity starts on the date that the application becomes effective (rule 5(3) of the *Director General of Fair Trading's Procedural Rules*).

Provisional decision

4.25 Where the Director General has conducted a preliminary investigation of an application for guidance or a decision in respect of an agreement and he considers it likely that the agreement concerned will infringe the Chapter I prohibition and that it would not be appropriate to grant an individual exemption, he may make a provisional decision notifying the parties of his preliminary conclusion.[7] The decision means that the provisional immunity from penalties which arose as a consequence of notification will be treated as never having applied in respect of that agreement. A similar procedure will be followed where the Director General considers it likely that conduct will infringe the Chapter II prohibition (although in such cases there is no immunity from financial penalties to be removed).

4.26 When the Director General proposes to make a provisional decision he must consult the applicant. The Director General must give written notice of his provisional decision to the applicant and the notice must include an account of the facts on which he bases his decision and the reasons for it (rule 9 in the *Director General of Fair Trading's Procedural Rules*).

4.27 A provisional decision does not affect the Director General's ability to proceed with the application for a decision.

Immunity after guidance or decision

4.28 Subject to paragraph 4.30 below, no penalty may be imposed in respect of any infringement of the Chapter I prohibition where the Director General has given guidance that the agreement is unlikely to infringe the Chapter I prohibition or that it is likely to be exempt from the Chapter I prohibition or where, following notification for a decision, he has made a decision that the agreement has not infringed the Chapter I prohibition.

PART III
OFT GUIDELINES

4.29 Subject to paragraph 4.30 below, no penalty may be imposed in respect of any infringement of the Chapter II prohibition where the Director General has given guidance that the conduct is unlikely to infringe the Chapter II prohibition or, following notification for a decision, he has made a decision that the conduct has not infringed the Chapter II prohibition.

4.30 The Director General may remove the immunity from penalties described in paragraphs 4.28 and 4.29 for favourable guidance or a favourable decision if—

— he takes further action with respect to the agreement or conduct in one of the following circumstances—

    (i) he has reasonable grounds for believing that there has been a material change of circumstance since he gave guidance or a decision, as the case may be; or

    (ii) he has a reasonable suspicion that the information on which he based his guidance or decision was incomplete, false or misleading in a material particular; or

    (iii) in the case of guidance only for Chapter I only, one of the parties to the agreement applies to him for a decision with respect to the agreement; or

    (iv) in the case of guidance only for Chapter I and Chapter II, a complaint about the agreement or conduct is made to him; and

— he considers that it is likely that the agreement or conduct will infringe the Chapter I or Chapter II prohibition; and

— he gives written notice to the undertaking on whose application the guidance was given or the decision was made that he is removing the immunity as from the date specified in the notice.

4.31 If the Director General has a reasonable suspicion that information on which he based the guidance or decision, as the case may be, which was provided to him by a party to the agreement or by an undertaking engaging in the conduct, was incomplete, false or misleading in a material particular, the date specified in the notice may be earlier than the date on which the notice is given. It is a criminal offence to provide information that is false or misleading in a material particular (see the Competition Act guideline *Powers of Investigation* for further treatment of offences)

Amount of a penalty

4.32 The Act places an obligation on the Director General to prepare and publish guidance (distinct from this **'guideline'**) as to the appropriate amount of any penalty. The purpose of such guidance is to inform and guide businesses on the level of penalties. The guidance explains the steps taken and the factors considered when setting the level of a penalty (*Guidance on Penalties* will be available in the form of a statutory instrument later in 1999).

4.33 The main steps set out in the guidance are as follows—

— step 1—an assessment of the gravity and duration of the infringement;

— step 2—an assessment of whether there should be an increase based on aggravating circumstances and if so, of the level of any such increase;

— step 3—an assessment of whether there should be a reduction based on mitigating circumstances, and if so, of the level of any such reduction;

— step 4—consideration of objective factors such as any economic or financial benefits derived and that the amount does not exceed 10 per cent of the undertaking's turnover in the UK.

4.34 When the Director General is setting the amount of any penalty he must have regard to the guidance.

Compliance programmes

4.35 When assessing the amount of any penalty the Director General may take into account, as a mitigating circumstance, the existence of a compliance programme. In order for a compliance programme to reduce a penalty as a mitigating circumstance, the parties will need to show that—

— the programme has been actively implemented;
— it has the visible and continuing support of, and is observed by, senior management;
— there are appropriate compliance policies and procedures in place;
— there is active and ongoing training for employees at all levels who may be involved in activities that are touched by competition law; and
— the programme is evaluated and formal audits are carried out at regular intervals to ensure that it is delivering its objectives.

4.36 Where the above conditions are satisfied, the Director General may make a reduction in the amount of any penalty.

Whistleblowers

4.37 The European Commission has published a notice on the non-imposition or reduction of fines in cartel cases which sets out the conditions under which undertakings which cooperate with the European Commission during an investigation into a cartel may be exempted from fines, or may be granted reductions in fines.

4.38 The Notice[8] applies only to **'secret cartels between enterprises aimed at fixing prices, production or sales quotas, sharing markets or banning imports or exports'**. It is therefore concerned only with certain types of agreements falling within Article 85.

4.39 The Director General will have regard to the Notice when imposing a penalty and deciding on the amount of any penalty for an infringement of the Chapter I prohibition. The Director General also intends to operate a policy of leniency for whistleblowers. An undertaking which comes forward with information and cooperates with an investigation by the Director General may be granted a reduction in the amount of a penalty which would have been imposed on it if it had not co-operated.

Double jeopardy

4.40 If a penalty or fine has already been imposed by the European Commission or by another Member State in respect of the same agreement or conduct under consideration for infringement of the prohibitions, the Director General, an appeal tribunal or the Court of Appeal in England and Wales and in Northern Ireland, and the Court of Session in Scotland must take that penalty or fine into account when setting the amount of a penalty in relation to that agreement or conduct. This is to ensure that where an anti-competitive agreement or conduct is subject to proceedings in more than one jurisdiction, an undertaking is not penalised more than once for the same infringement.

Payment

4.41 Where the Director General proposes to require the payment of a financial penalty he must give written notice to the applicant of the matters to which he has taken objection, the action he proposes and his reasons for it (rule 14 of the *Director General of Fair Trading's Procedural Rules*). Where he imposes a penalty he must serve a written notice on the undertaking required to pay the penalty, specifying the date before which the penalty is required to be paid. It is likely that payment will be required within a period of 3 months from the date of the notice. The date for payment must not be earlier than the end of the period within which an appeal against the notice may be brought.

Enforcement of penalty decision

4.42 The Director General may require any undertaking which is a party to an agreement which has infringed the Chapter I prohibition to pay a penalty. In respect of an infringement of the Chapter II prohibition, the Director General may require the undertaking concerned to pay a penalty. Where there has been a finding of joint dominance, so that more than one undertaking has infringed the Chapter II prohibition, the Director General can require each undertaking to pay a penalty.

4.43 The term **undertaking** is not defined in the Act, but the meaning has been set out in Community law under Article 85 and it extends to any natural or legal person carrying on commercial or economic activities, whatever its legal status.[9] Undertakings engaged in the supply of goods or services are clearly covered. A parent and subsidiary company are regarded as a single economic unit as long as the subsidiary has no economic independence. The Director General may need to consider the respective responsibility of both parent and subsidiary for an infringement and therefore for consequent liability to pay a penalty. Where the Director General decides to impose a penalty on both parent and subsidiary, it may be imposed jointly and severally.

4.44 A penalty may be imposed on a company that takes over the undertaking that has committed an infringement.[10] Changes in legal identity of an undertaking will not prevent it or its component parts from being penalised. As far as possible, liability for penalties will follow responsibility for actions. Thus, a subsequent transfer of a business from one economically distinct undertaking to another will not automatically absolve the transferor from responsibility. Where the original undertaking has ceased to exist by the time a penalty comes to be imposed, a successor undertaking may be liable.

4.45 The involvement of a trade association in an infringement of the Chapter I or Chapter II prohibition could result in financial penalties being imposed on the association itself, its members or both.

4.46 If an undertaking fails to pay within the date specified in the penalty notice, and it has not brought an appeal against the imposition or amount of the penalty within the time allowed or such an appeal has been made and determined, the Director General can commence proceedings to recover the required amount as a civil debt.

Appeals

4.47 The decision to impose a penalty and the decision as to the amount of that penalty can be appealed to an appeal tribunal of the Competition Commission by any party to the agreement in question or by the person who engaged in the conduct in question. Third parties cannot appeal decisions on penalties (see the Competition Act guideline *The Major Provisions*). Such an appeal must be brought within a specified period.

4.48 The appeal tribunal can impose, revoke or vary the amount of a penalty. A decision by the appeal tribunal as to the amount of a penalty can be appealed with leave to the Court of Appeal in England and Wales and in Northern Ireland, and the Court of Session in Scotland.

4.49 An appeal to the Competition Commission against the imposition or amount of a penalty will suspend the penalty until the appeal is determined. The infringement decision itself will remain in effect.

4.50 The Secretary of State may make rules with respect to appeals and appeal tribunals. These rules may include a provision for an appeal tribunal to order that interest is payable and the manner in which, and the periods by reference to which, interest is to be calculated and paid. The rules may provide, in particular, that interest is payable if the tribunal upholds the Director General's decision to impose a penalty or does not reduce the penalty imposed by more than a specified percentage.

[3060]

NOTES

1 *Musique Diffusion Francaise SA v European Commission* [1983] 3 CMLR 221.
2 Section 36(3).
3 See footnote 3 above at para 97.
4 Case 27/76 *United Brands Co and United Brands Continental BV v Commission* [1978] 1 CMLR 429 at paras 298-301, [1977] ECR 207.
5 *Tipp-ex* OJ 1987 L222/1.
6 *Commissioners of Inland Revenue v Alexander von Glehn & Co Ltd* (12 TC 232).
7 Schedule 5 paragraph 3.
8 [1996] OJ C207/4; [1996] 5 CMLR 362.
9 *Höfner and Elser v Macrotron* [1993] 4 CMLR 306.
10 *Suiker Unie v Commission* [1976] 1 CMLR 295.

5   Enforcement in the courts

5.1   Third parties who consider that they have suffered loss as a result of any unlawful agreement or conduct have a claim for damages in the courts. Section 60 provides for the United Kingdom authorities to handle cases in such a way as to ensure consistency with Community law, and expressly refers to decisions of the European Court and the European Commission as to the civil liability of an undertaking for harm caused by its infringement of Community law.[1]

[3061]

NOTES

1 Section 60(6)(b).

TRADE ASSOCIATIONS, PROFESSIONS AND SELF-REGULATING BODIES

(OFT 408, March 1999)

1   What this guideline is about

1.1   The Competition Act 1998 (**'the Act'**) prohibits agreements between undertakings, decisions by associations of undertakings, or concerted practices which may affect trade in the United Kingdom and have as their object or effect the prevention, restriction or distortion of competition within the United Kingdom (the Chapter I prohibition). This guideline deals with how the Chapter I prohibition applies to trade associations, professions and other self-regulating bodies. It must be read in conjunction with the Competition Act guideline *The Chapter I Prohibition*.

1.2   This guideline refers to trade associations, professions and other self-regulating bodies but there are no definitions of these terms in the Act. The boundaries between the three may be imprecise. The term used in the Act is an **'association of undertakings'**. Any body formed to represent the interests of its members in commercial matters may be an 'association of undertakings'. An association of undertakings is deemed to represent the interests of those undertakings which have chosen to join, and it is therefore irrelevant how the association is organised. It is not necessary for it to have any formal constitution for its activities to come within the scope of the Act. An association of undertakings will infringe the Chapter I prohibition if its decisions, rules, recommendations or other activities lead to an appreciable restriction of competition, regardless of the exact form that the association takes.

1.3 Part 2 of this guideline focuses on the application of the Chapter I prohibition to the **decisions of associations of undertakings** although, as explained above, the prohibition applies equally to **agreements between undertakings**. The definition of **'undertaking'** is wide and may include an association of undertakings (see the Competition Act guideline *The Major Provisions*). The relationship of an association of undertakings with third parties is likely to be considered an agreement between undertakings for the purposes of the Chapter I prohibition. The internal relationship between the undertakings which form the association is likely to be considered as a decision of that association, although this will depend upon the facts of the case. Other activities of an association of undertakings may also fall within the Chapter I prohibition, either as a decision or because they constitute agreements (or both), and this too will depend upon the circumstances of the case. (See also paragraph 2.1 below.)

1.4 Examples of the decisions, rules, recommendations or other activities of associations of undertakings that may prevent, restrict or distort competition and therefore breach the Chapter I prohibition are described in part 3 of this guideline and the possibility of exemption for such activities is explained in part 4. The specific relevance of the application of the prohibitions to associations of undertakings and of the exclusions from the prohibitions to trade associations, professions and other self-regulating bodies is described in parts 5, 6 and 7 respectively of this guideline.

1.5 The Chapter II prohibition may also apply to conduct of trade associations, professions and self-regulating bodies and/or their members. The Chapter II prohibition applies to **'conduct on the part of *one or more undertakings* which amounts to the abuse of a dominant position'** (emphasis added); therefore such organisations themselves may constitute undertakings, or their members may comprise **'one or more undertakings'** the conduct of which may fall within the scope of the prohibition. This is not covered in detail in this guideline and further reference should be made to the Competition Act guideline *The Chapter II Prohibition*.

1.6 The involvement of an association of undertakings in an infringement of the Chapter I or Chapter II prohibition could result in financial penalties being imposed on the association itself, its members, or both. Further information on financial penalties is given in the Competition Act guideline *Enforcement*.

1.7 Section 60 of the Act sets out principles which provide for the United Kingdom authorities to handle cases in such as way as to ensure consistency with Community law. This is considered in more detail in the Competition Act guideline *The Major Provisions*.

1.8 The new regime under the Act, which replaces the Restrictive Trade Practices Act 1976, fundamentally changes the way in which the constitutions and rules of associations of undertakings are regulated under competition law. It is not appropriate for changes in such rules or constitutions to be submitted to the Director General of Fair Trading for approval under the Act as a matter of course: as this guideline explains, they should be notified to the Director General of Fair Trading only where they have an appreciable effect on competition.

2 Application of the Chapter I prohibition to associations of undertakings

Decisions by associations of undertakings and agreements between undertakings

2.1 The Chapter I prohibition covers **'decisions by associations of undertakings'** in addition to **'agreements between undertakings'** and **'concerted practices'**. It will be a matter of fact in each case if an agreement between undertakings which is carried out within the structure of an association (for example, an agreement to abide by the rules of the association) is considered to be a **'decision'** or an **'agreement'** for the purposes of the Chapter I prohibition (see also paragraph 1.3 above). This part explains the nature of decisions for the purposes of the Chapter I prohibition; elsewhere the guideline deals with the application of the Chapter I prohibition to associations of undertakings by virtue of their activities more generally.

Decisions

2.2 **'Decision'** has a wide meaning. It may include, for example, the constitution or rules of an association of undertakings or its recommendations or other activities.[1] In the day to day conduct of the business of an association, resolutions of the management committee or of the full membership in general meeting, binding decisions of the management or executive committee of the association, or rulings of its chief executive, the effect of which are to limit the commercial freedom of action of the members in some respect, will all be 'decisions' of the association. The key consideration is whether the effect of the decision, whatever form it takes, is to limit the freedom of action of the members in some commercial matter.

Recommendations

2.3 A recommendation of an association of undertakings may be a decision, as may an oral exhortation which it is intended that members should follow. This will be the case even if the recommendation is not binding on the members or has not been fully complied with.[2] Any recommendation which has an appreciable effect on competition within the United Kingdom will therefore be caught by the Chapter I prohibition.

Rules

2.4 The rules of an association may also constitute a decision of the association, as may any co-ordination of the members' conduct in accordance with its constitution. A rule which has an appreciable effect on competition within the United Kingdom will therefore be caught by the Chapter I prohibition.

Other activities

2.5 Other activities which are organised by or through associations of undertakings may infringe the Chapter I prohibition if they lead to an appreciable restriction of competition. As noted in paragraph 2.1 above, these may take the form of decisions of the associations of undertakings or agreements between the undertakings which form part of the association. For example, this would cover the exchange of specific price information as discussed in part 3 opposite.

[3063]

NOTES

[1]   Re *the Application by the National Sulphuric Acid Association* OJ [1980] L260/24, [1980] 3 CMLR 429.

[2]   *IAZ International Belgium NV v Commission* [1984] 3 CMLR 276, [1983] ECR 3369.

3 Scope of the Chapter I prohibition

3.1   The fact that members of an association of undertakings are acting through the association does not affect the way in which the Act applies to their decisions, rules, recommendations or other activities: their position is no better and no worse than if they were acting in the same manner outside the forum of such an association. In each case the Chapter I prohibition applies only if the relevant activity has an appreciable effect on competition in the relevant United Kingdom market. Any such activity which does fall within the Chapter I prohibition may be considered for exemption: a number of the examples below will often be candidates for exemption (further details on exemptions are given in part 4 below).

3.2   The remainder of this part sets out examples of the decisions, rules, recommendations or other activities of associations of undertakings that have the potential to breach the Chapter I prohibition. This is a non-exhaustive list: it includes *types* of activities which would generally fall within the Chapter I prohibition, although the particular circumstances of a case may mean that an activity of one of these types does not do so. Equally, there will clearly be instances of activities not listed in the types shown below which are prohibited. More general examples of anti-competitive behaviour which may fall within the Chapter I prohibition can be found in the Competition Act guideline *The Chapter I Prohibition*.

Pricing

3.3   Collective price-fixing or price co-ordination of any product or service is likely to breach the Chapter I prohibition, whatever form it takes. The Director General believes that any decisions including any recommendation as to prices and charges, including discounts and allowances, is likely to have an appreciable effect on competition.

Information exchange

General

3.4   As a general principle, the more information made publicly available to market participants, the more effective competition is likely to be. In the normal course of business, undertakings exchange information on a variety of matters legitimately and with no risk to the competitive process. Indeed, competition may be enhanced by the sharing of information, for example on new technologies or market opportunities.

3.5   There are circumstances where there can be no objection to the exchange of information, whoever the exchange is made by, even between competitors, and whether or not under the aegis of an association of undertakings. For example, the collection and publication of statistics are legitimate functions of associations of undertakings.

3.6   The exchange of information may, however, have an appreciable effect on competition where it serves to remove any uncertainties in the market and therefore eliminate any competition between undertakings. This will be the case even though the exchange might appear innocuous. It does not matter that the information could have been obtained from other sources. Whether or not the information exchange has such an appreciable effect will depend on the circumstances of each individual case: the market characteristics, the type of information and the way in which it is exchanged. As a general principle, the Director General will consider that there is more likely to be an appreciable effect on competition the smaller the number of undertakings operating in the market, the more frequent the exchange and the more sensitive and confidential the nature of the information which is exchanged.

3.7 The general approach of the Director General to information exchange, based on the relevant principles established by the European Court[1] as appropriate, is set out below.

Exchange of price information

3.8 The exchange of information on prices may lead to price co-ordination and therefore eliminate any competition which would otherwise be present between the undertakings. This will be the case whether the information exchanged relates directly to the prices charged or to the elements of a pricing policy, for example, discounts, costs, terms of trade and rates and dates of change.

3.9 The circulation of historical information or the collation of price trends may be less likely to have an appreciable effect on competition. An example may be where it forms part of a structured scheme of inter-firm comparison which is intended to spread best industrial practice, in particular if the information is collected, aggregated and disseminated by an independent body. Many associations of undertakings organise the exchange of such information among members. For example, **bench-marking** exercises are often operated by associations of undertakings on behalf of their members. Much of this activity may have little effect on competition and therefore not be caught by the Chapter I prohibition.

3.10 The regular and systematic exchange of specific information on prices between competitors is, however, likely to reduce the uncertainties inherent in the competitive process and to facilitate the coordination of market conduct, whether the exchange is organised by the members themselves or, as is often the case, by or through an association of undertakings. While the compilation of general information, for example general price trends for an industry, may not have an appreciable effect on competition, it must not cover (or enable undertakings to divine) confidential information relating to individual undertakings.[2]

Exchange of non-price information

3.11 The exchange of information on matters other than price may have an appreciable effect on competition depending on the type of information exchanged and the market to which it relates. The exchange of statistical data, market research and general industry studies, for example, are unlikely to have an effect on competition provided that the information exchanged relates to what the European Commission has called **'opinion and experience'**[3] and does not enable confidential or sensitive business information to be shared.

3.12 In general, the exchange of information on output and sales should not affect competition provided that it is sufficiently historic and cannot influence future competitive market behaviour. There may however be an appreciable effect on competition if it is possible to disaggregate the information and identify the participants. This may also be the case if the exchange relates to recent, current or future information.

3.13 As an example of this, in *United Kingdom Agricultural Tractor Registration Exchange*, the exchange of information by members of the trade association on sales and market shares, broken down by territory, product line and time period, was found to have infringed Article 85(1) of the EC Treaty.[4] Significant to this decision was the detail of the information exchanged and the fact that the market was concentrated, with four undertakings accounting for 80 per cent of total sales. It was held that the information exchanged created a degree of transparency in such an oligopolistic market which could destroy any remaining competition and enhance entry barriers by identifying any newcomers to the market thus facilitating a strategic response by the established undertakings.

Advertising

3.14 Restrictions on advertising, whether relating to the amount, nature or form of advertising, restrict competition to some degree. Whether the effect is appreciable depends on the purpose and nature of the restriction, and on the market in which it is to apply. Rules or decisions of associations of undertakings aimed at curbing misleading advertising, or at ensuring that advertising is legal, truthful and decent are unlikely to have an appreciable effect on competition, but restrictions which more generally prevent members from using advertising are another matter. Rules or decisions of associations of undertakings prohibiting members from soliciting for business, from competing with other members, or from advertising prices, or prices below a minimum or recommended level, are all likely to be caught by the Chapter I prohibition.

Joint buying/selling

3.15 Any joint activity, for example joint buying, joint selling or joint research, coordinated through an association of undertakings will be subject to the Chapter I prohibition to the same extent as if they were done outside the medium of an association of undertakings, for example, by the undertakings individually in an agreement.

Codes of conduct

3.16 A code of conduct may seek to introduce **best practice** into a particular sector and may include provisions, for example, for dealing with consumer complaints and a redress procedure. A code is unlikely to be successful in promoting consumer protection unless it is widely adopted and effectively enforced, but at the same time it may limit the way participants can compete. If, however, the structure of the market is competitive and the code does not deal with prices or involve any element of market sharing, the effects on competition are less likely to be appreciable.

Technical standards

3.17 Associations of undertakings may play a role in the negotiation and promulgation of technical standards in an industry. This will limit the members in the make-up of the products or services that they can offer and there is therefore a restriction of competition. If entry barriers were to be significantly raised as a result of adoption of the standard, the effects on competition could be appreciable.

Standard terms and conditions

3.18 Associations may be involved in the formulation of standard terms and conditions to be applied by members. This may be no more than a useful simplification of what otherwise might be complex and, to the customer, potentially confusing conditions. If an association imposes on its members an obligation to use common terms and conditions of sale or purchase, this will inevitably restrict competition to some degree. Standard conditions, however, are less likely to have an appreciable effect on competition where members remain free to adopt different conditions if they so wish.

Terms of membership

3.19 Rules of admission as a member of an association should be transparent, proportionate, non-discriminatory and based on objective standards. Those that are not may breach the Chapter I prohibition. Terms of membership will have an appreciable effect on competition where the effect of exclusion from membership is to put the undertaking(s) concerned at a competitive disadvantage. Similarly, procedures for expelling members of an association may have an appreciable effect on competition, particularly where they are not based on reasonable and objective standards or where there is no proper appeals procedure in the event of refusal of membership or expulsion.

Certification

3.20 An association may certify or award quality labels to its members to demonstrate that they have met minimum industry standards. While such a scheme has benefits for consumers in the form of quality assurances, it may lead to a restriction of competition. A scheme is less likely to have an appreciable effect on competition and breach the Chapter I prohibition where certification is available to all manufacturers that meet objective quality requirements. However, the standards must be objective and reasonable. Where manufacturers must accept additional obligations governing the products which they can buy or sell, or restrictions as to pricing or marketing, the scheme is likely to have an appreciable effect on competition and be caught by the Chapter I prohibition.

[3064]

NOTES

[1]   For example, *United Kingdom Agricultural Tractor Registration Exchange* OJ [1992] L 68/19, [1993] 4 CMLR 358, upheld by the Court of First Instance, case T34/92; Case C-8/95 *New Holland Ford Limited v Commission* [1998] 5 CMLR 311 and Case T-35/92 *John Deere v Commission* [1994] II ECR 957.

[2]   *Bundesverband Deutscher Stahlhandel eV* [1980] 3 CMLR 193.

[3]   *Notice on Cooperation Agreements* OJ [1968] C 75/3.

[4]   See footnote 3 [above]. Article 85 of the EC Treaty (Article 85) is [now] renumbered Article 81 following ratification of the Treaty of Amsterdam.

4   Exemption

General

4.1   Any agreement between undertakings, decisions of an association of undertakings or concerted practices which fall within the Chapter I prohibition can be considered for exemption (see also the Competition Act guideline *The Chapter I Prohibition* for general guidance).

4.2   The Director General will consider any application for an exemption of a decision, rule, recommendation or other activity of an association of undertakings against the criteria laid down in section 9 of the Act which provide that, to qualify for exemption, it must—

'(a)   *contribute to*
    (i)   *improving production or distribution, or*
    (ii)   *promoting technical or economic progress,*
    while allowing consumers a fair share of the resulting benefit; but
(b)   *not*
    (i)   *impose on the undertakings concerned restrictions which are not indispensable to the attainment of those objectives; or*
    (ii)   *afford the undertakings concerned the possibility of eliminating competition in respect of a substantial part of the products in question.'*

4.3   The following paragraphs provide examples of the kinds of activities of associations of undertakings that, where they have an appreciable effect, might be considered suitable for individual exemption. Candidates for exemption will be judged on the facts of each case against the criteria set out in paragraph 4.2 above.

Standard terms and conditions

4.4   Given the potential benefit to consumers from clearly expressed standard terms and conditions, exemption of such terms may be possible notwithstanding that competition is inevitably restricted to some degree. The restrictions on competition are, however, likely to outweigh the benefits to consumers—and thus not qualify for exemption—if the standardisation covers terms that are likely to be relevant to a customer in choosing between competing suppliers, for example, if they indirectly affect the prices to be charged.

Technical standards

4.5   Technical standards can help to promote safety and protect consumers and are therefore likely to be candidates for exemption. The benefits would, however, have to be assessed against any effects on competition in deciding whether exemption would be ultimately justified.

Codes of conduct

4.6   Codes of conduct have been drawn up by many associations of undertakings, often with the support of the Office of Fair Trading or a regulator in its consumer protection role. If a code is considered to have an appreciable effect on competition there may still be the opportunity, in the light of the purpose of the code, for exemption.

Restrictive Trade Practices Act 1976

4.7   Any agreement, decision or practice which, *before* the Chapter I prohibition comes into force, is the subject of a direction under section 21(2) of the Restrictive Trade Practices Act that the Director General need not refer the agreement to the Restrictive Practices Court, is excluded from the Chapter I prohibition unless and until there is a **material variation** to the agreement. A variation will be material if, as a result of the variation, the agreement has an appreciable effect on competition. Agreements which are the subject of a section 21(2) direction are recorded in the Public Register of Registrable Agreements kept at the Office of Fair Trading. This exclusion, in Schedule 3 to the Act, is subject to a **clawback** by the Director General (enabling him to apply the Chapter I prohibition) in certain circumstances. Further details on the inter-relationship between the Restrictive Trade Practices Act and the Act is found in the Competition Act guideline *Transitional Arrangements*.

[3065]

5   Trade associations

5.1   Trade associations are the commonest form of association of undertakings. There are trade associations in almost every sector of the United Kingdom economy. Their functions in furthering the trade interests of their members are diverse but they can be broadly categorised as—

— representing to Government, the European Commission and other public bodies the interests of members on legislation, regulations, taxation and policy matters likely to affect them;
— promoting and protecting the interests of members in the media;
— collecting and disseminating statistics and market information, and information about legislation and Government policy;
— promulgating standards, codes of practice or standard terms and conditions of sale;
— providing a range of services of an advisory or consultancy nature on, for example, legal, accounting, training or environmental matters;
— providing advice of a more commercial nature.

5.2   The functions of trade associations are clearly useful to members—especially, perhaps, to smaller firms—and they may also be beneficial in increasing the efficiency of the market system as a whole. While the Act strengthens the law on anti-competitive agreements, activities of trade associations which have no appreciable effect on competition will be of no concern. A trade association may, however, provide directly or indirectly the vehicle for anti-competitive, or even collusive, activity, and any decision, rule or recommendation of a trade association or agreement between its members which has an appreciable effect on competition will infringe the Chapter I prohibition. It may nevertheless still qualify for an exemption.

5.3   The nature of the membership of a trade association is likely to be relevant in assessing whether an activity does have an appreciable effect. An association will usually seek to make its membership as comprehensive as possible to maximise its influence on behalf of its members. A wide membership will also increase the effectiveness of any code of practice on members' conduct, devised and implemented by a trade association in its self regulatory role. However, the wider the membership among those engaged in a market within the United Kingdom, the greater the risk that any anti-competitive behaviour carried on by the association will have an appreciable effect. This will be of greater significance where membership of a trade association is limited to a particular stage in the chain of production or distribution when members are likely to be actual or potential competitors. The appreciable effect test is looked at in more detail in the Competition Act guideline *The Chapter I Prohibition*.

[3066]

6   Professions

6.1   A professional body may lay down educational and experience qualifications for membership, keep a register of members, promulgate standards of conduct to be maintained by the members, and enforce the standards through a complaints and disciplinary procedure. A professional body represents its members' interests in dealing with Government and other public bodies and the media. Organisationally, the functions of representation and of registration and the establishment and enforcement of standards may be separated, as, for example, in the medical profession, between the British Medical Association and the General Medical Council. Increasingly, professional bodies have involved themselves in wider matters of professional practice such as professional indemnity insurance and relationships with other professions.

6.2   The Chapter I prohibition applies to rules and decisions of professional bodies in the same way as it does to those of other associations of undertakings, except that it does not apply to the extent to which an agreement—
— constitutes a **designated** professional rule;
— imposes obligations arising from such designated professional rules; or
— constitutes an agreement to act in accordance with such rules.
Professional rules are the rules regulating a professional service or the persons providing, or wishing to provide, that service. Rules include regulations, codes of practice and statements of principle.

6.3   This exclusion from the Chapter I prohibition applies only to those rules of the professional services listed in Part II of Schedule 4 to the Act (set out in paragraph 6.4 below) which are notified to, and designated by, the Secretary of State for Trade and Industry. Rules or decisions (including recommendations) of any body relating to a profession not listed in Schedule 4 could potentially be prohibited under the Act, whatever their avowed purpose. These could include, for example, rules or decisions affecting fees or other charges, advertising, the organisational form of a professional practice and the employment of non-professionals, and any rules or decisions restricting the way in which the professional can conduct the commercial aspects of his practice.

6.4   The exclusion in Schedule 4 applies to the professional rules (which are notified to, and designated by, the Secretary of State) of the following professional services—

— **legal**—the services of **barristers**, **advocates** or **solicitors**;
— **medical**—the provision of medical or surgical advice or attendance and the performance of surgical operations; the services of **nurses**, **midwives**, **physiotherapists** and **chiropodists**;
— **dental**—any services falling within the practice of dentistry;
— **ophthalmic**—the testing of sight;
— **veterinary**—any services which constitute veterinary surgery;
— the services of **architects**, and of **surveyors of land, quantity surveyors, buildings surveyors**, and **ship surveyors**;
— **accounting and auditing**—the making or preparation of accounts or accounting records and the examination, verification and auditing of financial statements, and **insolvency services**;
— the services of registered **patent agents**;
— the services of registered **parliamentary agents**;
— **engineers and technologists**—the services of persons practising or employed as consultants in the field of civil, mechanical, aeronautical, marine, electrical or electronic engineering; mining, quarrying, soil analysis, or other forms of mineralogy or geology; agronomy, forestry, livestock rearing or ecology, metallurgy, chemistry, biochemistry or physics; or any other analogous forms of engineering or technology;
— the provision of **education** or **training**;
— the services of **ministers of religion**.

6.5   Where there is no exclusion under Schedule 4 as described above, and a rule or decision of a professional body has an appreciable effect on competition, an individual exemption from the Chapter I prohibition may be applied for if the statutory criteria set out in the Act (referred to in paragraph 4.2 above) are met.

6.6   The exclusion under Schedule 4 does not, of course, preclude any action by the European Commission should the professional rules breach Article 85.

6.7   The Director General is required to keep the list of designated professional rules under review and to advise the Secretary of State if he considers that changes should be made to the list.

Restrictive Trade Practices Act 1976

6.8   The professions listed in Schedule 4 match those whose services were exempt from the Restrictive Trade Practices Act. The scope of the exclusion from the Chapter I prohibition is, however, narrower than that from the Restrictive Trade Practices Act in that it is limited to the designated rules of the profession rather than applying to any restrictive agreement relating to the supply of the professional service in question. Therefore, for example, an agreement on fees made between a local group of practitioners may still be caught by the Chapter I prohibition.

[3067]

7   Self-regulating bodies

7.1   There are self-regulating bodies outside the field of the professions. An example is the Committee on Advertising Practice which devises and enforces the British Codes of Advertising and Sales Promotion and the members of which include organisations representing the advertising and sales promotion industries and most media businesses. Self-regulating bodies may have statutory backing, such as those concerned with investment business set up under the Financial Services Act 1986. The essence of any system of self-regulation is that the conduct of the members of a profession, trade or industry is subject to a degree of monitoring and control by its representative body, or an organisation set up by that body or its members, to ensure that users or consumers are protected from unethical or otherwise unacceptable behaviour.

7.2 Self-regulating bodies are associations of undertakings and the Chapter I prohibition applies to their rules and decisions in exactly the same way as to those of any other association of undertakings. The guidance as to the scope of the Chapter I prohibition and the possibility of exemption set out in parts 2, 3 and 4 above applies equally to self-regulating bodies. The Chapter I prohibition applies to self-regulating bodies only where their decisions or rules have an appreciable effect on competition and, where they have such an effect, they will be able to apply for individual exemption.

7.3 Schedule 2 to the Act excludes from the Chapter I prohibition a number of self-regulating bodies, notably those operating under the Financial Services Act and those regulating the practice of auditing under the Companies Act 1989. In these cases, competition scrutiny of the self-regulating body's rules is already provided for under its own specific legislation. The Director General's functions and duties in relation to competition scrutiny under such legislation are not changed by the Act.

[3068]

FORM N

(OFT 409, March 2000)

NOTES

This form is set out in the Competition Act 1998 (Director's rules) Order 2000, SI 2000/293, Schedule at **[2025]**.

ASSESSMENT OF INDIVIDUAL AGREEMENTS AND CONDUCT

(OFT 414, September 1999)

1 Introduction

1.1 The Competition Act 1998 ('**the Act**') introduces two prohibitions: one of agreements which prevent, restrict or distort competition and which may affect trade within the United Kingdom ('**the Chapter I prohibition**'); the other of conduct by undertakings which amounts to an abuse of a dominant position in a market which may affect trade within the United Kingdom ('**the Chapter II prohibition**'). cAssessing whether either prohibition has been infringed will involve an assessment of the whole economic impact and circumstances of the individual case. This guideline explains how the Director General makes such an assessment. The assessment cannot, however, be carried out independently of an overall competition assessment which includes the boundaries of the relevant market (see the Competition Act guideline *Market Definition*) and whether undertakings possess, or will possess, market power within that market (see the Competition Act guideline *Assessment of Market Power*). This guideline should therefore be read in conjunction with those and other guidelines in the series.

1.2 This guideline provides guidance on how certain actions which might be prohibited under the Act will be assessed by the Director General. However, no guidelines can be exhaustive, and agreements or conduct which are not covered by, or referred to in, this guideline should not be assumed to be beyond the scope of the prohibitions. This guideline provides a more detailed and technical explanation of some issues covered in the Competition Act guidelines *The Chapter I Prohibition* and *The Chapter II Prohibition*.

1.3 Parts 2 and 3 of this guideline explain the assessment of prices that are alleged to be excessive and conduct that discriminates between different customers respectively. Part 4 covers predatory prices, including cross-subsidy, and part 5 looks at other pricing issues that may be alleged to be anti-competitive. Part 6 considers vertical arrangements and part 7 the refusal to supply products or grant access to an **essential facility**. Lastly, part 8 deals with situations where a dominant undertaking is alleged to be abusing its position in a related market.

1.4 Broadly speaking, the issues covered in parts 2 and 3 involve undertakings exploiting existing market power, and the issues in parts 3 to 8 consider anti-competitive behaviour designed to exclude competitors from a market in order to enhance market power. Some issues can involve both exploitative and anti-competitive behaviour, however. There is also some overlap between the topics because many of them are interrelated. Price discrimination, for example, covered in part 3, may involve issues of excessive prices or predatory prices. The issues discussed in this guideline are perhaps most likely to be potential infringements of the Chapter II prohibition, but could involve infringements of the Chapter I prohibition if they arose from agreements or concerted practices between undertakings.

1.5 This guideline refers to some technical concepts, such as particular measures of an undertaking's costs. These terms are explained in the glossary at the end of this guideline.

Section 60

1.6 The Director General has a duty under section 60 of the Act to handle cases in such a way as to ensure consistency with European Community law. This is described further in the Competition Act guideline *The Major Provisions*.

[3069]

2 Excessive prices

Introduction

2.1 The charging of excessive selling prices (or conversely the extraction of unfair or excessively low buying prices) by a dominant undertaking may be an infringement of the Chapter II prohibition.[1] The European Court of Justice has held that—

> 'charging a price which is excessive because it has no reasonable relation to the economic value of the product supplied . . . is an abuse'.[2]

2.2 The Court went on to declare that a detailed analysis of costs would be required before any judgment could be reached and added that the question to be asked was—

> '. . . whether the difference between the costs actually incurred and the price actually charged is excessive, and if the answer to this question is in the affirmative to consider whether a price has been charged which is either unfair in itself or when compared to other competing products.'

2.3 An important area where excessive prices might be viewed as an abuse is where a dominant undertaking is exploiting its ownership of an **essential facility**,[3] an important network facility which is unlikely to face competition in the foreseeable future. In addition to having no relation to the economic value of the product supplied, such excessive prices might make it more difficult for undertakings (that require the product as an input) to enter and compete in related markets.[4]

2.4 Excessive prices might also involve an infringement of the Chapter I prohibition where they result from an agreement between undertakings which is capable of having **appreciable effects** on competition (see the Competition Act guideline *The Chapter I Prohibition*). This part of this guideline concentrates on when excessive prices might infringe the Chapter II prohibition (although the analysis of when prices may be considered to be excessive and infringe either the Chapter I or the Chapter II prohibition is common to both).

2.5   The paragraphs below explain how the concept of **excessive prices** can be defined, the evidence that might be used to identify them, and issues such as markets where undertakings might be jointly dominant.

When prices may be considered to be excessive

2.6   An undertaking's prices in a particular market can be regarded as excessive if they allow the undertaking to sustain profits higher than it could expect to earn in a competitive market (in this guideline called **supra-normal profits**). All undertakings clearly need to earn some level of profits in order to remain in business and to provide a sufficient return to shareholders and lenders, on whom they depend for capital. The return required by shareholders (the equity cost of capital) is at least the return they could earn elsewhere, having regard to the relative risks incurred by investing in the particular undertaking. Prices within a particular market can be excessive if they allow shareholders to yield a rate of return that is significantly and persistently greater than this equity cost of capital. Similarly, lenders will have their own cost of capital and, by analogy, prices can be excessive if lenders' returns persistently exceed this level. Taken together, the return required by shareholders and lenders from an undertaking is that undertaking's weighted average cost of capital (WACC).

2.7   In principle, high returns might be shown by analysing the share price of an undertaking. In most cases, however, this will be difficult because the majority of undertakings operate in more than one relevant market and share prices are influenced by other factors. It is not the overall profitability of the undertaking which is at issue, but rather the profits it earns in a particular market where it enjoys a dominant position. Profitability of an individual line of business can provide a more direct measure of whether excess returns are being earned in a particular market.

2.8   Prices which, at first sight, might appear to be excessive will not always, of course, amount to an abuse. First, high prices (leading to supra-normal profits) will often occur for short periods within competitive markets. If demand were to increase in an industry where capacity was fixed in the short run, for example, prices (and profits) will initially rise. If high prices and profits encouraged new entry or investment in new capacity by existing undertakings, supra-normal profits would be eroded and competition problems would be unlikely to arise.

2.9   Secondly, undertakings in competitive markets may be able to sustain supra-normal profits for a period if they are more efficient than their competitors and thus would not be acting in an anti-competitive manner; if, for example, an undertaking had developed lower-cost techniques of production, supplied higher quality products or was more effective at identifying market opportunities. This might be shown by the fact that other undertakings charging the same prices were not earning high profits relative to their cost of capital. In the long run, however, the initial advantages that led to supra-normal profits would be incorporated into industry common practice if the market were truly competitive.

2.10   Thirdly, prices and profits may be high in markets where there is innovation. Innovation leads to new and improved products and processes being introduced into the market. In turn, this can lower costs to business and increase choice for customers. Innovation is also a spur to competition; the rewards of innovation attract new entry, and innovation itself provides a means to compete with incumbents. Innovation generally makes a beneficial impact on economic welfare.

2.11   Successful innovation will, at any single point in time, allow a firm to earn profits significantly higher than its competitors. Whether the Director General considers such profits to be excessive (and therefore abusive) will depend on two factors: first, he would consider whether the profits earned were necessary to provide a fair return on the costs of the innovation itself and a fair reward for the risks faced in bringing that innovation to the market. Secondly, he would consider whether the profits were temporary; in a dynamic market, high prices and profits should act as a spur to competitors to innovate further and to the incumbent to innovate to maintain its position. Such persistently high prices and profits are unlikely to be of concern to the Director General if they result from on-going successful innovations.[5]

2.12 In industries where there may be no prospect of new entry or of innovation to replace existing monopolists, consistently excessive prices (and profits) will, however, be of concern. This is one reason why special regimes exist to regulate the prices of certain utilities, whose functions are natural monopolies, or who are in transition to more competitive structures. For the same reason, some other undertakings, which do not face sufficient existing or potential competition, have given undertakings on price levels following investigations by the Monopolies and Mergers Commission (now the Competition Commission).

2.13 The Director General will be mindful of the need not to interfere in natural market mechanisms where high prices will encourage new entry or innovation and thereby increase competition. In such markets, excessive prices will be regarded as an abuse only where it is clear that high profits will not stimulate successful new entry within a reasonable period.

Measuring supra-normal profits

2.14 As explained above, supra-normal profits are profits earned in a particular market which are sustained at a level in excess of the risk-adjusted cost of capital for investment in the business serving that market. There are a number of ways to estimate the rate of supra-normal profitability. One approach is to compare an undertaking's return on capital with its weighted average cost of capital estimated using the Capital Asset Pricing Model. Another is to compare the Certainty Equivalent Accounting Rate of Return (CARR) over a number of years with the risk free rate of interest. No presumption should be made about the measure the Director General will use in any particular case; in deciding which measure to use, however, he will take into account the undertaking's views on how its profitability should be measured and its sensitivity to different measures of profitability.[6]

2.15 The Director General recognises that judgment is needed to estimate relevant rates of return and it may be difficult for an undertaking in a dominant position to know whether a particular rate indicates supra-normal profitability. There can be legitimate uncertainty in the estimation of the appropriate cost of capital, the valuation of net assets, and their attribution to the business. It is unlikely, however, that the Director General would conclude that an undertaking was abusing a dominant position solely on the evidence of supra-normal profitability.

2.16 An alternative to the two approaches to estimating supra-normal profits referred to above is to look at the stand-alone costs of the activity in question. The stand-alone cost of an activity is the least cost which would be incurred by a hypothetical efficient undertaking supplying only that product or service from a fully utilised plant of optimum size. The revenues of an undertaking significantly and consistently exceeding its stand-alone cost in a particular activity may indicate that excessive prices have been charged. The stand-alone cost will, of course, have to include an appropriate allowance for the undertaking's cost of capital (as described above). In regulated sectors the regulator may already possess some of the cost information needed to calculate an activity's stand-alone cost.

2.17 A particular difficulty when analysing the prices and profitability of a multi-product undertaking in respect of one or more of its business activities is that certain functions contribute costs to more than one business activity. For example, undertakings will generally have a number of head-office functions. These 'joint' or 'common' costs are those which are incurred in the supply of a group of products, and that cannot be attributed uniquely to one product. To ensure full cost recovery the undertaking will try to allocate common costs between its various services and there are a number of ways of achieving this. Common costs are therefore included in their entirety when calculating the stand-alone cost of an activity. The stand-alone cost assumes that the hypothetical efficient competitor will not be able to cover the common costs from another activity.

2.18 As well as information on an undertaking's profitability, the Director General might take note of relevant recent price changes: how the undertaking had adjusted its prices in response to increases in costs or taxes, for example, or how it had reacted to reductions in demand or increases in competitive pressures.

2.19 Whichever approach is used, the Director General would not normally be concerned by periods of transiently high prices. Excessive prices may be considered to be an abuse only if they have persisted in the absence of continuing successful innovation and/or without stimulating successful new entry or a significant loss of market share. The Director General will consider action under the Chapter II prohibition where the evidence suggests that prices are persistently and, for no objective reason, significantly above the level that could be sustained if the undertaking were subject to more effective competition.

Other issues

Excessive prices and joint dominance

2.20 In some markets two or more undertakings may both set excessive prices. Any agreement between them on their pricing policies will almost certainly be prohibited under the Chapter I prohibition. Excessive prices may occur, however, without any explicit agreement between the companies: when undertakings decide to follow each others' prices (parallel pricing) or when they follow the pricing policy of a market leader (price leadership), for example. These forms of behaviour may be considered as tacit collusion. Such behaviour might be prohibited as a concerted practice under the Chapter I prohibition or an abuse of dominance (or joint dominance) under the Chapter II prohibition. **Tacit collusion** might be indicated if price changes were not related to changes in costs, in particular, if the prices of all undertakings had risen when costs had not, or cost reductions had not been passed on to customers via lower prices. Such evidence would normally need to be supplemented by evidence of excess profits.[7]

2.21 The fact that undertakings are charging the same or similar prices, or have increased their prices at the same time, does not of itself, however, provide evidence of tacit collusion. In highly competitive markets, undertakings will be forced by competition to reduce their prices to their minimum costs. If all undertakings sell identical products or services and incur the same level of costs they will tend to charge identical prices. If input costs rise they will all be forced to increase prices by the same amount. Similar price levels and price increases can therefore occur in both collusive and in highly competitive markets.

Excessive prices and inefficiency

2.22 Although excessive prices should normally result in high profits, this will not always be the case: an undertaking protected from competition might be able to sustain higher costs. It would then be more difficult to establish that prices were excessive (because profits would not be particularly high), although the possibility cannot be ruled out. Information used to establish stand-alone cost (see above) may help to indicate whether costs have been incurred efficiently.

Excessive prices as evidence of market power

2.23 The ability of an undertaking to charge excessive prices or to earn excessive profits may provide evidence that it possesses some degree of market power, one of the factors used in assessing whether an agreement has an 'appreciable' effect on competition under the Chapter I prohibition and in identifying 'dominance' in relation to the Chapter II prohibition. This might occur if consistently high prices or profits had not stimulated successful new entry or a significant loss of market share. Evidence on profitability and excessive prices can be largely independent of evidence derived from an analysis of the market and can sometimes be more easily and efficiently obtained than other evidence of market power. The Director General would, however, still expect to identify the barriers which had prevented new entry. (A fuller discussion of market power and barriers to entry can be found in the Competition Act guideline *Assessment of Market Power.*)

[3070]

NOTES
¹ The European Commission's decision to initiate proceedings against Deutsche Telecom suggests that the Commission would be willing to take action under Article 82 where it found that prices were excessive (see European Commission's XXVIIth Report on Competition Policy: 1997, point 77). Deutsche Telecom subsequently agreed to reduce certain tariffs.
² Case 27/76 *United Brands v Commission* [1978] ECR 207, [1978] 1 CMLR 429.
³ See part 7 below.
⁴ In the extreme, the price of an essential facility may be so high that it is equivalent to the essential facility operator refusing to supply the services provided by the essential facility. Refusal to supply is discussed more fully in part 7.
⁵ The law of intellectual property rights also provides an incentive to firms to innovate by preventing the appropriation of commercial ideas that they have developed. (A fuller description of the relationship between the Competition Act and the laws of intellectual property rights can be found in the Competition Act guideline *Intellectual Property Rights.*)
⁶ For further background information and discussion on estimating the rate of supra-normal profitability see Martin Graham and Anthony Steele, The Assessment of Profitability by Competition Authorities, OFT Research Paper No 10, February 1997.
⁷ In Cases T-68/69 etc *Società Italiano Vetro SpA v Commission* [1992] II ECR 1403, [1992] 5 CMLR 302, the Court found that collusive price setting could be an abuse of a joint dominant position.

3 Price discrimination or undue preference

3.1 Price discrimination, and discrimination more generally, may be an abuse under the Chapter II prohibition.¹ Whether it is an abuse depends on the effect of any discrimination on the market.

3.2 The Director General considers price discrimination to be an abuse only where there is evidence that prices were also excessive or that the discrimination was used to reduce competition significantly (for example, because it was predatory or because it involved discounts designed to foreclose markets—these issues are considered in the parts of this guideline on predation and vertical restraints). The remainder of this part looks at the concept of price discrimination, the relationship between price discrimination and costs, how price discrimination might affect competition and the position of undertakings in regulated industries.

What is price discrimination?

3.3 An undertaking can be said to be discriminating when it applies dissimilar conditions to equivalent transactions with other trading parties. The most direct way is through the prices charged to different sets of customers. It can take two basic forms—

— an undertaking might charge different prices to different customers, or categories of customers, for the same product²—where the differences in prices do not reflect any differences in relative cost, quantity, quality or any other characteristics of the products supplied;

— an undertaking might charge different customers, or categories of customers, the same price even though the costs of supplying the product are in fact very different. A policy of uniform delivered prices throughout the country, for example, could be discriminatory if differences in transport costs were significant.

3.4   For price discrimination to be feasible an undertaking not only has to be able to **segment** the market in some way, but also has to be able to enforce the segmentation, so that trading between the different categories of customer who are charged different prices is not possible.

3.5   Where there are objective reasons for an undertaking charging different prices to different customers, such as obviously different transport costs— **price differentiation** as distinct from **price discrimination**—the pricing structure would not be considered discriminatory. The term price discrimination hereafter refers to situations where differences in prices cannot be justified by differences in costs.

Price discrimination and costs

3.6   It is normally efficient from an economic point of view for the prices of products to reflect the incremental costs of production (the cost of an additional increment of output).[3] It is possible that at any given point in time the price of a product may not reflect these incremental costs even in a competitive market. Such divergences are, nevertheless, likely to be temporary because price discrimination is not sustainable in a competitive market: if an undertaking were to try to maintain different prices for the same product it would be vulnerable to undercutting by competitors in the segment of the market where its prices were higher than the competitive level.

3.7   Cost structures inevitably differ between different industries, however, and there can be legitimate reasons why an undertaking might practise price discrimination. This guideline cannot, therefore, be prescriptive. In some industries (network industries such as telecommunications, for example), the presence of economies of scale and economies of scope can mean that marginal costs are below average costs to the extent that at a particular time the cost of an additional unit of output may be extremely low and in certain cases might even be zero. Prices set persistently at this level can clearly not be sustained indefinitely (as other costs must be recovered—see below). In some other industries (such as water), costs may be rising such that marginal cost may be above average cost.

3.8   In general, undertakings will need to set prices above their incremental costs so that common costs, for example, can be recovered. Price discrimination between different customer groups can be a means of achieving this; it can increase output and lead to customers who might otherwise be priced out of the market being served. In particular, in industries with high fixed or common costs and low marginal costs (such as those described above), it may be more efficient to set higher prices to customers with a higher willingness to pay.

3.9   A relevant example of this is peak and off-peak rail travel. Charging commuters (who have a higher willingness to pay than leisure travellers) a higher price so as to recover a bigger proportion of fixed and common costs may allow the train operating company to reduce the share of joint and common costs (and hence the prices) for off-peak travellers. This may increase output overall since if both categories of customers were charged the same price, off-peak travellers might switch to another mode of transport or not travel at all. This would leave peak travellers to pay all the joint and common costs. In the extreme, this may lead to both peak and off-peak travellers switching to another mode of transport. In general, price discrimination will not be an abuse if it leads to a higher level of output in the relevant market(s) than could be achieved if all customers were charged the same price. Similarly, charging the same price when costs are different may also be more efficient in some cases.

3.10 There is therefore no presumption that price discrimination by a dominant undertaking is necessarily an abuse of its dominant position. Discrimination which is clearly aimed at excluding competitors *will*, however, be considered as a potential abuse. Price discrimination issues need to be examined according to the circumstances of each case and the circumstances of each industry.

Effects on competition

3.11 Price discrimination raises two potential issues—
— it may be anti-competitive, excluding competitors from a market; or
— it may allow an undertaking (or group of undertakings) to exploit market power by charging excessively high prices to certain customers.

Anti-competitive effects

3.12 There are two ways in which price discrimination could exclude competitors. First, if it involved predatory pricing in one segment of the market (considered in detail in part 4 of this guideline); and secondly, if there were effects in downstream markets. This might occur if a vertically integrated company were dominant in the upstream market while, at the same time, being a competitor in the downstream market. An anti-competitive strategy by such an undertaking would be to sell the upstream monopoly input to its own downstream associate on more favourable terms than it would sell to others. This could have the effect of distorting competition in the downstream market, in a way that might result in higher prices and reduced output.[4]

Exploitation of customers

3.13 Even though price discrimination may not be anti-competitive in the way described above, some customers might still be worse off as a result of such a price structure. It might then be necessary to consider whether the pricing structure represented an abuse of a dominant position because it involved setting excessive prices to some customers. Where marginal costs are below average costs, however, discriminatory pricing arrangements are likely to be preferable to (that is, more efficient than) uniform prices, as explained above. The more that price discrimination results in increased output or indeed opens up new markets (for example, off-peak rail travel for price-sensitive travellers, such as students, pensioners, families), the more likely it is to have a beneficial impact on economic welfare. Nevertheless, not all discriminatory pricing structures are more economically efficient than uniform prices—it is usually possible to choose some discriminatory prices which are less efficient than others.

Regulated industries

3.14 In the regulated industries, an assessment of the pricing structure (and its effect on competition) will take account of the structure of any price regulation in force. If there were price caps on individual tariffs, for example, the ability of a dominant incumbent to reduce prices to one set of customers while at the same time raising prices to others would be likely to be much more constrained than if the price control system were based on the regulation of average revenues across a range of services.

3.15 In a number of regulated industries there are already restrictions on the ability of certain undertakings to discriminate between customers either in terms of prices or indeed other factors such as the terms and conditions for the supply of a product. In the case of the telecommunications, electricity, gas and railway industries in the United Kingdom and the water industry in England and Wales a number of licences contain conditions that prevent **undue discrimination** or **undue preference**. More detail of the interaction between utility legislation and the Competition Act is given in the guidelines issued by the respective regulators.

Exclusions

3.16 Agreements or conduct to the extent that either is necessary in order to comply with a legal requirement or to provide services of **general economic interest** are excluded from both the Chapter I and Chapter II prohibitions. This exclusion applies to all sectors but is most likely to be of relevance to regulated industries. A number of undertakings within regulated markets are required to offer uniform national prices for a range of products and services (as part of a universal service obligation, for example) even though the costs of providing those services in remote geographical areas is greater than the cost in urban areas. In these circumstances, such a pricing structure would not be regarded as an abuse. (For more detail see the Competition Act guideline *Services of General Economic Interest*.)

Non-price issues

3.17 As noted at the beginning of this part, discrimination should be regarded as applying dissimilar conditions to equivalent transactions; it is not concerned solely with the specific issue of price discrimination. Discrimination on terms other than price can also have anti-competitive effects. If an undertaking which controlled the supply of a key input were to supply a downstream undertaking with a poorer quality of service than it provided to its own business competing in the same downstream market (repairs took longer, for example), and if the difference in service quality were not reflected in the pricing by the upstream undertaking, the undertaking could be regarded as acting in a discriminatory way. Again, however, these practices are not necessarily an abuse. The Director General will need to assess their impact on competition before reaching a conclusion on the question.

[3071]

NOTES

[1]   Price discrimination has been considered by the European Court to be an abuse under Article 82 in a number of cases. For example: Case 27/76 *United Brands v Commission* [1978] ECR 207, [1978] 1 CMLR 429; Napier Brown/British Sugar OJ 1988 L 284/41, [1990] 4 CMLR 196; Case C-333/94P *Tetra Pak II* [1996] I ECR 5951, [1997] 4 CMLR 662; and Case T-229/94 *Deutsche Bahn v Commission* [1998] 4 CMLR 220.

[2]   **Product** here means either goods or services.

[3]   Most economic textbooks, when discussing the efficient output level, refer in certain circumstances to prices reflecting *marginal cost*, a particular type of incremental cost where the increment is one unit of output.

[4]   In its Notice on the Application of Competition Rules to Access Agreements in the Telecommunications Sector (1998), the European Commission refers to this concept as a **price squeeze**. A similar effect could be achieved if a vertically integrated undertaking reduced its downstream retail prices (although such an action may be predatory if the downstream price resulted in losses; see part 4 of this guideline). Indeed, the two actions may be combined.

4 Predation

4.1 Predation is strategic behaviour where an undertaking deliberately incurs short term losses in order to eliminate a competitor so as to be able to charge excessive prices in the future. It occurs where prices are so low that they could force some undertakings out of the market and threaten the competitive process itself. Although consumers may benefit in the short term from such lower prices, in the longer term weakened competition will lead to higher prices, reduced quality and less choice. Since one objective of competition policy is to create conditions where consumers benefit from low prices, there is a distinction between low prices which result from predatory behaviour and low prices which result from legitimate competitive behaviour.

4.2   In assessing predation, a key issue which the Director General will consider is whether the dominant undertaking is covering its costs. The fact that an activity is being run at a loss[1] is not in itself an infringement of the Act: the key question is whether it has an anti-competitive effect. Evidence on the undertaking's intentions is also relevant, therefore. The following paragraphs explain how the Director General assesses evidence on three issues—

— the undertaking's costs;
— the intentions of the undertaking; and
— the feasibility of an undertaking recouping its losses.

Costs

4.3   The European Court of Justice has stated[2] that where prices are below the average variable cost of production,[3] predation should be presumed (variable costs being those which vary directly with the amount of output produced).[4] The Court also held that if prices are above average variable costs but below average total costs, conduct is to be regarded as predatory where it can be established that the purpose of the conduct was to eliminate a competitor.[5]

4.4   The following broad guidelines can be drawn from the judgments of the European Court of Justice cases cited above—

Price below average variable costs	Predation can be assumed
Price above average variable costs, but below average total costs	Evidence on costs may indicate predation, but the Director General would need to establish evidence that the dominant undertaking intended to eliminate a competitor before predation could be found
Price above average total costs	Evidence does not indicate predation

Variable costs

4.5   Before variable costs can be discussed in detail, the relevant time frame must be clarified, as the variability of a cost and hence the magnitude of variable costs will depend crucially on the time frame under consideration—given enough time, for instance, a machine can be replaced by a smaller or larger machine. In *AKZO* the Court did not discuss explicitly the timescale appropriate for analysing predation.

4.6   In general, the Director General will consider that the relevant timescale for the analysis of costs in assessing allegations of predation is the time period over which the alleged predatory price or set of prices prevailed or could reasonably be expected to prevail.

Variable costs as a test for predation

4.7   Prices below average variable costs could be taken as conclusive proof of predation. Generally, sustained selling at below average variable costs is unlikely to be rational. An undertaking failing to cover its variable costs (or if its price is below its average variable costs), is on average making losses on each unit of output it supplies. A rational undertaking could increase its profitability by, for instance, increasing its price, or ceasing supply altogether. Therefore, prices below average variable costs may indicate that predation was occurring in the absence of convincing evidence that the undertaking's behaviour could be objectively justified.

4.8   The Director General will consider any evidence that may justify prices below average variable cost. A policy of loss leading, for example, might be objectively justifiable and would not therefore normally be predatory. A retailer cutting the price of one product in order to increase sales of complementary products would not be acting in a predatory manner unless it was clear that the real intention was to eliminate a competitor. Other possible justifications include—

— **short run promotions**: these often involve selling below average variable costs for a limited period and are widely used in many markets. A dominant undertaking which adopts a one-off short term promotion of this type is unlikely to be found to be in contravention of the Chapter II prohibition. However, a series of short term promotions could, taken together, amount to a predatory strategy. The time period which may be regarded as **short term** will inevitably vary from case to case, and it is not possible to provide general guidance as to what may and may not be acceptable;

— **inefficient entry**: some markets are able to support only one or two undertakings because, for example, there are significant economies of scale. If a new entrant mistakenly believes there is a profitable entry opportunity, its entry may force all undertakings in the market to sell below average variable costs. The incumbent undertakings would then have the choice of remaining in the market, and incurring losses, or exiting the market, perhaps leaving the market to be supplied by a less efficient new entrant. In such circumstances the incumbent's decision to remain in the market, and match the entrant's prices, would not necessarily be considered to be predatory;

— **mistakes**: in some markets demand and/or costs can be volatile and difficult to anticipate. In some cases an undertaking may find itself selling at below its variable costs because of unanticipated increases in input costs, or unanticipated reductions in demand. In such cases the Director General would expect the undertaking to be able to demonstrate that there had indeed been a misunderstanding and that it was taking action to remedy it;

— **externalities**: there are some services (such as telecommunications networks) where the addition of more customers adds to the value of the service sold to other customers. In these circumstances, it can be profitable for the undertaking to sell part of the service to customers at below average variable cost. This will encourage expansion of the network, which benefits all connected customers who then have access to a larger number of subscribers. The undertaking can recoup the loss by charging higher prices elsewhere, thereby increasing its overall profitability. Connection charges to a telecommunications network, for example, might be reduced to below average variable cost to encourage more subscribers to join the network. These losses can then be recovered through, for instance, higher rental charges or higher call charges;

— **the undertaking is making an incremental profit**: if the particular action being complained about is incrementally profitable (see the section below), it is unlikely that it is predatory. The Director General still needs to be convinced, however, that the reduction in losses will shortly result in the undertaking covering its average variable costs.

PART III
OFT GUIDELINES

Alternative cost floors

4.9   Average variable costs may not always be relevant to an analysis of predation, particularly for regulated industries. Such industries may, for example, exhibit economies of scale and scope which can mean that their variable costs may be extremely low, or indeed zero. In such cases, average variable cost may have no relevance to the analysis of predation. Such a cost structure is common to a number of the regulated industries.[6] The sector regulators have generally indicated that they consider that an alternative approach may be required when assessing allegations of predation (within the requirement for consistency with Community law imposed on the Director General and regulators by section 60 of the Act—see the Competition Act guideline *The Major Provisions*). Details can be found in the relevant sector-specific Competition Act guidelines issued by the regulators.

Avoidable costs

4.10   Where prices are above average *variable* costs but below average total costs the Director General may consider other evidence on costs. He might, for example, consider whether the undertaking is covering its avoidable costs, those which could be avoided if the undertaking were to cease the activity in question (the **activity** being the part of the business accused of predating) over the relevant time period. Avoidable costs include both the fixed costs and the variable costs of the activity in question, but they do not include—

- **common costs**: some undertakings have costs which are common across a number of different activities. If the alleged predation relates to only some of the undertaking's activities, the Director General generally does not include common costs in his assessment of whether predation is occurring because they are not avoidable costs unless the undertaking ceases its activities elsewhere. A large corporation will typically have substantial management overheads which will often be common to all the undertaking's activities. The Director General may, however, expect the undertaking to cover common costs through the activities to which these costs contribute: if an airline offers first class seats and economy seats on a particular flight, and if only the market for economy seats were under consideration, the avoidable costs would be fairly low since the undertaking must continue to operate the aeroplane if it is to sustain its first class business. The Director General might, however, want to verify that the undertaking would cover the avoidable costs of the aeroplane across both the economy and first class businesses;[7]

- **sunk costs**: costs which have already been incurred and are sunk are, by definition, not avoidable. There may be exceptions to this rule if sunk costs are incurred as part of the alleged predatory strategy, since the undertaking could then have avoided them by not incurring them in the first place.

4.11   Prices below average avoidable costs might, therefore, be evidence of predation. It would not be as strong as evidence that prices were below average variable costs, however, although pricing below average avoidable costs may not always constitute evidence of predation in regulated industries.

Intentions

4.12   Evidence on the intentions of the undertaking may be relevant in an investigation of predation. On the basis of the *AKZO* and *Tetra Pak II* judgments,[8] the fact that undertakings set prices below average variable costs is itself evidence of an intent to remove competitors.

4.13   In contrast, where prices fall between average variable costs and average total costs, the Director General may consider other evidence on the intentions of the dominant undertaking before establishing whether its behaviour is predatory. Pricing in this range for short periods will often be a rational strategy and represent legitimate competition. In those circumstances, it would not be an abuse. Prices set at this level as part of a strategy to eliminate a competitor would, however, be an abuse.

4.14 In addition to the evidence on costs explained above, the following areas of evidence on the undertaking's intentions may be relevant.

Incremental losses

4.15 Predation is strategic behaviour where an undertaking accepts short term losses in order to eliminate a competitor so as to be able to charge excessive prices in the future. It follows that the alleged predatory strategy should lead to incremental losses for the undertaking in the short term. If the alleged behaviour results in higher profits (or lower losses) than it otherwise would, that behaviour would be legitimate competition and would not be an abuse. Thus, where an undertaking can demonstrate that its behaviour is increasing its profits (or reducing its losses) that particular behaviour should not be treated as predatory.[9]

4.16 An incremental profit is made if the action results in higher profits, or lower losses, than would otherwise have been the case.[10] When a dominant undertaking cuts its prices, the price cut is likely to result in higher demand for the undertaking's product, either because consumers switch away from its competitors or because the overall demand for the product increases as a result of the lower prices. If the price cut resulted in an increase in revenue, large enough to cover the additional costs incurred in meeting the greater demand, the price cut would be incrementally profit-making. Even if the undertaking's competitors were harmed by the price cut (as occurs whenever an undertaking cuts its prices), the action would not be predatory. A shop cutting its price of one product to below its average variable cost of supplying that product, for example, might still be incrementally profitable if the price cut led to a significant increase in sales of complementary products. Assessing whether a price cut is incrementally profitable is sometimes referred to as a **net-revenue test**.

4.17 In practice, assessing whether an action has resulted in higher or lower profits is not straightforward. Difficulties can arise in determining the appropriate comparison: where the action is a simple price cut the best comparison is between the undertaking's profits before and after the price cut. Where the price cut occurred at the same time as a new entrant entered the market, however, the incumbent undertaking's profitability prior to the price cut is less useful, since its profitability would have been reduced by the new entrant in any event. If the price cut occurred during a period of volatile demand or costs, the undertaking's profits would also have changed irrespective of the price cut.

Other evidence on the behaviour of the undertaking

4.18 In some cases the behaviour of the undertaking will indicate whether there is intent to predate against a rival. The targeting of price cuts against a new entrant, while prices were maintained elsewhere, would be consistent with predation. Conversely, an across-the-board price cut, not restricted to areas where new competition existed, is not evidence of intent. Other evidence might include the timing of the action, whether it followed a pattern of aggressive pricing or was a one-off, whether the undertaking engaged in **dirty tricks**, or any other relevant evidence. In some instances documentary evidence may be used to determine whether an undertaking intended to predate.

Feasibility of recouping losses

4.19 Predation is an abuse because undertakings intend to eliminate competitors, which could then allow them to charge excessive prices (or offer less favourable terms or service quality below the competitive level) in the future. At a minimum, such excessive prices must recoup the losses incurred from the predatory strategy. If the undertaking would not be able to recoup these losses because it would still face competition, from existing or potential competitors, the strategy will be bound to fail. Predation can be an abuse only if practised by a dominant undertaking.

4.20 Undertakings are dominant only if they possess a substantial level of market power allowing them to act independently of competitors and customers (see the Competition Act guideline *Assessment of Market Power*). A dominant undertaking can therefore be expected to be able to recoup losses in a market where it is already dominant as the existence of barriers to entry will enable it to raise prices in the future. The fact that the undertaking is dominant means that predation is feasible and so does not require explicit analysis. If, however, an undertaking is attempting to predate in a related market where it does not currently have a dominant position, the feasibility of predation will need to be analysed explicitly. It will be necessary to take into account whether barriers to entry in that market would enable the undertaking to raise prices sufficiently to enable it to recoup the losses from predation.

4.21 In *AKZO*, the European Court of Justice found the dominant undertaking's conduct in the market in which it was dominant to be an abuse without explicitly considering whether recouping losses would be feasible. The Director General therefore does not consider that he would necessarily be required to establish that predation was feasible if the alleged predatory behaviour was undertaken by a dominant undertaking in the market in which it was dominant (that is, in circumstances similar to those found by the European Court in the *AKZO* case). The question of feasibility will still arise, however, where a dominant undertaking is alleged to be acting in a predatory way in a related market where it is not currently dominant.

Cross-subsidies

4.22 The term cross-subsidy is usually used when there is an implication that an undertaking has financed under-performing activity from another area of its business where revenues from one market are used to subsidise losses in another market. Cross-subsidy can often be viewed as an abuse in itself, however, and this is discussed below. Where an undertaking is financing losses in one market from profits made in another market where it has market power, there could be a significant effect on competition.

4.23 In its guidelines covering the telecommunications sector, for example, the European Commission has stated that a cross-subsidy represents an abuse of a dominant position in the following situation—

'*subsidising activities under competition, whether concerning services or equipment, by allocating their costs to monopoly activities . . . is likely to distort competition in violation of Article 86.*'[11]

4.24 Virtually the same principle is used in its guidelines on postal services,[12] and the same principles might be expected to apply elsewhere. The statement refers to monopoly activities, but it seems likely that an abuse could also occur where an undertaking was dominant, short of holding an absolute monopoly.

4.25 In the United Kingdom, the issue of cross-subsidy is of particular importance in regulated industries, especially where competition is being introduced into some product markets currently supplied by dominant incumbents. In a number of regulated industries there are specific licence requirements which prohibit cross-subsidy.

Effect of cross-subsidy on competition

4.26 In general, the assessment of cross-subsidy is similar to the assessment of predatory pricing and will follow the principles described above. However, cross-subsidy (or any subsidy, however it is financed) may significantly affect competition without necessarily being predatory.

4.27 When considering whether an undertaking is receiving a subsidy in a particular market, the Director General adopts the approach to assessing costs explained in parts 2 and 4 above. The use of stand-alone cost as a price ceiling together with an appropriate cost floor for predatory pricing (such as average variable costs or some other alternative) implies that a **subsidy-free** price for a product could lie in the range between this cost floor and its stand-alone cost.

Exclusions

4.28 As already noted in part 3 above, an agreement or conduct to the extent that either is necessary in order to comply with a legal requirement or to provide services of **general economic interest** are excluded from both the Chapter I and the Chapter II prohibitions. This exclusion applies to all sectors but is likely to be of particular relevance to regulated industries. Cross-subsidies between different classes of customers or even between different products are, therefore, unlikely to be considered to be anti-competitive behaviour or an abuse of dominance where they are required as a result of the regulatory framework. Where, for example, a cross-subsidy arises as a result of a formal requirement on an incumbent undertaking to offer uniform prices across the country (in the context, say, of some form of universal service obligation) it is possible that urban users could be subsidising rural consumers or that business users could be subsidising residential customers (see the Competition Act guideline *Services of General Economic Interest*).

[3072]

NOTES

1 The terms 'making a loss' and 'low rate of return' are used interchangeably in this part.

2 Case C62/86 *AKZO Chemie BV v Commission* [1993] 5 CMLR 215 and Case C-333/94P *Tetra Pak II* [1997] 4 CMLR 662.

3 As explained in paragraph 4.9 et seq, in some industries a cost floor other than average variable cost may be more appropriate.

4 In *AKZO*, the Court stated that labour did not vary directly with output and so could not be considered as a variable cost. It is worth noting that the variability of a cost may depend on the definition of output used. In transport markets for example, costs may not vary greatly with passenger miles even though they may vary significantly with vehicle miles.

5 A further case involving the use of non-price predation ('fighting ships') (Cases T24–26 & 28/93 *Compagnie Maritime Belge Transports SA and Others v Commission* [1997] 4 CMLR 273) is currently on appeal to the ECJ.

6 In its Notice on the Application of Competition Rules to Access Agreements in the Telecommunications Sector (1998), for example, the European Commission indicated that in the telecommunications sector average incremental costs (the cost of an increment in output) might be used as a cost floor for analysing allegations of predation (see the Competition Act guideline *The Application of the Competition Act in the Telecommunications Sector*).

7 In cases of this type, the Director General would still consider whether the airline was acting anti-competitively by cross-subsidising its economy business through excess returns earned on its first class business.

8 See footnote 1 to para 4.3.

9 For example, in Cases T24–26 & 28/93 *Compagnie Maritime Belge Transports SA and Others v Commission* [1997] 4 CMLR 273, the Court cited the fact that the parties 'admit having reduced their earnings' as evidence of an abuse (paragraph 141). This case is on appeal to the ECJ.

10 For more information on the assessment of incremental losses see Geoffrey Myers Predatory Behaviour in UK Competition Policy, OFT Research Paper No 5, November 1994.

11 Guidelines on the Application of the EC Competition Rules in the Telecommunications Sector, 1991.

12 Postal Services (Competition and State Measures) Guidelines, 1998.

5 Discounts

5.1 The offering of discounts to certain customers is a form of price competition and is therefore generally to be encouraged. Discounts often simply reflect the lower costs of supplying certain customers or groups of customers and in these circumstances do not raise any competition issues.

5.2 As with other pricing issues, discounts will infringe the prohibitions only if they are anti-competitive—if prices are set at predatory levels, or if they are used to foreclose a market, for example. Foreclosure can occur when discounts are conditional on customers buying all or a large proportion of their purchases from the dominant undertaking (**fidelity discounts**), or where they are conditional on the purchase of tied products (see part 6 below). Foreclosure effects, and other effects of vertical restraints, are explained in more detail in the next part (see also the Competition Act guideline *Vertical Agreements and Restraints*).

[3073]

6 Vertical restraints

6.1 In general, vertical restraints are provisions made between undertakings operating at different levels in the economic process in relation to any particular agreement which restricts the commercial freedom of one or more parties. The agreement might, for example, be between a manufacturer and a retailer, a manufacturer and a wholesaler, a wholesaler and a retailer, a retailer and a customer or even between two wholesalers which, for the purposes of the agreement, operate at different stages in the supply chain. In this guideline reference is made to agreements between a manufacturer and a retailer, but the same principles apply to agreements between any two parties which, for the purposes of the agreement, operate at different stages in the supply chain and in the supply of goods, services or property rights (for more on property rights see the Competition Act guidelines *Land Agreements* and *Intellectual Property Rights*).

6.2 Because competition is affected only if market power is present at one or both stages in the supply chain, few of the many contracts between manufacturers and retailers which place some restriction on the commercial freedom of one or both parties raise competition concerns. Nevertheless, even if none of the undertakings possesses market power individually, there may be a series of similar agreements which cover a group of undertakings that collectively possess substantial market power. Such **networks** of agreements may have appreciable effects on competition.

6.3 Even if they do restrict competition, vertical restraints can also produce benefits which can outweigh any anti-competitive effects they produce. An assessment of the effects of a vertical restraint needs to take account of both its potential anti-competitive effects and any countervailing benefits it produces.[1]

6.4 Vertical restraints are often part of an agreement and may therefore fall within the scope of the Chapter I prohibition. It is intended, however, that an Order will be introduced so that the Chapter I prohibition will not apply to certain specified categories of vertical agreements, subject to a **clawback** provision. The Chapter II prohibition will, however, apply to vertical restraints.

6.5 The following paragraphs provide a brief explanation of how vertical restraints imposed by dominant undertakings will be assessed under the Chapter II prohibition, and how networks of agreements will be assessed where the exclusion from the Chapter I prohibition is clawed back. Further details of how the exclusion will operate can be found in the Competition Act guideline *Vertical Agreements and Restraints*.

Types of vertical restraint

6.6   There is a wide range of restrictions which might appear in vertical agreements. The following list is not exhaustive but covers the main types of restriction which might potentially affect competition—

— **resale price maintenance (RPM)**: where the manufacturer specifies the resale price of the product. Commonly the manufacturer will specify only a minimum or a maximum price (it is expected that RPM will not be excluded from the Chapter I prohibition under the proposed vertical agreement exclusion order referred to above);

— **selective distribution**: where a manufacturer supplies only a limited number of retailers who are restricted in their ability to re-sell products. **Exclusive distribution** is a particular form of selective distribution where the manufacturer supplies only one retailer in a particular territory or allows only one retailer to supply a particular class of customer, such as businesses or consumers;

— **exclusive purchasing** or **dealing**: where the retailer agrees to purchase, or deal in, goods from only one manufacturer;

— **tie-in sales** and **bundling**: where the manufacturer makes the purchase of one product (the **tying** product) conditional on the purchase of a second product (the **tied** product). A set of tied products is sometimes referred to as a **bundle** of products;

— **full-line forcing**: an extreme form of tie-in sale where the retailer must stock the full range of the manufacturer's product range;

— **quantity forcing**: where the retailer is required to purchase a minimum quantity of a certain product; and

— **fidelity discounts**: where the retailer receives discounts based on the proportion of its sales which come from the manufacturer.

6.7   These arrangements are common business practices and are not prohibited unless they lead to a significant reduction in competition. The following paragraphs explain briefly—

— the possible anti-competitive effects of vertical restraints;
— the countervailing benefit they might produce; and
— how their overall effect will be assessed.

Competition effects

6.8   RPM can have direct effects on competition. Where prices are fixed absolutely, or minimum prices are specified, there will be no price competition between the retailers affected. The Director General expects to find all such restrictions in breach of the Chapter I prohibition and unlikely to benefit from an exemption.

6.9   In most other cases contractual terms in vertical agreements will not raise competition concerns, but they can produce appreciable effects on competition when combined with market power. They can also represent an abuse when imposed by dominant undertakings. The main effects are market foreclosure, raising rivals' costs and competition dampening.

Market foreclosure and raising rivals' costs

6.10   Markets are foreclosed when undertakings are unable to enter the market either completely or partially. A market might be partially foreclosed if, for example, undertakings had a much lower market share than they would in the absence of the vertical restraint, or if smaller undertakings were prevented from entering the market. Partial foreclosure often results when the vertical restraint raises rivals' costs, thereby raising entry barriers or forcing existing competitors out of the market. Vertical restraints can foreclose markets at either the manufacturer or retailer level.

PART III
OFT GUIDELINES

Foreclosure to manufacturers

6.11 The following are examples of vertical restraints that might foreclose a market to a manufacturer—

— **exclusive purchasing** or **dealing** may foreclose a market to a new manufacturer if potential retail outlets are tied to existing manufacturers and if they restrict appreciably the ability of new competitors to enter the market or the ability of existing competitors to expand their market share;[2]

— **tie-in sales** and **full-line forcing** can have similar effects as they can discourage a retailer from stocking the products of new manufacturers if the new products would displace sales of the tied products;[3]

— **quantity forcing** and **fidelity discounts** can have similar effects because a retailer will be reluctant to stock and promote the products of a rival manufacturer if, for example, it must purchase a high proportion of its products, or a large quantity, from one manufacturer to obtain a large discount.[4] A similar abuse may occur where the discounts are dependent on dealers meeting sales targets based on their previous year's sales.[5]

6.12 In all such cases, an important first question is the degree of competition between retailers: whether a manufacturer could avoid the restrictions by using alternative retailers, or by setting up its own retail operation. Foreclosure at the manufacturing level will occur only if retailers have market power, or if there is a network of agreements covering a significant proportion of retailers, and barriers to new entry in retailing exist.[6]

6.13 A second factor is the opportunities to renegotiate contracts. If one or more exclusive dealing contracts will shortly be reviewed it may be possible for a rival manufacturer to use that opportunity to secure the distribution of its products.

6.14 A third factor is the market power of the manufacturer. The extent to which a manufacturer can foreclose a significant proportion of retailers is likely to depend on its own market power. A dominant manufacturer foreclosing all potential retail outlets—unless the first two factors above indicate otherwise—is likely to be found to be behaving in an abusive way. Where a number of manufacturers with collective market power have foreclosed the market to new entry by competing manufacturers, the Director General may wish to withdraw the benefit of the special treatment given to the manufacturers' vertical agreements under the Chapter I prohibition (clawback), described more fully in the Competition Act guideline *Vertical Agreements and Restraints*.

Foreclosure to retailers

6.15 The following restraints might foreclose markets to retailers—

— **exclusive distribution** can foreclose the market if practised by a sufficient proportion of manufacturers. **Selective distribution** can also foreclose markets to retailers, depending on the conditions they have to meet. If a manufacturer imposed an absolute restriction on the number of retailers the effect would be likely to be more significant than if it set objective standards for all its retailers to meet. However, such objective standards may still prevent entry by new innovative retail operations and the Director General might become concerned if standards were clearly designed to favour existing retailers over new entrants;

— **tie-in sales** and **full-line** forcing can restrict entry by smaller retailers or undertakings which wish to specialise in more limited product ranges. **Quantity forcing** can also prevent entry by small-scale retailers.

6.16 In these examples the key factor is likely to be the market power of the manufacturer, or manufacturers, imposing the restraints.[7] The size of any networks will also be important: even where a manufacturer has a relatively small market share individually, the network of agreements may cover a high percentage of the market. In situations where a network of agreements exists, the Director General may wish to withdraw the benefit of the special treatment given to the agreements under the Chapter I prohibition by using the power of claw-back.

6.17 A further consideration in assessing the market power of the manufacturers is likely to be the strength of their brands. These brands may enjoy market power even when they are not market leaders. Retailers may find it difficult to establish themselves if they are unable to stock certain leading brands which customers expect to find available.

Competition dampening

6.18 The assessment of the foreclosure effects above involves establishing whether the restraints created a significant or absolute barrier to new entry, or would force existing competitors out of the market. Vertical restraints can also affect competition by reducing its intensity, or **dampening** competition.

6.19 The effects of foreclosure to manufacturers described above can reduce competition between manufacturers, **inter-brand** competition. This is likely to occur when the restraints lead to different retailers becoming tied to different products; or when retailers are differentiated by their location; or when the costs to customers of shopping around between retailers are high relative to product values (high search costs). Customers are less likely to shop around for low-value items than they are for high-value items, for example. This reduction in inter-brand competition can lead to higher prices or lower quality products.

6.20 The effects of foreclosure to retailers described above may similarly reduce competition between retailers of the same product, **intra-brand** competition. Selective distribution, for example, reduces the number of competing retailers in a particular product, reducing the intensity of retail competition in that product. This can lead to higher retail margins and less innovation in retailing and distribution.

Other effects

6.21 The list is not exhaustive and vertical restraints can have other anti-competitive effects, particularly when they reinforce other competition problems. Tie-in sales, for example, can be used to extend the scope of excessive prices.[8]

Benefits of vertical restraints

6.22 While vertical restraints, in the presence of market power, can lead to anti-competitive effects, they may also produce economic benefits which outweigh the anti-competitive effects. Vertical restraints are often used to overcome failures in the operation of the market. The most frequently cited benefits of vertical restraints are that they overcome **free-rider** problems which arise in the distribution of certain products. These benefits might allow an agreement to receive an individual exemption from the Chapter I prohibition (if it were not already excluded from the prohibition) or provide an objective justification which would prevent the imposition of the restraint being an abuse of dominance under the Chapter II prohibition.

Free-riding between retailers

6.23 In some markets, retailers provide services such as demonstrating products, and providing advice to potential purchasers. These services bring benefits to the customer and help to increase sales of the product. The benefits of providing the services can, however, spill over to other retailers not providing the services: they avoid the inherent costs, and are therefore able to undercut the full-service retailers. Customers may then opt to use the demonstration facilities at the high-service retailer but purchase the products from the lower-cost, **discount** retailer. The discount retailer would then be free-riding on the demonstration services of the high-cost retailer who would lose sales and therefore be likely to cut back on its demonstration services, possibly to a level below which the manufacturer stipulated.

6.24 These problems are most likely to arise in products which are relatively expensive to the customer, which are complex and technical, lacking in strong brands, or which are one-off purchases, and where the customer will have limited knowledge of the product. Similar issues can arise when retailers invest in advertising or promotion which may generate sales for competing retailers.

6.25 Manufacturers may use vertical restraints to overcome the problems resulting from free-riding by, for example, imposing selective distribution conditions which would require all retailers selling their products to provide the necessary demonstration services. At the extreme, the manufacturer could use a system of exclusive distribution to ensure there was only one outlet in a particular area and therefore no prospect of free-riding.

Free-riding between manufacturers

6.26 Free-riding between manufacturers normally arises when a manufacturer provides support to a retailer. This might include providing information on potential customers, financing investment in equipment, or technical support for staff training and servicing and repair facilities. If the retailer sells the products of a number of competing manufacturers, this support may benefit the sales of rival products as well as the manufacturer's own. Other manufacturers are able to free-ride on the investments and support provided by one manufacturer. Manufacturers may also free-ride on the brand image of a rival manufacturer. For some manufacturers, retail services form part of the product's brand image on which rival manufacturers, selling through the same outlet, could free-ride.

6.27 Manufacturers may try to remedy this problem by requiring the retailer to commit to an exclusive purchasing obligation, or by using some form of quantity or line forcing.

Other benefits from vertical restraints

6.28 Manufacturers may wish to control the numbers of retailers to ensure that economies of scale in distribution are achieved. This may lead them to impose selective distribution. They may wish to ensure that retailers stock a full range of products in order to achieve certain economies of scope between these products in production or distribution. This could be achieved by imposing tie-ins or full-line forcing. They may also wish to control retail margins to prevent retailers exploiting any downstream market power, which can lead to the imposition of maximum RPM. They may also wish to share the risks faced by retailers necessary to distribute their products (if the retailer has to invest in sunk costs, for example). In return a manufacturer may charge a higher unit price to the retailer or require the retailer to deal exclusively in its products.

Assessing the effects of vertical restraints

6.29 As with other issues, the Director General will assess the impact of a vertical restraint only if market power is present. This may occur if, for example, one undertaking is dominant or if there is a network of agreements covering undertakings which will collectively possess market power, leading to appreciable effects on competition.

6.30 Where market power exists, the Director General will assess the impact of the restraint on competition to see if any of the effects described above do occur.

This will depend on the form of the restraint and the degree of market power which exists. The key issues will be the extent to which the restraint forecloses the market, raises rivals' costs or dampens competition between existing competitors. This will normally depend on the scope of the restrictions, the market power of the other parties to the agreement, and the duration of the restrictions.

6.31 Where, however, a vertical restraint is likely to produce economic benefits even if an appreciable anti-competitive effect does occur, the Director General will assess whether any such benefits outweigh that effect. In general, the benefits of vertical restraints are more likely to outweigh any anti-competitive effects where the markets involve—

— complex, technical, and relatively expensive products;
— new products with weak branding;
— one-off rather than repeat purchases;
— customers who will have little knowledge of the product; and
— few economies of scope in retailing between the products of different manufacturers and low barriers to entry in retailing.

6.32 In practice, the Director General will not normally conduct a detailed cost-benefit analysis balancing anti-competitive effects against countervailing benefits. Instead, where both anti-competitive effects and significant benefits exist, the issue will be whether the form of the restraint is the least anti-competitive way to achieve the benefits. A vertical restraint might still be a breach of the Chapter I prohibition if there were clearly less anti-competitive ways to achieve the same benefits. In particular, to qualify for an exemption from the Chapter I prohibition an agreement must meet the specific criteria set out in the Act and the objective and appreciable advantages must be sufficient to outweigh any disadvantages to competition (see the Competition Act guideline *The Chapter I Prohibition*).

Vertical restraints as a barrier to entry

6.33 The analysis above considered the effects on competition of the imposition or acceptance of a vertical restraint and whether it might be in breach of the prohibitions in the Act. However, in some circumstances—where a restraint is not itself prohibited—it might still increase entry barriers and therefore be viewed as evidence of market power when assessing some other potential infringement (see the Competition Act guideline *Assessment of Market Power*).

[3074]

NOTES

[1] See Chapter 2 of Paul Dobson and Michael Waterson, Vertical Restraints in Competition Policy, OFT Research Paper No 12, December 1996.

[2] This has been found to be the case by the European Court: see, for example, Case C-234/89 *Stergios Delimitis v Henninger Bräu* [1991] I ECR 935, [1992] 5 CMLR 210. The imposition of exclusive dealing requirements by dominant undertakings could also be an abuse, see Case 85/76 *Hoffman-La Roche v Commission* [1979] ECR 461, [1979] 3 CMLR 211.

[3] Tying restrictions have been found to be an abuse under Article 82: see, for example, Case C-53/92P *Hilti v Commission* [1994] I ECR 667, [1994] 4 CMLR 614.

[4] This was found to be a potential abuse by the European Court in Case 85/76 *Hoffman-La Roche v Commission* [1979] ECR 461, [1979] 3 CMLR 211.

[5] This was found to be the case by the European Court in, for example, Case 322/81 *Michelin v Commission* [1983] ECR 3461, [1985] 1 CMLR 282.

[6] In practice there are often significant sunk costs involved in establishing a significant retail operation so the main issue in assessing the impact of a restriction is often the extent to which the existing retail sector is foreclosed to a new manufacturer.

[7] It may be that incumbent retailers are themselves forcing manufacturers to impose the vertical restraint. In such circumstances the market power of the incumbent retailers must also be considered.

[8] In some circumstances two different vertical restraints may have a similar effect. In some circumstances, it is possible to combine two vertical restraints and thereby reproduce the effect of a third.

7   Refusal to supply and access to essential facilities

Refusal to supply

7.1   The Director General takes the view that refusal to supply an existing customer by a dominant undertaking can be an abuse if no objective justification for the behaviour can be provided.[1] Obvious justifications might include the fact that the customer had a poor creditworthiness, or that supplies were cut for a temporary period due to capacity constraints. The Director General might conclude that similar behaviour—deliberately delaying supplies or supplying products of an inferior quality, for example—could also be an abuse. In some limited circumstances the refusal to supply a new customer might be an abuse.[2]

7.2   Refusal to supply might be used to impose a vertical restraint. A manufacturer imposing a selective distribution system, for example, would, by definition, be refusing to supply outlets which were not within the system, as considered above. In other cases, refusal to supply may be used to exclude certain competitors, particularly in upstream or downstream markets. Such behaviour by a dominant undertaking is clearly likely to be an abuse in the absence of objective justification. More recent cases of this type have raised the question of whether the dominant undertaking is abusing ownership of an essential facility.

An essential facility

7.3   Whether a particular facility is **essential** has to be assessed on a case-by-case basis.[3] Potential examples include ports,[4] bus stations, utility distribution networks (for example, electricity wires, water and gas pipelines) and some telecommunications networks. In some cases an intellectual property right might be considered to be an essential facility. Competitors may, for example, be able to develop alternative intellectual property in order to compete in a related market (the Competition Act guideline *Intellectual Property Rights* provides further information on the relationship between intellectual property rights and dominant positions).

7.4   Market definition is crucial to the determination of whether a particular facility is **essential**. An asset will not be an essential facility if other similar facilities compete within the same relevant market: a port will not be an essential facility if other ports compete within the same geographic market or if other modes of transport compete with the ferry services under consideration (see the Competition Act guideline *Market Definition*).

Access to essential facilities

7.5   If a facility is considered to be essential, the Director General would expect competitors to have access at economically efficient prices in order to compete in a related market (see part 2 above regarding excessive pricing). If this were not the case, the facility owner would be likely to be acting anti-competitively, unless the lack of access could be justified objectvely.[5] This is likely to be rare (other than for normal commercial reasons, such as creditworthiness). The ease with which third party access is afforded to an essential facility will, however, depend on the availability of spare capacity within the facility.

NOTES
¹   Cases 6 & 7/73 *Instituto Chemioterapico Italiano SpA & Commercial Solvents Corp v Commission* [1974] ECR 223, [1974] 1 CMLR 309.
²   Cases C-241 & 242/91 *RTE and ITP v Commission ('Magill')* [1995] 1 ECR 743, [1995] 4 CMLR 718, which involved the refusal to license copyright. In general refusal to license an intellectual property right is not an abuse. Examples of the circumstances where it would be are described in the Competition Act guideline *Intellectual Property Rights*.

³   A facility can be viewed as essential if access to it is indispensable in order to compete in a related market; and duplication is impossible or extremely difficult owing to physical, geographic or legal constraints (or is highly undesirable for reasons of public policy). See, for example, the judgement of the ECJ in Case C-7/79 *Oscar Bronner v Mediaprint and others*, [1998] and in particular the opinion of AG Jacobs, paragraphs 47 & 65.

⁴   The principal vehicle for the development of the essential features doctrine by the European Commission has been ports. The use of the port of Holyhead has been considered, for example: in *Sealink v B&I*, [1992] 5 CMLR 255, B&I's operation of a ferry service out of Holyhead was said to be compromised by the itinerary of the ferry services of Sealink, the owner of the port facility. In another case, *Sea Containers v Stena Sealink*, OJ 1994 No L 15/8, [1995] 4 CMLR 84, Sea Containers had requested use of the harbour for a new ferry service.

⁵   In order to plead the existence of abuse, the refusal of access to the facility must be likely to eliminate all competition in the market on the part of the person requiring access, and the refusal must be incapable of objective justification: see, for example, Case C-7/79 *Oscar Bronner v Mediaprint and others* [1998].

8   Actions in related markets

8.1   An investigation under the Act will usually need to establish that an undertaking possesses or would possess some degree of market power within a relevant market in order to assess whether an agreement would have an appreciable effect on competition or, in the case of dominance, whether the relevant undertaking has substantial market power.[1] It is not, however, necessary to show that the anti-competitive agreement or conduct under investigation existed in the same market as the one where the undertaking possessed market power. In certain circumstances the Chapter II prohibition may apply where an undertaking, dominant in one market, commits an abuse in a different but closely associated market. This principle has been set out by the European Court of Justice in the case of *Tetra Pak II*.[2]

8.2   There are two principal ways in which an undertaking that has a dominant position in one product market might then be able to exploit that position to behave anti-competitively in another market—

— **vertical links**: where an undertaking has control of a key input into a downstream market in which it is competing with other undertakings, control over a key input might enable the undertaking to foreclose the downstream market to other competitors (see part 6 of this guideline covering 'Vertical restraints' and part 7 on 'Refusal to supply and access to essential facilities'); and

— **horizontal links**: where an undertaking has dominance in one product market and uses it to acquire dominance or to strengthen an existing dominant position in a separate—and not vertically related—market.

8.3   The process of extending market power in one market into another, separate, market through horizontal links is often referred to as the leverage of market power. There are a number of mechanisms, considered in part 6 above, by which an undertaking might be able to leverage its market power—

— **pricing and discount structures**: the dominant undertaking could offer discounts based on total expenditure on the two products;

— **tie-ins** or **bundling**: the dominant undertaking makes purchases of the product where it has market power dependent on purchases of the product where it does not; and,

— **cross-subsidy**: the dominant undertaking uses its profits from its dominant position in the first market to cross-subsidise its activities in the second market.

8.4   Leverage of market power covers activities in two distinct product markets where the products in question are not necessarily complementary. Where two activities are complementary (the sale of a product and the provision of maintenance services associated with the product, for example) there may be grounds for including them within the same relevant product market, in which case the issue of leverage of market power, as such, would not arise. The Competition Act guideline *Market Definition* includes further discussion of the treatment of complementary products.

8.5 Where there are distinct product markets, the issue of determining whether an undertaking's conduct in one market might be considered to be an abuse of a dominant position in another market has to be taken together with an assessment of the extent to which it is feasible for action in one market to have an anti-competitive effect in another market. The most obvious way to assess the feasibility of an undertaking leveraging market power would be to consider the proximity of the two markets. Where they were not at all related, it is unlikely that market power in one market would confer any sort of influence in the other. Where they were closely linked, leverage of market power becomes more feasible.

8.6 In between the two extreme categories there may well be a third category where products could be loosely related. For example, there might be a similar set of customers but, say, little overlap in terms of functionality between products. In this situation the ability to leverage market power would probably have to depend on other additional factors, not just the fact that the goods were linked in some way. Such issues are perhaps more likely to arise in the context of technology-based sectors such as telecommunications, broadcasting, and information technology, where technological convergence can mean that the distinctions between the services become increasingly blurred. Technological developments may mean that products which were formerly supplied separately could then be integrated into a single product so that an undertaking with market power in one of the markets might be able to establish a dominant position in the new, converged, market.

[3076]

NOTES

¹ It is important to emphasise that although the tests for appreciability and dominance are different, in both cases the Director General will be interested in the competitive constraints that act on the undertaking (or undertakings). Furthermore, the assessment of market power is simply part of the Director General's overall analysis of whether there has been a breach of either or both of the prohibitions in the Act. It is neither a new concept nor a new test in addition to those which are set out in the Act itself or imported from Community law under section 60 of the Act.

² Case C-333/94P *Tetra Pak II* [1996] I ECR 5951, [1997] 4 CMLR 662: the Court found that Tetra Pak's activities in relation to the markets in non-aseptic machines and cartons constituted an abuse of its dominant position in the distinct, but closely associated, markets for aseptic machines and cartons intended for the packaging of liquid foods.

9 Glossary of terms

Terms used in a definition which are themselves defined are italicised.

Average costs	An undertaking's *total costs* divided by its output.
Average avoidable costs	An undertaking's *total avoidable costs* divided by its output.
Average variable costs	An undertaking's total *variable costs* divided by its output.
Avoidable costs	The costs avoided if an undertaking ceases supplying a particular market.
Bundling	See *tie-in sales*.

Common costs	Costs incurred when supplying a group of products or services, and which would not be reduced if the undertaking ceased supplying one of these products.
Economies of scale	Where *average costs* decline as output increases.
Economies of scope	Where *average costs* are lower if two or more products are produced jointly (for example, by the same undertaking) rather than separately (for example, by two separate undertakings). Economies of scope occur where there are *common costs*.
Essential facility	A facility to which access is indispensable in order to compete on the market and duplication of which is impossible or extremely difficult owing to physical, geographic or legal constraints, or is highly undesirable for reasons of public policy.
Exclusive distribution	A particular form of *selective distribution* where the manufacturer supplies only one retailer in a particular territory or allows one retailer to supply a particular class of customer, such as businesses or consumers.
Exclusive purchasing or dealing	Where the retailer agrees to purchase, or 'deal' in, goods from only one manufacturer.
Fidelity discounts	Where the retailer receives discounts based on the proportion of its sales which come from the manufacturer.
Fixed costs	Costs which do not vary with an undertaking's output.
Free-riding	A free-rider is a person who benefits from the provision of a good or service without paying for it. The free-riding problem arises because the quantity of a good or service consumed is not influenced by the amount paid for it. Markets fail to supply a good that is subject to free-riding because there is no incentive to pay for the good.
Full-line forcing	An extreme form of *tie-in sale* under which the retailer must stock the full range of the manufacturer's product range. It may be an absolute requirement, or the manufacturer may charge higher prices if only part of the range is stocked.
Incremental costs	The cost of producing a specified additional product, service or increment of output. *Marginal cost* is a particular type of incremental cost where the increment is one unit of output.
Incremental profit or loss	The change in profits resulting from a particular change in prices, or other decision of the undertaking.
Leverage of market power	Where an undertaking with market power in one market uses that market power to create or enhance market power in a separate market.

PART III
OFT GUIDELINES

Long run	The period when there are no fixed costs.
Marginal cost	The cost of producing one additional unit of output (see also *incremental costs*).
Net-revenue test	An assessment of whether an undertaking has incurred an *incremental loss*.
Quantity forcing	Where the retailer is required to purchase a minimum quantity of a certain product.
Resale price maintenance RPM	Where the manufacturer specifies the resale price of the product, commonly only a minimum or a maximum price.
Selective distribution	Where a manufacturer supplies only a limited number of retailers who are restricted in their ability to re-sell products and who may have to meet certain standards of service.
Short run	The period when some costs are *fixed*.
Stand-alone cost	The lowest cost which could be faced by a hypothetical supplier of only a particular product or service. Stand-alone costs include all *common costs*.
Sunk costs	Costs which cannot be recovered when an undertaking leaves a market, that is, they are not *avoidable*.
Supra-normal profits	Profits higher than an undertaking would earn in the long term in a competitive market.
Tie-in sales	Where the manufacturer makes the purchase of one product (the *tying* product) conditional on the purchase of a second (*tied*) product. A set of tied products is sometimes referred to as a *bundle*. Alternatively, customers might receive a discount conditional on purchasing a tied product.
Total costs	The sum of *variable* costs plus *fixed* costs.
Variable costs	Costs which vary with an undertaking's output.

[3077]

ASSESSMENT OF MARKET POWER

(OFT 415, September 1999)

1 Introduction

1.1 The Competition Act 1998 ('**the Act**') introduces two prohibitions: one of agreements which prevent, restrict or distort competition and which may affect trade within the United Kingdom ('**the Chapter I prohibition**'); the other of conduct by undertakings which amounts to an abuse of a dominant position in a market which may affect trade within the United Kingdom ('**the Chapter II prohibition**'). The prohibitions are described in the Competition Act guidelines *The Chapter I Prohibition* and *The Chapter II Prohibition*.

1.2 The concept of market power is not part of the statutory framework of the Act but it is a useful tool in assessing potentially anti-competitive behaviour. This guideline explains how the Director General will assess whether undertakings possess market power when investigating cases under the Act. Market power describes a situation where the constraints which would usually ensure that an undertaking behaves in a competitive manner are not working effectively. As a matter of convenience, however, this guideline usually refers to market power as the ability to raise prices consistently and profitably above competitive levels. This is not to suggest that market power is solely about increasing prices. For example, an undertaking with market power as defined above would also be able to supply goods of a lower quality, or restrict output to a lower level than would be supplied in a competitive environment. Market power can exist in a variety of other contexts and in a variety of degrees, some of which are discussed in this guideline. In some markets, a single undertaking may possess market power. In others—where, for example, the market is very concentrated, or where a number of undertakings have agreed not to compete with each other—a group of undertakings may collectively possess market power.

1.3   The approach described in this guideline is not a mechanical test, it is a conceptual framework within which evidence can be organised. It is not possible to give a prescriptive guide to market power since whether and the extent to which it exists will depend on the circumstances of each case.

1.4   The assessment of market power is complex: there are many theoretical and practical considerations involved, many of them interlinked. Assessing whether market power exists is not, however, an end in itself: it is one of the factors the Director General takes into account when carrying out an investigation into whether either of the prohibitions in the Act has been breached. Market power is neither a new concept nor is it a new test in addition to those which are set out in the Act itself or imported from European Community law under section 60 of the Act. The nature of market power and the evidence needed to establish its existence can be assessed only on a case-by-case basis; the Director General will consider a wide range of relevant evidence on market definition, market structure, the conduct of undertakings and their financial performance before coming to a view of market power. This guideline should therefore be read in conjunction with the Competition Act guidelines *Market Definition* and *Assessment of Individual Agreements and Conduct*.

1.5   Part 2 of this guideline describes why the assessment of market power can be useful under both the Chapter I prohibition of the Act in considering **appreciability** and under the Chapter II prohibition to assist in the identification of **dominance**. Although the concepts of appreciability and dominance are different, in both cases the Director General will be interested in the competitive constraints that act on the undertaking (or undertakings). This guideline refers to these constraints as the factors which affect whether or not undertakings have market power.

1.6   Parts 3 to 6 of this guideline look at the theoretical considerations and relevant evidence considered when assessing market power. Part 3 sets out a framework for assessing market power: defining the relevant market, assessing the structure of that market and assessing the conduct and performance of undertakings within that market. These issues are interlinked: evidence on conduct and performance is therefore important when assessing market definition and market structure. Part 4 considers market shares and how they may be measured. It considers what sort of evidence will be relevant and what potential problems may arise. Market shares on their own, however, are not a wholly reliable guide to market power because of the need to take into account the issues described in parts 5 and 6.

1.7   Part 5 considers three main types of entry barriers and how they may be assessed in practice. Part 6 considers other factors that are important in the assessment of market power. First, it discusses buyer power and the circumstances under which the influence of strong buyers may prevent undertakings from raising prices to unduly high levels. Secondly, it considers the extent to which evidence of unduly high prices or unduly high profits may indicate that the constraints provided by existing competition, potential competition and buyer power are weak. Thirdly, it looks at how market power might be affected in industry sectors where undertakings' economic behaviour may be subject to controls by the government or industry sector regulators.

Section 60

1.8 The Director General has a duty under section 60 of the Act to handle cases in such a way as to ensure consistency with Community law. This is described further in the Competition Act guideline *The Major Provisions*.

[3078]

2 The Chapter I and Chapter II prohibitions

2.1 This part describes why the assessment of market power can be useful under both the Chapter I prohibition of the Act in considering **appreciability** and under the Chapter II prohibition to assist in the identification of **dominance**.

The Chapter I prohibition

The 'appreciable effect' test

2.2 An agreement will infringe the Chapter I prohibition only if it has as its object or effect an appreciable prevention, restriction or distortion of competition in the United Kingdom. This follows from established case law of the European Court which the Director General and the United Kingdom courts will be bound to follow under section 60 of the Act. **Any agreement which does not have an appreciable effect on competition in the United Kingdom should not be notified to the Director General** (see the Competition Act guideline *The Chapter I Prohibition*).

2.3 The Director General takes the view that an agreement will generally have no appreciable affect on competition if the parties' combined market share of the relevant market does not exceed 25 per cent, although there will be circumstances in which this is not the case.

2.4 The Director General will, in addition, generally regard any agreement between undertakings which—

— directly or indirectly fixes prices or shares markets; or
— imposes minimum resale prices; or
— is one of a network of similar agreements which have a cumulative effect on the market in question

as being capable of having an appreciable effect even where the combined market share falls below the 25 per cent threshold. Examples of agreements which fall into these categories are given in the Competition Act guideline *The Chapter I Prohibition* and further details on networks of agreements are given in the Competition Act guideline *Vertical Agreements and Restraints*.

2.5 Other factors

Even where the parties' combined market share is higher than 25 per cent, the Director General may find that the effect on competition is not appreciable. Other factors, for example the content of the agreement and the structure of the market or markets affected by the agreement (such as entry conditions or the characteristics of buyers and the structure of the buyers' side of the market), will be considered in determining whether the agreement has an appreciable effect (entry conditions and buyer power are considered in parts 5 and 6 of this guideline).

2.6 Calculating market shares

When applying the market share thresholds, the relevant market share will be the combined market share not only of the parties to the agreement but also of other undertakings belonging to the same group of undertakings as the parties to the agreement. These will include, in the case of each party to the agreement, first, undertakings over which it exercises control and, secondly, both undertakings that exercise control over it and any other undertakings that are controlled by those undertakings. Further details on defining the relevant market are given in the Competition Act guideline *Market Definition*.

2.7 Market power

If it is clear that none of the parties to the agreement already possesses market power (either individually or collectively) and that market power would not arise as a result of the agreement, it is unlikely that the Director General will take further action unless he is considering one of the agreements described in paragraph 2.4 above.

The Chapter II prohibition

2.8   The Chapter II prohibition prohibits conduct by one or more undertakings which amounts to the abuse of a dominant position in a market in the United Kingdom (or a part thereof) and which may affect trade within the United Kingdom.

Dominance

2.9   The European Court has defined a dominant market position as—

   'a position of economic strength enjoyed by an undertaking which enables it to prevent effective competition being maintained on the relevant market by affording it the power to behave to an appreciable extent independently of its competitors, customers and ultimately of consumers.'[1]

2.10   An undertaking is unlikely to be dominant if it does not have substantial market power. Market power is not, however, an absolute term but a matter of degree; the degree of market power will depend on the circumstances of each case. In assessing whether there is dominance, the Director General considers whether and the extent to which an undertaking faces constraints on its ability to behave independently. Those constraints might be existing competitors, potential competitors and other factors such as strong buyer power from the undertaking's customers (which may include distributors, processors and commercial users). These constraints are discussed further in parts 3 to 6 of this guideline.

Market shares

2.11   The Act does not set any market share thresholds for defining 'dominance'. Market share is an important factor but does not, on its own, determine whether an undertaking is dominant. For example, it is also necessary to consider the position of other undertakings operating in the same market and how market shares have changed over time. An undertaking is more likely to be dominant if its competitors enjoy relatively weak positions or if it has enjoyed both a high, and stable, market share. The European Court has stated that dominance can be presumed in the absence of evidence to the contrary if an undertaking has a market share persistently above 50 per cent.[2] The Director General considers it unlikely that an undertaking will be individually dominant if its market share is below 40 per cent, although dominance could be established below that figure if other relevant factors (such as the weak position of competitors in that market) provided strong evidence of dominance (see the Competition Act guideline *The Chapter II Prohibition*).

Collective dominance under the Chapter II prohibition

2.12 The Chapter II prohibition prohibits conduct on the part of 'one or more' undertakings that amounts to the abuse of a dominant position (a collective dominant position). Although the behaviour of undertakings that operate as a single economic unit within the same corporate group will usually be treated as that of a single undertaking, those not so treated may be considered to hold a collectively dominant position.

2.13 In addition, a dominant position may be collective when two or more legally independent undertakings are linked in such a way that they adopt the same conduct in the market. The Court of First Instance confirmed the principle of collective dominance in the 'Italian Flat Glass' case—

'There is nothing, in principle, to prevent two or more independent economic entities from being, on a specific market, united by such economic links that, by virtue of that fact, together they hold a dominant position vis-à-vis the other operators on the same market.'[3]

2.14 The links may be structural or they may be such that the undertakings adopt the same conduct on the market.

[3079]

NOTES

[1] Case 27/76 *United Brands v Commission*, [1978] ECR207, [1978] 1 CMLR 429; the definition has been used in other cases.

[2] Case C62/86 *AKZO Chemie BV v Commission* [1993] 5 CMLR 215.

[3] Case T-68/69 etc *Società Italiano Vetro SpA v Commission* [1992] II ECR 1403, [1992] 5 CMLR 302.

---

3 A framework for assessing market power

3.1 As described in paragraph 1.2 above, one definition of market power describes a situation where the constraints which would usually ensure that an undertaking behaves in a competitive manner are not working effectively. For convenience the framework below refers to the ability of an undertaking or undertakings consistently and profitably to charge prices higher than if it or they faced effective competition. An undertaking with market power would not necessarily increase prices in such a way, however; it might, for example, reduce the level of services provided or adopt some other form of behaviour made possible only by the fact that it did not face effective competition.

3.2 When assessing whether market power exists and its extent, the Director General will consider any evidence—
— of any constraints that might prevent an undertaking from persistently raising prices either directly or implicitly above competitive levels;[1]
— and indicating how effective the constraints might be.

3.3 Examples of the sort of constraints that may prevent an undertaking from persistently raising prices in such a way include—
— **existing competitors**: undertakings already in the market[2] may undercut any undertaking (or group of undertakings) that increases prices above competitive levels. One measure of existing competition is the extent to which market shares of all undertakings in the market have moved over time. This issue is explored further in part 4 of this guideline;
— **potential competitors**: undertakings that would be able to enter the market and gain market share at the expense of any existing undertaking which raised prices above competitive levels. Potential competition will not necessarily prevent undertakings from increasing prices above competitive levels for a short period of time, but high prices should attract new entry

which will drive the price down again. Where the evidence suggests that entry barriers are low, potential competition should ensure that prices would not persistently remain above competitive levels. Entry barriers are the subject of part 5 of this guideline;

— **buyer power** may offset the potential market power of a seller when, in the absence of that buyer, prices would have been higher. This is discussed further in part 6 of this guideline.

3.4   **Economic regulation** is a further relevant factor when assessing market power in industry sectors where, for example, prices and/or services are subject to controls by the government or an industry sector regulator. This is also discussed further in part 6 of this guideline.

3.5   The Director General will consider evidence about the conduct and the financial performance of undertakings. The ability of an undertaking persistently to raise prices significantly above costs or persistently to earn an 'excessive' profit may provide evidence that it is setting prices above competitive levels and so has market power. In this case, the potential constraints on market power identified above are not effective. Conduct and performance are dealt with further in part 6 and discussed in greater detail in the Competition Act guideline *Assessment of Individual Agreements and Conduct*.

3.6   The approach described here is not a mechanical test, it is a conceptual framework within which evidence can be organised. Competition—and hence the extent of market power—is an ongoing process. It is not possible to give a prescriptive guide to market power since whether and the extent to which it exists will depend on the circumstances of each case. Many of the issues are interlinked: evidence that is relevant in market definition, for example, may also be relevant when assessing market power. The Director General will therefore take into account a wide range of relevant evidence. He will consider evidence over time on market structure, on the conduct of undertakings and on their financial performance before completing his assessment of market power. He will also take into account the competitive constraints that act on the undertaking (or undertakings) when he comes to his final assessment on whether the prohibitions in the Act apply.

[3080]

NOTES

1   An undertaking with market power would be able to lower services or lower quality below the level that would obtain in a competitive environment. This would mean that customers would pay more for a given level of service or quality and so, implicitly, the price of the good increases beyond competitive levels.

2   These may include undertakings which could move very quickly into the market; it will depend on market definition and in particular supply-side substitution—see the Competition Act guideline *Market Definition*.

4   Market shares

4.1   As part of the framework for assessing market power, the Director General will define the market and assess how market shares have developed over time. This part considers the extent to which market shares indicate market power, how market shares may be measured, the sort of evidence likely to be relevant and the potential problems. These issues are important when considering the intensity of existing competition.

Market shares and market power

4.2   In general, market power is more likely to exist if an undertaking (or group of undertakings) has a persistently high market share. Likewise, market power is less likely to exist if an undertaking has a persistently low market share. In these cases, 'high' and 'low' could be relative to absolute thresholds or relative to other competitors. The Director General will usually look at the history of the market shares of all undertakings within the relevant market (see the Competition Act guideline *Market Definition*). This is more informative than considering market shares at a single point in time, partly because such a snapshot might hide the dynamic nature of a market. In aerospace or defence products markets, for example, there are large, often long-term, irregularly-timed contracts. In these instances, the Director General might look at shares over a period of perhaps five years, as well as at how they have changed during the recent history of the market as part of the assessment of market power. Volatile market shares for the largest undertakings, or successful entry and expanding market shares for many small undertakings, for example, may indicate that a market is relatively competitive.

4.3   Nevertheless, market shares are not always a reliable guide to market power both for conceptual reasons and because of potential shortcomings with the data discussed below. An undertaking with a persistently high market share may not necessarily hold market power for two reasons: first, if entry into the market is easy, the incumbent undertaking is likely to be constrained to act competitively so as to avoid attracting entry over time by potential competitors. Secondly, in a market where undertakings regularly improve the quality of their products, a persistently high market share may indicate no more than persistently successful innovation. While consideration of market shares over time is important when assessing market power, an analysis of entry conditions and other factors is therefore equally important. These are discussed in parts 5 and 6 of this guideline respectively.

Measuring market shares

Evidence

4.4   The Director General may collect data on market shares from a number of sources including—
— information provided by undertakings themselves. The Director General will normally ask undertakings for data on their own market shares, and to estimate the shares of their competitors (this information is requested on Form N, the form by which notifications are made);
— trade associations, customers or suppliers who may be able to provide estimates of market shares; and
— market research reports.

4.5   The Director General will use whichever available method of calculating market share data is most appropriate for the case in hand. If sales data by value and by volume are both available for a market where goods are differentiated, for example, data by value may provide a better proxy of market share, although both measures may provide useful information. Sales data by value will not always be the preferred measure, however—data on passenger volumes may be preferred when looking at the transport sector, for example.

4.6   The following issues may arise when measuring market shares—
— **production and sales**—market share is determined by an undertaking's sales to customers. The Director General will therefore normally measure market share using the value of sales to direct customers rather than the value of an undertaking's production (which can vary from sales when stocks increase or decrease). Market share is valued at the price charged to an undertaking's direct customers. When measuring a manufacturer's market share, for example, the Director General will try to look at the value of its sales to retailers or wholesalers, not at market shares based on the prices at which the retailers sell to final consumers;

— **choice of exchange rates**—although the Chapter I prohibition applies only to an agreement which is or is intended to be implemented in the UK, the relevant geographic market may be international and this may complicate the calculation of market shares, as exchange rates often vary over time. The Director General may then look at a range of exchange rates over time, including an assessment of the sensitivity of the analysis to the use of different exchange rates;

— **internal production**—some vertically-integrated undertakings produce for both their own consumption and for external customers. Others produce only for internal consumption. In both situations the Director General would need to decide whether to include internal sales in an undertaking's market share. This will depend on the ease with which production can or could be switched from internal to external sales. If an undertaking could not easily produce for external customers (if all its capacity were committed to internal requirements for the foreseeable future, for example), internal consumption would not normally be included within the market;

— **imports**—if the market is international, market shares will be calculated to cover the whole geographic market. If the market is purely domestic, imports may nevertheless still account for a small share. If information is available, the Director General normally focuses on the sales of each importing undertaking and calculates market shares accordingly, rather than lumping them all together as if they were a single competitor. Where a domestic producer is also an importer (or is part of the same group as an importer), the Director General will include both its domestic sales and its importations as part of its market share.

Alternative market definitions

4.7   Given the complex issues involved in defining markets, the Director General will normally look at market share data under all potential definitions of the market. It may be that all definitions lead to a similar pattern. If the market definition does not alter the assessment of other relevant issues, particularly existing and potential competition, it may not be necessary to decide which market definition should be used: an undertaking may have a persistently low (or high) market share, which has remained significantly lower (or higher) than its closest competitors, whatever the definition.

4.8   Conversely, entry conditions and changes in market shares over time may differ substantially according to market definition. The Director General will then consider carefully the implications of the conceivable alternative definitions and may seek more detailed evidence. Information submitted by undertakings will therefore be of most use if it includes market shares under plausible alternative market definitions and an explanation of why one definition might be more relevant than another, rather than providing information using only the market definition most favourable to the undertaking's (undertakings') cause.

[3081]

5   Entry barriers

5.1   This part considers three main types of entry barriers and how they may be assessed in practice. It concentrates on establishing dominance under the Chapter II prohibition, but the Director General will take the same approach when considering the effect of agreements under the Chapter I prohibition. Entry barriers are important in the assessment of potential competition. The lower the entry barriers, the more likely it is that potential competition will prevent undertakings within the market from persistently raising prices above competitive levels. Prices set above, or services set below, competitive levels for even a short period of time should, provided entry barriers are insignificant, still attract new entry into the market and restore prices or services to their competitive levels.[1] An undertaking with a large market share in a market with very low entry barriers would be unlikely to have market power.

5.2 One definition of an entry barrier is that it is a cost that must be borne by an undertaking entering a market that does not need to be borne by an incumbent undertaking already operating in the market. The existence of entry barriers may reduce the scope for competition, so that incumbents are able to raise prices above competitive levels.[2] Entry barriers do not arise from cost advantages derived solely from the efficiency of the incumbent, and when assessing barriers to entry the Director General will therefore aim to distinguish between such efficiency-based cost advantages and other cost advantages. In practice, however, this may not be easy.

5.3 There are many ways in which different types of entry barrier can be classified, but it is useful to distinguish between three sources—

— absolute advantages;
— strategic advantages; and
— exclusionary behaviour.

At times they will overlap: exclusionary behaviour by an incumbent might, for example, have the effect of strengthening a pre-existing absolute or strategic advantage.

Absolute advantages

5.4 In some markets an incumbent owns or has access to important assets or resources which are not accessible to the potential entrant. This bestows an **absolute advantage** on the incumbent so that the entrant cannot gain access to an asset or resource at any cost or only at a cost substantially higher than that of the incumbent. The following paragraphs consider three examples of absolute advantages: regulation; essential facilities; and intellectual property rights.

5.5 **Regulation** may affect barriers to entry. There is a distinction, however, between regulation which sets objective standards and that which places a limit on the number of competitors in a market. Objective standards which apply equally to all undertakings, such as health and safety regulations, should not, in general, be an absolute barrier to entry, although the position may be different if they were drawn up largely under the influence of incumbents with a view to making entry more difficult. Conversely, some regulation may limit the number of undertakings which can operate in a market—through the granting of licences, for example. When the numbers of licences are restricted, there may be an absolute limit to the number of undertakings that can operate in the market. This will act as an entry barrier unless licences are tradeable in a competitive market, in which case a potential entrant could purchase a licence and enter the market if a profitable opportunity arose.

5.6 In some cases, entry to a market might require the use of an **essential facility**, an asset or facility with two key characteristics. First, access to it must be indispensable in order to compete on the market and, secondly, duplication of the facility is impossible or extremely difficult owing to physical, geographic or legal constraints, or is highly undesirable for reasons of public policy (see the Competition Act guideline *Assessment of Individual Agreements and Conduct*). If, for example, there were only one port serving a particular shipping market, and other forms of transport were not close substitutes to shipping, that port would probably be regarded as an essential facility. Furthermore, limited access to the port—perhaps because it was already fully utilised—would create an absolute entry barrier, unless a competitive market in the rights to use the port existed.[3]

5.7   **Intellectual property rights (IPRs)** may provide an incumbent with an absolute cost advantage. An incumbent might have an IPR over a state-of-the-art production process, for example, which allowed it to produce at a lower cost than any potential entrant. This is more likely to be the case the wider the coverage of the IPR with respect to the market.

5.8   Assessing the effect of IPRs on competition can be complex. Although an IPR may constitute an entry barrier in the short term, in the long term a rival undertaking may be able to overcome it by its own innovation. Thus, the short term profit which the IPR provides can act as an incentive to innovate and so can promote competition in innovation. This is important in a knowledge-driven economy. On the other hand, an undertaking holding the IPR using its cost advantage as a barrier to entry in a neighbouring market, where innovation was not the main force of competition, may be viewed as acting anti-competitively (see the Competition Act guideline *Intellectual Property Rights*).

Strategic advantages

5.9   The second source of entry barriers arises when an undertaking gains an advantage from being in the market first, sometimes called a 'first-mover advantage'. First-mover advantage can allow an undertaking to shape the way the market develops, by, for example, reducing or completely deterring the potential for other undertakings to enter the market. For simplicity, most of the following examples refer to a situation where there is one incumbent and one potential entrant. In reality, the existence of several incumbents and several potential entrants may complicate the analysis but the principles remain valid.

5.10   When an undertaking contemplates entering a market, it weighs up its expected revenue from entering against the expected costs of entering and exiting (which may be necessary if entry is unsuccessful). Expected revenues depend on how the entrant expects the incumbent to react when it enters the market: the potential entrant might believe that the incumbent would, for example, reduce prices substantially if it entered and so reduce the prospective revenue available from entering the market.

5.11   Predation (which is also discussed in the part of this guideline on exclusionary behaviour) may lead to a strategic entry barrier arising. If an incumbent has adopted a predatory strategy against and driven out a new entrant (or existing competitor) in the past, it may have secured for itself a reputation for aggressive behaviour. Any future potential entrants to this market (or any other market where the incumbent operates) might then attach a higher likelihood to facing an 'aggressive' response, where the incumbent reduces prices substantially in response to new entry.[4]

Sunk costs

5.12   As explained above, the expected revenue from entry will be compared with the expected costs of entry and exit. A key concept affecting the entrant's decision is the role of sunk costs, the costs incurred when an undertaking enters a market which it cannot recover if it exits. An entrant to the market for long distance coach services, for example, will have to obtain vehicles. The entrant will compare the cost of buying the vehicles with the price it would expect to receive for them in the second-hand market if it subsequently decided to pull out. The difference in the two prices (in net present value terms) is 'sunk'. Sunk costs will differ across markets, due to the different nature of the assets involved. Thus, while an undertaking starting up a coach service may expect to be able to resell its vehicles at a fair price, an undertaking that has built and paid for expensive steel plant may not be able to recover much of its initial costs should it decide to stop producing steel, because it would be difficult to find either a buyer or an alternative use for the plant.

5.13 The importance of sunk costs in relation to the first mover advantage of an incumbent is twofold. First, to the extent that an incumbent has already made its sunk investments it may not need to earn as high a rate of return as a potential entrant, because the potential entrant still has a choice not to enter and so could avoid incurring all costs if it stayed out of the market. Secondly, an incumbent may decide to use its own sunk costs strategically in a way that raises entry barriers. An incumbent may, for example, be able to sink costs in a way that sends a credible signal as to how it would behave if another undertaking decided to enter a market: it might 'over-invest' in sunk assets so that when it operated as the only undertaking in the market, it had significant spare capacity. From the potential entrant's point of view, the mere existence of that capacity might imply that the incumbent could adopt an 'aggressive' stance and manufacture large quantities of product at a very low unit cost. The entrant might decide not to enter if it believed that the incumbent was likely to respond to entry aggressively by pushing down the price to such a low level that the entrant would earn insufficient revenue to cover its sunk costs.[5]

Exogenous and endogenous sunk costs

5.14 There are two types of sunk costs: exogenous sunk costs are determined solely by the technology of a particular industry, for example, where before a firm can produce a certain good, it must purchase a plant or machine which has no resale value. Endogenous sunk costs are determined by the behaviour of incumbent undertakings, for example, the non-recoverable components of spending on advertising and on research and development (R&D). Endogenous sunk costs are set by incumbents in order to influence demand for their own products: incumbents may therefore compete with others partly by incurring sunk costs. The existence of large endogenous sunk costs may make it harder to enter the market, but it does not necessarily mean that competition within the market is not intense.

5.15 The Director General will assess to what extent sunk costs give an incumbent undertaking cost advantages over potential new entrants and to what extent sunk costs might affect entry barriers. The mere existence of sunk costs in any particular industry, however, does not necessarily mean that entry barriers are high.

Economies of scale, information constraints and time lags

5.16 Economies of scale mean that average costs fall as output rises.[6] Thus, a potential entrant would prefer to enter the market on a large scale (in relation to the size of the market), but such entry may be riskier, to the extent that it involves a larger commitment on the part of the entrant especially when a substantial share of costs are sunk, and more likely to attract an aggressive response from incumbents. These factors may constitute a barrier to entry.

5.17 An incumbent is likely to have more information on the existing costs of production than an entrant and this, in conjunction with sunk costs, may constitute a barrier to entry. Lack of information itself may deter entry when production technology is complex: obtaining the information may involve large sunk expenditures in R&D or in 'learning by doing'. The incumbent may seek to exploit its information advantage to deter entry by, for example, over-investing in sunk costs in an attempt to signal that the industry is one characterised by high sunk costs, when in reality it is not. Even when entry is not fully deterred, entrants may take time in acquiring the relevant information, raising capital and building the necessary plant and machinery. Thus, the incumbent may attract entry but retain market power for a substantial amount of time. This may be particularly relevant when there are economies of scale, so that time-consuming and expensive large scale entry is necessary.

Access to finance

5.18 Entry, particularly large scale entry, has to be financed. In the United Kingdom there are well-developed financial markets to finance new entry where it would be profitable. New entrants may, however, lack the same access to finance as incumbents—

— **experience and track record**—an incumbent may be a lower-risk investment if it can present a proven track record in the market. It may also have better information about the market and therefore be able to present a more convincing business case;

— **size**—any fixed costs involved in raising finance will bear disproportionately on smaller undertakings, although this need not deter entry by subsidiaries of larger undertakings.

5.19 A potential entrant may therefore face a higher cost of finance (whether obtained from borrowing or sales of equity) than an incumbent. This may deter new entry, even when costs of raising finance are not sunk. Access to finance is not likely to be an entry barrier, however, where potential entrants are relatively large or diversified, or where it is possible to lease equipment necessary for entry.

Exclusionary behaviour

5.20 The third source of entry barrier is created by exclusionary behaviour by the incumbent such as vertical restraints, predatory behaviour, and refusal to supply. (This is not an exhaustive list: other types of behaviour may be considered to be exclusionary.)

5.21 A vertical restraint between a manufacturer and a group of retailers may deter entry into manufacturing by foreclosing any potential retail outlets for a new manufacturer. A manufacturer who reached a series of exclusive purchasing agreements tying up all the retailers in a particular geographic market may take away the ability of a new manufacturer to sell any of its goods, if there were substantial barriers to entry in retailing, even if no other entry barriers existed at the manufacturing level. The manufacturer could exploit the existence of the retail barriers to entry to strengthen its own dominant position upstream. Some vertical restraints may, however, be beneficial or benign, especially if there is strong competition at both the upstream and downstream levels. These issues are discussed further in the Competition Act guidelines *Vertical Agreements and Restraints and Assessment of Individual Agreements and Conduct*.

5.22 Predation might deter entry if an undertaking secured a reputation for aggressive behaviour. Thus, successful predation may confer a dominant position on the undertaking.

5.23 Refusal to supply may also constitute a barrier to entry. If, for example, an upstream manufacturer were the sole supplier of inputs to a downstream industry and if there were barriers to entering the upstream market, the manufacturer's refusal to supply a potential entrant in the downstream market could constitute a barrier to entry in the downstream market, even if no other entry barriers existed at that level. As with vertical restraints, however, refusal to supply can sometimes be beneficial or benign, especially if there is strong competition at both upstream and downstream levels.

Combined effects of entry barriers

5.24 In some instances there will be more than one entry barrier to a market. Exclusionary behaviour by an incumbent (or a network of vertical restraints imposed by a number of manufacturers) can strengthen the effect of a pre-existing absolute or strategic advantage, for example. As the examples of vertical restraints and refusal to supply given above show, exclusionary behaviour sometimes requires the prior existence of entry barriers either in the relevant market or in a neighbouring market. These issues are considered in further detail in the Competition Act guidelines *Assessment of Individual Agreements and Conduct and Vertical Agreements and Restraints*.

Assessing entry barriers

5.25 Assessing the effects of entry barriers and the advantages they give to incumbents is complex. A variety of factors are involved. Whether in respect of a notification to the Director General of an agreement or conduct, or as part of an investigation following a complaint or on his own initiative, the Director General may ask potential entrants as well as incumbent undertakings about entry barriers; to estimate the costs associated with a commitment to entry; the cost of obtaining, say, a five per cent market share; or the cost of operating at the minimum efficient scale (the size of plant that an entrant would need to be able to produce in scale terms as efficiently as an incumbent).

5.26 Entry and exit conditions are important in assessing whether an undertaking possesses market power. While an incumbent with apparent market power may claim that potential competition is waiting in the wings, a more objective judgement can be made by the Director General if hard evidence of successful entry in the recent history of the market is provided. Such evidence might include a historical record of entry into and exit from the market (or closely related markets) or, if possible, fully documented evidence of plans to enter.

5.27 It is important, if not necessarily straightforward, to assess the time that may elapse before successful (that is, profitable) entry will occur. Some producers, most likely those in neighbouring markets, may be able to enter speedily by switching the use of existing facilities. Where this is possible it will usually be taken into account in defining the market (as supply-side substitutability, see the Competition Act guideline *Market Definition*). New entry from scratch tends to be slower than entry from a neighbouring market, for a variety of reasons—obtaining planning permission, recruiting and training staff, ordering equipment, appointing distributors and so on.

5.28 The Director General will consider whether overseas competitors provide an effective constraint on the ability of domestic undertakings to raise prices above competitive levels, even if only as a prospect of new entry. Imports into the United Kingdom may compete with the products of domestic undertakings and it is therefore important to assess whether trade barriers of any kind may dampen the effectiveness of overseas competition.

5.29 Growth, or prospective growth, in a market will usually have a bearing on the likelihood of entry: entry will usually be more likely in a growing market than in a static or declining one because it will be easier for an entrant to be accommodated without any precipitous collapse in prices and profits. The rate of innovation is also important: in markets where high rates of innovation occur, or are expected, innovation may overcome barriers to entry relatively quickly. Indeed, any profits that result from an entry barrier created by successful innovation may be an important incentive to innovate.

[3082]

NOTES

¹ New entry into an industry requires that both a new undertaking is established in the industry and that new productive capacity is set up in that industry.

² An exit barrier is a similar concept: a cost borne by an undertaking leaving a market that an undertaking remaining in the market does not have to bear. The existence of exit barriers can be important when considering sunk costs (see below) since exit costs reduce the disposal value of an incumbent's assets if it chooses to leave a market and may therefore equally deter new entry (see paragraph 5.12 below).

³   There may be circumstances in which difficulties accessing assets or resources will constitute an entry barrier without those assets or resources meeting the strict criteria required to be defined as 'essential facilities'.

⁴   It is interesting to note that over time market structure may depend on conduct and vice versa. For example, if predation drives out a competitor and enhances or creates an entry barrier by giving the incumbent a reputation for aggressive behaviour, then both existing competition and potential competition may be reduced for the foreseeable future. Here, anti-competitive conduct affects the structure of the market which in turn could increase the potential for more anti-competitive conduct.

⁵   In the economics literature there are many models which describe how an incumbent—due to its first mover advantage—might use sunk costs strategically to deter entry or, if entry is accommodated, reduce the share of the market available to the new entrant. However, the existence of sunk costs, per se, will not necessarily mean that entry barriers are high or that competition is weak; it depends upon the case in hand.

⁶   Economies of scope mean that average costs fall as more types of products are produced. They may have similar implications to economies of scale as a potential entrant would prefer to enter the market on a large scale in relation to the number of products in the market.

6   Other factors in the assessment of market power

Buyer power

6.1   The main potential constraint on market power of a seller is the strength of buyers and the structure of the buyers' side of the market. The potential market power of a seller is offset by the buying power of a buyer if, in the absence of that buyer, prices would have been higher.[1] Buyer power allows an undertaking (or a group of undertakings acting together) to exert a substantial influence on the price, quality or the terms of supply of a good purchased. It requires that a buyer should be large in relation to the relevant market, well informed about alternative sources of supply and that the buyer could readily, and at little cost to itself, switch from one supplier to another, or even commence production of the item himself.

6.2   In general, buyer power is beneficial in two circumstances: when it exerts downward pressure on a supplier's prices and the lower prices are passed on to the consumer; and when there are large efficiency gains that result from the buyer being large in relation to the market. Countervailing buyer power does not always benefit the consumer, however: if, for example, the buyer also has market power as a seller in the downstream market, it may not pass on lower prices to the consumer; it could even use its combined power strategically to the detriment of competition. Conversely, buyer power may have adverse consequences in the upstream market if it is used to foreclose entry or if it threatens the viability of suppliers.[2] A careful analysis of vertical relationships in the market, on a case-by-case basis, is therefore required to assess buyer power.

Conduct and performance

6.3   An undertaking's conduct in a market or its financial performance may, in itself, provide evidence that it possesses market power. It might, for example, be reasonable to infer that an undertaking possesses market power from evidence that it has—

    — consistently raised prices in excess of costs; or
    — persistently earned an 'excessive' rate of profit.

6.4   High prices or profits alone are not sufficient proof that an undertaking has market power— high profits may represent a return on previous innovation, or result from changing demand conditions. As such, they may be consistent with a competitive market, which requires that undertakings are able to take advantage of profitable opportunities when they exist. However, persistent significantly high returns, relative to those which would prevail in a competitive market of similar risk and rate of innovation, may suggest that market power does exist. This would be especially so if they did not stimulate new entry or innovation.

6.5 The assessment of excess prices or profits is discussed further in the Competition Act guideline *Assessment of Individual Agreements and Conduct*.

Economic regulation

6.6 In some industry sectors the economic behaviour of undertakings (such as the prices they set or the level of services they provide) is regulated by the government or an industry sector regulator, and an assessment of market power may need to take that into account. Although an undertaking might not face effective constraints from existing competitors, potential competitors or the nature of buyers in the market, it may still be constrained from, say, raising prices persistently above competitive levels by an industry sector regulator. However, that is not to say that market power cannot exist when there is economic regulation. It is feasible, for example, that a price control which is averaged across several markets supplied by an undertaking may still leave room for the undertaking to raise prices persistently above competitive levels in one (or some) of these markets.

6.7 The application of the Act to industry sectors where a regulator has concurrent powers with the Director General of Fair Trading is discussed in the Competition Act guideline *Concurrent Application to Regulated Industries* and in the sector-specific guidelines produced by the relevant regulators.

[3083]

NOTES

¹ If the issue is whether an undertaking has market power as a buyer, the structure of the sellers' side of the market may provide an offsetting force.

² The Chapter II prohibition catches abuses of buyer power by dominant undertakings. An agreement between customers to suppress prices would be likely to be prohibited under Chapter I, although any substantial efficiency gains might permit exemption.

EXCLUSION FOR MERGERS AND ANCILLARY RESTRICTIONS

(OFT 416, September 1999)

1 Introduction

1.1 The Competition Act 1998 ('**the Act**') introduces two prohibitions: one of agreements which prevent, restrict or distort competition and which may affect trade within the United Kingdom ('**the Chapter I prohibition**'); the other of conduct by undertakings which amounts to abuse of a dominant position in a market which may affect trade within the United Kingdom ('**the Chapter II prohibition**'). There are certain specific exclusions from the prohibitions, listed in Schedules 1 to 4 to the Act. This guideline describes the exclusion in Schedule 1 from the Chapter I and the Chapter II prohibitions to the extent to which an agreement or conduct would result in a merger (including a joint venture) within the merger provisions of the Fair Trading Act 1973.

1.2 The Competition Act has no direct effect on the United Kingdom's system of merger control. Mergers (including joint ventures) continue, where appropriate, to be assessed under the merger provisions of the Fair Trading Act although there may be some indirect effect on mergers through the operation of Schedule 1.

1.3 Under Schedule 1, to the extent that agreements and conduct give rise to mergers or joint ventures within the meaning of the Fair Trading Act, they are generally excluded from the provisions of the Competition Act, as are any restrictions that are 'directly related and necessary to the implementation of the merger' (**ancillary restrictions**). A merger does not have to qualify for reference to the Competition Commission under either the assets or market share tests in the Fair Trading Act to benefit from the exclusion.

1.4   The aim of the exclusion is to prevent agreements or conduct from being subject to control under both the Competition Act and the merger provisions of the Fair Trading Act. In order to ensure that the exclusion does not have the effect of allowing significantly anti-competitive transactions to escape scrutiny altogether, however, it can be withdrawn in certain limited circumstances.

1.5   This guideline explains how the exclusion works in practice. It gives advice on the types of restriction that are likely to be deemed ancillary and an indication of the circumstances in which the Director General of Fair Trading might withdraw the benefit of the exclusion. Further guidance on mergers is set out in the Office of Fair Trading booklet Mergers—A guide to procedures under the Fair Trading Act 1973, copies of which are available from [the following address: Office of Fair Trading, PO Box 366, Hayes, UB3 1XB.]

1.6   Information obtained by the Director General of Fair Trading under the merger provisions of the Fair Trading Act may be used by the Director General or by any of the sector regulators who have concurrent jurisdiction under the Competition Act for the purposes of facilitating the performance of their functions under either the Competition Act or, in the case of the regulators, under their respective sector-specific legislation. Information is, however, passed to a regulator only where it is necessary to do so to facilitate the performance of a function of that regulator or of the Director General.

[3084]

2   Exclusion for mergers

General

2.1   Under Schedule 1 to the Competition Act, an agreement does not fall within the scope of the Chapter I prohibition to the extent that it gives rise to a merger situation within the meaning of Part V of the Fair Trading Act. Similarly, to the extent to which conduct results in a merger situation, the conduct does not fall within the scope of the Chapter II prohibition.

2.2   Under the Fair Trading Act, a merger situation can arise where two or more enterprises cease to be distinct from each other. This usually occurs where they are brought under common ownership or common control.[1] The Fair Trading Act distinguishes three levels of control—

- material influence over policy;
- control of policy (known as *de facto* control); and
- a controlling interest (known as *de jure* or legal control)—usually more than 50 per cent of the voting rights.

2.3   The level of control relating to a particular merger is relevant to the Schedule 1 exclusion as it is one of the factors which determine whether the benefit of the exclusion can be withdrawn (see part 3 below). The concept of control is explained more fully in Mergers.

2.4   A merger situation qualifies for investigation under the Fair Trading Act where the gross value of the worldwide assets being taken over exceeds a certain value[2] (**the assets test**) or where, as a result of the merger, the merged enterprises together account for more than 25 per cent of the supply or acquisition of goods or services of a particular description in the United Kingdom or a substantial part of it (**the share of supply test**). Where one of the parties already supplies or acquires 25 per cent of particular goods or services, the test is satisfied as long as its share increases as a result of the merger. The Schedule 1 exclusion applies to any merger situation as defined in paragraph 2.2 above, whether or not it meets the assets or share of supply test.

2.5   The exclusion is automatic and no notification under the Competition Act therefore needs to be made to the Director General.

Newspaper mergers

2.6   The Fair Trading Act makes special provision for certain mergers involving newspapers. These are excluded from the prohibitions in the Competition Act. Nothing in this guideline applies to newspaper mergers.

The EC Merger Regulation

2.7   Under Council Regulation 4064/89[3] ('**the Merger Regulation**'), the European Commission normally has exclusive jurisdiction to deal with mergers which involve concentrations with a Community dimension. The Competition Act prohibitions do not apply to such cases.

[3085]

NOTES
1   See section 2.3 of Mergers.
2   Currently £70 million.
3   As amended by Council Regulation 1310/97.

3   Withdrawal of the exclusion

3.1   The Schedule 1 exclusion is defined so as to ensure that as many mergers as possible are not required to be considered under both the Competition Act and the Fair Trading Act. This means, however, that some significantly anti-competitive agreements, such as price fixing, might escape scrutiny altogether: if, for example, such an arrangement were to be deliberately structured in such a way that it fell within the definition of a merger situation in the Schedule 1 exclusion but beneath the qualification thresholds for investigation under the Fair Trading Act, it could not ordinarily be challenged under either piece of legislation. Schedule 1 therefore includes a mechanism which allows the Director General to give a direction withdrawing the benefit of the exclusion of specified agreements from the Chapter I prohibition in relation to specified agreements. He may, however, give such a direction only in certain limited circumstances, as set out below, and not at all in the case of those newspaper mergers that are dealt with exclusively by the Secretary of State for Trade and Industry (see paragraph 2.6 above), or in respect of those mergers which fall within the EC Merger Regulation. There is no provision for the exclusion to be withdrawn in relation to the Chapter II prohibition.

Failure to comply with a request for information

3.2   In considering whether to withdraw the benefit of the exclusion, Schedule 1 allows the Director General, by written notice, to require any party to the agreement to provide him with certain information. If, without reasonable excuse, that party fails to comply with this request within a specified period,[1] the Director General can withdraw the benefit of the exclusion. This is the case even where the agreement is protected (see paragraphs 3.4 to 3.6 below).

Infringement of the Chapter I prohibition

3.3   The only other circumstance in which the Director General can withdraw the benefit of the exclusion is where the agreement is not a 'protected agreement' and he considers that—
    — it will otherwise infringe the Chapter I prohibition; and
    — he would not be likely to grant it an unconditional individual exemption.

Protected agreements

3.4   An agreement is protected if—
— the Secretary of State has announced his decision not to refer the agreement to the Competition Commission under the merger provisions of the Fair Trading Act;[2] or
— the Secretary of State has referred the agreement to the Competition Commission which has confirmed that it gives rise to a merger situation qualifying for investigation; or
— it does not fall into either of the above categories but gives rise to a merger situation as a result of the acquisition of a controlling interest, but not as a result of the acquisition of control of policy or material influence; or
— it has been referred to the Competition Commission under section 32 of the Water Industry Act and the Commission has confirmed that the agreement gives rise to a merger situation to which that section applies.

3.5   One effect of these provisions is that the Director General can withdraw the benefit of the Schedule 1 exclusion only where the merger situation results from the acquisition of material influence or control of policy, including a move from material influence to control of policy (that is, it falls short of the acquisition of a controlling interest) and either has been found, after a preliminary examination by the Director General, not to qualify for investigation under the Fair Trading Act or has not been brought to his attention.

3.6   In practice, it is likely that the Director General will exercise this power only rarely. This is because, even where an agreement is not protected, he must believe that it will infringe the Chapter I prohibition and is unlikely to qualify for an unconditional exemption before he can withdraw the benefit of the exclusion. To infringe the Chapter I prohibition, the agreement must have an appreciable effect on competition which is generally unlikely to be the case where the combined market share of the parties to the agreement is less than 25 per cent (see the Competition Act guideline *The Chapter I Prohibition*).

Procedural issues

3.7   Where the Director General intends to withdraw the benefit of the exclusion, he will consult the parties to the agreement.

3.8   Withdrawal of the exclusion from a particular agreement does not mean that it is automatically deemed to infringe the Chapter I prohibition: it merely allows the Director General to apply the Chapter I prohibition to the agreement. This means that he can use the information-gathering powers in the Competition Act to require the parties to the agreement, and any relevant third parties, to provide certain information. He will analyse the effect of the agreement on competition and decide whether it infringes the prohibition. If he concludes that it does, he will consider whether it qualifies for exemption.

[3086]

NOTES
1   The draft procedural rules set this period at 10 working days.
2   This category includes a case where undertakings are accepted in lieu of a reference.

4   Exclusion for ancillary restrictions

General

4.1   Many merger cases involve the acceptance of restrictions which go beyond the merger agreement itself. A seller of a business, for example, sometimes accepts a **non-competition** obligation which prevents him from competing with that business.

Where such restrictions are '*directly related and necessary to the implementation of* the merger agreement, they are known as ancillary restrictions, and are covered by the Schedule 1 exclusion, whether or not the merger qualifies for investigation by the Competition Commission.

4.2 The concept of ancillary restrictions is well developed in European Community law under the Merger Regulation, which provides that ancillary restrictions are covered by any decision declaring a merger to be '*compatible with the common market*' (that is, a clearance decision). This provision aims to avoid the need for parallel proceedings under the Merger Regulation and Articles 81 and/or 82 of the EC Treaty. While no equivalent provision is made for ancillary restrictions under the merger provisions of the Fair Trading Act, the combined operation of that Act and Schedule 1 to the Competition Act will have a similar effect. Thus, if restrictions are ancillary to a merger, they will not fall to be considered under the Competition Act.

The Director General's approach

4.3 The Director General's approach to ancillary restrictions follows the European Commission's Notice regarding restrictions ancillary to concentrations,[1] as this constitutes a statement of the European Commission to which the United Kingdom authorities must have regard under section 60 of the Competition Act. As the Director General's practice of applying the Schedule 1 exclusion develops, he may issue additional guidance on the treatment of ancillary restrictions.

Definition of ancillary restriction

4.4 Schedule 1 provides that a restriction must be **directly related** *and* **necessary** to the implementation of the merger if it is to benefit from the exclusion.

4.5 In order to be directly related, the restriction must be connected with the merger, but ancillary or subordinate to its main object. The main object of a merger agreement may be for one company to buy a particular manufacturing operation from another, for example. The added obligation of supplying certain raw materials to enable the manufacturing operation to continue is directly related to the merger agreement, but subordinate to it.

4.6 Any contractual arrangements which go to the heart of the merger, such as the setting up of a holding company to facilitate joint control by two independent companies of a new joint venture company, are not classed as subordinate. Such arrangements are part of the merger agreement itself and will form part of the assessment of the merger under the Fair Trading Act.

4.7 A restriction is not automatically deemed directly related to the merger merely because it is agreed at the same time as the merger or is expressed to be so related. If there is little or no connection with the merger, such a restriction will not be ancillary.

4.8 In addition to deciding whether a restriction is to be considered to be directly related, it must also be established whether it is necessary to the implementation of the merger. This is likely to be the case where, for example, in the absence of the restriction, the merger would not go ahead, might have less chance of succeeding if it did, or would proceed only at considerable extra cost or over a considerably longer period. In determining the necessity of the restriction, account will also be taken of whether its duration and geographical scope are proportionate to the overall requirements of the merger. The Director General will consider all of these factors in the context of each case.

Examples of ancillary restrictions

4.9   Although the answer to the question whether a restriction satisfies the requirements of the Schedule 1 exclusion depends on the circumstances of the case, it is possible, drawing on the European Commission's notice, to set out some general points on how commonly arising restrictions—non-competition clauses, licences of industrial property and know-how, and purchase and supply agreements—will be handled.

Non-competition clauses

4.10   Non-competition clauses often arise in the context of the acquisition by one undertaking of all or part of another undertaking. Such clauses, if properly limited, are generally accepted as essential if the purchaser is to receive the full benefit of any goodwill and/or know-how acquired with any tangible assets.

4.11   The terms of the clause must not, however, exceed what is necessary to attain that objective. The Director General will consider the duration of the clause, its geographical coverage, and the products affected. In general terms, a five year period[2] will normally be acceptable where both goodwill and know-how have been acquired, and a period of two years where only goodwill is involved. Longer periods may be acceptable depending on individual circumstances. Any restriction must relate only to the goods and services of the acquired business and to the area in which the goods and services were established under the previous owner.

Licences of industrial property and know-how

4.12   Where an undertaking acquires all or part of another undertaking, the transaction often includes the transfer of rights to industrial or commercial property or know-how. In some instances, the seller may need to retain ownership of such rights to exploit them in the remaining parts of his business. In such cases the purchaser will normally be granted access to the rights under licensing arrangements.

4.13   In this context, restrictions in exclusive or simple licences of patents, trade-marks, know-how and similar rights may be accepted as necessary to the implementation of the merger and, therefore, covered by the definition of ancillary restrictions in Schedule 1. The licences may be limited in terms of their field of use to the activities of the business acquired and may be granted for the entire duration of the patents, trade-marks or similar rights, or the normal economic life of any know-how.

4.14   If the licences contain restrictions not within any of the above categories, they are likely to fall outside the definition of an ancillary restriction and, therefore, will not be covered by the Schedule 1 exclusion.

Purchase and supply agreements

4.15   Purchase and supply agreements may be acceptable where an acquired business was formerly part of an integrated group of companies and relied on another company in the group for raw materials, or where it represented a guaranteed outlet for the company's products. In such circumstances purchase and supply agreements between the new and former owners may be considered ancillary for a transitional period so that the businesses concerned can adapt to their new circumstances. Exclusivity will not, however, be acceptable save in exceptional circumstances.

PART III
OFT GUIDELINES

Other types of restriction

4.16 Restrictions other than in one of the above three categories may be considered ancillary. There may be other types of restriction that are directly related and necessary to the implementation of a merger and which may, therefore, be covered by the Schedule 1 exclusion, depending on the circumstances of the particular case.

Establishing whether restrictions are ancillary

4.17 The information given in this guideline and in the European Commission's notice should be sufficient in most cases to enable undertakings to determine whether a restriction related to a merger is ancillary and, therefore, whether it is covered by the Schedule 1 exclusion. Any restrictions not considered to be ancillary remain subject to the Chapter I prohibition.

4.18 Issues relating to ancillary restrictions will be dealt with by the Office's Mergers Branch in conjunction with the assessment of the merger to which the restrictions relate. If parties to a merger require a view as to whether restrictions are ancillary for the purposes of the Schedule 1 exclusion, they should so indicate when making a merger submission. To enable the request to be considered, the following information must be provided—

— details of each restriction which is considered to be ancillary and a copy of the relevant agreement(s); and

— an explanation of why each restriction is 'directly related' and 'necessary' to the implementation of the merger.

The Office may seek the views of third parties on the ancillary elements of the merger. If parties seeking Confidential Guidance from Ministers through the Mergers Branch as to the likelihood of a merger situation being referred to the Competition Commission also seek a view as to whether any particular provisions may amount to ancillary restrictions, any view expressed on the latter will be only the view of the Mergers Branch and will not form part of the Confidential Guidance (explained in more detail in Mergers).[3]

4.19 On the basis of the information provided, the parties will be advised in writing whether the restrictions are considered to be ancillary and covered by the Schedule 1 exclusion. This applies even where the merger is found not to qualify for investigation under the Fair Trading Act because it does not meet the share of supply or assets test (see paragraph 2.4 above or section 2.2 of Mergers). As far as possible, this assessment will be carried out within the Mergers Branch's timetable for considering the merger.

4.20 If some or all of the restrictions are not considered to be ancillary, the parties will need to consider whether the relevant restriction infringes the Chapter I prohibition and whether notification for guidance or a decision is appropriate. In so doing, they will need to bear in mind that an agreement will be caught by the prohibition only where it has an appreciable effect on competition within the United Kingdom (see the Competition Act guideline *The Chapter I Prohibition*).

4.21 It may be the case that a restriction is considered not to be ancillary because, for example, its duration is excessive. In such cases it will be possible to discuss with the Mergers Branch what would be acceptable.

Involvement of sector regulators

4.22 The regulators for gas and electricity, water, telecommunications and railways have concurrent powers under the Competition Act but no jurisdiction under the merger provisions of the Fair Trading Act, although they are routinely invited to comment on a merger that affects their particular sector. Where the Office is considering restrictions ancillary to such a merger, the relevant regulator will be consulted in relation to the ancillary elements. In general, any case where restrictions are not considered to be ancillary and fall to be examined under the Competition Act and relate to the industry sector of a regulator will be dealt with by that regulator (see the Competition Act guideline ***Concurrent Application to Regulated Industries***).

[3087]

NOTES

[1] OJ C203, 14.8.90, p 5.

[2] Currently subject to a review and consultation by the European Commission.

[3] This procedure will not be available for newspaper mergers dealt with exclusively by the Secretary of State for Trade and Industry and not considered by the Office (see paragraph 2.6 above).

THE APPLICATION OF THE COMPETITION ACT IN THE TELECOMMUNICATIONS SECTOR

(OFT 417, February 2000)

1 Introduction

1.1 This guideline explains how the Competition Act 1998 ('the Competition Act') will be applied and enforced in the telecommunications sector. It also explains the relationship between the Competition Act and the Telecommunications Act 1984 ('the Telecommunications Act').

1.2 The guideline refers to other Competition Act guidelines where relevant and where appropriate avoids duplication. There is, however, a certain amount of duplication to ensure that the guideline is as self–contained as possible, making it a useful point of reference for the industry.

1.3 The Competition Act is based on Articles 81 and 82 of the EC Treaty. It contains two prohibitions:

— **of anti-competitive agreements**

a prohibition of agreements between undertakings, decisions by associations of undertakings or concerted practices which have the object or effect of preventing, restricting or distorting competition in the United Kingdom (or a part thereof) and which may affect trade within the United Kingdom *('the Chapter I prohibition')*;

— **of abuses of dominance**

a prohibition of conduct by one or more undertakings which amounts to the abuse of a dominant position, in a market in the United Kingdom (or a part thereof) which may affect trade within the United Kingdom *('the Chapter II prohibition')*.

1.4 Articles 81 and 82 of the EC Treaty will continue to apply to:

— anti-competitive agreements, decisions or concerted practices; and

— abuses of a dominant position;

which may affect trade between Member States of the European Union.

1.5 In the telecommunications sector the Director General of Telecommunications ('DGT') and the Director General of Fair Trading ('DGFT') have concurrent jurisdiction to apply and enforce the Competition Act. References hereafter to 'the Director General' should therefore be read as meaning either the DGT or the DGFT.

[3088]

2 The Major Provisions of the Competition Act

The Chapter I Prohibition

2.1 The Chapter I prohibition prohibits agreements between undertakings, decisions by associations of undertakings or concerted practices which have the object or effect of preventing, restricting or distorting competition in the United Kingdom (or a part thereof) and which may affect trade within the United Kingdom. Unless stated otherwise, any reference to an 'agreement' should be read as a reference to an 'agreement between undertakings, decision by an association of undertakings or concerted practice' and any reference to 'agreements' should be read as a reference to 'agreements between undertakings, decisions by associations of undertakings or concerted practices'.

2.2 An agreement may be anti-competitive even though it is not clearly expressed or overt. The Chapter I prohibition is subject to certain exclusions and exemptions. Further details can be found in the Competition Act guidelines *The Major Provisions* and *The Chapter I Prohibition*.

The Chapter II Prohibition

2.3 The Chapter II prohibition prohibits conduct by one or more undertakings which amounts to the abuse of a dominant position in a market in the United Kingdom (or a part thereof) and which may affect trade within the United Kingdom.

2.4 The *holding* of a dominant position is not prohibited. It is the *abuse* of a dominant position that is prohibited.

2.5 The Chapter II prohibition is subject to certain limited exclusions. It is not possible to obtain an exemption from the Chapter II prohibition. Further details can be found in the Competition Act guidelines *The Major Provisions* and *The Chapter II Prohibition*.

Concurrent Jurisdiction

2.6 The DGT is able to exercise, concurrently with the DGFT, almost all of the functions of the DGFT under the Competition Act,[1] in so far as those functions relate to 'commercial activities connected with telecommunications'. References hereafter to 'Competition Act functions' should be read as meaning Competition Act functions exercisable concurrently by the DGT and the DGFT. 'Commercial activities connected with telecommunications' is defined in section 4(3) of the Telecommunications Act as:

'. . . . the provision of telecommunication services, the supply or export of telecommunications apparatus and the production or acquisition of such apparatus and the production or acquisition of such apparatus for supply or export.'

2.7 Throughout this guideline the DGT and the DGFT are described as having concurrent jurisdiction in relation to 'the telecommunications sector', that is, commercial activities connected with telecommunications, as defined in paragraph 2.6 above. Agreements or conduct that relate to the telecommunications sector will normally be dealt with by the DGT. However, the DGT and the DGFT will always consult with each other before a decision is made as to who will deal with a case in respect of which there is concurrent jurisdiction. Further information on how concurrency will work in practice and the extent of the DGT's concurrent jurisdiction can be found in the Competition Act guideline *Concurrent Application to Regulated Industries*.

Notifications

2.8   There is no statutory requirement to notify agreements or conduct. Undertakings are responsible for ensuring that their agreements and conduct are lawful and deciding whether notification is appropriate in any particular case.

2.9   Undertakings may make a notification for guidance or a decision, although the Director General will not provide guidance or decisions in respect of prospective agreements or conduct. In the telecommunications sector the DGFT and the DGT have concurrent jurisdiction to provide guidance or decisions. Notifications must be made to the DGFT by submitting Form N, plus an extra copy for the DGT, and enclosing the relevant fee. A further copy of Form N should also be sent directly to the DGT, but failure to send an additional copy of the form to or for the DGT will not render the notification incomplete. Notifications in respect of agreements or conduct relating to the telecommunications sector will normally be passed to the DGT. As soon as practicable, the DGFT will inform applicants who is dealing with the case, and applicants will also be informed if the case is subsequently transferred to another regulator or to the DGFT.

2.10 Guidance may indicate:
— whether or not the agreement or conduct would be likely to infringe the relevant prohibition; and
— in the case of agreements only, whether or not the agreement would be likely to be granted an exemption if an application for a decision were to be made.

2.11 The Director General is not able to reopen a case once guidance has been given unless:
— he has reasonable grounds for believing that there has been a material change of circumstances since the guidance was given; or
— he has a reasonable suspicion that materially incomplete, misleading or false information was given; or
— a complaint is received from a third party; or
— in respect of the Chapter I prohibition only, one of the parties to an agreement applies for a decision with respect to that agreement.

2.12 A decision may indicate that the agreement or conduct:
— is outside the relevant prohibition; or
— is prohibited; or
— in the case of agreements only, is exempt.

2.13 The Director General is not able to reopen a case once a decision has been given unless:
— he has reasonable grounds for believing that there has been a material change in circumstances; or
— he has a reasonable suspicion that materially incomplete, misleading or false information was given.

Complaints

2.14 In respect of agreements or conduct relating to the telecommunications sector, a complaint that there has been a breach of the Chapter I and/or the Chapter II prohibitions may be made to either the DGFT or the DGT. Complaints in respect of agreements or conduct relating to the telecommunications sector will normally be dealt with by the DGT.

Own-Initiative Investigations

2.15 The Director General may also carry out investigations on his own initiative.

PART III
OFT GUIDELINES

Powers of Investigation

2.16 If the Director General has reasonable grounds for suspecting that an undertaking is infringing either of the prohibitions he (or authorised officials) can exercise his powers of investigation. This means that he can, among other things:

— require the production of any document or information that is specified or that falls within a specified category, which he considers relates to any matter relevant to the investigation, at a time and place, and in the manner or form specified;

— take copies of, or extracts from, any document produced;

— require an explanation of any such document; and

— if a document is not produced, require a statement as to where it can be found;

— enter premises without a warrant and, among other things, require the production of any document that he considers relates to any matter relevant to the investigation and require any relevant information held in a computer to be produced in a form in which it can be read and can be taken away;

— enter premises with a warrant and, amongst other things, search the premises and take copies of, or extracts from, any documents appearing to be the kind in respect of which the warrant was granted and require any relevant information held in a computer to be produced in a form in which it can be read and can be taken away.

2.17 The Competition Act creates a number of criminal offences. It would, for example, be an offence, subject to certain defences, not to produce a specified document. Further details of the powers of investigation and the offences created by the Act are given in the Competition Act guideline *Powers of Investigation*.

Enforcement powers

2.18 Where the Director General proposes to make a decision that a breach of either prohibition has occurred ('an infringement decision') he will set out in a written statement the matters to which he has taken objection ('statement of objections'), the action he proposes to take and his reasons. Persons receiving the statement of objections will then have the opportunity to make representations.

2.19 Where the Director General then makes an infringement decision, he may give a direction to such persons as he considers appropriate, requiring them to bring the infringement to an end. This may include a direction to modify or terminate an agreement or to modify or cease the conduct in question.

2.20 If a person fails to comply with a direction, the Director General may seek a court order compelling him to do so. Non-compliance with such an order is a contempt of court punishable by fine and/or imprisonment.

2.21 Infringement of either of the prohibitions may result in a financial penalty of up to 10 per cent of an undertaking's turnover in the United Kingdom for each year that the infringement lasted, up to a maximum of 3 years.

2.22 Further details can be found in the Competition Act guideline *Enforcement* and in the DGFT's *Guidance on Penalties*.

Appeals

2.23 Appeals against decisions of the Director General are heard by the Competition Commission. In addition to acting as an appeals tribunal, the Competition Commission has assumed the reporting role previously fulfilled by the Monopolies and Mergers Commission pursuant to the monopolies and mergers provisions of the Fair Trading Act 1973.

Transitional arrangements

2.24 Agreements made before the Chapter I prohibitions came into force on 1 March 2000 benefit, in general, from a further one year transitional period before the Chapter I prohibition can be applied. Certain types of agreements qualify for different transitional periods and details of these can be found in the Competition Act Guideline *Transitional Arrangements*.

[3089]

NOTES
¹ Only the DGFT is able to issue guidance on penalties and the DGFT's procedural rules.

3   Relationship between the Competition Act and EC Law

Consistency

3.1 Section 60 of the Competition Act sets out certain principles with a view to ensuring that the United Kingdom authorities handle cases in such a way as to ensure consistency with Community law.

3.2 The Competition Act places a dual obligation on the United Kingdom authorities in applying the Chapter I and II prohibitions. First, they must ensure that there is no inconsistency with either the principles laid down by the EC Treaty and the European Court or any relevant decision of the European Court. Secondly, the United Kingdom authorities must have regard to any relevant decision or statement of the European Commission. In the Director General's view this is limited to decisions or statements which have the authority of the European Commission as a whole, such as, for example, decisions on individual cases under Articles 81 and 82. It would also include clear statements about the Commission's policy approach which it has published in the Annual Report on Competition Policy and the Commission's two notices on the application of EC competition law to the telecommunications sector:
— EC Notice on the application of the competition rules to access agreements in the telecommunications sector[1] ('the EC Access Notice');
— Guidelines on the application of EEC competition rules in the telecommunications sector.[2]

3.3 The EC Access Notice is of particular relevance as it was published after the telecommunications markets in most member states had been liberalised.

3.4 The obligation to ensure consistency applies only to the extent that this is possible, having regard to any relevant differences between the provisions concerned. This means that there will be certain areas where the Community principles will not be relevant. For example, the Community single market objectives, which were designed to establish a European common market, would not be relevant to the domestic prohibition system.

3.5 The provisions of section 60 apply to all United Kingdom authorities which are involved with the application and enforcement of the Competition Act: the Director General, the Competition Commission and the domestic courts.

EC Telecommunications Legislation

3.6 A number of EC Directives (including the Licensing Directive,[3] the Interconnection Directive,[4] the Revised Voice Telephony Directive,[5] and the Amended Leased Lines Directive)[6] require Member States to impose obligations on telecommunications operators. The EC Access Notice, to which the Director General must have regard, states that such legislation may be relevant to the application of Articles 81 and 82 of the EC Treaty (and therefore to the application of the Chapter I and II prohibitions):

'When appropriate, legislation such as the ONP [Open Network Provision] framework will be used as an aid in the interpretation of the competition rules. Given the duty resting on the National Regulatory Authority to ensure that effective competition is possible, application of the competition rules is likewise required for an appropriate interpretation of the ONP principles.'

3.7 The Access Notice provides a number of examples of how this might work in practice:

— accounting separation requirements may assist in investigating 'price squeezing' (see paragraph 7.26 below) by vertically integrated operators. They may also assist in the calculation of market shares;

— transparent cost-accounting systems may assist in the consideration of cases involving pricing issues, including, for example, an allegation of excessive pricing (see paragraphs 7.32 to 7.37 below).

3.8 Many of the obligations contained in the EC directives mentioned above are incorporated in the Telecommunications Act licences of operators. The relationship between the obligations contained in Telecommunications Act licences and the Chapter I and II prohibitions is explained below.

[3090]

NOTES
[1] OJ 98/C 265/02.
[2] OJ 91/C 233/02.
[3] EC Directive 97/13/EC.
[4] EC Directive 97/33/EC.
[5] EC Directive 98/10/EC.
[6] EC Directive 97/51/EC.

4 Relationship between the Competition Act and other relevant statutes

a. The Competition Act and the Telecommunications Act

Relationship between the Chapter I and II prohibitions and conditions contained in Telecommunications Act licences

4.1 An agreement or conduct that is prohibited by the Competition Act may also be in breach of one or more of the conditions contained in the Telecommunications Act licence of a public telecommunications operator ('PTO'). The prohibitions therefore co-exist with the conditions contained in the licences of PTOs. This means that licensees must ensure that they do not breach the Chapter I and II prohibitions, as well as complying with specific licence conditions. For example, all licences granted to PTOs prohibit undue discrimination against any person, or any class of person, in relation to the supply of certain services. In supplying those services a PTO must therefore ensure that it does not breach:

— the condition in its licence that prohibits undue discrimination; and

— the Chapter I prohibition and/or the Chapter II prohibition.

Legal requirements

4.2 To the extent to which an agreement or conduct is required 'in order to comply with a legal requirement'[1] it is excluded from the Chapter I and the Chapter II prohibitions. A licence condition may impose a legal requirement and behaviour specifically required in order to comply with such a condition would not be prohibited by the Competition Act. For example, in certain circumstances a telecoms operator may be required to set prices between a floor and a ceiling. Choosing the precise price within that range does not, however, amount to compliance by the operator with a 'legal requirement'.

An agreement or conduct in breach of both the Competition Act and a licence condition

4.3   As mentioned above, an agreement or conduct may be in breach of both the Competition Act and a licence condition. Price discrimination may, for example, breach the licence condition prohibiting undue discrimination and may also constitute an abuse of a dominant position contrary to the Chapter II prohibition as discussed in paragraphs 7.27 to 7.29 below. In such a case, the DGT may choose to take enforcement action under either the Competition Act or the Telecommunications Act.

4.4   Generally, the DGT has a duty to take enforcement action under the Telecommunications Act in response to a licence breach, but that duty does not apply if he is satisfied that the more appropriate way of proceeding is under the Competition Act. He must then give notice to that effect in accordance with section 16(5) of the Telecommunications Act.

4.5   The DGT cannot fetter his discretion in advance. This means that where he has a choice, he must decide whether to proceed under the Telecommunications Act or the Competition Act on a case by case basis.

4.6   If it appears to the DGT that there is a breach of a licence condition and he has reasonable grounds to suspect that there is also a breach of the Competition Act, he will generally take enforcement action under the Competition Act rather than the Telecommunications Act.

4.7   Whether or not it would be possible for an agreement or conduct to be dealt with under either the Competition Act or the Telecommunications Act may, however, become apparent only after an investigation has commenced. When launching an investigation the DGT may therefore use his powers under both the Competition Act and the Telecommunications Act. He may also use information obtained under the Telecommunications Act in a case dealt with under the Competition Act, and vice versa.

Fair Trading Condition

4.8   The Fair Trading Condition ('FTC') is at present contained in the PTO licences of all major operators. The FTC, like the Competition Act, is based on Articles 81 and 82 of the EC Treaty and contains a clause stating that it shall cease to apply to any behaviour prohibited by new legislation that:

'(i)   contains a prohibition enforceable by the . . . [DGT] . . . of any behaviour prohibited [under the FTC];

(ii)   gives to third parties in respect of a breach of that prohibition at least the rights they have under section 18 of the [Telecommunications Act 1984] in respect of a breach of a provisional or final Order; and

(iii)   permits the imposition on the licensee of monetary penalties in respect of the breach of that prohibition.'

4.9   The DGT believes that the Competition Act meets these criteria and the FTC therefore ceases to apply to agreements and conduct that would otherwise be in breach of both the FTC and the Competition Act. The FTC ceases, in any event, to have effect on 31 July 2001.

Sectoral duties

4.10 Section 3 of the Telecommunications Act sets out the DGT's general ('sectoral') duties. The Competition Act has amended the Telecommunications Act so that when the DGT is exercising his Competition Act functions his sectoral duties do not apply. When exercising any function under the Competition Act, the DGT may nevertheless have regard to any matter in respect of which a sectoral duty is imposed if it is a matter to which the DGFT could have regard when exercising that function.

b. The Competition Act and the Fair Trading Act 1973

4.11 As a general rule, agreements relating to mergers are excluded from the Chapter I prohibition. Specifically, paragraph 1(1) of Schedule 1 of the Competition Act provides that the Chapter I prohibition will not apply to an agreement to the extent to which the agreement would result in two companies ceasing to be distinct enterprises for the purposes of Part V of the Fair Trading Act 1973. Further details are given in the Competition Act guideline *Exclusion of Mergers and Ancillary Restraints*.

4.12 The complex monopoly provisions of the Fair Trading Act continue to apply because there may be activities which are anti-competitive, but which are not caught by the prohibitions. Undertakings may engage in parallel behaviour, for example, which appears to be anti-competitive even though there is no evidence of collusion or agreement. The scale monopoly provisions are retained to deal with the situation where a prior infringement of the Competition Act prohibitions has already been proven, but where the Director General believes that there is a real prospect of further abuse by the same undertaking. The structural remedies available under the scale monopoly provisions may provide the only effective means of preventing those further abuses. Further information about the provisions of the Fair Trading Act that have been retained are given in the Competition Act guideline *The Major Provisions*.

[3091]

NOTES
[1] See Schedule 3(5) of the Competition Act.

5   Market Definition

5.1 In order to determine whether a particular agreement or form of conduct is in breach of the Chapter I and/or the Chapter II prohibitions the Director General will:
— first, seek to define the market to which the agreement or conduct in question relates;
— secondly, consider whether the undertaking or undertakings in question have market power, (although an agreement may breach the Chapter I prohibition where the parties do not have market power—see paragraph 6.4 below);
— thirdly, determine whether there is a breach of the Chapter I and/or the Chapter II prohibitions.

5.2 Defining the relevant market is therefore the first step in any investigation under the Competition Act. Until the market has been defined it is not possible to determine whether the undertaking or undertakings in question have market power. The way that the Director General approaches market definition is outlined below and further details are given in the Competition Act guideline *Market Definition*.

The relevant market

5.3 In the context of a Competition Act investigation a market is defined by reference to:
— the products that are sold in the market ('the product market');
— the geographical area within which the products are sold ('the geographical market').[1]

5.4 The product market consists of the product[2] (or group of products) to which the agreement or conduct relates *plus* any demand-side substitutes[3] and/or supply-side substitutes,[4] the availability of which prevents the undertaking or undertakings from sustaining a small but significant increase in the price of the product above the competitive level. Unless stated otherwise, any reference below to 'undertaking' should be read as a reference to 'undertaking or undertakings'.

5.5   The geographical market may be a part of the United Kingdom, the whole of the United Kingdom, or a larger geographical area. The boundaries of the geographical market will depend on the extent to which:
— customers are able to switch to substitutes supplied by undertakings in different areas; and
— undertakings in different areas are able to supply substitute products.

5.6   The Director General defines the relevant market by identifying the constraints on the freedom of the undertaking to raise the price of the product in question. One way to achieve this is to apply the 'hypothetical monopolist test'.

The hypothetical monopolist test

5.7   The Director General will generally start by taking a narrow view of the market. He will normally assume that there is a separate market for the product in question. He will also assume that there is only one supplier of that product ('the hypothetical monopolist'). He will then consider whether the monopolist supplier could sustain a 'small but significant non-transitory increase in the price' (see paragraphs 5.14 to 5.16 below) of the product above the 'competitive level' (see paragraphs 5.17 to 5.19 below).

5.8   To determine whether the price rise could be sustained the Director General will consider the extent to which customers would switch to demand-side substitutes[5] and whether suppliers that did not currently supply the product could start to supply the product within a relatively short time period, say, within a year. If the Director General decided that the price rise could be sustained, in that there was little scope for demand-side or supply-side substitution, he would assume that there was a separate market for the product in question.

5.9   If the price rise could not be sustained, due to the existence of demand-side and/or supply-side substitutes, the test would be applied again, including those substitutes in the potential market. The Director General would consider whether a monopolist supplier of all the products in the enlarged market could sustain a small but significant increase in the price of the products above the competitive level. Any demand-side and/or supply-side substitute products that would prevent the price rise being sustained would then be added to the market. The Director General would continue to apply the test until the hypothetical monopolist would be unable to sustain the price rise. In this way the Director General will be assisted in identifying the relevant product market.

5.10   Normally, the hypothetical monopolist test will also be used to define the scope of the geographical market. The Director General will generally start by defining the market as the area in which the undertaking or the agreement in question operates. He will then consider whether a hypothetical monopolist in that area would be prevented from sustaining a small but significant non-transitory increase in the price above the competitive level by the availability of demand-side and/or supply-side substitutes supplied by undertakings from other areas. The areas in which any such undertakings operate would then be added to the geographical market. The hypothetical monopolist test would then be applied to the enlarged geographical market. The Director General would continue to apply the test until the hypothetical monopolist would no longer be constrained by the availability of substitutes supplied by undertakings from other areas.

5.11   In defining the product market, the area within which the suppliers of substitute products operate will normally be apparent, making the application of the hypothetical monopolist test to the geographical market more straightforward. In the telecommunications sector, however, some product markets might have a narrow geographical scope. A customer that wished to lease a private circuit connecting city A to city B, for example, would not consider a private circuit linking city A to city C to be a substitute. On the supply side, it might not be feasible (at reasonable cost) for a supplier of circuits between cities A and C to extend its network also to supply city B. In such circumstances, the hypothetical monopolist supplier of circuits between cities A and B would not face any constraints on its price-setting behaviour and circuits on that route would constitute a distinct market.

5.12 In some telecommunications markets, however, there is a requirement for some operators (usually BT) to offer geographically averaged prices. This may act as an indirect constraint on the prices of operators, even where they do not compete directly in the same geographic area. A cable operator in one local franchise area, for example, may not compete directly with a cable operator in another local franchise area, suggesting that local franchise areas are distinct geographic markets. Cable operators also compete with BT, however, which offers geographically averaged prices. This means that if a cable operator in one local franchise area changed its price, any pricing response from BT would not be confined to that local area but would apply nation-wide. This would then have implications for cable operators in other local franchise areas who would have to change their prices. Consequently, markets that appear to be local may actually be wider.

5.13 Details of the types of evidence that the Director General will consider in defining a relevant market are given in the Competition Act guideline *Market Definition*.

'A small but significant non-transitory increase in price'

5.14 The Director General will normally consider whether the hypothetical monopolist would be able to sustain a price increase of between 5 and 10 per cent above the competitive level. However, what is a 'significant' price increase will vary from case to case.

5.15 Generally, if the hypothetical monopolist would be able to raise the price of a product a small but significant amount above the competitive level for more than a year the price rise will be regarded as non-transitory and sustainable. In other words, to prevent the hypothetical monopolist from sustaining a price rise the Director General would normally expect demand-side and/or supply-side substitution to take place within that time.

5.16 This will not always be the case, however, as the Director General will also take into account the ease with which substitutes can be obtained or provided. If customers could switch to a substitute product within a year, for example, but in order to do so they would have to incur significant switching costs, the availability of the substitute product might not be regarded as sufficient to prevent the hypothetical monopolist from sustaining a price rise. The Director General would not normally take into account supply-side substitutes that could be supplied only as a result of significant investment in fixed assets.

The 'competitive level'

5.17 Prices are at the competitive level when no supernormal profits are being made in the long run. Although OFTEL has used price controls to reduce the prices of products in respect of which there was not the prospect of effective competition, it may still be the case that some prices are above competitive levels.

5.18 An undertaking with market power may already have sought to maximise profits by raising the price of the product above the competitive level. If this is the case the application of the hypothetical monopolist test might produce a different market definition from that which would be produced if the price were at the competitive level. The hypothetical monopolist might be prevented from sustaining a price increase by the availability of substitutes that would not form part of the relevant market if the price were raised from a competitive level.

5.19 The Director General will normally proceed on the basis that the current price is at a competitive level *unless* there is evidence to the contrary. Evidence that prices are above competitive levels might include excess profits or past price movements. Further details are contained in the Competition Act guideline *Assessment of Individual Agreements and Conduct*.

Previous cases

5.20 Although a market definition used in a previous case may provide a useful reference point, it will not necessarily be the correct market definition to use subsequently. This is particularly true in the telecommunications sector, which is characterised by rapid technological change. The Director General will not therefore be bound by previous market definitions when carrying out Competition Act investigations, although they will usually provide a useful starting point.

5.21 Further details are given in the Competition Act guideline *Market Definition*.

[3092]

NOTES

[1] In certain circumstances a market may also be defined by reference to time. It is possible, for example, that there could be separate markets for peak and off-peak telephone calls. It is also conceivable that a market could be defined by reference to a particular group of customers to which the product is supplied. This might be appropriate if, for example, an undertaking were able to discriminate between business and residential customers.

[2] Any reference to a 'product' should be read as a reference to a product, service or property right.

[3] A substitute product will not necessarily be identical or be sold at the same price or even be of the same quality as the product for which it is substituted.

[4] It may be possible for other undertakings that supply related products to switch production capacity so as to begin supplying the product. In certain circumstances, however, supply-side substitution might be technically possible, but barriers to entry, such as the need to incur marketing costs to create brand awareness, would prevent supply-side substitution taking place within a reasonably short timescale.

[5] Not all customers, or even a majority of them, would necessarily need to switch to substitutes in order to prevent an undertaking from sustaining a small but significant price increase. Indeed, some of the customers may be captive in that they are unable to switch to other products. Provided, however, that there were a significant number of non-captive customers who could switch to substitute products and that the hypothetical monopolist could not price discriminate by charging the remaining captive customers a higher price, the hypothetical monopolist would not be able to sustain a price increase.

6 Assessment of Market Power

6.1 In order to determine whether there is a breach of either prohibition the Director General will first, define the relevant market and secondly, assess whether the undertaking or undertakings in question have market power. An agreement may, however, breach the Chapter I prohibition where the parties do not have market power as explained in paragraph 6.4 below. The approach to the assessment of market power that the Director General will take is outlined below, and further details are given in the Competition Act guideline *Assessment of Market Power*.

6.2 An undertaking has market power if it is not constrained effectively by competition. In practice, an undertaking with market power will be able to raise prices consistently and profitably above the competitive level. It may also be able consistently to supply goods of a lower quality than it would be able to supply in a competitive market. As is explained below, in determining whether an undertaking has market power the Director General will take into account a range of factors, including:

— the undertaking's market share and changes in that share over time;

— whether there are constraints that would prevent the undertaking from acting anti-competitively, even where it does have a high market share.

The Chapter I prohibition

6.3　While the Chapter I prohibition prohibits agreements that have the object or effect of preventing, restricting or distorting competition in the United Kingdom (or a part thereof) and which may affect trade within the United Kingdom, an agreement will infringe the Chapter I prohibition only if it has an 'appreciable' effect on competition. In practice, if the parties to an agreement do not already have market power—either individually or collectively—and could not acquire such power as a result of the agreement, it is unlikely that the agreement would have an appreciable effect on competition.

6.4　However, the following types of agreement may have an appreciable effect on competition even though the parties to the agreement do not have market power, namely an agreement that:

　(a)　has the object or effect of:

　　　(i)　directly or indirectly fixing prices or sharing markets; or

　　　(ii)　imposing minimum resale prices;or

　(b)　is one of a network of similar agreements that cumulatively have an appreciable effect on competition.

6.5　Subject to the preceding paragraph, if the parties to an agreement have a combined share of the relevant market that does not exceed 25 per cent it is unlikely that they will have market power—individually or collectively—and consequently, it is unlikely that the agreement would have an appreciable effect on competition. Further information on how the Director General will calculate market shares is given at paragraphs 6.13 to 6.16 below.

6.6　Even where the parties' combined market share does exceed 25 per cent, the Director General may find that the agreement would not have an appreciable effect on competition. The other factors that the Director General will take into account are set out at paragraphs 6.17 to 6.32 below.

The Chapter II prohibition

6.7　The Chapter II prohibition prohibits conduct by one or more undertakings which amounts to the abuse of a dominant position in a market in the United Kingdom (or a part thereof), which may affect trade within the United Kingdom. The European Court has defined a dominant position as:

　'a position of economic strength enjoyed by an undertaking which enables it to prevent effective competition being maintained on the relevant market by affording it the power to behave to an appreciable extent independently of its competitors, customers and ultimately of consumers.'[1]

6.8　A dominant undertaking will possess a substantial degree of market power that is in excess of any market power held by any of its competitors. It is not, however, necessarily the case that a firm with market power, or even the firm with the greatest degree of market power in any particular market, will be dominant.

6.9　The European Court has stated that if an undertaking's market share has persistently exceeded 50 per cent, it will, unless there is evidence to the contrary, be presumed to be dominant.[2] In the absence of other factors, however, the Director General considers it unlikely that an undertaking will be dominant individually if its market share is below 40 per cent. Even where an undertaking has a market share in excess of 40 per cent it may not have a dominant position as there may be other factors that would prevent the undertaking acting anti-competitively. Further information on how the Director General will calculate market shares is given at paragraphs 6.13 to 6.16 below and the other factors he will take into account in assessing market power are set out at paragraphs 6.17 to 6.32 below.

Collective dominance

6.10 Conduct on the part of *one or more* undertakings that amounts to the abuse of a dominant position is prohibited. Undertakings may therefore be dominant collectively.

6.11 Undertakings in the same corporate group may have collective dominance. Collective dominance may also exist when two or more undertakings are linked in such a way that they adopt the same conduct in the market. The Court of First Instance has stated that:

> 'There is nothing in principle, to prevent two or more independent economic entities from being, on a specific market, united by such economic links that, by virtue of that fact, together they hold a dominant position vis-à-vis the other operators on the market.' [3]

6.12 A recent decision of the Court of First Instance[4] under the EC Merger Regulation suggests that collective dominance (at least for the purpose of that Regulation) may also exist where there are no such links between the undertakings in question, but where they are acting in the same way on the market. This is likely, however, to be the case only in oligopolistic markets characterised by homogeneous products and high entry barriers. It is not yet clear whether this broader definition of collective dominance under the Merger Regulation will also be applied to Article 82 of the EC Treaty (on which the Chapter II prohibition is based).

Calculating market shares

6.13 In determining whether an undertaking has market power the Director General will take into account the undertaking's market share, although even where an undertaking has a high market share there may be constraints that would prevent the undertaking acting anti-competitively.

6.14 Market share will normally be measured in terms of either value or volume of sales. The Director General will use whichever measure of market share is more appropriate, although it will generally be useful to obtain information in respect of both the value and volume of sales.

6.15 When calculating an undertaking's share of the relevant market the Director General will also take into account the market share of any undertakings in the same group:
— over which it exercises control directly or indirectly;
— which exercise control over it directly or indirectly.

6.16 In calculating an undertaking's market share the Director General will take into account not just its market share at a given point in time. As mentioned above, an undertaking will be presumed to be dominant if its market share has been *persistently* above 50 per cent. The Director General will therefore look at how the market shares of all undertakings in the relevant market have changed over time. In order to calculate market shares the Director General will normally consider information from a variety of sources, including:
— information from the undertaking or undertakings that he is investigating;
— information from competitors, customers, suppliers and trade associations;
— market research reports.

Other factors

6.17 An undertaking with a persistently high market share may not necessarily have market power. First, there may be constraints that prevent the undertaking from acting anti-competitively:
— existing and potential competitors;
— barriers to entry or exit;
— buyer power;
— the undertaking's conduct/performance.

PART III
OFT GUIDELINES

Secondly, in a market where undertakings regularly improve the quality of their products, a persistently high market share may be the consequence of persistently successful innovation.

Short-run constraints: existing competitors and supply-side substitution

6.18 Existing competitors may be able to prevent an undertaking from behaving anti-competitively, for example, by undercutting an undertaking that increases the price of its product above the competitive level.

6.19 An undertaking may also be constrained in the short run by the prospect of supply-side substitution. As mentioned in part 5 above, other undertakings may be able to increase production or switch capacity quickly and easily. As a rule of thumb, supply-side substitution should take place within a year and ought not to require significant investment in fixed assets.

Barriers to entry

6.20 An entry barrier is a cost borne by an undertaking entering a market that is not borne by an undertaking already operating in the market. The lower the barriers to entry, the more likely it is that the threat of competition will prevent an undertaking from acting anti-competitively. There are three types of barrier to entry:
— absolute advantages;
— strategic advantages;
— exclusionary behaviour.

Absolute advantages

6.21 An undertaking has an absolute advantage if it has access to important assets and/or resources that are not accessible to a potential entrant or are accessible only at a substantially higher cost. Until December 1996, for example, BT and Cable & Wireless had an absolute advantage in the handling of international telecoms traffic in that only they were licensed to own and operate international facilities, the infrastructure for handling international traffic. Also, the fact that there is a finite amount of radio spectrum means that only four undertakings are currently licensed to operate mobile networks. Those operators therefore have an absolute advantage.

Strategic advantages

6.22 A strategic advantage typically results from being the first to enter a market. An undertaking may have a strategic advantage over potential entrants, for example, as a result of its reputation for engaging in predatory pricing (see paragraphs 7.13 to 7.19 below) so as to drive competitors out of the market—something which would also fall within the category of exclusionary behaviour (see paragraph 6.26 below).

6.23 An undertaking may also have a strategic advantage over potential entrants if, in order to enter the market, undertakings would have to incur a high level of sunk costs, costs that would not be recoverable if it proved necessary to exit the market. Given that most telecommunications' services are based on or around networks that require substantial investment, a number of telecommunications markets are characterised by a high degree of sunk costs. The level of sunk costs is likely to be higher where there are significant economies of scale and/or scope,[5] because in order to compete undertakings would need to enter the market on a scale large enough for them to obtain the same economies of scale and/or scope as incumbents.

6.24 New entrants will also have to incur sunk costs in an effort to influence demand for their products—they may need to incur marketing costs in order to create brand awareness and to overcome customer inertia towards switching from a long-established incumbent operator. Incumbents may also be able to influence the level of sunk costs faced by the entrant.

6.25 An undertaking may also have a strategic advantage over potential entrants as a result of having more information on the existing costs of production. Potential entrants may not have the same access to finance as an undertaking that is already operating in the market and may therefore have a strategic disadvantage.

Exclusionary behaviour

6.26 Entry barriers may be created by exclusionary behaviour on the part of an undertaking that is already operating in the market. Competing telecommunications operators, for example, need to be able to interconnect with other networks in order to provide a full service to their customers. In particular, a small network with only a few subscribers that is competing with a large dominant network operator will need to be able to terminate calls on the latter's network. This is because the small network is unlikely to be able to attract customers if they are unable to make calls to the large number of subscribers remaining with the dominant operator. By contrast, there is little cost to the dominant operator if its subscribers are unable to call the relatively small number of customers of the small competing network. A dominant operator can exploit this asymmetry in order to exclude rivals by refusing to allow other network operators to interconnect with its network or allowing interconnection only on unfavourable terms.

Assessing barriers to entry

6.27 The Director General will generally seek information regarding the costs of entering the market from undertakings already operating in the market and from potential entrants. He might, for example, ask for an estimate of the cost of obtaining a 5 per cent share of the market. He might also ask for an estimate of the cost of operating at the 'minimum efficient scale'—the size of plant that an entrant would need in order to obtain the same economies of scale as undertakings already operating in the market.

6.28 The Director General will also look at the history of entry to, and exit from, the market (or closely related markets). The level of profits that have been earned will also be relevant. If an undertaking has consistently earned excess profits this might suggest that there are high barriers to entry, but they may also be a reward for persistently successful innovation, and might therefore encourage market entry.

6.29 The level of growth or prospective growth in the market will also be relevant. Entry will be more likely in a growing market than in a static or declining market because it will be easier for new entrants to gain market share. The rate of innovation is important too. In markets where high rates of innovation occur, or are expected to occur, innovation may enable barriers to entry to be overcome relatively quickly. Indeed, profit that results from a barrier to entry created by successful innovation may create an incentive to innovate.

Buyer power

6.30 An undertaking's ability to behave anti-competitively may also be affected by the power of a buyer (or group of buyers) to exert a substantial influence on the price, quality or terms of supply of a product. In order to have such power a buyer is likely to account for a large proportion of the producer's total output, be well-informed about alternative sources of supply, be able to switch to other suppliers readily at little cost to itself, and may even be able to begin producing the relevant product itself. The existence of countervailing buyer power does not, however, guarantee a more beneficial outcome in terms of, for example, lower prices to end consumers. If the buyer itself has market power in the downstream markets, it may not be sufficiently constrained by competition to pass on any benefits it obtains from its suppliers to its end customers.

PART III
OFT GUIDELINES

Conduct and performance

6.31 An undertaking's conduct or financial performance may in itself provide evidence of market power. The Director General will examine whether the undertaking has been able consistently to charge a price that is in excess of costs. In analysing the extent of price competition the Director General will take into account the impact of any price controls. It is feasible, however, that a price control which is averaged across several markets may still leave room for an undertaking to raise prices persistently above competitive levels in one or more of the markets in question.

6.32 As well as being relevant to the issue of whether barriers to entry exist, the fact that an undertaking has been able consistently to earn excess profits may also indicate that there is a lack of price competition.

Significant Market Power and Market Influence

6.33 The concepts of Significant Market Power ('SMP') and Market Influence are regulatory concepts. Telecommunications operators that are designated as having SMP and/or Market Influence must fulfil certain regulatory obligations. Further details are given in OFTEL's *Draft guidelines on Market Influence Determinations* (April 1999).[6]

6.34 In the context of an investigation under the Competition Act, the fact that an operator has been determined as having SMP and/or Market Influence status in a particular market does not imply that it will have market power in all markets in which it operates. In particular, it does not imply that it will have market power in the market that is the subject of the Competition Act investigation. This will have to be considered fully as part of the investigation, with the Director General first defining the relevant market and then assessing whether the operator has market power, using the approach outlined above.

[3093]

NOTES
1   Case C27/76 *United Brands v. Commission*, [1978] ECR 207, [1978] 1 CMLR 429.
2   Case C62/86 AKZO *Chemie BV v. Commission*, [1993] 5 CMLR 215.
3   Case T–68/69 etc *Societa Italiano Vetro SpA v. Commission* [1992] 2 ECR 1403, [1992] 5 CMLR 302.
4   Case T–102/96 *Gencor v. Commission* [1999] 4 CMLR 971.
5   Economies of scale exist where average costs fall as output increases; economies of scope exist where average costs fall as more types of product are produced.
6   These guidelines are not guidelines within the meaning of section 52 of the Competition Act.

7   Assessment of Agreements and Conduct

7.1 If having defined the relevant market the Director General determines that the undertaking or undertakings in question have market power, he will then consider whether there is a breach of the Chapter I prohibition, which prohibits anti-competitive agreements, and/or the Chapter II prohibition, which prohibits abuses of a dominant position. This is subject to the proviso that certain types of agreement may have an appreciable effect on competition and be in breach of the Chapter I prohibition even though the parties to the agreement do not have market power individually or collectively as referred to in paragraph 6.4 above. Further details are given in the Competition Act guideline *Assessment of Individual Agreements and Conduct*.

7.2 This part provides guidance on how the Director General will assess whether certain types of agreement and conduct are in breach of either prohibition. It concentrates on the types of agreement and conduct that are likely to be of concern in the telecommunications sector. Emphasis is placed on types of conduct rather than types of agreement, but there may be a breach of the Chapter I prohibition where conduct of the type mentioned below forms the subject matter of an agreement. It is also possible that by entering into an agreement that is in breach of the Chapter I prohibition an undertaking may also be in breach of the Chapter II prohibition.

Leveraging dominance into upstream or downstream markets

7.3   In assessing whether agreements and conduct are in breach of either prohibition, it is important to bear in mind that if an undertaking is dominant in one market and is vertically integrated into markets upstream or downstream of that market, it may have the ability adversely to affect competition in the upstream or downstream markets. The EC Access Notice, to which, in accordance with section 60 of the Competition Act, the Director General must have regard, states that the European Court of Justice's analysis in *Tetra Pak II*,[1] which concerned the leverage of dominance into closely related horizontal markets, is 'equally applicable . . . to closely related vertical markets'. The EC Access Notice goes on to state that where an operator has:

> 'a very high degree of market power on at least one of those [closely related markets] . . . it may be appropriate . . . to find that the particular operator was in a situation comparable to that of holding a dominant position on the markets in question as a whole.'

7.4   Telecommunications operators and/or independent service providers may rely on an operator for the provision of network inputs ('the upstream market'), while at the same time competing with that operator in downstream markets. If the vertically integrated operator were dominant in the upstream market there could be scope for it to leverage its position of dominance into the downstream market (see, for example, the discussion on price squeezing in paragraph 7.26 below).

Measuring the cost of providing telecommunications services

Background

7.5   Before dealing with specific types of pricing behaviour that may be anti-competitive it is necessary to explain how the Director General will measure the cost of providing telecommunications services.

7.6   The supply of telecommunications services is characterised by economies of scale[2] in the provision of networks, (which stem partly from the fact that there are some large elements of cost that do not vary with the number of customers or calls, even in the long run), and economies of scope[3] in the provision of services (stemming from common costs).[4] This means that telecommunications companies tend to be multi-product firms and that their pricing policies have to take into account the need to recover both the fixed costs of supplying a service and the common costs. In particular, the incidence of low marginal costs[5] and the existence of substantial common costs mean that an undertaking that is involved in a range of markets has, subject to regulatory constraints, a great deal of freedom to offer a range of prices and to choose the markets from which to recover its costs. This can put such an undertaking at a significant advantage over competitors that do not have the same degree of freedom because of their size and/or because they supply a more limited range of services. There is nothing wrong with a dominant undertaking having such advantages provided that it does not abuse its dominant position.

The use of long run incremental cost

7.7   In considering the appropriate cost base against which prices should be assessed, it is first of all necessary to distinguish between the short run and the long run. In the short run some costs, in particular capital costs, are fixed. In the long run, however, all costs, including capital costs, are variable.

7.8   The long run incremental cost[6] ('LRIC') measure takes into account the total long run costs (that is, both capital and operating costs) of supplying a specified additional unit of output ('the increment'). The increment could be, for example, the provision of a new service. If the price of a service covers all its LRIC, including the costs of capital (and with any common costs being recovered through charges for the undertaking's other services), it will be profitable for the undertaking to offer the service. As the provision of telecommunications services is characterised by high levels of capital costs it will generally be appropriate to use LRIC as the cost base.

7.9   In contrast, short run marginal cost, which includes only the short run cost of producing an additional unit of output, excludes capital costs. The use of short run marginal cost as a cost base tends, therefore, to result in prices that are very low. Where the costs of production include a large proportion of costs that do not vary with output, as is the case in telecommunications, the short run marginal cost of an additional unit of output could even be as low as zero. Setting prices in relation to short run marginal cost would therefore tend to underestimate the costs of supplying telecommunications services, whereas prices that are derived from incremental costs reflect the actual costs of supply. Prices that are derived from LRIC should also enable potential new entrants to make informed pricing and investment decisions.

7.10   The use of LRIC as the cost base for the supply of telecommunications services is also consistent with the view that in network industries it is generally inappropriate to measure the cost of supplying a service by reference to average variable costs.[7] The EC Access Notice states that:

'a price which equates to the variable cost of a service may be substantially lower than the price the operator needs in order to cover the cost of providing the service . . . the costs considered should include the total costs which are incremental to the provision of the service . . . [Therefore,] the Commission will often need to consider the average incremental costs of providing a service, and may need to examine average incremental costs over a longer period than one year.'

Common costs

7.11   When examining pricing issues in the telecommunications sector, LRIC is generally therefore a more satisfactory cost base than marginal or average variable cost. However, the existence of economies of scope means that if the prices of each of an undertaking's services are all equal to each service's LRIC, the undertaking will not recover its common costs. To ensure that such a situation could not have an anti-competitive effect, the undertaking would need to be able to demonstrate two things, first, that its individual prices are set at or above LRIC and secondly, that the combined prices of services in groups that share common costs cover both LRIC and the common costs of supplying those services. OFTEL usually refers to this as a 'combinatorial' test.

The use of LRIC in practice

7.12   Under the Network Charge Control arrangements, BT's charges for interconnection services are derived from the LRIC of conveyance, with an appropriate mark up to cover common costs. In relation to retail services, BT has, in consultation with OFTEL, recently developed a methodology to produce cost information based on LRIC. When dealing with cases concerning the supply of telecommunications services the Director General proposes to request that BT provides cost information produced in accordance with this methodology. The Director General will also ask other operators to provide cost information based on LRIC when dealing with cases that are concerned with the supply of telecommunications services.

Pricing behaviour that may be anti-competitive

Predatory pricing

7.13 Predatory pricing is a strategy whereby an undertaking deliberately incurs short term losses so as to eliminate a competitor and be able to charge excessive prices in the future. Customers and/or consumers may benefit in the short term from lower prices, but in the longer term weakened competition will lead to higher prices, reduced quality and reduced choice. Predatory pricing is therefore likely to be in breach of the Chapter II prohibition.

7.14 In assessing whether an undertaking is engaging in predatory pricing the Director General will consider whether:
— in the short run the undertaking will make an incremental profit,[8] which will enable it to cover its costs;[9]
— it is the undertaking's intention to eliminate a competitor;
— it would be feasible for the undertaking to recover its losses.

Further details are given in the Competition Act guideline *Assessment of Individual Agreements and Conduct*.

7.15 For the Director General to examine whether an undertaking is covering its LRIC is consistent with the approach set out in the EC Access Notice, which recognises that cost structures in network industries tend to be different from most other industries and that a straightforward application of the test established by the European Court of Justice in the *AKZO* case[10] (using average variable cost as the cost floor) is inappropriate. Further details of the *AKZO* case and the costs tests the Court established are given in the Competition Act guideline *Assessment of Individual Agreements and Conduct*. If a dominant undertaking is pricing below LRIC the Director General will therefore presume that it is intending to engage in predatory pricing. It will be for the undertaking in question to rebut this presumption, which, the Director General recognises, will be possible in certain circumstances. It may, for example, be rational to price below LRIC where an operator has excess capacity and this has not been reflected in existing prices.

7.16 If an undertaking's individual prices are above LRIC but revenue overall fails to cover total costs, it will be regarded as intending to engage in predatory pricing if it can be established that the purpose of the conduct is to eliminate a competitor. The existence of common costs will also mean that it will be appropriate to undertake the tests outlined in paragraph 7.11 above, to establish whether total revenue covers total costs.

7.17 An undertaking may seek to justify its pricing strategy by arguing that it will result in an incremental profit that will enable it to cover its costs. As stated in the EC Access Notice, however, pricing below average total costs would not be justifiable if a dominant operator would benefit only if one or more of its competitors were weakened.

7.18 In assessing whether an undertaking's pricing strategy would result in an incremental profit that would enable it to cover its costs, it will often be appropriate to use a net revenue test, which compares the profitability of a particular decision (for example, to adopt a lower price) with the alternative 'benchmark' strategy (for example, to maintain prices at their existing level). If profitability were not adversely affected by the reduction in price because the demand increased sufficiently to offset the price reduction and at the same time, the price remained sufficiently high to cover the incremental costs of the increase in output, the price reduction might be viewed as legitimate competitive behaviour. If, however, an undertaking had no realistic expectation that a profit would be made or had made no attempt to assess the impact on profitability that the pricing strategy would have, the price reduction is likely to be taken as evidence of an intention to eliminate a competitor.

PART III
OFT GUIDELINES

7.19 An additional factor that will need to be taken into account is the extent to which there is strong complementarity between two or more services in respect of which there are different supply and demand conditions. Where there is strong complementarity, in applying the relevant tests it may be more appropriate to take into account the costs and revenues of all the complementary services rather than require each individual service to cover its costs. For example, access (that is, line rentals and connections) and calls are likely to be strong complements in that customers would probably have a demand only for access services, primarily because they wished to make and receive calls. In general, however, the Director General would expect each individual service to be priced above LRIC because although a consumer may require two or more services, they need not be obtained from the same supplier.

Cross-subsidies

7.20 A cross subsidy occurs where an undertaking uses revenues from one market to subsidise losses in another market. Where the undertaking uses revenues from a market where it is dominant there may be a breach of the Chapter II prohibition.

7.21 A cross-subsidy will normally be judged to occur where an undertaking's revenues from an activity (for example, a new service) may be expected to fail to cover the costs associated with that activity over its *economic lifetime*. The Director General will consider whether the revenue over the lifetime of a service would exceed the LRIC, including the cost of capital. If the revenue would exceed the LRIC, the service would be sustainable in the long term, that is, providing the service would not require a cross-subsidy.

7.22 A group of services may share common costs which, although the services are individually priced above LRIC, are not covered. A combinatorial test would establish whether the prices of services in groups that share common costs cover both the incremental and common costs of supplying those services. If they did not, this would indicate that the group of services is being cross-subsidised.

7.23 In assessing whether the revenue from providing a service would exceed the LRIC it may be useful to perform a Discounted Cash Flow ('DCF') analysis.[11] This is a forward-looking analysis of the incremental cash flows (in terms of both costs and revenues) that are expected to arise from a service. It may be particularly useful to perform a DCF analysis in relation to new services or for a service in its start-up phase, when it is often reasonable to expect initial losses to be incurred. A DCF analysis is one of the standard methods of investment appraisal. It should be based on assumptions that are consistent with those made in an undertaking's business plan in relation to, for example, the competitive conditions to be expected in the market. It will not always be possible for an undertaking to meet all the targets set out in its business plan. Evidence of an abuse of dominance may be provided, however, where a business case is based on unjustified and implausible assumptions or where there has been a failure by the undertaking to take remedial action once it became apparent that it would not meet the targets.

7.24 For mature services there will be circumstances where a profitability analysis based on accounting data (with an allowance for the return on capital) may be used to assess whether there is a cross-subsidy. An undertaking would be expected to be able to justify the cost of capital figure that it has chosen to use in relation to the product in question and will be expected to earn at least that cost of capital. If there is a high level of risk it might be appropriate to allow the undertaking to earn a higher rate of return than would normally be assumed for products of average risk.

7.25 Further details are given in the Competition Act guideline *Assessment of Individual Agreements and Conduct*.

Price squeezing

7.26 Where a vertically integrated undertaking is dominant in an upstream market and supplies a key input to undertakings that compete with it in a downstream market, there is scope for it to abuse its dominance in the upstream market. The vertically integrated undertaking could subject its competitors in the downstream market to a price or a margin squeeze by raising the cost of the key input (see paragraph 7.32 to 7.37 below on excessive pricing) and/or by lowering its prices in the downstream market. The integrated undertaking's *total* revenue may remain unchanged. The effect would be to reduce the gross margin available to its competitors, which might well make them unprofitable. In considering whether an undertaking is engaging in price squeezing in breach of the Competition Act, the Director General will consider whether the dominant undertaking would be profitable in the relevant downstream market if it had to pay the same input prices as its competitors. A dominant undertaking may try to conceal a price squeeze by allocating to its upstream activities costs that are actually incurred as a result of its downstream activities. The Director General will give close consideration to the method of cost allocation where he believes that it may be being used to aid anti-competitive behaviour.

Price discrimination

7.27 An undertaking can be said to be discriminating when it applies dissimilar conditions to equivalent transactions. There may, however, be objective reasons for an undertaking charging different prices to different customers, where, for instance, there are different transport costs. The Director General recognises that where the demand for a service is different among different customers or groups of customers, price discrimination may be an efficient method of recovering substantial fixed costs.

7.28 Price discrimination, and discrimination more generally, may be an abuse of the Chapter II prohibition, where, for example:

— its effect is to exclude competitors from the market in question;

— an undertaking (or group of undertakings) exploits its market power by charging excessively high prices to certain customers.

7.29 Further details are given in the Competition Act guideline *Assessment of Individual Agreements and Conduct*.

Discounts

7.30 Discounts are a form of price competition. They can sometimes reflect the lower costs of supplying certain customers or groups of customers and, in general, such discounts would not normally be in breach of the Competition Act. Where discounts are offered to certain customers that do not reflect underlying cost differences they represent a form of price discrimination. There may be legitimate reasons for offering such discounts, even when they do not reflect underlying cost differences. They may, for example, represent an efficient way of recovering fixed or common costs.

7.31 There are some types of discounts, however, that, when offered by a dominant undertaking, would be likely to cause concern in the telecommunications sector:

— loyalty rebates, where the discount (or its level) is dependent on the customer not taking (or restricting) supplies from competitors, whether this is *de facto* (for example, the customer must meet certain expenditure targets) or by agreement;

— discounts which are calculated across, and applied to products offered in, a range of markets including those where the undertaking is dominant;

— volume rebates that are calculated on the basis of total telecommunications expenditure across a range of competitive and regulated markets even though the discounts are applied to spending only in competitive markets;

— discounts which are targeted at a narrow group of customers, particularly where the group consists of only those customers who have the ability to switch to alternative suppliers.

Excessive pricing

7.32 The charging of excessive selling prices (or, conversely, the extraction of unfair or excessively low buying prices) by a dominant undertaking may be an infringement of the Chapter II prohibition.[12] The European Court of Justice has held that:

'... charging a price which is excessive because it has no reasonable relation to the economic value of the product supplied ... is an abuse.'[13]

7.33 The Court stated that a detailed analysis of costs would be required before any judgement could be reached and said that the question to be asked was:

'... whether the difference between the costs actually incurred and the price actually charged is excessive, and if the answer to this question is in the affirmative to consider whether a price has been charged which is either unfair in itself or when compared to other competing products.'

7.34 Excessive prices charged by a dominant undertaking for the supply of network inputs required by competitors in a downstream market would be of particular concern (see also paragraph 7.26 above in relation to price squeezing). In addition to having no relation to the economic value of the product supplied, such excessive prices might make it more difficult for undertakings to compete and could deter market entry at the downstream level. This may be less of a concern, however, if the excessive prices attract new entry at the network level, although whether this can happen and how quickly will depend on the extent to which there are entry barriers at the network level.

7.35 An undertaking's prices in a particular market can be regarded as excessive if they allow the undertaking to sustain profits higher than it would expect to earn in a competitive market ('supra-normal profits'). Essentially, excessive prices will be abusive only if they have persisted in the absence of continuing successful innovation and/or without stimulating successful new entry or significant loss of market share. Excessive prices will not always, however, result in supra-normal profits as an undertaking protected from competition might be able to sustain higher costs.

7.36 An agreement between two or more undertakings to set excessive prices might be in breach of the Chapter I prohibition if it has an appreciable effect on competition. Undertakings might also engage in tacit collusion by, for example, deciding to follow each others' prices ('parallel pricing') or following the pricing policy of a market leader ('price leadership'). Such behaviour might also be in breach of the Chapter I prohibition if it has an appreciable effect on competition. It might also amount to an abuse of dominance or joint dominance under the Chapter II prohibition. In determining whether tacit collusion had occurred the Director General would consider whether price changes were related to costs. In particular, he would look at whether the prices of undertakings had risen when costs had not and whether cost reductions had been passed on to customers in the form of lower prices.

7.37 Further details are given in the Competition Act guideline *Assessment of Individual Agreements and Conduct*. The guideline also explains how the Director General will determine whether an undertaking is making supra-normal profits.

Other types of conduct and agreements

Refusal to supply

7.38 A dominant undertaking's refusal to supply may be in breach of the Chapter II prohibition if it cannot be justified objectively, for example, for safety reasons, to protect network integrity, because of the lack of creditworthiness of the operator seeking access or because of a lack of capacity. Various types of refusal to supply are dealt with below. As mentioned above, where a refusal to supply is the subject of an agreement, there may be a breach of the Chapter II and/or the Chapter I prohibitions.

Refusal to grant access to facilities

7.39 A refusal to grant access to certain facilities may be a breach of either prohibition. The EC Access Notice sets out three types of refusal to supply:
'(a) a refusal to grant access for the purposes of a service where another operator has been given access by the access provider to operate on that services market;
(b) a refusal to grant access for the purposes of a service where no other operator has been given access by the access provider to operate on that services market;
(c) a withdrawal of access from an existing customer.'

Type (a) refusal to grant access—discriminatory refusal

7.40 The EC Access Notice states that:
'a refusal to supply . . . where a dominant facilities owner is already supplying one or more customers operating in the same downstream market would constitute discriminatory treatment which, if it would restrict competition on the downstream market, would be an abuse . . . The dominant company's duty is to provide access in such a way that the goods and services offered to downstream companies are available on terms no less favourable than those given to other parties including its own corresponding downstream operations.'

7.41 Thus, where a discriminatory refusal by a dominant operator to grant the access required by a competing operator restricts competition in a downstream market it is likely to be an abuse of dominance in breach of the Chapter II prohibition. A discriminatory refusal to supply by a dominant operator might not be an abuse, however, if an objective justification for the refusal can be demonstrated.

Type (b) refusal to grant access—access required to supply new services

7.42 The EC Access Notice recognises that there is considerable scope for a refusal to supply to have serious anti-competitive consequences where, 'if there were no commercially feasible alternatives to the access being requested, then unless access is granted, the party requesting access would not be able to operate on the service market.' The Notice recognises that a refusal to grant access in such circumstances would limit the development of new services or impede the development of competition and would be likely to have abusive effects.

7.43 In accordance with the decision of the ECJ in *Oscar Bronner*,[14] a refusal to grant access required to supply new services will be prohibited under the Competition Act only if:
— it is likely to eliminate all competition on the part of the undertaking that is seeking access in the relevant downstream market;
— the refusal is incapable of objective justification.

7.44 Whether a refusal to grant access to a facility is in breach of the Competition Act will need to be assessed on a case by case basis. In respect of the launch of one service, a refusal to grant access to a facility may be prohibited, but the refusal to grant access for the launch of another service may not be. The Director General considers that a refusal by a dominant undertaking to grant access might be an abuse of dominance where, for example, the refusal prevents the supply of a new service that has one or more of the following characteristics:

— the service requires end to end capability across the dominant undertaking's network;

— the service requires interconnection in order to be economically viable;

— the service requires that equipment on customers' premises be capable of interacting with the network.

Type (c) refusal to grant access—withdrawal of access from an existing customer

7.45 The unilateral termination of access agreements raises similar issues to type (a) and type (b) refusals to grant access. The Director General will follow the approach of the European Commission as set out in the EC Access Notice:

'withdrawal of access from an existing customer will usually be abusive . . . objective reasons may be provided to justify the termination. Any such reasons must be proportionate to the effects on competition of the withdrawal.'

Refusal to supply information

7.46 A refusal by a dominant undertaking to supply information generated by its network, for example, calling line identification information, might be an abuse of a dominant position if the refusal means that services based on the availability of the information could be provided only by the dominant operator.

7.47 The refusal by a dominant operator to supply technical information may also be an abuse of dominance. The refusal by a dominant operator to inform a new operator where it can interconnect with its network, for example, would be likely to be prohibited.

7.48 Intellectual property rights ('IPRs') may exist in relation to technical information, and there are circumstances in which an IPR might be exercised in a manner that would constitute an abuse of a dominant position. A refusal by a dominant operator to supply interface information, for example, may have an effect on competition in the market for the supply of customer equipment designed to take advantage of the new interface. The Director General recognises, however, that the ability to obtain IPRs encourages innovation and therefore the circumstances in which the exercise of an IPR would constitute an abuse are likely to be limited.

Behaviour short of refusal to supply

7.49 In the absence of an objective justification, behaviour that falls short of a refusal to supply might be an abuse of dominance. A dominant undertaking might in principle be prepared to grant access to one of its facilities, for example, but might seek to impose unreasonable terms and conditions, delay access or refuse to allow testing. Guidance on what the Director General will regard as reasonable time scales for resolving interconnection disputes is contained in OFTEL's *Guidelines on Interconnection and Interoperability* (July 1999)[15] and *Guidelines on the Operation of the Network Charge Controls* (October 1997).[16]

Bundling

7.50 Bundling generally involves the tying of the supply of one product to the supply of other products. Bundling does not raise competition concerns when it is carried out by undertakings without any market power. It can also benefit consumers where, for example, it allows two or more products to be offered at a lower, combined price than if they had been supplied separately or where products are produced which otherwise would not be. In such cases, consumers may benefit from being able to consume products that would otherwise not be available to them.

Bundling by a dominant undertaking can, however, affect competition in both retail and wholesale markets. The assessment of whether bundling has anti-competitive effects can raise complex issues, although the main concern will be to determine whether the bundling has any exclusionary effects on competition. The Director General will balance any exclusionary effects against any countervailing benefits, such as lower prices resulting from the exploitation of economies of scope. He will also take into account the possibility that unbundling the products in question may not be feasible for economic or technical reasons.

7.51 There are a number of forms of bundling that are likely to be prohibited under the Competition Act:

— where a dominant telecommunications operator ties the supply of products in a market in which it is dominant to the supply of products that are (at least potentially) supplied competitively, for example, where a dominant operator ties the supply of access to its network to the supply of its own telephone equipment. This could be enforced through contractual means by, for example, making it a condition of the sale of the non-competitive product that the competitive product is purchased as well. Alternatively, it could be enforced through non-contractual means by, for example, offering more favourable terms for the non-competitive product if the competitive product is purchased as well. Such a practice could have the effect of foreclosing the market to other suppliers of the competitive product, even where the dominant undertaking also offered to supply the different elements of the bundle separately. There could still be an anti-competitive effect if the (implicit) price of the competitive product as part of the bundle were below cost. This would mean that other suppliers of the competitive product would not be able to compete;

— where a dominant operator bundles together physically services that could be supplied separately, for example, where a switch is supplied to a customer with the software already installed, when it is technically possible for it to be supplied separately and competitively. This could have the same foreclosure effects on other suppliers of the competitive service as mentioned above.

Vertical restraints

7.52 In general, a vertical restraint is a provision in an agreement made between undertakings operating at different stages in the supply chain that restricts the commercial freedom of one or more of the parties. A vertical restraint might, for example, be contained in an agreement between a network operator and a telecommunications service provider which, for the purposes of the agreement, operate at different stages in the supply chain. The restraint could take the form of an exclusive purchasing agreement whereby the service provider agreed only to purchase the network services of one operator. Vertical agreements are excluded from the scope of the Chapter I prohibition, although the Director General has the power to claw back agreements so that the Chapter I prohibition will apply. The Chapter II prohibition will apply to vertical agreements. Certain agreements in the telecommunications sector are likely to be classified as vertical, for example, non-reciprocal access agreements and agreements between mobile operators and service providers.

7.53 Further information on types of vertical restraints and how the Director General will assess whether they are prohibited is contained in the Competition Act guideline *Assessment of Individual Agreements and Conduct* and *Vertical Agreements and Restraints*.

Interconnection agreements

7.54 Interconnection agreements are an essential pre-requisite of network and services competition. It is possible, however, that an interconnection agreement may be in breach of the Chapter I and/or Chapter II prohibitions. The EC Access Notice recognises that an interconnection agreement may be anti-competitive where:

— it restricts competition between the parties to the agreement by, for example, price fixing or market sharing;
— it restricts competition from those not party to the agreement where, for example, it provides for interconnection on an exclusive basis;
— commercially sensitive information is used for other purposes.[17]

7.55 Operators with Significant Market Power ('SMP') (see paragraph 6.33 above) are required by the Interconnection Directive to:

— publish a standard 'interconnection agreement' containing standard prices for access to and use of its network; and
— offer interconnection on the same terms and conditions as are offered to their own downstream operations.

7.56 The Director General therefore considers it unlikely that standard interconnection agreements will be caught by the Chapter I prohibition.

7.57 Notification of interconnection agreements to OFTEL to meet the requirements of the Interconnection Directive does not amount to a notification for guidance or a decision under the Competition Act.

[3094]

NOTES
1 Case C–333/94P *Tetra Pak II* [1996] 1 ECR 595, [1997] 4 CMLR 662.
2 Economies of scale exist where average costs fall as output increases
3 Economies of scope exist where average costs fall as more types of products are produced.
4 Common costs are costs of production that are shared between two or more products.
5 The marginal cost is the cost of producing an additional unit of output.
6 Incremental costs should be calculated on the basis of 'forward-looking costs', taking into account the current valuation of assets.
7 Average variable costs are calculated by dividing an undertaking's total variable costs by its output. Average variable costs are normally used as a proxy for short run marginal costs, which can be difficult to estimate.
8 An incremental profit is the change in profit that results from a particular decision such as a price reduction.
9 It should be noted that an undertaking could respond to competition by reducing its prices and running at a lower level of profitability. In such circumstances, the undertaking would make an incremental loss, but might still be covering its costs.
10 Case C62/86 AKZO *Chemie BV v. Commission*, [1993] 5 CMLR 215.
11 The detailed information required to perform such an analysis will usually be available in the telecommunications sector, but may not be available in other sectors.
12 The European Commission's decision to initiate proceedings against Deutsche Telecom (see *XXVIIth Report on Competition Policy: 1997*, European Commission, point 77) suggests that the Commission would be willing to take action under Article 82 of the EC Treaty if it found that prices in the telecoms sector were excessive. Deutsche Telecom subsequently agreed to reduce certain tariffs.
13 Case C 27/76 *United Brands v. Commission*, [1978] ECR 207, [1978] 1 CMLR 429.
14 Case C 7/79 *Oscar Bronner v Mediaprint and others* [1999] 4 CMLR 112.
15 These guidelines are not guidelines within the meaning of section 52 of the Competition Act.
16 These guidelines are not guidelines within the meaning of section 52 of the Competition Act.
17 The Interconnection Directive (see paragraph 3.7) requires that information received by a network operator from an undertaking seeking interconnection be used only for the purposes for which it is supplied. Operators should therefore introduce safeguards to ensure that confidential information is only disclosed to those staff who are involved in making the interconnection agreements and that the information is not used for anti-competitive purposes.

VERTICAL AGREEMENTS AND RESTRAINTS

(OFT 419, February 2000)

1   Introduction

1.1   This guideline explains how the Director General expects the Competition Act 1998 (**'the Act'**) to operate in relation to vertical agreements and restraints. In particular, it explains the application of The Competition Act 1998 (Land and Vertical Agreements Exclusion) Order 2000[1] (**'the Exclusion Order'**) to vertical agreements.

1.2   The Act prohibits:

— agreements between undertakings, decisions by associations of undertakings or concerted practices which have the object or effect of preventing, restricting or distorting competition in the United Kingdom (or a part thereof) and which may affect trade within the United Kingdom (**'the Chapter I prohibition'**); and

— conduct by one or more undertakings which amounts to the abuse of a dominant position in a market in the United Kingdom (or a part thereof) and which may affect trade within the United Kingdom (**'the Chapter II prohibition'**).

1.3   Details of how the Director General expects these prohibitions to be applied and enforced are contained in the Competition Act guidelines *The Major Provisions*, *The Chapter I Prohibition* and *The Chapter II Prohibition*.

1.4   The Exclusion Order, made under section 50 of the Act, excludes vertical agreements (as defined in the Exclusion Order) from the application of the Chapter I prohibition.

1.5   Vertical agreements do not generally give rise to competition concerns unless one or more of the undertakings involved possesses market power on the relevant market or the agreement forms part of a network of similar agreements. The purpose of the Exclusion Order, therefore, is to provide certainty for business about the scope of the Chapter I prohibition. It avoids an unnecessary burden on business of scrutinising a large number of essentially benign agreements and of making precautionary notifications of such agreements. It also helps to ensure that the Director General is able to concentrate his resources on matters of significant competition concern.

1.6   Part 2 of this guideline describes the scope and effects of the exclusion provided in the Exclusion Order.[2] It also explains how the Exclusion Order covers certain provisions relating to the assignment or use of intellectual property rights which may be included in a vertical agreement. Part 3 describes the limits to the scope of the exclusion.

1.7   Part 4 describes the relationship between the Exclusion Order and the relevant European Community block exemptions. At European Community level many vertical agreements benefit from the block exemption from the prohibition contained in Article 81(1) of the EC Treaty set out in the EC Verticals Block Exemption.[3] There are also a number of other EC block exemption regulations which may be relevant.

1.8   Part 5 of the guideline explains the limited circumstances in which the benefit of the exclusion for vertical agreements provided in the Exclusion Order may be withdrawn by the Director General and the consequences of such withdrawal.

1.9   There is no exclusion from the Chapter II prohibition for vertical agreements and restraints. The Chapter II prohibition applies to conduct which amounts to an abuse of a dominant position. Part 6 describes the possible application of the Chapter II prohibition and the Fair Trading Act 1973 to vertical agreements and restraints.

1.10 Agreements[4] that do not benefit from the exclusion for vertical agreements because they do not fall within the definition of a vertical agreement in the Exclusion Order are subject to the Chapter I prohibition. Such agreements do not, however, necessarily fall within its scope. Agreements will fall within the scope of the Chapter I prohibition only where they may have an appreciable effect on competition within the UK.

1.11 The Director General takes the view that an agreement will generally have no appreciable effect on competition if the parties' combined share of the relevant market[5] does not exceed 25 per cent, although there will be circumstances in which this is not the case.

1.12 The Director General will, in addition, generally regard any agreement between undertakings which:
— directly or indirectly fixes prices or shares markets; or
— imposes minimum resale prices; or
— is one of a network of similar agreements which have a cumulative effect on the market in question

as being capable of having an appreciable effect even where the combined market share falls below the 25 per cent threshold.

1.13 Further guidance on appreciability is given in the Competition Act guidelines *The Chapter I Prohibition* and *Assessment of Market Power*.

1.14 Agreements which do not benefit from the exclusion provided by the Exclusion Order will not infringe the Chapter I prohibition if they benefit from another exclusion or an exemption (see the Competition Act guideline *The Chapter I Prohibition*) even if they may have an appreciable effect on competition. Additionally, agreements made prior to the starting date (1 March 2000) may, for an initial period, benefit from a transitional period during which the Chapter I prohibition will not apply.[6]

1.15 The Director General's approach to assessing whether vertical agreements and restraints infringe either of the prohibitions under the Act is described in the Competition Act guideline *Assessment of Individual Agreements and Conduct*. Categories of agreements likely to benefit from the exclusion for vertical agreements in the Exclusion Order include exclusive distribution agreements, exclusive purchasing agreements, selective distribution agreements and franchise agreements.

[3095]

NOTES

[1]   SI 2000/310.

[2]   The Competition Act guideline *Land Agreements* explains how the Director General expects the Exclusion Order to operate in relation to land agreements.

[3]   *Commission Regulation (EC) No 2790/1999 of 22 December 1999 on the application of Article 81(3) of the Treaty to categories of vertical agreements and concerted practices*, OJ L336/21, 29/12/1999.

[4]   Agreement is used in the guideline to cover decisions by associations of undertakings and concerted practices. The meaning of the terms 'undertakings', 'agreement', 'decisions by associations of undertakings' and 'concerted practices' in the context of the Act are described in the Competition Act guideline *The Chapter I Prohibition*.

[5]   The Competition Act guideline *Market Definition* gives details on defining the relevant market.

[6]   Transitional periods will normally last for one year, although some may last for five years. A transitional period may be withdrawn by the Director General in limited circumstances. Details are given in the Competition Act guideline *Transitional Arrangements*.

---

2   The UK Exclusion for Vertical Agreements

2.1   The Exclusion Order states: 'The Chapter I prohibition shall not apply to an agreement to the extent that it is a vertical agreement'. This exclusion is automatic and no individual notification needs to be made to the Director General to benefit from its provisions.

2.2   The Exclusion Order states that **'vertical agreement'**:

> *'means an agreement between undertakings, each of which operates, for the purposes of the agreement, at a different level of the production or distribution chain, and relating to the conditions under which the parties may purchase, sell or resell certain goods or services and includes provisions contained in such agreements which relate to the assignment to the buyer or use by the buyer of intellectual property rights, provided that those provisions do not constitute the primary object of the agreement and are directly related to the use, sale or resale of goods or services by the buyer or its customers.'*

The Director General considers that there are two elements to this definition:
—   the economic relationship between the undertakings involved in the agreement; and
—   the provisions of the agreement, which may include certain provisions relating to the assignment or use of intellectual property rights.

These two elements are considered below.

Economic Relationship Between the Undertakings Involved

2.3   For an agreement to fall within the definition of a 'vertical agreement' in the Exclusion Order and benefit from the exclusion, the economic relationship between the parties must be such that each of the undertakings involved in the agreement operates **'at a different level of the production or distribution chain'**. Examples of activities at different levels of the production or distribution chain include supplying raw materials, manufacturing, wholesaling and retailing. An agreement between a wood supplier and a paper manufacturer for the supply of wood to make paper would be an example of a vertical agreement between undertakings operating at different levels of the production or distribution chain.

2.4   Different levels of the production or distribution chain may be found within each of the broad categories mentioned above. Within manufacturing, for example, one undertaking may manufacture a component part of a final product (such as a light bulb) and make an agreement to sell that part to a second undertaking which uses that part in its manufacture of the final product (such as a car). Although each of these undertakings is a manufacturer (one of light bulbs and one of cars), they would be regarded as operating at different levels of the production or distribution chain when they entered into an agreement for the supply of light bulbs to be incorporated into a car. Such an agreement may, therefore, benefit from the exclusion.

2.5   **'Each'** undertaking must operate at a different level of the production or distribution chain for an agreement to benefit from the exclusion. Therefore, for example, an agreement between one manufacturer and a group of six competing wholesalers (where each of the six wholesalers operates at the same level of the production or distribution chain), while being an agreement between undertakings at different levels of the production or distribution chain (that is, manufacturing and wholesaling), would not benefit from the exclusion. The agreement would involve more than one undertaking at one particular level of the production or distribution chain (wholesaling). An agreement between a supplier of raw materials, a manufacturer, a distributor and a retailer could, however, benefit from the exclusion because each undertaking operates at a different level of the production or distribution chain.

2.6 Undertakings often operate at more than one level of the production or distribution chain. An agreement between undertakings that operate at one or more of the same levels of the production or distribution chain may benefit from the exclusion for vertical agreements. This will only be the case, however, where the agreement concerns only respective activities of those undertakings which are at different levels of the production or distribution chain. The agreement can benefit from the exclusion because the undertakings involved each operate at different levels of the production or distribution chain **'for the purposes of the agreement'**.

2.7 If, for example, a manufacturer which also distributes its product enters into a supply agreement with a distributor, that supply agreement may benefit from the exclusion even though the manufacturer also has sales activities which operate at the same level of the production or distribution chain as the distributor's activities. The two undertakings are operating at different levels of the production or distribution chain for the purposes of the agreement: the first is acting as a manufacturer and the second as a distributor. A supply agreement between them in these respective capacities (that is, as a manufacturer and as a distributor) may fall within the definition of a vertical agreement in the Exclusion Order and may therefore benefit from the exclusion.

Provisions of the Agreement

Conditions of the agreement

2.8 The agreement must relate to the conditions under which the undertakings involved may purchase, sell or resell certain goods or services to benefit from the exclusion. This covers final and intermediate goods and services. The goods or services may be resold by the buyer or may be used as an input by the buyer in producing its own goods or services. Conditions which relate to matters other than the conditions of purchase, sale and resale are not covered by the exclusion.

Intellectual property rights provisions

2.9 The definition of a vertical agreement in the Exclusion Order refers to certain provisions relating to the assignment to, or use by, the buyer of intellectual property rights. Where such provisions are included, however, they will fall within the definition of a vertical agreement and may therefore benefit from the exclusion. There is no requirement that an agreement which otherwise falls within the definition of a vertical agreement as described above must contain such provisions for it to fall within the definition of a vertical agreement.

2.10 In addition to being part of a vertical agreement, there are three additional elements to the definition of a vertical agreement with which provisions relating to intellectual property rights must comply in order to benefit from the exclusion. They must:

— relate to the assignment to the buyer or use by the buyer of intellectual property rights;

— not constitute the primary object of the agreement; and

— be directly related to the use, sale or resale of the goods or services by the buyer or its customers.

These elements are considered below.

2.11 In order to benefit from the exclusion, any provisions relating to intellectual property rights must relate to the assignment of the rights to the buyer or the use by the buyer of those rights. An agreement under which a licence is given to, for example, a software buyer to reproduce that software in order to sell it on may benefit from the exclusion.

2.12 The assignment of the intellectual property rights must not be the primary object of the agreement. A simple patent licence, for example, would not benefit from the exclusion since the purpose of the agreement is to license the patent. (It may, however, benefit from a parallel exemption if it falls within the EC technology transfer block exemption.)[1]

2.13 The provisions must relate directly to the activity of the buyer in relation to the use, sale or resale of goods or services. A trade mark licence to a distributor or franchisor, for example, may benefit from the exclusion if it relates to the distribution of goods or services and forms part of the distribution arrangements.

[3096]

NOTES

  [1]   *Commission Regulation (EC) No 240/1996 of 31 January 1996 on the application of Article 85(3) of the Treaty to certain categories of technology transfer agreements*, OJ L31/2, 9/2/1996.

3   Limits to the Scope of the Exclusion

Price-Fixing

3.1 The benefit of the exclusion does not apply to vertical agreements that fix prices. The Exclusion Order provides that the exclusion for vertical agreements does not apply to any vertical agreement which directly or indirectly has the object or effect of restricting a buyer's ability to determine its sale price.

3.2 Agreements where the seller imposes a maximum or recommended sale price may benefit from the exclusion except where such a maximum or recommended sale price results, in practice, in a fixed or minimum sale price because of pressure from, or any incentives offered by, any of the undertakings involved. Where recommended or maximum prices have such an effect the agreements will not benefit from the exclusion for vertical agreements. Examples of types of practices that may result in fixed or minimum sale prices include:

  — agreements fixing the maximum level of discount a distributor can grant;
  — intimidation, delay or suspension of deliveries and contract terminations in relation to the observance of a certain price level; and
  — measures aimed at identifying price-cutting distributors, such as the implementation of a price monitoring system.

3.3 Price-fixing agreements that do not benefit from the exclusion are subject to scrutiny under the Chapter I prohibition and are capable of having an appreciable effect on competition even if the parties' combined share of the relevant market is less than 25 per cent. Details of how agreements that fix prices will be treated by the Director General under the Act are given in the Competition Act guideline *The Chapter I Prohibition*.

Extent of the Exclusion

3.4 The Exclusion Order provides that the Chapter I prohibition does not apply to an agreement **'to the extent that'** it is a vertical agreement. The exclusion may therefore apply to only certain parts of an agreement rather than an agreement in its entirety. It is therefore possible for some provisions in an agreement to benefit from the exclusion while others do not.

3.5 Where an agreement is only partly covered by the exclusion, and the Director General has competition concerns about the object or effect of the agreement, he will be able to have regard to the whole agreement (including those parts of the agreement that benefit from the exclusion for vertical agreements) to assess whether the Chapter I prohibition has been infringed. The Director General will not, however, be able to take any action against the parts which benefit from the exclusion without first withdrawing it (see part 5 below).

[3097]

4   Relationship Between the UK and EC Treatment of Vertical Agreements

4.1   Article 81(1) of the EC Treaty prohibits anti-competitive agreements which 'may affect trade between Member States', whereas the Chapter I prohibition applies only to anti-competitive agreements which 'may affect trade within the United Kingdom'. The phrase 'may affect trade between Member States' has been broadly interpreted by the European Court which has found that even where the parties to an agreement are within the same Member State inter-state trade may still be affected.[1] Many agreements will therefore be caught by both Article 81(1) and the Chapter I prohibition.

4.2   Agreements that benefit from a European Commission individual or block exemption, or would do so if the agreement had an effect on trade between Member States, are automatically exempt from the Chapter I prohibition under the Act without the need for notification to the Director General. Such agreements benefit from a 'parallel exemption' (see the Competition Act guideline *The Chapter I Prohibition*).

4.3   An exclusion (or exemption) from the Chapter I prohibition does not, however, preclude the application of Article 81(1).

4.4   The exclusion from the Chapter I prohibition for vertical agreements provided in the Exclusion Order is intended to follow closely the treatment of vertical agreements in the European Community so that the burden on business of operating under different systems is minimised. At European Community level a broad range of vertical agreements is exempted from the Article 81(1) prohibition by the EC Verticals Block Exemption which applies from 1 June 2000. The EC Verticals Block Exemption does not apply to agreements whose subject matter is dealt with by other EC block exemptions.[2]

4.5   The definition of a vertical agreement in the Exclusion Order reflects that in the EC Verticals Block Exemption. The most significant differences between the scope of the Exclusion Order and that of the EC Verticals Block Exemption are that:

—   the EC Verticals Block Exemption applies only to agreements where the market share of the supplier (or buyer, in the case of an agreement with an exclusive supply obligation) does not exceed 30 per cent of the relevant market. There is no market share cap in order to benefit from the Exclusion Order; and

—   the EC Verticals Block Exemption contains a number of 'hardcore' restrictions which, if included in the vertical agreement, have the effect of taking the agreement outside its scope. The only equivalent restriction in the Exclusion Order relates to price-fixing vertical agreements.

4.6   Further details on the application of the EC Verticals Block Exemption are given by the European Commission in *Guidelines on Vertical Restraints*.[3]

[3098]

NOTES

[1]   Case 56/65 *Société Technique Minière v Maschinenbau Ulm GmbH* [1966] ECR 235; and Case 8/72 *Vereeniging van Cementhandelaren v Commission* [1972] ECR 977, [1973] CMLR 7.

[2]   The most relevant European Commission block exemptions are: Commission Regulation (EEC) No 417/85 on the application Article 85(3) to categories of specialisation agreements; Commission Regulation (EEC) No 418/85 on the application of Article 85(3) to categories of research and development agreements as amended and extended by Regulation No 151/93; Commission Regulation (EEC) No 1475/95

on the application of Article 85(3) to certain categories of motor vehicle distribution and servicing agreements; and Commission Regulation (EEC) No 240/96 on the application of Article 85(3) to certain categories of technology transfer agreements.

   3   At time of publication of this guideline these are in draft form, OJ C 270/12, 24/9/99. They are due to be finalised before 1 June 2000.

5   Withdrawal of the Exclusion for Vertical Agreements

5.1   The Exclusion Order excludes vertical agreements because they do not generally give rise to competition concerns unless one of the parties to the agreement has significant market power or a network of similar agreements exists which has a cumulative effect on the market. The Director General does, however, have the power to remove the benefit of the exclusion from individual vertical agreements which will enable them to be considered under the Chapter I prohibition. He can exercise this power only:

— if he is considering whether to withdraw the benefit of the exclusion, and, by written notice, requires any party to the agreement to provide him with information in connection with the agreement, and, without reasonable excuse, that party fails to comply with such requirement within 10 working days; or

where he considers that a vertical agreement will, if not excluded, infringe the Chapter I prohibition, and he is not likely to grant it an unconditional individual exemption.[1]

5.2   In practice, it is likely that the Director General will exercise these powers only rarely. To infringe the Chapter I prohibition, the agreement must have an 'appreciable' effect on competition (see part 1 above and the Competition Act guidelines *The Chapter I Prohibition* and *Assessment of Market Power*). The Director General will consider carefully complaints in respect of agreements which have the benefit of the exclusion.

5.3   Where the Director General intends to give a direction withdrawing the benefit of the exclusion from an agreement he must consult the parties to that agreement. Such a direction must specify the date from which it is to take effect; it may not take effect from a date earlier than the date on which it was given. If the Director General gives such a direction he will publish it on the public register that he maintains.

Consequences of Withdrawal

5.4   If the benefit of the exclusion is withdrawn from a particular agreement, the agreement does not automatically infringe the Chapter I prohibition. A withdrawal direction merely allows the Director General to consider the application of the Chapter I prohibition to the agreement. He may then be able to use the information-gathering powers in the Act to require the parties to the agreement (and any third parties) to provide information. He will be able to consider the effect of the whole of an agreement on competition and decide whether it infringes the Chapter I prohibition.

5.5   If the Director General withdraws the benefit of the exclusion from an agreement, and finds that it does infringe the Chapter I prohibition, such an infringement finding can have effect only from the date of the withdrawal. The agreement will be void only from the date of withdrawal and any financial penalties imposed in respect of that agreement can relate only to the period after the withdrawal of the exclusion.

5.6   The Exclusion Order prevents undertakings from avoiding the consequences of a withdrawal direction. If, following a direction withdrawing the benefit of the exclusion from an agreement, the undertakings enter into another agreement which is to the like object or effect as the agreement which was the subject of the withdrawal direction that subsequent agreement will not benefit from the exclusion.

[3099]

NOTES

¹ An individual exemption is unconditional if no conditions or obligations are attached to it by the Director General—see the Competition Act guideline *The Chapter I Prohibition*.

6 Other Possible UK Competition Scrutiny of Vertical Agreements

The Chapter II Prohibition

6.1 A vertical agreement entered into by an undertaking which holds a dominant position in a market is subject to the Chapter II prohibition. The Exclusion Order excludes vertical agreements only from the scope of the Chapter I prohibition. Abuse of a dominant position by an undertaking which takes the form of a vertical agreement or restraint is assessed in exactly the same way as any other type of conduct under the Chapter II prohibition. This is considered in the Competition Act guideline *The Chapter II Prohibition*.

The Fair Trading Act 1973

6.2 The scale and complex monopoly provisions in the Fair Trading Act 1973 (see part 13 of the Competition Act guideline *The Major Provisions*) may, in certain circumstances, be relevant for dealing with possible competition problems in relation to vertical agreements. A complex monopoly investigation may, for example, be appropriate where vertical agreements are prevalent in a market as a result of the structure of that market and have the effect of preventing the entry of new competitors into the market but there is no evidence of an agreement or collusion between the undertakings involved which might have caused this situation to arise.

[3100]

LAND AGREEMENTS

(OFT 420, February 2000)

Introduction

1.1 This guideline explains how the Director General expects the Competition Act 1998 ('**the Act**') to operate in relation to agreements and conduct relating to land. In particular, it explains the application of The Competition Act 1998 (Land and Vertical Agreements Exclusion) Order 2000¹ ('**the Exclusion Order**') to land agreements.

1.2 The Act prohibits:

— agreements between undertakings, decisions by associations of undertakings or concerted practices which have the object or effect of preventing, restricting or distorting competition in the United Kingdom (or a part thereof) and which may affect trade within the United Kingdom ('**the Chapter I prohibition**'); and

— conduct by one or more undertakings which amounts to the abuse of a dominant position in a market in the United Kingdom (or a part thereof) and which may affect trade within the United Kingdom ('**the Chapter II prohibition**').

1.3   Details on how the Director General expects these prohibitions to be applied and enforced are contained in the Competition Act guidelines *The Major Provisions*, *The Chapter I Prohibition* and *The Chapter II Prohibition*.

1.4   The Exclusion Order, made under section 50 of the Act, excludes land agreements (as defined in the Exclusion Order) from the application of the Chapter I prohibition.

1.5   Land agreements do not generally give rise to competition concerns. The purpose of the Exclusion Order is to provide certainty for business concerning the scope of the Chapter I prohibition. It avoids an unnecessary burden on business of scrutinising a large number of agreements that raise no competition concerns and of making precautionary notifications in respect of such agreements. It also helps to ensure that the Director General is able to concentrate his resources on matters of significant competition concern.

1.6   Part 2 of this guideline describes the scope and effects of the exclusion provided in the Exclusion Order[2] and part 3 describes the limits to the scope of the exclusion.

1.7   Part 4 explains the limited circumstances in which the benefit of the exclusion for land agreements provided in the Exclusion Order may be withdrawn by the Director General and the consequences of such withdrawal.

1.8   There is no exclusion from the Chapter II prohibition for land agreements. The Chapter II prohibition applies to conduct which amounts to the abuse of a dominant position. Part 5 describes the possible application of the Chapter II prohibition to conduct relating to land.

1.9   Agreements[3] that do not benefit from the exclusion for land agreements because they do not fall within the definition of a land agreement in the Exclusion Order are subject to the Chapter I prohibition. Such agreements do not, however, necessarily fall within its scope. Agreements will fall within the scope of the Chapter I prohibition only where they may have an appreciable effect on competition within the UK.

1.10   The Director General takes the view that an agreement will generally have no appreciable effect on competition if the parties' combined share of the relevant market[4] does not exceed 25 per cent, although there will be circumstances in which this is not the case.

1.11   The Director General will, in addition, generally regard any agreement between undertakings which:

— directly or indirectly fixes prices or shares markets; or
— imposes minimum resale prices; or
— is one of a network of similar agreements which have a cumulative effect on the market in question

as being capable of having an appreciable effect even where the combined market share falls below the 25 per cent threshold.

1.12   Further guidance on appreciability is given in the Competition Act guidelines *The Chapter I Prohibition* and *Assessment of Market Power*.

1.13   Agreements which do not benefit from the exclusion provided by the Exclusion Order will not infringe the Chapter I prohibition if they benefit from another exclusion or an exemption (see the Competition Act guideline *The Chapter I Prohibition*) even if they may have an appreciable effect on competition. The Act contains, for example, an exclusion for agreements to the extent that they are planning obligations.[5] This includes planning obligations made, for example, under section 106 of the Town and Country Planning Act 1990. Additionally, agreements made prior to the starting date (1 March 2000) may, for an initial period, benefit from a transitional period during which the Chapter I prohibition will not apply.[6]

1.14 The Director General's approach to assessing whether agreements and conduct infringe either of the prohibitions under the Act is described in the Competition Act guideline *Assessment of Individual Agreements and Conduct*.

[3101]

NOTES

[1]   SI 2000/310.

[2]   The Competition Act guideline *Vertical Agreements and Restraints* explains how the Director General expects the Exclusion Order to operate in relation to vertical agreements.

[3]   Agreement is used in this guideline to cover also decisions by associations of undertakings and concerted practices. The meaning of the terms 'undertakings', 'agreement', 'decisions by associations of undertakings' and 'concerted practices' in the context of the Act are described in the Competition Act guideline *The Chapter I Prohibition*.

[4]   The Competition Act guideline *Market Definition* gives details on defining the relevant market.

[5]   Schedule 3, paragraph 1.

[6]   Transitional periods will normally last for one year, although some may last for five years. A transitional period may be withdrawn by the Director General in limited circumstances. Details are given in the Competition Act guideline *Transitional Arrangements*.

2   The Exclusion for Land Agreements

2.1   The Exclusion Order states: 'The Chapter I prohibition shall not apply to an agreement to the extent that it is a land agreement'. The exclusion is automatic and no individual notification needs to be made to the Director General to benefit from its provisions.

2.2   The Exclusion Order defines a **'land agreement'** in terms of:
— the creation, alteration, transfer or termination of an interest in land; and
— certain obligations and restrictions.

These elements are considered below.

Interest in Land

2.3   A land agreement is defined in the Exclusion Order as an agreement which creates, alters, transfers or terminates an interest in land. Only agreements which have such results benefit from the exclusion. This includes, for example, transfers of freeholds, leases or assignments of leasehold interests and easements. The term **'interest in land'** is defined in the Exclusion Order. This covers what is usually understood to be an interest in land and includes licences, and, in Scotland, interests under a lease and other heritable rights in or over land including heritable securities. The exclusion also covers agreements to enter into land agreements.

2.4   The exclusion does not cover agreements which relate to land but which do not create, alter, transfer or terminate an interest in land. An agreement, for example, between landowners in a particular area to fix levels of rent to be charged to tenants or an agreement between tenants as to the nature of goods they will each sell in a particular area are not land agreements as defined in the Exclusion Order because they do not create, alter, transfer or terminate an interest in land and therefore do not benefit from the exclusion.

Obligations and Restrictions

2.5   Obligations and restrictions set out in the Exclusion Order benefit from the exclusion for land agreements where they are part of an agreement that creates, alters, transfers or terminates an interest in land. Such obligations and restrictions are defined in the Exclusion Order in relation to the concepts of **'capacity'** and '**activity**' which are described below. Those obligations and restrictions set out in the Exclusion Order are ones which are generally included in agreements which have the effect of creating, altering, transferring or terminating an interest in land and will benefit from the exclusion. These include, for example, covenants in commercial property agreements relating to payment of rent, service charges, user clauses and alienation. Restrictions on a tenant relating to alterations, repairs, applications for planning permission, the presence of shop signs, advertisements or the hours of use of the premises may also benefit from the exclusion.

Capacity

2.6   For an obligation or restriction to benefit from the exclusion, it must be either accepted in, or for the benefit of, an undertaking's capacity as holder of an interest in land. This requirement ensures that such obligation or restriction relates to the interest in land, as opposed to any trading capacity or other (non-land) business interests of the undertaking.

2.7   Whether an undertaking is acting in its capacity as holder of an interest in land will depend on the relationship between the undertakings which are parties to the agreement by which an interest in land is created, altered, transferred or terminated. Where their relationship is based solely on the creation, alteration, transfer or termination of the interest in land it is likely that the Director General will take the view that the undertakings are acting in their capacity as holders of interests in land. Where their relationship is also based on other trading interests and where the obligations and/or restrictions included are relevant to those other interests it is unlikely that the Director General will view the undertakings as acting in their capacity as holders of interests in land. Where undertakings do not act in their capacity as holders of interests in land any obligations and/or restrictions they accept, and any of which they have the benefit, will not have the benefit of the exclusion.

2.8   If, for example, a widgets and blodgets manufacturer sells its only blodgets factory to another undertaking and accepts a restriction not to open another blodgets factory and not to produce blodgets from its widgets factory, such a restriction would not be covered by the exclusion.[1] Equally, a restriction in a lease which required that the tenant of a petrol station must buy the petrol he sells only from the landlord would not be covered by the exclusion.[2]

2.9   Similarly, an obligation in a lease for a tenant to insure the leased property *with* its landlord, which is an insurance company, would not have the benefit of the exclusion. Such an obligation would be regarded by the Director General as relating to the trading interests of the insurance company and the insurance company would be regarded as acting in its capacity as an insurer. An obligation to insure a property *through* an insurance company landlord, however, would be likely to benefit from the exclusion. Such an obligation would be likely to be regarded by the Director General as relating solely to the relevant interests in land of the undertakings involved and the insurance company would be regarded as acting in its capacity as holder of an interest in land.

Activity

2.10   Certain restrictions may, in relevant circumstances, be placed on the activity which may be carried out from relevant land or other relevant land as defined in the Exclusion Order. Such restrictions can be expressed in positive (the premises may be used only as a wet fish shop) or negative (the premises may not be used for the sale of greetings cards) language. Restrictions on activity which will be likely to have the benefit of the exclusion include, for example in the context of a parade of shops, restrictions on the types of goods that may be sold from each premises, including restrictions relating to quality of goods.

2.11 Restrictions as to the conditions on which a trade or activity may be carried out, however, are not covered by the exclusion for land agreements provided in the Exclusion Order. These include, for example, restrictions which have the effect of fixing minimum resale prices at which goods may be sold, the quantity of goods which may be sold or the suppliers or sources of goods sold or services provided on or from the premises.

Reciprocal restrictions

2.12 Reciprocal restrictions may benefit from the exclusion. A lease in a shopping centre, for example, that restricts the tenant to selling wet fish, and accepted by the tenant on the basis that no other tenant in the centre will be permitted to sell wet fish, may benefit from the exclusion. Such a restriction can be either mutually enforceable or the landlord may covenant to enforce it.

[3102]

NOTES

¹   Such a restriction may, however, benefit from a different exclusion from the Chapter I prohibition. If the sale of the factory is excluded by the provisions relating to mergers in Schedule 1 to the Act, the restriction could be regarded as an ancillary restraint and may therefore be excluded; see the Competition Act guideline *Exclusion for Mergers and Ancillary Restrictions.*

²   Such a restriction may, however, benefit from the exclusion for vertical agreements also provided in the Exclusion Order; see part 3 below and the Competition Act guideline *Vertical Agreements and Restraints.*

3   Limits to the Scope of the Exclusion

3.1   The Exclusion Order provides that the Chapter I prohibition does not apply to an agreement **'to the extent that'** it is a land agreement. The exclusion may therefore benefit only certain provisions of an agreement rather than an agreement in its entirety. An agreement which transfers an interest in land may, for example, include provisions relating to the financing of the transaction. The financing provisions fall outside the definition of a land agreement and do not therefore benefit from the exclusion. Because an agreement does not fall within the exclusion does not, however, mean that it is likely to be caught by the Chapter I prohibition. It is likely that most agreements relating to land which fall outside the scope of the exclusion will not have an appreciable effect on competition within the United Kingdom and will therefore not be caught by the Chapter I prohibition.

3.2   Where an agreement is only partly covered by the exclusion, and the Director General has competition concerns about the object or effect of that agreement, he will be able to have regard to the whole agreement (including those parts of the agreement that benefit from the exclusion) to assess whether the Chapter I prohibition has been infringed. The Director General will not, however, be able to take any action against the parts which benefit from the exclusion without first withdrawing it (see part 4 below).

Vertical Agreements

3.3   Agreements covered by the exclusion for vertical agreements also provided in the Exclusion Order will not benefit from the exclusion for land agreements provided in the Exclusion Order.¹ Details on how the Director General expects the exclusion for vertical agreements to operate are given in the Competition Act guideline *Vertical Agreements and Restraints.*

3.4   There is no overlap between the exclusion for land agreements provided in the Exclusion Order and the exclusion for vertical agreements provided in the same order. A single agreement may, however, benefit from both exclusions as each exclusion could apply to different parts of the same agreement. Both exclusions will not apply to the same parts of the same agreement. Beer tie and petrol solus agreements are examples of agreements which may benefit from both the land exclusion and the exclusion for vertical agreements. The key elements of such agreements include a transfer of an interest in land between undertakings and an agreement for one undertaking to supply goods (beer or petrol) to another for retail. The provisions relating to the transfer of the interest in land may benefit from the exclusion for land agreements and those relating to the supply of goods may benefit from the exclusion for vertical agreements.

[3103]

NOTES

1　　Article 2 of the Exclusion Order defines a 'vertical agreement' and provides that 'to the extent that an agreement is a vertical agreement it is not a land agreement'.

4　Withdrawal of the Exclusion for Land Agreements

4.1　The term land agreement is widely defined in the Exclusion Order to provide certainty for business. This means that some agreements which potentially raise competition concerns may escape scrutiny by the Director General. The Director General therefore has the power to remove the benefit of the exclusion from individual agreements which will enable them to be considered under the Chapter I prohibition. He can exercise this power only:

— if he is considering whether to withdraw the benefit of the exclusion, and, by written notice, requires any party to the agreement to provide him with information in connection with the agreement, and, without reasonable excuse, that party fails to comply with such requirement within 10 working days; or

— where he considers that the land agreement in question will, if not excluded, infringe the Chapter I prohibition, and he is not likely to grant it an unconditional individual exemption.[1]

4.2　In practice, it is likely that the Director General will exercise these powers only rarely. To infringe the Chapter I prohibition, the agreement must have an appreciable effect on competition (see part 1 above and the Competition Act guidelines *The Chapter I Prohibition* and *Assessment of Market Power*). The Director General will consider carefully complaints in respect of agreements which have the benefit of the exclusion.

4.3　Where the Director General intends to give a direction withdrawing the benefit of the exclusion from an agreement he must consult the parties to that agreement. Such a direction must specify the date from which it is to take effect; it may not take effect from a date earlier than the date on which it was given. If the Director General gives such a direction he will publish it on the public register that he maintains.

Consequences of Withdrawal

4.4　If the benefit of the exclusion is withdrawn from a particular agreement that agreement does not automatically infringe the Chapter I prohibition. A withdrawal direction merely allows the Director General to consider the application of the Chapter I prohibition to the agreement. He may then be able to use the information-gathering powers in the Act to require the parties to the agreement (and any third parties) to provide information. He will be able to consider the effect of the whole of an agreement on competition and decide whether it infringes the Chapter I prohibition.

4.5　If the Director General withdraws the benefit of the exclusion from a land agreement, and finds that it does infringe the Chapter I prohibition, such an infringement finding can have effect only from the date of the withdrawal. The agreement will be void only from the date of withdrawal and any financial penalties imposed in respect of that agreement can relate only to the period after the withdrawal of the exclusion.

4.6 The Exclusion Order prevents undertakings from avoiding the consequences of a withdrawal direction. If, following a direction withdrawing the benefit of the exclusion from an agreement, the undertakings enter into another agreement which is to the like object or effect as the agreement which was the subject of the withdrawal direction, that subsequent agreement will not benefit from the exclusion.

[3104]

NOTES

  1   An individual exemption is unconditional if no conditions or obligations are attached to it by the Director General—see the Competition Act guideline *The Chapter I Prohibition.*

5   Application of the Chapter II Prohibition to Land Agreements

5.1 The Chapter II prohibition applies to any conduct by one or more undertakings which amounts to the abuse of a dominant position in a market in the United Kingdom (or a part thereof) and which may affect trade within the United Kingdom. This applies equally to conduct relating to land as it does to any other conduct. The Exclusion Order provides no exclusion from the Chapter II prohibition for land agreements.

5.2 There are two tests in assessing whether the Chapter II prohibition applies:
— whether an undertaking is dominant;
— and, if it is, whether it is abusing that dominant position.

Dominant Position

5.3 Whether an undertaking is dominant raises two questions which are considered below: the definition of the market in which the undertaking is alleged to be dominant and whether it is dominant within that market.

Market Definition

5.4 A market definition should normally contain two dimensions: a product and a geographic area.[1] Market definition is important because, first, market shares can be calculated only after the boundaries of a market have been defined and, secondly, it is important in the rest of the Director General's analysis because it sets the stage on which competition takes place. The issue in market definition is usually to determine products or areas to which customers might switch and also whether undertakings which do not currently supply the product or area might be able to start supplying it at relatively short notice.[2]

5.5 In relation to land, market definition will depend in part on the availability of substitute premises suitable for similar purposes and the propensity of customers to go elsewhere. Market definition will vary from case to case, but the Director General considers that, in most cases, it is unlikely that a geographic market would be defined as narrowly as, for example, a single town centre.

Dominance

5.6 An undertaking may be dominant if it possesses a substantial level of market power. The essence of dominance is the power to behave independently of competitive pressures. A dominant position may be held by one undertaking on its own or by a group of undertakings where those undertakings are linked in such a way that they adopt the same conduct in the market ('joint' or 'collective' dominance).[3]

5.7   The Director General will assess the degree of market power of the allegedly dominant undertaking by looking at the competitive constraints it faces in the relevant market. Those constraints will include, but will not be limited to, the bargaining power of customers (including tenants) and the possibility of new entry onto the market by, for instance, converting other premises or building new premises to act as a substitute. The market share of an undertaking is an important factor in assessing market power but it does not, on its own, determine whether an undertaking is dominant. The Director General considers it unlikely that an undertaking will be individually dominant if its market share is below 40 per cent, although dominance could be established below that figure if other relevant factors (such as the weak position of competitors in that market) provided strong evidence of dominance. Further details of the way in which market power will be assessed are contained in the Competition Act guideline *Assessment of Market Power*.

5.8   In general, ownership by an undertaking of an 'essential facility' confers a dominant position. A facility can be viewed as essential if access to it is indispensable in order to compete in the market and duplication is impossible or extremely difficult owing to physical, geographic or legal constraints (or is highly undesirable for reasons of public policy).[4] Potential examples include ports, bus stations, utility distribution networks and some telecommunications networks (see the Competition Act guidelines *The Chapter II Prohibition* and *Assessment of Individual Agreements and Conduct*).

Abuse

5.9   The prohibition is of the *abuse* of the dominant position, not the *holding* of the position. The Act sets out examples of conduct which may amount to abuse of a dominant position, but the list is not exhaustive and is for illustration only. The important issue is whether the dominant undertaking is using its dominant position in an abusive way. This may occur if it uses practices different from those normally adopted in the course of competition in the market, with the effect of restricting the degree of competition which it faces, or of exploiting its market position unjustifiably.

5.10 Examples of conduct which may be considered to be an abuse of a dominant position are given in the Competition Act guideline *The Chapter II Prohibition*. In relation to land, examples of conduct which could be an abuse of a dominant position may include charging excessive rents which are above the market level, discrimination between tenants, charging predatory rents, vertical restrictions that tie or otherwise affect the buying or selling of goods and services by occupants of the land in question (for example by fixing resale prices) or limiting access to an 'essential facility'. They may also include the possibility of abuse in a related market. Where the Director General has a reasonable suspicion that an abuse of a dominant position is or has been taking place he will carry out the kind of assessment described in the Competition Act guidelines *Assessment of Individual Agreements and Conduct* and *The Chapter II Prohibition*.

[3105]

NOTES

[1]   The term 'product' includes services and property rights.

[2]   See the Competition Act guideline *Market Definition*.

[3]   See the Competition Act guidelines *The Chapter II Prohibition* and *Assessment of Market Power*.

[4]   See, for example, the judgment of the European Court in Case C-7/97 *Oscar Bronner v Mediaprint and Others*, judgment of 26 November 1998.

APPLICATION IN THE WATER AND SEWERAGE SECTORS

(OFT 422, January 2000)

1 Introduction

1.1 The Competition Act 1998 (**'the Act'**) is applied and enforced by the Director General of Fair Trading and, in relation to regulated utility sectors, concurrently with the regulators for telecommunications, gas, electricity, water and sewerage, and railway services.

1.2 The Act introduces two prohibitions:
- a prohibition of agreements between undertakings, decisions by associations of undertakings or concerted practices which have the object or effect of preventing, restricting or distorting competition in the United Kingdom (or a part thereof) and which may affect trade within the United Kingdom (the Chapter I prohibition); and
- a prohibition of conduct by one or more undertakings which amounts to the abuse of a dominant position, in a market in the United Kingdom (or a part thereof), which may affect trade within the United Kingdom (the Chapter II prohibition).

1.3 Further details about the prohibitions are contained in the Competition Act guidelines *The Major Provisions*, *The Chapter I Prohibition*, and *The Chapter II Prohibition*.

1.4 The purpose of this guideline is to explain how the Director General of Water Services (**'the Director'**) and the Director General of Fair Trading expect to apply the provisions of the Act to the water and sewerage sectors in England and Wales. It outlines the powers that the Director holds to ensure that competitive processes are unhindered, and provides examples of how these powers may be applied in relation to the water and sewerage sectors. It is designed to increase understanding of the relevance and application of the Act to undertakings, customers, suppliers and new entrants (potential and actual).

1.5 The Director's jurisdiction under the Water Industry Act 1991 extends only to England and Wales. Thus, the concurrent jurisdiction under the Act, conferred by amendments to the Water Industry Act 1991 inserted under paragraph 5 of Schedule 10 to the Act, has the same geographic extent. Only the Director General of Fair Trading may apply the provisions of the Act in the water and sewerage sectors elsewhere in the United Kingdom. If the Director General of Fair Trading applies the provisions of the Act in the water and sewerage sectors, he will do so in the same manner as the Director, as set out in this guideline.

1.6 The Director's concurrent jurisdiction extends to all commercial activities connected with the supply of water or securing of a supply of water or with the provision or securing of sewerage services in England and Wales. The Director's concurrent jurisdiction, therefore, applies to activities within the scope of this definition irrespective of whether they are carried out by water and sewerage companies appointed under the Water Industry Act 1991 (**'undertakers'**) or by other undertakings.

1.7 Part 2 of this guideline sets out the powers and duties of the Director with regard to the Act and their relationship with his powers and duties under the Water Industry Act 1991.

1.8 Part 3 briefly summarises the approach the Director will adopt in undertaking investigations under the Act.

1.9   Part 4 identifies a number of issues particularly relevant to the water and sewerage sectors in England and Wales where the Director may apply his powers under the Act. In particular, the Director's powers under the Act extend to investigating complaints and initiating investigations where he has 'reasonable grounds for suspecting' that either the Chapter I prohibition or the Chapter II prohibition has been infringed.

1.10 Part 5 contains details about the processes and procedures that will be important in the application and enforcement of the Act by the Director.

1.11 Annexe A contains details of the legal framework for economic regulation of the water and sewerage industries in England and Wales and its relationship to the Act.

[3106]

2   Powers and duties

Concurrent powers under the Act

2.1   Under the Act, the Director has, with two exceptions,[1] all the powers of the Director General of Fair Trading to apply and enforce its provisions with respect to commercial activities connected with the supply of water or securing a supply of water or with the provision or securing of sewerage services in England and Wales. This means, for example, that the Director's concurrent jurisdiction extends to conduct by undertakings that are not appointed under the Water Industry Act 1991, to the extent that the conduct falls within this definition. In general, the Director will deal with any agreement or conduct that falls within his concurrent jurisdiction. The Director will use the powers to ensure that the competition process is unhindered by anti-competitive activity in the water and sewerage sectors. The Competition Act guidelines *The Major Provisions, Powers of Investigation, Enforcement* and *Concurrent Application to Regulated Industries* provide further details of the powers contained in the Act. Concurrent powers allow the Director to:

— give guidance on the application of the Act;
— consider complaints about breach of the prohibitions;
— impose interim measures to prevent serious and irreparable damage;
— consider notifications for a decision and give decisions on the application of the Act;
— grant exemptions to the Chapter I prohibition (subject, where appropriate, to conditions);
— carry out investigations both on his own initiative and in response to complaints. The Director has the same powers to require the production of documents and information and to search premises as the Director General of Fair Trading;
— impose financial penalties, taking account of the statutory guidance on penalties issued by the Director General of Fair Trading;
— give and enforce directions to bring an infringement to an end; and
— issue general advice and information on how the Act applies to his sectors.

2.2   Section 60 of the Act places an obligation on the Director to ensure consistency with principles established in Community law in the way cases are handled and to ensure that there is no inconsistency with either the principles laid down by the EC Treaty and the European Court or any relevant decision of the European Court. He must also have regard to any relevant decision or statement of the European Commission. The obligation to ensure consistency applies only to the extent that this is possible, 'having regard to any relevant differences between the provisions concerned' (see the Competition Act guideline *The Major Provisions*).

2.3   In giving directions to bring an infringement to an end or in giving interim measures directions, the courses of action available to the Director include:

PART III
OFT GUIDELINES

— requiring an undertaking to terminate an unlawful agreement or to cease unlawful conduct (for example, an unreasonable refusal to grant access or services); or

— requiring an undertaking to modify conduct or agreements so as to prevent existing (and future) breaches of the prohibitions in the Act.

2.4 Directions given and penalties imposed are subject to appeal to the Competition Commission.

Relationship of concurrent powers with duties under the Water Industry Act 1991

2.5 The Director's general duties under the Water Industry Act 1991 remain unchanged in relation to his regulatory functions in the water and sewerage industries. Instead, the Act amends his duty in relation to competition.

2.6 Specifically, the Act[2] amends the Water Industry Act 1991 to provide that the Director should not have regard to his general duties when exercising any function under the Act, except that he may have regard to any matter to which the Director General of Fair Trading could have regard when exercising that function. This means, for example, that when imposing financial penalties under the Act the Director will take account of the statutory guidance issued by the Director General of Fair Trading, and will not have regard to his duty under the Water Industry Act 1991 to secure that undertakers are able to finance the proper carrying out of their functions.

2.7 Where a particular agreement or practice falls within the scope of the Water Industry Act 1991 as well as one of the prohibitions in the Act, the Director is able to decide to use his powers under either the Water Industry Act 1991 or the Act. In such cases he will make use of whichever statutory powers he judges to be the more appropriate to address the specific conduct. Where he takes action using his powers under the Act, his duty to take enforcement action under the Water Industry Act 1991 does not apply. The Director will keep concerned parties informed regarding the statutory basis for his approach in handling a case.

2.8 The Director may make use of information made available to him for the purposes of sector regulatory duties under the Water Industry Act 1991 in relation to the application of the Act, and vice versa. Information made available to the Director for sector regulatory duties may, for example, be material in providing reasonable grounds for suspecting an infringement prior to the initiation of an investigation under the Act. Where information obtained in performing any of his statutory duties gives rise to such reasonable grounds, the Director will initiate further investigations.

2.9 The Director will seek to apply consistent policy principles to related subject matter irrespective of whether a matter is addressed through powers under the Competition Act or through his powers under the Water Industry Act 1991.

The Fair Trading Act 1973

2.10 Some cases may fall within the complex monopoly and scale monopoly provisions in the Fair Trading Act 1973 which are retained in addition to the Competition Act. Further details are contained in the Competition Act guideline *The Major Provisions*. The Director has a separate concurrent jurisdiction with the Director General of Fair Trading under the Fair Trading Act. It is not intended that the prohibitions in the Competition Act and the monopoly provisions in the Fair Trading Act should be used in parallel to investigate the same matters.

2.11 The complex monopoly provisions are retained for activities which are not caught by the Competition Act prohibitions: where, for example, a group of companies all adopt similar practices or engage in parallel behaviour which appears to be anti-competitive, but there is no evidence of collusion or agreement. The scale monopoly provisions are intended for dealing with the situation where a prior infringement of the prohibitions in the Competition Act has already been proven but where the Director believes that there is a real prospect of further abuse by the same company. The structural remedies available under the scale monopoly powers may be the only effective means of preventing those further abuses.

2.12 Because of the special circumstances of the utility sectors, and the difficulty of establishing competition, the full use of the scale monopoly provisions is retained for the regulated utility sectors. This means that the scale monopoly provisions may be used in the water and sewerage sectors whether or not there has been a prior infringement of the prohibitions in the Competition Act.

[3107]

NOTES

[1] The exceptions are that only the Director General of Fair Trading may issue guidance on penalties and make and amend the Director General of Fair Trading's Procedural Rules.

[2] Paragraph 5(4) of schedule 10 to the Act.

3 Approach to investigations

3.1 In determining whether a particular agreement or particular conduct constitutes a breach of either of the Act's prohibitions, the Director (or the Director General of Fair Trading, as appropriate) will generally consider:

— the definition of the market to which the agreement or conduct in question relates (market definition is important because market power can only be analysed in the context of the relevant market);

— whether the undertaking or undertakings in question have market power, although certain types of agreement may breach the Chapter I prohibition, even where the parties do not have market power (the concept of market power is not part of the statutory framework of the Act but it is a useful tool in assessing potentially anti-competitive behaviour); and

— whether the individual agreement or conduct is a breach of the Act's prohibitions.

3.2 The Competition Act guidelines *Market Definition*, *Assessment of Market Power* and *Assessment of Individual Agreements and Conduct* contain detailed guidance on these stages of investigations. The sections below summarise details that are particularly relevant to investigations of possible infringements in the water and sewerage sectors.

Market definition

3.3 The prohibitions in the Act are designed primarily to prevent undertakings from exploiting market power. In defining the relevant market the Director will make use of the conceptual framework outlined in the Competition Act guideline *Market Definition*, which emphasises product and geographic definitions of markets. Product and geographic market definitions are derived from consideration of an undertaking's freedom to raise the price of the product or service in question. The definition of the relevant market in cases arising in the water and sewerage sectors may not always be immediately obvious.

3.4 When considering the product definition of a market, the Director will analyse the specific nature of the product or service in question: for example, a distinction between services for domestic and industrial customers may be appropriate. In some cases, the Director may define markets for products or services that are inputs to, or components of, the provision of water or sewerage services.

PART III
OFT GUIDELINES

3.5   While geographical factors are likely to be of critical importance in market definition, the Director will not be bound in all cases by geographical patterns inherited at privatisation. The development of inset appointments, private supplies, on-site services, bulk supplies and common carriage arrangements may be important influences on geographic market definitions, and geographic market definitions will therefore require detailed analysis. In relation to water or sewerage services for domestic customers, for example, the Director may find that the licensed area of a water or sewerage undertaker constitutes the relevant geographic market. However, this same geographic market definition may not apply in the case of water supply or trade effluent disposal for large customers.

3.6   High market shares are not themselves prohibited, and do not necessarily indicate a competition problem.

Assessment of market power

3.7   The assessment of market power can be useful under both the Chapter I prohibition of the Act in considering the concept of 'appreciability' (see the Competition Act guideline *The Chapter I Prohibition*) and under the Chapter II prohibition to assist in the identification of 'dominance' (see the Competition Act guideline *The Chapter II Prohibition*). Thus, having defined the relevant market, the Director will normally assess whether the undertaking or undertakings in question have market power.

3.8   An agreement will infringe the Chapter I prohibition only if it has as its object or effect an 'appreciable' prevention, restriction or distortion of competition in the United Kingdom. The Director takes the view that an agreement will generally have no appreciable effect on competition if the parties' combined share of the relevant market does not exceed 25 per cent, although there will be circumstances in which this is not the case. The Director will, in addition, generally regard any agreement between undertakings which:
— directly or indirectly fix prices or share markets;
— imposes minimum resale prices; or
— is one of a network of similar agreements which have a cumulative effect on the market in question

as being capable of having an appreciable effect even where the combined market share falls below the 25 per cent threshold.

3.9   In respect of the Chapter II prohibition, the Director will assess whether the undertaking or undertakings in question occupy a dominant position in the relevant market. The European Court has defined a dominant position as:

'a position of economic strength enjoyed by an undertaking which enables it to prevent effective competition being maintained on the relevant market by affording it the power to behave to an appreciable extent independently of its competitors, customers and ultimately of consumers.'

3.10   The Act does not set any market share thresholds for defining 'dominance', but the European Court has stated that dominance can be presumed in the absence of evidence to the contrary if an undertaking has a market share persistently above 50 per cent.[1] The Director considers it unlikely that an undertaking will be individually dominant if its market share is below 40 per cent, although dominance could be established below that figure if other relevant factors (such as the weak position of competitors in that market) provided strong evidence of dominance. Market share on its own does not, however, determine whether an undertaking is dominant.

3.11   In assessing whether there is dominance, the Director will consider whether and the extent to which an undertaking faces constraints on its ability to behave independently. Those constraints might be:

— existing competitors, according to their strength in the market. This may be shown by market shares;

— potential competitors. This may be shown by a lack of significant entry barriers and the existence of other undertakings which might easily enter the market; and

— other constraints such as strong buyer-power from the undertaking's customers or the effect of government regulation.

3.12 In many circumstances in the water and sewerage sectors, entry barriers will be important factors in the Director's assessment of dominance. This is discussed in more detail in the Competition Act guideline *Assessment of Market Power.* Entry barriers that may be of particular relevance in the water and sewerage sectors include the existence of large sunk costs in many markets and absolute advantages arising from the regulation of water abstractions and discharges to the environment.

Assessment of individual agreements and conduct

3.13 The analysis of an individual agreement or conduct is a key stage in investigating whether there is a breach of the Chapter I or Chapter II prohibition. The overall approach in this regard is described in the Competition Act guideline *Assessment of Individual Agreements and Conduct.* Part 4 of this guideline contains a number of examples of issues relevant to the water and sewerage sectors where the Director's powers may be applied. Many of the examples concern possible abuses of a dominant position, but there may also be a breach of the Chapter I prohibition where abusive conduct is the subject of an agreement between undertakings.

Services of general economic interest

3.14 The prohibitions do not apply to 'an undertaking entrusted with the operation of services of general economic interest or having the character of a revenue-producing monopoly in so far as the prohibition would obstruct the performance, in law or in fact, of the particular tasks assigned to that undertaking'.[2] The Director considers that water and sewerage undertakers may fall within the category of undertakings entrusted with the operation of services of general economic interest, but the exclusion applies only in so far as the prohibition would obstruct the performance of tasks assigned to an undertaking, and does not apply to an undertaking or its activities generally. The Director considers that there are many aspects of undertakers' conduct where the exclusion is unlikely to apply. A number of these aspects are described further in Section 4. The Competition Act guideline *Services of General Economic Interest* provides further details of the exclusion, and relevant European case law.

[3108]

NOTES

1   *AKZO Chemie BV v Commission Case* [1993] 5 CMLR 215.
2   The exclusion contained in paragraph 4 of Schedule 3 to the Act.

4   Specific applications

4.1 This part identifies a number of issues specific to the water and sewerage sectors where the Director may apply his powers under the Act to enforce the Chapter I and Chapter II prohibitions. The issues identified here are not exhaustive: some indications are given of how the Director may approach investigations and the application of his powers in relation to the identified issues. The Director will impose financial penalties on infringing undertakings, where appropriate. Further details are contained in the Competition Act guideline *Enforcement.*

Issues in pricing of water and sewerage services

4.2   Until now, competition on price terms for water and sewerage services has been relevant mainly to large users, although this form of competition may be extended further in future. The Water Industry Act 1991[1] allows customers who are supplied (or likely to be supplied) with a quantity of water at or above a specified volumetric threshold the opportunity to secure a supply of water or sewerage service from an undertaker other than the one in whose area they are situated.[2] The volumetric threshold is currently 250,000 cubic metres per year. Most undertakers have responded to the threat of losing their large volume customers by introducing lower charges for these customers. In some cases, undertakers have offered lower tariffs as a direct result of competitive action by new entrants.

4.3   The tariff basket mechanism permits undertakers to rebalance tariffs between categories of customers (for example, between customers on a meter and those charged by other means, such as rateable values). Undertakers have been able to offer tariffs for their large users without reducing overall revenues, and have therefore been able to compete on price in a manner that could be predatory or exclusionary, without significant risk to their revenue. Tariffs for users whose supply of water is above the large user threshold will be removed from the tariff basket from 1 April 2000. This will prevent undertakers from rebalancing tariffs to recover lost revenues from other groups of customers. Undertakers could, however, still breach the Chapter II prohibition if they set predatory prices or if they set prices at excessively high levels.

Approach to pricing conduct

4.4   The pricing conduct of water and sewerage undertakers is currently subject to detailed regulation under the licence conditions. Condition E of the licence, for example, prohibits undertakers from exercising undue preference or undue discrimination in the charging of customers (and categories of customers). The Director's view is that large user tariffs should normally be set with reference to a robust estimate of the long run marginal costs of supply.

4.5   Furthermore, under the Water Industry Act 1999, undertakers' charges schemes are subject to approval by the Director. The exercise of the power to approve charges schemes takes effect from 1 April 2000 and involves the consideration of a number of criteria, including undue preference and undue discrimination.

4.6.   In addition, the pricing conduct of undertakers (and other undertakings involved in commercial activities connected with the supply of water or securing a supply of water or with the provision or securing of sewerage services) may infringe the prohibitions in the Act. The Director may use both sets of powers in addressing issues raised by the pricing conduct of undertakings in the water and sewerage sectors. Some aspects of pricing conduct may be effectively dealt with in terms of compliance with the licence conditions, while other types of pricing conduct may be addressed through the use of the Director's powers under the Act.

4.7.   The Director will consider the detailed circumstances of each case in deciding how to address pricing conduct, and whether or not the conduct involves breach of one of the Act's prohibitions. The relevant market and physical and technical circumstances are subject to change over time, however, and the Director's view of pricing conduct will take account of the prevailing circumstances.

4.8   The power to approve charges schemes will be exercised on an annual basis and will involve review of many aspects of the pricing conduct of undertakers, again in the light of prevailing circumstances. Following the coming into force of the Water Industry Act 1999, once the Director has approved a charges scheme he would not normally expect to re-open any of its contents before the undertaker submitted its proposals for the following year. He may, however, in some circumstances, investigate and conclude that the undertaker's conduct warrants further action under the Act.

Approach to cost assessment

4.9   Costs will be a key consideration in the assessment of pricing conduct in relation to the Act's prohibitions: their assessment will follow the approach outlined in the Competition Act guideline *Assessment of Individual Agreements and Conduct*. Where the Director has grounds to suspect that pricing conduct breaches either of the prohibitions in the Act, he will investigate the costs of providing the product or service in question. He will make use of cost information already available to him and will examine the consistency of approach used by undertakers in cost analyses for the purposes of setting tariffs and special agreements, arrangements for bulk supplies, resource development, leakage control and demand management.

4.10   In some cases water and sewerage undertakers may be judged to serve a number of markets, which are subject to varying levels of competition. It may then be necessary for the assessment of costs to involve consideration of undertakers as multi-product companies, with examination of methods of cost allocation to different products or services. An undertaker might, for example, exploit a dominant position in one market to subsidise predatory behaviour in another market.

Predation

4.11   Section 60 of the Act sets out certain principles with a view to ensuring that the United Kingdom authorities handle cases in such a way as to ensure consistency with Community law (see paragraph 2.2 above). When the Director considers allegations of possible predatory pricing, the judgments of the European Court of Justice referred to in the Competition Act guidelines *The Chapter II Prohibition* and *Assessment of Individual Agreements and Conduct* may be relevant decisions,[3] in that they relate to a corresponding question arising in Community law. Broad guidelines for the assessment of costs in relation to predatory pricing may be drawn from these judgments. These focus on average variable costs and average total costs.

4.12   The European Commission's *Notice on the Application of Competition Rules to Access Agreements in the Telecommunications Sector* [4] states that 'in network industries a simple application of the above rule [that is, use of average variable costs and average total costs] would not reflect the economic reality of network industries'. In many circumstances the water and sewerage industries may be regarded as network industries. The Director considers that the network industry characteristics of water and sewerage industries include the high proportion of common costs and the large fixed costs associated with network infrastructure, and the potential importance of access to network facilities for service markets. There may, therefore, be circumstances where the Director might consider that the judgments of the European Court of Justice referred to above do not address corresponding questions in terms of section 60 of the Act because of the specific nature of the water industry as a network industry, and the implications of this for the assessment of costs.

4.13   Where appropriate, therefore, the Director will assess the total costs that are incremental to the provision of a service, and will have regard to the relevant time frame over which costs should be analysed. In many circumstances, the Director considers that long run marginal costs will be an appropriate framework for the analysis of costs, due to the typically high proportion of total costs which are accounted for by long-lived capital assets in the provision of water and sewerage services. Prices set at or above long run marginal costs would not normally present concerns in relation to predation.

Excessive prices

4.14 Where an undertaking is dominant in a market, it is possible that prices may be set at excessively high levels. Prices may be considered excessively high when the price charged bears no reasonable relation to the economic value of the good or service supplied. In this instance, such behaviour could be an abuse of a dominant market position under the Chapter II prohibition. In cases where there may be excessive pricing, the Director may have regard to measures of the profitability or the 'stand-alone costs' of an activity.

Other relevant information

4.15 In addition to cost-based information, the Director will consult with Ofwat Customer Service Committees[5] and have regard to other evidence regarding the structure of markets and the effects of pricing conduct on competition. Evidence of intention, for example, may strengthen the case for regarding some instances of pricing conduct as predatory. A dominant undertaking which was unable to justify its pricing policy in commercial terms, and which would benefit only if one or more of its competitors were weakened, would normally be considered to be abusing its position. Similarly, the persistence of supra-normal profits or the introduction of significant price increases in the absence of commensurate cost increases may be regarded as indicators of excessively high prices.

Common carriage

4.16 The Director regards 'common carriage' as the shared use of assets by undertakings. In many circumstances it would be uneconomic for a competitor to duplicate the provision of large assets, such as a pipe network or treatment facility. Common carriage, therefore, has the potential to increase customer choice by facilitating the entry of competitors (whether existing undertakers or new entrants) into a local market.

4.17 There is no specific statutory framework for common carriage, but this does not prevent undertakings from agreeing to such arrangements, including the associated terms and conditions.[6] In general, however, incumbent undertakers may have little incentive to offer access to their facilities to other suppliers. In some cases refusal to allow a competitor to access or share facilities may be objectively justifiable—where, for example, the competitor refused to give adequate assurances on water quality or refused to make a reasonable contribution to necessary reinforcement costs. In other cases the refusal may be without any objective justification. Under the Act, such a refusal by a dominant undertaking to grant access to facilities that would allow another undertaking to compete in a related market may be an abuse of a dominant position. Similarly, the imposition of unreasonable price or non-price terms for access could infringe the Chapter II prohibition.

4.18 The Water Industry Act 1991 provides an effective legal framework for the development of common carriage in a manner that safeguards customers' interests. Undertakers' approaches to the development of common carriage should not endanger the ability of the Director or of undertakers to fulfil their respective statutory duties. In this regard there are a number of issues that undertakers should address in any common carriage agreements. These include:

— the protection of water quality standards;
— establishing liability in the event of supply failures or quality incidents;
— responsibility for leakage and maintenance; and
— reasonable terms of access (including price).

4.19 None of these issues should, however, be used merely as a means of restricting competition via common carriage. The Director recognises that undertakers currently address many of these issues within their own operations.

4.20 The Director will, therefore, use his powers under the Act to deal with abusive conduct by dominant undertakings. This will allow common carriage to develop where there are genuine opportunities for improved services to customers.

Refusal to supply and essential facilities

4.21 Refusal to supply by a dominant undertaking may, in some circumstances, be an infringement of the Chapter II prohibition. In particular, the doctrine of 'essential facilities' may be material to the application of the Act in cases regarding common carriage. The Competition Act guideline *Assessment of Individual Agreements and Conduct* provides more detailed guidance.

4.22 A facility can be viewed as essential if access to it is indispensable in order to compete in a market, and duplication is impossible or extremely difficult owing to physical, geographic or legal constraints (or is highly undesirable for reasons of public policy).[7] A facility cannot be deemed to be essential if other facilities compete in the same relevant market. The principle of common carriage may be applied to all providers of water and sewerage services, but the doctrine of essential facilities is most likely to apply where water or sewerage undertakers are the providers, as they control most of the networks in England and Wales. While the definition of an essential facility must be undertaken on a case by case basis, many of the capital assets of water and sewerage undertakers could be regarded as essential facilities.

4.23 Where it has been demonstrated that a facility is essential, it would be for the dominant undertaking to show that a refusal to share access can be justified objectively, and that the refusal is proportionate to the justification. In some circumstances, an unreasonable refusal to expand the capacity of an essential facility to meet the demands placed on facilities by an undertaking requesting common carriage, or to offer reasonable terms for network expansion, may be regarded as an abuse.

4.24 Where the Director has reasonable grounds for suspecting that an infringement of the Chapter II prohibition has occurred, he will ask the owner of the facility to justify his offer of terms for network access or expansion. He may also require the owner of the facility and the person seeking access to provide expert assessments of the matters relevant to the case. This may include supported opinions on the effects on competition of any refusal to grant access, the basis of any objective justification for refusing to grant access and an assessment of what would be reasonable terms to achieve access. If the parties involved cannot agree terms, the Director may find that there has been a breach of the prohibition, and use his powers under the Act to apply a remedy. Where the Director decides that an infringement has occurred he will publish his reasoning and may include analysis of the relevant network costs.

Competition in providing contestable services

4.25 Many of the functions currently carried out by undertakers (for example, engineering design, project management, billing, meter reading and call service operation) could be carried out by specialised sub-contractors through out-sourcing arrangements. These functions can be said to be 'contestable'. Out-sourcing may be more efficient than carrying out the function within the undertaker.

4.26 Many undertakers make use of out-sourcing arrangements for a number of services, but giving preference to associated companies, or choosing suppliers on subjective grounds, may restrict or distort competition. In the past, the Director has received a number of complaints about tendering procedures used by undertakers, including allegations of special preference given to associated companies. The issue of transfer pricing is already receiving scrutiny by the Director and some aspects of out-sourcing conduct involving preference to associated companies may be more appropriately addressed through licence enforcement action. Some types of conduct may nevertheless still be considered under the Act.

4.27 Some undertakers may prefer to continue to provide contestable services themselves. However, the Chapter II prohibition might be breached if, for example, undertakers are manifestly not in a position to satisfy the demand prevailing on a market to the detriment of customers and they prevent third parties from meeting this demand. There might also be a breach of the Chapter II prohibition if undertakers refuse to use modern technology (such as, for example, technology used by third parties who would be prepared to do the work) in providing contestable services which results in increased costs and/or delays in doing the work.

4.28 In addition, an undertaking may be found to be a dominant buyer in a market, and conduct by a dominant buyer directly or indirectly to impose unfair purchase prices or other unfair trading conditions may breach the Chapter II prohibition.

4.29 If he finds that an infringement has occurred, the Director will use his powers under the Act to apply a remedy by, for example, giving directions requiring undertakings to modify conduct in relation to the procurement of contestable services.

Conduct relating to non-price terms

4.30 Service agreements and contracts between undertakers and their customers contain a variety of non-price terms and conditions, including terms of payment, length of contract, the structuring of charges, and requirements to purchase linked services.

4.31 There may be circumstances where undertakings attach non-price terms to contracts or service agreements in a manner that infringes one of the prohibitions in the Act. This can be either by forcing customers to accept terms that restrict their ability to seek competitive offers, or by offering short-run benefits to customers which, in the long run, restrict the development of competition by predation or foreclosure of market entry. Similarly, non-price terms may be exploitative, in that a dominant undertaking may offer an unacceptably low quality of service, or unreasonable non-price terms.

4.32 In judging whether non-price terms infringe the prohibitions, the Director will take into account the specific conditions of the market in question, any technical or economic justification for the conduct, and evidence concerning the intent of the undertaking. In the case of long-term contracts, for example, the Director may have regard to the level of investment associated with the provision of a service, and any other objective justification for the terms. The undertaking will be asked to explain the reason for requesting or offering the non-price conditions. Evidence of an intention to behave anti-competitively, however, is not required for conduct to constitute an abuse.

4.33 The Competition Act guideline *Assessment of Individual Agreements and Conduct* provides more detailed guidance on these issues. The following paragraphs indicate some examples of possible non-price conduct by water and sewerage service providers that could breach the prohibitions in the Act.

Examples

4.34 Tariffs may be offered to customers on the condition that the customer agrees to a long-term commitment, without recourse to competitive suppliers. This may constitute an attempt to foreclose the market, and therefore an abuse of a dominant position under the Chapter II prohibition.

4.35 Preferential tariffs or non-price terms such as extended credit facilities may be offered, on the condition that the customer does not seek competitive supplies. This would make it more difficult for competitors to enter the market. Preferential terms offered on long-term contracts are likely to be of concern where it is judged that they do not reflect underlying real cost differences.

4.36 Non-price terms may also be used in an anti-competitive manner to discriminate between customers who share similar supply characteristics. Preferential levels of service or the provision of 'free' services, for example, could be offered to customers, in place of price reductions, when responding to competitive threats. The effect on competition of this conduct may be the same as predatory price reductions. A related form of conduct would be the offering of preferential terms by undertakings falling under linked ownership arrangements, conditional on loyalty to, or acceptance of, a particular supplier of services. These practices may constitute an infringement of the Chapter II prohibition.

4.37 An undertaking may provide a service subject to acceptance of other obligations, tying the supply of one product or service to the supply of others. This approach could be used by undertakings that are dominant in the supply of one service or product to prevent the emergence of competition in the supply of a separate product or service.

Licensed access to water resources

The Abstraction Licensing Regime

4.38 Access to, and the use of, water resources is currently governed by a licensing regime operated by the Environment Agency, the Secretary of State for the Environment, Transport and the Regions, and the Welsh Assembly. Those who wish to abstract and use water from rivers or the ground must be licensed by the Environment Agency. This confers protected rights on the licensee, preventing the grant of further licences in derogation of the earlier right without that licence holder's consent. Under current rules, licensed entitlements are not directly tradable, although the Environment Agency and the Secretary of State may revoke or modify a licence. If that happens, or if the Environment Agency grants a new abstraction licence in derogation of protected rights and without the abstraction licensee's consent, the Environment Agency is liable to pay compensation.[8]

4.39 The Government has announced the changes it intends to make to this regime.[9] Some will be made within existing legislation (the Water Resources Act 1991), but others will require new legislation which the Government will bring forward when Parliamentary time allows. The Environment Agency will draw up Abstraction Management Strategies on a catchment basis. New licences will be time-limited, generally to around 15 years, although longer periods will be appropriate in certain circumstances at the discretion of the Agency. Most existing licences will gradually be converted to time-limited status on a prioritised basis. There will be a general presumption of renewal of any time-limited licence, and the Agency will be expected to do this in accordance with its Abstraction Management Strategies and will take account of needs for emergency reserves. The Agency will be empowered to compel one water undertaker to seek a bulk supply from another or the transfer of licences where that is necessary to secure proper use of water resources.

Application of competition rules

4.40 The Director considers that an abstraction licensee's conduct in exploiting (or seeking to protect) its licensed entitlements could be a breach of the Chapter II prohibition. The fact that an abstraction licensee is entitled under the abstraction licence to use a resource in a particular way does not remove its actions from consideration under the Act.

PART III
OFT GUIDELINES

4.41 There may be circumstances in which an abstraction licensee's reliance on protected rights could have an anti-competitive effect. For example, it may be using only a proportion of the licensed entitlement but rely on its protected rights to resist an application from a third party to abstract from a neighbouring borehole in derogation of the abstraction licensee's unused entitlement. Such conduct could be regarded as an abuse if it would be likely to eliminate all competition in a related market.

4.42 Reliance on protected rights to abstract from a river to defeat an application from a potential upstream abstractor may also constitute an abuse. In particular, this may constitute a breach of the Chapter II prohibition where the conduct meant that customers could deal only with the downstream abstraction licensee.

4.43 In some circumstances a resource could be an 'essential facility', and unreasonable denial of access, or a refusal to supply, may amount to an abuse. Even if a resource were not regarded as an essential facility, the question as to whether an incumbent abstraction licensee's conduct was a breach of the Chapter II prohibition could still arise, depending on the particular circumstances of the case. Where the Director decides that an abstraction licensee's reliance upon protected rights or refusal to supply constitutes an abuse of a dominant position, he will consult with the Environment Agency in order to determine the most effective means of bringing the infringement to an end, having regard both to his powers under the Act and to relevant provisions governing the use and allocation of water resources.

Connections to water mains

4.44 Water undertakers have a duty under Section 45 of the Water Industry Act 1991 to make connections to the water mains to enable provision of water supplies for domestic purposes. They are entitled to recover expenses reasonably incurred in carrying out such work.[11] Some undertakers allow contractors to do some of the preparatory work.

4.45 As a result of complaints to the Director about the level of expenses requested by the undertakers for doing this work, he has found that some undertakers have overcharged the customers. Such behaviour may constitute an abuse of a dominant position especially when there is little or no competitive alternative.

4.46 The reasonableness of costs incurred for connections to water mains is likely to remain an issue where water undertakers continue to insist on making the connections themselves. The application of connection charges that are, for example, not cost-reflective might be found to be in breach of the Chapter II prohibition. In assessing the reasonableness of costs the Director may have regard to evidence about the level of costs that would have been incurred if the undertaker had followed a competitive tendering process. When assessing whether an undertaker has abused its dominant position, the Director will have regard to the fact that some undertakers allow customers to make arrangements for some of the preparatory work, while some do all the work themselves.

4.47 The Director will continue to use his powers of determination under the Water Industry Act 1991[12] to consider individual complaints about the cost of specific connections made by the undertakers. In addition, he may use his powers under the Act to judge whether an undertaker may have abused its dominant position by consistently overcharging customers.

4.48 If the Director has reasonable grounds for suspecting that an infringement of the Chapter II prohibition has occurred, undertakers will be required to provide information concerning their policies and requirements on the use of contractors, the costs of making the connection, and the process for deriving costs and charges. If the Director finds that an undertaker has abused its dominant position, he will use his powers under the Act to apply a remedy.

Requisitions

4.49 The Water Industry Act 1991 requires undertakers to install public mains and sewers within set timescales when requisitioned by the owner or occupier of premises or by the local authority. Similarly, developers who want to develop land can require undertakers to move mains or sewers. The undertaker is entitled to recover its expenses reasonably incurred for installing or diverting the infrastructure. The Water Industry Act 1991 also provides that disputes about costs incurred in installing mains or sewers may be resolved by arbitration. Although the Director has no role in that process, complaints have still been received by the Director about the level of costs imposed by undertakers (mainly where the undertaker has offered to receive a one-off payment instead of recovering the cost over 12 years, as provided for under the Water Industry Act 1991). Other areas of concern include the length of time taken to carry out the work, excessive levels of overheads charged, and delays in responding to requests for requisitions.

4.50 Developers often find it efficient and economic to provide their own on-site services. Some undertakers will agree to adopt systems that the developer has laid, but, in the case of water facilities, there is no procedure under which a developer may appeal to the Director if a water undertaker refuses to conclude such an agreement. An undertaker's refusal to enter into such an arrangement could be an abuse of a dominant position, in that the undertaker's insistence on doing the work at the developer's cost would foreclose the market for such works. In assessing whether such conduct breaches the Chapter II prohibition, the Director will consider any justification offered by the undertaker, but will also take into account the ability of other undertakers to co-operate effectively with developers in comparable circumstances. Any agreement between undertakers, either explicit or implicit, not to co-operate with developers may be an infringement of the Chapter I prohibition.

4.51 The Director considers that excessively high prices, unjustified delays or unreasonable terms imposed by undertakers for requisitions or infrastructure diversions may constitute an abuse of a dominant position under the Chapter II prohibition. The key test will be that expenses incurred by undertakers should be 'reasonable'. In making that judgement, the Director will have regard to the relationship between the amounts charged by undertakers and the costs of carrying out the work. He will also consider whether the works paid for were reasonably required for the requisition in question.

4.52 The Director will use his powers under the Act to remedy abuses in relation to requisitions or infrastructure diversions. A direction could, for example, require an undertaker to allow developers to engage their own contractors for water installations or infrastructure diversions (subject to appropriate verification of standards, at reasonable cost, by undertakers), or that charges for a particular requisition or infrastructure diversion be modified.

Examples of agreements that may restrict, distort or prevent competition

4.53 Competition in water and sewerage service provision may be prevented, restricted or distorted by formal or informal agreements among undertakings, to the detriment of customers or those who trade with them, in breach of the Chapter I prohibition. Examples of such agreements include those:

— between undertakers not to compete in each other's areas of appointment, for example, in relation to cross-border supplies, common carriage or inset appointments;

— between undertakings to collude on pricing conduct;

— leading to collusion in bidding for contracts (including agreements not to bid);

— leading to preference for related, or each other's related, suppliers in procurement or the out-sourcing of contestable services;

PART III
OFT GUIDELINES

— leading to collusion with the intention of preventing, restricting or distorting comparative competition;[12] and

— leading to the restriction of access by third parties to essential facilities.

4.54 The Director will use his powers under the Act to investigate suspected cases of anti-competitive agreements or concerted practices, and apply remedies where an agreement breaches the Chapter I prohibition. Further guidance on the Chapter I prohibition and on the criteria for exemption is given in the Competition Act guideline *The Chapter I Prohibition*.

[3109]

NOTES

[1] As amended by the Competition and Services (Utilities) Act 1992.

[2] This opportunity is also open to customers where the area is a greenfield site or where the incumbent undertaker consents to change its boundary. Further details are contained in the Ofwat publication *Inset appointments – Guidance for applicants*.

[3] Including, for example, Case C62/86 *AKZO Chemie BV v Commission* [1993] 5 CMLR 215, and *Tetra Pak II* [1997] 4 CMLR 662.

[4] European Commission *Notice on the Application of the Competition Rules to Access Agreements in the Telecommunications Sector Framework, relevant markets and principles*, Notice 98/C265/02.

[5] Ofwat Customer Service Committees are charged to represent the interests of customers and potential customers of the appointed water or sewerage undertakers.

[6] Parties to common carriage agreements must, of course, comply with other relevant statutory requirements, including the abstraction licensing regime and other water resource planning measures administered by the Environment Agency, and the requirements of the Drinking Water Inspectorate.

[7] See, for example, the judgment of the European Court of Justice in Case C–7/79 *Oscar Bronner v Mediaprint and others*, [1998] and in particular the opinion of AG Jacobs, paragraphs 47, 65 and 66.

[8] The Environment Agency is not permitted to grant new abstraction licences that are known to be in derogation of existing protected rights. Compensation must be provided if the grant of a new licence is later shown to be in derogation of protected rights.

[9] *Taking Water Responsibly: Government decisions following consultation on changes to the water abstraction licensing system in England and Wales*, Department of Environment, Transport and the Regions/Welsh Office, March 1999.

[10] Sections 106 and 107 of the Water Industry Act 1991 contain similar provisions relating to connections to public sewers, such that if undertakers insist on carrying out connection work they are entitled to recover expenses reasonably incurred.

[11] Water Industry Act 1991 Section 45 (6A), as amended by the Competition and Services (Utilities) Act 1992. Under section 107 (4A) of the Water Industry Act 1991 the Director also has powers of determination in relation to disputes about the cost of connections to public sewers. The Director is still able to apply his powers under the Act to such abusive conduct.

[12] The broad approach to regulation used to deliver improvements in prices and services for customers, whereby price limits and service standards are set with reference to comparisons based on the past performance of companies.

5   Process and Procedures

5.1   This part provides a brief indication of the elements of process and procedures that the Director will follow in enforcing the Act under his concurrent powers. Further details are contained in the Competition Act guidelines *Concurrent Application to Regulated Industries* and *The Major Provisions*.

Responsibility for case-handling

5.2   In general, any agreement or conduct which relates to commercial activities connected with the supply of water or securing a supply of water or with the provision or securing of sewerage services in England and Wales will be dealt with by the Director. This may include conduct in specific markets for inputs or services that are components of the wider provision of water or sewerage services.

5.3   The Director and the Director General of Fair Trading will always consult each other where it appears that there is a possibility of concurrent jurisdiction before either acts in a case, and will avoid a matter being addressed by both. They will consult each other during the course of an investigation as appropriate, regardless of which is responsible for handling a case.

Complaints

5.4   Complaints may be made to the Director or to the Director General of Fair Trading, but **should not be made to both** (although complaints about licence conditions only should continue to be sent direct to the Director). Guidance on the information that should be included in a complaint can be obtained from the Office of Fair Trading or any regulator.

5.5   Where the complaint concerns subject matter that may involve breach of both the prohibitions in the Act and sector-specific licence conditions, it will normally be considered by the Director.

Notifications

5.6   Parties to an agreement or conduct may notify the Director General of Fair Trading for guidance or a decision for clearance or (in the case of the Chapter I prohibition) for exemption decision. A standard form (Form N) must be used for notifications. A copy should also be sent to the Director where the case falls under his concurrent jurisdiction.

Interim measures directions

5.7   The Director has the power to impose interim measures directions during an investigation when he has a reasonable suspicion that one of the prohibitions has been infringed and he considers that it is necessary for him to act as a matter of urgency, to prevent serious, irreparable damage to a person or category of persons, or to protect the public interest. He may give such directions as he considers appropriate, which may include modification or termination of an agreement or conduct (see the Competition Act guideline *The Major Provisions*).

Appeals

5.8   Any party to an agreement in respect of which the Director has made a decision, and any person in respect of whose conduct the Director has made a decision, may appeal to the Competition Commission. Appeals against decisions made under the Act are possible both on the substance of the decision and on any penalties imposed. Any appeal made to the Competition Commission against a decision of the Director will be determined by an appeal tribunal.

Third party rights

5.9   The Act provides for a third party who has 'sufficient interest' in the decision to appeal against a decision made by the Director. Further details are contained in the Competition Act guideline *The Major Provisions*.

5.10 Third parties who consider that they have suffered loss as a result of any unlawful agreement or conduct may claim for damages in the courts.

Compliance

5.11 The Director General of Fair Trading has recommended that programmes for compliance with the Act should form an integral part of businesses' preparation for the new regime. This guideline outlines how the introduction of the new prohibitions under the Act will have significant implications for undertakings involved in the water and sewerage industries. In some cases, it is possible that aspects of current conduct may require modification to ensure that the prohibitions are not infringed.

5.12 The Director expects that water and sewerage undertakings will find it prudent to implement a corporate compliance programme to minimise the risk of infringements. In order to be effective, compliance programmes will require the introduction of appropriate compliance procedures, thorough initial and on-going training programmes for all relevant staff, and continuous evaluation and feedback supported by personal commitment from senior management.

5.13 As outlined in the Competition Act guideline *Enforcement* and the Director General of Fair Trading's *Guidance on Penalties,* the degree to which undertakings can demonstrate a genuine commitment to compliance with the provisions of the Act will be an important factor in determining the severity of any penalties imposed. Part 4 of this guideline highlights a number of specific issues that, together with the general guidance contained in the full series of Competition Act guidelines, should be taken into account by undertakings in considering compliance. Further details on compliance are contained in the Office of Fair Trading booklet *How your business can achieve compliance.*

[3110]

ANNEXE A

Legal framework for economic regulation of the water and sewerage industries in England and Wales and its relationship to the Competition Act 1998

Structure of the water and sewerage industry

In 1989 the ten water authorities in England and Wales were privatised and licences were granted to operate geographical monopolies for all aspects of water and sewerage services. The effect of privatisation was that these authorities became statutory water and sewerage **undertakers**. The water only companies, that were already operating under statute, also became undertakers and subject to the regulatory regime set out in the Water Act 1989.

Every area of England and Wales is allocated one water undertaker and one sewerage undertaker. However, undertakers are not statutory monopolies, in that some customers receive their water and sewerage services from private suppliers who did not become part of the regulatory regime at privatisation. These private suppliers were, and still are, able to supply water and sewerage services as long as they have the resources and assets to do so. They serve a range of customers, from single premises to towns. They are not appointed under the Water Industry Act 1991 and are not regulated by the Director. It is possible for people to develop their own supply and service. Private and individual suppliers and services are regulated, however, by local authorities. They monitor quality standards to the same regulations as licensed undertakers are monitored by the Drinking Water Inspectorate. The Environment Agency regulates water abstractions and discharges of wastewater.

The Director's duties

Among other requirements, Section 2 of the Water Industry Act 1991 requires the Director to carry out his principal functions in the manner that he considers best calculated to:
— secure that the functions of a water undertaker and a sewerage undertaker are properly carried out for every part of England and Wales and to secure that undertakers are able to finance the proper carrying out of their functions. This gives rise to the need for the Director to ensure that he is satisfied that inset applicants have managerial competence and financial viability to carry out their functions as an undertaker;

— protect the interests of every person who is a customer or potential customer of a company which has been or may be appointed to be an undertaker. This applies principally to the charges applied by the undertaker and to the quality of its service;

— promote economy and efficiency on the part of any undertaker in the carrying out of its functions;

— facilitate effective competition, both between undertakers and those seeking to become undertakers.

These requirements will not apply to the exercise by the Director of his concurrent powers under the Act (see paragraphs 2.5 to 2.9 above).

Principal features of the regulatory regime

There are ten water and sewerage companies and 17 water companies (undertakers). The conditions of their Appointments are generally similar, although a few have been modified to reflect an undertaker's membership of a larger group of companies, especially if that group contains another licensed utility, such as a Public Electricity Supplier.

The standard conditions provide the detailed means whereby the Director regulates the undertaker's activities, especially their financial and operational performance and their conduct towards customers. There is provision for the setting and revision of price limits (which from 1 April 2000 will take place automatically every five years) as well as for checking that year-on-year price increases comply with each undertaker's limit.

At the same time, the licence prohibits undertakers from levying charges that are unduly preferential or discriminatory, as between classes of customers (or, in the case of individual agreements, between the customers covered by them).

Paragraph 4.4 of this guideline describes the Director's approach to validation of charges by reference to long run marginal cost. Whenever the issue arises the undertaker should be able to show that particular charges are broadly related to the appropriate measure of cost. Failing that, the Director will consider whether the charges are unduly preferential or discriminatory and, at the same time, whether they (or any associated terms) may breach the Chapter II prohibition of abuse of a dominant position.

The Water Industry Act 1999

Under the Water Industry Act 1999, undertakers are required to obtain the Director's approval of their charges schemes, under which they customarily raise much of their revenue. This takes effect from 1 April 2000.

In deciding whether to approve a charges scheme, the Director will have regard to any ministerial guidance received about the social and environmental objectives, which the charges schemes ought to reflect. At the same time, each undertaker is required to include in its charges scheme items that have been specified in regulations (made by statutory instrument). These will deal particularly with the protection of the interests of disadvantaged customers, such as larger families on low incomes and persons whose illness or disability dictates larger-than-normal consumption of water (for example, those using kidney dialysis machines).

The Director's function in approving charges schemes will not be limited to the matters just described and he will examine each scheme, to satisfy himself that there is no evidence of inappropriate charges. As noted above, this may include charges which are not reflective of costs, or which appear to have an anti-competitive effect, for example if a tariff were made available only to selected customers where the undertaker anticipated the threat of competition.

Once the Director has approved a charges scheme, he would not normally expect to re-open any of its contents before the undertaker submitted its proposals for the following year. However, in some circumstances he may investigate and conclude that the undertaker's conduct warrants further action under the Act.

Enforcement

The Director is required to take action against any breach of an undertaker's licence obligations, unless he is satisfied that it is trivial or an undertaker has given an undertaking not to repeat it; or that some aspect of his other duties precludes him from taking that action. In addition, he will be relieved of that obligation if he concludes that it would be more appropriate to take action under the Act.

Competition

There is provision for competitive entry into the water and sewerage industries in England and Wales. The Director is authorised to appoint new undertakers in either (or both) capacities. This might happen with the agreement of the incumbent undertaker or, failing that, when the new appointment covers an undeveloped ('greenfield') site or the customer concerned uses, or is expected to use, at least 250,000 cubic metres per year. In making such an appointment, the Director is empowered to require an incumbent undertaker to provide a bulk transfer of water to the new undertaker or to permit it to connect its sewerage system to the incumbent's system, including the use of its treatment works. Further guidance may be found in *Inset Appointments—Guidance for applicants* published by Ofwat in February 1999.

The Director has proposed to the Secretary of State that the large user threshold of 250,000 cubic metres per year should be reduced to 100,000 cubic metres per year, so that the prospect of competition might be available to more large water users.

Since these competitive opportunities were introduced in 1992, many undertakers have revised large user tariffs, no doubt in anticipation of the threat of competition. The Director tests these proposals to see whether there is any evidence of unduly preferential or discriminatory charges (bearing in mind the importance of the broad relationship between charges and the relevant measure of cost). He will also consider whether there is any evidence of a breach of the Chapter II prohibition; but he does not believe that the adjustment of tariffs in response to a competitive threat must be improper in either case, provided that it can be justified against the appropriate measure of cost and the undertaker applies the charge, or makes it available, to all customers sharing similar supply characteristics.

Other dispute resolution powers

Apart from the charges that undertakers make to their customers for the provision of water and sewerage services, they have separate entitlements to recover various types of expenses. For example, if a domestic customer asks the undertaker to connect the customer's service pipe to the undertaker's water main, it is entitled to recover the expenses which it reasonably incurs in doing so. Any dispute will be settled by the Director.

Developers, owners of property and local authorities may require the provision of new mains and public sewers to serve their developments. The 'relevant deficit' formula entitles undertakers to recover their costs over 12 years, after giving credit for the water and sewerage charges which accrue from the new development. Any disputes must be referred to arbitration, in which the Director has no role.

The Director may, however, assess the conduct of an undertaker to see whether there is any evidence of an infringement of the Act. He considers that undertakers should allow developers (under appropriate supervision) to make connections between new service pipes and the undertaker's water main (for connections to public sewers, the developer may do that, unless the undertaker opts into the process). On requisitioning, he will examine an undertaker's conduct, especially if it has departed from the relevant deficit by requiring payment of capital sums which are not obviously commutations of the relevant deficit. He will also be alert to complaints about undertakers that will not properly justify the capital charges they are seeking to recover. The underlying issue may be an abuse of a dominant position, bearing in mind that a requisitioner's interests may not be served by potentially lengthy and uncertain arbitration. The Director does not therefore believe that the existence of an arbitration mechanism prevents him from scrutinising such conduct under the Act.

The Director's concurrent jurisdiction with the Director General of Fair Trading under the Fair Trading Act 1973

The Director has the same jurisdiction as the Director General of Fair Trading to investigate and refer to the Competition Commission cases regarding the existence of scale or complex monopolies. These may arise when either one undertaking, or several, supplies or acquires at least one quarter of the market for goods or services in the relevant part of the United Kingdom. The issue will be whether the existence of the monopoly operates (or may be expected to operate) against the public interest.

The Director has concurrent powers to require information for the purpose of assisting him in determining whether to make a monopoly reference. He may also propose that the Secretary of State accept undertakings in lieu of the Director making a monopoly reference. Part 13 of the Competition Act guideline *The Major Provisions* notes the interface with the Competition Act and some of the circumstances in which resort to this jurisdiction might be appropriate.

[3111]

ANNEX B
GLOSSARY OF TERMS

Terms used in a definition that are themselves defined are italicised.

Abstraction licence: a licence issued by the Environment Agency granting a party the right to abstract water from the environment.

Appointee: the company which carries out the business of providing *water* or *sewerage services*, acting under a licence granted under the Water Industry Act 1991.

Associated company: a company that is part of the same group of companies as the licensed *undertaker*.

Average costs: an undertaking's total costs divided by its output.

Bulk supply agreement: an agreement between two *undertakers* for a supply of water from one to the other.

Capital asset: the infrastructure vested in a company on which it can earn a return.

Charges scheme: it is a condition of an undertaker's licence that it must publish a scheme detailing the charges it will make for providing its services.

Common carriage: shared use of assets by undertakings for provision of *water* or *sewerage services*.

Common costs: costs that are incurred when supplying a group of products or services, and which would not be reduced if the *undertaking* ceased supplying one of the products.

Concurrency: the application of the Competition Act by the Director General of Fair Trading and the sector regulators.

Concurrency Working Party: a forum consisting of representatives of the sector regulators and the Director General of Fair Trading, set up with a view to ensuring the consistent application of the Act.

Conduct: the actions of a party in the carrying out of its business.

Connection charge: a charge payable to an *undertaker* to cover the direct cost of works and materials required to connect a premises to its main or sewer.

Contestable: products, services or markets which are open to competition.

Cross-border supply: where an *undertaker* makes available a supply of water for domestic purposes to a customer outside the *undertaker's* area of appointment. NB This is a water industry term and does not refer to international borders.

Demand management: the use of strategies to control the demand for water by customers. Such strategies include selective metering, water efficiency, and leakage control.

Distribution network: the pipe system by which water is delivered to customers, including service reservoirs and pumping apparatus.

Environment Agency: the non-departmental public body established by the Environment Act 1995. As part of its water resources function, it is responsible for the *abstraction licensing* regime.

Essential facility: a facility to which access is indispensable in order to compete in the market and duplication is impossible or extremely difficult owing to physical, geographic or legal constraints (or is highly undesirable for reasons of public policy).

Inset appointee: an *undertaker* that replaces another as a supplier of water and/or sewerage services for one or more customers within a specified geographical area.

Licence conditions: conditions contained in the licence by which an *undertaker* operates, which the Director is required to enforce.

Linked Ownership Arrangement: where one *undertaker* has an interest in another undertaker either directly or indirectly through another company.

Long run marginal cost (LRMC): the costs imposed on a water or sewerage company in supplying or treating an additional increment of water. Long run marginal costs comprise operating and capital costs.

New entrant: a new provider of services to customers, which was not an existing *undertaker*.

Non-price terms: terms in an agreement which relate to matters other than price, such as the duration of agreement, level of service or provisions relating to liability.

Out-sourcing: where provision of goods or services is contracted out to a third party.

Predation: strategic behaviour where an *undertaking* deliberately incurs short-term losses in order to eliminate a competitor so as to be able to charge excessive prices in the future.

Protected rights: rights conferred by an *abstraction licence* by which the licensee is entitled to abstract water up to the limit of its *abstraction licence* without let or hindrance.

Requisition: a request by one or more customers for an *undertaker* to provide a main for the provision of water for domestic purposes or a public sewer for drainage for domestic purposes.

Sewerage services: the collection, treatment and disposal of wastewater.

Special agreement: an *undertaker* may charge a customer by agreement rather than in accordance with a charges scheme. The agreement can cover price and/or non-*price terms*.

Stand-alone costs: the lowest cost which could be faced by a hypothetical supplier of only a particular product or service. Stand-alone costs include **all** common costs (that is those incurred when supplying a group of products or services, and which would not be reduced if the *undertaking* ceased supplying one of the products).

Tendering process: the bidding process in which a company submits a tender for a contract that is offered by another company.

Undertaker: a company appointed to provide *water* and/or *sewerage services* to a defined geographical area. The term is used in the Water Industry Act 1991.

Undertaking: any natural or legal person capable of carrying on commercial or economic activities relating to goods or services, irrespective of its legal status. *Undertakers* fall within this general definition.

Water Industry Act 1999: an Act which received Royal Assent on 30 June 1999, to make, *inter alia*, further provision in relation to England and Wales as to charges in respect of the supply of *water* and provision of *sewerage services*.

Water quality: properties of water defined by reference to specific criteria specified by the Secretary of State for the Environment, Transport and the Regions. Water Quality is regulated by the Drinking Water Inspectorate in respect of *undertakers*, and by local authorities for private suppliers.

Water services: the collection, treatment and distribution of water for domestic and non-domestic purposes.

[3112]

DIRECTOR GENERAL OF FAIR TRADING'S GUIDANCE AS TO THE APPROPRIATE AMOUNT OF A PENALTY

(OFT 423, March 2000)

INTRODUCTION

1　Statutory Background

1.1　Section 38(1) of the Competition Act 1998 ("the Act") requires the Director General of Fair Trading to prepare and publish guidance as to the appropriate amount of any penalty.

1.2　Under section 36 of the Act the Director General of Fair Trading may impose a financial penalty on an undertaking[1] which has intentionally or negligently committed an infringement of the Chapter I or Chapter II prohibition.

1.3　The sector regulators[2] have concurrent powers with the Director General of Fair Trading to apply and enforce the Act in their designated sector under section 54 of the Act. They also have the power to impose financial penalties on undertakings. References to the "Director" (but not references to the "Director General of Fair Trading") throughout this guidance should therefore be taken to include the regulators in relation to their designated sector.

1.4 The financial penalty may not exceed 10% of the "section 36(8) turnover" of the undertaking. The "section 36(8) turnover" of an undertaking for the purposes of this cap on penalties is to be calculated in accordance with the Determination of Turnover for Penalties Order.[3]

1.5 By virtue of section 38(8) of the Act, the Director must have regard to the guidance for the time being in force when setting the amount of any penalty imposed for infringement of the Chapter I or Chapter II prohibition.

1.6 This guidance was approved by the Secretary of State as required under section 38(4) of the Act on 29th January, 2000.

1.7 Section 38(2) of the Act provides that the Director General of Fair Trading may alter the guidance at any time. Any such alterations must be made with the approval of the Secretary of State and following consultation with such persons as the Director General of Fair Trading considers appropriate. This guidance on penalties will be reviewed in the light of experience in applying it over time.

[3113]

NOTES
[1] The meaning of "undertaking" may include both a parent and subsidiary where they operate as a single economic entity.
[2] These are regulators for telecommunications, gas and electricity, water and sewerage and railway services (as set out in Schedule 10 to the Act).
[3] The Competition Act 1998 (Determination of Turnover for Penalties) Order 2000, SI 2000/309.

2 Policy objectives

2.1 The twin objectives of the Director's policy on financial penalties are to impose penalties on infringing undertakings which reflect the seriousness of the infringement and to ensure that the threat of penalties will deter undertakings from engaging in anti-competitive practices. The Director therefore intends, where appropriate, to impose financial penalties which are severe, in particular in respect of agreements[1] between undertakings which fix prices or share markets and other cartel activities,[2] as well as serious abuses of a dominant position, which the Director considers are among the most serious infringements caught under the Act. The deterrent is not aimed solely at the undertakings which are subject to the decision, but also at other undertakings which might be considering activities that are contrary to the Chapter I and Chapter II prohibitions.

2.2 The Director also wishes to encourage members of cartels to come forward with evidence on the existence and activities of any cartel in which they are involved and therefore the guidance sets out in Part II a clear policy on when lenient treatment will be given to such undertakings.

2.3 The guidance has been drafted to increase transparency by setting out the steps which the Director will follow when calculating the amount of a penalty.

[3114]

NOTES
[1] The term "agreement" includes a concerted practice and decision by an association of undertakings.
[2] For the purposes of this guidance, cartel activities are agreements, decisions by associations of undertakings or concerted practices which infringe the Act and involve price fixing, bid rigging (collusive tendering), the establishment of output restrictions or quotas and/or market sharing or market dividing (based on the OECD definition of "hard core cartels").

PART I : STEPS FOR DETERMINING THE LEVEL OF A PENALTY

3 Method of calculation

3.1 Any financial penalty imposed by the Director under section 36 of the Act will be calculated following a five step approach:
— calculation of the starting point by applying a percentage determined by the nature of the infringement to the "relevant turnover" of the undertaking (see paragraph 4.1 below)
— adjustment for duration
— adjustment for other factors
— adjustment for further aggravating or mitigating factors
— adjustment if the maximum penalty of 10% of the "section 36(8) turnover" of the undertaking is exceeded and to avoid double jeopardy.

Details on each of these steps are set out in paragraphs 4 to 8 below.

3.2 A member of a cartel may benefit from total immunity from, or a significant reduction in the level of, a financial penalty, if the requirements set out in Part II of this guidance are satisfied.

[3115]

4 Step 1: Starting point

4.1 The starting point for determining the level of financial penalty which will be imposed on an undertaking is calculated by applying a percentage rate to the "relevant turnover" of the undertaking, up to a maximum of 10%.[1] The "relevant turnover" is the turnover of the undertaking in the relevant product market and relevant geographic market[2] affected by the infringement in the last financial year[3]. This may include turnover generated outside the United Kingdom if the relevant geographic market for the relevant product is wider than the United Kingdom.

4.2 The actual percentage rate which will be applied to the "relevant turnover" will depend upon the nature of the infringement. The more serious the infringement, the higher the percentage rate is likely to be. Price-fixing or market-sharing agreements and other cartel activities are among the most serious infringements caught under the Chapter I prohibition. Conduct which infringes the Chapter II prohibition and which by virtue of the undertaking's dominant position and the nature of the conduct has, or is likely to have a particularly serious effect on competition, for example, predatory pricing, is also one of the most serious infringements under the Act. The starting point for such activities and conduct will be calculated by applying a percentage likely to be at or near 10% of the "relevant turnover" of the infringing undertakings.

4.3 It is the Director's assessment of the seriousness of the infringement which will determine the percentage of "relevant turnover" which is chosen as the starting point for the financial penalty. When making his assessment, the Director will consider a number of factors, including the nature of the product, the structure of the market, the market share(s) of the undertaking(s) involved in the infringement, entry conditions and the effect on competitors and third parties. The damage caused to consumers whether directly or indirectly will also be an important consideration. The assessment will be made on a case by case basis for all types of infringement.

4.4 Where an infringement involves several undertakings, an assessment of the appropriate starting point will be carried out for each of the undertakings concerned, in order to take account of the real impact of the infringing activity of each undertaking on competition.

[3116]

NOTES

 1   In this Guidance, the expression "turnover" is used in two separate contexts: "relevant turnover" used to calculate the starting point and "section 36(8) turnover" (calculated in accordance with The Competition Act 1998 (Determination of Turnover for Penalties) Order 2000 (SI 2000/309)) which is used in Step 5 in the adjustment of the penalty figure to prevent the maximum amount for the penalty being exceeded. The "section 36(8) turnover" of the undertaking is not restricted to the turnover in the relevant product and relevant geographic market.

 2   See the Competition Act guideline *Market Definition* (OFT 403, published March 1999) for further information on the relevant product market and relevant geographic market. The relevant product market and relevant geographic market will be determined as part of the Director's decision that an infringement has taken place.

 3   "Relevant turnover" will be calculated after the deduction of sales rebates and value added tax and other taxes directly related to turnover.

5   Step 2: adjustment for duration

5.1   The starting point may be increased to take into account the duration of the infringement. Penalties for infringements which last for more than one year may be multiplied by not more than the number of years of the infringement. Part years may be treated as full years for the purpose of calculating the number of years of the infringement.

[3117]

6   Step 3: adjustment for other factors

6.1   The penalty figure reached after the calculations in steps 1 and 2 may be adjusted as appropriate to achieve the policy objectives, outlined in paragraph 2.1 above, in particular, of imposing penalties on infringing undertakings in order to deter undertakings from engaging in anti-competitive practices. The deterrent is not aimed solely at the undertakings which are subject to the decision, but also at other undertakings which might be considering activities which are contrary to the Chapter I and Chapter II prohibitions. Considerations at this stage may include, for example, the Director's estimate of the gain made or likely to be made by the infringing undertaking from the infringement. Where relevant, the Director's estimate would account for any gains which might accrue to the undertaking in other product or geographic markets as well as the "relevant" market under consideration.[1] The assessment of the need to adjust the penalty will be made on a case by case basis for each individual infringing undertaking.

6.2   This step may result in a substantial adjustment of the financial penalty calculated at the earlier steps. The consequence may be that the penalty which is imposed is much larger than would otherwise have been imposed. The result of any one of steps 2 or 3 above or 4 below may well be to take the penalty over 10% of the "relevant turnover" identified at step 1, but the overall cap on penalties is 10% of the "section 36(8) turnover" referred to in step 5 below and must not be exceeded.

[3118]

NOTES

 1   For example, in a predation case the relevant market may be very small. However, the act of predation might provide an undertaking with a reputation for aggressive behaviour which it could use to its advantage in many other markets across the UK.

7   Step 4: adjustment for further aggravating and mitigating factors

7.1   The basic amount of the financial penalty, adjusted as appropriate at steps 2 and 3, may be increased where there are other aggravating factors, or decreased where there are mitigating factors.

7.2   Aggravating factors include:

— role of the undertaking as a leader in, or an instigator of, the infringement;

— involvement of directors or senior management;

— retaliatory measures taken against other undertakings aimed at ensuring the continuation of the infringement;

— continuing the infringement after the start of the investigation;

— repeated infringements by the same undertaking or other undertakings in the same group.

7.3   Mitigating factors include:

— role of the undertaking, for example, where the undertaking is acting under severe duress or pressure;

— genuine uncertainty as to whether the agreement or conduct constituted an infringement;

— adequate steps having been taken with a view to ensuring compliance with the Act;[1]

— infringements which are committed negligently rather than intentionally;

— cooperation which enables the enforcement process to be concluded more effectively and/or speedily than would otherwise be the case, over and above that expected of any undertaking.

Note: in cartel cases an undertaking which cooperates fully with the investigation may benefit from total immunity from, or a significant reduction in the level of, a financial penalty, if it meets the requirements set out in Part II of this guidance.

[3119]

NOTES

    [1]   See the Office of Fair Trading's booklet on "How your business can achieve compliance—A guide to achieving compliance with the Competition Act 1998" (OFT 424, published August 1999) which does not form part of this guidance for more information on compliance issues.

8   Step 5: adjustment to prevent maximum penalty being exceeded and to avoid double jeopardy

8.1   The final amount of the penalty calculated according to the method set out above may not in any event exceed 10% of the "section 36(8) turnover" of the undertaking.[1]

8.2   The penalty will be adjusted if necessary to ensure that it does not exceed this maximum. This adjustment will be made *after* all the relevant adjustments have been made in steps 2 to 4 above and also, in cartel cases, *before* any adjustments are made under paragraph 9.4.1 of this guidance.

8.3   If a penalty or fine has been imposed by the European Commission, or by a court or other body in another Member State in respect of an agreement or conduct, the Director must take that penalty or fine into account when setting the amount of a penalty in relation to that agreement or conduct.

[3120]

NOTES

    [1]   See note to para **[3116]** regarding the terms "relevant turnover" and "section 36(8) turnover".

PART II: LENIENT TREATMENT FOR UNDERTAKINGS COMING FORWARD WITH INFORMATION

9 Immunity from or reduction in financial penalty for undertakings coming forward with information in cartel cases

9.1 Undertakings participating in cartel activities[1] might wish to terminate their involvement and inform the Director of the existence of the cartel, but be deterred from doing so by the risk of incurring large financial penalties. To encourage such undertakings to come forward the Director will offer total immunity from financial penalties for an infringement of the Chapter I prohibition to a member of a cartel who is the first to come forward and who satisfies the requirements set out in paragraph 9.3.2. Alternatively, the Director may offer total immunity from financial penalties to a member of a cartel who is the first to come forward and who satisfies the requirements set out in paragraph 9.3.4. An undertaking which is not the first to come forward, or does not satisfy these requirements may benefit from a reduction in the amount of the penalty imposed if it satisfies the requirements set out in paragraph 9.4.1 below.

9.2 The Director considers that it is in the interest of the economy of the United Kingdom to grant favourable treatment to undertakings which inform him of cartels and which then cooperate with him in the circumstances set out below. It is the secret nature of cartels which justifies such a policy. The interests of customers and consumers in ensuring that such practices are detected and prohibited outweigh the policy objectives of imposing financial penalties on those undertakings which are members of the cartel and which cooperate with the Director.

9.3 Total immunity from financial penalties in cartel cases

9.3.1 Where an undertaking participating in a cartel is the **first to come forward** to provide evidence of the existence and activities of the cartel, and it fulfils all the requirements in paragraph 9.3.2, it will benefit from **total immunity** from financial penalties in respect of that infringement; if it is the first to come forward to provide such evidence and it fulfils all the requirements of paragraph 9.3.4 below, it may benefit from **total immunity** from financial penalties in respect of that infringement.

9.3.2 **Total immunity for the first to come forward before an investigation has commenced:** In order to benefit from total immunity under this paragraph, the undertaking must be the **first** to provide the Director with evidence of the existence and activities of a cartel **before** he has commenced an investigation[2] of the undertakings involved; provided that the Director does not already have sufficient information to establish the existence of the alleged cartel, and the following conditions are satisfied:

the undertaking must:

(a) provide the Director with all the information, documents and evidence available to it regarding the existence and activities of the cartel;

(b) maintain continuous and complete cooperation throughout the investigation;

(c) not have compelled another undertaking to take part in the cartel and not have acted as the instigator or played the leading role in the cartel; and

(d) refrain from further participation in the cartel from the time it discloses the cartel.

9.3.3 If an undertaking does **not** fulfil all the requirements in paragraph 9.3.2 above, it may still benefit from total immunity from financial penalties if it fulfils all the requirements in paragraph 9.3.4 below.

9.3.4 Total immunity for the first to come forward <u>after</u> an investigation[3] has commenced: In order to benefit from the possibility of total immunity under this paragraph:

— the undertaking seeking immunity under this paragraph must be the **first**[4] to provide the Director with evidence of the existence and activities of a cartel **before** the Director has given written notice of his proposal to make a decision that the Chapter I prohibition has been infringed;[5] and

— conditions (a) to (d) in paragraph 9.3.2 above must be satisfied.

The grant of immunity by the Director in these circumstances is, however, **discretionary**. In order for the Director to exercise his discretion to grant immunity to the undertaking he must be satisfied that the undertaking should benefit from immunity, taking into account the stage at which the undertaking comes forward and whether or not at that stage the Director has sufficient evidence to make a decision that the Chapter I prohibition has been infringed.

9.4   Reduction in the level of financial penalties in cartel cases

9.4.1 Undertakings which provide evidence of the existence and activities of a cartel **before written notice of a proposed infringement decision is given**, but are not the first to come forward, or do not meet all the requirements under paragraphs 9.3.2 or 9.3.4 above, will be granted a **reduction** in the amount of a financial penalty which would otherwise be imposed of up to 50%, if the following conditions are met:

the undertakings must:
(a) provide the Director with all the information, documents and evidence available to them regarding the existence and activities of the cartel;
(b) maintain continuous and complete cooperation throughout the investigation; and
(c) refrain from further participation in the cartel from the time they disclose the cartel.

9.5   Procedure for requesting immunity or a reduction in the level of penalties

9.5.1 An undertaking which wishes to take advantage of the favourable treatment set out in this Part must contact the office of the Director of Cartel Investigations at the Office of Fair Trading, or his equivalent at the appropriate regulator. This step has to be taken by a person who has the power to represent the undertaking for that purpose.

9.6   Additional reduction in financial penalties

9.6.1 An undertaking cooperating with an investigation by the Director under the Act in relation to cartel activities in one market (the "first market") may also be involved in a separate cartel in another market (the "second market") which also infringes the Chapter I prohibition.

9.6.2 If the undertaking obtains total immunity from financial penalties under either paragraph 9.3.2 or 9.3.4 in relation to its activities in the second market, it will also receive a reduction in the financial penalties imposed on it which is additional to the reduction which it would have received for its cooperation in the first market alone.

9.7   Confidentiality

9.7.1 An undertaking coming forward with evidence of a cartel may be concerned about the disclosure of its identity as an undertaking which has volunteered information. The Director will therefore endeavour, where possible, to keep the identity of such undertakings confidential throughout the course of the investigation.

[3121]

PART III
OFT GUIDELINES

NOTES
1   See meaning of cartel activities as set out in note 2 to para **[3114]**.
2   By the exercise of powers under sections 26-28 of the Act.
3   See note 2 above.
4   Ie there must not be any undertaking which is benefitting from total immunity under paragraph 9.3.2
in relation to the same cartel.
5   Under Rule 14 in the Competition Act 1998 (Director's rules) Order 2000, SI 2000/293.

THE APPLICATION IN THE ENERGY SECTOR

(OFT 428, March 2001)

1   Introduction

1.1   The substantive provisions of the Competition Act 1998 (the Act) came into force on 1 March 2000. The Office of Fair Trading (OFT) and the sector regulators, including the Office of Gas and Electricity Markets (Ofgem), will enforce the Chapter I and II prohibitions using their concurrent powers. Chapter I prohibits agreements between undertakings, decisions by associations of undertakings or concerted practices which have the object or effect of preventing, restricting or distorting competition in the United Kingdom (or a part thereof) and which may affect trade within the United Kingdom (the Chapter I prohibition). Chapter II prohibits conduct by one or more undertakings which amounts to the abuse of a dominant position in a market in the United Kingdom (or a part thereof) which may affect trade within the United Kingdom (the Chapter II prohibition).

1.2   This guideline (the guideline) provides advice and information about the factors which the Gas and Electricity Markets Authority (the Authority)[1] will take into account when considering whether, and if so how, to exercise its powers under the Act.[2] This guideline is not exhaustive. It will be necessary to consider the circumstances of each case on an individual basis, with reference to the guideline.

1.3   The guideline will need to be updated from time to time to take account of relevant developments in the energy sector. It will also need to take account of any changes in the other guidelines issued by OFT and the sector regulators and the development of relevant case law under the Act and under the EC Treaty. Consultation with interested parties, including the OFT and other sector regulators, will take place before making any changes to the guideline.[3]

1.4   Part 2 of the guideline sets out the legal context within which Ofgem will be operating. It explains Ofgem's powers under the Act and the relationship of these powers with other relevant legal provisions. Part 3 provides an economic analysis of the application of the Act, with reference to the specific economic characteristics of the energy sector. The process for carrying out investigations, and in particular, how Ofgem intends to use its powers under the Act, the Gas Act 1986 (as amended) and the Electricity Act 1989 (as amended) is discussed in Part 4. Part 5 describes Ofgem's approach to considering agreements covered by the transitional arrangements in Schedule 13 to the Act.

2   Legal context

The Competition Act 1998

2.1   The Act replaces or amends legislation, including the Restrictive Trade Practices Act 1976, the Resale Prices Act 1976 and the majority of the Competition Act 1980. The Chapter I and II prohibitions of the Act are based on the provisions of Articles 81 and 82 of the EC Treaty. The Act gives the Authority and the other sector regulators new concurrent powers with the Director General of Fair Trading. These new powers include the ability to impose financial penalties of up to 10 per cent of turnover on undertakings infringing a prohibition in the Act, for every year of the infringement up to a maximum of three years.

2.2   The Act amends the Gas Act 1986 and the Electricity Act 1989, so that, while Ofgem should continue to have regard to its sectoral duties when carrying out its utility functions, Ofgem should not do so when exercising concurrent powers under the Act. Ofgem may, however, have regard to matters covered by its sectoral duties provided they are matters to which the Director General of Fair Trading could have regard in exercising his powers under the Act. The Annexe sets out Ofgem's statutory duties under the Gas Act 1986 and the Electricity Act 1989.

Community law—section 60

2.3   Section 60 of the Act sets out certain principles with a view to ensuring that the UK authorities (including the Authority) handle cases in such a way as to ensure consistency with Community law.

2.4   The Act therefore places a dual obligation on the UK authorities (including the Authority) in considering and dealing with the application of the Chapter I and Chapter II prohibitions. First, they must ensure that there is no inconsistency with either the principles laid down by the EC Treaty and the European Court or any relevant decision of the European Court. Secondly, the UK authorities (including the Authority) must have regard to any relevant decision or statement of the European Commission. The obligation to ensure consistency applies only to the extent that this is possible, having regard to any relevant differences between the provisions concerned.

2.5   The Competition Act guideline *The Major Provisions* contains further detail on how section 60 will be applied.

EC directives

2.6   There are two EC directives, which are directly related to the electricity and gas industries. There may also be other EC directives, which are relevant to the electricity and gas industries.

EC Directive concerning common rules for the internal market in electricity[4]

2.7   This directive provides a framework for EC member states to open up part of their electricity markets to competition. It addresses a number of issues, including—
— the role of public service obligations in a competitive market;
— open, non-discriminatory and transparent rules of access to electricity networks;
— transparency of vertically integrated electricity transmission or distribution companies (for example, through separate accounts); and
— the interaction of electricity networks across the EC.

EC Directive concerning the common rules for the internal market in natural gas[5]

2.8   This directive provides a framework for EC Member States to open up part of their gas markets to competition. It addresses a number of issues, including—
— the role of public service obligations in a competitive market;
— open, non-discriminatory and transparent rules of access to gas networks;
— transparency of vertically integrated gas transportation companies (for example, through separate accounts); and
— the possibility of making special provisions for undertakings adversely affected by long term take or pay contracts when competition is introduced.

2.9 Consistent with the principle of subsidiarity, each EC member state can determine how to implement these directives bearing in mind their particular circumstances.

2.10 Ofgem will take account of the provisions of the EC directives when applying the Act.

The Fair Trading Act 1973

2.11 The Fair Trading Act 1973 allows scale or complex monopolies to be examined by the United Kingdom authorities (including the Authority). A reference can be made to the Competition Commission in order to establish whether a monopoly situation exists, and if so, whether it operates, or may be expected to operate, against the public interest. Further details of the Authority's powers under the Fair Trading Act 1973 are set out in the Competition Act guideline *The Major Provisions*.

3 Economic analysis

The importance of regulating dominant incumbents[6]

3.1 The scope of monopoly and of public ownership in the electricity and gas industries (and other utility sectors) prior to privatisation gave rise to patterns of activity that were not subject to normal market disciplines. Not only was there a lack of competitive pressures on cost and price levels, but products, services, marketing methods, etc, tended to be relatively standardised, and incentives to respond to the varied requirements of different electricity and gas customers were weak. The subsequent introduction of competition to parts of these industries has enabled incumbents and new entrants alike to take advantage of the opportunities to better serve the interests of customers via a range of innovative activities, including

— lower costs and prices;
— new tariff structures;
— new products and services;
— new combinations of products and services;
— the offering of alternative billing and payment methods; and
— new marketing methods.

3.2 Such innovations are particularly important in the transition from statutory or *de facto* monopoly to effective competition in gas and electricity supply and a range of related services. In its application of the Act, and in particular the Chapter II prohibition, Ofgem will therefore be particularly vigilant in seeking to ensure that the conduct of dominant incumbent undertakings does not have an anti-competitive effect by restricting the opportunities for others to address markets in innovative ways. This could occur, for example, by preventing the introduction of new products or services or by artificially restricting the profits that could be made by new entrants from the introduction of new products and services.

Characteristics specific to the gas and electricity sector

3.3 Application of the Act to the gas and electricity industries will raise a number of challenges associated with the specific economic conditions to be found in the sectors. It may take some time for the sector specific case law to develop. The relatively advanced state of energy liberalisation in the UK compared with most other member states of the EC may, however, mean that the UK is at the forefront of the application of competition law to competitive energy markets. Where appropriate, Ofgem will ensure that it applies its powers under the Act in a manner that is consistent with relevant EC jurisprudence on corresponding questions in relation to competition, from other sectors.

3.4   Ofgem believes that there is a range of characteristics of the gas and electricity industries, which, when taken together, affect how the Act is applied to the energy sector as compared to other sectors in Great Britain. The relevant factors include—

— the importance of 'unbundling', business separation, divestment and structural change more generally in the transition from monopoly to competition across a range of activities;

— the existence of monopoly providers of gas transportation, and electricity transmission and distribution networks, which are unlikely to be replicated due to the cost conditions faced by any undertaking seeking to duplicate such networks (including the costs arising from planning and environmental constraints);

— the extent of incumbent market power in parts of the gas and electricity industries, including supply, metering, meter reading, connections and storage markets;

— the existence of price controls for gas transportation and electricity transmission and distribution, and in some other parts of the industries where market power is particularly strong;

— the limited storability of electricity, and to some extent gas, which limits the opportunities to substitute between time periods on either the supply side or the demand side;

— the low elasticity of demand for electricity and gas, particularly over short periods; the relative inelasticity of supply at some periods, in particular in electricity;

— the complexity of the rules for system balancing in electricity;[7]

— the economic linkages between different parts of the networks, which imply that the existence of market power in one set of activities or markets can have substantial effects on other (related) activities or markets; and

— the significance and complexity of the various codes and agreements, which govern connection to and use of electricity and gas systems, which are required to ensure the safe, secure and effective operation of those systems, for example, the Master Connection Use of System Agreement for electricity transmission and the Network Codes for gas transportation and shipping.

3.5   All of these factors may not be relevant for every case that Ofgem considers under the Act. For example, the limited storability of electricity, the low elasticity of demand for electricity, particularly over short periods, the relative inelasticity of supply for electricity at some periods and the complexity of the system balancing rules for determining wholesale electricity prices are likely to be factors that are highly relevant to an investigation of electricity generation activities. A different mix of considerations would apply in cases focused on the supply of gas to domestic customers.

3.6   Ofgem will not adopt approaches to applying the Act that are different from those set out in other Competition Act guidelines. The particular characteristics of the energy sector identified above, will, however, affect the emphasis that is placed on, and the weight given to, particular aspects of the analysis set out in other guidelines.

3.7   Ofgem considers that, in enforcing the Act, the specific economic conditions of the energy sector (including the relatively recent introduction of competition into many of the markets) will give rise to a particular emphasis on certain issues connected with—

— pre-emptive behaviour by dominant incumbents;

— the time dimension of dominance;

— the effects of agreements covering the use of networks; and

— the effects of conduct in relation to one activity or market on other related activities or markets.

3.8 These economic conditions and issues will affect at least six main aspects of the application of the Act—
—   market definition;
—   the assessment of market power,[8] and in particular, the assessment of dominance, including joint dominance;
—   the assessment as to whether an abuse of a dominant position has occurred;
—   the assessment of whether a dominant incumbent is engaging in pre-emptive behaviour;
—   the assessment of agreements between undertakings, decisions by associations of undertakings and concerted practices under the Chapter I prohibition; and
—   the exclusion from the Act's prohibitions, for services of general economic interest, under Paragraph 4 of Schedule 3 to the Act.

3.9 The remainder of this part of the guideline explains how Ofgem intends to approach these six issues when applying the Act to the specific combination of circumstances in the gas and electricity industries, identified above.

Market definition

3.10 In considering whether one of the prohibitions of the Act has been infringed it is necessary to define a relevant market or markets, since European competition law has required this in similar cases. A market definition normally contains two dimensions, a product and a geographic area.

Duration

3.11 In defining markets, one of the standard procedures to identify the extent of substitutability between products is to ask whether prices could profitably be sustained at levels significantly above competitive levels for a non-transitory period. As explained in the Competition Act guideline *Market Definition*, 'non-transitory' has generally been interpreted as a duration of a year, but could be shorter where appropriate.

3.12 Inelastic supply and demand, coupled with variations in levels of supply and demand, imply that both electricity and gas wholesale prices can be relatively volatile. Such volatility does not in itself raise problems. However, it is also the case that the combination of inelastic supply and demand can provide significantly enhanced opportunities for the exploitation of market power, which may infringe the prohibitions of the Act. This is particularly significant since limited storability means that one of the standard mitigating constraints on the abuse of very short-term market power—the ability of firms and their customers to substitute transactions in one time period with transactions in another time period—is largely absent. The absence of substitutability constraints means that, in certain circumstances, the appropriate definition of the market may be limited to a shorter duration than has generally been used for analysis in many other industries.

Combined effect of duration and magnitude

3.13 The Competition Act guideline *Market Definition* refers to tests based on hypothetical price increases of 5-10 per cent. In electricity and gas markets the price 'spikes' that occur can be many times higher than these benchmark numbers, irrespective of their causes in particular instances (for example, demand and supply fluctuations or the exploitation of market power). Very high wholesale prices, even if they hold for only short durations, can have significant effects on customers and, since customers may include other rival companies, on future competition. As discussed in the Competition Act guideline *Market Definition*, the consideration of hypothetical price increases where a dominant firm is present may be particularly difficult because of the problems of identifying clear competitive benchmarks.

Hence, as explained in that guideline, the process of defining a market cannot be carried out in isolation, but needs to be considered alongside other evidence on market power and the undertaking's conduct.

3.14 For reasons that are also explained in that guideline, Ofgem considers that, in defining markets, it is appropriate to take account of the combined effects both of the magnitude of potential deviations of prices from competitive levels and, simultaneously, of the likely duration for which such deviations can be sustained. Effects on customers and on competition of similar magnitudes can be caused either by large price increases that can be sustained only for a short period or small price increases that can be sustained for a long period. It is appropriate, given the emphasis placed by the Act on economic effects, that market assessments reflect this fact in the specific circumstances of gas and electricity markets.

Sequencing in the analysis

3.15 At an early stage of any investigation under the Act, and on the basis of the information then available, Ofgem will arrive at a preliminary view of the scope of the economic issues involved and of the analysis that will need to be done. It will then proceed to more detailed consideration of the various conditions of demand and supply that are relevant both to assessing competitive pressures on the undertaking(s) concerned and to evaluating the effects of the relevant conduct, including the appreciability of those effects. In the course of the investigation, as the detailed analysis proceeds, it may be appropriate to revisit the question of the scope of the economic issues involved.

3.16 Among the factors that will be considered during the investigation will be the demand and supply side substitution possibilities that are relevant in defining markets. Since these substitution possibilities are also directly relevant to the analysis of market power, market definition and the assessment of dominance will be overlapping exercises in Chapter II cases. New information obtained during the investigation about, say, demand conditions, might potentially affect the final conclusions reached in either or both of these exercises, for example.

3.17 Evaluation of the economic effects of the conduct of concern will also be undertaken as the investigation proceeds. In Chapter II cases, however, only after the market definition and assessment of dominance exercises have been completed, and only if the undertaking or undertakings has or have been found to be dominant, will conclusions be reached on whether or not the prohibition has been breached, that is, whether a dominant position has been abused.

Related markets

3.18 It is recognised in competition law that in many situations there may not be a single relevant market. An important class of cases concerns behaviour in one relevant market or market segment that may have anti-competitive effects in other related markets or market segments.[9] Such cases are likely to be particularly important in gas and electricity markets, bearing in mind the economic linkages between the different activities in the sectors. For example, a particular entry point on a transportation network may initially be defined as a relevant market because customers using that particular entry point are likely to have limited substitution possibilities. The effects of conduct at that entry point, however, are likely to have economic effects on other parts of the network. In such circumstances it is appropriate that any market definition exercise does not unduly restrict the scope of an investigation and that it takes fully into account all of the relevant economic effects.

3.19 As explained in the Competition Act guideline *The Assessment of Individual Agreements and Conduct*, there will also be cases where undertakings may be able to leverage market power in a relevant market or markets to abuse their dominance in another market. Again, such cases are likely to be particularly important in gas and electricity markets. The incumbent gas and electricity suppliers are now active in the supply of other products, for example.

3.20 Ofgem will therefore have regard to the actual or potential effects of a firm's conduct on different activities, in deciding the scope of an investigation and in defining relevant markets. Often the behaviour of competitors will provide practical examples of the relevant activities to consider in an investigation.[10]

The assessment of market power, and in particular, the assessment of dominance, including joint dominance

3.21 Dominance has been defined by the European Court as "a position of economic strength enjoyed by an undertaking which enables it to prevent effective competition being maintained on the relevant market by affording it the power to behave to an appreciable extent independently of its competitors, customers and ultimately of consumers".[11] Dominance may involve more than one undertaking ('joint dominance'). One important indicator of dominance on the supply side is to consider whether a firm or firms has or have the ability persistently to raise prices above competitive levels. In cases involving a potentially dominant buyer, the test is reversed by considering whether a firm or firms has or have the ability persistently to reduce prices below competitive levels.

3.22 When considering whether undertakings can act to an appreciable extent independently of their customers and competitors, Ofgem will look at a range of factors including—

— customers' behaviour and options (for example, awareness of competition, the extent to which alternative providers are chosen, the extent to which substitutes are available);
— competitors' behaviour and capacities (for example, their range of offers, their ability to increase output within the relevant time period);
— market operation (for example, the extent of barriers to entry and exit); and
— market share.[12]

3.23 Consistent with the Competition Act guideline *Assessment of Market Power*, Ofgem considers that market share on its own will only be an indicator of dominance, but would not be considered sufficient evidence on its own to determine whether an undertaking or group of undertakings is or are dominant, not least because the economic implications of any market share are likely to be heavily conditioned by a range of other relevant factors, including the magnitudes of demand and supply elasticities. In general, Ofgem will seek, wherever possible, to assess both substitution possibilities and actual behaviour directly, rather than rely on proxies, such as market share.

3.24 In developing the case law on dominance, the European Court and the European Commission have tended to assume that a dominant firm will be the largest firm (or group of firms) operating in a particular sector.[13] In the Great Britain gas and electricity sectors, due to the particular economic characteristics to be found there and due to some of the price setting rules, there are circumstances where firms may have the ability substantially and persistently to influence prices, and therefore to act independently of customers and competitors, even though they are not the largest firm in the market and even though their market shares fall below normal thresholds for considering dominance. This may particularly apply to markets for wholesale gas and electricity and to markets for capacity on gas and electricity networks.

The assessment of whether an abuse of a dominant position has occurred

3.25 It is the abuse of, not the existence of, a dominant position that is prohibited by the Act. Therefore, where an abuse of a dominant position is alleged or suspected and it is found that an enterprise or group of enterprises has the ability to act, to an appreciable extent, independently of its customers and competitors (as manifested, for example, by an ability to raise prices above competitive levels to an extent that can cause significant harm), Ofgem will investigate further, to determine whether or not any infringement has occurred. Such an investigation will focus on the commercial conduct of the relevant enterprise(s) and on the effects of that conduct, or agreements entered into by undertakings, on customers and on competition. The Competition Act guideline *The Chapter II Prohibition*, discusses the types of conduct that may breach the prohibition. Ofgem's approach to considering predatory pricing, which is one possible infringement, is set out below.

3.26 As noted earlier, unlike many sectors in the UK, the gas and electricity sectors are characterised by the widespread presence of historic incumbent dominance or market power, which previously was promoted as a matter of public policy, but is now, in many cases, being eroded through the development of competition. Ofgem, will therefore, pay particular attention to the possibility of pre-emptive[14] behaviour by incumbents, designed adversely to affect the development of competition in, for example, the relatively newly opened domestic gas and electricity markets. Pre-emptive behaviour may also occur through actions in related markets, for example, electricity distributors or gas transporters may use their dominance in these markets to prevent, restrict or distort competition in the provision of metering, meter reading, connections or storage services. This again highlights the importance of considering the effect of actions across all the potentially affected activities.

The assessment of whether a dominant incumbent is engaging in pre-emptive behaviour

3.27 The incumbent suppliers of gas and electricity have reacted to the recent introduction of competition by introducing a range of initiatives, including new payment methods, the offering of 'dual fuel' supply and the linking of other products to the supply of gas and electricity. Many of these initiatives have improved customers' choice. However, it is important for Ofgem to consider whether these initiatives are merely a response to competition that could be expected in any industry and which will benefit customers, or pre-emptive behaviour designed to prevent competition developing or continuing to develop, and to prevent new entrants establishing themselves in the market. It is necessary to consider incumbents' behaviour in each individual case, bearing in mind the circumstances of the initiative.

3.28 One example of such pre-emptive behaviour is predatory pricing. Ofgem will follow the approach set out in the Competition Act guideline *Assessment of Individual Agreements and Conduct*, when assessing whether a dominant undertaking is engaging in predatory pricing. That guideline explains that in considering predatory behaviour, three factors will be considered—

— the intentions of the undertaking alleged to be engaging in predatory pricing;
— the feasibility of the undertaking recovering the losses it incurs when engaging in predatory pricing; and
— the level of the undertaking's prices relative to its costs.

3.29 Bearing in mind the particular concerns about pre-emptive behaviour in the gas and electricity industries, Ofgem considers that it will be appropriate in considering whether an undertaking is engaging in predatory pricing, to apply a relatively strict cost-based test. Ofgem will follow the approach set out in the Competition Act guideline *Assessment of Individual Agreements and Conduct*, paying particular attention to whether undertakings are covering their avoidable costs, which include elements of costs that are often described as fixed costs that would not be included in a variable cost test.

The assessment of agreements between undertakings, decisions by associations of undertakings and concerted practices under the Chapter I prohibition

3.30 Chapter I of the Act prohibits those agreements between undertakings, decisions by associations of undertakings, and concerted practices which may affect trade within the United Kingdom and which prevent, restrict or distort competition, or are intended to do so. The Act includes a list of illustrative examples of agreements, decisions or practices, which—

— directly or indirectly fix purchase or selling prices or any other trading conditions;

— limit or control production, markets, technical development or investment;

— share markets or sources of supply;

— apply dissimilar conditions to equivalent transactions with other trading parties, thereby placing them at a competitive disadvantage;

— make the conclusion of contracts subject to acceptance by the other parties of supplementary obligations, which, by their nature or according to commercial usage, have no connection with the subject of such contracts.

3.31 There are a number of problems that arise in gas and electricity markets as a result of the statutory requirements for arrangements to ensure safe, secure and efficient operation of gas and electricity networks that are used by many market participants. These arrangements may involve restrictions on competition to achieve their objectives in relation to safety, security and efficiency.

3.32 As a result of their contribution to safety, security and efficiency, such agreements may qualify for exemption from the Chapter I prohibition. The criteria for exemption are set out in section 9 of the Act. All of these must be satisfied. The agreement must not impose on the parties restrictions which are not indispensable to achieving the desired effects (the indispensability test). More specifically, since a variety of different types of agreement may serve to achieve safety, security and efficiency objectives, and since different agreements may have different implications for competition, simply demonstrating that a particular agreement will achieve the stated objectives will be insufficient to warrant exemption. The agreement should constitute the least restrictive means of achieving its aims.

3.33 Ofgem can consider agreements involving 'dominant' undertakings under the Chapter II prohibition, subject to any exclusions that may apply.

3.34 Under section 5 of the Act, the Authority can cancel an individual exemption, or vary or remove any condition or obligation of an individual exemption, or impose additional conditions or obligations of an individual exemption if—[15]

— the Authority has reasonable grounds for believing that there has been a material change in circumstances since the individual exemption was granted; or

— the Authority has a reasonable suspicion that the information on which the decision to grant an individual exemption was made, was incomplete, false or misleading in a material particular.

The exclusion from the Act's prohibitions for services of general economic interest, under paragraph 4 of Schedule 3 to the Act

3.35 Neither the Chapter I prohibition nor the Chapter II prohibition of the Act applies to an undertaking entrusted with the operation of *services of general economic interest* or having the character of a revenue-producing monopoly in so far as the prohibition would obstruct the performance, in law or in fact, of the particular tasks assigned to that undertaking. Ofgem will therefore be required to assess whether or not, in a particular case, this exclusion is applicable.

3.36 As explained in the Competition Act guideline *Services of General Economic Interest*, the exclusion's application is particularly narrow, with undertakings seeking to benefit from the exclusion having to prove that they meet all the requirements of the exclusion. Amongst other requirements, the Authority will only consider undertakings that are able to show that they have been 'entrusted' with the operation of a service of general economic interest. The undertaking must also show that the operation of the service or the revenue-producing monopoly, and the resulting restriction on competition, is the least restrictive means for the undertaking to meet its obligations.

4 Process for investigation

Sector specific regulation

4.1 Unlike most sectors covered by the Act, undertakings' behaviour in the gas and electricity markets, including that of dominant companies, is regulated by sector specific Acts of Parliament that have created a licensing regime, as explained in Appendix 1. Among other things, these Acts and the licences regulate and attempt to prevent various types of anti-competitive behaviour that may have detrimental effects on gas and electricity customers. This includes restrictions on some undertakings' level and structure of charges and the prevention of unduly discriminatory behaviour by network operators and dominant suppliers. The Gas Act 1986 and the Electricity Act 1989 set out the factors the Authority should consider when deciding whether to use its powers under these Acts to address anti-competitive behaviour. In particular, the Authority may not take enforcement action under the sector specific Acts if it is satisfied that it would be more appropriate to address the issue under the Act.

4.2 Ofgem believes that the provisions of the sector specific forms of regulation are generally consistent with the Act and Ofgem will continue to use them to fulfil its statutory duties and obligations under the Gas Act 1986 and Electricity Act 1989. When applying the Act, the Authority can only take account of its duties under the Gas Act 1986 and the Electricity Act 1989 to the extent that they are factors of which the Director General of Fair Trading could take account when applying the Act.

4.3 The following part of this guideline is about how Ofgem will distinguish between complaints that are trivial and non-trivial in nature. It also explains how the Authority intends to use its powers under the Gas Act 1986, the Electricity Act 1989, the Fair Trading Act 1973 and the Act to ensure that any anti-competitive behaviour is most effectively addressed without undertakings facing 'double jeopardy'.[16]

Guidance for the gas and electricity sectors trivial or non-trivial complaints

4.4 Once it has been decided that Ofgem is responsible for a case,[17] Ofgem will attempt as quickly as possible to determine whether the complaint is trivial or non-trivial in nature. As part of this process Ofgem will consider whether the requirements of section 25 of the Act, that is, that there are reasonable grounds for suspecting that one of the prohibitions has been infringed, has been met and the potential economic effect of the agreement or conduct in the particular case. To the extent that it is relevant, Ofgem will use its existing knowledge of the issues to determine the nature of the complaint. If there is a doubt about whether the complaint is trivial or non-trivial that cannot be resolved quickly by Ofgem, it may seek information from undertakings to determine whether to commence an investigation.

Information gathering

4.5 When investigating potential infringements under the Act, the Gas Act 1986, the Electricity Act 1989 or issues under the Fair Trading Act 1973, Ofgem may need to seek information from various undertakings. When requesting information,

Ofgem will specify the potential infringement it is investigating and the power(s) it may use to address the suspected infringement. Where more than one of the powers explained in part 2 of this guideline (competition law powers) or Appendix 1 (sector specific powers) are considered to be potentially appropriate, it is likely that Ofgem will specify all the relevant powers. It may not be possible for Ofgem to decide which specific power(s) are likely to be the most appropriate to address the suspected infringement at the commencement of an investigation.

4.6 If it becomes clear to Ofgem when conducting its investigation that a particular power is no longer appropriate to the particular case, it will cease to request information under the respective power and inform the undertaking concerned. Also, where possible, Ofgem will inform an undertaking if a new infringement is suspected after the investigation has commenced, which may affect the powers Ofgem considers could be appropriate to address the suspected infringement(s).

4.7 Where information has been gathered using powers under one of the Acts described in part 2 (competition law powers) or Appendix 1 (sector specific powers), Ofgem may use information gathered to investigate other matters under the Act, the Gas Act 1986, the Electricity Act 1989 or the Fair Trading Act 1973, subject to and in accordance with the provisions of these various Acts.

Consultation

4.8 Section 31 of the Act requires the Authority, if it proposes to make a decision that one of the prohibitions has been infringed, to give written notice to the person or persons likely to be affected by the proposed decision and to give that person or persons an opportunity to make representations. In any event, Ofgem would normally expect to consult affected parties on decisions following non-trivial complaints, own initiative investigations or notifications of agreements.

Enforcement action and the imposition of penalties

4.9 As early as possible in the course of an investigation where infringements of more than one provision are under consideration, Ofgem will determine the most appropriate power to remedy the anti-competitive behaviour identified. Section 28 of the Gas Act 1986 and section 25 of the Electricity Act 1989 require the Authority not to make a provisional or final order or confirm a provisional order under either sector specific Act, if it is satisfied that the Act is the most appropriate way of proceeding to address the issue. Section 30A(2) of the Gas Act 1986 and section 27A(2) of the Electricity Act 1989 prevent the Authority levying a financial penalty for a matter for which a penalty under the Act has already been levied.

4.10 The Authority is required to have regard to the Director General of Fair Trading's guidance on the appropriate level of a penalty, prepared under section 38 of the Act, when setting a penalty, after an undertaking has been found to have infringed the Act. When setting penalties under the Act, the Authority will not have the ability to take into account its duty under the Gas Act 1986 and the Electricity Act 1989 to have regard to the ability of licensees to finance their activities, to the extent that this is not a factor to which the Director General of Fair Trading could have regard when applying the Act.

4.11 When publishing any decisions following investigations, Ofgem will have regard to the need to maintain propriety with regard to market sensitive information when deciding on the timing of announcements, as is currently the case for some announcements, for example, price control proposals. This is in accordance with Ofgem's voluntary agreement with the London Stock Exchange.[18]

Compliance

4.12 When setting penalties, in accordance with the Director General of Fair Trading's guidance, Ofgem will consider the extent to which the undertaking has taken reasonable steps, bearing in mind its resources, to put in place programmes to ensure compliance with the requirements of the Act. The OFT has produced a range of material to assist companies in developing compliance programmes.[19]

4.13 Ofgem expects companies within the gas and electricity sectors to implement corporate compliance programmes if they do not already have them. Ofgem expects that such programmes will minimise the risk of infringing the prohibitions by systematically ensuring that all relevant employees are sufficiently knowledgeable about the provisions of the law, and that they will put that knowledge to good effect.

4.14 The details of compliance programmes are likely to vary between companies, particularly with regard to their resources. A minimum programme might be expected to comprise at least four elements, with the depth with which each element is covered being dependent on a company's resources. The four elements are described below—

— support and personal commitment from senior management, both visible and continuous, will be essential to ensure that compliance is treated with the importance it deserves and to ensure acceptance by other employees who will be more receptive to an initiative which is seen to be applied equally to senior managers;

— appropriate compliance policy and procedures will include a clear policy commitment to comply with the legislation by not engaging in anti-competitive behaviour or condoning such behaviour in other parties. This policy could feed through into personal development performance objectives, contracts and disciplinary arrangements. Procedures could include a framework within which employees can check whether or not a particular contract or deal is in breach of the law. This might involve a nominated expert or compliance officer. An effective mechanism to communicate the policy and procedures supported by a review process is a necessity, part of which is likely to be a manual or handbook provided to all relevant staff;

— training will form an essential aspect of any compliance programme. It should be designed to ensure that all relevant staff are given proper training on both the law and the company policy and procedures. It will not be sufficient to limit training to the implementation phase. It must be offered on a regular basis to reinforce and update the message. Such training is likely to be an essential element of any induction programme for new staff; and

— evaluation of the effectiveness of the overall compliance programme is the final essential ingredient. This might include informal feedback at an individual level and perhaps as part of individual performance appraisal. At a broader level formal audits, both with and without warning, could be undertaken. A transparent approach to the correction of any revealed infringements would serve as a constant reminder to employees that their business dealings are subject to review and will thereby deter complacency.

Transitional arrangements

5.1 Provisions for the transition from existing competition law to the Act are set out in Schedule 13 to the Act. Those provisions are described further in the Competition Act guideline *Transitional Arrangements*. Certain provisions in Schedule 13 to the Act relate particularly to provisions of the Gas Act 1986 or the Electricity Act 1989. There are no transitional periods available in respect of the Chapter II prohibition, which applies to the behaviour of dominant undertakings immediately from 1 March 2000.

PART III
OFT GUIDELINES

Agreements benefiting from the transitional periods

5.2 Schedule 13 to the Act provides for transitional periods for particular agreements in the electricity and gas industries. In summary, the existing arrangements under the Restrictive Trade Practices Act will be retained for a further five years from the starting date, in that agreements currently exempt from the application of that Act and similar future agreements will benefit from transitional periods excluding them from the Chapter 1 prohibition during that period.

5.3 There are three categories of agreement that will benefit from the transitional periods in the gas and electricity industries—

— agreements to which, immediately before 1 March 2000, the Restrictive Trade Practices Act does not apply by virtue of section 100 of the Electricity Act 1989 or section 62 of the Gas Act 1986 respectively, or orders made thereunder. These agreements will receive a five year transitional period from 1 March 2000;

— agreements made during the five year period beginning on 1 March 2000 which are of a type such that, even if the Restrictive Trade Practices Act had not been repealed, it would not have applied to them because they would have been like those agreements in the category above, and agreements, whether made before or after the starting date, that are varied to become of that type in the five year period. These will receive a transitional period applying from the date that the agreement or variation is made and for the remaining part of the five year period; and

— agreements of a description specified in a transitional order by the Secretary of State. These will receive a transitional period beginning at such time as is specified in the order and, again, applying for the remaining part of the five year period beginning on 1 March 2000.

5.4 The benefit of these transitional periods will be lost if the agreement is varied in such a way that it ceases to be one to which the Restrictive Trade Practices Act would not have applied or one to which a transitional order applies.

5.5 The question of whether or not the Restrictive Trade Practices Act does or does not apply to an agreement requires, in some instances, an assessment by the Authority of the extent to which an agreement is likely to have a significant effect in preventing, restricting or distorting competition.[20] In making such assessments during the transitional period the Authority will, to the extent appropriate, take into account matters addressed in this guideline, and particularly, the issues raised in paragraphs 3.30–3.34 above.

Extending or terminating the transitional period

5.6 The Authority may extend for up to six months the transitional period during which the Chapter I prohibition will not apply to an agreement. The Authority may do so either on application by one of the parties to the agreement or under the Authority's own initiative. More details of the procedures in relation to the extension of transitional periods are given in the Competition Act guideline *Transitional Arrangements*.

5.7 It is unlikely that an agreement, which the Authority considers would infringe the Chapter I prohibition of the Act, would be granted an extension unless there are good reasons why an extension is required—for example, the agreement is being re-negotiated or is due to expire shortly after the end of the unextended transitional period, or the parties have a legitimate need for more time to prepare a notification. In deciding whether to extend the transitional period the Authority will apply the approach described above and set out in the Competition Act guideline *Transitional Arrangements* and the issues discussed in paragraphs 3.30–3.34 above.

5.8　The Authority may by direction terminate the transitional period in relation to any agreement if either—

— the Authority has required any party to that agreement to give it such information about that agreement as it may require and, at the end of the period specified in 'the Director General of Fair Trading's Procedural Rules'[21] for providing such information, any party has failed, without reasonable excuse, to do so; or

— if the Authority considers:

— that the agreement would, but for the transitional period, infringe the Chapter I prohibition; and

— that the Authority would not be likely to grant the agreement an unconditional individual exemption.

5.9　Any direction terminating a transitional period is subject to revocation, before it takes effect, either by the Authority or the Secretary of State.

ANNEXE: ENERGY SECTOR REGULATORY LAW

1　The Utilities Act 2000 establishes a new corporate body, the Gas and Electricity Markets Authority (the Authority), which assumes the responsibilities previously held by the Director General of Gas Supply and the Director General of Electricity Supply. The Authority is also responsible for carrying out other functions established by the Utilities Act. This annexe sets out the Authority's duties and powers under the Gas Act 1986 (as amended) and the Electricity Act 1989 (as amended).

Electricity Act 1989 (as amended)

2　The general duties of the Authority are set out in section 3 of the Electricity Act 1989. The Authority's functions are set out in sections 1 and 47 to 50 of the Electricity Act 1989. The principle objective of the Authority in carrying out its functions is to protect the interests of consumers, both present and future, in relation to electricity conveyed by distribution systems, wherever appropriate by promoting effective competition, having regard to the need to secure that all reasonable demands for electricity are met and the need to secure that licence holders are able to finance the activities which are subject to obligations under the Electricity Act 1989. In performing these duties the Authority should have regard to the interests of, amongst others, individuals who are disabled or chronically sick, of pensionable age, of low income and those living in rural areas.

3　The Authority has the power to obtain information from licensees and others in relation to potential breaches of licence, under section 28 of the Electricity Act 1989. However, the Authority cannot require information to be produced, which the holder of that information would not be required to produce in civil proceedings in court. A person who refuses to comply with a notice requiring information to be furnished to the Authority is liable on conviction to face a fine and a court order to provide the information.

4　If the Authority is satisfied that a licence holder is contravening or has contravened a condition or requirement, or has failed or is failing to achieve any standard of performance, the Authority can impose a penalty of not more than 10% of the licence holders' turnover.

The Gas Act 1986 (as amended)

5　The general duties of the Authority are set out in sections 4 and 4A of the Gas Act 1986. The principal objective of the Authority in carrying out its function is to protect the interests of consumers, both present and future, in relation to gas conveyed through pipes, wherever appropriate by promoting effective competition, having regard to the need to ensure that all reasonable demands for gas are met and the need to secure that licence holders are able to finance their activities which are subject to obligations under the Gas Act 1986. In performing these duties, the Authority should have regard to the interests of, amongst others, individuals who are disabled or chronically sick, of pensionable age, of low income and those living in rural areas.

6　The Authority has the power to obtain information in relation to potential breaches of licence under section 38 of the Gas Act 1986. However, the Authority cannot require information to be produced, which the holder of the information would not be required to produce in civil proceedings in court. A person who refuses to comply with a notice requiring information to be furnished to the Authority is liable on conviction to face a fine and a court order to provide the information.

7 If the Authority is satisfied that a licence holder is contravening or has contravened a condition or requirement, or has failed or is failing to achieve any standard of performance, the Authority can impose a penalty of not more than 10% of licence holders' turnover.

The Electricity Act 1989 licensing regime

8 Section 6 of the Electricity Act 1989 allows the Authority to grant licences for transmission, generation, supply and distribution activities. One person cannot hold both a supply and a distribution licence. These licences impose a number of obligations on their holders.

9 Where the Authority is satisfied that a licensee is contravening, or is likely to contravene, a licence condition, the Electricity Act 1989 requires the Authority (except in certain specified circumstances) to issue an enforcement order against the licensee. Failure to comply with the order can expose the licensee to action (including a claim for damages) by any person who suffers loss or damage as a result of that failure.

10 The Electricity Act 1989 empowers the Authority to modify the conditions of a licence with the licensee's consent (and after consultation). In the case of modifications to standard conditions, the Authority can modify the standard condition with licence holders' consent (and after consultation) providing that the Authority has received no objection from the Secretary of State. If one or more licence holder objects to the amendment, the Authority may only make the amendment if the proportion of those who object is less than a percentage as is prescribed, unless the Authority is satisfied that the amendment of the standard condition would reduce the burden of the standard condition without removing any necessary protection, or that the modification is such that no holder of a licence of the type in question would be unduly disadvantaged in competing with other holders of such licences. The Authority may also refer to the Competition Commission questions as to whether any matters relating to a licence operate, or may be expected to operate, against the public interest. In certain circumstances the Authority may, following a report from the Competition Commission, modify that licence.

11 The transmission, generation and supply licences include conditions requiring the licensees to provide information requested by the Authority to fulfil its duties under the Electricity Act 1989 and to enforce the requirements of the licences.

The Gas Act 1986 licensing regime

12 The Gas Act 1986 provides for the licensing of public gas transporters, shippers and suppliers of gas. These licences impose a number of obligations on their holders.

13 Where the Authority is satisfied that a licensee is contravening, or is likely to contravene, a licence condition, the Gas Act 1986 requires the Authority (except in certain specified circumstances) to issue an enforcement order against the licensee. An enforcement order may include a requirement for the licensee to pay a monetary penalty of an appropriate amount. Failure to comply with the order can expose the licensee to action (including a claim for damages) by any person who suffers loss or damage as a result of that failure.

14 The Authority can modify any standard condition with licence holders' consent (and after consultation) providing that the Authority has received no objection from the Secretary of State. If one or more licence holder objects to the amendment, the Authority may only make the amendment if the proportion of those who object is less than a percentage as may be prescribed, unless the Authority is satisfied that the amendment of the standard condition would reduce the burden of the standard condition without removing any necessary protection, or that the modification is such that no holder of a licence of the type in question would be unduly disadvantaged in competing with other holders of such licences. The Authority may also refer to the Competition Commission questions as to whether any matters relating to a licence operate, or may be expected to operate, against the public interest. In certain circumstances the Authority may, following a report from the Competition Commission, modify that licence.

15 The transportation, shipping and supply licences include conditions requiring the licensees to provide information requested by the Authority to fulfil its duties under the Gas Act 1986 and to enforce the requirements of the licences.

NOTES

[1]   The functions of the Director General of Gas Supply and the Director General of Electricity Supply were transferred to the Gas and Electricity Markets Authority on 20 December 2000 under section 3 of the Utilities Act 2000. Ofgem is the office of the Authority. The terms Ofgem and the Authority are used interchangeably in this guideline.

[2]   This guideline should be read in conjunction with the guidelines listed [at page 318].

[3]   The latest version of the guideline will be kept in the Ofgem library and will be available on Ofgem's website at www.ofgem.gov.uk and the OFT's website at www.oft.gov.uk.

[4]   Directive 96/92/EC of the European Parliament and the Council of 19 December 1996 concerning common rules for the internal market in electricity.

[5]   Directive 98/30/EC of the European Parliament and the Council of 22 June 1998 concerning common rules for the internal market in natural gas.

[6]   Ofgem notes that incumbents may not necessarily be dominant as competition develops and new entrants erode their dominance. New entrants may develop a position of dominance over time.

[7]   The system balancing mechanism sets the cash out price paid by suppliers whose demand and supply positions are out of balance.

[8]   The concept of market power is not part of the statutory framework of the act, but it is a useful tool in assessing potentially anti-competitive behaviour.

[9]   Ofgas' investigation in 1997 into BGT's Goldfish credit card joint venture (*'Goldfish: British Gas Trading's credit card joint venture, A Decision Document'*, Ofgas, October 1997) is an example of a case where the effect of behaviour by an undertaking with market power in one market (gas supply) on another (financial services) has been considered. Ofgas concluded that, while the 'Goldfish' credit card constituted a discount on BGT's gas bills, which might persuade customers to stay with BGT, it was a strategy that rivals could in principle, and if they so wished, also choose to adopt. Ofgas concluded that the ability to redeem points accrued against a final BGT gas bill was an important safeguard against a potential tie-in of the customer, and therefore required BGT to explain this facility on its gas bills and marketing literature.

[10]   Ofgas' investigation into the market for storage and related services in 1998 (*'Review of the supply of gas storage and related services, The Director General's final proposals'*, Ofgas, September 1999), showed the importance of considering all relevant markets when assessing market power. The investigation concluded that the conduct of BG plc, including its pricing, was affected by and could affect the related markets for spot and peak gas ('swing') and interruptible supply contracts.

[11]   Case 27/76 *United Brands v EC Commission* [1978] ECR 207, [1978] 1 CMLR 429.

[12]   In case 85/76 *Hoffman-La Roche & Co AG v Commission* [1979] ECR 461, [1979] 3 CMLR 211, and a number of other cases, the Court and the Commission have considered other factors as well as market share when determining dominance, including competitors' positions; barriers to entry; the resources, size and commercial superiority of the undertaking; and technical superiority and the possession of know-how and intellectual property.

[13]   Joint dominance may not involve the largest firm in a market.

[14]   'Pre-emptive behaviour' describes abuses by dominant incumbents in markets that are being opened to competition or are relatively newly opened to competition, which are designed to adversely affect the development of competition.

[15]   The provisions for exclusions for agreements that were covered or would be covered by the RTPA within the gas and electricity industries are discussed in Part 5.

[16]   'Double jeopardy' would occur where an undertaking faced the possibility of being subject to a penalty more than once for the same infringement.

[17]   See the Competition Act guideline *Concurrent Application to Regulated Industries*.

[18]   The voluntary agreement was published by the London Stock Exchange on 2 January 1996.

[19]   These can be obtained directly from the OFT.

[20]   For example, The Restrictive Trade Practices (Gas Conveyance and Storage) Order 1996, SI 1996/385 or the Electricity (Restrictive Trade Practices Act 1976) (Exemption) Order 1993, SI 1993/912.

[21]   The Competition Act 1998 (Director's rules) Order 2000 (SI 2000/293).

PART III
OFT GUIDELINES

GUIDANCE NOTES ON COMPLETING FORM N

(OFT 431, March 2000)

INTRODUCTION

These guidance notes are intended to assist you if you are considering notifying an agreement or conduct to the Director[1] and applying to him for guidance or a decision in relation to either the Chapter I prohibition (under section 13 or 14) or the Chapter II prohibition (under section 21 or 22) of the Competition Act 1998 (the "Act"). They are not part of Form N.

These guidance notes set out—
— general information that should be considered before submitting Form N;[2] and
— guidance on the specific information required by Form N.

NOTES
　[1]　The Act is applied and enforced by the Director General of Fair Trading and, in relation to the regulated utility sectors, concurrently with the regulators for telecommunications, gas, electricity, water and sewerage and railway services (under schedule 10 to the Competition Act). References throughout to the 'Director' should be taken to include the regulators in relation to their respective sectors. Note, however, that all notifications should be made to the Director General of Fair Trading. These will then be passed on to the appropriate regulator(s) with concurrent jurisdiction.
　[2]　See the section on Form N below for details on how to obtain a copy of Form N.

GENERAL INFORMATION

Purpose of the application

Sections 2 and 18 of the Act introduce two prohibitions: (i) of agreements (whether written or not) between undertakings that have the object or effect of preventing, restricting or distorting competition in the United Kingdom or a part thereof and which may affect trade within the United Kingdom ("the Chapter I prohibition"); and (ii) of conduct by one or more undertakings which amounts to the abuse of a dominant position in a market in the United Kingdom if it may affect trade within the United Kingdom or a part thereof ("the Chapter II prohibition").

Undertakings are not required to apply to the Director for guidance or a decision. However, parties to an agreement or conduct who have serious concerns about their position under the Act may notify their agreement or conduct to the Director and apply to him for:
— **guidance** as to whether or not, in his view:
　　the agreement is likely to infringe the Chapter I prohibition and, if so, whether the agreement is likely to be exempt (under a block exemption, parallel exemption or a section 11 exemption) or whether he would be likely to grant the agreement an individual exemption; or
　　the conduct is likely to infringe the Chapter II prohibition; or
— **a decision** as to whether:
　　the agreement has infringed the Chapter I prohibition and, if so, whether he would grant an individual exemption; or
　　the conduct has infringed the Chapter II prohibition.

The Director wishes to discourage the making of failsafe applications, that is, applications made by undertakings in relation to agreements or conduct which do not raise any real concerns about a possible infringement of the prohibitions. If the Director receives applications of this nature, he may determine the application by exercising his discretion not to give guidance or make a decision. Notification cannot be made in respect of prospective agreements (that is, where the parties have not yet entered into the agreement) or prospective conduct.

Form N

Applications must be made on Form N. Applicants should provide the information required to complete Form N using its paragraph numbers. Form N can be found at Annex 1 to the **Director's rules**.[1] Form N is also available on the OFT website at http://www.oft.gov.uk.

In some cases, it may be possible for the Director General of Fair Trading[2] (the "DGFT") to dispense with the obligation to submit any particular information forming part of Form N (Rule 4(3) of the **Director's rules**) where the DGFT considers that such information is unnecessary for the examination of the agreement or the consideration of the conduct in question. This should be discussed with OFT officials before making the application.

All applications for guidance or a decision should be sent to the DGFT at the address given below:

> Co-Ordination Unit CB 3
> The Office of Fair Trading
> Fleetbank House
> 2-6 Salisbury Square
> London
> EC4Y 8JX

NOTES
[1] The Competition Act 1998 (Director's rules) Order 2000, SI 2000/293.
[2] The regulators cannot dispense with the obligation to submit any particular information.

Copies

Applicants must provide the original version of Form N with two further copies. This means Applicants must also supply two further copies of any supporting documents provided as part of Form N.

The application may be dealt with by a regulator that has concurrent jurisdiction if that regulator is best placed to consider it. If an Applicant considers that a regulator, or more than one regulator, has or may have concurrent jurisdiction, he must still submit Form N to the DGFT but must also submit an additional copy of Form N and its supporting documents for each such regulator. It would also be helpful if an additional copy of Form N were sent directly to the relevant regulator(s). Failure to send an additional copy to or for the relevant regulator(s) will not render the application incomplete but may cause delay in the initial allocation of the application. For guidance on when a regulator may have concurrent jurisdiction, see paragraph 3.6 below and the Competition Act guideline **Concurrent Application to Regulated Industries**. Applicants should also refer to the **Concurrency Regulations**[1] for the procedures that apply in determining which Director will exercise jurisdiction in cases when questions of concurrency arise.

Before completing Form N, reference should be made to the **Director's rules** and to the guidelines which have been issued which provide general advice and information about the Act. The guidelines can be found on the OFT's website at http://www.oft.gov.uk or requested by:

Phone: 0870 60 60 321

Fax: 0870 60 70 321

Email: oft@echristian.co.uk

Post: OFT, PO Box 366, Hayes, UB3 1XB

NOTES
[1] The Competition Act (Concurrency) Regulations 2000, SI 2000/260.

Incomplete applications

The information provided by the Applicant in Form N must be correct and complete. Applicants will be notified within one month of receipt of the application if it is found to be incomplete and will be asked to provide the missing information. Where the application is incomplete it will be treated as being made on the date that the outstanding information is received (see Rule 5(5) of the **Director's rules**) and the appropriate fee has been paid and immunity from penalties will not arise until this date.

The Director may require an Applicant to provide further information after a complete application has been made.

The DGFT will acknowledge receipt of all applications by returning the Acknowledgement of Receipt in Part 3 of Form N if this is filled in by the Applicant. The Acknowledgement of Receipt does not confirm that the application is correct and complete.

Ongoing obligation

The Director dealing with the application must be informed of any material changes in the information contained in the application which occur after the application has been made (see Rule 4(4) of the **Director's rules**).

GUIDANCE ON THE INFORMATION REQUIRED BY FORM N

The numbering in the paragraphs below corresponds with the numbering of the relevant sections in Form N.

Part 1:   Introduction

The Act imposes a general duty on the Director not to disclose information obtained under or as a result of Part 1 of the Act that relates to the affairs of any individual or to any particular business of an undertaking (Section 55(1) of the Act). There are a number of exceptions to this general duty of non-disclosure. In particular, the Director may disclose information for the purpose of facilitating the performance of his functions under Part 1 of the Act. Before making such disclosure, the Director must have regard to the factors set out in section 56 of the Act.

Applicants are requested to put any information which they consider the Director would find to be confidential (within the meaning Rule 30(1)(c) of the **Director's rules**) in a separate annex to the application marked "confidential information" and give reasons why it should be treated as such. The information put into the annex should not be confused with the non-confidential summary provided by Applicants in response to Part 4 of Form N. If a decision has been applied for, this summary will be used to produce a summary of the application to appear on the public register and possibly for publication elsewhere. Further information on the issue of confidentiality can be found in part 9 of the Competition Act guideline **The Major Provisions**.

Part 2:   Information to be Provided by the Undertaking(s) Making the Application

1   Information about the Undertaking(s) Submitting the Application (the "Applicants") and the Other Parties to the Agreement

1.1   The submission of joint applications on behalf of two or more parties to the agreement or conduct is encouraged as it is useful to have the views of all of the parties concerned at the same time.

Where a joint application has been submitted, it would be helpful if the Applicants could appoint a joint representative to act on behalf of all the Applicants.

1.2   For the purposes of this form and these guidance notes, references to "agreement" (in question 1.5 and elsewhere) shall be read as referring equally to a decision by an association of undertakings or a concerted practice. The meaning of the terms "agreement", "decision by an association of undertakings" and "concerted practices" in the context of the Act are described in part 2 of the Competition Act guideline **The Chapter I Prohibition**.

1.3   For the purposes of this form and these guidance notes, an "undertaking" means any natural or legal person capable of carrying on commercial or economic activities relating to goods or services, whatever its legal status. It includes companies, firms, businesses, partnerships, individuals operating as sole traders, agricultural co-operatives, trade associations and non profit-making organisations.

1.4   A party to an agreement or conduct who makes an application is required to take all reasonable steps to notify all other parties to the agreement or conduct of whom he is aware that the application has been made and whether it is for guidance or a decision (paragraphs 2(2) of Schedules 5 and 6 to the Act).

The notification to such other undertakings must be (a) made in writing and (b) given within seven working days from the date on which the notifying undertaking receives the Acknowledgement of Receipt. A copy of such notification must be provided to the DGFT (Rule 7 of the **Director's rules**).

2   Purpose of the Application

2.1   The Chapter I prohibition does not apply unless the agreement has an "appreciable effect", ie, if it has as its object or effect an appreciable prevention, restriction or distortion of competition in the United Kingdom. The Director takes the view that an agreement will generally not have an appreciable effect on competition (and therefore will not be caught by the Chapter I prohibition) if the parties' combined share of the relevant market does not exceed 25%, although there will be circumstances in which this is not the case. The Director will, in addition, generally regard any agreement between undertakings which:
— directly or indirectly fixes prices or shares markets; or
— imposes minimum resale prices; or
— is one of a network of similar agreements which have a cumulative effect on the market in question

as being capable of having an appreciable effect even where the combined market share falls below the 25 per cent threshold.

Further information on appreciability is given in part 3 of the Competition Act guideline **The Major Provisions**.

2.3   The Director will consider whether an agreement qualifies for an individual exemption only if an individual exemption is specifically requested by the Applicant. The conditions which must be satisfied in order for an individual exemption to be granted are set out in Section 9 of the Act and guidance on satisfying these conditions is given in part 4 of the Competition Act guideline **The Chapter I Prohibition**.

2.4   This question requires Applicants to show why they consider that the agreement or conduct that is notified raises questions of compatibility with one of the prohibitions. In particular, Applicants must demonstrate why an agreement may have an appreciable effect (see paragraph 2.1 above). Guidance on the factors to be taken into account in assessing whether either of the prohibitions has been infringed is contained in the Competition Act guideline **Assessment of Individual Agreements and Conduct**.

In some cases there may be genuine uncertainty about whether an agreement or conduct is likely to infringe the Chapter I or Chapter II prohibitions. In such cases, Applicants may wish to include counter arguments that are relevant to the assessment of whether the agreement or conduct infringes one of the prohibitions.

Undertakings should avoid submitting an application where the agreement or conduct which is the subject of the application does not raise concerns about a possible infringement of the Chapter I and Chapter II prohibitions. If applications are made in such circumstances, the Director may determine the application by exercising his discretion not to give guidance or a decision.

It would be helpful if Applicants could refer in their application to any principles laid down by the EC Treaty and the European Court, any relevant decision of the European Court or any relevant decision of statement of the European Commission which they consider may be relevant to the determination of their application under section 60 of the Act. Further information on the scope of section 60 is given in part 6 of the Competition Act guideline **The Major Provisions**.

2.6   An agreement may qualify for one of the following exemptions:
  — Parallel exemption: this applies to an agreement which is covered by an EC individual or an EC block exemption or would be covered by an EC block exemption if the agreement had an effect on trade between EC Member States. A summary of the main EC block exemptions is given in part 4 of the Competition Act guideline **The Chapter I Prohibition**. An agreement which benefits from a parallel exemption will be exempt from the Chapter I prohibition automatically and no application needs to be made.
  — Block exemption: The Act enables the Secretary of State to make domestic block exemptions which exempt particular categories of agreement which he considers are likely to satisfy the statutory exemption criteria. An agreement which falls within a domestic block exemption will be exempt from the Chapter I prohibition automatically and no application needs to be made. Further information concerning the effect of a block exemption can be found in part 4 of the Competition Act guideline **The Chapter I Prohibition**. Applicants should check whether any domestic block exemptions have been adopted before submitting an application.
  — Section 11 exemption: The Secretary of State may make regulations exempting from the scope of the Chapter I prohibition agreements of a particular kind which have been the subject of a ruling given by virtue of Article 88 of the EC Treaty. Applicants should check whether any such regulations have been made before submitting an application.

Applications should not be made unless the Applicants have real concerns that the Chapter I prohibition has been infringed and there is real doubt that the agreement concerned benefits from one of these exemptions.

2.7   Details of the exclusions which are available from the Chapter I and/or Chapter II prohibitions are set out in part 5 of the Competition Act guideline **The Major Provisions**. Applications for guidance or a decision should not be made unless the Applicants have real concerns that one of the prohibitions has been infringed and there is real doubt that an exclusion from that prohibition applies.

3   Jurisdiction

3.1   An agreement which might be caught by the Chapter I prohibition may also be caught by Article 81(1) of the EC Treaty if it 'may affect trade between Member States' of the European Community. The European Court has interpreted this phrase broadly to apply to an agreement which "may have an influence, direct or indirect, actual or potential, on the pattern of trade between Member States."[1] It has found that even where the parties to an agreement are confined to the same country, inter-state trade may still be affected.[2] In general, when an agreement is also caught by Article 81 of the EC Treaty, the Director considers that the European Commission is the more appropriate authority to whom an application should be made. See part 7 of the Competition Act guideline, **The Chapter I Prohibition** for further information on the overlap of Article 81 and the Chapter I prohibition.

3.2 This question asks Applicant(s) to identify any regulator which they consider has or may have concurrent jurisdiction with the DGFT to deal with the application. A regulator may have concurrent jurisdiction if the agreement or conduct being notified relates to any one or more of:

(a) commercial activities connected with telecommunications;

(b) the shipping, conveyance, or supply of gas and activities ancillary thereto;

(c) commercial activities connected with the generation, transmission or supply of electricity;

(d) commercial activities connected with the supply of water or securing a supply of water or with the provision or securing of sewerage services;

(e) the supply of railway services;

(f) commercial activities connected with the generation, transmission or supply of electricity in Northern Ireland;

(g) the conveyance, storage or supply of gas in Northern Ireland.

NOTES

1   Case 56/65 Société Technique Minière v Maschinenbau Ulm GmbH [1966] ECR 235.

2   Case 8/72 Vereeniging van Cementhandelaren v Commission [1972] ECR 977, [1973] CMLR 7.

4   Details of the Arrangement or Conduct

4.3 Types of provisions or aspects of the conduct which may restrict the parties in their freedom to take independent commercial decision or to act on those decisions include provisions or conduct relating to the following:

— buying or selling prices, discounts or other trading conditions;

— the quantities of goods to be manufactured or distributed or services to be offered;

— technical development or investment;

— the choice of markets or sources of supply;

— purchases from or sales to third parties;

— whether to apply similar terms for the supply of equivalent goods or services;

— whether to offer different services separately or together.

5   Information on the Parties to the Arrangement or Conduct and the Groups to which they Belong

5.1 The question refers to "applicable turnover" and "business year". These terms are defined in the **Determination of Turnover for Penalties Order**.[1]

Applicants are requested to provide copies of annual reports and accounts. These must be copies of the most recent <u>audited</u> annual reports and accounts unless the undertakings concerned are exempted from the requirement to file audited accounts under the Companies Act 1985. Where the original version of the accounts and/or report is in a language other than English, it would assist the Director if Applicants could provide an English translation.

NOTES

1   Competition Act 1998 (Determination of Turnover for Penalties) Order 2000, SI 2000/309.

6   The Relevant Product and Geographic Markets

6.1 Applicants should use the definitions of the relevant product and geographic markets in question 6.1 when identifying the relevant markets in questions 6.2 and 6.3.

The definitions in 6.1 refer solely to demand side factors. The ability of other suppliers to move into the relevant markets ("supply-side substitution) is, however, also a factor which should be taken into consideration by Applicants when analysing the relevant markets for the purposes of questions 6.2 and 6.3. More detail is set out in paragraphs 3.13 et seq and paragraphs 4.7 et seq of the Competition Act guideline **Market Definition**.

6.2　There is rarely one clear boundary for a specific product's market. The relevant definition is likely to differ according to the competition problem under investigation. It would be helpful if Applicants could refer to the alternative market definitions and explain why one definition might be more appropriate than another. See paragraph 5.16 et seq of the Competition Act guideline **Market Definition** and paragraph 4.7 et seq of the Competition Act guideline **Assessment of Market Power**.

By way of example, the following factors may be taken into account by Applicants (together with any others considered to be relevant) when determining the relevant product market:
— the degree of physical similarity between the products in question;
— any differences in end-use to which the products are or may be put;
— differences in price between the products (although products' prices do not need to be identical for them to be in the same market);
— the cost of switching between two potentially competing products;
— the possibility of supply-side substitution;
— the existence of entry barriers;
— established or entrenched consumer preferences for one type or category of product over another; and
— industry wide product classifications (eg classifications maintained by trade associations).

Further guidance on defining the relevant product market is given in part 3 of the Competition Act guideline **Market Definition**.

6.3　By way of example, the following factors may be taken into account by Applicants (together with any others considered to be relevant) when determining the relevant geographic market:
— the nature and characteristics of the products or services concerned;
— the existence of entry barriers or consumer preferences;
— appreciable differences of the undertakings' market share or substantial price differences between neighbouring areas; and
— transport costs.

The geographic scope of the market may be an area smaller or larger than the whole of the UK.

Further guidance on defining the relevant geographic market is given in part 4 of the Competition Act guideline **Market Definition**.

6.4(a)　Applicants are asked to provide details of the level of concentration in the markets (for instance by providing the market shares of each of the five largest firms in the market, see question 7.1(b)).

6.4(b)　Applicants are asked to give details of the nature and extent of vertical integration, that is the degree to which undertakings operate at more than one level of the production process, combining for example production, distribution or retail.

7　The Position of the Undertakings in the Relevant Product Markets

7.1　The information requested in this section should be given in respect of the parties to the agreement or conduct <u>and</u> other undertakings belonging to the same group of undertakings as the parties to the agreement or conduct. Applicants should include all the undertakings identified as being in the group in 1.8.

Questions 7.1(a), (b) and (d) ask Applicants to provide estimates of market shares. Market shares may be calculated on the basis of value or volume. However, if the market share calculated by the alternative method would differ by 5 per cent or more, then both sets of figures should be provided.

An agreement will only infringe the Chapter I prohibition if it has as its object or effect an <u>appreciable</u> prevention, restriction or distortion of competition in the United Kingdom. See paragraph 2.1 above for further information on appreciability.

The market share estimates given by the parties will also be taken into account in assessing whether an undertaking has a dominant position for the purposes of determining whether the Chapter II prohibition applies. The Director has indicated that it is unlikely that an undertaking will be individually dominant if its market share is below 40 per cent. However, dominance could be established below that figure if other relevant factors (such as the weak position of competitors in that market) provided strong evidence of dominance. For further information on establishing dominance, see part 3 of the Competition Act guideline **The Chapter II Prohibition**.

Further information on measuring market shares is provided in part 4 of the Competition Act guideline **Assessment of Market Power**.

8. Market Entry and Potential Competition in the Relevant Product and Geographic Markets

8.1   This question requests Applicants to describe the barriers to entry which exist in the relevant product and geographic markets identified in 6.2 and 6.3. The form gives <u>examples</u> of barriers to entry which may be relevant. Further information on these factors and others which may be relevant (such as the effect of essential facilities on the ability of competing undertakings to enter the market) are given in part 5 of the Competition Act guideline **Assessment of Market Power**. Applicants should not limit their answer to the examples given in this section and in the guideline. They should refer to all the barriers to entry which exist in the relevant product and geographic markets concerned. Such evidence may also be useful in assessing the possibilities of supply-side substitution in paragraph 6.2 and 6.3 above.

8.2   Applicants are requested to identify whether the amount of time required for entry into the relevant product and geographic markets(s) would constitute 'quick and easy substitution' or is more likely to be considered to be 'longer term entry' (see paragraph 3.19 of the Competition Act guideline **Market Definition**).

9 Exemption

An Applicant must state in Form N if an individual exemption is sought and explain how the agreement meets each of the four conditions set out in section 9 of the Act.

It is particularly important that Applicants explain how the perceived benefits are expected to result from the agreement. It would be helpful if Applicants could give details of any studies or documents which have been produced to assess the feasibility of the operation of the agreement and the benefits likely to result from the agreement and whether these studies or documents give estimates of the savings and efficiencies likely to result. Please provide copies of any studies or documents referred to in this section.

Please also explain how the perceived benefits could not be achieved, or could not be achieved so quickly or efficiently or only at a higher cost or with less certainty of success (i) without the conclusion of the agreement which is the subject of the agreement as a whole and (ii) without those particular clauses and provisions of the agreement identified which the Applicant considers may breach the Chapter I prohibition.

Further information on the exemption criteria is given in part 4 of the Competition Act guideline **The Chapter I Prohibition**.

An individual exemption may be granted to have effect from a date which is earlier than that on which it is granted.

10 Transitional Periods

The Chapter I prohibition will not apply to the extent to which the agreement concerned is covered by a transitional period (Schedule 13, paragraph 19(2)).[1] Details of the transitional periods, which are available, and the procedures, which apply, are set out in the Competition Act guideline **Transitional Arrangements**.

NOTES
[1] Note that there are no transitional periods available in respect of the Chapter II prohibition.

11 Other Information:

11.3 A fee is payable for applications for guidance or a decision. An application will not be validly made (and the immunity from penalties will not begin) until the appropriate fee has been paid. The amount of the fee is set out in Annex 2 of the **Director's rules**.

Payment can be made either by cheque or by using the Bank Automated Clearing System (BACS). In either case, Applicants must complete the details on the relevant payment slip at Part 5 of Form N.

12 Supporting Documents

Supporting documents submitted as part of Form N must be either original or certified copies.

DECLARATION

The application must conclude with the declaration which is to be signed by or on behalf of all the Applicants. Unsigned applications are invalid. Where Form N is signed by a solicitor or other representative, written proof of authority to act on behalf of the undertaking submitting the application must be provided.

Part 3: Acknowledgement of Receipt

The Acknowledgement of Receipt which is sent to the Applicant will show the date on which the application was received by the DGFT. The Acknowledgement of Receipt does not prejudice the question of whether the application is correct and complete.

Part 4: To be Completed by the Applicant(s)

Following receipt of an application for a decision (but not guidance), the Director will place a brief summary of the application on the public register maintained at:

> The Office of Fair Trading
> Fleetbank House
> 2-6 Salisbury Square
> London EC4Y 8JX

The Director may also publish a notice inviting comments on an application for a decision in a suitable trade journal and/or the national press. The public register entry and any notice published will be made without consultation with the Applicant.

The summary provided by Applicants in this section may be used in the summary that appears on the public register or in any published notice.

Part 5: Payment Details for Fees Payable Under Rule 6

If payment is to be made by cheque it should be made payable to "The Office of Fair Trading" and crossed "AC Payee only". Please enclose the cheque with the application as required by Rule 6(5) of the **Director's rules**.

If payment is made using BACS please complete the Applicant's name[1] in the square brackets after the heading 'Reference No:' and before the letters '-CP/ CA1998'. Please note that failure to provide this information will mean that payment cannot be verified and may result in delay in processing the application. Please note on the slip the date that payment details were passed to the bank and enclose the payment details with the application.

28 February 2000

[3123]

NOTES

[1] The 'applicant's name' is the name of the undertaking(s) submitting the application and specified in section 1.1 of Part 2 of Form N and **not** the solicitor or other representative authorised to act on behalf of the applicant.

PUBLIC TRANSPORT TICKETING SCHEMES BLOCK EXEMPTION

(OFT 439, August 2002)

NOTES

On 16 June 1999, the former regulatory offices, Ofgas and OFFER, were renamed the Office of Gas and Electricity Markets (Ofgem). References in the text to documents and events before this date use the name of the original regulatory office.

1 Introduction

1.1   This guidance explains the application of The Competition Act 1998 (Public Transport Ticketing Schemes Block Exemption) Order 2001 (SI 2001 No 319) ('the block exemption').

1.2   While paragraphs 1.3 to 1.14 below explain the Competition Act 1998 ('the Act') in broad terms, this guideline has to assume some knowledge of the Act. The Director General, in conjunction with the sector regulators, has published a series of general guidelines and booklets about the Act and its application and enforcement. A list of all the guidelines in the series is on the inside back cover of this guideline. These are available by telephoning 0870 60 60 321 or faxing 0870 60 70 321. The guidelines are also available on the Office of Fair Trading's Internet web-site www.oft.gov.uk.

The Competition Act 1998

1.3   The Act prohibits:
   — agreements between undertakings, decisions by associations of undertakings or concerted practices which have the object or effect of preventing, restricting or distorting competition in the United Kingdom (or a part thereof) and which may affect trade within the United Kingdom ('the Chapter I prohibition'); and

— conduct by one or more undertakings which amounts to the abuse of a
dominant position in a market in the United Kingdom (or a part thereof)
and which may affect trade within the United Kingdom ('the Chapter II
prohibition').[1]

1.4 An agreement will infringe the Chapter I prohibition only if it has as its
object or effect an 'appreciable' prevention, restriction or distortion of competition
in the United Kingdom. The Director General takes the view that an agreement
generally has no appreciable effect on competition if the parties' combined share of
the relevant market does not exceed 25 per cent, although there are circumstances
inwhich this is not the case. Other factors, for example the content of the agreement
and the structure of the market or markets affected by the agreement (such as entry
conditions), are taken into account in considering whether the agreement has, or
may have, an 'appreciable' effect on competition.

1.5 In addition, the Director General generally regards any agreement between
undertakings which:

— directly or indirectly fixes prices or shares markets; or

— imposes minimum resale prices; or

— is one of a network of similar agreements which have a cumulative effect
on the market in question

as being capable of having an appreciable effect even where the combined market
share of the parties falls below the 25 per cent threshold. Further guidance on
appreciability is given in the Competition Act guidelines *The Chapter I Prohibition*
and *Assessment of Market Power.*

1.6 The term 'undertaking' includes any natural or legal person capable of
carrying on commercial or economic activities relating to goods or services,
irrespective of its legal status. It includes, for example, companies, firms, businesses,
partnerships, individuals operating as sole traders, agricultural co-operatives, trade
associations and non-profit making organisations. Depending on the facts of each
case, a parent company and its subsidiaries are usually treated as a single
undertaking if they operate as a single economic unit.

1.7 The Chapter I prohibition applies to local authorities insofar as they act as
undertakings. In assessing whether a local authority is acting as an undertaking in a
particular set of circumstances, the key question is whether or not it is engaging in
economic or commercial activities. A bus company co-owned by a local authority is
an undertaking. If the local authority merely owns shares in the bus company the
authority is not necessarily an undertaking, but if the local authority is involved in
the day to day running of the bus business it may be regarded as an undertaking. The
judgment of the Competition Commission Appeal Tribunal in BetterCare[2] may
mean that a local authority is acting as an undertaking when, for example, inviting
and accepting tenders under section 89 or 91 of the Transport Act 1985. If that is the
case, the activity may fall for consideration under the Competition Act and also
under the competition test contained in the Transport Act 2000 and the Transport
(Scotland) Act 2001.

1.8 Agreements[3] which do not benefit from the block exemption are subject to
the normal application of the Act by the Director General. Such agreements do not,
however, necessarily infringe the Chapter I prohibition. Agreements infringe the
Chapter I prohibition only where they have an appreciable effect on competition
within the United Kingdom, as described in paragraphs 1.4 and 1.5 above.[4]

1.9 In addition, agreements which do not benefit from the block exemption do
not infringe the Chapter I prohibition if they fall within another exemption or
exclusion (see the Competition Act guideline *The Chapter I Prohibition* and
paragraph 1.20 below), even if they have an appreciable effect on competition.

Exemption

1.10 Although the prohibition applies to agreements which prevent, restrict or distort competition, the Act recognises that some such agreements should, nevertheless, be permissible because of, among other things, the benefits they bring to consumers. Section 4 of the Act therefore provides that the Director General may grant an individual exemption from the Chapter I prohibition if the agreement meets the criteria specified in section 9 of the Act. An individual exemption must be applied for by notifying it to the OFT using Form N, with payment of the required fee.

1.11 There is, however, no obligation to obtain an exemption from the Director General. If the parties to an agreement are confident that it meets the criteria for exemption they are free to continue to operate the agreement without notifying it to the OFT. If necessary, an exemption can be applied for in the future and, provided the agreement does indeed satisfy the criteria for exemption, it can then receive a backdated exemption.[5] An agreement will satisfy the criteria for exemption only if it:

(i)   contributes to improving production or distribution or promoting technical or economic progress;

(ii)   allows consumers a fair share of the resulting benefit;

(iii)   does not impose on the undertakings concerned restrictions which are not indispensable to the attainment of those objectives; and

(iv)   does not afford the undertakings concerned the possibility of eliminating competition in respect of a substantial part of the products in question.[6]

1.12 In order to reduce the need for notification of large numbers of similar agreements for individual exemption, the Act provides that the Director General may recommend to the Secretary of State for Trade and Industry that he should make an Order exempting from the Chapter I prohibition agreements which fall within a particular category and which are likely to meet the exemption criteria in section 9 of the Act. These Orders are known as 'block exemptions'.

An agreement which falls within a category specified in a block exemption (and which does not breach any of the conditions specified in the block exemption) is automatically exempt from the Chapter I prohibition, and there is no need to notify such an agreement to the Director General.

1.13 A block exemption may include conditions or obligations. Breach of a **condition** imposed in a block exemption has the immediate effect of cancelling the exemption in relation to a particular agreement. Failure to comply with an **obligation** specified in a block exemption allows the Director General to cancel the block exemption in relation to a particular agreement. The conditions and obligation in the ticketing scheme block exemption are set out in part 3 below. The Act also allows the Director General to cancel the block exemption in relation to a particular agreement if he considers that the exemption criteria set out in section 9 of the Act, paraphrased in paragraph 1.11 above, are not satisfied (see paragraphs 3.52 and 3.53 below). This might be, for example, if the Director General considered that a particular agreement allowed the parties to eliminate existing competition, or to prevent new entry to the market.

1.14 A block exemption exempts agreements meeting the criteria specified in the Order only from the Chapter I prohibition. There is no provision for exemption from the Chapter II prohibition and public transport operators therefore remain subject to the Chapter II prohibition when making and considering ticketing arrangements. A dominant operator which sets excessive or predatory fares, for example, may still infringe the Chapter II prohibition whether or not the fares were set in the context of an exempt agreement.

Public transport ticketing schemes

1.15 Agreements between local public transport operators are subject to the terms of the Act in the same way as agreements in other sectors of the economy in the

United Kingdom. The Director General considers that certain public transport ticketing schemes are likely to prevent, restrict or distort competition to an appreciable extent and therefore to infringe the Chapter I prohibition. Examples of public transport ticketing schemes which are likely to fall within the prohibition include agreements which:

— fix fares for tickets sold under the schemes;

— carve-up routes between participants;

— raise barriers to entry and keep out new competitors, for example through exclusivity provisions, thus allowing incumbents to raise prices;

— eliminate single and return tickets,[7] the fares for which were set at the discretion of individual operators in order to compete on price; or

— facilitate price-fixing by resulting in exchanges of commercially sensitive information between operators.

These examples are not exhaustive: they include types of agreements that would **generally** fall within the prohibition, but the circumstances of a particular agreement may mean that it does not do so. Equally, there will clearly be instances of agreements not listed above which are prohibited because of their particular terms.

1.16 The Director General has, however, noted the benefits to consumers from certain types of integrated public transport ticketing schemes, described, for example, in the Government's consultation document *From Workhorse to Thoroughbred: A better role for bus travel*, issued in March 1999. These benefits include improvements in the efficient use of resources, thus promoting economic progress. Where the benefits accrue to consumers through, for example, cost or time savings, or reductions in external costs such as atmospheric or noise pollution, and provided that the restrictive provisions are indispensable and do not go so far as to make possible the elimination of competition, such schemes should meet the criteria for exemption.

1.17 Some public transport ticketing schemes meet these criteria more clearly than others. Particular care needs to be taken over schemes which risk eliminating competition on particular routes, to ensure that the basic building blocks of competition on price and quality remain intact. On the other hand, some schemes such as those providing only for onward travel on complementary routes may not infringe the prohibition at all.

1.18 The Director General therefore advised the Secretary of State that certain public transport ticketing schemes for local public transport services are categories of agreements in respect of which a block exemption should be made. The Secretary of State agreed with this advice and the block exemption was laid before Parliament on 8 February 2001 and came into effect on 1 March 2001.

The Articles

1.19 Article 1 gives the full title of the Order (the 'citation'); Article 2 states the length of time for which the Order shall be in place (the Order is effective from 1 March 2001 and ceases to have effect after 28 February 2006); Article 3 defines terms used in the Order. The remaining Articles are as follows:

Article 4: specifies the categories of agreements for the sale of tickets covered by the exemption and provides that there must be a written agreement;

Article 6: prevents any operator or potential operator from being excluded from the scheme without 'objective, transparent and non-discriminatory' reasons;

Article 7: prevents any restriction of any operator's ability to decide which routes to serve or to fix its own single, return or individual operator season tickets;

Article 8: prevents any restriction of the ability of operators to take independent commercial decisions on the number of vehicles operated, timetables or headways;

Article 9: prevents the exchange of commercially sensitive information, but allows the exchange of information that is 'directly related and indispensable' to the effective operation of the scheme;

Article 10: provides that any breach of Articles 6, 7, 8 or 9 results in the cancellation of the block exemption;

Article 11: requires that revenue under a scheme for a multi-operator travelcard ('MTC') must be distributed, 'as far as is reasonably practicable', to reflect actual passenger miles travelled;

Article 12: provides for cancellation of the block exemption if Article 11 is not met;

Article 13: prohibits price fixing for multi-operator individual tickets ('MITs'), through tickets ('TTs') and add-ons, but allows a 'posted price' arrangement for TTs and add-ons;

Article 14: provides for cancellation of the block exemption if Article 13 is not met;

Article 15: requires operators who offer a MIT to make own operator tickets concurrently available (that is, singles and/or returns, as appropriate) and requires revenue from MITs to lie where it falls;

Article 16: provides for cancellation of the block exemption if Article 15 is not met;

Article 17: specifies that a request for information must be complied with within 10 working days of receipt;

Article 18: provides for cancellation of the block exemption for failure to comply with Article 17;

Article 19: provides for the Director General to cancel the block exemption in relation to a particular scheme if the scheme does not meet the exemption criteria specified in section 9 of the Act;

Articles 20–21: specify the mechanism for cancelling the block exemption in the circumstances set out in Articles 18 or 19.

Exclusion

1.20 Certain agreements are excluded from the Chapter I prohibition completely by the Act. In particular, an agreement is excluded[8] if it is covered by a direction under section 21(2) of the Restrictive Trade Practices Act 1976 which was in force immediately before the Competition Act came into effect on 1 March 2000. The exclusion applies only to agreements made prior to 9 November 1998 (the enactment date of the Competition Act) and continues in force until or unless the agreement is 'materially' varied. In this context, 'material' is likely to mean that the change to the agreement would cause the agreement then to have an appreciable effect on competition. Minor adjustments to, for example the parties trading relationship – such as a change in delivery dates, mode of transportation, credit terms, or method of payment – would not normally be considered to be 'material'.[9] Variations to an agreement involving, for example, the change of a joint marketing area to segregated markets, or the addition of a significant competitor as a party to the agreement, are likely to be considered to be 'material'.[10]

[3124]

3   The term 'agreement' is not defined in the Act, but it is taken to include a decision by an association of undertakings or a concerted practice. The meanings of the terms 'undertakings', 'agreement', 'decisions by associations of undertakings' and 'concerted practices' in the context of the Act are described in the Competition Act guideline The Chapter I Prohibition. The block exemption, however, specifies that only written agreements can benefit from it. This is to encourage transparency between parties and potential parties on the terms of their particular public transport ticketing scheme.

4   The Director General will consider any public transport ticketing scheme which does not fall within the terms of the block exemption in accordance with the analytical framework provided in the European Commission's Guidelines on the applicability of Article 81 of the EC Treaty to horizontal cooperation agreements [2001/C 3/02 OJ: C3, 6.1.2001, p 2] (to which the Director General must have regard, in accordance with section 60 of the Act) for assessing whether the agreement breaches Chapter I and for assessing whether it is capable of being granted an individual exemption.

5   See Note 4 above.
6   Section 9 of the Act.
7   These tickets provide the 'building blocks' for competition.
8   By virtue of paragraph 2 of Schedule 3 to the Act.
9   Explained fully in the Competition Act Guideline 406, Transitional Arrangements, paragraph 4.16.
10   The Ticketing and Settlement Agreement ('TSA'), the agreement in the railway industry under which all train operating companies agree fares and procedures, which does not fall within the block exemption, received a direction under section 21(2) of the Restrictive Trade Practices Act and has therefore been covered by this exclusion. As at August 2002 no material variations have been made to the agreement so the TSA remains covered by the exclusion.

2 Application of the Block Exemption

2.1   Generally, the block exemption exempts agreements which:
— have an 'appreciable' effect on competition and which therefore fall within the scope of the Chapter I prohibition, and which are not otherwise exempted or excluded;
— fall within the categories of agreements specified in Article 4 of the block exemption, as set out in paragraph 2.4 below; and
— do not breach the conditions in the block exemption.[1]

Local public transport services

2.2   The block exemption applies principally to written agreements relating to the supply of local public transport services. In relation to bus services, these are local services that are registered under the Transport Act 1985.[2] Any other form of public transport service will be 'local'[3] if it meets the following criteria:
— broadly, one or more passengers travels less than fifteen miles on the service,[4]
— it is a scheduled, rather than a 'chartered', service, and
— it is not a local guided tour service.[5]

2.3   The block exemption applies to five types of public transport ticketing scheme[6] any of which could contain any one or more of the anti-competitive elements described in paragraph 1.15 above. Other than to the extent that long distance add-ons are issued under an agreement, long distance services – for example air services, international ferry services, or long distance rail or coach services – are not covered by the block exemption.

Categories of agreements covered by the block exemption

2.4   Schemes covered by the block exemption involve the following ticket types: **multi-operator travel cards** ('MTCs'): these entitle ticket holders to make multiple journeys on a number of different operators' services across a number of different routes (see paragraph 3.16 below). Bus zonal tickets and travel cards, for example, are likely to be types of MTC;

- **through tickets** ('TTs'): these entitle ticket holders to make a particular journey using two or more connecting services run by different operators where those operators do not compete with each other over a substantial part of the route covered by the particular journey[7] (see paragraph 3.28 below;
- **multi-operator individual tickets** ('MITs'): where two or more different operators provide services on the same route, these tickets entitle ticket holders to use whichever service they choose (see paragraph 3.36 below);
- **short distance add-ons:** these allow passengers to purchase an MTC as an extension to a ticket on an individual **local** route – for example, a route between two local towns (see paragraph 3.44 below); and
- **long distance add-ons:** these allow passengers to purchase a single ticket, MTC or TT as an extension to a ticket on an individual **long distance** route – for example, a route between two cities (see paragraph 3.45 below).[8]

2.5 Ticketing agreements containing only clauses that have a neutral or benign effect on competition do not infringe the Chapter I prohibition. For example, where a local bus company and a train operating company are not actual or potential competitors in a particular market, or where operators merely standardise the format of their ticketing documents, it is unlikely that an agreement between them will infringe the Chapter I prohibition because there will be no 'appreciable' effect on competition.

2.6 Some public transport ticketing schemes may include arrangements covering more than one ticket type. If the agreement contains a provision that breaches one of the conditions relating to one of the ticket types,[9] the arrangement for that particular ticket type is 'severed' and is not block exempted even though the rest of the agreement is exempted. If, for example, an agreement covered an MTC and a MIT and the MIT arrangement breached Article 15, that MIT arrangement would not benefit from the block exemption. However, providing that the MTC still met all the conditions in the block exemption, the MTC part of the arrangement would continue to benefit from the block exemption.

2.7 If an agreement falls outside the scope of the block exemption because, for example, it fails to meet one or more of the conditions set out in the block exemption, it might still meet the criteria for an individual exemption.

2.8 The category of agreements and the conditions contained in the block exemption[10] allow local transport operators to decide whether existing or potential agreements benefit from the block exemption or whether the terms of the agreement would need to be changed to fall within the block exemption. It is for operators to make that decision. There are two situations to consider:

- where an agreement falls within the terms of the block exemption, it is automatically exempted from the Chapter I prohibition, and no further action is necessary. The agreement does not need to be notified to the Director General. The parties may wish to consider whether it is appropriate to seek legal advice to confirm whether the agreement falls within the block exemption, however; and
- where an agreement does not fall within the terms of the block exemption consideration will need to be given as to whether:
  - it has an appreciable effect on competition. If it **does not**, no further action is necessary;
  - if it **does** have an appreciable effect on competition, whether it should be amended to bring it within the terms of the block exemption; or
  - whether it meets the criteria for individual exemption as set out in section 9 of the Act and paraphrased in paragraph 1.11 above.

2.9 If operators consider that an agreement does not benefit from the block exemption but that it does meet the criteria for individual exemption, it is not essential to notify an agreement for individual exemption immediately, as an exemption can be back-dated. A notification for individual exemption may, therefore, be made at a later date, but the parties to the agreement will need to consider whether they can be confident that the exemption criteria are, in fact, met, or whether they wish to notify the agreement for either guidance or a decision (see part 7 of the Competition Act guideline *The Major Provisions*).[11]

2.10 The situation can be represented graphically as follows:

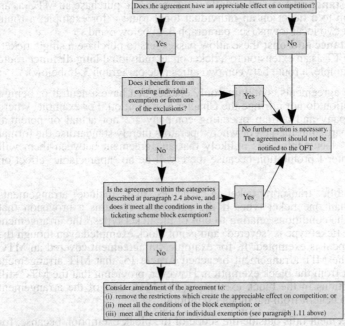

2.11 The block exemption does not cover agreements relating to, for example, joint marketing of tickets or routes. Such agreements will need careful consideration by the parties as to whether the agreements have an 'appreciable' effect on competition, and the action then to be taken.

[3125]

NOTES

1 Articles 6, 7, 8, 9, 11, 13 or 15.

2 Other than those on which the passengers travel together on a journey, with or without breaks, from one or more places to one or more places and back (section 159(1) of the Transport Act 1968), and other than local guided tour services (defined as 'tourist services' in Article 3 of the block exemption).

3 Defined more fully in paragraph (b) of the definition of 'local public transport service' in Article 3 of the block exemption. This definition reflects the approach in the Transport Acts 1968 and 1985 in relation to local bus services.

4 That is, that it is not a 'long distance service' as defined in Article 3 of the block exemption.

5 Defined as 'tourist services' in Article 3 in the block exemption.

6 A similar approach to defining ticket types has been taken in section 135 of the Transport Act 2000 and section 28 of the Transport (Scotland) Act 2001. The block exemption, however, applies to public transport ticketing schemes, that is, agreements or arrangements as a result of which the various tickets are issued; it is also more prescriptive as to the types of tickets that fall within it.

7 See paragraphs 3.3 to 3.6 below.

8 Unlike short distance add-ons, agreements that include long distance operators cannot be potentially exempted as other ticket types. This is why long distance add-ons can include single operator tickets or TTs on local public transport services and MTCs.

9 Articles 11, 13 or 15.

10 In Article 4 (and defined in Article 3), and the conditions listed in Articles 6–9, 11, 13 and 15.

3 The Scope of the Block Exemption

General

3.1   The block exemption applies to the public transport ticketing schemes set out in paragraph 2.4 above. The agreement must be in writing to benefit from the block exemption. There are a number of other conditions which apply to the application of the exemption. These are explained below.

3.2   Each ticket type can be purchased by any person other than an operator, long distance operator or potential operator or long distance operator. This means that each ticket type must be sold to a consumer although this person may then transfer the ticket to someone else. This includes, for example, parents buying tickets to be given to children, educational establishments buying tickets to be given or sold to students, and, for example, manufacturing firms buying tickets for onward sale to employees. This also includes family-type tickets where passengers travel together with only one document as evidence of their right to travel.

3.3   To benefit from the block exemption, MTCs cannot be available for journeys **only** on routes which are 'substantially' the same. Similarly, TTs cannot exist for journeys on services which are in competition with each other over a 'substantial' part of the route in question. Multi-operator tickets for these sorts of journeys are MITs and must satisfy the conditions in the block exemption for MITs in order to fall within its scope. A book of single tickets or a 'carnet' will be either an MTC if it is valid across a specified geographical area or a MIT if it is valid for a particular journey on a particular route. The distinction is important as it determines which conditions must be met for the scheme to fall within the scope of the block exemption.

3.4   For many routes which operators will wish to include in any MTC or TT scheme, however, there will be at least a **minimal** overlap between the component legs of any journey. This is because, for example, all services in a town may have to pass down one particular street in order to reach the bus station. Where two services have a few bus stops in common, for example, provided that these bus stops do not form a 'substantial' part of either route, then issuing an MTC or TT valid on both of these services should not diminish competition on any part of either route. This is therefore permitted by the block exemption.

3.5   In assessing whether a ticket is an MTC or a MIT, it is generally likely that a ticket that is valid over an entire geographical area, with many routes and many services, will be an MTC. Where, however, an MTC is relatively small-scale, covering only a small number of routes and services in a small town, for example, operators will have to consider carefully whether the MTC genuinely covers at least three substantially different routes and services. This guideline cannot give a definitive formula which will enable operators always to decide whether any two particular routes are 'substantially' competing or not. Common sense and local knowledge will play an important role in making this assessment. However, generally, it can be said that common stops would form a substantial part of any route where, for example:

— they account for all or most of the stops on the route itself;
— they account for all or most of the stops in a particular fare zone; or
— the pattern of usage (in terms of their location and/or the volume of passengers travelling between them, for example), means that the common stops could form a stand-alone route in their own right.

3.6 Operators should assess whether two routes do compete with each other from the passenger's point of view.[1] If they do, they will be 'substantially' the same and are in competition with one another. This is likely to be the case when common stops form a substantial part of any relevant route.

Conditions that apply to all public transport ticketing schemes

3.7 The Act provides that a block exemption may include 'conditions', breach of which has the effect of cancelling, without notice, the exemption in respect of the particular agreement. There are a number of conditions in the public transport ticketing schemes block exemption. Some apply only to specific types of ticketing schemes and are explained from paragraph 3.16 onwards below. Others apply to all types of scheme and, broadly, require that, in order to benefit from the block exemption, schemes shall not:

— have the object or effect of preventing any operator (existing or potential) from taking part in the scheme, without 'objective, transparent and non-discriminatory' reasons (Article 6);
— limit the variety or number of routes, or the price or availability of any single operator tickets offered by individual operators (Article 7);
— limit the frequency or timing of any public transport services operated by individual operators except where doing so is indispensable to providing effective onward travel connections for passengers (Article 8); or
— facilitate an exchange of information between the parties except where the exchange of information is directly related, and indispensable, to the effective operation of the scheme, and where the provision requiring the exchange of information is 'objective, transparent and non-discriminatory' (Article 9).

Each condition is considered in more detail below.

Article 6

3.8 This condition requires that any public transport ticketing scheme must be accessible to any local public transport operator, or potential operator, wishing to join it. A scheme which prevents an operator from joining it will benefit from the block exemption only if there is an objective, transparent and non-discriminatory reason for the exclusion. This condition is to ensure that public transport ticketing schemes do not exclude operators from the market, or form barriers that restrict the ability of new operators to enter the market. Examples (the list is not exhaustive) of reasons for excluding operators or potential operators which are **not** objective, transparent or non-discriminatory include:

— requiring an operator to incur costs on joining a public transport ticketing scheme which are not indispensable to the effective operation of that scheme. Such costs may include, for example:
 — requiring unreasonable investment in on-board hardware for recording the data required to administer the scheme; or
 — requiring unreasonable investment in advertising to the public the existence of the scheme;
— apportioning between the parties to a public transport ticketing scheme the fixed or variable costs of administering the scheme on terms which do not reflect, as far as is reasonably practicable,[2] the passenger miles travelled on the vehicles (or vessels) of the parties. This is to ensure that costs are apportioned in line with actual usage of services in the scheme;
— failing to distribute between the parties to a public transport ticketing scheme the revenue received through the scheme as regularly as reasonably

practicable.[3] This is to ensure that the cash flows of smaller operators are not unduly restricted by the scheme;

— requiring any operator to incur costs on leaving a public transport ticketing scheme which are not indispensable to the effective operation of the scheme. Such costs may include:

— requiring an unreasonable notice period to be given; or

— imposing an unreasonable financial or other penalty on a party for leaving the scheme; or

— requiring any party to a public transport ticketing scheme not to participate in any other such scheme.

Article 7

3.9   A public transport ticketing scheme must not limit the variety or number of routes each operator operates, nor must it limit the ability of the operators to make commercial decisions about their own single or return fares or the price of single-operator season tickets. A scheme must not interfere with, for example, price and availability of single-operator tickets. This is to preserve the competition existing between operators on the basic 'building blocks' of single and return tickets and to preserve the freedom of operators to provide services that meet passengers' needs.

Article 8

3.10   Operators must be free to take independent commercial decisions about the number of vehicles to be operated on any particular route, the headways to be used or the times of services, for example. The only exception is that a scheme may include agreement on schedules if it is indispensable for providing connecting services through, for example, a long distance add-on or a TT.

Article 9

3.11   Article 9(1) prevents a scheme from facilitating the exchange of commercially confidential information between operators. Such exchanges of information may 'dampen' the competitive process and may facilitate collusion.

3.12   Clearly, however, some exchange of information between the parties to a scheme is essential to the operation of many schemes. Article 9(2), therefore, allows the exchange of information which is 'directly related and indispensable' to the effective operation of the scheme itself, provided it is carried out on an 'objective, transparent and non-discriminatory' basis. Parties to public transport ticketing schemes will have to consider whether exchange of a particular type of information meets these criteria.

3.13   Article 9(2) does not give examples of the sort of information which could be exchanged. Given that revenue from MITs must lie where it falls it is likely that these schemes will require little or no information exchange.[4] Similarly the need for information exchange for TTs should be limited to informing participants of the posted prices and providing information relating to such reimbursement.[5] The OFT therefore expects that the need to exchange information will arise principally in the case of MTC schemes and will relate to the price of the MTC, the distribution of revenue received through the scheme and the apportionment of administration costs. The parties will clearly have to exchange information regarding the passenger numbers and revenues relating to the usage of the MTC but it should **not** be necessary to exchange information on revenues and passenger numbers relating to their own ticket sales, or for information to be (directly or by inference) identified as relating to a particular route.

PART III
OFT GUIDELINES

3.14 The parties to large scale MTC schemes in metropolitan areas are likely to have to exchange such information only by means of a strictly confidential bilateral exchange of information with an impartial person who is neither an operator nor a potential operator (an 'information referee'). A less stringent approach is likely to be suitable for small-scale schemes where the revenue or potential revenue does not allow for the appointment of an impartial third person to act as an information referee.

Article 10

3.15 Article 10 provides that breach of any of the conditions in Articles 6, 7, 8 or 9 will result in the block exemption being automatically cancelled in relation to the scheme to which the breach relates. This includes all the public transport ticketing schemes which are part of the same 'agreement' within the broad meaning of section 2 of the Act.[6]

Conditions that apply to multi-operator travelcard schemes

3.16 An MTC is a ticket valid:
— for three or more journeys (including unlimited travel for a particular period of time);
— on any of three or more services;
— operating on three or more routes;
— provided that those routes and services are not 'substantially' the same; and
— passenger usage and revenue received from the ticket demonstrate that it is not a MIT or a TT. It is likely that, in most cases, subject to any local conditions imposed, a '+Bus' add-on ticket[7] will be an MTC.

3.17 As explained in paragraphs 3.8 to 3.14 above, the scheme must not:
— prevent any operator from participating (except in limited circumstances);
— limit the variety or number of routes on which individual operators provide services;
— limit the individual operator's right to set its own fares and ticket validity;
— limit the frequency or timing of individual operator's services (except where schedule co-ordination is indispensable to providing onward travel connections for TTs and add-ons); or
— facilitate an exchange of information unless it is directly related and indispensable to the effective operation of the scheme.

3.18 The price of an MTC can, however, be fixed by the parties. Because of the flexibility of passenger use of MTCs and the consequence that operators will not know what journeys have been made using each ticket, it is clearly not possible to use a 'posted price' mechanism for revenue reimbursement for MTCs in the same way as for other ticket types (see paragraph 3.32 below). The operators could conceivably each agree to participate in an MTC in exchange for a fixed fee which could then form the basis of the price at which each operator decided to sell the MTC in the light of that commitment. That would be cumbersome, at the least, however, and would impose some risk on operators. It would also mean that the revenue received from the scheme would bear no resemblance to usage of the services of each operator. It seems, therefore, that the only satisfactory solution is for a common agreed price for an MTC.

3.19 While Article 13 prohibits price fixing for TTs, MITs, and add-ons, Article 13(2)(b) allows parties to an MTC scheme to agree the price at which they sell that MTC to other operators on a wholesale basis as an add-on.

The 'passenger miles' measure

3.20 Revenue distribution in an MTC scheme must reflect, 'as far as is reasonably practicable', the passenger miles travelled on the vehicles or vessels of each party to the agreement by passengers using tickets issued under the scheme. This condition provides incentives for operators to continue to compete for customers even though they have agreed a common price for the MTC. Such incentives would be dampened if revenues were allocated on the basis of revenue forgone as operators may find it advantageous to raise their individual single and return fares in order to attract a greater share of the MTC revenue pot. The condition includes the term 'as far as is reasonably practicable' to reflect the fact that it is likely to be difficult to measure passenger miles travelled completely accurately and because some types of schemes may require a modification to this approach or a different approach to be used.

3.21 In assessing passenger usage of MTCs it is likely that reliance will be placed on passenger surveys. The aim of these surveys should be to enable a representative sample of usage (that is, the actual passenger miles travelled during the accounting period in which the revenue was received) to be compiled which is statistically robust and defensible. It is not feasible, or desirable, to specify here how frequently such surveys should be carried out, but it is not expected that a full survey of every route involved in the scheme will be necessary in each accounting period.

3.22 In some cases it may be necessary to modify the passenger miles approach to take account of significant variations in the costs of providing different services included within the scheme. Reasons why a modified approach may be necessary could include, for example:

— the cost of carrying passengers does not vary in direct proportion to the distance travelled so that distribution by passenger miles would unfairly disadvantage operators, for example, catering principally for short trips;

— services on routes within the geographical area covered by a scheme are offered on different modes of transport (for example, the scheme covers trains as well as buses) that have very different cost structures; or

— one or more modes within a scheme receives a network subsidy so the operators are less reliant on revenues from ticket sales which results in lower basic single and return fares for that mode.

3.23 In such situations, it would clearly be inequitable for both or all the operators to receive a flat reimbursement based purely on passenger miles. In such circumstances, it may be appropriate for reimbursement to be based on a system of 'weighted' miles. Where any 'weighting' system is employed, the terms of the system must be objective, transparent and non-discriminatory. It will be necessary for the parties to be able to demonstrate that a weighting system has to be employed in the light of the circumstances of a particular scheme to allow adequate and fair reimbursement, and that the weighting scheme adopted is appropriate in the circumstances of the scheme.

3.24 In some circumstances it may be impractical for a scheme to use passenger miles, whether weighted or not, because the revenues from the scheme are too small to justify incurring the costs involved in setting up a method of collecting passenger miles data. Cases where alternative methods of allocating revenue may be acceptable include, for example:

— one-day, leisure-based 'explorer'-type MTCs, which permit travel on several operators' services, but which have irregular sales and make up a very small proportion of the total revenue of the network of services concerned. For this type of ticket it will generally be acceptable for revenue to lie with the operator that sells the ticket;

— where operators are already required to calculate amounts owing under local authority concessionary fares schemes under the Transport Act 1985 by reference to 'revenue forgone' and it is not feasible (because of the limited revenue obtained) for the schemes to apportion revenue by two different methods. In these limited circumstances, it would be acceptable for revenue from an MTC scheme to be apportioned according to revenue forgone; and

— where an MTC takes the form of a 'carnet' of tickets, each of which is valid for a single trip across a specified geographical area. For this type of ticket it will generally be acceptable for the value of each trip to accrue to the operator of the journey in question, regardless of its length.

3.25 If the parties to a scheme decide to apportion revenue and costs on a basis other than passenger miles they must be able to show that the cost of obtaining passenger miles data would be disproportionate to the overall revenue arising from the scheme. This balance would need to be reviewed if the size of the scheme changed materially or if new, more cost-effective, means of data collection became available.

3.26 Where allocation of revenue by reference to passenger miles is not possible, however, allowing the revenue to lie where it falls is the next best option, because it maintains the incentive for operators to compete to attract revenue. Such a view assumes that one operator would not receive a disproportionate share of the revenue because, for example, it ran the service during the day and another operated it in the evenings when sales would be likely to be significantly fewer. If operators are content to allow revenue to lie where it falls, the OFT is, generally, likely to view such a method of revenue-sharing as acceptable. The parties to an MTC scheme should, however, be able to demonstrate that, in the particular case, it was not 'reasonably practicable' to distribute revenue by reference to passenger miles travelled.

3.27 Breach of the condition requiring revenue in an MTC to be distributed reflecting actual passenger miles will cancel the block exemption in relation to the scheme only to the extent that MTCs are offered for sale under the scheme. This means that any MTCs sold under the particular scheme will not benefit from the block exemption, and that part of the scheme may, therefore, be in breach of the Chapter I prohibition unless it meets the criteria for individual exemption. If, however, other ticket types are offered under the scheme and these arrangements satisfy the relevant conditions, the block exemption will continue to apply to the provisions for these other tickets.

Conditions that apply to through ticket schemes

3.28 A TT is a ticket:
— which is valid on more than one operator's services;
— for completion of a particular journey (whether single or return);
— on two or more services;
— provided the journey is made on 'complementary' services, that is services where the operators do not compete with each other over a 'substantial' part of the route covered by that particular journey.

3.29 As explained in paragraphs 3.8 to 3.14 above, the scheme must not:
— prevent any operator from participating (except in limited circumstances);
— limit the variety or number of routes on which individual operators provide services;
— limit the individual operator's right to set its own fares and ticket validity;
— limit the frequency or timing of individual operator's services unless it is indispensable to providing onward travel connections; or
— facilitate an exchange of information unless it is directly related and indispensable to the effective operation of the scheme.

3.30 Other points to note about TTs are:
— price fixing is prohibited;

— but operators can agree to charge each other non-discriminatory posted prices, which should be related to the cost of carrying the additional passenger;

— they cannot exist for routes which are in competition with each other over a 'substantial' part of the route in question[8] because this would otherwise make them MITs;

— minimal overlaps are acceptable;

— if routes compete from the passenger's perception, they **are** in competition, and the TT would not fall within the block exemption;

— operators may limit the frequency or timing of a service only if it is indispensable to a TT which provides connecting services; and

— any information exchange is likely to be limited to posted prices.

3.31 Article 13(1) prohibits price fixing for, among other things, TTs. While an MTC clearly cannot operate without agreed common prices, it is not 'indispensable' for operators to agree the prices of TTs. The risks of anti-competitive collusion between parties to TT schemes will also be reduced if communication between parties to the agreement is kept to the minimum necessary. In order to retain the benefits of the block exemption, operators must not, therefore, agree the price of a TT.

3.32 Article 13(2)(a), however, allows each party in a TT scheme to set the 'posted' prices that it can charge another operator for accepting a ticket the other participant has issued. The 'posted price' is the reimbursement that an operator independently decides it requires for any passenger that it carries who uses a ticket purchased from another operator.[9]

3.33 The amount of reimbursement will clearly be related to the cost of carrying the additional passenger. Parties to the scheme are not likely to set the amount for reimbursement excessively, since to do so might mean that it would make it more attractive for passengers to purchase two single operator tickets instead of buying a TT. So long as single tickets are priced competitively, a posted pricing scheme should provide the minimum possible distortion of competition required to allow these tickets to be offered.

3.34 It is important to note that the condition is satisfied only if the relevant operators do not charge **discriminatory** posted prices. This means that an operator must have a single posted price for carrying passengers between any two points which it charges **any** other operator or long distance operator who has sold a TT valid for travel between those two points.

3.35 Breach of the conditions in Article 13 will cancel the block exemption in relation to the scheme only to the extent that the respective TTs are offered for sale under that scheme. This means that any TTs sold under the particular scheme will not benefit from the block exemption, and that part of the scheme may, therefore, be in breach of the Chapter I prohibition unless it meets the criteria for individual exemption. If, however, other ticket types are offered under the scheme and these arrangements satisfy the relevant conditions, the block exemption will continue to apply to the provisions for these other tickets.

Conditions that apply to multi-operator individual ticket schemes

3.36 A MIT is a ticket:

— which is valid on more than one operator's services;

— for the completion of a particular journey (single or return) on whichever service the passenger chooses, where that journey could be made on services provided by any of two or more operators where those operators' services are in competition with each other.

3.37 As explained in paragraphs 3.8 to 3.14 above, the scheme must not:

— prevent any operator from participating (except in limited circumstances);

— limit the variety or number of routes on which individual operators provide services;

— limit the individual operator's right to set its own fares and ticket validity;

— limit the frequency or timing of individual operator's services (schedule coordination is allowed where it is indispensable to providing onward travel connections but this will not be relevant to MITs); or

— facilitate an exchange of information unless it is directly related and indispensable to the effective operation of the scheme. As noted above, it is unlikely that **any** information exchange will be required for MITs.

3.38 Points to note about a MIT are:

— price fixing is prohibited;

— operators who offer a MIT **must** also concurrently make available tickets for travel on only their own services (that is, single and/or return tickets) for the same routes and the same ticket-types as the MIT (see paragraph 3.40 below); and

— revenue must lie where it falls (see paragraph 3.41 below).

3.39 Article 13(1) prohibits price fixing for, among other things, MITs. While an MTC clearly cannot operate without agreed common prices, it is not indispensable for operators to agree the prices of MITs. The risks of anti-competitive collusion between parties to MIT schemes will also be reduced if communication between parties to the agreement is kept to the minimum necessary. In order to retain the benefits of the block exemption, operators must not, therefore, agree the price of a MIT.

3.40 Article 15(a) requires that operators who offer a MIT must also concurrently make available single and return tickets for travel on only their own services, for the same routes and the same ticket-types as the MIT. Single and return tickets offered by individual operators provide the price discipline for all other tickets and prevent those other tickets from being priced above the competitive level. Competition will therefore be greater if individual operator tickets continue to be offered alongside the MIT on the route:

— 'offered', in this context, means that individual operator tickets must be made available and passengers must be aware that such tickets are available. It is, therefore, necessary that some publicity is given to the availability of the individual operator ticket. This may be achieved by providing notices or publicity material at enquiry points and bus stations/stops etc. It would not, however, be necessary, for example, for a bus driver to make each passenger who asks for a return ticket aware that a return ticket was available for use on only the buses of that operator in addition to the MIT, in order to meet the condition. The fact that the former ticket was, in fact, available, and that passengers could ascertain that it was available, is considered sufficient to maintain the competitive price discipline;

— the condition in Article 15(a) does not specify the price at which the tickets should be sold. This is a matter for the commercial judgement of the companies involved; and

— it is likely that most MITs will be return tickets which means that there must be an individual operator return ticket 'concurrently' made available. However, if the scheme provides for both single and return MITs, both single and return individual operator tickets must 'concurrently' be made available.

3.41 Article 15(b) requires that the revenue must 'lie where it falls' for schemes under which MITs are issued – in other words, the operator who collects the money keeps it and, over time, the revenues will balance themselves out. This is a very low-cost method of organising public transport ticketing schemes and is already in common usage for MIT schemes.[10]

3.42　Breach of the price-fixing condition for MITs in Article 13 will cancel the block exemption in relation to the scheme only to the extent that the respective MITs are offered for sale under that scheme (Article 14). This means that any MITs sold under the particular scheme will not benefit from the block exemption, and that part of the scheme may, therefore, be in breach of the Chapter I prohibition.

3.43　Breach of Article 15 will similarly cancel the block exemption in relation to the scheme but only insofar as it relates to the MIT (Article 16). This means that any MITs sold under the particular scheme will not benefit from the block exemption, and that part of the scheme may, therefore, be in breach of the Chapter I prohibition unless it meets the criteria for individual exemption. If, however, other ticket types are offered under the scheme and these arrangements satisfy the relevant conditions, the block exemption will continue to apply to the provisions for these other tickets.

Conditions that apply to short distance and long distance add-on ticket schemes

3.44　A short distance add-on is a ticket:
— where an MTC (for example, a bus zonal ticket) is provided as an add-on:
  — to another **local** public transport service (for example, a local train journey;
  — providing onward travel connections for passengers on 'complementary' services.

Short distance add-ons stem from agreements which provide for an operator who is supplying a **local** public transport service between two towns to offer passengers an MTC as an 'add-on' to a single or return ticket for travel between those two towns. This 'add-on' would be for travel within the destination town, for example.[11]

3.45　A long distance add-on is a ticket under which:
— a long distance operator offers:
  — a single operator ticket;
  — an MTC; or
  — a TT

as an add-on, for example, to a single or return ticket for travel on a **long distance** service between two cities (where every passenger on that service is set down only after 15 miles or more – that is, **not** a local service). For services where passengers are set down more frequently than every 15 miles, the ticket will be a short distance add-on or a TT.

3.46　As explained in paragraphs 3.8 to 3.14 above, the scheme must not:
— prevent any operator from participating (except in limited circumstances);
— limit the variety or number of routes on which individual operators provide services or limit the individual operator's right to set its own fares and ticket validity;
— limit the frequency or timing of individual operator's services unless it is indispensable to providing onward travel connections;
— facilitate an exchange of information unless it is directly related and indispensable to the effective operation of the scheme; or
— include a MIT (as defined in the block exemption) as an add-on.[12]

3.47　Other points to note about add-ons are that:
— price-fixing is prohibited;
— but operators may agree to charge each other non-discriminatory posted prices which should be related to the cost of carrying the additional passenger;
— short distance add-ons cover MTCs. Other short distance add-ons may operate as TTs. In contrast, there is no potential for agreements that include long distance operators to be potentially exempted as other ticket

types. This is why long distance add-ons can include single operator tickets or TTs on local public transport services as well as MTCs;
— operators may limit the frequency or timing of a service only if it is indispensable to an add-on which provides onward travel connections for passengers on complementary services; and
— any information exchange is likely to be limited to posted prices.

3.48 Article 13(1) prohibits price fixing for, among other things, short and long distance add-on tickets. While an MTC clearly cannot operate without agreed common prices, it is not 'indispensable' for operators to agree the prices of addons. The risks of anti-competitive collusion between parties to add-on schemes will also be reduced if communication between parties to the agreement is kept to the minimum necessary. In order to retain the benefits of the block exemption, operators must not, therefore, agree the total price of an add-on.

3.49 Article 13(2)(a), however, allows parties in an add-on scheme to set the 'posted' prices that they can charge one another for accepting a ticket another participant has issued. The 'posted price' is the reimbursement that an operator independently decides it requires for any passenger that it carries who uses a ticket purchased from another operator.[13] Article 13(2)(b) allows operators in a town to fix the price of an MTC provided that they do this in accordance with the conditions explained above.

3.50 Breach of the price-fixing condition for add-ons will cancel the block exemption in relation to the scheme only to the extent that the add-ons are offered for sale under that scheme (Article 14). This means that any add-ons sold under the particular scheme will not benefit from the block exemption, and that part of the scheme may, therefore, be in breach of the Chapter I prohibition. If, however, other ticket types are offered under the scheme and these arrangements satisfy the relevant conditions, the block exemption will continue to apply to the provisions for these other tickets.

Obligation to provide information to the Director General

3.51 Article 17 requires any person (which includes any undertaking) to provide the Director General with any information he may request concerning public transport ticketing schemes to which that person is a party. This is to facilitate monitoring of schemes and to require operators and others to provide information in the event that a complaint is made about the scheme. Requests for information will be made in writing and must be complied with within ten working days from the date on which the request is received. If the request is not complied with, the Director General may cancel the block exemption for any public transport ticketing scheme to which the request relates.[14]

Withdrawal of the block exemption

3.52 Under Article 19, the Director General may cancel the block exemption in respect of a particular agreement if he considers that the agreement does not meet the exemption criteria contained in section 9 of the Act (as set out in paragraph 1.11 above). This might happen where, for example, the introduction of a scheme resulted in an unreasonable increase in fares by any or all of the operators which were party to the agreement. In those circumstances, the agreement would not confer a fair share of the benefits on consumers, and would not meet the requirements for the exemption.

3.53 The Director General will therefore monitor the operation of public transport ticketing schemes with particular regard to the effect on prices for single and return fares offered by individual operators. If those fares rise at a rate that passengers consider to be excessive, they should inform the Director General so that the reasons for the price increases can be investigated.

NOTES

1   In other words, operators should assess whether routes are substitutes from the passengers' point of view (the demand side). In this particular instance, substitution from the operator's point of view (the supply side) is not taken into account. Any schemes which resulted in operators carving up routes in order to raise prices would not, however, meet the requirements of the block exemption.

2   See paragraph 3.20 onwards below for further information on 'as far as is reasonably practicable'.

3   It is recognised that it is helpful for operators to receive revenue from annual season ticket sales, for example, in one instalment in the accounting period in which the ticket is bought: 'regularly', in this instance, does not mean that distribution of the revenue from the sale of the ticket should be spread over the 12 months' validity of the ticket, unless the operational requirements of the ticketing scheme otherwise require it.

4   See paragraph 3.41 below regarding revenue lying where it falls.

5   See paragraph 3.32 below.

6   See Note 3 above.

7   An add-on option to single and return rail tickets starting and/or finishing at any station where a +Bus scheme exists through the Journey Solutions initiative.

8   See paragraphs 3.3 to 3.6 above.

9   The following example shows how this 'posted prices' system works. Suppose the TT is for a journey from A to C via B, where operator 1 provides the service from A to B and operator 2 provides the service from B to C. Each operator will independently set a 'posted price' which is the revenue it requires for carrying a passenger using a TT on its leg of the journey. Each operator will also set a price at which it sells the TT for the complete journey. The prices for the TT will also be determined independently by the two operators taking into account the costs and demand each faces for the leg of the journey it provides and the posted price each must pay to the other operator. If a passenger journeying from A to C purchases her ticket at A, she will pay the price that has been set by operator 1. Operator 1 will initially receive all the revenue but will pay operator 2 the posted price that operator 2 has set for the journey from B to C. Similarly, if the passenger starts her journey and purchases her ticket at C, operator 2 will receive the price that he has set for the complete journey from C to A but will pay operator 1 the posted price that operator 1 has set for the journey from A to B.

10   If sales are made through independent third party outlets – such as newsagents – under an agreement with a particular operator and the third party outlet bears no financial risk under that agreement, this is likely to be a sales agency agreement and outside the scope of the Chapter I prohibition (see part II, section 2 of the European Commission's Guidelines on Vertical Restraints OJ No C 291 13.10.2000 p 1). The analysis is, however, more complicated if a MIT is sold through a third party outlet.

11   There are two agreements that may be caught by section 2 of the Act. First, there is the agreement between the operators that are providing the MTC. Assuming that the relevant conditions are met, this agreement would benefit from the block exemption under Article 4(2)(a) described above. Secondly, there is an agreement between operators providing the MTC and the operator providing the service(s) to which the MTC is an add-on. Assuming that the relevant conditions are met, it will benefit from the block exemption under Article 4(2)(d).

12   This is because revenue must lie where it falls with a MIT.

13   See paragraph 3.32.

14   Article 18.

4 Duration

4.1   The block exemption applies from 1 March 2001 until 28 February 2006.[1] It is envisaged that the operation of the block exemption will be reviewed before its expiry. The Director General will then advise the Secretary of State as to whether the block exemption should be renewed, and, if so, the terms on which it should be renewed.

NOTES

1   Article 2.

5 Other United Kingdom Competition Scrutiny

The Chapter II prohibition

5.1   The block exemption exempts agreements only from the scope of the Chapter I prohibition. If an undertaking that participates in a ticketing scheme holds a dominant position in a market, it must comply with the Chapter II prohibition. Abuse of a dominant position by an undertaking which enters into a public transport ticketing scheme is assessed in exactly the same way as any other type of conduct under the Chapter II prohibition. This is considered in the Competition Act guideline *The Chapter II Prohibition*.

The Fair Trading Act 1973

5.2   The scale and complex monopoly provisions in the Fair Trading Act 1973 (see part 13 of the Competition Act guideline *The Major Provisions*) may, in certain circumstances, be relevant for dealing with possible competition problems in relation to public transport ticketing scheme agreements.[1] A complex monopoly investigation may, for example, be appropriate where, as a result of the structure of a market, agreements prevalent in that market have the effect of preventing the entry of new competitors into the market but where there is no evidence of an agreement or collusion between the undertakings involved which might have caused this situation to arise.

[3128]

NOTES

[1]   The Enterprise Bill, if enacted in its present form, will repeal the monopoly provisions in the Fair Trading Act and will introduce market investigation powers instead (this is discussed more fully in the OFT draft guidance on market investigations available on the OFT's web site www.oft.gov.uk).

6 The Relationship with EC Law

6.1   Article 81(1) of the EC Treaty prohibits anti-competitive agreements which 'may affect trade between Member States', whereas the Chapter I prohibition applies only to anti-competitive agreements which 'may affect trade within the United Kingdom'. The phrase 'may affect trade between Member States' has been broadly interpreted by the European Court of Justice which has found that even where the parties to an agreement are within the same Member State, inter-state trade may still be affected by the terms of that agreement. It is possible that some agreements will be caught by both Article 81(1) and the Chapter I prohibition. The public transport ticketing scheme block exemption under the Act does not apply outside the United Kingdom nor does it preclude the application of Article 81(1) of the EC Treaty.

[3129]

Addresses of the Regulators—

Office of Fair Trading Fleetbank House 2–6 Salsbury Square London EC4Y 8JX Tel: 020 7211 8000 Competition Act enquiries: 020 7211 8989 Cartels Task Force: 020 7211 8888 Fax: 020 7211 8800 Web: www.oft.gov.uk	Office of Gas and Electricity Markets 9 Millbank London SW1P 3GE Tel: 020 7901 7000 Fax: 020 7901 7066 Web: www.ofgem.gov.uk
Office of Telecommunications Compliance Directorate 50 Ludgate Hill London EC4M 7JJ Tel: 020 7634 8833 Fax: 020 7634 8949 Web: www.oftel.gov.uk	Office of the Rail Regulator 1 Waterhouse Square 138-142 Holborn London EC1N 2TQ Tel: 020 7282 2000 Fax: 020 7282 2045 Web: www.rail-reg.gov.uk
Office for the Regulation of Electricity and Gas Brookmount Buildings 42 Fountain Street Belfast BT1 5EE Northern Ireland Tel: 028 9031 1575 Fax: 028 9031 1740 Web: www.ofreg.nics.gov.uk	Office of Water Services Centre City Tower 7 Hill Street Birmingham B5 4UA Tel: 0121 625 1300 Fax: 0121 625 1400 Web: www.ofwat.gov.uk
Civil Aviation Authority CAA House 45–59 Kingsway London WC2B 6TE Tel: 020 7453 6225 Fax: 020 7453 6224 Web: www.caa.co.uk	

PART III
OFT GUIDELINES

[3130]–[4000]

PART IV
EC MATERIALS

PART IV

EC MATERIALS

A. GENERAL

TREATY ESTABLISHING THE EUROPEAN COMMUNITY (TREATY OF ROME)

NOTES

The Treaty is set out as consolidated by the Treaty of Amsterdam amending the Treaty on European Union, the Treaties establishing the European Communities and certain related acts, signed at Amsterdam, 2 October 1997, OJ C340, 10.11.97, p 1. The Treaty of Amsterdam takes effect from 1 May 1999.

PART THREE
COMMUNITY POLICIES

TITLE VI
COMMON RULES ON COMPETITION, TAXATION AND APPROXIMATION OF LAWS

CHAPTER 1
RULES ON COMPETITION

SECTION 1
RULES APPLYING TO UNDERTAKINGS

Article 81

1.   The following shall be prohibited as incompatible with the common market: all agreements between undertakings, decisions by associations of undertakings and concerted practices which may affect trade between Member States and which have as their object or effect the prevention, restriction or distortion of competition within the common market, and in particular those which—

    (a) directly or indirectly fix purchase or selling prices or any other trading conditions;

    (b) limit or control production, markets, technical development, or investment;

    (c) share markets or sources of supply;

    (d) apply dissimilar conditions to equivalent transactions with other trading parties, thereby placing them at a competitive disadvantage;

    (e) make the conclusion of contracts subject to acceptance by the other parties of supplementary obligations which, by their nature or according to commercial usage, have no connection with the subject of such contracts.

2.   Any agreements or decisions prohibited pursuant to this Article shall be automatically void.

3.   The provisions of paragraph 1 may, however, be declared inapplicable in the case of—

    — any agreement or category of agreements between undertakings;

    — any decision or category of decisions by associations of undertakings;

    — any concerted practice or category of concerted practices;

which contributes to improving the production or distribution of goods or to promoting technical or economic progress, while allowing consumers a fair share of the resulting benefit, and which does not—

    (a) impose on the undertakings concerned restrictions which are not indispensable to the attainment of these objectives;

    (b) afford such undertakings the possibility of eliminating competition in respect of a substantial part of the products in question.

[4001]

PART IV
EC MATERIALS

Article 82

Any abuse by one or more undertakings of a dominant position within the common market or in a substantial part of it shall be prohibited as incompatible with the common market in so far as it may affect trade between Member States.

Such abuse may, in particular, consist in—
  (a) directly or indirectly imposing unfair purchase or selling prices or other unfair trading conditions;
  (b) limiting production, markets or technical development to the prejudice of consumers;
  (c) applying dissimilar conditions to equivalent transactions with other trading parties, thereby placing them at a competitive disadvantage;
  (d) making the conclusion of contracts subject to acceptance by the other parties of supplementary obligations which, by their nature or according to commercial usage, have no connection with the subject of such contracts.

[4002]

Article 83

1. The appropriate regulations or directions to give effect to the principles set out in Articles 81 and 82 shall be laid down by the Council, acting by a qualified majority on a proposal from the Commission and after consulting the European Parliament.

2. The regulations or directives referred to in paragraph 1 shall be designed in particular—
  (a) to ensure compliance with the prohibitions laid down in Article 81(1) and in Article 82 by making provision for fines and periodic penalty payments;
  (b) to lay down detailed rules for the application of Article 81(3), taking into account the need to ensure effective supervision on the one hand, and to simplify administration to the greatest possible extent on the other;
  (c) to define, if need be, in the various branches of the economy, the scope of the provisions of Articles 81 and 82;
  (d) to define the respective functions of the Commission and of the Court of Justice in applying the provisions laid down in this paragraph;
  (e) to determine the relationship between national laws and the provisions contained in this Section or adopted pursuant to this Article.

[4003]

Article 84

Until the entry into force of the provisions adopted in pursuance of Article 83, the authorities in Member States shall rule on the admissibility of agreements, decisions and concerted practices and on abuse of a dominant position in the common market in accordance with the law of their country and with the provisions of Article 81, in particular paragraph 3, and of Article 82.

[4004]

Article 85

1. Without prejudice to Article 84, the Commission shall ensure the application of the principles laid down in Articles 81 and 82. On application by a Member State or on its own initiative, and in co-operation with the competent authorities in the Member States, who shall give it their assistance, the Commission shall investigate cases of suspected infringement of these principles. If it finds that there has been an infringement, it shall propose appropriate measures to bring it to an end.

2.   If the infringement is not brought to an end, the Commission shall record such infringement of the principles in a reasoned decision. The Commission may publish its decision and authorise Member States to take the measures, the conditions and details of which it shall determine, needed to remedy the situation.

[4005]

Article 86

1.   In the case of public undertakings and undertakings to which Member States grant special or exclusive rights, Member States shall neither enact nor maintain in force any measure contrary to the rules contained in this Treaty, in particular to those rules provided for in Article 6 and Articles 81 to 89.

2.   Undertakings entrusted with the operation of services of general economic interest or having the character of a revenue-producing monopoly shall be subject to the rules contained in this Treaty, in particular to the rules on competition, insofar as the application of such rules does not obstruct the performance, in law or in fact, of the particular tasks assigned to them. The development of trade must not be affected to such an extent as would be contrary to the interests of the Community.

3.   The Commission shall ensure the application of the provisions of this Article and shall, where necessary, address appropriate directives or decisions to Member States.

[4006]

Article 87

1.   Save as otherwise provided in this Treaty, any aid granted by a Member State or through State resources in any form whatsoever which distorts or threatens to distort competition by favouring certain undertakings or the production of certain goods shall, in so far as it affects trade between Member States, be incompatible with the common market.

2.   The following shall be compatible with the common market—
   (a) aid having a social character, granted to individual consumers, provided that such aid is granted without discrimination related to the origin of the products concerned;
   (b) aid to make good the damage caused by natural disasters or other exceptional occurrences;
   (c) aid granted to the economy of certain areas of the Federal Republic of Germany affected by the division of Germany, in so far as such aid is required in order to compensate for the economic disadvantages caused by that division.

3.   The following may be considered to be compatible with the common market—
   (a) aid to promote the economic development of areas where the standard of living is abnormally low or where there is serious underemployment;
   (b) aid to promote the execution of an important project of common European interest or to remedy a serious disturbance in the economy of a Member State;
   (c) aid to facilitate the development of certain economic activities or of certain economic areas, where such aid does not adversely affect trading conditions to an extent contrary to the common interest;
   (d) aid to promote culture and heritage conservation where such aid does not affect trading conditions and competition in the Community to an extent that is contrary to the common interest;
   (e) such other categories of aid as may be specified by decision of the Council acting by a qualified majority on a proposal from the Commission.

[4007]

PART IV
EC MATERIALS

Article 88

1.   The Commission shall, in cooperation with Member States, keep under constant review all systems of aid existing in those States. It shall propose to the latter any appropriate measures required by the progressive development or by the functioning of the common market.

2.   If, after giving notice to the parties concerned to submit their comments, the Commission finds that aid granted by a State or through State resources is not compatible with the common market having regard to Article 87, or that such aid is being misused, it shall decide that the State concerned shall abolish or alter such aid within a period of time to be determined by the Commission.

If the State concerned does not comply with this decision within the prescribed time, the Commission or any other interested State may, in derogation from the provisions of Articles 226 and 227, refer the matter to the Court of Justice direct.

On application by a Member State, the Council may, acting unanimously, decide that aid which that State is granting or intends to grant shall be considered to be compatible with the common market, in derogation from the provisions of Article 87 or from the regulations provided for in Article 89, if such a decision is justified by exceptional circumstances. If, as regards the aid in question, the Commission has already initiated the procedure provided for in the first subparagraph of this paragraph, the fact that the State concerned has made its application to the Council shall have the effect of suspending that procedure until the Council has made its attitude known.

If, however, the Council has not made its attitude known within three months of the said application being made, the Commission shall give its decision on the case.

3.   The Commission shall be informed, in sufficient time to enable it to submit its comments, of any plans to grant or alter aid. If it considers that any such plan is not compatible with the common market having regard to Article 87, it shall without delay initiate the procedure provided for in paragraph 2. The Member State concerned shall not put its proposed measures into effect until this procedure has resulted in a final decision.

[4008]

Article 89

The Council, acting by a qualified majority on a proposal from the Commission and after consulting the European Parliament, may make any appropriate regulations for the application of Articles 87 and 88 and may in particular determine the conditions in which Article 88(3) shall apply and the categories of aid exempted from this procedure.

[4009]

COUNCIL REGULATION
First Regulation implementing Articles 85 and 86 of the Treaty

(17/62/EEC)

NOTES
    Date of publication in OJ: OJ L13, 21.2.62, p 204 (S edn, 1959–62, p 87).

THE COUNCIL OF THE EUROPEAN ECONOMIC COMMUNITY,

Having regard to the Treaty establishing the European Economic Community, and in particular Article 87 thereof;
    Having regard to the proposal from the Commission;

Having regard to the Opinion of the Economic and Social Committee;

Having regard to the Opinion of the European Parliament;

Whereas, in order to establish a system ensuring that competition shall not be distorted in the common market, it is necessary to provide for balanced application of Articles 85 and 86 in a uniform manner in the Member States;

Whereas in establishing the rules for applying Article 85(3) account must be taken of the need to ensure effective supervision and to simplify administration to the greatest possible extent;

Whereas it is accordingly necessary to make it obligatory, as a general principle, for undertakings which seek application of Article 85(3) to notify to the Commission their agreements, decisions and concerted practices;

Whereas, on the one hand, such agreements, decisions and concerted practices are probably very numerous and cannot therefore all be examined at the same time and, on the other hand, some of them have special features which may make them less prejudicial to the development of the common market;

Whereas there is consequently a need to make more flexible arrangements for the time being in respect of certain categories of agreement, decision and concerted practice without prejudging their validity under Article 85;

Whereas it may be in the interest of undertakings to know whether any agreements, decisions or practices to which they are party, or propose to become party, may lead to action on the part of the Commission pursuant to Article 85(1) or Article 86;

Whereas, in order to secure uniform application of Articles 85 and 86 in the common market, rules must be made under which the Commission, acting in close and constant liaison with the competent authorities of the Member States, may take the requisite measures for applying those Articles;

Whereas for this purpose the Commission must have the co-operation of the competent authorities of the Member States and be empowered, throughout the common market, to require such information to be supplied and to undertake such investigations as are necessary to bring to light any agreement, decision or concerted practice prohibited by Article 85(1) or any abuse of a dominant position prohibited by Article 86;

Whereas, in order to carry out its duty of ensuring that the provisions of the Treaty are applied, the Commission must be empowered to address to undertakings or associations of undertakings recommendations and decisions for the purpose of bringing to an end infringements of Articles 85 and 86;

Whereas compliance with Articles 85 and 86 and the fulfilment of obligations imposed on undertakings and associations of undertakings under this Regulation must be enforceable by means of fines and periodic penalty payments;

Whereas undertakings concerned must be accorded the right to be heard by the Commission, third parties whose interests may be affected by a decision must be given the opportunity of submitting their comments beforehand, and it must be ensured that wide publicity is given to decisions taken;

Whereas all decisions taken by the Commission under this Regulation are subject to review by the Court of Justice under the conditions specified in the Treaty; whereas it is moreover desirable to confer upon the Court of Justice, pursuant to Article 172, unlimited jurisdiction in respect of decisions under which the Commission imposes fines or periodic penalty payments;

Whereas this Regulation may enter into force without prejudice to any other provisions that may hereafter be adopted pursuant to Article 87;

HAS ADOPTED THIS REGULATION—

Article 1

Basic provision

Without prejudice to Articles 6, 7 and 23 of this Regulation, agreements, decisions and concerted practices of the kind described in Article 85(1) of the Treaty and the abuse of a dominant position in the market, within the meaning of Article 86 of the Treaty, shall be prohibited, no prior decision to that effect being required.

[4010]

Article 2

Negative clearance

Upon application by the undertakings or associations of undertakings concerned, the Commission may certify that, on the basis of the facts in its possession, there are no grounds under Article 85(1) or Article 86 of the Treaty for action on its part in respect of an agreement, decision or practice.

[4011]

Article 3

Termination of infringements

1.   Where the Commission, upon application or upon its own initiative, finds that there is infringement of Article 85 or Article 86 of the Treaty, it may by decision require the undertakings or associations of undertakings concerned to bring such infringement to an end.

2.   Those entitled to make application are—
   (a) Member States;
   (b) natural or legal persons who claim a legitimate interest.

3.   Without prejudice to the other provisions of this Regulation, the Commission may, before taking a decision under paragraph 1, address to the undertakings or associations of undertakings concerned recommendations for termination of the infringement.

[4012]

Article 4

Notification of new agreements, decisions and practices

1.   Agreements, decisions and concerted practices of the kind described in Article 85(1) of the Treaty which come into existence after the entry into force of this Regulation and in respect of which the parties seek application of Article 85(3) must be notified to the Commission. Until they have been notified, no decision in application of Article 85(3) may be taken.

2.   Paragraph 1 shall not apply to agreements, decisions or concerted practices where—
   (1) the only parties thereto are undertakings from one Member State and the agreements, decisions or practices do not relate either to imports or to exports between Member States;
   [(2) (a) the agreements or concerted practices are entered into by two or more undertakings, each operating, for the purposes of the agreement, at a different level of the production or distribution chain, and relate to the conditions under which the parties may purchase, sell or resell certain goods or services;
   (b) not more than two undertakings are party thereto, and the agreements only impose restrictions on the exercise of the rights of the assignee or user of industrial property rights, in particular patents, utility models, designs or trade marks, or of the person entitled under a contract to the assignment, or grant, of the right to use a method of manufacture or knowledge relating to the use and to the application of industrial processes]
   (3) they have as their sole object—
   (a) the development or uniform application of standards or types; or
   [(b) joint research and development;

(c) specialisation in the manufacture of products, including agreements necessary for the achievement thereof;
— where the products which are the subject of specialisation do not, in a substantial part of the common market, represent more than 15% of the volume of business done in identical products or those considered by consumers to be similar by reason of their characteristics, price and use, and
— where the total annual turnover of the participating undertakings does not exceed 200 million units of account.

These agreements decisions and concerted practices may be notified to the Commission].

[4013]

NOTES

Para 2: sub-para (2) substituted by Council Regulation 1216/99/EC, Art 1; sub-para (3)(b) substituted and sub-para (3)(c) and the remaining words added by Council Regulation 2822/71/EEC.

Article 5

Notification of existing agreements, decisions and practices

1.   Agreements, decisions and concerted practices of the kind described in Article 85(1) of the Treaty which are in existence at the date of entry into force of this Regulation and in respect of which the parties seek application of Article 85(3) shall be notified to the Commission [before 1 November 1962]. [However, notwithstanding the foregoing provisions, any agreements, decisions and concerted practices to which not more than two undertakings are party shall be notified before 1 February 1963].

2.   Paragraph 1 shall not apply to agreements, decisions or concerted practices falling within Article 4(2); these may be notified to the Commission.

[4014]

NOTES

Para 1: words in first pair of square brackets substituted, words in second pair of square brackets added, by Council Regulation 59/62/EEC, Art 1(1), (2).

Article 6

Decisions pursuant to Article 85(3)

1.   Whenever the Commission takes a decision pursuant to Article 85(3) of the Treaty, it shall specify therein the date from which the decision shall take effect. Such date shall not be earlier than the date of notification.

2.   The second sentence of paragraph 1 shall not apply to agreements, decisions or concerted practices falling within Article 4(2) and Article 5(2), nor to those falling within Article 5(1) which have been notified within the time limit specified in Article 5(1).

[4015]

Article 7

Special provisions for existing agreements, decisions and practices

1.   Where agreements, decisions and concerted practices in existence at the date of entry into force of this Regulation and notified [within the limits specified in Article 5(1)] do not satisfy the requirements of Article 85(3) of the Treaty and the

undertakings or associations of undertakings concerned cease to give effect to them or modify them in such manner that they no longer fall within the prohibition contained in Article 85(1) or that they satisfy the requirements of Article 85(3), the prohibition contained in Article 85(1) shall apply only for a period fixed by the Commission. A decision by the Commission pursuant to the foregoing sentence shall not apply as against undertakings and associations of undertakings which did not expressly consent to the notification.

2. Paragraph 1 shall apply to agreements, decisions and concerted practices falling within Article 4(2) which are in existence at the date of entry into force of this Regulation if they are notified [before 1 January 1967].

[4016]

NOTES

Para 1: words in square brackets substituted by Council Regulation 59/62/EEC, Art 1(3).
Para 2: words in square brackets substituted by Council Regulation 118/63/EEC, Art 1.

Article 8

Duration and revocation of decisions under Article 85(3)

1. A decision in application of Article 85(3) of the Treaty shall be issued for a specified period and conditions and obligations may be attached thereto.

2. A decision may on application be renewed if the requirements of Article 85(3) of the Treaty continue to be satisfied.

3. The Commission may revoke or amend its decision or prohibit specified acts by the parties—
    (a) where there has been a change in any of the facts which were basic to the making of the decision;
    (b) where the parties commit a breach of any obligation attached to the decision;
    (c) where the decision is based on incorrect information or was induced by deceit;
    (d) where the parties abuse the exemption from the provisions of Article 85(1) of the Treaty granted to them by the decision.

In cases to which subparagraphs (b), (c) or (d) apply, the decision may be revoked with retroactive effect.

[4017]

Article 9

Powers

1. Subject to review of its decision by the Court of Justice, the Commission shall have sole power to declare Article 85(1) inapplicable pursuant to Article 85(3) of the Treaty.

2. The Commission shall have power to apply Article 85(1) and Article 86 of the Treaty; this power may be exercised notwithstanding that the time limits specified in Article 5(1) and in Article 7(2) relating to notification have not expired.

3. As long as the Commission has not initiated any procedure under Articles 2, 3 or 6, the authorities of the Member States shall remain competent to apply Article 85(1) and Article 86 in accordance with Article 88 of the Treaty; they shall remain competent in this respect notwithstanding that the time limits specified in Article 5(1) and in Article 7(2) relating to notification have not expired.

[4018]

Article 10

Liaison with the authorities of the Member States

1.   The Commission shall forthwith transmit to the competent authorities of the Member States a copy of the applications and notifications together with copies of the most important documents lodged with the Commission for the purpose of establishing the existence of infringements of Articles 85 or 86 of the Treaty or of obtaining negative clearance or a decision in application of Article 85(3).

2.   The Commission shall carry out the procedure set out in paragraph 1 in close and constant liaison with the competent authorities of the Member States; such authorities shall have the right to express their views upon that procedure.

3.   An Advisory Committee on Restrictive Practices and Monopolies shall be consulted prior to the taking of any decision following upon a procedure under paragraph 1, and of any decision concerning the renewal, amendment or revocation of a decision pursuant to Article 85(3) of the Treaty.

4.   The Advisory Committee shall be composed of officials competent in the matter of restrictive practices and monopolies. Each Member State shall appoint an official to represent it who, if prevented from attending, may be replaced by another official.

5.   The consultation shall take place at a joint meeting convened by the Commission; such meeting shall be held not earlier than fourteen days after dispatch of the notice convening it. The notice shall, in respect of each case to be examined, be accompanied by a summary of the case together with an indication of the most important documents, and a preliminary draft decision.

6.   The Advisory Committee may deliver an opinion notwithstanding that some of its members or their alternates are not present. A report of the outcome of the consultative proceedings shall be annexed to the draft decision. It shall not be made public.

[4019]

Article 11

Requests for information

1.   In carrying out the duties assigned to it by Article 89 and by provisions adopted under Article 87 of the Treaty, the Commission may obtain all necessary information from the Governments and competent authorities of the Member States and from undertakings and associations of undertakings.

2.   When sending a request for information to an undertaking or association of undertakings, the Commission shall at the same time forward a copy of the request to the competent authority of the Member State in whose territory the seat of the undertaking or association of undertakings is situated.

3.   In its request the Commission shall state the legal basis and the purpose of the request and also the penalties provided for in Article 15(1)(b) for supplying incorrect information.

4.   The owners of the undertakings or their representatives and, in the case of legal persons, companies or firms, or of associations having no legal personality, the persons authorised to represent them by law or by their constitution shall supply the information requested.

5.   Where an undertaking or association of undertakings does not supply the information requested within the time limit fixed by the Commission, or supplies incomplete information, the Commission shall by decision require the information

to be supplied. The decision shall specify what information is required, fix an appropriate time limit within which it is to be supplied and indicate the penalties provided for in Article 15(1)(b) and Article 16(1)(c) and the right to have the decision reviewed by the Court of Justice.

6.   The Commission shall at the same time forward a copy of its decision to the competent authority of the Member State in whose territory the seat of the undertaking or association of undertakings is situated.

[4020]

Article 12

Inquiry into sectors of the economy

1.   If in any sector of the economy the trend of trade between Member States, price movements, inflexibility of prices or other circumstances suggest that in the economic sector concerned competition is being restricted or distorted within the common market, the Commission may decide to conduct a general inquiry into that economic sector and in the course thereof may request undertakings in the sector concerned to supply the information necessary for giving effect to the principles formulated in Articles 85 and 86 of the Treaty and for carrying out the duties entrusted to the Commission.

2.   The Commission may in particular request every undertaking or association of undertakings in the economic sector concerned to communicate to it all agreements, decisions and concerted practices which are exempt from notification by virtue of Article 4(2) and Article 5(2).

3.   When making inquiries pursuant to paragraph 2, the Commission shall also request undertakings or groups of undertakings whose size suggests that they occupy a dominant position within the common market or a substantial part thereof to supply to the Commission such particulars of the structure of the undertakings and of their behaviour as are requisite to an appraisal of their position in the light of Article 86 of the Treaty.

4.   Article 10(3) to (6) and Articles 11, 13 and 14 shall apply correspondingly.

[4021]

Article 13

Investigations by the authorities of the Member States

1.   At the request of the Commission, the competent authorities of the Member States shall undertake the investigations which the Commission considers to be necessary under Article 14(1), or which it has ordered by decision pursuant to Article 14(3). The officials of the competent authorities of the Member States responsible for conducting these investigations shall exercise their powers upon production of an authorisation in writing issued by the competent authority of the Member State in whose territory the investigation is to be made. Such authorisation shall specify the subject matter and purpose of the investigation.

2.   If so requested by the Commission or by the competent authority of the Member State in whose territory the investigation is to be made, the officials of the Commission may assist the officials of such authorities in carrying out their duties.

[4022]

Article 14

Investigating powers of the Commission

1.   In carrying out the duties assigned to it by Article 89 and by provisions adopted under Article 87 of the Treaty, the Commission may undertake all necessary investigations into undertakings and associations of undertakings. To this end the officials authorised by the Commission are empowered—
   (a) to examine the books and other business records;
   (b) to take copies of or extracts from the books and business records;
   (c) to ask for oral explanations on the spot;
   (d) to enter any premises, land and means of transport of undertakings.

2.   The officials of the Commission authorised for the purpose of these investigations shall exercise their powers upon production of an authorisation in writing specifying the subject matter and purpose of the investigation and the penalties provided for in Article 15(1)(c) in cases where production of the required books or other business records is incomplete. In good time before the investigation, the Commission shall inform the competent authority of the Member State in whose territory the same is to be made of the investigation and of the identity of the authorised officials.

3.   Undertakings and associations of undertakings shall submit to investigations ordered by decision of the Commission. The decision shall specify the subject matter and purpose of the investigation, appoint the date on which it is to begin and indicate the penalties provided for in Article 15(1)(c) and Article 16(1)(d) and the right to have the decision reviewed by the Court of Justice.

4.   The Commission shall take decisions referred to in paragraph 3 after consultation with the competent authority of the Member State in whose territory the investigation is to be made.

5.   Officials of the competent authority of the Member State in whose territory the investigation is to be made may, at the request of such authority or of the Commission, assist the officials of the Commission in carrying out their duties.

6.   Where an undertaking opposes an investigation ordered pursuant to this Article, the Member State concerned shall afford the necessary assistance to the officials authorised by the Commission to enable them to make their investigation. Member States shall, after consultation with the Commission, take the necessary measures to this end before 1 October 1962.

[4023]

Article 15

Fines

1.   The Commission may by decision impose on undertakings or associations of undertakings fines of from 100 to 5000 units of account where, intentionally or negligently—
   (a) they supply incorrect or misleading information in an application pursuant to Article 2 or in a notification pursuant to Articles 4 or 5; or
   (b) they supply incorrect information in response to a request made pursuant to Article 11(3) or (5) or to Article 12, or do not supply information within the time limit fixed by a decision taken under Article 11(5); or
   (c) they produce the required books or other business records in incomplete form during investigations under Article 13 or 14, or refuse to submit to an investigation ordered by decision issued in implementation of Article 14(3).

2.   The Commission may by decision impose on undertakings or associations of undertakings fines of from 1 000 to 1 000 000 units of account, or a sum in excess thereof but not exceeding 10% of the turnover in the preceding business year of each of the undertakings participating in the infringement where, either intentionally or negligently—

    (a) they infringe Article 85(1) or Article 86 of the Treaty; or

    (b) they commit a breach of any obligation imposed pursuant to Article 8(1).

In fixing the amount of the fine, regard shall be had both to the gravity and to the duration of the infringement.

3.   Article 10(3) to (6) shall apply.

4.   Decisions taken pursuant to paragraphs 1 and 2 shall not be of a criminal law nature.

5.   The fines provided for in paragraph 2(a) shall not be imposed in respect of acts taking place—

    (a) after notification to the Commission and before its decision in application of Article 85(3) of the Treaty, provided they fall within the limits of the activity described in the notification;

    (b) before notification and in the course of agreements, decisions or concerted practices in existence at the date of entry into force of this Regulation, provided that notification was effected within the time limits specified in Article 5(1) and Article 7(2).

6.   Paragraph 5 shall not have effect where the Commission has informed the undertakings concerned that after preliminary examination it is of opinion that Article 85(1) of the Treaty applies and that application of Article 85(3) is not justified.

[4024]

Article 16

Periodic penalty payments

1.   The Commission may by decision impose on undertakings or associations of undertakings periodic penalty payments of from 50 to 1000 units of account per day, calculated from the date appointed by the decision, in order to compel them—

    (a) to put an end to an infringement of Article 85 or 86 of the Treaty, in accordance with a decision taken pursuant to Article 3 of this Regulation;

    (b) to refrain from any act prohibited under Article 8(3);

    (c) to supply complete and correct information which it has requested by decision taken pursuant to Article 11(5);

    (d) to submit to an investigation which it has ordered by decision taken pursuant to Article 14(3).

2.   Where the undertakings or associations of undertakings have satisfied the obligation which it was the purpose of the periodic penalty payment to enforce, the Commission may fix the total amount of the periodic penalty payment at a lower figure than that which would arise under the original decision.

3.   Article 10(3) to (6) shall apply.

[4025]

Article 17

Review by the Court of Justice

The Court of Justice shall have unlimited jurisdiction within the meaning of Article 172 of the Treaty to review decisions whereby the Commission has fixed a fine or periodic penalty payment; it may cancel, reduce or increase the fine or periodic penalty payment imposed.

[4026]

Article 18

Unit of account

For the purposes of applying Articles 15 to 17 the unit of account shall be that adopted in drawing up the budget of the Community in accordance with Articles 207 and 209 of the Treaty.

[4027]

Article 19

Hearing of the parties and of third persons

1.   Before taking decisions as provided for in Articles 2, 3, 6, 7, 8, 15 and 16, the Commission shall give the undertakings or associations of undertakings concerned the opportunity of being heard on the matters to which the Commission has taken objection.

2.   If the Commission or the competent authorities of the Member States consider it necessary, they may also hear other natural or legal persons. Applications to be heard on the part of such persons shall, where they show a sufficient interest, be granted.

3.   Where the Commission intends to give negative clearance pursuant to Article 2 or take a decision in application of Article 85(3) of the Treaty, it shall publish a summary of the relevant application or notification and invite all interested third parties to submit their observations within a time limit which it shall fix being not less than one month. Publication shall have regard to the legitimate interest of undertakings in the protection of their business secrets.

[4028]

Article 20

Professional secrecy

1.   Information acquired as a result of the application of Articles 11, 12, 13 and 14 shall be used only for the purpose of the relevant request or investigation.

2.   Without prejudice to the provisions of Articles 19 and 21, the Commission and the competent authorities of the Member States, their officials and other servants shall not disclose information acquired by them as a result of the application of this Regulation and of the kind covered by the obligation of professional secrecy.

3.   The provisions of paragraphs 1 and 2 shall not prevent publication of general information or surveys which do not contain information relating to particular undertakings or associations of undertakings.

[4029]

Article 21

Publication of decisions

1.   The Commission shall publish the decisions which it takes pursuant to Articles 2, 3, 6, 7 and 8.

2.   The publication shall state the names of the parties and the main content of the decision; it shall have regard to the legitimate interest of undertakings in the protection of their business secrets.

[4030]

Article 22

Special provisions

1.   The Commission shall submit to the Council proposals for making certain categories of agreement, decision and concerted practice falling within Article 4(2) or Article 5(2) compulsorily notifiable under Article 4 or 5.

2.   Within one year from the date of entry into force of this Regulation, the Council shall examine, on a proposal from the Commission, what special provisions might be made for exempting from the provisions of this Regulation agreements, decisions and concerted practices falling within Article 4(2) or Article 5(2).

[4031]

Article 23

Transitional provisions applicable to decisions of authorities of the Member States

1.   Agreements, decisions and concerted practices of the kind described in Article 85(1) of the Treaty to which, before the entry into force of this Regulation, the competent authority of a Member State has declared Article 85(1) to be inapplicable pursuant to Article 85(3) shall not be subject to compulsory notification under Article 5. The decision of the competent authority of the Member State shall be deemed to be a decision within the meaning of Article 6; it shall cease to be valid upon expiration of the period fixed by such authority but in any event not more than three years after the entry into force of this Regulation. Article 8(3) shall apply.

2.   Applications for renewal of decisions of the kind described in paragraph 1 shall be decided upon by the Commission in accordance with Article 8(2).

[4032]

Article 24

Implementing provisions

The Commission shall have power to adopt implementing provisions concerning the form, content and other details of applications pursuant to Articles 2 and 3 and of notifications pursuant to Articles 4 and 5, and concerning hearings pursuant to Article 19(1) and (2).

[4033]

[Article 25

1.   As regards agreements, decisions and concerted practices to which Article 85 of the Treaty applies by virtue of accession, the date of accession shall be substituted for the date of entry into force of this regulation in every place where reference is made in this Regulation to this latter date.

2.   Agreements, decisions and concerted practices existing at the date of accession to which Article 85 of the Treaty applies by virtue of accession shall be notified pursuant to Article 5(1) or Article 7(1) and (2) within six months from the date of accession.

3.   Fines under Article 15(2)(a) shall not be imposed in respect of any act prior to notification of the agreements, decisions and practices to which paragraph 2 applies and which have been notified within the period therein specified.

4.   New Member States shall take the measures referred to in Article 14(6) within six months from the date of accession after consulting the Commission.]

[5.   The provisions of paragraphs (1) to (4) above still apply in the same way in the case of accession of the Hellenic Republic, the Kingdom of Spain and of the Portuguese Republic.]

[6.   The provisions of paragraphs 1 to 4 still apply in the same way in the case of the accession of Austria, Finland and Sweden. However, they do not apply to agreements, decisions and concerted practices which at the date of the accession already fall under Article 53 of the EEA Agreement.]

[4034]

NOTES

Paras 1–4: added by the 1972 Act of Accession of Denmark, Ireland and the United Kingdom, Annex I(V)(1).

Para 5: added by the 1979 Act of Accession of the Hellenic Republic, Annex I(V)(1); substituted by the 1985 Act of Accession of the Kingdom of Spain and the Portuguese Republic, Annex I(IV)(5).

Para 6: added by the 1994 Act of Accession of the Kingdom of Norway, the Republic of Austria, the Republic of Finland and the Kingdom of Sweden, Annex I(III)(B)(1), as adjusted by Council Decision 95/1/EC, Annex I(III)(B)(1).

This Regulation shall be binding in its entirety and directly applicable in all Member States.

Done at Brussels, 6 February 1962.

COUNCIL REGULATION

applying certain rules of competition to production of and trade in agricultural products

(26/62/EEC)

NOTES

Date of publication in OJ: OJ L30, 21.4.62, p 993 (S edn, 1959–1962, p 129).

THE COUNCIL OF THE EUROPEAN ECONOMIC COMMUNITY,

Having regard to the Treaty establishing the European Economic Community, and in particular Articles 42 and 43 thereof;

Having regard to the proposal from the Commission;

Having regard to the Opinion of the European Parliament;

Whereas by virtue of Article 42 of the Treaty one of the matters to be decided under the common agricultural policy is whether the rules on competition laid down in the Treaty are to apply to production of and trade in agricultural products, and accordingly the provisions hereinafter contained will have to be supplemented in the light of developments in that policy;

Whereas the proposals submitted by the Commission for the formulation and implementation of the common agricultural policy show that certain rules on competition must forthwith be made applicable to production of and trade in agricultural products in order to eliminate practices contrary to the principles of the common market and prejudicial to attainment of the objectives set out in Article 39 of the Treaty and in order to provide a basis for the future establishment of a system of competition adapted to the development of the common agricultural policy;

Whereas the rules on competition relating to the agreements, decisions and practices referred to in Article 85 of the Treaty and to the abuse of dominant positions must be applied to production of and trade in agricultural products, in so far as their application does not impede the functioning of national organisations of agricultural markets or jeopardise attainment of the objectives of the common agricultural policy;

Whereas special attention is warranted in the case of farmers' organisations which are particularly concerned with the joint production or marketing of agricultural products or the use of joint facilities, unless such joint action excludes competition or jeopardises attainment of the objectives of Article 39 of the Treaty;

Whereas, in order both to avoid compromising the development of a common agricultural policy and to ensure certainty in the law and non-discriminatory treatment of the undertakings concerned, the Commission must have sole power, subject to review by the Court of Justice, to determine whether the conditions provided for in the two preceding recitals are fulfilled as regards the agreements, decisions and practices referred to in Article 85 of the Treaty;

Whereas, in order to enable the specific provisions of the Treaty regarding agriculture, and in particular those of Article 39 thereof, to be taken into consideration, the Commission must, in questions of dumping, assess all the causes of the practices complained of and in particular the price level at which products from other sources are imported into the market in question; whereas it must, in the light of its assessment, make recommendations and authorise protective measures as provided in Article 91(1) of the Treaty;

Whereas, in order to implement, as part of the development of the common agricultural policy, the rules on aids for production of or trade in agricultural products, the Commission should be in a position to draw up a list of existing, new or proposed aids, to make appropriate observations to the Member States and to propose suitable measures to them;

HAS ADOPTED THIS REGULATION—

Article 1

From the entry into force of this Regulation, Articles 85 to 90 of the Treaty and provisions made in implementation thereof shall, subject to Article 2 below, apply to all agreements, decisions and practices referred to in Articles 85(1) and 86 of the Treaty which relate to production of or trade in the products listed in Annex II to the Treaty.

[4035]

Article 2

1.   Article 85(1) of the Treaty shall not apply to such of the agreements, decisions and practices referred to in the preceding Article as form an integral part of a national market organisation or are necessary for attainment of the objectives set out in Article 39 of the Treaty. In particular, it shall not apply to agreements, decisions and practices of farmers, farmers' associations, or associations of such associations belonging to a single Member State which concern the production or sale of agricultural products or the use of joint facilities for the storage, treatment or processing of agricultural products, and under which there is no obligation to charge identical prices, unless the Commission finds that competition is thereby excluded or that the objectives of Article 39 of the Treaty are jeopardised.

2.   After consulting the Member States and hearing the undertakings or associations of undertakings concerned and any other natural or legal person that it considers appropriate, the Commission shall have sole power, subject to review by the Court of Justice, to determine, by decision which shall be published, which agreements, decisions and practices fulfil the conditions specified in paragraph 1.

3.   The Commission shall undertake such determination either on its own initiative or at the request of a competent authority of a Member State or of an interested undertaking or association of undertakings.

4.   The publication shall state the names of the parties and the main content of the decision; it shall have regard to the legitimate interest of undertakings in the protection of their business secrets.

[4036]

Article 3

1.   Without prejudice to Article 46 of the Treaty, Article 91(1) thereof shall apply to trade in the products listed in Annex II to the Treaty.

2.   With due regard for the provisions of the Treaty relating to agriculture, and in particular those of Article 39, the Commission shall assess all the causes of the practices complained of, in particular the price level at which products from other sources are imported into the market in question.

In the light of its assessment, it shall make recommendations and authorise protective measures as provided in Article 91(1) of the Treaty.

[4037]

Article 4

The provisions of Article 93(1) and of the first sentence of Article 93(3) of the Treaty shall apply to aids granted for production of or trade in the products listed in Annex II to the Treaty.

[4038]

Article 5

This Regulation shall enter into force on the day following its publication in the *Official Journal of the European Communities*, with the exception of Articles 1 to 3, which shall enter into force on [30 July 1962].

[4039]

NOTES

Words in square brackets substituted by Council Regulation 49/62/EEC.

This Regulation shall be binding in its entirety and directly applicable in all Member States.

Done at Brussels, 4 April 1962.

COUNCIL REGULATION

of 2 March 1965

on application of Article 85(3) of the Treaty to certain categories of agreements and concerted practices

(19/65/EEC)

NOTES

Date of publication in OJ: OJ L36, 6.3.65, p 533 (S edn 1965–66, p 35).

THE COUNCIL OF THE EUROPEAN ECONOMIC COMMUNITY,

Having regard to the Treaty establishing the European Economic Community, and in particular Article 87 thereof;

Having regard to the proposal from the Commission;[1]

Having regard to the Opinion of the European Parliament;[2]

Having regard to the Opinion of the Economic and Social Committee;

Whereas Article 85(1) of the Treaty may in accordance with Article 85(3) be declared inapplicable to certain categories of agreements, decisions and concerted practices which fulfil the conditions contained in Article 85(3);

Whereas the provisions for implementation of Article 85(3) must be adopted by way of regulation pursuant to Article 87;

Whereas in view of the large number of notifications submitted in pursuance of Regulation No 17[3] it is desirable that in order to facilitate the task of the Commission it should be enabled to declare by way of regulation that the provisions of Article 85(1) do not apply to certain categories of agreements and concerted practices;

Whereas it should be laid down under what conditions the Commission, in close and constant liaison with the competent authorities of the Member States, may exercise such powers after sufficient experience has been gained in the light of individual decisions and it becomes possible to define categories of agreements and concerted practices in respect of which the conditions of Article 85(3) may be considered as being fulfilled;

Whereas the Commission has indicated by the action it has taken, in particular by Regulation No 153,[4] that there can be no easing of the procedures prescribed by Regulation No 17 in respect of certain types of agreements and concerted practices that are particularly liable to distort competition in the common market;

Whereas under Article 6 of Regulation No 17 the Commission may provide that a decision taken pursuant to Article 85(3) of the Treaty shall apply with retroactive effect; whereas it is desirable that the Commission be also empowered to adopt, by regulation, provisions to the like effect;

Whereas under Article 7 of Regulation No 17 agreements, decisions and concerted practices may, by decision of the Commission, be exempted from prohibition in particular if they are modified in such manner that they satisfy the requirements of Article 85(3); whereas it is desirable that the Commission be enabled to grant like exemption by regulation to such agreements and concerted practices if they are modified in such manner as to fall within a category defined in an exempting regulation;

Whereas, since there can be no exemption if the conditions set out in Article 85(3) are not satisfied, the Commission must have power to lay down by decision the conditions that must be satisfied by an agreement or concerted practice which owing to special circumstances has certain effects incompatible with Article 85(3);

HAS ADOPTED THIS REGULATION—

NOTES

[1]   OJ 81, 27.5.64, p 1275/64.

[2]   OJ 197, 30.11.64, p 3320/64.

[3]   OJ 13, 21.12.62, p 204/62 (Regulation No 17 as amended by Regulation No 59—OJ 58, 10.7.62, p 1655/62—and Regulation No 118/63/EEC—OJ 162, 7.11.63, p 2696/63).

[4]   OJ 139, 24.12.62, p 2918/62.

Article 1

[1.   Without prejudice to the application of Regulation No 17 and in accordance with Article 81(3) of the Treaty the Commission may by regulation declare that Article 81(1) shall not apply to—

   (a) categories of agreements which are entered into by two or more undertakings, each operating, for the purposes of the agreement, at a different level of the production or distribution chain, and which relate to the conditions under which the parties may purchase, sell or resell certain goods or services,

   (b) categories of agreements to which only two undertakings are party and which include restrictions imposed in relation to the acquisition or use of industrial property rights, in particular of patents, utility models, designs or trade marks, or to the rights arising out of contracts for assignment of, or the right to use, a method of manufacture or knowledge relating to the use or to the application of industrial processes.]

2.   The regulation shall define the categories of agreements to which it applies and shall specify in particular—

(a) the restrictions or clauses which must not be contained in the agreements;

(b) . . . the other conditions which must be satisfied.

[3.   Paragraphs 1 and 2 shall apply by analogy to categories of concerted practices.]

[4040]

NOTES

Paras 1, 3 substituted and words omitted from para 2 repealed by Council Regulation 1215/99/EC, Art 1(1).

[Article 1a

A regulation pursuant to Article 1 may stipulate the conditions which may lead to the exclusion from its application of certain parallel networks of similar agreements or concerted practices operating on a particular market; when these circumstances are fulfilled the Commission may establish this by means of regulation and fix a period at the expiry of which the Regulation pursuant to Article 1 would no longer be applicable in respect of the relevant agreements or concerted practices on that market; such period must not be shorter than six months.]

[4041]

NOTES

Inserted by Council Regulation 1215/99/EC, Art 1(2).

Article 2

1.   A regulation pursuant to Article 1 shall be made for a specified period.

2.   It may be repealed or amended where circumstances have changed with respect to any factor which was basic to its being made; in such case, a period shall be fixed for modification of the agreements and concerted practices to which the earlier regulation applies.

[4042]

Article 3

A regulation pursuant to Article 1 may stipulate that it shall apply with retroactive effect to agreements and concerted practices to which, at the date of entry into force of that regulation, a decision issued with retroactive effect in pursuance of Article 6 of Regulation No 17 would have applied.

[4043]

Article 4

1.   A regulation pursuant to Article 1 may stipulate that the prohibition contained in Article 85(1) of the Treaty shall not apply, for such period as shall be fixed by that regulation, to agreements and concerted practices already in existence on 13 March 1962 which do not satisfy the conditions of Article 85(3), where—

[A regulation pursuant to Article 1 may stipulate that the prohibition contained in Article 85(1) of the Treaty shall not apply, for such period as shall be fixed by that regulation, to agreements and concerted practices already in existence at the date of

accession to which Article 85 applies by virtue of accession and which do not satisfy the conditions of Article 85(3), where:]
— within three months from the entry into force of the regulation, they are so modified as to satisfy the said conditions in accordance with the provisions of the regulation; and
— the modifications are brought to the notice of the Commission within the time limit fixed by the regulation.

[The provisions of the preceding subparagraph shall apply in the same way in the case of the accession of the Hellenic Republic, the Kingdom of Spain and of the Portuguese Republic.]

[The provisions of the preceding subparagraphs shall apply in the same way in the case of the accession of Austria, Finland and Sweden.]

2. Paragraph 1 shall apply to agreements and concerted practices which had to be notified before 1 February 1963, in accordance with Article 5 of Regulation No 17, only where they have been so notified before that date.

[Paragraph 1 shall not apply to agreements and concerted practices to which Article 85(1) of the Treaty applies by virtue of accession and which must be notified before 1 July 1973, in accordance with Articles 5 and 25 of Regulation No 17, unless they have been so notified before that date.]

[Paragraph 1 shall not apply to agreements and concerted practices to which Article 85(1) of the Treaty applies by virtue of the accession of the Hellenic Republic and which must be notified before 1 July 1981, in accordance with Articles 5 and 25 of Regulation No 17, unless they have been so notified before that date.]

[Paragraph 2 shall not apply to agreements and concerted practices to which Article 85(1) of the Treaty applies by virtue of the accession of the Kingdom of Spain and of the Portuguese Republic and which must be notified before 1 July 1986, in accordance with Articles 5 and 25 of Regulation No 17, unless they have been so notified before that date.]

[Paragraph 1 shall not apply to agreements and concerted practices to which Article 85(1) of the Treaty applies by virtue of the accession of Austria, Finland and Sweden and which must be notified within six months of accession, in accordance with Articles 5 and 25 of Regulation No 17, unless they have been so notified within that period. The present paragraph shall not apply to agreements and concerted practices which at the date of accession already fall under Article 53(1) of the EEA agreement.]

3. The benefit of the provisions laid down pursuant to paragraph 1 may not be claimed in actions pending at the date of entry into force of a regulation adopted pursuant to Article 1; neither may it be relied on as grounds for claims for damages against third parties.

NOTES

Para 1: words in first pair of square brackets inserted by the 1972 Act of Accession of Denmark, Ireland and the United Kingdom; words in second pair of square brackets added by the 1979 Act of Accession of the Hellenic Republic, substituted by the 1985 Act of Accession of the Kingdom of Spain and the Portuguese Republic; words in third pair of square brackets inserted by the 1994 Act of Accession of the Kingdom of Norway, the Republic of Austria, the Republic of Finland and the Kingdom of Sweden, Annex I(III)(A)(1), as adjusted by Council Decision 95/1/EC, Annex I(III)(A)(1).

Para 2: words in first pair of square brackets inserted by the 1972 Act of Accession of Denmark, Ireland and the United Kingdom; words in second pair of square brackets inserted by the 1979 Act of Accession of the Hellenic Republic; words in third pair of square brackets added by the 1985 Act of Accession of the Kingdom of Spain and the Portuguese Republic; words in fourth pair of square brackets inserted by the 1994 Act of Accession of the Kingdom of Norway, the Republic of Austria, the Republic of Finland and the Kingdom of Sweden, Annex I(III)(A)(1), as adjusted by Council Decision 95/1/EC, Annex I(III)(A)(1).

Article 5

Before adopting a regulation, the Commission shall publish a draft thereof and invite all persons concerned to submit their comments within such time limit, being not less than one month, as the Commission shall fix.

[4045]

Article 6

[1. The Commission shall consult the Advisory Committee on Restrictive Practices and Monopolies—
  (a) with regard to a regulation pursuant to Article 1 before publishing a draft regulation and before adopting a regulation;
  (b) with regard to a regulation pursuant to Article 1a before publishing a draft regulation if requested by a Member State, and before adopting a regulation.]

2. Article 10(5) and (6) of Regulation No 17, relating to consultation with the Advisory Committee, shall apply by analogy, it being understood that joint meetings with the Commission shall take place not earlier than one month after dispatch of the notice convening them.

[4046]

NOTES

Para 1: substituted by Council Regulation 1215/99/EC, Art 1(3).

Article 7

[1.] Where the Commission, either on its own initiative or at the request of a Member State or of natural or legal persons claiming a legitimate interest, finds that in any particular case agreements or concerted practices to which a regulation adopted pursuant to Article 1 of this Regulation applies have nevertheless certain effects which are incompatible with the conditions laid down in Article 85(3) of the Treaty, it may withdraw the benefit of application of that regulation and issue a decision in accordance with Articles 6 and 8 of Regulation No 17, without any notification under Article 4(1) of Regulation No 17 being required.

[2. When in any particular case agreements or concerted practices to which a regulation adopted pursuant to Article 1 applies have certain effects which are incompatible with the conditions laid down in Article 81(3) of the Treaty in the territory of a Member State, or in part thereof, which has all the characteristics of a distinct market, the competent authority in that Member State may on its own initiative or at the request of the Commission or of natural or legal persons claiming a legitimate interest withdraw the benefit of application of that regulation.]

[4047]

NOTES

Existing text renumbered as para 1 and para 2 added by Council Regulation 1215/99/EC, Art 1(4).

Article 8

The Commission shall, before 1 January 1970, submit to the Council a proposal for a Regulation for such amendment of this Regulation as may prove necessary in the light of experience.

[4048]

This Regulation shall be binding in its entirety and directly applicable in all Member States.

Done at Brussels, 2 March 1965.

COMMISSION NOTICE

on the definition of relevant market for the purposes of Community competition law

(97/C 372/03)

NOTES

Date of publication in OJ: OJ C372, 9.12.97, p 5.

I Introduction

1.   The purpose of this notice is to provide guidance as to how the Commission applies the concept of relevant product and geographic market in its ongoing enforcement of Community competition law, in particular the application of Council Regulation 17/62 and (EEC) 4064/89, their equivalents in other sectoral applications such as transport, coal and steel, and agriculture, and the relevant provisions of the EEA Agreement.[1] Throughout this notice, references to Articles 85 and 86 of the Treaty and to merger control are to be understood as referring to the equivalent provisions in the EEA Agreement and the ECSC Treaty.

2.   Market definition is a tool to identify and define the boundaries of competition between firms. It serves to establish the framework within which competition policy is applied by the Commission. The main purpose of market definition is to identify in a systematic way the competitive constraints that the undertakings involved[2] face. The objective of defining a market in both its product and geographic dimension is to identify those actual competitors of the undertakings involved that are capable of constraining those undertakings' behaviour and of preventing them from behaving independently of effective competitive pressure. It is from this perspective that the market definition makes it possible inter alia to calculate market shares that would convey meaningful information regarding market power for the purposes of assessing dominance or for the purposes of applying Article 85.

3.   It follows from point 2 that the concept of "relevant" market is different from other definitions of market often used in other contexts. For instance, companies often use the term "market" to refer to the area where it sells its products or to refer broadly to the industry or sector where it belongs.

4.   The definition of the relevant market in both its product and its geographic dimensions often has a decisive influence on the assessment of a competition case. By rendering public the procedures which the Commission follows when considering market definition and by indicating the criteria and evidence on which it relies to reach a decision, the Commission expects to increase the transparency of its policy and decision-making in the area of competition policy.

5.   Increased transparency will also result in companies and their advisers being able to better anticipate the possibility that the Commission may raise competition concerns in an individual case. Companies could, therefore, take such a possibility into account in their own internal decision-making when contemplating, for instance, acquisitions, the creation of joint ventures, or the establishment of certain agreements. It is also intended that companies should be in a better position to understand what sort of information the Commission considers relevant for the purposes of market definition.

6.   The Commission's interpretation of "relevant" market is without prejudice to the interpretation which may be given by the Court of Justice or the Court of First Instance of the European Communities.

II Definition of relevant market

Definition of relevant product market and relevant geographic market

7.   The Regulations based on Articles 85 and 86 of the Treaty, in particular in section 6 of Form A/B with respect to Regulation No 17, as well as in section 6 of Form CO with respect to Regulation (EEC) 4064/89 on the control of concentrations having a Community dimension have laid down the following definitions. "Relevant product markets" are defined as follows—

> "A relevant product market comprises all those products and/or services which are regarded as interchangeable or substitutable by the consumer, by reason of the products' characteristics, their prices and their intended use."

8.   "Relevant geographic markets" are defined as follows—

> "The relevant geographic market comprises the area in which the undertakings concerned are involved in the supply and demand of products or services, in which the conditions of competition are sufficiently homogeneous and which can be distinguished from neighbouring areas because the conditions of competition are appreciably different in those areas".

9.   The relevant market within which to assess a given competition issue is therefore established by the combination of the product and geographic markets. The Commission interprets the definitions in paragraphs 7 and 8 (which reflect the case law of the Court of Justice and the Court of First Instance as well as its own decision-making practice) according to the orientations defined in this notice.

Concept of relevant market and objectives of Community competition policy

10.   The concept of relevant market is closely related to the objectives pursued under Community competition policy. For example, under the Community's merger control, the objective in controlling structural changes in the supply of a product/ service is to prevent the creation or reinforcement of a dominant position as a result of which effective competition would be significantly impeded in a substantial part of the common market. Under the Community's competition rules, a dominant position is such that a firm or group of firms would be in a position to behave to an appreciable extent independently of its competitors, customers and ultimately of its consumers.[3] Such a position would usually arise when a firm or group of firms accounted for a large share of the supply in any given market, provided that other factors analysed in the assessment (such as entry barriers, customers' capacity, etc) point in the same direction.

11.   The same approach is followed by the Commission in its application of Article 86 of the Treaty to firms that enjoy a single or collective dominant position. Within the meaning of Regulation No 17, the Commission has the power to investigate and bring to an end abuses of such a dominant position, which must also be defined by reference to the relevant market. Markets may also need to be defined in the application of Article 85 of the Treaty, in particular, in determining whether an appreciable restriction of competition exists or in establishing if the condition pursuant to Article 85(3)(b) for an exemption from the application of Article 85(1) is met.

12.   The criteria for defining the relevant market are applied generally for the analysis of certain types of behaviour in the market and for the analysis of structural changes in the supply of products. This methodology, though, might lead to different results depending on the nature of the competition issue being examined. For instance, the scope of the geographic market might be different when analysing a concentration, where the analysis is essentially prospective, from an analysis of past behaviour. The different time horizon considered in each case might lead to the

PART IV
EC MATERIALS

result that different geographic markets are defined for the same products depending on whether the Commission is examining a change in the structure of supply, such as a concentration or a cooperative joint venture, or examining issues relating to certain past behaviour.

Basic principles for market definition

Competitive constraints

13.   Firms are subject to three main sources of competitive constraints: demand substitutability, supply substitutability and potential competition. From an economic point of view, for the definition of the relevant market, demand substitution constitutes the most immediate and effective disciplinary force on the suppliers of a given product, in particular in relation to their pricing decisions. A firm or a group of firms cannot have a significant impact on the prevailing conditions of sale, such as prices, if its customers are in a position to switch easily to available substitute products or to suppliers located elsewhere. Basically, the exercise of market definition consists in identifying the effective alternative sources of supply for the customers of the undertakings involved, in terms both of products/services and of geographic location of suppliers.

14.   The competitive constraints arising from supply side substitutability other than those described in paras 20–23 and from potential competition are in general less immediate and in any case require an analysis of additional factors. As a result such constraints are taken into account at the assessment stage of competition analysis.

Demand substitution

15.   The assessment of demand substitution entails a determination of the range of products which are viewed as substitutes by the consumer. One way of making this determination can be viewed as a speculative experiment, postulating a hypothetical small, lasting change in relative prices and evaluating the likely reactions of customers to that increase. The exercise of market definition focuses on prices for operational and practical purposes, and more precisely on demand substitution arising from small, permanent changes in relative prices. This concept can provide clear indications as to the evidence that is relevant to define markets.

16.   Conceptually, this approach means that, starting from the type of products that the undertakings involved sell and the area in which they sell them, additional products and areas will be included in, or excluded from, the market definition depending on whether competition from these other products and areas affect or restrain sufficiently the pricing of the parties' products in the short term.

17.   The question to be answered is whether the parties' customers would switch to readily available substitutes or to suppliers located elsewhere in response to a hypothetical small (in the range 5%–10%) but permanent relative price increase in the products and areas being considered. If substitution were enough to make the price increase unprofitable because of the resulting loss of sales, additional substitutes and areas are included in the relevant market. This would be done until the set of products and geographical areas is such that small, permanent increases in relative prices would be profitable. The equivalent analysis is applicable in cases concerning the concentration of buying power, where the starting point would then be the supplier and the price test serves to identify the alternative distribution channels or outlets for the supplier's products. In the application of these principles, careful account should be taken of certain particular situations as described within paragraphs 56 and 58.

18.   A practical example of this test can be provided by its application to a merger of, for instance, soft-drink bottlers. An issue to examine in such a case would be to decide whether different flavours of soft drinks belong to the same market. In

practice, the question to address would be whether consumers of flavour A would switch to other flavours when confronted with a permanent price increase of 5% to 10% for flavour A. If a sufficient number of consumers would switch to, say, flavour B, to such an extent that the price increase for flavour A would not be profitable owing to the resulting loss of sales, then the market would comprise at least flavours A and B. The process would have to be extended in addition to other available flavours until a set of products is identified for which a price rise would not induce a sufficient substitution in demand.

19.   Generally, and in particular for the analysis of merger cases, the price to take into account will be the prevailing market price. This might not be the case where the prevailing price has been determined in the absence of sufficient competition. In particular for the investigation of abuses of dominant positions, the fact that the prevailing price might already have been substantially increased will be taken into account.

Supply substitution

20.   Supply-side substitutability may also be taken into account when defining markets in those situations in which its effects are equivalent to those of demand substitution in terms of effectiveness and immediacy. This requires that suppliers be able to switch production to the relevant products and market them in the short term[4] without incurring significant additional costs or risks in response to small and permanent changes in relative prices. When these conditions are met, the additional production that is put on the market will have a disciplinary effect on the competitive behaviour of the companies involved. Such an impact in terms of effectiveness and immediacy is equivalent to the demand substitution effect.

21.   These situations typically arise when companies market a wide range of qualities or grades of one product; even if, for a given final customer or group of consumers, the different qualities are not substitutable, the different qualities will be grouped into one product market, provided that most of the suppliers are able to offer and sell the various qualities immediately and without the significant increases in costs described above. In such cases, the relevant product market will encompass all products that are substitutable in demand and supply, and the current sales of those products will be aggregated so as to give the total value or volume of the market. The same reasoning may lead to group different geographic areas.

22.   A practical example of the approach to supply-side substitutability when defining product markets is to be found in the case of paper. Paper is usually supplied in a range of different qualities, from standard writing paper to high quality papers to be used, for instance, to publish art books. From a demand point of view, different qualities of paper cannot be used for any given use, ie an art book or a high quality publication cannot be based on lower quality papers. However, paper plants are prepared to manufacture the different qualities, and production can be adjusted with negligible costs and in a short time-frame. In the absence of particular difficulties in distribution, paper manufacturers are able therefore, to compete for orders of the various qualities, in particular if orders are passed with sufficient lead time to allow for modification of production plans. Under such circumstances, the Commission would not define a separate market for each quality of paper and its respective use. The various qualities of paper are included in the relevant market, and their sales added up to estimate total market value and volume.

23.   When supply-side substitutability would entail the need to adjust significantly existing tangible and intangible assets, additional investments, strategic decisions or time delays, it will not be considered at the stage of market definition. Examples where supply-side substitution did not induce the Commission to enlarge the market are offered in the area of consumer products, in particular for branded beverages. Although bottling plants may in principle bottle different beverages, there are costs

and lead times involved (in terms of advertising, product testing and distribution) before the products can actually be sold. In these cases, the effects of supply-side substitutability and other forms of potential competition would then be examined at a later stage.

Potential competition

24. The third source of competitive constraint, potential competition, is not taken into account when defining markets, since the conditions under which potential competition will actually represent an effective competitive constraint depend on the analysis of specific factors and circumstances related to the conditions of entry. If required, this analysis is only carried out at a subsequent stage, in general once the position of the companies involved in the relevant market has already been ascertained, and when such position gives rise to concerns from a competition point of view.

III Evidence relied on to define relevant markets

The process of defining the relevant market in practice

Product dimension

25. There is a range of evidence permitting an assessment of the extent to which substitution would take place. In individual cases, certain types of evidence will be determinant, depending very much on the characteristics and specificity of the industry and products or services that are being examined. The same type of evidence may be of no importance in other cases. In most cases, a decision will have to be based on the consideration of a number of criteria and different items of evidence. The Commission follows an open approach to empirical evidence, aimed at making an effective use of all available information which may be relevant in individual cases. The Commission does not follow a rigid hierarchy of different sources of information or types of evidence.

26. The process of defining relevant markets may be summarised as follows: on the basis of the preliminary information available or information submitted by the undertakings involved, the Commission will usually be in a position to broadly establish the possible relevant markets within which, for instance, a concentration or a restriction of competition has to be assessed. In general, and for all practical purposes when handling individual cases, the question will usually be to decide on a few alternative possible relevant markets. For instance, with respect to the product market, the issue will often be to establish whether product A and product B belong or do not belong to the same product market. It is often the case that the inclusion of product B would be enough to remove any competition concerns.

27. In such situations it is not necessary to consider whether the market includes additional products, or to reach a definitive conclusion on the precise product market. If under the conceivable alternative market definitions the operation in question does not raise competition concerns, the question of market definition will be left open, reducing thereby the burden on companies to supply information.

Geographic dimension

28. The Commission's approach to geographic market definition might be summarised as follows: it will take a preliminary view of the scope of the geographic market on the basis of broad indications as to the distribution of market shares between the parties and their competitors, as well as a preliminary analysis of

pricing and price differences at national and Community or EEA level. This initial view is used basically as a working hypothesis to focus the Commission's enquiries for the purposes of arriving at a precise geographic market definition.

29.   The reasons behind any particular configuration of prices and market shares need to be explored. Companies might enjoy high market shares in their domestic markets just because of the weight of the past, and conversely, a homogeneous presence of companies throughout the EEA might be consistent with national or regional geographic markets. The initial working hypothesis will therefore be checked against an analysis of demand characteristics (importance of national or local preferences, current patterns of purchases of customers, product differentiation/brands, other) in order to establish whether companies in different areas do indeed constitute a real alternative source of supply for consumers. The theoretical experiment is again based on substitution arising from changes in relative prices, and the question to answer is again whether the customers of the parties would switch their orders to companies located elsewhere in the short term and at a negligible cost.

30.   If necessary, a further check on supply factors will be carried out to ensure that those companies located in differing areas do not face impediments in developing their sales on competitive terms throughout the whole geographic market. This analysis will include an examination of requirements for a local presence in order to sell in that area the conditions of access to distribution channels, costs associated with setting up a distribution network, and the presence or absence of regulatory barriers arising from public procurement, price regulations, quotas and tariffs limiting trade or production, technical standards, monopolies, freedom of establishment, requirements for administrative authorisations, packaging regulations, etc. In short, the Commission will identify possible obstacles and barriers isolating companies located in a given area from the competitive pressure of companies located outside that area, so as to determine the precise degree of market interpenetration at national, European or global level.

31.   The actual pattern and evolution of trade flows offers useful supplementary indications as to the economic importance of each demand or supply factor mentioned above, and the extent to which they may or may not constitute actual barriers creating different geographic markets. The analysis of trade flows will generally address the question of transport costs and the extent to which these may hinder trade between different areas, having regard to plant location, costs of production and relative price levels.

Market integration in the Community

32.   Finally, the Commission also takes into account the continuing process of market integration, in particular in the Community when defining geographic markets, especially in the area of concentrations and structural joint ventures. The measures adopted and implemented in the internal market programme to remove barriers to trade and further integrate the Community markets cannot be ignored when assessing the effects on competition of a concentration or a structural joint venture. A situation where national markets have been artificially isolated from each other because of the existence of legislative barriers that have now been removed will generally lead to a cautious assessment of past evidence regarding prices, market shares or trade patterns. A process of market integration that would, in the short term, lead to wider geographic markets may therefore be taken into consideration when defining the geographic market for the purposes of assessing concentrations and joint ventures.

The process of gathering evidence

33.   When a precise market definition is deemed necessary, the Commission will often contact the main customers and the main companies in the industry to enquire into their views about the boundaries of product and geographic markets and to obtain the necessary factual evidence to reach a conclusion. The Commission might also contact the relevant professional associations, and companies active in upstream markets, so as to be able to define, in so far as necessary, separate product and geographic markets, for different levels of production or distribution of the products/services in question. It might also request additional information to the undertakings involved.

34.   Where appropriate, the Commission will address written requests for information to the market players mentioned above. These requests will usually include questions relating to the perceptions of companies about reactions to hypothetical price increases and their views of the boundaries of the relevant market. They will also ask for provision of the factual information the Commission deems necessary to reach a conclusion on the extent of the relevant market. The Commission might also discuss with marketing directors or other officers of those companies to gain a better understanding on how negotiations between suppliers and customers take place and better understand issues relating to the definition of the relevant market. Where appropriate, they might also carry out visits or inspections to the premises of the parties, their customers and/or their competitors, in order to better understand how products are manufactured and sold.

35.   The type of evidence relevant to reach a conclusion as to the product market can be categorised as follows:

Evidence to define markets—product dimension

36.   An analysis of the product characteristics and its intended use allows the Commission, as a first step, to limit the field of investigation of possible substitutes. However, product characteristics and intended use are insufficient to show whether two products are demand substitutes. Functional interchangeability or similarity in characteristics may not, in themselves, provide sufficient criteria, because the responsiveness of customers to relative price changes may be determined by other considerations as well. For example, there may be different competitive constraints in the original equipment market for car components and in spare parts, thereby leading to a separate delineation of two relevant markets. Conversely, differences in product characteristics are not in themselves sufficient to exclude demand substitutability, since this will depend to a large extent on how customers value different characteristics.

37.   The type of evidence the Commission considers relevant to assess whether two products are demand substitutes can be categorised as follows:

38.   *Evidence of substitution in the recent past* In certain cases, it is possible to analyse evidence relating to recent past events or shocks in the market that offer actual examples of substitution between two products. When available, this sort of information will normally be fundamental for market definition. If there have been changes in relative prices in the past (all else being equal), the reactions in terms of quantities demanded will be determinant in establishing substitutability. Launches of new products in the past can also offer useful information, when it is possible to precisely analyse which products have lost sales to the new product.

39.   There are a number of *quantitative tests* that have specifically been designed for the purpose of delineating markets. These tests consist of various econometric and statistical approaches estimates of elasticities and cross-price elasticities[5] for the demand of a product, tests based on similarity of price movements over time, the analysis of causality between price series and similarity of price levels and/or their

convergence. The Commission takes into account the available quantitative evidence capable of withstanding rigorous scrutiny for the purposes of establishing patterns of substitution in the past.

40.   *Views of customers and competitors* The Commission often contacts the main customers and competitors of the companies involved in its enquiries, to gather their views on the boundaries of the product market as well as most of the factual information it requires to reach a conclusion on the scope of the market. Reasoned answers of customers and competitors as to what would happen if relative prices for the candidate products were to increase in the candidate geographic area by a small amount (for instance of 5%–10%) are taken into account when they are sufficiently backed by factual evidence.

41.   *Consumer preferences* In the case of consumer goods, it may be difficult for the Commission to gather the direct views of end consumers about substitute products. *Marketing studies* that companies have commissioned in the past and that are used by companies in their own decision-making as to pricing of their products and/or marketing actions may provide useful information for the Commission's delineation of the relevant market. Consumer surveys on usage patterns and attitudes, data from consumers' purchasing patterns, the views expressed by retailers and more generally, market research studies submitted by the parties and their competitors are taken into account to establish whether an economically significant proportion of consumers consider two products as substitutable, also taking into account the importance of brands for the products in question. The methodology followed in consumer surveys carried out ad-hoc by the undertakings involved or their competitors for the purposes of a merger procedure or a procedure pursuant to Regulation No 17 will usually be scrutinised with utmost care. Unlike pre-existing studies, they have not been prepared in the normal course of business for the adoption of business decisions.

42.   *Barriers and costs associated with switching demand to potential substitutes* There are a number of barriers and costs that might prevent the Commission from considering two prima facie demand substitutes as belonging to one single product market. It is not possible to provide an exhaustive list of all the possible barriers to substitution and of switching costs. These barriers or obstacles might have a wide range of origins, and in its decisions, the Commission has been confronted with regulatory barriers or other forms of State intervention, constraints arising in downstream markets, need to incur specific capital investment or loss in current output in order to switch to alternative inputs, the location of customers, specific investment in production process, learning and human capital investment, retooling costs or other investments, uncertainty about quality and reputation of unknown suppliers, and others.

43.   *Different categories of customers and price discrimination* The extent of the product market might be narrowed in the presence of distinct groups of customers. A distinct group of customers for the relevant product may constitute a narrower, distinct market when such a group could be subject to price discrimination. This will usually be the case when two conditions are met: (a) it is possible to identify clearly which group an individual customer belongs to at the moment of selling the relevant products to him, and (b) trade among customers or arbitrage by third parties should not be feasible.

Evidence for defining markets—geographic dimension

44.   The type of evidence the Commission considers relevant to reach a conclusion as to the geographic market can be categorised as follows:

45.   *Past evidence of diversion of orders to other areas* In certain cases, evidence on changes in prices between different areas and consequent reactions by

customers might be available. Generally, the same quantitative tests used for product market definition might as well be used in geographic market definition, bearing in mind that international comparisons of prices might be more complex due to a number of factors such as exchange rate movements, taxation and product differentiation.

46. *Basic demand characteristics* The nature of demand for the relevant product may in itself determine the scope of the geographical market. Factors such as national preferences or preferences for national brands, language, culture and life style, and the need for a local presence have a strong potential to limit the geographic scope of competition.

47. *Views of customers and competitors* Where appropriate, the Commission will contact the main customers and competitors of the parties in its enquiries, to gather their views on the boundaries of the geographic market as well as most of the factual information it requires to reach a conclusion on the scope of the market when they are sufficiently backed by factual evidence.

48. *Current geographic pattern of purchases* An examination of the customers' current geographic pattern of purchases provides useful evidence as to the possible scope of the geographic market. When customers purchase from companies located anywhere in the Community or the EEA on similar terms, or they procure their supplies through effective tendering procedures in which companies from anywhere in the Community or the EEA submit bids, usually the geographic market will be considered to be Community-wide.

49. *Trade flows/pattern of shipments* When the number of customers is so large that it is not possible to obtain through them a clear picture of geographic purchasing patterns, information on trade flows might be used alternatively, provided that the trade statistics are available with a sufficient degree of detail for the relevant products. Trade flows, and above all, the rationale behind trade flows provide useful insights and information for the purpose of establishing the scope of the geographic market but are not in themselves conclusive.

50. *Barriers and switching costs associated to divert orders to companies located in other areas* The absence of trans-border purchases or trade flows, for instance, does not necessarily mean that the market is at most national in scope. Still, barriers isolating the national market have to be identified before it is concluded that the relevant geographic market in such a case is national. Perhaps the clearest obstacle for a customer to divert its orders to other areas is the impact of transport costs and transport restrictions arising from legislation or from the nature of the relevant products. The impact of transport costs will usually limit the scope of the geographic market for bulky, low-value products, bearing in mind that a transport disadvantage might also be compensated by a comparative advantage in other costs (labour costs or raw materials). Access to distribution in a given area, regulatory barriers still existing in certain sectors, quotas and custom tariffs might also constitute barriers isolating a geographic area from the competitive pressure of companies located outside that area. Significant switching costs in procuring supplies from companies located in other countries constitute additional sources of such barriers.

51. On the basis of the evidence gathered, the Commission will then define a geographic market that could range from a local dimension to a global one, and there are examples of both local and global markets in past decisions of the Commission.

52. The paragraphs above describe the different factors which might be relevant to define markets. This does not imply that in each individual case it will be necessary to obtain evidence and assess each of these factors. Often in practice the evidence provided by a subset of these factors will be sufficient to reach a conclusion, as shown in the past decisional practice of the Commission.

IV Calculation of market share

53.   The definition of the relevant market in both its product and geographic dimensions allows the identification of the suppliers and the customers/consumers active on that market. On that basis, a total market size and market shares for each supplier can be calculated on the basis of their sales of the relevant products in the relevant area. In practice, the total market size and market shares are often available from market sources, ie companies' estimates, studies commissioned from industry consultants and/or trade associations. When this is not the case, or when available estimates are not reliable, the Commission will usually ask each supplier in the relevant market to provide its own sales in order to calculate total market size and market shares.

54.   If sales are usually the reference to calculate market shares, there are nevertheless other indications that, depending on the specific products or industry in question, can offer useful information such as, in particular, capacity, the number of players in bidding markets, units of fleet as in aerospace, or the reserves held in the case of sectors such as mining.

55.   As a rule of thumb, both volume sales and value sales provide useful information. In cases of differentiated products, sales in value and their associated market share will usually be considered to better reflect the relative position and strength of each supplier.

V Additional considerations

56.   There are certain areas where the application of the principles above has to be undertaken with care. This is the case when considering primary and secondary markets, in particular, when the behaviour of undertakings at a point in time has to be analysed pursuant to Article 86. The method of defining markets in these cases is the same, ie assessing the responses of customers based on their purchasing decisions to relative price changes, but taking into account as well, constraints on substitution imposed by conditions in the connected markets. A narrow definition of market for secondary products, for instance, spare parts, may result when compatibility with the primary product is important. Problems of finding compatible secondary products together with the existence of high prices and a long lifetime of the primary products may render relative price increases of secondary products profitable. A different market definition may result if significant substitution between secondary products is possible or if the characteristics of the primary products make quick and direct consumer responses to relative price increases of the secondary products feasible.

57.   In certain cases, the existence of chains of substitution might lead to the definition of a relevant market where products or areas at the extreme of the market are not directly substitutable. An example might be provided by the geographic dimension of a product with significant transport costs. In such cases, deliveries from a given plant are limited to a certain area around each plant by the impact of transport costs. In principle, such an area could constitute the relevant geographic market. However, if the distribution of plants is such that there are considerable overlaps between the areas around different plants, it is possible that the pricing of those products will be constrained by a chain substitution effect, and lead to the definition of a broader geographic market. The same reasoning may apply if product B is a demand substitute for products A and C. Even if products A and C are not direct demand substitutes, they might be found to be in the same relevant product market since their respective pricing might be constrained by substitution to B.

58.   From a practical perspective, the concept of chains of substitution has to be corroborated by actual evidence, for instance related to price interdependence at the

extremes of the chains of substitution, in order to lead to an extension of the relevant market in an individual case. Price levels at the extremes of the chains would have to be of the same magnitude as well.

[4049]

NOTES

1   The focus of assessment in State aid cases is the aid recipient and the industry/sector concerned rather than identification of competitive constraints faced by the aid recipient. When consideration of market power and therefore of the relevant market are raised in any particular case, elements of the approach outlined here might serve as a basis for the assessment of State aid cases.

2   For the purposes of this notice, the undertakings involved will be, in the case of a concentration, the parties to the concentration, in investigations within the meaning of Article 86 of the Treaty, the undertaking being investigated or the complainants; for investigations within the meaning of Article 85, the parties to the Agreement.

3   Definition given by the Court of Justice in its judgment of 13 February 1979 in Case 85/76 [1979] ECR 461 *Hoffmann La Roche*, and confirmed in subsequent judgments.

4   That is such a period that does not entail a significant adjustment of existing tangible and intangible assets (see para 23).

5   Own-price elasticity of demand for product X is a measure of the responsiveness of demand for X to percentage change in its own price. Cross-price elasticity between products X and Y is the responsiveness of demand for product X to percentage change in the price of product Y.

COMMISSION REGULATION

of 21 December 1994

on the form, content and other details of applications and notifications provided for in Council Regulation No 17

(3385/94/EEC)

(Text with EEA relevance)

NOTES

Date of publication in OJ: OJ L377, 31.12.94, p 28.

THE COMMISSION OF THE EUROPEAN COMMUNITIES,

Having regard to the Treaty establishing the European Community,

Having regard to the Agreement on the European Economic Area,

Having regard to Council Regulation No 17 of 6 February 1962, First Regulation implementing Articles 85 and 86 of the Treaty,[1] as last amended by the Act of Accession of Spain and Portugal, and in particular Article 24 thereof,

Whereas Commission Regulation No 27 of 3 May 1962, First Regulation implementing Council Regulation No 17,[2] as last amended by Regulation (EC) No 3666/93,[3] no longer meets the requirements of efficient administrative procedure; whereas it should therefore be replaced by a new regulation;

Whereas, on the one hand, applications for negative clearance under Article 2 and notifications under Articles 4, 5 and 25 of Regulation No 17 have important legal consequences, which are favourable to the parties to an agreement, a decision or a practice, while, on the other hand, incorrect or misleading information in such applications or notifications may lead to the imposition of fines and may also entail civil law disadvantages for the parties; whereas it is therefore necessary in the interests of legal certainty to define precisely the persons entitled to submit applications and notifications, the subject matter and content of the information which such applications and notifications must contain, and the time when they become effective;

Whereas each of the parties should have the right to submit the application or the notification to the Commission; whereas, furthermore, a party exercising the right should inform the other parties in order to enable them to protect their interests; whereas applications and notifications relating to agreements, decisions or practices of associations of undertakings should be submitted only by such association;

Whereas it is for the applicants and the notifying parties to make full and honest disclosure to the Commission of the facts and circumstances which are relevant for coming to a decision on the agreements, decisions or practices concerned;

Whereas, in order to simplify and expedite their examination, it is desirable to prescribe that a form be used for applications for negative clearance relating to Article 85(1) and for notifications relating to Article 85(3); whereas the use of this form should also be possible in the case of applications for negative clearance relating to Article 86;

Whereas the Commission, in appropriate cases, will give the parties, if they so request, an opportunity before the application or the notification to discuss the intended agreement, decision or practice informally and in strict confidence; whereas, in addition, it will, after the application or notification, maintain close contact with the parties to the extent necessary to discuss with them any practical or legal problems which it discovers on a first examination of the case and if possible to remove such problems by mutual agreement;

Whereas the provisions of this Regulation must also cover cases in which applications for negative clearance relating to Article 53(1) or Article 54 of the EEA Agreement, or notifications, relating to Article 53(3) of the EEA Agreement are submitted to the Commission,

---

NOTES

1 OJ 13, 21.2.62, p 204/62.
2 OJ 35, 10.5.62, p 1118/62.
3 OJ L336, 31.12.93, p 1.

HAS ADOPTED THIS REGULATION—

Article 1

Persons entitled to submit applications and notifications

1. The following may submit an application under Article 2 of Regulation No 17 relating to Article 85(1) of the Treaty or a notification under Articles 4, 5 and 25 of Regulation No 17—

(a) any undertaking and any association of undertakings being a party to agreements or to concerted practices; and

(b) any association of undertakings adopting decisions or engaging in practices;

which may fall within the scope of Article 85(1).

Where the application or notification is submitted by some, but not all, of the parties, referred to in point (a) of the first subparagraph, they shall give notice to the other parties.

2. Any undertaking which may hold, alone or with other undertakings, a dominant position within the common market or in a substantial part of it, may submit an application under Article 2 of Regulation No 17 relating to Article 86 of the Treaty.

3. Where the application or notification is signed by representatives of persons, undertakings or associations of undertakings, such representatives shall produce written proof that they are authorised to act.

4. Where a joint application or notification is made, a joint representative should be appointed who is authorised to transmit and receive documents on behalf of all the applicants or notifying parties.

Article 2

Submission of applications and notifications

1.   Applications under Article 2 of Regulation No 17 relating to Article 85(1) of the Treaty and notifications under Articles 4, 5 and 25 of Regulation No 17 shall be submitted in the manner prescribed by Form A/B as shown in the Annex to this Regulation. Form A/B may also be used for applications under Article 2 of Regulation No 17 relating to Article 86 of the Treaty. Joint applications and joint notifications shall be submitted on a single form.

2.   Seventeen copies of each application and notification and three copies of the Annexes thereto shall be submitted to the Commission at the address indicated in Form A/B.

3.   The documents annexed to the application or notification shall be either originals or copies of the originals; in the latter case the applicant or notifying party shall confirm that they are true copies of the originals and complete.

4.   Applications and notifications shall be in one of the official languages of the Community. This language shall also be the language of the proceeding for the applicant or notifying party. Documents shall be submitted in their original language. Where the original language is not one of the official languages, a translation into the language of the proceeding shall be attached.

5.   Where applications for negative clearance relating to Article 53(1) or Article 54 of the EEA Agreement or notifications relating to Article 53(3) of the EEA Agreement are submitted, they may also be in one of the official languages of the EFTA States or the working language of the EFTA Surveillance Authority. If the language chosen for the application or notification is not an official language of the Community, the applicant or notifying party shall supplement all documentation with a translation into an official language of the Community. The language which is chosen for the translation shall be the language of the proceeding for the applicant or notifying party.

[4051]

Article 3

Content of applications and notifications

1.   Applications and notifications shall contain the information, including documents, required by Form A/B. The information must be correct and complete.

2.   Applications under Article 2 of Regulation No 17 relating to Article 86 of the Treaty shall contain a full statement of the facts, specifying, in particular, the practice concerned and the position of the undertaking or undertakings within the common market or a substantial part thereof in regard to the products or services to which the practice relates.

3.   The Commission may dispense with the obligation to provide any particular information, including documents, required by Form A/B where the Commission considers that such information is not necessary for the examination of the case.

4.   The Commission shall, without delay, acknowledge in writing to the applicant or notifying party receipt of the application or notification, and of any reply to a letter sent by the Commission pursuant to Article 4(2).

[4052]

Article 4

Effective date of submission of applications and notifications

1.   Without prejudice to paragraphs 2 to 5, applications and notifications shall become effective on the date on which they are received by the Commission. Where, however, the application or notification is sent by registered post, it shall become effective on the date shown on the postmark of the place of posting.

2.   Where the Commission finds that the information, including documents, contained in the application or notification is incomplete in a material respect, it shall, without delay, inform the applicant or notifying party in writing of this fact and shall fix an appropriate time limit for the completion of the information. In such cases, the application or notification shall become effective on the date on which the complete information is received by the Commission.

3.   Material changes in the facts contained in the application or notification which the applicant or notifying party knows or ought to know must be communicated to the Commission voluntarily and without delay.

4.   Incorrect or misleading information shall be considered to be incomplete information.

5.   Where, at the expiry of a period of one month following the date on which the application or notification has been received, the Commission has not provided the applicant or notifying party with the information referred to in paragraph 2, the application or notification shall be deemed to have become effective on the date of its receipt by the Commission.

[4053]

Article 5

Repeal

Regulation No 27 is repealed.

[4054]

Article 6

Entry into force

This Regulation shall enter into force on 1 March 1995.

[4055]

This Regulation shall be binding in its entirety and directly applicable in all Member States.

Done at Brussels, 21 December 1994.

FORM A/B

INTRODUCTION

Form A/B, and its Annex, is an integral part of Commission Regulation (EC) No 3385/94 of 21 December 1994 on the form, content and other details of applications and notifications provided for in Council Regulation No 17 (hereinafter referred to as "the Regulation"). It allows undertakings and associations of undertakings to apply to the Commission for negative clearance of agreements or practices which may fall within the prohibitions of Article 85(1) and Article 86 of the EC Treaty, or within Articles 53(1) and 54 of the EEA Agreement or to notify such agreement and apply to have it exempted from the prohibition set out in Article 85(1) by virtue of the provisions of Article 85(3) of the EC Treaty or from the prohibition of Article 53(1) by virtue of the provisions of Article 53(3) of the EEA Agreement.

To facilitate the use of the Form A/B the following pages set out—

- — in which situations it is necessary to make an application or a notification (Point A),
- — to which authority (the Commission or the EFTA Surveillance Authority) the application or notification should be made (Point B),
- — for which purposes the application or notification can be used (Point C),
- — what information must be given in the application or notification (Points D, E and F),
- — who can make an application or notification (Point G),
- — how to make an application or notification (Point H),
- — how the business secrets of the undertakings can be protected (Point I),
- — how certain technical terms used in the operational part of the Form A/B should be interpreted (Point J), and
- — the subsequent procedure after the application or notification has been made (Point K).

A. IN WHICH SITUATIONS IS IT NECESSARY TO MAKE AN APPLICATION OR A NOTIFICATION?

I. *Purpose of the competition rules of the EC Treaty and the EEA Agreement*

1. Purpose of the EC Competition Rules

The purpose of the competition rules is to prevent the distortion of competition in the common market by restrictive practices or the abuse of dominant positions. They apply to any enterprise trading directly or indirectly in the common market, wherever established.

Article 85(1) of the EC Treaty (the text of Articles 85 and 86 is reproduced in Annex I to this form) prohibits restrictive agreements, decisions or concerted practices (arrangements) which may affect trade between Member States, and Article 85(2) declares agreements and decisions containing such restrictions void (although the Court of Justice has held that if restrictive terms of agreements are severable, only those terms are void); Article 85(3), however, provides for exemption of arrangements with beneficial effects, if its conditions are met. Article 86 prohibits the abuse of a dominant position which may affect trade between Member States. The original procedures for implementing these Articles, which provide for "negative clearance" and exemption pursuant to Article 85(3), were laid down in Regulation No 17.

2. Purpose of the EEA competition rules

The competition rules of the Agreement on the European Economic Area (concluded between the Community, the Member States and the EFTA States[1]) are based on the same principles as those contained in the Community competition rules and have the same purpose, ie to prevent the distortion of competition in the EEA territory by cartels or the abuse of dominant position. They apply to any enterprise trading directly or indirectly in the EEA territory, wherever established.

Article 53(1) of the EEA Agreement (the text of Articles 53, 54 and 56 of the EEA Agreement is reproduced in Annex I) prohibits restrictive agreements, decisions or concerted practices (arrangements) which may affect trade between the Community and one or more EFTA States (or between EFTA States), and Article 53(2) declares agreements or decisions containing such restrictions void; Article 53(3), however, provides for exemption of arrangements with beneficial effects, if its conditions are met. Article 54 prohibits the abuse of a dominant position which may affect trade between the Community and one or more EFTA States (or between EFTA States). The procedures for implementing these Articles, which provide for "negative clearance" and exemption pursuant to Article 53(3), are laid down in Regulation No 17, supplemented for EEA purposes, by Protocols 21, 22 and 23 to the EEA Agreement.[2]

NOTES

[1]   See list of Member States and EFTA States in Annex III.

[2]   Reproduced in Annex I.

II. *The scope of the competition rules of the EC Treaty and the EEA Agreement*

The applicability of Articles 85 and 86 of the EC Treaty and Articles 53 and 54 of the EEA Agreement depends on the circumstances of each individual case. It presupposes that the arrangement or behaviour satisfies all the conditions set out in the relevant provisions. This question must consequently be examined before any application for negative clearance or any notification is made.

1. Negative clearance

The negative clearance procedure allows undertakings to ascertain whether the Commission considers that their arrangement or their behaviour is or is not prohibited by Article 85(1), or Article 86 of the EC Treaty or by Article 53(1) or Article 54 of the EEA Agreement. This procedure is governed by Article 2 of Regulation No 17. The negative clearance takes the form of a decision by which the Commission certifies that, on the basis of the facts in its possession, there are no grounds pursuant to Article 85(1) or Article 86 of the EC Treaty or under Article 53(1) or Article 54 of the EEA Agreement for action on its part in respect of the arrangement or behaviour.

There is, however, no point in making an application when the arrangements or the behaviour are manifestly not prohibited by the abovementioned provisions. Nor is the Commission obliged to give negative clearance. Article 2 of Regulation No 17 states that ". . . the Commission may certify . . .". The Commission issues negative clearance decisions only where an important problem of interpretation has to be solved. In the other cases it reacts to the application by sending a comfort letter.

The Commission has published several notices relating to the interpretation of Article 85(1) of the EC Treaty. They define certain categories of agreement which, by their nature or because of their minor importance, are not caught by the prohibition.[1]

NOTES
[1] See Annex II.

2. Exemption

The procedure for exemption pursuant to Article 85(3) of the EC Treaty and Article 53(3) of the EEA Agreement allows companies to enter into arrangements which, in fact, offer economic advantages but which, without exemption, would be prohibited by Article 85(1) of the EC Treaty or by Article 53(1) of the EEA Agreement. This procedure is governed by Articles 4, 6 and 8 and, for the new Member States, also by Articles 5, 7 and 25 of Regulation No 17. The exemption takes the form of a decision by the Commission declaring Article 85(1) of the EC Treaty or Article 53(1) of the EEA Agreement to be inapplicable to the arrangements described in the decision. Article 8 requires the Commission to specify the period of validity of any such decision, allows the Commission to attach conditions and obligations and provides for decisions to be amended or revoked or specified acts by the parties to be prohibited in certain circumstances, notably if the decisions were based on incorrect information or if there is any material change in the facts.

The Commission has adopted a number of regulations granting exemptions to categories of agreements.[1] Some of these regulations provide that some agreements may benefit from exemption only if they are notified to the Commission pursuant to Article 4 or 5 of Regulation No 17 with a view to obtaining exemption, and the benefit of the opposition procedure is claimed in the notification.

NOTES
[1] See Annex II.

A decision granting exemption may have retroactive effect, but, with certain exceptions, cannot be made effective earlier than the date of notification (Article 6 of Regulation No 17). Should the Commission find that notified arrangements are indeed prohibited and cannot be exempted and, therefore, take a decision condemning them, the participants are nevertheless protected, between the date of the notification and the date of the decision, against fines for any infringement described in the notification (Article 3 and Article 15(5) and (6) of Regulation No 17).

Normally the Commission issues exemption decisions only in cases of particular legal, economic or political importance. In the other cases it terminates the procedure by sending a comfort letter.

B. TO WHICH AUTHORITY SHOULD APPLICATION OR NOTIFICATION BE MADE?

The applications and notifications must be made to the authority which has competence for the matter. The Commission is responsible for the application of the competition rules of the EC Treaty. However there is shared competence in relation to the application of the competition rules of the EEA agreement.

The competence of the Commission and of the EFTA Surveillance Authority to apply the EEA competition rules follows from Article 56 of the EEA Agreement. Applications and notifications relating to agreements, decisions or concerted practices liable to affect trade between Member States should be addressed to the Commission unless their effects on trade between Member States or on competition within the Community are not appreciable within the meaning of the Commission notice of 1986 on agreements of minor importance.[1] Furthermore, all restrictive agreements, decisions or concerted practices affecting trade between one Member State and one or more EFTA States fall within the competence of the Commission, provided that the undertakings concerned achieve more than 67% of their combined EEA-wide turnover within the Community.[2] However, if the effects of such agreements, decisions or concerted practices on trade between Member States or on competition within the Community are not appreciable, the notification should, where necessary, be addressed to the EFTA Surveillance Authority. All other agreements, decisions and concerted practices falling under Article 53 of the EEA Agreement should be notified to the EFTA Surveillance Authority (the address of which is given in Annex III).

NOTES

[1]   OJ C231, 12.9.1986, p 2.

[2]   For a definition of "turnover" in this context, see Articles 2, 3 and 4 of Protocol 22 to the EEA Agreement reproduced in Annex I.

Applications for negative clearance regarding Article 54 of the EEA Agreement should be lodged with the Commission if the dominant position exists only in the Community, or with the EFTA Surveillance Authority, if the dominant position exists only in the whole of the territory of the EFTA States, or a substantial part of it. Only where the dominant position exists within both territories should the rules outlined above with respect to Article 53 be applied.

The Commission will apply, as a basis for appraisal, the competition rules of the EC Treaty. Where the case falls under the EEA Agreement and is attributed to the Commission pursuant to Article 56 of that Agreement, it will simultaneously apply the EEA rules.

C. THE PURPOSE OF THIS FORM

Form A/B lists the questions that must be answered and the information and documents that must be provided when applying for the following—

— a negative clearance with regard to Article 85(1) of the EC Treaty and/or Article 53(1) of the EEA Agreement, pursuant to Article 2 of Regulation No 17, with respect to agreements between undertakings, decisions by associations of undertakings and concerted practices,

— an exemption pursuant to Article 85(3) of the EC Treaty and/or Article 53(3) of the EEA Agreement with respect to agreements between undertakings, decisions by associations of undertakings and concerted practices,

— the benefit of the opposition procedure contained in certain Commission regulations granting exemption by category.

This form allows undertakings applying for negative clearance to notify, at the same time, in order to obtain an exemption in the event that the Commission reaches the conclusion that no negative clearance can be granted.

Applications for negative clearance and notifications relating to Article 85 of the EC Treaty shall be submitted in the manner prescribed by Form A/B (see Article 2(1), first sentence of the Regulation).

This form can also be used by undertakings that wish to apply for a negative clearance from Article 86 of the EC Treaty or Article 53 of the EEA Agreement, pursuant to Article 2 of

Regulation No 17. Applicants requesting negative clearance from Article 86 are not required to use Form A/B. They are nonetheless strongly recommended to give all the information requested below to ensure that their application gives a full statement of the facts (see Article 2(1), second sentence of the Regulation).

The applications or notifications made on the Form A/B issued by the EFTA side are equally valid. However, if the agreements, decisions or practices concerned fall solely within Articles 85 or 86 of the EC Treaty, ie have no EEA relevance whatsoever, it is advisable to use the present form established by the Commission.

D. WHICH CHAPTERS OF THE FORM SHOULD BE COMPLETED?

The operational part of this form is sub-divided into four chapters. Undertakings wishing to make an application for a negative clearance or a notification must complete Chapters I, II and IV. An exception to this rule is provided for in the case where the application or notification concerns an agreement concerning the creation of a cooperative joint venture of a structural character if the parties wish to benefit from an accelerated procedure. In this situation Chapters I, III and IV should be completed.

In 1992, the Commission announced that it had adopted new internal administrative rules that provided that certain applications and notifications—those of cooperative joint ventures which are structural in nature—would be dealt with within fixed deadlines. In such cases the services of the Commission will, within two months of receipt of the complete notification of the agreement, inform the parties in writing of the results of the initial analysis of the case and, as appropriate, the nature and probable length of the administrative procedure they intend to engage.

The contents of this letter may vary according to the characteristics of the case under investigation—

— in cases not posing any problems, the Commission will send a comfort letter confirming the compatibility of the agreement with Article 85(1) or (3),

— if a comfort letter cannot be sent because of the need to settle the case by formal decision, the Commission will inform the undertakings concerned of its intention to adopt a decision either granting or rejecting exemption,

— if the Commission has serious doubts as to the compatibility of the agreement with the competition rules, it will send a letter to the parties giving notice of an in-depth examination which may, depending on the case, result in a decision either prohibiting, exempting subject to conditions and obligations, or simply exempting the agreement in question.

This new accelerated procedure, applicable since 1 January 1993, is based entirely on the principle of self-discipline. The deadline of two months from the complete notification—intended for the initial examination of the case—does not constitute a statutory term and is therefore in no way legally binding. However, the Commission will do its best to abide by it. The Commission reserves the right, moreover, to extend this accelerated procedure to other forms of cooperation between undertakings.

A cooperative joint venture of a structural nature is one that involves an important change in the structure and organisation of the business assets of the parties to the agreement. This may occur because the joint venture takes over or extends existing activities of the parent companies or because it undertakes new activities on their behalf. Such operations are characterised by the commitment of significant financial, material and/or non-tangible assets such as intellectual property rights and know how. Structural joint ventures are therefore normally intended to operate on a medium- or long-term basis.

This concept includes certain "partial function" joint ventures which take over one or several specific functions within the parents' business activity without access to the market, in particular research and development and/or production. It also covers those "full function" joint ventures which give rise to coordination of the competitive behaviour of independent undertakings, in particular between the parties to the joint venture or between them and the joint venture.

In order to respect the internal deadline, it is important that the Commission has available on notification all the relevant information reasonably available to the notifying parties that is necessary for it to assess the impact of the operation in question on competition. Form A/B therefore contains a special section (Chapter III) that must be completed only by persons notifying cooperative joint ventures of a structural character that wish to benefit from the accelerated procedure.

Persons notifying joint ventures of a structural character that wish to claim the benefit of the aforementioned accelerated procedure should therefore complete Chapters I, III and IV of this form. Chapter III contains a series of detailed questions necessary for the Commission to assess the relevant market(s) and the position of the parties to the joint venture on that (those) market(s).

Where the parties do not wish to claim the benefit of an accelerated procedure for their joint ventures of a structural character they should complete Chapters I, II and IV of this form. Chapter II contains a far more limited range of questions on the relevant market(s) and the position of the parties to the operation in question on that (those) market(s), but sufficient to enable the Commission to commence its examination and investigation.

E. THE NEED FOR COMPLETE INFORMATION

The receipt of a valid notification by the Commission has two main consequences. First, it affords immunity from fines from the date that the valid notification is received by the Commission with respect to applications made in order to obtain exemption (see Article 15(5) of Regulation No 17). Second, until a valid notification is received, the Commission cannot grant an exemption pursuant to Article 85(3) of the EC Treaty and/or Article 53(3) of the EEA Agreement, and any exemption that is granted can be effective only from the date of receipt of a valid notification.[1] Thus, whilst there is no legal obligation to notify as such, unless and until an arrangement that falls within the scope of Article 85(1) and/or Article 53(1) has not been notified and is, therefore, not capable of being exempted, it may be declared void by a national court pursuant to Article 85(2) and/or Article 53(2).[2]

NOTES

[1] Subject to the qualification provided for in Article 4(2) of Regulation No 17.

[2] For further details of the consequences of non-notification see the Commission notice on cooperation between national Courts and the Commission (OJ C39, 13.2.1993, p 6).

Where an undertaking is claiming the benefit of a group exemption by recourse to an opposition procedure, the period within which the Commission must oppose the exemption by category only applies from the date that a valid notification is received. This is also true of the two months' period imposed on the Commission services for an initial analysis of applications for negative clearance and notifications relating to cooperative joint ventures of a structural character which benefit from the accelerated procedure.

A valid application or notification for this purpose means one that is not incomplete (see Article 3(1) of the Regulation). This is subject to two qualifications. First, if the information or documents required by this form are not reasonably available to you in part or in whole, the Commission will accept that a notification is complete and thus valid notwithstanding the failure to provide such information, providing that you give reasons for the unavailability of the information, and provide your best estimates for missing data together with the sources for the estimates. Indications as to where any of the requested information or documents that are unavailable to you could be obtained by the Commission must also be provided. Second, the Commission only requires the submission of information relevant and necessary to its inquiry into the notified operation. In some cases not all the information required by this form will be necessary for this purpose. The Commission may therefore dispense with the obligation to provide certain information required by this form (see Article 3(3) of the Regulation). This provision enables, where appropriate, each application or notification to be tailored to each case so that only the information strictly necessary for the Commission's examination is provided. This avoids unnecessary administrative burdens being imposed on undertakings, in particular on small and medium-sized ones. Where the information or documents required by this form are not provided for this reason, the application or notification should indicate the reasons why the information is considered to be unnecessary to the Commission's investigation.

Where the Commission finds that the information contained in the application or notification is incomplete in a material respect, it will, within one month from receipt, inform the applicant or the notifying party in writing of this fact and the nature of the missing information. In such cases, the application or notification shall become effective on the date on which the complete information is received by the Commission. If the Commission has not informed the applicant or the notifying party within the one month period that the application or notification is incomplete in a material respect, the application or notification will be deemed to be complete and valid (see Article 4 of the Regulation).

It is also important that undertakings inform the Commission of important changes in the factual situation including those of which they become aware after the application or notification has been submitted. The Commission must, therefore, be informed immediately of any changes to an agreement, decision or practice which is the subject of an application or notification (see Article 4(3) of the Regulation). Failure to inform the Commission of such relevant changes could result in any negative clearance decision being without effect or in the withdrawal of any exemption decision[1] adopted by the Commission on the basis of the notification.

NOTES

[1]   See point (a) of Article 8(3) of Regulation No 17.

F. THE NEED FOR ACCURATE INFORMATION

In addition to the requirement that the application or notification be complete, it is important that you ensure that the information provided is accurate (see Article 3(1) of the Regulation). Article 15(1)(a) of Regulation No 17 states that the Commission may, by decision, impose on undertakings or associations of undertakings fines of up to ECU 5000 where, intentionally or negligently, they supply incorrect or misleading information in an application for negative clearance or notification. Such information is, moreover, considered to be incomplete (see Article 4(4) of the Regulation), so that the parties cannot benefit from the advantages of the opposition procedure or accelerated procedure (see above, Point E).

G. WHO CAN LODGE AN APPLICATION OR A NOTIFICATION?

Any of the undertakings party to an agreement, decision or practice of the kind described in Articles 85 or 86 of the EC Treaty and Articles 53 or 54 of the EEA Agreement may submit an application for negative clearance, in relation to Article 85 and Article 53, or a notification requesting an exemption. An association of undertakings may submit an application or a notification in relation to decisions taken or practices pursued in the operation of the association.

In relation to agreements and concerted practices between undertakings it is common practice for all the parties involved to submit a joint application or notification. Although the Commission strongly recommends this approach, because it is helpful to have the views of all the parties directly concerned at the same time, it is not obligatory. Any of the parties to an agreement may submit an application or notification in their individual capacities, but in such circumstances the notifying party should inform all the other parties to the agreement, decision or practice of that fact (see Article 1(3) of the Regulation). They may also provide them with a copy of the completed form, where relevant once confidential information and business secrets have been deleted (see below, operational part, question 1.2).

Where a joint application or notification is submitted, it has also become common practice to appoint a joint representative to act on behalf of all the undertakings involved, both in making the application or notification, and in dealing with any subsequent contacts with the Commission (see Article 1(4) of the Regulation). Again, whilst this is helpful, it is not obligatory, and all the undertakings jointly submitting an application or a notification may sign it in their individual capacities.

H. HOW TO SUBMIT AN APPLICATION OR NOTIFICATION

Applications and notifications may be submitted in any of the official languages of the European Community or of an EFTA State (see Article 2(4) and (5) of the Regulation). In order to ensure rapid proceedings, it is, however, recommended to use, in case of an application or notification to the EFTA Surveillance Authority one of the official languages of an EFTA State or the working language of the EFTA Surveillance Authority, which is English, or, in case of an application or notification to the Commission, one of the official languages of the Community or the working language of the EFTA Surveillance Authority. This language will thereafter be the language of the proceeding for the applicant or notifying party.

Form A/B is not a form to be filled in. Undertakings should simply provide the information requested by this form, using its sections and paragraph numbers, signing a declaration as stated in Section 19 below, and annexing the required supporting documentation.

Supporting documents shall be submitted in their original language; where this is not an official language of the Community they must be translated into the language of the proceeding. The supporting documents may be originals or copies of the originals (see Article 2(4) of the Regulation).

All information requested in this form shall, unless otherwise stated, relate to the calendar year preceding that of the application or notification. Where information is not reasonably available on this basis (for example if accounting periods are used that are not based on the calendar year, or the previous year's figures are not yet available) the most recently available information should be provided and reasons given why figures on the basis of the calendar year preceding that of the application or notification cannot be provided.

Financial data may be provided in the currency in which the official audited accounts of the undertaking(s) concerned are prepared or in Ecus. In the latter case the exchange rate used for the conversion must be stated.

Seventeen copies of each application or notification, but only three copies of all supporting documents must be provided (see Article 2(2) of the Regulation).

The application or notification is to be sent to—

> Commission of the European Communities,
> Directorate-General for Competition (DG IV),
> The Registrar,
> 200, Rue de la Loi,
> B–1049 Brussels.

or be delivered by hand during Commission working days and official working hours at the following address—

> Commission of the European Communities
> Directorate-General for Competition (DG IV),
> The Registrar,
> 158, Avenue de Cortenberg,
> B–1040 Brussels.

I. CONFIDENTIALITY

Article 214 of the EC Treaty, Article 20 of Regulation No 17, Article 9 of Protocol 23 to the EEA Agreement, Article 122 of the EEA Agreement and Articles 20 and 21 of Chapter II of Protocol 4 to the Agreement between the EFTA States on the establishment of a Surveillance Authority and of a Court of Justice require the Commission, the Member States, the EEA Surveillance Authority and EFTA States not to disclose information of the kind covered by the obligation of professional secrecy. On the other hand, Regulation No 17 requires the Commission to publish a summary of the application or notification, should it intend to take a favourable decision. In this publication, the Commission "... shall have regard to the legitimate interest of undertakings in the protection of their business secrets" (Article 19(3) of Regulation No 17; see also Article 21(2) in relation to the publication of decisions). In this connection, if an undertaking believes that its interests would be harmed if any of the information it is asked to supply were to be published or otherwise divulged to other undertakings, it should put all such information in a separate annex with each page clearly marked "Business Secrets". It should also give reasons why any information identified as confidential or secret should not be divulged or published. (See below, Section 5 of the operational part that requests a non-confidential summary of the notification).

J. SUBSEQUENT PROCEDURE

The application or notification is registered in the Registry of the Directorate-General for Competition (DG IV). The date of receipt by the Commission (or the date of posting if sent by registered post) is the effective date of the submission (see Article 4(1) of the Regulation). However, special rules apply to incomplete applications and notifications (see above under Point E).

The Commission will acknowledge receipt of all applications and notifications in writing, indicating the case number attributed to the file. This number must be used in all future correspondence regarding the notification. The receipt of acknowledgement does not prejudge the question whether the application or notification is valid.

Further information may be sought from the parties or from third parties (Articles 11 to 14 of Regulation No 17) and suggestions might be made as to amendments to the arrangements that might make them acceptable. Equally, a short preliminary notice may be published in the C series of the *Official Journal of the European Communities*, stating the names of the interested undertakings, the groups to which they belong, the economic sectors involved and the nature of the arrangements, and inviting third party comments (see below, operational part, Section 5).

Where a notification is made for the purpose of the application of the opposition procedure, the Commission may oppose the grant of the benefit of the group exemption with respect to the notified agreement. If the Commission opposes the claim, and unless it subsequently withdraws its opposition, that notification will then be treated as an application for an individual exemption.

If, after examination, the Commission intends to grant the application for negative clearance or exemption, it is obliged (by Article 19(5) of Regulation No 17) to publish a summary and invite comments from third parties. Subsequently, a preliminary draft decision has to be submitted to and discussed with the Advisory Committee on Restrictive Practices and Dominant Positions composed of officials of the competent authorities of the Member States in the matter of restrictive practices and monopolies (Article 10 of Regulation No 17) and attended where the case falls within the EEA Agreement, by representatives of the EFTA Surveillance Authority and the EFTA States which will already have received a copy of the application or notification. Only then, and providing nothing has happened to change the Commission's intention, can it adopt the envisaged decision.

Files are often closed without any formal decision being taken, for example, because it is found that the arrangements are already covered by a block exemption, or because they do not call for any action by the Commission, at least in circumstances at that time. In such cases comfort letters are sent. Although not a Commission decision, a comfort letter indicates how the Commission's departments view the case on the facts currently in their possession which means that the Commission could where necessary—for example, if it were to be asserted that a contract was void under Article 85(2) of the EC Treaty and/or Article 53(2) of the EEA Agreement—take an appropriate decision to clarify the legal situation.

K. DEFINITIONS USED IN THE OPERATIONAL PART OF THIS FORM

Agreement: The word "agreement" is used to refer to all categories of arrangements, ie agreements between undertakings, decisions by associations of undertakings and concerted practices.

Year: All references to the word "year" in this form shall be read as meaning calendar year, unless otherwise stated.

Group: A group relationship exists for the purpose of this form where one undertaking—
— owns more than half the capital or business assets of another undertaking, or
— has the power to exercise more than half the voting rights in another undertaking, or
— has the power to appoint more than half the members of the supervisory board, board of directors or bodies legally representing the undertaking, or
— has the right to manage the affairs of another undertaking.

An undertaking which is jointly controlled by several other undertakings (joint venture) forms part of the group of each of these undertakings.

Relevant product market: questions 6.1 and 11.1 of this form require the undertaking or individual submitting the notification to define the relevant product and/or service market(s) that are likely to be affected by the agreement in question. That definition(s) is then used as the basis for a number of other questions contained in this form. The definition(s) thus submitted by the notifying parties are referred to in this form as the relevant product market(s). These words can refer to a market made up either of products or of services.

Relevant geographic market: questions 6.2 and 11.2 of this form require the undertaking or individual submitting the notification to define the relevant geographic market(s) that are likely to be affected by the agreement in question. That definition(s) is then used as the basis for a number of other questions contained in this form. The definition(s) thus submitted by the notifying parties are referred to in this form as the relevant geographic market(s).

Relevant product and geographic market: by virtue of the combination of their replies to questions 6 and 11 the parties provide their definition of the relevant market(s) affected by the notified agreement(s). That (those) definition(s) is (are) then used as the basis for a number of other questions contained in this form. The definition(s) thus submitted by the notifying parties is referred to in this form as the relevant geographic and product market(s).

Notification: this form can be used to make an application for negative clearance and/or a notification requesting an exemption. The word "notification" is used to refer to either an application or a notification.

Parties and notifying party: the word "party" is used to refer to all the undertakings which are party to the agreement being notified. As a notification may be submitted by only one of the undertakings which are party to an agreement, "notifying party" is used to refer only to the undertaking or undertakings actually submitting the notification.

OPERATIONAL PART
PLEASE MAKE SURE THAT THE FIRST PAGE OF YOUR APPLICATION OR
NOTIFICATION CONTAINS THE WORDS "APPLICATION FOR NEGATIVE
CLEARANCE/NOTIFICATION IN ACCORDANCE WITH FORM A/B"

CHAPTER I
SECTIONS CONCERNING THE PARTIES, THEIR GROUPS AND THE AGREEMENT

(TO BE COMPLETED FOR ALL NOTIFICATIONS)

Section 1—Identity of the undertakings or persons submitting the notification

1.1.   Please list the undertakings on behalf of which the notification is being submitted and indicate their legal denomination or commercial name, shortened or commonly used as appropriate (if it differs from the legal denomination).

1.2.   If the notification is being submitted on behalf of only one or some of the undertakings party to the agreement being notified, please confirm that the remaining undertakings have been informed of that fact and indicate whether they have received a copy of the notification, with relevant confidential information and business secrets deleted.[1] (In such circumstances a copy of the edited copy of the notification which has been provided to such other undertakings should be annexed to this notification.)

NOTES
[1]   The Commission is aware that in exceptional cases it may not be practicable to inform non-notifying parties to the notified agreement of the fact that it has been notified, or to provide them a copy of the notification. This may be the case, for example, where a standard agreement is being notified that is concluded with a large number of undertakings. Where this is the case you should state the reasons why it has not been practicable to follow the standard procedure set out in this question.

1.3.   If a joint notification is being submitted, has a joint representative[1] been appointed?[2]

If yes, please give the details requested in 1.3.1 to 1.3.3 below.

If no, please give details of any representatives who have been authorised to act for each or either of the parties to the agreement indicating who they represent.

1.3.1.   Name of representative.
1.3.2.   Address of representative.
1.3.3.   Telephone and fax number of representative.

NOTES
[1]   *Note:* For the purposes of this question a representative means an individual or undertaking formally appointed to make the notification or application on behalf of the party or parties submitting the notification. This should be distinguished from the situation where the notification is signed by an officer of the company or companies in question. In the latter situation no representative is appointed.

 2   *Note:* It is not mandatory to appoint representatives for the purpose of completing and/or submitting this notification. This question only requires the identification of representatives where the notifying parties have chosen to appoint them.

1.4.   In cases where one or more representatives have been appointed, an authority to act on behalf of the undertaking(s) submitting the notification must accompany the notification.

Section 2—Information on the parties to the agreement and the groups to which they belong

2.1.   State the name and address of the parties to the agreement being notified, and the country of their incorporation.

2.2.   State the nature of the business of each of the parties to the agreement being notified.

2.3.   For each of the parties to the agreement, give the name of a person that can be contacted, together with his or her name, address, telephone number, fax number and position held in the undertaking.

2.4.   Identify the corporate groups to which the parties to the agreement being notified belong. State the sectors in which these groups are active, and the world-wide turnover of each group.[1]

NOTES
[1]   For the calculation of turnover in the banking and insurance sectors see Article 3 of Protocol 22 to the EEA Agreement.

Section 3—Procedural matters

3.1.   Please state whether you have made any formal submission to any other competition authorities in relation to the agreement in question. If yes, state which authorities, the individual or department in question, and the nature of the contact. In addition to this, mention any earlier proceedings or informal contacts, of which you are aware, with the Commission and/or the EFTA Surveillance Authority and any earlier proceedings with any national authorities or courts in the Community or in EFTA states concerning these or any related agreements.

3.2.   Please summarise any reasons for any claim that the case involves an issue of exceptional urgency.

3.3.   The Commission has stated that where notifications do not have particular political, economic or legal significance for the Community they will normally be dealt with by means of comfort letter.[1] Would you be satisfied with a comfort letter? If you consider that it would be inappropriate to deal with the notified agreement in this manner, please explain the reasons for this view.

3.4.   State whether you intend to produce further supporting facts or arguments not yet available and, if so, on which points.[2]

NOTES
[1]   See paragraph 14 of the notice on cooperation between national courts and the Commission in applying Articles 85 and 86 of the EC Treaty (OJ C39, 13.2.1993, p 6).
[2]   *Note:* In so far as the notifying parties provide the information required by this form that was reasonably available to them at the time of notification, the fact that the parties intend to provide further supporting facts or documentation in due course does not prevent the notification being valid at the time of notification and, in the case of structural joint ventures where the accelerated procedure is being claimed, the two month deadline commencing.

Section 4—Full details of the arrangements

4.1.   Please summarise the nature, content and objectives pursued by the agreement being notified.

4.2. Detail any provisions contained in the agreements which may restrict the parties in their freedom to take independent commercial decisions, for example regarding—
— buying or selling prices, discounts or other trading conditions,
— the quantities of goods to be manufactured or distributed or services to be offered,
— technical development or investment,
— the choice of markets or sources of supply,
— purchases from or sales to third parties,
— whether to apply similar terms for the supply of equivalent goods or services,
— whether to offer different services separately or together.

If you are claiming the benefit of the opposition procedure, identify in this list the restrictions that exceed those automatically exempted by the relevant regulation.

4.3. State between which Member States of the Community and/or EFTA States[1] trade may be affected by the arrangements. Please give reasons for your reply to this question, giving data on trade flows where relevant. Furthermore please state whether trade between the Community or the EEA territory and any third countries is affected, again giving reasons for your reply.

NOTES
[1] See list in Annex III.

Section 5—Non-confidential Summary

Shortly following receipt of a notification, the Commission may publish a short notice inviting third party comments on the agreement in question.[1] As the objective pursued by the Commission in publishing an informal preliminary notice is to receive third party comments as soon as possible after the notification has been received, such a notice is usually published without first providing it to the notifying parties for their comments. This section requests the information to be used in an informal preliminary notice in the event that the Commission decides to issue one. It is important, therefore, that your replies to these questions do not contain any business secrets or other confidential information.

1. State the names of the parties to the agreement notified and the groups of undertakings to which they belong.

2. Give a short summary of the nature and objectives of the agreement. As a guideline this summary should not exceed 100 words.

3. Identify the product sectors affected by the agreement in question.

NOTES
[1] An example of such a notice figures in Annex I to this Form. Such a notice should be distinguished from a formal notice published pursuant to Article 19(3) of Regulation No 17. An Article 19(3) notice is relatively detailed, and gives an indication of the Commission's current approach in the case in question. Section 5 only seeks information that will be used in a short preliminary notice, and not a notice published pursuant to Article 19(3).

CHAPTER II
SECTION CONCERNING THE RELEVANT MARKET (TO BE COMPLETED FOR ALL NOTIFICATIONS EXCEPT THOSE RELATING TO STRUCTURAL JOINT VENTURES FOR WHICH ACCELERATED TREATMENT IS CLAIMED)

Section 6—The relevant market

A relevant product market comprises all those products and/or services which are regarded as interchangeable or substitutable by the consumer, by reason of the products' characteristics, their prices and their intended use.

The following factors are normally considered to be relevant to the determination of the relevant product market and should be taken into account in this analysis[1]—
— the degree of physical similarity between the products/services in question,
— any differences in the end use to which the goods are put,
— differences in price between two products,
— the cost of switching between two potentially competing products,

— established or entrenched consumer preferences for one type or category of product over another,

— industry-wide product classifications (eg classifications maintained by trade associations).

The relevant geographic market comprises the area in which the undertakings concerned are involved in the supply of products or services, in which the conditions of competition are sufficiently homogeneous and which can be distinguished from neighbouring areas because, in particular, conditions of competition are appreciably different in those areas.

Factors relevant to the assessment of the relevant geographic market include[2] the nature and characteristics of the products or services concerned, the existence of entry barriers or consumer preferences, appreciable differences of the undertakings' market shares or substantial price differences between neighbouring areas, and transport costs.

NOTES

[1] This list is not, however, exhaustive, and notifying parties may refer to other factors.

[2] This list is not, however, exhaustive, and notifying parties may refer to other factors.

6.1.   In the light of the above please explain the definition of the relevant product market or markets that in your opinion should form the basis of the Commission's analysis of the notification.

In your answer, please give reasons for assumptions or findings, and explain how the factors outlined above have been taken into account. In particular, please state the specific products or services directly or indirectly affected by the agreement being notified and identify the categories of goods viewed as substitutable in your market definition.

In the questions figuring below, this (or these) definition(s) will be referred to as "the relevant product market(s)".

6.2.   Please explain the definition of the relevant geographic market or markets that in your opinion should form the basis of the Commission's analysis of the notification. In your answer, please give reasons for assumptions or findings, and explain how the factors outlined above have been taken into account. In particular, please identify the countries in which the parties are active in the relevant product market(s), and in the event that you consider the relevant geographic market to be wider than the individual Member States of the Community or EFTA on which the parties to the agreement are active, give the reasons for this.

In the questions below, this (or these) definition(s) will be referred to as "the relevant geographic market(s)".

Section 7—Group members operating on the same markets as the parties

7.1.   For each of the parties to the agreement being notified, provide a list of all undertakings belonging to the same group which are—

7.1.1.   active in the relevant product market(s);

7.1.2.   active in markets neighbouring the *relevant product market(s)* (ie active in products and/or services that represent imperfect and partial substitutes for those included in your definition of the relevant product market(s)).

Such undertakings must be identified even if they sell the product or service in question in other geographic areas than those in which the parties to the notified agreement operate. Please list the name, place of incorporation, exact product manufactured and the geographic scope of operation of each group member.

Section 8—The position of the parties on the affected relevant product markets

Information requested in this section must be provided for the groups of the parties as a whole. It is not sufficient to provide such information only in relation to the individual undertakings directly concerned by the agreement.

8.1.   In relation to each relevant product market(s) identified in your reply to question 6.1 please provide the following information—

8.1.1.   the market shares of the parties on the *relevant geographic market* during the previous three years;

8.1.2. where different, the market shares of the parties in (a) the EEA territory as a whole, (b) the Community, (c) the territory of the EFTA States and (d) each EC Member State and EFTA State during the previous three years.[1] For this section, where market shares are less than 20%, please state simply which of the following bands are relevant: 0 to 5%, 5 to 10%, 10 to 15%, 15 to 20%.

NOTES

[1] Ie where the relevant geographic market has been defined as world wide, these figures must be given regarding the EEA, the Community, the territory of the EFTA States, and each EC Member State. Where the relevant geographic market has been defined as the Community, these figures must be given for the EEA, the territory of the EFTA States, and each EC Member State. Where the market has been defined as national, these figures must be given for the EEA, the Community and the territory of the EFTA States.

For the purpose of answering these questions, market share may be calculated either on the basis of value or volume. Justification for the figures provided must be given. Thus, for each answer, total market value volume must be stated, together with the sales/turnover of each of the parties in question. The source or sources of the information should also be given (eg official statistics, estimates, etc), and where possible, copies should be provided of documents from which information has been taken.

Section 9—The position of competitors and customers on the relevant product market(s)

Information requested in this section must be provided for the group of the parties as a whole and not in relation to the individual companies directly concerned by the agreement notified.

For the (all) relevant product and geographic market(s) in which the parties have a combined market share exceeding 15%, the following questions must be answered.

9.1. Please identify the five main competitors of the parties. Please identify the company and give your best estimate as to their market share in the relevant geographic market(s). Please also provide address, telephone and fax number, and, where possible, the name of a contact person at each company identified.

9.2. Please identify the five main customers of each of the parties. State company name, address, telephone and fax numbers, together with the name of a contact person.

Section 10—Market entry and potential competition in product and geographic terms

For the (all) relevant product and geographic market(s) in which the parties have a combined market share exceeding 15%, the following questions must be answered.

10.1. Describe the various factors influencing entry in product terms into the *relevant product market(s)* that exist in the present case (ie what barriers exist to prevent undertakings that do not presently manufacture goods within the relevant product market(s) entering this market(s)). In so doing take account of the following where appropriate—
— to what extent is entry to the markets influenced by the requirement of government authorisation or standard setting in any form? Are there any legal or regulatory controls on entry to these markets?
— to what extent is entry to the markets influenced by the availability of raw materials?
— to what extent is entry to the markets influenced by the length of contracts between an undertaking and its suppliers and/or customers?
— describe the importance of research and development and in particular the importance of licensing patents, know-how and other rights in these markets.

10.2. Describe the various factors influencing entry in geographic terms into the relevant geographic market(s) that exist in the present case (ie what barriers exist to prevent undertakings already producing and/or marketing products within the relevant product market(s) but in areas outside the relevant geographic market(s) extending the scope of their sales into the relevant geographic market(s)?). Please give reasons for your answer, explaining, where relevant, the importance of the following factors—
— trade barriers imposed by law, such as tariffs, quotas etc,
— local specification or technical requirements,
— procurement policies,
— the existence of adequate and available local distribution and retailing facilities,

— transport costs,
— entrenched consumer preferences for local brands or products,
— language.

10.3. Have any new undertakings entered the relevant product market(s) in geographic areas where the parties sell during the last three years? Please provide this information with respect to both new entrants in product terms and new entrants in geographic terms. If such entry has occurred, please identify the undertaking(s) concerned (name, address, telephone and fax numbers, and, where possible, contact person), and provide your best estimate of their market share in the relevant product and geographic market(s).

CHAPTER III
SECTION CONCERNING THE RELEVANT MARKET ONLY FOR STRUCTURAL JOINT VENTURES FOR WHICH ACCELERATED TREATMENT IS CLAIMED

Section 11—The relevant market

A relevant product market comprises all those products/or services which are regarded as interchangeable or substitutable by the consumer, by reason of the products' characteristics, their prices and their intended use.

The following factors are normally considered to be relevant[1] to the determination of the relevant product market and should be taken into account in this analysis—
— the degree of physical similarity between the products/services in question,
— any differences in the end use to which the goods are put,
— differences in price between two products,
— the cost of switching between two potentially competing products,
— established or entrenched consumer preferences for one type or category of product over another,
— different or similar industry-wide product classifications (eg classifications maintained by trade associations).

The relevant geographic market comprises the area in which the undertakings concerned are involved in the supply of products or services, in which the conditions of competition are sufficiently homogeneous and which can be distinguished from neighbouring areas because, in particular, conditions of competition are appreciably different in those areas.

Factors relevant to the assessment of the relevant geographic market include[2] the nature and characteristics of the products or services concerned, the existence of entry barriers or consumer preferences, appreciable differences of the undertakings' market share or substantial price differences between neighbouring areas, and transport costs.

NOTES
[1] This list is not, however, exhaustive, and notifying parties may refer to other factors.
[2] This list is not, however, exhaustive, and notifying parties may refer to other factors.

Part 11.1—The notifying parties' analysis of the relevant market

11.1.1. In the light of the above, please explain the definition of the relevant product market or markets that in the opinion of the parties should form the basis of the Commission's analysis of the notification.

In your answer, please give reasons for assumptions or findings, and explain how the factors outlined above have been taken into account.

In the questions figuring below, this (or these) definition(s) will be referred to as "the relevant product market(s)".

11.1.2. Please explain the definition of the relevant geographic market or markets that in the opinion of the parties should form the basis of the Commission's analysis of the notification.

In your answer, please give reasons for assumptions or findings, and explain how the factors outlined above have been taken into account.

Part 11.2—Questions on the relevant product and geographic market(s)

Answers to the following questions will enable the Commission to verify whether the product and geographic market definitions put forward by you in Section 11.1 are compatible with definitions figuring above.

Product market definition

11.2.1.   List the specific products or services directly or indirectly affected by the agreement being notified.

11.2.2.   List the categories of products and/or services that are, in the opinion of the notifying parties, close economic substitutes for those identified in the reply to question 11.2.1. Where more than one product or service has been identified in the reply to question 11.2.1, a list for each product must be provided for this question.

The products identified in this list should be ordered in their degree of substitutability, first listing the most perfect substitute for the products of the parties, finishing with the least perfect substitute.[1]

Please explain how the factors relevant to the definition of the relevant product market have been taken into account in drawing up this list and in placing the products/services in their correct order.

NOTES

[1]   Close economic substitute; most perfect substitute; least perfect substitute: these definitions are only relevant to those filling out Chapter III of the form, ie those notifying structural joint ventures requesting the accelerated procedure).

For any given product (for the purposes of this definition "product" is used to refer to products or services) a chain of substitutes exists. This chain is made up of all conceivable substitutes for the product in question, ie all those products that will, to a greater or lesser extent, fulfil the needs of the consumer in question. The substitutes will range from very close (or perfect) ones (products to which consumers would turn immediately in the event of, for example, even a very small price increase for the product in question) to very distant (or imperfect) substitutes (products to which customers would only turn to in the event of a very large price rise for the product in question). When defining the relevant market, and calculating market shares, the Commission only takes into account close economic substitutes of the products in question. Close economic substitutes are ones to which customers would turn to in response to a small but significant price increase for the product in question (say 5%). This enables the Commission to assess the market power of the notifying companies in the context of a relevant market made up of all those products that consumers of the products in question could readily and easily turn to.

However, this does not mean that the Commission fails to take into account the constraints on the competitive behaviour of the parties in question resulting from the existence of imperfect substitutes (those to which a consumer could not turn to in response to a small but significant price increase (say 5%) for the products in question). These effects are taken into account once the market has been defined, and the market shares determined.

It is therefore important for the Commission to have information regarding both close economic substitutes for the products in question, as well as less perfect substitutes.

For example, assume two companies active in the luxury watch sector conclude a research and development agreement. They both manufacture watches costing ECU 1800 to 2000. Close economic substitutes are likely to be watches of other manufacturers in the same or similar price category, and these will be taken into account when defining the relevant product market. Cheaper watches, and in particular disposable plastic watches, will be imperfect substitutes, because it is unlikely that a potential purchaser of a ECU 2000 watch will turn to one costing ECU 20 if the expensive one increased its price by 5%.

Geographic market definition

11.2.3.   List all the countries in which the parties are active in the relevant product market(s). Where they are active in all countries within any given groups of countries or trading area (eg the whole Community or EFTA, the EEA countries, world-wide) it is sufficient to indicate the area in question.

11.2.4.   Explain the manner in which the parties produce and sell the goods and/or services in each of these various countries or areas. For example, do they manufacture locally, do they sell through local distribution facilities, or do they distribute through exclusive, or non-exclusive, importers and distributors?

11.2.5.   Are there significant trade flows in the goods/services that make up the relevant product market(s) (i) between the EC Member States (please specify which and estimate the percentage of total sales made up by imports in each Member State in which the parties are active), (ii) between all or part of the EC Member States and all or part of the EFTA States (again, please specify and estimate the percentage of total sales made up by imports), (iii) between the EFTA States (please specify which and estimate the percentage of total sales made up by imports in each such State in which the parties are active), and (iv) between all or part of the EEA territory and other countries? (again, please specify and estimate the percentage of total sales made up by imports.)

11.2.6.   Which producer undertakings based outside the Community or the EEA territory sell within the EEA territory in countries in which the parties are active in the affected products? How do these undertakings market their products? Does this differ between different EC Member States and/or EFTA States?

Section 12—Group members operating on the same markets as the parties to the notified agreement

12.1.   For each of the parties to the agreement being notified, provide a list of all undertakings belonging to the same group which are—

12.1.1.   active in the relevant product market(s);

12.1.2.   active in markets neighbouring the relevant product market(s) (ie active in products/services that represent imperfect and partial substitutes[1] for those included in your definition of the relevant product market(s);

12.1.3.   active in markets upstream and/or downstream from those included in the relevant product market(s).

Such undertakings must be identified even if they sell the product or service in question in other geographic areas than those in which the parties to the notified agreement operate. Please list the name, place of incorporation, exact product manufactured and the geographic scope of operation of each group member.

NOTES

[1]   The following are considered to be partial substitutes: products and services which may replace each other solely in certain geographic areas, solely during part of the year or solely for certain uses.

Section 13—The position of the parties on the relevant product market(s)

Information requested in this section must be provided for the group of the parties as a whole and not in relation to the individual companies directly concerned by the agreement notified.

13.1. In relation to each relevant product market(s), as defined in your reply to question 11.1.2, please provide the following information—

13.1.1.   the market shares of the parties on the relevant geographic market during the previous three years;

13.1.2.   where different, the market shares of the parties in (a) the EEA territory as a whole, (b) the Community, (c) the territory of the EFTA States and (d) each EC Member State and EFTA State during the previous three years.[1] For this section, where market shares are less than 20%, please state simply which of the following bands are relevant: 0 to 5%, 5 to 10%, 10 to 15%, 15 to 20% in terms of value or volume.

For the purpose of answering these questions, market share may be calculated either on the basis of value or volume. Justification for the figures provided must be given. Thus, for each answer, total market value/volume must be stated, together with the sales/turnover of each of the parties in question. The source or sources of the information should also be given, and where possible, copies should be provided of documents from which information has been taken.

13.2.   If the market shares in question 13.1 were to be calculated on a basis other than that used by the parties, would the resultant market shares differ by more than 5% in any market (ie if the parties have calculated market shares on the basis of volume, what would be the relevant figure if it was calculated on the basis of value?) If the figure were to differ by more than 5% please provide the information requested in question 13.1 on the basis of both value and volume.

13.3. Give your best estimate of the current rate of capacity utilisation of the parties and in the industry in general in the relevant product and geographic market(s).

___

NOTES

 [1] Ie where the relevant geographic market has been defined as world wide, these figures must be given regarding the EEA, the Community, the territory of the EFTA States, and each EC Member State and EFTA State. Where the relevant geographic market has been defined as the Community, these figures must be given for the EEA, the territory of the EFTA States, and each EC Member State and EFTA State. Where the market has been defined as national, these figures must be given for the EEA, the Community and the territory of the EFTA States.

___

Section 14—The position of competitors and customers on the relevant product market(s)

Information requested in this section must be provided for the group of the parties as a whole and not in relation to the individual companies directly concerned by the agreement notified.

For the (all) relevant product market(s) in which the parties have a combined market share exceeding 10% in the EEA as a whole, the Community, the EFTA territory or in any EC Member State or EFTA Member State, the following questions must be answered.

14.1. Please identify the competitors of the parties on the relevant product market(s) that have a market share exceeding 10% in any EC Member State, EFTA State, in the territory of the EFTA States, in the EEA, or world-wide. Please identify the company and give your best estimate as to their market share in these geographic areas. Please also provide the address, telephone and fax numbers, and, where possible, the name of a contact person at each company identified.

14.2. Please describe the nature of demand on the relevant product market(s). For example, are there few or many purchasers, are there different categories of purchasers, are government agencies or departments important purchasers?

14.3. Please identify the five largest customers of each of the parties for each *relevant product market(s)*. State company name, address, telephone and fax numbers, together with the name of a contact person.

Section 15—Market entry and potential competition

For the (all) relevant product market(s) in which the parties have a combined market share exceeding 10% in the EEA as a whole, the Community, the EFTA territory or in any EC Member State or EFTA State, the following questions must be answered.

15.1. Describe the various factors influencing entry into the relevant product market(s) that exist in the present case. In so doing take account of the following where appropriate—

— to what extent is entry to the markets influenced by the requirement of government authorisation or standard setting in any form? Are there any legal or regulatory controls on entry to these markets?

— to what extent is entry to the markets influenced by the availability of raw materials?

— to what extent is entry to the markets influenced by the length of contracts between an undertaking and its suppliers and/or customers?

— what is the importance of research and development and in particular the importance of licensing patents, know-how and other rights in these markets.

15.2. Have any new undertakings entered the relevant product market(s) in geographic areas where the parties sell during the last three years? If so, please identify the undertaking(s) concerned (name, address, telephone and fax numbers, and, where possible, contact person), and provide your best estimate of their market share in each EC Member State and EFTA State that they are active and in the Community, the territory of the EFTA States and the EEA territory as a whole.

15.3.   Give your best estimate of the minimum viable scale for the entry into the relevant product market(s) in terms of appropriate market share necessary to operate profitably.

15.4.   Are there significant barriers to entry preventing companies active on the relevant product market(s)—

15.4.1.   in one EC Member State or EFTA State selling in other areas of the EEA territory;

15.4.2.   outside the EEA territory selling into all or parts of the EEA territory.

Please give reasons for your answers, explaining, where relevant, the importance of the following factors—

— trade barriers imposed by law, such as tariffs, quotas etc,
— local specification or technical requirements,
— procurement policies,
— the existence of adequate and available local distribution and retailing facilities,
— transport costs,
— entrenched consumer preferences for local brands or products,
— language.

CHAPTER IV
FINAL SECTIONS TO BE COMPLETED FOR ALL NOTIFICATIONS

Section 16—Reasons for the application for negative clearance

If you are applying for negative clearance state—

16.1.   why, ie state which provision or effects of the agreement or behaviour might, in your view, raise questions of compatibility with the Community's and/or the EEA rules of competition. The object of this subheading is to give the Commission the clearest possible idea of the doubts you have about your agreement or behaviour that you wish to have resolved by a negative clearance.

Then, under the following three references, give a statement of the relevant facts and reasons as to why you consider Article 85(1) or 86 of the EC Treaty and/or Article 53(1) or 54 of the EEA Agreement to be inapplicable, ie—

16.2.   why the agreements or behaviour do not have the object or effect of preventing, restricting or distorting competition within the common market or within the territory of the EFTA States to any appreciable extent, or why your undertaking does not have or its behaviour does not abuse a dominant position; and/or

16.3.   why the agreements or behaviour do not have the object or effect of preventing, restricting or distorting competition within the EEA territory to any appreciable extent, or why your undertaking does not have or its behaviour does not abuse a dominant position; and/or

16.4.   why the agreements or behaviour are not such as may affect trade between Member States or between the Community and one or more EFTA States, or between EFTA States to any appreciable extent.

Section 17—Reasons for the application for exemption

If you are notifying the agreement, even if only as a precaution, in order to obtain an exemption under Article 85(3) of the EC Treaty and/or Article 53(3) of the EEA Agreement, explain how—

17.1.   the agreement contributes to improving production or distribution, and/or promoting technical or economic progress. In particular, please explain the reasons why these benefits are expected to result from the collaboration; for example, do the parties to the agreement possess complementary technologies or distribution systems that will produce important synergies? (if, so, please state which). Also please state whether any documents or studies were drawn up by the notifying parties when assessing the feasibility of the operation and the benefits likely to result therefrom, and whether any such documents or studies provided estimates of the savings or efficiencies likely to result. Please provide copies of any such documents or studies;

17.2.   a proper share of the benefits arising from such improvement or progress accrues to consumers;

17.3.   all restrictive provisions of the agreement are indispensable to the attainment of the aims set out under 17.1 (if you are claiming the benefit of the opposition procedure, it is particularly important that you should identify and justify restrictions that exceed those automatically exempted by the relevant Regulations). In this respect please explain how the benefits resulting from the agreement identified in your reply to question 17.1 could not be achieved, or could not be achieved so quickly or efficiently or only at higher cost or with less certainty of success (i) without the conclusion of the agreement as a whole and (ii) without those particular clauses and provisions of the agreement identified in your reply to question 4.2;

17.4.   the agreement does not eliminate competition in respect of a substantial part of the goods or services concerned.

Section 18—Supporting documentation

The completed notification must be drawn up and submitted in one original. It shall contain the last versions of all agreements which are the subject of the notification and be accompanied by the following—

(a)   sixteen copies of the notification itself;

(b)   three copies of the annual reports and accounts of all the parties to the notified agreement, decision or practice for the last three years;

(c)   three copies of the most recent in-house or external long-term market studies or planning documents for the purpose of assessing or analysing the affected markets with respect to competitive conditions, competitors (actual and potential), and market conditions. Each document should indicate the name and position of the author;

(d)   three copies of reports and analyses which have been prepared by or for any officer(s) or director(s) for the purposes of evaluating or analysing the notified agreement.

Section 19—Declaration

The notification must conclude with the following declaration which is to be signed by or on behalf of all the applicants or notifying parties.[1]

"The undersigned declare that the information given in this notification is correct to the best of their knowledge and belief, that complete copies of all documents requested by form A/B have been supplied to the extent that they are in the possession of the group of undertakings to which the applicant(s) or notifying party(ies) belong(s) and are accessible to the latter, that all estimates are identified as such and are their best estimates of the underlying facts and that all the opinions expressed are sincere.

They are aware of the provisions of Article 15(1)(a) of Regulation No 17.

Place and date:

Signatures:"

Please add the name(s) of the person(s) signing the application or notification and their function(s).

[4056]

NOTES

[1]   Applications and notifications which have not been signed are invalid.

(Annex I contains the text of the EC Treaty, Arts 85, 86 (now renumbered Arts 81, 82, reproduced at **[4001]**, **[4002]**, *and the text of the EEA Agreement, Arts 53, 54, 56, Protocol 22, Arts 2, 3, 4 (outside of the scope of this work).)*

ANNEX II
LIST OF RELEVANT ACTS
(AS OF 1 MARCH 1995)

(if you think it possible that your arrangements do not need to be notified by virtue of any of these regulations or notices it may be worth your while to obtain a copy.)

IMPLEMENTING REGULATIONS[1]

Council Regulation No 17 of 6 February 1962: First Regulation implementing Articles 85 and 86 of the Treaty (OJ L13, 21.2.1962, p 204/62, English Special Edition 1959–1962, November 1972, p 87) as amended (OJ L58, 10.7.1962, p 1655/62; OJ L162, 7.11.1963, p 2696/63; OJ L285, 29.12.1971, p 49; OJ L73, 27.3.1972, p 92; OJ L291, 19.11.1979, p 94 and OJ L302, 15.11.1985, p 165).

Commission Regulation (EC) No 3385/94 of 21 December 1994 on the form, content and other details of applications and notifications provided for in Council Regulation No 17.

NOTES

[1] As regards procedural rules applied by the EFTA Surveillance Authority, see Article 3 of Protocol 21 to the EEA Agreement and the relevant provisions in Protocol 4 to the Agreement between the EFTA States on the establishment of a Surveillance Authority and a Court of Justice.

REGULATIONS GRANTING BLOCK EXEMPTION IN RESPECT OF A WIDE RANGE OF AGREEMENTS

Commission Regulation (EC) No 1983/83 of 22 June 1983 on the application of Article 85(3) of the Treaty to categories of exclusive distribution agreements (OJ No L 173, 30.6.1983, p 1, as corrected in OJ No L 281, 13.10.1983, p 24), as well as this Regulation as adapted for EEA purposes (see point 2 of Annex XIV to the EEA Agreement).

Commission Regulation (EEC) No 1984/83 of 22 June 1983 on the application of Article 85(3) of the Treaty to categories of exclusive purchasing agreements (OJ No L 173, 30.6.1983, p 5, as corrected in OJ No L 281, 13.10.1983, p 24), as well as this Regulation as adapted for EEA purposes (see point 3 of Annex XIV to the EEA Agreement).

See also the Commission notices concerning Regulations (EEC) No 1983/93 and (EEC) No 1984/83 (OJ No C 101, 13.4.1984, p 2 and OJ No C 121, 13.5.1992, p 2).

Commission Regulation (EEC) No 2349/84 of 23 July 1984 on the application of Article 85(3) of the Treaty to certain categories of patent licensing agreements (OJ No L 219,16.8.1984, p 15, as corrected in OJ No L 113, 26.4.1985, p 34), as amended (OJ No L 12, 18.1.1995, p 13), as well as this Regulation as adapted for EEA purposes (see point 5 of Annex XIV to the EEA Agreement). Article 4 of this Regulation provides for an opposition procedure.

Commission Regulation (EEC) No 123/85 of 12 December 1984 on the application of Article 85(3) of the Treaty to certain categories of motor vehicle distribution and servicing agreements (OJ No L 15, 18.1.1985, p 16); as well as this Regulation as adapted for EEA purposes (see point 4 of Annex XIV to the EEA Agreement). See also the Commission notices concerning this Regulation (OJ No C 17, 18.1.1985, p 4 and OJ No C 329, 18.12.1991, p 20).

Commission Regulation (EEC) No 417/85 of 19 December 1984 on the application of Article 85(3) of the Treaty to categories of specialisation agreements (OJ No L 53, 22.2.1985, p 1), as amended (OJ No L 21, 29.1.1993, p 8), as well as this Regulation as adapted for EEA purposes (see point 6 of Annex XIV to the EEA Agreement). Article 4 of this Regulation provides for an opposition procedure.

Commission Regulation (EEC) No 418/85 of 19 December 1984 on the application of Article 85(3) of the Treaty to categories of research and development agreements (OJ No L 53, 22.2.1985, p 5), as amended (OJ No L 21, 29.1.1993, p 8), as well as this

Regulation as adapted for EEA purposes (see point 7 of Annex XIV to the EEA Agreement). Article 7 of this Regulation provides for an opposition procedure.

Commission Regulation (EEC) No 4087/88 of 30 November 1988 on the application of Article 85(3) of the Treaty to categories of franchise agreements (OJ No L 359, 28.12.1988, p 46), as well as this Regulation as adapted for EEA purposes (see point 8 of Annex XIV to the EEA Agreement). Article 6 of this Regulation provides for an opposition procedure.

Commission Regulation (EEC) No 556/89 of 30 November 1988 on the application of Article 85(3) of the Treaty to certain categories of know-how licensing agreements (OJ No L 61, 4.3.1989, p 1), as amended (OJ No L 21, 29.1.1993, p 8), as well as this Regulation as adapted for EEA purposes (see point 9 of Annex XIV to the EEA Agreement). Article 4 of this Regulation provides for an opposition procedure.

Commission Regulation (EEC) No 3932/92 of 21 December 1992 on the application of Article 85(3) of the Treaty to certain categories of agreements, decisions and concerted practices in the insurance sector (OJ No L 398, 31.12.1992, p 7). This Regulation will be adapted for EEA purposes.

NOTICES OF A GENERAL NATURE[1]

Commission notice on exclusive dealing contracts with commercial agents (OJ No 139, 24.12.1962, p 2921/62). This states that the Commission does not consider most such agreements to fall under the prohibition of Article 85(1).

Commission notice concerning agreements, decisions and concerted practices in the field of cooperation between enterprises (OJ No C 75, 29.7.1968, p 3, as corrected in OJ No C 84, 28.8.1968, p 14). This defines the sorts of cooperation on market studies, accounting, R & D, joint use of production, storage or transport, ad hoc consortia, selling or after-sales service, advertising or quality labelling that the Commission considers not to fall under the prohibition of Article 85(1).

Commission notice concerning its assessment of certain subcontracting agreements in relation to Article 85(1) of the Treaty (OJ No C 1, 3.1.1979, p 2).

Commission notice on agreements, decisions and concerted practices of minor importance which do not fall under Article 85(1) of the Treaty (OJ No C 231, 12.9.1986, p 2) as amended by Commission notice (OJ No C 368, 23.12.1994, p 20)—in the main, those where the parties have less than 5% of the market between them, and a combined annual turnover of less than ECU 300 million.

Commission guidelines on the application of EEC competition rules in the telecommunications sector (OJ No C 233, 6.9.1991, p 2). These guidelines aim at clarifying the application of Community competition rules to the market participants in the telecommunications sector.

Commission notice on cooperation between national courts and the Commission in applying Articles 85 and 86 (OJ No C 39, 13.2.1993, p 6). This notice sets out the principles on the basis of which such cooperation takes place.

Commission notice concerning the assessment of cooperative joint ventures pursuant to Article 85 of the EC Treaty (OJ No C 43, 16.2.1993, p 2). This notice sets out the principles of the assessment of joint ventures.

A collection of these texts (as at 31 December 1989) was published by the Office for Official Publications of the European Communities (references Vol I: ISBN 92–826–1307–0, catalogue No: CV–42–90–001–EN–C). An updated collection is in preparation.

Pursuant to the Agreement, these texts will also cover the European Economic Area.

[4057]

NOTES
[1]   See also the corresponding notices published by the EFTA Surveillance Authority.

ANNEX III
LIST OF MEMBER STATES AND EFTA STATES, ADDRESS OF THE COMMISSION AND
OF THE EFTA SURVEILLANCE AUTHORITY, LIST OF COMMISSION INFORMATION
OFFICES WITHIN THE COMMUNITY AND IN EFTA STATES AND ADDRESSES OF
COMPETENT AUTHORITIES IN EFTA STATES

The Member States as at the date of this Annex are: Austria, Belgium, Denmark, Finland, France, Germany, Greece, Ireland, Italy, Luxembourg, the Netherlands, Portugal, Spain, Sweden and the United Kingdom.

The EFTA States which will be Contracting Parties of the EEA Agreement, as at the date of this Annex, are: Iceland, Liechtenstein and Norway.

The address of the Commission's Directorate-General for Competition is—
Commission of the European Communities
Directorate-General for Competition
200 rue de la Loi
B-1049 Brussels
Tel (322) 299 11 11

The address of the EFTA Surveillance Authority's Competition Directorate is—

EFTA Surveillance Authority
Competition Directorate
1–3 rue Marie-Thérèse
B–1040 Brussels
Tel (322) 286 17 11

The addresses of the Commission's Information Offices in the Community are—

BELGIUM
73 rue Archimède
B–1040 Bruxelles
Tel (322) 299 11 11

DENMARK
Højbrohus
Østergade 61
Postb
DK–1004 København K
Tel (4533)14 41 40

FEDERAL REPUBLIC OF GERMANY
Zitelmannstraße 22
D–53113 Bonn
Tel (49228) 53 00 90
Kurfürstendamm 102
D–10711 Berlin 31
Tel (4930) 896 09 30
Erhardtstraße 27
D–80331 München
Tel (4989) 202 10 11

GREECE
2 Vassilissis Sofias
Case Postale 11002
GR–Athina 10674
Tel (301) 724 39 82/83/84

SPAIN
Calle de Serrano 41
5a Planta
E–28001 Madrid
Tel (341) 435 17 00
Av Diagonal, 407 bis
18 Planta
E–08008 Barcelona

FRANCE
288, boulevard Saint-Germain
F–75007 Paris
Tel (331) 40 63 38 00
CMCI
2, rue Henri Barbusse
F–13241 Marseille, Cedex 01
Tel (3391) 91 46 00

IRELAND
39 Molesworth Street
IRL–Dublin 2
Tel (3531) 71 22 44

ITALY
Via Poli 29
I–00187 Roma
Tel (396) 699 11 60
Corso Magenta 61
I–20123 Milano
Tel (392) 480 15 05

LUXEMBOURG
Bâtiment Jean-Monnet
rue Alcide de Gasperi
L–2920 Luxembourg
Tel (352) 430 11

NETHERLANDS
Postbus 30465
NL–2500 GL Den Haag
Tel (3170) 346 93 26

AUSTRIA
Hoyosgasse 5
A–1040 Wien
Tel (431) 505 33 79

PORTUGAL
Centro Europeu Jean Monnet
Largo Jean Monnet, 1-10°
P–1200 Lisboa
Tel (3511) 54 11 44

FINLAND
31 Pohjoisesplanadi
00100 Helsinki
Tel (3580) 65 64 20

SWEDEN
PO Box 16396
Hamngatan 6
11147 Stockholm
Tel (468) 611 11 72

UNITED KINGDOM
8 Storey's Gate
UK–London SW1P 3AT
Tel (4471) 973 19 92
Windsor House
9/15 Bedford Street
UK–Belfast BT2 7EG
Tel (44232)24 07 08

4 Cathedral Road
UK–Cardiff CF1 9SG
Tel (44222) 37 16 31
9 Alva Street
UK–Edinburgh EH2 4PH
Tel (4431) 225 20 58

The addresses of the Commission's Information Offices in the EFTA States are—

NORWAY
Postboks 1643 Vika 0119 Oslo 1
Haakon's VII Gate No 6
0161 Oslo 1
Tel (472) 83 35 83

Forms for notifications and applications, as well as more detailed information on the EEA competition rules, can also be obtained from the following offices—

AUSTRIA
Federal Ministry for Economic Affairs
Tel (431) 71 100

FINLAND
Office of Free Competition
Tel (3580) 73 141

ICELAND
Directorate of Competition and Fair Trade
Tel (3541) 27 422

LIECHTENSTEIN
Office of National Economy
Division of Economy and Statistics
Tel (4175) 61 11

NORWAY
Price Directorate
Tel (4722) 40 09 00

SWEDEN
Competition Authority
Tel (468) 700 16 00

[4058]

COMMISSION NOTICE

**on agreements of minor importance which do not appreciably restrict competition
under Article 81(1) of the Treaty establishing the European Community**
(de minimis)[1]

(2001/C 368/07)

(Text with EEA relevance)

NOTES

Date of publication in OJ: OJ C368, 22.12.01, p 13.

I

1.   Article 81(1) prohibits agreements between undertakings which may affect trade between Member States and which have as their object or effect the prevention, restriction or distortion of competition within the common market. The Court of Justice of the European Communities has clarified that this provision is not applicable where the impact of the agreement on intra-Community trade or on competition is not appreciable.

2.   In this notice the Commission quantifies, with the help of market share thresholds, what is not an appreciable restriction of competition under Article 81 of the EC Treaty. This negative definition of appreciability does not imply that agreements between undertakings which exceed the thresholds set out in this notice appreciably restrict competition. Such agreements may still have only a negligible effect on competition and may therefore not be prohibited by Article 81(1).[2]

3.   Agreements may in addition not fall under Article 81(1) because they are not capable of appreciably affecting trade between Member States. This notice does not deal with this issue. It does not quantify what does not constitute an appreciable effect on trade. It is however acknowledged that agreements between small and medium-sized undertakings, as defined in the Annex to Commission Recommendation 96/280/EC,[3] are rarely capable of appreciably affecting trade between Member States. Small and medium-sized undertakings are currently defined in that recommendation as undertakings which have fewer than 250 employees and have either an annual turnover not exceeding EUR 40 million or an annual balance-sheet total not exceeding EUR 27 million.

4.   In cases covered by this notice the Commission will not institute proceedings either upon application or on its own initiative. Where undertakings assume in good faith that an agreement is covered by this notice, the Commission will not impose fines. Although not binding on them, this notice also intends to give guidance to the courts and authorities of the Member States in their application of Article 81.

5.   This notice also applies to decisions by associations of undertakings and to concerted practices.

6.   This notice is without prejudice to any interpretation of Article 81 which may be given by the Court of Justice or the Court of First Instance of the European Communities.

II

7.   The Commission holds the view that agreements between undertakings which affect trade between Member States do not appreciably restrict competition within the meaning of Article 81(1)—

(a) if the aggregate market share held by the parties to the agreement does not exceed 10% on any of the relevant markets affected by the agreement, where the agreement is made between undertakings which are actual or potential competitors on any of these markets (agreements between competitors);[4] or

(b) if the market share held by each of the parties to the agreement does not exceed 15% on any of the relevant markets affected by the agreement, where the agreement is made between undertakings which are not actual or potential competitors on any of these markets (agreements between non-competitors).

In cases where it is difficult to classify the agreement as either an agreement between competitors or an agreement between non-competitors the 10% threshold is applicable.

8.   Where in a relevant market competition is restricted by the cumulative effect of agreements for the sale of goods or services entered into by different suppliers or distributors (cumulative foreclosure effect of parallel networks of agreements having similar effects on the market), the market share thresholds under point 7 are reduced to 5%, both for agreements between competitors and for agreements between non-competitors. Individual suppliers or distributors with a market share not exceeding 5% are in general not considered to contribute significantly to a cumulative foreclosure effect.[5] A cumulative foreclosure effect is unlikely to exist if less than 30% of the relevant market is covered by parallel (networks of) agreements having similar effects.

9.   The Commission also holds the view that agreements are not restrictive of competition if the market shares do not exceed the thresholds of respectively 10%, 15% and 5% set out in point 7 and 8 during two successive calendar years by more than 2 percentage points.

10.   In order to calculate the market share, it is necessary to determine the relevant market. This consists of the relevant product market and the relevant geographic market. When defining the relevant market, reference should be had to the notice on the definition of the relevant market for the purposes of Community competition law.[6] The market shares are to be calculated on the basis of sales value data or, where appropriate, purchase value data. If value data are not available, estimates based on other reliable market information, including volume data, may be used.

11.   Points 7, 8 and 9 do not apply to agreements containing any of the following hardcore restrictions—

(1)   as regards agreements between competitors as defined in point 7, restrictions which, directly or indirectly, in isolation or in combination with other factors under the control of the parties, have as their object—[7]

(a)   the fixing of prices when selling the products to third parties;

(b)   the limitation of output or sales;

(c)   the allocation of markets or customers;

(2)   as regards agreements between non-competitors as defined in point 7, restrictions which, directly or indirectly, in isolation or in combination with other factors under the control of the parties, have as their object:

(a)   the restriction of the buyer's ability to determine its sale price, without prejudice to the possibility of the supplier imposing a maximum sale price or recommending a sale price, provided that they do not amount to a fixed or minimum sale price as a result of pressure from, or incentives offered by, any of the parties;

(b)   the restriction of the territory into which, or of the customers to whom, the buyer may sell the contract goods or services, except the following restrictions which are not hardcore—

— the restriction of active sales into the exclusive territory or to an exclusive customer group reserved to the supplier or allocated by the supplier to another buyer, where such a restriction does not limit sales by the customers of the buyer,

— the restriction of sales to end users by a buyer operating at the wholesale level of trade,

— the restriction of sales to unauthorised distributors by the members of a selective distribution system, and

— the restriction of the buyer's ability to sell components, supplied for the purposes of incorporation, to customers who would use them to manufacture the same type of goods as those produced by the supplier;

(c)   the restriction of active or passive sales to end users by members of a selective distribution system operating at the retail level of trade, without prejudice to the possibility of prohibiting a member of the system from operating out of an unauthorised place of establishment;

    (d) the restriction of cross-supplies between distributors within a selective distribution system, including between distributors operating at different levels of trade;

    (e) the restriction agreed between a supplier of components and a buyer who incorporates those components, which limits the supplier's ability to sell the components as spare parts to end users or to repairers or other service providers not entrusted by the buyer with the repair or servicing of its goods;

  (3) as regards agreements between competitors as defined in point 7, where the competitors operate, for the purposes of the agreement, at a different level of the production or distribution chain, any of the hardcore restrictions listed in paragraph (1) and (2) above.

12.—(1) For the purposes of this notice, the terms "undertaking", "party to the agreement", "distributor", "supplier" and "buyer" shall include their respective connected undertakings.

  (2) "Connected undertakings" are—

    (a) undertakings in which a party to the agreement, directly or indirectly:

      — has the power to exercise more than half the voting rights, or

      — has the power to appoint more than half the members of the supervisory board, board of management or bodies legally representing the undertaking, or

      — has the right to manage the undertaking's affairs;

    (b) undertakings which directly or indirectly have, over a party to the agreement, the rights or powers listed in (a);

    (c) undertakings in which an undertaking referred to in (b) has, directly or indirectly, the rights or powers listed in (a);

    (d) undertakings in which a party to the agreement together with one or more of the undertakings referred to in (a), (b) or (c), or in which two or more of the latter undertakings, jointly have the rights or powers listed in (a);

    (e) undertakings in which the rights or the powers listed in (a) are jointly held by—

      — parties to the agreement or their respective connected undertakings referred to in (a) to (d), or

      — one or more of the parties to the agreement or one or more of their connected undertakings referred to in (a) to (d) and one or more third parties.

  (3) For the purposes of paragraph 2(e), the market share held by these jointly held undertakings shall be apportioned equally to each undertaking having the rights or the powers listed in paragraph 2(a).

[4059]–[4250]

NOTES

[1] This notice replaces the notice on agreements of minor importance published in OJ C372, 9.12.1997.

[2] See, for instance, the judgment of the Court of Justice in Joined Cases C-215/96 and C-216/96 *Bagnasco (Carlos)* v *Banca Popolare di Novara and Casa di Risparmio di Genova e Imperia* (1999) ECR I-135, points 34–35. This notice is also without prejudice to the principles for assessment under Article 81(1) as expressed in the Commission notice "Guidelines on the applicability of Article 81 of the EC Treaty to horizontal cooperation agreements", OJ C3, 6.1.2001, in particular points 17–31 inclusive, and in the Commission notice "Guidelines on vertical restraints", OJ C291, 13.10.2000, in particular points 5–20 inclusive.

[3] OJ L107, 30.4.1996, p 4. This recommendation will be revised. It is envisaged to increase the annual turnover threshold from EUR 40 million to EUR 50 million and the annual balance-sheet total threshold from EUR 27 million to EUR 43 million.

[4] On what are actual or potential competitors, see the Commission notice "Guidelines on the applicability of Article 81 of the EC Treaty to horizontal cooperation agreements", OJ C3, 6.1.2001,

paragraph 9. A firm is treated as an actual competitor if it is either active on the same relevant market or if, in the absence of the agreement, it is able to switch production to the relevant products and market them in the short term without incurring significant additional costs or risks in response to a small and permanent increase in relative prices (immediate supply-side substitutability). A firm is treated as a potential competitor if there is evidence that, absent the agreement, this firm could and would be likely to undertake the necessary additional investments or other necessary switching costs so that it could enter the relevant market in response to a small and permanent increase in relative prices.

[5] See also the Commission notice "Guidelines on vertical restraints", OJ C291, 13.10.2000, in particular paragraphs 73, 142, 143 and 189. While in the guidelines on vertical restraints in relation to certain restrictions reference is made not only to the total but also to the tied market share of a particular supplier or buyer, in this notice all market share thresholds refer to total market shares.

[6] OJ C372, 9.12.1997, p 5.

[7] Without prejudice to situations of joint production with or without joint distribution as defined in Article 5, paragraph 2, of Commission Regulation (EC) No 2658/2000 and Article 5, paragraph 2, of Commission Regulation (EC) No 2659/2000, OJ L304, 5.12.2000, pp 3 and 7 respectively.

B. TRANSPORT

COUNCIL REGULATION
exempting transport from the application of Council Regulation No 17

(141/62/EEC)

NOTES
Date of publication in OJ: OJ L62, 29.11.62, p 2751 (S edn, 1959–62, p 291).

THE COUNCIL OF THE EUROPEAN ECONOMIC COMMUNITY,

Having regard to the Treaty establishing the European Economic Community, and in particular Article 67 thereof;

Having regard to the first Regulation made in implementation of Articles 85 and 86 of the Treaty (Regulation No 17) of 6 February 1962, as amended by Regulation No 59 of 3 July 1962;

Having regard to the proposal from the Commission;

Having regard to the Opinion of the Economic and Social Committee;

Having regard to the Opinion of the Assembly;

Whereas, in pursuance of the common transport policy, account being taken of the distinctive features of the transport sector, it may prove necessary to lay down rules governing competition different from those laid down or to be laid down for other sectors of the economy, and whereas Regulation No 17 should not therefore apply to transport;

Whereas, in the light of work in hand on the formulation of a common transport policy, it is possible, as regards transport by rail, road and inland waterway, to envisage the introduction within a foreseeable period of rules of competition; whereas, on the other hand, as regards sea and air transport it is impossible to foresee whether and at what date the Council will adopt appropriate provisions; whereas accordingly a limit to the period during which Regulation No 17 shall not apply can be set only for transport by rail, road and inland waterway;

Whereas the distinctive features of transport make it justifiable to exempt from the application of Regulation No 17 only agreements, decisions and concerted practices directly relating to the provision of transport services;

HAS ADOPTED THIS REGULATION—

Article 1

Regulation No 17 shall not apply to agreements, decisions or concerted practices in the transport sector which have as their object or effect the fixing of transport rates and conditions, the limitation or control of the supply of transport or the sharing of transport markets; nor shall it apply to the abuse of a dominant position, within the meaning of Article 86 of the Treaty, within the transport market.

[4251]

Article 2

The Council, taking account of any measures that may be taken in pursuance of the common transport policy, shall adopt appropriate provisions in order to apply rules of competition to transport by rail, road and inland waterway. To this end, the Commission shall, before 30 June 1964, submit proposals to the Council.

[4252]

Article 3

Article 1 of this Regulation shall remain in force, as regards transport by rail, road and inland waterway, until 31 December 1965.

[4253]

Article 4

This Regulation shall enter into force on 13 March 1962. These provisions shall not be invoked against undertakings or associations of undertakings which, before the day following the date of publication of this Regulation in the *Official Journal of the European Communities*, shall have terminated any agreement, decision or concerted practice covered by Article 1.

[4254]

This Regulation shall be binding in its entirety and directly applicable in all Member States.

Done at Paris, 26 November 1962.

COUNCIL REGULATION

of 19 July 1968

applying rules of competition to transport by rail, road and inland waterway

(1017/68/EEC)

NOTES

Date of publication in OJ: OJ L175, 22.7.68, p 1 (S edn, 1968(I), p 302).

THE COUNCIL OF THE EUROPEAN COMMUNITIES,

Having regard to the Treaty establishing the European Economic Community, and in particular Articles 75 and 87 thereof;

Having regard to the proposal from the Commission;

Having regard to the Opinion of the European Parliament;[1]

Having regard to the Opinion of the Economic and Social Committee;[2]

Whereas Council Regulation No 141[3] exempting transport from the application of Regulation No 17 provides that the said Regulation No 17[4] shall not apply to agreements, decisions and concerted practices in the transport sector the effect of which is to fix transport rates and conditions, to limit or control the supply of transport or to share transport markets, nor to dominant positions, within the meaning of Article 86 of the Treaty, on the transport market;

Whereas, for transport by rail, road and inland waterway, Regulation No 1002/67/CEE[5] provides that such exemption shall not extend beyond 30 June 1968;

Whereas the establishing of rules of competition for transport by rail, road and inland waterway is part of the common transport policy and of general economic policy;

Whereas, when rules of competition for these sectors are being settled, account must be taken of the distinctive features of transport;

Whereas, since the rules of competition for transport derogate from the general rules of competition, it must be made possible for undertakings to ascertain what rules apply in any particular case;

Whereas, with the introduction of a system of rules on competition for transport, it is desirable that such rules should apply equally to the joint financing or acquisition of transport equipment for the joint operation of services by certain groupings of undertakings, and also to certain operations in connection with transport by rail, road or inland waterway of providers of services ancillary to transport;

Whereas, in order to ensure that trade between Member States is not affected or competition within the common market distorted, it is necessary to prohibit in principle for the three modes of transport specified above all agreements between undertakings, decisions of associations of undertakings and concerted practices between undertakings and all instances of abuse of a dominant position within the common market which could have such effects;

Whereas certain types of agreement, decision and concerted practice in the transport sector the object and effect of which is merely to apply technical improvements or to achieve technical co-operation may be exempted from the prohibition on restrictive agreements since they contribute to improving productivity; whereas, in the light of experience following application of this Regulation, the Council may, on a proposal from the Commission, amend the list of such types of agreement;

Whereas, in order that an improvement may be fostered in the sometimes too dispersed structure of the industry in the road and inland waterway sectors, there should also be exempted from the prohibition on restrictive agreements those agreements, decisions and concerted practices providing for the creation and operation of groupings of undertakings in these two transport sectors whose object is the carrying on of transport operations, including the joint financing or acquisition of transport equipment for the joint operation of services; whereas such overall exemption can be granted only on condition that the total carrying capacity of a grouping does not exceed a fixed maximum, and that the individual capacity of undertakings belonging to the grouping does not exceed certain limits so fixed as to ensure that no one undertaking can hold a dominant position within the grouping; whereas the Commission must, however, have power to intervene if, in specific cases, such agreements should have effects incompatible with the conditions under which a restrictive agreement may be recognised as lawful, and should constitute an abuse of the exemption; whereas, nevertheless, the fact that a grouping has a total carrying capacity greater than the fixed maximum, or cannot claim the overall exemption because of the individual capacity of the undertakings belonging to the grouping, does not in itself prevent such a grouping from constituting a lawful agreement, decision or concerted practice if it satisfies the conditions therefor laid down in this Regulation;

Whereas, where an agreement, decision or concerted practice contributes towards improving the quality of transport services, or towards promoting greater continuity and stability in the satisfaction of transport needs on markets where supply and demand may be subject to considerable temporal fluctuation, or towards increasing the productivity of undertakings, or towards furthering technical or economic progress, it must be made possible for the prohibition to be declared not to apply, always provided, however, that the agreement, decision or concerted practice takes fair account of the interests of transport users, and neither imposes on the undertakings concerned any restriction not indispensable to the attainment of the above objectives nor makes it possible for such undertakings to eliminate competition in respect of a substantial part of the transport market concerned, having regard to competition from alternative modes of transport;

Whereas it is desirable until such time as the Council, acting in pursuance of the common transport policy, introduces appropriate measures to ensure a stable transport market, and subject to the condition that the Council shall have found that a state of crisis exists, to authorise, for the market in question, such agreements as are needed in order to reduce disturbance resulting from the structure of the transport market;

Whereas, in respect of transport by rail, road and inland waterway, it is desirable that Member States should neither enact nor maintain in force measures contrary to this Regulation concerning public undertakings or undertakings to which they grant special or exclusive rights; whereas it is also desirable that undertakings entrusted with the operation of services of general economic importance should be subject to the provisions of this Regulation in so far as the application thereof does not obstruct, in law or in fact, the accomplishment of the particular tasks assigned to them, always provided that the development of trade is not thereby affected to such an extent as would be contrary to the interests of the Community; whereas the Commission must have power to see that these principles are applied and to address the appropriate directives or decisions for this purpose to Member States;

Whereas the detailed rules for application of the basic principles of this Regulation must be so drawn that they not only ensure effective supervision while simplifying administration as far as possible but also meet the needs of undertakings for certainty in the law;

Whereas it is for the undertakings themselves, in the first instance, to judge whether the predominant effects of their agreements, decisions or concerted practices are the restriction of competition or the economic benefits acceptable as justification for such restriction and to decide accordingly, on their own responsibility, as to the illegality or legality of such agreements, decisions or concerted practices;

Whereas, therefore, undertakings should be allowed to conclude or operate agreements without declaring them; whereas this exposes such agreements to the risk of being declared void with retroactive effect should they be examined following a complaint or on the Commission's own initiative, but does not prevent their being retroactively declared lawful in the event of such subsequent examination;

Whereas, however, undertakings may, in certain cases, desire the assistance of the competent authorities to ensure that their agreements, decisions or concerted practices are in conformity with the rules applicable; whereas for this purpose there should be made available to undertakings a procedure whereby they may submit applications to the Commission and a summary of each such application is published in the *Official Journal of the European*

Communities, enabling any interested third parties to submit their comments on the agreement in question; whereas, in the absence of any complaint from Member States or interested third parties and unless the Commission notifies applicants within a fixed time limit, that there are serious doubts as to the legality of the agreement in question, that agreement should be deemed exempt from the prohibition for the time already elapsed and for a further period of three years;

Whereas, in view of the exceptional nature of agreements needed in order to reduce disturbances resulting from the structure of the transport market, once the Council has found that a state of crisis exists undertakings wishing to obtain authorisation for such an agreement should be required to notify it to the Commission; whereas authorisation by the Commission should have effect only from the date when it is decided to grant it; whereas the period of validity of such authorisation should not exceed three years from the finding of a state of crisis by the Council; whereas renewal of the decision should depend upon renewal of the finding of a state of crisis by the Council; whereas, in any event, the authorisation should cease to be valid not later than six months from the bringing into operation by the Council of appropriate measures to ensure the stability of the transport market to which the agreement relates;

Whereas, in order to secure uniform application within the common market of the rules of competition for transport, rules must be made under which the Commission, acting in close and constant liaison with the competent authorities of the Member States, may take the measures required for the application of such rules of competition;

Whereas for this purpose the Commission must have the co-operation of the competent authorities of the Member States and be empowered throughout the common market to request such information and to carry out such investigations as are necessary to bring to light any agreement, decision or concerted practice prohibited under this Regulation, or any abuse of a dominant position prohibited under this Regulation;

Whereas, if, on the application of the Regulation to a specific case, a Member State is of the opinion that a question of principle concerning the common transport policy is involved, it should be possible for such questions of principle to be examined by the Council; whereas it should be possible for any general questions raised by the implementation of the competition policy in the transport sector to be referred to the Council; whereas a procedure must be provided for which ensures that any decision to apply the Regulation in a specific case will be taken by the Commission only after the questions of principle have been examined by the Council, and in the light of the policy guidelines that emerge from that examination;

Whereas, in order to carry out its duty of ensuring that the provisions of this Regulation are applied, the Commission must be empowered to address to undertakings or associations of undertakings recommendations and decisions for the purpose of bringing to an end infringements of the provisions of this Regulation prohibiting certain agreements, decisions or practices;

Whereas compliance with the prohibitions laid down in this Regulation and the fulfilment of obligations imposed on undertakings and associations of undertakings under this Regulation must be enforceable by means of fines and periodic penalty payments;

Whereas undertakings concerned must be accorded the right to be heard by the Commission, third parties whose interests may be affected by a decision must be given the opportunity of submitting their comments beforehand, and it must be ensured that wide publicity is given to decisions taken;

Whereas it is desirable to confer upon the Court of Justice, pursuant to Article 172, unlimited jurisdiction in respect of decisions under which the Commission imposes fines or periodic penalty payments;

Whereas it is expedient to postpone for six months, as regards agreements, decisions and concerted practices in existence at the date of publication of this Regulation in the *Official Journal of the European Communities*, the entry into force of the prohibition laid down in the Regulation, in order to make it easier for undertakings to adjust their operations so as to conform to its provisions;

Whereas, following discussions with the third countries signatories to the Revised Convention for the Navigation of the Rhine, and within an appropriate period of time from the conclusion of those discussions, this Regulation as a whole should be amended as necessary in the light of the obligations arising out of the Revised Convention for the Navigation of the Rhine;

Whereas the Regulation should be amended as necessary in the light of the experience gained over a three-year period; whereas it will in particular be desirable to consider whether, in the light of the development of the common transport policy over that period, the scope of the Regulation should be extended to agreements, decisions and concerted practices, and to instances of abuse of a dominant position, not affecting trade between Member States;

NOTES
1   OJ 205, 11.12.64, p 3505/64.
2   OJ 103, 12.6.65, p 1792/65.
3   OJ 124, 28.11.62, p 2751/62.
4   OJ 13, 21.2.62, p 204/62.
5   OJ 306, 16.12.67, p 1.

HAS ADOPTED THIS REGULATION—

Article 1

Basic provision

The provisions of this Regulation shall, in the field of transport by rail, road and inland waterway, apply both to all agreements, decisions and concerted practices which have as their object or effect the fixing of transport rates and conditions, the limitation or control of the supply of transport, the sharing of transport markets, the application of technical improvements or technical co-operation, or the joint financing or acquisition of transport equipment or supplies where such operations are directly related to the provision of transport services and are necessary for the joint operation of services by a grouping within the meaning of Article 4 of road or inland waterway transport undertakings, and to the abuse of a dominant position on the transport market. These provisions shall apply also to operations of providers of services ancillary to transport which have any of the objects or effects listed above.

[4255]

Article 2

Prohibition of restrictive practices

Subject to the provisions of Articles 3 to 6, the following shall be prohibited as incompatible with the common market, no prior decision to that effect being required: all agreements between undertakings, decisions by associations of undertakings and concerted practices liable to affect trade between Member States which have as their object or effect the prevention, restriction or distortion of competition within the common market, and in particular those which—

   (a) directly or indirectly fix transport rates and conditions or any other trading conditions;
   (b) limit or control the supply of transport, markets, technical development or investment;
   (c) share transport markets;
   (d) apply dissimilar conditions to equivalent transactions with other trading parties, thereby placing them at a competitive disadvantage;
   (e) make the conclusion of contracts subject to acceptance by the other parties of additional obligations which, by their nature or according to commercial usage, have no connection with the provision of transport services.

[4256]

Article 3

Exception for technical agreements

   1.   The prohibition laid down in Article 2 shall not apply to agreements, decisions or concerted practices the object and effect of which is to apply technical improvements or to achieve technical co-operation by means of—
   (a) the standardisation of equipment, transport supplies, vehicles or fixed installations;

(b) the exchange or pooling, for the purpose of operating transport services, of staff, equipment, vehicles or fixed installations;

(c) the organisation and execution of successive, complementary, substitute or combined transport operations, and the fixing and application of inclusive rates and conditions for such operations, including special competitive rates;

(d) the use, for journeys by a single mode of transport, of the routes which are most rational from the operational point of view;

(e) the co-ordination of transport timetables for connecting routes;

(f) the grouping of single consignments;

(g) the establishment of uniform rules as to the structure of tariffs and their conditions of application, provided such rules do not lay down transport rates and conditions.

2. The Commission shall, where appropriate, submit proposals to the Council with a view to extending or reducing the list in paragraph 1.

[4257]

Article 4

Exemption for groups of small and medium-sized undertakings

1. The agreements, decisions and concerted practices referred to in Article 2 shall be exempt from the prohibition in that Article where their purpose is—
— the constitution and operation of groupings of road or inland waterway transport undertakings with a view to carrying on transport activities;
— the joint financing or acquisition of transport equipment or supplies, where these operations are directly related to the provision of transport services and are necessary for the joint operations of the aforesaid groupings;

always provided that the total carrying capacity of any grouping does not exceed—
— 10 000 metric tons in the case of road transport,
— 500 000 metric tons in the case of transport by inland waterway.

The individual capacity of each undertaking belonging to a grouping shall not exceed 1 000 metric tons in the case of road transport or 50 000 metric tons in the case of transport by inland waterway.

2. If the implementation of any agreement, decision or concerted practice covered by paragraph 1 has, in a given case, effects which are incompatible with the requirements of Article 5 and which constitute an abuse of the exemption from the provisions of Article 2, undertakings or associations of undertakings may be required to make such effects cease.

[4258]

Article 5

Non-applicability of the prohibition

The prohibition in Article 2 may be declared inapplicable with retroactive effect to—
— any agreement or category of agreement between undertakings,
— any decision or category of decision of an association of undertakings, or
— any concerted practice or category of concerted practice which contributes towards—
— improving the quality of transport services; or
— promoting greater continuity and stability in the satisfaction of transport needs on markets where supply and demand are subject to considerable temporal fluctuation; or

— increasing the productivity of undertakings; or
— furthering technical or economic progress;

and at the same time takes fair account of the interests of transport users and neither—

(a) imposes on the transport undertakings concerned any restriction not essential to the attainment of the above objectives; nor

(b) makes it possible for such undertakings to eliminate competition in respect of a substantial part of the transport market concerned.

[4259]

Article 6

Agreements intended to reduce disturbances resulting from the structure of the transport market

1. Until such time as the Council, acting in pursuance of the common transport policy, introduces appropriate measures to ensure a stable transport market, the prohibition laid down in Article 2 may be declared inapplicable to any agreement, decision or concerted practice which tends to reduce disturbances on the market in question.

2. A decision not to apply the prohibition laid down in Article 2, made in accordance with the procedure laid down in Article 14, may not be taken until the Council, either acting by a qualified majority or, where any Member State considers that the conditions set out in Article 75(3) of the Treaty are satisfied, acting unanimously, has found, on the basis of a report by the Commission, that a state of crisis exists in all or part of a transport market.

3. Without prejudice to the provisions of paragraph 2, the prohibition in Article 2 may be declared inapplicable only where—

(a) the agreement, decision or concerted practice in question does not impose upon the undertakings concerned any restriction not indispensable to the reduction of disturbances; and

(b) does not make it possible for such undertakings to eliminate competition in respect of a substantial part of the transport market concerned.

[4260]

Article 7

Invalidity of agreements and decisions

Any agreement or decision prohibited under the foregoing provisions shall be automatically void.

[4261]

Article 8

Prohibition of abuse of dominant positions

Any abuse by one or more undertakings of a dominant position within the common market or in a substantial part of it shall be prohibited as incompatible with the common market in so far as trade between Member States may be affected thereby.

Such abuse may, in particular, consist in—

(a) directly or indirectly imposing unfair transport rates or conditions;

(b) limiting the supply of transport, markets or technical development to the prejudice of consumers;

(c) applying dissimilar conditions to equivalent transactions with other trading parties, thereby placing them at a competitive disadvantage;

(d) making the conclusion of contracts subject to acceptance by the other parties of supplementary obligations which, by their nature or according to commercial usage, have no connection with the provision of transport services.

[4262]

Article 9

Public undertakings

1.   In the case of public undertakings and undertakings to which Member States grant special or exclusive rights, Member States shall neither enact nor maintain in force any measure contrary to the provisions of the foregoing Articles.

2.   Undertakings entrusted with the operation of services of general economic importance shall be subject to the provisions of the foregoing Articles, in so far as the application thereof does not obstruct, in law or in fact, the accomplishment of the particular tasks assigned to them. The development of trade must not be affected to such an extent as would be contrary to the interests of the Community.

3.   The Commission shall see that the provisions of this Article are applied and shall, where necessary, address appropriate directives or decisions to Member States.

[4263]

Article 10

Procedures on complaint or on the Commission's own initiative

Acting on receipt of a complaint or on its own initiative, the Commission shall initiate procedures to terminate any infringement of the provisions of Article 2 or of Article 8 or to enforce Article 4(2).

Complaints may be submitted by—
(a) Member States;
(b) natural or legal persons who claim a legitimate interest.

[4264]

Article 11

Result of procedures on complaint or on the Commission's own initiative

1.   Where the Commission finds that there has been an infringement of Article 2 or Article 8, it may by decision require the undertakings or associations of undertakings concerned to bring such infringement to an end.

Without prejudice to the other provisions of this Regulation, the Commission may, before taking a decision under the preceding subparagraph, address to the undertakings or associations of undertakings concerned recommendations for termination of the infringement.

2.   Paragraph 1 shall apply also to cases falling within Article 4(2).

3.   If the Commission, acting on a complaint received, concludes that on the evidence before it there are no grounds for intervention under Article 2, Article 4(2) or Article 8 in respect of any agreement, decision or practice, it shall issue a decision rejecting the complaint as unfounded.

4.   If the Commission, whether acting on a complaint received or on its own initiative, concludes that an agreement, decision or concerted practice satisfies the provisions both of Article 2 and of Article 5, it shall issue a decision applying

Article 5. Such decision shall indicate the date from which it is to take effect. This date may be prior to that of the decision.

Article 12

Application of Article 5—objections

1.   Undertakings and associations of undertakings which seek application of Article 5 in respect of agreements, decisions and concerted practices falling within the provisions of Article 2 to which they are parties may submit applications to the Commission.

2.   If the Commission judges an application admissible and is in possession of all the available evidence, and no action under Article 10 has been taken against the agreement, decision or concerted practice in question, then it shall publish as soon as possible in the *Official Journal of the European Communities* a summary of the application and invite all interested third parties to submit their comments to the Commission within thirty days. Such publication shall have regard to the legitimate interest of undertakings in the protection of their business secrets.

3.   Unless the Commission notifies applicants, within ninety days from the date of such publication in the *Official Journal of the European Communities*, that there are serious doubts as to the applicability of Article 5, the agreement, decision or concerted practice shall be deemed exempt, in so far as it conforms with the description given in the application, from the prohibition for the time already elapsed and for a maximum of three years from the date of publication in the *Official Journal of the European Communities.*

If the Commission finds, after expiry of the ninety-day time limit, but before expiry of the three-year period, that the conditions for applying Article 5 are not satisfied, it shall issue a decision declaring that the prohibition in Article 2 is applicable. Such decision may be retroactive where the parties concerned have given inaccurate information or where they abuse the exemption from the provisions of Article 2.

4.   If, within the ninety-day time limit, the Commission notifies applicants as referred to in the first subparagraph of paragraph 3, it shall examine whether the provisions of Article 2 and of Article 5 are satisfied.

If it finds that the provisions of Article 2 and of Article 5 are satisfied it shall issue a decision applying Article 5. The decision shall indicate the date from which it is to take effect. This date may be prior to that of the application.

Article 13

Duration and revocation of decisions applying Article 5

1.   Any decision applying Article 5 taken under Article 11(4) or under the second sub-paragraph of Article 12(4) shall indicate the period for which it is to be valid; normally such period shall not be less than six years. Conditions and obligations may be attached to the decision.

2.   The decision may be renewed if the conditions for applying Article 5 continue to be satisfied.

3.   The Commission may revoke or amend its decision or prohibit specified acts by the parties—
   (a) where there has been a change in any of the facts which were basic to the making of the decision;

(b) where the parties commit a breach of any obligation attached to the decision;

(c) where the decision is based on incorrect information or was induced by deceit;

(d) where the parties abuse the exemption from the provisions of Article 2 granted to them by the decision.

In cases falling within (b), (c) or (d), the decision may be revoked with retroactive effect.

[4267]

Article 14

Decisions applying Article 6

1.   Any agreement, decision or concerted practice covered by Article 2 in respect of which the parties seek application of Article 6 shall be notified to the Commission.

2.   Any decision by the Commission to apply Article 6 shall have effect only from the date of its adoption. It shall state the period for which it is to be valid. Such period shall not exceed three years from the finding of a state of crisis by the Council provided for in Article 6(2).

3.   Such decision may be renewed by the Commission if the Council again finds, acting under the procedure provided for in Article 6(2), that there is a state of crisis and if the other conditions laid down in Article 6 continue to be satisfied.

4.   Conditions and obligations may be attached to the decision.

5.   The decision of the Commission shall cease to have effect not later than six months from the coming into operation of the measures referred to in Article 6(1).

6.   The provisions of Article 13(3) shall apply.

[4268]

Article 15

Powers

Subject to review of its decision by the Court of Justice, the Commission shall have sole power—

— to impose obligations pursuant to Article 4(2);
— to issue decisions pursuant to Articles 5 and 6.

The authorities of the Member States shall retain the power to decide whether any case falls within the provisions of Article 2 or Article 8, until such time as the Commission has initiated a procedure with a view to formulating a decision in the case in question or has sent notification as provided for in the first subparagraph of Article 12(3).

[4269]

Article 16

Liaison with the authorities of the Member States

1.   The Commission shall carry out the procedures provided for in this Regulation in close and constant liaison with the competent authorities of the Member States; these authorities shall have the right to express their views on such procedures.

2.   The Commission shall immediately forward to the competent authorities of the Member States copies of the complaints and applications and of the most important documents sent to it or which it sends out in the course of such procedures.

3.   An Advisory Committee on Restrictive Practices and Monopolies in the Transport Industry shall be consulted prior to the taking of any decision following upon a procedure under Article 10 or of any decision under the second subparagraph of Article 12(3), or under the second subparagraph of paragraph 4 of the same Article, or under paragraph 2 or paragraph 3 of Article 14. The Advisory Committee shall also be consulted prior to adoption of the implementing provisions provided for in Article 29.

4.   The Advisory Committee shall be composed of officials competent in the matter of restrictive practices and monopolies in transport. Each Member State shall appoint two officials to represent it, each of whom, if prevented from attending, may be replaced by some other official.

5.   Consultation shall take place at a joint meeting convened by the Commission; such meeting shall be held not earlier than fourteen days after dispatch of the notice convening it. This notice shall, in respect of each case to be examined, be accompanied by a summary of the case together with an indication of the most important documents, and a preliminary draft decision.

6.   The Advisory Committee may deliver an opinion notwithstanding that some of its members or their alternates are not present. A report of the outcome of the consultative proceedings shall be annexed to the draft decision. It shall not be made public.

[4270]

Article 17

Consideration by the Council of questions of principle concerning the common transport policy raised in connection with specific cases

1.   The Commission shall not give a decision in respect of which consultation as laid down in Article 16 is compulsory until after the expiry of twenty days from the date on which the Advisory Committee has delivered its Opinion.

2.   Before the expiry of the period specified in paragraph 1, any Member State may request that the Council be convened to examine with the Commission any question of principle concerning the common transport policy which such Member State considers to be involved in the particular case for decision.

The Council shall meet within thirty days from the request by the Member State concerned for the sole purpose of considering such questions of principle.

The Commission shall not give its decision until after the Council meeting.

3.   Further, the Council may at any time, at the request of a Member State or of the Commission, consider general questions raised by the implementation of the competition policy in the transport sector.

4.   In all cases where the Council is asked to meet to consider under paragraph 2 questions of principle or under paragraph 3 general questions, the Commission shall, for the purposes of this Regulation, take into account the policy guidelines which emerge from that meeting.

[4271]

Article 18

Inquiries into transport sectors

1.   If trends in transport, fluctuations in or inflexibility of transport rates, or other circumstances, suggest that competition in transport is being restricted or distorted within the common market in a specific geographical area, or over one or more transport links, or in respect of the carriage of passengers or goods belonging to one or more specific categories, the Commission may decide to conduct a general inquiry into the sector concerned, in the course of which it may request transport undertakings in that sector to supply the information and documentation necessary for giving effect to the principles formulated in Articles 2 to 8.

2.   When making inquiries pursuant to paragraph 1, the Commission shall also request undertakings or groups of undertakings whose size suggests that they occupy a dominant position within the common market or a substantial part thereof to supply such particulars of the structure of the undertakings and of their behaviour as are requisite to an appraisal of their position in the light of the provisions of Article 8.

3.   Article 16(2) to (6) and Articles 17, 19, 20 and 21 shall apply.

[4272]

Article 19

Requests for information

1.   In carrying out the duties assigned to it by this Regulation, the Commission may obtain all necessary information from the Governments and competent authorities of the Member States and from undertakings and associations of undertakings.

2.   When sending a request for information to an undertaking or association of undertakings, the Commission shall at the same time forward a copy of the request to the competent authority of the Member State in whose territory the seat of the undertakings is situated.

3.   In its request, the Commission shall state the legal basis and the purpose of the request, and also the penalties provided for in Article 22(1)(b) for supplying incorrect information.

4.   The owners of the undertakings or their representatives and, in the case of legal persons, companies or firms, or of associations having no legal personality, the person authorised to represent them by law or by their constitution, shall be bound to supply the information requested.

5.   Where an undertaking or association of undertakings does not supply the information requested within the time limit fixed by the Commission, or supplies incomplete information, the Commission shall by decision require the information to be supplied. The decision shall specify what information is required, fix an appropriate time limit within which it is to be supplied and indicate the penalties provided for in Article 22(1)(b) and Article 23(1)(c), and the right to have the decision reviewed by the Court of Justice.

6.   The Commission shall at the same time forward a copy of its decision to the competent authority of the Member State in whose territory the seat of the undertaking or association of undertakings is situated.

[4273]

Article 20

Investigations by the authorities of the Member States

1.   At the request of the Commission, the competent authorities of the Member States shall undertake the investigations which the Commission considers to be necessary under Article 21(1), or which it has ordered by decision pursuant to Article 21(3). The officials of the competent authorities of the Member States responsible for conducting these investigations shall exercise their powers upon production of an authorisation in writing issued by the competent authority of the Member State in whose territory the investigation is to be made. Such authorisation shall specify the subject matter and purpose of the investigation.

2.   If so requested by the Commission or by the competent authority of the Member State in whose territory the investigation is to be made, the officials of the Commission may assist the officials of such authority in carrying out their duties.

[4274]

Article 21

Investigating powers of the Commission

1.   In carrying out the duties assigned to it by this Regulation, the Commission may undertake all necessary investigations into undertakings and associations of undertakings. To this end the officials authorised by the Commission are empowered—
   (a) to examine the books and other business records;
   (b) to take copies of or extracts from the books and business records;
   (c) to ask for oral explanations on the spot;
   (d) to enter any premises, land and vehicles of undertakings.

2.   The officials of the Commission authorised for the purpose of these investigations shall exercise their powers upon production of an authorisation in writing specifying the subject matter and purpose of the investigation and the penalties provided for in Article 22(1)(c) in cases where production of the required books or other business records is incomplete.

In good time before the investigation, the Commission shall inform the competent authority of the Member State in whose territory the same is to be made of the investigation and of the identity of the authorised officials.

3.   Undertakings and associations of undertakings shall submit to investigations ordered by decision of the Commission. The decision shall specify the subject matter and purpose of the investigation, appoint the date on which it is to begin and indicate the penalties provided for in Article 22(1)(c) and Article 23(1)(d) and the right to have the decision reviewed by the Court of Justice.

4.   The Commission shall take decisions referred to in paragraph 3 after consultation with the competent authority of the Member State in whose territory the investigation is to be made.

5.   Officials of the competent authority of the Member State in whose territory the investigation is to be made, may at the request of such authority or of the Commission, assist the officials of the Commission in carrying out their duties.

6.   Where an undertaking opposes an investigation ordered pursuant to this Article, the Member State concerned shall afford the necessary assistance to the officials authorised by the Commission to enable them to make their investigation. Member States shall, after consultation with the Commission, take the necessary measures to this end before 1 January 1970. [New Member States shall, after consulting the Commission, take the necessary measures to this end within six

months from the date of accession.] [The Hellenic Republic shall, after consultation with the Commission, take the necessary measures to this end within a period of six months following the Accession.]

[4275]

NOTES

    Para 6: words in first pair of square brackets added by the 1972 Act of Accession of Denmark, Ireland and the United Kingdom, Annex I(V)(3); words in second pair of square brackets inserted by the 1979 Act of Accession of the Hellenic Republic, Annex I(IV)(1).

Article 22

Fines

    1.   The Commission may by decision impose on undertakings or associations of undertakings fines of from one hundred to five thousand units of account where, intentionally or negligently—

    (a) they supply incorrect or misleading information in an application pursuant to Article 12 or in a notification pursuant to Article 14; or

    (b) they supply incorrect information in response to a request made pursuant to Article 18 or to Article 19(3) or (5), or do not supply information within the time limit fixed by a decision taken under Article 19(5); or

    (c) they produce the required books or other business records in incomplete form during investigations under Article 20 or Article 21, or refuse to submit to an investigation ordered by decision issued in implementation of Article 21(3).

    2.   The Commission may by decision impose on undertakings or associations of undertakings fines of from one thousand to one million units of account, or a sum in excess thereof but not exceeding 10% of the turnover in the preceding business year of each of the undertakings participating in the infringement, where either intentionally or negligently—

    (a) they infringe Article 2 or Article 8; or

    (b) they commit a breach of any obligation imposed pursuant to Article 13(1) or Article 14(4).

    In fixing the amount of the fine, regard shall be had both to the gravity and to the duration of the infringement.

    3.   Article 16(3) to (6) and Article 17 shall apply.

    4.   Decisions taken pursuant to paragraphs 1 and 2 shall not be of a criminal law nature.

[4276]

Article 23

Periodic penalty payments

    1.   The Commission may by decision impose on undertakings or associations of undertakings periodic penalty payments of from fifty to one thousand units of account per day, calculated from the date appointed by the decision, in order to compel them—

    (a) to put an end to an infringement of Article 2 or Article 8 of this Regulation the termination of which it has ordered pursuant to Article 11 or to comply with an obligation imposed pursuant to Article 4(2);

    (b) to refrain from any act prohibited under Article 13(3);

    (c) to supply complete and correct information which it has requested by decision taken pursuant to Article 19(5);

(d) to submit to an investigation which it has ordered by decision taken pursuant to Article 21(3).

2.   Where the undertakings or associations of undertakings have satisfied the obligation which it was the purpose of the periodic penalty payment to enforce, the Commission may fix the total amount of the periodic penalty payment at a lower figure than that which would arise under the original decision.

3.   Article 16(3) to (6) and Article 17 shall apply.

[4277]

Article 24

Review by the Court of Justice

The Court of Justice shall have unlimited jurisdiction within the meaning of Article 172 of the Treaty to review decisions whereby the Commission has fixed a fine or periodic penalty payment; it may cancel, reduce or increase the fine or periodic penalty payment imposed.

[4278]

Article 25

Unit of account

For the purpose of applying Articles 23 to 24 the unit of account shall be that adopted in drawing up the budget of the Community in accordance with Articles 207 and 209 of the Treaty.

[4279]

Article 26

Hearing of the parties and of third persons

1.   Before taking decisions as provided for in Articles 11, 12(3), second subparagraph, and 12(4), 13(3), 14(2) and (3), 22 and 23, the Commission shall give the undertakings or associations of undertakings concerned the opportunity of being heard on the matters to which the Commission has taken objection.

2.   If the Commission or the competent authorities of the Member States consider it necessary, they may also hear other natural or legal persons. Applications to be heard on the part of such persons where they show a sufficient interest shall be granted.

3.   Where the Commission intends to give negative clearance pursuant to Article 5 or Article 6, it shall publish a summary of the relevant agreement, decision or concerted practice and invite all interested third parties to submit their observations within a time limit which it shall fix being not less than one month. Publication shall have regard to the legitimate interest of undertakings in the protection of their business secrets.

[4280]

Article 27

Professional secrecy

1.   Information acquired as a result of the application of Articles 18, 19, 20 and 21 shall be used only for the purpose of the relevant request or investigation.

2. Without prejudice to the provisions of Articles 26 and 28, the Commission and the competent authorities of the Member States, their officials and other servants shall not disclose information acquired by them as a result of the application of this Regulation and of the kind covered by the obligation of professional secrecy.

3. The provisions of paragraphs 1 and 2 shall not prevent publication of general information or surveys which do not contain information relating to particular undertakings or associations of undertakings.

[4281]

Article 28

Publication of decisions

1. The Commission shall publish the decisions which it takes pursuant to Articles 11, 12(3), second subparagraph, 12(4), 13(3) and 14(2) and (3).

2. The publication shall state the names of the parties and the main content of the decision; it shall have regard to the legitimate interest of undertakings in the protection of their business secrets.

[4282]

Article 29

Implementing provisions

The Commission shall have power to adopt implementing provisions concerning the form, content and other details of complaints pursuant to Article 10, applications pursuant to Article 12, notifications pursuant to Article 14(1) and the hearings provided for in Article 26(1) and (2).

[4283]

Article 30

Entry into force, existing agreements

1. This Regulation shall enter into force on 1 July 1968.

2. Notwithstanding the provisions of paragraph 1, Article 8 shall enter into force on the day following the publication of this Regulation in the *Official Journal of the European Communities*.

3. The prohibition in Article 2 shall apply from 1 January 1969 to all agreements, decisions and concerted practices falling within Article 2 which were in existence at the date of entry into force of this Regulation or which came into being between that date and the date of publication of this Regulation in the *Official Journal of the European Communities*.

[The prohibition in Article 85(1) of the Treaty shall not apply to agreements, decisions and concerted practices which were in existence at the date of accession of Austria, Finland and Sweden and which, by reason of that accession, fall within the scope of Article 85(1) if, within six months from the date of accession, they are so amended that they comply with the conditions laid down in Articles 4 and 5 of this Regulation. This subparagraph does not apply to agreements, decisions and concerted practices which at the date of accession already fall under Article 53(1) of the EEA Agreement.]

4.   Paragraph 3 shall not be invoked against undertakings or associations of undertakings which, before the day following publication of this Regulation in the *Official Journal of the European Communities*, shall have terminated any agreements, decisions or concerted practices to which they are party.

[4284]

NOTES

Para 3: words in square brackets inserted by the 1994 Act of Accession of the Kingdom of Norway, the Republic of Austria, the Republic of Finland and the Kingdom of Sweden, Annex I(III)(B)(2), as adjusted by Council Decision 95/1/EC, Annex I(III)(B)(2).

Article 31

Review of the Regulation

1.   Within six months of the conclusion of discussions with the third countries signatories to the Revised Convention for the Navigation of the Rhine, the Council, on a proposal from the Commission, shall make any amendments to this Regulation which may prove necessary in the light of the obligations arising out of the Revised Convention for the Navigation of the Rhine.

2.   The Commission shall submit to the Council, before 1 January 1971, a general report on the operation of this Regulation and, before 1 July 1971, a proposal for a Regulation to make the necessary amendments to this Regulation.

[4285]

This Regulation shall be binding in its entirety and directly applicable in all Member States.

Done at Brussels, 19 July 1968.

COUNCIL REGULATION

of 26 November 1974

concerning limitation periods in proceedings and the enforcement of sanctions under the rules of the European Economic Community relating to transport and competition

(2988/74/EEC)

NOTES

Date of publication in OJ: OJ L319, 29.11.74, p 1.

THE COUNCIL OF THE EUROPEAN COMMUNITIES,

Having regard to the Treaty establishing the European Economic Community, and in particular Articles 75, 79 and 87 thereof;

Having regard to the proposal from the Commission;[1]

Having regard to the Opinion of the European Parliament;[2]

Having regard to the Opinion of the Economic and Social Committee;

Whereas under the rules of the European Economic Community relating to transport and competition the Commission has the power to impose fines, penalties and periodic penalty payments on undertakings or associations of undertakings which infringe Community law relating to information or investigation, or to the prohibition on discrimination, restrictive practices and abuse of dominant position; whereas those rules make no provision for any limitation period;

Whereas it is necessary in the interests of legal certainty that the principle of limitation be introduced and that implementing rules be laid down; whereas, for the matter to be covered fully, it is necessary that provision for limitation be made not only as regards the power to impose fines or penalties, but also as regards the power to enforce decisions, imposing fines, penalties or periodic penalty payments; whereas such provisions should specify the length of limitation periods, the date on which time starts to run and the events which have the effect of interrupting or suspending the limitation period; whereas in this respect the interests of undertakings and associations of undertakings on the one hand, and the requirements imposed by administrative practice, on the other hand, should be taken into account;

Whereas this Regulation must apply to the relevant provisions of Regulation No 11 concerning the abolition of discrimination in transport rates and conditions, in implementation of Article 79(3) of the Treaty[3] establishing the European Economic Community, of Regulation No 17:[4] first Regulation implementing Articles 85 and 86 of the Treaty, and of Council Regulation (EEC) No 1017/68[5] of 19 July 1968 applying rules of competition to transport by rail, road and inland waterway; whereas it must also apply to the relevant provisions of future regulations in the fields of European Economic Community law relating to transport and competition,

NOTES

[1]   OJ C129, 11.12.72, p 10.
[2]   OJ C89, 23.8.72, p 21.
[3]   OJ 52, 16.8.60, p 1121/60.
[4]   OJ 13, 21.2.62, p 204/62.
[5]   OJ L175, 23.7.68, p 1.

HAS ADOPTED THIS REGULATION—

Article 1

Limitation periods in proceedings

1.   The power of the Commission to impose fines or penalties for infringements of the rules of the European Economic Community relating to transport or competition shall be subject to the following limitation periods—

(a) three years in the case of infringements of provisions concerning applications or notifications of undertakings or associations of undertakings, requests for information, or the carrying out of investigations;

(b) five years in the case of all other infringements.

2.   Time shall begin to run upon the day on which the infringement is committed. However, in the case of continuing or repeated infringements, time shall begin to run on the day on which the infringement ceases.

[4286]

Article 2

Interruption of the limitation period in proceedings

1.   Any action taken by the Commission, or by any Member State, acting at the request of the Commission, for the purpose of the preliminary investigation or proceedings in respect of an infringement shall interrupt the limitation period in proceedings. The limitation period shall be interrupted with effect from the date on which the action is notified to at least one undertaking or association of undertakings which have participated in the infringement.

Actions which interrupt the running of the period shall include in particular the following—

(a) written requests for information by the Commission, or by the competent authority of a Member State acting at the request of the Commission; or a Commission decision requiring the requested information;

    (b) written authorisations to carry out investigations issued to their officials by the Commission or by the competent authority of any Member State at the request of the Commission; or a Commission decision ordering an investigation;

    (c) the commencement of proceedings by the Commission;

    (d) notification of the Commission's statement of objections.

2.   The interruption of the limitation period shall apply for all the undertakings or associations of undertakings which have participated in the infringement.

3.   Each interruption shall start time running afresh. However, the limitation period shall expire at the latest on the day on which a period equal to twice the limitation period has elapsed without the Commission having imposed a fine or a penalty; that period shall be extended by the time during which limitation is suspended pursuant to Article 3.

[4287]

Article 3

Suspension of the limitation period in proceedings

The limitation period in proceedings shall be suspended for as long as the decision of the Commission is the subject of proceedings pending before the Court of Justice of the European Communities.

[4288]

Article 4

Limitation period for the enforcement of sanctions

1.   The power of the Commission to enforce decisions imposing fines, penalties or periodic payments for infringements of the rules of the European Economic Community relating to transport or competition shall be subject to a limitation period of five years.

2.   Time shall begin to run on the day on which the decision becomes final.

[4289]

Article 5

Interruption of the limitation period for the enforcement of sanctions

1.   The limitation period for the enforcement of sanctions shall be interrupted—

    (a) by notification of a decision varying the original amount of the fine, penalty or periodic penalty payments or refusing an application for variation;

    (b) by any action of the Commission, or of a Member State at the request of the Commission, for the purpose of enforcing payments of a fine, penalty or periodic penalty payment.

2.   Each interruption shall start time running afresh.

[4290]

Article 6

Suspension of the limitation period for the enforcement of sanctions

The limitation period for the enforcement of sanctions shall be suspended for so long as—

    (a) time to pay is allowed; or

(b) enforcement of payment is suspended pursuant to a decision of the Court of Justice of the European Communities.

[4291]

Article 7

Application to transitional cases

This Regulation shall also apply in respect of infringements committed before it enters into force.

[4292]

Article 8

Entry into force

This Regulation shall enter into force on 1 January 1975.

[4293]

This Regulation shall be binding in its entirety and directly applicable in all Member States.

Done at Brussels, 26 November 1974.

COUNCIL REGULATION

of 22 December 1986

laying down detailed rules for the application of Articles 85 and 86 of the Treaty to maritime transport

(4056/86/EEC)

NOTES

Date of publication on OJ: OJ L378, 31.12.86, p 1.

THE COUNCIL OF THE EUROPEAN COMMUNITIES,

Having regard to the Treaty establishing the European Economic Community, and in particular Articles 84(2) and 87 thereof,

Having regard to the proposal from the Commission,

Having regard to the opinion of the European Parliament,[1]

Having regard to the opinion of the Economic and Social Committee,[2]

Whereas the rules on competition form part of the Treaty's general provisions which also apply to maritime transport; whereas detailed rules for applying those provisions are set out in the Chapter of the Treaty dealing with the rules on competition or are to be determined by the procedures laid down therein;

Whereas according to Council Regulation No 141,[3] Council Regulation No 17[4] does not apply to transport; whereas Council Regulation (EEC) No 1017/68[5] applies to inland transport only; whereas, consequently, the Commission has no means at present of investigating directly cases of suspected infringement of Articles 85(1) and 86 in maritime transport; whereas, moreover, the Commission lacks such powers of its own to take decisions or impose penalties as are necessary for it to bring to an end infringements established by it;

Whereas this situation necessitates the adoption of a Regulation applying the rules of competition to maritime transport; whereas Council Regulation (EEC) No 954/79 of 15 May 1979 concerning the ratification by Member States of, or their accession to, the United Nations Convention on a Code of Conduct for Liner Conferences[6] will result in the application of the Code of Conduct to a considerable number of conferences serving the Community; whereas the Regulation applying the rules of competition to maritime transport foreseen in the last recital of Regulation (EEC) No 954/79 should take account of the adoption of the Code;

Whereas, as far as conferences subject to the Code of Conduct are concerned, the Regulation should supplement the Code or make it more precise;

Whereas it appears preferable to exclude tramp vessel services from the scope of this Regulation, rates for these services being freely negotiated on a case-by-case basis in accordance with supply and demand conditions;

Whereas this Regulation should take account of the necessity, on the one hand to provide for implementing rules that enable the Commission to ensure that competition is not unduly distorted within the common market, and on the other hand to avoid excessive regulation of the sector;

Whereas this Regulation should define the scope of the provisions of Articles 85 and 86 of the Treaty, taking into account the distinctive characteristics of maritime transport; whereas trade between Member States may be affected where restrictive practices or abuses concern international maritime transport, including intra-Community transport, from or to Community ports; whereas such restrictive practices or abuses may influence competition, firstly, between ports in different Member States by altering their respective catchment areas, and secondly, between activities in those catchment areas, and disturb trade patterns within the common market;

Whereas certain types of technical agreement, decisions and concerted practices may be excluded from the prohibition on restrictive practices on the ground that they do not, as a general rule, restrict competition;

Whereas provision should be made for block exemption of liner conferences; whereas liner conferences have a stabilising effect, assuring shippers of reliable services; whereas they contribute generally to providing adequate efficient scheduled maritime transport services and give fair consideration to the interests of users; whereas such results cannot be obtained without the cooperation that shipping companies promote within conferences in relation to rates and, where appropriate, availability of capacity or allocation of cargo for shipment, and income; whereas in most cases conferences continue to be subject to effective competition from both non-conference scheduled services and, in certain circumstances, from tramp services and from other modes of transport; whereas the mobility of fleets, which is a characteristic feature of the structure of availability in the shipping field, subjects conferences to constant competition which they are unable as a rule to eliminate as far as a substantial proportion of the shipping services in question is concerned;

Whereas, however, in order to prevent conferences from engaging in practices which are incompatible with Article 85(3) of the Treaty, certain conditions and obligations should be attached to the exemption;

Whereas the aim of the conditions should be to prevent conferences from imposing restrictions on competition which are not indispensable to the attainment of the objectives on the basis of which exemption is granted; whereas, to this end, conferences should not, in respect of a given route, apply rates and conditions of carriage which are differentiated solely by reference to the country of origin or destination of the goods carried and thus cause within the Community deflections of trade that are harmful to certain ports, shippers, carriers or providers of services ancillary to transport; whereas, furthermore, loyalty arrangements should be permitted only in accordance with rules which do not restrict unilaterally the freedom of users and consequently competition in the shipping industry, without prejudice, however, to the right of a conference to impose penalties on users who seek by improper means to evade the obligation of loyalty required in exchange for the rebates, reduced freight rates or commission granted to them by the conference; whereas users must be free to determine the undertakings to which they have recourse in respect of inland transport or quayside services not covered by the freight charge or by other charges agreed with the shipping line;

Whereas certain obligations should also be attached to the exemption; whereas in this respect users must at all times be in a position to acquaint themselves with the rates and conditions of carriage applied by members of the conference, since in the case of inland transports organised by shippers, the latter continue to be subject to Regulation (EEC) No 1017/68; whereas provision should be made that awards given at arbitration and recommendations made by conciliators and accepted by the parties be notified forthwith to the Commission in order to enable it to verify that conferences are not thereby exempted from the conditions provided for in the Regulation and thus do not infringe the provisions of Articles 85 and 86;

Whereas consultations between users or associations of users and conferences are liable to secure a more efficient operation of maritime transport services which takes better account of users' requirements; whereas, consequently, certain restrictive practices which could ensue from such consultations should be exempted;

Whereas there can be no exemption if the conditions set out in Article 85(3) are not satisfied; whereas the Commission must therefore have power to take the appropriate measures where an agreement or concerted practice owing to special circumstances proves to have certain effects incompatible with Article 85(3); whereas, in view of the specific role fulfilled by the conferences in the sector of the liner services, the reaction of the Commission should be progressive and proportionate; whereas the Commission should consequently have the power first to address recommendations, then to take decisions;

Whereas the automatic nullity provided for in Article 85(2) in respect of agreements or decisions which have not been granted exemption pursuant to Article 85(3) owing to their discriminatory or other features applies only to the elements of the agreement covered by the prohibition of Article 85(1) and applies to the agreement in its entirety only if those elements do not appear to be severable from the whole of the agreement; whereas the Commission should therefore, if it finds an infringement of the block exemption, either specify what elements of the agreement are covered by the prohibition and consequently automatically void, or indicate the reasons why those elements are not severable from the rest of the agreement and why the agreement is therefore void in its entirety;

Whereas, in view of the characteristics of international maritime transport, account should be taken of the fact that the application of this Regulation to certain restrictive practices or abuses may result in conflicts with the laws and rules of certain third countries and prove harmful to important Community trading and shipping interests; whereas consultations and, where appropriate, negotiations authorised by the Council should be undertaken by the Commission with those countries in pursuance of the maritime transport policy of the Community;

Whereas this Regulation should make provision for the procedures, decision-making powers and penalties that are necessary to ensure compliance with the prohibitions laid down in Article 85(1) and Article 86, as well as the conditions governing the application of Article 85(3);

Whereas account should be taken in this respect of the procedural provisions of Regulation (EEC) No 1017/68 applicable to inland transport operations which takes account of certain distinctive features of transport operations viewed as a whole;

Whereas, in particular, in view of the special characteristics of maritime transport, it is primarily the responsibility of undertakings to see to it that their agreements, decisions and concerted practices conform to the rules on competition, and consequently their notification to the Commission need not be made compulsory;

Whereas in certain circumstances undertakings may, however, wish to apply to the Commission for confirmation that their agreements, decisions and concerted practices are in conformity with the provisions in force; whereas a simplified procedure should be laid down for such cases,

NOTES

1   OJ C172, 2.7.84, p 178; OJ C255, 13.10.86, p 169.
2   OJ C77, 21.3.83, p 13; OJ C344, 31.12.85, p 31.
3   OJ 124, 28.11.62, p 2751/62.
4   OJ 13, 21.2.62, p 204/62.
5   OJ L175, 23.7.68, p 1.
6   OJ L121, 17.5.79, p 1.

HAS ADOPTED THIS REGULATION—

SECTION I

Article 1

Subject-matter and scope of the Regulation

1.   This Regulation lays down detailed rules for the application of Articles 85 and 86 of the Treaty to maritime transport services.

2.   It shall apply only to international maritime transport services from or to one or more Community ports, other than tramp vessel services.

3.   For the purposes of this Regulation—
    (a) "tramp vessel services" means the transport of goods in bulk or in break-bulk in a vessel chartered wholly or partly to one or more shippers on the basis of a voyage or time charter or any other form of contract for non-regularly scheduled or non-advertised sailings where the freight rates are freely negotiated case by case in accordance with the conditions of supply and demand;
    (b) "liner conference" means a group of two or more vessel-operating carriers which provides international liner services for the carriage of cargo on a particular route or routes within specified geographical limits and which has an agreement or arrangement, whatever its nature, within the framework of which they operate under uniform or common freight rates and any other agreed conditions with respect to the provision of liner services;
    (c) "transport user" means an undertaking (eg shippers, consignees, forwarders, etc) provided it has entered into, or demonstrates an intention to enter into, a contractual or other arrangement with a conference or shipping line for the shipment of goods, or any association of shippers.

[4294]

Article 2

Technical agreements

1.   The prohibition laid down in Article 85(1) of the Treaty shall not apply to agreements, decisions and concerted practices whose sole object and effect is to achieve technical improvements or cooperation by means of—
    (a) the introduction or uniform application of standards or types in respect of vessels and other means of transport, equipment, supplies or fixed installations;
    (b) the exchange or pooling for the purpose of operating transport services, of vessels, space on vessels or slots and other means of transport, staff, equipment or fixed installations;
    (c) the organisation and execution of successive or supplementary maritime transport operations and the establishment or application of inclusive rates and conditions for such operations;
    (d) the co-ordination of transport timetables for connecting routes;
    (e) the consolidation of individual consignments;
    (f) the establishment or application of uniform rules;
concerning the structure and the conditions governing the application of transport tariffs.

2.   The Commission shall, if necessary, submit to the Council proposals for the amendment of the list contained in paragraph 1.

[4295]

Article 3

Exemption for agreements between carriers concerning the operation of scheduled maritime transport services

Agreements, decisions and concerted practices of all or part of the members of one or more liner conferences are hereby exempted from the prohibition in Article 85(1) of the Treaty, subject to the condition imposed by Article 4 of this Regulation, when they have as their objective the fixing of rates and conditions of carriage, and, as the case may be, one or more of the following objectives—
    (a) the co-ordination of shipping timetables, sailing dates or dates of calls;
    (b) the determination of the frequency of sailings or calls;

(c) the co-ordination or allocation of sailings or calls among members of the conference;

(d) the regulation of the carrying capacity offered by each member;

(e) the allocation of cargo or revenue among members.

[4296]

Article 4

Condition attaching to exemption

The exemption provided for in Article 3 and 6 shall be granted subject to the condition that the agreement, decision or concerted practice shall not, within the common market, cause detriment to certain ports, transport users or carriers by applying for the carriage of the same goods and in the area covered by the agreement, decision or concerted practice, rates and conditions of carriage which differ according to the country of origin or destination or port of loading or discharge, unless such rates or conditions can be economically justified.

Any agreement or decision or, if it is severable, any part of such an agreement or decision not complying with the preceding paragraph shall automatically be void pursuant to Article 85(2) of the Treaty.

[4297]

Article 5

Obligations attaching to exemption

The following obligations shall be attached to the exemption provided for in Article 3—

1. Consultations

There shall be consultations for the purpose of seeking solutions on general issues of principle between transport users on the one hand and conferences on the other concerning the rates, conditions and quality of scheduled maritime transport services.

These consultations shall take place whenever requested by any of the abovementioned parties.

2. Loyalty arrangements

The shipping lines' members of a conference shall be entitled to institute and maintain loyalty arrangements with transport users, the form and terms of which shall be matters for consultation between the conference and transport users' organisations. These loyalty arrangements shall provide safeguards making explicit the rights of transport users and conference members. These arrangements shall be based on the contract system or any other system which is also lawful.

Loyalty arrangements must comply with the following conditions—

(a) Each conference shall offer transport users a system of immediate rebates or the choice between such a system and a system of deferred rebates—

— under the system of immediate rebates each of the parties shall be entitled to terminate the loyalty arrangement at any time without penalty and subject to a period of notice of not more than six months; this period shall be reduced to three months when the conference rate is the subject of a dispute;

— under the system of deferred rebates neither the loyalty period on the basis of which the rebate is calculated nor the subsequent loyalty period required before payment of the rebate may exceed six months;

this period shall be reduced to three months where the conference rate is the subject of a dispute.

(b) The conference shall, after consulting the transport users concerned, set out—

    (i) a list of cargo and any portion of cargo agreed with transport users which is specifically excluded from the scope of the loyalty arrangement; 100% loyalty arrangements may be offered but may not be unilaterally imposed;

    (ii) a list of circumstances in which transport users are released from their obligation of loyalty; these shall include—

      — circumstances in which consignments are dispatched from or to a port in the area covered by the conference but not advertised and where the request for a waiver can be justified, and

      — those in which waiting time at a port exceeds a period to be determined for each port and for each commodity or class of commodities following consultation of the transport users directly concerned with the proper servicing of the port.

The conference must, however, be informed in advance by the transport user, within a specified period, of his intention to dispatch the consignment from a port not advertised by the conference or to make use of a non-conference vessel at a port served by the conference as soon as he has been able to establish from the published schedule of sailings that the maximum waiting period will be exceeded.

3. Services not covered by the freight charges

Transport users shall be entitled to approach the undertakings of their choice in respect of inland transport operations and quayside services not covered by the freight charge or charges on which the shipping line and the transport user have agreed.

4. Availability of tariffs

Tariffs, related conditions, regulations and any amendments thereto shall be made available on request to transport users at reasonable cost, or they shall be available for examination at offices of shipping lines and their agents. They shall set out all the conditions concerning loading and discharge, the exact extent of the services covered by the freight charge in proportion to the sea transport and the land transport or by any other charge levied by the shipping line and customary practice in such matters.

5. Notification to the Commission of awards at arbitration and recommendations

Awards given at arbitration and recommendations made by conciliators that are accepted by the parties shall be notified forthwith to the Commission when they resolve disputes relating to the practices of conferences referred to in Article 4 and in points 2 and 3 above.

[4298]

Article 6

Exemption for agreements between transport users and conferences concerning the use of scheduled maritime transport services

Agreements, decisions and concerted practices between transport users, on the one hand, and conferences, on the other hand, and agreements between transport users which may be necessary to that end, concerning the rates, conditions and quality of liner services, as long as they are provided for in Article 5(1) and (2) are hereby exempted from the prohibition laid down in Article 85(1) of the Treaty.

[4299]

Article 7

Monitoring of exempted agreements

1.   Breach of an obligation

Where the persons concerned are in breach of an obligation which, pursuant to Article 5, attaches to the exemption provided for in Article 3, the Commission may, in order to put an end to such breach and under the conditions laid down in Section 11—

— address recommendations to the persons concerned;
— in the event of failure by such persons to observe those recommendations and depending upon the gravity of the breach concerned, adopt a decision that either prohibits them from carrying out or requires them to perform specific acts or, while withdrawing the benefit of the block exemption which they enjoyed, grants them an individual exemption according to Article 11(4) or withdraws the benefit of the block exemption which they enjoyed.

2.   Effects incompatible with Article 85(3)
    (a) Where, owing to special circumstances as described below, agreements, decisions and concerted practices which qualify for the exemption provided for in Articles 3 and 6 have nevertheless effects which are incompatible with the conditions laid down in Article 85(3) of the Treaty, the Commission, on receipt of a complaint or on its own initiative, under the conditions laid down in Section 11, shall take the measures described in (c) below. The severity of these measures must be in proportion to the gravity of the situation.
    (b) Special circumstances are, inter alia, created by—
      (i) acts of conferences or a change of market conditions in a given trade resulting in the absence or elimination of actual or potential competition such as restrictive practices whereby the trade is not available to competition; or
      (ii) acts of conference which may prevent technical or economic progress or user participation in the benefits;
      (iii) acts of third countries which—
        — prevent the operation of outsiders in a trade,
        — impose unfair tariffs on conference members,
        — impose arrangements which otherwise impede technical or economic progress (cargo-sharing, limitations on types of vessels).
    (c) (i) If actual or potential competition is absent or may be eliminated as a result of action by a third country, the Commission shall enter into consultations with the competent authorities of the third country concerned, followed if necessary by negotiations under directives to be given by the Council, in order to remedy the situation.
        If the special circumstances result in the absence or elimination of actual or potential competition contrary to Article 85(3)(b) of the Treaty the Commission shall withdraw the benefit of the block exemption. At the same time it shall   rule on whether and, if so, under what additional conditions and obligations an individual exemption should be granted to the relevant conference agreement with a view, inter alia, to obtaining access to the market for non-conference lines;
      (ii) If, as a result of special circumstances as set out in (b), there are effects other than those referred to in (i) hereof, the Commission shall take one or more of the measures described in paragraph 1.

[4300]

Article 8

Effects incompatible with Article 86 of the Treaty

1.   The abuse of a dominant position within the meaning of Article 86 of the Treaty shall be prohibited, no prior decision to that effect being required.

2.   Where the Commission, either on its own initiative or at the request of a Member State or of natural or legal persons claiming a legitimate interest, finds that in any particular case the conduct of conferences benefiting from the exemption laid down in Article 3 nevertheless has effects which are incompatible with Article 86 of the Treaty, it may withdraw the benefit of the block exemption and take, pursuant to Article 10, all appropriate measures for the purpose of bringing to an end infringements of Article 86 of the Treaty.

3.   Before taking a decision under paragraph 2, the Commission may address to the conference concerned recommendations for termination of the infringement.

[4301]

Article 9

Conflicts of international law

1.   Where the application of this Regulation to certain restrictive practices or clauses is liable to enter into conflict with the provisions laid down by law, regulation or administrative action of certain third countries which would compromise important Community trading and shipping interests, the Commission shall, at the earliest opportunity, undertake with the competent authorities of the third countries concerned, consultations aimed at reconciling as far as possible the abovementioned interest with the respect of Community law. The Commission shall inform the Advisory Committee referred to in Article 15 of the outcome of these consultations.

2.   Where agreements with third countries need to be negotiated, the Commission shall make recommendations to the Council, which shall authorise the Commission to open the necessary negotiations.

The Commission shall conduct these negotiations in consultation with an Advisory Committee as referred to in Article 15 and within the framework of such directives as the Council may issue to it.

3.   In exercising the powers conferred on it by this Article, the Council shall act in accordance with the decision-making procedure laid down in Article 84(2) of the Treaty.

[4302]

SECTION II
RULES OF PROCEDURE

Article 10

Procedures on complaint or on the Commission's own initiative

Acting on receipt of a complaint or on its own initiative, the Commission shall initiate procedures to terminate any infringement of the provisions of Articles 85(1) or 86 of the Treaty or to enforce Article 7 of this Regulation.

Complaints may be submitted by—
(a) Member States;
(b) natural or legal persons who claim a legitimate interest.

[4303]

Article 11

Result of procedures on complaint or on the Commission's own initiative

1.   Where the Commission finds that there has been an infringement of Articles 85(1) or 86 of the Treaty, it may by decision require the undertakings or associations of undertakings concerned to bring such infringement to an end.

Without prejudice to the other provisions of this Regulation, the Commission may, before taking a decision under the preceding subparagraph, address to the undertakings or associations of undertakings concerned recommendations for termination of the infringement.

2.   Paragraph 1 shall apply also to cases falling within Article 7 of this Regulation.

3.   If the Commission, acting on a complaint received, concludes that on the evidence before it there are no grounds for intervention under Articles 85(1) or 86 of the Treaty or Article 7 of this Regulation, in respect of any agreement, decision or practice, it shall issue a decision rejecting the complaint as unfounded.

4.   If the Commission, whether acting on a complaint received or on its own initiative, concludes that an agreement, decision or concerted practice satisfies the provisions both of Article 85(1) and of Article 85(3) of the Treaty, it shall issue a decision applying Article 85(3). Such decision shall indicate the date from which it is to take effect. This date may be prior to that of the decision.

[4304]

Article 12

Application of Article 85(3)—objections

1.   Undertakings and associations of undertakings which seek application of Article 85(3) of the Treaty in respect of agreements, decisions and concerted practices falling within the provisions of Article 85(1) to which they are parties shall submit applications to the Commission.

2.   If the Commission judges an application admissible and is in possession of all the available evidence, and no action under Article 10 has been taken against the agreement, decision or concerted practice in question, then it shall publish as soon as possible in the *Official Journal of the European Communities* a summary of the application and invite all interested third parties and the Member States to submit their comments to the Commission within 30 days. Such publications shall have regard to the legitimate interest of undertakings in the protection of their business secrets.

3.   Unless the Commission notifies applicants, within 90 days from the date of such publication in the *Official Journal of the European Communities*, that there are serious doubts as to the applicability of Article 85(3), the agreement, decision or concerted practice shall be deemed exempt, insofar as it conforms with the description given in the application, from the prohibition for the time already elapsed and for a maximum of six years from the date of publication in the *Official Journal of the European Communities*.

If the Commission finds, after expiry of the 90-day time limit, but before expiry of the six year period, that the conditions for applying Article 85(3) are not satisfied, it shall issue a decision declaring that the prohibition in Article 85(1) is applicable. Such decision may be retroactive where the parties concerned have given inaccurate information or where they abuse the exemption from the provisions of Article 85(1).

4.   The Commission may notify applicants as referred to in the first subparagraph of paragraph 3 and shall do so if requested by a Member State within 45 days of the forwarding to the Member State of the application in accordance with Article 15(2). This request must be justified on the basis of considerations relating to the competition rules of the Treaty.

If it finds that the conditions of Article 85(1) and of Article 85(3) are satisfied, the Commission shall issue a decision applying Article 85(3). The decision shall indicate the date from which it is to take effect. This date may be prior to that of the application.

[4305]

Article 13

Duration and revocation of decisions applying Article 85(3)

1.   Any decision applying Article 85(3) taken under Article 11(4) or under the second subparagraph of Article 12(4) shall indicate the period for which it is to be valid; normally such period shall not be less than six years. Conditions and obligations may be attached to the decision.

2.   The decision may be renewed if the conditions for applying Article 85(3) continue to be satisfied.

3.   The Commission may revoke or amend its decision or prohibit specified acts by the parties—
   (a)   where there has been a change in any of the facts which were basic to the making of the decision;
   (b)   where the parties commit a breach of any obligation attached to the decision;
   (c)   where the decision is based on incorrect information or was induced by deceit, or
   (d)   where the parties abuse the exemption from the provisions of Article 85(1) granted to them by the decision.

In cases falling within (b), (c) or (d), the decision may be revoked with retroactive effect.

[4306]

Article 14

Powers

Subject to review of its decision by the Court of Justice, the Commission shall have sole power—
   —   to impose obligations pursuant to Article 7;
   —   to issue decisions pursuant to Article 85(3).

The authorities of the Member States shall retain the power to decide whether any case falls within the provisions of Article 85(1) or Article 86, until such time as the Commission has initiated a procedure with a view to formulating a decision in the case in question or has sent notification as provided for in the first subparagraph of Article 12(3).

[4307]

Article 15

Liaison with the authorities of the Member States

1.   The Commission shall carry out the procedures provided for in this Regulation in close and constant liaison with the competent authorities of the Member States; these authorities shall have the right to express their views on such procedures.

2.   The Commission shall immediately forward to the competent authorities of the Member States copies of the complaints and applications, and of the most important documents sent to it or which it sends out in the course of such procedures.

3.   An Advisory Committee on agreements and dominant positions in maritime transport shall be consulted prior to the taking of any decision following upon a procedure under Article 10 or of any decision issued under the second subparagraph of Article 12(3), or under the second subparagraph of paragraph 4 of the same Article. The Advisory Committee shall also be consulted prior to the adoption of the implementing provisions provided for in Article 26.

4.   The Advisory Committee shall be composed of officials competent in the sphere of maritime transport and agreements and dominant positions. Each Member State shall nominate two officials to represent it, each of whom may be replaced, in the event of his being prevented from attending, by another official.

5.   Consultation shall take place at a joint meeting convened by the Commission; such meeting shall be held not earlier than fourteen days after dispatch of the notice convening it. This notice shall, in respect of each case to be examined, be accompanied by a summary of the case together with an indication of the most important documents, and a preliminary draft decision.

6.   The Advisory Committee may deliver an opinion notwithstanding that some of its members or their alternates are not present. A report of the outcome of the consultative proceedings shall be annexed to the draft decision. It shall not be made public.

[4308]

Article 16

Requests for information

1.   In carrying out the duties assigned to it by this Regulation, the Commission may obtain all necessary information from the Governments and competent authorities of the Member States and from undertakings and associations of undertakings.

2.   When sending a request for information to an undertaking or association of undertakings, the Commission shall at the same time forward a copy of the request to the competent authority of the Member State in whose territory the seat of the undertaking or association of undertakings is situated.

3.   In its request, the Commission shall state the legal basis and the purpose of the request, and also the penalties provided for in Article 19(1)(b) for supplying incorrect information.

4.   The owners of the undertakings or their representatives and, in the case of legal persons, companies or firms, or of associations having no legal personality, the person authorised to represent them by law or by their constitution, shall be bound to supply the information requested.

5.   Where an undertaking or association of undertakings does not supply the information requested within the time limit fixed by the Commission, or supplies incomplete information, the Commission shall by decision require the information to be supplied. The decision shall specify what information is required, fix an appropriate time limit within which it is to be supplied and indicate the penalties provided for in Article 19(1)(b) and Article 20(1)(c) and the right to have the decision reviewed by the Court of Justice.

6.   The Commission shall at the same time forward a copy of its decision to the competent authority of the Member State in whose territory the seat of the undertaking or association of undertakings is situated.

[4309]

Article 17

Investigations by the authorities of the Member States

1.   At the request of the Commission, the competent authorities of the Member States shall undertake the investigations which the Commission considers to be necessary under Article 18(1), or which it has ordered by decision pursuant to Article 18(3). The officials of the competent authorities of the Member States responsible for conducting these investigations shall exercise their powers upon production of an authorisation in writing issued by the competent authority of the Member State in whose territory the investigation is to be made. Such authorisation shall specify the subject matter and purpose of the investigation.

2.   If so requested by the Commission or by the competent authority of the Member State in whose territory the investigation is to be made, Commission officials may assist the officials of such authority in carrying out their duties.

The officials of the Commission authorised for the purpose of these investigations shall exercise their powers upon production of an authorisation in writing specifying the subject matter and purpose of the investigation and the penalties provided for in Article 19(1)(c) in cases where production of the required books or other business records is incomplete. In good time before the investigation, the Commission shall inform the competent authority of the Member State in whose territory the same is to be made of the investigation and of the identity of the authorised officials.

3.   Undertakings and associations of undertakings shall submit to investigations ordered by decision of the Commission. The decision shall specify the subject matter and purpose of the investigation, appoint the date on which it is to begin and indicate the penalties provided for in Article 19(1)(c) and Article 20(1)(d) and the right to have the decision reviewed by the Court of Justice.

4.   The Commission shall take decisions referred to in paragraph 3 after consultation with the competent authority of the Member State in whose territory the investigation is to be made.

5.   Officials of the competent authority of the Member State in whose territory the investigation is to be made, may at the request of such authority or of the Commission, assist the officials of the Commission in carrying out their duties.

6.   Where an undertaking opposes an investigation ordered pursuant to this Article, the Member State concerned shall afford the necessary assistance to the officials authorised by the Commission to enable them to make their investigation. To this end, Member States shall take the necessary measures, after consulting the Commission, before 1 January 1989.

[4310]

Article 18

Investigating powers of the Commission

1.   In carrying out the duties assigned to it by this Regulation, the Commission may undertake all necessary investigations into undertakings and associations of undertakings.

To this end the officials authorised by the Commission are empowered—
    (a) to examine the books and other business records;

(b) to take copies of or extracts from the books and business records;
(c) to ask for oral explanations on the spot;
(d) to enter any premises, land and vehicles of undertakings.

2.   The officials of the Commission authorised for the purpose of these investigations shall exercise their powers upon production of an authorisation in writing specifying the subject matter and purpose of the investigation and the penalties provided for in Article 19(1)(c) in cases where production of the required books or other business records is incomplete. In good time before the investigation, the Commission shall inform the competent authority of the Member State in whose territory the same is to be made of the investigation and of the identity of the authorised officials.

3.   Undertakings and associations of undertakings shall submit to investigations ordered by decision of the Commission. The decision shall specify the subject matter and purpose of the investigation, appoint the date on which it is to begin and indicate the penalties provided for in Article 19(1)(c) and Article 20(1)(d) and the right to have the decision reviewed by the Court of Justice.

4.   The Commission shall take decisions referred to in paragraph 3 after consultation with the competent authority of the Member State in whose territory the investigation is to be made.

5.   Officials of the competent authority of the Member State in whose territory the investigation is to be made, may at the request of such authority or of the Commission, assist the officials of the Commission in carrying out their duties.

6.   Where an undertaking opposes an investigation ordered pursuant to this Article, the Member State concerned shall afford the necessary assistance to the officials authorised by the Commission to enable them to make their investigation. To this end, Member States shall take the necessary measures, after consulting the Commission, before 1 January 1989.

[4311]

Article 19

Fines

1.   The Commission may by decision impose on undertakings or associations of undertakings fines of from 100 to 5000 ECU where, intentionally or negligently—
(a) they supply incorrect or misleading information, either in a communication pursuant to Article 5(5) or in an application pursuant to Article 12; or
(b) they supply incorrect information in response to a request made pursuant to Article 16(3) or (5), or do not supply information within the time limit fixed by a decision taken under Article 16(5); or
(c) they produce the required books or other business records in incomplete form during investigations under Article 17 or Article 18, or refuse to submit to an investigation ordered by decision issued in implementation of Article 18(3).

2.   The Commission may by decision impose on undertakings or associations of undertakings fines of from 1 000 to one million ECU, or a sum in excess thereof but not exceeding 10% of the turnover in the preceding business year of each of the undertakings participating in the infringement, where either intentionally or negligently—
(a) they infringe Article 85(1) or Article 86 of the Treaty, or do not comply with an obligation imposed under Article 7 of this Regulation;
(b) they commit a breach of any obligation imposed pursuant to Article 5 or to Article 13(1).

In fixing the amount of the fine, regard shall be had both to the gravity and to the duration of the infringement.

3. Article 15(3) and (4) shall apply.

4. Decisions taken pursuant to paragraphs 1 and 2 shall not be of criminal law nature.

The fines provided for in paragraph 2(a) shall not be imposed in respect of acts taking place after notification to the Commission and before its Decision in application of Article 85(3) of the Treaty, provided they fall within the limits of the activity described in the notification.

However, this provision shall not have effect where the Commission has informed the undertakings concerned that after preliminary examination it is of the opinion that Article 85(1) of the Treaty applies and that application of Article 85(3) is not justified.

[4312]

Article 20

Periodic penalty payments

1. The Commission may by decision impose on undertakings or associations of undertakings periodic penalty payments of from 50 to 1 000 ECU per day, calculated from the date appointed by the decision, in order to compel them—
   (a) to put an end to an infringement of Article 85(1) or Article 86 of the Treaty the termination of which it has ordered pursuant to Article 11, or to comply with an obligation imposed pursuant to Article 7;
   (b) to refrain from any act prohibited under Article 13(3);
   (c) to supply complete and correct information which it has requested by decision taken pursuant to Article 16(5);
   (d) to submit to an investigation which it has ordered by decision taken pursuant to Article 18(3).

2. Where the undertakings or associations of undertakings have satisfied the obligation which it was the purpose of the periodic penalty payment to enforce, the Commission may fix the total amount of the periodic penalty payment at a lower figure than that which would arise under the original decision.

3. Article 15(3) and (4) shall apply.

[4313]

Article 21

Review by the Court of Justice

The Court of Justice shall have unlimited jurisdiction within the meaning of Article 172 of the Treaty to review decisions whereby the Commission has fixed a fine or periodic penalty payment; it may cancel, reduce or increase the fine or periodic penalty payment imposed.

[4314]

Article 22

Unit of account

For the purpose of applying Articles 19 to 21 the ECU shall be that adopted in drawing up the budget of the Community in accordance with Articles 207 and 209 of the Treaty.

[4315]

Article 23

Hearing of the parties and of third persons

1.   Before taking decisions as provided for in Articles 11, 12(3) second subparagraph, and 12(4), 13(3), 19 and 20, the Commission shall give the undertakings or associations of undertakings concerned the opportunity of being heard on the matters to which the Commission has taken objection.

2.   If the Commission or the competent authorities of the Member States consider it necessary, they may also hear other natural or legal persons. Applications to be heard on the part of such persons where they show a sufficient interest shall be granted.

3.   Where the Commission intends to give negative clearance pursuant to Article 85(3) of the Treaty, it shall publish a summary of the relevant agreement, decision or concerted practice and invite all interested third parties to submit their observations within a time limit which it shall fix being not less than one month. Publication shall have regard to the legitimate interest of undertakings in the protection of their business secrets.

[4316]

Article 24

Professional secrecy

1.   Information acquired as a result of the application of Articles 17 and 18 shall be used only for the purpose of the relevant request or investigation.

2.   Without prejudice to the provisions of Articles 23 and 25, the Commission and the competent authorities of the Member States, their officials and other servants shall not disclose information acquired by them as a result of the application of this Regulation and of the kind covered by the obligation of professional secrecy.

3.   The provisions of paragraphs 1 and 2 shall not prevent publication of general information or surveys which do not contain information relating to particular undertakings or associations of undertakings.

[4317]

Article 25

Publication of decisions

1.   The Commission shall publish the decisions which it takes pursuant to Articles 11, 12(3), second paragraph, 12(4) and 13(3).

2.   The publication shall state the names of the parties and the main content of the decision; it shall have regard to the legitimate interest of undertakings in the protection of their business secrets.

[4318]

Article 26

Implementing provisions

The Commission shall have power to adopt implementing provisions concerning the scope of the obligation of communication pursuant to Article 5(5), the form, content and other details of complaints pursuant to Article 10, applications pursuant to Article 12 and the hearings provided for in Article 23(1) and (2).

[4319]

[Article 26a

The prohibition in Article 85(1) of the Treaty shall not apply to agreements, decisions and concerted practices which were in existence at the date of accession of Austria, Finland and Sweden and which, by reason of that accession, fall within the scope of Article 85(1) if, within six months from the date of accession, they are so amended that they comply with the conditions laid down in Articles 3 to 6 of this Regulation. However, this Article shall not apply to agreements, decisions and concerted practices which at the date of accession already fall under Article 53(1) of the EEA Agreement.]

[4320]

NOTES
    Inserted by the 1994 Act of Accession of the Kingdom of Norway, the Republic of Austria, the Republic of Finland and the Kingdom of Sweden, Annex I(III)(B)(3), as adjusted by Council Decision 95/1/EC, Annex I(III)(B)(3).

Article 27

Entry into force

This Regulation shall enter into force on 1 July 1987.

[4321]

    This Regulation shall be binding in its entirety and directly applicable in all Member States.

    Done at Brussels, 22 December 1986.

COUNCIL REGULATION

of 12 December 1986

on unfair pricing practices in maritime transport

(4057/86/EEC)

NOTES
    Date of publication in OJ: OJ L378, 31.12.86, p 14.

THE COUNCIL OF THE EUROPEAN COMMUNITIES,

    Having regard to the Treaty establishing the European Economic Community, and in particular Article 84(2) thereof,
    Having regard to the draft Regulation submitted by the Commission,
    Having regard to the opinion of the European Parliament,[1]
    Having regard to the opinion of the Economic and Social Committee,[2]
    Whereas there is reason to believe, inter alia on the basis of the information system set up by Council Decision 78/774/EEC,[3] that the competitive participation of Community shipowners in international liner shipping is adversely affected by certain unfair practices of shipping lines of third countries;
    Whereas the structure of the Community shipping industry is such as to make it appropriate that the provisions of this Regulation should also apply to nationals of Member States established outside the Community or cargo shipping companies established outside the Community and controlled by nationals of Member States, if their ships are registered in a Member State in accordance with its legislation;

Whereas such unfair practices consist of continuous charging of freight rates for the transport of selected commodities which are lower than the lowest freight rates charged for the same commodities by established and representative shipowners;

Whereas such pricing practices are made possible by non-commercial advantages granted by a State which is not a member of the Community;

Whereas the Community should be able to take redressive action against such pricing practices;

Whereas there are no internationally agreed rules as to what constitutes an unfair price in the maritime transport field;

Whereas, in order to determine the existence of unfair pricing practices, provision should therefore be made for an appropriate method of calculation; whereas when calculating the "normal freight rate" account should be taken of the comparable rate actually charged by established and representative companies operating within or outside conferences or otherwise of a constructed rate based on the costs of comparable companies plus a reasonable margin of profit;

Whereas appropriate factors relevant for the determination of injury should be laid down;

Whereas it is necessary to lay down the procedures for those acting on behalf of the Community shipping industry who consider themselves injured or threatened by unfair pricing practices to lodge a complaint; whereas it seems appropriate to make it clear that in the case of withdrawal of a complaint, proceedings may, but need not necessarily, be terminated;

Whereas there should be cooperation between the Member States and the Commission both as regards information about the existence of unfair pricing practices and injury resulting therefrom, and as regards the subsequent examination of the matter at Community level; whereas, to this end, consultations should take place within an Advisory Committee;

Whereas it is appropriate to lay down clearly the rules of procedure to be followed during the investigation, in particular the rights and obligations of the Community authorities and the parties involved, and the conditions under which interested parties may have access to information and may ask to be informed of the principal facts and considerations on the basis of which it is intended to propose the introduction of a redressive duty;

Whereas, in order to discourage unfair pricing practices, but without preventing, restricting or distorting price competition by non-conference lines, providing that they are working on a fair and commercial basis, it is appropriate to provide, in cases where the facts as finally established show that there is an unfair pricing practice and injury, for the possibility of imposing redressive duties on particular grounds;

Whereas it is essential, in order to ensure that redressive duties are levied in a correct and uniform manner, that common rules for the application of such duties be laid down; whereas, by reason of the nature of the said duties, such rules may differ from the rules for the levying of normal import duties;

Whereas open and fair procedures should be provided for the review of measures taken and for the investigation to be reopened when circumstances so require;

Whereas appropriate procedures should be established for examining applications for refund of redressive duties,

---

NOTES

[1] OJ C255, 15.10.86, p 169.
[2] OJ C344, 31.12.85, p 31.
[3] OJ L258, 21.9.78, p 35.

HAS ADOPTED THIS REGULATION—

Article 1

Objective

This Regulation lays down the procedure to be followed in order to respond to unfair pricing practices by certain third country shipowners engaged in international cargo liner shipping, which cause serious disruption of the freight pattern on a particular route to, from or within the Community and cause or threaten to cause major injury to Community shipowners operating on that route and to Community interests.

[4322]

Article 2

In response to unfair pricing practices as described in Article 1 which cause major injury, a redressive duty may be applied by the Community. A threat of major injury may only give rise to an examination within the meaning of Article 4.

[4323]

Article 3

For the purposes of this Regulation—
  (a) "third country shipowner" means cargo liner shipping companies other than those mentioned under (d);
  (b) "unfair pricing practices" means the continuous charging on a particular shipping route to, from or within the Community of freight rates for selected or all commodities which are lower than the normal freight rates charged during a period of at least six months, when such lower freight rates are made possible by the fact that the shipowner concerned enjoys non-commercial advantages which are granted by a State which is not a member of the Community;
  (c) the "normal freight rate" shall be determined taking into account—
    (i) the comparable rate actually charged in the ordinary course of shipping business for the like service on the same or comparable route by established and representative companies not enjoying the advantages in (b);
    (ii) or otherwise the constructed rate which is determined by taking the costs of comparable companies not enjoying the advantages in (b) plus a reasonable margin of profit. This cost shall be computed on the basis of all costs incurred in the ordinary course of shipping business, both fixed and variable, plus a reasonable amount for overhead expenses.
  (d) "Community shipowners" means—
    — all cargo shipping companies established under the Treaty in a Member State of the Community;
    — nationals of Member States established outside the Community or cargo shipping companies established outside the Community and controlled by nationals of Member States, if their ships are registered in a Member State in accordance with its legislation.

[4324]

Article 4

Examination of injury

  1. Examination of injury shall cover the following factors—
    (a) the freight rates offered by Community shipowners' competitors on the route in question, in particular in order to determine whether they have been significantly lower than the normal freight rate offered by Community shipowners, taking into account the level of service offered by all the Companies concerned;
    (b) the effect of the above factor on Community shipowners as indicated by trends in a number of economic indicators such as—
      — sailings,
      — utilisation of capacity,
      — cargo bookings,
      — market share,
      — freight rates (that is depression of freight rates or prevention of freight rate increases which would normally have occurred),
      — profits,

— return of capital,
— investment,
— employment.

2.   Where a threat of injury is alleged, the Commission may also examine whether it is clearly foreseeable that a particular situation is likely to develop into actual injury. In this regard, account may also be taken of factors such as—

(a) the increase in tonnage deployed on the shipping route where the competition with Community shipowners is taking place;

(b) the capacity which is already available or is to become available in the foreseeable future in the country of the foreign shipowners and the extent to which the tonnage resulting from that capacity is likely to be used on the shipping route referred to in (a).

3.   Injury caused by other factors which, either individually or in combination, are also adversely affecting Community shipowners must not be attributed to the practices in question.

[4325]

Article 5

Complaint

1.   Any natural or legal person, or any association not having legal personality, acting on behalf of the Community shipping industry who consider themselves injured or threatened by unfair pricing practices may lodge a written complaint.

2.   The complaint shall contain sufficient evidence of the existence of the unfair pricing practice and injury resulting therefrom.

3.   The complaint may be submitted to the Commission, or a Member State, which shall forward it to the Commission. The Commission shall send Member States a copy of any complaint it receives.

4.   The complaint may be withdrawn, in which case proceedings may be terminated unless such termination would not be in the interest of the Community.

5.   Where it becomes apparent after consultation that the complaint does not provide sufficient evidence to justify initiating an investigation, then the complainant shall be so informed.

6.   Where, in the absence of any complaint, a Member State is in possession of sufficient evidence both of unfair pricing practices and of injury resulting therefrom for Community shipowners, it shall immediately communicate such evidence to the Commission.

[4326]

Article 6

Consultations

1.   Any consultations provided for in this Regulation shall take place within an Advisory Committee, which shall consist of representatives of each Member State, with a representative of the Commission as Chairman. Consultations shall be held immediately on request by a Member State or on the initiative of the Commission.

2.   The Committee shall meet when convened by its Chairman. He shall provide the Member States, as promptly as possible, with all relevant information.

3.   Where necessary, consultation may be in writing only; in such case the Commission shall notify the Member States and shall specify a period within which they shall be entitled to express their opinions or to request an oral consultation.

4.   Consultation shall in particular cover—
   (a) the existence of unfair pricing practices and the amount thereof;
   (b) the existence and extent of injury;
   (c) the causal link between the unfair pricing practices and injury;
   (d) the measures which, in the circumstances, are appropriate to prevent or
        remedy the injury caused by unfair pricing practices and the ways and
        means for putting such measures into effect.

                                                                          [4327]

Article 7

Initiation and subsequent investigation

1.   Where, after consultation, it is apparent that there is sufficient evidence to
justify initiating a proceeding the Commission shall immediately—
   (a) announce the initiation of a proceeding in the *Official Journal of the
        European* Communities; such announcements shall indicate the foreign
        shipowner concerned and his country of origin, give a summary of the
        information received, and provide that all relevant information is to be
        communicated to the Commission; it shall state the period within which
        interested parties may make known their views in writing and may apply to
        be heard orally by the Commission in accordance with paragraph 5;
   (b) so advise the shipowners, shippers and freight forwarders known to the
        Commission to be concerned and the complainants;
   (c) commence the investigation at Community level, acting in cooperation
        with the Member States; such investigation shall cover both unfair pricing
        practices and injury resulting therefrom and shall be carried out in
        accordance with paragraphs 2 to 8; the investigation of unfair pricing
        practices shall normally cover a period of not less than six months
        immediately prior to the initiation of the proceeding.

2. (a) Where appropriate the Commission shall seek all the information it deems
        necessary and attempt to check this information with the shipowners,
        agents, shippers, freight forwarders, conferences, associations and other
        organisations, provided that the undertakings or organisations concerned
        give their consent.
   (b) Where necessary the Commission shall, after consultation, carry out
        investigations in third countries, provided that the firms concerned give
        their consent and the government of the country in question has been
        officially notified and raises no objection. The Commission shall be
        assisted by officials of those Member States which so request.

3. (a) The Commission may request Member States—
        — to supply information,
        — to carry out all necessary checks and inspections, particularly amongst
          shippers, freight forwarders, Community shipowners and their agents,
        — to carry out investigations in third countries, provided the firms
          concerned give their consent and the government of the country in
          question has been officially notified and raises no objection.
   (b) Member States shall take whatever steps are necessary in order to give
        effect to requests from the Commission. They shall send to the
        Commission the information requested together with the results of all
        inspections, checks or investigations carried out.
   (c) Where this information is of general interest or where its transmission
        has been requested by a Member State, the Commission shall forward it
        to the Member States provided it is not confidential, in which case a
        non-confidential summary shall be forwarded.

(d) Officials of the Commission shall be authorised, if the Commission or a Member State so requests, to assist the officials of Member States in carrying out their duties.

4. (a) The complainant and the shippers and shipowners known to be concerned may inspect all information made available to the Commission by any party to an investigation as distinct from internal documents prepared by the authorities of the Community or its Member States provided that it is relevant to the defence of their interests and not confidential within the meaning of Article 8 and that it is used by the Commission in the investigation. To this end, they shall address a written request to the Commission, indicating the information required.

(b) Shipowners subject to investigation and the complainant may request to be informed of the essential facts and considerations on the basis of which it is intended to recommend the imposition of redressive duties.

(c) (i) Requests for information pursuant to (b) shall—
    — be addressed to the Commission in writing,
    — specify the particular issues on which information is sought.

(ii) The information may be given either orally or in writing, as considered appropriate by the Commission. It shall not prejudice any subsequent decision which may be taken by the Council. Confidential information shall be treated in accordance with Article 8.

(iii) Information shall normally be given no later than 15 days prior to the submission by the Commission of any proposal for action pursuant to Article 11. Representations made after the information is given may be taken into consideration only if received within a period to be set by the Commission in each case, which shall be at least 10 days, due consideration being given to the urgency of the matter.

5.   The Commission may hear the interested parties. It shall so hear them if they have, within the periods prescribed in the notice published in the *Official Journal of the European Communities*, made a written request for a hearing showing that they are an interested party likely to be affected by the result of the proceeding and that there are particular reasons why they should be given a hearing.

6.   Furthermore, the Commission shall, on request, give the parties directly concerned an opportunity to meet, so that opposing views may be presented and any argument put forward by way of rebuttal. In providing this opportunity the Commission shall take account of the need to preserve confidentiality and of the convenience of the parties. There shall be no obligation on any party to attend a meeting and failure to do so shall not be prejudicial to that party's case.

7. (a) This Article shall not preclude the Council from reaching preliminary determinations or from applying measures expeditiously.

(b) In cases in which any interested party refuses access to, or otherwise does not provide, necessary information within a reasonable period, or significantly impedes the investigation, findings, affirmative or negative, may be made on the basis of the facts available.

8.   Proceedings on unfair pricing practices shall not constitute a bar to customs clearance of the goods to which the freight rates concerned apply.

9. (a) An investigation shall be concluded either by its termination or by action pursuant to Article 11. Conclusion should normally take place within one year of the initiation of the proceeding.

(b) A proceeding shall be concluded either by the termination of the investigation without the imposition of duties and without the acceptance of undertakings or by the expiry or repeal of such duties or by the lapse of undertakings in accordance with Articles 14 or 15.

[4328]

Article 8

Confidentiality

1.   Information received in pursuance of this Regulation shall be used only for the purpose for which it was requested.

2. (a) Neither the Council, nor the Commission, nor Member States, nor the officials of any of these, shall reveal any information received in pursuance of this Regulation of which confidential treatment has been requested by its supplier, without specific permission from the supplier.

   (b) Each request for confidential treatment shall indicate why the information is confidential and shall be accompanied by a non-confidential summary of the information, or a statement of the reasons why the information is not susceptible of such summary.

3.   Information will ordinarily be considered to be confidential if its disclosure is likely to have a significantly adverse effect upon the supplier or the source of such information.

4.   However, if it appears that a request for confidentiality is not warranted and if the supplier is either unwilling to make the information public or to authorise its disclosure in generalised or summary form, the information in question may be disregarded.

The information may also be disregarded where such request is warranted and where the supplier is unwilling to submit a non-confidential summary, provided that the information is susceptible of such summary.

5.   This Article shall not preclude the disclosure of general information by the Community authorities and in particular of the reasons on which decisions taken in pursuance of this Regulation are based, or disclosure of the evidence relied on by the Community authorities in so far as necessary to explain those reasons in court proceedings. Such disclosure must take into account the legitimate interest of the parties concerned that their business secrets should not be divulged.

[4329]

Article 9

Termination of proceedings where protective measures are unnecessary

1.   If it becomes apparent after consultation that protective measures are unnecessary, then, where no objection is raised within the Advisory Committee referred to in Article 6(1), the proceeding shall be terminated. In all other cases the Commission shall submit to the Council forthwith a report on the results of the consultation, together with a proposal that the proceeding be terminated. The proceeding shall stand terminated if, within one month, the Council, acting by a qualified majority, has not decided otherwise.

2.   The Commission shall inform the parties known to be concerned and shall announce the termination in the *Official Journal of the European Communities* setting forth its basic conclusions and a summary of the reasons therefor.

[4330]

Article 10

Undertakings

1.   Where, during the course of investigation, undertakings are offered which the Commission, after consultation, considers acceptable, the investigation may be terminated without the imposition of redressive duties.

Save in exceptional circumstances, undertakings may not be offered later than the end of the period during which representations may be made under Article 7(4)(c)(iii). The termination shall be decided in conformity with the procedure laid down in Article 9(1) and information shall be given and notice published in accordance with Article 9(2).

2. The undertakings referred to under paragraph 1 are those under which rates are revised to an extent such that the Commission is satisfied that the unfair pricing practice, or the injurious effects thereof, are eliminated.

3. Undertakings may be suggested by the Commission, but the fact that such undertakings are not offered or an invitation to do so is not accepted, shall not prejudice consideration of the case. However, the continuation of unfair pricing practices may be taken as evidence that a threat of injury is more likely to be realised.

4. If the undertakings are accepted, the investigation of injury shall nevertheless be completed if the Commission, after consultation, so decides or if request is made by the Community shipowners concerned. In such a case, if the Commission, after consultation, makes a determination of no injury, the undertaking shall automatically lapse. However, where a determination of no threat of injury is due mainly to the existence of an undertaking, the Commission may require that the undertaking be maintained.

5. The Commission may require any party from whom an undertaking has been accepted to provide periodically information relevant to the fulfilment of such undertakings, and to permit verification of pertinent data. Non-compliance with such requirements shall be construed as a violation of the undertaking.

[4331]

Article 11

Redressive duties

Where investigation shows that there is an unfair pricing practice, that injury is caused by it and that the interests of the Community make Community intervention necessary, the Commission shall propose to the Council, after the consultations provided for in Article 6, that it introduce a redressive duty. The Council, acting by a qualified majority, shall take a Decision within two months.

[4332]

Article 12

In deciding on the redressive duties, the Council shall also take due account of the external trade policy considerations as well as the port interests and the shipping policy considerations of the Member States concerned.

[4333]

Article 13

General provisions on duties

1. Redressive duties shall be imposed on the foreign shipowners concerned by regulation.

2. Such regulation shall indicate in particular the amount and type of duty imposed, the commodity or commodities transported, the name and the country of origin of the foreign shipowner concerned and the reasons on which the Regulation is based.

3.   The amount of the duties shall not exceed the difference between the freight rate charged and the normal freight rate referred to in Article 3(c). It shall be less if such lesser duty would be adequate to remove the injury.

4. (a) Duties shall be neither imposed nor increased with retroactive effect and shall apply to the transport of commodities which, after entry into force of such duties, are loaded or discharged in a Community port.

   (b) However, where the Council determines that an undertaking has been violated or withdrawn, the redressive duties may be imposed, on a proposal from the Commission, on the transport of commodities which were loaded or discharged in a Community port not more than 90 days prior to the date of application of these duties, except that in the case of violation or withdrawal of an undertaking such retroactive assessment shall not apply to the transport of commodities which were loaded or discharged in a Community port before the violation or withdrawal. These duties may be calculated on the basis of the facts established before the acceptance of the undertaking.

5.   Duties shall be collected by Member States in the form, at the rate and according to the other criteria laid down when the duties were imposed, and independently of the customs duties, taxes and other charges normally imposed on imports of goods transported.

6.   Permission to load or discharge cargo in a Community port may be made conditional upon the provision of security for the amount of the duties.

[4334]

Article 14

Review

1.   Regulations imposing redressive duties and decisions to accept undertakings shall be subject to review in whole or in part, where warranted. Such review may be held either at the request of a Member State or on the initiative of the Commission. A review shall also be held where an interested party so requests and submits evidence of changed circumstances sufficient to justify the need for such review, provided that at least one year has elapsed since the conclusion of the investigation. Such requests shall be addressed to the Commission, which shall inform the Member States.

2.   Where, after consultation, it becomes apparent that review is warranted, the investigation shall be re-opened in accordance with Article 7, where the circumstances so require. Such reopening shall not per se affect the measures in operation.

3.   Where warranted by the review, carried out either with or without reopening of the investigation, the measures shall be amended, repealed or annulled by the Community institution competent for their adoption.

[4335]

Article 15

1.   Subject to paragraph 2, redressive duties and undertakings shall lapse after five years from the date on which they entered into force or were last amended or confirmed.

2.   The Commission shall normally, after consultation and within six months prior to the expiry of the five year period, publish in the *Official Journal of the European Communities* a notice of the impending expiry of the measure in question and inform Community shipowners known to be concerned. This notice

shall state the period within which interested parties may make known their views in writing and may apply to be given a hearing by the Commission in accordance with Article 7(5).

Where an interested party shows that the expiry of the measure would again lead to injury or threat of injury, the Commission shall carry out a review of the measure. The measure shall remain in force pending the outcome of this review.

Where redressive duties and undertakings lapse under this Article the Commission shall publish a notice to that effect in the *Official Journal of the European Communities*.

[4336]

Article 16

Refund

1.   Where the shipowner concerned can show that the duty collected exceeds the difference between the freight rate charged and the normal freight rate referred to in Article 3(c) the excess amount shall be reimbursed.

2.   In order to request the reimbursement referred to in paragraph 1, the foreign shipowner may submit an application to the Commission. The application shall be submitted via the Member State within the territory of which the commodities transported were loaded or discharged and within three months of the date on which the amount of the redressive duties to be levied was duly determined by the competent authorities.

The Member State shall forward the application to the Commission as soon as possible, either with or without an opinion as to its merits.

The Commission shall inform the other Member States forthwith and give its opinion on the matter. If the Member States agree with the opinion given by the Commission or do not object to it within one month of being informed, the Commission may decide in accordance with the said opinion. In all other cases, the Commission shall, after consultation, decide whether and to what extent the application should be granted.

[4337]

Article 17

Final provisions

This Regulation shall not preclude the application of any special rules laid down in agreements concluded between the Community and third countries.

[4338]

Article 18

Entry into force

This Regulation shall enter into force on 1 July 1987.

[4339]

This Regulation shall be binding in its entirety and directly applicable in all Member States.

Done at Brussels, 22 December 1986.

COUNCIL REGULATION

of 14 December 1987

laying down the procedure for the application of the rules on competition to undertakings in the air transport sector

(3975/87/EEC)

NOTES

Date of publication in OJ: OJ L374, 31.12.87, p 1. The text of this Regulation incorporates the corrigenda published in OJ L30, 2.2.88, p 40, and OJ L43, 15.2.89, p 56.

THE COUNCIL OF THE EUROPEAN COMMUNITIES,

Having regard to the Treaty establishing the European Economic Community, and in particular Article 87 thereof,

Having regard to the proposal from the Commission,[1]

Having regard to the opinions of the European Parliament,[2]

Having regard to the opinion of the Economic and Social Committee,[3]

Whereas the rules on competition form part of the Treaty's general provisions which also apply to air transport; whereas the rules for applying these provisions are either specified in the Chapter on competition or fall to be determined by the procedures laid down therein;

Whereas, according to Council Regulation No 141,[4] Council Regulation No 17[5] does not apply to transport services; whereas Council Regulation (EEC) No 1017/68[6] applies only to inland transport; whereas Council Regulation (EEC) No 4056/86[7] applies only to maritime transport; whereas consequently the Commission has no means at present of investigating directly cases of suspected infringement of Articles 85 and 86 of the Treaty in air transport; whereas moreover the Commission lacks such powers of its own to take decisions or impose penalties as are necessary for it to bring to an end infringements established by it;

Whereas air transport is characterised by features which are specific to this sector; whereas, furthermore, international air transport is regulated by a network of bilateral agreements between States which define the conditions under which air carriers designated by the parties to the agreements may operate routes between their territories;

Whereas practices which affect competition relating to air transport between Member States may have a substantial effect on trade between Member States; whereas it is therefore desirable that rules should be laid down under which the Commission, acting in close and constant liaison with the competent authorities of the Member States, may take the requisite measures for the application of Articles 85 and 86 of the Treaty to international air transport between Community airports;

Whereas such a regulation should provide for appropriate procedures, decision-making powers and penalties to ensure compliance with the prohibitions laid down in Articles 85(1) and 86 of the Treaty; whereas account should be taken in this respect of the procedural provisions of Regulation (EEC) No 1017/68 applicable to inland transport operations, which takes account of certain distinctive features of transport operations viewed as a whole;

Whereas undertakings concerned must be accorded the right to be heard by the Commission, third parties whose interests may be affected by a decision must be given the opportunity of submitting their comments beforehand and it must be ensured that wide publicity is given to decisions taken;

Whereas all decisions taken by the Commission under this Regulation are subject to review by the Court of Justice under the conditions specified in the Treaty; whereas it is moreover desirable, pursuant to Article 172 of the Treaty, to confer upon the Court of Justice unlimited jurisdiction in respect of decisions under which the Commission imposes fines or periodic penalty payments;

Whereas it is appropriate to except certain agreements, decisions and concerted practices from the prohibition laid down in Article 85(1) of the Treaty, insofar as their sole object and effect is to achieve technical improvements or cooperation;

Whereas, given the specific features of air transport, it will in the first instance be for undertakings themselves to see that their agreements, decisions and concerted practices conform to the competition rules, and notification to the Commission need not be compulsory;

Whereas undertakings may wish to apply to the Commission in certain cases for confirmation that their agreements, decisions and concerted practices conform to the law, and a simplified procedure should be laid down for such cases;

Whereas this Regulation does not prejudice the application of Article 90 of the Treaty,

NOTES
1   OJ C182, 9.7.84, p 2.
2   OJ C182, 19.7.82, p 120 and OJ C345, 21.12.87.
3   OJ C77, 21.3.83, p 20.
4   OJ 124, 28.11.62, p 2751/62.
5   OJ 13, 21.2.62, p 204/62.
6   OJ L175, 23.7.68, p 1.
7   OJ L378, 31.12.86, p 4.

HAS ADOPTED THIS REGULATION—

Article 1

Scope

1.   This Regulation lays down detailed rules for the application of Articles 85 and 86 of the Treaty to air transport services.

2.   This Regulation shall apply only to . . . air transport between Community airports.

[4340]

NOTES
Para 2: words omitted deleted by Council Regulation 2410/92/EEC, Art 1, with effect from 25 August 1992.

Article 2

Exceptions for certain technical agreements

1.   The prohibition laid down in Article 85(1) of the Treaty shall not apply to the agreements, decisions and concerted practices listed in the Annex, in so far as their sole object and effect is to achieve technical improvements or cooperation. This list is not exhaustive.

2.   If necessary, the Commission shall submit proposals to the Council for the amendment of the list in the Annex.

[4341]

Article 3

Procedures on complaint or on the Commission's own initiative

1.   Acting on receipt of a complaint or on its own initiative, the Commission shall initiate procedures to terminate any infringement of the provisions of Articles 85(1) or 86 of the Treaty.

Complaints may be submitted by—
   (a) Member States;
   (b) natural or legal persons who claim a legitimate interest.

2.   Upon application by the undertakings or associations of undertakings concerned, the Commission may certify that, on the basis of the facts in its possession, there are no grounds under Article 85(1) or Article 86 of the Treaty for action on its part in respect of an agreement, decision or concerted practice.

[4342]

Article 4

Result of procedures on complaint or on the Commission's own initiative

1.   Where the Commission finds that there has been an infringement of Articles 85(1) or 86 of the Treaty, it may by decision require the undertakings or associations of undertakings concerned to bring such an infringement to an end.

Without prejudice to the other provisions of this Regulation, the Commission may address recommendations for termination of the infringement to the undertakings or associations of undertakings concerned before taking a decision under the preceding subparagraph.

2.   If the Commission, acting on a complaint received, concludes that, on the evidence before it, there are no grounds for intervention under Articles 85(1) or 86 of the Treaty in respect of any agreement, decision or concerted practice, it shall take a decision rejecting the complaint as unfounded.

3.   If the Commission, whether acting on a complaint received or on its own initiative, concludes that an agreement, decision or concerted practice satisfies the provisions of both Article 85(1) and 85(3) of the Treaty, it shall take a decision applying paragraph 3 of the said Article. Such a decision shall indicate the date from which it is to take effect. This date may be prior to that of the decision.

[4343]

[Article 4a

Interim measures against anti-competitive practices

1.   Without prejudice to the application of Article 4(1), where the Commission has clear *prima facie* evidence that certain practices are contrary to Article 85 or 86 of the Treaty and have the object or effect of directly jeopardising the existence of an air service, and where recourse to normal procedures may not be sufficient to protect the air service or the airline company concerned, it may by decision take interim measures to ensure that these practices are not implemented or cease to be implemented and give such instructions as are necessary to prevent the occurrence of these practices until a decision under Article 4(1) is taken.

2.   A decision taken pursuant to paragraph 1 shall apply for a period not exceeding six months. Article 8(5) shall not apply.

The Commission may renew the initial decision, with or without modification, for a period not exceeding three months. In such case, Article 8(5) shall apply.]

[4344]

NOTES

Inserted by Council Regulation 1284/91/EEC, Art 1(1).

Article 5

Application of Article 85(3) of the Treaty: Objections

1.   Undertakings and associations of undertakings which wish to seek application of Article 85(3) of the Treaty in respect of agreements, decisions and concerted practices falling within the provisions of paragraph 1 of the said Article to which they are parties shall submit applications to the Commission.

2.   If the Commission judges an application admissible and is in possession of all the available evidence and no action under article 3 has been taken against the agreement, decision or concerted practice in question, then it shall publish as soon as possible in the *Official Journal of the European Communities* a summary of the

application and invite all interested third parties and the Member States to submit their comments to the Commission within 30 days. Such publication shall have regard to the legitimate interest of undertakings in the protection of their business secrets.

3.   Unless the Commission notifies applicants, within 90 days of the date of such publication in the *Official Journal of the European Communities*, that there are serious doubts as to the applicability of Article 85(3) of the Treaty, the agreement, decision or concerted practice shall be deemed exempt, in so far as it conforms with the description given in the application, from the prohibition for the time already elapsed and for a maximum of six years from the date of publication in the *Official Journal of the European Communities*.

If the Commission finds, after expiry of the 90-day time limit, but before expiry of the six-year period, that the conditions for applying Article 85(3) of the Treaty are not satisfied, it shall issue a decision declaring that the prohibition in Article 85(1) applies. Such decision may be retroactive where the parties concerned have given inaccurate information or where they abuse an exemption from the provisions of Article 85(1) or have contravened Article 86.

4.   The Commission may notify applicants as referred to in the first subparagraph of paragraph 3; it shall do so if requested by a Member State within 45 days of the forwarding to the Member State of the application in accordance with Article 8(2). This request must be justified on the basis of considerations relating to the competition rules of the Treaty.

If it finds that the conditions of Article 85(1) and (3) of the Treaty are satisfied, the Commission shall issue a decision applying Article 85(3). The decision shall indicate the date from which it is to take effect. This date may be prior to that of the application.

[4345]

Article 6

Duration and revocation of decisions applying Article 85(3)

1.   Any decision applying Article 85(3) of the Treaty adopted under Articles 4 or 5 of this Regulation shall indicate the period for which it is to be valid; normally such period shall not be less than six years. Conditions and obligations may be attached to the decision.

2.   The decision may be renewed if the conditions for applying Article 85(3) of the Treaty continue to be satisfied.

3.   The Commission may revoke or amend its decision or prohibit specific acts by the parties—
   (a) where there has been a change in any of the facts which were basic to the making of the decision; or
   (b) where the parties commit a breach of any obligation attached to the decision; or
   (c) where the decision is based on incorrect information or was induced by deceit; or
   (d) where the parties abuse the exemption from the provisions of Article 85(1) of the Treaty granted to them by the decision.

In cases falling under subparagraphs (b), (c) or (d), the decision may be revoked with retroactive effect.

[4346]

Article 7

Powers

Subject to review of its decision by the Court of justice, the Commission shall have sole power to issue decisions pursuant to Article 85(3) of the Treaty.

The authorities of the Member States shall retain the power to decide whether any case falls under the provisions of Article 85(1) or Article 86 of the Treaty, until such time as the Commission has initiated a procedure with a view to formulating a decision on the case in question or has sent notification as provided by the first subparagraph of Article 5(3) of this Regulation.

[4347]

Article 8

Liaison with the authorities of the Member States

1.   The Commission shall carry out the procedures provided for in this Regulation in close and constant liaison with the competent authorities of the Member States; these authorities shall have the right to express their views on such procedures.

2.   The Commission shall immediately forward to the competent authorities of the Member States copies of the complaints and applications and of the most important documents sent to it or which it sends out in the course of such procedures.

3.   An Advisory Committee on Agreements and Dominant Positions in Air Transport shall be consulted prior to the taking of any decision following upon a procedure under Article 3 or of any decision under the second subparagraph of Article 5(3), or under the second subparagraph of paragraph 4 of the same Article or under Article 6. The Advisory Committee shall also be consulted prior to adoption of the implementing provisions provided for in Article 19.

4.   The Advisory Committee shall be composed of officials competent in the sphere of air transport and agreements and dominant positions. Each Member State shall nominate two officials to represent it, each of whom may be replaced, in the event of his being prevented from attending, by another official.

5.   Consultation shall take place at a joint meeting convened by the Commission; such a meeting shall be held not earlier than 14 days after dispatch of the notice convening it. In respect of each case to be examined, this notice shall be accompanied by a summary of the case, together with an indication of the most important documents, and a preliminary draft decision.

6.   The Advisory Committee may deliver an opinion notwithstanding that some of its members or their alternates are not present. A report of the outcome of the consultative proceedings shall be annexed to the draft decision. It shall not be made public.

[4348]

Article 9

Requests for information

1.   In carrying out the duties assigned to it by this Regulation, the Commission may obtain all necessary information from the governments and competent authorities of the Member States and from undertakings and associations of undertakings.

2.   When sending a request for information to an undertaking or association of undertakings, the Commission shall forward a copy of the request at the same time to the competent authority of the Member State in whose territory the head office of the undertaking or association of undertakings is situated.

3.   In its request, the Commission shall state the legal basis and purpose of the request and also the penalties for supplying incorrect information provided for in Article 12(1)(b).

4.   The owners of the undertakings or their representatives and, in the case of legal persons or of companies, firms or associations having no legal personality, the person authorised to represent them by law or by their rules shall be bound to supply the information requested.

5.   When an undertaking or association of undertakings does not supply the information requested within the time limit fixed by the Commission, or supplies incomplete information, the Commission shall by decision require the information to be supplied. The decision shall specify what information is required, fix an appropriate time limit within which it is to be supplied and indicate the penalties provided for in Article 12(1)(b) and Article 13(1)(c), as well as the right to have the decision reviewed by the Court of Justice.

6.   At the same time the Commission shall send a copy of its decision to the competent authority of the Member State in whose territory the head office of the undertaking or association of undertakings is situated.

[4349]

Article 10

Investigations by the authorities of the Member States

1.   At the request of the Commission, the competent authorities of the Member States shall undertake the investigations which the Commission considers to be necessary under Article 11(1) or which it has ordered by decision adopted pursuant to Article 11(3). The officials of the competent authorities of the Member States responsible for conducting these investigations shall exercise their powers upon production of an authorisation in writing issued by the competent authority of the Member State in whose territory the investigation is to be made. Such an authorisation shall specify the subject matter and purpose of the investigation.

2.   If so requested by the Commission or by the competent authority of the Member State in whose territory the investigation is to be made, Commission officials may assist the officials of the competent authority in carrying out their duties.

[4350]

Article 11

Investigating powers of the Commission

1.   In carrying out the duties assigned to it by this Regulation, the Commission may undertake all necessary investigations into undertakings and associations of undertakings. To this end the officials authorised by the Commission shall be empowered—

    (a)   to examine the books and other business records;

    (b)   to take copies of, or extracts from, the books and business records;

    (c)   to ask for oral explanations on the spot;

    (d)   to enter any premises, land and vehicles used by undertakings or associations of undertakings.

2.   The authorised officials of the Commission shall exercise their powers upon production of an authorisation in writing specifying the subject matter and purpose of the investigation and the penalties provided for in Article 12(1)(c) in cases where production of the required books or other business records is incomplete. In good time, before the investigation, the Commission shall inform the competent authority of the Member State, in whose territory the same is to be made, of the investigation and the identity of the authorised officials.

3.   Undertakings and associations of undertakings shall submit to investigations ordered by decision of the Commission. The decision shall specify the subject matter and purpose of the investigation, appoint the date on which it is to begin and indicate the penalties provided for in Articles 12(1)(c) and 13(1)(d) and the right to have the decision reviewed by the Court of Justice.

4.   The Commission shall take the decisions mentioned in paragraph 3 after consultation with the competent authority of the Member State in whose territory the investigation is to be made.

5.   Officials of the competent authority of the Member State in whose territory the investigation is to be made may assist the Commission officials in carrying out their duties, at the request of such authority or of the Commission.

6.   Where an undertaking opposes an investigation ordered pursuant to this Article, the Member State concerned shall afford the necessary assistance to the officials authorised by the Commission to enable them to make their investigation. To this end, Member States shall take the necessary measures after consultation of the Commission by 31 July 1989.

Article 12

Fines

1.   The Commission may, by decision, impose fines on undertakings or associations of undertakings of from 100 to 5000 ECU where, intentionally or negligently—
   (a) they supply incorrect or misleading information in connection with an application pursuant to Article 3(2) or Article 5; or
   (b) they supply incorrect information in response to a request made pursuant to Article 9(3) or (5), or do not supply information within the time limit fixed by a decision adopted under Article 9(5); or
   (c) they produce the required books or other business records in incomplete form during investigations under Article 10 or Article 11, or refuse to submit to an investigation ordered by decision taken pursuant to Article 11(3).

2.   The Commission may, by decision, impose fines on undertakings or associations of undertakings of from 1 000 to 1 000 000 ECU, or a sum in excess thereof but not exceeding 10% of the turnover in the preceding business year of the undertakings participating in the infringement, where either intentionally or negligently they—
   (a) infringe Article 85(1) or Article 86 of the Treaty; or
   (b) commit a breach of any obligation imposed pursuant to Article 6(1) of this Regulation.

In fixing the amount of the fine, regard shall be had both to the gravity and to the duration of the infringement.

3.   Article 8 shall apply.

4.   Decisions taken pursuant to paragraphs 1 and 2 shall not be of a penal nature.

5.   The fines provided for in paragraph 2(a) shall not be imposed in respect of acts taking place after notification to the Commission and before its decision in application of Article 85(3) of the Treaty, provided they fall within the limits of the activity described in the notification.

However, this provision shall not have effect where the Commission has informed the undertakings or associations of undertakings concerned that, after preliminary examination, it is of the opinion that Article 85(1) of the Treaty applies and that application of Article 85(3) is not justified.

[4352]

Article 13

Periodic penalty payments

1.   By decision, the Commission may impose periodic penalty payments on undertakings or associations of undertakings of from 50 ECU to 1 000 ECU per day, calculated from the date appointed by the decision, in order to compel them—

    (a)   to put an end to an infringement of Article 85(1) or Article 86 of the Treaty, the termination of which has been ordered pursuant to Article 4 of this Regulation;

    (b)   to refrain from any act prohibited under Article 6(3);

    (c)   to supply complete and correct information which has been requested by decision, taken pursuant to Article 9(5);

    (d)   to submit to an investigation which has been ordered by decision taken pursuant to Article 11(3).

    [(e)   to comply with any measure imposed by decision taken under Article 4a.]

2.   When the undertakings or associations of undertakings have satisfied the obligation which it was the purpose of the periodic penalty payment to enforce, the Commission may fix the total amount of the periodic penalty payment at a lower figure than that which would result from the original decision.

3.   Article 8 shall apply.

[4353]

NOTES

Para 1: sub-para (e) added by Council Regulation 1284/91/EEC, Art 2(2).

Article 14

Review by the Court of Justice

The Court of Justice shall have unlimited jurisdiction within the meaning of Article 172 of the Treaty to review decisions whereby the Commission has fixed a fine or periodic penalty payment; it may cancel, reduce or increase the fine or periodic penalty payment imposed.

[4354]

Article 15

Unit of account

For the purpose of applying Articles 12 to 14, the ECU shall be adopted in drawing up the budget of the Community in accordance with Articles 207 and 209 of the Treaty.

[4355]

PART IV
EC MATERIALS

Article 16

Hearing of the parties and of third persons

1.   Before refusing the certificate mentioned in Article 3(2), or taking decisions as provided for in Articles 4, [4a,] 5(3) second sub-paragraph and 5(4), 6(3), 12 and 13, the Commission shall give the undertakings or associations of undertakings concerned the opportunity of being heard on the matters to which the Commission takes, or has taken, objection.

2.   If the Commission or the competent authorities of the Member States consider it necessary, they may also hear other natural or legal persons. Applications by such persons to be heard shall be granted when they show a sufficient interest.

3.   When the Commission intends to take a decision pursuant to Article 85(3) of the Treaty, it shall publish a summary of the relevant agreement, decision or concerted practice in the *Official Journal of the European Communities* and invite all interested third parties to submit their observations within a period, not being less than one month, which it shall fix. Publication shall have regard to the legitimate interest of undertakings in the protection of their business secrets.

[4356]

NOTES

Para 1: figure in square brackets inserted by Council Regulation 1284/91/EEC, Art 2(3).

Article 17

Professional secrecy

1.   Information acquired as a result of the application of Articles 9 to 11 shall be used only for the purpose of the relevant request or investigation.

2.   Without prejudice to the provisions of Articles 16 and 18, the Commission and the competent authorities of the Member States, their officials and other servants shall not disclose information of a kind covered by the obligation of professional secrecy and which has been acquired by them as a result of the application of this Regulation.

3.   The provisions of paragraphs 1 and 2 shall not prevent publication of general information or of surveys which do not contain information relating to particular undertakings or associations of undertakings.

[4357]

Article 18

Publication of decisions

1.   The Commission shall publish the decisions which it adopts pursuant to Articles 3(2), 4, 5(3) second subparagraph, 5(4) and 6(3).

2.   The publication shall state the names of the parties and the main contents of the decision; it shall have regard to the legitimate interest of undertakings in the protection of their business secrets.

[4358]

Article 19

Implementing provisions

The Commission shall have the power to adopt implementing provisions concerning the form, content and other details of complaints pursuant to Article 3, applications pursuant to Articles 3(2) and 5 and the hearings provided for in Article 16(1) and (2).

[4359]

Article 20

Entry into force

This Regulation shall enter into force on 1 January 1988.

[4360]

This Regulation shall be binding in its entirety and directly applicable in all Member States.

Done at Brussels, 14 December 1987.

ANNEX
LIST REFERRED TO IN ARTICLE 2

(a)   The introduction or uniform application of mandatory or recommended technical standards for aircraft, aircraft parts, equipment and aircraft supplies, where such standards are set by an organisation normally accorded international recognition, or by an aircraft or equipment manufacturer;

(b)   the introduction or uniform application of technical standards for fixed installations for aircraft, where such standards are set by an organisation normally accorded international recognition;

(c)   the exchange, leasing, pooling, or maintenance of aircraft, aircraft parts, equipment or fixed installations for the purpose of operating air services and the joint purchase of aircraft parts, provided that such arrangements are made on a non-discriminatory basis;

(d)   the introduction, operation and maintenance of technical communication networks, provided that such arrangements are made on a non-discriminatory basis;

(e)   the exchange, pooling or training of personnel for technical or operational purposes;

(f)   the organisation and execution of substitute transport operations for passengers, mail and baggage, in the event of breakdown/delay of aircraft, either under charter or by provision of substitute aircraft under contractual arrangements;

(g)   the organisation and execution of successive or supplementary air transport operations, and the fixing and application of inclusive rates and conditions for such operations;

(h)   the consolidation of individual consignments;

(i)   the establishment or application of uniform rules concerning the structure and the conditions governing the application of transport tariffs, provided that such rules do not directly or indirectly fix transport fares and conditions;

(j)   arrangements as to the sale, endorsement and acceptance of tickets between air carriers (interlining) as well as the refund, pro-rating and accounting schemes established for such purposes;

(k)   the clearing and settling of accounts between air carriers by means of a clearing house, including such services as may be necessary or incidental thereto; the clearing and settling of accounts between air carriers and their appointed agents by means of a centralised and automated settlement plan or system, including such services as may be necessary or incidental thereto.

**PART IV
EC MATERIALS**

[4361]

COUNCIL REGULATION

of 14 December 1987

on the application of Article 85(3) of the Treaty to certain categories of agreements and concerted practices in the air transport sector

(3976/87/EEC)

NOTES

Date of publication in OJ: OJ L374, 31.12.87, p 9.

THE COUNCIL OF THE EUROPEAN COMMUNITIES,

Having regard to the Treaty establishing the European Economic Community and in particular Article 87 thereof,

Having regard to the proposal from the Commission,[1]

Having regard to the opinions of the European Parliament,[2]

Having regard to the opinions of the Economic and Social Committee,[3]

Whereas Council Regulation (EEC) No 3975/87[4] lays down the procedure for the application of the rules on competition to undertakings in the air transport sector; whereas Regulation No 17 of the Council[5] lays down the procedure for the application of these rules to agreements, decisions and concerted practices other than those directly relating to the provision of air transport services;

Whereas Article 85(1) of the Treaty may be declared inapplicable to certain categories of agreements, decisions and concerted practices which fulfil the conditions contained in Article 85(3);

Whereas common provisions for the application of Article 85(3) should be adopted by way of Regulation pursuant to Article 87; whereas, according to Article 87(2)(b), such a Regulation must lay down detailed rules for the application of Article 85(3), taking into account the need to ensure effective supervision, on the one hand, and to simplify administration to the greatest possible extent, on the other; whereas, according to Article 87(2)(d), such a Regulation is required to define the respective functions of the Commission and of the Court of Justice;

Whereas the air transport sector has to date been governed by a network of international agreements, bilateral agreements between States and bilateral and multilateral agreements between air carriers; whereas the changes required to this international regulatory system to ensure increased competition should be effected gradually so as to provide time for the air transport sector to adapt;

Whereas the Commission should be enabled for this reason to declare by way of Regulation that the provisions of Article 85(1) do not apply to certain categories of agreements between undertakings, decisions by associations of undertakings and concerted practices;

Whereas it should be laid down under what specific conditions and in what circumstances the Commission may exercise such powers in close and constant liaison with the competent authorities of the Member States;

Whereas it is desirable, in particular, that block exemptions be granted for certain categories of agreements, decisions and concerted practices; whereas these exemptions should be granted for a limited period during which air carriers can adapt to a more competitive environment; whereas the Commission, in close liaison with the Member States, should be able to define precisely the scope of these exemptions and the conditions attached to them;

Whereas there can be no exemption if the conditions set out in Article 85(3) are not satisfied; whereas the Commission should therefore have power to take the appropriate measures where an agreement proves to have effects incompatible with Article 85(3); whereas the Commission should consequently be able first to address recommendations to the parties and then to take decisions;

Whereas this Regulation does not prejudice the application of Article 90 of the Treaty;

Whereas the Heads of State and Government, at their meeting in June 1986, agreed that the internal market in air transport should be completed by 1992 in pursuance of Community actions leading to the strengthening of its economic and social cohesion; whereas the provisions of this Regulation, together with those of Council Directive 87/601/EEC of 14 December 1987 on fares for scheduled air services between Member States[6] and those of Council Decision 87/602/EEC of 14 December 1987 on the sharing of passenger capacity between air carriers on scheduled air services between Member States and on access for air carriers to scheduled air service routes between Member States,[7] are a first step in this direction and the Council will therefore, in order to meet the objective set by the Heads of State and Government, adopt further measures of liberalisation at the end of a three year initial period,

NOTES

[1]   OJ C182, 9.7.84, p 3.
[2]   OJ C262, 14.10.85, p 44.
[3]   OJ C190, 20.7.87, p 182 and OJ C345, 21.12.87.
[4]   OJ C374, 31.12.87, p 1.
[5]   OJ 13, 21.2.62, p 204/62.
[6]   OJ L374, 31.12.87, p 12.
[7]   OJ L374, 31.12.87, p 19.

HAS ADOPTED THIS REGULATION—

Article 1

This Regulation shall apply to . . . air transport between Community airports.

[4362]

NOTES

Words omitted deleted by Council Regulation 2411/92/EEC, Art 1(1).

Article 2

1.   Without prejudice to the application of Regulation (EEC) No 3975/87 and in accordance with Article 85(3) of the Treaty, the Commission may by regulation declare that Article 85(1) shall not apply to certain categories of agreements between undertakings, decisions of associations of undertakings and concerted practices.

[2.   The Commission may, in particular, adopt such Regulations in respect of agreements, decisions or concerted practices which have as their object any of the following—

— joint planning and coordination of airline schedules,
— consultations on tariffs for the carriage of passengers and baggage and of freight on scheduled air services,
— joint operations on new less busy scheduled air services,
— slot allocation at airports and airport scheduling; the Commission shall take care to ensure consistency with the Code of Conduct adopted by the Council,
— common purchase, development and operation of computer reservation systems relating to timetabling, reservations and ticketing by air transport undertakings; the Commission shall take care to ensure consistency with the Code of Conduct adopted by the Council.]

3.   Without prejudice to paragraph 2, such Commission regulations shall define the categories of agreements, decisions or concerted practices to which they apply and shall specify in particular—

(a) the restrictions or clauses which may, or may not, appear in the agreements, decisions and concerted practices;
(b) the clauses which must be contained in the agreements, decisions and concerted practices, or any other conditions which must be satisfied.

[4363]

NOTES

Para 2: substituted by Council Regulation 2411/92/EEC, Art 1(2).

[Article 3

Any Regulation adopted pursuant to Article 2 shall be for a specified period.

It may be repealed or amended where circumstances have changed with respect to any of the factors which prompted its adoption; in such case, a period shall be fixed for amendment of the agreements and concerted practices to which the earlier Regulation applied before repeal or amendment.]

[4364]

NOTES

Substituted by Council Regulation 2411/92/EEC, Art 1(3).

Article 4

Regulations adopted pursuant to Article 2 shall include a provision that they apply with retroactive effect to agreements, decisions and concerted practices which were in existence at the date of the entry into force of such Regulations.

[4365]

[Article 4a

A Regulation pursuant to Article 2 may stipulate that the prohibition contained in Article 85(1) of the Treaty shall not apply, for such period as fixed by that Regulation, to agreements, decisions and concerted practices already in existence at the date of accession to which Article 85(1) applies by virtue of the accession of Austria, Finland and Sweden and which do not satisfy the conditions of Article 85(3). However, this Article shall not apply to agreements, decisions and concerted practices which at the date of accession already fall under Article 53(1) of the EEA Agreement.]

[4366]

NOTES

Inserted by the 1994 Act of Accession of the Kingdom of Norway, the Republic of Austria, the Republic of Finland and the Kingdom of Sweden, Annex I(III)(A)(3), as adjusted by Council Decision 95/1/EC, Annex I(III)(A)(3).

Article 5

Before adopting a regulation, the Commission shall publish a draft thereof and invite all persons and organisations concerned to submit their comments within such reasonable time limit, being not less than one month, as the Commission shall fix.

[4367]

Article 6

The Commission shall consult the Advisory Committee on Agreements and Dominant Positions in Air Transport established by Article 8(3) of Regulation (EEC) No 3975/87 before publishing a draft Regulation and before adopting a Regulation.

[4368]

Article 7

Where the persons concerned are in breach of a condition or obligation which attaches to an exemption granted by a Regulation adopted pursuant to Article 2, the Commission may, in order to put an end to such a breach—

— address recommendations to the persons concerned, and

— in the event of failure by such persons to observe those recommendations, and depending on the gravity of the breach concerned, adopt a decision that either prohibits them from carrying out, or requires them to perform, specific acts or, while withdrawing the benefit of the block exemption which they enjoyed, grants them an individual exemption in accordance with Article 4(2) of Regulation (EEC) No 3975/87 or withdraws the benefit of the block exemption which they enjoyed.

2.   Where the Commission, either on its own initiative or at the request of a Member State or of natural or legal persons claiming a legitimate interest, finds that in any particular case an agreement, decision or concerted practice to which a block exemption granted by a regulation adopted pursuant to Article 2(2) applies, nevertheless has effects which are incompatible with Article 85(3) or are prohibited by Article 86, it may withdraw the benefit of the block exemption from those agreements, decisions or concerted practices and take, pursuant to Article 13 of Regulation (EEC) No 3975/87, all appropriate measures for the purpose of bringing these infringements to an end.

3.   Before taking a decision under paragraph 2, the Commission may address recommendations for termination of the infringement to the persons concerned.

[4369]

Article 8

(*Deleted by Council Regulation 2411/92/EEC, Art 1(4).*)

Article 9

This Regulation shall enter into force on 1 January 1988.

[4370]

This Regulation shall be binding in its entirety and directly applicable in all Member States.

Done at Brussels, 14 December 1987

COUNCIL REGULATION

of 24 July 1989

on a code of conduct for computerised reservation systems

(2299/89/EEC)

NOTES

Date of publication in OJ: OJ L220, 29.07.89, p 1.

THE COUNCIL OF THE EUROPEAN COMMUNITIES,

Having regard to the Treaty establishing the European Economic Community, and in particular Article 84(2) thereof,

Having regard to the proposal from the Commission,[1]

Having regard to the opinion of the European Parliament,[2]

Having regard to the opinion of the Economic and Social Committee,[3]

Whereas the bulk of airline reservations are made through computerised reservation systems;

Whereas such systems can, if properly used, provide an important and useful service to air carriers, travel agents and the travelling public by affording easy access to up-to-date and accurate information on flights, fares and seat availability, making reservations and, in some cases, issuing tickets and boarding passes;

Whereas abuses in the form of denial of access to the systems or discrimination in the provision, loading or display of data or unreasonable conditions imposed on participants or subscribers can seriously disadvantage air carriers, travel agents and ultimately consumers;

Whereas this Regulation is without prejudice to the application of Articles 85 and 86 of the Treaty;

Whereas Commission Regulation (EEC) No 2672/88[4] exempts for the provisions of Article 85(1) of the Treaty agreements for the common purchase, development and operation of computerised reservation systems;

Whereas a mandatory code of conduct applicable to all computerised reservation systems and/or distribution facilities offered for use and/or used in the Community could ensure that such systems are used in a nondiscriminatory and transparent way, subject to certain safeguards, so avoiding their misuse while reinforcing undistorted competition between air carriers and between computerised reservation systems and thereby protecting the interests of consumers;

Whereas it would not be appropriate to impose obligations on a computerised reservation system vendor or on a parent or participating carrier in respect of an air carrier of a third country which, alone or jointly with others, owns and/or controls another such system which does not conform with this code or offer equivalent treatment;

Whereas a complaints investigation and enforcement procedure for non-compliance with such a code is desirable,

NOTES
[1]   OJ C294, 18.11.88, p 12.
[2]   OJ C158, 26.6.89.
[3]   OJ C56, 6.3.89, p 32.
[4]   OJ L239, 30.8.88, p 13.

HAS ADOPTED THIS REGULATION—

[Article 1

This Regulation shall apply to any computerised reservation system, insofar as it contains air-transport products and insofar as rail-transport products are incorporated in its principal display, when offered for use or used in the territory of the Community, irrespective of—
— the status or nationality of the system vendor,
— the source of the information used or the location of the relevant central data processing unit,
— the geographical location of the airports between which air carriage takes place.]

[4371]

NOTES
Substituted by Council Regulation 323/99/EC, Art 1(1).

[Article 2

For the purposes of this Regulation—
   (a) "unbundled air transport product" means the carriage by air of a passenger between two airports, including any related ancillary services and additional benefits offered for sale and/or sold as an integral part of that product;
   (b) "bundled air transport product" means a pre-arranged combination of an unbundled air transport product with other services not ancillary to air transport, offered for sale and/or sold at an inclusive price;

(c) "air transport product" means both unbundled and bundled air transport products;

(d) "scheduled air service" means a series of flights all possessing the following characteristics;
   — performed by aircraft for the transport of passengers or passengers and cargo and/or mail for remuneration, in such a manner that seats are available on each flight for individual purchase by consumers either directly from the air carrier or from its authorised agents,
   — operated so as to serve traffic between the same two or more points, either;
      1. according to a published timetable: or
      2. with flights so regular or frequent that they constitute a recognisably systematic series;

(e) "fare" means the price to be paid for unbundled air transport products and the conditions under which this price applies;

(f) "computerised reservation system" (CRS) means a computerised system containing information about, inter alia, air carriers'
   — schedules,
   — availability,
   — fares, and
   — related services,
   with or without facilities through which—
   — reservations may be made, or
   — tickets may be issued,
   to the extent that some or all of these services are made available to subscribers;

(g) "distribution facilities" means facilities provided by a system vendor for the provision of information about air carriers' schedules, availability, fares and related services and for making reservations and/or issuing tickets, and for any other related services;

(h) "system vendor" means any entity and its affiliates which is or are responsible for the operation or marketing of a CRS;

(i) "parent carrier" means any air carrier which directly or indirectly, alone or jointly with others, owns or effectively controls a system vendor, as well as any air carrier which it owns or effectively controls;

(j) "effective control" means a relationship constituted by rights, contracts or any other means which, either separately or jointly and having regard to the considerations of fact or law involved, confer the possibility of directly or indirectly exercising a decisive influence on an undertaking, in particular by:
   — the right to use all or part of the assets of an undertaking,
   — rights or contracts which confer a decisive influence on the composition, voting or decisions of the bodies of an undertaking or otherwise confer a decisive influence on the running of the business of the undertaking;

(k) "participating carrier" means an air carrier which has an agreement with a system vendor for the distribution of air transport products through a CRS. To the extent that a parent carrier uses the facilities of its own CRS which are covered by this Regulation, it shall be considered a participating carrier;

[(l) "subscriber" shall mean a person, other than a consumer, or an undertaking, other than a participating carrier, using a CRS under contract or other financial arrangement with a system vendor. A financial arrangement shall be deemed to exist where a specific payment is made for the services of the system vendor or where an air-transport product is purchased;

(m) "consumer" shall mean any person seeking information about or intending to purchase an air-transport product for private use;]

(n) "principal display" means a comprehensive neutral display of data concerning air services between city-pairs, within a specified time period;

(o) "elapsed journey time" means the time difference between scheduled departure and arrival time;

(p) "service enhancement" means any product or service offered by a system vendor on its own behalf to subscribers in conjunction with a CRS, other than distribution facilities.

[(q) "unbundled rail-transport product" shall mean the carriage of a passenger between two stations by rail, including any related ancillary services and additional benefits offered for sale or sold as an integral part of that product;

(r) "bundled rail-transport product" shall mean a pre-arranged combination of an unbundled rail-transport product with other services not ancillary to rail transport, offered for sale or sold at an inclusive price;

(s) "rail-transport product" shall mean both unbundled and bundled rail-transport products;

(t) "ticket" shall mean a valid document giving entitlement to transport or an equivalent in paperless, including electronic, form issued or authorised by the carrier or its authorised agent;

(u) "duplicate reservation" shall mean a situation which arises when two or more reservations are made for the same passenger when it is evident that the passenger will not be able to use more than one.]]

[4372]

NOTES

Substituted by Council Regulation 3089/93/EEC, Art 1(1).
Paras (l), (m) substituted, paras (q)–(u) added by Council Regulation 323/99/EEC, Art 1(2).

[Article 3

1. A system vendor shall have the capacity, in its own name as a separate entity from the parent carrier, to have rights and obligations of all kinds, to make contracts, *inter alia* with parent carriers, participating carriers and subscribers, or to accomplish other legal acts and to sue and be sued.

2. A system vendor shall allow any air carrier the opportunity to participate, on an equal and non-discriminatory basis, in its distribution facilities within the available capacity of the system concerned and subject to any technical constraints outside the control of the system vendor.

3. (a) A system vendor shall not—
— attach unreasonable conditions to any contract with a participating carrier,
— require the acceptance of supplementary conditions which, by their nature or according to commercial usage, have no connection with participation in its CRS and shall apply the same conditions for the same level of service.

(b) A system vendor shall not make it a condition of participation in its CRS that a participating carrier may not at the same time be a participant in another system.

(c) A participating carrier may terminate its contract with a system vendor on giving notice which need not exceed six months, to expire not before the end of the first year.

In such a case a system vendor shall be entitled to recover more than the costs directly related to the termination of the contract.

4.   If a system vendor has decided to add any improvement to the distribution facilities provided or the equipment used in the provision of the facilities, it shall provide information on and offer these improvements to all participating carriers, including parent carriers, with equal timelines and on the same terms and conditions, subject to any technical constraints outside the control of the system vendor, and in such a way that there will be no difference in leadtime for the implementation of the new improvements between parent and participating carriers.]

[4373]

NOTES

Substituted by Council Regulation 3089/93/EEC, Art 1(1).

[Article 3a

1. (a) A parent carrier may not discriminate against a competing CRS by refusing to provide the latter, on request and with equal timeliness, with the same information on schedules, fares and availability relating to its own air services as that which it provides to its own CRS or to distribute its air transport products through another CRS, or by refusing to accept or to confirm with equal timeliness a reservation made through a competing CRS for any of its air transport products which are distributed through its own CRS. The parent carrier shall be obliged to accept and to confirm only those bookings which are in conformity with its fares and conditions.

   [(b) The parent carrier shall not be obliged to accept any costs in this connection except for reproduction of the information to be provided and for accepted bookings. The booking fee payable to a CRS for an accepted booking made in accordance with this Article shall not exceed the fee charged by the same CRS to participating carriers for an equivalent transaction.]

   (c) The parent carrier shall be entitled to carry out controls to ensure that Article 5(1) is respected by the competing CRS.]

[2.   The obligation imposed by this Article shall not apply in favour of a competing CRS when, in accordance with the procedures of Article 11, it has been decided that that CRS is in breach of Article 4a or of Article 6 concerning parent carriers' unauthorised access to information.]

[4374]

NOTES

Inserted by Council Regulation 3089/93/EEC, Art 1(2).
Paras 1(b), 2: substituted by Council Regulation 323/99/EC, Art 1(3).

[Article 4

1.   Participating carriers and other providers of air transport products shall ensure that the data which they decide to submit to a CRS are accurate, non-misleading, transparent and no less comprehensive than for any other CRS. The data shall, *inter alia*, enable a system vendor to meet the requirements of the ranking criteria as set out in the Annex.

Data submitted via intermediaries shall not be manipulated by them in a manner which would lead to inaccurate, misleading or discriminatory information.

[The principles stated in the first and second subparagraphs shall apply to rail services in respect of data provided for inclusion in the principal display.]

2.   A system vendor shall not manipulate the material referred to in paragraph 1 in a manner which would lead to the provision of inaccurate, misleading or discriminatory information.

3.   A system vendor shall load and process data provided by participating carriers with equal care and timeliness, subject only to the constraints of the loading method selected by individual participating carriers and to the standard formats used by the said vendor.]

[4375]

NOTES
Substituted by Council Regulation 3089/93/EEC, Art 1(3).
Para 1: words in square brackets added by Council Regulation 323/99/EC, Art 1(4).

[Article 4a

1.   Loading and/or processing facilities provided by a system vendor shall be offered to all parent and participating carriers without discrimination. Where relevant and generally accepted air transport industry standards are available, system vendors shall offer facilities compatible with them.

2.   A system vendor shall not reserve any specific loading and/or processing procedure or any other distribution facility for one or more of its parent carrier(s).

3.   A system vendor shall ensure that its distribution facilities are separated, in a clear and verifiable manner, from any carrier's private inventory and management and marketing facilities. Separation may be established either logically by means of software or physically in such a way that any connection between the distribution facilities and the private facilities may be achieved by means of an application-to-application interface only. Irrespective of the method of separation adopted, any such interface shall be made available to all parent and participating carriers on a non-discriminatory basis and shall provide equality of treatment in respect of procedures, protocols, inputs and outputs. Where relevant and generally accepted air transport industry standards are available, system vendors shall offer interfaces compatible with them.

[4.   The system vendor shall ensure that any third parties providing CRS services in whole or in part on its behalf comply with the relevant provisions of this Regulation.]]

[4376]

NOTES
Inserted by Council Regulation 3089/93/EEC, Art 1(4).
Para 4: added by Council Regulation 323/99/EC, Art 1(5).

[Article 5

1. (a) Displays generated by a CRS shall be clear and non-discriminatory.
   (b) A system vendor shall not intentionally or negligently display inaccurate or misleading information in its CRS.

2. (a) A system vendor shall provide a principal display or displays for each individual transaction through its CRS and shall include therein the data provided by participating carriers on flight schedules, fare types and seat availability in a clear and comprehensive manner and without discrimination or bias, in particular as regards the order in which information is presented.
   (b) A consumer shall be entitled to have, on request, a principal display limited to scheduled or non-scheduled services only.

(c) No discrimination on the basis of airports serving the same city shall be exercised in constructing and selecting flights for a given city-pair for inclusion in a principal display.

(d) Ranking of flight options in a principal display shall be as set out in the Annex.

(e) Criteria to be used for ranking shall not be based on any factor directly or indirectly relating to carrier identity and shall be applied on a non-discriminatory basis to all participating carriers.

3.   Where a system vendor provides information on fares, the display shall be neutral and non-discriminatory and shall contain at least the fares provided for all flights of participating carriers shown in the principal display. The source of such information shall be acceptable to the participating carrier(s) and system vendor concerned.

4.   Information on bundled products regarding, *inter alia*, who is organising the tour, availability and prices, shall not be featured in the principal display.

5.   A CRS shall not be considered in breach of this Regulation to the extent that it changes a display in order to meet the specific request(s) of a consumer.]

[4377]

NOTES

Substituted by Council Regulation 3089/93/EEC, Art 1(5).

[**Article 6**

1.   The following provisions shall govern the availability of information, statistical or otherwise, by a system vendor from its CRS—

[(a) information concerning identifiable individual bookings shall be provided on an equal basis and only to the air carrier or carriers participating in the service covered by and to the subscribers involved in the booking.]

Information under the control of the system vendor concerning identifiable individual bookings shall be archived off-line within seventy-two hours of the completion of the last element in the individual booking and destroyed within three years. Access to such data shall be allowed only for billing-dispute reasons.]

(b) any marketing, booking and sales data made available shall be on the basis that—

(i) such data are offered with equal timeliness and on a non-discriminatory basis to all participating carriers, including parent carriers;

[(ii) such data may and, on request, shall cover all participating carriers and/or subscribers, but shall include no identification, either directly or indirectly, of, or personal information on a passenger or a corporate user;]

(iii) all requests for such data are treated with equal care and timeless, subject to the transmission method selected by the individual carrier;

[(iv) information is made available on request to participating carriers and subscribers both globally and selectively with regard to the market in which they operate;

(v) a group of airlines and/or subscribers is entitled to purchase data for common processing.]

2.   A system vendor shall not make personal information concerning a passenger available to others not involved in the transaction without the consent of the passenger.

3.   A system vendor shall ensure that the provisions in paragraphs 1 and 2 above are complied with, by technical means and/or appropriate safeguards

regarding at least software, in such a way that information provided by or created for air carriers can in no way be accessed by one or more of the parent carriers except as permitted by this Article.

    4, 5. ...]

[4378]

NOTES

    Substituted by Council Regulation 3089/93/EEC, Art 1(5).

    Para 1: sub-paras (a), (b)(ii) substituted, sub-para (b)(iv), (v) inserted by Council Regulation 323/99/EC, Art 1(6), (7).

    Paras 4, 5: repealed by Council Regulation 323/99/EC, Art 1(8).

Article 7

[1.   The obligations of a system vendor under Articles 3 and 4 to 6 shall not apply in respect of a parent carrier of a third country to the extent that its CRS outside the territory of the Community does not offer Community air carriers equivalent treatment to that provided under this Regulation and under Commission Regulation (EEC) No 83/91.[1]

2.   The obligations of parent or participating carriers under Articles 3a, 4 and 8 shall not apply in respect of a CRS controlled by (an) air carrier(s) of one or more third country (countries) to the extent that outside the territory of the Community the parent or participating carrier(s) is (are) not accorded equivalent treatment to that provided under this Regulation and under Commission Regulation (EEC) No 83/91.]

3.   A system vendor or an air carrier proposing to avail itself of the provisions of paragraphs 1 or 2 must notify the Commission of its intentions and the reasons therefor at least 14 days in advance of such action. In exceptional circumstances, the Commission may, at the request of the vendor or the air carrier concerned, grant a waiver from the 14-day rule.

4.   Upon receipt of a notification, the Commission shall without delay determine whether discrimination within the meaning of paragraphs 1 and 2 exists. If this is found to be the case, the Commission shall so inform all system vendors or the air carriers concerned in the Community as well as Member States. If discrimination within the meaning of paragraph 1 or 2 does not exist, the Commission shall so inform the system vendor or air carriers concerned.

    [5. (a)   In cases where serious discrimination within the meaning of paragraph 1 or 2 is found to exist, the Commission may by decision instruct CRSs to modify their operations approximately in order to terminate such discrimination. The Commission shall immediately inform Member States of such a decision.

        (b)   Unless the Council, at the request of a Member State, takes another decision within two months of the date of the Commission's decision, the latter shall enter into force.]

[4379]

NOTES

    Paras 1, 2: substituted by Council Regulation 3089/93/EEC, Art 1(6).

    Para 5: added by Council Regulation 3089/93/EEC, Art 1(7).

    [1]   OJ L10, 15.1.91, p 9.

[Article 8

1.   A parent carrier shall neither directly nor indirectly link the use of any specific CRS by a subscriber with the receipt of any commission or other incentive or disincentive for the sale of air transport products available on its flights.

2.   A parent carrier shall neither directly nor indirectly require use of any specific CRS by a subscriber for sale or issue of tickets for any air transport products provided either directly or indirectly by itself.

3.   Any condition which an air carrier may require of a travel agent when authorising it to sell and issue tickets for its air transport products shall be without prejudice to paragraphs 1 and 2.]

[4380]

NOTES
    Substituted by Council Regulation 3089/93/EEC, Art 1(8).

Article 9

1.   A system vendor shall make any of the distribution facilities of a CRS available to any subscriber on a non-discriminatory basis.

2.   A system vendor shall not require a subscriber to sign an exclusive contract, nor directly or indirectly prevent a subscriber from subscribing to, or using, any other system or systems.

3.   A service enhancement offered to any other subscriber shall be offered by the system vendor to all subscribers on a non-discriminatory basis.

[4. (a)   A system vendor shall not attach unreasonable conditions to any subscriber contract allowing for the use of its CRS and, in particular, a subscriber may terminate its contract with a system vendor by giving notice which need not exceed three months, to expire not before the end of the first year.

   In such a case, a system vendor shall not be entitled to recover more than the costs directly related to the termination of the contract.
   (b)   Subject to paragraph 2, the supply of technical equipment is not subject to the conditions set out in (a).

5.   A system vendor shall provide in each subscriber contract for—
   (a)   the principal display, conforming to Article 5, to be accessed for each individual transaction, except where a consumer requests information for only one air carrier or where the consumer requests information for bundled air transport products alone;
   (b)   the subscriber not to manipulate material supplied by CRSs in a manner which would lead to inaccurate, misleading or discriminatory presentation of information to consumers.

6.   A system vendor shall not impose an obligation on a subscriber to accept an offer of technical equipment or software, but may require that equipment and software used be compatible with its own system.]

[4381]

NOTES
    Paras 4–6: substituted by Council Regulation 3089/93/EEC, Art 1(9).

[Article 9a

1. (a)   In the case of information provided by a CRS, a subscriber shall use a neutral display in accordance with Article 5(2)(a) and (b) unless another display is required to meet a preference indicated by a consumer.

(b) No subscriber shall manipulate information provided by a CRS in a manner that leads to inaccurate, misleading or discriminatory presentation of that information to any consumer.

(c) A subscriber shall make reservations and issue tickets in accordance with the information contained in the CRS used, or as authorised by the carrier concerned.

(d) A subscriber shall inform each consumer of any en route changes of equipment, the number of scheduled en route stops, the identity of the air carrier actually operating the flight, and of any changes of airport required in any itinerary provided, to the extent that that information is present in the CRS. The subscriber shall inform the consumer of the name and address of the system vendor, the purposes of the processing, the duration of the retention of individual data and the means available to the data subject of exercising his access rights.

(e) A consumer shall be entitled at any time to have a print-out of the CRS display or to be given access to a parallel CRS display reflecting the image that is being displayed to the subscriber.

(f) A person shall be entitled to have effective access free of charge to his own data regardless of whether the data is stored by the CRS or by the subscriber.

2.   A subscriber shall use the distribution facilities of a CRS in accordance with Annex II.]

[4382]

NOTES

Inserted by Council Regulation 323/99/EC, Art 1(9).

[Article 10

1. (a) Any fee charged to a participating carrier by a system vendor shall be non-discriminatory, reasonably structured and reasonably related to the cost of the service provided and used and shall, in particular, be the same for the same level of service.

The billing for the services of a CRS shall be sufficiently detailed to allow the participating carriers to see exactly which services have been used and the fees therefor; as a minimum, booking fee bills shall include the following information for each segment—

— type of CRS booking,
— passenger name,
— country,
— IATA/ARC agency identification code,
— city-code,
— city pair of segment,
— booking date (transaction date),
— flight date,
— flight number,
— status code (booking status),
— service type (class of service),
— passenger name record (PNR) locator, and
— booking/cancellation indicator.

The billing information shall be offered on magnetic media. The fee to be charged for the billing information provided in the form chosen by the carrier shall not exceed the cost of the medium itself together with its transportation costs.

A participating air carrier shall be offered the facility of being informed when any booking or transaction is made for which a booking fee will be charged. Where a carrier elects to be so informed, it shall be offered the option of disallowing any such booking or transaction, unless the latter has already been accepted. In the event of such a disallowance, the air carrier shall not be charged for that booking or transaction.

(b) Any fee for equipment rental or other service charged to a subscriber by a system vendor shall be non-discriminatory, reasonably structured and reasonably related to the cost of the service provided and used and shall, in particular, be the same for the same level of service. Productivity benefits awarded to subscribers by system vendors in the form of discount on rental charges or commission payments shall be deemed to be distribution costs of the system vendors and shall be based on ticketed segments. When, subject to paragraph 5 of Annex II the system vendor does not know whether a ticket has been issued or not, then that system vendor shall be entitled to rely upon notification of the ticket number from the subscriber.

The billing for the services of a CRS shall be sufficiently detailed to allow subscribers to see exactly which services have been used and what fees have been charged therefor.

2. A system vendor shall, on request, provide interested parties, including consumers, with details of current procedures, fees and system facilities, including interfaces, editing and display criteria used. For consumers that information shall be free of charge and cover the processing of individual data. This provision shall not, however, require a system vendor to disclose proprietary information such as software.]

3. Any changes to fee levels, conditions or facilities offered and the basis therefor shall be communicated to all participating carriers and subscribers on a nondiscriminatory basis.

[4383]

NOTES

Paras 1, 2: substituted by Council Regulation 323/99/EEC, Art 1(10).

Article 11

1. Acting on receipt of a complaint or on its own initiative, the Commission shall initiate procedures to terminate infringement of the provisions of this Regulation.

2. Complaints may be submitted by—
   (a) Member States;
   (b) natural or legal persons who claim a legitimate interest.

3. The Commission shall immediately forward to the Member States copies of the complaints and applications and of all relevant documents sent to it or which it sends out in the course of such procedures.

[4384]

Article 12

1. In carrying out the duties assigned to it by this Regulation, the Commission may obtain all necessary information from the Member States and from undertakings and associations of undertakings.

2. The Commission may fix a time limit of not less than one month for the communication of the information requested.

3.   When sending a request for information to an undertaking or association of undertakings, the Commission shall forward a copy of the request at the same time to the Member State in whose territory the head office of the undertaking or association of undertakings is situated.

4.   In its request, the Commission shall state the legal basis and purpose of the request and also the penalties for supplying incorrect information provided for in Article 16(1).

5.   The owners of the undertakings or their representatives and, in the case of legal persons or of companies, firms or associations not having legal personality, the person authorised to represent them by law or by their rules shall be bound to supply the information requested.

Article 13

1.   In carrying out the duties assigned to it by this Regulation, the Commission may undertake all necessary investigations into undertakings and associations of undertakings. To this end, officials authorised by the Commission shall be empowered—

    (a) to examine the books and other business records;

    (b) to take copies of, or extracts from, the books and business records;

    (c) to ask for oral explanations on the spot;

    (d) to enter any premises, land and vehicles used by undertakings or associations of undertakings.

2.   The authorised officials of the Commission shall exercise their powers upon production of an authorisation in writing specifying the subject matter and purpose of the investigation and the penalties provided for in Article 16(1) in cases where production of the required books or other business records is incomplete. In good time before the investigation, the Commission shall inform the Member State, in whose territory the same is to be made, of the investigation and the identity of the authorised officials.

3.   Undertakings and associations of undertakings shall submit to investigations ordered by decision of the Commission. The decision shall specify the subject matter and purpose of the investigation, appoint the date on which it is to begin and indicate the penalties provided for in Article 16(1) and the right to have the decision reviewed in the Court of Justice.

4.   The Commission shall take the decisions mentioned in paragraph 3 after consultation with the Member State in the territory of which the investigation is to be made.

5.   Officials of the Member State in the territory of which investigation is to be made may assist the Commission officials in carrying out their duties, at the request of the Member State or of the Commission.

6.   Where an undertaking opposes an investigation ordered pursuant to this Article, the Member State concerned shall afford the necessary assistance to the officials authorised by the Commission to enable them to make their investigation.

Article 14

1.   Information acquired as a result of the application of Articles 12 and 13 shall be used only for the purposes of the relevant request or investigation.

2. Without prejudice to Articles 11 and 20, the Commission and the competent authorities of the Member States, their officials and other servants shall not disclose information of a kind covered by the obligation of professional secrecy which has been acquired by them as a result of the application of this Regulation.

3. Paragraphs 1 and 2 shall not prevent publication of general information or of surveys which do not contain information relating to particular undertakings or associations of undertakings.

[4387]

Article 15

1. When an undertaking or association of undertakings does not supply the information requested within the time limit fixed by the Commission or supplies incomplete information, the Commission shall by decision require the information to be supplied. The decision shall specify what information is required, fix an appropriate time limit within which it is to be supplied and indicate the penalties provided for in Article 16(1) as well as the right to have the decision reviewed by the Court of Justice.

2. At the same time the Commission shall send a copy of its decision to the competent authority of the Member State in the territory of which the head office of the undertaking or association of undertakings is situated.

[4388]

Article 16

1. The Commission may, by decision, impose fines on undertakings or associations of undertakings from ECU 1 000 to 50 000 where, intentionally or negligently—
  (a) they supply incorrect information in response to a request made pursuant to Article 12 or do not supply information within the time limit fixed;
  (b) they produce the required books or other business records in incomplete form during investigations or refuse to submit to an investigation pursuant to Article 13(1).

2. The Commission may, by decision, impose fines on system vendors, parent carriers, participating carriers and/or subscribers for infringements of this Regulation up to a maximum of 10% of the annual turnover for the relevant activity of the undertaking concerned.

In fixing the amount of the fine, regard shall be had both to the seriousness and to the duration of the infringement.

3. Decisions taken pursuant to paragraphs 1 and 2 shall not be of a penal nature.

[4389]

Article 17

The Court of Justice shall have unlimited jurisdiction within the meaning of Article 172 of the Treaty to review decisions whereby the Commission has imposed a fine; it may cancel, reduce or increase the fine.

[4390]

Article 18

For the purposes of applying Article 16, the ecu shall be that adopted in drawing up the general budget of the European Communities in accordance with Articles 207 and 209 of the Treaty.

[4391]

Article 19

[1.   Before taking decisions pursuant to Article 11 or 16, the Commission shall give the undertakings or associations of undertakings concerned the opportunity of being heard on the matters to which the Commission takes or has taken objection.]

2.   Should the Commission or the competent authorities of the Member States consider it necessary, they may also hear other natural or legal persons. Applications by such persons to be heard shall be granted when they show a sufficient interest.

[4392]

NOTES

Para 1: substituted by Council Regulation 323/99/EC, Art 1(11).

Article 20

1.   The Commission shall publish the decisions which it adopts pursuant to Article 16.

2.   Such publication shall state the names of the parties and the main content of the decision; it shall have regard to the legitimate interest of undertakings in the protection of their business secrets.

[4393]

[Article 21

1.   Neither Article 5, Article 9(5) nor the Annexes shall apply to a CRS used by an air carrier or a group of air carriers—

    (a) in its or their own office or offices and sales counters clearly identified as such;
        or
    (b) to provide information and/or distribution facilities accessible through a public telecommunications network, clearly and continuously identifying the information provider or providers as such.

2.   Where booking is performed directly by an air carrier, that air carrier shall be subject to Article 9a(d) and (f).]

[4394]

NOTES

Substituted by Council Regulation 323/99/EC, Art 1(12).

[Article 21a

[1.   The system vendor shall ensure that the technical compliance of its CRS with Articles 4a and 6 is monitored by an independent auditor on a calendar year basis. For that purpose, the auditor shall be granted access at all times to any programmes, procedures, operations and safeguards used on the computers or computer systems through which the system vendor provides its distribution facilities. Each system vendor shall submit its auditor's report on his inspection and findings to the Commission within four months of the end of the calendar year under review. The Commission shall examine those reports with a view to taking any action necessary in accordance with Article 11(1).]

2.   The system vendor shall inform participating carriers and the Commission of the identity of the auditor at least three months before confirmation of an appointment and at least three months before each annual reappointment. If, within one month of notification, any of the participating carriers objects to the capability of the auditor to carry out the tasks as required under this Article, the Commission

shall, within a further two months and after consultation with the auditor, the system vendor and any other party claiming a legitimate interest, decide whether or not the auditor is to be replaced.]

[4395]

NOTES

Inserted by Council Regulation 3089/93/EEC, Art 1(12).

Para 1: substituted by Council Regulation 323/99/EC, Art 1(13).

[Article 21b

1.   Subject to this Article, this Regulation shall apply to the inclusion of rail-transport products.

2.   A system vendor may decide to include rail services in the principal display of its CRS.

3.   Where a system vendor decides to include rail products in the principal display of its CRS, it shall choose to include certain well-defined categories of rail services, while respecting the principles stated in Article 3(2).

4.   A rail-transport operator shall be deemed to be a participating or parent carrier, as appropriate, for the purposes of the code, insofar as it has an agreement with a system vendor for the distribution of its products through the principal display of a CRS or its own reservation system is a CRS as defined in Article 2(f). Subject to paragraph 5, those products shall be treated as air-transport products and shall be incorporated in the principal display in accordance with the criteria set out in Annex I.

5. (a) When applying the rules laid down in paragraphs 1 and 2 of Annex I to rail services the system vendor shall adjust the ranking principles for the principal display in order to take due account of the needs of consumers to be adequately informed of rail services that represent a competitive alternative to the air services. In particular, system vendors may rank rail services with a limited number of short stops with non-stop direct air services.

   (b) System vendors shall define clear criteria for the application of this Article to rail services. Such criteria shall cover elapsed journey time and reflect the need to avoid excessive screen padding. At least two months before their application those criteria shall be submitted to the Commission for information.

6.   For the purposes of this Article, all references to "flights" in this Regulation shall be deemed to include references to "rail services" and references to "air-transport products" shall be deemed to include references to "rail products".

7.   Particular attention shall be given to an assessment of the application of this Article in the Commission's report under Article 23(1).]

[4396]

NOTES

Inserted by Council Regulation 323/99/EC, Art 1(14).

[Article 22

[1.   This Regulation shall be without prejudice to national legislation on security, public-order and data-protection measures taken in implementation of Directive 95/46/EC.[1]]

2.   The beneficiaries of rights arising under Article 3(4), Articles 4a, 6 and 21(a) cannot renounce these rights by contractual or any other means.]

[4397]

NOTES
Substituted by Council Regulation 3089/93/EEC, Art 1(13).
Para 1: substituted by Council Regulation 323/99/EC, Art 1(15).
¹   OJ L281, 23.11.95, p 31.

[Article 23

Within two years of the entry into force of this Regulation, the Commission shall draw up a report on the application of this Regulation which shall, *inter alia*, take account of economic developments in the relevant market. That report may be accompanied by proposals for the revision of this Regulation.]

[4398]

NOTES
Substituted by Council Regulation 323/99/EEC, Art 1(16).

This Regulation shall be binding in its entirety and directly applicable in all Member States.

Done at Brussels, 24 July 1989.

[ANNEX I]

Principal display ranking criteria for flights¹ offering unbundled air transport products

1.   Ranking of flight options in a principal display, for the day or days requested, must be in the following order unless requested in a different way by a consumer for an individual transaction—
     (i) all non-stop direct flights between the city-pairs concerned;
     (ii) all other direct flights, not involving a change of aircraft or train, between the city pairs concerned;
     (iii) connecting flights.

2.   A consumer must at least be afforded the possibility of having, on request, a principal display ranked by departure or arrival time and/or elapsed journey time. Unless otherwise requested by a consumer, a principal display must be ranked by departure time for group (i) and elapsed journey time for groups (ii) and (iii).

3.   Where a system vendor chooses to display information for any city-pair in relation to the schedules or fares of non-participating carriers, but not necessarily all such carriers, such information must be displayed in an accurate, non-misleading and non-discriminatory manner between carriers displayed.

4.   If, to the system vendor's knowledge, information on the number of direct scheduled air services and the identity of the air carriers concerned is not comprehensive, that must be clearly stated on the relevant display.

5.   Flights other than scheduled air services must be clearly identified.

6.   Flights involving stops en route must be clearly identified.

7.   Where flights are operated by an air carrier which is not the air carrier identified by the carrier designator code, the actual operator of the flight must be clearly identified. That requirement will apply in all cases, except for short-term ad hoc arrangements.

8.   A system vendor must not use the screen space in a principal display in a manner which gives excessive exposure to one particular travel option or which displays unrealistic travel options.

9.   Except as provided in paragraph 10, the following will apply:
   (a) for direct services, no flight may be featured more than once in any principal display;
   (b) for multi-sector services involving a change of aircraft, no combination of flights may be featured more than once in any principal display;
   (c) flights involving a change of aircraft must be treated and displayed as connecting flights, with one line per aircraft segment.

Nevertheless, where the flights are operated by the same carrier with the same flight number and where a carrier requires only one flight coupon and one reservation, a CRS should issue only one coupon and should charge for only one reservation.

10—1.   Where participating carriers have joint-venture or other contractual arrangements requiring two or more of them to assume separate responsibility for the offer and sale of air-transport products on a flight or combination of flights, the terms "flight" (for direct services) and "combination of flights" (for multi-sector services) used in paragraph 9 must be interpreted as allowing each of the carriers concerned—not more than two—to have a separate display using its individual carrier-designator code.

   2.   Where more than two carriers are involved, designation of the two carriers entitled to avail themselves of the exception provided for in subparagraph 1 must be a matter for the carrier actually operating the flight. In the absence of information from the operating carrier sufficient to identify the two carriers to be designated, a system vendor must designate the carriers on a non-discriminatory basis.

11.   A principal display must, wherever practicable, include connecting flights on scheduled services which are operated by participating carriers and are constructed by using a minimum number of nine connecting points. A system vendor must accept a request by a participating carrier to include an indirect service, unless the routing is in excess of 130% of the great circle distance between the two airports or unless that would lead to the exclusion of services with a shorter elapsed journey time. Connecting points with routings in excess of 130% of that great circle distance need not be used.]

[4399]

NOTES

   Substituted, together with Annex II, for original Annex, by Council Regulation 323/99/EEC, Art 1(17).

   [1]   All references to "flights" in this Annex are in accordance with Article 21b(6).

[ANNEX II

Use of distribution facilities by subscribers

1.   A subscriber must keep accurate records covering all CRS reservation transactions. Those records must include flight numbers, reservations booking designators, date of travel, departure and arrival times, status of segments, names and initials of passengers with their contact addresses and/or telephone numbers and ticketing status. When booking or cancelling space, the subscriber must ensure that the reservation designator being used corresponds to the fare paid by the passenger.

2.   A subscriber should not deliberately make duplicate reservations for the same passenger. Where confirmed space is not available on the customer's choice, the passenger may be wait-listed on that flight (if wait-list is available) and confirmed on an alternative flight.

3.   When a passenger cancels a reservation, the subscriber must immediately release that space.

4.   When a passenger changes an itinerary, the subscriber must ensure that all space and supplementary services are cancelled when the new reservations are made.

5.   A subscriber must, where practicable, request or process all reservations for a specific itinerary and all subsequent changes through the same CRS.

6.   No subscriber may request or sell airline space unless requested to do so by a consumer.

7.   A subscriber must ensure that a ticket is issued in accordance with the reservation status of each segment and in accordance with the applicable time limit. A subscriber must not issue a ticket indicating a definite reservation and a particular flight unless confirmation of that reservation has been received.]

[4400]

NOTES

Substituted as noted to Annex I at **[4399]**.

EXPLANATORY NOTE ON THE EEC CODE OF CONDUCT FOR COMPUTER RESERVATION SYSTEMS

(90/C 184/02)

1.   Introduction

During the first few months of the implementation phase of Regulation (EEC) No 2299/89 on a code of conduct for computerised reservation systems[1] a number of questions have been raised on the way in which the provisions of the code have to be applied in practical terms with respect to the programming and operation of systems. The resulting clarification would seem to be of interest to system vendors in general since it would give some guidelines in particular to the programming by the system vendors. However, the solutions outlined may not be exhaustive and other approaches may in some instances comply with the provisions of the Annex. Furthermore, other elements in a total system may well influence unfavourably solutions which otherwise would be acceptable. The Commission, therefore, must reserve to itself the possibility of examining any system in its totality with a view to assessing its total compatibility with the code of conduct. It is important, therefore, that the Commission is kept up to date with the problems and the solutions found to them in the application of the code of conduct.

Reference is made to the block exemption Regulation[2] on the application of Article 85(3) of the EEC Treaty to certain categories of agreements between undertakings relating to computer reservation systems for air transport services.

2.   Existing contracts

Existing contracts with air carriers, travel agents and subscribers may not be fully in compliance with the code. How should they be treated?

Since the code of conduct is a Regulation and directly legally binding in the Community, all relevant contracts will have to be brought in line with the provisions of the code. This does not essentially mean a renegotiation of these contracts. An additional clause to the contract sent by the system vendors to the other contracting parties, referring to the direct applicability of the code of conduct and indicating the way in which certain clauses of the contracts would consequently have to be understood, is sufficient to bring all contracting parties up to date with the effects of the code on their contractual situation.

It goes without saying that the abovementioned procedure can only be followed for amendments to those provisions in the contracts which are in contravention of the code of conduct.

3. Responsibility for information

According to Article 4(1) participating carriers and other providers of information (eg OAG or ABC) are responsible for the quality of the information. The system vendors might, in their contracts with information suppliers, adopt a clause in this respect.

It is, for example, the responsibility of participating carriers and others to ensure that system vendors can recognise and consequently indicate that there is a change of aircraft and not just a stop en route (otherwise a connecting flight might be displayed as an indirect flight).

This would mean that participating carriers and others are responsible for the submission of data in such a way that the system vendors are given sufficient information to enable them to rank the services in accordance with the requirements of the code.

If a system vendor is aware or should be aware of inaccurate or misleading information, Article 5(2) of the code of conduct comes into play.

The system vendor should ensure that the information concerning direct flights of participating carriers is comprehensive. If schedules of non-participating carriers are not displayed and it can be reasonably expected that the system vendor is aware that services of non-participating carriers on the requested route exist (that is the case when these flights are mentioned in ABC/OAG guides), then this must be clearly indicated. A general statement is not sufficient; specific messages should be displayed wherever this is the case.

4. Secondary displays

The code applies primarily to principal displays. However, the responsibility of system vendors, in respect of displays, is not limited to principal displays. In particular Article 4(2) applies to secondary displays.

5. Use of principal displays

The system vendor shall ensure that the principal display is accessed first by the subscribers, either by technical means or through the contract. Unless a consumer, that is any person seeking information about and/or intending to purchase an air transport product, expressly requests another display, the principal displays shall be used for the provision of information and consequent transactions.

When preference has been expressed for a specific flight then a direct access display may be used to indicate a certain seat availability even when this display does not respect the display principles. A consumer can express a preference for a specific secondary display for more than one transaction, eg a company can request a travel agent to book its employees only on a specific airline for their business travel. This can be considered as an express request for each individual booking. In such cases secondary displays can be used for information and booking purposes.

6. Information on fares

Information on fares in relation to the principal display must be complete and not misleading. This means that all publicly available air fares for the air services displayed must be included in the database (see paragraph 3) and must be displayed on a non-discriminatory basis.

7.   Exclusive use of computerised reservation systems

The code of conduct does not create ticketing authorisation for system vendors. A system vendor may get that authorisation through the agreement with the participating air carrier. Article 8 stipulates that the basic ticketing authorisation is a matter for agreement between the airline in question and the travel agent. When an agent has been given authorisation to issue printed tickets by an air carrier he can then use stock for that purpose which the air carrier either has given to him or which the authorisation indicates he can use (eg bank settlement plan tickets). For the purpose of printing the tickets the agent can use any printer which can do the job and the air carrier cannot specify only the use of own printer. However, no printing fee to the system vendor can be incurred for the air carrier which is not participating. In other words the ticket is issued by the travel agent and not by the system vendor.

If an air carrier does participate fully in a computerised reservation system then an authorised travel agent is free to use that computerised reservation system for ticketing on that airline. However, if an air carrier does not participate in or accept reservations or tickets from a computerised reservation system, then Article 8 does not create a right for the travel agent to use that computerised reservation system for those purposes anyway. Neither does Article 8 in any way create a right for a travel agent to make reservations or issue tickets for an air carrier.

8.   Exclusivity clauses

A system vendor can link in its contracts with subscribers the fee levels with the number of bookings processed through its computerised reservation system, as long as the fee levels are cost-related.

The linkage of fee levels with a certain percentage of bookings made by the subscriber is not permitted, since the difference in fee level could not be justified by differences in costs.

9.   Termination of contracts

Article 9(4) gives subscribers the right to terminate contracts with system vendors without any penalty on three months' notice irrespective of the agreed termination date. Contracts may be concluded for a period exceeding one year. If a contract is terminated before the first year has expired, real damages may be claimed. In other cases system vendors can only charge the costs directly related to the termination of the contract.

10.   Relationship of fees to costs

It should be acknowledged that some costs may differ in different countries. Therefore, in order to comply with the provision of Article 10(1), it is possible, for example, to make a distinction between costs for the service and costs for communication. The fee level should be the same for the same level of service, but communication and other costs can differ from one country to another. Fee levels may reflect the differences in such costs only if these differences can be adequately demonstrated.

11.   Sample for display

The system vendor should always bear in mind that the purpose is to provide the consumer with accurate and non-misleading information. It is this basic criterion which prohibits the subscribers and/or the system vendors from constructing or displaying flight options with the purpose of discriminating against and/or of giving advantage to one or more carriers or airports.

The selection of the sample of flights of participating carriers which is to be displayed on one or more pages in response to a consumer request must respect at least the following principles—

— all direct services within the time limits between the two airports or cities in question must be included, ie both nonstop services and services with intermediate stops;

— the time limits within which the sample of connecting flights is to be selected may be a specific departure time around which a bracket is then constructed or the same principle applied to arrival time. It is also possible for a system to sample according to elapsed journey time on the day in question.

A minimum number of nine connecting points shall, if possible, be used for the construction of connecting flights for inclusion in the sample for the principal display. This does not mean, however, that unrealistic travel options are included.

A routing with an elapsed journey time which is considerably longer than alternative connections and which does not offer specific advantages may be considered as unrealistic, for example.

A system vendor is obliged to include in a sample for a principal display indirect services requested by participating carriers and falling within the time limits of the consumer request, unless the routing is in excess of 130% of the great circle distance between the two airports.

Routing in excess of 130% may, at the option of the system vendor, be included. However, this must be done in a non-discriminatory way. This means in fact that objective parameters should be set to determine which of these routes are to be included. The system vendor must take all practical measures to ensure that no unrealistic travel options are included.

Paragraph 2 of the general part of the Annex is aimed to prohibit the so-called "screen padding" practice. A system vendor is not allowed to give excessive exposure to one particular travel option or to display unrealistic travel options. This means in practice that similar flights should be displayed in a comparable format; that flight options should be displayed without discrimination and without giving advantage to particular carriers or airports and that unnecessary information should be avoided, for example, when a code-shared flight is displayed then the basic individual flights of the two carriers should not be sampled and shown as well as a connection; likewise, when a through flight is displayed with one flight number.

A system vendor has the option to sample and display information of any non-participating carrier in any or all of the three categories of flights set out in the Annex to the code. This information has to be displayed in an accurate, non-misleading and non-discriminatory manner as between the non-participating carriers. Within the three different categories of flights, participating carriers may be treated more favourably then non-participating carriers. Since the non-participating carrier is not providing information directly to the system vendor, it cannot be held directly responsible for the quality of the data. However, Article 4(1) of the code also refers to other information providers such as OAG or ABC. These information providers should ensure the quality of the information of non-participating airlines if they are providing the information under contract to the system vendor (see paragraph 3).

12. Ranking and quality of information in display

The ranking of the sample shall, unless the consumer requests otherwise, be in the following order:

first group: all direct non-stop flights in order of departure time;

second group: all direct flights with intermediate stop(s) in order of elapsed journey time:

— no change of aircraft may take place,
— only one flight number must be used,
— the fact that there are intermediate stops must be clearly indicated;

third group: all connecting flights in order of elapsed journey time:

— all on-line flights including a change of aircraft or a change of flight number, all interline and all code-shared flights fall within this category,
— change of aircraft and/or intermediate stops and/or change of airport must be clearly indicated. Special attention should be given to flights involving a change of aircraft where the same type of equipment is used for the different segments,
— code sharing is possible, but should be clearly indicated,
— code-shared flights may be displayed on one line or two lines but a system must be consistent in its practice. It must be quite clear that more than one airline is involved. The clearest way of doing this would be by displaying the flights on two or more lines,
— one flight number may be used for connecting flights, unless the different segments are displayed separately on a connection,
— one flight number may be used if there is a change of aircraft and/or change of terminal building involved,
— the use of one flight number when there is a change of airport included is not acceptable.

It should be noted that elapsed journey time should be realistic. The participating carriers are primarily responsible for the accurate and non-misleading scheduling of departure and arrival time. The use of penalty points by the system vendor is not in conformity with the provisions of the code, for instance for a change of terminal. However, it is the responsibility of the airline or the vendor to consider a realistic connecting time when providing or constructing a connection.

In addition to the abovementioned default display there shall be a possibility for the consumer to request displays:

1. ranked by departure time:
2. ranked by arrival time, and
3. ranked by elapsed journey time.

Any combination of—

1. departure time and elapsed journey time, and
2. arrival time and elapsed journey time is also possible.

[4401]

NOTES
[1]   OJ L220, 29.7.89.
[2]   OJ L239, 30.8.89.

COUNCIL REGULATION

of 24 July 1990

on access for air carriers to scheduled intra-Community air service routes and on the sharing of passenger capacity between air carriers on scheduled air services between Member States

(2343/90/EEC)

NOTES

Date of publication in OJ: OJ L217, 11.8.80, p 8.

Replaced, except for Art 2(a)(ii) and Annex I, printed below, by Council Regulation 2408/92/EEC, Art 15, at **[4458]**.

Article 2

(a)–(d) ...

   (e) Community air carrier means—
      (i) ...
     (ii) an air carrier which, at the time of adoption of this Regulation, . . .—
        1. either has its central administration and principal place of business in the Community and has been providing scheduled or non-scheduled air services in the Community during the 12 months prior to adoption of this Regulation;
        2. or has been providing scheduled air services between Member States on the basis of third-and fourth-freedom traffic rights during the 12 months prior to adoption of this Regulation.
          The air carriers which meet the criteria set out in this point (ii) are listed in Annex I;

(f)–(n) ...

[4402]

ANNEX I
AIR CARRIERS REFERRED TO IN ARTICLE 2(E)(II)

The following air carriers meet the criteria referred to in Article 2(e)(ii) as long as they are recognised as national carriers by the Member State which so recognises them at the time of the adoption of this Regulation—

— Scandinavian Airlines System,
— Britannia Airways,
— Monarch Airlines.

[4403]

COUNCIL REGULATION

of 4 February 1991

on the operation of air cargo services between Member States

(294/91/EEC)

NOTES

Date of publication in OJ: OJ L36, 8.2.91, p 1.

Replaced, except for Art 2(b) and the Annex, printed below, by Council Regulation 2408/92/EEC, Art 15, at **[4458]**.

Article 2

(a) ...

(b) "Community air cargo carrier" shall mean—

    (i) an air cargo carrier which has, and maintains, its central administration and principal place of business in the Community, and the majority of whose shares are, and continue to be, held by Member States and/or by nationals of Member States and which is, and continues to be, effectively controlled by such States or persons; or

    (ii) an air cargo carrier which meets the definition in Article, 2(e)(ii) of Regulation (EEC) No 2343/90 and is listed in the Annex hereto;

[4404]

ANNEX
AIR CARGO CARRIERS REFERRED TO IN ARTICLE 2(B)(II)

— Scandinavian Airlines System,
— Britannia Airways,
— Monarch Airlines.

[4405]

COUNCIL REGULATION

of 4 February 1991

establishing common rules for a denied-boarding compensation system in scheduled air transport

(295/91/EEC)

NOTES

Date of publication in OJ: OJ L36, 8.2.91, p 5.

THE COUNCIL OF THE EUROPEAN COMMUNITIES,

Having regard to the Treaty establishing the European Economic Community, and in particular Article 84(2) thereof,

Having regard to the proposal from the Commission,[1]

Having regard to the opinion of the European Parliament,[2]

Having regard to the opinion of the Economic and Social Committee,[3]

Whereas liberalisation measures adopted by the Council in July 1990 represent a further step towards a fully developed common air transport policy;

Whereas common action in the field of the protection of the interests of air transport users is required, in order to ensure a well-balanced development in the light of the radically changing environment in which air carriers have to operate;

Whereas current practice in the field of denied-boarding compensation differs substantially between air carriers;

Whereas certain common minimum standards in the field of denied-boarding compensation should ensure that the quality of air carriers' services is maintained in a context of increased competition;

Whereas an air carrier should be obliged to establish rules for boarding in the event of an overbooked flight;

Whereas in the event of boarding being denied the rights of passengers should be defined;

Whereas air carriers should be obliged to pay compensation and to provide additional services to passengers who are denied boarding;

Whereas passengers should be clearly informed about applicable rules,

NOTES
1   OJ C129, 24.5.90, p 15.
2   OJ C19, 28.1.91.
3   OJ C31, 6.2.91.

HAS ADOPTED THIS REGULATION—

Article 1

This Regulation establishes common minimum rules applicable where passengers are denied access to an overbooked scheduled flight for which they have a valid ticket and a confirmed reservation departing from an airport located in the territory of a Member State to which the Treaty applies, irrespective of the State where the air carrier is established, the nationality of the passenger and the point of destination.

[4406]

Article 2

For the purposes of this Regulation—
   (a) "denied boarding" means a refusal to accommodate passengers on a flight although they have—
       — a valid ticket,
       — a confirmed reservation on that flight, and
       — presented themselves for check-in within the required time limit and as stipulated;
   (b) "confirmed reservation" means that a ticket sold by the air carrier or its authorised travel agent contains—
       — a specification of the number, date and time of the flight, and
       — the notation "OK", or any other entry, in the appropriate space on the ticket signifying the registration by the air carrier as well as the express confirmation by the air carrier of the reservation;
   (c) "scheduled flight" means a flight possessing all of the following characteristics—
       — it is performed by aircraft for the transport of passengers or passengers and cargo and/or mail for remuneration, in such a manner that, for each flight, seats are available for purchase by members of the public, either directly from the carrier or from its authorised agents,
       — it is operated to serve traffic between two or more points, either—
           (i) according to a published timetable; or
           (ii) with flights so regular or frequent that they constitute a recognisably systematic series;
   (d) "overbooked flight" means a flight where the number of passengers holding a confirmed reservation and presenting themselves for check-in within the required time limit and as stipulated exceeds the number of available seats on that flight;
   (e) "volunteer" means a person who has—
       — a valid ticket,
       — a confirmed reservation, and
       — presented himself for check-in within the required time limit and as stipulated and who responds positively to the air carrier's call for passengers being prepared to surrender their confirmed reservation in exchange for compensation;

PART IV
EC MATERIALS

(f) "final destination" means the destination on the flight coupon presented at the check-in counter or, in the case of successive flights, on the last flight coupon of the ticket. Connecting flights which can be carried out without difficulties although a delay has been caused by denied boarding are not taken into account.

[4407]

Article 3

1.   The air carrier must lay down the rules which it will follow for boarding in the event of an overbooked flight. It shall notify these rules and any changes therein to the Member State concerned and to the Commission, which shall make them available to the other Member States. Any such changes shall enter into force one month after their notification.

2.   The rules referred to in paragraph 1 shall be made available to the public at the carrier's agencies and check-in counters.

3.   The rules referred to in paragraph 1 should include the possibility of a call for volunteers prepared not to board.

4.   In any event the air carrier should take into consideration the interests of passengers who must be given boarding priority for legitimate reasons, such as handicapped persons and unaccompanied children.

[4408]

Article 4

1.   In the event of boarding being denied, a passenger shall have the choice between:
— reimbursement without penalty of the cost of the ticket for the part of the journey not made, or
— re-routing to his final destination at the earliest opportunity, or
— re-routing at a later date at the passenger's convenience.

2.   Irrespective of the passenger's choice mentioned in the case referred to in paragraph 1, the air carrier shall, immediately after boarding has been denied, pay minimum compensation, without prejudice to paragraphs 3 and 4, amounting to:
— ECU 150 for flights of up to 3500 km,
— ECU 300 for flights of more than 3500 km,
having regard to the final destination specified in the ticket.

3.   Where the air carrier offers re-routing to the final destination on an alternative flight, the arrival time of which does not exceed the scheduled arrival time of the flight originally booked by two hours for flights of up to 3500 km, and by four hours for flights of more than 3500 km, the compensation provided for in paragraph 2 above may be reduced by 50%.

4.   The amounts of compensation need not exceed the price of the ticket in respect of the final destination.

5.   The compensation shall be paid in cash or, in agreement with the passenger, in travel vouchers and/or other services.

6.   If, on an overbooked flight, a passenger agrees to be placed in a class lower than that for which a ticket has been purchased, he shall be entitled to reimbursement of the difference in price.

7.   The distances given in paragraphs 2 and 3 shall be measured by the great circle track method (great circle route).

[4409]

Article 5

1.   In the event of boarding being denied on a flight sold as part of a package tour, the air carrier shall be obliged to compensate the tour operator who has concluded a contract with the passenger and who is liable to him for the proper performance of the contract for the said package tour under Council Directive 90/314/EEC of 13 June 1990 on package travel, package holidays and package tours.

2.   Without prejudice to the rights and obligations arising under Directive 90/314/EEC, the tour operator shall be obliged to pass on to the passenger the sums collected under paragraph 1.

[4410]

Article 6

1.   Apart from the minimum compensation amounts set out in Article 4, the air carrier shall offer free of charge to passengers who are denied boarding:
   (a) the expenses for a telephone call and/or telex/fax message to the point of destination;
   (b) meals and refreshments in a reasonable relation to the waiting time;
   (c) hotel accommodation in cases where an additional stay of one or more nights is necessary.

2.   When a town, city or region is served by several airports and an air carrier offers a passenger, who has been denied boarding, a flight to an airport other than the destination airport that the passenger had booked, the cost of travelling between the alternative airports or to an alternative close-by destination, agreed with the passenger, shall be borne by the air carrier.

[4411]

Article 7

The air carrier shall not be obliged to pay denied-boarding compensation in cases where the passenger is travelling free of charge or at reduced fares not available directly or indirectly to the public.

[4412]

Article 8

Air carriers shall provide each passenger affected by denied boarding with a form setting out the denied-boarding compensation rules.

[4413]

Article 9

1.   This Regulation shall apply without prejudice to subsequent application to the courts having jurisdiction with a view to further compensation.

2.   Paragraph 1 shall not apply to the volunteers as defined in Article 2(e) who have accepted compensation under the rules referred to in Article 3.

[4414]

Article 10

This Regulation shall enter into force two months after the date of its publication in the *Official Journal of the European Communities.*

[4415]

This Regulation shall be binding in its entirety and directly applicable in all Member States.

Done at Brussels, 4 February 1991.

COUNCIL REGULATION

of 25 February 1992

on the application of Article 85(3) of the Treaty to certain categories of agreements, decisions and concerted practices between liner shipping companies (consortia)

(479/92/EEC)

NOTES

Date of publication in OJ: OJ L55, 29.2.92, p 3.

THE COUNCIL OF THE EUROPEAN COMMUNITIES,

Having regard to the Treaty establishing the European Economic Community, and in particular Article 87 thereof,

Having regard to the proposal from the Commission,[1]

Having regard to the opinion of the European Parliament,[2]

Having regard to the opinion of the Economic and Social Committee,[3]

Whereas Article 85(1) of the Treaty may in accordance with Article 85(3) thereof be declared inapplicable to categories of agreements, decisions and concerted practices which fulfil the conditions contained in Article 85(3);

Whereas, pursuant to Article 87 of the Treaty, the provisions for the application of Article 85(3) of the Treaty should be adopted by way of Regulation; whereas, according to Article 87(2)(b), such a Regulation must lay down detailed rules for the application of Article 85(3), taking into account the need to ensure effective supervision, on the one hand, and to simplify administration to the greatest possible extent on the other; whereas, according to Article 87(2)(d), such a Regulation is required to define the respective functions of the Commission and of the Court of Justice;

Whereas liner shipping is a capital intensive industry; whereas containerisation has increased pressures for cooperation and rationalisation; whereas the Community shipping industry needs to attain the necessary economies of scale in order to compete successfully on the world liner shipping market;

Whereas joint-service agreements between liner shipping companies with the aim of rationalising their operations by means of technical, operational and/or commercial arrangements (described in shipping circles as consortia) can help to provide the necessary means for improving the productivity of liner shipping services and promoting technical and economic progress;

Having regard to the importance of maritime transport for the development of the Community's trade and the role which consortia agreements can fulfil in this respect, taking account of the special features of international liner shipping;

Whereas the legalisation of these agreements is a measure which can make a positive contribution to improving the competitiveness of shipping in the Community;

Whereas users of the shipping services offered by consortia can obtain a share of the benefits resulting from the improvements in productivity and service, by means of, *inter alia*, regularity, cost reductions derived from higher levels of capacity utilisation, and better service quality stemming from improved vessels and equipment;

Whereas the Commission should be enabled to declare by way of Regulation that the provisions of Article 85(1) of the Treaty do not apply to certain categories of consortia agreements, decisions and concerted practices, in order to make it easier for undertakings to cooperate in ways which are economically desirable and without adverse effect from the point of view of competition policy;

Whereas the Commission, in close and constant liaison with the competent authorities of the Member States, should be able to define precisely the scope of these exemptions and the conditions attached to them;

Whereas consortia in liner shipping are a specialised and complex type of joint venture; whereas there is a great variety of different consortia agreements operating in different circumstances; whereas the scope, parties, activities or terms of consortia are frequently altered; whereas the Commission should therefore be given the responsibility of defining from time to time the consortia to which a group exemption should apply;

Whereas, in order to ensure that all the conditions of Article 85(3) of the Treaty are met, conditions should be attached to group exemptions to ensure in particular that a fair share of the benefits will be passed on to shippers and that competition is not eliminated;

Whereas pursuant to Article 11(4) of Council Regulation (EEC) No 4056/86 of 22 December 1986 laying down detailed rules for the application of Articles 85 and 86 of the Treaty to maritime transport[4] the Commission may provide that a decision taken in accordance with Article 85(3) of the Treaty shall apply with retroactive effect; whereas it is desirable that the Commission be empowered to adopt, by Regulation, provisions to that effect;

Whereas notification of agreements, decisions and concerted practices falling within the scope of this Regulation must not be made compulsory, it being primarily the responsibility of undertakings to see to it that they conform to the rules on competition, and in particular to the conditions laid down by the subsequent Commission Regulation implementing this Regulation;

Whereas there can be no exemption if the conditions set out in Article 85(3) of the Treaty are not satisfied; whereas the Commission should therefore have power to take the appropriate measures where an agreement proves to have effects incompatible with Article 85(3) of the Treaty; whereas the Commission should be able first to address recommendations to the parties and then to take decisions,

NOTES

1   OJ C167, 10.7.90, p 9.
2   OJ C305, 25.11.91, p 39.
3   OJ C69, 18.3.91, p 16.
4   OJ L378, 31.12.86, p 4.

HAS ADOPTED THIS REGULATION—

Article 1

1.   Without prejudice to the application of Regulation (EEC) No 4056/86, the Commission may by regulation and in accordance with Article 85(3) of the Treaty, declare that Article 85(1) of the Treaty shall not apply to certain categories of agreements between undertakings, decisions of associations of undertakings and concerted practices that have as an object to promote or establish cooperation in the joint operation of maritime transport services between liner shipping companies, for the purpose of rationalising their operations by means of technical, operational and/or commercial arrangements—with the exception of price fixing (consortia).

2.   Such regulation adopted pursuant to paragraph 1 shall define the categories of agreements, decisions and concerted practices to which it applies and shall specify the conditions and obligations under which, pursuant to Article 85(3) of the Treaty, they shall be considered exempted from the application of Article 85(1) of the Treaty.

[4416]

Article 2

1.   The regulation adopted pursuant to Article 1 shall apply for a period of five years, calculated as from the date of its entry into force.

2.   It may be repealed or amended where circumstances have changed with respect to any of the facts which were basic to its adoption.

[4417]

PART IV
EC MATERIALS

Article 3

The regulation adopted pursuant to Article 1 may include a provision stating that it applies with retroactive effect to agreements, decisions and concerted practices which were in existence at the date of entry into force of such regulation, provided they comply with the conditions established in that regulation.

[4418]

[Article 3a

A regulation pursuant to Article 1 may stipulate that the prohibition contained in Article 85(1) of the Treaty shall not apply, for such period as fixed by that Regulation, to agreements, decisions and concerted practices already in existence at the date of accession to which Article 85(1) applies by virtue of the accession of Austria, Finland and Sweden and which do not satisfy the conditions of Article 85(3). However, this Article shall not apply to agreements, decisions and concerted practices which at the date of accession already fall under Article 53(1) of the EEA Agreement.]

[4419]

NOTES
    Inserted by the 1994 Act of Accession of the Kingdom of Norway, the Republic of Austria, the Republic of Finland and the Kingdom of Sweden, Annex I(III)(A)(4), as adjusted by Council Decision 95/1/EC, Annex I(III)(A)(4).

Article 4

Before adopting its regulation, the Commission shall publish a draft thereof to enable all the persons and organisations concerned to submit their comments within such reasonable time limit as the Commission shall fix, but in no case less than one month.

[4420]

Article 5

1.   Before publishing the draft regulation and before adopting the regulation, the Commission shall consult the Advisory Committee on Agreements and Dominant Positions in Maritime Transport established by Article 15(3) of Regulation (EEC) No 4056/86.

2.   Paragraphs 5 and 6 of Article 15 of Regulation (EEC) No 4056/86 relating to consultation with the Advisory Committee shall apply, it being understood that joint meetings with the Commission shall take place not earlier than one month after dispatch of the notice convening them.

[4421]

Article 6

1.   Where the persons concerned are in breach of a condition or obligation attaching to an exemption granted by the Regulation adopted pursuant to Article 1, the Commission may, in order to put an end to such a breach:
    — address recommendations to the persons concerned, and
    — in the event of failure by such persons to observe those recommendations, and depending on the gravity of the breach concerned, adopt a decision that either prohibits them from carrying out, or requires them to perform specific acts or, while withdrawing the benefit of the group exemption which they enjoyed, grants them an individual exemption in accordance with Article 11(4) of Regulation (EEC) No 4056/86, or withdraws the benefit of the group exemption which they enjoyed.

2.   Where the Commission, either on its own initiative or at the request of a Member State or of natural or legal persons claiming a legitimate interest, finds that in a particular case an agreement, decision or concerted practice to which the group exemption granted by the Regulation adopted pursuant to Article 1 applies, nevertheless has effects which are incompatible with Article 85(3) of the Treaty or with the prohibition laid down in Article 86 of the Treaty, it may withdraw the benefit of the group exemption from those agreements, decisions or concerted practices and take all appropriate measures for the purpose of bringing these infringements to an end, pursuant to Article 13 of Regulation (EEC) No 4056/86.

3.   Before taking a decision under paragraph 2, the Commission may address recommendations for termination of the infringement to the persons concerned.

[4422]

Article 7

This Regulation shall enter into force on the day following its publication in the *Official Journal of the European Communities*.

[4423]

This Regulation shall be binding in its entirety and directly applicable in all Member States.

Done at Brussels, 25 February 1992.

COUNCIL REGULATION

of 23 July 1992

on licensing of air carriers

(2407/92/EEC)

NOTES

Date of publication in OJ: OJ L240, 24.8.92, p 1.

THE COUNCIL OF THE EUROPEAN COMMUNITIES,

Having regard to the Treaty establishing the European Economic Community, and in particular Article 84(2) thereof,

Having regard to the proposal from the Commission,[1]

Having regard to the opinion of the European Parliament,[2]

Having regard to the opinion of the Economic and Social Committee,[3]

Whereas it is important to establish an air transport policy for the internal market over a period expiring on 31 December 1992 as provided for in Article 8a of the Treaty;

Whereas the internal market shall comprise an area without internal frontiers in which the free movement of goods, persons, services and capital is ensured;

Whereas the application in the air transport sector of the principle of the freedom to provide services needs to take into account the specific characteristics of that sector;

Whereas in Council Regulation (EEC) No 2343/90 of 24 July 1990 on access for air carriers to scheduled intra-Community air service routes and on the sharing of passenger capacity between air carriers on scheduled air services between Member States[4] the Council decided to adopt for implementation not later than 1 July 1992 common rules governing the licensing of air carriers;

Whereas, however, it is necessary to allow Member States a reasonable period, until 1 January 1993, for the application of this Regulation;

Whereas it is important to define non-discriminatory requirements in relation to the location and control of an undertaking applying for a licence;

Whereas in order to ensure dependable and adequate service it is necessary to ensure that an air carrier is at all times operating at sound economic and high safety levels;

Whereas for the protection of users and other parties concerned it is important to ensure that air carriers are sufficiently insured in respect of liability risks;

Whereas within the internal market air carriers should be able to use aircraft owned anywhere in the Community, without prejudice to the responsibilities of the licensing Member State with respect to the technical fitness of the carrier;

Whereas it should also be possible to lease aircraft registered outside the Community for a short term or in exceptional circumstances, providing safety standards are equivalent to those applicable within the Community;

Whereas procedures for the granting of licences to air carriers should be transparent and non-discriminatory,

NOTES
1   OJ C258, 4.10.91, p 2.
2   OJ C125, 18.5.92, p 140.
3   OJ C169, 6.7.92, p 15.
4   OJ L217, 11.8.90, p 8.

HAS ADOPTED THIS REGULATION—

Article 1

1.   This Regulation concerns requirements for the granting and maintenance of operating licences by Member States in relation to air carriers established in the Community.

2.   The carriage by air of passengers, mail and/or cargo, performed by non-power driven aircraft and/or ultra-light power driven aircraft, as well as local flights not involving carriage between different airports, are not subject to this Regulation. In respect of these operations, national law concerning operating licences, if any, and Community and national law concerning the air operator's certificate (AOC) shall apply.

[4424]

Article 2

For the purposes of this Regulation—
(a)   "undertaking" means any natural person, any legal person, whether profit-making or not, or any official body whether having its own legal personality or not;
(b)   "air carrier" means an air transport undertaking with a valid operating licence;
(c)   "operating licence" means an authorisation granted by the Member State responsible to an undertaking, permitting it to carry out carriage by air of passengers, mail and/or cargo, as stated in the operating licence, for remuneration and/or hire;
(d)   "air operator's certificate (AOC)" means a document issued to an undertaking or a group of undertakings by the competent authorities of the Member States which affirms that the operator in question has the professional ability and organisation to secure the safe operation of aircraft for the aviation activities specified in the certificate;
(e)   "business plan" means a detailed description of the air carrier's intended commercial activities for the period in question, in particular in relation to the market development and investments to be carried out, including the financial and economic implications of these activities;
(f)   "management account" means a detailed statement of income and costs for the period in question including a breakdown between air-transport-related and other activities as well as between pecuniary and non-pecuniary elements;

(g) "effective control" means a relationship constituted by rights, contracts or any other means which, either separately or jointly and having regard to the considerations of fact or law involved, confer the possibility of directly or indirectly exercising a decisive influence on an undertaking, in particular by—

  (a) the right to use all or part of the assets of an undertaking;

  (b) rights or contracts which confer a decisive influence on the composition, voting or decisions of the bodies of an undertaking or otherwise confer a decisive influence on the running of the business of the undertaking.

[4425]

Article 3

1.   Without prejudice to Article 5(5), Member States shall not grant operating licences or maintain them in force where the requirements of this Regulation are not complied with.

2.   An undertaking meeting the requirements of this Regulation shall be entitled to receive an operating licence. Such licence does not confer in itself any rights of access to specific routes or markets.

3.   Without prejudice to Article 1(2), no undertaking established in the Community shall be permitted within the territory of the Community to carry by air passengers, mail and/or cargo for remuneration and/or hire unless the undertaking has been granted the appropriate operating licence.

[4426]

Article 4

Operating licence

1.   No undertaking shall be granted an operating licence by a Member State unless—

  (a) its principal place of business and, if any, its registered office are located in that Member State; and

  (b) its main occupation is air transport in isolation or combined with any other commercial operation of aircraft or repair and maintenance of aircraft.

2.   Without prejudice to agreements and conventions to which the Community is a contracting party, the undertaking shall be owned and continue to be owned directly or through majority ownership by Member States and/or nationals of Member States. It shall at all times be effectively controlled by such States or such nationals.

3. (a) Notwithstanding paragraphs 2 and 4, air carriers which have already been recognised in Annex I to Council Regulation (EEC) No 2343/90 and Council Regulation (EEC) No 294/91 of 4 February 1991 on the operation of air cargo services between Member States[1] shall retain their rights under this and associated Regulations as long as they meet the other obligations in this Regulation and they continue to be controlled directly or indirectly by the same third countries and/or by nationals of the same third country as those exercising such control at the time of adoption of this Regulation. Such control may, however, be transferred to Member States and/or to Member State nationals at any time.

  (b) The possibility of buying and selling shares under subparagraph (a) does not cover nationals who have a significant interest in an air carrier of a third country.

4.   Any undertaking which directly or indirectly participates in a controlling shareholding in an air carrier shall meet the requirements of paragraph 2.

5.   An air carrier shall at all times be able on request to demonstrate to the Member State responsible for the operating licence that it meets the requirements of this Article. The Commission acting at the request of a Member State shall examine compliance with the requirements of this Article and take a decision if necessary.

[4427]

NOTES
¹   OJ L36, 8.2.91, p 1.

Article 5

1.   An applicant air transport undertaking to which an operating licence is granted for the first time must be able to demonstrate to the reasonable satisfaction of the competent authorities of the licensing Member State that—
   (a) it can meet at any time its actual and potential obligations, established under realistic assumptions, for a period of 24 months from the start of operations; and
   (b) it can meet its fixed and operational costs incurred from operations according to its business plan and established under realistic assumptions, for a period of three months from the start of operations, without taking into account any income from its operations.

2.   For the purpose of paragraph 1, each application shall submit a business plan for, at least, the first two years of operation. The business plan shall also detail the applicant's financial links with any other commercial activities in which the applicant is engaged either directly or through related undertakings. The applicant shall also provide all relevant information, in particular the data referred to in part A of the Annex.

3.   An air carrier shall notify in advance to its licensing authority plans for operation of a new scheduled service or a non-scheduled service to a continent or world region not previously served, changes in the type or number of aircraft used or a substantial change in the scale of its activities. It shall also notify in advance any intended mergers or acquisitions and shall notify its licensing authority within fourteen days of any change in the ownership of any single shareholding which represents 10% or more of the total shareholding of the air carrier or of its parent or ultimate holding company. The submission of a 12-month business plan two months in advance of the period to which it refers shall constitute sufficient notice under this paragraph for the purpose of changes to current operations and/or circumstances which are included in that business plan.

4.   If the licensing authority deems the changes notified under paragraph 3 to have a significant bearing on the finances of the air carrier, it shall require the submission of a revised business plan incorporating the changes in question and covering, at least, a period of 12 months from its date of implementation, as well as all the relevant information, including the data referred to in part B of the Annex, to assess whether the air carrier can meet its existing and potential obligations during that period of 12 months. The licensing authority shall take a decision on the revised business plan not later than three months after all the necessary information has been submitted to it.

5.   Licensing authorities may, at any time and in any event whenever there are clear indications that financial problems exist with an air carrier licensed by them, assess its financial performance and may suspend or revoke the licence if they are no longer satisfied that the air carrier can meet its actual and potential obligations for

a 12-month period. Licensing authorities may also grant a temporary licence pending financial reorganisation of the air carrier provided safety is not at risk.

6.   An air carrier shall provide to its licensing authority every financial year without undue delay the audited accounts relating to the previous financial year. At any time upon request of the licensing authority an air carrier shall provide the information relevant for the purposes of paragraph 5 and, in particular, the data referred to in part C of the Annex.

7. (a) Paragraphs 1, 2, 3, 4 and 6 of this Article shall not apply to air carriers exclusively engaged in operations with aircraft of less than 10 tonnes mtow (maximum take off weight) and/or less than 20 seats. Such air carriers shall at all times be able to demonstrate that their net capital is at least ECU 80 000 or to provide when required by the licensing authority the information relevant for the purposes of paragraph 5. A Member State may nevertheless apply paragraphs 1, 2, 3, 4 and 6 to air carriers licensed by it that operate scheduled services or whose turnover exceeds ECU 3 million per year.

(b) The Commission may, after consulting the Member States, increase as appropriate the values referred to in subparagraph (a) if economic developments indicate the necessity of such a decision. Such change shall be published in the *Official Journal of the European Communities*.

(c) Any Member State may refer the Commission's decision to the Council within a time limit of one month. The Council, acting by a qualified majority, may in exceptional circumstances take a different decision within a period of one month.

[4428]

Article 6

1.   Where the competent authorities of a Member State require, for the purpose of issuing an operating licence, proof that the persons who will continuously and effectively manage the operations of the undertaking are of good repute or that they have not been declared bankrupt, or suspend or revoke the licence in the event of serious professional misconduct or a criminal offence, that Member State shall accept as sufficient evidence in respect of nationals of other Member States the production of documents issued by competent authorities in the Member State of origin or the Member State from which the foreign national comes showing that those requirements are met.

Where the competent authorities of the Member State of origin or of the Member State from which the foreign national comes do not issue the documents referred to in the first subparagraph, such documents shall be replaced by a declaration on oath—or, in Member States where there is no provision for declaration on oath, by a solemn declaration—made by the person concerned before a competent judicial or administrative authority or, where appropriate, a notary or qualified professional body of the Member State of origin or the Member State from which the person comes; such authority or notary shall issue a certificate attesting the authenticity of the declaration on oath or solemn declaration.

2.   The competent authorities of Member States may require that the documents and certificates referred to in paragraph 1 be presented no more than three months after their date of issue.

[4429]

Article 7

An air carrier shall be insured to cover liability in case of accidents, in particular in respect of passengers, luggage, cargo, mail and third parties.

[4430]

Article 8

1.   Ownership of aircraft shall not be a condition for granting or maintaining an operating licence but a Member State shall require, in relation to air carriers licensed by it that they have one or more aircraft at their disposal, through ownership or any form of lease agreement.

2.   (a) Without prejudice to paragraph 3, aircraft used by an air carrier shall be registered, at the option of the Member State issuing the operating licence, in its national register or within the Community.

   (b)   If a lease agreement for an aircraft registered within the Community has been deemed acceptable under Article 10, a Member State shall not require the registration of that aircraft on its own register if this would require structural changes to the aircraft.

3.   In the case of short-term lease agreements to meet temporary needs of the air carrier or otherwise in exceptional circumstances, a Member State may grant waivers to the requirement of paragraph 2(a).

4.   When applying paragraph 2(a) a Member State shall, subject to applicable laws and regulations, including those relating to airworthiness certification, accept on its national register, without any discriminatory fee and without delay, aircraft owned by nationals of other Member States and transfers from aircraft registers of other Member States. No fee shall be applied to transfer of aircraft in addition to the normal registration fee.

[4431]

Air operator's certificate (AOC)

Article 9

1.   The granting and validity at any time of an operating licence shall be dependent upon the possession of a valid AOC specifying the activities covered by the operating licence and complying with the criteria established in the relevant Council Regulation.

2.   Until such time as the Council Regulation referred to in paragraph 1 is applicable, national regulations concerning the AOC, or equivalent title concerning the certification of air transport operators, shall apply.

[4432]

Article 10

1.   For the purposes of ensuring safety and liability standards an air carrier using an aircraft from another undertaking or providing it to another undertaking shall obtain prior approval for the operation from the appropriate licensing authority. The conditions of the approval shall be part of the lease agreement between the parties.

2.   A Member State shall not approve agreements leasing aircraft with crew to an air carrier to which it has granted an operating licence unless safety standards equivalent to those imposed under Article 9 are met.

[4433]

General provisions

Article 11

1.   An operating licence shall be valid as long as the air carrier meets the obligations of this Regulation. However, a Member State may make provision for a review one year after a new operating licence has been granted and every five years thereafter.

2.   When an air carrier has ceased operations for six months or has not started operations for six months after the granting of an operating licence, the Member State responsible shall decide whether the operating licence shall be resubmitted for approval.

3.   In relation to air carriers licensed by them, Member States shall decide whether the operating licence shall be resubmitted for approval in case of change in one or more elements affecting the legal situation of the undertaking and, in particular, in the case of mergers or takeovers. The air carrier(s) in question may continue its (their) operations unless the licensing authority decides that safety is at risk, stating the reasons.

[4434]

Article 12

An air carrier against which insolvency or similar proceedings are opened shall not be permitted by a Member State to retain its operating licence if the competent body in that Member State is convinced that there is no realistic prospect of a satisfactory financial reconstruction within a reasonable time.

[4435]

Article 13

1.   Procedures for the granting of operating licences shall be made public by the Member State concerned and the Commission shall be informed.

2.   The Member State concerned shall take a decision on an application as soon as possible, and not later than three months after all the necessary information has been submitted, taking into account all available evidence. The decision shall be communicated to the applicant air transport undertaking. A refusal shall indicate the reasons therefor.

3.   An undertaking whose application for an operating licence has been refused may refer the question to the Commission. If the Commission finds that the requirements of this Regulation have not been fulfilled it shall state its views on the correct interpretation of the Regulation without prejudice to Article 169 of the Treaty.

4.   Decisions by Member States to grant or revoke operating licences shall be published in the *Official Journal of the European Communities*.

[4436]

Article 14

1.   In order to carry out its duties under Article 4 the Commission may obtain all necessary information from the Member States concerned, which shall also ensure the provision of information by air carriers licensed by them.

2.   When the information requested is not supplied within the time limit fixed by the Commission, or is supplied in incomplete form, the Commission shall by decision addressed to the Member State concerned require the information to be supplied. The decision shall specify what information is required and fix an appropriate time limit within which it is to be supplied.

3.   If the information required under paragraph 2 is not provided by the time limit set or the air carrier has not otherwise demonstrated that it meets the requirements of Article 4, the Commission shall, except where special circumstances exist, forthwith inform all Member States of the situation. Member States may, until notified by the Commission that documentation has been provided to demonstrate the fulfilment of the requirements in question, suspend any

market access rights to which the air carrier is entitled under Council Regulation (EEC) No 2408/92 of 23 July 1992 on access for Community air carriers to intra-Community air routes.[1]

[4437]

NOTES
[1] OJ L240, 24.8.92, p 5.

Article 15

In addition to the rules of this Regulation the air carrier shall also respect the requirements of national law compatible with Community law.

[4438]

Article 16

Notwithstanding Article 3(1), operating licences in force in a Member State at the date of entry into force of the Regulation shall remain valid, subject to the laws on the basis of which they granted, for a maximum period of one year except in the case of Article 4(1)(b) for which a maximum period of three years shall apply, during which periods the air carriers holding such licences shall make the necessary arrangements to conform with all the requirements of this Regulation. For the purposes of this Article, carriers holding operating licences shall be deemed to include carriers legitimately operating with a valid AOC at the date of entry into force of this Regulation but without holding such licences.

This Article shall be without prejudice to Article 4(2), (3), (4) and (5) and Article 9, except that air carriers which operated by virtue of exemptions prior to the entry into force of this Regulation may continue to do so, for a period not exceeding the maximum periods specified above, pending enquiries by Member States as to their compliance with Article 4.

[4439]

Article 17

Member States shall consult the Commission before adopting laws, regulations or administrative provisions in implementation of this Regulation. They shall communicate any such measures to the Commission when adopted.

[4440]

Article 18

1.   Member States and the Commission shall cooperate in implementing this Regulation.

2.   Confidential information obtained in application of this Regulation shall be covered by professional secrecy.

[4441]

Article 19

This Regulation shall enter into force on 1 January 1993.

[4442]

This Regulation shall be binding in its entirety and directly applicable in all Member States.

Done at Brussels, 23 July 1992.

ANNEX
INFORMATION FOR USE IN ASSOCIATION WITH ARTICLE 5 OF FINANCIAL FITNESS OF AIR CARRIERS

A   Information to be provided by a first-time applicant from a financial fitness point of view

1.   The most recent internal management accounts and, if available, audited accounts for the previous financial year.

2.   A projected balance sheet, including profit and loss account, for the following two years.

3.   The basis for projected expenditure and income figures on such items as fuel, fares and rates, salaries, maintenance, depreciation, exchange rate fluctuations, airport charges, insurance, etc. Traffic/revenue forecasts.

4.   Details of the start-up costs incurred in the period from submission of application to commencement of operations and an explanation of how it is proposed to finance these costs.

5.   Details of existing and projected sources of finance.

6.   Details of shareholders, including nationality and type of shares to be held, and the Articles of Association. If part of a group of undertakings, information on the relationship between them.

7.   Projected cash-flow statements and liquidity plans for the first two years of operation.

8.   Details of the financing of aircraft purchase/leasing including, in the case of leasing, the terms and conditions of contract.

B   Information to be provided for assessment of the continuing financial fitness of existing licence holders planning a change in their structures or in their activities with a significant bearing on their finances

1.   If necessary, the most recent internal management balance sheet and audited accounts for the previous financial year.

2.   Precise details of all proposed changes eg change of type of service, proposed takeover or merger, modifications in share capital, changes in shareholders, etc.

3.   A projected balance sheet, with a profit and loss account, for the current financial year, including all proposed changes in structure or activities with a significant bearing on finances.

4.   Past and projected expenditure and income figures on such items as fuel, fares and rates, salaries, maintenance, depreciation, exchange rate fluctuations, airport charges, insurance, etc. Traffic/revenue forecasts.

5.   Cash-flow statements and liquidity plans for the following year, including all proposed changes in structure or activities with a significant bearing on finances.

6.   Details of the financing of aircraft purchase/leasing including, in the case of leasing, the terms and conditions of contract.

C   Information to be provided for assessment of the continuing financial fitness of existing licence holders

1.   Audited accounts not later than six months after the end of the relevant period and, if necessary, the most recent internal management balance sheet.

2.   A projected balance sheet, including profit and loss account, for the forthcoming year.

3.   Past and projected expenditure and income figures on such items as fuel, fares and rates, salaries, maintenance, depreciation, exchange rate fluctuations, airport charges, insurance, etc. Traffic/revenue forecasts.

4.   Cash-flow statements and liquidity plans for the following year.

[4443]

COUNCIL REGULATION

of 23 July 1992

on access for Community air carriers to intra-Community air routes

(2408/92/EEC)

NOTES

Date of publication in OJ: OJ L240, 24.8.92, p 8.

THE COUNCIL OF THE EUROPEAN COMMUNITIES,

Having regard to the Treaty establishing the European Economic Community, and in particular Article 84(2) thereof,

Having regard to the proposal from the Commission,[1]

Having regard to the opinion of the European Parliament,[2]

Having regard to the opinion of the Economic and Social Committee,[3]

Whereas it is important to establish an air transport policy for the internal market over a period expiring on 31 December 1992 as provided for in Article 8a of the Treaty;

Whereas the internal market shall comprise an area without internal frontiers in which the free movement of goods, persons, services and capital is ensured;

Whereas Council Decision 87/602/EEC of 14 December 1987 on the sharing of passenger capacity between air carriers on scheduled air services between Member States and on access for air carriers to scheduled air service routes between Member States[4] and Council Regulation (EEC) No 2343/90 of 24 July 1990 on access for air carriers to scheduled intra-Community air service routes and on the sharing of passenger capacity between air carriers on scheduled air services between Member States[5] constitute the first steps towards achieving the internal market in respect of access for Community air carriers to scheduled intra-Community air routes;

Whereas Regulation (EEC) No 2343/90 provides that the Council shall decide on the revision of that Regulation by 30 June 1992 at the latest;

Whereas in Regulation (EEC) No 2343/90 the Council decided to adopt rules governing route licensing for implementation not later than 1 July 1992;

Whereas in Regulation (EEC) No 2343/90 the Council decided to abolish capacity restrictions between Member States by 1 January 1993;

Whereas in Regulation (EEC) No 2343/90 the Council confirmed that cabotage traffic rights are an integral part of the internal market;

Whereas arrangements for greater cooperation over the use of Gibraltar airport were agreed in London on 2 December 1987 by the Kingdom of Spain and the United Kingdom in a joint declaration by the Ministers of Foreign Affairs of the two countries, and such arrangements have yet to come into operation;

Whereas the development of the air traffic system in the Greek islands and in the Atlantic islands comprising the autonomous region of the Azores is at present inadequate and for this reason airports situated on these islands should be temporarily exempted from the application of this Regulation;

Whereas it is necessary to abolish restrictions concerning multiple designation and fifth-freedom traffic rights and phase in cabotage rights in order to stimulate the development of the Community air transport sector and improve services for users;

Whereas it is necessary to make special provision, under limited circumstances, for public service obligations necessary for the maintenance of adequate air services to national regions;

Whereas it is necessary to make special provision for new air services between regional airports;

Whereas for air transport planning purposes it is necessary to give Member States the right to establish non-discriminatory rules for the distribution of air traffic between airports within the same airport system;

Whereas the exercise of traffic rights has to be consistent with operational rules relating to safety, protection of the environment and conditions concerning airport access and has to be treated without discrimination;

Whereas, taking into account problems of congestion or environment problems, it is necessary to include the possibility of imposing certain limitations on the exercise of traffic rights;

Whereas, taking into account the competitive market situation, provision should be made to prevent unjustifiable economic effects on air carriers;

Whereas it is necessary to specify the duties of Member States and air carriers for the purposes of providing necessary information;

Whereas it is appropriate to ensure identical assessment and evaluation of market access for the same types of air services;

Whereas it is appropriate to deal with all matters of market access in the same Regulation;

Whereas this Regulation partially replaces Regulation (EEC) No 2343/90 and Council Regulation (EEC) No 294/91 of 4 February 1991 on the operation of air cargo services between Member States,[6]

NOTES
[1]   OJ C258, 4.10.91, p 2.
[2]   OJ C125, 18.5.92, p 146.
[3]   OJ C169, 6.7.92, p 15.
[4]   OJ L374, 31.12.87, p 19.
[5]   OJ L217, 11.8.90, p 8.
[6]   OJ L36, 8.2.91, p 1.

HAS ADOPTED THIS REGULATION—

Article 1

1.   This Regulation concerns access to routes within the Community for scheduled and non-scheduled air services.

2.   The application of this Regulation to the airport of Gibraltar is understood to be without prejudice to the respective legal positions of the Kingdom of Spain and the United Kingdom with regard to the dispute over sovereignty over the territory in which the airport is situated.

3.   Application of the provisions of this Regulation to Gibraltar airport shall be suspended until the arrangements in the joint declaration made by the Foreign Ministers of the Kingdom of Spain and the United Kingdom on 2 December 1987 have come into operation. The Governments of Spain and the United Kingdom will so inform the Council on that date.

4.   Airports in the Greek islands and in the Atlantic islands comprising the autonomous region of the Azores shall be exempted from the application of this Regulation until 30 June 1993. Unless otherwise decided by the Council, on a proposal from the Commission, this exemption shall apply for a further period of five years and may be continued for five years thereafter.

[4444]

Article 2

For the purposes of this Regulation—
    (a)   "air carrier" means an air transport undertaking with a valid operating licence;
    (b)   "Community air carrier" means an air carrier with a valid operating licence granted by a Member State in accordance with Council Regulation (EEC) No 2407/92 of 23 July 1992 on licensing of air carriers;[1]

(c) "air service" means a flight or a series of flights carrying passengers, cargo and/or mail for remuneration and/or hire;

(d) "scheduled air service" means a series of flights possessing all the following characteristics—

   (i) it is performed by aircraft for the transport of passengers, cargo and/or mail for remuneration, in such a manner that on each flight seats are available for individual purchase by members of the public (either directly from the air carrier or from its authorised agents);

   (ii) it is operated so as to serve traffic between the same two or more airports, either—

      1. according to a published timetable; or

      2. with flights so regular or frequent that they constitute a recognisably systematic series;

(e) "flight" means a departure from a specified airport towards a specified destination airport;

(f) "traffic right" means the right of an air carrier to carry passengers, cargo and/or mail on an air service between two Community airports;

(g) "seat-only sales" means the sale of seats, without any other service bundled, such as accommodation, directly to the public by the air carrier or its authorised agent or a charterer;

(h) "Member State(s) concerned" means the Member State(s) between or within which an air service is operated;

(i) "Member State(s) involved" means the Member State(s) concerned and the Member State(s) where the air carrier(s) operating the air service is (are) licensed;

(j) "State of registration" means the Member State in which the licence referred to in (b) is granted;

(k) "airport" means any area in a Member State which is open for commercial air transport operations;

(l) "regional airport" means any airport other than one listed in Annex I as a category 1 airport;

(m) "airport system" means two or more airports grouped together as serving the same city or conurbation, as indicated in Annex II;

(n) "capacity" means the number of seats offered to the general public on a scheduled air service over a given period;

(o) "public service obligation" means any obligation imposed upon an air carrier to take, in respect of any route which it is licensed to operate by a Member State, all necessary measures to ensure the provision of a service satisfying fixed standards of continuity, regularity, capacity and pricing, which standards the air carrier would not assume if it were solely considering its commercial interest.

[4445]

NOTES

   [1]   OJ L240, 24.8.92, p 1.

Article 3

1.   Subject to this Regulation, Community air carriers shall be permitted by the Member State(s) concerned to exercise traffic rights on routes within the Community.

2.   Notwithstanding paragraph 1, before 1 April 1997 a Member State shall not be required to authorise cabotage traffic rights within its territory by Community air carriers licensed by another Member State, unless—

    (i) the traffic rights are exercised on a service which constitutes and is scheduled as an extension of a service from, or as a preliminary of a service to, the State of registration of the carrier;

   (ii) the air carrier does not use, for the cabotage service, more than 50% of its seasonal capacity on the same service of which the cabotage service constitutes the extension or the preliminary.

3.   An air carrier operating cabotage services in accordance with paragraph 2 shall furnish on request to the Member State(s) involved all information necessary for the implementation of the provisions of that paragraph.

4.   Notwithstanding paragraph 1, before 1 April 1997 a Member State may, without discrimination on grounds of nationality of ownership and air carrier identity, whether incumbent or applicant on the routes concerned, regulate access to routes within its territory for air carriers licensed by it in accordance with Regulation (EEC) No 2407/92 while otherwise not prejudging Community law and, in particular, competition rules.

[4446]

Article 4

1. (a) A Member State, following consultations with the other Member States concerned and after having informed the Commission and air carriers operating on the route, may impose a public service obligation in respect of scheduled air services to an airport serving a peripheral or development region in its territory or on a thin route to any regional airport in its territory, any such route being considered vital for the economic development of the region in which the airport is located, to the extent necessary to ensure on that route the adequate provision of scheduled air services satisfying fixed standards of continuity, regularity, capacity and pricing, which standards air carriers would not assume if they were solely considering their commercial interest. The Commission shall publish the existence of this public service obligation in the *Official Journal of the European Communities.*

  (b) The adequacy of scheduled air services shall be assessed by the Member States having regard to—

    (i) the public interest;

   (ii) the possibility, in particular for island regions, of having recourse to other forms of transport and the ability of such forms to meet the transport needs under consideration;

  (iii) the air fares and conditions which can be quoted to users;

  (iv) the combined effect of all air carriers operating or intending to operate on the route.

  (c) In instances where other forms of transport cannot ensure an adequate and uninterrupted service, the Member States concerned may include in the public service obligation the requirement that any air carrier intending to operate the route gives a guarantee that it will operate the route for a certain period, to be specified, in accordance with the other terms of the public service obligation.

  (d) If no air carrier has commenced or is about to commence scheduled air services on a route in accordance with the public service obligation which has been imposed on that route, then the Member State may limit access to that route to only one aircarrier for a period of up to three years, after which the situation shall be reviewed. The right to operate such services shall be offered by public tender either singly or for a group of such routes to any Community air carrier entitled to operate such air services. The invitation to tender shall be published in the *Official Journal of the European Communities* and the deadline for submission of tenders not be earlier than one month after the day of publication. The submissions made by air carriers shall forthwith be communicated to the other Member States concerned and to the Commission.

(e) The invitation to tender and subsequent contract shall cover, *inter alia*, the following points—

    (i) the standards required by the public service obligation;

    (ii) rules concerning amendment and termination of the contract, in particular to take account of unforeseeable changes;

    (iii) the period of validity of the contract;

    (iv) penalties in the event of failure to comply with the contract.

(f) The selection among the submissions shall be made as soon as possible taking into consideration the adequacy of the service, including the prices and conditions which can be quoted to users, and the cost of the compensation required from the Member State(s) concerned, if any.

(g) Notwithstanding subparagraph (f), a period of two months shall elapse after the deadline for submission of tenders before any selection is made, in order to permit other Member States to submit comments.

(h) A Member State may reimburse an air carrier, which has been selected under subparagraph (f), for satisfying standards required by a public service obligation imposed under this paragraph; such reimbursement shall take into account the costs and revenue generated by the service.

(i) Member States shall take the measures necessary to ensure that any decision taken under this Article can be reviewed effectively and, in particular, as soon as possible on the grounds that such decisions have infringed Community law or national rules implementing that law.

(j) When a public service obligation has been imposed in accordance with subparagraphs (a) and (c) then air carriers shall be able to offer seat-only sales only if the air service in question meets all the requirements of the public service obligation. Consequently that air service shall be considered as a scheduled air service.

(k) Subparagraph (d) shall not apply in any case in which another Member State concerned proposes a satisfactory alternative means of fulfilling the same public service obligation.

2.   Paragraph 1(d) shall not apply to routes where other forms of transport can ensure an adequate and uninterrupted service when the capacity offered exceeds 30 000 seats per year.

3.   At the request of a Member State which considers that the development of a route is being unduly restricted by the terms of paragraph 1, or on its own initiative, the Commission shall carry out an investigation and within two months of receipt of the request shall take a decision on the basis of all relevant factors on whether paragraph 1 shall continue to apply in respect of the route concerned.

4.   The Commission shall communicate its decision to the Council and to the Member States. Any Member State may refer the Commission's decision to the Council within a time limit of one month. The Council, acting by a qualified majority, may take a different decision within a period of one month.

[4447]

Article 5

On domestic routes for which at the time of entry into force of this Regulation an exclusive concession has been granted by law or contract, and where other forms of transport cannot ensure an adequate and uninterrupted service, such a concession may continue until its expiry date or for three years, whichever deadline comes first.

[4448]

Article 6

1.   Notwithstanding Article 3, a Member State may, where one of the air carriers licensed by it has started to operate a scheduled passenger air service with aircraft of no more than 80 seats on a new route between regional airports where the capacity does not exceed 30 000 seats per year, refuse a scheduled air service by another air carrier for a period of two years, unless it is operated with aircraft of not more than 80 seats, or it is operated in such a way that not more than 80 seats are available for sale between the two airports in question on each flight.

2.   Article 4(3) and (4) shall apply in relation to paragraph 1 of this Article.

[4449]

Article 7

In operating air services, a Community air carrier shall be permitted by the Member State(s) concerned to combine air services and use the same flight number.

[4450]

Article 8

1.   This Regulation shall not affect a Member State's right to regulate without discrimination on grounds of nationality or identity of the air carrier, the distribution of traffic between the airports within an airport system.

2.   The exercise of traffic rights shall be subject to published Community, national, regional or local operational rules relating to safety, the protection of the environment and the allocation of slots.

3.   At the request of a Member State or on its own initiative the Commission shall examine the application of paragraphs 1 and 2 and, within one month of receipt of a request and after consulting the Committee referred to in Article 11, decide whether the Member State may continue to apply the measure. The Commission shall communicate its decision to the Council and to the Member States.

4.   Any Member State may refer the Commission's decision to the Council within a time limit of one month. The Council, acting by a qualified majority, may in exceptional circumstances take a different decision within a period of one month.

5.   When a Member State decides to constitute a new airport system or modify an existing one it shall inform the other Member States and the Commission. After having verified that the airports are grouped together as serving the same city or conurbation the Commission shall publish a revised Annex II in the *Official Journal of the European Communities*.

[4451]

Article 9

1.   When serious congestion and/or environmental problems exist the Member State responsible may, subject to this Article, impose conditions on, limit or refuse the exercise of traffic rights, in particular when other modes of transport can provide satisfactory levels of service.

2.   Action taken by a Member State in accordance with paragraph 1 shall—
— be non-discriminatory on grounds of nationality or identity of air carriers,
— have a limited period of validity, not exceeding three years, after which it shall be reviewed,
— not unduly affect the objectives of this Regulation,
— not unduly distort competition between air carriers,
— not be more restrictive than necessary in order to relieve the problems.

3. When a Member State considers that action under paragraph 1 is necessary it shall, at least three months before the entry into force of the action, inform the other Member States and the Commission, providing adequate justification for the action. The action may be implemented unless within one month of receipt of the information a Member State concerned contests the action or the Commission, in accordance with paragraph 4, takes it up for further examination.

4. At the request of a Member State or on its own initiative the Commission shall examine action referred to in paragraph 1. When the Commission, within one month of having been informed under paragraph 3, takes the action up for examination it shall at the same time indicate whether the action may be implemented, wholly or partially, during the examination taking into account in particular the possibility of irreversible effects. After consulting the Committee referred to in Article 11 the Commission shall, one month after having received all necessary information, decide whether the action is appropriate and in conformity with this Regulation and not in any other way contrary to Community law. The Commission shall communicate its decision to the Council and the Member States. Pending such decision the Commission may decide on interim measures including the suspension, in whole or in part, of the action, taking into account in particular the possibility of irreversible effects.

5. Notwithstanding paragraphs 3 and 4, a Member State may take the necessary action to deal with sudden problems of short duration provided that such action is consistent with paragraph 2. The Commission and the Member State(s) shall be informed without delay of such action with its adequate justification. If the problems necessitating such action continue to exist for more than 14 days the Member State shall inform the Commission and the other Member States accordingly and may, with the agreement of the Commission, prolong the action for further periods of up to 14 days. At the request of the Member State(s) involved or on its own initiative the Commission may suspend this action if it does not meet the requirements of paragraphs 1 and 2 or is otherwise contrary to Community law.

6. Any Member State may refer the Commission's decision under paragraph 4 or 5 to the Council within a time limit of one month. The Council, acting by a qualified majority, may in exceptional circumstances take a different decision within a period of one month.

7. When a decision taken by a Member State in accordance with this Article limits the activity of a Community air carrier on an intra-Community route, the same conditions or limitation shall apply to all Community air carriers on the same route. When the decision involves the refusal of new or additional services, the same treatment shall be given to all requests by Community air carriers for new or additional services on that route.

8. Without prejudice to Article 8(1) and except with the agreement of the Member State(s) involved, a Member State shall not authorise an air carrier—

    (a) to establish a new service, or

    (b) to increase the frequency of an existing service,

between a specific airport in its territory and another Member State for such time as an air carrier licensed by that other Member State is not permitted, on the basis of slot-allocation rules as provided for in Article 8(2), to establish a new service or to increase frequencies on an existing service to the airport in question, pending the adoption by the Council and the coming into force of a Regulation on a code of conduct on slot-allocation based on the general principle of non-discrimination on the grounds of nationality.

Article 10

1.   Capacity limitations shall not apply to air services covered by this Regulation except as set out in Articles 8 and 9 and in this Article.

2.   Where the application of paragraph 1 has led to serious financial damage for the scheduled air carrier(s) licensed by a Member State, the Commission shall carry out a review at the request of that Member State and, on the basis of all relevant factors, including the market situation and in particular whether a situation exists whereby the opportunities of air carriers of that Member State to effectively compete in the market are unduly affected, the financial position of the air carrier(s) concerned and the capacity utilisation achieved, shall take a decision on whether the capacity for scheduled air services to and from that State should be stabilised for a limited period.

3.   The Commission shall communicate its decision to the Council and to the Member States. Any Member State may refer the Commission's decision to the Council within a time limit of one month. The Council, acting by a qualified majority, may in exceptional circumstances take a different decision within a period of one month.

[4453]

Article 11

1.   The Commission shall be assisted by an Advisory Committee composed of the representatives of the Member States and chaired by the representative of the Commission.

2.   The Committee shall advise the Commission on the application of Articles 9 and 10.

3.   Furthermore, the Committee may be consulted by the Commission on any other question concerning the application of this Regulation.

4.   The Committee shall draw up its rules of procedure.

[4454]

Article 12

1.   In order to carry out its duties under this Regulation the Commission may obtain all necessary information from the Member States concerned, which shall also ensure the provision of information by air carriers licensed by them.

2.   When the information requested is not supplied within the time limit fixed by the Commission, or is supplied in incomplete form, the Commission shall by decision addressed to the Member State concerned require the information to be supplied. The decision shall specify what information is required and fix an appropriate time limit within which it is to be supplied.

[4455]

Article 13

The Commission shall publish a report on the application of this Regulation by 1 April 1994 and periodically thereafter.

[4456]

Article 14

1.   Member States and the Commission shall cooperate in implementing this Regulation.

2.   Confidential information obtained in application of this Regulation shall be covered by professional secrecy.

[4457]

Article 15

Regulation (EEC) No 2343/90 and 294/91 are hereby replaced with the exceptions of Article 2(e)(ii) and of Annex I to Regulation (EEC) No 2343/90, as interpreted by Annex II to this Regulation, and Article 2(b) of and the Annex to Regulation (EEC) No 294/91.

[4458]

Article 16

This Regulation shall enter into force on 1 January 1993.

[4459]

This Regulation shall be binding in its entirety and directly applicable in all Member States.

Done at Brussels, 23 July 1992

ANNEX I
LIST OF CATEGORY 1 AIRPORTS

BELGIUM:	Brussels-Zaventem	IRELAND:	Dublin
DENMARK:	Copenhagen airport system	ITALY:	Rome airport system
			Milan airport system
GERMANY:	Frankfurt-Rhein/Main	NETHERLANDS:	Amsterdam-Schiphol
	Düsseldorf-Lohausen	PORTUGAL:	Lisbon
	Munich		Faro
	Berlin airport system	UNITED KINGDOM:	London airport system
SPAIN:	Palma-Mallorca		Luton
	Madrid-Barajas	[AUSTRIA:	Vienna
	Malaga	Finland:	Helsinki-Vantaab
	Las Palmas		Helsingfors Vanda
GREECE:	Athens-Hellinikon	Sweden:	Stockholm
	Thessalonika-Macedonia		airport system]
FRANCE:	Paris airport system		

[4460]

NOTES

    Words in square brackets inserted by the 1994 Act of Accession of the Kingdom of Norway, the Republic of Austria, the Republic of Finland and the Kingdom of Sweden, Annex I(VI)(D)(1)(a), as adjusted by Council Decision 95/1/EC, Annex I(VI)(D)(1)(a).

ANNEX II
LIST OF AIRPORT SYSTEMS

DENMARK:	Copenhagen–Kastrup/Roskilde
GERMANY:	Berlin–Tegel/Schönefeld/Tempelhof
FRANCE:	Paris–Charles De Gaulle/Orly/Le Bourget
	Lyon–Bron–Satolas
ITALY:	Rome–Fiumicino/Ciampino
	Milan–Linate/Malpensa/Bergamo (Orio al Serio)
	Venice–Tessera/Treviso
UNITED KINGDOM:	London–Heathrow/Gatwick/Stansted
[Sweden:	Stockholm –Arlanda/Bromma]

[4461]

NOTES
Words in square brackets inserted by the 1994 Act of Accession of the Kingdom of Norway, the Republic of Austria, the Republic of Finland and the Kingdom of Sweden, Annex I(VI)(D)(1)(a), as adjusted by Council Decision 95/1/EC, Annex I(VI)(D)(1)(a).

ANNEX III
INTERPRETATION REFERRED TO IN ARTICLE 15

Under the terms of Annex I to Regulation (EEC) No 2343/90 the air carrier Scanair, which is structured and organised exactly as Scandinavian Airlines System, is to be considered in the same way as the air carrier Scandinavian Airlines System.

[4462]

COUNCIL REGULATION

of 23 July 1992

on fares and rates for air services

(2409/92/EEC)

NOTES
Date of publication in OJ: OJ L240, 24.8.92, p 15.

THE COUNCIL OF THE EUROPEAN COMMUNITIES,

Having regard to the Treaty establishing the European Economic Community, and in particular Article 84(2) thereof,

Having regard to the proposal from the Commission,[1]

Having regard to the opinion of the European Parliament,[2]

Having regard to the opinion of the Economic and Social Committee,[3]

Whereas it is important to establish an air transport policy for the internal market over a period expiring on 31 December 1992 as provided for in Article 8a of the Treaty;

Whereas the internal market shall comprise an area without internal frontiers in which the free movement of goods, persons and capital is ensured;

Whereas Council Decision 87/601/EEC of 14 December 1987 on fares for scheduled air services between Member States[4] and Council Regulation (EEC) No 2342/90 of 24 July 1990 on fares for scheduled air services[5] constitute the first steps towards achieving the internal market in respect of air fares;

Whereas air fares should normally be determined freely by market forces;

Whereas it is appropriate to complement price freedom with adequate safeguards for the interests of consumers and industry;

Whereas it is appropriate to deal with all matters of pricing in the same Regulation;

Whereas this Regulation replaces Regulation (EEC) No 2342/90 and partially replaces Council Regulation (EEC) No 294/91 of 4 February 1991 on the operation of air cargo services between Member States,[6]

NOTES
[1]   OJ C258, 4.10.91, p 2.
[2]   OJ C125, 18.5.92, p 150.
[3]   OJ C169, 6.7.92, p 15.
[4]   OJ L374, 31.12.87, p 12.
[5]   OJ L217, 11.8.90, p 1.
[6]   OJ L36, 8.2.91, p 1.

HAS ADOPTED THIS REGULATION—

Article 1

1.   This Regulation concerns the criteria and procedures to be applied for the establishment of fares and rates on air services for carriage wholly within the Community.

2.   Without prejudice to paragraph 3, this Regulation shall not apply—
   (a) to fares and rates charged by air carriers other than Community air carriers;
   (b) to fares and rates established by public service obligation, in accordance with Council Regulation (EEC) No 2408/92 of 23 July 1992 on access for Community air carriers to intra-Community air routes.[1]

3.   Only Community air carriers shall be entitled to introduce new products or lower fares than the ones existing for identical products.

[4463]

NOTES
[1]   OJ L240, 24.8.92, p 8.

Article 2

For the purpose of this Regulation—
   (a) "air fares" means the prices expressed in ecus or in local currency to be paid by passengers to air carriers or their agents for the carriage of them and for the carriage of their baggage on air services and any conditions under which those prices apply, including remuneration and conditions offered to agency and other auxiliary services;
   (b) "seat rates" means the prices expressed in ecus or in local currency to be paid by charterers to air carriers for the carriage on air services of the charterer or its customers and their baggage and any conditions under which those prices apply, including remuneration and conditions offered to agency and other auxiliary services;
   (c) "charter fares" means the prices expressed in ecus or in local currency to be paid by passengers to charterers for services which constitute or include their carriage and the carriage of their baggage on air services and any

conditions under which those prices apply, including remuneration and conditions offered to agency or other auxiliary services;

(d) "cargo rates" means the prices expressed in ecus or in local currency to be paid for the carriage of cargo and the conditions under which those prices apply, including remuneration and conditions offered to agency and other auxiliary services;

(e) "standard cargo rates" means the rates which the air carrier would normally quote including the availability of normal discounts;

(f) "air service" means a flight or a series of flights carrying passengers, cargo and/or mail for remuneration and/or hire;

(g) "air carrier" means an air transport undertaking with a valid operating licence;

(h) "Community air carrier" means an air carrier with a valid operating licence issued by a Member State in accordance with Council Regulation (EEC) No 2407/92 of 23 July 1992 on licensing of air carriers;[1]

(i) "Member State(s) concerned" means the Member State(s) between or within which the fare or rate is applied;

(j) "Member State(s) involved" means the Member State(s) concerned and the Member State(s) where the air carrier(s) operating the air service is (are) licensed;

(k) "basic fare" means the lowest fully flexible fare, available on a one way and return basis, which is offered for sale at least to the same extent as that of any other fully flexible fare offered on the same air service.

[4464]

NOTES

[1]   OJ L240, 24.8.92, p 1.

Article 3

Charter fares and seat and cargo rates charged by Community air carriers shall be set by free agreement between the parties to the contract of carriage.

[4465]

Article 4

Air carriers operating within the Community shall inform the general public, on request, of all air fares and standard cargo rates.

[4466]

Article 5

1.   Without prejudice to this Regulation, Community air carriers shall freely set air fares.

2.   Member State(s) concerned may, without discrimination on grounds of nationality or identity of air carriers, require air fares to be filed with them in the form prescribed by them. Such filing shall not be required to be submitted more than 24 hours (including a working day) before the air fares come into effect, except in the case of matching of an existent fare for which no more than prior notification is required.

3.   Before 1 April 1997, a Member State may require that air fares on domestic routes where no more than one carrier licensed by it, or two carriers licensed by it under a joint operation, operate have to be filed more than one working day but no more than one month before the air fares come into effect.

4. An air fare may be available for sale and carriage as long as it is not withdrawn in accordance with Article 6 or Article 7.

Article 6

1. Subject to the procedures of this Article, a Member State concerned may decide, at any moment—
  (a) to withdraw a basic fare which, taking into account the whole fare structure for the route in question and other relevant factors including the competitive market situation, is excessively high to the disadvantage of users in relation to the long term fully-allocated relevant costs of the air carrier including a satisfactory return on capital;
  (b) to stop, in a non-discriminatory way, further fare decreases in a market, whether on a route or a group of routes, when market forces have led to sustained downward development of air fares deviating significantly from ordinary seasonal pricing movements and resulting in widespread losses among all air carriers concerned for the air services concerned, taking into account the long term fully-allocated relevant costs of the air carriers.

2. A decision taken pursuant to paragraph 1 shall be notified with reasons to the Commission and to all other Member State(s) involved, as well as to the air carrier(s) concerned.

3. If within fourteen days of the date of receiving notification no other Member State concerned or the Commission has notified disagreement stating its reasons on the basis of paragraph 1, the Member State which has taken the decision pursuant to paragraph 1 may instruct the air carrier(s) concerned to withdraw the basic fare or to abstain from further fare decreases, as appropriate.

4. In the case of disagreement, any Member State involved may require consultations to review the situation. The consultations shall take place within 14 days of being requested, unless otherwise agreed.

Article 7

1. At the request of a Member State involved the Commission shall examine whether a decision to act or not to act pursuant to Article 6 complies with the criteria of Article 6(1). The Member State shall at the same time inform the other Member State(s) concerned and the air carrier(s) concerned. The Commission shall forthwith publish in the *Official Journal of the European Communities* that the air fare(s) have been submitted for examination.

2. Notwithstanding paragraph 1, the Commission may, on the basis of a complaint made by a party with a legitimate interest, investigate whether air fares comply with the criteria of Article 6(1). The Commission shall forthwith publish in the *Official Journal of the European Communities* that the air fare(s) have been submitted for examination.

3. An air fare in force at the time of its submission for examination in accordance with paragraph 1 shall remain in force during the examination. However, where the Commission, or the Council in accordance with paragraph 8, has decided within the previous six months that a similar or lower level of the basic fare on the city-pair concerned does not comply with the criteria of Article 6(1)(a), the air fare shall not remain in force during the examination.

Furthermore, where paragraph 6 has been applied, the air carrier concerned may not, during the examination by the Commission, apply a higher basic fare than the one which was applicable immediately before the basic fare under examination.

4.   Following consultations with the Member States concerned, the Commission shall take a decision as soon as possible and in any event not later than twenty working days after having received sufficient information from the air carrier(s) concerned. The Commission shall take into account all information received from interested parties.

5.   When an air carrier does not supply the information requested within the time limit fixed by the Commission, or supplies it in incomplete form, the Commission shall by decision require the information to be supplied. The decision shall specify what information is required and fix an appropriate time limit within which it is to be supplied.

6.   The Commission may, by decision, decide that an air fare in force shall be withdrawn pending its final determination where an air carrier supplies incorrect information or produces it in incomplete form or does not supply it within the time limit fixed by decision under paragraph 5.

7.   The Commission shall without delay communicate its reasoned decision under paragraphs 4 and 6 to the Member State(s) concerned and to the air carrier(s) concerned.

8.   A Member State concerned may refer the Commission's decision under paragraph 4 to the Council within a time limit of one month. The Council, acting by a qualified majority, may take a different decision within a period of one month.

9.   The Member States concerned shall ensure that the Commission's decision is enforced, unless the decision is under examination by the Council or the Council has taken a different decision in accordance with paragraph 8.

[4469]

Article 8

At least once a year the Commission shall consult on air fares and related matters with representatives of air transport user organisations in the Community, for which purpose the Commission shall supply appropriate information to participants.

[4470]

Article 9

The Commission shall publish a report on the application of this Regulation by 1 April 1994 and periodically thereafter.

[4471]

Article 10

1.   Member States and the Commission shall cooperate in implementing this Regulation, particularly as regards collection of information for the report referred to in Article 9.

2.   Confidential information obtained in application of this Regulation shall be covered by professional secrecy.

[4472]

Article 11

Regulation (EEC) No 2342/90 is hereby repealed.

[4473]

Article 12

This Regulation shall enter into force on 1 January 1993.

[4474]

This Regulation shall be binding in its entirety and directly applicable in all Member States.

Done at Brussels, 23 July 1992

COUNCIL REGULATION

of 18 January 1993

on common rules for the allocation of slots at Community airports

(95/93/EEC)

NOTES

Date of publication in OJ: OJ L14, 22.1.93, p 1.

THE COUNCIL OF THE EUROPEAN COMMUNITIES,

Having regard to the Treaty establishing the European Economic Community, and in particular Article 84(2) thereof,

Having regard to the proposal from the Commission,[1]

Having regard to the opinion of the European Parliament,[2]

Having regard to the opinion of the Economic and Social Committee,[3]

Whereas there is a growing imbalance between the expansion of the air transport system in Europe and the availability of adequate airport infrastructure to meet that demand; whereas there is, as a result, an increasing number of congested airports in the Community;

Whereas the allocation of slots at congested airports should be based on neutral, transparent and non-discriminatory rules;

Whereas the requirement of neutrality is best guaranteed when the decision to coordinate an airport is taken by the Member State responsible for that airport on the basis of objective criteria;

Whereas under certain conditions, in order to facilitate operations, it is desirable that a Member State should be able to designate an airport as coordinated provided that principles of transparency, neutrality and non-discrimination are met;

Whereas the Member State responsible for the coordinated airport should ensure the appointment of a coordinator whose neutrality should be unquestioned;

Whereas transparency of information is an essential element for ensuring an objective procedure for slot allocation;

Whereas the principles governing the existing system of slot allocation could be the basis of this Regulation provided that this system evolves in harmony with the evolution of new transport developments in the Community;

Whereas it is Community policy to facilitate competition and to encourage entrance into the market, as provided for in Council Regulation (EEC) No 2408/92 of 23 July 1992 on access for Community air carriers to intra-Community air routes,[4] and whereas these objectives require strong support for carriers who intend to start operations on intra-Community routes;

Whereas the existing system makes provision for grandfather rights;

Whereas there should also be provisions to allow new entrants into the Community market;

Whereas it is necessary to make special provisions, under limited circumstances, for the maintenance of adequate domestic air services to regions of the Member State concerned;

Whereas it is also necessary to avoid situations where, owing to a lack of available slots, the benefits of liberalisation are unevenly spread and competition is distorted;

Whereas it is desirable to make the best use of the existing slots in order to meet the objectives set out above;

Whereas it is desirable that third countries offer Community carriers equivalent treatment;

Whereas the application of the provisions of this Regulation shall be without prejudice to the competition rules of the Treaty, in particular Articles 85 and 86;

Whereas arrangements for greater cooperation over the use of Gibraltar airport were agreed in London on 2 December 1987 by the Kingdom of Spain and the United Kingdom in a joint declaration by the Ministers of Foreign Affairs of the two countries, and such arrangements have yet to come into operation;

Whereas this Regulation should be reviewed after a fixed period of operation to assess its functioning,

---

NOTES
1   OJ C43, 19.2.91, p 3.
2   OJ C13, 20.1.92, p 446.
3   OJ C339, 31.12.91, p 41.
4   OJ L240, 24.8.92, p 8.

HAS ADOPTED THIS REGULATION—

Article 1

Scope

1.   This Regulation shall apply to the allocation of slots at Community airports.

2.   The application of this Regulation to the airport of Gibraltar is understood to be without prejudice to the respective legal positions of the Kingdom of Spain and the United Kingdom with regard to the dispute over sovereignty over the territory in which the airport is situated.

3.   Application of the provisions of this Regulation to Gibraltar airport shall be suspended until the arrangements in the joint declarations made by the Foreign Ministers of the Kingdom of Spain and the United Kingdom on 2 December 1987 have come into operation. The Governments of Spain and the United Kingdom will so inform the Council of that date.

[4475]

Article 2

Definitions

For the purpose of this Regulation—
  (a) "slot" shall mean the scheduled time of arrival or departure available or allocated to an aircraft movement on a specific date at an airport coordinated under the terms of this Regulation;
  (b) "new entrant" shall mean—
    (i) an air carrier requesting slots at an airport on any day and holding or having been allocated fewer than four slots at that airport on that day, or,
    (ii) an air carrier requesting slots for a non-stop service between two Community airports where at most two other air carriers operate a direct service between these airports or airport systems on that day and holding or having been allocated fewer than four slots at that airport on that day for that non-stop service.
  An air carrier holding more than 3% of the total slots available on the day in question at a particular airport, or more than 2% of the total slots available on the day in question in an airport system of which that airport forms part, shall not be considered as a new entrant at that airport;
  (c) "direct air service" shall mean a service between two airports including stopovers with the same aircraft and same flight number;
  (d) "scheduling period" shall mean either the summer or winter season as used in the schedules of air carriers;

(e) "Community air carrier" shall mean an air carrier with a valid operating licence issued by a Member State in accordance with Council Regulation (EEC) No 2407/92 of 23 July 1992 on licensing of air carriers;[1]

(f) "coordinated airport" shall mean an airport where a coordinator has been appointed to facilitate the operations of air carriers operating or intending to operate at that airport;

(g) "fully coordinated airport" shall mean a coordinated airport where, in order to land or take off, during the periods for which it is fully coordinated, it is necessary for an air carrier to have a slot allocated by a coordinator;

(h) "airport system" shall mean two or more airports grouped together and serving the same city or conurbation, as indicated in Annex II to Regulation (EEC) No 2408/92.

[4476]

NOTES
[1] OJ L240, 24.8.92, p 1.

Article 3

Conditions for airport coordination

1.   A Member State shall be under no obligation to designate any airport as coordinated save in accordance with the provisions of this Article.

2.   A Member State may, however, provide for any airport to be designated as a coordinated airport provided that principles of transparency, neutrality and non-discrimination are met.

3. (i) When air carriers representing more than a half of the operations at an airport and/or the airport authority consider that capacity is insufficient for actual or planned operations at certain periods or

   (ii) when new entrants encounter serious problems in securing slots or

   (iii) when a Member State considers it necessary,

the Member State shall ensure that a thorough capacity analysis is carried out, having regard to commonly recognised methods, as soon as possible at the airport with the purpose of determining possibilities of increasing the capacity in the short term through infrastructure or operational changes, and to determine the time frame envisaged to resolve the problems. The analysis shall be updated periodically. Both the analysis and the method underlying it shall be made available to interested parties.

4.   If, after consultation with the air carriers using the airport regularly, their representative organisations, the airport authorities, air traffic control authorities and passengers' organisations where such organisations exist, the analysis does not indicate possibilities of resolving the serious problems in the short term, the Member State shall ensure that the airport shall be designated as fully coordinated for the periods during which capacity problems occur.

5.   When a capacity sufficient to meet actual or planned operations is provided at a fully coordinated airport, its designation as a fully coordinated airport shall be lifted.

[4477]

Article 4

The coordinator

1.   The Member State responsible for a coordinated or fully coordinated airport shall ensure the appointment of a natural or legal person with detailed knowledge of

air carrier scheduling coordination as airport coordinator after having consulted the air carriers using the airport regularly, their representative organisations and the airport authorities. The same coordinator may be appointed for more than one airport.

2.   A Member State shall ensure that the coordinator carries out his duties under this Regulation in an independent manner.

3.   The coordinator shall act in accordance with this Regulation in a neutral, non-discriminatory and transparent way.

4.   The coordinator shall participate in such international scheduling conferences of air carriers as are permitted by Community law.

5.   The coordinator shall be responsible for the allocation of slots.

6.   The coordinator shall monitor the use of slots.

7.   Where slots are allocated, the coordinator shall, on request and within a reasonable time, make available for review to all interested parties the following information—
   (a) historical slots by airline, chronologically, for all air carriers at the airport,
   (b) requested slots (initial submissions), by air carriers and chronologically, for all air carriers,
   (c) all allocated slots, and outstanding slot requests, listed individually in chronological order, by air carriers, for all air carriers,
   (d) remaining available slots,
   (e) full details on the criteria being used in the allocation.

8.   The information in paragraph 7 shall be made available at the latest at the time of the relevant scheduling conferences and as appropriate during the conferences and thereafter.

[4478]

Article 5

Coordination committee

1.   A Member State shall ensure that in an airport that has been designated as fully coordinated a coordination committee is set up to assist, in a consultative capacity, the coordinator referred to in Article 4. Participation in this committee shall be open to at least the air carriers and/or their representative organisations using the airport(s) regularly, the airport authorities concerned and representatives of the air traffic control. The same coordination committee may be designated for more than one airport.

The tasks of the coordination committee shall be, *inter alia*, to advise on—
   — possibilities for increasing the capacity determined in accordance with Article 6,
   — improvements to traffic conditions prevailing at the airport in question,
   — complaints on the allocation of slots as provided for in Article 8(7),
   — the methods of monitoring the use of allocated slots,
   — guidelines for allocation of slots, taking into account local conditions,
   — serious problems for new entrants as provided for in Article 10.

2.   Paragraph 1 may be applied to airports designated as coordinated under the provisions of Article 3.

[4479]

Article 6

Airport capacity

1. At an airport where slot allocation takes place, the competent authorities shall determine the capacity available for slot allocation twice yearly in cooperation with representatives of air traffic control, customs and immigration authorities and air carriers using the airport and/or their representative organisations and the airport coordinator, according to commonly recognised methods. Where the competent authority is not the airport authority it shall also be consulted.

This exercise shall be based on an objective analysis of possibilities of accommodating the air traffic, taking into account the different types of traffic at that airport.

The results of this exercise shall be provided to the airport coordinator in good time before the initial slot allocation takes place for the purpose of scheduling conferences.

2. Paragraph 1 may be applied to airports designated as coordinated under the provisions of Article 3.

[4480]

Article 7

Information for the coordinator

Air carriers operating or intending to operate at a coordinated or fully coordinated airport shall submit to the coordinator relevant information requested by the coordinator.

[4481]

Article 8

Process of slot allocation

1. (a) Subject to the provisions of Article 10, a slot that has been operated by an air carrier as cleared by the coordinator shall entitle that air carrier to claim the same slot in the next equivalent scheduling period.
   (b) In a situation where all slot requests cannot be accommodated to the satisfaction of the air carriers concerned, preference shall be given to commercial air services and in particular to scheduled services and programmed non-scheduled services.
   (c) The coordinator shall also take into account additional priority rules established by the air carrier industry and if possible additional guidelines recommended by the coordination committee allowing for local conditions, provided such guidelines respect Community law.

2. If a requested slot cannot be accommodated, the coordinator shall inform the requesting air carrier of the reasons therefor and shall indicate the nearest alternative slot.

3. The coordinator shall, at all times, endeavour to accommodate *ad hoc* slot requests for any type of aviation including general aviation. To this end, the slots available in the pool referred to in Article 10 but not yet allocated may be used, as may slots liberated at short notice.

4. Slots may be freely exchanged between air carriers or transferred by an air carrier from one route, or type of service, to another, by mutual agreement or as a result of a total or partial takeover or unilaterally. Any such exchanges or transfers shall be transparent and subject to confirmation of feasibility by the coordinator that—
   (a) airport operations would not be prejudiced;

(b) limitations imposed by a Member State according to Article 9 are respected;

(c) a change of use does not fall within the scope of Article 11.

5.   Slots allocated to new entrants operating a service between two Community airports may not be exchanged or transferred between air carriers or by an air carrier from one route to another as provided for in paragraph 4 for a period of two seasons.

6.   The Commission may establish, after consultations with air carriers, coordinators, and airport authorities, recommended standards for the automated systems which are used by the coordinators in order to ensure the proper implementation of Articles 4 and 7.

7.   Where there are complaints about the allocation of slots, the coordination committee shall consider the matter and may make proposals to the coordinator in an attempt to resolve the problems.

8.   If the problems cannot be resolved after consideration by the coordination committee, the Member State concerned may provide for mediation by an air carriers' representative organisation or other third party.

[4482]

Article 9

Regional services

1.   A Member State may reserve certain slots at a fully coordinated airport for domestic scheduled services—

   (a) on a route to an airport serving a peripheral or development region in its territory, any such route being considered vital for the economic development of the region in which the airport is located, on condition that—

      (i) the slots concerned are being used on that route at the time of entry into force of this Regulation;

      (ii) only one air carrier is operating on the route;

      (iii) no other mode of transport can provide an adequate service;

      (iv) the reservation of slots shall end when a second air carrier has established a domestic scheduled service on the route with the same number of frequencies as the first air carrier and operated it for at least a season;

   (b) on routes where public service obligations have been imposed under Community legislation.

2.   The procedures in Article 4(1)(d) to 4(1)(i) of Regulation (EEC) No 2408/92 shall be applied if another Community air carrier is interested in servicing the route and has not been able to obtain slots within one hour before or after the times requested of the coordinator.

3.   The Member State shall communicate to the Commission a list of routes for which slots have been so reserved at a fully coordinated airport. This shall first be done at the entry into force of this Regulation. The Commission shall publish an overview of the routes concerned in the *Official Journal of the European Communities* not later than two months after the communication.

[4483]

Article 10

Slot pool

1.   At an airport where slot allocation takes place, a pool shall be set up for each coordinated period and shall contain newly created slots, unused slots and slots which have been given up by a carrier during, or by the end of, the season or which otherwise become available.

2.   Any slot not utilised shall be withdrawn and placed in the appropriate slot pool unless the non-utilisation can be justified by reason of the grounds of the grounding of an aircraft type, or the closure of an airport or airspace or other similarly exceptional case.

3.   Slots which are allocated to an air carrier for the operation of a scheduled service or a programmed non-scheduled service on a particular moment of a day and for the same day of the week over a recognisable period up to one scheduling period shall not entitle that air carrier to the same series of slots in the next equivalent period, unless the air carrier can demonstrate to the satisfaction of the coordinator that they have been operated, as cleared by the coordinator, by that air carrier for at least 80% of the time during the period for which they have been allocated.

4.   Slots allocated to an air carrier before 31 January for the following summer season, or before 31 August for the following winter season, but which are returned to the coordinator for reallocation before those dates shall not be taken into account for the purposes of the usage calculation.

5.   If the 80% usage of the series of slots cannot be demonstrated, all the slots constituting that series shall be placed in the slot pool, unless the non-utilisation can be justified on the basis of any of the following reasons—

(a) unforeseeable and irresistible cases outside the air carrier's control leading to, for example—
    — grounding of the aircraft type generally used for the service in question, or
    — closure of an airport or airspace;

(b) problems relating to the starting up of a new scheduled passenger service with aircraft of no more than eighty seats on a route between a regional airport and the coordinated airport and where the capacity does not exceed 30 000 seats per year, or

(c) serious financial damage for a Community air carrier concerned, with, as a result, the granting of a temporary licence by the licensing authorities pending financial reorganisation of the air carrier in accordance with Article 5(5) of Regulation (EEC) No 2407/92;

(d) an interruption of a series of non-scheduled services due to cancellations by tour operators, in particular outside the usual peak period provided that overall slot usage does not fall below 70%;

(e) an interruption of a series of services due to action intended to affect these services, which makes it practically and/or technically impossible for the air carrier to carry out operations as planned.

6.   If serious problems continue to exist for new entrants, the Member State shall ensure that a meeting of the airport coordination committee is convened. The purpose of the meeting shall be to examine possibilities for remedying the situation. The Commission shall be invited to such a meeting.

7.   Without prejudice to Article 8(1) of Regulation (EEC) No 2408/92, slots placed in the pools shall be distributed among applicant carriers. 50% of these slots shall be allocated to new entrants unless requests by new entrants are less than 50%.

8.   A new entrant which has been offered slots within two hours before or after the time requested but has not accepted this offer shall not retain the new entrant status.

[4484]

[Article 10a

The events of 11 September 2001

For the purposes of Article 10(3), coordinators shall accept that air carriers are entitled to the same series of slots during summer scheduling season 2002 and winter scheduling season 2002/2003 as had been allocated to them on the date of 11 September 2001 for the summer scheduling season 2001 and the winter scheduling season 2001/2002 respectively.]

[4485]

NOTES

    Inserted by Regulation of the European Parliament and of the Council 894/2002/EC, Art 1.

Article 11

Safeguard mechanism

1.   Where a solution cannot be found under paragraph 2 and taking into account that competition between the air carriers concerned should not be distorted, an air carrier shall not be allowed to use the flexibility provided for in Article 8(4) for the purpose of introducing one or more additional frequencies on a route between a fully coordinated airport within the Community and an airport in another Member State, if another Community air carrier, licensed by another Member State, has not been able, despite serious and consistent efforts, to obtain landing and departure slots which can reasonably be used for providing one or more additional frequencies on the route within two hours before or after the times requested of the coordinator.

This provision shall not apply if the air carrier using the flexibility provided for in Article 8(4) does not exceed the frequencies of the other air carrier.

2.   Taking into account that competition between the air carriers concerned should not be distorted, the Member States responsible for the fully co-ordinated airport referred to in paragraph 1 shall endeavour to facilitate an agreement between the air carriers concerned.

An alternative solution to the problem should be sought such as—
—   endeavouring to ensure that the request for slots of the air carrier licensed by the other Member State is accommodated,
—   the reasonable use by that carrier of the flexibility provided for in Article 8(4).

3.   A Member State concerned may request the Commission to investigate the application of this Article within two months of an air carrier informing the coordinator of its intention to use the flexibility provided for in Article 8(4).

[4486]

Article 12

General provisions

1.   Whenever it appears that a third country, with respect to the allocation of slots at airports,

(a) does not grant Community air carriers treatment comparable to that granted by Member States to air carriers from that country, or

(b) does not grant Community air carriers *de facto* national treatment, or

(c) grants air carriers from other third countries more favourable treatment than Community air carriers,

appropriate action may be taken to remedy the situation in respect of the airport or airports concerned, including the suspension wholly or partially of the obligations of this Regulation in respect of an air carrier of that third country, in accordance with Community law.

2. Member States shall inform the Commission of any serious difficulties encountered, in law or in fact, by Community air carriers in obtaining slots at airports in third countries.

[4487]

Article 13

Report and cooperation

1. The Commission shall submit a report to the European Parliament and the Council on the operation of this Regulation three years after its entry into force. This report should include *inter alia* the following elements—

(a) the structure of the airline industry;

(b) progress made by the industry in reducing the non-use of slots;

(c) size of the slot pool, as defined in Article 10(1), each season at selected airports;

(d) volume of unsuccessful applications for slots each season at selected airports;

(e) number of new entrants applying for slots each season at selected airports;

(f) use of dispute procedures established within the terms of Article 8.

2. Member States and the Commission shall cooperate in the application of this Regulation, particularly as regards the collection of information for the report mentioned in paragraph 1.

[4488]

Article 14

Revision

The Council shall decide on the continuation or revision of this Regulation by 1 July 1997, on the basis of a proposal from the Commission to be submitted no later than 1 January 1996.

[4489]

Article 15

Entry into force

This Regulation shall enter into force on the thirtieth day following that of its publication in the *Official Journal of the European Communities*.

[4490]

This Regulation shall be binding in its entirety and directly applicable in all Member States.

Done at Brussels, 18 January 1993.

COMMISSION REGULATION

of 25 June 1993

on the application of Article 85(3) of the Treaty to certain categories of agreements and concerted practices concerning joint planning and coordination of schedules, joint operations, consultations on passenger and cargo tariffs on scheduled air services and slot allocation at airports

(1617/93/EEC)

NOTES

Date of publication in OJ: OJ L155, 26.6.93, p 18.

THE COMMISSION OF THE EUROPEAN COMMUNITIES,

Having regard to the Treaty establishing the European Economic Community,

Having regard to Council Regulation (EEC) No 3976/87 of 14 December 1987 on the application of Article 85(3) of the Treaty to certain categories of agreements and concerted practices in the air transport sector,[1] as last amended by Regulation (EEC) No 2411/92,[2] and in particular Article 2 thereof,

Having published a draft of this Regulation,[3]

Having consulted the Advisory Committee on Agreements and Dominant Positions in Air Transport,

Whereas—

(1) Regulation (EEC) No 3976/87 empowers the Commission to apply Article 85(3) of the Treaty by regulation to certain categories of agreements, decisions or concerted practices relating directly or indirectly to the provision of air transport services.

(2) Agreements, decisions or concerted practices concerning joint planning and coordination of schedules, joint operations, consultations on tariffs and slot allocation at airports are liable to restrict competition and affect trade between Member States.

(3) Joint planning and coordination of the schedule of an air service can help to ensure the maintenance of services at less busy times of the day, during less busy periods or on less busy routes, and to develop onward connections, thus benefiting air transport users. However, any clauses concerning extra flights must not require the approval of the other parties or involve financial penalties. The arrangements must also allow parties to withdraw from them at reasonably short notice.

(4) Arrangements whereby a smaller airline receives marketing and financial support from another airline may help that smaller airline to operate air services on new or less busy routes. However, in order to avoid restrictions which are not indispensable to the attainment of that aim, the duration of such joint operations must be limited to the time necessary to gain sufficient commercial standing. The block exemption must not be granted to joint operations where both parties could reasonably be expected to operate the air service independently. Those conditions are without prejudice to the possibility, in appropriate cases, of an application made under Article 5 of Council Regulation (EEC) No 3975/87,[4] as last amended by Regulation (EEC) No 2410/92,[5] with a view to obtaining an individual exemption where the conditions are not met or where the parties need to extend the duration of the joint operation. In particular where the parties wish to avail themselves, through a joint operation, of the market access opportunities created by Council Regulation (EEC) No 2408/92[6] on routes which are neither new nor less busy, but which otherwise fulfil the conditions set forth herein, an individual exemption may be warranted.

(5) Consultations on passenger and cargo tariffs may contribute to the generalised acceptance of interlinable fares and rates to the benefit of air carriers as well as air transport users. However, consultations must not exceed the aim of facilitating interlining. Council Regulation (EEC) No 2409/92 of 23 July 1992 on fares and rates for air services,[7] is based on the principle of free pricing and therefore increases the possibility of price competition in air transport. Hence, competition may not be eliminated thereby. Consultations between air carriers on passenger and cargo tariffs may therefore be permitted for the time being, provided that they are limited to fares and rates which give rise to actual interlining, that the participation in such consultations is optional, that they do not lead to an agreement in respect of fares, rates or related conditions, that in the interests of transparency

the Commission and the Member States concerned can send observers to them, and that air carriers participating in the consultation mechanism are obliged to interline with all other carriers concerned, at the tariffs applied by the carrying airline for the tariff category under discussion.

The Commission will reassess the effects of tariff consultations on price competition in the light of the operation of Regulation (EEC) No 2409/92 and in the light of the development of the Community air transport industry, and may make appropriate changes to the exemption in the course of its lifetime;

(6) Arrangements on slot allocation at airports and airport scheduling can improve the utilisation of airport capacity and airspace, facilitate air-traffic control and help to spread the supply of air transport services from the airport. However, if competition is to be eliminated, entry to congested airports must remain possible. In order to provide a satisfactory degree of security and transparency, such arrangements can only be accepted if all air carriers concerned can participate in the negotiations, and if the allocation is made on a non-discriminatory and transparent basis.

(7) In accordance with Article 4 of Regulation (EEC) No 3976/87, this Regulation should apply with retroactive effect to agreements, decisions and concerted practices in existence on the date of entry into force of this Regulation, provided that they meet the conditions for exemption set out in this Regulation.

(8) In conformity with Article 7 of Regulation (EEC) No 3976/87, this Regulation should also specify the circumstances in which the Commission may withdraw the block exemption in individual cases.

(9) No applications under Article 3 or 5 of Regulation (EEC) No 3975/87 need be made in respect of agreements automatically exempted by this Regulation. However, when real doubt exists, undertakings may request the Commission to declare whether their arrangements comply with this Regulation.

(10) This Regulation is without prejudice to the application of Article 86 of the Treaty,

---

NOTES

1   OJ L374, 31.12.87, p 9.
2   OJ L240, 24.8.92, p 19.
3   OJ C253, 30.9.92, p 5.
4   OJ L374, 31.12.87, p 1.
5   OJ L240, 24.8.92, p 18.
6   OJ L240, 24.8.92, p 8.
7   OJ L240, 24.8.92, p 15.

HAS ADOPTED THIS REGULATION—

TITLE I
EXEMPTIONS

Article 1

Pursuant to Article 85(3) of the Treaty and subject to the provisions of this Regulation, it is hereby declared that Article 85(1) of the Treaty shall not apply to agreements between undertakings in the air transport sector, decisions by associations of such undertakings and concerted practices between such undertakings which have as their purpose one or more of the following—

   —   . . . ,

   [—   the holding of consultations on tariffs for the carriage of passengers, with their baggage, on scheduled air services between Community airports,]

   —   slot-allocation and airport scheduling in so far as they concern air services between airports in the Community.

[4491]

NOTES
   Words omitted repealed by Commission Regulation 1083/99/EC, Art 1(1); words in square brackets substituted by Commission Regulation 1523/96/EC, Art 1(1).

TITLE II
SPECIAL PROVISIONS

Articles 2, 3

(Repealed by Commission Regulation 1083/99/EC, Art 1(2).)

Article 4

[Special provisions for consultations on passenger tariffs]

1.   [The exemption concerning the holding of consultations on passenger tariffs shall apply only if the following conditions are met—]

[(a) the participants only discuss air fares to be paid by air transport users directly to a participating air carrier or to its authorised agents, for carriage as passengers on a scheduled service, as well as the conditions relating to those fares and rates. The consultations shall not extend to the capacity for which such tariffs are to be available;]

(b) the consultations give rise to interlining, that is to say, air transport users must be able, in respect of the types of fares or rates and of the seasons which were the subject of the consultations—

   (i) to combine on a single transportation document the service which was the subject of the consultations, with services on the same or on connecting routes operated by other air carriers, whereby the applicable fares, rates and conditions are set by the airline(s) effecting carriage; and

   (ii) in so far as is permitted by the conditions governing the initial reservation, to change a reservation on a service which was the subject of the consultations onto a service on the same route operated by another air carrier at the fares, rates and conditions applied by that other carrier;

provided that an air carrier may refuse to allow such combinations and changes of reservation for objective and non-discriminatory reasons of a technical or commercial nature, in particular where the air carrier effecting carriage is concerned with the credit worthiness of the air carrier who would be collecting payment for this carriage; in such case the latter air carrier must be notified thereof in writing;

[(c) the passenger tariffs which are the subject of the consultations are applied by participating air carriers without discrimination on grounds of passenger nationality or place of residence;]

(d) participation in the consultations is voluntary and open to any air carrier who operates or intends to operate direct or indirect services on the route concerned;

[(e) the consultations are not binding on participants, that is to say, following the consultations the participants retain the right to act independently in respect of passenger tariffs;]

(f) the consultations do not entail agreement on agents' remuneration or other elements of the tariffs discussed;

(g) where filing of tariffs is required, each participant individually files each tariff which was not the subject of the consultations, with the competent authorities of the Member States concerned; in so doing it may act itself or through its filing agent or through its general sales agent.

2. (a) The Commission and the Member States concerned shall be entitled to send observers to tariff consultations. For this purpose, air carriers shall give the Member States concerned and the Commission the same notice as

is given to participants, but not less than 10 days' notice, of the date, venue and subject matter of the consultations.
(b) Such notice shall be given—
  (i) to the Member States concerned according to procedures to be established by the competent authorities of those Member States;
  (ii) to the Commission according to procedures to be published in the *Official Journal of the European Communities.*
(c) A full report on these consultations shall be submitted to the Commission by or on behalf of the air carriers involved at the same time as it is submitted to participants, but not later than six weeks after those consultations were held.

3. Air carriers participating in consultations on passenger tariffs shall collect data as from 1 September 2002 with regard to—
  (a) the relative part of tariffs set in the consultations of all fare traffic within the EEA;
  (b) the extent to which tickets at tariffs set in the consultations are actually used for interlining;
  (c) the extent to which tickets which are not at tariffs set in the consultations are actually used for interlining.

The data collected shall be provided to the Commission by or on behalf of the air carriers involved at six-monthly intervals.]

[4492]

NOTES
Para 1: words in square brackets substituted by Commission Regulation 1523/96/EC, Art 1(2).
Para 3: added by Commission Regulation 1105/2002/EC, Art 1(1).

Article 5

Special provisions for slot allocation and airport scheduling

1. The exemption concerning slot allocation and airport scheduling shall apply only if the following conditions are met—
  (a) the consultations on slot allocation and airport scheduling are open to all air carriers having expressed an interest in the slots which are the subject of the consultations;
  (b) rules of priority are established and supplied without discrimination, that is to say that they neither directly nor indirectly relate to carrier identity or nationality or category of service, take into account constraints or air traffic distribution rules laid down by competent national or international authorities and give due consideration to the needs of the travelling publics and of the airport concerned. Subject to paragraph (d), such rules of priority may take account of rights acquired by air carriers through the use of particular slots in the previous corresponding season;
  (c) the rules of priority, once established, are made available on request to any interested party;
  (d) new entrants as defined in Article 2(b) of Council Regulation (EEC) No 95/93[1] are allocated 50% of newly created or unused slots and slots which have been given up by a carrier during or by the end of the season or which otherwise become available, to the extent that those new entrants have outstanding slot requests;
  (e) air carriers participating in the consultations have access, at the time of the consultations at the latest, to information relating to—
  — historical slots by airline, chronologically, for all air carriers at the airport,

— requested slots (initial submissions) by air carriers and chronologically for all air carriers,

— allocated slots, and outstanding slot requests listed individually in chronological order, by air carriers, for air carriers,

— remaining slots available,

— full details on the criteria being used in the allocation.

If a request for slots is not accepted, the air carrier concerned shall be entitled to a statement of the reasons therefor.

2. (a) The Commission and the Member States concerned shall be entitled to send observers to consultations on slot allocation and airport scheduling held in the context of a multilateral meeting in advance of each season. For this purpose, air carriers shall give the Member States concerned and the Commission the same notice as is given to participants, but not less than 10 days' notice, of the date, venue and subject matter of the consultations.

(b) Such notice shall be given—

(i) to the Member States concerned according to procedures to be established by the competent authorities of those Member States;

(ii) to the Commission according to procedures to be published in the *Official Journal of the European Communities*.

[4493]

NOTES

[1] OJ L14, 22.1.93, p 1.

TITLE III
FINAL PROVISIONS

Article 6

Withdrawal of the block exemption

The Commission may withdraw the benefit of the block exemption under this Regulation, pursuant to Article 7 of Regulation (EEC) No 3976/87 where it finds in a particular case that an agreement, decision or concerted practice exempted by this Regulation nevertheless has certain effects which are incompatible with the conditions laid down by Article 85(3) or are prohibited by Article 86 of the Treaty, and in particular where—

(i) there is no effective price competition on any route or group of routes which was the subject of tariff consultations. In such cases the benefit of this Regulation shall be withdrawn in respect of the air carriers which participated in the tariff consultations concerning such routes;

(ii) . . . ;

(iii) the operation of Article 5 has not enabled new entrants to obtain such slots as may be required at a congested airport in order to establish schedules which enable those carriers to compete effectively with established carriers on any route to and from that airport, and where competition on those routes is thereby substantially impaired. In such cases the withdrawal of the benefit of this Regulation shall be in respect of the slot allocation at the airport in question.

[4494]

NOTES

Words omitted repealed by Commission Regulation 1083/99/EC, Art 1(3).

[Article 6a

The prohibition in Article 85(1) of the Treaty shall not apply to agreements, decisions and concerted practices which were in existence at the date of accession of Austria, Finland and Sweden and which, by reason of that accession, fall within the scope of Article 85(1) if, within six months from the date of accession, they are so amended that they comply with the conditions laid down in this Regulation. However, this Article shall not apply to agreements, decisions and concerted practices which at the date of accession already fall under Article 53(1) of the EEA Agreement.]

[4495]

NOTES

Inserted by the 1994 Act of Accession of the Kingdom of Norway, the Republic of Austria, the Republic of Finland and the Kingdom of Sweden, Annex I(III)(D)(10), as adjusted by Council Decision 95/1/EC, Annex I(III)(D)(10).

Article 7

This Regulation shall enter into force on 1 July 1993.

[It shall apply until 30 June 2005.]

This Regulation shall apply with retroactive effect to agreements, decisions and concerted practices in existence when it enters into force, from the time when the conditions of application of this Regulation were fulfilled.

[4496]

NOTES

Second paragraph substituted by Commission Regulation 1105/2002/EC, Art 1(2).

This Regulation shall be binding in its entirety and directly applicable in all Member States.

Done at Brussels, 25 June 1993.

COMMISSION REGULATION

of 22 December 1998

on the form, content and other details of applications and notifications provided for in Council Regulations (EEC) No 1017/68, (EEC) No 4056/86 and (EEC) No 3975/87 applying the rules on competition to the transport sector

(2843/98/EC)

NOTES

Date of publication in OJ: OJ L354, 30.12.98, p 22.

THE COMMISSION OF THE EUROPEAN COMMUNITIES,

Having regard to the Treaty establishing the European Community,

Having regard to the Agreement on the European Economic Area,

Having regard to Council Regulation (EEC) No 1017/68 of 19 July 1968 applying rules of competition to transport by rail, road and inland waterway,[1] as last amended by the Act of Accession of Austria, Finland and Sweden, and in particular Article 29 thereof,

Having regard to Council Regulation (EEC) No 4056/86 of 22 December 1986 laying down detailed rules for the application of Articles 85 and 86 of the Treaty to maritime transport,[2] as last amended by the Act of Accession of Austria, Finland and Sweden, and in particular Article 26 thereof,

Having regard to Council Regulation (EEC) No 3975/87 of 14 December 1987 laying down the procedure for the application of the rules on competition to undertakings in the air transport sector,[3] as last amended by Regulation (EEC) No 2410/92,[4] and in particular Article 19 thereof,

Having consulted the Advisory Committee on restrictive practices and monopolies in the transport industry, the Advisory Committee on agreements and dominant positions in maritime transport, and the Advisory Committee on agreements and dominant positions in air transport,

(1) Whereas experience in the application of Commission Regulation (EEC) No 1629/69 of 8 August 1969 on the form, content and other detail of complaints pursuant to Article 10, applications pursuant to Article 12 and notifications pursuant to Article 14(1) of Council Regulation (EEC) No 1017/68 of 19 July 1968,[5] as last amended by the Act of Accession of Austria, Finland and Sweden, and of Section I of Commission Regulation (EEC) No 4260/88 of 16 December 1988 on the communications, complaints and applications and the hearings provided for in Council Regulation (EEC) No 4056/86 laying down detailed rules for the application of Articles 85 and 86 of the Treaty to maritime transport,[6] as last amended by the Act of Accession of Austria, Finland and Sweden and also of Section I of Commission Regulation (EEC) No 4261/88 of 16 December 1988 on the complaints, applications and hearings provided for in Council Regulation (EEC) No 3975/87 laying down the procedure for the application of the rules on competition to undertakings in the air transport sector,[7] as last amended by the Act of Accession of Austria, Finland and Sweden, has shown the need to improve certain procedural aspects of those Regulations;

(2) Whereas it is appropriate, for the sake of clarity, to adopt a single Regulation on the procedures for applications and notifications in the transport sector; whereas, accordingly, Regulation (EEC) No 1629/69 and Regulations (EEC) No 4260/88 and (EEC) No 4261/88 should be replaced;

(3) Whereas the submission of applications under Article 12 of Regulation (EEC) No 1017/68 and notifications under Article 14(1) of that Regulation, and applications under Article 12 of Regulation (EEC) No 4056/86 and Articles 3(2) and 5 of Regulation (EEC) No 3975/87, may have important legal consequences for each undertaking which is a party to an agreement, a decision or a practice; whereas each party should therefore have the right to submit such applications or notifications to the Commission; whereas, furthermore, a party exercising the right should inform the other parties in order to enable them to protect their interests;

(4) Whereas it is for the applicants and the notifying parties to make full and honest disclosure to the Commission of the facts and circumstances which are relevant to reaching a decision on the agreements, decisions or practices concerned;

(5) Whereas, in order to simplify and expedite their examination, it is desirable to prescribe that a form be used for applications for negative clearance relating to Article 85(1) and for applications relating to Article 5 of Regulation (EEC) No 1017/68 and to Article 85(3); whereas the use of this form should also be possible in the case of applications for negative clearance relating to Article 86;

(6) Whereas, in order to simplify their handling, it is appropriate to introduce a single form for applications under Article 12 of Regulation (EEC) No 1017/68, under Article 12 of Regulation (EEC) No 4056/86 and under Articles 3(2) and 5 of Regulation (EEC) No 3975/87; whereas, in the case of notifications under Article 14(1) of Regulation (EEC) No 1017/68, it is appropriate to provide a separate form;

(7) Whereas the Commission, in appropriate cases, should continue to give the parties, if they so request, an opportunity before the application or the notification to discuss the intended agreement, decision or practice informally and in strict confidence; whereas, in addition, it should, after the application or notification, continue to maintain close contact with the parties to the extent necessary to discuss with them any practical or legal problems which it discovers on a first examination of the case and if possible to remove such problems by mutual agreement;

(8) Whereas the obligation of communication to the Commission, pursuant to point 5 of Article 5 of Regulation (EEC) No 4056/86, of awards at arbitration and recommendations by conciliators concerns the settlement of disputes relating to the practices of conferences referred to in Article 4 and in points 2 and 3 of Article 5 of that Regulation; whereas it seems appropriate to make the procedure for this notification as simple as possible; whereas it is appropriate, therefore, to provide for notifications to be made in writing, attaching the documents containing the text of the awards and recommendations concerned;

(9) Whereas the provisions of this Regulation should also cover cases in which complaints, applications and notifications are made under Articles 53 and 54 of the Agreement on the European Economic Area,

NOTES
1   OJ L175, 23.7.68, p 1.
2   OJ L378, 31.12.86, p 4.
3   OJ L374, 31.12.87, p 1.
4   OJ L240, 24.8.92, p 18.
5   OJ L209, 21.8.69, p 1.
6   OJ L376, 31.12.88, p 1.
7   OJ L376, 31.12.88, p 10.

HAS ADOPTED THIS REGULATION—

Article 1

Entitled persons

1.   Any undertaking and any association of undertakings being a party to agreements or to concerted practices, or any association of undertakings adopting decisions, shall be permitted to submit applications or notifications to the Commission under any of the following provisions—

(a) Article 2 or Article 14(1) of Regulation (EEC) No 1017/68;
(b) Article 12 of Regulation (EEC) No 4056/86;
(c) Articles 3(2) and 5 of Regulation (EEC) No 3975/87.

2.   Where the application or notification is submitted by some, but not all, of the parties referred to in paragraph 1, they shall give notice to the other parties.

3.   Where the application or notification is signed by representatives of persons, undertakings or associations of undertakings, such representatives shall produce written proof that they are authorised to act.

4.   Where a joint application or notification is made, a joint representative shall be appointed who is authorised to transmit and receive documents on behalf of all the applicants or notifying parties.

[4497]

Article 2

Submission of applications and notifications

1.   Applications under Article 3(2) of Regulation (EEC) No 3975/87 relating to Article 85(1) of the Treaty and applications under Article 12 of Regulation (EEC) No 1017/68, Article 12 of Regulation (EEC) No 4056/86 and Article 5 of Regulation (EEC) No 3975/87 shall be submitted in the manner prescribed by Form TR as shown in Annex I to this Regulation.

Form TR may also be used for applications under Article 3(2) of Regulation (EEC) No 3975/87 relating to Article 86 of the Treaty.

Notifications under Article 14(1) of Regulation (EEC) No 1017/68 shall be submitted on Form TR(B) shown in Annex II to this Regulation.

2.   Joint applications and joint notifications shall be submitted on a single form.

3.   One original and 17 copies of each application and notification, and three copies of the supporting documents, shall be submitted to the Commission at the address indicated on the forms.

4. The supporting documents shall be either originals or copies of the originals; in the latter case the applicant or notifying party shall certify that they are true and complete copies of the originals.

5. Applications and notifications shall be in one of the official languages of the Union. This language shall also be the language of the proceeding for the applicant or notifying party. Documents shall be submitted in their original language. Where the original language is not one of the official Union languages, a translation into the language of the proceeding shall be attached.

6. Where an application which purports to be submitted under Article 12 of Regulation (EEC) No 1017/68, Article 12 of Regulation (EEC) No 4056/86 or Articles 3(2) and 5 of Regulation (EEC) No 3975/87 is found to fall outside the scope of the Regulation or Regulations under which it has been submitted, the Commission shall without delay inform the applicant that it intends to examine the application under the provisions of such other Regulation or Regulations as is or are applicable to the case; however, the date of submission of the application shall be the date resulting from Article 4. The Commission shall inform the applicant of its reasons and fix a period for the applicant to submit any comments in writing before it conducts its appraisal pursuant to that other Regulation or those other Regulations. The period fixed by the Commission shall be not less than two weeks; it may be extended.

[4498]

Article 3

Content of applications and notifications

1. Applications and notifications shall contain the information, including the documents, required by the forms. The information shall be correct and complete.

2. The Commission may dispense with the obligation to provide any particular information, including documents, required by the forms where the Commission considers that such information is not necessary for the examination of the case.

3. The Commission shall, without delay, acknowledge in writing to the applicant or notifying party receipt of the application or notification, and of any reply to a letter sent by the Commission pursuant to Article 4(2).

[4499]

Article 4

Effective date of submission of applications and notifications

1. Without prejudice to paragraphs 2 to 5, applications and notifications shall become effective on the date on which they are received by the Commission. Where, however, the application or notification is sent by registered post, it shall become effective on the date shown on the postmark of the place of posting.

2. Where the Commission finds that the information, including documents, contained in the application or notification is incomplete in any material respect, it shall, without delay, inform the applicant or notifying party in writing of this fact and shall fix an appropriate time limit for the supply of full information. In such cases, the application or notification shall become effective on the date on which the complete information is received by the Commission.

3.   Material changes in the facts contained in the application or notification which the applicant or notifying party knows or ought to know shall be communicated to the Commission voluntarily and without delay.

4.   Incorrect or misleading information shall be considered to be incomplete information.

5.   Where, at the expiry of a period of one month following the date on which the application or notification has been received, the Commission has not provided the applicant or notifying party with the information referred to in paragraph 2, the application or notification shall be deemed to have become effective on the date of its receipt by the Commission.

[4500]

Article 5

Notifications of awards given at arbitration and recommendations

1.   Awards at arbitration and recommendations by conciliators accepted by the parties shall be notified to the Commission when they concern the settlement of disputes relating to the practices of conferences referred to in Article 4 and points 2 and 3 of Article 5 of Regulation (EEC) No 4056/86.

2.   The obligation of notification applies to any party to the dispute resolved by the award or recommendation.

3.   Notifications shall be submitted forthwith by registered letter with an acknowledgement of receipt or shall be delivered by hand against receipt. They shall be written in one of the official languages of the Union.

4.   Supporting documents shall be either originals or copies. Copies shall be certified as true copies of the original. They shall be submitted in their original language. Where the original language is not one of the official languages of the Union, a translation in one of the official Union languages shall be attached.

5.   When representatives of undertakings, of associations of undertakings, or of natural or legal persons sign such notifications, they shall produce written proof that they are authorised to act.

[4501]

Article 6

Applications and notifications under Articles 53 and 54 of the EEA Agreement

Where applications and notifications as provided for in Articles 2(1) and 5(1) are made under Articles 53 or 54 of the Agreement on the European Economic Area, they may be made in one of the official Union languages or in one of the official languages of the EFTA States.

[4502]

Article 7

Repeal

Regulations (EEC) No 1629/69, (EEC) No 4260/88 and (EEC) No 4261/88 are repealed.

[4503]

Article 8

Entry into force

This Regulation shall enter into force on 1 February 1999.

[4504]

This Regulation shall be binding in its entirety and directly applicable in all Member States.

Done at Brussels, 22 December 1998.

ANNEX I
FORM TR

INTRODUCTION

Form TR, as its Annex, is an integral part of Commission Regulation (EC) No 2843/98 of 22 December 1998 on the form, content and other details of applications and notifications provided for in Council Regulations (EEC) No 1017/68, (EEC) No 4056/86 and (EEC) No 3975/87 applying the rules on competition to the transport sector (hereinafter referred to as "the Regulation"). It allows undertakings and associations of undertakings to make applications under Article 12 of Regulation (EEC) No 4056/86 and under Articles 3(2) and 5 of Regulation (EEC) No 3975/87.

Form TR is not a form to be filled in.

To facilitate the use of the Form TR the following pages set out—
— in which situations it is necessary to make an application (point A);
— to which authority (the Commission or the EFTA Surveillance Authority) the application should be made (point B);
— for which purposes the application can be used (point C);
— what information must be given in the application (points D, E, and F);
— who can make an application (point G);
— how to make an application (point H);
— how the business secrets of the undertakings can be protected (point I);
— the subsequent procedure after the application has been made (point J); and
— how certain technical terms used in the operational part of the Form TR should be interpreted (point K).

A. In which situations is it necessary to make an application?

I. Purpose of the competition of the EC Treaty and the EEA Agreement.

1. Purpose of the EC competition rules

The purpose of the competition rules is to prevent the distortion of competition in the common market by restrictive practices or the abuse of dominant positions. They apply to any enterprise trading directly or indirectly in the common market, wherever established.

Article 85(1) of the EC Treaty (the text of Articles 85 and 86 is reproduced in Appendix I to this form) prohibits restrictive agreements, decisions or concerted practices (arrangements) which may affect trade between Member States, and Article 85(2) declares agreements and decisions containing such restrictions void (although the Court of Justice has held that if restrictive terms of agreements are severable, only those terms are void); Article 85(3), however, provides for exemption of arrangements with beneficial effects, if its conditions are met. Article 86 prohibits the abuse of a dominant position which may affect trade between Member States.

The original procedures for implementation Articles 85 and 86, which provide for "negative clearance" and exemption pursuant to Article 85(3), were laid down in Regulation No 17. However, Council Regulation No 14[1] rendered Regulation No 17 inapplicable in the transport sector. The procedures for implementing the EC competition rules in the transport sector have subsequently been laid down for transport by rail, road and inland waterway in Regulation (EEC) No 1017/68, for maritime transport by Regulation (EEC) No 4056/86 and for the air transport sector by Regulation (EEC) No 3975/87 (the references to these and other acts mentioned in this form or relevant to applications made on this form are listed in Appendix II to this form).

Regulations (EEC) No 4056/86 and (EEC) No 3975/87, like Regulation No 17, make reference to Articles 85 and 86 of the EC Treaty. By contrast, Regulation (EEC) No 1017/68 enacts substantive competition rules for the inland transport sector. Articles 2, 5, 7 and 8 of Regulation (EEC) No 1017/68 contain provisions which, with minor variations, mirror those respectively of Articles 85(1), (2) and (3) and 86 of the EC Treaty. Those provisions of Regulation (EEC) No 1017/68 are to be interpreted in the same way as Articles 85 and 86 of the Treaty.[2]

2. Purpose of the EEA competition rules

The competition rules of the Agreement on the European Economic Area (concluded between the Community, the Member States and the EFTA States[3] are based on the same principles as those contained in the Community competition rules and have the same purpose, ie to prevent the distortion of competition in the EEA by cartels or the abuse of dominant positions. They apply to any enterprise trading directly or indirectly in the EEA, wherever established.

Article 53(1) of the EEA Agreement (the text of Articles 53, 54 and 56 of the EEA Agreement is reproduced in Appendix I) prohibits restrictive agreements, decisions or concerted practices (arrangements) which may affect trade between the Community and one or more EFTA States (or between EFTA States), and Article 53(2) declares agreements or decisions containing such restrictions void; Article 53(3), however, provides for exemption of arrangements with beneficial effects, if its conditions are met. Article 54 prohibits the abuse of a dominant position which may affect trade between the Community and one or more EFTA States (or between EFTA States). The procedures for implementing the EEA competition rules in the transport sector are laid down for transport by rail, road and inland waterway in Regulation (EEC) No 1017/68, for maritime transport by Regulation (EEC) No 4056/86 and for the air transport sector by Regulation (EEC) No 3975/87, supplemented for EEA purposes, by Protocols 21, 22 and 23 to the EEA Agreement.

II. The scope of the competition rules of the EC Treaty and the EEA Agreement

The applicability of Articles 2, 5 and 8 of Regulation (EEC) No 1017/68, Articles 85 and 86 of the EC Treaty and Articles 53 and 54 of the EEA Agreement depends on the circumstances of each individual case. It presupposes that the arrangement or behaviour satisfies all the conditions set out in the relevant provisions. This question must consequently be examined before any application is made.

1. Negative clearance

In the transport sector, the negative clearance procedure has been provided for only in the air transport sector. Its purpose is to allow undertakings to ascertain whether the Commission considers that their arrangement or their behaviour is or is not prohibited by Article 85(1), or Article 86 of the EC Treaty or by Article 53(1) or Article 54 of the EEA Agreement. This procedure is governed by Article 3(2) of Regulation (EEC) No 3975/87. The negative clearance takes the form of a decision by which the Commission certifies that, on the basis of the facts in its possession, there are no grounds pursuant to Article 85(1) or Article 86 of the EC Treaty or under Article 53(1) or Article 54 of the EEA Agreement for action on its part in respect of the arrangement or behaviour.

There is, however, no point in making an application when the arrangements or the behaviour are manifestly not prohibited by the abovementioned provisions. Nor is the Commission obliged to give negative clearance. Article 3(2) of Regulation (EEC) No 3975/87 states that ". . . the Commission may certify . . .". The Commission issues negative clearance decisions only where an important problem of interpretation has to be solved. In the other cases it reacts to the application by sending a comfort letter.

The Commission has published several notices relating the interpretation of Article 85(1) of the EC Treaty. They define certain categories of agreements which, by their nature or because of their minor importance, are not caught by the prohibition.[4]

2. Exemption

The procedure for exemption pursuant to Article 5 of Regulation (EEC) No 1017/68, Article 85(3) of the EC Treaty and Article 53(3) of the EEA Agreement allows companies to enter into arrangements which, in fact, offer economic advantages but which, without exemption, would be prohibited by Article 2 of Regulation (EEC) No 1017/68, Article 85(1) of the EC Treaty or by Article 53(1) of the EEA Agreement. This procedure is governed by Articles 12 and 13 of Regulation (EEC) No 1017/68, Articles 12 and 13 of Regulation (EEC) No 4056/86 and Articles 5 and 6 of Regulation (EEC) No 3975/87. The exemption takes the form of a decision by the Commission declaring Article 2 of Regulation (EEC) No 1017/68, Article 85(1) of the EC Treaty or Article 53(1) of the EEA Agreement to be inapplicable to the arrangements described in the decision. The Commission is required to specify the period of validity of any such decision, it can attach conditions and obligations and it can amend or revoke decisions or prohibit specified acts by the parties in certain circumstances, notably if the decisions were based on incorrect information or if there is any material change in the facts.

Regulations (EEC) No 1017/68, (EEC) No 4056/86 and (EEC) No 3975/87 provide for an objections procedure under which applications can be handled expeditiously. If an application is admissible pursuant to the relevant Regulation, if it is complete and if the arrangement which is the subject of the application has not given rise to a procedure as a result of a complaint or on the Commission's own initiative, the Commission publishes a summary of the request in the Official Journal of the European Communities and invites comments from interested third parties, from Member States and from EFTA States where requests relate to the EEA Agreement. Unless the Commission notifies the applicants within 90 days of the date of such publication that there are serious doubts as to the applicability of Article 5 of Regulation (EEC) No 1017/68, Article 85(3) of the EC Treaty or Article 53(3) of the EEA Agreement, the arrangement will be deemed exempt for the time already elapsed and for a maximum of three years from the date of publication, in the case of applications under Regulation (EEC) No 1017/68, and for a maximum of six years from the date of publication in the case of applications under Regulations (EEC) No 4056/86 and (EEC) No 3975/87.

The Commission has adopted a number of regulations granting exemptions to categories of agreements in the air transport sector and in the maritime sector.[5]

A decision granting exemption under Regulations (EEC) No 1017/68, (EEC) No 4056/86 or (EEC) No 3975/87 may have retroactive effect. Should the Commission find that notified arrrangements are indeed prohibited and cannot be exempted and, therefore, take a decision condemning them, the participants are nevertheless protected, between the date of the application of the date of the decision, against fines for any infringement described in the application (Article 19(4) of Regulation (EEC) No 4056/86 and Article 12(5) of Regulation (EEC) No 3975/87). Regulation (EEC) No 1017/68 does not provide for such immunity from fines.

B. To which authority should an application be made?

The applications must be made to the authority which has competence for the matter. The Commission is responsible for the application of the competition rules of the EC Treaty. However there is shared competence in relation to the application of the competition rules of the EEA Agreement.

The competence of the Commission and of the EFTA Surveillance Authority to apply the EEA competition rules follows from Article 56 of the EEA Agreement. Applications relating to agreements, decisions or concerted practices liable to affect trade between Member States should be addressed to the Commission unless their effects on trade between Member States or on competition within the Community are not appreciable within the meaning of the Commission notice of 1997 on agreements of minor importance.[6] Furthermore, all restrictive agreements, decisions or concerted practices affecting trade between one Member State and one or more EFTA States fall within the competence of the Commission, provided that the undertakings concerned achieve more than 67% of their combined EEA-wide turnover within the Community.[7] However, if the effects of such agreements, decisions or concerted practices on trade between Member States or on competition within the Community are not appreciable, the application should, where necessary, be addressed to the EFTA Surveillance Authority. All other agreements, decisions and concerted practices falling under Article 53 of the EEA Agreement should be notified to the EFTA Surveillance Authority (the address of which is given in Appendix III).

Applications for negative clearance regarding Article 54 of the EEA Agreement should be lodged with the Commission if the dominant position exists only in the Community, or with the EFTA Surveillance authority, if the dominant position exists only in the whole of the territory of the EFTA States, or a substantial part of it. Only where the dominant position exists within both territories should the rules outlined above with respect to Article 53 be applied.

The Commission will apply, as a basis for appraisal, the competition rules of the EC Treaty. Where the case falls under the EEA Agreement and is attributed to the Commission pursuant to Article 56 of that Agreement, it will simultaneously apply the EEA rules.

C. The purpose of this form

Form TR lists the questions that must be answered and the information and documents that must be provided when applying for the following—
- a negative clearance with regard to Article 85(1) of the EC Treaty and/or Article 53(1) of the EEA Agreement, pursuant to Article 3(2) of Regulation (EEC) No 3975/87, with respect to agreements between undertakings, decisions by associations of undertakings and concerted practices,
- an exemption pursuant to Article 5 of Regulation (EEC) No 1017/68, or Article 85(3) of the EC Treaty and/or Article 53(3) of the EEA Agreement with respect to agreements between undertakings, decisions by associations of undertakings and concerted practices.

Applications for exemption pursuant to Regulations (EEC) No 1017/68, (EEC) No 4056/86 and (EEC) No 3975/87 shall be submitted in the manner prescribed by form TR (see Article 2(1) of the Regulation).

This form can also be used by undertakings that wish to apply for a negative clearance from Article 86 of the EC Treaty or Article 53 of the EEA Agreement, pursuant to Article 3(2) of Regulation (EEC) No 3975/87. Applicants requesting negative clearance from Article 86 are not required to use form TR. They are none the less strongly recommended to give all the information requested below to ensure that their application gives a full statement of the facts (see Article 2(1)(a), second sentence of the Regulation).

The applications or notifications made on the form TR issued by the EFTA side are equally valid. However, if the agreements, decisions or practices concerned fall solely within Article 85 or 86 of the EC Treaty, ie have no EEA relevance whatsoever, it is advisable to use the present form established by the Commission.

D. Which chapters of the form should be completed?

Undertakings wishing to make an application must complete all three chapters of the operational part of this form. Notifications under Regulation No 17 of agreements concerning the creation of a cooperative joint venture of a structural character can benefit from an accelerated procedure. The accelerated procedure is not applied to applications under Regulations (EEC) No 1017/68, (EEC) No 4056/86 and (EEC) No 3975/87 because those Regulations provide for an objections procedure containing a specific timetable.

E. The need for complete information

The receipt by the Commission of a valid application has two main consequences. First, under Regulations (EEC) No 4056/86 and (EEC) No 3975/87, it affords immunity from fines from the date that the valid application is received by the Commission with regard to applications made in order to obtain exemption (see Article 19(4) of Regulation (EEC) No 4056/86 and Article 12(5) of Regulation (EEC) No 3975/87).

Second, until a valid application is received, the Commission is not "in possession of all the available evidence" which is necessary before it can publish a summary of the application under the opposition procedure in Article 12 of Regulation (EEC) No 1017/68, Article 12 of Regulation (EEC) No 4056/86 and Article 5 of Regulation (EEC) No 3975/87.

A valid application for this purpose means one that is not incomplete (see Article 3(1) of this Regulation). This is subject to two qualifications. First, if the information or documents required by this form are not reasonably available to you in part or in whole, the Commission will accept that an application is complete and thus valid notwithstanding the failure to provide such information, providing that you give reasons for the unavailability of the information, and provide your best estimates for missing data together with the sources for the

this publication, the Commission ". . . shall have regard to the legitimate interest of undertakings in the protection of their business secrets" (Article 12(2) of Regulation (EEC) No 1017/68, Article 12(2) of Regulation (EEC) No 4056/86 and Article 5(2) of Regulation (EEC) No 3975/87).

Before publishing a summary of an application, the Commission will show the applicant(s) a copy of the proposed text.

In this connection, if an undertaking believes that its interests would be harmed if any of the information it is asked to supply were to be published or otherwise divulged to other undertakings, it should put all such information in one or more separate annexes with each page clearly marked "Business secrets". It should also give reasons why any information identified as confidential or secret should not be divulged or published.

J.　Subsequent procedure

The application is registered in the Registry of the Directorate-General for Competition (DG IV). The date of receipt by the Commission (or the date of posting if sent by registered post) is the effective date of the submission (see Article 4(1) of the Regulation). However, special rules apply to incomplete applications (see under point E).

The Commission will acknowledge receipt of all applications in writing, indicating the case number attributed to the file. This number must be used in all future correspondence regarding the application. The receipt of acknowledgement does not prejudice the question whether the application is valid.

Further information may be sought from the parties or from third parties and suggestions may be made as to amendments to the arrangements that might make them acceptable.

An application for an exemption decision may be opposed by the Commission if it has serious doubts as to whether the arrangements should benefit from an exemption decision.

If, after having raised serious doubts under the opposition procedure, the Commission intends to issue an exemption decision, it is obliged to publish a summary and invite comments from third parties (Article 26(3) of Regulation (EEC) No 1017/68, Article 23(3) of Regulation (EEC) No 4056/86 and Article 16(3) of Regulation (EEC) No 3975/87). Subsequently, a preliminary draft decision has to be submitted to and discussed with the appropriate Advisory Committee composed of officials of the competent authorities of the Member States. Where the case falls under the EEA Agreement, representatives of the EFTA Surveillance Authority and the EFTA States will be invited to attend. Only then, and providing nothing has happened to change the Commission's intention, can it adopt a decision.

Sometimes files are closed without any formal decision being taken, for example, because it is found that the arrangements are already covered by a block exemption, or because they do not call for any action by the Commission, at least in circumstances at that time. In such cases comfort letters are sent. Although not a Commission decision, a comfort letter indicates how the Commission's Directorate-General for Competition (DG IV) views the case on the facts currently in their possession which means that the Commission could where necessary, for example, if it were to be asserted that a contract was void under Article 85(2) of the EC Treaty and/or Article 53(2) of the EEA Agreement, take an appropriate decision to clarify the legal situation.

K.　Definitions used in the operational part of this form

Agreement: the word "agreement" is used to refer to all categories of arrangements, ie agreements between undertakings, decisions by associations of undertakings and concerted practices.

Year: all references to the word "year" in this form shall be read as meaning calendar year, unless otherwise stated.

Group: a group relationship exists for the purpose of this form where one undertaking—
— owns more than half the capital or business assets of another undertaking, or
— has the power to exercise more than half the voting rights in another undertaking, or
— has the power to appoint more than half the members of the supervisory board, board of directors or bodies legally representing the undertaking, or
— has the right to manage the affairs of another undertaking.

An undertaking which is jointly controlled by several other undertakings (joint venture) forms part of the group of each of these undertakings.

Notified agreement: a notified agreement is one that is the subject of an application using this form.

Relevant product market: question 5.1 of this form requires the undertaking or individual submitting the application to define the relevant product and/or service market(s) that are likely to be affected by the agreement in question. That definition(s) is then used as the basis for a number of other questions contained in this form. The definition(s) thus submitted by the applicants are referred to in this form as the relevant product market(s).

Relevant geographic market: question 5.2 of this form requires the undertaking or individual submitting the application to define the relevant geographic market(s) that are likely to be affected by the agreement in question. That definition(s) is then used as the basis for a number of other questions contained in this form. The definition(s) thus submitted by the applicants are referred to in this form as the relevant geographic market(s).

Relevant product and geographic market: by virtue of the combination of their replies to question 5 the parties provide their definition of the relevant market(s) affected by the notified agreement(s). That (those) definition(s) is (are) then used as the basis for a number of other questions contained in this form. The definition(s) thus submitted by the notifying parties is referred to in this form as the relevant geographic and product market(s).

Parties and applicant: the word "party" is used to refer to all the undertakings which are party to the agreement being notified. As an application may be submitted by only one of the undertakings which are party to an agreement, "applicant" is used to refer only to the undertaking or undertakings actually submitting the application.

FORM TR — OPERATIONAL PART

The first page of your application must contain the words "Application in accordance with form TR", and also one or more of the following indications as the case may be—
— "Application for exemption under Article 12 of Regulation (EEC) No 1017/68",
— "Application for exemption under Article 12 of Regulation (EEC) No 4056/86",
— "Application for negative clearance under Article 3(2) and/or exemption under Article 5 of Regulation (EEC) No 3975/87".

CHAPTER I
SECTIONS CONCERNING THE PARTIES, THEIR GROUPS AND THE AGREEMENT

Section 1

Identity of the undertakings or persons submitting the application

1.1.   Please list the undertakings on behalf of which the application is being submitted and indicate their legal denomination or commercial name, shortened or commonly used as appropriate (if it differs from the legal denomination).

1.2.   If the application is being submitted on behalf of only one or some of the undertakings party to the agreement being notified, please confirm that the remaining undertakings have been informed of that fact and indicate whether they have received a copy of the application, with relevant confidential information and business secrets deleted.[9] (In such circumstances a copy of the edited copy of the application which has been provided to such other undertakings should be annexed to this application).

1.3.   If a joint application is being submitted, has a joint representative[10] been appointed?[11]

If yes, please give the details requested in 1.3.1 to 1.3.3.

If no, please give details of any representatives who have been authorised to act for each or either of the parties to the agreement indicating who they represent.

1.3.1.   Name of representative.

1.3.2.   Address of representative.

1.3.3.   Telephone and fax number of representative.

1.4.   In cases where one or more representatives have been appointed, an authority to act on behalf of the undertaking(s) submitting the application must accompany the application.

Section 2

Information on the parties to the agreement and the groups to which they belong

2.1.   State the name and address of the parties to the agreement being notified, and the country of their incorporation.

2.2.   State the nature of the business of each of the parties to the agreement being notified.

2.3.   For each of the parties to the agreement, give the name of a person that can be contacted, together with his or her name, address, telephone number, fax number and position held in the undertaking.

2.4.   Identify the corporate groups to which the parties to the agreement being notified belong. State the sectors in which these groups are active, and the worldwide turnover of each group.[12]

Section 3

Procedural matters

3.1.   Please state whether you have made any formal submission to any other competition authorities in relation to the agreement in question. If yes, state which authorities, the individual or department in question, and the nature of the contact. In addition to this, mention any earlier proceedings or informal contacts, of which you are aware, with the Commission and/or the EFTA Surveillance Authority and any earlier proceedings with any national authorities or courts in the Community or in the territory of the EFTA States concerning these or any related agreements.

3.2.   Please summarise any reasons for any claim that the case involves an issue of exceptional urgency.

3.3.   State whether you intend to produce further supporting facts or arguments not yet available and, if so, on which points.[13]

Section 4

Full details of the arrangements

4.1.   Please summarise the nature, content and objectives pursued by the agreement being notified.

4.2.   Detail any provisions contained in the agreements which may restrict the parties in their freedom to take independent commercial decisions, for example regarding—
— buying or selling prices, discounts or other trading conditions,
— the quantities of services to be offered,
— technical development or investment,
— the choice of markets or sources of supply,
— purchases from or sales to third parties,
— whether to apply similar terms for the supply of equivalent services,
— whether to offer different services separately or together.

If you are claiming the benefit of an opposition procedure under a block exemption regulation, identify in this list the restrictions that exceed those automatically exempted by the relevant regulation.

4.3.   State between which Member States of the Community and/or EFTA States[14] trade may be affected by the arrangements. Please give reasons for your reply to this question, giving data on trade flows where relevant. Furthermore please state whether trade between the Community or the EEA and any third countries is affected, again giving reasons for your reply.

CHAPTER II
SECTION CONCERNING THE RELEVANT MARKET

Section 5

The relevant market

A relevant product market comprises all those products and/or services which are regarded as interchangeable or substitutable by the consumer, by reason of the products' characteristics, their prices and their intended use.[15]

The following factors are normally considered to be relevant to the determination of the relevant product market and should be taken into account in this analysis—[16]

— the degree of similarity between the services in question,
— differences in price between two services,
— the cost of switching between two potentially competing services,
— established or entrenched consumer preferences for one type or category of service over another,
— industry-wide service classifications (eg classifications maintained by trade associations).

The relevant geographic market comprises the area in which the undertakings concerned are involved in the supply of products or services, in which the conditions of competition are sufficiently homogenous and which can be distinguished from neighbouring areas because, in particular, conditions of competition are appreciably different in those areas.

Factors relevant to the assessment of the relevant geographic market include[17] the nature and characteristics of the services concerned, the existence of entry barriers or consumer preferences, and appreciable differences for the undertakings' market share or substantial price differences between neighbouring areas.

5.1.   In the light of the above please explain the definition of the relevant product market or markets that in your opinion should form the basis of the Commission's analysis of the application.

In your answer, please give reasons for assumptions or findings, and explain how the factors outlined above have been taken into account. In particular, please state the specific products or services directly or indirectly affected by the agreement being notified and identify the categories of services viewed as substitutable in your market definition.

In the questions figuring below, this (or these) definition(s) will be referred to as "the relevant product market(s)".

5.2.   Please explain the definition of the relevant geographic market or markets that in your opinion should form the basis of the Commission's analysis of the application.

In your answer, please give reasons for assumptions or findings, and explain how the factors outlined above have been taken into account. In particular, please identify the countries in which the parties are active in the relevant product market(s), and in the event that you consider the relevant geographic market to be wider than the individual Member States of the Community or the territory of the EFTA States on which the parties to the agreement are active, give the reasons for this.

In the questions below, this (or these) definitions will be referred to as "the relevant geographic market(s)".

Section 6

Group members operating on the same markets as the parties

6.1.   For each of the parties to the agreement being notified, provide a list of all undertakings belonging to the same group which are—

6.1.1.   active in the relevant product market(s);

6.1.2.   active in markets neighbouring the relevant product market(s) (ie active in products and/or services that represent imperfect and partial substitutes for those included in your definition of the relevant product market(s)).

Such undertakings must be identified even if they sell the product or service in question in other geographic areas than those in which the parties to the notified agreement operate. Please list the name, country of incorporation, exact products or services provided and the geographic scope of operation of each group member.

Section 7

The position of the parties on the relevant product market(s)

Information requested in this section must be provided for the groups of the parties as a whole. It is not sufficient to provide such information only in relation to the individual undertakings directly concerned by the agreement.

7.1.   In relation to each relevant product market(s) identified in your reply to question 5.1 please provide the following information—

7.1.1.   the market shares of the parties on the relevant geographic market during the previous three years;

7.1.2.   where different, the market shares of the parties in (a) the EEA as a whole, (b) the Community, (c) the territory of the EFTA States and (d) each EC Member State and EFTA State during the previous three years.[18] For this section, where market shares are less than 20%, please state simply which of the following bands are relevant: 0 to 5%, 5 to 10%, 10 to 15%, 15 to 20%.

For the purpose of answering these questions, market share may be calculated either on the basis of value or volume. Justification for the figures provided must be given. Thus, for each answer, total market value/volume must be stated, together with the sales/turnover of each of the parties in question. The source or sources of the information should also be given (eg official statistics, estimates, etc), and where possible, copies should be provided of documents from which information has been taken.

Section 8

The position of competitors and customers on the relevant product market(s)

Information requested in this section must be provided for the group of the parties as a whole and not in relation to the individual companies directly concerned by the agreement notified.

For the (all) relevant product and geographic market(s) in which the parties have a combined market share exceeding 15%, the following questions must be answered.

8.1.   Please identify the five main competitors of the parties. Please identify the company and give your best estimate as to their market share in the relevant geographic market(s). Please also provide address, telephone and fax number, and, where possible, the name of a contact person at each company identified.

8.2.   Please identify the five main customers of each of the parties. State company name, address, telephone and fax numbers, together with the name of a contact person.

Section 9

Market entry and potential competition in product and geographic terms

For the (all) relevant product and geographic market(s) in which the parties have a combined market share exceeding 15%, the following questions must be answered.

9.1.   Describe the various factors influencing entry in product terms into the relevant product market(s) that exist in the present case (ie what barriers exist to prevent undertakings that do not presently provide services within the relevant product market(s) entering this market(s)). In so doing take account of the following where appropriate—

— to what extent is entry to the markets influenced by the requirement of government authorisation or standard setting in any form? Are there any legal or regulatory controls on entry to these markets?

— to what extent is entry to the markets influenced by the need to have access to transport infrastructure?

— to what extent is entry to the markets influenced by the availability of rolling-stock vessels, aircraft, or other vehicles required for providing the services?

— to what extent is entry to the market influenced by the length of contracts between an undertaking and its suppliers and/or customers?

— describe the importance of research and development and in particular the importance of licensing patents, know-how and other rights in these markets.

9.2.   Describe the various factors influencing entry in geographic terms into the relevant geographic market(s) that exist in the present case (ie what barriers exist to prevent undertakings already providing services within the relevant product market(s) but in areas outside the relevant geographic market(s) extending the scope of their activities into the relevant geographic market(s)?) Please give reasons for your answer, explaining, were relevant, the importance of the following factors—

— trade barriers imposed by law, such as tariffs, quotas etc,

— local specification or technical requirements,

— procurement policies,

— the existence of adequate and available local distribution and retailing facilities,
— the need to have access to transport infrastructure,
— entrenched consumer preferences for local brands or products,
— language.

9.3. Have any new undertakings entered the relevant product market(s) in geographic areas where the parties are active during the last three years? Please provide this information with respect to both new entrants in product terms and new entrants in geographic terms. If such entry has occurred, please identify the undertaking(s) concerned (name, address, telephone and fax numbers, and, where possible, contact person), and provide your best estimate of their market share in the relevant product and geographic market(s).

CHAPTER III
FINAL SECTIONS

Section 10

Reasons for the application for negative clearance

If you are applying for negative clearance state—

10.1. why, ie state which provision or effects of the agreement or behaviour might, in your view, raise questions of compatibility with the Community's and/or the EEA rules of competition. The object of this subheading is to give the Commission the clearest possible idea of the doubts you have about your agreement or behaviour that you wish to have resolved by a negative clearance.

Then, under the following three references, give a statement of the relevant facts and reasons as to why you consider Article 85(1) or 86 of the EC Treaty and/or Article 53(1) or 54 of the EEA Agreement to be inapplicable, ie—

10.2. why the agreements or behaviour do not have the object or effect of preventing, restricting or distorting competition within the common market or within the territory of the EFTA States to any appreciable extent, or why your undertaking does not have or its behaviour does not abuse a dominant position, and/or

10.3. why the agreements or behaviour do not have the object or effect of preventing, restricting or distorting competition within the EEA to any appreciable extent, or why your undertaking does not have or its behaviour does not abuse a dominant position, and/or

10.4. why the agreements or behaviour are not such as may affect trade between Member States or between the Community and one or more EFTA States, or between EFTA States to any appreciable extent.

Section 11

Reasons for the application for exemption

If you are applying for an exemption under Article 5 of Regulation (EEC) No 1017/68, Article 85(3) of the EC Treaty and/or Article 53(3) of the EEA Agreement, explain how—

11.1. the agreement contributes to improving production or distribution, and/or promoting technical or economic progress. Explain in particular how the agreement contributes towards improving the quality of transport services, or promoting greater continuity and stability in the satisfaction of transport needs on markets where supply and demand are subject to considerable temporal fluctuation, or increasing the productivity of undertakings.

In particular, please explain the reasons why these benefits are expected to result form the collaboration; for example, do the parties to the agreement possess complementary technologies or distribution systems that will produce important synergies? (if so, please state which). Also please state whether any documents or studies were drawn up by the applicants when assessing the feasibility of the operations and the benefits likely to result therefrom, and whether any such documents or studies provided estimates of the savings or efficiencies likely to result. Please provide copies of any such documents or studies;

11.2. a proper share of the benefits arising from such improvement or progress accrues to consumers. Explain in particular how the agreement takes fair account of the interest of transport users;

11.3. all restrictive provisions of the agreement are indispensable to the attainment of the aims set out under 11.1 (if you are claiming the benefit of the opposition procedure, it is particularly important that you should identify and justify restrictions that exceed those automatically exempted by the relevant Regulations). In this respect please explain how the benefits resulting from the agreement identified in your reply to question 11.1 could not be achieved, or could not be achieved so quickly or efficiently or only at higher cost or with less certainty of success (i) without the conclusion of the agreement as a whole and (ii) without those particular clauses and provisions of the agreement identified in your reply to question 4.2;

11.4. the agreement does not eliminate competition in respect of a substantial part of the goods or services concerned.

Section 12

Supporting documentation

The completed application must be drawn up and submitted in one original. It shall contain the last versions of all agreements which are the subject of the application and be accompanied by the following—

(a) 17 copies of the application itself;

(b) three copies of the annual reports and accounts of all the parties to the notified agreement, decision or practice for the last three years;

(c) three copies of the most recent in-house or external long-term market studies or planning documents for the purpose of assessing or analysing the affected market(s) with respect to competitive conditions, competitors (actual and potential), and market conditions. Each document should indicate the name and position of the author;

(d) three copies of reports and analyses which have been prepared by or for any officer(s) or director(s) for the purposes of evaluating or analysing the notified agreement.

Section 13

Declaration

The application must conclude with the following declaration which is to be signed by or on behalf of all the applicants.

"The undersigned declare that the information given in this application is correct to the best of their knowledge and belief, that complete copies of all documents requested by form TR have been supplied to the extent that they are in the possession of the group pf undertakings to which the applicant(s) belong(s) and are accessible to the latter, that all estimates are identified as such and are their best estimates of the underlying facts and that all the opinions expressed are sincere.

They are aware of the provisions of Article 22(1)(a) of Regulation (EEC) No 1017/68, Article 19(1)(a) of Regulation (EEC) No 4056/86 and Article 12(1)(a) of Regulation (EEC) No 3975/87.

Place and date:

Signatures:"

Please add the name(s) of the person(s) signing the application and their function(s).

Applications which have not been signed are invalid.

[4505]

NOTES

1   Council Regulation No 141/62 of 26 November 1962 exempting transport from the application of Council Regulation No 17, (OJ 124, 28.11.62, p 2753); Regulation as last amended by Regulation No 1002/67/EEC, (OJ 306, 16.12.67, p 1).

2   See Case T-224/94 Deutsche Bahn v Commission [1997] ECR II-1689, at paragraph 77. The Court of First Instance held that Article 8 of the Regulation does not have a purpose which is substantially different from that of Article 86 of the Treaty.

3   See list of Member States and EFTA States in Appendix III at **[4508]**.

4   See Appendix II at **[4507]**.

5   See Appendix II at **[4507]**.

⁶   OJ C372, 9.12.97, p 13.
⁷   For a definition of "turnover" in this context, see Articles 2, 3 and 4 of Protocol 22 to the EEA Agreement reproduced in Appendix I at **[4506]**.
⁸   See points (a) Article 13(3) of Regulation (EEC) No 1017/68, Article 13(3) of Regulation (EEC) No 4056/86 and Article 6(3) of Regulation (EEC) No 3975/87.
⁹   The Commission is aware that in exceptional cases it may not be practicable to inform non-notifying parties to the notified agreement of the fact that it has been notified, or to provide them with a copy of the application. This may be the case, for example, where a standard agreement is being notified that is concluded with a large number of undertakings. Where this is the case you should state the reasons why it has not been practicable to follow the standard procedure set out in this question.
¹⁰   For the purposes of this question a representative means an individual or undertaking formally appointed to make the application on behalf of the party or parties submitting the application. This should be distinguished from the situation where the application is signed by an officer of the company or companies in question. In the latter situation no representative is appointed.
¹¹   It is not mandatory to appoint representatives for the purpose of completing and/or submitting this application. This question only requires the identification of representatives where the applicants have chosen to appoint them.
¹²   For the calculation of turnover in the banking and insurance sectors see Article 3 of Protocol 22 to the EEA Agreement.
¹³   In so far as the notifying parties provide the information required by this form that was reasonably available to them at the time of notification, the fact that the parties intend to provide further supporting facts or documentation in due course does not prevent the notification being valid at the time of notification.
¹⁴   See list in Appendix II at **[4507]**.
¹⁵   See Commission notice on the definition of relevant market for the purposes of Community competition law (OJ C372, 9.12.97, p 5).
¹⁶   This is not, however, exhaustive, and applicants may refer to other factors.
¹⁷   This list is not, however, exhaustive, and applicants may refer to other factors.
¹⁸   That is where the relevant geographic market has been defined as worldwide, these figures must be given regarding the EEA, the Community, the territory of the EFTA States, and each EC Member State. Where the relevant geographic market has been defined as the Community, these figures must be given for the EEA, the territory of the EFTA States, and each EC Member State. Where the market has been defined as national, these figures must be given for the EEA, the Community and the territory of the EFTA States.

APPENDIX I
TEXT OF ARTICLES 85 AND 86 OF THE EC TREATY, ARTICLES 53, 54 AND 56 OF THE EEA AGREEMENT, AND OF ARTICLES 2, 3 AND 4 OF PROTOCOL 22 TO THAT AGREEMENT

Article 85 of the EC Treaty

1.   The following shall be prohibited as incompatible with the common market: all agreements between undertakings, decisions by associations of undertakings and concerted practices which may affect trade between Member States and which have as their object or effect the prevention, restriction or distortion of competition within the common market, and in particular those which—

(a) directly or indirectly fix purchase or selling prices or any other trading conditions;
(b) limit or control production, markets, technical development, or investment;
(c) share markets or sources of supply;
(d) apply dissimilar conditions to equivalent transactions with other trading parties, thereby placing them at a competitive disadvantage;
(e) make the conclusion of contracts subject to acceptance by the other parties of supplementary obligations which, by their nature or according to commercial usage, have no connection with the subject of such contracts.

2.   Any agreements or decisions prohibited pursuant to this Article shall be automatically void.

3.   The provisions of paragraph 1 may, however, be declared inapplicable in the case of—
— any agreement or category of agreements between undertakings,
— any decision or category of decisions by associations or undertakings,
— any concerted practice or category of concerted practices,

which contributes to improving the production or distribution of goods or to promoting technical or economic progress, while allowing consumers a fair share of the resulting benefit, and which does not—

(a) impose on the undertakings concerned restrictions which are not indispensable to the attainment of these objectives;

(b) afford such undertakings the possibility of eliminating competition in respect of a substantial part of the products in question.

Article 86 of the EC Treaty

Any abuse by one or more undertakings of a dominant position within the common market or in a substantial part of it shall be prohibited as incompatible with the common market in so far as it may affect trade between Member States.

Such abuse may, in particular, consist in—

(a) directly or indirectly imposing unfair purchase or selling prices or other unfair trading conditions;

(b) limiting production, markets or technical development to the prejudice of consumers;

(c) applying dissimilar conditions to equivalent transactions with other trading parties, thereby placing them at a competitive disadvantage;

(d) making the conclusion of contracts subject to acceptance by the other parties of supplementary obligations which, by their nature or according to commercial usage, have no connection with the subject of such contracts.

Article 53 of the EEA Agreement

1. The following shall be prohibited as incompatible with the functioning of this Agreement: all agreements between undertakings, decisions by associations of undertakings and concerted practices which may affect trade between Contracting Parties and which have as their object or effect the prevention, restriction or distortion of competition within the territory covered by this Agreement, and in particular those which—

(a) directly or indirectly fix purchase or selling prices or any other trading conditions;

(b) limit or control production, markets, technical development, or investment;

(c) share markets or sources of supply;

(d) apply dissimilar conditions to equivalent transactions with other trading parties, thereby placing them at a competitive disadvantage;

(e) make the conclusion of contracts subject to acceptance by the other parties of supplementary obligations which, by their nature or according to commercial usage, have no connection with the subject of such contracts.

2. Any agreements or decisions prohibited pursuant to this Article shall be automatically void.

3. The provisions of paragraph 1 may, however, be declared inapplicable in the case of—

— any agreement or category of agreements between undertakings,

— any decision or category of decisions by associations of undertakings,

— any concerted practice or category of concerted practices,

which contributes to improving the production or distribution of goods or to promoting technical or economic progress, while allowing consumers a fair share of the resulting benefit, and which does not

(a) impose on the undertakings concerned restrictions which are not indispensable to the attainment of these objectives;

(b) afford such undertakings the possibility of eliminating competition in respect of a substantial part of the products in question.

Article 54 of the EEA Agreement

Any abuse by one or more undertakings of a dominant position within the territory covered by this Agreement or in a substantial part of it shall be prohibited as incompatible with the functioning of this Agreement in so far as it may affect trade between Contracting Parties.

Such abuse may, in particular, consist in—

(a) directly or indirectly imposing unfair purchase or selling prices or other unfair trading conditions;

(b) limiting production, markets or technical development to the prejudice of consumers;

PART IV
EC MATERIALS

    (c) applying dissimilar conditions to equivalent transactions with other trading parties, thereby placing them at a competitive disadvantage;

    (d) making the conclusion of contracts subject to acceptance by the other parties of supplementary obligations which, by their nature or according to commercial usage, have no connection with the subject of such contracts.

Article 56 of the EEA Agreement

1.   Individual cases falling under Article 53 shall be decided on by the Surveillance Authorities in accordance with the following provisions—

    (a) individual cases where only trade between EFTA States is affected shall be decided on by the EFTA Surveillance Authority;

    (b) without prejudice to subparagraph (c), the EFTA Surveillance Authority decides, as provided for in the provisions set out in Article 58, Protocol 21 and the rules adopted for its implementation, Protocol 23 and Annex XIV, on cases where the turnover of the undertakings concerned in the territory of the EFTA States equals 33% or more of their turnover in the territory covered by this Agreement;

    (c) the EC Commission decides on the other cases as well as on cases under (b) where trade between EC Member States is affected, taking into account the provisions set out in Article 58, Protocol 21, Protocol 23 and Annex XIV.

2.   Individual cases falling under Article 54 shall be decided on by the Surveillance Authority in the territory of which a dominant position is found to exist. The rules set out in paragraph 1(b) and (c) shall apply only if dominance exists within the territories of both Surveillance Authorities.

3.   Individual cases falling under subparagraph (c) of paragraph 1, whose effects on trade between EC Member States or on competition within the Community are not appreciable, shall be decided on by the EFTA Surveillance Authority.

4.   The terms "undertaking" and "turnover" are, for the purpose of this Article, defined in Protocol 22.

Articles 2, 3 and 4 of Protocol 22 to the EEA Agreement

Article 2

"Turnover" within the meaning of Article 56 of the Agreement shall comprise the amounts derived by the undertaking concerned, in the territory covered by this Agreement, in the preceding financial year from the sale of products and the provision of services falling within the undertaking's ordinary scope of activities after deduction of sales rebates and of value-added tax and other taxes directly related to turnover.

Article 3

In place of turnover the following shall be used—

    (a) for credit institutions and other financial institutions, their total assets multiplied by the ratio between loans and advances to credit institutions and customers in transactions with residents in the territory covered by this Agreement and the total sum of those loans and advances;

    (b) for insurance undertakings, the value of gross premiums received from residents in the territory covered by this Agreement, which shall comprise all amounts received and receivable in respect of insurance contracts issued by or on behalf of the insurance undertakings, including also outgoing reinsurance premiums, and after deduction of taxes and parafiscal contributions or levies charged by reference to the amounts of individual premiums or the total value of premiums.

Article 4

1.   In derogation from the definition of the turnover relevant for the application of Article 56 of the Agreement, as contained in Article 2 of this Protocol, the relevant turnover shall be constituted—

    (a) as regards agreements, decisions of associations of undertakings and concerted practices related to distribution and supply arrangements between non-competing undertakings, of the amounts derived from the sale of goods or the provision of services which are the subject matter of the agreements, decisions or concerted practices, and from the other goods or services which are considered by users to be equivalent in view of their characteristics, price and intended use;

(b) as regards agreements, decisions of associations of undertakings and concerted practices related to arrangements on transfer of technology between non-competing undertakings, of the amounts derived from the sale of goods or the provision of services which result from the technology which is the subject matter of the agreements, decisions or concerted practices, and of the amounts derived from the sale of those goods or the provision of those services which that technology is designed to improve or replace.

2.   However, where at the time of the coming to existence of arrangements as described in paragraph 1(a) and (b) turnover as regards the sale of products or the provision of services is not in evidence, the general provision as contained in Article 2 shall apply.

[4506]

APPENDIX II
LIST OF RELEVANT ACTS

(as of 1 February 1999)

(If you think it possible that your arrangements do not need to be notified by virtue of any of these regulations or notices it may be worth your while to obtain a copy.)

Implementing regulations[1]

— Council Regulation (EEC) No 1017/68 of 19 July 1968 applying rules of competition to transport by rail, road and inland waterway (OJ L175, 23.7.1968, p 1), as last amended by the Act of Accession of Austria, Finland and Sweden,

— Council Regulation (EEC) No 4056/86 of 22 December 1986 laying down detailed rules for the application of Articles 85 and 86 of the Treaty to maritime transport (OJ L378, 31.12.1986, p 4), as last amended by the Act of Accession of Austria, Finland and Sweden,

— Council Regulation (EEC) No 3975/87 of 14 December 1987 laying down the procedure for the application of the rules on competition to undertakings in the air transport sector (OJ L374, 31.12.1987, p 1), as last amended by Regulation (EEC) No 2410/92 (OJ L240, 24.8.1992, p 18),

— Commission Regulation (EC) No 2843/98 of 22 December 1998 on the form, content and other details of applications and notifications provided for in Council Regulation (EEC) No 1017/68, (EEC) No 4056/86 and (EEC) No 3975/87 applying the rules on competition to the transport sector.

Regulations granting block exemption

— Article 4 of Council Regulation (EEC) No 1017/68 of 19 July 1968 applying rules of competition to transport by rail, road and inland waterway, as last amended by the Act of Accession of Austria, Finland and Sweden (exemption for groups of small and medium-sized undertakings),

— Articles 3 and 6 of Council Regulation (EEC) No 4056/86 of 22 December 1986 laying down detailed rules for the application of Articles 85 and 86 of the Treaty to maritime transport, as last amended by the Act of Accession of Austria, Finland and Sweden (exemption for agreements between carriers concerning the operation of scheduled maritime transport services, and exemption for agreements between transport users and conferences concerning the use of scheduled maritime transport services),

— Commission Regulation (EC) No 870/95 of 20 April 1995 on the application of Article 85(3) of the Treaty to certain categories of agreements, decisions and concerted practices between liner shipping companies (consortia) pursuant to Council Regulation (EEC) No 479/92 (OJ L89, 21.4.1992, p 7). Article 7 of this Regulation provides for an opposition procedure,

— Commission Regulation (EEC) No 1617/93 of 25 June 1993 on the application of Article 85(3) of the Treaty to certain categories of agreements and concerted practices concerning joint planning and coordination of schedules, joint operations, consultations on passenger and cargo tariffs on scheduled air services and slot allocation at airports (OJ L155, 26.6.1993, p 18), as last amended by Regulation (EC) No 1523/96 (OJ L190, 31.7.1996, p 11). See also the notice concerning procedures for communications to the Commission pursuant to Articles 4 and 5 of Commission Regulation (EEC) No 1617/93 (OJ C177, 29.6.1993, p 6).

Notices of a general nature[2]

— Commission notice concerning agreements, decisions and concerted practices in the field of cooperation between enterprises (OJ C75, 29.7.1968, p 3, as corrected in OJ C84, 28.8.1968, p 17). This defines the sorts of cooperation on market studies, accounting, R & D, joint use of production, storage or transport, ad hoc consortia, selling or after-sales service, advertising or quality labelling that the Commission considers not to fall under the prohibition of Article 85(1),

— Commission notice concerning its assessment of certain subcontracting agreements in relation to Article 85(1) of the Treaty (OJ C1, 3.1.1979, p 2),

— Commission notice concerning the assessment of cooperative joint ventures pursuant to Article 85 of the EC Treaty (OJ C43, 16.12.1993, p 2). This notice sets out the principles on the assessment of joint ventures,

— Commission communication on clarification of the Commission recommendations on the application of the competition rules to new transport infrastructure projects (OJ C298, 30.9.1997, p 5),

— Commission notice on the non-imposition or reduction of fines in cartel cases (OJ C207, 18.7.1996, p 4),

— Commission notice on the internal rules of procedure for processing requests for access to the file in cases under Articles 85 and 86 of the EC Treaty, Articles 65 and 66 of the ECSC Treaty and Council Regulation (EEC) No 4064/89 (OJ C23, 23.1.1997, p 3),

— notice on agreements of minor importance which do not fall under Article 85(1) of the Treaty establishing the European Community (OJ C372, 9.12.1997, p 13),

— Commission notice on the definition of the relevant market for the purposes of Community competition law (OJ C372, 9.12.1997, p 5).

A collection of these texts (as at 30 June 1994) was published by the Office or Official Publications of the European Communities (references Vol I: ISBN 92-826-6759-6, catalogue No CM-29-93-A01-EN-C). These texts can also be found at DGIV homepage "DGIV— Competition on Europa": http://europa.eu.int/comm/dg4home.htm

Pursuant to the Agreement, these texts will also cover the European Economic Area.

[4507]

NOTES
[1] As regards procedural rules applied by the EFTA Surveillance Authority, see Article 3 of Protocol 21 to the EEA Agreement and the relevant provisions in Protocol 4 to the Agreement between the EFTA States on the establishment of a Surveillance Authority and a Court of Justice.
[2] See also the corresponding notices published by the EFTA Surveillance Authority.

APPENDIX III
LIST OF MEMBER STATES AND EFTA STATES, ADDRESS OF THE COMMISSION AND OF THE EFTA SURVEILLANCE AUTHORITY, LIST OF COMMISSION INFORMATION OFFICES WITHIN THE COMMUNITY AND IN EFTA STATES AND ADDRESSES OF COMPETENT AUTHORITIES IN EFTA STATES

The Member States as at the date of this Annex are: Austria, Belgium, Denmark, Finland, France, Germany, Greece, Ireland, Italy, Luxembourg, the Netherlands, Portugal, Spain, Sweden and the United Kingdom.

The EFTA States which will be Contracting Parties to the EEA Agreement, as at the date of this Annex, are: Iceland, Liechtenstein and Norway.

The address of the Commission's Directorate-General for Competition is—

European Commission,
Directorate-General for Competition,
Rue de la Loi/Wetstraat 200,
B-1049 Brussels.
Tel. (32-2) 299 11 11
http://europa.eu.int/comm/dg04

The address of the EFTA Surveillance Authority's Competition Directorate is—

EFTA Surveillance Authority - ESA,
Competition and State Aid Directorate,
Rue de Trèves, 74,
B-1040 Brussels.
Tel. (32-2) 286 18 11
Fax (32-2) 286 18 00
http://www.efta.int

The addresses of the Commission's Information Offices in the Community are—

BELGIUM
Commission Européenne
Bureau en Belgique
Europese Commissie
Bureau in België
Rue Archiméde/Archimedesstraat 73
B-1040 Bruxelles/Brussel
Tel. (32-2) 295 38 44
Fax (32-2) 295 01 66
http://europa.eu.int/comm/represent/be

DENMARK
Europa-Kommissionen
Repræsentation i Danmark
Østergade 61 (Højbrohus)
Postboks 144
DK-1004 København K
Tel. (45) 33 14 41 40
Fax (45-33) 11 12 03
http://europa.eu.int/dk

FEDERAL REPUBLIC OF GERMANY
Europäische Kommission
Vertretung in der Bundesrepublik Deutschland
Zitelmannstraße 22
D-53113 Bonn
Tel. (49-228) 530 09-0
Fax (49-228) 530 09-50, 530 09-12

Europäische Kommission
Vertretung in der Bundesrepublik Deutschland
- Vertretung in Berlin
Kurfürstendamm 102
D-10711 Berlin 31
Tel. (49-30) 896 09 30
Fax (49-30) 892 20 59

Europäische Kommission
Vertretung in der Bundesrepublik Deutschland
- Vertretung in München
Erhardtstraße 27
D-80331 München
Tel. (49-89) 202 10 11
Fax (49-89) 202 10 15
http://www.eu-kommission.de

GREECE
Evropaiki Epitropi
Antiprosopia stin Ellada
2 Vassilissis Sofias
GR-10674 Athina
Tel. (30-1) 725 10 00
Fax (30-1) 724 46 20
http://www.forthnet.gr/ee

SPAIN
Comisión Europea
Representación en España
Paseo de la Castellana, 46
E-28046 Madrid
Tel. (34-1) 431 57 11
Fax (34-1) 432 17 64

Comisión Europea
Representación en Barcelona
Av. Diagonal, 407 bis, Planta 18
E-08008 Barcelona
Tel. (34-3) 415 81 77
Fax (34-3) 415 63 11
http://www.euroinfo.cce.es

FRANCE
Commission Européenne
Représentation en France
288, boulevard Saint-Germain
F-75007 Paris
Tel. (33-1) 40 63 38 00
Fax (33-1) 45 56 94 17/18/19

Commission Européenne
Représentation à Marseille
2, rue Henri Barbusse (CMCI)
F-13241 Marseille, Cedex 01
Tel. (33-4) 91 91 46 00
Fax (33-4) 91 90 98 07
http://europa.eu.int/france

IRELAND
European Commission
Representation in Ireland
18 Dawson Street
Dublin 2
Ireland
Tel. (353-1) 662 51 13
Fax (353-1) 662 51 18

ITALY
Commissione Europea
Rappresentanza in Italia
Via Poli 29
I-00187 Roma
Tel. (39-6) 69 99 91
Fax (39-6) 679 16 58, 679 36 52

Commissione Europea
Ufficio di Milano
Corso Magenta 59
I-20123 Milano
Tel. (39-2) 467 51 41
Fax (39-2) 480 12 535

LUXEMBOURG
Commission Européenne
Représentation au Luxembourg
Bâtiment Jean-Monnet
Rue Alcide de Gasperi
L-2920 Luxembourg
Tel. (352) 43 01-34935
Fax (352) 43 01-34433

NETHERLANDS
Europese Commissie
Bureau in Nederland
Korte Vijverberg 5
NL-2513 AB Den Haag
Nederland
Tel. (31-70) 346 93 26
Fax (31-70) 364 66 19
http://www.dds.nl/plein/europa

AUSTRIA
Europäische Kommission
Vertretung in Österreich
Kärtner Ring 5-7
A-1010 Wien
Tel: (43-1) 516 18
Fax (43-1) 513 42 25
http://www.europa.or.at

PORTUGAL
Comissão Europeia
Gabinete em Portugal
Centro Europeu Jean Monnet
Largo Jean Monnet, 1-10°
P-1250 Lisboa
Tel. (351-1) 350 98 00
Fax (351-1) 350 98 01/02/03
http://euroinfo.ce.pt

FINLAND
Euroopan komissio
Suomen edustusto
Europeiska kommissüonen
Representationen i Finland
31 Pohjoisesplanadi/Norra esplanaden 31
FIN-00100 Helsinki/Helsingfors
Tel. (358-9) 622 65 44
Fax (358-9) 65 67 28 (lehdistö ja tiedotus/press och information)

SWEDEN
Europeiska Kommissionen
Representation i Sverige
Nybrogatan 11, Box 7323
S-10390 Stockholm
Tel. (46-8) 562 444 11
Fax (46-8) 562 444 12
http://www.eukomm.se

UNITED KINGDOM
European Commission
Representation in the United Kingdom
Jean Monnet House
8 Storey's Gate
London SW1 P3 AT
United Kingdom
Tel. (44-171) 973 19 92
Fax (44-171) 973 19 00, 973 19 10

European Commission
Representation in Northern Ireland
9/15 Bedford Street (Windsor House)
Belfast BT2 7EG
United Kingdom
Tel. (44-1232) 24 07 08
Fax (44-1232) 24 82 41

European Commission
Representation in Wales
4 Cathedral Road
Cardiff CF1 9SG
United Kingdom
Tel. (44-1222) 37 16 31
Fax (44-1222) 39 54 89

European Commission
Representation in Scotland
9 Alva Street
Edinburgh EH2 4PH
United Kingdom
Tel. (44-131) 225 20 58
Fax (44-131) 226 41 05
http://www.cec.org.uk

The addresses of the Commission's Information Offices in the EFTA States are—

NORWAY
European Commission Delegation in Norway
Haakon VII's Gate 10 (9th floor)
N-0161 Oslo
Tel. (47-22) 83 35 83
Fax (47-22) 83 40 55

Forms for notifications and applications, as well as more detailed information on the EEA competition rules, can also be obtained from the following offices—

ICELAND
Samkeppnisstofnun (Icelandic Competition Authority)
Laugavegi 118
Pósthólf 5120
IS-125 Reykjavík
Iceland
Tel. (354-5) 527 422
Fax (354-5) 627 442

LIECHTENSTEIN
Amt Für Volkswirtschaft (Office of National Economy)
Gerberweg 5
FL-9490 Vaduz
Tel. (41-75) 236 68 73
Fax (41-75) 236 68 89

NORWAY
Norwegian Competition Authority
PO Box 8132 Dep. 0033 Oslo
Norway
Tel. (47-22) 40 09 00
Fax (47-22) 40 09 99

[4508]

ANNEX II
FORM TR(B)[1]

This form and the supporting documents should be forwarded in one original and 17 copies together with proof in a single copy of the representative's authority to act.

If the space opposite each question is insufficient, please use extra pages, specifying to which item on the form they relate.

TO THE EUROPEAN COMMISSION
Directorate-General for Competition
Rue de la Loi/Wetstraat 200
B-1049 Brussels.

Notification of an agreement, decision or concerted practice pursuant to Article 14(1) of Council Regulation (EEC) No 1017/68 with a view to obtaining a declaration of non-applicability of the prohibition in Article 2, available in states of crisis, pursuant to Article 6 of that Regulation.[2]

I. Information regarding parties

1.   Name, forenames and address of person submitting the notification. If such person is acting as representative, state also the name and address of the undertaking or association of undertakings represented and the name, forenames and address of the proprietors or partners or, in the case of legal persons, of their legal representatives.

Proof of representative's authority to act must be supplied.

If the notification is submitted by a number of persons or on behalf of a number of undertakings, the information must be given in respect of each person or undertaking.

2.   Name and address of the undertakings which are parties to the agreement, decision or concerted practice and name, forenames and address of the proprietors or partners, in the case of legal persons, of their legal representatives (unless this information has been given under I.1).

If the undertakings which are parties are not all associated in submitting the notification, state what steps have been taken to inform the other undertakings.

This information is not necessary in respect of standard contracts (see II.2(b)).

3.   If a firm or joint agency has been formed in pursuance of the agreement, decision or concerted practice, state the name and address of such firm or agency and the names, forenames and addresses of its representatives.

4.   If a firm or joint agency is responsible for operating the agreement, decision or concerted practice, state the name and address of such firm or agency and the names, forenames and addresses of its representatives.

Attach a copy of the statutes.

5.   In the case of a decision of an association of undertakings, state the name and address of the association and the names, forenames and addresses of its representatives.

Attach a copy of the statutes.

6.   If the undertakings are established or have their seat outside the EEA, state the name and address of a representative or branch established in the EEA.

II. Information regarding contents of agreement, decision or concerted practice

1.   Does the agreement, decision or concerted practice concern transport—
— by rail,
— by road,
— by inland waterway,
or operations of providers of services ancillary to transport?

2.   If the contents were reduced to writing, attach a copy of the full text unless (a) or (b) below provides otherwise.
    (a) Is there only an outline agreement or outline decision?
         If so, attach also copy of the full text of the individual agreements and implementing provisions.
    (b) Is there a standard contract, ie a contract which the undertaking submitting the notification regularly concludes with particular persons or groups of persons?

If so, only the text of the standard contract need be attached.

3.   If the contents were not, or were only partially, reduced to writing, state the contents in the space opposite.

4.   In all cases give the following additional information—
    (a) date of agreement, decision or concerted practice;
    (b) date when it came into force and, where applicable, proposed period of validity;
    (c) subject: exact description of the transport service or services involved, or of any other subject to which the agreement, decision or concerted practice relates;
    (d) aims of the agreement, decision or concerted practice;
    (e) terms of adherence, termination or withdrawal;

(f) sanctions which may be taken against participating undertakings (penalty clause, exclusion, etc).

III. Means of achieving the aims of the agreement, decision or concerted practice

1. State whether and how far the agreement, decision or concerted practice relates to—
   — adherence to certain rates and conditions of transport or other operating conditions,
   — restriction or control of the supply of transport, technical development or investment,
   — sharing of transport markets,
   — restrictions on freedom to conclude transport contracts with third parties (exclusive contracts),
   — application of different terms for supply of equivalent services.

2. Is the agreement, decision or concerted practice with transport services—
   (a) within one Member State or EFTA State only?
   (b) between Member States?
   (c) between EFTA States?
   (d) between the Community and one or more EFTA States?
   (e) between a Member State or an EFTA State and third countries?
   (f) between third countries in transit through one or more EC Member States and/or one or more EFTA States?

IV. Description of the conditions to be fulfilled by the agreement, decision or concerted practice so as to be exempt from the prohibition in Article 2

Describe to what extent—

1. the transport market is disturbed;

2. the agreement, decision or concerted practice is essential for reducing that disturbance;

3. the agreement, decision or concerted practice does not eliminate competition in respect of substantial parts of the transport market concerned.

V. State whether you intend to produce further supporting arguments and, if so, on which points

The undersigned declare that the information given above and in the Annexes attached hereto is correct. They are aware of the provisions of Article 22(1)(a) of Regulation (EEC) No 1017/68.

Place and date:

Signatures:

[4509]

NOTES
1   Notifications made by using form TR(B) issued by the Commission and the equivalent form issued by the EFTA side are equally valid. Any reference to EFTA States shall be understood to mean those EFTA States which are Contracting Parties to the Agreement on the European Economic Area.
2   See also this Regulation as adapted for EEA purposes (point 10 of Annex XIV to the Agreement on the European Economic Area, hereinafter referred to as "the EEA Agreement").

COMMISSION REGULATION

of 19 April 2000

on the application of Article 81(3) of the Treaty to certain categories of agreements, decisions and concerted practices between liner shipping companies (consortia)

(823/2000/EC)

(Text with EEA relevance)

NOTES
Date of publication in OJ: OJ L100, 20.4.2000, p 24.

THE COMMISSION OF THE EUROPEAN COMMUNITIES,

Having regard to the Treaty establishing the European Community,

Having regard to Council Regulation (EEC) No 479/92 of 25 February 1992 on the application of Article 85(3) of the Treaty to certain categories of agreements, decisions and concerted practices between liner shipping companies (consortia),[1] as amended by the Act of Accession of Austria, Finland and Sweden, and in particular Article 1 thereof,

Having published a draft of this Regulation,[2]

Having consulted the Advisory Committee on Restrictive Practices and Dominant Positions in Maritime Transport,

Whereas:

(1) Regulation (EEC) No 479/92 empowers the Commission to apply Article 81(3) of the Treaty to certain categories of agreements, decisions and concerted practices between shipping companies (consortia) relating to the joint operation of liner transport services, which, through the cooperation they bring about between the shipping companies that are parties thereto, are liable to restrict competition within the common market and to affect trade between Member States and may therefore be caught by the prohibition contained in Article 81(1) of the Treaty.

(2) The Commission has made use of this power by adopting Commission Regulation (EC) No 870/95.[3] In the light of experience thus acquired so far, it is possible to define a category of consortia which are capable of falling within the scope Article 81(1) but which can normally be regarded as satisfying the conditions laid down in Article 81(3).

(3) The Commission has taken due account of the special features of maritime transport. Those features will also constitute a material factor in any Commission assessment of consortia not covered by this block exemption.

(4) Consortia, as defined in this Regulation, generally help to improve the productivity and quality of available liner shipping services by reason of the rationalisation they bring to the activities of member companies and through the economies of scale they allow in the operation of vessels and utilisation of port facilities. They also help to promote technical and economic progress by facilitating and encouraging greater utilisation of containers and more efficient use of vessel capacity.

(5) Users of the shipping services provided by consortia generally obtain a fair share of the benefits resulting from the improvements in productivity and service quality which they bring about. Those benefits may also take the form of an improvement in the frequency of sailings and port calls, or an improvement in scheduling as well as better quality and personalised services through the use of more modern vessels and other equipment, including port facilities. Users can benefit effectively from consortia only if there is sufficient competition in the trades in which the consortia operate.

(6) Those agreements should therefore enjoy a block exemption, provided that they do not give the companies concerned the possibility of eliminating competition in a substantial part of the trades in question. In order to take account of the constant fluctuations in the maritime transport market and the frequent changes made by the parties to the terms of consortium agreements or to the activities covered by the agreements, one of the objects of this Regulation is to clarify the conditions to be met by consortia in order to benefit from the block exemption it grants.

(7) For the purpose of establishing and running a joint service, an essential feature inherent in consortia is the ability to make capacity adjustments. The non-utilisation of a certain percentage of vessel capacity within a consortium is not an essential feature of consortia.

(8) The block exemption granted by this Regulation should cover both consortia operating within a liner conference and consortia operating outside such conferences, except that it does not cover the joint fixing of freight rates.

(9) Rate-fixing activities come under Council Regulation (EEC) No 4056/86 of 22 December 1986 laying down detailed rules for the application of Articles 85 and 86 of the Treaty to maritime transport,[4] as amended by the Act of Accession of Austria, Finland and Sweden. Consortium members that wish to fix rates jointly and do not satisfy the criteria of Regulation (EEC) No 4056/86 must apply for individual exemption.

(10) The first of the conditions attaching to the block exemption should be that a fair share of the benefits resulting from the improved efficiency, as well as the other benefits offered by consortia, are passed on to transport users.

(11) This requirement of Article 81(3) should be regarded as being met when a consortium is in one or more of the three situations described below—

—there is effective price competition between the members of the conference within which the consortium operates as a result of independent rate action,

—there exists within the conference within which the consortium operates a sufficient degree of effective competition in terms of services provided between consortium members and other conference members that are not members of the consortium, as a result of the fact that the conference agreement expressly allows consortia to offer their own service arrangements, eg the provision by the consortium alone of a "just-in-time delivery" service or an advanced "electronic data interchange" (EDI) service allowing users to be kept informed at all times of the whereabouts of their goods, or a significant increase in the frequency of sailings and calls in the service offered by a consortium compared with that offered by the conference,

—consortium members are subject to effective, actual or potential competition from non-consortium lines, whether or not a conference operates in the trade or trades in question.

(12) In order to satisfy this same requirement of Article 81(3), provision should be made for a further condition aimed at promoting individual competition as to quality of service between consortium members as well as between consortium members and other shipping companies operating in the trade or trades.

(13) It should be a condition that consortia and their members do not, in respect of a given route, apply rates and conditions of carriage which are differentiated solely by reference to the country of origin or destination of the goods carried and thus cause within the Community deflections of trade that are harmful to certain ports, shippers, carriers or providers of services ancillary to transport, unless such rates or conditions can be economically justified.

(14) The aim of the conditions should also be to prevent consortia from imposing restrictions on competition which are not indispensable to the attainment of the objectives justifying the grant of the exemption. To this end, consortium agreements should contain a provision enabling each shipping line party to the agreement to withdraw from the consortium provided that it gives reasonable notice. However, provision should be made for a longer notice period in the case of highly integrated and/or high-investment consortia in order to take account of the higher investments undertaken to set them up and the more extensive reorganisation entailed in the event of a member's leaving. It should also be stipulated that, where a consortium operates with a joint marketing structure, each member should have the right to engage in independent marketing activities provided that it gives reasonable notice.

(15) Exemption must be limited to consortia which do not have the possibility of eliminating competition in a substantial part of the services in question.

(16) In order to determine for the purposes of exemption whether effective competition exists on each market upon which the consortium operates, account should be taken not only of direct trade between the ports served by a consortium but also of any competition from other liner services sailing from ports which may be substituted for those served by the consortium and, where appropriate, of other modes of transport.

(17) The block exemption granted by this Regulation is therefore applicable only on condition that on each market upon which the consortium operates the market share held by a consortium does not exceed a given size.

(18) The market share held by a consortium within a conference should be smaller in view of the fact that the agreements in question are superimposed on an existing restrictive agreement.

(19) However, it is appropriate to offer consortia which exceed the limits laid down in this Regulation by a given percentage but which continue to be subject to effective competition in the trades in which they operate a simplified procedure so that they may benefit from the legal certainty afforded by block exemptions. Such a procedure should also enable the Commission to carry out effective monitoring and simplify the administrative control of agreements.

(20) However, consortia which exceed the limit should be able to obtain exemption by individual decision, provided that they satisfy the tests of Article 81(3), regard being had to the special features of maritime transport.

(21) This Regulation should apply only to agreements concluded between the members of a consortium. Therefore, the block exemption should not cover restrictive agreements concluded between, on the one hand, consortia or one or more of their members, and, on the other hand, other shipping companies. Nor should it apply to restrictive agreements between different consortia operating in the same trade or between the members of such consortia.

(22) Certain obligations should also be attached to the exemption. In this respect, transport users should at all times be in a position to acquaint themselves with the conditions for the provision of the maritime transport services jointly operated by the members of the consortium. Provision should be made for real and effective consultations between the consortia and transport users on the activities covered by the agreements. This Regulation also specifies what is meant by "real and effective consultations" and what main procedural stages are to be followed for such consultations. Provision should be made for such mandatory consultation, limited to the activities of consortia as such.

(23) Such consultations are likely to secure a more efficient operation of maritime transport services which takes account of users' requirements. Consequently, certain restrictive practices which could ensue from such consultations should be exempted.

(24) For the purposes of this Regulation, the concept of *force majeure* is that laid down by the Court of Justice of the European Communities in its established case-law.

(25) Provision should be made whereby awards given at arbitration and recommendations made by conciliators and accepted by the parties are to be notified to the Commission forthwith, in order to enable it to verify that consortia are not thereby exempted from the conditions and obligations provided for in the Regulation and thus do not infringe the provisions of Articles 81 and 82.

(26) It is necessary to specify, in accordance with Article 6 of Regulation (EEC) No 479/92, the cases in which the Commission may withdraw from companies the benefit of the block exemption.

(27) 11 consortia benefited from the block exemption contained in Regulation (EC) No 870/95 by application of the opposition procedure in that Regulation which enabled the Commission in particular to check that they were subject to effective competition. There is no indication that circumstances have since become such that those consortia are no longer subject to effective competition. Those consortia should therefore continue to be exempted on the terms laid down in this Regulation.

(28) No applications under Article 12 of Regulation (EEC) No 4056/86 should need to be made in respect of agreements automatically exempted by this Regulation. However, when real doubts exist, companies should be permitted to request the Commission to declare whether their agreements comply with this Regulation.

(29) This Regulation is without prejudice to the application of Article 82 of the Treaty.

(30) In view of the expiry of Regulation (EC) No 870/95, it is appropriate to adopt a new Regulation renewing the block exemption,

NOTES

    1   OJ L55, 29.2.92, p 3.
    2   OJ C379, 31.12.99, p 13.
    3   OJ L89, 21.4.95, p 7.
    4   OJ L378, 31.12.86, p 4.

HAS ADOPTED THIS REGULATION:

CHAPTER I
SCOPE AND DEFINITIONS

Article 1

Scope

This Regulation shall apply to consortia only in so far as they provide international liner transport services from or to one or more Community ports.

[4510]

Article 2

Definitions

For the purposes of this Regulation—

    1.   "consortium" means an agreement between two or more vessel-operating carriers which provide international liner shipping services exclusively for the carriage of cargo, chiefly by container, relating to one or more trades, and the object of which is to bring about cooperation in the joint operation of a maritime transport service, and which improves the service that would be offered individually by each

of its members in the absence of the consortium, in order to rationalise their operations by means of technical, operational and/or commercial arrangements, with the exception of price fixing;

2. "liner shipping" means the transport of goods on a regular basis on a particular route or routes between ports and in accordance with timetables and sailing dates advertised in advance and available, even on an occasional basis, to any transport user against payment;

3. "service arrangement" means a contractual arrangement concluded between one or more transport users and an individual member of a consortium or a consortium itself under which, in return for an undertaking to commission the transportation of a certain quantity of goods over a given period of time, a user receives an individual undertaking from the consortium member or the consortium to provide an individualised service which is of a given quality and specially tailored to its needs;

4. "transport user" means any undertaking (such as shipper, consignee, forwarder) which has entered into, or demonstrated an intention to enter into, a contractual agreement with a consortium (or one of its members) for the shipment of goods, or any association of shippers;

5. "independent rate action" means the right of a maritime conference member to offer, on a case-by-case basis and in respect of goods, freight rates which differ from those laid down in the conference tariff, provided that notice is given to the other conference members.

[4511]

CHAPTER II
EXEMPTIONS

Article 3

Exempted agreements

1. Pursuant to Article 81(3) of the Treaty and subject to the conditions and obligations laid down in this Regulation, it is hereby declared that Article 81(1) of the Treaty shall not apply to the activities listed in paragraph 2 of this Article when contained in consortium agreements as defined in Articles 1 and 2 of this Regulation.

2. The declaration of non-applicability shall apply only to the following activities—
    (a) the joint operation of liner shipping transport services which comprise solely the following activities—
        (i) the coordination and/or joint fixing of sailing timetables and the determination of ports of call;
        (ii) the exchange, sale or cross-chartering of space or slots on vessels;
        (iii) the pooling of vessels and/or port installations;
        (iv) the use of one or more joint operations offices;
        (v) the provision of containers, chassis and other equipment and/or the rental, leasing or purchase contracts for such equipment;
        (vi) the use of a computerised data exchange system and/or joint documentation system;
    (b) temporary capacity adjustments;
    (c) the joint operation or use of port terminals and related services (such as lighterage or stevedoring services);
    (d) the participation in one or more of the following pools: cargo, revenue or net revenue;

  (e) the joint exercise of voting rights held by the consortium in the conference within which its members operate, in so far as the vote being jointly exercised concerns the consortium's activities as such;

  (f) a joint marketing structure and/or the issue of a joint bill of lading;

  (g) any other activity ancillary to those referred to above in points (a) to (f) which is necessary for their implementation.

3.   The following clauses shall in particular be considered ancillary activities within the meaning of paragraph 2(g)—

  (a) an obligation on members of the consortium to use on the trade or trades in question vessels allocated to the consortium and to refrain from chartering space on vessels belonging to third parties;

  (b) an obligation on members of the consortium not to assign or charter space to other vessel-operating carriers on the trade or trades in question except with the prior consent of the other members of the consortium.

[4512]

Article 4

Non-utilisation of capacity

The exemption provided for in Article 3 shall not apply to a consortium when the consortium includes arrangements concerning the non-utilisation of existing capacity whereby shipping line members of the consortium refrain from using a certain percentage of the capacity of vessels operated within the framework of the consortium.

[4513]

CHAPTER III
CONDITIONS FOR EXEMPTION

Article 5

Basic condition for the grant of exemption

The exemption provided for in Article 3 shall apply only if one or more of the conditions set out below are met—

  (a) there is effective price competition between the members of the conference within which the consortium operates, due to the fact that the members are expressly authorised by the conference agreement, whether by virtue of a statutory obligation or otherwise, to apply independent rate action to any freight rate provided for in the conference tariff; or

  (b) there exists within the conference within which the consortium operates a sufficient degree of effective competition between the conference members in terms of the services provided, due to the fact that the conference agreement expressly allows the consortium to offer its own service arrangements, irrespective of form, concerning the frequency and quality of transport services provided as well as freedom at all times to adapt the services it offers in response to specifc requests from transport users; or

  (c) whether or not a conference operates in the trade or trades in question, the consortium members are subject to effective competition, actual or potential, from shipping lines which are not members of that consortium.

[4514]

Article 6

Conditions relating to market share

1.   In order to qualify for the exemption provided for in Article 3, a consortium must possess on each market upon which it operates a market share of under 30% calculated by reference to the volume of goods carried (freight tonnes or 20-foot equivalent units) when it operates within a conference, and under 35% when it operates outside a conference.

2.   The exemption provided for in Article 3 shall continue to apply if the market share referred to in paragraph 1 of this Article is exceeded during any period of two consecutive calendar years by not more than one tenth.

3.   Where one of the limits specified in paragraphs 1 and 2 is exceeded, the exemption provided for in Article 3 shall continue to apply for a period of six months following the end of the calendar year during which it was exceeded. This period shall be extended to 12 months if the excess is due to the withdrawal from the market of a carrier which is not a member of the consortium.

[4515]

Article 7

Opposition procedure

1.   The exemption provided for in Articles 3 and 10 shall also apply to consortia whose market share on any market upon which it operates exceeds the limits laid down in Article 6 but does not, however, exceed 50% on any market, on condition that the agreements in question are notified to the Commission in accordance with the provisions of Commission Regulation (EC) No 2843/98,[1] and that the Commission does not oppose such exemption within a period of six months.

The period of six months shall run from the date on which notification takes effect in accordance with Article 4 of Regulation (EC) No 2843/98.

2.   Paragraph 1 shall apply only if express reference is made to this Article in the notification or in a communication accompanying it.

3.   The Commission may oppose the exemption.

It shall oppose the exemption if it receives a request to do so from a Member State within three months of the forwarding to the Member State of the notification referred to in paragraph 1. The request must be justified on the basis of considerations relating to the competition rules of the Treaty.

4.   The Commission may withdraw its opposition to the exemption at any time. However, where the opposition was raised at the request of a Member State and the request is maintained, it may be withdrawn only after consultation of the Advisory Committee on Restrictive Practices and Dominant Positions in Maritime Transport.

5.   If the opposition is withdrawn because the undertakings concerned have shown that the conditions of Article 81(3) are fulfilled, the exemption shall apply from the date of notification.

6.   If the opposition is withdrawn because the undertakings concerned have amended the agreement so that the conditions of Article 81(3) are fulfilled, the exemption shall apply from the date on which the amendments take effect.

7.   If the Commission opposes exemption and its opposition is not withdrawn, the effects of the notification shall be governed by the provisions of Section II of Regulation (EEC) No 4056/86.

[4516]

NOTES
1   OJ L354, 30.12.98, p 22.

Article 8

Other conditions

Eligibility for the exemptions provided for in Articles 3 and 10 shall be subject to the following conditions—

  (a) the consortium must allow each of its members to offer, on the basis of an individual contract, its own service arrangements;

  (b) the consortium agreement must give member companies the right to withdraw from the consortium without financial or other penalty such as, in particular, an obligation to cease all transport activity in the trade or trades in question, whether or not coupled with the condition that such activity may be resumed only after a certain period has elapsed. This right shall be subject to a maximum notice period of six months which may be given after an initial period of 18 months starting from the entry into force of the agreement.

      However, in the case of a highly integrated consortium which has a net revenue pool and/or high level of investment due to the purchase or charter by its members of vessels specifically for the purpose of setting up the consortium, the maximum notice period shall be six months, which may be given after an initial period of 30 months starting from the entry into force of the agreement;

  (c) where a consortium operates with a joint marketing structure, each member of the consortium must be free to engage in independent marketing without penalty subject to a maximum period of notice of six months;

  (d) neither the consortium nor consortia members shall, within the common market, cause detriment to certain ports, users or carriers by applying to the carriage of the same goods and in the area covered by the agreement, rates and conditions of carriage which differ according to the country of origin or destination or port of loading or discharge, unless such rates or conditions can be economically justified.

[4517]

CHAPTER IV
OBLIGATIONS

Article 9

Obligations attaching to exemption

1.   The obligations provided for in paragraphs 2 to [5] of this Article shall be attached to the exemptions provided for in Article 3 and Article 13(1).

2.   There shall be real and effective consultations between users or their representative organisations, on the one hand, and the consortium, on the other hand, for the purpose of seeking solutions on all important matters, other than purely operational matters of minor importance, concerning the conditions and quality of scheduled maritime transport services offered by the consortium or its members.

These consultations shall take place whenever requested by any of the abovementioned parties.

The consultations must take place, except in cases of *force majeure*, prior to the implementation of the measure forming the subject of the consultation. If, for reasons of *force majeure*, the members of the consortium are obliged to put a decision into effect before consultations have taken place, any consultations requested shall take place within 10 working days of the date of the request. Save in the case of such force majeure, to which reference shall be made in the notice announcing the measure, no public announcement of the measure shall be made before the consultations.

The consultations shall take place in accordance with the following procedural stages—

    (a) prior to the consultation, details of the subject matter of the consultation shall be notified in writing by the consortium to the other party;

    (b) an exchange of views shall take place between the parties either in writing or at meetings or both in the course of which the representatives of the consortium members and of the shippers taking part shall have authority to reach a common point of view and the parties shall use their best efforts to achieve that end;

    (c) where no common point of view can be reached despite the efforts of both parties, the disagreement shall be acknowledged and publicly announced. It may be brought to the Commission's attention by either party;

    (d) a reasonable period for the completion of consultations may be fixed, if possible, by common agreement between the two parties. That period shall be not less than one month, save in exceptional cases or by agreement between the parties.

    3.   The conditions concerning the maritime transport services provided by the consortium and its members, including those relating to the quality of such services and all relevant modifications, shall be made available on request to transport users at reasonable cost and shall be available for examination without cost at the offices of the consortium members, or the consortium itself, and their agents.

    4.   Arbitration awards and recommendations of conciliators, which have been accepted by the parties and which settle disputes concerning practices of consortia covered by this Regulation, shall be notified forthwith to the Commission by the consortium.

    5.   Any consortium claiming the benefit of this Regulation must be able, on being given a period of notice which the Commission shall determine on a case-by-case basis and which shall be not less than one month, to demonstrate at the Commission's request that the conditions and obligations imposed by Articles 5 to 8 and paragraphs 2 and 3 of this article are met and must submit to it the consortium agreement in question within this period.

[4518]

Article 10

Exemption for agreements between transport users and consortia on the use of scheduled maritime transport services

Agreements, decisions and concerted practices between transport users or their representative organisations, on the one hand, and a consortium exempted under Article 3, on the other hand, concerning the conditions and quality of liner shipping services provided by the consortium and all general questions connected with such services in so far as they arise out of the consultations provided for in paragraph 2 of Article 9, are hereby exempted from the prohibition laid down in Article 81(1) of the Treaty.

[4519]

CHAPTER V
MISCELLANEOUS PROVISIONS

Article 11

Professional secrecy

1.   Information acquired as a result of the application of Article 7 and paragraph 5 of Article 9 shall be used only for the purposes of this Regulation.

2.   The Commission and the authorities of the Member States, their officials and other servants shall not disclose information acquired by them as a result of the application of this Regulation which is of the kind covered by the obligation of professional secrecy.

3.   The provisions of paragraphs 1 and 2 shall not prevent publication of general information or studies which do not contain information relating to particular undertakings or associations of undertakings.

[4520]

Article 12

Withdrawal of block exemption

The Commission may withdraw the benefit of this Regulation, in accordance with Article 6 of Regulation (EEC) No 479/92, where it finds in a particular case that an agreement, decision or concerted practice exempted under Article 3 or Article 13(1) of this Regulation nevertheless has certain effects which are incompatible with the conditions laid down by Article 81(3) or are prohibited by Article 82 of the Treaty, in particular where—

   (a)   in a given trade, competition from outside the conference within which the consortium operates or from outside a particular consortium is not effective;

   (b)   a consortium fails repeatedly to comply with the obligations provided for in Article 9;

   (c)   the behaviour of a consortium produces effects that are incompatible with Article 82 of the Treaty;

   (d)   such effects result from an arbitration award.

[4521]

Article 13

Transitional provisions

1.   Article 81(1) of the Treaty shall not apply to agreements in force on 25 April 2000 which fulfil, on that date, the exemption requirements laid down by Regulation (EC) No 870/95 and to which the opposition procedure provided for by Article 7 of that Regulation was applied.

2.   A notification made before the entry into force of this Regulation pursuant to Article 7 of Regulation (EC) No 870/95 and in respect of which the period of six months has not expired on 25 April 2000 shall be deemed to have been made pursuant to Article 7 of this Regulation.

[4522]

Article 14

Entry into force

This Regulation shall enter into force on 26 April 2000.

It shall apply until 25 April 2005.

This Regulation shall be binding in its entirety and directly applicable in all Member States.

[4523]–[4700]

Done at Brussels, 19 April 2000.

C. INSURANCE

COUNCIL REGULATION

of 31 May 1991

on the application of Article 85(3) of the Treaty to certain categories of agreements, decisions and concerted practices in the insurance sector

(1534/91/EEC)

NOTES
Date of publication in OJ: OJ L143, 7.6.91, p 1.

THE COUNCIL OF THE EUROPEAN COMMUNITIES,

Having regard to the Treaty establishing the European Economic Community, and in particular Article 87 thereof,

Having regard to the proposal from the Commission,[1]

Having regard to the opinion of the European Parliament,[2]

Having regard to the opinion of the Economic and Social Committee,[3]

Whereas Article 85(1) of the Treaty may, in accordance with Article 85(3), be declared inapplicable to categories of agreements, decisions and concerted practices which satisfy the requirements of Article 85(3);

Whereas the detailed rules for the application of Article 85(3) of the Treaty must be adopted by way of a Regulation based on Article 87 of the Treaty;

Whereas cooperation between undertakings in the insurance sector is, to a certain extent, desirable to ensure the proper functioning of this sector and may at the same time promote consumers' interests;

Whereas the application of Council Regulation (EEC) No 4064/89 of 21 December 1989 on the control of concentrations between undertakings[4] enables the Commission to exercise close supervision on issues arising from concentrations in all sectors, including the insurance sector;

Whereas exemptions granted under Article 85(3) of the Treaty cannot themselves affect Community and national provisions safeguarding consumers' interests in this sector;

Whereas agreements, decisions and concerted practices serving such aims may, in so far as they fall within the prohibition contained in Article 85(1) of the Treaty, be exempted therefrom under certain conditions; whereas this applies in particular to agreements, decisions and concerted practices relating to the establishment of common risk premium tariffs based on collectively ascertained statistics or the number of claims, the establishment of standard policy conditions, common coverage of certain types of risks, the settlement of claims, the testing and acceptance of security devices, and registers of, and information on, aggravated risks;

Whereas in view of the large number of notifications submitted pursuant to Council Regulation No 17 of 6 February 1962: First Regulation implementing Articles 85 and 86 of the Treaty,[5] as last amended by the Act of Accession of Spain and Portugal, it is desirable that in order to facilitate the Commission's task, it should be enabled to declare, by way of Regulation, that the provisions of Article 85(1) of the Treaty are inapplicable to certain categories of agreements, decisions and concerted practices;

Whereas it should be laid down under which conditions the Commission, in close and constant liaison with the competent authorities of the Member States, may exercise such powers;

Whereas, in the exercise of such powers, the Commission will take account not only of the risk of competition being eliminated in a substantial part of the relevant market and of any benefit that might be conferred on policyholders resulting from the agreements, but also of the risk which the proliferation of restrictive clauses and the operation of accommodation companies would entail for policyholders;

Whereas the keeping of registers and the handling of information on aggravated risks should be carried out subject to the proper protection of confidentiality;

Whereas, under Article 6 of Regulation No 17, the Commission may provide that a decision taken in accordance with Article 85(3) of the Treaty shall apply with retroactive effect; whereas the Commission should also be able to adopt provisions to such effect in a Regulation;

Whereas, under Article 7 of Regulation No 17, agreements, decisions and concerted practices may, by decision of the Commission, be exempted from prohibition, in particular if they are modified in such manner that they satisfy the requirements of Article 85(3) of the Treaty; whereas it is desirable that the Commission be enabled to grant by Regulation like exemption to such agreements, decisions and concerted practices if they are modified in such manner as to fall within a category defined in an exempting Regulation;

Whereas it cannot be ruled out that, in specific cases, the conditions set out in Article 85(3) of the Treaty may not be fulfilled; whereas the Commission must have the power to regulate such cases pursuant to Regulation No 17 by way of a Decision having effect for the future,

NOTES

1   OJ C16, 23.1.90, p 13.
2   OJ C260, 15.10.90, p 57.
3   OJ C182, 23.7.90, p 27.
4   OJ L395, 30.12.89, p 1.
5   OJ 13, 21.2.62, p 204/62.

HAS ADOPTED THIS REGULATION—

Article 1

1.   Without prejudice to the application of Regulation No 17, the Commission may, by means of a Regulation and in accordance with Article 85(3) of the Treaty, declare that Article 85(1) shall not apply to categories of agreements between undertakings, decisions of associations of undertakings and concerted practices in the insurance sector which have as their object cooperation with respect to—

   (a)   the establishment of common risk premium tariffs based on collectively ascertained statistics or the number of claims;
   (b)   the establishment of common standard policy conditions;
   (c)   the common coverage of certain types of risks;
   (d)   the settlement of claims;
   (e)   the testing and acceptance of security devices;
   (f)   registers of, and information on, aggravated risks, provided that the keeping of these registers and the handling of this information is carried out subject to the proper protection of confidentiality.

2.   The Commission Regulation referred to in paragraph 1, shall define the categories of agreements, decisions and concerted practices to which it applies and shall specify in particular—

   (a)   the restrictions or clauses which may, or may not, appear in the agreements, decisions and concerted practices;
   (b)   the clauses which must be contained in the agreements, decisions and concerted practices or the other conditions which must be satisfied.

[4701]

Article 2

Any Regulation adopted pursuant to Article 1 shall be of limited duration.

It may be repealed or amended where circumstances have changed with respect to any of the facts which were essential to its being adopted; in such case, a period shall be fixed for modification of the agreements, decisions and concerted practices to which the earlier Regulation applies.

[4702]

Article 3

A Regulation adopted pursuant to Article 1 may provide that it shall apply with retroactive effect to agreements, decisions and concerted practices to which, at the date of entry into force of the said Regulation, a Decision taken with retroactive effect pursuant to Article 6 of Regulation No 17 would have applied.

[4703]

Article 4

1.   A Regulation adopted pursuant to Article 1 may provide that the prohibition contained in Article 85(1) of the Treaty shall not apply, for such period as shall be fixed in that Regulation, to agreements, decisions and concerted practices already in existence on 13 March 1962 which do not satisfy the conditions of Article 85(3) where—

—   within six months from the entry into force of the said Regulation, they are so modified as to satisfy the said conditions in accordance with the provisions of the said Regulation and

—   the modifications are brought to the notice of the Commission within the time limit fixed by the said Regulation.

The provisions of the first subparagraph shall apply in the same way to those agreements, decisions and concerted practices existing at the date of accession of new Member States to which Article 85(1) of the Treaty applies by virtue of accession and which do not satisfy the conditions of Article 85(3).

2.   Paragraph 1 shall apply to agreements, decisions and concerted practices which had to be notified before 1 February 1963, in accordance with Article 5 of Regulation No 17, only where they have been so notified before that date.

Paragraph 1 shall not apply to agreements, decisions and concerted practices existing at the date of accession of new Member States to which Article 85(1) of the Treaty applies by virtue of accession and which had to be notified within six months from the date of accession in accordance with Articles 5 and 25 of Regulation No 17, unless they have been so notified within the said period.

3.   The benefit of provisions adopted pursuant to paragraph 1 may not be invoked in actions pending at the date of entry into force of a Regulation adopted pursuant to Article 1; neither may it be invoked as grounds for claims for damages against third parties.

[4704]

Article 5

Where the Commission proposes to adopt a Regulation, it shall publish a draft thereof to enable all persons and organisations concerned to submit to it their comments within such time limit, being not less than one month, as it shall fix.

[4705]

Article 6

1.   The Commission shall consult the Advisory Committee on Restrictive Practices and Monopolies—

(a) before publishing a draft Regulation;

(b) before adopting a Regulation.

2.   Article 10(5) and (6) of Regulation No 17, relating to consultation of the Advisory Committee, shall apply. However, joint meetings with the Commission shall take place not earlier than one month after dispatch of the notice convening them.

[4706]

Article 7

Where the Commission, either on its own initiative or at the request of a Member State or of natural or legal persons claiming a legitimate interest, finds that, in any particular case, agreements, decisions and concerted practices, to which a Regulation adopted pursuant to Article 1 applies, have nevertheless certain effects which are incompatible with the conditions laid down in Article 85(3) of the Treaty, it may withdraw the benefit of application of the said regulation and take a decision in accordance with Articles 6 and 8 of Regulation No 17, without any notification under Article 4(1) of Regulation No 17 being required.

[4707]

Article 8

Not later than six years after the entry into force of the Commission Regulation provided for in Article 1, the Commission shall submit to the European Parliament and the Council a report on the functioning of this Regulation, accompanied by such proposals for amendments to this Regulation as may appear necessary in the light of experience.

[4708]

This Regulation shall be binding in its entirety and directly applicable in all Member States.

Done at Brussels, 31 May 1991.

COMMISSION REGULATION

of 21 December 1992

on the application of Article 85(3) of the Treaty to certain categories of agreements, decisions and concerted practices in the insurance sector

(3932/92/EEC)

NOTES

Date of publication in OJ: OJ L398, 31.12.92, p 7.

THE COMMISSION OF THE EUROPEAN COMMUNITIES,

Having regard to the Treaty establishing the European Economic Community,

Having regard to Council Regulation (EEC) No 1534/91 of 31 May 1991 on the application of Article 85(3) of the Treaty to certain categories of agreements, decisions and concerted practices in the insurance sector,[1]

Having published a draft of this Regulation,[2]

Having consulted the Advisory Committee on Restrictive Practices and Dominant Positions,

Whereas—

(1) Regulation (EEC) No 1534/91 empowers the Commission to apply Article 85(3) of the Treaty by regulation to certain categories of agreements, decisions and concerted practices in the insurance sector which have as their object—

    (a)   cooperation with respect to the establishment of common risk premium tariffs based on collectively ascertained statistics or the number of claims;

    (b)   the establishment of common standard policy conditions;

    (c)   the common coverage of certain types of risks;

    (d)   the settlement of claims;

    (e)   the testing and acceptance of security devices;

    (f)   registers of, and information on, aggravated risks.

(2) The Commission by now has acquired sufficient experience in handling individual cases to make use of such power in respect of the categories of agreements specified in points (a), (b), (c) and (e) of the list.

(3)   In many cases, collaboration between insurance companies in the aforementioned fields goes beyond what the Commission has permitted in its notice concerning cooperation between enterprises,[3] and is caught by the prohibition in Article 85(1). It is therefore appropriate to specify the obligations restrictive of competition which may be included in the four categories of agreements covered by it.

(4)   It is further necessary to specify for each of the four categories the conditions which must be satisfied before the exemption can apply. These conditions have to ensure that the collaboration between insurance undertakings is and remains compatible with Article 85(3).

(5)   It is finally necessary to specify for each of these categories the situations in which the exemption does not apply. For this purpose it has to define the clauses which may not be included in the agreements covered by it because they impose undue restrictions on the parties, as well as other situations falling under Article 85(1) for which there is no general presumption that they will yield the benefits required by Article 85(3).

(6)   Collaboration between insurance undertakings or within associations of undertakings in the compilation of statistics on the number of claims, the number of individual risks insured, total amounts paid in respect of claims and the amount of capital insured makes it possible to improve the knowledge of risks and facilitates the rating of risks for individual companies. The same applies to their use to establish indicative pure premiums or, in the case of insurance involving capitalisation, frequency tables. Joint studies on the probable impact of extraneous circumstances that may influence the frequency or scale of claims, or the yield of different types of investments, should also be included. It is, however, necessary to ensure that the restrictions are only exempted to the extent to which they are necessary to attain these objectives. It is therefore appropriate to stipulate that concerted practices on commercial premiums—that is to say, the premiums actually charged to policyholders, comprising a loading to cover administrative, commercial and other costs, plus a loading for contingencies or profit margins—are not exempted, and that even pure premiums can serve only for reference purposes.

(7)   Standard policy conditions or standard individual clauses for direct insurance and standard models illustrating the profits of a life assurance policy have the advantage of improving the comparability of cover for the consumer and of allowing risks to be classified more uniformly. However, they must not lead either to the standardisation of products or to the creation of too captive a customer base. Accordingly, the exemptions should apply on condition that they are not binding, but serve only as models.

(8)   Standard policy conditions may in particular not contain any systematic exclusion of specific types of risk without providing for the express possibility of including that cover by agreement and may not provide for the contractual relationship with the policyholder to be maintained for an excessive period or go beyond the initial object to the policy. This is without prejudice to obligations arising from Community or national law.

(9)   In addition, it is necessary to stipulate that the common standard policy conditions must be generally accessible to any interested person, and in particular to the policyholder, so as to ensure that there is real transparency and therefore benefit for consumers.

(10)   The establishment of co-insurance or co-reinsurance groups designed to cover an unspecified number of risks must be viewed favourably in so far as it allows a greater number of undertakings to enter the market and, as a result, increases the capacity for covering, in particular, risks that are difficult to cover because of their scale, rarity or novelty.

(11)   However, so as to ensure effective competition it is appropriate to exempt such groups subject to the condition that the participants shall not hold a share of the relevant market in excess of a given percentage. The percentage of 15% appears appropriate in the case of co-reinsurance groups. The percentage should be reduced to 10% in the case of co-insurance groups. This is because the mechanism of co-insurance requires uniform policy conditions and commercial premiums, with the result that residual competition between members of a co-insurance group is particularly reduced. As regards catastrophe risks or aggravated risks, those figures shall be calculated only with reference to the market share of the group itself.

(12)   In the case of co-reinsurance groups, it is necessary to cover the determination of the risk premium including the probable cost of covering the risks. It is further necessary to cover the determination of the operating cost of the co-reinsurance and the remuneration of the participants in their capacity as co-reinsurers.

(13)   It should be legitimate in both cases to declare group cover for the risks brought into the group to be subject to (a) the application of common or accepted conditions of cover, (b) the requirement that agreement be obtained prior to the settlement of all (or all large) claims, (c) joint negotiation of retrocession, and (d) a ban on retroceding individual shares. The requirement that all risks be brought into the group should however be excluded because that would be an excessive restriction of competition.

(14) The establishment of groups constituted only by reinsurance companies need not be covered by this Regulation due to lack of sufficient experience in this field.

(15) The new approach in the realm of technical harmonisation and standardisation, as defined in the Council resolution of 7 May 1985,[4] and also the global approach to certification and testing, which was presented by the Commission in its communication to the Council of 15 June 1989[5] and which was approved by the Council in its resolution of 21 December 1989,[6] are essential to the functioning of the internal market because they promote competition, being based on standard quality criteria throughout the Community.

(16) It is in the hope of promoting those standard quality criteria that the Commission permits insurance undertakings to collaborate in order to establish technical specifications and rules concerning the evaluation and certification of the compliance of security devices, which as far as possible should be uniform at a European level, thereby ensuring their use in practice.

(17) Cooperation in the evaluation of security devices and of the undertakings installing and maintaining them is useful in so far as it removes the need for repeated individual evaluation. Accordingly, the Regulation should define the conditions under which the formulation of technical specifications and procedures for certifying such security devices and the undertakings installing or maintaining them are authorised. The purpose of such conditions is to ensure that all manufacturers and installation and maintenance undertakings may apply for evaluation, and that the evaluation and certification are guided by objective and well-defined criteria.

(18) Lastly, such agreements must not result in an exhaustive list; each undertaking must remain free to accept devices and installation and maintenance undertakings not approved jointly.

(19) If individual agreements exempted by this Regulation nevertheless have effects which are incompatible with Article 85(3), as interpreted by the administrative practice of the Commission and the case-law of the Court of Justice, the Commission must have the power to withdraw the benefit of the block exemption. This applies for example where studies on the impact of future developments are based on unjustifiable hypotheses; or where recommended standard policy conditions contain clauses which create, to the detriment of the policyholder, a significant imbalance between the rights and obligations arising from the contract; or where groups are used or managed in such a way as to give one or more participating undertakings the means of acquiring or reinforcing a preponderant influence on the relevant market, or if these groups result in market sharing, or if policyholders encounter unusual difficulties in finding cover for aggravated risks outside a group. This last consideration would normally not apply where a group covers less than 25% of those risks.

(20) Agreements which are exempted pursuant to this Regulation need not be notified. Undertakings may nevertheless in cases of doubt notify their agreements pursuant to Council Regulation No 17,[7] as last amended by the Act of Accession of Spain and Portugal,

NOTES

[1] OJ L143, 7.6.91, p 1.
[2] OJ C207, 14.8.92, p 2.
[3] OJ C75, 29.7.68, p 3; corrigendum OJ C84, 28.8.68, p 14.
[4] OJ C136, 4.6.85, p 1.
[5] OJ C267, 19.10.89, p 3.
[6] OJ C10, 16.1.90, p 1.
[7] OJ 13, 21.2.62, p 204/62.

HAS ADOPTED THIS REGULATION—

TITLE I
GENERAL PROVISIONS

Article 1

Pursuant to Article 85(3) of the Treaty and subject to the provisions of this Regulation, it is hereby declared that Article 85(1) of the Treaty shall not apply to agreements, decisions by associations of undertakings and concerted practices in the insurance sector which seek cooperation with respect to—

(a) the establishment of common risk-premium tariffs based on collectively ascertained statistics or on the number of claims;

    (b) the establishment of standard policy conditions;
    (c) the common coverage of certain types of risks;
    (d) the establishment of common rules on the testing and acceptance of security devices.

[4709]

TITLE II
CALCULATION OF THE PREMIUM

Article 2

The exemption provided for in Article 1(a) hereof shall apply to agreements, decisions and concerted practices which relate to—

    (a) the calculation of the average cost of risk cover (pure premiums) or the establishment and distribution of mortality tables, and tables showing the frequency of illness, accident and invalidity, in connection with insurance involving an element of capitalisation—such tables being based on the assembly of data, spread over a number of risk-years chosen as an observation period, which relate to identical or comparable risks in sufficient number to constitute a base which can be handled statistically and which will yield figures on (*inter alia*)—
        — the number of claims during the said period,
        — the number of individual risks insured in each risk-year of the chosen observation period,
        — the total amounts paid or payable in respect of claims arisen during the said period,
        — the total amount of capital insured for each risk-year during the chosen observation period,

    (b) the carrying-out of studies on the probable impact of general circumstances external to the interested undertakings on the frequency or scale of claims, or the profitability of different types of investment, and the distribution of their results.

[4710]

Article 3

The exemption shall apply on condition that—

    (a) the calculations, tables or study results referred to in Article 2, when compiled and distributed, include a statement that they are purely illustrative;
    (b) the calculations or tables referred to in Article 2(a) do not include in any way loadings for contingencies, income deriving from reserves, administrative or commercial costs comprising commissions payable to intermediaries, fiscal or para-fiscal contributions or the anticipated profits of the participating undertakings;
    (c) the calculations, tables or study results referred to in Article 2 do not identify the insurance undertakings concerned.

[4711]

Article 4

The exemption shall not benefit undertakings or associations of undertakings which enter into an undertaking or commitment among themselves, or which oblige other undertakings, not to use calculations or tables that differ from those established pursuant to Article 2(a), or not to depart from the results of the studies referred to in Article 2(b).

[4712]

TITLE III
STANDARD POLICY CONDITIONS FOR DIRECT INSURANCE

Article 5

1.   The exemption provided for in Article 1(b) shall apply to agreements, decisions and concerted practices which have as their object the establishment and distribution of standard policy conditions for direct insurance.

2.   The exemption shall also apply to agreements, decisions and concerted practices which have as their object the establishment and distribution of common models illustrating the profits to be realised from an insurance policy involving an element of capitalisation.

[4713]

Article 6

1.   The exemption shall apply on condition that the standard policy conditions referred to in Article 5(1)—
- (a)   are established and distributed with an explicit statement that they are purely illustrative; and
- (b)   expressly mention the possibility that different conditions may be agreed; and
- (c)   are accessible to any interested person and provided simply upon request.

2.   The exemption shall apply on condition that the illustrative models referred to in Article 5(2) are established and distributed only by way of guidance.

[4714]

Article 7

1.   The exemption shall not apply where the standard policy conditions referred to in Article 5(1) contain clauses which—
- (a)   exclude from the cover losses normally relating to the class of insurance concerned, without indicating explicitly that each insurer remains free to extend the cover to such events;
- (b)   make the cover of certain risks subject to specific conditions, without indicating explicitly that each insurer remains free to waive them;
- (c)   impose comprehensive cover including risks to which a significant number of policyholders is not simultaneously exposed, without indicating explicitly that each insurer remains free to propose separate cover;
- (d)   indicate the amount of the cover or the part which the policyholder must pay himself (the "excess");
- (e)   allow the insurer to maintain the policy in the event that he cancels part of the cover, increases the premium without the risk or the scope of the cover being changed (without prejudice to indexation clauses), or otherwise alters the policy conditions without the express consent of the policyholder;
- (f)   allow the insurer to modify the term of the policy without the express consent of the policyholder;
- (g)   impose on the policyholder in the non-life assurance sector a contract period of more than three years;
- (h)   impose a renewal period of more than one year where the policy is automatically renewed unless notice is given upon the expiry of a given period;
- (i)   require the policyholder to agree to the reinstatement of a policy which has been suspended on account of the disappearance of the insured risk, if he is once again exposed to a risk of the same nature;

(j) require the policyholder to obtain cover from the same insurer for different risks;

(k) require the policyholder, in the event of disposal of the object of insurance, to make the acquirer take over the insurance policy.

2.   The exemption shall not benefit undertakings or associations of undertakings which concert or undertake among themselves, or oblige other undertakings not to apply conditions other than those referred to in Article 5(1).

[4715]

Article 8

Without prejudice to the establishment of specific insurance conditions for particular social or occupational categories of the population, the exemption shall not apply to agreements, decisions and concerted practices which exclude the coverage of certain risk categories because of the characteristics associated with the policyholder.

[4716]

Article 9

1.   The exemption shall not apply where, without prejudice to legally imposed obligations, the illustrative models referred to in Article 5(2) include only specified interest rates or contain figures indicating administrative costs;

2.   The exemption shall not benefit undertakings or associations of undertakings which concert or undertake among themselves, or oblige other undertakings not to apply models illustrating the benefits of an insurance policy other than those referred to in Article 5(2).

[4717]

TITLE IV
COMMON COVERAGE OF CERTAIN TYPES OF RISKS

Article 10

1.   The exemption under Article 1(c) hereof shall apply to agreements which have as their object the setting-up and operation of groups of insurance undertakings or of insurance undertakings and reinsurance undertakings for the common coverage of a specific category of risks in the form of co-insurance or co-reinsurance.

2.   For the purposes of this Regulation—

(a) "co-insurance groups" means groups set up by insurance undertakings which—

— agree to underwrite in the name and for the account of all the participants the insurance of a specified risk category, or

— entrust the underwriting and management of the insurance of a specified risk category in their name and on their behalf to one of the insurance undertakings, to a common broker or to a common body set up for this purpose;

(b) "co-reinsurance groups" means groups set up by insurance undertakings, possibly with the assistance of one or more re-insurance undertakings—

— in order to reinsure mutually all or part of their liabilities in respect of a specified risk category,

— incidentally, to accept in the name and on behalf of all the participants the re-insurance of the same category of risks.

3.   The agreements referred to in paragraph 1 may determine—

(a) the nature and characteristics of the risks covered by the co-insurance or co-reinsurance;

  (b) the conditions governing admission to the group;
  (c) the individual own-account shares of the participants in the risks co-insured or co-reinsured;
  (d) the conditions for individual withdrawal of the participants;
  (e) the rules governing the operation and management of the group.

4. The agreements alluded to in paragraph 2(b) may further determine—
  (a) the shares in the risks covered which the participants do not pass on for co-reinsurance (individual retentions);
  (b) the cost of co-reinsurance, which includes both the operating costs of the group and the remuneration of the participants in their capacity as co-reinsurers.

[4718]

Article 11

1. The exemption shall apply on condition that—
  (a) the insurance products underwritten by the participating undertakings or on their behalf do not, in any of the markets concerned, represent—
      — in the case of co-insurance groups, more than 10% of all the insurance products that are identical or regarded as similar from the point of view of the risks covered and of the cover provided,
      — in the case of co-reinsurance groups, more than 15% of all the insurance products that are identical or regarded as similar from the point of view of the risks covered and of the cover provided;
  (b) each participating undertaking has the right to withdraw from the group, subject to a period of notice of not more than six months, without incurring any sanctions.

2. By way of derogation from paragraph 1, the respective percentages of 10 and 15% apply only to the insurance products brought into the group, to the exclusion of identical or similar products underwritten by the participating companies or on their behalf and which are not brought into the group, where this group covers—
    — catastrophe risks where the claims are both rare and large,
    — aggravated risks which involve a higher probability of claims because of the characteristics of the risk insured.

This derogation is subject to the following conditions—
    — that none of the concerned undertakings shall participate in another group that covers risks on the same market, and
    — with respect to groups which cover aggravated risks, that the insurance products brought into the group shall not represent more than 15% of all identical or similar products underwritten by the participating companies or on their behalf on the market concerned.

[4719]

Article 12

Apart from the obligations referred to in Article 10, no restriction on competition shall be imposed on the undertakings participating in a co-insurance group other than—
  (a) the obligation, in order to qualify for the co-insurance cover within the group, to
      — take preventive measures into account,
      — use the general or specific insurance conditions accepted by the group,
      — use the commercial premiums set by the group;
  (b) the obligation to submit to the group for approval any settlement of a claim relating to a co-insured risk;

    (c) the obligation to entrust to the group the negotiation of reinsurance agreements on behalf of all concerned;

    (d) a ban on reinsuring the individual share of the co-insured risk.

[4720]

Article 13

Apart from the obligations referred to in Article 10, no restriction on competition shall be imposed on the undertakings participating in a co-reinsurance group other than—

    (a) the obligation, in order to qualify for the co-reinsurance cover, to
- take preventive measures into account,
- use the general or specific insurance conditions accepted by the group,
- use a common risk-premium tariff for direct insurance calculated by the group, regard being had to the probable cost of risk cover or, where there is not sufficient experience to establish such a tariff, a risk premium accepted by the group,
- participate in the cost of the co-reinsurance;

    (b) the obligation to submit to the group for approval the settlement of claims relating to the co-reinsured risks and exceeding a specified amount, or to pass such claims on to it for settlement;

    (c) the obligation to entrust to the group the negotiation of retrocession agreements on behalf of all concerned;

    (d) a ban on reinsuring the individual retention or retroceding the individual share.

[4721]

TITLE V
SECURITY DEVICES

Article 14

The exemption provided for in Article 1(d) shall apply to agreements, decisions and concerted practices which have as their object the establishment, recognition and distribution of—
- technical specifications, in particular technical specifications intended as future European norms, and also procedures for assessing and certifying the compliance with such specifications of security devices and their installation and maintenance,
- rules for the evaluation and approval of installation undertakings or maintenance undertakings.

[4722]

Article 15

The exemption shall apply on condition that—

    (a) the technical specifications and compliance assessment procedures are precise, technically justified and in proportion to the performance to be attained by the security device concerned;

    (b) the rules for the evaluation of installation undertakings and maintenance undertakings are objective, relate to their technical competence and are applied in a non-discriminatory manner;

    (c) such specifications and rules are established and distributed with the statement that insurance undertakings are free to accept other security devices or approve other installation and maintenance undertakings which do not comply with these technical specifications or rules;

    (d) such specifications and rules are provided simply upon request to any interested person;

(e) such specifications include a classification based on the level of performance obtained;
(f) a request for an assessment may be submitted at any time by any applicant;
(g) the evaluation of conformity does not impose on the applicant any expenses that are disproportionate to the costs of the approval procedure;
(h) the devices and installation undertakings and maintenance undertakings that meet the assessment criteria are certified to this effect in a non-discriminatory manner within a period of six months of the date of application, except where technical considerations justify a reasonable additional period;
(i) the fact of compliance or approval is certified in writing;
(j) the grounds for a refusal to issue the certificate of compliance are given in writing by attaching a duplicate copy of the records of the tests and controls that have been carried out;
(k) the grounds for a refusal to take into account a request for assessment are provided in writing;
(l) the specifications and rules are applied by bodies observing the appropriate provisions of norms in the series EN 45 000.

[4723]

TITLE VI
MISCELLANEOUS PROVISIONS

Article 16

1.   The provisions of this Regulation shall also apply where the participating undertakings lay down rights and obligations for the undertakings connected with them. The market shares, legal acts or conduct of the connected undertakings shall be considered to be those of the participating undertakings.

2.   "Connected undertakings" for the purposes of this Regulation means—
  (a) undertakings in which a participating undertaking, directly or indirectly—
    — owns more than half the capital or business assets, or
    — has the power to exercise more than half the voting rights, or
    — has the power to appoint more than half the members of the supervisory board, board of directors or bodies legally representing the undertaking, or
    — has the right to manage the affairs of the undertaking;
  (b) undertakings which directly or indirectly have in or over a participating undertaking the rights or powers listed in (a);
  (c) undertakings in which an undertaking referred to in (b) directly or indirectly has the rights or powers listed in (a).

3.   Undertakings in which the participating undertakings or undertakings connected with them have directly or indirectly the rights or powers set out in paragraph 2(a) shall be considered to be connected with each of the participating undertakings.

[4724]

Article 17

The Commission may withdraw the benefit of this Regulation, pursuant to Article 7 of 1534/91, where it finds in a particular case that an agreement, decision or concerted practice exempted under this Regulation nevertheless has certain effects which are incompatible with the conditions laid down in Article 85(3) of the EEC Treaty, and in particular where,
    — in the cases referred to in Title II, the studies are based on unjustifiable hypotheses,

— in the cases referred to in Title III, the standard policy conditions contain clauses other than those listed in Article 7(1) which create, to the detriment of the policyholder, a significant imbalance between the rights and obligations arising from the contract,

— in the cases referred to in Title IV—

   (a) the undertakings participating in a group would not, having regard to the nature, characteristics and scale of the risks concerned, encounter any significant difficulties in operating individually on the relevant market without organising themselves in a group;

   (b) one or more participating undertakings exercise a determining influence on the commercial policy of more than one group on the same market;

   (c) the setting-up or operation of a group may, through the conditions governing admission, the definition of the risks to be covered, the agreements on retrocession or by any other means, result in the sharing of the markets for the insurance products concerned or for neighbouring products;

   (d) an insurance group which benefits from the provisions of Article 11(2) has such a position with respect to aggravated risks that the policyholders encounter considerable difficulties in finding cover outside this group.

[4725]

Article 18

1.   As regards agreements existing on 13 March 1962 and notified before 1 February 1963 and agreements, whether notified or not, to which Article 4(2)(1) of Regulation No 17 applies, the declaration of inapplicability of Article 85(1) of the Treaty contained in this Regulation shall have retroactive effect from the time at which the conditions for application of this Regulation were fulfilled.

2.   As regards all other agreements notified before this Regulation entered into force, the declaration of inapplicability of Article 85(1) of the Treaty contained in this Regulation shall have retroactive effect from the time at which the conditions for application of this Regulation were fulfilled, or from the date of notification, whichever is later.

[4726]

Article 19

If agreements existing on 13 March 1962 and notified before 1 February 1963, or agreements covered by Article 4(2)(1) of Regulation No 17 and notified before 1 January 1967, are amended before 31 December 1993 so as to fulfil the conditions for application of this Regulation, and if the amendment is communicated to the Commission before 1 April 1994, the prohibition in Article 85(1) of the Treaty shall not apply in respect of the period prior to the amendment. The communication shall take effect from the time of its receipt by the Commission. Where the communication is sent by registered post, it shall take effect from the date shown on the postmark of the place of posting.

[4727]

Article 20

1.   As regards agreements covered by Article 85 of the Treaty as a result of the accession of the United Kingdom, Ireland and Denmark, Articles 18 and 19 shall apply, on the understanding that the relevant dates shall be 1 January 1973 instead of 13 March 1962 and 1 July 1973 instead of 1 February 1963 and 1 January 1967.

2.   As regards agreements covered by Article 85 of the Treaty as a result of the accession of Greece, Articles 18 and 19 shall apply, on the understanding that the relevant dates shall be 1 January 1981 instead of 13 March 1962 and 1 July 1981 instead of 1 February 1963 and 1 January 1967.

3.   As regards agreements covered by Article 85 of the Treaty as a result of the accession of Spain and Portugal, Articles 18 and 19 shall apply, on the understanding that the relevant dates shall be 1 January 1986 instead of 13 March 1962 and 1 July 1986 instead of 1 February 1963 and 1 January 1967.

[4.   As regards agreements covered by Article 85 of the Treaty as a result of the accession of Austria, Finland and Sweden, Articles 18 and 19 shall apply mutatis mutandis on the understanding that the relevant dates shall be the date of accession instead of 13 March 1962 and six months after the date of accession instead of 1 February 1963, 1 January 1967, 31 December 1993 and 1 April 1994. The amendments made to the agreements in accordance with Article 19 need not be notified to the Commission. However, the present paragraph shall not apply to agreements which at the date of accession already fall under Article 53(1) of the EEA Agreement.]

[4728]

_____

NOTES

    Para 4: added by the 1994 Act of Accession of the Kingdom of Norway, the Republic of Austria, the Republic of Finland and the Kingdom of Sweden, Annex I(III)(D)(9), as adjusted by Council Decision 95/1/EC, Annex I(III)(D)(9).

_____

Article 21

This Regulation shall enter into force on 1 April 1993.

    It shall apply until 31 March 2003.

[4729]–[4900]

    This Regulation shall be binding in its entirety and directly applicable in all Member States.

    Done at Brussels, 21 December 1992.

D. COOPERATION AGREEMENTS

COUNCIL REGULATION

of 20 December 1971

on application of Article 85(3) of the Treaty to categories of agreements, decisions and concerted practices

(2821/71/EEC)

NOTES

Date of publication in OJ: OJ L285, 29.12.71, p 46 (S edn 1971 (III), p 1032).

THE COUNCIL OF THE EUROPEAN COMMUNITIES,

Having regard to the Treaty establishing the European Economic Community, and in particular Article 87 thereof;

Having regard to the proposal from the Commission;

Having regard to the Opinion of the European Parliament;

Having regard to the Opinion of the Economic and Social Committee;

Whereas Article 85(1) of the Treaty may in accordance with Article 85(3) be declared inapplicable to categories of agreements, decisions and concerted practices which fulfil the conditions contained in Article 85(3);

Whereas the provisions for implementation of Article 85(3) must be adopted by way of regulation pursuant to Article 87;

Whereas the creation of a common market requires that undertakings be adapted to the conditions of the enlarged market and whereas cooperation between undertakings can be a suitable means of achieving this;

Whereas agreements, decisions and concerted practices for co-operation between undertakings which enable the undertakings to work more rationally and adapt their productivity and competitiveness to the enlarged market may, in so far as they fall within the prohibition contained in Article 85(1), be exempted therefrom under certain conditions; whereas this measure is necessary in particular as regards agreements, decisions and concerted practices relating to the application of standards and types, research and development of products or processes up to the stage of industrial application, exploitation of the results thereof and specialisation;

Whereas it is desirable that the Commission be enabled to declare by way of regulation that the provisions of Article 85(1) do not apply to those categories of agreements, decisions and concerted practices, in order to make it easier for undertakings to co-operate in ways which are economically desirable and without adverse effect from the point of view of competition policy;

Whereas it should be laid down under what conditions the Commission, in close and constant liaison with the competent authorities of the Member States, may exercise such powers;

Whereas under Article 6 of Regulation No 17[1] the Commission may provide that a decision taken in accordance with Article 85(3) of the Treaty shall apply with retroactive effect; whereas it is desirable that the Commission be empowered to issue regulations whose provisions are to the like effect;

Whereas under Article 7 of Regulation No 17 agreements, decisions and concerted practices may by decision of the Commission be exempted from prohibition, in particular if they are modified in such manner that Article 85(3) applies to them; whereas it is desirable that the Commission be enabled to grant by regulation like exemption to such agreements, decisions and concerted practices if they are modified in such manner as to fall within a category defined in an exempting regulation;

Whereas the possibility cannot be excluded that, in a specific case, the conditions set out in Article 85(3) may not be fulfilled; whereas the Commission must have power to regulate such a case in pursuance of Regulation No 17 by way of decision having effect for the future;

NOTES
1 OJ 13, 21.2.62, p 204/62.

HAS ADOPTED THIS REGULATION—

Article 1

1. Without prejudice to the application of Regulation No 17 the Commission may, by regulation and in accordance with Article 85(3) of the Treaty, declare that Article 85(1) shall not apply to categories of agreements between undertakings, decisions of associations of undertakings and concerted practices which have as their object—

    (a) the application of standards or types;

    (b) the research and development of products or processes up to the stage of industrial application, and exploitation of the results, including provisions regarding industrial property rights and confidential technical knowledge;

    (c) specialisation, including agreements necessary for achieving it.

2. Such regulation shall define the categories of agreements, decisions and concerted practices to which it applies and shall specify in particular—

    (a) the restrictions or clauses which may, or may not, appear in the agreements, decisions and concerted practices;

    (b) the clauses which must be contained in the agreements, decisions and concerted practices or the other conditions which must be satisfied.

[4901]

Article 2

1. Any regulation pursuant to Article 1 shall be made for a specified period.

2. It may be repealed or amended where circumstances have changed with respect to any of the facts which were basic to its being made; in such case, a period shall be fixed for modification of the agreements, decisions and concerted practices to which the earlier regulation applies.

[4902]

Article 3

A regulation pursuant to Article 1 may provide that it shall apply with retroactive effect to agreements, decisions and concerted practices to which, at the date of entry into force of that regulation, a decision issued with retroactive effect in pursuance of Article 6 of Regulation No 17 would have applied.

[4903]

Article 4

1. A regulation pursuant to Article 1 may provide that the prohibition contained in Article 85(1) of the Treaty shall not apply, for such period as shall be fixed by that regulation, to agreements, decisions and concerted practices already in existence on 13 March 1962 which do not satisfy the conditions of Article 85(3), where—

    — within six months from the entry into force of the regulation, they are so modified as to satisfy the said conditions in accordance with the provisions of the regulation; and

    — the modifications are brought to the notice of the Commission within the time limit fixed by the regulation.

[A regulation adopted pursuant to Article 1 may lay down that the prohibition referred to in Article 85(1) of the Treaty shall not apply, for the period fixed in the same regulation, to agreements and concerted practices which existed at the date of accession and which, by virtue of accession, come within the scope of Article 85 and do not fulfil the conditions set out in Article 85(3).]

[The provisions of the preceding sub-paragraph shall apply in the same way in the case of the accession of the Hellenic Republic, the Kingdom of Spain and of the Portuguese Republic.]

[The provisions of the preceding subparagraphs shall apply in the same way in the case of the accession of Austria, Finland and Sweden.]

2.   Paragraph 1 shall apply to agreements, decisions and concerted practices which had to be notified before 1 February 1963, in accordance with Article 5 of Regulation No 17, only where they have been so notified before that date.

[Paragraph 1 shall be applicable to those agreements and concerted practices which, by virtue of the accession, come within the scope of Article 85(1) of the Treaty and for which notification before 1 July 1973 is mandatory, in accordance with Articles 5 and 25 of Regulation 17, only if notification was given before that date.]

[Paragraph 1 shall not apply to agreements and concerted practices to which Article 85(1) of the Treaty applies by virtue of the accession of the Hellenic Republic and which must be notified before 1 July 1981, in accordance with Articles 5 and 25 of Regulation 17, unless they have been so notified before that date.]

[Paragraph 1 shall not apply to agreements and concerted practices to which Article 85(1) of the Treaty applies by virtue of the accession of the Kingdom of Spain and the Portuguese Republic and which must be notified before 1 July 1986, in accordance with Articles 5 and 25 of Regulation 17, unless they have been so notified before that date.]

[Paragraph 1 shall not apply to agreements and concerted practices to which Article 85(1) of the Treaty applies by virtue of the accession of Austria, Finland and Sweden and which must be notified within six months of accession, in accordance with Articles 5 and 25 of Regulation No 17, unless they have been so notified within that period. The present paragraph shall not apply to agreements and concerted practices which at the date of accession already fall under Article 53(1) of the EEA Agreement.]

3.   The benefit of the provisions laid down pursuant to paragraph 1 may not be claimed in actions pending at the date of entry into force of a regulation adopted pursuant to Article 1; neither may it be relied on as grounds for claims for damages against third parties.

[4904]

NOTES

Para 1: words in first pair of square brackets added by EEC Council Regulation No 2743/72, Art 1; words in second pair of square brackets originally added by the 1979 Act of Accession of the Hellenic Republic, Annex I(V)(5), substituted by the 1985 Act of Accession of the Kingdom of Spain and the Portuguese Republic, Annex I(IV)(9); words in third pair of square brackets added by the 1994 Act of Accession of the Kingdom of Norway, the Republic of Austria, the Republic of Finland and the Kingdom of Sweden, Annex I(III)(A)(2), as adjusted by Council Decision 95/1/EC, Annex I(III)(A)(2).

Para 2: words in first pair of square brackets added by EEC Council Regulation No 2743/72; words in second pair of square brackets added by the 1979 Act of Accession of the Hellenic Republic; words in third pair of square brackets added by the 1985 Act of Accession of the Kingdom of Spain and the Portuguese Republic; words in final pair of square brackets added by the 1994 Act of Accession of the Kingdom of Norway, the Republic of Austria, the Republic of Finland and the Kingdom of Sweden, Annex I(III)(A)(2), as adjusted by Council Decision 95/1/EC, Annex I(III)(A)(2).

Article 5

Before making a regulation, the Commission shall publish a draft thereof to enable all persons and organisations concerned to submit their comments within such time limit, being not less than one month, as the Commission shall fix.

[4905]

Article 6

1. The Commission shall consult the Advisory Committee on Restrictive Practices and Monopolies—
    (a) before publishing a draft regulation;
    (b) before making a regulation.

2. Paragraphs 5 and 6 of Article 10 of Regulation No 17, relating to consultation with the Advisory Committee, shall apply by analogy, it being understood that joint meetings with the Commission shall take place not earlier than one month after dispatch of the notice convening them.

[4906]

Article 7

Where the Commission, either on its own initiative or at the request of a Member State or of natural or legal persons claiming a legitimate interest, finds that in any particular case agreements, decisions or concerted practices to which a regulation made pursuant to Article 1 of this Regulation applies have nevertheless certain effects which are incompatible with the conditions laid down in Article 85(3) of the Treaty, it may withdraw the benefit of application of that regulation and take a decision in accordance with Articles 6 and 8 of Regulation No 17, without any notification under Article 4(1) of Regulation No 17 being required.

[4907]

This Regulation shall be binding in its entirety and directly applicable in all Member States.

Done at Brussels, 20 December 1971.

COMMISSION REGULATION

of 29 November 2000

on the application of Article 81(3) of the Treaty to categories of specialisation agreements

(2658/2000/EC)

(Text with EEA relevance)

NOTES
Date of publication in OJ: OJ L304, 5.12.2000, p 3.

THE COMMISSION OF THE EUROPEAN COMMUNITIES,

Having regard to the Treaty establishing the European Community,

Having regard to Council Regulation (EEC) No 2821/71 of 20 December 1971 on the application of Article 85(3) of the Treaty to categories of agreements, decisions and concerted practices,[1] as last amended by the Act of Accession of Austria, Finland and Sweden, and in particular Article 1(1)(c) thereof,

Having published a draft of this Regulation,[2]

Having consulted the Advisory Committee on Restrictive Practices and Dominant Positions,

Whereas:

(1) Regulation (EEC) No 2821/71 empowers the Commission to apply Article 81(3) (formerly Article 85(3)) of the Treaty by regulation to certain categories of agreements, decisions and concerted practices falling within the scope of Article 81(1) which have as their object specialisation, including agreements necessary for achieving it.

(2) Pursuant to Regulation (EEC) No 2821/71, in particular, the Commission has adopted Regulation (EEC) No 417/85 of 19 December 1984 on the application of Article 85(3) of the Treaty to categories of specialisation agreements,[3] as last amended by Regulation (EC) No 2236/97.[4] Regulation (EEC) No 417/85 expires on 31 December 2000.

(3) A new regulation should meet the two requirements of ensuring effective protection of competition and providing adequate legal security for undertakings. The pursuit of these objectives should take account of the need to simplify administrative supervision and the legislative framework to as great an extent as possible. Below a certain level of market power it can, for the application of Article 81(3), in general be presumed that the positive effects of specialisation agreements will outweigh any negative effects on competition.

(4) Regulation (EEC) No 2821/71 requires the exempting regulation of the Commission to define the categories of agreements, decisions and concerted practices to which it applies, to specify the restrictions or clauses which may, or may not, appear in the agreements, decisions and concerted practices, and to specify the clauses which must be contained in the agreements, decisions and concerted practices or the other conditions which must be satisfied.

(5) It is appropriate to move away from the approach of listing exempted clauses and to place greater emphasis on defining the categories of agreements which are exempted up to a certain level of market power and on specifying the restrictions or clauses which are not to be contained in such agreements. This is consistent with an economics-based approach which assesses the impact of agreements on the relevant market.

(6) For the application of Article 81(3) by regulation, it is not necessary to define those agreements which are capable of falling within Article 81(1). In the individual assessment of agreements under Article 81(1), account has to be taken of several factors, and in particular the market structure on the relevant market.

(7) The benefit of the block exemption should be limited to those agreements for which it can be assumed with sufficient certainty that they satisfy the conditions of Article 81(3).

(8) Agreements on specialisation in production generally contribute to improving the production or distribution of goods, because the undertakings concerned can concentrate on the manufacture of certain products and thus operate more efficiently and supply the products more cheaply. Agreements on specialisation in the provision of services can also be said to generally give rise to similar improvements. It is likely that, given effective competition, consumers will receive a fair share of the resulting benefit.

(9) Such advantages can arise equally from agreements whereby one participant gives up the manufacture of certain products or provision of certain services in favour of another participant ("unilateral specialisation"), from agreements whereby each participant gives up the manufacture of certain products or provision of certain services in favour of another participant ("reciprocal specialisation") and from agreements whereby the participants undertake to jointly manufacture certain products or provide certain services ("joint production").

(10) As unilateral specialisation agreements between non-competitors may benefit from the block exemption provided by Commission Regulation (EC) No 2790/1999 of 22 December 1999 on the application of Article 81(3) of the Treaty to categories of vertical agreements and concerted practices,[5] the application of the present Regulation to unilateral specialisation agreements should be limited to agreements between competitors.

(11) All other agreements entered into between undertakings relating to the conditions under which they specialise in the production of goods and/or services should fall within the scope of this Regulation. The block exemption should also apply to provisions contained in specialisation agreements which do not constitute the primary object of such agreements, but are directly related to and necessary for their implementation, and to certain related purchasing and marketing arrangements.

(12) To ensure that the benefits of specialisation will materialise without one party leaving the market downstream of production, unilateral and reciprocal specialisation agreements should only be covered by this Regulation where they provide for supply and purchase obligations. These obligations may, but do not have to, be of an exclusive nature.

(13) It can be presumed that, where the participating undertakings' share of the relevant market does not exceed 20%, specialisation agreements as defined in this Regulation will, as a general rule, give rise to economic benefits in the form of economies of scale or scope or better production technologies, while allowing consumers a fair share of the resulting benefits.

(14) This Regulation should not exempt agreements containing restrictions which are not indispensable to attain the positive effects mentioned above. In principle certain severe anti-competitive restraints relating to the fixing of prices charged to third parties, limitation of output or sales, and allocation of markets or customers should be excluded from the benefit of the block exemption established by this Regulation irrespective of the market share of the undertakings concerned.

(15) The market share limitation, the non-exemption of certain agreements and the conditions provided for in this Regulation normally ensure that the agreements to which the block exemption applies do not enable the participating undertakings to eliminate competition in respect of a substantial part of the products or services in question.

(16) In particular cases in which the agreements falling under this Regulation nevertheless have effects incompatible with Article 81(3) of the Treaty, the Commission may withdraw the benefit of the block exemption.

(17) In order to facilitate the conclusion of specialisation agreements, which can have a bearing on the structure of the participating undertakings, the period of validity of this Regulation should be fixed at 10 years.

(18) This Regulation is without prejudice to the application of Article 82 of the Treaty.

(19) In accordance with the principle of the primacy of Community law, no measure taken pursuant to national laws on competition should prejudice the uniform application throughout the common market of the Community competition rules or the full effect of any measures adopted in implementation of those rules, including this Regulation,

NOTES
1   OJ L285, 29.12.71, p 46.
2   OJ C118, 27.4.2000, p 3.
3   OJ L53, 22.2.85, p 1.
4   OJ L306, 11.11.97, p 12.
5   OJ L336, 29.12.99, p 21.

HAS ADOPTED THIS REGULATION:

Article 1

Exemption

1.   Pursuant to Article 81(3) of the Treaty and subject to the provisions of this Regulation, it is hereby declared that Article 81(1) shall not apply to the following agreements entered into between two or more undertakings (hereinafter referred to as "the parties") which relate to the conditions under which those undertakings specialise in the production of products (hereinafter referred to as "specialisation agreements")—

  (a) unilateral specialisation agreements, by virtue of which one party agrees to cease production of certain products or to refrain from producing those products and to purchase them from a competing undertaking, while the competing undertaking agrees to produce and supply those products; or

  (b) reciprocal specialisation agreements, by virtue of which two or more parties on a reciprocal basis agree to cease or refrain from producing certain but different products and to purchase these products from the other parties, who agree to supply them; or

  (c) joint production agreements, by virtue of which two or more parties agree to produce certain products jointly.

This exemption shall apply to the extent that such specialisation agreements contain restrictions of competition falling within the scope of Article 81(1) of the Treaty.

2.   The exemption provided for in paragraph 1 shall also apply to provisions contained in specialisation agreements, which do not constitute the primary object of such agreements, but are directly related to and necessary for their implementation, such as those concerning the assignment or use of intellectual property rights.

The first subparagraph does, however, not apply to provisions which have the same object as the restrictions of competition enumerated in Article 5(1).

[4908]

Article 2

Definitions

For the purposes of this Regulation—

1.   "Agreement" means an agreement, a decision of an association of undertakings or a concerted practice.

2.   "Participating undertakings" means undertakings party to the agreement and their respective connected undertakings.

3.   "Connected undertakings" means—
   (a) undertakings in which a party to the agreement, directly or indirectly:
     (i) has the power to exercise more than half the voting rights, or
     (ii) has the power to appoint more than half the members of the supervisory board, board of management or bodies legally representing the undertaking, or
     (iii) has the right to manage the undertaking's affairs;
   (b) undertakings which directly or indirectly have, over a party to the agreement, the rights or powers listed in (a);
   (c) undertakings in which an undertaking referred to in (b) has, directly or indirectly, the rights or powers listed in (a);
   (d) undertakings in which a party to the agreement together with one or more of the undertakings referred to in (a), (b) or (c), or in which two or more of the latter undertakings, jointly have the rights or powers listed in (a);
   (e) undertakings in which the rights or the powers listed in (a) are jointly held by—
     (i) parties to the agreement or their respective connected undertakings referred to in (a) to (d), or
     (ii) one or more of the parties to the agreement or one or more of their connected undertakings referred to in (a) to (d) and one or more third parties.

4.   "Product" means a good and/or a service, including both intermediary goods and/or services and final goods and/or services, with the exception of distribution and rental services.

5.   "Production" means the manufacture of goods or the provision of services and includes production by way of subcontracting.

6.   "Relevant market" means the relevant product and geographic market(s) to which the products, which are the subject matter of a specialisation agreement, belong.

7.   "Competing undertaking" means an undertaking that is active on the relevant market (an actual competitor) or an undertaking that would, on realistic grounds, undertake the necessary additional investments or other necessary switching costs so that it could enter the relevant market in response to a small and permanent increase in relative prices (a potential competitor).

8.   "Exclusive supply obligation" means an obligation not to supply a competing undertaking other than a party to the agreement with the product to which the specialisation agreement relates.

PART IV
EC MATERIALS

9. "Exclusive purchase obligation" means an obligation to purchase the product to which the specialisation agreement relates only from the party which agrees to supply it.

[4909]

Article 3

Purchasing and marketing arrangements

The exemption provided for in Article 1 shall also apply where—
   (a) the parties accept an exclusive purchase and/or exclusive supply obligation in the context of a unilateral or reciprocal specialisation agreement or a joint production agreement, or
   (b) the parties do not sell the products which are the object of the specialisation agreement independently but provide for joint distribution or agree to appoint a third party distributor on an exclusive or non-exclusive basis in the context of a joint production agreement provided that the third party is not a competing undertaking.

[4910]

Article 4

Market share threshold

The exemption provided for in Article 1 shall apply on condition that the combined market share of the participating undertakings does not exceed 20% of the relevant market.

[4911]

Article 5

Agreements not covered by the exemption

1.   The exemption provided for in Article 1 shall not apply to agreements which, directly or indirectly, in isolation or in combination with other factors under the control of the parties, have as their object—
   (a) the fixing of prices when selling the products to third parties;
   (b) the limitation of output or sales; or
   (c) the allocation of markets or customers.

2.   Paragraph 1 shall not apply to—
   (a) provisions on the agreed amount of products in the context of unilateral or reciprocal specialisation agreements or the setting of the capacity and production volume of a production joint venture in the context of a joint production agreement;
   (b) the setting of sales targets and the fixing of prices that a production joint venture charges to its immediate customers in the context of point (b) of Article 3.

[4912]

Article 6

Application of the market share threshold

1.   For the purposes of applying the market share threshold provided for in Article 4 the following rules shall apply—
   (a) the market share shall be calculated on the basis of the market sales value; if market sales value data are not available, estimates based on other reliable market information, including market sales volumes, may be used to establish the market share of the undertaking concerned;

(b) the market share shall be calculated on the basis of data relating to the preceding calendar year;

(c) the market share held by the undertakings referred to in point 3(e) of Article 2 shall be apportioned equally to each undertaking having the rights or the powers listed in point 3(a) of Article 2.

2. If the market share referred to in Article 4 is initially not more than 20% but subsequently rises above this level without exceeding 25%, the exemption provided for in Article 1 shall continue to apply for a period of two consecutive calendar years following the year in which the 20% threshold was first exceeded.

3. If the market share referred to in Article 4 is initially not more than 20% but subsequently rises above 25%, the exemption provided for in Article 1 shall continue to apply for one calendar year following the year in which the level of 25% was first exceeded.

4. The benefit of paragraphs 2 and 3 may not be combined so as to exceed a period of two calendar years.

[4913]

Article 7

Withdrawal

The Commission may withdraw the benefit of this Regulation, pursuant to Article 7 of Regulation (EEC) No 2821/71, where, either on its own initiative or at the request of a Member State or of a natural or legal person claiming a legitimate interest, it finds in a particular case that an agreement to which the exemption provided for in Article 1 applies nevertheless has effects which are incompatible with the conditions laid down in Article 81(3) of the Treaty, and in particular where—

(a) the agreement is not yielding significant results in terms of rationalisation or consumers are not receiving a fair share of the resulting benefit, or

(b) the products which are the subject of the specialisation are not subject in the common market or a substantial part thereof to effective competition from identical products or products considered by users to be equivalent in view of their characteristics, price and intended use.

[4914]

Article 8

Transitional period

The prohibition laid down in Article 81(1) of the Treaty shall not apply during the period from 1 January 2001 to 30 June 2002 in respect of agreements already in force on 31 December 2000 which do not satisfy the conditions for exemption provided for in this Regulation but which satisfy the conditions for exemption provided for in Regulation (EEC) No 417/85.

[4915]

Article 9

Period of validity

This Regulation shall enter into force on 1 January 2001.

It shall expire on 31 December 2010.

This Regulation shall be binding in its entirety and directly applicable in all Member States.

[4916]

Done at Brussels, 29 November 2000.

PART IV
EC MATERIALS

COMMISSION REGULATION

of 29 November 2000

on the application of Article 81(3) of the Treaty to categories of research and development agreements

(2659/2000/EC)

(Text with EEA relevance)

NOTES

Date of publication in OJ: OJ L304, 5.12.2000, p 7.

THE COMMISSION OF THE EUROPEAN COMMUNITIES,

Having regard to the Treaty establishing the European Community,

Having regard to Council Regulation (EEC) No 2821/71 of 20 December 1971 on application of Article 85(3) of the Treaty to categories of agreements, decisions and concerted practices,[1] as last amended by the Act of Accession of Austria, Finland and Sweden, and in particular Article 1(1)(b) thereof,

Having published a draft of this Regulation,[2]

Having consulted the Advisory Committee on Restrictive Practices and Dominant Positions,

Whereas:

(1) Regulation (EEC) No 2821/71 empowers the Commission to apply Article 81(3) (formerly Article 85(3)) of the Treaty by regulation to certain categories of agreements, decisions and concerted practices falling within the scope of Article 81(1) which have as their object the research and development of products or processes up to the stage of industrial application, and exploitation of the results, including provisions regarding intellectual property rights.

(2) Article 163(2) of the Treaty calls upon the Community to encourage undertakings, including small and medium-sized undertakings, in their research and technological development activities of high quality, and to support their efforts to cooperate with one another. Pursuant to Council Decision 1999/65/EC of 22 December 1998 concerning the rules for the participation of undertakings, research centres and universities and for the dissemination of research results for the implementation of the fifth framework programme of the European Community (1998-2002)[3] and Commission Regulation (EC) No 996/1999[4] on the implementation of Decision 1999/65/EC, indirect research and technological development (RTD) actions supported under the fifth framework programme of the Community are required to be carried out cooperatively.

(3) Agreements on the joint execution of research work or the joint development of the results of the research, up to but not including the stage of industrial application, generally do not fall within the scope of Article 81(1) of the Treaty. In certain circumstances, however, such as where the parties agree not to carry out other research and development in the same field, thereby forgoing the opportunity of gaining competitive advantages over the other parties, such agreements may fall within Article 81(1) and should therefore be included within the scope of this Regulation.

(4) Pursuant to Regulation (EEC) No 2821/71, the Commission has, in particular, adopted Regulation (EEC) No 418/85 of 19 December 1984 on the application of Article 85(3) of the Treaty to categories of research and development agreements,[5] as last amended by Regulation (EC) No 2236/97.[6] Regulation (EEC) No 418/85 expires on 31 December 2000.

(5) A new regulation should meet the two requirements of ensuring effective protection of competition and providing adequate legal security for undertakings. The pursuit of these objectives should take account of the need to simplify administrative supervision and the legislative framework to as great an extent possible. Below a certain level of market power it can, for the application of Article 81(3), in general be presumed that the positive effects of research and development agreements will outweigh any negative effects on competition.

(6) Regulation (EEC) No 2821/71 requires the exempting regulation of the Commission to define the categories of agreements, decisions and concerted practices to which it applies, to specify the restrictions or clauses which may, or may not, appear in the agreements, decisions and concerted practices, and to specify the clauses which must be contained in the agreements, decisions and concerted practices or the other conditions which must be satisfied.

(7) It is appropriate to move away from the approach of listing exempted clauses and to place greater emphasis on defining the categories of agreements which are exempted up to a certain level of market power and on specifying the restrictions or clauses which are not to be contained in such agreements. This is consistent with an economics based approach which assesses the impact of agreements on the relevant market.

(8) For the application of Article 81(3) by regulation, it is not necessary to define those agreements which are capable of falling within Article 81(1). In the individual assessment of agreements under Article 81(1), account has to be taken of several factors, and in particular the market structure on the relevant market.

(9) The benefit of the block exemption should be limited to those agreements for which it can be assumed with sufficient certainty that they satisfy the conditions of Article 81(3).

(10) Cooperation in research and development and in the exploitation of the results generally promotes technical and economic progress by increasing the dissemination of know-how between the parties and avoiding duplication of research and development work, by stimulating new advances through the exchange of complementary know-how, and by rationalising the manufacture of the products or application of the processes arising out of the research and development.

(11) The joint exploitation of results can be considered as the natural consequence of joint research and development. It can take different forms such as manufacture, the exploitation of intellectual property rights that substantially contribute to technical or economic progress, or the marketing of new products.

(12) Consumers can generally be expected to benefit from the increased volume and effectiveness of research and development through the introduction of new or improved products or services or the reduction of prices brought about by new or improved processes.

(13) In order to attain the benefits and objectives of joint research and development the benefit of this Regulation should also apply to provisions contained in research and development agreements which do not constitute the primary object of such agreements, but are directly related to and necessary for their implementation.

(14) In order to justify the exemption, the joint exploitation should relate to products or processes for which the use of the results of the research and development is decisive, and each of the parties is given the opportunity of exploiting any results that interest it. However, where academic bodies, research institutes or undertakings which supply research and development as a commercial service without normally being active in the exploitation of results participate in research and development, they may agree to use the results of research and development solely for the purpose of further research. Similarly, non-competitors may agree to limit their right to exploitation to one or more technical fields of application to facilitate cooperation between parties with complementary skills.

(15) The exemption granted under this Regulation should be limited to research and development agreements which do not afford the undertakings the possibility of eliminating competition in respect of a substantial part of the products or services in question. It is necessary to exclude from the block exemption agreements between competitors whose combined share of the market for products or services capable of being improved or replaced by the results of the research and development exceeds a certain level at the time the agreement is entered into.

(16) In order to guarantee the maintenance of effective competition during joint exploitation of the results, provision should be made for the block exemption to cease to apply if the parties' combined share of the market for the products arising out of the joint research and development becomes too great. The exemption should continue to apply, irrespective of the parties' market shares, for a certain period after the commencement of joint exploitation, so as to await stabilisation of their market shares, particularly after the introduction of an entirely new product, and to guarantee a minimum period of return on the investments involved.

(17) This Regulation should not exempt agreements containing restrictions which are not indispensable to attain the positive effects mentioned above. In principle certain severe anti-competitive restraints such as limitations on the freedom of parties to carry out research and development in a field unconnected to the agreement, the fixing of prices charged to third parties, limitations on output or sales, allocation of markets or customers, and limitations on effecting passive sales for the contract products in territories reserved for other parties should be excluded from the benefit of the block exemption established by this Regulation irrespective of the market share of the undertakings concerned.

(18) The market share limitation, the non-exemption of certain agreements, and the conditions provided for in this Regulation normally ensure that the agreements to which the block exemption applies do not enable the participating undertakings to eliminate competition in respect of a substantial part of the products or services in question.

(19) In particular cases in which the agreements falling under this Regulation nevertheless have effects incompatible with Article 81(3) of the Treaty, the Commission may withdraw the benefit of the block exemption.

(20) Agreements between undertakings which are not competing manufacturers of products capable of being improved or replaced by the results of the research and development will only eliminate effective competition in research and development in exceptional circumstances. It is therefore appropriate to enable such agreements to benefit from the block exemption irrespective of market share and to address such exceptional cases by way of withdrawal of its benefit.

(21) As research and development agreements are often of a long-term nature, especially where the cooperation extends to the exploitation of the results, the period of validity of this Regulation should be fixed at 10 years.

(22) This Regulation is without prejudice to the application of Article 82 of the Treaty.

(23) In accordance with the principle of the primacy of Community law, no measure taken pursuant to national laws on competition should prejudice the uniform application throughout the common market of the Community competition rules or the full effect of any measures adopted in implementation of those rules, including this Regulation,

NOTES

1   OJ L285, 29.12.71, p 46.
2   OJ C118, 27.4.2000, p 3.
3   OJ L26, 1.2.99, p 46.
4   OJ L122, 12.5.99, p 9.
5   OJ L53, 22.2.85, p 5.
6   OJ L306, 11.11.97, p 12.

HAS ADOPTED THIS REGULATION:

Article 1

Exemption

1.   Pursuant to Article 81(3) of the Treaty and subject to the provisions of this Regulation, it is hereby declared that Article 81(1) shall not apply to agreements entered into between two or more undertakings (hereinafter referred to as "the parties") which relate to the conditions under which those undertakings pursue—

  (a) joint research and development of products or processes and joint exploitation of the results of that research and development;

  (b) joint exploitation of the results of research and development of products or processes jointly carried out pursuant to a prior agreement between the same parties; or

  (c) joint research and development of products or processes excluding joint exploitation of the results.

This exemption shall apply to the extent that such agreements (hereinafter referred to as "research and development agreements") contain restrictions of competition falling within the scope of Article 81(1).

2.   The exemption provided for in paragraph 1 shall also apply to provisions contained in research and development agreements which do not constitute the primary object of such agreements, but are directly related to and necessary for their implementation, such as an obligation not to carry out, independently or together with third parties, research and development in the field to which the agreement relates or in a closely connected field during the execution of the agreement.

The first subparagraph does, however, not apply to provisions which have the same object as the restrictions of competition enumerated in Article 5(1).

[4917]

Article 2

Definitions

For the purposes of this Regulation:

1.   "agreement" means an agreement, a decision of an association of undertakings or a concerted practice;

2.   "participating undertakings" means undertakings party to the research and development agreement and their respective connected undertakings;

3.   "connected undertakings" means—
   (a)   undertakings in which a party to the research and development agreement, directly or indirectly—
      (i)   has the power to exercise more than half the voting rights,
      (ii)   has the power to appoint more than half the members of the supervisory board, board of management or bodies legally representing the undertaking, or
      (iii)   has the right to manage the undertaking's affairs;
   (b)   undertakings which directly or indirectly have, over a party to the research and development agreement, the rights or powers listed in (a);
   (c)   undertakings in which an undertaking referred to in (b) has, directly or indirectly, the rights or powers listed in (a);
   (d)   undertakings in which a party to the research and development agreement together with one or more of the undertakings referred to in (a), (b) or (c), or in which two or more of the latter undertakings, jointly have the rights or powers listed in (a);
   (e)   undertakings in which the rights or the powers listed in (a) are jointly held by—
      (i)   parties to the research and development agreement or their respective connected undertakings referred to in (a) to (d), or
      (ii)   one or more of the parties to the research and development agreement or one or more of their connected undertakings referred to in (a) to (d) and one or more third parties;

4.   "research and development" means the acquisition of know-how relating to products or processes and the carrying out of theoretical analysis, systematic study or experimentation, including experimental production, technical testing of products or processes, the establishment of the necessary facilities and the obtaining of intellectual property rights for the results;

5.   "product" means a good and/or a service, including both intermediary goods and/or services and final goods and/or services;

6.   "contract process" means a technology or process arising out of the joint research and development;

7.   "contract product" means a product arising out of the joint research and development or manufactured or provided applying the contract processes;

8.   "exploitation of the results" means the production or distribution of the contract products or the application of the contract processes or the assignment or licensing of intellectual property rights or the communication of know-how required for such manufacture or application;

9.   "intellectual property rights" includes industrial property rights, copyright and neighbouring rights;

10.   "know-how" means a package of non-patented practical information, resulting from experience and testing, which is secret, substantial and identified: in this context, "secret" means that the know-how is not generally known or easily

accessible; "substantial" means that the know-how includes information which is indispensable for the manufacture of the contract products or the application of the contract processes; "identified" means that the know-how is described in a sufficiently comprehensive manner so as to make it possible to verify that it fulfils the criteria of secrecy and substantiality;

11. research and development, or exploitation of the results, are carried out "jointly" where the work involved is—
    (a) carried out by a joint team, organisation or undertaking,
    (b) jointly entrusted to a third party, or
    (c) allocated between the parties by way of specialisation in research, development, production or distribution;

12. "competing undertaking" means an undertaking that is supplying a product capable of being improved or replaced by the contract product (an actual competitor) or an undertaking that would, on realistic grounds, undertake the necessary additional investments or other necessary switching costs so that it could supply such a product in response to a small and permanent increase in relative prices (a potential competitor);

13. "relevant market for the contract products" means the relevant product and geographic market(s) to which the contract products belong.

[4918]

Article 3

Conditions for exemption

1. The exemption provided for in Article 1 shall apply subject to the conditions set out in paragraphs 2 to 5.

2. All the parties must have access to the results of the joint research and development for the purposes of further research or exploitation. However, research institutes, academic bodies, or undertakings which supply research and development as a commercial service without normally being active in the exploitation of results may agree to confine their use of the results for the purposes of further research.

3. Without prejudice to paragraph 2, where the research and development agreement provides only for joint research and development, each party must be free independently to exploit the results of the joint research and development and any pre-existing know-how necessary for the purposes of such exploitation. Such right to exploitation may be limited to one or more technical fields of application, where the parties are not competing undertakings at the time the research and development agreement is entered into.

4. Any joint exploitation must relate to results which are protected by intellectual property rights or constitute know-how, which substantially contribute to technical or economic progress and the results must be decisive for the manufacture of the contract products or the application of the contract processes.

5. Undertakings charged with manufacture by way of specialisation in production must be required to fulfil orders for supplies from all the parties, except where the research and development agreement also provides for joint distribution.

[4919]

Article 4

Market share threshold and duration of exemption

1. Where the participating undertakings are not competing undertakings, the exemption provided for in Article 1 shall apply for the duration of the research and

development. Where the results are jointly exploited, the exemption shall continue to apply for seven years from the time the contract products are first put on the market within the common market.

2.   Where two or more of the participating undertakings are competing undertakings, the exemption provided for in Article 1 shall apply for the period referred to in paragraph 1 only if, at the time the research and development agreement is entered into, the combined market share of the participating undertakings does not exceed 25% of the relevant market for the products capable of being improved or replaced by the contract products.

3.   After the end of the period referred to in paragraph 1, the exemption shall continue to apply as long as the combined market share of the participating undertakings does not exceed 25% of the relevant market for the contract products.

[4920]

Article 5

Agreements not covered by the exemption

1.   The exemption provided for in Article 1 shall not apply to research and development agreements which, directly or indirectly, in isolation or in combination with other factors under the control of the parties, have as their object—

(a) the restriction of the freedom of the participating undertakings to carry out research and development independently or in cooperation with third parties in a field unconnected with that to which the research and development relates or, after its completion, in the field to which it relates or in a connected field;

(b) the prohibition to challenge after completion of the research and development the validity of intellectual property rights which the parties hold in the common market and which are relevant to the research and development or, after the expiry of the research and development agreement, the validity of intellectual property rights which the parties hold in the common market and which protect the results of the research and development, without prejudice to the possibilty to provide for termination of the research and development agreement in the event of one of the parties challenging the validity of such intellectual property rights;

(c) the limitation of output or sales;

(d) the fixing of prices when selling the contract product to third parties;

(e) the restriction of the customers that the participating undertakings may serve, after the end of seven years from the time the contract products are first put on the market within the common market;

(f) the prohibition to make passive sales of the contract products in territories reserved for other parties;

(g) the prohibition to put the contract products on the market or to pursue an active sales policy for them in territories within the common market that are reserved for other parties after the end of seven years from the time the contract products are first put on the market within the common market;

(h) the requirement not to grant licences to third parties to manufacture the contract products or to apply the contract processes where the exploitation by at least one of the parties of the results of the joint research and development is not provided for or does not take place;

(i) the requirement to refuse to meet demand from users or resellers in their respective territories who would market the contract products in other territories within the common market; or

(j) the requirement to make it difficult for users or resellers to obtain the contract products from other resellers within the common market, and in particular to exercise intellectual property rights or take measures so as to

PART IV
EC MATERIALS

prevent users or resellers from obtaining, or from putting on the market within the common market, products which have been lawfully put on the market within the Community by another party or with its consent.

2. Paragraph 1 shall not apply to—
(a) the setting of production targets where the exploitation of the results includes the joint production of the contract products;
(b) the setting of sales targets and the fixing of prices charged to immediate customers where the exploitation of the results includes the joint distribution of the contract products.

[4921]

Article 6

Application of the market share threshold

1. For the purposes of applying the market share threshold provided for in Article 4 the following rules shall apply—
(a) the market share shall be calculated on the basis of the market sales value; if market sales value data are not available, estimates based on other reliable market information, including market sales volumes, may be used to establish the market share of the undertaking concerned;
(b) the market share shall be calculated on the basis of data relating to the preceding calendar year;
(c) the market share held by the undertakings referred to in point 3(e) of Article 2 shall be apportioned equally to each undertaking having the rights or the powers listed in point 3(a) of Article 2.

2. If the market share referred to in Article 4(3) is initially not more than 25% but subsequently rises above this level without exceeding 30%, the exemption provided for in Article 1 shall continue to apply for a period of two consecutive calendar years following the year in which the 25% threshold was first exceeded.

3. If the market share referred to in Article 4(3) is initially not more than 25% but subsequently rises above 30%, the exemption provided for in Article 1 shall continue to apply for one calendar year following the year in which the level of 30% was first exceeded.

4. The benefit of paragraphs 2 and 3 may not be combined so as to exceed a period of two calendar years.

[4922]

Article 7

Withdrawal

The Commission may withdraw the benefit of this Regulation, pursuant to Article 7 of Regulation (EEC) No 2821/71, where, either on its own initiative or at the request of a Member State or of a natural or legal person claiming a legitimate interest, it finds in a particular case that a research and development agreement to which the exemption provided for in Article 1 applies nevertheless has effects which are incompatible with the conditions laid down in Article 81(3) of the Treaty, and in particular where:
(a) the existence of the research and development agreement substantially restricts the scope for third parties to carry out research and development in the relevant field because of the limited research capacity available elsewhere;
(b) because of the particular structure of supply, the existence of the research and development agreement substantially restricts the access of third parties to the market for the contract products;

(c) without any objectively valid reason, the parties do not exploit the results of the joint research and development;

(d) the contract products are not subject in the whole or a substantial part of the common market to effective competition from identical products or products considered by users as equivalent in view of their characteristics, price and intended use;

(e) the existence of the research and development agreement would eliminate effective competition in research and development on a particular market.

[4923]

Article 8

Transitional period

The prohibition laid down in Article 81(1) of the Treaty shall not apply during the period from 1 January 2001 to 30 June 2002 in respect of agreements already in force on 31 December 2000 which do not satisfy the conditions for exemption provided for in this Regulation but which satisfy the conditions for exemption provided for in Regulation (EEC) No 418/85.

[4924]

Article 9

Period of validity

This Regulation shall enter into force on 1 January 2001.

It shall expire on 31 December 2010.

This Regulation shall be binding in its entirety and directly applicable in all Member States.

[4925]

Done at Brussels, 29 November 2000.

COMMISSION NOTICE

Guidelines on the applicability of Article 81 of the EC Treaty to horizontal cooperation agreements

(2001/C 3/02)

(Text with EEA relevance)

NOTES

Date of publication in OJ: C3, 6.1.2001, p 2.

1. INTRODUCTION

1.1. Purpose

1.   These guidelines set out the principles for the assessment of horizontal cooperation agreements under Article 81 of the Treaty. A cooperation is of a "horizontal nature" if an agreement or concerted practice is entered into between companies operating at the same level(s) in the market. In most instances, horizontal cooperation amounts to cooperation between competitors. It covers for example areas such as research and development (R & D), production, purchasing or commercialisation.

PART IV
EC MATERIALS

2.   Horizontal cooperation may lead to competition problems. This is for example the case if the parties to a cooperation agree to fix prices or output, to share markets, or if the cooperation enables the parties to maintain, gain or increase market power and thereby causes negative market effects with respect to prices, output, innovation or the variety and quality of products.

3.   On the other hand, horizontal cooperation can lead to substantial economic benefits. Companies need to respond to increasing competitive pressure and a changing market place driven by globalisation, the speed of technological progress and the generally more dynamic nature of markets. Cooperation can be a means to share risk, save costs, pool know-how and launch innovation faster. In particular for small and medium-sized enterprises cooperation is an important means to adapt to the changing market place.

4.   The Commission, while recognising the economic benefits that can be generated by cooperation, has to ensure that effective competition is maintained. Article 81 provides the legal framework for a balanced assessment taking into account both anti-competitive effects as well as economic benefits.

5.   In the past, two Commission notices and two block exemption regulations provided guidance for the assessment of horizontal cooperation under Article 81. Commission Regulation (EEC) No 417/85,[1] as last amended by Regulation (EC No 2236/97[2] and Commission Regulation (EEC) No 418/85,[3] as last amended by Regulation (EC) No 2236/97, provided for the exemption of certain forms of specialisation agreement and research and development agreement (R & D) respectively. Those two Regulations have now been replaced by Commission Regulation (EC) No 2658/2000 of 29 November 2000 on the application of Article 81(3) of the Treaty to categories of specialisation agreements[4] ("the Specialisation block exemption Regulation") and Commission Regulation (EC) No 2659/2000 of 29 November 2000 on the application of Article 81(3) of the Treaty to categories of research and development agreements[5] ("the R & D block exemption Regulation"). The two notices provided guidance in respect of certain types of cooperation agreement falling outside Article 81[6] and the assessment of cooperative joint ventures.[7]

6.   Changing markets have generated an increasing variety and use of horizontal cooperation. More complete and updated guidance is needed to improve clarity and transparency regarding the applicability of Article 81 in this area. Within the assessment greater emphasis has to be put on economic criteria to better reflect recent developments in enforcement practice and the case law of the Court of Justice and Court of First Instance of the European Communities.

7.   The purpose of these guidelines is to provide an analytical framework for the most common types of horizontal cooperation. This framework is primarily based on criteria that help to analyse the economic context of a cooperation agreement. Economic criteria such as the market power of the parties and other factors relating to the market structure, form a key element of the assessment of the market impact likely to be caused by a cooperation and therefore for the assessment under Article 81. Given the enormous variety in types and combinations of horizontal cooperation and market circumstances in which they operate, it is impossible to provide specific answers for every possible scenario. The present analytical framework based on economic criteria will nevertheless assist businesses in assessing the compatibility of an individual cooperation agreement with Article 81.

8.   The guidelines not only replace the Notices referred to in paragraph 5, but also cover a wider range of the most common types of horizontal agreements. They complement the R & D block exemption Regulation and the Specialisation block exemption Regulation.

1.2. Scope of the guidelines

9.   These guidelines cover agreements or concerted practices (hereinafter referred to as "agreements") entered into between two or more companies operating at the same level(s) in the market, eg at the same level of production or distribution. Within this context the focus is on cooperation between competitors. The term "competitors" as used in these guidelines includes both actual[8] and potential.[9]

10.   The present guidelines do not, however, address all possible horizontal agreements. They are only concerned with those types of cooperation which potentially generate efficiency gains, namely agreements on R & D, production, purchasing, commercialisation, standardisation, and environmental agreements. Other types of horizontal agreements between competitors, for example on the exchange of information or on minority shareholdings, are to be addressed separately.

11.   Agreements that are entered into between companies operating at a different level of the production or distribution chain, that is to say vertical agreements, are in principle excluded from these guidelines and dealt with in Commission Regulation (EC) No 2790/1999[10] (the "Block Exemption Regulation on Vertical Restraints") and the Guidelines on vertical restraints.[11] However, to the extent that vertical agreements, eg distribution agreements, are concluded between competitors, the effects of the agreement on the market and the possible competition problems can be similar to horizontal agreements. Therefore, these agreements have to be assessed according to the principles described in the present guidelines. This does not exclude the additional application of the Guidelines on Vertical Restraints to these agreements to assess the vertical restraints included in such agreements.[12]

12.   Agreements may combine different stages of cooperation, for example R & D and the production of its results. Unless they fall under Council Regulation (EEC) No 4064/89 of 21 December 1989 on the control of concentrations between undertakings,[13] as last amended by Regulation (EC) No 1310/97[14] ("the Merger Regulation"), these agreements are covered by the guidelines. The centre of gravity of the cooperation determines which section of the present guidelines applies to the agreement in question. In the determination of the centre of gravity, account is taken in particular of two factors: firstly, the starting point of the cooperation, and, secondly, the degree of integration of the different functions which are being combined. A cooperation involving both joint R & D and joint production of the results would thus normally be covered in the section on "Agreements on Research and Development", as the joint production will only take place if the joint R & D is successful. This implies that the results of the joint R & D are decisive for production. The R & D agreement can thus be regarded as the starting point of the cooperation. This assessment would change if the agreement foresaw a full integration in the area of production and only a partial integration of some R & D activities. In this case, the possible anti-competitive effects and economic benefits of the cooperation would largely relate to the joint production, and the agreement would therefore be examined according to the principles set out in the section on "Production Agreements". More complex arrangements such as strategic alliances that combine a number of different areas and instruments of cooperation in varying ways are not covered by the guidelines. The assessment of each individual area of cooperation within an alliance may be carried out with the help of the corresponding chapter in the guidelines. However, complex arrangements must also be analysed in their totality. Due to the variety of areas an alliance may combine, it is impossible to give general guidance for such an overall assessment. Alliances or other forms of cooperation that primarily declare intentions are impossible to assess under the competition rules as long as they lack a precise scope.

13.   The criteria set out in these guidelines apply to cooperation concerning both goods and services, collectively referred to as "products". However, the guidelines

do not apply to the extent that sector-specific rules apply, as is the case for agriculture, transport or insurance.[15] Operations that come under the Merger Regulation are also not the subject of the present guidelines.

14.   Article 81 only applies to those horizontal cooperation agreements which may affect trade between Member States. These guidelines are not concerned with the analysis of the capability of a given agreement to affect trade. The following principles on the applicability of Article 81 are therefore based on the assumption that trade between Member States is affected. In practice, however, this issue needs to be examined on a case-by-case basis.

15.   Article 81 does not apply to agreements which are of minor importance because they are not capable of appreciably restricting competition by object or effect. These guidelines are without prejudice to the application of the present or any future "de minimis" notice.[16]

16.   The assessment under Article 81 as described in these guidelines is without prejudice to the possible parallel application of Article 82 of the Treaty to horizontal cooperation agreements. Furthermore, these guidelines are without prejudice to the interpretation that may be given by the Court of First Instance and the Court of Justice of the European Communities in relation to the application of Article 81 to horizontal cooperation agreements.

1.3. Basic principles for the assessment under Article 81

1.3.1. *Article 81(1)*

17.   Article 81(1) applies to horizontal cooperation agreements which have as their object or effect the prevention, restriction or distortion of competition (hereinafter referred to as "restrictions of competition").

18.   In some cases the nature of a cooperation indicates from the outset the applicability of Article 81(1). This is the case for agreements that have as their object a restriction of competition by means of price fixing, output limitation or sharing of markets or customers. These agreements are presumed to have negative market effects. It is therefore not necessary to examine their actual effects on competition and the market in order to establish that they fall within Article 81(1).

19.   Many horizontal cooperation agreements, however, do not have as their object a restriction of competition. Therefore, an analysis of the effects of the agreement is necessary. For this analysis it is not sufficient that the agreement limits competition between the parties. It must also be likely to affect competition in the market to such an extent that negative market effects as to prices, output, innovation or the variety or quality of goods and services can be expected.

20.   Whether the agreement is able to cause such negative market effects depends on the economic context taking into account both the nature of the agreement and the parties' combined market power which determines—together with other structural factors—the capability of the cooperation to affect overall competition to such a significant extent.

Nature of the agreement

21.   The nature of an agreement relates to factors such as the area and objective of the cooperation, the competitive relationship between the parties and the extent to which they combine their activities. These factors indicate the likelihood of the parties coordinating their behaviour in the market.

22.   Certain types of agreement, for instance most R & D agreements or cooperation to set standards or improve environmental conditions, are less likely to include restrictions with respect to prices and output. If these types of agreements

have negative effects at all these are likely to be on innovation or the variety of products. They may also give rise to foreclosure problems.

23.   Other types of cooperation such as agreements on production or purchasing typically cause a certain degree of commonality in (total) costs. If this degree is significant, the parties may more easily coordinate market prices and output. A significant degree of commonality in costs can only be achieved under certain conditions: First, the area of cooperation, eg production and purchasing, has to account for a high proportion of the total costs in a given market. Secondly, the parties need to combine their activities in the area of cooperation to a significant extent. This is, for instance, the case, where they jointly manufacture or purchase an important intermediate product or a high proportion of their total output of a final product.

Agreements that do not fall under Article 81(1)

24.   Some categories of agreements do not fall under Article 81(1) because of their very nature. This is normally true for cooperation that does not imply a coordination of the parties' competitive behaviour in the market such as—

— cooperation between non-competitors,
— cooperation between competing companies that cannot independently carry out the project or activity covered by the cooperation,
— does not influence the relevant parameters of competition.

These categories of cooperation could only come under Article 81(1) if they involve firms with significant market power[17] and are likely to cause foreclosure problems vis-à-vis third parties.

Agreements that almost always fall under Article 81(1)

25.   Another category of agreements can be assessed from the outset as normally falling under Article 81(1). This concerns cooperation agreements that have the object to restrict competition by means of price fixing, output limitation or sharing of markets or customers. These restrictions are considered to be the most harmful, because they directly interfere with the outcome of the competitive process. Price fixing and output limitation directly lead to customers paying higher prices or not receiving the desired quantities. The sharing of markets or customers reduces the choice available to customers and therefore also leads to higher prices or reduced output. It can therefore be presumed that these restrictions have negative market effects. They are therefore almost always prohibited.[18]

Agreements that may fall under Article 81(1)

26.   Agreements that do not belong to the above-mentioned categories need further analysis in order to decide whether they fall under Article 81(1). The analysis has to include market-related criteria such as the market position of the parties and other structural factors.

Market power and market structure

27.   The starting point for the analysis is the position of the parties in the markets affected by the cooperation. This determines whether or not they are likely to maintain, gain or increase market power through the cooperation, ie have the ability to cause negative market effects as to prices, output, innovation or the variety or quality of goods and services. To carry out this analysis the relevant market(s) have to be defined by using the methodology of the Commission's market definition notice.[19] Where specific types of markets are concerned such as purchasing or technology markets, these guidelines will provide additional guidance.

28.   If the parties together have a low combined market share,[20] a restrictive effect of the cooperation is unlikely and no further analysis normally is required. If one of just two parties has only an insignificant market share and if it does not

possess important resources, even a high combined market share normally cannot be seen as indicating a restrictive effect on competition in the market.[21] Given the variety of cooperation types and the different effects they may cause in different market situations, it is impossible to give a general market share threshold above which sufficient market power for causing restrictive effects can be assumed.

29. In addition to the market position of the parties and the addition of market shares, the market concentration, ie the position and number of competitors, may have to be taken into account as an additional factor to assess the impact of the cooperation on market competition. As an indicator the Herfindahl-Hirshman Index ("HHI"), which sums up the squares of the individual market shares of all competitors,[22] can be used: With an HHI below 1 000 the market concentration can be characterised as low, between 1 000 and 1 800 as moderate and above 1 800 as high. Another possible indicator would be the leading firm concentration ratio, which sums up the individual market shares of the leading competitors.[23]

30. Depending on the market position of the parties and the concentration in the market, other factors such as the stability of market shares over time, entry barriers and the likelihood of market entry, the countervailing power of buyers/suppliers or the nature of the products (eg homogeneity, maturity) have to be considered as well. Where an impact on competition in innovation is likely and can not be assessed adequately on the basis of existing markets, specific factors to analyse these impacts may have to be taken into account (see Chapter 2, R & D agreements).

1.3.2. *Article 81(3)*

31. Agreements that come under Article 81(1) may be exempted provided the conditions of Article 81(3) are fulfilled. This is the case if the agreement—
  — contributes to improving the production or distribution of products or to promoting technical or economic progress
  — allows consumers a fair share of the resulting benefit
and does not
  — impose restrictions which are not indispensable to the attainment of the above listed objectives
  — afford the possibility of eliminating competition in respect of a substantial part of the products in question.

Economic benefits

32. The first condition requires that the agreement contributes to improving the production or distribution of products or to promoting technical or economic progress. As these benefits relate to static or dynamic efficiencies, they can be referred to as "economic benefits". Economic benefits may outweigh restrictive effects on competition. For instance, a cooperation may enable firms to offer goods or services at lower prices, better quality or to launch innovation more quickly. Most efficiencies stem from the combination and integration of different skills or resources. The parties must demonstrate that the efficiencies are likely to be caused by the cooperation and cannot be achieved by less restrictive means (see also below). Efficiency claims must be substantiated. Speculations or general statements on cost savings are not sufficient.

33. The Commission does not take into account cost savings that arise from output reduction, market sharing, or from the mere exercise of market power.

Fair share for the consumers

34. Economic benefits have to favour not only the parties to the agreement, but also the consumers. Generally, the transmission of the benefits to the consumers will depend on the intensity of competition within the relevant market. Competitive pressures will normally ensure that cost-savings are passed on by way of lower prices

or that companies have an incentive to bring new products to the market as quickly as possible. Therefore, if sufficient competition which effectively constrains the parties to the agreement is maintained on the market, the competitive process will normally ensure that the consumers receive a fair share of the economic benefits.

Indispensability

35.   The restriction of competition must be necessary to achieve the economic benefits. If there are less restrictive means to achieve similar benefits, the claimed efficiencies cannot be used to justify the restrictions of competition. Whether or not individual restrictions are necessary depends on market circumstances and on the duration of the agreement. For instance, exclusivity agreements may prevent a participating party from free riding and may therefore be acceptable. Under certain circumstances they may, however, not be necessary and worsen a restrictive effect.

No elimination of competition

36.   The last criterion of elimination of competition for a substantial part of the products in question is related to the question of dominance. Where an undertaking is dominant or becoming dominant as a consequence of a horizontal agreement, an agreement which produces anti-competitive effects in the meaning of Article 81 can in principle not be exempted.

Block Exemption Regulations for R&D and Specialisation

37.   Under certain conditions the criteria of Article 81(3) can be assumed to be fulfilled for specified categories of agreements. This is in particular the case for R & D and production agreements where the combination of complementary skills or assets can be the source of substantial efficiencies. These guidelines should be seen as a complement to the R & D and Specialisation block exemption Regulations. Those block exemption Regulations exempt most common forms of agreements in the fields of production/specialisation up to a market share threshold of 20% and in the field of R & D up to a market share threshold of 25% provided that the agreements fulfil the conditions for application of the block exemption and do not contain "hard core" restrictions ("black clauses") that render the block exemption inapplicable. The block exemption Regulations do not provide severability for hardcore restrictions. If there are one or more hardcore restrictions, the benefit of the block exemption Regulation is lost for the entire agreement.

1.4. Structure of the following chapters on types of cooperation

38.   The guidelines are divided into chapters relating to certain types of agreements. Each chapter is structured according to the analytical framework described above under point 1.3. Where necessary, specific guidance on the definition of relevant markets is given (eg in the field of R & D or with respect to purchasing markets).

[4926]

2. AGREEMENTS ON RESEARCH AND DEVELOPMENT

2.1. Definition

39.   R & D agreements may vary in form and scope. They range from outsourcing certain R & D activities to the joint improvement of existing technologies or to a cooperation concerning the research, development and marketing of completely new products. They may take the form of a cooperation agreement or of a jointly controlled company. This chapter applies to all forms of R & D agreements including related agreements concerning the production or commercialisation of the R & D results provided that the cooperation's centre of gravity lies in R & D, with the exception of mergers and joint ventures falling under the Merger Regulation.

40.   Cooperation in R & D may reduce duplicative, unnecessary costs, lead to significant cross fertilisation of ideas and experience and thus result in products and technologies being developed more rapidly than would otherwise be the case. As a general rule, R & D cooperation tends to increase overall R & D activities.

41.   Small and medium-sized enterprises (SMEs) form a dynamic and heterogeneous community which is confronted by many challenges, including the growing demands of larger companies for which they often work as sub-contractors. In R & D intensive sectors, fast growing SMEs, more often called "start-up companies", also aim at becoming a leader in fast-developing market segments. To meet those challenges and to remain competitive, SMEs need constantly to innovate. Through R & D cooperation there is a likelihood that overall R & D by SMEs will increase and that they will be able to compete more vigorously with stronger market players.

42.   Under certain circumstances, however, R & D agreements may cause competition problems such as restrictive effects on prices, output, innovation, or variety or quality of products.

2.2. Relevant markets

43.   The key to defining the relevant market when assessing the effects of an R & D agreement is to identify those products, technologies or R & D efforts, that will act as a competitive constraint on the parties. At one end of the spectrum of possible situations, the innovation may result in a product (or technology) which competes in an existing product (or technology) market. This is the case with R & D directed towards slight improvements or variations, such as new models of certain products. Here, possible effects concern the market for existing products. At the other end, innovation may result in an entirely new product which creates its own new market (eg of the spectrum of a new vaccine for a previously incurable disease). In such a case, existing markets are only relevant if they are somehow related to the innovation in question. Consequently, and if possible, the effects of the cooperation on innovation have to be assessed. However, most of the cases probably concern situations in between these two extremes, ie situations in which innovation efforts may create products (or technology) which, over time, replace existing ones (eg CDs which have replaced records). A careful analysis of those situations may have to cover both existing markets and the impact of the agreement on innovation.

Existing markets

(a) *Product markets*

44.   When the cooperation concerns R & D for the improvement of existing products, these existing products including its close substitutes form the relevant market concerned by the cooperation.[24]

45.   If the R & D efforts aim at a significant change of an existing product or even at a new product replacing existing ones, substitution with the existing products may be imperfect or long-term. Consequently, the old and the potentially emerging new products are not likely to belong to the same relevant market. The market for existing products may nevertheless be concerned, if the pooling of R & D efforts is likely to result in the coordination of the parties' behaviour as suppliers of existing products. An exploitation of power in the existing market, however, is only possible if the parties together have a strong position with respect to both the existing product market and R & D efforts.

46.   If the R & D concerns an important component of a final product, not only the market for this component may be relevant for the assessment, but the existing market for the final product as well. For instance, if car manufacturers cooperate in R & D related to a new type of engine, the car market may be affected by this R & D cooperation. The market for final products, however, is only relevant for the

assessment, if the component at which the R & D is aimed, is technically or economically a key element of these final products and if the parties to the R & D agreement are important competitors with respect to the final products.

(b) *Technology markets*

47.   R & D cooperation may not only concern products but also technology. When rights to intellectual property are marketed separately from the products concerned to which they relate, the relevant technology market has to be defined as well. Technology markets consist of the intellectual property that is licensed and its close substitutes, ie other technologies which customers could use as a substitute.

48.   The methodology for defining technology markets follows the same principles as product market definition.[25] Starting from the technology which is marketed by the parties, one needs to identify those other technologies to which customers could switch in response to a small but permanent increase in relative prices. Once these technologies are identified, one can calculate market shares by dividing the licensing income generated by the parties with the total licensing income of all sellers of substitutable technologies.

49.   The parties' position in the market for existing technology is a relevant assessment criterion where the R & D cooperation concerns the significant improvement of existing technology or a new technology that is likely to replace the existing technology. The parties' market share can however only be taken as a starting point for this analysis. In technology markets, particular emphasis must be put on potential competition. If companies, who do not currently license their technology, are potential entrants on the technology market they could constrain the ability of the parties to raise the price for their technology (see Example 3 below).

Competition in innovation (R & D efforts)

50.   R & D cooperation may not—or not only—affect competition in existing markets, but competition in innovation. This is the case where cooperation concerns the development of new products/technology which either may—if emerging—one day replace existing ones or which are being developed for a new intended use and will therefore not replace existing products but create a completely new demand. The effects on competition in innovation are important in these situations, but can in some cases not be sufficiently assessed by analysing actual or potential competition in existing product/technology markets. In this respect, two scenarios can be distinguished, depending on the nature of the innovative process in a given industry.

51.   In the first scenario, which is for instance present in the pharmaceutical industry, the process of innovation is structured in such a way that it is possible at an early stage to identify R & D poles. R & D poles are R & D efforts directed towards a certain new product or technology, and the substitutes for that R & D, ie R & D aimed at developing substitutable products or technology for those developed by the cooperation and having comparable access to resources as well as a similar timing. In this case, it can be analysed if after the agreement there will be a sufficient number of R & D poles left. The starting point of the analysis is the R & D of the parties. Then credible competing R & D poles have to be identified. In order to assess the credibility of competing poles, the following aspects have to be taken into account: the nature, scope and size of possible other R & D efforts, their access to financial and human resources, know-how/patents, or other specialised assets as well as their timing and their capability to exploit possible results. An R & D pole is not a credible competitor if it can not be regarded as a close substitute for the parties' R & D effort from the viewpoint of, for instance, access to resources or timing.

52.   In the second scenario, the innovative efforts in an industry are not clearly structured so as to allow the identification of R & D poles. In this situation, the Commission would, absent exceptional circumstances, not try to assess the impact

of a given R & D cooperation on innovation, but would limit its assessment to product and/or technology markets which are related to the R & D cooperation in question.

Calculation of market shares

53.   The calculation of market shares, both for the purposes of the R & D block exemption Regulation and of these guidelines, has to reflect the distinction between existing markets and competition in innovation. At the beginning of a cooperation the reference point is the market for products capable of being improved or replaced by the products under development. If the R & D agreement only aims at improving or refining existing products, this market includes the products directly concerned by the R & D. Market shares can thus be calculated on the basis of the sales value of the existing products. If the R & D aims at replacing an existing product, the new product will, if successful, become a substitute to the existing products. To assess the competitive position of the parties, it is again possible to calculate market shares on the basis of the sales value of the existing products. Consequently, the R & D block exemption Regulation bases its exemption of these situations on the market share in "the relevant market for the products capable of being improved or replaced by the contract products". For an automatic exemption, this market share may not exceed 25%.[26]

54.   If the R & D aims at developing a product which will create a complete new demand, market shares based on sales cannot be calculated. Only an analysis of the effects of the agreement on competition in innovation is possible. Consequently, the R & D block exemption Regulation exempts these agreements irrespective of market share for a period of seven years after the product is first put on the market.[27] However, the benefit of the block exemption may be withdrawn if the agreement would eliminate effective competition in innovation.[28] After the seven year period, market shares based on sales value can be calculated, and the market share threshold of 25% applies.[29]

2.3.   Assessment under Article 81(1)

2.3.1.   *Nature of the agreement*

2.3.1.1.   Agreements that do not fall under Article 81(1)

55.   Most R & D agreements do not fall under Article 81(1). First, this can be said for agreements relating to cooperation in R & D at a rather theoretical stage, far removed from the exploitation of possible results.

56.   Moreover, R & D cooperation between non-competitors does generally not restrict competition.[30] The competitive relationship between the parties has to be analysed in the context of affected existing markets and/or innovation. If the parties are not able to carry out the necessary R & D independently, there is no competition to be restricted. This can apply, for example, to firms bringing together complementary skills, technologies and other resources. The issue of potential competition has to be assessed on a realistic basis. For instance, parties cannot be defined as potential competitors simply because the cooperation enables them to carry out the R & D activities. The decisive question is whether each party independently has the necessary means as to assets, know-how and other resources.

57.   R & D cooperation by means of outsourcing of previously captive R & D is often carried out by specialised companies, research institutes or academic bodies which are not active in the exploitation of the results. Typically such agreements are combined with a transfer of know-how and/or an exclusive supply clause concerning possible results. Due to the complementary nature of the cooperating parties in these scenarios, Article 81(1) does not apply.

58.   R & D cooperation which does not include the joint exploitation of possible results by means of licensing, production and/or marketing rarely falls under Article 81(1). Those "pure" R & D agreements can only cause a competition problem, if effective competition with respect to innovation is significantly reduced.

2.3.1.2. Agreements that almost always fall under Article 81(1)

59.   If the true object of an agreement is not R & D but the creation of a disguised cartel, ie otherwise prohibited price fixing, output limitation or market allocation, it falls under Article 81(1). However, an R & D agreement which includes the joint exploitation of possible future results is not necessarily restrictive of competition.

2.3.1.3. Agreements that may fall under Article 81(1)

60.   R & D agreements that cannot be assessed from the outset as clearly non-restrictive may fall under Article 81(1)[31] and have to be analysed in their economic context. This applies to R & D cooperation which is set up at a stage rather close to the market launch and which is agreed between companies that are competitors on either existing product/technology markets or on innovation markets.

2.3.2. *Market power and market structures*

61.   R & D cooperation can cause negative market effects in three respects: First, it may restrict innovation, secondly it may cause the coordination of the parties' behaviour in existing markets and thirdly, foreclosure problems may occur at the level of the exploitation of possible results. These types of negative market effects, however, are only likely to emerge when the parties to the cooperation have significant power on the existing markets and/or competition with respect to innovation is significantly reduced. Without market power there is no incentive to coordinate behaviour on existing markets or to reduce or slow down innovation. A foreclosure problem may only arise in the context of cooperation involving at least one player with significant market power for a key technology and the exclusive exploitation of results.

62.   There is no absolute market share threshold which indicates that an R & D agreement creates some degree of market power and thus falls under Article 81(1). However, R & D agreements are exempted provided that they are concluded between parties with a combined market share not exceeding 25% and that the other conditions for the application of the R & D Block Exemption Regulation are fulfilled. Therefore, for most R & D agreements, restrictive effects only have to be analysed if the parties' combined market share exceeds 25%.

63.   Agreements falling outside the R & D Block Exemption Regulation due to a stronger market position of the parties do not necessarily restrict competition. However, the stronger the combined position of the parties on existing markets and/or the more competition in innovation is restricted, the more likely is the application of Article 81(1) and the assessment requires a more detailed analysis.

64.   If the R & D is directed at the improvement or refinement of existing products/technology possible effects concern the relevant market(s) for these existing products/technology. Effects on prices, output and/or innovation in existing markets are, however, only likely if the parties together have a strong position, entry is difficult and few other innovation activities are identifiable. Furthermore, if the R & D only concerns a relatively minor input of a final product, effects as to competition in these final products are, if invariably, very limited. In general, a distinction has to be made between pure R & D agreements and more comprehensive cooperation involving different stages of the exploitation of results (ie licensing, production, marketing). As said above, pure R & D agreements rarely come under Article 81(1). This is in particular true for R & D directed towards a limited improvement of existing products/technology. If, in such a scenario, the R & D cooperation includes joint

exploitation only by means of licensing, restrictive effects such as foreclosure problems are unlikely. If, however, joint production and/or marketing of the slightly improved products/technology are included, the cooperation has to be examined more closely. First, negative effects as to prices and output in existing markets are more likely if strong competitors are involved in such a situation. Secondly, the cooperation may come closer to a production agreement because the R & D activities may de facto not form the centre of gravity of such a collaboration.

65.   If the R & D is directed at an entirely new product (or technology) which creates its own new market, price and output effects on existing markets are rather unlikely. The analysis has to focus on possible restrictions of innovation concerning, for instance, the quality and variety of possible future products/technology or the speed of innovation. Those restrictive effects can arise where two or more of the few firms engaged in the development of such a new product, start to cooperate at a stage where they are each independently rather near to the launch of the product. In such a case, innovation may be restricted even by a pure R & D agreement. In general, however, R & D cooperation concerning entirely new products is pro-competitive. This principle does not change significantly if the joint exploitation of the results, even joint marketing, is involved. Indeed, the issue of joint exploitation in these situations is only relevant where foreclosure from key technologies plays a role. Those problems would, however, not arise where the parties grant licences to third parties.

66.   Most R & D agreements will lie somewhere in between the two situations described above. They may therefore have effects on innovation as well as repercussions on existing markets. Consequently, both the existing market and the effect on innovation may be of relevance for the assessment with respect to the parties' combined positions, concentration ratios, number of players/ innovators and entry conditions. In some cases there can be restrictive price/output effects on existing markets and a negative impact on innovation by means of slowing down the speed of development. For instance, if significant competitors on an existing technology market cooperate to develop a new technology which may one day replace existing products, this cooperation is likely to have restrictive effects if the parties have significant market power on the existing market (which would give an incentive to exploit it), and if they also have a strong position with respect to R & D. A similar effect can occur, if the major player in an existing market cooperates with a much smaller or even potential competitor who is just about to emerge with a new product/technology which may endanger the incumbent's position.

67.   Agreements may also fall outside the block exemption irrespective of the market power of the parties. This applies for instance to agreements which restrict access of a party to the results of the work because they do not, as a general rule, promote technical and economic progress by increasing the dissemination of technical knowledge between the parties.[32] The block exemption provides for a specific exception to this general rule in the case of academic bodies, research institutes or specialised companies which provide R & D as a service and which are not active in the industrial exploitation of the results of research and development.[33] Nevertheless, it should be noted that agreements containing exclusive access rights may, where they fall under Article 81(1), meet the criteria for exemption under Article 81(3), particularly where exclusive access rights are economically indispensable in view of the market, risks and scale of the investment required to exploit the results of the research and development.

2.4. Assessment under Article 81(3)

2.4.1. *Economic benefits*

68.   Most R & D agreements—with or without joint exploitation of possible results—bring about economic benefits by means of cost savings and cross

fertilisation of ideas and experience, thus resulting in improved or new products and technologies being developed more rapidly than would otherwise be the case. Under these conditions it appears reasonable to provide for the exemption of such agreements which result in a restriction of competition up to a market share threshold below which it can, for the application of Article 81(3), in general, be presumed that the positive effects of research and development agreements will outweigh any negative effects on competition. Therefore, the R & D Block Exemption Regulation exempts those R & D agreements which fulfill certain conditions (see Article 3) and which do not include hard core restrictions (see Article 5), provided that the combined market share of the parties in the affected existing market(s) does not exceed 25%.

69.   If considerable market power is created or increased by the cooperation, the parties have to demonstrate significant benefits in carrying out R & D, a quicker launch of new products/technology or other efficiencies.

2.4.2. *Indispensability*

70.   An R & D agreement can not be exempted if it imposes restrictions that are not indispensable to the attainment of the above-mentioned benefits. The individual clauses listed in Article 5 of the R & D block exemption Regulation will in most cases render an exemption impossible following an individual assessment too, and can therefore be regarded as a good indication of restrictions that are not indispensable to the cooperation.

2.4.3. *No elimination of competition*

71.   No exemption will be possible, if the parties are afforded the possibility of eliminating competition in respect of a substantial part of the products (or technologies) in question. Where as a consequence of an R & D agreement an undertaking is dominant or becoming dominant either on an existing market or with respect to innovation, such an agreement which produces anti-competitive effects in the meaning of Article 81 can in principle not be exempted. For innovation this is the case, for example, if the agreement combines the only two existing poles of research.

Time of the assessment and duration of the exemption

72.   R & D agreements extending to the joint production and marketing of new products/technology require particular attention as to the time of the assessment.

73.   At the beginning of an R & D cooperation, its success and factors such as the parties' future market position as well as the development of future product or technology markets are often not known. Consequently, the assessment at the point in time when the cooperation is formed is limited to the (then) existing product or technology markets and/or innovation markets as described in this chapter. If, on the basis of this analysis, competition is not likely to be eliminated, the R & D agreement can benefit from an exemption. This will normally cover the duration of the R & D phase plus, in as far as the joint production and marketing of the possible results is concerned, an additional phase for a possible launch and market introduction. The reason for this additional exemption phase is that the first companies to reach the market with a new product/technology will often enjoy very high initial market shares and successful R & D is also often rewarded by intellectual property protection. A strong market position due to this "first mover advantage" cannot normally be interpreted as elimination of competition. Therefore, the block exemption covers R & D agreements for an additional period of seven years (ie beyond the R & D phase) irrespective of whether or not the parties obtain with their new products/technology a high share within this period. This also applies to the individual assessment of cases falling outside the block exemption provided that the criteria of Article 81(3) as to the other aspects of the agreement are fulfilled.

This does not exclude the possibility that a period of more than 7 years also meets the criteria of Article 81(3) if it can be shown to be the minimum period of time necessary to guarantee an adequate return on the investment involved.

74.   If a new assessment of an R & D cooperation is made after that period—for instance, following a complaint—the analysis has to be based on the (then) existing market situation. The block exemption still continues to apply if the parties' share on the (then) relevant market does not exceed 25%. Similarly, Article 81(3) continues to apply to R & D agreements falling outside the block exemption provided that the criteria for an exemption are fulfilled.

2.5. Examples

75.   Example 1

Situation: There are two major companies on the European market for the manufacture of existing electronic components: A (30%) and B (30%). They have each made significant investment in the R & D necessary to develop miniaturised electronic components and have developed early prototypes. They now agree to pool these R & D efforts by setting up a JV to complete the R & D and produce the components, which will be sold back to the parents, who will commercialise them separately. The remainder of the market consists of small firms without sufficient resources to undertake the necessary investments.

Analysis: Miniaturised electronic components, while likely to compete with the existing components in some areas, are essentially a new technology and an analysis must be made of the poles of research destined towards this future market. If the JV goes ahead then only one route to the necessary manufacturing technology will exist, whereas it would appear likely that A and B could reach the market individually with separate products. While the agreement could have advantages in bringing a new technology forward quicker, it also reduces variety and creates a commonality of costs between the parties. Furthermore, the possibility for the parties to exploit their strong position on the existing market must be taken into account. Since they would face no competition at the R & D level, their incentives to pursue the new technology at a high pace could be severely reduced. Although some of these concerns could be remedied by requiring the parties to license key know-how for manufacturing miniature components to third parties on reasonable terms, it may not be possible to remedy all concerns and fulfil the conditions for an exemption.

76. Example 2

Situation: A small research company A which does not have its own marketing organisation has discovered and patented a pharmaceutical substance based on new technology that will revolutionise the treatment of a certain disease. Company A enters into an R&D agreement with a large pharmaceutical producer B of products that have so far been used for treating the disease. Company B lacks any similar R & D programme. For the existing products company B has a market share of around 75% in all Member States, but patents are expiring over the next five-year period. There exist two other poles of research at approximately the same stage of development using the same basic new technology. Company B will provide considerable funding and know-how for product development, as well as future access to the market. Company B is granted a license for the exclusive production and distribution of the resulting product for the duration of the patent. It is expected that the parties could jointly bring the product to market in five to seven years.

Analysis: The product is likely to belong to a new relevant market. The parties bring complementary resources and skills to the cooperation, and the probability of the product coming to market increases substantially. Although Company B is likely to have considerable market power on the existing market, this power will be decreasing shortly and the existence of other poles of research are likely to eliminate any incentive to reduce R & D efforts. The exploitation rights during the remaining patent period are likely to be necessary for Company B to make the considerable investments needed and Company A has no own marketing resources. The agreement is therefore unlikely to restrict competition.

77. Example 3

Situation: Two engineering companies that produce vehicle components, agree to set up a JV to combine their R & D efforts to improve the production and performance of an existing component. They also pool their existing technology licensing businesses in this area, but will continue to manufacture separately. The two companies have market shares in Europe of 15% and 20% on the OEM product market. There are two other major competitors together with several in-house research programmes by large vehicle manufacturers. On the world-wide market for the licensing of technology for these products they have shares of 20% and 25%, measured in terms of revenue generated, and there are two other major technologies. The product life cycle for the component is typically two to three years. In each of the last five years one of the major firms has introduced a new version or upgrade.

Analysis: Since neither company's R & D effort is aimed at a completely new product, the markets to consider are for the existing components and for the licensing of relevant technology. Although their existing R & D programmes broadly overlap, the reduced duplication through the cooperation could allow them to spend more on R & D than individually. Several other technologies exist and the parties' combined market share on the OEM market does not bring them into a dominant position. Although their market share on the technology market, at 45%, is very high, there are competing technologies. In addition, the vehicle manufacturers, who do not currently licence their technology, are also potential entrants on this market thus constraining the ability of the parties to raise price. As described, the JV is likely to benefit from an exemption.

[4927]

3. PRODUCTION AGREEMENTS (INCLUDING SPECIALISATION AGREEMENTS)

3.1. Definition

78.   Production agreements may vary in form and scope. They may take the form of joint production through a joint venture,[34] ie a jointly controlled company that runs one or several production facilities, or can be carried out by means of specialisation or subcontracting agreements whereby one party agrees to carry out the production of a certain product.

79.   Generally, one can distinguish three categories of production agreements: Joint production agreements, whereby the parties agree to produce certain products jointly, (unilateral or reciprocal) specialisation agreements, whereby the parties agree unilaterally or reciprocally to cease production of a product and to purchase it from the other party, and subcontracting agreements whereby one party (the "contractor") entrusts to another party (the "subcontractor") the production of a product.

80.   Subcontracting agreements are vertical agreements. They are therefore, to the extent that they contain restrictions of competition, covered by the Block Exemption Regulation and the Guidelines on Vertical Restraints. There are however two exceptions to this rule: Subcontracting agreements between competitors,[35] and subcontracting agreements between non-competitors involving the transfer of know-how to the subcontractor.[36]

81.   Subcontracting agreements between competitors are covered by these guidelines.[37] Guidance for the assessment of subcontracting agreements between non-competitors involving the transfer of know-how to the subcontractor is given in a separate Notice.[38]

3.2.   Relevant markets

82.   In order to assess the competitive relationship between the cooperating parties, the relevant product and geographic market(s) directly concerned by the cooperation (ie the market(s) to which products subject to the agreement belong) must first be defined. Secondly, a production agreement in one market may also affect the competitive behaviour of the parties in a market which is downstream or upstream or a neighbouring market closely related to the market directly concerned by the cooperation[39] (so-called "spill-over markets"). However, spill-over effects only occur if the cooperation in one market necessarily results in the coordination of competitive behaviour in another market, ie if the markets are linked by interdependencies, and if the parties are in a strong position on the spill-over market.

3.3.   Assessment under Article 81(1)

3.3.1.   *Nature of the agreement*

83.   The main source of competition problems that may arise from production agreements is the coordination of the parties' competitive behaviour as suppliers. This type of competition problem arises where the cooperating parties are actual or potential competitors on at least one of these relevant market(s), ie on the markets directly concerned by the cooperation and/or on possible spill-over markets.

84.   The fact that the parties are competitors does not automatically cause the coordination of their behaviour. In addition, the parties normally need to cooperate with regard to a significant part of their activities in order to achieve a substantial degree of commonality of costs. The higher the degree of commonality of costs, the greater the potential for a limitation of price competition, especially in the case of homogenous products.

85.   In addition to coordination concerns, production agreements may also create foreclosure problems and other negative effects towards third parties. They are not caused by a competitive relationship between the parties, but by a strong market position of at least one of the parties (eg on an upstream market for a key component, which enables the parties to raise the costs of their rivals in a downstream market) in the context of a more vertical or complementary relationship between the cooperating parties. Therefore, the possibility of foreclosure mainly needs to be examined in the case of joint production of an important component and of subcontracting agreements (see below).

3.3.1.1.   Agreements that do not fall under Article 81(1)

86.   Unless foreclosure problems arise, production agreements between non-competitors are not normally caught by Article 81(1). This is also true for agreements whereby inputs or components which have so far been manufactured for own consumption (captive production) are purchased from a third party by way of subcontracting or unilateral specialisation, unless there are indications that the company which so far has only produced for own consumption could have entered the merchant market for sales to third parties without incurring significant additional costs or risks in response to small, permanent changes in relative market prices.

87.   Even production agreements between competitors do not necessarily come under Article 81(1). First, cooperation between firms which compete on markets closely related to the market directly concerned by the cooperation, cannot be

defined as restricting competition, if the cooperation is the only commercially justifiable possible way to enter a new market, to launch a new product or service or to carry out a specific project.

88.   Secondly, an effect on the parties' competitive behaviour as market suppliers is highly unlikely if the parties have a small proportion of their total costs in common. For instance, a low degree of commonality in total costs can be assumed where two or more companies agree on specialisation/joint production of an intermediate product which only accounts for a small proportion of the production costs of the final product and, consequently, the total costs. The same applies to a subcontracting agreement between competitors where the input which one competitor purchases from another only accounts for a small proportion of the production costs of the final product. A low degree of commonality of total costs can also be assumed where the parties jointly manufacture a final product, but only a small proportion as compared to their total output of the final product. Even if a significant proportion is jointly manufactured, the degree of commonality of total costs may nevertheless be low or moderate, if the cooperation concerns heterogeneous products which require costly marketing.

89.   Thirdly, subcontracting agreements between competitors do not fall under Article 81(1) if they are limited to individual sales and purchases on the merchant market without any further obligations and without forming part of a wider commercial relationship between the parties.[40]

3.3.1.2.   Agreements that almost always fall under Article 81(1)

90.   Agreements which fix the prices for market supplies of the parties, limit output or share markets or customer groups have the object of restricting competition and almost always fall under Article 81(1). This does, however, not apply to cases

— where the parties agree on the output directly concerned by the production agreement (eg the capacity and production volume of a joint venture or the agreed amount of outsourced products), or

— where a production joint venture that also carries out the distribution of the manufactured products sets the sales prices for these products, provided that the price fixing by the joint venture is the effect of integrating the various functions.[41]

In both scenarios the agreement on output or prices will not be assessed separately, but in light of the overall effects of the joint venture on the market in order to determine the applicability of Article 81(1).

3.3.1.3.   Agreements that may fall under Article 81(1)

91.   Production agreements that cannot be characterised as clearly restrictive or non-restrictive on the basis of the above factors may fall under Article 81(1)[42] and have to be analysed in their economic context. This applies to cooperation agreements between competitors which create a significant degree of commonality of costs, but do not involve hard core restrictions as described above.

3.3.2.   *Market power and market structures*

92.   The starting point for the analysis is the position of the parties in the market(s) concerned. This is due to the fact that without market power the parties to a production agreement do not have an incentive to coordinate their competitive behaviour as suppliers. Secondly, there is no effect on competition in the market without market power of the parties, even if the parties would coordinate their behaviour.

93.   There is no absolute market share threshold which indicates that a production agreement creates some degree of market power and thus falls under

Article 81(1). However, agreements concerning unilateral or reciprocal specialisation as well as joint production are block exempted provided that they are concluded between parties with a combined market share not exceeding 20% in the relevant market(s) and that the other conditions for the application of the Specialisation block exemption Regulation are fulfilled. Therefore, for agreements covered by the block exemption, restrictive effects only have to be analysed if the parties combined market share exceeds 20%.

94.   Agreements which are not covered by the block exemption Regulation require a more detailed analysis. The starting point is the market position of the parties. This will normally be followed by the concentration ratio and the number of players as well as by other factors as described in Chapter 1.

95.   Usually the analysis will only involve the relevant market(s) with which the cooperation is directly concerned. Under certain circumstances, eg if the parties have a very strong combined position on up- or downstream markets or on markets otherwise closely related to the markets with which the cooperation is directly concerned, these spill-over markets may however have to be analysed as well. This applies in particular to cooperation in upstream markets by firms which also enjoy a strong combined market position further downstream. Similarly, problems of foreclosure may need to be examined if the parties individually have a strong position as either suppliers or buyers of an input.

Market position of the parties, concentration ratio, number of players and other structural factors

96.   If the parties' combined market share is larger than 20%, the likely impact of the production agreement on the market must be assessed. In this respect market concentration as well as market shares will be a significant factor. The higher the combined market share of the parties, the higher the concentration in the market concerned. However, a moderately higher market share than allowed for in the block exemption does not necessarily imply a high concentration ratio. For instance, a combined market share of the parties of slightly more than 20% may occur in a market with a moderate concentration (HHI below 1800). In such a scenario a restrictive effect is unlikely. In a more concentrated market, however, a market share of more than 20% may, alongside other elements, lead to a restriction of competition (see also example 1 below). The picture may nevertheless change, if the market is very dynamic with new participants entering the market and market positions changing frequently.

97.   For joint production, network effects, ie links between a significant number of competitors, can also play an important role. In a concentrated market the creation of an additional link may tip the balance and make collusion in this market likely, even if the parties have a significant, but still moderate, combined market share (see example 2 below).

98.   Under specific circumstances a cooperation between potential competitors may also raise competition concerns. This is, however, limited to cases where a strong player in one market cooperates with a realistic potential entrant, for instance, with a strong supplier of the same product or service in a neighbouring geographic market. The reduction of potential competition creates particular problems if actual competition is already weak and threat of entry is a major source of competition.

Cooperation in upstream markets

99.   Joint production of an important component or other input to the parties' final product can cause negative market effects under certain circumstances:
 — Foreclosure problems (see example 3 below) provided that the parties have a strong position on the relevant input market (non-captive use) and that switching between captive and non-captive use would not occur in the presence of a small but permanent relative price increase for the product in question.

— Spill-over effects (see example 4 below) provided that the input is an important component of costs and that the parties have a strong position in the downstream market for the final product.

Subcontracting agreements between competitors

100. Similar problems can arise if a competitor subcontracts an important component or other input to its final product from a competitor. This can also lead to—

— Foreclosure problems provided that the parties have a strong position as either suppliers or buyers on the relevant input market (non-captive use). Subcontracting could then either lead to other competitors not being able to obtain this input at a competitive price or to other suppliers not being able to supply the input competitively if they will be losing a large part of their demand.

— Spill-over effects provided that the input is an important component of costs and that the parties have a strong position in the downstream market for the final product.

Specialisation agreements

101. Reciprocal specialisation agreements with market shares beyond the threshold of the block exemption will almost always fall under Article 81(1) and have to be examined carefully because of the risk of market partitioning (see example 5 below).

3.4. Assessment under Article 81(3)

3.4.1. *Economic benefits*

102. Most common types of production agreements can be assumed to cause some economic benefits in the form of economies of scale or scope or better production technologies unless they are an instrument for price fixing, output restriction or market and customer allocation. Under these conditions it appears reasonable to provide for the exemption of such agreements which result in a restriction of competition up to a market share threshold below which it can, for the application of Article 81(3), in general, be presumed that the positive effects of production agreements will outweigh any negative effects on competition. Therefore, agreements concerning unilateral or reciprocal specialisation as well as joint production are block exempted (Specialisation block exemption Regulation) provided that they do not contain hard core restrictions (see Article 5) and that they are concluded between parties with a combined market share not exceeding 20% in the relevant market(s).

103. For those agreements not covered by the block exemption the parties have to demonstrate improvements of production or other efficiencies. Efficiencies that only benefit the parties or cost savings that are caused by output reduction or market allocation cannot be taken into account.

3.4.2. *Indispensability*

104. Restrictions that go beyond what is necessary to achieve the economic benefits described above will not be accepted. For instance, parties should not be restricted in their competitive behaviour on output outside the cooperation.

3.4.3. *No elimination of competition*

105. No exemption will be possible, if the parties are afforded the possibility of eliminating competition in respect of a substantial part of the products in question. Where as a consequence of a production agreement an undertaking is dominant or becoming dominant, such an agreement which produces anti-competitive effects in

the meaning of Article 81 can in principle not be exempted. This has to be analysed on the relevant market to which the products subject to the cooperation belong and on possible spill-over markets.

3.5. Examples

Joint production

106. The following two examples concern hypothetical cases causing competition problems on the relevant market to which the jointly manufactured products belong.

107. Example 1

Situation: Two suppliers, A and B, of the basic chemical product X decide to build a new production plant controlled by a joint venture. This plant will produce roughly 50% of their total output. X is a homogeneous product and is not substitutable with other products, ie forms a relevant market on its own. The market is rather stagnant. The parties will not significantly increase total output, but close down two old factories and shift capacity to the new plant. A and B each have a market share of 20%. There are three other significant suppliers each with 10–15% market share and several smaller players.

Analysis: It is likely that this joint venture would have an effect on the competitive behaviour of the parties because coordination would give them considerable market power, if not even a dominant position. Severe restrictive effects in the market are probable. High efficiency gains which may outweigh these effects are unlikely in such a scenario where a significant increase in output cannot be expected.

108. Example 2

Situation: Two suppliers, A and B, form a production joint venture on the same relevant market as in example 1. The joint venture also produces 50% of the parties' total output. A and B each have 15% market share. There are 3 other players: C with a market share of 30%, D with 25% and E with 15%. B already has a joint production plant with E.

Analysis: Here the market is characterised by very few players and rather symmetric structures. The joint venture creates an additional link between the players. Coordination between A and B would de facto further increase concentration and also link E to A and B. This cooperation is likely to cause a severe restrictive effect, and—as in example 1—high efficiency gains cannot be expected.

109. Example 3 also concerns the relevant market to which the jointly manufactured products belong, but demonstrates the importance of criteria other than market share (here: switching between captive and non-captive production).

110. Example 3

Situation: A and B set up a production joint venture for an intermediate product X through restructuring current plants. The joint venture sells X exclusively to A and B. It produces 40% of A's total output of X and 50% of B's total output. A and B are captive users of X and are also suppliers of the non-captive market. A's share of total industry output of X is 10%, B's share amounts to 20% and the share of the joint venture to 14%. On the non-captive market, however, A and B have respectively 25% and 35% market share.

Analysis: Despite the parties' strong position on the non-captive market the cooperation may not eliminate effective competition in the market for X, if switching costs between captive and non-captive use are small. However, only very rapid switching would counteract the high market share of 60%. Otherwise this production venture raises serious competition concerns which cannot be outweighed even by significant economic benefits.

111. Example 4 concerns cooperation regarding an important intermediate product with spill-over effects on a downstream market.

112. Example 4

Situation: A and B set up a production joint venture for an intermediate product X. They will close their own factories, which have been manufacturing X, and will cover their needs of X exclusively from the joint venture. The intermediate product accounts for 50% of the total costs of the final product Y. A and B each have a share of 20% in the market for Y. There are two other significant suppliers of Y each with 15% market share and several smaller competitors.

Analysis: Here the commonality of costs is high; furthermore, the parties would gain market power through coordination of their behaviour on the market Y. The case raises competition problems and the assessment is almost identical to example 1 although here the cooperation is taking place in an upstream market.

Reciprocal specialisation

113. Example 5

Situation: A and B each manufacture and supply the homogeneous products X and Y, which belong to different markets. A's market share of X is 28% and of Y it is 10%. B's share of X is 10% and of Y it is 30%. Because of scale economies they conclude a reciprocal specialisation agreement according to which A will in future only produce X and B will produce only Y. Both agree on cross-supplies so that they will both remain in the markets as suppliers. Due to the homogeneous nature of the products, distribution costs are minor. There are two other manufacturing suppliers of X and Y with market shares of roughly 15% each, the remaining suppliers have 5–10% shares.

Analysis: The degree of commonality of costs is extremely high, only the relatively minor distribution costs remain separate. Consequently, there is very little room for competition left. The parties would gain market power through coordination of their behaviour on the markets for X and Y. Furthermore, it is likely that the market supplies of Y from A and X from B will diminish over time. The case raises competition problems which the economies of scale are unlikely to outweigh.

The scenario may change if X and Y were heterogeneous products with a very high proportion of marketing and distribution costs (eg 65–70% of total costs). Furthermore, if the offer of a complete range of the differentiated products was a condition for competing successfully, the withdrawal of one or more parties as suppliers of X and/or Y would be unlikely. In such a scenario the criteria for exemption may be fulfilled (provided that the economies are significant), despite the high market shares.

Subcontracting between competitors

114. Example 6

Situation: A and B are competitors in the market for the final product X. A has a market share of 15%, B of 20%. Both also produce the intermediate product Y, which is an input into the production of X, but is also used to produce other products. It accounts for 10% of the cost of X. A only produces Y for internal consumption, while B is also selling Y to third party customers. Its market share for Y is 10%. A and B agree on a subcontracting agreement, whereby A will purchase

60% of its requirements of Y from B. It will continue to produce 40% of its requirements internally to not lose the know-how related to the production of Y.

Analysis: As A has only produced Y for internal consumption, it first needs to be analysed if A is a realistic potential entrant into the merchant market for sales of Y to third parties. If this is not the case, then the agreement does not restrict competition with respect to Y. Spill-over effects into the market for X are also unlikely in view of the low degree of commonality of costs created by the agreement.

If A were to be regarded a realistic potential entrant into the merchant market for sales of Y to third parties, the market position of B in the market for Y would need to be taken into account. As B's market share is rather low, the result of the analysis would not change.

[4928]

4. PURCHASING AGREEMENTS

4.1. Definition

115. This chapter focuses on agreements concerning the joint buying of products. Joint buying can be carried out by a jointly controlled company, by a company in which many firms hold a small stake, by a contractual arrangement or even looser form of cooperation.

116. Purchasing agreements are often concluded by small and medium-sized enterprises to achieve volumes and discounts similar to their bigger competitors. These agreements between small and medium-sized enterprises are therefore normally pro-competitive. Even if a moderate degree of market power is created, this may be outweighed by economies of scale provided the parties actually bundle volume.

117. Joint purchasing may involve both horizontal and vertical agreements. In these cases a two-step analysis is necessary. First, the horizontal agreements have to be assessed according to the principles described in the present guidelines. If this assessment leads to the conclusion that a cooperation between competitors in the area of purchasing is acceptable, a further assessment will be necessary to examine the vertical agreements concluded with suppliers or individual sellers. The latter assessment will follow the rules of the Block Exemption Regulation and the Guidelines on Vertical Restraints.[43]

118. An example would be an association formed by a group of retailers for the joint purchasing of products. Horizontal agreements concluded between the members of the association or decisions adopted by the association have to be assessed first as a horizontal agreement according to the present guidelines. Only if this assessment is positive does it become relevant to assess the resulting vertical agreements between the association and individual members or between the association and suppliers. These agreements are covered—up to a certain limit—by the block exemption for vertical restraints.[44] Those agreements falling outside the vertical block exemption will not be presumed to be illegal but may need individual examination.

4.2. Relevant markets

119. There are two markets which may be affected by joint buying: First, the market(s) with which the cooperation is directly concerned, ie the relevant purchasing market(s). Secondly, the selling market(s), ie the market(s) downstream where the participants of the joint purchasing arrangement are active as sellers.

120. The definition of relevant purchasing markets follows the principles described in the Commission Notice on the definition of the relevant market and is based on the concept of substitutability to identify competitive constraints. The only difference to the definition of "selling markets" is that substitutability has to be

defined from the viewpoint of supply and not from the viewpoint of demand. In other words: the suppliers' alternatives are decisive in identifying the competitive constraints on purchasers. These could be analysed for instance by examining the suppliers' reaction to a small but lasting price *decrease*. If the market is defined, the market share can be calculated as the percentage for which the purchases by the parties concerned account out of the total sales of the purchased product or service in the relevant market.

121. Example 1

A group of car manufacturers agree to buy product X jointly. Their combined purchases of X account for 15 units. All the sales of X to car manufacturers account for 50 units. However, X is also sold to manufacturers of products other than cars. All sales of X account for 100 units. Thus, the (purchasing) market share of the group is 15%.

122. If the parties are in addition competitors on one or more selling markets, these markets are also relevant for the assessment. Restrictions of competition on these markets are more likely if the parties will achieve market power by coordinating their behaviour and if the parties have a significant proportion of their total costs in common. This is, for instance, the case if retailers which are active in the same relevant retail market(s) jointly purchase a significant amount of the products they offer for resale. It may also be the case if competing manufacturers and sellers of a final product jointly purchase a high proportion of their input together. The selling markets have to be defined by applying the methodology described in the Commission Notice on the definition of the relevant market.

4.3. Assessment under Article 81(1)

4.3.1. *Nature of the agreement*

4.3.1.1. Agreements that do not fall under Article 81(1)

123. By their very nature joint buying agreements will be concluded between companies that are at least competitors on the purchasing markets. If, however, competing purchasers cooperate who are not active on the same relevant market further downstream (eg retailers which are active in different geographic markets and cannot be regarded as realistic potential competitors), Article 81(1) will rarely apply unless the parties have a very strong position in the buying markets, which could be used to harm the competitive position of other players in their respective selling markets.

4.3.1.2. Agreements that almost always fall under Article 81(1)

124. Purchasing agreements only come under Article 81(1) by their nature if the cooperation does not truly concern joint buying, but serves as a tool to engage in a disguised cartel, ie otherwise prohibited price fixing, output limitation or market allocation.

4.3.1.3. Agreements that may fall under Article 81(1)

125. Most purchasing agreements have to be analysed in their legal and economic context. The analysis has to cover both the purchasing and the selling markets.

4.3.2. *Market power and market structures*

126. The starting point for the analysis is the examination of the parties' buying power. Buying power can be assumed if a purchasing agreement accounts for a sufficiently large proportion of the total volume of a purchasing market so that prices can be driven down below the competitive level or access to the market can be foreclosed to competing buyers. A high degree of buying power over the suppliers of a market may bring about inefficiencies such as quality reductions, lessening of innovation efforts, or ultimately sub-optimal supply. However, the primary concerns

in the context of buying power are that lower prices may not be passed on to customers further downstream and that it may cause cost increases for the purchasers' competitors on the selling markets because either suppliers will try to recover price reductions for one group of customers by increasing prices for other customers or competitors have less access to efficient suppliers. Consequently, purchasing markets and selling markets are characterised by interdependencies as set out below.

Interdependencies between purchasing and selling market(s)

127. The cooperation of competing purchasers can appreciably restrict competition by means of creating buying power. Whilst the creation of buying power can lead to lower prices for consumers, buying power is not always pro-competitive and may even, under certain circumstances, cause severe negative effects on competition.

128. First, lower purchasing costs resulting from the exercise of buying power cannot be seen as pro-competitive, if the purchasers together have power on the selling markets. In this case, the cost savings are probably not passed on to consumers. The more combined power the parties have on their selling markets, the higher is the incentive for the parties to coordinate their behaviour as sellers. This may be facilitated if the parties achieve a high degree of commonality of costs through joint purchasing. For instance, if a group of large retailers buys a high proportion of their products together, they will have a high proportion of their total cost in common. The negative effects of joint buying can therefore be rather similar to joint production.

129. Secondly, power on the selling markets may be created or increased through buying power which is used to foreclose competitors or to raise rivals' costs. Significant buying power by one group of customers may lead to foreclosure of competing buyers by limiting their access to efficient suppliers. It can also cause cost increases for its competitors because suppliers will try to recover price reductions for one group of customers by increasing prices for other customers (eg rebate discrimination by suppliers of retailers). This is only possible if the suppliers of the purchasing markets also have a certain degree of market power. In both cases, competition in the selling markets can be further restricted by buying power.

130. There is no absolute threshold which indicates that a buying cooperation creates some degree of market power and thus falls under Article 81(1). However, in most cases, it is unlikely that market power exists if the parties to the agreement have a combined market share of below 15% on the purchasing market(s) as well as a combined market share of below 15% on the selling market(s). In any event, at that level of market share it is likely that the conditions of Article 81(3) explained below are fulfilled by the agreement in question.

131. A market share above this threshold does not automatically indicate that a negative market effect is caused by the cooperation but requires a more detailed assessment of the impact of a joint buying agreement on the market, involving factors such as the market concentration and possible countervailing power of strong suppliers. Joint buying that involves parties with a combined market share significantly above 15% in a concentrated market is likely to come under Article 81(1), and efficiencies that may outweigh the restrictive effect have to be shown by the parties.

4.4. Assessment under Article 81(3)

4.4.1. *Economic benefits*

132. Purchasing agreements can bring about economic benefits such as economies of scale in ordering or transportation which may outweigh restrictive effects. If the parties together have significant buying or selling power, the issue of

efficiencies has to be examined carefully. Cost savings that are caused by the mere exercise of power and which do not benefit consumers cannot be taken into account.

4.4.2. *Indispensability*

133. Purchasing agreements cannot be exempted if they impose restrictions that are not indispensable to the attainment of the above mentioned benefits. An obligation to buy exclusively through the cooperation can in certain cases be indispensable to achieve the necessary volume for the realisation of economies of scale. However, such an obligation has to be assessed in the context of the individual case.

4.4.3. *No elimination of competition*

134. No exemption will be possible, if the parties are afforded the possibility of eliminating competition in respect of a substantial part of the products in question. This assessment has to cover buying and selling markets. The combined market shares of the parties can be regarded as a starting point. It then needs to be evaluated whether these market shares are indicative of a dominant position, and whether there are any mitigating factors, such as countervailing power of suppliers on the purchasing markets or potential for market entry in the selling markets. Where as a consequence of a purchasing agreement an undertaking is dominant or becoming dominant on either the buying or selling market, such an agreement which produces anti-competitive effects in the meaning of Article 81 can in principle not be exempted.

4.5. Examples

135. Example 2

Situation: Two manufacturers, A and B, decide to jointly buy component X. They are competitors on their selling market. Together their purchases represent 35% of the total sales of X in the EEA, which is assumed to be the relevant geographic market. There are 6 other manufacturers (competitors of A and B on their selling market) accounting for the remaining 65% of the purchasing market; one having 25%, the others accounting for significantly less. The supply side is rather concentrated with 6 suppliers of component X, two with 30% market share each, and the rest with between 10 and 15% (HHI of 2300-2500). On their selling market, A and B achieve a combined market share of 35%.

Analysis: Due to the parties' market power in their selling market, the benefits of possible cost savings may not be passed on to final consumers. Furthermore, the joint buying is likely to increase the costs of the parties' smaller competitors because the two powerful suppliers probably recover price reductions for the group by increasing smaller customers' prices. Increasing concentration in the downstream market may be the result. In addition, the cooperation may lead to further concentration among suppliers because smaller ones, which may already work near or below minimum optimal scale, may be driven out of business if they cannot reduce prices further. Such a case probably causes a significant restriction of competition which may not be outweighed by possible efficiency gains from bundling volume.

136. Example 3

Situation: 150 small retailers conclude an agreement to form a joint buying organisation. They are obliged to buy a minimum volume through the organisation which accounts for roughly 50% of each retailer's total costs. The retailers can buy more than the minimum volume through the organisation, and they may also buy outside the cooperation. They have a combined market share of 20% on each of the purchasing and the selling market(s). A and B are their two large competitors, A has a 25% share on each of the markets concerned, B 35%. The remaining smaller competitors have also formed a buying group. The 150 retailers achieve economies by combining a significant amount of volume and buying tasks.

Analysis: The retailers may achieve a high degree of commonality of costs if they ultimately buy more than the agreed minimum volume together. However, together they only have a moderate market position on the buying and the selling market. Furthermore, the cooperation brings about some economies of scale. This cooperation is likely to be exempted.

137. Example 4

Situation: Two supermarket chains conclude an agreement to jointly buy products which account for roughly 50% of their total costs. On the relevant buying markets for the different categories of products the parties have shares between 25% and 40%, on the relevant selling market (assuming there is only one geographic market concerned) they achieve 40%. There are five other significant retailers each with 10–15% market share. Market entry is not likely.

Analysis: It is likely that this joint buying arrangement would have an effect on the competitive behaviour of the parties because coordination would give them significant market power. This is particularly the case if entry is weak. The incentive to coordinate behaviour is higher if the costs are similar. Similar margins of the parties would add an incentive to have the same prices. Even if efficiencies are caused by the cooperation, it is not likely to be exempted due to the high degree of market power.

138. Example 5

Situation: small cooperatives conclude an agreement to form a joint buying organisation(s). They are obliged to buy a minimum volume through the organisation. The parties can buy more than the minimum volume through the organisation, but they may also buy outside the cooperation. Each of the parties has a total market share of 5% on each of the purchasing and selling markets, giving a combined market share of 25%. There are two other significant retailers each with 20–25% market share and a number of smaller retailers with market shares below 5%.

Analysis: The setting up of the joint buying organisation is likely to give the parties a market position on both the purchasing and selling markets of a degree which enables them to compete with the two largest retailers. Moreover, the presence of these two other players with similar levels of market position is likely to result in the efficiencies of the agreement being passed on to consumers. In such a scenario the agreement is likely to be exempted.

[4929]

5. COMMERCIALISATION AGREEMENTS

5.1. Definition

139. The agreements covered in this section involve cooperation between competitors in the selling, distribution or promotion of their products. These agreements can have a widely varying scope, depending on the marketing functions which are being covered by the cooperation. At one end of the spectrum, there is joint selling that leads to a joint determination of all commercial aspects related to the sale of the product including price. At the other end, there are more limited agreements that only address one specific marketing function, such as distribution, service, or advertising.

140. The most important of these more limited agreements would seem to be distribution agreements. These agreements are generally covered by the Block Exemption Regulation and Guidelines on Vertical Restraints unless the parties are actual or potential competitors. In this case, the Block Exemption Regulation only

covers non-reciprocal vertical agreements between competitors, if (a) the buyer, together with its connected undertakings, has an annual turnover not exceeding EUR 100 million, or (b) the supplier is a manufacturer and a distributor of products and the buyer is a distributor who is not also a manufacturer of products competing with the contract products, or (c) the supplier is a provider of services at several levels of trade, while the buyer does not provide competing services at the level of trade where it purchases the contract services.[45] If competitors agree to distribute their products on a reciprocal basis there is a possibility in certain cases that the agreements have as their object or effect the partitioning of markets between the parties or that they lead to collusion. The same is true for non-reciprocal agreements between competitors exceeding a certain size. These agreements have thus first to be assessed according to the principles set out below. If this assessment leads to the conclusion that a cooperation between competitors in the area of distribution would in principle be acceptable, a further assessment will be necessary to examine the vertical restraints included in such agreements. This assessment should be based on the principles set out in the Guidelines on Vertical Restraints.

141. A further distinction should be drawn between agreements where the parties agree only on joint commercialisation and agreements where the commercialisation is related to another cooperation. This can be for instance the case as regards joint production or joint purchasing. These agreements will be dealt with as in the assessment of those types of cooperation.

5.2. Relevant markets

142. To assess the competitive relationship between the cooperating parties, first the relevant product and geographic market(s) directly concerned by the cooperation (ie the market(s) to which products subject to the agreement belong) have to be defined. Secondly, a commercialisation agreement in one market may also affect the competitive behaviour of the parties in a neighbouring market closely related to the market directly concerned by the cooperation.

5.3. Assessment under Article 81(1)

5.3.1. *Nature of the agreement*

5.3.1.1. Agreements that do not fall under Article 81(1)

143. The commercialisation agreements covered by this section only fall under the competition rules if the parties to the agreements are competitors. If the parties clearly do not compete with regard to the products or services covered by the agreement, the agreement cannot create competition problems of a horizontal nature. However, the agreement can fall under Article 81(1) if it contains vertical restraints, such as restrictions on passive sales, resale price maintenance, etc. This also applies if a cooperation in commercialisation is objectively necessary to allow one party to enter a market it could not have entered individually, for example because of the costs involved. A specific application of this principle would be consortia arrangements that allow the companies involved to mount a credible tender for projects that they would not be able to fulfil, or would not have bid for, individually. As they are therefore not potential competitors for the tender, there is no restriction of competition.

5.3.1.2. Agreements that almost always fall under Article 81(1)

144. The principal competition concern about a commercialisation agreement between competitors is price fixing. Agreements limited to joint selling have as a rule the object and effect of coordinating the pricing policy of competing manufacturers. In this case they not only eliminate price competition between the parties but also restrict the volume of products to be delivered by the participants within the framework of the system for allocating orders. They therefore restrict competition between the parties on the supply side and limit the choice of purchasers and fall under Article 81(1).

145. This appreciation does not change if the agreement is non-exclusive. Article 81(1) continues to apply even where the parties are free to sell outside the agreement, as long as it can be presumed that the agreement will lead to an overall coordination of the prices charged by the parties.

5.3.1.3. Agreements that may fall under Article 81(1)

146. For commercialisation arrangements that fall short of joint selling there will be two major concerns. The first is that the joint commercialisation provides a clear opportunity for exchanges of sensitive commercial information particularly on marketing strategy and pricing. The second is that, depending on the cost structure of the commercialisation, a significant input to the parties' final costs may be common. As a result the actual scope for price competition at the final sales level may be limited. Joint commercialisation agreements therefore can fall under Article 81(1) if they either allow the exchange of sensitive commercial information, or if they influence a significant part of the parties' final cost.

147. A specific concern related to distribution arrangements between competitors which are active in different geographic markets is that they can lead to or be an instrument of market partitioning. In the case of reciprocal agreements to distribute each other's products, the parties to the agreement allocate markets or customers and eliminate competition between themselves. The key question in assessing an agreement of this type is if the agreement in question is objectively necessary for the parties to enter each other's market. If it is, the agreement does not create competition problems of a horizontal nature. However, the distribution agreement can fall under Article 81(1) if it contains vertical restraints, such as restrictions on passive sales, resale price maintenance, etc. If the agreement is not objectively necessary for the parties to enter each other's market, it falls under 81(1). If the agreement is not reciprocal, the risk of market partitioning is less pronounced. It needs however to be assessed if the non-reciprocal agreement constitutes the basis for a mutual understanding to not enter each other's market or is a means to control access to or competition on the "importing" market.

5.3.2. *Market power and market structure*

148. As indicated above, agreements that involve price fixing will always fall under Article 81(1) irrespective of the market power of the parties. They may, however, be exemptable under Article 81(3) under the conditions described below.

149. Commercialisation agreements between competitors which do not involve price fixing are only subject to Article 81(1) if the parties to the agreement have some degree of market power. In most cases, it is unlikely that market power exists if the parties to the agreement have a combined market share of below 15%. In any event, at that level of market share it is likely that the conditions of Article 81(3) explained below are fulfilled by the agreement in question.

150. If the parties' combined market share is greater than 15%, the likely impact of the joint commercialisation agreement on the market must be assessed. In this respect market concentration, as well as market shares will be a significant factor. The more concentrated the market the more useful information about prices or marketing strategy to reduce uncertainty and the greater the incentive for the parties to exchange such information.[46]

5.4. Assessment under Article 81(3)

5.4.1. *Economic benefits*

151. The efficiencies to be taken into account when assessing whether a joint commercialisation agreement can be exempted will depend upon the nature of the activity. Price fixing can generally not be justified, unless it is indispensable for the integration of other marketing functions, and this integration will generate

substantial efficiencies. The size of the efficiencies generated depends *inter alia* on the importance of the joint marketing activities for the overall cost structure of the product in question. Joint distribution is thus more likely to generate significant efficiencies for producers of widely distributed consumer products than for producers of industrial products which are only bought by a limited number of users.

152. In addition, the claimed efficiencies should not be savings which result only from the elimination of costs that are inherently part of competition, but must result from the integration of economic activities. A reduction of transport cost which is only a result of customer allocation without any integration of the logistical system can therefore not be regarded as an efficiency that would make an agreement exemptable.

153. Claimed efficiency benefits must be demonstrated. An important element in this respect would be the contribution by both parties of significant capital, technology, or other assets. Cost savings through reduced duplication of resources and facilities can also be accepted. If, on the other hand, the joint commercialisation represents no more than a sales agency with no investment, it is likely to be a disguised cartel and as such cannot fulfil the conditions of Article 81(3).

5.4.2. *Indispensability*

154. A commercialisation agreement cannot be exempted if it imposes restrictions that are not indispensable to the attainment of the abovementioned benefits. As discussed above, the question of indispensability is especially important for those agreements involving price fixing or the allocation of markets.

5.4.3. *No elimination of competition*

155. No exemption will be possible, if the parties are afforded the possibility of eliminating competition in respect of a substantial part of the products in question. In making this assessment, the combined market shares of the parties can be regarded as a starting point. One then needs to evaluate whether these market shares are indicative of a dominant position, and whether there are any mitigating factors, such as the potential for market entry. Where as a consequence of a commercialisation agreement an undertaking is dominant or becoming dominant, such an agreement which produces anti-competitive effects in the meaning of Article 81 can in principle not be exempted.

5.5.   Examples

156. Example 1

Situation: 5 small food producers, each with 2% market share of the overall food market, agree to, combine their distribution facilities, market under a common brand name; and sell their products at a common price. This involves significant investment in warehousing, transport, advertising, marketing and a sales force. It significantly reduces their cost base, representing typically 50% of the price at which they sell, and allows them to offer a quicker, more efficient distribution system. The customers of the food producers are large retail chains.

Three large multinational food groups dominate the market, each with 20% market share. The rest of the market is made up of small independent producers. The product ranges of the parties to this agreement overlap in some significant areas, but in no product market does their combined market share exceed 15%.

Analysis: The agreement involves price fixing and thus falls under Article 81(1), even though the parties to the agreement cannot be considered as having market power. However, the integration of the marketing and distribution appears to provide significant efficiencies which are of benefit to customers both in terms of improved service, and lower costs. The question is therefore whether the agreement is exemptable under Article 81(3). To answer this question it must be established whether the price fixing is indispensable for the integration of the other marketing functions and the attainment of the economic benefits. In this case, the price fixing can be regarded as indispensable, as the clients—large retail chains—do not want to deal with a multitude of prices. It is also indispensable, as the aim—a common brand—can only be credibly achieved if all aspects of marketing, including price, are standardised. As the parties do not have market power and the agreement creates significant efficiencies it is compatible with Article 81.

157. Example 2

Situation: 2 producers of ball bearings, each having a market share of 5%, create a sales joint venture which will market the products, determine the prices and allocate orders to the parent companies. They retain the right to sell outside this structure. Deliveries to customers continue to be made directly from the parents' factories. They claim that this will create efficiencies as the joint sales force can demonstrate the parties' products at the same time to the same client thus eliminating a wasteful duplication of sales efforts. In addition, the joint venture would, wherever possible, allocate orders to the closest factory possible, thus reducing transport costs.

Analysis: The agreement involves price fixing and thus falls under Article 81(1), even though the parties to the agreement cannot be considered as having market power. It is not exemptable under Article 81(3), as the claimed efficiencies are only cost reductions derived from the elimination of competition between the parties.

158. Example 3

Situation: 2 producers of soft drinks are active in 2 different, neighbouring Member States. Both have a market share of 20% in their home market. They agree to reciprocally distribute each other's product in their respective geographic market.

Both markets are dominated by a large multi-national soft drink producer, having a market share of 50% in each market.

Analysis: The agreement falls under Article 81(1) if the parties can be presumed to be potential competitors. Answering this question would thus require an analysis of the barriers to entry into the respective geographic markets. If the parties could have entered each other's market independently, then their agreement eliminates competition between them. However, even though the market shares of the parties indicate that they could have some market power, an analysis of the market structure indicates that this is not the case. In addition, the reciprocal distribution agreement benefits customers as it increases the available choice in each geographic market. The agreement would thus be exemptable even if it were considered to be restrictive of competition.

[4930]

6. AGREEMENT ON STANDARDS

6.1. Definition

159. Standardisation agreements have as their primary objective the definition of technical or quality requirements with which current or future products, production processes or methods may comply.[47] Standardisation agreements can cover various issues, such as standardisation of different grades or sizes of a particular product or technical specifications in markets where compatibility and interoperability with other products or systems is essential. The terms of access to a particular quality mark or for approval by a regulatory body can also be regarded as a standard.

160. Standards related to the provision of professional services, such as rules of admission to a liberal profession, are not covered by these guidelines.

6.2. Relevant markets

161. Standardisation agreements produce their effects on three possible markets, which will be defined according to the Commission notice on market definition. First, the product market(s) to which the standard(s) relates. Standards on entirely new products may raise issues similar to those raised for R & D agreements, as far as market definition is concerned (see Point 2.2). Second, the service market for standard setting, if different standard setting bodies or agreements exist. Third, where relevant, the distinct market for testing and certification.

6.3. Assessment under Article 81(1)

162. Agreements to set standards[48] may be either concluded between private undertakings or set under the aegis of public bodies or bodies entrusted with the operation of services of general economic interest, such as the standards bodies recognised under Directive 98/34/EC.[49] The involvement of such bodies is subject to the obligations of Member States regarding the preservation of non-distorted competition in the Community.

6.3.1. *Nature of the agreement*

6.3.1.1. Agreements that do not fall under Article 81(1)

163. Where participation in standard setting is unrestricted and transparent, standardisation agreements as defined above, which set no obligation to comply with the standard or which are parts of a wider agreement to ensure compatibility of products, do not restrict competition. This normally applies to standards adopted by the recognised standards bodies which are based on non-discriminatory, open and transparent procedures.

164. No appreciable restriction exists for those standards that have a negligible coverage of the relevant market, as long as it remains so. No appreciable restriction is found either in agreements which pool together SMEs to standardise access forms or conditions to collective tenders or those that standardise aspects such as minor product characteristics, forms and reports, which have an insignificant effect on the main factors affecting competition in the relevant markets.

6.3.1.2. Agreements that almost always fall under Article 81(1)

165. Agreements that use a standard as a means amongst other parts of a broader restrictive agreement aimed at excluding actual or potential competitors will almost always be caught by Article 81(1). For instance, an agreement whereby a national association of manufacturers set a standard and put pressure on third parties not to market products that did not comply with the standard would be in this category.

6.3.1.3. Agreements that may fall under Article 81(1)

166. Standardisation agreements may be caught by Article 81(1) insofar as they grant the parties joint control over production and/or innovation, thereby restricting their ability to compete on product characteristics, while affecting third parties like suppliers or purchasers of the standardised products. The assessment of each agreement must take into account the nature of the standard and its likely effect on the markets concerned, on the one hand, and the scope of possible restrictions that go beyond the primary objective of standardisation, as defined above, on the other.

167. The existence of a restriction of competition in standardisation agreements depends upon the extent to which the parties remain free to develop alternative standards or products that do not comply with the agreed standard. Standardisation agreements may restrict competition where they prevent the parties from either developing alternative standards or commercialising products that do not comply with the standard. Agreements that entrust certain bodies with the exclusive right to test compliance with the standard go beyond the primary objective of defining the

standard and may also restrict competition. Agreements that impose restrictions on marking of conformity with standards, unless imposed by regulatory provisions, may also restrict competition.

6.3.2. *Market power and market structures*

168. High market shares held by the parties in the market(s) affected will not necessarily be a concern for standardisation agreements. Their effectiveness is often proportional to the share of the industry involved in setting and/or applying the standard. On the other hand, standards that are not accessible to third parties may discriminate or foreclose third parties or segment markets according to their geographic scope of application. Thus, the assessment whether the agreement restricts competition will focus, necessarily on an individual basis, on the extent to which such barriers to entry are likely to be overcome.

6.4. **Assessment under Article 81(3)**

6.4.1. *Economic benefits*

169. The Commission generally takes a positive approach towards agreements that promote economic interpenetration in the common market or encourage the development of new markets and improved supply conditions. To materialise those economic benefits, the necessary information to apply the standard must be available to those wishing to enter the market and an appreciable proportion of the industry must be involved in the setting of the standard in a transparent manner. It will be for the parties to demonstrate that any restrictions on the setting, use or access to the standard provide economic benefits.

170. In order to reap technical or economic benefits, standards should not limit innovation. This will depend primarily on the lifetime of the associated products, in connection with the market development stage (fast growing, growing, stagnant . . .). The effects on innovation must be analysed on a case-by-case basis. The parties may also have to provide evidence that collective standardisation is efficiency-enhancing for the consumer when a new standard may trigger unduly rapid obsolescence of existing products, without objective additional benefits.

6.4.2. *Indispensability*

171. By their nature, standards will not include all possible specifications or technologies. In some cases, it would be necessary for the benefit of the consumers or the economy at large to have only one technological solution. However, this standard must be set on a non-discriminatory basis. Ideally, standards should be technology neutral. In any event, it must be justifiable why one standard is chosen over another.

172. All competitors in the market(s) affected by the standard should have the possibility of being involved in discussions. Therefore, participation in standard setting should be open to all, unless the parties demonstrate important inefficiencies in such participation or unless recognised procedures are foreseen for the collective representation of interests, as in formal standards bodies.

173. As a general rule there should be a clear distinction between the setting of a standard and, where necessary, the related R & D, and the commercial exploitation of that standard. Agreements on standards should cover no more than what is necessary to ensure their aims, whether this is technical compatibility or a certain level of quality. For instance, it should be very clearly demonstrated why it is indispensable to the emergence of the economic benefits that an agreement to disseminate a standard in an industry where only one competitor offers an alternative should oblige the parties to the agreement to boycott the alternative.

6.4.3. *No elimination of competition*

174. There will clearly be a point at which the specification of a private standard by a group of firms that are jointly dominant is likely to lead to the creation of a de facto industry standard. The main concern will then be to ensure that these standards are as open as possible and applied in a clear non-discriminatory manner. To avoid elimination of competition in the relevant market(s), access to the standard must be possible for third parties on fair, reasonable and non-discriminatory terms.

175. To the extent that private organisations or groups of companies set a standard or their proprietary technology becomes a de facto standard, then competition will be eliminated if third parties are foreclosed from access to this standard.

6.5. Examples

176. Example 1

Situation: EN 60603-7:1993 defines the requirements to connect television receivers to video-generating accessories such as video recorders and video games. Although the standard is not legally binding, in practice manufacturers both of television receivers and of video games use the standard, as the market requires so.

Analysis: Article 81(1) is not infringed. The standard has been adopted by recognised standards bodies, at national, European and international level, through open and transparent procedures, and is based on national consensus reflecting the position of manufacturers and consumers. All manufacturers are allowed to use the standard.

177. Example 2

Situation: A number of videocassette manufacturers agree to develop a quality mark or standard to denote the fact that the videocassette meets certain minimum technical specifications. The manufacturers are free to produce videocassettes which do not conform to the standard and the standard is freely available to other developers.

Analysis: Provided that the agreement does not otherwise restrict competition, Article 81(1) is not infringed, as participation in standard setting is unrestricted and transparent, and the standardisation agreement does not set an obligation to comply with the standard. If the parties agreed only to produce videocassettes which conform to the new standard, the agreement would limit technical development and prevent the parties from selling different products, which would infringe Article 81(1).

178. Example 3

Situation: A group of competitors active in various markets which are interdependent with products that must be compatible, and with over 80% of the relevant markets, agree to jointly develop a new standard that will be introduced in competition with other standards already present in the market, widely applied by their competitors. The various products complying with the new standard will not be compatible with existing standards. Because of the significant investment needed to shift and to maintain production under the new standard, the parties agree to commit a certain volume of sales to products complying with the new standard so as to create a "critical mass" in the market. They also agree to limit their individual production volume of products not complying with the standard to the level attained last year.

Analysis: This agreement, owing to the parties' market power and the restrictions on production, falls under Article 81(1) while not being likely to fulfil the conditions of paragraph 3, unless access to technical information were provided on a non-discriminatory basis and reasonable terms to other suppliers wishing to compete.

[4931]

7. ENVIRONMENTAL AGREEMENTS

7.1. Definition

179. Environmental agreements[50] are those by which the parties undertake to achieve pollution abatement, as defined in environmental law, or environmental objectives, in particular, those set out in Article 174 of the Treaty. Therefore, the target or the measures agreed need to be directly linked to the reduction of a pollutant or a type of waste identified as such in relevant regulations.[51] This excludes agreements that trigger pollution abatement as a by-product of other measures.

180. Environmental agreements may set out standards on the environmental performance of products (inputs or outputs) or production processes.[52] Other possible categories may include agreements at the same level of trade, whereby the parties provide for the common attainment of an environmental target such as recycling of certain materials, emission reductions, or the improvement of energy-efficiency.

181. Comprehensive, industry-wide schemes are set up in many Member States for complying with environmental obligations on take-back or recycling. Such schemes usually comprise a complex set of arrangements, some of which are horizontal, while others are vertical in character. To the extent that these arrangements contain vertical restraints they are not subject to these guidelines.

7.2. Relevant markets

182. The effects are to be assessed on the markets to which the agreement relates, which will be defined according to the Notice on the definition of the relevant market for the purposes of Community competition law. When the pollutant is not itself a product, the relevant market encompasses that of the product into which the pollutant is incorporated. As for collection/recycling agreements, in addition to their effects on the market(s) on which the parties are active as producers or distributors, the effects on the market of collection services potentially covering the good in question must be assessed as well.

7.3. Assessment under Article 81(1)

183. Some environmental agreements may be encouraged or made necessary by State authorities in the exercise of their public prerogatives. The present guidelines do not deal with the question of whether such State intervention is in conformity with the Member State's obligations under the Treaty. They only address the assessment that must be made as to the compatibility of the agreement with Article 81.

7.3.1. *Nature of the agreement*

7.3.1.1. Agreements that do not fall under Article 81(1).

184. Some environmental agreements are not likely to fall within the scope of the prohibition of Article 81(1), irrespective of the aggregated market share of the parties.

185. This may arise if no precise individual obligation is placed upon the parties or if they are loosely committed to contributing to the attainment of a sector-wide environmental target. In this latter case, the assessment will focus on the discretion left to the parties as to the means that are technically and economically available in order to attain the environmental objective agreed upon. The more varied such means, the less appreciable the potential restrictive effects.

186. Similarly, agreements setting the environmental performance of products or processes that do not appreciably affect product and production diversity in the relevant market or whose importance is marginal for influencing purchase decisions do not fall under Article 81(1). Where some categories of a product are banned or phased out from the market, restrictions cannot be deemed appreciable in so far as

their share is minor in the relevant geographic market or, in the case of Community-wide markets, in all Member States.

187. Finally, agreements which give rise to genuine market creation, for instance recycling agreements, will not generally restrict competition, provided that and for as long as, the parties would not be capable of conducting the activities in isolation, whilst other alternatives and/or competitors do not exist.

7.3.1.2. Agreements that almost always come under Article 81(1)

188. Environmental agreements come under Article 81(1) by their nature if the cooperation does not truly concern environmental objectives, but serves as a tool to engage in a disguised cartel, ie otherwise prohibited price fixing, output limitation or market allocation, or if the cooperation is used as a means amongst other parts of a broader restrictive agreement which aims at excluding actual or potential competitors.

7.3.1.3. Agreements that may fall under Article 81(1)

189. Environmental agreements covering a major share of an industry at national or EC level are likely to be caught by Article 81(1) where they appreciably restrict the parties' ability to devise the characteristics of their products or the way in which they produce them, thereby granting them influence over each other's production or sales. In addition to restrictions between the parties, an environmental agreement may also reduce or substantially affect the output of third parties, either as suppliers or as purchasers.

190. For instance, environmental agreements, which may phase out or significantly affect an important proportion of the parties' sales as regards their products or production processes, may fall under Article 81(1) when the parties hold a significant proportion of the market. The same applies to agreements whereby the parties allocate individual pollution quotas.

191. Similarly, agreements whereby parties holding significant market shares in a substantial part of the common market appoint an undertaking as exclusive provider of collection and/or recycling services for their products, may also appreciably restrict competition, provided other actual or realistic potential providers exist.

7.4. Assessment under Article 81(3)

7.4.1. *Economic benefits*

192. The Commission takes a positive stance on the use of environmental agreements as a policy instrument to achieve the goals enshrined in Article 2 and Article 174 of the Treaty as well as in Community environmental action plans,[53] provided such agreements are compatible with competition rules.[54]

193. Environmental agreements caught by Article 81(1) may attain economic benefits which, either at individual or aggregate consumer level, outweigh their negative effects on competition. To fulfil this condition, there must be net benefits in terms of reduced environmental pressure resulting from the agreement, as compared to a baseline where no action is taken. In other words, the expected economic benefits must outweigh the costs.[55]

194. Such costs include the effects of lessened competition along with compliance costs for economic operators and/or effects on third parties. The benefits might be assessed in two stages. Where consumers individually have a positive rate of return from the agreement under reasonable payback periods, there is no need for the aggregate environmental benefits to be objectively established. Otherwise, a cost-benefit analysis may be necessary to assess whether net benefits for consumers in general are likely under reasonable assumptions.

7.4.2. *Indispensability*

195. The more objectively the economic efficiency of an environmental agreement is demonstrated, the more clearly each provision might be deemed indispensable to the attainment of the environmental goal within its economic context.

196. An objective evaluation of provisions which might "prima facie" be deemed not to be indispensable must be supported with a cost-effectiveness analysis showing that alternative means of attaining the expected environmental benefits, would be more economically or financially costly, under reasonable assumptions. For instance, it should be very clearly demonstrated that a uniform fee, charged irrespective of individual costs for waste collection, is indispensable for the functioning of an industry-wide collection system.

7.4.3. *No elimination of competition*

197. Whatever the environmental and economic gains and the necessity of the intended provisions, the agreement must not eliminate competition in terms of product or process differentiation, technological innovation or market entry in the short or, where relevant, medium run. For instance, in the case of exclusive collection rights granted to a collection/recycling operator who has potential competitors, the duration of such rights should take into account the possible emergence of an alternative to the operator.

7.5. **Examples**

198. Example

Situation: Almost all Community producers and importers of a given domestic appliance (eg washing machines) agree, with the encouragement of a public body, to no longer manufacture and import into the Community products which do not comply with certain environmental criteria (eg energy efficiency). Together, the parties hold 90% of the Community market. The products which will be thus phased out of the market account for a significant proportion of total sales. They will be replaced with more environmentally friendly, but also more expensive products. Furthermore, the agreement indirectly reduces the output of third parties (eg electric utilities, suppliers of components incorporated in the products phased out).

Analysis: The agreement grants the parties control of individual production and imports and concerns an appreciable proportion of their sales and total output, whilst also reducing third parties' output. Consumer choice, which is partly focused on the environmental characteristics of the product, is reduced and prices will probably rise. Therefore, the agreement is caught by Article 81(1). The involvement of the public authority is irrelevant for this assessment.

However, newer products are more technically advanced and by reducing the environmental problem indirectly aimed at (emissions from electricity generation), they will not inevitably create or increase another environmental problem (eg water consumption, detergent use). The net contribution to the improvement of the environmental situation overall outweighs increased costs. Furthermore, individual purchasers of more expensive products will also rapidly recoup the cost increase as the more environmentally friendly products have lower running costs. Other alternatives to the agreement are shown to be less certain and less cost-effective in delivering the same net benefits. Varied technical means are economically available to the parties in order to manufacture products which do comply with the environmental characteristics agreed upon and competition will still take place for other product characteristics. Therefore, the conditions for an exemption under Article 81(3) are fulfilled.

[4932]–[5100]

NOTES

[1]   OJ L53, 22.2.85, p 1.

[2]   OJ L306, 11.11.97, p 12.

[3]   OJ L53, 22.2.85, p 5.

[4]   OJ L304, 5.12.2000, p 3.

[5]   OJ L304, 5.12.2000, p 7.

[6]   OJ C75, 29.7.68, p 3.

[7]   OJ C43, 16.2.93, p 2.

[8]   A firm is treated as an actual competitor if it is either active on the same relevant market or if, in the absence of the agreement, it is able to switch production to the relevant products and market them in the short term without incurring significant additional costs or risks in response to a small and permanent increase in relative prices (immediate supply-side substitutability). The same reasoning may lead to the grouping of different geographic areas. However, when supply-side substitutability would entail the need to adjust significantly existing tangible and intangible assets, to make additional investments, to take strategic decisions or to incur time delays, a company will not be treated as a competitor but as a potential competitor (see below). See Commission Notice on the definition of the relevant market for the purposes of Community competition law (OJ C372, 9.12.97, p 5, paragraphs 20–23).

[9]   A firm is treated as a potential competitor if there is evidence that, absent the agreement, this firm could and would be likely to undertake the necessary additional investments or other necessary switching costs so that it could enter the relevant market in response to a small and permanent increase in relative prices. This assessment has to be based on realistic grounds, the mere theoretical possibility to enter a market is not sufficient (see Commission Notice on the definition of the relevant market for the purposes of Community competition law (paragraph 24); see also the Commission's Thirteenth Report on Competition Policy, point 55 and Commission Decision 90/410/EEC in case Elopak/Metal Box-Odin (OJ L209, 8.8.90, p 15). Market entry needs to take place sufficiently fast so that the threat of potential entry is a constraint on the market participants' behaviour. Normally, this means that entry has to occur within a short period. The Guidelines on Vertical Restraints (OJ C291, 13.10.2000, p 1, paragraph 26) consider a period of maximum 1 year for the purposes of application of the Block Exemption Regulation on Vertical Restraints (see footnote 11). However, in individual cases longer time periods can be taken into account. The time period needed by companies already active on the market to adjust their capacities can be used as a yardstick to determine this period.

[10]   OJ L336, 29.12.99, p 21.

[11]   OJ C291, 13.10.2000, p 1.

[12]   The delineation between horizontal and vertical agreements will be further developed in the chapters on joint purchasing (Chapter 4) and joint commercialisation (Chapter 5). See also the Guidelines on Vertical Restraints, paragraph 26 and 29.

[13]   OJ L395, 30.12.89, p 1. Corrected version OJ L257, 21.9.90, p 13.

[14]   OJ L180, 9.7.97, p 1.

[15]   Council Regulation 26/62 (OJ 30, 20.4.62, p 993) (agriculture);
Council Regulation (EEC) No 1017/68, (OJ L 175, 23.7.68, p 1) (transport by rail road and inland waterway);
Council Regulation (EEC) No 4056/86, (OJ L378, 31.12.86, p 4) (maritime transport);
Council Regulation (EEC) No 3975/87, (OJ L374, 31.12.87, p 1) (air transport);
Commission Regulation (EEC) No 3976/87, (OJ L374, 31.12.87, p 9) (air transport);
Commission Regulation (EEC) No 1617/93, (OJ L155, 26.6.93, p 18) (Block exemption concerning joint planning and coordination of schedules, joint operations, consultation on passenger and cargo tariffs on scheduled air services and slot allocation as airports);
Council Regulation (EEC) No 479/92, (OJ L55, 29.2.92 p 3) (Liner shipping companies);
Commission Regulation (EC) No 870/95, (OJ L89, 21.4.95, p 7) (Block exemption covering certain agreements between liner shipping companies);
Council Regulation (EEC) No 1534/91, (OJ L143, 7.6.1991, p 1) (insurance sector);
Commission Regulation (EEC) No 3932/92, (OJ L398, 31.12.92, p 7) (Block exemption covering certain agreements in the insurance sector).

[16]   See Notice on agreements of minor importance (OJ C372, 9.12.97, p 13).

[17]   Companies may have significant market power below the level of market dominance, which is the threshold for the application of Article 82.

[18]   This does, however, exceptionally not apply to a production joint venture. It is inherent to the functioning of such a joint venture that decisions on output are taken jointly by the parties. If the joint venture also markets the jointly manufactured goods, then decisions on prices need to be taken jointly by the parties to such an agreement. In this case, the inclusion of provisions on prices or output does not automatically cause the agreement to fall under Article 81(1). The provisions on prices or output will have to be assessed together with the other effects of the joint venture on the market to determine the applicability of Article 81(1) (see paragraph 90).

[19]   See Commission Notice on the definition of the relevant market for the purposes of Community competition law (OJ C372, 9.12.97, p 5).

[20]   Market shares should normally be calculated on the basis of the market sales value (see Article 6 of the R & D Block Exemption Regulation and Article 6 of the Specialisation Block Exemption Regulation). In determining the market share of a party in a given market, account must be taken of the undertakings which are connected to the parties (see point 2 of Article 2 of the R & D Block Exemption Regulation and point 2 of Article 2 of the Specialisation Block Exemption Regulation).

21   If there are more than two parties, then the collective share of all cooperating competitors has to be significantly greater than the share of the largest single participating competitor.

22   A market consisting of four firms with shares of 30%, 25%, 25% and 20%, has a HHI of 2550 (900+625+625+400) pre-cooperation. If the first two market leaders would cooperate, the HHI would change to 4050 (3025+625+400) post-cooperation. The HHI post-cooperation is relevant for the assessment of the possible market effects of a cooperation.

23   Eg the three-firm concentration ratio CR3 is the sum of the market shares of the leading three competitors in a market.

24   For market definition see the Commission Notice on the definition of the relevant market.

25   See Commission Notice on the definition of the relevant market; see also, for example, Commission Decision 94/811/EC of 8 June 1994 in Case No IV/M269—Shell/Montecatini (OJ L332, 22.12.94 p 48).

26   Article 4(2) of the R & D Block Exemption Regulation.

27   Article 4(1) of the R & D Block Exemption Regulation.

28   Article 7(e) of the R & D Block Exemption Regulation.

29   Article 4(3) of the R & D Block Exemption Regulation.

30   An R & D cooperation between non-competitors can however produce foreclosure effects under Article 81(1) if it relates to an exclusive exploitation of results and if it is concluded between firms, one of which has significant market power with respect to key technology.

31   Pursuant to Article 4(2)(3) of Regulation No 17, agreements which have as their sole object joint research and development need not , but may, be notified to the Commission.

32   See Art 3(2) of the R & D Block Exemption Regulation.

33   See Art 3(2) of the R & D Block Exemption Regulation.

34   As indicated above, joint ventures which fall under the Merger Regulation are not the subject of these guidelines. Full-function joint ventures below Community dimension are normally dealt with by the competition authorities of the Member States. The application of Regulation No 17 could be relevant only where such a full-function joint venture would lead to a restriction of competition resulting from the coordination of the parent companies outside the joint venture ("spill-over effect"). In this respect, the Commission has declared that it will leave the assessment of such operations to the Member States as far as possible (see Statement for the Council Minutes on Regulation (EC) No 1310/97, pt 4).

35   Article 2(4) of the Block Exemption Regulation on Vertical Restraints.

36   Article 2(3) of the Block Exemption Regulation on Vertical Restraints. See also Guidelines on Vertical Restraints, paragraph 33, which notes that subcontracting arrangements between non-competitors under which the buyer provides only specifications to the supplier which describe the goods or services to be supplied are covered by the Block Exemption Regulation on Vertical Restraints.

37   If a subcontracting agreement between competitors stipulates that the contractor will cease production of the product to which the agreement relates, the agreement constitutes a unilateral specialisation agreement which is covered, subject to certain conditions, by the Specialisation Block Exemption Regulation.

38   Notice concerning the assessment of certain subcontracting agreements in relation to Article 85(1) of the EEC Treaty, OJ C1, 3.1.79, p 2.

39   As also referred to in Article 2(4) of the Merger Regulation.

40   As any subcontracting agreement such an agreement can however fall under Article 81(1) if it contains vertical restraints, such as restrictions on passive sales, resale price maintenance, etc.

41   A production joint venture which also carries out joint distribution is, however, in most of the cases a full-function joint venture.

42   Pursuant to Article 4(2)(3) of Council Regulation No 17, agreements which have as their sole object specialisation in the manufacture of products need, under certain conditions, not to be notified to the Commission. They may, however, be notified.

43   See Guidelines on Vertical Restraints, paragraph 29.

44   Article 2(2) of Block Exemption Regulation on Vertical Restraints.

45   Article 2(4) of Block Exemption Regulation on Vertical Restraints.

46   The exchange of sensitive and detailed information which takes place in an oligopolistic market might as such be caught by Article 81(1). The judgments of 28 May 1998 in the "Tractor" cases (C-8/958 P: New Holland Ford and C-7/95 P: John Deere) and of 11 March 1999 in the "Steel Beams" cases (T-134/94, T-136/94, T-137/94, T-138/94, T-141/94, T-145/94, T-147/94, T-148/94, T-151/94, T-156/94 and T-157/94) provide useful clarification in this respect.

47   Standardisation can take different forms, ranging from the adoption of national consensus based standards by the recognised European or national standards bodies, through consortia and fora, to agreements between single companies. Although Community law defines standards in a narrow way, these guidelines qualify as standards all agreements as defined in this paragraph.

48   Pursuant to Article 4(2)(3) of Regulation No 17, agreements which have as their sole object the development or the uniform application of standards and types need not to, but may, be notified to the Commission.

49   Directive 98/34/EC of the European Parliament and of the Council on 22 June 1998 laying down a procedure for the provision of information in the field of technical standards and regulations (OJ L204, 21.7.98, p 37).

50   The term "agreement" is used in the sense defined by the Court of Justice and the Court of First Instance in the case law on Article 81. It does not necessarily correspond to the definition of an 'agreement' in Commission documents dealing with environmental issues such as the Communication on environmental agreements COM(96) 561 final of 27.11.96.

⁵¹ For instance, a national agreement phasing out a pollutant or waste identified as such in relevant Community directives may not be assimilated to a collective boycott on a product which circulates freely in the Community.

⁵² To the extent that some environmental agreements could be assimilated to standardisation, the same assessment principles for standardisation apply to them.

⁵³ Vth Environmental Action Programme (OJ C138, 17.5.93), p 1; European Parliament and Council Decision No 2179/98/EC of 24 September 1998 (OJ L275, 10.10.98, p 1).

⁵⁴ Communication on environmental agreements COM(96) 561 final of 27.11.96, paragraphs 27–29 and Article 3(1)f of EP and Council Decision *ut supra*. The communication includes a "Checklist for Environmental Agreements" identifying the elements that should generally be included in such an agreement.

⁵⁵ This is consistent with the requirement to take account of the potential benefits and costs of action or lack of action set forth in Article 174(3) of the Treaty and Article 7(d) of European Parliament and Council Decision *ut supra*.

E. VERTICAL AGREEMENTS

COMMISSION NOTICE

of 18 December 1978

concerning its assessment of certain subcontracting agreements in relation to Article 85(1) of the EEC Treaty

---

NOTES

Date of publication in OJ: OJ C1, 3.1.79, p 2.

---

1. In this notice the Commission of the European Communities gives its view as to subcontracting agreements in relation to Article 85(1) of the Treaty establishing the European Economic Community. This class of agreement is at the present time a form of work distribution which concerns firms of all sizes, but which offers opportunities for development in particular to small and medium sized firms.

The Commission considers that agreements under which one firm, called "the contractor", whether or not in consequence of a prior order from a third party, entrusts to another, called "the subcontractor", the manufacture of goods, the supply of services or the performance of work under the contractor's instructions, to be provided to the contractor or performed on his behalf, are not of themselves caught by the prohibition in Article 85(1).

To carry out certain subcontracting agreements in accordance with the contractor's instructions, the subcontractor may have to make use of particular technology or equipment which the contractor will have to provide. In order to protect the economic value of such technology or equipment, the contractor may wish to restrict their use by the subcontractor to whatever is necessary for the purpose of the agreement. The question arises whether such restrictions are caught by Article 85(1). They are assessed in this notice with due regard to the purpose of such agreements, which distinguishes them from ordinary patent and know-how licensing agreements.

[5101]

2. In the Commission's view, Article 85(1) does not apply to clauses whereby—
   — technology or equipment provided by the contractor may not be used except for the purposes of the subcontracting agreement,
   — technology or equipment provided by the contractor may not be made available to third parties,
   — the goods, services or work resulting from the use of such technology or equipment may be supplied only to the contractor or performed on his behalf,

provided that and in so far as this technology or equipment is necessary to enable the subcontractor under reasonable conditions to manufacture the goods, to supply the services or to carry out the work in accordance with the contractor's instructions. To that extent the subcontractor is providing goods, services or work in respect of which he is not an independent supplier in the market.

The above proviso is satisfied where performance of the subcontracting agreement makes necessary the use by the subcontractor of—
   — industrial property rights of the contractor or at his disposal, in the form of patents, utility models, designs protected by copyright, registered designs or other rights, or

— secret knowledge or manufacturing processes (know-how) of the contractor or at his disposal, or of

— studies, plans or documents accompanying the information given which have been prepared by or for the contractor, or

— dies, patterns or tools, and accessory equipment that are distinctively the contractor's,

which, even though not covered by industrial property rights nor containing any element of secrecy, permit the manufacture of goods which differ in form, function or composition from other goods manufactured or supplied on the market.

However, the restrictions mentioned above are not justifiable where the subcontractor has at his disposal or could under reasonable conditions obtain access to the technology and equipment needed to produce the goods, provide the services or carry out the work. Generally, this is the case when the contractor provides no more than general information which merely describes the work to be done. In such circumstances the restrictions could deprive the subcontractor of the possibility of developing his own business in the fields covered by the agreement.

[5102]

3.   The following restrictions in connection with the provision of technology by the contractor may in the Commission's view also be imposed by subcontracting agreements without giving grounds for objection under Article 85(1)—

— an undertaking by either of the parties not to reveal manufacturing processes or other know-how of a secret character, or confidential information given by the other party during the negotiation and performance of the agreement, as long as the know-how or information in question has not become public knowledge,

— an undertaking by the subcontractor not to make use, even after expiry of the agreement, of manufacturing processes or other know-how of a secret character received by him during the currency of the agreement, as long as they have not become public knowledge,

— an undertaking by the subcontractor to pass on to the contractor on a non-exclusive basis any technical improvements which he has made during the currency of the agreement, or, where a patentable invention has been discovered by the subcontractor, to grant non-exclusive licences in respect of inventions relating to improvements and new applications of the original invention to the contractor for the term of the patent held by the latter.

This undertaking by the subcontractor may be exclusive in favour of the contractor in so far as improvements and inventions made by the subcontractor during the currency of the agreement are incapable of being used independently of the contractor's secret know-how or patent, since this does not constitute an appreciable restriction of competition.

However, any undertaking by the subcontractor regarding the right to dispose of the results of his own research and development work may restrain competition, where such results are capable of being used independently. In such circumstances, the subcontracting relationship is not sufficient to displace the ordinary competition rules on the disposal of industrial property rights or secret know-how.

[5103]

4.   Where the subcontractor is authorised by a subcontracting agreement to use a specified trade mark, trade name or get up, the contractor may at the same time forbid such use by the subcontractor in the case of goods, services or work which are not to be supplied to the contractor.

[5104]

5.   Although this notice should in general obviate the need for firms to obtain a ruling on the legal position by an individual Commission Decision, it does not affect the right of the firms concerned to apply for negative clearance as defined by Article 2 of Regulation No 17 or to notify the agreement to the Commission under Article 4(1) of that Regulation.[1]

The 1968 notice on cooperation between enterprises,[2] which lists a number of agreements that by their nature are not to be regarded as anti-competitive, is thus supplemented in the subcontracting field. The Commission also reminds firms that, in order to promote co-operation between small and medium sized businesses, it has published a notice concerning agreements of minor importance which do not fall under Article 85(1) of the Treaty establishing the European Economic Community.[3]

This notice is without prejudice to the view that may be taken of subcontracting agreements by the Court of Justice of the European Communities.

[5105]

NOTES
    The 1968 notice on cooperation between enterprises: Commission Notice of 29 July 1968.
    Notice concerning agreements of minor importance which do not fall under Article 85(1) of the Treaty: see now the Commission Notice on agreements of minor importance at **[4059]**.
    [1]   First Regulation implementing Articles 85 and 86 of the EEC Treaty (OJ 13, 21.2.62, p 204/62.)
    [2]   Notice concerning agreements, decisions and concerted practices relating to cooperation between enterprises (OJ C75, 29.7.68, p 3).
    [3]   OJ C313, 29.12.77, p 3.

COMMISSION REGULATION

of 31 January 1996

on the application of Article 85(3) of the Treaty to certain categories of technology transfer agreements

(240/96/EC)

(Text with EEA relevance)

NOTES
    Date of publication in OJ: OJ L31, 9.2.96, p 2.

THE COMMISSION OF THE EUROPEAN COMMUNITIES,

Having regard to the Treaty establishing the European Community,
    Having regard to Council Regulation No 19/65/EEC of 2 March 1965 on the application of Article 85(3) of the Treaty to certain categories of agreements and concerted practices,[1] as last amended by the Act of Accession of Austria, Finland and Sweden, and in particular Article 1 thereof,
    Having published a draft of this Regulation,[2]
    After consulting the Advisory Committee on Restrictive Practices and Dominant Positions,
    Whereas—
    (1)   Regulation No 19/65/EEC empowers the Commission to apply Article 85(3) of the Treaty by regulation to certain categories of agreements and concerted practices falling within the scope of Aricle 85(1) which include restrictions imposed in relation to the acquisition or use of industrial property rights—in particular of patents, utility models, designs or trademarks—or to the rights arising out of contracts for assignment of, or the right to use, a method of manufacture or knowledge relating to use or to the application of industrial processes.

(2)　The Commission has made use of this power by adopting Regulation (EEC) No 2349/84 of 23 July 1984 on the application of Article 85(3) of the Treaty to certain categories of patent licensing agreements,[3] as last amended by Regulation (EC) No 2131/95,[4] and Regulation (EEC) No 556/89 of 30 November 1988 on the application of Article 85(3) of the Treaty to certain categories of know-how licensing agreements,[5] as last amended by the Act of Accession of Austria, Finland and Sweden.

(3)　These two block exemptions ought to be combined into a single regulation covering technology transfer agreements, and the rules governing patent licensing agreements and agreements for the licensing of know-how ought to be harmonised and simplified as far as possible, in order to encourage the dissemination of technical knowledge in the Community and to promote the manufacture of technically more sophisticated products. In those circumstances Regulation (EEC) No 556/89 should be repealed.

(4)　This Regulation should apply to the licensing of Member States' own patents, Community patents[6] and European patents[7] ("pure" patent licensing agreements). It should also apply to agreements for the licensing of non-patented technical information such as descriptions of manufacturing processes, recipes, formulae, designs or drawings, commonly termed "know-how" ("pure" know-how licensing agreements), and to combined patent and know-how licensing agreements ("mixed" agreements), which are playing an increasingly important role in the transfer of technology. For the purposes of this Regulation, a number of terms are defined in Article 10.

(5)　Patent or know-how licensing agreements are agreements whereby one undertaking which holds a patent or know-how ("the licensor") permits another undertaking ("the licensee") to exploit the patent thereby licensed, or communicates the know-how to it, in particular for purposes of manufacture, use or putting on the market. In the light of experience acquired so far, it is possible to define a category of licensing agreements covering all or part of the common market which are capable of falling within the scope of Article 85(1) but which can normally be regarded as satisfying the conditions laid down in Article 85(3), where patents are necessary for the achievement of the objects of the licensed technology by a mixed agreement or where know-how—whether it is ancillary to patents or independent of them—is secret, substantial and identified in any appropriate form. These criteria are intended only to ensure that the licensing of the know-how or the grant of the patent licence justifies a block exemption of obligations restricting competition. This is without prejudice to the right of the parties to include in the contract provisions regarding other obligations, such as the obligation to pay royalties, even if the block exemption no longer applies.

(6)　It is appropriate to extend the scope of this Regulation to pure or mixed agreements containing the licensing of intellectual property rights other than patents (in particular, trademarks, design rights and copyright, especially software protection), when such additional licensing contributes to the achievement of the objects of the licensed technology and contains only ancillary provisions.

(7)　Where such pure or mixed licensing agreements contain not only obligations relating to territories within the common market but also obligations relating to non-member countries, the presence of the latter does not prevent this Regulation from applying to the obligations relating to territories within the common market. Where licensing agreements for non-member countries or for territories which extend beyond the frontiers of the Community have effects within the common market which may fall within the scope of Article 85(1), such agreements should be covered by this Regulation to the same extent as would agreements for territories within the common market.

(8)　The objective being to facilitate the dissemination of technology and the improvement of manufacturing processes, this Regulation should apply only where the licensee himself manufactures the licensed products or has them manufactured for his account, or where the licensed product is a service, provides the service himself or has the service provided for his account, irrespective of whether or not the licensee is also entitled to use confidential information provided by the licensor for the promotion and sale of the licensed product. The scope of this Regulation should therefore exclude agreements solely for the purpose of sale. Also to be excluded from the scope of this Regulation are agreements relating to marketing know-how communicated in the context of franchising arrangements and certain licensing agreements entered into in connection with arrangements such as joint ventures or patent pools and other arrangements in which a licence is granted in exchange for other licences not related to improvements to or new applications of the licensed technology. Such agreements pose different problems which cannot at present be dealt with in a single regulation (Article 5).

(9)　Given the similarity between sale and exclusive licensing, and the danger that the requirements of this Regulation might be evaded by presenting as assignments what are in fact exclusive licenses restrictive of competition, this Regulation should apply to agreements concerning the assignment and acquisition of patents or know-how where the risk associated with exploitation remains with the assignor. It should also apply to licensing agreements in which the licensor is not the holder of the patent or know-how but is authorised by the holder to grant the licence (as in the case of sub-licences) and to licensing agreements in which the parties' rights or obligations are assumed by connected undertakings (Article 6).

(10) Exclusive licensing agreements, ie agreements in which the licensor undertakes not to exploit the licensed technology in the licensed territory himself or to grant further licences there, may not be in themselves incompatible with Article 85(1) where they are concerned with the introduction and protection of a new technology in the licensed territory, by reason of the scale of the research which has been undertaken, of the increase in the level of competition, in particular inter-brand competition, and of the competitiveness of the undertakings concerned resulting from the dissemination of innovation within the Community. In so far as agreements of this kind fall, in other circumstances, within the scope of Article 85(1), it is appropriate to include them in Article 1 in order that they may also benefit from the exemption.

(11) The exemption of export bans on the licensor and on the licensees does not prejudice any developments in the case law of the Court of Justice in relation to such agreements, notably with respect to Articles 30 to 36 and Article 85(1). This is also the case, in particular, regarding the prohibition on the licensee from selling the licensed product in territories granted to other licensees (passive competition).

(12) The obligations listed in Article 1 generally contribute to improving the production of goods and to promoting technical progress. They make the holders of patents or know-how more willing to grant licences and licensees more inclined to undertake the investment required to manufacture, use and put on the market a new product or to use a new process. Such obligations may be permitted under this Regulation in respect of territories where the licensed product is protected by patents as long as these remain in force.

(13) Since the point at which the know-how ceases to be secret can be difficult to determine, it is appropriate, in respect of territories where the licensed technology comprises know-how only, to limit such obligations to a fixed number of years. Moreover, in order to provide sufficient periods of protection, it is appropriate to take as the starting-point for such periods the date on which the product is first put on the market in the Community by a licensee.

(14) Exemption under Article 85(3) of longer periods of territorial protection for know-how agreements, in particular in order to protect expensive and risky investment or where the parties were not competitors at the date of the grant of the licence, can be granted only by individual decision. On the other hand, parties are free to extend the term of their agreements in order to exploit any subsequent improvement and to provide for the payment of additional royalties. However, in such cases, further periods of territorial protection may be allowed only starting from the date of licensing of the secret improvements in the Community, and by individual decision. Where the research for improvements results in innovations which are distinct from the licensed technology the parties may conclude a new agreement benefitting from an exemption under this Regulation.

(15) Provision should also be made for exemption of an obligation on the licensee not to put the product on the market in the territories of other licensees, the permitted period for such an obligation (this obligation would ban not just active competition but passive competition too) should, however, be limited to a few years from the date on which the licensed product is first put on the market in the Community by a licensee, irrespective of whether the licensed technology comprises know-how, patents or both in the territories concerned.

(16) The exemption of territorial protection should apply for the whole duration of the periods thus permitted, as long as the patents remain in force or the know-how remains secret and substantial. The parties to a mixed patent and know-how licensing agreement must be able to take advantage in a particular territory of the period of protection conferred by a patent or by the know-how, whichever is the longer.

(17) The obligations listed in Article 1 also generally fulfil the other conditions for the application of Article 85(3). Consumers will, as a rule, be allowed a fair share of the benefit resulting from the improvement in the supply of goods on the market. To safeguard this effect, however, it is right to exclude from the application of Article 1 cases where the parties agree to refuse to meet demand from users or resellers within their respective territories who would resell for export, or to take other steps to impede parallel imports. The obligations referred to above thus only impose restrictions which are indispensable to the attainment of their objectives.

(18) It is desirable to list in this Regulation a number of obligations that are commonly found in licensing agreements but are normally not restrictive of competition, and to provide that in the event that because of the particular economic or legal circumstances they should fall within Article 85(1), they too will be covered by the exemption. This list, in Article 2, is not exhaustive.

(19) This Regulation must also specify what restrictions or provisions may not be included in licensing agreements if these are to benefit from the block exemption. The restrictions listed in Article 3 may fall under the prohibition of Article 85(1), but in their case there can be no general presumption that, although they relate to the transfer of technology, they will lead to the positive effects required by Article 85(3), as would be necessary for the granting of a block exemption. Such restrictions can be declared exempt only by an individual decision, taking account of the market position of the undertakings concerned and the degree of concentration on the relevant market.

(20) The obligations on the licensee to cease using the licensed technology after the termination of the agreement (Article 2(1)(3)) and to make improvements available to the licensor (Article 2(1)(4)) do not generally restrict competition. The post-term use ban may be regarded as a normal feature of licensing, as otherwise the licensor would be forced to transfer his know-how or patents in perpetuity. Undertakings by the licensee to grant back to the licensor a licence for improvements to the licensed know-how and/or patents are generally not restrictive of competition if the licensee is entitled by the contract to share in future experience and inventions made by the licensor. On the other hand, a restrictive effect on competition arises where the agreement obliges the licensee to assign to the licensor rights to improvements of the originally licensed technology that he himself has brought about (Article 3(6)).

(21) The list of clauses which do not prevent exemption also includes an obligation on the licensee to keep paying royalties until the end of the agreement independently of whether or not the licensed know-how has entered into the public domain through the action of third parties or of the licensee himself (Article 2(1)(7)). Moreover, the parties must be free, in order to facilitate payment, to spread the royalty payments for the use of the licensed technology over a period extending beyond the duration of the licensed patents, in particular by setting lower royalty rates. As a rule, parties do not need to be protected against the foreseeable financial consequences of an agreement freely entered into, and they should therefore be free to choose the appropriate means of financing the technology transfer and sharing between them the risks of such use. However, the setting of rates of royalty so as to achieve one of the restrictions listed in Article 3 renders the agreement ineligible for the block exemption.

(22) An obligation on the licensee to restrict his exploitation of the licensed technology to one or more technical fields of application ("fields of use") or to one or more product markets is not caught by Article 85(1) either, since the licensor is entitled to transfer the technology only for a limited purpose (Article 2(1)(8)).

(23) Clauses whereby the parties allocate customers within the same technological field of use or the same product market, either by an actual prohibition on supplying certain classes of customer or through an obligation with an equivalent effect, would also render the agreement ineligible for the block exemption where the parties are competitors for the contract products (Article 3(4)). Such restrictions between undertakings which are not competitors remain subject to the opposition procedure. Article 3 does not apply to cases where the patent or know-how licence is granted in order to provide a single customer with a second source of supply. In such a case, a prohibition on the second licensee from supplying persons other than the customer concerned is an essential condition for the grant of a second licence, since the purpose of the transaction is not to create an independent supplier in the market. The same applies to limitations on the quantities the licensee may supply to the customer concerned (Article 2(1)(13)).

(24) Besides the clauses already mentioned, the list of restrictions which render the block exemption inapplicable also includes restrictions regarding the selling prices of the licensed product or the quantities to be manufactured or sold, since they seriously limit the extent to which the licensee can exploit the licensed technology and since quantity restrictions particularly may have the same effect as export bans (Article 3(1) and (5)). This does not apply where a licence is granted for use of the technology in specific production facilities and where both a specific technology is communicated for the setting-up, operation and maintenance of these facilities and the licensee is allowed to increase the capacity of the facilities or to set up further facilities for its own use on normal commercial terms. On the other hand, the licensee may lawfully be prevented from using the transferred technology to set up facilities for third parties, since the purpose of the agreement is not to permit the licensee to give other producers access to the licensor's technology while it remains secret or protected by patent (Article 2(1)(12)).

(25)   Agreements which are not automatically covered by the exemption because they contain provisions that are not expressly exempted by this Regulation and not expressly excluded from exemption, including those listed in Article 4(2), may, in certain circumstances, nonetheless be presumed to be eligible for application of the block exemption. It will be possible for the Commission rapidly to establish whether this is the case on the basis of the information undertakings are obliged to provide under Commission Regulation (EC) No 3385/94.[8] The Commission may waive the requirement to supply specific information required in form A/B but which it does not deem necessary. The Commission will generally be content with communication of the text of the agreement and with an estimate, based on directly available data, of the market structure and of the licensee's market share. Such agreements should therefore be deemed to be covered by the exemption provided for in this Regulation where they are notified to the Commission and the Commission does not oppose the application of the exemption within a specified period of time.

(26)   Where agreements exempted under this Regulation nevertheless have effects incompatible with Article 85(3), the Commission may withdraw the block exemption, in particular where the licensed products are not faced with real competition in the licensed territory (Article 7). This could also be the case where the licensee has a strong position on the market. In assessing the competition the Commission will pay special attention to cases where the licensee has more than 40% of the whole market for the licensed products and of all the products or services which customers consider interchangeable or substitutable on account of their characteristics, prices and intended use.

(27)   Agreements which come within the terms of Articles 1 and 2 and which have neither the object nor the effect of restricting competition in any other way need no longer be notified. Nevertheless, undertakings will still have the right to apply in individual cases for negative clearance or for exemption under Article 85(3) in accordance with Council Regulation No 17,[9] as last amended by the Act of Accession of Austria, Finland and Sweden. They can in particular notify agreements obliging the licensor not to grant other licences in the territory, where the licensee's market share exceeds or is likely to exceed 40%,

---

NOTES

[1]   OJ 36, 6.3.65, p 533/65.
[2]   OJ C178, 30.6.94, p 3.
[3]   OJ L219, 16.8.84, p 15.
[4]   OJ L214, 8.9.95, p 6.
[5]   OJ L61, 4.3.89, p 1.
[6]   Convention for the European patent for the common market (Community Patent Convention) of 15 December 1975, OJ L17, 26.1.76, p 1.
[7]   Convention on the grant of European patents (European Patent Convention) of 5 October 1973.
[8]   OJ L377, 31.12.94, p 28.
[9]   OJ 13, 21.2.62, p 204/62.

HAS ADOPTED THIS REGULATION—

Article 1

1.   Pursuant to Article 85(3) of the Treaty and subject to the conditions set out below, it is hereby declared that Article 85(1) of the Treaty shall not apply to pure patent licensing or know-how licensing agreements and to mixed patent and know-how licensing agreements, including those agreements containing ancillary provisions relating to intellectual property rights other than patents, to which only two undertakings are party and which include one or more of the following obligations—

   (1)   an obligation on the licensor not to license other undertakings to exploit the licensed technology in the licensed territory;

   (2)   an obligation on the licensor not to exploit the licensed technology in the licensed territory himself;

   (3)   an obligation on the licensee not to exploit the licensed technology in the territory of the licensor within the common market;

(4) an obligation on the licensee not to manufacture or use the licensed product, or use the licensed process, in territories within the common market which are licensed to other licensees;

(5) an obligation on the licensee not to pursue an active policy of putting the licensed product on the market in the territories within the common market which are licensed to other licensees, and in particular not to engage in advertising specifically aimed at those territories or to establish any branch or maintain a distribution depot there;

(6) an obligation on the licensee not to put the licensed product on the market in the territories licensed to other licensees within the common market in response to unsolicited orders;

(7) an obligation on the licensee to use only the licensor's trademark or get up to distinguish the licensed product during the term of the agreement, provided that the licensee is not prevented from identifying himself as the manufacturer of the licensed products;

(8) an obligation on the licensee to limit his production of the licensed product to the quantities he requires in manufacturing his own products and to sell the licensed product only as an integral part of or a replacement part for his own products or otherwise in connection with the sale of his own products, provided that such quantities are freely determined by the licensee.

2. Where the agreement is a pure patent licensing agreement, the exemption of the obligations referred to in paragraph 1 is granted only to the extent that and for as long as the licensed product is protected by parallel patents, in the territories respectively of the licensee (points (1), (2), (7) and (8)), the licensor (point (3)) and other licensees (points (4) and (5)). The exemption of the obligation referred to in point (6) of paragraph 1 is granted for a period not exceeding five years from the date when the licensed product is first put on the market within the common market by one of the licensees, to the extent that and for as long as, in these territories, this product is protected by parallel patents.

3. Where the agreement is a pure know-how licensing agreement, the period for which the exemption of the obligations referred to in points (1) to (5) of paragraph 1 is granted may not exceed ten years from the date when the licensed product is first put on the market within the common market by one of the licensees.

The exemption of the obligation referred to in point (6) of paragraph 1 is granted for a period not exceeding five years from the date when the licensed product is first put on the market within the common market by one of the licensees.

The obligations referred to in points (7) and (8) of paragraph 1 are exempted during the lifetime of the agreement for as long as the know-how remains secret and substantial.

However, the exemption in paragraph 1 shall apply only where the parties have identified in any appropriate form the initial know-how and any subsequent improvements to it which become available to one party and are communicated to the other party pursuant to the terms of the agreement and to the purpose thereof, and only for as long as the know-how remains secret and substantial.

4. Where the agreement is a mixed patent and know-how licensing agreement, the exemption of the obligations referred to in points (1) to (5) of paragraph 1 shall apply in Member States in which the licensed technology is protected by necessary patents for as long as the licensed product is protected in those Member States by such patents if the duration of such protection exceeds the periods specified in paragraph 3.

The duration of the exemption provided in point (6) of paragraph 1 may not exceed the five-year period provided for in paragraphs 2 and 3.

However, such agreements qualify for the exemption referred to in paragraph 1 only for as long as the patents remain in force or to the extent that the know-how is identified and for as long as it remains secret and substantial whichever period is the longer.

5.　　The exemption provided for in paragraph 1 shall also apply where in a particular agreement the parties undertake obligations of the types referred to in that paragraph but with a more limited scope than is permitted by that paragraph.

[5106]

Article 2

1.　　Article 1 shall apply notwithstanding the presence in particular of any of the following clauses, which are generally not restrictive of competition—

(1)　an obligation on the licensee not to divulge the know-how communicated by the licensor; the licensee may be held to this obligation after the agreement has expired;

(2)　an obligation on the licensee not to grant sublicences or assign the licence;

(3)　an obligation on the licensee not to exploit the licensed know-how or patents after termination of the agreement in so far and as long as the know-how is still secret or the patents are still in force;

(4)　an obligation on the licensee to grant to the licensor a licence in respect of his own improvements to or his new applications of the licensed technology, provided—

— that, in the case of severable improvements, such a licence is not exclusive, so that the licensee is free to use his own improvements or to license them to third parties, in so far as that does not involve disclosure of the know-how communicated by the licensor that is still secret,

— and that the licensor undertakes to grant an exclusive or non-exclusive licence of his own improvements to the licensee;

(5)　an obligation on the licensee to observe minimum quality specifications, including technical specifications, for the licensed product or to procure goods or services from the licensor or from an undertaking designated by the licensor, in so far as these quality specifications, products or services are necessary for—

(a)　a technically proper exploitation of the licensed technology; or

(b)　ensuring that the product of the licensee conforms to the minimum quality specifications that are applicable to the licensor and other licensees;

and to allow the licensor to carry out related checks;

(6)　obligations—

(a)　to inform the licensor of misappropriation of the know-how or of infringements of the licensed patents; or

(b)　to take or to assist the licensor in taking legal action against such misappropriation or infringements;

(7)　an obligation on the licensee to continue paying the royalties—

(a)　until the end of the agreement in the amounts, for the periods and according to the methods freely determined by the parties, in the event of the know-how becoming publicly known other than by action of the licensor, without prejudice to the payment of any additional damages in the event of the know-how becoming publicly known by the action of the licensee in breach of the agreement;

(b)　over a period going beyond the duration of the licensed patents, in order to facilitate payment;

(8)　an obligation on the licensee to restrict his exploitation of the licensed technology to one or more technical fields of application covered by the licensed technology or to one or more product markets;

(9)　an obligation on the licensee to pay a minimum royalty or to produce a minimum quantity of the licensed product or to carry out a minimum number of operations exploiting the licensed technology;

(10) an obligation on the licensor to grant the licensee any more favourable terms that the licensor may grant to another undertaking after the agreement is entered into;

(11) an obligation on the licensee to mark the licensed product with an indication of the licensor's name or of the licensed patent;

(12) an obligation on the licensee not to use the licensor's technology to construct facilities for third parties; this is without prejudice to the right of the licensee to increase the capacity of his facilities or to set up additional facilities for his own use on normal commercial terms, including the payment of additional royalties;

(13) an obligation on the licensee to supply only a limited quantity of the licensed product to a particular customer, where the licence was granted so that the customer might have a second source of supply inside the licensed territory; this provision shall also apply where the customer is the licensee, and the licence which was granted in order to provide a second source of supply provides that the customer is himself to manufacture the licensed products or to have them manufactured by a subcontractor;

(14) a reservation by the licensor of the right to exercise the rights conferred by a patent to oppose the exploitation of the technology by the licensee outside the licensed territory;

(15) a reservation by the licensor of the right to terminate the agreement if the licensee contests the secret or substantial nature of the licensed know-how or challenges the validity of licensed patents within the common market belonging to the licensor or undertakings connected with him;

(16) a reservation by the licensor of the right to terminate the licence agreement of a patent if the licensee raises the claim that such a patent is not necessary;

(17) an obligation on the licensee to use his best endeavours to manufacture and market the licensed product;

(18) a reservation by the licensor of the right to terminate the exclusivity granted to the licensee and to stop licensing improvements to him when the licensee enters into competition within the common market with the licensor, with undertakings connected with the licensor or with other undertakings in respect of research and development, production, use or distribution of competing products, and to require the licensee to prove that the licensed know-how is not being used for the production of products and the provision of services other than those licensed.

2.   In the event that, because of particular circumstances, the clauses referred to in paragraph 1 fall within the scope of Article 85(1), they shall also be exempted even if they are not accompanied by any of the obligations exempted by Article 1.

3.   The exemption in paragraph 2 shall also apply where an agreement contains clauses of the types referred to in paragraph 1 but with a more limited scope than is permitted by that paragraph.

[5107]

Article 3

Article 1 and Article 2(2) shall not apply where—

(1) one party is restricted in the determination of prices, components of prices or discounts for the licensed products;

(2) one party is restricted from competing within the common market with the other party, with undertakings connected with the other party or with other undertakings in respect of research and development, production, use or

distribution of competing products without prejudice to the provisions of Article 2(1)(17) and (18);

(3) one or both of the parties are required without any objectively justified reason—

 (a) to refuse to meet orders from users or resellers in their respective territories who would market products in other territories within the common market;

 (b) to make it difficult for users or resellers to obtain the products from other resellers within the common market, and in particular to exercise intellectual property rights or take measures so as to prevent users or resellers from obtaining outside, or from putting on the market in the licensed territory products which have been lawfully put on the market within the common market by the licensor or with his consent;

or do so as a result of a concerted practice between them;

(4) the parties were already competing manufacturers before the grant of the licence and one of them is restricted, within the same technical field of use or within the same product market, as to the customers he may serve, in particular by being prohibited from supplying certain classes of user, employing certain forms of distribution or, with the aim of sharing customers, using certain types of packaging for the products, save as provided in Article 1(1)(7) and Article 2(1)(13);

(5) the quantity of the licensed products one party may manufacture or sell or the number of operations exploiting the licensed technology he may carry out are subject to limitations, save as provided in Article (1)(8) and Article 2(1)(13);

(6) the licensee is obliged to assign in whole or in part to the licensor rights to improvements to or new applications of the licensed technology;

(7) the licensor is required, albeit in separate agreements or through automatic prolongation of the initial duration of the agreement by the inclusion of any new improvements, for a period exceeding that referred to in Article 1(2) and (3) not to license other undertakings to exploit the licensed technology in the licensed territory, or a party is required for a period exceeding that referred to in Article 1(2) and (3) or Article 1(4) not to exploit the licensed technology in the territory of the other party or of other licensees.

[5108]

Article 4

1. The exemption provided for in Articles 1 and 2 shall also apply to agreements containing obligations restrictive of competition which are not covered by those Articles and do not fall within the scope of Article 3, on condition that the agreements in question are notified to the Commission in accordance with the provisions of Articles 1, 2 and 3 of Regulation (EC) No 3385/94 and that the Commission does not oppose such exemption within a period of four months.

2. Paragraph 1 shall apply, in particular, where—

 (a) the licensee is obliged at the time the agreement is entered into to accept quality specifications or further licences or to procure goods or services which are not necessary for a technically satisfactory exploitation of the licensed technology or for ensuring that the production of the licensee conforms to the quality standards that are respected by the licensor and other licensees;

 (b) the licensee is prohibited from contesting the secrecy or the substantiality of the licensed know-how or from challenging the validity of patents licensed within the common market belonging to the licensor or undertakings connected with him.

3.   The period of four months referred to in paragraph 1 shall run from the date on which the notification takes effect in accordance with Article 4 of Regulation (EC) No 3385/94.

4.   The benefit of paragraphs 1 and 2 may be claimed for agreements notified before the entry into force of this Regulation by submitting a communication to the Commission referring expressly to this Article and to the notification. Paragraph 3 shall apply *mutatis mutandis.*

5.   The Commission may oppose the exemption within a period of four months. It shall oppose exemption if it receives a request to do so from a Member State within two months of the transmission to the Member State of the notification referred to in paragraph 1 or of the communication referred to in paragraph 4. This request must be justified on the basis of considerations relating to the competition rules of the Treaty.

6.   The Commission may withdraw the opposition to the exemption at any time. However, where the opposition was raised at the request of a Member State and this request is maintained, it may be withdrawn only after consultation of the Advisory Committee on Restrictive Practices and Dominant Positions.

7.   If the opposition is withdrawn because the undertakings concerned have shown that the conditions of Article 85(3) are satisfied, the exemption shall apply from the date of notification.

8.   If the opposition is withdrawn because the undertakings concerned have amended the agreement so that the conditions of Article 85(3) are satisfied, the exemption shall apply from the date on which the amendments take effect.

9.   If the Commission opposes exemption and the opposition is not withdrawn, the effects of the notification shall be governed by the provisions of Regulation No 17.

[5109]

Article 5

1.   This Regulation shall not apply to—
   (1) agreements between members of a patent or know-how pool which relate to the pooled technologies;
   (2) licensing agreements between competing undertakings which hold interests in a joint venture, or between one of them and the joint venture, if the licensing agreements relate to the activities of the joint venture;
   (3) agreements under which one party grants the other a patent and/or know-how licence and in exchange the other party, albeit in separate agreements or through connected undertakings, grants the first party a patent, trademark or know-how licence or exclusive sales rights, where the parties are competitors in relation to the products covered by those agreements;
   (4) licensing agreements containing provisions relating to intellectual property rights other than patents which are not ancillary;
   (5) agreements entered into solely for the purpose of sale.

2.   This Regulation shall nevertheless apply—
   (1) to agreements to which paragraph 1(2) applies, under which a parent undertaking grants the joint venture a patent or know-how licence, provided that the licensed products and the other goods and services of the participating undertakings which are considered by users to be interchangeable or substitutable in view of their characteristics, price and intended use represent—
      — in case of a licence limited to production, not more than 20%, and
      — in case of a licence covering production and distribution, not more than 10%;

of the market for the licensed products and all interchangeable or substitutable goods and services;

    (2) to agreements to which paragraph 1(1) applies and to reciprocal licences within the meaning of paragraph 1(3), provided the parties are not subject to any territorial restriction within the common market with regard to the manufacture, use or putting on the market of the licensed products or to the use of the licensed or pooled technologies.

3.   This Regulation shall continue to apply where, for two consecutive financial years, the market shares in paragraph 2(1) are not exceeded by more than one-tenth; where that limit is exceeded, this Regulation shall continue to apply for a period of six months from the end of the year in which the limit was exceeded.

[5110]

Article 6

This Regulation shall also apply to—

    (1) agreements where the licensor is not the holder of the know-how or the patentee, but is authorised by the holder or the patentee to grant a licence;

    (2) assignments of know-how, patents or both where the risk associated with exploitation remains with the assignor, in particular where the sum payable in consideration of the assignment is dependent on the turnover obtained by the assignee in respect of products made using the know-how or the patents, the quantity of such products manufactured or the number of operations carried out employing the know-how or the patents;

    (3) licensing agreements in which the rights or obligations of the licensor or the licensee are assumed by undertakings connected with them.

[5111]

Article 7

The Commission may withdraw the benefit of this Regulation, pursuant to Article 7 of Regulation No 19/65/EEC, where it finds in a particular case that an agreement exempted by this Regulation nevertheless has certain effects which are incompatible with the conditions laid down in Article 85(3) of the Treaty, and in particular where—

    (1) the effect of the agreement is to prevent the licensed products from being exposed to effective competition in the licensed territory from identical goods or services or from goods or services considered by users as interchangeable or substitutable in view of their characteristics, price and intended use, which may in particular occur where the licensee's market share exceeds 40%;

    (2) without prejudice to Article 1(1)(6), the licensee refuses, without any objectively justified reason, to meet unsolicited orders from users or resellers in the territory of other licensees;

    (3) the parties—

        (a) without any objectively justified reason, refuse to meet orders from users or resellers in their respective territories who would market the products in other territories within the common market; or

        (b) make it difficult for users or resellers to obtain the products from other resellers within the common market, and in particular where they exercise intellectual property rights or take measures so as to prevent resellers or users from obtaining outside, or from putting on the market in the licensed territory products which have been lawfully put on the market within the common market by the licensor or with his consent;

(4) the parties were competing manufacturers at the date of the grant of the licence and obligations on the licensee to produce a minimum quantity or to use his best endeavours as referred to in Article 2(1), (9) and (17) respectively have the effect of preventing the licensee from using competing technologies.

[5112]

Article 8

1.   For purposes of this Regulation—
  (a) patent applications;
  (b) utility models;
  (c) applications for registration of utility models;
  (d) topographies of semiconductor products;
  (e) *certificats d'utilité* and *certificats d'addition* under French law;
  (f) applications for *certificats d'utilité* and *certificats d'addition* under French law;
  (g) supplementary protection certificates for medicinal products or other products for which such supplementary protection certificates may be obtained;
  (h) plant breeder's certificates,

shall be deemed to be patents.

2.   This Regulation shall also apply to agreements relating to the exploitation of an invention if an application within the meaning of paragraph 1 is made in respect of the invention for a licensed territory after the date when the agreements were entered into but within the time-limits set by the national law or the international convention to be applied.

3.   This Regulation shall furthermore apply to pure patent or know-how licensing agreements or to mixed agreements whose initial duration is automatically prolonged by the inclusion of any new improvements, whether patented or not, communicated by the licensor, provided that the licensee has the right to refuse such improvements or each party has the right to terminate the agreement at the expiry of the initial term of an agreement and at least every three years thereafter.

[5113]

Article 9

1.   Information acquired pursuant to Article 4 shall be used only for the purposes of this Regulation.

2.   The Commission and the authorities of the Member States, their officials and other servants shall not disclose information acquired by them pursuant to this Regulation of the kind covered by the obligation of professional secrecy.

3.   The provisions of paragraphs 1 and 2 shall not prevent publication of general information or surveys which do not contain information relating to particular undertakings or associations of undertakings.

[5114]

Article 10

For purposes of this Regulation—
  (1) "know-how" means a body of technical information that is secret, substantial and identified in any appropriate form;
  (2) "secret" means that the know-how package as a body or in the precise configuration and assembly of its components is not generally known or easily accessible, so that part of its value consists in the lead which the licensee gains when it is communicated to him; it is not limited to the

narrow sense that each individual component of the know-how should be totally unknown or unobtainable outside the licensor's business;

(3) "substantial" means that the know-how includes information which must be useful, ie can reasonably be expected at the date of conclusion of the agreement to be capable of improving the competitive position of the licensee, for example by helping him to enter a new market or giving him an advantage in competition with other manufacturers or providers of services who do not have access to the licensed secret know-how or other comparable secret know-how;

(4) "identified" means that the know-how is described or recorded in such a manner as to make it possible to verify that it satisfies the criteria of secrecy and substantiality and to ensure that the licensee is not unduly restricted in his exploitation of his own technology, to be identified the know-how can either be set out in the licence agreement or in a separate document or recorded in any other appropriate form at the latest when the know-how is transferred or shortly thereafter, provided that the separate document or other record can be made available if the need arises;

(5) "necessary patents" are patents where a licence under the patent is necessary for the putting into effect of the licensed technology in so far as, in the absence of such a licence, the realisation of the licensed technology would not be possible or would be possible only to a lesser extent or in more difficult or costly conditions. Such patents must therefore be of technical, legal or economic interest to the licensee;

(6) "licensing agreement" means pure patent licensing agreements and pure know-how licensing agreements as well as mixed patent and know-how licensing agreements;

(7) "licensed technology" means the initial manufacturing know-how or the necessary product and process patents, or both, existing at the time the first licensing agreement is concluded, and improvements subsequently made to the know-how or patents, irrespective of whether and to what extent they are exploited by the parties or by other licensees;

(8) "the licensed products" are goods or services the production or provision of which requires the use of the licensed technology;

(9) "the licensee's market share" means the proportion which the licensed products and other goods or services provided by the licensee, which are considered by users to be interchangeable or substitutable for the licensed products in view of their characteristics, price and intended use, represent the entire market for the licensed products and all other interchangeable or substitutable goods and services in the common market or a substantial part of it;

(10) "exploitation" refers to any use of the licensed technology in particular in the production, active or passive sales in a territory even if not coupled with manufacture in that territory, or leasing of the licensed products;

(11) "the licensed territory" is the territory covering all or at least part of the common market where the licensee is entitled to exploit the licensed technology;

(12) "territory of the licensor" means territories in which the licensor has not granted any licences for patents and/or know-how covered by the licensing agreement;

(13) "parallel patents" means patents which, in spite of the divergences which remain in the absence of any unification of national rules concerning industrial property, protect the same invention in various Member States;

(14) "connected undertakings" means—

  (a) undertakings in which a party to the agreement, directly or indirectly—

    — owns more than half the capital or business assets, or

    — has the power to exercise more than half the voting rights, or

     — has the power to appoint more than half the members of the supervisory board, board of directors or bodies legally representing the undertaking, or

     — has the right to manage the affairs of the undertaking;

(b) undertakings which, directly or indirectly, have in or over a party to the agreement the rights or powers listed in (a);

(c) undertakings in which an undertaking referred to in (b), directly or indirectly, has the rights or powers listed in (a);

(d) undertakings in which the parties to the agreement or undertakings connected with them jointly have the rights or powers listed in (a): such jointly controlled undertakings are considered to be connected with each of the parties to the agreement;

(15) "ancillary provisions" are provisions relating to the exploitation of intellectual property rights other than patents, which contain no obligations restrictive of competition other than those also attached to the licensed know-how or patents and exempted under this Regulation;

(16) "obligation" means both contractual obligation and a concerted practice;

(17) "competing manufacturers" or manufacturers of "competing products" means manufacturers who sell products which, in view of their characteristics, price and intended use, are considered by users to be interchangeable or substitutable for the licensed products.

[5115]

Article 11

1.   Regulation (EEC) No 556/89 is hereby repealed with effect from 1 April 1996.

2.   Regulation (EEC) No 2349/84 shall continue to apply until 31 March 1996.

3.   The prohibition in Article 85(1) of the Treaty shall not apply to agreements in force on 31 March 1996 which fulfil the exemption requirements laid down by Regulation (EEC) No 2349/84 or (EEC) No 556/89.

[5116]

Article 12

1.   The Commission shall undertake regular assessments of the application of this Regulation, and in particular of the opposition procedure provided for in Article 4.

2.   The Commission shall draw up a report on the operation of this Regulation before the end of the fourth year following its entry into force and shall, on that basis, assess whether any adaptation of the Regulation is desirable.

[5117]

Article 13

This Regulation shall enter into force on 1 April 1996.

It shall apply until 31 March 2006.

Article 11(2) of this Regulation shall, however, enter into force on 1 January 1996.

[5118]

This Regulation shall be binding in its entirety and directly applicable in all Member States.

Done at Brussels, 31 January 1996.

COMMISSION REGULATION

of 22 December 1999

on the application of Article 81(3) of the Treaty to categories of vertical agreements and concerted practices

(2790/99/EC)

(Text with EEA relevance)

NOTES

Date of publication in OJ: OJ L336, 29.12.99, p 21.

THE COMMISSION OF THE EUROPEAN COMMUNITIES,

Having regard to the Treaty establishing the European Community,

Having regard to Council Regulation No 19/65/EEC of 2 March 1965 on the application of Article 85(3) of the Treaty to certain categories of agreements and concerted practices,[1] as last amended by Regulation (EC) No 1215/1999,[2] and in particular Article 1 thereof,

Having published a draft of this Regulation,[3]

Having consulted the Advisory Committee on Restrictive Practices and Dominant Positions,

Whereas—

(1) Regulation No 19/65/EEC empowers the Commission to apply Article 81(3) of the Treaty (formerly Article 85(3)) by regulation to certain categories of vertical agreements and corresponding concerted practices falling within Article 81(1).

(2) Experience acquired to date makes it possible to define a category of vertical agreements which can be regarded as normally satisfying the conditions laid down in Article 81(3).

(3) This category includes vertical agreements for the purchase or sale of goods or services where these agreements are concluded between non-competing undertakings, between certain competitors or by certain associations of retailers of goods; it also includes vertical agreements containing ancillary provisions on the assignment or use of intellectual property rights; for the purposes of this Regulation, the term "vertical agreements" includes the corresponding concerted practices.

(4) For the application of Article 81(3) by regulation, it is not necessary to define those vertical agreements which are capable of falling within Article 81(1); in the individual assessment of agreements under Article 81(1), account has to be taken of several factors, and in particular the market structure on the supply and purchase side.

(5) The benefit of the block exemption should be limited to vertical agreements for which it can be assumed with sufficient certainty that they satisfy the conditions of Article 81(3).

(6) Vertical agreements of the category defined in this Regulation can improve economic efficiency within a chain of production or distribution by facilitating better coordination between the participating undertakings; in particular, they can lead to a reduction in the transaction and distribution costs of the parties and to an optimisation of their sales and investment levels.

(7) The likelihood that such efficiency-enhancing effects will outweigh any anti-competitive effects due to restrictions contained in vertical agreements depends on the degree of market power of the undertakings concerned and, therefore, on the extent to which those undertakings face competition from other suppliers of goods or services regarded by the buyer as interchangeable or substitutable for one another, by reason of the products' characteristics, their prices and their intended use.

(8) It can be presumed that, where the share of the relevant market accounted for by the supplier does not exceed 30%, vertical agreements which do not contain certain types of severely anti-competitive restraints generally lead to an improvement in production or distribution and allow consumers a fair share of the resulting benefits; in the case of vertical agreements containing exclusive supply obligations, it is the market share of the buyer which is relevant in determining the overall effects of such vertical agreements on the market.

(9) Above the market share threshold of 30%, there can be no presumption that vertical agreements falling within the scope of Article 81(1) will usually give rise to objective advantages of such a character and size as to compensate for the disadvantages which they create for competition.

(10) This Regulation should not exempt vertical agreements containing restrictions which are not indispensable to the attainment of the positive effects mentioned above; in particular, vertical agreements containing certain types of severely anti-competitive restraints such as minimum and fixed resale-prices, as well as certain types of territorial protection, should be excluded from the benefit of the block exemption established by this Regulation irrespective of the market share of the undertakings concerned.

(11) In order to ensure access to or to prevent collusion on the relevant market, certain conditions are to be attached to the block exemption; to this end, the exemption of non-compete obligations should be limited to obligations which do not exceed a definite duration; for the same reasons, any direct or indirect obligation causing the members of a selective distribution system not to sell the brands of particular competing suppliers should be excluded from the benefit of this Regulation.

(12) The market-share limitation, the non-exemption of certain vertical agreements and the conditions provided for in this Regulation normally ensure that the agreements to which the block exemption applies do not enable the participating undertakings to eliminate competition in respect of a substantial part of the products in question.

(13) In particular cases in which the agreements falling under this Regulation nevertheless have effects incompatible with Article 81(3), the Commission may withdraw the benefit of the block exemption; this may occur in particular where the buyer has significant market power in the relevant market in which it resells the goods or provides the services or where parallel networks of vertical agreements have similar effects which significantly restrict access to a relevant market or competition therein; such cumulative effects may for example arise in the case of selective distribution or non-compete obligations.

(14) Regulation No 19/65/EEC empowers the competent authorities of Member States to withdraw the benefit of the block exemption in respect of vertical agreements having effects incompatible with the conditions laid down in Article 81(3), where such effects are felt in their respective territory, or in a part thereof, and where such territory has the characteristics of a distinct geographic market; Member States should ensure that the exercise of this power of withdrawal does not prejudice the uniform application throughout the common market of the Community competition rules or the full effect of the measures adopted in implementation of those rules.

(15) In order to strengthen supervision of parallel networks of vertical agreements which have similar restrictive effects and which cover more than 50% of a given market, the Commission may declare this Regulation inapplicable to vertical agreements containing specific restraints relating to the market concerned, thereby restoring the full application of Article 81 to such agreements.

(16) This Regulation is without prejudice to the application of Article 82.

(17) In accordance with the principle of the primacy of Community law, no measure taken pursuant to national laws on competition should prejudice the uniform application throughout the common market of the Community competition rules or the full effect of any measures adopted in implementation of those rules, including this Regulation,

---

NOTES

1   OJ 36, 6.3.65, p 533/65.
2   OJ L148, 15.6.99, p 1.
3   OJ C270, 24.9.99, p 7.

HAS ADOPTED THIS REGULATION—

Article 1

For the purposes of this Regulation—

    (a) "competing undertakings" means actual or potential suppliers in the same product market; the product market includes goods or services which are regarded by the buyer as interchangeable with or substitutable for the contract goods or services, by reason of the products' characteristics, their prices and their intended use;

    (b) "non-compete obligation" means any direct or indirect obligation causing the buyer not to manufacture, purchase, sell or resell goods or services which compete with the contract goods or services, or any direct or indirect obligation on the buyer to purchase from the supplier or from another undertaking designated by the supplier more than 80% of the buyer's total purchases of the contract goods or services and their substitutes on the relevant market, calculated on the basis of the value of its purchases in the preceding calendar year;

(c) "exclusive supply obligation" means any direct or indirect obligation causing the supplier to sell the goods or services specified in the agreement only to one buyer inside the Community for the purposes of a specific use or for resale;

(d) "Selective distribution" system means a distribution system where the supplier undertakes to sell the contract goods or services, either directly or indirectly, only to distributors selected on the basis of specified criteria and where these distributors undertake not to sell such goods or services to unauthorised distributors;

(e) "intellectual property rights" includes industrial property rights, copyright and neighbouring rights;

(f) "know-how" means a package of non-patented practical information, resulting from experience and testing by the supplier, which is secret, substantial and identified: in this context, "secret" means that the know-how, as a body or in the precise configuration and assembly of its components, is not generally known or easily accessible; "substantial" means that the know-how includes information which is indispensable to the buyer for the use, sale or resale of the contract goods or services; "identified" means that the know-how must be described in a sufficiently comprehensive manner so as to make it possible to verify that it fulfils the criteria of secrecy and substantiality;

(g) "buyer" includes an undertaking which, under an agreement falling within Article 81(1) of the Treaty, sells goods or services on behalf of another undertaking.

Article 2

1.   Pursuant to Article 81(3) of the Treaty and subject to the provisions of this Regulation, it is hereby declared that Article 81(1) shall not apply to agreements or concerted practices entered into between two or more undertakings each of which operates, for the purposes of the agreement, at a different level of the production or distribution chain, and relating to the conditions under which the parties may purchase, sell or resell certain goods or services ("vertical agreements").

This exemption shall apply to the extent that such agreements contain restrictions of competition falling within the scope of Article 81(1) ("vertical restraints").

2.   The exemption provided for in paragraph 1 shall apply to vertical agreements entered into between an association of undertakings and its members, or between such an association and its suppliers, only if all its members are retailers of goods and if no individual member of the association, together with its connected undertakings, has a total annual turnover exceeding EUR 50 million; vertical agreements entered into by such associations shall be covered by this Regulation without prejudice to the application of Article 81 to horizontal agreements concluded between the members of the association or decisions adopted by the association.

3.   The exemption provided for in paragraph 1 shall apply to vertical agreements containing provisions which relate to the assignment to the buyer or use by the buyer of intellectual property rights, provided that those provisions do not constitute the primary object of such agreements and are directly related to the use, sale or resale of goods or services by the buyer or its customers. The exemption

applies on condition that, in relation to the contract goods or services, those provisions do not contain restrictions of competition having the same object or effect as vertical restraints which are not exempted under this Regulation.

4.   The exemption provided for in paragraph 1 shall not apply to vertical agreements entered into between competing undertakings; however, it shall apply where competing undertakings enter into a non-reciprocal vertical agreement and—

    (a)   the buyer has a total annual turnover not exceeding EUR 100 million, or

    (b)   the supplier is a manufacturer and a distributor of goods, while the buyer is a distributor not manufacturing goods competing with the contract goods, or

    (c)   the supplier is a provider of services at several levels of trade, while the buyer does not provide competing services at the level of trade where it purchases the contract services.

5.   This Regulation shall not apply to vertical agreements the subject matter of which falls within the scope of any other block exemption regulation.

[5120]

Article 3

1.   Subject to paragraph 2 of this Article, the exemption provided for in Article 2 shall apply on condition that the market share held by the supplier does not exceed 30% of the relevant market on which it sells the contract goods or services.

2.   In the case of vertical agreements containing exclusive supply obligations, the exemption provided for in Article 2 shall apply on condition that the market share held by the buyer does not exceed 30% of the relevant market on which it purchases the contract goods or services.

[5121]

Article 4

The exemption provided for in Article 2 shall not apply to vertical agreements which, directly or indirectly, in isolation or in combination with other factors under the control of the parties, have as their object—

    (a)   the restriction of the buyer's ability to determine its sale price, without prejudice to the possibility of the supplier's imposing a maximum sale price or recommending a sale price, provided that they do not amount to a fixed or minimum sale price as a result of pressure from, or incentives offered by, any of the parties;

    (b)   the restriction of the territory into which, or of the customers to whom, the buyer may sell the contract goods or services, except—

        — the restriction of active sales into the exclusive territory or to an exclusive customer group reserved to the supplier or allocated by the supplier to another buyer, where such a restriction does not limit sales by the customers of the buyer,

        — the restriction of sales to end users by a buyer operating at the wholesale level of trade,

        — the restriction of sales to unauthorised distributors by the members of a selective distribution system, and

        — the restriction of the buyer's ability to sell components, supplied for the purposes of incorporation, to customers who would use them to manufacture the same type of goods as those produced by the supplier;

    (c)   the restriction of active or passive sales to end users by members of a selective distribution system operating at the retail level of trade, without prejudice to the possibility of prohibiting a member of the system from operating out of an unauthorised place of establishment;

   (d) the restriction of cross-supplies between distributors within a selective distribution system, including between distributors operating at different levels of trade;

   (e) the restriction agreed between a supplier of components and a buyer who incorporates those components, which limits the supplier to selling the components as spare parts to end-users or to repairers or other service providers not entrusted by the buyer with the repair or servicing of its goods.

[5122]

Article 5

The exemption provided for in Article 2 shall not apply to any of the following obligations contained in vertical agreements—

   (a) any direct or indirect non-compete obligation, the duration of which is indefinite or exceeds five years. A non-compete obligation which is tacitly renewable beyond a period of five years is to be deemed to have been concluded for an indefinite duration. However, the time limitation of five years shall not apply where the contract goods or services are sold by the buyer from premises and land owned by the supplier or leased by the supplier from third parties not connected with the buyer, provided that the duration of the non-compete obligation does not exceed the period of occupancy of the premises and land by the buyer;

   (b) any direct or indirect obligation causing the buyer, after termination of the agreement, not to manufacture, purchase, sell or resell goods or services, unless such obligation:

      — relates to goods or services which compete with the contract goods or services, and

      — is limited to the premises and land from which the buyer has operated during the contract period, and

      — is indispensable to protect know-how transferred by the supplier to the buyer,

and provided that the duration of such non-compete obligation is limited to a period of one year after termination of the agreement; this obligation is without prejudice to the possibility of imposing a restriction which is unlimited in time on the use and disclosure of know-how which has not entered the public domain;

   (c) any direct or indirect obligation causing the members of a selective distribution system not to sell the brands of particular competing suppliers.

[5123]

Article 6

The Commission may withdraw the benefit of this Regulation, pursuant to Article 7(1) of Regulation No 19/65/EEC, where it finds in any particular case that vertical agreements to which this Regulation applies nevertheless have effects which are incompatible with the conditions laid down in Article 81(3) of the Treaty, and in particular where access to the relevant market or competition therein is significantly restricted by the cumulative effect of parallel networks of similar vertical restraints implemented by competing suppliers or buyers.

[5124]

Article 7

Where in any particular case vertical agreements to which the exemption provided for in Article 2 applies have effects incompatible with the conditions laid down in Article 81(3) of the Treaty in the territory of a Member State, or in a part thereof, which has all the characteristics of a distinct geographic market, the competent authority of that Member State may withdraw the benefit of application of this Regulation in respect of that territory, under the same conditions as provided in Article 6.

[5125]

Article 8

1.   Pursuant to Article 1(a) of Regulation No 19/65/EEC, the Commission may by regulation declare that, where parallel networks of similar vertical restraints cover more than 50% of a relevant market, this Regulation shall not apply to vertical agreements containing specific restraints relating to that market.

2.   A regulation pursuant to paragraph 1 shall not become applicable earlier than six months following its adoption.

[5126]

Article 9

1.   The market share of 30% provided for in Article 3(1) shall be calculated on the basis of the market sales value of the contract goods or services and other goods or services sold by the supplier, which are regarded as interchangeable or substitutable by the buyer, by reason of the products' characteristics, their prices and their intended use; if market sales value data are not available, estimates based on other reliable market information, including market sales volumes, may be used to establish the market share of the undertaking concerned. For the purposes of Article 3(2), it is either the market purchase value or estimates thereof which shall be used to calculate the market share.

2.   For the purposes of applying the market share threshold provided for in Article 3 the following rules shall apply—
  (a) the market share shall be calculated on the basis of data relating to the preceding calendar year;
  (b) the market share shall include any goods or services supplied to integrated distributors for the purposes of sale;
  (c) if the market share is initially not more than 30% but subsequently rises above that level without exceeding 35%, the exemption provided for in Article 2 shall continue to apply for a period of two consecutive calendar years following the year in which the 30% market share threshold was first exceeded;
  (d) if the market share is initially not more than 30% but subsequently rises above 35%, the exemption provided for in Article 2 shall continue to apply for one calendar year following the year in which the level of 35% was first exceeded;
  (e) the benefit of points (c) and (d) may not be combined so as to exceed a period of two calendar years.

[5127]

Article 10

1.   For the purpose of calculating total annual turnover within the meaning of Article 2(2) and (4), the turnover achieved during the previous financial year by the relevant party to the vertical agreement and the turnover achieved by its connected undertakings in respect of all goods and services, excluding all taxes and other duties, shall be added together. For this purpose, no account shall be taken of dealings between the party to the vertical agreement and its connected undertakings or between its connected undertakings.

2.   The exemption provided for in Article 2 shall remain applicable where, for any period of two consecutive financial years, the total annual turnover threshold is exceeded by no more than 10%.

[5128]

Article 11

1.   For the purposes of this Regulation, the terms "undertaking", "supplier" and "buyer" shall include their respective connected undertakings.

2.   "Connected undertakings" are—
   (a) undertakings in which a party to the agreement, directly or indirectly—
      — has the power to exercise more than half the voting rights, or
      — has the power to appoint more than half the members of the supervisory board, board of management or bodies legally representing the undertaking, or
      — has the right to manage the undertaking's affairs;
   (b) undertakings which directly or indirectly have, over a party to the agreement, the rights or powers listed in (a);
   (c) undertakings in which an undertaking referred to in (b) has, directly or indirectly, the rights or powers listed in (a);
   (d) undertakings in which a party to the agreement together with one or more of the undertakings referred to in (a), (b) or (c), or in which two or more of the latter undertakings, jointly have the rights or powers listed in (a);
   (e) undertakings in which the rights or the powers listed in (a) are jointly held by—
      — parties to the agreement or their respective connected undertakings referred to in (a) to (d), or
      — one or more of the parties to the agreement or one or more of their connected undertakings referred to in (a) to (d) and one or more third parties.

3.   For the purposes of Article 3, the market share held by the undertakings referred to in paragraph 2(e) of this Article shall be apportioned equally to each undertaking having the rights or the powers listed in paragraph 2(a).

[5129]

Article 12

1.   The exemptions provided for in Commission Regulations (EEC) No 1983/83,[1] (EEC) No 1984/83[2] and (EEC) No 4087/88[3] shall continue to apply until 31 May 2000.

2.   The prohibition laid down in Article 81(1) of the EC Treaty shall not apply during the period from 1 June 2000 to 31 December 2001 in respect of agreements already in force on 31 May 2000 which do not satisfy the conditions for exemption provided for in this Regulation but which satisfy the conditions for exemption provided for in Regulations (EEC) No 1983/83, (EEC) No 1984/83 or (EEC) No 4087/88.

[5130]

NOTES
   [1]   OJ L173, 30.6.83, p 1.
   [2]   OJ L173, 30.6.83, p 5.
   [3]   OJ L359, 28.12.88, p 46.

Article 13

This Regulation shall enter into force on 1 January 2000.

It shall apply from 1 June 2000, except for Article 12(1) which shall apply from 1 January 2000.

This Regulation shall expire on 31 May 2010.

[5131]

This Regulation shall be binding in its entirety and directly applicable in all Member States.

Done at Brussels, 22 December 1999.

COMMISSION NOTICE

(2000/C 291/01)

Guidelines on Vertical Restraints

(Text with EEA relevance)

NOTES

Date of publication in OJ: OJ C291, 13.10.2000, p 1.

I. INTRODUCTION

1. Purpose of the Guidelines

(1)   These Guidelines set out the principles for the assessment of vertical agreements under Article 81 of the EC Treaty. What are considered vertical agreements is defined in Article 2(1) of Commission Regulation (EC) No 2790/1999 of 22 December 1999 on the application of Article 81(3) of the Treaty to categories of vertical agreements and concerted practices[1] (Block Exemption Regulation) (see paragraphs 23 to 45). These Guidelines are without prejudice to the possible parallel application of Article 82 of the Treaty to vertical agreements. The Guidelines are structured in the following way—

— Section II (paragraphs 8 to 20) describes vertical agreements which generally fall outside Article 81(1);

— Section III (paragraphs 21 to 70) comments on the application of the Block Exemption Regulation;

— Section IV (paragraphs 71 to 87) describes the principles concerning the withdrawal of the block exemption and the disapplication of the Block Exemption Regulation;

— Section V (paragraphs 88 to 99) addresses market definition and market share calculation issues;

— Section VI (paragraphs 100 to 229) describes the general framework of analysis and the enforcement policy of the Commission in individual cases concerning vertical agreements.

(2)   Throughout these Guidelines the analysis applies to both goods and services, although certain vertical restraints are mainly used in the distribution of goods. Similarly, vertical agreements can be concluded for intermediate and final goods and services. Unless otherwise stated, the analysis and arguments in the text apply to all types of goods and services and to all levels of trade. The term "products" includes both goods and services. The terms "supplier" and "buyer" are used for all levels of trade.

(3)   By issuing these Guidelines the Commission aims to help companies to make their own assessment of vertical agreements under the EC competition rules. The standards set forth in these Guidelines must be applied in circumstances specific to each case. This rules out a mechanical application. Each case must be evaluated in the light of its own facts. The Commission will apply the Guidelines reasonably and flexibly.

(4)   These Guidelines are without prejudice to the interpretation that may be given by the Court of First Instance and the Court of Justice of the European Communities in relation to the application of Article 81 to vertical agreements.

2. Applicability of Article 81 to vertical agreements

(5)   Article 81 of the EC Treaty applies to vertical agreements that may affect trade between Member States and that prevent, restrict or distort competition (hereinafter referred to as "vertical restraints").[2] For vertical restraints, Article 81 provides an appropriate legal framework for assessment, recognising the distinction between anti-competitive and pro-competitive effects: Article 81(1) prohibits those agreements which appreciably restrict or distort competition, while Article 81(3) allows for exemption of those agreements which confer sufficient benefits to outweigh the anti-competitive effects.

(6)   For most vertical restraints, competition concerns can only arise if there is insufficient inter-brand competition, ie if there is some degree of market power at the level of the supplier or the buyer or at both levels. If there is insufficient inter-brand competition, the protection of inter- and intra-brand competition becomes important.

(7)   The protection of competition is the primary objective of EC competition policy, as this enhances consumer welfare and creates an efficient allocation of resources. In applying the EC competition rules, the Commission will adopt an economic approach which is based on the effects on the market; vertical agreements have to be analysed in their legal and economic context. However, in the case of restrictions by object as listed in Article 4 of the Block Exemption Regulation, the Commission is not required to assess the actual effects on the market. Market integration is an additional goal of EC competition policy. Market integration enhances competition in the Community. Companies should not be allowed to recreate private barriers between Member States where State barriers have been successfully abolished.

[5132]

NOTES
  [1]   OJ L336, 29.12.99, p 21.
  [2]   See inter alia judgment of the Court of Justice of the European Communities in Joined Cases 56/64 and 58/64 Grundig-Consten v Commission [1966] ECR 299; Case 56/65 Technique Minière v Machinenbau Ulm [1966] ECR 235; and of the Court of First Instance of the European Communities in Case T-77/92 Parker Pen v Commission [1994] ECR II 549.

II. VERTICAL AGREEMENTS WHICH GENERALLY FALL OUTSIDE ARTICLE 81(1)

1. Agreements of minor importance and SMEs

(8)   Agreements which are not capable of appreciably affecting trade between Member States or capable of appreciably restricting competition by object or effect are not caught by Article 81(1). The Block Exemption Regulation applies only to agreements falling within the scope of application of Article 81(1). These Guidelines are without prejudice to the application of the present or any future "*de minimis*" notice.[1]

(9) Subject to the conditions set out in points 11, 18 and 20 of the "*de minimis*" notice concerning hardcore restrictions and cumulative effect issues, vertical agreements entered into by undertakings whose market share on the relevant market does not exceed 10% are generally considered to fall outside the scope of Article 81(1). There is no presumption that vertical agreements concluded by undertakings having more than 10% market share automatically infringe Article 81(1). Agreements between undertakings whose market share exceeds the 10% threshold may still not have an appreciable effect on trade between Member States or may not constitute an appreciable restriction of competition.[2] Such agreements need to be assessed in their legal and economic context. The criteria for the assessment of individual agreements are set out in paragraphs 100 to 229.

(10) As regards hardcore restrictions defined in the "*de minimis*" notice, Article 81(1) may apply below the 10% threshold, provided that there is an appreciable effect on trade between Member States and on competition. The applicable case-law of the Court of Justice and the Court of First Instance is relevant in this respect.[3] Reference is also made to the particular situation of launching a new product or entering a new market which is dealt with in these Guidelines (paragraph 119, point 10).

(11) In addition, the Commission considers that, subject to cumulative effect and hardcore restrictions, agreements between small and medium-sized undertakings as defined in the Annex to Commission Recommendation 96/280/EC[4] are rarely capable of appreciably affecting trade between Member States or of appreciably restricting competition within the meaning of Article 81(1), and therefore generally fall outside the scope of Article 81(1). In cases where such agreements nonetheless meet the conditions for the application of Article 81(1), the Commission will normally refrain from opening proceedings for lack of sufficient Community interest unless those undertakings collectively or individually hold a dominant position in a substantial part of the common market.

2. Agency agreements

(12) Paragraphs 12 to 20 replace the Notice on exclusive dealing contracts with commercial agents of 1962.[5] They must be read in conjunction with Council Directive 86/653/EEC.[6]

Agency agreements cover the situation in which a legal or physical person (the agent) is vested with the power to negotiate and/or conclude contracts on behalf of another person (the principal), either in the agent's own name or in the name of the principal, for the—

— purchase of goods or services by the principal, or
— sale of goods or services supplied by the principal.

(13) In the case of genuine agency agreements, the obligations imposed on the agent as to the contracts negotiated and/or concluded on behalf of the principal do not fall within the scope of application of Article 81(1). The determining factor in assessing whether Article 81(1) is applicable is the financial or commercial risk borne by the agent in relation to the activities for which he has been appointed as an agent by the principal. In this respect it is not material for the assessment whether the agent acts for one or several principals. Non-genuine agency agreements may be caught by Article 81(1), in which case the Block Exemption Regulation and the other sections of these Guidelines will apply.

(14) There are two types of financial or commercial risk that are material to the assessment of the genuine nature of an agency agreement under Article 81(1). First there are the risks which are directly related to the contracts concluded and/or negotiated by the agent on behalf of the principal, such as financing of stocks. Secondly, there are the risks related to market-specific investments. These are

investments specifically required for the type of activity for which the agent has been appointed by the principal, ie which are required to enable the agent to conclude and/or negotiate this type of contract. Such investments are usually sunk, if upon leaving that particular field of activity the investment cannot be used for other activities or sold other than at a significant loss.

(15) The agency agreement is considered a genuine agency agreement and consequently falls outside Article 81(1) if the agent does not bear any, or bears only insignificant, risks in relation to the contracts concluded and/or negotiated on behalf of the principal and in relation to market-specific investments for that field of activity. In such a situation, the selling or purchasing function forms part of the principal's activities, despite the fact that the agent is a separate undertaking. The principal thus bears the related financial and commercial risks and the agent does not exercise an independent economic activity in relation to the activities for which he has been appointed as an agent by the principal. In the opposite situation the agency agreement is considered a non-genuine agency agreement and may fall under Article 81(1). In that case the agent does bear such risks and will be treated as an independent dealer who must remain free in determining his marketing strategy in order to be able to recover his contract- or market-specific investments. Risks that are related to the activity of providing agency services in general, such as the risk of the agent's income being dependent upon his success as an agent or general investments in for instance premises or personnel, are not material to this assessment.

(16) The question of risk must be assessed on a case-by-case basis, and with regard to the economic reality of the situation rather than the legal form. Nonetheless, the Commission considers that Article 81(1) will generally not be applicable to the obligations imposed on the agent as to the contracts negotiated and/or concluded on behalf of the principal where property in the contract goods bought or sold does not vest in the agent, or the agent does not himself supply the contract services and where the agent—

— does not contribute to the costs relating to the supply/purchase of the contract goods or services, including the costs of transporting the goods. This does not preclude the agent from carrying out the transport service, provided that the costs are covered by the principal;

— is not, directly or indirectly, obliged to invest in sales promotion, such as contributions to the advertising budgets of the principal;

— does not maintain at his own cost or risk stocks of the contract goods, including the costs of financing the stocks and the costs of loss of stocks and can return unsold goods to the principal without charge, unless the agent is liable for fault (for example, by failing to comply with reasonable security measures to avoid loss of stocks);

— does not create and/or operate an after-sales service, repair service or a warranty service unless it is fully reimbursed by the principal;

— does not make market-specific investments in equipment, premises or training of personnel, such as for example the petrol storage tank in the case of petrol retailing or specific software to sell insurance policies in the case of insurance agents;

— does not undertake responsibility towards third parties for damage caused by the product sold (product liability), unless, as agent, he is liable for fault in this respect;

— does not take responsibility for customers' non-performance of the contract, with the exception of the loss of the agent's commission, unless the agent is liable for fault (for example, by failing to comply with reasonable security or anti-theft measures or failing to comply with reasonable measures to report theft to the principal or police or to communicate to the principal all necessary information available to him on the customer's financial reliability).

(17) This list is not exhaustive. However, where the agent incurs one or more of the above risks or costs, then Article 81(1) may apply as with any other vertical agreement.

(18) If an agency agreement does not fall within the scope of application of Article 81(1), then all obligations imposed on the agent in relation to the contracts concluded and/or negotiated on behalf of the principal fall outside Article 81(1). The following obligations on the agent's part will generally be considered to form an inherent part of an agency agreement, as each of them relates to the ability of the principal to fix the scope of activity of the agent in relation to the contract goods or services, which is essential if the principal is to take the risks and therefore be in a position to determine the commercial strategy—

— limitations on the territory in which the agent may sell these goods or services;
— limitations on the customers to whom the agent may sell these goods or services;
— the prices and conditions at which the agent must sell or purchase these goods or services.

(19) In addition to governing the conditions of sale or purchase of the contract goods or services by the agent on behalf of the principal, agency agreements often contain provisions which concern the relationship between the agent and the principal. In particular, they may contain a provision preventing the principal from appointing other agents in respect of a given type of transaction, customer or territory (exclusive agency provisions) and/or a provision preventing the agent from acting as an agent or distributor of undertakings which compete with the principal (non-compete provisions). Exclusive agency provisions concern only intra-brand competition and will in general not lead to anti-competitive effects. Non-compete provisions, including post-term non-compete provisions, concern inter-brand competition and may infringe Article 81(1) if they lead to foreclosure on the relevant market where the contract goods or services are sold or purchased (see Section VI.2.1).

(20) An agency agreement may also fall within the scope of Article 81(1), even if the principal bears all the relevant financial and commercial risks, where it facilitates collusion. This could for instance be the case when a number of principals use the same agents while collectively excluding others from using these agents, or when they use the agents to collude on marketing strategy or to exchange sensitive market information between the principals.

[5133]

NOTES
1   See Notice on agreements of minor importance of 9 December 1997, OJ C372, 9.12.97, p 13.
2   See judgment of the Court of First Instance in Case T-7/93 Langnese-Iglo v Commission [1995] ECR II-1533, paragraph 98.
3   See judgment of the Court of Justice in Case 5/69 Völk v Vervaecke [1969] ECR 295; Case 1/71 Cadillon v Höss [1971] ECR 351 and Case C-306/96 Javico v Yves Saint Laurent [1998] ECR I-1983, paragraphs 16 and 17.
4   OJ L107, 30.4.96, p 4.
5   OJ 139, 24.12.62, p 2921/62.
6   OJ L382, 31.12.86, p 17.

III. APPLICATION OF THE BLOCK EXEMPTION REGULATION

1. Safe harbour created by the Block Exemption Regulation

(21) The Block Exemption Regulation creates a presumption of legality for vertical agreements depending on the market share of the supplier or the buyer. Pursuant to Article 3 of the Block Exemption Regulation, it is in general the market share of the supplier on the market where it sells the contract goods or services which determines the applicability of the block exemption. This market share may not exceed the threshold of 30% in order for the block exemption to apply.

Only where the agreement contains an exclusive supply obligation, as defined in Article 1(c) of the Block Exemption Regulation, is it the buyer's market share on the market where it purchases the contract goods or services which may not exceed the threshold of 30% in order for the block exemption to apply. For market share issues see Section V (paragraphs 88 to 99).

(22) From an economic point of view, a vertical agreement may have effects not only on the market between supplier and buyer but also on markets downstream of the buyer. The simplified approach of the Block Exemption Regulation, which only takes into account the market share of the supplier or the buyer (as the case may be) on the market between these two parties, is justified by the fact that below the threshold of 30% the effects on downstream markets will in general be limited. In addition, only having to consider the market between supplier and buyer makes the application of the Block Exemption Regulation easier and enhances the level of legal certainty, while the instrument of withdrawal (see paragraphs 71 to 87) remains available to remedy possible problems on other related markets.

2. Scope of the Block Exemption Regulation

(i) Definition of vertical agreements

(23) Vertical agreements are defined in Article 2(1) of the Block Exemption Regulation as "agreements or concerted practices entered into between two or more undertakings each of which operates, for the purposes of the agreement, at a different level of the production or distribution chain, and relating to the conditions under which the parties may purchase, sell or resell certain goods or services".

(24) There are three main elements in this definition—
— the agreement or concerted practice is between two or more undertakings. Vertical agreements with final consumers not operating as an undertaking are not covered; More generally, agreements with final consumers do not fall under Article 81(1), as that article applies only to agreements between undertakings, decisions by associations of undertakings and concerted practices. This is without prejudice to the possible application of Article 82 of the Treaty;
— the agreement or concerted practice is between undertakings each operating, for the purposes of the agreement, at a different level of the production or distribution chain. This means for instance that one undertaking produces a raw material which the other undertaking uses as an input, or that the first is a manufacturer, the second a wholesaler and the third a retailer. This does not preclude an undertaking from being active at more than one level of the production or distribution chain;
— the agreements or concerted practices relate to the conditions under which the parties to the agreement, the supplier and the buyer, "may purchase, sell or resell certain goods or services". This reflects the purpose of the Block Exemption Regulation to cover purchase and distribution agreements. These are agreements which concern the conditions for the purchase, sale or resale of the goods or services supplied by the supplier and/or which concern the conditions for the sale by the buyer of the goods or services which incorporate these goods or services. For the application of the Block Exemption Regulation both the goods or services supplied by the supplier and the resulting goods or services are considered to be contract goods or services. Vertical agreements relating to all final and intermediate goods and services are covered. The only exception is the automobile sector, as long as this sector remains covered by a specific block exemption such as that granted by Commission Regulation (EC) No 1475/95.[1] The goods or services provided by the supplier may be resold by the buyer or may be used as an input by the buyer to produce his own goods or services.

(25) The Block Exemption Regulation also applies to goods sold and purchased for renting to third parties. However, rent and lease agreements as such are not covered, as no good or service is being sold by the supplier to the buyer. More generally, the Block Exemption Regulation does not cover restrictions or obligations that do not relate to the conditions of purchase, sale and resale, such as an obligation preventing parties from carrying out independent research and development which the parties may have included in an otherwise vertical agreement. In addition, Articles 2(2) to (5) directly or indirectly exclude certain vertical agreements from the application of the Block Exemption Regulation.

(ii) Vertical agreements between competitors

(26) Article 2(4) of the Block Exemption Regulation explicitly excludes from its application "vertical agreements entered into between competing undertakings". Vertical agreements between competitors will be dealt with, as regards possible collusion effects, in the forthcoming Guidelines on the applicability of Article 81 to horizontal cooperation.[2] However, the vertical aspects of such agreements need to be assessed under these Guidelines. Article 1(a) of the Block Exemption Regulation defines competing undertakings as "actual or potential suppliers in the same product market", irrespective of whether or not they are competitors on the same geographic market. Competing undertakings are undertakings that are actual or potential suppliers of the contract goods or services or goods or services that are substitutes for the contract goods or services. A potential supplier is an undertaking that does not actually produce a competing product but could and would be likely to do so in the absence of the agreement in response to a small and permanent increase in relative prices. This means that the undertaking would be able and likely to undertake the necessary additional investments and supply the market within 1 year. This assessment has to be based on realistic grounds; the mere theoretical possibility of entering a market is not sufficient.[3]

(27) There are three exceptions to the general exclusion of vertical agreements between competitors, all three being set out in Article 2(4) and relating to non-reciprocal agreements. Non-reciprocal means, for instance, that while one manufacturer becomes the distributor of the products of another manufacturer, the latter does not become the distributor of the products of the first manufacturer. Non-reciprocal agreements between competitors are covered by the Block Exemption Regulation where (1) the buyer has a turnover not exceeding EUR 100 million, or (2) the supplier is a manufacturer and distributor of goods, while the buyer is only a distributor and not also a manufacturer of competing goods, or (3) the supplier is a provider of services operating at several levels of trade, while the buyer does not provide competing service at the level of trade where it purchases the contract services. The second exception covers situations of dual distribution, ie the manufacturer of particular goods also acts as a distributor of the goods in competition with independent distributors of his goods. A distributor who provides specifications to a manufacturer to provide particular goods under the distributor's brand name is not to be considered a manufacturer of such own-brand goods. The third exception covers similar situations of dual distribution, but in this case for services, when the supplier is also a provider of services at the level of the buyer.

(iii) Associations of retailers

(28) Article 2(2) of the Block Exemption Regulation includes in its application vertical agreements entered into by an association of undertakings which fulfils certain conditions and thereby excludes from the Block Exemption Regulation vertical agreements entered into by all other associations. Vertical agreements entered into between an association and its members, or between an association and its suppliers, are covered by the Block Exemption Regulation only if all the members are retailers of goods (not services) and if each individual member of the association has a turnover not exceeding EUR 50 million. Retailers are distributors

reselling goods to final consumers. Where only a limited number of the members of the association have a turnover not significantly exceeding the EUR 50 million threshold, this will normally not change the assessment under Article 81.

(29) An association of undertakings may involve both horizontal and vertical agreements. The horizontal agreements have to be assessed according to the principles set out in the forthcoming Guidelines on the applicability of Article 81 to horizontal cooperation. If this assessment leads to the conclusion that a cooperation between undertakings in the area of purchasing or selling is acceptable, a further assessment will be necessary to examine the vertical agreements concluded by the association with its suppliers or its individual members. The latter assessment will follow the rules of the Block Exemption Regulation and these Guidelines. For instance, horizontal agreements concluded between the members of the association or decisions adopted by the association, such as the decision to require the members to purchase from the association or the decision to allocate exclusive territories to the members have to be assessed first as a horizontal agreement. Only if this assessment is positive does it become relevant to assess the vertical agreements between the association and individual members or between the association and suppliers.

(iv) Vertical agreements containing provisions on intellectual property rights (IPRs)

(30) Article 2(3) of the Block Exemption Regulation includes in its application vertical agreements containing certain provisions relating to the assignment of IPRs to or use of IPRs by the buyer and thereby excludes from the Block Exemption Regulation all other vertical agreements containing IPR provisions. The Block Exemption Regulation applies to vertical agreements containing IPR provisions when five conditions are fulfilled—
- The IPR provisions must be part of a vertical agreement, ie an agreement with conditions under which the parties may purchase, sell or resell certain goods or services;
- The IPRs must be assigned to, or for use by, the buyer;
- The IPR provisions must not constitute the primary object of the agreement;
- The IPR provisions must be directly related to the use, sale or resale of goods or services by the buyer or his customers. In the case of franchising where marketing forms the object of the exploitation of the IPRs, the goods or services are distributed by the master franchisee or the franchisees;
- The IPR provisions, in relation to the contract goods or services, must not contain restrictions of competition having the same object or effect as vertical restraints which are not exempted under the Block Exemption Regulation.

(31) These conditions ensure that the Block Exemption Regulation applies to vertical agreements where the use, sale or resale of goods or services can be performed more effectively because IPRs are assigned to or transferred for use by the buyer. In other words, restrictions concerning the assignment or use of IPRs can be covered when the main object of the agreement is the purchase or distribution of goods or services.

(32) The first condition makes clear that the context in which the IPRs are provided is an agreement to purchase or distribute goods or an agreement to purchase or provide services and not an agreement concerning the assignment or licensing of IPRs for the manufacture of goods, nor a pure licensing agreement. The Block Exemption Regulation does not cover for instance—
- agreements where a party provides another party with a recipe and licenses the other party to produce a drink with this recipe;
- agreements under which one party provides another party with a mould or master copy and licenses the other party to produce and distribute copies;
- the pure licence of a trade mark or sign for the purposes of merchandising;

— sponsorship contracts concerning the right to advertise oneself as being an official sponsor of an event;

— copyright licensing such as broadcasting contracts concerning the right to record and/or the right to broadcast an event.

(33) The second condition makes clear that the Block Exemption Regulation does not apply when the IPRs are provided by the buyer to the supplier, no matter whether the IPRs concern the manner of manufacture or of distribution. An agreement relating to the transfer of IPRs to the supplier and containing possible restrictions on the sales made by the supplier is not covered by the Block Exemption Regulation. This means in particular that subcontracting involving the transfer of know-how to a subcontractor[4] does not fall within the scope of application of the Block Exemption Regulation. However, vertical agreements under which the buyer provides only specifications to the supplier which describe the goods or services to be supplied are covered by the Block Exemption Regulation.

(34) The third condition makes clear that in order to be covered by the Block Exemption Regulation the primary object of the agreement must not be the assignment or licensing of IPRs. The primary object must be the purchase or distribution of goods or services and the IPR provisions must serve the implementation of the vertical agreement.

(35) The fourth condition requires that the IPR provisions facilitate the use, sale or resale of goods or services by the buyer or his customers. The goods or services for use or resale are usually supplied by the licensor but may also be purchased by the licensee from a third supplier. The IPR provisions will normally concern the marketing of goods or services. This is for instance the case in a franchise agreement where the franchisor sells to the franchisee goods for resale and in addition licenses the franchisee to use his trade mark and know-how to market the goods. Also covered is the case where the supplier of a concentrated extract licenses the buyer to dilute and bottle the extract before selling it as a drink.

(36) The fifth condition signifies in particular that the IPR provisions should not have the same object or effect as any of the hardcore restrictions listed in Article 4 of the Block Exemption Regulation or any of the restrictions excluded from the coverage of the Block Exemption Regulation by Article 5 (see paragraphs 46 to 61).

(37) Intellectual property rights which may be considered to serve the implementation of vertical agreements within the meaning of Article 2(3) of the Block Exemption Regulation generally concern three main areas: trade marks, copyright and know-how.

Trade mark

(38) A trade mark licence to a distributor may be related to the distribution of the licensor's products in a particular territory. If it is an exclusive licence, the agreement amounts to exclusive distribution.

Copyright

(39) Resellers of goods covered by copyright (books, software, etc.) may be obliged by the copyright holder only to resell under the condition that the buyer, whether another reseller or the end user, shall not infringe the copyright. Such obligations on the reseller, to the extent that they fall under Article 81(1) at all, are covered by the Block Exemption Regulation.

(40) Agreements under which hard copies of software are supplied for resale and where the reseller does not acquire a licence to any rights over the software but only has the right to resell the hard copies, are to be regarded as agreements for the supply of goods for resale for the purpose of the Block Exemption Regulation. Under this form of distribution the licence of the software only takes place between

the copyright owner and the user of the software. This may take the form of a "shrink wrap" licence, ie a set of conditions included in the package of the hard copy which the end user is deemed to accept by opening the package.

(41) Buyers of hardware incorporating software protected by copyright may be obliged by the copyright holder not to infringe the copyright, for example not to make copies and resell the software or not to make copies and use the software in combination with other hardware. Such use-restrictions, to the extent that they fall within Article 81(1) at all, are covered by the Block Exemption Regulation.

Know-how

(42) Franchise agreements, with the exception of industrial franchise agreements, are the most obvious example where know-how for marketing purposes is communicated to the buyer. Franchise agreements contain licences of intellectual property rights relating to trade marks or signs and know-how for the use and distribution of goods or the provision of services. In addition to the licence of IPR, the franchisor usually provides the franchisee during the life of the agreement with commercial or technical assistance, such as procurement services, training, advice on real estate, financial planning etc. The licence and the assistance are integral components of the business method being franchised.

(43) Licensing contained in franchise agreements is covered by the Block Exemption Regulation if all five conditions listed in point 30 are fulfilled. This is usually the case, as under most franchise agreements, including master franchise agreements, the franchisor provides goods and/or services, in particular commercial or technical assistance services, to the franchisee. The IPRs help the franchisee to resell the products supplied by the franchisor or by a supplier designated by the franchisor or to use those products and sell the resulting goods or services. Where the franchise agreement only or primarily concerns licensing of IPRs, such an agreement is not covered by the Block Exemption Regulation, but it will be treated in a way similar to those franchise agreements which are covered by the Block Exemption Regulation.

(44) The following IPR-related obligations are generally considered to be necessary to protect the franchisor's intellectual property rights and are, if these obligations fall under Article 81(1), also covered by the Block Exemption Regulation:

    (a) an obligation on the franchisee not to engage, directly or indirectly, in any similar business;

    (b) an obligation on the franchisee not to acquire financial interests in the capital of a competing undertaking such as would give the franchisee the power to influence the economic conduct of such undertaking;

    (c) an obligation on the franchisee not to disclose to third parties the know-how provided by the franchisor as long as this know-how is not in the public domain;

    (d) an obligation on the franchisee to communicate to the franchisor any experience gained in exploiting the franchise and to grant it, and other franchisees, a non-exclusive licence for the know-how resulting from that experience;

    (e) an obligation on the franchisee to inform the franchisor of infringements of licensed intellectual property rights, to take legal action against infringers or to assist the franchisor in any legal actions against infringers;

    (f) an obligation on the franchisee not to use know-how licensed by the franchisor for purposes other than the exploitation of the franchise;

    (g) an obligation on the franchisee not to assign the rights and obligations under the franchise agreement without the franchisor's consent.

(v) Relationship to other block exemption regulations

(45) Article 2(5) states that the Block Exemption Regulation does "not apply to vertical agreements the subject matter of which falls within the scope of any other block exemption regulation." This means that the Block Exemption Regulation does not apply to vertical agreements covered by Commission Regulation (EC) No 240/96[5] on technology transfer, Commission Regulation (EC) No 1475/1995[6] for car distribution or Regulations (EEC) No 417/85[7] and (EEC) No 418/85[8] exempting vertical agreements concluded in connection with horizontal agreements, as last amended by Regulation (EC) No 2236/97[9] or any future regulations of that kind.

3. Hardcore restrictions under the Block Exemption Regulation

(46) The Block Exemption Regulation contains in Article 4 a list of hardcore restrictions which lead to the exclusion of the whole vertical agreement from the scope of application of the Block Exemption Regulation. This list of hardcore restrictions applies to vertical agreements concerning trade within the Community. In so far as vertical agreements concern exports outside the Community or imports/re-imports from outside the Community see the judgment in Javico v Yves Saint Laurent. Individual exemption of vertical agreements containing such hardcore restrictions is also unlikely.

(47) The hardcore restriction set out in Article 4(a) of the Block Exemption Regulation concerns resale price maintenance (RPM), that is agreements or concerted practices having as their direct or indirect object the establishment of a fixed or minimum resale price or a fixed or minimum price level to be observed by the buyer. In the case of contractual provisions or concerted practices that directly establish the resale price, the restriction is clear cut. However, RPM can also be achieved through indirect means. Examples of the latter are an agreement fixing the distribution margin, fixing the maximum level of discount the distributor can grant from a prescribed price level, making the grant of rebates or reimbursement of promotional costs by the supplier subject to the observance of a given price level, linking the prescribed resale price to the resale prices of competitors, threats, intimidation, warnings, penalties, delay or suspension of deliveries or contract terminations in relation to observance of a given price level. Direct or indirect means of achieving price fixing can be made more effective when combined with measures to identify price-cutting distributors, such as the implementation of a price monitoring system, or the obligation on retailers to report other members of the distribution network who deviate from the standard price level. Similarly, direct or indirect price fixing can be made more effective when combined with measures which may reduce the buyer's incentive to lower the resale price, such as the supplier printing a recommended resale price on the product or the supplier obliging the buyer to apply a most-favoured-customer clause. The same indirect means and the same "supportive" measures can be used to make maximum or recommended prices work as RPM. However, the provision of a list of recommended prices or maximum prices by the supplier to the buyer is not considered in itself as leading to RPM.

(48) In the case of agency agreements, the principal normally establishes the sales price, as the agent does not become the owner of the goods. However, where an agency agreement falls within Article 81(1) (see paragraphs 12 to 20), an obligation preventing or restricting the agent from sharing his commission, fixed or variable, with the customer would be a hardcore restriction under Article 4(a) of the Block Exemption Regulation. The agent should thus be left free to lower the effective price paid by the customer without reducing the income for the principal.[10]

(49) The hardcore restriction set out in Article 4(b) of the Block Exemption Regulation concerns agreements or concerted practices that have as their direct or indirect object the restriction of sales by the buyer, in as far as those restrictions relate to the territory into which or the customers to whom the buyer may sell the contract goods or services. That hardcore restriction relates to market partitioning by territory or by customer. That may be the result of direct obligations, such as the obligation not to sell to certain customers or to customers in certain territories or the obligation to refer orders from these customers to other distributors. It may also result from indirect measures aimed at inducing the distributor not to sell to such customers, such as refusal or reduction of bonuses or discounts, refusal to supply, reduction of supplied volumes or limitation of supplied volumes to the demand within the allocated territory or customer group, threat of contract termination or profit pass-over obligations. It may further result from the supplier not providing a Community-wide guarantee service, whereby all distributors are obliged to provide the guarantee service and are reimbursed for this service by the supplier, even in relation to products sold by other distributors into their territory. These practices are even more likely to be viewed as a restriction of the buyer's sales when used in conjunction with the implementation by the supplier of a monitoring system aimed at verifying the effective destination of the supplied goods, eg the use of differentiated labels or serial numbers. However, a prohibition imposed on all distributors to sell to certain end users is not classified as a hardcore restriction if there is an objective justification related to the product, such as a general ban on selling dangerous substances to certain customers for reasons of safety or health. It implies that also the supplier himself does not sell to these customers. Nor are obligations on the reseller relating to the display of the supplier's brand name classified as hardcore.

(50) There are four exceptions to the hardcore restriction in Article 4(b) of the Block Exemption Regulation. The first exception allows a supplier to restrict active sales by his direct buyers to a territory or customer group which has been allocated exclusively to another buyer or which the supplier has reserved to itself. A territory or customer group is exclusively allocated when the supplier agrees to sell his product only to one distributor for distribution in a particular territory or to a particular customer group and the exclusive distributor is protected against active selling into his territory or to his customer group by the supplier and all the other buyers of the supplier inside the Community. The supplier is allowed to combine the allocation of an exclusive territory and an exclusive customer group by for instance appointing an exclusive distributor for a particular customer group in a certain territory. This protection of exclusively allocated territories or customer groups must, however, permit passive sales to such territories or customer groups. For the application of Article 4(b) of the Block Exemption Regulation, the Commission interprets "active" and "passive" sales as follows—

— "Active" sales mean actively approaching individual customers inside another distributor's exclusive territory or exclusive customer group by for instance direct mail or visits; or actively approaching a specific customer group or customers in a specific territory allocated exclusively to another distributor through advertisement in media or other promotions specifically targeted at that customer group or targeted at customers in that territory; or establishing a warehouse or distribution outlet in another distributor's exclusive territory.

— "Passive" sales mean responding to unsolicited requests from individual customers including delivery of goods or services to such customers. General advertising or promotion in media or on the Internet that reaches customers in other distributors' exclusive territories or customer groups but which is a reasonable way to reach customers outside those territories or customer groups, for instance to reach customers in non-exclusive territories or in one's own territory, are passive sales.

(51) Every distributor must be free to use the Internet to advertise or to sell products. A restriction on the use of the Internet by distributors could only be compatible with the Block Exemption Regulation to the extent that promotion on the Internet or sales over the Internet would lead to active selling into other distributors' exclusive territories or customer groups. In general, the use of the Internet is not considered a form of active sales into such territories or customer groups, since it is a reasonable way to reach every customer. The fact that it may have effects outside one's own territory or customer group results from the technology, ie the easy access from everywhere. If a customer visits the web site of a distributor and contacts the distributor and if such contact leads to a sale, including delivery, then that is considered passive selling. The language used on the website or in the communication plays normally no role in that respect. Insofar as a web site is not specifically targeted at customers primarily inside the territory or customer group exclusively allocated to another distributor, for instance with the use of banners or links in pages of providers specifically available to these exclusively allocated customers, the website is not considered a form of active selling. However, unsolicited e-mails sent to individual customers or specific customer groups are considered active selling. The same considerations apply to selling by catalogue. Notwithstanding what has been said before, the supplier may require quality standards for the use of the Internet site to resell his goods, just as the supplier may require quality standards for a shop or for advertising and promotion in general. The latter may be relevant in particular for selective distribution. An outright ban on Internet or catalogue selling is only possible if there is an objective justification. In any case, the supplier cannot reserve to itself sales and/or advertising over the Internet.

(52) There are three other exceptions to the second hardcore restriction set out in Article 4(b) of the Block Exemption Regulation. All three exceptions allow for the restriction of both active and passive sales. Thus, it is permissible to restrict a wholesaler from selling to end users, to restrict an appointed distributor in a selective distribution system from selling, at any level of trade, to unauthorised distributors in markets where such a system is operated, and to restrict a buyer of components supplied for incorporation from reselling them to competitors of the supplier. The term "component" includes any intermediate goods and the term "incorporation" refers to the use of any input to produce goods.

(53) The hardcore restriction set out in Article 4(c) of the Block Exemption Regulation concerns the restriction of active or passive sales to end users, whether professional end users or final consumers, by members of a selective distribution network. This means that dealers in a selective distribution system, as defined in Article 1(d) of the Block Exemption Regulation, cannot be restricted in the users or purchasing agents acting on behalf of these users to whom they may sell. For instance, also in a selective distribution system the dealer should be free to advertise and sell with the help of the Internet. Selective distribution may be combined with exclusive distribution provided that active and passive selling is not restricted anywhere. The supplier may therefore commit itself to supplying only one dealer or a limited number of dealers in a given territory.

(54) In addition, in the case of selective distribution, restrictions can be imposed on the dealer's ability to determine the location of his business premises. Selected dealers may be prevented from running their business from different premises or from opening a new outlet in a different location. If the dealer's outlet is mobile ("shop on wheels"), an area may be defined outside which the mobile outlet cannot be operated.

(55) The hardcore restriction set out in Article 4(d) of the Block Exemption Regulation concerns the restriction of cross-supplies between appointed distributors within a selective distribution system. This means that an agreement or concerted practice may not have as its direct or indirect object to prevent or restrict the active or passive selling of the contract products between the selected distributors. Selected

distributors must remain free to purchase the contract products from other appointed distributors within the network, operating either at the same or at a different level of trade. This means that selective distribution cannot be combined with vertical restraints aimed at forcing distributors to purchase the contract products exclusively from a given source, for instance exclusive purchasing. It also means that within a selective distribution network no restrictions can be imposed on appointed wholesalers as regards their sales of the product to appointed retailers.

(56) The hardcore restriction set out in Article 4(e) of the Block Exemption Regulation concerns agreements that prevent or restrict end-users, independent repairers and service providers from obtaining spare parts directly from the manufacturer of these spare parts. An agreement between a manufacturer of spare parts and a buyer who incorporates these parts into his own products (original equipment manufacturer (OEM)), may not, either directly or indirectly, prevent or restrict sales by the manufacturer of these spare parts to end users, independent repairers or service providers. Indirect restrictions may arise in particular when the supplier of the spare parts is restricted in supplying technical information and special equipment which are necessary for the use of spare parts by users, independent repairers or service providers.

However, the agreement may place restrictions on the supply of the spare parts to the repairers or service providers entrusted by the original equipment manufacturer with the repair or servicing of his own goods. In other words, the original equipment manufacturer may require his own repair and service network to buy the spare parts from it.

4. Conditions under the Block Exemption Regulation

(57) Article 5 of the Block Exemption Regulation excludes certain obligations from the coverage of the Block Exemption Regulation even though the market share threshold is not exceeded. However, the Block Exemption Regulation continues to apply to the remaining part of the vertical agreement if that part is severable from the non-exempted obligations.

(58) The first exclusion is provided in Article 5(a) of the Block Exemption Regulation and concerns non-compete obligations. Non-compete obligations are obligations that require the buyer to purchase from the supplier or from another undertaking designated by the supplier more than 80% of the buyer's total purchases during the previous year of the contract goods and services and their substitutes (see the definition in Article 1(b) of the Block Exemption Regulation), thereby preventing the buyer from purchasing competing goods or services or limiting such purchases to less than 20% of total purchases. Where for the year preceding the conclusion of the contract no relevant purchasing data for the buyer are available, the buyer's best estimate of his annual total requirements may be used. Such non-compete obligations are not covered by the Block Exemption Regulation when their duration is indefinite or exceeds five years. Non-compete obligations that are tacitly renewable beyond a period of five years are also not covered by the Block Exemption Regulation. However, non-compete obligations are covered when their duration is limited to five years or less, or when renewal beyond five years requires explicit consent of both parties and no obstacles exist that hinder the buyer from effectively terminating the non-compete obligation at the end of the five year period. If for instance the agreement provides for a five-year non-compete obligation and the supplier provides a loan to the buyer, the repayment of that loan should not hinder the buyer from effectively terminating the non-compete obligation at the end of the five year period; the repayment needs to be structured in equal or decreasing instalments and should not increase over time. This is without prejudice to the possibility, in the case for instance of a new distribution outlet, to delay repayment for the first one or two years until sales have reached a certain level. The buyer must

have the possibility to repay the remaining debt where there is still an outstanding debt at the end of the non-compete obligation. Similarly when the supplier provides the buyer with equipment which is not relationship specific, the buyer should have the possibility to take over the equipment at its market asset value at the end of the non-compete obligation.

(59) The five-year duration limit does not apply when the goods or services are resold by the buyer "from premises and land owned by the supplier or leased by the supplier from third parties not connected with the buyer." In such cases the non-compete obligation may be of the same duration as the period of occupancy of the point of sale by the buyer (Article 5(a) of the Block Exemption Regulation). The reason for this exception is that it is normally unreasonable to expect a supplier to allow competing products to be sold from premises and land owned by the supplier without his permission. Artificial ownership constructions intended to avoid the five-year limit cannot benefit from this exception.

(60) The second exclusion from the block exemption is provided for in Article 5(b) of the Block Exemption Regulation and concerns post term non-compete obligations. Such obligations are normally not covered by the Block Exemption Regulation, unless the obligation is indispensable to protect know-how transferred by the supplier to the buyer, is limited to the point of sale from which the buyer has operated during the contract period, and is limited to a maximum period of one year. According to the definition in Article 1(f) of the Block Exemption Regulation the know-how needs to be "substantial", meaning "that the know-how includes information which is indispensable to the buyer for the use, sale or resale of the contract goods or services".

(61) The third exclusion from the block exemption is provided for in Article 5(c) of the Block Exemption Regulation and concerns the sale of competing goods in a selective distribution system. The Block Exemption Regulation covers the combination of selective distribution with a non-compete obligation, obliging the dealers not to resell competing brands in general. However, if the supplier prevents his appointed dealers, either directly or indirectly, from buying products for resale from specific competing suppliers, such an obligation cannot enjoy the benefit of the Block Exemption Regulation. The objective of the exclusion of this obligation is to avoid a situation whereby a number of suppliers using the same selective distribution outlets prevent one specific competitor or certain specific competitors from using these outlets to distribute their products (foreclosure of a competing supplier which would be a form of collective boycott).[11]

5. No presumption of illegality outside the Block Exemption Regulation

(62) Vertical agreements falling outside the Block Exemption Regulation will not be presumed to be illegal but may need individual examination. Companies are encouraged to do their own assessment without notification. In the case of an individual examination by the Commission, the latter will bear the burden of proof that the agreement in question infringes Article 81(1). When appreciable anti-competitive effects are demonstrated, undertakings may substantiate efficiency claims and explain why a certain distribution system is likely to bring about benefits which are relevant to the conditions for exemption under Article 81(3).

6. No need for precautionary notification

(63) Pursuant to Article 4(2) of Council Regulation No 17 of 6 February 1962, First Regulation implementing Articles 85 and 86 of the Treaty,[12] as last amended by Regulation (EC) No 1216/1999,[13] vertical agreements can benefit from an exemption under Article 81(3) from their date of entry into force, even if notification occurs after that date. This means in practice that no precautionary notification needs to be made. If a dispute arises, an undertaking can still notify, in which case the Commission can

exempt the vertical agreement with retroactive effect from the date of entry into force of the agreement if all four conditions of Article 81(3) are fulfilled. A notifying party does not have to explain why the agreement was not notified earlier and will not be denied retroactive exemption simply because it did not notify earlier. Any notification will be reviewed on its merits. This amendment to Article 4(2) of Regulation No 17 should eliminate artificial litigation before national courts and thus strengthen the civil enforceability of contracts. It also takes account of the situation where undertakings have not notified because they assumed the agreement was covered by the Block Exemption Regulation.

(64) Since the date of notification no longer limits the possibility of exemption by the Commission, national courts have to assess the likelihood that Article 81(3) will apply in respect of vertical agreements falling within Article 81(1). If such likelihood exists, they should suspend proceedings pending adoption of a position by the Commission. However, national courts may adopt interim measures pending the assessment by the Commission of the applicability of Article 81(3), in the same way as they do when they refer a preliminary question to the Court of Justice under Article 234 of the EC Treaty. No suspension is necessary in respect of injunction proceedings, where national courts themselves are empowered to assess the likelihood of application of Article 81(3).[14]

(65) Unless there is litigation in national courts or complaints, notifications of vertical agreements will not be given priority in the Commission's enforcement policy. Notifications as such do not provide provisional validity for the execution of agreements. Where undertakings have not notified an agreement because they assumed in good faith that the market share threshold under the Block Exemption Regulation was not exceeded, the Commission will not impose fines.

7. Severability

(66) The Block Exemption Regulation exempts vertical agreements on condition that no hardcore restriction, as set out in Article 4, is contained in or practised with the vertical agreement. If there are one or more hardcore restrictions, the benefit of the Block Exemption Regulation is lost for the entire vertical agreement. There is no severability for hardcore restrictions.

(67) The rule of severability does apply, however, to the conditions set out in Article 5 of the Block Exemption Regulation. Therefore, the benefit of the block exemption is only lost in relation to that part of the vertical agreement which does not comply with the conditions set out in Article 5.

8. Portfolio of products distributed through the same distribution system

(68) Where a supplier uses the same distribution agreement to distribute several goods/services some of these may, in view of the market share threshold, be covered by the Block Exemption Regulation while others may not. In that case, the Block Exemption Regulation applies to those goods and services for which the conditions of application are fulfilled.

(69) In respect of the goods or services which are not covered by the Block Exemption Regulation, the ordinary rules of competition apply, which means—
— there is no block exemption but also no presumption of illegality;
— if there is an infringement of Article 81(1) which is not exemptable, consideration may be given to whether there are appropriate remedies to solve the competition problem within the existing distribution system;
— if there are no such appropriate remedies, the supplier concerned will have to make other distribution arrangements.

This situation can also arise where Article 82 applies in respect of some products but not in respect of others.

9. Transitional period

(70) The Block Exemption Regulation applies from 1 June 2000. Article 12 of the Block Exemption Regulation provides for a transitional period for vertical agreements already in force before 1 June 2000 which do not satisfy the conditions for exemption provided in the Block Exemption Regulation, but which do satisfy the conditions for exemption under the Block Exemption Regulations which expired on 31 May 2000 (Commissions Regulations (EEC) No 1983/83, (EEC) No 1984/83 and (EEC) No 4087/88). The Commission Notice concerning Regulations (EEC) Nos 1983/83 and 1984/83 also ceases to apply on 31 May 2000. The latter agreements may continue to benefit from these outgoing Regulations until 31 December 2001. Agreements of suppliers with a market share not exceeding 30% who signed with their buyers non-compete agreements with a duration exceeding five years are covered by the Block Exemption Regulation if on 1 January 2002 the non-compete agreements have no more than five years to run.

[5134]

NOTES

[1] OJ L145, 29.6.95, p 25.

[2] Draft text published in OJ C118, 27.4.2000, p 14.

[3] See Commission Notice on the definition of the relevant market for the purposes of Community competition law, OJ C372, 9.12.97, p 5 at paras 20–24, the Commission's Thirteenth Report on Competition Policy, point 55, and Commission Decision 90/410/EEC in Case No IV/32.009—Elopak/Metal Box—Odin, OJ L209, 8.8.90, p 15.

[4] See Notice on subcontracting, OJ C1, 3.1.79, p 2.

[5] OJ L31, 9.2.96, p 2.

[6] OJ L145, 29.6.95, p 25.

[7] OJ L53, 22.2.85, p 1.

[8] OJ L53, 22.2.85, p 5.

[9] OJ L306, 11.11.97, p 12.

[10] See, for instance, Commission Decision 91/562/EEC in Case No IV/32.737—Eirpage, OJ L306, 7.11.91, p 22, in particular point (6).

[11] An example of indirect measures having such exclusionary effects can be found in Commission Decision 92/428/EEC in Case No IV/33.542—Parfum Givenchy (OJ L236, 19.8.92, p 11).

[12] OJ 13, 21.2.62, p 204/62.

[13] OJ L148, 15.6.99, p 5.

[14] Case C-234/89 Delimitis v Henninger Brau [1991] ECR 1-935, at paragraph 52.

IV. WITHDRAWAL OF THE BLOCK EXEMPTION AND DISAPPLICATION OF THE BLOCK EXEMPTION REGULATION

1. Withdrawal procedure

(71) The presumption of legality conferred by the Block Exemption Regulation may be withdrawn if a vertical agreement, considered either in isolation or in conjunction with similar agreements enforced by competing suppliers or buyers, comes within the scope of Article 81(1) and does not fulfil all the conditions of Article 81(3). This may occur when a supplier, or a buyer in the case of exclusive supply agreements, holding a market share not exceeding 30%, enters into a vertical agreement which does not give rise to objective advantages such as to compensate for the damage which it causes to competition. This may particularly be the case with respect to the distribution of goods to final consumers, who are often in a much weaker position than professional buyers of intermediate goods. In the case of sales to final consumers, the disadvantages caused by a vertical agreement may have a stronger impact than in a case concerning the sale and purchase of intermediate goods. When the conditions of Article 81(3) are not fulfilled, the Commission may withdraw the benefit of the Block Exemption Regulation under Article 6 and establish an infringement of Article 81(1).

(72) Where the withdrawal procedure is applied, the Commission bears the burden of proof that the agreement falls within the scope of Article 81(1) and that the agreement does not fulfil all four conditions of Article 81(3).

(73) The conditions for an exemption under Article 81(3) may in particular not be fulfilled when access to the relevant market or competition therein is significantly restricted by the cumulative effect of parallel networks of similar vertical agreements practised by competing suppliers or buyers. Parallel networks of vertical agreements are to be regarded as similar if they contain restraints producing similar effects on the market. Similar effects will normally occur when vertical restraints practised by competing suppliers or buyers come within one of the four groups listed in paragraphs 104 to 114. Such a situation may arise for example when, on a given market, certain suppliers practise purely qualitative selective distribution while other suppliers practise quantitative selective distribution. In such circumstances, the assessment must take account of the anti-competitive effects attributable to each individual network of agreements. Where appropriate, withdrawal may concern only the quantitative limitations imposed on the number of authorised distributors. Other cases in which a withdrawal decision may be taken include situations where the buyer, for example in the context of exclusive supply or exclusive distribution, has significant market power in the relevant downstream market where he resells the goods or provides the services.

(74) Responsibility for an anti-competitive cumulative effect can only be attributed to those undertakings which make an appreciable contribution to it. Agreements entered into by undertakings whose contribution to the cumulative effect is insignificant do not fall under the prohibition provided for in Article 81(1)[1] and are therefore not subject to the withdrawal mechanism. The assessment of such a contribution will be made in accordance with the criteria set out in paragraphs 137 to 229.

(75) A withdrawal decision can only have ex nunc effect, which means that the exempted status of the agreements concerned will not be affected until the date at which the withdrawal becomes effective.

(76) Under Article 7 of the Block Exemption Regulation, the competent authority of a Member State may withdraw the benefit of the Block Exemption Regulation in respect of vertical agreements whose anti-competitive effects are felt in the territory of the Member State concerned or a part thereof, which has all the characteristics of a distinct geographic market. Where a Member State has not enacted legislation enabling the national competition authority to apply Community competition law or at least to withdraw the benefit of the Block Exemption Regulation, the Member State may ask the Commission to initiate proceedings to this effect.

(77) The Commission has the exclusive power to withdraw the benefit of the Block Exemption Regulation in respect of vertical agreements restricting competition on a relevant geographic market which is wider than the territory of a single Member State. When the territory of a single Member State, or a part thereof, constitutes the relevant geographic market, the Commission and the Member State concerned have concurrent competence for withdrawal. Often, such cases lend themselves to decentralised enforcement by national competition authorities. However, the Commission reserves the right to take on certain cases displaying a particular Community interest, such as cases raising a new point of law.

(78) National decisions of withdrawal must be taken in accordance with the procedures laid down under national law and will only have effect within the territory of the Member State concerned. Such national decisions must not prejudice the uniform application of the Community competition rules and the full effect of the measures adopted in implementation of those rules.[2] Compliance with this

principle implies that national competition authorities must carry out their assessment under Article 81 in the light of the relevant criteria developed by the Court of Justice and the Court of First Instance and in the light of notices and previous decisions adopted by the Commission.

(79) The Commission considers that the consultation mechanisms provided for in the Notice on cooperation between national competition authorities and the Commission[3] should be used to avert the risk of conflicting decisions and duplication of procedures.

2. Disapplication of the Block Exemption Regulation

(80) Article 8 of the Block Exemption Regulation enables the Commission to exclude from the scope of the Block Exemption Regulation, by means of regulation, parallel networks of similar vertical restraints where these cover more than 50% of a relevant market. Such a measure is not addressed to individual undertakings but concerns all undertakings whose agreements are defined in the regulation disapplying the Block Exemption Regulation.

(81) Whereas the withdrawal of the benefit of the Block Exemption Regulation under Article 6 implies the adoption of a decision establishing an infringement of Article 81 by an individual company, the effect of a regulation under Article 8 is merely to remove, in respect of the restraints and the markets concerned, the benefit of the application of the Block Exemption Regulation and to restore the full application of Article 81(1) and (3). Following the adoption of a regulation declaring the Block Exemption inapplicable in respect of certain vertical restraints on a particular market, the criteria developed by the relevant case-law of the Court of Justice and the Court of First Instance and by notices and previous decisions adopted by the Commission will guide the application of Article 81 to individual agreements. Where appropriate, the Commission will take a decision in an individual case, which can provide guidance to all the undertakings operating on the market concerned.

(82) For the purpose of calculating the 50% market coverage ratio, account must be taken of each individual network of vertical agreements containing restraints, or combinations of restraints, producing similar effects on the market. Similar effects normally result when the restraints come within one of the four groups listed in paragraphs 104 to 114.

(83) Article 8 does not entail an obligation on the part of the Commission to act where the 50% market-coverage ratio is exceeded. In general, disapplication is appropriate when it is likely that access to the relevant market or competition therein is appreciably restricted. This may occur in particular when parallel networks of selective distribution covering more than 50% of a market make use of selection criteria which are not required by the nature of the relevant goods or discriminate against certain forms of distribution capable of selling such goods.

(84) In assessing the need to apply Article 8, the Commission will consider whether individual withdrawal would be a more appropriate remedy. This may depend, in particular, on the number of competing undertakings contributing to a cumulative effect on a market or the number of affected geographic markets within the Community.

(85) Any regulation adopted under Article 8 must clearly set out its scope. This means, first, that the Commission must define the relevant product and geographic market(s) and, secondly, that it must identify the type of vertical restraint in respect of which the Block Exemption Regulation will no longer apply. As regards the latter aspect, the Commission may modulate the scope of its regulation according to the competition concern which it intends to address. For instance, while all parallel

networks of single-branding type arrangements shall be taken into account in view of establishing the 50% market coverage ratio, the Commission may nevertheless restrict the scope of the disapplication regulation only to non-compete obligations exceeding a certain duration. Thus, agreements of a shorter duration or of a less restrictive nature might be left unaffected, in consideration of the lesser degree of foreclosure attributable to such restraints. Similarly, when on a particular market selective distribution is practised in combination with additional restraints such as non-compete or quantity-forcing on the buyer, the disapplication regulation may concern only such additional restraints. Where appropriate, the Commission may also provide guidance by specifying the market share level which, in the specific market context, may be regarded as insufficient to bring about a significant contribution by an individual undertaking to the cumulative effect.

(86) The transitional period of not less than six months that the Commission will have to set under Article 8(2) should allow the undertakings concerned to adapt their agreements to take account of the regulation disapplying the Block Exemption Regulation.

(87) A regulation disapplying the Block Exemption Regulation will not affect the exempted status of the agreements concerned for the period preceding its entry into force.

[5135]

NOTES

¹   Judgment in the Delimitis case.
²   Judgment of the Court of Justice in Case 14/68 Walt Wilhelm and Others v Bundeskartellamt [1969] ECR 1, paragraph 4, and judgment in Delimitis.
³   OJ C313, 15.10.97, p 3, points 49 to 53.

V. MARKET DEFINITION AND MARKET SHARE CALCULATION ISSUES

1. Commission Notice on definition of the relevant market

(88) The Commission Notice on definition of the relevant market for the purposes of Community competition law¹ provides guidance on the rules, criteria and evidence which the Commission uses when considering market definition issues. That Notice will not be further explained in these Guidelines and should serve as the basis for market definition issues. These Guidelines will only deal with specific issues that arise in the context of vertical restraints and that are not dealt with in the general notice on market definition.

2. The relevant market for calculating the 30% market share threshold under the Block Exemption Regulation

(89) Under Article 3 of the Block Exemption Regulation, it is in general the market share of the supplier that is decisive for the application of the block exemption. In the case of vertical agreements concluded between an association of retailers and individual members, the association is the supplier and needs to take into account its market share as a supplier. Only in the case of exclusive supply as defined in Article 1(c) of the Block Exemption Regulation is it the market share of the buyer, and only that market share, which is decisive for the application of the Block Exemption Regulation.

(90) In order to calculate the market share, it is necessary to determine the relevant market. For this, the relevant product market and the relevant geographic market must be defined. The relevant product market comprises any goods or services which are regarded by the buyer as interchangeable, by reason of their

characteristics, prices and intended use. The relevant geographic market comprises the area in which the undertakings concerned are involved in the supply and demand of relevant goods or services, in which the conditions of competition are sufficiently homogeneous, and which can be distinguished from neighbouring geographic areas because, in particular, conditions of competition are appreciably different in those areas.

(91) For the application of the Block Exemption Regulation, the market share of the supplier is his share on the relevant product and geographic market on which he sells to his buyers.[2] In the example given in paragraph 92, this is market A. The product market depends in the first place on substitutability from the buyers' perspective. When the supplied product is used as an input to produce other products and is generally not recognisable in the final product, the product market is normally defined by the direct buyers' preferences. The customers of the buyers will normally not have a strong preference concerning the inputs used by the buyers. Usually the vertical restraints agreed between the supplier and buyer of the input only relate to the sale and purchase of the intermediate product and not to the sale of the resulting product. In the case of distribution of final goods, what are substitutes for the direct buyers will normally be influenced or determined by the preferences of the final consumers. A distributor, as reseller, cannot ignore the preferences of final consumers when he purchases final goods. In addition, at the distribution level the vertical restraints usually concern not only the sale of products between supplier and buyer, but also their resale. As different distribution formats usually compete, markets are in general not defined by the form of distribution that is applied. Where suppliers generally sell a portfolio of products, the entire portfolio may determine the product market when the portfolios and not the individual products are regarded as substitutes by the buyers. As the buyers on market A are professional buyers, the geographic market is usually wider than the market where the product is resold to final consumers. Often, this will lead to the definition of national markets or wider geographic markets.

(92) In the case of exclusive supply, the buyer's market share is his share of all purchases on the relevant purchase market.[3] In the example below, this is also market A.

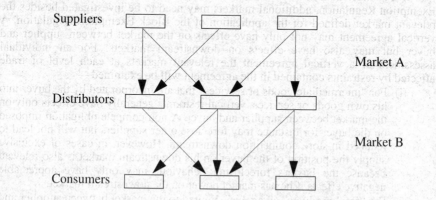

(93) Where a vertical agreement involves three parties, each operating at a different level of trade, their market shares will have to be below the market share threshold of 30% at both levels in order to benefit from the block exemption. If for instance, in an agreement between a manufacturer, a wholesaler (or association of retailers) and a retailer, a non-compete obligation is agreed, then the market share of both the manufacturer and the wholesaler (or association of retailers) must not exceed 30% in order to benefit from the block exemption.

(94) Where a supplier produces both original equipment and the repair or replacement parts for this equipment, the supplier will often be the only or the major supplier on the after-market for the repair and replacement parts. This may also arise where the supplier (OEM supplier) subcontracts the manufacturing of the repair or replacement parts. The relevant market for application of the Block Exemption Regulation may be the original equipment market including the spare parts or a separate original equipment market and after-market depending on the circumstances of the case, such as the effects of the restrictions involved, the lifetime of the equipment and importance of the repair or replacement costs.[4]

(95) Where the vertical agreement, in addition to the supply of the contract goods, also contains IPR provisions—such as a provision concerning the use of the supplier's trademark—which help the buyer to market the contract goods, the supplier's market share on the market where he sells the contract goods is decisive for the application of the Block Exemption Regulation. Where a franchisor does not supply goods to be resold but provides a bundle of services combined with IPR provisions which together form the business method being franchised, the franchisor needs to take account of his market share as a provider of a business method. For that purpose, the franchisor needs to calculate his market share on the market where the business method is exploited, which is the market where the franchisees exploit the business method to provide goods or services to end users. The franchisor must base his market share on the value of the goods or services supplied by his franchisees on this market. On such a market the competitors may be providers of other franchised business methods but also suppliers of substitutable goods or services not applying franchising. For instance, without prejudice to the definition of such market, if there was a market for fast-food services, a franchisor operating on such a market would need to calculate his market share on the basis of the relevant sales figures of his franchisees on this market. If the franchisor, in addition to the business method, also supplies certain inputs, such as meat and spices, then the franchisor also needs to calculate his market share on the market where these goods are sold.

3. The relevant market for individual assessment

(96) For individual assessment of vertical agreements not covered by the Block Exemption Regulation, additional markets may need to be investigated besides the relevant market defined for the application of the Block Exemption Regulation. A vertical agreement may not only have effects on the market between supplier and buyer but may also have effects on downstream markets. For an individual assessment of a vertical agreement the relevant markets at each level of trade affected by restraints contained in the agreement will be examined—

(i) For "intermediate goods or services" that are incorporated by the buyer into his own goods or services, vertical restraints generally have effects only on the market between supplier and buyer. A non-compete obligation imposed on the buyer for instance may foreclose other suppliers but will not lead to reduced in-store competition downstream. However, in cases of exclusive supply the position of the buyer on his downstream market is also relevant because the buyer's foreclosing behaviour may only have appreciable negative effects if he has market power on the downstream market.

(ii) For "final products" an analysis limited to the market between supplier and buyer is less likely to be sufficient since vertical restraints may have negative effects of reduced inter-brand and/or intra-brand competition on the resale market, that is on the market downstream of the buyer. For instance, exclusive distribution may not only lead to foreclosure effects on the market between the supplier and the buyer, but may above all lead to less intra-brand competition in the resale territories of the distributors. The resale market is in particular important if the buyer is a retailer selling to final consumers. A non-compete obligation agreed between a manufacturer and a wholesaler may foreclose this wholesaler to other manufacturers but a loss of in-store competition is not very likely at the wholesale level. The same agreement concluded with a retailer may however cause this added loss of in-store inter-brand competition on the resale market.

(iii) In cases of individual assessment of an "after-market", the relevant market may be the original equipment market or the after-market depending on the circumstances of the case. In any event, the situation on a separate after-market will be evaluated taking account of the situation on the original equipment market. A less significant position on the original equipment market will normally reduce possible anti-competitive effects on the after-market.

4. Calculation of the market share under the Block Exemption Regulation

(97) The calculation of the market share needs to be based in principle on value figures. Where value figures are not available substantiated estimates can be made. Such estimates may be based on other reliable market information such as volume figures (see Article 9(1) of the Block Exemption Regulation).

(98) In-house production, that is production of an intermediate product for own use, may be very important in a competition analysis as one of the competitive constraints or to accentuate the market position of a company. However, for the purpose of market definition and the calculation of market share for intermediate goods and services, in-house production will not be taken into account.

(99) However, in the case of dual distribution of final goods, ie where a producer of final goods also acts as a distributor on the market, the market definition and market share calculation need to include the goods sold by the producer and competing producers through their integrated distributors and agents (see Article 9(2)(b) of the Block Exemption Regulation). "Integrated distributors" are connected undertakings within the meaning of Article 11 of the Block Exemption Regulation.

                                                                        [5136]

NOTES

¹ OJ C372, 9.12.97, p 5.

² For example, the Dutch market for new replacement truck and bus tyres in the Michelin case (Case 322/81 Nederlandsche Banden-Industrie Michelin v Commission [1983] ECR 3461), the various meat markets in the Danish slaughter-house case: Commission Decision 2000/42/EC in Case No IV/M.1313—Danish Crown/Vestjyske Slagterier, OJ L20 25.1.2000, p 1.

³ For an example of purchase markets, see Commission Decision 1999/674/EC in Case No IV/M.1221—Rewe/Meinl. OJ L274, 23.10.99, p 1.

⁴ See for example Pelikan/Kyocera in XXV Report on Competition Policy, point 87, and Commission Decision 91/595/EEC in Case No IV/M.12—Varta/Boach, OJ L320, 22.11.91, p 26, Commission Decision in Case No IV/M.1094—Caterpillar/Perkins Engines, OJ C 94, 28.3.98, p 23, and Commission Decision in Case No IV/M.768—Lucas/Varity, OJ C 266, 13.9.96, p 6. See also Eastman Kodak Co v Image Technical Services, Inc et al, Supreme Court of the United States, No 90 1029. See also point 56 of the Commission Notice on the definition of relevant market for the purposes of Community competition law.

VI. ENFORCEMENT POLICY IN INDIVIDUAL CASES

(100) Vertical restraints are generally less harmful than horizontal restraints. The main reason for treating a vertical restraint more leniently than a horizontal restraint lies in the fact that the latter may concern an agreement between competitors producing identical or substitutable goods or services. In such horizontal relationships the exercise of market power by one company (higher price of its product) may benefit its competitors. This may provide an incentive to competitors to induce each

other to behave anti-competitively. In vertical relationships the product of the one is the input for the other. This means that the exercise of market power by either the upstream or downstream company would normally hurt the demand for the product of the other. The companies involved in the agreement therefore usually have an incentive to prevent the exercise of market power by the other.

(101) However, this self-restraining character should not be over-estimated. When a company has no market power it can only try to increase its profits by optimising its manufacturing and distribution processes, with or without the help of vertical restraints. However, when it does have market power it can also try to increase its profits at the expense of its direct competitors by raising their costs and at the expense of its buyers and ultimately consumers by trying to appropriate some of their surplus. This can happen when the upstream and downstream company share the extra profits or when one of the two uses vertical restraints to appropriate all the extra profits.

(102) In the assessment of individual cases, the Commission will adopt an economic approach in the application of Article 81 to vertical restraints. This will limit the scope of application of Article 81 to undertakings holding a certain degree of market power where inter-brand competition may be insufficient. In those cases, the protection of inter-brand and intra-brand competition is important to ensure efficiencies and benefits for consumers.

1. The framework of analysis

1.1. Negative effects of vertical restraints

(103) The negative effects on the market that may result from vertical restraints which EC competition law aims at preventing are the following—

   (i) foreclosure of other suppliers or other buyers by raising barriers to entry;

  (ii) reduction of inter-brand competition between the companies operating on a market, including facilitation of collusion amongst suppliers or buyers; by collusion is meant both explicit collusion and tacit collusion (conscious parallel behaviour);

 (iii) reduction of intra-brand competition between distributors of the same brand;

 (iv) the creation of obstacles to market integration, including, above all, limitations on the freedom of consumers to purchase goods or services in any Member State they may choose.

(104) Such negative effects may result from various vertical restraints. Agreements which are different in form may have the same substantive impact on competition. To analyse these possible negative effects, it is appropriate to divide vertical restraints into four groups: a single branding group, a limited distribution group, a resale price maintenance group and a market partitioning group. The vertical restraints within each group have largely similar negative effects on competition.

(105) The classification into four groups is based upon what can be described as the basic components of vertical restraints. In paragraphs 103 to 136, the four different groups are analysed. In 137 to 229, vertical agreements are analysed as they are used in practice because many vertical agreements make use of more than one of these components.

Single branding group

(106) Under the heading of "single branding" come those agreements which have as their main element that the buyer is induced to concentrate his orders for a particular type of product with one supplier. This component can be found amongst others in non-compete and quantity-forcing on the buyer, where an obligation or

incentive scheme agreed between the supplier and the buyer makes the latter purchase his requirements for a particular product and its substitutes only, or mainly, from one supplier. The same component can be found in tying, where the obligation or incentive scheme relates to a product that the buyer is required to purchase as a condition of purchasing another distinct product. The first product is referred to as the "tied" product and the second is referred to as the "tying" product.

(107) There are four main negative effects on competition: (1) other suppliers in that market cannot sell to the particular buyers and this may lead to foreclosure of the market or, in the case of tying, to foreclosure of the market for the tied product; (2) it makes market shares more rigid and this may help collusion when applied by several suppliers; (3) as far as the distribution of final goods is concerned, the particular retailers will only sell one brand and there will therefore be no inter-brand competition in their shops (no in-store competition); and (4) in the case of tying, the buyer may pay a higher price for the tied product than he would otherwise do. All these effects may lead to a reduction in inter-brand competition.

(108) The reduction in inter-brand competition may be mitigated by strong initial competition between suppliers to obtain the single branding contracts, but the longer the duration of the non-compete obligation, the more likely it will be that this effect will not be strong enough to compensate for the reduction in inter-brand competition.

Limited distribution group

(109) Under the heading of "limited distribution" come those agreements which have as their main element that the manufacturer sells to only one or a limited number of buyers. This may be to restrict the number of buyers for a particular territory or group of customers, or to select a particular kind of buyers. This component can be found amongst others in—

— exclusive distribution and exclusive customer allocation, where the supplier limits his sales to only one buyer for a certain territory or class of customers;
— exclusive supply and quantity-forcing on the supplier, where an obligation or incentive scheme agreed between the buyer and supplier makes the former sell only or mainly to one buyer;
— selective distribution, where the conditions imposed on or agreed with the selected dealers usually limit their number;
— after-market sales restrictions which limit the component supplier's sales possibilities.

(110) There are three main negative effects on competition: (1) certain buyers within that market can no longer buy from that particular supplier, and this may lead in particular in the case of exclusive supply, to foreclosure of the purchase market, (2) when most or all of the competing suppliers limit the number of retailers, this may facilitate collusion, either at the distributor's level or at the supplier's level, and (3) since fewer distributors will offer the product it will also lead to a reduction of intra-brand competition. In the case of wide exclusive territories or exclusive customer allocation the result may be total elimination of intra-brand competition. This reduction of intra-brand competition can in turn lead to a weakening of inter-brand competition.

Resale price maintenance group

(111) Under the heading of "resale price maintenance" (RPM) come those agreements whose main element is that the buyer is obliged or induced to resell not below a certain price, at a certain price or not above a certain price. This group comprises minimum, fixed, maximum and recommended resale prices. Maximum and recommended resale prices, which are not hardcore restrictions, may still lead to a restriction of competition by effect.

(112) There are two main negative effects of RPM on competition: (1) a reduction in intra-brand price competition, and (2) increased transparency on prices. In the case of fixed or minimum RPM, distributors can no longer compete on price for that brand, leading to a total elimination of intra-brand price competition. A maximum or recommended price may work as a focal point for resellers, leading to a more or less uniform application of that price level. Increased transparency on price and responsibility for price changes makes horizontal collusion between manufacturers or distributors easier, at least in concentrated markets. The reduction in intra-brand competition may, as it leads to less downward pressure on the price for the particular goods, have as an indirect effect a reduction of inter-brand competition.

Market partitioning group

(113) Under the heading of "market partitioning" come agreements whose main element is that the buyer is restricted in where he either sources or resells a particular product. This component can be found in exclusive purchasing, where an obligation or incentive scheme agreed between the supplier and the buyer makes the latter purchase his requirements for a particular product, for instance beer of brand X, exclusively from the designated supplier, but leaving the buyer free to buy and sell competing products, for instance competing brands of beer. It also includes territorial resale restrictions, the allocation of an area of primary responsibility, restrictions on the location of a distributor and customer resale restrictions.

(114) The main negative effect on competition is a reduction of intra-brand competition that may help the supplier to partition the market and thus hinder market integration. This may facilitate price discrimination. When most or all of the competing suppliers limit the sourcing or resale possibilities of their buyers this may facilitate collusion, either at the distributors' level or at the suppliers' level.

1.2. Positive effects of vertical restraints

(115) It is important to recognise that vertical restraints often have positive effects by, in particular, promoting non-price competition and improved quality of services. When a company has no market power, it can only try to increase its profits by optimising its manufacturing or distribution processes. In a number of situations vertical restraints may be helpful in this respect since the usual arm's length dealings between supplier and buyer, determining only price and quantity of a certain transaction, can lead to a sub-optimal level of investments and sales.

(116) While trying to give a fair overview of the various justifications for vertical restraints, these Guidelines do not claim to be complete or exhaustive. The following reasons may justify the application of certain vertical restraints—

(1) To "solve a 'free-rider' problem". One distributor may free-ride on the promotion efforts of another distributor. This type of problem is most common at the wholesale and retail level. Exclusive distribution or similar restrictions may be helpful in avoiding such free-riding. Free-riding can also occur between suppliers, for instance where one invests in promotion at the buyer's premises, in general at the retail level, that may also attract customers for its competitors. Non-compete type restraints can help to overcome this situation of free-riding.

For there to be a problem, there needs to be a real free-rider issue. Free-riding between buyers can only occur on pre-sales services and not on after-sales services. The product will usually need to be relatively new or technically complex as the customer may otherwise very well know what he or she wants, based on past purchases. And the product must be of a reasonably high value as it is otherwise not attractive for a customer to go to one shop for information and to another to buy. Lastly, it must not be practical for the supplier to impose on all buyers, by contract, effective service requirements concerning pre-sales services.

Free-riding between suppliers is also restricted to specific situations, namely in cases where the promotion takes place at the buyer's premises and is generic, not brand specific.

(2) To "open up or enter new markets". Where a manufacturer wants to enter a new geographic market, for instance by exporting to another country for the first time, this may involve special "first time investments" by the distributor to establish the brand in the market. In order to persuade a local distributor to make these investments it may be necessary to provide territorial protection to the distributor so that he can recoup these investments by temporarily charging a higher price. Distributors based in other markets should then be restrained for a limited period from selling in the new market. This is a special case of the free-rider problem described under point (1).

(3) The "certification free-rider issue". In some sectors, certain retailers have a reputation for stocking only "quality" products. In such a case, selling through these retailers may be vital for the introduction of a new product. If the manufacturer cannot initially limit his sales to the premium stores, he runs the risk of being de-listed and the product introduction may fail. This means that there may be a reason for allowing for a limited duration a restriction such as exclusive distribution or selective distribution. It must be enough to guarantee introduction of the new product but not so long as to hinder large-scale dissemination. Such benefits are more likely with "experience" goods or complex goods that represent a relatively large purchase for the final consumer.

(4) The so-called "hold-up problem". Sometimes there are client-specific investments to be made by either the supplier or the buyer, such as in special equipment or training. For instance, a component manufacturer that has to build new machines and tools in order to satisfy a particular requirement of one of his customers. The investor may not commit the necessary investments before particular supply arrangements are fixed.

However, as in the other free-riding examples, there are a number of conditions that have to be met before the risk of under-investment is real or significant. Firstly, the investment must be relationship-specific. An investment made by the supplier is considered to be relationship-specific when, after termination of the contract, it cannot be used by the supplier to supply other customers and can only be sold at a significant loss. An investment made by the buyer is considered to be relationship-specific when, after termination of the contract, it cannot be used by the buyer to purchase and/or use products supplied by other suppliers and can only be sold at a significant loss. An investment is thus relationship-specific because for instance it can only be used to produce a brand-specific component or to store a particular brand and thus cannot be used profitably to produce or resell alternatives. Secondly, it must be a long-term investment that is not recouped in the short run. And thirdly, the investment must be asymmetric; ie one party to the contract invests more than the other party. When these conditions are met, there is usually a good reason to have a vertical restraint for the duration it takes to depreciate the investment. The appropriate vertical restraint will be of the non-compete type or quantity-forcing type when the investment is made by the supplier and of the exclusive distribution, exclusive customer-allocation or exclusive supply type when the investment is made by the buyer.

(5) The "specific hold-up problem that may arise in the case of transfer of substantial know-how". The know-how, once provided, cannot be taken back and the provider of the know-how may not want it to be used for or by his competitors. In as far as the know-how was not readily available to the buyer, is substantial and indispensable for the operation of the agreement, such a transfer may justify a non-compete type of restriction. This would normally fall outside Article 81(1).

PART IV
EC MATERIALS

(6) "Economies of scale in distribution". In order to have scale economies exploited and thereby see a lower retail price for his product, the manufacturer may want to concentrate the resale of his products on a limited number of distributors. For this he could use exclusive distribution, quantity forcing in the form of a minimum purchasing requirement, selective distribution containing such a requirement or exclusive purchasing.

(7) "Capital market imperfections". The usual providers of capital (banks, equity markets) may provide capital sub-optimally when they have imperfect information on the quality of the borrower or there is an inadequate basis to secure the loan. The buyer or supplier may have better information and be able, through an exclusive relationship, to obtain extra security for his investment. Where the supplier provides the loan to the buyer this may lead to non-compete or quantity forcing on the buyer. Where the buyer provides the loan to the supplier this may be the reason for having exclusive supply or quantity forcing on the supplier.

(8) "Uniformity and quality standardisation". A vertical restraint may help to increase sales by creating a brand image and thereby increasing the attractiveness of a product to the final consumer by imposing a certain measure of uniformity and quality standardisation on the distributors. This can for instance be found in selective distribution and franchising.

(117) The eight situations mentioned in paragraph 116 make clear that under certain conditions vertical agreements are likely to help realise efficiencies and the development of new markets and that this may offset possible negative effects. The case is in general strongest for vertical restraints of a limited duration which help the introduction of new complex products or protect relationship-specific investments. A vertical restraint is sometimes necessary for as long as the supplier sells his product to the buyer (see in particular the situations described in paragraph 116, points (1), (5), (6) and (8).

(118) There is a large measure of substitutability between the different vertical restraints. This means that the same inefficiency problem can be solved by different vertical restraints. For instance, economies of scale in distribution may possibly be achieved by using exclusive distribution, selective distribution, quantity forcing or exclusive purchasing. This is important as the negative effects on competition may differ between the various vertical restraints. This plays a role when indispensability is discussed under Article 81(3).

1.3. General rules for the evaluation of vertical restraints

(119) In evaluating vertical restraints from a competition policy perspective, some general rules can be formulated—

(1) For most vertical restraints competition concerns can only arise if there is insufficient inter-brand competition, ie if there exists a certain degree of market power at the level of the supplier or the buyer or both. Conceptually, market power is the power to raise price above the competitive level and, at least in the short term, to obtain supra-normal profits. Companies may have market power below the level of market dominance, which is the threshold for the application of Article 82. Where there are many firms competing in an unconcentrated market, it can be assumed that non-hardcore vertical restraints will not have appreciable negative effects. A market is deemed unconcentrated when the HHI index, ie the sum of the squares of the individual market shares of all companies in the relevant market, is below 1000.

(2) Vertical restraints which reduce inter-brand competition are generally more harmful than vertical restraints that reduce intra-brand competition. For instance, non-compete obligations are likely to have more net negative effects than exclusive distribution. The former, by possibly foreclosing the market to other brands, may prevent those brands from reaching the

market. The latter, while limiting intra-brand competition, does not prevent goods from reaching the final consumer.

(3) Vertical restraints from the limited distribution group, in the absence of sufficient inter-brand competition, may significantly restrict the choices available to consumers. They are particularly harmful when more efficient distributors or distributors with a different distribution format are foreclosed. This can reduce innovation in distribution and denies consumers the particular service or price-service combination of these distributors.

(4) Exclusive dealing arrangements are generally worse for competition than non-exclusive arrangements. Exclusive dealing makes, by the express language of the contract or its practical effects, one party fulfil all or practically all its requirements from another party. For instance, under a non-compete obligation the buyer purchases only one brand. Quantity forcing, on the other hand, leaves the buyer some scope to purchase competing goods. The degree of foreclosure may therefore be less with quantity forcing.

(5) Vertical restraints agreed for non-branded goods and services are in general less harmful than restraints affecting the distribution of branded goods and services. Branding tends to increase product differentiation and reduce substitutability of the product, leading to a reduced elasticity of demand and an increased possibility to raise price. The distinction between branded and non-branded goods or services will often coincide with the distinction between intermediate goods and services and final goods and services.

Intermediate goods and services are sold to undertakings for use as an input to produce other goods or services and are generally not recognisable in the final goods or services. The buyers of intermediate products are usually well-informed customers, able to assess quality and therefore less reliant on brand and image. Final goods are, directly or indirectly, sold to final consumers who often rely more on brand and image. As distributors (retailers, wholesalers) have to respond to the demand of final consumers, competition may suffer more when distributors are foreclosed from selling one or a number of brands than when buyers of intermediate products are prevented from buying competing products from certain sources of supply. The undertakings buying intermediate goods or services normally have specialist departments or advisers who monitor developments in the supply market. Because they effect sizeable transactions, search costs are in general not prohibitive. A loss of intra-brand competition is there-fore less important at the intermediate level.

(6) In general, a combination of vertical restraints aggravates their negative effects. However, certain combinations of vertical restraints are better for competition than their use in isolation from each other. For instance, in an exclusive distribution system, the distributor may be tempted to increase the price of the products as intra-brand competition has been reduced. The use of quantity forcing or the setting of a maximum resale price may limit such price increases.

(7) Possible negative effects of vertical restraints are reinforced when several suppliers and their buyers organise their trade in a similar way. These so-called cumulative effects may be a problem in a number of sectors.

(8) The more the vertical restraint is linked to the transfer of know-how, the more reason there may be to expect efficiencies to arise and the more a vertical restraint may be necessary to protect the know-how transferred or the investment costs incurred.

(9) The more the vertical restraint is linked to investments which are relationship-specific, the more justification there is for certain vertical restraints. The justified duration will depend on the time necessary to depreciate the investment.

(10) In the case of a new product, or where an existing product is sold for the first time on a different geographic market, it may be difficult for the company to define the market or its market share may be very high. However, this should not be considered a major problem, as vertical restraints linked to opening up new product or geographic markets in general do not restrict competition. This rule holds, irrespective of the market share of the company, for two years after the first putting on the market of the product. It applies to all non-hardcore vertical restraints and, in the case of a new geographic market, to restrictions on active and passive sales imposed on the direct buyers of the supplier located in other markets to intermediaries in the new market. In the case of genuine testing of a new product in a limited territory or with a limited customer group, the distributors appointed to sell the new products on the test market can be restricted in their active selling outside the test market for a maximum period of 1 year without being caught by Article 81(1).

1.4. Methodology of analysis

(120) The assessment of a vertical restraint involves in general the following four steps:

(1) First, the undertakings involved need to define the relevant market in order to establish the market share of the supplier or the buyer, depending on the vertical restraint involved (see paragraphs 88 to 99, in particular 89 to 95).

(2) If the relevant market share does not exceed the 30% threshold, the vertical agreement is covered by the Block Exemption Regulation, subject to the hardcore restrictions and conditions set out in that regulation.

(3) If the relevant market share is above the 30% threshold, it is necessary to assess whether the vertical agreement falls within Article 81(1).

(4) If the vertical agreement falls within Article 81(1), it is necessary to examine whether it fulfils the conditions for exemption under Article 81(3).

1.4.1. Relevant factors for the assessment under Article 81(1)

(121) In assessing cases above the market share threshold of 30%, the Commission will make a full competition analysis. The following factors are the most important to establish whether a vertical agreement brings about an appreciable restriction of competition under Article 81(1)—

(a) market position of the supplier;
(b) market position of competitors;
(c) market position of the buyer;
(d) entry barriers;
(e) maturity of the market;
(f) level of trade;
(g) nature of the product;
(h) other factors.

(122) The importance of individual factors may vary from case to case and depends on all other factors. For instance, a high market share of the supplier is usually a good indicator of market power, but in the case of low entry barriers it may not indicate market power. It is therefore not possible to provide strict rules on the importance of the individual factors. However the following can be said:

Market position of the supplier

(123) The market position of the supplier is established first and foremost by his market share on the relevant product and geographic market. The higher his market share, the greater his market power is likely to be. The market position of the supplier is further strengthened if he has certain cost advantages over his competitors. These competitive advantages may result from a first mover advantage

(having the best site, etc), holding essential patents, having superior technology, being the brand leader or having a superior portfolio.

Market position of competitors

(124) The same indicators, that is market share and possible competitive advantages, are used to describe the market position of competitors. The stronger the established competitors are and the greater their number, the less risk there is that the supplier or buyer in question will be able to foreclose the market individually and the less there is a risk of a reduction of inter-brand competition. However, if the number of competitors becomes rather small and their market position (size, costs, R & D potential, etc) is rather similar, this market structure may increase the risk of collusion. Fluctuating or rapidly changing market shares are in general an indication of intense competition.

Market position of the buyer

(125) Buying power derives from the market position of the buyer. The first indicator of buying power is the market share of the buyer on the purchase market. This share reflects the importance of his demand for his possible suppliers. Other indicators focus on the market position of the buyer on his resale market including characteristics such as a wide geographic spread of his outlets, own brands of the buyer/distributor and his image amongst final consumers. The effect of buying power on the likelihood of anti-competitive effects is not the same for the different vertical restraints. Buying power may in particular increase the negative effects in case of restraints from the limited distribution and market partitioning groups such as exclusive supply, exclusive distribution and quantitative selective distribution.

Entry barriers

(126) Entry barriers are measured by the extent to which incumbent companies can increase their price above the competitive level, usually above minimum average total cost, and make supra-normal profits without attracting entry. Without any entry barriers, easy and quick entry would eliminate such profits. In as far as effective entry, which would prevent or erode the supra-normal profits, is likely to occur within one or two years, entry barriers can be said to be low.

(127) Entry barriers may result from a wide variety of factors such as economies of scale and scope, government regulations, especially where they establish exclusive rights, state aid, import tariffs, intellectual property rights, ownership of resources where the supply is limited due to for instance natural limitations,[1] essential facilities, a first mover advantage and brand loyalty of consumers created by strong advertising. Vertical restraints and vertical integration may also work as an entry barrier by making access more difficult and foreclosing (potential) competitors. Entry barriers may be present at only the supplier or buyer level or at both levels.

(128) The question whether certain of these factors should be described as entry barriers depends on whether they are related to sunk costs. Sunk costs are those costs that have to be incurred to enter or be active on a market but that are lost when the market is exited. Advertising costs to build consumer loyalty are normally sunk costs, unless an exiting firm could either sell its brand name or use it somewhere else without a loss. The more costs are sunk, the more potential entrants have to weigh the risks of entering the market and the more credibly incumbents can threaten that they will match new competition, as sunk costs make it costly for incumbents to leave the market. If, for instance, distributors are tied to a manufacturer via a non-compete obligation, the foreclosing effect will be more significant if setting up its own distributors will impose sunk costs on the potential entrant.

(129) In general, entry requires sunk costs, sometimes minor and sometimes major. Therefore, actual competition is in general more effective and will weigh more in the assessment of a case than potential competition.

Maturity of the market

(130) A mature market is a market that has existed for some time, where the technology used is well known and widespread and not changing very much, where there are no major brand innovations and in which demand is relatively stable or declining. In such a market negative effects are more likely than in more dynamic markets.

Level of trade

(131) The level of trade is linked to the distinction between intermediate and final goods and services. As indicated earlier, negative effects are in general less likely at the level of intermediate goods and services.

Nature of the product

(132) The nature of the product plays a role in particular for final products in assessing both the likely negative and the likely positive effects. When assessing the likely negative effects, it is important whether the products on the market are more homogeneous or heterogeneous, whether the product is expensive, taking up a large part of the consumer's budget, or is inexpensive and whether the product is a one-off purchase or repeatedly purchased. In general, when the product is more heterogeneous, less expensive and resembles more a one-off purchase, vertical restraints are more likely to have negative effects.

Other factors

(133) In the assessment of particular restraints other factors may have to be taken into account. Among these factors can be the cumulative effect, ie the coverage of the market by similar agreements, the duration of the agreements, whether the agreement is "imposed" (mainly one party is subject to the restrictions or obligations) or "agreed" (both parties accept restrictions or obligations), the regulatory environment and behaviour that may indicate or facilitate collusion like price leadership, pre-announced price changes and discussions on the "right" price, price rigidity in response to excess capacity, price discrimination and past collusive behaviour.

1.4.2. Relevant factors for the assessment under Article 81(3)

(134) There are four cumulative conditions for the application of Article 81(3)—
— the vertical agreement must contribute to improving production or distribution or to promoting technical or economic progress;
— the vertical agreement must allow consumers a fair share of these benefits;
— the vertical agreement must not impose on the undertakings concerned vertical restraints which are not indispensable to the attainment of these benefits;
— the vertical agreement must not afford such undertakings the possibility of eliminating competition in respect of a substantial part of the products in question.

(135) The last criterion of elimination of competition for a substantial part of the products in question is related to the question of dominance. Where an undertaking is dominant or becoming dominant as a consequence of the vertical agreement, a vertical restraint that has appreciable anti-competitive effects can in principle not be exempted. The vertical agreement may however fall outside Article 81(1) if there is an objective justification, for instance if it is necessary for the protection of

relationship-specific investments or for the transfer of substantial know-how without which the supply or purchase of certain goods or services would not take place.

(136) Where the supplier and the buyer are not dominant, the other three criteria become important. The first, concerning the improvement of production or distribution and the promotion of technical or economic progress, refers to the type of efficiencies described in paragraphs 115 to 118. These efficiencies have to be substantiated and must produce a net positive effect. Speculative claims on avoidance of free-riding or general statements on cost savings will not be accepted. Cost savings that arise from the mere exercise of market power or from anti-competitive conduct cannot be accepted. Secondly, economic benefits have to favour not only the parties to the agreement, but also the consumer. Generally the transmission of the benefits to consumers will depend on the intensity of competition on the relevant market. Competitive pressures will normally ensure that cost-savings are passed on by way of lower prices or that companies have an incentive to bring new products to the market as quickly as possible. Therefore, if sufficient competition which effectively constrains the parties to the agreement is maintained on the market, the competitive process will normally ensure that consumers receive a fair share of the economic benefits. The third criterion will play a role in ensuring that the least anti-competitive restraint is chosen to obtain certain positive effects.

2. Analysis of specific vertical restraints

(137) Vertical agreements may contain a combination of two or more of the components of vertical restraints described in paragraphs 103 to 114. The most common vertical restraints and combinations of vertical restraints are analysed below following the methodology of analysis developed in paragraphs 120 to 136.

2.1. Single branding

(138) A non-compete arrangement is based on an obligation or incentive scheme which makes the buyer purchase practically all his requirements on a particular market from only one supplier. It does not mean that the buyer can only buy directly from the supplier, but that the buyer will not buy and resell or incorporate competing goods or services. The possible competition risks are foreclosure of the market to competing suppliers and potential suppliers, facilitation of collusion between suppliers in case of cumulative use and, where the buyer is a retailer selling to final consumers, a loss of in-store inter-brand competition. All three restrictive effects have a direct impact on inter-brand competition.

(139) Single branding is exempted by the Block Exemption Regulation when the supplier's market share does not exceed 30% and subject to a limitation in time of five years for the non-compete obligation. Above the market share threshold or beyond the time limit of five years, the following guidance is provided for the assessment of individual cases.

(140) The "market position of the supplier" is of main importance to assess possible anti-competitive effects of non-compete obligations. In general, this type of obligation is imposed by the supplier and the supplier has similar agreements with other buyers.

(141) It is not only the market position of the supplier that is of importance but also the extent to and the duration for which he applies a non-compete obligation. The higher his tied market share, ie the part of his market share sold under a single branding obligation, the more significant foreclosure is likely to be. Similarly, the longer the duration of the non-compete obligations, the more significant foreclosure is likely to be. Non-compete obligations shorter than one year entered into by non-dominant companies are in general not considered to give rise to appreciable anti-competitive effects or net negative effects. Non-compete obligations between

one and five years entered into by non-dominant companies usually require a proper balancing of pro- and anti-competitive effects, while non-compete obligations exceeding five years are for most types of investments not considered necessary to achieve the claimed efficiencies or the efficiencies are not sufficient to outweigh their foreclosure effect. Dominant companies may not impose non-compete obligations on their buyers unless they can objectively justify such commercial practice within the context of Article 82.

(142) In assessing the supplier's market power, the "market position of his competitors" is important. As long as the competitors are sufficiently numerous and strong, no appreciable anti-competitive effects can be expected. It is only likely that competing suppliers will be foreclosed if they are significantly smaller than the supplier applying the non-compete obligation. Foreclosure of competitors is not very likely where they have similar market positions and can offer similarly attractive products. In such a case foreclosure may however occur for potential entrants when a number of major suppliers enter into non-compete contracts with a significant number of buyers on the relevant market (cumulative effect situation). This is also a situation where non-compete agreements may facilitate collusion between competing suppliers. If individually these suppliers are covered by the Block Exemption Regulation, a withdrawal of the block exemption may be necessary to deal with such a negative cumulative effect. A tied market share of less than 5% is not considered in general to contribute significantly to a cumulative foreclosure effect.

(143) In cases where the market share of the largest supplier is below 30% and the market share of the five largest suppliers (concentration rate (CR) 5) is below 50%, there is unlikely to be a single or a cumulative anti-competitive effect situation. If a potential entrant cannot penetrate the market profitably, this is likely to be due to factors other than non-compete obligations, such as consumer preferences. A competition problem is unlikely to arise when, for instance, 50 companies, of which none has an important market share, compete fiercely on a particular market.

(144) "Entry barriers" are important to establish whether there is real foreclosure. Wherever it is relatively easy for competing suppliers to create new buyers or find alternative buyers for the product, foreclosure is unlikely to be a real problem. However, there are often entry barriers, both at the manufacturing and at the distribution level.

(145) "Countervailing power" is relevant, as powerful buyers will not easily allow themselves to be cut off from the supply of competing goods or services. Foreclosure which is not based on efficiency and which has harmful effects on ultimate consumers is therefore mainly a risk in the case of dispersed buyers. However, where non-compete agreements are concluded with major buyers this may have a strong foreclosure effect.

(146) Lastly, "the level of trade" is relevant for foreclosure. Foreclosure is less likely in case of an intermediate product. When the supplier of an intermediate product is not dominant, the competing suppliers still have a substantial part of demand that is "free". Below the level of dominance a serious foreclosure effect may however arise for actual or potential competitors where there is a cumulative effect. A serious cumulative effect is unlikely to arise as long as less than 50% of the market is tied. When the supplier is dominant, any obligation to buy the products only or mainly from the dominant supplier may easily lead to significant foreclosure effects on the market. The stronger his dominance, the higher the risk of foreclosure of other competitors.

(147) Where the agreement concerns supply of a final product at the wholesale level, the question whether a competition problem is likely to arise below the level of dominance depends in large part on the type of wholesaling and the entry barriers

at the wholesale level. There is no real risk of foreclosure if competing manufacturers can easily establish their own wholesaling operation. Whether entry barriers are low depends in part on the type of wholesaling, ie whether or not wholesalers can operate efficiently with only the product concerned by the agreement (for example ice cream) or whether it is more efficient to trade in a whole range of products (for example frozen foodstuffs). In the latter case, it is not efficient for a manufacturer selling only one product to set up his own wholesaling operation. In that case anti-competitive effects may arise below the level of dominance. In addition, cumulative effect problems may arise if several suppliers tie most of the available wholesalers.

(148) For final products, foreclosure is in general more likely to occur at the retail level, given the significant entry barriers for most manufacturers to start retail outlets just for their own products. In addition, it is at the retail level that non-compete agreements may lead to reduced in-store inter-brand competition. It is for these reasons that for final products at the retail level, significant anti-competitive effects may start to arise, taking into account all other relevant factors, if a non-dominant supplier ties 30% or more of the relevant market. For a dominant company, even a modest tied market share may already lead to significant anti-competitive effects. The stronger its dominance, the higher the risk of foreclosure of other competitors.

(149) At the retail level a cumulative foreclosure effect may also arise. When all companies have market shares below 30% a cumulative foreclosure effect is unlikely if the total tied market share is less than 40% and withdrawal of the block exemption is therefore unlikely. This figure may be higher when other factors like the number of competitors, entry barriers etc. are taken into account. When not all companies have market shares below the threshold of the Block Exemption Regulation but none is dominant, a cumulative foreclosure effect is unlikely if the total tied market share is below 30%.

(150) Where the buyer operates from premises and land owned by the supplier or leased by the supplier from a third party not connected with the buyer, the possibility of imposing effective remedies for a possible foreclosure effect will be limited. In that case intervention by the Commission below the level of dominance is unlikely.

(151) In certain sectors the selling of more than one brand from a single site may be difficult, in which case a foreclosure problem can better be remedied by limiting the effective duration of contracts.

(152) A so-called "English clause", requiring the buyer to report any better offer and allowing him only to accept such an offer when the supplier does not match it, can be expected to have the same effect as a non-compete obligation, especially when the buyer has to reveal who makes the better offer. In addition, by increasing the transparency of the market it may facilitate collusion between the suppliers. An English clause may also work as quantity-forcing. Quantity-forcing on the buyer is a weaker form of non-compete, where incentives or obligations agreed between the supplier and the buyer make the latter concentrate his purchases to a large extent with one supplier. Quantity-forcing may for example take the form of minimum purchase requirements or non-linear pricing, such as quantity rebate schemes, loyalty rebate schemes or a two-part tariff (fixed fee plus a price per unit). Quantity-forcing on the buyer will have similar but weaker foreclosure effects than a non-compete obligation. The assessment of all these different forms will depend on their effect on the market. In addition, Article 82 specifically prevents dominant companies from applying English clauses or fidelity rebate schemes.

(153) Where appreciable anti-competitive effects are established, the question of a possible exemption under Article 81(3) arises as long as the supplier is not dominant. For non-compete obligations, the efficiencies described in paragraph 116, points 1 (free riding between suppliers), 4, 5 (hold-up problems) and 7 (capital market imperfections) may be particularly relevant.

(154) In the case of an efficiency as described in paragraph 116, points 1, 4 and 7, quantity forcing on the buyer could possibly be a less restrictive alternative. A non-compete obligation may be the only viable way to achieve an efficiency as described in paragraph 116, point 5 (hold-up problem related to the transfer of know-how).

(155) In the case of a relationship-specific investment made by the supplier (see efficiency 4 in paragraph 116), a non-compete or quantity forcing agreement for the period of depreciation of the investment will in general fulfil the conditions of Article 81(3). In the case of high relationship-specific investments, a non-compete obligation exceeding five years may be justified. A relationship-specific investment could, for instance, be the installation or adaptation of equipment by the supplier when this equipment can be used afterwards only to produce components for a particular buyer. General or market-specific investments in (extra) capacity are normally not relationship specific investments. However, where a supplier creates new capacity specifically linked to the operations of a particular buyer, for instance a company producing metal cans which creates new capacity to produce cans on the premises of or next to the canning facility of a food producer, this new capacity may only be economically viable when producing for this particular customer, in which case the investment would be considered to be relationship-specific.

(156) Where the supplier provides the buyer with a loan or provides the buyer with equipment which is not relationship-specific, this in itself is normally not sufficient to justify the exemption of a foreclosure effect on the market. The instances of capital market imperfection, whereby it is more efficient for the supplier of a product than for a bank to provide a loan, will be limited (see efficiency 7 in paragraph 116). Even if the supplier of the product were to be the more efficient provider of capital, a loan could only justify a non-compete obligation if the buyer is not prevented from terminating the non-compete obligation and repaying the outstanding part of the loan at any point in time and without payment of any penalty. This means that the repayment of the loan should be structured in equal or decreasing instalments and should not increase over time and that the buyer should have the possibility to take over the equipment provided by the supplier at its market asset value. This is without prejudice to the possibility, in case for example of a new point of distribution, to delay repayment for the first one or two years until sales have reached a certain level.

(157) The transfer of substantial know-how (efficiency 5 in paragraph 116) usually justifies a non-compete obligation for the whole duration of the supply agreement, as for example in the context of franchising.

(158) Below the level of dominance the combination of non-compete with exclusive distribution may also justify the non-compete obligation lasting the full length of the agreement. In the latter case, the non-compete obligation is likely to improve the distribution efforts of the exclusive distributor in his territory (see paragraphs 161 to 177).

(159) Example of non-compete

The market leader in a national market for an impulse consumer product, with a market share of 40%, sells most of its products (90%) through tied retailers (tied market share 36%). The agreements oblige the retailers to purchase only from the market leader for at least four years. The market leader is especially strongly represented in the more densely populated areas like the capital. Its competitors, 10 in number, of which some are only locally available, all have much smaller market shares, the biggest having 12%. These 10 competitors together supply another 10% of the market via tied outlets. There is strong brand and product differentiation in the market. The market leader has the strongest brands. It is the only one with regular national advertising campaigns. It provides its tied retailers with special stocking cabinets for its product.

The result on the market is that in total 46% (36% + 10%) of the market is foreclosed to potential entrants and to incumbents not having tied outlets. Potential entrants find entry even more difficult in the densely populated areas where foreclosure is even higher, although it is there that they would prefer to enter the market. In addition, owing to the strong brand and product differentiation and the high search costs relative to the price of the product, the absence of in-store inter-brand competition leads to an extra welfare loss for consumers. The possible efficiencies of the outlet exclusivity, which the market leader claims result from reduced transport costs and a possible hold-up problem concerning the stocking cabinets, are limited and do not outweigh the negative effects on competition. The efficiencies are limited, as the transport costs are linked to quantity and not exclusivity and the stocking cabinets do not contain special know-how and are not brand specific. Accordingly, it is unlikely that the conditions for exemption are fulfilled.

(160) Example of quantity forcing

A producer X with a 40% market share sells 80% of its products through contracts which specify that the reseller is required to purchase at least 75% of its requirements for that type of product from X. In return X is offering financing and equipment at favourable rates. The contracts have a duration of five years in which repayment of the loan is foreseen in equal instalments. However, after the first two years buyers have the possibility to terminate the contract with a six-month notice period if they repay the outstanding loan and take over the equipment at its market asset value. At the end of the five-year period the equipment becomes the property of the buyer. Most of the competing producers are small, twelve in total with the biggest having a market share of 20%, and engage in similar contracts with different durations. The producers with market shares below 10% often have contracts with longer durations and with less generous termination clauses. The contracts of producer X leave 25% of requirements free to be supplied by competitors. In the last three years, two new producers have entered the market and gained a combined market share of around 8%, partly by taking over the loans of a number of resellers in return for contracts with these resellers.

Producer X's tied market share is 24% (0,75 x 0,80 x 40%). The other producers' tied market share is around 25%. Therefore, in total around 49% of the market is foreclosed to potential entrants and to incumbents not having tied outlets for at least the first two years of the supply contracts. The market shows that the resellers often have difficulty in obtaining loans from banks and are too small in general to obtain capital through other means like the issuing of shares. In addition, producer X is able to demonstrate that concentrating his sales on a limited number of resellers allows him to plan his sales better and to save transport costs. In the light of the 25% non-tied part in the contracts of producer X, the real possibility for early termination of the contract, the recent entry of new producers and the fact that around half the resellers are not tied, the quantity forcing of 75% applied by producer X is likely to fulfil the conditions for exemption.

2.2. *Exclusive distribution*

(161) In an exclusive distribution agreement the supplier agrees to sell his products only to one distributor for resale in a particular territory. At the same time the distributor is usually limited in his active selling into other exclusively allocated territories. The possible competition risks are mainly reduced intra-brand competition and market partitioning, which may in particular facilitate price discrimination. When most or all of the suppliers apply exclusive distribution this may facilitate collusion, both at the suppliers' and distributors' level.

(162) Exclusive distribution is exempted by the Block Exemption Regulation when the supplier's market share does not exceed 30%, even if combined with other

non-hardcore vertical restraints, such as a non-compete obligation limited to five years, quantity forcing or exclusive purchasing. A combination of exclusive distribution and selective distribution is only exempted by the Block Exemption Regulation if active selling in other territories is not restricted. Above the 30% market share threshold, the following guidance is provided for the assessment of exclusive distribution in individual cases.

(163) The market position of the supplier and his competitors is of major importance, as the loss of intra-brand competition can only be problematic if inter-brand competition is limited. The stronger the "position of the supplier", the more serious is the loss of intra-brand competition. Above the 30% market share threshold there may be a risk of a significant reduction of intra-brand competition. In order to be exemptable, the loss of intra-brand competition needs to be balanced with real efficiencies.

(164) The "position of the competitors" can have a dual significance. Strong competitors will generally mean that the reduction in intra-brand competition is out-weighed by sufficient inter-brand competition. However, if the number of competitors becomes rather small and their market position is rather similar in terms of market share, capacity and distribution network, there is a risk of collusion. The loss of intra-brand competition can increase this risk, especially when several suppliers operate similar distribution systems. Multiple exclusive dealerships, ie when different suppliers appoint the same exclusive distributor in a given territory, may further increase the risk of collusion. If a dealer is granted the exclusive right to distribute two or more important competing products in the same territory, inter-brand competition is likely to be substantially restricted for those brands. The higher the cumulative market share of the brands distributed by the multiple dealer, the higher the risk of collusion and the more inter-brand competition will be reduced. Such cumulative effect situations may be a reason to withdraw the benefit of the Block Exemption Regulation when the market shares of the suppliers are below the threshold of the Block Exemption Regulation.

(165) "Entry barriers" that may hinder suppliers from creating new distributors or finding alternative distributors are less important in assessing the possible anti-competitive effects of exclusive distribution. Foreclosure of other suppliers does not arise as long as exclusive distribution is not combined with single branding.

(166) Foreclosure of other distributors is not a problem if the supplier which operates the exclusive distribution system appoints a high number of exclusive distributors in the same market and these exclusive distributors are not restricted in selling to other non-appointed distributors. Foreclosure of other distributors may however become a problem where there is "buying power" and market power downstream, in particular in the case of very large territories where the exclusive distributor becomes the exclusive buyer for a whole market. An example would be a supermarket chain which becomes the only distributor of a leading brand on a national food retail market. The foreclosure of other distributors may be aggravated in the case of multiple exclusive dealership. Such a case, covered by the Block Exemption Regulation when the market share of each supplier is below 30%, may give reason for the block exemption.

(167) "Buying power" may also increase the risk of collusion on the buyers' side when the exclusive distribution arrangements are imposed by important buyers, possibly located in different territories, on one or several suppliers.

(168) "Maturity of the market" is important, as loss of intra-brand competition and price discrimination may be a serious problem in a mature market but may be less relevant in a market with growing demand, changing technologies and changing market positions.

(169) "The level of trade" is important as the possible negative effects may differ between the wholesale and retail level. Exclusive distribution is mainly applied in the distribution of final goods and services. A loss of intra-brand competition is especially likely at the retail level if coupled with large territories, since final consumers may be confronted with little possibility of choosing between a high price/high service and a low price/low service distributor for an important brand.

(170) A manufacturer which chooses a wholesaler to be his exclusive distributor will normally do so for a larger territory, such as a whole Member State. As long as the wholesaler can sell the products without limitation to downstream retailers there are not likely to be appreciable anti-competitive effects if the manufacturer is not dominant. A possible loss of intra-brand competition at the wholesale level may be easily outweighed by efficiencies obtained in logistics, promotion etc, especially when the manufacturer is based in a different country. Foreclosure of other wholesalers within that territory is not likely as a supplier with a market share above 30% usually has enough bar-gaining power not to choose a less efficient wholesaler. The possible risks for inter-brand competition of multiple exclusive dealerships are however higher at the wholesale than at the retail level.

(171) The combination of exclusive distribution with single branding may add the problem of foreclosure of the market to other suppliers, especially in case of a dense network of exclusive distributors with small territories or in case of a cumulative effect. This may necessitate application of the principles set out above on single branding. However, when the combination does not lead to significant foreclosure, the combination of exclusive distribution and single branding may be pro-competitive by increasing the incentive for the exclusive distributor to focus his efforts on the particular brand. Therefore, in the absence of such a foreclosure effect, the combination of exclusive distribution with non-compete is exemptable for the whole duration of the agreement, particularly at the wholesale level.

(172) The combination of exclusive distribution with exclusive purchasing increases the possible competition risks of reduced intra-brand competition and market partitioning which may in particular facilitate price discrimination. Exclusive distribution already limits arbitrage by customers, as it limits the number of distributors and usually also restricts the distributors in their freedom of active selling. Exclusive purchasing, requiring the exclusive distributors to buy their supplies for the particular brand directly from the manufacturer, eliminates in addition possible arbitrage by the exclusive distributors, who are prevented from buying from other distributors in the system. This enhances the possibilities for the supplier to limit intra-brand competition while applying dissimilar conditions of sale. The combination of exclusive distribution and exclusive purchasing is therefore unlikely to be exempted for suppliers with a market share above 30% unless there are very clear and substantial efficiencies leading to lower prices to all final consumers. Lack of such efficiencies may also lead to withdrawal of the block exemption where the market share of the supplier is below 30%.

(173) The "nature of the product" is not very relevant to assessing the possible anti-competitive effects of exclusive distribution. It is, however, relevant when the issue of possible efficiencies is discussed, that is after an appreciable anti-competitive effect is established.

(174) Exclusive distribution may lead to efficiencies, especially where investments by the distributors are required to protect or build up the brand image. In general, the case for efficiencies is strongest for new products, for complex products, for products whose qualities are difficult to judge before consumption (so-called experience products) or of which the qualities are difficult to judge even after consumption (so

called credence products). In addition, exclusive distribution may lead to savings in logistic costs due to economies of scale in transport and distribution.

(175) Example of exclusive distribution at the wholesale level

In the market for a consumer durable, A is the market leader. A sells its product through exclusive wholesalers. Territories for the wholesalers correspond to the entire Member State for small Member States, and to a region for larger Member States. These exclusive distributors take care of sales to all the retailers in their territories. They do not sell to final consumers. The wholesalers are in charge of promotion in their markets. This includes sponsoring of local events, but also explaining and promoting the new products to the retailers in their territories. Technology and product innovation are evolving fairly quickly on this market, and pre-sale service to retailers and to final consumers plays an important role. The wholesalers are not required to purchase all their requirements of the brand of supplier A from the producer himself, and arbitrage by wholesalers or retailers is practicable because the transport costs are relatively low compared to the value of the product. The wholesalers are not under a non-compete obligation. Retailers also sell a number of brands of competing suppliers, and there are no exclusive or selective distribution agreements at the retail level. On the European market of sales to wholesalers A has around 50% market share. Its market share on the various national retail markets varies between 40% and 60%. A has between 6 and 10 competitors on every national market: B, C and D are its biggest competitors and are also present on each national market, with market shares varying between 20% and 5%. The remaining producers are national producers, with smaller market shares. B, C and D have similar distribution networks, whereas the local producers tend to sell their products directly to retailers.

On the wholesale market described above, the risk of reduced intra-brand competition and price discrimination is low. Arbitrage is not hindered, and the absence of intra-brand competition is not very relevant at the wholesale level. At the retail level neither intra-nor inter-brand competition are hindered. Moreover, inter-brand competition is largely unaffected by the exclusive arrangements at the wholesale level. This makes it likely, if anti-competitive effects exist, that the conditions for exemption are fulfilled.

(176) Example of multiple exclusive dealerships in an oligopolistic market

In a national market for a final product, there are four market leaders, who each have a market share of around 20%. These four market leaders sell their product through exclusive distributors at the retail level. Retailers are given an exclusive territory which corresponds to the town in which they are located or a district of the town for large towns. In most territories, the four market leaders happen to appoint the same exclusive retailer ("multiple dealership"), often centrally located and rather specialised in the product. The remaining 20% of the national market is composed of small local producers, the largest of these producers having a market share of 5% on the national market. These local producers sell their products in general through other retailers, in particular because the exclusive distributors of the four largest suppliers show in general little interest in selling less well-known and cheaper brands. There is strong brand and product differentiation on the market. The four market leaders have large national advertising campaigns and strong brand images, whereas the fringe producers do not advertise their products at the national level. The market is rather mature, with stable demand and no major product and technological innovation. The product is relatively simple.

In such an oligopolistic market, there is a risk of collusion between the four market leaders. This risk is increased through multiple dealerships. Intra-brand competition is limited by the territorial exclusivity. Competition between the four leading brands is reduced at the retail level, since one retailer fixes the price of all four brands in each territory. The multiple dealership implies that, if one producer cuts the price for its brand, the retailer will not be eager to transmit this price cut to the final consumer as it would reduce its sales and profits made with the other brands. Hence, producers have a reduced interest in entering into price competition with one another. Inter-brand price competition exists mainly with the low brand image goods of the fringe producers. The possible efficiency arguments for (joint) exclusive distributors are limited, as the product is relatively simple, the resale does not require any specific investments or training and advertising is mainly carried out at the level of the producers.

Even though each of the market leaders has a market share below the threshold, exemption under Article 81(3) may not be justified and withdrawal of the block exemption may be necessary.

(177) Example of exclusive distribution combined with exclusive purchasing

Manufacturer A is the European market leader for a bulky consumer durable, with a market share of between 40% and 60% in most national retail markets. In every Member State, it has about seven competitors with much smaller market shares, the largest of these competitors having a market share of 10%. These competitors are present on only one or two national markets. A sells its product through its national subsidiaries to exclusive distributors at the retail level, which are not allowed to sell actively into each other's territories. In addition, the retailers are obliged to purchase manufacturer A's products exclusively from the national subsidiary of manufacturer A in their own country. The retailers selling the brand of manufacturer A are the main resellers of that type of product in their territory. They handle competing brands, but with varying degrees of success and enthusiasm. A applies price differences of 10% to 15% between markets and smaller differences within markets. This is translated into smaller price differences at the retail level. The market is relatively stable on the demand and the supply side, and there are no significant technological changes.

In these markets, the loss of intra-brand competition results not only from the territorial exclusivity at the retail level but is aggravated by the exclusive purchasing obligation imposed on the retailers. The exclusive purchase obligation helps to keep markets and territories separate by making arbitrage between the exclusive retailers impossible. The exclusive retailers also cannot sell actively into each other's territory and in practice tend to avoid delivering outside their own territory. This renders price discrimination possible. Arbitrage by consumers or independent traders is limited due to the bulkiness of the product.

The possible efficiency arguments of this system, linked to economies of scale in transport and pro-motion efforts at the retailers' level, are unlikely to outweigh the negative effect of price discrimination and reduced intra-brand competition. Consequently, it is unlikely that the conditions for exemption are fulfilled.

2.3. *Exclusive customer allocation*

(178) In an exclusive customer allocation agreement, the supplier agrees to sell his products only to one distributor for resale to a particular class of customers. At the same time, the distributor is usually limited in his active selling to other exclusively allocated classes of customers. The possible competition risks are mainly reduced intra-brand competition and market partitioning, which may in particular facilitate price discrimination. When most or all of the suppliers apply exclusive customer allocation, this may facilitate collusion, both at the suppliers' and the distributors' level.

(179) Exclusive customer allocation is exempted by the Block Exemption Regulation when the supplier's market share does not exceed the 30% market share threshold, even if combined with other non-hardcore vertical restraints such as

non-compete, quantity-forcing or exclusive purchasing. A combination of exclusive customer allocation and selective distribution is normally hardcore, as active selling to end-users by the appointed distributors is usually not left free. Above the 30% market share threshold, the guidance provided in paragraphs 161 to 177 applies mutatis mutandis to the assessment of exclusive customer allocation, subject to the following specific remarks.

(180) The allocation of customers normally makes arbitrage by the customers more difficult. In addition, as each appointed distributor has his own class of customers, non-appointed distributors not falling within such a class may find it difficult to obtain the product. This will reduce possible arbitrage by non-appointed distributors. Therefore, above the 30% market share threshold of the Block Exemption Regulation exclusive customer allocation is unlikely to be exemptable unless there are clear and substantial efficiency effects.

(181) Exclusive customer allocation is mainly applied to intermediate products and at the wholesale level when it concerns final products, where customer groups with different specific requirements concerning the product can be distinguished.

(182) Exclusive customer allocation may lead to efficiencies, especially when the distributors are required to make investments in for instance specific equipment, skills or know-how to adapt to the requirements of their class of customers. The depreciation period of these investments indicates the justified duration of an exclusive customer allocation system. In general the case is strongest for new or complex products and for products requiring adaptation to the needs of the individual customer. Identifiable differentiated needs are more likely for intermediate products, that is products sold to different types of professional buyers. Allocation of final consumers is unlikely to lead to any efficiencies and is therefore unlikely to be exempted.

(183) Example of exclusive customer allocation

A company has developed a sophisticated sprinkler installation. The company has currently a market share of 40% on the market for sprinkler installations. When it started selling the sophisticated sprinkler it had a market share of 20% with an older product. The installation of the new type of sprinkler depends on the type of building that it is installed in and on the use of the building (office, chemical plant, hospital etc). The company has appointed a number of distributors to sell and install the sprinkler installation. Each distributor needed to train its employees for the general and specific requirements of installing the sprinkler installation for a particular class of customers. To ensure that distributors would specialise the company assigned to each distributor an exclusive class of customers and prohibited active sales to each others' exclusive customer classes. After five years, all the exclusive distributors will be allowed to sell actively to all classes of customers, thereby ending the system of exclusive customer allocation. The supplier may then also start selling to new distributors. The market is quite dynamic, with two recent entries and a number of technological developments. Competitors, with market shares between 25% and 5%, are also upgrading their products.

As the exclusivity is of limited duration and helps to ensure that the distributors may recoup their investments and concentrate their sales efforts first on a certain class of customers in order to learn the trade, and as the possible anti-competitive effects seem limited in a dynamic market, the conditions for exemption are likely to be fulfilled.

2.4. Selective distribution

(184) Selective distribution agreements, like exclusive distribution agreements, restrict on the one hand the number of authorised distributors and on the other the possibilities of resale. The difference with exclusive distribution is that the

restriction of the number of dealers does not depend on the number of territories but on selection criteria linked in the first place to the nature of the product. Another difference with exclusive distribution is that the restriction on resale is not a restriction on active selling to a territory but a restriction on any sales to non-authorised distributors, leaving only appointed dealers and final customers as possible buyers. Selective distribution is almost always used to distribute branded final products.

(185) The possible competition risks are a reduction in intra-brand competition and, especially in case of cumulative effect, foreclosure of certain type(s) of distributors and facilitation of collusion between suppliers or buyers. To assess the possible anti-competitive effects of selective distribution under Article 81(1), a distinction needs to be made between purely qualitative selective distribution and quantitative selective distribution. Purely qualitative selective distribution selects dealers only on the basis of objective criteria required by the nature of the product such as training of sales personnel, the service provided at the point of sale, a certain range of the products being sold etc.[2] The application of such criteria does not put a direct limit on the number of dealers. Purely qualitative selective distribution is in general considered to fall outside Article 81(1) for lack of anti-competitive effects, provided that three conditions are satisfied. First, the nature of the product in question must necessitate a selective distribution system, in the sense that such a system must constitute a legitimate requirement, having regard to the nature of the product concerned, to preserve its quality and ensure its proper use. Secondly, resellers must be chosen on the basis of objective criteria of a qualitative nature which are laid down uniformly for all potential resellers and are not applied in a discriminatory manner. Thirdly, the criteria laid down must not go beyond what is necessary.[3] Quantitative selective distribution adds further criteria for selection that more directly limit the potential number of dealers by, for instance, requiring minimum or maximum sales, by fixing the number of dealers, etc.

(186) Qualitative and quantitative selective distribution is exempted by the Block Exemption Regulation up to 30% market share, even if combined with other non-hardcore vertical restraints, such as non-compete or exclusive distribution, provided active selling by the authorised distributors to each other and to end users is not restricted. The Block Exemption Regulation exempts selective distribution regardless of the nature of the product concerned. However, where the nature of the product does not require selective distribution, such a distribution system does not generally bring about sufficient efficiency enhancing effects to counterbalance a significant reduction in intra-brand competition. If appreciable anti-competitive effects occur, the benefit of the Block Exemption Regulation is likely to be withdrawn. In addition, the following guidance is provided for the assessment of selective distribution in individual cases which are not covered by the Block Exemption Regulation or in the case of cumulative effects resulting from parallel networks of selective distribution.

(187) The market position of the supplier and his competitors is of central importance in assessing possible anti-competitive effects, as the loss of intra-brand competition can only be problematic if inter-brand competition is limited. The stronger the position of the supplier, the more problematic is the loss of intra-brand competition. Another important factor is the number of selective distribution networks present in the same market. Where selective distribution is applied by only one supplier in the market which is not a dominant undertaking, quantitative selective distribution does not normally create net negative effects provided that the contract goods, having regard to their nature, require the use of a selective distribution system and on condition that the selection criteria applied are necessary to ensure efficient distribution of the goods in question. The reality, however, seems to be that selective distribution is often applied by a number of the suppliers in a given market.

(188) The position of competitors can have a dual significance and plays in particular a role in case of a cumulative effect. Strong competitors will mean in general that the reduction in intra-brand competition is easily outweighed by sufficient inter-brand competition. However, when a majority of the main suppliers apply selective distribution there will be a significant loss of intra-brand competition and possible foreclosure of certain types of distributors as well as an increased risk of collusion between those major suppliers. The risk of foreclosure of more efficient distributors has always been greater with selective distribution than with exclusive distribution, given the restriction on sales to non-authorised dealers in selective distribution. This is designed to give selective distribution systems a closed character, making it impossible for non-authorised dealers to obtain supplies. This makes selective distribution particularly well suited to avoid pressure by price discounters on the margins of the manufacturer, as well as on the margins of the authorised dealers.

(189) Where the Block Exemption Regulation applies to individual networks of selective distribution, withdrawal of the block exemption or disapplication of the Block Exemption Regulation may be considered in case of cumulative effects. However, a cumulative effect problem is unlikely to arise when the share of the market covered by selective distribution is below 50%. Also, no problem is likely to arise where the market coverage ratio exceeds 50%, but the aggregate market share of the five largest suppliers (CR5) is below 50%. Where both the CR5 and the share of the market covered by selective distribution exceed 50%, the assessment may vary depending on whether or not all five largest suppliers apply selective distribution. The stronger the position of the competitors not applying selective distribution, the less likely the foreclosure of other distributors. If all five largest suppliers apply selective distribution, competition concerns may in particular arise with respect to those agreements that apply quantitative selection criteria by directly limiting the number of authorised dealers. The conditions of Article 81(3) are in general unlikely to be fulfilled if the selective distribution systems at issue prevent access to the market by new distributors capable of adequately selling the products in question, especially price discounters, thereby limiting distribution to the advantage of certain existing channels and to the detriment of final consumers. More indirect forms of quantitative selective distribution, resulting for instance from the combination of purely qualitative selection criteria with the requirement imposed on the dealers to achieve a minimum amount of annual purchases, are less likely to produce net negative effects, if such an amount does not represent a significant proportion of the dealer's total turnover achieved with the type of products in question and it does not go beyond what is necessary for the supplier to recoup his relationship-specific investment and/or realise economies of scale in distribution. As regards individual contributions, a supplier with a market share of less than 5% is in general not considered to contribute significantly to a cumulative effect.

(190) "Entry barriers" are mainly of interest in the case of foreclosure of the market to non-authorised dealers. In general entry barriers will be considerable as selective distribution is usually applied by manufacturers of branded products. It will in general take time and considerable investment for excluded retailers to launch their own brands or obtain competitive supplies elsewhere.

(191) "Buying power" may increase the risk of collusion between dealers and thus appreciably change the analysis of possible anti-competitive effects of selective distribution. Foreclosure of the market to more efficient retailers may especially result where a strong dealer organisation imposes selection criteria on the supplier aimed at limiting distribution to the advantage of its members.

(192) Article 5(c) of the Block Exemption Regulation provides that the supplier may not impose an obligation causing the authorised dealers, either directly or indirectly, not to sell the brands of particular competing suppliers. This condition

aims specifically at avoiding horizontal collusion to exclude particular brands through the creation of a selective club of brands by the leading suppliers. This kind of obligation is unlikely to be exemptable when the CR5 is equal to or above 50%, unless none of the suppliers imposing such an obligation belongs to the five largest suppliers in the markets.

(193) Foreclosure of other suppliers is normally not a problem as long as other suppliers can use the same distributors, ie as long as the selective distribution system is not combined with single branding. In the case of a dense network of authorised distributors or in the case of a cumulative effect, the combination of selective distribution and a non-compete obligation may pose a risk of foreclosure to other suppliers. In that case the principles set out above on single branding apply. Where selective distribution is not combined with a non-compete obligation, foreclosure of the market to competing suppliers may still be a problem when the leading suppliers apply not only purely qualitative selection criteria, but impose on their dealers certain additional obligations such as the obligation to reserve a minimum shelf-space for their products or to ensure that the sales of their products by the dealer achieve a minimum percentage of the dealer's total turnover. Such a problem is unlikely to arise if the share of the market covered by selective distribution is below 50% or, where this coverage ratio is exceeded, if the market share of the five largest suppliers is below 50%.

(194) Maturity of the market is important, as loss of intra-brand competition and possible foreclosure of suppliers or dealers may be a serious problem in a mature market but is less relevant in a market with growing demand, changing technologies and changing market positions.

(195) Selective distribution may be efficient when it leads to savings in logistical costs due to economies of scale in transport and this may happen irrespective of the nature of the product (efficiency 6 in paragraph 116). However, this is usually only a marginal efficiency in selective distribution systems. To help solve a free-rider problem between the distributors (efficiency 1 in paragraph 116) or to help create a brand image (efficiency 8 in paragraph 116), the nature of the product is very relevant. In general the case is strongest for new products, for complex products, for products of which the qualities are difficult to judge before consumption (so-called experience products) or of which the qualities are difficult to judge even after consumption (so-called credence products). The combination of selective and exclusive distribution is likely to infringe Article 81 if it is applied by a supplier whose market share exceeds 30% or in case of cumulative effects, even though active sales between the territories remain free. Such a combination may exceptionally fulfil the conditions of Article 81(3) if it is indispensable to protect substantial and relationship-specific investments made by the authorised dealers (efficiency 4 in paragraph 116).

(196) To ensure that the least anti-competitive restraint is chosen, it is relevant to see whether the same efficiencies can be obtained at a comparable cost by for instance service requirements alone.

(197) Example of quantitative selective distribution:

In a market for consumer durables, the market leader (brand A), with a market share of 35%, sells its product to final consumers through a selective distribution network. There are several criteria for admission to the network: the shop must employ trained staff and provide pre-sales services, there must be a specialised area in the shop devoted to the sales of the product and similar hi-tech products, and the shop is required to sell a wide range of models of the supplier and to display them in an attractive manner. Moreover, the number of admissible retailers in the network is directly limited through the establishment of a maximum number of retailers per number of inhabitants in each province or urban area. Manufacturer A has

6 competitors in this market. Its largest competitors, B, C and D, have market shares of respectively 25, 15 and 10%, whilst the other producers have smaller market shares. A is the only manufacturer to use selective distribution. The selective distributors of brand A always handle a few competing brands. However, competing brands are also widely sold in shops which are not members of A's selective distribution network. Channels of distribution are various: for instance, brands B and C are sold in most of A's selected shops, but also in other shops providing a high quality service and in hypermarkets. Brand D is mainly sold in high service shops. Technology is evolving quite rapidly in this market, and the main suppliers maintain a strong quality image for their products through advertising.

In this market, the coverage ratio of selective distribution is 35%. Inter-brand competition is not directly affected by the selective distribution system of A. Intra-brand competition for brand A may be reduced, but consumers have access to low service/low price retailers for brands B and C, which have a comparable quality image to brand A. Moreover, access to high service retailers for other brands is not foreclosed, since there is no limitation on the capacity of selected distributors to sell competing brands, and the quantative limitation on the number of retailers for brand A leaves other high service retailers free to distribute competing brands, In this case, in view of the service requirements and the efficiencies these are likely to provide and the limited effect on intra-brand competition the conditions for exempting A's selective distribution network are likely to be fulfilled.

(198) Example of selective distribution with cumulative effects:

On a market for a particular sports article, there are seven manufacturers, whose respective market shares are: 25%, 20%, 15%, 15%, 10%, 8% and 7%. The five largest manufacturers distribute their products through quantitative selective distribution, whilst the two smallest use different types of distribution systems, which results in a coverage ratio of selective distribution of 85%. The criteria for access to the selective distribution networks are remarkably uniform amongst manufacturers: shops are required to have trained personnel and to provide pre-sale services, there must be a specialised area in the shop devoted to the sales of the article and a minimum size for this area is specified. The shop is required to sell a wide range of the brand in question and to display the article in an attractive manner, the shop must be located in a commercial street, and this type of article must represent at least 30% of the total turnover of the shop. In general, the same dealer is appointed selective distributor for all five brands. The two brands which do not use selective distribution usually sell through less specialised retailers with lower service levels. The market is stable, both on the supply and on the demand side, and there is strong brand image and product differentiation. The five market leaders have strong brand images, acquired through advertising and sponsoring, whereas the two smaller manufacturers have a strategy of cheaper products, with no strong brand image.

In this market, access by general price discounters to the five leading brands is denied. Indeed, the requirement that this type of article represents at least 30% of the activity of the dealers and the criteria on presentation and pre-sales services rule out most price discounters from the network of authorised dealers. As a consequence, consumers have no choice but to buy the five leading brands in high service/high price shops. This leads to reduced inter-brand competition between the five leading brands. The fact that the two smallest brands can be bought in low service/low price shops does not compensate for this, because the brand image of the five market leaders is much better. Inter-brand competition is also limited through multiple dealership. Even though there exists some degree of intra-brand competition and the number of retailers is not directly limited, the criteria for admission are strict enough to lead to a small number of retailers for the five leading brands in each territory.

The efficiencies associated with these quantitative selective distribution systems are low: the product is not very complex and does not justify a particularly high service. Unless the manufacturers can prove that there are clear efficiencies linked to their network of selective distribution, it is probable that the block exemption will have to be withdrawn because of its cumulative effects resulting in less choice and higher prices for consumers.

2.5. Franchising

(199) Franchise agreements contain licences of intellectual property rights relating in particular to trade marks or signs and know-how for the use and distribution of goods or services. In addition to the licence of IPRs, the franchisor usually provides the franchisee during the life of the agreement with commercial or technical assistance. The licence and the assistance are integral components of the business method being franchised. The franchisor is in general paid a franchise fee by the franchisee for the use of the particular business method. Franchising may enable the franchisor to establish, with limited investments, a uniform network for the distribution of his products. In addition to the provision of the business method, franchise agreements usually contain a combination of different vertical restraints concerning the products being distributed, in particular selective distribution and/or non-compete and/or exclusive distribution or weaker forms thereof.

(200) The coverage by the Block Exemption Regulation of the licensing of IPRs contained in franchise agreements is dealt with in paragraphs 23 to 45. As for the vertical restraints on the purchase, sale and resale of goods and services within a franchising arrangement, such as selective distribution, non-compete or exclusive distribution, the Block Exemption Regulation applies up to the 30% market share threshold for the franchisor or the supplier designated by the franchisor.[4] The guidance provided earlier in respect of these types of restraints applies also to franchising, subject to the following specific remarks—

  (1) In line with general rule 8 (see paragraph 119), the more important the transfer of know-how, the more easily the vertical restraints fulfil the conditions for exemption.

  (2) A non-compete obligation on the goods or services purchased by the franchisee falls outside Article 81(1) when the obligation is necessary to maintain the common identity and reputation of the franchised network. In such cases, the duration of the non-compete obligation is also irrelevant under Article 81(1), as long as it does not exceed the duration of the franchise agreement itself.

(201) Example of franchising:

A manufacturer has developed a new format for selling sweets in so-called fun shops where the sweets can be coloured specially on demand from the consumer. The manufacturer of the sweets has also developed the machines to colour the sweets. The manufacturer also produces the colouring liquids. The quality and freshness of the liquid is of vital importance to producing good sweets. The manufacturer made a success of its sweets through a number of own retail outlets all operating under the same trade name and with the uniform fun image (style of lay-out of the shops, common advertising etc). In order to expand sales the manufacturer started a franchising system. The franchisees are obliged to buy the sweets, liquid and colouring machine from the manufacturer, to have the same image and operate under the trade name, pay a franchise fee, contribute to common advertising and ensure the confidentiality of the operating manual prepared by the franchisor. In addition, the franchisees are only allowed to sell from the agreed premises, are only allowed to sell to end users or other franchisees and are not allowed to sell other sweets. The franchisor is obliged not to appoint another franchisee nor operate a retail outlet himself in a given contract territory. The franchisor is also under the obligation to update and further develop its products, the business outlook and the operating manual and make these improvements available to all retail franchisees. The franchise agreements are concluded for a duration of 10 years.

Sweet retailers buy their sweets on a national market from either national producers that cater for national tastes or from wholesalers which import sweets from foreign producers in addition to selling products from national producers. On this market the franchisor's products compete with other brands of sweets. The franchisor has a market share of 30% on the market for sweets sold to retailers. Competition comes from a number of national and international brands, sometimes produced by large diversified food companies. There are many potential points of sale of sweets in the form of tobacconists, general food retailers, cafeterias and specialised sweet shops. On the market for machines for colouring food the franchisor's market share is below 10%.

Most of the obligations contained in the franchise agreements can be assessed as being necessary to protect the intellectual property rights or maintain the common identity and reputation of the franchised network and fall outside Article 81(1). The restrictions on selling (contract territory and selective distribution) provide an incentive to the franchisees to invest in the colouring machine and the franchise concept and, if not necessary for, at least help to maintain the common identity, thereby offsetting the loss of intra-brand competition. The non-compete clause excluding other brands of sweets from the shops for the full duration of the agreements does allow the franchisor to keep the outlets uniform and prevent competitors from benefiting from its trade name. It does not lead to any serious foreclosure in view of the great number of potential outlets available to other sweet producers. The franchise agreements of this franchisor are likely to fulfil the conditions for exemption under Article 81(3) in as far as the obligations contained therein fall under Article 81(1).

2.6. Exclusive supply

(202) Exclusive supply as defined in Article 1(c) of the Block Exemption Regulation is the extreme form of limited distribution in as far as the limit on the number of buyers is concerned: in the agreement it is specified that there is only one buyer inside the Community to which the supplier may sell a particular final product. For intermediate goods or services, exclusive supply means that there is only one buyer inside the Community or that there is only one buyer inside the Community for the purposes of a specific use. For intermediate goods or services, exclusive supply is often referred to as industrial supply.

(203) Exclusive supply as defined in Article 1(c) of the Block Exemption Regulation is exempted by Article 2(1) read in conjunction with Article 3(2) of the Block Exemption Regulation up to 30% market share of the buyer, even if combined with other non-hardcore vertical restraints such as non-compete. Above the market share threshold the following guidance is provided for the assessment of exclusive supply in individual cases.

(204) The main competition risk of exclusive supply is foreclosure of other buyers. The market share of the buyer on the upstream purchase market is obviously important for assessing the ability of the buyer to "impose" exclusive supply which forecloses other buyers from access to supplies. The importance of the buyer on the downstream market is however the factor which determines whether a competition problem may arise. If the buyer has no market power downstream, then no appreciable negative effects for consumers can be expected. Negative effects can however be expected when the market share of the buyer on the downstream supply market as well as the upstream purchase market exceeds 30%. Where the market share of the buyer on the upstream market does not exceed 30%, significant foreclosure effects may still result, especially when the market share of the buyer on

his downstream market exceeds 30%. In such cases withdrawal of the block exemption may be required. Where a company is dominant on the downstream market, any obligation to supply the products only or mainly to the dominant buyer may easily have significant anti-competitive effects.

(205) It is not only the market position of the buyer on the upstream and downstream market that is important but also the extent to and the duration for which he applies an exclusive supply obligation. The higher the tied supply share, and the longer the duration of the exclusive supply, the more significant the foreclosure is likely to be. Exclusive supply agreements shorter than five years entered into by non-dominant companies usually require a balancing of pro- and anti-competitive effects, while agreements lasting longer than five years are for most types of investments not considered necessary to achieve the claimed efficiencies or the efficiencies are not sufficient to outweigh the foreclosure effect of such long-term exclusive supply agreements.

(206) The market position of the competing buyers on the upstream market is important as it is only likely that competing buyers will be foreclosed for anti-competitive reasons, ie to increase their costs, if they are significantly smaller than the foreclosing buyer.

Foreclosure of competing buyers is not very likely where these competitors have similar buying power and can offer the suppliers similar sales possibilities. In such a case, foreclosure could only occur for potential entrants, who may not be able to secure supplies when a number of major buyers all enter into exclusive supply contracts with the majority of suppliers on the market. Such a cumulative effect may lead to withdrawal of the benefit of the Block Exemption Regulation.

(207) Entry barriers at the supplier level are relevant to establishing whether there is real foreclosure. In as far as it is efficient for competing buyers to provide the goods or services themselves via upstream vertical integration, foreclosure is unlikely to be a real problem. However, often there are significant entry barriers.

(208) Countervailing power of suppliers is relevant, as important suppliers will not easily allow themselves to be cut off from alternative buyers. Foreclosure is therefore mainly a risk in the case of weak suppliers and strong buyers. In the case of strong suppliers the exclusive supply may be found in combination with non-compete. The combination with non-compete brings in the rules developed for single branding. Where there are relationship-specific investments involved on both sides (hold-up problem) the combination of exclusive supply and non-compete ie reciprocal exclusivity in industrial supply agreements is usually justified below the level of dominance.

(209) Lastly, the level of trade and the nature of the product are relevant for foreclosure. Foreclosure is less likely in the case of an intermediate product or where the product is homogeneous. Firstly, a foreclosed manufacturer that uses a certain input usually has more flexibility to respond to the demand of his customers than the wholesaler/retailer has in responding to the demand of the final consumer for whom brands may play an important role. Secondly, the loss of a possible source of supply matters less for the foreclosed buyers in the case of homogeneous products than in the case of a heterogeneous product with different grades and qualities.

(210) For homogeneous intermediate products, anti-competitive effects are likely to be exemptable below the level of dominance. For final branded products or differentiated intermediate products where there are entry barriers, exclusive supply may have appreciable anti-competitive effects where the competing buyers are relatively small compared to the foreclosing buyer, even if the latter is not dominant on the downstream market.

(211) Where appreciable anti-competitive effects are established, an exemption under Article 81(3) is possible as long as the company is not dominant. Efficiencies can be expected in the case of a hold-up problem (paragraph 116, points 4 and 5), and this is more likely for intermediate products than for final products. Other efficiencies are less likely. Possible economies of scale in distribution (paragraph 116, point 6) do not seem to justify exclusive supply.

(212) In the case of a hold-up problem and even more so in the case of scale economies in distribution, quantity forcing on the supplier, such as minimum supply requirements, could well be a less restrictive alternative.

(213) Example of exclusive supply:

On a market for a certain type of components (intermediate product market) supplier A agrees with buyer B to develop, with his own know-how and considerable investment in new machines and with the help of specifications supplied by buyer B, a different version of the component. B will have to make considerable investments to incorporate the new component. It is agreed that A will supply the new product only to buyer B for a period of five years from the date of first entry on the market. B is obliged to buy the new product only from A for the same period of five years. Both A and B can continue to sell and buy respectively other versions of the component elsewhere. The market share of buyer B on the upstream component market and on the downstream final goods market is 40%. The market share of the component supplier is 35%. There are two other component suppliers with around 20–25% market share and a number of small suppliers.

Given the considerable investments, the agreement is likely to fulfil the conditions for exemption in view of the efficiencies and the limited foreclosure effect. Other buyers are foreclosed from a particular version of a product of a supplier with 35% market share and there are other component suppliers that could develop similar new products. The foreclosure of part of buyer B's demand to other suppliers is limited to maximum 40% of the market.

(214) Exclusive supply is based on a direct or indirect obligation causing the supplier only to sell to one buyer. Quantity forcing on the supplier is based on incentives agreed between the supplier and the buyer that make the former concentrate his sales mainly with one buyer. Quantity forcing on the supplier may have similar but more mitigated effects than exclusive supply. The assessment of quantity forcing will depend on the degree of foreclosure of other buyers on the upstream market.

2.7. Tying

(215) Tying exists when the supplier makes the sale of one product conditional upon the purchase of another distinct product from the supplier or someone designated by the latter. The first product is referred to as the tying product and the second is referred to as the tied product. If the tying is not objectively justified by the nature of the products or commercial usage, such practice may constitute an abuse within the meaning of Article 82.[5] Article 81 may apply to horizontal agreements or concerted practices between competing suppliers which make the sale of one product conditional upon the purchase of another distinct product. Tying may also constitute a vertical restraint falling under Article 81 where it results in a single branding type of obligation (see paragraphs 138 to 160) for the tied product. Only the latter situation is dealt with in these Guidelines.

(216) What is to be considered as a distinct product is determined first of all by the demand of the buyers. Two products are distinct if, in the absence of tying, from the buyers' perspective, the products are purchased by them on two different markets. For instance, since customers want to buy shoes with laces, it has become commercial usage for shoe manufacturers to supply shoes with laces. Therefore, the

sale of shoes with laces is not a tying practice. Often combinations have become accepted practice because the nature of the product makes it technically difficult to supply one product without the supply of another product.

(217) The main negative effect of tying on competition is possible foreclosure on the market of the tied product. Tying means that there is at least a form of quantity-forcing on the buyer in respect of the tied product. Where in addition a non-compete obligation is agreed in respect of the tied product, this increases the possible foreclosure effect on the market of the tied product. Tying may also lead to supra-competitive prices, especially in three situations. Firstly, when the tying and tied product are partly substitutable for the buyer. Secondly, when the tying allows price discrimination according to the use the customer makes of the tying product, for example the tying of ink cartridges to the sale of photocopying machines (metering). Thirdly, when in the case of long-term contracts or in the case of after-markets with original equipment with a long replacement time, it becomes difficult for the customers to calculate the consequences of the tying. Lastly, tying may also lead to higher entry barriers both on the market of the tying and on the market of the tied product.

(218) Tying is exempted by Article 2(1) read in conjunction with Article 3 of the Block Exemption Regulation when the market share of the supplier on both the market of the tied product and the market of the tying product does not exceed 30%. It may be combined with other non-hardcore vertical restraints such as non-compete or quantity forcing in respect of the tying product, or exclusive purchasing. Above the market share threshold the following guidance is provided for the assessment of tying in individual cases.

(219) The market position of the supplier on the market of the tying product is obviously of main importance to assess possible anti-competitive effects. In general this type of agreement is imposed by the supplier. The importance of the supplier on the market of the tying product is the main reason why a buyer may find it difficult to refuse a tying obligation.

(220) To assess the supplier's market power, the market position of his competitors on the market of the tying product is important. As long as his competitors are sufficiently numerous and strong, no anti-competitive effects can be expected, as buyers have sufficient alternatives to purchase the tying product without the tied product, unless other suppliers are applying similar tying. In addition, entry barriers on the market of the tying product are relevant to establish the market position of the supplier. When tying is combined with a non-compete obligation in respect of the tying product, this considerably strengthens the position of the supplier.

(221) Buying power is relevant, as important buyers will not easily be forced to accept tying without obtaining at least part of the possible efficiencies. Tying not based on efficiency is therefore mainly a risk where buyers do not have significant buying power.

(222) Where appreciable anti-competitive effects are established, the question of a possible exemption under Article 81(3) arises as long as the company is not dominant. Tying obligations may help to produce efficiencies arising from joint production or joint distribution. Where the tied product is not produced by the supplier, an efficiency may also arise from the supplier buying large quantities of the tied product. For tying to be exemptable, it must, however, be shown that at least part of these cost reductions are passed on to the consumer. Tying is therefore normally not exemptable when the retailer is able to obtain, on a regular basis, supplies of the same or equivalent products on the same or better conditions than those offered by the supplier which applies the tying practice. Another efficiency may exist where tying helps to ensure a certain uniformity and quality

standardisation (see efficiency 8 in paragraph 116). However, it needs to be demonstrated that the positive effects cannot be realised equally efficiently by requiring the buyer to use or resell products satisfying minimum quality standards, without requiring the buyer to purchase these from the supplier or someone designated by the latter. The requirements concerning minimum quality standards would not normally fall within Article 81(1). Where the supplier of the tying product imposes on the buyer the suppliers from which the buyer must purchase the tied product, for instance because the formulation of minimum quality standards is not possible, this may also fall outside Article 81(1), especially where the supplier of the tying product does not derive a direct (financial) benefit from designating the suppliers of the tied product.

(223) The effect of supra-competitive prices is considered anti-competitive in itself. The effect of foreclosure depends on the tied percentage of total sales on the market of the tied product. On the question of what can be considered appreciable foreclosure under Article 81(1), the analysis for single branding can be applied. Above the 30% market share threshold exemption of tying is unlikely, unless there are clear efficiencies that are transmitted, at least in part, to consumers. Exemption is even less likely when tying is combined with non-compete, either in respect of the tied or in respect of the tying product.

(224) Withdrawal of the block exemption is likely where no efficiencies result from tying or where such efficiencies are not passed on to the consumer (see paragraph 222). Withdrawal is also likely in the case of a cumulative effect where a majority of the suppliers apply similar tying arrangements without the possible efficiencies being transmitted at least in part to consumers.

2.8 Recommended and maximum resale prices

(225) The practice of recommending a resale price to a reseller or requiring the reseller to respect a maximum resale price is—subject to the comments in paragraphs 46 to 56 concerning RPM—covered by the Block Exemption Regulation when the market share of the supplier does not exceed the 30% threshold. For cases above the market share threshold and for cases of withdrawal of the block exemption the following guidance is provided.

(226) The possible competition risk of maximum and recommended prices is firstly that the maximum or recommended price will work as a focal point for the resellers and might be followed by most or all of them. A second competition risk is that maximum or recommended prices may facilitate collusion between suppliers.

(227) The most important factor for assessing possible anti-competitive effects of maximum or recommended resale prices is the market position of the supplier. The stronger the market position of the supplier, the higher the risk that a maximum resale price or a recommended resale price leads to a more or less uniform application of that price level by the resellers, because they may use it as a focal point. They may find it difficult to deviate from what they perceive to be the preferred resale price proposed by such an important supplier on the market. Under such circumstances the practice of imposing a maximum resale price or recommending a resale price may infringe Article 81(1) if it leads to a uniform price level.

(228) The second most important factor for assessing possible anti-competitive effects of the practice of maximum and recommended prices is the market position of competitors. Especially in a narrow oligopoly, the practice of using or publishing maximum or recommended prices may facilitate collusion between the suppliers by exchanging information on the preferred price level and by reducing

the likelihood of lower resale prices. The practice of imposing a maximum resale price or recommending resale prices leading to such effects may also infringe Article 81(1).

2.9. Other vertical restraints

(229) The vertical restraints and combinations described above are only a selection. There are other restraints and combinations for which no direct guidance is provided here. They will however be treated according to the same principles, with the help of the same general rules and with the same emphasis on the effect on the market.

[5137]

NOTES

1 See Commission Decision 97/26/EC (Case No IV/M.619—Gencor/Lonrho), (OJ L11, 14.1.97, p 30).
2 See for example judgment of the Court of First Instance in Case T-88/92 Groupement d'achat Édouard Leclerc v Commission [1996] ECR II-1961.
3 See judgments of the Court of Justice in Case 31/80 L'Oréal v PVBA [1980] ECR 3775, paragraphs 15 and 16; Case 26/76 Metro I [1977] ECR 1875, paragraphs 20 and 21; Case 107/82 AEG [1983] ECR 3151, paragraph 35; and of the Court of First Instance in Case T-19/91 Vichy v Commission [1992] ECR II-415, paragraph 65.
4 See also paragraphs AEG [1983] ECR 3151, paragraph 35; and of the Court of First Instance in Case T-19/91 Vichy v Commission [1992] ECR II-415, paragraph 65. See also paragraphs 89 to 95, in particular paragraph 95.
5 Judgment of the Court of Justice in Case C-333/94 P Tetrapak v Commission [1996] ECR 1-5951, paragraph 37.

COMMISSION REGULATION

of 31 July 2002

on the application of Article 81(3) of the Treaty to categories of vertical agreements and concerted practices in the motor vehicle sector

(1400/2002/EC)

NOTES

Date of publication in OJ: OJ L203, 1.8.02, p 30.

THE COMMISSION OF THE EUROPEAN COMMUNITIES,

Having regard to the Treaty establishing the European Community,
Having regard to Council Regulation No 19/65/EEC of 2 March 1965 on the application of Article 85(3) of the Treaty to certain categories of agreements and concerted practices,[1] as last amended by Regulation (EC) No 1215/1999,[2] and in particular Article 1 thereof,
Having published a draft of this Regulation,[3]
Having consulted the Advisory Committee on Restrictive Practices and Dominant Positions,
Whereas—

(1) Experience acquired in the motor vehicle sector regarding the distribution of new motor vehicles, spare parts and after sales services makes it possible to define categories of vertical agreements which can be regarded as normally satisfying the conditions laid down in Article 81(3).

(2) This experience leads to the conclusion that rules stricter than those provided for by Commission Regulation (EC) No 2790/1999 of 22 December 1999 on the application of Article 81(3) of the Treaty to categories of vertical agreements and concerted practices,[4] are necessary in this sector.

(3) These stricter rules for exemption by category (the exemption) should apply to vertical agreements for the purchase or sale of new motor vehicles, vertical agreements for the purchase or sale of spare parts for motor vehicles and vertical agreements for the purchase or sale of repair and maintenance services for such vehicles where these agreements are concluded between non-competing undertakings, between certain competitors, or by certain

associations of retailers or repairers. This includes vertical agreements concluded between a distributor acting at the retail level or an authorised repairer and a (sub)distributor or repairer. This Regulation should also apply to these vertical agreements when they contain ancillary provisions on the assignment or use of intellectual property rights. The term "vertical agreements" should be defined accordingly to include both such agreements and the corresponding concerted practices.

(4) The benefit of the exemption should be limited to vertical agreements for which it can be assumed with sufficient certainty that they satisfy the conditions of Article 81(3).

(5) Vertical agreements falling within the categories defined in this Regulation can improve economic efficiency within a chain of production or distribution by facilitating better coordination between the participating undertakings. In particular, they can lead to a reduction in the transaction and distribution costs of the parties and to an optimisation of their sales and investment levels.

(6) The likelihood that such efficiency-enhancing effects will outweigh any anti-competitive effects due to restrictions contained in vertical agreements depends on the degree of market power held by the undertakings concerned and therefore on the extent to which those undertakings face competition from other suppliers of goods or services regarded by the buyer as interchangeable or substitutable for one another, by reason of the products' characteristics, prices or intended use.

(7) Thresholds based on market share should be fixed in order to reflect suppliers', market power. Furthermore, this sector-specific Regulation should contain stricter rules than those provided for by Regulation (EC) No 2790/1999, in particular for selective distribution. The thresholds below which it can be presumed that the advantages secured by vertical agreements outweigh their restrictive effects should vary with the characteristics of different types of vertical agreement. It can therefore be presumed that in general, vertical agreements have such advantages where the supplier concerned has a market share of upto 30% on the markets for the distribution of new motor vehicles or spare parts, or of up to 40% where quantitative selective distribution is used for the sale of new motor vehicles. As regards after sales services it can be presumed that, in general, vertical agreements by which the supplier sets criteria on how its authorised repairers have to provide repair or maintenance services for the motor vehicles of the relevant make and provides them with equipment and training for the provision of such services have such advantages where the network of authorised repairers of the supplier concerned has a market share of up to 30%. However, in the case of vertical agreements containing exclusive supply obligations, it is the market share of the buyer which is relevant for determining the overall effects of such vertical agreements on the market.

(8) Above those market share thresholds, there can be no presumption that vertical agreements falling within the scope of Article 81(1) will usually give rise to objective advantages of such a character and magnitude as to compensate for the disadvantages which they create for competition. However, such advantages can be anticipated in the case of qualitative selective distribution, irrespective of the supplier's market share.

(9) In order to prevent a supplier from terminating an agreement because a distributor or a repairer engages in pro-competitive behaviour, such as active or passive sales to foreign consumers, multi-branding or subcontracting of repair and maintenance services, every notice of termination must clearly set out in writing the reasons, which must be objective and transparent. Furthermore, in order to strengthen the independence of distributors and repairers from their suppliers, minimum periods of notice should be provided for the non-renewal of agreements concluded for a limited duration and for the termination of agreements of unlimited duration.

(10) In order to foster market integration and to allow distributors or authorised repairers to seize additional business opportunities, distributors or authorised repairers have to be allowed to purchase other undertakings of the same type that sell or repair the same brand of motor vehicles within the distribution system. To this end, any vertical agreement between a supplier and a distributor or authorised repairer has to provide for the latter to have the right to transfer all of its rights and obligations to any other undertaking of its choice of the same type that sell or repairs the same brand of motor vehicles within the distribution system.

(11) In order to favour the quick resolution of disputes which arise between the parties to a distribution agreement and which might otherwise hamper effective competition, agreements should only benefit from exemption if they provide for each party to have a right of recourse to an independent expert or arbitrator, in particular where notice is given to terminate an agreement.

(12) Irrespective of the market share of the undertakings concerned, this Regulation does not cover vertical agreements containing certain types of severely anti-competitive restraints (hardcore restrictions) which in general appreciably restrict competition even at low market shares and which are not indispensable to the attainment of the positive effects mentioned above. This concerns in particular vertical agreements containing restraints such as minimum

or fixed resale prices and, with certain exceptions, restrictions of the territory into which, or of the customers to whom, a distributor or repairer may sell the contract goods or services. Such agreements should not benefit from the exemption.

(13) It is necessary to ensure that effective competition within the common market and between distributors located in different Member States is not restricted if a supplier uses selective distribution in some markets and other forms of distribution in others. In particular selective distribution agreements which restrict passive sales to any end user or unauthorised distributor located in markets where exclusive territories have been allocated should be excluded from the benefit of the exemption, as should those selective distribution agreements which restrict passive sales to customer groups which have been allocated exclusively to other distributors. The benefit of the exemption should also be withheld from exclusive distribution agreements if active or passive sales to any end user or unauthorised distributor located in markets where selective distribution is used are restricted.

(14) The right of any distributor to sell new motor vehicles passively or, where relevant, actively to end users should include the right to sell such vehicles to end users who have given authorisation to an intermediary or purchasing agent to purchase, take delivery of, transport or store a new motor vehicle on their behalf.

(15) The right of any distributor to sell new motor vehicles or spare parts or of any authorised repairer to sell repair and maintenance services to any end user passively or, where relevant, actively should include the right to use the Internet or Internet referral sites.

(16) Limits placed by suppliers on their distributors' sales to any end user in other Member States, for instance where distributor remuneration or the purchase price is made dependent on the destination of the vehicles or on the place of residence of the end users, amount to an indirect restriction on sales. Other examples of indirect restrictions on sales include supply quotas based on a sales territory other than the common market, whether or not these are combined with sales targets. Bonus systems based on the destination of the vehicles or any form of discriminatory product supply to distributors, whether in the case of product shortage or otherwise, also amount to an indirect restriction on sales.

(17) Vertical agreements that do not oblige the authorised repairers within a supplier's distribution system to honour warranties, perform free servicing and carry out recall work in respect of any motor vehicle of the relevant make sold in the common market amount to an indirect restriction of sales and should not benefit from the exemption. This obligation is without prejudice to the right of a motor vehicle supplier to oblige a distributor to make sure as regards the new motor vehicles that he has sold that the warranties are honoured and that free servicing and recall work is carried out, either by the distributor itself or, in case of subcontracting, by the authorised repairer(s) to whom these services have been subcontracted. Therefore consumers should in these cases be able to turn to the distributor if the above obligations have not been properly fulfilled by the authorised repairer to whom the distributor has subcontracted these services. Furthermore, in order to allow sales by motor vehicle distributors to end users throughout the common market, the exemption should apply only to distribution agreements which require the repairers within the supplier's network to carry out repair and maintenance services for the contract goods and corresponding goods irrespective of where these goods are sold in the common market.

(18) In markets where selective distribution is used, the exemption should apply in respect of a prohibition on a distributor from operating out of an additional place of establishment where he is a distributor of vehicles other than passenger cars or light commercial vehicles. However, this prohibition should not be exempted if it limits the expansion of the distributor's business at the authorised place of establishment by, for instance, restricting the development or acquisition of the infrastructure necessary to allow increases in sales volumes, including increases brought about by Internet sales.

(19) It would be inappropriate to exempt any vertical agreement that restricts the sale of original spare parts or spare parts of matching quality by members of the distribution system to independent repairers which use them for the provision of repair or maintenance services. Without access to such spare parts, these independent repairers would not be able to compete effectively with authorised repairers, since they could not provide consumers with good quality services which contribute to the safe and reliable functioning of motor vehicles.

(20) In order to give end users the right to purchase new motor vehicles with specifications identical to those sold in any other Member State, from any distributor selling corresponding models and established in the common market, the exemption should apply only to vertical agreements which enable a distributor to order, stock and sell any such vehicle which corresponds to a model within its contract range. Discriminatory or objectively unjustified supply conditions, in particular those regarding delivery times or prices, applied by the supplier to corresponding vehicles, are to be considered a restriction on the ability of the distributor to sell such vehicles.

(21) Motor vehicles are expensive and technically complex mobile goods which require repair and maintenance at regular and irregular intervals. However, it is not indispensable for distributors of new motor vehicles also to carry out repair and maintenance. The legitimate interests of suppliers and end users can be fully satisfied if the distributor subcontracts these services, including the honouring of warranties, free servicing and recall work, to a repairer or to a number of repairers within the supplier's distribution system. It is nevertheless appropriate to facilitate access to repair and maintenance services. Therefore, a supplier may require distributors who have subcontracted repair and maintenance services to one or more authorised repairers to give end users the name and address of the repair shop or shops in question. If any of these authorised repairers is not established in the vicinity of the sales outlet, the supplier may also require the distributor to tell end users how far the repair shop or shops in question are from the sales outlet. However, a supplier can only impose such obligations if he also imposes similar obligations on distributors whose own repair shop is not on the same premises as their sales outlet.

(22) Furthermore, it is not necessary, in order to adequately provide for repair and maintenance services, for authorised repairers to also sell new motor vehicles. The exemption should therefore not cover vertical agreements containing any direct or indirect obligation or incentive which leads to the linking of sales and servicing activities or which makes the performance of one of these activities dependent on the performance of the other; this is in particular the case where the remuneration of distributors or authorised repairers relating to the purchase or sale of goods or services necessary for one activity is made dependent on the purchase or sale of goods or services relating to the other activity, or where all such goods or services are indistinctly aggregated into a single remuneration or discount system.

(23) In order to ensure effective competition on the repair and maintenance markets and to allow repairers to offer end users competing spare parts such as original spare parts and spare parts of matching quality, the exemption should not cover vertical agreements which restrict the ability of authorised repairers within the distribution system of a vehicle manufacturer, independent distributors of spare parts, independent repairers or end users to source spare parts from the manufacturer of such spare parts or from another third party of their choice. This does not affect spare part manufacturers' liability under civil law.

(24) Furthermore, in order to allow authorised and independent repairers and end users to identify the manufacturer of motor vehicle components or of spare parts and to choose between competing spare parts, the exemption should not cover agreements by which a manufacturer of motor vehicles limits the ability of a manufacturer of components or original spare parts to place its trade mark or logo on these parts effectively and in a visible manner. Moreover, in order to facilitate this choice and the sale of spare parts, which have been manufactured according to the specifications and production and quality standards provided by the vehicle manufacturer for the production of components or spare parts, it is presumed that spare parts constitute original spare parts, if the spare part producer issues a certificate that the parts are of the same quality as the components used for the assembly of a motor vehicle and have been manufactured according to these specifications and standards. Other spare parts for which the spare part producer can issue a certificate at any moment attesting that they match the quality of the components used for the assembly of a certain motor vehicle, may be sold as spare parts of matching quality.

(25) The exemption should not cover vertical agreements which restrict authorised repairers from using spare parts of matching quality for the repair or maintenance of a motor vehicle. However, in view of the vehicle manufacturers' direct contractual involvement in repairs under warranty, free servicing, and recall operations, agreements containing obligations on authorised repairers to use original spare parts supplied by the vehicle manufacturer for these repairs should be covered by the exemption.

(26) In order to protect effective competition on the market for repair and maintenance services and to prevent foreclosure of independent repairers, motor vehicle manufacturers must allow all interested independent operators to have full access to all technical information, diagnostic and other equipment, tools, including all relevant software, and training required for the repair and maintenance of motor vehicles. Independent operators who must be allowed such access include in particular independent repairers, manufacturers of repair equipment or tools, publishers of technical information, automobile clubs, roadside assistance operators, operators offering inspection and testing services and operators offering training for repairers. In particular, the conditions of access must not discriminate between authorised and independent operators, access must be given upon request and without undue delay, and the price charged for the information should not discourage access to it by failing to take into account the extent to which the independent operator uses it. A supplier of motor vehicles should be required to give independent operators access to technical information on new motor

vehicles at the same time as such access is given to its authorised repairers and must not oblige independent operators to purchase more than the information necessary to carry out the work in question. Suppliers should be obliged to give access to the technical information necessary for re-programming electronic devices in a motor vehicle. It is, however, legitimate and proper for them to withhold access to technical information which might allow a third party to bypass or disarm on-board anti-theft devices, to recalibrate electronic devices or to tamper with devices which for instance limit the speed of a motor vehicle, unless protection against theft, re-calibration or tampering can be attained by other less restrictive means. Intellectual property rights and rights regarding know-how including those which relate to the aforementioned devices must be exercised in a manner which avoids any type of abuse.

(27) In order to ensure access to and to prevent collusion on the relevant markets and to give distributors opportunities to sell vehicles of brands from two or more manufacturers that are not connected undertakings, certain specific conditions are attached to the exemption. To this end, the exemption should not be accorded to non-compete obligations. In particular, without prejudice to the ability of the supplier to require the distributor to display the vehicles in brand-specific areas of the showroom in order to avoid brand confusion, any prohibition on sales of competing makes should not be exempted. The same applies to an obligation to display the full range of motor vehicles if it makes the sale or display of vehicles manufactured by undertakings which are not connected impossible or unreasonably difficult. Furthermore, an obligation to have brand-specific sales personnel is considered to be an indirect non-compete obligation and therefore should not be covered by the exemption, unless the distributor decides to have brand-specific sales personnel and the supplier pays all the additional costs involved.

(28) In order to ensure that repairers are able to carry out repairs or maintenance on all motor vehicles, the exemption should not apply to any obligation limiting the ability of repairers of motor vehicles to provide repair or maintenance services for brands of competing suppliers.

(29) In addition, specific conditions are required to exclude certain restrictions, sometimes imposed in the context of a selective distribution system, from the scope of the exemption. This applies in particular to obligations which have the effect of preventing the members of a selective distribution system from selling the brands of particular competing suppliers, which could easily lead to foreclosure of certain brands. Additional conditions are necessary in order to foster intra-brand competition and market integration within the common market, to create opportunities for distributors and authorised repairers who wish to seize business opportunities outside their place of establishment, and to create conditions which allow the development of multi-brand distributors. In particular a restriction on operating out of an unauthorised place of establishment for the distribution of passenger cars and light commercial vehicles or the provision of repair and maintenance services should not be exempted. The supplier may require additional sales or delivery outlets for passenger cars and light commercial vehicles or repair shops to comply with the relevant qualitative criteria applicable for similar outlets located in the same geographic area.

(30) The exemption should not apply to restrictions limiting the ability of a distributor to sell leasing services for motor vehicles.

(31) The market share limitations, the fact that certain vertical agreements are not covered, and the conditions provided for in this Regulation, should normally ensure that the agreements to which the exemption applies do not enable the participating undertakings to eliminate competition in respect of a substantial part of the goods or services in question.

(32) In particular cases in which agreements which would otherwise benefit from the exemption nevertheless have effects incompatible with Article 81(3), the Commission is empowered to withdraw the benefit of the exemption; this may occur in particular where the buyer has significant market power on the relevant market on which it resells the goods or provides the services or where parallel networks of vertical agreements have similar effects which significantly restrict access to a relevant market or competition thereon; such cumulative effects may for example arise in the case of selective distribution. The Commission may also withdraw the benefit of the exemption if competition is significantly restricted on a market due to the presence of a supplier with market power or if prices and conditions of supply to motor vehicle distributors differ substantially between geographic markets. It may also withdraw the benefit of the exemption if discriminatory prices or sales conditions, or unjustifiably high supplements, such as those charged for right hand drive vehicles, are applied for the supply of goods corresponding to the contract range.

(33) Regulation No 19/65/EEC empowers the national authorities of Member States to withdraw the benefit of the exemption in respect of vertical agreements having effects incompatible with the conditions laid down in Article 81(3), where such effects are felt in their territory, or in a part thereof, and where such territory has the characteristics of a distinct geographic market; the exercise of this national power of withdrawal should not prejudice the

uniform application throughout the common market of the Community competition rules or the full effect of the measures adopted in implementation of those rules.

(34) In order to allow for better supervision of parallel networks of vertical agreements which have similar restrictive effects and which cover more than 50% of a given market, the Commission should be permitted to declare the exemption inapplicable to vertical agreements containing specific restraints relating to the market concerned, thereby restoring the full application of Article 81(1) to such agreements.

(35) The exemption should be granted without prejudice to the application of the provisions of Article 82 of the Treaty on the abuse by an undertaking of a dominant position.

(36) Commission Regulation (EC) No 1475/95 of 28 June 1995 on the application of Article 85(3) of the Treaty to certain categories of motor vehicle distribution and servicing agreements,[5] is applicable until 30 September 2002. In order to allow all operators time to adapt vertical agreements which are compatible with that regulation and which are still in force when the exemption provided for therein expires, it is appropriate for such agreements to benefit from a transition period until 1 October 2003, during which time they should be exempted from the prohibition laid down in Article 81(1) under this Regulation.

(37) In order to allow all operators within a quantitative selective distribution system for new passenger cars and light commercial vehicles to adapt their business strategies to the non-application of the exemption to location clauses, it is appropriate to stipulate that the condition set out in Article 5(2)(b) shall enter into force on 1 October 2005.

(38) The Commission should monitor the operation of this Regulation on a regular basis, with particular regard to its effects on competition in motor vehicle retailing and in after sales servicing in the common market or relevant parts of it. This should include monitoring the effects of this Regulation on the structure and level of concentration of motor vehicle distribution and any resulting effects on competition. The Commission should also carry out an evaluation of the operation of this Regulation and draw up a report not later than 31 May 2008.

NOTES
[1] OJ 36, 6.3.1965, p 533/65.
[2] OJ L148, 15.6.1999, p 1.
[3] OJ C67, 16.3.2002, p 2.
[4] OJ L336, 29.12.1999, p 21.
[5] OJ L145, 29.6.1995, p 25.

HAS ADOPTED THIS REGULATION—

Article 1

Definitions

1. For the purposes of this Regulation—
   (a) "competing undertakings" means actual or potential suppliers on the same product market; the product market includes goods or services which are regarded by the buyer as interchangeable with or substitutable for the contract goods or services, by reason of the products' characteristics, their prices and their intended use;
   (b) "non-compete obligation" means any direct or indirect obligation causing the buyer not to manufacture, purchase, sell or resell goods or services which compete with the contract goods or services, or any direct or indirect obligation on the buyer to purchase from the supplier or from another undertaking designated by the supplier more than 30% of the buyer's total purchases of the contract goods, corresponding goods or services and their substitutes on the relevant market, calculated on the basis of the value of its purchases in the preceding calendar year. An obligation that the distributor sell motor vehicles from other suppliers in separate areas of the showroom in order to avoid confusion between the makes does not constitute a non-compete obligation for the purposes of this Regulation. An obligation that the distributor have brand-specific sales personnel for different brands of

motor vehicles constitutes a non-compete obligation for the purposes of this Regulation, unless the distributor decides to have brand-specific sales personnel and the supplier pays all the additional costs involved;

(c) "vertical agreements" means agreements or concerted practices entered into by two or more undertakings, each of which operates, for the purposes of the agreement, at a different level of the production or distribution chain;

(d) "vertical restraints" means restrictions of competition falling within the scope of Article 81(1), when such restrictions are contained in a vertical agreement;

(e) "exclusive supply obligation" means any direct or indirect obligation causing the supplier to sell the contract goods or services only to one buyer inside the common market for the purposes of a specific use or for resale;

(f) "selective distribution system" means a distribution system where the supplier undertakes to sell the contract goods or services, either directly or indirectly, only to distributors or repairers selected on the basis of specified criteria and where these distributors or repairers undertake not to sell such goods or services to unauthorised distributors or independent repairers, without prejudice to the ability to sell spare parts to independent repairers or the obligation to provide independent operators with all technical information, diagnostic equipment, tools and training required for the repair and maintenance of motor vehicles or for the implementation of environmental protection measures;

(g) "quantitative selective distribution" system means a selective distribution system where the supplier uses criteria for the selection of distributors or repairers which directly limit their number;

(h) "qualitative selective distribution" system means a selective distribution system where the supplier uses criteria for the selection of distributors or repairers which are only qualitative in nature, are required by the nature of the contract goods or services, are laid down uniformly for all distributors or repairers applying to join the distribution system, are not applied in a discriminatory manner, and do not directly limit the number of distributors or repairers;

(i) "intellectual property rights" includes industrial property rights, copyright and neighbouring rights;

(j) "know-how" means a package of non-patented practical information, derived from experience and testing by the supplier, which is secret, substantial and identified; in this context, "secret" means that the know-how, as a body or in the precise configuration and assembly of its components, is not generally known or easily accessible; "substantial" means that the know-how includes information which is indispensable to the buyer for the use, sale or resale of the contract goods or services; "identified" means that the know-how must be described in a sufficiently comprehensive manner so as to make it possible to verify that it fulfils the criteria of secrecy and substantiality;

(k) "buyer", whether distributor or repairer, includes an undertaking which sells goods or services on behalf of another undertaking;

(l) "authorised repairer" means a provider of repair and maintenance services for motor vehicles operating within the distribution system set up by a supplier of motor vehicles;

(m) "independent repairer" means a provider of repair and maintenance services for motor vehicles not operating within the distribution system set up by the supplier of the motor vehicles for which it provides repair or maintenance. An authorised repairer within the distribution system of a given supplier shall be deemed to be an independent repairer for the purposes of this Regulation to the extent that he provides repair or maintenance services for motor vehicles in respect of which he is not a member of the respective supplier's distribution system;

(n) "motor vehicle" means a self propelled vehicle intended for use on public roads and having three or more road wheels;

(o) "passenger car" means a motor vehicle intended for the carriage of passengers and comprising no more than eight seats in addition to the driver's seat;

(p) "light commercial vehicle" means a motor vehicle intended for the transport of goods or passengers with a maximum mass not exceeding 3.5 tonnes; if a certain light commercial vehicle is also sold in a version with a maximum mass above 3.5 tonnes, all versions of that vehicle are considered to be light commercial vehicles;

(q) the "contract range" means all the different models of motor vehicles available for purchase by the distributor from the supplier;

(r) a "motor vehicle which corresponds to a model within the contract range" means a vehicle which is the subject of a distribution agreement with another undertaking within the distribution system set up by the manufacturer or with his consent and which is—
— manufactured or assembled in volume by the manufacturer, and
— identical as to body style, drive-line, chassis, and type of motor to a vehicle within the contract range;

(s) "spare parts" means goods which are to be installed in or upon a motor vehicle so as to replace components of that vehicle, including goods such as lubricants which are necessary for the use of a motor vehicle, with the exception of fuel;

(t) "original spare" parts means spare parts which are of the same quality as the components used for the assembly of a motor vehicle and which are manufactured according to the specifications and production standards provided by the vehicle manufacturer for the production of components or spare parts for the motor vehicle in question. This includes spare parts which are manufactured on the same production line as these components. It is presumed, unless the contrary is proven, that parts constitute original spare parts if the part manufacturer certifies that the parts match the quality of the components used for the assembly of the vehicle in question and have been manufactured according to the specifications and production standards of the vehicle manufacturer;

(u) "spare parts of matching quality" means exclusively spare parts made by any undertaking which can certify at any moment that the parts in question match the quality of the components which are or were used for the assembly of the motor vehicles in question;

(v) "undertakings within the distribution system" means the manufacturer and undertakings which are entrusted by the manufacturer or with the manufacturer's consent with the distribution or repair or maintenance of contract goods or corresponding goods;

(w) "end user" includes leasing companies unless the leasing contracts used provide for a transfer of ownership or an option to purchase the vehicle prior to the expiry of the contract.

2. The terms "undertaking", "supplier", "buyer", "distributor" and "repairer" shall include their respective connected undertakings.

"Connected undertakings" are—

(a) undertakings in which a party to the agreement, directly or indirectly—
   (i) has the power to exercise more than half the voting rights, or
   (ii) has the power to appoint more than half the members of the supervisory board, board of management or bodies legally representing the undertaking, or jointly have the rights or powers listed in (a);
   (iii) has the right to manage the undertaking's affairs;

(b) undertakings which directly or indirectly have, over a party to the agreement, the rights or powers listed in (a);

(c) undertakings in which an undertaking referred to in (b) has, directly or indirectly, the rights or powers listed in (a);

(d) undertakings in which a party to the agreement together with one or more of the undertakings referred to in (a), (b) or (c), or in which two or more of the latter undertakings, jointly have the rights or powers listed in (a);

(e) undertakings in which the rights or the powers listed in (a) are jointly held by—

    (i) parties to the agreement or their respective connected undertakings referred to in (a) to (d), or

    (ii) one or more of the parties to the agreement or one or more of their connected undertakings referred to in (a) to (d) and one or more third parties.

[5138]

Article 2

Scope

1. Pursuant to Article 81(3) of the Treaty and subject to the provisions of this Regulation, it is hereby declared that the provisions of Article 81(1) shall not apply to vertical agreements where they relate to the conditions under which the parties may purchase, sell or resell new motor vehicles, spare parts for motor vehicles or repair and maintenance services for motor vehicles.

The first subparagraph shall apply to the extent that such vertical agreements contain vertical restraints.

The exemption declared by this paragraph shall be known for the purposes of this Regulation as "the exemption".

2. The exemption shall also apply to the following categories of vertical agreements—

  (a) Vertical agreements entered into between an association of undertakings and its members, or between such an association and its suppliers, only if all its members are distributors of motor vehicles or spare parts for motor vehicles or repairers and if no individual member of the association, together with its connected undertakings, has a total annual turnover exceeding EUR 50 million; vertical agreements **entered into by such associations shall be covered by this Regulation without** prejudice to the application of Article 81 to horizontal agreements concluded between the members of the association or decisions adopted by the association;

  (b) vertical agreements containing provisions which relate to the assignment to the buyer or use by the buyer of intellectual property rights, provided that those provisions do not constitute the primary object of such agreements and are directly related to the use, sale or resale of goods or services by the buyer or its customers. The exemption shall apply on condition that those provisions do not contain restrictions of competition relating to the contract goods or services which have the same object or effect as vertical restraints which are not exempted under this Regulation.

3. The exemption shall not apply to vertical agreements entered into between competing undertakings.

However, it shall apply where competing undertakings enter into a non-reciprocal vertical agreement and—

  (a) the buyer has a total annual turnover not exceeding EUR 100 million, or

  (b) the supplier is a manufacturer and a distributor of goods, while the buyer is a distributor not manufacturing goods competing with the contract goods, or

(c) the supplier is a provider of services at several levels of trade, while the buyer does not provide competing services at the level of trade where it purchases the contract services.

[5139]

Article 3

General conditions

1. Subject to paragraphs 2, 3, 4, 5, 6 and 7, the exemption shall apply on condition that the supplier's market share on the relevant market on which it sells the new motor vehicles, spare parts for motor vehicles or repair and maintenance services does not exceed 30%.

However, the market share threshold for the application of the exemption shall be 40% for agreements establishing quantitative selective distribution systems for the sale of new motor vehicles.

Those thresholds shall not apply to agreements establishing qualitative selective distribution systems.

2. In the case of vertical agreements containing exclusive supply obligations, the exemption shall apply on condition that the market share held by the buyer does not exceed 30% of the relevant market on which it purchases the contract goods or services.

3. The exemption shall apply on condition that the vertical agreement concluded with a distributor or repairer provides that the supplier agrees to the transfer of the rights and obligations resulting from the vertical agreement to another distributor or repairer within the distribution system and chosen by the former distributor or repairer.

4. The exemption shall apply on condition that the vertical agreement concluded with a distributor or repairer provides that a supplier who wishes to give notice of termination of an agreement must give such notice in writing and must include detailed, objective and transparent reasons for the termination, in order to prevent a supplier from ending a vertical agreement with a distributor or repairer because of practices which may not be restricted under this Regulation.

5. The exemption shall apply on condition that the vertical agreement concluded by the supplier of new motor vehicles with a distributor or authorised repairer provides

    (a) that the agreement is concluded for a period of at least five years; in this case each party has to undertake to give the other party at least six months' prior notice of its intention not to renew the agreement;

    (b) or that the agreement is concluded for an indefinite period; in this case the period of notice for regular termination of the agreement has to be at least two years for both parties; this period is reduced to at least one year where—

        (i) the supplier is obliged by law or by special agreement to pay appropriate compensation on termination of the agreement, or

        (ii) the supplier terminates the agreement where it is necessary to re-organise the whole or a substantial part of the network.

6. The exemption shall apply on condition that the vertical agreement provides for each of the parties the right to refer disputes concerning the fulfilment of their contractual obligations to an independent expert or arbitrator. Such disputes may relate, *inter alia*, to any of the following—

    (a) supply obligations;

    (b) the setting or attainment of sales targets;

    (c) the implementation of stock requirements;
    (d) the implementation of an obligation to provide or use demonstration vehicles;
    (e) the conditions for the sale of different brands;
    (f) the issue whether the prohibition to operate out of an unauthorised place of establishment limits the ability of the distributor of motor vehicles other than passenger cars or light commercial vehicles to expand its business, or
    (g) the issue whether the termination of an agreement is justified by the reasons given in the notice.

The right referred to in the first sentence is without prejudice to each party's right to make an application to a national court.

7. For the purposes of this Article, the market share held by the undertakings referred to in Article 1(2)(e) shall be apportioned equally to each undertaking having the rights or the powers listed in Article 1(2)(a).

[5140]

Article 4

Hardcore restrictions

(Hardcore restrictions concerning the sale of new motor vehicles, repair and maintenance services or spare parts)

1. The exemption shall not apply to vertical agreements which, directly or indirectly, in isolation or in combination with other factors under the control of the parties, have as their object—
    (a) the restriction of the distributor's or repairer's ability to determine its sale price, without prejudice to the supplier's ability to impose a maximum sale price or to recommend a sale price, provided that this does not amount to a fixed or minimum sale price as a result of pressure from, or incentives offered by, any of the parties;
    (b) the restriction of the territory into which, or of the customers to whom, the distributor or repairer may sell the contract goods or services; however, the exemption shall apply to—
        (i) the restriction of active sales into the exclusive territory or to an exclusive customer group reserved to the supplier or allocated by the supplier to another distributor or repairer, where such a restriction does not limit sales by the customers of the distributor or repairer;
        (ii) the restriction of sales to end users by a distributor operating at the wholesale level of trade;
        (iii) the restriction of sales of new motor vehicles and spare parts to unauthorised distributors by the members of a selective distribution system in markets where selective distribution is applied, subject to the provisions of point (i);
        (iv) the restriction of the buyer's ability to sell components, supplied for the purposes of incorporation, to customers who would use them to manufacture the same type of goods as those produced by the supplier;
    (c) the restriction of cross-supplies between distributors or repairers within a selective distribution system, including between distributors or repairers operating at different levels of trade;
    (d) the restriction of active or passive sales of new passenger cars or light commercial vehicles, spare parts for any motor vehicle or repair and maintenance services for any motor vehicle to end users by members of a selective distribution system operating at the retail level of trade in markets where selective distribution is used. The exemption shall apply to agreements containing a prohibition on a member of a selective

distribution system from operating out of an unauthorised place of establishment. However, the application of the exemption to such a prohibition is subject to Article 5(2)(b);

(e) the restriction of active or passive sales of new motor vehicles other than passenger cars or light commercial vehicles to end users by members of a selective distribution system operating at the retail level of trade in markets where selective distribution is used, without prejudice to the ability of the supplier to prohibit a member of that system from operating out of an unauthorised place of establishment;

(Hardcore restrictions only concerning the sale of new motor vehicles)

(f) the restriction of the distributor's ability to sell any new motor vehicle which corresponds to a model within its contract range;

(g) the restriction of the distributor's ability to subcontract the provision of repair and maintenance services to authorised repairers, without prejudice to the ability of the supplier to require the distributor to give end users the name and address of the authorised repairer or repairers in question before the conclusion of a sales contract and, if any of these authorised repairers is not in the vicinity of the sales outlet, to also tell end users how far the repair shop or repair shops in question are from the sales outlet; however, such obligations may only be imposed provided that similar obligations are imposed on distributors whose repair shop is not on the same premises as their sales outlet;

(Hardcore restrictions only concerning the sale of repair and maintenance services and of spare parts)

(h) the restriction of the authorised repairer's ability to limit its activities to the provision of repair and maintenance services and the distribution of spare parts;

(i) the restriction of the sales of spare parts for motor vehicles by members of a selective distribution system to independent repairers which use these parts for the repair and maintenance of a motor vehicle;

(j) the restriction agreed between a supplier of original spare parts or spare parts of matching quality, repair tools or diagnostic or other equipment and a manufacturer of motor vehicles, which limits the supplier's ability to sell these goods or services to authorised or independent distributors or to authorised or independent repairers or end users;

(k) the restriction of a distributor's or authorised repairer's ability to obtain original spare parts or spare parts of matching quality from a third undertaking of its choice and to use them for the repair or maintenance of motor vehicles, without prejudice to the ability of a supplier of new motor vehicles to require the use of original spare parts supplied by it for repairs carried out under warranty, free servicing and vehicle recall work;

(l) the restriction agreed between a manufacturer of motor vehicles which uses components for the initial assembly of motor vehicles and the supplier of such components which limits the latter's ability to place its trade mark or logo effectively and in an easily visible manner on the components supplied or on spare parts.

2. The exemption shall not apply where the supplier of motor vehicles refuses to give independent operators access to any technical information, diagnostic and other equipment, tools, including any relevant software, or training required for the repair and maintenance of these motor vehicles or for the implementation of environmental protection measures.

Such access must include in particular the unrestricted use of the electronic control and diagnostic systems of a motor vehicle, the programming of these systems in accordance with the supplier's standard procedures, the repair and training instructions and the information required for the use of diagnostic and servicing tools and equipment.

Access must be given to independent operators in a non-discriminatory, prompt and proportionate way, and the information must be provided in a usable form. If the relevant item is covered by an intellectual property right or constitutes know-how, access shall not be withheld in any abusive manner.

For the purposes of this paragraph "independent operator" shall mean undertakings which are directly or indirectly involved in the repair and maintenance of motor vehicles, in particular independent repairers, manufacturers of repair equipment or tools, independent distributors of spare parts, publishers of technical information, automobile clubs, roadside assistance operators, operators offering inspection and testing services and operators offering training for repairers.

[5141]

Article 5

Specific conditions

1. As regards the sale of new motor vehicles, repair and maintenance services or spare parts, the exemption shall not apply to any of the following obligations contained in vertical agreements—

    (a) any direct or indirect non-compete obligation;

    (b) any direct or indirect obligation limiting the ability of an authorised repairer to provide repair and maintenance services for vehicles from competing suppliers;

    (c) any direct or indirect obligation causing the members of a distribution system not to sell motor vehicles or spare parts of particular competing suppliers or not to provide repair and maintenance services for motor vehicles of particular competing suppliers;

    (d) any direct or indirect obligation causing the distributor or authorised repairer, after termination of the agreement, not to manufacture, purchase, sell or resell motor vehicles or not to provide repair or maintenance services.

2. As regards the sale of new motor vehicles, the exemption shall not apply to any of the following obligations contained in vertical agreements—

    (a) any direct or indirect obligation causing the retailer not to sell leasing services relating to contract goods or corresponding goods;

    (b) any direct or indirect obligation on any distributor of passenger cars or light commercial vehicles within a selective distribution system, which limits its ability to establish additional sales or delivery outlets at other locations within the common market where selective distribution is applied.

3. As regards repair and maintenance services or the sale of spare parts, the exemption shall not apply to any direct or indirect obligation as to the place of establishment of an authorised repairer where selective distribution is applied.

[5142]

Article 6

Withdrawal of the benefit of the Regulation

1. The Commission may withdraw the benefit of this Regulation, pursuant to Article 7(1) of Regulation No 19/65/EEC, where it finds in any particular case that vertical agreements to which this Regulation applies nevertheless have effects which

are incompatible with the conditions laid down in Article 81(3) of the Treaty, and in particular—

(a) where access to the relevant market or competition therein is significantly restricted by the cumulative effect of parallel networks of similar vertical restraints implemented by competing suppliers or buyers, or

(b) where competition is restricted on a market where one supplier is not exposed to effective competition from other suppliers, or

(c) where prices or conditions of supply for contract goods or for corresponding goods differ substantially between geographic markets, or

(d) where discriminatory prices or sales conditions are applied within a geographic market.

2. Where in any particular case vertical agreements to which the exemption applies have effects incompatible with the conditions laid down in Article 81(3) of the Treaty in the territory of a Member State, or in a part thereof, which has all the characteristics of a distinct geographic market, the relevant authority of that Member State may withdraw the benefit of application of this Regulation in respect of that territory, under the same conditions as those provided in paragraph 1.

[5143]

Article 7

Non-application of the Regulation

1. Pursuant to Article 1a of Regulation No 19/65/EEC, the Commission may by regulation declare that, where parallel networks of similar vertical restraints cover more than 50% of a relevant market, this Regulation shall not apply to vertical agreements containing specific restraints relating to that market.

2. A regulation pursuant to paragraph 1 shall not become applicable earlier than one year following its adoption.

[5144]

Article 8

Market share calculation

1. The market shares provided for in this Regulation shall be calculated

(a) for the distribution of new motor vehicles on the basis of the volume of the contract goods and corresponding goods sold by the supplier, together with any other goods sold by the supplier which are regarded as interchangeable or substitutable by the buyer, by reason of the products' characteristics, prices and intended use;

(b) for the distribution of spare parts on the basis of the value of the contract goods and other goods sold by the supplier, together with any other goods sold by the supplier which are regarded as interchangeable or substitutable by the buyer, by reason of the products' characteristics, prices and intended use;

(c) for the provision of repair and maintenance services on the basis of the value of the contract services sold by the members of the supplier's distribution network together with any other services sold by these members which are regarded as interchangeable or substitutable by the buyer, by reason of their characteristics, prices and intended use.

If the volume data required for those calculations are not available, value data may be used or vice versa. If such information is not available, estimates based on other reliable market information may be used. For the purposes of Article 3(2), the market purchase volume or the market purchase value respectively, or estimates thereof shall be used to calculate the market share.

2. For the purposes of applying the market share thresholds of 30% and 40% provided for in this Regulation the following rules shall apply—

   (a) the market share shall be calculated on the basis of data relating to the preceding calendar year;

   (b) the market share shall include any goods or services supplied to integrated distributors for the purposes of sale;

   (c) if the market share is initially not more than 30% or 40% respectively but subsequently rises above that level without exceeding 35% or 45% respectively, the exemption shall continue to apply for a period of two consecutive calendar years following the year in which the market share threshold of 30% or 40% respectively was first exceeded;

   (d) if the market share is initially not more than 30% or 40% respectively but subsequently rises above 35% or 45% respectively, the exemption shall continue to apply for one calendar year following the year in which the level of 30% or 40% respectively was first exceeded;

   (e) the benefit of points (c) and (d) may not be combined so as to exceed a period of two calendar years.

[5145]

Article 9

Turnover calculation

1. For the purposes of calculating total annual turnover figures referred to in Article 2(2)(a) and 2(3)(a) respectively, the turnover achieved during the previous financial year by the relevant party to the vertical agreement and the turnover achieved by its connected undertakings in respect of all goods and services, excluding all taxes and other duties, shall be added together. For this purpose, no account shall be taken of dealings between the party to the vertical agreement and its connected undertakings or between its connected undertakings.

2. The exemption shall remain applicable where, for any period of two consecutive financial years, the total annual turnover threshold is exceeded by no more than 10%.

[5146]

Article 10

Transitional period

The prohibition laid down in Article 81(1) shall not apply during the period from 1 October 2002 to 30 September 2003 in respect of agreements already in force on 30 September 2002 which do not satisfy the conditions for exemption provided for in this Regulation but which satisfy the conditions for exemption provided for in Regulation (EC) No 1475/95.

[5147]

Article 11

Monitoring and evaluation report

1. The Commission shall monitor the operation of this Regulation on a regular basis, with particular regard to its effects on—

   (a) competition in motor vehicle retailing and in after sales servicing in the common market or relevant parts of it;

   (b) the structure and level of concentration of motor vehicle distribution and any resulting effects on competition.

2. The Commission shall draw up a report on this Regulation not later than 31 May 2008 having regard in particular to the conditions set out in Article 81(3).

Article 12

Entry into force and expiry

1. This Regulation shall enter into force on 1 October 2002.

2. Article 5(2)(b) shall apply from 1 October 2005.

3. This Regulation shall expire on 31 May 2010.

This Regulation shall be binding in its entirety and directly applicable in all Member States.

Done at Brussels, 31 July 2002.

F. MERGERS AND JOINT VENTURES

COUNCIL REGULATION

of 21 December 1989

on the control of concentrations between undertakings

(4064/89/EEC)

NOTES

Date of publication in OJ: OJ L257, 21.9.90, p 13.

The text of this Regulation is the corrected version, replacing the original version published in OJ L395, 30.12.89, p 1.

Set out as amended by Corrigendum of 7 January 1998, see OJ L3, 7.1.98, p 16.

This Regulation should be read together with the preamble to the amending Council Regulation 1310/97/EC, the text of which is set out after this Regulation.

THE COUNCIL OF THE EUROPEAN COMMUNITIES,

Having regard to the Treaty establishing the European Economic Community, and in particular Articles 87 and 235 thereof,

Having regard to the proposal from the Commission,[1]

Having regard to the opinion of the European Parliament,[2]

Having regard to the opinion of the Economic and Social Committee,[3]

(1) Whereas, for the achievement of the aims of the Treaty establishing the European Economic Community, Article 3(f) gives the Community the objective of instituting "a system ensuring that competition in the common market is not distorted";

(2) Whereas this system is essential for the achievement of the internal market by 1992 and its further development;

(3) Whereas the dismantling of internal frontiers is resulting and will continue to result in major corporate reorganisations in the Community, particularly in the form of concentrations;

(4) Whereas such a development must be welcomed as being in line with the requirements of dynamic competition and capable of increasing the competitiveness of European industry, improving the conditions of growth and raising the standard of living in the Community;

(5) Whereas, however, it must be ensured that the process of reorganisation does not result in lasting damage to competition; whereas Community law must therefore include provisions governing those concentrations which may significantly impede effective competition in the common market or in a substantial part of it;

(6) Whereas Articles 85 and 86, while applicable, according to the case-law of the Court of Justice, to certain concentrations, are not, however, sufficient to control all operations which may prove to be incompatible with the system of undistorted competition envisaged in the Treaty;

(7) Whereas a new legal instrument should therefore be created in the form of a Regulation to permit effective control of all concentrations from the point of view of their effect on the structure of competition in the Community and to be the only instrument applicable to such concentrations;

(8) Whereas this Regulation should therefore be based not only on Article 87 but, principally, on Article 235 of the Treaty, under which the Community may give itself the additional powers of action necessary for the attainment of its objectives, including with regard to concentrations on the markets for agricultural products listed in Annex II to the Treaty;

(9) Whereas the provisions to be adopted in this Regulation should apply to significant structural changes the impact of which on the market goes beyond the national borders of any one Member State;

(10) Whereas the scope of application of this Regulation should therefore be defined according to the geographical area of activity of the undertakings concerned and be limited by quantitative thresholds in order to cover those concentrations which have a Community dimension; whereas, at the end of an initial phase of the application of this Regulation, these thresholds should be reviewed in the light of the experience gained;

(11) Whereas a concentration with a Community dimension exists where the combined aggregate turnover of the undertakings concerned exceeds given levels worldwide and within the Community and where at least two of the undertakings concerned have their sole or main

fields of activities in different Member States or where, although the undertakings in question act mainly in one and the same Member State, at least one of them has substantial operations in at least one other Member State; whereas that is also the case where the concentrations are effected by undertakings which do not have their principal fields of activities in the Community but which have substantial operations there;

(12) Whereas the arrangements to be introduced for the control of concentrations should, without prejudice to Article 90(2) of the Treaty, respect the principle of non-discrimination between the public and the private sectors; whereas, in the public sector, calculation of the turnover of an undertaking concerned in a concentration needs, therefore, to take account of undertakings making up an economic unit with an independent power of decision, irrespective of the way in which their capital is held or of the rules of administrative supervision applicable to them;

(13) Whereas it is necessary to establish whether concentrations with a Community dimension are compatible or not with the common market from the point of view of the need to maintain and develop effective competition in the common market; whereas, in so doing, the Commission must place its appraisal within the general framework of the achievement of the fundamental objectives referred to in Article 2 of the Treaty, including that of strengthening the Community's economic and social cohesion, referred to in Article 130a;

(14) Whereas this Regulation should establish the principle that a concentration with a Community dimension which creates or strengthens a position as a result of which effective competition in the common market or in a substantial part of it is significantly impeded is to be declared incompatible with the common market;

(15) Whereas concentrations which, by reason of the limited market share of the undertakings concerned, are not liable to impede effective competition may be presumed to be compatible with the common market; whereas, without prejudice to Articles 85 and 86 of the Treaty, an indication to this effect exists, in particular, where the market share of the undertakings concerned does not exceed 25% either in the common market or in a substantial part of it;

(16) Whereas the Commission should have the task of taking all the decisions necessary to establish whether or not concentrations with a Community dimension are compatible with the common market, as well as decisions designed to restore effective competition;

(17) Whereas to ensure effective control undertakings should be obliged to give prior notification of concentrations with a Community dimension and provision should be made for the suspension of concentrations for a limited period, and for the possibility of extending or waiving a suspension where necessary; whereas in the interests of legal certainty the validity of transactions must nevertheless be protected as much as necessary;

(18) Whereas a period within which the Commission must initiate proceedings in respect of a notified concentration and periods within which it must give a final decision on the compatibility or incompatibility with the common market of a notified concentration should be laid down;

(19) Whereas the undertakings concerned must be afforded the right to be heard by the Commission when proceedings have been initiated; whereas the members of the management and supervisory bodies and the recognised representatives of the employees of the undertakings concerned, and third parties showing a legitimate interest, must also be given the opportunity to be heard;

(20) Whereas the Commission should act in close and constant liaison with the competent authorities of the Member States from which it obtains comments and information;

(21) Whereas, for the purposes of this Regulation, and in accordance with the case-law of the Court of Justice, the Commission must be afforded the assistance of the Member States and must also be empowered to require information to be given and to carry out the necessary investigations in order to appraise concentrations;

(22) Whereas compliance with this Regulation must be enforceable by means of fines and periodic penalty payments; whereas the Court of Justice should be given unlimited jurisdiction in that regard pursuant to Article 172 of the Treaty;

(23) Whereas it is appropriate to define the concept of concentration in such a manner as to cover only operations bringing about a lasting change in the structure of the undertakings concerned; whereas it is therefore necessary to exclude from the scope of this Regulation those operations which have as their object or effect the coordination of the competitive behaviour of undertakings which remain independent, since such operations fall to be examined under the appropriate provisions of the Regulations implementing Articles 85 and 86 of the Treaty; whereas it is appropriate to make this distinction specifically in the case of the creation of joint ventures;

(24) Whereas there is no coordination of competitive behaviour within the meaning of this Regulation where two or more undertakings agree to acquire jointly control of one or more other undertakings with the object and effect of sharing amongst themselves such undertakings or their assets;

(25) Whereas this Regulation should still apply where the undertakings concerned accept restrictions directly related and necessary to the implementation of the concentration;

(26) Whereas the Commission should be given exclusive competence to apply this Regulation, subject to review by the Court of Justice;

(27) Whereas the Member States may not apply their national legislation on competition to concentrations with a Community dimension, unless this Regulation makes provision therefor; whereas the relevant powers of national authorities should be limited to cases where, failing intervention by the Commission, effective competition is likely to be significantly impeded within the territory of a Member State and where the competition interests of that Member State cannot be sufficiently protected otherwise by this Regulation; whereas the Member States concerned must act promptly in such cases; whereas this Regulation cannot, because of the diversity of national law, fix a single deadline for the adoption of remedies;

(28) Whereas, furthermore, the exclusive application of this Regulation to concentrations with a Community dimension is without prejudice to Article 223 of the Treaty, and does not prevent the Member States from taking appropriate measures to protect legitimate interests other than those pursued by this Regulation, provided that such measures are compatible with the general principles and other provisions of Community law;

(29) Whereas concentrations not covered by this Regulation come, in principle, within the jurisdiction of the Member States; whereas, however, the Commission should have the power to act, at the request of a Member State concerned, in cases where effective competition could be significantly impeded within that Member State's territory;

(30) Whereas the conditions in which concentrations involving Community undertakings are carried out in non-member countries should be observed, and provision should be made for the possibility of the Council giving the Commission an appropriate mandate for negotiation with a view to obtaining non-discriminatory treatment for Community undertakings;

(31) Whereas this Regulation in no way detracts from the collective rights of employees as recognised in the undertakings concerned,

NOTES
1   OJ C130, 19.5.88, p 4.
2   OJ C309, 5.12.88, p 55.
3   OJ C208, 8.8.88, p 11.

HAS ADOPTED THIS REGULATION—

Article 1

Scope

[1.   Without prejudice to Article 22, this Regulation shall apply to all concentrations with a Community dimension as defined in paragraphs 2 and 3.]

2.   For the purposes of this Regulation, a concentration has a Community dimension where—

   (a) the combined aggregate worldwide turnover of all the undertakings concerned is more than ECU 5000 million; and

   (b) the aggregate Community-wide turnover of each of at least two of the undertakings concerned is more than ECU 250 million,

unless each of the undertakings concerned achieves more than two-thirds of its aggregate Community-wide turnover within one and the same Member State.

[3.   For the purposes of this Regulation, a concentration that does not meet the thresholds laid down in paragraph 2 has a Community dimension where—

   (a) the combined aggregate worldwide turnover of all the undertakings concerned is more than ECU 2 500 million;

   (b) in each of at least three Member States, the combined aggregate turnover of all the undertakings concerned is more than ECU 100 million;

   (c) in each of at least three Member States included for the purpose of point (b), the aggregate turnover of each of at least two of the undertakings concerned is more than ECU 25 million; and

(d) the aggregate Community-wide turnover of each of at least two of the undertakings concerned is more than ECU 100 million;

unless each of the undertakings concerned achieves more than two-thirds of its aggregate Community-wide turnover within one and the same Member State.]

[4. Before 1 July 2000 the Commission shall report to the Council on the operation of the thresholds and criteria set out in paragraphs 2 and 3.]

[5. Following the report referred to in paragraph 4 and on a proposal from the Commission, the Council, acting by a qualified majority, may revise the thresholds and criteria mentioned in paragraph 3.]

[5401]

NOTES

Para 1: substituted by Council Regulation 1310/97/EC, Arts 1(1)(a), 2, as from 1 March 1998, except in relation to any concentration which was the subject of an agreement or announcement or where control was acquired within the meaning of Art 4(1) post before 1 March 1998 or to any concentration in respect of which proceedings were initiated by a Member State's authority with responsibility for competition before 1 March 1998. Original text read as follows—

"1. Without prejudice to Article 22, this Regulation shall apply to all concentrations with a Community dimension as defined in paragraph 2."

Para 3: substituted by Council Regulation 1310/97/EC, Arts 1(1)(b), 2, as from 1 March 1998, except in relation to any concentration which was the subject of an agreement or announcement or where control was acquired within the meaning of Art 4(1) post before 1 March 1998 or to any concentration in respect of which proceedings were initiated by a Member State's authority with responsibility for competition before 1 March 1998. Original text read as follows—

"3. The thresholds laid down in paragraph 2 will be reviewed before the end of the fourth year following that of the adoption of this Regulation by the Council acting by a qualified majority on a proposal from the Commission."

Paras 4, 5: added by Council Regulation 1310/97/EC, Arts 1(1)(c), 2, as from 1 March 1998, except in relation to any concentration which was the subject of an agreement or announcement or where control was acquired within the meaning of Art 4(1) post before 1 March 1998 or to any concentration in respect of which proceedings were initiated by a Member State's authority with responsibility for competition before 1 March 1998.

Article 2

Appraisal of concentrations

1. Concentrations within the scope of this Regulation shall be appraised in accordance with the following provisions with a view to establishing whether or not they are compatible with the common market.

In making this appraisal, the Commission shall take into account—
(a) the need to maintain and develop effective competition within the common market in view of, among other things, the structure of all the markets concerned and the actual or potential competition from undertakings located either within or outwith the Community;
(b) the market position of the undertakings concerned and their economic and financial power, the alternatives available to suppliers and users, their access to supplies or markets, any legal or other barriers to entry, supply and demand trends for the relevant goods and services, the interests of the intermediate and ultimate consumers, and the development of technical and economic progress provided that it is to consumers' advantage and does not form an obstacle to competition.

2. A concentration which does not create or strengthen a dominant position as a result of which effective competition would be significantly impeded in the common market or in a substantial part of it shall be declared compatible with the common market.

3.   A concentration which creates or strengthens a dominant position as a result of which effective competition would be significantly impeded in the common market or in a substantial part of it shall be declared incompatible with the common market.

[4.   To the extent that the creation of a joint venture constituting a concentration pursuant to Article 3 has as its object or effect the coordination of the competitive behaviour of undertakings that remain independent, such coordination shall be appraised in accordance with the criteria of Article 85(1) and (3) of the Treaty, with a view to establishing whether or not the operation is compatible with the common market.

In making this appraisal, the Commission shall take into account in particular—
— whether two or more parent companies retain to a significant extent activities in the same market as the joint venture or in a market which is downstream or upstream from that of the joint venture or in a neighbouring market closely related to this market,
— whether the coordination which is the direct consequence of the creation of the joint venture affords the undertakings concerned the possibility of eliminating competition in respect of a substantial part of the products or services in question.]

[5402]

NOTES

Para 4: added by Council Regulation 1310/97/EC, Arts 1(2), 2, as from 1 March 1998, except in relation to any concentration which was the subject of an agreement or announcement or where control was acquired within the meaning of Art 4(1) post before 1 March 1998 or to any concentration in respect of which proceedings were initiated by a Member State's authority with responsibility for competition before 1 March 1998.

Article 3

Definition of concentration

1.   A concentration shall be deemed to arise where—
(a) two or more previously independent undertakings merge, or
(b) — one or more persons already controlling at least one undertaking, or
— one or more undertakings acquire, whether by purchase of securities or assets, by contract or by any other means, direct or indirect control of the whole or parts of one or more other undertakings.

2.   . . .

The creation of a joint venture performing on a lasting basis all the functions of an autonomous economic entity, . . . , shall constitute a concentration within the meaning of paragraph 1(b).

3.   For the purposes of this Regulation, control shall be constituted by rights, contracts or any other means which, either separately or in combination and having regard to the considerations of fact or law involved, confer the possibility of exercising decisive influence on an undertaking, in particular by—
(a) ownership or the right to use all or part of the assets of an undertaking;
(b) rights or contracts which confer decisive influence on the composition, voting or decisions of the organs of an undertaking.

4.   Control is acquired by persons or undertakings which—
(a) are holders of the rights or entitled to rights under the contracts concerned, or
(b) while not being holders of such rights or entitled to rights under such contracts, have the power to exercise the rights deriving therefrom.

5.   A concentration shall not be deemed to arise where—

(a) credit institutions or other financial institutions or insurance companies, the normal activities of which include transactions and dealing in securities for their own account or for the account of others, hold on a temporary basis securities which they have acquired in an undertaking with a view to reselling them, provided that they do not exercise voting rights in respect of those securities with a view to determining the competitive behaviour of that undertaking or provided that they exercise such voting rights only with a view to preparing the disposal of all or part of that undertaking or of its assets or the disposal of those securities and that any such disposal takes place within one year of the date of acquisition; that period may be extended by the Commission on request where such institutions or companies can show that the disposal was not reasonably possible within the period set;

(b) control is acquired by an office-holder according to the law of a Member State relating to liquidation, winding up, insolvency, cessation of payments, compositions or analogous proceedings;

(c) the operations referred to in paragraph 1(b) are carried out by the financial holding companies referred to in Article 5(3) of the Fourth Council Directive 78/660/EEC of 25 July 1978 on the annual accounts of certain types of companies,[1] as last amended by Directive 84/569/EEC,[2] provided however that the voting rights in respect of the holding are exercised, in particular in relation to the appointment of members of the management and supervisory bodies of the undertakings in which they have holdings, only to maintain the full value of those investments and not to determine directly or indirectly the competitive conduct of those undertakings.

[5403]

NOTES

[1]   OJ L222, 14.8.78, p 11.

[2]   OJ L314, 4.12.84, p 28.

Para 2: first paragraph and, in the second paragraph, words "which does not give rise to coordination of the competitive behaviour of the parties amongst themselves or between them and the joint venture" repealed by Council Regulation 1310/97/EC, Arts 1(3), 2, as from 1 March 1998, except in relation to any concentration which was the subject of an agreement or announcement or where control was acquired within the meaning of Art 4(1) post before 1 March 1998 or to any concentration in respect of which proceedings were initiated by a Member State's authority with responsibility for competition before 1 March 1998. The first paragraph read as follows—

"An operation, including the creation of a joint venture, which has as its object or effect the coordination of the competitive behaviour of undertakings which remain independent shall not constitute a concentration within the meaning of paragraph 1(b)."

Article 4

Prior notification of concentrations

1.   Concentrations with a Community dimension defined in this Regulation shall be notified to the Commission not more than one week after the conclusion of the agreement, or the announcement of the public bid, or the acquisition of a controlling interest. That week shall begin when the first of those events occurs.

2.   A concentration which consists of a merger within the meaning of Article 3(1)(a) or in the acquisition of joint control within the meaning of Article 3(1)(b) shall be notified jointly by the parties to the merger or by those acquiring joint control as the case may be. In all other cases, the notification shall be effected by the person or undertaking acquiring control of the whole or parts of one or more undertakings.

3.   Where the Commission finds that a notified concentration falls within the scope of this Regulation, it shall publish the fact of the notification, at the same time indicating the names of the parties, the nature of the concentration and the economic sectors involved. The Commission shall take account of the legitimate interest of undertakings in the protection of their business secrets.

[5404]

Article 5

Calculation of turnover

1.   Aggregate turnover within the meaning of Article 1(2) shall comprise the amounts derived by the undertakings concerned in the preceding financial year from the sale of products and the provision of services falling within the undertakings' ordinary activities after deduction of sale rebates and of value added tax and other taxes directly related to turnover. The aggregate turnover of an undertaking concerned shall not include the sale of products or the provision of services between any of the undertakings referred to in paragraph 4.

Turnover, in the Community or in a Member State, shall comprise products sold and services provided to undertakings or consumers, in the Community or in that Member State as the case may be.

2.   By way of derogation from paragraph 1, where the concentration consists in the acquisition of parts, whether or not constituted as legal entities, of one or more undertakings, only the turnover relating to the parts which are the subject of the transaction shall be taken into account with regard to the seller or sellers.

However, two or more transactions within the meaning of the first subparagraph which take place within a two-year period between the same persons or undertakings shall be treated as one and the same concentration arising on the date of the last transaction.

[3.   In place of turnover the following shall be used—

(a) for credit institutions and other financial institutions, as regards Article 1(2) and (3), the sum of the following income items as defined in Council Directive 86/635/EEC of 8 December 1986 on the annual accounts and consolidated accounts of banks and other financial institutions, after deduction of value added tax and other taxes directly related to those items, where appropriate—

   (i) interest income and similar income;

   (ii) income from securities—

     — income from shares and other variable yield securities,

     — income from participating interests,

     — income from shares in affiliated undertakings;

   (iii) commissions receivable;

   (iv) net profit on financial operations;

   (v) other operating income.

   The turnover of a credit or financial institution in the Community or in a Member State shall comprise the income items, as defined above, which are received by the branch or division of that institution established in the Community or in the Member State in question, as the case may be;

(b) for insurance undertakings, the value of gross premiums written which shall comprise all amounts received and receivable in respect of insurance contracts issued by or on behalf of the insurance undertakings, including also outgoing reinsurance premiums, and after deduction of taxes and parafiscal contributions or levies charged by reference to the amounts of individual premiums or the total volume of premiums; as regards

Article 1(2)(b) and (3)(b), (c) and (d) and the final part of Article 1(2) and (3), gross premiums received from Community residents and from residents of one Member State respectively shall be taken into account.]

[4.   Without prejudice to paragraph 2, the aggregate turnover of an undertaking concerned within the meaning of Article 1(2) and (3) shall be calculated by adding together the respective turnovers of the following—]
   (a) the undertaking concerned;
   (b) those undertakings in which the undertaking concerned, directly or indirectly—
       — owns more than half the capital or business assets, or
       — has the power to exercise more than half the voting rights, or
       — has the power to appoint more than half the members of the supervisory board, the administrative board or bodies legally representing the undertakings, or
       — has the right to manage the undertakings' affairs;
   (c) those undertakings which have in the undertaking concerned the rights or powers listed in (b);
   (d) those undertakings in which an undertaking as referred to in (c) has the rights or powers listed in (b);
   (e) those undertakings in which two or more undertakings as referred to in (a) to (d) jointly have the rights or powers listed in (b).

[5.   Where undertakings concerned by the concentration jointly have the rights or powers listed in paragraph 4(b), in calculating the aggregate turnover of the undertakings concerned for the purposes of Article 1(2) and (3)—]
   (a) no account shall be taken of the turnover resulting from the sale of products or the provision of services between the joint undertaking and each of the undertakings concerned or any other undertaking connected with any one of them, as set out in paragraph 4(b) to (e);
   (b) account shall be taken of the turnover resulting from the sale of products and the provision of services between the joint undertaking and any third undertakings. This turnover shall be apportioned equally amongst the undertakings concerned.

[5405]

NOTES

Para 3: substituted by Council Regulation 1310/97/EC, Arts 1(4), 2, as from 1 March 1998, except in relation to any concentration which was the subject of an agreement or announcement or where control was acquired within the meaning of Art 4(1) ante before 1 March 1998 or to any concentration in respect of which proceedings were initiated by a Member State's authority with responsibility for competition before 1 March 1998. Original text read as follows—

"3.   In place of turnover the following shall be used—
   (a) for credit institutions and other financial institutions, as regards Article 1(2)(a), one-tenth of their total assets.
       As regards Article 1(2)(b) and the final part of Article 1(2), total Community-wide turnover shall be replaced by one-tenth of total assets multiplied by the ratio between loans and advances to credit institutions and customers in transactions with Community residents and the total sum of those loans and advances.
       As regards the final part of Article 1(2), total turnover within one Member State shall be replaced by one-tenth of total assets multiplied by the ratio between loans and advances to credit institutions and customers in transactions with residents of that Member State and the total sum of those loans and advances;
   (b) for insurance undertakings, the value of gross premiums written which shall comprise all amounts received and receivable in respect of insurance contracts issued by or on behalf of the insurance undertakings, including also outgoing reinsurance premiums, and after deduction of taxes and parafiscal contributions or levies charged by reference to the amounts of individual premiums or the total volume of premiums; as regards Article 1(2)(b) and the final part of Article 1(2), gross premiums received from Community residents and from residents of one Member State respectively shall be taken into account."

Paras 4, 5: introductory sentences substituted by Council Regulation 1310/97/EC, Arts 1(4), 2, as from 1 March 1998, except in relation to any concentration which was the subject of an agreement or announcement or where control was acquired within the meaning of Art 4(1) ante before 1 March 1998 or to any concentration in respect of which proceedings were initiated by a Member State's authority with responsibility for competition before 1 March 1998. Original text read as follows—

"4. Without prejudice to paragraph 2, the aggregate turnover of an undertaking concerned within the meaning of Article 1(2) shall be calculated by adding together the respective turnovers of the following—" and

"5. Where undertakings concerned by the concentration jointly have the rights or powers listed in paragraph 4(b), in calculating the aggregate turnover of the undertakings concerned for the purposes of Article 1(2)—"

Article 6

Examination of the notification and initiation of proceedings

1. The Commission shall examine the notification as soon as it is received.
   (a) Where it concludes that the concentration notified does not fall within the scope of this Regulation, it shall record that finding by means of a decision.
   (b) Where it finds that the concentration notified, although falling within the scope of this Regulation, does not raise serious doubts as to its compatibility with the common market, it shall decide not to oppose it and shall declare that it is compatible with the common market.

   [The decision declaring the concentration compatible shall also cover restrictions directly related and necessary to the implementation of the concentration.]
   [(c) Without prejudice to paragraph 1(a), where the Commission finds that the concentration notified falls within the scope of this Regulation and raises serious doubts as to its compatibility with the common market, it shall decide to initiate proceedings.]

[1a. Where the Commission finds that, following modification by the undertakings concerned, a notified concentration no longer raises serious doubts within the meaning of paragraph 1(c), it may decide to declare the concentration compatible with the common market pursuant to paragraph 1(b).

The Commission may attach to its decision under paragraph 1(b) conditions and obligations intended to ensure that the undertakings concerned comply with the commitments they have entered into vis-à-vis the Commission with a view to rendering the concentration compatible with the common market.]

[1b. The Commission may revoke the decision it has taken pursuant to paragraph 1(a) or (b) where—
   (a) the decision is based on incorrect information for which one of the undertakings is responsible or where it has been obtained by deceit,
or
   (b) the undertakings concerned commit a breach of an obligation attached to the decision.]

[1c. In the cases referred to in paragraph 1(b), the Commission may take a decision under paragraph 1, without being bound by the deadlines referred to in Article 10(1).]

2. The Commission shall notify its decision to the undertakings concerned and the competent authorities of the Member States without delay.

[5406]

PART IV
EC MATERIALS

NOTES

Para 1: in sub-para (b), paragraph added and sub-para (c) substituted by Council Regulation 1310/97/EC, Arts 1(5)(a), 2, as from 1 March 1998, except in relation to any concentration which was the subject of an agreement or announcement or where control was acquired within the meaning of Art 4(1) ante before 1 March 1998 or to any concentration in respect of which proceedings were initiated by a Member State's authority with responsibility for competition before 1 March 1998. Original text read as follows—

"(c) If, on the other hand, it finds that the concentration notified falls within the scope of this Regulation and raises serious doubts as to its compatibility with the common market, it shall decide to initiate proceedings."

Paras 1a, 1b, 1c: inserted by Council Regulation 1310/97/EC, Arts 1(5)(b), 2, as from 1 March 1998, except in relation to any concentration which was the subject of an agreement or announcement or where control was acquired within the meaning of Art 4(1) ante before 1 March 1998 or to any concentration in respect of which proceedings were initiated by a Member State's authority with responsibility for competition before 1 March 1998.

Article 7

Suspension of concentrations

[1. A concentration as defined in Article 1 shall not be put into effect either before its notification or until it has been declared compatible with the common market pursuant to a decision under Article 6(1)(b) or Article 8(2) or on the basis of a presumption according to Article 10(6).]

2. . . .

3. [Paragraph 1] shall not prevent the implementation of a public bid which has been notified to the Commission in accordance with Article 4(1), provided that the acquirer does not exercise the voting rights attached to the securities in question or does so only to maintain the full value of those investments and on the basis of a derogation granted by the Commission under paragraph 4.

[4. The Commission may, on request, grant a derogation from the obligations imposed in paragraphs 1 or 3. The request to grant a derogation must be reasoned. In deciding on the request, the Commission shall take into account inter alia the effects of the suspension on one or more undertakings concerned by a concentration or on a third party and the threat to competition posed by the concentration. That derogation may be made subject to conditions and obligations in order to ensure conditions of effective competition. A derogation may be applied for and granted at any time, even before notification or after the transaction.]

[5. The validity of any transaction carried out in contravention of paragraph 1 shall be dependent on a decision pursuant to Article 6(1)(b) or Article 8(2) or (3) or on a presumption pursuant to Article 10(6).

This Article shall, however, have no effect on the validity of transactions in securities including those convertible into other securities admitted to trading on a market which is regulated and supervised by authorities recognised by public bodies, operates regularly and is accessible directly or indirectly to the public, unless the buyer and seller knew or ought to have known that the transaction was carried out in contravention of paragraph 1.]

NOTES

Para 1: substituted by Council Regulation 1310/97/EC, Arts 1(6)(a), 2, as from 1 March 1998, except in relation to any concentration which was the subject of an agreement or announcement or where control was acquired within the meaning of Art 4(1) ante before 1 March 1998 or to any concentration in respect of which proceedings were initiated by a Member State's authority with responsibility for competition before 1 March 1998. Original text read as follows—

"1. For the purposes of paragraph 2 a concentration as defined in Article 1 shall not be put into effect either before its notification or within the first three weeks following its notification."

Para 2: repealed by Council Regulation 1310/97/EC, Arts 1(6)(b), 2, as from 1 March 1998, except in relation to any concentration which was the subject of an agreement or announcement or where control was acquired within the meaning of Art 4(1) ante before 1 March 1998 or to any concentration in respect of which proceedings were initiated by a Member State's authority with responsibility for competition before 1 March 1998. Original text read as follows—

"2. Where the Commission, following a preliminary examination of the notification within the period provided for in paragraph 1, finds it necessary in order to ensure the full effectiveness of any decision taken later pursuant to Article 8(3) and (4), it may decide on its own initiative to continue the suspension of a concentration in whole or in part until it takes a final decision, or to take other interim measures to that effect."

Para 3: words in square brackets substituted for original words "Paragraphs 1 and 2" by Council Regulation 1310/97/EC, Arts 1(6)(c), 2, as from 1 March 1998, except in relation to any concentration which was the subject of an agreement or announcement or where control was acquired within the meaning of Art 4(1) ante before 1 March 1998 or to any concentration in respect of which proceedings were initiated by a Member State's authority with responsibility for competition before 1 March 1998.

Para 4: substituted by Council Regulation 1310/97/EC, Arts 1(6)(d), 2, as from 1 March 1998, except in relation to any concentration which was the subject of an agreement or announcement or where control was acquired within the meaning of Art 4(1) ante before 1 March 1998 or to any concentration in respect of which proceedings were initiated by a Member State's authority with responsibility for competition before 1 March 1998. Original text read as follows—

"4. The Commission may, on request, grant a derogation from the obligations imposed in paragraphs 1, 2 or 3 in order to prevent serious damage to one or more undertakings concerned by a concentration or to a third party. That derogation may be made subject to conditions and obligations in order to ensure conditions of effective competition. A derogation may be applied for and granted at any time, even before notification or after the transaction."

Para 5: substituted by Council Regulation 1310/97/EC, Arts 1(6)(e), 2, as from 1 March 1998, except in relation to any concentration which was the subject of an agreement or announcement or where control was acquired within the meaning of Art 4(1) ante before 1 March 1998 or to any concentration in respect of which proceedings were initiated by a Member State's authority with responsibility for competition before 1 March 1998. Original text read as follows—

"5. The validity of any transaction carried out in contravention of paragraph 1 or 2 shall be dependent on a decision pursuant to Article 6(1)(b) or Article 8(2) or (3) or on a presumption pursuant to Article 10(6).

This Article shall, however, have no effect on the validity of transactions in securities including those convertible into other securities admitted to trading on a market which is regulated and supervised by authorities recognised by public bodies, operates regularly and is accessible directly or indirectly to the public, unless the buyer and seller knew or ought to have known that the transaction was carried out in contravention of paragraph 1 or 2."

Article 8

Powers of decision of the Commission

1. Without prejudice to Article 9, all proceedings initiated pursuant to Article 6(1)(c) shall be closed by means of a decision as provided for in paragraphs 2 to 5.

[2. Where the Commission finds that, following modification by the undertakings concerned if necessary, a notified concentration fulfils the criterion laid down in Article 2(2) and, in the cases referred to in Article 2(4), the criteria laid down in Article 85(3) of the Treaty, it shall issue a decision declaring the concentration compatible with the common market.

It may attach to its decision conditions and obligations intended to ensure that the undertakings concerned comply with the commitments they have entered into *vis-à-vis* the Commission with a view to rendering the concentration compatible with the common market. The decision declaring the concentration compatible with the common market shall also cover restrictions directly related and necessary to the implementation of the concentration.]

[3. Where the Commission finds that a concentration fulfils the criterion defined in Article 2(3) or, in the cases referred to in Article 2(4), does not fulfil the criteria laid down in Article 85(3) of the Treaty, it shall issue a decision declaring that the concentration is incompatible with the common market.]

4. Where a concentration has already been implemented, the Commission may, in a decision pursuant to paragraph 3 or by separate decision, require the undertakings or assets brought together to be separated or the cessation of joint control or any other action that may be appropriate in order to restore conditions of effective competition.

5. The Commission may revoke the decision it has taken pursuant to paragraph 2 where—

(a) the declaration of compatibility is based on incorrect information for which one of the undertakings is responsible or where it has been obtained by deceit; or

(b) the undertakings concerned commit a breach of an obligation attached to the decision.

6. In the cases referred to in paragraph 5, the Commission may take a decision under paragraph 3, without being bound by the deadline referred to in Article 10(3).

[5408]

NOTES

Para 2: substituted by Council Regulation 1310/97/EC, Arts 1(7)(a), 2, as from 1 March 1998, except in relation to any concentration which was the subject of an agreement or announcement or where control was acquired within the meaning of Art 4(1) ante before 1 March 1998 or to any concentration in respect of which proceedings were initiated by a Member State's authority with responsibility for competition before 1 March 1998. Original text read as follows—

"2. Where the Commission finds that, following modification by the undertakings concerned if necessary, a notified concentration fulfils the criterion laid down in Article 2(2), it shall issue a decision declaring the concentration compatible with the common market.

Para 3: substituted by Council Regulation 1310/97/EC, Arts 1(7)(b), 2, as from 1 March 1998, except in relation to any concentration which was the subject of an agreement or announcement or where control was acquired within the meaning of Art 4(1) ante before 1 March 1998 or to any concentration in respect of which proceedings were initiated by a Member State's authority with responsibility for competition before 1 March 1998. Original text read as follows—

"3. Where the Commission finds that a concentration fulfils the criterion laid down in Article 2(3), shall issue a decision declaring that the concentration is incompatible with the common market."

Article 9

Referral to the competent authorities of the Member States

1. The Commission may, by means of a decision notified without delay to the undertakings concerned and the competent authorities of the other Member States, refer a notified concentration to the competent authorities of the Member State concerned in the following circumstances.

[2. Within three weeks of the date of receipt of the copy of the notification a Member State may inform the Commission, which shall inform the undertakings concerned, that—

(a) a concentration threatens to create or to strengthen a dominant position as a result of which effective competition will be significantly impeded on a market within that Member State, which presents all the characteristics of a distinct market, or

(b) a concentration affects competition on a market within that Member State, which presents all the characteristics of a distinct market and which does not constitute a substantial part of the common market.]

3.   If the Commission considers that, having regard to the market for the products or services in question and the geographical reference market within the meaning of paragraph 7, there is such a distinct market and that such a threat exists, either—

(a) it shall itself deal with the case in order to maintain or restore effective competition on the market concerned; or

[(b) it shall refer the whole or part of the case to the competent authorities of the Member State concerned with a view to the application of that State's national competition law.

In cases where a Member State informs the Commission that a concentration affects competition in a distinct market within its territory that does not form a substantial part of the common market, the Commission shall refer the whole or part of the case relating to the distinct market concerned, if it considers that such a distinct market is affected.]

If, however, the Commission considers that such a distinct market or threat does not exist it shall adopt a decision to that effect which it shall address to the Member State concerned.

4.   A decision to refer or not to refer pursuant to paragraph 3 shall be taken—

(a) as a general rule within the six-week period provided for in Article 10(1), second subparagraph, where the Commission, pursuant to Article 6(1)(b), has not initiated proceedings; or

(b) within three months at most of the notification of the concentration concerned where the Commission has initiated proceedings under Article 6(1)(c), without taking the preparatory steps in order to adopt the necessary measures under Article 8(2), second subparagraph, (3) or (4) to maintain or restore effective competition on the market concerned.

5.   If within the three months referred to in paragraph 4(b) the Commission, despite a reminder from the Member State concerned, has not taken a decision on referral in accordance with paragraph 3 nor has taken the preparatory steps referred to in paragraph 4(b), it shall be deemed to have taken a decision to refer the case to the Member State concerned in accordance with paragraph 3(b).

6.   The publication of any report or the announcement of the findings of the examination of the concentration by the competent authority of the Member State concerned shall be effected not more than four months after the Commission's referral.

7.   The geographical reference market shall consist of the area in which the undertakings concerned are involved in the supply and demand of products or services, in which the conditions of competition are sufficiently homogeneous and which can be distinguished from neighbouring areas because, in particular, conditions of competition are appreciably different in those areas. This assessment should take account in particular of the nature and characteristics of the products or services concerned, of the existence of entry barriers or of consumer preferences, of appreciable differences of the undertakings' market shares between the area concerned and neighbouring areas or of substantial price differences.

8.   In applying the provisions of this Article, the Member State concerned may take only the measures strictly necessary to safeguard or restore effective competition on the market concerned.

9.   In accordance with the relevant provisions of the Treaty, any Member State may appeal to the Court of Justice, and in particular request the application of Article 186, for the purpose of applying its national competition law.

PART IV
EC MATERIALS

[10. This Article may be re-examined at the same time as the thresholds referred to in Article 1.]

[5409]

NOTES

Para 2: substituted by Council Regulation 1310/97/EC, Arts 1(8)(a), 2, as from 1 March 1998, except in relation to any concentration which was the subject of an agreement or announcement or where control was acquired within the meaning of Art 4(1) ante before 1 March 1998 or to any concentration in respect of which proceedings were initiated by a Member State's authority with responsibility for competition before 1 March 1998. Original text read as follows—

"2. Within three weeks of the date of receipt of the copy of the notification a Member State may inform the Commission, which shall inform the undertakings concerned, that a concentration threatens to create or to strengthen a dominant position as a result of which effective competition would be significantly impeded on a market, within that Member State, which presents all the characteristics of a distinct market, be it a substantial part of the common market or not."

Para 3: words in square brackets substituted for original para (b) by Council Regulation 1310/97/EC, Arts 1(8)(b), 2, as from 1 March 1998, except in relation to any concentration which was the subject of an agreement or announcement or where control was acquired within the meaning of Art 4(1) ante before 1 March 1998 or to any concentration in respect of which proceedings were initiated by a Member State's authority with responsibility for competition before 1 March 1998. Original text read as follows—

"(b) it shall refer the case to the competent authorities of the Member State concerned with a view to the application of that State's national competition law."

Para 10: substituted by Council Regulation 1310/97/EC, Arts 1(8)(c), 2, as from 1 March 1998, except in relation to any concentration which was the subject of an agreement or announcement or where control was acquired within the meaning of Art 4(1) ante before 1 March 1998 or to any concentration in respect of which proceedings were initiated by a Member State's authority with responsibility for competition before 1 March 1998. Original text read as follows—

"10. This Article will be reviewed before the end of the fourth year following that of the adoption of this Regulation."

Article 10

Time limits for initiating proceedings and for decisions

1.   The decisions referred to in Article 6(1) must be taken within one month at most. That period shall begin on the day following that of the receipt of a notification or, if the information to be supplied with the notification is incomplete, on the day following that of the receipt of the complete information.

That period shall be increased to six weeks if the Commission receives a request from a Member State in accordance with Article 9(2) [or where, after notification of a concentration, the undertakings concerned submit commitments pursuant to Article 6(1a), which are intended by the parties to form the basis for a decision pursuant to Article 6(1)(b).]

2.   Decisions taken pursuant to Article 8(2) concerning notified concentrations must be taken as soon as it appears that the serious doubts referred to in Article 6(1)(c) have been removed, particularly as a result of modifications made by the undertakings concerned, and at the latest by the deadline laid down in paragraph 3.

3.   Without prejudice to Article 8(6), decisions taken pursuant to Article 8(3) concerning notified concentrations must be taken within not more than four months of the date on which proceedings are initiated.

4.   [The periods set by paragraphs 1 and 3] shall exceptionally be suspended where, owing to circumstances for which one of the undertakings involved in the concentration is responsible, the Commission has had to request information by decision pursuant to Article 11 or to order an investigation by decision pursuant to Article 13.

5.   Where the Court of Justice gives a Judgement which annuls the whole or part of a Commission decision taken under this Regulation, the periods laid down in this Regulation shall start again from the date of the Judgement.

6.   Where the Commission has not taken a decision in accordance with Article 6(1)(b) or (c) or Article 8(2) or (3) within the deadlines set in paragraphs 1 and 3 respectively, the concentration shall be deemed to have been declared compatible with the common market, without prejudice to Article 9.

[5410]

NOTES

Para 1: words in square brackets added by Council Regulation 1310/97/EC, Arts 1(9)(a), 2, as from 1 March 1998, except in relation to any concentration which was the subject of an agreement or announcement or where control was acquired within the meaning of Art 4(1) ante before 1 March 1998 or to any concentration in respect of which proceedings were initiated by a Member State's authority with responsibility for competition before 1 March 1998.

Para 4: words in square brackets substituted for original words "The period set by paragraph 3" by Council Regulation 1310/97/EC, Arts 1(9)(b), 2, as from 1 March 1998, except in relation to any concentration which was the subject of an agreement or announcement or where control was acquired within the meaning of Art 4(1) ante before 1 March 1998 or to any concentration in respect of which proceedings were initiated by a Member State's authority with responsibility for competition before 1 March 1998.

Article 11

Requests for information

1.   In carrying out the duties assigned to it by this Regulation, the Commission may obtain all necessary information from the Governments and competent authorities of the Member States, from the persons referred to in Article 3(1)(b), and from undertakings and associations of undertakings.

2.   When sending a request for information to a person, an undertaking or an association of undertakings, the Commission shall at the same time send a copy of the request to the competent authority of the Member State within the territory of which the residence of the person or the seat of the undertaking or association of undertakings is situated.

3.   In its request the Commission shall state the legal basis and the purpose of the request and also the penalties provided for in Article 14(1)(c) for supplying incorrect information.

4.   The information requested shall be provided, in the case of undertakings, by their owners or their representatives and, in the case of legal persons, companies or firms, or of associations having no legal personality, by the persons authorised to represent them by law or by their statutes.

5.   Where a person, an undertaking or an association of undertakings does not provide the information requested within the period fixed by the Commission or provides incomplete information, the Commission shall by decision require the information to be provided. The decision shall specify what information is required, fix an appropriate period within which it is to be supplied and state the penalties provided for in Articles 14(1)(c) and 15(1)(a) and the right to have the decision reviewed by the Court of Justice.

6.   The Commission shall at the same time send a copy of its decision to the competent authority of the Member State within the territory of which the residence of the person or the seat of the undertaking or association of undertakings is situated.

[5411]

Article 12

Investigations by the authorities of the Member States

1.   At the request of the Commission, the competent authorities of the Member States shall undertake the investigations which the Commission considers to be necessary under Article 13(1), or which it has ordered by decision pursuant to Article 13(3). The officials of the competent authorities of the Member States responsible for conducting those investigations shall exercise their powers upon production of an authorisation in writing issued by the competent authority of the Member State within the territory of which the investigation is to be carried out. Such authorisation shall specify the subject matter and purpose of the investigation.

2.   If so requested by the Commission or by the competent authority of the Member State within the territory of which the investigation is to be carried out, officials of the Commission may assist the officials of that authority in carrying out their duties.

[5412]

Article 13

Investigative powers of the Commission

1.   In carrying out the duties assigned to it by this Regulation, the Commission may undertake all necessary investigations into undertakings and associations of undertakings.

To that end the officials authorised by the Commission shall be empowered—
   (a) to examine the books and other business records;
   (b) to take or demand copies of or extracts from the books and business records;
   (c) to ask for oral explanations on the spot;
   (d) to enter any premises, land and means of transport of undertakings.

2.   The officials of the Commission authorised to carry out the investigations shall exercise their powers on production of an authorisation in writing specifying the subject matter and purpose of the investigation and the penalties provided for in Article 14(1)(d) in cases where production of the required books or other business records is incomplete. In good time before the investigation, the Commission shall inform, in writing, the competent authority of the Member State within the territory of which the investigation is to be carried out of the investigation and of the identities of the authorised officials.

3.   Undertakings and associations of undertakings shall submit to investigations ordered by decision of the Commission. The decision shall specify the subject matter and purpose of the investigation, appoint the date on which it shall begin and state the penalties provided for in Articles 14(1)(d) and 15(1)(b) and the right to have the decision reviewed by the Court of Justice.

4.   The Commission shall in good time and in writing inform the competent authority of the Member State within the territory of which the investigation is to be carried out of its intention of taking a decision pursuant to paragraph 3. It shall hear the competent authority before taking its decision.

5.   Officials of the competent authority of the Member State within the territory of which the investigation is to be carried out may, at the request of that authority or of the Commission, assist the officials of the Commission in carrying out their duties.

6.   Where an undertaking or association of undertakings opposes an investigation ordered pursuant to this Article, the Member State concerned shall afford the necessary assistance to the officials authorised by the Commission to enable them to carry out their investigation. To this end the Member States shall, after consulting the Commission, take the necessary measures within one year of the entry into force of this Regulation.

[5413]

Article 14

Fines

1.   The Commission may by decision impose on the persons referred to in Article 3(1)(b), undertakings or associations of undertakings fines of from ECU 1000 to 50 000 where intentionally or negligently—
(a) they fail to notify a concentration in accordance with Article 4;
(b) they supply incorrect or misleading information in a notification pursuant to Article 4;
(c) they supply incorrect information in response to a request made pursuant to Article 11 or fail to supply information within the period fixed by a decision taken pursuant to Article 11;
(d) they produce the required books or other business records in incomplete form during investigations under Article 12 or 13, or refuse to submit to an investigation ordered by decision taken pursuant to Article 13.

2.   The Commission may by decision impose fines not exceeding 10% of the aggregate turnover of the undertakings concerned within the meaning of Article 5 on the persons or undertakings concerned where, either intentionally or negligently, they—
(a) fail to comply with an obligation imposed by decision pursuant to Article 7(4) or 8(2), second subparagraph;
(b) put into effect a concentration in breach of Article 7(1) or disregard a decision taken pursuant to Article 7(2);
(c) put into effect a concentration declared incompatible with the common market by decision pursuant to Article 8(3) or do not take the measures ordered by decision pursuant to Article 8(4).

3.   In setting the amount of a fine, regard shall be had to the nature and gravity of the infringement.

4.   Decisions taken pursuant to paragraphs 1 and 2 shall not be of criminal law nature.

[5414]

Article 15

Periodic penalty payments

1.   The Commission may by decision impose on the persons referred to in Article 3(1)(b), undertakings or associations of undertakings concerned periodic penalty payments of up to ECU 25 000 for each day of delay calculated from the date set in the decision, in order to compel them—
(a) to supply complete and correct information which it has requested by decision pursuant to Article 11;
(b) to submit to an investigation which it has ordered by decision pursuant to Article 13.

2.   The Commission may by decision impose on the persons referred to in Article 3(1)(b) or on undertakings periodic penalty payments of up to ECU 100 000

for each day of delay calculated from the date set in the decision, in order to compel them—

    (a) to comply with an obligation imposed by decision pursuant to Article 7(4) or Article 8(2), second subparagraph, or

    (b) to apply the measures ordered by decision pursuant to Article 8(4).

3. Where the persons referred to in Article 3(1)(b), undertakings or associations of undertakings have satisfied the obligation which it was the purpose of the periodic penalty payment to enforce, the Commission may set the total amount of the periodic penalty payments at a lower figure than that which would arise under the original decision.

              [5415]

Article 16

Review by the Court of Justice

The Court of Justice shall have unlimited jurisdiction within the meaning of Article 172 of the Treaty to review decisions whereby the Commission has fixed a fine or periodic penalty payments; it may cancel, reduce or increase the fine or periodic penalty payments imposed.

              [5416]

Article 17

Professional secrecy

1. Information acquired as a result of the application of Article 11, 12, 13 and 18 shall be used only for the purposes of the relevant request, investigation or hearing.

2. Without prejudice to Articles 4(3), 18 and 20, the Commission and the competent authorities of the Member States, their officials and other servants shall not disclose information they have acquired through the application of this Regulation of the kind covered by the obligation of professional secrecy.

3. Paragraphs 1 and 2 shall not prevent publication of general information or of surveys which do not contain information relating to particular undertakings or associations of undertakings.

              [5417]

Article 18

Hearing of the parties and of third persons

1. Before taking any decision provided for in [Article 7(4)], Article 8(2), second subparagraph, and (3) to (5), and Articles 14 and 15, the Commission shall give the persons, undertakings and associations of undertakings concerned the opportunity, at every stage of the procedure up to the consultation of the Advisory Committee, of making known their views on the objections against them.

[2. By way of derogation from paragraph 1, a decision to grant a derogation from suspension as referred to in Article 7(4) may be taken provisionally, without the persons, undertakings or associations of undertakings concerned being given the opportunity to make known their views beforehand, provided that the Commission gives them that opportunity as soon as possible after having taken its decision.]

3. The Commission shall base its decision only on objections on which the parties have been able to submit their observations. The rights of the defence shall be fully respected in the proceedings. Access to the file shall be open at least to the

parties directly involved, subject to the legitimate interest of undertakings in the protection of their business secrets.

4.   In so far as the Commission or the competent authorities of the Member States deem it necessary, they may also hear other natural or legal persons. Natural or legal persons showing a sufficient interest and especially members of the administrative or management bodies of the undertakings concerned or the recognised representatives of their employees shall be entitled, upon application, to be heard.

[5418]

NOTES

Para 1: words in square brackets substituted for original words "Articles 7(2) and (4)" by Council Regulation 1310/97/EC, Arts 1(10)(a), 2, as from 1 March 1998, except in relation to any concentration which was the subject of an agreement or announcement or where control was acquired within the meaning of Art 4(1) ante before 1 March 1998 or to any concentration in respect of which proceedings were initiated by a Member State's authority with responsibility for competition before 1 March 1998.

Para 2: substituted by Council Regulation 1310/97/EC, Arts 1(10)(b), 2, as from 1 March 1998, except in relation to any concentration which was the subject of an agreement or announcement or where control was acquired within the meaning of Art 4(1) ante before 1 March 1998 or to any concentration in respect of which proceedings were initiated by a Member State's authority with responsibility for competition before 1 March 1998. Original text read as follows—

"2. By way of derogation from paragraph 1, a decision to continue the suspension of a concentration or to grant a derogation from suspension as referred to in Article 7(2) or (4) may be taken provisionally, without the persons, undertakings or associations of undertakings concerned being given the opportunity to make known their views beforehand, provided that the Commission gives them that opportunity as soon as possible after having taken its decision."

Article 19

Liaison with the authorities of the Member States

1.   The Commission shall transmit to the competent authorities of the Member States copies of notifications within three working days and, as soon as possible, copies of the most important documents lodged with or issued by the Commission pursuant to this Regulation.

[Such documents shall include commitments which are intended by the parties to form the basis for a decision pursuant to Articles 6(1)(b) or 8(2).]

2.   The Commission shall carry out the procedures set out in this Regulation in close and constant liaison with the competent authorities of the Member States, which may express their views upon those procedures. For the purposes of Article 9 it shall obtain information from the competent authority of the Member State as referred to in paragraph 2 of that Article and give it the opportunity to make known its views at every stage of the procedure up to the adoption of a decision pursuant to paragraph 3 of that Article; to that end it shall give it access to the file.

3.   An Advisory Committee on concentrations shall be consulted before any decision is taken pursuant to Article 8(2) to (5), 14 or 15, or any provisions are adopted pursuant to Article 23.

4.   The Advisory Committee shall consist of representatives of the authorities of the Member States. Each Member State shall appoint one or two representatives; if unable to attend, they may be replaced by other representatives. At least one of the representatives of a Member State shall be competent in matters of restrictive practices and dominant positions.

5.   Consultation shall take place at a joint meeting convened at the invitation of and chaired by the Commission. A summary of the case, together with an indication of the most important documents and a preliminary draft of the decision to be taken

for each case considered, shall be sent with the invitation. The meeting shall take place not less than 14 days after the invitation has been sent. The Commission may in exceptional cases shorten that period as appropriate in order to avoid serious harm to one or more of the undertakings concerned by a concentration.

6. The Advisory Committee shall deliver an opinion on the Commission's draft decision, if necessary by taking a vote. The Advisory Committee may deliver an opinion even if some members are absent and unrepresented. The opinion shall be delivered in writing and appended to the draft decision. The Commission shall take the utmost account of the opinion delivered by the Committee. It shall inform the Committee of the manner in which its opinion has been taken into account.

7. The Advisory Committee may recommend publication of the opinion. The Commission may carry out such publication. The decision to publish shall take due account of the legitimate interest of undertakings in the protection of their business secrets and of the interest of the undertakings concerned in such publications taking place.

[5419]

NOTES

Para 1: subparagraph added by Council Regulation 1310/97/EC, Arts 1(11), 2, as from 1 March 1998, except in relation to any concentration which was the subject of an agreement or announcement or where control was acquired within the meaning of Art 4(1) ante before 1 March 1998 or to any concentration in respect of which proceedings were initiated by a Member State's authority with responsibility for competition before 1 March 1998.

Article 20

Publication of decisions

1. The Commission shall publish the decisions which it takes pursuant to Article 8(2) to (5) in the *Official Journal of the European Communities*.

2. The publication shall state the names of the parties and the main content of the decision; it shall have regard to the legitimate interest of undertakings in the protection of their business secrets.

[5420]

Article 21

Jurisdiction

1. Subject to review by the Court of Justice, the Commission shall have sole jurisdiction to take the decisions provided for in this Regulation.

2. No Member State shall apply its national legislation on competition to any concentration that has a community dimension.

The first subparagraph shall be without prejudice to any Member State's power to carry out any enquiries necessary for the application of Article 9(2) or after referral, pursuant to Article 9(3), first subparagraph, indent (b), or (5), to take the measures strictly necessary for the application of Article 9(8).

3. Notwithstanding paragraphs 1 and 2, Member States may take appropriate measures to protect legitimate interests other than those taken into consideration by this Regulation and compatible with the general principles and other provisions of Community law.

Public security, plurality of the media and prudential rules shall be regarded as legitimate interests within the meaning of the first subparagraph.

Any other public interest must be communicated to the Commission by the Member State concerned and shall be recognised by the Commission after an assessment of its compatibility with the general principles and other provisions of Community law before the measures referred to above may be taken. The Commission shall inform the Member State concerned of its decision within one month of that communication.

[5421]

Article 22

Application of the Regulation

[1.   This Regulation alone shall apply to concentrations as defined in Article 3, and Regulations No 17, (EEC) No 1017/68, (EEC) No 4056/86 and (EEC) No 3975/87 shall not apply, except in relation to joint ventures that do not have a Community dimension and which have as their object or effect the coordination of the competitive behaviour of undertakings that remain independent.]

[3.   If the Commission finds, at the request of a Member State or at the joint request of two or more Member States, that a concentration as defined in Article 3 that has no Community dimension within the meaning of Article 1 creates or strengthens a dominant position as a result of which effective competition would be significantly impeded within the territory of the Member State or States making the joint request, it may, in so far as that concentration affects trade between Member States, adopt the decisions provided for in Article 8(2), second subparagraph, (3) and (4).]

[4.   Articles 2(1)(a) and (b), 5, 6, 8 and 10 to 20 shall apply to a request made pursuant to paragraph 3. Article 7 shall apply to the extent that the concentration has not been put into effect on the date on which the Commission informs the parties that a request has been made.

The period within which proceedings may be initiated pursuant to Article 10(1) shall begin on the day following that of the receipt of the request from the Member State or States concerned. The request must be made within one month at most of the date on which the concentration was made known to the Member State or to all the Member States making a joint request or effected. This period shall begin on the date of the first of those events.]

5.   Pursuant to paragraph 3 the Commission shall take only the measures strictly necessary to maintain or restore effective competition within the territory of the Member State [or States] at the request of which it intervenes.

6.   . . .

[5422]

NOTES

Para 1: substituted for original paras 1, 2 by Council Regulation 1310/97/EC, Arts 1(12)(a), 2, as from 1 March 1998, except in relation to any concentration which was the subject of an agreement or announcement or where control was acquired within the meaning of Art 4(1) ante before 1 March 1998 or to any concentration in respect of which proceedings were initiated by a Member State's authority with responsibility for competition before 1 March 1998. Original text read as follows—

"1.   This Regulation alone shall apply to concentrations as defined in Article 3.

2.   Regulations No 17,[1] (EEC) No 1017/68,[2] (EEC) No 4056/86[3] and (EEC) No 3975/87[4] shall not apply to concentrations as defined in Article 3."

[1]   OJ L13, 21.2.62, p 204.
[2]   OJ L175, 23.7.68, p 1.
[3]   OJ L378, 31.12.86, p 4.
[4]   OJ L374, 31.12.87, p 1.

Para 3: substituted by Council Regulation 1310/97/EC, Arts 1(12)(b), 2, as from 1 March 1998, except in relation to any concentration which was the subject of an agreement or announcement or where control was acquired within the meaning of Art 4(1) ante before 1 March 1998 or to any concentration in respect of which proceedings were initiated by a Member State's authority with responsibility for competition before 1 March 1998. Original text read as follows—

"3. If the Commission finds, at the request of a Member State, that a concentration as defined in Article 3 that has no Community dimension within the meaning of Article 1 creates or strengthens a dominant position as a result of which effective competition would be significantly impeded within the territory of the Member State concerned it may, in so far as the concentration affects trade between Member States, adopt the decisions provided for in Article 8(2), second subparagraph, (3) and (4)."

Para 4: substituted by Council Regulation 1310/97/EC, Arts 1(12)(c), 2, as from 1 March 1998, except in relation to any concentration which was the subject of an agreement or announcement or where control was acquired within the meaning of Art 4(1) ante before 1 March 1998 or to any concentration in respect of which proceedings were initiated by a Member State's authority with responsibility for competition before 1 March 1998. Original text read as follows—

"4. Articles 2(1)(a) and (b), 5, 6, 8 and 10 to 20 shall apply. The period within which proceedings may be initiated pursuant to Article 10(1) shall begin on the date of the receipt of the request from the Member State. The request must be made within one month at most of the date on which the concentration was made known to the Member State or effected. This period shall begin on the date of the first of those events."

Para 5: words in square brackets inserted by Council Regulation 1310/97/EC, Arts 1(12)(d), 2, as from 1 March 1998, except in relation to any concentration which was the subject of an agreement or announcement or where control was acquired within the meaning of Art 4(1) ante before 1 March 1998 or to any concentration in respect of which proceedings were initiated by a Member State's authority with responsibility for competition before 1 March 1998.

Para 6: repealed by Council Regulation 1310/97/EC, Arts 1(12)(e), 2, as from 1 March 1998, except in relation to any concentration which was the subject of an agreement or announcement or where control was acquired within the meaning of Art 4(1) ante before 1 March 1998 or to any concentration in respect of which proceedings were initiated by a Member State's authority with responsibility for competition before 1 March 1998. Original text read as follows—

"6. Paragraphs 3 to 5 shall continue to apply until the thresholds referred to in Article 1(2) have been reviewed."

Article 23

Implementing provisions

The Commission shall have the power to adopt implementing provisions concerning the form, content and other details of notifications pursuant to Article 4, [time limits pursuant to Articles 7, 9, 10 and 22], and hearings pursuant to Article 18.

[The Commission shall have the power to lay down the procedure and time limits for the submission of commitments pursuant to Articles 6(1a) and 8(2).]

[5423]

NOTES

Words in square brackets substituted for original words "time limits pursuant to Article 10" by Council Regulation 1310/97/EC, Arts 1(13)(a), 2, as from 1 March 1998, except in relation to any concentration which was the subject of an agreement or announcement or where control was acquired within the meaning of Art 4(1) ante before 1 March 1998 or to any concentration in respect of which proceedings were initiated by a Member State's authority with responsibility for competition before 1 March 1998.

Subparagraph added by Council Regulation 1310/97/EC, Arts 1(13)(b), 2, as from 1 March 1998, except in relation to any concentration which was the subject of an agreement or announcement or where control was acquired within the meaning of Art 4(1) ante before 1 March 1998 or to any concentration in respect of which proceedings were initiated by a Member State's authority with responsibility for competition before 1 March 1998.

Article 24

Relations with non-member countries

1.   The Member States shall inform the Commission of any general difficulties encountered by their undertakings with concentrations as defined in Article 3 in a non-member country.

2.   Initially not more than one year after the entry into force of this Regulation and thereafter periodically the Commission shall draw up a report examining the treatment accorded to Community undertakings, in the terms referred to in paragraphs 3 and 4, as regards concentrations in non-member countries. The Commission shall submit those reports to the Council, together with any recommendations.

3.   Whenever it appears to the Commission, either on the basis of the reports referred to in paragraph 2 or on the basis of other information, that a non-member country does not grant Community undertakings treatment comparable to that granted by the Community to undertakings from that non-member country, the Commission may submit proposals to the Council for an appropriate mandate for negotiation with a view to obtaining comparable treatment for Community undertakings.

4.   Measures taken under this Article shall comply with the obligations of the Community or of the Member States, without prejudice to Article 234 of the Treaty, under international agreements, whether bilateral or multilateral.

[5424]

Article 25

Entry into force

1.   This Regulation shall enter into force on 21 September 1990.

2.   This Regulation shall not apply to any concentration which was the subject of an agreement or announcement or where control was acquired within the meaning of Article 4(1) before the date of this Regulation's entry into force and it shall not in any circumstances apply to any concentration in respect of which proceedings were initiated before that date by a Member State's authority with responsibility for competition.

[3.   As regards concentrations to which this Regulation applies by virtue of accession, the date of accession shall be substituted for the date of entry into force of this Regulation. The provision of paragraph 2, second alternative, applies in the same way to proceedings initiated by a competition authority of the new Member States or by the EFTA Surveillance Authority.]

[5425]

NOTES

Para 3: added by the 1994 Act of Accession of the Kingdom of Norway, the Republic of Austria, the Republic of Finland and the Kingdom of Sweden, Annex I(III)(B)(4), as adjusted by Council Decision 95/1/EC, Annex I(III)(B)(4).

This Regulation shall be binding in its entirety and directly applicable in all Member States.

Done at Brussels, 21 December 1989.

COUNCIL REGULATION

of 30 June 1997

amending Regulation (EEC) No 4064/89 on the control of concentrations between undertakings

(1310/97/EC)

NOTES
Date of publication in OJ; OJ L 180, 9/7/97, p 1.

THE COUNCIL OF THE EUROPEAN UNION,

Having regard to the Treaty establishing the European Community, and in particular Articles 87 and 235 thereof,

Having regard to the proposal from the Commission,[1]

Having regard to the opinion of the European Parliament,[2]

Having regard to the opinion of the Economic and Social Committee,[3]

(1) Whereas concentrations with a significant impact in several Member States that fall below the thresholds referred to in Council Regulation (EEC) No 4064/89 of 21 December 1989 on the control of concentrations between undertakings[4] may qualify for examination under a number of national merger control systems; whereas multiple notification of the same transaction increases legal uncertainty, effort and cost for companies and may lead to conflicting assessments;

(2) Whereas extending the scope of Community merger control to concentrations with a significant impact in several Member States will ensure that a "one-stop shop" system applies and will allow, in compliance with the subsidiarity principle, for an appreciation of the competition impact of such concentrations in the Community as a whole;

(3) Whereas additional criteria should be established for the application of Community merger control in order to meet the abovementioned objectives; whereas those criteria should consist of new thresholds established in terms of the total turnover of the undertakings concerned achieved world-wide, at Community level and in at least three Member States;

(4) Whereas at the end of the initial phase of application of this Regulation the Commission should report to the Council on the implementation of all applicable thresholds and criteria, so that the Council is in a position, acting in accordance with Article 145 of the Treaty, to change the criteria or adjust the thresholds laid down in this Regulation;

(5) Whereas it is appropriate to define the concept of concentration in such a manner as to cover operations bringing about a lasting change in the structure of the undertakings concerned; whereas in the specific case of joint ventures it is appropriate to include within the scope and procedure of Regulation (EEC) No 4064/89 all full-function joint ventures; whereas, in addition to the dominance test set out in Article 2 of that Regulation, it should be provided that the Commission apply the criteria of Article 85(1) and (3) of the Treaty to such joint ventures, to the extent that their creation has as its direct consequence an appreciable restriction of competition between undertakings that remain independent; whereas, if the effects of such joint ventures on the market are primarily structural, Article 85(1) does not as a general rule apply; whereas Article 85(1) may apply if two or more parent companies remain active in the market of the joint venture, or, possibly, if the creation of the joint venture has as its object or effect the prevention, restriction or distortion of competition between the parent companies in upstream, downstream or neighbouring markets; whereas, in this context, the appraisal of all competition aspects of the creation of the joint venture must be made within the same procedure;

(6) Whereas, for the purposes of calculating the turnover of credit and financial institutions, banking income is a better criterion than a proportion of assets, because it reflects more accurately the economic reality of the whole banking sector;

(7) Whereas it should be expressly provided that decisions taken at the end of the first phase of the procedure cover restrictions directly related and necessary for the implementation of a concentration;

(8) Whereas the Commission may declare a concentration compatible with the common market in the second phase of the procedure, following commitments by the parties that are proportional to and would entirely eliminate the competition problem; whereas it is also appropriate to accept commitments in the first phase of the procedure where the competition problem is readily identifiable and can easily be remedied; whereas it should be expressly provided that in these cases the Commission may attach to its decision conditions and

obligations; whereas transparency and effective consultation of Member States and interested third parties should be ensured in both phases of the procedure;

(9) Whereas, to ensure effective control, concentrations should be suspended until a final decision has been taken; whereas, on the other hand, it should be possible to waive a suspension, where appropriate; whereas, in deciding whether or not to grant a waiver, the Commission should take account of all pertinent factors, such as the nature and gravity of damage to the undertakings concerned by a concentration or to third parties, and the threat to competition posed by the concentration;

(10) Whereas the rules governing the referral of concentrations between the Commission and Member States should be reviewed at the same time as the additional criteria for implementation of Community merger control are established; whereas these rules protect the competition interests of the Member States in an adequate manner and take due account of legal security and the "one-stop shop" principle; whereas, however, certain aspects of the referral procedures should be improved or clarified;

(11) Whereas, in particular, the Commission can declare a concentration incompatible with the common market only if it impedes effective competition in a substantial part thereof; whereas the application of national competition law is, therefore, particularly appropriate where a concentration affects competition on a distinct market within a Member State that does not constitute a substantial part of the common market; whereas in this case it should not be necessary to demonstrate, in the request for referral, that the concentration threatens to create or to strengthen a dominant position on this distinct market;

(12) Whereas it should be possible to suspend exceptionally the period within which the Commission must take a decision within the first phase of the procedure;

(13) Whereas it should be expressly provided that two or more Member States may make a joint request pursuant to Article 22 of Regulation (EEC) No 4064/89; whereas to ensure effective control, provision should be made for the suspension of concentrations referred to the Commission by one or more Member States;

(14) Whereas the Commission should be given the power to adopt implementing provisions where necessary,

NOTES
1   OJ C 350, 21.11.96, pp 8 and 10.
2   OJ C 362, 2.12.96, p 130.
3   OJ C 56, 24.2.97, p 71.
4   OJ L 395, 30.12.89, p 1. Regulation rectified by OJ L 257, 21.9.90, p 13 and amended by the 1994 Act of Accession.

HAS ADOPTED THIS REGULATION—

Articles 1–3

(Amend Council Regulation 4064/89/EEC, at **[5401]** *et seq.)*

COMMISSION REGULATION

of 1 March 1998

on the notifications, time limits and hearings provided for in Council Regulation (EEC) No 4064/89 on the control of concentrations between undertakings

(447/98/EC)

(Text with EEA relevance)

NOTES
Date of publication in OJ: OJ L61, 2.3.98, p 1.

THE COMMISSION OF THE EUROPEAN COMMUNITIES,

Having regard to the Treaty establishing the European Community,

Having regard to the Agreement on the European Economic Area,

Having regard to Council Regulation (EEC) No 4064/89 of 21 December 1989 on the control of concentrations between undertakings,[1] as last amended by Regulation (EC) No 1310/97,[2] and in particular Article 23 thereof,

Having regard to Council Regulation No 17 of 6 February 1962, First Regulation implementing Articles 85 and 86 of the Treaty,[3] as last amended by the Act of Accession of Austria, Finland and Sweden, and in particular Article 24 thereof,

Having regard to Council Regulation (EEC) No 1017/68 of 19 July 1968 applying rules of competition to transport by rail, road and inland waterway,[4] as last amended by the Act of Accession of Austria, Finland and Sweden, and in particular Article 29 thereof,

Having regard to Council Regulation (EEC) No 4056/86 of 22 December 1986 laying down detailed rules for the application of Articles 85 and 86 of the Treaty to maritime transport,[5] as amended by the Act of Accession of Austria, Finland and Sweden, and in particular Article 26 thereof,

Having regard to Council Regulation (EEC) No 3975/87 of 14 December 1987 laying down the procedure for the application of the rules on competition to undertakings in the air transport sector,[6] as last amended by Regulation (EEC) No 2410/92,[7] and in particular Article 19 thereof,

Having consulted the Advisory Committee on Concentrations,

(1) Whereas Regulation (EEC) No 4064/89 and in particular Article 23 thereof has been amended by Regulation (EC) No 1310/97;

(2) Whereas Commission Regulation (EC) No 3384/94,[8] implementing Regulation (EEC) No 4064/89, must be modified in order to take account of those amendments; whereas experience in the application of Regulation (EC) No 3384/94 has revealed the need to improve certain procedural aspects thereof; whereas for the sake of clarity it should therefore be replaced by a new regulation;

(3) Whereas the Commission has adopted Decision 94/810/ECSC, EC of 12 December 1994 on the terms of reference of hearing officers in competition procedures before the Commission,[9]

(4) Whereas Regulation (EEC) No 4064/89 is based on the principle of compulsory notification of concentrations before they are put into effect; whereas, on the one hand, a notification has important legal consequences which are favourable to the parties to the concentration plan, while, on the other hand, failure to comply with the obligation to notify renders the parties liable to a fine and may also entail civil law disadvantages for them; whereas it is therefore necessary in the interests of legal certainty to define precisely the subject matter and content of the information to be provided in the notification;

(5) Whereas it is for the notifying parties to make full and honest disclosure to the Commission of the facts and circumstances which are relevant for taking a decision on the notified concentration;

(6) Whereas in order to simplify and expedite examination of the notification, it is desirable to prescribe that a form be used;

(7) Whereas since notification sets in motion legal time limits pursuant to Regulation (EEC) No 4064/89, the conditions governing such time-limits and the time when they become effective must also be determined;

(8) Whereas rules must be laid down in the interests of legal certainty for calculating the time limits provided for in Regulation (EEC) No 4064/89; whereas in particular, the beginning and end of the period and the circumstances suspending the running of the period must be determined, with due regard to the requirements resulting from the exceptionally short legal time-limits referred to above; whereas in the absence of specific provisions the determination of rules applicable to periods, dates and time-limits should be based on the principles of Council Regulation (EEC, Euratom) No 1182/71;[10]

(9) Whereas the provisions relating to the Commission's procedure must be framed in such a way as to safeguard fully the right to be heard and the rights of defence; whereas for these purposes the Commission should distinguish between the parties who notify the concentration, other parties involved in the concentration plan, third parties and parties regarding whom the Commission intends to take a decision imposing a fine or periodic penalty payments;

(10) Whereas the Commission should give the notifying parties and other parties involved, if they so request, an opportunity before notification to discuss the intended concentration informally and in strict confidence; whereas in addition it should, after notification, maintain close contact with those parties to the extent necessary to discuss with them any practical or legal problems which it discovers on a first examination of the case and if possible to remove such problems by mutual agreement;

(11)   Whereas in accordance with the principle of the rights of defence, the notifying parties must be given the opportunity to submit their comments on all the objections which the Commission proposes to take into account in its decisions; whereas the other parties involved should also be informed of the Commission's objections and granted the opportunity to express their views;

(12)   Whereas third parties having sufficient interest must also be given the opportunity of expressing their views where they make a written application;

(13)   Whereas the various persons entitled to submit comments should do so in writing, both in their own interest and in the interest of good administration, without prejudice to their right to request a formal oral hearing where appropriate to supplement the written procedure; whereas in urgent cases, however, the Commission must be able to proceed immediately to formal oral hearings of the notifying parties, other parties involved or third parties;

(14)   Whereas it is necessary to define the rights of persons who are to be heard, to what extent they should be granted access to the Commission's file and on what conditions they may be represented or assisted;

(15)   Whereas the Commission must respect the legitimate interest of undertakings in the protection of their business secrets and other confidential information;

(16)   Whereas, in order to enable the Commission to carry out a proper assessment of commitments that have the purpose of rendering the concentration compatible with the common market, and to ensure due consultation with other parties involved, third parties and the authorities of the Member States as provided for in Regulation (EEC) No 4064/89, in particular Article 18(1) and (4) thereof, the procedure and time-limits for submitting such commitments as provided for in Article 6(2) and Article 8(2) of Regulation (EEC) No 4064/89 must be laid down;

(17)   Whereas it is also necessary to define the rules for fixing and calculating the time limits for reply fixed by the Commission;

(18)   Whereas the Advisory Committee on Concentrations must deliver its opinion on the basis of a preliminary draft decision; whereas it must therefore be consulted on a case after the inquiry into that case has been completed; whereas such consultation does not, however, prevent the Commission from reopening an inquiry if need be,

---

NOTES

1   OJ L395, 30.12.89, p 1; corrected version, OJ L257, 21.9.90, p 13.
2   OJ L180, 9.7.97, p 1.
3   OJ 13, 21.2.62, p 204/62.
4   OJ L175, 23.7.68, p 1.
5   OJ L378, 31.12.86, p 4.
6   OJ L374, 31.12.87, p 1.
7   OJ L240, 24.8.92, p 18.
8   OJ L377, 31.12.94, p 1.
9   OJ L330, 21.12.94, p 67.
10   OJ L124, 8.6.71, p 1.

HAS ADOPTED THIS REGULATION—

CHAPTER I
NOTIFICATIONS

Article 1

Persons entitled to submit notifications

1.   Notifications shall be submitted by the persons or undertakings referred to in Article 4(2) of Regulation (EEC) No 4064/89.

2.   Where notifications are signed by representatives of persons or of undertakings, such representatives shall produce written proof that they are authorised to act.

3.   Joint notifications should be submitted by a joint representative who is authorised to transmit and to receive documents on behalf of all notifying parties.

[5426]

Article 2

Submission of notifications

1.   Notifications shall be submitted in the manner prescribed by form CO as shown in the Annex. Joint notifications shall be submitted on a single form.

2.   One original and 23 copies of the form CO and the supporting documents shall be submitted to the Commission at the address indicated in form CO.

3.   The supporting documents shall be either originals or copies of the originals; in the latter case the notifying parties shall confirm that they are true and complete.

4.   Notifications shall be in one of the official languages of the Community. This language shall also be the language of the proceeding for the notifying parties. Supporting documents shall be submitted in their original language. Where the original language is not one of the official languages of the Community, a translation into the language of the proceeding shall be attached.

5.   Where notifications are made pursuant to Article 57 of the EEA Agreement, they may also be in one of the official languages of the EFTA States or the working language of the EFTA Surveillance Authority. If the language chosen for the notifications is not an official language of the Community, the notifying parties shall simultaneously supplement all documentation with a translation into an official language of the Community. The language which is chosen for the translation shall determine the language used by the Commission as the language of the proceedings for the notifying parties.

[5427]

Article 3

Information and documents to be provided

1.   Notifications shall contain the information, including documents, requested by form CO. The information must be correct and complete.

2.   The Commission may dispense with the obligation to provide any particular information, including documents, requested by form CO where the Commission considers that such information is not necessary for the examination of the case.

3.   The Commission shall without delay acknowledge in writing to the notifying parties or their representatives receipt of the notification and of any reply to a letter sent by the Commission pursuant to Article 4(2) and (4).

[5428]

Article 4

Effective date of notification

1.   Subject to paragraphs 2, 3 and 4, notifications shall become effective on the date on which they are received by the Commission.

2.   Where the information, including documents, contained in the notification is incomplete in a material respect, the Commission shall inform the notifying parties or their representatives in writing without delay and shall set an appropriate time-limit for the completion of the information. In such cases, the notification shall

become effective on the date on which the complete information is received by the Commission.

3.   Material changes in the facts contained in the notification which the notifying parties know or ought to have known must be communicated to the Commission without delay. In such cases, when these material changes could have a significant effect on the appraisal of the concentration, the notification may be considered by the Commission as becoming effective on the date on which the information on the material changes is received by the Commission; the Commission shall inform the notifying parties or their representatives of this in writing and without delay.

4.   Incorrect or misleading information shall be considered to be incomplete information.

5.   When the Commission publishes the fact of the notification pursuant to Article 4(3) of Regulation (EEC) No 4064/89, it shall specify the date upon which the notification has been received. Where, further to the application of paragraphs 2, 3 and 4, the effective date of notification is later than the date specified in this publication, the Commission shall issue a further publication in which it will state the later date.

[5429]

Article 5

Conversion of notifications

1.   Where the Commission finds that the operation notified does not constitute a concentration within the meaning of Article 3 of Regulation (EEC) No 4064/89, it shall inform the notifying parties or their representatives in writing. In such a case, the Commission shall, if requested by the notifying parties, as appropriate and subject to paragraph 2 of this Article, treat the notification as an application within the meaning of Article 2 or a notification within the meaning of Article 4 of Regulation No 17, as an application within the meaning of Article 12 or a notification within the meaning of Article 14 of Regulation (EEC) No 1017/68, as an application within the meaning of Article 12 of Regulation (EEC) No 4056/86 or as an application within the meaning of Article 3(2) or of Article 5 of Regulation (EEC) No 3975/87.

2.   In cases referred to in paragraph 1, second sentence, the Commission may require that the information given in the notification be supplemented within an appropriate time-limit fixed by it in so far as this is necessary for assessing the operation on the basis of the Regulations referred to in that sentence. The application or notification shall be deemed to fulfil the requirements of such Regulations from the date of the original notification where the additional information is received by the Commission within the time-limit fixed.

[5430]

CHAPTER II
TIME-LIMITS

Article 6

Beginning of periods

1.   The period referred to in Article 9(2) of Regulation (EEC) No 4064/89 shall start at the beginning of the working day following the date of the receipt of the copy of the notification by the Member State.

2.   The period referred to in Article 9(4)(b) of Regulation (EEC) No 4064/89 shall start at the beginning of the working day following the effective date of the notification, within the meaning of Article 4 of this Regulation.

3.   The period referred to in Article 9(6) of Regulation (EEC) No 4064/89 shall start at the beginning of the working day following the date of the Commission's referral.

4.   The periods referred to in Article 10(1) of Regulation (EEC) No 4064/89 shall start at the beginning of the working day following the effective date of the notification, within the meaning of Article 4 of this Regulation.

5.   The period referred to in Article 10(3) of Regulation (EEC) No 4064/89 shall start at the beginning of the working day following the day on which proceedings were initiated.

6.   The period referred to in Article 22(4), second subparagraph, second sentence, of Regulation (EEC) No 4064/89 shall start at the beginning of the working day following the date of the first of the events referred to.

[5431]

Article 7

End of periods

1.   The period referred to in Article 9(2) of Regulation (EEC) No 4064/89 shall end with the expiry of the day which in the third week following that in which the period began is the same day of the week as the day from which the period runs.

2.   The period referred to in Article 9(4)(b) of Regulation (EEC) No 4064/89 shall end with the expiry of the day which in the third month following that in which the period began falls on the same date as the day from which the period runs. Where such a day does not occur in that month, the period shall end with the expiry of the last day of that month.

3.   The period referred to in Article 9(6) of Regulation (EEC) No 4064/89 shall end with the expiry of the day which in the fourth month following that in which the period began falls on the same date as the day from which the period runs. Where such a day does not occur in that month, the period shall end with the expiry of the last day of that month.

4.   The period referred to in Article 10(1), first subparagraph, of Regulation (EEC) No 4064/89 shall end with the expiry of the day which in the month following that in which the period began falls on the same date as the day from which the period runs. Where such a day does not occur in that month, the period shall end with the expiry of the last day of that month.

5.   The period referred to in Article 10(1), second subparagraph, of Regulation (EEC) No 4064/89 shall end with the expiry of the day which in the sixth week following that in which the period began is the same day of the week as the day from which the period runs.

6.   The period referred to in Article 10(3) of Regulation (EEC) No 4064/89 shall end with the expiry of the day which in the fourth month following that in which the period began falls on the same date as the day from which the period runs. Where such a day does not occur in that month, the period shall end with the expiry of the last day of that month.

7.   The period referred to in Article 22(4), second subparagraph, second sentence, of Regulation (EEC) No 4064/89 shall end with the expiry of the day which in the month following that in which the period began falls on the same date

as the day from which the period runs. Where such a day does not occur in that month, the period shall end with the expiry of the last day of that month.

8.   Where the last day of the period is not a working day, the period shall end with the expiry of the following working day.

[5432]

Article 8

Recovery of holidays

Once the end of the period has been determined in accordance with Article 7, if public holidays or other holidays of the Commission referred to in Article 23 fall within the periods referred to in Articles 9, 10 and 22 of Regulation (EEC) No 4064/89, a corresponding number of working days shall be added to those periods.

[5433]

Article 9

Suspension of time limit

1.   The periods referred to in Article 10(1) and (3) of Regulation (EEC) No 4064/89 shall be suspended where the Commission, pursuant to Article 11(5) and Article 13(3) of that Regulation, has to take a decision because—
   (a) information which the Commission has requested pursuant to Article 11(1) of Regulation (EEC) No 4064/89 from one of the notifying parties or another involved party, as defined in Article 11 of this Regulation, is not provided or not provided in full within the time limit fixed by the Commission;
   (b) information which the Commission has requested pursuant to Article 11(1) of Regulation (EEC) No 4064/89 from a third party, as defined in Article 11 of this Regulation, is not provided or not provided in full within the time limit fixed by the Commission owing to circumstances for which one of the notifying parties or another involved party, as defined in Article 11 of this Regulation, is responsible;
   (c) one of the notifying parties or another involved party, as defined in Article 11 of this Regulation, has refused to submit to an investigation deemed necessary by the Commission on the basis of Article 13(1) of Regulation (EEC) No 4064/89 or to cooperate in the carrying out of such an investigation in accordance with that provision;
   (d) the notifying parties have failed to inform the Commission of material changes in the facts contained in the notification.

2.   The periods referred to in Article 10(1) and (3) of Regulation (EEC) No 4064/89 shall be suspended—
   (a) in the cases referred to in paragraph 1(a) and (b), for the period between the end of the time limit fixed in the request for information and the receipt of the complete and correct information required by decision;
   (b) in the cases referred to in paragraph 1(c), for the period between the unsuccessful attempt to carry out the investigation and the completion of the investigation ordered by decision;
   (c) in the cases referred to in paragraph 1(d), for the period between the occurrence of the change in the facts referred to therein and the receipt of the complete and correct information requested by decision or the completion of the investigation ordered by decision.

3.   The suspension of the time limit shall begin on the day following that on which the event causing the suspension occurred. It shall end with the expiry of the day on which the reason for suspension is removed. Where such a day is not a

working day, the suspension of the time limit shall end with the expiry of the following working day.

[5434]

Article 10

Compliance with the time-limits

1.   The time limits referred to in Article 9(4) and (5), and Article 10(1) and (3) of Regulation (EEC) No 4064/89 shall be met where the Commission has taken the relevant decision before the end of the period.

2.   The time limit referred to in Article 9(2) of Regulation (EEC) No 4064/89 shall be met where a Member State informs the Commission before the end of the period in writing.

3.   The time limit referred to in Article 9(6) of Regulation (EEC) No 4064/89 shall be met where the competent authority of the Member State concerned publishes any report or announces the findings of the examination of the concentration before the end of the period.

4.   The time limit referred to in Article 22(4), second subparagraph, second sentence, of Regulation (EEC) No 4064/89 shall be met where the request made by the Member State or the Member States is received by the Commission before the end of the period.

[5435]

CHAPTER III
HEARING OF THE PARTIES AND OF THIRD PARTIES

Article 11

Parties to be heard

For the purposes of the rights to be heard pursuant to Article 18 of Regulation (EEC) No 4064/89, the following parties are distinguished—

   (a)   notifying parties, that is, persons or undertakings submitting a notification pursuant to Article 4(2) of Regulation (EEC) No 4064/89;

   (b)   other involved parties, that is, parties to the concentration plan other than the notifying parties, such as the seller and the undertaking which is the target of the concentration;

   (c)   third parties, that is, natural or legal persons showing a sufficient interest, including customers, suppliers and competitors, and especially members of the administration or management organs of the undertakings concerned or recognised workers' representatives of those undertakings;

   (d)   parties regarding whom the Commission intends to take a decision pursuant to Article 14 or 15 of Regulation (EEC) No 4064/89.

[5436]

Article 12

Decisions on the suspension of concentrations

1.   Where the Commission intends to take a decision pursuant to Article 7(4) of Regulation (EEC) No 4064/89 which adversely affects one or more of the parties, it shall, pursuant to Article 18(1) of that Regulation, inform the notifying parties and other involved parties in writing of its objections and shall fix a time limit within which they may make known their views.

2.   Where the Commission, pursuant to Article 18(2) of Regulation (EEC) No 4064/89, has taken a decision referred to in paragraph 1 of this Article provisionally without having given the notifying parties and other involved parties the opportunity to make known their views, it shall without delay send them the text of the provisional decision and shall fix a time limit within which they may make known their views.

Once the notifying parties and other involved parties have made known their views, the Commission shall take a final decision annulling, amending or confirming the provisional decision. Where they have not made known their views within the time limit fixed, the Commission's provisional decision shall become final with the expiry of that period.

3.   The notifying parties and other involved parties shall make known their views in writing or orally within the time limit fixed. They may confirm their oral statements in writing.

[5437]

Article 13

Decisions on the substance of the case

1.   Where the Commission intends to take a decision pursuant to Article 8(2), second subparagraph, or Article 8(3), (4) or (5) of Regulation (EEC) No 4064/89, it shall, before consulting the Advisory Committee on Concentrations, hear the parties pursuant to Article 18(1) and (3) of that Regulation.

2.   The Commission shall address its objections in writing to the notifying parties.

The Commission shall, when giving notice of objections, set a time limit within which the notifying parties may inform the Commission of their views in writing.

The Commission shall inform other involved parties in writing of these objections.

The Commission shall also set a time limit within which those other involved parties may inform the Commission of their views in writing.

3.   After having addressed its objections to the notifying parties, the Commission shall, upon request, give them access to the file for the purpose of enabling them to exercise their rights of defence.

The Commission shall, upon request, also give the other involved parties who have been informed of the objections access to the file in so far as this is necessary, for the purposes of preparing their observations.

4.   The parties to whom the Commission's objections have been addressed or who have been informed of those objections shall, within the time limit fixed, make known in writing their views on the objections. In their written comments, they may set out all matters relevant to the case and may attach any relevant documents in proof of the facts set out. They may also propose that the Commission hear persons who may corroborate those facts. They shall submit one original and 29 copies of their response to the Commission at the address indicated in form CO.

5.   Where the Commission intends to take a decision pursuant to Article 14 or 15 of Regulation (EEC) No 4064/89 it shall, before consulting the Advisory Committee on Concentrations, hear pursuant to Article 18(1) and (3) of that Regulation the parties regarding whom the Commission intends to take such a decision.

The procedure provided for in paragraph 2, first and second subparagraphs, paragraph 3, first subparagraph, and paragraph 4 is applicable, *mutatis mutandis*.

[5438]

Article 14

Oral hearings

1.   The Commission shall afford the notifying parties who have so requested in their written comments the opportunity to put forward their arguments orally in a formal hearing if such parties show a sufficient interest. It may also in other cases afford such parties the opportunity of expressing their views orally.

2.   The Commission shall afford other involved parties who have so requested in their written comments the opportunity to express their views orally in a formal hearing if they show a sufficient interest. It may also in other cases afford such parties the opportunity of expressing their views orally.

3.   The Commission shall afford parties on whom it proposes to impose a fine or periodic penalty payment who have so requested in their written comments the opportunity to put forward their arguments orally in a formal hearing. It may also in other cases afford such parties the opportunity of expressing their views orally.

4.   The Commission shall invite the persons to be heard to attend on such date as it shall appoint.

5.   The Commission shall invite the competent authorities of the Member States to take part in the hearing.

[5439]

Article 15

Conduct of formal oral hearings

1.   Hearings shall be conducted by the Hearing Officer.

2.   Persons invited to attend shall either appear in person or be represented by legal representatives or by representatives authorised by their constitution as appropriate. Undertakings and associations of undertakings may be represented by a duly authorised agent appointed from among their permanent staff.

3.   Persons heard by the Commission may be assisted by their legal adviser or other qualified persons admitted by the Hearing Officer.

4.   Hearings shall not be public. Each person shall be heard separately or in the presence of other persons invited to attend. In the latter case, regard shall be had to the legitimate interest of the undertakings in the protection of their business secrets and other confidential information.

5.   The statements made by each person heard shall be recorded.

[5440]

Article 16

Hearing of third parties

1.   If third parties apply in writing to be heard pursuant to Article 18(4), second sentence, of Regulation (EEC) No 4064/89, the Commission shall inform them in writing of the nature and subject matter of the procedure and shall fix a time limit within which they may make known their views.

2.   The third parties referred to in paragraph 1 shall make known their views in writing within the time limit fixed. The Commission may, where appropriate, afford the parties who have so requested in their written comments the opportunity to

participate in a formal hearing. It may also in other cases afford such parties the opportunity of expressing their views orally.

3.   The Commission may likewise afford to any other third parties the opportunity of expressing their views.

[5441]

Article 17

Confidential information

1.   Information, including documents, shall not be communicated or made accessible in so far as it contains business secrets of any person or undertaking, including the notifying parties, other involved parties or of third parties or other confidential information the disclosure of which is not considered necessary by the Commission for the purpose of the procedure, or where internal documents of the authorities are concerned.

2.   Any party which makes known its views under the provisions of this Chapter shall clearly identify any material which it considers to be confidential, giving reasons, and provide a separate non-confidential version within the time limit fixed by the Commission.

[5442]

CHAPTER IV
COMMITMENTS RENDERING THE CONCENTRATION COMPATIBLE

Article 18

Time limits for commitments

1.   Commitments proposed to the Commission by the undertakings concerned pursuant to Article 6(2) of Regulation (EEC) No 4064/89 which are intended by the parties to form the basis for a decision pursuant to Article 6(1)(b) of that Regulation shall be submitted to the Commission within not more than three weeks from the date of receipt of the notification.

2.   Commitments proposed to the Commission by the undertakings concerned pursuant to Article 8(2) of Regulation (EEC) No 4064/89 which are intended by the parties to form the basis for a decision pursuant to that Article shall be submitted to the Commission within not more than three months from the date on which proceedings were initiated. The Commission may in exceptional circumstances extend this period.

3.   Articles 6 to 9 shall apply *mutatis mutandis* to paragraphs 1 and 2 of this Article.

[5443]

Article 19

Procedure for commitments

1.   One original and 29 copies of commitments proposed to the Commission by the undertakings concerned pursuant to Article 6(2) or Article 8(2) of Regulation (EEC) No 4064/89 shall be submitted to the Commission, at the address indicated in form CO.

2. Any party proposing commitments to the Commission pursuant to Article 6(2) or Article 8(2) of Regulation (EEC) No 4064/89 shall clearly identify any material which it considers to be confidential, giving reasons, and provide a separate non-confidential version within the time limit fixed by the Commission.

[5444]

CHAPTER V
MISCELLANEOUS PROVISIONS

Article 20

Transmission of documents

1. Transmission of documents and invitations from the Commission to the addressees may be effected in any of the following ways—
  (a) delivery by hand against receipt;
  (b) registered letter with acknowledgement of receipt;
  (c) fax with a request for acknowledgement of receipt;
  (d) telex;
  (e) electronic mail with a request for acknowledgement of receipt.

2. Unless otherwise provided in this Regulation, paragraph 1 also applies to the transmission of documents from the notifying parties, from other involved parties or from third parties to the Commission.

3. Where a document is sent by telex, by fax or by electronic mail, it shall be presumed that it has been received by the addressee on the day on which it was sent.

[5445]

Article 21

Setting of time limits

In fixing the time limits provided for pursuant to Article 4(2), Article 5(2), Article 12(1) and (2), Article 13(2) and Article 16(1), the Commission shall have regard to the time required for preparation of statements and to the urgency of the case. It shall also take account of working days as well as public holidays in the country of receipt of the Commission's communication.

These time limits shall be set in terms of a precise calendar date.

[5446]

Article 22

Receipt of documents by the Commission

1. In accordance with the provisions of Article 4(1) of this Regulation, notifications must be delivered to the Commission at the address indicated in form CO or have been dispatched by registered letter to the address indicated in form CO before the expiry of the period referred to in Article 4(1) of Regulation (EEC) No 4064/89.

Additional information requested to complete notifications pursuant to Article 4(2) and (4) or to supplement notifications pursuant to Article 5(2) must reach the Commission at the aforesaid address or have been dispatched by registered letter before the expiry of the time limit fixed in each case.

Written comments on Commission communications pursuant to Article 12(1) and (2), Article 13(2) and Article 16(1) must have reached the Commission at the aforesaid address before the expiry of the time limit fixed in each case.

2.   Time limits referred to in subparagraphs two and three of paragraph 1 shall be determined in accordance with Article 21.

3.   Should the last day of a time limit fall on a day which is not a working day or which is a public holiday in the country of dispatch, the time limit shall expire on the following working day.

[5447]

Article 23

Definition of working days

The expression "working days" in this Regulation means all days other than Saturdays, Sundays, public holidays and other holidays as determined by the Commission and published in the *Official Journal of the European Communities* before the beginning of each year.

[5448]

Article 24

(Repeals Regulation 3384/94/EEC.)

Article 25

Entry into force

This Regulation shall enter into force on 2 March 1998.

[5449]

This Regulation shall be binding in its entirety and directly applicable in all Member States.

NOTES

Article as amended by Corrigenda of 6 March 1998; see OJL66, 6.3.98, p 25.

Done at Brussels, 1 March 1998.

ANNEX

FORM CO RELATING TO THE NOTIFICATION OF A CONCENTRATION PURSUANT TO REGULATION (EEC) NO 4064/89

INTRODUCTION

A.   The purpose of this form

This form specifies the information that must be provided by an undertaking or undertakings when notifying the Commission of a concentration with a Community dimension. A "concentration" is defined in Article 3 of Regulation (EEC) No 4064/89 (hereinafter referred to as "the Merger Regulation") and "Community dimension" in Article 1 thereof.

Your attention is drawn to the Merger Regulation and to Regulation (EC) No 447/98 (hereinafter referred to as "the Implementing Regulation") and to the corresponding provisions of the Agreement on the European Economic Area.[1]

Experience has shown that prenotification meetings are extremely valuable to both the notifying parties and the Commission in determining the precise amount of information required in a notification and, in the large majority of cases, will result in a significant reduction of the information required. Accordingly, notifying parties are encouraged to consult the Commission regarding the possibility of dispensing with the obligation to provide certain information (see Section B(g) on the possibility of dispensation).

B.   The need for a correct and complete notification

All information required by this form must be correct and complete. The information required must be supplied in the appropriate section of this form. Annexes to this form shall only be used to supplement the information supplied in the form itself.

In particular you should note that—

(a) In accordance with Article 10(1) of the Merger Regulation and Article 4(2) and (4) of the Implementing Regulation, the time limits of the Merger Regulation linked to the notification will not begin to run until all the information that has to be supplied with the notification has been received by the Commission. This requirement is to ensure that the Commission is able to assess the notified concentration within the strict time-limits provided by the Merger Regulation.

(b) The notifying parties should check carefully, in the course of preparing their notification, that contact names and numbers, and in particular fax numbers, provided to the Commission are accurate, relevant and up-to-date.

(c) Incorrect or misleading information in the notification will be considered to be incomplete information (Article 4(4) of the Implementing Regulation).

(d) If a notification is incomplete, the Commission will inform the notifying parties or their representatives of this in writing and without delay. The notification will only become effective on the date on which the complete and accurate information is received by the Commission (Article 10(1) of the Merger Regulation, Article 4(2) and (4) of the implementing Regulation).

(e) Article 14(1)(b) of the Merger Regulation provides that incorrect or misleading information, where supplied intentionally or negligently, can make the notifying party or parties liable to fines of up to ECU 50000. In addition, pursuant to Article 6(3)(a) and Article 8(5)(a) of the Merger Regulation the Commission may also revoke its decision on the compatibility of a notified concentration where it is based on incorrect information for which one of the undertakings is responsible.

(f) You may request that the Commission accept that the notification is complete notwithstanding the failure to provide information required by this form, if such information is not reasonably available to you in part or in whole (for example, because of the unavailability of information on a target company during a contested bid).

The Commission will consider such a request, provided that you give reasons for the unavailability of that information, and provide your best estimates for missing data together with the sources for the estimates. Where possible, indications as to where any of the requested information that is unavailable to you could be obtained by the Commission should also be provided.

(g) You may request that the Commission accept that the notification is complete notwithstanding failure to provide information required by this form, if you consider that any particular information requested by this form, in the full or short form version, may not be necessary for the Commission's examination of the case.

The Commission will consider such a request, provided that you give reasons why that information is not relevant and necessary to its inquiry into the notified operation. You may explain this during your pre-notification contacts with the Commission and/or in your notification and ask the Commission to dispense with the obligation to provide that information, pursuant to Article 3(2) of the Implementing Regulation.

C.   Notification in short form

(a) In cases where a joint venture has no, or *de minimis,* actual or foreseen activities within the EEA territory, the Commission intends to allow notification of the operation by means of short form. Such cases occur where joint control is acquired by two or more undertakings, and where—

  (i)   the turnover[2] of the joint venture and/or the turnover of the contributed activities,[3] is less than ECU 100 million in the EEA territory; and

  (ii)   the total value of assets[4] transferred to the joint venture is less than ECU 100 million in the EEA territory.[5]

(b)   If you consider that the operation to be notified meets these qualifications, you may explain this in your notification and ask the Commission to dispense with the obligation to provide the full-form notification, pursuant to Article 3(2) of the Implementing Regulation, and to allow you to notify by means of short form.

(c)   Short-form notification allows the notifying parties to limit the information provided in the notification to the following sections and questions:

—   Section 1,

—   Section 2, except questions 2.1 (a, b and d), 2.3.4, and 2.3.5,

—   Section 3, only questions 3.1 and 3.2 (a),

—   Section 5, only questions 5.1 and 5.3,

—   Section 6,

—   Section 10,

—   Section 11 (optional for the convenience of the parties), and

—   Section 12,

—   the five largest independent customers, the five largest independent suppliers, and the five largest competitors in the markets in which the joint venture will be active. Provide the name, address, telephone number, fax number and appropriate contact person of each such customer, supplier and competitor.

(d)   In addition, with respect to the affected markets of the joint venture as defined in Section 6, indicate for the EEA territory, for the Community as a whole, for each Member State and EFTA State, and where different, in the opinion of the notifying parties, for the relevant geographic market, the sales in value and volume, as well as the market shares, for the year preceding the operation.

(e)   The Commission may require full, or where appropriate partial, notification under the form CO where—

—   the notified operation does not meet the short-form thresholds, or

—   this appears to be necessary for an adequate investigation with respect to possible competition problems.

In such cases, the notification may be considered incomplete in a material respect pursuant to Article 4(2) of the Implementing Regulation. The Commission will inform the notifying parties or their representatives of this in writing and without delay and will fix a deadline for the submission of a full or, where appropriate, partial notification. The notification will only become effective on the date on which all information required is received.

D.   Who must notify

In the case of a merger within the meaning of Article 3(1)(a) of the Merger Regulation or the acquisition of joint control in an undertaking within the meaning of Article 3(1)(b) of the Merger Regulation, the notification shall be completed jointly by the parties to the merger or by those acquiring joint control as the case may be.

In case of the acquisition of a controlling interest in one undertaking by another, the acquirer must complete the notification.

In the case of a public bid to acquire an undertaking, the bidder must complete the notification.

Each party completing the notification is responsible for the accuracy of the information which it provides.

E.   How to notify

The notification must be completed in one of the official languages of the European Community. This language will thereafter be the language of the proceeding for all notifying parties. Where notifications are made in accordance with Article 12 of Protocol 24 to the EEA Agreement in an official language of an EFTA State which is not an official language of the Community, the notification must simultaneously be supplemented with a translation into an official language of the Community.

The information requested by this form is to be set out using the sections and paragraph numbers of the form, signing a declaration as provided in Section 12, and annexing supporting documentation.

Supporting documents are to be submitted in their original language; where this is not an official language of the Community, they must be translated into the language of the proceeding (Article 2(4) of the Implementing Regulation).

Supporting documents may be originals or copies of the originals. In the latter case, the notifying party must confirm that they are true and complete.

One original and 23 copies of the form CO and all supporting documents must be provided.

The notification must be delivered to the Commission on working days as defined by Article 23 of the Implementing Regulation. In order to enable it to be registered on the same day, it must be delivered before 17.00 on Mondays to Thursdays and before 16.00 on Fridays, at the following address—

Commission of the European Communities
Directorate-General for Competition (DG IV)
Merger Task Force
150 avenue de Cortenberg/Kortenberglaan 150
B-1049 Brussels.

F. Confidentiality

Article 214 of the Treaty and Article 17(2) of the Merger Regulation as well as the corresponding provisions of the EEA Agreement[6] require the Commission, the Member States, the EFTA Surveillance Authority and the EFTA States, their officials and other servants not to disclose information they have acquired through the application of the Regulation of the kind covered by the obligation of professional secrecy. The same principle must also apply to protect confidentiality between notifying parties.

If you believe that your interests would be harmed if any of the information you are asked to supply were to be published or otherwise divulged to other parties, submit this information separately with each page clearly, marked "Business Secrets". You should also give reasons why this information should not be divulged or published.

In the case of mergers or joint acquisitions, or in other cases where the notification is completed by more than one of the parties, business secrets may be submitted under separate cover, and referred to in the notification as an annex. All such annexes must be included in the submission in order for a notification to be considered complete.

G. Definitions and instructions for purposes of this form

Notifying party or parties: in cases where a notification is submitted by only one of the undertakings party to an operation, "notifying parties" is used to refer only to the undertaking actually submitting the notification.

Party (parties) to the concentration: these terms relate to both the acquiring and acquired parties, or to the merging parties, including all undertakings in which a controlling interest is being acquired or which is the subject of a public bid.

Except where otherwise specified, the terms "notifying party (parties)" and "party (parties) to the concentration" include all the undertaking which belong to the same groups as those "parties".

Affected markets: Section 6 of this form requires the notifying parties to define the relevant product markets, and further to identify which of those relevant markets are likely to be affected by the notified operation. This definition of affected market is used as the basis for requiring information for a number of other questions contained in this form. The definitions thus submitted by the notifying parties are referred to in this form as the affected market(s). This term can refer to a relevant market made up either of products or of services.

Year: all references to the word "year" in this form should be read as meaning calendar year, unless otherwise stated. All information requested in this form must, unless otherwise specified, relate to the year preceding that of the notification.

The financial data requested in Sections 2.3 to 2.5 must be provided in **ecus** at the average conversion rates prevailing for the years or other periods in question.

All references contained in this form are to the relevant Articles and paragraphs of Council Regulation (EEC) No 4064/89, unless otherwise stated.

NOTES

[1] Hereinafter referred to as "the EEA Agreement"; see in particular Article 57 of the EEA Agreement (point 1 of Annex XIV to the EEA Agreement and Protocol 4 to the Agreement between the EFTA States on the establishment of a Surveillance Authority and a Court of Justice), as well as Protocols 21 and 24 to the EEA Agreement and Article 1, and the Agreed Minutes of the Protocol adjusting the EEA Agreement. In particular, any reference to EFTA States shall be understood to mean those EFTA States which are Contracting Parties to the EEA Agreement.

[2] The turnover of the joint venture should be determined according to the most recent audited accounts of the parent companies, or the joint venture itself, depending upon the availability of separate accounts for the resources combined in the joint venture.

[3] The expression "and/or" refers to the variety of situations covered by the short form; for example—

— in the case of the joint acquisition of a target company, the turnover to be taken into account is the turnover of this target (the joint venture),
— in the case of the creation of a joint venture to which the parent companies contribute their activities, the turnover to be taken into account is that of the contributed activities,
— in the case of entry of a new controlling party into existing joint venture, the turnover of the joint venture and the turnover of the activities contributed by the new parent company (if any) must be taken into account.

[4] The total value of assets of the joint venture should be determined according to the last regularly prepared and approved balance sheet of each parent company. The term "asset" includes: (1) all tangible and intangible assets that will be transferred to the joint venture (examples of tangible assets include production plants, wholesale or retail outlets, and inventory of goods), and (2) any amount of credit or any obligations of the joint venture which any parent company of the joint venture has agreed to extend or guarantee.

[5] Where the assets transferred generate turnover, then neither the value of the assets nor that of the turnover may exceed ECU 100 million.

[6] See, in particular, Article 122 of the EEA Agreement, Article 9 of Protocol 24 to the EEA Agreement and Article 17(2) of Chapter XIII of Protocol 4 to the Agreement between the EFTA States on the establishment of a Surveillance Authority and a Court of Justice (ESA Agreement).

SECTION 1

Background information

1.1 *Information on notifying party (or parties)*

Give details of—
    1.1.1. name and address of undertaking;
    1.1.2. nature of the undertaking's business;
    1.1.3. name, address, telephone number, fax number and/or telex of, and position held by, the appropriate contact person.

1.2. *Information on other parties[1] to the concentration*

For each party to the concentration (except the notifying party or parties) give details of—
    1.2.1. name and address of undertaking;
    1.2.2. nature of undertaking's business;
    1.2.3. name, address, telephone number, fax number and/or telex of, and position held by the appropriate contact person.

1.3. *Address for service*

Give an address (in Brussels if available) to which all communications may be made and documents delivered.

1.4. *Appointment of representatives*

Where notifications are signed by representatives of undertakings, such representatives must produce written proof that they are authorised to act.

If a joint notification is being submitted, has a joint representative been appointed?

If yes, please give the details requested in Sections 1.4.1 to 1.4.4.

If no, please give details of information of any representatives who have been authorised to act for each of the parties to the concentration, indicating whom they represent—

    1.4.1. name of representative;

    1.4.2. address of representative;

    1.4.3. name of person to be contacted (and address, if different from 1.4.2);

    1.4.4. telephone number, fax number and/or telex.

NOTES

[1]   This includes the target company in the case of a contested bid, in which case the details should be completed as far as is possible.

SECTION 2

Details of the concentration

  2.1.   *Describe the nature of the concentration being notified. In doing so state—*

    (a) whether the proposed concentration is a full legal merger, an acquisition of sole or joint control, a full-function joint venture within the meaning of Article 3(2) of the Merger Regulation or a contract or other means of conferring direct or indirect control within the meaning of Article 3(3) of the Merger Regulation;

    (b) whether the whole or parts of parties are subject to the concentration;

    (c) a brief explanation of the economic and financial structure of the concentration;

    (d) whether any public offer for the securities of one party by another party has the support of the former's supervisory boards of management or other bodies legally representing that party;

    (e) the proposed or expected date of any major events designed to bring about the completion of the concentration;

    (f) the proposed structure of ownership and control after the completion of the concentration;

    (g) any financial or other support received from whatever source (including public authorities) by any of the parties and the nature and amount of this support.

  2.2.   *List the economic sectors involved in the concentration*

  2.3.   *For each of the undertakings concerned by the concentration[1] provide the following data[2] for the last financial year—*

    2.3.1. worldwide turnover;

    2.3.2. Community-wide turnover;

    2.3.3. EFTA-wide turnover;

    2.3.4. turnover in each Member State;

    2.3.5. turnover in each EFTA State;

    2.3.6. the Member State, if any, in which more than two thirds of Community-wide turnover is achieved;[3]

    2.3.7. the EFTA State, if any, in which more than two thirds of EFTA-wide turnover is achieved.

  2.4.   *For the purposes of Article 1(3) of the Merger Regulation, if the operation does not meet the thresholds set out in Article 1(2), provide the following data for the last financial year—*

    2.4.1. the Member States, if any, in which the combined aggregate turnover of all the undertakings concerned is more than ECU 100 million;

    2.4.2. the Member States, if any, in which the aggregate turnover of each of at least two of the undertakings concerned is more than ECU 25 million.

  2.5.   *Provide the following information with respect to the last financial year—*

    2.5.1. does the combined turnover of the undertakings concerned in the territory of the EFTA States equal 25% or more of their total turnover in the EEA territory?

    2.5.2. does each of at least two undertakings concerned have a turnover exceeding ECU 250 million in the territory of the EFTA States?

NOTES
¹ See Commission notice on the concept of undertakings concerned.
² See, generally, the Commission notice on calculation of turnover. Turnover of the acquiring party or parties to the concentration should include the aggregated turnover of all undertakings within the meaning of Article 5(4). Turnover of the acquired party or parties should include the turnover relating to the parts subject to the transaction within the meaning of Article 5(2). Special provisions are contained in Article 5(3), (4) and (5) for credit, insurance, other financial institutions and joint undertakings.
³ See Guidance Note III for the calculation of turnover in one Member State with respect to Community-wide turnover.

SECTION 3
OWNERSHIP AND CONTROL¹

For each of the parties to the concentration provide a list of all undertakings belonging to the same group.

This list must include—

3.1. all undertakings or persons controlling these parties, directly or indirectly;

3.2. all undertakings active on any affected market² that are controlled, directly or indirectly—
    (a) by these parties;
    (b) by any other undertaking identified in 3.1.

For each entry listed above, the nature and means of control should be specified.

The information sought in this section may be illustrated by the use of organisation charts or diagrams to show the structure of ownership and control of the undertakings.

NOTES
¹ See Article 3(3), (4) and (5) and Article 5(4).
² See Section 6 for the definition of affected markets.

SECTION 4

Personal and financial links and previous acquisitions

With respect to the parties to the concentration and each undertaking or person identified in response to Section 3, provide—
  4.1. a list of all other undertakings which are active on affected markets (affected markets are defined in Section 6) in which the undertakings, or persons, of the group hold individually or collectively 10% or more of the voting rights, issued share capital or other securities;
    in each case identify the holder and state the percentage held;
  4.2. a list for each undertaking of the members of their boards of management who are also members of the boards of management or of the supervisory boards of any other undertaking which is active on affected markets; and (where applicable) for each undertaking a list of the members of their supervisory boards who are also members of the boards of management of any other undertaking which is active on affected markets;
    in each case identify the name of the other undertaking and the positions held;
  4.3. details of acquisitions made during the last three years by the groups identified above (Section 3) of undertakings active in affected markets as defined in Section 6.
Information provided here may be illustrated by the use of organisation charts or diagrams to give a better understanding.

SECTION 5

Supporting documentation

Notifying parties must provide the following—
  5.1. copies of the final or most recent versions of all documents bringing about the concentration, whether by agreement between the parties to the concentration, acquisition of a controlling interest or a public bid;

5.2. in a public bid, a copy of the offer document; if it is unavailable at the time of notification, it should be submitted as soon as possible and not later than when it is posted to shareholders;

5.3. copies of the most recent annual reports and accounts of all the parties to the concentration;

5.4. where at least one affected market is identified:

copies of analyses, reports, studies and surveys submitted to or prepared for any member(s) of the board of directors, the supervisory board, or the shareholders' meeting, for the purpose of assessing or analysing the concentration with respect to competitive conditions, competitors (actual and potential), and market conditions.

SECTION 6

Market definitions

The relevant product and geographic markets determine the scope within which the market power of the new entity resulting from the concentration must be assessed.[1]

The notifying party or parties must provide the data requested having regard to the following definitions—

I.   *Relevant product markets*

A relevant product market comprises all those products and/or services which are regarded as interchangeable or substitutable by the consumer, by reason of the products' characteristics, their prices and their intended use. A relevant products market may in some cases be composed of a number of individual products and/or services which present largely identical physical characteristics and are interchangeable.

Factors relevant to the assessment of the relevant product market include the analysis of why the products or services in these markets are included and why others are excluded by using the above definition, and having regard to, for example, substitutability, conditions of competition, prices, cross-price elasticity of demand or other factors relevant for the definition of the product markets.

II.   *Relevant geographic markets*

The relevant geographic market comprises the area in which the undertakings concerned are involved in the supply and demand of relevant products or services, in which the conditions of competition are sufficiently homogenous and which can be distinguished from neighbouring geographic areas because, in particular, conditions of competition are appreciably different in those areas.

Factors relevant to the assessment of the relevant geographic market include the nature and characteristics of the products or services concerned, the existence of entry barriers, consumer preferences, appreciable differences in the undertakings' market shares between neighbouring geographic areas or substantial price differences.

III.   *Affected markets*

For purposes of information required in this form, affected markets consist of relevant product markets where, in the EEA territory, in the Community, in the territory of the EFTA States, in any Member State or in any EFTA State—

(a) two or more of the parties to the concentration are engaged in business activities in the same product market and where the concentration will lead to a combined market share of 15% or more. These are horizontal relationships;

(b) one or more of the parties to the concentration are engaged in business activities in a product market, which is upstream or downstream of a product market in which any other party to the concentration is engaged, and any of their individual or combined market shares is 25% or more, regardless of whether there is or is not any existing supplier/customer relationship between the parties to the concentration. These are vertical relationships.

On the basis of the above definitions and market share thresholds, provide the following information—

6.1.   Identify each affected market within the meaning of Section III, at—

(a) the EEA, Community or EFTA level;

(b) the individual Member States or EFTA States level.

IV.   Markets related to affected markets within the meaning of Section III

6.2.   Describe the relevant product and geographic markets concerned by the notified operation, which are closely related to the affected market(s) (in upstream, downstream and horizontal neighbouring markets), where any of the parties to the concentration are active and which are not themselves affected markets within the meaning of Section III.

V.   Non-affected markets

6.3.   In case there are no affected markets [within] the meaning of Section 6.1, describe the product and geographic scope of the markets on which the notified operation would have an impact.

NOTES

   [1]   See Commission notice on the definition of the relevant market for the purposes of Community competition law.

SECTION 7

Information on affected markets

For each affected relevant product market, for each of the last three financial years—[1]
   (a)   for the EEA territory,
   (b)   for the Community as a whole,
   (c)   for the territory of the EFTA States as a whole,
   (d)   individually for each Member State and EFTA State where the parties to the concentration do business,
   (e)   and, where in the opinion of the notifying parties, the relevant geographic market is different,

   provide the following—

7.1.   an estimate of the total size of the market in terms of sales value (in ecus) and volume (units).[2] Indicate the basis and sources for the calculations and provide documents where available to confirm these calculations;

7.2.   the sales in value and volume, as well as an estimate of the market shares, of each of the parties to the concentration;

7.3.   an estimate of the market share in value (and where appropriate volume) of all competitors (including importers) having at least 10% of the geographic market under consideration. Provide documents where available to confirm the calculation of these market shares and provide the name, address, telephone number, fax number and appropriate contact person, of these competitors;

7.4.   an estimate of the total value and volume and source of imports from outside the EEA territory and identify—
   (a)   the proportion of such imports that are derived from the groups to which the parties to the concentration belong,
   (b)   an estimate of the extent to which any quotas, tariffs or non-tariff barriers to trade, affect these imports, and
   (c)   an estimate of the extent to which transportation and other costs affect these imports;

7.5.   the extent to which trade among States within the EEA territory is affected by—
   (a)   transportation and other costs, and
   (b)   other non-tariff barriers to trade;

7.6.   the manner in which the parties to the concentration produce and sell the products and/or services; for example, whether they manufacture locally, or sell through local distribution facilities;

7.7.   a comparison of price levels in each Member State and EFTA State by each party to the concentration and a similar comparison of price levels between the Community, the EFTA States and other areas where these products are produced (eg eastern Europe, the United States of America, Japan, or other relevant areas);

7.8.   the nature and extent of vertical integration of each of the parties to the concentration compared with their largest competitors.

PART IV
EC MATERIALS

NOTES
   [1] Without prejudice to Article 3(2) of the Implementing Regulation, the information required under 7.1 and 7.2 below must be provided with regard to all the territories under (a), (b), (c), (d) and (e).
   [2] The value and volume of a market should reflect output less imports for the geographic areas under consideration.

SECTION 8
GENERAL CONDITIONS IN AFFECTED MARKETS

8.1. Identify the five largest independent[1] suppliers to the parties and their individual shares of purchases from each of these suppliers (of raw materials or goods used for purposes of producing the relevant products). Provide the name, address, telephone number, fax number and appropriate contact person, of these suppliers.

NOTES
   [1] That is suppliers which are not subsidiaries, agents or undertakings forming part of the group of the party in question. In addition to those five independent suppliers the notifying parties can, if they consider it necessary for a proper assessment of the case, identify the intra-group suppliers. The same will apply in 8.5 in relation with customers.

Structure of supply in affected markets

8.2. Explain the distribution channels and service networks that exist on the affected markets. In so doing, take account of the following where appropriate—
   (a) the distribution systems prevailing on the market and their importance. To what extent is distribution performed by third parties and/or undertakings belonging to the same group as the parties identified in Section 3?
   (b) the service networks (for example, maintenance and repair) prevailing and their importance in these markets. To what extent are such services performed by third parties and/or undertakings belonging to the same group as the parties identified in Section 3?

8.3. Where appropriate, provide an estimate of the total Community-wide and EFTA-wide capacity for the last three years. Over this period what proportion of this capacity is accounted for by each of the parties to the concentration, and what have been their respective rates of capacity utilisation.

8.4. If you consider any other supply-side considerations to be relevant, they should be specified.

Structure of demand in affected markets

8.5. Identify the five largest independent customers of the parties in each affected market and their individual share of total sales for such products accounted for by each of those customers. Provide the name, address, telephone number, fax number and appropriate contact person, of each of these customers.

8.6. Explain the structure of demand in terms of—
   (a) the phases of the markets in terms of, for example, take-off, expansion, maturity and decline, and a forecast of the growth rate of demand;
   (b) the importance of customer preferences, in terms of brand loyalty, product differentiation and the provision of a full range of products;
   (c) the degree of concentration or dispersion of customers;
   (d) segmentation of customers into different groups with a description of the "typical customer" of each group;
   (e) the importance of exclusive distribution contracts and other types of long-term contracts;
   (f) the extent to which public authorities, government agencies, State enterprises or similar bodies are important participants as a source of demand.

Market entry

8.7. Over the last five years, has there been any significant entry into any affected markets? If the answer is "yes", where possible provide their name, address, telephone number, fax number and appropriate contact person, and an estimate of their current market shares.

8.8. In the opinion of the notifying parties are there undertakings (including those at present operating only in extra-Community or extra-EEA markets) that are likely to enter the market? If the answer is "yes", please explain why and identify such entrants by name, address, telephone number, fax number and appropriate contact person, and an estimate of the time within which such entry is likely to occur.

8.9. Describe the various factors influencing entry into affected markets that exist in the present case, examining entry from both a geographical and product viewpoint. In so doing, take account of the following where appropriate—

    (a) the total costs of entry (R & D, establishing distribution systems, promotion, advertising, servicing, etc) on a scale equivalent to a significant viable competitor, indicating the market share of such a competitor;

    (b) any legal or regulatory barriers to entry, such as government authorisation or standard setting in any form;

    (c) any restrictions created by the existence of patents, know-how and other intellectual property rights in these markets and any restrictions created by licensing such rights;

    (d) the extent to which each of the parties to the concentration are licensees or licensors of patents, know-how and other rights in the relevant markets;

    (e) the importance of economies of scale for the production of products in the affected markets;

    (f) access to sources of supply, such as availability of raw materials.

Research and development

8.10. Give an account of the importance of research and development in the ability of a firm operating on the relevant market(s) to compete in the long term. Explain the nature of the research and development in affected markets carried out by the parties to the concentration.

In so doing, take account of the following, where appropriate—

    (a) trends and intensities of research and development[1] in these markets and for the parties to the concentration;

    (b) the course of technological development for these markets over an appropriate time period (including developments in products and/or services, production processes, distribution systems, etc);

    (c) the major innovations that have been made in these markets and the undertakings responsible for these innovations;

    (d) the cycle of innovation in these markets and where the parties are in this cycle of innovation.

NOTES
[1] Research and development intensity is defined as research and development expenditure as a proportion of turnover.

Cooperative agreements

8.11. To what extent do cooperative agreements (horizontal or vertical) exist in the affected markets?

8.12. Give details of the most important cooperative agreements engaged in by the parties to the concentration in the affected markets, such as research and development, licensing, joint production, specialisation, distribution, long term supply and exchange of information agreements.

Trade associations

8.13. With respect to the trade associations in the affected markets—

    (a) identify those in which the parties to the concentration are members;

    (b) identify the most important trade associations to which the customers and suppliers of the parties to the concentration belong.

Provide the name, address, telephone number, fax number and appropriate contact person of all trade associations listed above.

SECTION 9

General market information

Market data on conglomerate aspects

Where any of the parties to the concentration hold individually a market share of 25% or more for any product market in which there is no horizontal or vertical relationship as described above, provide the following information—

9.1. a description of each product market and explain why the products and/or services in these markets are included (and why others are excluded) by reason of their characteristics, prices and their intended use;

9.2. an estimate of the value of the market and the market shares of each of the groups to which the parties belong for each product market identified in 9.1 for the last financial year—

(a) for the EEA territory as a whole;

(b) for the Community as a whole;

(c) for the territory of the EFTA States as a whole;

(d) individually for each Member State and EFTA State where the groups to which the parties belong do business;

(e) and, where different, for the relevant geographic market.

Overview of the markets

9.3. Describe the worldwide context of the proposed concentration, indicating the position of each of the parties to the concentration outside of the EEA territory in terms of size and competitive strength.

9.4. Describe how the proposed concentration is likely to affect the interests of intermediate and ultimate consumers and the development of technical and economic progress.

SECTION 10

Cooperative effects of a joint venture

10. For the purpose of Article 2(4) of the Merger Regulation please answer the following questions—

(a) Do two or more parents retain to a significant extent activities in the same market as the joint venture or in a market which is downstream or upstream from that of the joint venture or in a neighbouring market closely related to this market?[1]

If the answer is affirmative, please indicate for each of the markets referred to here—

the turnover of each parent company in the preceding financial year,

the economic significance of the activities of the joint venture in relation to this turnover,

the market share of each parent.

If the answer is negative, please justify your answer.

(b) If the answer to (a) is affirmative and in your view the creation of the joint venture does not lead to coordination between independent undertakings that restricts competition within the meaning of Article 85(1) of the EC Treaty, give your reasons.

(c) Without prejudice to the answers to (a) and (b) and in order to ensure that a complete assessment of the case can be made by the Commission, please explain how the criteria of Article 85(3) apply.

Under Article 85(3), the provisions of Article 85(1) may be declared inapplicable if the operation:

(i) contributes to improving the production or distribution of goods, or to promoting technical or economic progress;

(ii) allows consumers a fair share of the resulting benefit;

(iii) does not impose on the undertakings concerned restrictions which are not indispensable to the attainment of these objectives; and

(iv) does not afford such undertakings the possibility of eliminating competition in respect of a substantial part of the products in question.

For guidance, please refer to form A/B, and in particular Sections 16 and 17 thereof, annexed to Commission Regulation (EC) No 3385/94.[2]

NOTES

¹   For market definitions refer to Section 6.

²   OJ L377, 31.12.94, p 28.

SECTION 11

General matters

Ancillary restraints

11.1. If the parties to the concentration and/or other involved parties (including the seller and minority shareholders), enter into ancillary restrictions directly related and necessary to the implementation of the concentration, these restrictions may be assessed in conjunction with the concentration itself (see Article 6(1)(b) and Article 8(2) of the Merger Regulation, recital 25 to the Merger Regulation, recital 7 to Regulation (EC) No 1310/97 and the Commission notice on restrictions ancillary to concentrations)— ¹

    (a)   identify each ancillary restriction in the agreements provided with the notification for which you request an assessment in conjunction with the concentration; and

    (b)   explain why these are directly related and necessary to the implementation of the concentration.

NOTES

¹   OJ L180, 9.7.97, p 1.

Conversion of notification

11.2. In the event that the Commission finds that the operation notified does not constitute a concentration within the meaning of Article 3 of the Merger Regulation, do you request that it be treated as an application for negative clearance from, or a notification to obtain an exemption from Article 85 of the EC Treaty?

SECTION 12

Declaration

Article 1(2) of the Implementing Regulation states that where notifications are signed by representatives of undertakings, such representatives must produce written proof that they are authorised to act. Such written authorisation must accompany the notification.

The notification must conclude with the following declaration which is to be signed by or on behalf of all the notifying parties.

The undersigned declare that, to the best of their knowledge and belief, the information given in this notification is true, correct, and complete, that complete copies of documents required by form CO have been supplied, and that all estimates are identified as such and are their best estimates of the underlying facts and that all the opinions expressed are sincere.

They are aware of the provisions of Article 14(1)(b) of the Merger Regulation.

Place and date:

Signatures:

Name/s:

On behalf of:

GUIDANCE NOTE I

Calculation of turnover for insurance undertakings

(Article 5(3)(a))

For the calculation of turnover for insurance undertakings, we give the following example (proposed concentration between insurance A and B):

I. *Consolidated profit and loss account*

(million ECU)

Income	Insurance A		Insurance B	
Gross premiums written	5000		300	
—gross premiums received from Community residents		(4500)		(300)
—gross premiums received from residents of one (and the same) Member State X		(3600)		(270)
Other income	500		50	
Total income	5500		350	

II. *Calculation of turnover*

1. Aggregate worldwide turnover is replaced by the value of gross premiums written worldwide, the sum of which is ECU 5 300 million.

2. Community-wide turnover is replaced, for each insurance undertaking, by the value of gross premiums written with Community residents. For each of the insurance undertakings, this amount is more than ECU 250 million.

3. Turnover within one (and the same) Member State X is replaced, for insurance undertaking, by the value of gross premiums written with residents of one (and the same) Member State X. For insurance A, it achieves 80% of its gross premiums written with Community residents within Member State X, whereas for insurance B, it achieves 90% of its gross premiums written with Community residents in that Member State X.

III. *Conclusion*

Since

   (a) the aggregate worldwide turnover of insurances A and B, as replaced by the value of gross premiums written worldwide, is more than ECU 5 000 million;

   (b) for each of the insurance undertakings, the value of gross premiums written with Community residents is more than ECU 250 million; but

   (c) each of the insurance undertakings achieves more than two thirds of its gross premiums written with Community residents in one (and the same) Member State X,

the proposed concentration would not fall under the scope of the Regulation.

GUIDANCE NOTE II

Calculation of turnover for joint undertakings

A. Creation of a joint undertaking (Article 3(2))

In a case where two (or more) undertakings create a joint undertaking that constitutes a concentration, turnover is calculated for the undertakings concerned.

B. Existence of a joint undertaking (Article 5(5))

For the calculation of turnover in case of the existence of a joint undertaking C between two undertakings A and B concerned in a concentration, we give the following example—

I.　*Profit and loss accounts*

(*million ECU*)

Turnover	Undertaking A	Undertaking B
Sales revenue worldwide	10 000	2 000
— Community	(8 000)	(1 500)
— Member State Y	(4 000)	(900)

(*million ECU*)

Turnover	Joint undertaking C
Sales revenues worldwide	100
— with undertaking A	(20)
— with undertaking B	(10)
Turnover with third undertakings	70
— Community-wide	(60)
— in Member State Y	(50)

II.　*Consideration of the joint undertaking*

(a) The undertaking C is jointly controlled (in the meaning of Article 3(3) and (4)) by the undertakings A and B concerned by the concentration, irrespective of any third undertaking participating in that undertaking C.

(b) The undertaking C is not consolidated by A and B in their profit and loss accounts.

(c) The turnover of C resulting from operations with A and B shall not be taken into account.

(d) The turnover of C resulting from operations with any third undertaking shall be apportioned equally amongst the undertakings A and B, irrespective of their individual shareholdings in C.

III.　*Calculation of turnover*

(a) Undertaking A's aggregate worldwide turnover shall be calculated as follows: ECU 10 000 million and 50% of C's worldwide turnover with third undertakings (ie ECU 35 million), the sum of which is ECU 10 035 million.

Undertaking B's aggregate worldwide turnover shall be calculated as follows: ECU 2 000 million and 50% of C's world-wide turnover with third undertakings (ie ECU 35 million), the sum of which is ECU 2 035 million.

(b) The aggregate worldwide turnover of the undertakings concerned is ECU 12 070 million.

(c) Undertaking A achieves ECU 4 025 million within Member State Y (50% of C's turnover in this Member State taken into account), and a Community-wide turnover of ECU 8 030 million (including 50% of C's Community-wide turnover).

Undertaking B achieves ECU 925 million within Member State Y (50% of C's turnover in this Member State taken into account), and a Community-wide turnover of ECU 1 530 million (including 50% of C's Community-wide turnover).

IV.　*Conclusion*

Since

(a) the aggregate worldwide turnover of undertakings A and B is more than ECU 5 000 million;

(b) each of the undertakings concerned by the concentration achieves more than ECU 250 million within the Community;

(c) each of the undertakings concerned (undertaking A 50,1% and undertaking B 60,5%) achieves less than two thirds of its Community-wide turnover in one (and the same) Member State Y;

the proposed concentration would fall under the scope of the Regulation.

GUIDANCE NOTE III

Application of the two-thirds rule

(Article 1)

For the application of the two thirds rule for undertakings, we give the following examples (proposed concentration between undertakings A and B):

I. *Consolidated profit and loss accounts*

Example 1 *(million ECU)*

Turnover	Undertaking A	Undertaking B
Sales revenues worldwide	10 000	500
— within the Community	(8 000)	(400)
— in Member State X	(6 000)	(200)

Example 2(a) *(million ECU)*

Turnover	Undertaking A	Undertaking B
Sale revenues worldwide	4 800	500
— within the Community	(2 400)	(400)
— in Member State X	(2 100)	(300)

Example 2(b)

Same figures as in example 2(a) but undertaking B achieves ECU 300 million in Member State Y.

II. *Application of the two-thirds rule*

Example 1

1.   Community-wide turnover is, for undertaking A, ECU 8 000 million and for undertaking B ECU 400 million.

2.   Turnover in one (and the same) Member State X is, for undertaking A (ECU 6 000 million), 75% of its Community-wide turnover and is, for undertaking B (ECU 200 million), 50% of its Community-wide-turnover.

3.   Conclusion: In this case, although undertaking A achieves more than two thirds of its Community-wide turnover in Member State X, the proposed concentration would fall under the scope of the Regulation due to the fact that undertaking B achieves less than two thirds of its Community-wide turnover in Member State X.

Example 2(a)

1.   Community-wide turnover of undertaking A is ECU 2 400 million and of undertaking B, ECU 400 million.

2.   Turnover in one (and the same) Member State X is, for undertaking A, ECU 2 100 million (ie 87,5% of its Community-wide turnover); and, for undertaking B, ECU 300 million (ie 75% of its Community-wide turnover).

3.   Conclusion: In this case, each of the undertakings concerned achieves more than two thirds of its Community-wide turnover in one (and the same) Member State X; the proposed concentration would not fall under the scope of the Regulation.

Example 2(b)

Conclusion: In this case, the two thirds rule would not apply due to the fact that undertakings A and B achieve more than two thirds of their Community-wide turnover in different Member States X and Y. Therefore, the proposed concentration would fall under the scope of the Regulation.

COMMISSION NOTICE

on the concept of concentration under Council Regulation (EEC) 4064/89 on the control of concentrations between undertakings

(98/C 66/02)

(Text with EEA relevance)

NOTES
Date of publication in OJ: OJ C66, 2.3.98, p 5.

I INTRODUCTION

1.   The purpose of this Notice is to provide guidance as to how the Commission interprets the term "concentration" used in Article 3 of Council Regulation (EEC) 4064/89[1] as last amended by Regulation (EC) 1310/97[2] (hereinafter referred to as "the Merger Regulation"). This formal guidance on the interpretation of Article 3 should enable firms to establish more quickly, in advance of any contact with the Commission, whether and to what extent their operations may be covered by Community merger control.

This Notice replaces the Notice on the notion of a concentration.[3]

This Notice deals with paragraphs (1), (3), (4) and (5) of Article 3. The interpretation of Article 3 in relation to joint ventures, dealt with in particular under Article 3(2), is set out in the Commission's Notice on the concept of full-function joint ventures.

NOTES
[1]   OJ L395, 30.12.89, p 1, corrected version OJ L257, 21.9.90, p 13.
[2]   OJ L180, 9.7.97, p 1.
[3]   OJ C385, 31.12.94, p 5.

2.   The guidance set out in this Notice reflects the Commission's experience in applying the Merger Regulation since it entered into force on 21 December 1990. The principles contained here will be applied and further developed by the Commission in individual cases.

3.   According to recital 23 to Regulation (EEC) 4064/89, the concept of concentration is defined as covering only operations which bring about a lasting change in the structure of the undertakings concerned. Article 3(1) provides that such a structural change is brought about either by a merger between two previously independent undertakings or by the acquisition of control over the whole or part of another undertaking.

4.   The determination of the existence of a concentration under the Merger Regulation is based upon qualitative rather than quantitative criteria, focusing on the concept of control. These criteria include considerations of both law and fact. It follows, therefore, that a concentration may occur on a legal or a *de facto* basis.

5.   Article 3(1) of the Merger Regulation defines two categories of concentration—
  — those arising from a merger between previously independent undertakings (point (a));
  — those arising from an acquisition of control (point (b)).

These are treated respectively in Sections II and III below.

II MERGERS BETWEEN PREVIOUSLY INDEPENDENT UNDERTAKINGS

6.   A merger within the meaning of Article 3(1)(a) of the Merger Regulation occurs when two or more independent undertakings amalgamate into a new undertaking and cease to exist as separate legal entities. A merger may also occur when an undertaking is absorbed by another, the latter retaining its legal identity while the former ceases to exist as a legal entity.

7.   A merger within the meaning of Article 3(1)(a) may also occur where, in the absence of a legal merger, the combining of the activities of previously independent undertakings results in the creation of a single economic unit.[1] This may arise in particular where two or more undertakings, while retaining their individual legal personalities, establish contractually a common economic management.[2] If this leads to a *de facto* amalgamation of the undertakings concerned into a genuine common economic unit, the operation is considered to be a merger. A prerequisite for the determination of a common economic unit is the existence of a permanent, single economic management. Other relevant factors may include internal profit and loss compensation as between the various undertakings within the group, and their joint liability externally. The *de facto* amalgamation may be reinforced by cross-shareholdings between the undertakings forming the economic unit.

[5452]

NOTES

[1]   In determining the previous independence of undertakings, the issue of control may be relevant. Control is considered generally in paragraphs 12 et seq below. For this specific issue, minority shareholders are deemed to have control if they have previously obtained a majority of votes on major decisions at shareholders meetings. The reference period in this context is normally three years.

[2]   This could apply for example, in the case of a "Gleichordnungskonzern" in German law, certain "Groupements d'Intérêt Economique" in French law, and certain partnerships.

III ACQUISITION OF CONTROL

8.   Article 3(1)(b) provides that a concentration occurs in the case of an acquisition of control. Such control may be acquired by one undertaking acting alone or by two or more undertakings acting jointly.

Control may also be acquired by a person in circumstances where that person already controls (whether solely or jointly) at least one other undertaking or, alternatively, by a combination of persons (which controls another undertaking) and/or undertakings. The term "person" in this context extends to public bodies[1] and private entities, as well as individuals.

As defined, a concentration within the meaning of the Merger Regulation is limited to changes in control. Internal restructuring within a group of companies, therefore, cannot constitute a concentration.

An exceptional situation exists where both the acquiring and acquired undertakings are public companies owned by the same State (or by the same public body). In this case, whether the operation is to be regarded as an internal restructuring depends in turn on the question whether both undertakings were formerly part of the same economic unit within the meaning of recital 12 to Regulation (EEC) 4064/89. Where the undertakings were formerly part of different economic units having an independent power of decision, the operation will be deemed to constitute a concentration and not an internal restructuring.[2] Such independent power of decision does not normally exist, however, where the undertakings are within the same holding company.[3]

9. Whether an operation gives rise to an acquisition of control depends on a number of legal and/or factual elements. The acquisition of property rights and shareholders' agreements are important, but are not the only elements involved: purely economic relationships may also play a decisive role. Therefore, in exceptional circumstances, a situation of economic dependence may lead to control on a *de facto* basis where, for example, very important long-term supply agreements or credits provided by suppliers or customers, coupled with structural links, confer decisive influence.[1]

There may also be acquisition of control even if it is not the declared intention of the parties.[2] Moreover, the Merger Regulation clearly defines control as having "the possibility of exercising decisive influence" rather than the actual exercise of such influence.

10. Control is nevertheless normally acquired by persons or undertakings which are the holders of the rights or are entitled to rights conferring control (Article 3(4)(a)). There may be exceptional situations where the formal holder of a controlling interest differs from the person or undertaking having in fact the rea power to exercise the rights resulting from this interest. This may be the case, for example, where an undertaking uses another person or undertaking for the acquisition of a controlling interest and exercises the rights through this person or undertaking, even though the latter is formally the holder of the rights. In such a situation, control is acquired by the undertaking which in reality is behind the operation and in fact enjoys the power to control the target undertaking (Article 3(4)(b)). The evidence needed to establish this type of indirect control may include factors such as the source of financing or family links.

11. The object of control can be one or more undertakings which constitute legal entities, or the assets of such entities, or only some of these assets.[1] The assets in question, which could be brands or licences, must constitute a business to which a market turnover can be clearly attributed.

12. The acquisition of control may be in the form of sole or joint control. In both cases, control is defined as the possibility of exercising decisive influence on an undertaking on the basis of rights, contracts or any other means (Article 3(3)).

1 Sole control

13. Sole control is normally acquired on a legal basis where an undertaking acquires a majority of the voting rights of a company. It is not in itself significant

that the acquired shareholding is 50% of the share capital plus one share[1] or that it is 100% of the share capital.[2] In the absence of other elements, an acquisition which does not include a majority of the voting rights does not normally confer control even if it involves the acquisition of a majority of the share capital.

NOTES

1   Case IV/M.296—Crédit Lyonnais/BFG Bank, of 11 January 1993.
2   Case IV/M.299—Sara Lee/BP Food Division, of 8 February 1993.

14.   Sole control may also be acquired in the case of a "qualified minority". This can be established on a legal and/or *de facto* basis.

On a legal basis it can occur where specific rights are attached to the minority shareholding. These may be preferential shares leading to a majority of the voting rights or other rights enabling the minority shareholder to determine the strategic commercial behaviour of the target company, such as the power to appoint more than half of the members of the supervisory board or the administrative board.

A minority shareholder may also be deemed to have sole control on a *de facto* basis. This is the case, for example, where the shareholder is highly likely to achieve a majority at the shareholders' meeting, given that the remaining shares are widely dispersed.[1] In such a situation it is unlikely that all the smaller shareholders will be present or represented at the shareholders' meeting. The determination of whether or not sole control exists in a particular case is based on the evidence resulting from the presence of shareholders in previous years. Where, on the basis of the number of shareholders attending the shareholders' meeting, a minority shareholder has a stable majority of the votes at this meeting, then the large minority shareholder is taken to have sole control.[2]

Sole control can also be exercised by a minority shareholder who has the right to manage the activities of the company and to determine its business policy.

NOTES

1   Case IV/M.025—Arjomari/Wiggins Teape, of 10 February 1990.
2   Case IV/M.343—Société Générale de Belgique/Générale de Banque, of 3 August 1993.

15.   An option to purchase or convert shares cannot in itself confer sole control unless the option will be exercised in the near future according to legally binding agreements.[1] However, the likely exercise of such an option can be taken into account as an additional element which, together with other elements, may lead to the conclusion that there is sole control.

NOTES

1   Judgment in Case T-2/93—Air France v EC Commission [1994] ECR II-323.

16.   A change from joint to sole control of an undertaking is deemed to be a concentration within the meaning of the Merger Regulation because decisive influence exercised alone is substantially different from decisive influence exercised jointly.[1] For the same reason, an operation involving the acquisition of joint control of one part of an undertaking and sole control of another part is in principle regarded as two separate concentrations under the Merger Regulation.[2]

NOTES

1   This issue is dealt with in paragraphs 30, 31 and 32 of the Notice on the concept of undertakings concerned.
2   Case IV/M.409—ABB/Renault Automation, of 9 March 1994.

17.   The concept of control under the Merger Regulation may be different from that applied in specific areas of legislation concerning, for example, prudential rules, taxation, air transport or the media. In addition, national legislation within a Member State may provide specific rules on the structure of bodies representing the organisation of decision-making within an undertaking, in particular, in relation to the rights of representatives of employees. While such legislation may confer some power of control upon persons other than the shareholders, the concept of control under the Merger Regulation is related only to the means of influence normally enjoyed by the owners of an undertaking. Finally, the prerogatives exercised by a State acting as a public authority rather than as a shareholder, in so far as they are limited to the protection of the public interest, do not constitute control within the meaning of the Merger Regulation to the extent that they have neither the aim nor the effect of enabling the State to exercise a decisive influence over the activity of the undertaking.[1]

NOTES
[1]   Case IV/M.493—Tractebel/Distrigaz II, of 1 September 1994.

2   Joint control

18.   As in the case of sole control, the acquisition of joint control (which includes changes from sole control to joint control) can also be established on a legal or *de facto* basis. There is joint control if the shareholders (the parent companies) must reach agreement on major decisions concerning the controlled undertaking (the joint venture).

19.   Joint control exists where two or more undertakings or persons have the possibility of exercising decisive influence over another undertaking. Decisive influence in this sense normally means the power to block actions which determine the strategic commercial behaviour of an undertaking. Unlike sole control, which confers the power upon a specific shareholder to determine the strategic decisions in an undertaking, joint control is characterized by the possibility of a deadlock situation resulting from the power of two or more parent companies to reject proposed strategic decisions. It follows, therefore, that these shareholders must reach a common understanding in determining the commercial policy of the joint venture.

2.1 *Equality in voting rights or appointment to decision-making bodies*

20.   The clearest form of joint control exists where there are only two parent companies which share equally the voting rights in the joint venture. In this case, it is not necessary for a formal agreement to exist between them. However, where there is a formal agreement, it must be consistent with the principle of equality between the parent companies, by laying down, for example, that each is entitled to the same number of representatives in the management bodies and that none of the members has a casting vote.[1] Equality may also be achieved where both parent companies have the right to appoint an equal number of members to the decision-making bodies of the joint venture.

NOTES
[1]   Case IV/M.272—Matra/CAP Gemini Sogeti, of 17 March 1993.

2.2 *Veto rights*

21.   Joint control may exist even where there is no equality between the two parent companies in votes or in representation in decision-making bodies or where there are more than two parent companies. This is the case where minority shareholders have additional rights which allow them to veto decisions which are

essential for the strategic commercial behaviour of the joint venture.[1] These veto rights may be set out in the statute of the joint venture or conferred by agreement between its parent companies. The veto rights themselves may operate by means of a specific quorum required for decisions taken at the shareholders' meeting or by the board of directors to the extent that the parent companies are represented on this board. It is also possible that strategic decisions are subject to approval by a body, eg supervisory board, where the minority shareholders are represented and form part of the quorum needed for such decisions.

NOTES
[1] Case T-2/93—Air France v EC Commission (ibid); Case IV/M.010—Conagra/Idea, of 3 May 1991.

22. These veto rights must be related to strategic decisions on the business policy of the joint venture. They must go beyond the veto rights normally accorded to minority shareholders in order to protect their financial interests as investors in the joint venture. This normal protection of the rights of minority shareholders is related to decisions on the essence of the joint venture, such as changes in the statute, an increase or decrease in the capital or liquidation. A veto right, for example, which prevents the sale or winding-up of the joint venture does not confer joint control on the minority shareholder concerned.[1]

NOTES
[1] Case IV/M.062—Eridania/ISI, of 30 July 1991.

23. In contrast, veto rights which confer joint control typically include decisions and issues such as the budget, the business plan, major investments or the appointment of senior management. The acquisition of joint control, however, does not require that the acquirer has the power to exercise decisive influence on the day-to-day running of an undertaking. The crucial element is that the veto rights are sufficient to enable the parent companies to exercise such influence in relation to the strategic business behaviour of the joint venture. Moreover, it is not necessary to establish that an acquirer of joint control of the joint venture will actually make use of its decisive influence. The possibility of exercising such influence and, hence, the mere existence of the veto rights, is sufficient.

24. In order to acquire joint control, it is not necessary for a minority shareholder to have all the veto rights mentioned above. It may be sufficient that only some, or even one such right, exists. Whether or not this is the case depends upon the precise content of the veto right itself and also the importance of this right in the context of the specific business of the joint venture.

Appointment of management and determination of budget

25. Normally the most important veto rights are those concerning decisions on the appointment of the management and the budget. The power to co-determine the structure of the management confers upon the holder the power to exercise decisive influence on the commercial policy of an undertaking. The same is true with respect to decisions on the budget since the budget determines the precise framework of the activities of the joint venture and, in particular, the investments it may make.

Business plan

26. The business plan normally provides details of the aims of a company together with the measures to be taken in order to achieve those aims. A veto right over this type of business plan may be sufficient to confer joint control even in the absence of any other veto right. In contrast, where the business plan contains merely

general declarations concerning the business aims of the joint venture, the existence of a veto right will be only one element in the general assessment of joint control but will not, on its own, be sufficient to confer joint control.

Investments

27.   In the case of a veto right on investments, the importance of this right depends, first, on the level of investments which are subject to the approval of the parent companies and, secondly, on the extent to which investments constitute an essential feature of the market in which the joint venture is active. In relation to the first criterion, where the level of investments necessitating approval of the parent companies is extremely high, this veto right may be closer to the normal protection of the interests of a minority shareholder than to a right conferring a power of co-determination over the commercial policy of the joint venture. With regard to the second, the investment policy of an undertaking is normally an important element in assessing whether or not there is joint control. However, there may be some markets where investment does not play a significant role in the market behaviour of an undertaking.

Market-specific rights

28.   Apart from the typical veto rights mentioned above, there exist a number of other veto rights related to specific decisions which are important in the context of the particular market of the joint venture. One example is the decision on the technology to be used by the joint venture where technology is a key feature of the joint venture's activities. Another example relates to markets characterised by product differentiation and a significant degree of innovation. In such markets, a veto right over decisions relating to new product lines to be developed by the joint venture may also be an important element in establishing the existence of joint control.

Overall context

29.   In assessing the relative importance of veto rights, where there are a number of them, these rights should not be evaluated in isolation. On the contrary, the determination of whether or not joint control exists is based upon an assessment of these rights as a whole. However, a veto right which does not relate either to commercial policy and strategy or to the budget or business plan cannot be regarded as giving joint control to its owner.[1]

NOTES
[1]   Case IV/M.295—SITA-RPC/SCORI, of 19 March 1993.

2.3 *Joint exercise of voting rights*

30.   Even in the absence of specific veto rights, two or more undertakings acquiring minority shareholdings in another undertaking may obtain joint control. This may be the case where the minority shareholdings together provide the means for controlling the target undertaking. This means that the minority shareholders, together, will have a majority of the voting rights; and they will act together in exercising these voting rights. This can result from a legally binding agreement to this effect, or it may be established on a *de facto* basis.

31.   The legal means to ensure the joint exercise of voting rights can be in the form of a holding company to which the minority shareholders transfer their rights, or an agreement by which they undertake to act in the same way (pooling agreement).

32.   Very exceptionally, collective action can occur on a *de facto* basis where strong common interests exist between the minority shareholders to the effect that they would not act against each other in exercising their rights in relation to the joint venture.

33. In the case of acquisitions of minority shareholdings, the prior existence of links between the minority shareholders or the acquisition of the shareholdings by means of concerted action will be factors indicating such a common interest.

34. In the case where a new joint venture is established, as opposed to the acquisition of minority shareholdings in a pre-existing company, there is a higher probability that the parent companies are carrying out a deliberate common policy. This is true, in particular, where each parent company provides a contribution to the joint venture which is vital for its operation (eg specific technologies, local know-how or supply agreements). In these circumstances, the parent companies may be able to operate the joint venture with full co-operation only with each other's agreement on the most important strategic decisions even if there is no express provision for any veto rights. The greater the number of parent companies involved in such a joint venture, however, the more remote is the likelihood of this situation occurring.

35. In the absence of strong common interests such as those outlined above, the possibility of changing coalitions between minority shareholders will normally exclude the assumption of joint control. Where there is no stable majority in the decision-making procedure and the majority can on each occasion be any of the various combinations possible amongst the minority shareholders, it cannot be assumed that the minority shareholders will jointly control the undertaking. In this context, it is not sufficient that there are agreements between two or more parties having an equal shareholding in the capital of an undertaking which establish identical rights and powers between the parties. For example, in the case of an undertaking where three shareholders each own one-third of the share capital and each elect one-third of the members of the Board of Directors, the shareholders do not have joint control since decisions are required to be taken on the basis of a simple majority. The same considerations also apply in more complex structures, for example, where the capital of an undertaking is equally divided between three shareholders and where the Board of Directors is composed of twelve members, each of the shareholders A, B and C electing two, another two being elected by A, B and C jointly, whilst the remaining four are chosen by the other eight members jointly. In this case also there is no joint control, and hence no control at all within the meaning of the Merger Regulation.

2.4 *Other considerations related to joint control*

36. Joint control is not incompatible with the fact that one of the parent companies enjoys specific knowledge of and experience in the business of the joint venture. In such a case, the other parent company can play a modest or even non-existent role in the daily management of the joint venture where its presence is motivated by considerations of a financial, long-term-strategy, brand image or general policy nature. Nevertheless, it must always retain the real possibility of contesting the decisions taken by the other parent company, without which there would be sole control.

37. For joint control to exist, there should not be a casting vote for one parent company only. However, there can be joint control when this casting vote can be exercised only after a series of stages of arbitration and attempts at reconciliation or in a very limited field.[1]

NOTES

[1] Case IV/M.425—British Telecom/Banco Santander, of 28 March 1994.

2.5 *Joint control for a limited period*

38. Where an operation leads to joint control for a starting-up period[1] but, according to legally binding agreements, this joint control will be converted to sole

control by one of the shareholders, the whole operation will normally be considered to be an acquisition of sole control.

NOTES
[1] This starting-up period must not exceed three years. Case IV/M.425—British Telecom/Banco Santander, ibid.

3 Control by a single shareholder on the basis of veto rights

39.   An exceptional situation exists where only one shareholder is able to veto strategic decisions in an undertaking, but this shareholder does not have the power, on his own, to impose such decisions. This situation occurs either where one shareholder holds 50% in an undertaking whilst the remaining 50% is held by two or more minority shareholders, or where there is a quorum required for strategic decisions which in fact confers a veto right upon only one minority shareholder.[1] In these circumstances, a single shareholder possesses the same level of influence as that normally enjoyed by several jointly-controlling shareholders, ie the power to block the adoption of strategic decisions. However, this shareholder does not enjoy the powers which are normally conferred on an undertaking with sole control, ie the power to impose strategic decisions. Since this shareholder can produce a deadlock situation comparable to that in normal cases of joint control, he acquires decisive influence and therefore control within the meaning of the Merger Regulation.[2]

NOTES
[1] Case IV/M.258—CCIE/GTE, of 25 September 1992, where the veto rights of only one shareholder were exercisable through a member of the board appointed by this shareholder.
[2] Since this shareholder is the only undertaking acquiring a controlling influence, only this shareholder is obliged to submit a notification under the Merger Regulation.

4 Changes in the structure of control

40.   A concentration may also occur where an operation leads to a change in the structure of control. This includes the change from joint control to sole control as well as an increase in the number of shareholders exercising joint control. The principles for determining the existence of a concentration in these circumstances are set out in detail in the Notice on the concept of undertakings concerned.[1]

[5453]

NOTES
[1] Paragraphs 30 to 48.

IV EXCEPTIONS

41.   Article 3(5) sets out three exceptional situations where the acquisition of a controlling interest does not constitute a concentration under the Merger Regulation.

42.   First, the acquisition of securities by companies whose normal activities include transactions and dealing in securities for their own account or for the account of others is not deemed to constitute a concentration if such an acquisition is made in the framework of these businesses and if the securities are held on only a temporary basis (Article 3(5)(a)). In order to fall within this exception, the following requirements must be fulfilled—

— the acquiring undertaking must be a credit or other financial institution or insurance company the normal activities of which are described above,
— the securities must be acquired with a view to their resale,

— the acquiring undertaking must not exercise the voting rights with a view to determining the strategic commercial behaviour of the target company or must exercise these rights only with a view to preparing the total or partial disposal of the undertaking, its assets or securities,

— the acquiring undertaking must dispose of its controlling interest within one year of the date of the acquisition, that is, it must reduce its shareholding within this one-year period at least to a level which no longer confers control. This period, however, may be extended by the Commission where the acquiring undertaking can show that the disposal was not reasonably possible within the one-year period;

43. Secondly, there is no change of control, and hence no concentration within the meaning of the Merger Regulation, where control is acquired by an office-holder according to the law of a Member State relating to liquidation, winding-up, insolvency, cessation of payments, compositions or analogous proceedings (Article 3(5)(b));

44. Thirdly, a concentration does not arise where a financial holding company within the meaning of the Fourth Council Directive 78/660/EEC[1] acquires control, provided that this company exercises its voting rights only to maintain the full value of its investment and does not otherwise determine directly or indirectly the strategic commercial conduct of the controlled undertaking.

NOTES
[1]   OJ L222, 14.8.78, p 11, as last amended by the Act of Accession of Austria, Finland and Sweden. Article 5(3) of this Directive defines financial holding companies as "those companies the sole objective of which is to acquire holdings in other undertakings, and to manage such holdings and turn them to profit, without involving themselves directly or indirectly in the management of those undertakings, the foregoing without prejudice to their rights as shareholders".

45. In the context of the exceptions under Article 3(5), the question may arise whether a rescue operation constitutes a concentration under the Merger Regulation. A rescue operation typically involves the conversion of existing debt into a new company, through which a syndicate of banks may acquire joint control of the company concerned. Where such an operation meets the criteria for joint control, as outlined above, it will normally be considered to be a concentration.[1] Although the primary intention of the banks is to restructure the financing of the undertaking concerned for its subsequent resale, the exception set out in Article 3(5)(a) is normally not applicable to such an operation. This is because the restructuring programme normally requires the controlling banks to determine the strategic commercial behaviour of the rescued undertaking. Furthermore, it is not normally a realistic proposition to transform a rescued company into a commercially viable entity and to resell it within the permitted one-year period. Moreover, the length of time needed to achieve this aim may be so uncertain that it would be difficult to grant an extension of the disposal period.

[5454]

NOTES
[1]   Case IV/M.116—Kelt/American Express, of 28 August 1991.

V FINAL

46. The Commission's interpretation of Article 3 as set out in this Notice is without prejudice to the interpretation which may be given by the Court of Justice or the Court of First Instance of the European Communities.

[5455]

COMMISSION NOTICE

on the concept of undertakings concerned under Council Regulation (EEC) 4064/89 on the control of concentrations between undertakings

(98/C 66/03)

(Text with EEC relevance)

NOTES
    Date of publication in OJ: OJ C66, 2.3.98, p 14.

I INTRODUCTION

1.   The purpose of this notice is to clarify the Commission's interpretation of the term "undertakings concerned" used in Articles 1 and 5 of Council Regulation (EEC) 4064/89[1] as last amended by Regulation (EC) 1310/97[2] (hereinafter referred to as "the Merger Regulation") and to help identify the undertakings concerned in the most typical situations which have arisen in cases dealt with by the Commission to date. The principles set out in this notice will be followed and further developed by the Commission's practice in individual cases.

This Notice replaces the Notice on the notion of undertakings concerned.[3]

NOTES
    [1]   OJ L395, 30.12.89, p 1; corrected version OJ L257, 21.9.90, p 13.
    [2]   OJ L180, 9.7.97, p 1.
    [3]   OJ C385, 31.12.94, p 12.

2.   According to Article 1 of the Merger Regulation, the Regulation only applies to operations that satisfy two conditions. First, several undertakings must merge, or one or more undertakings must acquire control of the whole or part of other undertakings through the proposed operation, which must qualify as a concentration within the meaning of Article 3 of the Regulation. Secondly, those undertakings must meet the turnover thresholds set out in Article 1.

3.   From the point of view of determining jurisdiction, the undertakings concerned are, broadly speaking, the actors in the transaction in so far as they are the merging, or acquiring and acquired parties; in addition, their total aggregate economic size in terms of turnover will be decisive in determining whether the thresholds are met.

4.   The Commission's interpretation of Articles 1 and 5 with respect to the concept of undertakings concerned is without prejudice to the interpretation which may be given by the Court of Justice or by the Court of First Instance of the European Communities.

[5456]

II THE CONCEPT OF UNDERTAKING CONCERNED

5.   Undertakings concerned are the direct participants in a merger or acquisition of control. In this respect, Article 3(1) of the Merger Regulation provides that—

"A concentration shall be deemed to arise where—
    (a) two or more previously independent undertakings merge, or
    (b) — one or more persons already controlling at least one undertaking, or
         — one or more undertakings

PART IV
EC MATERIALS

acquire, whether by purchase of securities or assets, by contract or by any other means, direct or indirect control of the whole or parts of one or more other undertakings".

6. In the case of a merger, the undertakings concerned will be the undertakings that are merging.

7. In the remaining cases, it is the concept of "acquiring control" that will determine which are the undertakings concerned. On the acquiring side, there can be one or more companies acquiring sole or joint control. On the acquired side, there can be one or more companies as a whole or parts thereof, when only one of their subsidiaries or some of their assets are the subject of the transaction. As a general rule, each of these companies will be an undertaking concerned within the meaning of the Merger Regulation. However, the particular features of specific transactions require some refinement of this principle, as will be seen below when analysing different possible scenarios.

8. In concentrations other than mergers or the setting-up of new joint ventures, ie in cases of sole or joint acquisition of pre-existing companies or parts of them, there is an important party to the agreement that gives rise to the operation who is to be ignored when identifying the undertakings concerned: the seller. Although it is clear that the operation cannot proceed without his consent, his role ends when the transaction is completed since, by definition, from the moment the seller has relinquished all control over the company, his links with it disappear. Where the seller retains joint control with the acquiring company (or companies), it will be considered to be one of the undertakings concerned.

9. Once the undertakings concerned have been identified in a given transaction, their turnover for the purposes of determining jurisdiction should be calculated according to the rules set out in Article 5 of the Merger Regulation.[1] One of the main provisions of Article 5 is that where the undertaking concerned belongs to a group, the turnover of the whole group should be included in the calculation. All references to the turnover of the undertakings concerned in Article 1 should therefore be understood as the turnover of their entire respective groups.

NOTES

[1] The rules for calculating turnover in accordance with Article 5 are detailed in the Commission Notice on calculation of turnover.

10. The same can be said with respect to the substantive appraisal of the impact of a concentration in the market place. When Article 2 of the Merger Regulation provides that the Commission is to take into account "the market position of the undertakings concerned and their economic and financial power", that includes the groups to which they belong.

11. It is important, when referring to the various undertakings which may be involved in a procedure, not to confuse the concept of "undertakings concerned" under Articles 1 and 5 with the terminology used in the Merger Regulation and in Commission Regulation (EC) 447/98 of 1 March 1998 on the notifications, time limits and hearings provided for in Council Regulation (EEC) 4064/89 (hereinafter referred to as the "Implementing Regulation")[1] referring to the various undertakings which may be involved in a procedure. This terminology refers to the notifying parties, other involved parties, third parties and parties who may be subject to fines or periodic penalty payments, and they are defined in Chapter III of the Implementing Regulation, along with their respective rights and duties.

[5457]

NOTES

[1] OJ L61, 2.3.98, p 1.

III IDENTIFYING THE UNDERTAKINGS CONCERNED IN DIFFERENT TYPES OF OPERATIONS

1 Mergers

12.   In a merger, several previously independent companies come together to create a new company or, while remaining separate legal entities, to create a single economic unit. As mentioned earlier, the undertakings concerned are each of the merging entities.

2 Acquisition of sole control

2.1 *Acquisition of sole control of the whole company*

13.   Acquisition of sole control of the whole company is the most straightforward case of acquisition of control; the undertakings concerned will be the acquiring company and the acquired or target company.

2.2 *Acquisition of sole control of part of a company*

14.   The first subparagraph of Article 5(2) of the Merger Regulation provides that when the operation concerns the acquisition of parts of one or more undertakings, only those parts which are the subject of the transaction shall be taken into account with regard to the seller. The concept of "parts" is to be understood as one or more separate legal entities (such as subsidiaries), internal subdivisions within the seller (such as a division or unit), or specific assets which in themselves could constitute a business (eg in certain cases brands or licences) to which a market turnover can be clearly attributed. In this case, the undertakings concerned will be the acquirer and the acquired part(s) of the target company.

15.   The second subparagraph of Article 5(2) includes a special provision on staggered operations or follow-up deals, whereby if several acquisitions of parts by the same purchaser from the same seller occur within a two-year period, these transactions are to be treated as one and the same operation arising on the date of the last transaction. In this case, the undertakings concerned are the acquirer and the different acquired part(s) of the target company taken as a whole.

2.3 *Acquisition of sole control after reduction or enlargement of the target company*

16.   The undertakings concerned are the acquiring company and the target company or companies, in their configuration at the date of the operation.

17.   The Commission bases itself on the configuration of the undertakings concerned at the date of the event triggering the obligation to notify under Article 4(1) of the Merger Regulation, namely the conclusion of the agreement, the announcement of the public bid or the acquisition of a controlling interest. If the target company has divested an entity or closed a business prior to the date of the event triggering notification or where such a divestment or closure is a pre-condition for the operation,[1] then sales of the divested entity or closed business are not to be included when calculating turnover. Conversely, if the target company has acquired an entity prior to the date of the event triggering notification, the sales of the latter are to be added.[2]

NOTES

[1]   See judgment of the Court of First Instance of 24 March 1994 in Case T-3/93—Air France v EC Commission [1994] ECR II-121.

[2]   The calculation of turnover in the case of acquisitions or divestments subsequent to the date of the last audited accounts is dealt with in the Commission Notice on calculation of turnover, paragraph 27.

2.4 *Acquisition of sole control through a subsidiary of a group*

18.   Where the target company is acquired by a group through one of its subsidiaries, the undertakings concerned for the purpose of calculating turnover are the target company and the acquiring subsidiary. However, regarding the actual notification, this can be made by the subsidiary concerned or by its parent company.

19.   All the companies within a group (parent companies, subsidiaries, etc) constitute a single economic entity, and therefore there can only be one undertaking concerned within the one group—ie the subsidiary and the parent company cannot each be considered as separate undertakings concerned, either for the purposes of ensuring that the threshold requirements are fulfilled (for example, if the target company does not meet the ECU 250 million Community turnover threshold), or that they are not (for example, if a group was split into two companies each with a Community turnover below ECU 250 million).

20.   However, even though there can only be one undertaking concerned within a group, Article 5(4) of the Merger Regulation provides that it is the turnover of the whole group to which the undertaking concerned belongs that shall be included in the threshold calculations.[1]

NOTES
  [1]   The calculation of turnover in the case of company groups is dealt with in the Commission Notice on calculation of turnover, paragraphs 36 to 42.

3   Acquisition of joint control

3.1 *Acquisition of joint control of a newly-created company*

21.   In the case of acquisition of joint control of a newly-created company, the undertakings concerned are each of the companies acquiring control of the newly set-up joint venture (which, as it does not yet exist, cannot be considered to be an undertaking concerned and moreover, as yet, has no turnover of its own).

3.2 *Acquisition of joint control of a pre-existing company*

22.   In the case of acquisition of joint control of a pre-existing company or business,[1] the undertakings concerned are each of the companies acquiring joint control on the one hand, and the pre-existing acquired company or business on the other.

NOTES
  [1]   Ie two or more companies (companies A, B, etc) acquire a pre-existing company (company X). For changes in the shareholding in cases of joint control of an existing joint venture, see Section III.6.

23.   However, where the pre-existing company was under the sole control of one company and one or several new shareholders acquire joint control while the initial parent company remains, the undertakings concerned are each of the jointly-controlling companies (including this initial shareholder). The target company in this case is not an undertaking concerned, and its turnover is part of the turnover of the initial parent company.

3.3 *Acquisition of joint control with a view to immediate partition of assets*

24.   Where several undertakings come together solely for the purpose of acquiring another company and agree to divide up the acquired assets according to a pre-existing plan immediately upon completion of the transaction, there is no effective concentration of economic power between the acquirers and the target company since the assets acquired are jointly held and controlled for only a "legal instant". This type of acquisition with a view to immediate partition of assets will in fact be considered to be several operations, whereby each of the acquiring

companies acquires its relevant part of the target company. For each of these operations, the undertakings concerned will therefore be the acquiring company and that part of the target which it is acquiring (just as if there was an acquisition of sole control of part of a company).

25.   This scenario is referred to in recital 24 of Regulation (EEC) 4064/89, which states that the Regulation applies to agreements whose sole object is to divide up the assets acquired immediately after the acquisition.

4   Acquisition of control by a joint venture

26.   In transactions where a joint venture acquires control of another company, the question arises whether or not, from the point of view of the acquiring party, the joint venture should be regarded as a single undertaking concerned (the turnover of which would include the turnover of its parent companies), or whether each of its parent companies should individually be regarded as undertakings concerned. In other words, the issue is whether or not to "lift the corporate veil" of the intermediate undertaking (the vehicle). In principle, the undertaking concerned is the direct participant in the acquisition of control. However, there may be circumstances where companies set up "shell" companies, which have little or no turnover of their own, or use an existing joint venture which is operating on a different market from that of the target company in order to carry out acquisitions on behalf of the parent companies. Where the acquired or target company has a Community turnover of less than ECU 250 million, the question of determining the undertakings concerned may be decisive for jurisdictional purposes.[1] In this type of situation, the Commission will look at the economic reality of the operation to determine which are the undertakings concerned.

NOTES
   [1]   The target company hypothetically has an aggregate Community turnover of less than ECU 250 million, and the acquiring parties are two (or more) undertakings, each with a Community turnover exceeding ECU 250 million. If the target is acquired by a "shell" company set up between the acquiring undertakings, there would only be one company (the "shell" company) with a Community turnover exceeding ECU 250 million, and thus one of the cumulative threshold conditions for Community jurisdiction would not be fulfilled (namely, the existence of at least two undertakings with a Community turnover exceeding ECU 250 million). Conversely, if instead of acting through a "shell" company, the acquiring undertakings acquire the target company themselves, then the turnover threshold would be met and the Merger Regulation would apply to this transaction. The same considerations apply to the national turnover thresholds referred to in Article 1(3).

27.   Where the acquisition is carried out by a full-function joint venture, ie a joint venture which has sufficient financial and other resources to operate a business activity on a lasting basis[1] and is already operating on a market, the Commission will normally consider the joint venture itself and the target company to be the undertakings concerned (and not the joint venture's parent companies).

NOTES
   [1]   The criteria determining the full-function nature of a joint venture are contained in the Commission Notice on the concept of full-function joint ventures.

28.   Conversely, where the joint venture can be regarded as a vehicle for an acquisition by the parent companies, the Commission will consider each of the parent companies themselves to be the undertakings concerned, rather than the joint venture, together with the target company. This is the case in particular where the joint venture is set up especially for the purpose of acquiring the target company, where the joint venture has not yet started to operate, where an existing joint venture has no legal personality or full-function character as referred to above or where the joint venture is an association of undertakings. The same applies where there are elements which demonstrate that the parent companies are in fact the real players

behind the operation. These elements may include a significant involvement by the parent companies themselves in the initiation, organisation and financing of the operation. Moreover, where the acquisition leads to a substantial diversification in the nature of the joint venture's activities, this may also indicate that the parent companies are the real players in the operation. This will normally be the case when the joint venture acquires a target company operating on a different product market. In those cases, the parent companies are regarded as undertakings concerned.

29.   In the TNT case,[1] joint control over a joint venture (JVC) was to be acquired by a joint venture (GD NET BV) between five postal administrations and another acquiring company (TNT Ltd). In this case, the Commission considered that the joint venture GD NET BV was simply a vehicle set up to enable the parent companies (the five postal administrations) to participate in the resulting JVC joint venture in order to facilitate decision-making amongst themselves and to ensure that the parent companies spoke and acted as one; this configuration would ensure that the parent companies could exercise a decisive influence with the other acquiring company, TNT, over the resulting joint venture JVC and would avoid the situation where that other acquirer could exercise sole control because of the postal administrations' inability to reach a unified position on any decision.

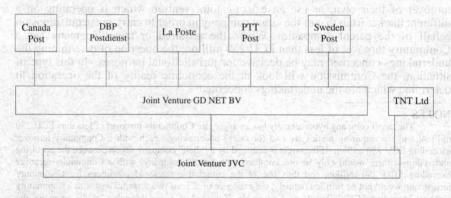

NOTES
1   Case IV/M.102—TNT/Canada Post, DBP Postdienst, La Poste, PTT Post and Sweden Post, of 2 December 1991.

5   Change from joint control to sole control

30.   In the case of a change from joint control to sole control, one shareholder acquires the stake previously held by the other shareholder(s). In the case of two shareholders, each of them has joint control over the entire joint venture, and not sole control over 50% of it; hence the sale of all of his shares by one shareholder to the other does not lead the sole remaining shareholder to move from sole control over 50% to sole control over 100% of the joint venture, but rather to move from joint control to sole control of the entire company (which, subsequent to the operation, ceases to be a "joint" venture).

31.   In this situation, the undertakings concerned are the remaining (acquiring) shareholder and the joint venture. As is the case for any other seller, the "exiting" shareholder is not an undertaking concerned.

32.   The ICI/Tioxide case[1] involved such a change from joint (50/50) control to sole control. The Commission considered that ". . . decisive influence exercised solely is substantially different to decisive influence exercised jointly, since the latter has to take into account the potentially different interests of the

other party or parties concerned . . . By changing the quality of decisive influence exercised by ICI on Tioxide, the transaction will bring about a durable change of the structure of the concerned parties . . .". In this case, the undertakings concerned were held to be ICI (as acquirer) and Tioxide as a whole (as acquiree), but not the seller Cookson.

NOTES
¹   Case IV/M.023—ICI/Tioxide, of 28 November 1990.

6   Change in the shareholding in cases of joint control of an existing joint venture

33.   The decisive element in assessing changes in the shareholding of a company is whether the operation leads to a change in the quality of control. The Commission assesses each operation on a case-by-case basis, but under certain hypotheses, there will be a presumption that the given operation leads, or does not lead, to such a change in the quality of control, and thus constitutes, or does not constitute, a notifiable concentration.

34.   A distinction must be made according to the circumstances of the change in the shareholding; firstly, one or more existing shareholders can exit; secondly, one or more new additional shareholders can enter; and thirdly, one or more existing shareholders can be replaced by one or more new shareholders.

6.1 *Reduction in the number of shareholders leading to a change from joint to sole control*

35.   It is not the reduction in the number of shareholders per se which is important, but rather the fact that if some shareholders sell their stakes in a given joint venture, these stakes are then acquired by other (new or existing) shareholders, and thus the acquisition of these stakes or additional contractual rights may lead to the acquisition of control or may strengthen an already existing position of control (eg additional voting rights or veto rights, additional board members, etc).

36.   Where the number of shareholders is reduced, there may be a change from joint control to sole control (see also Section III.5), in which case the remaining shareholder acquires sole control of the company. The undertakings concerned will be the remaining (acquiring) shareholder and the acquired company (previously the joint venture).

37.   In addition to the shareholder with sole control of the company, there may be other shareholders, for example with minority stakes, but who do not have a controlling interest in the company; these shareholders are not undertakings concerned as they do not exercise control.

6.2 *Reduction in the number of shareholders not leading to a change from joint to sole control*

38.   Where the operation involves a reduction in the number of shareholders having joint control, without leading to a change from joint to sole control and without any new entry or substitution of shareholders acquiring control (see Section III.6.3), the proposed transaction will normally be presumed not to lead to a change in the quality of control and will therefore not be a notifiable concentration. This would be the case where, for example, five shareholders initially have equal stakes of 20% each and where, after the operation, one shareholder exits and the remaining four shareholders each have equal stakes of 25%.

39.   However, this situation would be different where there is a significant change in the quality of control, notably where the reduction in the number of shareholders gives the remaining shareholders additional veto rights or additional

board members, resulting in a new acquisition of control by at least one of the shareholders, through the application of either the existing or a new shareholders' agreement. In this case, the undertakings concerned will be each of the remaining shareholders which exercise joint control and the joint venture. In Avesta II,[1] the fact that the number of major shareholders decreased from four to three led to one of the remaining shareholders acquiring negative veto rights (which it had not previously enjoyed) because of the provisions of the shareholders' agreement which remained in force.[2] This acquisition of full veto rights was considered by the Commission to represent a change in the quality of control.

NOTES

[1]   Case IV/M.452—Avesta II, of 9 June 1994.

[2]   In this case, a shareholder who was a party to the shareholders' agreement sold its stake of approximately 7%. As the exiting shareholder had shared veto rights with another shareholder who remained, and as the shareholders' agreement remained unchanged, the remaining shareholder now acquired full veto rights.

6.3 *Any other changes in the composition of the shareholding*

40.   Finally, in the case where, following changes in the shareholding, one or more shareholders acquire control, the operation will constitute a notifiable operation as there is a presumption that it will normally lead to a change in the quality of control.

41.   Irrespective of whether the number of shareholders decreases, increases or remains the same subsequent to the operation, this acquisition of control can take any of the following forms—

— entry of one or more new shareholders (change from sole to joint control, or situation of joint control both before and after the operation),

— acquisition of a controlling interest by one or more minority shareholders (change from sole to joint control, or situation of joint control both before and after the operation),

— substitution of one or more shareholders (situation of joint control both before and after the operation).

42.   The question is whether the undertakings concerned are the joint venture and the new shareholder(s) who would together acquire control of a pre-existing company, or whether all of the shareholders (existing and new) are to be regarded as undertakings concerned acquiring control of a new joint venture. This question is particularly relevant when there is no express agreement between one (or more) of the existing shareholders and the new shareholder(s), who might only have had an agreement with the "exiting" shareholder(s), ie the seller(s).

43.   A change in the shareholding through the entry or substitution of shareholders is considered to lead to a change in the quality of control. This is because the entry of a new parent company, or the substitution of one parent company for another, is not comparable to the simple acquisition of part of a business as it implies a change in the nature and quality of control of the whole joint venture, even when, both before and after the operation, joint control is exercised by a given number of shareholders.

44.   The Commission therefore considers that the undertakings concerned in cases where there are changes in the shareholding are the shareholders (both existing and new) who exercise joint control and the joint venture itself. As mentioned earlier, non-controlling shareholders are not undertakings concerned.

45.   An example of such a change in the shareholding is the Synthomer/Yule Catto case[1] in which one of two parent companies with joint control over the pre-existing joint venture was replaced by a new parent company. Both parent

companies with joint control (the existing one and the new one) and the joint venture were considered to be undertakings concerned.

NOTES
    [1]   Case IV/M.376—Synthomer/Yule Catto, of 22 October 1993.

7   "Demergers" and the break-up of companies

46.   When two undertakings merge or set up a joint venture, then subsequently demerge or break up their joint venture, and in particular the assets[1] are split between the "demerging" parties, particularly in a configuration different from the original, there will normally be more than one acquisition of control (see the Annex).

NOTES
    [1]   The term "assets" as used here means specific assets which in themselves could constitute a business (eg a subsidiary, a division of a company or, in some cases, brands or licences) to which a market turnover can be clearly attributed.

47.   For example, undertakings A and B merge and then subsequently demerge with a new asset configuration. There will be the acquisition by undertaking A of various assets (assets which may previously have been owned by itself or by undertaking B and assets jointly acquired by the entity resulting from the merger), with similar acquisitions by undertaking B. Similarly, a break-up of a joint venture can be deemed to involve a change from joint control over the joint venture's entire assets to sole control over the divided assets.[1]

NOTES
    [1]   Case IV/M.197—Solvay-Laporte/Interox, of 30 April 1997.

48.   A break-up of a company in this way is "asymmetrical". For such a demerger, the undertakings concerned (for each break-up operation) will be, on the one hand, the original parties to the merger and, on the other, the assets that each original party is acquiring. For the break-up of a joint venture, the undertakings concerned (for each break-up operation) will be, on the one hand, the original parties to the joint venture, each as acquirer, and, on the other, that part of the joint venture that each original party is acquiring.

8   Exchange of assets

49.   In those transactions where two (or more) companies exchange assets, regardless of whether these constitute legal entities or not, each acquisition of control constitutes an independent concentration. Although it is true that both transfers of assets in a swap are usually considered by the parties to be interdependent, that they are often agreed in a single document and that they may even take place simultaneously, the purpose of the Merger Regulation is to assess the impact of the operation resulting from the acquisition of control by each of the companies. The legal or even economic link between those operations is not sufficient for them to qualify as a single concentration.

50.   Hence the undertakings concerned will be, for each property transfer, the acquiring companies and the acquired companies or assets.

9   Acquisitions of control by individual persons

51.   Article 3(1) of the Merger Regulation specifically provides that a concentration is deemed to arise, inter alia, where "one or more persons already controlling at least one undertaking" acquire control of the whole or parts of one or

more undertakings. This provision indicates that acquisitions of control by individuals will bring about a lasting change in the structure of the companies concerned only if those individuals carry out economic activities of their own. The Commission considers that the undertakings concerned are the target company and the individual acquirer (with the turnover of the undertaking(s) controlled by that individual being included in the calculation of the individual's turnover).

52. This was the view taken in the Commission decision in the Asko/Jacobs/Adia case,[1] where Asko, a German holding company with substantial retailing assets, and Mr Jacobs, a private Swiss investor, acquired joint control of Adia, a Swiss company active mainly in personnel services. Mr Jacobs was considered to be an undertaking concerned because of the economic interests he held in the chocolate, confectionery and coffee sectors.

NOTES
  [1]   Case IV/M.082—Asko/Jacobs/Adia, of 16 May 1991.

10   Management buy-outs

53. An acquisition of control of a company by its own managers is also an acquisition by individuals, and what has been said above is therefore also applicable here. However, the management of the company may pool its interests through a "vehicle company", so that it acts with a single voice and also to facilitate decision-making. Such a vehicle company may be, but is not necessarily, an undertaking concerned. The general rule on acquisitions of control by a joint venture applies here (see Section III.4).

54. With or without a vehicle company, the management may also look for investors in order to finance the operation. Very often, the rights granted to these investors according to their shareholding may be such that control within the meaning of Article 3 of the Merger Regulation will be conferred on them and not on the management itself, which may simply enjoy minority rights. In the CWB/Goldman Sachs/Tarkett decision,[1] the two companies managing the investment funds taking part in the transaction were those acquiring joint control, and not the managers.

NOTES
  [1]   Case IV/M.395—CWB/Goldman Sachs/Tarkett, of 21 February 1994.

11   Acquisition of control by a State-owned company

55. In those situations where a State-owned company merges with or acquires control of another company controlled by the same State,[1] the question arises as to whether these transactions really constitute concentrations within the meaning of Article 3 of the Merger Regulation or rather internal restructuring operations of the "public sector group of companies".[2] In this respect, recital 12 of Regulation (EEC) 4064/89 sets out the principle of non-discrimination between public and private sectors and declares that "in the public sector, calculation of the turnover of an undertaking concerned in a concentration needs, therefore, to take account of undertakings making up an economic unit with an independent power of decision, irrespective of the way in which their capital is held or of the rules of administrative supervision applicable to them".

NOTES
  [1]   The term "State" as used here means any legal public entity, ie not only Member States, but also regional or local public entities such as provinces, departments, Länder, etc.
  [2]   See also Commission Notice on the concept of concentration, paragraph 8.

56.   A merger or acquisition of control arising between two companies owned by the same State may constitute a concentration and, if so, both of them will qualify as undertakings concerned, since the mere fact that two companies are both owned by the same State does not necessarily mean that they belong to the same "group". Indeed, the decisive issue will be whether or not these companies are both part of the same industrial holding and are subject to a coordinated strategy. This was the approach taken in the SGS-Thomson decision.[1]

[5458]

NOTES

[1]   Case IV/M.216—CEA Industrie/France Telecom/Finmeccanica/SGS-Thomson, of 22 February 1993.

ANNEX

"DEMERGERS" AND BREAK-UP OF COMPANIES[1]

Merger scenario

Before merger

Company A		Company B

After merger

Merged company
Combined assets

After breaking up the merger

Company A: Divided assets of merged company: — some (initial) assets of A — some (initial) assets of B — some (subsequent) assets of the merged-company	Company B: Divided assets of merged company: — some (initial) assets of A — some (initial) assets of B — some (subsequent) assets of the merged-company

Joint venture scenario (JV)

Before JV

Company A	Assets of A for the JV		Assets of B for the JV	Company B

After JV

Company A	——	Joint venture	——	Company B
		Combined assets		

After breaking up the JV

Company A	Divided assets of joint venture: — some (initial) assets of A — some (initial) assets of B — some (subsequent) assets of the JV	Divided assets of joint venture: — some (initial) assets of A — some (initial) assets of B — some (subsequent) assets of the JV	Company B

[5459]

NOTES

[1]   The term "assets" as used here means specific assets which in themselves could constitute a business (eg a subsidiary, a division of a company or, in some cases, brands or licences) to which a market turnover can be clearly attributed.

COMMISSION NOTICE

on calculation of turnover under Council Regulation (EEC) 4064/89 on the control of concentrations between undertakings

(98/C 66/04)

(Text with EEA relevance)

NOTES
Date of publication in OJ: OJ C66, 2.3.98, p 25.

1. The purpose of this Notice is to expand upon the text of Articles 1 and 5 of Council Regulation (EEC) 4064/89[1] as last amended by Council Regulation (EC) 1310/97[2] (hereinafter referred to as "the Merger Regulation") and in so doing to elucidate certain procedural and practical questions which have caused doubt or difficulty.

NOTES
[1]   OJ L395, 30.12.89, p 1; corrected version OJ L257, 21.9.90, p 13.
[2]   OJ L180, 9.7.97, p 1.

2. This Notice is based on the experience gained by the Commission in applying the Merger Regulation to date. The principles it sets out will be followed and further developed by the Commission's practice in individual cases.

This Notice replaces the Notice on calculation of turnover.[1]

NOTES
[1]   OJ C385, 31.12.94, p 21.

3. The Merger Regulation has a two fold test for Commission jurisdiction. One test is that the transaction must be a concentration within the meaning of Article 3.[1] The second comprises the turnover thresholds contained in Article 1 and designed to identify those transactions which have an impact upon the Community and can be deemed to be of "Community interest". Turnover is used as a proxy for the economic resources being combined in a concentration, and is allocated geographically in order to reflect the geographic distribution of those resources.

Two sets of thresholds are set out in Article 1, in paragraph 2 and paragraph 3 respectively. Article 1(2) sets out the thresholds which must first be checked in order to establish whether the transaction has a Community dimension. In this respect, the worldwide turnover threshold is intended to measure the overall dimension of the undertakings concerned; the Community turnover threshold seeks to determine whether the concentration involves a minimum level of activities in the Community; and the two-thirds rule aims to exclude purely domestic transactions from Community jurisdiction.

Article 1(3) must only be applied in the event that the thresholds set out in Article 1(2) are not met. This second set of thresholds is designed to tackle those transactions which fall short of achieving Community dimension under Article 1(2), but would need to be notified under national competition rules in at least three Member States (so called "multiple notifications"). For this purpose, Article 1(3) provides for lower turnover thresholds, both worldwide and Community-wide, to be achieved by the undertakings concerned. A concentration has a Community dimension if these lower thresholds are fulfilled and the undertakings concerned achieve jointly and individually a minimum level of activities in at least three Member States. Article 1(3) also contains a two-thirds rule similar to that of Article 1(2), which aims to identify purely domestic transactions.

NOTES
1   See the Notice on the concept of concentration.

4.   The thresholds as such are designed to establish jurisdiction and not to assess the market position of the parties to the concentration nor the impact of the operation. In so doing they include turnover derived from, and thus the resources devoted to, all areas of activity of the parties, and not just those directly involved in the concentration. Article 1 of the Merger Regulation sets out the thresholds to be used to determine a concentration with a "Community dimension" while Article 5 explains how turnover should be calculated.

5.   The fact that the thresholds of Article 1 of the Merger Regulation are purely quantitative, since they are only based on turnover calculation instead of market share or other criteria, shows that their aim is to provide a simple and objective mechanism that can be easily handled by the companies involved in a merger in order to determine if their transaction has a Community dimension and is therefore notifiable.

6.   The decisive issue for Article 1 of the Merger Regulation is to measure the economic strength of the undertakings concerned as reflected in their respective turnover figures, regardless of the sector where such turnover was achieved and of whether those sectors will be at all affected by the transaction in question. The Merger Regulation has thereby given priority to the determination of the overall economic and financial resources that are being combined through the merger in order to decide whether the latter is of Community interest.

7.   In this context, it is clear that turnover should reflect as accurately as possible the economic strength of the undertakings involved in a transaction. This is the purpose of the set of rules contained in Article 5 of the Merger Regulation which are designed to ensure that the resulting figures are a true representation of economic reality.

8.   The Commission's interpretation of Articles 1 and 5 with respect to calculation of turnover is without prejudice to the interpretation which may be given by the Court of Justice or the Court of First Instance of the European Communities.

[5460]

I "ACCOUNTING" CALCULATION OF TURNOVER

1   Turnover as a reflection of activity

1.1 *The concept of turnover*

9.   The concept of turnover as used in Article 5 of the Merger Regulation refers explicitly to "the amounts derived from the sale of products and the provision of services". Sale, as a reflection of the undertaking's activity, is thus the essential criterion for calculating turnover, whether for products or the provision of services. "Amounts derived from sale" generally appear in company accounts under the heading "sales".

10.   In the case of products, turnover can be determined without difficulty, namely by identifying each commercial act involving a transfer of ownership.

11.   In the case of services, the factors to be taken into account in calculating turnover are much more complex, since the commercial act involves a transfer of "value".

12.   Generally speaking, the method of calculating turnover in the case of services does not differ from that used in the case of products: the Commission takes into consideration the total amount of sales. Where the service provided is sold directly by the provider to the customer, the turnover of the undertaking concerned consists of the total amount of sales for the provision of services in the last financial year.

13.   Because of the complexity of the service sector, this general principle may have to be adapted to the specific conditions of the service provided. Thus, in certain sectors of activity (such as tourism and advertising), the service may be sold through the intermediary of other suppliers. Because of the diversity of such sectors, many different situations may arise. For example, the turnover of a service undertaking which acts as an intermediary may consist solely of the amount of commissions which it receives.

14.   Similarly, in a number of areas such as credit, financial services and insurance, technical problems in calculating turnover arise which will be dealt with in Section III.

1.2 *Ordinary activities*

15.   Article 5(1) states that the amounts to be included in the calculation of turnover must correspond to the "ordinary activities" of the undertakings concerned.

16.   With regard to aid granted to undertakings by public bodies, any aid relating to one of the ordinary activities of an undertaking concerned is liable to be included in the calculation of turnover if the undertaking is itself the recipient of the aid and if the aid is directly linked to the sale of products and the provision of services by the undertaking and is therefore reflected in the price.[1] For example, aid towards the consumption of a product allows the manufacturer to sell at a higher price than that actually paid by consumers.

NOTES
[1]   See Case IV/M.156—Cereol/Continentale Italiana, of 27 November 1991. In this case, the Commission excluded Community aid from the calculation of turnover because the aid was not intended to support the sale of products manufactured by one of the undertakings involved in the merger, but the producers of the raw materials (grain) used by the undertaking, which specialized in the crushing of grain.

17.   With regard to services, the Commission looks at the undertaking's ordinary activities involved in establishing the resources required for providing the service. In its Decision in the Accor/Wagons-Lits case,[1] the Commission decided to take into account the item "other operating proceeds" included in Wagons-Lits's profit and loss account. The Commission considered that the components of this item which included certain income from its car-hire activities were derived from the sale of products and the provision of services by Wagons-Lits and were part of its ordinary activities.

NOTES
[1]   Case IV/M.126—Accor/Wagons-Lits, of 28 April 1992.

2   "Net" turnover

18.   The turnover to be taken into account is "net" turnover, after deduction of a number of components specified in the Regulation. The Commission's aim is to adjust turnover in such a way as to enable it to decide on the real economic weight of the undertaking.

2.1 *The deduction of rebates and taxes*

19.   Article 5(1) provides for the "deduction of sales rebates and of value added tax and other taxes directly related to turnover". The deductions thus relate to business components (sales rebates) and tax components (value added tax and other taxes directly related to turnover).

20.   "Sales rebates" should be taken to mean all rebates or discounts which are granted by the undertakings during their business negotiations with their customers and which have a direct influence on the amounts of sales.

21.   As regards the deduction of taxes, the Merger Regulation refers to VAT and "other taxes directly related to turnover". As far as VAT is concerned, its deduction does not in general pose any problem. The concept of "taxes directly related to turnover" is a clear reference to indirect taxation since it is directly linked to turnover, such as, for example, taxes on alcoholic beverages.

2.2 *The deduction of "internal" turnover*

22.   The first subparagraph of Article 5(1) states that "the aggregate turnover of an undertaking concerned shall not include the sale of products or the provision of services between any of the undertakings referred to in paragraph 4", ie those which have links with the undertaking concerned (essentially parent companies or subsidiaries).

23.   The aim is to exclude the proceeds of business dealings within a group so as to take account of the real economic weight of each entity. Thus, the "amounts" taken into account by the Merger Regulation reflect only the transactions which take place between the group of undertakings on the one hand and third parties on the other.

3   Adjustment of turnover calculation rules for the different types of operations

3.1 *The general rule*

24.   According to Article 5(1) of the Merger Regulation, aggregate turnover comprises the amounts derived by the undertakings concerned in the preceding financial year from the sale of products and the provision of services. The basic principle is thus that for each undertaking concerned the turnover to be taken into account is the turnover of the closest financial year to the date of the transaction.

25.   This provision shows that since there are usually no audited accounts of the year ending the day before the transaction, the closest representation of a whole year of activity of the company in question is the one given by the turnover figures of the most recent financial year.

26.   The Commission seeks to base itself upon the most accurate and reliable figures available. As a general rule therefore, the Commission will refer to audited or other definitive accounts. However, in cases where major differences between the Community's accounting standards and those of a non-member country are observed, the Commission may consider it necessary to restate these accounts in accordance with Community standards in respect of turnover. The Commission is, in any case, reluctant to rely on management or any other form of provisional accounts in any but exceptional circumstances (see the next paragraph). Where a concentration takes place within the first months of the year and audited accounts are not yet available for the most recent financial year, the figures to be taken into account are those relating to the previous year. Where there is a major divergence between the two sets of accounts, and in particular, when the final draft figures for the most recent years are available, the Commission may decide to take those draft figures into account.

27.   Notwithstanding paragraph 26, an adjustment must always be made to account for acquisitions or divestments subsequent to the date of the audited

accounts. This is necessary if the true resources being concentrated are to be identified. Thus if a company disposes of part of its business at any time before the signature of the final agreement or the announcement of the public bid or the acquisition of a controlling interest bringing about a concentration, or where such a divestment or closure is a pre-condition for the operation[1] the part of the turnover to be attributed to that part of the business must be subtracted from the turnover of the notifying party as shown in its last audited accounts. Conversely, the turnover to be attributed to assets of which control has been acquired subsequent to the preparation of the most recent audited accounts must be added to a company's turnover for notification purposes.

NOTES
  [1] See Judgment of the Court of First Instance in Case T-3/93—Air France v EC Commission [1994] ECR II-121.

28. Other factors that may affect turnover on a temporary basis such as a decrease in orders for the product or a slow-down in the production process within the period prior to the transaction will be ignored for the purposes of calculating turnover. No adjustment to the definitive accounts will be made to incorporate them.

29. Regarding the geographical allocation of turnover, since audited accounts often do not provide a geographical breakdown of the sort required by the Merger Regulation, the Commission will rely on the best figures available provided by the companies in accordance with the rule laid down in Article 5(1) of the Merger Regulation (see Section II.1).

3.2 *Acquisitions of parts of companies*

30. Article 5(2) of the Merger Regulation provides that "where the concentration consists in the acquisition of parts, whether or not constituted as legal entities, of one or more undertakings, only the turnover relating to the parts which are the subject of the transaction shall be taken into account with regard to the seller or sellers".

31. This provision states that when the acquirer does not purchase an entire group, but only one, or part, of its businesses, whether or not constituted as a subsidiary, only the turnover of the part acquired should be included in the turnover calculation. In fact, although in legal terms the seller as a whole (with all its subsidiaries) is an essential party to the transaction, since the sale-purchase agreement cannot be concluded without him, he plays no role once the agreement has been implemented. The possible impact of the transaction on the market will depend only on the combination of the economic and financial resources that are the subject of a property transfer with those of the acquirer and not on the remaining business of the seller who remains independent.

3.3 *Staggered operations*

32. Sometimes certain successive transactions are only individual steps within a wider strategy between the same parties. Considering each transaction alone, even if only for determining jurisdiction, would imply ignoring economic reality. At the same time, whereas some of these staggered operations may be designed in this fashion because they will better meet the needs of the parties, others could be structured like this in order to circumvent the application of the Merger Regulation.

33. The Merger Regulation has foreseen these scenarios in Article 5(2), second subparagraph, which provides that "two or more transactions within the meaning of the first subparagraph which take place within a two-year period between the same persons or undertakings shall be treated as one and the same concentration arising on the date of the last transaction".

34.   In practical terms, this provision means that if company A buys a subsidiary of company B that represents 50% of the overall activity of B and one year later it acquires the other subsidiary (the remaining 50% of B), both transactions will be taken as one. Assuming that each of the subsidiaries attained a turnover in the Community of only ECU 200 million, the first transaction would not be notifiable unless the operation fulfilled the conditions set out in Article 1(3). However, since the second transaction takes place within the two-year period, both have to be notified as a single transaction when the second occurs.

35.   The importance of the provision is that previous transactions (within two years) become notifiable with the most recent transaction once the thresholds are cumulatively met.

3.4   *Turnover of groups*

36.   When an undertaking concerned in a concentration within the meaning of Article 1 of the Merger Regulation[1] belongs to a group, the turnover of the group as a whole is to be taken into account in order to determine whether the thresholds are met. The aim is again to capture the total volume of the economic resources that are being combined through the operation.

NOTES
[1]   See the Commission Notice on the concept of undertakings concerned.

37.   The Merger Regulation does not define the concept of group in abstract terms but focuses on whether the companies have the right to manage the undertaking's affairs as the yardstick to determine which of the companies that have some direct or indirect links with an undertaking concerned should be regarded as part of its group.

38.   Article 5(4) of the Merger Regulation provides the following—

"Without prejudice to paragraph 2 [acquisitions of parts], the aggregate turnover of an undertaking concerned within the meaning of Article 1(2) and (3) shall be calculated by adding together the respective turnovers of the following—

(a)   the undertaking concerned;

(b)   those undertakings in which the undertaking concerned directly or indirectly—

— owns more than half the capital or business assets, or

— has the power to exercise more than half the voting rights, or

— has the power to appoint more than half the members of the supervisory board, the administrative board or bodies legally representing the undertakings, or

— has the right to manage the undertaking's affairs;

(c)   those undertakings which have in an undertaking concerned the rights or powers listed in (b);

(d)   those undertakings in which an undertaking as referred to in (c) has the rights or powers listed in (b);

(e)   those undertakings in which two or more undertakings as referred to in (a) to (d) jointly have the rights or powers listed in (b)."

This means that the turnover of the company directly involved in the transaction (point (a)) should include its subsidiaries (point (b)), its parent companies (point (c)), the other subsidiaries of its parent companies (point (d)) and any other undertaking jointly controlled by two or more of the companies belonging to the group (point (e)). A graphic example is as follows—

The undertaking concerned and its group—

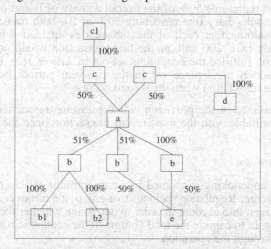

a: The undertaking concerned
b: Its subsidiaries and their own subsidiaries (b1 and b2)
c: Its parent companies and their own parent companies (c1)
d: Other subsidiaries of the parent companies of the undertaking concerned
e: Companies jointly controlled by two (or more) companies of the group

Note: these letters correspond to the relevant points of Article 5(4).

Several remarks can be made from this chart—

1. As long as the test of control of point (b) is fulfilled, the whole turnover of the subsidiary in question will be taken into account regardless of the actual shareholding of the controlling company. In the example, the whole turnover of the three subsidiaries (called b) of the undertaking concerned (a) will be included.

2. When any of the companies identified as belonging to the group also controls others, these should also be incorporated into the calculation. In the example, one of the subsidiaries of a (called b) has in turn its own subsidiaries b1 and b2.

3. When two or more companies jointly control the undertaking concerned (a) in the sense that the agreement of each and all of them is needed in order to manage the undertaking's affairs, the turnover of all of them should be included.[1] In the example, the two parent companies (c) of the undertaking concerned (a) would be taken into account as well as their own parent companies (c1 in the example). Although the Merger Regulation does not explicitly mention this rule for those cases where the undertaking concerned is in fact a joint venture, it is inferred from the text of Article 5(4)(c), which uses the plural when referring to the parent companies. This interpretation has been consistently applied by the Commission.

4. Any intra-group sale should be subtracted from the turnover of the group (see paragraph 22).

NOTES
[1]   See Commission Notice on the concept of undertakings concerned (paragraphs 26–29).

39.   The Merger Regulation also deals with the specific scenario that arises when two or more undertakings concerned in a transaction exercise joint control of another company. Pursuant to point (a) of Article 5(5), the turnover resulting from the sale of products or the provision of services between the joint venture and each

of the undertakings concerned or any other company connected with any one of them in the sense of Article 5(4) should be excluded. The purpose of such a rule is to avoid double counting. With regard to the turnover of the joint venture generated from activities with third parties, point (b) of Article 5(5) provides that it should be apportioned equally amongst the undertakings concerned, to reflect the joint control.[1]

NOTES

[1]   For example, company A and company B set up a joint venture C. These two parent companies exercise at the same time joint control of company D, although A has 60% and B 40% of the capital. When calculating the turnover of A and B at the time they set up the new joint venture C, the turnover of D with third parties is attributed in equal parts to A and B.

40.   Following the principle of point (b) of Article 5(5) by analogy, in the case of joint ventures between undertakings concerned and third parties, the Commission's practice has been to allocate to each of the undertakings concerned the turnover shared equally by all the controlling companies in the joint venture. In all these cases, however, joint control has to be demonstrated.

The practice shows that it is impossible to cover in the present Notice the whole range of scenarios which could arise in respect of turnover calculation of joint venture companies or joint control cases. Whenever ambiguities arise, an assessment should always give priority to the general principles of avoiding double counting and of reflecting as accurately as possible the economic strength of the undertakings involved in the transaction.[1]

NOTES

[1]   See for example Case IV/M.806—BA/TAT, of 26 August 1996.

41.   It should be noted that Article 5(4) refers only to the groups that already exist at the time of the transaction, ie the group of each of the undertakings concerned in an operation, and not to the new structures created as a result of the concentration. For example, if companies A and B, together with their respective subsidiaries, are going to merge, it is A and B, and not the new entity, that qualify as undertakings concerned, which implies that the turnover of each of the two groups should be calculated independently.

42.   Since the aim of this provision is simply to identify the companies belonging to the existing groups for the purposes of turnover calculation, the test of having the right to manage the undertaking's affairs in Article 5(4)[1] is somewhat different from the test of control set out in Article 3(3), which refers to the acquisition of control carried out by means of the transaction subject to examination. Whereas the former is simpler and easier to prove on the basis of factual evidence, the latter is more demanding because in the absence of an acquisition of control no concentration arises.

NOTES

[1]   See for example Case IV/M.126—Accor/Wagons-Lits, of 28 April 1992, and Case IV/M.940—UBS/Mister Minit, of 9 July 1997.

3.5 *Turnover of State-owned companies*

43.   While Article 5(4) sets out the method for determining the economic grouping to which an undertaking concerned belongs for the purpose of calculating turnover, it should be read in conjunction with recital 12 to Regulation (EEC) 4064/89 in respect of State-owned enterprises. This recital states that in order to avoid discrimination between the public and private sector, account should be taken "of undertakings making up an economic unit with an independent power of decision,

irrespective of the way in which their capital is held or of the rules of administrative supervision applicable to them". Thus the mere fact that two companies are both State-owned should not automatically lead to the conclusion that they are part of a group for the purposes of Article 5. Rather, it should be considered whether there are grounds to consider that each company constitutes an independent economic unit.

44. Thus where a State-owned company is not part of an overall industrial holding company and is not subject to any coordination with other State-controlled holdings, it should be treated as an independent group for the purposes of Article 5, and the turnover of other companies owned by that State should not be taken into account. Where, however, a Member State's interests are grouped together in holding companies, or are managed together, or where for other reasons it is clear that State-owned companies form part of an "economic unit with an independent power of decision", then the turnover of those businesses should be considered part of the group of the undertakings concerned for the purposes of Article 5.

[5461]

II GEOGRAPHICAL ALLOCATION OF TURNOVER

1 General rule

45. The thresholds other than those set by Article 1(2)(a) and Article 1(3)(a) select cases which have sufficient turnover within the Community in order to be of Community interest and which are primarily cross-border in nature. They require turnover to be allocated geographically to achieve this. The second subparagraph of Article 5(1) provides that the location of turnover is determined by the location of the customer at the time of the transaction—

> "Turnover, in the Community or in a Member State, shall comprise products sold and services provided to undertakings or consumers, in the Community or in that Member State as the case may be."

46. The reference to "products sold" and "services provided" is not intended to discriminate between goods and services by focusing on where the sale takes place in the case of goods but the place where a service is provided (which might be different from where the service was sold) in the case of services. In both cases, turnover should be attributed to the place where the customer is located because that is, in most circumstances, where a deal was made, where the turnover for the supplier in question was generated and where competition with alternative suppliers took place.[1] The second subparagraph of Article 5(1) does not focus on where a good or service is enjoyed or the benefit of the good or service derived. In the case of a mobile good, a motor car may well be driven across Europe by its purchaser but it was purchased at only one place—Paris, Berlin or Madrid say. This is also true in the case of those services where it is possible to separate the purchase of a service from its delivery. Thus in the case of package holidays, competition for the sale of holidays through travel agents takes place locally, as with retail shopping, even though the service may be provided in a number of distant locations. This turnover is, however, earned locally and not at the site of an eventual holiday.

NOTES

[1] If the place where the customer was located when purchasing the goods or service and the place where the billing was subsequently made are different, turnover should be allocated to the former.

47. This applies even where a multinational corporation has a Community buying strategy and sources all its requirements for a good or service from one location. The fact that the components are subsequently used in ten different plants in a variety of Member States does not alter the fact that the transaction with a company outside the group occurred in only one country. The

subsequent distribution to other sites is purely an internal question for the company concerned.

48.   Certain sectors do, however, pose very particular problems with regard to the geographical allocation of turnover (see Section III).

2   Conversion of turnover into ecu

49.   When converting turnover figures into ecu great care should be taken with the exchange rate used. The annual turnover of a company should be converted at the average rate for the twelve months concerned. This average can be obtained from the Commission. The audited annual turnover figures should not be broken down into component quarterly, monthly, or weekly sales figures which are converted individually at the corresponding average quarterly, monthly or weekly rates, with the ecu figures then added to give a total for the year.

50.   When a company has sales in a range of currencies, the procedure is no different. The total turnover given in the consolidated audited accounts and in that company's reporting currency is converted into ecu at the average rate for the twelve months. Local currency sales should not be converted directly into ecu since these figures are not from the consolidated audited accounts of the company.

[5462]

III CREDIT AND OTHER FINANCIAL INSTITUTIONS AND INSURANCE UNDERTAKINGS

1   Definitions

51.   The specific nature of banking and insurance activities is formally recognized by the Merger Regulation which includes specific provisions dealing with the calculation of turnover for these sectors.[1] Although the Merger Regulation does not provide a definition of the terms, "credit institutions and other financial institutions" within the meaning of point (a) of Article 5(3), the Commission in its practice has consistently adopted the definitions provided in the First and Second Banking Directives—

— "Credit institution means an undertaking whose business is to receive deposits or other repayable funds from the public and to grant credits for its own account".[2]

— "Financial institution shall mean an undertaking other than a credit institution, the principal activity of which is to acquire holdings or to carry on one or more of the activities listed in points 2 to 12 in the Annex".[3]

NOTES

[1]   See Article 5(3) of the Merger Regulation.

[2]   Article 1 of First Council Directive 77/780/EEC of 12 December 1977 on the coordination of laws, regulations and administrative provisions relating to the taking up and pursuit of the business of credit institutions (OJ L322, 17.12.77, p 30).

[3]   Article 1(6) of Second Council Directive 89/646/EEC of 15 December 1989 on the coordination of laws, regulations and administrative provisions relating to the taking up and pursuit of the business of credit institutions (OJ L386, 30.12.89, p 1).

52.   From the definition of "financial institution" given above, it is clear that on the one hand holding companies must be regarded as financial institutions and, on the other hand, that undertakings which perform on a regular basis as a principal activity one or more activities expressly mentioned in points 2 to 12 of the abovementioned Annex must also be regarded as financial institutions within the meaning of point (a) of Article 5(3) of the Merger Regulation. These activities include—

— lending (inter alia, consumer credit, mortgage credit, factoring, . . .),

- financial leasing,
- money transmission services,
- issuing and managing instruments of payment (credit cards, travellers' cheques and bankers' drafts),
- guarantees and commitments,
- trading on own account or on account of customers in money market instruments, foreign exchange, financial futures and options, exchange and interest rate instruments, and transferable securities,
- participation in share issues and the provision of services related to such issues,
- advice to undertakings on capital structure, industrial strategy and related questions and advice and services relating to mergers and the purchase of undertakings,
- money broking,
- portfolio management and advice,
- safekeeping and administration of securities.

2   Calculation of turnover

53.   The methods of calculation of turnover for credit and other financial institutions and for insurance undertakings are described in Article 5(3) of the Merger Regulation. The purpose of this Section is to provide an answer to supplementary questions related to turnover calculation for the abovementioned types of undertakings which were raised during the first years of the application of the Merger Regulation.

2.1 *Credit and financial institutions (other than financial holding companies)*

2.1.1 General

54.   There are normally no particular difficulties in applying the banking income criterion for the definition of the worldwide turnover to credit institutions and other kinds of financial institutions. Difficulties may arise for determining turnover within the Community and also within individual Member States. For this purpose, the appropriate criterion is that of the residence of the branch or division, as provided by Article 5(3)(a)(v), second subparagraph, of the Merger Regulation.

2.1.2 Turnover of leasing companies

55.   There is a fundamental distinction to be made between financial leases and operating leases. Basically, financial leases are made for longer periods than operating leases and ownership is generally transferred to the lessee at the end of the lease term by means of a purchase option included in the lease contract. Under an operating lease, on the contrary, ownership is not transferred to the lessee at the end of the lease term and the costs of maintenance, repair and insurance of the leased equipment are included in the lease payments. A financial lease therefore functions as a loan by the lessor to enable the lessee to purchase a given asset. A financial leasing company is thus a financial institution within the meaning of point (a) of Article 5(3) and its turnover has to be calculated by applying the specific rules related to the calculation of turnover for credit and other financial institutions. Given that operational leasing activities do not have this lending function, they are not considered as carried out by financial institutions, at least as primary activities, and therefore the general turnover calculation rules of Article 5(1) should apply.[1]

NOTES
  [1]   See Case IV/M.234—GECC/Avis Lease, of 15 July 1992.

2.2 Insurance undertakings

2.2.1 Gross premiums written

56. The application of the concept of gross premiums written as a measure of turnover for insurance undertakings has raised supplementary questions notwithstanding the definition provided in point (b) of Article 5(3) of the Merger Regulation. The following clarifications are appropriate—

— "gross" premiums written are the sum of received premiums (which may include received reinsurance premiums if the undertaking concerned has activities in the field of reinsurance). Outgoing or outward reinsurance premiums, ie all amounts paid and payable by the undertaking concerned to get reinsurance cover, are already included in the gross premiums written within the meaning of the Merger Regulation,

— wherever the word "premiums" is used (gross premiums, net (earned) premiums, outgoing reinsurance premiums, etc), these premiums are related not only to new insurance contracts made during the accounting year being considered but also to all premiums related to contracts made in previous years which remain in force during the period taken into consideration.

2.2.2 Investments of insurance undertakings

57. In order to constitute appropriate reserves allowing for the payment of claims, insurance undertakings, which are also considered as institutional investors, usually hold a huge portfolio of investments in shares, interest-bearing securities, land and property and other assets which provide an annual revenue which is not considered as turnover for insurance undertakings.

58. With regard to the application of the Merger Regulation, a major distinction should be made between pure financial investments, in which the insurance undertaking is not involved in the management of the undertakings where the investments have been made, and those investments leading to the acquisition of an interest giving control in a given undertaking thus allowing the insurance undertaking to exert a decisive influence on the business conduct of the subsidiary or affiliated company concerned. In such cases Article 5(4) of the Merger Regulation would apply, and the turnover of the subsidiary or affiliated company should be added to the turnover of the insurance undertaking for the determination of the thresholds laid down in the Merger Regulation.[1]

NOTES

[1] See Case IV/M.018—AG/AMEV, of 21 November 1990.

2.3 Financial holding companies[1]

59. A financial holding company is a financial institution and therefore the calculation of its turnover should follow the criteria established in point (a) of Article 5(3) for the calculation of turnover for credit and other financial institutions. However, since the main purpose of a financial holding [company] is to acquire and manage participation in other undertakings, Article 5(4) also applies, (as for insurance undertakings), with regard to those participations allowing the financial holding company to exercise a decisive influence on the business conduct of the undertakings in question. Thus, the turnover of a financial holding [company] is basically to be calculated according to Article 5(3), but it may be necessary to add turnover of undertakings falling within the categories set out in Article 5(4) ("Article 5(4) companies").

In practice, the turnover of the financial holding company (non-consolidated) must first be taken into account. Then the turnover of the Article 5(4) companies must be added, whilst taking care to deduct dividends and other income distributed by those companies to the financial holding [company]. The following provides an example for this kind of calculation—

	ECU million
1. Turnover related to financial activities (from non-consolidated P&L)	3,000
2. Turnover related to insurance Article 5(4) companies (gross premiums written)	300
3. Turnover of industrial Article 5(4) companies	2,000
4. Deduct dividends and other income derived from Article 5(4) companies 2 and 3	(200)
5. Total turnover financial holding [company] and its group	5,100

NOTES
  ¹ The principles set out in this paragraph for financial holdings may to a certain extent be applied to fund management companies.

60.   In such calculations different accounting rules, in particular those related to the preparation of consolidated accounts, which are to some extent harmonised but not identical within the Community, may need to be taken into consideration. Whilst this consideration applies to any type of undertaking concerned by the Merger Regulation, it is particularly important in the case of financial holding companies¹ where the number and the diversity of enterprises controlled and the degree of control the holding [company] holds on its subsidiaries, affiliated companies and other companies in which it has shareholdings requires careful examination.

NOTES
  ¹ See for example Case IV/M.166—Torras/Sarrió, of 24 February 1992; Case IV/M.213—Hong Kong and Shanghai Bank/Midland, of 21 May 1992; Case IV/M.192—Banesto/Totta, of 14 April 1992.

61.   Turnover calculation for financial holding companies as described above may in practice prove onerous. Therefore a strict and detailed application of this method will be necessary only in cases where it seems that the turnover of a financial holding company is likely to be close to the Merger Regulation thresholds; in other cases it may well be obvious that the turnover is far from the thresholds of the Merger Regulation, and therefore the published accounts are adequate for the establishment of jurisdiction.

[5463]

COMMISSION NOTICE

on the concept of full-function joint ventures under Council Regulation (EEC) 4064/89 on the control of concentrations between undertakings

(98/C 66/01)

(Text with EEA relevance)

NOTES
  Date of publication in OJ: OJ C66, 2.3.98, p 1.

I INTRODUCTION

1.   The purpose of this notice is to provide guidance as to how the Commission interprets Article 3 of Council Regulation (EEC) 4064/89¹ as last amended by Regulation (EC) 1310/97² (hereinafter referred to as the Merger Regulation) in relation to joint ventures.³

NOTES

1   OJ L395, 30.12.89, p 1, corrected version OJ L257, 21.9.90, p 13.

2   OJ L180, 9.7.97, p 1.

3   The Commission intends, in due course, to provide guidance on the application of Article 2(4) of the Merger Regulation. Pending the adoption of such guidance, interested parties are referred to the principles set out in paragraphs 17 to 20 of Commission Notice on the distinction between concentrative and co-operative joint ventures, OJ C385, 31.12.94, p 1.

2.   This Notice replaces the Notice on the distinction between concentrative and cooperative joint ventures. Changes made in this Notice reflect the amendments made to the Merger Regulation as well as the experience gained by the Commission in applying the Merger Regulation since its entry into force on 21 September 1990. The principles set out in this Notice will be followed and further developed by the Commission's practice in individual cases.

3.   Under the Community competition rules, joint ventures are undertakings which are jointly controlled by two or more other undertakings.[1] In practice joint ventures encompass a broad range of operations, from merger-like operations to cooperation for particular functions such as R & D, production or distribution.

NOTES

1   The concept of joint control is set out in the Notice on the concept of concentration.

4.   Joint ventures fall within the scope of the Merger Regulation if they meet the requirements of a concentration set out in Article 3 thereof.

5.   According to recital 23 to Council Regulation (EEC) 4064/89 it is appropriate to define the concept of concentration in such a manner as to cover only operations bringing about a lasting change in the structure of the undertakings concerned.

6.   The structural changes brought about by concentrations frequently reflect a dynamic process of restructuring in the markets concerned. They are permitted under the Merger Regulation unless they result in serious damage to the structure of competition by creating or strengthening a dominant position.

7.   The Merger Regulation deals with the concept of full-function joint ventures in Article 3(2) as follows:

> "The creation of a joint venture performing on a lasting basis all the functions of an autonomous economic entity shall constitute a concentration within the meaning of paragraph 1(b)."

[5464]

II JOINT VENTURES UNDER ARTICLE 3 OF THE MERGER REGULATION

8.   In order to be a concentration within the meaning of Article 3 of the Merger Regulation, an operation must fulfil the following requirements:

1 Joint control

9.   A joint venture may fall within the scope of the Merger Regulation where there is an acquisition of joint control by two or more undertakings, that is, its parent companies (Article 3(1)(b)). The concept of control is set out in Article 3(3). This provides that control is based on the possibility of exercising decisive influence over an undertaking, which is determined by both legal and factual considerations.

10.   The principles for determining joint control are set out in detail in the Commission's Notice on the concept of concentration.[1]

PART IV EC MATERIALS

NOTES
   [1]   Paragraphs 18 to 39.

2   Structural change of the undertakings

11.   Article 3(2) provides that the joint venture must perform, on a lasting basis, all the functions of an autonomous economic entity. Joint ventures which satisfy this requirement bring about a lasting change in the structure of the undertakings concerned. They are referred to in this Notice as "full-function" joint ventures.

12.   Essentially this means that a joint venture must operate on a market, performing the functions normally carried out by undertakings operating on the same market. In order to do so the joint venture must have a management dedicated to its day-to-day operations and access to sufficient resources including finance, staff, and assets (tangible and intangible) in order to conduct on a lasting basis its business activities within the area provided for in the joint-venture agreement.[1]

NOTES
   [1]   Case IV/M.527—Thomson CSF/Deutsche Aerospace, of 2 December 1994 (paragraph 10)—intellectual rights; Case IV/M.560—EDS/Lufthansa, of 11 May 1995 (paragraph 11)—outsourcing; Case IV/M.585—Voest Alpine Industrieanlagenbau GmbH/Davy International Ltd, of 7 September 1995 (paragraph 8)—joint venture's right to demand additional expertise and staff from its parent companies; Case IV/M.686—Nokia/Autoliv, of 5 February 1996 (paragraph 7), joint venture able to terminate "service agreements" with parent company and to move from site retained by parent company; Case IV/M.791—British Gas Trading Ltd/Group 4 Utility Services Ltd, of 7 October 1996 (paragraph 9) joint venture's intended assets will be transferred to leasing company and leased by joint venture.

13.   A joint venture is not full-function if it only takes over one specific function within the parent companies' business activities without access to the market. This is the case, for example, for joint ventures limited to R & D or production. Such joint ventures are auxiliary to their parent companies' business activities. This is also the case where a joint venture is essentially limited to the distribution or sales of its parent companies' products and, therefore, acts principally as a sales agency. However, the fact that a joint venture makes use of the distribution network or outlet of one or more of its parent companies normally will not disqualify it as "full-function" as long as the parent companies are acting only as agents of the joint venture.[1]

NOTES
   [1]   Case IV/M.102—TNT/Canada Post etc, of 2 December 1991 (paragraph 14).

14.   The strong presence of the parent companies in upstream or downstream markets is a factor to be taken into consideration in assessing the full-function character of a joint venture where this presence leads to substantial sales or purchases between the parent companies and the joint venture. The fact that the joint venture relies almost entirely on sales to its parent companies or purchases from them only for an initial start-up period does not normally affect the full-function character of the joint venture. Such a start-up period may be necessary in order to establish the joint venture on a market. It will normally not exceed a period of three years, depending on the specific conditions of the market in question.[1]

Where sales from the joint venture to the parent companies are intended to be made on a lasting basis, the essential question is whether, regardless of these sales, the joint venture is geared to play an active role on the market. In this respect the relative proportion of these sales compared with the total production of the joint venture is an important factor. Another factor is whether sales to the parent companies are made on the basis of normal commercial conditions.[2]

In relation to purchases made by the joint venture from its parent companies, the full-function character of the joint venture is questionable in particular where little value is added to the products or services concerned at the level of the joint venture itself. In such a situation, the joint venture may be closer to a joint sales agency. However, in contrast to this situation where a joint venture is active in a trade market and performs the normal functions of a trading company in such a market, it normally will not be an auxiliary sales agency but a full-function joint venture. A trade market is characterised by the existence of companies which specialise in the selling and distribution of products without being vertically integrated in addition to those which are integrated, and where different sources of supply are available for the products in question. In addition, many trade markets may require operators to invest in specific facilities such as outlets, stockholding, warehouses, depots, transport fleets and sales personnel. In order to constitute a full-function joint venture in a trade market, an undertaking must have the necessary facilities and be likely to obtain a substantial proportion of its supplies not only from its parent companies but also from other competing sources.[3]

NOTES

[1]   Case IV/M.560—EDS/Lufthansa, of 11 May 1995 (paragraph 11); Case IV/M.686—Nokia/Autoliv, of 5 February 1996 (paragraph 6); to be contrasted with Case IV/M.904—RSB/Tenex/Fuel Logistics, of 2 April 1997 (paragraphs 15–17) and Case IV/M.979—Preussag/Voest-Alpine, of 1 October 1997 (paragraphs 9–12). A special case exists where sales by the joint venture to its parent are caused by a legal monopoly downstream of the joint venture: Case IV/M.468—Siemens/Italtel of 17 February 1995 (paragraph 12), or where the sales to a parent company consist of by-products, which are of minor importance to the joint venture: Case IV/M.550—Union Carbide/Enichem, of 13 March 1995 (paragraph 14).

[2]   Case IV/M.556—Zeneca/Vanderhave of 9 April 1996 (paragraph 8); Case IV/M.751—Bayer/Hüls, of 3 July 1996 (paragraph 10).

[3]   Case IV/M.788—AgrEVO/Marubeni of 3 September 1996 (paragraphs 9 and 10).

15.   Furthermore, the joint venture must be intended to operate on a lasting basis. The fact that the parent companies commit to the joint venture the resources described above normally demonstrates that this is the case. In addition, agreements setting up a joint venture often provide for certain contingencies, for example, the failure of the joint venture or fundamental disagreement as between the parent companies.[1] This may be achieved by the incorporation of provisions for the eventual dissolution of the joint venture itself or the possibility for one or more parent companies to withdraw from the joint venture. This kind of provision does not prevent the joint venture from being considered as operating on a lasting basis. The same is normally true where the agreement specifies a period for the duration of the joint venture where this period is sufficiently long in order to bring about a lasting change in the structure of the undertakings concerned,[2] or where the agreement provides for the possible continuation of the joint venture beyond this period. By contrast, the joint venture will not be considered to operate on a lasting basis where it is established for a short finite duration. This would be the case, for example, where a joint venture is established in order to construct a specific project such as a power plant, but it will not be involved in the operation of the plant once its construction has been completed.

[5465]

NOTES

[1]   Case IV/M.891—Deutsche Bank/Commerzbank/J M Voith, of 23 April 1997 (paragraph 7).

[2]   Case IV/M.791—British Gas Trading Ltd/Group 4 Utility Services Ltd, of 7 October 1996 (paragraph 10); to be contrasted with Case IV/M.722—Teneo/Merill Lynch/Bankers Trust, of 15 April 1996 (paragraph 15).

III FINAL

16.   The creation of a full-function joint venture constitutes a concentration within the meaning of Article 3 of the Merger Regulation. Restrictions accepted by the parent companies of the joint venture that are directly related and necessary for the implementation of the concentration ("ancillary restrictions"), will be assessed together with the concentration itself.[1]

Further, the creation of a full-function joint venture may as a direct consequence lead to the co-ordination of the competitive behaviour of undertakings that remain independent. In such cases Article 2(4) of the Merger Regulation provides that those cooperative effects will be assessed within the same procedure as the concentration. This assessment will be made in accordance with the criteria of Article 85(1) and (3) of the Treaty with a view to establishing whether or not the operation is compatible with the common market.

The applicability of Article 85 of the Treaty to other restrictions of competition, that are neither ancillary to the concentration, nor a direct consequence of the creation of the joint venture, will normally have to be examined by means of Regulation No 17.

NOTES
1   See Commission Notice regarding restrictions ancillary to concentrations, OJ C203, 14.8.90, p 5.

17.   The Commission's interpretation of Article 3 of the Merger Regulation with respect to joint ventures is without prejudice to the interpretation which may be given by the Court of Justice or the Court of First Instance of the European Communities.

[5466]

MERGER: BEST PRACTICE GUIDELINES

NOTES
The text of these Guidelines is taken from the European Commission website at http://europa.eu.int/comm/competition/mergers/others/best_practice_gl.html.

One of the fundamental principles underlying the EC Merger Regulation is that in all cases that do not involve "serious doubts", a clearance decision is taken by the Commission within one month from notification. The confidence of European industry and of legal practitioners in the Commission's regulation of mergers is dependent on the Commission being able to process the majority of cases that do not raise competition issues within the one month period.

Declarations of incompleteness under Article 4(2) of the Implementing Regulation have only been made in a few cases (17 cases out of a total of 172 notifications in 1997 and 17 cases out of a total of 196 notifications until 13.11.1998).

However there has been a certain increase in declarations of incompleteness in recent years. Members of the ECLF Committee have had an open discussion with the Merger Task Force with a view to coming to a better understanding of the reasons for these declarations.

We have been informed that declarations according to Article 4(2) are still only made in exceptional circumstances. The Merger Task Force has explained that notifications have been declared incomplete for principally the following reasons—

— In some cases it was not technically possible to accept a notification. These cases include for example notifications made by two parties while they should have been made by three or more parties, or notifications made before there were sufficiently clear legally binding agreements.
— A number of notifications have been poor in terms of the drafting and adequacy of the information provided.

— In some cases the Merger Task Force has identified late during the one month period potential affected markets that should have been identified by the notifying parties in good faith during the pre-notification stage and in the notification itself.

As a more general point, it was explained that in a number of cases in which the notification has been declared incomplete the notification was not preceded by a pre-notification contact, or such contact has been very limited. The consequence of this is that in the absence of any pre-notification discussions there is a higher risk of a declaration of incompleteness.

It is in the interests of the Commission, European business and the legal community to ensure that declarations of incompleteness are kept to the minimum. With this in mind, we have developed the following best practice guidelines in consultation with the Merger Task Force. We recognise that it will not be possible for notifying parties to follow these guidelines in all circumstances.

GUIDELINES

It is always appropriate even in straightforward cases to have pre-notification contacts with the Merger Task Force case team. Notifying parties should submit a briefing memorandum at least three working days before a first meeting. This first meeting should take place preferably at least one or two weeks before the expected date of notification. In more difficult cases, a more protracted pre-notification period may well be appropriate.

Following this first meeting, the parties should provide before notification the Merger Task Force with a substantially complete draft Form CO. The Merger Task Force should be given in general one week to review the draft before a further meeting or being asked to comment on the phone on the adequacy of the draft.

At pre-notification meetings, a discussion should take place on what should and what should not be included in the notification. Indeed, it may not be necessary to provide all information specified in Form CO. However all requests to omit any part of the information specified should be discussed in detail and agreed with the Merger Task Force beforehand.

Potentially affected markets should be openly discussed with the case team in good faith, even if the notifying parties take a different view on market definition. Furthermore, wherever there may be uncertainty or differences of view over market definitions, it will be more prudent to produce market shares on one or more alternative basis—eg by national markets as well as by an EU-wide one.

Notifying parties and their advisers should take care to ensure that the information contained in Form CO has been carefully prepared and verified. Contact details for customers and competitors should be carefully checked to ensure that the Merger Task Force's investigations are not delayed.

At meetings in general (both at the pre-notification stage and during notification), it is preferable that cases are discussed with both legal advisers and business representatives who have a good understanding of the relevant markets.

Provided these guidelines are complied with, the Merger Task Force case team will in principle be prepared to confirm informally the adequacy of a draft notification at the pre-notification stage or, if appropriate to identify in what specific respects it is incomplete.

Despite these guidelines, we recognise that it will not be possible for the Merger Task Force to exclude the fact that it may have to declare a notification incomplete in appropriate cases.

COMMISSION NOTICE

on a simplified procedure for treatment of certain concentrations under Council Regulation (EEC) No 4064/89

(2000/C 217/11)

(Text with EEA relevance)

NOTES

Date of publication in OJ: OJ C247, 29.7.2000, p 32.

1. This Notice sets out a simplified procedure under which the Commission intends to treat certain concentrations that do not raise competition concerns. The Notice is based on experience gained by the Commission in applying Council Regulation (EEC) No 4064/89 of 21 December 1989 on the control of concentrations between undertakings,[1] as amended by Regulation (EC) No 1310/97[2] (the "Merger Regulation") to date, which has shown that certain categories of notified concentrations are normally cleared without having raised any substantive doubts, provided that there were no special circumstances.

2. By following the procedure outlined in the following sections, the Commission aims to make Community merger control more focused and effective.

I. OVERVIEW OF THE SIMPLIFIED PROCEDURE

3. This Notice sets out the conditions under which the simplified procedure will be applied, together with the procedure itself. Pre-notification contact between the notifying parties and the Commission in such cases is encouraged. When all necessary conditions are met, and provided there are no special circumstances, the Commission will adopt a short-form clearance decision within one month from the date of notification, pursuant to Article 6(1)(b) of the Merger Regulation. Where it considers it appropriate in any particular case, the Commission may, naturally, launch an investigation and/or adopt a full decision within the time-limits laid down in Article 10(1) of the Merger Regulation.

II. CATEGORIES OF CONCENTRATIONS SUITABLE FOR TREATMENT UNDER THE SIMPLIFIED PROCEDURE

Eligible concentrations

4. The simplified procedure will apply to the following categories of concentrations—

    (a) two or more undertakings acquire joint control of a joint venture, provided that the joint venture has no, or negligible, actual or foreseen activities within the territory of the European Economic Area (EEA). Such cases occur where—

        (i) the turnover[3] of the joint venture and/or the turnover of the contributed activities[4] is less than EUR 100 million in the EEA territory; and

        (ii) the total value of assets[5] transferred to the joint venture is less than EUR 100 million in the EEA territory;[6]

    (b) two or more undertakings merge, or one or more undertakings acquire sole or joint control of another undertaking, provided that none of the parties to the concentration are engaged in business activities in the same product and geographical market, or in a product market which is upstream or downstream of a product market in which any other party to the concentration is engaged;[7]

(c) two or more undertakings merge, or one or more undertakings acquire sole or joint control of another undertaking and—

    (i) two or more of the parties to the concentration are engaged in business activities in the same product and geographical market (horizontal relationships); or

    (ii) one or more of the parties to the concentration are engaged in business activities in a product market which is upstream or downstream of a product market in which any other party to the concentration is engaged (vertical relationships),[8]

    provided that their combined market share is not 15% or more for horizontal and 25% or more for vertical relationships.[9]

5.   The Commission's experience in applying the Merger Regulation to date has shown that, except in exceptional circumstances, concentrations falling into the above categories do not combine market positions in a way that would give rise to competition concerns.

Safeguards and exclusions

6.   In assessing whether a concentration falls into one of the above categories, the Commission will ensure that all relevant circumstances are established with sufficient clarity. Given that market definitions may be a key element in this assessment, the parties are invited to provide information on possible alternative market definitions during the pre-notification phase (see point 10). Notifying parties are responsible for describing all alternative relevant product and geographic markets on which the notified concentration could have an impact and for providing data and information relating to the definition of such markets.[10] The Commission retains the discretion to take the ultimate decision on market definition, basing its decision on an analysis of the facts of the case. Where it is difficult to define the relevant markets or to determine the parties' market shares, the Commission will not apply the simplified procedure.

7.   While it can normally be assumed that concentrations falling into the above categories will not raise serious doubts as to their compatibility with the common market, there may nonetheless be certain situations, which exceptionally require a closer investigation and/or full decision. In such cases, the Commission may refrain from applying the simplified procedure.

8.   The following are indicative examples of types of cases which may be excluded from the simplified procedure. Certain types of concentrations may increase the parties' market power, for instance by combining technological, financial or other resources, even if the parties to the concentration do not operate in the same market. Concentrations involving conglomerate aspects may also be unsuitable for the simplified procedure, in particular, where one or more of the parties to the concentration holds individually a market share of 25% or more in any product market in which there is no horizontal or vertical relationship between the parties. In other cases, it may not be possible to determine the parties' precise market shares. This is often the case when the parties operate in new or little developed markets. Concentrations in markets with high entry barriers, with a high degree of concentration or other known competition problems may also be unsuitable. Finally, the Commission may not apply the simplified procedure where an issue of coordination as referred to in Article 2(4) of the Merger Regulation arises.

9.   If a Member State expresses substantiated concerns about the notified concentration within three weeks of receipt of the copy of the notification, or if a third party expresses substantiated concerns within the time-limit laid down for such comments, the Commission will adopt a full decision. The time-limits set out in Article 10(1) of the Merger Regulation apply. The simplified procedure will not be applied if a Member State requests the referral of a notified concentration pursuant to Article 9 of the Merger Regulation.

III. PROCEDURAL PROVISIONS

Pre-notification contacts

10. Experience has shown that the business community has found pre-notification contacts between notifying parties and the Commission beneficial.[11] In particular, such contacts allow the Commission and the notifying parties to determine the precise amount of information to be provided in a notification. Notifying parties are therefore advised to engage in pre-notification contacts, particularly where they request the Commission to waive full-form notification in accordance with Article 3(2) of Commission Regulation (EC) No 447/98[12] on the grounds that the operation to be notified will not raise competition concerns.

Publication of the fact of notification

11. The information to be published in the *Official Journal of the European Communities* upon receipt of a notification[13] will include: the names of the parties to the concentration, the nature of the concentration and the economic sectors involved, as well as an indication that, on the basis of the information provided by the notifying party, the concentration may qualify for a simplified procedure. Interested parties will then have the opportunity to submit observations, in particular on circumstances which might require an investigation.

Short-form decision

12. If the Commission is satisfied that the concentration qualifies for the simplified procedure, it will normally issue a short-form decision. The concentration will thus be declared compatible with the common market, within one month from the date of notification, pursuant to Article 10(1) and (6) of the Merger Regulation. However, in the period leading up to the one-month deadline, the option of reverting to a normal first phase merger procedure and thus launching investigations and/or adopting a full decision remains open to the Commission, should it judge such action appropriate in the case in question.

Publication of the short-form decision

13. The Commission will publish a notice of the fact of the decision in the *Official Journal of the European Communities* as it does for full clearance decisions. The public version of the decision will be made available on the Internet for a limited period. The short-form decision will contain the information about the notified concentration published in the Official Journal at the time of notification (names of the parties, nature of the concentration and economic sectors concerned) and a statement in the decision that the concentration is declared compatible with the common market because it falls within one or more of the categories described in the Notice on simplified procedure, with the applicable category(ies) being explicitly identified.

IV. RESTRICTIONS DIRECTLY RELATED TO AND NECESSARY FOR THE IMPLEMENTATION OF THE CONCENTRATION

14. Unless otherwise decided by the Commission, the simplified procedure for the approval of concentrations will also apply to restrictions directly related and necessary to the implementation of the concentration. The approval of a concentration by a short-form decision will cover, pursuant to Article 6(1)(b), second subparagraph, of the Merger Regulation, restrictions which are specified by the notifying parties and which are directly related and necessary to the implementation of the concentration. It should be noted in this regard that the criteria of direct relation and necessity are objective in nature;[14] restrictions are not ancillary simply because the parties regard them as such.

NOTES

1   OJ L395, 30.12.89, p 1; Corrigendum: OJ L257, 21.9. 90, p 13.

2   OJ L180, 9.7.97, p 1; Corrigendum: OJ L40, 13.2.98, p 17.

3   The turnover of the joint venture should be determined according to the most recent audited accounts of the parent companies, or the joint venture itself, depending upon the availability of separate accounts for the resources combined in the joint venture.

4   The expression "and/or" refers to the variety of situations covered; for example:

—in the case of a joint acquisition of a target company, the turnover to be taken into account is the turnover of this target (the joint venture),

—in the case of the creation of a joint venture to which the parent companies contribute their activities, the turnover to be taken into account is that of the contributed activities,

—in the case of entry of a new controlling party into an existing joint venture, the turnover of the joint venture and the turnover of the activities contributed by the new parent company (if any) must be taken into account.

5   The total value of assets of the joint venture should be determined according to the last regularly prepared and approved balance sheet of each parent company. The term "assets" includes: (1) all tangible and intangible assets that will be transferred to the joint venture (examples of tangible assets include production plants, wholesale or retail outlets, and inventory of goods; examples of intangible assets include intellectual property, goodwill, etc), and (2) any amount of credit or any obligations of the joint venture which any parent company of the joint venture has agreed to extend or guarantee.

6   Where the assets transferred generate turnover, then neither the value of the assets nor that of the turnover may exceed EUR 100 million.

7   See Commission Notice on the definition of relevant market for the purposes of Community competition law (OJ C372, 9.12.97, p 5).

8   See footnote 7.

9   This means that only concentrations, which do not lead to affected markets, as defined in Section 6 III of Form CO, fall into this category. The thresholds for horizontal and vertical relationships apply to market shares both at national and at EEA levels and to any alternative product market definition that may have to be considered in a given case. It is important that the underlying market definitions set out in the notification are precise enough to justify the assessment that these thresholds are not met, and that all possible alternative market definitions are mentioned (including geographic markets narrower than national).

10   As with all other notifications, the Commission may revoke the short-form decision if it is based on incorrect information for which one of the undertakings concerned is responsible (Article 6(3)(a) of the Merger Regulation).

11   See the ECLF Committee's best practice guidelines, reproduced on the Commission's website at: http://europa.eu.int/comm/competition/mergers/others/best_practice_gl.html.

12   OJ L61, 2.3.98, p 1.

13   Article 4, paragraph 3, of the Merger Regulation.

14   See Commission Notice on restrictions directly related and necessary to concentrations (OJ C203, 14.8.90, p 5. This Notice sets out those categories of restrictions that, on the basis of the Commission's experience of applying the Merger Regulation to date, can be considered directly related and necessary to the implementation of a concentration.

COMMISSION NOTICE

on remedies acceptable under Council Regulation (EEC) No 4064/89 and under Commission Regulation (EC) No 447/98

(2001/C 68/03)

(Text with EEA relevance)

NOTES

Date of publication in OJ: OJ C68, 2.3.2001, p 3.

I. INTRODUCTION

1. Council Regulation (EEC) No 4064/89 of 21 December 1989 on the control of concentrations between undertakings,[1] as last amended by Regulation (EC) No 1310/97[2] (hereinafter referred to as "the Merger Regulation") expressly provides

that the Commission may decide to declare a concentration compatible with the common market following modification by the parties.[3] Recital 8 of Council Regulation (EC) No 1310/97 states that *"the Commission may declare a concentration compatible with the common market in the second phase[4] of the procedure, following commitments by the parties that are proportional to and would entirely eliminate the competition problem ...."* Recital 8 also provides for *"commitments in the first phase[5] of the procedure where the competition problem is readily identifiable and can easily be remedied. . . . Transparency and effective consultation of Member States and interested third parties should be ensured in both phases of the procedure."*

2.   The purpose of this Notice is to provide guidance on modifications to concentrations, including, in particular, commitments to modify a concentration. Such modifications are more commonly described as "remedies" since their object is to reduce the merging parties' market power and to restore conditions for effective competition which would be distorted as a result of the merger creating or strengthening a dominant position. The guidance set out in this Notice reflects the Commission's evolving experience with the assessment, acceptance and implementation of remedies under the Merger Regulation since its entry into force on 21 September 1990. The principles contained here will be applied and further developed and refined by the Commission in individual cases. The guidance provided on commitments is without prejudice to the interpretation which may be given by the Court of Justice or by the Court of First Instance of the European Communities.

3.   This Notice sets out the general principles applicable to remedies acceptable to the Commission, the main types of commitments that have been accepted by the Commission in cases under the Merger Regulation, the specific requirements which proposals of commitments need to fulfil in both phases of the procedure, and the main requirements for the implementation of commitments.

II. GENERAL PRINCIPLES

4.   Under the Merger Regulation, the Commission assesses the compatibility of a notified concentration with the common market on the basis of its effect on the structure of competition in the Community.[6] The test for compatibility under Article 2(2) and (3) of the Merger Regulation is whether or not a concentration would create or strengthen a dominant position as a result of which effective competition would be significantly impeded in the common market or a substantial part of it.[7] A concentration that creates or strengthens a dominant position as described above is incompatible with the common market and the Commission is required to prohibit it.

5.   Where a concentration raises competition concerns in that it could lead to the creation or strengthening of a dominant position, the parties may seek to modify the concentration in order to resolve the competition concerns raised by the Commission and thereby gain clearance of their merger. Such modifications may be offered and implemented in advance of a clearance decision. However, it is more common that the parties submit commitments with a view to rendering the concentration compatible with the common market within a specific period following clearance.

6.   It is the responsibility of the Commission to show that a concentration creates or strengthens market structures which are liable to impede significantly effective competition in the common market. It is the responsibility of the parties to show that the proposed remedies, once implemented, eliminate the creation or strengthening of such a dominant position identified by the Commission. To this end, the parties are required to show clearly, to the Commission's satisfaction in accordance with its obligations under the Merger Regulation, that the remedy restores conditions of effective competition in the common market on a permanent basis.

7. In assessing whether or not a remedy will restore effective competition the Commission will consider all relevant factors relating to the remedy itself, including *inter alia* the type, scale and scope of the remedy proposed, together with the likelihood of its successful, full and timely implementation by the parties. Moreover, these factors have to be judged by reference to the structure and particular characteristics of the market in which the competition concerns arise, including of course the position of the parties and other players on the market. It follows that it is incumbent on the parties from the outset to remove any uncertainties as to any of these factors which might cause the Commission to reject the remedy proposed.

8. More generally, the Commission will take into account the fact that any remedy, so long as it remains a commitment which is not yet fulfilled, carries with it certain uncertainties as to its eventual outcome. This general factor must also be taken into consideration by the parties when presenting a remedy to the Commission.

9. In the *Gencor* case,[8] the Court of First Instance established the principle that the basic aim of commitments is to ensure competitive market structures. Accordingly, commitments that would amount merely to a promise to behave in a certain way, for example a commitment not to abuse a dominant position created or strengthened by the proposed concentration, are as such not considered suitable to render the concentration compatible with the common market. According to the Court,[9] commitments which are structural in nature, such as the commitment to sell a subsidiary, are, as a rule, preferable from the point of view of the Regulation's objective, inasmuch as such a commitment prevents the creation or strengthening of a dominant position previously identified by the Commission and does not, moreover, require medium or long-term monitoring measures. Nevertheless, the possibility cannot automatically be ruled out that other types of commitments may themselves also be capable of preventing the emergence or strengthening of a dominant position. However, whether such commitments can be accepted has to be determined on a case-by-case basis.

10. Once the concentration has been implemented, despite the possibility of some interim safeguards, the desired conditions of competition on the market cannot actually be restored until the commitments have been fulfilled. Therefore, commitments must be capable of being implemented effectively and within a short period. Commitments should not require additional monitoring once they have been implemented.[10]

11. The Commission may accept commitments in either phase of the procedure. However, given the fact that an in-depth market investigation is only carried out in phase II, commitments submitted to the Commission in phase I must be sufficient to clearly rule out "serious doubts" within the meaning of Article 6(1)(c) of the Merger Regulation.[11] Pursuant to Article 10(2) of the Merger Regulation, the Commission has to take a clearance decision as soon as the serious doubts established in the decision pursuant to Article 6(1)(c) of the Merger Regulation are removed as a result of commitments submitted by the parties. This rule applies in particular to commitments proposed at an early stage of phase II-proceedings.[12] After an in-depth investigation and where the Commission in a Statement of Objections has reached the preliminary view that the merger leads to the creation or strengthening of a dominant position within the meaning of Article 2(3) of the Merger Regulation, the commitments have to eliminate the creation or strengthening of such a dominant position.

12. Whilst commitments have to be offered by the parties, the Commission may ensure the enforceability of commitments by making its authorisation subject to compliance with them.[13] A distinction must be made between conditions and obligations. The requirement for achievement of each measure that gives rise to the structural change of the market is a condition—for example, that a business is to be divested. The implementing steps which are necessary to achieve this result are generally obligations on the parties, such as the appointment of a trustee with an irrevocable mandate to sell the business. Where the undertakings concerned commit a breach of an obligation, the Commission may revoke clearance decisions issued either

under Article 6(2) or Article 8(2) of the Merger Regulation, acting pursuant to Article 6(3) or Article 8(5)(b), respectively. The parties may also be subject to fines and periodic penalty payments as provided in Article 14(2)(a) and 15(2)(a) respectively of the Merger Regulation. Where, however, the situation rendering the concentration compatible with the common market does not materialise,[14] that is, where the condition is not fulfilled, the compatibility decision no longer stands. In such circumstances, the Commission may, pursuant to Article 8(4) of the Merger Regulation, order any appropriate action necessary to restore conditions of effective competition.[15] In addition, the parties may also be subject to fines as provided in Article 14(2)(c).

[5470]

III. TYPES OF REMEDY ACCEPTABLE TO THE COMMISSION[16]

1. Divestiture

13. Where a proposed merger threatens to create or strengthen a dominant position which would impede effective competition, the most effective way to restore effective competition, apart from prohibition, is to create the conditions for the emergence of a new competitive entity or for the strengthening of existing competitors via divestiture.

Viable business

14. The divested activities must consist of a **viable business** that, if operated by a suitable purchaser, can compete effectively with the merged entity on a lasting basis. Normally a viable business is an **existing** one that can operate on a **stand-alone-basis**, which means independently of the merging parties as regards the supply of input materials or other forms of co-operation other than during a transitory period.

15. In proposing a viable business for divestiture, the parties must take into account the uncertainties and risks related to the transfer of a business to a new owner. These risks may limit the competitive impact of the divested business, and, therefore, may lead to a market situation where the competition concerns of the Commission will not necessarily be eliminated.

Object of the divestiture

16. Where the competition problem results from horizontal overlap, the most appropriate business has to be divested.[17] This might be the business of the acquiring company in cases of a hostile bid where the notifying party's knowledge of the business to be acquired is more limited. A commitment to divest activities of the target company might, in such circumstances, increase the risk that this business might not result in a viable competitor which could effectively compete in the market on a lasting basis.

17. In determining which overlapping business should be divested, the ability of the business to be operated on a stand-alone-basis is an important consideration.[18] In order to assure a viable business, it might be necessary to include in a divestiture those activities which are related to markets where the Commission did not raise competition concerns because this would be the only possible way to create an effective competitor in the affected markets.[19]

18. Although it has been accepted in certain specific circumstances,[20] a divestiture consisting of a combination of certain assets from both the purchaser and the target may create additional risks as to the viability and efficiency of the resulting business. It will, therefore, be assessed with great care. In exceptional cases, a divestiture package including only brands and supporting production assets may be sufficient to create the conditions for effective competition.[21] In such circumstances, the Commission would have to be convinced that the buyer could integrate these assets effectively and immediately.

Suitable purchaser

19. The condition for a clearance decision by the Commission is that the viable business will have been transferred to a suitable purchaser[22] within a specific deadline. The two elements of the viable business and the suitable purchaser are thus inter-linked. The potential of a business to attract a suitable purchaser is, therefore, an important element of the Commission's assessment of the appropriateness of the proposed commitment.[23]

20. There are cases where the viability of the divestiture package depends, in view of the assets being part of the business, to a large extent on the identity of the purchaser. In such circumstances, the Commission will not clear the merger unless the parties undertake not to complete the notified operation before having entered into a binding agreement with a purchaser for the divested business (known as the "upfront buyer"), approved by the Commission.[24]

21. Once a divestiture of a business is made a condition of the clearance decision, it is a matter for the parties to find a suitable purchaser for this business. The parties may therefore add, on their own initiative, other assets to make the package more attractive to buyers.[25]

Alternative divestiture commitments

22. In certain cases, the implementation of the parties' preferred divestiture option (of a viable business solving the competition concerns) might be uncertain or difficult in view of, for instance, third parties' pre-emption rights or uncertainty as to the transferability of key contracts, intellectual property rights or employees, as the case may be. Nevertheless, the parties may consider that they would be able to divest this business within the appropriate short time period.

23. In such circumstances, the Commission cannot take the risk that, in the end, effective competition will not be restored. Accordingly, it is up to the parties to set out in the commitment an alternative proposal, which has to be at least equal if not better suited to restore effective competition, as well as a clear timetable as to how and when the other alternative will be implemented.[26]

Removal of structural links

24. Divestiture commitments may not be limited to overcoming competition problems created by horizontal overlaps. The divestiture of an existing shareholding in a joint venture may be necessary in order to sever a structural link with a major competitor.[27]

25. In other cases, a possible remedy could be the divestiture of minority shareholdings or the elimination of interlocking directorates in order to increase the incentives for competing on the market.[28]

2. Other remedies

26. Whilst being the preferred remedy, divestiture is not the only remedy acceptable to the Commission. First, there may be situations where a divestiture of a business is impossible.[29] Secondly, competition problems can also result from specific features, such as the existence of exclusive agreements, the combination of networks ("network effects") or the combination of key patents. In such circumstances, the Commission has to determine whether or not other types of remedy may have a sufficient effect on the market to restore effective competition.

27. The change in the market structure resulting from a proposed concentration can cause existing contractual arrangements to be inimical to effective competition. This is in particular true for exclusive long-term supply and distribution agreements if such agreements limit the market potential available for competitors. Where the merged entity will have a considerable market share, the foreclosure effects resulting from **existing exclusive agreements** may contribute to the creation of a dominant position.[30] In such circumstances, the termination of existing exclusive agreements[31]

may be considered appropriate to eliminate the competitive concerns if there is clearly no evidence that de facto exclusivity is being maintained.

28. The change in the market structure resulting from a proposed concentration can lead to major barriers or impediments to entry into the relevant market. Such barriers may arise from control over infrastructure, in particular networks, or key technology including patents, know-how or other intellectual property rights. In such circumstances, remedies may aim at facilitating market entry by ensuring that competitors will have **access to the necessary infrastructure**[32] or **key technology**.

29. Where the competition problem is created by control over key technology, a divestiture of such technology[33] is the preferable remedy as it eliminates a lasting relationship between the merged entity and its competitors. However, the Commission may accept licensing arrangements (preferably exclusive licences without any field-of-use restrictions on the licensee) as an alternative to divestiture where, for instance, a divestiture would have impeded efficient, on-going research. The Commission has pursued this approach in mergers involving, for example, the pharmaceutical industry.[34]

30. Owing to the specifics of the competition problems raised by a given concentration in several markets, the parties may have to offer **remedy packages** which comprise a combination of divestiture remedies and other remedies that facilitate market entry by granting network access or access to specific content.[35] Such packages may be appropriate to remedy specific foreclosure problems arising, for instance, in concentrations in the telecommunication and media sectors. In addition, there may be transactions affecting mainly one product market where, however, only a package including a variety of other commitments will be able to remedy the competitive concerns raised by the specific concentration on an overall basis.[36]

[5471]

IV. SITUATIONS WHERE REMEDIES ARE DIFFICULT, IF NOT IMPOSSIBLE

31. The Commission is willing to explore solutions to the competition problems raised by a concentration, provided that these solutions are convincing and effective. There are, however, concentrations where remedies adequate to eliminate competition concerns within the common market cannot be found.[37] In such circumstances, the only possibility is prohibition.

32. Where the parties submit proposed remedies that are so extensive and complex that it is not possible for the Commission to determine with the required degree of certainty that effective competition will be restored in the market, an authorisation decision cannot be granted.[38]

[5472]

V. SPECIFIC REQUIREMENTS FOR SUBMISSION OF COMMITMENTS

1. Phase I

33. Pursuant to Article 6(2) of the Merger Regulation the Commission may declare a concentration compatible with the common market, where it is confident that following modification a notified concentration no longer raises serious doubts within the meaning of paragraph 1(c). Parties can submit proposals for commitments to the Commission on an informal basis, even before notification. Where the parties submit proposals for commitments together with the notification or within three weeks from the date of receipt of the notification,[39] the deadline for the Commission's decision pursuant to Article 6(1) of the Merger Regulation is extended from one month to six weeks.

34. In order to form the basis of a decision pursuant to Article 6(2), proposals for commitments must meet the following requirements—
  (a) They shall be submitted in due time, at the latest on the last day of the three-week period.
  (b) They shall specify the commitments entered into by the parties in a sufficient degree of detail to enable a full assessment to be carried out.
  (c) They shall explain how the commitments offered solve the competition concerns identified by the Commission.

At the same time as submitting the commitments, the parties need to supply a non-confidential version of the commitments, for purposes of market testing.[40]

35. Proposals submitted by the parties in accordance with these requirements will be assessed by the Commission. The Commission will consult the authorities of the Member States on the proposed commitments and, when considered appropriate, also third parties in the form of a market test. In addition, in cases involving a geographic market that is wider than the European Economic Area ("EEA") or where, for reasons related to the viability of the business, the scope of the business to be divested is wider than the EEA territory, the proposed remedies may also be discussed with non-EEA competition authorities in the framework of the Community's bilateral co-operation agreements with these countries.

36. Where the assessment confirms that the proposed commitments remove the grounds for serious doubts, the Commission clears the merger in phase I.

37. Where the assessment shows that the commitments offered are not sufficient to remove the competitive concerns raised by the merger, the parties will be informed accordingly. Given that phase I remedies are designed to provide a straightforward answer to a readily identifiable competition concern,[41] only limited modifications can be accepted to the proposed commitments. Such modifications, presented as an immediate response to the result of the consultations, include clarifications, refinements and/or other improvements which ensure that the commitments are workable and effective.

38. If the parties have not removed the serious doubts, the Commission will issue an Article 6(1)(c) decision and open proceedings.

2. Phase II

39. Pursuant to Article 8(2) of the Merger Regulation, the Commission must declare a concentration compatible with the common market, where following modification a notified concentration no longer creates or strengthens a dominant position within the meaning of Article 2(3) of the Merger Regulation. Commitments proposed to the Commission pursuant to Article 8(2) must be submitted to the Commission within not more than three months from the day on which proceedings were initiated. An extension of this period shall only be taken into consideration on request by the parties setting forth the exceptional circumstances which, according to them, justify it. The request for extension must be received within the three-month-period. An extension is only possible in case of exceptional circumstances and where in the particular case there is sufficient time to make a proper assessment of the proposal by the Commission and to allow adequate consultation with Member States and third parties.[42]

40. The Commission is available to discuss suitable commitments prior to the end of the three-month period. The parties are encouraged to submit draft proposals dealing with both substantive and procedural aspects which are necessary to ensure that the commitments are fully workable.

41. Proposals for commitments submitted in order to form the basis for a decision pursuant to Article 8(2) must meet the following requirements—

    (a) They shall be submitted in due time, at the latest on the last day of the three-month period.

    (b) They shall address all competition problems raised in the Statement of Objections and not subsequently abandoned. In this respect, they must specify the substantive and implementing terms entered into by the parties in sufficient detail to enable a full assessment to be carried out.

    (c) They shall explain how the commitments offered solve the competition concerns.

At the same time as submitting the commitments, the parties shall supply a non-confidential version of the commitments, for purposes of market testing.

42. Proposals submitted by the parties in accordance with these requirements will be assessed by the Commission. If the assessment confirms that the proposed commitments remove the competition concerns, following consultation with the authorities of the Member States, discussions with non-Member States authorities[43] and, when considered appropriate, with third parties in the form of a market test, a clearance decision will be submitted for Commission approval.

43. Conversely, where the assessment leads to the conclusion that the proposed commitments appear not to be sufficient to resolve the competition concerns raised by the concentration, the parties will be informed accordingly. Where the parties subsequently modify the proposed commitments, the Commission may only accept these modified commitments[44] where it can clearly determine—on the basis of its assessment of information already received in the course of the investigation, including the results of prior market testing, and without the need for any other market test—that such commitments, once implemented, resolve the competition problems identified and allow sufficient time for proper consultation of Member States.

[5473]

VI. REQUIREMENTS FOR IMPLEMENTATION OF COMMITMENTS

44. Commitments are offered as a means of securing a clearance, with the implementation normally taking place after the decision. These commitments require safeguards to ensure their successful and timely implementation. These implementing provisions will form part of the commitments entered into by the parties vis-à-vis the Commission. They have to be considered on a case-by-case basis. This is in particular true for the fixed time periods laid down for the implementation, which should in general be as short as is feasible. Consequently, it is not possible to standardise these requirements totally.

45. The following guidance is intended to assist the parties in framing commitment proposals. The principles are based on the framework of a divestiture commitment, which, as was seen above, is the most typical commitment. However, many of the principles discussed below are equally applicable to other types of commitments.

1. Essential features of divestment commitments

46. In a typical divestment commitment, the business to be divested normally consists of a combination of tangible and intangible assets, which could take the form of a pre-existing company or group of companies, or of a business activity which was not previously incorporated in its own right. Thus the parties,[45] when submitting a divestiture commitment, have to give a precise and exhaustive definition of the intended subject of divestment (hereafter referred to as "the description of the business" or "the description"). The description has to contain all the elements of the business that are necessary for the business to act as a viable competitor in the market: tangible (such as R&D, production, distribution, sales and marketing activities) and

intangible (such as intellectual property rights, goodwill) assets, personnel, supply and sales agreements (with appropriate guarantees about the transferability of these), customer lists, third party service agreements, technical assistance (scope, duration, cost, quality) and so forth. In order to avoid any misunderstanding about the business to be divested, assets that are used within the business but that should not, according to the parties, be divested, have to be identified separately.

47. The description has to provide for a mechanism whereby the acquirer of the business can retain and select the appropriate personnel. Such a mechanism is required both for the personnel that are currently working in the business unit as it is operated and for the personnel that provide essential functions for the business such as, for instance, group R&D and information technology staff even where such personnel are currently employed by another business unit of the parties. This mechanism is without prejudice to the application of the Council Directives on collective redundancies;[46] on safeguarding employees rights in the event of transfers of undertakings;[47] and on informing and consulting employees[48] as well as national provisions implementing those Directives.

48. The divestment has to be completed within a fixed time period agreed between the parties and the Commission, which takes account of all relevant circumstances. The package will specify what kind of agreement—binding letter of intent, final agreement, transfer of legal title—is required by what date. The deadline for the divestment should start on the day of the adoption of the Commission decision.

49. In order to ensure the effectiveness of the commitment, the sale to a proposed purchaser is subject to prior approval by the Commission. The purchaser is normally required to be a viable existing or potential competitor, independent of and unconnected to the parties, possessing the financial resources,[49] proven expertise and having the incentive to maintain and develop the divested business as an active competitive force in competition with the parties. In addition, the acquisition of the business by a particular proposed purchaser must neither be likely to create new competition problems nor give rise to a risk that the implementation of the commitment will be delayed. These conditions are hereinafter referred to as "the purchaser standards". In order to maintain the structural effect of a remedy, the merged entity cannot, even in the absence of an explicit clause in the commitments, subsequently acquire influence over the whole or parts of the divested business unless the Commission has previously found that the structure of the market has changed to such an extent that the absence of influence over the divested business is no longer necessary to render the concentration compatible with the common market.

2. Interim preservation of the business to be divested – the hold-separate trustee

50. It is the parties' responsibility to reduce to the minimum any possible risk of loss of competitive potential of the business to be divested resulting from the uncertainties inherent to the transfer of a business. Pending divestment, the Commission will require the parties to offer commitments to maintain the independence, economic viability, marketability and competitiveness of the business.

51. These commitments will be designed to keep the business separate from the business retained by the parties, and to ensure that it is managed as a distinct and saleable business. The parties will be required to ensure that all relevant tangible and intangible assets of the divestiture package are maintained, pursuant to good business practice and in the ordinary course of business. This relates in particular to the maintenance of fixed assets, know-how or commercial information of a confidential or proprietary nature, the customer base and the technical and commercial competence of the employees. Furthermore, the parties must maintain the same conditions of competition as regards the divestiture package as those applied before the merger, so as to continue the business as it is currently conducted. This includes providing relevant administrative and management functions, sufficient capital, and a line of credit, and it may include other conditions specific to maintaining competition in an industry.

52. As the Commission cannot, on a daily basis, be directly involved in overseeing compliance with these interim preservation measures, it therefore approves the appointment of a trustee to oversee the parties' compliance with such preservation measures (a so-called "hold-separate trustee"). The hold-separate trustee will act in the best interests of the business to be divested. The commitment will set out the specific details of the trustee's mandate. The trustee's mandate, to be approved by the Commission, together with the trustee appointment, will include for example, responsibilities for supervision, which include the right to propose, and, if deemed necessary, impose, all measures which the trustee considers necessary to ensure compliance with any of the commitments, and periodic compliance reports.

3. Implementation of the commitments – the divestiture trustee

53. The commitment will also set out the specific details and procedures relating to the Commission's oversight of the implementation of the divestiture: for example, criteria for approval of the purchaser, periodic reporting requirements, and approval of the prospectus or advertising material. Here, too, it is noted that the Commission cannot, on a daily basis, be directly involved in managing the divestment. Consequently, in most cases, the Commission considers it appropriate to approve the appointment [of] a trustee with responsibilities for overseeing the implementation of the commitments (the "divestiture trustee").

54. The divestiture trustee's role will vary on a case-by-case basis, but will generally include supervision which includes the right to propose, and if deemed necessary, impose, all measures which the trustee requires to ensure compliance with any of the commitments, and reporting at regular intervals. Where appropriate, the trustee's role will span two phases: in the first phase, he or she will be responsible for overseeing the parties' efforts to find a potential purchaser. If the parties do not succeed in finding an acceptable purchaser within the time frame set out in their commitments, then in the second phase, the trustee will be given an irrevocable mandate to dispose of the business within a specific deadline at any price, subject to the prior approval of the Commission.

4. Approval of the trustee and the trustee mandate

55. Depending on the types of commitments involved and the facts of the case, the divestiture trustee may or may not be the same person or institution as the hold-separate trustee. The trustee will normally be an investment bank, management consulting or accounting company or similar institution. The parties shall suggest the trustee (or a number of trustees) to the Commission. The trustee shall be independent of the parties, possess the necessary qualifications to carry out the job and shall not be, or become, exposed to a conflict of interests. It is the parties' responsibility to supply the Commission with adequate information for it to verify that the trustee fulfils these requirements. The Commission will review and approve the terms of the trustee's appointment, which should be irrevocable unless "good cause" is shown to the Commission for the appointment of a new trustee.

56. The parties are responsible for remuneration of each trustee for all services rendered in the execution of their responsibilities, and the remuneration structure must be such as to not impede the trustee's independence and effectiveness in fulfilling his mandate. The trustee will assume specified duties designed to ensure compliance in good faith with the commitments on behalf of the Commission, and these duties will be defined in the trustee's mandate. The mandate must include all provisions necessary to enable the trustee to fulfil its duties under the commitments accepted by the Commission. It is subject to [the] Commission's approval.

57. When the specific commitments with which the trustee has been entrusted have been implemented—that is to say, when legal title for the divestiture package to be divested has passed or at the end of some specific obligations which continue

post-divestiture—the mandate will provide for the trustee to request the Commission for a discharge from further responsibilities. Even after the discharge has been given, the Commission has the discretion to require the reappointment of the trustee, if subsequently it appears to the Commission that the relevant commitments might not have been fully and properly implemented.

5. Approval of the purchaser and the purchase agreement

58. The parties or the trustee can only proceed with the sale if the Commission approves a proposed purchaser and the purchase agreement on the basis of the arrangements set out in the commitment. The parties or the trustee will be required to demonstrate satisfactorily to the Commission that the proposed buyer meets the requirements of the commitments, which means the purchaser's standards, and that the business is sold in a manner consistent with the commitment. The Commission will formally communicate its view to the parties. Before doing so, the Commission officials may have discussed with the proposed purchaser its incentives for competing with the merged entity on the basis of its business plans. Where different purchasers are being proposed for different parts of the package, the Commission will assess whether each individual proposed purchaser is acceptable and that the total package solves the competition problem.

59. Where the Commission determines that the acquisition of the divestiture package by the proposed purchaser, in the light of the information available to the Commission, threatens to create *prima facie* competition problems[50] or other difficulties, which may delay the timely implementation of the commitment or indicate the lack of appropriate incentives for the purchaser to compete with the merged entity, the proposed purchaser will not be considered acceptable. In this case, the Commission will formally communicate its view that the buyer does not satisfy the purchaser's standards.[51]

60. Where the purchase results in a concentration that has a Community dimension, this new operation will have to be notified under the Merger Regulation and cleared under the normal procedures.[52] Where this is not the case, the Commission's approval of a purchaser is without prejudice to the jurisdiction of merger control of the national authorities.

[5474]

NOTES

1 OJ L395, 30.12.89, p 1; corrected version OJ L257, 21.9.90, p 13.
2 OJ L180, 9.7.97, p 1.
3 The references to 'parties' and 'merging parties' also cover situations with one notifying party.
4 Referred to hereinafter as "phase II".
5 Referred to hereinafter as "phase I".
6 Recital 7 of the Merger Regulation.
7 In the case of the creation of a joint venture, the Commission will also examine the concentration under Article 2(4) of the Merger Regulation. In this respect, the Commission examines whether or not the creation of the joint venture has as its object or effect the coordination of the competitive behaviour of undertakings that remain independent. Such coordination will be appraised in accordance with the criteria of Article 81(1) and (3) of the Treaty, with a view to establishing whether or not the operation is compatible with the common market. The principles set out in this Notice would normally also apply to cases dealt with under Article 2(4).
8 Judgment of the Court of First Instance of 25 March 1999 in Case T-102/96 *Gencor v Commission* [1999] ECR II-753, at paragraph 316.
9 *Op.cit.*, at paragraph 319.
10 Only in exceptional circumstances will the Commission consider commitments which require further monitoring: Commission Decision 97/816/EC (IV/M.877—*Boeing/McDonnell Douglas*; OJ L336, 8.12.97, p 16).
11 Commitments in phase I can only be accepted in certain types of situation. The competition problem needs to be so straightforward and the remedies so clear-cut that it is not necessary to enter into an in-depth investigation.
12 Commission decision of 30 March 1999 (IV/JV.15—*BT/AT&T*); Commission Decision 2000/45/EC (IV/M.1532—*BP Amoco/Arco;* OJ L18, 19.1.2001, p 1).

¹³   If the Commission's final assessment of a case shows that there are no competition concerns or that the resolution of the concerns does not depend on a particular element of the submitted commitments, the parties, being informed, may withdraw them. If the parties do not withdraw them, the Commission may either take note of their proposals in the decision or ignore them. Where the Commission takes note of them, it will explain in its decision that they do not constitute a condition for clearance.

¹⁴   The same principle applies where the situation that originally rendered the concentration compatible is subsequently reversed; see the last sentence of paragraph 49.

¹⁵   These measures may also lead to periodic penalty payments as provided in Article 15(2)(b).

¹⁶   The following overview is non-exhaustive.

¹⁷   Where the competition problem arises in vertical integration cases, divestiture may also resolve the competition concern.

¹⁸   Commission Decision of 29 September 1999 (IV/M.1383—*Exxon/Mobil*, at paragraph 860); Commission Decision of 9 February 2000 (COMP/M.1641—*Linde/AGA*, at paragraph 94).

¹⁹   Commission Decision 1999/229/EC (IV/M.913—*Siemens/Elektrowatt*; OJ L88, 31.3.99, p 1, at paragraph 134); Commission Decision 2000/718/EC (COMP/M.1578—*Sanitec/Sphinx*; OJ L294, 22.11.2000, p 1, at paragraph 255); Commission Decision of 8 March 2000 (COMP/M.1802—*Unilever/Amora Maille*); Commission Decision of 28 September 2000 (COMP/M.90—*Unilever/Bestfoods*; OJ C311, 31.10.2000, p 6).

²⁰   Commission Decision 96/222/EC (IV/M.603—*Crown Cork & Seal/CarnaudMetalbox*; OJ L75, 23.3.96, p 38).

²¹   Commission Decision 96/435/EC (IV/M.623—*Kimberly-Clark/Scott Paper*; OJ L183, 23.7.96, p 1).

²²   See paragraph 49 for the purchaser standards.

²³   IV/M.913—*Siemens/Elektrowatt*: cited above.

²⁴   Commission Decision of 13 December 2000 (COMP/M.2060—*Bosch/Rexroth*).

²⁵   IV/M.1532—*BP Amoco/Arco* (cited above) where the commitment was to divest the interests in certain gas pipelines and processing facilities in the North Sea, also the interests in the related gas fields were divested.

²⁶   Commission Decision of 8 April 1999 (COMP/M.1453—*AXA/GRE*; OJ C 30, 2.2.2000, p 6).

²⁷   Commission Decision 98/455/EC (IV/M.942—*VEBA/Degussa*; OJ L201, 17.7.98, p 102).

²⁸   Commission Decision of 9 February 2000 (COMP/M.1628—*TotalFina/Elf*); Commission Decision of 13 June 2000 (COMP/M.1673—*VEBA/VIAG*); Commission Decision of 1 September 2000 (COMP/M.80—*Volvo/Renault*; OJ C 301, 21.10.2000, p 23).

²⁹   IV/M.877—*Boeing/McDonnell Douglas* (cited above). The Commission's investigations revealed that no existing aircraft manufacturer was interested in acquiring Douglas Aircraft Company (DAC, the commercial aircraft division of McDonnell Douglas) from Boeing, nor was it possible to find a potential entrant to the commercial jet aircraft market who might achieve entry through the acquisition of DAC.

³⁰   Commission Decision 98/475/EC (IV/M. 986—*AGFA Gevaert/DuPont*; OJ L211, 29.7.98, p 22)

³¹   Commission Decision of 28 October 1999 (IV/M.1571—*New Holland/Case*; OJ C130, 11.5.2000, p 11); Commission Decision of 19 April 1999 (IV/M.1467—*Rohm and Haas/Morton*; OJ C157, 4.6.99, p 7).

³²   Commission Decision of 5 October 1992 (IV/M.157—*Air France/SABENA*; OJ C 272, 21.10.92, p 1; Commission Decision of 27 November 1992 (IV/M.259—*British Airways/TAT*; OJ C 326, 11.12.92, p 1); Commission Decision of 20 July 1995 (IV/M.616—*Swissair/SABENA*; OJ C 200, 4.8.95, p 10); Commission Decision of 13 October 1999 (IV/M.1439—*Telia/Telenor*); Commission Decision of 12 April 2000 (COMP/M.1795—*Vodafone/Mannesmann*).

³³   Commission Decision of 9 August 1999 (IV/M.1378—*Hoechst/Rhône-Poulenc*; OJ C254, 7.9.99, p 5); Commission Decision of 1 December 1999 (COMP/M.1601—*AlliedSignal/Honeywell*); Commission Decision of 3 May 2000 (COMP/M.1671—*Dow/UCC*).

³⁴   Commission Decision of 28 February 1995 (IV/M.555—*Glaxo/Wellcome*; OJ C 65, 16.3.95, p 3).

³⁵   COMP/M.1439—*Telia/Telenor*; COMP/M.1795—*Vodafone Airtouch/Mannesmann* (cited above); Commission Decision of 13 October 2000 (COMP/M.2050—*Vivendi/Canal+/Seagram*; OJ C311, 31.10.2000, p 3).

³⁶   Commission Decision 97/816/EC (IV/M.877—*Boeing/McDonnell Douglas*; OJ L336, 8.12.97, p 16); COMP/M.1673—*VEBA/VIAG*.

³⁷   Commission Decision 94/922/EC (*MSG Media Service*, OJ L364, 31.12.94, p 1); Commission Decision 96/177/EC (*Nordic Satellite Distribution*, OJ L53, 2.3.96, p 20); Commission Decision 96/342/EC (*RTL/Veronica/Endemol*, OJ L134, 5.6.96, p 32); Commission Decision 1999/153/EC (*Bertelsmann/Kirch/Premiere*; OJ L53, 27.2.99, p 1); Commission Decision 1999/154/EC (*Deutsche Telekom BetaResearch*; OJ L53, 27.2.99, p 31); Commission Decision 97/610/EC (*St. Gobain/Wacker Chemie/NOM*; OJ L247, 10.9.97, p 1); Commission Decision 91/619/EEC (*Aerospatiale/Alenia/De Havilland*, OJ L334, 5.12.91, p 42); Commission Decision 97/26/EC*Gencor/Lonrho*, OJ L11, 14.1.97, p 30); Commission Decision 2000/276/EC (M.1524—*Airtours/First Choice*; OJ L93, 13.4.2000, p 1).

³⁸   Commission Decision of 15 March 2000 (COMP/M.1672—*Volvo/Scania*); Commission Decision of 28 June 2000 (COMP/M.1741—*WorldCom/Sprint*).

[39] Article 18(1) of Commission Regulation (EC) No 447/98 (Implementing Regulation), OJ L61, 2.3.98, p 1.

[40] By way of a market test, customers, competitors, suppliers and other companies which might be affected or have specific expertise are requested to indicate to the Commission their reasoned opinion as to the effectiveness of the commitment.

[41] See recital 8 of Council Regulation (EC) No 1310/97 referred to in paragraph 1.

[42] M.1439—*Telia/Telenor*; and in Commission Decision 98/335/EC (M.754—*Anglo American/Lonrho*; OJ L149, 20.5.98, p 21).

[43] See paragraph 35.

[44] COMP/M.1628—*TotalFina/Elf*, LPG, cited above, at paragraph 345.

[45] Commitments must be signed by a person duly authorised to do so.

[46] Council Directive 98/59/EC of 20 July 1998 on the approximation of the laws of the Member States relating to collective redundancies (OJ L225, 12.8.98, p 16).

[47] Council Directive 77/187/EEC of 14 February 1977 on the approximation of the laws of the Member States relating to the safeguarding of employees rights in the event of transfers of undertakings, businesses or parts of a business (OJ L61, 5.3.77, p 26) as amended by Council Directive 98/50/EC (OJ L201, 17.7.98, p 88).

[48] Council Directive 94/45/EC of 22 September 1994 on the establishment of a European Works Council or a procedure in Community-scale undertakings and Community-scale groups of undertakings for the purposes of informing and consulting employees (OJ L254, 30.9.94, p 64), as amended by Directive 97/74/EC (OJ L10, 16.1.98, p 22).

[49] The Commission does not accept seller-financed divestitures because of the impact this has on the divested company's independence.

[50] This is most likely to arise where the market structure is already highly concentrated and where the remedy would transfer the market share to another market player.

[51] COMP/M.1628—*TotalFina/Elf*—motorway service stations.

[52] Commission Decision of 29 September 1999 (Case M.1383—*Exxon/Mobil*) and the Commission Decisions of 2 February 2000 in the follow-up Cases M.1820—*BP/JV Dissolution* (not published) and M.1822—*Mobil/JV Dissolution* (OJ C 112, 19.4.2000, p 6).

COMMISSION NOTICE

on restrictions directly related and necessary to concentrations

(2001/C 188/03)

(Text with EEA relevance)

NOTES

Date of publication in OJ: OJ C188, 4.7.01, p 5.

I. INTRODUCTION

1.   Council Regulation (EEC) No 4064/89 of 21 December 1989 on the control of concentrations between undertakings[1] (hereinafter: "the Merger Regulation") provides in Article 6(1)(b), second subparagraph, and in Article 8(2), second subparagraph, second sentence, that a decision declaring a concentration compatible with the Common Market shall also cover "restrictions which are directly related and necessary to the implementation of the concentration". This concept is also referred to in the 25th recital of the Merger Regulation. The decision declaring the concentration compatible with the Common Market shall also cover this type of restrictions. According to Article 22(1) of the Merger Regulation, that Regulation alone applies, to the exclusion of Council Regulation No 17[2] as well as Council Regulations (EEC) No 1017/68 of 19 July 1968 applying rules of competition to transport by rail, road and inland waterway,[3] (EEC) No 4056/86 of 22 December 1986 laying down detailed rules for the application of Articles 81 and 82 of the Treaty to maritime transport[4] and (EEC) No 3975/87 of 14 December 1987 laying down the procedure for the application of the rules on competition to undertakings in the air transport sector.[5]

2.   This legal framework does not impose an obligation on the Commission to assess and formally address such restrictions. Any such assessment is only of a declaratory nature, as all restrictions meeting the criteria set by the Merger Regulation are already covered by Article 6(1)(b), second subparagraph, and Article 8(2), second subparagraph, second sentence, and are therefore cleared by operation of law, whether or not explicitly addressed in the Commission's decision. The Commission does not intend to make such an assessment in its merger decisions any more. This approach is consistent with the Commission's administrative practice introduced for cases qualifying for simplified treatment since 1 September 2000.[6]

3.   Disputes between the parties to a concentration as to whether restrictions are directly related and necessary to its implementation and thus automatically covered by the Commission's clearance decision fall under the jurisdiction of national courts.

4.   This Notice outlines the Commission's interpretation of the notion of "restrictions directly related and necessary to the implementation of the concentration". The guidance given in the following sections reflects past Commission experience and practice in this field.

This Notice replaces the Commission Notice regarding restrictions ancillary to concentrations.[7]

5.   The Commission's interpretation of Article 6(1)(b), second subparagraph, and Article 8(2), second subparagraph, second sentence, of the Merger Regulation is without prejudice to the interpretation which may be given by the Court of Justice or the Court of First Instance of the European Communities.

[5475]

NOTES

[1]   OJ L395, 30.12.1989, p 1; Corrigendum: OJ L257, 21.9.1990, p 13. Regulation as amended by Council Regulation (EC) No 1310/97 (OJ L180, 9.7.1997, p 1, Corrigendum: OJ L40, 13.2.1998, p 17, and OJ L199, 26.7.1997, p 69).
[2]   First Regulation implementing Articles 81 and 82 of the Treaty (OJ L13, 21.2.1962, p 204/62); Regulation as last amended by Council Regulation (EC) No 1216/1999 (OJ L148, 15.6.1999, p 5).
[3]   OJ L175, 23.7.1968, p 1; Regulation as last amended by the Act of Accession of Austria, Finland and Sweden.
[4]   OJ L378, 31.12.1986, p 4; Regulation as last amended by the Act of Accession of Austria, Finland and Sweden.
[5]   OJ L374, 31.12.1987, p 1; Regulation as last amended by Council Regulation (EEC) No 2410/92 (OJ L240, 24.8.1992, p 18).
[6]   See paragraph 14 of the Commission Notice on a simplified procedure for treatment of certain concentrations under Council Regulation (EEC) No 4064/89 (OJ C217, 29.7.2000, p 32).
[7]   OJ C 203, 14.8.1990, p 5.

II. GENERAL PRINCIPLES

6.   A concentration may consist of contractual arrangements and agreements establishing control within the meaning of Article 3(3) of the Merger Regulation. All agreements related to assets necessary to carry out the main object of the concentration are also integral parts of the concentration. In addition to these arrangements and agreements, the parties to the concentration may enter into other agreements which do not form an integral part of the concentration and limit the parties' freedom of action in the market. If such agreements contain restrictions directly related and necessary to the implementation of the concentration itself, these are covered by the decision declaring the concentration compatible with the common market; if not, their restrictive effects may need to be assessed under Articles 81 and 82 of the EC Treaty.

7.   For restrictions to be considered 'directly related to the implementation of the concentration', it is not sufficient that an agreement has been entered into at the same time or in the same context as the concentration.

8.   Agreements must be 'necessary to the implementation of the concentration', which means that in the absence of those agreements, the concentration could not be implemented or could only be implemented under more uncertain conditions, at substantially higher cost, over an appreciably longer period or with considerably higher difficulty[1] agreements aimed at protecting the value transferred,[2] maintaining the continuity of supply after the break-up of a former economic entity,[3] or enabling the start-up of a new entity[4] usually meet these criteria.

9.   In determining whether a restriction is necessary, it is appropriate not only to take account of its nature, but also to ensure that its duration, subject matter and geographical field of application do not exceed what the implementation of the concentration reasonably requires. If equally effective alternatives are available for attaining the legitimate aim pursued, the undertakings must choose the one which is objectively the least restrictive of competition.

10.   For concentrations which are carried out in stages, the contractual arrangements relating to the stages before the establishment of control within the meaning of Article 3(1) and (3) of the Merger Regulation cannot be considered directly related and necessary to the implementation of the concentration. For these agreements, Articles 81 and 82 of the EC Treaty remain applicable. However, agreements which serve to facilitate the acquisition of control can be considered directly related and necessary.

11.   The criteria of direct relation and necessity are objective in nature. Restrictions are not directly related and necessary to the implementation of a concentration simply because the parties regard them as such.

[5476]

NOTES

[1]   Commission Decision of 18 December 2000 (COMP/M.1863—Vodafone/BT/Airtel JV, recital 20).
[2]   Commission Decision of 30 July 1998 (IV/M.1245—Valeo/ITT Industries, recital 59); Commission Decision of 3 March 1999 (IV/M.1442—MMP/AFP, recital 17); Commission Decision of 9 March 2001 (COMP/M.2330—Cargill/Banks, recital 30); Commission Decision of 20 March 2001 (COMP/M.2227—Goldman Sachs/Messer Griesheim, recital 11).
[3]   Commission Decision of 25 February 2000 (COMP/M.1841—Celestica/IBM).
[4]   Commission Decision of 30 March 1999 (IV/JV.15—BT/AT & T, recitals 207 to 214); Commission Decision of 22 December 2000 (COMP/M.2243—Stora Enso/AssiDomän/JV, recitals 49, 56 and 57).

III. PRINCIPLES APPLICABLE TO COMMON CLAUSES IN CASES OF ACQUISITION OF AN UNDERTAKING

12.   Restrictions agreed between the parties in the context of a transfer of an undertaking may be to the benefit of the acquirer or of the vendor. In general terms, the need for the acquirer to benefit from certain protection is more compelling than the corresponding need for the vendor. It is the acquirer who needs to be assured that she/he will be able to acquire the full value of the acquired business. Thus, as a general rule, restrictions which benefit the vendor are either not directly related and necessary to the implementation of the concentration at all, or their scope and/or duration need to be more limited than that of clauses which benefit the acquirer.

A. Non-competition clauses

13.   Non-competition obligations which are imposed on the vendor in the context of the transfer of an undertaking or of part of it can be directly related and necessary to the implementation of the concentration. In order to obtain the full

value of the assets transferred, the acquirer must be able to benefit from some protection against competition from the vendor in order to gain the loyalty of customers and to assimilate and exploit the know-how. Such non-competition clauses guarantee the transfer to the acquirer of the full value of the assets transferred, which in general include both physical assets and intangible assets, such as the goodwill accumulated by the vendor or the know-how[1] she/he has developed.[2] These are not only directly related to the concentration, but are also necessary to its implementation because, without them, there would be reasonable grounds to expect that the sale of the undertaking or of part of it could not be accomplished.

14.   However, such non-competition clauses are only justified by the legitimate objective of implementing the concentration when their duration, their geographical field of application, their subject matter and the persons subject to them do not exceed what is reasonably necessary to achieve that end. Such protection cannot generally be considered necessary when the transfer is in fact limited to physical assets (such as land, buildings or machinery) or to exclusive industrial and commercial property rights (the holders of which could immediately take action against infringements by the transferor of such rights).

15.   Past Commission experience and practice have shown that when the transfer of the undertaking includes both elements of goodwill and know-how, non-competition clauses are generally justified for periods of up to three years[3]; when only goodwill is included, they are generally justified for periods of up to two years.[4] Longer durations can only be justified in a limited range of circumstances, for example where it can be shown that customer loyalty to the seller will persist for more than two years, or for more than three years where the scope or nature of the know-how transferred justifies an additional period of protection.[5]

16.   The geographical scope of a non-competition clause should normally be limited to the area in which the vendor offered the relevant products or services before the transfer.[6] The presumption is that the acquirer does not need to be protected against competition from the vendor in territories not previously penetrated by the vendor, unless it can be shown that such protection is required by particular circumstances of the case, eg for territories the vendor was planning to enter at the time of the transaction, provided that she/he had already invested in preparing this move.

17.   Similarly, non-competition clauses must remain limited to products (including improved versions or updates of products as well as successor models) and services forming the economic activity of the undertaking transferred. This can include products and services at an advanced stage of development at the time of the transaction, or products which are fully developed but not yet marketed. The acquirer does not need to be protected against competition from the vendor in product or service markets in which the transferred undertaking was not active before the transfer.[7]

18.   The vendor may bind herself/himself, her/his subsidiaries and commercial agents. However, an obligation to impose similar restrictions on others would not be regarded as directly related and necessary to the implementation of the concentration. This applies, in particular, to clauses which would restrict the freedom of resellers or users to import or export.

19.   Clauses which limit the vendor's right to purchase or hold shares in a company competing with the business transferred shall be considered directly related and necessary to the implementation of the concentration under the same conditions as outlined above for non-competition clauses, unless they prevent the vendor from purchasing or holding shares for investment purposes, without granting him/her, directly or indirectly, management functions or a material influence in the competing company.[8]

20. Non-solicitation and confidentiality clauses should be evaluated the same way as non-competition clauses, to the extent that their restrictive effect does not exceed that of a non-competition clause. However, since the scope of these clauses may be narrower than that of non-competition clauses, they are more likely to be found to be directly related and necessary to the implementation of the concentration. Confidentiality clauses can, if justified by particular circumstances of the case, be accepted for periods of longer than three years, taking into account companies' interests in protecting valuable business secrets.[9]

NOTES
[1]   As defined in Article 10 of Commission Regulation (EC) No 240/96 of 31 January 1996 on the application of Article 81(3) of the Treaty to certain categories of technology transfer agreements (OJ L31, 9.2.1996, p. 2).
[2]   Commission Decision of 2 March 2001 (COMP/M.2305—Vodafone Group plc/Eircell, recital 22).
[3]   Commission Decision of 2 April 1998 (IV/M.1127—Nestlé/Dalgety, recital 33); Commission Decision of 1 September 2000 (COMP/M.2077—Clayton Dubilier & Rice/Iteltel, recital 15); Commission Decision of 2 March 2001 (COMP/M.2305—Vodafone Group plc/Eircell, recitals 21 and 22).
[4]   Commission Decision of 12 April 1999 (IV/M.1482—Kingfisher/Großlabor, recital 26); Commission Decision of 14 December 1997 (IV/M.884—KNP BT/Bunzl/Wilhelm Seiler, recital 17).
[5]   Commission Decision of 1 September 2000 (COMP/M.1980—Volvo/Renault VI, recital 56).
[6]   Commission Decision of 14 December 1997 (IV/M.884—KNP BT/Bunzl/Wilhelm Seiler, recital 17); Commission Decision of 12 April 1999 (IV/M.1482—Kingfisher/Großlabor, recital 27); Commission Decision of 6 April 2001 (COMP/M.2355—Dow/Enichem Polyurethane, recital 28); Commission Decision of 4 August 2000 (COMP/M.1979—CDC/Banco Urquijo/JV, recital 18).
[7]   Commission Decision of 14 December 1997 (IV/M.884—KNP BT/Bunzl/Wilhelm Seiler, recital 17); Commission Decision of 2 March 2001 (COMP/M.2305—Vodafone Group plc/Eircell, recital 22); Commission Decision of 6 April 2001 (COMP/M.2355—Dow/Enichem Polyurethane, recital 28); Commission Decision of 4 August 2000 (COMP/M.1979—CDC/Banco Urquijo/JV, recital 18).
[8]   Commission Decision of 4 February 1993 (IV/M.304—Tesco/Catteau, recital 14); Commission Decision of 14 December 1997 (IV/M.884—KNP BT/Bunzl/Wilhelm Seiler, recital 19); Commission Decision of 12 April 1999 (IV/M.1482—Kingfisher/Großlabor, recital 27); Commission Decision of 6 April 2000 (COMP/M.1832—Ahold/ICA Förbundet/Canica, recital 26); Commission Decision of 22 June 2000 (COMP/JV.40—Canal+/Lagardère/Canalsatellite, recital 61).
[9]   Commission Decision of 12 April 1999 (IV/M.1482—Kingfisher/Großlabor, recital 28); Commission Decision of 1 September 2000 (COMP/M.1980—Volvo/Renault VI, recital 56); Commission Decision of 6 April 2001 (COMP/M.2355—Dow/Enichem Polyurethane, recital 28).

B. Licence agreements

21. The transfer of an undertaking or of part of it generally includes the transfer to the acquirer, with a view to the full exploitation of the assets transferred, of intellectual property rights or know-how. However, the vendor may remain the owner of the rights in order to exploit them for activities other than those transferred. In these cases, the usual means for ensuring that the acquirer will have the full use of the assets transferred is to conclude licensing agreements in his/her favour. Likewise, where the vendor has transferred intellectual property rights with the business, she/he may still want to continue using some or all of these rights for activities other than those transferred; in such a case the acquirer will grant a licence to the vendor.

22. Licences of patents,[1] of similar rights, or of know-how,[2] can be considered necessary to the implementation of the concentration. They may equally be considered an integral part of the concentration and, in any event, need not be limited in time. These licences can be simple or exclusive and may be limited to certain fields of use, to the extent that they correspond to the activities of the undertaking transferred. However, territorial limitations on manufacture reflecting the territory of the transferred activity are normally not necessary to the implementation of the operation. Restrictions in licence agreements going beyond the above provisions, such as those which protect the licensor rather than the licensee, are not usually necessary to the implementation of the concentration.

Instead, they may be assessed in accordance with Article 81 of the EC Treaty. Agreements which contain restrictions on competition may nevertheless fall under Commission Regulation (EC) No 240/96. In the case of a licence granted by the seller of a business to the buyer, the seller can be made subject to a territorial restriction in the licence agreement under the same conditions as are laid down for non-competition clauses in the context of the sale of a business.

23. Similarly, in the case of licences of trademarks, business names, design rights, copyrights or similar rights, there may be situations in which the vendor wishes to remain the owner of such rights in relation to activities retained, but the acquirer needs those rights in order to market the goods or services produced by the undertaking or part of the undertaking transferred. Here, the same considerations as above apply.[3]

24. Agreements relating to the use of business names or trademarks should normally be analysed in the context of the corresponding licence of the relevant intellectual property right.

NOTES

[1] Including patent applications, utility models, topographies of semi-conductor products, certificats d'utilité and certificats d'addition under French law and applications for these, supplementary protection certificates for medicinal products or other products for which supplementary protection certificates may be obtained, and plant breeder's certificates (as referred to in Article 8 of Commission Regulation (EC) No 240/96).

[2] As defined in Article 10 of Commission Regulation (EC) No 240/96.

[3] Commission Decision of 1 September 2000 (COMP/M.1980—Volvo/Renault VI, recital 54).

C. Purchase and supply obligations

25. In many cases, the transfer of an undertaking or of part of it can entail the disruption of traditional lines of purchase and supply which existed as a result of the previous integration of activities within the economic unity of the vendor. In order to enable the break-up of the economic unity of the vendor and the partial transfer of the assets to the acquirer under reasonable conditions, it is often necessary to maintain, at least for a transitional period, the existing or similar links between the vendor and the acquirer. This objective is normally attained by purchase and supply obligations for the vendor and/or the acquirer of the undertaking or of part of it. Taking into account the particular situation resulting from the break-up of the economic unity of the vendor, such obligations, which may lead to restrictions of competition, can be recognised as directly related and necessary to the implementation of the concentration. They may be in favour of the vendor as well as the acquirer, depending on the particular circumstances of the case.

26. The aim of such obligations may be to ensure the continuity of supply to either of the parties of products necessary for carrying out the activities retained by the vendor or taken over by the acquirer.[1] Thus, there are grounds for recognising, for a transitional period,[2] the need for supply obligations aimed at guaranteeing the quantities previously supplied within the vendor's integrated business, including, where appropriate, the possibility for their adjustment to foreseeable demand forecasts.

27. Likewise, the aim may also be to provide continuity of sales, as they were previously assured within the single economic entity. Purchase obligations which benefit the supplier of a product will require particularly careful justification, depending on the circumstances of the case.

28. Both supply and purchase obligations providing for fixed quantities, possibly with a variation clause, may be recognised as directly related and necessary to the implementation of the concentration. However, obligations providing for unlimited quantities, or conferring preferred supplier or purchaser status, are

presumed not to be necessary to the implementation of the concentration. Any such obligations would need to be justified by particular circumstances of the case.

29.   Likewise, there is no general justification for exclusive purchase or supply obligations.[3] Save under exceptional circumstances, for example resulting from the absence of a market or the specificity of the products in question, such exclusivity is not necessary to the implementation of a concentration.

30.   Past Commission experience and practice have shown that the duration of purchase and supply obligations must be limited to a period necessary for the replacement of the relationship of dependency by autonomy in the market.[4]

The duration of purchase and supply contracts for complex industrial products is normally justified for a transitional period of three years and must, in any event, be justified by particular circumstances of the case, taking into account the goods or services in question.[5]

31.   Service agreements can be equivalent in their effect to supply arrangements; in this case, the same considerations as above shall apply. As for distribution arrangements, they may also be regarded as restrictions directly related and necessary to the implementation of the concentration.[6] If this is not the case, agreements containing restrictions on competition may fall within the scope of Commission Regulation (EC) No 2790/1999 of 22 December 1999 on the application of Article 81(3) of the Treaty to categories of vertical agreements and concerted practices.[7]

[5477]

NOTES
[1]   Commission Decision of 6 April 2001 (COMP/M.2355—Dow/Enichem Polyurethane, recital 31).
[2]   Commission Decision of 30 July 1998 (IV/M.1245—Valeo/ITT Industries, recitals 63 and 64); Commission Decision of 30 March 1999 (IV/JV.15—BT/AT & T, recitals 209, 210 and 212); Commission Decision of 1 September 2000 (COMP/M.1980—Volvo/Renault VI, recital 55); Commission Decision of 6 April 2001 (COMP/M.2355—Dow/Enichem Polyurethane, recital 28).
[3]   Commission Decision of 30 July 1998 (IV/M.1245—Valeo/ITT Industries, recital 64).
[4]   Commission Decision of 30 March 1999 (IV/JV.15—BT/AT & T, recital 209).
[5]   Commission Decision of 2 February 1997 (IV/M. 984—Dupont/ICI, recital 55); Commission Decision of 30 July 1998 (IV/M.1245—Valeo/ITT Industries, recital 64); Commission Decision of 6 April 2001 (COMP/M.2355—Dow/Enichem Polyurethane, recital 31).
[6]   Commission Decision of 30 March 1999 (IV/JV.15—BT/AT & T, recitals 207 and 211).
[7]   OJ L336, 29.12.1999, p 21.

IV. PRINCIPLES APPLICABLE TO COMMON CLAUSES IN CASES OF JOINT ACQUISITION

32.   The Merger Regulation is applicable when two or more undertakings agree to acquire jointly the control of one or more other undertakings, in particular by means of a public tender offer, where the object or effect is the division among themselves of the undertakings or their assets. This is a concentration implemented in two successive stages. The common strategy is limited to the acquisition of control. For this purpose, in the context of a joint bid, an agreement by the joint acquirers of an undertaking to abstain from making separate competing offers for the same undertaking, or otherwise acquiring control, may be considered directly related and necessary to the implementation of the concentration.

33.   Furthermore, restrictions aimed at implementing the division of assets are to be considered directly related and necessary to the implementation of the concentration. This will apply to arrangements made between the parties for the joint acquisition of control in order to divide among themselves the production facilities or distribution networks, together with the existing trademarks of the undertaking acquired jointly.

34. To the extent that such a division involves the break-up of a pre-existing economic entity, arrangements that make the break-up possible under reasonable conditions can be considered directly related and necessary to the implementation of the concentration. In this regard, the principles explained above in relation to purchase and supply arrangements for a transitional period in cases of transfer of undertakings should be applied by analogy.

[5478]

V. PRINCIPLES APPLICABLE TO COMMON CLAUSES IN CASES OF JOINT VENTURES WITHIN THE MEANING OF ARTICLE 3(2) OF THE MERGER REGULATION

A. Non-competition obligations

35. A non-competition obligation between the parent undertakings and a joint venture may be considered directly related and necessary to the implementation of the concentration. Non-competition clauses may reflect, *inter alia*, the need to ensure good faith during negotiations; they may also reflect the need to fully utilise the joint venture's assets or to enable the joint venture to assimilate know-how and goodwill provided by its parents; or the need to protect the parents' interests in the joint venture against competitive acts facilitated, *inter alia*, by the parents' privileged access to the know-how and goodwill transferred to or developed by the joint venture.

36. As a general rule, such clauses can, in case of joint-ventures, be justified for periods of up to five years. However, the Commission considers that non-competition clauses whose duration exceeds three years need to be duly justified by particular circumstances of the case.[1] Moreover, non-competition obligations between the parent undertakings and a joint venture extending beyond the lifetime of the joint venture may never be regarded as directly related and necessary to the implementation of the concentration.[2]

37. The geographical scope of a non-competition clause must be limited to the area in which the parents offered the relevant products or services before establishing the joint venture.[3] That geographical scope can be extended to territories which the parent companies were planning to enter at the time of the transaction, provided that they had already invested in preparing this move.

38. Similarly, non-competition clauses must be limited to products and services constituting the economic activity of the joint venture. This may include products and services at an advanced stage of development at the time of the transaction, as well as products and services which are fully developed but not yet marketed.

39. If the joint venture is set up to enter a new market, reference will be made to the products, services and territories in which it is to operate under the joint venture agreement or by-laws. The presumption is that one parent's interest in the joint venture does not need to be protected against competition from the other parent in markets other than those in which the joint venture will be active at its outset.

40. Additionally, it will be presumed as a general rule that non-competition obligations between non-controlling parents and a joint venture are not directly related and necessary to the implementation of the concentration.

41. The same principles apply to non-solicitation and confidentiality clauses, to the extent that their restrictive effect does not exceed that of a non-competition clause. However, since the scope of these clauses may be narrower than that of non-competition clauses, they may be considered directly related and necessary to the implementation of the concentration in a larger number of circumstances. Moreover, the duration of confidentiality clauses may exceed five years, depending on the

particular circumstances of the case, taking into account companies' interests in protecting valuable business secrets.

[5479]

_____

NOTES

¹   Commission Decision of 16 October 2000 (COMP/M.2137—SLDE/NTL/MSCP/Noos, recital 41); Commission Decision of 4 August 2000 (COMP/M.1979—CDC/Banco Urquijo/JV, recitals 18 and 19); Commission Decision of 22 December 2000 (COMP/M.2243—Stora Enso/AssiDomän/JV, recital 49).

²   Commission Decision of 10 July 2000 (COMP/M.1964—Planet Internet/Fortis Bank/Mine JV, recital 16); Commission Decision of 29 August 2000 (COMP/M.1913—Lufthansa Menzies/LGS/JV; recital 18).

³   Commission Decision of 29 August 2000 (COMP/M.1913—Lufthansa Menzies/LGS/JV; recital 18); Commission Decision of 22 December 2000 (COMP/M.2243—Stora Enso/AssiDomän/JV, recital 49).

_____

B. Licence agreements

42.   A licence granted by the parents to the joint venture may be considered directly related and necessary to the implementation of the concentration. This applies regardless of whether or not the licence is an exclusive one and whether or not it is limited in time. The licence may be restricted to a particular field of use which corresponds to the activities of the joint venture.

43.   Licences granted by the joint venture to one of its parents, or cross-licence agreements, can be regarded as directly related and necessary to the implementation of the concentration under the same conditions as in the case of the sale of a business. Licence agreements between the parents, however, are not considered directly related and necessary to the implementation of a joint venture.

44.   Licence agreements which contain a restriction on competition but are not considered directly related and necessary to the implementation of the concentration may nevertheless fall under Commission Regulation (EC) No 240/96.

C. Purchase and supply obligations

45.   If the parent undertakings remain present in a market upstream or downstream of that of the joint venture, any purchase and supply agreements, including distribution agreements, are subject to the principles applicable in the case of the transfer of an undertaking.

[5480]–[5700]

G. ENFORCEMENT

COMMISSION NOTICE

of 23 December 1992

on cooperation between national courts and the Commission in applying Articles 85 and 86 of the EEC Treaty

(93/C 39/05)

NOTES

Date of publication in OJ: OJ C39, 13.2.93, p 6.

I INTRODUCTION

1.   The abolition of internal frontiers enables firms in the Community to embark on new activities and Community consumers to benefit from increased competition. The Commission considers that these advantages must not be jeopardised by restrictive or abusive practices of undertakings and that the completion of the internal market thus reaffirms the importance of the Community's competition policy and competition law.

2.   A number of national and Community institutions have contributed to the formulation of Community competition law and are responsible for its day-to-day application. For this purpose, the national competition authorities, national and Community courts and the Commission each assume their own tasks and responsibilities, in line with the principles developed by the case-law of the Court of Justice of the European Communities.

3.   If the competition process is to work well in the internal market, effective cooperation between these institutions must be ensured. The purpose of this Notice is to achieve this in relations between national courts and the Commission. It spells out how the Commission intends to assist national courts by closer cooperation in the application of Articles 85 and 86 of the EEC Treaty in individual cases.

[5701]

II POWERS

4.   The Commission is the administrative authority responsible for the implementation and for the thrust of competition policy in the Community and for this purpose has to act in the public interest. National courts, on the other hand, have the task of safeguarding the subjective rights of private individuals in their relations with one another.[1]

5.   In performing these different tasks, national courts and the Commission possess concurrent powers for the application of Article 85(1) and Article 86 of the Treaty. In the case of the Commission, the power is conferred by Article 89 and by the provisions adopted pursuant to Article 87. In the case of the national courts, the power derives from the direct effect of the relevant Community rules. In BRT v Sabam, the Court of Justice considered that "as the prohibitions of Articles 85(1) and 86 tend by their very nature to produce direct effects in relations between individuals, these Articles create direct rights in respect of the individuals concerned which the national courts must safeguard".[2]

6.   In this way, national courts are able to ensure, at the request of the litigants or on their own initiative, that the competition rules will be respected for the benefit of private individuals. In addition, Article 85(2) enables them to determine, in

accordance with the national procedural law applicable, the civil law effects of the prohibition set out in Article 85.[3]

7.   However, the Commission, pursuant to Article 9 of Regulation No 17,[4] has sole power to exempt certain types of agreements, decisions and concerted practices from this prohibition. The Commission may exercise this power in two ways. It may take a decision exempting a specific agreement in an individual case. It may also adopt regulations granting block exemptions for certain categories of agreements, decisions or concerted practices, where it is authorised to do so by the Council, in accordance with Article 87.

8.   Although national courts are not competent to apply Article 85(3), they may nevertheless apply the decisions and regulations adopted by the Commission pursuant to that provision. The Court has on several occasions confirmed that the provisions of a regulation are directly applicable.[5] The Commission considers that the same is true for the substantive provisions of an individual exemption decision.

9.   The powers of the Commission and those of national courts differ not only in their objective and content, but also in the ways in which they are exercised. The Commission exercises its powers according to the procedural rules laid down by Regulation No 17, whereas national courts exercise theirs in the context of national procedural law.

10.   In this connection, the Court of Justice has laid down the principles which govern procedures and remedies for invoking directly applicable Community law.

> "Although the Treaty has made it possible in a number of instances for private persons to bring a direct action, where appropriate, before the Court of Justice, it was not intended to create new remedies in the national courts to ensure the observance of Community law other than those already laid down by national law. On the other hand . . . it must be possible for every type of action provided for by national law to be available for the purpose of ensuring observance of Community provisions having direct effect, on the same conditions concerning the admissibility and procedure as would apply were it a question of ensuring observance of national law".[6]

11.   The Commission considers that these principles apply in the event of breach of the Community competition rules; individuals and companies have access to all procedural remedies provided for by national law on the same conditions as would apply if a comparable breach of national law were involved. This equality of treatment concerns not only the definitive finding of a breach of competition rules, but embraces all the legal means capable of contributing to effective legal protection. Consequently, it is the right of parties subject to Community law that national courts should take provisional measures, that an effective end should be brought, by injunction, to the infringement of Community competition rules of which they are victims, and that compensation should be awarded for the damage suffered as a result of infringements, where such remedies are available in proceedings relating to similar national law.

12.   Here the Commission would like to make it clear that the simultaneous application of national competition law is compatible with the application of Community law, provided that it does not impair the effectiveness and uniformity of Community competition rules and the measures taken to enforce them. Any conflicts which may arise when national and Community competition law are applied simultaneously must be resolved in accordance with the principle of the precedence of Community law.[7] The purpose of this principle is to rule out any national measure which could jeopardise the full effectiveness of the provisions of Community law.

PART IV
EC MATERIALS

NOTES
    [1]   Case C-234/89 Delimitis v Henninger Bräu [1991] ECR I-935, paragraph 44; Case T-24/90, Automec v Commission, judgment of 17 September 1992, paragraphs 73 and 85 (not yet reported).
    [2]   Case 127/73 BRT v Sabam [1974] ECR 51, paragraph 16.
    [3]   Case 56/65 LTM v MBU [1966] ECR 337; Case 48/72, Brasserie De Haecht v Wilkin-Janssen [1973] ECR 77; Case 319/82, Ciments et Bétons v Kerpen & Kerpen, [1983] ECR 4173.
    [4]   Council Regulation No 17 of 6 February 1962: First Regulation implementing Articles 85 and 86 of the Treaty (OJ 13, 21.2.1962, p 204/62; Special Edition 1959-62, p 87).
    [5]   Case 63/75 Fonderies Roubaix v Fonderies Roux [1976] ECR 111; Case C-234/89 Delimitis v Henninger Bräu, [1991] ECR I-935.
    [6]   Case 158/80 Rewe v Hauptzollamt Kiel [1981] ECR 1805, paragraph 44; see also Case 33/76 Rewe v Landwirtschaftskammer Saarland, [1976] ECR 1989; Case 79/83 Harz v Deutsche Tradax, [1984] ECR 1921; Case 199/82 Amministrazione delle Finanze dello Stato v San Giorgio [1983] ECR 3595.
    [7]   Case 14/68 Walt Wilhelm and Others v Bundeskartellamt, [1969] ECR 1; Joined Cases 253/78 and 1 to 3/79 Procureur de la République v Giry and Guerlain, [1980] ECR 2327.

III THE EXERCISE OF POWERS BY THE COMMISSION

13.   As the administrative authority responsible for the Community's competition policy, the Commission must serve the Community's general interest. The administrative resources at the Commission's disposal to perform its task are necessarily limited and cannot be used to deal with all the cases brought to its attention. The Commission is therefore obliged, in general, to take all organisational measures necessary for the performance of its task and, in particular, to establish priorities.[1]

14.   The Commission intends, in implementing its decision-making powers, to concentrate on notifications, complaints and own-initiative proceedings having particular political, economic or legal significance for the Community. Where these features are absent in a particular case, notifications will normally be dealt with by means of comfort letter and complaints should, as a rule, be handled by national courts or authorities.

15.   The Commission considers that there is not normally a sufficient Community interest in examining a case when the plaintiff is able to secure adequate protection of his rights before the national courts.[2] In these circumstances the complaint will normally be filed.

16.   In this respect the Commission would like to make it clear that the application of Community competition law by the national courts has considerable advantages for individuals and companies—
    — the Commission cannot award compensation for loss suffered as a result of an infringement of Article 85 or Article 86. Such claims may be brought only before the national courts. Companies are more likely to avoid infringements of the Community competition rules if they risk having to pay damages or interest in such an event,
    — national courts can usually adopt interim measures and order the ending of infringements more quickly than the Commission is able to do,
    — before national courts, it is possible to combine a claim under Community law with a claim under national law. This is not possible in a procedure before the Commission,
    — in some Member States, the courts have the power to award legal costs to the successful applicant. This is never possible in the administrative procedure before the Commission.

NOTES
    [1]   Case T-24/90 Automec v Commission, judgment of 17 September 1992, paragraph 77 (not yet reported).
    [2]   Case T-24/90, cited above, paragraphs 91 to 94.

IV APPLICATION OF ARTICLES 85 AND 86 BY NATIONAL COURTS

17.   The national court may have to reach a decision on the application of Articles 85 and 86 in several procedural situations. In the case of civil law proceedings, two types of action are particularly frequent: actions relating to contracts and actions for damages. Under the former, the defendant usually relies on Article 85(2) to dispute the contractual obligations invoked by the plaintiff. Under the latter, the prohibitions contained in Articles 85 and 86 are generally relevant in determining whether the conduct which has given rise to the alleged injury is illegal.

18.   In such situations, the direct effect of Article 85(1) and Article 86 gives national courts sufficient powers to comply with their obligation to hand down judgment. Nevertheless, when exercising these powers, they must take account of the Commission's powers in order to avoid decisions which could conflict with those taken or envisaged by the Commission in applying Article 85(1) and Article 86, and also Article 85(3).[1]

19.   In its case-law the Court of Justice has developed a number of principles which make it possible for such contradictory decisions to be avoided.[2] The Commission feels that national courts could take account of these principles in the following manner.

1 Application of Article 85(1) and (2) and Article 86

20.   The first question which national courts have to answer is whether the agreement, decision or concerted practice at issue infringes the prohibitions laid down in Article 85(1) or Article 86. Before answering this question, national courts should ascertain whether the agreement, decision or concerted practice has already been the subject of a decision, opinion or other official statement issued by an administrative authority and in particular by the Commission. Such statements provide national courts with significant information for reaching a judgment, even if they are not formally bound by them. It should be noted in this respect that not all procedures before the Commission lead to an official decision, but that cases can also be closed by comfort letters. Whilst it is true that the Court of Justice has ruled that this type of letter does not bind national courts, it has nevertheless stated that the opinion expressed by the Commission constitutes a factor which the national courts may take into account in examining whether the agreements or conduct in question are in accordance with the provisions of Article 85.[3]

21.   If the Commission has not ruled on the same agreement, decision or concerted practice, the national courts can always be guided, in interpreting the Community law in question, by the case-law of the Court of Justice and the existing decisions of the Commission. It is with this in view that the Commission has, in a number of general notices,[4] specified categories of agreements that are not caught by the ban laid down in Article 85(1).

22.   On these bases, national courts should generally be able to decide whether the conduct at issue is compatible with Article 85(1) and Article 86. Nevertheless, if the Commission has initiated a procedure in a case relating to the same conduct, they may, if they consider it necessary for reasons of legal certainty, stay the proceedings while awaiting the outcome of the Commission's action.[5] A stay of proceedings may also be envisaged where national courts wish to seek the Commission's views in accordance with the arrangements referred to in this Notice.[6] Finally, where national courts have persistent doubts on questions of compatibility, they may stay proceedings in order to bring the matter before the Court of Justice, in accordance with Article 177 of the Treaty.

23.   However, where national courts decide to give judgment and find that the conditions for applying Article 85(1) or Article 86 are not met, they should pursue their proceedings on the basis of such a finding, even if the agreement, decision or concerted practice at issue has been notified to the Commission. Where the assessment of the facts shows that the conditions for applying the said Articles are met, national courts must rule that the conduct at issue infringes Community competition law and take the appropriate measures, including those relating to the consequences that attach to infringement of a statutory prohibition under the civil law applicable.

2 Application of Article 85(3)

24.   If the national court concludes that an agreement, decision or concerted practice is prohibited by Article 85(1), it must check whether it is or will be the subject of an exemption by the Commission under Article 85(3). Here several situations may arise.

25.(a) The national court is required to respect the exemption decisions taken by the Commission. Consequently, it must treat the agreement, decision or concerted practice at issue as compatible with Community law and fully recognise its civil law effects. In this respect mention should be made of comfort letters in which the Commission services state that the conditions for applying Article 85(3) have been met. The Commission considers that national courts may take account of these letters as factual elements.

26.(b) Agreements, decisions and concerted practices which fall within the scope of application of a block exemption regulation are automatically exempted from the prohibition laid down in Article 85(1) without the need for a Commission decision or comfort letter.[7]

27.(c) Agreements, decisions and concerted practices which are not covered by a block exemption regulation and which have not been the subject of an individual exemption decision or a comfort letter must, in the Commission's view, be examined in the following manner.

28.   The national court must first examine whether the procedural conditions necessary for securing exemption are fulfilled, notably whether the agreement, decision or concerted practice has been duly notified in accordance with Article 4(1) of Regulation No 17. Where no such notification has been made, and subject to Article 4(2) of Regulation No 17, exemption under Article 85(3) is ruled out, so that the national court may decide, pursuant to Article 85(2), that the agreement, decision or concerted practice is void.

29.   Where the agreement, decision or concerted practice has been duly notified to the Commission, the national court will assess the likelihood of an exemption being granted in the case in question in the light of the relevant criteria developed by the case law of the Court of Justice and the Court of First Instance and by previous regulations and decisions of the Commission.

30.   Where the national court has in this way ascertained that the agreement, decision or concerted practice at issue cannot be the subject of an individual exemption, it will take the measures necessary to comply with the requirements of Article 85(1) and (2). On the other hand, if it takes the view that individual exemption is possible, the national court should suspend the proceedings while awaiting the Commission's decision. If the national court does suspend the proceedings, it nevertheless remains free, according to the rules of the applicable national law, to adopt any interim measures it deems necessary.

31.   In this connection, it should be made clear that these principles do not apply to agreements, decisions and concerted practices which existed before Regulation No 17 entered into force or before that Regulation became applicable as a result of the accession of a new Member State and which were duly notified to the Commission. The national courts must consider such agreements, decisions and concerted practices to be valid so long as the Commission or the authorities of the Member States have not taken a prohibition decision or sent a comfort letter to the parties informing them that the file has been closed.[8]

32.   The Commission realises that the principles set out above for the application of Articles 85 and 86 by national courts are complex and sometimes insufficient to enable those courts to perform their judicial function properly. This is particularly so where the practical application of Article 85(1) and Article 86 gives rise to legal or economic difficulties, where the Commission has initiated a procedure in the same case or where the agreement, decision or concerted practice concerned may become the subject of an individual exemption within the meaning of Article 85(3). National courts may bring such cases before the Court of Justice for a preliminary ruling, in accordance with Article 177. They may also avail themselves of the Commission's assistance according to the procedures set out below.

[5704]

NOTES

[1]   Case C-234/89 Delimitis v Henninger Bräu [1991] ECR I-935, paragraph 47.

[2]   Case 48/72 Brasserie de Haecht v Wilkin-Janssen [1973] ECR 77; Case 127/73 BRT v Sabam, [1974] ECR 51; Case C-234/89, Delimitis v Henninger Bräu, [1991] ECR I-935.

[3]   Case 99/79, Lancôme v Etos, (1980) ECR 2511, paragraph 11.

[4]   See the notices on—
        —   exclusive dealing contracts with commercial agents (OJ 139, 24.12.1962, p 2921/62),
        —   agreements, decisions and concerted practices in the field of cooperation between enterprises (OJ C 75, 29.7.1968, p 3, as corrected in OJ C84, 28.8.1968, p 14),
        —   assessment of certain subcontracting agreements (OJ C1, 3.1.1979, p 2),
        —   agreements of minor importance (OJ C231, 12.9.1986, p 2).

[5]   Case 127/73 BRT v Sabam, [1974] ECR 51, paragraph 21. The procedure before the Commission is initiated by an authoritative act. A simple acknowledgement of receipt cannot be considered an authoritative act as such; Case 48/72 Brasserie de Haecht v Wilkin-Janssen, [1973] ECR 77, paragraphs 16 and 17.

[6]   Case C-234/89 Delimitis v Henninger Bräu [1991] ECR I-935, paragraph 53, Part V of this Notice.

[7]   A list of the relevant regulations and of the official explanatory comments relating to them is given in the Annex to this Notice.

[8]   Case 48/72 Brasserie de Haecht v Wilkin-Janssen, [1973] ECR 77; Case 59/77 De Bloss v Bouyer [1977] ECR 2359; Case 99/79, Lancôme v Etos [1980] ECR 2511.

V COOPERATION BETWEEN NATIONAL COURTS AND THE COMMISSION

33.   Article 5 of the EEC Treaty establishes the principle of constant and sincere cooperation between the Community and the Member States with a view to attaining the objectives of the Treaty, including implementation of Article 3(f), which refers to the establishment of a system ensuring that competition in the common market is not distorted. This principle involves obligations and duties of mutual assistance, both for the Member States and for the Community institutions. The Court has thus ruled that, under Article 5 of the EEC Treaty, the Commission has a duty of sincere cooperation vis-à-vis judicial authorities of the Member States, who are responsible for ensuring that Community law is applied and respected in the national legal system.[1]

34.   The Commission considers that such cooperation is essential in order to guarantee the strict, effective and consistent application of Community competition law. In addition, more effective participation by the national courts in the day-to-day

application of competition law gives the Commission more time to perform its administrative task, namely to steer competition policy in the Community.

35. In the light of these considerations, the Commission intends to work towards closer cooperation with national courts in the following manner.

36. The Commission conducts its policy so as to give the parties concerned useful pointers to the application of competition rules. To this end, it will continue its policy in relation to block exemption regulations and general notices. These general texts, the case-law of the Court of Justice and the Court of First Instance, the decisions previously taken by the Commission and the annual reports on competition policy are all elements of secondary legislation or explanations which may assist national courts in examining individual cases.

37. If these general pointers are insufficient, national courts may, within the limits of their national procedural law, ask the Commission and in particular its Directorate-General for Competition for the following information.

First, they may ask for information of a procedural nature to enable them to discover whether a certain case is pending before the Commission, whether a case has been the subject of a notification, whether the Commission has officially initiated a procedure or whether it has already taken a position through an official decision or through a comfort letter sent by its services. If necessary, national courts may also ask the Commission to give an opinion as to how much time is likely to be required for granting or refusing individual exemption for notified agreements or practices, so as to be able to determine the conditions for any decision to suspend proceedings or whether interim measures need to be adopted.[2] The Commission, for its part, will endeavour to give priority to cases which are the subject of national proceedings suspended in this way, in particular when the outcome of a civil dispute depends on them.

38. Next, national courts may consult the Commission on points of law. Where the application of Article 85(1) and Article 86 causes them particular difficulties, national courts may consult the Commission on its customary practice in relation to the Community law at issue. As far as Articles 85 and 86 are concerned, these difficulties relate in particular to the conditions for applying these Articles as regards the effect on trade between Member States and as regards the extent to which the restriction of competition resulting from the practices specified in these provisions is appreciable. In its replies, the Commission does not consider the merits of the case. In addition, where they have doubts as to whether a contested agreement, decision or concerted practice is eligible for an individual exemption, they may ask the Commission to provide them with an interim opinion. If the Commission says that the case in question is unlikely to qualify for an exemption, national courts will be able to waive a stay of proceedings and rule on the validity of the agreement, decision or concerted practice.

39. The answers given by the Commission are not binding on the courts which have requested them. In its replies the Commission makes it clear that its view is not definitive and that the right for the national court to refer to the Court of Justice, pursuant to Article 177, is not affected. Nevertheless, the Commission considers that it gives them useful guidance for resolving disputes.

40. Lastly, national courts can obtain information from the Commission regarding factual data: statistics, market studies and economic analyses. The Commission will endeavour to communicate these data, within the limits laid down in the following paragraph, or will indicate the source from which they can be obtained.

41. It is in the interests of the proper administration of justice that the Commission should answer requests for legal and factual information in the shortest

possible time. Nevertheless, the Commission cannot accede to such requests unless several conditions are met. First, the requisite data must actually be at its disposal. Secondly, the Commission may communicate this data only in so far as permitted by the general principle of sound administrative practice.

42.　For example, Article 214 of the Treaty, as spelt out in Article 20 of Regulation No 17 for the purposes of the competition rules, requires the Commission not to disclose information of a confidential nature. In addition, the duty of sincere cooperation deriving from Article 5 is one applying to the relationship between national courts and the Commission and cannot concern the position of the parties to the dispute pending before those courts. As *amicus curiae*, the Commission is obliged to respect legal neutrality and objectivity. Consequently, it will not accede to requests for information unless they come from a national court, either directly, or indirectly through parties which have been ordered by the court concerned to provide certain information. In the latter case, the Commission will ensure that its answer reaches all the parties to the proceedings.

43.　Over and above such exchange of information, required in specific cases, the Commission is anxious to develop as far as possible a more general information policy. To this end, the Commission intends to publish an explanatory booklet regarding the application of the competition rules at national level.

44.　Lastly, the Commission also wishes to reinforce the effect of national competition judgments. To this end, it will study the possibility of extending the scope of the Convention on jurisdiction and the enforcement of judgments in civil and commercial matters to competition cases assigned to administrative courts.[3] It should be noted that, in the Commission's view, competition judgments are already governed by this Convention where they are handed down in cases of a civil and commercial nature.

[5705]

NOTES
[1]　Case C-2/88, Imm., Zwartveld, [1990] ECR I-3365, paragraph 18; Case C-234/89, Delimitis v Henninger Bräu, [1991] ECR I-935, paragraph 53.
[2]　See paragraphs 22 and 30 of this Notice.
[3]　Convention of 27 September 1968 (OJ L304, 30.10.1978, p 77).

VI FINAL REMARKS

45.　This Notice does not relate to the competition rules governing the transport sector.[1] Nor does it relate to the competition rules laid down in the Treaty establishing the European Coal and Steel Community.

46.　This Notice is issued for guidance and does not in any way restrict the rights conferred on individuals or companies by Community law.

47.　This Notice is without prejudice to any interpretation of the Community competition rules which may be given by the Court of Justice of the European Communities.

48.　A summary of the answers given by the Commission pursuant to this Notice will be published annually in the Competition Report.

[5706]

NOTES
[1]　Competition rules governing the transport sector: Regulation No 141/62 of the Council of 26 November 1962 exempting transport from the application of Council Regulation No 17 (OJ 124, 28.11.1962, p 2751/62), as amended by Regulations Nos 165/65/EEC (OJ 210,11.12.1965, p 3141/65) and 1002/67/EEC (OJ 306, 16.12.1967, p 1); Regulation (EEC) No 1017/68 of the Council of 19 July 1968 applying rules of competition to transport by rail, road and inland waterway (OJ L175, 23.7.1968, p 1);

Council Regulation (EEC) No 4056/86 of 22 December 1986 laying down detailed rules for the application of Articles 85 and 86 of the Treaty to maritime transport (OJ L378, 31.12.1986, p 4); Council Regulation (EEC) No 3975/87 of 14 December 1987 laying down the procedure for the application of the rules on competition to undertakings in the air transport sector (OJ L374, 31.12.1987, p 1).

ANNEX
BLOCK EXEMPTIONS

A.   ENABLING COUNCIL REGULATIONS

I   Vertical agreements (see under B.I and B.II)

Council Regulation No 19/65/EEC of 2 March 1965 on the application of Article 85(3) of the Treaty to certain categories of agreements and concerted practices (OJ, Special Edition 1965–66, p 35).

II   Horizontal agreements (see under B.III)

Council Regulation (EEC) No 2821/71 of 20 December 1971 on the application of Article 85(3) of the Treaty to categories of agreements, decisions and concerted practices (OJ, Special Edition 1971–III, p 1032), modified by Regulation (EEC) No 2743/72 of 19 December 1972 (OJ, Special Edition 1972, 28–30.12.1972, p 60).

B.   COMMISSION BLOCK EXEMPTION REGULATIONS AND EXPLANATORY NOTICES

I   Distribution agreements

1.   Commission Regulation (EEC) No 1983/83 of 22 June 1983 concerning exclusive distribution agreements (OJ No L 173, 30.6.1983, p 1).

2.   Commission Regulation (EEC) No 1984/83 of 22 June 1983 concerning exclusive purchasing agreements (OJ No L 173, 30.6.1983, p 5).

3.   Commission Notice concerning Commission Regulations (EEC) No 1983/83 and (EEC) No 1984/83 (OJ No C 101, 13.4.1984, p 2).

4.   Commission Regulation (EEC) No 123/85 of 12 December 1984 concerning motor vehicle distribution and servicing agreements (OJ No L 15, 18.1.1985, p 16).

5.   Commission Notice concerning Regulation (EEC) No 123/85 (OJ No C 17, 18.1.1985, p 4).

6.   Commission Notice on the clarification of the activities of motor vehicle intermediaries (OJ No C 329, 18.12.1991, p 20).

II   Licensing and franchising agreements

1.   Commission Regulation (EEC) No 2349/84 of 23 July 1984 concerning patent licensing agreements (OJ No L 219, 16.8.1984, p 15; corrigendum OJ No L 280, 22.10.1985, p 32).

2.   Commission Regulation (EEC) No 4087/88 of 30 November 1988 concerning franchising agreements (OJ No L 359, 28.12.1988, p 46).

3.   Commission Regulation (EEC) No 556/89 of 30 November 1988 concerning know-how licensing agreements (OJ No L 61, 4.3.1989, p 1).

III   Cooperative agreements

1.   Commission Regulation (EEC) No 417/85 of 19 December 1984 concerning specialisation agreements (OJ No L 53, 22.2.1985, p 1).

2.   Commission Regulation (EEC) No 418/85 of 19 December 1984 concerning research and development agreements (OJ No L 53, 22.2.1985, p 5).

PRESS RELEASE

of 23 December 1992

commission adopts notice aimed at decentralising application of EC anti-trust rules

The Commission has adopted a Notice clarifying the application of the EC's competition rules (Articles 85 and 86) by national courts. The aim of the Notice is to encourage national courts to apply EC competition rules more frequently and more efficiently, ensuring a more decentralised policy while seeking to establish a clearer delineation of responsibilities between the Commission and the national courts. Community law will therefore be applied nearer to the citizen, fully in line with the concept of subsidiarity. The Notice, which forms an integral part of the procedural reforms explained recently by Sir Leon Brittan, EC Commissioner for competition policy (Speech to CEPS on 8 December 1992), is addressed to national courts, competition authorities, lawyers and to other interested parties.

The Notice sets out to do the following: to codify the case-law of the Court of Justice on the relation between the Commission and national courts; to identify their respective fields of competence; to specify how the Commission takes account of national procedures when it establishes its priorities; and to explain how the Commission intends to assist national courts, for example by offering legal advice and access to information on statistics and on the state of its own inquiries. It also aims to reinforce the effect of national competition judgments.

Encouraging complainants to use national courts

The strengthened role of national courts brings with it several advantages. Recourse to national courts enables individuals to obtain adequate injunctions and immediate interim measures. They may also award damages that the Commission is not empowered to provide. In some member states, national courts have the power to award legal costs to the successful applicant, unlike the Commission. It is also possible to combine a claim under Community law with a claim under national law, something which cannot be done in a procedure before the Commission.

The Commission states in the Notice that it intends to concentrate on notifications, complaints and own-initiative proceedings which have a particular political, economic or legal significance for the Community. The Commission will encourage complainants to go to the national courts in cases where adequate redress exists there.

Avoiding conflicts with the Commission

Articles 85(1) and 86 give national courts sufficient powers to hand down judgments, most frequently on actions relating to contracts and actions for damages. When exercising these powers, they must take account of the Commission's powers in order to avoid decisions which conflict with those taken or envisaged by the Commission. The national courts should therefore find out whether the Commission, or any other administrative authority, has already issued a decision, opinion or official statement on a case before reaching their own decision. If the Commission has not ruled on the same case, the national courts can always be guided by the case law of the Court of Justice or by existing Commission decisions. If the Commission has opened a procedure in a case relating to the same conduct, the national courts may see fit to suspend their own proceedings while awaiting the outcome of the Commission's action. They may of course also seek the opinion of the Court of Justice directly.

If the national courts do find an infringement of Articles 85 or 86, they should pursue their proceedings, even if the case has already been notified to the Commission. They must then rule whether the business conduct at issue infringes EC competition law, and take appropriate measures.

However, it is important to note that the Commission remains the sole authority with the jurisdiction to grant individual exemptions pursuant to Article 85(3) of the Treaty. Thus, in individual cases where an alleged infringement of Article 85(1) is being considered, national courts must check whether an agreement in breach of Article 85(1) could qualify for an exemption by the Commission under Article 85(3). National courts should always assess the likelihood of an exemption being granted by the Commission. If they think it is possible, they should suspend their proceedings where appropriate while awaiting the Commission's decision. They remain free to adopt any interim measures they deem necessary.

Cooperation between Commission and national courts

Both Commission and national courts are governed by obligations and duties of mutual assistance. More effective participation by the national courts in the day-to-day application of competition law gives the Commission more time to perform its administrative task of steering the EC's competition policy. Where possible, the Commission will give useful pointers to the national courts, and will continue its policy of publishing block exemption regulations and general notices.

National courts may ask the Commission for procedural information which would enable them to discover whether a case is pending before the Commission, whether it has been notified, whether the Commission has officially opened an investigation, whether it has taken a position officially or through a "comfort letter", and how much time the Commission expects to take to decide, thus enabling the national courts to plan the length of their own suspension or interim measures. The Commission will strive to give priority to cases which have been suspended by the national courts. National courts may also consult the Commission on points of law, particularly regarding its view on the effect on intra-Community trade whilst the Commission will not get involved in the merits of such cases. It will be able to provide a court with an opinion on its customary practice in relation to relevant Community law. They may also ask the Commission to provide them with an interim statement on whether a contested agreement is eligible for an individual exemption from the competition rules. The Commission answers are not binding on the national courts.

National courts can also obtain statistics, market studies and economic analyses from the Commission, which will reply in the shortest possible time. It will also publish an explanatory booklet on the application of EC competition rules at national level. The Notice covers neither the transport sector nor the ECSC Treaty.

[5708]

COMMISSION NOTICE

on co-operation between national competition authorities and the Commission in handling cases falling within the scope of Articles 85 or 86 of the EC Treaty

(97/C 313/03)

(Text with EEA relevance)

NOTES

Date of publication in OJ: OJ C313, 15.10.97, p 3.

I ROLE OF THE MEMBER STATES AND OF THE COMMUNITY

1.   In competition policy the Community and the Member States perform different functions. Whereas the Community is responsible only for implementing the Community rules, Member States not only apply their domestic law but also have a hand in implementing Articles 85 and 86 of the EC Treaty.

2.   This involvement of the Member States in Community competition policy means that decisions can be taken as closely as possible to the citizen (Article A of the Treaty on European Union). The decentralised application of Community competition rules also leads to a better allocation of tasks. If, by reason of its scale or effects, the proposed action can best be taken at Community level, it is for the Commission to act. Otherwise, it is for the competition authority of the Member State concerned to act.

3.   Community law is implemented by the Commission and national competition authorities, on the one hand, and national courts, on the other, in accordance with the principles developed by the Community legislature and by the Court of Justice and the Court of First Instance of the European Communities.

It is the task of national courts to safeguard the rights of private persons in their relations with one another.[1] Those rights derive from the fact that the prohibitions in Articles 85(1) and 86[2] and the exemptions granted by regulation[3] have been recognised by the Court of Justice as being directly applicable. Relations between national courts and the Commission in applying Articles 85 and 86 were spelt out in a Notice published by the Commission in 1993.[4] This Notice is the counterpart, for relations with national authorities, to that of 1993 on relations with national courts.

4.   As administrative authorities, both the Commission and national competition authorities act in the public interest in performing their general task of monitoring and enforcing the competition rules.[5] Relations between them are determined primarily by this common role of protecting the general interest. Although similar to the Notice on co-operation with national courts, this Notice accordingly reflects this special feature.

5.   The specific nature of the role of the Commission and of national competition authorities is characterised by the powers conferred on those bodies by the Council regulations adopted under Article 87 of the Treaty. Article 9(1) of Regulation No 17[6] thus provides: "Subject to review of its decision by the Court of Justice,[7] the Commission shall have sole power to declare Article 85(1) inapplicable pursuant to Article 85(3) of the Treaty". And Article 9(3) of the same Regulation provides: "As long as the Commission has not initiated any procedure under Article 2,[8] 3[9] or 6,[10] the authorities of the Member States shall remain competent to apply Article 85(1) and Article 86 in accordance with Article 88 of the Treaty."

It follows that, provided their national law has conferred the necessary powers on them, national competition authorities are empowered to apply the prohibitions in Articles 85(1) and 86. On the other hand, for the purposes of applying Article 85(3), they do not have any powers to grant exemptions in individual cases; they must abide by the decisions and regulations adopted by the Commission under that provision. They may also take account of other measures adopted by the Commission in such cases, in particular comfort letters, treating them as factual evidence.

6.   The Commission is convinced that enhancing the role of national competition authorities will boost the effectiveness of Articles 85 and 86 of the Treaty and, generally speaking, will bolster the application of Community competition rules throughout the Community. In the interests of safeguarding and

developing the single market, the Commission considers that those provisions should be used as widely as possible. Being closer to the activities and businesses that require monitoring, national authorities are often in a better position than the Commission to protect competition.

7.   Co-operation must therefore be organised between national authorities and the Commission. If this co-operation is to be fruitful, they will have to keep in close and constant touch.

8.   The Commission proposes to set out in this Notice the principles it will apply in future when dealing with the cases described herein. The Notice also seeks to induce firms to approach national competition authorities more often.

9.   This Notice describes the practical co-operation which is desirable between the Commission and national authorities. It does not affect the extent of the powers conferred by Community law on either the Commission or national authorities for the purpose of dealing with individual cases.

10.   For cases falling within the scope of Community law, to avoid duplication of checks on compliance with the competition rules which are applicable to them, which is costly for the firms concerned, checks should wherever possible be carried out by a single authority (either a Member State's competition authority or the Commission). Control by a single authority offers advantages for businesses.

Parallel proceedings before the Commission, on the one hand, and a national competition authority, on the other, are costly for businesses whose activities fall within the scope both of Community law and of Member States' competition laws. They can lead to the repetition of checks on the same activity, by the Commission, on the one hand, and by the competition authorities of the Member States concerned, on the other.

Businesses in the Community may therefore in certain circumstances find it to their advantage if some cases falling within the scope of Community competition law were dealt with solely by national authorities. In order that this advantage may be enjoyed to the full, the Commission thinks it is desirable that national authorities should themselves apply Community law directly or, failing that, obtain, by applying their domestic law, a result similar to that which would have been obtained had Community law been applied.

11.   What is more, in addition to the resulting benefits accruing to competition authorities in terms of mobilisation of their resources, co-operation between authorities reduces the risk of divergent decisions and hence the opportunities for those who might be tempted to do so to seek out whichever authority seemed to them to be the most favourable to their interests.

12.   Member States' competition authorities often have a more detailed and precise knowledge than the Commission of the relevant markets (particularly those with highly specific national features) and the businesses concerned. Above all, they may be in a better position than the Commission to detect restrictive practices that have not been notified or abuses of a dominant position whose effects are essentially confined to their territory.

13.   Many cases handled by national authorities involve arguments based on national law and arguments drawn from Community competition law. In the interests of keeping proceedings as short as possible, the Commission considers it preferable that national authorities should directly apply Community law themselves, instead of making firms refer the Community-law aspects of their cases to the Commission.

14.   An increasing number of major issues in the field of Community competition law have been clarified over the last thirty years through the case-law of the Court of Justice and the Court of First Instance and through decisions taken on questions of principle and the exemption regulations adopted by the Commission. The application of that law by national authorities is thereby simplified.

15.   The Commission intends to encourage the competition authorities of all Member States to engage in this co-operation. However, the national legislation of several Member States does not currently provide competition authorities with the procedural means of applying Articles 85(1) and 86. In such Member States conduct caught by the Community provisions can be effectively dealt with by national authorities only under national law.

In the Commission's view, it is desirable that national authorities should apply Articles 85 or 86 of the Treaty, if appropriate in conjunction with their domestic competition rules, when handling cases that fall within the scope of those provisions.

16.   Where authorities are not in a position to do this and hence can apply only their national law to such cases, the application of that law should "not prejudice the uniform application throughout the common market of the Community rules on cartels and of the full effect of the measures adopted in implementation of those rules".[11] At the very least, the solution they find to a case falling within the scope of Community law must be compatible with that law, Member States being forbidden, given the primacy of Community law over national competition law[12] and the obligation to co-operate in good faith laid down in Article 5 of the Treaty,[13] to take measures capable of defeating the practical effectiveness of Articles 85 and 86.

17.   Divergent decisions are more likely to be reached where a national authority applies its national law rather than Community law. Where a Member State's competition authority applies Community law, it is required to comply with any decisions taken previously by the Commission in the same proceedings. Where the case has merely been the subject of a comfort letter, then, according to the Court of Justice, although this type of letter does not bind national courts, the opinion expressed by the Commission constitutes a factor which the national courts may take into account in examining whether the agreements on conduct in question are in accordance with the provisions of Article 85.[14] In the Commission's view, the same holds true for national authorities.

18.   Where an infringement of Articles 85 or 86 is established by Commission decision, that decision precludes the application of a domestic legal provision authorising what the Commission has prohibited. The objective of the prohibitions in Articles 85(1) and 86 is to guarantee the unity of the common market and the preservation of undistorted competition in that market. They must be strictly complied with if the functioning of the Community regime is not to be endangered.[15]

19.   The legal position is less clear as to whether national authorities are allowed to apply their more stringent national competition law where the situation they are assessing has previously been the subject of an individual exemption decision of the Commission or is covered by a block exemption Regulation. In Walt Wilhelm, the Court stated that the Treaty "permits the Community authorities to carry out certain positive, though indirect, actions with a view to promoting a harmonious development of economic activities within the whole Community" (paragraph 5 of the judgment). In Bundeskartellamt v Volkswagen and VAG Leasing,[16] the Commission contended that national authorities may not prohibit exempted agreements. The uniform application of Community law would be frustrated every time an exemption granted under Community law was made to depend on the relevant national rules. Otherwise, not only would a given agreement be treated differently depending on the law of each Member State, thus detracting from the

uniform application of Community law, but the full effectiveness of an act giving effect to the Treaty—which an exemption under Article 85(3) undoubtedly is— would also be disregarded. In the case in point, however, the Court did not have to settle the question.

20.   If the Commission's Directorate-General for Competition sends a comfort letter in which it expresses the opinion that an agreement or a practice is incompatible with Article 85 of the Treaty but states that, for reasons to do with its internal priorities, it will not propose to the Commission that it take a decision thereon in accordance with the formal procedures laid down in Regulation No 17, it goes without saying that the national authorities in whose territory the effects of the agreement or practice are felt may take action in respect of that agreement or practice.

21.   In the case of a comfort letter in which the Directorate-General for Competition expresses the opinion that an agreement does restrict competition within the meaning of Article 85(1) but qualifies for exemption under Article 85(3), the Commission will call upon national authorities to consult it before they decide whether to adopt a different decision under Community or national law.

22.   As regards comfort letters in which the Commission expresses the opinion that, on the basis of the information in its possession, there is no need for it to take any action under Article 85(1) or Article 86 of the Treaty, "that fact cannot by itself have the result" of preventing the national authorities from applying to those agreements" or practices "provisions of national competition law which may be more rigorous than Community law in this respect. The fact that a practice has been held by the Commission not to fall within the ambit of the prohibition contained in Article 85(1) and (2)" or Article 86, "the scope of which is limited to agreements" or dominant positions "capable of affecting trade between Member States, in no way prevents that practice from being considered by the national authorities from the point of view of the restrictive effects which it may produce nationally". (Judgment of the Court of Justice in Procureur de la République v Giry and Guerlain).[17]

[5709]

NOTES

[1]   Case T-24/90 Automec v EC Commission ("Automec II") [1992] ECR II-2223, paragraph 85.
[2]   Case 127/733 BRT v SABAM [1974] ECR 51, paragraph 16.
[3]   Case 63/75 Fonderies Roubaix-Wattrelos v Fonderies A Roux [1976] ECR 111.
[4]   Notice on co-operation between national courts and the Commission in applying Articles 85 and 86 of the EEC Treaty (OJ C39, 13.2.93, p 6).
[5]   Automec II, see footnote 1, paragraph 85.
[6]   Council Regulation 17 of 6 February 1962: First Regulation implementing Articles 85 and 86 of the Treaty; OJ 13, 21.2.62, p 204/62 (English Special Edition 1959-62, p 87).
[7]   Now by the Court of First Instance and, on appeal, by the Court of Justice.
[8]   Negative clearance.
[9]   Termination of infringements—prohibition decisions.
[10]   Decisions pursuant to Article 85(3).
[11]   Case 14/68 Walt Wilhelm and Others v Bundeskartellamt [1969] ECR 1, paragraph 4.
[12]   Walt Wilhelm, see footnote 11, paragraph 6; Case 66/86 Ahmed Saeed Flugreisen and Others v Zentrale Zur Bekämpfung Unlauteren Wettbewerbs [1989] ECR 803, paragraph 48.
[13]   Case C-165/91 Van Munster v Rijksdienst voor Pensioenen [1994] ECR I-4661, paragraph 32.
[14]   Case 99/79 Lancôme v Etos [1980] ECR 2511, paragraph 11, cited in the abovementioned notice on co-operation between national courts and the Commission in applying Articles 85 and 86.
[15]   Fourth Report on Competition Policy 1974, point 45.
[16]   Case C-266/93 [1995] ECR I-3477; see also the Opinion of Advocate-General Tesauro in the same case, paragraph 51.
[17]   Joined Cases 253/78 and 1 to 3/79 Procureur de la République v Giry and Guerlain [1980] ECR 2327, paragraph 18.

II GUIDELINES ON CASE ALLOCATION

23.   Co-operation between the Commission and national competition authorities has to comply with the current legal framework. First, if it is to be caught by Community law and not merely by national competition law, the conduct in question must be liable to have an appreciable effect on trade between Member States. Secondly, the Commission has sole power to declare Article 85(1) of the Treaty inapplicable under Article 85(3).

24.   In practice, decisions taken by a national authority can apply effectively only to restrictions of competition whose impact is felt essentially within its territory. This is the case in particular with the restrictions referred to in Article 4(2)(1) of Regulation No 17, namely agreements, decisions or concerted practices the only parties to which are undertakings from one Member State and which, though they do not relate either to imports or to exports between Member States, may affect intra-Community trade.[1] It is extremely difficult from a legal standpoint for such an authority to conduct investigations outside its home country, such as when on-the-spot inspections need to be carried out on businesses, and to ensure that its decisions are enforced beyond its national borders. The upshot is that the Commission usually has to handle cases involving businesses whose relevant activities are carried on in more than one Member State.

25.   A national authority having sufficient resources in terms of manpower and equipment and having had the requisite powers conferred on it, also needs to be able to deal effectively with any cases covered by the Community rules which it proposes to take on. The effectiveness of a national authority's action is dependent on its powers of investigation, the legal means it has at its disposal for settling a case—including the power to order interim measures in an emergency—and the penalties it is empowered to impose on businesses found guilty of infringing the competition rules. Differences between the rules of procedure applicable in the various Member States should not, in the Commission's view, lead to outcomes which differ in their effectiveness when similar cases are being dealt with.

26.   In deciding which cases to handle itself, the Commission will take into account the effects of the restrictive practice or abuse of a dominant position and the nature of the infringement.

In principle, national authorities will handle cases the effects of which are felt mainly in their territory and which appear upon preliminary examination unlikely to qualify for exemption under Article 85(3). However, the Commission reserves the right to take on certain cases displaying a particular Community interest.

Mainly national effects

27.   First of all, it should be pointed out that the only cases at issue here are those which fall within the scope of Articles 85 and 86.

That being so, the existing and foreseeable effects of a restrictive practice or abuse of a dominant position may be deemed to be closely linked to the territory in which the agreement or practice is applied and to the geographic market for the goods or services in question.

28.   Where the relevant geographic market is limited to the territory of a single Member State and the agreement or practice is applied only in that State, the effects of the agreement or practice must be deemed to occur mainly within that State even if, theoretically, the agreement or practice is capable of affecting trade between Member States.

Nature of the infringement: cases that cannot be exempted

29.   The following considerations apply to cases brought before the Commission, to cases brought before a national competition authority and to cases which both may have to deal with.

A distinction should be drawn between infringements of Article 85 of the Treaty and infringements of Article 86.

30.   The Commission has exclusive powers under Articles 85(3) of the Treaty to declare the provisions of Article 85(1) inapplicable. Any notified restrictive practice that prima facie qualifies for exemption must therefore be examined by the Commission, which will take account of the criteria developed in this area by the Court of Justice and the Court of First Instance and also by the relevant regulations and its own previous decisions.

31.   The Commission also has exclusive responsibility for investigation of complaints against decisions it has taken under its exclusive powers, such as a decision to withdraw an exemption previously granted by it under Article 85(3).[2]

32.   No such limitation exists, however, on implementation of Article 86 of the Treaty. The Commission and the Member States have concurrent competence to investigate complaints and to prohibit abuses of dominant positions.

Cases of particular significance to the Community

33.   Some cases considered by the Commission to be of particular Community interest will more often be dealt with by the Commission even if, inasmuch as they satisfy the requirements set out above (points 27–28 and 29–32), they can be dealt with by a national authority.

34.   This category includes cases which raise a new point of law, that is to say, those which have not yet been the subject of a Commission decision or a judgment of the Court of Justice or Court of First Instance.

35.   The economic magnitude of a case is not in itself sufficient reason for its being dealt with by the Commission. The position might be different where access to the relevant market by firms from other Member States is significantly impeded.

36.   Cases involving alleged anti-competitive behaviour by a public undertaking, an undertaking to which a Member State has granted special or exclusive rights within the meaning of Article 90(1) of the Treaty, or an undertaking entrusted with the operation of services of general economic interest or having the character of a revenue-producing monopoly within the meaning of Article 90(2) of the Treaty may also be of particular Community interest.

[5710]

NOTES

[1]   It is possible that an agreement, "although it does not relate either to imports or to exports between Member States" within the meaning of Article 4 of Regulation No 17, "may affect trade between Member States" within the meaning of Article 85(1) of the Treaty (judgment of the Court of Justice in Case 43/69 Bilger v Jehle [1970] ECR 127, paragraph 5).

[2]   Case T-24/90 Automec v EC Commission (Automec II) [1992] ECR II-2223, paragraph 75.

III   CO-OPERATION IN CASES WHICH THE COMMISSION DEALS WITH FIRST

37.   Cases dealt with by the Commission have three possible origins: own-initiative proceedings, notifications and complaints. By their very nature, own-initiative proceedings do not lend themselves to decentralised processing by national competition authorities.

38. The exclusivity of the Commission's powers to apply Article 85(3) of the Treaty in individual cases means that cases notified to the Commission under Article 4(1) of Regulation No 17 by parties seeking exemption under Article 85(3) cannot be dealt with by a national competition authority on the Commission's initiative. According to the case-law of the Court of First Instance, these exclusive powers confer on the applicant the right to obtain from the Commission a decision on the substance of his request for exemption.[1]

39. National competition authorities may deal, at the Commission's request, with complaints that do not involve the application of Article 85(3), namely those relating to restrictive practices which must be notified under Articles 4(1), 5(1) and 25 of Regulation No 17 but have not been notified to the Commission and those based on alleged infringement of Article 86 of the Treaty. On the other hand, complaints concerning matters falling within the scope of the Commission's exclusive powers, such as withdrawal of exemption, cannot be usefully handled by a national competition authority.[2]

40. The criteria set out at points 23 to 36 above in relation to the handling of a case by the Commission or a national authority, in particular as regards the territorial extent of the effects of a restrictive practice or dominant position (points 27–28), should be taken into account.

Commission's right to reject a complaint

41. It follows from the case-law of the Court of First Instance that the Commission is entitled under certain conditions to reject a complaint which does not display sufficient Community interest to justify further investigation.[3]

42. The Commission's resultant right to reject a complaint stems from the concurrent competence of the Commission, national courts and—where they have the power—national competition authorities to apply Articles 85(1) and 86 and from the consequent protection available to complainants before the courts and administrative authorities. With regard to that concurrent competence, it has been consistently held by the Court of Justice and the Court of First Instance that Article 3 of Regulation No 17 (the legal basis for the right to lodge a complaint with the Commission for alleged infringement of Article 85 or Article 86) does not entitle an applicant under that Article to obtain from the Commission a decision within the meaning of Article 189 of the Treaty as to whether or not the alleged infringement has occurred.[4]

Conditions for rejecting a complaint

43. The investigation of a complaint by a national authority presupposes that the following specific conditions, derived from the case-law of the Court of First Instance, are met.

44. The first of these conditions is that, in order to assess whether or not there is a Community interest in having a case investigated further, the Commission must first undertake a careful examination of the questions of fact and law set out in the complaint.[5] In accordance with the obligation imposed on it by Article 190 of the Treaty to state the reasons for its decisions, the Commission has to inform the complainant of the legal and factual considerations which have induced it to conclude that the complaint does not display a sufficient Community interest to justify further investigation. The Commission cannot therefore confine itself to an abstract reference to the Community interest.[6]

45. In assessing whether it is entitled to reject a complaint for lack of any Community interest, the Commission must balance the significance of the alleged infringement as regards the functioning of the common market, the probability of its being able to establish the existence of the infringement, and the extent of the

investigative measures required for it to perform, under the best possible conditions, its task of making sure that Articles 85 and 86 are complied with.[7] In particular, as the Court of First Instance held in BEMIM,[8] where the effects of the infringements alleged in a complaint are essentially confined to the territory of one Member State and where proceedings have been brought before the courts and competent administrative authorities of that Member State by the complainant against the body against which the complaint was made, the Commission is entitled to reject the complaint for lack of any sufficient Community interest in further investigation of the case, provided however that the rights of the complainant can be adequately safeguarded. As to whether the effects of the restrictive practice are localised, such is the case in particular with practices to which the only parties are undertakings from one Member State and which, although they do not relate either to imports or to exports between Member States, within the meaning of point 1 of Article 4(2) of Regulation No 17,[9] are capable of affecting intra-Community trade. As regards the safeguarding of the complainant's rights, the Commission considers that the referral of the matter to the national authority concerned needs must protect them quite adequately. On this latter point, the Commission takes the view that the effectiveness of the national authority's action depends notably on whether that authority is able to take interim measures if it deems it necessary, without prejudice to the possibility, found in the law of certain Member States, that such measures may be taken with the requisite degree of effectiveness by a court.

Procedure

46. Where the Commission considers these conditions to have been met, it will ask the competition authority of the Member State in which most of the effects of the contested agreement or practice are felt if it would agree to investigate and decide on the complaint. Where the competition authority agrees to do so, the Commission will reject the complaint pending before it on the ground that it does not display sufficient Community interest and will refer the matter to the national competition authority, either automatically or at the complainant's request. The Commission will place the relevant documents in its possession at the national authority's disposal.[10]

47. With regard to investigation of the complaint, it should be stressed that, in accordance with the ruling given by the Court of Justice in Case C-67/91[11] (the Spanish banks case), national competition authorities are not entitled to use as evidence, for the purposes of applying either national rules or the Community competition rules, unpublished information contained in replies to requests for information sent to firms under Article 11 of Regulation No 17 or information obtained as a result of any inspections carried out under Article 14 of that Regulation. This information can nevertheless be taken into account, where appropriate, to justify instituting national proceedings.[12]

[5711]

NOTES
[1]   Case T-23/90 Peugeot v EC Commission [1991] ECR II-653, paragraph 47.
[2]   Case T-24/90 Automec v EC Commission (Automec II) [1992] ECR II-2223, paragraph 75.
[3]   Automec II, see footnote 2, paragraph 85; cited in Case T-114/92 BEMIM v EC Commission [1995] ECR II-147, paragraph 80, and in Case T-77/95 SFEI and Others v EC Commission [1997] ECR II-1, paragraphs 29 and 55.
[4]   See in particular Case 125/78 GEMA v EC Commission [1979] ECR 3173, paragraph 17, and Case T-16/91 Rendo and Others v EC Commission [1992] ECR II-2417, paragraph 98.
[5]   Automec II, see footnote 2, paragraph 82.
[6]   Automec II, see footnote 2, paragraph 85.
[7]   Automec II, see footnote 2, paragraph 86, cited in BEMIM, paragraph 80.
[8]   See footnote 3, paragraph 86.
[9]   See footnote 1.

10   However, in the case of information accompanied by a request for confidentiality with a view to protecting the informant's anonymity, an institution which accepts such information is bound, under Article 214 of the Treaty, to comply with such a condition (Case 145/83 Adams v EC Commission [1985] ECR 3539). The Commission will thus not divulge to national authorities the name of an informant who wishes to remain anonymous unless the person concerned withdraws, at the Commission's request, his request for anonymity vis-à-vis the national authority which may be dealing with his complaint.

11   Case C-67/91 Dirección General de Defensa de la Competencia v Asociación Española de Banca Privada (AEB) and Others [1992] ECR I-4785, operative part.

12   See footnote 11, paragraphs 39 and 43.

IV   CO-OPERATION IN CASE WHICH A NATIONAL AUTHORITY DEALS WITH FIRST

Introduction

48.   At issue here are cases falling within the scope of Community competition law which a national competition authority handles on its own initiative, applying Articles 85(1) or 86, either alone or in conjunction with its national competition rules, or, where it cannot do so, its national rules alone. This covers all cases within this field which a national authority investigates before the Commission—where appropriate—does so, irrespective of their procedural origin (own-initiative proceedings, notification, complaint, etc). These cases are therefore those which fulfil the conditions set out in Part II (Guidelines on case allocation) of this Notice.

49.   As regards cases which they deal with under Community law, it is desirable that national authorities should systematically inform the Commission of any proceedings they initiate. The Commission will pass on this information to the authorities in the other Member States.

50.   This co-operation is especially necessary in regard to cases of particular significance to the Community within the meaning of points 33–36. This category includes (a) all cases raising a new point of law, the aim being to avoid decisions, whether based on national law or on Community law, which are incompatible with the latter; (b) among cases of the utmost importance from an economic point of view, only those in which access by firms from other Member States to the relevant national market is significantly impeded; and (c) certain cases in which a public undertaking or an undertaking treated as equivalent to a public undertaking (within the meaning of Article 90(1) and (2) of the Treaty) is suspected of having engaged in an anti-competitive practice. Each national authority must determine, if necessary after consulting the Commission, whether a given case fits into one of these sub-categories.

51.   Such cases will be investigated by national competition authorities in accordance with the procedures laid down by their national law, whether they are acting with a view to applying the Community competition rules or applying their national competition rules.[1]

52.   The Commission also takes the view that, like national courts to which competition cases involving Articles 85 or 86 have been referred, national competition authorities applying those provisions are always at liberty, within the limits of their national procedural rules and subject to Article 214 of the Treaty, to seek information from the Commission on the state of any proceedings which the Commission may have set in motion and as to the likelihood of its giving an official ruling, pursuant to Regulation No 17, on cases which they are investigating on their own initiative. Under the same circumstances, national competition authorities may contact the Commission where the concrete application of Article 85(1) or of Article 86 raises particular difficulties, in order to obtain the economic and legal information which the Commission is in a position to supply to them.[2]

53. The Commission is convinced that close co-operation with national authorities will forestall any contradictory decisions. But if, "during national proceedings, it appears possible that the decision to be taken by the Commission at the culmination of a procedure still in progress concerning the same agreement may conflict with the effects of the decision of the national authorities, it is for the latter to take the appropriate measures" (Walt Wilhelm) to ensure that measures implementing Community competition law are fully effective. The Commission takes the view that these measures should generally consist in national authorities staying their proceedings pending the outcome of the proceedings being conducted by the Commission. Where a national authority applies its national law, such a stay of proceedings would be based on the principles of the primacy of Community law (Walt Wilhelm)[3] and legal certainty, and where it applies Community law, on the principle of legal certainty alone. For its part, the Commission will endeavour to deal as a matter of priority with cases subject to national proceedings thus stayed. A second possibility may, however, be envisaged, whereby the Commission is consulted before adopting the national decision. The consultations would consist, due regard being had to the judgment in the Spanish banks case, in exchanging any documents preparatory to the decisions envisaged, so that Member States' authorities might be able to take account of the Commission's position in their own decision without the latter having to be deferred until such time as the Commission's decision has been taken.

Procedure

In respect of complaints

54. Since complainants cannot force the Commission to take a decision as to whether the infringement they allege has actually occurred, and since the Commission is entitled to reject a complaint which lacks a sufficient Community interest, national competition authorities should not have any special difficulty in handling complaints submitted initially to them involving matters that fall within the scope of the Community competition rules.

In respect of notifications

55. Although they form a very small percentage of all notifications to the Commission, special consideration needs to be given to notifications to the Commission of restrictive practices undergoing investigation by a national authority made for dilatory purposes. A dilatory notification is one where a firm, threatened with a decision banning a restrictive practice which a national authority is poised to take following an investigation under Article 85(1) or under national law, notifies the disputed agreement to the Commission and asks for it to be exempted under Article 85(3) of the Treaty. Such a notification is made in order to induce the Commission to initiate a proceeding under Articles 2, 3 or 6 of Regulation No 17 and hence, by virtue of Article 9(3) of that Regulation, to remove from Member States' authorities the power to apply the provisions of Article 85(1). The Commission will not consider a notification to be dilatory until after it has contacted the national authority concerned and checked that the latter agrees with its assessment. The Commission calls upon national authorities, moreover, to inform it of their own accord of any notifications they receive which, in their view, are dilatory in nature.

56. A similar situation arises where an agreement is notified to the Commission with a view to preventing the imminent initiation of national proceedings which might result in the prohibition of that agreement.[4]

57. The Commission recognises, of course, that a firm requesting exemption is entitled to obtain from it a decision on the substance of its request (see point 38).

However, if the Commission takes the view that such notification is chiefly aimed at suspending the national proceedings, given its exclusive powers to grant exemptions it considers itself justified in not examining it as a matter of priority.

58.   The national authority which is investigating the matter and has therefore initiated proceedings should normally ask the Commission for its provisional opinion on the likelihood of its exempting the agreement now notified to it. Such a request will be superfluous where, "in the light of the relevant criteria developed by the case-law of the Court of Justice and the Court of First Instance and by previous regulations and decisions of the Commission, the national authority has ascertained that the agreement, decision or concerted practice at issue cannot be the subject of an individual exemption".[5]

59.   The Commission will deliver its provisional opinion on the likelihood of an exemption being granted, in the light of a preliminary examination of the questions of fact and law involved, as quickly as possible once the complete notification is received. Examination of the notification having revealed that the agreement in question is unlikely to qualify for exemption under Article 85(3) and that its effects are mainly confined to one Member State, the opinion will state that further investigation of the matter is not a Commission priority.

60.   The Commission will transmit this opinion in writing to the national authority investigating the case and to the notifying parties. It will state in its letter that it will be highly unlikely to take a decision on the matter before the national authority to which it was referred has taken its final decision and that the notifying parties retain their immunity from any fines the Commission might impose.

61.   In its reply, the national authority, after taking note of the Commission's opinion, should undertake to contact the Commission forthwith if its investigation leads it to a conclusion which differs from that opinion. This will be the case if, following its investigation, the national authority concludes that the agreement in question should not be banned under Article 85(1) of the Treaty or, if that provision cannot be applied, under the relevant national law. The national authority should also undertake to forward a copy of its final decision on the matter to the Commission. Copies of the correspondence will be sent to the competition authorities of the other Member States for information.

62.   The Commission will not itself initiate proceedings in the same case before the proceedings pending before the national authority have been completed; in accordance with Article 9(3) of Regulation No 17, such action would have the effect of taking the matter out of the hands of the national authority. The Commission will do this only in quite exceptional circumstances—in a situation where, against all expectations, the national authority is liable to find that there has been no infringement of Articles 85 or 86 or of its national competition law, or where the national proceedings are unduly long drawn-out.

63.   Before initiating proceedings the Commission will consult the national authority to discover the factual or legal grounds for that authority's proposed favourable decision or the reasons for the delay in the proceedings.

[5712]

NOTES
1   Case C-67/91 Dirección General de Defensa de la Competencia v Asociación Española de Banca Privada (AEB) and Others [1992] ECR I-4785, paragraph 32.
2   Case C-234/89 Delimitis v Henninger Bräu [1991] ECR I-935, paragraph 53.
3   Case 14/68 Walt Wilhelm v Bundeskartellamt [1969] ECR I, paragraphs 8, 9, 5 respectively.
4   With respect to agreements not subject to notification pursuant to point 1 of Article 4(2) of Regulation No 17, points 56 and 57 of this Notice also apply mutatis mutandis to express requests for exemption.
5   Points 29 and 30 of the Notice on co-operation between national courts and the Commission.

V CONCLUDING REMARKS

64.   This Notice is without prejudice to any interpretation by the Court of First Instance and the Court of Justice.

65.   In the interests of effective, consistent application of Community law throughout the Union, and legal simplicity and certainty for the benefit of undertakings, the Commission calls upon those Member States which have not already done so to adopt legislation enabling their competition authority to implement Articles 85(1) and 86 of the Treaty effectively.

66.   In applying this Notice, the Commission and the competent authorities of the Member States and their officials and other staff will observe the principle of professional secrecy in accordance with Article 20 of Regulation No 17.

67.   This Notice does not apply to competition rules in the transport sector, owing to the highly specific way in which cases arising in that sector are handled from a procedural point of view.[1]

68.   The actual application of this Notice, especially in terms of the measures considered desirable to facilitate its implementation, will be the subject of an annual review carried out jointly by the authorities of the Member States and the Commission.

69.   This Notice will be reviewed no later than at the end of the fourth year after its adoption.

[5713]

NOTES

[1]   Council Regulation No 141/62 of 26 November 1962 exempting transport from the application of Council Regulation No 17 (OJ 124, 28.11.62, p 2753; English Special Edition 1959-62, p 291), as amended by Regulations Nos 165/65/EEC (OJ 210, 11.12.65, p 314) and 1002/67/EEC (OJ 306, 16.12.67, p 1); Council Regulation (EEC) No 1017/68 of 19 July 1968 applying rules of competition to transport by rail, road and inland waterway (OJ L175, 23.7.68. p 1; English Special Edition 1968 I, p 302); Council Regulation (EEC) No 4056/86 of 22 December 1986 laying down detailed rules for the application of Articles 85 and 86 of the Treaty to maritime transport (OJ L378, 31.12.86, p 4); Council Regulation (EEC) 3975/87 of 14 December 1987 laying down the procedure for the application of the rules on competition to undertakings in the air transport sector (OJ L374, 31.12.87, p 1); and Commission Regulation (EC) No 870/95 of 20 April 1995 on the application of Article 85(3) of the Treaty to certain categories of agreements, decisions and concerted practices between liner shipping companies (consortia) pursuant to Council Regulation (EEC) No 479/92 (OJ L89, 21.4.95, p 7).

GUIDELINES

on the method of setting fines imposed pursuant to Article 15(2) of Regulation No 17 and Article 65(5) of the ECSC Treaty

(98/C 9/03)

NOTE

Date of publication in OJ: OJ C9, 14.1.98, p 3.

The principles outlined here should ensure the transparency and impartiality of the Commission's decisions, in the eyes of the undertakings and of the Court of Justice alike, while upholding the discretion which the Commission is granted under the relevant legislation to set fines within the limit of 10% of overall turnover. This discretion must, however, follow a coherent and non-discriminatory policy which is consistent with the objectives pursued in penalising infringements of the competition rules.

The new method of determining the amount of a fine will adhere to the following rules, which start from a basic amount that will be increased to take account of aggravating circumstances or reduced to take account of attenuating circumstances.

1. Basic amount

The basic amount will be determined according to the gravity and duration of the infringement, which are the only criteria referred to in Article 15(2) of Regulation No 17.

A. *Gravity*

In assessing the gravity of the infringement, account must be taken of its nature, its actual impact on the market, where this can be measured, and the size of the relevant geographic market.

Infringements will thus be put into one of three categories: minor infringements, serious infringements and very serious infringements

— *minor infringements*:

These might be trade restrictions, usually of a vertical nature, but with a limited market impact and affecting only a substantial but relatively limited part of the Community market.

Likely fines: ECU 1 000 to ECU 1 million.

— *serious infringements*:

These will more often than not be horizontal or vertical restrictions of the same type as above, but more rigorously applied, with a wider market impact, and with effects in extensive areas of the common market. There might also be abuse of a dominant position (refusals to supply, discrimination, exclusion, loyalty discounts made by dominant firms in order to shut competitors out of the market, etc).

Likely fines: ECU 1 million to ECU 20 million.

— *very serious infringements*:

These will generally be horizontal restrictions such as price cartels and market-sharing quotas, or other practices which jeopardise the proper functioning of the single market, such as the partitioning of national markets and clear-cut abuse of a dominant position by undertakings holding a virtual monopoly (see Decisions 91/297/EEC, 91/298/EEC, 91/299/EEC, 91/300/EEC and 91/301/EEC[1]–Soda Ash, 94/815/EC[2]–Cement, 94/601/EC[3]–Cartonboard, 92/163/EC[4]–Tetra Pak, and 94/215/ ECSC[5]–Steel beams).

Likely fines: above ECU 20 million

Within each of these categories, and in particular as far as serious and very serious infringements are concerned, the proposed scale of fines will make it possible to apply differential treatment to undertakings according to the nature of the infringement committed.

It will also be necessary to take account of the effective economic capacity of offenders to cause significant damage to other operators, in particular consumers, and to set the fine at a level which ensures that it has a sufficiently deterrent effect.

Generally speaking, account may also be taken of the fact that large undertakings usually have legal and economic knowledge and infrastructures which enable them more easily to recognise that their conduct constitutes an infringement and be aware of the consequences stemming from it under competition law.

Where an infringement involves several undertakings (eg cartels), it might be necessary in some cases to apply weightings to the amounts determined within each of the three categories in order to take account of the specific weight and, therefore, the real impact of the offending conduct of each undertaking on competition, particularly where there is considerable disparity between the sizes of the undertakings committing infringements of the same type.

Thus, the principle of equal punishment for the same conduct may, if the circumstances so warrant, lead to different fines being imposed on the undertakings concerned without this differentiation being governed by arithmetic calculation.

B. Duration
— infringements of short duration (in general, less than one year): no increase in amount,
— infringements of medium duration (in general, one to five years): increase of up to 50 % in the amount determined for gravity,
— infringements of long duration (in general, more than five years): increase of up to 10 % per year in the amount determined for gravity.

This approach will therefore point to a possible increase in the amount of the fine.

Generally speaking, the increase in the fine for long-term infringements represents a considerable strengthening of the previous practice with a view to imposing effective sanctions on restrictions which have had a harmful impact on consumers over a long period. Moreover, this new approach is consistent with the expected effect of the notice of 18 July 1996 on the non-imposition or reduction of fines in cartel cases[6]. The risk of having to pay a much larger fine, proportionate to the duration of the infringement, will necessarily increase the incentive to denounce it or to cooperate with the Commission.

The basic amount will result from the addition of the two amounts established in accordance with the above:

$$x \text{ gravity} + y \text{ duration} = \text{basic amount}$$

2. Aggravating circumstances

The basic amount will be increased where there are aggravating circumstances such as—
— repeated infringement of the same type by the same undertaking(s),
— refusal to cooperate with or attempts to obstruct the Commission in carrying out its investigations,
— role of leader in, or instigator of the infringement,
— retaliatory measures against other undertakings with a view to enforcing practices which constitute an infringement,
— need to increase the penalty in order to exceed the amount of gains improperly made as a result of the infringement when it is objectively possible to estimate that amount,
— other.

3. Attenuating circumstances

The basic amount will be reduced where there are attenuating circumstances such as—
— an exclusively passive or "follow-my-leader" role in the infringement,
— non-implementation in practice of the offending agreements or practices,
— termination of the infringement as soon as the Commission intervenes (in particular when it carries out checks),
— existence of reasonable doubt on the part of the undertaking as to whether the restrictive conduct does indeed constitute an infringement,
— infringements committed as a result of negligence or unintentionally,
— effective cooperation by the undertaking in the proceedings, outside the scope of the Notice of 18 July 1996 on the non-imposition or reduction of fines in cartel cases,
— other.

4. Application of the Notice of 18 July 1996 on the non-imposition or reduction of fines [7]

5. General comments

(a) It goes without saying that the final amount calculated according to this method (basic amount increased or reduced on a percentage basis) may not in any case exceed 10% of the worldwide turnover of the undertakings, as laid down by

Article 15(2) of Regulation No 17. In the case of agreements which are illegal under the ECSC Treaty, the limit laid down by Article 65(5) is twice the turnover on the products in question, increased in certain cases to a maximum of 10% of the undertaking's turnover on ECSC products.

The accounting year on the basis of which the worldwide turnover is determined must, as far as possible, be the one preceding the year in which the decision is taken or, if figures are not available for that accounting year, the one immediately preceding it.

(b)   Depending on the circumstances, account should be taken, once the above calculations have been made, of certain objective factors such as a specific economic context, any economic or financial benefit derived by the offenders (see Twenty-first Report on Competition Policy, point 139), the specific characteristics of the undertakings in question and their real ability to pay in a specific social context, and the fines should be adjusted accordingly.

(c)   In cases involving associations of undertakings, decisions should as far as possible be addressed to and fines imposed on the individual undertakings belonging to the association. If this is not possible (eg where there are several thousands of affiliated undertakings), and except for cases falling within the ECSC Treaty, an overall fine should be imposed on the association, calculated according to the principles outlined above but equivalent to the total of individual fines which might have been imposed on each of the members of the association.

(d)   The Commission will also reserve the right, in certain cases, to impose a "symbolic" fine of ECU 1 000, which would not involve any calculation based on the duration of the infringement or any aggravating or attenuating circumstances. The justification for imposing such a fine should be given in the text of the decision.

[5714]

NOTES

1   OJ L152, 15.6.91, p 54.
2   OJ L343, 30.12.94, p 1.
3   OJ L243, 19.9.94, p 1.
4   OJ L72, 18.3.92, p 1.
5   OJ L116, 6.5.94, p 1.
6   OJ C207, 18.7.96, p 4.
7   See footnote 6.

COMMISSION NOTICE ON IMMUNITY FROM FINES AND REDUCTION OF FINES IN CARTEL CASES

(2002/C 45/03)

(Text with EEA relevance)

NOTES

Date of publication in OJ: OJ C45, 19.2.02, p 3.

INTRODUCTION

1.   This notice concerns secret cartels between two or more competitors aimed at fixing prices, production or sales quotas, sharing markets including bid-rigging or restricting imports or exports. Such practices are among the most serious restrictions of competition encountered by the Commission and ultimately result in increased prices and reduced choice for the consumer. They also harm European industry.

2.   By artificially limiting the competition that would normally prevail between them, undertakings avoid exactly those pressures that lead them to innovate, both in terms of product development and the introduction of more efficient production

methods. Such practices also lead to more expensive raw materials and components for the Community companies that purchase from such producers. In the long term, they lead to a loss of competitiveness and reduced employment opportunities.

3.   The Commission is aware that certain undertakings involved in this type of illegal agreements are willing to put an end to their participation and inform it of the existence of such agreements, but are dissuaded from doing so by the high fines to which they are potentially exposed. In order to clarify its position in this type of situation, the Commission adopted a notice on the non-imposition or reduction of fines in cartel cases,[1] hereafter "the 1996 notice".

4.   The Commission considered that it is in the Community interest to grant favourable treatment to undertakings which cooperate with it. The interests of consumers and citizens in ensuring that secret cartels are detected and punished outweigh the interest in fining those undertakings that enable the Commission to detect and prohibit such practices.

5.   In the 1996 notice, the Commission announced that it would examine whether it was necessary to modify the notice once it had acquired sufficient experience in applying it. After five years of implementation, the Commission has the experience necessary to modify its policy in this matter. Whilst the validity of the principles governing the notice has been confirmed, experience has shown that its effectiveness would be improved by an increase in the transparency and certainty of the conditions on which any reduction of fines will be granted. A closer alignment between the level of reduction of fines and the value of a company's contribution to establishing the infringement could also increase this effectiveness. This notice addresses these issues.

6.   The Commission considers that the collaboration of an undertaking in the detection of the existence of a cartel has an intrinsic value. A decisive contribution to the opening of an investigation or to the finding of an infringement may justify the granting of immunity from any fine to the undertaking in question, on condition that certain additional requirements are fulfilled.

7.   Moreover, cooperation by one or more undertakings may justify a reduction of a fine by the Commission. Any reduction of a fine must reflect an undertaking's actual contribution, in terms of quality and timing, to the Commission's establishment of the infringement. Reductions are to be limited to those undertakings that provide the Commission with evidence that adds significant value to that already in the Commission's possession.

[5715]

NOTES
[1]   OJ C207, 18.7.1996, p 4.

A. IMMUNITY FROM FINES

8.   The Commission will grant an undertaking immunity from any fine which would otherwise have been imposed if—
   (a) the undertaking is the first to submit evidence which in the Commission's view may enable it to adopt a decision to carry out an investigation in the sense of Article 14(3) of Regulation No 17,[1] in connection with an alleged cartel affecting the Community; or
   (b) the undertaking is the first to submit evidence which in the Commission's view may enable it to find an infringement of Article 81 EC,[2] in connection with an alleged cartel affecting the Community.

9.   Immunity pursuant to point 8(a) will only be granted on the condition that the Commission did not have, at the time of the submission, sufficient evidence to adopt a decision to carry out an investigation in the sense of Article 14(3) of Regulation No 17 in connection with the alleged cartel.

10.   Immunity pursuant to point 8(b) will only be granted on the cumulative conditions that the Commission did not have, at the time of the submission, sufficient evidence to find an infringement of Article 81 EC in connection with the alleged cartel and that no undertaking had been granted conditional immunity from fines under point 8(a) in connection with the alleged cartel.

11.   In addition to the conditions set out in points 8(a) and 9 or in points 8(b) and 10, as appropriate, the following cumulative conditions must be met in any case to qualify for any immunity from a fine—

(a)   the undertaking cooperates fully, on a continuous basis and expeditiously throughout the Commission's administrative procedure and provides the Commission with all evidence that comes into its possession or is available to it relating to the suspected infringement. In particular, it remains at the Commission's disposal to answer swiftly any request that may contribute to the establishment of the facts concerned;

(b)   the undertaking ends its involvement in the suspected infringement no later than the time at which it submits evidence under points 8(a) or 8(b), as appropriate;

(c)   the undertaking did not take steps to coerce other undertakings to participate in the infringement.

Procedure

12.   An undertaking wishing to apply for immunity from fines should contact the Commission's Directorate-General for Competition. Should it become apparent that the requirements set out in points 8 to 10, as appropriate, are not met, the undertaking will immediately be informed that immunity from fines is not available for the suspected infringement.

13.   If immunity from fines is available for a suspected infringement, the undertaking may, in order to meet conditions 8(a) or 8(b), as appropriate—

(a)   immediately provide the Commission with all the evidence relating to the suspected infringement available to it at the time of the submission; or

(b)   initially present this evidence in hypothetical terms, in which case the undertaking must present a descriptive list of the evidence it proposes to disclose at a later agreed date. This list should accurately reflect the nature and content of the evidence, whilst safeguarding the hypothetical nature of its disclosure. Expurgated copies of documents, from which sensitive parts have been removed, may be used to illustrate the nature and content of the evidence.

14.   The Directorate-General for Competition will provide a written acknowledgement of the undertaking's application for immunity from fines, confirming the date on which the undertaking either submitted evidence under 13(a) or presented to the Commission the descriptive list referred to in 13(b).

15.   Once the Commission has received the evidence submitted by the undertaking under point 13(a) and has verified that it meets the conditions set out in points 8(a) or 8(b), as appropriate, it will grant the undertaking conditional immunity from fines in writing.

16.   Alternatively, the Commission will verify that the nature and content of the evidence described in the list referred to in point 13(b) will meet the conditions set out in points 8(a) or 8(b), as appropriate, and inform the undertaking accordingly. Following the disclosure of the evidence no later than on the date agreed and having verified that it corresponds to the description made in the list, the Commission will grant the undertaking conditional immunity from fines in writing.

17.   An undertaking which fails to meet the conditions set out in points 8(a) or 8(b), as appropriate, may withdraw the evidence disclosed for the purposes of its

immunity application or request the Commission to consider it under section B of this notice. This does not prevent the Commission from using its normal powers of investigation in order to obtain the information.

18.   The Commission will not consider other applications for immunity from fines before it has taken a position on an existing application in relation to the same suspected infringement.

19.   If at the end of the administrative procedure, the undertaking has met the conditions set out in point 11, the Commission will grant it immunity from fines in the relevant decision.

[5716]

NOTES
¹   OJ 13, 21.2.1962, p 204/62. (Or the equivalent procedural regulations: Article 21(3) of Regulation (EEC) No 1017/68 of the Council; Article 18(3) of Council Regulation (EEC) No 4056/86 and Article 11(3) of Council Regulation (EEC) No 3975/87).
²   Reference in this text to Article 81 EC also covers Article 53 EEA when applied by the Commission according to the rules laid down in Article 56 of the EEA Agreement.

B. REDUCTION OF A FINE

20.   Undertakings that do not meet the conditions under section A above may be eligible to benefit from a reduction of any fine that would otherwise have been imposed.

21.   In order to qualify, an undertaking must provide the Commission with evidence of the suspected infringement which represents significant added value with respect to the evidence already in the Commission's possession and must terminate its involvement in the suspected infringement no later than the time at which it submits the evidence.

22.   The concept of "added value" refers to the extent to which the evidence provided strengthens, by its very nature and/or its level of detail, the Commission's ability to prove the facts in question. In this assessment, the Commission will generally consider written evidence originating from the period of time to which the facts pertain to have a greater value than evidence subsequently established. Similarly, evidence directly relevant to the facts in question will generally be considered to have a greater value than that with only indirect relevance.

23.   The Commission will determine in any final decision adopted at the end of the administrative procedure:
   (a) whether the evidence provided by an undertaking represented significant added value with respect to the evidence in the Commission's possession at that same time;
   (b) the level of reduction an undertaking will benefit from, relative to the fine which would otherwise have been imposed, as follows. For the—
        — first undertaking to meet point 21: a reduction of 30–50%,
        — second undertaking to meet point 21: a reduction of 20–30%,
        — subsequent undertakings that meet point 21: a reduction of up to 20%.

In order to determine the level of reduction within each of these bands, the Commission will take into account the time at which the evidence fulfilling the condition in point 21 was submitted and the extent to which it represents added value. It may also take into account the extent and continuity of any cooperation provided by the undertaking following the date of its submission.

In addition, if an undertaking provides evidence relating to facts previously unknown to the Commission which have a direct bearing on the gravity or duration of the suspected cartel, the Commission will not take these elements into account when setting any fine to be imposed on the undertaking which provided this evidence.

Procedure

24.   An undertaking wishing to benefit from a reduction of a fine should provide the Commission with evidence of the cartel in question.

25.   The undertaking will receive an acknowledgement of receipt from the Directorate-General for Competition recording the date on which the relevant evidence was submitted. The Commission will not consider any submissions of evidence by an applicant for a reduction of a fine before it has taken a position on any existing application for a conditional immunity from fines in relation to the same suspected infringement.

26.   If the Commission comes to the preliminary conclusion that the evidence submitted by the undertaking constitutes added value within the meaning of point 22, it will inform the undertaking in writing, no later than the date on which a statement of objections is notified, of its intention to apply a reduction of a fine within a specified band as provided in point 23(b).

27.   The Commission will evaluate the final position of each undertaking which filed an application for a reduction of a fine at the end of the administrative procedure in any decision adopted.

[5717]

GENERAL CONSIDERATIONS

28.   From 14 February 2002, this notice replaces the 1996 notice for all cases in which no undertaking has contacted the Commission in order to take advantage of the favourable treatment set out in that notice. The Commission will examine whether it is necessary to modify this notice once it has acquired sufficient experience in applying it.

29.   The Commission is aware that this notice will create legitimate expectations on which undertakings may rely when disclosing the existence of a cartel to the Commission.

30.   Failure to meet any of the requirements set out in sections A or B, as the case may be, at any stage of the administrative procedure may result in the loss of any favourable treatment set out therein.

31.   In line with the Commission's practice, the fact that an undertaking cooperated with the Commission during its administrative procedure will be indicated in any decision, so as to explain the reason for the immunity or reduction of the fine. The fact that immunity or reduction in respect of fines is granted cannot protect an undertaking from the civil law consequences of its participation in an infringement of Article 81 EC.

32.   The Commission considers that normally disclosure, at any time, of documents received in the context of this notice would undermine the protection of the purpose of inspections and investigations within the meaning of Article 4(2) of Regulation (EC) No 1049/2001 of the European Parliament and of the Council.

33.   Any written statement made vis-à-vis the Commission in relation to this notice, forms part of the Commission's file. It may not be disclosed or used for any other purpose than the enforcement of Article 81 EC.

[5718]–[5900]

H. RIGHTS OF THE DEFENCE

COMMISSION NOTICE

on the internal rules of procedure for processing requests for access to the file in cases pursuant to Articles 85 and 86 of the EC Treaty, Articles 65 and 66 of the ECSC Treaty and Council Regulation (EEC) No 4064/89

(97/C 23/03)

(Text with EEA relevance)

NOTES
Date of publication in OJ: OJ C23, 23.1.97, p 3.

INTRODUCTION

Access to the file is an important procedural stage in all contentious competition cases (prohibitions with or without a fine, prohibitions of mergers, rejection of complaints, etc). The Commission's task in this area is to reconcile two opposing obligations, namely that of safeguarding the rights of the defence and that of protecting confidential information concerning firms.

The purpose of this notice is to ensure compatibility between current administrative practice regarding access to the file and the case-law of the Court of Justice of the European Communities and the Court of First Instance, in particular the "Soda-ash" cases.[1] The line of conduct thus laid down concerns cases dealt with on the basis of the competition rules applicable to enterprises: Articles 85 and 86 of the EC Treaty, Regulation (EEC) No 4064/89[2] (hereinafter "the Merger Regulation"), and Articles 65 and 66 of the ECSC Treaty.

Access to the file, which is one of the procedural safeguards designed to ensure effective exercise of the right to be heard[3] provided for in Article 19(1) and (2) of Council Regulation No 17[4] and Article 2 of Commission Regulation No 99/63/EEC,[5] as well as in the corresponding provisions of the Regulations governing the application of Articles 85 and 86 in the field of transport, must be arranged in all cases involving decisions on infringements, decisions rejecting complaints, decisions imposing interim measures and decisions adopted on the basis of Article 15(6) of Regulation No 17.

The guidelines set out below, however, essentially relate to the rights of the undertakings which are the subject of investigations into alleged infringements; they do not relate to the rights of third parties, and complainants in particular.

In merger cases, access to the file by parties directly concerned is expressly provided for in Article 18(3) of the Merger Regulation and in Article 13(3)(a) of Regulation (EC) No 3384/94[6] ("the Implementing Regulation").

[5901]

I. SCOPE AND LIMITS OF ACCESS TO THE FILE

As the purpose of providing access to the file is to enable the addressees of a statement of objections to express their views on the conclusions reached by the Commission, the firms in question must have access to all the documents making up the "file" of the Commission (DG IV), apart from the categories of documents identified in the Hercules judgment,[7] namely the business secrets of other undertakings, internal Commission documents[8] and other confidential information.

Thus not all the documents collected in the course of an investigation are communicable and a distinction must be made between non-communicable and communicable documents.

A. Non-communicable documents

1. *Business secrets*

Business secrets means information (documents or parts of documents) for which an undertaking has claimed protection as "business secrets", and which are recognized as such by the Commission.

The non-communicability of such information is intended to protect the legitimate interest of firms in preventing third parties from obtaining strategic information on their essential interests and on the operation or development of their business.[9]

The criteria for determining what constitutes a business secret have not as yet been defined in full. Reference may be made, however, to the case-law, especially the Akzo and the BAT and Reynolds judgments,[10] to the criteria used in anti-dumping procedures,[11] and to decisions on the subject by the Hearing Officer. The term "business secret" must be construed in its broader sense: according to Akzo, Regulation No 17 requires the Commission to have regard to the legitimate interest of firms in the protection of their business secrets.

Business secrets need no longer be protected when they are known outside the firm (or group or association of firms) to which they relate. Nor can facts remain business secrets if, owing to the passage of time or for any other reason, they are no longer commercially important.

Where business secrets provide evidence of an infringement or tend to exonerate a firm, the Commission must reconcile the interest in the protection of sensitive information, the public interest in having the infringement of the competition rules terminated, and the rights of the defence. This calls for an assessment of—
- (i) the relevance of the information to determining whether or not an infringement has been committed;
- (ii) its probative value;
- (iii) whether it is indispensable;
- (iv) the degree of sensitivity involved (to what extent would disclosure of the information harm the interests of the firm?);
- (v) the seriousness of the infringement.

Each document must be assessed individually to determine whether the need to disclose it is greater than the harm which might result from disclosure.

2. *Confidential documents*

It is also necessary to protect information for which confidentiality has been requested.

This category includes information making it possible to identify the suppliers of the information who wish to remain anonymous to the other parties, and certain types of information communicated to the Commission on condition that confidentiality is observed, such as documents obtained during an investigation which form part of a firm's property and are the subject of a non-disclosure request (such as a market study commissioned by the firm and forming part of its property). As in the preceding case (business secrets), the Commission must reconcile the legitimate interest of the firm in protecting its assets, the public interest in having breaches of the competition rules terminated, and the rights of the defence. Military secrets also belong in the category of "other confidential information".

As a rule, the confidential nature of documents is not a bar to their disclosure[12] if the information in question is necessary in order to prove an alleged infringement ("inculpatory documents") or if the papers invalidate or rebut the reasoning of the Commission set out in its statement of objections ("exculpatory documents").

3. Internal documents

Internal documents are, by their nature, not the sort of evidence on which the Commission can rely in its assessment of a case. For the most part they consist of drafts, opinions or memos from the departments concerned and relating to ongoing procedures.

The Commission departments must be able to express themselves freely within their institution concerning ongoing cases. The disclosure of such documents could also jeopardize the secrecy of the Commission's deliberations.

It should, moreover, be noted that the secrecy of proceedings is also protected by the code of conduct on public access to Commission and Council documents as set out in Commission Decision 94/90/ECSC, EC, Euratom,[13] as amended by Decision 96/567/ECSC, EC, Euratom[14] as are internal documents relating to inspections and investigations and those whose disclosure could jeopardize the protection of individual privacy, business and industrial secrets or the confidentiality requested by a legal or natural person.

These considerations justify the non-disclosure of this category of documents, which will, in future, be placed in the file of internal documents relating to cases under investigation, which is, as a matter of principle, inaccessible (see point II.A.2).

B. Communicable documents

All documents not regarded as "non-communicable" under the abovementioned criteria are accessible to the parties concerned.

Thus, access to the file is not limited to documents which the Commission regards as "relevant" to an undertaking's rights of defence.

The Commission does not select accessible documents in order to remove those which may be relevant to the defence of an undertaking. This concept, already outlined in the Court of First Instance judgments in Hercules and Cimenteries CBR,[15] was confirmed and developed in the Soda-ash case, where the Court held that "in the defended proceedings for which Regulation No 17 provides it cannot be for the Commission alone to decide which documents are of use for the defence. . . . The Commission must give the advisers of the undertaking concerned the opportunity to examine documents which may be relevant so that their probative value for the defence can be assessed." (Case T-30/91, paragraph 81).

Special note concerning studies:

It should be stressed that studies commissioned in connection with proceedings or for a specific file, whether used directly or indirectly in the proceedings, must be made accessible irrespective of their intrinsic value. Access must be given not only to the results of a study (reports, statistics, etc), but also to the Commission's correspondence with the contractor, the tender specifications and the methodology of the study.[16]

However, correspondence relating to the financial aspects of a study and the references concerning the contractor remain confidential in the interests of the latter.

II. PROCEDURES FOR IMPLEMENTING ACCESS TO THE FILE

A. Preparatory procedure—Cases investigated pursuant to Articles 85 and 86

1. *Investigation file*

1.1 *Return of certain documents after inspection visits*

In the course of its investigations under Article 14(2) and (3) of Regulation No 17, the Commission obtains a considerable number of documents, some of which may, following a detailed examination, prove to be irrelevant to the case in question. Such documents are normally returned to the firm as rapidly as possible.

1.2 *Request for a non-confidential version of a document*

In order to facilitate access to the file at a later stage in proceedings, the undertakings concerned will be asked systematically to—

- detail the information (documents or parts of documents) which they regard as business secrets and the confidential documents whose disclosure would injure them,
- substantiate their claim for confidentiality in writing,
- give the Commission a non-confidential version of their confidential documents (where confidential passages are deleted).

As regards documents taken during an inspection (Article 14(2) and (3)), requests are made only after the inspectors have returned from their mission.

When an undertaking, in response to a request from the Commission, claims that the information supplied is confidential, the following procedure will be adopted—

    (a) at that stage of the proceedings, claims of confidentiality which at first sight seem justified will be accepted provisionally. The Commission reserves the right, however, to reconsider the matter at a later stage of the proceedings;

    (b) where it is apparent that the claim of confidentiality is clearly unjustified, for example where it relates to a document already published or distributed extensively, or is excessive where it covers all, or virtually all the documents obtained or sent without any plausible justification, the firm concerned will be informed that the Commission does not agree with the scope of the confidentiality that is claimed. The matter will be dealt with when the final assessment is made of the accessibility of the documents (see below).

1.3 *Final assessment of the accessibility of documents*

It may prove necessary to grant other undertakings involved access to a document even where the undertaking that has issued it objects, if the document serves as a basis for the decision[17] or is clearly an exculpatory document.

If an undertaking states that a document is confidential but does not submit a non-confidential version, the following procedure applies—

- the undertaking claiming confidentiality will be contacted again and asked for a reasonably coherent non-confidential version of the document,
- if the undertaking continues to object to the disclosure of the information, the competent department applies to the Hearing Officer, who will if necessary implement the procedure leading to a decision pursuant to Article 5(4) of Commission Decision 94/810/ECSC, EC of 12 December 1994 on the terms of reference of hearing officers in competition procedures before the Commission.[18] The undertaking will be informed by letter that the Hearing Officer is examining the question.

1.4 *Enumerative list of documents*

An enumerative list of documents should be drawn up according to the following principles—

    (a) the list should include uninterrupted numbering of all the pages in the investigation file and an indication (using a classification code) of the degree of accessibility of the document and the parties with authorized access;

    (b) an access code is given to each document on the list—

        — accessible document

        — partially accessible document

        — non-accessible document;

    (c) the category of completely non-accessible documents essentially consists of documents containing "business secrets" and other confidential documents. In view of the "Soda-ash" case-law, the list will include a summary enabling the content and subject of the documents to be identified, so that any firm having requested access to the file is able to determine in full knowledge of the facts whether the documents are likely to be relevant to its defence and to decide whether to request access despite that classification;

    (d) accessible and partially accessible documents do not call for a description of their content in the list as they can be "physically" consulted by all firms, either in their full version or in their non-confidential version. In the latter event, only the sensitive passages are deleted in such a way that the firm with access is able to determine the nature of the information deleted (eg turnover).

2. *File of internal documents relating to ongoing cases*

In order to simplify administration and increase efficiency, internal documents will, in future, be placed in the file of internal documents relating to cases under investigation (non-accessible) containing all internal documents in chronological order. Classification in this category is subject to the control of the Hearing Officer, who will if necessary certify that the papers contained therein are "internal documents".

The following, for example, will be deemed to be internal documents—

    (a) requests for instructions made to, and instructions received from, hierarchical superiors on the treatment of cases;

    (b) consultations with other Commission departments on a case;

    (c) correspondence with other public authorities concerning a case;[19]

    (d) drafts and other working documents;

    (e) individual technical assistance contracts (languages, computing, etc) relating to a specific aspect of a case.

B. Preparatory procedure—Cases examined within the meaning of the Merger Regulation

1. *Measures common to the preparatory procedure in cases investigated pursuant to Articles 85 and 86*

    (a) *Return of certain documents after an inspection*

On-the-spot inspections are specifically provided for in Article 13 of the Merger Regulation: in such cases, the procedure provided for above in point II.A.1.1 for cases examined on the basis of Articles 85 and 86 is applicable.

    (b) *Enumerative list of documents*

The enumerative list of the documents in the Commission file with the access codes will be drawn up in accordance with the criteria set out in point II.A.1.4.

(c)   *Request for a non-confidential version of a document*

In order to facilitate access to the file, firms being investigated will be asked to—
— detail the information (documents or parts of documents) they regard as business secrets and the confidential documents whose disclosure would injure them,
— substantiate their request for confidentiality in writing,
— give the Commission a reasonably coherent non-confidential version of their confidential documents (where confidential passages are deleted).

This procedure will be followed in stage II cases (where the Commission initiates proceedings in respect of the notifying parties) and in stage I cases (giving rise to a Commission decision without initiation of proceedings).

2.   *Measures specific to preparatory procedures in merger cases*

(a)   *Subsequent procedure in stage II cases*

In stage II cases the subsequent procedure is as follows.

Where a firm states that all or part of the documents it has provided are business secrets, the following steps should be taken—
— if the claim appears to be justified, the documents or parts of documents concerned will be regarded as non-accessible to third parties,
— if the claim does not appear to be justified, the competent Commission department will ask the firm, in the course of the investigation and no later than the time at which the statement of objections is sent, to review its position. The firm must either state in writing which documents or parts of documents must be regarded as confidential, or send a non-confidential version of the documents.

If disagreement regarding the extent of the confidentiality persists, the competent department refers the matter to the Hearing Officer, who may if necessary take the decision provided for in Article 5(4) of Decision 94/810/ECSC, EC.

(b)   *Specific cases*

Article 9(1) of the Merger Regulation provides that "the Commission may, by means of a decision notified without delay to the undertakings concerned . . . refer a notified concentration to the competent authorities of the Member State concerned". In the context of access to the file, the parties concerned should, as a general rule be able to see the request for referral from a national authority, with the exception of any business secrets or other confidential information it may contain.

Article 22(3) of the Merger Regulation provides that "If the Commission finds, at the request of a Member State, that a concentration . . . that has no Community dimension . . . creates or strengthens a dominant position . . . it may . . . adopt the decisions provided for in the second subparagraph of Article 8(2), (3) and (4)". Such requests have the effect of empowering the Commission to deal with mergers which would normally fall outside its powers of review. Accordingly, the parties concerned should be granted right of access to the letter from the Member State requesting referral, after deletion of any business secrets or other confidential information.

C. Practical arrangements for access to the file

1.   *General rule: access by way of consultation on the Commission's premises*

Firms are invited to examine the relevant files on the Commission's premises.

If the firm considers, on the basis of the list of documents it has received, that it requires certain non-accessible documents for its defence, it may make a reasoned request to that end to the Hearing Officer.[20]

2.   If the file is not too bulky, however, the firm has the choice of being sent all the accessible documents, apart from those already sent with the statement of objections or the letter rejecting the complaint, or of consulting the file on the Commission's premises.

As regards Articles 85 and 86 cases, contrary to a common previous practice, the statement of objections or letter of rejection will in future be accompanied only by the evidence adduced and documents cited on which the objections/rejection letter is based.

Any request for access made prior to submission of the statement of objections will in principle be inadmissible.

D. Particular questions which may arise in connection with complaints and procedures relating to abuse of a dominant position (Articles 85 and 86)

1.   *Complaints*

Whilst complainants may properly be involved in proceedings, they do not have the same rights and guarantees as the alleged infringers. A complainant's right to consult the files does not share the same basis as the rights of defence of the addressees of a statement of objections, and there are no grounds for treating the rights of the complainant as equivalent to those of the firms objected to.

Nevertheless, a complainant who has been informed of the intention to reject his complaint may request access to the documents on which the Commission based its position. Complainants may not, however, have access to any confidential information or other business secrets belonging to the firms complained of, or to third-party firms, which the Commission has obtained in the course of its investigations (Articles 11 and 14 of Regulation No 17).

Clearly, it is even more necessary here to respect the principle of confidentiality as there is no presumption of infringement. In accordance with the judgment in Fedetab,[21] Article 19(2) of Regulation No 17 gives complainants a right to be heard and not a right to receive confidential information.

2.   *Procedures in cases of abuse of a dominant position*

The question of procedures in cases of abuse of a dominant position was referred to by the Court of First Instance and the Court of Justice in the BPB Industries and British Gypsum v Commission case.[22]

By definition, firms in a dominant position on a market are able to place very considerable economic or commercial pressure on their competitors or on their trading partners, customers or suppliers.

The Court of First Instance and the Court of Justice thus acknowledged the legitimacy of the reluctance displayed by the Commission in revealing certain letters received from customers of the firm being investigated.

Although it is of value to the Commission for giving a better understanding of the market concerned, the information does not in any way constitute inculpatory evidence, and its disclosure to the firm concerned might easily expose the authors to the risk of retaliatory measures.

NOTES

[1] Court of First Instance judgments in Cases T-30/91, Solvay v Commission, T-36/91, ICI v Commission, and T-37/91, ICI v Commission [1995] ECR II-1775, II-1847 and II-1901.

[2] OJ No L395, 30.12.1989, p 1, as corrected in OJ No L257, 21.9.1990, p 13.

[3] Judgment of the Court of First Instance in Joined Cases T-10, 11, 12 and 15/92, CBR and Others [1992] ECR II-2667, at paragraph 38.

[4] OJ No 13, 21.2.1962, p 204/62.

[5] OJ No 127, 20.8.1963, p 2268/63.

[6] OJ No L377, 31.12.1994, p 1.

[7] Court of First Instance judgment in Case T-7/89, Hercules Chemicals v Commission [1991] ECR II-1711, paragraph 54.

[8] Internal Commission documents do not form part of the investigation file and are placed in the file of internal documents relating to the case under examination (see points I.A.3 and II.A.2 below).

[9] For example methods of assessing manufacturing and distribution costs, production secrets and processes, supply sources, quantities produced and sold, market shares, customer and distributor lists, marketing plants, cost price structure, sales policy, and information on the internal organization of the firm.

[10] Case 53/85, Akzo [1986] ECR 1965, paragraphs 24 to 28, and paragraph 28 in particular on pp 1991–1992. Cases 142 and 156/84, BAT and Reynolds v Commission [1987] ECR 4487, paragraph 21.

[11] Order of the Court of 30.3.1982 in Case 236/81, Celanese v Commission and Council [1982] ECR 1183.

[12] Here the procedure described in point II.A.1.3 should be followed.

[13] OJ No L46, 18.2.1994, p 58.

[14] OJ No L247, 28.9.1996, p 45.

[15] In paragraph 54 of Hercules, referred to in paragraph 41 of the Cimenteries judgment, the Court of First Instance held that the Commission has an obligation to make available to the undertakings all documents, whether in their favour or otherwise, which it has obtained during the course of the investigation, save where the business secrets of other undertakings, the internal documents of the Commission or other confidential information are involved.

[16] As a result of this provision, it is necessary, when drawing up a study contract, to include a specific clause stipulating that the study and the relevant documents (methodology, correspondence with the Commission) may be disclosed by the Commission to third parties.

[17] For example, documents which help to define the scope, duration and nature of the infringement, the identity of participants, the harm to competition, the economic context, etc.

[18] OJ No L330, 21.12.1994, p 67.

[19] It is necessary to protect the confidentiality of documents obtained from public authorities; this rule applies not only to documents from competition authorities, but also to those from other public authorities, Member States or non-member countries.

Any exception to the principle of non-disclosure of these documents must be firmly justified on the grounds of safeguarding the rights of the defence (eg complaint lodged by a Member State pursuant to Article 3 of Regulation No 17). Letters simply expressing interest, whether from a public authority of a Member State or of a third country, are non-communicable in principle.

A distinction must be made, however, between the opinions or comments expressed by other public authorities, which are afforded absolute protection, and any specific documents they may have furnished, which are not always covered by the exception. In the latter case, it is advisable in any event to proceed with circumspection, especially if the documents are from a non-member country, as it is considered of prime importance for the development of international cooperation in the application of the competition rules, to safeguard the relationship of trust between the Commission and non-member countries.

There are two possibilities in this context—

(a) There may already be an agreement governing the confidentiality of the information exchanged.

Article VIII(2) of the Agreement between the European Communities and the Government of the United States of America regarding the application of their competition laws (OJ No L95, 27.4.1995, p 45) stipulates that exchanges of information and information received under the Agreement must be protected "to the fullest extent possible". The article lays down a point of international law which must be complied with.

(b) If there is no such agreement, the same principle of guaranteed confidentiality should be observed.

[20] Special procedure provided for in Decision 94/810/ECSC, EC.

[21] Cases 209-215 and 218/78, Fedetab [1980] ECR 3125, paragraph 46.

[22] Judgment of the Court of First Instance in Case T-65/89, BPB Industries and British Gypsum [1993] ECR II-389, and judgment of the Court of Justice in Case C-310/93 P in BPB Industries and British Gypsum [1995] ECR I-865.

COMMISSION REGULATION

of 22 December 1998

on the hearing of parties in certain proceedings under Articles 85 and 86 of the EC Treaty

(2842/98/EC)

NOTES

Date of publication in OJ: OJ L354, 30.12.98, p 18.

THE COMMISSION OF THE EUROPEAN COMMUNITIES,

Having regard to the Treaty establishing the European Community,

Having regard to the Agreement on the European Economic Area,

Having regard to Council Regulation No 17 of 6 February 1962, First Regulation implementing Articles 85 and 86 of the Treaty,[1] as last amended by the Act of Accession of Austria, Finland and Sweden, and in particular Article 24 thereof,

Having regard to Council Regulation (EEC) No 1017/68 of 19 July 1968 applying rules of competition to transport by rail, road and inland waterway,[2] as last amended by the Act of Accession of Austria, Finland and Sweden, and in particular Article 29 thereof,

Having regard to Council Regulation (EEC) No 4056/86 of 22 December 1986 laying down detailed rules for the application of Articles 85 and 86 of the Treaty to maritime transport,[3] as last amended by the Act of Accession of Austria, Finland and Sweden, and in particular Article 26 thereof,

Having regard to Council Regulation (EEC) No 3975/87 of 14 December 1987 laying down the procedure for the application of the rules on competition to undertakings in the air transport sector,[4] as last amended by Regulation (EEC) No 2410/92,[5] and in particular Article 19 thereof,

Having consulted the appropriate Advisory Committees on Restrictive Practices and Dominant Positions,

(1) Whereas a great deal of experience has been acquired in the application of Commission Regulation No 99/63/EEC of 25 July 1963 on the hearings provided for in Article 19(1) and (2) of Regulation No 17,[6] Commission Regulation (EEC) No 1630/69 of 8 August 1969 on the hearings provided for in Article 26(1) and (2) of Council Regulation (EEC) No 1017/68 of 19 July 1968,[7] Section II of Commission Regulation (EEC) No 4260/88 of 16 December 1988 on the communications, complaints and applications and the hearings provided for in Council Regulation (EEC) No 4056/86 laying down detailed rules for the application of Articles 85 and 86 of the Treaty to maritime transport,[8] as last amended by the Act of Accession of Austria, Finland and Sweden, and Section II of Commission Regulation (EEC) No 4261/88 of 16 December 1988 on the complaints, applications and hearings provided for in Council Regulation (EEC) No 3975/87 laying down the procedure for the application of the rules on competition to undertakings in the air transport sector;[9]

(2) Whereas that experience has revealed the need to improve certain procedural aspects of those Regulations; whereas it is appropriate for the sake of clarity to adopt a single Regulation on the various hearing procedures laid down by Regulation No 17, Regulation (EEC) No 1017/68, Regulation (EEC) No 4056/86 and Regulation (EEC) No 3975/87; whereas, accordingly, Regulations No 99/63/EEC and (EEC) No 1630/69 should be replaced, and Sections II of Regulations (EEC) No 4260/88 and (EEC) No 4261/88 should be deleted and replaced;

(3) Whereas the provisions relating to the Commission's procedure under Decision 94/810/ECSC, EC of 12 December 1994 on the terms of reference of hearing officers in competition procedures before the Commission[10] should be framed in such a way as to safeguard fully the right to be heard and the rights of defence; whereas for these purposes, the Commission should distinguish between the respective rights to be heard of the parties to which the Commission has addressed objections, of the applicants and complainants, and of other third parties;

(4) Whereas in accordance with the principle of the rights of defence, the parties to which the Commission has addressed objections should be given the opportunity to submit their

comments on all the objections which the Commission proposes to take into account in its decisions;

(5) Whereas the applicants and complainants should be granted the opportunity of expressing their views, if the Commission considers that there are insufficient grounds for granting the application or acting on the complaint; whereas the applicant or complainant should be provided with a copy of the non-confidential version of the objections and should be permitted to make known its views in writing where the Commission raises objections;

(6) Whereas other third parties having sufficient interest should also be given the opportunity of expressing their views in writing where they make a written application to do so;

(7) Whereas the various parties entitled to submit comments should do so in writing, both in their own interest and in the interests of sound administration, without prejudice to the possibility of an oral hearing where appropriate to supplement the written procedure;

(8) Whereas it is necessary to define the rights of persons who are to be heard and on what conditions they may be represented or assisted;

(9) Whereas the Commission should continue to respect the legitimate interest of undertakings in the protection of their business secrets and other confidential information;

(10) Whereas compatibility should be ensured between the Commission's current administrative practices and the case-law of the Court of Justice and the Court of First Instance of the European Communities in accordance with the Commission notice on the internal rules of procedure for processing requests for access to the file in cases pursuant to Articles 85 and 86 of the Treaty, Articles 65 and 66 of the ECSC Treaty and Council Regulation (EEC) No 4064/89;[11]

(11) Whereas to facilitate the proper conduct of the hearing it is appropriate to allow statements made by each person at a hearing to be recorded;

(12) Whereas in the interest of legal certainty, it is appropriate to set the time limit for the submissions by the various persons pursuant to this Regulation by defining the date by which the submission must reach the Commission;

(13) Whereas the appropriate Advisory Committee under Article 10(3) of Regulation No 17, Article 16(3) of Regulation (EEC) No 1017/68, Article 15(3) of Regulation (EEC) No 4056/86 or Article 8(3) of Regulation (EEC) No 3975/87 must deliver its opinion on the basis of a preliminary draft decision; whereas it should therefore be consulted on a case after the inquiry in that case has been completed; whereas such consultation should not prevent the Commission from reopening an inquiry if need be,

---

NOTES

[1] OJ 13, 21.2.62, p 204/62.
[2] OJ L175, 23.7.68, p 1.
[3] OJ L378, 31.12.86, p 4.
[4] OJ L374, 31.12.87, p 1.
[5] OJ L240, 24.8.92, p 18.
[6] OJ 127, 20.8.63, p 2268/63.
[7] OJ L209, 21.8.69, p 11.
[8] OJ L376, 31.12.88, p 1.
[9] OJ L376, 31.12.88, p 10.
[10] OJ L330, 21.12.94, p 67.
[11] OJ C23, 23.1.97, p 3.

HAS ADOPTED THIS REGULATION—

CHAPTER I
SCOPE

Article 1

This Regulation shall apply to the hearing of parties under Article 19(1) and (2) of Regulation No 17, Article 26(1) and (2) of Regulation (EEC) No 1017/68, Article 23(1) and (2) of Regulation (EEC) No 4056/86 and Article 16(1) and (2) of Regulation (EEC) No 3975/87.

[5904]

CHAPTER II
HEARING OF PARTIES TO WHICH THE COMMISSION HAS ADDRESSED OBJECTIONS

Article 2

1.   The Commission shall hear the parties to which it has addressed objections before consulting the appropriate Advisory Committee under Article 10(3) of Regulation No 17, Article 16(3) of Regulation (EEC) No 1017/68, Article 15(3) of Regulation (EEC) No 4056/86 or Article 8(3) of Regulation (EEC) No 3975/87.

2.   The Commission shall in its decisions deal only with objections in respect of which the parties have been afforded the opportunity of making their views known.

[5905]

Article 3

1.   The Commission shall inform the parties in writing of the objections raised against them. The objections shall be notified to each of them or to a duly appointed agent.

2.   The Commission may inform the parties by giving notice in the Official Journal of the European Communities, if from the circumstances of the case this appears appropriate, in particular where notice is to be given to a number of undertakings but no joint agent has been appointed. The notice shall have regard to the legitimate interests of the undertakings in the protection of their business secrets and other confidential information.

3.   A fine or a periodic penalty payment may be imposed on a party only if the objections have been notified in the manner provided for in paragraph 1.

4.   The Commission shall, when giving notice of objections, set a date by which the parties may inform it in writing of their views.

5.   The Commission shall set a date by which the parties may indicate any parts of the objections which in their view contain business secrets or other confidential material. If they do not do so by that date, the Commission may assume that the objections do not contain such information.

[5906]

Article 4

1.   Parties which wish to make known their views on the objections raised against them shall do so in writing and by the date referred to in Article 3(4). The Commission shall not be obliged to take into account written comments received after that date.

2.   The parties may in their written comments set out all matters relevant to their defence. They may attach any relevant documents as proof of the facts set out and may also propose that the Commission hear persons who may corroborate those facts.

[5907]

Article 5

The Commission shall afford to parties against which objections have been raised the opportunity to develop their arguments at an oral hearing, if they so request in their written comments.

[5908]

CHAPTER III
HEARING OF APPLICANTS AND COMPLAINANTS

Article 6

Where the Commission, having received an application made under Article 3(2) of Regulation No 17 or a complaint made under Article 10 of Regulation (EEC) No 1017/68, Article 10 of Regulation (EEC) No 4056/86 or Article 3(1) of Regulation (EEC) No 3975/87, considers that on the basis of the information in its possession there are insufficient grounds for granting the application or acting on the complaint, it shall inform the applicant or complainant of its reasons and set a date by which the applicant or complainant may make known its views in writing.

[5909]

Article 7

Where the Commission raises objections reating to an issue in respect of which it has received an application on a complaint as referred to in Article 6, it shall provide an applicant or complainant with a copy of the non-confidential version of the objections and set a date by which the applicant or complainant may make known its views in writing.

[5910]

Article 8

The Commission may, where appropriate, afford to applicants and complainants the opportunity of orally expressing their views, if they so request in their written comments.

[5911]

CHAPTER IV
HEARING OF OTHER THIRD PARTIES

Article 9

1.   If parties other than those referred to in Chapters II and III apply to be heard and show a sufficient interest, the Commission shall inform them in writing of the nature and subject matter of the procedure and shall set a date by which they may make known their views in writing.

2.   The Commission may, where appropriate, invite parties referred to in paragraph 1 to develop their arguments at the oral hearing of the parties against which objections have been raised, if they so request in their written comments.

3.   The Commission may afford to any other third parties the opportunity of orally expressing their views.

[5912]

CHAPTER V
GENERAL PROVISIONS

Article 10

Hearings shall be conducted by the Hearing Officer.

[5913]

Article 11

1.   The Commission shall invite the persons to be heard to attend the oral hearing on such date as it shall appoint.

PART IV
EC MATERIALS

2.   The Commission shall invite the competent authorities of the Member States to take part in the oral hearing.

[5914]

Article 12

1.   Persons invited to attend shall either appear in person or be represented by legal representatives or by representatives authorised by their constitution as appropriate. Undertakings and associations of undertakings may be represented by a duly authorised agent appointed from among their permanent staff.

2.   Persons heard by the Commission may be assisted by their legal advisers or other qualified persons admitted by the Hearing Officer.

3.   Oral hearings shall not be public. Each person shall be heard separately or in the presence of other persons invited to attend. In the latter case, regard shall be had to the legitimate interest of the undertakings in the protection of their business secrets and other confidential information.

4.   The statements made by each person heard shall be recorded on tape. The recording shall be made available to such persons on request, by means of a copy from which business secrets and other confidential information shall be deleted.

[5915]

Article 13

1.   Information, including documents, shall not be communicated or made accessible in so far as it contains business secrets of any party, including the parties to which the Commission has addressed objections, applicants and complainants and other third parties, or other confidential information or where internal documents of the authorities are concerned. The Commission shall make appropriate arrangements for allowing access to the file, taking due account of the need to protect business secrets, internal Commission documents and other confidential information.

2.   Any party which makes known its views under the provisions of this Regulation shall clearly identify any material which it considers to be confidential, giving reasons, and provide a separate non-confidential version by the date set by the Commission. If it does not do so by the set date, the Commission may assume that the submission does not contain such material.

[5916]

Article 14

In setting the dates provided for in Articles 3(4), 6, 7 and 9(1), the Commission shall have regard both to the time required for preparation of the submission and to the urgency of the case. The time allowed in each case shall be at least two weeks; it may be extended.

[5917]

CHAPTER VI
FINAL PROVISIONS

Article 15

1.   Regulations No 99/63/EEC and (EEC) No 1630/69 are repealed.

2.   Sections II of Regulations (EEC) No 4260/88 and (EEC) No 4261/88 are deleted.

[5918]

Article 16

This Regulation shall enter into force on 1 February 1999.

[5919]

This Regulation shall be binding in its entirety and directly applicable in all Member States.

Done at Brussels, 22 December 1998.

COMMISSION DECISION

of 23 May 2001

on the terms of reference of hearing officers in certain competition proceedings

(notified under document number C(2001) 1461)

(Text with EEA relevance)

(2001/462/EC, ECSC)

NOTES

Date of publication in OJ: OJ L162, 19.6.01, p 21.

THE COMMISSION OF THE EUROPEAN COMMUNITIES,

Having regard to the Treaty establishing the European Community,

Having regard to the Treaty establishing the European Coal and Steel Community,

Having regard to the Agreement on the European Economic Area,

Having regard to the Rules of Procedure of the Commission,[1] and in particular Article 20 thereof,

Whereas—

(1) The right of the parties concerned and of third parties to be heard before a final decision affecting their interests is taken is a fundamental principle of Community law. That right is also set out in Council Regulation (EEC) No 4064/89 of 21 December 1989 on the control of concentrations between undertakings,[2] as last amended by Regulation (EC) No 1310/97,[3] Commission Regulation (EC) No 2842/98 of 22 December 1998 on the hearing of parties in certain proceedings under Articles 85 and 86 of the EC Treaty,[4] and Commission Regulation (EC) No 447/98 of 1 March 1998 on the notifications, time limits and hearings provided for in Council Regulation (EEC) No 4064/89 on the control of concentrations between undertakings.[5]

(2) The Commission must ensure that that right is guaranteed in its competition proceedings, having regard in particular to the Charter of Fundamental Rights of the European Union.[6]

(3) The conduct of administrative proceedings should therefore be entrusted to an independent person experienced in competition matters who has the integrity necessary to contribute to the objectivity, transparency and efficiency of those proceedings.

(4) The Commission created the post of hearing officer for these purposes in 1982 and last laid down the terms of reference for that post in Commission Decision 94/810/ ECSC, EC of 12 December 1994 on the terms of reference of hearing officers in competition procedures before the Commission.[7]

(5) It is necessary to further strengthen the role of the hearing officer and to adapt and consolidate those terms of reference in the light of developments in competition law.

(6) In order to ensure the independence of the hearing officer, he should be attached, for administrative purposes, to the member of the Commission with special responsibility for competition. Transparency as regards the appointment, termination of appointment and transfer of hearing officers should be increased.

(7) The hearing officer should be appointed in accordance with the rules laid down in the Staff Regulations of Officials and the Conditions of Employment of Other Servants of the European Communities. In accordance with those rules, consideration may be given to candidates who are not officials of the Commission.

(8) The terms of reference of the hearing officer in competition proceedings should be framed in such a way as to safeguard the right to be heard throughout the whole procedure.

(9) When disclosing information on natural persons, particular attention should be paid to Regulation (EC) No 45/2001 of the European Parliament and of the Council of 18 December 2000 on the protection of individuals with regard to the processing of personal data by the Community institutions and bodies and on the free movement of such data[8].

(10) This Decision should be without prejudice to the general rules granting or excluding access to Commission documents.

(11) Decision 94/810/ECSC, EC should be repealed,

NOTES

[1] OJ L308, 8.12.2000, p 26.
[2] OJ L395, 30.12.1989, p 1 (corrected version in OJ L257, 21.9.1990, p 13).
[3] OJ L180, 9.7.1997, p 1.
[4] OJ L354, 30.12.1998, p 18.
[5] OJ L61, 2.3.1998, p 1.
[6] OJ C364, 18.12.2000, p 1.
[7] OJ L330, 21.12.1994, p 67.
[8] OJ L8, 12.1.2001, p 1.

HAS DECIDED AS FOLLOWS—

Article 1

The Commission shall appoint one or more hearing officers (hereinafter "the hearing officer"), who shall ensure that the effective exercise of the right to be heard is respected in competition proceedings before the Commission under Articles 81 and 82 of the EC Treaty, Articles 65 and 66 of the ECSC Treaty, and Regulation (EEC) No 4064/89.

[5920]

Article 2

1. The appointment of the hearing officer shall be published in the *Official Journal of the European Communities*. Any interruption, termination of appointment or transfer by whatever procedure, shall be the subject of a reasoned decision of the Commission. That decision shall be published in the *Official Journal of the European Communities*.

2. The hearing officer shall be attached, for administrative purposes, to the member of the Commission with special responsibility for competition (hereinafter "the competent member of the Commission").

3. Where the hearing officer is unable to act, the competent member of the Commission, where appropriate after consultation of the hearing officer, shall designate another official, who is not involved in the case in question, to carry out the hearing officer's duties.

[5921]

Article 3

1. In performing his duties, the hearing officer shall take account of the need for effective application of the competition rules in accordance with the Community legislation in force and the principles laid down by the Court of Justice and the Court of First Instance of the European Communities.

2. The hearing officer shall be kept informed by the director responsible for investigating the case (hereinafter "the director responsible") about the development of the procedure up to the stage of the draft decision to be submitted to the competent member of the Commission.

3.   The hearing officer may present observations on any matter arising out of any Commission competition proceeding to the competent member of the Commission.

[5922]

Article 4

1.   The hearing officer shall organise and conduct the hearings provided for in the provisions implementing Articles 81 and 82 of the EC Treaty, Articles 65 and 66 of the ECSC Treaty and Regulation (EEC) No 4064/89, in accordance with Articles 5 to 13 of this Decision.

2.   The provisions referred to in paragraph 1 are—
   (a) the first paragraph of Article 36 of the ECSC Treaty;
   (b) Regulation (EC) No 2842/98;
   (c) Regulation (EC) No 447/98.

[5923]

Article 5

The hearing officer shall ensure that the hearing is properly conducted and contributes to the objectivity of the hearing itself and of any decision taken subsequently. The hearing officer shall seek to ensure in particular that, in the preparation of draft Commission decisions, due account is taken of all the relevant facts, whether favourable or unfavourable to the parties concerned, including the factual elements related to the gravity of any infringement.

[5924]

Article 6

1.   Applications to be heard from third parties, be they persons, undertakings or associations of persons or undertakings, shall be submitted in writing, together with a written statement explaining the applicant's interest in the outcome of the procedure.

2.   Decisions as to whether third parties are to be heard shall be taken after consulting the director responsible.

3.   Where it is found that an application has not shown a sufficient interest to be heard, he shall be informed in writing of the reasons for such finding. A time limit shall be fixed within which he may submit any further written comments.

[5925]

Article 7

1.   Applications to be heard orally shall be made in the applicant's written comments on letters which the Commission has addressed to him.

2.   The letters referred to in paragraph 1 are those:
   (a) communicating a statement of objections;
   (b) inviting the written comments of a third party having shown sufficient interest to be heard;
   (c) informing a complainant that in the Commission's view there are insufficient grounds for finding an infringement and inviting him to submit any further written comments.

3.   Decisions as to whether applicants are to be heard orally shall be taken after consulting the director responsible.

[5926]

PART IV
EC MATERIALS

Article 8

1.   Where a person, an undertaking or an association of persons or undertakings has received one or more of the letters listed in Article 7(2) and has reason to believe that the Commission has in its possession documents which have not been disclosed to it and that those documents are necessary for the proper exercise of the right to be heard, access to those documents may be sought by means of a reasoned request.

2.   The reasoned decision on any such request shall be communicated to the person, undertaking or association that made the request and to any other person, undertaking or association concerned by the procedure.

[5927]

Article 9

Where it is intended to disclose information which may constitute a business secret of an undertaking, it shall be informed in writing of this intention and the reasons for it. A time limit shall be fixed within which the undertaking concerned may submit any written comments.

Where the undertaking concerned objects to the disclosure of the information but it is found that the information is not protected and may therefore be disclosed, that finding shall be stated in a reasoned decision which shall be notified to the undertaking concerned. The decision shall specify the date after which the information will be disclosed. This date shall not be less than one week from the date of notification.

The first and second paragraphs shall apply *mutatis mutandis* to the disclosure of information by publication in the *Official Journal of the European Communities*.

[5928]

Article 10

Where a person, undertaking or association of persons or undertakings considers that the time limit imposed for its reply to a letter referred to in Article 7(2) is too short, it may, within the original time limit, seek an extension of that time limit by means of a reasoned request. The applicant shall be informed in writing whether the request has been granted.

[5929]

Article 11

Where appropriate, in view of the need to ensure that the hearing is properly prepared and particularly that questions of fact are clarified as far as possible, the hearing officer may, after consulting the director responsible, supply in advance to the parties invited to the hearing a list of the questions on which he wishes them to make known their views.

For this purpose, after consulting the director responsible, the hearing officer may hold a meeting with the parties invited to the hearing and, where appropriate, the Commission staff, in order to prepare for the hearing itself.

The hearing officer may also ask for prior written notification of the essential contents of the intended statement of persons whom the parties invited to the hearing have proposed for hearing.

[5930]

Article 12

1.   After consulting the director responsible, the hearing officer shall determine the date, the duration and the place of the hearing. Where a postponement is requested, the hearing officer shall decide whether or not to allow it.

2.   The hearing officer shall be fully responsible for the conduct of the hearing.

3.   The hearing officer shall decide whether fresh documents should be admitted during the hearing, what persons should be heard on behalf of a party and whether the persons concerned should be heard separately or in the presence of other persons attending the hearing.

4.   Where appropriate, in view of the need to ensure the right to be heard, the hearing officer may, after consulting the Director responsible, afford persons, undertakings, and associations of persons or undertakings the opportunity of submitting further written comments after the oral hearing. The hearing officer shall fix a date by which such submissions may be made. The Commission shall not be obliged to take into account written comments received after that date.

[5931]

Article 13

1.   The hearing officer shall report to the competent member of the Commission on the hearing and the conclusions he draws from it, with regard to the respect of the right to be heard. The observations in this report shall concern procedural issues, including disclosure of documents and access to the file, time limits for replying to the statement of objections and the proper conduct of the oral hearing.

A copy of the report shall be given to the Director-General for Competition and to the director responsible.

2.   In addition to the report referred to in paragraph 1, the hearing officer may make observations on the further progress of the proceedings. Such observations may relate among other things to the need for further information, the withdrawal of certain objections, or the formulation of further objections.

[5932]

Article 14

Where appropriate, the hearing officer may report on the objectivity of any enquiry conducted in order to assess the competition impact of commitments proposed in relation to any proceeding initiated by the Commission in application of the provisions referred to in Article 1. This shall cover in particular the selection of respondents and the methodology used.

[5933]

Article 15

The hearing officer shall, on the basis of the draft decision to be submitted to the Advisory Committee in the case in question, prepare a final report in writing on the respect of the right to be heard, as referred to in Article 13(1). This report will also consider whether the draft decision deals only with objections in respect of which the parties have been afforded the opportunity of making known their views, and, where appropriate, the objectivity of any enquiry within the meaning of Article 14.

The final report shall be submitted to the competent member of the Commission, the Director-General for Competition and the director responsible. It shall be communicated to the competent authorities of the Member States and, in accordance with the provisions on cooperation laid down in Protocol 23 and Protocol 24 of the EEA Agreement, to the EFTA Surveillance Authority.

[5934]

Article 16

1.   The hearing officer's final report shall be attached to the draft decision submitted to the Commission, in order to ensure that, when it reaches a decision on an individual case, the Commission is fully apprised of all relevant information as regards the course of the procedure and respect of the right to be heard.

PART IV
EC MATERIALS

2.   The final report may be modified by the hearing officer in the light of any amendments to the draft decision up to the time the decision is adopted by the Commission.

3.   The Commission shall communicate the hearing officer's final report, together with the decision, to the addressees of the decision. It shall publish the hearing officer's final report in the *Official Journal of the European Communities*, together with the decision, having regard to the legitimate interest of undertakings in the protection of their business secrets.

[5935]

Article 17

Decision 94/810/ECSC, EC is repealed.

Procedural steps already taken under that Decision shall continue to have effect.

Done at Brussels, 23 May 2001.

[5936]-[6150]

I. STATE AIDS

COMMISSION NOTICE

on cooperation between national courts and the Commission in the State aid field

(95/C 312/07)

NOTES

Date of publication in OJ: OJ C312, 23.11.95, p 8.

The purpose of this notice is to offer guidance on cooperation between national courts and the Commission in the State aid field. The notice does not in any way limit the rights conferred on Member States, individuals or undertakings by Community law. It is without prejudice to any interpretation of Community law which may be given by the Court of Justice and the Court of First Instance of the European Communities. Finally, it does not seek to interfere in any way with the fulfilment by national courts of their duties.

I. INTRODUCTION

1. The elimination of internal frontiers between Member States enables undertakings in the Community to expand their activities throughout the internal market and consumers to benefit from increased competition. These advantages must not be jeopardised by distortions of competition caused by aid granted unjustifiably to undertakings. The completion of the internal market thus reaffirms the importance of enforcement of the Community's competition policy.

2. The Court of Justice has delivered a number of important judgments on the interpretation and application of Articles 92 and 93 of the EC Treaty. The Court of First Instance now has jurisdiction over actions by private parties against the Commission's State aid decisions and will thus also contribute to the development of case-law in this field. The Commission is responsible for the day-to-day application of the competition rules under the supervision of the Court of First Instance and the Court of Justice. Public authorities and courts in the Member States, together with the Community's courts and the Commission each assume their own tasks and responsibilities for the enforcement of the EC Treaty's State aid rules, in accordance with the principles laid down by the case-law of the Court of Justice.

3. The proper application of competition policy in the internal market may require effective cooperation between the Commission and national courts. This notice explains how the Commission intends to assist national courts by instituting closer cooperation in the application of Articles 92 and 93 in individual cases. Concern is frequently expressed that the Commission's final decisions in State aid cases are reached some time after the distortions of competition have damaged the interests of third parties. While the Commission is not always in a position to act promptly to safeguard the interests of third parties in State aid matters, national courts may be better placed to ensure that breaches of the last sentence of Article 93(3) are dealt with and remedied.

II. POWERS[1]

4. The Commission is the administrative authority responsible for the implementation and development of competition policy in the Community's public interest. National courts are responsible for the protection of rights and the enforcement of duties, usually at the behest of private parties. The Commission must examine all aid measures which fall under Article 92(1) in order to assess their

compatibility with the common market. National courts must make sure that Member States comply with their procedural obligations.

5.   The last sentence of Article 93(3) (in bold below) has direct effect in the legal order of the Member States.

"The Commission shall be informed, in sufficient time to enable it to submit its comments, of any plans to grant or alter aid. If it considers that any such plan is not compatible with the common market having regard to Article 92, it shall without delay initiate the procedure provided for in paragraph 2. **The Member State concerned shall not put its proposed measures into effect until this procedure has resulted in a final decision.**"

6.   The prohibition on implementation referred to in the last sentence of Article 93(3) extends to all aid which has been implemented without being notified[2] and, in the event of notification, operates during the preliminary period and, if the Commission sets in motion the contentious procedure, until the final decision.[3]

7.   Of course a court will have to consider whether the "proposed measures" constitute State aid within the meaning of Article 92(1)[4] before reaching a decision under the last sentence of Article 93(3). The Commission's Decisions and the Court's case-law devote considerable attention to this important question. Accordingly, the notion of State aid must be interpreted widely to encompass not only subsidies, but also tax concessions and investments from public funds made in circumstances in which a private investor would have withheld support.[5] The aid must come from the "State", which includes all levels, manifestations and emanations of public authority.[6] The aid must favour certain undertakings or the production of certain goods: this serves to distinguish State aid to which Article 92(1) applies from general measures to which it does not.[7] For example, measures which have neither as their object nor as their effect the favouring of certain undertakings or the production of certain goods, or which apply to persons in accordance with objective criteria without regard to the location, sector or undertaking in which the beneficiary may be employed, are not considered to be State aid.

8.   Only the Commission can decide that State aid is "compatible with the common market", ie authorised.

9.   In applying Article 92(1), national courts may of course refer preliminary questions to the Court of Justice pursuant to Article 177 of the EC Treaty and indeed must do so in certain circumstances. They must also request assistance from the Commission by asking it for "legal or economic information" by analogy with the Court's Delimitis[8] judgment in respect of Article 85 of the EC Treaty.

10.   The national court's role is to safeguard rights which individuals enjoy as a result of the direct effect of the prohibition laid down in the last sentence of Article 93(3). The court should use all appropriate devices and remedies and apply all relevant provisions of national law to implement the direct effect of this obligation placed by the Treaty on Member States.[9] A national court must, in a case within its jurisdiction, apply Community law in its entirety and protect rights which that law confers on individuals; it must therefore set aside any provision of national law which may conflict with it, whether prior or subsequent to the Community rule.[10] The judge may, as appropriate and in accordance with applicable rules of national law and the developing case-law of the Court of Justice,[11] grant interim relief, for example by ordering the freezing or return of monies illegally paid, and award damages to parties whose interests are harmed.

11.   The Court of Justice has held that the full effectiveness of Community rules would be impaired and the protection of the rights which they grant would be weakened if individuals were unable to obtain redress when their rights are infringed by a breach of Community law for which a Member State can be held responsible;[12]

the principle whereby a State must be liable for loss and damage caused to individuals as a result of breaches of Community law for which the State can be held responsible is inherent in the system of the Treaty;[13] a national court which considers, in a case concerning Community law, that the sole obstacle precluding it from granting interim relief is a rule of national law, must set aside that rule.[14]

12. These principles apply in the event of a breach of the Community's competition rules. Individuals and undertakings must have access to all procedural rules and remedies provided for by national law on the same conditions as would apply if a comparable breach of national law were involved. This equality of treatment concerns not only the definitive finding of a breach of directly effective Community law, but extends also to all legal means capable of contributing to effective legal protection.

III. THE COMMISSION'S LIMITED POWERS

13. The application of Community competition law by the national courts has considerable advantages for individuals and undertakings. The Commission cannot award damages for loss suffered as a result of an infringement of Article 93(3). Such claims may be brought only before the national courts. National courts can usually adopt interim measures and order the termination of infringements quickly. Before national courts, it is possible to combine a claim under Community law with a claim under national law. This is not possible in a procedure before the Commission. In addition, courts may award costs to the successful applicant. This is never possible in the administrative procedure before the Commission.

IV. APPLICATION OF ARTICLE 93(3)

14. Member States are required to notify to the Commission all plans to grant aid or to alter aid plans already approved. This also applies to aid that may qualify for automatic approval under Article 92(2), because the Commission has to check that the requisite conditions are met. The only exception to the notification obligation is for aid classed as *de minimis* because it does not affect trade between Member States significantly and thus does not fall within Article 92(1).[15]

15. The Commission receives notification of general schemes or programmes of aid, as well as of plans to grant aid to individual firms. Once a scheme has been authorised by the Commission, individual awards of aid under the scheme do not normally have to be notified. However, under some of the aid codes or frameworks for particular industries or particular types of aid, individual notification is required of all awards of aid or of awards exceeding a certain amount. Individual notification may also be required in some cases by the terms of the Commission's authorisation of a given scheme. Member States must notify aid which they wish to grant outside the framework of an authorised scheme. Notification is required in respect of planned measures, including plans to make financial transfers from public funds to public or private sector enterprises, which may involve aid within the meaning of Article 92(1).

16. The first question which national courts have to consider in an action under the last sentence of Article 93(3) is whether the measure constitutes new or existing State aid within the meaning of Article 92(1). The second question to be answered is whether the measure has been notified either individually or under a scheme and if so, whether the Commission has had sufficient time to come to a decision.[16]

17. With respect to aid schemes, a period of two months is considered by the Court of Justice to be "sufficient time", after which the Member State concerned may, after giving the Commission prior notice, implement the notified measure.[17] This period is reduced by the Commission voluntarily to 30 working days for individual cases and 20 working days under the "accelerated" procedure. The

periods run from the time the Commission is satisfied that the information provided by the Member State is sufficient to enable it to reach a decision.[18]

18. If the Commission has decided to initiate the procedure provided for in Article 93(2), the period during which the implementation of an aid measure is prohibited runs until the Commission has reached a positive decision. For non-notified aid measures, no deadline exists for the Commission's decision-making process, although the Commission will act as speedily as possible. Aid may not be awarded before the Commission's final decision.

19. If the Commission has not ruled on an aid measure, national courts can always be guided, in interpreting Community law, by the case-law of the Court of First Instance and the Court of Justice, as well as by decisions issued by the Commission. The Commission has published a number of general notices which may be of assistance in this regard.[19]

20. National courts should thus be able to decide whether or not the measure at issue is illegal under Article 93(3). Where national courts have doubts, they may and in some cases must request a preliminary ruling from the Court of Justice in accordance with Article 177.

21. Where national courts give judgment finding that Article 93(3) has not been complied with, they must rule that the measure at issue infringes Community law and take the appropriate measures to safeguard the rights enjoyed by individuals and undertakings.

V. EFFECTS OF COMMISSION DECISIONS

22. The Court of Justice has held[20] that a national court is bound by a Commission Decision addressed to a Member State under Article 93(2) where the beneficiary of the aid in question seeks to question the validity of the decision of which it had been informed in writing by the Member State concerned and where it had failed to bring an action for annulment of the decision within the time limits prescribed by Article 173 of the EC Treaty.

VI. COOPERATION BETWEEN NATIONAL COURTS AND THE COMMISSION

23. The Commission realises that the principles set out above for the application of Articles 92 and 93 by national courts are complex and may sometimes be insufficiently developed to enable them to carry out their judicial duties properly. National courts may therefore ask the Commission for assistance.

24. Article 5 of the EC Treaty establishes the principle of loyal and constant cooperation between the Community institutions and the Member States with a view to attaining the objectives of the Treaty, including implementation of Article 3(g), which provides for the establishment of a system ensuring that competition in the internal market is not distorted. This principle involves obligations and duties of mutual assistance, both for the Member States and for the Community institutions. Under Article 5, the Commission has a duty of cooperation with the judicial authorities of the Member States which are responsible for ensuring that Community law is applied and respected in the national legal order.

25. The Commission considers that such cooperation is essential in order to guarantee the strict, effective and consistent application of Community competition law. In addition, participation by the national courts in the application of competition law in the field of State aid is necessary to give effect to Article 93(3). The Treaty obliges the Commission to follow the procedure laid down in Article 93(2) before it can order reimbursement of aid which is incompatible with the common market.[21] The Court has ruled that Article 93(3) has direct effect and

that the illegality of an aid measure, and the consequences that flow therefrom, can never be validated retroactively by a positive decision of the Commission on an aid measure. Application of the rules on notification in the field of State aid therefore constitutes an essential link in the chain of possible legal action by individuals and undertakings.

26.   In the light of these considerations, the Commission intends to work towards closer cooperation with national courts in the following manner.

27.   The Commission is committed to a policy of openness and transparency. The Commission conducts its policy so as to give the parties concerned useful information on the application of competition rules. To this end, it will continue to publish as much information as possible about State aid cases and policy. The case-law of the Court of Justice and Court of First Instance, general texts on State aid published by the Commission, decisions taken by the Commission, the Commission's annual reports on competition policy and the monthly Bulletin of the European Union may assist national courts in examining individual cases.

28.   If these general pointers are insufficient, national courts may, within the limits of their national procedural law, ask the Commission for information of a procedural nature to enable them to discover whether a certain case is pending before the Commission, whether a case has been the subject of a notification or whether the Commission has officially initiated a procedure or taken any other decision.

29.   National courts may also consult the Commission where the application of Article 92 (1) or Article 93(3) causes particular difficulties. As far as Article 92(1) is concerned, these difficulties may relate in particular to the characterisation of the measure as State aid, the possible distortion of competition to which it may give rise and the effect on trade between Member States. Courts may therefore consult the Commission on its customary practice in relation to these issues. They may obtain information from the Commission regarding factual data, statistics, market studies and economic analyses. Where possible, the Commission will communicate these data or will indicate the source from which they can be obtained.

30.   In its answer, the Commission will not go into the substance of the individual case or the compatibility of the measure with the common market. The answer given by the Commission will not be binding on the requesting court. The Commission will make it clear that its view is not definitive and that the court's right to request a preliminary ruling from the Court of Justice pursuant to Article 177 is unaffected.

31.   It is in the interests of the proper administration of justice that the Commission should answer requests for legal and factual information in the shortest possible time. Nevertheless, the Commission cannot accede to such requests unless several conditions are met. The requisite data must actually be at its disposal and the Commission may communicate only non-confidential information.

32.   Article 214 of the EC Treaty requires the Commission not to disclose information of a confidential nature. In addition, the duty of loyal cooperation under Article 5 applies to the relationship between courts and the Commission, and does not concern the parties to the dispute pending before those courts. The Commission is obliged to respect legal neutrality and objectivity. Consequently, it will not accede to requests for information unless they come from a national court, either directly, or indirectly through parties which have been ordered by the court concerned to request certain information.

VII. FINAL REMARKS

33. This notice applies *mutatis mutandis* to relevant State aid rules, in so far as they have direct effect in the legal order of Member States, of—
  — the Treaty establishing the European Coal and Steel Community and provisions adopted thereunder, and
  — the Agreement on the European Economic Area.

34. This notice is issued for guidance and does not in any way limit the rights conferred on Member States, individuals or undertakings by Community law.

35. This notice is without prejudice to any interpretation of Community law which may be given by the Court of Justice and Court of First Instance of the European Communities.

36. A summary of the answers given by the Commission pursuant to this notice will be published annually in the Report on Competition Policy.

[6151]

NOTES

[1] The Court of Justice has described the roles of the Commission and the national courts in the following way—

  "9. As far as the role of the Commission is concerned, the Court pointed out in its judgment in Case 78/96, Steinlike and Weinlig v Germany (1977) ECR 595, at paragraph 9, that the intention of the Treaty, in providing through Article 93 for aid to be kept under constant review and supervised by the Commission, is that the finding that aid may be incompatible with the common market is to be arrived at, subject to review by the Court, by means of an appropriate procedure which it is the Commission's responsibility to set in motion.

  10. As far as the role of national courts is concerned, the Court held in the same judgment that proceedings may be commenced before national courts requiring those courts to interpret and apply the concept of aid contained in Article 92 in order to determine whether State aid introduced without observance of the preliminary examination procedure provided for in Article 93(3) ought to have been subject to this procedure.

  11. The involvement of national courts is the result of the direct effect which the last sentence of Article 93(3) of the Treaty has been held to have. In this respect, the Court stated in its judgment of 11 December 1973 in Case 120/73, Lorenz v Germany, (1973) ECR p 1471 that the immediate enforceability of the prohibition on implementation referred to in that Article extends to all aid which has been implemented without being notified and, in the event of notification, operates during the preliminary period, and if the Commission sets in motion the contentious procedure, until the final decision.

  14. ... The principal and exclusive role conferred on the Commission by Articles 92 and 93 of the Treaty, which is to hold aid to be incompatible with the common market where this is appropriate, is fundamentally different from the role of national courts in safeguarding rights which individuals enjoy as a result of the direct effect of the prohibition laid down in the last sentence of Article 93(3) of the Treaty. Whilst the Commission must examine the compatibility of the proposed aid with the common market, even where the Member State has acted in breach of the prohibition on giving effect to aid, national courts do no more than preserve, until the final decision of the Commission, the rights of individuals faced with a possible breach by State authorities of the prohibition laid down by the last sentence of Article 93(3)."

  Case C-354/90, Fédération nationale du commerce exterieur des produits alimentaires and Syndicat national des négociants et transformateurs de saumon v France (1991) ECR I-5505, paragraphs 9, 10, 11 and 14, at pp 5527 and 5528.

[2] With the exception of "existing" aid. Such aid may be implemented until the Commission has decided that it is incompatible with the common market: see Case C-387/92, Banco de Crédito Industrial, now Banco Exterior de Espana v Ayuntamiento de Valencia (1994) ECR I-877 and Case C-44/93, Namur-Les Assurances du Crédit v Office National du Ducroire and Belgium (1994) ECR I-3829.

[3] Case C-354/90, cited at footnote 1, paragraph 11 at p 5527.

[4] See the Court of Justice's judgment in Case 78/76, Steinlike and Weinlig v Germany (1977) ECR 595, paragraph 14: " ... a national court may have cause to interpret and apply the concept of aid contained in Article 92 in order to determine whether State aid introduced without observance of the preliminary examination procedure provided for in Article 93(3) ought to have been subject to this procedure".

⁵ For a recent formulation, see Advocate-General Jacob's opinion in Joined Cases C-278/92, C-279/92 and C-280/92, Spain v Commission, paragraph 28: " . . . State aid is granted whenever a Member State makes available to an undertaking funds which in the normal course of events would not be provided by a private investor applying normal commercial criteria and disregarding other considerations of a social, political or philanthropic nature".

⁶ The Court of Justice held in Case 290/83, Commission v France (1985) ECR p 439, that " . . . The prohibition contained in Article 92 covers all aid granted by a Member State or through State resources and there is no necessity to draw any distinction according to whether the aid is granted directly by the State or by public or private bodies established or appointed by it to administer the aid" (paragraph 14 at p 449).

⁷ A clear statement of this distinction is to be found in Advocate-General Darmon's opinion in Joined Cases C-72 and C-73/91, Sloman Neptun, (1993) ECR I-887.

⁸ Case C-234/89, Delimitis v Henninger Bräu (1991) ECR I-935; Commission notice on cooperation between national courts and the Commission in applying Articles 85 and 86 of the EC Treaty (OJ C39, 13.12.93, p 6). See Advocate-General Lenz's opinion in Case C-44/93, cited at footnote 2 (paragraph 106). See also Case C-2/88, Imm, Zwartveld (1990) ECR I-3365 and I-4405: "the Community institutions are under a duty of sincere cooperation with the judicial authorities of the Member States, which are responsible for ensuring that Community law is applied and respected in the national legal system" (paragraph 1 at p I-3366 and paragraph 10 at pp 4410 and 4411, respectively).

⁹ As the Court of Justice held in Case C-354/90, cited at footnote 1, paragraph 12 at p 5528: " . . . the validity of measures giving effect to aid is affected if national authorities act in breach of the last sentence of Article 93(3) of the Treaty. National Courts must offer to individuals in a position to rely on such breach the certain prospect that all the necessary inferences will be drawn, in accordance with their national law, as regards the validity of measures giving effect to the aid, the recovery of financial support granted in disregard of that provision and possible interim measures.".

¹⁰ Case 106/77, Amministrazione delle Finanze dello Stato v Simmenthal, (1978) ECR 629, (paragraph 21 at p 644). See also Case C-213/89, The Queen v Secretary of State for Transport, ex parte Factortame Ltd, et al, (1990) ECR I-2433, at p 2475.

¹¹ Joined Cases C-6/90 and C-9/90, Andrea Francovich et al v Italy, (1991) ECR I-5357. Other important cases are pending before the Court concerning the responsibilities of national courts in the application of Community law: Case C-48/93, The Queen v Secretary of State for Transport ex parte Factortame Ltd and others, (OJ C94, 3.4.93, p 13); Case C-46/93, Brasserie du Pêcheur SA v Germany (OJ C92, 2.4.93, p 4); Case C-312/93, SCS Peterbroeck, Van Campenhout & Cie v Belgian State (OJ C189, 13.7.93, p 9); Cases C-430 and C-431/93, J Van Schindel and JNC Van Veen v Stichting Pensioenfonds voor Fysiotherapeuten (OJ C338, 15.12.93, p 10).

¹² Francovich, cited at footnote 11, paragraph 33 at p 5414.

¹³ Francovich, cited at footnote 11, paragraph 35 at p 5414.

¹⁴ The Queen v Secretary of State for Transport ex parte Factortame Ltd, et al, cited at footnote 10.

¹⁵ See point 3.2 of the Community guidelines on State aid for SMEs (OJ C213, 19.8.92, p 2) and the letter to the Member States ref. IV/D/06878 of 23 March 1993, Competition Law in the European Communities, Volume II.

¹⁶ Case 120/73, Lorenz v Germany, (1973) ECR 1471.

¹⁷ Case 120/73, Lorenz v Germany, cited at footnote 16, paragraph 4 at p 1481; see also Case 84/42, Germany v Commission, (1984) ECR 1451, paragraph 11 at p 1488.

¹⁸ The Commission has issued a guide to its procedures in State aid cases: see Competition Law in the European Communities, Volume II.

¹⁹ The Commission publishes and updates from time to time a compendium of State aid rules (Competition Law in the European Communities, Volume II).

²⁰ Case C-188/92, TWD Textilwerke Deggendorf GmbH v Germany (1994) ECR I-833; see also Case 77/72, Capolongo v Maya, (1973) ECR 611.

²¹ The Commission has informed the Member States that " . . . in appropriate cases it may after giving the Member State concerned the opportunity to comment and to consider alternatively the granting of rescue aid, as defined by the Community guidelines — adopt a provisional decision ordering the Member State to recover any monies which have been disbursed in infringement of the procedural requirements. The aid would have to be recovered in accordance with the requirements of domestic law; the sum repayable would carry interest running from the time the aid was paid out." (Commission communication to the Member States supplementing the Commission's letter No SG(91) D/4577 of 4 March 1991 concerning the procedures for the notification of aid plans and procedures applicable when aid is provided in breach of the rules of Article 93(3) of the EC Treaty), not yet published.

GUIDELINES

on National Regional Aid

(1998/C 74/06)

(Text with EEA relevance)

NOTES
Date of publication in OJ: OJ C74, 10.3.98, p 9.

1. Introduction

The criteria applied by the Commission when examining the compatibility of national regional aid with the common market under Articles 92(3)(a) and 92(3)(c) of the EC Treaty have been set out in a number of documents of various sorts brought to the attention of the Member States and other interested parties.[1]

The growing number of these documents, their heterogeneous nature and the long time-frame involved, the changes in thinking and practice both within the Commission and within Member States and the need to concentrate aid and reduce distortions of competition make it necessary to aim for transparency, up-to-dateness and simplification by revising all the criteria currently applied and replacing the said document[2] with a single text. The text that follows seeks to meet this need.

The aid measures which form the subject-matter of these Guidelines ("regional aid") differ from the other categories of government support (in particular aid for R&D, environmental protection, or firms in difficulty) in that they are reserved for particular regions and have as their specific aim the development of those regions.[3]

Regional aid is designed to develop the less-favoured regions by supporting investment and job creation in a sustainable context. It promotes the expansion, modernisation and diversification of the activities of establishments located in those regions and encourages new firms to settle there. In order to foster this development and reduce the potential negative effects of any relocation, it is necessary to make the granting of such aid conditional on the maintenance of the investment and the jobs created during a minimum period in the less-favoured region.

In exceptional cases, such aid may not be enough to trigger a process of regional development, if the structural handicaps of the region concerned are too great. Only in such cases may regional aid be supplemented by operating aid.

The Commission considers that regional aid can play the role that is assigned to it effectively and hence justify the consequent distortions of competition, provided that it adheres to certain principles and obeys certain rules. Foremost among these principles is the exceptional nature of the instrument, in keeping with the letter and spirit of Article 92.

In fact, such aid is conceivable in the European Union only if it is used sparingly and remains concentrated on the most disadvantaged regions.[4] If aid were to become generalised and, as it were, the norm, it would lose all its incentive quality and its economic impact would be nullified. At the same time, the aid would interfere with the normal interplay of market forces and reduce the efficacy of the Community economy as a whole.

[6152]

NOTES
[1]   See Commission of the European Communities, Competition law in the European Communities, Volume IIA: Rules applicable to State aids, Brussels—Luxembourg, 1995, p 187 et seq.
[2]   The documents replaced by these Guidelines, including the annexes thereto, are as follows—
— Commission Communication to the Council (OJ C111, 4.11.1971, p 7);

— Commission Communication to the Council (COM(73) 1110, 27.6.1973);
— Commission Communication to the Council (COM(75) 77 final, 26.2.1975);
— Commission Communication to the Member States (OJ C31, 3.2.1979, p 9);
— Commission Communication to the Member States on the method for the application of Article 92(3)(a) and (c) to regional aid (OJ C212, 12.8.1988, p 2);
— Commission Communication to the Member States on the reference and discount rates applicable in France, Ireland and Portugal (OJ C10, 16.1.1990, p 8);
— Commission Communication to the Member States on the method of application of Article 92(3)(a) to regional aid (OJ C163, 4.7.1990, p 6);
— Commission Notice, addressed to Member States and other interested parties, concerning an amendment to Part II of the Communication on the method for the application of Article 92(3)(a) and (c) to regional aid (OJ C364, 20.12.1994, p 8).

The Guidelines are consistent with the criteria in the Council Resolution of 20 October 1971 (OJ C111, 4.11.1971, p 1).

As to the Notice concerning the reference and discount rate (OJ C273, 9.9.1997, p 3), this is no longer part of the documents relating to regional aid, since it concerns all State aid.

[3] Also regarded as regional aid is aid to SMEs that provides for increases to assist regional development.

[4] See the conclusions of the Council of 6–7 November 1995 on competition policy and industrial competitiveness.

2. Scope

The Commission will apply these Guidelines to regional aid granted in every sector of the economy apart from the production, processing and marketing of the agricultural products listed in Annex II of the Treaty, fisheries and the coal industry. In addition, some of the sectors they cover are also governed by rules aimed specifically at the sectors in question.[1]

A derogation from the incompatibility principle established by Article 92(1) of the Treaty may be granted in respect of regional aid only if the equilibrium between the resulting distortions of competition and the advantages of the aid in terms of the development of a less-favoured region[2] can be guaranteed. The weight given to the advantages of the aid is likely to vary according to the derogation applied, having a more adverse effect on competition in the situations described in Article 92(3)(a) than in those described in Article 92(3)(c).[3]

An individual *ad hoc* aid payment[4] made to a single firm, or aid confined to one area of activity, may have a major impact on competition in the relevant market, and its effects on regional development are likely to be too limited. Such aid generally comes within the ambit of specific or sectoral industrial policies and is often not in keeping with the spirit of regional aid policy as such.[5] The latter must remain neutral towards the allocation of productive resources between the various economic sectors and activities.

The Commission considers that, unless it can be shown otherwise, such aid does not fulfil the requirements set out in the preceding paragraph.[6]

Consequently, the derogations in question will normally be granted only for multisectoral aid schemes open, in a given region, to all firms in the sectors concerned.

[6153]

NOTES

[1] The sectors covered by special rules over and above those set out here are currently as follows: transport, steel, ship-building, synthetic fibres, and motor vehicles. In addition, specific rules apply to investment covered by the multi-sectoral framework for regional aid to large projects.

[2] See in this respect the judgment of the Court of Justice in Case 730/79 Philip Morris [1980] ECR 2671, at paragraph 17 and in Case C-169/95 Spain v Commission [1997] ECR I-135, at paragraph 20.

[3] See in this respect the judgment of the Court of First Instance in T-380/94 AIUFFASS and AKT [1996] ECR II-2169, at paragraph 54.

[4] See in this respect the judgment of the Court of Justice in Joined Cases C-278/92, C-279/92 and C-280/92, Spain v Commission [1994] ECR I-4103.

⁵ As a result, under the WTO Agreement on subsidies and countervailing measures, this type of aid has been expressly excluded from the category of non-actionable regional aid (authorized without scrutiny).

⁶ Ad hoc aid for firms in difficulty is governed by specific rules and is not conceived of as regional aid as such. The rules currently in force are those published in OJ C368, 23.12.1994, p 12.

3. Demarcation of regions

3.1. In order that the aid schemes directed at them may benefit from one of the derogations, the regions concerned must satisfy the conditions set forth in those derogations. The Commission establishes whether the conditions are met by applying predetermined analytical criteria.

3.2. In the light of the principle stated in the introduction to these Guidelines (that of the exceptional nature of the aid), the Commission considers *prima facie* that the total extent of assisted regions in the Community must remain smaller than that of unassisted regions. In practice, and using the most common unit of measurement of the scale of the aid (the percentage of population covered), this means that the total coverage of regional aid in the Community must be less than 50% of the Community population.

3.3 As the two derogations in question relate to regional problems of a different nature and intensity, priority must be given, within the limits of the total aid coverage referred to in point 3.2, to regions affected by the most acute problems.[1]

3.4. The demarcation of eligible regions must therefore lead to a spatial concentration of aid in accordance with the principles mentioned in points 3.2 and 3.3.

The derogation in Article 92(3)(a)

3.5. Article 92(3)(a) provides that aid to promote the economic development of areas where the standard of living is abnormally low or where there is serious underemployment may be considered compatible with the common market. As the Court of Justice of the European Communities has held, "the use of the words 'abnormally' and 'serious' in the exemption contained in Article 92(3)(a) shows that it concerns only areas where the economic situation is extremely unfavourable in relation to the Community as a whole".[2]

The Commission accordingly considers, following a tried and tested approach, that the conditions laid down are fulfilled if the region, being a NUTS[3] level II geographical unit, has a per capita gross domestic product (GDP), measured in purchasing power standards (PPS), of less than 75.0% of the Community average.[4] The GDP/PPS of each region and the Community average to be used in the analysis must relate to the average of the last three years for which statistics are available. These amounts are calculated on the basis of data furnished by the Statistical Office for the European Communities.

The derogation in Article 92(3)(c)

3.6. In contrast to Article 92(3)(a), where the situation in view is identified precisely and formally, Article 92(3)(c) allows greater latitude when it comes to defining the difficulties of a region that can be alleviated with the help of aid measures. The relevant indicators do not therefore necessarily boil down in this case to standards of living and underemployment. In any case, the appropriate framework for evaluating these difficulties may be provided not only by the Community as a whole but also by the relevant Member State in particular.

The Court of Justice, in Case 248/84 (see footnote 12), has expressed its views on these two matters (range of problems covered and reference framework for the analysis), as follows: "The exemption in Article 92(3)(c), on the other hand, is wider in scope inasmuch as it permits the development of certain areas without being restricted by the economic conditions laid down in Article 92(3)(a), provided such aid 'does not adversely affect trading conditions to an extent contrary to the common interest'. That provision gives the Commission power to authorise aid intended to further the economic development of areas of a Member State which are disadvantaged in relation to the national average".

3.7.　The regional aid covered by the derogation in point (c) must, however, form part of a coherent regional policy of the Member State and adhere to the principles of geographical concentration set out above. Inasmuch as it is intended for regions which are less disadvantaged than those to which point (a) relates, such aid is, to a greater extent than the latter, exceptional and can be allowed only to a very limited degree. This being so, only a small part of the national territory of a Member State may *prima facie* qualify for the aid in question. This is why the population coverage of regions falling under Article 92(3)(c) must not exceed 50% of the national population not covered by the derogation under Article 92(3)(a).[5]

On the other hand, the fact that the nature of such aid makes it possible to take account of the national peculiarities of a Member State does not exempt the aid from the need for scrutiny from the viewpoint of Community interests. The determination of the regions eligible in each Member State must therefore fit into a framework guaranteeing the overall coherence of such determination at Community level.[6]

3.8.　So as to afford national authorities sufficient latitude when it comes to choosing eligible regions without jeopardising the effectiveness of the system of checks operated by the Commission in respect of this type of aid and the equal treatment of all Member States, the determination of the regions eligible under the derogation in question consists of two parts—

— the fixing by the Commission, for each country, of a ceiling on the coverage of such aid,
— the selection of eligible regions.

The latter part will obey transparent rules but will also be sufficiently flexible to allow for the diversity of situations potentially justifying the application of the derogation. The aid coverage ceiling is designed to be conducive to the abovementioned flexibility in the choice of eligible regions whilst ensuring the uniform treatment required by acceptance of such aid from the Community point of view.

3.9.　To guarantee effective control of regional aid while contributing to the achievement of the objectives set out in Article 3 of the Treaty, in particular under points (g) and (j), the Commission sets an overall ceiling for the coverage of regional aid in the Community in terms of population. The overall ceiling covers all the regions eligible under the 92(3)(c) and 92(3)(a) derogations. Since the regions eligible for regional aid under the Article 92(3)(a) derogation and their global coverage at Community level are determined exogenously and automatically by applying the criterion of 75% of per capita GDP/PPS, it follows that the Commission decision on the overall ceiling defines, simultaneously, the ceiling on coverage under the Article 92(3)(c) derogation, at Community level. The Article 92(3)(c) ceiling is obtained by deducting from the overall ceiling the population of the regions eligible under the 92(3)(a) derogation. It is then distributed among the different Member States in the light of the relative socio-economic situation of the regions within each Member State, assessed in the context of the Community. The method of determining this percentage in each Member State is described in Annex III.

3.10.　The Member States notify to the Commission, under Article 93(3), the methodology and the quantitative indicators which they wish to use to determine the eligible regions, and the list of regions they propose for the (c) derogation and the relative intensities.[7] The percentage for the population of the regions concerned may not exceed the said ceiling on coverage for the purposes of the 92(3)(c) derogation.

3.10.1.The methodology must satisfy the following conditions—
— it must be objective,
— it must make it possible to measure the disparities in the socio-economic circumstances of the regions in question in the Member State concerned, highlighting significant differences,
— it must be presented in a clear, detailed fashion, to enable the Commission to assess its merits.

3.10.2.The indicators must satisfy the following conditions—
— their number, including both simple indicators and combinations of indicators, must be limited to five,
— they must be objective and relevant to the examination of the socio-economic circumstances of the regions,
— they must either be based on statistical series relating to the indicators used over a period including at least the three years prior to the moment of notification, or be derived from the last survey carried out, if the relevant statistics are not available on an annual basis,
— they must be drawn up by reliable statistical sources.

3.10.3.The list of regions must satisfy the following conditions—
— the regions must conform to NUTS level III or, in justified circumstances, to a different homogeneous geographical unit. Only one type of geographical unit may be submitted by each Member State,
— the individual regions proposed or the groups of contiguous regions must form compact zones, each of which must have a population of at least 100,000. If the population of the regions is less, a fictitious figure of 100,000 inhabitants will be used for the calculation of the percentage of the population covered. Exceptions to this rule are the NUTS level III regions with a population of less than 100,000, islands and other regions characterised by similar geographical isolation.[8] Where one region adjoins regions eligible for regional aid in other Member States, the rule applies to the whole complex formed by those regions,
— the list of regions must be arranged on the basis of the indicators set out at point 3.10.2. The regions proposed must show significant disparities (half of the standard deviation) compared with the average of the potential 92(3)(c) regions of the Member State concerned, in respect of one or other indicator used in the method.

3.10.4.Regions with a low population density—
— subject to the ceiling for each Member State mentioned at point 3.9, regions with a population density of less than 12.5 inhabitants per square kilometre[9] may also qualify for the derogation in question.

3.10.5.Consistency with the Structural Funds—
— to encourage the Member States to ensure consistency between the choice of such regions and the selection of those qualifying for Community assistance the regions eligible under the Structural Funds may also qualify for the derogation in question subject to the ceilings mentioned at point 3.9, and in accordance with the conditions set out in the second indent of point 3.10.3.

[6154]

NOTES

[1] The regions eligible under the derogation in paragraph (a) currently account for 22.7% of the Community population, compared with 24% for the regions eligible under the derogation in paragraph (c)

[2] Case 248/84 Germany v Commission [1987] ECR 4013, at paragraph 19.

[3] Nomenclature of Statistical Territorial Units.

[4] The underlying assumption being that the GDP indicator is capable of reflecting synthetically both the phenomena mentioned.

[5] Barring a transitional exception arising from the application of point 8 of Annex III to the Guidelines.

6   See, in this connection, the judgments of the Court of Justice in Cases 730/79 Philip Morris, at paragraph 26, and 310/85 Deufil [1987] ECR 901, at paragraph 18.

7   See points 4.8 and 4.9.

8   Because of the size of its population, Luxembourg is also exempt from this rule.

9   Eligibility criterion established by the Commission Notice cited at footnote 2, eighth indent.

4. Object, form and level of aid

4.1.   The object of regional aid is to secure either productive investment (initial investment) or job creation which is linked to investment. Thus this method favours neither the capital factor nor the labour factor.

4.2.   To ensure that the productive investment aided is viable and sound, the recipient's contribution[1] to its financing must be at least 25%.

The form of the aid is variable: grant, low-interest loan or interest rebate, government guarantee or purchase of a State shareholding on favourable terms, tax exemption, reduction in social security contributions, supply of goods and services at a concessionary price, etc.

In addition, aid schemes must lay down that an application for aid must be submitted before work is started on the projects.

4.3.   The level of the aid is defined in terms of intensity compared with reference costs. (see 4.5, 4.6 and 4.13)

Aid for initial investment

4.4.   Initial investment means an investment in fixed capital relating to the setting-up of a new establishment, the extension of an existing establishment, or the starting-up of an activity involving a fundamental change in the product or production process of an existing establishment (through rationalisation, diversification or modernisation).[2]

An investment in fixed capital undertaken in the form of the purchase of an establishment which has closed or which would have closed had it not been purchased may also be regarded as initial investment, unless the establishment concerned belongs to a firm in difficulty. In the latter case, aid for the purchase of an establishment may include an advantage for the firm in difficulty, which must be examined in accordance with the Guidelines on State aid for rescuing and restructuring firms in difficulty.[3]

4.5.   Aid for initial investment is calculated as a percentage of the investment's value. This value is established on the basis of a uniform set of items of expenditure (standard base) corresponding to the following elements of the investment: land, buildings and plant/machinery.[4]

In the event of a purchase, only the costs of buying these assets[5] should be taken into consideration (the transaction must take place under market conditions). Assets for whose acquisition aid has already been granted prior to the purchase should be deducted.

4.6.   Eligible expenditure may also include certain categories of intangible investment up to a limit of 25% of the standard base in the case of large firms.[6]

Such expenditure must be confined to expenditure entailed by the transfer of technology through the acquisition of—

— patents,

— operating or patented know-how licences,

— unpatented know-how.

Eligible intangible assets will be subject to the necessary conditions for ensuring that they remain associated with the recipient region eligible for the regional aid and, consequently, that they are not the subject of a transfer benefiting other regions, especially other regions not eligible for regional aid. To this end, eligible intangible assets will have to satisfy the following conditions in particular—

— they must be used exclusively in the establishment receiving the regional aid,

— they must be regarded as amortisable assets,

— they must be purchased from third parties under market conditions,

— they must be included in the assets of the firm and remain in the establishment receiving the regional aid for at least five years.

4.7.   Aid notified by the Member States must normally be expressed in gross terms, ie before tax.

In order to make (i) the various forms of aid comparable with one another and (ii) aid intensities comparable from one Member State to another, the Commission converts aid notified by Member States into aid expressed in net grant equivalent (NGE).[7]

4.8.   The intensity of the aid must be adapted to take account of the nature and intensity of the regional problems that are being addressed. A distinction must therefore be drawn from the outset between the intensities allowed in regions eligible under the derogation in point (a) and those allowed in regions eligible under the derogation in point (c). Regard has to be had in this connection to the fact that regions which are eligible under the derogation in Article 92(3)(c) are not characterised by an abnormally low standard of living or serious underemployment in the sense in which these terms are used in the derogation in point (a) of that paragraph. The distorting effects of aid are accordingly less justified there than in regions qualifying for exemption under point (a). This means that the admissible aid intensities are from the outset less high in regions qualifying for exemption under point (c) than in those qualifying for exemption under point (a).

In the case of regions falling under Article 92(3)(a), the Commission thus considers that the intensity of regional aid must not exceed the rate of 50% NGE except in the outermost regions,[8] where it may be as much as 65% NGE. In the Article 92(3)(c) regions, the ceiling on regional aid must not exceed 20% NGE in general, except in the low population density regions or in the outermost regions where it may be as high as 30% NGE.

In the NUTS level II regions eligible under Article 92(3)(a) whose per capita GDP/PPS is greater than 60% of the Community average, the intensity of regional aid must not exceed 40% NGE, except in the outermost regions, where it may be as high as 50% NGE.

In the regions eligible under Article 92(3)(c) which have both a higher per capita GDP/PPS and a lower unemployment rate than the respective Community average, the intensity of regional aid must not exceed 10% NGE except in the low population density regions or in the outermost regions, where it may be as high as 20% NGE. Exceptionally in the case of regions subject to the said ceiling of 10% NGE, higher intensities not exceeding the normal ceiling of 20% NGE may be approved for region (corresponding to NUTS level III or smaller) adjoining a region with Article 92(3)(a) status.

All the abovementioned ceilings constitute upper limits. Beneath these ceilings the Commission will ensure that the regional aid intensity is adjusted to reflect th seriousness and intensity of the regional problems addressed when examined in Community context.

4.9. The ceilings indicated in point 4.8 may be raised by the supplements for SMEs provided for in the Commission notice on aid for SMEs,[10] ie by 15 percentage points gross[11] in the case of regions qualifying for exemption under point (a) and by 10 percentage points gross in the case of regions qualifying for exemption under point (c). The final ceiling applies to the base for SMEs. These supplements for SMEs do not apply to transport firms.

4.10. Aid for initial investment must be made conditional, through its method of payment or through the conditions associated with its acquisition, on the maintenance of the investment in question for a minimum period of five years.

Aid for job creation

4.11. As was indicated in point 4.1, regional aid may also focus on job creation. However, unlike aid for job creation, which is defined in the Guidelines on aid to employment and relates to jobs not linked to an investment project,[12] we are concerned here solely with jobs linked to the carrying-out of an initial investment project.[13]

4.12. Job creation means a net increase in the number of jobs[14] in a particular establishment compared with the average over a period of time. Any jobs lost during that period must therefore be deducted from the apparent number of jobs created during the same period.[15]

4.13. As with investment aid, the aid for job creation provided for in these Guidelines must be tailored to the nature and intensity of the regional problems it addresses. The Commission considers that the amount of aid must not exceed a certain percentage of the wage cost[16] of the person hired, calculated over a period of two years. The percentage is equal to the intensity allowed for investment aid in the area in question.

4.14. Aid for job creation must be made conditional, through its method of payment or through the conditions associated with its acquisition, on the maintenance of the employment created during a minimum period of five years.

Operating aid

4.15. Regional aid aimed at reducing a firm's current expenses (operating aid) is normally prohibited. Exceptionally, however, such aid may be granted in regions eligible under the derogation in Article 92(3)(a) provided that (i) it is justified in terms of its contribution to regional development and its nature and (ii) its level is proportional to the handicaps it seeks to alleviate.[17] It is for the Member State to demonstrate the existence of any handicaps and gauge their importance.

4.16. In the outermost regions qualifying for exemption under Article 92(3)(a) and (c), and in the regions of low population density qualifying either for exemption under Article 92(3)(a) or under 92(3)(c) on the basis of the population density test referred to at point 3.10.4, aid intended partly to offset additional transport costs[18] may be authorised under special conditions.[19] It is up to the Member State to prove that such additional costs exist and to determine their amount.

4.17. With the exception of the cases mentioned in point 4.16, operating aid must be both limited in time and progressively reduced. In addition, operating aid intended to promote exports[20] between Member States is ruled out.

Rules on the cumulation of aid

4.18. The aid intensity ceilings laid down in accordance with the criteria set out at points 4.8 and 4.9, apply to the total aid—
— where assistance is granted concurrently under several regional schemes,
— whether the aid comes from local, regional, national or Community sources.

4.19. The job creation aid described in points 4.11 to 4.14 and the investment aid described in points 4.4 to 4.10 may be combined,[21] subject to the intensity ceiling laid down for the region.[22]

4.20. Where the expenditure eligible for regional aid is eligible in whole or in part for aid for other purposes, the common portion will be subject to the most favourable ceiling under the schemes in question.

4.21. Where the Member State lays down that State aid under one scheme may be combined with aid under other schemes, it must specify, for each scheme, the method by which it will ensure compliance with the conditions listed above.

[6155]

NOTES

[1] This minimum contribution of 25% must not contain any aid. This is not the case, for instance, where a loan carries an interest-rate subsidy or is backed by government guarantees containing elements of aid.

[2] Replacement investment is thus excluded from the concept. Aid for this type of investment falls within the category of operating aid, to which the rules described at points 4.15 to 4.17 apply.

Also excluded from this concept is aid for the financial restructuring of a firm in difficulty within the meaning of the Community Guidelines on State aid for rescuing and restructuring firms in difficulty (OJ C368, 23.12.1994, p 12).

Restructuring aid within the meaning of point 2.5 of the said Guidelines may be granted, in so far as it relates to investment measures (rationalisation, modernisation, diversification), without needing separate notification, under a scheme of regional aid. However, since such regional aid is part of proposed aid for the restructuring of a firm in difficulty, it must be taken into account in the examination carried out under the said Guidelines.

[3] For the text currently applicable, see footnote 10.

[4] In the transport sector, expenditure on the purchase of transport equipment (movable assets) cannot be included in the uniform set of items of expenditure (standard base). Such expenditure, therefore, is not eligible for aid for initial investment.

[5] Where a purchase is accompanied by other initial investment, the expenditure relating to the latter should be added to the cost of the purchase.

[6] For SMEs, the criteria and conditions applying are defined in the Community Guidelines on State aid for small and medium-sized enterprises, OJ C213, 23.7.1996, p 4.

[7] For the method used to calculate NGE, see Annex I.

[8] The outermost regions are: the French overseas departments (FOD), the Azores, Madeira and the Canary Islands (see Declaration 26 on the Outermost Regions of the Community, annexed to the Treaty on European Union).

[9] GDP and unemployment must be measured at NUTS level III.

[10] Regional aid supplements are also provided for in the case of aid for R&D and aid for environmental protection. The basis on which such aid is calculated is, however, different from that for regional aid (including the SME variant). The supplements in question, therefore, are added, not to the regional aid, but to the other type of aid concerned. The texts currently applicable to the two types of aid mentioned are, in the case of R&D, that published in OJ C45, 17.2.1996, p 5 and, in the case of environmental protection, that published in OJ C72, 10.3.1994, p 3.

[11] Aid intensity supplements in gross terms are used, as defined in the guidelines on aid for SMEs.

[12] For the version currently in force, see OJ C334, 12.12.1995, p 4.

[13] A job is deemed to be linked to the carrying-out of an investment project if it concerns the activity to which the investment relates and if it is created within three years of the investment's completion. During this period, the jobs created following an increase in the utilisation rate of the capacity created by the investment are also linked to the investment.

[14] The number of jobs corresponds to the number of annual labour units (ALU), ie the number of persons employed full time in one year, part-time and seasonal work being ALU fractions.

[15] It goes without saying that such a definition holds true as much for an existing establishment as for a new establishment.

[16] The wage cost comprises the gross wage, ie before tax, and the compulsory social security contributions. The Commission retains the right to use Community statistics on the average wage cost in the different Member States as a reference.

[17] Operating aid takes the form in particular of tax exemptions or reductions in social security contributions.

[18] Additional transport costs mean the extra costs occasioned by movements of goods within the borders of the country concerned. In no circumstances may such aid constitute export aid, nor must it

constitute measures having an equivalent effect to quantitative restrictions on imports, within the meaning of Article 30 of the EC Treaty.

[19] With regard to the special conditions for regions qualifying for the Article 92(3)(c) derogation under the population density criterion, see Annex II. As for the other regions eligible for aid to offset in part additional transport costs, the conditions applicable are similar to those in Annex II.

[20] See footnote 3 of the Notice on *de minimis* aid, OJ C68, 6.3.1996, p 9.

[21] The job creation aid and the investment aid provided for in these Guidelines may not be combined with the job creation aid defined in the Guidelines on aid to employment indicated in footnote 31, since it applies in different circumstances and at different times. However, increases in aid for particularly less-favoured categories of beneficiaries will be acceptable under arrangements to be laid down in the Guidelines on aid to employment.

[22] This condition is deemed to be met if the sum of the aid for the initial investor, expressed as a percentage of the investment, and of the job creation aid, expressed as a percentage of wage costs, does not exceed the most favourable amount resulting from application of either the ceiling set for the region in accordance with the criteria indicated at points 4.8 and 4.9 or the ceiling set for the region in accordance with the criteria indicated at point 4.13.

5. Regional aid map and declaration of compatibility of aid

5.1. The regions of a Member State eligible under the derogations and the ceilings on the intensity of aid for initial investment or the aid for job creation approved for each region together form a Member State's regional aid map.

5.2. Under Article 93(3) of the Treaty, the Member States notify the draft map drawn up in accordance with the criteria set out above in points 3.5, 3.10, 4.8 and 4.9. The Commission adopts the map in accordance with the procedure laid down in Article 93 of the Treaty, normally by a single decision for all the relevant regions of a Member State and for a fixed period. National regional aid maps will thus be reviewed periodically.

5.3. In the interests of consistency between the Commission's competition policy decisions and decisions concerning regions eligible under the Structural Funds, the period of validity of the maps is in principle aligned on the timetable for Structural Fund assistance.

5.4. Draft aid schemes are approved by the Commission either when the map is drawn up or subsequently, subject to the regions, ceilings and duration defined for the map.

5.5. The implementation of the schemes mentioned in point 5.4 forms the subject matter, on the part of Member States, of annual reports to the Commission in accordance with the rules in force.[1]

5.6. During the period of validity of the map, Member States may request adjustments to it, if it is shown that socio-economic conditions have changed significantly. Such changes may relate to the rates of intensity and the eligible regions, provided that the possible inclusion of new regions is offset by the exclusion of regions having the same population. The validity of the adjusted map expires on the date already set for the original map.

5.7. For regions losing their Article 92(3)(a) status as a result of the review of the regional aid map, and acquiring Article 92(3)(c) status, the Commission could accept, during a transitional period, a progressive reduction of the aid intensities for which such regions had been eligible under Article 92(3)(a), at a linear or faster rate, until the intensity ceiling corresponding to the application of points 4.8 and 4.9 above is reached.[2, 3] The transitional period should not exceed two years in the case of operating aid and four years in the case of aid for initial investment and job creation.

5.8. With a view to drawing up the map, Member States are invited to notify to the Commission under Article 93(3) of the Treaty, in addition to the list of regions they propose as being eligible for the derogations in question and the ceilings on intensity, any other factors that need to be taken into account in determining a framework scheme for aid schemes (purpose and form of the aid, size of firms, etc) which they propose to adopt, whether at central or regional and local level. During the period of validity of the map and within the limits of its duration, all schemes conforming to this framework scheme may be notified in the context of an accelerated procedure.

[6156]

NOTES

¹ For the rules currently in force, see the Commission letter to the Member States of 22 February 1994 as modified by Commission letter to Member States of 2 August 1995.

² The transitional provisions do not apply to the parts of NUTS II regions losing their Article 92(3)(a) status which, where the additional population-density percentage obtained by applying the second adjustment at point 8 of Annex III to these Guidelines is not available, would have had to be excluded from the new aid map.

³ In view of its particularly difficult situation, Northern Ireland will retain its status as an exceptional region and its ceiling will be 40%.

6. Entry into force, implementation and review

6.1. Except for the transitional provisions set out in points 6.2 and 6.3 below, the Commission will assess the compatibility of regional aid with the common market on the basis of these Guidelines as soon as they are applicable. However, aid proposals which are notified before these Guidelines are communicated to the Member States and on which the Commission has not yet adopted a final decision will be assessed on the basis of criteria in force at the time of notification.

In addition, the Commission will propose appropriate measures under Article 93(1) of the EC Treaty to the Member States to ensure that all the regional aid maps and all the regional aid schemes in force on 1 January 2000 are compatible with these Guidelines.

In this connection, the Commission will propose, as an appropriate measure under Article 93(1), that the Member States limit the validity of all lists of assisted regions approved by the Commission without an expiry date, or with an expiry date after 31 December 1999, to 31 December 1999.

The Commission will also propose, as an appropriate measure under Article 93(1), that the Member States amend all existing regional aid schemes which will be in force after 31 December 1999, so as to make them compatible with these Guidelines from 1 January 2000, and that they communicate the proposed changes within six months.

6.2. Since the eligibility for regional aid under the Article 92(3)(a) and (c) derogations of most of the assisted regions has been approved until 31 December 1999, and with a view to ensuring equitable treatment of the Member States until that date, the Commission may derogate from these Guidelines until 31 December 1999, with regard to examination of the eligibility of the lists of assisted regions (new lists or amendments) notified prior to 1 January 1999, provided that the validity of the said lists expires on 31 December 1999. In such cases, the Commission will continue to base itself on the method laid down in its Communication.¹

6.3. Also with a view to ensuring equitable treatment of the Member States, the Commission may derogate from these Guidelines until 31 December 1999, with regard to the examination of the compatibility of the aid intensities and ceilings on combination proposed in new schemes, *ad hoc* cases and modifications of existing schemes notified prior to 1 January 1999, provided that the validity of the said intensities and ceilings on combination expires on 31 December 1999 or that the intensities and ceilings on combination proposed from 1 January 2000 are compatible with these Guidelines.

6.4 The Commission will review these Guidelines within five years of their becoming applicable. It may, in addition, decide to amend them at any time, if this should be necessary for reasons associated with competition policy or in order to take account of other Community policies and international commitments.

[6157]

NOTES

1 Commission Communication on the method for the application of Article 92(3)(a) and (c) to regional aid: see footnote 2, fifth indent.

ANNEX I
NET GRANT EQUIVALENT OF INVESTMENT AID

The method of calculating the net grant equivalent (NGE) is used by the Commission in its assessment of aid schemes notified by the Member States. In principle, therefore, the Member States do not have to apply it, and it is published here simply for reasons of transparency.

1. GENERAL PRINCIPLES

The calculation of net grant equivalent (NGE) consists in reducing all the forms of aid connected with an investment[1] to a common measure irrespective of the country concerned, ie the net intensity, for the purposes of comparing them with each other or with a predetermined ceiling. What is involved is an *ex ante* comparative method that does not always reflect accounting practice.

The net intensity represents the final benefit which a firm is deemed to derive from the value without tax of the aid in relation to the assisted investment. This calculation may take account only of fixed capital expenditure corresponding to land, building and plant, which represent the standard base.

In the case of schemes whose base includes supplementary expenditure, the latter must be limited to a certain proportion of the standard base. Thus, all schemes will be examined, in the light of their intensities reduced to the expenditure appearing in the standard base, as shown in the following examples.[2]

Example 1

— Base of scheme: plant
— Maximum intensity of scheme: 30%

As all the expenditure eligible for the scheme appears in the standard base, the Commission will take the maximum intensity of the scheme, ie 30%, into account without further ado. If the intensity ceiling authorised by the Commission in the region in question is 30%, the scheme will be considered compatible in this respect.

Example 2

— Base of scheme: plant, buildings + patents up to 20% of the preceding expenditure
— Maximum intensity of scheme: 30%

All the expenditure eligible for the scheme appears either in the standard base (plant, buildings) or in the list of eligible intangible expenditure (patents). The latter expenditure may not exceed 25% of the standard base. In these circumstances, the Commission will take the maximum intensity of the scheme, ie 30%, into account without further ado. If the intensity ceiling authorised by the Commission in the region in question is 30%, the scheme will be considered compatible in this respect.

Example 3

— Base of scheme: buildings, plant, land + stocks up to 50% of the preceding expenditure

— Maximum intensity of scheme: 30%

The Commission will take into account the maximum intensity of the scheme reduced to the standard base, ie 30% x 1.5 = 45%. If the intensity ceiling authorised by the Commission in the region in question is 30%, the scheme will not be considered compatible, unless its intensity is reduced to 30%/1.5 = 20%.

Example 4

— Base of scheme: buildings

— Maximum intensity of scheme: 60%

If the regional ceiling authorised by the Commission is 30%, there is nothing to ensure that the aid will comply with the ceiling. The intensity provided for by the scheme is higher than the regional ceiling, but it is applied to a reduced base. The scheme will therefore not be considered compatible in this respect, unless an express condition is added concerning compliance with the regional ceiling applied to the complete base.

The determination of the NGE is based solely on calculation of tax and present value, except in the case of certain forms of aid which require specific treatment. Such calculations are based on elements supplied by the aid scheme or the tax law of the country concerned and on certain parameters established by convention.

1.1. **Taxation**

The intensity of aid must be calculated after taxation, ie after having deducted the taxes payable on it, and in particular taxes on company profits. This is the basis for the term Net Grant Equivalent (NGE), which represents the aid accruing to the recipient after payment of the relevant tax, assuming that the enterprise makes a profit right from the first year, so that maximum tax is charged on the aid.

1.2. **Discounting**

Present value is calculated at various stages in the determination of an NGE. First, when aid and/or investment expenditure is staggered over time, the actual timing of aid disbursement and expenditure must be taken into account. Consequently, the investment expenditure and aid payments are discounted back to the end of the year in which the enterprise made its first depreciation write-off. Second, the present value is calculated of benefits obtained on repayment of a subsidised loan, or of the tax charged on a grant.

The rate used in such cases is the reference/discount rate determined by the Commission for each Member State. In addition to being used as the discount rate, it is also used to calculate the interest subsidy on a low-interest loan.

1.3. **Specific cases**

In addition to the taxation and discounting calculations described above, some forms of aid require specific handling. Thus, in the case of aid for the renting of a building, the aid is measured by discounting the differences between the rent paid by the enterprise and a theoretical rent equivalent to the reference rate applied to the value of the building, plus an amount corresponding to depreciation for the building in the year in question. A similar method is used for aid to finance leasing.[3]

In the case of aid for the renting of land, the theoretical rent is calculated on the basis of the reference rate, minus the rate of inflation, applied to the value of the land.

[6158]

NOTES

[1] Tax aid may be considered to be aid connected with an investment where it is based on an amount invested in the region. In addition, any tax aid may be connected with an investment if one sets a ceiling expressed as a percentage of the amount invested in the region. Where the grant of tax aid is spread over

several years, any balance remaining at the end of a given year may be carried over to the following year and increased in accordance with the reference rate.

   [2] This system of recalculating intensities does not apply to the intangible investments referred to at point 4.6 of the main text.

   [3] It should be noted that the expenditure associated with the purchase of the land or the building by the renting firm may be considered as eligible, provided that the need for the aid in question is demonstrated.

2. NET GRANT EQUIVALENT OF INVESTMENT AID IN THE FORM OF A CAPITAL GRANT

2.1. General

Investment aid given to an enterprise in the form of a capital grant is expressed first as a percentage of the investment, representing the nominal grant equivalent or the gross grant equivalent.

According to the common assessment method, the Net Grant Equivalent (NGE) of aid is the benefit accruing to the recipient after payment of taxes on company profits.

In most cases, grants are not taxable in themselves, but are deducted from the value of the depreciable investment. This means that the investor depreciates a smaller amount each year than if he had not received aid. Since depreciation amounts are deductible from taxable profits, a grant increases the proportion taken by the State each year in the form of tax on company profits.

The taxation method applying to grants described above, which consists in adding the grant to profits in step with depreciation, is the one most commonly used in all the Member States, but other taxation methods are encountered in certain schemes.

2.2. Calculation examples

Example 1: The aid is not subject to tax

In all Member States, grants are generally entered in the accounts as income and are made subject to tax. It may be, however, particularly in the case of certain R&D aid, that they are exempt from tax. In this case, the NGE is equal to the nominal grant.

Example 2: The investment involves only one category of expenditure and the grant is fully subject to tax at the end of the first financial years

This means that the full grant is subject to corporate profits tax from the first year onward. This convention is not excessive, if one remembers that firms, which generally record a loss in their first years of operation, can carry over their losses for several financial years.

To calculate the NGE of the grant, the amount of tax charged is deducted from it.

For instance: investment: 100

                  nominal grant: 20

                  rate of tax: 40.0%

[The tax charged on the grant is thus $20 \times 40\% = 8$

The NGE will thus be: $(20 - 8)/100 = 12\%$

Example 3: The investment involves only one category of expenditure and the grant is subject to tax on a straight-line basis over five years.

Here the grant is subject to tax in equal portions over five years. One fifth of the aid will thus be added to profits each year for five years. To calculate the NGE, the discounted amounts of tax charged each year on each fifth under the tax arrangements applicable are deducted from the grant.

For instance: investment: 100
                 nominal grant: 20
                 rate of tax: 40.0%
                 discount rate: 8%

The table below shows how the taxes charged each year, and the discounted values, are calculated—

Period	Tax charged on grant (1)	Discount factor (2)	Discounted value (1) x (2)
End of 1st year	(20/5) x 40%	1.0	1.600
End of 2nd year	(20/5) x 40%	$1/(1 + 0.08)^1$	1.481
End of 3rd year	(20/5) x 40%	$1/(1 + 0.08)^2$	1.372
End of 4th year	(20/5) x 40%	$1/(1 + 0.08)^3$	1.270
End of 5th year	(20/5) x 40%	$1/(1 + 0.08)^4$	1.176
		Total	6.900

The total in the last column represents the sum of the discounted taxes charged each year. It has to be deducted from the nominal grant to obtain the Net Grant Equivalent.

Thus the NGE is: $(20 - 6.9)/100 = 13.1\%$

Note: The tax charged on the grant is discounted at the end of the first year on the assumption that this is the date when the enterprise makes its first depreciation write-off.

Example 4: The investment involves three categories of capital expenditure: land, buildings and plant, taxed over different timescales

The three types of expenditure constitute what is referred to as the standard base for aid. Expenditure is apportioned within the standard base using a breakdown which differs by Member State, as shown in the following table.

	Land	Buildings	Plant
Belgium	5	40	55
Germany	5	30	65
France	5	50	45
Italy	5	30	65
Luxembourg	5	50	45
Netherlands	5	40	55
United Kingdom	10	20	70
Denmark	5	45	50
Greece	3	27	70
Spain	5	40	55
Ireland	5	50	45
Portugal	3	25	72
Austria	5	30	65
Finland	1	19	80
Sweden	5	45	50

These factors are used to calculate the theoretical NGEs under aid schemes. In individual cases of aid, on the other hand, the actual apportionment breakdown of the three categories of expenditure in the standard base is used.

As the timescale over which a grant is subject to tax differs according to the category of expenditure, the first step is to allocate the grant proportionally among the items forming the base of the aid.

The next step is to calculate the amounts charged as tax, separately for each category of expenditure (the calculations are of the same kind as those in Example 3).

Lastly, the taxes are deducted from the nominal grant in order to arrive at the NGE—

NGE = Nominal grant less—
— The tax charged on aid allocated to land
— The tax charged on aid allocated to buildings
— The tax charged on aid allocated to plant

For instance:	investment:	100
	of which:	— land: 3 not depreciable
		— buildings: 33 straight-line depreciation over 20 years
		— plant: 64 decreasing-line depreciation over 5 years
	normal grant:	20
	rate of tax:	55%
	discount rate:	8%

To calculate the tax on aid allocated to land

In general, land is not depreciable. Assuming that the aid is to be subject to tax at the same pace as depreciation, aid granted to land is not taxed and no tax is to be deducted from the grant made in respect of land.

To calculate the tax on aid allocated to buildings

Assuming that the aid allocated to buildings is to be subject to tax in equal portions at the same pace as depreciation, ie over 20 years—
— the nominal grant allocated to buildings would be: 20 x 33% = 6.6
— each year, the portion of the grant included in profits would be: 6.6/20 = 0.33
— the amount of tax charged on that portion would be: 0.33 x 55% = 0.18

An amount of 0.18 would be due from profits each year for 20 years in respect of the grant made for buildings. If this stream of amounts is discounted at the end of the first year (same kind of calculation as in the table in Example 3), the total tax charged in the period on the aid grant to buildings will be 1.925.

To calculate the tax on aid allocated to plant

Let us assume that the aid allocated to plant is to be subject to tax at the same pace as depreciation, ie by the decreasing-line method, over five years, at the following rates: 40%, 24%, 14.4%, 10.8% and 10.8%.

Unlike the case of buildings, taxation here is different each year. The tax will therefore have to be calculated year by year. The share of the nominal grant allocated to plant is 20 x 64% = 12.8.

To calculate the tax charges

Period	Tax charged on grant (1)	Discount factor (2)	Discounted value (1) x (2)
End of 1st year	12.8 x 40% x 55%	1.0	2.816
End of 2nd year	12.8 x 24% x 55%	$1/(1 + 0.08)^1$	1.564
End of 3rd year	12.8 x 14.4% x 55%	$1/(1 + 0.08)^2$	0.869

End of 4th year	12.8 x 10.8% x 55%	$1/(1 + 0.08)^3$	0.604
End of 5th year	12.8 x 10.8% x 55%	$1/(1 + 0.08)^4$	0.559
		Total	6.412

To calculate the NGE—

— nominal grant   20

less—

— tax charged on aid allocated to land   0

— tax charged on aid allocated to buildings   –1.925

x

— tax charged on aid allocated to plant   –6.412

                    NGE   11.6%

Notes:

1. The taxation of grants, referred to in the common method of assessing aid, is governed both by the tax laws of the Member States concerned and by any special arrangements under the scheme in question.

2. For the purposes of determining an NGE, it is therefore necessary to have precise information on—
   — the scale of tax rates on profits in the country concerned,
   — the depreciation rules in force, or the specific method of incorporating aid into profits prescribed by the scheme in question.

[6159]

3. NET GRANT EQUIVALENT OF INVESTMENT AID IN THE FORM OF A SUBSIDISED LOAN

3.1. General

Investment aid given to an enterprise in the form of a subsidised loan is expressed first as the number of percentage points of the rebate, ie the difference between the reference rate and the rate charged by the lender.

The sole effect of the interest rebate is to reduce interest charges, since it is assumed that capital repayments are carried out in the same way whether the interest rate is normal or reduced.

This benefit obtained on repayment of the loan is expressed as a percentage of the investment, as for capital grants. This gives the nominal grant equivalent or gross grant equivalent.

This does not represent the final benefit which the enterprise derives from the interest subsidy. Since interest charges are deductible from taxable profits, an interest subsidy means the loss of part of such tax benefit by increasing the share taken by the State in the form of tax on company profits.

Consequently, the net grant equivalent (NGE) is obtained by deducting from the gross grant equivalent the tax charged by the State on the increase in taxable profits that is attributable to the rebate.

As in the case of a grant, the NGE of a subsidised loan is based on elements supplied either by the aid scheme or by the tax law of the country in question, plus any other factors established by convention.

The following elements are needed to calculate the NGE of investment aid in the form of a subsidised loan—
   — period of the loan,

— length of the grace period, ie the initial period when no repayments need to be made, interest being paid on the total amount of principal,
— number of percentage points of the rebate,
— duration of the rebate, not necessarily the same as the loan,
— amount of the loan as a percentage or proportion of the investment,
— reference/discount rate,
— rate of tax.

It is also necessary to know the terms for repayment of the loan. In most cases the loan is repaid on a straight-line basis, in equal portions, interest being due on the balance outstanding. Repayment is occasionally by constant annual instalments, in which case this is taken into account in calculating the NGE.

3.2. Calculation examples

Example 1

1. *Parameters*
— the loan is for ten years with straight-line repayment and no grace period,
— the rebate is three percentage points throughout the period of the loan,
— the loan is for 40% of the investment,
— the reference/discount rate is 8%,
— the rate of tax is 35%.

2. *Calculation of the unit gift element*

The unit gift element is the nominal grant equivalent of a one-point interest rabete on a loan of 100% of the investment, taking account of the characteristics of the aid used as parameters. It is calculated as follows—

End of year No	Loan: balance outstanding	1-point rebate	Benefit obtained	Discount factor	Discounted value (*)
	(1)	(2)	(1) x (2)	(3)	(1) x (2) x (3)
1	100	1%	1	$1/(1+0.08)^1$	0.926
2	90	1%	0.9	$1/(1+0.08)^2$	0.772
3	80	1%	0.8	$1/(1+0.08)^3$	0.635
4	70	1%	0.7	$1/(1+0.08)^4$	0.515
5	60	1%	0.6	$1/(1+0.08)^5$	0.408
6	50	1%	0.5	$1/(1+0.08)^6$	0.315
7	40	1%	0.4	$1/(1+0.08)^7$	0.233
8	30	1%	0.3	$1/(1+0.08)^8$	0.162
9	20	1%	0.2	$1/(1+0.08)^9$	0.100
10	10	1%	0.1	$1/(1+0.08)^{10}$	0.046
				Unit gift element:	4.112

(*) Discounting starts at the beginning of the first year.

3. *Calculation of net grant equivalent*

The net grant equivalent is obtained simply by multiplying the unit gift element by the characteristics of the aid (three-point rebate, 40% share, non-taxable portion of aid: $(1 - 35\%)$—

$$NGE = 4.112 \times 3 \times 40\% \times (1 - 35\%) = 3.21\%$$

Example 2

1. *Parameters*

The parameters are the same as in Example 1, but with a two-year grace period from repayment. This means that capital is not repaid in the first two years. The ten-year loan will thus be repaid in eight equal portions from the third to the tenth year. Interest is payable during the ten years on the balance outstanding.

2. *Calculation of unit gift element*

End of year No	Loan: balance outstanding	1-point rebate	Benefit obtained	Discount factor	Discounted value (*)
	(1)	(2)	(1) x (2)	(3)	(1) x (2) x (3)
1	100	1%	1	$1/(1 + 0.08)^1$	0.926
2	100	1%	1	$1/(1 + 0.08)^2$	0.857
3	100	1%	1	$1/(1 + 0.08)^3$	0.794
4	87.5	1%	0.875	$1/(1 + 0.08)^4$	0.643
5	75.0	1%	0.750	$1/(1 + 0.08)^5$	0.510
6	62.5	1%	0.625	$1/(1 + 0.08)^6$	0.394
7	50	1%	0.500	$1/(1 + 0.08)^7$	0.292
8	37.5	1%	0.375	$1/(1 + 0.08)^8$	0.203
9	25.0	1%	0.250	$1/(1 + 0.08)^9$	0.125
10	12.5	1%	0.125	$1/(1 + 0.08)^{10}$	0.058
				Unit gift element:	4.802%

(*) Discounting starts at the beginning of the first year.

3. *To calculate the net grant equivalent*

As in Example 1, the unit gift element is multiplied by the number of rebate points, the proportion of expenditure covered by the loan and the complement to unity of the rate of tax—

$$NGE = 4.802 \times 3 \times 40\% \times (1 - 35\%) = 3.75\%$$

Note: It will be seen that, other things being equal, the result of introducing a grace period from capital repayments is to increase the NGE. The grace period increases the balance due each year and hence the benefit attributable to the rebate and, consequently, the unit gift element.

Example 3

1. *Parameters*

The same facts as in Example 2, but the loan is to be repaid in constant annual instalments.

In this case, the calculation method differs fundamentally from that used in the preceding two examples: first the "normal" annual instalments excluding the interest rebate are calculated, then the "rebated" instalments; the difference between the two series is established year by year, and the results discounted in order to obtain the grant equivalent.

2. *To calculate the grant equivalent*

The constant annual instalments, expressed as a percentage of the loan, are calculated as follows—

$$A = i/(1 - r^n)$$

where $r = 1/(1 + i)$

i being the interest rate and n the number of years for which the instalment is calculated. The calculations below are based on a loan of 100 units—

Year	Normal instalment	Rebated annual instalment	Benefit obtained	Discount factor	Discounted value (*)
	(1)	(2)	(3)	(4)	(3) x (4)
1	8	5	3	$1/(1 + 0.08)^1$	2.778
2	8	5	3	$1/(1 + 0.08)^2$	2.572
3	17.401	15.472	1.929	$1/(1 + 0.08)^3$	1.532

4	17.401	15.472	1.929	$1/(1 + 0.08)^4$	1.418
5	17.401	15.472	1.929	$1/(1 + 0.08)^5$	1.313
6	17.401	15.472	1.929	$1/(1 + 0.08)^6$	1.216
7	17.401	15.472	1.929	$1/(1 + 0.08)^7$	1.126
8	17.401	15.472	1.929	$1/(1 + 0.08)^8$	1.042
9	17.401	15.472	1.929	$1/(1 + 0.08)^9$	0.965
10	17.401	15.472	1.929	$1/(1 + 0.08)^{10}$	0.894
				Grant equivalent:	14.85%

(*) Discounting starts at the beginning of the first year.

3. To calculate the net grant equivalent

The net grant equivalent is obtained by multiplying the grant equivalent by the proportion, then deducting the portion charged as tax—

$$NGE = 14.85 \times 40\% \times (1 - 35\%) = 3.86\%$$

Note: If there is no grace period from repayment, the NGE calculated in the same way is 3.41%.

3.3. Formula for calculating the NGE of a subsidised loan

The preceding methods, which can easily be transposed to a spreadsheet, make it possible to calculate the NGE of a low-interest loan according to the characteristics of the case in question. In standard cases, the NGE may also be calculated direct by means of the following formulae.

1. Terms
  — i is the reference rate per interval and $r = 1/(1 + i)$
  — i' is the subsidised rate per maturity interval and $r' = 1/(1 + i')$
  — P is the period (in number of maturity intervals) of the loan
  — Q is the proportion
  — T is the rate of tax
  — F is the period, in number of intervals, of any grace period from repayment of principal: during the grace period, only interest on the loan is repaid, at the subsidised rate.
    (F = 0 where there is no grace period)

2. Straight-line repayment

$$NGE = (1 - T)\, Q\, (1 - i'/i)\, (1 + (r^P - r^F)/i \times (P - F))$$

3. Repayment in constant annual instalments

$$NGE = (1 - T)\, Q\, [1 - (i'/i) \times (1 - r^F + (r^F - r^P)/1 - r'^{P-F})]$$

[6160]

ANNEX II
AID TO OFFSET ADDITIONAL TRANSPORT COSTS IN REGIONS QUALIFYING FOR EXEMPTION UNDER ARTICLE 92(3)(C) ON THE BASIS OF THE POPULATION DENSITY TEST

Conditions to be met
— aid may serve only to compensate for the additional cost of transport. The Member State concerned will have to show that compensation is needed on objective grounds. There must never be overcompensation. Account will have to be taken here of other schemes of assistance to transport,
— aid may be given only in respect of the extra cost of transport of goods inside the national borders of the country concerned. It must not be allowed to become export aid,

— aid must be objectively quantifiable in advance, on the basis of an aid-per-kilometre ratio or on the basis of an aid-per-kilometre and an aid-per-unit-weight ratio, and there must be an annual report drawn up which, among other things, shows the operation of the ratio or ratios,

— the estimate of additional cost must be based on the most economical form of transport and the shortest route between the place of production or processing and commercial outlets,

— aid may be given only to firms located in areas qualifying for regional aid on the basis of the new population density test. Such areas will be made up essentially of NUTS level III geographic regions with a population density of less than 12.5 inhabitants per square kilometre. However, a certain flexibility is allowed in the selection of areas, subject to the following limitations—

— flexibility in the selection of areas must not mean an increase in the population covered by transport aid,

  — the NUTS III parts qualifying for flexibility must have a population density of less than 12.5 inhabitants per square kilometre,

  — they must be contiguous with NUTS III regions which satisfy the low population density test,

  — their population must remain low compared with the total coverage of the transport aid,

— no aid may be given towards the transport or transmission of the products of businesses without an alternative location (products of the extractive industries, hydroelectric power stations, etc),

— transport aid given to firms in industries which the Commission considers sensitive (motor vehicles, synthetic fibres, shipbuilding and steel) must always be notified in advance and will be subject to the industry guidelines in force.

[6161]

ANNEX III

METHOD OF DETERMINING THE CEILINGS ON THE POPULATION COVERED BY
THE 92(3)(C) DEROGATION

1.   The Commission first fixes an overall ceiling on the coverage of regional aid in the Community. This determines the maximum percentage of the population which the regions eligible for the Article 92(3) regional derogations in the Community may together account for.

2.   The regions eligible for regional aid under the derogation in Article 92(3)(a), and their overall coverage at Community level, are determined exogenously and automatically by the application of the criterion of 75.0% of per capita GDP expressed in purchasing power standards (PPS). The Commission's decision on the overall ceiling, therefore, simultaneously defines the ceiling on coverage under the Article 92(3)(c) derogation, at Community level. The Article 92(3)(c) ceiling is obtained by deducting from the overall ceiling the population of the regions eligible under the 92(3)(a) derogation.

3.   The distribution of the Article 92(3)(c) Community ceiling between the different Member States is effected by using a distribution key (see section I), which takes account of regional disparities in a national and Community context.

The results thus obtained are then adjusted to take account of certain other aspects (see section II).

1. DISTRIBUTION KEY

4.   The distribution key for the Article 92(3)(c) Community ceiling is calculated on the basis of the population of the regions which, at national level, have a minimum disparity in terms of per capita GDP/PPS and/or unemployment, defined in relation to certain thresholds (see point 5).

The geographical unit used is NUTS level III. For each NUTS III region, an average value over three years is calculated for per capita GDP/PPS and unemployment indices, defined in relation to the national average. The per capita GDP/PPS and unemployment rate indicators are supplied by Eurostat.

5. The abovementioned thresholds are calculated for each of the two criteria (per capital GDP/PPS and unemployment), and for each of the Member States concerned. The calculation is carried out in two stages. The first establishes an identical basic threshold for all Member States, set at 85 for per capita GDP and 115 for the unemployment rate. In the second stage, the basic thresholds are adjusted to take account of the relative situation of each of the Member States compared with the average for the Community. The formula applied is as follows—

$$\text{Threshold} = 1/2 \text{ x (Basic threshold + (Basic threshold x 100/European index))}$$

where the European index expresses the position of the different Member States, in terms of unemployment or per capita GDP/PPS, as a percentage of the corresponding Community average. The European index is calculated as an average value over the same three-year period as for the regional indices.

Thus, the more favourable a Member State's situation as regards unemployment or the standard of living, the more selective the thresholds used for the distribution of the ceiling on 92(3)(c) coverage, and vice versa.

However, so that the unemployment criterion does not become too rigorous, the corresponding threshold is subject to a ceiling of 150. This facilitates the granting of regional aid in Member States which show considerable disparities in domestic unemployment but whose situation does not seem that unfavourable at Community level. Since for the per capita GDP/PPS threshold the differences observed between the Member States are small, it has not been thought necessary to establish a minimum level.

6. The regional indices are then compared with the abovementioned thresholds, which makes it possible to determine whether the region concerned shows a sufficient regional disparity to be taken into account in the calculation of the distribution key.

The population of all the regions not eligible for regional aid under the Article 92(3)(a) derogation which show a sufficient regional disparity compared with at least one of the two abovementioned thresholds is aggregated for each of the Member States. The distribution key for the Article 92(3)(c) Community ceiling is defined as each Member State's share of the corresponding total Community population.

7. Subject to the corrections mentioned above, the population ceiling for each Member State under the Article 92(3)(c) derogation is calculated by directly applying the distribution key, ie by multiplying the Article 92(3)(c) Community ceiling, expressed in terms of population, by the share of the Member State concerned in the total sum obtained.

2. CORRECTIONS

8. The results thus obtained are corrected, if necessary, in order—

— to guarantee to each Member State that the population assisted under the 92(3)(c) derogation is at least equal to 15% and does not exceed 50% of its population not covered by the 92(3)(a) derogation,

— to attain, in each Member State, a sufficient level to include all the regions which have just lost 92(3)(c) status and the areas with a low population density,

— to limit the reduction in the total coverage (under the two Article 92(3) regional derogations) of a Member State to 25% of its previous coverage.

9. The results obtained for the Member States not directly concerned by the abovementioned corrections are then adjusted proportionately so that the sum of the individual ceilings equals the Article 92(3)(c) ceiling set for the Community.

[6162]

COUNCIL REGULATION

of 7 May 1998

on the application of Articles 92 and 93 of the Treaty establishing the European Community to certain categories of horizontal State aid

(994/98/EC)

NOTES

Date of publication in OJ: OJ L142, 14.5.98, p 1.

THE COUNCIL OF THE EUROPEAN UNION,

Having regard to the Treaty establishing the European Community, and in particular Article 94 thereof,

Having regard to the proposal from the Commission,[1]

After consulting the European Parliament,[2]

Having regard to the opinion of the Economic and Social Committee,[3]

(1) Whereas, pursuant to Article 94 of the Treaty, the Council may make any appropriate regulations for the application of Articles 92 and 93 and may, in particular, determine the conditions in which Article 93(3) shall apply and the categories of aid exempted from this procedure;

(2) Whereas, under the Treaty, the assessment of compatibility of aid with the common market essentially rests with the Commission;

(3) Whereas the proper functioning of the internal market requires strict and efficient application of the rules of competition with regard to State aids;

(4) Whereas the Commission has applied Articles 92 and 93 of the Treaty in numerous decisions and has also stated its policy in a number of communications; whereas, in the light of the Commission's considerable experience in applying Articles 92 and 93 of the Treaty and the general texts issued by the Commission on the basis of those provisions, it is appropriate, with a view to ensuring efficient supervision and simplifying administration, without weakening Commission monitoring, that the Commission should be enabled to declare by means of regulations, in areas where the Commission has sufficient experience to define general compatibility criteria, that certain categories of aid are compatible with the common market pursuant to one or more of the provisions of Article 92(2) and (3) of the Treaty and are exempted from the procedure provided for in Article 93(3) thereof;

(5) Whereas group exemption regulations will increase transparency and legal certainty; whereas they can be directly applied by national courts, without prejudice to Articles 5 and 177 of the Treaty;

(6) Whereas it is appropriate that the Commission, when it adopts regulations exempting categories of aid from the obligation to notify provided for in Article 93(3) of the Treaty, specifies the purpose of the aid, the categories of beneficiaries and thresholds limiting the exempted aid, the conditions governing the cumulation of aid and the conditions of monitoring, in order to ensure the compatibility with the common market of aid covered by this Regulation;

(7) Whereas it is appropriate to enable the Commission, when it adopts regulations exempting certain categories of aid from the obligation to notify in Article 93(3) of the Treaty, to attach further detailed conditions in order to ensure the compatibility with the common market of aid covered by this Regulation;

(8) Whereas it may be useful to set thresholds of other appropriate conditions requiring the notification of awards of aid in order to allow the Commission to examine individually the effect of certain aid on competition and trade between Member States and its compatibility with the common market;

(9) Whereas the Commission, having regard to the development and the functioning of the common market, should be enabled to establish by means of a regulation that certain aid does not fulfil all the criteria of Article 92(1) of the Treaty and is therefore exempted from the notification procedure laid down in Article 93(3), provided that aid granted to the same undertaking over a given period of time does not exceed a certain fixed amount;

(10) Whereas in accordance with Article 93(1) of the Treaty the Commission is under an obligation, in cooperation with Member States, to keep under constant review all systems of existing aid; whereas for this purpose and in order to ensure the largest possible degree of transparency and adequate control it is desirable that the Commission ensures the

establishment of a reliable system of recording and storing information about the application of the regulations it adopts, to which all Member States have access, and that it receives all necessary information from the Member States on the implementation of aid exempted from notification to fulfil this obligation, which may be examined and evaluated with the Member States within the Advisory Committee; whereas for this purpose it is also desirable that the Commission may require such information to be supplied as is necessary to ensure the efficiency of such review;

(11) Whereas the control of the granting of aid involves factual, legal and economic issues of a very complex nature and great variety in a constantly evolving environment; whereas the Commission should therefore regularly review the categories of aid which should be exempted from notification; whereas the Commission should be able to repeal or amend regulations it has adopted pursuant to this Regulation where circumstances have changed with respect to any important element which constituted grounds for their adoption or where the progressive development or the functioning of the common market so requires;

(12) Whereas the Commission, in close and constant liaison with the Member States, should be able to define precisely the scope of these regulations and the conditions attached to them; whereas, in order to provide for cooperation between the Commission and the competent authorities of the Member States, it is appropriate to set up an advisory committee on State aid to be consulted before the Commission adopts regulations pursuant to this Regulation,

NOTES

[1]   OJ C262, 28.8.1997, p 6.
[2]   OJ C138, 4.5.1998.
[3]   OJ C129, 27.4.1998, p.70.

HAS ADOPTED THIS REGULATION—

Article 1

Group exemptions

1.   The Commission may, by means of regulations adopted in accordance with the procedures laid down in Article 8 of this Regulation and in accordance with Article 92 of the Treaty, declare that the following categories of aid should be compatible with the common market and shall not be subject to the notification requirements of Article 93(3) of the Treaty—

    (a) aid in favour of—
        (i)   small and medium-sized enterprises;
        (ii) research and development;
        (iii) environmental protection;
        (iv) employment and training;
    (b) aid that complies with the map approved by the Commission for each Member State for the grant of regional aid.

2.   The Regulations referred to in paragraph 1 shall specify for each category of aid—

    (a) the purpose of the aid;
    (b) the categories of beneficiaries;
    (c) thresholds expressed either in terms of aid intensities in relation to a set of eligible costs or in terms of maximum aid amounts;
    (d) the conditions governing the cumulation of aid;
    (e) the conditions of monitoring as specified in Article 3.

3.   In addition, the regulations referred to in paragraph 1 may, in particular—

    (a) set thresholds or other conditions for the notification of awards of individual aid;
    (b) exclude certain sectors from their scope;
    (c) attach further conditions for the compatibility of aid exempted under such regulations.

[6163]

Article 2

De minimis

1.   The Commission may, by means of a Regulation adopted in accordance with the procedure laid down in Article 8 of this Regulation, decide that, having regard to the development and functioning of the common market, certain aids do not meet all the criteria of Article 92(1) and that they are therefore exempted from the notification procedure provided for in Article 93(3), provided that aid granted to the same undertaking over a given period of time does not exceed a certain fixed amount.

2.   At the Commission's request, Member States shall, at any time, communicate to it any additional information relating to aid exempted under paragraph 1.

[6164]

Article 3

Transparency and monitoring

1.   When adopting regulations pursuant to Article 1, the Commission shall impose detailed rules upon Member States to ensure transparency and monitoring of the aid exempted from notification in accordance with those regulations. Such rules shall consist, in particular, of the requirements laid down in paragraphs 2, 3 and 4.

2.   On implementation of aid systems or individual aids granted outside any system, which have been exempted pursuant to such regulations, Member States shall forward to the Commission, with a view to publication in the *Official Journal of the European Communities*, summaries of the information regarding such systems of aid or such individual aids as are not covered by exempted aid systems.

3.   Member States shall record and compile all the information regarding the application of the group exemptions. If the Commission has information which leads it to doubt that an exemption regulation is being applied properly, the Member States shall forward to it any information it considers necessary to assess whether an aid complies with that regulation.

4.   At least once a year, Member States shall supply the Commission with a report on the application of group exemptions, in accordance with the Commission's specific requirements, preferably in computerised form. The Commission shall make access to those reports available to all the Member States. The Advisory Committee referred to in Article 7 shall examine and evaluate those reports once a year.

[6165]

Article 4

Period of validity and amendment of regulations

1.   Regulations adopted pursuant to Articles 1 and 2 shall apply for a specific period. Aid exempted by a regulation adopted pursuant to Articles 1 and 2 shall be exempted for the period of validity of that regulation and for the adjustment period provided for in paragraphs 2 and 3.

2.   Regulations adopted pursuant to Articles 1 and 2 may be repeated or amended where circumstances have changed with respect to any important element that constituted grounds for their adoption or where the progressive development or the functioning of the common market so requires. In that case the new regulation shall set a period of adjustment of six months for the adjustment of aid covered by the previous regulation.

3.   Regulations adopted pursuant to Articles 1 and 2 shall provide for a period as referred to in paragraph 2, should their application not be extended when they expire.

[6166]

Article 5

Evaluation report

Every five years the Commission shall submit a report to the European Parliament and to the Council on the application of this Regulation. It shall submit a draft report for consideration by the Advisory Committee referred to in Article 7.

[6167]

Article 6

Hearing of interested parties

Where the Commission intends to adopt a regulation, it shall publish a draft thereof to enable all interested persons and organisations to submit their comments to it within a reasonable time limit to be fixed by the Commission and which may not under any circumstances be less than one month.

[6168]

Article 7

Advisory committee

An advisory committee, hereinafter referred to as the Advisory Committee on State Aid, shall be set up. It shall be composed of representatives of the Member States and chaired by the representative of the Commission.

[6169]

Article 8

Consultation of the Advisory Committee

1.   The Commission shall consult the Advisory Committee on State Aid—
   (a)   before publishing any draft regulation;
   (b)   before adopting any regulation.

2.   Consultation of the Committee shall take place at a meeting called by the Commission. The drafts and documents to be examined shall be annexed to the notification. The meeting shall take place no earlier than two months after notification has been sent.

This period may be reduced in the case of the consultations referred to in paragraph 1(b), when urgent or for simple extension of a regulation.

3.   The representative of the Commission shall submit to the Committee a draft of the measures to be taken. The Committee shall deliver its opinion on the draft, within a time limit which the Chairman may lay down according to the urgency of the matter, if necessary by taking a vote.

4.   The opinion shall be recorded in the minutes; in addition, each Member State shall have the right to ask to have its position recorded in the minutes. The Advisory Committee may recommend publication of the opinion in the *Official Journal of the European Communities*.

5.   The Commission shall take the utmost account of the opinion delivered by the Committee. It shall inform the Committee of the manner in which its opinion has been taken into account.

[6170]

Article 9

Final provisions

This Regulation shall enter into force on the day following its publication in the *Official Journal of the European Communities*.

[6171]

This Regulation shall be binding in its entirety and directly applicable in all Member States.

Done at Brussels, 7 May 1998.

COUNCIL REGULATION

of 22 March 1999

laying down detailed rules for the application of Article 93 of the EC Treaty

(659/99/EC)

NOTES

Date of publication in OJ: OJ L83, 27.03.99, p 1.

THE COUNCIL OF THE EUROPEAN UNION,

Having regard to the Treaty establishing the European Community, and in particular Article 94 thereof,

Having regard to the proposal from the Commission,[1]

Having regard to the opinion of the European Parliament,[2]

Having regard to the opinion of the Economic and Social Committee,[3]

(1) Whereas, without prejudice to special procedural rules laid down in regulations for certain sectors, this Regulation should apply to aid in all sectors; whereas, for the purpose of applying Articles 77 and 92 of the Treaty, the Commission has specific competence under Article 93 thereof to decide on the compatibility of State aid with the common market when reviewing existing aid, when taking decisions on new or altered aid and when taking action regarding non-compliance with its decisions or with the requirement as to notification;

(2) Whereas the Commission, in accordance with the case-law of the Court of Justice of the European Communities, has developed and established a consistent practice for the application of Article 93 of the Treaty and has laid down certain procedural rules and principles in a number of communications; whereas it is appropriate, with a view to ensuring effective and efficient procedures pursuant to Article 93 of the Treaty, to codify and reinforce this practice by means of a regulation;

(3) Whereas a procedural regulation on the application of Article 93 of the Treaty will increase transparency and legal certainty;

(4) Whereas, in order to ensure legal certainty, it is appropriate to define the circumstances under which aid is to be considered as existing aid; whereas the completion and enhancement of the internal market is a gradual process, reflected in the permanent development of State aid policy; whereas, following these developments, certain measures, which at the moment they were put into effect did not constitute State aid, may since have become aid;

(5) Whereas, in accordance with Article 93(3) of the Treaty, any plans to grant new aid are to be notified to the Commission and should not be put into effect before the Commission has authorised it;

(6) Whereas, in accordance with Article 5 of the Treaty, Member States are under an obligation to cooperate with the Commission and to provide it with all information required to allow the Commission to carry out its duties under this Regulation;

(7) Whereas the period within which the Commission is to conclude the preliminary examination of notified aid should be set at two months from the receipt of a complete notification or from the receipt of a duly reasoned statement of the Member State concerned that it considers the notification to be complete because the additional information requested by the Commission is not available or has already been provided; whereas, for reasons of legal certainty, that examination should be brought to an end by a decision;

(8) Whereas in all cases where, as a result of the preliminary examination, the Commission cannot find that the aid is compatible with the common market, the formal investigation procedure should be opened in order to enable the Commission to gather all the information it needs to assess the compatibility of the aid and to allow the interested parties to submit their comments; whereas the rights of the interested parties can best be safeguarded within the framework of the formal investigation procedure provided for under Article 93(2) of the Treaty;

(9) Whereas, after having considered the comments submitted by the interested parties, the Commission should conclude its examination by means of a final decision as soon as the doubts have been removed; whereas it is appropriate, should this examination not be concluded after a period of 18 months from the opening of the procedure, that the Member State concerned has the opportunity to request a decision, which the Commission should take within two months;

(10) Whereas, in order to ensure that the State aid rules are applied correctly and effectively, the Commission should have the opportunity of revoking a decision which was based on incorrect information;

(11) Whereas, in order to ensure compliance with Article 93 of the Treaty, and in particular with the notification obligation and the standstill clause in Article 93(3), the Commission should examine all cases of unlawful aid; whereas, in the interests of transparency and legal certainty, the procedures to be followed in such cases should be laid down; whereas when a Member State has not respected the notification obligation or the standstill clause, the Commission should not be bound by time limits;

(12) Whereas in cases of unlawful aid, the Commission should have the right to obtain all necessary information enabling it to take a decision and to restore immediately, where appropriate, undistorted competition; whereas it is therefore appropriate to enable the Commission to adopt interim measures addressed to the Member State concerned; whereas the interim measures may take the form of information injunctions, suspension injunctions and recovery injunctions; whereas the Commission should be enabled in the event of non-compliance with an information injunction, to decide on the basis of the information available and, in the event of non-compliance with suspension and recovery injunctions, to refer the matter to the Court of Justice direct, in accordance with the second subparagraph of Article 93(2) of the Treaty;

(13) Whereas in cases of unlawful aid which is not compatible with the common market, effective competition should be restored; whereas for this purpose it is necessary that the aid, including interest, be recovered without delay; whereas it is appropriate that recovery be effected in accordance with the procedures of national law; whereas the application of those procedures should not, by preventing the immediate and effective execution of the Commission decision, impede the restoration of effective competition; whereas to achieve this result, Member States should take all necessary measures ensuring the effectiveness of the Commission decision;

(14) Whereas for reasons of legal certainty it is appropriate to establish a period of limitation of 10 years with regard to unlawful aid, after the expiry of which no recovery can be ordered;

(15) Whereas misuse of aid may have effects on the functioning of the internal market which are similar to those of unlawful aid and should thus be treated according to similar procedures; whereas unlike unlawful aid, aid which has possibly been misused is aid which has been previously approved by the Commission; whereas therefore the Commission should not be allowed to use a recovery injunction with regard to misuse of aid;

(16) Whereas it is appropriate to define all the possibilities in which third parties have to defend their interests in State aid procedures;

(17) Whereas in accordance with Article 93(1) of the Treaty, the Commission is under an obligation, in cooperation with Member States, to keep under constant review all systems of existing aid; whereas in the interests of transparency and legal certainty, it is appropriate to specify the scope of cooperation under that Article;

(18) Whereas, in order to ensure compatibility of existing aid schemes with the common market and in accordance with Article 93(1) of the Treaty, the Commission should propose appropriate measures where an existing aid scheme is not, or is no longer, compatible with the common market and should initiate the procedure provided for in Article 93(2) of the Treaty if the Member State concerned declines to implement the proposed measures;

(19) Whereas, in order to allow the Commission to monitor effectively compliance with Commission decisions and to facilitate cooperation between the Commission and Member States for the purpose of the constant review of all existing aid schemes in the Member States in accordance with Article 93(1) of the Treaty, it is necessary to introduce a general reporting obligation with regard to all existing aid schemes;

(20) Whereas, where the Commission has serious doubts as to whether its decisions are being complied with, it should have at its disposal additional instruments allowing it to obtain the information necessary to verify that its decisions are being effectively complied with; whereas for this purpose on-site monitoring visits are an appropriate and useful instrument, in particular for cases where aid might have been misused; whereas therefore the Commission must be empowered to undertake on-site monitoring visits and must obtain the cooperation of the competent authorities of the Member States where an undertaking opposes such a visit;

(21) Whereas, in the interests of transparency and legal certainty, it is appropriate to give public information on Commission decisions while, at the same time, maintaining the principle that decisions in State aid cases are addressed to the Member State concerned; whereas it is therefore appropriate to publish all decisions which might affect the interests of interested parties either in full or in a summary form or to make copies of such decisions available to interested parties, where they have not been published or where they have not been published in full; whereas the Commission, when giving public information on its decisions, should respect the rules on professional secrecy, in accordance with Article 214 of the Treaty;

(22) Whereas the Commission, in close liaison with the Member States, should be able to adopt implementing provisions laying down detailed rules concerning the procedures under this Regulation; whereas, in order to provide for cooperation between the Commission and the competent authorities of the Member States, it is appropriate to create an Advisory Committee on State aid to be consulted before the Commission adopts provisions pursuant to this Regulation,

NOTES
1 OJ C116, 16.4.1998, p 13.
2 Opinion delivered on 14 January 1999 (not yet published in the Official Journal).
3 OJ C284, 14.9.1998, p 10.

HAS ADOPTED THIS REGULATION—

CHAPTER I
GENERAL

Article 1

Definitions

For the purpose of this Regulation—
- (a) "aid" shall mean any measure fulfilling all the criteria laid down in Article 92(1) of the Treaty;
- (b) "existing aid" shall mean—
  - (i) without prejudice to Articles 144 and 172 of the Act of Accession of Austria, Finland and Sweden, all aid which existed prior to the entry into force of the Treaty in the respective Member States, that is to say, aid schemes and individual aid which were put into effect before, and are still applicable after, the entry into force of the Treaty;
  - (ii) authorised aid, that is to say, aid schemes and individual aid which have been authorised by the Commission or by the Council;
  - (iii) aid which is deemed to have been authorised pursuant to Article 4(6) of this Regulation or prior to this Regulation but in accordance with this procedure;

    (iv) aid which is deemed to be existing aid pursuant to Article 15;

    (v) aid which is deemed to be an existing aid because it can be established that at the time it was put into effect it did not constitute an aid, and subsequently became an aid due to the evolution of the common market and without having been altered by the Member State. Where certain measures become aid following the liberalisation of an activity by Community law, such measures shall not be considered as existing aid after the date fixed for liberalisation;

  (c) "new aid" shall mean all aid, that is to say, aid schemes and individual aid, which is not existing aid, including alterations to existing aid;

  (d) "aid scheme" shall mean any act on the basis of which, without further implementing measures being required, individual aid awards may be made to undertakings defined within the act in a general and abstract manner and any act on the basis of which aid which is not linked to a specific project may be awarded to one or several undertakings for an indefinite period of time and/or for an indefinite amount;

  (e) "individual aid" shall mean aid that is not awarded on the basis of an aid scheme and notifiable awards of aid on the basis of an aid scheme;

  (f) "unlawful aid" shall mean new aid put into effect in contravention of Article 93(3) of the Treaty;

  (g) "misuse of aid" shall mean aid used by the beneficiary in contravention of a decision taken pursuant to Article 4(3) or Article 7(3) or (4) of this Regulation;

  (h) "interested party" shall mean any Member State and any person, undertaking or association of undertakings whose interests might be affected by the granting of aid, in particular the beneficiary of the aid, competing undertakings and trade associations.

[6172]

CHAPTER II
PROCEDURE REGARDING NOTIFIED AID

Article 2

Notification of new aid

   1.   Save as otherwise provided in regulations made pursuant to Article 94 of the Treaty or to other relevant provisions thereof, any plans to grant new aid shall be notified to the Commission in sufficient time by the Member State concerned. The Commission shall inform the Member State concerned without delay of the receipt of a notification.

   2.   In a notification, the Member State concerned shall provide all necessary information in order to enable the Commission to take a decision pursuant to Articles 4 and 7 (hereinafter referred to as "complete notification").

[6173]

Article 3

Standstill clause

Aid notifiable pursuant to Article 2(1) shall not be put into effect before the Commission has taken, or is deemed to have taken, a decision authorising such aid.

[6174]

Article 4

Preliminary examination of the notification and decisions of the Commission

1.   The Commis6sion shall examine the notification as soon as it is received. Without prejudice to Article 8, the Commission shall take a decision pursuant to paragraphs 2, 3 or 4.

2.   Where the Commission, after a preliminary examination, finds that the notified measure does not constitute aid, it shall record that finding by way of a decision.

3.   Where the Commission, after a preliminary examination, finds that no doubts are raised as to the compatibility with the common market of a notified measure, in so far as it falls within the scope of Article 92(1) of the Treaty, it shall decide that the measure is compatible with the common market (hereinafter referred to as a "decision not to raise objections"). The decision shall specify which exception under the Treaty has been applied.

4.   Where the Commission, after a preliminary examination, finds that doubts are raised as to the compatibility with the common market of a notified measure, it shall decide to initiate proceedings pursuant to Article 93(2) of the Treaty (hereinafter referred to as a "decision to initiate the formal investigation procedure").

5.   The decisions referred to in paragraphs 2, 3 and 4 shall be taken within two months. That period shall begin on the day following the receipt of a complete notification. The notification will be considered as complete if, within two months from its receipt, or from the receipt of any additional information requested, the Commission does not request any further information. The period can be extended with the consent of both the Commission and the Member State concerned. Where appropriate, the Commission may fix shorter time limits.

6.   Where the Commission has not taken a decision in accordance with paragraphs 2, 3 or 4 within the period laid down in paragraph 5, the aid shall be deemed to have been authorised by the Commission. The Member State concerned may thereupon implement the measures in question after giving the Commission prior notice thereof, unless the Commission takes a decision pursuant to this Article within a period of 15 working days following receipt of the notice.

Article 5

Request for information

1.   Where the Commission considers that information provided by the Member State concerned with regard to a measure notified pursuant to Article 2 is incomplete, it shall request all necessary additional information. Where a Member State responds to such a request, the Commission shall inform the Member State of the receipt of the response.

2.   Where the Member State concerned does not provide the information requested within the period prescribed by the Commission or provides incomplete information, the Commission shall send a reminder, allowing an appropriate additional period within which the information shall be provided.

3.   The notification shall be deemed to be withdrawn if the requested information is not provided within the prescribed period, unless before the expiry of that period, either the period has been extended with the consent of both the Commission and the Member State concerned, or the Member State concerned, in a duly reasoned statement, informs the Commission that it considers the notification

to be complete because the additional information requested is not available or has already been provided. In that case, the period referred to in Article 4(5) shall begin on the day following receipt of the statement. If the notification is deemed to be withdrawn, the Commission shall inform the Member State thereof.

[6176]

Article 6

Formal investigation procedure

1.   The decision to initiate the formal investigation procedure shall summarise the relevant issues of fact and law, shall include a preliminary assessment of the Commission as to the aid character of the proposed measure and shall set out the doubts as to its compatibility with the common market. The decision shall call upon the Member State concerned and upon other interested parties to submit comments within a prescribed period which shall normally not exceed one month. In duly justified cases, the Commission may extend the prescribed period.

2.   The comments received shall be submitted to the Member State concerned. If an interested party so requests, on grounds of potential damage, its identity shall be withheld from the Member State concerned. The Member State concerned may reply to the comments submitted within a prescribed period which shall normally not exceed one month. In duly justified cases, the Commission may extend the prescribed period.

[6177]

Article 7

Decisions of the Commission to close the formal investigation procedure

1.   Without prejudice to Article 8, the formal investigation procedure shall be closed by means of a decision as provided for in paragraphs 2 to 5 of this Article.

2.   Where the Commission finds that, where appropriate following modification by the Member State concerned, the notified measure does not constitute aid, it shall record that finding by way of a decision.

3.   Where the Commission finds that, where appropriate following modification by the Member State concerned, the doubts as to the compatibility of the notified measure with the common market have been removed, it shall decide that the aid is compatible with the common market (hereinafter referred to as a "positive decision"). That decision shall specify which exception under the Treaty has been applied.

4.   The Commission may attach to a positive decision conditions subject to which an aid may be considered compatible with the common market and may lay down obligations to enable compliance with the decision to be monitored (hereinafter referred to as a "conditional decision").

5.   Where the Commission finds that the notified aid is not compatible with the common market, it shall decide that the aid shall not be put into effect (hereinafter referred to as a "negative decision").

6.   Decisions taken pursuant to paragraphs 2, 3, 4 and 5 shall be taken as soon as the doubts referred to in Article 4(4) have been removed. The Commission shall as far as possible endeavour to adopt a decision within a period of 18 months from the opening of the procedure. This time limit may be extended by common agreement between the Commission and the Member State concerned.

7.   Once the time limit referred to in paragraph 6 has expired, and should the Member State concerned so request, the Commission shall, within two months, take a decision on the basis of the information available to it. If appropriate, where the information provided is not sufficient to establish compatibility, the Commission shall take a negative decision.

[6178]

Article 8

Withdrawal of notification

1.   The Member State concerned may withdraw the notification within the meaning of Article 2 in due time before the Commission has taken a decision pursuant to Article 4 or 7.

2.   In cases where the Commission initiated the formal investigation procedure, the Commission shall close that procedure.

[6179]

Article 9

Revocation of a decision

The Commission may revoke a decision taken pursuant to Article 4(2) or (3), or Article 7(2), (3), (4), after having given the Member State concerned the opportunity to submit its comments, where the decision was based on incorrect information provided during the procedure which was a determining factor for the decision. Before revoking a decision and taking a new decision, the Commission shall open the formal investigation procedure pursuant to Article 4(4). Articles 6, 7 and 10, Article 11(1), Articles 13, 14 and 15 shall apply *mutatis mutandis*.

[6180]

CHAPTER III
PROCEDURE REGARDING UNLAWFUL AID

Article 10

Examination, request for information and information injunction

1.   Where the Commission has in its possession information from whatever source regarding alleged unlawful aid, it shall examine that information without delay.

2.   If necessary, it shall request information from the Member State concerned. Article 2(2) and Article 5(1) and (2) shall apply *mutatis mutandis*.

3.   Where, despite a reminder pursuant to Article 5(2), the Member State concerned does not provide the information requested within the period prescribed by the Commission, or where it provides incomplete information, the Commission shall by decision require the information to be provided (hereinafter referred to as an "information injunction"). The decision shall specify what information is required and prescribe an appropriate period within which it is to be supplied.

[6181]

Article 11

Injunction to suspend or provisionally recover aid

1.   The Commission may, after giving the Member State concerned the opportunity to submit its comments, adopt a decision requiring the Member State to suspend any unlawful aid until the Commission has taken a decision on the compatibility of the aid with the common market (hereinafter referred to as a "suspension injunction").

2.   The Commission may, after giving the Member State concerned the opportunity to submit its comments, adopt a decision requiring the Member State provisionally to recover any unlawful aid until the Commission has taken a decision on the compatibility of the aid with the common market (hereinafter referred to as a "recovery injunction"), if the following criteria are fulfilled—

—   according to an established practice there are no doubts about the aid character of the measure concerned and

—   there is an urgency to act and

—   there is a serious risk of substantial and irreparable damage to a competitor.

Recovery shall be effected in accordance with the procedure set out in Article 14(2) and (3). After the aid has been effectively recovered, the Commission shall take a decision within the time limits applicable to notified aid.

The Commission may authorise the Member State to couple the refunding of the aid with the payment of rescue aid to the firm concerned.

The provisions of this paragraph shall be applicable only to unlawful aid implemented after the entry into force of this Regulation.

[6182]

Article 12

Non-compliance with an injunction decision

If the Member State fails to comply with a suspension injunction or a recovery injunction, the Commission shall be entitled, while carrying out the examination on the substance of the matter on the basis of the information available, to refer the matter to the Court of Justice of the European Communities direct and apply for a declaration that the failure to comply constitutes an infringement of the Treaty.

[6183]

Article 13

Decisions of the Commission

1.   The examination of possible unlawful aid shall result in a decision pursuant to Article 4(2), (3) or (4). In the case of decisions to initiate the formal investigation procedure, proceedings shall be closed by means of a decision pursuant to Article 7. If a Member State fails to comply with an information injunction, that decision shall be taken on the basis of the information available.

2.   In cases of possible unlawful aid and without prejudice to Article 11(2), the Commission shall not be bound by the time-limit set out in Articles 4(5), 7(6) and 7(7).

3.   Article 9 shall apply *mutatis mutandis*.

[6184]

Article 14

Recovery of aid

1.   Where negative decisions are taken in cases of unlawful aid, the Commission shall decide that the Member State concerned shall take all necessary measures to recover the aid from the beneficiary (hereinafter referred to as a "recovery decision"). The Commission shall not require recovery of the aid if this would be contrary to a general principle of Community law.

2.   The aid to be recovered pursuant to a recovery decision shall include interest at an appropriate rate fixed by the Commission. Interest shall be payable from the date on which the unlawful aid was at the disposal of the beneficiary until the date of its recovery.

3. Without prejudice to any order of the Court of Justice of the European Communities pursuant to Article 185 of the Treaty, recovery shall be effected without delay and in accordance with the procedures under the national law of the Member State concerned, provided that they allow the immediate and effective execution of the Commission's decision. To this effect and in the event of a procedure before national courts, the Member States concerned shall take all necessary steps which are available in their respective legal systems, including provisional measures, without prejudice to Community law.

[6185]

Article 15

Limitation period

1. The powers of the Commission to recover aid shall be subject to a limitation period of ten years.

2. The limitation period shall begin on the day on which the unlawful aid is awarded to the beneficiary either as individual aid or as aid under an aid scheme. Any action taken by the Commission or by a Member State, acting at the request of the Commission, with regard to the unlawful aid shall interrupt the limitation period. Each interruption shall start time running afresh. The limitation period shall be suspended for as long as the decision of the Commission is the subject of proceedings pending before the Court of Justice of the European Communities.

3. Any aid with regard to which the limitation period has expired, shall be deemed to be existing aid.

[6186]

CHAPTER IV
PROCEDURE REGARDING MISUSE OF AID

Article 16

Misuse of aid

Without prejudice to Article 23, the Commission may in cases of misuse of aid open the formal investigation procedure pursuant to Article 4(4). Articles 6, 7, 9 and 10, Article 11(1), Articles 12, 13, 14 and 15 shall apply *mutatis mutandis*.

[6187]

CHAPTER V
PROCEDURE REGARDING EXISTING AID SCHEMES

Article 17

Cooperation pursuant to Article 93(1) of the Treaty

1. The Commission shall obtain from the Member State concerned all necessary information for the review, in cooperation with the Member State, of existing aid schemes pursuant to Article 93(1) of the Treaty.

2. Where the Commission considers that an existing aid scheme is not, or is no longer, compatible with the common market, it shall inform the Member State concerned of its preliminary view and give the Member State concerned the opportunity to submit its comments within a period of one month. In duly justified cases, the Commission may extend this period.

[6188]

Article 18

Proposal for appropriate measures

Where the Commission, in the light of the information submitted by the Member State pursuant to Article 17, concludes that the existing aid scheme is not, or is no longer, compatible with the common market, it shall issue a recommendation proposing appropriate measures to the Member State concerned. The recommendation may propose, in particular—

(a) substantive amendment of the aid scheme, or

(b) introduction of procedural requirements, or

(c) abolition of the aid scheme.

[6189]

Article 19

Legal consequences of a proposal for appropriate measures

1.   Where the Member State concerned accepts the proposed measures and informs the Commission thereof, the Commission shall record that finding and inform the Member State thereof. The Member State shall be bound by its acceptance to implement the appropriate measures.

2.   Where the Member State concerned does not accept the proposed measures and the Commission, having taken into account the arguments of the Member State concerned, still considers that those measures are necessary, it shall initiate proceedings pursuant to Article 4(4). Articles 6, 7 and 9 shall apply *mutatis mutandis.*

[6190]

CHAPTER VI
INTERESTED PARTIES

Article 20

Rights of interested parties

1.   Any interested party may submit comments pursuant to Article 6 following a Commission decision to initiate the formal investigation procedure. Any interested party which has submitted such comments and any beneficiary of individual aid shall be sent a copy of the decision taken by the Commission pursuant to Article 7.

2.   Any interested party may inform the Commission of any alleged unlawful aid and any alleged misuse of aid. Where the Commission considers that on the basis of the information in its possession there are insufficient grounds for taking a view on the case, it shall inform the interested party thereof. Where the Commission takes a decision on a case concerning the subject 659/1999/EC, Art 1 matter of the information supplied, it shall send a copy of that decision to the interested party.

3.   At its request, any interested party shall obtain a copy of any decision pursuant to Articles 4 and 7, Article 10(3) and Article 11.

[6191]

PART IV
EC MATERIALS

CHAPTER VII
MONITORING

Article 21

Annual reports

1. Member States shall submit to the Commission annual reports on all existing aid schemes with regard to which no specific reporting obligations have been imposed in a conditional decision pursuant to Article 7(4).

2. Where, despite a reminder, the Member State concerned fails to submit an annual report, the Commission may proceed in accordance with Article 18 with regard to the aid scheme concerned.

[6192]

Article 22

On-site monitoring

1. Where the Commission has serious doubts as to whether decisions not to raise objections, positive decisions or conditional decisions with regard to individual aid are being complied with, the Member State concerned, after having been given the opportunity to submit its comments, shall allow the Commission to undertake on-site monitoring visits.

2. The officials authorised by the Commission shall be empowered, in order to verify compliance with the decision concerned—
    (a) to enter any premises and land of the undertaking concerned;
    (b) to ask for oral explanations on the spot;
    (c) to examine books and other business records and take, or demand, copies.

The Commission may be assisted if necessary by independent experts.

3. The Commission shall inform the Member State concerned, in good time and in writing, of the on-site monitoring visit and of the identities of the authorised officials and experts. If the Member State has duly justified objections to the Commission's choice of experts, the experts shall be appointed in common agreement with the Member State. The officials of the Commission and the experts authorised to carry out the on-site monitoring shall produce an authorisation in writing specifying the subject-matter and purpose of the visit.

4. Officials authorised by the Member State in whose territory the monitoring visit is to be made may be present at the monitoring visit.

5. The Commission shall provide the Member State with a copy of any report produced as a result of the monitoring visit.

6. Where an undertaking opposes a monitoring visit ordered by a Commission decision pursuant to this Article, the Member State concerned shall afford the necessary assistance to the officials and experts authorised by the Commission to enable them to carry out the monitoring visit. To this end the Member States shall, after consulting the Commission, take the necessary measures within eighteen months after the entry into force of this Regulation.

[6193]

Article 23

Non-compliance with decisions and judgments

1. Where the Member State concerned does not comply with conditional or negative decisions, in particular in cases referred to in Article 14, the Commission

may refer the matter to the Court of Justice of the European Communities direct in accordance with Article 93(2) of the Treaty.

2.   If the Commission considers that the Member State concerned has not complied with a judgment of the Court of Justice of the European Communities, the Commission may pursue the matter in accordance with Article 171 of the Treaty.

[6194]

CHAPTER VIII
COMMON PROVISIONS

Article 24

Professional secrecy

The Commission and the Member States, their officials and other servants, including independent experts appointed by the Commission, shall not disclose information which they have acquired through the application of this Regulation and which is covered by the obligation of professional secrecy.

[6195]

Article 25

Addressee of decisions

Decisions taken pursuant to Chapters II, III, IV, V and VII shall be addressed to the Member State concerned. The Commission shall notify them to the Member State concerned without delay and give the latter the opportunity to indicate to the Commission which information it considers to be covered by the obligation of professional secrecy.

[6196]

Article 26

Publication of decisions

1.   The Commission shall publish in the *Official Journal of the European Communities* a summary notice of the decisions which it takes pursuant to Article 4(2) and (3) and Article 18 in conjunction with Article 19(1). The summary notice shall state that a copy of the decision may be obtained in the authentic language version or versions.

2.   The Commission shall publish in the *Official Journal of the European Communities* the decisions which it takes pursuant to Article 4(4) in their authentic language version. In the Official Journal published in languages other than the authentic language version, the authentic language version will be accompanied by a meaningful summary in the language of that Official Journal.

3.   The Commission shall publish in the *Official Journal of the European Communities* the decisions which it takes pursuant to Article 7.

4.   In cases where Article 4(6) or Article 8(2) applies, a short notice shall be published in the *Official Journal of the European Communities*.

5.   The Council, acting unanimously, may decide to publish decisions pursuant to the third subparagraph of Article 93(2) of the Treaty in the *Official Journal of the European Communities*.

[6197]

Article 27

Implementing provisions

The Commission, acting in accordance with the procedure laid down in Article 29, shall have the power to adopt implementing provisions concerning the form, content and other details of notifications, the form, content and other details of annual reports, details of time-limits and the calculation of time-limits, and the interest rate referred to in Article 14(2).

[6198]

Article 28

Advisory Committee on State aid

An Advisory Committee on State aid (hereinafter referred to as the "Committee") shall be set up. It shall be composed of representatives of the Member States and chaired by the representative of the Commission.

[6199]

Article 29

Consultation of the Committee

1.   The Commission shall consult the Committee before adopting any implementing provision pursuant to Article 27.

2.   Consultation of the Committee shall take place at a meeting called by the Commission. The drafts and documents to be examined shall be annexed to the notification. The meeting shall take place no earlier than two months after notification has been sent. This period may be reduced in the case of urgency.

3.   The Commission representative shall submit to the Committee a draft of the measures to be taken. The Committee shall deliver an opinion on the draft, within a time-limit which the chairman may lay down according to the urgency of the matter, if necessary by taking a vote.

4.   The opinion shall be recorded in the minutes; in addition, each Member State shall have the right to ask to have its position recorded in the minutes. The Committee may recommend the publication of this opinion in the *Official Journal of the European Communities*.

5.   The Commission shall take the utmost account of the opinion delivered by the Committee. It shall inform the Committee on the manner in which its opinion has been taken into account.

[6200]

Article 30

Entry into force

This Regulation shall enter into force. on the twentieth day following that of its publication in the *Official Journal of the European Communities*.

[6201]

This Regulation shall be binding in its entirety and directly applicable in all Member States.

Done at Brussels, 22 March 1999.

COMMUNITY GUIDELINES ON STATE AID FOR RESCUING AND RESTRUCTURING FIRMS IN DIFFICULTY

(Notice to Member States including proposals for appropriate measures)

(1999/C 288/02)

(Text with EEA relevance)

NOTES
  Date of publication in OJ: OJ C288, 9.10.99, p 2.

1. INTRODUCTION

(1)   The Commission adopted its original Guidelines on State aid for rescuing and restructuring firms in difficulty[1] in 1994. Their validity was extended until 31 December 1999.[2] In 1997, the Commission added specific rules for agriculture.[3]

(2)   The Commission wishes through this version of the Guidelines, the text of which builds on previous versions, to make certain changes and clarifications prompted by a number of factors. First, completion of the internal market calls for a closer watch to be kept on State aid. The sixth and seventh surveys on State aid in the European Union in the manufacturing and certain other sectors[4] reveal an increase in the volume of ad hoc aid, chiefly for rescuing and restructuring firms in difficulty, without taking into account aid granted in the new German *Länder* by the *Treuhandanstalt* or the *Bundesanstalt für vereinigungsbedingte Sonderaufgaben*. The advent of the single currency will also speed up the trend towards increased intra-Community trade, which will make the impact of rescue and restructuring aid on competitive conditions within the Community felt all the more keenly. In addition, the Commission committed itself in its action plan for the single market[5] to further tightening the rules on rescue and restructuring aid, while taking account of the role of appropriate levels of aid in cushioning the social effects of restructuring. The Commission therefore set about clarifying the rules applicable to rescue and restructuring aid and framing more strictly the Guidelines according to which it will examine such aid.

(3)   State aid for rescuing firms in difficulty from bankruptcy and helping them to restructure may only be regarded as legitimate subject to certain conditions. It may be justified, for instance, by social or regional policy considerations, by the need to take into account the beneficial role played by small and medium-sized enterprises (SMEs) in the economy or, exceptionally, by the desirability of maintaining a competitive market structure when the disappearance of firms could lead to a monopoly or to a tight oligopolistic situation.

[6202]

NOTES
  [1]   OJ C368, 23.12.1994, p 12.
  [2]   OJ C67, 10.3.1999, p 11.
  [3]   OJ C283, 19.9.1997, p 2. See also the footnote relating to the heading of Chapter 5.
  [4]   COM(1998) 417 final; COM(1999) 148 final.
  [5]   CSE(97) 1 final.

2. DEFINITIONS AND SCOPE OF THE GUIDELINES AND LINKS WITH OTHER TEXTS ON STATE AID

2.1. CONCEPT OF "A FIRM IN DIFFICULTY"

(4)   There is no Community definition of what constitutes "a firm in difficulty". However, for the purposes of these Guidelines, the Commission regards a firm as being in difficulty where it is unable, whether through its own resources or with the funds it is able to obtain from its owner/shareholders or creditors, to stem losses which, without outside intervention by the public authorities, will almost certainly condemn it to go out of business in the short or medium term.

(5)   In particular, a firm is, in any event and irrespective of its size, regarded as being in difficulty for the purposes of these Guidelines—
   (a) in the case of a limited company,[1] where more than half of its registered capital has disappeared[2] and more than one quarter of that capital has been lost over the preceding 12 months; or
   (b) in the case of an unlimited company,[3] where more than half of its capital as shown in the company accounts has disappeared and more than one quarter of that capital has been lost over the preceding 12 months; or
   (c) whatever the type of company concerned, where it fulfils the criteria under its domestic law for being the subject of collective insolvency proceedings.

(6)   The usual signs of a firm being in difficulty are increasing losses, diminishing turnover, growing stock inventories, excess capacity, declining cash flow, mounting debt, rising interest charges and falling or nil net asset value. In acute cases the company may already have become insolvent or may be the subject of collective insolvency proceedings brought under its domestic law. In the latter case, these Guidelines apply to any aid granted in the context of such proceedings which leads to the firm continuing in business. In any event, a firm in difficulty is eligible only where, demonstrably, it cannot recover through its own resources or with the funds it obtains from its owners/shareholders or creditors.

(7)   For the purposes of these Guidelines, a newly created firm[4] is not eligible for rescue or restructuring aid, even if its initial financial position is insecure. This is the case, for instance, where a new firm emerges from the liquidation of a previous firm or merely takes over such firm's assets.[5]

(8)   A company belonging to a larger business group is not normally eligible for rescue or restructuring aid, except where it can be demonstrated that the company's difficulties are its own and are not the result of an arbitrary allocation of costs within the group, and that the difficulties are too serious to be dealt with by the group itself.

2.2. DEFINITION OF RESCUE AND RESTRUCTURING AID

(9)   Rescue aid and restructuring aid are covered by the same set of guidelines, because in both cases the public authorities are faced with a firm in difficulties and the rescue and the restructuring are often two parts of a single operation, even if they involve different processes.

(10)   Rescue aid is by nature temporary assistance. It should make it possible to keep an ailing firm afloat for the time needed to work out a restructuring or liquidation plan and/or for the length of time the Commission needs to be able to reach a decision on that plan.

(11)   Restructuring, on the other hand, will be based on a feasible, coherent and far-reaching plan to restore a firm's long-term viability. Restructuring usually involves one or more of the following elements: the reorganisation and rationalisation of the firm's activities on to a more efficient basis, typically involving

the withdrawal from loss-making activities, the restructuring of those existing activities that can be made competitive again and, possibly, diversification in the direction of new and viable activities. Financial restructuring (capital injections, debt reduction) usually has to accompany the physical restructuring. Restructuring operations within the scope of these Guidelines cannot, however, be limited to financial aid designed to make good past losses without tackling the reasons for those losses.

2.3. SCOPE

(12) These Guidelines apply to firms in all sectors (except those covered by the ECSC Treaty), without prejudice to any specific rules relating to firms in difficulty in the sector concerned.[6] Chapter 5 incorporates the specific rules for agriculture adopted in 1997.

2.4. APPLICABILITY OF ARTICLE 87(1) OF THE EC TREATY

(13) State aid for rescuing or restructuring firms in difficulty will, by its very nature, tend to distort competition. In so far as it affects trade between Member States, it falls within the scope of Article 87(1) of the EC Treaty.

(14) Aid for restructuring can take different forms, such as capital injections, debt write-offs, loans, relief from taxes or social security contributions, or loan guarantees. For rescues, however, unless it is expressly stipulated otherwise in some other Community text on State aid, assistance should be limited to loans or loan guarantees (see points 23 to 27).

(15) The source of the aid can be any level of government,[7] central, regional and local, and any "public undertaking", as defined in Article 2 of the 1980 Commission Directive 80/723/EEC of 25 June 1980 on the transparency of financial relations between Member States and public undertakings.[8] Thus, for example, rescue or restructuring aid may come from State holding companies or public investment companies.[9]

(16) To determine when injections of new capital by public authorities into companies which they own involve elements of aid, the criterion applied is the "market-economy private investor" principle.[10] This provides that in circumstances where a rational private investor operating in a market economy would have made the finance available the provision or guarantee of funding to a company is not regarded as involving aid.

(17) Where funding is provided or guaranteed by the State to an enterprise that is in financial difficulties, however, it must be deemed likely that the financial transfers involve State aid. Therefore, such financial transactions must be communicated to the Commission in advance, where appropriate through the notification of a general scheme, in accordance with Article 88(3) of the Treaty.[11] The presumption of aid is stronger in cases where there is a Community-wide or EEA-wide structural excess of production capacity on a market in which the recipient firm is active or where the industry as a whole is in difficulties.

(18) The assessment of rescue or restructuring aid should not be affected by changes in the ownership of the business aided.

2.5. COMPATIBILITY WITH THE COMMON MARKET

(19) Article 87(2) and (3) of the Treaty provide for the possibility of aid falling within the scope of Article 87(1) being regarded as compatible with the common market. Apart from cases of aid to make good the damage caused by national disasters or exceptional occurrences (Article 87(2)(b)), which are not covered here, the only basis whereby aid for rescuing or restructuring firms in difficulty can be

deemed compatible is Article 87(3)(c). Under this provision the Commission has the power to authorise "aid to facilitate the development of certain economic activities . . . where such aid does not adversely affect trading conditions to an extent contrary to the common interest."

(20) The Commission considers that aid for rescue and restructuring may contribute to the development of economic activities without adversely affecting trade to an extent contrary to the Community interest if the conditions set out in these Guidelines are met. Where the firms to be rescued or restructured are located in assisted areas, the Commission will take the regional considerations referred to in Article 87(3)(a) and (c) into account as described in points 53 and 54.

2.6. OTHER PROVISIONS OF COMMUNITY LAW

(21) It should be stressed that the Commission cannot authorise aid for rescuing or restructuring firms in difficulty where the terms and conditions of the aid infringe Treaty provisions other than Articles 87 and 88 or secondary legislation.

NOTES

[1] This refers in particular to the types of company mentioned in the first subparagraph of Article 1(1) of Council Directive 78/660/EEC (OJ L222, 14.8.1978, p 11), as amended in particular by Directive 90/605/EEC (OJ L317, 16.11.1990, p 60).

[2] By analogy with the provisions of Council Directive 77/91/EEC (OJ L26, 30.1.1977, p 1).

[3] This refers in particular to the types of company mentioned in Article 1 of Directive 90/605/EEC.

[4] The creation by a company of a subsidiary merely as a vehicle for receiving its assets and possibly its liabilities is not regarded as the creation of a new firm.

[5] The only exceptions of this rule are any cases dealt with by the *Bundesanstalt für vereinigungsbedingte Sonderaufgaben* in the context of its privatisation remit and other similar cases in the new *Länder*, involving companies emerging from a liquidation or a take-over of assets occurring up to 31 December 1999.

[6] Specific rules of this nature exist for shipbuilding (Regulation (EC) No 1540/98, OJ L202, 18.7.1998, p 1), the motor vehicle industry (OJ C279, 15.9.1997, p 1) and the aviation sector (OJ C350, 10.12.1994, p 5).

[7] Including in the case of aid co-financed from Community funds.

[8] OJ L195, 29.7.1980, p 35, as amended by Directive 93/84/EEC (OJ L254, 12.10.1993, p 16).

[9] See judgment of the Court of Justice of 22 March 1977 in Case 78/76 Steinike und Weinlig v Germany, [1977] ECR 595; Crédit Lyonnais/Usinor-Sacilor, Commission press release IP(91) 1045.

[10] See the Communication on public undertakings in the manufacturing sector (OJ C307, 13.11.1993, p 3).

[11] See in particular point 27 of the Communication on public undertakings in the manufacturing sector.

3. GENERAL CONDITIONS FOR THE AUTHORISATION OF RESCUE AND/OR RESTRUCTURING AID NOTIFIED INDIVIDUALLY TO THE COMMISSION

(22) This chapter deals exclusively with aid measures that are notified individually to the Commission. Under certain conditions, the Commission may authorise rescue or restructuring aid schemes: those conditions are set out in Chapter 4.

3.1. RESCUE AID

(23) In order to be approved by the Commission, rescue aid as defined in point 12 must—

(a) consist of liquidity support in the form of loan guarantees or loans.[1] In both cases, the loan must be granted at an interest rate at least comparable to those observed for loans to healthy firms, and in particular the reference rates adopted by the Commission;

(b) be linked to loans that are to be reimbursed over a period of not more than twelve months after disbursement of the last instalment to the firm;[2]

(c) be warranted on the grounds of serious social difficulties and have no unduly adverse spillover effects on other Member States;

(d) be accompanied on notification by an undertaking on the part of the Member State concerned to communicate to the Commission, not later than six months after the rescue aid measure has been authorised, a restructuring plan or a liquidation plan or proof that the loan has been reimbursed in full and/or that the guarantee has been terminated;

(e) be restricted to the amount needed to keep the firm in business for the period during which the aid is authorised (for example, covering wage and salary costs or routine supplies).

(24) The rescue aid will initially be authorised for not more than six months or, where the Member State concerned has submitted a restructuring plan within that period, until the Commission reaches its decision on the plan. In duly substantiated exceptional circumstances and at the request of the Member State concerned, the Commission may extend the initial six-month period.

(25) Rescue aid is a one-off operation designed to keep a company in business for a limited period, during which its future can be assessed. On the other hand, repeated rescues that would merely maintain the status quo, postpone the inevitable and in the meantime shift the attendant economic and social problems on to other, more efficient producers or other Member States cannot be allowed.

(26) If the Member State fails to communicate the information stipulated in (d) of point 23 before the six-month deadline expires and does not make a duly substantiated request for the deadline to be extended, the Commission will initiate proceedings under Article 88(2).

(27) The approval of rescue aid does not necessarily mean that aid under a restructuring plan will subsequently be approved; such aid will have to be assessed on its own merits.

3.2. RESTRUCTURING AID

3.2.1. Basic principle

(28) Aid for restructuring raises particular competition concerns as it can shift an unfair share of the burden of structural adjustment and the attendant social and economic problems onto other producers who are managing without aid and to other Member States. The general principle should therefore be to allow the grant of restructuring aid only in circumstances in which it can be demonstrated that it does not run counter to the Community interest. This will only be possible if strict criteria are met, and if it is certain that any distortions of competition will be offset by the benefits flowing from the firm's survival (in particular, where it is clear that the net effect of redundancies resulting from the firm going out of business, combined with the effects on its suppliers, would exacerbate local, regional or national employment problems or, exceptionally, where the firm's disappearance would result in a monopoly or tight oligopolistic situation) and, where appropriate, there are adequate compensatory measures in favour of competitors.

3.2.2. Conditions for the authorisation of aid

(29) Subject to the special provisions for assisted areas, SMEs and the agricultural sector (see points 53, 54 and 55 and Chapter 5), the Commission will approve aid only under the following conditions—

(a) *Eligibility of the firm*

(30) The firm must qualify as a firm in difficulty within the meaning of these Guidelines (see points 4 to 8).

(b) *Restoration of viability*

(31) The grant of the aid is conditional on implementation of the restructuring plan which must be endorsed by the Commission in the case of all individual aid measures.

(32) The restructuring plan, the duration of which must be as short as possible, must restore the long-term viability of the firm within a reasonable timescale and on the basis of realistic assumptions as to future operating conditions. Restructuring aid must therefore be linked to a viable restructuring plan to which the Member State concerned commits itself. The plan must be submitted in all relevant detail to the Commission and include, in particular, a market survey.[3] The improvement in viability must derive mainly from internal measures contained in the restructuring plan and may be based on external factors such as variations in prices and demand over which the company has no great influence if the market assumptions made are generally acknowledged. Restructuring must involve the abandonment of activities which would remain structurally loss-making even after restructuring.

(33) The restructuring plan should describe the circumstances that led to the company's difficulties, thereby providing a basis for assessing whether the proposed measures are appropriate. It should take account, *inter alia*, of the present state of and future prospects for supply and demand on the relevant product market, with scenarios reflecting best-case, worst-case and intermediate assumptions and the firm's specific strengths and weaknesses. It should enable the firm to progress towards a new structure that offers it prospects for long-term viability and enables it to stand on its own feet.

(34) The plan should provide for a turnaround that will enable the company, after completing its restructuring, to cover all its costs including depreciation and financial charges. The expected return on capital should be enough to enable the restructured firm to compete in the marketplace on its own merits.

(c) *Avoidance of undue distortions of competition*

(35) Measures must be taken to mitigate as far as possible any adverse effects of the aid on competitors. Otherwise, the aid should be regarded as "contrary to the common interest" and therefore incompatible with the common market.

(36) This condition usually takes the form of a limitation on the presence which the company can enjoy on its market or markets after the end of the restructuring period. Where the size of the relevant market(s)[4] is negligible at Community and at EEA level, or the firm's share of the relevant market(s) is negligible it should be considered that there is no undue distortion of competition. This condition should accordingly be regarded as not normally applying to small or medium-sized enterprises, except where otherwise provided by rules on State aid in a particular sector.

(37) The compulsory limitation or reduction of the company's presence on the relevant market(s) represents a compensatory factor in favour of its competitors. It should be in proportion to the distortive effects of the aid and, in particular, to the relative importance of the firm on its market or markets. The Commission will determine the extent of the limitation or reduction on the basis of the market survey attached to their structuring plan and, where the procedure has been initiated, on the basis of information supplied by interested parties. The reduction in the firm's presence is to be put into effect through the restructuring plan and any conditions attached thereto.

(38) A relaxation of the need for compensatory measures may be contemplated if such a reduction or limitation is likely to cause a manifest deterioration in the structure of the market, for example by having the indirect effect of creating a monopoly or a tight oligopolistic situation.

(39) Compensatory measures can take different forms according to whether or not the firm is operating in a market where there is excess capacity. In assessing whether or not there is excess capacity on a given market, the Commission can take into account all the relevant data in its possession—

   (i) where there is a Community-wide or EEA-wide structural excess of production capacity in a market served by the recipient, the restructuring plan must make a contribution, in proportion to the amount of aid received and its impact on that market, to the improvement of market conditions by irreversibly reducing production capacity. A capacity reduction is irreversible when the relevant assets are rendered permanently incapable of achieving the previous rate of output, or are permanently converted to another use. The sale of capacity to competitors is not sufficient in this case, except if the plant is sold for use in a geographic market in which its continued operation is unlikely to have significant effects on the competitive situation in the Community. The capacity reduction requirements must contribute to a reduction in the recipient firm's presence on its market or markets;

  (ii) where, on the other hand, there is no Community-wide or EEA-wide structural excess of production capacity in a market served by the recipient, the Commission will nevertheless examine whether compensatory measures should be required. Where any such compensatory measures involve a reduction in the capacity of the firm concerned, the necessary reduction could be achieved through the hiving-off of assets or subsidiaries. The Commission will have to examine the compensatory measures proposed by the Member State concerned, whatever form they take, and determine whether they are sufficient in scope to mitigate the potentially distortive effects of the aid on competition. In examining the necessary compensatory measures, the Commission will take account of the state of the market, and in particular its level of growth and the extent to which demand is met.

(d)   *Aid limited to the minimum*

(40) The amount and intensity of the aid must be limited to the strict minimum needed to enable restructuring to be undertaken in the light of the existing financial resources of the company, its shareholders or the business group to which it belongs. Aid beneficiaries will be expected to make a significant contribution to the restructuring plan from their own resources, including through the sale of assets that are not essential to the firm's survival, or from external financing at market conditions. To limit the distortive effect, the amount of the aid or the form in which the aid is granted must be such as to avoid providing the company with surplus cash which could be used for aggressive, market-distorting activities not linked to the restructuring process. The Commission will accordingly examine the level of the firm's liabilities after restructuring, including the situation after any postponement or reduction of its debts, particularly in the context of its continuation in business following collective insolvency proceedings brought against it under national law.[5] Neither should any of the aid go to finance new investment that is not essential for restoring the firm's viability.

(41) In any event, it must be demonstrated to the Commission that the aid will be used only for the purpose of restoring the firm's viability and that it will not enable the recipient during the implementation of the restructuring plan to expand production capacity, except in so far as this is essential for restoring viability without unduly distorting competition.

(e)   *Specific conditions attached to the authorisation of aid*

(42) In addition to the compensatory measures described in points 35 to 39, and in the event that such provisions have not been adopted by the Member State concerned, the Commission may impose any conditions and obligations it considers

necessary in order to ensure that the aid does not distort competition to an extent contrary to the common interest. For example, it may require the Member State—
  (i) to take certain measures itself (eg to open up certain markets to other Community operators);
  (ii) to impose certain obligations on the recipient firm (eg to refrain from acting as price leader on certain markets);
  (iii) to refrain from granting other types of aid to the recipient firm during the restructuring period.

(f) *Full implementation of restructuring plan and observance of conditions*

(43) The company must fully implement the restructuring plan that has been accepted by the Commission and must discharge any other obligations laid down in the Commission Decision. The Commission will regard any failure to implement the plan or to fulfil the other obligations as misuse of the aid.

(44) Where restructuring operations cover several years and involve substantial amounts of aid, the Commission may require payment of the restructuring aid to be split into instalments and may make payment of each instalment, subject to—
  (i) confirmation, prior to each payment, of the satisfactory implementation of each stage in the restructuring plan, in accordance with the planned timetable; or
  (ii) its approval, prior to each payment, after verification that the plan is being satisfactorily implemented.

(g) *Monitoring and annual report*

(45) The Commission must be put in a position to make certain that the restructuring plan is being implemented properly, through detailed regular reports communicated by the Member State concerned.

(46) In the case of aid to large firms, the first of these reports will normally have to be submitted to the Commission not later than six months after approval of the aid. Reports will subsequently have to be sent to the Commission at least once a year, at a fixed date, until the objectives of the restructuring plan can be deemed to have been achieved. They must contain all the information the Commission needs in order to be able to monitor the implementation of the restructuring programme, the timetable for payments to the company and its financial position and the observance of any conditions or obligations laid down in the decision approving the aid. They must in particular include all relevant information on any aid for any purpose which the company has received, either on an individual basis or under a general scheme, during the restructuring period (see points 90 to 93). Where the Commission needs timely confirmation of certain key items of information, eg on closures or capacity reductions, it may require more frequent reports.

(47) In the case of aid to small or medium-sized enterprises, transmission each year of a copy of the recipient firm's balance sheet and profit and loss account will normally be sufficient, except where stricter conditions have been laid down in the decision approving the aid.

3.2.3. "One time, last time" condition

(48) In order to prevent firms from being unfairly assisted, restructuring aid should be granted once only. When planned restructuring aid is notified to the Commission, the Member State must specify whether the firm concerned has in the past already received restructuring aid, including aid granted before entry into force of these Guidelines and any unnotified aid.[6] If so, and where less than 10 years has elapsed since the restructuring period came to an end[7] or implementation of the plan has been halted, the Commission will normally[8] allow further restructuring aid only in exceptional and unforeseeable circumstances for which the company is not

responsible.[9] An unforeseeable circumstance is one which could in no way be anticipated when the restructuring plan was drawn up.

(49) The application of this rule will in no way be affected by any changes in ownership of the recipient firm following the grant of aid or by any judicial or administrative procedure which has the effect of putting its balance sheet on a sounder footing, reducing its liabilities or wiping out its previous debts where it is the same firm that is continuing in business.

(50) Where a firm over assets of another firm, and in particular one that has been the subject of one of the procedures listed in point 49 or of collective insolvency proceedings brought under national law, and has itself already received rescue or restructuring aid, the purchaser is not subject to the "one time, last time" requirement, provided that the following three conditions are met—

   (a) the purchaser is clearly separate from the old firm;
   (b) the purchaser has acquired the old firm's assets at market prices (thereby avoiding any shifting to the new company of aid paid to the old one);
   (c) the winding-up or court-supervised administration and purchase of the old company are not merely devices aimed at evading application of the "one time, last time" principle (the Commission could determine that this is the case if, for example, the difficulties encountered by the purchaser were clearly foreseeable when it took over the assets of the old company).

(51) It should, however, be stressed here that, since it constitutes aid for initial investment, aid for the purchase of the assets cannot be authorised under these Guidelines (see also point 7).

3.2.4. Amendment of the restructuring plan

(52) Where restructuring aid has been approved, the Member State concerned may, during the restructuring period, ask the Commission to agree to changes being made to the restructuring plan and the amount of the aid. The Commission may allow such changes where they meet the following conditions—

   (a) the revised plan must still show a return to viability within a reasonable timescale;
   (b) if the amount of the aid is increased, any requisite compensatory measures must be more extensive than those initially imposed;
   (c) if the proposed compensatory measures are smaller than those initially planned, the amount of the aid must be correspondingly reduced;
   (d) the new timetable for implementation of the compensatory measures may be delayed with respect to the timetable initially adopted only for reasons outside the company's or the Member State's control. If that is not the case, the amount of the aid must be correspondingly reduced.

3.2.5. Restructuring aid in assisted areas

(53) Economic and social cohesion being a priority objective of the Community under Article 158 of the EC Treaty and other policies being required to contribute to this objective under Article 159,[10] the Commission must take the needs of regional development into account when assessing restructuring aid in assisted areas. The fact that an ailing firm is located in an assisted area does not, however, justify a permissive approach to aid for restructuring: in the medium to long term it does not help a region to prop up companies artificially. Furthermore, given the limited resources available to promote regional development it is in the regions' own best interest to apply these scarce resources to develop as soon as possible alternative activities that are viable and sustainable. Finally, distortions of competition must be minimised even in the case of aid to firms in assisted areas.

(54) Thus, the criteria listed in points 29 to 52 are equally applicable to assisted areas, even when the needs of regional development are considered. In assisted areas however, and unless otherwise stipulated in rules on State aid in a particular sector, the conditions for authorising aid may be less stringent as regards the implementation of compensatory measures. If regional development needs justify it, the required capacity reduction will be smaller in assisted areas than in non-assisted areas and a distinction will be drawn between areas eligible for regional aid under Article 87(3)(a) of the Treaty and those eligible under Article 87(3)(c) so as to take account of the greater severity of the regional problems in the former areas.

3.2.6. Aid for restructuring small and medium-sized enterprises

(55) Aid to firms in the small to medium-sized category[11] tends to affect trading conditions less than that granted to large firms. This also applies to aid to help restructuring, so that the conditions laid down in points 29 to 47 are applied less strictly: the grant of restructuring aid to SMEs will not usually be linked to compensatory measures (see points 35 to 39), unless this is otherwise stipulated in rules on State aid in a particular sector; and the requirements regarding the content of reports will be less stringent (see points 45, 46 and 47). On the other hand, the "one time, last time" principle (points 48 to 51) applies in full to SMEs.

3.2.7. Aid to cover the social costs of restructuring

(56) Restructuring plans normally entail reductions in or abandonment of the affected activities. Such retrenchments are often necessary in the interests of rationalisation and efficiency, quite apart from any capacity reductions that may be required as a condition for granting aid (particularly in cases where there is a Community-wide or EEA-wide structural excess of production capacity—see points 35 to 39). Whatever the reason for them, such measures will generally lead to reductions in the company's workforce.

(57) Member States' labour legislation may comprise general social security schemes under which redundancy benefits and early retirement pensions are paid direct to redundant employees. Such schemes are not to be regarded as State aid falling within the scope of Article 87(1) in so far as the State deals direct with employees, and the company is not involved.

(58) Besides direct redundancy benefit and early retirement provision for employees, general social support schemes frequently provide for the government to cover the cost of benefits which the company grants to redundant workers and which go beyond its statutory or contractual obligations. Where such schemes are available generally without sectoral limitations to any worker meeting predefined and automatic eligibility conditions, they are not deemed to involve aid under Article 87(1) for firms undertaking restructuring. On the other hand, if the schemes are used to support restructuring in particular industries, they may well involve aid because of the selective way in which they are used.[12]

(59) The obligations a company itself bears under employment legislation or collective agreements with trade unions, to provide redundancy benefits and/or early retirement pensions are part of the normal costs of a business which a firm has to meet from its own resources. That being so, any contribution by the State to these costs must be counted as aid. This is true regardless of whether the payments are made direct to the firm or are administered through a government agency to the employees.

(60) The Commission has a positive approach to such aid, for it brings economic benefits above and beyond the interests of the firm concerned, facilitating structural

change and reducing hardship, and often only serves to even out differences in the obligations placed on companies by national legislation.

(61) Besides meeting the cost of redundancy payments and early retirement, aid is commonly provided in connection with a particular restructuring case for training, counselling and practical help with finding alternative employment, assistance with relocation, and professional training and assistance for employees wishing to start new businesses. The Commission consistently takes a favourable view of such aid.

(62) The type of aid described in points 56 to 61 should be clearly identified in the restructuring plan, since aid for social measures exclusively for the benefit of redundant employees is disregarded for the purposes of determining the extent of the compensatory measures referred to in points 35 to 39.

(63) In the common interest, the Commission will ensure in the context of the restructuring plan that social effects of the restructuring in Member States other than the one granting aid are kept to the minimum.

[6204]

NOTES

¹ An exception may be made in the case of rescue aid in the banking sector, in order to enable the credit institution in question to continue temporarily carrying on its banking business in accordance with the prudential legislation in force (Council Directive 89/647/EEC of 18 December 1989 on a solvency ratio for credit institutions, OJ L386, 30.12.1989, p 14). Any aid granted in a form other than that described in subparagraph (b), for example a capital injection or a subordinated loan, will be taken into account when any compensatory measures under a restructuring plan are examined in accordance with points 35 to 39.

² Reimbursement of the loan linked to the rescue aid may possibly be covered by the restructuring aid subsequently approved by the Commission.

³ The items of information which the Commission needs in order to examine the aid satisfactorily are listed in Annex I.

⁴ As defined in point 7.6 of the multisectoral framework on regional aid for large investment projects (OJ C107, 7.4.1998, p 7): "The relevant product market(s) for determining market share comprises the products envisaged by the investment project and, where appropriate, its substitutes considered by the consumer (by reason of the products' characteristics, their prices and their intended use) or by the producer (through flexibility of the production installations). The relevant geographic market comprises usually the EEA or, alternatively, any significant part of it if the conditions of competition in that area can be sufficiently distinguished from other areas of the EEA. Where appropriate the relevant market(s) may be considered to be global". A footnote states that, where the investment concerns the production of intermediate goods, the relevant market may be the market for the final product if most of the production is not sold on the open market.

⁵ See the third paragraph of point 6.

⁶ With regard to unnotified aid, the Commission will take account in its analysis of the possibility that the aid could have been declared compatible with the common market other than as restructuring aid.

⁷ Unless otherwise specified, the restructuring period will normally come to an end when the deadline for implementation of the various measures provided for in the restructuring plan expires (see the sixth indent in point IV of Annex I).

⁸ Given the degree of liberalisation and specific features of each sector, two situations should be noted—

—in the air transport sector, entirely liberalised since 1997, the Commission will apply the "one time, last time" principle within the limits and conditions of the guidelines on State aid in the aviation sector.

—in other sectors, if the effects of the liberalisation of Community markets that were previously closed to competition have created new economic conditions, derogations may be considered.

⁹ For the purposes of this paragraph, aid granted before 1 January 1996 to enterprises in the former GDR and declared compatible with the common market by the Commission is not taken into account. In addition, the paragraph does not apply to cases of aid to such enterprises notified before 31 December 2000. However, the Commission considers that restructuring aid should normally only need to be granted once and will examine such cases in the light of this principle.

¹⁰ Article 159 of the EC Treaty provides *inter alia* that "the formulation and implementation of the Community's policies and actions and the implementation of the internal market shall take into account the objectives set out in Article 158 and shall contribute to their achievement".

¹¹ As defined in the Commission recommendation of 3 April 1996 concerning the definition of small and medium-sized enterprises (OJ L107, 30.4.1996, p 4).

[12] In its judgment of 26 September 1996 in Case C-241/94, *(France v Commission* [1996] ECR I-4551), *(Kimberly Clark Sopalin)*, the Court of Justice confirmed that the system of financing on a discretionary basis by the French authorities, through the National Employment Fund, was liable to place certain undertakings in a more favourable situation than others and thus to qualify as aid within the meaning of Article 87(1) of the Treaty. (The Court's judgment did not call into question the Commission's conclusion that the aid was compatible with the common market.)

4. AID SCHEMES FOR SMES

4.1. GENERAL PRINCIPLES

(64) The Commission will authorise aid schemes for rescuing and/or restructuring small or medium-sized enterprises in difficulty only where the firms concerned correspond to the Community definition of SMEs. Subject to the following specific provisions, the compatibility of such schemes will be assessed in the light of the conditions set out in Chapters 2 and 3. Any aid which is granted under a scheme and does not meet one of those conditions must be notified individually and approved in advance by the Commission.

4.2. ELIGIBILITY

(65) Unless otherwise stipulated in rules on State aid in a particular sector, awards of aid, under schemes authorised from now on, to small or medium-sized enterprises will be exempted from individual notification only where the enterprise concerned meets at least one of the three criteria set out in point 5. Aid to enterprises that do not meet any of those three criteria must be notified individually to the Commission so that it can assess whether they qualify as firms in difficulty.

4.3. CONDITIONS FOR THE AUTHORISATION OF RESCUE AID SCHEMES

(66) In order to be approved by the Commission, rescue aid schemes must satisfy the conditions set out in (a), (b), (c) and (e) of point 23. Condition (d) set out in point 23 is replaced by the following, for the purposes of this Chapter—

(d) Rescue aid may be granted for not more than six months, during which time an analysis must be made of the firm's position. Before the end of that period the Member State should either approve a restructuring plan or a liquidation plan, or demand reimbursement of the loan and the aid corresponding to the risk premium from the beneficiary.

Any rescue aid granted for longer than six months must be individually notified to the Commission.

4.4. CONDITIONS FOR THE AUTHORISATION OF RESTRUCTURING AID SCHEMES

(67) The Commission will authorise restructuring aid schemes only if the grant of aid is conditional on full implementation by the recipient of a restructuring plan that has been approved by the Member State concerned and meets the following conditions—

(a) *Restoration of viability*: the criteria set out in points 31 to 34 apply;
(b) *Avoidance of undue distortions of competition*: since aid to SMEs tends to distort competition less, the principle set out in points 35 to 39, namely that the recipient firm's presence on the relevant market(s) should be reduced, does not apply unless it is otherwise stipulated in rules on State aid in a particular sector. Schemes should nevertheless provide that recipient firms must not increase their capacity during the restructuring plan;

(c) *Aid limited to the minimum necessary*: the principles set out in points 40 and 41 apply;

(d) *"One time, last time" principle*: the rule laid down in points 48 to 51 applies. However, Member States must notify measures individually to the Commission where an exception is made to this principle—

    (i) in exceptional and unforeseeable circumstances for which the company is not responsible;

    (ii) where a firm takes over assets of another firm which has itself already received rescue or restructuring aid;

(e) *Amendment of the restructuring plan*: any changes to the plan must comply with the rules set out in point 52.

4.5. COMMON CONDITION FOR THE AUTHORISATION OF RESCUE AND/OR RESTRUCTURING AID SCHEMES

(68) Schemes must specify the maximum amount of aid that can be awarded to any one firm as part of a rescue and/or restructuring operation, including where the plan is modified. Any aid exceeding that amount must be notified individually to the Commission. The maximum amount of aid may not be more than EUR 10 million, including any aid from other sources or under other schemes.

4.6. MONITORING AND ANNUAL REPORTS

(69) Points 45, 46 and 47 do not apply to aid schemes. However, a condition of approval will be that reports are presented on the scheme's operation, normally on an annual basis, containing the information specified in the Commission's instructions on standardised reports.[1] The reports must also include a list of all beneficiary firms indicating, for each of them—

(a) the company name;

(b) its sectoral code, using the NACE[2] two-digit sectoral classification codes;

(c) the number of employees;

(d) annual turnover and balance sheet value;

(e) the amount of aid granted;

(f) where appropriate, any restructuring aid, or other support treated as such, which it has received in the past;

(g) whether or not the beneficiary company has been wound up or subject to collective insolvency proceedings before the end of the restructuring period.

[6205]

NOTES

[1]   See letter to the Member States of 22 February 1994: Competition law in the European Communities, Vol IIA.

[2]   Statistical classification of economic activities in the European Community, published by the Statistical Office of the European Communities.

5. PROVISIONS APPLICABLE TO AID FOR RESTRUCTURING IN THE AGRICULTURAL SECTOR[1]

5.1. CAPACITY REDUCTIONS

(70) Points 35 to 39, and 55 and 67(b) provide that the requirement for compensatory measures is not normally applied in the case of small and medium-sized enterprises, unless otherwise stipulated in sector-specific State aid rules. In the agricultural sector, the Commission will normally require compensatory measures, in accordance with the principles set out in points 35 to 39, to be carried

out by all recipients of restructuring aid, whatever their size. However, Member States may alternatively apply the special rules for agriculture set out in points 73 to 82.

5.2. DEFINITION OF EXCESS CAPACITY

(71) In the agricultural sector and for the purposes of these Guidelines, structural excess capacity is defined by the Commission on a case-by-case basis taking account in particular of—

(a) the extent and trend for the relevant product category over the past three years of market stabilisation measures, especially export refunds and withdrawals from the market, development of world market prices, and the presence of sector limits in Community legislation. Primary products subject to production quotas shall be deemed not to have excess capacity;

(b) as regards fisheries and aquaculture, the specific features of the sector and the Community rules governing it, and in particular the Guidelines for the examination of State aid to fisheries and aquaculture[2] and Council Regulation (EC) No 2468/98.[3]

5.3. ELIGIBILITY FOR RESCUE AND RESTRUCTURING AID SCHEMES

(72) Point 65, concerning eligibility for rescue and restructuring aid schemes for SMEs and more specifically the exemption from the requirement to notify individually any awards of such aid, does not apply to the agricultural sector (production, processing and marketing). In that sector and under aid schemes authorised from now on, awards of aid to SMEs that do not fulfil the conditions set out in the point may nevertheless be exempted from individual notification.

5.4. CAPACITY REDUCTIONS

(73) The Commission will, at the request of the Member State concerned, and as an alternative to the general provisions of these Guidelines concerning capacity reduction, apply the following provisions for operators in the agricultural sector.

(a) *General case*

(74) Where there is a structural excess of production capacity, the requirement of irreversibly reducing or closing capacity set out in points 35 to 39 applies. However, in the case of primary agricultural production, this requirement is replaced by the requirement that the capacity reduction or closure continues for at least five years, as follows—

(i) for measures targeted on particular products or operators the production capacity reduction must normally attain 16%[4] of that for which the restructuring aid is effectively granted;

(ii) for other measures not so targeted the abovementioned capacity reduction must normally attain 8%[4] of the value of output of products with structural excess for which the restructuring aid is effectively granted.

(75) In determining eligibility for, and amounts of, restructuring aid, no account shall be taken of the burdens of compliance with Community quota and related provisions applicable at the level of individual operators.

(b) *Special case for small agricultural enterprises (SAEs)*

(76) For the purposes of these Guidelines SAEs are defined as those operators in the agricultural sector with no more than 10 annual work units.

(77) For SAEs, the requirement of irreversibly reducing or closing capacity may be deemed to be achieved at the relevant market level (not necessarily involving

exclusively or even any of the beneficiaries of the restructuring aid). Subject to compliance with common agricultural policy provisions, Member States may choose whatever capacity reduction system they wish to apply to SAEs. In such cases, Member States must, as a general rule, demonstrate that—

  (i) for measures targeted on particular products or operators the system would in the relevant Member State, reduce production capacity of product(s) with structural excess by 10%[4] of that which the restructuring aid is effectively granted;

 (ii) for other measures not so targeted, this capacity reduction must attain 5%[4] of the value of output of products with structural excess for which the restructuring aid is actually granted. This reduction may be either products which actually benefit from the restructuring aid or any other Annex I products with structural excess.

The Member State must also demonstrate that the capacity reduction would be supplementary to any applicable in the absence of the restructuring aid.

(78) Where the capacity reduction is not sought at the level of the beneficiary of the aid, measures to achieve the reduction must be implemented no later than two years after the threshold set out in points 79, 80 and 81 has been attained.

  (c)   *Particular circumstances for all operators in the agricultural sector*

(79) In this sector even very small amounts of aid are capable of fulfilling the conditions of Article 87(1) of the Treaty. However, in recognition of the practical problems associated with capacity reduction at the level of primary agricultural production (and indirectly in the processing and marketing of products under Annex I of the Treaty), yet recognising the common interest to be eligible for exemption under Article 87(3)(c), the Commission, subject to adherence to all other conditions, will waive the capacity reduction requirements in the following situations—

  (i) for measures aimed at any particular category of products or operators, where the totality of decisions taken in favour of all beneficiaries over any consecutive twelve-month period does not involve a quantity of products which exceeds 3% of the total annual production of such products in that country;

 (ii) for other measures not so aimed, where the totality of decisions taken in favour of all beneficiaries over any consecutive twelve-month period does not involve a value of product which exceeds 1.5% of the total annual value of agricultural production in that country.

(80) At the request of the Member State concerned, the geographic references under (i) and (ii) of point 79 may, for any measure, be determined at a regional level. In all cases, measurement of the production of a country (or a region) shall be based on normal production levels (in general, the average of the previous three years), and, as regards the quantity or the value of production of beneficiaries, be representative of that of their enterprises prior to the decision to grant aid.

(81) Exemption from the capacity reduction requirement shall in no case imply tolerance of investment aid related to activities subject to sectoral limits.

(82) In cases where the limits for exemption from capacity reduction pursuant to points 79, 80 and 81 are exceeded—

  (i) the capacity reduction to be achieved shall be determined on the basis of total aided capacity, not only that part exceeding the thresholds;

 (ii) as regards beneficiaries other than SAEs which already have been accepted for aid prior to the thresholds being attained, the capacity reduction may be achieved through measures analogous to those for SAEs under points 76, 77 and 78.

5.5. "ONE TIME, LAST TIME" CONDITION

(83) The principle that restructuring aid should be granted once only also applies to the agricultural sector. However, by way of derogation from points 48 to 51 and 67, as regards individual awards of aid and rescue and restructuring schemes concerning primary agricultural production, the period during which further aid may not be granted except in exceptional and unforeseeable circumstances for which the company is not responsible is reduced to five years. Derogations from this principle do not need to be notified individually to the Commission, provided that they are made in accordance with conditions set out in the scheme and approved by the Commission. Amendments to rescue and restructuring schemes which are intended to take account of market developments that were not foreseeable at the time the schemes were approved by the Commission will be examined on a case-by-case basis.

5.6. MONITORING AND ANNUAL REPORT

(84) The rules set out in Chapters 3 and 4 apply to monitoring and annual reports in the agricultural sector, except for the obligation to supply a list of all aid beneficiaries and certain items of information on each of them (points 69(a) to (g)). The latter obligation does not apply to schemes for SAEs.

(85) Where recourse has been had to the provisions of points 73 to 82, the report must also include data showing either—

    (a) the quantity (or value) of production which has effectively benefited from the restructuring aid, and data on capacity reduction achieved pursuant to those points; or

    (b) that the conditions for exemption from capacity reduction according to points 79, 80 and 81 have been fulfilled.

5.7. DEFINITION OF "ASSISTED AREAS"

(86) For the purposes of these Guidelines, "assisted areas" (see points 53 and 54) shall also include, for operators in the agricultural sector, the less favoured areas defined in Council Regulation (EC) No 1257/1999 of 17 May 1999 on support for rural development from the European Agricultural Guidance and Guarantee Fund (EAGGF) and amending and repealing certain Regulations.[5]

[6206]

NOTES

[1] Covering, for the purposes of the Guidelines, all operators involved in the production of, and/or trade in, products of Annex I to the Treaty, including fisheries and aquaculture, but having due regard to the specific features of the sector and the Community rules governing it.

[2] OJ C100, 27.3.1997, p 12.

[3] OJ L312, 20.11.1998, p 19.

[4] For restructuring aid granted in assisted areas, including less favoured regions, the capacity reduction requirement will be reduced by two percentage points.

[5] OJ L160, 26.6.1999, p 80.

6. APPROPRIATE MEASURES UNDER ARTICLE 88(1)

(87) The Commission is proposing, under Article 88(1) of the Treaty, that the Member States adopt appropriate measures as set out below, with regard to their existing aid schemes. The Commission will make authorisation of any future scheme conditional on compliance with the provisions below.

6.1. INDIVIDUAL NOTIFICATION OF ANY AID FOR TANGIBLE INVESTMENT DURING THE RESTRUCTURING PERIOD

(88) Where a large enterprise receives restructuring aid examined under these Guidelines, the grant of any other investment aid during the restructuring period, even in accordance with a scheme that has already been authorised, is liable to influence the Commission's assessment of the extent of the compensatory measures required.

(89) During the period for restructuring such an enterprise, any aid intended to encourage tangible investment (whether it be to promote regional development, environmental protection or any other objective) awarded after 30 June 2000 must be notified individually, unless it is covered by the *de minimis* rule.[1]

6.2. NEED TO INFORM THE COMMISSION OF ANY AID GRANTED TO THE RECIPIENT FIRM

(90) Where a large enterprise receives restructuring aid examined under these Guidelines, monitoring of the satisfactory implementation of the Commission's decisions on such aid requires a large measure of transparency with regard to any further aid which the firm might receive, even in accordance with a scheme that has already been authorised and even where such aid is not subject to individual notification under points 88 and 89.

(91) With effect from 30 June 2000, notifications of aid for restructuring a large enterprise must indicate, for information, all other aid of any kind which is planned to be granted to the recipient firm during the restructuring period, unless it is covered by the *de minimis* rule.

(92) Likewise, the reports to be submitted in accordance with points 45, 46 and 47 of these Guidelines must indicate any other aid granted to the recipient firm during the period covered, and any other aid which is planned to be granted to the recipient firm during the restructuring period, unless it is covered by the *de minimis* rule.

(93) The Commission reserves the right to initiate proceedings under Article 88(2) of the Treaty against all aid to a particular firm if the grant of aid under approved schemes is liable to circumvent the requirements of these Guidelines.

6.3. ADAPTATION OF EXISTING RESCUE OR RESTRUCTURING AID SCHEMES IN THE LIGHT OF THESE GUIDELINES

(94) Member States must adapt their existing rescue and restructuring aid schemes which are to remain in operation after 30 June 2000 in order to bring them into line with these Guidelines, and in particular with the requirements of Chapter 4, after that date.

(95) To enable the Commission to monitor the adaptation process, Member States must let it have a list of all such schemes before 31 December 1999. They must subsequently, and in any event before 30 June 2000, provide it with sufficient information to enable it to check that the schemes have indeed been modified in accordance with these Guidelines.

[6207]

PART IV
EC MATERIALS

NOTES
  [1] OJ C68, 6.3.1996, p 9.

7. ENTRY INTO FORCE; DURATION AND REVIEW OF THE GUIDELINES

7.1. AMENDMENT OF THE REGIONAL AID GUIDELINES

(96) Point 4.4 of the Guidelines on national regional aid[1] is hereby amended by deleting the text from the word "unless" up to the end of that point. That text excluded from the scope of "initial investment" the purchase of an establishment from a firm in difficulty, and thus disqualified it for regional aid. That exclusion therefore no longer operates. However, where an establishment is purchased from a firm in difficulty, it must be demonstrated in particular that the condition laid down in point 4.5, namely that the transaction takes place at market conditions, has been fulfilled.

7.2. ENTRY INTO FORCE AND DURATION

(97) Subject to the provisions set out below, these Guidelines shall enter into force on the date of their publication in the *Official Journal of the European Communities*. They shall remain in force, unless otherwise stipulated in any new decision, for five years.

7.3. AID TO SMES

(98) Aid for rescuing and restructuring SMEs individually notified before 30 April 2000 will be assessed in the light of the guidelines in force before adoption of this text. The extension of those guidelines, which was notified to Member States and published in the *Official Journal of the European Communities* on 10 March 1999 (see footnote 2) is therefore renewed for such aid.

(99) Any scheme is nevertheless subject to the appropriate measure referred to in points 94 and 95 where the scheme is intended to remain in operation after 30 June 2000.

7.4. AID TO LARGE ENTERPRISES

(100) Subject to the provisions set out below, the Commission will assess the compatibility with the common market of any aid for rescuing or restructuring large enterprises, on the basis of these Guidelines once they are published in the *Official Journal of the European Communities*.

However, notifications registered by the Commission before that date will be examined in the light of the criteria in force at the time of notification.

7.5. NON-NOTIFIED AID

(101) The Commission will examine the compatibility with the common market of any rescue or restructuring aid granted without its authorisation and therefore in breach of Article 88(3) of the Treaty—

    (a) on the basis of these Guidelines if some or all of the aid is granted after their publication in the *Official Journal of the European Communities*;

    (b) on the basis of the Guidelines in force at the time the aid is granted in all other cases.

NOTES
   [1]   OJ C74, 10.3.1998, p 9.

ANNEX I
NOTIFICATION FORM FOR INDIVIDUAL GRANTS OF RESTRUCTURING AID

I. Information on the company

- —Company name;
- —Legal status;
- —Sector in which it operates, with corresponding NACE code;
- —Names of the main shareholders and extent of their holdings;
- —List of shareholders' agreements (creation of a hard core, purchase option, etc);
- —If the company belongs to a group, copy of the full, up-to-date organisation chart of the whole of the group, showing the links between its members (capital and voting rights);
- —If the company originates from a purchase of assets following liquidation or court-supervised administration proceedings, also give the above details for the firm(s) concerned;
- —Location of all main production sites throughout the world, with workforce;
- —If the company is treated as an SME, the Member State must supply evidence that it fulfils all the criteria of the Community definition. If that is the case, it must explain why the company does not qualify for a restructuring aid scheme for SMEs (either there is no such scheme or the company does not meet the eligibility criteria);
- —A copy of the last three profit and loss accounts (if possible) or at least of the most recent one;
- —A copy of any court decision appointing an administrator or opening an investigation into the company.

II. Market surveys

The Member State must supply a copy of the survey of the market(s) served by the firm in difficulty, with the name of the organisation which carried it out. The market survey must give in particular—

- —a precise definition of the market covered by the survey;
- —the names of the company's main competitors with their shares of the world, Community or domestic market, as appropriate;
- —the evolution of the company's market shares in recent years;
- —an assessment of total production capacity and demand at Community level, concluding whether or not there is excess capacity on the market;
- —Community-wide forecasts for trends in demand, aggregate capacity and prices on the market over the five years ahead.

III. Description of the aid

- —Demonstrate that the company's difficulties are its own and are not the result of an arbitrary allocation of costs within a group;
- —State whether the company has already received rescue aid and, if so, give the approval date and attach the Member State's commitment to submit a restructuring or liquidation plan;
- —State whether the company or any of its subsidiaries in which it holds not less than 25% of the capital or the voting rights have in the past already received restructuring aid or aid regarded as such. If so, give the references of the previous Commission decisions;
- —Indicate the form to be taken by the aid and the total amount of the financial benefit involved;
- —Describe the compensatory measures proposed with a view to mitigating the distortive effects on competition at Community level;
- —Specify all the aid of any kind which the firm is likely to receive before the end of its restructuring period, unless it is covered by the "*de-minimis*" rule.

IV. Restructuring plan

The Member State must supply a restructuring plan drawn up in accordance with points 29 to 47 and containing at least the following information—

- —presentation of the different market assumptions arising from the market survey;
- —analysis of the reason why the firm has run into difficulty;
- —presentation of the proposed future strategy for the firm;
- —description of the different restructuring measures planned and their cost;
- —comparative assessment of the economic and social consequences, at regional and/or national level, of disappearance of the firm in difficulty and of implementation of the restructuring plan;
- —timetable for implementing the different measures and final deadline for implementing the restructuring plan in its entirety;
- —very precise description of the financial arrangements for the restructuring—
  - —use of capital still available,
  - —sale of assets or subsidiaries to help finance the restructuring,
  - —financial commitment by the different private shareholders and the main lending banks,
  - —amount of public assistance and demonstration of the need for that amount,
  - —where appropriate, grant of repayable loans or insertion of a "better fortunes" clause to secure reimbursement of the aid;
- —projected profit and loss accounts for the next five years with estimated return on capital and sensitivity study based on several scenarios;
- —record of the discussion on the planned restructuring held with the trade unions representing the firm's employees;
- —name(s) of the author(s) of the restructuring plan and date on which it was drawn up.

V. Undertaking by the Member State

The Member State must undertake to give, in the reports on restructuring aid that has been allowed, all relevant information on aid of any kind granted to the firm receiving restructuring aid, whether under a scheme or not, until the restructuring period comes to an end.

[6209]

ANNEX II
NOTIFICATION FORM FOR RESCUE AID

Essential information on the company

Company name:

Legal status:

Sector in which it operates:

Workforce (consolidated where appropriate):

Operating costs and financial charges over the last 12 months:

Maximum amount to be loaned:

Name of lender:

Essential supporting documents to be supplied

- —latest profit and loss account with balance sheet, or court decision opening an investigation into the company under national company law;
- —an undertaking by the Member State to submit to the Commission, within not more than six months of the date of approval of the rescue aid, either a restructuring plan, or a liquidation plan, or proof that both the loan and the aid have been reimbursed in full;
- —a liquidity plan for the six months ahead, indicating the amounts to be borrowed in the short term;
- —a copy of the offer of a loan (linked to the rescue aid) to the firm in difficulty, specifying the conditions for the payment of the amounts loaned and the terms of reimbursement;
- —a copy of the draft guarantee covering the loan in question where it is to be guaranteed.

[6210]

COMMISSION NOTICE

on the application of Articles 87 and 88 of the EC Treaty to State aid in the form of guarantees

(2000/C 71/07)

NOTES
Date of publication in OJ: OJ C71, 11.3.00, p 14.

1. INTRODUCTION

1.1.   This notice outlines the Commission's approach to State aid granted in the form of guarantees. Guarantees are usually associated with a loan or other financial obligation to be contracted by a borrower with a lender. However, this notice covers all forms of guarantees, irrespective of their legal basis and the transaction covered. Guarantees may be granted as individual guarantees or within guarantee schemes. If aid is involved, this aid in most cases benefits the borrower. However, in certain circumstances, there may also be an aid to the lender.

1.2.   This notice applies without prejudice to Article 295 and thus does not prejudice the rules in Member States governing the system of property ownership. The Commission is neutral as regards public or private ownership. This notice does not apply to export credit guarantees.

1.3.   In 1989 the Commission addressed two letters on State guarantees to the Member States. In the first letter,[1] it pointed out that it regards all guarantees given by a State as falling within the scope of Article 87(1). According to this letter, the Commission must therefore be notified of any plans to give or alter such guarantees in sufficient time to enable it to submit its comments. In the second letter,[2] the Commission made it clear that it intended to examine the establishment of State guarantee schemes, and that individual guarantees given under an approved scheme would not need to be notified. In 1993 the Commission adopted a communication,[3] which addressed the subject of guarantees as well.

1.4.   Experience gained in the meantime suggests that the Commission's policy in this area should be reviewed. This notice replaces the two Commission letters of 1989 and paragraph 38 of the Commission communication of 1993. Its purpose is to give Member States more detailed explanations about the principles on which the Commission intends to base its interpretation of Articles 87 and 88 and their application to State guarantees. The Commission intends in this way to make its policy in this area as transparent as possible, thereby ensuring that its decisions are predictable and that equal treatment is guaranteed.

[6211]

NOTES
  [1]   Commission letter to the Member States, SG(89) D/4328 of 5 April 1989.
  [2]   Commission letter to the Member States, SG(89) D/12772 of 12 October 1989.
  [3]   Commission Communication to the Member States on the application of Articles 92 and 93 of the EEC Treaty and of Article 5 of Commission Directive 80/723/EEC to public undertakings in the manufacturing sector (OJ C307, 13.11.1993, p 3).

2. APPLICABILITY OF ARTICLE 87(1)

2.1.   Aid to the borrower

2.1.1.   Usually, the aid beneficiary is the borrower. The State guarantee enables the borrower to obtain better financial terms for a loan than those normally available on the financial markets. Typically, with the benefit of the State guarantee, the borrower can obtain lower rates and/or offer less security. In some cases, the borrower would not, without a State guarantee, find a financial institution prepared to lend on any terms. State guarantees may thus facilitate the creation of new businesses and enable certain undertakings to raise money in order to pursue new activities or simply remain active instead of being eliminated or restructured, thereby creating distortions of competition. State guarantees thus generally fall within the scope of Article 87(1), if trade between Member States is affected and no market premium is paid.

2.1.2. The benefit of a State guarantee is that the risk associated with the guarantee is carried by the State. This carrying of a risk by the State should normally be remunerated by an appropriate premium. Where the State forgoes such a premium, there is both a benefit for the undertaking and a drain on the resources of the State. Thus, even if no payments are ever made by the State under a guarantee, there may nevertheless be a State aid under Article 87(1). The aid is granted at the moment when the guarantee is given, not the moment at which the guarantee is invoked or the moment at which payments are made under the terms of the guarantee. Whether or not a guarantee constitutes State aid, and, if so, what the amount of that State aid may be, must be assessed at the moment the guarantee is given.

2.1.3. The Commission also regards as aid in the form of a guarantee, the more favourable funding terms obtained by enterprises whose legal form rules out bankruptcy or other insolvency procedures or provides an explicit State guarantee or coverage of losses by the State. The same applies to the acquisition by a State of a holding in an enterprise if unlimited liability is accepted instead of the usual limited liability.[1]

2.1.4. Article 87(1) covers aid granted by a Member State or through State resources. Therefore, in the same way as other forms of potential aid, guarantees given by the State directly, namely by central, regional or local authorities, as well as guarantees given by undertakings under the dominant influence of public authorities, may constitute State aid.

2.2. Aid to the lender

2.2.1. Even if usually the aid beneficiary is the borrower it cannot be ruled out that under certain circumstances the lender, too, will benefit from the aid. In such a case the Commission will certainly pursue the matter accordingly.

2.2.2. In particular, for example, if a State guarantee is given *ex post* in respect of a loan or other financial obligation already entered into without the terms of this loan or financial obligation being adjusted, or if one guaranteed loan is used to pay back another, non-guaranteed loan to the same credit institution, then there may also be an aid to the lender, in so far as the security of the loans is increased. Such aid is capable of favouring the lender and distorting competition, and generally falls within the scope of Article 87(1), if trade between Member States is affected.

[6212]

NOTES
  [1]   See footnote 3, paragraph 38.1 and 38.2.

3. AMOUNT OF THE AID

3.1. In the case of an individual State guarantee, the aid element must be assessed by reference to the details of the guarantee and loan (or other financial obligation). The relevant factors include in particular the duration and amount of the guarantee and loan, the risk of default by the borrower, the price paid by the borrower for the guarantee, the nature of any security given, how and when the State could be called upon to pay a debt and the means (eg declaration of bankruptcy) to be used by the State to recover amounts owed by the borrower once the guarantee has been invoked.

3.2.   The cash grant equivalent of a loan guarantee in a given year can be:
— calculated in the same way as the grant equivalent of a soft loan, the interest subsidy representing the difference between the market rate and the rate obtained thanks to the State guarantee after any premiums paid have been deducted, or
— taken to be the difference between (a) the outstanding sum guaranteed, multiplied by the risk factor (the probability of default) and (b) any premium paid, ie (guaranteed sum × risk) – premium, or
— calculated by any other objectively justifiable and generally accepted method.

For individual guarantees, the first method should in principle be the standard form of calculation, for guarantee schemes the second one.

The risk factor should be based on the past experience of defaults on loans given in similar circumstances (sector, size of firm, level of general economic activity). The yearly grant equivalents should be discounted to their present value using the reference rate, then added up to obtain the total grant equivalent.

Where, at the time the loan is granted, there is a strong probability that the borrower will default, eg because he is in financial difficulty, the value of the guarantee may be as high as the amount effectively covered by that guarantee.

3.3.   If a financial obligation is wholly covered by a State guarantee, the lender has less incentive to assess properly, secure and minimise the risk arising from the lending operation, and in particular to assess properly the borrower's creditworthiness. Such risk assessment might also not always be taken over by the guarantor, for lack of means. This lack of incentive to minimise the risk of non-repayment of the loan might encourage lenders to contract loans with a greater than normal commercial risk and could thus increase the amount of higher-risk guarantees in the State's portfolio.

3.4.   The Commission suggests that a percentage of at least 20% not covered by a State guarantee will serve as an appropriate limit for inducing the lender to properly assess the creditworthiness of the borrower,[1] to properly secure its loans and to minimise the risk associated with the transaction.[2] The Commission will therefore, in general, examine critically any guarantees covering the entirety (or nearly the entirety) of a financial transaction.

3.5.   In the case of State guarantee schemes, the specific features of the individual cases may not be known at the time when the scheme is to be assessed. In these circumstances, the aid element must be assessed by reference to the provisions of the scheme concerning amongst others the maximum amount and duration of loans, the category of enterprise and type of project eligible, the security required from the borrowers, the premium to be paid and the interest rates obtained by them.

[6213]

NOTES
[1]   This is under the assumption that the same level of security is provided by the company to the State and the credit institution.
[2]   From the answers to the questionnaire on State guarantees it can be seen that several Member States already apply this rule. The percentage covered varies widely from 20% to 100%. Nevertheless, a multitude of guarantees cover the full amount of the underlying financial operation, thereby exempting the lending institution from the necessity to assess properly the creditworthiness of the beneficiary in its own interest.

4. CONDITIONS EXCLUDING THE EXISTENCE OF AID

4.1. An individual guarantee or a guarantee scheme entered into by the State will be outside the scope of Article 87(1) when there is no aid which favours certain undertakings or the production of certain goods. In such cases, notification by the Member State is not necessary. Also, a guarantee does not constitute State aid under Article 87(1) when the measure does not affect trade between Member States.

4.2. The Commission considers that the fulfilment of all the following conditions ensures that an individual State guarantee does not constitute State aid under Article 87(1)—

   (a) the borrower is not in financial difficulty;
   (b) the borrower would in principle be able to obtain a loan on market conditions from the financial markets without any intervention by the State;
   (c) the guarantee is linked to a specific financial transaction, is for a fixed maximum amount, does not cover more than 80% of the outstanding loan or other financial obligation (except for bonds and similar instruments) and is not open-ended;
   (d) the market price for the guarantee is paid (which reflects, amongst others, the amount and duration of the guarantee, the security given by the borrower, the borrower's financial position, the sector of activity and the prospects, the rates of default, and other economic conditions).

4.3. The Commission considers that the fulfilment of all the following conditions ensures that a State guarantee scheme does not constitute State aid under Article 87(1)—

   (a) the scheme does not allow guarantees to be granted to borrowers who are in financial difficulty;
   (b) the borrowers would in principle be able to obtain a loan on market conditions from the financial markets without any intervention by the State;
   (c) the guarantees are linked to a specific financial transaction, are for a fixed maximum amount, do not cover more than 80 % of each outstanding loan or other financial obligation (except for bonds and similar instruments) and are not open-ended;
   (d) the terms of the scheme are based on a realistic assessment of the risk so that the premiums paid by the beneficiary enterprises make it, in all probability, self-financing;
   (e) the scheme provides for the terms on which future guarantees are granted and the overall financing of the scheme to be reviewed at least once a year;
   (f) the premiums cover both the normal risks associated with granting the guarantee and the administrative costs of the scheme, including, where the State provides the initial capital for the start-up of the scheme, a normal return on that capital.

4.4. Failure to comply with any one of the above conditions set out in points 4.2 and 4.3 does not mean that such guarantee or guarantee scheme is automatically regarded as State aid. If there is any doubt as to whether a planned guarantee or scheme does constitute State aid, it should be notified.

4.5. There may be circumstances in which it is planned to use State guarantees to enable enterprises, and in particular small and medium-sized enterprises, to obtain loans that the market would not supply. The enterprises may be starting up, expanding fast or be small and hence unable to furnish the necessary security to secure a loan or obtain a guarantee. They may fall into the category of high-risk enterprises (expected to move into profitability only in the long term and/or having a particularly high failure rate). This may be the case, for example, with projects concerning new, innovative products or processes. The Commission considers that such circumstances will generally not take State guarantees outside the scope of

Article 87(1). State guarantees given in such circumstances should therefore be notified to the Commission in sufficient time, in the same way as State guarantees given in other circumstances.

[6214]

5 COMPATIBILITY OF STATE AID IN THE FORM OF GUARANTEES WITH THE COMMON MARKET

5.1. State guarantees within the scope of Article 87(1) must be examined by the Commission with a view to determining whether or not they are compatible with the common market. Before such assessment of compatibility can be made, the beneficiary of the aid must be identified. As has been explained under point 2, this can be either the borrower, or the lender, or both.

5.2. In most cases the guarantee contains aid to the borrower (point 2.1). Whether or not this aid is compatible with the common market will be examined by the Commission according to the same rules as are applied to aid measures taking other forms. The concrete criteria for the compatibility assessment have been clarified and detailed by the Commission in frameworks and guidelines concerning horizontal, regional and sectoral aid.[1] The examination will take into account, in particular, the aid intensity, the characteristics of the beneficiaries and the objectives pursued.

5.3. The Commission will accept guarantees only if their mobilisation is contractually linked to specific conditions which may go as far as the compulsory declaration of bankruptcy of the beneficiary undertaking, or any similar procedure. These conditions will have to be agreed at the initial examination by the Commission of the proposed guarantee within the normal procedures of Article 88(3), at the stage when it is granted. In the event that a Member State wants to mobilise the guarantee under conditions other than those initially agreed at the granting stage, then the Commission will regard the mobilisation of the guarantee as creating a new aid which has to be notified under Article 88(3).

5.4. Where the guarantee contains aid to the lender (point 2.2), attention should be drawn to the fact that such aid might, in principle, constitute operating aid.

[6215]

NOTES
[1] See Competition law in the European Community, Volume IIA, Rules applicable to State aid, published by the Office for Official Publications of the European Communities. Certain texts have also been published in the *Official Journal of the European Communities* and are available on the Internet.

6. CONSEQUENCES OF THE INFRINGEMENT OF ARTICLE 88(3)

6.1. Where Member States do not observe the obligations of prior notification and suspension laid down in Article 88(3), the aid element of the guarantee is to be qualified as unlawful in accordance with Article 1(f) of Council Regulation (EC) No 659/1999 of 22 March 1999 laying down detailed rules for the application of Article 93 of the EC Treaty.[1] As to the consequences of infringement of the third sentence of Article 88(3), various distinctions should be drawn. In the following the position of the aid beneficiary and that of lenders not being a beneficiary will be examined in turn.

6.2. First, where aid has been illegally granted, the beneficiaries of the aid contained in the guarantee will run a risk. The Commission may take interim measures in accordance with Article 11 of Regulation (EC) No 659/1999 pending the outcome of the examination as to the compatibility of the aid. If, after this examination, the Commission finds that the State aid is incompatible with the common market, it shall be recovered from the beneficiary in accordance with Article 14 of Regulation (EC) No 659/1999, even if this means the declaration of bankruptcy of the enterprise.

6.3.   Moreover, aid beneficiaries also run a risk at national level, inasmuch as the third sentence of Article 88(3) has direct effect. The Court of Justice of the European Communities has repeatedly confirmed that it is the duty of national courts to safeguard the rights of the individuals concerned, such as competitors of firms receiving illegal aid, against breaches of the third sentence of Article 88(3). National courts have to draw all the appropriate conclusions from the illegality of State aid granted in breach of the procedural rules of the Treaty. If a national court is requested to order recovery of the unlawful aid, it must normally grant that application.[2]

6.4.   Secondly, guarantees differ from other State aid measures, such as grants or tax exemptions, in the sense that in the case of a guarantee the State also enters into a legal relation with the lender. Therefore, consideration has to be given to whether the fact that a State aid has been illegally granted also has consequences for third parties. In the case of State guarantees for loans, this concerns mainly the financial lending institutions. In the case of guarantees for bonds issued to obtain financing for undertakings, this concerns the financial institutions involved in the issuance of the bonds.

6.5.   The question whether the illegality of the aid affects the legal relations between the State and third parties is a matter which has to be examined under national law. National courts may have to examine whether national law prevents the guarantee contracts from being honoured, and in that assessment the Commission considers that they should take account of the breach of Community law. Accordingly, lenders may have an interest in verifying, as a standard precaution, that the Community rules on State aid have been observed, whenever guarantees are granted. The Member State should be able to provide a case number issued by the Commission for an individual case or a scheme and eventually a non-confidential copy of the Commission's decision together with the relevant reference to the *Official Journal of the European Communities*. The Commission for its part will do its utmost to make available in a transparent manner information on cases and schemes approved by it.

[6216]

NOTES

[1]   OJ L83, 27.3.1999, p 1.

[2]   See Case C-39/94 Syndicat Français de l'Express International (SFEI) and Others v La Poste and Others [1996] ECR I-3547.

7. REPORTS TO BE PRESENTED TO THE COMMISSION BY THE MEMBER STATES

7.1.   As there may be new developments on the financial markets and as the value of State guarantees is difficult to assess, the constant review pursuant to Article 88(1) of State guarantee schemes approved by the Commission is of particular importance. In addition to the usual data on expenditure, the reports to be presented annually to the Commission should give (for schemes and individual guarantees as well) data on the total amount of State guarantees outstanding, the total amount paid in the preceding year by the State to defaulting debtors (net of any funds recovered), and the premiums paid for State guarantees in the same year. This information will help in calculating the rate of default and will be used to reassess the value of future guarantees and, if necessary, the premium to be paid in the future.

7.2.   The Commission does not intend to use information supplied in the above mentioned reports and not known or foreseeable when it took an earlier decision, in order to revise its initial conclusions concerning the existence or scale of aid contained in State guarantee schemes. The Commission may, however, use such information to propose appropriate measures to a Member State under Article 88(1) in order to alter an existing State guarantee scheme.

[6217]

COMMISSION REGULATION

of 12 January 2001

on the application of Articles 87 and 88 of the EC Treaty to training aid

(68/2001/EC)

NOTES

Date of publication in OJ: OJ L10, 13.1.2001, p 20.

THE COMMISSION OF THE EUROPEAN COMMUNITIES,

Having regard to the Treaty establishing the European Community,

Having regard to Council Regulation (EC) No 994/98 of 7 May 1998 on the application of Articles 92 and 93 of the Treaty establishing the European Community to certain categories of horizontal State aid,[1] and in particular point (a)(iv) of Article 1(1) thereof,

Having published a draft of this Regulation,[2]

Having consulted the Advisory Committee on State Aid,

Whereas:

(1) Regulation (EC) No 994/98 empowers the Commission to declare, in accordance with Article 87 of the Treaty, that under certain conditions training aid is compatible with the common market and not subject to the notification requirement of Article 88(3) of the Treaty.

(2) The Commission has applied Articles 87 and 88 of the Treaty to training aid in numerous decisions and has also stated its policy, most recently in the Community framework on training aid.[3] In the light of the Commission's considerable experience in applying those Articles to training aid, it is appropriate, with a view to ensuring efficient supervision and simplifying administration without weakening Commission monitoring, that the Commission should make use of the powers conferred by Regulation (EC) No 994/98.

(3) In order to establish a transparent and coherent policy for all sectors, it is appropriate that the scope of this Regulation be as broad as possible and include the agricultural sector, fisheries and aquaculture.

(4) This Regulation is without prejudice to the possibility for Member States to notify training aid. Such notifications will be assessed by the Commission in particular in the light of the criteria set out in this Regulation, or in accordance with the applicable Community guidelines and frameworks, if such guidelines and frameworks exist. This is currently the case for activities relating to the production, processing and marketing of products listed in Annex I to the Treaty and for the sector of maritime transport. The framework on training aid should be abolished from the date of entry into force of this Regulation, since its contents are replaced by this Regulation.

(5) For reasons of transparency, it should be recalled that in accordance with the second subparagraph of Article 51(1), of Council Regulation (EC) No 1257/1999 of 17 May 1999 on support for rural development from the European Agricultural Guidance and Guarantee Fund (EAGGF) and amending and repealing certain Regulations,[4] Articles 87 to 89 of the Treaty do not apply to financial contributions provided by the Member States for measures subject to Community support for training according to Article 9 of the said Regulation.

(6) For reasons of transparency it should be underlined that this Regulation should only apply to training measures which constitute State aid within the meaning of Article 87(1) of the Treaty. Many training measures are not caught by that Article, but constitute general measures because they are open to all enterprises in all sectors without discrimination and without discretionary power for the authorities applying the measure, eg general tax incentive schemes, such as automatic tax credits, open to all firms investing in employee training. Other training measures do not fall within the scope of Article 87(1) of the Treaty because they directly benefit people everywhere and do not grant an advantage to certain enterprises or sectors. Examples are: schooling and initial training (such as apprenticeships and day-release schemes); the training or re-training of unemployed people, including traineeships in enterprises; measures directly targeted at workers or even at certain categories of workers, affording them the opportunity of receiving training unconnected with the firm or industry in which they work (for example the "learning account"). On the other hand, it should be recalled that contributions from sectoral funds, if they are made compulsory by the State, are not considered as private resources, but constitute State resources within the meaning of Article 87(1) of the Treaty.

(7) This Regulation should exempt any aid that meets all the relevant requirements of this Regulation, and any aid scheme, provided that any aid that could be granted under such scheme meets all the relevant requirements of this Regulation. With a view to ensuring efficient supervision and simplifying administration without weakening Commission monitoring, aid schemes and individual grants, outside any aid scheme, should contain an express reference to this Regulation.

(8) In order to eliminate differences that might give rise to distortions of competition, in order to facilitate coordination between different Community and national initiatives concerning small and medium-sized enterprises, and for reasons of administrative clarity and legal certainty, the definition of "small and medium-sized enterprises" used in this Regulation should be that laid down in Commission Recommendation 96/280/EC of 3 April 1996 concerning the definition of small and medium-sized enterprises.[5]

(9) In order to determine whether or not aid is compatible with the common market pursuant to this Regulation, it is necessary to take into consideration the aid intensity and thus the aid amount expressed as a grant equivalent. Calculation of the grant equivalent of aid payable in several instalments, and calculation of aid in the form of a soft loan, require the use of market interest rates prevailing at the time of grant. With a view to a uniform, transparent and simple application of the State aid rules, the market rates for the purposes of this Regulation should be deemed to be the reference rates, provided that, in the case of a soft loan, the loan is backed by normal security and does not involve abnormal risk. The reference rates should be those which are periodically fixed by the Commission on the basis of objective criteria and published in the *Official Journal of the European Communities* and on the Internet.

(10) Training usually has positive external effects for society as a whole since it increases the pool of skilled workers from which other firms may draw, improves the competitiveness of Community industry and plays an important role in employment strategy. In view of the fact that enterprises in the Community generally underinvest in the training of their workers, State aid might help to correct this market imperfection and therefore can be considered under certain conditions to be compatible with the common market and therefore exempted from prior notification.

(11) In order to ensure that State aid is limited to the minimum necessary to obtain the Community objective which market forces alone would not make possible, the permissible intensities of exempted aid should be modulated according to the type of training provided, the size of the enterprise and its geographical location.

(12) General training provides transferable qualifications and substantially improves the employability of the trained worker. Aid for this purpose has less distortive effects on competition, so that higher intensities of aid can be considered compatible with the common market and exempted from prior notification. Specific training, on the other hand, which mainly benefits the enterprise, involves a greater risk of distortion of competition so that the intensity of aid which can be considered compatible and exempted from prior notification should be much lower.

(13) In view of the handicaps with which SMEs are confronted and the higher relative costs that they have to bear when they invest in the training of their workers, the intensities of aid exempted by this Regulation should be increased for SMEs.

(14) In assisted areas under Article 87(3)(a) and (c) of the Treaty, training has a relatively greater external impact, since there is a substantial underinvestment in training in those regions and a higher unemployment rate. Consequently, the intensities of aid exempted by this Regulation should be increased for those areas.

(15) The characteristics of training in the maritime transport sector justify a specific approach for that sector.

(16) It is appropriate that large amounts of aid remain subject to an individual assessment by the Commission before they are put into effect. Accordingly, aid amounts exceeding a fixed amount, which should be set at EUR 1 000 000, are excluded from the exemption provided for in this Regulation and remain subject to the requirements of Article 88(3) of the Treaty.

(17) This Regulation should not exempt aid cumulated with other State aid, including aid granted by national, regional and local authorities, or with Community assistance, in relation to the same eligible costs when such cumulation exceeds the thresholds fixed in this Regulation.

(18) In order to ensure transparency and effective monitoring in accordance with Article 3 of Regulation (EC) No 994/98, it is appropriate to establish a standard format in which Member States should provide the Commission with summary information whenever, in pursuance of this Regulation, an aid scheme is implemented or an individual aid outside such schemes is granted, with a view to publication in the *Official Journal of the European Communities*. For the same reasons, it is appropriate to establish rules concerning the records that Member States

should keep regarding the aid exempted by this Regulation. For the purposes of the annual reports to be submitted to the Commission by Member States, it is appropriate for the Commission to establish its specific requirements, including, in view of the wide availability of the necessary technology, information in computerised form.

(19) Having regard to the Commission's experience and in particular the frequency with which it is generally necessary to revise State aid policy, it is appropriate to limit the period of application of this Regulation. Should this Regulation expire without being extended, aid schemes already exempted by this Regulation should continue to be exempted for six months,

NOTES
1   OJ L142, 14.5.98, p 1.
2   OJ C89, 28.3.2000, p 8.
3   OJ C343, 11.11.98, p 10.
4   OJ L160, 26.6.99, p 80.
5   OJ L107, 30.4.96, p 4.

HAS ADOPTED THIS REGULATION:

Article 1

Scope

This Regulation applies to aid in all sectors, including the activities relating to the production, processing and marketing of products listed in Annex I of the Treaty.

[6218]

Article 2

Definitions

For the purpose of this Regulation—
  (a) "aid" shall mean any measure fulfilling all the criteria laid down in Article 87(1) of the Treaty;
  (b) "small and medium-sized enterprises" shall mean enterprises as defined in Annex I;
  (c) "large enterprises" shall mean enterprises not coming under the definition of SME in Annex I;
  (d) "specific training" shall mean training involving tuition directly and principally applicable to the employee's present or future position in the assisted firm and providing qualifications which are not or only to a limited extent transferable to other firms or fields of work;
  (e) "general training" shall mean training involving tuition which is not applicable only or principally to the employee's present or future position in the assisted firm, but which provides qualifications that are largely transferable to other firms or fields of work and thereby substantially improve the employability of the employee. Training shall be considered "general" if, for example,
    — it is jointly organised by different independent enterprises, or if employees of different enterprises may avail themselves of the training,
    — it is recognised, certified or validated by public authorities or bodies or by other bodies or institutions on which a Member State or the Community has conferred the necessary powers.
  (f) "aid intensity" shall mean the gross aid amount expressed as a percentage of the project's eligible costs. All figures used shall be taken before any deduction for direct taxation. Where aid is awarded in a form other than a grant, the aid amount shall be the grant equivalent of the aid. Aid payable in several instalments shall be discounted to its value at the time of

granting. The interest rate to be used for discounting purposes and for calculating the aid amount in a soft loan shall be the reference rate applicable at the time of grant;

(g) "disadvantaged worker" shall mean—

— any young person under 25 who has not previously obtained his first regular paid employment,

— any person with serious disabilities which result from physical, mental or psychological impairments and yet capable of entering the labour market,

— any migrant worker who moves or has moved within the Community or becomes resident in the Community to take up work and who needs professional and/or language training,

— any person wishing to re-enter working life after a break of at least three years, and particularly any person who gave up work on account of the difficulty of reconciling his working life and family life, for the first six months after recruitment,

— any person older than 45 who has not attained an upper secondary educational qualification or its equivalent,

— any long-term unemployed person, ie any person who was without work for 12 consecutive months, for the first six months after recruitment.

[6219]

Article 3

Conditions for exemption

1.　Individual aid outside any scheme, fulfilling all the conditions of this Regulation, shall be compatible with the common market within the meaning of Article 87(3) of the Treaty and shall be exempt from the notification requirement of Article 88(3) of the Treaty provided that it contains an express reference to this Regulation, by citing its title and publication reference in the *Official Journal of the European Communities.*

2.　Aid schemes fulfilling all the conditions of this Regulation shall be compatible with the common market within the meaning of Article 87(3) of the Treaty and shall be exempt from the notification requirement of Article 88(3) of the Treaty provided that—

(a) any aid that could be awarded under such scheme fulfils all the conditions of this Regulation;

(b) the scheme contains an express reference to this Regulation, by citing its title and publication reference in the *Official Journal of the European Communities.*

3.　Aid granted under the schemes referred to in paragraph 2 shall be compatible with the common market within the meaning of Article 87(3) of the Treaty and shall be exempt from the notification requirement of Article 88(3) of the Treaty provided that the aid granted directly fulfils all the conditions of this Regulation.

[6220]

Article 4

Exempted training aid

1.　Aid schemes and individual aid for training must fulfil the conditions laid down in paragraphs 2 to 7.

2.   Where the aid is granted for specific training, its intensity shall not exceed 25% for large enterprises and 35% for small and medium-sized enterprises.

These intensities shall be increased by five percentage points for enterprises in areas which qualify for regional aid pursuant to Article 87(3)(c) of the Treaty and by 10 percentage points for enterprises in areas which qualify for regional aid pursuant to Article 87(3)(a) of the Treaty.

3.   Where the aid is granted for general training, its intensity shall not exceed 50% for large enterprises and 70% for small and medium-sized enterprises.

These intensities shall be increased by five percentage points for enterprises in areas which qualify for regional aid pursuant to Article 87(3)(c) of the Treaty and by 10 percentage points for enterprises in areas which qualify for regional aid pursuant to Article 87(3)(a) of the Treaty.

4.   The maximum intensities referred to in paragraphs 2 and 3 shall be increased by 10 percentage points if the training is given to disadvantaged workers.

5.   In cases where the aid project involves both specific and general training components which cannot be separated for the calculation of the aid intensity, and in cases where the specific or general character of the training aid project cannot be established, the intensities applicable to specific training pursuant to paragraph 2 shall apply.

6.   Where the aid is granted in the maritime transport sector, it may reach an intensity of 100%, whether the training project concerns specific or general training, provided that the following conditions are met—

    (a) the trainee shall not be an active member of the crew but shall be supernumerary on board, and

    (b) the training shall be carried out on board ships entered on Community registers.

7.   The eligible costs of a training aid project shall be—

    (a) trainers' personnel costs,

    (b) trainers' and trainees' travel expenses,

    (c) other current expenses such as materials and supplies,

    (d) depreciation of tools and equipment, to the extent that they are used exclusively for the training project,

    (e) cost of guidance and counselling services with regard to the training project,

    (f) trainees' personnel costs up to the amount of the total of the other eligible costs referred to in (a) to (e). Only the hours during which the trainees actually participate in the training, after deduction of any productive hours or of their equivalent, may be taken into account.

The eligible costs shall be supported by documentary evidence, which shall be transparent and itemised.

[6221]

Article 5

Large individual aid grants

The exemption shall not apply if the amount of aid granted to one enterprise for a single training project exceeds EUR 1 000 000.

[6222]

Article 6

Cumulation

1.   The aid ceilings fixed in Articles 4 and 5 shall apply regardless of whether the support for the project is financed entirely from State resources or is partly financed by the Community.

2. Aid exempted by this Regulation shall not be cumulated with any other State aid within the meaning of Article 87(1) of the Treaty, or with other Community funding, in relation to the same eligible costs, if such cumulation would result in an aid intensity exceeding that fixed by this Regulation.

[6223]

Article 7

Transparency and monitoring

1. On implementation of an aid scheme, or grant of individual aid outside any scheme, exempted by this Regulation, Member States shall, within 20 working days, forward to the Commission, with a view to its publication in the *Official Journal of the European Communities*, a summary of the information regarding such aid scheme or individual aid according to the model laid down in Annex II.

2. Member States shall maintain detailed records regarding the aid schemes exempted by this Regulation, the individual aid granted under those schemes, and the individual aid exempted by this Regulation that is granted outside any existing aid scheme. Such records shall contain all information necessary to establish that the conditions for exemption, as laid down in this Regulation, are fulfilled. Member States shall keep a record regarding an individual aid for 10 years from the date on which it was granted, and regarding an aid scheme, for 10 years from the date on which the last individual aid was granted under such scheme. On written request, the Member State concerned shall provide the Commission, within a period of 20 working days or such longer period as may be fixed in the request, with all the information which the Commission considers necessary to assess whether the conditions of this Regulation have been complied with.

3. Member States shall compile a report on the application of this Regulation in respect of each whole or part calendar year during which this Regulation applies, in the form laid down in Annex III, also in computerised form. Member States shall provide the Commission with such report no later than three months after the expiry of the period to which the report relates.

[6224]

Article 8

Entry into force and period of validity

1. This Regulation shall enter into force on the 20th day following its publication in the *Official Journal of the European Communities*.

It shall remain in force until 31 December 2006.

2. At the end of the period of validity of this Regulation, aid schemes exempted under this Regulation shall remain exempted during an adjustment period of six months.

This Regulation shall be binding in its entirety and directly applicable in all Member States.

[6225]

Done at Brussels, 12 January 2001.

ANNEX I

Definition of small and medium-sized enterprises

(extract from Commission Recommendation 96/280/EC of 3 April 1996 concerning the definition of small and medium-sized enterprises (OJ L107, 30.4.96, p 4))

"Article 1

1.   Small and medium-sized enterprises, hereinafter referred to as "SMEs", are defined as enterprises which—
— have fewer than 250 employees, and
— have either,
— an annual turnover not exceeding EUR 40 million, or
— an annual balance-sheet total not exceeding EUR 27 million,
— conform to the criterion of independence as defined in paragraph 3.

2.   Where it is necessary to distinguish between small and medium-sized enterprises, the "small enterprise" is defined as an enterprise which—
— has fewer than 50 employees and
— has either,
— an annual turnover not exceeding EUR 7 million, or
— an annual balance-sheet total not exceeding EUR 5 million,
— conforms to the criterion of independence as defined in paragraph 3.

3.   Independent enterprises are those which are not owned as to 25% or more of the capital or the voting rights by one enterprise, or jointly by several enterprises, falling outside the definitions of an SME or a small enterprise, whichever may apply. This threshold may be exceeded in the following two cases—
— if the enterprise is held by public investment corporations, venture capital companies or institutional investors, provided no control is exercised either individually or jointly,
— if the capital is spread in such a way that it is not possible to determine by whom it is held and if the enterprise declares that it can legitimately presume that it is not owned as to 25% or more by one enterprise, or jointly by several enterprises, falling outside the definitions of an SME or a small enterprise, whichever may apply.

4.   In calculating the thresholds referred to in paragraphs 1 and 2, it is therefore necessary to cumulate the relevant figures for the beneficiary enterprise and for all the enterprises that it directly or indirectly controls through possession of 25% or more of the capital or of the voting rights.

5.   Where it is necessary to distinguish microenterprises from other SMEs, these are defined as enterprises having fewer than 10 employees.

6.   Where, at the final balance-sheet date, an enterprise exceeds or falls below the employee thresholds or financial ceilings, this is to result in its acquiring or losing the status of "SME", "medium-sized enterprise", "small enterprise" or "microenterprise" only if the phenomenon is repeated over two consecutive financial years.

7.   The number of persons employed corresponds to the number of annual working units (AWU), that is to say, the number of full-time workers employed during one year with part-time and seasonal workers being fractions of AWU. The reference year to be considered is that of the last approved accounting period.

8.   The turnover and balance-sheet total thresholds are those of the last approved 12-month accounting period. In the case of newly established enterprises whose accounts have not yet been approved, the thresholds to apply shall be derived from a reliable estimate made in the course of the financial year."

ANNEX II

Form of summary information to be provided whenever an aid scheme exempted by this regulation is implemented and whenever an individual aid exempted by this regulation is granted outside any aid scheme

Summary information on State aid granted in conformity with Commission Regulation (EC) No 68/2001

Summary information to be filled in	Explanatory remarks
Member State	
Region	Indicate the name of the region if the aid is granted by a subcentral authority
Title of aid scheme or name of company receiving an individual aid	Indicate the name of the aid scheme or in the case of individual aid, the name of the beneficiary. In the latter case, no subsequent annual report is necessary!
Legal basis	Indicate the precise national legal reference for the aid scheme or for the individual aid
Annual expenditure planned under the scheme or overall amount of individual aid granted to the company	Amounts are to be given in euro or, if applicable, national currency. In the case of an aid scheme: indicate the annual overall amount of the budget appropriation(s) or the estimated tax loss per year for all aid instruments contained in the scheme. In the case of an individual aid award: indicate the overall aid amount/tax loss. If appropriate, indicate also for how many years the aid will be paid in instalments or over how many years tax losses will be incurred. For guarantees in both cases, indicate the (maximum) amount of loans guaranteed
Maximum aid intensity	Indicate the maximum aid intensity or the maximum aid amount per eligible item
Date of implementation	Indicate the date from which aid may be granted under the scheme or when the individual aid is granted
Duration of scheme or individual aid award	Indicate the date (year and month) until which aid may be granted under the scheme or in the case of an individual aid and if appropriate the expected date (year and month) of the last instalment to be paid
Objective of aid	In the case of training aid, indicate whether the training is specific or general. In the case of general training, documentary evidence (eg description of the contents of the training) must be attached regarding the qualification of the training as general

Summary information to be filled in	Explanatory remarks
Economic sector(s) concerned	Choose from the list, where relevant
☐ All sectors	
or	
☐ Agriculture	
☐ Fisheries and aquaculture	
☐ Coalmining	
☐ All manufacturing	
or	
☐ Steel	
☐ Shipbuilding	
☐ Synthetic fibres	
☐ Motor vehicles	
☐ Other manufacturing	
☐ All services	
or	
☐ Maritime transport services	
☐ Other transport services	
☐ Financial services	
☐ Other services	
Remarks:	
Name and address of the granting authority	
Other information	

[6227]

ANNEX III

Form of the periodic report to be provided to the Commission

Annual reporting format on aid schemes exempted under a group exemption regulation adopted pursuant to Article 1 of Council Regulation (EC) No 994/98

Member States are required to use the format below for their reporting obligations to the Commission under group exemption regulations adopted on the basis of Council Regulation (EC) No 994/98.

The reports should also be provided in computerised form.

Information required for all aid schemes exempted under group exemption regulations adopted pursuant to Article 1 of Council Regulation (EC) No 994/98

1. Title of aid scheme

2. Commission exemption regulation applicable

3. Expenditure

Separate figures have to be provided for each aid instrument within a scheme or individual aid (eg grant, soft loans, etc). The figures have to be expressed in euro or, if applicable, national currency. In the case of tax expenditure, annual tax losses have to be reported. If precise figures are not available, such losses may be estimated.

These expenditure figures should be provided on the following basis—

for the year under review indicate separately for each aid instrument within the scheme (eg grant, soft loan, guarantee, etc):

3.1.   amounts committed, (estimated) tax losses or other revenue forgone, data on guarantees, etc for new assisted projects. In the case of guarantee schemes, the total amount of new guarantees handed out should be provided;

3.2.   actual payments, (estimated) tax losses or other revenue forgone, data on guarantees, etc. for new and current projects. In the case of guarantee schemes, the following should be provided: total amount of outstanding guarantees, premium income, recoveries, indemnities paid out, operating result of the scheme under the year under review;

3.3.   number of new assisted projects;

3.4.   estimated overall number of jobs created or maintained by new projects (if appropriate);

3.5.   estimated overall amount of investment aided by new projects;

3.6.   regional breakdown of amounts under point 3.1 either by regions defined at NUTS[1] level 2 or below or by Article 87(3)(a) regions, Article 87(3)(c) regions and non-assisted regions;

3.7.   sectorial breakdown of amounts under point 3.1. by beneficiaries' sectors of activity (if more than one sector is covered, indicate the share of each)—

— agriculture

— fisheries and/or aquaculture

— coalmining

— manufacturing

of which—

steel

shipbuilding

synthetic fibres

motor vehicles

other manufacturing (please specify)

— services

of which—

maritime transport services

other transport services

financial services

other services (please specify)

— other sectors (please specify)

4.   Other information and remarks

[6228]

NOTES
> [1]   NUTS is the nomenclature of territorial units for statistical purposes in the EC.

COMMISSION REGULATION

of 12 January 2001

on the application of Articles 87 and 88 of the EC Treaty to de minimis aid

(69/2001/EC)

NOTES
Date of publication in OJ: OJ L10, 13.1.2001, p 30.

THE COMMISSION OF THE EUROPEAN COMMUNITIES,

Having regard to the Treaty establishing the European Community,

Having regard to Council Regulation (EC) No 994/98 of 7 May 1998 on the application of Articles 92 and 93 of the Treaty establishing the European Community to certain categories of horizontal State aid,[1] and in particular Article 2 thereof,

Having published a draft of this Regulation,[2]

Having consulted the Advisory Committee on State aid,

Whereas:

(1) Regulation (EC) No 994/98 empowers the Commission to set out in a regulation a threshold under which aid measures are deemed not to meet all the criteria of Article 87(1) of the Treaty and therefore do not fall under the notification procedure provided for in Article 88(3) of the Treaty.

(2) The Commission has applied Articles 87 and 88 of the Treaty and in particular clarified, in numerous decisions, the notion of aid within the meaning of Article 87(1) of the Treaty. The Commission has also stated its policy with regard to a *de minimis* ceiling, under which Article 87(1) can be considered not to apply, most recently in the notice on the *de minimis* rule for State aid.[3] In the light of this experience and with a view to increasing transparency and legal certainty, it is appropriate that the *de minimis* rule be laid down in a Regulation.

(3) In view of the special rules which apply in the sectors of agriculture, fisheries and aquaculture, and transport, and of the risk that even small amounts of aid could fulfil the criteria of Article 87(1) of the Treaty in those sectors, it is appropriate that this Regulation should not apply to those sectors.

(4) In the light of the World Trade Organisation (WTO) Agreement on Subsidies and Countervailing Measures,[4] this Regulation should not exempt export aid or aid favouring domestic over imported products. Aid towards the cost of participating in trade fairs, or of studies or consultancy services needed for the launch of a new or existing product on a new market does not normally constitute export aid.

(5) In the light of the Commission's experience, it can be established that aid not exceeding a ceiling of EUR 100 000 over any period of three years does not affect trade between Member States and/or does not distort or threaten to distort competition and therefore does not fall under Article 87(1) of the Treaty. The relevant period of three years has a mobile character, so that for each new grant of *de minimis* aid, the total amount of *de minimis* aid granted during the previous three years needs to be determined. The *de minimis* aid should be considered to be granted at the moment the legal right to receive the aid is conferred to the beneficiary. The *de minimis* rule is without prejudice to the possibility that enterprises receive, also for the same project, State aid authorised by the Commission or covered by a group exemption Regulation.

(6) For the purpose of transparency, equal treatment and the correct application of the *de minimis* ceiling, it is appropriate that Member States should apply the same method of calculation. In order to facilitate this calculation and in accordance with the present practice of application of the *de minimis* rule, it is appropriate that aid amounts not taking the form of a cash grant should be converted into their gross grant equivalent. Calculation of the grant equivalent of aid payable in several instalments, and calculation of aid in the form of a soft loan, require the use of market interest rates prevailing at the time of grant. With a view to a uniform, transparent and simple application of the State aid rules, the market rates for the purposes of this Regulation should be deemed to be the reference rates, provided that, in the case of a soft loan, the loan is backed by normal security and does not involve abnormal risk. The reference rates should be those which are periodically fixed by the Commission on the basis of objective criteria and published in the *Official Journal of the European Communities* and on the Internet.

(7) The Commission has a duty to ensure that State aid rules are respected and in particular that aid granted under the *de minimis* rules adheres to the conditions thereof. In accordance with the cooperation principle laid down in Article 10 of the Treaty, Member States should facilitate the achievement of this task by establishing the necessary machinery in order to ensure that the total amount of aid, granted to the same beneficiary under the *de minimis* rule, does not exceed the ceiling of EUR 100 000 over a period of three years. To that end, it is appropriate that Member States, when granting a *de minimis* aid, should inform the enterprise concerned of the *de minimis* character of the aid, receive full information about other *de minimis* aid received during the last three years and carefully check that the *de minimis* ceiling will not be exceeded by the new *de minimis* aid. Alternatively respect of the ceiling may also be ensured by means of a central register.

(8) Having regard to the Commission's experience and in particular the frequency with which it is generally necessary to revise State aid policy, it is appropriate to limit the period of application of this Regulation. Should this Regulation expire without being extended, Member States should have an adjustment period of six months with regard to *de minimis* aid schemes which were covered by this Regulation,

NOTES
1　OJ L142, 14.5.98, p 1.
2　OJ C89, 28.3.2000, p 6.
3　OJ C68, 6.3 96, p 9.
4　OJ L336, 23.12.94, p 156.

HAS ADOPTED THIS REGULATION:

Article 1

Scope

This Regulation applies to aid granted to enterprises in all sectors, with the exception of—
　　(a) the transport sector and the activities linked to the production, processing or marketing of products listed in Annex I to the Treaty;
　　(b) aid to export-related activities, namely aid directly linked to the quantities exported, to the establishment and operation of a distribution network or to other current expenditure linked to the export activity;
　　(c) aid contingent upon the use of domestic over imported goods.

[6229]

Article 2

De minimis aid

1.　Aid measures shall be deemed not to meet all the criteria of Article 87(1) of the Treaty and shall therefore not fall under the notification requirement of Article 88(3) of the Treaty, if they fulfil the conditions laid down in paragraphs 2 and 3.

2.　The total *de minimis* aid granted to any one enterprise shall not exceed EUR 100 000 over any period of three years. This ceiling shall apply irrespective of the form of the aid or the objective pursued.

3.　The ceiling in paragraph 2 shall be expressed as a cash grant. All figures used shall be gross, that is, before any deduction for direct taxation. Where aid is awarded in a form other than a grant, the aid amount shall be the gross grant equivalent of the aid.

Aid payable in several instalments shall be discounted to its value at the moment of its being granted. The interest rate to be used for discounting purposes and to calculate the aid amount in a soft loan shall be the reference rate applicable at the time of grant.

[6230]

Article 3

Cumulation and monitoring

1.　Where a Member State grants *de minimis* aid to an enterprise, it shall inform the enterprise about the *de minimis* character of the aid and obtain from the enterprise concerned full information about other *de minimis* aid received during the previous three years.

The Member State may only grant the new *de minimis* aid after having checked that this will not raise the total amount of *de minimis* aid received during the relevant period of three years to a level above the ceiling set out in Article 2(2).

2.   Where a Member State has set up a central register of *de minimis* aid containing complete information on all *de minimis* aid granted by any authority within that Member State, the requirement in the first subparagraph of paragraph 1 no longer applies from the moment the register covers a period of three years.

3.   Member States shall record and compile all the information regarding the application of this Regulation. Such records shall contain all information necessary to demonstrate that the conditions of this Regulation have been respected. Records regarding an individual *de minimis* aid shall be maintained for 10 years from the date on which it was granted and regarding a *de minimis* aid scheme, for 10 years from the date on which the last individual aid was granted under such scheme. On written request the Member State concerned shall provide the Commission, within a period of 20 working days, or such longer period as may be fixed in the request, with all the information that the Commission considers necessary for assessing whether the conditions of this Regulation have been complied with, in particular the total amount of *de minimis* aid received by any enterprise.

[6231]

Article 4

Entry into force and period of validity

1.   This Regulation shall enter into force on the 20th day following that of its publication in the *Official Journal of the European Communities*.

It shall remain in force until 31 December 2006.

2.   At the end of the period of validity of this Regulation, *de minimis* aid schemes falling under this Regulation shall continue to benefit from it during an adjustment period of six months.

During the adjustment period, these schemes may continue to be applied under the conditions of this Regulation.

This Regulation shall be binding in its entirety and directly applicable in all Member States.

[6232]

Done at Brussels, 12 January 2001.

COMMISSION REGULATION

of 12 January 2001

on the application of Articles 87 and 88 of the EC Treaty to State aid to small and medium-sized enterprises

(70/2001/EC)

NOTES

Date of Publication in OJ: OJ L10, 13.1.2001, p 33.

THE COMMISSION OF THE EUROPEAN COMMUNITIES,

Having regard to the Treaty establishing the European Community,
Having regard to Council Regulation (EC) No 994/98 of 7 May 1998 on the application of Articles 92 and 93 of the Treaty establishing the European Community to certain categories of horizontal State aid,[1] and in particular points (a)(i) and (b) of Article 1(1) thereof,

Having published a draft of this Regulation,[2]
Having consulted the Advisory Committee on State Aid,
Whereas:

(1) Regulation (EC) No 994/98 empowers the Commission to declare, in accordance with Article 87 of the Treaty, that under certain conditions aid to small and medium-sized enterprises is compatible with the common market and not subject to the notification requirement of Article 88(3) of the Treaty.

(2) Regulation (EC) No 994/98 also empowers the Commission to declare, in accordance with Article 87 of the Treaty, that aid that complies with the map approved by the Commission for each Member State for the grant of regional aid is compatible with the common market and is not subject to the notification requirement of Article 88(3) of the Treaty.

(3) The Commission has applied Articles 87 and 88 of the Treaty to small and medium-sized enterprises in and outside assisted areas in numerous decisions and has also stated its policy, most recently in the Community guidelines on State aid for small and medium-sized enterprises[3] and in the guidelines on national regional aid.[4] In the light of the Commission's considerable experience in applying those Articles to small and medium-sized enterprises and in the light of the general texts relating to small and medium-sized enterprises and to regional aid issued by the Commission on the basis of those provisions, it is appropriate, with a view to ensuring efficient supervision and simplifying administration without weakening Commission monitoring, that the Commission should make use of the powers conferred by Regulation (EC) No 994/98.

(4) This Regulation is without prejudice to the possibility for Member States of notifying aid to small and medium-sized enterprises. Such notifications will be assessed by the Commission in particular in the light of the criteria set out in this Regulation. The guidelines on State aid for small and medium-sized enterprises should be abolished from the date of entry into force of this Regulation, since their contents are replaced by this Regulation.

(5) Small and medium-sized enterprises play a decisive role in job creation and, more generally, act as a factor of social stability and economic drive. However, their development may be limited by market imperfections. They often have difficulties in obtaining capital or credit, given the risk-shy nature of certain financial markets and the limited guarantees that they may be able to offer. Their limited resources may also restrict their access to information, notably regarding new technology and potential markets. Having regard to those considerations, the purpose of the aid exempted by this Regulation should be to facilitate the development of the economic activities of small and medium-sized enterprises, provided that such aid does not adversely affect trading conditions to an extent contrary to the common interest.

(6) This Regulation should exempt any aid that meets all the relevant requirements of this Regulation, and any aid scheme, provided that any aid that could be granted under such scheme meets all the relevant requirements of this Regulation. With a view to ensuring efficient supervision and simplifying administration without weakening Commission monitoring, aid schemes and individual grants outside any aid scheme should contain an express reference to this Regulation.

(7) This Regulation should apply without prejudice to special rules in regulations and directives concerning State aid in certain sectors, such as currently exist for shipbuilding, and should not apply to agriculture and fisheries and aquaculture.

(8) In order to eliminate differences that might give rise to distortions of competition, in order to facilitate coordination between different Community and national initiatives concerning small and medium-sized enterprises, and for reasons of administrative clarity and legal certainty, the definition of "small and medium-sized enterprises' used in this Regulation should be that laid down in Commission Recommendation 96/280/EC of 3 April 1996 concerning the definition of small and medium-sized enterprises.[5] That definition was also used in the Community guidelines on State aid for small and medium-sized enterprises.[6]

(9) In accordance with the established practice of the Commission, and with a view to better ensuring that aid is proportionate and limited to the amount necessary, thresholds should be expressed in terms of aid intensities in relation to a set of eligible costs, rather than in terms of maximum aid amounts.

(10) In order to determine whether or not aid is compatible with the common market pursuant to this Regulation, it is necessary to take into consideration the aid intensity and thus the aid amount expressed as a grant equivalent. The calculation of the grant equivalent of aid payable in several instalments and aid in the form of a soft loan requires the use of market interest rates prevailing at the time of grant. With a view to a uniform, transparent, and simple application of the State aid rules, the market rates for the purposes of this Regulation should

e deemed to be the reference rates, provided that, in the case of a soft loan, the loan is backed y normal security and does not involve abnormal risk. The reference rates should be those hich are periodically fixed by the Commission on the basis of objective criteria and published the *Official Journal of the European Communities* and on the Internet.

(11) Having regard to the differences between small enterprises and medium-sized nterprises, different ceilings of aid intensity should be set for small enterprises and for medium-sized enterprises.

(12) The ceilings of aid intensity should be fixed, in the light of the Commission's experience, at a level that strikes the appropriate balance between minimising distortions of competition in the aided sector and the objective of facilitating the development of the economic activities of small and medium-sized enterprises.

(13) It is appropriate to establish further conditions that should be fulfilled by any aid scheme or individual aid exempted by this Regulation. Having regard to Article 87(3)(c) of the Treaty, such aid should not normally have the sole effect of continuously or periodically reducing the operating costs which the beneficiary would normally have to bear, and should be proportionate to the handicaps that have to be overcome in order to secure the socioeconomic benefits deemed to be in the Community interest. It is therefore appropriate to limit the scope of this Regulation to aid granted in relation to certain tangible and intangible investments, certain services supplied to beneficiaries and certain other activities. In the light of Community overcapacity in the transport sector, with the exception of railway rolling stock, eligible investment costs for enterprises having their main economic activity in the transport sector should not include transport means and equipment.

(14) This Regulation should exempt aid to small and medium-sized enterprises regardless of location. Investment and job creation can contribute to the economic development of less favoured regions in the Community. Small and medium-sized enterprises in those regions suffer from both the structural disadvantage of the location and the difficulties deriving from their size. It is therefore appropriate that small and medium-sized enterprises in assisted regions should benefit from higher ceilings.

(15) In order not to favour the capital factor of an investment over the labour factor, provision should be made for the possibility of measuring aid to investment on the basis of either the costs of the investment or the costs of new employment linked to the carrying-out of the investment project.

(16) In the light of the World Trade Organisation (WTO) Agreement on Subsidies and Countervailing Measures,[7] this Regulation should not exempt export aid or aid favouring domestic over imported products. Aid towards the costs of participation in trade fairs or of studies or consultancy services needed for the launch of a new or existing product on a new market does not normally constitute export aid.

(17) Having regard to the need to strike the appropriate balance between minimising distortions of competition in the aided sector and the objectives of this Regulation, it should not exempt individual aid grants which exceed a fixed maximum amount, whether or not made under an aid scheme exempted by this Regulation.

(18) In order to ensure that the aid is necessary and acts as an incentive to develop certain activities, this Regulation should not exempt aid for activities in which the beneficiary would already engage under market conditions alone.

(19) This Regulation should not exempt aid cumulated with other State aid, including aid granted by national, regional or local authorities, or with Community assistance, in relation to the same eligible costs, when such cumulation exceeds the thresholds fixed in this Regulation.

(20) In order to ensure transparency and effective monitoring, in accordance with Article 3 of Regulation (EC) No 994/98, it is appropriate to establish a standard format in which Member States should provide the Commission with summary information whenever, in pursuance of this Regulation, an aid scheme is implemented or an individual aid outside such schemes is granted, with a view to publication in the *Official Journal of the European Communities*. For the same reasons, it is appropriate to establish rules concerning the records that Member States should keep regarding the aid exempted by this Regulation. For the purposes of the annual report to be submitted to the Commission by Member States, it is appropriate for the Commission to establish its specific requirements, including, in view of the wide availability of the necessary technology, information in computerised form.

(21) Having regard to the Commission's experience in this area, and in particular the frequency with which it is generally necessary to revise State aid policy, it is appropriate to limit the period of application of this Regulation. Should this Regulation expire without being extended, aid schemes already exempted by this Regulation should continue to be exempted for six months,

NOTES
1   OJ L142, 14.5.98, p 1.
2   OJ C89, 28.3.2000, p 15.
3   OJ C213, 23.7.96, p 4.
4   OJ C74, 10.3.98, p 9.
5   OJ L107, 30.4.96, p 4.
6   See footnote 3.
7   OJ L336, 23.12.94, p 156.

HAS ADOPTED THIS REGULATION:

Article 1

Scope

1.   Without prejudice to special Community Regulations or Directives under the EC Treaty governing the granting of State aid in specific sectors, whether more or less restrictive than this Regulation, this Regulation applies to aid granted to small and medium-sized enterprises in all sectors.

2.   This Regulation shall not apply—
   (a) to activities linked to the production, processing or marketing of products listed in Annex I to the Treaty;
   (b) to aid to export-related activities, namely aid directly linked to the quantities exported, to the establishment and operation of a distribution network or to other current expenditure linked to the export activity;
   (c) to aid contingent upon the use of domestic over imported goods.

[6233]

Article 2

Definitions

For the purpose of this Regulation—
   (a) "aid" shall mean any measure fulfilling all the criteria laid down in Article 87(1) of the Treaty;
   (b) "small and medium-sized enterprises" shall mean enterprises as defined in Annex I;
   (c) "investment in tangible assets" shall mean an investment in fixed physical assets relating to the creation of a new establishment, the extension of an existing establishment, or the engagement in an activity involving a fundamental change in the product or production process of an existing establishment (in particular through rationalisation, diversification or modernisation). An investment in fixed assets undertaken in the form of the takeover of an establishment which has closed or which would have closed had it not been purchased shall also be regarded as tangible investment;
   (d) "investment in intangible assets" shall mean investment in transfer of technology by the acquisition of patent rights, licences, know-how or unpatented technical knowledge;
   (e) "gross aid intensity" shall mean the aid amount expressed as a percentage of the project's eligible costs. All figures used shall be taken before any deduction for direct taxation. Where aid is awarded in a form other than a grant, the aid amount shall be the grant equivalent of the aid. Aid payable in several instalments shall be discounted to its value at the moment of granting. The interest rate to be used for discounting purposes and for calculating the aid amount in a soft loan shall be the reference rate applicable at the time of grant;

  (f) "net aid intensity" shall mean the aid amount net of tax expressed as a percentage of the project's eligible costs;

  (g) "number of employees" shall mean the number of annual labour units (ALU), namely the number of persons employed full time in one year, part-time and seasonal work being ALU fractions.

[6234]

Article 3

Conditions for exemption

1.   Individual aid outside any scheme, fulfilling all the conditions of this Regulation, shall be compatible with the common market within the meaning of Article 87(3) of the Treaty and shall be exempt from the notification requirement of Article 88(3) of the Treaty provided that it contains an express reference to this Regulation, by citing its title and publication reference in the *Official Journal of the European Communities.*

2.   Aid schemes fulfilling all the conditions of this Regulation shall be compatible with the common market within the meaning of Article 87(3) of the Treaty and shall be exempt from the notification requirement of Article 88(3) of the Treaty provided that—

  (a) any aid that could be awarded under such scheme fulfils all the conditions of this Regulation;

  (b) the scheme contains an express reference to this Regulation, by citing its title and publication reference in the *Official Journal of the European Communities.*

3.   Aid granted under the schemes referred to in paragraph 2 shall be compatible with the common market within the meaning of Article 87(3) of the Treaty and shall be exempt from the notification requirement of Article 88(3) of the Treaty provided that the aid granted directly fulfils all the conditions of this Regulation.

[6235]

Article 4

Investment

1.   Aid for investment in tangible and intangible assets inside or outside the Community shall be compatible with the common market within the meaning of Article 87(3) of the Treaty and shall be exempt from the notification requirement of Article 88(3) of the Treaty if it fulfils the conditions of paragraphs 2 to 6.

2.   The gross aid intensity shall not exceed—

  (a) 15% in the case of small enterprises;

  (b) 7,5% in the case of medium-sized enterprises.

3.   Where the investment takes place in areas which qualify for regional aid, the aid intensity shall not exceed the ceiling of regional investment aid determined in the map approved by the Commission for each Member State by more than—

  (a) 10 percentage points gross in areas covered by Article 87(3)(c), provided that the total net aid intensity does not exceed 30%; or

  (b) 15 percentage points gross in areas covered by Article 87(3)(a), provided that the total net aid intensity does not exceed 75%.

    The higher regional aid ceilings shall only apply if the aid is granted under the condition that the investment is maintained in the recipient region for at least five years and that the beneficiary's contribution to its financing is at least 25%.

4. The ceilings fixed in paragraphs 2 and 3 shall apply to intensity of the calculated either as a percentage of the investment's eligible costs or as a percen of the wage costs of employment created by the carrying-out of an investment (a job creation) or a combination thereof, provided the aid does not exceed the i favourable amount resulting from the application of either calculation.

5. In cases where the aid is calculated on the basis of the investment's co the eligible costs of tangible investment shall be the costs relating to investment land, buildings, machinery and equipment. In the transport sector, except for railwa rolling stock, transport means and transport equipment shall not be included in the eligible costs. The eligible costs of intangible investment shall be the costs of acquisition of the technology.

6. In cases where the aid is calculated on the basis of jobs created, the amount of the aid shall be expressed as a percentage of the wage costs over a period of two years relating to the employment created under the following conditions—
   (a) job creation shall be linked to the carrying-out of a project of investment in tangible or intangible assets. Jobs shall be created within three years of the investment's completion;
   (b) the investment project shall lead to a net increase in the number of employees in the establishment concerned, compared with the average over the previous twelve months; and
   (c) the employment created shall be maintained during a minimum period of five years.

[6236]

Article 5

Consultancy and other services and activities

Aid to small and medium-sized enterprises that fulfil the following conditions shall be compatible with the common market within the meaning of Article 87(3) of the Treaty and shall be exempt from the notification requirement of Article 88(3) of the Treaty—
   (a) for services provided by outside consultants, the gross aid shall not exceed 50% of the costs of such services. The services concerned shall not be a continuous or periodic activity nor relate to the enterprise's usual operating expenditure, such as routine tax consultancy services, regular legal services, or advertising;
   (b) for participation in fairs and exhibitions, the gross aid shall not exceed 50% of the additional costs incurred for renting, setting up and running the stand. This exemption shall only apply to the first participation of an enterprise in a particular fair or exhibition.

[6237]

Article 6

Large individual aid grants

This Regulation shall not exempt an individual aid grant where one of the following thresholds is met—
   (a) the total eligible costs of the whole project are at least EUR 25 000 000 and
       (i) in areas which do not qualify for regional aid, the gross aid intensity is at least 50% of the ceilings laid down in Article 4(2);
       (ii) in areas which qualify for regional aid, the net aid intensity is at least 50% of the net aid ceiling as determined in the regional aid map for the area concerned; or
   (b) the total gross aid amount is at least EUR 15 000 000.

[6238]

cle 7

ssity for the aid

Regulation shall only exempt aid if, before work on the aided project is started—
— either an application for aid has been submitted to the Member State by the
  beneficiary, or
— the Member State has adopted legal provisions establishing a legal right to
  aid according to objective criteria and without further exercise of discretion
  by the Member State.

[6239]

Article 8

Cumulation

1.   The aid ceilings fixed in Articles 4, 5 and 6 shall apply regardless of whether
the support for the aided project is financed entirely from State resources or is partly
financed by the Community.

2.   Aid exempted by this Regulation shall not be cumulated with any other State
aid within the meaning of Article 87(1) of the Treaty, or with other Community
funding, in relation to the same eligible costs, if such cumulation would result in an
aid intensity exceeding that fixed by this Regulation.

[6240]

Article 9

Transparency and monitoring

1.   On implementation of an aid scheme, or grant of individual aid outside any
scheme, exempted by this Regulation, Member States shall, within 20 working days,
forward to the Commission, with a view to its publication in the *Official Journal of
the European Communities*, a summary of the information regarding such aid
scheme or individual aid in the form laid down in Annex II.

2.   Member States shall maintain detailed records regarding the aid schemes
exempted by this Regulation, the individual aid granted under those schemes, and
the individual aid exempted by this Regulation that is granted outside any existing
aid scheme. Such records shall contain all information necessary to establish that the
conditions for exemption, as laid down in this Regulation, are fulfilled, including
information on the status of the company as an SME. Member States shall keep a
record regarding an individual aid for 10 years from the date on which it was
granted, and regarding an aid scheme, for 10 years from the date on which the last
individual aid was granted under such scheme. On written request, the Member
State concerned shall provide the Commission, within a period of 20 working days
or such longer period as may be fixed in the request, with all the information which
the Commission considers necessary to assess whether the conditions of this
Regulation have been complied with.

3.   Member States shall compile a report on the application of this Regulation
in respect of each whole or part calendar year during which this Regulation applies,
in the form laid down in Annex III, also in computerised form. Member States shall
provide the Commission with such report no later than three months after the expiry
of the period to which the report relates.

[6241]

PART IV
EC MATERIALS

Article 10

Entry into force and period of validity

1.   This Regulation shall enter into force on the 20th day following that of publication in the *Official Journal of the European Communities*.

It shall remain in force until 31 December 2006.

2.   At the end of the period of validity of this Regulation, aid scheme exempted under this Regulation shall remain exempted during an adjustment period of six months.

This Regulation shall be binding in its entirety and directly applicable in all Member States.

Done at Brussels, 12 January 2001.

[6242]

ANNEX I
DEFINITION OF SMALL AND MEDIUM-SIZED ENTERPRISES

(extract from the Commission Recommendation 96/280/EC of 3 April 1996 concerning the definition of small and medium-sized enterprises (OJ L 107, 30.4.96, p 4))

"Article 1

1. Small and medium-sized enterprises, hereinafter referred to as "SMEs", are defined as enterprises which—
— have fewer than 250 employees, and
— have either,
— an annual turnover not exceeding EUR 40 million, or
— an annual balance-sheet total not exceeding EUR 27 million,
— conform to the criterion of independence as defined in paragraph 3.

2. Where it is necessary to distinguish between small and medium-sized enterprises, the "small enterprise" is defined as an enterprise which—
— has fewer than 50 employees and
— has either,
— an annual turnover not exceeding EUR 7 million, or
— an annual balance-sheet total not exceeding EUR 5 million,
— conforms to the criterion of independence as defined in paragraph 3.

3. Independent enterprises are those which are not owned as to 25% or more of the capital or the voting rights by one enterprise, or jointly by several enterprises, falling outside the definitions of an SME or a small enterprise, whichever may apply. This threshold may be exceeded in the following two cases—
— if the enterprise is held by public investment corporations, venture capital companies or institutional investors, provided no control is exercised either individually or jointly,
— if the capital is spread in such a way that it is not possible to determine by whom it is held and if the enterprise declares that it can legitimately presume that it is not owned as to 25% or more by one enterprise, or jointly by several enterprises, falling outside the definitions of an SME or a small enterprise, whichever may apply.

4. In calculating the thresholds referred to in paragraphs 1 and 2, it is therefore necessary to cumulate the relevant figures for the beneficiary enterprise and for all the enterprises that it directly or indirectly controls through possession of 25% or more of the capital or of the voting rights.

5. Where it is necessary to distinguish microenterprises from other SMEs, these are defined as enterprises having fewer than 10 employees.

6. Where, at the final balance sheet date, an enterprise exceeds or falls below the employee thresholds or financial ceilings, this is to result in its acquiring or losing the status of "SME", "medium-sized enterprise", "small enterprise" or "microenterprise" only if the phenomenon is repeated over two consecutive financial years.

The number of persons employed corresponds to the number of annual working AWU), that is to say, the number of full-time workers employed during one year with me and seasonal workers being fractions of AWU. The reference year to be considered t of the last approved accounting period.

The turnover and balance sheet total thresholds are those of the last approved 12-month unting period. In the case of newly-established enterprises whose accounts have not yet approved, the thresholds to apply shall be derived from a reliable estimate made in the rse of the financial year."

[6243]

ANNEX II

m of summary information to be provided whenever an aid scheme exempted by this gulation is implemented and whenever an individual aid exempted by this Regulation is granted outside any aid scheme

Summary information on State aid granted in conformity with Commission Regulation (EC) No 70/2001

Summary information to be filled in	Explanatory remarks
Member State	
Region	Indicate the name of the region if the aid is granted by a subcentral authority
Title of aid scheme or name of company receiving an individual aid	Indicate the name of the aid scheme or in the case of individual aid, the name of the beneficiary. In the latter case, no subsequent annual report is necessary!
Legal basis	Indicate the precise national legal reference for the aid scheme or for the individual aid
Annual expenditure planned under the scheme or overall amount of individual aid granted to the company	Amounts are to be given in euro or, if applicable, national currency. In the case of an aid scheme: indicate the annual overall amount of the budget appropriation(s) or the estimated tax loss per year for all aid instruments contained in the scheme. In the case of an individual aid award: indicate the overall aid amount/tax loss. If appropriate, indicate also for how many years the aid will be paid in instalments or over how many years tax losses will be incurred. For guarantees in both cases, indicate the (maximum) amount of loans guaranteed
Maximum aid intensity	Indicate the maximum aid intensity or the maximum aid amount per eligible item
Date of implementation	Indicate the date from which aid may be granted under the scheme or when the individual aid is granted
Duration of scheme or individual aid award	Indicate the date (year and month) until which aid may be granted under the scheme or in the case of an individual aid and if appropriate the expected date (year and month) of the last instalment to be paid

Summary information to be filled in	Explanatory remarks
Objective of aid	It is understood that the primary obje is aid to SME. This field gives opportunity to indicate further (second objectives pursued (eg small enterpri only or SME; investment aid consultancy)
Economic sector(s) concerned □ All sectors or □ Coalmining □ All manufacturing or □ Steel □ Shipbuilding □ Synthetic fibres □ Motor vehicles □ Other manufacturing □ All services or □ Transport services □ Financial services □ Other services Remarks:	Choose from the list, where relevant
Name and address of the granting authority	
Other information	

[6244]

ANNEX III

Form of the periodic report to be provided to the Commission

Annual reporting format on aid schemes exempted under a group exemption regulation adopted pursuant to Article 1 of Council Regulation (EC) No 994/98

Member States are required to use the format below for their reporting obligations to the Commission under group exemption regulations adopted on the basis of Council Regulation (EC) No 994/98.

The reports should also be provided in computerised form.

Information required for all aid schemes exempted under group exemption regulations adopted pursuant to Article 1 of Council Regulation (EC) No 994/98

1. Title of aid scheme

2. Commission exemption regulation applicable

3. Expenditure

arate figures have to be provided for each aid instrument within a scheme or individual grant, soft loans, etc) The figures have to be expressed in euro or, if applicable, al currency. In the case of tax expenditure, annual tax losses have to be reported. If e figures are not available, such losses may be estimated.

ese expenditure figures should be provided on the following basis.

or the year under review indicate separately for each aid instrument within the scheme grant, soft loan, guarantee, etc)—

.1. amounts committed, (estimated) tax losses or other revenue forgone, data on antees, etc. for new assisted projects. In the case of guarantee schemes, the total amount w guarantees handed out should be provided;

2. actual payments, (estimated) tax losses or other revenue forgone, data on guarantees, for new and current projects. In the case of guarantee schemes, the following should be vided: total amount of outstanding guarantees, premium income, recoveries, indemnities d out, operating result of the scheme under the year under review;

3.3. number of new assisted projects;

3.4. estimated overall number of jobs created or maintained by new projects (if appropriate);

3.5. estimated overall amount of investment aided by new projects;

3.6. Regional breakdown of amounts under point 3.1 either by regions defined at NUTS[1] level 2 or below or by Article 87(3)(a) regions, Article 87(3)(c) regions and non-assisted regions;

3.7. Sectorial breakdown of amounts under point 3.1. by beneficiaries' sectors of activity (if more than one sector is covered, indicate the share of each)—

coalmining

manufacturing

of which—

     steel

     shipbuilding

     synthetic fibres

     motor vehicles

     other manufacturing (please specify)

services

of which—

     transport services

     financial services

     other services (please specify)

other sectors (please specify)

4. Other information and remarks.

[6245]–[6300]

NOTES

[1]   NUTS is the nomenclature of territorial units for statistical purposes in the Community.

APPENDIX

PROPOSAL FOR A COUNCIL REGULATION
on the implementation of the rules on competition laid down in Articles 81 an
of the Treaty and amending Regulations (EEC) No 1017/68, (EEC) No 2988/
(EEC) No 4056/86 and (EEC) No 3975/87
("Regulation implementing Articles 81 and 82 of the Treaty")

(presented by the Commission)

EXPLANATORY MEMORANDUM

1. GENERAL

A. Context

The Community competition rules were established in its founding Treaty of 1957. Article 81 sets out the rules applicable to restrictive agreements, decisions and concerted practices, while Article 82 concerns abuses of dominant positions.

In 1962, the Council adopted Regulation No 17, which sets out the rules of procedure for the application of Articles 81 and 82 of the Treaty which have been applied till today without any significant modifications. Regulation No 17 was based on direct applicability of the prohibition rule of Article 81(1) and prior notification of restrictive agreements and practices for exemption under Article 81(3). While the Commission, national courts and national competition authorities can all apply Article 81(1), the power to apply Article 81(3) was granted exclusively to the Commission. Regulation No 17 thus established a highly centralised authorisation system for all restrictive agreements requiring exemption. In contrast, Article 82 has always been enforced in parallel by the Commission, national courts and national authorities.

This system was well suited for a Community of six Member States in which there was little competition culture. It allowed the development of Community competition law and its consistent application throughout the Community. However, today the context has changed fundamentally. The European Union now has 15 Member States, whose markets have already been extensively integrated, 380 million inhabitants, and 11 official languages. National competition authorities have been set up in the Member States and national competition laws have been enacted, many reflecting the content of Articles 81 and 82.

In this new context, the current system presents two major deficiencies. First, it no longer ensures the effective protection of competition. The Commission's monopoly on the application of Article 81(3) is a significant obstacle to the effective application of the rules by national competition authorities and courts. And in a wide Community, the Commission alone cannot bear the responsibility for enforcing the competition rules throughout the Union. Furthermore, the notification regime no longer constitutes an effective tool for the protection of competition. It only rarely reveals cases that pose a real threat to competition. In fact, the notification system prevents the Commission's resources from being used for the detection and punishment of serious infringements.

The second deficiency of the current system is that it imposes an excessive burden on industry by increasing compliance costs and preventing companies from enforcing their agreements without notifying them to the Commission even if they fulfil the conditions of Article 81(3). This is particularly detrimental to SMEs for whom the cost of notification and in the absence of notification, the difficulty of enforcing their agreements can constitute a competitive disadvantage compared with larger firms.

perspective of the enlargement of the Community makes it even more urgent
ceed with a reform of Regulation No 17. A Union with 25 or even more
ber States is now in prospect. A notification system with prior authorisation by
dministrative body would be completely unsustainable in an enlarged Community,
, potentially, thousands of agreements would require administrative clearance in
r to be enforceable. Direct application of Article 81(3) would ensure that
ements fulfilling the conditions of that provision were legally enforceable
hout recourse to an administrative body being necessary.

The White Paper and the consultation process

rder to prepare Community competition law for the challenges of the coming
s, the Commission initiated the reform process by adopting and publishing
1999 a White Paper on modernisation of the rules implementing Articles 81
l 82 of the EC Treaty.

The White Paper examines various options for reform and proposes the adoption of
fundamentally different enforcement system called a directly applicable exception
system. Such a system is based on the direct applicability of the exception rule of
Article 81(3), implying that the Commission and national competition authorities and
courts would apply Article 81(3) in all proceedings in which they are called upon to
apply the prohibition rule of Article 81(1), which is already directly applicable.

The White Paper was adopted on 28 April 1999. Interested parties were invited to
submit comments by 30 September 1999. The European Parliament organised a
public hearing on 22 September 1999. It adopted a resolution on 18 January 2000.
The Economic and Social Committee adopted an opinion on 8 December 1999. The
Commission has received and carefully examined submissions from all Member
States and more than 100 interested parties, including submissions from EFTA
countries, the ESA, and competition authorities from Estonia, Hungary and the
Czech Republic. A working group composed of Commission officials and experts
from the national competition authorities has discussed the content of the White
Paper in a number of meetings.

The European Parliament and the Economic and Social Committee support the
Commission's proposal while insisting on the importance of ensuring consistent
application of Community competition law in a system of parallel powers and of
maintaining an adequate level of legal certainty.

The positions of industry associations and lawyers are varied. Many welcome the
Commission's approach as a more efficient and less bureaucratic alternative to the
present system of implementation, which is almost universally considered
unsatisfactory. However, many also stress the need to ensure that the reform does not
lead to inconsistent application and renationalisation of Community competition law
and that the reform does not reduce legal certainty for companies.

The proposal for a new regulation is in its main parts based on the White Paper,
taking due account, however, of the major preoccupations expressed in the
consultation process. The question of extending the procedures of the Merger
Regulation to partial-function production joint ventures, that was also raised in the
White Paper (nos 79–81), will be further examined in the context of forthcoming
reflections on the revision of that regulation.

[6301]

2. PROPOSAL FOR A NEW COUNCIL REGULATION

A. Subject

The subject of the proposal is the reform of the implementing regulations for
Articles 81 and 82 of the EC Treaty, ie Regulation No 17 and the corresponding
transport regulations. It is proposed to create a new enforcement system referred to

as a "directly applicable exception system". In such a system, both the prohib
rule set out in Article 81(1) and the exception rule contained in Article 81(3) a
directly applied by not only the Commission but also national courts and nat
competition authorities. Agreements are legal or void depending on whether
satisfy the conditions of Article 81(3). No authorisation decision is required
enforcing agreements complying with Article 81 as a whole. This is already
existing enforcement system for Article 82 of the EC Treaty.

B. Legal basis

The legal basis for the present proposal is Article 83 of the EC Treaty. Article
empowers the Council to lay down the appropriate regulations or directives to
effect to the principles set out in Articles 81 and 82. In a non-exhaustive
Article 83(2) mentions elements that should in particular be covered by implement
rules created on this basis.

The legal basis in Article 83 covers the application of Articles 81 and 82 i
general. In particular, it is not limited to the application of the rules by specific
decision-makers. The Community legislature, within the limits of the general
principles of the Treaty, is therefore empowered to lay down rules on the application
of Articles 81 and 82 by bodies other than the Community institutions as well as
rules on the interaction between the different decision-makers. Accordingly, the
proposed Regulation provides for certain rules to be respected by national
competition authorities and/or courts when applying Articles 81 and 82 as well as
rules on cooperation between them and with the Commission.

Article 83(2)(b) expressly provides for the Community legislature to lay down
detailed rules for the application of Article 81(3), taking into account the need to
ensure effective supervision on the one hand, and to simplify administration to the
greatest extent possible on the other. The legal basis in Article 83 thereby enjoins the
Community legislature to fill a lacuna left by Article 81. Leaving aside Article 81(2),
Article 81 is divided into a prohibition rule (Article 81(1)) and a rule according to
which the prohibition may be declared inapplicable if stated conditions are satisfied
(Article 81(3)). It does not, however, lay down by what procedure the prohibition
may be declared inapplicable, and by whom. In particular, the words "may be
declared inapplicable", unlike the words "the High Authority shall authorise" used
by the ECSC Treaty (see Article 65 of the ECSC Treaty), do not define a specific
procedure.

The existing Regulation No 17 granted exclusive power to the Commission to
apply Article 81(3) in the framework of an administrative procedure aiming at an
authorisation decision. Article 81(3) is however suitable for direct application.
While leaving a certain margin of appreciation as to its interpretation, Article 81(3)
does not imply discretionary powers that could only be exercised by an administrative
body. A limited margin of appreciation does not make a Treaty provision unsuitable
for direct application, as is clear from the case-law on for instance Article 81(1) and
Article 82, which are already directly applied by national courts.

There is no indication in the Treaty to contradict this conclusion. In particular, the
words "to simplify administration to the greatest extent possible" in Article 83(2)(b),
while imposing on the legislature the objective of a minimum of procedural
bureaucracy, do not exclude the application of Article 81(3) by courts in addition to
administrative bodies. Under the powers granted to it by Article 83, the Community
legislature can choose an implementing system that is based on direct application of
Article 81(3).

Article 83(2)(e) states that the Community legislature is also empowered to define
the relationship between national laws and the Community rules on competition.
Regulation No 17 refrained from regulating this relationship, which has led to
long-standing debates and to legal uncertainty. The Court of Justice was able to

some of the issues involved by applying the principle of primacy of
unity law over national law. Given the specificity of Article 81 in particular,
lutions found on that basis do not, however, cover the entirety of cases in
conflicts can arise. In addition, the change to a new implementing system
to reopening the debate and creating new legal uncertainties as to this
amental issue. The proposed Regulation therefore lays down a rule regulating
elationship between Community competition law and national law.

inally, Article 83 is also the appropriate legal basis for regulating the application
rticles 81 and 82 to the transport sector. This was not yet clear when Regulation
C) No 1017/68 was adopted: it had two legal bases, the former Articles 75 and 87,
Articles 71 and 83. However, the Court of Justice has since held that the
munity competition rules apply in full to the transport sector.[1] The Community
slature can therefore provide that the application of Articles 81 and 82 to
eements and decisions presently governed by Regulation (EEC) No 1017/68 is
egrated into the proposed Regulation on the legal basis of Article 83. The same
es for the application of Articles 81 and 82 to the maritime transport sector
resently governed by Regulation (EEC) No 4056/86. The latter regulation,
although adopted subsequently to the abovementioned case-law of the Court of
Justice, and in contrast to the Commission proposal (based on Article 87 (now 83)
alone), was also based by Council on the former Article 84(2) (now 80(2)), owing to
the inclusion of Article 9 of that Regulation concerning relations with third
countries. The difference of opinion between the Council and the Commission does
not need to be resolved in the present instance, as the proposed Regulation leaves
Article 9 of Regulation (EEC) No 4056/86 untouched.

C. Characteristics of the proposed system

1. More efficient protection of competition

The proposal aims at increasing the protection of competition in the Community.

This will be achieved by the proposal in three ways.

(a) More enforcers

The proposed system will result in increased enforcement of Community
competition rules, as in addition to the Commission, national competition
authorities and national courts will also be able to apply Articles 81 and 82 in their
entirety.

National competition authorities, which have been set up in all Member States,
are generally well equipped to deal with Community competition law cases. In
general, they have the necessary resources and are close to the markets.

As regards the applicant countries, considerable progress has already been made
in establishing national competition authorities. Even if initially they may not all
possess sufficient resources to ensure the effective protection of competition, the
proposed reform will allow the Commission to step up enforcement in those parts of
the enlarged Community. The proposed discontinuation of the notification and
exemption system ensures that all available resources can be used for the effective
protection of competition.

It is a core element of the Commission's proposal that the Commission and the
national competition authorities should form a network and work closely together in
the application of Articles 81 and 82. The network will provide an infrastructure for
mutual exchange of information, including confidential information, and assistance,
thereby expanding considerably the scope for each member of the network to
enforce Articles 81 and 82 effectively. The network will also ensure an efficient
allocation of cases based on the principle that cases should be dealt with by the best
placed authority.

National courts will also play an important and enhanced role in the enforc of Community competition rules. Unlike national authorities or the Comm which act in the public interest, the function of national courts is to prote rights of individuals. They can grant damages and order the performan non-performance of contracts. They are the necessary complement to actio public authorities.

The Commission's proposal aims at promoting private enforcement thro national courts. Both Article 81(1) and Article 81(3) confer rights on individu which should be protected by national courts. The present division of powers ur Article 81 is not in line with the important role that national courts play in enforcement of Community law in general. In the present Regulation N the authorisation system and the Commission's monopoly on the applicatio Article 81(3) make application of Article 81(1) by national courts very difficult. fact that the elimination of this obstacle may lead to more application of Article and thereby increase the case load on national courts is not a valid argument agai the reform. Such considerations should not be allowed to hamper the implementatio of a reform that aims at strengthening the enforcement of the rules and at enhancing the protection of individual rights.

(b) Refocusing the Commission's action

The second way in which the proposal will increase the protection of competition is by allowing the Commission to concentrate on the detection of the most serious infringements. Experience in the last decades has shown that notifications do not bring to the attention of the Commission serious violations of the competition rules.

The handling of a large number of notifications prevents the Commission from focusing on the detection and the punishment of the most serious restrictions such as cartels, foreclosure of the market and abuses of dominant positions. In the proposed system, the abolition of the notification and authorisation system will allow the Commission to focus on complaints and own-initiative proceedings that lead to prohibition decisions, rather than establishing what is not prohibited. The Commission intends to issue a notice providing potential complainants with guidance on the treatment of complaints. The notice will *inter alia* set a deadline within which the Commission should inform the complainant whether it intends to deal with its complaint.

(c) Increased powers of investigation for the Commission

In order to guarantee the protection of competition, it is also necessary to ensure that the Commission's powers of investigation are sufficient and effective. Under the existing Regulation No 17, the Commission can conduct inspections on the premises of companies and make written requests for information. It can fine companies for infringements of substantive and procedural rules and impose periodic penalty payments.

Three main improvements of the current system are required to ensure a more effective application of Articles 81 and 82.

First, the rules governing the obtaining of judicial orders at national level in order to overcome any opposition on the part of an undertaking to an inspection should be codified. This will clarify the intervention of national judges in accordance with the limits established by the Court of Justice.

Secondly, it is necessary to adapt the powers vested in Commission officials during inspections: they must be empowered, subject to judicial authorisation, to search private homes if professional documents are likely to be kept there. The experience of the national competition authorities and the Commission shows that incriminating documents are ever more frequently kept and discovered in private homes. Commission inspectors should also be empowered to seal cupboards or

in order to ensure that documents are not removed and destroyed. Finally,
ould be entitled to ask oral questions relating to the subject matter of the
tion.

rdly, the fines for breaches of procedural rules and the periodic penalty
ents, which were set in absolute terms in the sixties, must be increased. A
m based on turnover percentage figures is considered the appropriate solution.

More level playing field

petition laws have an immediate impact on the commercial activities of
anies, as they have to adapt to the prevailing standard in any given area. For
anies that engage in activities having cross-border effects it is therefore
rtant that there be a level playing field throughout the European Union,
wing them to reap the full benefits of the single market.

he present proposal will create a more level playing field in two ways. First,
ommunity competition law will be applied to more cases, thereby limiting the
cope for inconsistencies caused by differences in national competition laws.
Secondly, a number of measures will ensure that Articles 81 and 82 are applied in a
consistent manner by the various decision-makers involved in their application.

(a) More application of Community competition law

In the present enforcement system, several national systems of competition law
and Community competition law may apply concurrently to the same transaction to
the extent that an agreement or practice is capable of affecting trade between
Member States. The application of national law is constrained only by the principle
of primacy of Community law.

Several national systems of competition law have been modelled on Articles 81
and 82. However, no formal harmonisation is in place, and differences remain both
in law and practice. Such differences can lead to different treatment of agreements
and practices that affect trade between Member States.

In order to promote a level playing field for companies that engage in agreements
or practices that have a cross-border effect, it is necessary to regulate the relationship
between national law and Community law, as provided in Article 83(2)(e) of the EC
Treaty. Accordingly, Article 3 of the proposed Regulation provides that only
Community competition law applies when an agreement, decision or concerted
practice within the meaning of Article 81 or abusive conduct within the meaning of
Article 82 is capable of affecting trade between Member States. This rule ensures in
a simple and effective way that all transactions with a cross-border effect are subject
to a single body of law.

The proposal not only creates a level playing field throughout the European
Union, it also facilitates an efficient allocation of cases within the network of
competition authorities, the aim being that cases should be dealt with by the best
placed authority. In several Member States the competition authority, once seized of
a case, is obliged to come to a formal decision. Such obligations may hinder
reallocation of cases to a better placed authority. To overcome this problem in
respect of the application of Articles 81 and 82 the Regulation empowers a
competition authority to suspend a proceeding or reject a complaint on grounds that
another competition authority is dealing with or has dealt with the case. However,
the scope of this provision is limited to the application of Community competition
law. Article 3 of the proposed Regulation ensures that an efficient allocation of cases
is not hindered by simultaneous application of national law in respect of which a
national competition authority may remain bound to come to a formal decision.
Parallel application of national and Community competition law should be avoided
because it leads to unnecessary parallel proceedings.

(b) Consistent application of Community competition law

The application of the same law and policy will in itself promote cons throughout the single market. The application of Articles 81 and 82 by n competition authorities and courts will be subject to Community block exen regulations, creating safe harbours for defined categories of agreements. Ft guidance will be provided by guidelines adopted by the Commission.

Application by national competition authorities and courts will also be subjee the case-law of the Court of Justice of the European Communities and the Cour First Instance as well as the administrative practice of the Commission. In the l respect, it is proposed in Article 16 of the proposed Regulation to impos national competition authorities and courts an obligation to use every effort r contradict a Commission decision.

More decision-makers also mean more case-law and administrative decisic which will further clarify the scope of the Community competition rules.

Moreover, there will be a number of additional instruments aiming at ensurin, that Articles 81 and 82 are applied in a consistent manner.

The application of the Community competition rules by national courts will be subject to the preliminary reference procedure of Article 234 of the EC Treaty. The Court of Justice of the European Communities will play the same important role in ensuring consistency as it has done and continues to do in other areas of Community law. As the proposal aims at increasing the level of private enforcement before national courts, an initial increase in Article 234 references can be expected. A significant increase, however, is unlikely, as it is expected that most litigation before national courts will concern areas where the law has been clearly established.

Article 15 of the proposed Regulation codifies the existing obligation of the Commission, based on Article 10 of the Treaty, to cooperate with national courts. This cooperation includes a right for national courts to ask the Commission for information in its possession or for its opinion on questions concerning the application of the Community competition rules. It is expected that the importance of this mechanism will increase once national courts are empowered to apply Article 81(3) as well.

Article 15 also proposes to vest in the Commission the power to submit written or oral submissions to national courts at its own initiative and in the Community public interest. This will allow the Commission to contribute to the consistent application of Community competition law by national courts. It is also proposed that the national competition authorities be empowered to make oral and written submissions to the courts of their Member State.

With regard to the national competition authorities, the creation of a network in which all members apply the same law and policy will greatly promote consistency and a level playing field throughout the single market. The formal basis for establishing the network is found in Article 11 of the proposed Regulation, according to which the national competition authorities and the Commission are to apply the Community competition rules in close cooperation. The details of this cooperation will be developed in a notice. The network will foster the development of a common competition culture throughout the Community.

In addition, certain formal mechanisms are established to ensure consistent application, including a consultation procedure for certain types of decisions adopted by national competition authorities (see Article 11(4) of the proposed Regulation). This provision requires national competition authorities to consult the Commission prior to the adoption of prohibition decisions, decisions accepting commitments and decisions withdrawing the benefit of a block exemption regulation. All such decisions have direct repercussions for the addressees. It is

ore important to ensure that these decisions are consistent with the general
e of the network. In case of substantial disagreement within the network, the
ssion retains the power to withdraw a case from a national competition
ity by itself initiating proceedings in the case.

s not necessary for consistency purposes to provide for prior consultation in
ct of other types of decisions adopted by national competition authorities, such
jections of complaints and decisions to take no action. These decisions bind
the deciding authority, and do not preclude subsequent action by any other
petition authority or before national courts.

regards decisions adopted by the Commission, it is proposed to maintain the
nt obligation for the Commission to consult the Advisory Committee on
rictive Practices and Dominant Positions.

*An adequate level of legal certainty for companies and a reduction of
reaucracy*

Jnder the existing Regulation No 17 an agreement or decision caught by Article 81(1)
an become valid, ie enforceable before a civil court, only if it is notified to the
Commission and is exempted by the Commission. In practice, most notified cases
are closed by a non-binding administrative letter from the Commission services (a
'comfort letter').

The proposed Regulation removes the bureaucratic obstacles connected with the
notification and authorisation procedure while maintaining an adequate degree of
legal certainty.

In particular, the proposed Regulation provides that agreements and decisions
which satisfy the conditions of Article 81(3) are valid and enforceable *ab initio* with
no administrative decision being required to that effect. Undertakings can therefore
rely on civil enforceability as an element of improved legal certainty independently
of any action by an administration.

The proposed Regulation does not remove the necessity for undertakings to assess
their business transactions to verify whether they are in compliance with the
competition rules. Under the present Regulation No 17, this analysis is carried out
by undertakings when preparing a notification. The proposal assimilates the
application of the Community competition rules to other areas of law where
undertakings are required to ascertain themselves that their behaviour is legal.

In the field of Community competition law, companies' task of assessing their
behaviour is facilitated by block exemptions and Commission notices and guidelines
clarifying the application of the rules. As a complementary element of the current
reform, the Commission commits itself to an even greater effort in this area. Article 28
of the proposed Regulation confers on the Commission a general power to adopt
block exemption regulations. This power will ensure that it is in a position to react
with sufficient speed to new developments and changing market conditions.

In addition, under the new system, with the larger number of decision-makers
applying Article 81(3), case-law and practice on its interpretation will rapidly
develop where they do not yet exist, thereby inherently reinforcing the framework
for assessment.

The Commission will further contribute to this development by continuing to set
policy through its own decisions in individual cases. In addition to prohibition
decisions, the proposed Regulation provides that in cases where it is in the
Community public interest to do so the Commission, acting on its own initiative, can
adopt decisions finding that no infringement has been committed. This will permit
the Commission to set out its position in a landmark case so as to clarify the law for
all companies that find themselves in similar situations.

PART IV
EC MATERIALS

Finally, the Commission will remain open to discuss specific cases wi[...] undertakings where appropriate. In particular, it will provide guidance reg[...] agreements, decisions or concerted practices that raise an unresolved, genuine[...] question of interpretation. To that effect, the Commission will publish a no[...] which it will set out the conditions under which it may issue reasoned opinions.[...] such system of opinions must not, however, lead to companies being entitle[...] obtain an opinion, as this would reintroduce a kind of notification system.

[63[...]

3. SUBSIDIARITY AND PROPORTIONALITY

In the interest of the single market, the proposed Regulation ensures[...] Community competition law should be applied to agreements and practices cap[...] of affecting trade between Member States, thereby creating a level playing f[...] throughout the Community. At the same time, the proposal ensures that[...] application of that law takes place at the most efficient level. Under the proposal, t[...] Commission shares the power to apply Article 81(3) with national competitio[...] authorities and national courts, thereby enabling these bodies to apply Articles 81[...] and 82 effectively.

The scope for effective intervention at national level is substantially increased by[...] the cooperation mechanisms contained in Articles 12 and 21 of the proposed[...] Regulation, which empower national competition authorities to exchange confidential information and to assist each other in respect of fact-finding. As a result of market integration evidence and information will increasingly be located in several Member States. Enhanced horizontal cooperation will make it easier for national competition authorities to obtain all the relevant facts.

The Commission's proposal is thus fully in line with the principle enshrined in Article 5 of the Treaty, according to which action should be taken at the most efficient level. While promoting the Community interest in a level playing field throughout the single market, the proposal ensures that national competition authorities and courts can apply Articles 81 and 82 fully and effectively to all cases in respect of which intervention at national level is more efficient.

The Commission, being the only authority that can act throughout the European Union, will necessarily continue to play a central role in the development of Community competition law and policy and in ensuring that it is applied consistently throughout the single market, thereby preventing any renationalisation of Community competition law. The development and application of the law and policy will, however, be a concern of all the competition authorities involved in the enforcement of Articles 81 and 82. Policy issues will be the subject of discussion within the network.

The proposal does not go beyond what is necessary to achieve the objectives of the Treaty. The Treaty aims, *inter alia*, to create an internal market and a system of undistorted competition. The very objective of the present proposal is to enhance the protection of competition and to create a level playing field throughout the Community.

The proposal to exclude the application of national competition law to agreements and practices that affect trade between Member States is necessary in order to ensure that such agreements and practices are subject to a single set of rules. This is essential in order to ensure that competition in the internal market is not distorted as a result of differences in the legal framework and to ensure that cases can be allocated efficiently within the network.

Effective case allocation also makes it necessary that the members of the network should inform each other of all new cases and exchange relevant case-related information. Moreover, provision must be made for prior consultation by the

l competition authorities in respect of prohibition decisions, decisions
g commitments and decisions withdrawing the benefit of a block exemption
on. Inconsistencies in respect of these types of decisions would be
ental to the single market and the objective of creating a level playing field
ghout the Community. Such decisions also have important implications for the
non competition policy of the network. The Commission will associate the
members of the network in the consultation process. The functioning of the
vork will be further elaborated upon in a notice on cooperation between
petition authorities.

e present proposal is based on the premise that national competition authorities
pply Articles 81 and 82 in accordance with their respective national procedural
. It is not necessary for the implementation of the reform to embark on a
scale harmonisation of national procedural laws. On the other hand, it is
essary to regulate at Community level a limited number of issues that have a
ect impact on the proper functioning of the proposed system.

First and foremost, it is necessary to oblige the Member States to empower their
national competition authorities to apply Articles 81 and 82.

It is also necessary to stipulate the content of the decisions that national
competition authorities may adopt in the application of Articles 81 and 82 (see
Article 5 of the proposed Regulation), in order to ensure a full and effective
implementation of the directly applicable exception system. No competition
authority forming part of the network can be empowered to adopt constitutive
exemption decisions when applying the Community competition rules.

Article 13 of the proposed Regulation empowers national competition authorities
and the Commission to suspend or terminate proceedings on the ground that another
member of the network is or has been dealing with the case; this is necessary to
ensure an efficient allocation of cases and use of resources within the network. It is,
however, neither necessary nor appropriate to oblige other competition authorities to
suspend or terminate their proceedings. It is the task of the network to ensure in
practice that resources are used efficiently.

The proposed Regulation provides a legal basis for the exchange of information
and assistance between national competition authorities. Such horizontal cooperation
is necessary in order to enable them to apply Articles 81 and 82 effectively.

The power of the Commission to make written and oral submissions in the
Community public interest before national courts hearing a case on the application
of Articles 81 and 82 (see Article 15) is necessary in order to allow the Commission
to contribute to their consistent application. Divergent application of Community
competition law by national courts would pose a threat to the proper functioning of
the single market and the coherence of the system. In accordance with the principle
of subsidiarity it is proposed that the power to make submissions before the courts
be shared between the Commission and the national competition authorities.
Furthermore, submissions will be made in accordance with the procedural rules in
force in the Member State in question. Thus, the proposal does not purport to
harmonise national procedural law, except that it grants the Commission and the
national competition authorities the power to make submissions on their own
initiative. In order to enable the Commission and the national competition
authorities to exercise this proposed new power effectively, it is necessary to oblige
national courts to furnish, upon request, relevant information pertaining to cases
before them in which the Commission or a national competition authority is
considering making a written or oral submission or has decided to do so.

[6303]

4. THE REGULATION, ARTICLE BY ARTICLE

CHAPTER I
PRINCIPLES

Article 1—Direct applicability

This Article sets out the general principle governing the new implementing r[ ]
outside the scope of block exemption regulations. In addition to the prohibitio[ ]
Article 81(1) and the prohibition of Article 82, it provides that Article 81(3)[ ]
also be directly applicable.

Under this rule, agreements, decisions or practices that fall under Article 8[ ]
and do not satisfy the conditions of Article 81(3) are prohibited and void *ab i[ ]*
in accordance with Article 81(1) and 81(2). On the other hand, agreeme[ ]
decisions and practices that fall under Article 81(1) but do satisfy the conditions[ ]
Article 81(3) are valid *ab initio*, no prior administrative decision to that effect bein[ ]
required.

When applying Article 81(1), all decision-makers, ie the Commission, national
courts and national competition authorities, are also obliged to consider whether the
conditions of Article 81(3) are met. In doing so, they must respect the interpretation
of Article 81(3) given by the Community Courts. In addition, they should take due
account of all other elements of interpretation including Commission guidelines,
notices and decisions.

On finding that the conditions of Article 81(3) are met or not met, decision-
makers are to draw the appropriate legal consequences in accordance with the
proposed Regulation and, where applicable, the relevant national procedural rules.

Article 2—Burden of proof

This Article clarifies which party bears the burden of proving the facts pertaining to
the fulfilment of the conditions of Article 81. It is based on the division in the Treaty
between the prohibition in Article 81(1) and the conditions under which it may be
declared inapplicable set out in Article 81(3). It is also in line with the principle,
widely observed in the laws of the Member States, that each party to litigation has to
prove the facts on which it relies.

The rule proposed ensures a fair balance between the parties. In particular, the
party invoking the benefit of Article 81(3) is generally best placed to supply the
information required to demonstrate that the conditions of Article 81(3) are satisfied
(eg regarding efficiencies). It is therefore appropriate that that party should bear the
burden of proof as regards Article 81(3).

Article 3—Relationship between Articles 81 and 82 and national competition laws

This Article stipulates that when an agreement or practice is capable of affecting
trade between Member States only Community competition law applies. National
competition authorities, being empowered to apply Articles 81 and 82 in their
entirety, will thus apply Community law in all cases affecting trade between
Member States.

In the present system the same agreement or conduct may be subject to
Community competition law and several national competition laws. In accordance
with the principle of primacy of Community competition law, established by the
Court of Justice in the *Walt Wilhelm* case,[2] national law can be applied only in so far
as it does not prejudice the uniform application of the Community competition rules

hout the single market. The primacy principle resolves clear conflicts in
of Community law. It does not, however, effectively prevent inconsistencies
fferences in the treatment of agreements and practices between Member
, even if such agreements and practices affect trade between Member States.

the present stage of development of the Community it is essential to ensure that
e is a level playing field throughout the European Union, allowing companies to
the full benefits of the single market. As is evident from the very content of
icle 81(3), many agreements have desirable effects on economic welfare. It is
nsistent with the notion of a single market that agreements and practices capable
ffecting cross-border trade should be subject to different standards and that an
ement which would be considered innocuous or beneficial under Community
can be prohibited under national competition law. To address this problem
ctively it is necessary to adopt the solution alluded to by the Court of Justice in
lt Wilhelm, namely to regulate the relationship between national law and
ommunity competition law as provided for in Article 83(2)(e) of the EC Treaty.

Article 3 ensures that agreements and practices capable of affecting cross-border
trade are scrutinised under a single set of rules, thereby promoting a level playing
field throughout the Community, and removing the costs attached to the parallel
application of Community law and national laws for both competition authorities
and business. The provision does not limit the scope for action of national
competition authorities, which will be able to apply Community law. Experience
gained at national level will contribute to the development of Community
competition policy within the network.

The Article also ensures that all cases concerning agreements and practices
affecting trade between Member States become subject to the mechanisms of
cooperation inside the network of competition authorities. It is a fundamental aim of
the proposed Regulation that the Commission and the national competition
authorities should form a network of competition authorities that cooperate closely
in the application of Articles 81 and 82. The network will incorporate mechanisms
that seek to ensure that the consistency of Community competition law is preserved.

The proposal eliminates the risk that the proper functioning of the network might
be affected by the concurrent application of Community competition law and
national competition law. The objective is to ensure an efficient allocation of cases,
generally to a single authority, which is considered the best placed to act. This
objective would be hampered if national authorities were bound to continue dealing
with the case under their own competition law. In several Member States the
competition authority that has received a complaint based on national law is obliged
to adopt a formal reasoned decision. These parallel proceedings should be avoided.

CHAPTER II
POWERS

Article 4—Powers of the Commission

Paragraph 1 establishes the Commission's power to take the measures provided for
in the Regulation.

Such measures may in the first place be individual decisions. The Commission
thus keeps an autonomous power of enforcement, which it will use not only to act
against infringements but also to set policy and to ensure consistent application of
Community competition law.

The measures provided for also include block exemptions. Article 28 confers on
the Commission a general power to adopt block exemption regulations.

PART IV
EC MATERIALS

The block exemption is one of the main tools, which the Commission u
ensure the consistent application of competition law throughout the single i
Together with the practice developed by the Commission in its decisions,
exemptions form the backbone of a common set of competition enforcement
that is complemented by the guidelines that the Commission issues. In the
system, where undertakings must, as a general rule, assess for themselves whe
their   behaviour complies with the law, the legislative framework that bi
exemptions offer will be of crucial importance in providing legal certainty
undertakings.

Block exemption regulations, while containing abstract rules, do not create
law for undertakings, but codify and clarify the interpretation of Article 81(3). V
drafting them, the Commission is able to base itself on the experience it has ga
in individual cases. Under Article 16 of the proposed Regulation, it will also l.
information about the application of Articles 81 and 82 by national courts in
Member States. It is therefore best placed to know in which areas it is necessary
enact or amend block exemption regulations in order to keep up with nev
developments and rapidly changing market conditions. In doing so, the Commission
will cooperate closely with the competition authorities of the Member States.

As block exemption regulations cannot authorise behaviour that is ultimately
prohibited by Article 81, the benefit of a block exemption can be withdrawn where it
is found that in an individual case an agreement, decision or concerted practice has
effects that are incompatible with Article 81(3). Under the proposed Regulation, in
the spirit of decentralised but consistent application, the national competition
authorities have the power to withdraw the benefit of a block exemption if the
relevant geographic market is no wider than the territory of their Member State (see
Article 29(2)). Decisions to that effect are, however, subject to consultation in
accordance with Article 11(4).

Paragraph 2 gives the Commission power to introduce a registration requirement
for types of agreements, decisions or practices that fall under Article 81(1) and are
not covered by block exemptions. In accordance with the conditions set out in this
paragraph, the Commission can lay down the details of such an obligation in a
Commission regulation, including possible penalties for failure to comply with the
registration obligation.

Article 5—Powers of the competition authorities of the Member States

This Article serves to establish and define the powers of the competition authorities
of the Member States to apply Articles 81 and 82. If additional measures to achieve
this objective are necessary under national law, Article 36 obliges Member States to
take such measures by a date to be determined.

The competition authorities of the Member States are to apply Article 81 as a whole:
each time they apply Article 81(1) they are also empowered to decide whether the
conditions of Article 81(3) are satisfied. They may also apply Article 82.

If they find that there is infringement of Article 81 as a whole, or of Article 82, the
competition authorities of the Member States are to take effective action against the
conduct in question, acting in accordance with the proposed Regulation and
applicable national procedural rules. Paragraph 3 lists the contents of the decisions
they may take in that respect. While the proposed regulation does not foresee
harmonisation of national sanctions, general principles of Community law require
that such sanctions ensure effective enforcement.

If the competition authority of a Member State finds that behaviour, acting on a
complaint or on its own initiative does not infringe Article 81 as a whole or
Article 82, it can close the proceedings or reject the complaint by decision, finding
that there are no grounds for action.

decisions bind only the authority adopting the decision.

effect of other types of decisions adopted by the national competition
ties within their own Member State is not regulated in the proposed
ation. This is a matter of national law. Decisions adopted by national
etition authorities do not have legal effects outside the territory of their
ber State, nor do they bind the Commission.

icle 6—Powers of the national courts

Article gives national courts jurisdiction to apply Article 81(3). When applying
le 81(1), a court will be empowered to apply Article 81(3). It is already
lished case-law that courts have jurisdiction to apply Article 81(1) and (2) and
cle 82.

f a national court finds that the conditions of Article 81(3) are satisfied it must—
the absence of other objections—hold that the agreement is valid with effect *ab*
nitio. It must then enforce the agreement and reject any claims for damages based
on an alleged violation of Article 81.

Conversely, if the conditions of Article 81(3) are not satisfied, national courts
must rule that an agreement or decision or part of it is void under Article 81(2), and
may order damages or take any other decision that follows from the violation of
Article 81(1).

CHAPTER III
COMMISSION DECISIONS

Article 7—Finding and termination of infringement

This Article is equivalent to Article 3 of the present Regulation No 17, with two
exceptions.

First, it makes it clear that the Commission is empowered to adopt a decision
finding an infringement not only when it orders the termination of an infringement
or imposes a fine, but also where the infringement has already come to an end and
no fine is imposed.

In conformity with the case-law of the Court of Justice, however,[3] the power of the
Commission to adopt an infringement decision in such circumstances is limited to
cases where it has a legitimate interest in doing so. This may be the case where there
is a danger that the addressee might re-offend, or where the case raises new issues
clarification of which is in the public interest.

Secondly, the Commission is empowered to impose all remedies necessary to
bring the infringement to an end, including structural remedies. Structural remedies
can be necessary in order to bring an infringement effectively to an end. This may in
particular be the case with regard to cooperation agreements and abuses of a
dominant position, where divestiture of certain assets may be necessary.

Article 8—Interim measures

According to this Article, the Commission is empowered to adopt interim
measures in cases where there is a risk of serious and irreparable harm to
competition and there is *prima facie* evidence of an infringement. It is further
stipulated that interim measures may be adopted for no more than one year, with a
possibility of renewal.

The Commission acts in the public interest and not in the interest of individual
operators. It is therefore appropriate to ensure that the Commission has an obligation

to adopt interim measures only in cases where there is a risk of seriou
irreparable harm to competition. Companies can always have recourse to n
courts, the very function of which is to protect the rights of individuals.

Article 9—Commitments

Paragraph 1 introduces a new provision empowering the Commission to ac
decisions accepting commitments offered by undertakings in the course of proceedi
in which the Commission intends to adopt a decision ordering termination of
alleged infringement. Such decisions constitute an appropriate remedy when
commitments offered meet the competition concerns identified by the Commiss
Decisions accepting commitments establish the material facts of the case and
prima facie evidence of the suspected infringement, and incorporate the acce
commitments.

The addressee of the Commission decision is bound by the decision containi
the commitments, which can be invoked by third parties before national courts.

The time-limit ensures that undertakings are not bound by the commitments for an
indefinite period, and that the Commission is in a position, if need be, to reassess the
agreement or practice and the effectiveness of the commitments after a certain
period of time.

Paragraph 2 provides that the decision makes no finding as to the existence of an
infringement prior to the commitments or as to the absence of an infringement
following the commitments. Following the acceptance of the commitments by
decision, the Commission closes the file.

Paragraph 3 stipulates that the Commission is entitled to reopen the procedure
only if the facts on the basis of which the Commission accepted the commitments
have materially changed, if the undertaking offering the commitments has supplied
incorrect, incomplete or misleading information, or if the undertaking violates the
commitments.

Article 10—Finding of inapplicability

In the proposed directly applicable exception system the main functions of the
Commission will be to take action against infringements and to develop competition
policy and promote consistent application of the rules by means of general measures
such as block exemption regulations and guidelines.

However, Article 10 of the proposed Regulation also empowers the Commission
to adopt decisions finding that Article 81 is inapplicable, either because the
conditions of Article 81(1) are not fulfilled or because the conditions of Article 81(3)
are satisfied, and decisions finding that Article 82 does not apply.

Such decisions can be adopted only at the Commission's own initiative and in the
Community public interest. These conditions ensure that decisions making a finding
of inapplicability cannot be obtained on demand by companies. Such a possibility
would seriously undermine the principal aim of the reform, which is to focus the
activities of all competition authorities on what is prohibited.

In the decentralised system the Commission, as the guardian of the Treaty and the
centrally placed authority, has a special role to play in setting competition policy and
in ensuring that Articles 81 and 82 are applied consistently throughout the single
market. To that end it is necessary to empower the Commission to adopt positive
decisions if the Community public interest so requires. This power allows the
Commission to adopt a decision making a finding of inapplicability, in particular in
respect of new types of agreements or practices or issues that have not been settled
in the existing case-law and administrative practice.

ch decisions will be of a declaratory nature. The proposed instrument thus
significantly from the exemption decisions currently adopted under
81(3), which create rights with effect *erga omnes* for the duration of the
on regardless of any material change in the facts. Non-infringement decisions
have the effects of Community acts. Article 16 of the proposed Regulation
tes a general obligation for national competition authorities and national courts
nake every effort to avoid decisions conflicting with decisions adopted by the
mmission. A finding of inapplicability by the Commission pursuant to Article 10
therefore make an important contribution to the uniform application of Community
petition law.

CHAPTER IV
COOPERATION WITH NATIONAL AUTHORITIES AND COURTS

rticle 11—Cooperation between the Commission and the competition authorities f the Member States

This Article establishes the principle of close cooperation aimed at enabling the
Commission and the Member States' competition authorities to function as a
network when applying Articles 81 and 82 under the proposed Regulation. It sets
out the basic information and consultation mechanisms; detailed rules will be laid
down in an implementing Commission regulation in accordance with Article 34 and
in a notice on cooperation between competition authorities.

Paragraph 1 establishes the principle of close cooperation, covering cooperation
between the Commission and the Member States' competition authorities on the one
hand and between the latter on the other hand.

Paragraph 2 takes over the rule of Article 10(1) of the existing Regulation No 17,
adapted to the new implementing system.

Paragraph 3 requires national competition authorities to inform the Commission
at an early stage of cases treated under Articles 81 and 82. In practice this will be
done by electronic means, and the information will be made accessible to all
Member States' authorities via the network. The objective is in particular to
facilitate case allocation, to initiate cooperation on cases at an early stage, and to
ensure effective handling of multiple complaints.

Paragraph 4 establishes a consultation obligation regarding all decisions by
Member States' authorities aimed at terminating or penalising an infringement of
Article 81 or 82. Its objective is to allow for coordination of prohibition decisions
and equivalent decisions in order to ensure consistent application.

Paragraph 5 makes it clear that the principle of close cooperation also includes
voluntary consultation on cases other than those covered by paragraph 4.

Paragraph 6 takes over the rule of Article 9(3) of the existing Regulation No 17,
the provision empowering the Commission to withdraw a case from a national
competition authority and deal with the case itself, adapted to the new implementing
system. This provision is of crucial importance in the new system; it serves
to ensure effective case allocation and consistent application of Community
competition law.

Article 12—Exchange of information

Paragraph 1 creates a legal basis for the exchange of any information between the
Commission and the Member States' competition authorities and its use as evidence
in proceedings applying Community competition law. It covers the transfer of
information from the Commission to a Member State's authority and vice versa, and
the transfer from one Member State authority to another. This provision also allows

the transfer of entire case files, including confidential documents, the obj[...]
being to render possible the transfer of a case from one authority to another
interest of effective case allocation.

Paragraph 2 introduces limits on the use of information transmitted [...]
paragraph 1, thereby ensuring that the undertakings concerned benefit f[...]
appropriate procedural safeguards. The first sentence limits the use of
information transferred to the application of the Community competition rules.
use for other purposes is possible. The second sentence further limits the use of t
information transferred with regard to penalties. The objective of this rule is
ensure an appropriate balance between the rights of defence the undertak[...]
concerned could invoke in the Member State from which the information origina[...]
and the penalties they may face in the prosecuting Member State. It is propose[...]
exclude the use of evidence exchanged for imposing penalties other than pecuni[...]
penalties.

Article 13—Suspension or termination of proceedings

This Article serves the purpose of effective case allocation within the network of
competition authorities. It gives all Member States' competition authorities and the
Commission the right to suspend a proceeding or reject a complaint if the same case
is or has been dealt with by another competition authority. It thereby removes risks
of duplication of work and incentives for multiple complaints.

Paragraph 1 creates a legal basis for the staying or closing of proceedings if a
complaint is already under examination by another competition authority. It
supersedes national law that might oblige some Member States' competition
authorities to rule on the substance of each complaint they receive. The provision is
without prejudice to other grounds for rejecting a complaint and without prejudice
to the power of the Commission to withdraw a case from national competition
authorities under Article 11(6).

Paragraph 2 contains an equivalent rule regarding complaints against an
agreement or practice that has previously been dealt with by another competition
authority.

Article 14—Advisory Committee

Article 14 maintains the Advisory Committee on Restrictive Practices and
Dominant Positions as set up by the existing Regulation No 17. It has worked well in
the past and is perfectly in line with the principle of close cooperation between the
Commission and Member States' competition authorities. The adaptations
proposed, namely written procedure and the possibility of discussing cases dealt
with by Member States authorities, serve to adapt it to the new enforcement system.

Paragraph 1 sets out the types of decisions on which the Commission has an
obligation to consult the Advisory Committee.

Paragraph 2 sets out the composition of the Committee. It is aligned on Article 10(4)
of the existing Regulation No 17.

Paragraph 3 defines the working methods of the Committee. It takes over the
elements set out in Article 10(5) of the existing Regulation No 17. In the interest of
efficient proceedings it introduces the possibility for the Member States to agree that
the meeting may be convened at shorter notice.

Paragraph 4 creates a legal basis for written procedure. The purpose of this
provision is to allow for more flexible and efficient working methods.

Paragraph 5 allows the opinion of the Advisory Committee to be published, along
the lines of the Merger Regulation.

graph 6 creates a legal basis for discussing a case dealt with by a Member
competition authority. Its purpose is to allow the Committee to serve as a
or discussion of all cases that may be of common interest, in particular cases
issues of consistent application of Articles 81 and 82. If requested by a
er State, the Commission will normally put a national case on the agenda.

cle 15—Cooperation with national courts

s Article aims at reinforcing cooperation between the Commission and national
ts in order to promote consistent application of Articles 81 and 82.

agraph 1 establishes a right for national courts to obtain from the Commission
nation in its possession for the purpose of applying Article 81 and 82. They
also ask for an opinion from the Commission on questions relating to the
lication of the Community competition rules. The Commission will set out
ailed rules on its practice in this field in a notice, replacing the existing notice on
ooperation between national courts and the Commission. These rules will include a
eadline within which the Commission must reply.

Paragraph 2 aims at facilitating the monitoring of the application of Articles 81
and 82 by national courts. It sets up an obligation for national courts to transmit a
copy of judgments applying Articles 81 or 82 to the Commission. The extent of this
information obligation is such that the amount of bureaucracy involved for the courts
and for the Commission is kept to a minimum. On the courts' side, in particular,
very little additional work is required, and what there is is purely clerical. As far as
possible, paper transmission should be replaced by electronic transmission.

Paragraph 3 introduces a right for the Commission and the national competition
authorities to make submissions to national courts in written or oral form. In the case
of the national competition authorities the power is limited to the courts of their own
Member State. The Commission may act under this provision only in the
Community public interest (as *amicus curiae*), ie not in the interest of one of the
parties. This provision aims in particular at permitting the Commission and the
national competition authorities to draw the courts' attention to issues of
considerable importance for the consistent application of Community competition
law. The national courts are not bound to follow an opinion expressed by the
Commission or a national competition authority. Paragraph 3 is without prejudice to
Article 234 of the EC Treaty.

The second subparagraph of paragraph 3 requires national courts to supply
information to the Commission or the national competition authorities, as the case
may be, in individual cases, but only upon specific request, in order to ensure that
they have all relevant information about proceedings before a national court to
which they intend to make written or oral submissions. It is essential for the
Commission and the national competition authorities to be fully informed about the
substance of the case, first in order to arrive at a well-founded decision about
whether they want to make a submission in accordance with paragraph 3, and
second in order to be able to make qualitatively satisfactory submissions.

Article 16—Uniform application of Community competition law

In the proposed new system Commission decisions will continue to play an
important role in defining competition policy and—given their Community-wide
effect—in maintaining consistency throughout the single market. Such decisions are
Community acts within the meaning of Article 249 of the EC Treaty and are subject
to a separate system of judicial control. National courts have no jurisdiction to
review the validity of Community acts. This is the prerogative of the Community
courts, which in the exercise of their jurisdiction ensure the uniform application of
Community law in the interest of the Community legal order and legal certainty.

Maintaining consistent application is essential in an enforcement system in
parallel powers to apply Articles 81 and 82 are exercised by the Comm
national competition authorities and national courts. If significant differences
application of these provisions were to develop the consistency of Comm
competition law and the proper functioning of the single market would be put a
It is therefore necessary to adopt measures addressing the danger of inconsi
application effectively.

Article 16 of the proposed Regulation imposes on national courts and natio
competition authorities an obligation to make every effort to avoid taking decisi
that conflict with decisions adopted by the Commission. This rule is wit
prejudice to the case-law of the Court of Justice.

The objective of this Article is to create a system that limits the scope
conflicting decisions. It is essential to prevent national courts and natio
competition authorities from adopting decisions that contradict Commiss
decisions, as it would be detrimental to the proper functioning of the Communi
legal order if contradicting decisions based on the same body of law were to persist

The potential for conflict depends on the operative part of the Commission
decision and the facts on which it is based. When the Commission has found that
there has been an infringement, national courts and national competition authorities
must use every effort to avoid conflicts to the extent that the material facts are the
same. This also applies to findings of inapplicability under Article 10 of the
proposed Regulation.

National courts can avoid taking contradictory decisions, in particular, by making
a preliminary reference to the Court of Justice under Article 234 of the EC Treaty or
—in cases where a Commission decision is pending before the Community courts—
by suspending their own proceedings. The outcome in both situations is that the
issue is clarified by the Community courts with effect for the whole of the
Community. National competition authorities can avoid taking conflicting decisions
by consulting the Commission and—in cases where a Commission decision is
pending before the Community courts—by suspending their own proceedings.

CHAPTER V
POWERS OF INVESTIGATION

Article 17—Inquiries into sectors of the economy

This Article takes over Article 12 of the existing Regulation No 17. The detection of
infringements is achieved partly by monitoring markets. The instrument of sector
enquiries, whereby the Commission can conduct general enquiries in a given sector
if the evolution of the market suggests that competition is restricted, should
therefore be maintained.

Article 18—Requests for information

This Article is based on Article 11 of the existing Regulation No 17.

The existing text does not require substantial modification. The proposed Article
introduces only one minor amendment—

Paragraph 3 allows duly authorised lawyers to answer requests for information on
behalf of their clients. However, companies remain responsible for the correctness
of the information provided.

Article 19—Power to take statements

This Article creates a legal basis for the Commission to interview natural or legal
persons, whether or not they are themselves the subject of the proceedings, and to

their statements. The provision fills a gap in the Commission's powers by g for oral submissions to be recorded and used as evidence in proceedings.

20—The Commission's powers of inspection

Article defines the Commission's powers of inspection. It is largely identical to le 14 of the existing Regulation No 17, but in order to increase the effectiveness spections it proposes certain amendments.

der the existing Regulation No 17, Commission officials are empowered to ine the books and other business records, take copies of or extracts from the and business records, ask for oral explanations on the spot, and enter any ses, land and means of transport of undertakings. The proposal contains the wing changes:

aragraph 2 of the proposed Article introduces three new elements to complement e Commission's powers in order to safeguard the effectiveness of inspections:

First, paragraph 2(b) provides for the extension of the powers of search to private homes if there is reason to suspect that professional documents are kept there. This extension is based on experience gained in recent cases where it appeared that company employees kept relevant documents in their private homes. Evidence was found suggesting that incriminatory documents were deliberately stored in private homes. Under the existing rules, this enables companies effectively to undermine inspections by the Commission. In order to ensure that the effectiveness of inspections against secret infringements is maintained, it is therefore necessary to extend the powers of the Commission inspectors to search private homes of companies' personnel where professional documents are likely to be kept. Paragraph 7 of Article 20 ensures that the exercise of this power is subject to authorisation by a national court.

Secondly, paragraph 2(e) empowers Commission inspectors to seal cupboards and offices in order to make sure that no documents disappear during the inspection. This power serves to ensure the efficiency of inspections, in particular in cases where an inspection is carried out over more than one day and where the officials have to leave the premises of the company without having finished the inspection. Breaking of the seals is punishable by fines under Article 22 paragraph 1(d).

Thirdly, paragraph 2(f) stipulates, without prejudice to the case-law of the Court of Justice, that all questions related to the subject matter of the inspection can be asked by the Commission inspectors in the course of the inspection. This is necessary to increase the effectiveness of the investigations, as the wording of the present Article 14 of Regulation No 17 allows inspectors to ask only for oral explanations relating to documents.

Paragraph 8 codifies the *Hoechst* case-law,[4] in order to ensure uniform conditions for companies subject to Commission inspections throughout the single market.

When the Commission decides to carry out inspections under the present Article 14(3), the national authorities assisting it must, in most Member States, obtain an order from a court in order to overcome any opposition on the part of the undertakings. The Court of Justice held in *Hoechst* that the national court cannot substitute its assessment for that of the Commission and cannot question the validity of the Commission decision. The review by the national court is limited to checking the authenticity of the Commission decision and balancing the measures of constraint envisaged (ie the possibility for the Commission to proceed without the consent of the undertaking) against the subject matter of the inspection. To allow the court to fulfil this task, the Commission decision ordering the inspection must give an adequate statement of the reasons on which it is based.

PART IV
EC MATERIALS

The powers of courts in respect of the application of domestic competitio
differ from those they can exercise in respect of the application of Con
competition law. This may introduce confusion in the proceedings, sinc
courts have a tendency to apply domestic standards to inspections bas
Community law. In order to ensure that inspections by the Commission are gov
by the same rules throughout the single market, it is considered indispensal
clearly state in the new Regulation the standards set out in the *Hoechst* judgmen

Article 21—Investigations by competition authorities of Member States

This Article is based on Article 13 of the existing Regulation No 17, adapted
new implementing system. While continuing to allow Member States to cc
investigations on their territory on behalf of the Commission, it also enables th
carry out fact-finding measures on behalf of a competition authority of anc
Member State. This provision is necessary in order to allow effective coopera.
between the competition authorities of the Member States. Such cooperati
enables national competition authorities to deal with cases where some evidence
to be found in other Member States. Without such mechanisms a rea
decentralisation of the application of Community competition rules would be
seriously hampered.

CHAPTER VI
PENALTIES

Article 22—Fines

There are two types of fine in Article 15 of the existing Regulation No 17: fines for
breaches of procedural rules (requests for information, refusal to submit to an
inspection, etc) and fines for substantive breaches of Articles 81 and 82.

Paragraph 1 modifies the fines for breaches of procedural rules, which in the
existing Regulation No 17 can be between EUR 100 and 5 000. These amounts no
longer have any deterrent effect. It is proposed that these procedural fines be aligned
on the ECSC Treaty, which provides for fines of up to 1% of the total annual
turnover for these kinds of infringements (Article 47). The proposed Regulation also
introduces penalties for refusing to answer oral questions during inspections or for
breaking seals.

Paragraph 2 concerns fines for breaches of the substantive rules. It is not proposed
that the level of this second category of fines should be changed (up to 10% of the
total annual turnover). It is simply necessary to add to the list of infringements the
violation of a decision granting interim measures and failure to comply with
commitments made binding by decision.

Paragraph 4 introduces a new rule concerning infringements committed by
associations of undertakings. The Treaty allows the imposition of fines on
associations for breach of Community competition law. The Court of Justice has
found that the fine can be calculated on the basis of the turnover of the members of
the association. However, in practice, it is often impossible to recover the fine
imposed: associations seldom have sufficient resources of their own to cover the
payment and there is currently no legal means to recover the fine from members of
the association. A new rule is therefore proposed permitting the Commission, in
case of default on the part of an association, to recover the fine from its members at
the time of the infringement.

Article 23 – Periodic penalty payments

Rules on periodic penalty payments also have to be amended with regard to the
amount stipulated in the Regulation (the existing Regulation No 17 provides for

ts of from EUR 50 to 1 000 per day). It is proposed that a ceiling should be e basis of the total turnover: 5% of the average daily turnover for each day's his is the amount provided for in the ECSC Treaty (Article 47).

hermore, the creation of new categories of decisions, ie decisions accepting itments and decisions adopting interim measures, requires that it be possible pose periodic penalty payments on undertakings if they fail to comply with decision.

CHAPTER VII
LIMITATION PERIODS

cle 24—Limitation periods for the imposition of penalties

s Article takes over the rules on prescription from Regulation (EEC) No 2988/74 d integrates them into the proposed Regulation. As a result, Regulation (EEC) o 2988/74 will no longer apply to fines or periodic penalty payments covered by he proposed Regulation.

The provisions on prescription have been adapted to the new enforcement system. The only significant aspect relates to decentralised application under the proposed Regulation: under Regulation (EEC) No 2988/74 prescription is interrupted by steps taken by the Member States only if they act at the Commission's request. The latter condition is here removed, so that prescription is also interrupted by measures taken by national competition authorities applying Articles 81 or 82, irrespective of any request from the Commission.

Article 25—Limitation period for the enforcement of penalties

Like Article 24, this Article takes over the rules on prescription from Regulation (EEC) No 2988/74 and integrates them into the proposed Regulation. The same adaptation has been made as for Article 24.

CHAPTER VIII
HEARINGS AND PROFESSIONAL SECRECY

Article 26—Hearing of the parties, complainants and others

On the basis of Article 19 of the existing Regulation No 17, the Commission has developed a practice of fair hearing and access to file which is partially set out in the 1997 notice on access to file. It is proposed that this Article should confirm the right of access to file, while leaving the detailed rules for a Commission notice.

Article 27—Professional secrecy

Paragraph 1 takes over the provision in Article 20(1) of the existing Regulation No 17. It confines the use of information gathered under Articles 17 to 21 to the purpose for which it was collected. Article 27(1) is subject to the application of the more specific rules of the Regulation, namely Article 12 and Article 15.

Paragraph 2 makes the obligation of professional secrecy laid down in Article 20(2) of the existing Regulation No 17 applicable to all confidential information exchanged by the national competition authorities under the proposed Regulation. This provision complements the safeguards set out in Article 12(2).

CHAPTER IX
BLOCK EXEMPTIONS

Article 28—Adoption of block exemption regulations

At present, the Commission has been empowered by the Council to adopt exemption regulations in the field of vertical agreements, intellectual pro, rights, specialisation and research and development agreements, insurance certain fields of transport.

This Article empowers the Commission to adopt block exemption regulation sets out the conditions with which it must comply. The adoption of block exer regulations requires that the Advisory Committee on Restrictive Practicc Dominant Positions be consulted twice.

Article 29—Withdrawal in particular cases

Paragraph 1 provides, in line with the existing legal framework, that th Commission is empowered to withdraw the benefit of a block exemption, for th future, if it finds upon an individual assessment that a specific agreement does no fulfil the conditions of Article 81(3).

Paragraph 2 proposes to give the national competition authorities the power to withdraw the benefit of block exemptions for their own territory on condition that the territory constitutes a distinct relevant geographic market. At present the national competition authorities have such a power only in respect of vertical agreements.[5] To ensure consistency in the application of block exemption regulations, which are Community acts, it is necessary to provide for prior consultation of the Commission in respect of national decisions withdrawing the benefit of a block exemption (see Article 11(4) of the proposed Regulation).

Article 30—Regulations ending the application of a block exemption

This Article provides that the Commission may include in block exemption regulations a clause entitling it to exclude, by way of regulation, from their scope certain agreements or practices that are applied within a particular relevant market. Often anti-competitive effects are caused by the existence of a number of parallel agreements or networks of agreements.[6] In such cases it is inefficient to proceed by way of individual withdrawal in respect of each agreement or network. The proper response is to end the application of the block exemption to the particular market.

CHAPTER X
GENERAL PROVISIONS

Article 31—Publication of decisions

This Article is equivalent to Article 21 of the existing Regulation No 17.

Article 32—Review by the Court of Justice

This Article is identical to Article 17 of the existing Regulation No 17.

Article 33—Exclusions

This Article sets out areas to which the Regulation does not apply. These are certain areas of the sea and air transport sectors that are not covered by the present rules implementing Articles 81 and 82 (see Regulations (EEC) Nos 4056/86 and 3975/87).

~~e~~ 34—Implementing provisions

~~A~~rticle establishes the right of the Commission to adopt implementing rules for ~~re~~gulation and lists certain particular areas that may be covered by such rules.

CHAPTER XI
TRANSITIONAL AND FINAL PROVISIONS

~~Artic~~le 35—Transitional provisions

~~Parag~~raph 1 makes it clear that notifications and equivalent applications submitted ~~under~~ the existing Regulation No 17, Regulations (EEC) Nos 1017/68, 4056/86 ~~and~~ 3975/87 serve no further purpose upon the date of application of the proposed ~~Re~~gulation.

Subparagraph 2 of paragraph 1 draws the conclusion of the introduction of the ~~n~~ew system by providing that existing exemption decisions cease to be valid on the ~~d~~ate of application of the Regulation.

Paragraph 2 ensures that procedural steps taken under the existing Regulation No 17, Regulations (EEC) Nos 1017/68, 4056/86 and 3975/87 remain valid under the proposed new Regulation. Proceedings started under Articles 3 and 15 of the existing Regulation No 17, for example, will continue under the proposed Regulation, and be governed by the new rules from the date of their application.

Article 36—Designation of competition authorities of Member States

This Article requires the Member States to empower their national competition authorities to apply Articles 81 and 82 in their entirety in so far as national measures in addition to Article 6 may be needed. Full empowerment of the Member States' competition authorities is an indispensable precondition for efficient application of Articles 81 and 82 in the new decentralised enforcement system. It is also the precondition for the proper functioning of the network of competition authorities. Without it, case allocation could not take place as envisaged, and the Commission might be forced to take up a disproportionate share of cases concerning the markets of a Member State whose authority is unable to apply Articles 81 and 82.

Article 37—Amendment of Regulation (EEC) No 1017/68

This Article repeals specific procedural rules contained in Regulation (EEC) No 1017/68, leaving in force the substantive rules the Regulation lays down. The amendments are required in order to create an implementing system which includes the transport sector.

Article 38—Amendment of Regulation (EEC) No 2988/74

This Article makes Regulation (EEC) No 2988/74 inapplicable to the fines and periodic penalty payments provided for in the proposed Regulation.

Article 39—Amendment of Regulation (EEC) No 4056/86

This Article repeals procedural rules contained in Regulation (EEC) No 4056/86, leaving in force the substantive rules the Regulation lays down. The amendments are required in order to create an implementing system which includes the transport sector.

Article 40—Amendment of Regulation (EEC) No 3975/87

This Article repeals specific procedural rules contained in Regulation
No 3975/87, leaving in force the substantive rules the Regulation lays dow
amendments are required in order to create an implementing system which inc
the transport sector.

Article 41—Repeals

This Article lists the Regulations to be replaced by the present Regulation.

Article 42—Entry into force

This Article regulates the entry into force of the Regulation.

[6

NOTES

[1] See Joined Cases 209 to 213/84 *Nouvelles Frontières* [1986] ECR 1425 and Case 66/86 *Ahm*
Saeed [1989] ECR 803.
[2] See Case 14/68 *Walt Wilhelm* [1969] ECR 1.
[3] See Case 7/82 *GVL* [1983] ECR 483.
[4] See Joined Cases 46/87 a.o. *Hoechst* [1989] ECR 2859.
[5] See Article 1(4) of Council Regulation (EC) No 1215/1999 amending Regulation No 19/65/EEC
on the application of Article 81(3) of the Treaty to certain categories of agreements and concerted practices.
[6] See in this respect Article 1(2) of Regulation (EC) No 1215/1999.

PROPOSAL FOR A COUNCIL REGULATION

on the implementation of the rules on competition laid down in Articles 81 and 82 of the Treaty and amending Regulations (EEC) No 1017/68, (EEC) No 2988/74, (EEC) No 4056/86 and (EEC) No 3975/87 ("Regulation implementing Articles 81 and 82 of the Treaty") (Text with EEA relevance)

THE COUNCIL OF THE EUROPEAN UNION,

Having regard to the Treaty establishing the European Community, and in particular
Article 83 thereof,
Having regard to the proposal from the Commission,[1]
Having regard to the opinion of the European Parliament,[2]
Having regard to the opinion of the Economic and Social Committee,[3]
Whereas:

(1) If a system is to be established which ensures that competition in the common market is
not distorted, Articles 81 and 82 must be applied effectively and uniformly in the Community.
Council Regulation No 17 of 6 February 1962, First Regulation implementing Articles 85 and
86 of the Treaty,[4] has allowed a Community competition policy to develop that has helped to
disseminate a competition culture within the Community. In the light of experience, however,
that Regulation should now be replaced by legislation designed to meet the challenges of an
integrated market and a future enlargement of the Community.

(2) In particular, there is a need to rethink the arrangements for applying the exception from
the prohibition on agreements, which restrict competition, laid down in Article 81(3). Under
Article 83(2)(b), account must be taken in this regard of the need to ensure effective
supervision, on the one hand, and to simplify administration to the greatest possible extent, on
the other.

(3) The centralised scheme set up by Regulation No 17 no longer secures a balance between
those two objectives. It hampers application of the Community competition rules by the courts
and competition authorities of the Member States, and the system of notification it involves
prevents the Commission from concentrating its resources on curbing the most serious
infringements. It also imposes considerable costs on undertakings.

(4) The present system should therefore be replaced by a directly applicable exception
system in which the competition authorities and courts of the Member States have the power
to apply not only Articles 81(1) and 82, which have direct applicability by virtue of the
case-law of the Court of Justice of the European Communities, but also Article 81(3).

should be specified here that, in line with the case-law developed in the framework of
on No 17, the burden of proving that the conditions of Article 81(3) are fulfilled rests
rty seeking to rely on that provision. That party is usually best placed to prove that the
ns of that paragraph are fulfilled.

n order to ensure that the Community competition rules are applied effectively, the
tition authorities of the Member States must be associated more closely with their
ation. To this end, they must be empowered to apply Community law.

National courts have an essential part to play in applying the Community competition
. When deciding disputes between private individuals, they protect the subjective rights
Community law, for example by awarding damages to the victims of infringements. The
he national courts here complements that of the competition authorities of the Member
They must therefore be allowed to apply Articles 81 and 82 of the Treaty in full.

n order to ensure that the same competition rules apply to businesses throughout the
unity, provision must be made pursuant to Article 83(2)(e) to regulate the relationship
een Articles 81 and 82 and national competition law by excluding the application of
onal law to agreements, decisions and practices within the scope of Articles 81 and 82.

9) Although, in the new system, application of the rules will be decentralised, the
iformity of Community law requires that the rules be laid down centrally. To this end, the
ommission must be given a general power to adopt block exemption regulations in order to
nable it to adapt and clarify the legislative framework. This power must be exercised in close
cooperation with the competition authorities of the Member States. It must be without
prejudice to the existing rules in Council Regulations (EEC) No 1017/68,[5] (EEC) No 4056/86[6]
and (EEC) No 3975/87.[7]

(10) As the system of notification will now come to an end, it may be expedient, in order to
improve transparency, to require registration of certain types of agreement. The Commission
should accordingly be empowered to require registration of certain types of agreement. If any
such requirement is introduced, it must not confer any entitlement to a decision on the
compatibility with the Treaty of the agreement registered, and must not be prejudicial to
effective action against infringements.

(11) For it to ensure that the provisions of the Treaty are applied, the Commission must be
able to address decisions to undertakings or associations of undertakings for the purpose of
bringing to an end infringements of Articles 81 and 82. Provided there is a legitimate interest
in doing so, the Commission must also be able to adopt decisions which find that an
infringement has been committed in the past even if it does not impose a fine. This Regulation
should also make explicit provision for the Commission's power to adopt decisions ordering
interim measures, which has been acknowledged by the Court of Justice.

(12) Where, in the course of proceedings which might lead to an agreement being prohibited,
undertakings offer the Commission commitments such as to meet its objections, the
Commission should be able to adopt decisions which make those commitments binding on the
undertakings concerned, without settling the question of the applicability of Article 81 or
Article 82, so that the commitments can be relied upon by third parties before national courts
and failure to comply with them can be punished by the imposition of fines and periodic
penalty payments.

(13) In exceptional cases where the public interest of the Community so requires, it may also
be expedient for the Commission to adopt a decision of a declaratory nature finding that the
prohibition in Article 81 or Article 82 does not apply, with a view to clarifying the law and
ensuring its consistent application throughout the Community.

(14) If the Commission and the competition authorities of the Member States are to form
together a network of public authorities applying the Community competition rules in close
cooperation, arrangements for information and consultation must be set up and the exchange
of information must be allowed between the members of the network even where the
information is confidential, subject to appropriate guarantees for undertakings.

(15) If the competition rules are to be applied consistently and, at the same time, the network
is to be managed in the best possible way, it is essential to retain the rule that the competition
authorities of the Member States are automatically relieved of their competence if the
Commission initiates its own proceedings.

(16) To ensure that cases are dealt with by the most appropriate authorities within the
network, a general provision should be laid down allowing a competition authority to suspend
or close a case on the ground that another authority is dealing with it or has already dealt with
it, the objective being that each case should be handled by a single authority. This provision

must not prevent the Commission from rejecting a complaint for lack of Community i
as the case-law of the Court of Justice has acknowledged it may do, even if n
competition authority has indicated its intention of dealing with the case.

(17) The Advisory Committee on Restrictive Practices and Dominant Positions se
Regulation No 17 has functioned in a very satisfactory manner. It will fit perfectly into th
system of decentralised application. It is necessary, therefore, to build upon the rules laid
by Regulation No 17, while improving the effectiveness of the organisational arrangen
To this end, it would be expedient to allow opinions to be delivered by written procedure
Advisory Committee should also be able to act as a forum for discussing cases handled b
competition authorities of the Member States, so as to help safeguard the consistent applic
of the Community competition rules.

(18) Consistency in the application of the competition rules also requires that arrang
be established for cooperation between the courts of the Member States and the Comm
In particular, it will be useful to allow national courts to ask the Commission for inforr
or for its opinion on points concerning the application of Community competition law
Commission and the competition authorities of the Member States must also be able to su
written or oral observations to courts called upon to apply Article 81 or Article 82. Steps n
therefore be taken to ensure that the Commission and the competition authorities of tl
Member States are kept sufficiently well informed of proceedings before national courts.

(19) In order to ensure compliance with the principles of legal certainty and the uniform
application of the Community competition rules in a system of parallel powers, conflicting
decisions must be avoided. When the Commission has adopted a decision, therefore, the
competition authorities and courts of the Member States must use every effort to avoid
contradicting it. In this context, it should be recalled that the courts may refer questions to the
Court of Justice for a preliminary ruling.

(20) The Commission must be empowered throughout the Community to require such
information to be supplied and to undertake such inspections as are necessary to detect any
agreement, decision or concerted practice prohibited by Article 81 or any abuse of a dominant
position prohibited by Article 82. The competition authorities of the Member States must
cooperate actively in the exercise of these powers.

(21) The detection of infringements of the competition rules is growing ever more difficult,
and, in order to protect competition effectively, the Commission's powers of investigation
need to be supplemented. The Commission must in particular be empowered to interview any
persons who may be in possession of useful information and to record the statements made. In
the course of an inspection, authorised Commission officials must be empowered to affix seals
and to ask for any information relevant to the subject matter and purpose of the inspection.

(22) It is expedient to clarify, in keeping with the case-law of the Court of Justice, the limits
to the power of review that the national courts may exercise when asked, under national law,
to order measures allowing assistance from law enforcement authorities in order to overcome
opposition on the part of an undertaking to an inspection ordered by decision.

(23) Experience has shown that business records are often kept in the homes of directors or
other people working for an undertaking. In order to safeguard the effectiveness of inspections,
therefore, authorised Commission officials should be empowered to enter any premises where
business records may be kept, including private homes. However, the exercise of this latter
power must be subject to the authorisation of the judicial authority.

(24) In order to help the competition authorities of the Member States to apply Articles 81
and 82 effectively, it is expedient to enable them to assist one another by carrying out
fact-finding measures.

(25) Compliance with Articles 81 and 82 and the fulfilment of the obligations imposed on
undertakings and associations of undertakings under this Regulation must be enforceable by
means of fines and periodic penalty payments. To that end, appropriate levels of fine should
also be laid down for infringements of the procedural rules.

(26) The rules on periods of limitation for the imposition of fines and periodic penalty
payments were laid down in Council Regulation (EEC) No 2988/74,[8] which also concerns
penalties in the field of transport. In a system of parallel powers, the acts, which may interrupt
a limitation period, should include procedural steps taken independently by the competition
authority of a Member State. To clarify the legal framework, Regulation (EEC) No 2988/74
should therefore be amended to prevent it applying to matters covered by this Regulation, and
this Regulation should include provisions on periods of limitation.

(27) The undertakings concerned must be accorded the right to be heard by the Commission,
third parties whose interests may be affected by a decision must be given the opportunity of
submitting their observations beforehand, and the decisions taken must be widely publicised.

nsuring the rights of defence of the undertakings concerned, in particular, the right of
the file, it is essential that business secrets be protected. The confidentiality of
on exchanged in the network must likewise be safeguarded.

ince all decisions taken by the Commission under this Regulation are subject to review
Court of Justice in accordance with the Treaty, the Court of Justice should, in
nce with Article 229 thereof be given unlimited jurisdiction in respect of decisions by
the Commission imposes fines or periodic penalty payments.

) The principles laid down in Articles 81 and 82 of the Treaty, as they have been applied
gulation No 17, have given a central role to the Community bodies.

central role should be retained, whilst associating the Member States more closely with
lication of the Community competition rules. In accordance with the principles of
rity and proportionality as set out in Article 5 of the Treaty, this Regulation confines
the minimum required in order to achieve its objective, which is to allow the
unity competition rules to be applied effectively, and does not go beyond what is
sary for that purpose.

0) As the case-law has made it clear that the competition rules apply to transport, that
tor should be made subject to the procedural provisions of this Regulation. Regulations
EC) No 1017/68, (EEC) No 4056/86 and (EEC) No 3975/87 should therefore be amended
order to delete the specific procedural provisions they contain.

(31) In order to take account of the new arrangements established by this Regulation,
he following Regulations should be repealed: Council Regulation No 141 of 26 November
1962 exempting transport from the application of Regulation No 17,[9] Council Regulation
No 19/65/EEC of 2 March 1965 on application of Article 85(3) of the Treaty to certain
categories of agreements and concerted practices,[10] Council Regulation (EEC) No 2821/71
of 20 December 1971 on application of Article 85(3) of the Treaty to categories of
agreements, decisions and concerted practices,[11] Council Regulation (EEC) No 3976/87 of
14 December 1987 on the application of Article 85(3) of the Treaty to certain categories of
agreements and concerted practices in the air transport sector,[12] Council Regulation (EEC)
No 1534/91 of 31 May 1991 on the application of Article 85(3) of the Treaty to certain
categories of agreements, decisions and concerted practices in the insurance sector,[13] and
Council Regulation (EEC) No 479/92 of 25 February 1992 on the application of Article
85(3) of the Treaty to certain categories of agreements, decisions and concerted practices
between liner shipping companies (consortia),[14]

NOTES

[1]   OJ C

[2]   OJ C

[3]   OJ C

[4]   OJ L3, 21.2.62, p 204/62; Regulation as last amended by Regulation (EC) No 1216/1999
(OJ L148, 15.6.99, p 5).

[5]   OJ L175, 23.7.68, p 1; Regulation as last amended by the Act of Accession of Austria, Finland
and Sweden.

[6]   OJ L378, 31.12.86, p 4; Regulation as amended by the Act of Accession of Austria, Finland and
Sweden.

[7]   OJ L374, 31.12.87, p 1; Regulation as last amended by Regulation (EC) No 2410/92 (OJ L240,
24.8.92, p 18).

[8]   OJ L319, 29.11.74, p 1.

[9]   OJ L24, 28.11.62, p 2751/62; Regulation as last amended by Regulation No 1002/67/EEC
(OJ 306, 16.12.67, p. 1).

[10]   OJ 36, 6.3.65, p. 533/65; Regulation as last amended by Regulation (EC) No 1215/1999
(OJ L148, 15.6.99, p 1).

[11]   OJ L285, 29.12.71, p 46; Regulation as last amended by the Act of Accession of Austria, Finland
and Sweden.

[12]   OJ L374, 31.12.87, p 9; Regulation as last amended by the Act of Accession of Austria, Finland
and Sweden.

[13]   OJ L143, 7.6.91, p 1.

[14]   OJ L55, 29.2.92, p 3; Regulation as amended by the Act of Accession of Austria, Finland and
Sweden.

HAS ADOPTED THIS REGULATION—

CHAPTER I
PRINCIPLES

Article 1

Direct applicability

Agreements, decisions and concerted practices caught by Article 81(1) of the
which do not satisfy the conditions of Article 81(3), and the abuse of a do
position referred to in Article 82, shall be prohibited, no prior decision to tha
being required.

Article 2

Burden of proof

In any national or Community proceedings for the application of Article 81 an
Article 82 of the Treaty, the burden of proving an infringement of Article 81(1) or o
Article 82 shall rest on the party alleging the infringement. A party claiming the
benefit of Article 81(3) shall bear the burden of proving that the conditions of that
paragraph are fulfilled.

Article 3

Relationship between Articles 81 and 82 and national competition laws

Where an agreement, a decision by an association of undertakings or a concerted
practice within the meaning of Article 81 of the Treaty or the abuse of a dominant
position within the meaning of Article 82 may affect trade between Member States,
Community competition law shall apply to the exclusion of national competition laws.

CHAPTER II
POWERS

Article 4

Powers of the Commission

1.   For the purpose of applying Articles 81 and 82 of the Treaty, the Commission
shall have the powers provided for by this Regulation.

2.   The Commission may, by regulation, determine types of agreements, decisions
of associations of undertakings and concerted practices caught by Article 81(1) of the
Treaty which must be registered by undertakings. In that event, it shall also
determine the procedures for such registration and the penalties applicable in the
event of failure to comply with the obligation. Registration of an agreement, a
decision of an association or a concerted practice shall confer no entitlement on the
registering undertakings or associations of undertakings and shall not form an
obstacle to the application of this Regulation.

Article 5

Powers of the competition authorities of the Member States

The competition authorities of the Member States shall have the power in individual
cases to apply the prohibition in Article 81(1) of the Treaty where the conditions of
Article 81(3) are not fulfilled, and the prohibition in Article 82. For this purpose,

on their own initiative or on a complaint, they may take any decision that an infringement be brought to an end, adopting interim measures, commitments or imposing fines, periodic penalty payments or any other provided for in their national law. Where on the basis of the information in ssession the conditions for prohibition are not met they may likewise decide re are no grounds for action on their part.

le 6

of the national courts

l courts before which the prohibition in Article 81(1) of the Treaty is d shall also have jurisdiction to apply Article 81(3).

CHAPTER III
COMMISSION DECISIONS

rticle 7

inding and termination of infringement

1. Where the Commission, acting on a complaint or on its own initiative, finds that there is an infringement of Article 81 or of Article 82 of the Treaty, it may by decision require the undertakings and associations of undertakings concerned to bring such infringement to an end. For this purpose, it may impose on them any obligations necessary, including remedies of a structural nature. If it has a legitimate interest in doing so, it may also find that an infringement has been committed in the past.

2. Those entitled to lodge a complaint for the purposes of paragraph 1 are Member States and natural or legal persons who can show a legitimate interest.

Article 8

Interim measures

1. In cases of urgency due to the risk of serious and irreparable damage to competition, the Commission, acting on its own initiative may, on the basis of a *prima facie* finding of infringement, by decision order interim measures.

2. A decision under paragraph 1 shall apply for a maximum of one year but shall be renewable.

Article 9

Commitments

1. Where the Commission intends to adopt a decision requiring that an infringement be brought to an end and the undertakings concerned offer commitments such as to meet the Commission's objections, the Commission may by decision make those commitments binding on the undertakings. Such a decision shall be adopted for a specified period.

2. Irrespective of whether or not there has been or still is an infringement of Article 81 or Article 82 of the Treaty, such a decision shall terminate the proceedings.

3. The Commission may reopen the proceedings—
   (a) where there has been a material change in any of the facts on which the decision was based;

PART IV
EC MATERIALS

(b) where the undertakings concerned act contrary to their commitmen[
(c) where the decision was based on incomplete, incorrect or m[
information.

Article 10

Finding of inapplicability

For reasons of the Community public interest, the Commission, acting on its
initiative, may by decision find that, on the basis of the information in its poss[
Article 81 of the Treaty is not applicable to an agreement, a decision of an ass[
of undertakings or a concerted practice, either because the conditions of Artic[
are not fulfilled, or because the conditions of Article 81(3) are satisfied.

The Commission may likewise make such a finding with reference to Artic[
of the Treaty.

CHAPTER IV
COOPERATION WITH NATIONAL AUTHORITIES AND COURTS

Article 11

Cooperation between the Commission and the competition authorities of the
Member States

1.   The Commission and the competition authorities of the Member States shall
apply the Community competition rules in close cooperation.

2.   The Commission shall forthwith transmit to the competition authorities of
the Member States copies of the most important documents it has collected with a
view to applying Articles 7 to 10.

3.   Where a matter involving the application of Article 81 or Article 82 of the
Treaty is referred to the competition authorities of the Member States or where they
act on their own initiative to apply those Articles, they shall inform the Commission
accordingly at the outset of their own proceedings.

4.   Where competition authorities of Member States intend to adopt a decision
under Article 81 or Article 82 of the Treaty requiring that an infringement be
brought to an end, accepting commitments or withdrawing the benefit of a block
exemption regulation, they shall first consult the Commission. For that purpose, they
shall no later than one month before adopting the decision provide the Commission
with a summary of the case and with copies of the most important documents drawn
up in the course of their own proceedings. At the Commission's request, they shall
provide it with a copy of any other document relating to the case.

5.   The competition authorities of the Member States may consult the
Commission on any other case involving the application of Community law.

6.   The initiation by the Commission of proceedings for the adoption of a
decision under this Regulation shall relieve the competition authorities of the
Member States of their competence to apply Articles 81 and 82 of the Treaty.

Article 12

Exchange of information

1.   Notwithstanding any national provision to the contrary, the Commission and
the competition authorities of the Member States may provide one another with and
use in evidence any matter of fact or of law, including confidential information.

Information provided under paragraph 1 may be used only for the purpose [of apply]ing Community competition law. Only financial penalties may be imposed [on the b]asis of information provided.

[Articl]e 13

[Susp]ension or termination of proceedings

Where competition authorities of two or more Member States have received [a comp]laint or are acting on their own initiative under Article 81 or Article 82 of the [Treaty] against the same agreement, decision of an association or practice, the fact [that on]e authority is dealing with the case shall be sufficient grounds for the others [to sus]pend the proceedings before them or to reject the complaint. The Commission [may] likewise reject a complaint on the ground that the competition authority of a [Me]mber State is dealing with the case.

[2.] Where the competition authority of a Member State or the Commission [h]as received a complaint against an agreement, decision of an association or [p]ractice which has already been dealt with by another competition authority, it may reject it.

Article 14

Advisory Committee

1. An Advisory Committee on Restrictive Practices and Dominant Positions shall be consulted prior to the taking of any decision under Articles 7, 9, 10, 22 and 23(2).

2. The Advisory Committee shall be composed of representatives of the competition authorities of the Member States. Each Member State shall appoint a representative who, if prevented from attending, may be replaced by another representative.

3. The consultation may take place at a meeting convened by the Commission, which shall supply the chairman, not earlier than fourteen days after dispatch of the notice convening it. The Member States may accept a period of notice of less than fourteen days. The Commission shall attach to the notice convening the meeting a summary of the case, together with an indication of the most important documents, and a preliminary draft decision. The Advisory Committee shall deliver an opinion on the Commission's preliminary draft decision. It may deliver an opinion even if some members are absent and are not represented.

4. Consultation may also take place by written procedure. In that case, the Commission shall determine a date by which the Member States are to put forward their observations. However, if any Member State so requests, the Commission shall convene a meeting.

5. The opinion of the Advisory Committee shall be delivered in writing and appended to the draft decision. The Advisory Committee may recommend publication of the opinion. The Commission may carry out such publication. The decision to publish shall take account of the legitimate interest of undertakings in the protection of their business secrets.

6. Acting on its own initiative or at the request of a Member State, the Commission may include a case being dealt with by the competition authority of a Member State on the agenda of the Advisory Committee for discussion before the final decision is adopted.

Article 15

Cooperation with national courts

1. In proceedings for the application of Article 81 or Article 82 of the courts of the Member States may ask the Commission for information possession or for its opinion on questions concerning the application o Community competition rules.

2. Courts of the Member States shall send the Commission copies of judgments applying Article 81 or Article 82 of the Treaty within one month date on which the judgment is delivered.

3. For reasons of the Community public interest, the Commission may, own initiative, submit written or oral observations to courts of the Member Stat the subject of proceedings in which questions concerning the application of Articl or Article 82 of the Treaty arise. It may have itself represented by competit authorities of Member States. Acting on their own initiative, competition authorit of Member States may likewise submit written or oral observations to the nation courts of their Member State.

To this end, the Commission and the competition authorities of the Member States may request the national courts to transmit to them any documents necessary.

Article 16

Uniform application of Community competition law

In accordance with Article 10 of the Treaty and the principle of the uniform application of Community law, national courts and the competition authorities of the Member States shall use every effort to avoid any decision that conflicts with decisions adopted by the Commission.

CHAPTER V
POWERS OF INVESTIGATION

Article 17

Inquiries into sectors of the economy

1. If, in any sector of the economy, the trend of trade between Member States, the rigidity of prices or other circumstances suggest that competition is being restricted or distorted within the common market, the Commission may conduct a general inquiry into that sector and, in the course of that inquiry, may request undertakings in the sector concerned to supply the information necessary for giving effect to Articles 81 and 82 of the Treaty and may carry out any inspections necessary for that purpose.

The Commission may in particular request any undertaking or association of undertakings in the sector concerned to communicate to it all agreements, decisions and concerted practices.

2. Articles 18 to 23 shall apply by analogy.

Article 18

Requests for information

1. In order to carry out the duties assigned to it by this Regulation, the Commission may request all necessary information from the governments and competition authorities of the Member States and from undertakings and associations of undertakings.

In its request for information the Commission shall state the legal bases of
est, the time-limit within which the information is to be provided, the
of the request, and the penalties provided for in Articles 22 and 23 for
ng incorrect, incomplete or misleading information.

The owners of the undertakings or their representatives and, in the case of
persons, companies or firms, or associations having no legal personality, the
ns authorised to represent them by law or by their constitution shall supply the
mation requested. Lawyers duly authorised to act may supply the information
alf of their clients. The latter shall remain fully responsible if the information
d is incomplete, incorrect or misleading.

Where an undertaking or association of undertakings does not supply the
nation requested within the time-limit fixed or supplies incomplete information,
Commission shall by decision require the information to be supplied. The
sion shall specify what information is required and fix an appropriate time-limit
hin which it is to be supplied. It shall indicate the penalties provided for in
rticle 22(1)(a), and indicate or impose the penalties provided for in Article 23(1)(d).
shall also indicate the right to have the decision reviewed by the Court of Justice
f the European Communities.

Article 19

Power to take statements

In order to carry out the duties assigned to it by this Regulation, the Commission
may interview any natural or legal person that may be in possession of useful
information, in order to ask questions relating to the subject-matter of an investigation
and recording the answers.

Article 20

The Commission's powers of inspection

1.   In order to carry out the duties assigned to it by this Regulation, the
Commission may conduct all necessary inspections of undertakings and associations
of undertakings.

2.   The officials authorised by the Commission to conduct an inspection are
empowered—
   (a) to enter any premises, land and means of transport of the undertakings and
       associations of undertakings concerned;
   (b) to enter any other premises, including the homes of directors, managers
       and other members of staff of the undertakings and associations of
       undertakings concerned, in so far as it may be suspected that business
       records are being kept there;
   (c) to examine the books and other business records, irrespective of the
       medium on which they are stored;
   (d) to take copies of or extracts from the documents examined;
   (e) to seal any premises or business records during the inspection;
   (f) to ask any representative or member of staff of the undertaking or
       association of undertakings for information relating to the subject-matter
       and purpose of the inspection and to record the answers.

3.   The officials authorised by the Commission to conduct an inspection shall
exercise their powers upon production of a written authorisation specifying the
subject matter and purpose of the inspection and the penalties provided for in
Article 22 in cases where production of the required books or other business records
is incomplete or where the answers to questions asked under paragraph 2 of this

Article are incorrect, incomplete or misleading. In good time before the insp
the Commission shall give notice of the inspection to the competition aut
the Member State in whose territory it is to be conducted.

4.   Undertakings and associations of undertakings are required to sut
inspections ordered by decision of the Commission. The decision shall spec.
subject matter and purpose of the inspection, appoint the date on which it is to
and indicate the penalties provided for in Articles 22 and 23 and the right to hav
decision reviewed by the Court of Justice. The Commission shall take
decisions after consulting the competition authority of the Member State in
territory the inspection is to be conducted.

5.   Officials of the competition authority of the Member State in
territory the inspection is to be conducted shall, at the request of that authority
the Commission, actively assist the officials of the Commission. To this end,
shall enjoy the powers specified in paragraph 2.

6.   Where the officials authorised by the Commission find that an undertaki
opposes an inspection ordered pursuant to this Article, the Member State concerne
shall afford them the necessary assistance, requesting where appropriate tl
assistance of the police, so as to enable them to conduct their inspection.

If national law requires authorisation from the judicial authority before the
assistance of the police can be called upon, such authorisation may be applied for as
a precautionary measure.

7.   Where the officials authorised by the Commission wish to exercise the
power provided for by paragraph 2(b), authorisation from the judicial authority must
be obtained beforehand.

8.   The lawfulness of the Commission decision shall be subject to review only
by the Court of Justice. The power of review of the national court shall extend only
to establishing that the Commission decision is authentic and that the enforcement
measures envisaged are neither arbitrary nor excessive having regard to the subject
matter of the inspection. The national court may not review the necessity for the
inspection or require information other than that out in the Commission decision.

Article 21

Investigations by competition authorities of Member States

1.   The competition authority of a Member State may in its own territory carry
out any fact-finding measure under its national law on behalf and for the account of
the competition authority of another Member State in order to establish whether
there has been an infringement of Article 81 or Article 82 of the Treaty. It shall
transmit the information collected to the requesting authority in accordance with
Article 12 of this Regulation.

2.   At the request of the Commission, the competition authorities of the
Member States shall undertake the inspections which the Commission considers to
be necessary under Article 20(1) or which it has ordered by decision pursuant to
Article 20(4). The officials of the competition authorities of the Member States who
are responsible for conducting these inspections shall exercise their powers upon
production of a written authorisation issued by the competition authority of the
Member State in whose territory the inspection is to be conducted. Such
authorisation shall specify the subject matter and purpose of the inspection.

If so requested by the Commission or by the competition authority of the Member
State in whose territory the inspection is to be conducted, the officials of the
Commission may assist the officials of the authority concerned.

CHAPTER VI
PENALTIES

22

The Commission may by decision impose on undertakings and associations of undertakings fines not exceeding 1% of the total turnover in the preceding business year, intentionally or negligently—

(a) they supply incorrect, incomplete or misleading information in response to a request made pursuant to Article 17 or Article 18(1) or (4), or do not supply information within the time-limit fixed by a decision adopted pursuant to Article 18(4);

(b) they produce the required books or other business records in incomplete form during inspections under Article 20 or Article 21(2), or refuse to submit to inspections ordered by a decision adopted pursuant to Article 20(4);

(c) they refuse to answer a question asked in accordance with Article 20(2)(f) or give an incorrect, incomplete or misleading answer;

(d) seals affixed by authorised officials of the Commission in accordance with Article 20(2)(e) have been broken.

2.   The Commission may by decision impose on undertakings and associations of undertakings fines not exceeding 10% of the total turnover in the preceding business year of each of the undertakings participating in the infringement where, either intentionally or negligently—

(a) they infringe Article 81 or Article 82 of the Treaty; or

(b) they contravene a decision ordering interim measures under Article 8 of this Regulation; or

(c) they fail to comply with a commitment made binding by a decision pursuant to Article 9 of this Regulation.

3.   In fixing the amount of the fine, regard shall be had both to the gravity and to the duration of the infringement.

4.   Where a fine is imposed on an association of undertakings under this Regulation and the association is not solvent, the Commission may require payment of the fine by any of the undertakings which were members of the association at the time the infringement was committed. The amount required to be paid by each individual member cannot exceed 10% of its total turnover in the preceding business year.

5.   Decisions taken pursuant to paragraphs 1 and 2 shall not be of a criminal law nature.

Article 23

Periodic penalty payments

1. The Commission may, by decision, impose on undertakings or associations of undertakings periodic penalty payments not exceeding 5% of the average daily turnover in the preceding business year per day and calculated from the date appointed by the decision, in order to compel them—

(a) to put an end to an infringement of Article 81 or Article 82 of the Treaty, in accordance with a decision taken pursuant to Article 7 of this Regulation;

(b) to comply with a decision ordering interim measures taken pursuant to Article 8;

    (c) to comply with a commitment made binding by a decision pursu
        Article 9;

    (d) to supply complete and correct information which it has reque
        decision taken pursuant to Article 18(4);

    (e) to submit to an inspection which it has ordered by decision taken pu
        to Article 20.

2. Where the undertakings or associations of undertakings have satisfied
obligation which the periodic penalty payment was intended to enforce.
Commission may fix the definitive amount of the periodic penalty paymer
figure lower than that which would arise under the original decision. Article
shall apply by analogy.

CHAPTER VII
LIMITATION PERIODS

Article 24

Limitation periods for the imposition of penalties

  1. The powers conferred on the Commission by Articles 22 and 23 shall be subject
to the following limitation periods—

    (a) three years in the case of infringements of provisions concerning requests
        for information or the conduct of inspections;

    (b) five years in the case of all other infringements.

  2. Time shall begin to run on the day on which the infringement is committed.
However, in the case of continuing or repeated infringements, time shall begin to run
on the day on which the infringement ceases.

  3. Any action taken by the Commission or by the competition authority of a
Member State for the purpose of the investigation or proceedings in respect of an
infringement shall interrupt the limitation period for the imposition of fines or
periodic penalty payments. The limitation period shall be interrupted with effect
from the date on which the action is notified to at least one undertaking or
association of undertakings which has participated in the infringement. Actions
which interrupt the running of the period shall include in particular the following—

    (a) written requests for information by the Commission or by the competition
        authority of a Member State;

    (b) written authorisations to conduct inspections issued to its officials by the
        Commission or by the competition authority of a Member State;

    (c) the initiation of proceedings by the Commission or by the competition
        authority of a Member State;

    (d) notification of the statement of objections of the Commission or of the
        competition authority of a Member State.

  4.   The interruption of the limitation period shall apply for all the undertakings
or associations of undertakings which have participated in the infringement.

  5.   Each interruption shall start time running afresh. However, the limitation
period shall expire at the latest on the day on which a period equal to twice the
limitation period has elapsed without the Commission having imposed a fine or a
periodic penalty payment. That period shall be extended by the time during which
limitation is suspended pursuant to paragraph 6.

  6.   The limitation period for the imposition of fines or periodic penalty
payments shall be suspended for as long as the decision of the Commission is the
subject of proceedings pending before the Court of Justice.

25

on period for the enforcement of penalties

e power of the Commission to enforce decisions taken pursuant to Articles 22
shall be subject to a limitation period of five years.

ime shall begin to run on the day on which the decision becomes final.

he limitation period for the enforcement of penalties shall be interrupted—
) by notification of a decision varying the original amount of the fine or
periodic penalty payment or refusing an application for variation;
by any action of the Commission or of a Member State, acting at the
request of the Commission, designed to enforce payment of the fine or
periodic penalty payment.

Each interruption shall start time running afresh.

. The limitation period for the enforcement of penalties shall be suspended for so
ng as—
(a) time to pay is allowed;
(b) enforcement of payment is suspended pursuant to a decision of the Court
of Justice.

CHAPTER VIII
HEARINGS AND PROFESSIONAL SECRECY

Article 26

Hearing of the parties, complainants and others

1.   Before taking decisions as provided for in Articles 7, 8, 22 and 23(2), the
Commission shall give the undertakings or associations of undertakings which are
the subject of the proceedings the opportunity of being heard on the matters to
which the Commission has taken objection. The Commission shall base its decisions
only on objections on which the parties concerned have been able to comment.
Complainants shall be associated closely with the proceedings.

2.   The rights of defence of the parties concerned shall be fully respected in the
proceedings. They shall be entitled to have access to the file, subject to the
legitimate interest of undertakings in the protection of their business secrets. That
legitimate interest may not constitute an obstacle to the disclosure and use by the
Commission of information necessary to prove an infringement.

The right of access to the file shall not extend to confidential information and
internal documents of the Commission or the competition authorities of the Member
States. In particular, any correspondence between the Commission and the
Competition Authority of the Member States, or between the latter, *inter alia*,
documents drawn up pursuant to Articles 8 and 11 are excluded.

3.   If the Commission or the competition authorities of the Member States
consider it necessary, they may also hear other natural or legal persons. Applications
to be heard on the part of such persons shall, where they show a sufficient interest,
be granted.

Article 27

Professional secrecy

1.   Without prejudice to Articles 12 and 15, information collected pursuant to
Articles 17 to 21 shall be used only for the purpose for which it was acquired.

2.   Without prejudice to Articles 11, 12, 14, 15 and 26, the Commission
competition authorities of the Member States, their officials and other serv;
not disclose information acquired or exchanged by them pursuant to this Re
and of the kind covered by the obligation of professional secrecy.

CHAPTER IX
BLOCK EXEMPTIONS

Article 28

Adoption of block exemption regulations

1.   In accordance with Article 81(3) of the Treaty, the Commission n
regulation, declare that Article 81(1) is not applicable to categories of agree;
decisions by associations of undertakings or concerted practices, subject t
conditions in paragraphs 2 to 5 of this Article.

2.   Exemption regulations must define the categories of agreements, decisic
or concerted practices to which they apply and specify in particular the restriction
which are not exempted, and any conditions that must be fulfilled.

3.   Exemption regulations must be limited in time.

4.   Before adopting an exemption regulation, the Commission must publish a
draft thereof and invite all interested parties concerned to submit their comments
within the time-limit it lays down, which may not be less than one month.

5.   Before publishing a draft exemption regulation and before adopting such a
regulation, the Commission shall consult the Advisory Committee on Restrictive
Practices and Dominant Positions.

Article 29

Withdrawal in individual cases

1.   Where, in any particular case, the Commission, acting on its own initiative
or on a complaint, finds that agreements, decisions or concerted practices to which a
block exemption regulation applies nevertheless have certain effects which are
incompatible with Article 81(3) of the Treaty, it may withdraw the benefit of the
regulation.

2.   Where in any particular case agreements, decisions or concerted practices to
which a block exemption regulation applies have effects which are incompatible
with Article 81(3) of the Treaty in the territory of a Member State, or in a part
thereof, which has all the characteristics of a distinct geographic market, the
competition authority of that Member State may withdraw the benefit of the
regulation in question in respect of that territory.

Article 30

Regulations ending the application of a block exemption

A block exemption regulation adopted pursuant to Article 28 may specify the
circumstances which may lead to the exclusion from its scope of certain types of
agreement, decision or concerted practice that are applied on a particular market.
Where those circumstances obtain, the Commission may establish this by way of
regulation, and fix a period on the expiry of which the block exemption regulation
will no longer be applicable to the relevant agreements, decisions or concerted
practices on that market. That period must not be less than six months. Article 28(4)
and (5) shall apply by analogy.

CHAPTER X
GENERAL PROVISIONS

e 31

cation of decisions

The Commission shall publish the decisions, which it takes pursuant to
les 7 to 10, 22 and 23.

The publication shall state the names of the parties and the main content of
ision, including any penalties imposed. It shall have regard to the legitimate
st of undertakings in the protection of their business secrets.

cle 32

view by the Court of Justice

he Court of Justice shall have unlimited jurisdiction to review decisions whereby
he Commission has fixed a fine or periodic penalty payment. It may cancel, reduce
or increase the fine or periodic penalty payment imposed.

Article 33

Exclusions

This Regulation shall not apply to agreements, decisions and concerted practices or
to the abuse of a dominant position within the meaning of Article 82 of the Treaty in
the following areas:
  (a) international sea transport of the tramp service type;
  (b) sea transport between ports in the same Member State;
  (c) air transport between the Community and third countries.

Article 34

Implementing provisions

The Commission shall be authorised to take such measures as may be appropriate in
order to apply this Regulation. The measures may concern *inter alia*:
  (a) the introduction of a registration requirement for certain types of agreement;
  (b) the form, content and other details of complaints lodged pursuant to Article 7
       and the procedure for rejecting complaints;
  (c) the practical arrangements for the exchange of information and consultations
       provided for in Article 11;
  (d) the practical arrangements for the hearings provided for in Article 26.

CHAPTER XI
TRANSITIONAL AND FINAL PROVISIONS

Article 35

Transitional provisions

  1. Applications made to the Commission under Article 2 of Regulation No 17,
notifications made under Articles 4 and 5 of that Regulation and the corresponding
applications and notifications made under Regulations (EEC) No 1017/68, (EEC)
No 4056/86 and (EEC) No 3975/87 shall lapse as from the date of application of this
Regulation.

The validity of decisions applying Article 81(3) of the Treaty adopted
Commission under those Regulations shall come to an end no later than the
application of this Regulation.

2.   Procedural steps taken under Regulation No 17 and Regulations
No 1017/68, (EEC) No 4056/86 and (EEC) No 3975/87 shall continue to have
for the purposes of applying this Regulation.

Article 36

Designation of competition authorities of Member States

The Member States shall designate the competition authorities responsible
application of Articles 81 and 82 of the Treaty, and shall take the mea
necessary to empower those authorities to apply those Articles before ***.

Article 37

Amendment of Regulation (EEC) No 1017/68

Regulation (EEC) No 1017/68 is amended as follows—

(1)   Article 2 is deleted.

(2)   In Article 3(1), the words "The prohibition laid down in Article 2" are
replaced by the words "The prohibition in Article 81(1) of the Treaty".

(3)   Articles 5 to 29 are deleted.

(4)   In Article 30, paragraphs 2 and 3 are deleted.

Article 38

Amendment of Regulation (EEC) No 2988/74

In Regulation (EEC) No 2988/74, the following Article 7a is inserted—

> **"Article 7a**
>
> **Exclusion**
>
> This Regulation shall not apply to measures taken under Council Regulation
> (EC) No . . .*

NOTES
     * OJ L . . ."

Article 39

Amendment of Regulation (EEC) No 4056/86

Regulation (EEC) No 4056/86 is amended as follows:

(1)   Article 7 is amended as follows:
   (a)   Paragraph 1 is replaced by the following:

> "1. Breach of an obligation
>
> Where the persons concerned are in breach of an obligation which, pursuant
> to Article 5, attaches to the exemption provided for in Article 3, the
> Commission may, in order to put an end to such breach and under the
> conditions laid down in Council Regulation (EC) No . . .*—
>
> —   address recommendations to the persons concerned;
>
> —   in the event of failure by such persons to observe those
>   recommendations and depending on the gravity of the breach

concerned, adopt a decision that either prohibits them from carrying out or requires them to perform certain specific acts, or withdraws the benefit of the block exemption which they enjoyed."

) Paragraph 2 is amended as follows:

(i) In point (a), the words "under the conditions laid down in Section II" are replaced by the words "under the conditions laid down in Regulation (EC) No . . . / . . . ";

(ii) The second sentence of the second subparagraph of point (c)(i) is replaced by the following:

"At the same time it shall decide, in accordance with Article 9 of Regulation (EC) No . . . / . . . , whether it accepts commitments offered by the undertakings concerned with a view, *inter alia*, to obtaining access to the market for non-conference lines."

ﻟ) In Article 8, paragraph 1 is deleted.

(3) Article 9 is amended as follows:

(a) In paragraph 1, the words "Advisory Committee referred to in Article 15" are replaced by the words "Advisory Committee referred to in Article 14 of Regulation (EC) No . . . / . . . ";

(b) In paragraph 2, the words "Advisory Committee as referred to in Article 15" are replaced by the words "the Advisory Committee referred to in Article 14 of Regulation (EC) No . . . / . . . ".

(4) Articles 10 to 25 are deleted.

(5) In Article 26, the words "the form, content and other details of complaints pursuant to Article 10, applications pursuant to Article 12 and the hearings provided for in Article 23(1) and (2)" are deleted.

NOTES

* OJ L . . ."

Article 40

Amendment of Regulation (EEC) No 3975/87

Articles 3 to 19 of Regulation (EEC) No 3975/87 are deleted.

Article 41

Repeals

Regulations No 17, No 141, No 19/65/EEC, (EEC) No 2821/71, (EEC) No 3976/87, (EEC) No 1534/91 and (EEC) No 479/92 are hereby repealed.

References to the repealed Regulations shall be construed as references to this Regulation.

Article 42

Entry into force

This Regulation shall enter into force on the twentieth day following that of its publication in the *Official Journal of the European Communities*.

It shall apply from xxx.

This Regulation shall be binding in its entirety and directly applicable Member States.

Done at Brussels,

For the Council

The President

[6

IMPACT ASSESSMENT FORM

THE IMPACT OF THE PROPOSAL ON BUSINESS WITH SPECIA REFERENCE TO SMALL AND MEDIUM-SIZED ENTERPRISES (SM

TITLE OF PROPOSAL

"Proposal for a Council Regulation implementing Articles 81 and 82 of the E Treaty"

DOCUMENT REFERENCE NUMBER

2000/018

THE PROPOSAL

1. *Taking account of the principle of subsidiarity, why is Community legislation necessary in this area and what are its main aims?*

Community legislation is required to give effect to Articles 81 and 82 of the Treaty. The implementation of these rules is presently based on Regulation No 17 of 1962 (together with the procedural rules contained in Regulations (EEC) No 1017/68, (EEC) No 4056/86 and (EEC) No 3975/87 regarding transport; certain specific issues are also regulated in other regulations). The proposed Regulation brings about a major reform of the implementing system. It aims at more effective application of the Community competition rules through a stronger involvement of Member States competition authorities and courts in the application of Articles 81 and 82. This is achieved in particular by rendering Article 81(3) directly applicable. To ensure consistent application of the Community competition rules, the proposed Regulation provides for rules on the relationship between Articles 81 and 82 and national competition law and for mechanisms for cooperation and consultation between the Commission and national competition authorities and national courts.

THE IMPACT ON BUSINESS

2. *Who will be affected by the proposal?*

   — *which sectors of business*

The proposed Regulation concerns the implementation of Articles 81 and 82 to all sectors of the economy subject to very limited exceptions. The proposed Regulation maintains certain exceptions of limited scope in the transport sector. Implementation in the agricultural sector remains governed by Regulation No 26 of 1962.

   — *which sizes of business (what is the concentration of small and medium-sized firms)*

The proposed Regulation applies to all businesses independent of their size as well as associations of undertakings, if they engage in behaviour that fulfils the conditions of Articles 81 or 82. The practical impact of the proposed Regulation on

and medium-sized companies however tends to be different from that on
usinesses. This question is further developed under point 5 below.

*– are there particular geographical areas of the Community where these
businesses are found*

. All undertakings doing business in the Community are concerned in the same
independent of the geographical area in which they operate.

What will business have to do to comply with the proposal?

proposal does not affect the basic obligation for companies to comply with
s 81 and 82 of the Treaty. But it does bring about a major change in the way
e 81 is implemented in individual cases, ie cases that are not covered by block
ption regulations. The companies most concerned by the reform will therefore
eneral be companies that have some degree of market power. These companies
generally the larger companies, and only rarely SMEs. Depending on their
urrent practices, these companies may have to review the processes by which they
nsure compliance of their transactions with Article 81 in individual cases and,
where necessary, adapt them.

Under the present Regulation No 17, agreements falling under Article 81(1) that
are not covered by a block exemption, and for which the parties wish to avail
themselves of Article 81(3), must be notified to the Commission in order to obtain
an individual exemption. Without such notification and exemption, the agreement is
legally void.

In the present system, companies (assisted by their legal advisors) evaluate the
business transactions they envisage in the light of Article 81 (on the basis of the
existing case-law and practice and of Commission guidelines and notices), and
decide whether or not to notify. They must weigh the risks entailed by the legal
invalidity of their agreements in the absence of an exemption decision against the
cost, duration and likely outcome of the notification procedure.

Under the proposed Regulation Article 81(3) becomes directly applicable.
Agreements that satisfy the conditions of Article 81(3) become valid *ab initio* and
can be enforced without the need to obtain an exemption decision. Only agreements
which do not satisfy the conditions of Article 81(3) will be invalid *ab initio* and
unenforceable. Companies will be able to invoke Article 81(3) as a defence in all
proceedings. Alongside the Commission, national competition authorities and
national courts will be able to apply Article 81 in its entirety.

The proposed Regulation thus eliminates the burden of notifications and prior
administrative authorisation and thereby considerably reduces bureaucracy for all
companies. This is particularly valuable for SMEs. The reform strongly improves
the civil enforceability of all agreements that fulfil the conditions of Article 81(3).
Invalidity of agreements based on the argument that an agreement has not been
notified, and is therefore void, will disappear.

The proposed Regulation, however, also implies that companies must assume a
higher degree of responsibility for their behaviour as regards compliance with
Article 81, as they can no longer apply to the Commission for formal exemption.
The body of existing secondary legislation and case-law which has been developed
over the last 40 years has put companies in a position to assess the legality of their
transactions. Under the present Regulation companies are already generally
confident of their assessment. This is demonstrated by the fact that the
implementation of an agreement is only very rarely postponed until the
Commission's view has been obtained. This shows that companies are able to carry
out their analysis in such a way that it can serve as a basis for an informed decision
on whether to go ahead with the transaction and if so, in which form.

Under both the present and the proposed new system, the assessment made company will require more care the closer the agreement or practice come scope of the prohibition. Where they envisage transactions bordering prohibition, businesses must be particularly careful in choosing to what exte are prepared to take the risk of seeing their transactions invalidated with eff *initio*, and the risk of claims for damages. It is in the nature of the prohibition that companies in these cases have to consider alternative solutions that pres different balance of restrictive and beneficial effects if they want to exclude all r

Under the new system, Article 81 will become directly applicable in its entir the Commission, national competition authorities and national courts (p powers). Business will not however be exposed to a significant risk of div decisions. Several aspects are important in this context—

—   The proposed Regulation provides that all decision-makers apply a si set of rules, ie Articles 81 and 82, to all transactions that may have impact on trade between Member States.

—   The proposal is complemented by a reinforced effort on the part of th Commission in the design of the legislative framework of block exemption regulations, guidelines and Commission notices that shape the application of Article 81 to a large extent and provide guidance to companies in the vast majority of cases (in particular cases involving small and medium-sized companies, cf point 5 below). To simplify the adoption of block exemption regulations, a general power in this field is to be vested in the Commission.

—   The proposed Regulation will bring about a change in approach in the enforcement of the rules. Without the present treatment of notifications, the Commission will have more time to clarify what is prohibited under Article 81. In addition to the reform of the enforcement rules, reform work is being undertaken on the substantive rules, aiming at a more economic and reasonable approach.

—   The proposed Regulation is designed to maintain a high degree of consistency in the application of Articles 81 and 82 in general. It sets up a range of mechanisms for consultation and cooperation between the various decision-makers that will ensure a high degree of consistency from the outset, and contribute to laying the foundations for a common interpretation practice that will be self-sustaining in the longer term. The Commission maintains the right to withdraw a case from a national competition authority if it considers that the case would be better dealt with by itself or that the direction taken in the case deviates from its own policy. National courts may there exists the possibility (and at last instance must) make a reference to the ECJ under Article 234. Furthermore, the Brussels Convention on Jurisdiction and Enforcement of Judgments in Civil and Commercial Matters largely prevents forum shopping and multiple litigation in civil courts.

—   In the rare cases presenting a genuine predictability problem because they raise new or unresolved questions the Commission will consider issuing reasoned opinions in order to provide guidance to companies. Details of this mechanism will be set out in a Commission notice.

4. *What economic effects is the proposal likely to have on employment, on investment and the creation of new businesses and on the competitiveness of businesses?*

The proposed Regulation is designed to reinforce the impact of the Community competition rules by ensuring more efficient enforcement. The abolition of the notification and authorisation system enables the Commission to step up enforcement action against serious infringements. The removal of the Commission monopoly on the application of Article 81(3) will release the enforcement potential of national courts and national competition authorities. Both elements taken together

rve to raise the deterrent effect of the Community competition rules, thereby
g more widespread compliance with the rules and furthering effective
ition in the markets.

no longer disputed that effective competition is of fundamental importance to
uropean economy. Effective competition is the best guarantor of efficient
ation of resources, laying the foundations of economic growth. Competitive
ure forces companies to adapt by implementing innovations and striving to
ase productivity. Companies exposed to vigorous competition become more
titive, and will generally be better equipped to compete internationally.
ve competition ensures a high degree of productive and therefore sustainable
cure employment. Competitive markets are open to new entrants; they invite
ment and job creation. This effect has been clearly demonstrated in recently
alised markets.

n addition, the proposal will serve to create a more level playing field for
mpanies in the internal market by ensuring more widespread application of the
Community competition rules rather than national competition law and by providing
a comprehensive set of mechanisms to ensure consistent application. A more level
playing field in terms of competition law encourages further market integration,
thereby enhancing competition through market entry.

*5. Does the proposal contain measures to take account of the specific situation of
small and medium-sized firms (reduced or different requirements etc)?*

The proposal does not make any specific provision for small and medium-sized
undertakings. However, the practical impact of the reform on small and medium-sized
companies will be positive, for several reasons.

First, a large number of small and medium-sized companies are not directly
concerned by the application of the Community competition rules, because they are
involved in agreements, decisions or practices that do not have an appreciable
impact on trade between Member States. In addition, the Commission is pursuing a
more economic and reasonable interpretation of Article 81(1). Under this approach,
companies that do not have a certain degree of market power are less likely to be
involved in transactions caught by the prohibition.

Secondly, small and medium-sized businesses with little market power are
generally more likely to be victims of infringements of the Community competition
rules than actively to engage in infringements themselves. The proposed Regulation
is designed to generate more efficient enforcement of the competition rules by the
Commission and the national competition authorities. It will in particular enable the
Commission to be more active in combating serious infringements at its own
initiative or following complaints. This effect therefore particularly benefits small
and medium-sized businesses.

Thirdly, the impact of removing the notification and authorisation system is
different with regard to small and medium-sized companies. Their activities very
often fall within the scope of block exemption regulations. This means that under the
present Regulation No 17 they are already generally much less concerned to notify
agreements with a view to individual exemption decisions.

Alongside the reform of the rules implementing Articles 81 and 82 through the
proposed Regulation, the Commission, pursuing the more economic and reasonable
approach mentioned earlier, has initiated a reform of the substantive rules in block
exemption regulations, Commission notices and guidelines. In particular, a new type
of block exemption regulation simplifies compliance for companies with little or no
market power by introducing market share thresholds (with the exception of certain
hard-core restrictions). Under this type of regulation, the vast majority of small and
medium-sized businesses are able to act within 'safe harbours'.

Finally, where agreements involving small and medium-sized businesses o
outside block exemptions, they will benefit fully from the direct effect of Artic
provided for in the proposed Regulation. Under the present system, th
particularly likely to fight shy of the cost of the notification procedure (in a
sense, ie including the resources required to prepare the information to be pres
etc), and thus to run the risk of legal invalidity of their agreements. This probl
removed by the reform. Most agreements of small and medium-sized undertak
will be rendered valid *ab initio* without the need for notification.

CONSULTATION

6. *List the organisations which have been consulted about the propos*
outline their main views.

The proposal is the result of an extensive consultation process and a wide pu
and academic debate. This debate was initiated by the Commission through
White Paper on modernisation of the rules implementing Articles 81 and 82 of t
EC Treaty of 28 April 1999.

Following the White Paper the Commission received and carefully examined
submissions from more than 100 interested parties, including numerous companies,
industry organisations and lawyers advising companies in competition law
proceedings. In addition, the Commission has had and continues to have numerous
contacts with industry, lawyers and their organisations, bilaterally and in a very large
number of conferences and similar events.

The European Parliament organised a public hearing on 22 September 1999. It
adopted a resolution, supporting the reform, on 18 January 2000. The Economic and
Social Committee adopted a generally favourable opinion on 8 December 1999.

The majority of comments received following the White Paper take a favourable
view on the Commission's approach. The position of industry associations and
lawyers are varied. Many welcome the Commission's approach as a more efficient
and less bureaucratic alternative to the present enforcement system, which is almost
universally considered unsatisfactory. However, many also stress the need to ensure
that the reform does not lead to inconsistent application and renationalisation of
Community competition law and that the reform does not reduce legal certainty for
companies.   **[6306]**

Index

estimates. Indications as to where any of the requested information or documents that are unavailable to you could be obtained by the Commission must also be provided. Secondly, the Commission only requires the submission of information relevant and necessary to its inquiry into the notified operation. In some cases not all the information required by this form will be necessary for this purpose. The Commission may therefore dispense with the obligation to provide certain information required by this form (see Article 3(2) of the Regulation). This provision enables, where appropriate, each application to be tailored to each case so that only the information strictly necessary for the Commission's examination is provided. This avoids unnecessary administrative burdens being imposed on undertakings, in particular on small and medium-sized ones. Where the information or documents required by this form are not provided for this reason, the application should indicate the reasons why the information is considered to be unnecessary to the Commission's investigation.

Where the Commission finds that the information contained in the application is incomplete in a material respect, it will, within one month from receipt, inform the applicant or the notifying party in writing of this fact and the nature of the missing information. In such cases, the application shall become effective on the date on which the complete information is received by the Commission. If the Commission has not informed the applicant or the notifying party within the one month period that the application is incomplete in a material respect, the application will be deemed to be complete and valid (see Article 4 of the Regulation).

It is also important that undertakings inform the Commission of important changes in the factual situation including those of which they become aware after the application has been submitted. The Commission must, therefore, be informed immediately of any changes to an agreement, decision or practice which is the subject of an application (see Article 4(3) of the Regulation). Failure to inform the Commission of such relevant changes could result in any negative clearance decision being without effect or in the withdrawal of any exemption decision[8] adopted by the Commission on the basis of the application.

F.   The need for accurate information

In addition to the requirement that the application be completed, it is important that you ensure that the information provided is accurate (see Article 3(1) of the Regulation). The Commission is empowered to impose, by decision, on undertakings or associations of undertakings, fines of up to EUR 5000 where, intentionally or negligently, they supply incorrect or misleading information in an application (Article 22(1)(a) of Regulation (EEC) No 1017/68, Article 19(1)(a) of Regulation (EEC) No 4056/86 and Article 12(1)(a) of Regulation (EEC) No 3975/87). Such information is, moreover, considered to be incomplete (see Article 4(4) of the Regulation).

G.   Who can lodge an application?

Any of the undertakings party to an agreement, decision or practice of the kind described in Articles 85 or 86 of the EC Treaty and Articles 53 or 54 of the EEA Agreement may submit an application for negative clearance pursuant to Article 3(2) of Regulation (EEC) No 3975/87. Any of the undertakings party to an agreement, decision or practice of the kind described in Articles 2 and 5 of Regulation (EEC) No 1017/68, or Article 85 of the EC Treaty and Article 53 of the EEA Agreement, may submit an application requesting an exemption. An association of undertakings may submit an application in relation to decisions taken or practices pursued in the operation of the association.

In relation to agreements and concerted practices between undertakings it is common practice for all the parties involved to submit a joint application. Although the Commission strongly recommends this approach, because it is helpful to have the views of all the parties directly concerned at the same time, it is not obligatory. Any of the parties to an agreement may submit an application in their individual capacities, but in such circumstances the notifying party should inform all the other parties to the agreement, decision or practice of that fact (see Article 1(2) of the Regulation). They may also provide them with a copy of the completed form, where relevant, once confidential information and business secrets have been deleted (see below, operational part, question 1.2).

Where a joint application is submitted, it has also become common practice to appoint a joint representative to act on behalf of all the undertakings involved, both in making the application or notification, and in dealing with any subsequent contacts with the Commission (see Article 1(4) of the Regulation). Again, while this is helpful, it is not obligatory, and all the undertakings jointly submitting an application may sign it in their individual capacities.

H. How to submit an application

Applications may be submitted in any of the official languages of the European Union or of an EFTA State (see Articles 2(5) and 6 of the Regulation). In order to ensure rapid proceedings, it is, however, recommended to use, in case of an application to the EFTA Surveillance Authority one of the official languages of an EFTA State or the working language of the EFTA Surveillance Authority, which is English, or, in case of an application to the Commission, one of the official languages of the Union or of the EFTA States or the working language of the EFTA Surveillance Authority. This language will thereafter be the language of the proceeding for the applicant.

Undertakings should provide the information requested by form TR, using its sections and paragraph numbers, signing a declaration as stated in Section 13, and annexing the required supporting documentation.

Supporting documents shall be submitted in their original language; where this is not an official language of the Union they must be translated into the language of the proceeding. The supporting documents may be originals or copies of the originals (see Article 2(4) of the Regulation).

All information requested in this form shall, unless otherwise stated, relate to the calendar year preceding that of the application. Where information is not reasonably available on this basis (for example if accounting periods are used that are not based on the calendar year, or the previous year's figures are not yet available), the most recently available information should be provided and reasons given why figures on the basis of the calendar year preceding that of the application cannot be provided.

Financial data may be provided in the currency in which the official audited accounts of the undertaking(s) concerned are prepared or in euros. In the latter case the exchange rate used for the conversion must be the average conversion rates prevailing for the years or other periods in question.

One original and 17 copies of each application, but only three copies of all supporting documents must be provided (see Article 2(3) of the Regulation).

The application is to be sent to—

European Commission
Directorate-General for Competition (DG IV),
The Registrar
Rue de la Loi/Wetstraat 200,
B-1049 Brussels,

or be delivered by hand during Commission working days and official working hours to the following address—

European Commission,
Directorate-General for Competition (DG IV),
The Registrar
Avenue de Cortenberg/Kortenberglaan 158,
B-1040 Brussels.

I. Confidentiality

Article 214 of the EC Treaty, Article 27 of Regulation (EEC) No 1017/68, Article 24 of Regulation (EEC) No 4056/86 and Article 17 of Regulation (EEC) No 3975/87, Article 9 of Protocol 23 to the EEA Agreement, Article 122 of the EEA Agreement and Article 27 of Chapter VI, Article 24 of Chapter IX and Article 17 of Chapter XI of Protocol 4 to the Agreement between the EFTA States on the establishment of a Surveillance Authority and of a Court of Justice require the Commission, the Member States, the EEA Surveillance Authority and EFTA States not to disclose information of the kind covered by the obligation of professional secrecy.

On the other hand, Regulations (EEC) No 1017/68, (EEC) No 4056/86 and (EEC) No 3975/87 require the Commission to publish a summary of an application for exemption. In

BUTTERWORTHS
COMPETITION LAW
HANDBOOK